RALPH E. McCOY

FREEDOM OF THE PRESS

A Bibliocyclopedia

TEN-YEAR SUPPLEMENT (1967–1977)

With a Foreword by Robert B. Downs

SOUTHERN ILLINOIS UNIVERSITY PRESS

Carbondale and Edwardsville

FEFFER & SIMONS, INC.

London and Amsterdam

Library of Congress Cataloging in Publication Data

McCoy, Ralph Edward, 1915-
  Freedom of the press, bibliocyclopedia.

  Includes index.
  1. Freedom of the press—Bibliography.   I. McCoy,
Ralph Edward, 1915-   Freedom of the press.   II.   Title.
III.   Title: A Bibliocyclopedia.
K3255.A12M3   016.32344'5   78-16573
ISBN 0-8093-0844-4

To Robert and David

CONTENTS

FOREWORD

by Robert B. Downs

Vital Issues of the Past Decade

THE OLD APHORISM that the more things change the more they remain the same applies to a considerable extent in the field of censorship and intellectual freedom. Nevertheless, old issues take new directions, legal aspects receive new interpretations, opposing forces re-group and fluctuate, while the objects of attack vary from perennial favorites to nine days' wonders. The overall impression is described by the French phrase *déjà vu*.

Dr. McCoy's monumental bibliography on *Freedom of the Press*, for which the present work provides an extensive supplement, is predominantly concerned with the American scene, but it contains a representative selection of British, Canadian, Australian, and other entries from English-speaking areas of the world to demonstrate the international nature of the struggle to maintain the freedom of the mind everywhere. The picture would be far grimmer, of course, in the repressive dictatorial regimes behind the Iron Curtain and among many nations of Africa, Asia, and Latin America, whose people remain helpless under the heels of ruthless tyrants.

It is refreshing and heartening to note the continued interest in the historical aspects of speech and press freedom. One who refuses to learn from the lessons of history is doomed to repeat its mistakes. We should never forget that the First Amendment's prohibition against interference with free speech and free press was a direct consequence of centuries of bitter experience living under extremely repressive English laws controlling speech and press. The authority of government was long regarded as supreme, irresistible, and absolute. Any criticism of the government was viewed as dangerous heresy which must be ruthlessly put down. That entire concept was rejected by the First Amendment. Thomas Jefferson's warning that the price of liberty is eternal vigilance is borne out by the unremitting efforts in the Supreme Court, the U.S. Congress, state legislatures, and other agencies to modify, soften, weaken, or redefine the simple principle that "Congress shall make no law . . . abridging the freedom of speech, or of the press."

Scattered throughout the McCoy record are numerous references to past events, such as the trial of Peter Zenger, the martyrdom of Elijah Lovejoy, and the fanaticism of Comstockery, as well as more recent happenings, such as the A. Mitchell Palmer "Red Raids" of the nineteen twenties and Senator Joseph McCarthy's witchhunts of the nineteen fifties. But recent writings on these historical matters have not been simply threshing over old straw. Through sound research and proper historical perspective, they have brought new interpretations and new insights to bear on familiar subjects.

Though we have continued to be preoccupied with the same or similar problems year after year, new issues have risen during the past decade, in response to new pressures, new legislation, and recent legal decisions, especially at the Supreme Court level. It will be the purpose of the present discussion to review and analyse a number of the most vital issues as they have developed during the ten-year period, 1967–77.

PENTAGON PAPERS

Complex issues relating to freedom of the press were raised in 1971 by publication of the Pentagon Papers, a collection of documents, totaling forty-seven volumes, on the "History of U.S. Decision-Making Process on Vietnam Policy." The principal questions at stake were the constitutional ban on prior restraint in publication, national security, and government censorship policies, especially excessive use of "classification" by the federal government to conceal information. The Pentagon Papers had been secretly taken from Defense Department files by a staff member, Daniel Ellsberg, and turned over to the *New York Times*, *Washington Post*, *Boston Globe*, and *St. Louis Post-Dispatch*. The study, which had been commissioned by DOD Secretary Robert McNamara, was a critique of U.S. Indochina policy up to 1968, plus texts of relevant documents. The papers showed that four successive administrations (Truman, Eisenhower, Kennedy, and Johnson) had made major military and political decisions without the knowledge of the Congress and of the American people.

The celebrated Pentagon Papers case opened in June 1971 after publication by the *New York Times* of three installments of the material. The Justice Department filed a civil suit in District Court seeking a permanent injunction against further publication. Judge Murray I. Gurfein issued a temporary restraining order against the newspaper, but four days later denied a permanent injunction, stating that "A cantankerous press, an obstinate press, an ubiquitous press must be suffered by those in authority in order to preserve the even greater values of freedom of expression and the right of the people to know."

The Justice Department refused to accept defeat, basing its arguments on violation of a statute by the *Times* against "unauthorized possession" of government documents, publication of which would cause irreparable injury to defense interests of the United States. The Espionage Act adopted by Congress in 1951, on which the Department rested its case, it was noted by one judge, "provides for criminal penalties, but not prior restraint." The New York Appellate Court ruled that the *Times* could resume publication, though it could not use any material deemed dangerous to national security. On the same day, the Washington Circuit Court ruled seven to two in favor of the *Washington Post*, holding that publication of the documents would not endanger national security.

The next act of the drama occurred at the Supreme Court level, to which both the *Times* and the Justice Department appealed. Newspaper executives in general took the view that the Pentagon Papers dealt with events long past and thus constituted a historical treatise that the public was entitled to read. The information in the documents was not damaging to national security, they held, though it was probably embarrassing to the high officials responsible for making Vietnamese policy. In any event, on June 30, 1971, in a split decision (Justices Burger, Blackmun, and Harlan dissenting), the Supreme Court found in favor of the *Times* and the *Post*, holding that any government attempt to block a news article prior to publication bears "a heavy burden of presumption against its constitutionality." In the Court's opinion, "the government had not met that burden," and so this first attempt to suppress publication of material held dangerous to national security was denied.

Despite the victory achieved in the Supreme Court's Pentagon Papers ruling, civil libertarians were inclined to view it as a flawed decision. They noted that all nine justices filed separate opinions on widely varying grounds. Furthermore, though the press had ultimately been permitted to publish, it had been silenced for fifteen days by the government, during which time the First Amendment guarantees of freedom from government control had been suspended.

CLASSIFIED INFORMATION

The tremendous effort by Federal Government officials to halt publication of the Pentagon Papers for political reasons made clear a fundamental democratic dilemma: how to reconcile demands for suppression of information in the name of national security with democratic beliefs in an open society and the people's right to know, or in other words to determine where to draw the line between the fullest flow of information and publication of material deemed contrary to national security. The legal arguments advanced by the Justice Department in the Pentagon Papers case grew out of an assertion that the President has "inherent" power to decide what information can be released, both military and political. In recent decades, the concept of "executive privilege," which has no constitutional or legal basis, has been frequently invoked by the President in refusing to release information requested by Congress, the press, or other agencies.

As the power of the Chief Executive has expanded, steadily and relentlessly, mountains of "Top-Secret Sensitive," "Top-Secret," and "Secret" documents have piled up, remaining concealed even from the eyes of historians, long after any possible justification for their "classified" status has ceased.

Controversy over the Pentagon Papers affair brought charges of excessive secrecy and improperly concealed information on the part of the executive branch of the government. The Department of Defense conceded that ninety-five percent of the material in the papers had already been published or declassified when the furor began. Nevertheless, administration spokesmen claimed that for the President or his representatives to withhold information was a right intrinsic in the doctrine of separation of powers. Adhering to that principle, efforts by Congress to obtain information on the Laotian campaign were blocked, together with data on the deployment of nuclear weapons abroad and the gross budget of the Central Intelligence Agency. President Nixon also denied a request of Congress to inspect the Defense Department's foreign military assistance plan.

Spearheaded by then Vice-President Spiro Agnew, attacks by the Nixon administration on news media became virulent. Evidence seemed convincing that the executive branch was attempting to intimidate the media, especially television, in order to stifle criticisms of administrative policies. A study by the American Civil Liberties Union characterized the situation as follows: "attacks on the press by officers of government have become so widespread and all pervasive that they constitute a massive federal-level attempt to subvert the letter and the intent of the First Amendment." Among the tactics used was the government's increased use of its subpoena power to force newsmen to turn over news notes and film footage from their files and to name sources of information. A natural consequence was self-censorship by the media, particularly radio and television stations operating under licenses, causing them to avoid discussion of controversial issues.

Somewhat analogous to the Pentagon Papers affair was a subsequent much-publicized case which brought on a confrontation with the House Ethics Committee. CBS television reporter Daniel Schorr had procured a copy of a House Intelligence Committee report and passed it on to a newspaper, the *Village Voice*, for publication. Schorr refused to turn over his copy of the report to the Ethics Committee or to name the person who gave it to him. In a statement to the House Committee, Schorr said: "For a journalist the most crucial kind of confidence is the identity of a source of information. To betray a confidential source would mean to dry up many future sources for many future reporters. The reporter and the news organization would be the immediate loser. I would submit to you that the ultimate losers would be the American people and their free institutions." The House Committee refused to cite Schorr for contempt of Congress, but the incident led to the loss of Schorr's position with CBS.

PRIOR RESTRAINT

The question of prior restraint, a key issue in the Pentagon Papers case, has cropped up in other connections during the past decade.

In 1974, a unique case of censorship arose when a book by

Victor Marchetti and John A. Marks, *The CIA and the Cult of Intelligence* was published with deletions demanded by the Central Intelligence Agency and approved by a federal district court judge. There had been several years of litigation preceding publication. Such prior restraint by government had never been imposed previously in the United States. Marchetti had been an agent of the CIA at one time, and it was claimed that as a condition of employment years before, he had signed an agreement not to reveal any information without the consent of CIA officials. In accordance with the court order, the manuscript was submitted to the agency, which deleted 339 passages. The publisher, Alfred Knopf, and the author prepared to sue for restoration, after which the number of deletions was reduced to 168. In a later court action, it was found that publication would affect national security in only 27 passages. Further legal appeals by the CIA, however, resulted in the book being issued with the full 168 deletions.

The Supreme Court refused to intervene in the Marchetti case, letting stand the lower court's ruling permitting extensive censorship by the CIA. Another dimension was added in 1975 by a second book about the CIA, *Inside the Company*, published in England. This work is subject to seizure on entering the United States.

At about the same time, a proposed revision of the federal criminal code was submitted to Congress containing a provision for press censorship that would have imposed heavy fines and long prison sentences on reporters, editors, and authors who released information considered damaging to national security or to the nation's foreign relations. Fortunately, because of wide protests, it appears that the legislation will not be approved by Congress.

The United States was not alone in practicing prior restraint. Britain's attorney general temporarily blocked publication of a deceased government official's diary, by asserting that its revelations would damage future confidential exchanges between officers of the government. The order was set aside later by a high court. National security was the claimed basis in Israel for banning publication of a book *Confrontation and Disengagement*; the author's manuscript and notes were seized.

PRESS GAG ORDERS

Another type of prior restraint, press gag orders by trial court judges, became an increasingly common practice during the decade. Judges sought to limit information by orders of silence to defense lawyers, prosecutors, and police officials and by restricting access of reporters to the proceedings. Artists for two television networks were forbidden to sketch courtroom scenes either in the courtroom or from memory outside it. Such orders have generally been held unconstitutional on appeal. In one instance, a New Orleans court restricted reporting of a murder trial until after the jury was seated and all editorial comment until the trial was concluded. The order was stayed by Justice Powell of the Supreme Court, who declared that it "imposes significant prior restraint on media publication," and therefore carried "a heavy presumption against its constitutional validity." In several instances, violators of secrecy orders were found guilty of contempt

by judges. A leading writer on censorship, Paul Fisher, Director of the University of Missouri's Freedom of Information Center, commented that "the strict enforcement of these restrictions raised judicial censoring power to heights not known in the last half century." The laudable motive behind the orders, the guarantee of a fair trial, came into direct conflict with guarantees of free speech and free press.

An important victory was won by the press in 1976 when the Supreme Court found a Nebraska court's order suppressing facts concerning a sensational murder case unconstitutional on grounds of prior restraint. The ruling described the order as "the most serious and least tolerable infringement on First Amendment rights," especially "as applied to reporting of criminal proceedings." A five-judge majority of the Court envisioned no situation in which the danger of prejudicial pretrial publicity would justify prior restraint or an injunction against publication of information obtained by the press concerning crimes of accused defendants, even if it was claimed that the facts might threaten the right to trial by an impartial jury. The court went on to hold that in balancing competing constitutional rights, a vague fear that publication of information may be harmful to a defendant's Sixth Amendment rights could not support violation of equally significant First Amendment principles.

FAIR TRIAL *vs.* FREE PRESS

Nevertheless, controversy continued over the rights of individuals as against the rights of the press in dealing with courtroom trials. A prime question is the apparent difference between the First and Sixth Amendments to the U.S. Constitution. The First Amendment states clearly that "Congress shall make no law . . . abridging the freedom of speech, or of the press," while the Sixth Amendment offers various kinds of protection to accused persons in court and to suspects in police custody. The best solution to this complex issue, it is generally agreed, is a strong sense of responsibility on the part of the media. However, as Paul M. Chalfin points out, "If we are to expect the press to exercise proper self-restraint, we also have a right to demand that the law enforcement officers, district attorneys and defense lawyers refrain from trying their cases in the newspapers. This is dictated not only by wise law enforcement and courtroom procedure but also by an adherence to the canons of professional ethics."

PRIVACY

Not necessarily involving criminal charges but somewhat related to the fair trial question is the privacy issue. A growing concern for an individual's right to privacy is shown by references in the McCoy bibliography—a right which sometimes seems to be in conflict with the public's right to know. Enactment of "sunshine laws" has resulted in revelations about public business. Noteworthy are the federal Freedom of Information Act and numerous similar laws in the states involving public records and public meetings. A far more touchy issue, however, is publicity relating to individual citizens.

In a 1967 decision involving *Life* magazine the Supreme Court ruled that a person seeking to collect damages for invasion of privacy must prove that the publicity was false and that it was published with knowledge of its falsity or with a reckless disregard of whether it was false or not. A 1975 decision had broad implications for publishers of newspapers, magazines, and books. In an eight to one decision (Justice Douglas dissenting), the Court ruled that the *Cleveland Plain Dealer* must pay $60,000 to a West Virginia family for invading its privacy because one of its reporters published two articles containing knowingly false statements. In March 1976, in a decision that narrowed the First Amendment shield protecting the news media against libel suits, the Court declared that a prominent Florida socialite could not be considered a "public figure" for the purpose of deciding libel claims against *Time* magazine, the charge being the alleged misquoting of a 1968 divorce decree. Justice Brennan dissented from the opinion in these words: "At stake in the present case is the ability of the press to report to the citizenry the events transpiring in the nation's judicial systems. There is no meaningful or constitutionally adequate way to report such events without reference to those persons and transactions that form the subject matter in controversy."

There is considerable evidence to the effect that the concept of privacy is being used increasingly to deny the public information that traditionally was fully available. Individuals' past records and convictions cannot be revealed without peril. The trend of recent Supreme Court decisions is effectively to narrow the definition of a "public figure," leaving publishers vulnerable to libel suits. The key issue is to find a proper balance between the privacy rights of individuals and the necessity for society to inform and govern itself.

A new agency, the Federal Privacy Protection Study Commission, was established in 1975, chiefly for the purpose of protecting the privacy of U.S. citizens by restricting access to personal information. The Commission has announced plans to recommend legislation dealing with personal data contained in medical records, federal income tax forms, and insurance company files, for example, and every person would be guaranteed the right to see, copy, and correct any files that any organization has concerning him or her.

The most flagrant and unjustifiable invasions of personal privacy, recent investigations reveal, have been the work of two federal agencies, the Central Intelligence Agency and the Federal Bureau of Investigation. Among illegal acts were the opening and photographing of mail, including the correspondence of many prominent Americans, spying on every black student union or group on U.S. college campuses, and efforts to break up so-called hate groups.

Such activities on the part of the CIA and FBI had been sanctioned and encouraged by the White House. The Nixon administration asserted its power to engage in wiretapping and eavesdropping, without prior judicial approval, of persons whom the Attorney General thought were a threat to the nation's domestic security. When the matter reached the Supreme Court, it was ruled that eavesdropping without a warrant is unconstitutional. Justice Powell noted that "The price of lawful public dissent must not be a dread of subjection to an unchecked surveillance power. Nor must the fear of unauthorized official eaves-

dropping deter vigorous citizen dissent and discussion of government action in private conversation. For private dissent, no less than open public discourse, is essential to our society."

RIGHTS OF SPECIAL GROUPS

Increasing concern has been shown during the past decade in the rights of special groups in society: prisoners, military personnel, mental patients, children, students, and teachers. It has been remarked that four public institutions in the United States have traditionally ignored the Bill of Rights—the military, the schools, mental "hospitals," and prisons. First Amendment rights are severely restricted and often prohibited in all four. They deny the right of free trial to persons accused of misconduct, and consider authority more important than freedom, order more precious than liberty, and discipline more valuable than individual expression. Military commanders, school principals, chief psychiatrists, and prison wardens, it is suggested, have similar characteristics in the governance of their respective organizations.

An estimated 1,500,000 Americans are presently confined in penal institutions. During the past few years, four principal issues concerning their rights have emerged in legal actions: 1] the right of a prisoner to have access to materials without prior screening or censorship, including receipt of personal correspondence and reading published literature; 2] the right of a prisoner to publish his own writings without restraint or interference with royalties; 3] the right of a prisoner to correspond with or to be interviewed by the public press; and 4] the right of a prisoner to have access to legal research materials.

A growing number of court decisions have been made clarifying these points. For example, U.S. District Court Judge Walter T. McGovern ruled that prisoners had the right to subscribe to newspapers, periodicals, and books, and specified that reading materials "can be denied an inmate only if such censorship furthers one or more of the substantial governmental interests of security against escape or unauthorized entry, or if the publication is obscene." Another District Court Judge, Wilbur D. Owens, Jr., joined other federal judges in California, Alabama, Florida, and Georgia in upholding the right of prisoners to law library service. If other suitable legal assistance is unavailable, Judge Owens declared, prison officials must make an adequate law library available as an aid in the preparation of prisoners' habeas corpus and civil rights petitions.

Writing in the *New Republic*, Peter Barnes declares that "For three-and-a-half million Americans in uniform, justice is what the brass says it is, damn the Constitution and full speed ahead." The author was commenting on the arrest and sentencing to four years hard labor and dishonorable discharge of two army privates for producing and distributing a mimeographed protest against the Vietnamese war to soldiers at Ford Ord, California.

Underground newspapers have proliferated at army bases during the past several years, especially before the end of the war in Vietnam. Invariably, they were suppressed. Dissent against the war was stamped out by military commanders. GI protestors were punished for leafleting, for distributing underground newspapers, for demonstrating, and for voicing unpopular opinions. According to the Uniform Code of Military Justice, words that are "unbecoming," "provocative," "defamatory," or "reproachful" are crimes. Actually, as a practical matter, the words mean anything the commanding officer wants them to mean. A commentator on one famous case, that of Captain Howard Levy, noted that during the trial the captain's "words were invested with meanings so terrible that the existence of the nation as well as the army seemed to be at stake."

A case before the Supreme Court in 1976 involved an attempt by Benjamin Spock and others to campaign at Fort Dix, New Jersey. In a six-to-two decision, the Court declared that the business of military bases is "to train soldiers, not to provide a public forum" for political debate. The decision cited the American tradition of "a politically neutral military" and drew a sharp distinction between the rights of civilians and those of military personnel, holding that base commanders have broad powers to bar political campaigning on United States installations. Later in the same year, U.S. District Court Judge Barrington D. Parker overturned as unconstitutional a Marine Corps regulation prohibiting the distribution of "political literature" on Marine bases without the approval of commanders, and remarked that "Perhaps encouragement of more freedom of thought would have sparked recognition of unlawful orders in the Vietnam War and prevented atrocities such as the massacre of civilians at My-lai."

Teachers' and students' rights also received judicial review at various levels. A series of articles in the *New Yorker* brought national notice to the case of Charles James, an eleventh-grade English teacher at Addison High School near Elmira, New York. James had been fired by his school board for wearing a black armband symbolizing his opposition to the Vietnam war. A lower court approved the right of a teacher to express political views in the classroom so long as there was no threat of disruption. Because the school board failed to show that his action disrupted classroom activities or interfered with his teaching, the court concluded that the board dismissed James simply because it disagreed with his political views, and ordered his reinstatement. The board appealed to the Supreme Court, which let stand the lower court ruling.

A prominent library educator, Martha Boaz, maintains that "the student has a right to read; he has a right to free access to books. He has a right to a wide variety and an extensive selection of materials. He has a right to examine all ideas, to explore all forms of learning, to investiage all cultures. He has a right to investigate every medium of art and every mode of expression of it. He has a right to search for truth wherever it may be found." Interference with student freedom has most frequently taken the form of censorship of student newspapers. The College Press Service has reported numerous instances of "overt acts of censorship" against campus newspapers, often involving the disciplining of editors and reporters and sometimes suppression of the papers. The principal issues, generally, were the extent to which student editors and reporters can legitimately express controversial views, whether they may use allegedly indecent words, and whether university and college administrators can censor or suppress student publications unacceptable to them. A University of California Special Commission on the Student Press, apparently reflecting the opinion of the American Society of Newspaper Editors, concluded: "It is the Commission's first and basic recommendation that it be accepted and made repeatedly clear to all concerned—regents, administrators, and campus newspaper staffs—that these newspapers are not 'official' organs of the University." Cases that have reached the courts have for the most part ended in rejection of attempts by campus administrators to censor the student press.

OBSCENITY AND PORNOGRAPHY

On June 21, 1973, the Supreme Court issued new obscenity guidelines. Henceforth, it was ruled, "community standards," as opposed to "national standards," would become the measure for determining whethere a work is "prurient." The basic criteria, the Court ruled, must be   *a)* whether "the average person applying contemporary community standards" would find that the work, taken as a whole, appeals to the prurient interest,   *b)* whether the work depicts or describes, in a patently offensive way, sexual conduct specifically defined by the applicable state law, and   *c)* whether the work, taken as a whole, lacks serious literary, artistic, political, or scientific value.

In the wake of the Court's decision, the question immediately arose: what is the "local" community? The state or the city, or county, or neighborhood? The question was not directly answered by the Court. Authors, publishers, and motion picture producers were concerned that "contemporary community standards" would become defined as "local community standards," reducing the range of ideas and expression to the least tolerant segment of the "community." Thus a single county might have the power to censor books for the entire country, since, from an economic point of view, publishers would be inclined to produce only titles acceptable everywhere.

In effect, the Court's new ruling substantively altered previous Supreme Court definitions of what constitutes the obscene and the nature of criminal proceedings against its purveyors. Most significant was the denial of any nationwide standard. "It is neither realistic nor constitutionally sound," declared Chief Justice Burger, "to read the First Amendment as requiring that the people of Maine or Mississippi accept public depiction of conduct found tolerable in Las Vegas or New York City." (Counting states, territories, counties, townships, etc., there are some 20,000 local jurisdictions in the United States.) Justice Burger stated further that in the prosecution of allegedly obscene works the testimony of expert witnesses need not be introduced; the defense may introduce such witnesses, but their testimony may be disregarded.

Justice Rehnquist, who delivered the opinion of the Court in *Miller vs. California*, the case establishing the concept of community standards, commenting on the meaning of "local community standards," held that the Court did not refer to any "precise geographical area." It was the Court's view, he stated, that the First and Fourteenth Amendments do not require uniform national standards and "A juror is entitled to draw on his own knowledge of the view of the average person in the community or vicinage from which he comes for making the required determination for obscenity."

A flood of new state laws and local ordinances followed the Supreme Court's *Miller vs. California* decision. Now that local rather than national standards may determine whether a publication is obscene or not, publishers were discovering how widely standards vary. Thus the movie *Deep Throat*, often a target for censors, plays without interference in some cities while it is banned in others. A notorious case arose in Memphis, Tennessee, where Larry Parrish, an assistant U.S. attorney, won convictions against sixteen defendants and four corporations on charges of conspiring to distribute *Deep Throat*, and sixteen persons (few, if any, of whom had ever been in Memphis) were indicted for conspiring to distribute a movie called *School Girl*. Actors and producers of *The Devil in Miss Jones* were next on the schedule. Serious constitutional questions are raised by the Memphis convictions. It appears that any person who contributes in any way to the production or distribution of a motion picture can be indicted and prosecuted, based on standards in some Bible Belt town. Such prosecutors as Parrish and other officials around the nation would impose on the entire country the standards of their own districts. Richard A. Blake, in an article entitled "Will Fig Leaves Blossom Again?" concluded that "Good state laws and sound judicial procedures might make it [the community standards decision] work; a new wave of suppression and neo-Victorian censorship will bring the debate back to zero."

COMMISSION REPORT

During the Johnson administration, a commission to investigate obscenity and pornography was appointed. The commission's report was not submitted until 1970, during President Richard Nixon's first term. The commission recommended the abolition of obscenity laws that prohibit the distribution of materials to adults who choose to receive them—a proposal in accord with Supreme Court decisions ruling that the First Amendment protects an adult's right to read and see whatever he chooses. The COP report found against all laws banning pornography, citing evidence gathered in the United States and Denmark to the effect that pornography did no discernible harm to man's character; it discovered no proof to the contrary.

President Nixon promptly disavowed the report's "morally bankrupt conclusions and major recommendations . . . American morality is not to be trifled with. The Commission on Pornography and Obscenity has performed a disservice and I totally reject its report." In response, the commission's chairman, William B. Lockhart, Dean of the University of Minnesota School of Law, suggested that President Nixon was unhappy with the report because its "scientific studies do not support the assumptions congenial to his viewpoint." Lockhart pointed out that the commission had been directed by Congress to test assumptions about the harmful effects of sexual materials, and "this we did through extensive scientific studies of many kinds." Since the commission's findings were politically unpopular, the long-range influence of its report has remained uncertain.

TEXTBOOKS

Another highly sensitive area in the field of free expression was textbooks for public schools. Pressures continued to be exerted on textbook publishers, school boards, and school librarians. A much publicized case in 1974 occurred in Kanawha County, West Virginia, where fundamentalists raised loud and demonstrative protests against the school board's adoption of "un-Godly and un-American" textbooks, deemed unfit for their children. At issue was a series of textbooks primarily for high school English literature and language skills—books which included selections from works by Eldridge Cleaver, Malcolm X, Allen Ginsberg, and Gwendolyn Brooks. Dissident parents kept their children out of school for over nine weeks, led boycotts, inspired coal mine strikes, and led a march on the state capital. The protests were marked by bombings and other violence. At the height of the controversy, the Heath textbooks, prime targets of the parents, were removed from classrooms and relegated to libraries, where only children with permission slips from home were allowed to use them. A series of alternative texts was adopted by the Kanawha County Board of Education in July 1975. The antitextbook forces were successful in forcing the removal of more than three hundred books from the schools and the development of new guidelines for the purchase of textbooks. By mid-1975, however, many of the books were returned to the schools, though some principals refused to accept them or placed them in storage.

Fifty years after the famous Scopes antievolution trial in Dayton, Tennessee, a new antievolution law was enacted by the Tennessee legislature. At about the same time, California and Texas passed laws requiring that equal time be given to the Book of Genesis when the theory of evolution was taught in the public schools. On the same day, in August 1975, a federal judge and the Tennessee Supreme Court declared unconstitutional the Tennessee law requiring textbooks to provide equal space to biblical and scientific theories on the creation of the universe. In finding the law unreasonable, U.S. District Court Judge Frank Gray, Jr. noted, "Every religious sect, from the worshipers of Apollo to the followers of Zoroaster, has its belief or theory. It is beyond the comprehension of this court how the legislature, if indeed it did, expected that all such theories should be included in any textbook of reasonable size." In California, when the State Board of Education adopted new science and social science textbooks in 1975, none of the works contained any reference to the biblical theory of the creation of the world.

A major decision affecting school libraries was rendered by the U.S. Court of Appeals for the Sixth Circuit (Kentucky, Michigan, Ohio, and Tennessee) in 1976. The Court ruled that school officials cannot go through a school library and arbitrarily remove and ban books they dislike. The decision elaborated on four principal points concerning what sort of books should be: 1] selected as high school textbooks, 2] purchased for a high school library, 3] removed from a high school library, and 4] forbidden to be taught or assigned in a high school classroom. In a stirring conclusion, the judges declared, "A library is a mighty resource in the free marketplace of ideas. It is specially dedicated to broad dissimination of ideas. It is a forum for silent speech. . . . Here we are concerned with the right of students to receive information which they and their teachers desire them to have."

THE EVIDENCE IS OVERWHELMING that censorship and governmental repression is on the increase throughout the world. A strong new voice speaking out for universal human rights is that of President Jimmy Carter. How much influence his outspoken sentiments will have outside the United States remains to be seen. Indeed, there are indications that President Carter's stand

has led to increased oppression of dissidents in the Soviet Union and other Iron Curtain nations.

The colossal nature of the problem of human freedom and human rights is revealed by reports issued by the Anti-Slavery Society for the Protection of Human Rights, founded in 1834, in Britain. As recently as 1955, the Society estimated that there were 62 million people classifiable as slaves. The United Nations failed to adopt a convention against the practice of slavery until 1956, after years of lobbying by the Anti-Slavery Society. Only 85 of the 147 UN members have ratified the convention.

PREFACE

by Ralph E. McCoy

IN THE DECADE since publication of *Freedom of the Press: An Annotated Bibliography* (1968) there has been an unprecedented volume of publishing in this area, reflecting several factors: an increased awareness of the importance of intellectual freedom in the democratic world, the emergence of new facets of concern, and greater complexities in the mass media. More than half as many publications relating to press freedom in the English-speaking world appeared in the past ten years as in the previous four hundred years. The literature of law and journalism account for a large part of the increase, but general interest publications also gave greater attention to freedom of the press. Watergate and the attacks on the press under the Nixon Administration were the events that brought forth the greatest avalanche of publications in both the general and scholarly press.

Heresy, blasphemy, and sedition, which loomed large in historical literature recorded in the 1968 volume, have almost disappeared in the supplement. They have been replaced by publications showing increased concern with public access to government information; the right of the people to know, sometimes pitted against the individual's right of privacy and the accused's right to a fair trial; and government's role in regulating both the newspaper and electronic press. Obscenity, well represented in the 1968 volume, continued to be a live issue during the past decade both in the United States and Great Britain as greater freedom of expression led to excesses and prompted demands for the revival of censorship. To this controversy has been added a concern over excessive violence in the media, particularly with respect to the effect of television on children. Personal libel, long a problem on both sides of the Atlantic, has taken on new dimensions as the issue has come before the courts and legislative bodies. And zealots, both on the right and the left have continued to advocate censorship to impose their respective social philosophies. The alternative (underground) press and the so-called journalism review which introduced self-criticism of the media, were among the new formats for expressing views on press freedom. Dean Robert B. Downs, in his Foreword to this volume, has analyzed these and other issues dealing with intellectual freedom as they are reflected in the published record of the past ten years.

The present supplement, which includes works published through 1976, follows the pattern and scope of the 1968 volume. It is an annotated bibliography of books, pamphlets, journal articles, dissertations, films, and other materials relating to freedom of the press in the English-speaking world. "Press" is used generically to include all media of mass communications: books, newspapers, and other printed matter; but also motion pictures, recordings, radio and television broadcasting, and, to a limited extent, stage plays. Annotations in the supplement are intended to be descriptive rather than critical and, within the stated scope of the work there has been little attempt at selectivity. Both positive and negative statements on press freedom have been included. Wherever possible the author's own words have been used to summarize the work or to present salient points of view. Background information has been supplied as necessary.

A number of reviewers of the 1968 work pointed out that, because of extensive annotations and additional information supplied by the compiler, the work assumed the character of an encyclopedia in the field of intellectual freedom. Consequently, I have used the term "bibliocyclopedia" in the title to more accurately describe the contents of the present volume. The format of the supplement follows the earlier work. It is arranged alphabetically by personal or corporate author or by title where the author is unknown. Efforts to arrange the work by subject, which might have been more useful, proved impractical because of the multifaceted nature of many of the entries. To facilitate a subject approach to the work, a comprehensive subject index identifies topics, concepts, countries, individuals, court decisions, and titles of censored works. Throughout the text cross-references are made to numbered entries in the 1968 volume, e.g., H240.

In addition to publications issued during the past decade (the bulk of the entries) I have included a number of older items discovered since preparation of the 1968 volume, particularly works in various British libraries located during a sabbatical leave. A number of older and obscure American works were discovered with the acquisition by Southern Illinois University Library of the papers of Theodore Schroeder (1864–1953), pioneer writer on press freedom and author of the 1922 *Free Speech Bibliography*. More than a score of reports of historic libel trials were located in an uncataloged collection in the Library of Congress, with the assistance of James W. Elder of the American-British Law Division.

While I made use of many libraries in the United States and Great Britain, either in person or through interlibrary borrowing, in the preparation of the bibliocyclopedia, my principle sources for new publications were my personal library on freedom of the press which now numbers some 7,000 items, and the libraries of Southern Illinois University, University of Illinois, and the Library of Congress. The publication of the National Union Catalog greatly facilitated the locating of copies of older works.

Several serial publications that attempt to keep abreast of current publishing in the area of press freedom have been useful: *Newsletter on Intellectual Freedom* issued by the Intellectual Freedom Committee of the American Library Association; *FOI Digest* issued by the Freedom of Information Center, School of Journalism, University of Missouri at Columbia; bibliographies in the *Free Speech Yearbook* (Commission on Freedom of Speech of the Speech Communication Association); and the book reviews and lists of journal articles appearing regularly in *Journalism Quarterly.* Also useful have been the accession lists of the Communication Library, University of Illinois, prepared by Eleanor Blum. In addition, I have systematically checked more than seventy indexes and abstracts and examined countless bibliographies that might provide clues to new publications.

I am indebted to many librarians, scholars, booksellers, and readers of the earlier volume who brought to my attention items (old and new) that I might have overlooked. Alan M. Cohn, Humanities Librarian, Southern Illinois University, has been particularly helpful. I have also received assistance from Roger F. Jacobs, Librarian, and Elizabeth S. Kelly, Reader Services Librarian, of the University's Law Library. (Mr. Jacobs has since become Librarian of the U.S. Supreme Court and Ms. Kelly has succeeded him as Librarian of the University Law Library.) Gordon Stein, fellow bibliographer and book collector in the related field of freethought has been generous in his assistance. My secretary, Henrietta Miller, handled most of the voluminous correspondence in searching for materials for both the 1968 volume and the supplement, and Beatrice R. Moore of Southern Illinois University Press edited the manuscript of both works, completing the supplement just before her retirement. I am pleased that Andor Braun, who did such a magnificent job in designing the 1968 volume, has also applied his talents to the supplement. Finally, my wife, Melba E. McCoy, was not only tolerant of my spending long hours on the book but did most of the manuscript typing and assisted with the proofreading. When the 1968 volume appeared, a friend asked her if she had read her husband's bulky book; she replied that she had not only read it but read it aloud.

While I had not intended to continue with the bibliographical project after having spent some ten years on the 1968 volume, I found myself still interested in keeping up with the field and still buying books on freedom of the press for my personal library. I was also encouraged to continue with the work by the favorable reviews of the earlier volume and by numerous letters received from persons who had found the work useful. One of the most gratifying uses has been by scholars in various fields who found in the volume clues for further research in untapped fields, resulting in a number of articles, dissertations, and books which I am pleased to include in the present supplement.

Just now there seems to be a curious publishing lull in the field of intellectual freedom, possibly the result of media and reader exhaustion from the tremendous volume of commentary that grew out of Watergate. But the issue of a free press is eternal and will continue in varying patterns, as its defenders, its reformers, and its detractors exercise their own right to speak and write freely.

Carbondale, Illinois
August 1977

Freedom of the Press

A

AIM Report. Washington, D.C., Accuracy in Media, Inc., 1972–date. Monthly.
1A1
Accuracy in Media is a nonprofit citizens organization which monitors the newspaper and electronic press to detect errors, serious omission of facts, and evidence of bias in news coverage. Each issue of its publication reports on its findings and efforts to restore what it feels is an imbalance in the mass media which favors liberal views. If the media, when informed, fail to take corrective action, AIM publicizes the facts through its own monthly report, through letters to the editor, paid advertisements, or complaints filed with the National News Council or the Federal Communications Commission.

Abbey, Thomas G. "Judicial Restraint of the Press." *Creighton Law Review*, 9:693–716, June 1976. **1A2**
Re: *Nebraska Press Association v. Stuart*, a 1976 case involving a series of restrictive (gag) orders on the news media in the coverage of a murder trial. "The purpose of this comment is not to predict the eventual outcome of the case in the United States Supreme Court [the gag order was found unconstitutional], but to identify interests, principles, and standards which are germane in the confrontation crystallized in the NPA situation."

Abbott, C. Michael. "The Student Press: Some First Impressions." *Wayne Law Review*, 16:1–36, Winter 1969. **1A3**
Questions considered: How far can student editors go in taking the establishment to task and incurring the wrath of the administration, the community, or perhaps the legislature, without fear of administrative or statutory reprisal being foist upon them through some form of authorized censorship? What constitutional equities lie on the side of the administration in dealing with the student-run fourth estate? Is the right of dissent in student publications coterminous with the First and Fourteenth amendments?

————. "The Student Press: Some Second Thoughts." *Wayne Law Review*, 16:989–1004, Summer 1970. **1A4**

In the months since the appearance of the author's article, The Student Press: Some First Impressions, events have occurred which both confirm and discount the impression that the lower courts were moving toward a restrictive reading of the U.S. Supreme Court's opinion in *Tinker v. Des Moines Independent Community School District*, 393 U.S. 503 (1969). "While there is still cause for concern among student publishers, recently decided cases have been especially hard-hitting in their assessment of the strength of the first amendment on campus. The present article reviews some of these new cases and using *Tinker* as a focal point, attempts to demonstrate why some of the reported decisions are inconsistent. It will also be argued that some courts are being unduly restrictive in not considering *Tinker* as a school-related version of the traditional first amendment 'clear and present danger' rule."

Abbott, James W. "Rowan v. United States Post Office Department: Pandering Advertisements and the Mail." *Willamette Law Journal*, 7:330–37, June 1971. **1A5**
An analysis of the U.S. Supreme Court ruling, 397 U.S. 728 (1970), upholding the act of Congress which enables a householder to prevent receipt of obscene advertising and, by extension, to protect his right of privacy from unwanted advertising through the mails.

Abel, Ekkehard. *Der Straf- und Zivilrechtliche Schutz bei Diffamierungen von Personengruppen im Anglo-Amerikanischen, Französischen, und Deutschen Recht.* [Munich, 1965.] 182p. (Inaugural Dissertation, Cologne) **1A6**
Legal defense for group defamation in Anglo-American, French, and German law.

Abelson, David, and Robert Crow. "The Scienter Element in California's Obscenity Laws: Is There a Way To Know?" *Hastings Law Journal*, 24:1303–25, May 1973. **1A7**
"The central contention of this note is that California's legislative and judicial interpretation of the scienter requirement is unconstitu-

tional. Furthermore, it is contended that the only scienter requirement which is constitutionally sound is one that requires the prosecution to prove that the defendant knew or had reason to know the material was *legally obscene*."

Abelson, H., R. Cohen, E. Heaton, and S. Suder. "Public Attitudes Towards and Experience with Erotic Materials: Findings." *Technical Report of the [U.S.] Commission on Obscenity and Pornography*, 6:1–137, 1971. **1A8**
A report of the findings from a nationwide study of adults and young people (1) to determine the extent of public exposure to and experience with erotic material, (2) to assess attitudes toward the desirability of controlling availability of erotic materials and the means for effecting such control, and (3) to examine some of the demographic and attitudinal correlates of experience with erotica as well as other relationships between individual and group characteristics and attitudes and behavior related to erotic materials.

Abraham, Henry J. "Censorship." In *International Encyclopedia of the Social Sciences*. New York, Macmillan, 1968, vol. 2, pp. 356–60. **1A9**
A brief history of censorship from classical antiquity to the present, followed by a critique. The author cites three bases often used to rationalize censorship in the western world: (1) the ideas presented are false and/or dangerous, (2) the people subjected to the ideas are not capable of seeing the "falsity" and would hence be led astray, and (3) the ideas expressed may lead to antisocial action. The last seems to stand on stronger ground and poses a dilemma as to where to draw the line.

————. "Freedom of Expression: A Constant Dilemma." *Social Education*, 23:364–70+, December 1959. **1A10**
The author reviews the historical constitutional position toward freedom of expression and summarizes a few well-known court cases in which the U.S. Supreme Court attempted to define the matter. He concludes that "the clear and present danger" test would appear to be the most workable decision.

———. "The Precious Freedom of Expression." In his *Freedom and the Court*. 2d ed. New York, Oxford University Press, 1972, pp. 144–205.   **1A11**
The author gives examples of "drawing lines" between Constitutional freedoms: press freedom vs. fair trial, free speech vs. freedom from noise, freedom of street corner exhortation vs. subversive activity, and obscenity vs. erotica. He considers such judicial tests as "clear and present danger," "bad tendency," and "preferred freedoms."

Abraham, Louis A. "Defamation as Contempt of Parliament." In Michael Rubinstein, *ed.*, *Wicked, Wicked Libels*, London, Routledge & Kegan Paul, 1972, pp. 146–67.   **1A12**
A history and current status of the use of Parliamentary contempt power to punish those who have published works defamatory to the British Parliament or its members.

Abrahams, Gerald. *The Law for Writers and Journalists*. London, Jenkins, 1958. 224p.   **1A13**
Privacy and publicity, copyright, defamatory words and publication, apologies and amends, varieties of privilege, and the journalist spectator and the courts.

Abrams, Floyd. "Judges and Journalists: Who Decides What?" *Nieman Reports*, 28(4): 34–41, Winter 1974. **1A14**
An attorney discusses cases in which he has defended the press in matters of libel and coverage of trials. "With respect to press coverage of the courts, it seems to me that the press and the entire publishing industry must be unremitting in telling the courts that they alone decide what is fit to print, and that prior restraints on what they decide to print about the courts are as improper as prior restraints about anything else."

Abse, Leo. "Emancipation Not Suppression: Pornography under Labour." *Spectator*, 7605:385–86, 30 March 1975.   **1A15**
A Labour Member of Parliament denounces recent efforts to enact antipornography laws as self-indulgent and futile. Libertarians in the Labour movement look with scepticism on efforts to legislate puritan morals. Another point of view is taken in an accompanying article by David Holbrook.

"The Abuses of Literacy." *Times Literary Supplement*, 3,645:12, 7 January 1972.   **1A16**
In this introduction to a series of seven articles on pornography, the editor remarks on the false importance of the subject in relation to other issues in society. He notes the confusion that exists in understanding and interpreting the law on obscenity, especially among psychologists in assessing the possible harm or value of the genre. He also notes the relationship of pornography to radical political movements and to the right of privacy. The following articles in the series are entered in this bibliography under author: (1) The Law and Its Application by Cecil R. Hewitt ⌜C. H. Rolph, *pseud.*⌟, (2) H. M. G.'s Secret Pornographer by Sefton Delmer, (3) Obscenity in Religion by Wendy O'Flaherty, (4) The Politics of Subversion and Rage by Masud R. Kahn, (5) The Porn Market by Norman Shrapnel, (6) The Death of Censorship by Peter Fryer, and (7) The Right to Be Left Alone by Alan Ryan.

Access. Washington, D.C., National Citizens Committee for Broadcasting. 1975–date. Biweekly.   **1A17**
An organ for the citizens media reform movement. "The citizens movement is the community video people, the full-time activists in station negotiation and federal regulation, the cable television people, listener-supported broadcasting, journalism reviews and underground newspapers, public interest law and advertising firms, and —most importantly— those mass-media organizations whose views have so far been underrepresented in media. . . . Throughout the various rallying cries of citizens involved in the media—'community control,' 'public access,' 'open media and open regulatory process'—there runs a common theme. . . . An emphasis on participation, a meaningful citizen input, runs throughout the 'movement'?" Taken from an editorial in a "model issue." The Committee's first periodic newsletter, *Media Watch*, was issued in March 1976.

"An Accommodation of Privacy Interests and First Amendment Rights in Public Disclosure Cases." *University of Pennsylvania Law Review*, 124:1385–417, June 1976.   **1A18**
"This Comment will address the broader question left open in Cox ⌜Cox Broadcasting Corp. v. Cohn, 420 U.S. 469 (1975)⌟; that is, the general accommodation of the individual's right under state law to be protected from public disclosure of private facts and the press' right under the first amendment to publish or broadcast truthful information. These two sets of conflicting interests will be analyzed, and their crucial components extracted and placed in the framework of a new test designed to afford maximum protection to both sets of interests."

The Accused. 16 mm. b/w movie, 25 min. Cincinnati, Distributed by Citizens for Decent Literature, 1958. **1A19**
Dramatizes the action of two members of a parent and teacher association to clean the newsstands of indecent literature. Stars Loretta Young.

Ace, Goodman. "The Dirty Five-Letter Word." *Saturday Review*, 53:10, 24 January 1970.   **1A20**
Columbia Broadcasting System censors cut PEACE out of a talk show.

———. "The Most Unkindest Cut of All." *Saturday Review*, 54(26):4, 26 June 1971.   **1A21**
Anecdotes of censorship of comedy lines in the golden days of radio.

Acharya, G. N. "A New Birth of Freedom." *Mainstream*, 8:51–53, Annual number, 1969.   **1A22**
"All talk of Freedom of the Press is unreal, as newspaper ownership rights are governed by the same, old, musty outmoded laws, principles and modes of thought, that apply to other species of property. There can be no property rights over the minds of men and women. The Press is Unfree because of these property laws. It can be made free only by freeing it from the power of property and profit."

"Achieving a Workable Definition of Free Speech: A Symposium on the Nature and Scope of the Constitutional Guarantee of Freedom of Expression." *Journal of Urban Law*, 47:395–521, 1969–70.   **1A23**
Selected essays written by students in a constitutional law seminar at the University of Detroit: The Reality of a Fair Trial by Thomas Law and Joseph Kramer, Freedom of Speech and the Communist Conspiracy: A Search for First Amendment Standards by Laurence Campbell and Vera Massey Jones. Black Militancy: A Clear and Present Danger? by Gerald D. Ducharme and John A. O'Leary, The Dissenter and Government Employment by David T. Coyle, and Obscenity by Susan Borman and William Rush.

Ackerman, Margaret B. "Arguments Against Censorship: Milton and Mill." *Arizona English Bulletin*, 11:23–27, February 1969.   **1A24**
A comparison of the arguments against censorship, given in two classic documents on freedom of expression—John Milton's *Areopagitica* and John Stuart Mill's *Of the Liberty of Thought and Discussion*.

"An Act to Protect Confidential Sources of News Media." *Harvard Journal on Legislation*, 6:341–45, March 1969.   **1A25**
Text and commentary on a proposed law providing that employees of news-gathering media cannot be compelled to disclose the source of news or information unless disclosure is essential to the public interest. "The proposed bill is based upon a recognition that in appropriate circumstances the public benefits more from protecting the journalist-informant relationship than it is injured by the impediments such privileges may cause to the administration of justice."

Adamo, S. J. "Let Freedom Zing." *America*, 127:346–47, 28 October 1972. **1A26**
An attack on the Nixon Administration's "bureaucratic bullying" of the press, noting the irony that "93 percent of the committed newspapers support an Administration which, wittingly or not, aims at enslaving them."

———. "Strange Coincidence: Concerning Editorial Freedom in the Catholic Press." *America*, 116:322–23, 4 March 1967. **1A27**
A brief article defending the priest-editor's right to editorial freedom, and criticism of the censorship of Father Herbert McCabe for an editorial in *New Blackfriers* charging corruption in the Church.

Adams, Charles J. "A Checklist of the Dissident Press." *RQ* (Reference Services Division of the American Library Association), 6:54–61, Winter 1966. **1A28**
Many reputable writers who espouse unpopular views are unable to get their work published in standard publications and must resort to dissident journals that are not indexed and not generally available in public libraries. The author cites some notable examples of curtailment of articles and provides a selected list of dissident periodicals not included in existing indexes.

———. "Is Your Generation Gap Showing?" *Focus on Indiana Libraries*, 22:56–57, June 1968. **1A29**
Introduction by the guest editor to a special issue dealing with censorship in Indiana libraries. "The thrust of this entire *Focus* issue assumes that Indiana libraries value our First Amendment Freedoms and that they want to live up to our professional ideals."

Adams, Charles J., and Clayton Shepherd. "Censorship or Selection? in Hoosier Libraries." *Focus on Indiana Libraries*, 22:58–66, June 1968. **1A30**
A report on results from a questionnaire study of flexibility and rigidity in book selection practices in Indiana public libraries. On the basis of findings the authors suggest the need for more training programs in book selection, adherance to minimum standards of education for librarians, encouragement of larger units of service, and research in various methods to upgrade book selection practices, particularly in libraries serving small towns and rural areas.

Adams, James W. "Newspaper Immunity in Reporting Judicial Proceedings." *Cleveland-Marshall Law Review*, 17:271–82, May 1968. **1A31**
The author recommends a modification of the Ohio law which would provide a temporary delay in a newspaper's informing the public. "This harm can be offset by the improved accuracy and quality possible in a report published at the conclusion of the proceedings where the entire record, including the result, is available for evaluation."

Adams, John B. *State Open Meetings Laws: An Overview*. Columbia, Mo., Freedom of Information Foundation, 1974. 31p. (Freedom of Information Foundation Series, no. 3) **1A32**
This paper looks at state laws on open meetings and the principles involved. The author identifies eleven desirable characteristics of a state open-meetings law and examines such laws of forty-seven states, giving points for each favorable characteristic represented. He concludes that "very few states, by law at least, go beyond minimal provisions for openness and three have no laws at all."

Adams, Michael. *Censorship: The Irish Experience*. University, Ala., University of Alabama Press, 1968. 265p. **1A33**
A chronicle of the Irish experience since the Censorship of Publications Bill was enacted in 1928. The study "recalls the original reasons for the introduction of a system which many people even in the 1920's saw as a sinister attempt to mould the mind of a young nation; it examines the application of the law over the years, avoiding wider constitutional and philosophical questions which might be asked and skirting literary and moral aspects with which I am not competent to deal; and in particular it indicates the extra-legal, social influences which have in various ways modified the behavior of the censors. It deals with the more influential side of formal censorship, making no more than passing reference to the censorship of films; and is only a partial contribution to the more general subject of Irish grundyism."

Adams, Roy. "The Press in a Black Robe." *Chicago-Kent Law Review*, 45:170–82, Fall-Winter 1968/69. (Reprinted in Donald G. Douglas, and Philip Noble, eds., *Justice on Trial*, pp. 198–208) **1A34**
"This article has devoted considerable space to demonstrate that the press is unwilling to curb its appetite for news in the interests of criminal defendants. The bar's record of self-imposed standards for the protection of an accused criminal is as ignoble as that of the press. There will be no remedy without penalties for misconduct."

Adams, Samuel Hopkins. "Bibliocide." In his *Incredible Era; the Life and Times of Warren Gamaliel Harding*. Boston, Houghton Mifflin, 1939, pp. 273–82. **1A35**
The story of the controversial book, *Warren Gamaliel Harding, President of the United States. A Review of Facts Collected from Anthropological, Historical, and Political Researches* by William Estabrook Chancellor, former professor at Wooster College, which purported to show that President Harding was part Negro. The book appeared early in 1922 and vanished. "The Government snuffed it out of existence."

———. "The Patent Medicine Conspiracy against the Freedom of the Press." In his *The Great American Fraud*. New York, Collier, 1906, pp. 123–46. (Reprinted from *Collier's Weekly*, 5 November 1905) **1A36**
How patent medicine advertisers enter into a "contract of silence" with the nation's newspaper publishers, to suppress the reporting of anything detrimental to the interests of the industry. This work, exposing fraudulent quack medicines, created a tremendous stir and contributed to the enactment of the Food and Drug Act of 1906.

Adams, Wilsie H., Jr. "Freedom of Information Act and Pretrial Discovery." *Military Law Review*, 43:1–35, January 1969. **1A37**
"This article discusses the 1966 amendment to 5 U.S.C. 1002, allowing greater access to government agency records, and authorizing federal courts to enjoin agencies with unreasonable withholding such records. . . . The author concludes that the new Act can be a useful discovery tool, provided that the 'exemptions' are not interpreted so as to continue the denial of needed information; and he suggests that a new all-encompassing discovery statute be enacted independent of any larger act."

Addison, Alexander. *Liberty of Speech, and of the Press. A Charge to the Grand Juries of the County Courts of the Fifth Circuit of the State of Pennsylvania*. [Boston, 1799.] Folio broadside, printed on both sides. **1A38**
This defense of the Sedition Act is published as a New Year's extra to the *Columbian Sentinel*. "It is impressed on a separate sheet, that it may be preserved with care, or carried in the pocket, to be produced whenever the necessity of convicting slander against the Government shall occur." Pupils who memorize the statement, the text reads, "shall be entitled to a Gold Medal from the Editor of the *Columbian Sentinel*." Same text as A32.

[———.] *The Trial of Alexander Addison, Esq., president of the Court of Common-Pleas . . . on an impeachment, by the House of Representatives, before the Senate of the Commonwealth of Pennsylvania, To which Is Affixed the Certificates Offered by Mr. Addison in His Defence, But by the Senate Refused a Reading. taken in short-hand by Thomas Lloyd*. 2d ed., with additions. Lancaster, Pa., Printed by William

Hamilton, 1803. 123p., 154p., 24p.
1A39
A defender of the Alien and Sedition Acts, Judge Addison was impeached and removed from the bench on charges of slander in court.

Addison, Roger G. "Can Offensive Language Be Punished in Oklahoma?" *Oklahoma Law Review*, 29:395–409, Spring 1976. **1A40**
"This note will discuss the impact of *Conchito* [*Conchito v. City of Tulsa*, 521 P.2d 1384 (1974)] and recent United States Supreme Court decisions on prior Oklahoma cases and currently applicable statutes. Examination will focus essentially upon court use of the 'fighting words' test and upon the doctrines of vagueness and Constitutional overbreadth as applied to statutes dealing with offensive language. This examination will tend to show that the applicable Oklahoma statutes are in need of reappraisal either by the legislature or by the court."

Adelson, Alan M. "The Barriers Fall: As Censorship Relaxes, Debate Grows on Impact of New Permissiveness; Effect of Erotica on Human Behavior Studied." *Wall Street Journal*, 173(48):1, 15, 10 March 1969. **1A41**
A federal court's approval of the import of the Swedish film, *I Am Curious (Yellow)*, prompts the author to review the trend toward relaxing the barriers against explicit sex in the mass media, and the debate, pro and con, over the effect of pornography on people's lives.

———. "The Subpoena Siege: Have the News Media Become Too Big To Fight?" *Saturday Review*, 53(11):106–8, 14 March 1970. **1A42**
Television networks and stations, newspapers and news magazines were besieged with subpoenas to turn over to grand juries in several states the raw material on their reporting about the Black Panthers and the SDS Weathermen. For some months the media neglected to defend the right to privacy with their sources and cooperated, until they realized the widespread implication to freedom of the press.

Adler, Mark S. "National Security Information under the Amended Freedom of Information Act: Historical Perspectives and Analysis." *Hofstra Law Review*, 4:759–804, Spring 1976. **1A43**
"Part I reviews the basis for governmental withholding of national security information prior to the Freedom of Information Act; part II examines the impact of the 1966 Act on the executive's privilege in this area; and part III discusses the 1974 amendments to the Act."

"Administrator's Forum: This Month's Problem: [Censorship]." *School Management*, various issues in 1967–69. **1A44**
Student editor of school newspaper suspended for editorial criticizing school, September 1967; censorship of Molière's *Tartuffe* production for high school students, April 1968; parents say teacher uses "obscene" books, November 1969; student editor charges unfair censorship, December 1969.

Agee, Warren K. "Is the Public Commission Idea Still Relevant Today?" *Bulletin of the American Society of Newspaper Editors*, 523:1, 8–10, October 1968. **1A45**

The dean of the William Allen White School of Journalism, University of Kansas, looks at the pros and cons of press councils.

———, ed. *The Press and the Public Interest*. Washington, D.C., Public Affairs, 1968. 220p. **1A46**
"The role of a free, responsible, and agressive press in making democracy work is the theme of these William Allen White lectures, which have been delivered annually [University of Kansas] by eighteen of America's leading reporters, editors, and publishers." The issues of secrecy, credibility gaps, managed news, and social responsibility of the press are either expressly stated or implicit in a number of the lectures.

Agnew, Spiro. "Another Challenge to the Television Industry." *TV Guide*, 18(20):6–10, 16 May 1970. **1A47**
Criticism of the television industry by the vice-president for overemphasizing controversy and participating in contrived action, with harmful social consequences.

———. [*Boston Speech.*] Boston, Middlesex Club, 1971. 10p. Processed news release. **1A48**
Vice-President Agnew continues his attacks on the nation's news media, disclaiming any intention of intimidation. He singles out for special criticism the Columbia Broadcasting System's documentaries—The Selling of the Pentagon, Hunger in America, and Project Nassau.

———. [*"The Des Moines Speech."*] In Michael C. Emery and Ted C. Smythe, *Readings in Mass Communications*, Dubuque, Iowa, Brown, 1972, pp. 309–18. **1A49**
In a speech written by Patrick J. Buchanan and approved by President Nixon, the vice-president launched an attack on the news media, particularly the television networks, for lack of objectivity in reporting the news of the Nixon Administration. The media considered the attack as demagoguery and an implied threat of censorship, as evidenced by the accompanying article, False Premises, Wrong Conclusions (pp. 319–23), and by interviews

with ABC's Howard K. Smith and CBS's Eric Sevareid (pp. 324–35).

———. [*"The Montgomery Speech."*] In Michael C. Emery and Ted C. Smythe, *Readings in Mass Communications*, Dubuque, Iowa, Brown, 1972 pp. 347–53. **1A50**
In a talk delivered before the Montgomery, Ala., Chamber of Commerce on 20 November 1969 Vice-President Agnew continued his attacks on the press, with particularly scathing remarks about the *New York Times* and the *Washington Post*. He accuses the press of overreacting to his Des Moines speech and disclaims any attempt to stifle dissent.

"Agnew Reviews His Views on News." *Broadcasting*, 80:25–26, 7 June 1971. **1A51**
"The Vice-President chides media as paranoid; goes on to hit Vietnam-related coverage as slanted."

Agoos, Lawrence D. *The Court's Use of the Contempt Power, Thereby Judicially Interpreting the First Amendment's Protective Clause, Its Status in Relation to the Other Constitutional Rights, and Its Relation to Protective State Statutes . . . As They Relate to the Denial of a News Source Privilege to Newsmen*. Athens, Ga., University of Georgia, 1973. 104p. (Unpublished Master's thesis) **1A52**

Aikin, Charles. "Freedom, Liberty, and Privacy in Modern Society: Speech, Press, Radio, Television, Religion and Their Brush with the Censor." In *Legal Thought in the United States of America under Contemporary Pressures. Report from the United States of America*. Brussels, Belgium, American Association for the Comparative Study of Law, 1970, pp. 563–81. **1A53**
A general discussion of freedom as established by the First Amendment and interpreted by the courts, including references to the cases of *Near v. Minnesota*, 283 U.S. 697 (1931), and *New York Times v. Sullivan*, 376 U.S. 254, 261 (1964), with a note that the task of defining obscenity remains confused.

Aims of Industry, Ltd., London. *BAN. The Attack on Press Freedom*. London, The Council, 1974. 5p. **1A54**
The pamphlet complains of the refusal by certain metropolitan press to accept advertising on the theme of the danger of communist influence in the British trade unions.

———. *Evidence for the Royal Commission on the Press* [London, Aims of Industry, Ltd., 1974?] 20p. **1A55**
"In our evidence we would like to look at two of

the factors which we believe threaten the future and the freedom of the Press. The first relates to an aspect of censorship which is, we feel, too often overlooked—that is, the way people working in the Press have been exercising censorship increasingly on the content of advertisements, comments, news and cartoons. This, we believe, has reached a stage where there is a threat to freedom of expression in the media because of pressures by the unions. The second concerns the very survival of the Press. Here we are concerned with what we see as the single most important factor—the industry's restrictive practices and overmanning and its inability to adopt the technical changes which could undoubtedly save it." The report calls on management and unions to cooperate in attacking the industry's basic economic problems.

Ainsworth, Robert A., Jr. "Fair Trial—Free Press." *Federal Rules Decisions*, 45:417–26, 1968. **1A56**
In an address before the Eighth Circuit Judicial Conference, Judge Ainsworth reviews the status of the fair trial–free press controversy, beginning with the recommendation of the Warren Commission "that representatives of the bar, law enforcement associations, and the news media work together to establish ethical standards concerning the collection and presentation of information to the public so that there will be no interference with pending criminal investigations, court proceedings, or the right of individuals to a fair trial," the report of the Reardon Committee which resulted in part from the Warren Commission's recommendation, and the several court decisions that resulted from prejudicial publicity. He calls on the federal judiciary to take leadership in the dialogue necessary to "establish an equitable position between the important but frequently conflicting rights to fair trial and free press."

———. "Fair Trial and Free Press." *Louisiana Bar Journal*, 15:7–13, June 1967. **1A57**
By constant seeking of remedies for the conflict between the basic rights under the First and Sixth Amendments, fair trial and free press can be a reality and the dispute which has arisen can subside.

Aitchison, Bill. "The Right to Receive and the Commercial Speech Doctrine: New Constitutional Considerations." *Georgetown Law Journal*, 63:775–803, February 1975. **1A58**
Re: *Virginia Citizens Consumer Council, Inc. v. State Board of Pharmacy*, 373 F. Supp. 683 (E.D. Va. 1974), challenging a Virginia statute prohibiting prescription drug price advertising. The court rejected the commercial speech argument and held the statute unconstitutionally violative of the right to receive. The author sees the use of this right as a tool for consumers to obtain information needed to make intelligent buying decisions.

Aitken, Jonathan. *Officially Secret.*
London, Weidenfeld and Nicholson, 1971. 236p. **1A59**
The author, one of the defendants in The Fleet Street Secrets Case, gives a full account of the affair which ended in his acquittal and a recommendation by the judge that section 2 of the Official Secrets Act of 1911 under which Aitken was tried "be pensioned off" in the interest of free speech. Part one of the book traces the development of the Official Secrets Act "up to the moment when the Attorney-General decided to instigate prosecutions over the publication of the Scott Report. Part two is the detailed account of my own case from its beginnings through to the final verdict and historic judgment by Mr. Justice Caulfield at the Old Bailey. Part three is a brief plea for the kind of legislative amendments which are necessary if Parliament is now to enact a meaningful reform of the Official Secrets Act."

Akamatsu, Muriel. *Electronic Coverage: Public Meetings*. Columbia, Mo., Freedom of Information Center, School of Journalism, University of Missouri at Columbia, 1972. 4p. (Report no. 279) **1A60**
"The issue of electronic coverage is far from settled despite gains in the area by broadcast journalists during the past two decades. Although there is better than a 50–50 chance of electronic access, the fate of the coverage lies in the hands of minor local and state officials who decide on a case by case basis."

———. *Looking Out for the Consumer*. Columbia, Mo., Freedom of Information Center, School of Journalism, University of Missouri at Columbia, 1972. 6p. (Report no. 285) **1A61**
"Consumer information of both a specific and general nature proliferates at the federal and state levels of government. However, largely ineffective distribution of this information allows only a small portion to be utilized by consumers."

———. *The Metamorphosis of the FTC*. Columbia, Mo., Freedom of Information Center, School of Journalism, University of Missouri at Columbia, 1971. 7p. (Report no. 263) **1A62**
The report deals with increased activities of the Federal Trade Commission in the curtailment of deceptive advertising practices.

———. *Presidents v. Press: F. D. R. to Nixon*. Columbia, Mo., Freedom of Information Center, School of Journalism, University of Missouri at Columbia, 1971. 7p. (Report no. 271) **1A63**
"The press today is saying that press freedom has sunken to an all-time low as the Nixon Administration continues its all-out attack aimed at discrediting the media through criticism, subpoenas and general harassment. This paper attempts to shed light on the problem by examining past instances in which the press

and the executive branch clashed, causing the same cries from the media that are being heard today."

[Alarcon, Arthur L.] "Gag Rules and a Free Press." *Review of Southern California Journalism*, 15:4–5, 1975. **1A64**
An interview with a Los Angeles Superior Court judge on the topic of restraining orders, conducted by Richard De Atley.

Albert, Jeffrey B. "Court May Permit Withholding of Information Not Exempted from Disclosure under Freedom of Information Act." *Harvard Civil Rights-Civil Liberties Law Review*, 5:121–33, January 1970. **1A65**
The effect of the holding in *Consumers Union of United States, Inc. v. Veterans Administration*, 301 F. Supp. 796 (S.D. N.Y., 1969), is "to shift discretionary authority to withhold information under FOIA from the administrative agency to the judiciary."

Alchin, Gordon. *Manual of Law for the Cinema Trade*. London, Pitman, 1934. 508p. **1A66**
Copyright, censorship, defamation, and licensing covering the fields of British cinema and sound recording. Tables of legal cases, offenses, and statutes and orders.

Alcott, Muriel. *Missouri's Access Law*. Columbia, Mo., Freedom of Information Center, School of Journalism, University of Missouri at Columbia, 1974. 7p. (Report no. 326) **1A67**
Missouri's access law is too recent to evaluate fully, whether it has opened doors and records or closed them more securely. "The law has generated a certain amount of confusion or connivance, with a measure of non-compliance, as illustrated in the activity taking place since the law's enforcement date, Sept. 28, 1973."

Alderman, Jeffrey D. "The Army Way: News Management at Fort Hood." *Columbia Journalism Review*, 7(4):22–24, Winter 1968/69. **1A68**
How the army suppresses news unfavorable to the service in its camp newspapers. The author suggests the use of the Freedom of Information Act as a means of forcing information the public has a right to know about the army.

Aldred, Guy A. ["Birth Control Agitation."] In *No Traitor's Gait! The Life and Times of Guy A. Aldred*. Glasgow, Strickland Press, 1963, pp. 439–42, 446–48, 450–56. **1A69**
An account of the arrest of the author and his

wife for the sale of Margaret Sanger's birth control pamphlet, *Family Limitations*.

―――. *The Devil's Chaplain; the Story of the Rev. Robert Taylor, M.A., M.R.C.S. (1784–1834)*. Glasgow, Strickland Press, 1942. 33p. (Revised from articles in the *Freethinker*, July–September 1923)   **1A70**
A brief biographical sketch of the freethought lecturer, twice jailed for blasphemy. In 1828 he was sentenced to a year in prison for a blasphemous sermon; in 1831 he was given a two-year sentence for publishing an allegedly blasphemous address in behalf of striking agricultural laborers.

―――. *Letters to the Editor*. Glasgow, Strickland Press, 1940. 59p. ("The Word" Library, no. 4)   **1A71**
A collection of "essays on revolt" written by this leading British anarchist over a period of thirty-five years (1904–39). Many deal with freedom of speech and the press.

[―――.] "Seized by Whom?" *Herald of Revolt*, 1(1):1–2, 5 October 1907.   **1A72**
The first issue of this anarchist paper is devoted entirely to reporting on the seizure from the print shop of the copy and forms of type for this first issue. The issue reprints only the title of articles that were to have been published in the eight-page paper.

―――, ed. *It Might Have Happened to You!* Glasgow, Strickland Press, December 1943. 39p. (*The Word* Special Investigation Report)   **1A73**
A series of notes and editorial comments gathered by J. Wynn and edited by Guy A. Aldred during the year 1942, describing the arrest and jailing without trial under wartime regulation 18B (1939) for danger to national security. The offenses generally involved possessing or distributing Fascist literature critical of Britain's war effort. Aldred, a leading British anarchist, had defended the internal Fascists on principle even though he himself was an avowed enemy of fascism.

Aldrich, Bailey. *Libel Handbook*. Boston, Massachusetts Newspaper Information Committee, 1950. 19p.   **1A74**
A simple guide for the use of newspapermen.

Aleinikoff, Eugene N. "Privacy in Broadcasting." *Indiana Law Journal*, 42:373–84, Spring 1967. (Reprinted in David G. Clark and Earl R. Hutchison, eds., *Mass Media and the Law*, pp. 210–23)   **1A75**
"As privacy has become less private and broadcasting more broad, it is not surprising that

privacy suits have finally begun to rival defamation suits against broadcasters in the state and federal courts across the country." The author discusses a number of significant cases and the legal bases on which they were resolved.

Alexander, David T. "Michigan 'Freedom of Information Act.'" *Prospectus*, 3:441–49, May 1970.   **1A76**
A description and analysis of the public inspection provisions of the Michigan Administrative Procedures Act.

Alfange, Dean, Jr. *The Role of the Supreme Court in the Protection of Freedom of Expression in the United States*. Ithaca, N.Y., Cornell University, 1967. 442p. (Ph.D. dissertation, University Microfilms, no. 67–8751)   **1A77**
A discussion of the doctrine of constitutional absolutism versus the doctrine of self-restraint as applied to First Amendment guarantees of freedom of expression. The first doctrine, espoused by Justice Black, dominated the Court in the 1940s; the second, associated with Justice Frankfurter, was applied notably in the years following World War I. A third doctrine, "balancing of interests" when properly practiced, the author believes, "would appear to be a sound technique for adjudication of First Amendment disputes because it permits judges to decide on the basis, not of abstract doctrine, but of the relative magnitudes in each particular case of the actual abridgment of expression and of the public interest underlying the abridgment."

Alisky, Marvin. "What Is Past May Be Prologue After All." *Journal of Broadcasting*, 1:131–38, Spring 1957. (Reprinted in John M. Kittross and Kenneth Harwood, eds., *Free and Fair*, pp. 171–78)   **1A78**
Discussion of the hazards of libel in giving background information to elucidate current controversial news. The main question is whether the past events are germane.

Alison, David. "Censorship—By Coincidence." In his *Searchlight: An Exposé of New York City Schools*. New York, Teachers Center, 1951, pp. 115–29.   **1A79**
Incidents of book banning in school libraries, particularly in the New York public school system.

Alkazin, John. "Defamation of a Public Official—After *Times v. Sullivan*." *University of San Francisco Law Review*, 1:356–68, April 1967. (Reprinted in David G. Clark and Earl R. Hutchison, eds., *Mass Media and the Law*, pp. 236–48)   **1A80**
"It is the purpose of this comment to examine how these [Supreme Court] decisions have af-

fected the law of defamation, to indicate the inadequacy of the rule enunciated in the *New York Times* [New York Times v. Sullivan, (1964)] and subsequent cases, and to discuss the effect of the decision on California law." He concludes that the "California courts seem inclined to extend the 'comment' privilege to include good-faith misstatements of fact about a person who is a 'public figure,' on a matter which is of public interest."

Allain, Alex P. "The First and Fourteenth Amendments As They Support Libraries, Librarians, Library Systems and Library Developments." *Illinois Libraries*, 56:3–14, January 1974. (Also published as a separate twenty-page reprint by the Illinois State Library)   **1A81**
On the occasion of the U.S. Supreme Court's 21 June 1973 obscenity decisions, the president of the Freedom to Read Foundation discusses the implication of these decisions on libraries and librarians. He presents "some of the practical and legal reasons why legislation drawn or amended by the states must include some careful reasoning as to the state action. This paper is addressed primarily to the state of Illinois, but the practical and legal reasoning is applicable to all states." Subjects concerned: Constitutional reasons why adults should have unrestricted freedom to read, why libraries must be excluded under any law involving the First Amendment rights to read, legal reasons why standards must be statewide and the law must preempt local ordinances, and why presumption of knowledge is unconstitutional.

―――. "Public Library Governing Bodies and Intellectual Freedom." *Library Trends*, 19:47–63, July 1970.   **1A82**
"It should be clear to all governing bodies of all public libraries, including those commissioned to govern the state libraries, that censorship is abhorrent in a free society." The author argues that obscenity, one of the chief issues in public library censorship, defies definition and there is no positive evidence that antisocial behavior results from its use. "In the face of such negative evidence the only plausible explanation for any attempt to impose restrictions on reading is the desire of the would-be censors to impose their own religious morality upon others." Library governing boards must recognize that "every adult has the right to read any printed matter . . . and that any attempts to prevent his doing so have been banned by the Supreme Court." Boards should oppose unlawful censorship by government officials and pressure for censorship from nongovernment individuals and groups. They should back their librarians in resisting such attempts and should not expect librarians to act as censors. They have no right to do so for adults and they are in no position to fulfill this function for minors. "Parents are the only persons who should properly say what their children can or cannot read." For those who fear for young adults or children he suggests: "Freedom may be the greatest safety for our young people, for it may be better for young people to be prepared by

books to meet the evil they will undoubtedly encounter sooner or later."

———, and Ervin J. Gaines. "Trustee and Censorship." In Virginia G. Young, *ed.*, *Library Trustee, A Practical Guidebook*. New York, Bowker, 1969, pp. 149–54. **1A83**
"Once the trustees have chosen a librarian and stated the book selection policy to be followed, they must be prepared to follow through and accept their share of the abuse, which may be heaped upon the hapless librarian. They must make it clear, both to the librarian and to the public that books selected by the librarian are considered to have been selected by the board." The text of the Library Bill of Rights is given on pages, 179–80, the Freedom to Read statement on pages 181–86.

Allen, Carla W. "Access to Public Documents in Kentucky." *Kentucky Law Journal*, 64:165–79, 1975–76. **1A84**

Allen, Donald L. "Coverage Problems in Libel, Slander, and Assault and Battery Cases." *American Bar Association, Section of Insurance, Negligence and Constitutional Law. Proceedings*, 1968:531–44, 1968. **1A85**
A discussion of liability insurance coverage for assault, battery, libel, and slander.

Allen, Jane, and Derek Guthrie. "Rockford Censorship." *New Art Examiner*, 2(8):1, 15, May 1975. **1A86**
"A number of recent incidents across the country . . . vividly demonstrate that artists still have to fight for the right to show their work without fear of censorship." An account of the censorship of artist Steve Dudek's nude painting in the Rockford (Ill.) Burpee Museum.

Allen, Richard B. "Validity of Restrictive Order of Prior Restraint Pending for Decision by the Supreme Court." *American Bar Association Journal*, 62:770–72, June 1976. **1A87**
Re: *Nebraska Press Association v. Stuart*, 1976, written before the U.S. Supreme Court had rendered a decision.

Allentuck, Barry N. *The Equal Time Provision of Section 315 of the Communications Act of 1934: An Analysis of the Official Policies of the NAB, the FCC, and the Political Parties*. Washington, D.C., American University, 1968. 111p. (Unpublished Master's thesis) **1A88**
Includes a prediction of the future of Section 315 and a proposal to amend it.

Alley, Geoffrey T. "[Censorship] Trends Abroad: New Zealand." *Library Trends*, 19:131–38, July 1970. **1A89**

"Censorship of books, periodicals, films, and other means of communication has always been, even in a disguised or minor form, a factor in the life of New Zealand society." While librarians have fought censorship, public officials who favor "dismantling all the seemingly preposterous apparatus of censorship" are still in a minority. A liberalizing of restrictions has been achieved through the Indecent Publications Act of 1963 which established a tribunal to judge whether or not a work is obscene. The tribunal has performed ably and well so that only those works "utterly without merit" could expect to be rejected. It is doubtful, however, that New Zealand will follow Denmark in scrapping all censorship of books.

Allison, Antony F., and D. M. Rogers. *A Catalogue of Catholic Books in English Printed Abroad or Secretly in England, 1558–1640*. Bognor Regis, England, Arundel, 1956; London, Dawson, 1964 (reprint). 187p. (Biographical Studies, vol. 3, nos. 3 and 4, 1956) **1A90**
Brief reference in introduction to the circumstances of the secret printing.

[Allison, George, and William G. Shepherd.] *Penal Servitude for Politics*. London, International Labour Defence, [1931?]. 18p. **1A91**
Text of speeches for the defense in *Rex v. George Allison and William George Shepherd*, accused of encouraging and inciting mutiny, based on a pamphlet which was never published. The accused charge the government with using an agent provocateur. They were found guilty and sentenced to three years and one year and eight months respectively. Tom Mann, in a preface, writes of his own conviction and imprisonment in 1912.

Allsop, Kenneth. "Iniquity?" *Encounter*, 29(1):62, 64–66, July 1967. **1A92**
Commentary on Pamela Hansford Johnson's book, *On Iniquity*.

[Almon, John?] *A Letter to J. Kidgell, Containing A full Answer to his Narrative*. London, J. Williams, 1763. 21p. (Reproduced in facsimile in Adrian Hamilton, *The Infamous Essay on Woman*, pp. 138–54) **1A93**
The author (probably John Almon) accuses the Reverend Mr. Kidgell of issuing his pamphlet (K96) attacking John Wilkes's *An Essay on Woman* (W263) in order to profit on obscenity, witness his signing each copy to be sure the bookseller doesn't cheat and take advantage of his clerical status. The author also criticizes Kidgell for dealing with stolen literary property, doubly despicable because of his status as a clergyman. It would have been enough to let the law take its course, but the Kidgell pamphlet was an act of defamation. "If a man, a *clergyman*, under the veil of religion, may publish with impunity, the contents of a book

which is deemed *obscene* and *blasphemous*; and may likewise go so far as to make extracts from it; if he may, by the strongest insinuation, impute the crime of it to a gentleman, *before* he is convicted of any thing relative to it; if he may by this means forestall the law, and attempt to bias the minds of a jury; if he may hang out to the public what was never intended for the public eye; if a man's servant may be bribed, to clandestinely take away from his master, papers to be made use of against him, *then* farewell Religion, Liberty, and Law."

[Almon, John.] *A Letter To the Right Honourable George Grenville, occasioned By his Publication of the Speech he made in the House of Commons on the Motion for expelling Mr. Wilkes, Friday, February 3, 1769. To which is added, A Letter on the Public Conduct of Mr. Wilkes, First Published November 1, 1768. With an Appendix*. London, Isaac Fell, 1769. 130p. **1A94**
A defense of John Wilkes and answer to the charges made against him by Grenville (G287). While Grenville had opposed expulsion of Wilkes from Parliament on practical grounds, he attacked him for publication of obscene and seditious works and favored the use of the General Warrant in his arrest. The *Letter on the Public Conduct of Mr. Wilkes* (W264) is believed to have been written by Wilkes himself, although attributed to A Friend. It complains of the ill-treatment by the House of Commons, but predicts that Wilkes will outlive his youthful dissipations and achieve greatness, a prediction realized.

Alpert, Hollis. "The Movies' New Sex-and-Violence Ratings." In David G. Clark and Earl R. Hutchison, *eds.*, *Mass Media and the Law*, New York, Wiley-Interscience, 1970, pp. 59–64. (Reprinted from *Woman's Day*, January 1969) **1A95**
The article "details the lastest effort to deal with movies that have content of dubious value to certain age groups. The new classification system, although it differs from previous attempts, is significant because it is clearly a form of extralegal prior restraint."

Alpert, Robert. "*Lloyd Corp. v. Tanner*: Handbilling Within a Shopping Mall Not Directed at a Store Is Not Protected by the First Amendment Unless No Adequate Alternative Location Exists." *New York University Review of Law & Social Change*, 3:70–82, Winter 1973. **1A96**
Re: *Lloyd Corp. v. Tanner*, 407 U.S. 551 (1972).

Alsbrooks, John H., Jr. "State Abridgement of Newsmen's Right of Access to News of Government Held Unconstitutional." *Cumberland-Samford Law Review*, 5:124–29, Spring 1974. **1A97**

Re: *Lewis v. Baxley*, 368 F. Supp. 768 (M.D. Ala. 1973), in which the Court ruled unconstitutional an Alabama law requiring newsmen to disclose their financial interests to a state ethics commission in order to be admitted to the legislature's public press gallery.

Alschuler, Martha. "Origins of the Law of Obscenity." *Technical Report of the [U.S.] Commission on Obscenity and Pornography*, 2:65–81, 1971. **1A98**

"This paper traces the development of laws regulating obscene publications in England and the United States. It treats obscenity and related offenses up until approximately the 1870's, by which time obscenity offenses had become well rooted in the laws of both countries."

———. "Theoretical Approach to 'Morals' Legislation." *Technical Report of the [U.S.] Commission on Obscenity and Pornography*, 2:82–89, 1971. **1A99**

The study provides perspective on the philosophical debate regarding whether or not the state should attempt to legislate private morals.

Alt, James D. "The Right to Record and Broadcast Public Legislative Proceedings." *University of Chicago Law Review*, 42:336–61, Winter 1975. **1A100**

"This comment suggests that the first amendment protects not only the right of the press to attend public legislative proceedings, but also its right to record and broadcast them."

Altick, Richard D. "The Destructive Elements" and "Shades of Mrs. Grundy." In his *The Scholar Adventurers*. New York, Macmillan, 1950, pp. 211–48. **1A101**

How the ravages of fire, vermin, damp, war, pilferage, and neglect have destroyed forever precious pieces of English literature is related in the chapter on Destructive Elements. In the Shades of Mrs. Grundy, the author relates instances of "bowdlerism" of literature by family, friends, and later editors.

Altman, Dennis. "How I Fought the Censors and (Partly) Won." *Meanjin Quarterly*, 29:236–39, Winter 1970. **1A102**

An account of the Australian trial of two books—Sanford Friedman's *Totempole* and Gore Vidal's *Myra Breckinridge*—that had been seized by the Customs Department. The former was cleared; the latter ban upheld. The authors charges that "censorship in Australia has strong political implications and this has increased as the use of obscenity as a political weapon has increased."

Alward, Jennifer. "Memoirs of a Censor." *Take One*, 4(10):14–16, 30 June 1975. **1A103**

A censor for Columbia Broadcasting System attempts to clarify some of the misconceptions people have about television censors, particularly with regard to films. Outside influences include advertisers, affiliates, writers, producers, directors, organized pressure groups, Nielsen ratings, the Federal Communications Commission, Congress, and critics. While advertisers have some influence, the local affiliates that buy the programs exert the greatest influence, usually of a conservative nature.

Amberg, Richard H. *Energy and Courage*. Carbondale, Ill., Southern Illinois University, 1963. 14p. **1A104**

In this Elijah Parish Lovejoy Lecture, the publisher of the St. Louis *Globe-Democrat* calls for newspaper editors to show energy and courage as exemplified by Lovejoy: Energy, to counteract government management of the news, and courage to editorialize against graft, corruption, and indifference in the community.

Ament, William S. "Bowdler and the Whale." *American Literature*, 4:39–46, March 1932. **1A105**

An account of the bowdlerizing of the British edition of *Moby-Dick*, in which some thirty-five passages were omitted for reasons of profanity, impropriety, or blasphemy.

Amerasinghe, A. R. B. *Defamation in the Law of South Africa and Ceylon*. Colombo, Ceylon, H. W. Cave [1969]. 595p. **1A106**

Content: Nature and interpretation of a defamatory statement, publication, reference to the plaintiff, *animus injuriandi*, damages.

American Association of School Librarians. *Policies and Procedures for Selection of Instructional Materials*. Chicago, AASL, 1970. 4p. **1A107**

This statement includes criteria for selecting materials for the school library media center, a procedure for handling challenged materials, the School Library Bill of Rights, and a sample statement of Policies for Selection of Instructional Materials, prepared by the North Carolina Department of Public Instruction.

———. *School Library Bill of Rights for School Library Media Center Programs*. Chicago, AASL, 1969. 1p. (Also in *Newsletter on Intellectual Freedom* [IFC-ALA], March 1972 and in American Library Association, *Intellectual Freedom Manual*, pt. 2, pp. 20–26) **1A108**

An extension of the American Library Association's Library Bill of Rights, applied to school libraries. This revision of a 1955 statement was adopted by the Board of Directors of the American Association of School Librarians in 1969.

American Bar Association. Committee on Cooperation of the Press and the Bar. *Report*. [Buffalo, N.Y.?], The Association, 1927. 11p. **1A109**

The report, presented at the Association's meeting, Buffalo, 30 August 1927, dealt with the "effect of newspaper publicity on the courts and matters pending therein."

American Bar Association. Legal Advisory Committee on Fair Trial and Free Press. *Fair Trial / Free Press: Voluntary Agreements*. Chicago, The Association, 1974. 61p. **1A110**

"A handbook of information about agreements entered into voluntarily by the bar and news media to strengthen constitutional safeguards in the administration of criminal justice."

———. *The Rights of Fair Trial and Free Press. An Information Manual for the Bar, News Media, Law Enforcement Officials and Courts*. Chicago, The Association, 1969. 34p., 28p. **1A111**

"The manual is intended to: (1) Acquaint all concerned with the intent and limitations of the ABA standards [of fair trial and free press]; (2) Clarify for lawyers, law enforcement officers and news media representatives the types of information which should be released promptly and also those types which the courts have held to be potentially prejudicial; (3) Assist bar-media committees in their joint consideration of voluntary codes of fair practice."

American Bar Association. Special Committee on Televising and Broadcasting Legislative and Judicial Proceedings. "Report [of the Special Committee]," *American Bar Association Annual Report*, 77:607–11, 1952. **1A112**

The Committee, headed by John W. Davis, recommended that the American Bar Association condemn the practice of televising or broadcasting the testimony of witnesses when called before investigating committees of Congress and take appropriate action to restrict or prevent it. The Association adopted the recommendation.

American Bar Association. Special Committee to Appraise Canon 35. *Brief in Support of Canon 35, of the Canons of Judicial Ethics, Prohibiting the Photographing, Broadcasting or Televising of Trial Court Proceedings*. Chicago, The Association, 1957. 20p. Processed. **1A113**

"Model brief prepared by Wayland B. Cedarquist of the Chicago Bar for the Committee on Public Relations of the American Bar Association. It is to be distributed to state and local bar associations for use in proceedings concerning Judicial Canon 35."

American Bar Foundation. Special Committee on Canons of Ethics. *Report and Recommendation on a Restatement of Canon 35 of the Canons of Judicial Ethics.* Chicago, The Foundation, 1957. 20p.
1A114

The Committee, chaired by Philbrick McCoy, reviewed the original canon as amended, examined cases and the literature on broadcasting, telecasting, and taking of motion pictures of court proceedings. It recommended the retention of the prohibitions in Canon 35 but with an emphasis on proper conduct of court proceedings rather than on "improper publicizing of court proceedings." Much of the report deals with counteracting the arguments of the media for abolition of the restrictions.

American Civil Liberties Union. *Beat the Kramer Sedition Bill! . . .* New York, ACLU, 1935. 8p.
1A115
A call for political action to defeat H. R. 6427 which would "prohibit statements and publications advocating overthrow of the Government by violence, and for other purposes."

———. *Constitutional Rights in War Time.* New York, National Civil Liberties Bureau, 1917. 8p.
1A116
How and to what extent the wartime Espionage Act places limits upon free speech and press.

———. *Old-Fashioned Free Speech.* New York, ACLU, n.d. 8p.
1A117
Quotations from Thomas Jefferson, Woodrow Wilson, William Allen White, Alfred E. Smith, and other famous Americans.

———. *What Do You Mean— "Free Speech"?* New York, ACLU, 1924. 7p.
1A118
The position of the ACLU in matters of free speech and a free press and how supporters of the principles can take effective action.

———. *Your Right to Government Information; How to Use the FOIA.* New York, ACLU, 1973. 22p.
1A119
What the Freedom of Information Act includes, what it exempts, how to request data, and how to appeal a denial of information.

———. Board of Directors. "Fair Trial and Free Press." *Law in Transition Quarterly,* 4:44–51, March 1967.
1A120
"No problem within the scope of its interest has proved more difficult for the American Civil Liberties Union than that raised by the publicizing of pending criminal trials. On the one hand, the Union has steadfastly held as its core principle the inviolability of first amendment freedoms, including freedom of the newspapers and electronic media to report all matters which they hold to be newsworthy. On the other, we have consistently urged throughout our history ever more rigorous standards of due process in criminal proceedings, including methods of insuring impartial judges and juries." This introduces the statement of the Board of Directors of the ACLU, December 1966. The statement lists arguments for not restricting information relating to trials and arguments in favor of news limitations. It concludes that "specific changes in our laws are necessary to preserve the historic right to a free trial without unduly limiting public discussion and public understanding of the machinery of justice." Six standards are suggested to apply to the release of information to news media from the time a person is arrested or is charged with a criminal offense until the proceedings have been terminated by trial or otherwise. Sanctions are proposed to be directed initially against law enforcement officers and prosecution and defense attorneys responsible for presenting a case to the press instead of to the court. "We feel at this time that it would be a mistake to enact sanctions directly against the press. We urge the press, the bar, the bench, and all law enforcement agencies to cooperate in working out effective measures as guarantees that neither of the great institutions of our society—the free press and the fair trial—will be sacrificed to the other."

American Civil Liberties Union *et al.* "Coalition Statement on COP Report." In *Newsletter on Intellectual Freedom* (IFC-ALA), 20:57, 74, May 1971.
1A121
Thirty-one organizations and individuals representing publishers, writers, teachers, churches, librarians, and leaders in public health, without endorsing the report of the United States Commission on Obscenity and Pornography, "commend it for serious study and debate by legislators, courts, community leaders, and the general public."

American Enterprise Institute for Policy Research. *Bills to Protect Newsmen from Compulsary Disclosures.* Washington, D.C., The Institute, 1971. 34p. (Legislative Analysis no. 11)
1A122
The analysis gives such background information as a brief legislative history of newsmen's privilege, subpoena of broadcast networks, state and federal laws and case decisions, and Justice Department Guidelines. The report describes pending legislation, summarizes arguments for and against a federal newsmen's privilege law, and offers a Model Newsmen's Privilege Statute.

———. *Newsmen's Privilege Legislation.* Washington, D.C., The Institute, 1973. 82p. (Legislative Analysis no. 8)
1A123
Content: Background, current status, and basic principles of newsmen's privilege; arguments for and against shield laws and whether they should apply to the states; pending legislation; and scope of privilege. Includes text of the Department of Justice Guidelines for Subpoenas to the News Media and the Newsman's Privilege Act of 1973 (S. 1128).

American Federation of Labor and Congress of Industrial Organizations. *The Threat to Press Freedom.* Washington, D.C., AFL-CIO, 1973. Broadside. (Sixth in a series, The Case for Impeachment of Richard M. Nixon)
1A124
"Richard M. Nixon has committed an impeachable offense by interfering with the constitutionally guaranteed freedom of the press by means of wiretaps, FBI investigations and threats of punitive action." There follow specific statements from officials in the Nixon Administration in support of the Union's contention.

American Historical Association and the Organization of American Historians. *Final Report of the Joint AHA-OAH Ad Hoc Committee to Investigate the Charges Against the Franklin D. Roosevelt Library and Related Matters.* Washington, D.C., Bloomington, Ind., AHA-OAH, 1970. 448p.
1A125
The report of an investigation of charges made by an historian that he had been improperly denied access to materials in the Franklin D. Roosevelt Library, a dispute lasting several years that severely jolted the historical and archival professions. A statement of rebuttal (93p.) was made by the complainant, Francis L. Loewenheim; replies were also made by James B. Rhoads, Archivist of the United States (10p.) and Herman Kahn, Yale archivist (9p). The report is reviewed by Richard Polenberg, *American Archivist,* July 1971. An article, The Long-Range Implications for Historians and Archivist of the Charges Against the Franklin D. Roosevelt Library, by Herman Kahn, also appears in the July 1971 issue.

American Institute for Political Communication. *The Credibility Problem.* Washington, D.C., The Institute, 1972. 85p.
1A126
"A report based on an in-depth study of the relationship between the Nixon Administration and the mass media with particular emphasis on the Administration's approach to informational policy-making and on the attitudes of government officials, the Washington press corps, daily newspaper editors and broadcast news executives." Recommendations in the study call for the creation of "a public corporation with both arbitration and ombudsman-like characteristics to mediate differences between government and media organizations and to serve as a forum whereby legitimate complaints relating to the dissemination of public affairs information can be aired."

———. *The Effects of Local Media Monopoly on the Mass Mind.* Washington, D.C., The Institute, 1971. 42p. **1A127**
A study of public attitudes, behavior, and knowledge of current events carried out in York, Pa. and Zanesville, Ohio, in 1970 reveals that a community served by a media monopoly is substantially less knowledgable about current events than where there are competing media.

———. *"Liberal Bias" as a Factor in Network Television News Reporting.* Washington, D.C., The Institute, 1972. 56p. **1A128**
A special report based on the monitoring of the three major television network evening news shows during the 1972 primary election campaign period. The survey found that the networks were pro-McGovern in the primaries and anti-Nixon on the war, but that "the great bulk of the reporting on the news shows was straight-forward and objective."

American Jewish Congress. Commission on Law and Social Action. *Censorship and Obscenity.* 62 min. tape recording. Berkeley, Calif., Pacifica Tape Library, 1962. **1A129**
Participants: Writer Mark Schorer, Father Eugene J. Boyle, and Coleman Blease, attorney for the American Civil Liberties Union. Attorney Lawrence Goldberg is moderator.

American Judicature Society. *News Media and the Administration of Justice.* Chicago, The Society, 1968. 13p. Processed. (Report no. 4) **1A130**
An annotated bibliography. Includes texts of American Bar Association Canons of Professional Ethics 20 and 35; the Colorado Judicial Canon 35, and the Fair Trial—Free Press Standards for Lawyers (Reardon Committee).

American Library Association. . . . *Brief Amicus Curiae of American Library Association [in the case of] Williams and Wilkins Company, Plaintiff, vs. United States, Defendant.* Chicago, ALA, 1972. 46p. (U.S. Court of Claims, Dockett no. 73-68) **1A131**
A defense of "fair use" of copyrighted material by libraries as conforming to the Constitutional clause empowering Congress "to promote the Progress of Science and the Useful Arts." Amicus curiae briefs were also filed by the National Education Association of the United States, and by a group of fifteen universities and professional societies.

———. . . . *Motion of the American Library Association to File an Amicus Curiae Brief in Support of Petition for Rehearing, With Brief Annexed. Murray Kaplan, Petitioner, vs. People of the State of California, Respondent. In the Supreme Court of the United States, October Term, 1971, No, 71-1422.* Chicago, ALA, 1973. 40p. **1A132**
The U.S. Supreme Court obscenity decisions of 21 June 1973 "permit the imposition of censorship functions on libraries and librarians which would fundamentally change their traditional role in support of intellectual freedom and would fundamentally alter the nature and content of their collections and the dissemination of such collections to the people." Among the problems left unsolved by the Court are: How does the Librarian determine whether a work of sexual content is to be used by the patron for permissable scientific purposes or impermissable recreational purposes? Must every work having sexual content be reviewed to determine whether it has serious literary, artistic, political, or scientific value? When a library serves more than one community with varying obscenity laws, what contemporary standards are to be applied? Three arguments are set forth in the brief: (1) The First Amendment is not limited to protecting works which, "taken as a whole, have serious literary, artistic, political or scientific value." (2) The Right to Read is a fundamental right which may be exercised in libraries as well as in the home. (3) To subject a distributor of books or other media to criminal prosecution before the work has been judicially determined obscene is a denial of due process of law and constitutes cruel and unusual punishment. The rehearing of the cases was denied by the Court.

———. "Proceedings and Findings Pertaining to a Request for Action Submitted by Mrs. Joan Bodger Under the Program of Action in Support of the Library Bill of Rights." *American Libraries*, 1:694–704, July–August 1970. **1A133**
A fact-finding subcommittee reports on its investigation and conclusions in the case of Mrs. Joan Bodger's departure from the staff of the Missouri State Library in a controversy which began over the distribution of an underground newspaper, *Free Press Underground*, on the University of Missouri campus, Columbia, Mo.

———. *Statement . . . Submitted to Subcommittee on Criminal Laws and Procedures, Senate Committee on the Judiciary, re: Criminal Code Revision (S. 1 and S. 1400), June 8, 1973.* Washington, D.C., ALA, 1973. 10p. Processed. **1A134**
Opposition to sections of the bill revising the criminal code, which relate to dissemination of so-called "obscene" materials and disclosure of classified information. "Section 1124 would simply give the legislative imprimateur to classification pursuant to Executive Order, and would even extend such classification beyond the limits of 18 U.S.C. 798. . . . The Associa-tion urges Congress to review the matter of classified information in order to give the people 'the power that knowledge gives.' "

American Library Association. Council. "Expurgation of Library Materials." In ALA's *Intellectual Freedom Manual*, pt. 1, pp. 23–24. **1A135**
On 2 February 1973 the ALA Council adopted a resolution interpreting expurgation of library materials as a violation of the Library Bill of Rights.

———. "Free Access to Libraries for Minors." *Newsletter on Intellectual Freedom* (IFC-ALA), 21:125–38. (Also in ALA's *Intellectual Freedom Manual*, pt. 1, pp. 14–17) **1A136**
An interpretation of the Association's Library Bill of Rights applied to minors. "All limitations on minors' access to library materials and services violate Article 5 of the 'Library Bill of Rights' which states, 'The rights of an individual to the use of a library should not be denied or abridged because of his age.' The American Library Association holds that it is the parent—and only the parent—who may restrict his children—and only *his* children—from access to library materials and services. The parent who would rather his child not have access to certain materials should so advise the child." Adopted by the ALA Council, 30 June 1972.

———. *Intellectual Freedom Statement; An Interpretation of the Library Bill of Rights.* Chicago, ALA, 1971. 4p. (Also in ALA's *Intellectual Freedom Manual*, pt. 1, pp. 46–50) **1A137**
A broad statement of the Association on intellectual freedom, designed "to meet challenges to unrestricted library service foreseen arising in the 1970s." Reflecting the growing militancy in the Association, the statement calls for legal means to challenge censorship and to protect librarians from "the threat of personal, economic, and legal reprisals resulting from our support and defense of the principle of intellectual freedom." Adopted by the ALA Council, 25 June 1971; endorsed by the Board of Trustees, Freedom to Read Foundation, 18 June 1971.

———. "Policy on Confidentiality of Library Records." In ALA's *Intellectual Freedom Manual*, pt. 2, pp. 27–31. **1A138**
The resolution urged all libraries to make circulation records confidential as a matter of policy and to make them available to government agencies only upon receipt of court order. The statement was adopted by the ALA Council, 20 January 1971; amended 4 July 1975.

———. "Policy on Sanctions." *Newsletter on Intellectual Freedom* (IFC-ALA), 19:71, September 1970. **1A139**

The American Library Association adopted on 3 July 1970 a policy on applying sanctions against violators of the Library Bill of Rights. In June 1971, the ALA council approved a Program of Action for Mediation, Arbitration, and Inquiry which outlines procedures for such action.

————. "Reevaluating Library Collections." In ALA's *Intellectual Freedom Manual*, pt. 1, pp. 30–31. **1A140**
This brief statement interprets the Library Bill of Rights to the effect that the continual reevaluation of library collections to ensure that they fulfill and remain responsive to the goals of the institution and the needs of library patrons should not be used "as a convenient means to remove materials thought to be too controversial or disapproved of by segments of the community." Adopted by the ALA Council, 3 February 1973.

————. "Resolution Concerning the Ownership of the Records of Public Officials." *Newsletter on Intellectual Freedom* (IFC-ALA), 24:153–54, September 1975. **1A141**
On 4 July 1975 the ALA Council adopted this resolution endorsing the principle "that records and documents produced by or on behalf of all federal officials in pursuit of the public business are and ought to be, by law, public property, and urges the Public Documents Commission to recommend legislation to this effect." A position paper accompanies the resolution.

————. "Resolution on Challenged Materials." *Newsletter on Intellectual Freedom* (IFC-ALA), 20:101, September 1971. (Also in ALA's *Intellectual Freedom Manual*, pt. 1, pp. 39–41) **1A142**
On 25 June 1971 the ALA Council adopted the statement which provided that "no challenged library material should be removed from any library under any legal or extra-legal pressure, save after an independent determination by a judicial officer in a court of competent jurisdiction and only after an adversary hearing, in accordance with well-established principles of law."

————. "Resolution on Governmental Intimidation." *Newsletter on Intellectual Freedom* (IFC-ALA), 22:1, March 1973. (Also in ALA's *Intellectual Freedom Manual*, pt. 2, pp. 32–36) **1A143**
The resolution, adopted by the ALA Council, 2 February 1973, was in response to the threat of government use of informers, electronic surveillance, grand juries, and indictments under the Conspiracy Act of 1968, to intimidate anti-Vietnam war activists.

————. "Restricted Access to Library Materials." In ALA's *Intellectual Freedom Manual*, pt. 1, pp. 42–45. **1A144**
Restricting access to certain titles and certain classes of library materials frequently violates the spirit of the Library Bill of Rights because it achieves *de facto* suppression and denies the rights of an individual to the use of a library because of his age. This interpretation of the Library Bill of Rights was adopted by the ALA Council, 2 February 1973.

————. "Sexism, Racism, and Other 'Isms' in Library Materials, an Interpretation of the Library Bill of Rights." *American Libraries*, 4:227–28, April 1973. (Also in ALA's *Intellectual Freedom Manual*, pt. 1, pp. 25–29) **1A145**
Removal of library materials that might convey a derogatory or false image of a minority, even though the librarian may feel a strong personal commitment to counteract injustices, is "in conflict with the professional responsibility of librarians to guard against encroachments upon intellectual freedom." This interpretation of the Library Bill of Rights was adopted by the ALA Council, 2 February 1973.

————. "Statement on Labeling; An Interpretation of the Library Bill of Rights." *Newsletter on Intellectual Freedom* (IFC-ALA), 21:50–51, March 1972. (Also in ALA's *Intellectual Freedom Manual*, pt. 1, pp. 18–22) **1A146**
On 13 July 1951 the ALA Council adopted a resolution to the effect that labeling of books by point of view was an act of censorship and should not be undertaken by any library. The statement was revised on 25 June 1971 to make it apply to a broader range of labeling problems including "harmful matter."

American Library Association. Intellectual Freedom Committee. "Proceedings of the Prototype Workshop, April 15–17, 1973, Chicago." *Newsletter on Intellectual Freedom* (IFC-ALA), 22:74–83, July 1973. **1A147**
The workshop considered two problems—applying the principles of intellectual freedom to library service, and planning local workshops and programs dealing with the issues. The opening remarks by Richard L. Darling, chairman of the Intellectual Freedom Committee, are included, followed by reports of group discussions on materials selection, handling complaints, public relations, and censorship.

American Library Association. Office for Intellectual Freedom. "How Libraries Can Resist Censorship." *Newsletter on Intellectual Freedom* (IFC-ALA), 21:49–50, March 1972. (Also in ALA's *Intellectual Freedom Manual*, pt. 1, pp. 32–38) **1A148**
Revision of a 1962 statement on what steps to take to avoid censorship and to resist it should it come about. The six principles and procedures recommended are supported by the National Education Association, the American Civil Liberties Union, and the National Council of Teachers of English. The revised statement

was adopted by the Council of the American Library Association, 28 January 1972.

————. *Intellectual Freedom Manual*. Chicago, ALA, 1974. Looseleaf. Six parts, various paging. **1A149**
"This manual is designed to answer the many practical questions that confront librarians in applying principles of intellectual freedom to library service." Introduction: ALA and Intellectual Freedom—A Historical Overview. Part 1: Library Bill of Rights and Its Interpretations (free access to minors; expurgation of library material; sexism, racism, and other -isms in library materials; reevaluating library collections; how libraries can resist censorship; resolution on challenged materials; and restricted access to library materials). Interpretative statements also appear in issues of *American Libraries* and the *Newsletter on Intellectual Freedom* (IFC-ALA) at the time of their adoption by the ALA Council. Part 2: Freedom to Read, School Library Bill of Rights, Policy on Confidentiality of Library Records, and Resolution on Government Intimidation. Part 3: A group of articles on application of intellectual freedom in various types of libraries. Part 4: What to Do Before the Censor Comes. Part 5: Intellectual Freedom and the Law. Part 6: Assistance from ALA.

————. *OIF-ALA Memorandum*. Chicago, The Association, 1970–date. Monthly. **1A150**
A newsletter to chairmen of state Intellectual Freedom Committees.

————. "Position Statement Regarding Proposition 18." *California Librarian*, 33:237–41, October 1972. **1A151**
An analysis of the proposed change in the California penal code relating to obscenity, changes which the Intellectual Freedom Committee believes would endanger freedom of expression and destroy the effectiveness of libraries in remaining as forums of open inquiry.

————. "State Obscenity Laws Compiled April 1976." In *OIF-ALA Memorandum*, May 1976. Seven-page addendum. **1A152**

————. "What to Do Before the Censor Comes—And After." *Newsletter on Intellectual Freedom* (IFC-ALA), 21:49–56, March 1972. **1A153**
Content: How Libraries Can Resist Censorship (revision of a 1962 statement), Library Bill of Rights, School Library Bill of Rights, Statement on Labeling, Resolution on Challenged Materials, and What the American Library Association Can Do For You to Help Combat Censorship. The last item includes a statement of the work of the Intellectual Free-

---

dom Committee, the Office of Intellectual Freedom, the Freedom to Read Foundation, and the Program of Action for Mediation, Arbitration and Inquiry, approved by the ALA Council, 25 June 1971.

American Newspaper Publishers Association Foundation. *Speaking of a Free Press: A Collection of Notable Quotations about Newspapers and a Free Press.* New York, The Foundation, 1970. 24p.
1A154

"The emphasis here is on quotes which have met the test of time and on those contemporary quotes which seem particularly apt and insightful."

American Society of Newspaper Editors. "Code of Ethics or Canons of Journalism." *Editor & Publisher*, 109(11):13, 15 March 1975.
1A155
A revision of the 1923 Code covering topics of responsibility, freedom of the press, independence, truth and accuracy, and impartiality and fair play. The new section on freedom of the press (Article II) reads: "Freedom of the press is a vital right of the people in a free society. It must be defended against infringement or assault, from any source, public and private. Journalists must be constantly alert to see that the public's business is conducted in public, and must oppose those who would use the press as a servant of government or any special interest." Comment on the new Code by Mark Ethridge, Jr., appears in the February 1975 issue of the *Bulletin of the American Society of Newspaper Editors*.

"America's News Industry: Responsible or Reckless?" *U.S. News & World Report*, 76(17):32–36, 29 April 1974.
1A156
An assessment of the widespread criticism of the nation's press in the wake of Watergate, including the questions of credibility, the rise of aggressive investigative reporting, the advent of advocacy journalism, and the pressures for right of access in newspaper and broadcast journalism.

America's Town Meetings of the Air. *What Should Be the Limits on Your Free Speech?* New York, Town Hall, 1949. 23p. (Bulletin vol. 15, no. 6)
1A157
Speakers: Norman Thomas, Bartley Crum, G. Bromley Oxnam, and Louis Waldman. Moderator: George V. Denny, Jr. The discussion revolved around the issue of "clear and present danger" and to what extent speakers, under the law of libel, should be held responsible for abuse of speech.

Amerman, John E. "Activities of State Attorney-General in Initiating Public-

ity Concerning Offense With Which an Accused Was Charged Did Not Necessarily Preclude Fair Trial." *Notre Dame Lawyer*, 42:976–83, Symposium 1967.
1A158

Re: *State v. Woodington*, 31 Wis. 2d 151, 142 N.W.2d 810.

Ames, William. *Stage-plays Arraigned and Condemned; by that eminent foreign theologist, namely William Ames, Doctor and Professor of Divinity of Francker in Friesland; in a solution by him given to this following question, Quest. What is to be thought of stage-plays?* London, A. Baldwin, 1702. 8p. (Lowe 341) **1A159**

Amoroso, Donald M. *et al.* "An Investigation of Behavioral, Psychological, and Physiological Reactions to Pornographic Stimuli." *Technical Report of the [U.S.] Commission on Obscenity and Pornography*, 8:1–40, 1971.
1A160
"Two studies are described in this report, the purpose of which was to investigate some of the behavioral, psychological, and physiological effects of exposure to pornographic stimuli. Sixty male subjects participated in the first study, individually and in groups, and rated 27 sexual slides along three dimensions: pornographic-nonpornographic, stimulating-nonstimulating, and pleasant-unpleasant. . . . In the second study, which employed 56 male subjects, the effects of the pornographic ratings of the slides on the time spent looking at them were examined under two conditions: when the subject viewed the slides alone and when he viewed them while observed by an audience."

Amoroso, Frank. "The Freedom of Information Act: Shredding the Paper Curtain." *St. John's Law Review*, 47:694–724, May 1973.
1A161
"The Act attempts to provide a workable balance among the people's right to know, the Government's right to a degree of confidentiality and the individual's right to privacy. In light of the all-inclusive objective, it is no wonder that the statutory scheme is replete with inconsistencies and ambiguities. . . . However, the most overwhelming impression that must emerge from studying the FOIA is a recognition that the Legislative, Executive and Judicial branches of Government must imbue in themselves and the agencies the general philosophy that the people *must* know how the government is discharging its duty as the steward of the people."

Anastaplo, George. " 'Abridging the Freedom of Speech.' " In his *The Constitutionalist: Notes on the First Amendment*. Dallas, Tex., Southern Methodist University Press, 1971, pp. 93–129.
1A162
An analysis and interpretation of the First Amendment of the Constitution, drawing

upon discussions that took place at the time of enactment and commenting on the interpretation of other scholars, especially Leonard Levy. Anastaplo finds that Congress has power to legislate against the political crimes of treason, espionage, and certain kinds of fraud which may rely primarily on words for their effectiveness. Obscenity, not being a "political matter" is not a First Amendment problem, but is protected by the rule of law. In earlier chapters he discusses the absoluteness of the First Amendment ("Congress Shall Make No Law") and Congress as the agency constrained ("All Legislative Powers Herein Granted").

———. "Obscenity and Common Sense: Toward a Definition of 'Community' and 'Individuality.' " *St. Louis University Law Journal*, 16:527–56, Summer 1972.
1A163
A philosophical discussion of problems of obscenity in relation to community interests and individual self-expression.

———. "Preliminary Reflections on the Pentagon Papers." *University of Chicago Magazine*, 64(3):2–11, January–February 1972; 64(4):16–28, March–April 1972.
1A164
In the first of a two-part examination of the implications of the publication of the Pentagon Papers, the author discusses "what may be learned from the papers about the way our government conducts our affairs and how our public servants conceive of our limitations—and hence of their duties." The second part deals with "what may be learned from the unprecedented litigation attending the publication," including the issue of prior restraint of the press, national security, and the responsibility of the press in handling information the government has tried to conceal from public view.

———. "Self-Government and the Mass Media: A Practical Man's Guide." In Harry M. Clor, *ed.*, *The Mass Media and Modern Democracy*, Chicago, Rand McNally, 1974, pp. 161–232.
1A165
"I propose to begin to examine what sense there is (with a view to the common good) in the extensive freedom we traditionally accord the press. That is, I propose to examine such things as the risks run and the safeguards provided as well as the advantages offered by our traditional way of regarding what the press may do. I also propose to consider the rationale of the extensive regulation of the television industry to which we are accustomed. . . . We will consider, first, how we live with an absolute prohibition (in practice) of previous restraints on the press, what that means, and why it should be that way. We will consider thereafter . . . what television is like and what should be done about it. I am prepared to defend the proposition that, for the sake of our way of life, there cannot be (in ordinary constitutional circumstances) *any* previous restraints of the press and that there should be

even more previous restraint than we now have of the television industry." The author believes that the abolition of television "would enlarge freedom of speech among us" and "would probably contribute *among us* to the preservation of self-government and hence genuine freedom." Since we are no more likely to abolish television than to curtail the use of the automobile, he suggests ways of curtailing and regulating television, including reduction of commercialization, curtailment of time on the air, and reserving television for entertainment and leaving the discussion of politics to more appropriate forums.

Anchell, Melvin. "Pornography Anyone?" *Social Justice*, 66:194–98, October 1973.   **1A166**
A California doctor believes that the notion that pornography causes no social or individual harm is fallacious. It is not only harmful for children but for adults as well. The cumulative result of pornography on a young person is equivalent to an actual attack by a child seducer; the effect on an adult is that it encourages sexual behavior characteristic of perverts. The repressive effect of pornography on sexual behavior brings on premature death. The entertainment media are seducing and ravaging millions of children, adolescents, and adults, and are making money on it.

Andersen, L. A. "*Horrocks v. Low*: Scope of Unqualified Privilege Redefined." *Otago Law Review*, 3:410–18, 1975.   **1A167**
The House of Lords, in *Horrocks v. Low*, has denied as grounds for loss of qualified privilege in a defamation allegation insufficient relevance to the interest or duty which gives rise to the privileged occasion.

Anderson, A. J. *Problems in Intellectual Freedom and Censorship*. Ann Arbor, Mich., Bowker, 1974. 195p. (Problem-Centered Approaches to Librarianship)   **1A168**
"The thirty instructional cases presented attempt to expose librarians and library science students to as many manifestations as possible of the kinds of intellectual freedom and censorship problems that occur or could occur in all types of libraries—public, academic, school and special. There are cases on the effects on people of reading and viewing pornographic and violence-oriented material; on whether librarians' personal philosophies and political beliefs are relevant to the successful discharge of their duties; on whether librarians should lend their weight to one side over another on controversial issues; on what community standards mean and what effects they can have on the selection of material; on whether librarians should turn over borrowing records to the police and other officials; on whether there should be 'restricted shelves' and 'adults only' sections; on how to inform school boards, trustees, or communities about the *Library Bill of Rights* and other documents on intellectual freedom; on how to convince a staff that a collection needs to become more contempo-

rary; on whether libraries do indeed have an obligation, as many feel, to represent all points of view; and much more."

Anderson, Anthony L. *Fairness: A Continuing Controversy*. Columbia, Mo., Freedom of Information Center, School of Journalism, University of Missouri at Columbia, 1972. 7p. (Report no. 278)   **1A169**
"The Fairness Doctrine continues to plague broadcasters who fear loss of broadcast license yet are afraid to dwell on controversial issues for fear of opening a Pandora's box filled with demands for free air time. As the issue is being debated, citizens' complaints to the FCC under the Fairness Doctrine are increasing to more than 60,000 yearly."

Anderson, Clinton P. " 'Top Secret'—But Should It Be?" *New York Times Magazine*, 108:14, 101, 104–5, 3 May 1959.   **1A170**
"The preoccupation with classification in the atomic energy program, says a Senator, violates the public's basic 'right to know' and hobbles scientific advances."—Editor

Anderson, David A. "Libel and Press Self-Censorship." *Texas Law Review*, 53:422–81, March 1975.   **1A171**
"Until *Gertz* [*Gertz v. Robert Welch, Inc.* (1974)], all of the [U.S. Supreme] Court's incursions into the defamation field had the effect of protecting the press from libel judgments. *Gertz*, however, was a retrenchment. . . . This article is concerned only with the effectiveness of the *Times—Gertz* privilege in preventing self-censorship; it does not attempt to assess its impact on reputation."

———. "A Response to Professor Robertson: The Issue Is Control of Press Power." *Texas Law Review*, 54:271–84, January 1976.   **1A172**
Response to David W. Robertson's defense of the U.S. Supreme Court's decision in *Gertz v. Robert Welch, Inc.*, 1974, appearing in the same issue (pp. 199–284). "Underlying our disagreement on this issue is a more fundamental difference concerning the appropriate roles of the law and the press in American life. He believes that to free the press from the restraints of libel law is to make the press 'a law unto itself.' I believe that permitting judges and juries to decide what the press may or may not publish, on pain of paying a libel judgment, is government control of the press, just as surely as would be a system permitting the executive to prohibit publication upon pain of paying a fine. Professor Robertson wants to retain significant control of the press through libel law, while I want to minimize it."

———. "The Selective Impact of Libel Law." *Columbia Journalism Review*, 14(1): 38–40, 42, May–June 1975. **1A173**
"The great power of libel lawyers in the coun-

try's newsrooms these days is the unintended result of a series of Supreme Court cases, ending with the important *Gertz v. Robert Welch, Inc.* [1974] decision last year. The legal system, as it now operates in matters of libel, favors the established media outlets over the newer ones, rich news subjects over poorer ones, and 'professional' reporting over advocacy." The author sees better libel insurance as the most promising solution to the situation. With a good insurance system "the decision to publish or not publish can be based more on journalistic grounds, and less on the cost of litigating."

Anderson, David A., and Jonathan Winer. "Corrective Advertising: The FTC's New Formula for Effective Relief." *Texas Law Review*, 50:312–33, January 1972.   **1A174**
"Corrective advertising is a potent remedy that falls within the statutory authority of the FTC when limited to the purpose of preventing deception. In the past, an advertiser could establish a deceptive claim in the consumer's mind before a cease and desist order could be made effective, and then continue to benefit from the deception by using new advertising messages that ostensibly abandon the deceptive claim but in fact recall that claim to the consumer's memory."

Anderson, David W. *Access; An Analysis of the Development of an Affirmative Concept of the First Amendment in Broadcasting*. Urbana, Ill., University of Illinois, 1974. 99p. (Unpublished Master's thesis)   **1A175**
"This study examines the development of regulatory policy affecting individual broadcaster's public service obligation and the public trustee concept of regulation. The access movement as defined in this study includes demands for expanded rights of individual expression over the airwaves, access for ideas, and reform of the license renewal process brought about by the movement for audience rights."

Anderson, Herbert M. "Fair Trial and Free Press." *Catholic Lawyer*, 15:238–47, Summer 1969.   **1A176**
A review of historical developments in efforts to resolve the conflict between press and bar.

Anderson, Jack. "Why I Blew the Whistle." *Parade*, 13 February 1972, pp. 6, 8.   **1A177**
"Like all investigative reporters, Anderson is provocative and controversial. Many government officials and politicians of both parties object to his ferreting out secrets they would rather keep hidden. In this article Anderson tells why he believes the people have a right to know."

Anderson, Jack, with George Clifford. *The Anderson Papers*. New York, Random House, 1973. 275p.   **1A178**
In this account of the struggle of a columnist to acquire news about the activities of the federal government, there is an underlying theme of secrecy. "Perhaps most important of all," writes Anderson in the epilogue, "Congress must rip aside the veil of censorship that prevents the American people from knowing what their government is doing. The United States now possesses more than twenty million documents that are hidden from public scrutiny by the censor's stamp. Men familiar with this hoard, insist that only ten to thirty percent of the papers have any genuine bearing on national security. The rest are classified to keep Americans from learning of malfeasance, bungling, or simply because the censor lacked the wit to make the papers public."

Anderson, James A. "The Alliance of Broadcast Stations and Newspapers." *Journal of Broadcasting*, 16:51–64, Winter 1971–72.   **1A179**
The author "examines the contents of both independent and newspaper-controlled broadcast stations and compares news treatment with that found in the same day's local newspapers."

Anderson, John. "Case against Censorship." *Honi Soit*, 43:8–9, 19 March 1971.   **1A180**
Re: Australian censorship.

[Anderson, John of Australia.] *Censorship in the Working-Class Movement*. [Sydney], Sydney University Freethought Society [1932]. 8p.   **1A181**
The Sydney University Freethought Society protests the censorship by the *Proletariat* of an article critical of the leadership of the Communist Party of Australia. The objectionable article is included.

Anderson, Joseph J. "State Library Agencies and Intellectual Freedom." In American Library Association, *Intellectual Freedom Manual*, Chicago, ALA, 1974, pt. 3, pp. 19–20.   **1A182**

Anderson, Karen G. "Attorney 'Gag' Rules: Reconciling the First Amendment and the Right to a Fair Trial." *University of Illinois Law Forum*, 1976:763–82, 1976.   **1A183**
"The purposes of this note are to illustrate the occasional conflict between freedom of expression and the fair administration of justice and to suggest a means of reconciling this conflict. The note will focus on the justifications and consequences of gag orders that restrict attorneys. First, the note will examine the relationship of the news media to the conflict between freedom of speech and the fair administration of justice. Second, it will discuss solutions proposed by several groups that have studied the conflict. Third, it will analyze judicial responses to the conflict. Finally, the note will present a detailed analytical framework for harmonizing the competing interests."

Anderson, Margaret. "Mr. Comstock and the Resourceful Police." *Little Review*, 2(2): 2–5, April 1915.   **1A184**
A fulmination against Anthony Comstock for his attacks on the distribution of birth control information, particularly the arrest of William Sanger for giving to Comstock's agent provocateur a copy of Mrs. Sanger's *Family Limitation*.

———. " 'Ulysses' in Court." *Little Review*, 7(4) 22–25, January–March 1921.   **1A185**
The publisher of *Little Review* describes the courtroom farce which led to her being fined $100 on obscenity charges for publishing serially James Joyce's *Ulysses*. John Cowper Powys testified that *Ulysses* was "too obscure and philosophical a work to be in any sense corrupting."

Anderson, Richard E. "Branzburg v. Hayes: A Need for Statutory Protection of News Sources." *Kentucky Law Journal*, 61:551–59, 1972/73.   **1A186**
"Stripped of the possibility of constitutional protection by the Supreme Court's [1972] decision in *Branzburg*, the newsman must now rely on Congress and the state legislatures to provide him with the protection he needs to satisfactorily perform his role as the 'guardian of the public interest.' The statutory privileges afforded newsmen should be absolute; if the reporter cannot consistently insure the anonymity of his sources, the fear of potential reprisals against informants would be sufficient to render any privilege less than absolute, valueless."

Anderson, Theodore A. "Public Figures Precluded from Recovering Punitive Damages When Liability Is Founded upon Actual Malice." *Western State University Law Review*, 2:305–17, Spring 1975.   **1A187**
Re: *Maheu v. Hughes Tool Co.*, 384 F. Supp. 166 (C.D. Cal. 1974).

Andich, David W. "The Freedom of Information Act; A Challenge to the Executive and the Judiciary." *John Marshall Journal of Practice and Procedure*, 7:293–331, Spring 1974.   **1A188**
Content: An Historical Perspective on Legislation Related to the Control of Government Information. The Freedom of Information Act in Perspective. The Judicial Branch's Position With Respect to the National Security Privilege. Determination of the Privilege.

Andrews, Edwin L. *Courtland Madison Asher, Editor and Publisher of The X-Ray: Seditionist, Extremist or Patriot?* Muncie, Ind., Ball State University, 1969. 271p. (Ed.D. dissertation, University Microfilms, no. 70-5268)   **1A189**
A study of the life and career of the publisher of a right-wing weekly newspaper in Muncie, Ind., who was indicted for sedition during World War II. Asher and his paper were labeled a subversive threat to the nation.

Andrist, Ralph K. "Paladin of Purity." *American Heritage*, 24(6):4–7, 84–89, October 1973.   **1A190**
The story of Anthony Comstock, the New York reformer who "spent a lifetime on a crusade to clean the nation's Augean stables of smut, vice, and nudity."

Anello, Douglas A., and Robert V. Cahill. "Legal Authority of the FCC to Place Limits on Broadcast Advertising Time." *Journal of Broadcasting*, 7:285–303, Fall 1963.   **1A191**
A discussion by an official of the National Association of Broadcasters of the legal background of the FCC's proposal of rules that would require limitations on advertising time. He argues that such an action might spell the difference between a free system of broadcasting and a controlled one.

Angle, Margaret S. "Media Freedom of Speech and Press—Defamation." *Wisconsin Law Review*, 1974:1167–79, 1974.   **1A192**
"On its face, *Gertz v. Robert Welch, Inc.* [1974], has restricted the first amendment freedoms of newspapers and broadcasters. It has eliminated the *Rosenbloom* 'public interest' doctrine, and reduced the standards of liability for false defamatory publications concerning matters of public interest. Yet the impact of the doctrine's loss may turn out to be slight since actual malice is still the required basis for an award of punitive damages."

Angstadt, Thomas F. "Broadcaster's Discretion—A Privilege Over Free Speech." *Loyola Law Review* (New Orleans), 20:89–104, 1974.   **1A193**
"This comment will first review the balance between free speech and those values which purportedly allow such constitutional deviation; second, review the broadcaster's duties, responsibilities and limitations as established by the courts, legislature and the Federal Communications Commission; and last, discuss the right of the public to seek and *gain access* to such broadcast facilities to present their views."

Antrim, Robert. "Sam Roth, Prometheus of the Unprintable." *Eros*, 1(3): 24–27, Autumn 1962.   **1A194**
"To the Supreme Court he was the key figure

in an important test case involving the First Amendment and the murky issue of obscenity (Roth lost, 5–4)."

App, Austin J. *The Law and Pornography*. St. Louis, Central Bureau Press [1969?]. 13p. (Reprinted from *Social Justice Review*, February 1969)   **1A195**
"What is needed is a new spirit in favor of decency in our courts reinforced by an aroused public opinion that simply will not tolerate permissiveness on pornography. . . . When we have once succeeded in protecting our young from the smut peddlers, we can hope to get hard core pornography banned for adults, too."

"The Applicability of General Public Lewdness Statutes to Live Theatrical Performances." *Valparaiso University Law Review*, 5:184–91, Fall 1970. **1A196**
In *Barrows v. Municipal Court*, 1Cal. 3d 821, 464P.2d 483 (1970), the Supreme Court of California ruled that the portion of the California Penal Code making it a misdemeanor to engage in lewd or dissolute conduct in a public place was inapplicable to live performances before an audience. The case involved a one-act play, *The Beard*.

"The Application of a Local or National Standard of Decency in the Use of the Roth-Memoirs Obscenity Test." *Washington University Law Quarterly*, 1971:691–95, Fall 1971.   **1A197**
In *Scuncio v. Columbus Theatre, Inc.*, 277 A.2d 924 (R.I. 1971) the Rhode Island Supreme Court held that the standard of decency by which the film involved is to be characterized should be a national rather than the Rhode Island standard.

Aptheker, Herbert. "Book Burning: Yesterday and Today." *Masses & Mainstream*, 6(8):1–5, August 1953.   **1A198**
The author compares book burning under the Eisenhower Administration and the McCarthy influence with book burning in Nazi Germany.

Archer, John F. "Advertising of Professional Fees: Does the Consumer Have a Right to Know?" *South Dakota Law Review*, 21:310–31, Spring 1976.   **1A199**
"Whether professionals should be able to advertise their fees has recently been the subject of intense controversy. This comment discusses the consumer's first amendment right to know these fees in light of statutes and regulations which prohibit access to professional fee information. The author examines the first amendment right-to-know principle as it is applied to the bans on advertising prescription drug prices, medical and legal fees."

Archibald, Samuel J. "Access to Government Information—The Right Before First Amendment." In Roscoe Pound–American Trial Lawyers Foundation, *The First Amendment and the News Media*, Cambridge, Mass., The Foundation, 1973, pp. 64–76.   **1A200**
A study of the operation of the Freedom of Information Act including the extent of its use (only one-tenth of requests for information came from the press), the extent of compliance on the part of agencies, the nature of the appeals and how they were settled by the courts. The author calls for minor improvements in the Act and a major overhaul of government information programs.

———. *The FOI Act Goes to Court*. Columbia, Mo., Freedom of Information Center, School of Journalism, University of Missouri at Columbia, 1972. 14p. (Report no. 280)   **1A201**
To determine how well the appeal provision of the Freedom of Information Act was working the Congressional Research Service of the Library of Congress prepared a digest of major court decisions under the Act. The Washington director of the Freedom of Information Center compared the significant cases with the affected sections of the U.S. Code and attempted to plot the trend in court interpretations. This report contains both the digest of cases and the analysis.

———. "Rules for the Game of Ghost." *Columbia Journalism Review*, 6(4):17–23, Winter 1968.   **1A202**
"In the cooperation—or conspiracy—between Washington reporters and unnamed government news sources, the public sometimes gets less candid news than it deserves."

———. "Whose FoI Law?" *Bulletin of the American Society of Newspaper Editors*, 536:10–12, December 1969.   **1A203**
"While the Freedom of Information law is not the exclusive property of the press, it can, if properly used, be a valuable tool to dig out the facts of government." The Washington "watchdog" for the University of Missouri Freedom of Information Center urges reporters to make use of the facility.

The Archibald Newsletter. (An Occasional Communication from Sam Archibald, Washington Office, Freedom of Information Center, School of Journalism, University of Missouri at Columbia) No. 1, July 1968–No. 7, September 1971.   **1A204**
News developments from Washington on such topics as secrecy in government, security classification, access to public records, and related federal legislation.

"Are the Prime Time Access Rule and Family Viewing Hour in the Public

Interest?" *Rutgers Law Review*, 29:902–20, Summer 1976.   **1A205**
"This Note will examine the PTAR [Prime Time Access Rule of the Federal Communications Commission] and consider the first amendment and public interest consequences of PTAR's interaction with Family Viewing Hour [on television]."

Arkansas. Legislative Council. *Censorship or Restriction of Motion Pictures*. [Memorandum] to Committee on Judiciary, *Arkansas Legislative Council from Research Staff. . . .* Little Rock, Ark., The Council, 1970. 4p. (Informational Memorandum no. 138)   **1A206**
The report concludes that "it would appear that either the State, county or city has the implied authority to establish [a motion picture censorship] board to assist in the enforcement of the [obscenity] laws of the State."

———. *Sale of Obscene Literature to Minors*. Little Rock, Ark., The Council, 1968. 8p. Processed. (Informational Memorandum no. 85)   **1A207**
A summary of state and federal laws and court decisions.

Arkes, Hadley. "Civility and the Restriction of Speech: Rediscovering the Defamation of Groups." *Supreme Court Review*, 1974:281–335, 1974.   **1A208**
The Problem of Group Libel—*Beauharnais v. Illinois*; On Libels, Injuries, and Political Speech; the Black Dissent; the Third Man—Enter the Jackson Dissent; The Decisive Role of Chaplinsky, Cohen and the Problem of *Chaplinsky*; The Flight from Legal Restraint; A Framework for Regulation.

Arkin, Stanley S., and Luther A. Granquist. "The Presumption of General Damages in the Law of Constitutional Libel." *Columbia Law Review*, 68:1482–95, December 1968.   **1A209**
"This article considers the ramifications of *Sullivan* [New York Times Company v. Sullivan, 1964] in an area of prime importance to every litigant in a libel suit—the presumption of general damages. Specifically, the issue discussed is whether the Constitution permits a public official to benefit from that rule when he brings a libel action." The author concludes that "a rule requiring the public official plaintiff to prove that some specific monetary, professional, or social loss results from the libelous publication would serve as an additional strong protection for the first amendment right with which the Supreme Court was concerned in *Sullivan*."

Armstrong, O. K. "How Coral Gables

Cleaned Up Its News Stands." *Parents Magazine*, 32(12):50, 76, 78, December 1957. **1A210**
How a Decent Literature Council in Coral Gables, Fla., prompted by the local women's club and supported by local officials and the press, led to the enforcement of a city obscenity ordinance and the passage of a state obscenity law.

———. "Landmark Decision in the War on Pornography." *Reader's Digest*, 91:93–97, September 1967. (Reprinted in U.S. House of Representatives, Post Office and Civil Service Committee, Postal Operations Subcommittee, Hearings on *Obscenity in the Mails*, 5–6 August 1969, pp. 173–77) **1A211**
A report on the successful prosecution of newsstand pornography in Cincinnati (the case of Polly King), backed by efforts of the Citizens for Decent Literature, whose headquarters is in that city. The author attributes the success to five factors: a vigilant citizens group, thorough police investigation, well-planned prosecution, anticipating the defense, and a careful judge who gave a clear explanation of the law to jurors.

———. "The Problems of Pornography." *American Legion Magazine*, 87:22–25+, August 1969. **1A212**
"How protective legal decisions encourage the growth of the smut business and saddle the nation with rampant open obscenity."

Armstrong, Robert D. "Today We Shall Discuss Sin." *Nevada Libraries*, 6(3):78–79, April 1969. **1A213**
Criticism of a bill before the Nevada legislature, patterned after a New York act, prohibiting the "exhibition and sale of obscene material to minors."

Armstrong, Rupert, and Max Toller. "Quarterly Quarrel: Should We Suppress Free Speech?" *Service in Life & Work* (Rotary International), 2:190–97, Winter 1933. **1A214**
Armstrong says "yes"; Toller, "no."

Arn, Robert. "Obscenity and Pornography." *Cambridge Review*, 89A:160–63, 2 December 1967. **1A215**
"In this paper I shall deal not with pornography but with obscenity, and then with only a few contemporary American examples. My interest here is with the significance of a certain type of diction used as a stylistic device to gain certain thematic ends." Examples include *Candy* by Terry Southern, *The Naked Lunch* by William Burroughs, and *Beautiful Losers* by Leonard Cohen. Arn accuses the literary critics

of being so tied up with legal and social arguments (in defending works in court) that they "have abdicated their professional function, which is to provide us with an accurate and convincing analysis of these works."

Arnett, Peter. "A Time to Tell the Truth About War." *Seminar (A Quarterly Review for Newspapermen by Copley Newspapers)*, 19:15–18, March 1971. **1A216**
Almost complete press freedom prevailed in the news coverage in Vietnam despite the attempts to muffle the reports when news was critical of military operations.

Arnold, Edmund R. "Intellectual Freedom: Imperative of the Free." *Iowa English Bulletin: Yearbook*, 25(3):4–11, November 1975. **1A217**
Intellectual freedom is difficult to live with because it requires tolerance of ideas sometimes diametrically opposed to our own and contrary to that which we hold dear, true, and beautiful. But democracy derives its strength from the diversity of its people. Censorship is the antithesis of intellectual freedom; it is the attempt to limit thought to certain "acceptable" channels. The author reviews the historic efforts to combat ideas in the areas of religion, politics, sex, and science. Librarians must have the freedom to acquire the record of our intellectual heritage and to make these materials available for use.

Arnold, Marc, and Andrew Kisseloff. "An Introduction to the Federal Privacy Act of 1974 and Its Effect on the Freedom of Information Act." *New England Law Review*, 11:463–96, Spring 1976. **1A218**

Arnold, Mark R. "Pressure on the Press Alarms Newsmen." *National Observer*, 11(53):20, 30 December 1972. **1A219**
Reporters go to jail in a growing battle over confidentiality of news sources.

Arnold, Thurman. "The Puzzling Problem of Obscenity in American Law." In his *Fair Fights and Foul*. New York, Harcourt, Brace, 1965, pp. 160–87. **1A220**
Comment on what is and what is not obscene, with texts of Judge Arnold's decision in the U.S. Court of Appeals in *Esquire v. Frank C. Walker* (1945) and his brief as an attorney for *Playboy* before the Vermont Supreme Court.

Arnott, Felix. "Censorship." *St. Mark's Review*, 77:11–15, March 1974. **1A221**
Censorship in Australia.

Arnott, James F., and John W. Robinson. *English Theatrical Literature*,

1559–1900. A Bibliography Incorporating Robert W. Lowe's A Bibliographical Account of English Theatrical Literature Published in 1888. London, Society for Theatre Research, 1970. 486p. **1A222**
Two sections cite works relating to British stage regulation and censorship: Government Regulation of the Theatre (item nos. 138–242) and the Morality of the Theatre (item nos. 243–679). The former section includes works dealing with licensing and suppression of the theater; the latter includes Prynne's *Histrio-Mastix* (1633), the Jeremy Collier controversy (1698–1707), Law's *Absolute Unlawfulness* (1726), and various other controversies over morality of stage plays. Ninety of the more important listed works have been reprinted in photo-facsimile in fifty volumes of a series, *The English Stage: Attack and Defense, 1577–1730*, edited by Arthur Freeman and published by Garland, New York, 1971.

Aronson, James. "Buddy—Buddy." *Nation*, 210:792–94, 29 June 1970. **1A223**
A review of two books: *The Information War* by Dale Minor and *The Adversaries: Politics and the Press* by William L. Rivers. "Rivers and Minor have between them done valuable service in adding to the body of contructive criticism of the press meaningful personal experience and carefully researched case histories that will help the reader gain insight into the communications industry."

———. *Deadline for the Media; Today's Challenges to Press, TV and Radio*. Indianapolis, Bobbs-Merrill, 1972. 327p. **1A224**
"Rarely in the history of the United States have the news media made so much news themselves as in the early 1970s." A veteran journalist writes about the crisis in American journalism, beginning with the public scepticism of the news that began with the "credibility gap" of the Johnson Administration over news of the Vietnam war. Scepticism widened into "a chasm of incredibility during the Nixon Administration," with the attempts to control the flow of news and commentary through assaults of Agnew, Justice Department subpoenas, the furor over the Pentagon Papers and other events. Aronson criticizes the media, especially the so-called liberal press, for unquestioned support of the government during the war and for failure to take an adversary stance to government even when the government was practicing a "policy of calculated deceit." He discusses the widespread dissatisfaction and frustration of working journalists and their efforts to have a greater role in media policy, the rise of the muckraking journalism reviews, and the history and effectiveness of the "alternative" radical press.

———. "The First Amendment Must be Reaffirmed: Congress, the Shield Law and the Press." *Grassroots Editor*, 14(4):9–11, July–August 1973. **1A225**
Testimony before the Senate Committee on

the Judiciary as a proponent of an absolute federal shield law for journalists. "My belief is that passage of an absolute law would be a clear statement from the Congress—in effect a resolution by the Congress—endorsing the bedrock protections and privileges of First Amendment for journalists, in the public interest."

———. "Meditations." *Antioch Review*, 31:267–82, Summer 1971.   **1A226**
The author contends that the summer of 1971 was a "crisis point" for the communications media. "The times and events called for the most searching kind of self-examination, not only of the factors behind the publication of the Pentagon Papers, but of the whole question of government-press relations, and the responsibility of the communications industry to the public."

———. *Packaging the News: A Critical Survey of Press, Radio, TV.* New York, International, 1971. 110p.   **1A227**
"The first year of the decade of the 1970's might well be termed a Time of the Toad for the communications industry. It was a time of frontal government assaults on the integrity and credibility of the press and the television networks under the field generalship of the Vice President, with the Commander in Chief issuing the directives from the White House. It was a time also of government subpoenas for the working press, and for newspapers, newsmagazines, and the television networks themselves; of reporters and photographers turning up as agents of the FBI on the home front, and of the CIA on the foreign fronts; of Army counterintelligence operatives being accredited as newspaper correspondents in Vietnam to snoop on legitimate reporters. . . . It was a time that was forcing decisions in the communications industry—from top to bottom. For the owners and operators of the media, the decision was whether to resist, individually and collectively, a direct encroachment on the freedom of the press by the national Administration; or whether to accede to the pressures and demands behind a dust storm of indignant rhetoric and double talk. For the men and women who work for the newspapers and the radio, television networks, the decision was whether to comply or to determine the extent to which they could use their power to persuade their employers to resist and, if persuasion failed, the extent to which they would use their own power to counter their employers' capitulation." The author presents a hard-hitting account of this assault on press freedom and the rebellion which, he believes, must take place if there is to be a fundamental change in American journalism. He concludes with the heartening fact that there is in American journalism today "a company of honest journalists of all ages, conscious of their own responsibility as journalists and human beings both, conscious of the potential power of an informed people, who will never give up the effort to establish an honorable and constructive communications network."

———. *The Press and the Cold War.* Indianapolis, Bobbs-Merrill, 1970. 308p.   **1A228**
"It is the contention of this book that the press of the United States has to a large degree become a voluntary arm of established power. . . . This thesis will be argued in an examination of the conduct of the press in time of crisis during the Cold War years, particularly as the crises concerned foreign policy. . . . The book is a study of the degree to which the newspaper industry has abdicated its role of public service." Leonard Granato reviews the book in *Grassroots Editor*, September–October 1971.

Aronson, Stephen D. "Constitutionality of Massachusetts Obscenity Statute." *Suffolk University Law Review*, 9:255–67, Fall 1974.   **1A229**
"Re: *Commonwealth v. George C. Horton*, 310 N.E.2d 316 (1974), in which the Supreme Judicial Court found that the Massachusetts obscenity law did not specifically define the sexual conduct whose displays or description in books and magazines the statute intended to prohibit.

Arthur, William B. "Freedom of the Press and the Phenomenon Called Agnewism." *Quill*, 59:22–27, June 1971.   **1A230**
The editor of *Look* magazine charges that "American journalism is the target of a uniquely broad and unrelenting attack. Some among us regard it as the bitterest attack in history." The assaults on the press are made in "a malignant atmosphere" nurtured and inflamed by the Nixon Administration. "In the Administration's war on truth Spiro Agnew is simply the chosen front man. His voice is the chosen voice. . . . Our danger, clearly, is not merely to our freedom, not merely to the freedom of the press. The danger is to the freedom of the people, the freedom of this society."

———. "The National News Council." *Mass Communications Review*, 2:3–7, December 1974.   **1A231**
The executive director of the National News Council describes the work of the organization at the end of its first year, drawing certain conclusions on its performance as a watchdog of the nation's press.

Arthurs, H. W. "Hate Propaganda: An Argument Against Attempts to Stop It By Legislation." *Chitty's Law Journal*, 18:1–5, January 1970.   **1A232**
The article is part of a presentation before the Standing Committee on Legal and Constitutional Affairs, Senate of Canada, opposing Bill S-21, an act to amend the Criminal Code to outlaw the dissemination of Hate Propaganda. Criminal legislation, the author maintains, is an ineffective and inappropriate method of fighting hate propaganda. Instead, we should "bend every effort toward eliminating real injustices, toward explaining and exploding fantasies, and toward stimulating respect for individuals and their differences, and for the use of

orderly processes for the resolution of grievances."

Arts Council of Great Britain. "Depravity and Corruption." In *The Theatre Today in England and Wales.* London, The Arts Council, 1970, pp. 57–59.   **1A233**
This chapter in the report of the Committee of Inquiry of the Arts Council deals with the Committee's conclusions with respect to stage censorship, including the recommendations of the Working Party of the Council's Conference on Obscenity, which recommends the repeal of the Obscene Publications Acts of 1959 and 1964, and that the Theatres Act of 1968 be brought into line.

———. *The Obscenity Laws. A Report by the Working Party set up by a Conference convened by the Chairman of the Arts Council of Great Britain.* With a Foreword by John Montgomerie. London, Deutsch, 1969. 124p.   **1A234**
On 6 June 1968 the Arts Council of Great Britain, concerned with the protection of artists and authors, voted to form a Working Party "to investigate the working of the Obscene Publications Acts of 1959 and 1964, and other relevant Acts, with special reference to literature, drama and the visual arts, and to consider such changes including the repeal of any such Acts as in their opinion shall be expedient." Their report calls for repeal of the Obscene Publications Acts which they concluded "while constituting a danger to the innocent private individual, provide no serious benefit to the public. The basic problem of founding a law that can be accepted on so subjective a concept as obscenity appears to be insuperable. Any formula of definition must be doomed to beg the question, so there can be little hope of formulating alternative legislation with more than peripheral improvements." The Working Party recommended a trial period of five years after repeal before considering whether further legislation was desirable. Appended to the report is a draft of a repeal bill, text of related laws, and a summary of testimony and statements from various experts and observers.

Asch, Sidney H. "Freedom of Expression." In his *Civil Rights and Responsibilities under the Constitution.* New York, Arco, 1968, pp. 57–73.   **1A235**
Limits of freedom of expression: the "clear and present danger" test; the "bad tendency" test; the "preferred position" test; obscenity; censorship and free press.

Ash, Gerald W. *The China News Ban: A Survey of Its History and Its Effect.* Morgantown, W.Va., West Virginia Uni-

versity, 1967. 138p. (Unpublished Master's thesis) **1A236**
"This work has attempted (1) to determine the validity of the charge that Americans are inadequately informed about Communist China; (2) to examine the charges and countercharges concerning the cause of alleged inadequate news coverage; and (3) to separate fact from emotion and to present an unbiased framework through which the China news problem can be better understood." The author found both the U.S. and China guilty of preventing American journalists from reporting from within China, but the blame has rested firmly on China since 1961.

Ash, Michael. "The Growth of Justice Black's Philosophy on Freedom of Speech, 1962–1966." *Wisconsin Law Review*, 1967:840–62, Fall 1967. **1A237**
Summing up a lengthy discussion, the author notes two areas where Black would limit the protection of the First Amendment: "He maintained (1) that the right to speak did not entail the right to speak on another's property; and (2) that the right to speak did not entail the right to engage in 'conduct' properly proscribed by law, even if such conduct had a communicative aspect. . . . Apart from these votes . . . Black gave every evidence of remaining a firm supporter of first amendment freedoms." In the area of obscenity, freedom of association, and state libel laws, he was an absolutist.

Asher, Thomas R. "A Lawyer Looks at Libraries and Censorship." *Library Journal*, 95:3247–49, 1 October 1970. **1A238**
"A workable balance between the risks of absolute censorship and the objectives of intellectual freedom" is suggested by a practicing lawyer, president of the American Civil Liberties Union of Maryland.

Ashley, Benedict M. "Ethical Pluralism in Our Schools." *Iowa English Bulletin Yearbook*, 25:34–40, November 1975. **1A239**
"The present controversy over censorship in the schools cannot be resolved either by supine submission to parental pressures, nor by talk about free speech. It reflects the fact that our schools have not faced squarely the problem of pluralism in values and in the symbolic expression on these values. The controversy will serve a very good purpose if it stimulates educators to provide a more positive program based on a frank acceptance of pluralism."

Ashmore, Harry S. *Fear in the Air*: *Broadcasting and the First Amendment: The Anatomy of a Constitutional Crisis*. New York, Norton, 1973. 180p. **1A240**
The book developed out of a two-day confer-

ence on broadcasting and the First Amendment held in January 1972 at the Center for the Study of Democratic Institutions to which were invited a select group of officials from the Nixon Administration, network officials, and station owners, meeting with the Center staff. The discussion began with consideration of the accommodation between the imperative of a licensing system and the First Amendment, followed by discussion of the adversary role of the broadcast press, the rising pressures for access to the broadcast channels, the role of public television and the political atmosphere presently bearing on news gathering. The conference concluded with a discussion of alternatives to regulation, principally the surveillance by a nongovernmental news council. Text of papers presented at the conference and commentary by Harry S. Ashmore, president of the Center, appear in Broadcasting and the First Amendment, *Center Magazine*, May–June 1973.

————. "Government by Public Relations. The Pentagon Papers as a Case History." *Center Magazine*, 4(5):21–28, September–October 1971. **1A241**
The president of the Center considers the lessons to be drawn from the publication of the Pentagon Papers and the confrontation between the U.S. government and press.

————. "The Pentagon Papers Revisited." *Center Magazine*, 4(6):52–56, November–December 1971. **1A242**
"The basic issue is the people's right to know what goes on in the corridors of power." The president of the Center considers the reaction of the intellectuals (those who "pursue their careers under the shelter of the rights and immunities set forth in the Bill of Rights") and their lack of alarm when the absolute bar of prior restraint of publication was weakened and clearly in peril.

————. "Public Commission or Government Intervention." *Journal of the Producers Guild of America*, 11(2):39–42, June 1969. **1A243**
The author urges that serious consideration be given to the proposal for a commission on the mass media, as recommended by the Hutchins Commission. Condensed and reprinted from his *Cause, Effect and Cure*, published by the Center for the Study of Democratic Institutions, 1966.

————. *et al*. "Broadcasting and the First Amendment; the Anatomy of a Constitutional Issue." *Center Magazine*, 6(3):19–68, May–June 1973. **1A244**
Report on a two-day conference held at the Center for the Study of Democratic Institutions, Santa Barbara, Calif., to consider whether the safeguards guaranteed to the press under the First Amendment apply to broadcast journalism as well as to the printed press. Special statements were presented by Rick J. Carlson (The State of the Law), Harry Kalven, Jr. (If This Be Asymmetry, Make the Most of It), Antonin Scalia (Asymmetry Is an Unbalanced

View), Harvey Wheeler (The Multi-Media Home), John Macy (The Short and Unhappy Life of P.B.S.), and Ronald Segal (Whose Fireball in the Night). Other participants: Blair Clark, Lloyd Cutler, Reuven Frank, James L. Loper, Newton Minow, Fred Warner Neal, Paul Porter, Lawrence Rogers, II, Richard Salant, Eric Sevareid, Harold Willens, Thomas H. Wolf, and Fellows of the Center. Harry S. Ashmore, president of the Center, edited the report and presents a synethesis of the ideas in his book *Fear in the Air*. (A portion of the conference was recorded on tape and is entered under 1C105.)

Ashmore, Richard D. *et al. Censorship as an Attitude Change Induction*. New Brunswick, N.J., Rutgers University, 1971. 7p. (Speech given before the Eastern Psychological Association Annual Meeting) (ED053 411) **1A245**
A study of the relationship between censorship and attitude change, testing a reaction theory. Results affirm the investigator's hypotheses that censorship of a speech which advocates a particular position arouses reaction in a person who could have heard the talk, producing a tendency for him to change his attitude on the issue toward greater agreement with the censored position.

Ashton, Thomas L. "The Censorship of Byron's *Marino Faliero*." *Huntington Library Quarterly*, 36:27–44, November 1972. **1A246**
An account of the emasculation of Lord Byron's five-act play, *Marino Faliero*, for production at Drury Lane Theater in 1821. The proprietors cut some 44 percent of the play, without the author's permission, to excise references to plebeian revolution, sexual innuendos, and criticism of the Church. The critics attributed the failure of the play to the literary butchery.

Aspen Institute Program on Communications and Society. *Control of the Direct Broadcast Satellite: Values in Conflict*. Palo Alto, Calif., Aspen Institute Program on Communications and Society, 1974. 156p. (An Occasional Paper, The Aspen Institute Program on Communications and Society Series on Communications) **1A247**
"The volume consists of a series of papers and documents examining the regulation, uses, and problems of direct satellite broadcasting in an international context. It examines the history of the broadcast satellite, describes the current status and explores the future possible uses of this global communications technology."

Associated Press. *Appeal! Why AP Must Appeal to the Supreme Court. Rights in Copy Challenge Opinion of Lower Court. In the Case of the United States, Plaintiff, vs. The Associated Press, et al, Defendants, decided in the District Court of the United*

States for the Southern District of New York, October 6, 1943. Chicago [The Chicago Times?], 1943. 47p.   **1A248**
The case for the Associated Press as defendants in an antitrust suit filed by the U.S. Attorney General to force the Associated Press to sell its services to any paper willing to pay.

Associated Press Managing Editors Association. *APME Fact Guide on Free Press—Fair Trial Debate*. n.p., 1965. 19p.   **1A249**

———. "Code of Ethics." *Editor & Publisher*, 108(16):11, 19 April 1975.   **1A250**
"This Code is a model against which newspaper men and women can measure their performance. It is meant to apply to news and editorial staff members and others who are involved in, or who influence news coverage and editorial policy. It has been formulated in the belief that newspapers and the people who produce them should adhere to the highest standards of ethical and professional conduct." The Code covers areas of responsibility, accuracy, integrity, and conflicts of interest.

Associated Press Managing Editors Association. Freedom of Information Committee. *1968 Annual Report*. . . . [Wenatchee, Wash., The Association, 1968.] 13p. Processed; *1969 Annual Report*. . . . [Cleveland, The Association, 1969.] 7p. Processed.   **1A251**
Reports on the state of press freedom as indicated by events of the year, including developments in the free press – fair trial controversy, freedom of information legislation, voluntary restraint in court coverage, nonattribution of news sources, right of access, and open meetings and records.

Association for Education in Journalism. Division of Mass Communications and Society. *The Hutchins Commission Revisited*. Iowa City, The Association, 1967. 26p. Processed.   **1A252**
A panel discussion of the reports of the Commission on Freedom of the Press twenty years after their issuance, considering "whether its recommendations still make sense in view of changes in the mass media system of our country, and whether there is need for a new Hutchins-type study of American communications in the context of contemporary society." Panelists: William E. Ames, Harry S. Ashmore, Ben H. Bagdikian, and Wayne A. Danielson. Moderator: H. Eugene Goodwin. The program was given at a meeting of the Society, University of Colorado, 30 August 1967.

Association of American Publishers. *Book Publishers Call for Repeal of All "Obscenity" Laws for Adults*. New York,

The Association, 1973. 5p. Processed.   **1A253**
A news release endorsing major recommendations of the Report of the Commission on Obscenity and Pornography, including repeal of all laws prohibiting the sale to consenting adults, but not opposing "carefully-drawn legislation regulating the commercial distribution of sexual materials to young persons or legislation to protect persons from having such materials thrust upon them without their consent through open public display."

———. Freedom to Read Committee. *Books and the Young Reader: A Statement for Communities, Schools and Libraries*. New York, The Committee, 1976. 4p. (One fold)   **1A254**
In this brief statement, the publishers of textbooks for children and young people urge that those who select school textbooks take into consideration that (1) "no community, no matter how small, is completely homogeneous" and what one parent will approve for a child, another will not, (2) that "the rights of children and young people to read books that seem relevant to their own lives and to society as they see it cannot be abridged without courting the danger that books themselves will seem to them obsolete," and (3) that "a publisher's total output should not be judged on the basis of one book." The Committee also issues a periodic newsletter—*The Free Reader*—reporting on events relating to censorship, freedom to publish, and freedom to read.

Association of the Bar of the City of New York. Committee on Federal Legislation. "Tinkering with the First." *Trial*, 9:34–38, May–June 1973.   **1A255**
A report on journalists' privilege legislation. Content: Is legislation needed? What information should be privileged? Scope of the privilege. To whom should the privilege extend?

Astley, George D. "Translating Libels." *Author*, 85:73–74, Summer 1974.   **1A256**
Concern of the Translators' Association over the liability of its members under British libel laws in light of action taken against the translator of Rolf Hochhuth's *Soldiers*. The Association believes a translator should not be held liable unless he had good reason to know that the original work was defamatory or that he introduced defamatory material into his translation not in the original.

Astor, Gerald. *Minorities and the Media*. New York, Office of Reports, Ford Foundation, 1974. 29p.   **1A257**
"Partly in response to the Kerner Commission findings [U.S. National Advisory Commission on Civil Disorders], partly as an outgrowth of its earlier efforts to widen minority opportunities and improve race relations, the Ford Foundation in the late 1960s and early 1970s supported a series of activities designed to enhance the content and the sensitivity of the media in

relation to minorities. The projects took three main directions: 1. Training of minority journalists. 2. Opening broadcasting to more and better coverage of minority affairs by means of advocacy in the administration and interpretation of broadcast law. 3. Supporting organizations committed to produce material about minorities and matters that concern them. This report summarizes the experience."

———. "No Recession in the Skin Trade." *Look*, 35(13):27–36, 29 June 1971.   **1A258**
A look at the nationwide pornography trade flourishing in a more permissive society.

Atkey, Ronald G. "The Law of the Press in Canada." *Gazette: International Journal for Mass Communications Studies*, 15:105–24, 1969; 15:185–200, 1969.   **1A259**
The paper reviews Canadian law of the press with respect to three areas: (1) freedom of the press; (2) control of the press in the administration of justice; and (3) the law of libel and the press. "Freedom of the press, as a legal right, is still a matter of some uncertainty in terms of its application in the courts. In the administration of justice, control of the press reporting is still subject to the application of a vague and inconsistent 'contempt' sanction, at common law, with small pockets of certainty carved out in the form of direct press prohibitions in the Canadian Criminal Code. And the law of libel is still partially dependent on English common law, interspersed with provincial statutory enactments which dabble in but do not blanket the field."

Atkins, Jeanni. *Chicano Media Challenge: Basta Ya!* Columbia, Mo., Freedom of Information Center, School of Journalism, University of Missouri at Columbia, 1972. 7p. (Report no. 282)   **1A260**
Through nonviolent challenges the Chicanos have exerted a degree of influence on American broadcasting media which promises to serve as an example for other groups.

———, and Belvel J. Boyd. *Classification Reexamined*. Columbia, Mo., Freedom of Information Center, School of Journalism, University of Missouri at Columbia, 1975. 11p. (Report no. 332)   **1A261**
"Abuses of government secrecy revealed when the Pentagon Papers were released precipitated congressional hearings. Witnesses testified that over-classification and inefficiency had undermined the original intent of the existing classification system; as a result, Congress has explored a statutory alternative."

Atkins, Thomas R., *ed. Movies and Sexuality*. Hollins College, Va., Film Journal, 1973. 31p. **1A262**
A special supplement to *Film Journal* dealing with screen sex and containing the following articles: Last Tango in Paris: The Skull Beneath the Skin Flick by Jack Fisher, How Do You Like Your Hero—Over Easy or Sunny-Side-Up? by George Garrett, Deep Throat: The Climax as Anti-Climax by Harry M. Geduld, The Death of the Flesh Film by Wayne A. Losano, and Sex, Morality and Film by Lawrence Becker.

———. *Sexuality in the Movies*. Bloomington, Ind., Indiana University Press, 1975. 244p. **1A263**
This book consists of a group of essays, with numerous illustrations, giving "a general picture of the treatment of sexuality in a wide variety of different kinds of movies, from the 1890s to the present, with special emphasis on the social and cultural context in which the movies were created." In part I, A History of Censorship of the American Films by Arthur Lennig deals with the influence of various censorship codes, laws, and groups that helped shape the content of American films; The Contemporary Movie Rating System in America by Evelyn Renold offers an inside view of the movie classification system from the vantage point of one who has served as an intern on the rating board of the Motion Picture Association of America; Sex Morality and the Movies by Lawrence Becker clarifies "some of the issues involved in understanding the complicated relationship between film aesthetics and moral values." In part II, five essays deal with various categories and genre of sex films. "Skin flicks and hard-core pornographic movies are evaluated, as well as the frequently disguised but powerful sexual ingredients of the classic horror movies." Part III presents appraisals of six representative movies of the late 1960s and '70s that have become centers of controversy: *I Am Curious—Yellow, Deep Throat, Midnight Cowboy, Carnal Knowledge, Cries and Whispers*, and *Last Tango in Paris*.

[Atkinson, Edward.] *The Anti-Imperialist*. Brookline, Mass., vol. 1, nos. 1/2–6, 3 June 1899–1 October 1900. Five numbers issued. **1A264**
In this short-lived journal the editor-publisher opposes the "tropical expansion and present warfare in the Philippines." Numerous references in the issues deal with accounts of censorship of news by the Army. Issue no. 2 was declared seditious by the Postmaster General and rejected for mailing.

Atkinson, Elliott W., Jr. "Free Press v. Fair Trial: Insulation Against Injustice." *Louisiana Law Review*, 33:547–59, Summer 1973. **1A265**
In a discussion of American Bar Association minimum standards, the author examines the record of free press and fair trial cases, the ABA standards, and Louisiana Guide to News Media and Bar Relations (text included), concluding that "alternative remedies must be sought for avoiding prejudicial publicity which are less disruptive of constitutional freedoms than bans on publication. Changes of venue, continuances, or granting new trials must first be used before any sanctions against the press and media will be tolerated."

An Attempt toward a Coalition of English Protestants . . . , to Which is added Reasons for Restraining the Licentiousness of the Pulpit and Press. London, Roberts, 1715. 40p. **1A266**
On pages 21–23 the author argues for suppressing "all argumentative Papers in a Political Way," unless they are addressed to the Parliament. Such arguments should not be presented directly to the people since they might be influenced to change their minds. "It is better to cut off a diseased member of the body (liberty of press) than to infect the whole."

"Attorney General's Memorandum on the Public Information Section of the Administrative Procedure Act." *Administrative Law Review*, 20:263–316, March 1968. **1A267**
The memorandum is intended as a guide to executive agencies in interpreting and implementing the Freedom of Information Act in line with the spirit and purpose of the act and the president's instructions.

Aubry, Claude B. "Intellectual Freedom." *Canadian Libraries*, 23:185–87, November 1966. **1A268**
The author writes of four fears which form the basis for censorship: (1) fear of interference with religious doctrines and dogmas, (2) fear of political leaders being criticized, (3) fear of those at the top of the ladder in organized society from losing their positions and privileges, and (4) fear of destroying purity and innocence in the young.

Auerbach, Erich. "State Censorship of Motion Pictures Shown by Television." *Southern California Law Review*, 24:486–89, July 1951. **1A269**
Re: *Allen B. DuMont Laboratories, Inc. v. Carroll*, 184 Fed. (2d) 1953 (C.A.3d 1950), 340 U.S. 929 (1951).

Auerbach, Jerald S. "Introduction" to Theodore Schroeder, *"Obscene" Literature and Constitutional Law; A Forensic Defense of Freedom of the Press*. New York, Da Capo, 1972, pp. vi–xvii. (Reprinting of 1911 edition with new introduction) **1A270**
The author of the introduction states that Theodore Schroeder, who languishes in obscurity today, was "a maverick radical" who "ventured further than any of his contemporaries in exploring the meaning of literary and political freedom of expression." Noting Schroeder's parodoxical character, he writes: "His was an intolerant crusade for tolerance, an authoritarian struggle for liberty, an emotional pursuit of reasoned truth." Schroeder called for judicial annulment of all laws against obscene literature, arguing that obscenity statutes violated the First Amendment, the due process clause, and contributed to ignorance, which, in turn, produced serious emotional disturbances.

———. "The Patrician as Libertarian: Zechariah Chafee, Jr. and Freedom of Speech." *New England Quarterly*, 42:511–31, December 1969. **1A271**
An account of how a conservative young member of the Harvard Law School faculty became a leading exponent of freedom of speech. It began with an interest, sparked by former Harvard Law School Dean Roscoe Pound, in an 1839 case, *Brandreth v. Lance*, in which the New York Court of Chancery refused a request for prior restraint on a publication as a violation of the First Amendment. Chafee's lifelong search for the boundaries of free expression was stimulated by the executive and judicial attacks on press freedom under the World War I Espionage Act. His 1920 book on *Freedom of Speech* (C244), reporting and analyzing these events, became a civil liberties classic. Chafee, who was himself an antiradical, was subjected to attack from antiradical components of the American Bar Association who attempted unsuccessfully to remove him from the Harvard faculty. He survived these efforts, to become the revered scholar of freedom of speech and press.

Aumente, Jerome. *Against Misinformation; A Media Action Program for Young People*. New York, Anti-Defamation League of B'nai B'rith, 1973. 126p. **1A272**
A monograph on the use and abuse of mass communications, aimed at high school students and designed to guide them in distinguishing between good and bad information. Included are discussions of the "isms," sex education, hatred on the left and on the right, editorial bias in newspapers and magazines, the significance of the Pentagon Papers case, censorship in the television industry, advertising and misinformation, and censorship of the mob on college campuses who shout down speakers, disrupt forums, and create chaos when views opposed to their own are expressed.

———. "Detroit's Year Without News." *Nation*, 207(12):363–66, 14 October 1968. **1A273**
An account of experiences of the city without its major newspapers during the 267-day strike. "As information dried up, the ability to make decisions, to bring about political and social change, or simply to achieve peace of mind, went with it."

Ausness, Richard C. "Libel *Per Quod* in Florida." *University of Florida Law Review*, 23:51–65, Fall 1970. **1A274**
"The purpose of this article is to trace the development of the rules of defamation with particular reference to extrinsic fact." Extrinsic facts may be required to establish the defamatory nature of the statement for action under either tort for libel or slander. "The discussion of Florida cases on the extrinsic-fact problem has demonstrated that no one aspect of the law of libel or slander can be modified without considering its effect on other areas involving defamation." The author calls for a thorough and systematic reform in Florida law of defamation.

Austin, Bradford L. "Newspaper or Broadcaster That Publishes Defamatory Falsehoods About Individual Who Is Neither Public Official Nor Public Figure May Not Claim Constitutional Privilege Against Liability for Injury Inflicted by Those Statements." *Drake Law Review*, 24:464–70, Winter 1975. **1A275**

Re: *Gertz v. Robert Welch, Inc.*, 418 U.S. 323 (1974).

Australia. Department of Customs and Excise. *Agreement Between the Governments of the Commonwealth and of the States of Australia in Relation to the Administration of Laws Relating to Blasphemous, Indecent or Obscene Literature.* Canberra, Australia, Government Printer, 1968. 11p. (Parliamentary Papers, 157 of 1968) **1A276**

———. *List of Publications Released after Examination in Terms of Customs (Prohibited Imports) Regulations.* Canberra, Australia, Government Printer, 1967. 53p. (Kept up-to-date by amendment pages) **1A277**

Australia. Department of Customs and Excise. General Customs Branch. *Commonwealth Film Censorship, 1917–1963.* Canberra, Australia, The Department, 1964. Various paging; typescript. **1A278**

Content: Authority for Commonwealth Film Censorship (legislation, regulations, standards). Film Censorship in the States. Commonwealth-State Cooperation. Working of Commonwealth Film Censorship. Sources of Reference. Attachments include various agreements with Victoria, Queensland, Western Australia, Tasmania, and Film Censorship, Classification and Advertising Control in South Australia.

Australia. New South Wales. Parliament. Legislative Assembly. *Theatre Censorship. Petition from Certain Citizens of New South Wales Praying That Action Be Taken to Have All Restrictions on the Performance of the Segment "Motel" of the New Theatre's Production of the Play "America Hurrah" Be Removed.* Sydney, Australia, Government Printer, 1969. 1p. (Parliamentary Papers, 75 of 1968) **1A279**

Australian School Library Association. "Australian School Library Bill of Rights." *Australian Library Journal*, 21:344, September 1972. **1A280**
Adopted by the Association's Council, May 1972.

Avery, Emmett L., and A. H. Scouten. "Opposition to Sir Robert Walpole, 1737–1739." *English Historical Review*, 83:331–36, April 1968. **1A281**
"A curious and previously unnoticed series of episodes wherein James Lacy, once a minor actor in Henry Fielding's company at the Little Haymarket Theatre before the Stage Licensing Act of 1737, became involved in defiance of the Act and in propaganda and demagoguery leading to the war with Spain in 1739. As the first person to attempt an evasion of Sir Robert Walpole's restrictions on playhouses, Lacy provocatively assisted a rising opposition in Parliament, and had a role in securing freedom of the press and in the evolution of civil rights and personal liberty in eighteenth-century England."

Ayer, Douglas, Roy E. Bates, and Peter J. Herman. "Self-Censorship in the Movie Industry: An Historical Perspective on Law and Social Change." *Wisconsin Law Review*, 1970:791–838, 1970. **1A282**

"We shall start by describing the old Code which effectively governed movie content until the 1950's and lingered on until it was replaced by the new rating system in 1968. We shall then examine the forces that brought about change and the reactions to that change, note the occasion for a new Code and describe its formulation. We shall conclude with an account of the factors that will determine the actual impact of the rating system on what all of us may see at the movies."

Ayotte, Peter. "Media under Fire: The October Crisis and Other Infamous Crimes of the Press." *Canadian Communications Law Review*, 4:55–97, 1972. **1A283**
The author examines recent government reactions to the role of the media in crisis situations, both real and imagined, "to arrive at solutions which the government, the media and society as a whole can live with." Three crisis situations in three countries are examined and compared: the Scott Report Affair in the United Kingdom, the Pentagon Papers Case in the United States, and, in greater detail, the October Crisis in Canada, which grew out of the kidnapping of the British Trade Commissioner and the kidnapping and murder of the Quebec Labour Minister. One of the solutions suggested is a conference of government leaders, media people, and a cross section of the public to reassess the role of government and the media in the area of information gathering and reporting. "In addition something like a Freedom of Information Act in the United States might be appropriate as a counterbalance to this censorship power." Above all, a greater sense of responsibility both in government and the media is essential.

Ayrton, Michael. "Talking About Censorship—1: Obscenity in Committee." *Author*, 81:69–70, Summer 1970. **1A284**
Reaction of members of the British Society of Authors to the Arts Council Report on Obscenity. The majority favored the report with reservations (one reservation was the failure of the report to address itself to the connection between sex and violence); a substantive minority favored no change in present obscenity laws, with a smaller minority favoring abolition of all obscenity censorship.

B

Baach, Martin R. "Classification of Files Pursuant to Executive Order Is Not Subject to Judicial Review under the Freedom of Information Act." *University of Cincinnati Law Review*, 42:529–39, 1973.   **1B1**

In *Environmental Protection Agency v. Mink* (1973), the U.S. Supreme Court ruled that *in camera* court review of executive documents is not authorized by the Freedom of Information Act. Moreover, the soundness of executive classification of documents is not subject to judicial review.

[Babcock, Mary K.] "State Statute Prohibiting Pharmacists from Publishing Prescription Drug Prices Violates Consumers' Right to Know." *University of Kansas Law Review*, 23:289–300, Winter 1975.   **1B2**

Re: *Virginia Citizens Consumer Council, Inc. v. State Board of Pharmacy*, 373 F. Supp. 683 (E.D. Va., 1974).

[Bacheler, Origen.] *Trial of The Commonwealth versus Origen Bacheler, for a Libel on the Character of George B. Beals, Deceased, at the Municipal Court, Boston, March Term, A.D. 1829. Before Hon. P. O. Thacher, Judge, Reported by John W. Whitman.* Boston, John H. Belcher, 1829. 47p.   **1B3**

The case involved the publication in the defendant's paper, *Anti-Universalist*, of an item contradicting an obituary statement that had appeared in the *Trumpet*, a Universalist paper. The latter article had praised the deceased as never using vulgar or profane words. Not so said the *Anti-Universalist*; he used profanity habitually. The defense, pleading a lack of malice and freedom to argue religious issues, persuaded the jury to find the defendant "not guilty."

Back, Gunnar. "The Role of the Communicator As Censor of the News." In Harry J. Skornia and Jack W. Kitson, eds., *Problems and Controversies in Television and Radio*, Palo Alto, Calif., Pacific Books, 1968, pp. 339–46.   **1B4**

The pressures of time, industry policy practices, lack of experience in news editing and in delivery, and reliance almost entirely on wire services, results in local newscasters (not news commentators) giving the "who," "what," "when," and "where," but not much of the "why."

Bacon, Kenneth H. "Press and Its Critics Tangle over Question of 'Access' to Media; Editors, Broadcasters View Drive for Citizens' Rights As Threat to Their Own." *Wall Street Journal*, 183(112):1, 27, 10 June 1974.   **1B5**

References to the Citizens Communications Center, the nation's first public-interest communications law firm to help citizens get their views into the public prints and on the airwaves, and to the impending *Tornillo* case, involving Florida's right of reply law, FCC restrictions on broadcasters, and the barrage of criticism from Spiro Agnew and others in the Nixon Administration.

Baer, Randy C., and Christopher Baffer. "TV Censorship of the Movies." *Take One*, 4(10):16–19, 30 June 1975.   **1B6**

The authors describe what takes place in the editing of films for television, giving numerous examples. "Please don't criticize the TV film prematurely and don't always expect the film to be ruined. If the TV film editor is really with it, you won't even be aware that the picture you are viewing has been cut unless you had seen the film before. Nothing of importance will be missing and the filmmaker's purpose in making that movie will not be lost. The commercials will not drastically interrupt the continuity of the story line."

Baer, Walter S. *et al. Concentration of Mass Media Ownership: Assessing the State of Current Knowledge*. Santa Monica, Calif., Rand, 1974. 202p. (Prepared under a grant from the National Science Foundation)   **1B7**

The report sifts the vast literature dealing with the ownership and control of radio, television, cable communications, and newspapers "to determine what factual evidence there is on the effect of media ownership and its relevance to present government policies" and "to suggest what additional data and analysis are needed to strengthen the basis for future policymaking." "Determining adequate measures of media performance remains a fundamental problem for serious research." The authors call for "some more fundamental studies of the economics of news gathering and presentation, and the determinants of advertising price and quantity."

Bagdikian, Ben H. "Considerations on the Future of American Journalism." In Charles C. Flippen, *ed. Liberating the Media; the New Journalism*, Washington, D.C., Acropolis, 1973, pp. 192–202.   **1B8**

"The future of journalism is not in the hands of the technologists and the social scientists and the city planners. It is in the hands of political leaders and the courts. And how the public, leaders, and courts emerge depends to a great degree on the determination of every journalist to remain free at any cost."

———. "Courts, Convicts & the Press." *Nation*, 219(5):145–46, 31 August 1974.   **1B9**

References to the decision of the U.S. Supreme Court (5–4) upholding the U.S. Bureau of Prisons' rule forbidding press interviews with inmates. The minority report emphasized the restriction on press freedom and the need for greater public accountability of a public institution.

———. "Don't Let Them Scare You." *Quill*, 60(8):12–15, August 1972. **1B10**

In an age of fear and uncertainty too many Americans are panicking before a faceless "them." The press has not done an adequate job of reporting on the evolution of official policies and the failure of these policies as they affect the individual. The citizen and the press that represents him has too often been considered by government as an intruder, and secrecy has increased to a degree unknown in the past.

The press is being pushed toward greater orthodoxy when it needs to be more diverse and open. It must not let itself be intimidated by "them."

———. *The Effete Conspiracy and Other Crimes of the Press.* New York, Harper & Row, 1972. 159p. **1B11**
A series of essays by a practicing journalist critical of the American press—its conservative bias, its catering to the political, financial, and even religious interests of its owners, the effect of conglomerates and monopolies, absentee ownership, press agentry and free advertising, suppression of news, presidential manipulation of news, and the recent attempts from high quarters (The Great Nixon—Agnew Media Con Game) to bring the press to heel. "If the mildly reformist *Post* and *Times* can be isolated and silenced (by the Nixon Administration), the progression toward total insignificance of the media will be complete."

———. "The First Amendment on Trial: What Did We Learn?" *Columbia Journalism Review*, 10 (3):45–50, September–October 1971. **1B12**
The U.S. Supreme Court decision in the Pentagon Papers case "signalizes not the triumphant end, but the start of a struggle. The astonishing cluster of major issues involved in the court case moves onward with an uncertain future: legitimacy of the war in Vietnam; deception by the Government; secrecy in government; and freedom of the press. . . . Having won in the Supreme Court, the press now must fight the more insidious self-censorship that comes when it tries to avoid future confrontations, when it concedes in the newsroom what it won in the courts."

———. "First Amendment Revisionism." *Columbia Journalism Review*, 13(1):39–46, May–June 1974. **1B13**
The author assesses the criticism of the press from the public, the courts, and the federal government. He examines the new philosophy of right of access, which shifts the meaning from the right of anyone to publish to the right of the author to have his ideas published. Government intervention, he believes, will not provide the answer. "When individuals and groups today lack equitable access and right of reply in the media they are usually precisely the same groups that government has either ignored or tried to silence." Publishers and broadcasters have been arrogant, but government regulation can be arrogant too.

———. "Governmental Suppression of the Media." *University of Miami Law Review*, 29:447–55, Spring 1975. **1B14**
A strong defense of a voluntary press council is the best guarantee against government suppression of the media. "Readers, listeners, and viewers clearly want someone they can trust to examine the complexities of specific journalistic problems that affect the public. If the public does not have this belief and trust, then the warnings of the Hutchins Commission in 1947 can come true. Government, using public

opinion, can circumvent the first amendment. The news establishment did not believe this in 1947; if they do not believe it now even after the attacks and the attempted suppression of the last five years, then we are all, journalists and laymen alike, in trouble."

———. "Right of Access: A Modest Proposal." *Columbia Journalism Review*, 8(1):10–13, Spring 1969. (Reprinted in Alfred Balk and James Boylan, *eds.*, *Our Troubled Press*, pp. 360–67) **1B15**
Comments on Professor Jerome A. Barron's proposal on the public's right of access to the press. "The Barron proposal is thoughtful and dramatic. But there are more modest possibilities." They include: start a new journalistic form with skilled journalists presenting a variety of ideas of experts on solution of problems, devote a full page a day to letters to the editor, appoint a full-time ombudsman, and organize a local press council.

Bailey, F. Lee, and Russell Fairbanks. *Free Press and Fair Trial.* 20 min. tape recording. North Hollywood, Calif., Center for Cassette Studies, 1971. (Legal Domain series) **1B16**
"The unfair practices of trial judges and the sensation seeking tactics of the press are probed and illustrated by the case of Sam Sheppard."

Bailey, George A., and Laurence W. Lichty. "Rough Justice on a Saigon Street: A Gatekeeper Study of NBC's Tet Execution Film." *Journalism Quarterly*, 49:221–29, 238, Summer 1972. **1B17**
"Step by step, person by person, decision by decision, the authors record the story of the filming and telecasting of General Loan's famed shot. The 'organization' proved to be the gatekeeper." A detailed account on how decisions are made on what to show and what not to show on television.

Bailey, H.S., Jr. "Staff Memo to Editorial Staff, Princeton University Press; Subject: Obscenity." *Scholarly Publishing*, 3:249–50, April 1972. **1B18**
The statement concludes: "The purpose of humanistic study is to enrich human life, to give it meaning and value. Any question of obscenity must be seen in these terms. We will not publish anything that is obscene just because it is true. We will publish something that is 'obscene by itself' only if it contributes to a larger whole that furthers our humanistic purpose." The policy statement was issued in 1966.

[Bain, Kenneth B. F.] *Comic Cuts; a Bedside Sampler of Censorship in Action, Compiled and introduced by Richard Findlater (pseud.), with drawings by William Rushton.* London, Deutsch, 1970. 126p. **1B19**

In a serious essay on censorship the compiler points out that "however sinister its potential power may be, most public censorship in a country like ours is ultimately absurd, and most of its cuts are comic." He follows with a collection of such comic cuts made by the censors—film, stage, and book—in Britain and the United States. Included are lists of taboo words and forbidden subjects, and the text (published in England for the first time) of fourteen of the suppressed poems by D. H. Lawrence in his book, *Pansies*.

Baird, Frank L. *Congress' Role in Regulation: Radio and Television Programming.* Austin, Tex., University of Texas, 1965. 439p. (Ph.D. dissertation, University Microfilms, no. 65-4291) **1B20**
"The purposes of this study were to determine the effect of Congressional activities on the Federal Communications Commission's efforts to formulate and implement policies for the regulation of radio and television program content—to ascertain whether or not Congress has given positive guidance to the FCC in the performance of this function and to discover whether Congressional intervention in FCC activities has tended to strengthen or weaken the agencies' policies and their enforcement."

———. "Program Regulation on the New Frontier." *Journal of Broadcasting*, 11:231–43, Summer 1967. **1B21**
The dilemma faced by the FCC in the Kennedy Administration by pressures to translate the spirit and substance of the New Frontier into more vigorous regulation of broadcast programming over against Section 326 of the Communications Act of 1943 which prohibits the Commission from censoring anything broadcast. When the FCC began to adopt more aggressive policies, Congress began to object and investigate. "From the standpoint of programming regulation, the New Frontier period has become yet another ghost town." Adapted from the author's doctoral dissertation.

Baistow, Tom. "Ill Judged." *New Statesman*, 78:682–83, 14 November 1969. **1B22**
Criticism of the actions of the British Press Council for lack of good judgment with respect to Christine Keeler's *News of the World.*

———. "Miss Keeler and the Establishment." *New Statesman*, 78:488–89, 10 October 1969. **1B23**
Censorship controversy in Britain over Christine Keeler's *News of the World.*

Baker, C. Edwin. "Commercial Speech: A Problem in the Theory of Freedom." *Iowa Law Review*, 62:1–56, October 1976. **1B24**

The thesis of this Article rejects the thrust of the Supreme Court's reasoning in these cases ₁*Bigelow v. Virginia* (1975) and *Virginia State Board of Pharmacy v. Virginia Citizens Consumer Council, Inc.* (1976)₁. It argues that, given the existing form of social and economic relationship in the United States, a complete denial of first amendment protection is not only consistent with, but is required by, first amendment theory." He argues that "profit-motivated or commercial speech lacks the crucial connections with individual liberty and self-realization which exist for speech generally, and which are central to justifications for the constitutional protection of speech, justifications which in turn define the proper scope of protection under the first amendment."

Baker, Frederick, E., and Victor Elting, Jr. "Proposals for Self-Regulation Administered by the American Advertising Federation." *Congressional Record*, 13 October 1970, pp. 36403–6. **1B25**
In separate addresses two officials of the American Advertising Federation make similar proposals to establish a voluntary and substantive program for effective self-regulation in the advertising business.

Baker, Joan, "Free Speech and Federal Control: The U.S. Approach to Broadcasting Regulation." *Modern Law Review*, 39:147–61, March 1976. **1B26**
"It is the major purpose of this article to explore the problem of control over programme content in the context of the United States broadcasting structure." The author sees no evidence of radical change in the regulatory structure in the near future. "It is much more realistic that American broadcasting will continue to operate much as it has in the past, developing without real guidance from Congress, on the basis of ad hoc regulatory determinations by a federal agency which exercises a severely restricted (but potent) form of purely negative control, supplemented by occasional decisions of the courts of appeals and the United States Supreme Court."

₁Baker, John F.₁ "Publishing and the Law: Some Perils, Some Controversies, Some Optimistic Prospects." *Publishers' Weekly*, 207 (17): 22–23, 28 April 1975. **1B27**
Copyright, obscenity and pornography, libel, and freedom of information are among the problems plaguing publishers.

Baker, R. J. S. "The Official Secrets Acts: Another View." *Political Quarterly* (Great Britain), 44:214–16, 1973. **1B28**
Comment on the proposal of the Franks Committee which studied the working of Section 2

of the Official Secrets Act. View differs from that of Gavin Drewry, pp. 88–93.

Baker, Richard T. "Subpoenaing Newsmen: What Effects?" *Columbia Journalism Review*, 10(6):52–53, March–April 1972. **1B29**
A brief report on a survey of newsmen's attitudes toward the subpoenaing of reporters and the effect on news coverage. The survey was conducted by Professors Richard T. Baker and Vince Blasi. The latter reported more fully on the results in the *Michigan Law Review*, December 1971.

Baker, Robert K., Sandra J. Ball *et al.* *Mass Media and Violence.* Washington, D.C., National Commission on the Causes and Prevention of Violence, 1969. 614p. (A Task Force Report to the National Commission on the Causes and Prevention of Violence, no. IX) **1B30**
This report of the Media Task Force brings together an extensive body of information on the nature of the mass media, their functions, and effect. The report denies the frequent accusation that the press is the source of most that is evil and considers fatuous the notion that the press ought to "accentuate the positive and eliminate the negative." Nevertheless, "the media have contributed to the widespread use of confrontation as an instrument of social change by their failure to report adequately the conditions underlining current protest, by the proposals for solutions of pressing social problems, and by their action-oriented coverage of conflict." While "the government's role of news is properly restricted," the policies of the First Amendment cannot be realized simply by keeping government out. The report recommends five specific government actions: (1) increased support for public broadcasting for news and public affairs programming, (2) greater scrutiny of industry mergers and license renewals to reduce concentration of media ownership, (3) establishment of an executive level department for communications planning with authority to appeal in regulatory proceedings, (4) clarification by the FCC of the ambiguity over the "fairness doctrine," requiring only that "the licensee give a representative portrayal of the arguments of various sides of an issue," and (5) development by the FCC of broad guidelines and standards for judging applications for license renewals. The report makes seven recommendations for action by the news media: (1) "Journalists should reexamine the degree to which existing news judgments incorporate obsolete standards, including a tendency to report violence because it is sensational, rather than because it is significant"; (2) give greater prominence to interpretive news stories that can be written with time for calm reflection and balanced judgment; (3) pay greater attention to the coverage of minority group action, enabling groups to have access to the media without use of confrontation and demonstration; (4) provide greater interaction between the news media and the community; (5) further up-grading of the journalism

profession; (6) establish a code to be followed in the coverage of riots or other events involving group violence; and (7) offer resistance to critics who would have the media deny coverage to protest groups, but make provision for more balanced treatment of such events. The report further recommends the creation of a nonprofit corporation, a Center for Media Study, to collect, study, store, and disseminate information about the performances, practices, and values of the mass media. The appendices carry text of various codes, canons, and guidelines employed by the mass media, and summaries of independent research, as well as research done for the Task Force. A general report of the National (Eisenhower) Commission is entered under U.S. National Commission on the Causes and Prevention of Violence, *To Establish Justice*. . . .

Baker, Russell. "Perfect Sensor." *New York Times Magazine*, 25 November 1973, p. 6. **1B31**
Comment on the appropriateness of selecting a blind man as one of the movie censors in Clarkstown, N.Y. "Censorship shelters the community from what it does not go to see ₁people are watching television, not attending movies₁. It is protection of the blind. It is right that it should be done by the blind."

Baker, Samm S. "The Attempted Suppression of *The Permissible Lie.*" *Censorship Today*, 1(2):11–13 ₁August–September₁ 1968. **1B32**
An account of the banning of the author's book by Reader's Digest Association, Inc., parent company of Funk & Wagnalls who had contracted for the book. The book was critical of the advertising industry and the magazine deemed it contrary to their best interests. The book, with plates changed, was issued by World Publishing Co. The author sees this as a serious form of corporate censorship, considering the growing number of book companies that have been taken over by conglomerates—RCA, Time, Inc., CBS, Dun & Bradstreet, and ITT.

———. *The Permissible Lie; the Inside Truth About Advertising.* Cleveland, World, 1968. 236p. **1B33**
A veteran advertising man exposes the situation in the industry where "lying copy is not only condoned but encouraged by many advertisers and agencies." Included in his book are accounts of the industry's war against government regulation of advertising and the extent of advertisers control of television programming. The related article in *Censorship Today* gives an account of efforts to suppress the book.

Baker, Warren E. "The Background and Status of CATV Industry Regulations." *TV and Communications*, 4 (12):58, 60, 65, December 1967. **1B34**
FCC regulation of CATV is largely for the purpose of protecting the television industry from competition.

Baldasty, Gerald J. *A Theory of Press Freedom: Massachusetts Newspapers and Law, 1782–1791.* Madison, Wis., University of Wisconsin–Madison, 1974. 106p. (Unpublished Master's thesis) **1B35**

"This study is an attempt to determine contemporary standards on press freedom in Massachusetts newspapers in the decade before the adoption of the First Amendment, to examine what legal constraints affected the press, and to see whether these constraints include the English common law on defamation." An article based on the thesis appears in the April 1976 issue of *Journalism History.*

Baldwin, Carl R. "Art & the Law: The Flag in Court Again." *Art in America,* 3:50–54, May–June 1974. **1B36**

An account of the case of Stephen Radich, New York art dealer, brought to trial for violating a state statute on flag-desecration. Objected to were three-dimensional works of art by Marc Morrel which used the American flag to express satirical or dissident sentiments. The case went to the U.S. Supreme Court where a divided opinion upheld Radich's conviction but failed to settle the issue whether the statute violated First Amendment freedom of expression for the creative artist.

[Baldwin, Charles.] *The Important Trial in the Common Pleas, Friday, February 16, 1816. Webster v. Baldwin, for a Libel Charging Adultery between the Most Noble Arthur Duke of Wellington and Lady Frances C. W. Webster, at Brussels, after the Battle of Waterloo.* London, Hone, 1816. 16p. **1B37**

The publisher of *St. James Chronicle,* Charles Baldwin, was found guilty of publishing libellous statements suggesting an affair between Lady Webster and the Duke of Wellington, and fined £2,000.

Bales, Waldo F. "Public Business Is Not Always Public." *Urban Lawyer,* 7:332–42, Spring 1975. **1B38**

The fourth estate is the public, not the media. Public officials must balance their rights with the right of the public, of which the media are a part. The public is entitled to information about public business, but not necessarily via the press.

Balk, Alfred. "Beyond Agnewism." *Columbia Journalism Review,* 8(4):14–19, Winter 1969–70. **1B39**

A discussion of the credibility problems of the media in response to the attacks of Vice-President Agnew. Following the article is: The Agnew Analysis: False Premises, Wrong Conclusions.

———. "Britain's Great Thalidomide Cover-up." *Columbia Journalism Review,* 14(1):24–27, May–June 1975. **1B40**

"A tough press gag rule virtually choked off coverage of a national scandal."

———. "Minnesota Launches a Press Council." *Columbia Journalism Review,* 10(4):22–27, November–December 1971. **1B41**

An account of the establishment of the first statewide press council in the United States, with widespread newspaper support. "The council is a voluntary, extralegal body with no enforcement powers. Its effectiveness will depend upon the cooperation of the press and the public," according to Associate Justice C. Donald Peterson of the Minnesota Supreme Court and chairman of the Council.

———. "What the Press Council Is All About." *Bulletin of the American Society of Newspaper Editors,* 566:19–21, February 1973. **1B42**

"Press Councils are not panaceas. But in no case where councils have been established have the worst fears of press council opponents been realized."

———, and James Boylan, *eds. Our Troubled Press: Ten Years of the Columbia Journalism Review.* Boston, Little, Brown, 1975. 393p. **1B43**

This collection of articles from the *Columbia Journalism Review* contains a number of pieces relating to freedom of the press: The Agnew Analysis: False Premises, Wrong Conclusions. The Subpoena Dilemma. Why We Lack a National Press Council by Norman E. Isaacs. Right of Access: A Modest Proposal by Ben H. Bagdikian. Must the Media Be "Used"? by James McCartney.

Ball, Revonda J. *An Examination of the Current Threat of Dismissal of Public High School Teachers Because of Controversy About Selected Reading Materials and Suggested Activities for Teachers.* Durham, N.C., Duke University, 1973. 157p. (Ph.D. dissertation, University Microfilms, no. 74–1121) **1B44**

"This study examines the question of using controversial literature in the secondary school classroom from legal and professional standpoints and provides suggestions for activities whereby English teachers may avoid dismissal. The contents include: (1) a discussion of the question of standards, both of the community and of the profession, which emphasizes the need for the teacher to become familiar with community standards in order to prepare himself more thoroughly for his work; (2) reasons for community objections to controversial literature and a discussion of why pressure groups have objected to some literary works; (3) a discussion of the legal aspects of the censorship problem and an examination of censorship controversies which were resolved out of court; and (4) several conclusions and suggestions for planning units of courses to meet the needs of students for literature."

Bambrick, John G., Jr. "FCC's Formal Rules Concerning Personal Attacks and Political Editorials Contravene the First Amendment." *Notre Dame Lawyer,* 44:447–57, February 1969. **1B45**

Comment on the decision of the Court in *Radio Television News Directors Association v. FCC,* 7th Cir., Sept. 10, 1968, which held that the personal attack and political editorial rules promulgated by the FCC contravene the First Amendment in view of their vagueness, the burden they impose on licensees, and the possibility they raise of both Commission censorship and licensee self-censorship. "Whether or not there is such a public interest in attaining fairness so as to sustain government regulation under the Fairness Doctrine is something the court has apparently left for the determination of the Supreme Court when it hears *Red Lion* [Red Lion Broadcasting Co. v. FCC, 1969]."

Bandura, Albert. "What TV Violence Can Do to Your Child." *Look,* 27(21): 46–52, 22 October 1963. (Reprinted in Otto N. Larsen, *ed., Violence and the Mass Media,* pp. 123–30) **1B46**

Today's youth are being raised on a heavy dosage of television aggression and violence. The author reports on a series of tests he conducted which "leave little doubt that exposure to violence heightens aggressive tendencies in children."

Bane, David. "We Are All Censors." *Minnesota English Journal,* 12(1):34–37, Winter 1976. **1B47**

The author argues that it is hypocritical for teachers to say they are not censors and that they have an edge on the truth not possessed by outsiders. In the effort to inculcate skills and morality in students—and the two cannot be separated in society—we are all censors. "If we are really serious about helping students to develop these value-skills, then we should be arguing that they have the chance to judge alternative modes of life, the chance to make real choices among those alternatives and the chance to bear the consequences of their choices. If students are to have real choices between sexist and non-sexist ways of behaving, they must somehow come into contact with both modes of behavior. Teachers may have to use sexist materials in the classroom to accomplish this."

Banerjee, Sumanta. *India's Monopoly Press: A Mirror of Distortion.* New Delhi, Indian Federation of Working Journalists, 1973. 95p. **1B48**

The author contends that the major English newspapers in India are controlled by a few big industrial houses and that their news reporting fails in objectivity and their editorials do not reflect independent thinking.

Bannerjee, D.N. "Freedom of Speech and Expression in India: Clear-and-Present-Danger Test." *Indian Law Review*, 6:90–103, 1952. **1B49**
A discussion of the American concept of "clear and present danger" as applied to Indian law, including a review of the various U.S. Supreme Court cases in which this concept was a factor.

"Banning Books: An Ancient Sport Makes a Rowdy Comeback among School Boards." *American School Board Journal*, 160:25–44, May 1973. **1B50**
Book banning is on the increase but "when a school board allows itself to become a combatant in a book banning war, it turns the leadership over to other forces." Also includes articles: The Debate: Whether and How to Censure "Objectionable" School Books. Not All "Dirty" Words in Student Publications Can (or Should) Be Bleeped, Say the Courts by M. Chester Nolte. Will the High Court Change the Rules on "Dirty" Books? The Books They Are Banning and Why: The List Has Something for Nearly Everyone. Try Out This Model School District Policy on Censorship.

Baragli, Enrico. *Codice Hays, Legion of Decency, Due Esperienze U.S.A.* Rome, Studio Romano Della Communicazione Sociale, 1968. 148p. (Contributi 2) **1B51**
Motion picture censorship in the United States: the Hays Office and the Catholic Legion of Decency.

Barbas, Rex M. "Perspective; Advocacy, Activist Journalism and the Law." *Loyola Law Review* (New Orleans), 20:105–19, 1974. **1B52**
"This article is an analysis of the conflict between government, the press and the people's right to know, with special emphasis on the part subjectivity plays in that conflict."

Barbeau, Clayton C., *ed. Art, Obscenity, and Your Children.* St. Meinrad, Ind., Abbey, 1967. 160p. (Marriage Paperback Library) **1B53**
Content: Four Letter Words and Art by Clayton C. Barbeau. Constitutional Tests for Obscenity by Patrick D. McAnany. Adults, Movies and Censorship by Simon Scanlon. Book, Bell and Scandal by Irving Sussman. Someone Please Restate the Question by Joseph W. Bird. The Use and Abuse of Children's Time by Isidore Ziferstein. His Image: Art or Pornography? by Margaret Krebs. The Parent's Role: Censor or Teacher? by John Ford. Family Camp Art by Don May. Ambassadors of Innocence by William H. Bishop.

Parents, Children and Art by Joan and Barry Ulanov.

Barber, D. F. *Pornography and Society.* London, Skilton, 1972. 192p. **1B54**
Following a discussion of the laws of obscene libel in Britain, an appraisal of various views on pornography, attempts to defend it, and causal relationships between pornography and antisocial acts, the author comes to the conclusion that there can only be "two honest and realistic ways of looking at pornography. Either we accept it as a minor facet of the whole complex structure of human sexuality . . . or we regard it as a symptom of a more general malaise. It is in the latter sense that it is a social problem and not because it presents a threat to society or the individual. . . . 'Pornography' as we commonly know it is the miasma of guilt and shame which obtrudes between us and the object perceived." Legalizing pornography would not automatically remove guilt and shame from our consciousness of sex, but the conditions for such a removal would be created. Legalizing pornography, which he recommends, would not mean complete lack of control. "Window displays, unsolicited receipt of pornographic material, the use of children as models and many other fears about pornography could easily be controlled with realistic and enforceable laws." The author concludes that: "The whole man is a sexual creature and we cannot legislate sexuality out of existence or suppress it. Our various attempts to do so have caused untold damage and it is time to stop." A postscript by the publisher, Charles Skilton, cites the long history of prosecution of publishers in the area of sex, and urges that authorities turn their attention to more serious issues.

Barber, John L. "The Geography of Obscenity's 'Contemporary Community Standard.' " *Wake Forest Law Review*, 8:81–92, December 1971. **1B55**
"This comment will attempt to analyze this confusion over the 'contemporary community standard' [referred to in the U.S. Supreme Court's decision in the obscenity case, *Miller v. California*] by (1) categorizing the court decisions by the particular community that they have selected, (2) setting out the rationale the courts have given for their choice in communities, and (3) evaluating the reasoning of the court."

Barber, Richard J. "Newspaper Monopoly in New Orleans: The Lessons for Antitrust Policy." *Louisiana Law Review*, 24:503–54, April 1964. **1B56**
To assess the role of antitrust policy in the newspaper industry a case study is made of the New Orleans newspaper market. "This article purports (1) to review the principal structural and performance characteristics of newspaper publication in New Orleans; (2) to survey the nature of the relevant antitrust litigation; (3) to analyze the merit of the government's action, directed as it was exclusively to certain practices in which the city's leading newspaper engaged; and (4) to consider the role of antitrust

policy generally in the newspaper industry. Most of the discussion deals with the period 1949–1958, with particular emphasis on the years 1949 and 1950 since they were at the heart of the pertinent antitrust litigation and exemplify the market's outstanding features over the past thirty years."

Barber, Stephan A. "The California Public Records Act: The Public's Right of Access to Governmental Information." *Pacific Law Journal*, 7:105–48, January 1976. **1B57**

Barbour, Alton B. *Free Speech Attitude Consistency.* Denver, Colo., University of Denver, 1968. 138p. (Ph.D. dissertation, University Microfilms, no. 68-17, 836) **1B58**
"The purpose of this investigation was to develop and test an instrument which would probe not only prevalent attitudes regarding freedom of speech, but the consistencies of such attitudes with stated beliefs about free speech and other attitude components, as well." Results of the study revealed that while 93 percent of the subjects claimed belief in free speech, "in all four topical areas, and on nearly every item, subjects revealed attitudes opposed to free speech as defined and delineated by U.S. Supreme Court decisions."

———. "Survey Research in Free Speech Attitudes." *Free Speech Yearbook*, *1971*. New York, Speech Communication Association, 1971, pp. 28–35. **1B59**
A summary of published research studies. The author concludes that "on the basis of literature available about free speech attitudes it is reasonable to conclude that Americans are poorly informed about their constitutional rights of free speech, and that a large number of Americans, young and old, are willing to restrict the free speech of others, particularly with regard to threatening issues."

Barendt, Eric M. "Official Secrecy in British Government: The Franks Report and the Future." *Round Table* (Great Britain), 250:183–92, 1973. **1B60**
An analysis of the report of the 1972 Franks Committee, appointed in 1971 to review Britain's Official Secrets Act, and a comparison of the recommendations with similar legislation in other Commonwealth countries.

Barilla, John. "Inherent Disciplinary Powers of a University Include Proscription of Student Distribution of Pamphlets Where There Is a Reasonable Forecast of Substantial Campus Disruption." *Syracuse Law Review*, 21:1260–70, Summer 1970. **1B61**
Re: *Norton v. Discipline Committee of East Tennessee State University*, 419 F.2d 195 (6th Cir. 1969). The Court refused to interfere in the disciplinary action taken against students who

issued pamphlets critical of the University administration on grounds that the school officials had reasonable concerns that disruption would result, that the pamphlets created a clear and present danger, and that the University had inherent authority to discipline students for such offenses.

Barilli, Andrea. *Basic Principles of Freedom of the Press in the United States and Italy: A Constitutional Survey.* Berkeley, Calif., University of California, 1960. 140p. (Unpublished Master's thesis) **1B62**

Barish, Lawrence. *Determining the Limits of Free Expression: A New Look at the Obscenity Issue.* Madison, Wis., Wisconsin Legislative Reference Bureau, 1971. 20p. Processed. (Information Bulletin, 71-5) **1B63**
(1) A summary of U.S. Supreme Court decisions which have attempted to define and categorize obscenity, which involve federal statutes, and those relating to motion pictures. (2) An overview of recently enacted state obscenity statutes dealing with such issues as prohibition of obscene materials to minors, pandering, scienter requirements, and regulation of motion pictures. (3) The Wisconsin experience: The impact of court decisions, measures considered by the 1969 legislature, and the new obscenity law (1969) prohibiting "harmful materials" to minors, text of which is included, and the impact of Wisconsin District Court decisions on local obscenity ordinances.

Barist, Jeffrey A. "The First Amendment and Regulation of Prejudicial Publicity—An Analysis." *Fordham Law Review,* 36:425–52, March 1968. **1B64**
A discussion of the case of *Bridges v. California* (1941), in which the U.S. Supreme Court drastically limited the common law power of a court to punish out-of-court publications for contempt. The decision related to judge-directed publication and, the author argues, does not apply to control of publications that might influence a jury. "It is the conclusion of this paper that limited regulation upon publicity affecting the impartiality of a jury in a criminal case can be constitutionally imposed." The central doctrine must be found in *New York Times Co. v. Sullivan* "not by rigidly applying the specific rule but by understanding that the primary function of the first amendment is to protect speech concerned with the political process and the exercise of that sovereignty which the Constitution vests in the electorate."

Barker, Carol M., and Matthew H. Fox. *Classified Files: The Yellowing Pages; A Report on Scholars' Access to Government Documents.* New York, Twentieth Century Fund, 1971. 115p. **1B65**
This report deals with the concern of "scholars and historians who must cope with the maze of security restrictions to gain access to govern-

ment records and archives in order to evaluate and understand past policies and activities. . . . This paper investigates the problems involved in independent research in diplomatic and military archives, the distortions that may result from unequal and privileged access to government records, and proposals for reform of the classification system, including Nixon's new order." The appendix includes the text of the Freedom of Information Act, and President Nixon's Executive Order on Security Classification.

Barker, Joel. "The Arkansas Law on Obscenity and *Gent v. Arkansas.*" *Arkansas Historical Quarterly,* 29(1):48–67, Spring 1970. **1B66**
An account of the testing of the Arkansas law on obscenity based on a model antiobscenity statute prepared by the national Council for Periodical Distributors Association. The case of *Gent v. Arkansas* (1967), reversed a lower court decision against the magazine, but failed to rule on the constitutionality of the statute.

Barletta, Robert T. "First Amendment Right of a Newsman Not to Reveal Confidential information." *Duquesne Law Review,* 9:506–14, Spring 1971. **1B67**
The case of Earl Caldwell, *Caldwell v. U.S.,* 434 F.2d 1081 (9th Cir. 1970).

Barlongay, Samilo N. "Censorship of the Mails." *Philippine Law Journal,* 35:1219–29, September 1960. **1B68**
The paper deals with relevant Philippine statutes on mail censorship, particularly that which relates to the seizure of communist propaganda. References are also made to United States law and practices.

Barlow, N.L.A. "Indecent and Obscene Language in New Zealand." *New Zealand Law Journal,* 1974:319–26, 30 July 1974. **1B69**
The author considers the recent Court of Appeals decision in *Drummond v. Police* (1973) 2 NZLR 263, which differentiated between offenses relating to public morality and offenses relating to public behavior, and which marked the demise of the 1868 *Hicklin* rule on obscenity in New Zealand. The Court acknowledged the assistance of an analysis made by Dr. J. J. Bray, Chief Justice of South Australia, whose lecture, The Juristic Basis of the Law Relating to Offenses Against Public Morality and Obscenity, deals with this issue.

Barnard, Warren E. *The Prime Time Access Rule.* Columbia, Mo., Freedom of Information Center, School of Journalism, University of Missouri at Columbia, 1971. 6p. (Report no. 267) **1B70**
"Under a barrage of criticism from broadcasters, independent producers and even FCC Chairman Dean Burch, the Federal Communications Commission enacted the 'prime time

access rule' after nearly 15 years of deliberation. The rule, which will become effective this October, is designed to curtail the role of the network in controlling television programming."

Barnds, William J. *The Right to Know, to Withhold, & to Lie.* New York, The Council on Religion and International Affairs, 1969. 86p. (Special Studies 207) **1B71**
"If a government is going to lie it can probably do so for a short period, and when that period is over it should generally admit what it did and why. For it is continual exaggeration and distortion rather than the individual lie that are really damaging to society." Commentary on Barnds' views by Wilson Carey McWilliams (Honesty and Political Authority), Daniel C. Maguire (Secrecy and the Myths of Power), and Paul W. Blackstock (Deception in Public Affairs: A Disestablishment View).

Barnes, Frances K. *Policies and Practices Governing Provision of Controversial Materials in the Public High School Libraries in Texas in 1965.* Austin, Tex., University of Texas, 1966. 170p. (Unpublished Master's thesis) **1B72**
"It is the purpose of this study to examine some of the factors which affect the inclusion or exclusion of potentially controversial titles in high school libraries; factors which free or restrain school librarians in their tasks of materials selection." The study was conducted by means of questionnaires sent to selected high school libraries in Texas, which sought to learn book selection policies, particularly in dealing with controversial materials, the prevalence of potentially controversial holdings in these libraries and the response of the community to them.

Barnes, Harry Elmer. *Blasting the Historical Blackout.* n.p., The Author, 1963. 42p. **1B73**
Further discussion on the theme (B69) that efforts have been made since the outbreak of World War II to suppress the truth about the circumstances of the U.S. entry into the war. Special references to A.J.P. Taylor's *The Origins of the Second World War,* which he praises for its revisionist views.

Barnes, Peter. "The Army and the First Amendment." *New Republic,* 160:13–14, 24 May 1969. **1B74**
"For three-and-a-half million American citizens in uniform, justice is what the brass say it is, damn the Constitution and full speed ahead." Comments on the arrest and sentencing to four years hard labor and dishonorable discharge of two army privates for running off a mimeographed protest to the war and distributing them to soldiers at Fort Ord, Calif.

———. "Farewell, Free Enterprise." *New Republic*, 163:15–18, 17 October 1970. **1B75**
Criticism of the Newspaper Preservation Act and an account of the filing of a lawsuit alleging that the act violates the Constitution.

Barnes, Richard L. "A changing View Toward Trial by Newspaper." *Oklahoma Law Review*, 16:337–50, August 1963. **1B76**
A review of recent cases involving prejudicial press coverage which have resulted in court action. The author suggests three measures that might prevent endangerment of fair trials: (1) self-imposed restraint on the part of the news media, (2) punishment by contempt conviction for improper publication, and (3) cutting off the source of the information to a limited extent. A combination of all three, the author suggests, would probably be the best answer.

Barnett, C.S. "Obscenity and S. 150 (8) of the Criminal Code." *Criminal Law Quarterly*, 12:10–29, December 1969. **1B77**
"The purpose of this paper is to determine, from the few relevant cases, the meaning of 'obscene' within the Criminal Code of Canada as it purports to be and as it really is."

———. "Regina v. Great West News, Ltd." *Criminal Law Quarterly*, 12:357–61, October 1970. **1B78**
The author concludes that the decision in this obscenity case established that expert evidence is not required to determine community standards.

Barnett, Lincoln. "The Case of John Peter Zenger." *American Heritage*, 23(1):33–41, 103–5, December 1971. **1B79**
A retelling of the story (with illustrations) of the New York colonial newspaper editor whose libel trial was a legal landmark of press freedom on both sides of the Atlantic. "The two great principles set forth by [Andrew] Hamilton [Zenger's attorney]—the validity of truth as a defense of libel and the right of the jury to decide libellousness—did eventually become universal in the English-speaking world."

Barnett, Stephen R. "The FCC's Nonbattle Against Media Monopoly." *Columbia Journalism Review*, 11:43–50, January–February 1973. **1B80**
A proposed FCC rule "requiring the owners of daily newspapers and TV stations in the same city—and also of daily newspapers and radio stations, of which there are some 230

instances—to sell either the station or the newspaper within five years" has never been adopted.

———. "Merger, Monopoly and a Free Press." *Nation*, 216:76–86, 15 January 1973. **1B81**
The media are keeping quiet about a "leading nonstory"—the proposal of the Federal Communications Commission to break up common ownership of newspapers and broadcast stations in cities throughout the country.

———. "Newspaper Lobby." *New Republic*, 163:11–12, 18 July 1970. **1B82**
Criticism of the Newspaper Preservation Bill which would grant exemption from the antitrust laws for the "joint-operating agreements" that exist between separately owned daily newspapers in twenty-two cities.

———. "Press Monopoly: Mr. Agnew's Oversights." *Nation*, 210(3):72–75, 26 January 1970. **1B83**
Mr. Agnew made front-page news challenging the monopoly power of certain newspapers, but he overlooked some roughly 1600 cities that have a complete daily-newspaper monopoly. Noted are the positions taken by various governmental and monopoly groups on the "newspaper preservation" bill being pushed through Congress to create an antitrust exemption.

———. "State, Federal, and Local Regulation of Cable Television." *Notre Dame Lawyer*, 47:685–814, April 1972. **1B84**
A comprehensive survey and critique of existing regulations of CATV.

———. "Televising the President: Equal Time and the Nixon Style." *Nation*, 214:807–11, 26 June 1972. **1B85**
The author examines the two legal doctrines which govern the use of television by the president and his opponents—the "equal opportunities" law, popularly known as "equal time," and the FCC's "fairness doctrine" and concludes there is a need for decisions, "either by the FCC or the courts, reversing the FCC's positions on the status of Presidential speeches and news conferences under the equal time law."

Barnett, Ursula. "Censorship in South Africa—From Bad to Worse." *Publishers' Weekly*, 208(12):78–80, 22 September 1975. **1B86**
The Censorship Act, which stipulates what South Africans may or may not read or use, has been strengthened so that it may be applied from a Christian point of view, and so that appeals to the courts from the Board of Censors are abolished. The author charges that the Board does not adequately represent the white population and has no representation from the blacks. "Like apartheid, the Censorship Act is a desperate measure by the Nationalist Af-

rikaner, not just to maintain the status quo, but to ensure survival of his identity. Otherwise, he fears that he will drown in the deluge of 20th-century ideas."

Barnett, Walter. "Corruption of Morals—the Underlying Issue of the Pornography Commission Report." *Law & Social Order*, 1971:189–243, 1971. **1B87**
"Beginning with the assumption that some moral tenets, such as prohibition against murder and rape, must be enforced because they are essential to communal life among human beings, this article examines whether as a matter of policy a society may enforce those morals which are peculiar to it, as compared with other societies. Professor Barnett analyzes the traditional theses which buttress each side of the argument, and agreeing with the principles articulated by John Stuart Mills' essay *On Liberty* concludes that society must limit itself to controlling that behavior which it can demonstrate is actually harmful to other people."

Barney, Ralph D. *News Access in the Southwest*. Columbia, Mo., Freedom of Information Center, School of Journalism, University of Missouri at Columbia, 1969. 6p. (Report no. 232) **1B88**
"The thirteen western states have passed more open meetings and open records laws than the national average. Led by the five most southwestern states, legislative and court actions have favored liberal interpretation and strengthening of these laws in favor of the press and individual citizens."

———. *The Right to Attend Public Trials*. Columbia, Mo., Freedom of Information Center, School of Journalism, University of Missouri at Columbia, 1969. 8p. (Report no. 225) **1B89**
The author explores the constitutional concept of a "speedy and public trial." "In the resulting give and take of court decisions, a body of law which is quite amorphous, has arisen—one which attempts to define 'public' trial and to explain just whom courts may exclude and just what circumstances may give rise to exclusions."

Barnouw, Erik. *The Golden Web: A History of Broadcasting in the United States. Volume II—1933 to 1953*. New York, Oxford University Press, 1968. 391p. **1B90**
This second volume in the history of broadcasting traces the rise of the American radio networks and ushers in an era dominated by television. The work covers the development of news broadcasting; the growing stranglehold of advertising agencies over programming; the blacklisting and purges of the early 1950s that ended the careers of many creative artists; the increased role of the Federal Communications Commission, operating under the Communications Act of 1934; wartime controls; the development of industry codes; monopoly

probes; and the development of the concept of public service responsibilities.

————. *The Image Empire: A History of Broadcasting in the United States. Volume III—from 1953.* New York, Oxford University Press, 1970. 396p.　**1B91**
The final volume in the series records the sweep of television throughout the world and United States involvement "of imperial scope." The work "shows the television industry, closely allied with American business and military interests," with a powerful and widespread influence on political and social opinions. Included are discussions of the McCarthy hearings, limitations on news coverage because of constraints of time, drama, business interests, and personal bias. He discusses the manipulation of public opinion by the CIA, the Defense Department, and the White House, with respect to the Bay of Pigs invasion and the Vietnam war.

————. *A Tower of Babel: A History of Broadcasting in the United States. Volume I—to 1933.* New York, Oxford University Press, 1966. 344p.　**1B92**
This history of American broadcasting from its birth through the Great Depression of the '30s includes such topics as ownership and control of radio, government regulations (text of the Radio Acts of 1912 and 1927 are given in the appendix), licensing standards, the adoption of a code of ethics, and the numerous efforts at censorship taken by a cautious industry. The latter includes use of an emergency cutoff switch when such topics as birth control or prostitution were mentioned and the banning of H. V. Kaltenborn's newscasts from the air in 1924 for his criticism of the State Department.

————. *Tube of Plenty; the Evolution of American Television.* New York, Oxford University Press, 1975. 573p.　**1B93**
The work is based on the author's trilogy, *A History of Broadcasting in the United States,* with material added that has taken place since their publication, including the 1972 presidential campaign and the Nixon resignation.

Barr, Henry L. "Using the FCC's Fairness Doctrine to Effect Environmental Reform." *Environmental Affairs,* 1:367–83, June 1972.　**1B94**
An analysis of the FCC's adverse decision in the case of the Friends of the Earth who had requested counter advertising from a New York television station under the fairness doctrine to counteract automobile and gasoline commercials.

Barrer, Bertram. "A Media Man's View of Dissent." (Abstract). In Speech Association of America. *Abstracts, 56th Annual Meeting,* New Orleans, The Association, 1970, p. 93.　**1B95**

An analysis of the right to dissent as practiced in broadcast journalism, whose role is to offer the public "a vast communication environment in which national dialogue and debate can take place."

Barrett, James K. "Inside the Mob's Smut Rackets." *Reader's Digest,* 103:128–32, November 1973.　**1B96**
"A former Mafia operative and FBI undercover man exposes the insidious involvement of organized crime in the billion-dollar-a-year pornography industry."

Barrett, John C., and Mary L. Frampton. "From the FCC's Fairness Doctrine to Red Lion's Fiduciary Principle." *Harvard Civil Rights–Civil Liberties Law Review,* 5:89–103, January 1970. (Reprinted in 1A100)　**1B97**
"In *Red Lion Broadcasting Co. v. FCC* and *U.S. v. Radio Television News Directors Association* [1969], the court faced squarely and for the first time the question whether the FCC relying on its 'fairness doctrine,' could constitutionally compel a licensee to adhere to certain minimal programming requisites." The Court ruled "that the specific application of the fairness doctrine in *Red Lion,* and . . . in *RTNDA,* are both authorized by Congress and enhance rather than abridge the freedoms of speech and press."

Barrett, Laurence I. *et al.* "Monitoring National News Suppliers." *Columbia Journalism Review,* 11(6):43–57, March–April 1973.　**1B98**
Reaction of the nation's press to proposals of a Twentieth Century Fund Task Force to establish a media council to monitor national news reporting. Included is the text of the report and questions and answers at a press conference that accompanied release of the report.

Barrett, Marvin, *ed. The Alfred I. duPont—Columbia University Survey of Broadcast Journalism, 1968–1969.* New York, Grosset & Dunlap, 1969. 132p.　**1B99**
The chapter on Government and Broadcast Journalism deals with such issues as pressures and interconnection of congressmen and the media, license renewal, media monopoly, the U.S. Supreme Court's upholding of the FCC's fairness doctrine, and the staging of documentaries. An article by Ruth Lieban, Trouble in Paradise, deals with a controversy in Paradise, Calif., over license renewal of radio station KEWQ.

————. *The Alfred I. duPont—Columbia University Survey of Broadcast Journalism, 1969–1970: Year of Challenge, Year of Crisis.* New York, Grosset & Dunlap, 1970. 156p.　**1B100**
Articles relating to freedom of the press: Agnew and the Tiny Fraternity of Privileged Men. Government and Broadcast Journalism. The FCC and the Future of Broadcast Jour-

nalism by Kenneth A. Cox, Subpoenas: Should Reporters Tell All by Marcus Cohn, Transcript of Spiro T. Agnew's Des Moines, Iowa Address.

————. *The Alfred I. duPont—Columbia University Survey of Broadcast Journalism, 1970–1971: A State of Siege.* New York, Grosset & Dunlap, 1971. 183p.　**1B101**
Articles relating to freedom of the press: The Selling of the Pentagon, Government and Broadcast Journalism, Truth and Public Television. Profits, Advertising and the News. The Inevitable Bias of Television by Michael Novak. From Fairness to Access by Jerome Barron. Women on the Air by Helen Epstein.

————. *The Alfred I. duPont—Columbia University Survey of Broadcast Journalism, 1971–1972: The Politics of Broadcasting.* New York, Crowell, 1973. 247p.　**1B102**
The theme of this year's survey of broadcasting was the confrontation between politics and broadcasting; between the Nixon Administration and particularly its spokesman, Spiro Agnew, and the networks over the fairness or lack of fairness of television to the Administration; and the proposals of Clay T. Whitehead, director, Office of Telecommunications Policy on the White House staff, to make certain changes in the system of commercial television. Texts of three Whitehead speeches are included.

————. *The Fifth Alfred I. duPont—Columbia University Survey of Broadcast Journalism: Moments of Truth?* New York, Crowell, 1974. 274p.　**1B103**
This survey covers "the most exciting and excruciating eighteen months in the history of the media"—the events of Watergate, the energy crisis, and the effect on public and commercial broadcasting "under an actively hostile Nixon regime." Separate articles: First Amendment: Challenge and Commitment by Senator Lowell P. Weicker. The People and the News by Michael Novak. Big Media—Free Press by Clay T. Whitehead. The appendix contains various noteworthy statements, some secret, from Nixon officials regarding the press; William Paley, CBS chairman's policy discontinuing "instant analysis" and a later statement rescinding the rule; the National News Council's statement on Nixon's charges against television news.

[Barrier, Mary L.] "Restriction of the First Amendment in an Academic Environment." *University of Kansas Law Review,* 22:597–605, Summer 1974.　**1B104**
Comment on the case, *Papish v. Board of Curators* (1973), in which the U.S. Supreme

Court reversed a lower court decision which had upheld the University of Missouri's expulsion of a journalism student for distributing an underground newspaper containing an allegedly obscene expression. The Court held that the university was bound by the same First Amendment standards which restrict the state's constitutional authority to regulate speech in the wider state community. The note considers "derivation and scope of the standards employed by the Court in its analysis of *Papish* and the possible effect, if any, which the new obscenity test set forth in *Miller v. California* [1973] might have on the scope of University control over speech content."

Barrier, N. Gerald. *Banned; Controversial Literature and Political Control in British India, 1907–1947.* Columbia, Mo., University of Missouri Press at Columbia, 1974. 324p. (University of Missouri Studies, 61)   **1B105**
The first part of the volume is an examination of the control of printed matter in British India growing from a concern with maintaining public order and confronting the dual threat of nationalism and religious disturbances. The second part of the book is a guide to four major collections of literature that have been banned in India, arranged under the headings "religious controversy," "national, secular politics," and "patriotic poetry, songs."

———, and G. R. Thursby. "South Asian Proscribed Publications, 1907–1947." *Indian Archives* (India), 18(2):24–53, 1969.   **1B106**
A discussion of British censorship of the press in India under the Indian Press Act of 1910 and other legislation which resulted in the banning of some 3,000 books and pamphlets and over 400 issues of newspapers.

[Barrister at Law.] *Considerations on Proceedings by Information and Attachment. Addressed to the Members of the House of Commons by a Barrister at Law.* . . . 2d ed. London, Printed for W. Harris, 1768. 48p.   **1B107**
Criticism of the use of "ex-officio informations" and "attachments" by the Attorney General in the prosecution of seditious libel. This practice sets aside the old common-law proceedings of indictment and presentment by Grand Juries. Chief Justice Hall, according to the author, considered the ex-officio information illegal. "Trial by Jury, is by Informations in part set aside; and by Attachments totally annihilated." Parliament should discuss this matter because it poses a threat to English liberties. "The Liberty of the Press is one of the most valuable privileges of Englishmen; and, when employed to patriotic purposes, merits the patronage of the courts and judicature. As the interests of every member of society is con-

cerned in the proper administration of public affairs, he has a right to publish his thoughts upon them. The freedom of writing and speaking has more than once preserved our constitution. An upright government can no more be injured by seditious publications than the interests of religion by heretical writings, which, when fairly brought to the test, establish its fundamental doctrines, and shew the futility of all endeavors to subvert it."

Barron, Jerome A. "Access—The Only Choice for the Media?" *Texas Law Review* 48:766–82, March 1970. (Reprinted in Donald M. Gillmor and Jerome A. Barron, *Mass Communication Law*, 2d ed., pp. 818–21; and in Kenneth S. Devol, ed., *Mass Media and the Supreme Court*, pp. 91–97)   **1B108**
The U.S. Supreme Court, in its *Red Lion* decision (*Red Lion Broadcasting Company v. FCC*, 1969) provided a legal stimulus for public access to the media by validating the fairness doctrine. Freedom of expression should no longer be defined by the legal immunities of publishers and broadcasters. "In broadcasting, both the fairness doctrine and the right of reply to groups and individuals attacked by the broadcast media have been held constitutionally authorized." The same rights of reply, "a fair price to extract for the new relative freedom from libel judgments (*New York Times v. Sullivan*) should be required of newspaper."

———. *Access: The Only Choice for the Media.* 46 min. tape recording. Berkeley, Calif., Pacifica Tape Library, 1969. (Law and the Free Society I)   **1B109**
Professor Barron argues for restoring to the people First Amendment right of access to the media, now controlled by the powerful few in the newspaper and broadcasting industry. He believes the media have an affirmative obligation to provide access for divergent ideas. He applauds the *Red Lion* decision of the U.S. Supreme Court (1969) which gave support to the FCC's fairness doctrine, and calls for a similar guarantee of fairness in the newspaper press. Clifton Daniel and John Pemberton respond to Professor Barron's remarks and that tape is entered under Daniel.

———. "Access to the Press." *Seminar (A Quarterly Review for Newspapermen by Copley Newspapers)*, 11:23–26, March 1969.   **1B110**
"Here, in a non-legal presentation, Professor Barron proposes that a new interpretation should be applied to the First Amendment to give the public a right of access to the press."

———. "Access to the Press—A New First Amendment Right." *Harvard Law Review*, 80(8):1641–77, June 1967. (Reprinted in Donald M. Gillmor and Jerome A. Barron, *Mass Communication Law*, 2d ed., pp. 553–72; in Michael C.

Emery and Ted C. Smythe, eds., *Readings in Mass Communications*, pp. 16–22; and in David G. Clark and Earl R. Hutchison, eds., *Mass Media and the Law*, pp. 421–61)   **1B111**
"The press, long enshrined among our most highly cherished institutions, was thought a cornerstone of democracy when its name was boldly inscribed in the Bill of Rights. Freed from governmental restraint, initially by the first amendment and later by the fourteenth, the press was to stand majestically as the champion of new ideas and the watch dog against governmental abuse. Professor Barron finds this conception of the first amendment, perhaps realistic in the eighteenth-century heyday of political pamphleteering, essentially romantic in an era marked by extraordinary technological developments in the communications industry. To make viable the time-honored 'marketplace' theory, he argues for a twentieth-century interpretation of the first amendment which will impose an affirmative responsibility on the monopoly newspaper to act as sounding board for new ideas and old grievances"—Editor. This article ushered in a nationwide debate over the "right of access."

———. "An Emerging First Amendment Right of Access to the Media?" *George Washington Law Review*, 37:487–509, March 1969. (Reprinted in Donald M. Gillmor and Jerome A. Barron, *Mass Communication Law*, pp. 178–86, 689–97; and in *Columbia Journalism Quarterly*, Spring 1969)   **1B112**
This article will examine the propriety of imposing an affirmative duty on the owners of the various media to provide access for the voices of dissent, with particular attention to the role which government should assume in promoting access in each area. The author expands on ideas of access to the media presented in the *Harvard Law Review*, June 1967.

———. "The Federal Communications Commission's Fairness Doctrine: An Evaluation." *George Washington Law Review*, 30:1–41, October 1961.   **1B113**
Content: (1) The Fairness Doctrine: Its Evolution (the FCC Report on Editorializing by Broadcast Licensees, 1949; methods of enforcement). (2) The Fairness Doctrine and Editorializing by Broadcast Licensees: the Objectives and the Performance (response of the industry; response of the Commission). (3) The Fairness Doctrine and Its Evasions. (4) The Fairness Doctrine and the First Amendment (constitutionality, rationale). (5) The Fairness Doctrine: Recent Trends in Its Development and Operation. (6) The Fairness Doctrine: Some Reflections and a Summary (including alternative proposals).

———. *Freedom of the Press for Whom? The Right of Access to Mass Media.* Bloomington, Ind., Indiana University Press, 1973. 368p.   **1B114**
The author, a professor of constitutional law,

argues that "freedom of expression is meaningless if all the important means of expression—press, television, and radio—are closed. In the past, freedom of the press was achieved by forbidding government censorship. Now the communications industry itself is the major censor, deciding which ideas will be conveyed and which will be unheard. With most American cities dependent upon a single newspaper ownership and the three broadcasting networks, that power of selection is in very few hands. Barron believes that the First Amendment, which now functions primarily to protect the property rights of media owners, must be given a positive interpretation to protect the right of readers, viewers, and listeners to have access to the full range of public opinion." Methods of opening up the media include group pressures, court action, the prodding of federal agencies, and the extension of the fairness doctrine now invoked for broadcasting to apply to the newspaper press. The views of the author have stirred a controversy in the field of mass communication.

———. "Opening Up the Media." *Trial*, 6:37–38, May 1970. **1B115**
Public access to broadcasting has been legitimized by the U.S. Supreme Court, *Red Lion v. FCC* (1969), which validated the fairness doctrine employed by the FCC. The print media should be required by law and court action to publish political advertisements if the normal rate is met, and public figures attacked by the press should have the right of reply.

———. "Public Access to the Media and Its Critics." In Charles C. Flippen, *ed., Liberating the Media: The New Journalism*, Washington, D.C., Acropolis, 1973, pp. 173–91. **1B116**
The author argues for a legal right of access that, under the First Amendment, the right of the public as well as the proprietors should be protected.

———. " 'The Selling of the Pentagon': Partisan Investments and Antagonisms." In National Association of Educational Broadcasters, *CBS and Congress: "The Selling of the Pentagon."* Washington, D.C., The NAEB in Cooperation with Ohio State University, 1971, pp. ix–xiv. (A special issue of *Educational Broadcasting Review*, Winter 1971/72; reprinted in Robert O. Blanchard, *ed., Congress and the News Media*, pp. 406–10) **1B117**
An introduction to a group of articles discussing the implication of the confrontation between Congress and the Columbia Broadcasting Co. over a Congressional investigating committee subpoenaing film outtakes in CBS's documentary, Selling of the Pentagon. When Congress referred the matter back to committee the contempt citation was dropped and the matter was never brought to court. The author states that there are three theories in conflict in the struggle over the First Amendment application to broadcasting: (1) the inherent limita-

tion of the broadcast spectrum, (2) laissez faire liberalism that the government should have no control over broadcasting, and (3) the idea that the pivotal interest should be that of the reader, listener, and viewer. The author favors the last theory.

Barrow, Roscoe L. "The Attainment of Balanced Program Service in Television." *Virginia Law Review*, 52:633–66, May 1966. **1B118**
"The author finds the cause of the poor quality of television programming in the use of this medium as an advertising instead of a communications tool. After noting the ineffectiveness of present FCC methods, and the inability of technological advances to change the underlying structure of the industry, Mr. Barrow suggests ways to improve the quality of program fare"—Editor. He suggests the adoption of the Office of Network Study recommendation "that networks be prohibited from owning more than 50 percent of the programs they exhibit in prime time ₁thus encouraging₁ the production by independent producers of programs designed to fulfill needs of substantial minority audiences." He also suggests expansion of educational television facilities and the appointment by the president of an advisory commission to evaluate broadcasting service in the public interest.

———. "The Equal Opportunities and Fairness Doctrines in Broadcasting: Pillars in the Forum of Democracy." *University of Cincinnati Law Review*, 37:447–549, Summer 1968. **1B119**
"The purpose of this Article is to describe the equal opportunities and fairness doctrines, to evaluate the criticism of them, to analyze the issues of their constitutionality, and to recommend changes which would render them more effective in promoting a viable political process."

———. "Fairness Doctrine: A Double Standard for Electronic and Print Media." *Hastings Law Journal*, 26:659–708, January 1975. (Reprinted in *Advertising Law Quarterly*, Fall 1975)**1B120**
"The author analyzes the fairness doctrine in broadcasting and criticizes the double standard which fails to support any such regulatory scheme for the print media, as evidenced by the recent Supreme Court decision in *Miami Herald Publishing Co. v. Tornillo.*"

———. "Program Regulation in Cable TV: Fostering Debate in a Cohesive Audience." *Virginia Law Review*, 61:515–39, April 1975. **1B121**
"The purpose of this article is to assess the merit of restoring mandatory program origination and retaining the application of the fairness and equal opportunity doctrines to cable television."

Barth, Thomas E. *Perception and Acceptance of Supreme Court Decisions at the*

State and Local Level: The Case of Obscenity Policy in Wisconsin. Madison, Wis., University of Wisconsin, 1968. 335p. (Ph.D. dissertation, University Microfilms, no. 68–13,616) **1B122**
"This study examines the impact of the Supreme Court's obscenity decisions on state and local policy-makers in Wisconsin. Its primary concerns are three. What, if any, patterns of policy exist at the local level on the question of obscenity? What is the perception of the local policy-makers with regard to the Supreme Court's policy on this subject? What are the attitudes of the local actors toward the Court's policy and its role in the political process?" The conclusion reached was that communication of Supreme Court decisions to the local level is sporadic and irregular at best.

Barthel, Joan. "The Panic in TV Censorship." *Life*, 67(5):51–54, 1 August 1969. **1B123**
Network reaction to censorship threats from the FCC and Congress, particularly to the proposals of Senator Pastore.

——— *et al.* "Sex, Shock and Sensuality." *Life*, 66(13):22–35, 4 April 1969. **1B124**
An examination of the uproar over the new freedom of sex expression in the movies, on the stage, and on television. The Barthel article deals largely with the issues faced by the networks and the FCC, including the case of the Smothers Brothers.

Bartlett, Norman. "Où Est le Porno?" *Meanjin Quarterly*, 30:102–7, Autumn 1971. **1B125**
A discussion of the "sexploitation" wave taking place in London—underground advertising, cinema, books, and newspapers. "Many people find London's current climate of 'anything goes' pleasant enough but it is a mistake to confuse a high degree of sophistication with a high state of civilization."

Bartlett, Richard A. "A Fire Bell in the Night." *Journal of Library History*, 2:56–57, January 1967. **1B126**
The lawsuit brought by Henry Clay Frick's daughter to prevent the sale and distribution of the book, *Pennsylvania: Birthplace of a Nation* by Sylvester K. Stevens, would amount to direct censorship if won and has frightening implications.

Barton, Ansley B. "*United States v. Nixon* and the Freedom of Information Act: New Impetus for Agency Disclosure?" *Emory Law Journal*, 24:405–24, Spring 1975. **1B127**
"The thesis of this paper is that the recent

decision in *United States v. Nixon* will likely have an important effect in increasing agency disclosure of material covered by the fifth exemption, inter- and intra-agency communications, leaving intact the exemption of material containing military secrets covered by the first exemption."

Barton, Richard L. "The Lingering Legacy of Pacifica: Broadcasters' Freedom of Silence." *Journalism Quarterly*, 53:429–33, Autumn 1976.   **1B128**
"A review of the Pacifica case [FCC's investigation of license renewal of Pacifica radio stations] suggests that commercial broadcasters are apparently less capable of identifying and reacting to violations of free speech in their own sphere of operations than are individuals who regulate and use their communication channels." The author concludes that "when confronted with issues of free speech the broadcast industry as a whole typically sought a role which lies within a range represented by silence on the one extreme and active opposition to free speech provisions on the other."

Bartz, Fredrica K. "An Immodest Proposal." *English Journal*, 59:43, January 1970.   **1B129**
A satirical answer to the letters of protest against books used in classrooms and the demands for their removal. Since parents evidently do not mind the obscene words their children read on the walls of their school buildings, she proposes that the teachers tear out the pages containing the filth and paste them on the rest-room walls.

Basinger, William K. "Privilege under New York Times Rule Extended to Suits by Private Individuals Engaged in Matters of Public or General Concern." *Journal of Urban Law*, 49:593–602, February 1972.   **1B130**
The case, *Rosenbloom v. Metromedia* (1971), involves a state civil libel action brought by a private individual against a radio station about the individual's involvement in an event of public interest.

Basta, Donald K. "Free Press—Fair Trial: How May a Defendant's Right to a Fair Criminal Trial Be Protected from Prejudicial Newspaper Publicity?" *Journal of Criminal Law*, 50:374–82, November–December 1959.   **1B131**
Among the possible remedies proposed are: constructive contempt ("may be too high a price to pay"); change of venue and continuance; court restriction on the issuing of news releases by defense, prosecution, and police; and education of the press toward a greater responsibility for justice.

[Bate, Henry]. *A Letter to John Dunning, Esq. . . . on the Trial of The Rev. Henry Bate, Clerk, upon the Information of his Grace, The Duke of Richmond, for a Libel. With an Apologetic Dedication to His Grace of Richmond.* London, Bladon, 1780. 68p.   **1B132**
A law student of the Middle Temple writes a scathing criticism of the conduct of the trial of the Reverend Henry Bates, editor of the *Morning Post*, who was convicted of libel at a trial conducted by Justice Buller. Bates had been brought to trial at the instigation of the Duke of Richmond for a letter to the editor that had criticized the Duke, to whom the student-writer offers a tongue-in-cheek laudatory dedication. The author, addressing his letter to the prosecutor, believes that evidence presented at the trial showed clearly that Bates didn't write the alleged libel, didn't print it, wasn't publisher, and had no malice toward the Duke. He was convicted only because he was editor of a paper of different political views. The author charges that there has been a miscarriage of justice and calls for a new trial. In the presentation are a number of observations about libel trials in general including the belief that juries should be empowered to judge the nature of the libel as well as the fact of publication, a right not enacted into law until 1793; that intent of the defendant should be considered; that newspaper editors should have the same privilege to discuss public issues as members of Parliament; that editors should not be subject to persecution because they were partisan and should have the same rights of partisanship as Ministers of the Crown; and that prosecutors should not be privileged to libel the defendant during the trial. He also stated his belief that newspapers should be sentinels "placed upon the out-posts of the constitution, who should never be punished but for sleeping, neglect of duty, or giving intelligence to the enemy."

Bateman, Carroll J. "Techniques of Managing the News." *Public Relations Journal*, 19(8):6–9, August 1963.   **1B133**
An examination of charges and condemnation of news management leveled at the Kennedy Administration, and reference to the problem under earlier presidents. The author concludes that while news management is not an evil per se, "there are proper moral objections to 'management' techniques that involve deliberate misstatement of facts, intentional distortion, suppression of pertinent information to hide administration errors or inefficiency, and the threatening, the intimidation or the harassment of correspondents or publications that have offended the man in power."

Bates, Alan. "The Sad History of Censorship." *Humanist*, 82:268–70, September 1967.   **1B134**
"Mankind faces three enormous problems: nuclear weapons, the population explosion, and world food shortage. As these problems become increasingly urgent it will, I imagine, become increasingly easy both to impose censorship and to acquiesce in its imposition. Our

duty then will be ever clearer than it is now to do neither."

Bates, Roy E. "Private Censorship of Movies." *Stanford Law Review*, 22:618–56, February 1970.   **1B135**
"This Note examines the contention of several critics that the Motion Picture Association of America (MPAA) classification system is a disguised form of censorship, utilizing impermissibly vague standards to restrict freedom of expression, and as such is unconstitutional under the first and fourteenth amendments to the Constitution." The author finds that the classification does constitute censorship and is a violation of constitutionally protected speech. He believes that "the federal courts should not allow powerful organizations to operate a comprehensive regulatory scheme in an area of governmental concern, where that operation effectively and unduly interferes with the flow of expression between citizens."

Baudouin, Jean-Louis. "La Responsabilité des Dommages Causés par les Moyens d'Information de Masse." *La Revue Juridique Thémis*, 1973:201–8 1973.   **1B136**
An analysis of Quebec libel law dealing with the two issues of damages to reputation and invasion of privacy.

Baugh, Edward. "Hubert Crackanthorpe and the Cause of 'Literary Freedom.'" *Notes and Queries*, 18 (n.s.): 105–7, March 1971.   **1B137**
Excerpts from the letters of the British author (1870–96) dealing with literary attacks, including the trial of Vizetelly and a proposal for an organization to defend literary freedom.

Baughman, Thomas H. "Obscene Publications—Pandering." *Case Western Reserve Law Review*, 19:748–56, April 1968. (Reprinted in Donald B. Sharp, *ed.*, *Commentaries on Obscenity*, pp. 313–22)   **1B138**
"It is the purpose of this article to examine the contribution of one recent per curiam decision, *Books, Inc. v. United States* [1967], toward reducing the confusion in the area of obscenity censorship. Briefly, it may be said that this case clarifies the rule announced in *Ginzburg v. United States* [1966], pertaining to evidential requirements in criminal prosecutions under obscenity statutes."

Baum, Daniel J. "Broadcasting Regulation in Canada: The Power of Decision." *Osgoode Hall Law Journal*, 13:693–733, December 1975.   **1B139**
A critique of the role and performance of the Canadian Radio-Television Commission, with conclusions that the days of the agency "as a broadcasting parliament" are numbered. The author suggests that the future national policy may be one that encourages regionalism.

———. "Controversial Broadcasting in Canada." *Osgood Hall Law Journal*, 8:159–70, August 1970. **1B140**
"Professor Baum uses political programming on television as an illustration of the complexity of issues involved in the regulatory control of controversial broadcasting. The author describes the direction Parliamant has chosen and records the Canadian Broadcasting Corporation's attempt to achieve fairness and objectivity in the entire sphere of broadcasting controversial matters."

———. "Self Regulation and Antitrust: Suppression of Deceptive Advertising by the Publishing Media." *Publishing, Entertainment, Advertising and Allied Fields Law Quarterly*, 2:330–53, December 1962. **1B141**
The author discusses the media's duty to eliminate deceptive advertising, various plans in use and their effectiveness, the right of media to refuse advertising, and the right of media to combine for the purpose of eliminating deceptive advertising.

———, ed. "Access to the Mass Media." *Osgoode Hall Law Journal*, 8:1–9, August 1970. **1B142**
An introduction to a series of papers dealing with the impact of the burgeoning television technology on society. Nicholas Johnson discusses Freedom to Create; Mary Gardiner Jones, The Cultural and Social Impact of Advertising on American Society; Stanley E. Cohen, The Advertiser's Influence in TV Programming; Harry J. Boyle, Responsibility in Broadcasting; D. H. W. Henry, The Combines Investigation Act and Mass Media; and Daniel J. Baum, Controversial Broadcasting in Canada. Papers are followed by commentary by various industry, government, and university representatives.

Bauman, Gus. "Private Business Districts and the First Amendment; From Marsh to Tanner." *Urban Law Annual*, 7:199–218, 1974. **1B143**
Consideration of three significant U.S. Supreme Court decisions concerning the right of free expression vs. property rights: *Marsh v. Alabama* (1946); *Amalgamated Food Employees Local 590 v. Logan Valley Plaza, Inc.* (1968); and *Lloyd Corp. v. Tanner* (1972).

Baumrin, Bernard. "Is There a Freedom Not to Speak?" *Metaphilosophy*, 6:25–34, January 1975. **1B144**
"Is there a freedom not to speak? As regards the law of evidence, the answer is 'no'. Neither when required to speak, nor when forbidden by privilege from speaking is one free not to speak. One has a duty to speak or a duty not to, and where there is a duty, there is no freedom."

Baxi, Upendra *et al. Vidura*, 11(6): 847–75, December 1974. **1B145**

In a attempt to evaluate freedom of the press in India, *Vidura* sent questionnaires to journalists, publishers, union leaders, and members of Parliament. They were asked if they thought the Indian press was free and, if not, how it was handicapped. They were also asked what could be done to maintain newspaper independence and ensure fair distribution of advertising. Statements from eighteen respondents are published.

Baxter, James A. "Testimonial Privilege of Newsmen." *Marquette Law Review*, 55:184–91, Winter 1972. **1B146**
Comment on the decision of the Supreme Court of Wisconsin in *State v. Knops*, 49 Wis. 2d 647, 183 N.W. 2d 94 (1971), granting the newsman a qualified testimonial privilege. Rather than adopt an absolute privilege, the court established a case-by-case approach which would require a balancing of the various interests. The case involved the editor of the Madison, Wis., *Kaleidoscope*.

Baxter, James E. *Selection and Censorship of Public School Textbooks. (A Descriptive Study).* Hattiesburg, Miss., University of Southern Mississippi, 1964. 178p. (Ed.D. dissertation, University Microfilms, no. 65–760) **1B147**
"This study is an attempt to describe state procedures for selecting textbooks and to analyze the criticisms. The attempt is made to determine the adequacy of selection procedures and the validity of the claim that lay people should participate in textbook selection." The author concludes that "selection of textbooks is a professional responsibility and should be accomplished by professional educators. Some lay participation may be desirable for good public understanding, but the responsibility is still professional. It should be completely removed from state or local politics."

Baylen, Joseph O. "William Archer, W. T. Stead, and the Theatre. Some Unpublished Letters." *Studies in English (University of Mississippi)*, 5:91–103, 1964. **1B148**
Much of the correspondence between Editor W. T. Stead and Dramatic Critic William Archer of the *Pall Mall Gazette* dealt with the issue of censorship of the stage by Britain's Lord Chamberlain.

Baynton, G. W. "Freedom of the Press; Will It Be Preserved?" *Saskatchewan Bar Review*, 30:17–32, March 1965. **1B149**
"Because of the phenomenal changes in the economics and character of the press, lack of government intervention [the classical concept of freedom of the press] will no longer ensure a free press. . . . The ideal solution would be for the press itself to take the initiative, to set up a Council composed of its own representatives to formulate and preserve high standards of conduct. . . . If the press will not take the initiative, . . . then a statutory Council will have to be created. . . . Positive action of this nature can be postponed no longer."

Bayston, B. D. "Christianity, Pornography and Censorship." *Interchange*, 3:15–28, June 1971. **1B150**

Bayus, Elaine. "The Constitutional Status of Commercial Expression." *Hastings Constitutional Law Quarterly*, 3:761–801, Summer 1976. **1B151**
The author "outlines the development of the commercial speech distinction and its subsequent judicial refinement and clarification . . . focuses on cases in which federal courts have employed the distinction to protect such interests as privacy, equal protection, and public health over the commercial interests of advertisers, while at the same time preserving various first amendment interests."

Bazelon, David L. "FCC Regulation of the Telecommunications Press." *Duke Law Journal*, 1975:213–51, May 1975. **1B152**
Content: Historical justifications for FCC regulation of the telecommunications press; the purpose of the free press guarantee; and alternative strategies to remedy present failures in telecommunications regulation (reform of the FCC itself, increasing private competition in the production and placement of programming, public broadcasting, and altering the economic structure of the telecommunications industry).

Bazzell, Charles. "Libraries and Theatre Owners Have Something in Common: The Threat of Censorship." *LLA Bulletin* (Louisiana Library Association), 36:6–10, Spring 1974. **1B153**
A theater owner recounts his experience with the censor, reviews the recent decisions on obscenity, and suggests that librarians and theater owners join forces in getting legislation that would remove censorship for "consenting adults."

Beach, Joseph W. "Bowdlerized Versions of Hardy." *PMLA* (Papers of the Modern Language Association), 36:632–43, December 1921. **1B154**
A documented account of alterations in several of Hardy's more important novels at the hands of English editors.

Beach, Richard. "Issues of Censorship and Research on Effects of and Response to Reading." *Journal of Research and Development in Education*, 9(3):3–21, Spring 1976. **1B155**
A survey of research findings on the response and effects of reading shows that there are no definitive answers as to the need for censorship. Several conclusions relating to censorship can be made: (1) Responses of individual

readers vary greatly so that predictions are questionable. (2) Differences in readers' age, personality values, sex, literary training, and previous reading experience result in highly unique meanings for different readers. (3) Most studies show little short-term changes resulting from the reading of a particular book. (4) There is little or no relationship between reading and deviant behavior. (5) Exposure to sex material may be part of adolescent development. (6) Some studies indicate that when a book is not available desire for it is enhanced.

Beach, Thomas P. *A Voice From the Jail* (Vol. I, no. 1). Newburyport (Mass.) Jail, The Author, 11 December 1842. 4p. **1B156**
Thomas Parnell Beach, an abolitionist, was imprisoned "for opening his mouth in behalf of two and a half million of his enslaved fellowmen, in the meeting-house of the Society of Friends, so called, in Lynn, Mass., and also for repeating the act in the house of the Baptist Society of Danvers. . . ." The issue contains editorials and resolutions on freedom of speech and the press and criticism of the action of the Friends and Baptists for persecution of Beach, reprinted from various abolitionist papers.

Beale, Howard K. *Are American Teachers Free? An Analysis of Restraints Upon the Freedom of Teaching in American Schools*. New York, Scribner's, 1936. 855p. (Report of the Commission on the Social Studies, Part 12) **1B157**
A documented study of the pressures—political, economic, and religious—that have threatened freedom to teach and to select appropriate textbooks. The hysteria of World War I, the pacifist movement that followed, the radical economic and social movements of the thirties, the conflict between religion and science, the rise of revisionist American history that did not coincide with views of patriotic societies—all were issues in which pressure groups operated to restrict teaching and control textbooks. A chapter on textbooks discusses the lack of freedom of teachers to select their own texts, the pressures exerted by patriotic, economic, and religious groups to adopt or reject textbooks, and pressures exerted on authors and publishers to rewrite books to meet objections of these groups. Among those forces that threaten freedom, the author cites the press itself which has not always been a champion of intellectual freedom.

————. "The Present State of Freedom." In John Dewey Society, *Educational Freedom and Democracy*. New York, Appleton-Century, 1938, pp. 50–91. **1B158**
Included is a discussion of the effect of pressure groups—religious, patriotic, political, and business—in the selection, modification, or banning of school textbooks. "Perhaps worse than the banning of good books has been the way in which reputable authors have changed their texts after attacks on them. . . . For men like [historians] Guitteau, Hart, McLaughlin, Muzzey, Van Tyne, and West to feel impelled quietly to change attacked passages indicates a deplorable situation." The author also cites cases of a civic book modified to placate a utility company, and two science books omitting any reference to evolution.

Beals, Robert L. "Freedom of Expression in the Media: The Public's Claim for a Right of Access." *Ohio State Law Journal*, 33:151–56, Winter 1972. **1B159**
This note explores the strengths of both sides of the controversy over the treatment of controversial issues by the electronic media—exclusive control over subject matter by the broadcasters versus a carefully supervised federal policy requiring fairness in presentation. The note analyzes one federal case, *Business Executives Move for Vietnam Peace v. FCC* (1973), which marks a significant breakthrough for those who advocate a right of access.

[Beals, William, and Charles G. Greene.] *Trial of William Beals & Charles G. Greene, for an alleged libel, published in the Boston Morning Post, on Alfred W. Pike, Preceptor of the Topsfield Academy, at the November Term of the Sup. J. Court, at Salem, before His Honor Judge Putnam. By the Reporter of the Boston Morning Post.* Boston, Beals & Greene, 1835. 52p. **1B160**
The alleged libel was for articles appearing in the *Boston Morning Post* in which Mr. Pike, a schoolmaster, was accused of brutally mistreating a young girl placed in his care. Eminent counsel argued the case—Rufus Choate and Asahel Huntington for the plaintiff, Everett Saltonstall and George Wheatland for the defendant. Judge Samuel Putnam gave a thoughtful and lucid summary of the issues in his instructions to the jury, which rendered a verdict for the plaintiff, with damages of one dollar.

Bean, Walton, E. *George Creel and His Critics; A Study of the Attack on the Committee on Public Information, 1917–1919*. Berkeley, Calif., University of California, 1941. 277p. (Unpublished Ph.D. dissertation) **1B161**
George Creel was chief United States censor in World War I and head of the Committee on Public Information.

Beasley, Joseph W. "Newsman's Privilege: The First Amendment Grants None." *University of Florida Law Review*, 25:381–87, Winter 1973. **1B162**
Re: *United States v. Caldwell*, 408 U.S. 665 (1972), the case of the reporter who refused to testify before the Grand Jury investigating the activities of the Black Panthers. The U.S. Supreme Court ruled 5–4 against the right of newsmen's privilege.

[Beattie, Francis S.] *A Report of the Trial of an Action for Libel, in Which Dr. Geo. M'Clellan Was Plaintiff, and Dr. Francis S. Beattie Was Defendant, at Philadelphia, March, 1829. Comprising the Whole of the Evidence and the Judges Charge. . . .* Philadelphia, 1829. 78p. **1B163**
Dr. Beattie, a professor of obstetrics at Jefferson Medical College was brought to trial for a pamphlet attacking the medical malpractice of Dr. George M'Clellan. The jury found for the plaintiff, and assessed five hundred dollars damage.

Béauté, J. "Liberté de la Presse et Sécurité Nationale: a Propos de l'Arrêt de la Cour Suprême Relatif aux Documents du Pentagone." *Revue du Droit Public et de la Science Politique (Paris)*, 90:721–87, May–June 1974. **1B164**
An analysis of the U.S. Supreme Court's decision in the case of the *Pentagon Papers*.

Beaver, James E. "The Newsman's Code; the Claim of Privilege and Everyman's Right to Evidence." *Oregon Law Review*, 47:243–59, April 1968. **1B165**
In commentary on the case, *State v. Buchanan* (1968), the author questions the desirability of creating a statutory privilege for journalists. "The creation of a 'special position' for newspapermen could encourage irresponsible reporting. Those occupational groups that presently possess the privilege have, for the most part, internal or other mechanisms for discipline and control that are not yet found in the journalist profession." The author fears the extension of the privilege would interfere with the administration of justice.

Becht, Arno C. "The Absolute Privilege of the Executive in Defamation." *Vanderbilt Law Review*, 15:1127–71, October 1962. **1B166**
"Should executive officers have an absolute privilege to commit defamation? This is Professor Becht's inquiry as he traces the evolution and application of this privilege from its origin in England through its development in American state and federal courts. After balancing the factors for and against absolute immunity, the writer reaches the conclusion that officials should be reduced to a qualified privilege in defamation."

Beck, James M. . . . *The Lewis Publishing Company, A Body Corporate in Law, Complainant-Appellant, against Edward M. Morgan, Postmaster in and for the City of New York, Defendant-Appellee. The Invalidity of a Federal Censorship of the Press. Brief for the Appellant. James M. Beck,*

Counsel for Appellant. New York, C. G. Burgoyne [1912], 52p. **1B167**
A brief for the Lewis Publishing Co. in a case before the U.S. Supreme Court in which counsel argues that the disclosure requirements and the label of advertising for second-class mailing privileges constitute a violation of the First Amendment. Lewis was a St. Louis promoter-publisher of the *Woman's Magazine* and *Woman's Farm Journal.*

Becker, Jerrold L. "The Supreme Court's Recent 'National Security' Decisions: Which Interests Are Being Protected?" *Tennessee Law Review,* 40:1–27, Fall 1972. **1B168**
It is the thesis of this article that "the Court has previously formulated discernible standards for adjudicating conflicts couched in terms of national security. That these standards are overhauled continually is a result attributed more to the composition of the Court than a lack of precedent. . . . Whether this has resulted in a change of emphasis, if not outright departure from its predecessor, the Warren Court, is the subject of this study. Specifically, the article will examine the Burger Court's response to the conflict between freedom and security by its opinions in *New York Times Co. v. United States* [1971], *United States v. United States District Court* [1972], and *Laird v. Tatum* [1972]."

Becker, Samuel L. "Mass Communication and the First Amendment: An American Dilemma." *Freedom of Speech Newsletter* (Western Speech Communication Association), 1(1):16–21, April 1975. **1B169**
The author considers three solutions or partial solutions to the lack of adequate and effective mass communications: (1) the establishment of "an independent, adequately financed, nongovernmental citizens advisory commission whose sole task would be to evaluate on a continuing basis whether the mass media are denying access to competing views," (2) enactment by Congress of a statute establishing "an enforceable right of equality of opportunity to advertise in all media which sell advertising space or time" (Professor Barron's proposal), and (3) the extension of the fairness doctrine, which now exists in broadcasting, to the print media.

Beckwith, Harry G., III. "Oregon's Obscenity Bill; New Fig Leaves, Old Faux Pas." *Oregon Law Review,* 53:375–92, Spring 1974. **1B170**
This comment "discusses the nature and shortcomings of obscenity laws in general, analyzes SB708 [an Oregon bill which prohibits the dissemination of obscene materials to anyone regardless of age; the existing law prohibits the dissemination to minors] according to its constitutional and practical implications, and suggests alternatives to the Oregon legislature." Adults may be protected from having obscene materials thrust upon them by means of nuisance laws or by laws restricting unsol-icited mailings to customers and requiring warning of the content of a book, movie, or magazine, without the broad prohibitions of SB708.

Bedi, Asit Singh. *Freedom of Expression and Security: A Comparative Study of the Function of the Supreme Courts of the United States of America and India.* London, Asia Publishing House, 1968. 483p. **1B171**
Content: Common law of England relating to licensing, censorship, and sedition; interpretation of the First Amendment by the United States Supreme Court in matters of sedition and espionage; freedom of expression and the function of the Supreme Court of India, principally as expressed in the twin cases of *Romesh Thappar v. State of Madras* (1950) and *Brij Bhusham v. State of Delhi* (1950) and the aftermath.

Bedner, Mark A. *A Case Study of Spiro Agnew's Relations with the National News Media.* Lawrence, Kan., University of Kansas, 1975. 126p. (Unpublished Master's thesis) **1B172**
"This thesis traces the development of Spiro Agnew's relationship with the press, from his election as governor of Maryland in 1966 to the 1969 speeches. It suggests that Agnew's resentment of the press was strong enough to motivate his attacks. But the major point is that Agnew's speeches were part of a campaign by the Nixon White House to discredit criticism by the press."

Beelar, Donald C. "Cables in the Sky and the Struggle for Their Control." *Federal Communications Bar Journal,* 21:26–41, 1967. **1B173**
An account of the struggle for control of domestic satellite communications. "The overall question remains whether the de facto monopoly condition prevailing in microwave and the private line markets can be reversed and reconstructed under a regulatory environment assuring effective free market competition."

Beeson, Trevor. "Pornophobia: The Longford Commission Report." *Christian Century,* 89:1032–33, 18 October 1972. **1B174**
Criticism of the Longford Committee Report on obscenity in Britain and its "crude and unsatisfactory" proposals for law reform. The author concludes that in "the present state of knowledge, those who campaign for further encroachment by the law into the realm of private behavior are a far greater threat to the well-being of society than the purveyors of 'dirty' books and 'blue' films."

Beeton, D. R. "Plea for a Return to Frankness." *South African Libraries,* 38:232–35, January 1971. **1B175**
"I believe that censorship is necessary, and that even when one has doubts about its results, it should be attempted. But, I believe, too, that it has been much abused, and that it is often grotesquely applied in this country."

[Beeton, William A., Jr.] "Virginia Recognizes a Newsman's Qualified First Amendment Privilege of Confidentiality of Information and Identity of Source." *University of Richmond Law Review,* 9:171–80, Fall 1974. **1B176**
Re: *Brown v. Commonwealth,* 214 Va. 755, 204 S.E.2d 429 (1974).

Behrens, John. "Legal Review [of Campus Newspapers]." *College Press Review,* 10(2):13–14, Spring 1971. **1B177**
A review of action by the courts on the status of campus newspapers and excerpts from the contract of Ithaca College with the student newspaper, *Ithacan,* to release the college from responsibility for libel of a student-edited paper.

Beirne, Raymond M. "Lawrence's Night-Letter on Censorship and Obscenity." *D. H. Lawrence Review,* 7:321–22, Fall 1974. **1B178**
The article quotes a letter from D. H. Lawrence to his publisher, Thomas Seltzer, that had appeared in the *New York Times,* 11 February 1923. It dealt with Justice John Ford of the New York Supreme Court who had found his daughter reading Lawrence's *Women in Love* and persuaded the New York Society for the Supression of Vice to go after the book and have the legislature introduce a "clean book" bill. Lawrence suggested that the Judge take away his daughter's library card "lest worse befall her."

Beke, A. John. "Government Regulation of Broadcasting in Canada." *Saskatchewan Law Review,* 36:39–109, 235–94, 1971/72. **1B179**
Content: The necessity of regulation, defining the public interest, the licensing procedure (new broadcasters, renewals, effectiveness of licensing as a regulatory tool), good balance and methods of achieving it, and the need for a different regulatory approach.

Belfrage, Cedric. *The American Inquisition, 1945–1960.* Indianapolis, Bobbs-Merrill, 1973. 316p. **1B180**
An account of the American "inquisition" against communism and particularly of the "heretics" who were subjected to persecution by the authorities during the period of hysteria that swept the nation following World War II. The work discusses the investigations of the House Un-American Activities Committee and the Senate Committee on Government

Operations under Joseph R. McCarthy and later John L. McClellan. It covers the operation of the McCarran (Internal Security) Act of 1950 requiring registration of organizations found subversive (including labeling of its printed matter), and the Smith Act (1940) which included a provision for making it a crime "to print, publish, edit, issue, circulate, sell, distribute, or publicly display any written or printed matter" advocating the overthrow of any government in the United States by force. The work includes frequent references to both overt and subtle attacks on intellectual freedom. The author was one of the "heretics" whose refusal to discuss his political views before the McCarthy Committee led to his deportation.

Belin, Alletta, Mercedes R. Bilotto, and Thaddeus Carhart. *A Legal Handbook for Billboard Control*. Palo Alto Calif., Stanford Environmental Law Society, 1976. 87p.   **1B181**
Includes sections on the power to control billboards through legislation and court decisions involving the issue of free speech.

Bell, Elouise. "Censorship—A Paradox in Governing." *Idaho Librarian*, 26:142–43, October 1974. (Reprinted from *Daily Universe*, Brigham Young University, 15 October 1973)   **1B182**
A plea for individual censorship, for the application of biblical stewardship on the part of teachers, bookstore operators, and students. "We must not seek a spelling-out of what we can or cannot read or see on film in the theater. We have no index of forbidden books. . . . In the Doctrine and Covenants the Lord speaks of the 'true independence of Heaven.' I plead for this independence to be exercised by each person who calls himself a Latter-day Saint. The responsibility is his and the consequences are his. Wholesale censorship from some central source is the easier path. It is not the path for men and women seeking ultimate godhood."

Bell, Joseph N. "Danger: Smut." *Good Housekeeping*, 172:85, 178–86, April 1971.   **1B183**
The author lists steps that a citizen may take to stop receiving pornography through the mails and considers legal and citizen campaigns against pornography. He raises the other issues involved, however, and questions: "Is the risk of censorship greater than the weakening of the social fabric that might result from giving them free market?"

Bell, Joy C. "The Anarchist Cookbook: Banned?" *Bay State Librarian*, 61(3):11–15, October 1972.   **1B184**
A report on the extent to which libraries and bookstores in the Boston area had copies of the *Anarchist Cookbook*, a manual of drugs, explosives, weapons, and sabotage, written by William Powell, and published by Lyle Stuart. The book was not involved in much controversy since few libraries acquired it, largely on the basis that it contained incorrect and/or dangerous information on drugs and explosives. "Perhaps librarians should consider Powell's book to be the unique work of a neoanarchist. As such the *Anarchist Cookbook* should be preserved in a number of libraries, if only to reflect that troubled period of American history of which it is a part."

Bellezza, Suzanne. "Definition of Obscenity in Printed Material: Minnesota and the U.S.A." *Minnesota Libraries*, 22:215–23, Winter 1968. **1B185**
Following a discussion of the status of obscenity under federal court ruling, the writer considers the effect of federal law on Minnesota. "The definition of obscenity in Minnesota cases—including Minnesota Supreme Court decisions and cases beginning in the Minnesota district court—have paralleled the U.S. Federal court definitions quite closely."

Bellows, Henry W. *The Relation of Public Amusements to Public Morality, Especially of the Theatre to the Highest Interests of Humanity. An Address Delivered at the Academy of Music, New York, before "The American Dramatic Fund Society."* New York, C. S. Francis, 1857. 53p. (Also published in Melbourne, Australia in 1859 with introductions on the drama of England and the Australian colonies)   **1B186**
The pastor of the All Soul's Church, New York, considers the evils of the stage to fall into four categories—(1) identification with frivolity, worldliness, and moral indifference, and a tendency to reproduce them, (2) association with intemperance and licentiousness, (3) immorality of plays, use of foul language and immodest costumes, and (4) bad effect on life of actors. He believes the Church is largely responsible for the condition because it has traditionally rejected the institution and left it to reflect the lowest levels of society and the tastes of the time. He calls on theater managers whose power over play selection is absolute "to exclude every kind of play or entertainment from your list, from which the heart must recoil, or at which an innocent cheek must blush. . . . The only effective censorship in a country like ours," he argues, is for "sober and virtuous people of this and every city" to go in moderation to the theater and demand virtuous entertainment.

Beloff, Max. "How 'Dangerous' Are the Crossman Diaries?" *Encounter*, 45(3):51–57, September 1975.   **1B187**
The British Attorney-General is seeking to halt publication in book form of the late Richard Crossman's dairies, while refraining from challenging the *Sunday Times* for publishing extracts. Crossman was a former member of Prime Minister Wilson's Cabinet and a keen student of the British political system. The question of government secrecy is involved.

Beloff, Michael. "Onward from 'Oz'." *Encounter*, 38(3):43–51, March 1972.   **1B188**
The author reviews British obscenity law in a permissive society, finding that it is "in a state of confusion so extreme that it violates in content and operation many of the most basic precepts of criminal justice." No one can know in advance whether any particular publication does or does not contravene the law; hard-core pornography flourishes in parts of London while works of literary merit such as *Lady Chatterley* and *Last Exit to Brooklyn* are challenged. The recent *Oz* trial opened up a new dimension—concern less with what was said than with who was saying it. *Oz* could not be seriously defended against charges of obscenity or on grounds of art (as were *Lady Chatterley* and *Ulysses*) but the real object of the prosecution seemed to be the radical life-style of the defendants. Any reform of the obscenity laws should be based on one factor only—public display of offensive materials, to be tried as a "nuisance" as is indecent exposure. This has the advantage of attacking profiteering and pandering; it supports privacy without intolerance to the interest of others; it encourages the promotion of aesthetic values, and enables enforcement to be judged on the basis of public complaint from those offended.

Belser, Clinch H., Jr. "Frontiers of Fairness in Broadcasting." *South Carolina Law Review*, 22:208–27, 1970.   **1B189**
"The purposes of this note are to examine the *Red Lion* decision [*Red Lion Broadcasting Co. v. FCC*, 1969], to survey briefly the law in this broad area, and to preview the aftermath of *Red Lion* not only in legal but also in practical and economic terms."

Belton, Peter J. "The Control of Group Defamation: A Comparative Study of Law and Its Limitations." *Tulane Law Review*, 34:299–342, February 1960; 34:469–504, April 1960.   **1B190**
The article considers the laws of Great Britain, the United States, and France as they relate to control by the imposition of criminal sanctions and civil liability for group defamation. "We have seen that neither the criminal nor the civil sanctions of the common law accord the groups of our society or their individual members any real protection against the harm caused by group defamation, and that only the civil sanctions of the French law may do so in France." The author believes the courts are motivated more or less consciously by the belief that legal sanctions are inappropriate and that "the price which would have to be paid for such control would be far too high a price to pay in a democratic society."

Bender, Paul. "Definition of 'Obscene' Under Existing Law." *Technical Report of the* [U.S.] *Commission on Obscenity and Pornography*, 2:5–27, 1971.   **1B191**
The author finds that there has been very little development of guidelines for determining what kinds of specific statutes would be permissible. Excessive vagueness must be avoided, and the specific prohibition must not sweep more broadly than necessary to achieve its objective. There needs to be at least a "rational relationship" between the definitional language in the specific prohibition and the harm which the legislature seeks to prevent, and the harm may be at least the offensiveness of uncontracted exposure to sexual materials, harm to juveniles, or harm through pandering.

————. "Implications of Stanley v. Georgia." *Technical Report of the* [U.S.] *Commission on Obscenity and Pornography*, 2:28–36, 1971.   **1B192**
The author considers the U.S. Supreme Court's decision in *Stanley v. Georgia* "easily the most important judicial decision since *Roth v. United States*, and it may well turn out to be even more important than *Roth* itself. The significance I find in the *Stanley* decision flows not from the actual 'holding' of the case . . . but from the stated underpinnings of that holding and from certain other statements about obscenity law made by the Court in the course of its opinion."

————. "The Obscenity Muddle: A Guide to the Supreme Court's Latest Sexual Crisis." *Harper's*, 246:46, 50–52, February 1973.   **1B193**
The U.S. Supreme Court faces a sexual crisis as it considers a group of obscenity cases—with antipornography forces asking the court to broaden the scope of the *Fanny Hill* test and the U.S. Commission on Obscenity and Pornography recommending that adults be permitted to see whatever sexual material they wish. The author suggests the court might appropriately move in two directions simultaneously— "broaden the permissible meaning of 'obscene,' while narrowing the permissible situations where that categorization is legally relevant." This would permit action to protect children and control pandering while freeing the sale of sexual materials to consenting adults. Ending obscenity for adults, however, might open up the liberalization of other "victimless" crimes.

Benedict, John. "Pornography, a Political Weapon." *American Mercury*, 90:3–21, February 1960.   **1B194**
"An alerted and determined public can fight obscenity and win." The author criticizes Supreme Court decisions relating to obscenity, lists organizations "fighting the forces of licentiousness today," and details specific ways individuals may protest against materials they consider obscene.

Benedict, Mary. "Freedom of the High School Press?" *NEA Journal*, 56:64–66, December 1967.   **1B195**

"Administrators have the final say on freedom of the high school newspaper. Let us hope they will permit enough freedom to encourage responsible, independent thought as we educate tomorrow's citizens."

———— *et al.* "Writing About Controversy: Use a Mature Approach." *Communication: Journalism Education Today*, 2(3):6, 21, Spring 1969.   **1B196**
One of a series of articles on advice to high school editors on how to deal with controversy in the school. There follows: Freedom to Make Mistakes, But Freedom Plus Responsibility Needed by Ron Bottini. School Press—A Sturdy Tool for Education, Silence Won't Work by Edmund Arnold. Underground Newspapers? Strengthen Editorial Policy by Sam Feldman. Learn Rights—Responsibilities Functionally by Elena Marcheschi. We Must Rejuvenate School Publications by Allan A. Glatthorn.

Bendix, Dorothy. "Teaching the Concept of Intellectual Freedom: The State of the Art." *ALA Bulletin*, 63:351–62, March 1969.   **B197**
A library school faculty member reports on results from a questionnaire to library schools inquiring what teaching was taking place in the area of intellectual freedom and censorship. She recommends that greater emphasis be given in the library school curriculum to self-censorship by librarians; that library school faculty consider making greater uses of films and role playing; that care be given to present conservative as well as liberal points of view on censorship; and that faculty consider how to narrow the gap between the official or professional objectives and the actual objectives in intellectual freedom.

Benjoya, Mitchell, Richard L. Zisson, and Dennis J. LaCroix. "Obscenity: The New Law and Its Enforcement—Two Views." *Suffolk University Law Review*, 8:1–37, Fall 1973.   **1B198**
"The following Article deals with recent Supreme Court obscenity decisions collectively identified as the *Miller v. California* series. The primary goal of the Article is to evaluate the decisions, which are concerned with both substantive and procedural obscenity law, in light of historical and socioscientific data. The first section of the Article is concerned with the substantive effect these decisions have had on the existing law. . . . The second portion of the Article deals with procedural aspects of the recent rulings. The Article concludes with the author's individual evaluation of the decisions, which emphasize the Article's intention to present a picture of the two main aspects of the recent cases from two views."

Bennet, William. *Report of the Trial by Jury, Anderson Against Rintoul and Others, for Libels Spoken at Public Meetings in Dundee, and Published in the Dundee, Perth, and Cupar Advertiser Newspaper.*

Edinburgh, John Lothian, 1824. 151p., 38p.   **1B199**
The case involved the publication of information questioning the financial honesty of the plaintiff, a merchant, appearing in the newspaper published by Robert S. Rintoul. The jury found for the defendant.

Bennett, Arnold. "Books Not for Daughters." In *Arnold Bennett: The Evening Standard Years. "Books and Persons," 1926–1931*. London, Chatto & Windus, 1974, pp. 186–88. (Reprinted from the *Evening Standard*, 16 August 1928)   **1B200**
Bennett does not recognize the need for the circulating libraries to protect the innocence of adolescents. But one way out of the difficulty is for the management to place a red seal on books that "some parents may regard as unsuitable for perusal by their children or themselves." He predicts, however, a rush for the red-sealed volumes.

————. "The Censor in the Library." In *Arnold Bennett: The* Evening Standard *Years. "Books and Persons," 1926–1931*. London, Chatto & Windus, 1974, pp. 167–69. (Reprinted from the *Evening Standard*, 21 June 1928) **1B201**
Criticism of the British circulating libraries for their ban of Isadora Duncan's *My Life*. He recommends that subscribers who want the library to censor their reading, request this service on their subscription form so that "the other 95 percent of subscribers would be spared a great deal of annoyance and the expletive use of a deal of bad language."

————. "A Censorship By All Means, But—." In *Arnold Bennett: The* Evening Standard *Years. "Books and Persons," 1926–1931*. London, Chatto & Windus, 1974, pp. 247–49. (Reprinted from the *Evening Standard*, 7 March 1929).   **1B202**
While granting the need to restrict circulation of James Joyce's *Ulysses* in England ("the most wonderful and original of modern novels") Bennett calls on a weakening of the Lord Campbell obscenity law to permit healthy and honest modern fiction.

————. "Who Should Select Books for Censorship?" In *Arnold Bennett: The Evening Standard Years. "Books and Persons," 1926–1931*. London, Chatto & Windus, 1974, pp. 217–19. (Reprinted from the *Evening Standard*, 29 November 1928).   **1B203**
"Children, if they are to be influenced, require something more concrete than books—

something more concrete even than films. . . . Give a nice child the *Newgate Calendar* . . . and he will remain nice. Give a nasty child the *Pilgrim's Progress*, and he will remain nasty. A child will only take from a book what he wants. The rest will slide off his intelligence like water off a duck's back. . . . I feel sure I should do more harm by forbidding any book than by permitting all books."

Bennett, Arnold. *Jackie, Bobby & Manchester; the Story Behind the Headlines!* New York, Bee-Line Books, 1967. 191p. **1B204**
The book deals in a somewhat sensational manner with the controversy over William Manchester's book, *The Death of a President*, authorized to be written by Jacqueline Kennedy, who later went to court in an effort to prevent publication. Settlement was made out of court.

Bennett, Charles L. "The Potential Dangers of Shield Legislation." In Robert O. Blanchard, *ed., Congress and the News Media*, New York, Hastings House, 1974, pp. 455–57. **1B205**
Remarks of the managing editor, *Daily Oklahoman*, at an American Society of Newspaper Editors' panel discussion, Washington, D.C., 4 May 1973.

Bennett, Charles P. "The Freedom of Information Act, Is It a Clear Public Records Law?" *Brooklyn Law Review*, 34:72–82, Fall 1967. **1B206**
"It is the purpose of this article to analyze the nine exemptions under subsection (e) of the [Freedom of Information] Act." The author concludes that, while the Act makes clear that the burden is on government to justify withholding a document and that one seeking information has the right to go to court for injunctive relief, "any curtailment of the former abuses in the field of disclosure of government records will not result from the clarity of the legislative history or the language but rather from the provision of the remedy in the District Court."

Bennett, De Robigne M. *The World's Sages, Thinkers and Reformers, Being Biographical Sketches of Leading Philosophers, Teachers, Skeptics, Innovators, Founders of New Schools of Thought, Eminent Scientists, Etc.* New York, D. M. Bennett, Liberal and Scientific Publishing House, 1876. 1075p. **1B207**
In this collection of biographical sketches of innovative thinkers, from Anaximander to Zeno, are a number who were involved in issues of freedom of the press: Annie Besant (pp. 1034–37), Charles Bradlaugh (pp. 1001–3), Richard Carlile (pp. 711–16), Edward Bliss

Foote (pp. 976–77), Thomas Herttell (pp. 1048–50), Ezra H. Heywood (pp. 976–77), Robert G. Ingersoll (pp. 1007–8), Abner Kneeland (pp. 696–97), Charles Knowlton (pp. 1051–56), Robert Taylor (pp. 685–90), and Matthew Tindal (pp. 414–16). A final biography (pp. 1060–75) is of the author, D. M. Bennett, editor of *The Truth Seeker* (T197) which frequently championed press freedom and attacked censorship in the areas of religion and obscenity. Two years after the publication of this book Bennett was sent to jail for selling a copy of Ezra Heywood's *Cupid's Yokes.*

Bennett, Edgar C. "Developments in Courtroom Publicity." *Journal of the Bar Association of Kansas*, 26:307–15, February 1958. **1B208**
A retired District Court judge discusses various celebrated cases where courtroom publicity was an issue—the Sheppard murder trial, the trial of Minot F. Jelke, the experiment with television coverage in Waco, Tex., and the recent Colorado decision which nullified in part Canon 35 of the American Bar Association by permitting television in the courtroom at the discretion of the judge. The final decision on whether to permit photography in the courtroom must depend on whether or not it will contribute to a fair trial.

[Bennett, James Gordon.] . . . *The People of the State of New York on the Complaint of Daniel Sickles vs. James Gordon Bennett*. New York, New York General Sessions, 1857. 90p. **1B209**
The case is one of a number of libel cases in which James Gordon Bennett, publisher of the *New York Herald*, was brought to trial. The plaintiff, counsel in a New York Street Commission case, objected to one sentence in a news story. John Graham was the prosecutor, James R. Whitney and David Dudley Field were attorneys for Bennett.

Bennett, John. *Freedom of Expression in Australia*. Melbourne, Australia, The Author, 1968. 39p. (A Civil Liberties Publication) **1B210**
The pamphlet deals with book censorship (federal and state, and proposed legislative changes), film censorship (objections to the present system and proposed legislative changes), censorship of television, radio and press, censorship of the live theater, freedom of speech and assembly, and invasion of privacy. The author concludes that "it is regrettable that neither of the major political parties are particularly interested in issues raised in this pamphlet" and extremists of both the "left" and "right" are generally concerned only with their own civil liberties and not of the community at large.

Bennett, Margaret, *pseud.* "The Case for 'The Compleat Dirty Book.'" *San Francisco Examiner & Chronicle*, 24 September 1967, pp. 35, 38. **1B211**
A satire in behalf of the publication of a well-indexed "Compleat Dirty Book," an unexpur-

gated compendium of obscenity and pornography that the librarian could put on the shelf and be forever relieved of censorship entanglements, because no other book could ever rise above, or fall below the "Compleat Dirty Book." If this experiment were successful we could follow it with "The Compleat Book of Communist Propaganda"—and the library could be used not as a center for voyeurism and witch-hunting but to educate and expand the human mind.

Bennett, Richard V. "Must Newsmen Reveal Their Confidential Sources to Grand Juries?" *Wake Forest Law Review*, 8:567–80, October 1972. **1B212**
Re: *Branzburg v. Hayes*, 408 U.S. 665 (1972).

Bennett, Robert W. "Broadcast Coverage of Administrative Proceedings." *Northwestern University Law Review*, 67:528–61, September–October 1972. **1B213**
A discussion of the issues, pro and con, regarding electronic media coverage of administrative proceedings. The discussion was prompted by a proposal encouraging such broadcasting, made by the Administrative Conference of the United States in 1972.

Bennett, Stephen A., Jack C. Landau, and Martin Shapiro. "Free Press v. Fair Trial; A Symposium." *Trial*, 12(8): 24–35, September 1976. **1B214**
A review of the issues raised by the press gag order imposed by a Nebraska judge in the Simants murder trial, reversed by unanimous decision of the U.S. Supreme Court. Bennett writes an introduction; Landau argues the free press side in the debate. Shapiro supports the "fair trial" point of view.

Bennis, Warren. "Have We Gone Overboard on 'The Right to Know'?" *Saturday Review*, 3(11):18–21, 6 March 1976. **1B215**
Requirements for complete disclosure of information could make it impossible for government to operate effectively. "The disclosure mania will make for more cliques that meet privately beforehand to agree on concerted actions subsequently revealed only at the public meetings." The author believes we are likely to get better government "if we focus our energies on finding leaders whose innate integrity, honesty, and openness will make it unnecessary for us to sue them or ransack their files later on."

Benson, George A. "The Essence of Our Freedom." *American Editor*, 2:24–30, July 1958. **1B216**
The editor of the *Toledo Times* criticizes the "brigade" of the American Society of Newspaper Editors who are defending the people's right to know. The government also has a stake in an informed public opinion and thus might reason that the people must not be misled or deceived by the press. He defends the right of privacy, the right of the government to with-

hold certain material, and denies that the exclusion of cameras in the courtroom is a violation of the First Amendment.

Benson, Ivor. *The Opinion Makers*. Pretoria, South Africa, Dolphin, 1967. 177p.   **1B217**
An attack on the liberal establishment press in African countries which operates behind a curtain of secrecy and fears the kind of criticism of itself that it metes out to others. Government censorship of such abuse of the power of the press is only effective in time of war, and press councils are useless. He calls for the creation of a rival conservative press and for stricter enforcement of the laws of defamation to protect politicians and others who have been marked for destruction by the liberal press.

Bentil, John K. "Parliamentary Sketch As a Privileged Publication." *Public Law*, 1974:4–9, Spring 1974.   **1B218**
The article considers the following points relating to the British law of defamation: "that which is privileged in a report of parliamentary proceedings; the nature and scope of a parliamentary sketch; the *Cook* case (*Cook v. Alexander* (1973) 3 W.L.R. 617); other relevant cases."

Bentley, Eric. *Are You Now or Have You Ever Been; An Investigation of Show Business by the Un-American Activities Committee, 1947–1958*. New York, Harper & Row, 1972. 160p. (Harper Colophon Book)   **1B219**
The dialogue in this dramatization has been taken from hearings before the House Un-American Activities Committee. "Hence no resemblance between the witness and the actual person is coincidental." The hearings involved investigation of Hollywood writers, actors, and directors suspected of being Communists.

———, ed. *Thirty Years of Treason. Excerpts from Hearings before the House Committee on Un-American Activities, 1938–1968*. New York, Viking, 1971. 991p.   **1B220**
A retelling of the story of the House Un-American Activities Committee which investigated alleged subversive activities in America. Many of the witnesses were from the field of the theater, the motion pictures, and journalism.

Benton, Elvin. "The FCC and Pollution of the Airwaves." *Liberty*, 63:8–12 +, May–June 1968.   **1B221**
"Is the Fairness Doctrine really fair? And are minority religious rights protected when Government can grant or deny a broadcasting license on the basis of what programming it believes to be in the public interest?"

Berbysse, Edward J. "Conflict in the Courts: Obscenity Control & First Amendment Freedoms." *Catholic Lawyer*, 20:1–29, Winter 1974.   **1B222**
"Contemporary society is confronted with the necessity of maintaining a balance between protecting freedom of expression and preventing the erosion of society's morality. The general purpose of this writing is to analyze the common law tradition—both English and American—and to discover the basic principles which preserve freedom and the moral health of society. More specifically, obscenity is the particular concern of this paper. It will study the legal conflict between those who advance the argument for greater individual permissiveness and those determined to prevent the destruction of society's moral order." The author concludes that "there is no present danger of writers and publishers having their freedom restricted. Rather, in the widespread pestilence of obscenity, where the law has become ineffective and the courts permissive to a dangerous degree, it is the public that has been left unprotected from the virulent and aggressive proliferation of obscenity in speech, writings, films and action."

Berdes, George R. *Friendly Adversaries: The Press and Government*. Milwaukee, Center for the Study of the American Press, College of Journalism, Marquette University, 1969. 187p.   **1B223**
"Complexity, news management, secrecy— these are the three external obstacles with which the Washington newsman must grapple daily. To the extent that he overcomes each of them prudently, wisely, intelligently he fulfills his mission. Whether, in fact, he is able to overcome them and if so how, was one of the primary concerns of this study." In a series of interviews with leading Washington correspondents and government news specialists, the author questions each with respect to these factors as well as general views of the quality of news coverage of the Washington scene.

Berg, Morton L. "Defenses to Defamation in Proxy Statements." *Defense Law Journal*, 18:673–701, 1969.   **1B224**
A discussion of possible conflicts between federal and state laws and policies dealing with defamation in the regulation of securities and persons dealing with them.

Berger, Margaret A. "How the Privilege for Governmental Information Met Its Watergate." *Case Western Reserve*, 25:747–95, Summer 1975.   **1B225**
"The author describes in detail the ill-starred course of Proposed Federal Rule of Evidence 509, which concerned state secrets and official information. . . . The author discusses *United States v. Nixon* and its role in the development of executive privilege, reasoning that the Supreme Court's decision may have affirmed the supremacy of the judiciary on questions of privilege at the expense of Congress' ability to obtain information from the executive branch."

Berger, Raoul. *Executive Privilege; A Constitutional Myth*. Cambridge, Mass., Harvard University Press, 1974. 430p.
                                    1B226
Content: History of Legislative Inquiries into Executive Conduct. Presidential Powers: The "Executive Power." Presidential Powers: The Commander-in-Chief. Presidential Powers: Foreign Relations. Presidential "Precedents." Executive Privilege Compared with Evidentiary Privilege. Withholding Interdepartmental Communications from Congress. The Cost of Secrecy (including suppression of the Pentagon Papers). Practical Arguments for Executive Privilege Examined. Judicial Review.

———. "Executive Privilege v. Congressional Inquiry." *UCLA Law Review*, 12:1043–1120, April 1965; 12:1287–1364, May 1965. (Also in U.S. Congress. Senate, Committee on the Judiciary. *Executive Privilege: The Withholding of Information by the Executive. Hearings . . .*, pp. 48–203)   **1B227**
"Resistance to the congressional claim to unlimited information from the executive branch presents a dispute about constitutional boundaries. Ascertainable boundries between the branches are a basic presupposition of the separation of powers, and Part I of this study conned the pages of history in a search for boundaries that obtained at the adoption of the Constitution. Parliamentary and colonial legislative inquiries, it was there concluded, were virtually unlimited, and the Framers gave no evidence of an intention to confer executive power to withhold information from Congress. Instead of assuming that history was conclusive in the process of constitutional interpretation, Part I posited minimally that exigencies of an expanding, changing nation required a departure from historical practices. Part II assays the practical reasons which have been advanced for a restrictive view of the inquiry power. Then, because conflicting constitutional boundary claims ought to be submitted to impartial arbitrament, and because it is traditionally the function of the courts to draw constitutional boundaries, there follows inquiry into whether constitutional obstacles to judicial resolution of the dispute exist."

———. "The Grand Inquest of the Nation." *Harper's*, 247:12–23, October 1973.   **1B228**
"The president can no more create a constitutional power to withhold information than he can pull himself up by his own bootstraps." The article is drawn from the author's book, *Executive Privilege*.

Bergman, Lincoln *et al.* "The Learning Tree" Incident. 30 min. tape recording. Berkeley, Calif., Pacifica Tape Library, 1970.   **1B229**

Lincoln Bergman of radio station KPFA interviews four teachers to provide their views on the controversy in Richmond, Calif., over the banning of Gordon Parks' novel, *The Learning Tree*, from school libraries. Teachers instituted grievance procedures to contest the censorship and at the same time investigated other instances of censorship and violation of academic freedom.

Berkby, Robert H. "Supreme Court Libertarians and the First Amendment: an Analysis of Voting and Opinion Agreement, 1956–1964." *Southwestern Social Science Quarterly*, 48:586–94, March 1968. **1B230**
"The libertarians reach substantially similar results in the free speech, press and assembly cases, but they present different explanations of the path their reasoning took. Divided on points of principle and strategy, this voting bloc has failed to establish a coherent doctrine in constitutional interpretation."

Berkman, Dave. "A Modest Proposal: Abolish the FCC." *Columbia Journalism Review*, 4(3):34–36, Fall 1965. **1B231**
A criticism of the record of the Federal Communications Commission in carrying out the mandate to regulate broadcasting "in the public interest." The author proposes a "rental fee" for the use of TV channels and the creation of a dual system of broadcasting, "a variation of the Canadian approach in which a government-owned but independently run network such as the Canadian (or British) Broadcasting Corporation, operates the alternatively programmed network." In an accompanying statement William Benton, although disagreeing with Berkman's proposal, recommends the creation of a commission with sole purpose of annually appraising the current status of broadcasting and making suggestions for its improvement to Congress, the president, the FCC, and the American people.

Berkman, Howard I. "The Right of Publicity—Protection for Public Figures and Celebrities." *Brooklyn Law Review*, 42:527–57, Winter 1976. **1B232**
"This Note will trace the development of the right of publicity, discuss the question whether this right may descend to a public figure's distributees, and describe the constitutional limitations on its assertion. The confusion that exists between the rights of privacy and publicity will be examined, and the distinctions that should be drawn between the two rights will be stressed."

Berman, Harriet K. "Federal Meddling; Censoring Public TV." *Civil Liberties*, 297:1–2, July 1973. **1B233**
The author charges that, despite strong admonitions in the Public Broadcasting Act, the Corporation for Public Broadcasting and the Public Broadcasting Service have acted as censors. She cites examples of cancellation of programs, issuing of warnings to local stations over controversial programs, and general interference with program content. Lack of adequate funding during the Nixon Administration and threats and pressures from the White House have also contributed to government control of the institution.

Bernardi, John A., and D. Peter De Bruyne. "The KWK Case: A History and Analysis." *St. Louis University Law Journal*, 15:126–55, Fall 1970. **1B234**
A history and criticism of the FCC's ten-year controversy over the license renewal case of radio station KWK, St. Louis.

Bernas, Joaquin G. "Contempt of Court by Publication: A Look at Philippine, English and American Practice." *Ateneo Law Journal* (Philippines), 13:251–76, January 1964. **1B235**
"This paper will review the historical course which freedom of expression has taken in the past sixty years of Philippine jurisprudence particularly as applied to the ever recurring issue of contempt of court by publication. An attempt also will be made to compare it with American and English constitutional doctrine, to criticize it and, in the process, to make suggestions as to the course of future developments."

———. "Problems and Principles toward a Legal Definition of Obscenity." *Ateneo Law Journal* (Philippines), 12:1–23, September 1962. **1B236**
The author considers the problems of defining obscenity as faced by the U.S. Supreme Court and by the Philippine Supreme Court and the Court of Appeals.

Berninghausen, David K. "Antithesis in Librarianship: Social Responsibility vs. *The Library Bill of Rights*." *Library Journal*, 97:3675–81, 15 November 1972. Comments: *Library Journal*, 98:6–7, 25–41, 1 January 1973; 98:106–7, 15 January 1973; 98:363, 1 February 1973. **1B237**
"It is not the purpose of ALA to take positions as to how men must resolve" the vital issues facing mankind today. "Vital though they are, it is essential that librarians, in their professional activities, shall view such issues as subordinate to the principles of intellectual freedom." The author charges the library press with supporting the "social responsibility" concept of librarianship by subjective and selective reporting of ALA activities. A chapter from the author's book, *The Flight from Reason*.

———. *The Flight from Reason. Essays on Intellectual Freedom in the Academy, the Press, and the Library*. Chicago, American Library Association, 1975. 175p. **1B238**
"These essays are concerned with threats to intellectual freedom from both left and right." The abuse and violence of the New Left during the 1960s and early 1970s fanned the flames of extremism from the Radical Right, enabling these fanatics to capitalize on the fears of the majority and both groups turned on the "liberal," who was identified as the enemy. "This is to be expected, for the fanatic, whether conservative or revolutionary, typically despises the liberal for being willing to tolerate the expression of 'wrong and objectionable' views, because the fanatic *knows* the truth. The fanatic's absolute conviction that he knows the truth seems to him to justify his attempts to make expressions that he dislikes inaccessible. Censors, whether they focus an attack upon the university, the press, or the library try to limit access to ideas." The essays are as follows: (1) Educating Librarians for Intellectual Freedom. (2) Intellectual Freedom and the Communications Process. (3) The Threat to Liberal Values in the Communications Institutions. (4) Problem Cases of Library Censorship: Film Censorship in Peoria; the Case of the *Nation;* Wrenshall Bans Orwell's *1984;* and the Report of the Commission on Obscenity and Pornography. (5) The Flight from Reason. (6) Theories of the Press as Bases for Intellectual Freedom. (7) The Social Responsibility Concept of Librarianship Versus the Library Bill of Rights Concept. (8) ALA's Program to Defenders of Intellectual Freedom. The Appendixes include: (1) The Bodger Report—A Landmark Case for ALA and (2) Free Press and Fair Trial—Statements of Ethical Principles, reprinted from an *Occasional Paper* of the Center for the Study of Democratic Institutions. Reviewed by Zoia Horn, *Newsletter on Intellectual Freedom* (IFC-ALA), November 1975.

———. "Intellectual Freedom and the Press." *Library Journal*, 97:3960–67, 15 December 1972. Reply by John Berry, 3d., 98:11, 1 January 1973. **1B239**
In this chapter from his forthcoming book, *The Flight from Reason*, the author concludes that "if scholars are not free to conduct honest objective research, if libraries are not free to collect and disseminate the reports of such scholarship, or if the press is controlled by government or by advocacy journalists of either Right or Left, then we face a bleak future. If any of these three professions reject the obligations to perform as objectively as is humanly possible, then decisions will be made by those who can command the biggest weapons. Violence can so easily replace dialogue. I believe it to be the special obligation of scholars, librarians, and journalists to keep the channels of communication open, as an essential condition for civilization."

———. "The Librarian's Commitment to the Library Bill of Rights." *Library Trends*, 19:19–38, July 1970. **1B240**
"This paper will discuss some of the events and issues that led the American Library Association to adopt the Library Bill of Rights, to

establish a Committee on Intellectual Freedom, and to continue to emphasize the vital importance of free inquiry. It will also include comments on some unfinished business regarding the protection of librarians who practice according to their commitment."

————. "Struggle for Intellectual Freedom in 1971." In the *Bowker Annual of Library & Book Trade Information*. New York, Bowker, 1972, pp. 66–71. **1B241**

This annual review includes references to the Pentagon Papers case, the Report of the U.S. Commission on Obscenity and Pornography, and the American Library Association's efforts in behalf of intellectual freedom.

————. "Teaching a Commitment to Intellectual Freedom." *Library Journal*, 92:3601–5, 15 October 1967. (Reprinted in Eric Moon, *ed.*, *Book Selection in the Sixties*, pp. 385–94) **1B242**

It is the responsibility of professors in library schools to persuade their students that they "have chosen a profession that commits them to the principle of intellectual freedom."

Berns, Edward. "Freedom of the Press on the College Campus." *New England Law Review*, 9:153–68, Fall 1973. **1B243**

An examination of recent court decisions involving freedom of the college press, including *Keyishian v. Board of Regents of the University of the State of New York*, 385 U.S. 589 (1967).

Berns, Walter. "Absurdity at the *New York Times:* The Confusion Between Art and Self-Righteousness." *Harper's*, 246:34–40, May 1973. **1B244**

The author considers the *New York Times* as absurd in its campaign against the pornographic condition of Times Square when "what it denounces as filth on the editorial page it praises as art or serious social comment on the film and drama pages."

————. "Beyond the (Garbage) Pale or Democracy, Censorship and the Arts." In Harry M. Clor, *ed.*, *Censorship and Freedom of Expression*. Chicago, Rand McNally, 1971, pp. 49–72. (Reprinted in Victor B. Cline, *ed.*, *Where Do We Draw the Line?* pp. 25–44; Ray C. Rist, *ed.*, *The Pornography Controversy*, pp. 40–63; *Public Interest*, Winter 1971; *Quadrant*, March–April 1972) **1B245**

An essay in defense of censorship of pornography and in opposition to the civil libertarian view that has been adopted by the courts in recent years with the result that pornography has become "a growth industry" in America. The excesses in explicit portrayal of sex in literature and on the screen and stage has led many liberals, including the *New York Times* and Morris Ernst, to denounce with disgust what is happening and appeal to the "laws of

common decency." Other liberals turn to the old faith that "when there is no lower depth to descend to, ennui will erase the problem." Censorship has gotten a bad name because it has been misused by zealots. "Just as it is no simple task to formulate a rule of law that distinguishes the nonobscene from the obscene, it is still more difficult to distinguish the obscene from the work of genuine literary merit . . . ," but failure to maintain the distinction in law will mean that "not only will we no longer be able to teach the distinction between the proper and the improper, but we will no longer be able to teach—and will therefore come to forget—the distinction between art and trash." While granting the difficulty in distinguishing between "the justified and unjustified employment of obscenity," Berns regards censorship in some degree as desirable "because it inhibits self-indulgence and supports the idea of propriety and impropriety, protects political democracy . . . [and] serves to maintain the distinction between art and trash and, therefore, to protect art and, thereby, to enhance the quality of this democracy." Dissenting and concurring opinions on Berns's viewpoint are expressed by Alexander Bickel, Stanley Kauffmann, W. Carey McWilliams, and Marshall Cohen.

————. "The Constitution and a Responsible Press." In Harry M. Clor, *ed.*, *The Mass Media and Modern Democracy*, Chicago, Rand McNally, 1974, pp. 113–35. **1B246**

The author's theme is that society and the courts have placed a primary value in recent years on freedom of speech and press, under the First Amendment, while the various laws designed to promote a responsible press (libel, privacy, fair trial, obscenity, and confidentiality of government papers) have been given a secondary place. He denies that the men who wrote the First Amendment intended freedom of speech and press to be applied as Justice Holmes said, "to the thought that we hate." They would not have tolerated the advocacy of monarchy, fascism, or communism as a Constitutional right. Laws promoting a responsible press are "not incompatible with free government; they may be a necessary condition of it."

————. *The First Amendment and the Future of American Democracy*. New York, Basic Books, 1976. 288p. **1B247**

"It is the thesis of this book that the [U.S. Supreme] Court, in the name of civil liberty, is steadily eroding the condition of civil liberty, to the point where it is appropriate to wonder about the future of liberal democracy in the United States." The Court's broad construction of the First Amendment which embraces freedom of speech to pornography, for example, departs from the intent of the Founding Fathers and, by undermining moral foundations, weakens the very liberties that the Amendment was created to protect. Chapters 1 and 5 on obscenity appeared in Harry M. Clore, *ed.*, *The Mass Media and Modern Democracy;* chapter 3 on the history of a free press appeared in Philip B. Kurland, *ed.*, *Supreme Court Reports, 1970.*

————. "Freedom of the Press and the Alien and Sedition Laws: A Reappraisal." In *Supreme Court Reports, 1970.* Chicago, University of Chicago Press, 1970, pp. 109–59. **1B248**

In his reappraisal of the political situation that gave rise to the Alien and Sedition Acts the author takes issue with a number of historians over the relation of the Acts to the concept of freedom of the press. "Contrary to Professor [Leonard] Levy, there is reason to believe that it was not really a 'broad libertarian theory' that emerged during the fight against the Alien and Sedition Laws; and that contrary to Professors [Adrienne] Koch and [Harry] Ammon, these laws were the occasion more than the cause of Madison and Jefferson's famous [Virginia and Kentucky] resolutions. The principle on which especially Jefferson and John Taylor and some other Republican leaders based their opposition was not 'a broad libertarian' version of civil liberties but the doctrine of states' rights, or nullification, or disunion. The men principally responsible for the development of a liberal law of free speech and press—for fashioning a remedy for the deprivation of the constitutional rights of freedom of speech and press—were the Federalists Alexander Hamilton and James Kent who were able to do this because, unlike Jefferson and his colleagues and successors, they were not inhibited by an attachment to the institution of slavery."

Bernstein, Jay H. "The Broadcast Media and the First Amendment: A Redefinition." *American University Law Review*, 22:180–222, Fall 1972. **1B249**

"In defining the first amendment interests in the broadcast media, two questions are germane. First, whether there is a constitutionally, as opposed to statutorily, mandated right of the public to receive information. Second, whether there is an individual right of access to the broadcast media. Resolution of this question is contingent upon whether the first amendment protects an individual interest in speech which frequently enhances the receiving of information by the public and sometimes is unrelated to it, and whether a broadcast station is a facility amenable to the concept of access and the notion of the public or quasi-public forum. Affirmative responses to these questions prompt an additional inquiry—namely, how must the manner in which the broadcast media is presently operated be altered to conform with the requirement of the first amendment."

Bernstein, Peter. "Reporting in Pretoria." *Index on Censorship*, 4(3):44–48, Autumn 1975. **1B250**

A young American who spent six months working as a reporter in South Africa, "gives an account of his experience in a country which has over 20 different laws restricting the freedom of the press and where 'the journalists are mostly white, the newspapers mostly interested in the affairs of the white community, the capital behind the papers is white, the readership is white and, above all, the perspective is white.' Yet all this does not fully explain why the newspapers do not carry all the news that should be printed. Peter Bernstein reveals some of the complex problems behind South African censorship and self-censorship."

Bernstein, Victor H. "TV Editorials: How Brave & Free?" *Nation*, 205(6):170–73, 4 September 1967. **1B251**
Television is a "near vacuum" in the field of editorials by the owner or management of the station presenting an opinion in such a way as the management of a newspaper presents an opinion.

————, and Jesse Gordon. "The Press and the Bay of Pigs." *Columbia University Forum*, 10(3):5–13, Fall 1967. **1B252**
A reconstruction of the relationship of the American press and the government in the Bay of Pigs affair. The authors conclude that "most of the press decides for or against cooperation with the government not on the basis of principle, but on the basis of the issue." They ask "who best served journalism and the public weal in the months before the Bay of Pigs—those who talked, or those who kept silent?"

Berry, Janis M. "Prison Regulation Limiting Press Access to Prisoners Held Unconstitutional." *Boston University Law Review*, 54:670–88, May 1974. **1B253**
Re: *Washington Post Co. v. Kleindienst, Globe Newspaper Co. v. Bork,* and *Hillery v. Procunier.* In the three recent cases the courts reached their decisions by markedly different constitutional paths. "*Globe* looked to the constitutionally protected right of news gathering; *Washington Post* relied on a public right to receive information and ideas; and *Hillery* sought to protect innate rights of free expression."

Berry, Paul M. *et al.* "A Right of Access to the Media: Some Canadian Reactions." *Canadian Communications Law Review*, 2:54–69, 1970. **1B254**
In this research study Graham R. Garton contributes a basic introduction to Jerome Barron's concept of "access" and relates it to Canadian law; Patricia Wallace examines the impact of the CRTC hearing into Air of Death on the question of access and responsibility; Richard G. Pyne examines the proposals of INTER-COM and Town Talk with respect to community cablecasting on CATV channels; Gerald D. Parkinson reviews some statistics on Ontario daily newspapers to see if more access could be provided in the print media on an economic basis; and, in the final section, Paul

M. Berry reexamines the arguments and offers some ominous conclusions on the governmental and institutional barriers to free access in Canada.

[Berry, Walter, and James Robertson.] *In the Criminal Prosecution at the Instance of His Majesty's Advocate, against James Robertson and Walter Berry.* Edinburgh, 1793. 7p. 5p. 12p., and 10p. **1B255**
Charges, evidence, and speeches of opposing counsels in the trial of two booksellers for publishing and selling James T. Callender's *The Political Progress of Britain; or an Impartial Account of this Country from the Revolution in 1688 . . . ,* charged as seditious.

Bertelsman, William O. "The First Amendment and Protection of Reputation and Privacy—New York Times Co. v. Sullivan and How It Grew." *Kentucky Law Journal,* 56:718–56, Summer 1967–68. **1B256**
"It is the purpose of this article to discuss in some detail the development of the *New York Times* doctrine, its logic and policy, its place in first amendment theory, its shortcomings, and finally some possibilities for channels of future growth."

————. "Injunctions Against Speech and Writing: A Re-evaluation." *Kentucky Law Journal,* 59:319–50, Winter 1971. **1B257**
"Positing that the public interest rule in defamation cases erected by *New York Times v. Sullivan* is applicable to injunctive as well as damages actions, and saying that the trade libel cases are long standing precedent that the doctrine against prior restraint is not applicable to all defamatory expression, Mr. Bertelsman develops an approach for allowing injunctions in what he denominates as the defamation-privacy areas."

[Besant, Annie, *plaintiff.*] *Report of Mrs. Annie Besant's Suit Against the "Daily Graphic."* London, Theosophical Publishing House [1921]. 35p. **1B258**
The trial was held before Lord Anderson and a special jury in the Court of Sessions at Edinburgh, against Messrs. H. R. Baines & Co., proprietors of the *Daily Graphic*, London, for alleged libel. At issue was an article entitled Unrest in India, published in 1917, charging Mrs. Besant with the advocacy of sedition. The Court ruled for the defendant. The pamphlet includes newspaper comment critical of the decision. Mrs. Besant had been interned during the war.

Beschle, Donald, Neil J. Fogarty, and Peter J. Niemiec. "Freedom of the Press: Libel." *Annual Survey of American Law,* 1974–75:282–90, Winter, 1975/76. **1B259**
Deals largely with the U.S. Supreme Court

decision in *Gertz v. Robert Welch, Inc.* (1974) and its implication on libel law.

Bessie, Alvah. *Inquisition in Eden.* New York, Macmillan, 1965. 278p. **1B260**
One of the "Hollywood Ten" writes of his experience with the House Un-American Activities Committee that found him guilty of contempt of Congress for taking the First Amendment when asked of his Communist affiliations, and about the blacklisting by the film industry.

Best, Geoffrey *et al.* " 'My Secret Life': Theme and Variations." *Victorian Studies,* 13:204–15, December 1969. **1B261**
"In January 1969 a jury determined, in the quietly conducted case of the *Queen v. Dobson* at Leeds Assizes, that *My Secret Life* was an obscene book without benefit of such academic interest as should entitle it nevertheless to be published 'for the public good' under the Obscene Publications Act of 1959." Here are brief statements of the points of view of three who gave evidence in defense of the book at the trial—Donald Thomas, J. A. Banks and Geoffrey Best, and of Michael Irvin who had used the book in his classes at University of Kent.

Bethea, Charles G. "The Fairness Doctrine and Entertainment Programming: All in the Family." *Georgia Law Review,* 7:554–70, Spring 1973. **1B262**
"This Note will present an argument for the inclusion of entertainment programming within the scope of the fairness doctrine and will suggest the manner in which a successful complaint concerning this type of programming may be made. The rationale for this conclusion will be considered first, and then this rationale will be applied to a variety of factual possibilities in an effort to analyze the effect of such an application upon both the licensee and the audience."

Bettelheim, Bruno. "Children Should Learn About Violence." *Saturday Evening Post,* 240(5):10, 12, 11 March 1967. **1B263**
A psychiatrist disagrees with those who insist that the depiction of violence on television and in print is harmful to children. "Children must be taught about violence so that they can learn to master it."

Betts, Robert. *Smut; Rising Tide of Pornographic Books, Magazines and Films Threaten to Swamp America.* San Diego, Calif., San Diego Union [1969?]. 12p. (Reprinted from the *San Diego Union*) **1B264**
A reporter for the Copley News Service "details pornography's origins, its vast scope and the sinister nature behind it" in a series of four articles: Smut Panel Report Awaited; Pornography on Campus Becomes Political Weapon; Subversion through Smut Seen Communists'

Aim; and Bills to Curb Obscenity Reflect
Growing Alarm.

Beytagh, Francis X. "Privacy and a
Free Press: A Contemporary Conflict
in Values." *New York Law Forum*,
20:453–514, Winter 1975.   **1B265**
The focus of this article will be on a "still
unsettled and important aspect of privacy—
control over public disclosure of information
about an individual by the news media and the
permissible scope of legal protection of that
aspect of privacy consistent with the first
amendment. . . . The privacy/press freedom
problem involves an infrequently appreciated
conflict of base values that, once understood,
makes its resolution extremely delicate and difficult."

Bhattacharjee, Arun. *The Indian Press
Profession to Industry*. Delhi, Published
for the Press Institute of India by Vikas
Publications, 1972. 216p.   **1B266**
The first part of the book deals with press
freedom: (1) Pressures on Mass Media (law,
political, news agencies). (2) Is State Finance
of Newspapers Compatible with the Freedom
Concept (ethics, fiscal magnitude). (3) Newsprint Crisis and Growth of the Press (production handicaps and problems of raw materials).

*The Bible and the Public Schools. The Il-
linois Supreme Court Decision Barring the
Bible from the Public Schools of the State*.
Elgin, Ill., Educational League [1913?],
64p.   **1B267**
An account of the Illinois Supreme Court decision of 29 June 1910, banning from the public
schools the reading of the Bible, the repeating
of the Lord's Prayer, and the singing of sacred
songs, in a case growing out of demands by five
members of the Roman Catholic Church. The
text of the decision follows a discussion of the
issue and the views of the State Teachers Association.

Bickel, Alexander M. "Domesticated
Civil Disobedience: The First
Amendment, from *Sullivan* to the Pentagon Papers." In his *The Morality of
Consent*. New Haven, Conn., Yale
University Press, 1976, pp. 57–88.
      1B268
"The First Amendment decisions of the Supreme Court, in part, incorporate a 'right to
disobey,' a right that has been controlled and
stylized. The amendment makes allowances
for domesticated civil disobedience much after
the fashion of exemptions for conscientious objection." While we cannot get along without
some restraint and self-discipline on the part of
both government and the press, "it is the contest that serves the interest of society as a
whole, which is identified neither with the interest of the government alone nor of the press.
The best resolution of this contest lies in an
untidy accommodation. . . . The accommodation works well only when there is forbearance
and continence on both sides. It threatens to

break down when the adversaries turn into
enemies, when they break diplomatic relations
with each other, gird for and wage war."

———. "On Pornography." *Public Interest*, 22:25–28, Winter 1971.   **1B269**
Commenting on an essay on pornography by
Walter Berns in the same issue (pp. 3–24), the
author concludes that the federal government
"should stay out of the business of censorship
altogether, because its idiocies, when they occur, affect the whole country. But the Supreme
Court, while exercising procedural oversight,
ought to let state and local governments run the
risks if they wish."

———. "Pornography, Censorship
and Common Sense." *Reader's Digest*,
104(2):115–18, February 1974.   **1B270**
In an interview conducted by George Denison,
a Yale law professor indicates why pornography is a serious social problem, defends the
U.S. Supreme Court's efforts to restrict hard-
core pornography, does not believe that the
Court's action endangers First Amendment
rights. "There comes a time, and I believe we
have reached it, when society is threatened by
unbridled obscenity. Societies polluted by
moral stench are not likely to survive. And that
is why the Supreme Court decision—and the
moral statement it permits law to make—are
important."

———. "The Press and Government:
Adversaries without Absolutes." *Freedom at Issue*, 19:5–6, 24, May–June
1973.   **1B271**
"A broad freedom to seek and report news
persists but there are no absolutes in a complex,
free society. Not for the news media and not
for government. The Constitution provides
only an adversary game—but an effective
one."—Editor

———. "The 'Uninhibited, Robust,
and Wide-Open' First Amendment:
From Sullivan to the Pentagon Papers." *Commentary*, 54(5):60–67,
November 1972. (Reprinted in Victor
B. Cline, *ed.*, *Where Do You Draw the
Line?* pp. 63–77; also tape-recorded and
issued in cassette form by the Committee on Continuing Education, State Bar
of California)   **1B272**
The term "uninhibited, robust, and wide-
open" as applied to the First Amendment is
taken from the decision of the U.S. Supreme
Court in *New York Times v. Sullivan* (1964). The
author considers the various rationales given
by the Court for press freedom and the limitations thereof under the First Amendment.
"The Court will not accept infringements on
free speech by administrative or executive action, and if the infringement occurs pursuant to
a statute, the Court will demand that the statute express the wish of the legislature in the
clearest, most precise, and narrowest fashion
possible. Essentially what the Court is exacting
is assurance that the judgment that speech

should be suppressed is that of the full,
pluralist, open political process, not of someone down the line, representing only one or
another particular segment of the society—and
assurance that the judgment has been made
closely and deliberately, with awareness of the
consequences and with clear focus on the sort
of speech that the legislature wished to suppress." In a brief commentary on Professor
Bickel's article, Norman Podhoretz (pp. 79–81
in Cline's reprinting) questions why the media
should be entitled to unchecked power, including the right to lie *(New York Times v. Sullivan)*,
when no other institution is given such
privilege. So long as we honor the First
Amendment, "we will continue to be burdened
as a political community with more freedom of
speech than may well be good for us to live
with." Despite the blurred line, we should attempt to draw distinctions between speech and
overt action.

———, Abraham Goldstein, William
Nelson, and John Fischer. "The Press
as Watchdog." *Yale Reports*, 625:1–4, 22
October 1972. (Reprinted in *Current*,
December 1972)   **1B273**
A broadcast discussion on the U.S. Supreme
Court decision denying reporters the privilege
to withhold information about their confiden-
tial news sources. Professor Bickel points out
that, unlike lawyers and priests, the newsman
is the only profession that can plausibly claim
First Amendment protection.

Bickel, Alexander M., Burke Marshall,
and Victor Navasky. "The Public's
Right to Know—An Unruly Contest."
Yale Reports, 624:1–4, 15 October 1972.
      1B274
A broadcast discussion on the operation of the
Freedom of Information Act from the point of
view of a professor of law, a government official, and a journalist. Agreement was reached
that the present system of security classification was irrational and intolerable.

*The Bill of Rights in Action: Freedom of
Speech*. 16 min. color movie. Los
Angeles, Released by Film Associates
of California, 1968. Directed by Bernard Wilets. (Accompanying study
guide)   **1B275**
The film explores the complex meaning of the
constitutional right of free speech by asking,
"Are there limits to this freedom or may an
individual's speech be controlled when it
threatens law and order?" Reviewed by Patricia B. Harris in the September 1972 issue of
Newsletter on Intellectual Freedom (IFC-ALA).

*The Bill of Rights in Action: Freedom of the
Press*. 16mm. color movie, 23 min.
Santa Monica, Calif., Released by BFA

Educational Media, 1973. Directed by Bernard Wilets.   **1B276**
Considers the conflicts over freedom of the press between the public's right to know, guaranteed by the First Amendment, and the duty of all citizens to cooperate with criminal investigations to discover and punish wrongdoers. Shows how a reporter's protection of confidential sources can lead to important Constitutional conflicts over these issues.

Bill of Rights Newsletter. Los Angeles, Constitutional Rights Foundation, 1967–date. Biennial.   **1B277**
The publication is intended to provide California social studies teachers with information and suggested teaching strategies in the area of the Constitution and the Bill of Rights. The April 1967 issue featured Fair Trial and Free Press; the Spring 1969 issue carried articles on academic freedom in the public schools; the Fall 1973 issue featured Problem of a Free Press; and the Fall 1975 issue included a case study involving freedom for student publications and an account of the West Virginia textbook controversy.

Billings, Thomas. *Anatomy of a Pressure Group.* Columbia, Mo., Freedom of Information Center, School of Journalism, University of Missouri at Columbia, 1972. 7p. (Report no. 284)
                                          1B278
"The Office of Communication of the United Church of Christ is in the vanguard of the movement challenging broadcasters. With a persistent, sophisticated approach, the small organization has chalked up some remarkable successes and helped to change the character of the broadcasters' license renewal process."

Billington, Ray A. *The Historian's Contribution to Anglo-American Misunderstanding. Report of a Committee on National Bias in Anglo-American History Textbooks.* London, Routledge & Kegan Paul, 1966. 118p. (With the collaboration of C. P. Hill, Angus J. Johnston II, C. L. Mowat, and Charles F. Mullett)
                                          1B279
A working party of historians analyzed thirty-eight widely used British and American school textbooks for their treatment of three episodes in history: the American Revolution, the War of 1812, and the First World War. They categorized the degree and variety of bias as (1) deliberate falsification, (2) bias by inertia, (3) unconscious falsification, (4) bias by omission, (5) bias in the use of language, and (6) bias by cumulative implication.

[Binder, L. James.] "Is It Really Censorship When the Boss Says No?" *Army*, 20(2):8, 10 February 1970. **1B280**
A defense of the army's action in suspending Spec. 5 Robert Lawrence who charged censorship of his newscasting. His superiors (news editors) were exercising their prerogative in deciding what would go on the air in a war zone (Vietnam).

Bingham, Jonathan. "Legislation to End Government Censorship by Injunction." *Congressional Record*, 121(116):H 7167–70, 21 July 1975. (Reprinted in *Free Speech*, Commission on Freedom of Speech, Speech Communication Association, November 1975)   **1B281**
The text of Congressman Bingham's speech in behalf of a bill to prohibit court injunctions which would prohibit freedom to speak, print, or publish. The legislation was in response to an injunction against publisher Knopf to prevent publication of the book *The CIA and the Cult of Intelligence* by Victor Marchetti and John D. Marks. The injunction grew out of a suit brought by the CIA. "My bill would do away with the peculiar doctrine that a free press may publish 'rumor and speculation'—in Judge Haynsworth's words—about an issue, but not the facts; it would eliminate from our law the notion that certain men—in particular, those in possession of the embarrassing facts—live outside the protection of the first amendment, in a jurisprudential nether-world where the Government may use injunctions to cut off their ability to communicate with the public."

Birchfield, James D. "Banned in Dublin: *The Parson's Horn-Book.*" *Journal of Library History*, 10:231–40, July 1975.
                                          1B282
A bibliographic study of the suppression of Thomas Egerton Browne's satire on the English clergy and clerical abuses in Ireland and the imprisonment of the author for seditious libel.

Bird, Allen W., II, Thomas W. Goldman, and Keith D. Lawrence. "Corporate Image Advertising: A Discussion of the Factors that Distinguish Those Corporate Image Advertising Practices Protected under the First Amendment From Those Subject to Control by the Federal Trade Commission." *Journal of Urban Law*, 51:405–20, February 1974.   **1B283**
"After considering the historical control of advertising in general and approaches to the control of image advertising in particular, a guideline to be used in construing the FTCA as it relates to image advertising by business concerns in view of the first amendment is proposed."

Birkhead, L. M. "How the Radio Suppresses Liberal Opinion." *Debunker*, 9(5):76–84, April 1929.   **1B284**
How reactions from the Fundamentalist public forced the discontinuance of the liberal religious broadcasts of the author, a Unitarian minister in Kansas City.

Birley, Robert. "Freedom of the Press." *Index on Censorship*, 5:32–40, Spring 1976.   **1B285**
A broad history of the development of press freedom in the western world (England, France, Germany, and the United States) from the time of the invention of printing and the Protestant Revolution to present-day Britain where the concern over freedom rests in the monopoly of the press by a few industrialists, on the one hand, and the control of unions, on the other. The author discusses the conflict over press freedom in Britain during the Commonwealth (including Milton's *Areopagitica*) and the role of the Levellers; the end of licensing (1695); the Fox Libel Act (1792) which gave juries rather than judges the right to designate a libel; and the nineteenth-century struggle to abolish the stamp tax on newspapers.

Birmingham, Stephen. "Does a Zionist Conspiracy Control the Media?" *MORE*, 6(7/8):12–17, July–August 1976.   **1B286**
The author debunks allegations made by Spiro Agnew in connection with the promotion of his novel that a powerful "Jewish cabel" controls the American news media and that this results in an unfair and pro-Israel slant to the news. The author concludes that Agnew fails to understand the Jews just as he failed to understand and deal with the media when he was vice-president. Not only do the leaders of the media not conspire, a number of them "barely tolerate one another, and a few do not even speak to one another."

"Birth Control Libel Action; Stopes v. Sutherland and Another." *Catholic Medical Guardian* (Middlesex, Eng.), 1:36–43, 1923.   **1B287**
A full account of the libel action brought by Dr. Marie Stopes against Dr. Halliday G. Sutherland for an alleged libel contained in the latter's book, *Birth Control: A Statement of Christian Doctrine against the Neo-Malthusians.* Dr. Sutherland had attacked the birth control clinic and methods employed by Dr. Stopes. The jury found the words were defamatory, that they were not fair but that they were true in substance and fact. The Lord Chief Justice, noting that truth in substance and fact was a good defense in libel, found for the defendant. Two leading authorities on libel law, Patrick Hastings and Sir Hugh Fraser, appeared for the plaintiff.

Birtles, William. "Big Brother Knows Best: The Franks Report on Section Two of the Official Secrets Act." *Public Law*, 1973:100–122, Summer 1973.
                                          1B288
"The Official Secrets Acts are based on the theory of privilege, according to which all official information, whether or not related to the

national defence and security, is the property of the Crown. It is therefore privileged and those who receive it officially may not divulge it without the Crown's authority. The same theory permeates the Franks Report on section 2. The thrust of the report is to show how the criminal law may be used to protect government information. It concedes that the existing law is too broad, and goes on to recommend a number of narrower criminal offenses to protect a wide range of government information. Its failure is that it virtually ignores any right of the citizen to access to information over a whole range of governmental activity." The author offers a model classification system, modeled on critical reflection of the United States Freedom of Information Act of 1967. The Franks Committee was appointed in 1971 by the Home Secretary to review the operation of Section 2 of the Official Secrets Act of 1911 and make recommendations.

Bishop, Robert L., and La Mar S. Mackay. *Mysterious Silence, Lyrical Scream: Government Information in World War II*. Lexington, Ky., Association for Education in Journalism, 1971. 39p. (Journalism Monographs, no. 19)   **1B289**
"This monograph is an attempt to outline the main problems encountered in setting up U.S. information agencies for World War II and to suggest some conclusions which may be relevant now. It is our hope that this effort may contribute to the larger question of how we may protect the historic right of the people to know about the politics and programs of their government while maintaining the security of the nation. The title was suggested by *The New Yorker*, whose anonymous 'Talk of The Town' once complained that news of World War II 'has undulated in the mysterious region somewhere between the mysterious silence of the censor and the lyrical scream of the propagandist.' "

[Black, Charles L., Jr.] "The Supreme Court, 1966 Term: Freedom of Speech and Association." *Harvard Law Review*, 81:160–66, November 1967.   **1B290**
Under the heading Libel and Privacy Actions, the survey considers the following cases: *Curtis Publishing Co. v. Butts, Associated Press v. Walker*, and *Time, Inc. v. Hill*.

Black, Eugene C. *The Association. British Extraparliamentary Political Organization, 1769–1793*. Cambridge, Mass., Harvard University Press, 1963. 344p. (Harvard Historical Monographs, 54)   **1B291**
Among the notable extraparliamentary political organizations formed during the latter part of the eighteenth century that dealt with issues of press freedom discussed in this study are: the Society for the Supporters of the Bill of Rights (1769) formed to support John Wilkes; the Society for Constitutional Information (1780); the Association for the Preservation of Liberty and Property against Republicans and Levellers,

founded by John Reeves in 1792 to support the government's campaign against seditious libel; and Friends to the Liberty of the Press, an opposing society formed the same year (1792) by Thomas Erskine, defense attorney for Thomas Paine's *Rights of Man*. When Erskine lost the case the Friends organization collapsed.

Black, Hugo L. "Democracy's Heritage; Free Thought, Free Speech, Free Press." In *1968 Britannica Book of the Year*. Chicago, Encyclopaedia Britannica, 1968, pp. 39–44.   **1B292**
A general history of the development of press freedom in the English-speaking world.

Blackburn, Gary M. *Legal Interpretation and Press Use of the Illinois Open Meetings Law*. Carbondale, Ill., Southern Illinois University at Carbondale, 1974. 96p. (Unpublished Master's thesis)   **1B293**
"The comprehensive study concludes that the number of exceptions to the law may have weakened its intent, that newspapers should more diligently pursue violations of the law in the courts, and that the media itself is its own best weapon in fighting behind-closed-door sessions."

Blackman, Samuel G. "The Strange Case of Libel." *Saturday Review*, 54(15):48–49, 56, 10 April 1971. **1B294**
Thanks to the *New York Times* [*New York Times v. Sullivan* (1964)], and other recent rulings of the U.S. Supreme Court, libel suits against newspapers are no longer as successful as they once were. "I contend that a newspaper or a magazine can publish with little risk any story that should be published if it follows the ground rules. For practical purposes, they can be reduced to two: (1) Is the material provably true? And (2) Is it privileged?" The author discusses the two forms of privilege—absolute and qualified.

Blackmun, Sally A. "The Press Cannot Be Restrained from Reporting Facts Contained in Official Court Records." *Emory Law Journal*, 24:1205–28, Fall 1975.   **1B295**
Re: *Cox Broadcasting Corp. v. Cohn*, 420 U.S. 469 (1975).

Blackshield, Anthony R. "Constitutionalism and Comstockery." *Kansas Law Review*, 14:403–52, March 1966.   **1B296**
On the occasion of the death of Connecticut's birth control law of 1879, *Griswold v. Connecticut* (1965), an Australian law professor discusses the history of contraceptive laws and efforts to repeal them in the legislatures and courts. He examines the *Griswold* decision and the philosophical and legal concepts on which it was based.

[Blacow, Richard.] *The Defence of the Rev. Richard Blacow, A. M. Addressed to the Jury, in the Court at Lancaster, September 14, 1821. On a Criminal Information for A Libel Against the Queen, with Notes on the Whig-Radical Faction. To Which Is Prefixed, The Sermon, That Was Read in Evidence by the Clerk in Court. With Introductory Remarks*. London, Printed and published for the Author, 1822. 132p. (Bound with . . . *Trial of the Rev. Richard Blacow*. . . .)   **1B297**
The Reverend Mr. Blacow restates his argument to the jury in his trial for libeling the Queen, including those comments he was not permitted to make in Court. The text of the objectionable sermon is included along with "extraordinary facts" dealing with Whig-Jacobin party politics in Liverpool.

[————.] . . . *Trial of the Rev. Richard Blacow, for Libels on Her Late Majesty, the Queen of England; Before Mr. Justice Holroyd and a Common Jury, at the Lancaster Summer Assizes. . . .* London, T. Dolby [1827?]. 16p. (Bound with *The Defence of the Rev. Richard Blacow*. . . .)   **1B298**
A Liverpool minister of the Church of England was charged with libeling the late Queen in a sermon which he later published. In the sermon he referred to the Queen as a "Goddess of Lust" who "polluted the Holy Sepulchure itself [the church at Hammersmith] with her presence." Blacow pleaded his own case before Justice Holroyd, using the occasion to further criticize the Queen's morals and impugn the reputation of the Whigs. When restrained by the Court, he cited the cases of Hone and Carlile who, though blasphemous and seditious, were given greater freedom to express themselves in Court. The jury found Blacow guilty of libel.

Blake, Gene. "The Purloined List." *Bulletin of the American Society of Newspaper Editors*, 546:6–7, November–December 1970.   **1B299**
Implications in the case of the *Los Angeles Free Press*, an underground newspaper brought to trial for publishing a confidential list of undercover narcotics agents.

Blake, Jonathan S. "Red Lion Broadcasting Co. v. FCC: Fairness and the Emperor's New Clothes." *Federal Communications Bar Journal*, 23:75–92, 1969.   **1B300**
"This article submits that the *Red Lion* decision [*Red Lion Broadcasting Co. v. FCC* (1969)] constitutes an unfortunate adoption by the Supreme Court of certain basic misconceptions underlying the fairness doctrine, and an extension of

those misconceptions with likely radical consequences for broadcast regulation generally."

Blake, Joseph M. *Libel Suit of Chief Justice ₁Samuel₁ Ames Against Thomas R. Hazard. Hon. Joseph M. Blake's Argument for Defendant upon Plaintiff's Demurrer.* Providence, A. Crawford Greene, 1862. 38p.   **1B301**
Samuel Ames, attorney for the successful plaintiff in the case of *Ives v. Hazard*, later was appointed Chief Justice of the Rhode Island Supreme Court and, in this capacity, published the official report of the case in which he had participated as prosecuting attorney. Thomas R. Hazard, brother of the defendant, accused Judge Ames of publishing a prejudicial account of the trial, a "gross forgery." Judge Ames sued Hazard for libel.

Blake, Richard A. "Will Fig Leaves Blossom Again?" *America*, 129:82–84, 18 August 1973.   **1B302**
"Recent Supreme Court obscenity rulings pose two major problems: What 'community standards' will obtain? How can allegedly obscene materials be tested for 'serious merit'? Both problems remain unsolved." The author concludes: "Good state laws and sound judicial procedures might make it work; a new wave of suppression and neo-Victorian censorship will bring the debate back to zero."

Blanchard, Robert O. "The Freedom of Information Act—Disappointment or Hope." *Columbia Journalism Review*, 6(3):16–20, Fall 1967.   **1B303**
"The Federal Public Records Law probably represents the best that Congress can or will do in the way of statutory FOI reform. The legislative means recommended by Harold L. Cross for libertarian ends have apparently reached their limit. It is not enough. It is now more obvious than ever that revived and more extensive press-Congress surveillance of executive policy is necessary."

———. *A History of the Federal Records Law.* Columbia, Mo., Freedom of Information Center, School of Journalism, University of Missouri at Columbia, 1967. 12p. (Report no. 189)   **1B304**
"The substance of the Federal Public Records Law is the work of Harold L. Cross and Jacob Scher, and the weaknesses of the law are largely the result of political actions in which Cross's and Scher's recommendations were compromised. One major victim of these compromises was the recommendation that only one exemption should be permitted: information protected by specific congressional statute"—Editor. The author of the article, a member of the Moss Committee staff, traces

the evolution of the law from 1955 until it was signed on 4 July 1966.

———. *The Moss Committee and a Federal Public Records Law (1955–1965).* Syracuse, N.Y., Syracuse University, 1966. 286p. (Ph.D. dissertation, University Microfilms, no. 67–7059)   **1B305**
A description of the Moss Committee's work on a proposed federal public records law over the first decade of its existence. The Committee's official name was the Foreign Operations and Government Information Subcommittee of the House Committee on Government Operations.

———. "Present at the Creation: The Media and the Moss Committee." *Journalism Quarterly*, 49:271–79, Summer 1972.   **1B306**
"In general media FoI leaders acted as public spokesmen for the media and, in this case, they publicly represented many newsmen who seemed to share complaints against the Eisenhower Administration's information policies, but who were reluctant to openly participate in a Congressional investigation. The Subcommittee was successful, however, in obtaining information from media FoI spokesmen."

———. "Remember the Freedom of Information Act? It's Practically in Mothballs Today." *Quill*, 60(8):16–18, August 1972. (Reprinted in Robert O. Blanchard, *ed., Congress and the News Media*, pp. 440–46)   **1B307**
Criticism of media freedom of information spokesmen for not keeping the pressure on Congress, particularly the Foreign Operations and Government Information Subcommittee of the House Operations Committee, so that it would function as a continuous check against executive secrecy and propaganda.

———, ed. *Congress and the News Media.* New York, Hastings House, 1974. 506p.   **1B308**
Part 1, Access and Accommodation, includes articles on the historical development of access, equal rights for broadcast journalism, and access of the underground press. Part 2, Interdependence and Interaction, includes the perspectives of congressmen on the role and performance of the press corps and public relations aspects of television and congressional hearings. Part 3, Conflict and Cooperation, discusses First Amendment rights of broadcast journalists, freedom of information and shield laws, and the issue of fair trial vs. free press. A number of the contributions with special bearing on freedom of the press are listed separately under the name of the author.

Blankenburg, William B. "The Adversaries and the News Ethics: Tensions Between Press and Government Are

Historic and Continuing." *Public Relations Quarterly*, 14(4):30–37, 1970. **1B309**
A defense of the adversary relationship between press and government. The journalist may be unhappy under the lash of official criticism, but if tension was not present "we should become uneasy."

———. "Local Press Councils: An Informal Accounting." *Columbia Journalism Review*, 8(1):14–17, Spring 1969.   **1B310**
A reporting on the work of the six local press councils, funded by the Mellett Fund—Bend, Ore.; Redwood City, Calif.; Cairo, and Sparta in Illinois; Seattle and St. Louis. These councils, the author concludes, "may have planted some good seeds in the weedy field of press responsibility."

Blanshard, Paul. "Censorship and Apartheid." *Reporter*, 38:37–39, 22 February 1968.   **1B311**
South Africa's nine-man Publications Control Board is an "autonomous body functioning under the Minister of Interior with broad powers of censorship over books, magazines, plays, films and radio programs." A double standard exists because most of the censoring involves works that "might 'pervert' the minds of the blacks because they discuss race or violence or are sexually provocative by Calvinistic standards." Paperbacks are particularly scrutinized because they are available to the blacks' pocketbook.

———. "Freda Kirchwey and The Nation Magazine on Religious Freedom." *Humanist*, 36(4):40–41, July–August 1976.   **1B312**
On the occasion of the death of Freda Kirchwey, former editor and publisher of the *Nation*, Paul Blanshard recalls the battle over the ban of that journal from New York public school libraries because of his articles critical of the Roman Catholic Church, a battle in which Blanshard was the victim and "Freda was the heroine." Reproduced with the article is the Appeal to Reason and Conscience signed by more than one hundred intellectuals and issued 16 October 1948 by an Ad Hoc Committee to lift the ban on the *Nation* (A22).

———. *Personal and Controversial; An Autobiography.* Boston, Beacon, 1973. 308p.   **1B313**
Includes chapters on the ban on the *Nation* for publication of Blanshard's articles criticizing the Catholic Church's policies on birth control and abortion, the attacks and boycotts against his book, *American Freedom and Catholic Power*, including refusal of the *New York Times* to carry advertisements of the book.

Blasi, Vincent A. "The Justice and the Journalist." *Nation*, 215:198–99, 18 September 1972.   **1B314**
The author, a professor at the University of Michigan Law School, has been director of the

Field Foundation Study of Press Subpoenas. He comments on the decision of the U.S. Supreme Court majority in recent cases involving newsmen's privilege: *United States v. Caldwell*, *Bransburg v. Hayes*, and *In re Pappas* (1972).

————. "The Newsman's Privilege: An Empirical Study." *Michigan Law Review*, 70:229–84, December 1971. **1B315**

Among the findings in this empirical study of newsman's privilege are: (1) The primary adverse impact in the subpoena threat is that it poisons the atmosphere in investigative reporting. (2) Understandings of confidentiality in reporter-source relationships are frequently unstated and imprecise. (3) Press subpoenas damage source relationships rather than reveal sensitive information. (4) Reporters often testify voluntarily, but are willing to go to jail to honor what they believe is an obligation of confidentiality. (5) Newsmen prefer a flexible ad hoc qualified privilege to an inflexible per se qualified privilege. (6) Newsmen believe press subpoenas too often have been issued in unnecessary circumstances.

————. "On the Question of Privilege: Newsmen May Have Little to Gain." *Quill*, 59(11):9–12, November 1971. **1B316**

A summary of results from a nationwide survey of opinions of editors and reporters on the matter of qualified privilege shows that journalists believe that the profession relies too much on off-the-record information acquired through a confidential source; that most information acquired in this way is already a matter of public record. But reporters consider the resistance of subpoenas as a matter of principle and 90 percent would accept a contempt citation. "On the whole, it appears that the increased subpoena threat in the last two years has significantly hampered only a small, rather specialized segment of the journalism profession."

————. *Press Subpoenas: An Empirical and Legal Analysis.* Washington, D.C., Reporters' Committee on Freedom of the Press [1973?]. 291p., 67p. Processed. **1B317**

The author recommends that newsmen "be granted absolute, unqualified privilege against subpoenas issued by grand juries, legislative bodies and administrative agencies"; that in a criminal trial newsmen be required to testify only concerning criminal behavior, not of the "victimless" variety to which they were eyewitnesses or in which they participated; that criminal defendants may subpoena the testimony or documentary evidence of reporters only when it has been established that the reporter has evidence relative to the case; and that the claimant of the privilege should have the burden of establishing that he is a "newsman."

————. "Privilege in a Time of Violence; Caldwell Ruling and Press Sub-

poenas." *Nation*, 211:653–56, 21 December 1970. **1B318**

"The Ninth Circuit's *Caldwell* opinion [*United States v. Caldwell* (1972)] can in no wise be considered a definitive resolution of the press subpoena controversy, and should even be viewed with some misgivings by reporters who seek a meaningful constitutional protection for their source relationships."

"Blasphemy." *Columbia Law Review*, 70:694–733, April 1970. **1B319**

The author reviews the history of blasphemy laws and court decisions, beginning with early English heritage, followed by a history of blasphemy in the United States. A constitutional analysis of blasphemy laws will undoubtedly involve three provisions of the First Amendment: the establishment clause, the free-exercise clause, and the free-speech clause, all made applicable to the states by virtue of the Fourteenth Amendment. The author discusses each provision, concluding: "Blasphemy laws are one of the last remnants of an established church, and in protecting the religious from verbal affront they significantly curtail the freedom of expression of others. . . . The Christian's interest in being free from the psychic attack caused by insult to his deeply held beliefs is, in light of the establishment clause, even less than that of the superpatriot; in any event, neither can be given more than the narrowest protection without infringing on the more vital national interests represented by the first amendment."

Blatt, Gloria T. "Children's Books: X or PG?" *Top of the News*, 32:61–66, November 1975. **1B320**

An examination of recent children's fiction suggests that writers have been able to provide realism which children demand without excessive violence, so that arguments for censorship are without foundation. The article is based on the author's doctoral dissertation.

————. *Violence in Children's Literature; a Content Analysis of a Select Sampling of Children's Literature and a Study of Children's Responses to Literary Episodes Depicting Violence.* East Lansing, Mich., Michigan State University, 1972. 358p. (Ph.D. dissertation, University Microfilms, no. 72-29,931) **1B321**

A content analysis of notable children's books published during 1960–70 revealed no substantial increase in violence; historical fiction was, on the average, two times as violent as modern realistic fiction. Half or more of the children indicated they liked the episodes; children from inner-city schools with real social disorders more often said they liked violent episodes than those from rural or suburban schools.

Blayney, Peter W. M. "*The Booke of Sir Thomas Moore* Re-Examined." *Studies in Philology*, 69(2):167–91, April 1972. **1B322**

"A reconstruction is attempted of the probable

history of the MS during the process of writing and revision. The present state of the MS is examined and is found to provide evidence suggesting two distinct stages of censorship by the Revels Office."

Bleiberg, Robert M. "Beware the Watchdogs; They Mean to Sink Their Teeth Into the Press." *Barron's*, 55(51):7–8, 22 December 1975. **1B323**

The article expresses concern over a legislative proposal for a study by the Securities and Exchange Commission which "looks like the first step in an exercise boldly aimed at ultimately compelling magazines and newspapers to register with the SEC, thereby—in a move neatly timed to coincide with the Bicentennial—effectively scrapping the First Amendment and restoring to the New World after more than two centuries, licensing of the press and censorship."

Bliss, Robert M. "Development of Fair Comment as a Defense to Libel." *Journalism Quarterly*, 44(4):627–38, Winter 1967. **1B324**

In analyzing the landmark decision in *New York Times v. Sullivan* (1964), the author traces the development of the doctrine in three earlier libel cases: *Wason v. Walter* (1868); *Coleman v. MacLennan* (1908); and *Star Publishing Company v. Donahoe* (1904).

————. *Some Implications for Mass Communications in New York Times Company v. Sullivan: Presumption of Privilege in Public Libel.* Iowa City, Iowa, University of Iowa, 1967. 397p. (Ph.D. dissertation, University Microfilms, no. 67-16,778) **1B325**

"This study includes the contextual and case history of *Times* [*New York Times v. Sullivan* (1964)], Supreme Court cases citing the case and rule in the 1963, 1964 and 1965 sessions; press and legal opinions respecting the *Times* case and rule; and the citation and application of the case and rule in state and federal courts in 1964–1965, together with antecedent developments in tort and constitutional law which were drawn on, or appeared analogous to, *New York Times v. Sullivan*."

Block, Bradford E. "Commercial Speech—An End in Sight to *Chrestensen?*" *De Paul Law Review*, 23:1258–75, Spring 1974. **1B326**

"This note will examine the [U.S. Supreme] Court's traditional approach to governmental abridgement of commercial speech, will analyze the treatment of commercial speech in *Pittsburgh Press* [*Pittsburgh Press Co. v. Pittsburgh Commission on Human Relations* (1973)] and will propose that the Court no longer exclude commercial speech from first amendment protection merely because of the commercial nature of the expression."

Block, Herbert. *Herblock's State of the Union.* New York, Simon & Schuster, 1972. 224p.   **1B327**
Three sections in "Herblock's" devastatingly witty cartoons and commentary deal with issues of press freedom: PRolitics, his term for public relations in government; the Secret Snooperstate, dealing with efforts of government officials to hide news under a "national security" blanket; and the Press Section, centered on the systematic attempts of the Nixon Administration to make news and to throttle the press. "When things begin to get rough," Herblock observes, "is when it's suggested that there's something wrong or unpatriotic about criticism of officials and policies, and that the press should mind its own business. Keeping an eye on government *is* our business. That's why the founders set up a free press—to serve, in our system of checks and balances, as a check on all government." Herblock compares the techniques of the Nixon-Agnew attacks on the media with those of Joseph McCarthy in the fifties. "What is needed is not only a defense of the media, but a recognition of the character of the assault and a vigorous effort to turn back the encroachments of government. The media need to regain their rightful initiative."

Block, Stephen M. "The Government Must Demonstrate Compelling Need for a Journalist's Presence at Secret Grand Jury Proceedings before His Attendance Can Be Required." *Texas Law Review,* 49:807–13, April 1971. **1B328**
Re: *Caldwell v. U.S.* (1970).

Blom-Cooper, Louis. "Freer Speech—and Privacy." In Michael Rubinstein, *ed., Wicked, Wicked Libels,* London, Routledge & Kegan Paul, 1972, pp. 40–53.   **1B329**
The author proposes a formula for resolving the conflict between free press and the right of privacy: "Leave the Press and other media of communication free to publish matters of public interest, unencumbered by any threats of libel damages (the criminal law would be the sole threat) and place a much tighter control (by way of a damper) on the publication of matters not within the public domain." While favoring greater protection of individuals from invasion of privacy by idle and prurient curiosity, the author would modify the Official Secrets Act so that governmental doors would be opened more widely to public scrutiny.

———. "What to Do About Libel?" *Encounter,* 30:88–90, May 1968. **1B330**
A British lawyer-journalist offers a radical change in the law of libel: "Abolish totally the civil action for defamatory statements, and

substitute an action for the invasion of the right to privacy."

Bloomberg, Mitchell R. "Pornography; An Obscene Clarification." *University of Miami Law Review,* 28:238–46, Fall 1973.   **1B331**
Re: *Miller v. California* (1973).

Bloomfield, Joy F. *An Investigation of Censorship in the Cuyahoga County (Ohio) Library System.* Kent, Ohio, Kent State University, 1968. 165p. (Unpublished Master's thesis)   **1B332**
Books selected for the survey: *Another Country* by James Baldwin, *The Arrangement* by Elia Kazan, *Autobiography* by Malcolm X, *Candy* by Terry Southern and Mason Hoffenberg, *A Choice Not an Echo* by Phyllis Schlafly, *The Confession of Nat Turner* by William Styron, *Dairy of a Mad Old Man* by Junichiro Tanizaki, *The Exhibitionist* by Henry Sutton, *Fanny Hill* by John Cleland, *God's Little Acre* by Erskine Caldwell, *The Group* by Mary McCarthy, *How to Avoid Probate* by Norman F. Dacey, *Justine* by Marquis de Sade, *Lady Chatterley's Lover* by D. H. Lawrence, *Last Exit to Brooklyn* by Hubert Selby, Jr., *Last Temptation of Christ* by Mikas Kazantzakis, *Lolita* by Vladimir Nabokov, *My Life and Loves* by Frank Harris, *Naked Lunch* by William Burroughs, *Quotations from Chairman Mao Tse-tung, Red Star over China* by Nathaniel West, *Tropic of Cancer* by Henry Miller, *Valley of the Dolls* by Jacqueline Susann, *Why Are We in Vietnam?* by Norman Mailer, and *Wretched of the Earth* by Frantz Fanon. The survey of twenty-five libraries revealed a general lack of a clear knowledge of court decisions and legislation involving freedom to read and a lack of clear principles of book selection. None of the libraries have had to face a genuine censorship crisis. While only one admitted to censorship, the number of restricted shelves and absence of books from the list indicated actual practice of censorship.

Blount, Winton M. "Case Against the Commission on Obscenity and Pornography." *Congressional Record,* 116:36943–45, 14 October 1970. **1B333**
"If it is true that a majority of Americans want pornography legalized, then I think they ought to vote men into office who will legalize it. But until that happens, until we have candidates running on a smut platform, until the people decide to embrace the politics of pornography, we are not going to raise legislative monuments to human degradation." Speech of the Postmaster General, Philadephia, 8 October 1970.

———. "Let's Put the Smut Merchants Out of Business." *Nation's Business,* 59:34–36, 39, September 1971. (Reprinted in *Marriage and Family Living,* February 1972)   **1B334**
Pornography is big business and is defended under the First Amendment only by "tunnel vision." Defenses against it include the postal obscenity statute and legislation passed by

Congress which enables homeowners to protect themselves from unsolicited obscene materials coming in the mail.

———. "Pornography and Its Effect on Society." *Florida Bar Journal,* 44:518–21, November 1970. (Reprinted from the *Congressional Record,* 29 September 1970)   **1B335**
The Postmaster General pleads for public support to stamp out pornography. "If the American people decide against pornography, we can do away with it. If we endorse stringent laws; if we elect and appoint discerning judges; and if, above all, we refuse to patronize the pornographer, then we can put him out of business. There is no room in American for those who use our freedoms to destroy the very habits of mind and spirit that give meaning to these freedoms." Speech before the Nashville Area of Chamber of Commerce, 28 September 1970.

———. *Remarks [Obscenity in Mails],* Greater Chamber of Commerce, Kansas City, October 1, 1970. Washington, D.C., U.S. Post Office Department, 1970. 14p. Processed.   **1B336**
Criticism of the cult of permissiveness which would allow unchecked distribution of pornography by mail. While criticizing the report of the U.S. Commission on Obscenity and Pornography he cautions against impugning the character of members of the Commission.

Boustein, Edward J. "The First Amendment and Privacy: The Supreme Court Justice and the Philosopher." *Rutgers Law Review,* 28:41–95, Fall 1974.   **1B337**
"This paper has attempted to demonstrate the successful application of the Meiklejohn theory to the mass publication privacy tort. The theory developed enables one to distinguish the public's governing interest from the public's curiosity and the publisher's private right. This, in turn, allows one to ask what constitutional interest is served by the actual identification of name or likeness in a particular instance of its mass publication. . . . As I see it, however, the increasing sensitivity of the Court to the distinction between public and private libels and public and private uses of speech suggests, to the contrary, that the *New York Times* case and its progeny will establish a firm constitutional foundation for the mass publication privacy tort. Meiklejohn's theory, by exposing the private and public uses of speech, enables us, I believe, to assure the robust exposition of public issues without inviting the lurid exploitation of private lives."

Blue, James, and Michael Gill. "Peter Watkins Discusses His Suppressed Nuclear Film, 'The War Game.'" *Film Comment,* 3(4):14–19, Fall 1965. **1B338**
The British Broadcasting Corp. had refused to televise this film depicting the outbreak of nu-

clear conflagration, which B.B.C. had itself commissioned.

Blum, Karen M. "A Look at Thought Control: Obscenity in the Eyes of the Supreme Court." *Suffolk University Law Review*, 7:649–72, Spring 1973. **1B339**
"This Note examines the leading cases dealing with the obscenity problem in an attempt to demonstrate the futility and the risks involved in the [U.S. Supreme] Court's struggle to provide a rational scheme for justifying, interpreting and applying legislation in the area of morals. In an effort to delineate guidelines for determining what is *not* constitutionally protected, the Court—in its role as what Justice Black has called the 'Super-Censor'—may well be endangering first amendment rights of individuals which deserve constitutional protection. Perhaps the problem of obscenity may best be disposed of by treating the idea in much the same manner as the equally elusive concept of beauty. After all, perhaps obscenity, too, is merely 'in the eye of the beholder,' in which case one can always close one's eyes."

Blum, Robert A. "Access to Governmental Information in California." *California Law Review*, 54:1650–80, October 1967. **1B340**
The article explains and evaluates accessibility to governmental information in California as established by the legislature under the open meetings acts and the public records acts, and as interpreted by the courts.

Blumenfeld, R. D. "The Freedom of the Press." In his *All in a Lifetime*. London, Benn, 1931, pp. 124–38. **1B341**
A British journalist reminisces about censorship of the press in Britain during World War I. "No sooner had the censorship got itself firmly fixed as a Government department . . . than all the retired Colonels who were too old to fight were decanted into the Censor's department to play hell and demoralisation with every newspaper in the country." Censorship eventually eased off and worked very well and when it was lifted after the war "we had become so accustomed to it that we hardly knew what to do with the Freedom of the Press which had been taken from us four years before."

Blumenthal, Ralph. "Porno Chic." *New York Times Magazine*, 21 January 1973, pp. 28, 30, 32–34. **1B342**
Commentary on the rise of the porno-films, with special attention to *Deep Throat* and its record in the courts.

Blumenthal, Walter H. "American Book Burnings." *American Book Collector*, 6(10):13–19, Summer 1956. **1B343**
A survey of the more notable incidents of book burning in American from the days of Colonial Massachusetts when heretical books were burned, to U.S. State Department book burning in the U.S. Information Service Libraries abroad during the Eisenhower Administration.

Boardman, Neil S. "—And Sweet Are the Uses of Adversity, Too." *Library News Letter (Indiana University)*, 8:10–11, December 1972. **1B344**
Notes on the history of censorship, including events illustrating the observation that censorship has sometimes encouraged good literature.

Boaz, Martha. "Censorship." In Allen Kent and Harold Lancour, *eds.*, *Encyclopedia of Library and Information Science*, New York, Dekker, 1970, vol. 4, pp. 328–38. **1B345**
Topics: Definition, historical background, censorship and the law, recent cases, pressure groups, tolerance and intellectual freedom, libraries and intellectual freedom, and perspective.

———. "The Student Does Have the Right to Read." *California School Libraries*, 41:63–67, January 1970. **1B346**
"The student has a right to read; he has a right to free access to books. He has a right to a wide variety and to an extensive selection of materials. He has a right to examine all ideas, to explore all forms of learning, to investigate all cultures. He has a right to investigate every medium of art and every mode of expression of it. He has a right to search for truth wherever it may be found."

Boccarosse, Ralph N. "Lloyd Corporation v. Tanner: Expression of First Amendment Rights in the Privately Owned Shopping Center—A Reevaluation by the Burger Court." *Catholic University Law Review*, 22:807–29, Summer 1973. **1B347**
Re: *Lloyd Corporation v. Tanner*, 406 U.S. 551 (1972).

Bock, Alan. "What Can Be Done About Media Bias?" *Human Events*, 33:406, 408, 411, 19 May 1973. **1B348**
"We will explore several questions: Is there bias in the media now? If so, what is the political nature of the bias? How is bias expressed in the media, and particularly in the electronic media? If there is bias in the news media, how can those whose views are ignored, slanted or slandered set about rectifying the situation? What will be effective short-term tactics and long-term strategies against bias in the existing news media?"

Bocking, D. H. "The Saskatchewan Board of Film Censors." *Saskatchewan History*, 24(2):51–62, Spring 1971. **1B349**
"Judging from the rejection reports the Saskatchewan censors over the years did maintain high standards or, alternatively, as some might prefer to put it, low standards of tolerance. Their work was apparently generally acceptable as there appears to have been little criti-

cism of it. Most of the criticism that was advanced came from people with special cases to plead."

Bode, Carl. *Mencken.* Carbondale, Ill., Southern Illinois University Press. 1969. 452p. **1B350**
Throughout the volume are references to Mencken's bouts with the censor—Anthony Comstock and John Sumner, the cases against Theodore Dreiser, and Mencken's own involvement in the "Hatrack" case, and coverage of the Scopes evolution trial.

Boffey, Philip M. "Improved Access to Government Papers." *Chronicle of Higher Education*, 10:1, 14 April 1975. **1B351**
The new Freedom of Information Act is a two-edged sword for the academic community. While it helps scholars pry out government documents previously denied them, it also opens many research documents and meetings that some academicians would prefer to keep out of public view.

Bogart, Leo. "Warning: The Surgeon General Has Determined That TV Violence Is Moderately Dangerous to Your Child's Mental Health." *Public Opinion Quarterly*, 36:491–521, Winter 1972/73. **1B352**
The author reviews the history of the Surgeon General's *Study of Television and Social Behavior*, and summarizes the findings and their significance.

Bogart, Max. *A Study of Certain Legally Banned Novels in the United States, 1900–1950.* New York, New York University, 1956. 501p. (Ph.D. dissertation, University Microfilms, no. 57–1356) **1B353**
"The problem was to investigate what novels of importance were legally banned in the United States from 1900 to 1950, on what grounds, the forces involved, the court decisions and their acknowledged influence, and the trends in literary censorship."

Bogen, David S. "The Supreme Court's Interpretation of the Guarantee of Freedom of Speech." *Maryland Law Review*, 35:555–616, 1976. **1B354**
"This paper has attempted to show that the clear and present danger standard for speech urging persons to commit unlawful acts and the multi-level approach to speech which inflicts harm are aspects of the same concept. The tests reflect the Supreme Court's insistence that government may not suppress ideas because it disapproves of those ideas. At the same time, government may incidentally impair speech in

the fulfillment of any of its legitimate functions. Since a direct test of government motivation where speech is impaired would be impossible to administer and would hamstring the government in its ability to engage in legitimate operations, the Court protects against the use of feigned legitimate interests to suppress speech by using tests of necessity; in order to be upheld governmental action impairing speech must be necessary to the accomplishment of legitimate governmental ends."

Bogin, Mary M. *An Examination of the Journalist's Claim to Testimonial Privilege, 1874–1971*. East Lansing, Mich., Michigan State University, 1971. 128p. (Unpublished Master's thesis)   **1B355**

"This thesis argues for an unwritten solution to the subpoena problem and urges the United States Supreme Court to recognize the privilege under the First Amendment's guarantee to freedom of the press."

Bogsch, Arpad. *The Law of Copyright under the Universal Convention*. New York, Bowker, 1964. 591p. 3d ed., 1969. 696p.   **1B356**
An analysis of the Universal Copyright Convention, adopted by a conference of fifty countries in Geneva, 1952, and which went into effect in 1955. The second part of the volume deals with copyright laws of member countries, including Canada, India, Ireland, Great Britain, and the United States.

Bogutz, Allan D. "Protection of the Adults' Right to Pornography." *Arizona Law Review*, 11:792–806, Winter 1969.   **1B357**
The author proposes the adoption of a self-rating system for published works, similar to that in effect for motion pictures. Such a system would exclude children from access to material on an adult level and permit everyone to avoid involuntary contact with material they may find offensive.

Boicourt, Michael L. "Pretrial Publicity." *Missouri Law Review*, 34:538–61, Fall 1969.   **1B358**
Content: Procedural Remedies (change of venue, continuance, voir dire examination, sequestration of the jury, closed preliminary hearings, waiver of jury, mistrial, instruction to the jury, habeas corpus, and appellate review). Constructive Contempt. Restriction of the Source. The author concludes that "an all-inclusive plan, such as the one represented by the American Bar Association recommendations of the Reardon Committee, are needed in the pretrial publicity area, more as a preventive than as a penalizing force.

Boisse, Joseph A. *et al.* "Intellectual Freedom in Wisconsin." *Wisconsin Library Bulletin*, 67:241–53, July–August 1971.   **1B359**
A collection of brief articles on censorship and libraries: "The subtleties of censorship and the thin line between selection and censorship are discussed by William L. Jambrek and Eugene G. McLane. Professor ₍Lee₎ Burress looks at selection and rejection in school libraries and Mrs. ₍Helen H.₎ Lyman presents the broad range choice in films. Mr. ₍Joseph A.₎ Boisse summarizes the censorship problems in Wisconsin during the past year and outlines the services available from the Wisconsin Library Association Intellectual Freedom Committee."

Bolden, C. E., and Thomas L. Dempsey, *comp. Free Press vs. Fair Trial—A Bibliography*. Olympia, Wash., Supreme Court Law Library, 1966. 50p. Processed.   **1B360**
Most, but not all, of the references are included in the McCoy bibliography or supplement.

Boldt, David. "Blue-Pencil Men: TV Censors Work Hard Screening Racy Humor of Bold Comedy Shows." *Wall Street Journal*, 173(20):1, 15, 29 January 1969.   **1B361**
How the network censors work to "allow the shows enough freedom to appeal to the younger set, while imposing enough restraint to avoid estranging the older, more conservative viewers" and to avoid provoking the wrath of the FCC.

₍Bole, John.₎ *Report of the Galway Libel Case: "The Rev. Patrick Lavelle versus John Bole." Tried Before Sergeant Howley In the Court-house of Galway, on the 27th, 28th, 30th, and 31st July, and the 1st and 2nd August, 1860*. Dublin, J. F. Fowler, 1860. 84p.   **1B362**
The case was an action for six alleged libels against the parish priest of Parlry contained in the defendant's newspaper, the *Mayo Constitution*, during May and June 1859. The case became enmeshed in Catholic-Protestant theological matters and was enlivened by the testy characters in the trial and the outspoken letters to the editors on both sides. Much of the controversy was over action of the Catholic priest who interfered between Lord Plunket and the tenants on his land. The jury was unable to reach a verdict and the case was dismissed. The trial lasted six days and was distinguished by florid rhetoric on both sides.

Bollinger, Lee C. "Freedom of the Press and Public Access: Toward a Theory of Partial Regulation of the Mass Media." *Michigan Law Review*, 75:1–42, November 1976.   **1B363**
"The purpose of this article is to examine critically these decisions ₍Supreme Court cases which consider limits of permissible regulation

of print and broadcast media₎ and to explore whether there is any rational basis for limiting to one sector of the media the legislature's power to impose access regulation."

Bolton, Charles K. *The Arrest of John Colman . . . With Notes by Henry Edes*. Cambridge, Mass., John Wilson, 1901. 14p. (Reprinted from *The Publications of the Colonial Society of Massachusetts*, vol. VI)   **1B364**
An account of the case of John Colman, charged with libel in 1720 by the Boston Council for his pamphlet, *The Distressed State of the Town of Boston &c Considered. In a Letter from a Gentleman in the Town, to his Friend in the Country.*

Bond, William K. *Speech of Mr. Bond, of Ohio, upon the Resolution to Correct Abuses in the Public Expenditures, and to Separate the Government from the Press. Delivered in the House of Representatives, April 1838*. ₍Washington, D.C., n.p., 1838.₎ 16p.   **1B365**
An attack in the House of Representatives on government patronage in general and printing patronage in particular, which the speaker considers a form of press subsidy leading to editorial support of the Jackson and Van Buren Administrations and libel of their opponents. Bond supported a reform measure introduced by Congressman Hopkins.

Bonfante, Jordan. "Lord Porn: A Noble Briton Leads a Battle Against 'Filth.'" *Life*, 73:57–58+, 3 November 1972.   **1B366**
"Francis Aungier Pakenham, the seventh earl of Longford—known as Lord Porn—is author of a controversial report on pornography and is surprised at the furor it has caused."

Bonnard, Georges A. *La Controverse de Martin Marprelate, 1588–1590; Épisode de l'histoire littéraire du puritanisme sous Elizabeth*. Geneva, A. Julien, 1916. 237p.   **1B367**
The Marprelate controversy involved a series of Puritan tracts issued secretly under the assumed name of Martin Marprelate, attacking the episcopacy system of church government. Discovery of the press led to the execution of John Penry and cruel imprisonment of John Udall (P159).

Bonniwell, Bernard L. "The Social Control of Pornography and Sexual Behavior." *Annals of the American Academy of Political and Social Science*, 397:97–104, September 1971.   **1B368**
"The law, cognizant of the problem but unable to effectively moderate the flow of pornography and demeaning sexual behavior in areas of public communication, suggests the need to establish some form of direct social control. In order to offset their cumulative and debasing

effect, it is tentatively proposed that the flexibility of the mass media be matched by an equally flexible monitoring-voting system ("monivoting"), under which public controls may be imposed within matter of hours. The proposals are perceived as a socio-cultural necessity for the continuing vitality of the nation."

Borchardt, D. H. "Ideas, Books and the Censor." *Australian Quarterly* (Australian Institute of Political Science), 1954:69–81, December 1954.   **1B369**

Borcher, Daniel E. "Fair Trial and Free Press: Preliminary Hearing—Gateway to Prejudice." *Law and Social Order*, 1973:903–17, 1973.   **1B370**
"In *Phoenix Newspapers; Inc. v. Jennings* ₍1971₎ the Arizona Supreme Court held that a preliminary hearing could not be closed to the public, including the press, unless there was a clear and present danger that the judicial process would be subverted. This Comment analyzes this holding in the light of the dangers of pre-trial publicity, and concludes that in order to strike a balance between fair trial and free press, a preliminary hearing should be closed upon the motion of the accused."

Bork, Robert H. "Neutral Principles and Some First Amendment Problems." *Indiana Law Journal*, 47:1–35, Fall 1971.   **1B371**
Concerned over the lack of First Amendment theory, the author offers a number of suggestions. "The first section centers upon the implications of Professor ₍Herbert₎ Wechsler's concept of 'neutral principles,' and the second attempts to apply those implications to some important and much-debated problems in the interpretation of the first amendment." One of the author's suggestions: "Constitutional protection should be accorded only to speech that is explicitly political. There is no basis for judicial intervention to protect any other form of expression, be it scientific, literary or that variety of expression we call obscene or pornographic. Moreover, within that category of speech we ordinarily call political, there should be no constitutional obstruction to laws making criminal any speech that advocates forcible overthrow of the government or the violation of any law." The author cites two problems arising from this interpretation, which he believes do not seem to raise crippling difficulties: (1) drawing a line between political and non-political speech and (2) much speech that is essential to the life of a civilized community would be left unprotected.

Borman, Susan, and William Rush. "Obscenity: A Matter of Individual Conscience?" *Journal of Urban Law*, 47:490–521, 1969–70.   **1B372**
"We do not believe in censorship for the most susceptible persons except for children. . . . We feel the present evidence does not compel a connection between pornography and dangerous or antisocial conduct. . . . No one factor, such as pornography, is responsible for criminal sexual conduct. Moreover, we feel repressive policies will only serve to push obscene materials underground. . . . In short, we would not restrict the absolute mandate of the First Amendment for what we consider at best a tenuous connection between pornography and any danger to society."

Born, Gerald M. "Public Libraries and Intellectual Freedom." In American Library Association, *Intellectual Freedom Manual*, Chicago, ALA, 1974, pt. 3, pp. 4–10.   **1B373**
"Because the public library ₍unlike many other educational institutions₎ seeks to enlighten rather than indoctrinate, a basic goal of the institution is the preservation of intellectual freedom. The public library offers the whole spectrum of man's knowledge without moralizing as to its use and without fear of its potential impact on users. . . . The best way to ensure the intellectual freedom of the library's public is to include controversial material that is relevant to the life of the community." The author notes six external forces at work in censorship: parents, religious groups, political groups, ethnic groups, patriotic groups, and emotionally unstable individuals. Pressures for censorship come from within the institution from such sources as trustees, library staff, management, neglect in selection, restrictive selective policies, circulation methods, and catalogers.

Boros, Jerome S., Duncan Darrow, and David Koslow. "Communications Law." *Annual Survey of American Law*, 1973–74:597–624, Summer 1974.   **1B374**
Recent developments in the interpretation of the Communications Act of 1934 are reported under the headings of license renewal challenges and regulation of programming.

Borrie, Gordon, and Nigel Lowe. *The Law of Contempt*. London, Butterworth, 1973. 401p.   **1B375**
Includes sections on publications prejudicial to a fair criminal trial, publications tending to prejudice civil proceedings, the timing of publication, and contempt by publication.

Bose, Mrinal K. "Freedom of the Press in India." *Indian Law Review*, 5:26–36, 1951.   **1B376**
An examination of some fifteen Indian laws affecting freedom of the press. Despite disclaimers by government officials, the author declares that India has placed more restrictions on the press, most of them dating to the period of British rule, than any other democracy. Interpretations by the Supreme Court have made a "mince-meat" of the entire structure.

Bose, Nemai S. "James Silk Buckingham and Indian Affairs." *Quarterly Review of Historical Studies*, 6 (2):90–94, 1966–67.   **1B377**

An account of the career of the nineteenth-century editor of the controversial *Calcutta Journal*, a staunch advocate of press freedom in India.

Bosmajian, Haig A. "First Amendment Crossword Puzzle." *Civil Liberties Review*, 3:70, April–May 1976.   **1B378**
This crossword puzzle ranges from the name of an editor tried for obscenity in the eighteenth century to obscenity decisions of the Supreme Court in the twentieth century.

————. "Freedom of Speech; *Cato's Letters* and the American Colonists." *Speaker and Gavel*, 6:43–48, January 1969.   **1B379**
"The libertarian persuasion of ₍Thomas₎ Gordon and ₍John₎ Trenchard ₍authors of *Cato's Letters*₎ was attractive and acceptable to the colonists to the extent that the 'founding fathers' incorporated the sentiments and arguments in that persuasion into the colonists' case justifying rebellion against what was viewed as English tyranny."

————. *The Language of Oppression*. Washington, D.C., Public Affairs, 1974. 156p.   **1B380**
"It is my hope that an examination of the language of oppression will result in a conscious effort by the reader to help cure this decadence in our language, especially that language which leads to dehumanization of the human being." Chapters deal with the language of anti-Semitism, white racism, Indian derision, sexism, and war. In a final chapter the author considers the enactment of antidefamation legislation, but concludes that "group libel prohibitions would not only be difficult to square with our First Amendment rights, but would be almost impossible to define and circumscribe. . . . The solution to the problem of the language of oppression does not lie in the legislatures or the courts." Instead, he proposes vigorous educational efforts involving publishers, personnel managers, judges, teachers, students, librarians, educational administrators, and television producers to discourage the use of defamatory and dehumanizing language, employing a variety of sanctions.

————. "Obscenity and Protest." *Today's Speech*, 18:9–14, Winter 1970.   **1B381**
"The purpose of this paper is to briefly establish the rhetorical awareness of the youthful protesters and examine the use of obscenities in their persuasion." The New Left has seemed unwilling or unable to resist the use of obscenities in their persuasions for several reasons. Obscenities (1) are evidence of their liberation, (2) will not be co-opted by the Establishment, (3) label Establishment men and actions for what they are seen as—obscene, (4) give dissenters the power to define their

adversaries, (5) provoke a response from their adversaries, (6) act as a release of frustrations, and (7) mask the fears plaguing youth.

———. " 'Speech' and the First Amendment." *Today's Speech*, 18(4):3–11, Fall 1970. (Reprinted in Michael H. Prosser, *ed.*, *Intercommunications among Nations and Peoples*. New York, Harper & Row, 1973, pp. 497–508)   **1B382**
A discussion of symbolic speech and the rhetorical strategies of dissenters during the past decade and the way in which symbolic speech has been interpreted by the courts.

———, *comp.* "Freedom of Speech Bibliography: January 1968–June 1969." In *1969 Yearbook of The Committee on Freedom of Speech of the Speech Association of America*. n.p., The Association, 1970, pp. 62–77.   **1B383**

———. "Freedom of Speech Bibliography: July 1969–June 1970." In *Free Speech Yearbook: 1970. A Publication of The Committee on Freedom of Speech of the Speech Communication Association*. New York, The Association, 1970, pp. 104–16.   **1B384**

———. "Freedom of Speech Bibliography: July 1970–June 1971. Articles, Books, and Court Decisions." In *Free Speech Yearbook: 1971. A Publication of the Committee on Freedom of Speech of the Speech Communication Association*. New York, The Association, 1971, pp. 97–115.   **1B385**

———. "Freedom of Speech Bibliography: July 1971–June 1972. Articles, Books, and Court Decisions." In *Free Speech Yearbook: 1972. A Publication of The Commission on Freedom of Speech of the Speech Communication Association*. New York, The Association, 1973, pp. 115–39.   **1B386**

———. "Freedom of Speech Bibliography: July 1972–June 1973. Articles, Books, and Court Decisions." In *Free Speech Yearbook: 1973. A Publication of The Commission on Freedom of Speech of the Speech Communication Association*. New York, The Association, 1974, pp. 87–106. The 1973–74 bibliography was compiled by David Eshelman.   **1B387**

———, *ed. The Principles and Practices of Freedom of Speech*. Boston, Houghton Mifflin, 1971. 448p.   **1B388**
Beginning with Milton's *Areopagitica*, this collection of readings includes the text of Mill's *Of the Liberty of Thought and Discussion*, "Cato's" Letter no. 15 (1720), the Alien and Sedition Acts of 1798, and such landmark court decisions on free speech as *Schenck v. U.S.* (1919), *Adams v. U.S.* (1919), *Gitlow v. New York* (1925) in the area of sedition and *Roth v. U.S.* (1957), *Alberts v. California* (1957) and *Ginzburg v. U.S.* (1966) in the area of obscenity. There are excerpts from Zechariah Chafee, Jr., *Blessings of Liberty*, and Thomas I. Emerson, *Toward a General Theory of the First Amendment*.

———, *ed. and comp. Obscenity and Freedom of Expression*. New York, Franklin, 1976. 348p.   **1B389**
The work consists of the text of nearly 100 key legal decisions on obscenity beginning with the British Hicklin case of 1868 and concluding with the U.S. Supreme Court decisions of the 1970s. The decisions are prefaced by a comprehensive historical survey revealing "how American law and society have attempted to solve the dilemma posed by constitutionally protected speech, on the one hand, and obscenity in literature, film, and speech on the other."

Boston, Bonny. "On Skids and Still Sliding." *Books*, 8:20–21, Summer 1972. (Reprinted in *DLAS Newsletter* [Defence of Literature and the Arts], February 1973)   **1B390**
"In weird times like the present when we are sliding into realms never before exposed, it seems to me the only thing to do, like skidding on ice, is to steer right into it. Don't fight it, that's suicidal." The answer is education. "A utopian situation is not necessarily one where the matter of censorship has been resolved but, rather, one where there is no need for it." The author doubts that children who are everyday exposed to pornography will be harmed by it. She recommends bringing sex out of the shadows.

Boston Public Library. *The Public Interest and the Right to Know; Access to Government Information and the Role of the Press*. Boston, The Library, 1971. 59p.   **1B391**
"This annotated bibliography was prepared to provide the layman with background reading on both sides of the debate over the public's right to know and the government's right to withhold information felt to be injurious to the public interest if revealed." Included is the text of the Freedom of Information Act of 1967 and a chronology of events, 1808–1971.

Botein, Michael. "Access to Cable Television." *Cornell Law Review*, 57:419–59, February 1972.   **1B392**
"Only an enforceable right of access will guarantee that all programmers can use the cable and, conversely, that viewers will see a wide range of programming. Implementing a right of access, however, is far more difficult than creating it. None of the three possible alternatives—marketplace regulation, administrative regulation, and formula regulation—is itself satisfactory. A combination of all three approaches thus seems most appropriate."

———. "CATV Regulation: A Jumble of Jurisdictions." *New York University Law Review*, 45:816–43, October 1970.   **1B393**
"Local, state and federal authorities were slow to recognize the need for CATV regulation and, when they finally entered the field, their efforts were uncoordinated and inadequate. But, recent activity in the field by city and state authorities, the Federal Communications Commission and the Congress signals the emergence of a multijurisdictional system of CATV regulation. The author describes this system and suggests improvements that will encourage CATV to realize its full potential."

———. "Clearing the Airwaves for Access." *American Bar Association Journal*, 59:38–41, January 1973.   **1B394**
"While the courts and the government grapple with the concepts and consequences of access, activist citizens press broadcasters to open the airwaves. In the resulting legal tangle, the effective means of securing access are essentially extralegal, while the legal means are essentially ineffective."

———. "The Federal Communications Commission's Fairness Regulations: A First Step Towards Creation of a Right of Access to the Mass Media." *Cornell Law Review*, 54:294–305, January 1969.   **1B395**
"Recently, the Federal Communications Commission codified two aspects of this traditional 'fairness doctrine'—the requirement of reply time to both personal attacks and editorial endorsements. A current challenge to these new regulations raises a compelling first amendment question. Are the regulations the unreasonable inhibition on free speech which the Seventh Circuit found them to be in *Radio Television News Directors Association v. United States* [1968], or are they instead the first step towards the creation of a right of access to the mass media?"

Botsford, Keith. "The Innocence of Oz." *Encounter*, 37(5):64–72, November 1971.   **1B396**
An American novelist living in London writes a critical analysis of the issues and tactics in the *Oz* magazine obscenity trial, concluding that none of the participants emerged with credit, that the whole proceedings were puerile and set "a poor precedent for future defense of press freedom." The real martyrs were not the defendants, whom he characterized as "mental celibates," but the words we use, the mind we need to think with, and the young on whose behalf *Oz* claimed to speak.

Bottini, Ronald L. *Access to the Press: A New Right?* Columbia, Mo., Freedom of Information Center, School of Journalism, University of Missouri at Columbia, 1969. 8p. (Report no. 216)
1B397
A summary of the drive for "right of access" of minority groups to newspapers, a proposal first advocated by law professor Jerome A. Barron (1967) and now taken up by the American Civil Liberties Union which may go to court in behalf of the right.

————. *Group Ownership of Newspapers.* Columbia, Mo., Freedom of Information Center, School of Journalism, University of Missouri at Columbia, 1967. 6p. (Report no. 190) **1B398**
"The number of U.S. daily newspaper groups (chains) has increased elevenfold since 1910. It is the purpose of this paper to discuss the growth, advantages and criticisms of such ownership."

————. *Self-Regulation of Motion Picture Content.* Columbia, Mo., University of Missouri, 1966. 242p. (Master's thesis, University Microfilms, no. M-1089)
1B399
The author recommends that the motion picture industry adopt some form of voluntary film classification system, labeling movies on the basis of their moral and emotional content so that the general public will know whether they are suitable or not for children.

Botto, Louis. "They Shoot Dirty Movies Don't They?" *Look*, 34(22):56, 58–60, 3 November 1970. **1B400**
A look at the production of X-rated "skin flicks," that have come with the sexual revolution in the United States.

Boutwell, George S. *et al.* . . . *Mass Meetings of Protest Against the Suppression of Truth About the Philippines. Faneuil Hall, Tuesday, March 19,* [1903] . . . *Addresses by the Hon. George S. Boutwell . . .* [et al.] *Testimony of some of the witnesses who were refused a hearing before the Senate Committee.* Boston, 1903. 60p.
1B401
In a mass meeting of protest, chaired by Col. Thomas Wentworth Higginson and addressed by ten speakers including Governor George S. Boutwell, charges were made that the United States Army suppressed truth about atrocities committed by American soldiers in the recent war in the Philippines and that the facts were further withheld by the U.S. Senate Committee headed by Massachusetts Senator Henry Cabot Lodge. Witnesses testified that prisoners were shot without trial, male children were slaughtered, priests were tortured, women and children were herded like animals into the deserts and mountains, and their homes were burned. The case was reminiscent of army action in the My Lei massacre in the Vietnam war. The testimony of some of the speakers had been refused by Senator Lodge's investigating committee. A resolution called for a censure of the Lodge Committee, a demand for full information on the war, and independence for the Philippines.

Bowden, Ann. "Thou Shalt Not Censor." *Texas Library Journal*, 50:60–68, May 1974. **1B402**
A report on responses to a questionnaire on "censorship by librarians" completed by 283 librarians attending a Texas Library Association program on the recent pornography decisions of the U.S. Supreme Court. The majority of librarians felt that the major responsibility for censorship of pornography was up to the family. There was a wide disparity between views on censorship by library school students and practicing school librarians, with 19.6 percent of the latter favoring internal censorship. Specific questions were asked concerning the purchase and circulation of *The Joy of Sex*.

Bowers, John. "The Porn Is Green." *Playboy*, 18(7):78–82, 182–88, July 1971. **1B403**
"In California, on the front lines of the sexual revolution, totally explicit and uncensored films and live 'exhibitions' have become not only a major spectator sport but a minor industry as well."

Bowers, Thomas A. "The Bankhead Bill: How a Threatened Press Subsidy Was Defeated." *Journalism Quarterly*, 53:21–27, Spring 1976. **1B404**
"In the midst of World War II . . . Congress gave serious consideration to a plan which would have required the government to purchase War Bond advertising in a manner which would have made it a thinly-disguised subsidy to the nation's smaller newspapers."

Bowie, Raymond J. "Between Candor and Shame: The Municipal Regulation of Obscenity . . . Concurrent or Preempted?" *Certiorari: A Journal of Law Students Research*, 2:10–15, 1976. **1B405**

Box, Muriel, *ed. Birth Control and Libel. The Trial of Marie Stopes.* New York, Barnes, 1968. 392p. **1B406**
In 1923 Dr. Marie Stopes brought libel charges against Dr. Halliday Sutherland for accusations in his book, *Birth Control*, that Dr. Stopes' "monstrous campaign of birth control" was taking advantage of the ignorance of the poor. This is an edited transcript of the sensational trial. The Lord Chief Justice ruled for the defendant; his ruling was reversed by the Court of Appeal, and Dr. Sutherland then took his case to the House of Lords which restored the verdict of the Lord Chief Justice against Dr. Stopes. While Dr. Stopes lost the case, the attendant publicity "served to bring about a social revolution which otherwise might have been delayed for many years."

Boyan, A. Stephen, Jr. "The Ability to Communicate: A First Amendment Right." In Harry M. Clor, *ed., The Mass Media and Modern Democracy*, Chicago, Rand McNally, 1974, pp. 137–66.
1B407
The thesis of this essay is that "the changes that have taken place in the means of communication in American public life require government action to protect First Amendment values. The character of this governmental action, procedural regulation of speech, was always permitted and sometimes required under the First Amendment. But this aspect of the First Amendment has historically been largely unrecognized because the thrust of its development was directed against *government* interference with the 'free competition of ideas.' Today, while government must continue not to restrict the expression of ideas, it can enact a variety of procedures to enable those who have something to say to the public to be heard."

Boyars, Marion. "Last Exit to Wonderland." *Twentieth Century*, 176(1035): 46–47, 1967–68. **1B408**
A satire written from the viewpoint of Alice in Wonderland about the British trial banning Selby's *Last Exit to Brooklyn*. After the trial Alice wishes herself back in her own world "where there is freedom of expression, where the artist is at liberty to depict and criticize the society in which he lives, where the publisher can publish seriously and not be banned, where one can rely on good sense in the law."

————. "Must We Censor Our Art?" *Books*, 8:3–6, Summer 1972. (Reprinted in *DLAS Newsletter* [Defence of Literature and the Arts Society], February 1973) **1B409**
"Pornography is written for amusement, and just as it describes excessive and unbelievable sexual exploits, so Mrs. Whitehouse's incredible claims for it are nothing if not funny, and Lord Longford's antics in Soho and Denmark are downright hilarious! Pornography is for laughter, and the exposures by these two protagonists have taught us first to laugh heartily at the whole thing and then to admit how boring it all is: both pornography and the controversy about pornography." The author believes the issue over pornography is dead, that the *Oz* case suggests that "no higher court will ever again be prepared to take on a case where sexual descriptions, having lewd thoughts, are the overt issue. In the future, such trials with political overtones, will have to find other excuses." The author considers hypocritical the concern over violence in art as harmful to children. "Children learn their morals from the example of those around them, not from works of art, films, or novels." The artist, like the scientist, should have the freedom to explore new natural phenomena—"the very stuff of

life, which is what makes us the human beings we are."

───── *et al.* ₁Censorship of Literature₁ *DLAS Newsletter* ₁Defence of Literature and the Arts Society₁, February 1973. Entire issue.   **1B410**
Content: Must We Censor Our Art? by Marion Boyars (reprinted from *Books*, Summer 1972). The Law in Action: The Little Red Schoolbook by Richard Handyside. The Festival of Light by Barbara Smoker. A Sorry Case (Mishan) by Anthony Grey. On Skids by Bonny Boston. A Review of the Longford Report (reprinted from *Books*, Summer 1972).

Boyce, Emily S. "The United States Supreme Court and North Carolina Obscenity Laws." *North Carolina Libraries*, 32:5–8, Winter 1974.   **1B411**

Boyce, Peter. "Snip, Snip, Snip . . ." *Masque*, 10:10–11, June–July 1969.   **1B412**
"Australian censors are among the world's best . . . but in New Zealand they are less successful."

Boyce, Ronald N. "Freedom of Speech and the Military." *Utah Law Review*, 1968:240–66, May 1968.   **1B413**
The author concludes that "in most cases there is little danger that the application of traditional military sanctions will infringe on the freedom of speech of persons in military service. The most serious threat of infringement lies in an extended application of articles 88, 133, and 134 of the Uniform Code of Military Justice. More conservative construction of these provisions would avoid serious constitutional problems. Indeed, the historical development of the case law as expressed in opinions of the United States Supreme Court would appear to reject the early World War I position and demand more modest limits on the speech of military personnel as well as on civilian speech." The concern over free speech in the military service grew out of the experience in the Vietnam war.

Boyd, Bruce M. "Film Censorship in India: A 'Reasonable Restriction' on Freedom of Speech and Expression." *Journal of the Indian Law Institute*, 14:501–61, October–December 1972.   **1B414**

Boyd, George N. "Movies and the Sexual Revolution: Should the Ratings be Revised?" *Christian Century*, 87:1124–25, 23 September 1970.**1B415**
In a review of the rating system for films, the author suggests that "the age restriction for R films was set unrealistically high" and should be lowered to include high school youth.

Boyer, Brian. "Reporters Threatened by Subpoena Actions." *Chicago Journalism Review*, 3(3):13–15, March 1970.   **1B416**
A general survey of the status of subpoenas against reporters and news media for notes, outtakes, tapes, and photographs. More than one hundred subpoenas have been issued against Chicago newspapers and television stations in the past twelve months; but the media have done very little to resist. The author recommends that "reporters should not allow anybody to keep their notes. They should not put in office files names, addresses and other identifications whose identities they wish to remain confidential. They should be prepared to go to jail to protect a confidential source if push comes to shove."

Boyer, John H. "Barron and the Courts." *Journalism Quarterly*, 52:120–24, Spring 1975.   **1B417**
"The Supreme Court ruling that overturned the Florida right-of-reply law also closed a door to a right-of-access to print-media," a position advocated by Professor Jerome Barron. Reference is to *Miami Herald v. Tornillo* (1974). "There seems to be an editor's right to edit, and the Barron idea of print access by Constitutional right seems to have been severely bruised."

─────. *Supreme Court and the Right to Know*. Columbia, Mo., Freedom of Information Center, School of Journalism, University of Missouri at Columbia, 1971. 7p. (Report no. 272)
                                                        1B418
"Although the Supreme Court has generally upheld a Constitutional interpretation that grants the people a right to know about the workings of their government, there has been no one ruling that specifically acknowledges such a right. This paper traces Supreme Court decisions that have had a bearing on the people's right to know."

─────, and Charles H. Marler. *Buckley v. AFTRA*. Columbia, Mo., Freedom of Information Center, School of Journalism, University of Missouri at Columbia, 1973. 6p. (Report no. 308)
                                                        1B419
"In broadcasting, is compulsory union membership a threat to the First Amendment rights? William F. Buckley thought so in his case, took on the American Federation of Radio and Television Artists in the courts, and won."

Boyer, Paul S. *Purity in Print. The Vice-Society Movement and Book Censorship in America*. New York, Scribner's, 1968. 362p.   **1B420**

In this volume the author attempts "to place in historical prospective the so-called 'vice-societies' of New York, Boston, and other cities—the organizations which were the source and target of so much of the censorship and anti-censorship activity of the 1920s" and "to trace the circumstances which spawned these groups, maintained them for decades, and finally destroyed them." In the conflict between obscenity and a free press Anthony Comstock, John Sumner, J. Frank Chase and other leaders of the vice societies were pitted against authors H. L. Mencken, Theodore Dreiser, Upton Sinclair, Margaret Anderson, Margaret Sanger, and lawyers Arthur Garfield Hays and Morris Ernst. Among the works of literature that became subjects of court cases and controversy were: *Hagar Revelly* (Daniel Carson Goodman), *Ulysses* (James Joyce), *An American Tragedy* (Theodore Dreiser), *Well of Loneliness* (Radclyffe Hall), *Oil* (Upton Sinclair), *Lady Chatterley's Lover* (D.H. Lawrence), *Replenishing Jessica* (Maxwell Bodenheim), *Jurgen* (James B. Cabell).

Boylan, James. "The Hutchins Report: A Twenty-Year View." *Columbia Journalism Review*, 6(2):5–20, Summer 1967.   **1B421**
The direct effect of the Report of the Hutchins Commission on A Free and Responsible Press has been slight; the direction of movement in the institutions of journalism have not changed. But the report has had a subtle effect on the terms and climate of the debate over freedom of press and it has served notice on the media that press performance is not merely an internal concern of the media as a business operation, but is a matter of serious public concern. There follows a listing of the thirteen recommendations of the Commission with comments from three experts.

─────. "Watchdog of the Press." *Lithopinion*, 3(1):15–18, 1968.   **1B422**
The editor of *Columbia Journalism Review* discusses the role of that journal as a critic of the print and broadcasting media, acting in behalf of readers and listeners.

Boyle, Harry J. "Responsibility in Broadcasting." *Osgoode Hall Law Journal*, 8:119–38, August 1970.   **1B423**
"The Broadcasting Act provides that Canadian broadcasters should promote national unity. Canadian broadcasting has failed to exclude hostile influences. TV should cater to a wide interest, through a great diversity of programmes, and let the public choose from the widest possible range of programme matter. Freedom of Information can only exist if the new forms of communication are protected from undue commercial, paternalistic or authoritarian influences."

Brackman, Jacob. "Films." *Esquire*, 76:114, 116, December 1971.   **1B424**
Consideration of film ratings particularly the need for lifting present restrictions for teenagers to give them easy access to some good pictures now rated R or X.

Brademas, John. "Don't Censor Textbooks; But Let's Keep Out Biased or Inaccurate Information." *Nation's Schools*, 79(6):38–39, June 1967. **1B425**
A congressman reports on recent congressional hearings to consider reading and other instructional materials used in the nation's schools and to the treatment in these materials of minority groups. Some of the findings were: (1) Federal control of the content of school books is neither legally possible nor desirable. (2) Most states and most publishers are giving serious thought to the need for textbooks which are integrated and have more authentic content. (3) There are still doubts on the subject of dual editions, one for the North and one for the South. (4) There is need for more consultation with the minority groups involved.

Bradlee, Benjamin C. "Ben Bradlee on Freedom of the Press." *Bulletin of the American Society of Newspaper Editors*, 578:10–13, May–June 1974. **1B426**
An adaptation of an address by the executive editor of the *Washington Post*.

Bradley, Edward F. "By Any Other Name: Meiklejohn. The First Amendment & School Desegregation." *Connecticut Law Review*, 3:299–315, Winter 1970/71. **1B427**
"This comment sets forth the conceptual content of Meiklejohn's First Amendment theory, shows how the Supreme Court has accepted it, and argues for its application to American public education."

Bradley, F. H. "On the Treatment of Sexual Detail in Literature." In his *Collected Essays*. Oxford, Oxford University Press, 1935, vol. 2, pp. 618–27. **1B428**
An essay written in 1912 to justify the use of sexual detail in literature against what he considered harsh and unjust strictures on certain books. In a later footnote he acknowledges the flood of erotic literature with its excessive treatment of sexual themes, but reiterates his belief in "freedom in art and literature, and against those who would adapt them to their weaknesses, real or supposed, of young persons, or estimate their character by its effect on their own uncultivated or perhaps vicious personality."

Bradley, Norman. "What Do You Care What I Read? or, What Do I Care What You Read?" *Tennessee Librarian*, 27:58–61, Spring 1975. **1B429**
The editor of the *Chattanooga Times* considers the common concerns of librarians and journalists "in presenting to the public free access to truthful accounts of what is taking place around us today, as well as to the ideas, concepts, and principles to be found within the covers of books."

Bradshaw, Jon. "The Death of a Re-porter Who Knew Too Much." *New York*, 9(36):29–36, 6 September 1976. **1B430**
An account of the murder of Don Bolles of the *Arizona Republic*, the result of his investigative reporting.

Bradshaw, Lillian M. "The 3 R's of Censorship vs. the 3 R's of Freedom to Teach." *English Journal*, 56:1007–10, October 1967. **1B431**
The 3 R's of censorship are represented by *Rigidity* of purpose, *Regimentation* of action, and *Resistance* to change. The 3 R's of freedom to read are: *Refinement* of taste, *Relevancy* for our time, and *Responsibility* for action. The author challenges teachers to have faith in man's ability to develop himself as an individual and faith that the American way of life provides the freedom for personal development.

Brady, Veronica. "Of Castles and Censorship." *Westerly*, 2:45–50, June 1974. **1B432**
It is important "to oppose censorship, that is, to suggest that there is one official way of looking at the world." The real dangers of pornography and violence degrading the human person "will not be lessened by censorship, they may even in fact be increased, since as Freud tells us, the return of the repressed is always disasterous."

Brahm, Walter. "Knights and Windmills." *Library Journal*, 96:3096–98, 1 October 1971. **1B433**
Librarians and their professional organizations give too much time and talent to provocation and promotion of intellectual freedom. "Let us give to intellectual freedom only the attention the censor forces us to give it." Time and society's changed viewpoint and not librarians' battles are responsible for eliminating censorship.

[Brainerd, Thomas.] *Influence of Theatres, or The True Nature and Tendency of Theatrical Amusements*. [Philadelphia], Presbyterian Board of Publication, 1840. 16p. (Introductory note signed T. B.) **1B434**
A sermon preached against the evils of the theater, which the author attacked as a waste of time and money. The theater has a pernicious moral tendency and a tendency to harden the heart against sympathy with real suffering, and presents impure plays. He accused the local press of commending stage plays in return for free season tickets.

Branch, Taylor. "The Odd Couple; Ellsberg and Otepka." *Washington Monthly*, 3(8):50–60, October 1971. **1B435**
An examination of the cases of two "whistle blowers"—Otto F. Otepka who "violated our national security by slipping classified documents to veteran Red-hunter Julien G. Sourwine, counsel to the Senate Internal Security

Subcommittee" and Daniel Ellsberg who "violated our national security by slipping classified documents, later to be called the Pentagon Papers, to numerous senators and newspapers."

Brannan, Richard G. "Freedom of the Press v. Pretrial News Release. A View from the Arena." *Police Chief*, 40(12):68–72, December 1973. **1B436**
A police captain looks at the issue from the point of view of those concerned with the responsibilities of the administration of criminal justice and the obligation of providing public information.

Branscomb, Anne W. "A Crisis of Identity: Public Broadcasting and the Law." *Public Telecommunications Review*, 3:10–23, February 1975. **1B437**
"A lawyer's searching examination of the fundamental, unresolved questions that public broadcasting must face: the meaning of 'non-commercial' service, the concept of objectivity and balance, the problem of political broadcasting, the reservation of channels, the role of ascertainment, the problem of who does what—and, underlying it all, the implications of a commitment to 'alternative programming.' "

————. *The First Amendment as a Shield or a Sword: An Integrated Look at Regulation of Multi-Media Ownership*. Santa Monica, Calif., Rand, 1975. 114p. **1B438**
"The purpose of this paper is to: (1) examine the different ways in which the First Amendment has been applied with respect to concentrations of control over the mass media—newspapers, radio and television broadcast facilities, and cable television systems, (2) review the existing and proposed regulations concerning monopoly, duopoly, multiple ownership, or cross-ownership of the media, (3) explore, in the light of a continued trend toward amalgamation of media ownership, the viability of alternative policies which would assure a diversity of information reaching the public regardless of ownership or control of the transmission facilities, and (4) project, from recent judicial decisions concerning media ownership, what directions government policy might take to promote a diverse marketplace of ideas."

————. "Should Political Broadcasting Be Fair or Equal? A Reappraisal of Section 315 of the Federal Communications Act." *George Washington Law Review*, 30:63–83, October 1961. **1B439**
"The purpose of this article is to analyze the impact of these 'firsts' [television usage in presidential election of 1960] on the function of the

broadcasting industry in a democratic society, to review the statutory standards imposed upon broadcasters with respect to political coverage, and to discuss possible legislative changes."

Brant, Irving. *The Constitution and the Right to Know*. Columbia, Mo., Freedom of Information Center, School of Journalism, University of Missouri at Columbia, [1968]. 20p. (Tenth Harold L. Cross Memorial Lecture Series, delivered 4 December 1967; reprinted in David G. Clark and Earl R. Hutchinson, *eds.*, *Mass Media and the Law*, pp. 73–85) **1B440**
In discussing the history of government secrecy and freedom in the United States, this historian of the Constitution observes that the convention which drafted the Constitution met in secret and even James Madison's voluminous personal notes of the deliberation were not published for more than fifty years. He also considers the discussions of the wording of the requirement for Congress to publish its own proceedings. He comments on the recent mounting pressures against government concealment and analyzes the case of *U.S. v. Reynolds* (1953).

Brant, Jonathan. "Prison Censorship Regulations versus the Constitution; An Analysis." *Loyola Law Review*, 19:25–39, 1972–73. **1B441**
The author believes that "the realistic needs for maintenance of prison security must be balanced against the scope of the first amendment protections which are retained by inmates. For the most part, present prison censorship regulations are unduly restrictive and, if they are to avoid being overturned in litigation, must be revised." A section of the article deals with the censorship of reading matter and with inmates' contact with the press.

Brantley, William R. "Censors Don't Protect Morals." In Ralph Brandon, *Witch Finder*, Fresno, Calif., Fabian Books, 1960, pp. 147–58. **1B442**
An exchange of letters between an English teacher, William R. Brantley, who discounts the harm to children of modern sex novels as charged by former vice chief John S. Sumner, and a concerned housewife. The exchange appeared in the *Miami Herald* during July 1959.

Braun, Saul. "How Television Cuts the Bleep Out of Shows." *TV Guide*, 21(18):6–10, 5 May 1973. **1B443**
"Deleting offensive language is no longer crude hatchetwork, but a sophisticated and sometimes touchy job."

Bravard, Robert S. "American Erotica at the Close of the Sixties." *Choice*, 7:1197–1205, November 1970. **1B444**
A look at the world of paperback erotic fiction results in six distinct impressions: (1) The number has increased to staggering proportions. (2) They are very expensive. (3) The era of reprinting Victorian "classics" is nearly over. (4) Major publishers are "tiptoeing into the area very carefully." (5) Erotic fiction is available at about any paperback stand. (6) There are literally no forbidden areas. There follows a bibliography of erotica appropriate for academic libraries.

Bray, J. J. "The Juristic Basis of the Law Relating to Offences Against Public Morality and Decency." *Australian Law Journal*, 46:100–108, March 1972. **1B445**
The Chief Justice of South Australia, in the Third Wilfred Fullagar Memorial Lecture, attempts to discover a rationale for Australian obscenity laws. He believes that distinctions should be made between public conduct and private conduct and between conduct intended to insult or offend and conduct not so intended. "People, it may be thought, have no right to complain of being shocked by something they deliberately seek out with advance notice of its nature." He calls upon the courts and academic jurists to define the bounds of the right not to be shocked.

[Breatnach, Deasún.] "How Your Films Are Censored. By Rex MacGall, *pseud.*" *Bell*, 10:493–501, September 1945. **1B446**
How Irish film censorship operates under the Censorship of Films Acts of 1923, 1925, and 1930, and under the Emergency Powers Orders of World War II.

Breckenridge, Adam C. *The Executive Privilege; Presidential Control Over Information*. Lincoln, Nebr., University of Nebraska Press, 1974. 188p. **1B447**
Content: Conflicts between Coequals. Development of the Executive Privilege. Congress and the Need to Know. Executive Privacy. Policing the Privilege. Watergate. Future Directions.

———. *The Right of Privacy*. Lincoln, Nebr., University of Nebraska Press, 1970. 155p. **1B448**
A discussion of the various aspects of the right of privacy and the conflicts with other rights such as the freedom to information. Includes citations to important cases and, as an appendix, the text of The Right to Privacy by Samuel D. Warren and Louis D. Brandeis. "The primary object and purpose is to show how far government in the United States has gone in invading the right to personal privacy and how far government has gone also to protect that right." The writer "is strongly in favor of the maximum protection to privacy which a free society can tolerate and should ensure."

[Breckinridge, Robert J.] "Trial for Libel.—State of Maryland vs. Robert J. Breckinridge with Annotations by the Traverser." In *The Baltimore Literary and Religious Magazine*, 65/66:193–300, May and June 1840. **1B449**
Breckinridge, editor of the magazine, was charged with libeling James L. Maguire, overseer of the alms house of Baltimore in the November 1839 issue of his magazine. Breckinridge, an anti-Catholic crusader, had accused Maguire of operating "a papal mass house" and a "papal prison." The jury could not agree and the state entered a *nolle prosqui*. Breckinridge noted that his account of the trial is a composite of three other published reports of the trial—in the *Baltimore Sun*, the *Baltimore Clipper*, and a pamphlet issued by John Reilly, "keeper of a Papal book store" in Baltimore.

Bredin, James. "Broadcasting Parliament: The British Radio Experiment." *EBU Review* (European Broadcasting Union), 26(5):17–19, September 1975. **1B450**
"The British Government has decided to support proposals for radio broadcasts of House of Commons proceedings on a permanent basis from early 1976." This follows a month's experiment of broadcasting House of Commons proceedings.

Brennan, John J., III. "The Journalist's Prerogative of Non-Disclosure: Fact or Fancy?" *Loyola Law Review* (New Orleans), 20:120–39, 1974. **1B451**
"The issue of the newsman's privilege arises in a variety of situations and authority for it may be found in either the common law, the Constitution or in statutes. This comment will survey these sources and analyze the arguments pro and con for the privilege's existence."

Brennan, William J., Jr. *An Affair with Freedom: A Collection of His Opinions and Speeches Drawn from His First Decade as a United States Supreme Court Justice*. Selected and Edited with an Introduction and Notes, by Stephen J. Friedman. Foreword by Arthur J. Goldberg. New York, Atheneum, 1967. 384p. **1B452**
Among the U.S. Supreme Court decisions written by Justice Brennan and included in this volume are the following relating to obscenity: *Roth v. United States* (1957); *Kingsley Books, Inc. v. Brown* (1957); *Smith v. California* (1959); *Marcus v. Search Warrant* (1961); *Bantam Books, Inc. v. Sullivan* (1963); *Jacobellis v. State of Ohio* (1964); and *Ginzberg v. United States* (1966). Also included are three decisions involving criticism of the government: *New York Times Co. v. Sullivan* (1964); *Garrison v. State of Louisiana* (1964); and *Rosenblatt v. Baer* (1966).

Brenner, Daniel L. "The Limits of Broadcast Self-Regulation Under the

First Amendment." *Stanford Law Review*, 27:1527–62, July 1975. **1B453**
"Part I of this Note discusses ₁National Association of Broadcaster's Television₁ Code development and administration. Part II considers the scope of first amendment protection of thematic advocacy on television, concluding that the level of constitutional alertness afforded to other media is fully warranted, and, accordingly, that the absolute thematic proscriptions found in the Television Code contravenes first amendment values. Finally, part III articulates the mechanisms by which courts or the FCC should evaluate this 'private' Code conduct if judicially or administratively contested."

————. "TV Access: The New Soapbox." *America*, 126:477–79, 6 May 1972. **1B454**
"Launched by the Supreme Court's fairness doctrine' decision in 1969, the emerging problem of citizen access to television time has become a contest between citizen groups and broadcasters—and some citizens are winning." Among the unsolved problems in implementing the right of access are: Who will decide who appears? What subjects should remain off-limits? Will a right of paid access provide availability of rich only? With a right of access does the fairness doctrine still apply?

————. "Toward a New Balance in License Renewals." *Journal of Broadcasting*, 17:63–76, Winter 1973. **1B455**
This paper analyzes two decisions by the District of Columbia Court of Appeals which challenge the traditional policy of the FCC in according an existing broadcaster an almost unassailable right to renewal of his license.

Bretnor, Reginald. "A Plea for Censorship." *Modern Age*, 11:35–44, Winter 1966/67. **1B456**
An attack on liberal interpretations of freedom of speech, on "leftist liberals beating the drums for the Communist Party," television programming, and pornography. "A sane censorship would certainly limit the license now enjoyed by the mass media and the mass movements. However, by doing so, it would restore some semblance of freedom of speech to the individual, and would guarantee him a freedom of choice and decision which he no longer enjoys."

Brett, Peter. "Free Speech, Supreme Court Style: A View from Overseas." *Texas Law Review*, 46:668–705, April 1968. **1B457**
The author compares the results achieved by the U.S. Supreme Court in interpreting and applying the free-speech and press aspects of the First Amendment with those achieved in England and Australia by using the method of legislative restraint. He considers four concepts used by the Supreme Court in judging First Amendment cases: prior restraint, taxes on knowledge, clear and present danger, and the balancing of interests.

Brewer, David J. "Libel." *Central Law Journal*, 22:363–65, 16 April 1886. **1B458**
In an address before the Kansas Bar Association, Judge Brewer draws the distinction between severe but honest criticism of public officials and libel. The former is a responsibility of the press; the latter should be severely punished.

Brich, George M. "Pentagon Papers: A Momentous Decision." *Newsletter on Intellectual Freedom* (IFC-ALA), 20:102, 116, September 1971. **1B459**
A concise review of legal events in the publication of the Pentagon Papers, which led to the 26 June 1971 decision of the U.S. Supreme Court.

Brickman, William W. "Freedom from Filth." *Intellect*, 102:149, December 1973. **1B460**
An editorial defending the U.S. Supreme Court decision decentralizing the control over the content of the mass media in the area of sex. Individuals who feel that their constitutional freedoms have been diminished if their community does not permit the public exhibition of pornographic art or of writings exploiting sex could obtain relief by travel to another area. He also suggests that hard-core pornographic materials might be reserved for private viewing, but kept from the public eye on the grounds that they are injurious or objectionable to many. Eli M. Oboler replies to the article in the January 1975 issue.

Bridge, Peter. "Absolute Immunity, Absolutely." *Quill*, 61(1):8–11, January 1973. (Reprinted in *Current*, March 1973) **1B461**
A reporter who spent twenty days in jail for refusing to divulge information to a grand jury argues for an absolute shield law for journalists.

————. "Is the Press All Too Willing to Be Neutralized?" *National Observer*, 11(50):15, 9 December 1972. **1B462**
An essay by the reporter for the now defunct *Newark Evening News* who went to jail for contempt of court after he refused to answer certain questions posed by a grand jury. Bridge explains why he chose to go to jail and relates his view of the principle involved in his and similar cases.

Bridgewater, Hope. "The Rabbit Hole." *Atlantic Province Library Association Bulletin*, 35:40–41, June 1971. **1B463**
The case of *Epaminondas* and pressures on Nova Scotia libraries to remove it as racist. The columnist defends the book. "In this story a mischievous little boy makes mistakes; I do not find it racist. It has its equivalent in the Silly Jack stories—Silly Jack being a stupid white boy." The columnist appeals to children's librarians to resist such pressures.

₁Briellat, Thomas.₁ *The Trial of Thomas Briellat, for Seditious Words, before Mr. Mainwaring, at the Sessions-House, Clerkenwell-Green, December 6, 1793. . . .* London, Printed for T. Briellat, 1794. 68p. (Also in Howell, *State Trials*, vol. 22, pp. 909 ff.) **1B464**
For his seditious expressions against the king, Briellat was sentenced to a year in prison.

Brien, Alan. "Battle of the Ban." *New Statesman*, 82:734–35, 26 November 1971. **1B465**
Charges of overt and covert censorship of the news media by the Establishment, and a tendency for the press to exercise self-censorship and to rely on official sources.

————. "I Am Still Curious (Blue)." *New Statesman*, 77:444, 28 March 1969. **1B466**
An analysis of New York publications, *Screw* and *Review of Sex*, which have gone so far in sex frankness that the pornographer has left nothing for an encore. "This is surely the end of pornography, which depends essentially on titillation and suspense, on not quite seeing all, on being always on the verge of making it."

————. "Make the Pubic Public." *New Statesman*, 73:446–47, 5 April 1968. **1B467**
A whimsical essay on censorship of pubic hair.

Brightman, Carol. "The Chicago Film Scene." *Film Comment*, 1(4):41–44, 1963. **1B468**
"The imported, classic or independent film in Chicago must contend with limited outlet, censorship and lack of intelligent criticism." Includes comments on the Chicago court cases involving *The Lovers, Don Juan*, and *The Miracle*, and the work of the Appeals Board.

Brignolo, Donald E. "Censorship Pressure Rising, Missouri Librarians Told." *Library Journal*, 94:2188–90, 1 June 1969. **1B469**
Brief review of ideas presented at a conference, entitled The Censor Always Rings Twice, dealing with "the problems of censorship in libraries, the schools, the mass media, political life and the writing of history."

————. *Community Press Councils.* Columbia, Mo., Freedom of Information Center, School of Journalism, University of Missouri at Columbia, 1969. 6p. (Report no. 217) (Reprinted in Michael C. Emery and Ted C. Smythe, *eds.,*

Readings in Mass Communications, pp. 65–76)   **1B470**
"At the start of 1969, permanent community press councils were meeting regularly to criticize press performance in Littleton, Colorado, Bend, Oregon, and Sparta and Cairo, Illinois. Catalyst for the current grassroots press council movement is the Mellett Fund for a Free and Responsible Press, a non-profit corporation, which financed press council experiments in 1967 and 1968. Preliminary results of the pilot projects indicate that a community press council can be a way of encouraging responsible press performance without infringing upon freedom of the newspapers."

Brilliant, Andrew P. "Cable Television: A Regulatory Dilemma." *Boston College Industrial and Commercial Law Review*, 13:326–68, December 1971.
                                                1B471
The author traces the history of the federal government's efforts to regulate CATV, concluding that "the government's unfavorable posture has resulted directly from its misguided attempts to preserve 'free' local television at all costs. Even now that a compromise proposal has been accepted, delays appear imminent. It is likely that acceptance of CATV will not be achieved until effective statutory regulation designed to promote the interests of the public, not those of the television industry, is established on a national scale."

Brine, Ruth. "Pornography Revisited: Where to Draw the Line." *Time*, 97:64–65, 5 April 1971.   **1B472**
Consideration of pornography in the light of new discussions, much of it in favor of some sort of censorship. Questions raised: (1) Does pornography really do anyone harm? (2) Does pornography have a deleterious effect upon the moral climate as a whole and on values generally? (3) Does the First Amendment, which guarantees free speech, protect obscenity? (4) Can obscenity laws be enforced? (5) What can be done about pornography?

Brink, André. "Censorship: Climate of Fear." *Contrast*, 7(2):17–22, June 1971.
                                                1B473
"It is easier to ban a book by an English writer than an Afrikaans book. . . . If it is true that Afrikaans writers do have greater freedom *vis-à-vis* censorship than others . . . What Have They Done With This Freedom?" The author believes that Afrikaans writers, who are generally pro-apartheid, lack compassion and are, therefore, badly equipped for the all-demanding task of writing.

————. "Censorship: Some Philosophical Issues: (1) Literature and Offence." *Philosophical Papers*, 5(1):53–66, May 1976.   **1B474**

"All significant art is offensive." The experienced reader or viewer is able to be liberated by the contemplation of the work while the less experienced person is trapped by the offensive elements and demands protection. The author explores the philosophical issues which prompt censorship, giving special attention to "offensiveness" in the area of sex. His analysis includes not only a consideration of the offending works, but the nature of the persons offended and the nature of those who feel obligated to protect the offended.

Briscoe, John. "*Reidel, 37 Photographs, and Luros*: The Disinterring of *Roth*." *University of San Francisco Law Review*, 6:399–417, April 1972.   **1B475**
"The Supreme Court's blessings to censorship, it seemed, were about to be retracted [*Stanley v. Georgia*, 1969]. But the *Luros, 37 Photographs*, and *Reidel* cases, doubtless having been met with the obscenities of smut purveyors throughout the country, have established that we cannot exercise our right to possess obscenity without manufacturing it ourselves, and have assured that the courts will continue to pour over mountains of pornography each term, dutifully searching for that whit of redeeming social value." *United States v. 37 Photographs* (1971); *United States v. Reidel* (1971); and *People v. Luros* (1971).

Brissenden, R. F. "Censorship in Australia." *Woroni*, 21:4–6, 11 March 1970.   **1B476**

British Association for the Advancement of Science. *Does Research Threaten Privacy or Does Privacy Threaten Research? Report of a Study Group*. London, The Association, 1974. 23p. (British Association Publication, 74/1)   **1B477**
Conclusion: "All research on individuals and groups threatens their privacy. This report is intended, in part, as a warning that people's jealousy for their privacy will come to be a threat to research if researchers cannot guarantee to defend that privacy. The greatest danger is not from conspiracy, but absentmindedness and public apathy. The possibility of leakage from an ever-increasing aggregation of data will sooner or later cause a public reaction with serious consequences for scientific research. Debate and responsible action are essential now so that research in the future can continue without harm being inflicted on an unsuspecting public."

British Board of Film Censors. *Annual Report*. London, The Board, 1915–35?
                                                1B478
A narrative report of activities of the Board, including special problems faced, given by the Board president. The 1934 report by Edward Shortt was in the form of an address.

British Broadcasting Corporation. *Taste and Standards in BBC Programmes, a Study by the BBC for Its General Advisory*

Council. London, BBC, 1973. 11p.
                                                1B479
In the introduction the report notes that "taste" and "standards" hold different meanings for different people at different times, and that, "because of the ways in which broadcasting reaches its audiences, there are constraints to be observed in the choice of material and its treatment which do not necessarily apply to other means of communications." Questions are raised concerning the treatment of the monarchy, Christianity, and the charges of paternalism. The report considers issues involved in setting standards for news programs, current affairs programs, the use of language, the treatment of drama and light entertainment, the arts, and education. Finally, there is a discussion of the system of editorial control including the practice of referring controversial issues upward.

————. *Violence on Television: Programme Content and Viewer Perception*. London, Audience Research Department, BBC, 1972. 220p.   **1B480**
The studies "do not of themselves, provide a basis for concluding *either* that those who criticize television for showing too much violence are justified, or that there is no cause for concern. There must always be some portrayal of violence both in news reporting and in fictional programmes. The problem arises in deciding *what* to include and how to present it honestly."

British Columbia Civil Liberties Association. *Censorship: Hate Literature: A Position Paper*. Vancouver, The Association, 1969. 5p.   **1B481**
The paper offers the Association's reaction to proposals for the legal suppression of "hate literature." A politically free, self-governing people cannot rightfully authorize its government to serve as censor, even if ideas are considered offensive, indecent, or dangerous. To do this even in one area "would thereby diminish the people's self-governing capacity and render them less fit for their civic role." Furthermore, it would be impossible to legally define the concept of "hate literature," much useful social, economic, and political literature would be found offensive to some, and "hatred" cannot be eliminated by cutting off its oral and written expressions.

————. *Censorship: Pornography and Obscenity*. Vancouver, The Association, 1963. 10p.   **1B482**
The Association opposes all institutions of censorship or suppression whether legal or extralegal, and espouses as its policy "principled opposition to all institutions and practices of censorship or suppression with regard to pornography and obscenity, and advocates the repeal of all laws supporting such institutions and practices." The policy calls for making the Association's views known to the public and for a program of education.

———. *Censorship: Submission to the Special Committee on the Classification of Motion Pictures, British Columbia Civil Liberties Association.* Vancouver, The Association, 1972. 4p.   **1B483**
"The Director appointed to administer the British Columbia Motion Pictures Act has the power not only to classify films but also to cut them, or to prohibit their showing altogether. We believe his duties should be limited strictly to the classification of films and that he should no longer have the power to cut or prohibit them."

Brittain, Vera. *Radclyffe Hall; A Case of Obscenity?* [London, Femina Books, 1968.] 186p.   **1B484**
The author, who as a rising young journalist was present at the trial of Radclyffe Hall's *The Well of Loneliness*, presents this study of her fellow novelist and the sensational censorship case. Radclyffe Hall, a self-confessed lesbian, wrote the book in defense of those who, like herself, were victims of a tendency to sexual inversion. The book was banned by the English courts until the passing of the Obscene Publications Act of 1959. It was successfully cleared by the American court. Introduction by C. H. Rolph [pseud. for Cecil R. Hewitt].

"Broadcast Journalism Under Siege." *Broadcasting*, 77:27–29, 17 November 1969.   **1B485**
Comments on the attack on television by Vice-President Spiro T. Agnew.

"Broadcasting: Limited Access to Purchase Public Advertising Time." *Rutgers Law Review*, 27:738–62, Spring 1974.   **1B486**
"This Comment examines the bases of 'journalistic discretion' identified by the Court to determine whether, contrary to the Court's conclusion, broadcasters are indeed required to grant access to the medium through the sale of air time to some people who wish to express their views on some issues of public importance." Re: *Columbia Broadcasting System, Inc. v. Democratic National Committee* (1973).

Broadfoot, John W. "Defamation in Radio and Television—Past and Present." *Mercer Law Review*, 15:450–66, Spring 1964.   **1B487**
The author's purpose is to bring some clarity to the maze of court decisions on defamation in radio by tracing the background of defamatory remarks and considering some of the recent solutions that may reform and revitalize this branch of the law.

Brock, Timothy C. "Erotic Materials: A Commodity Theory Analysis of Availability and Desirability." *Technical Report of the [U.S.] Commission on Obscenity and Pornography*, 1:131–37, 1971.   **1B488**

"The purpose of the present essay is to analyze one specific dimension of the pornography control issue, namely, the probable reactions of individuals who desire information which is not freely available."

Broderick, Dorothy M. "Censorship—Reevaluated." *Library Journal*, 96:3816–18, 15 November 1971.   **1B489**
The author is critical of the use of the current stance of the American Library Association's Office of Intellectual Freedom to defend materials "that perpetuate attitudes that hinder the growth of individuals who are intellectually free." In book selection we should ask "How does this book reflect the sanctity of life?"

———. "Racism, Sexism, Intellectual Freedom and Youth Librarians." *PLA Bulletin* (Pennsylvania Library Association), 31:122–25, November 1976.   **1B490**
The author discusses the debate within the American Library Association (Intellectual Freedom Committee and Children's Services Division) over the selection and reevaluation of children's literature in the area of racism and sexism, defending the right (and obligation) of children's librarians to exercise judgments on accuracy and suitability of books for children's collections.

———. "A Study in Conflicting Values." *Library Journal*, 91:2557–64, 15 May 1966.   **1B491**
"What are the characteristics of the books which cause otherwise gentle ladies to remove their white gloves and come out swinging?" The author reviews some of the provocative books for children and young people and the need for them. "What I want from the librarians of the world is the guts to provide a book collection that allows children and young people to make their own decisions."

———. "When the Censor Knocks . . ." *Phi Delta Kappan*, 52:462–64, April 1971.   **1B492**
"Battles for intellectual freedom are never fought in the abstract. Most Americans favor freedom of speech and press. Certain ideas presented in specific books, however, may stir up another set of feelings. Here are presented old and contemporary materials that cause many to support censorship."

Brogan, Denis. "On Pornography and Censorship." *Spectator*, 220:263–64, 1 March 1968.   **1B493**
Commentary on the case for and against censorship of pornography by a writer who finds "the humbug of both sides equally irritating and equally misleading."

Broin, Leo O. "Amending Irish Broadcasting Law." *EBU Review* (European Broadcasting Union), 26(5):39–41, September 1975.   **1B494**

A bill before the Irish Senate involves control over programming by government agencies, overall responsibility for broadcasting, and assurance of objectivity and impartiality.

Bromberger, Bryan. "Australia. [Censorship of Obscene Literature]." *Technical Report of the [U.S.] Commission on Obscenity and Pornography*, 2:109–26, 1971.   **1B495**
Content: Commonwealth Censorship. State Obscenity Laws. Informal Censorship. Film Censorship. Radio and Television. Censorship of the Live Theater. Movements toward Reform. Criminal Sanctions for Offences against State Antiobscenity Legislation.

———. "United Kingdom [Censorship of Obscene Literature]." *Technical Report of the [U.S.] Commission on Obscenity and Pornography*, 2:206–21, 1971.   **1B496**
Content: Activities Covered (importation, distribution, display, conspiracy, and definitions of "obscene"). Special Juvenile Legislation. Obscenity Laws and Mass Media (theater, radio, and television). Sanctions. Movements toward Reform. Draft of the Working Party's Obscene Publication Bill.

Bronson, Peter C. "New Prosecutorial Techniques and Continued Judicial Vagueness: An Argument for Abandoning Obscenity as a Legal Concept." *UCLA Law Review*, 21:181–241, October 1973.   **1B497**
"This Comment will begin with a brief survey of the proffered social justifications for controlling obscenity. The evolution of the Supreme Court's approach to this problem then will be examined, followed by a critical evaluation of the current obscenity standards. Prosecutorial and statutory efforts to deal with the problem—which often employ techniques outside the scope of the obscenity laws—will be assessed in terms of both legitimacy and advisability. Finally, it will be suggested that, as an alternative to the present general prohibition of obscene conduct, specific legislation be enacted to define and prohibit particular conduct in films and plays."

Brook, Charles W. *Carlile and the Surgeons.* Glasgow, Strickland, 1943. 78p.   **1B498**
An account of the intellectual and personal association of Richard Carlile, lifelong crusader for a free press in England during the early nineteenth century, with certain surgeons of his time: Christopher Arden, surgeon of the Dorchester Jail where Carlile spent three years for his publishing activities and with whom he quarreled; William Lawrence, the controversial medical professor whose book, *Lectures on Physiology*, was condemned and who

later recanted (Carlile republished the *Lectures*); Thomas Wakley, founder of *Lancet*, leader in medical reform, and a frequent target of libel charges for revealing the unethical practices of doctors; Joseph Hume, a member of Parliament and sponsor of a petition to release Carlile from jail, and who, along with Wakley, was a leader in the fight to abolish the tax on newspapers; and Robert Taylor ("the devil's chaplain") who started out as a surgeon, became a priest, then turned freethinker and spent a year in jail for blasphemy. The account reveals as much about Carlile's crusade for freedom of thought and the press as about the unorthodox surgeons.

Brooke, Henry. "A Prefatory Dedication to the Subscribers." In his *Gustavus Vasa, the Deliverer of his Country. A Tragedy*. London, Printed for R. Dodsley, 1739, pp. iii–viii.   **1B499**
Brooke's play was banned by the Lord Chamberlain after it had been in rehearsal for five weeks and hundreds of tickets had been sold, the first such ban under the Stage Licensing Act of 1737. The author, in the preface to this first publication of the play, defends his work and objects to being condemned and punished without being accused of any crime. His purpose in publishing the play is to prove to all that there is nothing in it either seditious or immoral. There follows a twelve-page list of subscribers to the book, which includes the name of Samuel Johnson, who wrote a satirical essay condemning the action of the Lord Chamberlain (J79). The John Bell edition (1778) includes the preface but not the list of subscribers.

Brooks, Carol F. "The Early History of the Anti-Contraceptive Laws in Massachusetts and Connecticut." *American Quarterly*, 18:3–23, Spring 1966. **1B500**
Early anticontraceptive laws were a by-product of the Comstock obscenity law of 1873 and the state laws that followed. Backed by the New England Society for Suppression of Vice, Massachusetts passed an obscenity law in 1879 and Connecticut, with the support of P. T. Barnum, the showman, amended its obscenity laws in 1879 to include an anticontraceptive section. There was little publicity to the passage, but subsequent convictions by jury trials suggested strong public support. The author discusses one segment of the public—the religious liberals—who protested passage: Ezra Heywood of Princeton, Mass., publisher of *The Word*, and D. M. Bennett of New York, publisher of *The Truth Seeker*, went to jail under the Comstock Act. Moses Harman of Chicago, publisher of *Lucifer, The Light-Bearer*, another opponent of restrictions on birth control information, went to jail in 1890. Controversy among liberals of the National Liberal League over the Comstock Acts led to a split in that organization in 1878. Most of the cases under the acts involved obscenity rather than con-

traceptive information. The strong Catholic support for the laws in Massachusetts and Connecticut as a prohibition of contraceptive information was a later development.

Brophy, Brigid. *The Longford Threat to Freedom*. Foreword by Barbara Smoker. London, National Secular Society. 1972. 12p.   **1B501**
"I do not believe the authors, subsidizers, publishers and distributors of the *Longford Report* ought to be put in prison for three years. This is the point which I and other protesters at this meeting [protest meeting in Conway Hall, 3 October 1972] differ from the Longford Committee. I do not believe that the mere fact that a book offends me is a sufficient reason to punish its authors and to deprive my 55 million fellow-citizens of the right to choose for themselves whether to read the book or avoid it." Reference is to the Longford Committee's report on pornography.

———. "Our Impermissive Society." *Mosaic*, 1(2):1–15, January 1968. **1B502**
The author observes the "one-eyed" obsession with sex and the indifference to violence in literature. A writer can treat violence without fear; discussion of fornication may result in prosecution. One may be prosecuted for writing about sexual intercourse, but not for indulging in it. There is a new concern over violence, but it is often linked with sex, as sadism. The author criticizes Pamela Hansford Johnson's work, *On Iniquity*, for its concern over frankness in sex and violence with sexual overtones, but with ignoring violence *per se*. Also, she objects to Johnson's proposal that Krafft-Ebing's *Psychopathia Sexualis* not be made available in paperback because it might fall into the hands of the ignorant. She equates wealth with education and sophistication.

———. "Victorian Pornography." *New Statesman*, 73:81–82, 20 January 1967. **1B503**
Commentary on Steven Marcus, *The Other Victorians*, and Peter Fryer, *Private Case–Public Scandal*.

Brosnahan, James J. "From Times v. Sullivan to Gertz v. Welch: Ten Years of Balancing Libel Law and the First Amendment." *Hastings Law Review*, 26:777–96, January 1975.   **1B504**
"This article will trace the development of constitutional protection of libelous and defamatory utterances beginning with the watershed case of *New York Times Co. v. Sullivan* [1964] through the Supreme Court's recent decision in *Gertz v. Robert Welch, Inc.* [1974]. Substantive and procedural developments since *New York Times* will be described with particular emphases given to the distinctive constitutional approach adopted by the majority of the Court in *Gertz*. The *Gertz* opinion brings about three major developments which substantially depart from the reasoning of the *New York Times* decision and its progeny: (1) adoption of a constitutional balancing test which weighs the

First Amendment interest in the institutional autonomy of the media against the state's interest in compensating an individual for wrongful injury to his reputation; (2) reformulation of the public figure concept and (3) significant alteration of the common law rules governing damages in libel actions."

Brothers, Joyce. "What Women Think of Pornography." *Good Housekeeping*, 170:54, 56, 58, May 1970.   **1B505**
The author's informal survey confirms a Danish survey that women are not the buyers of hard-core pornography, in fact that they are more apt to be repelled by it.

Brothers, Sue *et al.* "If You've Seen One, Have You Seen Them All? Sex Instruction Collections in Five Public Libraries." *Bay State Librarian*, 6(5):12–14, 16, December 1974. **1B506**
How five Massachusetts public libraries handle material in the controversial area of sex education.

Brough, James C. "Defamation by Radio and Television." *South Texas Law Journal*, 4:253–76, Summer 1959. **1B507**
The purpose of the article is to analyze the difference between libel and slander with respect to radio and television, with special attention to the case of *Gibler v. The Houston Post*, 310 S.W.2d 377.

[Brougham and Vaux, Henry Peter Brougham, *1st Baron*.] "Abuses of the Press." *Edinburgh Review*, 22:72–88, October 1813.   **1B508**
A review of John George, *A Treatise on the Offence of Libel* (G71). The reviewer is concerned with the uncertainty in the execution of the law of libel and questions the aspersion commonly made of the increased licentiousness of the present-day press. Houghton's *Wellesley Index* attributes this unsigned review to Brougham.

———. "Taxes on Knowledge." *Edinburgh Review*, 62:66–70, October 1835.   **1B509**
An essay on the evil of the newspaper stamp tax and criticism of the establishment press in London for suppressing discussion of the matter.

Broun, Heywood. "What Shakespeare Missed." In his *Pieces of Hate and Other Enthusiasms*. New York, Doran, 1922, pp. 207–21.   **1B510**
An imaginary story of what a Pennsylvania State Board of Censors of Motion Pictures might do to *Macbeth* in following the Standards of the Board. "As a matter of fact, it is pretty hard to see just how *Macbeth* could possibly come to the screen in Pennsylvania." The author describes the almost insurmountable difficulty in announcing the arrival of babies on the screen—how to inform adults without creating

impressions in the minds of children. Even the showing of mothers knitting baby socks has been eliminated in Pennsylvania as too shocking.

Brown, Alan W. *Editorial Advertising: A Means of Free Expression?* Orlando, Fla., Florida Technological University, 1974. 92p. (Unpublished Master's thesis) **1B511**
"The thesis calls for a view of editorial advertising within the context of the First Amendment. It suggests that, with today's rapidly increasing communication processes and technologies, editorial advertising is a modern way for citizens to express themselves to their community."

Brown, Bob W., and Henry A. Buchanan. "We Learned What Pornography Really Is." *Liberty*, 61:7–11, March–April 1966. **1B512**
Two Lexington, Ky., clergymen who became concerned over pornography being peddled in their community, "learned to distinguish it—even by smell—from literature that simply treats sex realistically." They concluded that the ultimate answer lies in the influence of the family itself. "Unless parents create the healthy family environment for the child's development of his sex drives and interests along socially acceptable, personally satisfying and creative lines, neither laws nor courts nor popular crusades, nor committees of concerned civic leaders, can compensate for their failure."

[Brown, Charles O.] *Brown vs. Ingersoll, Did the Great Infidel Petition for Repeal of the Laws against Obscenity? Rev. C. O. Brown Gives the Promised Proofs to Sustain His Charges. . . .* Dubuque, Iowa, Dubuque Daily Times, 1888. 8p. (Reprinted from the *Dubuque Daily Times*, 14 February 1888) **1B513**
An address of the Reverend Charles O. Brown to a Dubuque audience, defending his earlier charges that the noted infidel, Robert G. Ingersoll, had headed a group and signed a petition to Congress in 1878 asking for the repeal of the Comstock law. Ingersoll had denied the charges, saying that he was opposed to obscenity but wanted the law changed so that infidel literature would not be suppressed as obscene. The Reverend Mr. Brown praised the good work of Comstock in enforcing the law and denounced the "liberals" who opposed Comstock and the law as, "an army of short-haired women and long-haired men."

Brown, Claude. "How to Deal with Censorship." In David R. Bender, *ed.*, *Issues in Media Management.* Baltimore, Division of Library Development and Services, Maryland State Department of Education, 1974, pp. 27–35. **1B514**
The author of *Manchild in the Promised Land* discusses the difficulties over the censorship of his own book, which only served to increase its

sales. He also refers to the purchase and destruction of copies of a private printing of Michael Selzer's *Aryanization of the Jewish State*. He urges librarians to resist the censor. "It's a cruel thing to tell people not to read. It's not only a violation of people's Constitutional rights, it's cruel. It is a waste of time telling students what not to read. They're going to get access to it anyway."

Brown, Dennis E. *Dilemmas of Film Classification.* Columbia, Mo., Freedom of Information Center, School of Journalism, University of Missouri at Columbia, 1967. 6p. (Report no. 192) **1B515**
"Growing 'permissiveness' in the film industry, coupled with a decline of state and municipal boards of censorship, is prompting support for municipal or state legislation which would provide a means of classifying motion pictures as 'suitable' or 'unsuitable' for minors. . . . In an effort to head off this possibility, the Motion Picture Association of America has established a voluntary system of classification operating under its new code of self-regulation. Success of the industry's move will depend upon the solution of problems at the operational level, as well as on the degree of public confidence and acceptance the new code receives."

———. *S1312: The Failing Newspaper Bill.* Columbia, Mo., Freedom of Information Center, School of Journalism, University of Missouri at Columbia, 1968. 6p. (Report no. 196) **1B516**
"This paper outlines the major arguments for and against S. 1312 as given in subcommittee hearings and explores some of the side issues raised in the testimony. . . . In its present form S. 1312 could have an important effect on patterns of press ownership and control. Whatever merit there may be in protecting joint operations seems, at this juncture, to be balanced off by possible dangers to small publishers and weaker segments of the industry."

———, and John C. Merrill. *Regulatory Pluralism in the Press.* Columbia, Mo., Freedom of Information Center, School of Journalism, University of Missouri at Columbia, 1967. 4p. (Report no. 005) **1B517**
Two journalism faculty members present arguments for and against the right of access to the use of the press as proposed by Professor Jerome A. Barron. They conclude that "a forced publishing concept will take root only when our society has proceeded much farther along the road toward Orwell's *1984*, wherein a paternalistic and omnipotent Power Structure makes our individual decisions for us."

Brown, Donald E. "The Invasion of Defamation by Privacy." *Stanford Law Review*, 23:547–68, February 1971. **1B518**

"This Note first examines the development of defamation law in the Supreme Court, focusing on *New York Times* [*New York Times v. Sullivan*, 1964] and the subsequent broadening of person and issue requirements for first amendment protection. Next, it discusses the relationship between the privacy and defamation torts and demonstrates that the Court intended to limit the *Hill* holding [*Time, Inc. v. Hill*, 1967] to private actions. Part III focuses on the lower court decisions extending the concepts of *Hill* into the defamation area. The final part proposes an analytic framework for defamation and recommends that the Court adopt different standards of proof for different types of plaintiffs and issues in defamation actions."

Brown, Edward R. "Fair Trial and Free Press: The ABA Recommendations—A Defense Lawyer's Viewpoint." *Western Reserve Law Review*, 18:1156–76, May 1967. **1B519**
The author "summarizes the process by which the ABA Committee reached its conclusions and discusses several of the more important findings. [He] concurs with the Committee that the existing devices available to the defense in eliminating prejudice—change of venue, continuance, jury selection, and mistrial—should be invoked more frequently and that the standards used to justify these remedies should be reduced." He also discusses the expansion of news blackouts and the use of closed-door hearings.

Brown, Elton R., III. "Direct Broadcast Satellites and Freedom of Speech." *California Western International Law Journal*, 4:374–93, Spring 1974. **1B520**
An analysis of regulatory proposals made by the Working Group on Direct Broadcast Satellites (United Nations). "The provisions dealing with regulation of program content will be measured against the standards of international law and the first amendment to the United States Constitution to determine whether the United States should become a Party to an agreement embodying these provisions."

Brown, Ivor. *I Commit to the Flames.* London, Hamilton, 1934. 240p. **1B521**
In his introductory remarks on book burning, the author states: "I do not believe in bonfires as the best means of dispatch for intellectual nuisances. I am old-fashioned enough to believe in freedom. . . . If arson there must be, let us burn such natural fuel as the fasces and the shafts of axes and leave the books on the shelf. . . . The flames to which I commit the enemy are those of argument, reinforced, I hope, by a little salutary rudeness and by a spark or two of insolent contempt. These are the only flames which can finally consume." There follows attacks on T. S. Eliot, D. H. Lawrence, and other modern literary persons, particularly those with a "ferocious domination of sex."

Brown, James J., and Carl L. Stern. "Group Defamation in the U.S.A." *Cleveland-Marshall Law Review*, 13:7–32, January 1964.   **1B522**
The article deplores the fact that there is no adequate law in the United States to defend racial or religious minority groups against falsehoods and vilification, no law to check bigots and fear peddlers.

Brown, James W. ["Freedom of the Press".] In Walter Williams, *ed.*, *The Press Congress of the World in Hawaii*. Columbia, Mo., E. W. Stephens, 1922, pp. 243–49.   **1B523**
The editor of *Editor and Publisher* reviews the status of press freedom in the United States, referring to three recent instances where government officials attempted to discipline the press: Postmaster General Burlison's attempt to withdraw second-class mailing privileges to the *New York Call*, a socialist paper critical of the government; a 10-million-dollar libel suit by the City of Chicago against the *Chicago Tribune* and the *Chicago Daily News*; and New York Mayor Hylan's efforts to get advertisers to boycott newspapers that had been critical of him.

Brown, Lee. *The Reluctant Reformation: On Criticizing the Press in America*. New York, McKay, 1974. 224p.   **1B524**
Chapters deal with the role of criticism and the social responsibility of the press, a history of press criticism drawing upon its British origin, a survey of various forms of press criticism and experiments in self-criticism, proposals for a national press council, and possible future developments. The appendix (more than half of the book) includes: the text of various press codes, Press Council Operating Rules (Minnesota), two surveys on the image of the newspaper, and results of a study on the newspapers' use of internal criticism.

Brown, Michael A. "Must the Soldier Be A Silent Member of Our Society?" *Military Law Review*, 43:71–109, January 1969.   **1B525**
"The author compares the rights of the individual soldier with the rights of the private citizen in the area of constitutionally protected speech. In addition, the author analyzes congressional and executive restraints upon freedom of speech and Department of the Army regulations implementing such restraints. He then compares these restraints with those extant in the civilian community. Conclusions are then proffered as to whether substantial differences in the freedom of speech rights exist between the civilian and military spheres."

Brown, Philip A. *The French Revolution in English History*. New York, Barnes & Noble, 1918. 234p. (Reprinted by Frank Cass, London, 1965)   **1B526**
An account of the hysteria that swept England in the wake of the French Revolution; the role of John Wilkes and Thomas Paine; the rise of the reform movement and their various societies; the prosecution of dissenters; the State Trials of 1794 against Thomas Hardy, John Horne Tooke, John Thelwal, and Thomas Fyshe Palmer; and the reform role of the Whigs during and after the Revolution.

Brown, Roy. "Literature and the Permissive Society." *Library World*, 72:257–62 March, 1971.   **1B527**
A history of censorship in England from the day of the Court of Star Chamber to recent decisions on obscenity (*Last Exit to Brooklyn* and *The Story of O*). The writer believes that if a valid case can be made for literary quality a book can circulate without difficulty. This is largely the result of a benevolent attitude of individuals in authority rather than leniency in the statutes. He cites three problems that remain despite the great freedom for literature: (1) to recognize new works of literary merit dealing with subjects hitherto taboo, (2) difficulty in defining "obscene," and (3) whether the obscene in literature is harmful socially.

Brown, Stanley M., and John W. Reed. "Regulation of Radio Broadcasting: Competitive Enterprise or Public Utility?" *Cornell Law Quarterly*, 27:249–66, January 1942.   **1B528**
The authors argue for treatment of radio broadcasting as a public utility.

Brown, Stephen J. "Concerning Censorship." *Irish Monthly*, 64:25–35, January 1936.   **1B529**
The author finds that "some sort of censorship over the printed word is . . . not only the right but the duty of Governments," and, in the case of pornography, "there are few who would question this right." He denies the claims that literature and other forms of art are independent of morality. Works that attack morality, regardless of their artistic merit, can justifiably be banned. "The repression of evil literature ought to be regarded as a matter of sanitation, of simple scavenging, more difficult, no doubt, than the cleansing of the streets but not less necessary."

Brown, Trevor. "Free Press Fair Game for South Africa's Government." *Journalism Quarterly*, 48:120–27, Spring 1971. (Reprinted in Michael H. Prosser, *ed.*, *Intercommunication Among Nations and People*. New York, Harper & Row, 1973, pp. 509–18)   **1B530**
"Author finds English newspapers practice libertarian ethic cautiously, but remain too vulnerable for effective opposition; non-white newsmen suffer under apartheid, while all lack professional perspective."—Editor

Brown, Wanda L. "Elimination of Sexually Segregated Employment Ads: A Step toward Equal Employment Opportunity." *University of Florida Law Review*, 26:577–86, Spring 1974.   **1B531**
Re: *Pittsburgh Press Co. v. Pittsburgh Commission on Human Relations* (1972). A discussion of the issue over the control of the format of classified ads in the interest of eliminating sex discrimination in employment.

Browne, Harry L., and Howard F. Sachs. "The End of Libel in Labor Cases?" *American Bar Association Journal*, 62:456–59, April 1976.   **1B532**
"The Supreme Court decision in *Gissel* [*NLRB v. Gissel Packing Co.* (1969)] and *Old Dominion* [*Old Dominion Branch No. 496, National Association of Letter Carriers v. Austin* (1974)] may have had a practical effect of ending libel actions for defamation arising in the context of a labor case. But the *Cantrell* decision [*Cantrell v. Forest City Publishing Co.* (1974)] may have breathed life into the privacy concept—a concept that may have some validity in the labor cases. At any rate, systematic harassment by defamation should not have immunity."

Browne, Terry W. "Censorship." In his *Playwright's Theatre: The English Stage Company of the Royal Court Theatre*. With Foreword by Martin Esslin. London, Pitman, 1975, pp. 56–71.   **1B533**
The author writes of the Royal Court Theatre's experience with the Lord Chamberlain's censorship of the stage, giving examples. He also discusses events leading to the abolition of the censorship system. "Censorship of the stage has been under attack for generations before the English Stage Company had come into being, but, partly as a result of the Company's willingness to fight for its right to deal seriously with contemporary problems, the whole idea of theatrical censorship had finally become too obviously stupid to be allowed to continue."

Bruce, Harry. "Me, Premier Regan and a Matter of Principle." *Saturday Night*, 87(8):9–11, August 1972.   **1B534**
The author of an article in *Saturday Night* which offended the Premier of Nova Scotia, who, the author charges, attempted unsuccessfully to get him fired from his job in a utility company. Bruce comments on the role of the press in questioning and criticizing actions of government officials.

Brucker, Herbert. "Can Printed News Save a Free Society?" *Saturday Review*, 53(41):52–55, 64, 10 October 1970.   **1B535**
Despite monopolies, the press is not a single behemoth; the tradition of objective reporting survives; and little of significance is ignored or suppressed. If democracy is to survive, "the newspaper reporter must continue to be an

observer on the sidelines, a detached and knowledgeable inquisitor into what is going on" not an activist-journalist who begins with opinions and looks for facts to bolster them. Editors "should be left on a long leash"—free to examine each issue and interest before determining which side to take.

———. *Communication Is Power.* New York, Oxford University Press, 1973. 385p. **1B536**
References to such issues as the government's claim to the right to lie, the press's responsibility to report the facts without suppression or distortion, trial by newspaper, the camera in the courtroom, and who should own the newspapers.

———. "A Conscience for the Press; An American Newspaper Council?" *Saturday Review*, 53:59–61, 9 May 1970. **1B537**
The press has been reluctant to accept outside criticism, witness its opposition to the report of the Commission on Freedom of the Press and proposals for watchdog action of a press council. "Newspapers and broadcasters had better do something themselves," the author concludes, "before some big, bad Spiro does it for them—with a majority of the American people cheering him on."

———. "Journalism by Lawyers." *Connecticut Bar Journal*, 29:40–50, March 1955. **1B538**
A discussion of a "tendency on the part of lawyers—judges, prosecuting attorneys, attorneys for the defense, and lawyers generally—to suppress what has hitherto been considered legitimate news." This tendency, the opposite of "trial by newspaper," the author terms "journalism by lawyers."

Brudnoy, David. "Comstock's Nemesis." *National Review*, 23:1065–66, 24 September 1971. **1B539**
In a review of the reprinting of three books on obscenity and free speech by Theodore Schroeder, the author discusses the conflict between the censorship ideas of Anthony Comstock and the libertarian views of Schroeder.

———. "How to Spot Public Broadcasting Bias." *Human Events*, 33:362, 373, 5 May 1973. **1B540**
How individual television viewers can monitor public television's public affairs and news programs to detect bias, and what action they can take. "Only when matters of importance are treated with scrupulous fairness and balance can they be said to have been presented in a spirit consistent with the Fairness Doctrine."

———. *Liberty's Bugler: The Seven Ages of Theodore Schroeder.* Waltham, Mass., Brandeis University, 1971. 544p.

(Ph.D. dissertation, University Microfilms, no. 71–30,119) **1B541**
The most important of the seven ages of Theodore Schroeder, presented in this biography, was that devoted to championing First Amendment freedoms. Schroeder, a New York lawyer, came to the defense of persons involved in blasphemy, sedition, and obscenity, serving as a nemesis to Anthony Comstock. He was one of the founders of the Free Speech League, and wrote numerous articles arguing for the abolition of all censorship. His writings in the field of obscenity, beginning at the turn of the century, were forerunners of present-day thinking on the subject.

———. "Theodore Schroeder and the Suppressers of Vice." *Civil Liberties Review*, 3 (2):48–56, June/July 1976. **1B542**
An account of the life work of Theodore Schroeder, who waged a war of words against the vice societies and was one of the earliest crusaders for the removal of all state and federal laws against obscene literature. In addition to his libertarian views on obscenity Schroeder believed that the separation of church and state relieved judges and juries of the responsibility to deal with blasphemy as a crime against the state. The author's research was based on the Schroeder papers at Southern Illinois University.

Bruggeman, Carl V. "Bases of Slander Per Se in Ohio." *Ohio State Law Journal*, 15:312–29, Summer 1954. **1B543**
A consideration of the narrow exceptions under Ohio law which are accepted as basis for slander *per se*, that is without proof of damages. The author concludes that "more good than harm would result from extending the number of actionable *per se* imputations whether it is done by a partial extension or a complete extension to all actions of slander."

Brundage, Gloria S. "Freedom of Speech in Radio Broadcasting." In Speech Association of America. *Abstracts, 55th Annual Meeting*, New York, 1969, p. 79. **1B544**
"The nature and development of the concept of freedom of radio is interpreted by the investigator within its historical context and the development of social responsibility in the other media."

———. "Rationale for the Application of the Fairness Doctrine in Broadcast News." *Journalism Quarterly*, 47:531–37, Autumn 1972. **1B545**
An examination of the origin and development of the fairness doctrine in broadcasting as an administrative attempt by the Federal Communications Commission to encourage the free flow of ideas essential for the development of an informed public opinion. "Recognition of the principles of free expression in the Fairness Doctrine might provide a rationale for 'news judgement' in future broadcast news."

Brunette, Robert A. "Rehabilitation, Privacy and Freedom of the Press—Striking a New Balance." *Loyola of Los Angeles Law Review*, 5:544–88, August 1972. **1B546**
Re: *Briscoe v. Reader's Digest Association* (1971). The author concludes that (1) the express application of the Meiklejohn theory to truthful disclosures of "private" facts lessens the scope of published matter absolutely protected by the First Amendment compared to the vague newsworthiness standard of past privacy decisions, (2) the implied rejection of the public-record doctrine also radically expands the class of disclosures which may constitute an invasion of privacy, and (3) a jury could still find that mere fact of disclosure was highly offensive to a reasonable man.

Brustein, Robert. "Freedom and Restraint." *New Republic*, 166:22 +, 6 May 1972; 166:30–32, 13 May 1972. (Also in abridged form in *Current*, July 1972) **1B547**
The American theater at the present time enjoys "a period of cultural autonomy unique in our history, and probably in the history of the world." The author attempts "to place our theatrical freedom in historical context, to make some effort to account for it, and to suggest what, aside from the omnipresent danger of government intervention, is now inhibiting its healthy expression."

Bryan, D. Tennant. "Of Trials and the Press." *Nieman Reports*, 22(2):25–27, June 1968. **1B548**
The American Bar Association "cannot unilaterally impose its will nationwide on the Press, on the judiciary or on law enforcement officers and police, and the Reardon recommendations [on press coverage of trials]—repugnant as they are to our concept of a free Press—can have no real impact on us unless or until they are adopted by the appropriate legal jurisdictions of the several states." The chairman of the American Newspaper Publishers Association calls upon representatives of the media to convince friends of the Bench and Bar "that, by adopting the Reardon Report, they will be doing a disservice to the people, the Press and to the cause of justice."

Bryan, William S. "The Trial of J. T. Scopes." *Truth Seeker*, 52:373–74, 13 June 1925; 52:426, 4 July 1925; 52:471–72, 25 July 1925; 52:487–88, 1 August 1925; 52:503–4, 8 August 1925; 52:522, 15 August 1925. **1B549**
In a series of articles in this freethinker journal, the writer discusses the events and implications of the Tennessee evolution trial in which William Jennings Bryan and Clarence Darrow were pitted as lawyers for the prosecution and the defense.

Bryant, Ashbrook P. "Regulation of Broadcast Networks." *St. Louis University Law Journal*, 15:3–47, Fall 1970.   1B550

"The purpose of this article is to summarize the history of broadcasting networks and the consideration of their regulation, to discuss various types and areas of regulation which have been suggested from time to time, to describe forms of network regulation adopted up to now, and to suggest possible courses of action for the future."

Bryant, Hilda M. *A Free and Responsible Press: A Three-Year Inquiry*. Seattle, University of Washington, 1969. 150p. (Unpublished Master's thesis)   1B551

The author examined the vast file of unpublished working papers of the Commission on Freedom of the Press to discover how the Commission arrived at its concept of the social responsibility of the press. The concept, the study showed, "arose, not out of the First Amendment, but out of a pragmatic new philosophy of freedom and responsibility that the commissioners derived from several older philosophical concepts to meet the new demands of the communications revolution. The results of this examination indicate that the commissioners rejected libertine freedom as offered by the First Amendment while stoutly defending the necessity for such unconditional liberty. They formulated a New Liberalism which required moral grounds for freedom of the press in modern society, thereby providing the potential basis for revocation of press freedom—moral delinquency."

Bryant, Kenneth C. "Newsmen's Immunity Needs a Shot in the Arm." *Santa Clara Lawyer*, 11:56–71, Fall 1970.   1B552

An examination of California's "reporters privilege" statute and the conflicting interpretations of it. The author finds that defects in the statute nullify any encouragement to news gathering it was intended to create, and suggests revisions which would carry out the intent of the legislature.

Bryant, Roscoe. "The History and Background of Public Law 90–23, The Freedom of Information Act." *North Carolina Central Law Journal*, 3:193–97, Spring 1972.   1B553

"With all the governmental safeguards to protect the public's right to know, the citizens and public interest groups still are unable to attain full access. The problem is that the very safeguards set up to protect the rights and to set out the limitations are still broad enough for putting any desired document out of reach."

Bryson, Verena L. "Banned Books."

South Carolina Librarian, 14(2):30–33, March 1970.   1B554

References to some of the important works at one time banned.

Buchanan, G. Sidney. "Obscenity and Brandenburg: The Missing Link?" *Houston Law Review*, 11:537–82, March 1974.   1B555

"This article will focus primarily on the premise underlying the *Chaplinsky* dictum (*Chaplinsky v. New Hampshire*, 1942) and the holdings in *Roth* (*Roth v. United States*, 1957) and *Miller* (*Miller v. California*, 1973) that certain categories of speech content are not protected by the first amendment. As applied to obscenity, this article will contend that the *Chaplinsky* dictum is wrong."

Buchanan, Patrick J. "Can Democracy Survive the New Journalism?" In his *Conservative Votes, Liberal Victories: Why the Right Has Failed*. New York, Quadrangle/New York Times, 1975, pp. 72–92.   1B556

The author, formerly on the staff of President Nixon, accuses the "new journalism" of permeating the press with strong liberal bias—against the military and big business and for federal social spending, and forced integration. The national press is "a silent partner of the political and social movements of liberalism—consumerism, civil rights, environmental, anti-war and women's liberation." Certain institutional biases also contribute to the predominance of liberal news: the location of the principal news bureaus in major cities, the brief time frame of television news, the tendency to favor the changing rather than that which endures, and an emphasis on conflict and controversy. He also criticizes the insistance of the new journalists on an "adversary relationship" with government and with adopting a chronic negativism that permeates their reporting.

————. "Were Two Networks Unfair in Refusing Oil Commercials?" *TV Guide*, 22(29):6–7, 20 July 1974. 1B557

The author accuses Columbia Broadcasting System and American Broadcasting Company of dictating the terms of the national debate on the energy crisis, and for failure to give the oil companies and industry in general fair treatment in news reporting.

Buckalew, James K. *The Television News Editor As A Gatekeeper*. Iowa City, Iowa, University of Iowa, 1967. 244p. (Ph.D. dissertation, University Microfilms, no. 68–908)   1B558

"This study set out to learn what factors influence the decisions made by television news editors in selecting from their input. It was done by observing the retention and rejection of items from the pool of input available to 12 television news editors and by relating the results to the characteristics of editors and their situation."

[Buckingham, Joseph T.] *A Correct Statement and Review of the Trial of Joseph T. Buckingham, for an alleged libel on the Rev. John N. Maffit, before the Hon. Josiah Quincy, Judge of the Municipal Court, Dec. 16, 1822*. Boston, William S. Spear, 1822. 16p.   1B559

Commentary on the trial and acquittal of the editor of the *New England Galaxy* (B613), with sympathy for the plaintiff who seemed to be the victim of public persecution.

Buckle, Henry T. *Letter to a Gentleman Respecting Pooley's Case*. London, John W. Parker, 1859. 16p.   1B560

Buckle had written a criticism of Sir John Coleridge's decision in the blasphemy trial of Thomas Pooley (*Frazer's Magazine*, May 1859), to which Justice Coleridge's son responded in a subsequent article. This pamphlet is Buckle's rejoinder to young Coleridge's attack on Buckle's views and his character. Buckle points out that Coleridge raises issues that Buckle had not addressed in his article, ignoring Buckle's chief criticism that the sentence of twenty-one months imprisonment was an "act of cruelty," alien to the spirit of the time, imposed on a poor man who was mentally deranged and had done no harm to any man. The real issue, Buckle states, is "whether language is to be refuted by language, or whether it is to be refuted by force."

Buckley, Frank W. *Judicial Interpretation of Powers and Responsibilities to Deal with Excessive Publicity in American Criminal Cases*. Carbondale, Ill., Southern Illinois University, 1966. 272p. (Ph.D. dissertation, University Microfilms, no. 67-3141)   1B561

"This study involved the tracing of the free press-fair trial dispute from the earliest cases through the appeal of Dr. Sam Sheppard decided by the United States Supreme Court in 1966, and the drawing of some conclusions as to possible resolution of the problem."

Buckley, Kenneth. "Censorship of Oz Publications Inc Limited." In *Offensive and Obscene: A Civil Liberties Casebook*. Sydney, Ure Smith, 1970, pp. 47–91.   1B562

An account of the obscenity prosecution in London against the publishers, printer, and cartoonist of the magazine *Oz* for its February 1964 issue. Although final decision of the court (February 1966) was in favor of the defendants (the magazine's emphasis upon sex was not undue within the meaning of the Obscene and Indecent Publications Act), the long term effect of the decision was "a set back for forces of freedom in the running war against censorship."

Buckley, William F., Jr. "Broadcasting Dilemma; Licensing and Censorship." *National Review*, 25:382–83, 30 March 1973.   1B563

Comment on Fred Friendly's criticism of the Nixon Administration and Clay T. Whitehead, director of the White House Telecommunications Office, for threats of censorship. Buckley favors permanent licensing and encouragement of cable and pay TV as a means of counteracting bias in television news.

―――. "Neglect of the First Amendment: Television Unions Impede Rights of Non-Members." *National Review*, 25:598, 25 May 1973.   **1B564**
A brief note of criticism of television unions for denying consumers of the news the right to get that news from nonmember television crews working for public broadcasting.

―――. "Shield Laws." *National Review*, 25:330, 16 March 1973.   **1B565**
Observations on the plea of Columbia Broadcasting System's Frank Stanton for absolute shield laws for reporters. "What is needed is not an 'absolute' privilege but the making of some distinctions." The author sees less danger to the free flow of information from government ("as always we need to keep an eye on the government") than from labor strikes that choke off all news.

Bucknell, Neal. "Libel Insurance." In Melbourne University. *The Law and the Printer, the Publisher and the Journalist. The Collected Papers of a Seminar at Melbourne University on August 12, 1971*. Melbourne, Antony Whitlock, 1971, pp. 29–33.   **1B566**
An insurance man gives practical information on libel insurance in Australia which, he notes, indemnifies the policyholder against damages awarded and covers the cost of defense; it requires that the insurance underwriter handle the claim. All libel insurance requires that the insured assume a portion of the risk (generally 10 to 25 percent), which discourages reckless publishing. He discusses how premiums are fixed, how claims are handled, and advantages and disadvantages of taking out libel insurance.

Bufford, Samuel. "Drug Songs and the Federal Communications Commission." *Journal of Law Reform (University of Michigan)*, 5:334–50, Winter 1972.   **1B567**
"This article will examine the notice ₁issued by the Federal Communications Commission concerning the broadcasting of drug-related popular songs₁ to ascertain its likely meaning, determine its legal status, and examine three constitutional issues it raises: whether the songs are protected as speech under the first amendment; whether the statement of the prohibition (if that be the import of the notice) is sufficiently precise to avoid due process problems of vagueness; and whether the notice is a kind of prior restraint on freedom of speech and press."

₁Bull, Nicholas B.₁ *Palmer v. Bull. The Speech of C. Phillips, Esq. as Delivered in the Sheriff's Court, in an Action Between Palmer versus Bull, to Recover Damages for a Libel, Published in the John Bull Newspaper, on Monday, April 7th, 1823, Before the Under-Sheriff and a Common Jury*. London, George Hebert, 1823. 8p.   **1B568**
An Irish barrister pleads the case brought by C. Fysche Palmer against the editor of the scandalous Tory newspaper, *John Bull*, for an article describing comments allegedly made by Palmer in a private billiard-room, derogatory to the recently deceased Lord Londonderry. The jury found Bull guilty and fined him $200.

Bumstead, Eben. *"Blessed are the pure in heart . . . "* Boston, The Author, ₁1906?₁. Broadside.   **1B569**
A Boston man defends Anthony Comstock's seizure of nude publications of a New York art school. "There is nothing noble but much that is hazardous in school teachers leading mixed classes of children through art museums where the nude abounds."

Bunge, Walter K. *Public Interest as a Function of the First Amendment in Broadcasting: A Study of the New Technology and Some Old Assumptions*. Minneapolis, University of Minnesota, 1972. 344p. (Ph.D. dissertation, University Microfilms, no. 72-27,732)   **1B570**
The study concluded that "the rights and duties of broadcasters must be reconciled with the traditional interpretations of the First Amendment and that these two come together in cable communications. The freedom of speech cases offer the legal basis for a reconciliation which has not been made heretofore because of the limited-channel nature of broadcasting and because of the unreliable and inconsistent interpretation that the FCC has put on the concept of the public interest."

Bunks, Abe. "Newspaperman's Privilege As to Sources." *Intermural Law Review*, 13:170–83, March 1958. **1B571**
On the occasion of the Marie Torre case, *Garland v. Torre*, the author reviews the history, current status, and prospects for newsman's claim of privilege to refuse to reveal news sources.

Burbidge, Dighton W. *Harvest of Mischief*. Melbourne, Australia, Celadon, 1947. 218p.   **1B572**
A novel about attempts to overcome Australian Customs' censorship by local reprinting of a banned American novel and the subsequent obscenity trial. The prosecution is abetted by the League for the Suppression of Vice; the defendant is supported by testimony given by two university professors. The verdict was "not guilty." The plot is similar to later efforts used in bringing *The Trial of Lady Chatterley* to the reading public.

Burch, Angelus T. "The Press and the Administration of Justice." *Michigan State Bar Journal*, 40:11–18, January 1961. (Reprinted in *PEAL Quarterly*, September 1962)   **1B573**
A newspaper editor discusses three problems of joint concern to editors and lawyers: public access to the courts and court records, photography and broadcasting in the courtroom, and reporting and comment prior to trials or during them. He suggests that photography in the courtroom begin with the appellate courts where there are no witnesses and jurors to be affected.

Burch, Dean. "Another Type of Air Pollution?" *Television Quarterly*, 9:5–10, Winter 1970.   **1B574**
The chairman of the Federal Communications Commission discusses obscene and indecent programming in broadcasting—not an overwhelming problem in the industry but a disturbing trend.

―――. "Can Stations Police the Fairness of Newscasters?" *TV Guide*, 21(17):36–39, 28 April 1973.   **1B575**
The second part of an interview with the chairman of the Federal Communications Commission in which there is discussion of such topics as the fairness doctrine, license renewal, advertising on children's shows, and the legislative proposals of Clay T. Whithead of President Nixon's staff.

―――. "How Permissive Do You Think Television Ought To Be?" *TV Guide*, 21(16):5–8, 21 April 1973. **1B576**
In an interview conducted by Richard K. Doan, FCC Chairman Burch discusses such topics as sex and violence on television, permissiveness, and cable and pay-TV. The interview is continued in the 28 April issue.

―――. ₁*State of the Fairness Doctrine*.₁ Washington, D.C., Federal Communications Commission, 1970. 70p. Processed.   **1B577**
"An honest mistake in judgment ₁in programming₁ doesn't in the least place your license in jeopardy. . . . What will place your license in jeopardy . . . is to avoid controversial issue programming because you have to be fair to engage in it." Address before the Radio & Television News Directors Association, Denver, Colo., 25 September 1970.

Burchell, J. M. "The Criteria of Defamation." *South African Law Journal*, 91:178–207, May 1974.   **1B578**
"The test evolved by our courts over the years for determining what constitutes defamatory matter is whether the imputation lowers the

plaintiff in the estimation of ordinary, right-thinking persons generally. In this article a reappraisal of these criteria is attempted in order to discern whether any refinement of the traditional test is justified and whether additional guidelines can be suggested in judging defamation. In essence the inquiry involves two basic questions: (a) whose opinion is decisive? and (b) what is meant by the phrase 'lowering in estimation'?"

Burda, Ronald E. *Photographic Libel: An Inquiry Into the Rights of Photographers.* San Jose, Calif., California State University, San Jose, 1973. 110p. (Unpublished Master's thesis)　**1B579**
"This thesis is an attempt to collect into one source all the federal legal cases where a photograph was involved in a libel. Nineteen such cases exist, spanning the years from 1850 to 1972. . . . The conclusion of this compilation is that a photojournalist has more to fear from identifying someone who is libeled by a writer in an accompanying article or caption, than he does from making someone appear foolish in his photograph."

Burdick, C. Gray. "Procedural Guidelines Involved in Municipal Control of Motion Pictures." *Mississippi Law Journal*, 41:611–18, Fall 1970.　**1B580**
"This note will . . . show some of the difficulties faced by a municipality in its attempt to regulate motion pictures, with special attention being given to the procedural guidelines set down by the courts."

Buresh, Bernice. "Boycott Turns on Wisconsin Publisher." *Chicago Journalism Review*, 2(9):7–8, 11, September 1969.　**1B581**
An account of the advertising boycott of three Wisconsin papers whose publisher printed the underground newspaper, *Kaleidoscope.* The crusade against the publisher was led by an arch-conservative, anti-Communist businessman.

Burger, Warren E. "Interdependence of Judicial and Journalistic Independence." *New York State Bar Journal*, 47:453–55, 476–78, October 1975.
1B582
"Whether or not we always agree with each other on every detail, we share a need for something fundamental that neither of us can maintain without the support of the other. Journalistic independence and judicial independence have served to maintain the unique American system of ordered liberty for two centuries. To continue that system we must both persist with a constant and vigilant pursuit of our respective functions, ours assigned by the Constitution and yours guaranteed by

the same Constitution." Remarks of the Chief Justice of the United States before the American Society of Newspaper Editors.

———. "An Interview with Chief Justice Burger on the Judiciary and the Press." *American Bar Association Journal*, 61:1352–53, November 1975.　**1B583**
An interview conducted by Burnett F. Anderson and recorded by the United States Information Agency for distribution throughout the world.

Burgett, George L. "Transit District May Not Constitutionally Restrict Paid Advertising So As to Exclude Opinions and Beliefs Within the Ambit of First Amendment Protection." *Notre Dame Lawyer*, 43:781–86, June 1968.
1B584
Re: *Wirta v. Alameda-Contra Costa Transit District*, 434 P.2d 982, 64 Cal. Rptr. 430 (1967).

Burke, John G., and H. Paxton Bowers. "Institutional Censorship; A Proposal for an Effective Mechanism to Protect the Researcher." *Library Journal*, 95:468–69, 1 February 1970. **1B585**
The authors call for an addition to the Library Bill of Rights which would contain the following elements to combat institutional censorship: "(1) No individual should be denied access to library material which is free of donor restrictions; (2) Libraries should not accept donations of library materials upon which unreasonable time limitations for access are attached; (3) A permanent subcommittee of the ALA's Intellectual Freedom Committee should consider reported abuses of institutional censorship on a regular basis and publicize a final determination of fact in each case; and (4) Librarians should instigate litigation to remove any unreasonable restriction that may exist upon library materials in their collections."

Burke, Roger. *The Murky Cloak; Local Authority–Press Relations.* London, Charles Knight, 1970. 141p.　**1B586**
"The book deals with the working of the 1960 [Admissions to Meetings] Act, the criticisms of the Press and the public, the opinions of the local authorities' associations, and considers complaints by and about local authorities which have been examined by the Press Council." The author suggests a strengthening of the working relationship between councils and their local papers, to persuade more councils to admit the Press to their meetings.

Burkley, Diane E. "Ungagging the Press: Expedited Relief from Prior Restraints on News Coverage of Criminal Proceedings." *Georgetown Law Journal*, 65:81–122, October 1976.　**1B587**
"The urgency of establishing a procedure for speedy relief stems from the Supreme Court's sanction of gag orders [in *Nebraska Press Associa-*

tion v. Stuart (1976)], making their increased imposition likely. It is important to examine the alternative procedures available to speedy review because various procedures are being advocated and adopted." While the Court invalidated the Nebraska gag order, it stated that "the guarantees of freedom of expression are not an absolute prohibition."

[Burks, Joseph.]. *Affidavit [of Joseph Burks, Bookseller].* London, 1798. 4p.
1B588
This London bookseller served two years in prison in Cold-bath-field for selling a work, *Duties of Citizenship.* In his affidavit Burks complains of his cruel and inhuman treatment and the unsanitary conditions of the prison.

Burley, Laurel, comp. *The President's Commission on Obscenity and Pornography: Preliminary Bibliography.* Sacramento, Calif., California Library Association, 1972. 12p. Processed.　**1B589**
Includes numerous references to the Commission and its work appearing in the *Congressional Record*, references not included in this bibliography.

Burnett, Arthur L. "Obscenity: Search and Seizure and the First Amendment." *Denver Law Journal*, 51:41–74, 1974.　**1B590**
"This article will examine the current state of the law on obscenity as a prelude to an analysis of the myriad issues that must be dealt with when the attempts of the federal or state governments to suppress allegedly obscene material conflict with an individual's wishes to retain freedoms guaranteed by the Constitution." Content: The State of the Law of Obscenity. First and Fourth Amendment Problems. The *Miller-Paris Adult Theatre* Sequel.

Burnett, M. Dallas. "The Utah Federal Court's Ban on Sketching of Courtroom Scenes." *Brigham Young University Law Review*, 1975:21–48, 1975.
1B591
"A recent example of judicial infringement on freedom of the press and expression took place in the United States District Court for the District of Utah in 1969 and 1973. That attack came in the form of a 1969 order prohibiting sketching in the courtroom and its environs and a 1973 amendment thereto extending the prohibition to drawings of courtroom scenes regardless of where made. . . . This article will discuss the constitutionality of that order, particularly the 1973 amendment that extends the authority of the judge from the courtroom and its environs to the desks of those who make news decisions for the press."

Burnham, James. "Open House; The Protracted Conflict." *National Review*, 24:90, 4 February 1972.　**1B592**
The author asserts the "need and right of the head of the government to have inviolate confi-

dential relations with his aids" and considers damaging aspects of leakages to the press. However "there is no justification for 99 percent of government 'classifying.' " If classifying stamps were restricted to the minimum and all items declassified after three years unless specifically excepted by executive order, secrecy would be simpler to sustain.

Burnham, Jeffrey M. *Freedom of Speech and the Public Interest in Broadcasting.* Chicago, University of Chicago, 1971. 294p. (Unpublished Ph.D. dissertation)   **1B593**

Burns, James MacGregor. "Speaking of Books; The Historian's Right to See." *New York Times Book Review,* 8 November 1970, pp. 2, 42–44. **1B594**
The author considers "the problem of access by historians and other scholars to classified Government records covering relatively recent military and diplomatic actions of the United States Government." He summarizes: "The need for withholding classified records after a span of a few years is largely a myth. The need for scholars to see and for the public to know is, in a great democracy, urgent and compelling."

Burns, P. T. "Defamatory Libel in Canada; a Recent Illustration of a Rare Crime." *Chitty's Law Journal,* 17:213–17, September 1969. **1B595**
Re: *R. v. Georgia Straight et al* (1969) in which the editors of a British Columbia underground newspaper were convicted under the criminal libel law for comparing the action of a magistrate to that of Pontius Pilate.

Burnside, Janet R. "Private Plaintiff Versus Member News Media—An Application of Gertz v. Robert Welch, Inc." *Ohio State Law Journal,* 36:929–46, 1975. **1B596**
Re: *Walker v. Colorado Springs Sun, Inc.* 538 P.2d 450 (Colo. Sup. Ct. 1975), representing the difficulties facing state courts in interpreting state libel law following the *Gertz* decision by the U.S. Supreme Court.

Burress, Lee A., Jr. *Basic Annotated Bibliography on Censorship.* Champaign, Ill., National Council of Teachers of English, 1970. 7p. Processed. (NCTE/ERIC: Clearinghouse on the Teaching of English) **1B597**
A selected listing of books and articles with special attention to school problems.

Burrows, J. F. "Another Aspect of Freedom of the Press." *New Zealand Law Journal,* 1975:621–27, 2 September 1975. **1B598**
"Recent criticism of the performance of the press in the field of investigative journalism prompts J. F. Burrows to examine the way in which the law hinders the press in the performance of this public duty."

Burt, Donald F. "Inflammatory Publicity in State Criminal Cases." *Nebraska Law Review,* 44:614–34, May 1965. **1B599**
The article summarizes the problem of trial by newspaper and considers the relative merits of such solutions as: "(1) amendment and/or enforcement of Canon 20; (2) adoption by the news media of enforceable codes of ethics; and (3) adoption of criminal legislation which would punish divulgence or publication of prejudicial material. . . . These are considered in light of the decision of the New Jersey Supreme Court in *State v. Van Duyne,* 43 N.J. 369, 204 A.2d 841 (1964)."

Burton, Dwight L. "Literature and the Liberated Spirit." *ALA Bulletin,* 60:904–8 +, October 1966. **1B600**
"I would impose very few restrictions on the kinds of books and other reading materials that we place in our libraries and classrooms. There is an invidious, and often unconscious, censorship on reading imposed at the very point where restriction of the right to read should be most vigorously resisted. I refer, for example, to teachers who insist that students should spend their time reading only 'great' books, literary masterpieces. . . . I refer, too, to policies in libraries of not stocking certain kinds of books, of not permitting some books to be in general circulation. . . . Frequently, though, we underestimate the power of emotion on the part of children and adolescents and their potential for coping with powerful emotion in what they read."

Burton, James A. "Prejudicial Pretrial and Trial Publicity." *Tulane Law Review,* 45:1043–49, June 1971. **1B601**
Re: *Hale v. United States* (1970), in which the Court held that, in the absence of demonstrable jury prejudice or highly pervasive and prejudicial publicity, there was no reversible error.

Buse, Isabel E. "F.T.C. Guide Banning TV Ads That Entice Children: Soft Decision or Assertive Policy?" *Capital University Law Review,* 4:109–22, 1975. **1B602**
"This note is specifically addressed to the limitation of the proposed F.T.C. Guide which bans premiums and similar devices directed over television networks to children. It includes an examination of the F.T.C.'s administrative functions with regard to children as a special group of consumers, and a discussion of the advisability of broadening such a guide in scope, or in the alternative, of elevating its status to an industry rule."

Buser, Paul J. "The Newsman's Privilege: Protection of Confidential Sources of Information Against Government Subpoenas." *St. Louis Univer-*

sity Law Journal, 15:181–201, Fall 1970. **1B603**
"It is the purpose of this comment to (1) document and analyze the events of the past year which indicate that the subpoena has been used by the government for political purposes to search out the sources of revolutionary dissent in order that it may be suppressed and perhaps to punish the press for publicizing the activities of the dissidents, and (2) to discuss the First Amendment limitations upon the use of the subpoena in such situations."

Bush, Chilton R., *ed. Free Press and Fair Trial; Some Dimensions of the Problem.* Athens, Ga., University of Georgia Press, 1970. 133p. **1B604**
"The relationship of jury verdicts in felony cases and pretrial publicity is a field of study that has been somewhat neglected by both legal scholars and communication specialists. To partially remedy the insufficiency of objective evidence, the American Newspaper Publishers Association Foundation in November 1947 commissioned three studies to measure the dimensions of the problem." The studies, conducted by Fred S. Siebert, George Hough, III, and Walter Wilcox, are reported here. They attempted to answer such questions as "How important, really, is the problem? Are there a good many or only a few cases in which it is possible for pretrial publicity to influence a jury verdict? Do judges who have tried felony cases believe that the problem is of great importance?" Each of the three studies is entered in this bibliography under the author. Bush summarizes the findings on pages 111–17. The appendix contains the text of press-bench-bar agreements from Burlington, Vt., and the states of Minnesota, Oregon, and Washington.

Busha, Charles H. *The Attitudes of Midwestern Public Librarians toward Intellectual Freedom and Censorship.* Bloomington, Ind., Indiana University, 1971. 175p. (Ph.D. dissertation, University Microfilms, no. 71-29, 561) **1B605**
"The purposes of this opinion research among Midwestern public librarians were the determination of: (1) the extent to which librarians accept intellectual freedom principles of the *Library Bill of Rights* and the *Freedom to Read* statement, (2) the attitudes of librarians toward censorship, (3) the relationship of librarians' censorship attitudes to their attitudes toward selected authoritarian beliefs, and (4) the relationship between librarians intellectual freedom and censorship attitudes." Major conclusions were: "(1) All of the librarians obtained either low or intermediate intellectual freedom scores, which indicates a very high degree of agreement among the respondents with statements favoring intellectual freedom; however, a marked disparity existed between the attitudes of some librarians toward intellec-

tual freedom as a concept and their attitudes toward censorship as an activity. (2) The attitudes of 14 percent of the librarians were predominantly sympathetic toward censorship; 22 percent expressed strong anticensorship attitudes; and the remaining 64 percent were neither highly favorable nor unfavorable toward censorship. (3) Librarians who agreed with authoritarian beliefs also tended, very strongly, to approve of censorship measures." The findings are also published as part of the author's book, *Freedom versus Suppression and Censorship*, and are summarized in *Newsletter on Intellectual Freedom* (IFC-ALA), September 1971.

————. *Authoritarianism and Censorship: Attitudes and Opinions of Students in the Graduate Library School of Indiana University. A Report of an Exploratory Project Conducted as a Preliminary for a Proposed Nationwide Study of American Public Librarians and Intellectual Freedom.* Bloomington, Ind., Indiana University, 1969. 48p. (Condensed in *Journal of Education for Librarianship*, Fall 1970)   **1B606**
"This study attempts to measure the attitudes toward intellectual freedom held by a group of future librarians and to correlate these findings with certain syndromes of authoritarianism as reported in 'The Authoritarian Personality,' by T. W. Adorno, and others."

————. *Freedom versus Suppression and Censorship: With a Study of the Attitudes of Midwestern Public Librarians and a Bibliography of Censorship.* Preface by Allan Pratt; Introduction by Peter Hiatt. Littleton, Colo., Libraries Unlimited, 1972. 240p. (Research Studies in Library Science, no. 8)   **1B607**
Part I deals with the nature of censorship: a discussion of censorship in action, including the *Ginzburg* case; the protection of individual rights (freedom of choice and conventionality vs. creativity); book selection in public libraries, including the handling of controversial issues; and the role of the public librarian in facing censorship. Part II is a report on the author's study of attitudes of midwestern public librarians toward intellectual freedom and censorship, drawn from his doctoral dissertation. Part III is a bibliography of censorship, 1950–71. Appended are a number of basic documents on intellectual freedom adopted by the American Library Association, including the Library Bill of Rights, the School Library Bill of Rights, and the Freedom to Read statement.

————. "Intellectual Freedom and Censorship: The Climate of Opinion in Midwestern Public Libraries." *Library Quarterly*, 42:283–301, July 1972. **1B608**
"An attempt to quantify the attitudes of more than 3,200 public librarians toward intellectual freedom, censorship, and certain antidemocratic ideas is reported in this article." The study revealed a positive, but far from perfect, relationship between the attitudes of librarians toward intellectual freedom and censorship. Women librarians were found to be more procensorship than men librarians; the greater the age the more the librarian tended to agree with censorship measures; the larger the community the less the support of censorship; anticensorship librarians had completed more years of formal education; and heads of public service departments were the most permissive and liberal of the five groups of job classifications.

Bustamante, Luis C., and Forrest W. Lewis. "Pornography, the Local Option." *Baylor Law Review*, 26:97–107, Winter 1974.   **1B609**
"The purpose of this article is to note the recent Supreme Court cases on obscenity; discuss their effect on prior decisions; familiarize the reader with the new guidelines; and reflect on the probable impact of these new developments."

Butler, Hubert. "The County Libraries and the Censorship." *Irish Writing*, 7:66–70, July 1949.   **1B610**
A county librarian of twenty years ago recalls the difficulty in getting the support of Irish county councils and the general public who looked upon public libraries as dangerous agencies. They have become so dominated and suppressed by local forces that competent librarians are difficult to obtain and libraries have failed to be centers of culture.

Button, John. "Obscenity and Indecency Laws." In Melbourne University. *The Law and the Printer, the Publisher and the Journalist. The Collected Papers of a Seminar at Melbourne University on August 12, 1971.* Melbourne, Antony Whitlock, 1971, pp. 65–72. **1B611**
A summary of Australian obscenity law in general and Victorian law in particular, noting that while Australian state laws are broadly similar, interpretations vary widely. Federal obscenity laws are administered through control of broadcasting, postal service, and Customs. The major defects in Customs censorship are the broad powers it gives to the Minister, the unreasonable distinctions in the handling of books over against magazines, plays, films, and other items, the difficulty in appeals, and the fact that a work cleared under federal laws may still be subject to state laws. The author recommends: (1) that obscenity laws be removed from the area of criminal prosecution; (2) that the *Roth* or similar test replace the existing obscenity definition; (3) that community standards be established by a panel broadly representing the community, rather than by a judge; (4) that elitism in a censorship panel should be avoided; and (5) that the ultimate decision whether a work is obscene should be removed from the Minister for Customs and Excise and vested in a National Literary Board of Review.

Button, Robert. "Michigan Paper Bears Censorship Threat." *Communication*, 5(1):10–13, Fall 1971.   **1B612**
Controversy over the student newspaper, *The Tower*, Grosse Pointe (Mich.) South High School. The case resulted in strong statements supporting responsible freedom for the student press being adopted by the Board of Education; and the staff of the paper put in writing a statement of philosophy and policy as guidelines for the future.

Byrne, Donn, and John Lambeth. "The Effect of Erotic Stimuli on Sex Arousal, Evaluative Responses, and Subsequent Behavior." *Technical Report of the ⸢U.S.⸣ Commission on Obscenity and Pornography*, 8:41–67, 1971.   **1B613**
"Within the very real limits of the present experiment, it may be seen that brief exposure to sexual stimuli elicits strong and quite divergent emotional responses, including sexual arousal, and that specific sexual themes are reliably different in their arousal qualities. Males and females do not differ in their overall sexual response to such stimuli but there are specific themes which members of each sex find more arousing than do members of the opposite sex. Among the more unusual findings was that instructions to imagine the activities of each theme led to much greater arousal than exposure to either pictorial or prose presentations of the themes. Sexual arousal and judgments of pornography appear to be independent dimensions. Judgments concerning what is and is not pornographic appear to be based on a negative affective response to the stimuli and to be related to the desire to impose legal restrictions on such stimuli. Despite the effects on emotional reactions and the wide range of beliefs concerning the necessity of legal restrictions against sexual stimuli, the effects of the stimuli of the present experiment on the reported sexual behavior of this particular group of subjects was negligible. It is possible that the emotional reactions to erotic stimuli are of greater interest and importance than the behavioral consequences of exposure to such stimuli."

Byrne, Edward T. "Government Seizures of Imported Obscene Matter: Section 305 of the Tariff Act of 1930 and Recent Supreme Court Obscenity Decisions." *Columbia Journal of Transnational Law*, 13:114–42, 1974. **1B614**
"This comment will examine the impact of the 1973 obscenity decisions on federal attempts to regulate the importation of obscene matter. Is it now possible for Macon, Georgia, to dictate the standards for determining obscenity which must be applied by customs officers in the New York port of entry? If it is, is it both administratively feasible and compatible with existing international obligations of the United States

relating to the suppression of obscene publications?"

[Byrne, Robert.] *Persecutions of Protestants in the Year 1845, as detailed in a full and correct report of the Trial at Tralee, on Thursday, March 20, 1845, for a Libel on the Rev. Charles Gayer.* . . . Dublin, Philip Dixon Hardy, 1845. 90p. **1B615**

Byrne was editor of the *Kerry Examiner*. The paper had carried several scurrilous articles describing a local protestant minister as an "itinerant liar, imposter," lying to obtain money for his own "animal wants." Byrne was found guilty and fined £40 damages, all the jury thought he could afford to pay.

Byrnes, J. V. "Our First Book: Trial and Conviction of Dr. William Bland

for the Composition of Seditious Libel Against Governor Macquarie." *Biblionews and Australian Notes & Queries* (Sydney), 15?:22–23, August 1962; 15?:25–27, September 1962. **1B616**

C

"CLA Regional Meetings, 'In Defense of the Freedom to Read.' " *Connecticut Libraries*, 12(1):24–28, Winter 1970. **1C1**
A report of panel discussions by librarians, booksellers, and Connecticut state representatives on the topic of censorship and the freedom to read.

"Cable Television and Content Regulation: The FCC, the First Amendment and the Electronic Newspaper." *New York University Law Review*, 51:133–47, April 1976. **1C2**
"Cable, potentially the greatest revolution in audiovisual communications since the invention of television, is in danger of regulatory strangulation. In protecting the status quo, the FCC has neglected to protect the public. . . . The current content regulations are unjustifiable and contrary to the FCC statutory duty. Most important, by constricting cable content the FCC is imposing prior restraints that stifle free speech. Government has very narrow authority to restrict the content of a newspaper. It should have no greater authority to restrict the content of cable television."

"Cable Television and the First Amendment." *Columbia Law Review*, 77:1008–38, June 1971. **1C3**
"This Note is concerned with the application of the first amendment to CATV. The first half examines the rationales that have been suggested to justify a control over television programming stricter than that constitutionally permissible in other media and the applicability of these theories to a cable-based system. A model for governmental regulation of CATV program content within constitutional bounds is proposed in the second half."

Cades, J. R. "Power of the Courts to Protect Journalists' Confidential Sources of Information: An Examination of Proposed Shield Legislation." *Hawaii Bar Journal*, 11:35–45, Summer 1974. **1C4**

Cage, Penelope B. *A Constitutional Dilemma: Censorship of the Obscene*. Charlottesville, Va., University of Virginia, 1967. 173p. (Ph.D. dissertation, University Microfilms, no. 67–17,594) **1C5**
"The Supreme Court has become entangled in a dilemma of its own making: by basing the *Roth* decision on the idea that obscene expression is not protected by the First Amendment, the Court made it imperative that the term 'obscene' be precisely defined. This has been found to be impossible. Then in an attempt to circumvent the demands of the *Roth* decision without disavowing it, the Court established a new test in which censorship did not depend upon the nature of the material. By so doing the majority has once again failed to adequately protect nonobscene material. The *Ginzburg* decision testifies to that."

Caginalp, Aydin S. "Newsman's Privilege." *Tulane Law Review*, 47:1184–91, June 1973. **1C6**
Re: *Branzburg v. Hayes*, 408 U.S. 665 (1972).

Cahill, Robert V. " 'Fairness' and the FCC." *Federal Communications Bar Journal*, 21:17–25, 1967. **1C7**
A clarification and defense of the fairness doctrine by the legal assistant to the FCC chairman.

Cain, Robert E., and Georgeanne Roe. "The Liberals, the Conservatives and the Seesaw." *Bay State Librarian*, 63:8–14, October 1974. **1C8**
The story of the passage of a state obscenity law in Massachusetts in the wake of the U.S. Supreme Court's decisions, and Massachusetts Library Association's efforts to see that the law was one they could live with.

[Caine, Hall.] *Statement of the evidence in chief of Hall Caine before the Joint-Committee on Stage-Plays (Censorship and Theatre Licensing)*. [Isle of Man?] Printed privately; Confidential, 1909. 32p. **1C9**

The author was one of forty–nine witnesses brought before the Select Committee to inquire into the censorship of stage plays under the Theatres Act of 1843 (G248). Caine argued that the present censorship implied that the theater was merely a place of amusement and that all serious drama was suspect. While recognizing the need of a central licensing authority, he would take it out of the hands of the Lord Chamberlain and give it to local authority with limited powers.

Cairns, Robert B., J. C. N. Paul, and J. Wishner. "Psychological Assumptions in Sex Censorship: An Evaluative Review of Recent Research (1961–1968)." *Technical Report of the [U.S.] Commission on Obscenity and Pornography*, 1:5–21, 1971. **1C10**
This review of empirical evidence relevant to the issue of sex censorship brings up to date a 1962 review by the same authors (C4) and was presented at the first meeting of the Commission.

"Calculated Misstatements of Fact Not Protected By First Amendment Guarantees of Free Speech and Press." *Utah Law Review*, 1969:118–39, January 1969. **1C11**
Comment on *St. Amant v. Thompson* (1968), in which the U.S. Supreme Court, reversing the Louisiana State Court, "held that the 'actual malice' test for defeating the free speech privilege against liability for defamation was misinterpreted and misapplied. 'Reckless disregard' was interpreted to signify that a defendant at the time of publication was either aware of falsity or entertained serious doubts as to the truth of his statement."

Calder, John. "Censorship and the Publisher." In Raymond Astbury, *ed.*, *Libraries & the Book Trade in Britain. Papers Delivered at a Symposium Held at Liverpool School of Librarianship, May 1967*. . . . London, Archon Books & Clive Bingley, 1968, pp. 105–15. **1C12**
The publisher of such controversial novels as

Tropic of Cancer, *Naked Lunch*, and *Last Exit to Brooklyn* discusses the present state of intellectual freedom, the difference between obscenity and pornography (the former reflecting the evils of life—murder, war, and cruelty of man—the latter a form of writing intended to titillate). There is no precensorship in England but every publisher must take his chance under the law. A serious publisher will not allow a lawyer to decide whether or not a book is to be published or to perform the role of censor. He denies that books corrupt the reader. Reading reflects the interests and inclinations of the reader and is more likely to restrain and broaden his knowledge than to inflame him. He refers to proposed legislation which would permit a jury rather than a magistrate to rule on obscenity, the former less likely to be prejudiced than the latter. The author believes censorship is on the way out. "The only genuine morality is that which the individual, through his own logical processes, decides is true and right for himself."

————. "A Reply to Pamela Hansford Johnson on 'The Pornography of Violence'." *Encounter*, 34:85–90, April 1970.   **1C13**
An answer to Pamela Hansford Johnson (*Encounter*, February 1970) who "is now leading the brigade that wants to swing the pendulum back" toward censorship of violence in the mass media. "We must stop worrying about the symptoms of our disease, the violence that portrays society, and look at the disease itself, the causes of that violence." The author was a member of the Working Party created by the Arts Council of Great Britain to study British obscenity laws.

————. "What Is Obscene?" *Spectator*, 221:194–95, 9 August 1968.   **1C14**
The publisher of *Last Exit to Brooklyn* discusses the case against the book, successfully appealed from a conviction under the Obscene Publications Act 1959. Contradictions in the law call for clear directions to the jury on vital semantic points.

Calder-Marshall, Arthur. *Lewd, Blasphemous & Obscene; Being the Trials and Tribulations of Sundry Founding Fathers of Today's Alternative Societies, Most Notably, William Hone . . . Richard Carlile . . . George Jacob Holyoake . . . & George William Foote. . . . To Which Is Appended the Strange History of Sexual Inversion Written by Havelock Ellis. . . .* London, Hutchinson, 1972. 248p.   **1C15**
The story of four nineteenth-century blasphemers who became martyrs to the freedom of the press: William Hone, tried for blasphemy on three successive days in 1817 and acquitted after speaking for twenty-one hours; Richard Carlile, who between 1819 and 1834 spent two days out of every three in jail; George Jacob Holyoake, imprisoned in Gloucester for six months for twenty-six words uttered in Cheltenham in 1842; and

George W. Foote, who, being sentenced by Mr. Justice North to twelve months hard labour for blasphemy in 1883, said "it is a sentence worthy of your creed." There is also a brief account of Charles Bradlaugh "who drove his ambitious young subaltern George William Foote to seek in prison the fame which he could not attract by ability alone"; and also the indictment of George Bedborough for publishing and selling "a certain lewd, wicked, bawdy, scandalous and obscene libel, in the form of a book entitled *Studies in the Psychology of Sex . . .* by Havelock Ellis."

Calderone, Mary S. " 'Pornography' As a Public Health Problem." *American Journal of Public Health*, 63:374–76, March 1972.   **1C16**
"When is the portrayal of explicit sexual behaviour a form of social 'pollution' with consequences for various members of the community? The need to deal with the problem in behavioral and value terms is stressed."

Caldwell, Earl. "Ask Me, I Know—I Was the Test Case." *Saturday Review*, 55(32):4–6, 5 August 1972.   **1C17**
The defendant in the case, *United States v. Caldwell* (1972), in which the U.S. Supreme Court in a 5–4 decision ruled against the right of a journalist's privilege, tells his own story, his associations with the Black Panthers, and the reasons for refusing to testify before the Grand Jury.

"Caldwell Aftermath: A National Shield Law." *Bulletin of the American Association of Newspaper Editors*, 562:12–15, September 1972.   **1C18**
"The heart of the problem is that any subpoena of a newsman tends to dry up news sources. And the publicizing of such subpoenas has a chain reaction with potential informants. A negative, silencing reaction. The court's opinion [in the *Caldwell* case] can't help but have such a multiplying effect."

Califano, Joseph A., Jr. "Shielding the Press: The First Amendment Is Enough." *New Republic*, 168:21–23, 5 May 1973.   **1C19**
The author examines what the Supreme Court did and did not decide in the *Branzburg* case [*Branzburg v. Hayes*, 1972], and opposes the variety of press shield laws before Congress. "In the long run the judiciary has been a more vigilant protector of First Amendment rights than either the executive or the legislative branches."

California. Assembly. Committee on Criminal Procedure. *The California Obscenity Laws*. San Francisco, The Committee, 1963. 113p. Processed.   **1C20**
Includes the following articles: Enforcement of Obscenity Laws by Murray L. Schwartz. Pornography and Juvenile Behavior by William Beach. Social Effect of Pornographic

Literature—Is It Criminal in Nature? by Leo Lowenthal. Free Speech and the First Amendment by Robert O'Neil. Redeeming Social Importance—Literary Fact or Fiction by Eugene Burdick.

California. Assembly. Interim Committee on Judiciary. Subcommittee on Free Press—Fair Trial. *Final Report*. Sacramento, Calif., The Assembly of the State of California, 1967. 48p. (Assembly Interim Committee Reports, vol. 23, no. 8)   **1C21**
The Committee recommended the discontinuance of the bar against photographers and broadcasters from courtrooms and proposed a joint legislative study of the most effective way of testing the "Colorado Plan" in California. The Committee heard testimony from thirty-eight witnesses from bar and press and viewed several experiments. Text of testimony is included with the report.

California. Senate. Special Committee on Pornographic Plays. *An Investigation of the Production of "The Beard" on the Campus of California State College at Fullerton*. [Sacramento, Calif.], Senate of the State of California, 1968. 200p.   **1C22**
A report of an investigation of the performance at California State College at Fullerton of *Beard*, "a most objectionable and notorious play containing hundreds of obscenities and depicting as its climax a perverted act of sexual intercourse, and constituting a situation of intolerable dimension . . . ," to determine whether present law was adequate to prevent such recurrence and to insure proper discipline of students and faculty should such an incident recur. A portion of the script is reproduced together with testimony from various witnesses, statements from college faculty and administrators, and pictures of a San Francisco performance taken by the police.

California. University. Special Commission on the Student Press. *The Student Newspaper. Report of the Special Commission on the Student Press to the President of the University of California*. Washington, D.C., American Council on Education, 1970. 58p.   **1C23**
The Commission, headed by Norman E. Isaacs, president of the American Society of Newspaper Editors, examined the student press on the campuses of the University of California and expanded its study to look at college journalism elsewhere in the nation. The Commission considered such questions as: How effective are campus newspapers in meeting student needs? How should the student paper be financed and supervised? What is obscene language, and how should its use in

campus publications be viewed? Is the student paper an "official" publication in the university? The Commission made eight recommendations. "It is the Commission's first and basic recommendation that it be accepted and made repeatedly clear to all concerned—regents, administrators, and campus newspaper staffs—that these newspapers are not 'official' organs of the university."

[California League Enlisting Action Now.] "Obscenity: A Report." *Los Angeles Times*, 6 November 1966. (Ten-page "political advertisement" supplement) **1C24**
The "Committee for YES on Proposition 16" issued this paid political supplement to the *Los Angeles Times* carrying arguments and testimonials favoring the antipornography proposition before the California voters.

California Library Association. "Intellectual Freedom Update." *California Library Association Newsletter*, 15(12):1–35, December 1973. **1C25**
The entire issue deals with intellectual freedom: Questions and Answers with the Supreme Court [regarding recent obscenity decisions], a letter from ALA president Edward G. Holley regarding the decisions, the ALA Council resolution, and various ALA documents relating to intellectual freedom including the Library Bill of Rights.

Camp, Laurie S. "Applying Due Process to Gag Rules and Orders: ABA Recommended Court Procedure to Accommodate Rights of Fair Trial and Free Press." *Nebraska Law Review*, 55:427–39, 1976. **1C26**
"This article will first explore the structure of the ABA[American Bar Association], proposal and how it could improve the current system of judicial restraints by reducing unneeded gag orders, preserving first amendment freedoms of speech and press without the expense and delay of traditional court procedures, and eliminating the hidden jeopardy of standing gag rules. It will then examine the two pressing issues left unsolved: When does the Constitution allow a judge to gag a journalist, lawyer, or other individual interested in a trial? Should one who violates an improper or erroneous order be punished?"

Campbell, Alexander. *Trial and Self-Defense of Alexander Campbell, Operative, before the Exchequer Court, Edinburgh, for Printing and Publishing "The Tradesman," Contrary to the Infamous Gagging Act. . . .* Glasgow, W. & W. Miller, 1835. 32p. **1C27**
The case involved the sale of a newspaper, *The*

Tradesman, without being duly stamped. The prosecution pointed out that the sole purpose of the tax was to collect revenue and not to interfere with freedom of the press. The proprietor, Alexander Campbell, argued his own case, declaring that the paper was not really sold but given away, with customers invited to make contributions; that it was intended for the poor workingman and was not in competition with the established press. He cited precedence in the recent trial of *King v. Hetherington* involving the *Poor Man's Guardian*. Judge Coburn was not convinced, although he commended Campbell for his efforts, and charged the jury to find Campbell guilty, which they did but recommended leniency.

Campbell, Brahm L. "The Quebec Moving Pictures Act: Some Constitutional Notes." *McGill Law Journal*, 11:131–36, 1965. **1C28**
Criticism of the Act and the Board of Film Censors which it created and which, the author believes, may be unconstitutional. The Act constitutes "a prior restraint of the worst kind and only succeeds in stifling the normal development of a free society."

Campbell, Dennis. "Free Press in Sweden and America: Who's the Fairest of Them All?" *Southwestern University Law Review*, 8:61–108, 1976. **1C29**
The article deals with the depth of similarity between the press in Sweden and the United States with respect to the guarantees of a free press. It begins with a summary of the broad legal basis for free press in the two countries, then analyzes the issues of common concern within three major subject areas: "(1) the flow of information, (2) the ability of the public to command space in the print media, and (3) the relationship of the press to the right of privacy."

Campbell, Enid. "Public Access to Government Documents." *Australian Law Journal*, 41:73–89, 31 July 1967. **1C30**
"The object of this essay is to examine the arguments for and against publicity, to outline the provisions by which American legislatures have attempted to reinforce the public's right to know, and to compare these provisions with English and Australian laws respecting official secrets." Americans enjoy distinctly better facilities for finding out what their government does than do Australians. There is a traditional characteristic of confidentiality in Australian public service, not so much prescribed by law as by custom. Government bureaus need to be more free with information and the news media need to be more aggressive in covering public affairs.

———, and Harry Whitmore. *Freedom in Australia*. Sydney, Sydney University Press, 1966. 298p. **1C31**
Chapters on Public Meetings, Radio and Television, Theatre and Cinema, The Press,

Obscenity, Defamation, Contempt of Court and Contempt of Parliament, Security of the State and Freedom of Speech, and Freedom of Religion.

Campbell, Laurence R. "Principals' Attitudes Toward Freedom of the Press." *Quill & Scroll*, 50(3):19–23, February–March, 1976. **1C32**
Do principals support freedom of the press for student journalists? What is the attitude of principals and advisers toward censorship of student publications, the enforcement of the First Amendment, and control of student journalists? The report compares the attitudes of 145 principals and 317 newspaper advisers as determined from a questionnaire survey.

Campbell, Lawrence, and Vera M. Jones. "Freedom of Speech and the Communist Conspiracy: A Search for First Amendment Standards." *Journal of Urban Law*, 47:427–51, 1969–70. **1C33**
"The purpose of this article is two-fold: (1) to present for evaluation the threat of the Communist conspiracy, and (2) to diagram the clear and present danger doctrine in the light of such a threat." The authors find such a threat "real and perhaps substantial" and suggest alternative methods for dealing with the threat and the implication of these methods to first amendment freedoms.

Campbell, Will D. "West Virginia Controversy. Whose Code Do We Follow?" *Christianity & Crisis*, 35:68–73, 31 March 1975. **1C34**
The news media that have widely castigated the West Virginia parents for their objections to the use of certain obscenities in school books have themselves avoided spelling out exactly what words were objectionable, often leaving blanks for the offending words, because the media themselves operate within a self-imposed code. The author argues that what the parents wanted in West Virginia was not so different from what parents want in other parts of the nation and what is routine in other public institutions. To attribute the complaints to their being ignorant and fundamentalist hillbillies is unfair. While there were elements of religious and racial bigotry in the controversy, the author questions whether there is any basic difference between those who are demanding changes in textbook treatment of racial minorities and women and those who want to remove books because they conflict with their codes of sexual morality. Both groups favor censorship. The West Virginia controversy raised the broader issue of providing public education in a pluralistic society.

Canada. Canadian Radio-Television and Telecommunications Commission. *Symposium on Television Violence*. Ottawa, The Commission, 1976. 252p. **1C35**
Representatives of the television industry,

writers, social scientists, and legal experts examine the issues in television violence and what is known about its effects, and express their opinions on the problem and possible solutions.

Canada. Law Reform Commission. Prohibited and Regulated Conduct Project. *Criminal Law: Obscenity. A Study Paper [by Richard G. Fox], Published by the Prohibited and Regulated Conduct Project*. Ottawa, The Commission, 1972. 20p., 134p. Bilingual. **1C36**
The Project staff, in a preface to the study paper by Professor Fox, notes the uncertainty of the law of obscenity, the unevenness of its interpretation and application throughout Canada, and the question of its relevance as part of the criminal law. They raise such questions as: How is obscenity to be defined? What possible effects are the concern of the criminal law? Should the audience be considered? They express these tentative views: that "the prohibition of obscene matter should be maintained and applied strictly where children are concerned"; that the "flood of advertising and public display of sexual material should be eliminated so that persons who have no interest in such material and who do not want access to it will be protected from the nuisance that it represents"; that films should be rated, not prohibited, "according to the extent to which they deal explicitly with sex, in order to determine whether children and adolescents can be admitted to them, and to enable the public to make an informed choice of entertainment"; that the present power of the Canadian Radio-Television Commission to regulate program content be continued, because of the general audience reached by broadcasting; and that "where adults are concerned, the possession, sale and distribution of 'sexually explicit material' should no longer be penalized. Adults should be free to determine their own conduct in this regard." The study paper by Professor Fox is entered under his name.

Canada. Privy Council. *To Know and Be Known: Report of the Task Force on Government Information*. Ottawa, Queen's Printer, 1969. 2 vols. **1C37**
Includes a discussion of the role of information in a participatory democracy, the right of access and government information systems, strategic gatekeepers of federal news, and case studies in current information process.

Canada. Senate. Committee on Mass Media. *Report on the Special Senate Committee on Mass Media*. Ottawa, Queen's Printer, 1970. 3 vols. **1C38**
The Committee was appointed "to consider and report upon the ownership and control of the major means of mass public communications in Canada, and in particular . . . to examine and report upon the extent and nature of their impact and influence on the Canadian public." The Committee concluded (vol. I) that there were "a number of aspects of the media's structure and performance which are

capable of improvement" but very little that government could or should do to bring them about. The job was for the media owners and the professionals in the media. One government action proposed, however, was the creation of a Press Ownership Review Board to represent the public interest in future newspaper mergers. Owners and operators were urged to give greater attention to program quality, to consider the establishment of a national Press Council, to support a serious study of the social consequences of advertising, and to identify newspaper ownership on their editorial pages. Advice was also given to the professional workers in the media and to the general public on ways of improving the media. Volume II, Words, Music, and Dollars, is a study of the economics of publishing and broadcasting in Canada, conducted by a private firm. The report deals with concentration of media, economics of the media (advertising, print industry, broadcasting industry, and cable television), and such factors affecting concentration and economics as taxation, salaries, technology, and postal rates. Volume III, Good, Bad, or Simply Inevitable? is a report on an audience and readership survey conducted by a private firm and indicating the views of the public in such matters as the use of sex, love, violence, and drugs in the media; censorship and controls; advertising; ownership; and general image.

Canada. Senate. Special Committee on the Criminal Code (Hate Propaganda). *First Proceedings on Bill S-5, Intitled an Act to Amend the Criminal Code. No. 1, Wednesday, February 14, 1968; No. 2, Thursday, February 29, 1968; No. 3, Thursday, March 7, 1968*. Ottawa, Queen's Printer, 1968. 16p., 61p., 22p. **1C39**
A Committee, chaired by J. Harper Prowse, held hearings on a proposal to amend the Canadian Criminal Code to outlaw hate propaganda. The witness at the first session was the director of the Criminal Law Section of the Department of Justice; witnesses at the second session were representatives from the Canadian Jewish Congress, and Professor Maxwell Cohen, Faculty of Law, McGill University; witnesses at the third session were representatives of the Quebec Conservative Party.

Canadian Jewish Congress. *Brief of the Canadian Jewish Congress on Bill S-21 (Hate Propaganda) to the Senate Standing Committee on Constitutional and Legal Affairs*. Ottawa, The Congress, 1969. 22p. **1C40**
The Canadian Jewish Congress believes that legislation curbing incitement to violence and hate propaganda is called for and, with some comments, supports Bill S-21.

Canadian Library Association. "Porn in the Nursery: Brief to the Prohibited and Regulated Conduct Project of the Law Reform Commission of

Canada. . . ." *Feliciter*, 20(12):16, 25–27, December 1974. **1C41**
Committee draft of a statement on the study paper on obscenity by Richard G. Fox and the Project's preface to that study paper. "Protecting youngsters from supposed risk of distorted sexual learning, moral danger and the potentiality of delinquency compromises their civil liberties, interferes with their freedom of expression and anyway, it's virtually impossible."—Editor

Canavan, Francis. "Freedom of Speech and Press: For What Purpose?" *American Journal of Jurisprudence*, 16:95–142, 1971. **1C42**
The thesis of this study is that to get at the real problem of defining or delimiting the right of free speech and press it is necessary to "start from the purposes which the right is intended to serve, taken in relation to other purposes which the Constitution also intends to achieve." The author concludes that "not everything that can be labelled 'speech' or 'expression,' or 'utterance' is worth protecting. Much of it must be granted immunity for the sake of preserving the freedom of speech and press that serves the ends of the First Amendment. But not all of it need be or should be rendered immune from legal regulation for the general good. . . . The quest for rationality in interpreting the Amendment's guarantees of freedom of speech and press forces us to ask, in the end, what the freedom is for."

Canby, William C., Jr. "The First Amendment and the State as Editor: Implications for Public Broadcasting." *Texas Law Review*, 52:1123–65, August 1974. **1C43**
"The editorial function in public television . . . may not receive exactly the same type of protection as in the case of the state university press. But there is good reason to protect the freedom of editors of public broadcasting programs from sporadic intervention from above or outside, particularly when the intervention is politically motivated." While the courts cannot protect the appropriations of public broadcasting, it can protect the editorial function below that level. "Public broadcasting cannot survive an operation performed with as blunt an instrument as the public forum approach suggested in *DNC [Columbia Broadcasting System, Inc. v. Democratic National Committee*, 1973] which admits of no content control, and therefore no editing, and which mandates virtually uncontrollable public access to public broadcasting channels."

———. "The First Amendment Right to Persuade: Access to Radio and Television." *UCLA Law Review*, 19:723–58, June 1972. **1C44**
While the courts have recognized the utility of

public access to the media for the purpose of providing information in public debate, to view access "wholly in informational terms is to distort the realities of broadcast advertising and to deny other fundamental first amendment interests. For the right of political association must ultimately include the opportunity to win power for one's cause or one's party. An essential step in this political fruition will often be a media advertising campaign likely to be repetitious and low in informational value. These attributes, however, do not make it undeserving of first amendment protection."

Canham, Erwin D. *The World Flow of News*. Tucson, Ariz., University of Arizona Press, 1970. 20p. (John Peter Zenger Award Lectures) **1C45**
The editor–in–chief of the *Christian Science Monitor* assesses the adequacy of the nation's press coverage of international affairs. Except for Communist China there is a fairly competent flow of news from the nations of the world, but high cost of covering world news is a limiting factor. He believes that, with some notable exceptions, the press did a creditable job in covering Vietnam. Most papers do not use as much international news as is available to them, and there is need for more in-depth coverage and interpretive reporting. He writes of his own fruitless efforts following World War II in behalf of intergovernmental agreements on free flow of information because of different philosophies of freedom; the more fruitful work of three international professional organizations; the International Federation of Newspaper Editors, the International Press Institute, and the Inter-American Press Association.

Cannady, Kenneth S. "Defamation and the First Amendment: The Elements and Application of the Reckless-Disregard Test." *North Carolina Law Review*, 50:390–403, February 1972. **1C46**
Comment on court interpretation of the "reckless-disregard" standard with respect to personal libel. Two factors must be considered in determining whether a defendant's conduct is justifiable: the magnitude of the public's interest, and the burden of verifying the truth or falsity of the subject matter. The author finds the standard complex and difficult to apply and believes the necessary fact-finding will place an unhappy burden on the courts.

Canon, Bradley C. "The FCC's Disposition of 'Fairness Doctrine' Complaints." *Journal of Broadcasting*, 13:315–24, Summer 1969. **1C47**
"This article reports the result of an investigation into the nature and disposition of all 'fairness' complaints received ₍by the Federal Communications Commission₎ over a two year period." The author concludes: "These com-

plaints have been lodged by political, economic, or religious interest groups. They are appealing from a denial of free air time to rebut a personal attack or a one-sided presentation concerning a specific controversial issue. They are primarily directed against syndicated, ideological programs that often espouse the causes of the 'far right.' And they are most often filed against radio stations in smaller communities."

————. *The FCC's "Fairness" Doctrine: Its Substance, Enforcement and Impact*. Madison, Wis., University of Wisconsin, 1967. 374p. (Ph.D. dissertation, University Microfilms, no. 67–16,903) **1C48**
The study revealed an extremely passive enforcement stance on the part of the Federal Communications Commission, leaving compliance with the fairness doctrine largely to the settling of complaints and showing timidity in punishing obvious violators. Inaction was attributed to a lack of adequate "middle range" sanctions, a low priority of the doctrine in allocation of enforcement resources, policy disagreement among the Commissioners, and fear of Congressional retribution.

Capaldi, Nicholas. "Censorship and Social Stability in J. S. Mill." *Mill Newsletter*, 9(1):12–16, Fall 1973. **1C49**
The author defends John Stuart Mill against charges of contradictions on freedom of discussion as expressed in his *On Liberty* (M339) and a passage in his *System of Logic*.

Cardno, J. A. "Censorship and Conformity." *Australian Psychologist*, 8:128–38, July 1973. **1C50**
"The paper will try to show how much conformity and, therefore, how much censorship is enough by relating conformity behavior to censorship mechanisms. Numerous examples are cited of self-censorship applied to works of literature."

Carlson, Elliot. "Now It Can Be Told: Declassifying Secrets, An Enormous Project, Turns Up Little So Far." *Wall Street Journal*, 180:1, 24, 6 September 1972. **1C51**
A popularly written account of the enormous bulk of classified documents in the National Archives, what is being done to declassify them, and the criticism by scholars of the difficulties in obtaining and using material.

Carlson, Glenn H. *Fair Trial vs. Free Press: Anxiety over Values in Conflict*. Washington, D.C., American University, 1968. 124p. (Unpublished Master's thesis) **1C52**
The author concludes that certain types of pretrial information are not protected by the First Amendment and violate the Sixth Amendment by interfering with the development of an impartial jury.

Carlson, John H. "Newspaper Preservation Act: A Critique." *Indiana Law Journal*, 46:392–412, Spring 1971. **1C53**
"The acclaimed need for exempting joint newspaper operating arrangements from the antitrust laws and the effects of such an exemption will be analyzed in evaluating the effectiveness of the NPA's ₍National Newspaper Preservation Act₎ objectives in promoting diverse, independent and competing sources of news."

Caron, Arthur J., Jr. "Federal Procurement and the Freedom of Information Act." *Federal Bar Journal*, 28:271–86, Summer 1968. **1C54**
Despite the ambiguities and deficiencies of the Act and the fact that its intent is revealed more through the committee reports, "it would seem that the mere promulgation of regulations identifying procedures and methods whereby requests will be entertained will in itself result in greater access to information."

Carp, Robert A. "Censorship Pressure on Social Studies Teachers." *Social Education*, 32:487–88, 492, May 1968. **1C55**
A survey of censorship pressures being brought to bear on high school social studies teachers in the state of Iowa. The author concludes that (1) important censorship groups are organized on a national basis and make much the same charges and demands wherever they are active, (2) the national groups are more active in urban than rural areas, and (3) many teachers turn to self-censorship, particularly in rural areas.

Carpenter, Edwin P. "Walton's Castle: The Spectrun of 'I Am Curious—Yellow.'" *Washburn Law Journal*, 10:163–76, Fall 1970. **1C56**
Criticism of the decision of Judge Walton in *State of Kansas v. A Motion Picture Film Entitled "I Am Curious Yellow*," Johnson County, Kansas, finding the motion picture to be obscene on the basis of three elements—prurient interest, community standard, and minimal social value.

Carpenter, James R., Jr. "Defamation under the First Amendment—The Actual Malice Test and 'Public Figures.'" *North Carolina Law Review*, 46:392–98, February 1968. **1C57**
The author looks at the actual malice test as promulgated in *New York Times* ₍*New York Times v. Sullivan*, 1964₎—knowledge of the falsity of a statement, and reckless disregard of the truth or falsity of the statement.

₍Carpenter, Robert E.₎ "The Shopping Center as a Forum for the Exercise of First Amendment Rights." *Albany Law Review*, 37:556–66, 1973. **1C58**
In the case of *Lloyd Corp. v. Tanner* (1972), the U.S. Supreme Court found that there was no

state deprivation of the asserted first amendment rights, resolving the issue in favor of the owner's property rights. The author believes the Court might have found in favor of the shopping center owner because there were other public forums available. At the same time the decision kept shopping centers open as a potential forum.

Carper, Donald L. "Obscenity, 1969: Another Attempt to Define Scienter." *Pacific Law Journal*, 1:364–72, January 1970.　　　**1C59**
An examination of the legal meaning of "knowingly" with respect to obscenity as defined by the California legislature in an attempt at codification of Supreme Court decisions.

Carr, Gary. "John Howard Lawson: Hollywood Craftsmanship and Censorship in the 1930s." *ICarbS* (Southern Illinois University), 3(1):37–48, Summer–Fall 1976.　　**1C60**
Despite his commitment to Marxism over the years, Lawson was able to work with the most reactionary elements of the Hollywood motion picture industry and there is no evidence of his ideologies permeating his film scripts, despite charges made to the contrary during the McCarthy witch-hunting. Lawson, blacklisted by the motion picture industry for his Marxian affiliations, "lived with studio censorship throughout his Hollywood career." He is probably best remembered for his defiance of the Un-American Activities Committee in the late forties which resulted in his imprisonment for contempt for taking the First Amendment in his defense.

[Carr, Thomas N.] *The People Ex Rel. Richard Busteed, vs. Thomas N. Carr. Indictment for Libel. Opening Speech of John Graham, Esq., to the Jury, on the Part of the Prosecution, May Term, 1858.* New York, William A. Townsend, 1858. 34p., 65p.　　**1C61**
John Graham, attorney for the prosecution, reviews the history of libel law in New York State, noting that, unlike criminal cases, the jury in libel cases is responsible for determining both the law and the facts. To escape libel a statement must not only be true but show good motive and a justifiable end. The case involved the writer of a letter to the editor of the *New York Herald*, accused of making false and malicious charges against the Corporation Counsel involving advertising of proposed street improvements.

Carroll, Dorothy C. "Cultural Boycott—Yes or No?" *Index on Censorship*, 4(1):35–43, Spring 1975.　　**1C62**
The journal conducted a survey of opinion among writers, artists, performing artists, and scholars about the propriety of a cultural boycott of South Africa in particular and cultural boycotts in general. The author discusses the issue. The text of the questionnaire is published (p.36) along with a selection of the re-

plies. "*Index* hopes, through its questionnaire, to stimulate discussion about South Africa and, more broadly, about ways the artist can and should manifest his opposition to tyranny wherever it has been institutionalized."

Carroll, Maurine A. "New York Times Co. v. United States: Confrontation Between Free Press and Presidential Power." *Loyola Law Review* (New Orleans), 20:140–47, 1974.　　**1C63**
An analysis of the issues and opinions rendered by the U.S. Supreme Court in the Pentagon Papers case. The author believes that a solution to the free press—executive power conflict lies in the development of a mutual respect between the two parties. "Neither the government nor the press should feel that it is given a preferred status by the Constitution."

Carroll, Thomas F. "The Evolution of the Theory of Freedom of Speech and of the Press." *Georgetown Law Journal*, 11:27–43, November 1922.　　**1C64**
The author looks at the concept of press freedom at the time of the adoption of the First Amendment (1791), and at the early controversy over the meaning of the First Amendment. He considers four definitions of press freedom that have been advanced: Sir William Blackstone's, Thomas M. Cooley's, Oliver Wendell Holmes', and Alexander Hamilton's. He shows how each interpretation has been modified by later writers and by decisions of the courts, concluding: "From the progress we have made toward a greater freedom of discussion, we may confidently expect a greater liberalism in the future."

———. *Freedom of Speech and the Press in the Critical Periods of American History.* Washington, D.C., American University, 1923. 204p. (Unpublished Ph.D. dissertation)　　**1C65**
Part I, Freedom of Speech and of the Press in the Federalist Period: The Sedition Act. Part II, Freedom of Speech and of the Press During the Civil War. Part III, Freedom of Speech and of the Press in War Time: The Espionage Act. Part IV, Federal Authority over the Mails, Its Exercise and Limitations.

Carroll, William R. "Constitutional Privilege for Defamation—Private Individual—Libel—Damages." *Duquesne Law Review*, 14:89–100, Fall 1975.　　**1C66**
Re: *Gertz v. Robert Welch, Inc.*, 418 U.S. 323 (1974).

Carter, Hodding, III. "The Deteriorating First Amendment." *Grassroots Editor*, 14(1):16–17, January–February 1973.　　**1C67**
The publisher of the *Delta Democrat–Times* of Greenville, Ga., in a speech before the Sigma Delta Chi convention in Dallas, questions "whether the men who own and run American

journalism today give enough of a damn to mobilize that 'powerful mechanism' [a term used by Mr. Justice White] and restore the First Amendment to the Bill of Rights."

Carter, James. "Censorship and the Librarian." In Raymond Astbury, *ed.*, *Libraries & the Book Trade. Papers Delivered at a Symposium Held at Liverpool School of Librarianship*, *May 1967*. London, Clive Bingley, 1968, pp. 131–46.　　**1C68**
In the United Kingdom it is sex, not politics, that brings out the censor. But British public libraries are less under siege than American public libraries. Some librarians may be tempted to avoid controversy and trouble by a cautious book-selection process and the misuse of a reserve shelf. The author lists six practical policies in book selection which should be adopted and made public. The policies are based on the 1963 British Library Association statement and the American Library Bill of Rights.

Carter, John. "Rainbow Prosecution." *Times Literary Supplement*, 68:216, 27 February, 1969.　　**1C69**
A reporting on correspondence recently uncovered in the files of the Society of Authors concerning the prosecution of D. H. Lawrence's *The Rainbow* in the autumn of 1915. Letters are from Lawrence, Methuen, his publisher, and J. B. Pinker, his agent.

———, and Percy Muir, *eds. Printing and the Mind of Man. A Descriptive Catalogue Illustrating the Impact of Print on the Evolution of Western Civilizations During Five Centuries. . . .* With an Introductory Essay by Denys Hay. London, Cassell, 1967. 280p.　　**1C70**
Among the great works considered were the following books, either banned or treating censorship: *Index Librorum Prohibitorum*, Tyndale's *New Testament*, the works of Erasmus, the works of Servetus, John Foxe's *Actes and Monuments* (°F19), Milton's *Areopagitica* (M378), Lilburne's *An Agreement of the Free People of England*, Paine's *Rights of Man*, and Hansard's *Parliamentary Debates*.

Carter, John M. "The Fructification Fulguration." *Library Journal*, 95:1001, 15 March 1970.　　**1C71**
"Fructification fulguration" (an alternative to the over-used phrase "sexual revolution") is causing a reaction in the form of a bill before the United States Senate (S. 1077) and the House (H.R. 7201) to amend titles 18 and 28 of the U.S. Code to "prohibit judicial review of any determination made by a jury on the question [of] whether something is obscene by any court in the United States." The author be-

lieves that "there should not be any laws at all against obscenity, simply because obscenity defies definition."

Carter, Joseph. *Freedom to Know; A Background Book*. New York, Parents' Magazine, 1974. 169p.   **1C72**
A popular presentation "to show the reader the strengths and weaknesses of the various media and the eternal conflict between the press and the government on the limits of freedom of information. . . . The battle for freedom of the press was waged by earlier men for at least three hundred years but now, at least in democratic countries, it seems safely won. The battle for freedom to know, however, seems to have just begun."

Carter, Mary D. *et al*. "Censorship and Selection." In their *Building Library Collections*. 4th ed. Metuchen, N.J., Scarecrow, 1974, pp. 177–202.   **1C73**
The author presents the fundamental problem of book selection and censorship in a democratic society, where attitudes shift over the years and where the librarian must be responsive to the society which supports it. "The library has the responsibility for making clear to the community that it represents the democratic idea of tolerance, that it has the duty to be many-sided, to give service to all of the citizens, and not just those of one particular shade of opinion. That this task will not always be easy, that on occasions it may be impossible, that sometimes it may not be worldly wise, is beyond doubt."

Carter, P. B. "The Journalist, His Informant and Testimonial Privilege." *New York University Law Review*, 35:1111–25, May 1960.   **1C74**
A British barrister believes that neither solicitude for the journalist nor concern with the free flow of news are adequate justification for testimonial privilege of newsmen. The central question should be whether the information given is so desirable that this kind of confidence should be demanded or accepted.

Carter-Ruck, Peter F. "The Law of Contempt." *Journalism Today*, 1(5):19–32, Autumn 1969.   **1C75**
The author discusses the legal concept of contempt of court, contempt of Parliament, and contempt of tribunals, with special attention to how these laws may operate unfairly against British journalists.

———. *Libel and Slander*. Foreward by Colin Duncan. London, Faber and Faber, 1972. 448p. (Archon Books, Hamden, Conn., 1973)   **1C76**
Revision of *The Law of Libel and Slander* by Oswald S. Hickson and P. F. Carter-Ruck, 1953 (H252).

———. "Privacy and the Press." *Journalism Today*, 2:5–26, Spring 1971.   **1C77**
In an address before the annual conference of the Institute of Journalists Carter-Ruck examines the present nature of privacy in Great Britain, explains why and to what extent the law has in recent years proved to be defective, and considers by what means, if at all, there ought to be legal protection in the event of privacy being infringed.

———. "Theatre Act 1968." *Solicitors' Journal*, 112:647–49, 16 August 1968.   **1C78**
The author analyzes the British Theatres Act of 1968 which abolishes the censorship functions of the Lord Chamberlain, transfers licensing of theater premises to local authorities, provides criminal proceedings for performance of a play which is obscene, amends the law of defamation so that publication by performance of a play should be treated as publication in permanent form for purpose of the law of libel and slander, provides for an offense in a public performance for use of abusive language against any racial group, or use of abusive language with intent to provoke a breach of the peace.

[Cary, Theodore.] *Report of the Libel Suit, Llewellyn Powers vs. Theodore Cary, Editor and Publisher of the Aroostook Times. Tried at the February Term, 1874, Supreme Judicial Court Held at Houlton, Me., Hon. John A. Peters, Jr., Presiding. . . .* Houlton, Me., Aroostook Times, 1874. 395p.   **1C79**
The *Aroostook Times*, 13 March 1873, had carried an affidavit from a Negro servant woman accusing the plaintiff of accosting her. No verdict is reported in the account.

The Case of the Stage in Ireland; Containing the Reasons for and against a Bill for limiting the Number of Theatres in the City of Dublin; wherin the Qualifications, Duty and Importance of a Manager Are carefully considered and explained, and the Conduct and Abilities of the present Manager [Mr. Sheridan] of the Theatre [Royal] in Smock-Alley Are particularly reviewed and examined. The Whole occasionally interspersed with critical Observations on Oratory; And a Summary of the principal Advantages that must necessarily accrue to this Kingdom from an Academy, Connected with the Theatre. Dublin, H. Saunders, 1758. 51p.   **1C80**
Sheridan had applied for an Act of Parliament to prohibit opening of any theater in Dublin except that over which he presided.

Casey, Ralph D., *ed. The Press in Perspective*. Baton Rouge, La., Louisiana State University Press, 1963. 271p.   **1C81**
This volume brings together a series of sixteen annual lectures given by distinguished journalists at the University of Minnesota School of Journalism under a grant from the Newspaper Guild of the Twin Cities. Recurring themes in the lectures were (1) the need for the nation's journalists to take a greater responsibility for serving the public interest, not only in reporting but interpreting the news; and (2) the need for constant vigilance to prevent government, newspaper owners, and public pressures from exercising controls over the news. Content: Which Direction for America? by Marquis Childs. Current Challenges to Our Free Press by Thomas L. Stokes, Jr. The Press and World Affairs by James B. Reston. The Role of the Newspaperman in America's Function as the Greatest World Power by Reinhold Niebuhr. Must We Mislead the Public? by Elmer Davis. The Government and the Press by Alan Barth. The Big Truth by Eric Sevareid. Foreign News: Weapon for World Peace? by George V. Ferguson. Federal Centralization and the Press by Henry S. Commanger. An Independent Press by Herbert L. Block. An Art to Be Practiced by Doris Fleeson. Personality in Journalism by Gerald W. Johnson. The Third Reader by Louis M. Lyons. Reporting Politics by Joseph W. Alsop, Jr. The Press and Presidential Leadership by Pierre Salinger and James Hagerty. Magazine and Newspaper Journalism: A Comparison by John Fischer.

Caskey, Marshall A. *Polls: Critics and Proposed Controls*. Columbia, Mo., Freedom of Information Center, School of Journalism, University of Missouri at Columbia, 1969. 6p. (Report no. 220)   **1C82**
Criticism of unchecked and sometimes slanted political polls have led to proposals for controls—both from the polling organizations themselves and from government

Casper, Gerhard. *Redefreiheit und Ehrenschutz; Anmerkungen zu den Grundlagen der Neuren Amerikanischen und Deutschen Rechtsprechung*. Karlsruhe, C. F. Müller, 1971. 39p. (Juristische Studiengesellschaft, Karlsruhe)   **1C83**
Freedom of speech and protection of reputation; notes to the foundation of new American and German administration of justice.

Castagna, Edwin. "Censorship, Intellectual Freedom and Libraries." In Melvin J. Voigt, *ed., Advances in Librarianship*. London, Seminar Press, 1971, pp. 215–51.   **1C84**
Content: Definitions, historical review, problems of censorship in libraries, the American Library Association's concern about censorship and intellectual freedom, and censorship in Australia and New Zealand.

Castan, Frances. "A Teacher vs. a

Town." *Scholastic Teacher*, no vol., pp. 22–23+, April–May, 1974. **1C85**
Controversy in Berkeley Springs, W. Va., over a book used in the local schools, *The Little Red Schoolbook* by Danish author Soren Hansen and edited for Americans by Wallace Roberts, former associate education editor of the *Saturday Review*. The author of the article has interviewed participants in the controversy.

Castanien, Anne T. *Censorship and Historiography in Elizabethan England: The Expurgation of Holinshed's Chronicles*. Davis, Calif., University of California, Davis, 1970. 343p. (Ph.D. dissertation, University Microfilms, no. 71–20,374) **1C86**
"This study examines the effects of the official censorship of the press established in Elizabethan England upon the preparation and publication of Holinshed's *Chronicles of England, Ireland and Scotland*, the last and most comprehensive of the Tudor chronicle histories."

Cater, Douglass, and Stephen Strickland. *TV Violence and the Child: The Evolution and Fate of the Surgeon General's Report*. New York, Russell Sage Foundation, 1975. 178p. **1C87**
The authors trace the history of the study of television violence from the request of Senator John Pastore, through the selection of the Committee, with the elimination of the seven social scientists objected to by the broadcasting industry; the work of the Committee and its staff; the "cautious" findings of causal relationship between television violence and actual behavior; the lack of recommendation of action to be taken; the agreement by the industry, the Federal Communications Commission, and the Department of Health, Education and Welfare to "take steps"; and the singular lack of progress in the two years that have passed. A critique of the critique appears in *Journalism Quarterly*, Summer 1975.

Catholic Truth Society of Ireland. *The Problem of Undesirable Printed Matter. Suggested Remedies. Evidence of the Catholic Truth Society of Ireland Presented to Departmental Committee of Enquiry, 1926*. Dublin, The Society, 1926. 99p. **1C88**
The Committee was charged with the mission "to consider and report whether it is necessary or advisable in the interest of public morality to extend the existing powers of the State to prohibit or restrict the sale and circulation of printed matter." The Catholic Truth Society testified that the present obscenity laws in Ireland were inadequate to control the various types of obscene literature flourishing in the country. The lengthy testimony cited five categories of publications that should be placed under more rigid state controls: (1) neomalthusian birth control propaganda, which should be placed under an absolute ban; (2) newspapers and periodicals which specialize in stories

of crime, divorce court trials, etc. (a list of examples is given), should be controlled by suspending publication—one month for the first offense, two months for the second offense, and one year for the third offense; (3) books of an immoral suggestive tendency or which depict scenes of a like tendency; (4) newspapers, magazines, and other publications which make a regular feature of "smutty" jokes and stories or which specialize in tales of undisguised sexual passion or print immorally suggestive pictures, reproductions, or representation; and (5) photographic prints and reproductions of the nude or semi-nude, designed to have an immorally suggestive appeal. A government censorship board is recommended for the control of books. Banned books and pictures required for professional or scientific purposes would be imported through specially approved booksellers and a record of names and addresses of all persons purchasing such works would be kept. The Society favored the adoption by law of the British "Hicklin rule" defining obscenity as any matter which is likely "to deprave and corrupt those whose minds are open to such immoral influences, and into whose hands a publication of this sort may fall." The appendix contains statements about control of obscene publications in Australia, Canada, France, Tasmania, and New Zealand.

Catledge, Turner. "Historic Confrontation between Government and Press." *Loyola Law Review* (New Orleans), 20:1–10, 1974. **1C89**
Thanks to Watergate, the American press was able to win the battle of the credibility gap and to cut off the intimidations by public officialdom in the Nixon Administration. The author examines the conflict between the press and the Nixon Administration in light of historic precedent. In the struggle for national goals "the media, in order to remain credible. . . ., operates with shifting standards of fair play and impartiality"; and "the government, both to survive and to govern, resorts to shifting standards of public accountability."

Caulfield [Malachy F.] *Mary Whitehouse*. By Max Caulfield. London, Mowbrays, 1975. 182p. **1C90**
An account of the career of Britain's self-appointed censor, founder of the Clean-Up TV Campaign and now secretary of the National Viewers and Listeners Association. Mrs. Whitehouse waged a successful fight to obtain recognition for "the other point of view" on obscenity, pornography, and violence on television in a permissive age.

[Caunt, James.] *An Editor on Trial. Rex v. Caunt. Alleged Seditious Libel*. Morecambe and Heysham, England, Morecambe Press [1974?]. 62p. **1C91**
Caunt was tried in the Liverpool Assize Court for alleged libel against the Jewish people, published in the *Morecambe and Heysham Visitor*, 6 August 1947. He was acquitted. Justice Birkett reviewed the history of libel laws and made a

strong plea for freedom of the press. The text of his remarks are included.

Cavallo, Robert M., and Stuart Kahn. *Photography: What's the Law?* New York, Crown, 1976. 139p. **1C92**
Includes discussion of what pictures the photographer can or cannot take, invasion of privacy, libel, releases, what is obscene, and truth in advertising.

Cavanagh, John E. "The Freedom of Information Act and Government Contractors—Problems in Protection of Confidential Information." *Public Contract Law Journal*, 2:225–35, January 1969. **1C93**
"Indiscriminate attempts to limit disclosure of contractor information will create more problems than they solve."

Cavanagh, John R. "Towards an Objective View of Pornographic Literature." *National Guild of Catholic Psychiatrists Bulletin*, 16:67–73, May 1969. **1C94**
A doctor is concerned with the harmful effect of pornographic literature, with its falseness and the emptiness of the specter of sex on the emotional maturity of young people. "When these subjects are looked at as primarily the portrayal of perversions, the prurient interest is more clearly seen. Such communications are likely to stimulate the usually repressed perverse sexual fantasies and may lead to their activation and the appearance of overt, painful and dangerous conduct. Adolescents are most likely to be affected by these publications."

Ceccarelli, Edwin M. "Television and Radio Commentators' Freedom of Speech Not Infringed by Dues Requirement of Union Shop Agreement." *Fordham Urban Law Journal*, 3:715–31, Spring 1975. **1C95**
Re: *Buckley v. American Federation of Television and Radio Artists*, 496 F.2d 305 (2d Cir.).

"The Censor Cometh." *Hibernia*, 40 (16): 4–5, 10 September 1976. **1C96**
An editorial attacking the Irish government's proposals for emergency powers which would include censorship of the press. The cover of the issue carries a caricature of a censor with scissors clipping the Irish Press.

Censoring Textbooks: Is West Virginia the Tip of the Iceberg? A Transcript of "Options on Education," December 11, 1974. Washington, D.C., Institute for Educational Leadership, George Washing-

ton University, 1974. 16p. (ED 105,518)   **1C97**
"Interviews with several individuals representing a variety of viewpoints about the recent controversy regarding textbooks and philosophy in the Kanawha County, West Virginia, public schools are presented in this transcript of a National Public Radio program broadcast in December 1974. . . . From these interviews it becomes clear that the controversy begun over textbooks envelops more than a few words or reading selections; it encompasses the foundations of American education and questions who, indeed, should run our schools."

"Censorship and Racism: A Dilemma for Librarians." *Interracial Books for Children*, 6(3/4):1, 10, 1975.   **1C98**
"The American Library Association has taken a firm position in opposition to 'all forms of censorship.' As an organization, the ALA has still to take an equally firm position opposing all forms of racism and sexism. Recognizing the difficulties an absence of guidelines poses for librarians . . . we herewith present some views on the censorship issue that we hope will lead to an expansion of the dialogue and ultimately, to a reconciliation of the various viewpoints which have emerged." Further censorship dialogue appears in subsequent issues.

"Censorship and the Indecent Publications Tribunal." *Auckland University Law Review*, 2:1–24, August 1972. **1C99**
"The aim of this article is to examine the attitude of the New Zealand Indecent Publications Tribunal . . . toward the basic issues in the area of literary censorship, and to consider what factors influence it in deciding where to draw the line between complete freedom and paternalistic control."

Censorship News. New York and Chicago, National Coalition Against Censorship, 1975–date. Published periodically. (Formerly National Ad Hoc Committee Against Censorship)
                                        1C100
Issue no. 1 (March 1975) dealt largely with state legislation; issue no. 2 (September 1975) reported on various threats of censorship and cases before the courts.

Censorship: The Death of a Free Press. Springfield, Mass., Victory Publishing Co. [1960]. 23p.   **1C101**
An anonymous author, who admits that many of his friends are in "the censorship brigade," attacks censorship and reviews historic and recent "attempts of the censor to dictate what books you may read, what movies you may attend, and what moral code you must follow." He writes particularly of the censorship efforts of the Post Office Department and the pressures of the Catholic Church. He asks readers

to send their names to enlist in a national battle against the censor.

"Censorship: The Malady Lingers On. Symposium." *Today's Education*, 65:48–54, March–April 1976   **1C102**
Views expressed by a librarian (Judith F. Krug), a teacher (Nell Wood), a parent, and two students.

Censorship Today; A Review of the Continuing Fight for Free Speech. Los Angeles, June–July 1968—October–November 1969. Ten numbers issued.
                                        1C103
During its short life *Censorship Today* carried numerous critical and analytical articles on censorship issues and reported on events—incidents of censorship, court decisions, and legislation. Individual articles are separately entered in this bibliography. Doris Fleishman was editor.

Center for National Security Studies. *The New Freedom of Information Act & National Security Secrecy*. Washington, D.C., The Center [1975?]. 16p. **1C104**
"The Center for National Security Studies is concerned with the menacing growth of state power in the name of 'national security.' It sponsors research and publishes reports on policies and practices of national security agencies—including the CIA, the FBI, and the military establishment. It is also working to curtail the present executive branch secrecy system and drastically reduce the secrecy which presently veils national security policies." This brochure gives specific advice (including form letters) on how to request government information under the amended Freedom of Information Act, passed by Congress in 1974 over President Ford's veto.

Center for the Study of Democratic Institutions. *Censorship by Manipulation*. Santa Barbara, Calif., The Center, 1973. 27 min. tape recording. (Broadcasting and the First Amendment, VI; serial no. 615)   **1C105**
"Censorship is not the only way to control the press. Many subtler tools are available to an administration wishing to use them. One participant, for example, points out that the FCC's antitrust function alone gives it great leverage in controlling the content of the media—not formally and openly—but informally, by intimidation and manipulation." Participants in this discussion and others in the series: Blair Clark, former director of CBS News and a director of the Center; Lloyd Cutler, a Washington, D.C. attorney; Reuven Frank, former president of NBC News; Harry Kalven, Jr., a University of Chicago law professor; James Loper, former chairman, Public Broadcasting System; John W. Macy, Jr., former president, Public Broadcasting Corporation; Newton Minow, former FCC chairman; Fred Warner Neal, a professor at the Claremont Graduate School; Paul Porter, former FCC chairman;

Lawrence Rogers, president, Taft Broadcasting Company; Richard Salant, president of CBS News; Antonin Scalia, former general counsel for the White House Office of Telecommunications; Eric Sevareid, CBS commentator; Roger Traynor, former chief justice of the California Supreme Court, now chairman of the National News Council; Harold Willens, co-chairman, Business Executives Move for Vietnam Peace and a Center director; Thomas H. Wolf, ABC-TV vice president for documentaries; and from the Center staff, Harry S. Ashmore, Rick J. Carlson, John Cogley, Thomas E. Cronin, Norton Ginsburg, Eduard Goldstücker, Laurence I. Hewes, Jr., Robert M. Hutchins, Frank K. Kelley, Donald McDonald, Wendell Mordy, Lord Ritchie-Calder, Ronald M. Segal, Rexford Guy Tugwell, Harvey Wheeler, and John Wilkinson. (A printed report of the conference is entered under 1A244.)

———. *The Heart of the Matter—Licensing*. Santa Barbara, Calif., The Center, 1973. 28 min. tape recording. (Broadcasting and the First Amendment, I; serial no. 610)   **1C106**
"How should the government decide which applicants should be granted broadcast licenses? In this program the question provokes conflicting answers: an apologist for Mr. [Clay T.] Whitehead's proposals concludes that the government is obliged to determine (and license) the 'better' applicants; a network official insists that this procedure is prohibited by the First Amendment; and a lawyer suggests that decisions could be made by lottery."

———. *How Good Is Television News Reporting?* Santa Barbara, Calif., The Center, 1973. 29 min. tape recording. (Broadcasting and the First Amendment, II, serial no. 611)   **1C107**
"Vice-President Agnew and Clay T. Whitehead are not the only ones to question the quality of network news and public affairs programs. Here conference participants face network representatives with such tough questions as these: Does the fact that the networks are private enterprises, run for profit, inhibit their ability to present the news fairly? Does national television offer adequate access for the presentation of minority and dissident opinion? Why do polls show that the public rates the broadcasting industry just above labor unions in terms of responsibility?"

———. *The National News Council—A Solution?* Santa Barbara, Calif., The Center, 1973. 28 min. tape recording. (Broadcasting and the First Amendment, IV; serial no. 613)   **1C108**
"One way to assure responsible and accurate television news may be to charge a private independent organization with evaluating media performance. Here Roger Traynor, head of the new National News Council, describes how his organization could just fit the bill; Lord Ritchie-Calder reports on the way a similar organization has improved the quality

of the English press; and Eduard Goldstücker comments on his experiences with both press and television in Czechoslovakia."

———. *National News, Local Control.* Santa Barbara, Calif., The Center, 1973. 27 min. tape recording. (Broadcasting and the First Amendment, VII; serial no. 616)   **1C 109**
"Ronald Segal, exiled South African journalist and revolutionary, triggers this discussion with the proposal that the people themselves should set the policies that govern their television stations. Ironically, this suggestion has much in common with Nixon administration proposals: each in its way favors local control of program content. But Eric Sevareid warns that enhancing localism may lead to 'the kind of political and intellectual anarchy' that marked the disintegration of France's Third Republic in the thirties."

———. *The Right to Be Unfair.* Santa Barbara, Calif., The Center, 1973. 28 min. tape recording. (Broadcasting and the First Amendment, V; serial no. 614)   **1C 110**
"Does the First Amendment give broadcasters the constitutional right to be unfair? Several conference participants insist that it does—that any other interpretation opens the door to government interference and control. The President of CBS News takes the lead in presenting this view and discusses with other participants the relationship that should exist between the government and the media."

———. *Television: The Exclusive Medium.* Santa Barbara, Calif., The Center, 1973. 27 min. tape recording. (Broadcasting and the First Amendment, VIII; serial no. 617)   **1C 111**
" 'This particular medium allows fewer and fewer of us to talk to more and more people, and I think it is inherently undemocratic.' This comment by one participant points up the concern that underlies much of this discussion. How can our television system provide reasonable access to both popular and unpopular opinion? Would additional networks or a tax-supported television system broaden access to the media so that people would not resort to bizarre, violent, or exotic behavior to obtain a hearing for their views?"

———. *The Whitehead Emancipation Proclamation.* Santa Barbara, Calif., The Center, 1973. 28 min. tape recording. (Broadcasting and the First Amendment, III; serial no. 612) **1C 112**
"Interpretations of Clay T. Whitehead's proposals vary almost as much as the responses they have provoked. Are they an attempt to impose more government restrictions on the media? Or, does Mr. Whitehead mean to relax present regulations? What led him to propose his changes when he did? Antonin Scalia, former General Counsel to Mr. Whitehead's office, sees the proposals as effecting few

changes in government regulations. His comments provoke one participant to remark with some irony that the proposals are 'sort of an emancipation proclamation for the broadcasting industry.' "

[Chadwick, Edwin.] "The Taxes on Knowledge." *Westminster Review*, 15:238–67, July 1831. (Reprinted as a separate pamphlet by Robert Heward, London, 1831)   **1C 113**
A Benthomite reformer, Chadwick was one of the leaders of the middle-class sponsors of repeal of the stamp tax. In this essay he reviews three publications: *The Moral and Political Evils of the Taxes on Knowledge* . . . , Francis Place's *Letter to a Minister of State, Respecting the Taxes on Knowledge* (P187), and his own *The Real Incendiaries and Promoters of Crime.* Chadwick considered repeal of the tax on newspapers as an inducement of free trade in politics and a deterrent to press monopoly. "A journalist would be bound to good behavior" by the operation of the law of supply and demand.

Chalfin, Paul M. "Free Press vs. Fair Trial." *Shingle* (Philadelphia Bar Association), 25:115–18, May 1962. **1C 114**
"If we are to expect the press to exercise proper self-restraint, we also have a right to demand that the law enforcement officers, district attorneys and defense lawyers refrain from trying their cases in the newspapers. This is dictated not only by wise law enforcement and courtroom procedure but also by an adherance to the canons of professional ethics."

Challies, G. S. "Reflexions sur la Liberté de Presse." *Justinien* (La Faculté de Droit de l'Université D'Ottawa), 4:53–59, 1967–68.   **1C 115**
(1) Commentaires sur les Causes Pendantes, (2) Critiques de l'Administration de la Justice.

Chamberlain, John. "Freedom of the Press and National Security." *Modern Age*, 17:234–42, Summer 1973. **1C 116**
A critique on the conduct of the nation's press in matters of national security, particularly with respect to the spread of communism and the Vietnam war. Throughout there is the implication of a liberal bias in the news media. Favorable comments and expansion on the ideas of the author are presented in an accompanying article, Advocacy Journalism by Peter B. Clark (pp. 243–47).

[Chamberlin, John F.] *The Answer of John F. Chamberlin to the Complaint of George Wilkes, in an Action to Recover Damages for Defamation of Character.* New York, William J. Read, 1873. 15p.   **1C 117**
The defendant, in a case of libel before the New York Supreme Court, repeats the charges he had made against the plaintiff and for which he was brought to court, including "frequenter of brothals, the companion of thieves, the confederate of knaves, himself a thief, a swindler, a forger and a felon; that he has been directly or

indirectly engaged in the publishing of scandalous, libelous and obscene newspapers, in which he has defamed and vilified good and respectable citizens, kept the community at large in terror of his filthy and envenomed falsehoods, levying black mail, poisoning the public morals, outraging public decency, debauching the minds of the young. . . . " Wilkes was publisher of a number of sensational papers—*The Sunday Flash, The Wasp, The Police Gazette,* the *Subterranean,* and *The Spirit of the Times.* The last named, according to the defendant, carried false and scurrilous articles about him as a means of blackmail for Chamberlin's refusal to take Wilkes into partnership in a "Paris Mutual" betting enterprise. The record shows that Wilkes had numerous convictions for libel, obscenity, theft, and had been brought to trial for the forgery of a will, but was acquitted on a technicality. In light of Wilkes's criminal record and the documented proof of Chamberlin's accusations, he asks that Wilkes's charges against him be dropped and the court agreed. Wilkes's account of thirty days in a New York City jail for publishing an obscene libel are described in his book, *Mystery of the Tombs* (W255).

Chambers, M. M. *Freedom of the College Student Press.* Normal, Ill., Department of Educational Administration, Illinois State University, 1971. 18p. (ED 51,772)   **1C 118**
"There is considerable debate on and off campus about the extent to which student editors and reporters can legitimately express controversial views and whether they may use allegedly indecent words; and whether university and college administrators can censor or suppress student publications unacceptable to them. This paper reviews some of the cases of freedom of the college and high school student press and court pronouncements related to these issues."

Chancellor, John. "Electronic Journalism." *Playboy* 19(1):121, 216–17, January 1972.   **1C 119**
The NBC television commentator assesses the Nixon-Agnew Administration's attacks on the press.

Chandler, Christopher. "Sun-Times Kills Exposé of Swibel Renewal Deal." *Chicago Journalism Review,* 2(11):3–6, November 1969.   **1C 120**
An account of the rejection of a news story dealing with a Chicago urban-renewal project headed by a protégé of Mayor Richard Daley. Includes the text of "the story that didn't fit in print."

Chapel, Charles S. "The First Amendment and Nonverbal Expres-

sion." *Tulsa Law Journal*, 5:213–17, May 1968. **1C121**
Deals with the case of *People v. Street* (1967) in which the incident combined a verbal statement plus public burning of the American flag. While Street was convicted on the basis that his conduct might have provoked a breach of peace, "the decision might well have rested upon the distinction between expression and criminal conduct." The United States Supreme Court (*Street v. New York*) reversed the decision.

Chaplin, George. "Free Press—Fair Trial." *Women Lawyers' Journal*, 61:12, 16–21, 32, Winter 1975. **1C122**
A Honolulu newspaper editor believes that some elements of the bar and bench have greatly overblown the whole prejudicial publicity issue. Today the record of self-restraint in journalism is the best in history, yet open season on the press is on the increase. He reports on the current efforts of bar and press to resolve the issues of free press and fair trial and is encouraged by the prospects.

Chapman, A. B. W. "The Imprisonment of the Treasurer." *The Individualist; A Magazine of Personal Rights*, 58(n.s.):13–14, April–June 1918. **1C123**
A brief account of the imprisonment of the treasurer of the Personal Rights Association for possessing pamphlets contrary to the Defence of the Realm Act and the imprisonment of three members of the Society of Friends for distributing a pacifist pamphlet, *A Challenge to Militarism*.

Chappelle, Pamela. "Can an Adult Theater or Bookstore Be Abated as a Public Nuisance in California?" *University of San Francisco Law Review*, 10:115–32, Summer 1975. **1C124**
"This comment will discuss the advantages of a civil public nuisance action as opposed to criminal obscenity action, whether 'public nuisance' includes such conduct as the exhibition of pornographic materials, and the limits which the first amendment guarantee of freedom of expression places upon such use of public nuisance concept."

[Chapple, Thomas L.] "*Friends of the Earth v. FCC*: Is It a Judicial Extension of the Fairness Doctrine?" *Albany Law Review*, 36:216–24, Fall 1971. **1C125**
Re: *Friends of the Earth v. FCC* (1971), involved the use of counter-commercials for automobile ads.

Charles, John. "Seizure of Allegedly Obscene Material—Requirement of a

Prior Adversary Hearing." *Ohio State Law Journal*, 32:668–73, Summer 1971. **1C126**
A discussion of two 1970 Ohio obscenity cases, *State v. Brooke*, and *State v. Miqdadi*. Though quite disparate in their outcomes, the two cases are representative of the range of decisions that have been reached by lower courts under existing Supreme Court guidelines.

Charleton, Gene. "Will a Free Watergate Press Allow Fair Watergate Trials?" *Grassroots Editor*, 15(3):3–9, May–June 1974. **1C127**
"By present legal standards, full and conscientious use of remedies against prejudicial publicity will allow for fair trials for Watergate defendants. But even after the safeguards have been applied, there is no way of knowing whether the jury reached a fair verdict."

Chase, J. Frank. "Literary Freedom and Its Limitations." *Zion's Herald*, 101:160–61, 31 January 1923. **1C128**
The secretary of the Watch and Ward Society describes the "gentlemen's agreement" by which Boston booksellers, at the instigation of the Society, voluntarily remove from sale any book that is "perversive of public chastity." If a book should escape them and get to the courts, it is the jury that must decide whether or not it is obscene, and works of literature must take their chances along with other works. Chase concludes with a quotation from the Apostle Paul as to the ultimate test of good literature.

Chaturvedi, J. P. "Diffusion of Ownership and Freedom of the Press." *Mainstream* (New Delhi), 9(52):11–12, 36–37, 28 August 1971. **1C129**
A discussion of the controversial draft bill on Diffusion of Ownership of Newspapers, recommended by the Press Commission. "It is possible today to pressurise the press by a government without any single law because of the leverage it has in the form of newsprint, advertisement import facilities, more business and presidential awards. When the management and ownership is distributed in a large number of people, the Government will be the worst sufferer and the people will be the best beneficiary."

Chatzky, Michael G., and William E. Robinson. "A Constitutional Right of Access to Newspapers: Is There Life After Tornillo?" *Santa Clara Law Review*, 16:453–94, Summer 1976. **1C130**
"This article will examine the constitutional underpinnings of a 'right of access' doctrine in relation to newspapers. The writers will sketch the pattern of dwindling competition in the newspaper industry, giving particular attention to the Newspaper Preservation Act as the culmination of that pattern. The article will consider the emergence of the first amendment-based rights to communicate in an effective manner and to receive information from diversified sources."

Chazen, Leonard, and Leonard Ross. "Federal Regulation of Cable Television: The Visible Hand." *Harvard Law Review*, 83:1820–41, June 1970. **1C131**
"Although cable television offers the potential of greatly increased television diversity, its possibilities have been left largely unrealized. The explanation, the authors argue, lies in the shifting but persistently adverse pattern of regulation which the FCC has imposed in order to protect a competing medium—UHF. These restrictions have been based on the mistaken notion that the interest of cable operators on the one hand and UHF outlets and program owners on the other are irreconcilable. The authors propose several plans which would accommodate the demand for CATV growth while at the same time leaving unharmed other interests which the FCC has deemed worthy of protection."—Editor.

Cheek, Leslie, III. "An Analysis of Proposals to Deregulate Commercial Radio Broadcasting." *Federal Communications Bar Journal*, 25:1–52, 1972. **1C132**
Some critics of Federal Communications Commission regulatory policies under the Communications Act of 1934 believe the act should be revised to "deregulate" radio broadcasting to free it from restraints no longer relevant or necessary. The article examines such proposals in the context of existing regulations, with emphasis on economic and policy considerations.

Cheever, George B. *A Defence in Abatement of Judgment for an Alleged Libel in the Story Entitled "Inquire at Amos Giles' Distillery." Addressed to The Hon. Chief Justice Shaw, at the Session of the Supreme Judicial Court of Massachusetts, Held at Salem, Dec. 4, 1835*. Salem, Mass., John W. Archer, 1836. 28p. **1C133**
The Reverend Mr. Cheever defends himself against libel charges from a Salem distiller, declaring that his temperance story was fictional, was not intended to reflect on a particular distillery but on the entire nefarious business; that the evils in the traffic were well known and that his charges were truthful.

[———.] *Stone versus Cheever. Great Temperance Case*. Belfast, Printed by Macaulay & Quin, 1835. 48p. (Reprinted from *New York Evangelist*) **1C134**
The Reverend Mr. Cheever, a temperance crusader, was brought to court (Court of Common Pleas, Essex County, Mass.) held in Salem, June 1835, on a libel charge for a piece of fiction entitled Inquire at Amos Giles' Distillery, appearing in the *Salem Landmark*. It was a story of Deacon Giles, a rum distiller who was also treasurer of the local Bible Society, and the trick played on him by a group of pranksters. They secretly marked each keg of rum with invisible ink with such labels as "death," "consumption," "delerium tremens," "hell-fire," etc. When the kegs were opened the

labels appeared and frightened potential drunkards. Deacon John Stone, a Salem distiller, charged that the story was intended to depict him. He was a deacon in the church and treasurer of the local Bible Society and there were other similarities including the fact that Deacon Stone's ads read: "Apply at John Stone's Distillery." An illustrious team of lawyers was engaged—John T. Austin and Leverett Salstonstall appeared for the plaintiff and Peleg Sprague and Rufus Choate for the defendant. Professor Reuben D. Mussey of the Dartmouth Medical School testified on the evil effects of alcohol. Cheever was convicted and the case was appealed to the Supreme Judicial Court of Massachusetts where Cheever pleaded guilty and was given a thirty-day jail sentence and required to give bonds of $1,000 for keeping the peace for two years. One of the side issues in the case was the attempt by a man with an axe to chop down the door of the shop that printed the offending issue of the *Landmark*.

————. *The True History of Deacon Giles' Distillery Reported for the Benefit of Posterity*. New York, 1844. 48p. **1C135**
One of the many editions of the Deacon Giles' Distillery libel case that were published by temperance groups in the United States and in Ireland. This edition gives the background of the case; the text of the offending story, Inquire at Amos Giles' Distillery, with illustrations; an account of the trial before the Court of Common Pleas; and Mr. Cheever's own defense statement read on appeal before the Supreme Judicial Court of Massachusetts. Cheever had alienated himself from many local citizens because of his attacks on Unitarianism.

Cherry, Jonathan B. "Obscenity and Ohio Nuisance Statutes." *University of Toledo Law Review*, 5:171–80, Fall 1973. **1C136**
Re: *Pursue, Ltd. v. Huffman* (1973), involving the constitutionality of Ohio nuisance statutes as they pertain to the exhibition of obscene motion pictures.

Chesterton, G. K. "Anonymity and Further Counsels." In his *All Things Considered*. London, Methuen, 1908, pp. 125–29. **1C137**
An appeal for an end to anonymity in newspaper articles. "I hope some day to see an anonymous article counted as dishonorable as an anonymous letter." The author also recommends that the names of the editor, proprietor, and stockholders of a newspaper be prominently published in each issue.

Chicago Civil Liberties Committee. *An Open Letter to the Mayor of Chicago protesting the attempt to ban A Diary of Love, the Novel by Maude Hutchins*. Chicago, The Committee [1950?]. 6p. **1C138**
Includes statements by the publisher (New Directions) and the author, and favorable reviews of the work. The case involves action by the

Police Bureau of Censorship against the novel on grounds of obscenity.

Chicago Journalism Review. Chicago, Association of Working Press, 1968–date. Monthly, except March–April. **1C139**
Launched during the 1968 Democratic convention by Chicago "working newsmen," the paper was the first of a growing number of so-called "journalism reviews" whose purpose is to comment on and criticize freely the operations of the established press. Over the years the review has carried articles dealing with efforts to suppress or distort the news, with special reference to the Chicago scene. Among the other "journalism reviews" with similar purpose are: *The Review of Southern California Journalism* (Long Beach), *St. Louis Journalism Review*, the *Philadelphia Journalism Review*, *The Unsatisfied Man* (Denver), and *Journalist Newsletter* (Providence).

[Chicago Times.] *The Suppression of The Chicago Times*. Chicago, [The Chicago Times? 1863?]. 32p. **1C140**
At eleven o'clock on 2 June 1863, General Ambrose E. Burnside, Civil War commander of the Department of the Ohio, issued the following telegram to the editor of the *Chicago Times* from his headquarters in Cincinnati: "You are hereby notified that I have issued an order stopping the publication of your paper, which order will be published in the morning papers of this city to day. You will please govern yourself accordingly." At twelve o'clock, U.S. Judge Thomas Drummond issued a restraining order to prevent the Army action. Despite the court order a military force invaded the newspaper office on the following day and stopped the presses. The General's action was taken "on account of the repeated expression of disloyal and incendiary sentiments" of the paper. On the day of the suppression a mass protest meeting was held at the Court House Square, presided over by Samuel W. Fuller, and numerous prominent citizens and public officials protested the action. A group of citizens petitioned President Lincoln to revoke the order. Later in the week, while the matter was before the federal court in Chicago, the editor received the following telegram from General Burnside: "By direction of the President of the United States, my order suppressing the circulation of your paper is revoked. You are at liberty to resume publication." The entire account, including speeches and documents, many taken from the columns of the *Chicago Times*, is contained in this contemporary pamphlet.

Chipp, D. L. "Aspects of Australian Censorship Laws." In Melbourne University, *The Law and the Printer, the Publisher and the Journalist. The Collected Papers of a Seminar at Melbourne University on August 12, 1971*. Melbourne, Antony Whitlock, 1971, pp. 58–64. **1C141**
The Minister of Customs and Excise, charged with responsibility for literature and film censorship of works coming into Australia, discusses the difficulties in interpreting and enforc-

ing regulations against obscenity, blasphemy, and other offensive matter. He favors less official censorship and more responsible self-censorship by individuals and units in society, including parents for their children.

Chitre, Dilip. "Aspects of Pornophobia." *Quest*, 59:71–73, October–December 1968. **1C142**
Criticism of the report on obscenity and the law eminating from the Select Committee of the Rajya Sabha, which is based on an unreasoned fear of pornography, which the author believes may result in more stringent laws. "The consequence of this is quite clear. The serious Indian creative writer will from now on be working in a far more oppressive climate than earlier." The author sees sadistic pornography, which combines violence with titillation, as the only area that could lead to socially dangerous consequences. "But in India sadistic pornography is remarkably absent."

Chittick, William O. "American Foreign Policy Elites; Attitudes toward Secrecy and Publicity." *Journalism Quarterly*, 47:689–96, Winter 1970. **1C143**
State Department officials are more likely than either reporters or nongovernmental organization leaders to accept manipulation of information to serve policy needs.

Chopra, Pran. " 'Freeing' the 'Free' Press." *Economic and Political Weekly*, 6(39):2053–59, 25 September 1971. (Reprinted in *Seminar*, November 1971) **1C144**
Criticism of current government proposals to diffuse the ownership of Indian newspapers by relying exclusively on the law and not on incentive. "To whom will the Press turn for protection if the government developed the same inclination which is suspected in the present keepers of the Press?"

Chorley, Robert S. T. Chorley, *baron*. "Freedom of Discussion Today." In *The Rationalist Annual for the Year 1956, Edited by Hector Hawton*. London, Watts, 1956, pp. 23–32. **1C145**
Lord Chorley finds little in the law or court decisions for rationalists to complain of since the demise of laws against blasphemy and sedition, although personal libel may be a problem. The main issue of concern is the monopoly control of the media which makes access difficult. He suggests the setting up of a quasi-judicial tribunal to which complaints that the media were infringing on defined civil liberties or were not in the public interest could be referred. In the area of obscenity he believes Britain should look to the experience in America where laws and court decisions have been liberalized.

Choudhury, Malay R. "An Obscenity Bust in—Would You Believe?—India." *Avant Garde*, 1:36–39, January 1968. **1C146**
A young Indian poet describes his arrest and trial for the publication of his poem, Stark Electric Jesus, in the *Hungry Generation Anthology*. The magistrate, after hearing evidence from those who considered the work depraved and corrupt and those literary critics who considered it a work of literature, found the work patently offensive, without redeeming social value and "dirt for dirt's sake." He sentenced Choudhury to one month in jail and fined him 200 rupees. Since then, the poet writes, he has been unable to find a publisher or a bookstore that will sell his works.

Christensen, William E. "The Library Bill of Rights." *Illinois Libraries*, 55:245–48, April 1973. **1C147**
An account of the background, origin, and various revisions of the American Library Association's Library Bill of Rights.

Christenson, Reo M. "Censorship and the Middle American." In *Obscenity in the Mails. Hearings . . .* , U.S. House of Representatives, Committee on the Post Office, 1969, pp. 381–88. **1C148**
"America's intellectuals and the 'Middle American' are on a collision course over pornography. The former, joined by most college youth, the entertainment industry and sexual nonconformists, are almost solidly opposed to the stiffening of censorship laws while an increasing percentage of average Americans favor a crackdown."

———, and A. S. Engel. "Censorship of Pornography?" *Progressive*, 34(9): 24–30, September 1970. (Reprinted in *Current*, November 1970; the Christenson half of the debate is reprinted in Victor B. Cline, *ed.*, *Where Do You Draw the Line?* pp. 309–11) **1C149**
A debate between two members of the Political Science Department of Miami University, Professor Christenson taking the affirmative and Proffessor Engel the negative. Christenson points out that polls indicate three-fourths of the American people want stricter censorship of pornography. "They are offended by books, magazines, movies, plays, erotic displays, pictures, and records which vulgarize, desecrate and cheapen sex, or which encourage or glamorize deviant sexual behavior." To the critics who contend that morals should not be legislated he points out that every criminal law represents a moral judgment. If the small minority who want no official censorship have their way we run the risk of private vigilantism. Engel believes that new censorship proposals will not be any more successful than

those of the past. "In exchange for keeping us safe from the devil of pornography, we can expect to pay a handsome price: the endless harassment of bookshops and theaters; the frustration of an effort to stamp out pornography, and only to succeed in driving up the profits . . . and the sheer waste of our precious talents and resources in so sterile a venture when so many truly important and compelling problems beset us."

Christian Action. *Moral Protest in Britain; A Guide to Action*. London, Christian Action, 1963. 28p. **1C150**
While recognizing the repugnance in Britain to official censorship, George E. Catlin notes in the preface that "experience has shown that it is not practical politics to dispense altogether with supervision and legal restriction." Between the two extremes of a single censor and total absence of control there have grown up a variety of bodies, official and unofficial, concerned in maintaining standards of propriety in print, film, and broadcasting. The pamphlet describes such bodies as a guide to public action. There are chapters on the Lord Chamberlain and stage censorship (since abolished), the British Board of Film Censors, the Press Council, B.B.C., Independent Television, Obscene Publications Act, and Private Vigilant Bodies.

Christie, George C. "Injury to Reputation and the Constitution: Confusion Amid Conflicting Approaches." *Michigan Law Review*, 75:43–67, November 1976. **1C151**
"It is the thesis of this article that the long-run implications of *Firestone* [*Time*, *Inc. v. Firestone* (1976)] and *Paul v. Davis* [1976] will force a radical reformulation of the circumstances under which an individual may obtain legal redress for injury to his reputation brought about by falsehoods."

Church, Bud. " 'Soul on Ice' Makes the School Board Agenda." *Media & Methods*, 6:54–58, 62–64, March 1970. **1C152**
A discussion on the use of Eldridge Cleaver's *Soul on Ice* by high school English students and the broader issues of teaching controversial modern literature to high school students. Appended are guidelines for selection and use of controversial materials, approved by a Connecticut school system.

Church League of America. Research Department. *Subversion By the Volume. The Sad State of the American Book Publishing Industry Today*. Wheaton, Ill., The League, 1970. 72p. **1C153**
A sampling of left-wing books issued by major American publishers documents the charge that "communists and their dupes and fellow travelers have penetrated into almost every publishing company in the United States."

Church of England. National Assem-

bly. Board for Social Responsibility. *Obscene Publications: Law and Practice*. London, General Synod of the Church of England (Board for Social Responsibility), 1970. 15p. **1C154**

[Cincinnati Board of Education *et al.*] *The Bible in the Public Schools. Arguments in the Case of John D. Minor et al. versus The Board of Education of the City of Cincinnati et al. Superior Court of Cincinnati. With the Opinions and Decision of the Court*. Cincinnati, Robert Clarke, 1870. 420p. **1C155**
The Cincinnati Board of Education had, on 1 November 1869, passed a resolution to the effect "that religious instruction, and the reading of religious books, including the Holy Bible, are prohibited in the Common Schools of Cincinnati, it being the true object and intent of this rule to allow the children of the parents of all sects and opinions, in matters of faith and worship, to enjoy alike the benefit of the Common School fund." A group of citizens challenged the action of the Board and secured an injunction against its enforcement, citing the long-standing practice of Bible reading, the fact that a large number of school texts had religious references in them and would have to be discarded, and that the action would deprive some children of any religious education. After extensive arguments the court decided 2 to 1 to uphold a perpetual injunction against the School Board's action.

"A Circulating Censorship." *Saturday Review* (London), 58:747–48, 13 December 1884. **1C156**
An attack on the British circulating libraries which regulate the sale, and indirectly the character of English literature. Their rules and regulations are absurd and anomalous; they have crushed out private purchases because "the managers of the libraries must make the scruples of the weakest bretheren their standard of admission or rejection."

Cirino, Robert. "Commercial Outlets Wouldn't Publish My Book." *Grassroots Editor*, 12(5):4–6, 18, September–October 1971. **1C157**
The author of *Don't Blame the People*, a criticism of the mass media for right-wing bias, describes his difficulty in getting his manuscript published, ending with his publishing the book himself.

———. *Don't Blame the People: How the News Media Use Bias, Distortion and Censorship to Manipulate Public Opinion*. Los Angeles, Diversity, 1971. 341p.; New York, Random House, 1972. 339p. **1C158**
The author, a high school history teacher, has assembled a considerable amount of data on coverage or lack of coverage of the news by the *New York Times*, the *Los Angeles Times*, the three

major television networks, four radio networks, and the *Reader's Digest*. He considers such subjects as the Vietnam war, pollution, cigarette smoking, the space program, meat inspection, hunger in America, the Roman Catholic Church, foreign policy, automobile safety, venereal diseases, prison conditions, and the military-industrial complex. "The establishment," he charges, "has prevented real public participation by not allowing all ideas to compete fairly for public acceptance." One of the tragic consequences of the manipulation of news was the Vietnam war. "Had those opposing our involvement had an equal use of communications technology, United States involvement could not have been initiated or carried out in the first place; it would have been revealed as unwise and unjust." The book has been praised by those critics who saw right-wing bias in the nation's press and criticized by those who supported the Agnew thesis that the press favored the dissidents. The book was also criticized for its simplistic approach to complex issues, and its lack of objectivity and discipline.

———. *Power to Persuade*: *Mass Media and the News*. New York, Bantam, 1974. 246p. **1C159**
"The purpose of this book is to help the citizen develop a better understanding of the production, control, and dissemination of information by the mass media. This understanding will enable him to detect and compensate for one-sided propaganda, to make better choices among information sources, and thus to participate more effectively on both an intellectual and practical level in the democratic process. . . . The method of this book is to provide actual case studies in the production, control, and dissemination of mass media products. Each case invites you to retrace the decision-making process just as if you were a media executive, editor, or reporter." A chart is provided for scoring publications and broadcasts.

Citizens Communications Center. *Primer on Citizens' Access to the Federal Communications Commission*. Washington, D.C., The Center, 1972. 52p. **1C160**
"The purpose of this booklet is to explore in a general and rudimentary way the forms of redress available to a citizen or community group at the Federal Communications Commission when it is dissatisfied with either a particular aspect of a broadcast licensee's performance or the licensee's overall performance."

———. *Progress Report*. Washington, D.C., The Center, 1971. 32p. Processed. **1C161**
"Citizens Communications Center is a law firm which provides free assistance to people interested in improving the quality of their local broadcasting service by gaining access to the regulatory process of the industry."

Citizens Conference on State Legislatures. *Legislative Openness*: *A Special Report on Press and Public Access to Information and Activities in State Legislatures*. Kansas City, Mo., The Conference, 1974. 141p. **1C162**
Includes four views on legislative openness: Government Belongs in the Sunshine by Alfred W. Baxter, Citizen Ownership of State Houses by Nan F. Waterman, Opening the Door into Nothing Is Not Enough by Henry Holcomb, and That Sheep Crying "Public Interest" Ain't No Sheep by R. Allan Hickman.

Citizens for Decency Through Law. *How to Start an Anti-Pornography Drive in Your Community*. Cleveland, CDL, [1975?]. 12p. **1C163**
"The complete guidebook for establishing an effective unit of Citizens for Decency through Law [formerly Citizens for Decent Literature]."

The Civil Liberties Review. New York, American Civil Liberties Union Foundation. 1973–date. Six times a year. **1C164**
"A national magazine of analysis, opinion, record, and debate," the journal frequently carries articles relating to freedom of the press.

Clancy, Paul. *Privacy and the First Amendment*. Columbia, Mo., Freedom of Information Center, 1976. 47p. (Freedom of Information Foundation Series, no. 5). **1C165**
A discussion of the issues involved in finding the proper balance between the privacy rights of individuals and the necessity that society inform and govern itself. "Legislation regulating the interstate exchange of personal information, including criminal records, is viewed as an absolute necessity. But the press has a strong interest in seeing that such laws and regulations do not touch its vital information channels and that the public record remains just that." The press has a responsibility to consider the bonds of propriety and decency; if it fails to do this it creates a climate favorable to curtailing the rights of the press.

Clancy, Phyllis E. *News Management in Vietnam*. Columbia, Mo., Freedom of Information Center, School of Journalism, University of Missouri at Columbia, 1969. 5p. (Report no. 228) **1C166**
"Throughout its history, the United States has placed increased pressure on the press in time of war to insure military security and to enlist the support of public opinion. The news coverage of the Vietnam war has illustrated once again the fine line between censorship of news for military security and management of news for propaganda purposes."

———. *Obscenity*: *From Ginzburg to Stanley*. Columbia, Mo., Freedom of Information Center, School of Jour-

nalism, University of Missouri at Columbia, 1970. 4p. (Report no. 239) **1C167**
"Supreme Court decisions since 1966 have expanded the guidelines used in judging obscenity, but conflicting opinions exist as to how clear and applicable they are. Adjunctive to these expanded guidelines are the Court's statements regarding state regulation and the possession of obscene material in an individual's home."

Clapp, Jane. *Art Censorship; A Chronology of Proscribed and Prescribed Art*. Metuchen, N.J., Scarecrow, 1972. 582p. **1C168**
"*Art Censorship* brings together from scattered sources a record of suppression, restriction and restraint of visual communication in the plastic arts—painting, sculpture, graphic arts, architecture—and the decorative arts. Photography, including motion pictures, is not considered in *Art Censorship*. 'Censorship' has been broadly construed to include artists or art works restricted for economic, social, moral or aesthetic reasons by state and church officials, and also by citizens or other groups, individuals, or society as a whole." The work begins with the Egyptian dynasty, 3400–2900 B.C. and ends with a U.S. Supreme Court ruling 3 May 1971. There is a subject index and an extensive bibliography.

Clapp, Verner W. *Copyright—A Librarian's View*. Prepared for the National Advisory Commission on Libraries. Washington, D.C., Copyright Committee, Association of Research Libraries, 1968. 40p. **1C169**
The author, long associated with the Library of Congress, concludes from his study of libraries and copyright that: a principle purpose for the existence of a research library is to facilitate copying of relevant documents; that copying is indispensable to library-based research; that no copyright proprietor has ever had an exclusive right to a copyrighted work; that prohibition of library copying is contrary to the public interest; that studies have failed to show that photocopying has led to significant loss of sales; and that libraries that have already paid once for material cannot be expected to pay additionally for the privilege of copying.

Clardy, J. V. "Communist Publications in the U.S. Mail." *Western Humanities Review*, 20:3–9, Winter 1966. **1C170**
A history of the effort by Congress to restrict the rights of American people to read certain types of printed materials—especially foreign Communist newspapers, magazines and pamphlets, beginning with the Espionage Act in 1917 down to the Supreme Court case, *Lamont v. Postmaster General* (1965), in which the Court

held that postal officials may not withhold foreign Communist material from an addressee.

Clark, David G. "H. V. Kaltenborn and His Sponsors: Controversial Broadcasting and the Sponsor's Role." *Journal of Broadcasting*, 12:309–21, Fall 1968. (Reprinted in Lawrence W. Lichty and Malachi C. Topping, *eds.*, *American Broadcasting*, pp. 236–44) **1C171**

An account of the role of the sponsors of a radio commentator who spoke frankly on controversial issues, including criticism of the Nazis and Spain's General Franco. Following pressures from German interests and Catholics, the sponsor, General Mills, terminated Kaltenborn's contract. Pure Oil Company took over sponsorship and for 15 years and through many controversies which resulted in boycott of the company's product, Pure Oil "never once tried to crack down on him, or even threatened seriously to do so." The author believes the case "seems strongly to reinforce the suggestion that successful airing of controversial public issues depends not so much on commentator or network willingness to speak out, as on sponsor willingness to stand the gaff." Pure Oil made the decision to resist pressure and "eventually troubles flew in the face of firm resolve."

————, and Earl R. Hutchison, *eds*. *Mass Media and the Law: Freedom and Restraint*. New York, Wiley-Interscience, 1970. 461p. **1C172**

An anthology of articles under the following categories: (1) Prior Restraint; (2) Right of Access; (3) The Flow of Ideas; (4) Conflict with the Courts; (5) Invasion of Privacy; (6) Libel; (7) Control of Ideas About Sex, Religion, Politics, and Commerce; (8) The Federal Government (Post Office, FTC, FCC); (9) Copyright; and (10) Future for Whom to Do What? Individual articles are listed in this bibliography under the name of the author.

Clark, Elias. "Holding Government Accountable: The Amended Freedom of Information Act: An Article in Honor of Fred Rodell." *Yale Law Journal*, 84:741–69, March 1975. **1C173**

Comments on the first seven years of experience under the Act and predictions about the effect of the amendments on the future. The author concludes that "the amended Act will affect fundamentally the way we govern ourselves. The individual citizen, either alone or in conjunction with others who share his concern, now has substantial access to information which was previously the exclusive possession of the handful of administrators who made the decisions on our behalf."

Clark, Miles. "Big Brother, 1976—Judges and the Gag Order." *Freedom of Speech Newsletter* (Western Speech Communication Association), 2(4):4–7, May 1976. **1C174**

The author reviews recent evidence on pretrial publicity in light of the impending "gag order" case before the U.S. Supreme Court.

Clark, Peter B. "The Opinion Machine: Intellectuals, the Mass Media and American Government." In Harry M. Clor, *ed.*, *The Mass Media and Modern Democracy*, Chicago, Rand McNally, 1974, pp. 37–84. **1C175**

The author develops the thesis that liberally biased news media have changed the goals of society, the functions of the economy, and the role and reliability of government. This has been accomplished by the cumulative efforts of thousands of newspaper, television, and magazine stories. This monolithic intellectual viewpoint "has to a great extent demoralized and overwhelmed the pragmatic functionaries of American political life and government in recent years." He suggests that the media "cease to advocate the intellectual viewpoint but again merely report it, as one among many diverse American perceptions." Specifically, he suggests care in the selection of staff to get greater balance in ideologies, breaking of the chain of academic influence on journalists, and less reliance by local newspapers and radio stations on the national media and their orthodox liberalism.

Clark, Robert L., Jr. "Book Burning Okies." *Oklahoma Librarian*, 22(2):4–5, 50–53, April 1972. **1C176**

Three men and a woman were sentenced to ten years in prison in the 1940s under the Oklahoma syndicalist law for displaying books. The books, some 10,000, were seized and publicly burned. The author of the article tells the story of an official witch-hunt in Oklahoma City in 1940, using a World War I law to stamp out subversive literature. Petitions to the governor protesting the sentence were turned over to the FBI.

Clark, Susan A. "Censorship: Utterly Without Redeeming Value." *Journal of Research and Development in Education*, 9:33–40, Spring 1976. **1C177**

The June 1973 obscenity decisions of the U.S. Supreme Court have resulted in "a rush of censorship attempts on all levels of government which has made its impact felt in schools and libraries around the country." The article traces the history of obscenity legislation and court decisions in the United States leading to the *Miller v. California* decision of 1973, which resulted in a surge of state legislative action reflecting varying interpretations of the Supreme Court's ruling. Three provisions should be present in any equitable state obscenity law—mandating prior civil proceedings, precise sexual conduct definitions, and statewide standards. Much of the state legislation does not contain these protections. The author calls

on teachers and librarians to change the tide of censorship by active participation in the legislative process through professional and community organizations.

Clark, Thomas P., and **Ronald J. Stites.** "The First Amendment: Congressional Investigations and the Speech or Debate Clause." *University of Missouri at Kansas City Law Review*, 40:108–28, Autumn 1971. **1C178**

An examination of the case of *Hentoff v. Ichord* (1970), in which Nat Hentoff, a political columnist, filed a class action suit to enjoin the publication of a report of the House Internal Security Committee which he alleged would encroach upon the First Amendment rights of sixty-six persons who were listed as speaking on college campuses. "The report inferred without offering any positive evidence that these speakers, 'Pied Pipers of pernicious propaganda,' were using the money they received for speaking to finance the listed (left-wing and radical) organizations." The Court ruled for the plaintiff, upholding an injunction against the printing and distribution of the report by the Public Printer. The authors consider the implications under the First Amendment. Congressman Ichord, chairman of the Committee, noted that this was the first time in English or American history that a legislative report has been judicially suppressed and called for Congress to "assert and defend" its supremacy over its own affairs against interference by the courts.

Clark, Todd. "The West Virginia Textbook Controversy: A Personal Account." *Social Education*, 39:216–19, April 1975. **1C179**

A member of the team of the National Council for the Social Studies that conducted a fact-finding study of the explosive textbook controversy in Kanawha County, W.Va., found a far from simple situation. The controversy involved sincere differences in philosophies of education, the consideration of minority ideologies, and the participation of parents in the education of their children. As part of a settlement, parents are now free to approve or disapprove of the use of the challenged books by their children, but not to force their views on other children. The writer sees the need for professional educators to be more aware of the value structure of their communities.

————*et al. Fair Trial v. Free Speech. A Resource Manual for Teachers and Students*. Pitman, N.J., Institute for Political/Legal Education, 1975. 66p. (ED 110,391) **1C180**

The manual was prepared to instruct high school students in political, governmental, and legal processes. The unit examines civil rights in relation to fair trial and free press. Case studies (three murder trials) are presented for students to analyze and render decisions.

Clarke, Jack. *Open Meeting Law: An Analysis*. Columbia, Mo., Freedom of

Information Center, School of Journalism, University of Missouri at Columbia, 1975. 12p. (Report no. 338) **1C181**
"Open meeting statutes vary from state to state; the author evaluates different characteristics with respect to their effectiveness in a democracy and presents a model FoI law."

"Clash of Absolutes." *New Republic*, 165 (1):5–7, 3 July 1971. **1C182**
This editorial examines the legal issues advanced by government prosecution and the defense in the case against the *New York Times* and the *Washington Post* over the publication of the Pentagon Papers.

Clayton, Charles C. "Bar Association Attempts to Regulate Press Ethics." *Grassroots Editor*, 10(2):12–15, March–April 1969. **1C183**
A review of the unsuccessful efforts by the journalism profession to agree upon a single code of ethics and the more successful efforts by the legal profession. In recent years the American Bar Association has attempted to impose its canons of ethics upon the profession of journalists and has also sought to invoke the power of the courts to compel compliance. The author discusses the two specific areas where the ABA canons conflict with the precepts of journalism: Canon 20 dealing with pretrial publicity and Canon 35 dealing with photographic coverage of trials.

———."The Reardon Report." *Grassroots Editor*, 9(2):5–8, March–April 1968. **1C184**
Criticism of the recommendation of the Reardon Commission to strengthen Canon 20 of the American Bar Association governing news coverage of trials. The muzzle imposed upon the press achieves nothing but "places a premium on ignorance and insults the intelligence of the average citizen." Neither side in a jury case wants intelligent jurors, and newsmen who are knowledgeable about public affairs are considered dangerous as jurymen. The supporters of the Reardon plan cite such celebrated incidents of prejudicial publicity as the cases of Dr. Samuel Sheppard and Jack Ruby; a study conducted by the American Newspaper Publishers Association shows that out of 40,000 felony jury trials in a two-year period, there were only two reversals on the basis of presumed prejudice. With the rising tide of crime the news media are needed to compliment the work of the police in law enforcement; they are also needed to insure that justice is carried out. Truth may be as beneficial to the accused as to the state.

Cleary, Thomas J., Jr. "Aid and Comfort to the Enemy." *Military Review*, 48:51–55, August 1968. **1C185**
An army colonel reviews the incident in which two American press representatives in Korea had their credentials revoked by General MacArthur's headquarters for writing news reports that purportedly "gave aid and comfort to the enemy." Although later reinstated, friction between press and military existed throughout the conflict. The author concludes that both journalists and the military should pursue their own viewpoints—"the press to seek and publish the truth, within the bounds of security, and the military services to provide for the security of its operations and personnel."

[Cleland, John.] "A Note on the American History of *Memoirs of a Woman of Pleasure*." In John Cleland, *Memoirs of a Woman of Pleasure*. New York, Putnam's, 1963, pp. xv–xxviii. **1C186**
This publisher's note traces the hectic publishing history of this often-banned book from 1789 when a New York bookseller offered a copy for sale until it was cleared by the courts in 1963.

Clifford, John. "Political Broadcasts and the Informed Electorate: A Call for Action." *Catholic University Law Review*, 22:177–87, Fall 1972. **1C187**
"The purpose of this paper is to examine the problems of lack of access to the broadcast media in political campaigns, to examine the lack of substance in political uses of the media, and to suggest corrective measures which could be taken by Congress or the Federal Communications Commission."

Clifton, James R. "Court of Appeals Review of Facts in First Amendment Cases Is De Novo." *Cumberland–Samford Law Review*, 4:182–89, Spring 1973. **1C188**
Re: *Firestone v. Time, Inc.* (1972), a libel case against *Time, Inc.* which was resolved in favor of the defendant on the basis of *New York Times Co. v. Sullivan* (1964).

Clifton, Shaw. "Defamation Defamed." *Solicitors Journal*, 115:357–60, 14 May 1971. **1C189**
The aim of the article is "to pinpoint three matters which are considered to be at the heart of reforming the [British] law of defamation: the attitude of lawyers to language both technical and non-technical, the distinction between libel and slander, and the possibility of a defamation code."

Cline, Timothy R., and Rebecca J. Cline. "Gaining Access to the Media: Some Issues and Cases." Speech Communication Association. *Free Speech Yearbook*, 1975, pp. 35–56. **1C190**
"A critical look at the cases made for and against a right to access uncovers the issues involved and suggests three departure points for analysis: from the view of the listener, the speaker, and the media."

Cline, Victor B. "Another View: Pornography Effects, the State of the Art."

In his *Where Do You Draw the Line?* Provo, Utah, Brigham Young University Press, 1974, pp. 203–44. **1C191**
"After carefully reviewing all the [Commission on Obscenity and Pornography] original research as well as the data in the open literature, it is my judgment that the Commission's final report was marked by certain ideological biases which, in Hans Eysenck's words, 'implied a slide from scientific discussion to propaganda.' It is this issue, as well as to a consideration of the current state of the art concerning effects of pornography that I address this review."

———."Censorship in a Free Society?" *Utah Libraries*, 14:10–14, Spring 1971. **1C192**
"There is probably sufficient evidence, along with logical reasoning, for suggesting that there is risk in exposing latency—age and adolescent youth—to excessive display of violence, pornography, and any extremes of antisocial behavior in the mass media, particularly in a widespread and extended fashion, and that some sort of modest restriction of dissemination of such materials would seem sensible. Restrictions should be developed only with the consent of the electorate, using the traditional processes of democratic government and law, through legitimately enacted legislation." The author is a professor of psychology, University of Utah.

———."The Pornography Commission: A Case Study of Scientists and Social Policy Decision Making." In his *Where Do You Draw the Line?* Provo, Utah, Brigham Young University Press, 1974, pp. 245–56. **1C193**
The effort to bring diverse views to the project resulted in a polarization among the participants "which led to a taking of sides and ultimately to an inability of the various factions to communicate effectively or to negotiate with each other. And the will of the side, or orthodoxy with the most members, prevailed." Since the findings were inconclusive, particularly with respect to adults, a "trade-off between perceived or real harm versus the benefits of greater freedom of expression" must ultimately be decided by ordinary citizens. "And it will usually be decided on the basis of shared community values and majoritarian ethical consensus."

———."The Problem of Pornography." *National Decency Reporter*, 4(4):2–4, September–October 1967. **1C194**
A psychologist concludes that "there are sufficient reasons and evidence which suggest that there are risks in exposing (especially in quantity) latency age and adolescent youth to pornography and that some sorts of restrictions on their dissemination would seem sensible."

———. "The Scientists vs. Pornography: An Untold Story." *Intellect*, 104:574–76, May–June 1976. Reply with rejoinder, E. M. Oboler, September 1976.   **1C195**
"A comprehensive review of the full report of the Pornography Commission [U.S. Commission on Obscenity and Pornography] plus the many thousands of pages of supporting scientific studies . . . and outside literature indicates that considerable data suggesting harms associated with pornography exposure were suppressed or covered up by several scientist-members of the Effects Panel and, possibly, their two-man support staff. The evidence strongly suggests that the non-scientist members of the commission and Chairman Lockhart were misled or decieved by withheld negative effects evidence. This undoubtedly influenced the decision of many of the commissioners to recommend repeal of nearly all pornography laws."

———, ed. *Where Do You Draw the Line? An Exploration into Media Violence, Pornography, and Censorship*. Provo, Utah, Brigham Young University Press, 1974. 365p.   **1C196**
It is the intention of this book, which consists of a collection of articles with commentary by the editor, to present "the dilemmas created by either total license or excessive censure, regarding the open expression of ideas and the free depiction of images and behavior in the various media." In the editor's introductory chapter he lists thirty-six traditional arguments against censorship, but follows with eighteen exceptions to free speech allowed by law and court decisions. In a summary chapter the editor suggests that "as long as we live in a pluralistic society, we may not reasonably expect an overwhelming consensus on most of these issues. . . . Some middle ground may ultimately be the most reasonable and judicious approach to media violence, pornography, and similar issues." In a final chapter he proposes a fourfold test for determining obscenity (an alternative to recent Supreme Court tests) that includes violence as well as sex. He favors a jury trial rather than decisions by a judge, if the obscenity law has been breached. He concludes that we must draw a line, because "both pornography and media violence assault taboos with persuasive force, especially taboos involving sexuality and injury/assault on fellow humans—taboos that are intrinsic to social order." Articles in the book are listed in this bibliography under the name of the author.

Cline, Victor B., Roger G. Croft, and Steven Courrier. "The Desensitization of Children to TV Violence." *Journal of Personality and Social Psychology*, 27:360–65, September 1973. (Reprinted in Victor B. Cline, ed., *Where*

Do We Draw the Line? pp. 147–55) **1C197**
"The result of these several studies using two different measures of automatic response corroborate each other and suggest that some children who are heavy TV watchers (and see more violence) may become, to some degree, habituated, or 'desensitized' to violence generally. This raises the possibility of a blunting of 'conscience and concern' when children are exposed to a great amount of filmed violence."

Clor, Harry M. "Effects of Obscenity: The Arguments and the Evidence." *Midway*, 8:3–25, Spring 1968.   **1C198**
A study of the effect of obscenity which "leads to two sets of conclusions. With regard to the direct effects of obscenity upon conduct, informed opinion is divided and the evidence is problematic. The social importance of such direct effects as can be shown remains open to dispute. The most socially significant issues concern the more subtle and longterm influences of obscenity upon mind and character—its moral standards and, ultimately, of moral character. The assertion of this truth does not, however, resolve all issues. If obscenity poses for society what is essentially a moral problem, it remains to be established that government and law can legitimately address themselves to this problem. To what extent, if any, is 'the state' legitimately concerned with the moral life of citizens and, more specifically, with that area of moral life which is related to sex?"

———."The Law and the Obscene." *Denver Quarterly*, 3(2):1–24, Summer 1968.   **1C199**
A case for stricter legal restraint of obscenity in literature.

———. *Legal Control of Obscenity*. Chicago, University of Chicago, 1967. 348p. (Unpublished Ph.D. dissertation)   **1C200**

———. "Obscenity and Freedom of Expression." In his *Censorship and Freedom of Expression*, Chicago, Rand McNally, 1971, pp. 97–129. (Reprinted in Victor B. Cline, ed., *Where Do We Draw the Line?* pp. 317–34)   **1C201**
The author defends the censorship of obscenity which he believes rests upon two propositions: "(1) that its unrestrained circulation endangers values and qualities of character that are indispensable for responsible citizenship and decent social relations; (2) that in society's effort to preserve values and qualities that are important to it, there is a legitimate role for the law. These presuppositions are not unreasonable. . . . By means of laws against the more extreme forms of obscenity [which he describes in detail], we are reminded . . . that 'We, the People' have an ethical order and moral limits. The individual is made aware that the community in which he lives regards some things as beyond the pale of civility. This educative function of obscenity laws is ultimately more significant than their coercive function."

———.*Obscenity and Public Morality: Censorship in a Liberal Society*. Chicago, University of Chicago Press, 1969. 315p.   **1C202**
A challenge to the libertarian point of view on censorship and an attempt to define obscenity and assess its influence precisely enough so that it can be dealt with. The author traces the successively more permissive decisions of the United States Supreme Court in the area of obscenity, which he believes, show greater concern with freedom of expression than in the control of a social vice. He rejects the notion that obscenity is harmless or, in fact, may have a cathartic value. He believes it is possible to distinguish between the erotic or realistic in art and literature and the obscene. In a foreward to the work (pp. ix–xii) C. Herman Pritchett states: "The essence of obscenity for him consists in making public that which is private, intruding on intimate physical processes and acts or physical-emotional states and hereby degrading the human dimensions of life to a subhuman or merely physical level. Not only the sex organs and sexual activities but all bodily functions, physical suffering, and death can be treated obscenely. . . . He believes it is possible to draft standards which will provide a barrier against the worst intrusions upon intimacies of the body and against some of the most obscene portrayals of sex, brute violence and death."

———. "Obscenity and the First Amendment: Round Three." *Loyola of Los Angeles Law Review*, 7:207–26, June 1974.   **1C203**
The article explores several of the more controversial themes in the June 1973 obscenity rulings of the U.S. Supreme Court [Miller v. California et al. 1973] "with a view to determining what has been accomplished, what remains to be done, and where the difficulties lie. The first part of the analysis is concerned with the legal standards established for determining obscenity and with related legal questions. The second part deals with the Court's rationale for censorship of obscenity and with the larger moral and philosophic dimensions of the subject, including those treated in the dissenting opinions."

———. "Science, Eros and the Law: A Critique of the Obscenity Commission Report." *Duquesne Law Review*, 10:63–76, Fall 1971.   **1C204**
The author finds that the U.S. Commission on Obscenity and Pornography has failed to resolve the obscenity problem with scientific facts, but has allowed the ideologies of its members to dictate the findings. The crucial battle is still that of opposing social ideologies and different ways of interpreting common experience.

———, ed. *Censorship and Freedom of Expression: Essays on Obscenity and the Law*. Chicago, Rand McNally, 1971. 175p.   **1C205**
Essays prepared for a Public Affairs Confer-

ence, Kenyon College. Judicial opinions by Judge Jerome Frank (*U.S. v. Roth*) and Associate Justice William J. Brennan (*Roth v. U.S.*) "introduce the problem of obscenity and censorship in its legal context from the perspective of American judges who must decide upon the constitutionality of obscenity censorship." Essays by Charles Rembar, Walter Berns, Richard F. Hettlinger, Harry M. Clor, Richard H. Kuh, and Willard M. Gaylin, "present diverse viewpoints on the constitutional issues and opposing arguments about the dangers of obscenity and the propriety of censorship as public policy in the United States."

————. *The Mass Media and Modern Democracy*. Chicago, Rand McNally, 1974. 232p.   **1C206**
A series of essays exploring basic issues in the conflict between the news media and the government—whether ideological biases in the journalistic profession result in distortion in the news, the extent to which the press (print and electronic) should be free under the First Amendment, the conflict between the people's right to know and the interest of national security and the privacy of the individual, the propriety of requiring newsmen to testify and divulge confidential information in criminal cases, and the effects of the mass media (particularly television) upon public morality, public opinion, and cultural values. Content: The New Journalism by Robert D. Novak. Why Does Nobody Love the Press by George E. Reedy. The Opinion Machine: Intellectuals, the Mass Media, and American Government by Peter B. Clark. The Politics of a News Story by Paul H. Weaver. The Constitution and a Responsible Press by Walter Berns. The Ability to Communicate: A First Amendment Right by A. Stephen Boyan, Jr. Self-Government and the Mass Media: A Practical Man's Guide by George Anastaplo.

Cloutman, Brett, and Francis W. Luck. *Law for Printers and Publishers. Second Edition Edited by E. H. Hale*. London, Staples, 1949. 341p. (First published in 1929)   **1C207**
Includes discussions of defamation, libel, copyright, and illegal publications.

Clune, Frank. *The Scottish Martyrs; Their Trials and Transportation to Botany Bay*. Sydney, Angus and Robertson, 1969. 191p.   **1C208**
The story of the Scottish sedition trials of Thomas Muir (M565–67), Thomas Fyshe Palmer (P25–27), William Skirving, Joseph Gerrald, and Maurice Margarot in the years 1793 and 1794 and their sentencing to be transported to New South Wales.

Clymer, Adam. "Further More: In Defense of Leaks." *MORE*, 4(8):22–23, August 1974.   **1C209**
"The problem of leaks on the impeachment story is not one of fairness. The leaks have made the President look bad because the secret evidence makes him look bad."

Cobb, Thomas C. "Venue: Florida Rejects Single Publication Rule." *University of Florida Law Review*, 19:654–59, Spring 1967   **1C210**
In the libel case, *Firstamerica Corp. v. News-Journal Corp.* (1967), the Florida Supreme Court ruled that venue could be laid at plaintiff's option in any county in which the newspaper circulated the alleged libel. The author suggests that the legislature amend the venue statutes to preclude "forum shopping" and multiple suits.

Cobbe, Frances P. "The Morals of Literature." *Fraser's Magazine*, 70:124–33, July 1864.   **1C211**
The author discusses the moral obligation of writers of biography (frankness v. invasion of privacy), fiction (resemblance of real persons, distortion of human nature), and criticism (fairness).

Coben, Stanley. *The Political Career of A. Mitchell Palmer*. New York, Columbia University, 1961. 417p. (Ph.D. dissertation, University Microfilms, no. 64–9157)   **1C212**
One of the objects of the study is to explain the enigma of the man who was, on the one hand, "an infamous violator of our civil liberties, responsible for the atrocious Palmer Raids [on subversive literature] of 1919–1920 and for the postwar labor injunctions," and on the other hand, "one of the most powerful advocates of advanced social legislation as a Congressman before World War I."

Cobin, David M. "CATV Regulation—A Complex Problem of Regulatory Jurisdiction." *Boston College Industrial and Commercial Law Review*, 9:429–43, Winter 1968.   **1C213**
"This comment will review CATV's impact on the television industry and, in the light of this recent litigation, examine the FCC's authority to regulate CATV under the powers granted by the Communications Act of 1934."

Cochran, Wendell R. *The Press at the Calley Trial*. Columbia, Mo., Freedom of Information Center, School of Journalism, University of Missouri at Columbia, 1974. 10p. (Report no. 320)   **1C214**
"Despite the difficulties inherent in press coverage of the complex and emotionally explosive trial of Lieutenant William Calley, media and government relations at Fort Benning generally worked well, establishing a precedent for similar future situations."

Code News. The Code Authority, National Association of Broadcasters. Washington, D.C., 1968–date. Monthly.   **1C215**
News and official announcements relating to

the administration of the radio-television code of ethics.

Coffin, Thomas E. *et al.* "Violence Ratings: A Dialogue." *Journal of Broadcasting*, 17:3–35, Winter 1972–73.   **1C216**
Five researchers (Thomas E. Coffin, Sam Tuchman, Michael F. Eleey, George Gerbner, and Nancy Tedesco) discuss the relative merits of a number of so-called indices of violence on television programming.

Coggin, Ted R. "Journalists' Privilege under the First Amendment Guarantee of Freedom of the Press." *Cumberland-Samford Law Review*, 2:223–28, Spring 1971.   **1C217**
Notes on the case of *Caldwell v. United States* (1970), involving contempt for refusal to reveal news sources. "Without question, the balance of interest heretofore required in construction of first amendment rights has been tipped in favor of the journalist." The decision was later reversed by the U.S. Supreme Court.

Cohen, Chapman. *Blasphemy: A Plea for Religious Equality*. London, Pioneer Press, 1922. 30p.   **1C218**
"The pamphlet is written with the object of calling attention to the existence of the law of blasphemy and to further the movement for the repeal of both the Statute and Common law dealing with the offense. . . . There is only one sure protection against the abuse of free speech, only one certain way of securing decency in controversy and that is to leave such matters wholly and entirely to the free play of public opinion and the development of public manners. The maintenance of the blasphemy laws prevent the one and they do not even lead to the other. They are an appeal to the principle of intolerance and persecution and they thrive only as long as intolerance and persecution are kept alive."

Cohen, Claudia. "Eclipse in Baltimore." *MORE*, 4(3):8–9, March 1974.   **1C219**
Reprinting of an article on the sale of Spiro Agnew's Maryland home, written by a reporter for the *Baltimore Sun*, but killed after Agnew complained to the newspaper's publisher, together with comment about the incident—Enterprise Reporting or "Invasion of Privacy"? by Claudia Cohen.

Cohen, David. " 'Be Prepared' Is Not Only for Boy Scouts! Or Coping with Censorship in Schools!" In Dominic Salvatore, *ed.*, *The Paperback Goes to School*. New York, Bureau of Independent Publishers and Distributors, 1972, pp. 91–112.   **1C220**

"Since World War II the tremendous surge of realistic literature, both fiction and nonfiction, has made the job of book selection for teachers and librarians a rewarding as well as a hazardous experience." The author cites a number of titles that have been the subject of censorship cases; he reproduces a model policy statement governing selection of instructional materials, the School Library Bill of Rights, forms prepared by the National Council of Teachers of English for citizens to use in asking for reconsideration of educational materials, the Library Bill of Rights, and the Freedom to Read Statement. He also summarizes the findings of the national Commission on Obscenity and Pornography.

Cohen, David S. "Current Freedom of Information Legislation." *Illinois Libraries*, 56:274–79, April 1974.   **1C221**
The vice-president of Common Cause pleads for an end to government secrecy, giving examples of continued secrecy in the areas of closed meetings, security classification, executive privilege, and exclusions from the Freedom of Information Act.

————."The Public's Right of Access to Government Information under the First Amendment." *Chicago-Kent Law Review*, 51:164–85, Summer 1974.   **1C222**
The author advocates that "where such interests of public access are in conflict with other rights, it is within the province of the court to balance these rights. A viable democracy cannot permit an official or government agency whose self-interest is at stake to make decisions regarding freedom of access to information."

Cohen, Mark C. "*United States v. Columbia Broadcasting System, Inc.*: Courtroom Sketching and the Right to Fair Trial." *New England Law Review*, 10:541–59, Spring 1975.   **1C223**
"Whether 'reporting' includes an unrestricted right to in-court sketching has not been definitively decided in *CBS*. It is conceivable that a limited restriction, requested by a defendant and within the discretion of the trial judge, might be upheld in the proper situation to reinforce the sanctity and inviolability of the courtroom, and insure the right of an accused to a fair trial."

Cohen, Marla. *FoI Attitudes of the 91st Congress*. Columbia, Mo., Freedom of Information Center, School of Journalism, University of Missouri at Columbia, 1969. 6p. (Report no. 214)   **1C224**
"The American Society of Newspaper Editors and the FoI Center queried members of the 91st Congress concerning their attitudes toward freedom of information legislation in Congress. The result appears to be qualified support for more access to the workings of the legislative branch."

————. *On Obtaining Syndicated Features*. Columbia, Mo., Freedom of Information Center, School of Journalism, University of Missouri at Columbia, 1969. 3p. (Report no. 221)   **1C225**
"Exclusive territory agreements limit access to certain features, a situation which has been noted by the Department of Justice, which has instituted proceedings in a number of cases under provisions of the Sherman and Clayton Acts."

————. *Shield Legislation in the United States*. Columbia, Mo., Freedom of Information Center, School of Journalism, University of Missouri at Columbia, 1968. 4p. (Report no. 212)   **1C226**
"Reporter guarantees of confidentiality have existed since 1896. To date, 15 states have passed such statutes. Recent court cases have stimulated reporter privilege proposals across the United States. These proposals usually have incorporated exceptions to the absolute guarantees of the older statutes."

Cohen, Marshall. "On Pornography." *Public Interest*, 22:38–44, Winter 1971.   **1C227**
Commenting on an essay on pornography by Walter Berns in the same issue (pp.3–24), the author asserts that "the concept of obscenity is a dangerously vague one to play so important a role in criminal legislation. The attempt to control pornography and obscenity, in addition to requiring an indeterminate sacrifice of general principle, endows the criminal authorities with an undesirable degree of discretion, especially unfortunate in so sensitive an area; and it does all this to protect us from harms that are generally exaggerated and often simply fabricated." Cohen would support legislation which would prevent obscenity from being forced upon people and that would prohibit sales to minors. The interpretation of the First Amendment that Berns has been circulating, if widely accepted, "would constitute a far greater threat to the Republic than all the pornography now in print, here and in Denmark."

Cohen, Peter. "Sex and the Censors." *New Nation*, 4(2):5–6, September 1970.   **1C228**
Criticism of the criteria used by the Publications Control Board in South Africa to censor publications and films coming into the country from abroad. The author calls for an enlightened approach, stating that under present policy "we are running the risk of becoming isolated from contemporary Western thought and entering a period of cultural stagnation."

Cohen, Richard E. "The Search for the King Assassin and the Fair-Trial Issue." *Columbia Journalism Review*, 8(2):31–35, Summer 1969.   **1C229**
"Despite all the debate of the last five years, did the press still convict James Earl Ray in print before he went to trial?" The author reviews the coverage of the trial by the *Memphis Commercial Appeal*, the *Boston Record-American*, and the *New York Times*. He concludes that it is not the business of the press to do the work of the court before the formal trial. "The press can attempt to improve the morality of the courts and has often been successful at doing so. Unfortunately, the courts may soon be attempting to enforce the morality of the press unless editors and reporters correct many of their serious infringements of the pretrial rights of the accused."

Cohen, Saul. "Is the Right to Lie Protected by the First Amendment?" *Journal of the Beverly Hills Bar Association*, 3(1):10–15, January 1969.   **1C230**
An examination of recent U.S. Supreme Court decisions involving defamation of public figures.

Cohen, Stanley E. "The Advertiser's Influence in TV Programming." *Osgoode Hall Law Journal*, 8:91–113, August 1970. (Also in *Law and Social Order*, 1970:405–22, 1970)   **1C231**
"Mr. Cohen describes the evolution of the advertiser's influence on programme content and the many trends in the Industry which have decreased the advertiser's leverage. He analyzes television's dilemma of trying to serve the public on one hand while selling that public to the advertiser on the other. Mr. Cohen concludes that direct pressure is at most a marginal problem but recognizes the subtle and complex conflicting interests inherent in the advertiser-supported, profit oriented system. Finally Mr. Cohen describes how the advertiser's awesome though unsought influence may be controlled by countervailing forces which must be used responsibly by the other participants with the uniqueness of the media and the advertiser's needs in mind."—Editor

Cohen, Stephen S. "Hate Propaganda: Amendments to the Criminal Code." *McGill Law Journal*, 17:740–91, December 1971.   **1C232**
The author discusses civil and criminal remedies for group libel in England and the United States, traces the background of antihate legislation in Canada, and analyzes the provisions of Bill C-3, now before the Canadian legislature. He concludes that antihate legislation is useful and necessary to deal with a serious social evil, far outweighing any publicity given to the hatemonger or any possible threat to freedom of speech or the press.

Cohen, Steven M. *The Pentagon Papers Case: Three Years of Interpretation in the Courts*. Columbia, Mo., University of

Missouri, 1974. 129p. (Unpublished Master's thesis) **1C233**
An analysis of prior-restraint cases since the U.S. Supreme Court's decision in the Pentagon Papers case, to determine how the decision made use of *New York Times v. United States* (1971).

Cohen, William. "A New Niche for the Fault Principle: A Forthcoming Newsworthiness Privilege in Libel Cases?" *UCLA Law Review*, 18:371–88, December 1970. **1C234**
"We may be on the verge of a major revolution in the law of libel, where the basis of publisher liability in routine defamation cases is the publisher's fault. . . . The belated recognition of the first amendment interest in the law of libel in *New York v. Sullivan*, however, has led a majority of the Court to embrace the fault standard as a compromise between the common law's absolute liability, and the argument of Justices Black and Douglas for the publisher's absolute privilege. . . . The most interesting question for the future may be whether the fault standard will be a mere verbal admonition to juries or a useful tool to accommodate the competing interests of individual reputation and freedom of the press."

[Cohlan, Richard M.] "Handbilling Unrelated to the Business Function of a Shopping Center Not Protected by First Amendment." *New York Law Forum*, 19:174–84, Summer 1973. **1C235**
Re: *Lloyd Corp. v. Tanner*, 407 U.S. 551 (1972).

Cohn, David S. "Access to Television to Rebut the President of the United States: An Analysis and Proposal." *Temple Law Quarterly*, 45:141–209, Winter 1972. **1C236**
"This article will analyze whether a right of access to radio and television could and should be recognized in circumstances such as these (Indochina War) so that spokesmen for viewpoints contrasting those of the President would be able to rebut him in the broadcast media after he had requested, received, and used time therein to address the Nation." The author concludes that "what is really needed is not an artificially balanced presentation in one licensee but either a large number of licensees covering the whole spectrum and each ably presenting its own side fairly or else a single highly visible station of genuine professional standards of impartiality on which Presidential speeches and rebuttals could be presented." Some degree of government regulation is necessary but "broadcast journalists should be left the discretion to choose the spokesmen, format, timing and electronic environment used in the presentation of contrasting viewpoints and the Commission should be given the role of reviewing the resulting balance."

Cohn, Marcus. "Problems in Maintaining Competition in Broadcasting." In

Don R. Le Duc, *ed.*, *Issues in Broadcast Regulation*. Washington, D.C., Broadcast Education Association, 1974, pp. 95–103. **1C237**
The author challenges many of the assumptions about competition in the broadcasting industry and questions some of the efforts of the Federal Communications Commission, abetted by the courts, at restructuring the industry. On the *Red Lion* decision of the U.S. Supreme Court (*Red Lion Broadcasting Co. v. FCC*, 1967), which requires the broadcaster to carry varying points of view on controversial issues, he comments: "The basic significance of the *Red Lion* case is that it elevates the FCC's concept of participatory democracy to a constitutional principle." He concludes that "the thrust of the present trend toward restructuring the industry is to dehumanize the licensee. It makes him impotent, sterile, and unimaginative. The whole concept of the public participation in what the licensee is doing, or can do, or should do, turns over to the public at large and relieves the licensee of all the ideas inherent in competition. It turns him into a common carrier."

———. "Who Really Controls Television?" *University of Miami Law Review*, 29:482–86, Spring 1975. **1C238**
"Broadcasting is no longer private enterprise in the sense that we formerly thought of it, but rather semi-private enterprise. The decision-making policies of broadcasters are caught up with such phrases as 'the public's right to know' and 'the public's right to access.' The public today does have access to broadcast media and the trend is toward greater and greater access."

Colberg, Don. "Are Librarians Enemies of Intellectual Freedom?" *Georgia Librarian*, 12:5–14, November 1975. **1C239**
"Looking closely at one's attitudes toward intellectual freedom, educating oneself to the philosophical bases of intellectual freedom as developed by ALA, working with library and other organizations for the attainment and advancement of intellectual freedom, helping to provide written selection policies containing positive statements on the need for materials on controversial subjects, are all important means of seeing that people have the right to read, view, and hear what they wish; such a right, however, is hollow, without 'the right of unrestricted access to all information and ideas regardless of the medium of communication use.'"

Colburn, William E. "The Vizetelly Extracts." *Princeton University Chronicle*, 33:54–59, Winter 1962. **1C240**
A bibliographical study of the small volume, *English Classics: Showing That the Legal Suppression of M. Zola's Novels Would Logically Involve the Bowdlerizing of Some of the Greatest Works in English Literature* (V60), issued by Henry Vizetelly in 1888 during his trial for publishing English translations of Zola novels. The author compares the original 1888 publication with a

"pirated reprint" probably issued in New York in the twenties.

Colby, W. E., and Alfred W. McCoy. "Commentary." *Harper's*, 245:116–20, October 1972. **1C241**
Following an introductory statement from the editor, there appears the text of a letter from W. E. Colby, executive director, Central Intelligence Agency, complaining of an article in the July issue, Flowers of Evil by Alfred W. McCoy. His article and subsequently published book describe CIA complicity in the heroin trade in Southeast Asia. McCoy's response that follows discloses that the CIA requested of Harper & Row an advance copy of the proof of the book. Despite criticisms by the CIA the publisher issued the book without change.

Colcord, Herbert. *Nebraska's Shield Law*. Columbia, Mo., Freedom of Information Center, School of Journalism, University of Missouri at Columbia, 1975. 7p. (Report no. 333) **1C242**
"Nebraska's 'Free Flow of Information Act' is one of the strongest shield laws in the nation. This report chronicles the statute's development and describes unsuccessful attempts to weaken it."

Cole, Barry G. *The Australian Broadcasting Control Board and the Regulation of Commercial Radio in Australia Since 1948*. Evanston, Ill., Northwestern University, 1966. 587p. (Ph.D. dissertation, University Microfilms, no. 67–4211) **1C243**
"This study examines the regulation of commercial radio in Australia since 1948, the year in which the Australian Broadcasting Control Board was created by Parliament statute to assume responsibility for almost all regulatory functions. . . . Particular attention is devoted to the Control Board and its relationship to the Government and the Federation of Australian Commercial Broadcasters."

———."License Renewal and Reform." In Don R. Le Duc, *ed.*, *Issues in Broadcast Regulation*. Washington, D.C., Broadcast Education Association, 1974, pp. 49–57. **1C244**
A consultant to the Federal Communications Commission discusses policies and procedures the Commission has considered and is considering in making its license renewal process more effective, including an attempt to define the "good" and "superior" broadcaster.

Cole, David W. *W. S. Gilbert's Contribution to the Freedom of the Stage*. Madison, Wis., University of Wisconsin, 1970. 260p. (Ph.D. dissertation, University Microfilms, no. 70-24,686) **1C245**

Gilbert's success in spite of his violation of Victorian dramatic taboos (treatment of certain moral and religious themes, use of coarse language, scriptural allusions, and personal and political satire) is attributed to his personal aggressiveness, his moderation and indirection on the stage, and the use of forms that tended to limit his satire and distract attention from it. "By adapting himself to the realities of the Victorian theatre, though, Gilbert was able to set precedents for freer dramatic expression in the late Victorian and Edwardian theatre, and to make significant dramatic statements of his own."

Cole, Jeffrey, and Michael I. Spak. "Defense Counsel and the First Amendment: 'A Time To Keep Silence, and a Time to Speak.'" *St. Mary's Law Journal*, 6:347–85, Summer 1974. **1C246**

Contrary to the U.S. Supreme Court ruling in *Sheppard v. Maxwell* (1966), which approved the proscription of extrajudicial statements by trial participants, the authors conclude that rules proscribing extrajudicial comments by counsel of record made during pending litigation, and for public dissemination, are perfectly consonant with the First Amendment.

[Cole, John W.] *A Defence of the Stage, or an Inquiry into the Real Qualities of Theatrical Entertainments, Their Scope and Tendency. Being a reply to a sermon entitled "The Evil of Theatrical Amusements Stated and Illustrated," lately published in Dublin, and preached in the Wesleyan Methodist Chapel in Lower Abbey Street, on Sunday, November 4th, 1838. By the Rev. Dr. John B. Bennett . . . By John William Calcraft* [*pseud. for John William Cole*]. . . . Dublin, Milliken, 1839. 175p. **1C247**

The manager of the Theatre Royal, Dublin, examines the various publications on the social and immoral tendencies of the stage from William Prynne to the present day, showing that the fanaticism of those who oppose the theater has led to false charges and immoderate views. "The severe opinions now disseminating, the harsh reprobation of every gay pursuit or cheerful employment, the constant demand for unintermitted devotion, the attempt to mysticize what in itself is simple and intelligible; all these tend to check the progress of active virtue . . . , to reduce the business of life exclusively to prayer and religious speculation." If opinions of this kind prevail, they will "chill all the powers of the mind" so that "reason itself will be regarded with a jealous eye as the rival of true religion; and learning, that sacred pledge of faith, will be considered as a vain idol, and all our studies idolatry."

Coles, Robert. "Stripped Bare at the Follies." *New Republic*, 158:18,28–30, 20 January 1968. **1C248**

The story of the suppression of the documentary film, *Titicut Follies*, in Massachusetts and the arrest of the producer, Frederick Wiseman. The film which had been widely acclaimed elsewhere was charged with violating the privacy of patients. The real reason for its suppression, according to the author, was that it showed "human life made cheap and betrayed . . . men needlessly stripped bare, insulted, herded about callously, mocked, taunted."

"College Papers Face Obscenity Charges, Censorship Threats." *Chronicle of Higher Education*, 3:1, 6, 9 December 1968. **1C249**

Comment on the use of four-letter words in campus publications and the strong reaction against them in some ten attempts to censor alleged obscenities. A brief review of the position of the College Press Service as an opponent of censorship.

Collier, Arlen. "Censorship of Ideas and I.B.M., or Swift's Moderns Are Winning Again." *Western Review*, 7(2):57–63, Winter 1970. **1C250**

"Only when we reject the I.B.M. syndrome in literature with its indirect censorship of ideas, can we hope to combat that overt censorship that threatens us from the right and from the left. For the fact-oriented computer mind is the real problem in the censorship of literature today." The reference to Swift is to his *A Tale of a Tub*, in which a hack writer (170 years ago) espouses modern scientific approaches to learning as opposed to the old-fashioned methods which call for reading books.

Collier, James L. "The Language of Censorship." In Neil Postman *et al.*, eds. *Language in America*. New York, Pegasus, 1969, pp. 57–70. **1C251**

"There exists in the United States today a freedom of speech in political matters which is almost absolute. . . . American political censorship is almost entirely concerned with . . . sexual materials." The author discusses how words and their definitions have played an important role in obscenity laws and their interpretation and how language has been used to measure language. He develops the thesis that censorship in the United States is "a residue of Victorian attitudes, and is still directed primarily against the working-class male."

Collier, Peter. "A Doily for Your Mind." *Ramparts*, 7:44, 46, 48–50, June 1969. **1C252**

A review of the censorship of the Smothers Brothers Comedy Hour over the Columbia Broadcasting System network and its eventual removal from the air, with particular reference to their case as seen by Tommy Smothers.

———. "Pirates of Pornography." *Ramparts*, 7:17–23, 10 August 1968. **1C253**

Publishing in the erotic and pornographic field in America is looked at in the article, particularly in reference to Maurice Girodias, his background in France and his activities since arriving in this country.

Collings, Rex. "Censors in Africa." *New Statesman*, 78:468, 3 October 1969. **1C254**

Written after the author spent eighteen months visiting seven African countries, in all of which he found some form of censorship. He gives particular attention to censorship in South Africa and Ethiopia.

Collingwood, C. A., Cecil B. Ramage, and E. C. Carus-Wilson. "Libel and Slander." In *The English and Empire Digest*. Replacement volume no. 32. London, Butterworth, 1964, pp. 1–250. **1C255**

Content: Parties to libel suits, identity of person defamed, the statement, publication, defenses, malice, damages and costs, injunction, pleading, practice and evidence, criminal proceedings, slander of title, and slander of goods.

Collins, Richard. "The Screen Writer and Censorship." *Screen Writer*, 3(5):15–17, October 1947. **1C256**

The author discusses industry censorship under the production code and the self-censorship of writers after a lifetime under thought control and the influence of pressure groups.

[Collins, Robert G.] "The Shopping Center As a Forum for the Exercise of First Amendment Rights." *Albany Law Review*, 37:556–66, 1973. **1C257**

Re: *Lloyd Corp. v. Tanner* (1972). In an examination of the conflict between property rights and First Amendment expression in the distribution of handbills, the Court ruled in favor of property rights and, in the view of the author, "dealt an unnecessary blow to first amendment rights."

Collins, Tom A. "Counter-Advertising in the Broadcast Media; Bringing the Administrative Process to Bear Upon a Theoretical Imperative." *William & Mary Law Review*, 15:799–844, Summer 1974. **1C258**

"Guided by the basic administrative qualities of flexibility and experimentation, the FTC and FCC can create, develop, and refine a scheme which can avoid the detrimental political and economic effects which opponents fear will result from the implementation of the FTC proposal."

———. "The Future of Cable Communication and the Fairness Doc-

trine." *Catholic University Law Review*, 24:833–53, Summer 1975.   **1C259**
"The legal basis of the fairness doctrine . . . has traditionally rested upon the scarcity of broadcast frequencies and the consequent intense competition for broadcast time. . . . This requires issuance of a limited number of broadcast licenses and other governmental regulations to create a viable system. In cable, the reverse applies. Rather than scarcity, abundance of channel capacity is likely. Nevertheless, the fairness doctrine presently applies to cable." The author examines the theory of the fairness doctrine as it applies to cable communications.

——. "Positing a Right of Access: Evaluations and Subsequent Developments." *William & Mary Law Review*, 15:339–52, Winter 1973.   **1C260**
Review of James A. Barron, *Freedom of the Press for Whom? The Right of Access to Mass Media*.

Collison, Robert. "Trends Abroad: Western Europe." *Library Trends*, 19:115–21, July 1970.   **1C261**
In a general discussion of European censorship there are references to recommended changes in Britain's obscenity laws, the abolition of stage censorship, and concern with invasion of privacy.

Colquitt, Roy. "The High School Press and Prior Restraint or 'Don't Stop the Presses.'" *Indiana English Journal*, 10(1):3–11, Fall 1975.   **1C262**
A look at recent court cases concerning the high school student press rather accurately defines the boundaries of school rules concerning student generated publications, and also suggests the advisability of certain rules.

Colton, Arthur S. "The Book Publisher and the Court." *Graphic Arts Monthly*, 43:104+, February 1971.
          1C263
"There are two basic kinds of law affecting the publication of books: those that protect the publisher, as copyright law, and those protecting others, as from libel, invasion of privacy, or exposure to objectionable material." A brief history of the acts protecting authors and publishers and what constitutes "a valid infringement, which is regarded as a tort, and must be prosecuted within three years after the claim accrues."

Colton, Douglas. "The Doctrine of Executive Privilege Limits Statutory Access to Information Held Within the Executive Office of the President." *Texas Law Review*, 49:780–91, April 1971.   **1C264**
In the case of *Soucie v. DuBridge* (1970) the plaintiffs brought suit under the Freedom of Information Act against the Office of Science and Technology to compel disclosure of a report on the proposed supersonic transport.

The case was dismissed on grounds that the court lacked jurisdiction over records under control of the Executive Office of the president. The doctrine of executive privilege protects "Presidential papers" and the Information Act does not apply.

Columbia Broadcasting System. "Memorandum: Criticism of the 'Selling of the Pentagon.'" *Congressional Record*, 117:E 13493–99, 15 December 1971; 117:E 13697–701, 17 December 1971. Also issued as an eleven-page reprint.   **1C265**
The Columbia Broadcasting System in this staff paper answers Congressional criticism of its documentary broadcast which criticizes the propaganda machine of the Pentagon. They take particular exception to the charges of bias in film editing. The statement was introduced into the House of Representatives by Congressman Ogden R. Reid.

Columbia Journalism Review. New York, Graduate School of Journalism, Columbia University, 1962–date. Quarterly 1962–71; bimonthly Spring 1971–date.   **1C266**
"To assess the performance of journalism in all its forms, to call attention to its shortcomings and strengths, and to help define—or redefine—standards of honest service . . . to help stimulate continuing improvements in the profession and to speak out for what is right, fair, and decent"—from founding editorial, Autumn 1961. Issues frequently contain articles on freedom of the press. Selected articles from ten years of the review are presented in *Our Troubled Press*, edited by Alfred Balk and James Boylan.

Columbia University. Graduate School of Journalism *et al. Access to the Air. A Conference on the Public Responsibility of Broadcast Licenses and the Ethical and Legal Considerations of Equal Time, Editorializing, Personal Attacks, Balanced Programming and the Fairness Doctrine*. New York, Columbia University, Graduate School of Journalism, 1968. 46p. **1C267**
Abstracts of presentations: The Fairness Doctrine and Its Challengers by Commissioner Kenneth A. Cox. If the Fairness Doctrine Were Struck Down by Robert M. Lowe. The Ethics of Mass Communications Practices by Everett C. Parker. The Public's Voice in Programming by Earle K. Moore. Overseers for F.C.C. by Marcus Cohn. The Critic and the Media by Lawrence Laurent. Open Mike Shows and Other Vehicles of Extremism by Commissioner Cox and Dr. Parker. Cablevision and the Public Interest by Sidney W. Dean, Jr. The Media and Race Conflict by John P. Spiegel.

Comeau, Reginald. "Nothing to Fear But . . ." *Bay State Librarian*, 59:11–18, October 1970.   **1C268**

In light of two instances in which state police visited Massachusetts libraries to investigate charges of pornography, the author and the editor conducted interviews with police officials. Discussion ranged "from police procedures in controlling obscenity to the viability of the concept of obscenity in an increasingly sophisticated society." The author concludes: "It would appear from this discussion that librarians have relatively little to fear legally from visits from law enforcement agencies, although the variation in training from officer to officer may well lead to some extralegal measures and the legality of some pictorial material is still very much an open question in the courts."

Comics Magazine Association of America. "Role of the Code Administrator." In Otto N. Larsen, *ed. Violence and the Mass Media*. New York, Harper & Row, 1968, pp. 244–49.   **1C269**
The Administrator of the Comics Code Authority reports on his sixteen-months experience in directing the program. A memorandum for Applying the Comic Book Code follows (pp. 250–52).

Commission of Inquiry into High School Journalism. *Captive Voices: The Report of the Commission of Inquiry into High School Journalism*. Convened by the Robert F. Kennedy Memorial. Prepared by Jack Nelson. New York, The Commission, 1974. 264p. (Distributed by Schocken Books)   **1C270**
Censorship was one of the four areas of investigation. The Commission recommended: (1) full discussion of the First Amendment as part of the school curriculum, (2) First Amendment rights for high school journalists, (3) out-of-school media be given First Amendment protection, (4) students be alert to First Amendment issues, (5) student journalists and teachers seek support of community organizations traditionally concerned with First Amendment rights, (6) established media keep special vigilance to protect rights of young journalists, (7) widespread discussion of free expression guidelines, and (8) all sectors of the school community share successful experiences based upon these guidelines. Case studies of high school censorship are presented on pages 3–24, followed by discussion of censorship from the top, advisors as censors, self-inflicted censorship by student editors, and a chapter on kinds of material censored. An article about the Commission's report appeared in *Communication: Journalism Education Today*, Winter 1974.

Commission on Educational and Cultural Films. "Censorship and Control." In *The Film in National Life*. London,

Allen & Unwin, 1932, pp. 28–40.
1C271

The report of an inquiry conducted by the Commission into the service which the cinematograph may render to education and social progress.

Committee for the First Amendment. [*Purpose, Signers, Quotations.*] Beverly Hills, Calif., The Committee, [1947?]. 23p.   **1C272**

"We the Committee for the First Amendment, espouse no political party. We represent no motion picture studios. We are in no way involved in attacking or defending any individuals connected with the [House Committee on Un-American Activities] hearings in Washington. We are a group of five hundred independent private citizens who believe we must take action to inform the American people of the danger to their liberties. Not only the freedom of the screen but also freedom of the press, radio, and publishing are in jeopardy." The Committee was formed to protest the "continuing attempt of the House Committee on Un-American Activities to smear the Motion Picture Industry." The brochure consists largely of reprints of newspaper articles and editorials, and a list of the signers.

Committee of First Amendment Defenders. *Behind the Bars for the First Amendment.* New York, The Committee, 1960. 33p.   **1C273**

"The story of 36 Americans, four of them already in jail, and the rest facing the possibility of imprisonment because they believe the First Amendment of the Constitution means what it says." Most of the defendants, called to account by the House Un-American Activities Committee for their beliefs and their writings, refused to testify, pleading the First Amendment rather than the Fifth. The latter would have protected them from charges of contempt, but in citing the First Amendment they challenged the right of the Committee to pry into their minds and to punish by exposure. Dalton Trumbo, one of the "Hollywood Ten," jailed in 1950 for upholding the First Amendment, wrote the foreword; the text was written by several of the defendants.

Committee to Evaluate the National News Council. *Report. . . .* New York, The Committee, 1976. 5p. Processed.   **1C274**

An independent appraisal of the work of the National News Council at the end of its third year of existence. The Committee found that there was a positive need for a national news council, that the Council had made a sound if not spectacular beginning, had been handicapped by opposition from important media elements and personalities, had often not had cooperation from the media, and had correctly refused jurisdiction involving editorial opinion labeled as such. The Committee recommended that the Council continue to use its limited resources on national media and national issues, but broaden its scope to cover the entire nation; that it take on important cases regardless of whether a specific complaint was filed. "The task of the Council is a complex and difficult one. But its importance to the national body politic is such that the Committee feels every effort should be made not only to continue the Council but actively to seek to deepen and broaden the opening pathway which it has hewed out."

A Commoner, *pseud. A Brief Appeal to the Royal Heir of the Throne, the Hereditary Noblemen, the Heads of the Church, the Judges, the Opulent Landholders, and the Members of the Parliament of the British Empire; occasioned by the Present Alarming Licentiousness of the Press As Evidenced by Some Late Attacks upon the . . . Royal Family!* . . . London, B. McMillan, 1809. 28p.   **1C275**

The author believes freedom of the press affords a proper check to immorality and corruption, but licentiousness of the press is something else and should not be tolerated. More severe laws against sedition are needed to deal with the revolutionary doctrines of the Jacobins. He particularly denounces a pamphlet entitled *Bandogs* which is contemptuous of the royal family.

"Community Standards, Class Actions, and Obscenity under *Miller v. California.*" *Harvard Law Review,* 88:1838–74, June 1975.   **1C276**

"This Note undertakes first to describe the configuration of the procedure *Miller* [*Miller v. California* (1973)] set up by considering, both in terms of their development in the case law to date and their theoretical implications, the three *Miller* rules in relationship to each other. Once that configuration is apparent, it will be seen that the impact of the process is overbroad, deterring the distribution of works of serious value ostensibly under the *Miller* rule. The Note concludes by examining the combined use of federal declaratory judgment and class action procedures as a corrective device."

Comstock, Anthony. "Foes to Society, Church and State." In *Social Purity, and Foes to Society, Church, and State by Rev. George Douglas and Mr. Anthony Comstock.* Boston, United Society of Christian Endeavor, 1893, pp. 11–14.   **1C277**

An attack on gambling, drinking, and evil reading. "Hark! What sound is this that drowns Niagara's? It is the whirl, the united whirl, of the devil's printing press—as it is striking off millions of pages of printed matter to infatuate our boys and girls; to defile their minds; to corrupt their thoughts; to pervert their imaginations; to sear their consciences, harden their hearts, and damn their souls." The head of the New York Society for the Suppression of Vice and inspector of obscene mail for the U.S. Post Office since 1872, reports on raids, arrests, and destruction of obscene publications.

———. "Indictable Art." *Household Guest (Our Day)* 1:44–48, October 1888.   **1C278**

"Between morals and art there is no conflict until art becomes indictable from indecency, and then law interposes against this corrupting element in art. . . . Law stands as a health officer, and quarantines this evil tendency, while the courts supply a remedy." Comstock describes the efforts of his New York Society for the Suppression of Vice in dealing with immoral art, most recently the vile French postcard, and attacks "Liberals" for supporting these "cancer planters." He concludes with this question: "Pure children or indictable French photographs, which shall it be?"

"Comstock's Fight for the Fig Leaf." *Brush and Pencil,* 1:167–72, October 1906. (Salon of the Dilettanti—XI)   **1C279**

An irreverent essay on the nude in art, occasioned by the controversy over Anthony Comstock's raid on the Art Students League of New York.

Comyn, Andrew F. "Censorship in Ireland." *Studies,* 58:42–50, Spring 1969.   **1C280**

In a review of Michael Adams' *Censorship: The Irish Experience,* the author makes his own assessment of the work of the Irish Censorship Board. While defending the need for censorship of indecent works under the Censorship of Publications Acts of 1929, 1946, and 1967, he criticizes the Board's interpretation of the Acts and some of its specific actions. "The practical approach to censorship would appear to be first to decide if a book is *prima facie* indecent. This is more a matter of common sense than an analysis of the definition in the Act. If it is, then one takes into account the general tenor, giving due regard to literary and historic merit, etc., and the type of reader likely to read it and decides whether it should be banned. This is inevitably a hit-or-miss method because it is not easy to set off a percentage of indecency against historic or literary merit, etc., and for that reason, too, the Board should err on the side of leniency."

"Concepts of the Broadcast Media Under the First Amendment: A Reevaluation and a Proposal." *New York University Law Review,* 47:83–109, April 1972.   **1C281**

The author considers four possible concepts of the broadcast media in relation to the First Amendment: (1) Because of unique technological and economic factors broadcasting should be limited in the public interest. (2) To the extent that radio and television have replaced or supplemented public forums, they should serve this function, with right of public access. (3) Since radio and television perform the communications function of the print media they should be afforded the same First Amendment protection. The author proposes a compromise: (1) A major part of the broadcast spectrum would be designated as private and sold or leased by the government, subject only to standards of technical competence. (2) *The government would own certain frequencies for public purposes—educational and cultural.* (3) Certain stations would be operated as public forums, with a constitutionally protected right of access.

Cone, Carl B. *The English Jacobins: Reformers in Late 18th-Century England.* New York, Scribner's, 1968. 248p.
1C282
This is the story of the English Jacobins who pressed for political and social reform in England during the period of the French Revolution. The right of free expression was basic to the movement and the reformers fought their battles through pamphlets and newspapers. Some of those who figure in the account are: John Almon, Major John Cartwright (portrait), Daniel I. Eaton, Thomas Erskine (portrait), John Frost, Thomas Hardy (portrait), Thomas Muir (portrait), Thomas Paine (portrait), Thomas F. Palmer, Francis Place, Thomas Spence, and John Thelwell (portrait). References are also made to the various competing political societies such as Friends of the Liberty of the Press and the Association for the Preservation of Liberty and Property.

Cone, John C. P. "A Rational View of Pornography." *Australian Rationalist* (Rationalist Society of Australia), 3:7–10, November 1973.
1C283

Conference on American Freedom, Washington, D.C., 1973. *Papers from the Conference on American Freedom: Press, Privacy, Religion, Speech. Washington, D.C., April 10 and 11, 1973.* Washington, D.C., The Conference, 1973. 63p.
1C284
Remarks by Sander Vanocur. First Amendment Overview by Thomas I. Emerson. Freedom of the Press by Jack Landau. Misuse of Grand Juries by Sanford Rosen. Privacy by John H. F. Shattuck. Freedom of Religion by Dean Kelley. Address by Congressman Charles W. Whalen, Jr.

Conference on Censorship, University of Missouri, 1969. *Conference on Censorship[Papers].* Columbia, Mo., Freedom of Information Center, School of Journalism, University of Missouri at Columbia [1969?]. 61p.
1C285
Milton Meltzer, the keynote speaker, discusses the battles with the censor experienced by the men and women he has written about— Langston Hughes, Mark Twain, Lydia Maria Child, and Margaret Sanger; Enid Olson, National Council of Teachers of English, reviews recent efforts at censorship in the schools and the work of the NCTE in behalf of the freedom to read; Margaret Twyman, Motion Picture

Association of America, discusses the "creativity gap" between those who wish to retain the status quo and those, generally the younger generation who are the moviegoers, who want to see change; Irving Levitas, Temple Emanu-el, believes that all the argument about pornography and violence is but a subterfuge for an actual political situation—that the censors are aiming at a social structure; Joan Bodger, Missouri State Library, speaks for the rights of the young reader; attorney Morris Ernst is more concerned with the way in which big television uses or abuses its power than in governmental censorship; and Anson Mount of *Playboy*, emphasizes that freedom is the key word in understanding the younger generation, including freedom to examine new ideas and to reject old ones.

Conference on News Media and Law Enforcement. "Fair Trial and Free Press." *New York State Bar Journal*, 41:7–43, January 1969.
1C286
At a conference held in New York, 18 October 1968, addresses were given by Justice Robert C. Finley; Howard C. Cleavenger, Spokane newspaperman; Robert Fichenberg, president of the New York State Society of Newspaper Editors; and Lyman M. Tondel, Jr., president of the New York State Bar Association.

"Conflict Within the First Amendment: A Right of Access to Newspapers." *New York Law Review*, 48:1200–1226, December 1973.
1C287
The article considers various proposals by which government creates a right of access to the press for the individual who wishes to express his views. Proposals are criticized against the standard that they will not "destroy the historic role of the independent press as a check upon abuses of power by all three branches of government."

"Conflicts of Interest in News Broadcasting." *Columbia Law Review*, 69:881–96, May 1969.
1C288
"This Note will concern itself with the conflicts created by the nonbroadcasting activities of broadcast licensees and their employees. These activities may provide motivation to use the airways for private economic benefit." An examination of Federal Communications Commission policy reveals a necessity for more effective regulation and control of conglomerate structures that threaten objective news presentation.

"Confronting the Censor: A Micro-Workshop." *Illinois Libraries*, 54:104–7, February 1972.
1C289
A report on a workshop of children's librarians and results of a survey of attitudes of those attending on book-selection policies and censorship.

"Congress Seeks to Outlaw Sale of Obscene Materials." *Congressional*

Quarterly Weekly Report, 28:755–57, 13 March 1970.
1C290
"Members of Congress, goaded by complaints from their constituents, have seized on pornography as an issue on which they can take a firm stand without fear of reprisal." The article reviews the recent events in Congress and in the nation which have resulted in more than 200 antiobscenity bills being introduced.

"Congressional Employees Enjoined from Printing and Distributing Report of House Internal Security Committee." *New York University Law Review*, 46:606–16, May 1971.
1C291
Re: *Hentoff v. Ichord* (1970), in which the district court enjoined the printing and distribution of the report of the House Internal Security Committee on grounds that it constituted a political blacklist and that its infringement of First Amendment freedoms outweighed genuine legislative purpose. The report had disclosed the honoraria of certain speakers on college campuses. The suit was brought by political columnist Nat Hentoff as a class action suit.

Conley, Thelma R. "Scream Silently: One View of the Kanawha County Textbook Controversy." *Journal of Research and Development in Education*, 9:93–101, Spring 1976.
1C292
The personal experience and perception of the Kanawha County, W.Va., textbook controversy by one of the teachers under attack. She concludes that "during the tumult of this almost unbelievable year in the Kanawha Valley, the students in our schools have learned—not only from books but [quoting Lord Chesterfield] from the 'various editons' of men."

Conlin, Joseph R., *ed. The American Radical Press, 1880–1960.* Westport, Conn., Greenwood, 1974. 2 vols.
1C293
A collection of 100 essays with five elaborative notes by various authorities on the American radical movement, convering 119 different radical journals published in America between 1880 and 1960. The work is an outgrowth of Walter Goldwater's *Radical Periodicals in America, 1890–1950* and the subsequent reprinting project, *Radical Periodicals in the United States, 1890–1960.* Periodicals include Socialist party papers, wobbly papers, journals of the Bolshevik crises, the Communist press, periodicals of various sects and splinter groups, anarchist publications, independent and personal radical journals, and theoretical journals and little magazines. Frequent references are made to episodes of censorship, particularly under the World War I Espionage Act, by the refusal of the U.S. Post Office to honor second-class mailing privileges, and

sometimes by the arrest of the editor and a raid on the printshop.

Connecticut. Commission for Standards of Decency in Materials Available for Sale to the Public. *Report . . . to the Governor, State of Connecticut and the General Assembly*. Hartford, 1971. Various paging.   **1C294**
The Commission was established in 1969 by Special Act no. 252.

Connecticut Library Association. "Intellectual Freedom in Libraries; A Statement of Policy Adopted. . . . May 1970." *Connecticut Libraries*, 12(3):13–14, Summer 1970.   **1C295**

"Connecticut's Birth Control Law: Reviewing a State Statute under the Fourteenth Amendment." *Yale Law Journal*, 70:322–34, December 1960.   **1C296**
The author discusses the constitutionality or lack of it in the Connecticut Birth Control Law, presently being tested by the U.S. Supreme Court in *Poe v. Ullman* (1961).

Connor, Harry L. *Democracy in the Newsroom*. Columbia, Mo., Freedom of Information Center, School of Journalism, University of Missouri at Columbia, 1974. 10p. (Report no. 328)   **1C297**
The report deals with "those aspects of editorial control which might serve to limit the true presentation of the facts and the movement by working reporters to have more of a say in how straight news, as opposed to features, is covered and edited."

Connor, Julia M. *The Boycott Against Schanen: Economic and Social Pressures at Work*. Madison, Wis., University of Wisconsin, 1972. 147p. (Unpublished Master's thesis)   **1C298**
An investigation of the social and economic pressures on freedom of the press in the boycotting of three Wisconsin newspapers because the publisher, William Schanen, Jr., refused to cancel a contract for printing the Milwaukee underground paper, *Kaleidoscope*.

Connors, Mary M. *Prejudicial Publicity: An Assessment*. Minneapolis, Association for Education in Journalism, 1975. 36p. (Journalism Monographs, no. 41)   **1C299**
"The sections [of this monograph] treat the historical evolution of decisions related to the fair trial/free press issue in the area of 'prejudicial' publicity, summarize the evidence con-

cerned with the effects of such publicity and give an assessment of the solutions proposed to deal with this problem." The author concludes that "press/bar agreements appear to be the best hope for preserving all the freedoms protected by the First and Sixth Amendments to the Constitution," but they depend upon the good will of the participants. "Whether or not these interactions can continue to provide an acceptable resolution of the conflict must await the test of time and the resolution of judicial decisions on media matters currently pending."

Conolly, Leonard W. "The Abolition of Theatre Censorship in Great Britain: The Theatres Act of 1968." *Queen's Quarterly*, 74:569–83, Winter 1968.   **1C300**
An account of the actions leading to the abolition of theater censorship by the Lord Chamberlain and some of the legal problems involved.

———. "A Case of Political Censorship at the Little Theatre in the Haymarket in 1794: John O'Keefe's *Jenny's Whim; or, the Roasted Emperor*." *Restoration and 18th-Century Theatre Research*, 10(2):34–40, November 1971.   **1C301**
O'Keefe's play was banned by the Lord Chamberlain under the Licensing Act of 1737 because it poked fun at Morocco and Spain, two of England's allies.

———. "The Censor and Early Nineteenth-Century English Pantomime." *Notes and Queries*, 22(n.s.):394–96, September 1975.   **1C302**
"Two recently discovered letters written by John Larpent attest to the care taken by the censor to see that theatre managers did not overlook the fact that pantomimes were just as subject to his scrutiny before their performance as the legitimate drama."

———. "The Censor's Wife at the Theatre: The Diary of Anna Margaretta Larpent, 1790–1800." *Huntington Library Quarterly*, 35:49–64, November 1971.   **1C303**
Extracts from the diaries of the wife of John Larpent, Examiner of Plays in the office of the Lord Chamberlain (1778–1824?), whose responsibility was to receive and censor all plays intended for public performance. These extracts record her visits to the theater, 1790–1800.

———. *The Censorship of English Drama, 1737–1824*. San Marino, Calif., Huntington Library, 1976. 233 p.   **1C304**
"This book is an attempt to describe in detail, for the first time, the nature, extent, and practice of theatrical censorship in England for almost a hundred years after the [Stage Licensing] Act [of 1737] was passed, and to assess the

significance of the censorship to the theater and society of that period. . . . The following chapters are an examination of the official censorship as it was operated under the Licensing Act between 1737 and 1824, the year of the death of England's longest-serving Examiner of Plays, John Larpent." The work is based in large part on the manuscripts of Larpent (and his wife's diary) in Huntington Library. The author gives an account of trends in political censorship and of the perils to the playwright of indulging in personal satire. Because of the turbulent political climate of the eighteenth and early nineteenth centuries there was surprisingly little opposition to censorship of the theater, even by the playwrights. "Denied the stimulus of personal or social satire, of participation in religious or moral debate, and, above all, of engagement in political controversy, the drama limped forward, seriously handicapped. The censors' defense of the social order evolved at the expense of the drama."

———. "Horace Walpole, Unofficial Play Censor." *English Language Notes*, 9:42–46, September 1971.   **1C305**
Horace Walpole's cousin Francis Seymour-Conway, Earl of Hertford, sought Walpole's advice in performing his duties as Lord Chamberlain, which included enforcing the 1737 Stage Licensing Act. Letters from Hertford indicate that Walpole tended to discourage the implementation of the law that his father, Robert Walpole, had sponsored.

———. "More on John O'Keefe and the Lord Chamberlain." *Notes & Queries*, 16:190–92, May 1969.   **1C306**
In an article by Stewart S. Morgan in the November 1958 issue of the *Huntington Library Quarterly* on public condemnation and government censorship of Thomas Holcroft's *Knave or Not?* and John O'Keefe's *She's Eloped*, Morgan refers to a series of letters bound with the manuscript copy submitted to the Lord Chamberlain for licensing and now in the Huntington Library. Conolly gives more complete evidence from the letters of the "manoeuvring that went on among the Lord Chamberlain, his Examiner of Plays, the theatre manager, and the author when the Examiner deemed a play objectionable."

———. "Pornography." *Dalhousie Review*, 54:698–709, Winter 1974/75.   **1C307**
The author finds the case against government censorship of pornography a convincing one: "such censorship abrogates a central principle of democratic society; it does so for no demonstrably sound reason; and it hinders and sometimes prevents the free circulation of the works of serious creative writers. . . . Perhaps the only attitude we can reasonably adopt is that pornography has established itself as a part of the popular culture of western civilization. . . . We really cannot be certain what it is doing or is likely to do to that culture. We are in no position to damn it or praise it."

Conrad, Thomas M. "The Politics of

Gullibility." *Commonweal*, 95:13–15, 1 October 1971. **1C308**
"It takes two parties to maintain a consistent pattern of deception." To combat government secrecy and deception, official policy will need to be forced to serve public interests. To do this we must "concentrate upon the patterns of behavior of the information media and the public itself which contributes to ignorance and deception."

"Conspiracy and the First Amendment." *Yale Law Journal*, 79:872–95, April 1970. **1C309**
Based on an analysis of the Constitution and the conspiracy laws, the author offers three rules to bring the use of conspiracy law into conformance with the principles of the First Amendment: (1) the First Amendment prohibits conspiracy indictments alleging agreements to engage in any form of expression; (2) "if the overt acts indicate that a nonexpressive conspiratorial objective was achieved, or was to be achieved, solely by means of expression and action incidental to that expression, the court should pierce the form of the indictment, interpret the conspiratorial objective as unlawful expression, and dismiss the conspiracy charge"; and (3) to prevent the use of conspiracy law to convict individuals on the basis of their ideas "courts should bar the use of constitutionally protected public expression as evidence either of an overt act or of an individual's specific intent." The author concludes that "if the First Amendment bars the use of protected public expression as overt acts in a conspiracy, then such expression should be barred as evidence of a defendant's intent."

"Constitutional Privilege Does Not Extend to Defamation Concerning a Private Individual on a Public Issue." *University of Richmond Law Review*, 9:394–99, Winter 1975. **1C310**
Re: *Gertz v. Robert Welch, Inc.*, 418 U.S. 323 (1974).

"Constitutionality of Proscribing Drug Related Songs." *New York Law Forum*, 19:902–15, Spring 1974. **1C311**
Yale Broadcasting Co. v. FCC, 478 F.2d 594 (D.C. Cir. 1973).

"Contempt by Publication." *Yale Law Journal*, 59:534–46, 1950. **1C312**
The author believes there is no justification for punishing the press and radio for reports relating to criminal trials unless they actually cause intimidation or violence. In most cases contempt by publication contributes little to a fair trial. He recommends that the U.S. Supreme Court make the federal contempt rule binding on the states, guaranteeing newsmen a jury trial for out-of-court activities alleged to be illegal. The "standard of guilt will be a concrete one of direct and tangible obstruction."

A Controversial Film: A Contemporary Case Study. 57 frame, color filmstrip.

New York, Guidance Associates, 1972. (For use with manual or automatic projectors, 10 in., 33⅓ rpm., 7 min. Also issued in phonotape in cassette form) **1C313**
"A dramatization of an incident involving the showing of a film considered bigoted and inflammatory by some people. The owner of the theater is ordered by police to stop showing the film after the audience attacks picketers. He is arrested after refusing, citing his first amendment right to freedom of expression. The open-end format allows the viewer to act as judge." A discussion guide and student manual is provided.

"Conversion As a Remedy for Injurious Publication—New Challenge to the *New York Times* Doctrine?" *Georgetown Law Journal*, 56:1223–30, June 1968. **1C314**
In the case of *Dodd v. Pearson* (1968), the court found that certain property rights of a public official outweighed the press's interest in obtaining and publishing incriminating information.

Cook, Bruce. "Irish Censorship: The Case of John McGahern." *Catholic World*, 206:176–79, January 1968. **1C315**
A discussion of Irish censorship, state action backed by the Catholic Church, and "notoriously conservative, paternalistic and narrow." Numerous Irish writers have had their works accepted as Catholic literature abroad while banned in Dublin. The author states the case of John McGahern, whose second novel, *The Dark*, published in England and favorably reviewed, was banned in Ireland and McGahern was removed from his teaching job. Despite economic persecution, McGahern has refused to leave Ireland and, unlike Brendan Behan, has refused to drown his misfortune in drink.

Cook, Cassius V. *A Statement and an Appeal Concerning the Latest Victims of Conspiracy Charges*. Chicago, Cook-Wallace Defense and Appeal Fund, 1918. 3p. Processed. **1C316**
Charges of conspiracy against author (Daniel H. Wallace) and publisher (Cassius V. Cook) for publication of *Shanghaied into the European War*, a book critical of America's entrance into World War I.

Cook, Robert F., and Robert H. Fosen. "Pornography and the Sex Offender: Patterns of Exposure and Immediate Arousal Effects of Pornographic Stimuli." *Technical Report of the ₍U.S.₎ Commission on Obscenity and Pornography*, 7:149–62, 1971. (Also reported in *Journal of Applied Psychology*, December 1971) **1C317**
"One hundred twenty-nine (63 sex offenders, 66 criminal code offenders) in the Wisconsin

State Prison were shown a series of 26 slides depicting sexual behavior, then interviewed about previous exposure to pornography. No differences were found between the two groups on the measure of rated sexual arousal to the slides. Numerous differences were found between the two groups in their past exposure to pornography. Sex offenders generally experienced less frequent and milder exposure to pornography than did the criminal code offenders."

₍Cook, Samuel.₎ *A Full Report of the Trial of Samuel Cook, Draper, Dudley, for an Alleged Seditious Libel, Tried at Worcester, Aug. 1, 1827, before Mr. Justice Littledale . . .* Dudley, Eng., Samuel Cook, 1827. 72p. **1C318**
The defendant, a linen draper, was found guilty of displaying in his shop window a seditious libel, a handbill accusing government ministers of contributing to the starvation of the people and recommending that they lose their heads on Tower Hill.

Cooke, Colin. " 'At Risk with Honour,' Censorship After the Lord Chamberlain." *Prompt*, 13:21–23, 1969. **1C319**
Speculation on the future of controversial theater productions under the law, now that the Lord Chamberlain is no longer censoring the Birtish stage. "It remains to be seen how far his removal will pose a challenge to playwright and theatre manager alike to risk court action in staging what they believe to be good and true."

Coombs, Frederick S., III. "Access vs. Fairness in Newspapers; the Implications of *Tornillo* for a Free and Responsible Press." *Ohio State Law Journal*, 35:954–73, 1974. **1C320**
Re: *Miami Herald Publishing Co. v. Tornillo* (1974). The first section of the article "presents the history and holdings of *Tornillo* as a framework within which the problem of governmental assurance of a balanced, yet free, press will be examined. The second section then traces the legal history of access, demonstrating how each of the various arguments employed to promote access has met with strong first amendment resistance. The second section concludes with an assessment of the effectiveness of access in achieving a balanced presentation of public issues in the press. The third section examines the groundwork *Tornillo* may have laid for the imposition of the 'Fairness Doctrine' upon newspapers."

Coon, Thomas F. "Free Press Need Not Be Trial by Newspaper." *Police*, 12:41–44, March–April, 1968. **1C321**
Following an examination of the pros and cons of the American Bar Association's report on

fair trial and free press (Reardon Report) and the reaction of the American Newspaper Publishers Association, the author concludes that "Guidelines of responsibility might be devised—but integrity and decency of publishers, with a free flow of news, is certainly preferable to star chamber proceedings which could result from unrealistic restrictions upon the press."

Cooney, Stuart. "An Annotated Bibliography of Articles on Broadcasting Law and Regulation in Law Periodicals, 1920–1955." *Journal of Broadcasting*, 1:290–302, Summer 1957; reprinted, 14:133–46, Winter 1969/70. **1C322**
Topics: Background of legislation, basic laws of broadcasting, administration, problems in regulating, and control of program content.

Coonradt, Frederic C. "The Courts Have All But Repealed the Libel Laws." *Center Report*, 4(5):26–27, December 1971. (Reprinted in *Quill*, February 1972) **1C323**
"What has happened to the law of libel in the past few years is that the concept of 'privilege' has been extended to cover, within limits, the journalist acting in his own right. At the same time the concept of what constitutes a 'public performance or offering' has been stretched to cover a multitude of matters previously considered private. And the insistance on 'absolute truth' as a necessary defense has been largely abondoned."

[Cooper, C. P.?] "The Liberty of the Press." *Dublin Review*, 7:518–40, November 1839. **1C324**
The author applauds the efforts in Malta to codify the laws of libel, something never attempted in England. Following a review of the long struggle for freedom of press and the stage in England, he criticizes the vague generalities of the present libel laws and the unsatisfactory method of criminal proceedings. He attacks the arbitrary use of *ex officio* informations by the Attorney General and the criminal informations filed with permission of the Court of Queen's Bench. Libel indictments should be left to action of a grand jury. The unsigned article is attributed to C. P. Cooper by the *Wellesley Index*.

Cooper, Grant B. "The Rationale of the ABA Recommendations." *Notre Dame Lawyer*, 42:857–64, Symposium 1967. **1C325**
A member of the Advisory Committee of Fair Trial and Free Press (Reardon Committee of the American Bar Association) discusses the thinking behind the proposals.

Cooper, H. H. A. "Deep Throat; Not All That Easy to Swallow." *Chitty's Law Journal*, 21:270–73, October 1973. **1C326**
Comment on the judgment in *People v. Mature Enterprises, Inc.*, involving the motion picture *Deep Throat*, in which the court attempted to examine the purpose and effect of hard-core pornography.

Coopersmith, Douglas P. "Requiring Newsmen to Testify Before State or Federal Grand Juries Held Not Violative of First Amendment." *Villanova Law Review*, 18:288–302, December 1972. **1C327**
Re: *Branzburg v. Hayes* (1972). The author concludes that the decision "will have little effect on bringing about more effective law enforcement through grand jury investigations, and it is unfortunate that news reporters will continue to be subject to contempt convictions." Qualified privilege, he believes, will both serve effective law enforcement and protect the public's right to know.

Coote, Anna, and Lawrence Grant. "Censorship." In their *The NCCL Guide*, 2d ed., Harmondsworth, England, Penguin, 1973, pp. 118–30. **1C328**
Brief information on the legal rights of British citizens with respect to obscenity, film and theater censorship, libel and slander, and national defense. The work was sponsored by the National Council for Civil Liberties.

Copley, Helen K. "Thoughts on Press Freedom." *Seminar (A Quarterly Review for Newspapermen by Copley Newspapers)*, 34:9–11, December 1974. **1C329**
"In its purest form, freedom of the press exists when the printing press is neither subservient nor responsive to the will of the state." The head of Copley newspapers discusses the recent attacks on the press, the pressures for shield laws, and the watchdog role of the press. She urges the press to put its own house in order by practicing restraint and responsibility, fairness and accuracy, and by confining its opinions to the editorial pages.

Corcoran, John S. "Libel and Private College Newspaper." *School and Society*, 98:354–56, October 1970. **1C330**
"Are private college administrators legally responsible for libel published in their student newspapers?" The article reviews conditions which qualify a private college and its administrators as the legal publisher of its newspaper, and also the legal defenses which protect the publisher against unjust legal suits.

Corliss, Richard. "Cinema Sex; From 'The Kiss' to 'Deep Throat.'" *Film Comment*, 9(1):4–5, January–February 1973. **1C331**

General observations on the nature and trend in hard-core pornographic films; speculations on the future. "Two factors seem operative: The Law of Supply and Demand, and the Law of the Land." On pages 19–29 of the same issue Corliss interviews Radley Metzger, the "aristocrat of erotic films." Metzger comments on the prospects of government repression.

———. "The Legion of Decency." *Film Comment*, 4(4):24–61, Summer 1968. **1C332**
An illustrated history of the Legion of Decency, a Catholic Church sponsored organization to regulate sexual morality in motion picture films. Illustrations include portraits of such Legion leaders as Martin Quigley, Father Daniel A. Lord (director until 1948), and Will Hays, head of the Motion Picture Association, who considered the Legion as an ally. The article discusses actions taken on specific films, court decisions, and includes a 1965 list of objectionable films.

———. "Still Legion, Still Decent?" *Commonweal*, 90:289–93, 23 May 1969. **1C333**
The author reviews the position of the National Catholic Office for Motion Pictures (successor to the Legion of Decency) in its attempt to impose limits on film-makers and guidelines for the faithful, but "to be relevant to a new, expanding film form and to the generation that finds art, entertainment, and identity in it."

Cornell, Greg. "Myth of the Free Press." *International Socialist Review*, 33(8):12–17, 36–37, September 1972. **1C334**
The only real freedom of the press in America is "the freedom" to distort, twist, and suppress information" in the interest of profitmaking. "It is only when we have a mass circulation socialist press in this country, arising out of the movements of workers, Blacks, Chicanos, women, and students, that we will have a press that can tell the truth and can be heard."

Cornell, Julien. *The Trial of Ezra Pound: A Documented Account of the Treason Case by the Defendant's Lawyer*. New York, Day, 1966. 215p. **1C335**
The poet was confined by the U.S. government for thirteen years on charges of wartime treason, being released in 1958. The charge was for making broadcasts over Italian radio that gave "aid and comfort" to the enemy. Includes text of two broadcasts and transcript of the trial.

Cornell University Libraries. "Access to Information." *Cornell University Libraries Bulletin*, 176:1–21, April 1972. **1C336**
The entire issue of the *Bulletin* explores some of the influences on open access to information: The Growth of Library Collections by Hen-

drik Edelman. Access to the Law by Robert L. Oakley. Comics As an Intellectual Resource by David H. R. Shearer. The Government and Access in the U.S.S.R. by Anna K. Stuliglowa. Access: Musing the Obscure by Gary Dellow. A Search Strategy for Freedom of Access by Thomas L. Bonn.

Cornish, Craig. "A First Amendment Right of Access—Denied." *Washburn Law Journal*, 13:518–23, Summer 1974.
1C337
Re: *Columbia Broadcasting System Inc. v. Democratic National Committee*, 412 U.S. 94 (1973).

"Corrective Advertising and the FTC: No, Virginia, Wonder Bread Doesn't Help Build Strong Bodies Twelve Ways." *Michigan Law Review*, 70:374–99, December 1871.
1C338
"This Note will outline the development and theory of corrective advertising. In particular, it will discuss the residual effects of deceptive advertising, which are the basis for a corrective remedy. The ₁Federal Trade₁ Commission's statutory authority to require corrective advertising, will then be explored; the analysis will compare corrective advertising with other types of affirmative disclosure required by the Commission and relate it to the present use of divestiture as a trade regulation remedy. Finally, the possible public benefit accruing from corrective advertising will be considered along with some thoughts on what policies the FTC should pursue in order to maximize that benefit."

" 'Corrective Advertising' Orders of the Federal Trade Commission." *Harvard Law Review*, 85:477–506, December 1971.
1C339
"It is the thesis of this Note that 'corrective advertising' orders are not beyond the FTC's statutory remedial authority, and that they represent a potentially viable solution to the past ineffectiveness of the Commission in dealing with certain kinds of false advertising. It is further suggested, however, that such orders should be employed, and upheld by reviewing courts, only when warranted by particular facts, and only when carefully suited to correcting the violation—conditions which may be more difficult to fulfill than the corresponding prerequisites of more typical FTC cease and desist orders."

"Corrective Advertising—the New Response to Consumer Deception." *Columbia Law Review*, 72:415–31, February 1972.
1C340
The author explores the legality and probable effectiveness of corrective advertising as a remedy for consumer deception, finding that it is within the broad scope of the Federal Trade Commission enabling act, and that it is probably a useful addition to the regulatory power of the Commission.

Correia, Eddie. "The Constitutionality of a Statute Prohibiting Advertising of Prescription Drug Prices." *Oklahoma Law Review*, 28:350–59, Spring 1975.
1C341
"This note discusses the social policy arguments for and against prohibiting the advertising of prescription drug prices, the trends in federal and state court decisions regarding the constitutionality of these statutes, and the likely constitutional status of the Oklahoma statute."

Corrigan, Robert A. "The Artist As Censor: J. P. Donleavy and *The Ginger Man*." *Midcontinent American Studies Journal*, 8(1):60–72, Spring 1967. **1C342**
An analysis of the changes made by the author of *The Ginger Man* to make the work less offensive to the general American reader. Changes include elimination of words, passages, and an entire chapter. The author of the article found that in general "the changes made by Mr. Donleavy to get his book published in the United States correspond to those elements Professor Kinsey found so repellant to the lower-educated group in his interviews."

———."Ezra Pound and the Bollinger Prize Controversy." *Midcontinent American Studies Journal*, 8(2):43–57, Fall 1967.
1C343
An account of the controversy involving the awarding of the Bollinger Prize for poetry to Ezra Pound in 1949 by the Library of Congress Fellows in American Literature. An extensive bibliography of the controversy is appended.

———. "*What's My Line*: Bennett Cerf, Ezra Pound and the *American* Poet." *American Quarterly*, 24:101–13, March 1972.
1C344
Deals with the 1946 controversy over Bennett Cerf's exclusion of Ezra Pound's poetry from a Modern Library anthology of American and British verse.

Corry, John. "Strom's Dirty Movies." *Harper's*, 237:30–40, December 1968.
1C345
Senator Strom Thurmond invited members of the press and the Senate Judiciary Committee to see a special screening of the movie "0–7" for which he said Justice Abe Fortas cast the deciding vote in a 5–4 Supreme Court decision, and which he used against him in the consideration of Fortas as Chief Justice.

Cors, Paul B. "Academic Libraries and Intellectual Freedom." In American Library Association's *Intellectual Freedom Manual*, Chicago, ALA, 1974, pt. 3, pp. 14–16.
1C346
"If the institution is firmly committed to freedom of inquiry in all areas of knowledge, and this commitment has been made a formal policy by the governing body, the library is unlikely to come under attack from would-be censors, and should be able to defend itself suc-

cessfully if an attack does come." The author recommends a written policy for collection development, incorporating the principles of the Library Bill of Rights; an established procedure for handling complaints about the absence or presence of titles; and a policy of free and equal access to materials.

———. "State Libraries and Intellectual Freedom." *American Libraries*, 1:944–45, November 1970. **1C347**
A five-point plan to remedy the apparent neglect of state libraries toward intellectual freedom, which includes establishing a program of direct aid to libraries requesting such in time of intellectual-freedom problems.

Cossham, Handel. *Mr. H. Cossham v. "Times and Mirror."* Action for Alleged Libel. High Court of Justice at Westminster. . . . Bristol, Leech and Taylor, 1875. 160p. **1C348**
A businessman charged the paper with publishing libelous statements about him in the course of a political campaign. The jury found for the defendants, after considerable evidence was presented to support the truth of the statements.

Costello, Mary. *Magazine Industry Shake-Out*. Washington, D.C., Editorial Research Reports, 1971. (*Editorial Research Reports*, 2:971–88, 15 December 1971) **1C349**
Content: The economic ills of American magazines, postal increases, TV advertising competition, *Look* and *Satevepost* casualties, origin and development of the periodical press through nineteenth-century mass circulation, political information and opinion-making editors versus business interests, present success of city and specialized magazines, survival methods, and group ownership.

———. *Newsmen's Rights*. Washington, D.C., Editorial Research Reports, 1972. (*Editorial Research Reports*, 2:949–68, 20 December 1972) **1C350**
Content: Fight over protecting news sources (government-press battle in jailing reporters, action to force reporters to reveal sources, Supreme Court's *Caldwell* ruling and its impact, and status of journalists cited for contempt of court); relationship of press and government (degrees of protection rights in time of war, the Pentagon Papers case, and previous conflicts involving press subpoenas); debate over privilege for journalists (inadequacy of state laws to protect news sources, continuing battle for passage of federal statute, argument over absolute vs. qualified privilege, and proposal for establishing a National Press Council).

———. *Pornography Control*. Washing-

ton, D.C., Editorial Research Reports, 1973. (*Editorial Research Reports*, 1:207–28, 21 March 1973)   **1C351**
Content: Reaction against sexual explicitness (hardening of public attitudes toward pornography, rejection of report by U.S. Commission on Obscenity and Pornography, local, state, and federal efforts to control smut, and criticism of court rulings as being permissive); past attempts to regulate obscenity (early influence of Puritan and Victorian ethics, Comstock and vice crusaders after the Civil War, question of art vs. pronography in this century, and recent breakdown of barriers against eroticism); debate over legalizing pornography (disputed claims as to harm of obscene material, Denmark's experience after legalization in 1969, and options for dealing with present glut of eroticism).

Cotham, Perry C. *Obscenity, Pornography, & Censorship*. Grand Rapids, Mich., Baker, 1973. 206p.   **1C352**
A "concerned Christian layman" studies the problems of obscenity and pornography, recognizing that the issue of morality in the media is so complex and confusing that it defies easy answers. Christians need to know the effects of pornography on individuals and society before an appropriate response can be given. He draws a distinction between pornography which is evil and dehumanizing, and erotic realism, which may be obscene, quoting from D. H. Lawrence's essay. He presents arguments for and against censorship, noting that official action is not the sole nor the most effective means of control and that the most dangerous forms of evil from the point of view of Christians will not be touched by censorship law. He offers seven suggestions for church action which include further study and attempt at understanding, encouragement of the arts, further guidelines and reviews of the media to help in decision making, wholesome church-sponsored recreation, a more active role of the church in sex education, compassionate attention to sex problems, and the encouragement of greater individual responsibility in decision making. He concludes that "the conflict must always be resolved in favor of the children."

Cotterell, Leslie E. "The Theatre Act, 1968." *New Law Journal*, 118:939–41, 3 October 1968.   **1C353**
An analysis of the British act which abolished licensing and censorship of plays by the Lord Chamberlain.

Cottle, Thomas J. "The Wellesley Incident: A Case of Obscenity." *Saturday Review*, 52(11):67–68, 75–77, 15 March 1969.   **1C354**
The incident involved a racial drama presented at the Wellesley Senior High School and objected to as being obscene. The incident re-

sulted in a community-wide controversy and a violent public hearing.

Council for Civil Liberties, Melbourne, Australia. *Judge Foster's Banned Speech*. Melbourne, Australia, The Council, 1938, 8p.   **1C355**
The uncensored text of a talk which was to have been broadcast through a national station on 2 May 1938 by Judge Foster of the Victorian County Court and which was withdrawn by him after censorship by officers of the Australian Broadcasting Commission. The pamphlet relates the events of the censorship of the talk, ironically entitled Freedom of Speech.

————. *Six Acts Against Civil Liberties*. Melbourne, Australia, The Council, 1937. 27p.   **1C356**
Censorship of books and films under the Customs Act of 1901; censorship of broadcasting under the Australian Broadcasting Commission Act of 1932; censorship of newspapers under the War Crimes Act and the War Precautions Act; and censorship of stage productions under the Theatres and Public Affairs Act. A sixth act dealt with immigration.

Council of Europe. European Committee on Crime Problems. *The Cinema and the Protection of Youth*. Strasbourg, France, 1968. 167p.   **1C357**
This report of a subcommittee on the mass media in relation to juvenile delinquency deals largely with the problems and experiences of European countries, but includes the United Kingdom. The report consists of a general study by Henri Michard, a report on censorship by Claude Brémond, a synthesis by James D. Halloran (University of Leicester), and a summary of legislation by various countries relating to the cinema, including laws to protect juveniles and laws creating censorship boards.

Council of Scientology Ministers. *How to Use the Freedom of Information Act*. Hollywood, Calif., The Council [1976?]. 18p.   **1C358**
"The booklet is designed to encourage the use of the FOIA by religious groups by clarifying (1) how to use the FOIA and (2) what to expect when it is used." Includes text of the act, sample FOIA request and appeal letters.

Council of State Governments. *Shield Laws: A Report on Freedom of the Press, of News Sources, and the Obligation to Testify*. Lexington, Ky., Council of State Governments, 1973. 33p.   **1C359**
A brief report on the historical background of shield laws, recent court decisions involving newsmen's privileges, types of shield laws in operation in the several states, and a sampling of the diverse opinion regarding the desirability of such laws. In view of the refinements and standards incorporated in some state shield laws and the inability of Congress to agree on a

law, there is now no pressing need for federal legislation.

"The Counter–Government and the Pentagon Papers." *National Review*, 23:739–41, 13 July 1971.   **1C360**
The author considers publication of the Pentagon Papers as an element in the antiwar campaign, an attempt to defeat Richard Nixon in his reelection in 1972. Those in opposition to the present administration serve as a counter-government and do not recognize the "authority of the regular government to determine policy."

Court, John H. *Law, Light, and Liberty*. Adelaide, Australia, Lutheran Publishing House, 1975. 144p.   **1C361**
An Australian psychologist states a case for "quality control" of publications in the area of sex and violence, a term which he prefers to "censorship" which has a negative connotation. This control would "preserve high standards by the exclusion of whatever does not measure up." The traditional standards of sexual morality as established by the courts and based on assumptions of Christian morality have been challenged and in some cases rejected. He calls for "a Christian stance" in restoring these standards. He is critical of the liberal interpretation of obscenity legislation by Don Chipp, Australia's Minister of Customs and Excise, particularly with respect to the introduction of "R" certificate films. The author challenges the so-called experts whose scientific findings on the effect of pornography do not always support their testimony, particularly in the so-called "catharsis" theory. In one chapter he answers the various charges made by opponents of censorship: (1) What right have you to interfere in the affairs of others? (2) The law has no place in the bedroom. (3) Censorship is antidemocratic. (4) Let a man go to hell in his own way if he wants to. (5) There are more important issues. (6) We've always had this kind of problem—what's new? In a final chapter the author suggests avenues of action to bring about the "quality control" of materials disseminated through the mass media. One of the appendices contains a statement on the work of the Festival of Light, a worldwide organization concerned with declining standards of morality. The present book supersedes two earlier pamphlets by the author: *In Defense of Censorship; a Christian View* (Adelaide, The Community Standards Organization, 1975) and *Changing Community Standards* (Adelaide, Lutheran Publishing House, 1972).

————. "The Place of Censored Material in the Treatment of Behavioral Disturbances." *Australian Psychologist*, 8:150–60, July 1973.   **1C362**
Summary of a paper given before the symposium, Psychological Impacts of Censorship, at the 7th annual Conferance of the Australian Psychological Society.

————. *Pornography and Sex Crimes*. Sydney, Australia, Australian Festival of Light, 1975. 41p. ("Light" Group

Resource Paper, Revised, no. 1) **1C363**
The author debunks four myths with respect to the effect of pornography as seen from the experience in Denmark where pornography laws have been repealed: (1) Make pornography freely available and people will quickly lose interest. (2) It's only for the tourist. (3) Children can be adequately protected while adults retain their right to freedom. (4) Sex crimes will go down.

————. *Pornography: Personal and Societal Effects*. Sydney, Australia, Australian Festival of Light, 1973. 26p.
1C364
A paper presented to the Geigy Symposium on Liberation Movements and Psychiatry, Prince Henry Hospital, University of New South Wales.

————, comp. *Pornography: Some Points of View*. Sydney, Australia, Australian Festival of Light, 1974. 11p. (Group Resource Paper, no. 3) **1C365**
A collection of forty-three statements on pornography from various documented sources, useful for those stating the case against pornography.

Courtney, Janet E. "A Library Censorship." In her *Recollected in Tranquility*. London, Heinemann, 1926, pp. 186–200.
1C366
A former member of the staff of the Times Book Club discusses the system of book censorship imposed by the Circulating Libraries Association to which her Club (under Lord Northcliffe's management) belonged. Among the 1,901 books banned was George Moore's *Memoirs of My Dead Life*; among those restricted was H. G. Wells' *Ann Veronica*. Miss Courtney's resignation in protest of the censorship provoked a general outcry in the literary world, and the circulating libraries "for the most part dropped their censorship in practice, though not in principle."

Cousens, Hilderic, *ed. Pros and Cons: A Newspaper-Reader's and Debater's Guide to the Leading Controversies of the Day*. 7th ed. London, Routledge, 1926. 211p. (First published in 1896) **1C367**
Opposing arguments are advanced on social, economic, and political topics, including: public control and taxation of advertising, abolition of the blasphemy laws, government control of broadcasting, censorship of the cinema, censorship of fiction, censorship of the stage, publicity of court proceedings, and anonymity of newspaper articles.

Cousins, Norman. "America's Need to Know." *Saturday Review–World*, 1(4):4–5, 23 October 1973. **1C368**
"Americans need not be grateful for being told the truth by their government; this is their natural right. In recent years, however, a strange new notion has gained ground. It is the

idea that government has options with respect to truth. A possible beginning date for this departure is 1947, when the government was authorized by Congress to practice secret violence, deceit, and subversion as essential parts of the conduct of U.S. foreign policy."

————. "The Uses of Boredom." *Saturday Review*, 53:16, 11 April 1970.
1C369
"The real issue emerging from the extreme new candor ["x"-rated films] is not whether society has been too rigid—it probably has—but whether many specimens of the new candor are anything more than a colossal invasion of privacy. As such, they are not a manifestation of freedom but an assault on it. For nothing is more essential to freedom than privacy." The author writes of the "corrective power of boredom," noting that "there is nothing like a slow box office to start a new trend." Sex has not ceased to be interesting, but there are many dimensions more meaningful and appealing.

Covert, Cathy. " 'Passion Is Ye Prevailing Motive': The Feud Behind the Zenger Case." *Journalism Quarterly*, 50:3–10, Spring 1973. **1C370**
"Zenger may have been mere pawn in a lengthy struggle between Governor Cosby and James Alexander. Their feud may have helped produce an expanded theory of press freedom."

Covington, John P. "Scheme to Defame Political Candidate Coupled with Unreasonable Headlines Is Evidence of Actual Malice." *St. Mary's Law Journal*, 7:416–23, 1975. **1C371**
Re: *Sprouse v. Clay Communication, Inc.*, 211 S.E.2d 674 (W.Va. 1975).

Cowley, Malcolm. "Dirty Books." *Virginia Librarian*, 14(4):8–17, Winter 1967. **1C372**
A literary critic reminisces about the use of dirty words in literature—the experience of Hemingway and Fitzgerald with their publisher over taboo words that would now be considered mild, the use of dirty words as a male idiom which first began to become public as the bawdy songs of World War I, Paris in the 1920s as a refuge for writers who wanted to use bad words in their books, the flourishing of publishers of English-language dirty books (e.g. Maurice Girodius), and the underground trade in pornographic works in the United States. He "laments the decline in prestige and power of what used to be bad words in language" as these words have become commonplace. Cowley considers the great upheaval in recent years to have brought about a reversal of attitudes, so that books which would have formerly been banned as pornographic are now widely circulated and approved by the courts. He discusses the *Lady Chatterley's Lover* and *Tropic of Cancer* cases and the erotic products of Grove Press and other major publishers. There is an increase in complaints from book reviewers on the use of sex as a form of

protest. Looking to the future, he predicts that "the change in the language itself will be permanent and that the bad words will never regain the power they had for our parents and grandparents. The new attitudes toward sex are likely to represent another permanent change for better or worse. . . . It is safe to predict, however, that there will be a reaction against the tasteless permissiveness that now prevails in writing and publishing. Yes, the censors will come back in some fashion, as they came back in France, and the Supreme Court of some future day will write new decisions to authorize their return."

Cowley, Susan C., and Loren Jenkins. "Censorship, Indian-Style." *Newsweek*, 86(5):50–51, 4 August 1975. **1C373**
"Since her constitutional coup of June 26, Indian Prime Minister Indira Gandhi has matched her purge of political dissidents with a censorship-and-harassment crackdown designed to muzzle the press as well. . . . She has imposed a set of draconian censorship 'guidelines' that make a mockery of a free press in a country with one of the liveliest traditions of journalistic independence in the Third World."

[Cox, Archibald.] "The Supreme Court, 1965 Term: Fair Trial; Freedom of Speech and Association; Libel of 'Public Official.' " *Harvard Law Review*, 80:180–98, November 1966.
1C374
Under the heading Fair Trial, the survey considers the case of *Sheppard v. Maxwell*; under Obscenity, the case of *Ginzburg v. United States*; under Libel of "Public Official," the case of *Rosenblatt v. Baer*.

Cox, Barry. "Freedom of Expression." In his *Civil Liberties in Britain*. Harmondsworth, England, Penguin, 1975, pp. 76–120. **1C375**
"Freedom of expression is perhaps the single most important civil liberty. The free play of ideas is the basis of all political, scientific and artistic activity." While the British have not established this freedom as an inalienable right as Americans have in their Constitution, so that some restrictions imposed in Britain would not be possible in America, dissent since 1960 has existed on an unprecedented scale and recent experience has demonstrated that threats to freedom can be resisted effectively. The author suggests abolition or reform of the official secrets laws, the obscenity laws, and the incitement to disaffection law.

Cox, John T., Jr. "Defamation: A Compendium." *Louisiana Law Review*, 28:82–109, December 1967. **1C376**
An examination of the Louisiana law of defamation in light of the development of English

common law torts of libel and slander and of the recent U.S. Supreme Court decisions.

Cox, Kenneth A. Broadcasters as Revolutionaries." *Television Quarterly*, 6:13–19, Winter 1967. (Reprinted in John H. Pennybacker and Waldo W. Braden, *eds. Broadcasting in the Public Interest*, pp. 57–64) **1C377**
"The First Amendment guards the broadcaster's right to say things of little importance to anyone; but it also guards his right to discuss matters of vital consequence to all, matters which will shape our lives and the destiny of our country. The choice, in the last analysis, is their own." The article, by a member of the Federal Communications Commission, discusses local public service programming.

Crabtree, James, and Daniel Kearney. "A Revised Standard of Obscenity?" *University of Florida Law Review*, 19:185–93, 1966. **1C378**
Re: *Ginzburg v. United States* (1966); *Mishkin v. State of New York* (1966); *Memoirs of a Woman of Pleasure v. Massachusetts* (1966).

"Crackdown on Smut; How It's Faring." *U.S. News & World Report*, 75(2):24–26, 30 July 1973. **1C379**
"Armed with new legal clout, city after city is clamping down on pornographers. It's being welcomed by many—but causing some concern, too."

Crago, Neville. "Lord Ellenborough's State Trials." *University of Western Australia Law Review*, 12:235–53, June 1976. **1C380**
An examination of the performance of Lord Ellenborough who presided over the British state trials for treason, libel, and seditous libel during the early years of the nineteenth century. Among the libel trials discussed are those of Jean Peltier (1803), William Cobbett (1805), James Perry, John Lambert, and John and Leigh Hunt (1810–11), and William Hone (1817).

[Crampton, Philip C.] *Report of the Speech of the Solicitor General on the Trial of the Case of the King v. Richard Barrett, in the Court of King's Bench, in Ireland, on the 27th of November, 1833. By James Mongan.* Dublin, Richard Milliken, 1834. 40p. **1C381**
Barrett, publisher of *The Pilot*, was brought to trial in Dublin on charges of seditious libel for publication of an article by Daniel O'Connor. O'Connor appeared in court as Barrett's defense attorney, giving a stirring address in defense of the sentiments of his article as well as the right to publish them. Solicitor General

Crampton, in response, asked the jury to consider three questions: Was the work published by the defendant? Was it a libel on the British parliament? and Was the intention to create dissention, to effect a repeal of the Union by force, and to bring the law and parliament into disrepute? Barrett was found guilty.

Cranberg, Gilbert. "Is 'Right of Access' Coming?" *Saturday Review*, 53(32):48–49, 57, 8 August 1970. **1C382**
Mounting attention is being given to the "right of access" theory in the mass media since it was proposed three years ago by Professor Jerome A. Barron.

———. "New Look at the First Amendment." *Saturday Review*, 51:136–37, 14 September 1968. **1C383**
"The American Civil Liberties Union, that most vigorous defender of First Amendment rights, is poised to do battle in the courts to establish Professor [Jerome A.] Barron's notion of a 'right of access' to the press." Barron had proposed government regulation through court rulings and laws to force the press to give space to novel and unpopular ideas. The ACLU Communications Media Committee, headed by New York attorney Harriet Pilpel, prepared a paper for the annual ACLU conference favoring Professor Barron's proposals.

———. "Voluntary Press Codes." *Saturday Review*, 52(19):71–72, 10 May 1969. **1C384**
The Warren Commission in 1964 recommended that the newspaper press promulgate "a code of professional conduct." The idea was rejected by the American Society of Newspaper Editors as impractical. This gave the clue to the bar associations to establish guidelines for fair trial–free press, resulting in the ABA's Reardon Report of 1966. Subsequently, press associations have taken a new look at guidelines; nearly two–thirds have either adopted them or have them under consideration.

Crane, Brian A. "Freedom of the Press and National Security." *McGill Law Journal*, 21:148–55, Spring 1975. **1C385**
A discussion of the Canadian Official Secrets Act and the Criminal Code as it applies not only to persons who release confidential information without authority but also to the journalist who publishes such information that comes into his hands.

Crane, Frank. "Nude or Undressed." In his *The Looking Glass*. London, Lane, 1921, pp. 240–42. **1C386**
Crane draws a distinction between "nude" which is a natural state and, therefore, innocent, and "undressed" which is the removal of clothing which is "indecent." Reference to the controversy over Paul Chabas's picture, *September Morn*, which portrays a nude and is, therefore, not obscene.

Crane, Stanley. "What Was and Will Be 5036, A Bill to Define Obscenity; A Personal Report." *Connecticut Libraries*, 14(3):7–9, Summer 1972. **1C387**
The chairman of the Intellectual Freedom Committee of the Connecticut Library Association calls for membership support in defeating a bill before the state legislature that would strike out the factor of "social value" from the state's obscenity law, a first step in carrying out the recommendation of the Commission on Standards of Decency. The establishing of an obscenity commission, the author states, is another step.

Cranston, Alan. "Senate Bill One." *Review of Southern California Journalism*, 4(16):1–2, 1975. **1C388**
"Under the guise of protecting national security, this dangerous measure would shelter those who hide incompetence, cover up waste, bury corruption, or peddle improper influence. If Senate Bill One had been law three years ago, the public never would have gotten the full story of Watergate." The Senator from California, a former newsman, discusses the six "pernicious provisions" of the bill to revise the Federal Criminal Code, provisions that, ironically, "on the eve of our bicentennial . . . could booby trap the first amendment and freedom of the press."

———. "Shield Laws? First Means First." *Trial*, 9:30–34, May–June 1973. **1C389**
"I believe strongly that Congress should give newsmen an absolute and unqualified privilege to refuse under all circumstances and without penalty to divulge to anyone any confidential information or confidential source obtained in the course of their professional newsgathering activities."

Crawford, Donald W. "Can Disputes Over Censorship Be Resolved?" *Ethics*, 78:93–108, January 1968. **1C390**
The author's "primary aim is to gain some understanding of the futility of arguments, disputes, and discussions on whether the practice of censorship is justified; and I think this requires, above all, exploring the framework in terms of which the arguments on both sides usually are presented and asking whether it is adequate." On exploring the framework, the author finds it inadequate and concludes that if "the courts and the many other parties involved address themselves to the real question at issue—the right of an electorate to impose restrictions on private morality—then and only then is a resolution possible."

Crawford, Kenneth. "Gap Prone." *Newsweek*, 70:39, 25 September 1967. **1C391**
There is a void in news from high government officials concerning the war in Southeast Asia. "This Administration is credibility-gap prone." There are questions, particularly concerning the bombing targets, calling for answers from the President.

Crawford, Nelson A. *The Ethics of Journalism*. New York, Knopf, 1924. 264p. (Reprinted, Johnson Reprint Corp., 1969) **1C392**
A consideration of the principles of objectivity in newspaper editing and of professional codes of ethics including the Canons of Journalism, adopted by the American Society of Newspaper Editors in 1923, and codes adopted by state press associations (Kansas, Missouri, Oregon, South Dakota, and Washington) and individual newspapers (including *Brooklyn Eagle*, *Christian Science Monitor*, *Springfield Republican*, *Detroit News*, and others).

Crawford, Twila J. *The Newsman and Confidential Sources: A Focus on the Earl Caldwell Case*. Manhatten, Kans., Kansas State University, 1971. 111p. (Unpublished Master's thesis) **1C393**
A study of the case of the newspaper reporter who was cited for contempt of court for refusal to obey a subpoena to appear before a federal grand jury investigating the Black Panther Party. *United States v. Caldwell* (1972).

Crawfurd, John. *Taxes on Knowledge: A Financial and Historical View of the Taxes Which Impede the Education of the People*. London, Charles Ely, 1836. 63p. **1C394**
"Taxes on knowledge" include stamp duty on newspapers, an advertisement duty, an import duty on the raw materials used in papermaking, writing, and printing, an excise duty on paper, duty on foreign books, and taxes imposed on the diffusion of books and printing through the monopoly of the Post Office. Some taxes were imposed for purposes of raising revenue; others to arrest the dissemination of political knowledge. On both scores, the laws are a mistake and should be abolished.

Crawley, John. "Censorship and the Media." *Political Quarterly*, 47:160–68, April–June 1976. **1C395**
"The case against censorship rests absolutely on the right of the editor to have the last word. And that right rests in turn on the responsibility that falls on the editor—a responsibility which is recognized by the law. . . . The ultimate reason for making a fuss about a free Press is the right of the public to know, but this cannot be secured without a general acceptance of the independence of the editor under the law."

Creel, H. G. *Tricks of the Press: A Lecture*. St. Louis, The National Rip-Saw Publishing Co., 1911. 32p. (Rip-Saw Series no. 5) **1C396**
In an address delivered at City Park, Kansas City, Kans., 10 September 1910, this Socialist lecturer reveals how news is suppressed because of the economic interest of the "capitalist" newspaper owner. He tells how tricky wording of headlines and stories is used to mislead the reader and to avoid libel suits and how newspapers propagandize through news stories, headlines, and editorials. Many

of his examples are taken from the *Chicago Tribune*. A second lecture, *Newspaper Frauds*, was published as no. 6 in the series.

Crick, Bernard. "How the Essay Came to Be Written." *Times Literary Supplement*, 3,680:3–4, 15 September 1972. Also in *New York Times*, 8 October 1972. **1C397**
An account of how George Orwell came to write the essay, "Freedom of the Press," as an introduction to his *Animal Farm*, and the story of the book's rejection by four leading British publishers because it might be offensive to the Russians.

Crick, Don. "Aspects of Censorship." *Australian Author*, 1:25–29, April 1969. **1C398**

Criley, Richard. "Sneaking Up on the Press: Nixon's 'Official Secrets' Act." *Nation*, 218:265–68, 2 March 1974. **1C399**
"Few Americans are aware that despite Watergate, the Nixon Administration is pressing to enact a sweeping plan for press censorship that would be more damaging than the infamous 'Alien and Sedition Laws' denounced by Thomas Jefferson." The Criminal Code Reform Act "provides detailed evidence of the Administration's intent to subvert the substance of our constitutional system." Special reference is made to penalties for disclosing national defense and classified information, an outgrowth of the government's failure to get a conviction in the Ellsberg case.

"Crisis in Britain." *Grassroots Editor*, 8(6):23–24, 26, November–December 1967. **1C400**
An unidentified "Source Close to the British Press Council" reports the curtailment of press freedom by provisions of the Criminal Justice Act which alters the practice of reporting committal proceedings. The act was passed despite vigorous protest from the British press and the Press Council.

Crist, Judith *et al. Pornography and Censorship*. North Hollywood, Calif., Center for Cassette Studies, 1971. Tape recording; part 1, 54 min.; part 2, 28 min. (Distributor's title: Censors and Free Speech; the Pornographic Mind) **1C401**
A panel discussion on pornography—its meaning, effect, and control. Panel members: Judith Crist, movie critic; Paul Krassner, editor; Richard Kuh and Herbert Schwartz, attorneys; Rabbi Julius G. Newmann; Dr. Isadore Rubin; and Irving Wallace, novelist. Panel members respond to questions from the audience.

Crist, Phyllis I. "The Freedom of Information Act and Equitable Discre-

tion." *Denver Law Journal*, 51:263–74, 1974. **1C402**
The article analyzes the language of the Freedom of Information Act and its legislative history "to determine whether Congress intended that Act to abrogate courts' equitable remedies, discusses the *Consumers Union* and *Hawkes* cases concerning the use of equitable principles to withhold disclosure which would otherwise be available under the Act, and proposes reconciliation through coexistence of the two seemingly conflicting viewpoints."

Crocker, Leslie J. "*Ginzburg et al.*—An Attack on Freedom of Expression." *Western Reserve Law Review*, 17:1325–41, 1966. (Reprinted in Donald B. Sharp, *ed.*, *Commentaries on Obscenity*, pp. 297–303) **1C403**
Criticism of the *Ginzburg* decision on obscenity, *Ginzburg v. United States* (1966), as a serious set-back to protection of free expression under the First Amendment.

Cronkite, Walter. *Broadcast News and Half-Free Speech*. Lawrence, Kans., William Allen White School of Journalism, University of Kansas, 1969. 19p. (Twentieth Annual William Allen White Memorial Lecture) **1C404**
The Columbia Broadcasting System commentator defends news broadcasting against its critics—newspaper critics, political critics, and critics in academia—and calls for a joint attack by the media against the encroachment on freedom. He argues that broadcasting be given the same rights as the press under the First Amendment. The original rationale for government regulation of broadcasting—limitation of channels and expense in starting a station—are no longer valid. Today with the opening of ultra-high frequencies in television there are more stations than there are newspapers and it is cheaper to start a television station than a newspaper. "Our experience in publishing in this nation guarantees that we can safely take our chances with *laissez-faire* broadcasting, that broadcasting entrepreneurs will provide a varied diet, a diet for each taste even as today, motion picture producers and book publishers offer products that run the gamut from the obscene to the glorious."

———. " 'Conspiracy' Against a Free Press." *Seminar* (*A Quarterly Review for Newspapermen by Copley Newspapers*), 22:21–24, December 1971. **1C405**
In remarks to the International Radio and Television Society, the CBS news commentator charges the Nixon Administration with a "conspiracy . . . to destroy the credibility of the press, mainly the electronic news." He urges journalists to "resist unflaggingly and with all our resources, every effort to intimidate, coerce and control us."

————.] "Playboy Interview. Walter Cronkite: A Candid Conversation with America's Most Trusted Television Newsman." *Playboy*, 20(6):67–68+, June 1973. **1C406**
Much of the interview deals with the issue of freedom of the press and the orchestrated efforts of the Nixon Administration to control the press, a campaign "agreed upon in secret by members of the Administration." He criticizes Clay T. Whitehead's plans to deflate the power of television network news programs; he favors eliminating the FCC's fairness doctrine which poses artificial controls on balance and objectivity; he discusses the Pentagon Papers case and government secrecy, the controversy over the CBS documentary, *The Selling of the Pentagon*, press coverage of the Vietnam war, and government surveillance of newsmen.

————. "Privilege: Broadcast News and the First Amendment." *Vital Speeches*, 39:521–24, 15 June 1973. **1C407**
A discussion of the role of the press in the Watergate affair. "The information that must flow freely from government to the people, also eddies around government itself. Good newspapers and broadcasters, through their diligence, can provide information about one branch of government to officials of another branch." The Nixon Administration might have avoided disgrace if it had put more faith in the press instead of waging a campaign against the credibility of the press.

————. *Testimony before the U.S. Senate Subcommittee on Constitutional Rights*. New York, The Author, 1971. 21p. Processed. **1C408**
The anchorman of CBS–TV evening news calls for Congress to grant to television the same protection of the First Amendment as given to publishing. "The difference between publishing and broadcasting is mostly a myth." While admitting the shortcomings of broadcast journalism, he decries the intimidation of government officials who are dissatisfied with the news. "The ultimate intimidation is to attempt, or even threaten to attempt, through licensing procedure to take a station away from its owners."

[Cross, Charles F.] "Withdrawal of Funds from College Newspaper Advocating Segregationalist Policy Deemed Violative of First and Fourteenth Amendments." *University of Richmond Law Review*, 8:297–302, Winter 1974. **1C409**
Re: *Joyner v. Whiting* (1973), involving withdrawal of financial support from *Campus Echo*, a student publication at North Carolina Central University, when the publication advocated a strong segregationalist policy, urging blacks to separate themselves from Caucasians in every way.

Cross, Fred M., Jr. "Delineation of Procedures Used in Seizing Obscene Films." *Journal of Urban Law*, 47:746–52, 1969–70. **1C410**
"The importance of *Tyrone* [*Tyrone, Inc. v. James B. Wilkinson*, 1969] is that within its written opinion is the summation of a common thread running through the various decisions on the seizure of allegedly obscene matter: the idea that because the line between protected and unprotected speech is so difficult to draw, the circulation of a particular form of expression should be completely unhampered, at least until an independent determination of obscenity is made by a judicial officer; complete restraint of any form of expression or communication, no matter what form this expression takes, must await final judicial determination of obscenity."

Cross, Robert. "All the Brave Bunnies." *New York*, 6(31):64–65, 30 July 1973. **1C411**
Reaction to the Supreme Court decision on obscenity, *Miller v. California* (1973), from *Playboy* publisher Hugh Hefner and his staff.

————. "Busting the Blue Movie." *Chicago Tribune Magazine*, 2 December 1973, pp. 38, 98+. **1C412**
An interview with a Chicago porn movie operator reveals the state of the business, the effect of Supreme Court decisions, and action of Chicago police, state's attorney, and the courts.

Cross, Scott. "Obscenity: Determined by Whose Standards?" *University of Florida Law Review*, 26:324–29, Winter 1974. **1C413**
Miller v. State of California (1973). "While the instant case conforms to the Supreme Court's consistent refusal to extend first amendment protection to all forms of expression and provides a long-needed means of relieving the Court of its burden of independently determining factual issues in obscenity cases, it creates new problems concerning the identity of the community from which contemporary community standards are to be derived."

Crossland, Hugh J. "The Rise and Fall of Fair Use: The Protection of Literary Materials Against Copyright Infringement by New and Developing Media." *South Carolina Law Review*, 20:153–242, 1968. **1C414**
The author suggests that a provision be added to the Copyright Act establishing a statutory licensing system with a private clearinghouse.

Crossley, D. J. "F. H. Bradley on Censorship and Psychical Distance." *Idealistic Studies*, 3:80–102, January 1973. **1C415**
The author explores the concept of "psychical distance" relating to sex censorship, as expressed by Edward Bullough in a 1959 article on art and aesthetics and by F. H. Bradley in an article written in 1912 but first published in his *Collected Essays* in 1935. The debate revolves around this hypothesis: "If a causal link is established between smut and antisocial behavior, then the practice of censorship is justified." Even though there is a causal link between idea and action, the concept holds that censorship is not justified because the link between the idea and antisocial behavior can be blocked.

Crowell, Joan. "The 99th Kind of Censorship." *American Pen*, 6:66–69, Spring 1974. **1C416**
Deals with the author's experience in being refused permission to interview jailed war dissenters in the preparation of a book, *The Moral Generation*, and her difficulty in getting a publisher for another book on conditions in the Fort Dix stockade.

Crowl, John A. "Time Lag in Release of Secret Documents Divides Historians." *Chronicle of Higher Education*, 6(14):1, 6, 10 January 1972. **1C417**
A report of the debate on historians' access to government documents which took place at the annual meeting of the American Historical Association.

[Crowley, David A.] "Distribution of Handbills in Mall of Private Shopping Center Is Not Constitutionally Protected When Purpose of Handbilling Is Unrelated to Shopping Center's Operations." *Alabama Law Review*, 25:76–97, Fall 1972. **1C418**
Re: *Lloyd Corp. v. Tanner*, 407 U.S. 551 (1972).

Crowley, Juanita A., and David F. B. Smith. "Constitutional Ramifications of a Repeal of the Fairness Doctrine." *Georgetown Law Journal*, 64:1293–321, July 1976. **1C419**
"Repeal of the fairness doctrine would raise important first amendment issues that courts have not yet confronted. Listeners seeking to protect their programming interests would attempt to persuade a court that the first amendment itself requires the broadcaster to provide adequate and balanced coverage. . . . A court will have to determine if the first amendment provides a listener's right; if it does, the court then would have to strike a balance between the competing first amendment right of the listener and broadcaster. A threshold issue in such a case would be whether the first amendment prohibition against government abridgment of speech governs conduct of the broadcaster."

Crown, Sidney. "Pornography and Sexual Promiscuity." *Medicine, Science, and the Law*, 13:239–43, October 1973.   **1C420**

A psychiatrist discusses pornography from the point of view of sociology and psychology, differentiating between sexual arousal and sexual behavior, relating it to other potentially damaging experiences, and considering it in the general context of individual freedom and control in society. "In so far as it produces sexual behavior at all it seems to me likely that pornography is overwhelmingly a stimulation to masturbation." Paper presented as part of a special program on The Role of Law in a Permissive Society.

Cruikshank, R. J. "Freedom of Thought and Expression." In *The Meaning of Freedom: Six Essays*. London, Pall Mall Features, 1956, pp. 62–72. (Supplement no. 7 to World Liberalism)   **1C421**

The author applauds the wisdom of our forefathers who looked upon freedom of the press as "the conditioning in enabling freedom—the medium through which the other liberties of man expressed themselves and by which they were protected." Of the various legal limitations on press freedom, he sees the increasingly strict libel laws most questionable. Britons are less free to criticize individuals today than during the days of Charles Dickens, who under present law would probably be up for libel or contempt of court. There is a potential danger in the monopoly of the press and broadcasting, but he believes the British system provides greater diversity of ideas than the free-enterprise system in the United States; it has been well administered. One of the hardest things to learn in life is to be tolerant of intolerance. "We should extend freedom to the utterance of teachings we abominate."

Crush, Marion. "Deselection Policy: How to Exclude Everything." *Wilson Library Bulletin*, 45:180–81, October 1970.   **1C422**

How a written book-selection policy can be used as a tool for censorship. The author reproduces such a policy with twenty reasons for excluding material, and illustrates how one or more of these reasons were used to reject a goodly number of major works of fiction. "A book selection policy must never be used as an *excuse* for not buying a book which, for some personal reason, the book selector does not want to buy."

Cuddy, Kevin M., and William Diller. "Fair Trial, Free Press, the Contempt Power: Its Historic and Modern Application." *Suffolk University Law Review*, 3:484–512, Summer 1969.   **1C423**

"The purpose of this Note will be to ascertain whether the court's power to punish, by contempt, out of court publications which prejudice a fair trial has been negated by the First Amendment. This will be accomplished through an analysis and comparison of this power in the United States and England, with emphasis on the historic development of the contempt power in both state and federal courts in the United States."

Cudlipp, Hugh. *Publish and Be Damned*. London, Dakers, 1953. 292p.   **1C424**

Includes several chapters dealing with government threats to control the British press and, in particular, to suppress the London *Daily Mirror* during World War II.

[Cullen, Richard.] "Newspaper Advertisement of Abortion Referral Service Entitled to First Amendment Protection." *University of Richmond Law Review*, 10:427–33, Winter 1976.   **1C425**

Re: *Bigelow v. Virginia* (1975), in which the U.S. Supreme Court ruled that the prior courts "erred in their assumptions that advertisement, as such, was entitled to no first amendment protection." The Court "felt compelled to decide the case by direct confrontation with the first amendment issue and balancing competing interests, rather than applying the overbreadth doctrine to the statute."

Cullinan, Eustace. "The Rights of Newspapers: May They Print Whatever They Choose?" *American Bar Association Journal*, 41:1020–23+, November 1955.   **1C426**

"To poison public opinion by falsehoods and half truths is in a fashion a form of treason in this country; especially if the deception bears on matters which tend to influence the popular decision on public affairs. Certainly it is no less a danger to the public than attempts at monopoly or unfair practices in trade or commerce."

Cultural Defence Committee. (Fellowship of Australian Writers.) *Mental Rubbish from Overseas; A Public Protest*. Sydney, Australia, The Committee, 1935. 14p. (Pamphlet no. 1)   **1C427**

"No objection is taken to bona fide cultural intercourse with other countries, nor to American culture as such, nor to American books and periodicals of an educational or at least a literary quality. Objection is taken to the 'dumped' import into Australia, of magazines, newspapers or syndicated features, radio dramas and music, and films, which normally-decent people in America would themselves condemn as being a travesty of American ideas and culture. This campaign is being organized to free Australian thought and education from the infection of a set of foreign ideas which are not only nasty but also literally cheap." The Committee proposes a tax on such material of overseas origin which will make the retail price at least equal to the price normally charged by Australian producers for similar material.

Cunningham, Ann M. " 'A Roller Coaster to Hell.' " *MORE*, 4(8):8, 10–11, August 1974.   **1C428**

"Visions of 'affairs-animal,' 'self-masturbation'

and something called 'hunger-thumps', brought the peaceful town of Bennington, Vt., to a boil over whether Mt. Anthony Union High School's copy of *Ms.* magazine should remain on the library shelf."

Cunningham, Ben. "It *Can* Happen Here; Ask Bill Farr." *Review of Southern California Journalism*, 2(2):2–4, December 1972.   **1C429**

The case of the Los Angeles reporter, cited for contempt of court for refusal to reveal his news sources in covering the Manson trial.

——. "The William Farr Case: In and Out of Jail—And In Again." *Quill*, 60:9–13, December 1972.   **1C430**

The author criticizes the nation's press for inadequate coverage of the Farr case.

Cunningham, Glenn. "New Way to Discourage Pornographers." *Catholic Digest*, 32:61–64, June 1968. (Condensed from *The Register*, 4 February 1968)   **1C431**

A sponsor of federal legislation which invokes the invasion of privacy concept in controlling obscenity in the mails, discusses the way in which the law will work.

"Cures for Corruption." *Times Literary Supplement*, 3,681:1083–84, 22 September 1972.   **1C432**

Reviews and commentary on four publications: *Pornography: The Longford Report; The Obscenity Report* edited by Maurice Girodias; *To Deprave and Corrupt* edited by Alan Burns; and *Censorship and the Limits of Permission* by Jonathan Miller.

[Curll, Edmund.] *The Humble Representation of Edmund Curll, Bookseller and Citizen of London, Concerning Five Books Complained of to the Secretary of State*. London, The Author, 1725. 12p.   **1C433**

The five books were: *Treatise on the Use of Flogging in Physical and Venereal Affairs* by John Henry Meibomius, M.D., *Venus in the Cloister; Or the Nun in Her Smock, The Praise of Drunkenness, Three New Poems (Family Duty, Or the Monk and the Merchant's Wife, The Curious Wife*, and *Buckingham-House*) edited by John Markland, and *De Secretis Mulierum, or, The Mysteries of Human Generation Fully Revealed* by Albertus Magnus. Attached is a catalog of Curll's publications.

Curran, Barbara A. *Fair Trial—Free Press*. Chicago, American Bar Foundation, 1964. 23p. Processed. (Research Memorandum Series, no. 33)   **1C434**

Barbara A. Curran – Robert E. Cushman

A brief review of the issues involved in the fair trial—free press conflict and suggested methods for dealing with it. The paper covers (1) controls imposed directly on the communication media, (2) controls imposed in respect to judicial proceedings to insure fair trial, and (3) controls imposed on members of the legal profession.

Curtis, Russell L., Jr., and Louis A. Zurcher, Jr. "Stable Resources of Protest Movements: The Multi-Organizational Field." *Social Forces*, 52:53–61, September 1973.   **1C435**
"The natural histories and membership characteristics of two protest organizations, both conducting antipornography crusades, were assembled from nonparticipant observation, document research, and structured interviews with active members and other knowledgeable individuals."

Cushman, Robert E., and Robert F. Cushman. "First Amendment Rights." In their *Cases in Constitutional Law*. 3d ed. New York, Appleton-Century-Crofts, 1968, pp. 812–1014.   **1C436**
Chapter 18 on First Amendment Rights contains the text of major court decisions in such areas as free speech and press, free press and fair trial, censorship and the right to publish, and postal censorship.

D

Dabb, Wayne C., Jr., and Peter A. Kelly. "The Newsman's Privilege: Protection of Confidential Associations and Private Communications." *Journal of Law Reform*, 4:85–120, Fall 1970. **1D1**
"The First Amendment guarantee of freedom of the press suggests a constitutional basis for a newsman's privilege. The decisions of the United States Supreme Court under that amendment make the conclusion that the confidential associations and private communications of newsmen are constitutionally protected inescapable. However, the Court has never decided the precise question, and the lower federal courts and state supreme courts which have considered it have, with one notable recent exception, held that there is no newsman's privilege as a matter of federal constitutional law. Nevertheless, their cases should be accorded little weight when the question is again presented as the reasoning behind their decisions is generally questionable and always unsatisfactory."

Dahlan, Muhammad A. *Anonymous Disclosure of Government Information As a Form of Political Communications*. Urbana, Ill., University of Illinois, 1967. 222p. (Ph.D. dissertation, University Microfilms, no. 68–1737) **1D2**
"This dissertation examines anonymous disclosure independent of the question of freedom of the press. The leak is viewed as a distinctive communication process by which the source of information may send a message to a particular target-receiver. This study describes the process, shows how it differs from related newsgathering practices (e.g. speculative reporting and unofficial 'leaks') and investigates its functions and operations."

Daily, Jay E. *The Anatomy of Censorship*. New York, Dekker, 1973. 403p. **1D3**
Following a decade of study of sex censorship, including watching scores of pornographic movies, wading through hundreds of pornographic books, and reading the vast amount of commentary on sex censorship, the author has produced this volume on sex censorship in the United States. Throughout the work he describes incidents of censorship and analyzes the factors which motivated the censor, governmental and private. He believes that sex-exploitation had about reached market-saturation in this country until it was given a restored vigor by the decision of the United States Supreme Court which turned over the matter of standards to local authorities. The author admits writing with a librarian's bias for intellectual freedom.

————. "Censorship, Contemporary and Controversial Aspects of." In Allen Kent and Harold Lancour, *eds.*, *Encyclopedia of Library and Information Science*. New York, Dekker, 1970, vol. 4, pp. 338–81. **1D4**
"The purpose of the present article is to examine the positions of both censors and anticensors, to ascertain whether some censorship is always necessary, to distinguish between selection and censorship as much as the scant illumination of this gray area will permit—and to examine the limits that have been reached in the publication of materials." The author concludes that it is up to the librarian more than any other member of the intellectual community "to form anticensorship groups and to counteract the propaganda of those who would limit the freedom of inquiry by making some subjects beyond the pale of honest research."

Dale, Francis L. "First and Sixth Amendments: Can They Co-exist?" *Tennessee Law Review*, 37:209–14, Fall 1969. **1D5**
The author believes that the two basic rights of fair trial and free press can exist together and have done so many years with only occasional overlap or conflict. The two amendments are supportive of each other.

D'Alemberte, Talbot. "Journalists Under the Axe: Protection of Confidential Sources of Information." *Harvard Journal on Legislation*, 6:307–45, March 1969. **1D6**
"It is the purpose of this article to consider the proper weight to be given to the public interests involved—the interests of society in the revelation of facts and in the maintenance of confidential news sources. The history and development of the journalist's privileged source of information will be traced from its early sources to the present and a statutory survey and analysis [by state] will be presented culminating with two proposed model statutes."

Dallas, A. R. C. *Correspondence of Lord Byron, with a Friend, Including His Letters to His Mother . . . also Recollections of the Poet by the Late R. C. Dallas, Esq. The Whole Forming An Original Memoir of Lord Byron's Life, from 1808 to 1814. And a Continuation and Preliminary Statement of the Proceedings by Which the Letters were Suppressed in England, at the Suit of Lord Byron's Executors*. Paris, A. and W. Galignani, 1825. 2 vols. (Preliminary statement of Mr. Dallas, vol. I, pp. i–cxvii). **1D7**
A lengthy account of the controversy over posthumous publication of Byron's letters to his mother. The late Rev. R. C. Dallas had been given the letters by Byron, with the understanding that they would be published, but the executors got an injunction against Dallas and his son, A. R. C. Dallas (*Hobhouse v. Dallas*) and Lord Eldon ruled for the plaintiff. The elder Dallas, in the meantime had died and the son arranged for publication in Paris. It was either a matter of running the risk of contempt of British courts or violation of a French contract which he had entered into prior to the lawsuit.

[Daly, Patrick T., *plaintiff*.] *P. T. Daly's Libel Action. A Report of the Legal Proceedings against "The Voice of Labour" and the Irish Transport and General Workers' Union*. Dublin, National Executive Council of the Irish Transport and General Workers' Union, 1925. 36p. **1D8**
The editor and printer of *The Voice of Labour* were brought to trial for alleged libels appearing in *The Voice* of 16 and 23 June 1923. The jury found that the statements published were true and awarded the verdict to the defendants.

Dance, Jim. "Meanwhile, Another Constitutional Crisis." *Bulletin of the American Society of Newspaper Editors*, 571:13–14, September 1973. **1D9**
Commentary on the case of *Tornillo v. The Miami Herald Publishing Co.* (1974), involving Florida's right of reply statute. The article was written before the case had been decided by the U.S. Supreme Court. Text of the law is included.

Daniel, Clifton. "Fair Trial and Freedom of the Press." *Case and Comment*, 71(5):3–4, 6, 8–9, September–October 1966. **1D10**
While recognizing the shortcomings and abuses of the press and applauding the efforts of the legal profession to discipline its members, the author itemizes the things the press will *not* do: It will not accept censorship or any legislative abridgment of a free press; it will not surrender the freedom to publish anything said or done in public provided it does not violate the laws of libel or offend existing standards of decency; it will not yield up the privilege of publishing anything said in open court or to criticize and expose the acts of public officials, including prosecutors and judge; and it will not accept any compulsory code.

———. "The Fairness of a Free Press." *Editor & Publisher*, 106(52):5, 27, 29 December 1973. **1D11**
Address by the associate editor of the *New York Times* at the New York Fair Trial–Free Press Conference, 2 November 1973, including comment on the role of the press in the Watergate and Agnew cases.

———. "Right of Access and Reply." In Michael C. Emery and Ted C. Smythe, *eds.*, *Readings in Mass Communications*. Dubuque, Iowa, Brown, 1972, pp. 23–29. (Reprinted from *Seminar Quarterly*, December 1969) **1D12**
Similar to the article appearing in the *Texas Law Review*, March 1970.

———. "Right of Access to Mass Media—Government Obligation to Enforce First Amendment?" *Texas Law Review*, 48:783–89, March 1970. (Reprinted in 1U100) **1D13**
"Mr. Daniel contends that any judicial or legislative regulation of access to the press would be unconstitutional. He admits that there is a problem, but his solution is intra-industry diversity or increased competition with the numerical growth of media voices." Based on Daniel's remarks in a panel discussion before the Section on Individual Rights and Responsibilities, 1969, American Bar Association convention.

——— *et al. Theater and Movies: Four Letter Rebellion.* 50 min. tape recording. n.p., Educational Research Group, 1970. (Publisher's title: Obscenity and Nudity). **1D14**
A panel discussion on the changing sexual morality as reflected in the permissiveness and explicitness of the theater and movies. Moderator Clifton Daniel; panelists Clive Barnes, Vincent Canby, Renata Adler, and Walter Kerr.

Daniel, Clifton, and John Pemberton. [Access to the Press: Response to Proposals by Jerome Barron.] 30 min. tape recording. Berkeley, Calif., Pacifica Tape Library, 1969. (Law and the Free Society, II) **1D15**
A panel discussion before the section on Individual Rights and Responsibilities, 1969, American Bar Association Convention. Mr. Daniel, associate editor of the *New York Times*, while recognizing the problem of access to the mass media, believes that the solution lies with the press itself rather than with government regulations, which would violate the First Amendment to the Constitution. Mr. Barron's proposals (presented in part I of the tape series) are impractical as well as unconstitutional. As it is, the *New York Times* is only able to publish about one-tenth of the news that comes to it each day, calling for discrimination on the part of editors. He proposes ways in which newspapers can do a better job of providing access, including the encouragement of greater media competition, to be preferred to government control of the existing press. He favors the principle of the right of reply, widely accepted by the press, but questions an absolute legal right. Mr. Pemberton, executive director of the American Civil Liberties Union, while agreeing with Professor Barron as to the large dimension of the problem of access and accepting his thesis that the press has the obligation to provide access, believes that great caution should be exercised in applying statutory and judicial remedies.

["The Daniel Schorr Case."] *Free Speech* (Commission on Freedom of Speech, Speech Communication Association), 38:2–6, May 1976. **1D16**
A collection of articles on the case of the Columbia Broadcasting System correspondent who leaked the CIA report to the press, including articles by Lawrence Stern, Martin Arnold, Congressman Michael Harrington, Tom Wicker, Richard D. Lyons, and Schorr's own speech to the Washington Press Club.

Danish, Roy, "Broadcast Freedom—Is It Still There?" In *Poor Richard's Almanac*. Philadelphia, Poor Richard Club, 1972. 6p. (Reprinted by Television Information Office, New York) **1D17**
In a speech before a combined meeting of the Poor Richard Club and Broadcast Pioneers, in Philadelphia, 9 November 1971, the director of the Television Information Office discusses the pressures being applied to the broadcasting industry which threaten to curtail the flow of news, information, and entertainment.

Danna, Sammy R. *The Press–Radio War*. Columbia, Mo., Freedom of Information Center, School of Journalism, University of Missouri at Columbia, 1968. 7p. (Report no. 213) **1D18**
A continuation of the press–radio war discussed in Center Report no. 211. An account of the so-called Press Radio Bureau through which newsmen forced the networks to limit their newscasting, and the breaking of this control when the news services offered their news for sale directly to the networks and stations.

———. *The Rise of Radio News*. Columbia, Mo., Freedom of Information Center, School of Journalism, University of Missouri at Columbia, 1968. 8p. (Report no. 211) **1D19**
An account of the early days of newscasting and the struggle between radio and newspapers, as radio encroached upon their domain.

———. *TV's Fight for Courtroom Access*. Columbia, Mo., Freedom of Information Center, University of Missouri at Columbia, 1968. 6p. (Report no. 200) **1D20**
The progress made from 1958 to 1965 in efforts to repeal or substantially modify Canon 35 of the American Bar Association barring photography from the courtroom was blocked by two U.S. Supreme Court decisions: The cases of Billie Sol Estes and Dr. Samuel Sheppard. The court ruled in the first instance that televising of the trial violated Estes' right of a fair trial; in the second, prejudicial publicity by print and electronic news media violated Sheppard's rights.

Darling, Richard L. "Censorship—an Old Story." *Elementary English*, 51:691–96, May 1974. **1D21**
"Censorship is peculiarly a new story as it relates to children's books," almost a twentieth-century phenomenon. Standards for juvenile literature began to be set in mid-nineteenth century with the Sunday School movement, and by the end of the century proper and improper books for children became a topic at conferences of librarians. Pressure groups in recent years, coupled with timid librarians, resulted in numerous censorship cases against textbooks, comic books, and, more recently, trade books written for children. But "there has never yet been a children's book declared illegal by a court of competent jurisdiction." The author reviews some of the recent attacks against children's books and reports on the strong stand of the American Library Association against such pressures.

———. *Intellectual Freedom and The Li-*

brarian. Ann Arbor, Mich., School of Library Science, University of Michigan, 1974. 24p. (The Fifth Annual Alumnus-in-Residence Program) (ED 93,202) **1D22**

A former chairman of the American Library Association's Intellectual Freedom Committee "emphasizes the librarian's important role in the guardianship of intellectual freedom. A brief overview of censorship attempts shows that suppression of a given work may be demanded for political or social motives, as well as for sexual content. Darling then outlines the growing militancy of librarians on this issue, dating from the American Library Association's 1939 statement of Libraries' Bill of Rights. Although library organizations are making a strong defense of intellectual freedom, Darling concludes that the real responsibility still rests with the individual librarian."

————. "School Libraries and Intellectual Freedom." In American Library Association's *Intellectual Freedom Manual*. Chicago, ALA, 1974, pt. 3, pp. 11–13. **1D23**

School libraries are particularly vulnerable to censorship attempts; consequently school librarians need to plan carefully to protect the integrity of their collections and the rights of their students. The author discusses the content of selection policy statements and procedures to follow in preparing them.

Darshini, Prem. "The Dilemma of Indian Film Censorship." *Vidura*, 6(3):6–11, August 1969. **1D24**

A critical review of the report of the Enquiry Committee on Film Censorship which considered the state of Indian cinema and the impact of the Indian Cinematograph (censorship) Rules.

Dart, Peter. "Breaking the Code: A Historical Footnote." *Cinema Journal*, 8:39–41, Fall 1968. **1D25**

Howard Hughes's use of the film, *Outlaw*, to break the Motion Picture Production Code.

Dart, W. J. "Film Censorship in New Zealand." *Landfall 93*, 24(1) 67–73, March 1970. **1D26**

A review of the work of New Zealand's chief film censor, describing the classification system and the banning and cutting of films. Unlike the open publication of the decisions of the Indecent Publications Tribunal, the business of film censorship is secretive, even furtive. The author calls for a complete revision of the censor's duties, with removal of the practice of cutting, and with much more careful grading and classification of films.

Dascha, Julius. "The White House Watch Over TV and The Press." *New York Times Magazine*, 121:9, 92, 20 August 1972. **1D27**

An account of the efforts of White House aid Patrick J. Buchanan to orchestrate the Nixon Administration's unprecedented attack on the press. Buchanan wrote Agnew's speeches criticizing the networks, suggested antitrust action to force the networks to produce the kind of news coverage and commentary wanted by the White House, and has marshaled Administration forces in opposition of public television.

David, Toby. "Censorship and Obscenity: An Outline for Beginners." *Author*, 79:129–34, Autumn 1968. **1D28**

Consideration of some of the facts of British censorship. Sometimes censorship starts with the printer who refuses to set the type on works dealing with sex, for fear of prosecution; next is censorship exercised by the distributive trade, e.g. W. H. Smith or by libraries; there may be random police raids, and Customs might confiscate a work from abroad. In radio and television, authors generally know the limitations and write to please; in cinema production, censorship is performed by the British Board of Film Censors, but local authorities are the ultimate censors of the finished product. It is unlikely that any attempts will be made to replace the Lord Chamberlain by another form of censorship of the theater.

Davidson, Stanley J. "New York Times Rule Extended to Statements Made About Matters of Public Concern." *Loyola University Law Review*, 1:343–58, Summer 1970. **1D29**

Comments on the case of *Farnsworth v. Tribune Co.* (1969), in which the Illinois Supreme Court ruled that all published statements concerning matters of public interest are constitutionally protected and do not depend on a public official or figure.

Davies, W. Rupert. *Speech of Senator W. Rupert Davies on Salacious and Indecent Literature Delivered in the Senate of Canada on May 5, 1953*. Ottawa, Queen's Printer, 1953. 12p. (Senate of Canada, Official Report of Debates) **1D30**

Davies, William B. "Use of the Mails: A Privilege or a Right?" *Boston University Law Review*, 50:285–96, Spring 1970. **1D31**

Re: *Hiett v. United States*, in which the U.S. Court of Appeals of the Fifth District held unconstitutional Section 1714, Chapter 18 of the U.S. Code. The section prohibited certain information on obtaining divorces from being conveyed in the mails. "The primary purpose of this comment is to consider the consequences flowing from the court's construction of the postal power and the limitations placed upon that power by the first amendment."

Davila, Andrés. *Libel Law and The Press*. Zurich, International Press Institute, 1971. 143p. **1D32**

A comparative study of the libel laws of eight countries: Argentina, Denmark, England, France, Germany, Japan, the Philippines, and the United States. Topics include: definition of libel and slander, the distinction between who may be defamed and who may bring a libel prosecution, the distinction between the author of the defamatory articles and the defendant in a libel case, what is an action for libel, the juristiction, the burden of proof, defenses available, the public interest, sanctions, and other remedies for libel.

Davis, A. G. "Parliamentary Broadcasting and the Law of Defamation." *University of Toronto Law Journal*, 7:385–94, 1948. **1D33**

Radio communication and particularly the broadcasting of parliamentary debates raise the question whether the rule laid down in 1689 "that the freedom of speech and debates or proceedings in Parliament ought not to be impeached or questioned in any court or place out of Parliament," applies as absolutely today as it has done in the last two and half centuries.

Davis, Chee. "Firestone Case: A Judicial Exercise in Press Censorship." *Emory Law Journal*, 25:705–36, Summer 1976. **1D34**

Re: *Time, Inc. v. Firestone*, 424 U.S. 448 (1976).

Davis, James E. "Recent Censorship Fires: Flareups or Holocaust?" *Journal of Research and Development in Education*, 9(3):22–32, Spring 1976. **1D35**

A summary of what is happening nationwide in censorship, taken from the 1975 issue of *Arizona English Bulletin*.

Davis, Keith E., and George N. Braucht. "Exposure to Pornography, Character, and Sexual Deviance: A Retrospective Survey." *Technical Report of the [U.S.] Commission on Obscenity and Pornography*, 7:173–243, 1971. (Also reported in *Journal of Social Issues*, vol. 29, no. 3, 1973) **1D36**

"The aim of this study is to evaluate critically hypotheses about the impact of exposure to pornography and erotically realistic materials upon moral character and deviant sexual behavior. The impetus of research comes partly from public concern about the consequences of exposure to pornography and partly from general theoretical ideas about character development. A guiding feature of our approach has been to formulate the psychological bases of public concern in the most cogent and testable manner possible." The study found that the "amount of exposure to pornography was positively related to self–acknowledged sexual 'deviance' at all ages of first exposure. . . . The pattern of obtained results leaves open the possibility that early exposure to pornography plays some causal role in the development of sexually deviant life styles or the possibility that exposure is merely part of or a product of adopting a sexually deviant life style."

———. "Reactions to Viewing Films of Erotically Realistic Heterosexual Behavior," *Technical Report of the ₁U.S.₁ Commission on Obscenity and Pornography*, 8:68–96, 1971.   **1D37**
"The impact of viewing films of erotically realistic heterosexual behavior on sexual arousal, physiological arousal, sexual behavior, sexual thoughts or discussions, emotional tension, judgments about availability of such films, and beliefs about the effects of pornography on oneself were evaluated using a pretest, post-test, no control group design."

Davis, Kenneth C. "The Information Act: A Preliminary Analysis." *University of Chicago Law Review*, 34:761–816, Summer 1967. (Also in U.S. Senate. Committee on the Judiciary. *Freedom of Information Act Source Book*, pp. 240–95)
                                                  1D38
The author analyzes the Act, looking into the legislative history to learn the intent of Congress. He finds the Act ambiguous and unworkable and that it "must be in large measure superseded by official and judicial understanding based on considerations beyond the Act."

——— *et al*. "Public Information Act and Interpretive and Advisory Rulings." *Administrative Law Review*, 20:1–54, December 1967.   **1D39**
A panel discussion at a conference of the Section of Administrative Law, American Bar Association.

Davis, Maxon R. "Publication of Libel in Montana: Lewis v. Reader's Digest Association." *Montana Law Review*, 36:120–28, Winter 1975.   **1D40**
A critique of the Montana Supreme Court decision in *Lewis v. Reader's Digest Association, Inc.*, in which it adopted the multiple publication rule. Under this rule every sale of a periodical is a separate basis for a cause of action and the publisher of a libelous statement risks potential liability in as many separate causes of action as he has readers. The author believes the court should reconsider its action and that the legislature should adopt a uniform single publication act.

Davis, Rex D. "False Advertising: The Expanding Presence of the FTC." *Baylor Law Review*, 25:650–59, Fall 1973.   **1D41**
"It is the purpose of this article to inform the

reader of the scope of the regulatory power of the FTC, to explore and analyze two remedial areas, and to ponder the possible influence on advertising that the Commission will have in the future."

Davis, Robert G. "An Impossible Innocence." *New Leader*, 50(25):15–16, 18 December 1967.   **1D42**
The British trial of Hubert Selby's *Last Exit to Brooklyn* was remarkable because it ended in a verdict of guilty and witnesses were found who stood up in court and said they had been depraved by the book. The author believes the jurors were not trying to save the young; "they were trying to save themselves in a doomed rearguard action. In a way—and thus to the paradox—they were responding to the moral intensity of *Last Exit to Brooklyn*."

Davis, Thomas L. "Defects in Indiana's Pornographic Nuisance Act." *Indiana Law Journal*, 49:320–33, Winter 1974.   **1D43**
Applying obscenity standards formulated by the U.S. Supreme Court in *Miller v. California* (1957), the Indiana Supreme Court recently held two state obscenity statutes unconstitutional. "Indiana's Pornographic Nuisance Act, now the state's sole obscenity statute, is also likely to fail."

Daws, S. O. "The Signal Has Been Denied Admission to 2nd Class Mail Rate and Effort is Made to Muzzle It." *Indiahoma Union Signal* (Shawnee, Oklahoma Territory). Special four-page supplement, 13 February 1906.
                                                  1D44
This "protest supplement" deals with the rejection of the paper by the Post Office Department on the grounds that it was the organ of a union and did not disseminate "information of a public character." The supplement carries an open letter to President Theodore Roosevelt protesting the decision of Third Assistant Postmaster General Edwin C. Madden.

Day, A. E. "More About Arnold Bennett's Attitude Regarding Censorship in Libraries." *Library World*, 68:337–38, June 1967.   **1D45**
A review of Arnold Bennett's criticism of censorship of the circulating libraries and the public libraries. His criticism was not directed at the foolish woman who, being shocked at her daughter's reading, took the matter to a cabinet minister, or against the cabinet minister who gave serious attention to the foolish woman, but rather against the publisher and authors who failed to stand up for their work. On the request to ban *The Harlot's Progress*, he observed that you could see harlots walking up and down the Strand, buy them on postcards, entertain them in fashionable restaurants, but couldn't read about them in a circulating library.

Day, Anthony. "Why Justice Black

Was Right: An Absolutist's View of the First Amendment." *Congressional Record*, 121:S13581–82, 24 July 1975. (Reprinted in *Free Speech*, Commission on Freedom of Speech, Speech Communication Association, November 1975)   **1D46**
In a commencement address delivered to graduates of the School of Journalism, University of California, Berkeley, a member of the staff of the *Los Angeles Times* argues that the First Amendment is preeminent among the rights guaranteed by the Bill of Rights. He believes that "just as an absolute interpretation of the First Amendment is the only sure defense for the press against the courts, so an absolute interpretation of the First Amendment in cases like the Pentagon Papers is the only sure defense for the press against the government." He attacks Senate Bill One, revision of the criminal code "that attempts to describe what may and may not be published," and he calls for an absolute shield law to protect journalists until the courts may some day affirm this right.

Day-Lewis, Sean. "Quarter." *Drama*, 89:37–40, Summer 1968.   **1D47**
The author discusses the Lord Chamberlain's action against plays of Edward Bond, *Saved* and *Early Morning*, and recommends the formation of a Defence of Literature and Arts society.

Deakin, James. *Lyndon Johnson's Credibility Gap*. Washington, D.C., Public Affairs Press, 1968. 65p.   **1D48**
Lyndon Johnson is a tragedy for the American people because "they have been led by a man who has diminished the institution of the presidency by his inability to be wholly candid with the electorate on the major issues confronting the nation." The author, Washington correspondent for the *St. Louis Post-Dispatch*, chronicles the history of the credibility gap in the Johnson Administration, beginning with Mr. Johnson's 1964 campaign as a Vietnam dove at a time when he had already set in motion the hawkish policies that were to dominate his administration.

Deal, Elizabeth M. "Responsible Freedom for the Secondary School Press: A Cooperative Effort." *English Journal*, 60:960–62, October 1971.   **1D49**
How greater freedom for high school journalists in Savannah, Ga., improved the school paper and discouraged shoddy underground journalism. There follows an Approved Code of Ethics for Secondary School Newspapers.

Dean, Barry. "Censorship in South Africa: (2) Censorship and the Law." *Philosophical Papers*, 5(1):34–52, May 1976.   **1D50**
"The comprehensive system of censorship which operates in South Africa today is a tribute to the belief, apparently held by our rulers, that the free circulation of ideas and knowledge

poses a serious threat to social stability in this country and that the dissemination of ideas and knowledge can be controlled effectively by governmental action. It reflects a view of South African society as basically unstable and of the average South African as incapable of making decisions in his own interests." Changes that take place in South Africa "must take place under the direction and control of the government." The author describes the legal basis for censorship in the areas of public morality and respect for religious beliefs, political ideas, and information about government and its activities. Appended is the text of a policy statement of the Publications Appeal Board, prepared by Professor J. C. W. van Rooyen, a member of the Board, and reprinted from the January 1976 issue of *De Rebus Procuratoriis*.

Dean, W. H. B. "Judging the Obscene: A Critical Analysis of the Criteria Used for Determining What are Undesirable Sexually Explicit Materials in South Africa." *Acta Juridica* (South Africa), 1972:61–150, 1972.   **1D51**

Dearlove, John. "The BBC and the Politicians." *Index on Censorship*, 3:23–33, Spring 1974.   **1D52**
"In my critique I am not seeking to defend rather poor programmes, and neither and I advocating some sort of anarchy within the BBC where young producers would do what they liked with a monopoly at public expense. Rather I wish simply to challenge an emerging orthodoxy which suggests that the BBC is unfair and overharsh in its treatment of established party politicians and should, therefore, be subject to more control." The discussion is prompted by an incident over a BBC broadcast, A Question of Confidence.

DeArmond, Anna J. *Andrew Bradford, Colonial Journalist*. Newark, Del., University of Delaware Press, 1949. 272p. (Based on a Ph.D. dissertation, University of Pennsylvania)   **1D53**
This account of the publishing career of the colonial editor of the *Philadelphia Mercury* contains frequent references to his conflict with the provisional government, his imprisonment, and his stubborn courage in resisting government control of the press.

Dearn, Ed. *Pornography Degrades*. Sydney, Australia, Renda Publication [1974?]. 82p.   **1D54**
An examination of the problem of pornography in the United States, Great Britain, Australia, and New Zealand, and, recognizing the danger to society, how the traffic can be controlled without violating due process or freedom of expression.

"Death of an Industry?" *Nation's Business*, 60:24–29, May 1972.   **1D55**
"Commercial broadcasting is the victim of foul blows struck under the guise of fairness, and it

faces an even greater threat—'counter-advertising.' "

"Death of Retraction Statutes." *University of Pittsburg Law Review*, 36:756–66, Spring 1975.   **1D56**
"The purpose of this Note is to demonstrate how *Gertz's* [*Gertz v. Robert Welch, Inc.*, 1974] limitations on punitive damages has a disabling effect upon the operation of the retraction statutes. Additionally, the Note demonstrates the similarity between retraction statutes and Florida's unconstitutional right to reply statute, such that the language of the Court in *Miami Herald* [*Miami Herald Publishing Co. v. Tornillo*, 1974] in effect invalidates retraction statutes."

Deay, Dwight O. *Libel Law, 1970–1973: The New York Times Rule and Stories of Public Interest*. Lawrence, Kans., University of Kansas, 1974. 113p. (Unpublished Master's thesis)   **1D57**
"The thesis concludes that newspapers publishing deliberate falsehoods can recklessly disregard the truth in at least seven ways and that, except for gossip mongering and invasion of a person's sex life, a reporter's right to report news of public interest is almost unlimited."

Debes, Cheryl. "The Impertinence of Being Earnest: Field on Libel." *Chicago Journalism Review*, 7(7/8):8–11, July–August 1974.   **1D58**
An account of a speech by Marshall Field, publisher of the *Chicago Sun-Times* and the *Chicago Daily News*, made before the Off The Street Club, in which he advocated a change in the libel laws to allow any person, especially public figures, to be able to sue for libel "even if there is no malice." Field further suggested that reporters as well as publishers suffer financial loss for libelous reporting. The author records the strong response, pro and con, to Field's remarks.

de Camp, L. Sprague. "The End of the Monkey War." *Scientific American*, 220:15–21, February 1969.   **1D59**
"The Fundamentalist crusade against the theory of evolution subsided soon after the Scopes Trial of 1925, but it was only three months ago that the last antievolution law of any consequence was killed." An illustrated account of the Scopes case and the aftermath.

———. *The Great Monkey Trial*. New York, Doubleday, 1968. 538p.   **1D60**
A dramatic retelling of the famous Scopes evolution trial of 1925, at Dayton, Tenn., in which a school teacher (John T. Scopes), an idea (the theory of evolution), and a high school textbook (*Civic Biology* by George W. Hunter) were on trial. The story is based on newspaper accounts, books and articles, archives, correspondence, and interviews. It is illustrated with contemporary newspaper cartoons.

"Deceptive Advertising." *Harvard Law Review*, 80:1005–1163, 1967.   **1D61**
Content: Advertising—A Theoretical Introduction, The Interests at Stake. History of Legal Controls. The Application of the First Amendment to Commercial Advertising. The Federal Trade Commission. Substantive Standards. The Federal Trade Commission. Modes of Administration. The Food and Drug Administration. The FDA and the FTC: Jurisdiction. State Regulation. Regulation by Local Governments. Private Regulation.

Decker, Jack W. "Commercial Speech and the First Amendment: Virginia State Board of Pharmacy v. Virginia Citizens Consumer Council." *Capital University Law Review*, 6:75–93, 1976.   **1D62**
Re: *Virginia State Board of Pharmacy v. Virginia Citizens Consumer Council*, 423 U.S. 815 (1976), in which the U.S. Supreme Court overturned a Virginia statute which prohibited advertising of prices of prescription drugs by pharmacists.

Decker, Raymond G. "Justice Hugo L. Black: The Balancer of Absolutes." *California Law Review*, 59:1335–55, November 1971.   **1D63**
This general appraisal of the contribution of Supreme Court Justice Black includes comments on his views of the First Amendment. "Although the majority of the Court never fully accepted his absolutist view of the First Amendment, his influence is certainly present in the Court's current position regarding libel, slander, and obscenity."

"Defamation Law in the Wake of Gertz v. Robert Welch, Inc.: The Impact on State Law and The First Amendment." *Northwestern University Law Review*, 69:960–82, February 1975.   **1D64**
"In *Gertz* [*Gertz v. Robert Welch, Inc.*, 1974], the U.S. Supreme Court for the first time since *New York Times* put a limit on the scope of first amendment protection in the defamation area. At the same time, it required a total restructuring of state libel laws in regard to the fundamental questions of liability and damages. This comment will examine the decision and evaluate its impact on state defamation laws and on the scope of first amendment protections."

"Defamation Since the New York Times Case—Editorial Comment and Annotations." *Defense Law Journal*, 18:703–14, 1969.   **1D65**
Topics discussed: "Actual malice" requirements, "public figures," "public officials," "reckless disregard," right of privacy, and U.S. Supreme Court cases.

Defouloy, Elizabeth A. "Obligation of Reporters, as Citizens, to Respond to a Grand Jury Subpoena and Answer Questions Relevant to a Criminal Investigation." *Journal of Urban Law*, 50:306–17, November 1972. **1D66**
Re: *Branzburg v. Hayes*, 408 U.S. 665 (1972).

De Grazia, Edward, *comp. Censorship Landmarks*. New York, Bowker, 1969. 657p. **1D67**
A compilation of texts of 144 precedent-setting court decisions and important minority decisions in the area of censorship in the United States. Beginning with the early British obscenity case, *King v. Sidley* (1663), the cases are arranged in chronological order concluding with *United States v. A Motion Picture Film Entitled "I Am Curious—Yellow"* (1968), a case in which the compiler argued successfully for the defense. A lengthy introduction reviews the evolution of legal decisions on censorship, placing the various cases in their proper historical and judicial perspective in what the author considers "the movement toward freedom of expression taking place in the United States."

De Hart, Florence E. "Subscription Libraries and Intellectual Freedom: A Case Study." *Newsletter on Intellectual Freedom* (IFC–ALA), 20:46, 49, March 1971. **1D68**
The author contrasts censorship practiced in past years by the New York Society Library (founded in 1754) and the lack of it by that library today.

———, and Roger N. Jaeger. "Wisconsin Librarians and Intellectual Freedom." *Wisconsin Library Bulletin*, 65:389–91, September–October 1969. **1D69**
Text of a resolution on intellectual freedom adopted by the Association of Beloit Librarians joined with the Association of Jonesville Librarians.

Dehler, David. "The Right of Information." *Revue de l'Université d'Ottawa*, 44:467–74, October–December 1974. **1D70**
"This article examines the 'right to information' in the context of human rights and the exercise of these rights in human society and in the Church."

Deitchler, M. Douglas, and Howard F. Hahn. "Legal Aspects of the Fair Trial–Free Press Controversy: The Reardon Report Considered." *Nebraska Law Review*, 48:1045–88, 1969. **1D71**
"This comment presents a critical analysis of the recommendations of the [American Bar Association's] Reardon Report. An attempt will be made to evaluate the recommendations with particular emphasis on whether they have struck a fair and constitutional balance between the constitutional guarantees of fair trial and free speech."

Delaney, Oliver J. "Libraries and 'Obscenity': Are First Amendment Rights in Jeopardy?" *Oklahoma Librarian*, 26(2):10–12, April 1976. **1D72**
The author expresses the concern of libraries over the application of the *Miller v. California* (1973) decision of the U.S. Supreme Court. Thirty-eight states have passed new laws dealing with obscenity since the *Miller* decision. He considers specifically a bill before the last session of the Oklahoma legislature which did not come up for a vote but which should be watched in the next session.

de Laurot, Edouard L. "The Price of Fear." *Film Culture*, 1(3):3–6, 23, May–June 1955. **1D73**
"The shots deleted from 'Wager of Fear' form an animated fresco of the many prejudices or taboos that still haunt our cinema." The author tabulates the deletions made for the American audience from this winner of the 1953 Grand Prix at the Cannes Festival.

de Leon, Dennis L., and Robert L. Naon. "The Regulation of Television Violence." *Stanford Law Review*, 26:1291–1325, June 1974. **1D74**
Congress, the viewing public, and the Federal Communications Commission are concerned with findings from experimental and correlational survey research that show that televised violence can instigate viewers to acts of specific physical aggression and can teach viewers a general aggressive strategy. "Part I of this Note summarizes and examines the studies that support the above conclusion. . . . Part II attempts to determine the elements that increase likelihood that television violence will lead to increased viewer aggression. Part II then uses this evidence to design a specific policy for eliminating the adverse effect of television violence while preserving the role such violence plays in encouraging discussion of public issues and in dramatic expression. Part III examines the most effective means of enacting the proposed restrictions on television violence. . . . Part III argues that new congressional legislation is necessary."

Dell, Floyd. "The Puritanism of Erotic Literature." *The Wide Way*, 1(3):30–34, February 1908. **1D75**
The novelist accuses such contemporaries as D'Annunzio, Swinburne, and Viereck as laboring under the same obsession as Anthony Comstock—that sex is indecent. While Comstock expresses his unwholesome views of sex by suppression, the neopagans manifest their unwholesome views of sex by expression. There is real need for decent erotic literature, following in the steps of Walt Whitman. Sex in literature should be treated with dignity, humor, and frankness.

Delmer, Sefton. "H.M.G.'s Secret Pornographer (The Abuses of Literacy—2)." *Times Literary Supplement*, 3,647:63–64, 21 January 1972. **1D76**
The use of radio pornography by the British as part of the psychological warfare against the Nazis in World War II, told by the director of the program.

Dembitz, Nanette. "Congressional Investigation of Newspapermen, Authors, and Others in the Opinion Field—Its Legality Under the First Amendment." *Minnesota Law Review*, 40:517–60, April 1956. **1D77**
"After discussing the impact on first amendment rights of congressional investigation of alleged Communists in the opinion field, consideration will be accorded to the circumstances in which such an investigation would nevertheless be constitutionally justified. In this connection, we shall give due regard to the fact that pro-Communists in opinion work may deliberately try to mislead public opinion on political questions. On the constitutional question, we shall also consider the case pending before the United States Supreme Court involving the order of the Subversive Activities Control Board requiring the Communist Party to register with the Attorney General as a Communist-action organization. . . . We shall also consider the contempt of Congress indictment now pending against author Harvey O'Connor, which offers the most imminent possibility of upper court consideration of the first amendment in connection with investigations in the opinion field, and we shall thereafter give attention to the 'informing' function of Congress, on which the investigations have been partly predicated."

Demeter, Thomas P. "Legal Perils of Parody and Burlesque." *Cleveland–Marshall Law Review*, 17:242–50, May 1968. **1D78**
"The doctrine of fair use must be expanded to allow the parodist substantial freedom to use the elements of the original work necessary to conjure up the object of the satire. While the property right of the author as composer must be protected, the courts should recognize that parody and burlesque are valid art forms, and as such are also deserving of protection."

Dempsey, David. "Social Comment and TV Censorship." *Saturday Review*, 52:53–55, 12 July 1969. **1D79**
Commentary of network censorship, particularly the efforts to restrict comment on social issues within an entertainment format, during prime time to an audience of middle-aged and middle class that has "locked out the young, the minorities, and the discontented." While dissent is portrayed on television newscasts as the dissenters create news, "prime time goes on

being good, censored, and largely irrelevant. It reflects not so much society as the image of society that TV has been instrumental in creating."

Dempster, Eleanor L. "The Librarian's Attitude Toward and Adherence to Principles of Intellectual Freedom." *Catholic Library World*, 46:112–15, October 1974.   **1D80**
"Freedom of access to information, by definition, denies censorship of any sort. The responsibility of librarians to provide opportunity for their patrons to exercise their freedoms is given a great deal of verbal applause, but how much real attention is intellectual freedom given in daily activities, particularly in material selection?"

Denby, David. "Dirty Movies—Hard-Core and Soft." *Atlantic*, 226:99–102, August 1970.   **1D81**
A description of pornographic movies as seen in San Francisco porn houses—why they are produced (money), what they are like (mostly joyless and ugly), who goes there (those who want to be sexually aroused), and their future (pornography is on the verge of becoming a permanent part of mass culture).

Dening, G. M. "Censorship: 2) Thoughts on a Randy Censor." *Meanjin Quarterly*, 28:503–7, Summer 1969.
1D82
An essay on the absurdities of public censorship in the realm of morals, with special reference to the Australian scene. The title is taken from a remark of a British censor that the criterion for prosecution of a book was how randy it made him feel. "The function of censorship," the author suggests, "is to provide a control system that relieves the individual and society of the necessity of moral judgment and provides an unequivocal model of idealized social behavior."

Denison, George. "Put Mail-Order Smut Merchants Out of Business!" *Reader's Digest*, 96(5):209–10, 214, 216, May 1970.   **1D83**
"An inside look at obscenity-by-mail and what can be done to break it up." The author recommends that the reader forward obscene ads to the Postmaster General, write his congressman, and urge the president to support the Dirksen bill (S 1077) on postal obscenity.

———. "Smut: The Mafia's Newest Racket; With an Editorial Comment." *Reader's Digest*, 99(12):157–60, December 1971.   **1D84**
"Three years ago mob leaders discovered pornography—and the astronomical profits to be made from it. Today, from coast to coast, they dominate what has become a multimillion–dollar business."

———. "Sultan of Smut." *Reader's Digest*, 107(11):105–9, November 1975.
1D85
"The life and times of Mike Thevis, operator of America's largest pornographic network."

Denning, Alfred T., *Baron Denning of Whitchurch*. "The Law of Libel with some Reference to Changing Judicial Attitudes." *Journalism Today*, 1(4):60–70, Spring 1969.   **1D86**
Lord Denning discovers the "delicate balance" between freedom of the press and abuse in the area of contempt of court, libel, right of privacy, and disclosure of sources. The press should be free to criticize the courts provided improper motives are not imputed. Wrongdoing can be criticized as long as the facts are right and the comment is not distorted by malice. The courts do not generally compel the press to disclose sources, but they may do so if national security or justice is at stake.

Dennis, Everette E. "Leaked Information as Property: Vulnerability of the Press to Criminal Prosecution." *Saint Louis University Law Journal*, 20:610–24, 1976.   **1D87**
"This article will briefly examine the vulnerability of the press to prosecution under both federal and state property crime statutes for publication of leaked information . . . . The discussion of subsequent punishment in the states will deal largely with a recent case in California involving the prosecution of a newspaper editor and reporter for receipt of stolen property" (*People v. Kunkin*, 1973).

———. "The Press and the Public Interest: A Definitional Dilemma." *De Paul Law Review*, 23:937–60, Spring 1974.   **1D88**
"Professor Dennis discusses the interests of the press and the public in terms of the content and manner of dissemination of mass information. Through analysis of opinions of noted political scientists, economists, and jurists, he defines the content of these widely divergent interests. Finally, he suggests an operational model for reconciling the rights and expectations of both."

———. "Purloined Information as Property: A New First Amendment Challenge." *Journalism Quarterly*, 50:456–62, 474, Autumn 1973.   **1D89**
"By defining information as property, courts on several widely-publicized cases since the mid-1960's have created a conflict with the rights of the press under the First Amendment. Each case involved purloined papers, and together they represent a new judicial concern with the way in which information is acquired . . . . It was the Pentagon Papers controversy of 1971 that brought the manner and method of information acquisition involving government property into sharp focus." Litigation has employed federal criminal statutes (*New York Times Co. v. United States* and four other cases, 1971); the common law of trover

and conversion (*Pearson v. Dodd*, 1969); and the California state criminal statutes for receiving stolen goods (*Kunkin v. People*, 1972).

Dennison, Lyle. "Free Press–Fair Trial in the Wake of Watergate." *Quill*, 63(2):22–23, February 1975.   **1D90**
An apparently classic case of conflict of press rights and rights of criminal defendants isn't expected to set any legal precedents in the area of prejudicial pretrial publicity.

Denniston, John B. *et al. Libel and Slander*. 29 min. tape recording. North Hollywood, Calif., Center for Cassette Studies, 1969.   **1D91**
A panel discussion of the limits imposed by the U.S. Supreme Court on the written and spoken word in the area of libel and slander. Moderator, John B. Denniston; panelists Jerome Barron and David Redman.

Denton, David E. "How Free Should School Press Be? Existentialist Asks." *Communication: Journalism Education Today*, 5:1–3, Summer 1972.   **1D92**
The author believes the high school press should be "absolutely free—to be the dialectician of dialogue within its particular world."

Derfer, George E. "A Philosopher on Censorship: An Inquiry Into Its Context and Criterion." *Arizona English Bulletin*, 8:70–74, May 1966.   **1D93**
"The discussion will be structured in terms of the following argument: 'Censorship, properly understood, is an inevitable facet of intellection, and it functions most constructively when it is informed by an explicit ethical concern and aesthetic awareness.'" The article "seeks only to stimulate thought: its goal is reflection, not resolution."

Derrick, Tyree C., Jr. "Obscenity in the Mails: Post Office Department Procedures and the First Amendment." *Northwestern University Law Review*, 58:664–84, November–December 1963.   **1D94**
Criticism of Post Office Department procedures in withdrawal from the mails materials that are considered obscene. Decisions are made by General Counsel without seeing the item as a whole and the flow of mail is held up an unreasonable length of time. The author recommends that judicial rather than administrative hearings be conducted and that expert witnesses be called upon to testify.

Deslonde, James. "Little Black Sambo vs. The Panther News: Apparent Dilemmas in Censorship." In Phil L. Nacke, *ed.*, *Diversity in Mature Reading*:

Theory and Research. Boone, N.C., National Reading Conference, 1973, pp. 219–23. (22d Yearbook, vol. 1) **1D95**
The author finds that "conflict and dilemmas on censorship can easily arise as revolutionaries, conservatives, and reactionaries attempt to use censorship as a means to achieve their ends. It would follow that this conflict is greatest in the school serving the most diverse mixture of groups." He also finds that the "various segments of society generally judge and/or censor literature to suit their own taste or to serve as a means of obtaining certain ends for their group." As an alternative to censorship he suggests the use of children's books labeled according to one of three categories or levels: level 1, literature which recognizes basic values in a pluralistic society; level 2, literature giving facts and unbiased information but which fails to recognize pluralistic values; and level 3, books blatantly stereotyped or biased (such as *Little Black Sambo*) which can be used in critical analysis.

Detmuld, Michael. "Censorship and Pornography," *Australian Humanist*, 8:5–12, Summer 1968. **1D96**

Detwiler, Richard M. "Managing the News for Freedom of the Press." *Public Relations Journal*, 30(2):6–8, February 1974. **1D97**
The author calls for the news media to improve their public relations with some intelligent news management, less self-flagellation and with public education on the nature and value of a free press.

———. "The Tragic Fallacy: The Press and Public Relations Under Seige." *Public Relations Journal*, 28(7):6–12, July 1972. **1D98**
The article expresses concern over the widening breach between a "discredited press" and business management and the need to rebuild confidence in a free press. The author deflates the myth that the press is antibusiness and antiestablishment and is in league with radicals and activists. It is government that is the more serious threat to a free press.

Devane, Richard S. "Indecent Literature: Some Legal Remedies." *Irish Ecclesiastical Record*, 25:182–204, February 1925. **1D99**
Father Devane calls for more strict laws to enforce Irish ideals and Catholic standards of sexual morality in literature and for the formation of vigilance committees to help in the enforcement of these laws. Specifically, the law should establish a more strict, less permissive, legal definition of obscenity than the British "Hicklin" rule; declare as obscene and illegal any literature on birth control, and make a mandatory jail sentence for violators. The law should establish a black list of indecent books and magazines, and forbid advertisements of drugs, appliances designed to prevent conception or procure abortion.

De Vault, John A., III, and Allan T. Geiger. "The Expanding Right to Criticize: A Post-*Times* Analysis." *University of Florida Law Review*, 19:700–729, Spring 1967. **1D100**
"This note will explore the holdings of the Supreme Court beginning with *Times* [*New York Times Co. v. Sullivan*, 1964] and subsequent cases, and then survey the impact of these decisions on the lower federal and state courts. An elaboration of the standards that these lower courts have developed will be undertaken as to who and what is a 'public official,' and the difficulties encountered with damages and 'actual malice' within the constitutional standards promulgated by the Court. Finally, a workable and fair set of standards will be suggested and applied to two cases awaiting decision by the Court [*Curtis Publishing Co. v. Butts*, 1967, and *Associated Press v. Walker*, 1967]."

"Developments in the Law of Defamation." *Harvard Law Review*, 69:876–960, March 1956. **1D101**
Content: The interest protected, actionable injuries to reputation, who may bring a defamation action, the standard of conduct and state of mind requisite to liability for defamation, privileges and other defenses, remedies (civil action for damages, retraction, right of reply, injunction, criminal libel), and problems of multiple defamation actions.

"Developments Under the Freedom of Information Act—1972." *Duke Law Journal*, 1973:178–206, April 1973. **1D102**
"Congressional hearings conducted in 1972 represent the first detailed review of agency performance under the Freedom of Information Act. As a result of these hearings, the House Committee on Government Operations concluded that many agencies either had failed to comply or had delayed in complying with the provisions of the Act. This recalcitrant attitude on the part of the federal agencies is reflected in the large volume of FOIA litigation in 1971."

Devirieux, Claude J. *Manifeste pour la Liberté de l'Information*. Montreal, Editions du Jour [1971]. 223p. **1D103**
Content: The Law of Information. The Freedom of Information. Journalists and the Public. Appendix: "Le Dossier 'Z' " (statement on the Intervention of the Administration of the Police and the Ministry of Justice in the Work of Journalists, prepared for the Professional Federation of Journalists of Quebec). The Pentagon Papers Case. Text of Canadian Laws Relating to the Press.

Devitt, Edward J. "An Appeal for Cooperation on the Fair Trial–Free Press Issue." *Oklahoma Law Review*, 22:155–62, May 1969. (Reprinted in David G. Clark and Earl R. Hutchison, eds., *Mass Media and the Law*, pp. 146–53) **1D104**
An address by the chief judge, U.S. District Court, District of Minnesota, and chairman of the Fair Trial–Free Press Advisory Committee of the American Bar Association, given before the Eastern Regional Conference of the Radio–Television News Directors Association, New York, 29 June 1968.

Devol, Kenneth S. "The Ginzburg Decision: Reactions in California." *Journalism Quarterly*, 45:271–78, Summer 1968. **1D105**
"Undertaken one year after the *Ginzburg* [*Ginzburg v. United States*] and *Mishkin* [*Mishkin v. State of New York*] decisions of 1966, this study found evidence to support those who predicted increasing legal activity aimed at obscene publication in following the Supreme Court action."

———, ed. *Mass Media and the Supreme Court: The Legacy of the Warren Years*. Edited with Commentaries and Special Notes. New York, Hastings House, 1971. 309p. 2d ed., 1976. 400p. (Studies in Public Communication) **1D106**
A book of readings, including text of cases and commentary under the following headings: The Role of the Supreme Court (*Schenck v. U.S.*, *Dennis v. U.S.*); Prior Restraint (*Near v. Minnesota*, *Grosjean v. American Press*, *Lovell v. Griffin*, *Mills v. Alabama*, *New York Times v. U.S.*); Prior Censorship (*Hannegan v. Esquire*, *Manual Enterprises v. Day*, *Lamont v. Postmaster General*, *Rowan v. Post Office*, *Blount v. Mail Box*); Control of Broadcasting (*NBC v. U.S.*, *FCC v. ABC*, *FTC v. Colgate Palmolive Co.*, *U.S. v. Southwestern Cable Co.*, *Fortnightly Corp. v. United Artists*, *Red Lion Broadcasting Co. v. FCC*); Obscenity Defined (*Butler v. Michigan*, *Kingsley Books v. Brown*, *Roth v. U.S.*); Obscenity Refined (*Smith v. California*, *Marcus v. Search Warrant*, *Bantam Books v. Sullivan*, *Memoirs v. Massachusetts*, *Ginzburg v. U.S.*, *Mishkin v. N.Y.*, *Ginsberg v. N.Y.*, *Stanley v. Georgia*, *U.S. v. Thirty-seven Photographs*, *U.S. v. Reidel*); Motion Picture Censorship (*Burstyn v. Wilson*, *Kingsley Pictures v. Regents*, *Times Film Corp. v. Chicago*, *Jacobellis v. Ohio*, *Freedman v. Maryland*, *Interstate Circuit, Inc. v. Dallas*); Libel (*New York Times v. Sullivan*, *Garrison v. Louisiana*, *Rosenblatt v. Baer*, *Curtis Publishing Co. v. Butts*, *St. Amant v. Thompson*, *Greenbelt Publishing Assn. v. Bresler*, *Monitor Patriot Co. v. Roy*, *Time, Inc. v. Pape*, *Rosenbloom v. Metromedia*); Right of Privacy (*Time, Inc. v. Hill*); Trial by Newspaper (*Bridges v. California*, *Irvin v. Dowd*, *Sheppard v. Maxwell*); and Trial by Television (*Rideau v. Louisiana*, *Estes v. Texas*). A second edition (1976) added Supreme Court decisions of the past five years including the

1973 obscenity decisions and the Nebraska gag-order decision.

De Volder, Arthur L. "A Short Guide to Censorship." *New Mexico Libraries*, 1:57–67, Fall 1968.　　**1D107**
Prepared by the chairman of the Intellectual Freedom Committee of the New Mexico Library Association.

De Vore, P. Cameron, and Marshall J. Nelson. "Commercial Speech and Paid Access to the Press." *Hastings Law Review*, 26:745–75, January 1975. **1D108**
"Limited constitutional protection for commercial advertising has traditionally been justified by the unexamined assumption that commercial speech involves few interests protected under the First Amendment. In an analysis of the history of the commercial speech doctrine, the authors demonstrate that the courts have, until recently, ignored broader issues concerning freedom of the press. While federal courts have begun to acknowledge that restrictions on commercial advertising pose serious threats to the independence of the press, many of the issues which transcend the commercial speech doctrine remain as yet unresolved."

Dewey, John. "Investigating Education: Search for 'Subversive' Textbooks Is Held Politically Dangerous." *New York Times*, 6 May 1940, p. 16. **1D109**
A letter to the editor opposing current state and federal searches for "subversive" textbooks. Replying in the 9 May 1940 issue, Mervin K. Hart of the New York State Economic Council defends the Binghamton community ban on Harold Rugg textbooks in the social sciences. Dewey's rejoinder, Censorship Not Wanted, appears in the 14 May 1940 issue.

——. "Our Un-Free Press." *Common Sense*, 4(11):6–7, November 1935.
　　1D110
Dewey charges that advertising, profit, and vested interests in the existing worn-out economic system, all warp the news we get. He suggests how freedom of the press can be realized along cooperative lines, with control in the hands of those who write rather than those who publish.

——, and Horace M. Kallen, *eds. The Bertrand Russell Case*. New York, Viking Press, 1941. 227p.　　**1D111**
A series of essays by distinguished scholars condemning the ousting of British philosopher-mathematician Bertrand Russell from the faculty of the College of the City of New York. A combination of "fundamentalist clerics [Catholic and Protestant], machine politicians, and professional patriots" demanded the ouster on the grounds that Russell was a propagandist against religion and morality. The lawyer for one of the critics who brought the case to court charged that Russell's writings were "lecherous, salacious, libidin-

ous, lustful, venerous, erotomaniac, aphrodisiac, atheistic, irreverent, narrow-minded, untruthful, and bereft of moral fiber." Besides, the suit charged two technicalities: Russell was not a citizen and he hadn't taken the civil service exam. Judge John E. McGeehan agreed with the charges, accused the Board of Education of using public funds for "establishing a chair of indecency," and sustained the order to discharge Russell. Contributors to the volume in addition to Kallen and Dewey are Walton H. Hamilton, Yale law professor; Richard McKeon, professor of philosophy, University of Chicago; Morris R. Cohen, emeritus professor of philosophy, College of the City of New York; Guy E. Shipler, editor of *The Churchman;* Carleton Washburn, Winnetka Superintendent of Schools; Yervant H. Krikorian, professor philosophy, College of the City of New York; and Professor Sidney Hook, chairman of the Department of Philosophy, New York University.

De Zutter, Henry. "Why SDS Banned Press at Coliseum." *Chicago Journalism Review*, 2(7):11–12, July 1969.　**1D112**
At the annual convention of the Students for a Democratic Society held in the Chicago Coliseum, the SDS tried to keep out the establishment media.

Dhutia, Gopel, Zarine Merchant, Bhaichand Patel, and Kobita Sarkar. [*Film Censorship in India.*] *Times of India Magazine*, 8 June 1973, p. 1. **1D113**
Dhutia states the problem and proposed solution. "If the abolition of censorship is not possible, the continuation of the current system is ludicrous." He recommends the establishment of "an autonomous censorship body with an eminent, liberal personage of unimpeachable moral and intellectual calibre at the head" and assisted by a professional staff. Merchant discusses censorship of political matters, noting that "if the censorship code is interpreted literally, no film with a political theme could ever be made." Patel discusses obscenity in the films, suggesting that until censorship can be abolished entirely, a producer should be given the freedom to exhibit a film without prior approval of censors, taking his chances under the Indian Penal Code. Films should be taken to the open courts where matters can be thrashed out in public view in accordance with the law. Sarkar considers the issue of violence in the Indian cinema. "Censors in India have been so obsessed with sex that they have usually let scenes of the most unprincipled and sadistic violence slip through without a murmur."

Diamond, Alan. "Declassification of Sensitive Information: A Comment on Executive Order 11652." *George Washington Law Review*, 41:1052–71, July 1973.　　**1D114**
Executive Order 11652 checks many abuses in security classification by requiring regular departmental reports, limiting the personnel who have authority to classify, and circumscribing the period during which classification will re-

main effective. It does not solve all the classification problems, which the author enumerates. The Order will be more useful to historians than to those concerned with current operation of government.

Diamond, Edwin. "The Atrocity Papers." *Chicago Journalism Review*, 3(8):3–4, 12–14, August 1970. **1D115**
"In the winter of media discontent initiated by Spiro Agnew, one news organization in particular has felt the icy winds of the Administration. The following is an account of CBS News' trial by intimidation, an innuendo told largely in documentary form." The case involves coverage of alleged atrocities in the Vietnam war.

——. "Multiplying Media Voices." *Columbia Journalism Review*, 8(4):22–27, Winter 1969/70. (Reprinted in Michael C. Emery and Ted C. Smythe, *eds.*, *Readings in Mass Communications*, pp. 7–16)　　**1D116**
A report on recent efforts to achieve diversity in news coverage and a widening of access to ideas. A number of ideas and techniques are suggested.

——. " 'Reporter Power' Takes Root." *Columbia Journalism Review*, 8(4):22–27, Winter 1969/70. (Reprinted in Michael C. Emery and Ted C. Smythe, *eds.*, *Readings in Mass Communications*, pp. 84–94)　　**1D117**
A report on the movement among young journalists for greater participation of reporters in the management and policy-making of newspapers, and for freedom to participate and take active stands on issues.

Diamond, Judith E. "First Amendment Onstage." *Boston University Law Review*, 53:1121–41, November 1973.
　　1D118
"The thesis of this Comment is that in the content of entertainment, where sexual themes are often presented by means of action, neither theory standing alone [obscenity theory or expressive conduct theory] is suitable for first amendment analysis. This Comment will focus upon *California v. La Rue* [1972], a case which serves as an appropriate vehicle for framing the first amendment issues where movement is the message."

Dickey, Anthony. "The Legal Concept of Obscenity in Western Australia." *University of Western Australia Law Review*, 10:223–42, 1972.　　**1D119**
Comment on *Mackinlay v. Wiley* [1971], the first reported case in Western Australia to be concerned with the meaning of the term

"obscene." It involved a newspaper, *Pelican*, at the University of Western Australia, which featured censorship as a theme.

Dickinson, Hugh. "The Esthetics of Self-Censorship." *Drama Critique*, 11:15–21, Winter 1968; 11:89–93, Spring 1968. **1D120**
"Aware that the sensational, and in particular the obscene in word or act, may hamper or endanger the spectator's esthetic responses by directing them away from the creation of that virtual illusion which is the life of his drama, he regards his esthetic freedom, not as absolute but as conditional; he accepts self-imposed 'censorship' as an esthetic principle basic to dramatic art."

Dickson, Paul. "Freedom of Information Act." *Writer's Digest*, 49:44–47, 96, November 1969. **1D121**
"Congress has given the writer a valuable tool for digging information out of the government, but few writers have used it."

Dienes, C. Thomas. *Law, Politics, and Birth Control*. Urbana, Ill., University of Illinois Press, 1974. 374p. **1D122**
"This study will encompass a time span of over a hundred years, stretching from the emergence of birth control as a social and legal problem in the early nineteenth century to the present fashioning of a policy for publicly supported fertility control. The focus will be on the activities of Anthony Comstock and his Puritan vice hunters in the Society for the Suppression of Vice as they waged their holy crusade against obscenity; the judicial martyrdom and legislative travails of the feminist reformer Margaret Sanger as she fought to tear down the legal and social barriers impeding the dissemination of family-planning services; the fervid resistance of the Roman Catholic Church to the birth-control movement and the changes within the Catholic 'monolith'; and the gradual emasculation and eradication of the legal prohibitions against birth control in response to changing social needs and values." Particularly related to freedom of the press are references to the suppression of birth-control literature by the vice societies under the Comstock laws, and the prosecution of such crusaders as Dr. Charles Knowlton, Ezra Heywood, de Robigne M. Bennett, Margaret Sanger, and Mary Ware Dennett.

————. "The Progeny of Comstockery—Birth Control Laws Return to Court." *American University Law Review*, 21:1–129, September 1971. **1D123**
Largely excerpted from Dienes's book, *Law, Politics, and Birth Control*.

Dieterich, Daniel J. "What News Is Fit to Print in the High School Press?"

English Journal, 61:296–301, February 1972. **1D124**
A review of the diversity of opinion on freedom and censorship of the high school press.

Dilley, Marilyn G. *Miami Herald v. Tornillo; Press Freedom and Public Access*. Madison, Wis., University of Wisconsin, Madison, 1975. 206p. (Unpublished Master's thesis) **1D125**
"The major conclusion of the thesis is that *Tornillo* [*Miami Herald Publishing Co. v. Tornillo*, 1974] has strengthened the free speech and press clause because of the Court's reliance on libertarian principles to reach the decision. If the Court decides to project this line of reasoning to television and radio free-press conflicts, the *Tornillo* decision would have a major impact on a case challenging the constitutionality of government regulation of broadcast media."

Dilts, Jon P. *Cry Treason: Testing Siebert's Proposition II*. Bloomington, Ind., Indiana University, 1974. 98p. (Unpublished Master's thesis). **1D126**
"This study analyzed the plight of Copperhead newspapers in Indiana during the Civil War as a test case of Frederick S. Siebert's proposition that newspaper suppression is related to stress on the government and society. It considered these major questions: (1) Were attempts to prevent publication limited to certain geographic areas? (2) Was suppression defended by the government, military officials, and citizen's organizations? (3) Did newspaper editors have the means and opportunity to redress grievances and defend their right to a free press? (4) Was repression confined to times of severe governmental stress?"

Di Matteo, Philip S. "*Times* Marches On: The Courts' Continuing Expansion of the Application of the 'Actual Malice' Standard." *Notre Dame Lawyer*, 47:153–71, October 1971. **1D127**
"It is the purpose of this note to examine the history and development (progression, if you will) of the scope of the First Amendment—qualified privilege in the law of defamation, together with an analysis of the current limits of the *Times* doctrine, and an examination of lower court applications of the 'actual malice' standard."

Dinsmore, Herman H. *All the News That Fits. A Critical Analysis of the News and Editorial Contents of the New York Times*. New Rochelle, N.Y., Arlington, 1969. 376p. **1D128**
The author develops the thesis that the *New York Times* is "deliberately pitched to the so-called liberal point of view, both in its news and editorial columns." He deals particularly with press and government withholding or slanting of information about the Korean War, Castro's rise to power, the Kennedy Assassination, and the Vietnam war.

————. "Controlled Press and TV." *Economic Council Letter*, 717:1–4, September 1972. **1D129**
An attack on the news media, in support of Vice-President Agnew's charges, for controlling, manipulating, and distorting the news. References are made to the *New York Times* and to press coverage of the Vietnam war in which, the author charges, denigration in the press of the various South Vietnamese governments.

Dionisopoulas, P. Allan. "Privacy and the Press." *Grassroots Editor*, 17 (1):8–9, January–March 1976. **1D130**
The author identifies three natural categories of persons entitled to different degrees of privacy: (1) the public official with the least claim on the right of privacy, but who should be protected in some areas of his life; (2) the public figure such as entertainers, athletes, and former officeholders, with a larger claim on privacy and "should be permitted to turn publicity on and off as they wish"; and (3) ordinary citizens who by accident of fate become newsworthy and should be given the greatest protection. The author considers recent Supreme Court decisions on privacy, noting that "the Court should acknowledge the true purpose for which freedom of expression was made a constitutional principle—the rights to speak and to publish were intended solely as protections against government and not to enhance the rights of some over the rights of others in the non–public sector."

"Direct Satellite Broadcasting and the First Amendment." *Harvard International Law Journal*, 15:514–27, Summer 1974. **1D131**
"This Comment will analyze the extent to which the free speech provision of the First Amendment to the Constitution may inhibit the United States from participating in an international agreement to regulate the control of direct satellite broadcasting."

Directors Guild of America. "Special Report: The Supreme Court and Creative Rights." *Action*, 9(2):5–25, March–April 1974. **1D132**
Content: Statement of Principle [on obscenity censorship], National Board of Directors. Viewpoints on Censorship by Eleven Directors. Obscenity—It started with Gutenberg by Charles Rembar. Excerpts from television discussion on the U.S. Supreme Court obscenity decisions by Robert Wise, president of the Guild. Those Good Old Bad Days by Bob Thomas. The Gospel According to Will Hays: Dialogue [on censorship] between two directors, Robert Aldrich and Bernardo Bertolucci. Rembar's speech traces the history of Anglo-American legal attitudes toward obscenity.

Dirksen, Everett M. "A New Plan to Fight Pornography." *Reader's Digest*, 95(11):113–16, November 1969. **1D133**
Senator Dirksen discusses his antiobscenity bill (S. 1077), which would free juries of local

citizens to make the final determination as to whether a book, magazine, or movie is obscene, and limiting U.S. Supreme Court review to the legal correctness of the prosecution.

"Dirty Digs in 'Dirty Play' Controversy Result in a London Suit for Libel." *Dramatists Guild Quarterly*, 13(2):6–14, Summer 1966. **1D134**
Excerpts from the *Times* (London) report of the libel case, *Littler v. British Broadcasting Corporation and Another*, involving charges by Emile Littler, theater director, against the broadcasting company for malicious libel for remarks made about his objections to the "theater of cruelty" and the use of filthy language and filthy situations. The jury was deadlocked.

"Dirty Words and Dirty Politics: Cognitial Dissonance in the First Amendment." *University of Chicago Law Review*, 34:367–86, Winter 1967. **1D135**
The author considers "cognative dissonance" in the protection afforded libel and obscenity under the First Amendment. In *New York Times Co. v. Sullivan* (1964), "the Supreme Court subjected the common law tests for libel to the scrutiny of the First Amendment, adding the element of intent to what had previously been a two-part test encompassing falsity and harm to reputation," giving more complete protection to those criticizing the government in print. In obscenity law the Court employed a somewhat similar three-part test: the materials must be "patently offensive," appeal to "prurient interest," and the seller must have some knowledge of the obscenity of his merchandise.

"Dissenting Servicemen and the First Amendment." *Georgia Law Review*, 58:534–68, February 1970. **1D136**
"This Note will explore three considerations . . . : the role of the first amendment in the armed forces, the issues involved in vindicating the communicative rights of servicemen in military and civilian courts, and the procedural problems encountered in protecting servicemen from retaliatory administrative action."

"Distribution of Handbills in a Privately Owned Shopping Mall Is Not Protected by the First Amendment when the Handbilling Is Unrelated to the Operations of the Shopping Mall, When the Mall Is Not Dedicated to a General Public Use and When There Is a Reasonable Alternative Place to Distribute the Handbills." *Georgia Law Review*, 7:177–88, Fall 1972. **1D137**
Re: *Lloyd Corp. v. Tanner*, 407 U.S. 551 (1972).

Divoky, Diane. "Revolt in the High Schools: The Way It's Going To Be." *Saturday Review*, 52(7):83–84, 89,

101–2, 15 February 1969. (A similar report in *Scholastic Teacher*, 6 October 1969) **1D138**
A story about the growing movement among high school students to gain complete freedom of the press through underground newspapers. Some 500 such papers exist and there is a national student-run press service. "The underground high school press represents attitudes that have generated a variety of organizations bent on changing the school and the society. Their tactics range from polite dialogue to picketing to direct confrontation with the authorities." A number of cases brought by parents and students challenge the right of school authorities to ban the publications and punish the editor.

———. "Textbook Censorship: New Hands Wielding Red Pencils." *Education News*, 2:1, 16, 10 June 1968. **1D139**
A National Education Association Commission on Professional Rights and Responsibilities notes that in the past two years parents have replaced the John Birch Society and other right wing groups as the leading critics of books, and English and literature overtook social studies texts as the subject of attacks.

Dixon, John W., Jr. "Art and Pornography." *Theology Today*, 25:474–77, January 1969. **1D140**
Philosophic reflections on art and pornography upon visiting a contemporary art show and a pornographic book shop—"the accidental juxtaposition of experiences."

Dixon, Robert G., Jr. "The Constitution Is Shield Enough for Newsmen." *American Bar Association Journal*, 60:707–10, June 1974. **1D141**
"National legislation granting newsmen an absolute privilege against disclosure through judicial processes would upset a delicate balancing of rights. Experience is showing that First Amendment rights will be guaranteed by the courts when the balance requires that action. The Constitution, not a statutory privilege, should be the newsman's shield."—Editor

Do We Really Have Freedom of the Press? An Inquiry Into the First Amendment. 2 color filmstrips (pt. 1, 101 frames; pt. 2, 105 frames); 2 phonodiscs (1 side for manual projector; 1 side for automatic projector) 16 min. each. Also issued with phonotape in cassette. Chicago, Denoyer-Geppert Audio Visuals, 1972. (Joan Troy, producer) **1D142**
"Explores the implications of the increased friction between government and the printed and broadcast news media, considering specifically the cases of the Pentagon Papers and the television documentary *The Selling of the Pentagon*. Outlines the broad issue of the conflict between a free press, first amendment guarantees, and governmental security." Issued with guide.

Doan, Richard K. "Report from a Quagmire." *TV Guide*, 21(4):6–9, 27 January 1973. **1D143**
"After a season and a half, the FCC's prime-time access rule seems to have produced nothing but problems."

Dobkin, James A. "The Release of Government-Owned Technical Data under the Freedom of Information Law: Between Scylla and Charybdis." *Villanova Law Review*, 14:74–85, Fall 1968. **1D144**
The author suggests that "numerous references in the legislative history of section 3 [Freedom of Information Act of 1966] prove that the section was promulgated to expose the executive machinery and that the disclosure of substantive data unrelated to agency function is beyond the intent of the legislators; the status of such data should be unaffected by the new law."

Dr. Robinson's Voice in the Wilderness; A Magazine of Sane Radicalism. New York, 1917–20. (Reprinted, with an introduction by Charles Leinenweber, Westport, Conn., Greenwood, 1970) **1D145**
In issues of his journal, the radical New York physician attacked America's participation in World War I, incurring the wrath of the Wilson Administration. The first four issues were confiscated by the Post Office Department and for seventeen months Robinson's journal ceased publication. In June 1919 *Voice* resumed publication. Almost every issue attacked a complaisant press and an oppressive government. The introduction to the reprint recounts the history of the journal's fight for survival. Robinson was also a crusader for free circulation of birth-control information and sex education, and opposed the oppressive Comstock laws in his journal, *Medical Critic and Guide* (R180–82).

[Dodd, Charles E.] "Law of Libel—State of the Press." *Quarterly Review*, 35:566–609, March 1827. **1D146**
In this anonymously published essay, attributed by the Wellesley Index to a barrister of Inner Temple, the author defends the existing law of libel against those who consider it harsh and severe. He favors retaining the rule that truth cannot be admitted in defense of a libel. He argues further that it may be appropriate to attack immorality and vice in the abstract or to attack a class, but objects to the exposure of the action of individuals, even though the truth of their actions can be ascertained.

Dodson, Daniel B. "Ulysses in America." *Columbia Library Columns*, 21(2):13–19, February 1972. **1D147**

The story of the Random House battle over publication of James Joyce's *Ulysses* in the United States as revealed in the Bennett Cerf papers at Columbia University. The article reports on the standard test of a reader's interest in *Ulysses*: Place the book on its spine and if it falls open between pages 723 to 768 (Modern Library edition) the assumption is that the reader's interest was not primarily scholarly.

[Doebler, Peter D.] "Viewpoint: The Printer and Censorship." *Book Production Industry*, 46(12):47, 50, December 1970. (Reprinted in *Newsletter on Intellectual Freedom* [IFC–ALA], May 1971) **1D148**

The author considers the serious threat to First Amendment freedom when printers for personal, moral, or political reasons refuse to print material with which they disagree. The discussion is prompted by the *Scanlan's Monthly* case.

Doiron, Peter M. "Responsibility: Books Dealing With Censorship and Society." *Choice*, 5:922–27, October 1968. **1D149**

The editor's comments on censorship are followed by an annotated list of twelve recent and relevant books.

Dolson, Hildegarde. *Please Omit Funeral*. Philadelphia, Lippincott, 1975. 237p. **1D150**

A mystery novel involving censorship of "dirty" books in a high school library.

Dominian, J. "Pornography: After the Longford Report." *Tablet: The International Catholic Weekly*, 226:1070–71, 11 November 1972. **1D151**

An appraisal of the Longford report on pornography by a one-time member of the Longford Committee. He advises that the report should be read in conjunction with David Holbrook's book, *The Case Against Pornography*. "The debate on pornography must not divert attention from this urgent task of wider education on sexuality which, in my view, can find the full answer only in the bosom of Christianity."

Donart, Arthur C. "The Books They're Banning and Why." *American School Board Journal*, 160:42–43, May 1973. **1D152**

A partial list of the current targets for schoolbook banning.

Donelson, Kenneth L. "A Brief Note on Censorship and Junior High Schools in Arizona, 1966–68." *Arizona English Bulletin*, 11:26–30, April 1969. **1D153**

———. "Censorship and Arizona Schools:1966–1968." *Arizona English Bulletin*, 11:28–44, February 1969. **1D154**

Report of a survey to determine the nature and extent of censorship in Arizona high schools. Some 115 incidents of direct or indirect censorship of books (11 of other materials) were reported; 59 books were objected to (a list of titles is appended). The questionnaire elicited responses on the seriousness of the problem and advice to universities in training English teachers in areas of book selection and the handling of censorship.

———. "Censorship and the Teaching of English: A Few Problems and Fewer Solutions." *Statement: The Journal of the Colorado Language Arts Society*, 4(1):5–15, 18–20, October 1968. **1D155**

"To deal effectively with censorship, an English teacher needs to know about (1) the history of censorship, (2) the nature of censorship and the censor, (3) the nature of literature and the purpose for teaching literature. Finally, the English teacher needs to have defenses or approaches to the censor, for without some guidelines, the English teacher will be unprepared for every attack and vulnerable to any attack."

———. "Censorship in the 1970's: Some Ways to Handle It When It Comes (And It Will)." *English Journal*, 63:47–51, February 1974. **1D156**

The author lists eight categories of "suspect" books where censorship is likely to strike in the public schools: sex, politics, an attack on the American Dream, war and peace, religion, sociology and race, language, drugs, and inappropriate adolescent behavior. He suggests six ways for English teachers and librarians to prepare to meet the censor: (1) develop statements of rationales for teaching literature; (2) establish a departmental committee to recommend books; (3) work for community support of academic freedom before the censor strikes; (4) let the public know what is going on in English classrooms and why; (5) have a formal policy for handling attempted censorship; and (6) expect each faculty member to give rationale for selection of any book used in the classroom.

———. "The Censorship of Non-Print Media Comes to the English Classroom." *English Journal*, 62:1226–27, December 1973. **1D157**

"Right now, censorship of non-print media threatens to become as big a problem for English teachers as censorship of printed matter." Among those short films coming under attack are: *Pas de Deux*, *Future Shock*, *The Lottery*, *Occurrence at Owl Creek Bridge*, *Timepiece*, and *Skater Dater*.

———. "Censorship: Some Issues and Problems." *Theory Into Practice*, 14:186–94, June 1975. **1D158**

The areas of greatest concern in school censorship, according to the author, are: sex, un-Americanism, war and peace, religion, race, offensive language, drugs, and inappropriate adolescent behavior. He makes seven observations: (1) any work is potentially censorable, (2) the newer the work the more likely it is to be censored, (3) censorship generally comes without warning, (4) censorship almost always produces a rippling effect, (5) censorship is capricious and arbitrary, (6) teachers do not always accept the reality of censorship, and (7) censorship stems more often than not from parents and people outside the school, but a significant number of attacks come from within. Among the reasons for increased school censorship are: the recent restrictive decisions of the U.S. Supreme Court, parent revolt from what they see as a decade of permissiveness, and a lack of understanding of the basic purpose of education.

———. "Court Decisions and Legal Arguments About Censorship and the Nature of Obscenity." *Arizona English Bulletin*, 11:45–49, February 1969. (ED 26,397) **1D159**

A selective bibliography including court decisions and quotations from the opinions of judges.

———. "Current Reading: A Scholarly and Pedagogical Bibliography of Articles and Books, Recent and Old, On Censorship." *Arizona English Bulletin*, 11:50–52, February 1969. (ED 26,398) **1D160**

Headings: Freedom and Censorship, histories of censorship, general comments, sex and censorship, and a basic book list.

———. "A Few Safe Assumptions About Censorship and the Censor." *Peabody Journal of Education*, 50:235–44, April 1973. (Reprinted in *Education Digest*, September 1973) **1D161**

The author suggests seven assumptions about the nature of censors and censorship that teachers and librarians "need to remember to act upon in their daily work": (1) Any book or idea or teaching method is potentially censorable; (2) new books or ideas or teaching methods are more likely to come under attack than established ones; (3) censorship is capricious and arbitrary; (4) censorship comes from within the school system as well as from outside; (5) most people are not willing to consider ideas about sex or sexually oriented literature when they conflict with folk wisdom; (6) censorship is a real threat that can happen to you; and (7) censorship usually strikes unexpectedly, and schools experiencing censorship often become fearful of trying anything new or different.

———. "Gore, Filth, and Communism: Censorship Comes to Non-Print Media." *Kentucky English Bulletin*, 24(2):5–10, Winter 1974/75. **1D162**

There is a growing sentiment for censorship of non-print media in the classrooms as more teachers become aware of new, exciting, provocative and stimulating short films, records, and tapes. The author gives examples of recent cases of censorship involving non-print media in English classrooms. "We must fight the censor of non-print media material just as we must fight the censor of print material."

————. "Obscenity and the Chill Factor: Court Decisions About Obscenity and Their Relationships to School Censorship." *Journal of Research and Development in Education*, 9(3):102–11, Spring 1976. **1D163**
"Sketching briefly over the history of meanings and tests of obscenity evolved through more than 200 years of court decisions and the influence these decisions have had and may have on censorship problems in the schools will suggest some inter-relationships. These two matters, court decisions and school censorship, are not always directly related, but neither are they totally separable, and they are more and more intertwined today."

————. "Some Responsibilities of the English Teacher Facing Censorship." *Arizona English Bulletin*, 11:13–22, February 1969. (ED 43,603) **1D164**
Demands for censorship can be expected in the study of contemporary literature in high school. The author proposes seven responsibilities that English teachers must accept in facing the forces of censorship: (1) to know literature, literary merit, and what is appealing to adolescents; (2) to understand the implications of arguments for and against censorship; (3) to develop competency in discussing controversial works and in defending a formal policy on attempted censorship; (4) to prepare a rationale of works taught; (5) to let the public know what is studied and why; (6) to enlist community support of academic freedom; and (7) to recognize that the censor may have a legitimate complaint and that the teacher may have made a bad judgment.

————. "Some Tentative Answers to Some Questions About Censorship." *English Journal*, 63(4):20–21, April 1974. **1D165**
The author suggests answers to a number of questions raised by Keith Wright and Roy Alin in the December 1973 issue: Does the individual parent have the right to object to his child's reading a specific literary work? Is a teacher presumptuous in identifying a specific literary work as one every student must read at a given time? What are the student's options regarding the selection of reading materials to which he is to be exposed? Although a parent may have something to say about the selection of a book for his child, can he prevent other members of the class from reading it? Is the number of parents an important consideration?

————. "These I Believe: Some Statements About Censorship." *Minnesota English Journal*, 12(1):15–19, Winter 1976. **1D166**
(1) The school must be the hotbed of intellectual ferment in a community; (2) English teachers who ask young people to think and challenge ideas must themselves be models of openmindedness and fairness; (3) students are far more aware of the censorship climate around them than we know; (4) literature can make students aware of their own personal worlds and the world around them and make them more discriminating readers; (5) we must involve the community in the selection of our teaching materials.

————. "What to Do When the Censor Comes." *Elementary English*, 51:403–9, March 1974. **1D167**
With more and more realism in children's and adolescent literature, the demand for censorship is becoming an increasingly serious problem in the schools. "When censorship strikes, the individual librarian or teacher puts his judgment and often his job squarely on the line." The author makes five recommendations for meeting this situation: (1) Language arts teachers, English teachers, and librarians should develop policy statements on teaching goals and book selection; (2) they should establish school or district committees to recommend books; (3) they should work toward community support for freedom to read; (4) they should let the public know what goes on in the classroom and in libraries; and (5) they should establish and implement some formal policy for handling any attempted censorship.

————. "White Walls and High Windows: Some Contemporary Censorship Problems." *English Journal*, 61:1191–98, November 1972. (Reprinted in *Education Digest*, April 1973) **1D168**
"The English teacher who tries to bring life into his English classes often risks his job and tenure, for some school officials, parents, and other teachers may not share his enthusiasm for reality in the schoolroom. He may likely face some form of censorship, some direct or indirect attempt to silence him or his 'controversial' or 'questionable' or 'un-American' materials or methods." The author cites six areas "which have come more and more under the eagle-eye of the censor": (1) the traditional controversial work such as *Catcher in the Rye*; (2) modern literature written for the adolescent such as Nat Hentoff's Vietnam book, *I'm Really Dragged But Nothing Gets Me Down*; (3) books about ethnic or racial minorities, such as Claude Brown's *Manchild in the Promised Land*; (4) magazines dealing with controversial issues; (5) films dealing with such topics as sex and war; and (6) student-made films or tapes.

————, *ed.* "Censorship and the Teaching of English." *Arizona English Bulletin*, 17(2):1–263, February 1975. (Entire issue) **1D169**
Content: Censorship and Arizona English Teaching, 1971–1974 by Kenneth L. Donel-

son. The Censor by George Benedict. Freedom for Readers and Other Endangered Species by Harriet McIntosh. I Wish I'd Had the Guts by Lee Barclay. Censorship in Pennsylvania by Edward R. Fagan. Censorship in the Classroom—Censure, Selection, or Both? by Ruth Stein. The Censor by Mason Williams. A Case for Censorship by Thomas J. Blee. Censorship, Sexism and Racism by John M. Kean. Censorship in Indiana by Richard Blough. How to Stack Firewood So Teachers and Books Aren't Burned by Censors by Sharon Crowley and George Redman. Scenario of Book Burning by Bruce Severy. Censorship: A Difference in Kind, Not Degree by Dennis Badeczewski. How Students Can Help Educate the Censors by Paul Janeczko. Censorship in Ohio by James E. Davis. Protecting the Gullible: The Supreme Court and Censorship by Judith F. Krug and Roger L. Funk. What in Blazes? by Joan Catmull. The English Teacher as Self-Censor by Ronald La Conte. The Censored Teacher as Scapegoat by James E. Davis. Biased? Irreverent? Censorship in Flagstaff by Retha Foster. Court Decisions and Legal Arguments about Censorship and the Nature of Obscenity. Censorship: A Publisher's View by Leo B. Kneer and Clement Stacy. 1975 Censorship Battleground: State Legislatures by Susan H. Clark. School Newspapers and Student Rights to Freedom of Thought and Expression by Suzanne H. Emery. Censorship and a False Assumption by Lucky Jacobs. Censorship and Racism: In Pursuit of a Relationship by Albert V. Schwartz. You Can't Tell the Players Without a Program: A Case Study in Censorship by Robert Stewart. Censorship and the High School Librarian by Jerry Mangan. Censorship in Louisiana by Charles Suhor. Films: Censorship or Education? by Ronald E. Sutton. School Boards Need Protection, Too! by Warren Packer. A Student's Right to Write by Robert E. Bartman. Censorship in Kansas by Ronald C. Stewart. Let's Get on with the Censored Story by John Donovan. Censorship in Kentucky: Kentucky's Council of Teachers of English Questionnaire by Alfred L. Crabb, Jr., and Alice Manchikes. The Liberal's Liberal: Morris L. Ernst by Saundra Harmon. Censorship in Virginia by Paul Slayton. Censorship: What to Do About It? A Modest Proposal by Rollin Douma. Arguments Against Censorship: Milton and Mill by Margaret B. Fleming. Censorship in Utah by Jewel J. Bindrup. A State-Minded View of Censorship by Edward R. Fagan. Children's Books That Have Met the Censor by M. Jean Greenlaw. A Note on Censorship During the Age of Reason in England by Stephen Jones. Censorship in Illinois by James Coe. Censorship! Who Wants It? More People Than We Think, Maybe by James W. Reith. Censorship in Maryland by Jean C. Sisk. Censorship Cases May Increase by Robert F. Hogan. Censorship: The English Teacher's Nemesis by Ray H. Lawson. Censorship: The Student's Non-Right to Learn by Louis M. Papes. A Brief Chronology of the West Virginia Textbook Crisis. Censorship in North Dakota by Michael H. Keedy. Exclusion and Invisibility: Chicano Literature Not in Textbooks by Raymund A. Paredes. Censorship and Paperbacks: Toward a Common Sense Policy by Gloria Steinberg Scott. Current Reading: A Scholarly and Pedagogical Bibliography of Articles and Books, Recent and Old, about Censorship.

Donelson, Kenneth L., Frances C. Dean, and H. Keith Sterzing. "What To Do Before the Censor Arrives." *Today's Education*, 64:22–25, January 1975. (Adapted from a longer article in *English Journal*, February 1974) **1D170**
Following the Donelson article are reactions from Frances C. Dean and H. Keith Sterzing. Dean observes that every area of the curriculum and the materials supporting it in today's schools are scrutinized for sexism. Home economics, industrial arts, and mathematics are no longer "safe" subjects. There are concerns over racism, treatment of minorities, and portrayal of life styles as well as such issues as abortion, genocide, divorce, and evolution. The author offers further advice on dealing with issues of censorship. Sterzing believes that conflict over the purpose of education is at the root of censorship pressures. "Should teachers simply teach what the local community . . . wishes taught in the manner in which it wishes it taught? Or, on the other hand, do teachers have a basic responsibility to help their students explore and weigh our traditional values?" So long as teaching materials deal with abstractions they are relatively "safe"; when they attempt to deal with real issues and values of today's world they are in danger.

Donlan, Dan. "Parent Versus Teacher: The Dirty Word." In Phil L. Nacke, *ed.*, *Diversity in Mature Reading: Theory and Research*. Boone, N.C., National Reading Conference, 1973, pp. 224–31. (22d Yearbook, vol. 1) **1D171**
The author reports on two surveys he conducted: one was a sampling of California English teachers to determine their experience with ten controversial books; the second was a survey of parents to learn their reactions to a list of fourteen galvanizing words selected from *The Catcher in the Rye*. He suggests two solutions to the censorship dilemma: dialogue between parents and teachers and arrangements for individualized reading assignments which would enable the use of alternative books.

Donovan, Paul F. "Private Individuals Defamed in Newspaper Need Only Prove Negligence for Recovery in Massachusetts." *Suffolk University Law Review*, 10:126–41, Fall 1975. **1D172**
Re: *Stone v. Essex County Newspapers, Inc.*, Mass., 330 N.E.2d 161 (1975).

Dorbin, Sanford M. "Morris Ernst and the Banned Books Collection." *Censorship Today*. 1(3):18–21 [October–November] 1968. **1D173**
A description of the Morris L. Ernst Banned Books Collection at the University of California, Santa Barbara.

Dorothy, Wade A. "Public Figure or Private Individual?" *Washburn Law Journal*, 16:184–89, Fall 1976. **1D174**
Re: *Time, Inc. v. Firestone*, 424 U.S. 448, (1976).

Dorricott, Jack W. "Free Speech and the Military." *Free Speech*, 19:3–8, February 1970. **1D175**
References to recent court decisions which have supported the liberalizing of free speech in the army and to a 1969 army memorandum, Guidance on Dissent, recognizing the increased rights of soldiers.

Dorsen, Norman. *Frontiers of Civil Liberties*. New York, Pantheon, 1968. 420p. **1D176**
Chapter 7, Censorship of "Foreign Communist Propaganda"; Chapter 8, Military Censorship; Chapter 9, Blacklisting; Chapter 10, Academic Freedom; Chapter 16, Trial by Television.

———, Paul Bender, and Burt Neuborne. *Emerson, Haber, and Dorsen's Political and Civil Rights in the United States*. Vol. 1. Boston, Little, Brown, 1976. 1695p. **1D177**
Part I of this expansion of the classic work (E90) deals with Freedom of Expression: theory and history, national security, government secrecy and the public's right to know, freedom of expression in the public forum, administration of justice, obscenity and offensive speech, actions for defamation and invasion of privacy, commercial speech, access to the media, academic freedom, religious freedom, individuals rights within private groups (unions, professional and trade associations), and the rights of groups within restricted categories (prisoners, mental patients, and military personnel).

Dorsen, Norman, and Stephen Gillers, *eds*. *None of Your Business: Government Secrecy in America*. Introduction by Anthony Lewis. New York, Viking, 1974. 362p. **1D178**
Content: Executive Privilege: The President Won't Tell by Norman Dorsen and John Shattuck. The Government's Classification System by William G. Phillips. What Is the Real Problem with the Classification System? by Stanley Futterman. Secrecy and Covert Intelligence Collection and Operations by Morton H. Halperin and Jeremy J. Stone. Legislative Secrecy by Albert Gore. The Secrets of Local Government by M. L. Stein. Administering the Freedom of Information Act: An Insider's View by Robert L. Saloschin. Rights of

People: The Freedom of Information Act by Harrison Wellford. Pressures on the Press by David Wise. Blowing the Whistle on the Pentagon by Ernest Fitzgerald. The Ellsberg Perspective: A Discussion. The Technology of Secrecy by Alan Westin. Government Secrecy in the United Kingdom. The book is based on the proceedings of a conference on government secrecy held in New York on May 18–19, 1973, sponsored jointly by the Committee for Public Justice and the Arthur Garfield Hays Civil Liberties Program of New York University School of Law.

Dorsey, Joseph L. "Changing Attitudes Toward The Massachusetts Birth Control Law." *New England Journal of Medicine*, 27:823–27, 15 October 1964. **1D179**
The author traces the Massachusetts birth-control law from the federal Comstock law of 1873 and the highly restrictive law of Connecticut and Massachusetts, to test cases in the courts, the 1942 and 1948 referenda in Massachusetts, the work of the Planned Parenthood League, and the recent climate for change.

Dotter, Glenn N. *A Review of the Controversy Over Newsmen's Privilege*. Chapel Hill, N.C., University of North Carolina, 1975. 58p. (Unpublished Master's thesis) **1D180**
"An examination of the controversy over newsmen's privilege is presented as a series of five articles intended for newspaper publication. The purpose of the articles is to present to the average reader the dimensions of this problem, which involves a newsman's right to keep his confidential sources of information secret."

Doty, Janet R. M. *A History of Oregon's Pre-Trial Publicity Guidelines and How They Are Used By 20 Daily Newspapers*. Eugene, Ore., University of Oregon, 1969. 127p. (Unpublished Master's thesis) **1D181**
In only two of the twenty daily newspapers in the study did both the editor and reporter know the content of and use the Guidelines. On only two other newspapers were the reporters familiar with the Guidelines.

Douberley, William M. "Resolving the Free Speech–Free Press Dichotomy: Access to the Press through Advertising." *University of Florida Law Review*, 22:293–316, Fall 1969. **1D182**
"This note is an attempt to describe the increasing incidence of suppression of free expression in the nation's newspapers. This suppression gives rise to the free presss-free speech dichotomy. It is asserted that a positive view of the first amendment requires that access to the press be afforded the individual. Furthermore, the right declared by newspapers to decline to accept advertisements at will cannot apply where the advertiser is exercising his constitutionally protected freedom of expression."

"A Double Standard of Obscenity: The Ginsberg Decision." *Valparaiso University Law Review*, 3:57–68, Fall 1968. **1D183**
"The approach used in Ginsberg—₍Ginsberg v. State of New York, 1968₎ setting a different standard for those under the age of seventeen—is the most pragmatic method yet devised to accomplish the interests of society in protecting children from material that they cannot yet deal with on a mature level, while yet allowing the more mature segments of society the pleasure of adult literature." The text of the pertinent New York Penal Code is included.

Douglas, Charles G., III. "The New Hampshire Right to Know Law—An Analysis." *New Hampshire Bar Journal*, 16:227–45, March 1975. **1D184**

Douglas, Donald G., and Philip Noble, comps. *Justice on Trial. A Collection of Critical Essays on the Subject of Judicial Reforms*. Skokie, Ill., National Textbook, 1971. 250p. (Contemporary Issues series) **1D185**
Content: Free Press vs. Fair Trial: The Press in Black Robe by Roy Adams. Journalistic Media and Fair Trial by William M. Ware and Gerard D. Di Marco. Pretrial Publicity by Michael L. Boicourt. Procedural Compromise and Contempt: Feasible Alternatives in the Fair Trial versus Free Press Controversy by Bruce A. Weihe.

Douglas, Emily Taft. *Margaret Sanger: Pioneer of the Future*. New York, Holt, Rinehart, and Winston, 1970. 274p. **1D186**
The dramatic story of Margaret Sanger (1879–1966) and her lifelong crusade in behalf of birth control in America and abroad. For her efforts she frequently faced censorship under the Comstock laws which considered birth-control information as a form of obscenity and prohibited it from the mails.

Douglas, William O. *The Bible and the Schools*. Boston, Little, Brown, 1966. 65p. **1D187**
The Associate Justice of the U.S. Supreme Court discusses the reasoning behind the Court's decision regarding religion in the public schools.

———. "Press and First Amendment Rights." *Idaho Law Review*, 7:1–15, Spring 1970. **1D188**
Justice Douglas traces the history of the First Amendment through the various interpretations by the courts, raising some of the questions on press freedoms that have come before the courts.

———et al. ₍"The First Amendment"₎ *Quill*, 64(8):16–45, September 1976. **1D189**

A special issue of *Quill* growing out of a resolution of Sigma Delta Chi to establish a national program on the role of the news media and the meaning and importance of the First Amendment. The issue is introduced by retired Supreme Court Justice William O. Douglas who writes that preserving the basic freedom spelled out in the First Amendment has been and will continue to be a challenge. Other contributions: Born of Struggle by J. Edward Gerald (the theory behind the First Amendment is not young). Sibling Rivalry by Richard M. Schmidt, Jr. (the First and Sixth Amendments—an often-strained, occasionally combative relationship). Milestones by J. Edward Gerald (a guide to landmark First Amendment cases). Treated Like Distant Cousins by William Small (the broadcast news media are free only some of the time). Today's Godfathers by Lyle Denniston (the First Amendment is what the Supreme Court says it is, and here's what the present Supreme Court is saying). The Child in Jeopardy by Ben H. Bagdikian (freedom of expression is withering away for lack of exercise).

Douglas–Home, Charles. "South Africa's Laws for Curbing Press Freedom." *The Times* (London), 57,418:9, 26 November 1968. **1D190**
"Two events this month have helped to raise doubts about the real, as opposed to apparent, freedom of the press in South Africa." They are the trial of Lawrence Gander of the *Rand Daily Mail* and a speech by the Minister of Interior warning of further laws to control the press.

Douma, Rollin G. *Book Selection Policies, Book Complaint Policies and Censorship in Selected Michigan Public High Schools*. Ann Arbor, Mich., University of Michigan, 1973. 163p. (Ph.D. dissertation, University Microfilms, no. 73–24,556; ED 78,448) **1D191**
"The purposes of this study were (1) to describe the content of the various book selection and book complaint policies used by a selected sample of Michigan public high school English Departments; (2) to compare the effects these policies have on the inhibition or resolution of censorship; and (3) to provide a complete, sample book selection and complaint policy modeled on the best characteristics of the policies examined during the writing of the study."

———. "Censorship in the English Classroom: A Review of Research." *Journal of Research and Development in Education*, 9(3):60–68, Spring 1976. **1D192**
A review of research on the nature of censorship incidents, the censor, and the material censored, with a less substantial portion on suggested and empirically tested procedures for remedying censorship pressures.

Dove, Linda M. *Actual Malice: The Application of a Judicial Doctrine*. Chapel

Hill, N.C., University of North Carolina, 1968. 104p. (Unpublished Master's thesis) **1D193**
Interviews with twenty North Carolina state legislators suggested that the effects of the actual malice rule, as indicated in *New York Times Co. v. Sullivan* (1964), would be subtle, setting informal boundaries to govern the behavior of the press and the politicians.

Dow, Orrin B. "When Birches Last in the Dooryard Swung." *ALA Bulletin*, 63:1237–39, October 1969. **1D194**
The librarian of the Farmingdale, Long Island, Public Library reports on the efforts of local citizens to remove Kazantzakis' *Last Temptation of Christ* from the library and the harassment campaign of a library board member, an ardent John Birch Society member. Action charged included the theft of an objectionable journal, for which the member was brought to trial and convicted; newspaper and bumper advertising (Support Your Local Degenerate, Vote Yes on the Library Budget); assault on a staff member; and foraging in the library's garbage can.

Dowd, Donald W. "The Press, Privacy, and 'Public Figures': A Symposium." *Villanova Law Review*, 12:725–29, Summer 1967. **1D195**
An introduction to a symposium on the implication of the recent cases of *New York Times v. Sullivan* (1964) and *Time, Inc. v. Hill* (1967), on the law of defamation, privacy, and the constitutional right of a free press. Participants were: Lewis C. Green, member of the Missouri Bar; Harold L. Nelson, director of the University of Minnesota School of Journalism; and Arthur B. Hanson, general counsel, American Newspaper Publishers Association.

Dowling, John. "Bigger and Better Censors." *Ireland Today*, 3:221–25, March 1938. **1D196**
A criticism of English and American writers who use the Irishman as villain, rogue, fool, or monster. While nothing can be done abroad, "we have the power, however, to protect our self-respect at home and to restore our tottering national morale. All we require is bigger and better censorship as well as censors who have some idea of the meaning of morale and who have, at least, heard of a place called Ireland."

Dowling, Ruth N. *William Cobbett, His Trials and Tribulations as an Alien Journalist, 1794–1800*. Carbondale, Ill., Southern Illinois University at Carbondale, 1972. 361p. (Ph.D. dissertation, University Microfilms, no. 73–3875) **1D197**
"The purpose of this study was to determine the pressures exerted against 'Bullish' William Cobbett when he expressed political views op-

posing prevailing sentiments of prominent Americans, particularly those of patriot [Benjamin] Rush; the political machinations used through the courts to stifle Cobbett's opinions; and the kinds of personal, political, and legal pressures."

Dowling, William J. "Fair Trial v. Free Press: Proposals for Statutory Reform." *University of San Francisco Law Review*, 3:49–74, October 1968. **1D198**
In an examination of court cases, the author concludes that "whether a defendant has suffered inherent prejudice is a question resolvable with any degree of accuracy only after the fact. Because of the many and sundry variables demanding consideration, it is impossible to foretell on the issue and in effect, foretelling is precisely the office which a statute would have to perform."

Downie, Currie S. *Barriers to the Flow of Technical Information: Limitation Statements—Legal Basis*. Arlington, Va. Office of Aerospace Research (Air Force), 1969. 16p. (ED 32,910) **1D199**
"The new 'Freedom of Information Act' and the more important reasons for limitations on the flow of information are discussed. The legal basis for these limitations can be found in the almost 100 statutory provisions which prohibit, exempt, or otherwise protect certain types of information from disclosure."

Downs, Robert B. "Freedom of Speech and Press: Development of a Concept." *Library Trends*, 19:8–18, July 1970. **1D200**
A retracing of the series of events in England and Colonial America that led to the adoption of the First Amendment to the Constitution. The author dispels the myth that freedom of the press was cherished in Colonial America; conflict over diversity of opinion was diverted by living in one of the closed enclaves with co-believers. Printing was strictly controlled in all the colonies and popular assemblies were more severe than royal governors. The author discusses the case of John Peter Zenger, the circumstances surrounding the adoption of the First Amendment, the first challenge to the Amendment by the Sedition Act of 1798, Senator Calhoun's attempt to keep abolitionist literature out of the mails, Comstock's use of the mails to censor obscenity, and the more recent efforts to suppress ideas considered politically subversive. While Americans have greater freedom of expression today than ever before, that freedom constantly must be guarded.

Doyle, M. W. "Obscenity Revisited: From Morality to Manners." *New Zealand University Law Review*, 6:68–73, April 1974. **1D201**

Re: *Police v. Drummond* (1973), in which the New Zealand Court of Appeals "rejected the older formulation which emphasized the moral damage to the listener or reader and clearly stated that it was more concerned with the manner of expression rather than the content of the matter that was being expressed."

Doyle, Vincent, and Hoyt Gimlin. "Prosecution and the Press." Washington, D.C., Editorial Research Reports, 1967. (*Editorial Research Reports*, 2:481–96, 1967) **1D202**
Content: Crime coverage and criminal justice (including references to Warren Commission's criticism of the press, and coverage of the Hauptmann and Sheppard trials); the law and free press and fair trial (including prejudicial publicity and contempt of court, and the ban on televising of court proceedings); and proposals for assuring fairer trials (including British rules, American proposals, and codes of conduct).

Drabelle, Dennis J., and William F. Taylor. "The President, the Fairness Doctrine, and Political Access to the Broadcast Media." *St. Louis University Law Journal*, 15:73–93, Fall 1970. **1D203**
"In recent months the President of the United States has far outstripped his predecessors in using prime-time television as a forum for expounding his views to the nation." In reaction, political parties, antiwar groups and other groups, disturbed at what they regard a presidential monopoly of access to the people, have filed complaints and petitions with the FCC. The purpose of this article is to analyze the Federal Communications Commission's decisions disposing of these petitions and to discuss the general application of the fairness doctrine.

Drake, Gordon V. *Is the School House the Proper Place to Teach Raw Sex?* Tulsa, Christian Crusade, 1968. 40p. **1D204**
A staff member of Rev. Billy James Hargis's Christian Crusade attacks the sex education program of SIECUS (Sex Information and Education Council of the U.S.) and recommends action to keep the materials and philosophy of SIECUS out of the schools.

———. *SIECUS, Corrupter of Youth*. Tulsa, Christian Crusade, 1969. 64p. **1D205**
An attack on the Sex Information and Education Council of the U.S. (SIECUS), conceived by Dr. Mary Calderone for the "humanistic sputum" of sex education introduced in high schools.

Drakeford, John W., and Jack Hamm. *Pornography: The Sexual Mirage*. Nashville, Tenn., Nelson, 1973. 189p. **1D206**
An attack on pornography which the authors believe is an insidious evil that fails to fulfill the promise of sexual stimulation. "In this volume we will focus on the phantasmagoria of por-

nography, its various forms, techniques, media, the activities it promotes, the amazing investigation by a presidential commission, the arguments for pornography and their answer, the legal mess, the indictments against pornography, and finally a plan of action for meeting the situation." The action called for: (1) make your voice heard; (2) present a positive view of sex; (3) mobilize public opinion; (4) hit them in the cash register; (5) enlist the women; (6) emphasize the consumer angle; and (7) utilize the legal channels. Cartoons throughout the book are by Jack Hamm.

Draper, Elizabeth. "Attitude of States and Their Laws." In her *Birth Control in the Modern World*. 2d ed., Harmondsworth, England, Penguin, 1972, pp. 217–63. **1D207**

Dresner, Hal. *The Man Who Wrote Dirty Books*. New York, Simon & Schuster, 1965. 192p. (Paperback edition, Fawcett World Library, 1966). **1D208**
"A novel written not by but about The Man Who Wrote Dirty Books." The dust jacket reads: The Man Who W——e Dirty B——s; and this jacket is covered by a plain brown wrapper bearing the printing, "This is a plain brown wrapper." In the copy acquired by the bibliographer is a red bookmark bearing the wording "Dirty Book Mark."

Dresser, Glen S. "First Amendment Protection Against Libel Actions: Distinguishing Media and Non-Media Defendants." *Southern California Law Review*, 47:902–42, May 1974. **1D209**
"This Note will argue that, because media and non-media speakers have different options and responsibilities, access to the constitutional privilege as a defense to libel should be different for each group. While media speakers would be entitled to full *Times* [New York Times v. Sullivan] protection, non-media speakers should be subject to a more restrictive standard." The author concludes that "since the non–media speaker does not share the same functional role or bear the same self-disciplining characteristics of the typical media speaker, he should be held to a higher standard of care than the *Times* standard. This proposed standard would allow for better accommodation of the conflicting interests of speech and individual reputation than would the possible extension of *Times* to private libels."

Drew, Donald J. "Censorship or Criticism?" In his *Images of Man; A Critique of the Contemporary Cinema*. Downers Grove, Ill., Inter–Varsity, 1974, pp. 91–97. **1D210**
In this view of film censorship from a Christian point of view, the writer believes the best form of censorship is refusal to see a film. But this calls for fair appraisals of a film's form, validity, and content from honest film criticism, which is often lacking. He charges many critics with dishonest and pernicious reviewing by

which "debauchery not only is glamorized but made to appear positive and virtuous."

Drew, Elizabeth B. "Is The FCC Dead?" *Atlantic*, 220:29–36, July 1967.
1D211
"The only obstacle to total domination of radio and television broadcasting in this country by self-interested corporate giants or provincial monopolies is the Federal Communications Commission. The role of the FCC in the communications field in general and its failure to influence the broadcasting industry in particular are explored in detail by Mrs. Drew."—Editor.

Drewry, Gavin. "The Official Secrets Acts." *Political Quarterly* (Great Britain), 44:88–93, 1973.
1D212
A discussion of the findings of the Franks Committee which studied the working of Section 2 of the Official Secrets Act of 1911. Another view is presented by R. J. S. Baker, pp. 214–16.

Dreyer, John J. "Whiteners for the Red, Black and Blue Library." *Library Journal*, 98:606–10, 15 February 1973; *School Library Journal*, 19:30–34, February 1973.
1D213
Censorship efforts of the Constitutional Heritage Club at the Cincinnati Public Library. The organization has directed its efforts against books by black authors, United Nations, fluoridation, sex education, and communism. CHC is supported in its campaign to reform the library by the Real Friends of the Library (RFL), headed by a member of the John Birch Society.

Drinnon, James E. *The Application of the First Amendment Right of Freedom of Expression to the Campus*. Knoxville, Tenn., University of Tennessee, 1971. 117p. (Ed. D. dissertation, University Microfilms, no. 72–5433)
1D214
"Does the First Amendment right of freedom of expression apply to the college or university campus? If it does apply to the campus, what variations are required because of the peculiar need of the campus community? What guidelines may an administrator use in developing rules and regulations which modify or limit the right of freedom of expression on the campus? These questions were the subject of this study."

"Drug Pricing and the Rx Police State." *Consumer Reports*, 37:136–40, March 1971.
1D215
A discussion of the laws of thirty-seven states that expressly prohibit drug-price advertising and the efforts of one drug chain, Osco, to challenge this threat to free competition in the courts.

Drummond, Alexander M., and Russell H. Wagner, *eds*. "Censorship." In

their *Problems and Opinions: A Book of Discussions of Persistent Questions for Classes in Speaking and Writing*. New York, Century, 1931, pp. 413–52.
1D216
Content: Censorship or Discussion by Joyce O. Hertzler. Freedom from Censorship by the National Council on Freedom from Censorship (N6o). The Absurdities of Censorship by Bronson Cutting. I Believe in Censorship by Hamlin Garland. Censorship and the Censors by George Jean Nathan. Censor and the "Movie Menace" by Ellis P. Oberholtzer (O5). Moving Pictures, Books, and Child Crime by R. C. Sheldon. Censorship and the Parents by Newell D. Hillis. The Christian Science Censor by Henry R. Mussey (M612).

Du Bester, Ernest W. "Florida Right to Reply Statute Does Not Violate First Amendment Freedom of Press." *Catholic University Law Review*, 23:621–31, Spring 1974.
1D217
Re: *Tornillo v. Miami Herald Publishing Co.*, 418 U.S. 241 (1974). "It is the purpose of this note to analyze the concept of first amendment freedoms in relation to a state-fashioned right of reply. The principal question to consider is whether a state 'right to reply' statute, which requires newspapers to publish, without charge, replies of political candidates whom they criticize during election campaigns is violative of the first amendment freedom of the press." The Florida court's upholding the state law was overturned by a subsequent decision of the U.S. Supreme Court which declared the Florida statute unconstitutional.

Dubois, Jules. *The Fight for Freedom in Latin America*. Lawrence, Kans., William Allen White School of Journalism, University of Kansas, 1960. 22p. (11th Annual William Allen White Memorial Lecture)
1D218
The Latin American correspondent of the *Chicago Tribune* and for ten years chairman of the Freedom of the Press Committee of the Inter American Press Association, reviews the struggle for press freedom in Latin American countries against dictatorship and Communist influence. In particular, he discusses the plunder of Buenos Aires' paper, *La Prensa*, by the Peron regime and the more recent events in Castro's Cuba.

Ducat, Craig R. *Dimensions of Jurisprudence and Judicial Decision-Making in the Law of Obscenity*. Minneapolis, University of Minnesota, 1970. 429p. (Ph.D. dissertation, University Microfilms, no. 71–8144)
1D219
A series of five separable studies which explore a number of questions fundamental to the study of public law in the context of observations drawn from the law of obscenity. "The end product of these studies is a dilemma; those standards most consistent with the proper role of the criminal law in a constitutional democracy seem to be least libertarian and least neutral; and those standards least compatible with the premises of law in the American constitutional system stimulate legal judgments which are most libertarian and also most independent of the decision-maker's value judgment."

Duchek, Douglas F. "The Right of Access to the Press." *Nebraska Law Review*, 50:120–36, Fall 1970.
1D220
"This comment will examine the status of editorial advertisements which depend on another's printing presses and established circulation to reach the public . . . . The similarities and distinctions between newspapers, private property and broadcasting provide the bases for this discussion."

Dudley, Bruce M. *Censorship and Control of the Small College Student Newspaper*. Athens, Ohio, Ohio University, 1967. 136p. (Unpublished Master's thesis)
1D221
A mail survey of 292 college newspapers, 218 responding, indicated about one-fourth of the papers experienced censorship. About one-half reported that a staff member had been forced to resign, to print a retraction, or had been called before a college administrator.

Dué, Paul H. "Prejudicial Publicity Versus The Rights of the Accused." *Louisiana Law Review*, 26:818–47, June 1966.
1D222
"The purpose of this Comment is to examine each of these types of prejudicial publicity [pretrial and during the trial] in detail, considering the effectiveness of various devices presently available to counteract the prejudice, requirements the accused must meet to obtain these remedies, and proposed solutions to the problem of prejudicial publicity."

"Due Process of Law." In Robert O. Blanchard, *ed.*, *Congress and the News Media*. New York, Hastings House, 1974, pp. 468–72. (Reprinted from the *Times* (London), 5 June 1973)
1D223
Criticism of the lack of due process in the three trials of former President Nixon—the Senate, the grand jury and the press. The press, the editorial charges, is publishing prejudicial matter that would be contempt under British law.

Duffield, Eugene S. "Does First Amendment Cover Business Activities of Press?" *Advertising Age*, 42:3, 28, 30, 25 October 1971.
1D224
In testimony before a U.S. Senate committee the president of Popular Science Publishing Co. argues for the freedom of the press to include freedom of government dictates on advertising and freedom from being starved into

impotence by direct or indirect government interference with its source of revenue.

[Duffy, Sir Charles G.]. *Mr. Holmes' Defence of "The Nation."A Special Report of the Proceedings in the Case of The Queen v. Charles Gavan Duffy, Esq. Editor and Proprietor of the Nation Newspaper, in the Court of Queen's Bench, Ireland, Trinity Term, 1846. On an Indictment for a Seditious Libel*. Dublin, James Duffy, 1846. **1D225**

Duffy was charged with publishing a libel on her Majesty's administration in Ireland. While disclaiming any intention of controlling the jury, the judge declared the work was in his opinion a libel. The jury was unable to agree, despite being sent back twice by the judge, and the defendant was released.

Dulaney, William L. *An Assessment of Some Assertions Made Relative to the Fair Trial and Free Press Controversy*. Evanston, Ill., Northwestern University, 1968. 144p. (Ph.D. dissertation, University Microfilms, no. 69–1823) **1D226**

"This study assessed through content analysis 13 hypotheses related to the free press-fair trial controversy. Most of the hypotheses were derived from public assertions made by those interested in securing a fair trial for a defendant as guaranteed by the Sixth Amendment to the United States Constitution and in also maintaining a free press as guaranteed by the First Amendment."

Dunaj, Sherryll M. "Private Possession of Obscene Films Where There Is No Intent to Sell, Circulate, or Distribute." *University of Miami Law Review*, 24:179–83, Fall 1969. **1D227**

Re: *Stanley v. Georgia*, 394 U.S. 557 (1969). "If the First Amendment means anything, it means that a state has no business telling a man, sitting alone in his house, what books he may read or what films he may watch."

Duncan, Colin, and A. T. Hoolahan. *A Guide to Defamation Practice*. 2d ed. London, Sweet & Maxwell, 1958. 94p. Foreword by Sir Valentine Holmes. **1D228**

The work deals with the "highly technical and important preliminaries [in British defamation law], and particularly with the manner in which they have been modified by the Defamation Act, 1952," to assist counsel and solicitors in the preparation of defamation cases.

Dunkovich, Dona R. *Fair Trial and Free Press: A Categorically Annotated Bibliog-* raphy of the Views of the American Press and Bar, 1965–1971. Fullerton, Calif., California State University, 1973. 114p. (Unpublished Master's thesis) **1D229**

"This thesis presents a categorically annotated bibliography of articles and studies from law reviews and press journals on specific areas of the general 'fair trial and free press' issue."

Dunn, Bill. "Hush, Hush Sweet Journalist." *Quill*, 57(1):18–19, January 1969. **1D230**

A Florida newspaperman explores the pros and cons of privileged communications for journalists. "Only after all the alternative benefits of free flow of news against the benefits of the forced obligation to testify are weighed may the court ever come up with an interpretation with clearcut guidelines."

Dunn, Robert W., *ed. The Palmer Raids. Prepared by Labor Research Association*. New York, International, 1948. 80p. **1D231**

An account of the 1920 raids of headquarters of radical organizations under the direction of Attorney General A. Mitchell Palmer.

Durbin, Ann, *comp*. "Pressure Groups and School Library Censorship: A Bibliography." *Catholic Library World*, 46:119–21, October 1974. **1D232**

"A selected, annotated bibliography designed to give the reader an overview of significant literature dealing with the censorship of library materials."

Duscha, Julius. "After Watergate: The Press Still Under Pressure." *Bulletin of the American Society of Newspaper Editors*, 573:7–10, November–December 1973. **1D233**

A recent Conference on the Media sponsored by the Washington Journalism Center revealed that there is a continuing crisis of credibility facing the media and other American institutions including the presidency, Congress, the Supreme Court, corporations, and labor unions; there is also a trend to provide by law greater access to the press, and there is continuing erosion of First Amendment rights through court decisions. "As the conference discussions demonstrated, the lessons coming out of Watergate for the media were many, but one wonders whether the press has learned any of them."

———. "A Free and Accessible Press." *Progressive*, 38(1):41–43, January 1974. **1D234**

A report on efforts by the media to meet public criticisms of lack of diversity and access resulting from monopoly ownership. References are made to op–ed pages, CBS "Spectrum," pro and con editorials, and to the Media Access Project.

———. "Whitehead? Who's Whitehead?" *Progressive*, 37(4):39–43, April 1973. **1D235**

With no background in communications, thirty-four-year-old Clay T. Whitehead has become a powerful figure in the control of the television industry by virtue of his heading the Nixon Administration's Office of Telecommunications Policy. He "fronts for an Administration which has mounted the most sustained attack on the press in modern times." The article discusses some of the proposals for control of television offered by Whitehead and his staff.

———, and Thomas Fischer. *The Campus Press: Freedom and Responsibility*. Washington, D.C., American Association of State Colleges and Universities, 1973. 115p. (Sponsored by the John and Mary R. Markle Foundation) **1D236**

This report includes a discussion of the historical perspective of freedom of speech and of the press, legal distinctions between public and private colleges and universities, legal distinction between campus press and the public press, three ways to operate a university newspaper and the legal consequences thereof, legal consequences resulting from the use of the institution's name, responsibilities of the campus press, consequences of selection and deselection of student newspaper personnel, limitations on free speech, and a review of the important court cases, including *Tinker v. Des Moines Independent Community School District*, (1969). The study concludes that "the University is not *ultimately* responsible for every word uttered and every publication distributed on the campus. Neither is every student editor or writer *completely* free to express himself." Better solutions can be worked out between the parties involved than to resort to the courts. Anticipation of potential conflict is better than "knee-jerk reaction."

[Dutton, Anne.] *A Letter to Such of the Servants of Christ, Who May Have Any Scruple About the Lawfulness of Printing Any Thing Written By a Woman: To Shew, That Book-Teaching is Private, With Respect to the Church, and Permitted to Private Christians; Yea, Commanded to Those, of Either Sex, Who Are Gifted for, and Inclined to Engage in this Service. By A. D.* London, Printed by J. Hart, 1743. 12p. **1D237**

The author defends her right as a woman to publish, citing scriptures in behalf of female authors. "If it is the Duty of Women to seek the Edification of Their Brethren and Sisters, then is it their Duty to use the Means of it, whether it be in speaking, writing, or printing." Certain brethren had objected to a woman author appearing in print as contrary to the revealed will of God.

Dutton, Geoffrey, and Max Harris,

eds. *Australia's Censorship Crises*. Melbourne, Sun Books, 1970. 224p. **1D238**
Content: Censorship and the Law by Anthony Blackshield. Two Case Histories (*The Carpetbaggers*, *Lady Chatterley's Lover*) by Gordon Hawkins. Censorship in the Theatre by John Tasker. Cultural Despotism—Film Censorship by Eric Williams. Censorship and Literary Studies by S. Murray–Smith. Moral Protectionism by Geoffrey Dutton. Censorship in Queensland by Judith Wright and David Lake. A Terror of Words by Max Harris. A Note from a Victim by Richard Walsh. The appendix contains erotic passages from nine literary works, indicates at the end which are prohibited by Customs, showing the vagaries of the law. There is also the text of the Report of the Working Party of the Arts Council of Great Britain dealing with the Obscene Publications Act, and finally, the text of the decision of Judge Stable in *Donald Bradbury v. Norman Aubrey Staines*, a case of stage censorship.

Du Val, Benjamin S., Jr. "Free Communication of Ideas and the Quest for Truth: Toward a Teleological Approach to First Amendment Adjudication." *George Washington Law Review*, 41:161–259, December 1972. **1D239**
"The thesis of this article is that the implementation of a system of free expression should begin with an inquiry into the purposes of the freedom as guaranteed by the first amendment."

Dworkin, Martin S. "Classified Matter." *Educational Forum*, 33:379–83, March 1969. **1D240**
A critique of the motion picture film classification system. "Self-classification by film makers of their own works could be valuable as one source of data contributing to public decision. As the only system, or the inevitably dominant one, however, the new order of industry classification is flawed in its functioning as a public agency, and is as inherently dangerous in its potential success as any institution that begs the grand old question of the guardianship of guardians: Quis custodiet ipsos custodes?"

Dyal, Robert A. "Is Pornography Good for You?" *Southwestern Journal of Philosophy*, 7(3):95–118, Fall 1976. **1D241**

The author calls for the removal of all legal and authoritarian restrictions and controls of pornography, citing fourteen arguments: (1) Pornography is not necessarily obscene nor does it exhaust the category of obscenity. (2) Its legal status is ambiguous. (3) Illegality and immorality are not synonymous. (4) Private consensual behavior ought not to be the business of the law. (5) The rights of the individual should be protected. (6) Community consensus is more assumed than known. (7) The negative impact of pornography is more myth than reality. (8) Behavior of contemporary society ought not be dictated by standards of past morality. (9) Morality requires a framework of freedom to act autonomously. (10) Erotica may not only be harmless but beneficial to social health. (11) Pornography and art are not mutually exclusive phenomena. (12) As a mode of exploring the frontiers of consciousness, pornography is a way of knowing. (13) Pornography may serve to reveal the tragic, demonic element in human sexuality. (14) Preoccupation with pornography by consumption or censorship testifies to a need for a more profound integration of sexuality and existence.

Dybikowski, J. C. "Law, Liberty, and Obscenity." *University of British Columbia Law Review*, 7:33–54, Summer 1972. **1D242**
The author suggests that obscenity may be positively valuable in a number of ways, but independent of such claims, the author has defended the right of the purveyor to purvey and of the receiver to receive obscene materials. "My case is underpinned by strong and forceful conceptions rooted in our ability to carry on the business of democratic self-government and in our powers to develop as individuals. The defenses offered of obscenity laws, such as they are, are inadequate to overpower these conceptions."

Dyer, Robert F., and Philip G. Kuehl. "The 'Corrective Advertising' Remedy of the FTC: An Experimental Evaluation." *Journal of Marketing*, 38:48–54, January 1974. **1D243**
"This study examined message source and strength effects of the FTC's corrective advertising remedy. Two significant results associated with *broadcast* media corrective messages are: (1) FTC-source messages increased brand recall; and (2) FTC high-strength and

company low-strength messages ranked highly as information sources."

Dyson, Allan J. "Ripping Off Young Minds: Textbooks, Propaganda, and Librarians." *Wilson Library Bulletin*, 46:260–67, November 1971. **1D244**
"How does this [textbook] propagandist work? What effect has he had? Should we fight him directly—or lock horns with the whole concept of the textbook? In this article I hope to answer these questions at least in part. I will also briefly discuss some trends in the social studies curriculum which may help defeat the censors, trends which also may radically expand the role of the school and academic librarian."

Dziamba, John A. "The Free Press–Fair Trial Controversy—An Empirical Approach." *Connecticut Law Review*, 2:351–74, Winter 1969. **1D245**
The article shows that the law regarding the prejudicial effect of news coverage on the rights of the defendant to a fair trial is based on "implied prejudice" of judges. This judicial intuition has resulted in restraints on the release and publication of certain information. The author finds no consensus about the effect of the mass media on the formation of beliefs. He suggests that all relevant social-psychological data on the subject needs to be considered and advises against legislation on the subject as tending to establish a rigidity, highly resistant to change.

Dzida, Steven J. "No Place for Equal Space in the First Amendment." *Loyola of Los Angeles University Law Review*, 7:370–84, June 1974. **1D246**
While the right to "equal time" over the airwaves has gained judicial recognition, an analogous right to "equal space" in the printed media has not developed. The author discusses the constitutional issues involved in the Florida right of access statute in the case of *Tornillo v. Miami Herald Publishing Co.* (1973), which had not yet gone to the U.S. Supreme Court, and an advisory decision of the Massachusetts Supreme Judicial Court on a proposed access statute.

E

Eads, Arthur C. "*Stanley v. Georgia*: A Private Look at Obscenity." *Baylor Law Review*, 21:503–11, Fall 1969. **1E1**
The author concludes that in the U.S. Supreme Court's ruling in *Stanley v. Georgia*, "commercial regulation of obscene material has now been brought into direct conflict with the individual's expanding right of privacy. . . . Where commercial regulation stands in the path of the individual's right of privacy, the regulation must be removed. It is only logical that the individual has a right to purchase that which he has the right to possess. The right to purchase can only be given the individual at the expense of commercial regulation."

Eagle, Kenneth L. "Prior Restraint Enforced Against Publication of Classified Material by CIA Employee." *North Carolina Law Review*, 51:865–74, March 1973. **1E2**
"The scope of the Pentagon Papers case has recently been narrowed by the Court of Appeals for the Fourth Circuit in *United States v. Marchetti* ₍1972₎, in which the court affirmed the issuance of an injunction enforcing a secrecy agreement which had been exacted by the Central Intelligence Agency (CIA) from an employee as a condition of employment."

Eagleton, Thomas F. "We Must Work to Preserve Press Freedom." *Grassroots Editor*, 14(3):27–28, May–June 1973. **1E3**
In support of shield laws Senator Eagleton states: "If the Constitution prohibits Congress from making any 'law . . . abridging the freedom . . . of the press' . . . then I submit that it is also our duty to prohibit any other institution from violating that same freedom." There follows editorials from weekly newspapers for and against shield laws.

Earnshaw, John. *Thomas Muir, Scottish Martyr. Some Account of his Exile to New South Wales, his Adventurous Escape in 1796 across the Pacific to California, and thence, by Way of New Spain, to France*. Cremorne, Australia, Stone Copying Co., 1959. 84p. (Studies in Australian and Pacific History, no. 1) **1E4**
The author has uncovered much new material about Muir from sources in New South Wales, England, Scotland, Spain, Mexico, California, and Washington, D.C. Accounts of Muir's sedition trial are given in M565–67.

East, P. D. *The Magnolia Jungle; The Life, Times and Education of a Southern Editor*. New York, Simon & Schuster, 1960. 243p. **1E5**
Autobiography of "the iconoclast of Petal, Miss.," editor of *The Petal Paper*, and his continuous struggle against boycott by subscribers and advertisers, personal abuse, and threats of violence for writing frankly on local issues.

Eastland, James, and Abner J. Mikva. "Should Congress Ban Obscenity from the Mail." *American Legion Magazine*, 91:22–23, October 1971. **1E6**
Senator Eastland presents the case *for* postal censorship; Congressman Mikva *against* postal censorship. The readers are asked to let their senators and congressmen know their wishes by mailing an attached ballot.

₍Eaton, Daniel I.?₎ *The Pernicious Effects of the Art of Printing upon Society, Exposed. A Short Essay. Addressed to the Friends of Social Order*. London, Printed for Daniel I. Eaton, 1794? 16p. (Signed at end: Antitype) (Reprinted in Stephen Parks, *ed. The English Book Trade, 1660–1853*. New York, Garland, 1974, vol. 29) **1E7**
A satire suggesting that all books and printing presses be destroyed.

Eaton, Joel D. "The American Law of Defamation through *Gertz v. Robert Welch, Inc.* and Beyond: An Analytical Primer." *Virginia Law Review*, 61:1349–1451, November 1975. **1E8**
An extensive discussion of the law of defamation as it has been defined by court decisions, with emphasis on *New York Times v. Sullivan* (1964) and subsequent decisions through *Gertz v. Robert Welch, Inc.* (1974).

Eaton, Robert E. L. "The Promotionary Chaos: The Three Major Catalysts." *Vital Speeches*, 37:687–90, 1 September 1971. **1E9**
One of the three elements contributing to chaos in America, according to the national vice-president of the American Legion, is the news media. Freedom of the press is not accompanied by a sense of responsibility and a code of ethics. The educational system and political leadership are the other two elements.

Ebert, Roger. "Russ Meyer, King of the Nudies." *Film Comment*, 9(1):35–45, January–February 1973. **1E10**
An interview with Russ Meyer by Stan Berkowitz appears on pages 47–51.

———. "Who Knows What Evil Lurks in the Minds of Men." *Chicago Journalism Review*, 4(9):12–13, September 1974. **1E11**
A brief story, with pictures, on the work of the "Mad Brassiere Artist" who touches up offending movie ads.

Eckhardt, Robert C. "Mr. Agnew, You Are Wrong About The Press." *Congressional Record*, 116:37209–11, 14 October 1970. **1E12**
Following Vice-President Agnew's charge that the press had lost its neutrality, a Texas congressman made a survey of the press, finding that 68 percent had supported Nixon but that on particular issues there was great diversity of opinion. Contrary to Agnew's charges, the Eastern establishment press agreed editorially with the nation as a whole.

₍Edell, Marc Z.₎ "Constitutionality of Proscribing Drug Related Songs." *New York Law Forum*, 19:902–15, Spring 1974. **1E13**
A discussion of the Federal Communications Commission's directives to radio and television stations proscribing drug-related lyrics, and

the response of the court in the case of *Yale Broadcasting Co. vs. FCC* (1973).

Edelstein, Stephen J., and Kenneth Mott. "Collateral Problems in Obscenity Regulation: A Uniform Approach to Prior Restraints, Community Standards, and Judgment Preclusion." *Seton Hall Law Review*, 7:543–87, Spring 1976. **1E14**
The article focuses on prehearing prior-restraint issues in obscenity litigation. It examines "the considerations in determining the relevant community from which community standards are to be drawn, primarily as that issue relates to the estoppel effect of judgments." Finally, the article analyzes "the judgment-preclusion effect of a judgment of obscenity or nonobscenity on a subsequent proceeding involving identical materials."

Eden, Van N. "Obscenity: A Quick Look at Stanley v. Georgia." *Tulsa Law Journal*, 6:277–87, August 1970. **1E15**
Re: *Stanley v. Georgia* (1969), in which the U.S. Supreme Court "stretched the first amendment beyond its traditional proportions to insulate the individual's right to possess obscenity."

Edgar, Harold, and Benno C. Schmidt, Jr. "The Espionage Statutes and Publication of Defense Information." *Columbia Law Review*, 73:929–1087, May 1973. **1E16**
A detailed analysis of the current espionage laws with respect to their mandate on communication and publication of defense information, with suggestions of general principles that should control legislative action.

Edgar, Jerry A. "Obscenity Standards: What Is Obscenity? What Is a Community?" *Wisconsin Library Bulletin*, 70:203–4+, September–October 1974. **1E17**
An opinion on the role of Wisconsin cities in combating obscenity, considering federal and state statutes and court decisions, given to the League of Wisconsin Municipalities by their legal counsel.

Edhlund, Sandra. "Candor or Shame? Defining Obscenity by Statute." *Oklahoma Bar Association Journal*, 38:1333–45, 24 June 1967; *Catholic Lawyer*, 13:131–44, 177, September 1967. (Also in Wisconsin Legislative Reference Bureau, *Informational Bulletin* 66–73, August 1966) **1E18**
A summary of various judicial tests and definitions of obscenity, including the British Hicklin rule, the *Roth* test, and more recent tests in common law; an examination of various state obscenity statutes, including Florida's definition by multiple synonyms. The prevailing view of the U.S. Supreme Court is based

on the *Roth* decision with its three specifications: (1) the dominant theme as a whole appeals to the prurient interest, (2) it is patently offensive to present community standards, and (3) it contains no redeeming social value.

Edlavitch, Susan T. "The Fairness Doctrine and Access to Reply to Product Commercials." *Indiana Law Journal*, 51:756–82, Spring 1976. **1E19**
"This note will demonstrate that the FCC is not free to insulate standard product advertising from fairness obligations. Rather the Constitution and the first amendment principles embodied in the public interest standard of the Communications Act require application of the fairness doctrine to certain categories of product commercials."

Edmondson, Ronnie. "Pandering, First Amendment Rights, and the Right of Privacy." *Baylor Law Review*, 22:442–55, Summer 1970. **1E20**
Re: *Rowan v. United States Post Office Department* 397 U.S. 728 (1970), in which the U.S. Supreme Court upheld the constitutionality of 39 U.S.C., Art. 4009, which allows the addressee of a "pandering advertisement" to determine in his sole discretion that material advertised is offensive and to cut his household off from all subsequent mailings from that source.

Edwards, George. "Violence on Television—Who Is Responsible?" *Journal of the Producers Guild of America*, 11(2):25–27, June 1969. **1E21**
While opposing bureaucratic censorship and questioning whether TV creates violence in any society, Judge Edwards would like to see "an emphasis in television on some nonviolent choices in relation to programming on the entertainment side," and "some care exercised in relation to what was actively newsworthy that is presented in terms of violence in the newscasts."

Edwards, June K. "The Textbook Controversy: A Political Confrontation." *Christian Century*, 91:1064–66, 13 November 1974. **1E22**
The textbook controversy in West Virginia raises moral and ethical problems over rights and roles of children, parents, and professional educators in a democracy. "As taxpaying citizens, as human beings in a democratic society, fundamentalist parents are entitled to the same consideration for their wishes as anyone else. And conversely, students who want to read books like the 'Responding' series should have an equal right to enjoy a stimulating class without interference from people who personally object to these books. The majority should not rule in either case, nor the minority. All children and all parents have the right to demand that their interests, needs and desires be respected in the schools—especially since they have no choice about being there."

Efron, Edith. "The Free Mind." *Vital*

Speeches, 40:522–27, 15 June 1974. **1E23**
In an address given at a business seminar at Pepperdine University, the speaker criticizes the anticapitalist bias among American television newsmen which prevails despite the fact that their industry and jobs depend upon the system. The same television leaders who support government control of business in general object to controls over their own business on grounds of First Amendment freedom. Intellectual and political freedom and capitalism, she maintains, are inextricably linked. "If you destroy capitalism, you will inextricably destroy intellectual and political freedom." The First Amendment actually protects the marketing process of the intellectual product; it guarantees laissez-faire capitalism for ideas. Broadcasting is the most dramatic example of the state's violation of the First Amendment through its regulation of the marketplace of ideas. She calls on American businessmen to fight for the free marketplace of ideas in the media.

———. *How CBS Tried to Kill a Book*. By Edith Efron with the assistance of Clytia Chambers. Los Angeles, Nash, 1972. 187p. **1E24**
"An exposé of CBS News President Richard Salant's public relations campaign against *The News Twisters*—the 1971 best-seller that revealed political and racist bias in network news."

———. "Is Speech on Television Really Free?" *TV Guide*, 12(15):4–9, 11 April 1964. (Reprinted in Barry G. Cole, *ed.*, *Television; a Selection of Readings from TV Guide Magazine*. New York, Free Press, 1970, pp. 303–9) **1E25**
Criticism of the fairness doctrine in broadcasting, which spokesmen from both left and right blame for suppressing their views and, at the same time, invoke for protection. By its middle-of-the-road interpretation of the doctrine the networks have produced a "soggy tyranny of 'medium' opinion" which has pleased no one. The author calls for adoption of the "spectrum theory" by which wide divergence of opinion is offered to the listening and viewing public.

[———.] "Is There Bias in T.V. News?" *Freedom Journal (Church of Scientology)*, 16:9, February–April, 1974. **1E26**
In an interview Efron talks about bias in television news, the evaluation of *The News Twisters*, and some of the changes brought about by it.

———. *The News Twisters*. Los Angeles, Nash, 1971. 355p. **1E27**
The author, a staff member of *TV Guide*, finds the three television networks guilty of severe bias against Richard Nixon in their coverage of

the 1968 presidential campaign. Her findings are the result of a content analysis of television news which she conducted under the auspices of the Historical Research Foundation. She accuses the networks of being controlled by a "ruling intellectual elite determined to hold onto a position of influence in which it is now entrenched." In an epilogue, the author comments on possible solutions to three network myths revealed in her study: (1) the nonexistent liberal, to be counteracted by "political labeling"; (2) the missing intellectuals, to be solved by "spectrum commentary"; and (3) the nonpartisan middle, to be solved by "spectrum hiring." The book was warmly praised by such conservative reviewers as William F. Buckley, Jr. ("Everyone who has ears to hear or eyes to see knows that the television networks are biased. . . . What Edith Efron came up with is 'the proof.' ") and criticized by most liberal reviewers. In a review appearing in *Harper's Magazine* for March 1972, Professor Nelson W. Polsby, University of California political scientist, found the book itself "so filled with bias [using the author's own scoring procedures] as to be unworthy of serious consideration." The response from Columbia Broadcasting System's President Richard S. Salant and from Professor Charles Winick, employed by CBS to examine the methodology of the study, are separately entered in this bibliography.

————. "So This Is 'Adversary' Journalism!" *TV Guide*, 23(3):A5–A6, 18 January 1975.   **1E28**
A look at "adversary" journalism as it is practiced in six major stories on the administration of President Ford—journalism by antagonists "who seek to knock off individuals and causes that (rightly or wrongly) they hate."

————. "TV's Sex Crisis." *TV Guide*, 23(42):4–8, 18 October 1975; 23(43): 26–32, 25 October 1975.   **1E29**
"A two-pronged drive for censorship of TV's dramatic content is going on," to meet the pressures against sex and violence, the former assault led by conservative religionists, the latter by liberal social scientists. The author discusses the effect of the current sexual revolution on TV programming and the response from the viewing public.

————. "There Is A Network News Bias." *TV Guide*, 18(9):6–11, 1 February 1970.   **1E30**
A report on the conclusion of American Broadcasting Company newscaster Howard K. Smith, who cites coverage of the race question, Vietnam, Russia, and conservatives as proof of network liberal political bias.

Egan, Beresford, and P. R. Stephensen. *The Sink of Solitude. Being a Series of Satirical Drawings Occasioned by some Recent Events performed by Beresford Egan,* *Gent, to which is added a Preface by P. R. Stephensen, Gent, and a Verse Lampoon composed by Several Hands and now set forth for the first time, the whole very proper to be read both on Family and Public Occasions.* London, Hermes Press, 1928. [30p.]   **1E31**
This satire in text and drawings was inspired by British censorship of Radclyffe Hall's novel, *The Well of Loneliness,* found offensive because of its lesbian theme. The attack is addressed particularly against James Douglas of the *London Daily Express* who demanded the book be banned for putting British morality in peril. He wrote that he "would rather give a healthy boy or a healthy girl a phial of prussic acid than this novel." Stephensen responds that he would rather give the censor, Sir William Joynson-Hicks, a copy of the *Sunday Express* than a dose of prussic acid, and calls for the repression of Mr. Douglas as a public nuisance. Using the reviewer's own logic, he calls on the Home Secretary to put a stop to Mr. Douglas on the basis of his misuse of the English language and his advocacy of moral standards not held by all Britons. If necessary an Enabling Act should be passed to withdraw him. Egan's caricatures are aimed largely at Sir William Joynson-Hicks.

Ehlers, D. L. "Die Bibliotekaris en Sensuur; 'n Teoretiese Siening [The Librarian and Censorship: A Theoretical View]." *South African Libraries,* 38:218–23, January 1971.   **1E32**
Even if censorship is necessary in the country as a whole, libraries should be largely exempted so that they can offer the reader a wide range of all possible viewpoints.

Eich, William F. "From Ulysses to Portnoy: A Pornography Primer." *Marquette Law Review,* 53:155–71, Summer 1970.   **1E33**
A survey of the development of recent obscenity law in the United States under the following headings: Roth: The Build-Up and Aftermath; The 1966 Trio: Mishkin, Ginzburg, and Fanny Hill; Stanley and Ginsberg—A New Direction; The Sum Total—Confusion; The New Wave: Some Speculation on the Future of Obscenity Legislation.

Eimermann, Thomas E. *Free Press–Fair Trial: An Empirical Look at the Problem and Its Solution.* Urbana, Ill., University of Illinois, 1971. 250p. (Ph.D. dissertation, University Microfilms, no. 71–21113)   **1E34**
The dissertation examines the question of whether pretrial criminal news does actually prejudice jury verdicts. Empirical data, gathered from a jury simulation, lend support to the proposition that some limited types of information do prejudice jurors. Further data derived from content analyses and mailed surveys indicate that traditional trial remedies for neutralizing prejudicial publicity do not provide an adequate solution to the problem.

————. "The Free Press–Fair Trial Controversy Rides Again." *Topic: A Journal of The Liberal Arts,* 26:48–58, 1973.   **1E35**
The author observes that in the Watergate affair with its extremely visable press coverage "you have a classic example of free press–fair trial dilemma." Since the press in recent years has failed to provide adequate self-restraint, and traditional court remedies for dealing with prejudicial publicity have been ineffective, "some type of expanded use of the contempt power" is recommended.

————, and Rita J. Simon. "Newspaper Coverage of Crimes and Trials: Another Empirical Look at Free Press–Fair Trial Controversy." *Journalism Quarterly,* 47:142–44, Spring 1970.   **1E36**
A brief report on a study of the length and type of news coverage given to criminal cases by two local newspapers published daily in a midwestern community of about 100 thousand people, both before and during the trial.

Eisenberg, Lawrence D. "The Constitutional Law of Defamation and Privacy: *Butts* and *Walker.*" *Cornell Law Review,* 53:649–62, April 1968.   **1E37**
The Supreme Court, beginning with *New York Times Co. v. Sullivan,* has formulated a broad doctrine of freedom of speech and the press to comment on public officials and public figures: "If the 'public figure' label is expanded beyond *Hill* [*Time, Inc. v. Hill,* 1967], *Butts* [*Curtis Publishing Co. v. Butts,* 1967], and *Walker* [*Associated Press v. Walker,* 1966], the press will be the recipient of a nearly unrestricted license against which the 'mores test' and the 'actual malice' doctrine will afford little protection. . . . . There is only one way to strike a balance between the first amendment freedoms of speech and press, and the common law protections of privacy, name, and reputation—very carefully."

Eitner, Walter H. *An Inquiry into the Effects of Censorship on Some Major Nineteenth-Century American Novelists.* Denver, University of Denver, 1959. 192p. (Unpublished Ph.D. dissertation)   **1E38**
The study attempts to ascertain the effects of censorship on the novelist. "To what extent, historically, did the censor intimidate the novelist into a concern for extraliterary considerations? To what extent did he bring about a spoiling of fictionality? A cleaving to outmoded class distinctions? A reticence in language? A diminution of protest? A circumspection regarding human behavior? An impetus toward commercialization? Or, on the other hand, to what extent did the censor help induce a more clever subtlety? A finer craftsmanship? A fuller aggressiveness? A greater determination? Or, again on the record, did the censor simply waste the novelist's time?" Novelists considered: Charles

Brockden Brown, James Fenimore Cooper, Nathaniel Hawthorne, Herman Melville, Mark Twain, William Dean Howells, and Henry James.

Ek, Richard A. "Victoria Woodhull and the Pharisees." *Journalism Quarterly*, 47:453–59, Autumn 1972. **1E39**
The story of the nineteenth-century woman's liberation advocate and publisher of the New York paper, *Woodhull & Claflin Weekly*. When the young woman and her sister exposed the Beecher-Tilton sex scandal their paper was suppressed and she was jailed on obscenity charges. Unable to take her case to the people through her paper, she turned to the lecture platform. The eighty-three-year-old millionaire industrialist, Peter Cooper, came to her rescue by providing the hall, despite strong public protest. Cooper, a stern Puritan, had long been an advocate of free speech. To avoid arrest by Comstock agents, Mrs. Woodhull arrived disguised as an old woman, throwing off her cape only when she reached the platform.

Eldredge, Laurence H. "Practical Problems in Preparation and Trial of Libel Cases." *Vanderbilt Law Review*, 15:1085–92, October 1962. **1E40**
"The author discusses some of the more frequent problems that arise in defamation proceedings. Mr. Eldredge, drawing on his own experience in private practice, treats the action for libel in all its critical stages: investigation, pleading, and trial of the case. He stresses the point that only the expert should handle a defamation action and gives convincing reasons."—Editor

———. "Recent Developments in the Law of Defamation." *Journal of the Trial Lawyers Association*, 33:113–21, 1970. **1E41**
Re: *New York Times v. Sullivan* (1964) and subsequent U.S. Supreme Court cases dealing with defamation.

———. "The Spurious Rule of Libel Per Quod." *Harvard Law Review*, 79:733–56, February 1966. **1E42**
"Libel has proved to be one of the most misunderstood torts. Among the questions that have caused the greatest confusion is that of determining whether special damages must be pleaded and proved by the plaintiff when an alleged libel involves extrinsic facts. In his article Mr. Eldredge probes the murky field of the law. After discussing some of the general problems that have perplexed the courts, he argues that section 569 of the Restatement of Torts, which declares that all libel claims are actionable without proof of special damages, represents the prevailing view of courts in the United States and should not be altered."—Editor

———. "Variation on Libel Per Quod." *Vanderbilt Law Review*, 25:79–92, January 1972. **1E43**

A discussion of changes in the interpretation of the law of libel in section 569 of the American Law Institute's *Restatement of Torts*, involving libel per quod, that is, in light of extrinsic facts.

Elias, Erwin A. "Sex Publications and Moral Corruption: The Supreme Court Dilemma." *William and Mary Law Review*, 9:302–26, Winter 1967. **1E44**
The author believes that the only tenable position the Court can take in fulfilling its responsibility is to take account of both the possible effect of sex publications on overt moral conduct or moral standards, and to preserve the essential values of the First Amendment. In the long run "the law will be better served by an express adoption and application of a balancing test in this area, even though this would require that the Court undertake the truly formidable task of candidly evaluating on a case to case basis the extent and nature of the state's interest in avoiding moral corruption and under what circumstances that interest will be paramount to free speech values."

Eliot, T. S. "Censorship." *Time and Tide*, 9:1131, 23 November 1928. **1E45**
A letter to the editor commenting on G. B. Shaw's article on the Irish censorship in the 16 November issue.

———. "Literature and the American Courts." *Egoist*, 3:39, March 1918. **1E46**
Concerns the suppression of a number of the *Little Review* containing a story by Wyndham Lewis.

Elison, Larry M., and Gary L. Graham. "Obscenity: A Compromise Proposal." *Montana Law Review*, 30:123–39, Spring 1969. **1E47**
Censorship is probably unjustified in the area of obscenity; at a minimum it should be removed from criminal law and placed in the field of general social sanction and tort law. A tort action could be predicated on the general right of privacy which the author defines as intrusion or penetration into the home. Under the proposed theory, the zone of privacy for those under the age of eighteen would be expanded to include any exposure to matters offensive to local community standards.

Elkins, W. F. "Marcus Garvey, the *Negro World*, and the British West Indies, 1919–1920." *Science and Society*, 36:63–77, Spring 1972. **1E48**
How a New York City paper, *Negro World*, published by Marcus Garvey, stimulated black nationalism and socialism in the British West Indies following World War I. The paper was banned in most of the British colonies in the West Indies and led to a successful campaign initiated by J. Edgar Hoover in the Department of Justice to have Garvey deported from the United States to the West Indies.

Elledge, Melinda. *Action for Children's*

Television (ACT). Columbia, Mo., Freedom of Information Center, School of Journalism, University of Missouri at Columbia, 1971. 7p. (Report no. 265) **1E49**
"Using legal principles to attack the vulnerable broadcast industry, citizen groups have met with unprecedented success in forcing broadcasters to program in the public interest. This is an in-depth study of one such group. Unlike the others, however, ACT is seeking sweeping changes in network programming rather than attempting to challenge the licenses of specific stations."

Ellenburg, F. C. "Phantasy and Facts: Censorship and Schools." *Clearing House*, 45:515–19, May 1971. **1E50**
A review of the status of censorship in the schools, followed by advice as to what school boards and principals can do in developing an intelligent policy on book selection and review.

Elliott, John R., Jr. " 'Feeling Hot': Victorian Drama and the Censors." *Victorian Newsletter*, 49:5–9, Spring 1976. **1E51**
One of the reasons for the lifeless quality of Victorian drama was the fact of censorship. After sifting through more than a hundred volumes of correspondence of the Lord Chamberlain's Office, the author gives "a brief outline of the history of theatre censorship during the period and a few of the jucier examples of the censor's art." Among the plays banned by the Lord Chamberlain during Queen Victoria's reign were Dickens's *Oliver Twist*, Dumas's *Lady of the Camelias*, Sophocles' *Oedipus Rex*, Shelley's *The Cenci*, Ibsen's *Ghosts*, Shaw's *Blanco Posnet* and *Mrs. Warren's Profession*, Granville-Barker's *Waste*, and Gilbert and Sullivan's *Mikado*.

Elliott, Osborn. "The Case for Total Privilege." *Bulletin of the American Society of Newspaper Editors*, 544:4–7, September 1970. **1E52**
"Nothing less than a full and unqualified privilege for newsmen, empowering them to decline to testify as to *any* information professionally obtained, will truly preserve and protect the newsgathering activities or the media."

Ellis, Anthony L. "The Queen's Minister." In E. M. Smith-Dampier, *The Queen's Minister*. London, Melrose, 1922, pp. v–viii. **1E53**
A letter to the editor of the *Times* objecting to the Lord Chamberlain's ban of *The Queen's Minister* because of possible offense to the Royal Family. The letter, reproduced as an introduction to the text of the play, evoked considerable press correspondence. "Is he [the dramatist] to be warned off and told that he

may not depict on the stage any monarch later than King Charles II, for whose political security the censorship came into being?"

Ellis, Havelock. "What Is Obscenity?" *Esquire*, 6:48, 196–97, September 1936. **1E54**
Shifting social practices prove that obscenity is an idea born of ignorance and superstition. "It is by diving into the multifarious facts and vigorous arguments contained in [Theodore] Schroeder's book [*"Obscene" Literature and Constitutional Law*] that we may still find the most suggestive answer to the question which here faces us."

Ellis, J. S. "Obscenity and Free Speech." *Secular Thought* (Toronto), 33:339–44, September 1907. **1E55**
The editor takes issue with Theodore Schroeder's thesis that, since there is nothing obscene in nature, no offense can be committed by the exhibition or discussion of the natural body. However, he recognizes the need to amend present obscenity laws so that the judge and jury, not a post office clerk, should decide what literature is obscene and therefore unmailable.

Ellis, Richard W. "Requirements for Collection of Substantial Damages in Actionable Per Se Defamation." *North Carolina Law Review*, 46:160–68, December 1967. **1E56**
Re: *R. H. Bouligny, Inc. v. United Steelworkers* 270 N.C. 160 (1967), a defamation action arising out of a labor organization campaign.

Ellman, Ira M. "And Now a Word Against Our Sponsor: Extending the FCC's Fairness Doctrine to Advertising." *California Law Review*, 60:1416–50, September 1972. **1E57**
"Part I briefly reviews the principles underlying the fairness doctrine and part II describes the FCC's application of these principles to commercials. Part III suggests how the [Federal Communications] Commission should deal with three possible categories of commercial announcements. Part IV discusses the complainant's difficulties in obtaining a quantity or quality of reply time comparable to that of the original announcements, a fairness problem that is especially difficult to resolve when the doctrine is applied to commercials. Finally, part V examines the financial impact an extension of the fairness doctrine to commercial announcements may have upon licenses."

Ellsberg, Daniel. "Ellsberg Talks." *Look*, 35(20):31–34, 39–42, 5 October 1971. **1E58**
An interview with the man who leaked the top-secret Pentagon Papers, "starting a battle in which the Supreme Court refused to stop the nation's press from making the papers public." Ellsberg is interviewed by J. Robert Moskin.

"Ellsberg: The Battle Over The Right to Know." *Time*, 98:6–12, 5 July 1971. **1E59**
"Regardless of the legal issues, the newspapers saw a higher morality in exposing the secret history of decisions that has led to a dangerously unpopular public policy. Appeal to a higher morality by an individual or an organization is often necessary—and always dangerous. No government of law can passively permit it—or simply repress it. Therein lies the Administration's dilemma." An extensive news report of the events in the Pentagon Papers case.

Elovitz, Mark H. "Libel Law: A Confused and Meandering State of Affairs." *Cumberland Law Review*, 6:667–87, Winter 1976. **1E60**
"It is the purpose of this Comment to review and attempt an identification of any definitive standard or broadly conceived first amendment rationale which the [U.S. Supreme] Court had called into operation when libel was at issue. It is with this scope and purpose in mind that *Austin* [*National Association of Letter Carriers v. Austin* (1974)] becomes pertinent."

Elstein, Herman, and Frederic R. Hartz. "Censorship Lives! Does Selection?" *New Jersey Libraries*, 2(3):14–18, Fall 1969. **1E61**
"Courts, legislatures and vigilante groups are not solely responsible for the difficulties writers encounter. The Victorian Mrs. Grundy image appears among librarians. Many librarians prove inept or fearful in dealing with controversial materials—whether political or sexual in nature. At the root of their failure may be a lack of ability to judge, and select, as well as the lack of a liberal education that promotes commitment to democracy and appreciation of literature."

"The Emerging Constitutional Privilege to Conceal Confidential News Sources." *University of Richmond Law Review*, 6:129–40, Fall 1971. **1E62**
"The purpose of this Comment is to evaluate the constitutional privilege to conceal confidential news sources, as expressed in *Caldwell v. United States* [1972] and to assess the probable impact of that decision upon the further development of a journalistic privilege."

Emerson, Thomas I. *The Bill of Rights Today*. New York, Public Affairs Pamphlets, 1973. 28p. **1E63**
In this concise popular presentation there are sections on freedom of expression and the right of privacy. Professor Emerson concludes that while attacks on freedom of expression have to some extent emanated from minority groups in our society, the real danger to the Bill of Rights comes from official authority. He cites evidence of government efforts to restrain publication of the Pentagon Papers, pressures against broadcasters, and demands of grand juries that newspaper reporters disclose information derived from confidential sources.

———. "Communication and Freedom of Expression." *Scientific American*, 227:163–64+, September 1972. **1E64**
Consideration of the entire subject of freedom of expression as a system based on "a series of fundamental rights, constitutive principles, working rules and social institutions that have an over all unity and are designed to perform specific functions in our society. . . . The system of freedom of expression, as it has developed in the U.S., is designed to achieve four separate but related objectives. The first is individual self–fulfillment. . . . Second, to borrow John Stuart Mill's formulation, freedom of expression is essential to the attainment of 'truth'. . . . Third, a system of freedom of expression is essential to popular decision-making in a democratic society. . . . Finally, a system of freedom of expression enables a society to find the proper balance between stability and change." The author concludes that, while a system of freedom of expression cannot alone save humanity, it may nonetheless help. "It provides the most civilized method devised so far for solving social problems while protecting the integrity of the individual."

———. "Freedom of Expression in Wartime." *University of Pennsylvania Law Review*, 116:975–1011, April 1968. **1E65**
"This article deals with the main problem areas concerning freedom of expression as it relates to war and defense. These areas include (1) the law of treason; (2) general criticism of the war effort; (3) more specific forms of expression which may lead to insubordination in the armed forces, obstruction of recruitment, or resistance to conscription; (4) other forms of protest; and (5) practical problems of protecting wartime dissent against illegitimate harassment." The author explores these problems, employing First Amendment doctrine that "maintenance of a system of freedom of expression requires recognition of the distinction between those forms of conduct which should be classified as 'expression' and those which should be classified as 'action'; and that conduct classifiable as 'expression' is entitled to complete protection against government infringement, while 'action' is subject to reasonable and non-discriminatory regulation designed to achieve a legitimate social objective."

———. "Information Is Power: The Danger of State Secrecy." *Nation*, 218:395–99, 30 March 1974. (Reprinted in *Current*, June 1974) **1E66**
In light of "the shocking peaks of government secrecy" in recent years and the baleful effect of secrecy on the operation of modern government, the author examines some of the basic philosophy and political considerations that underlie the use of secrecy in government,

makes note of some constitutional and statutory tools for dealing with the problem, and suggests some working rules for achieving a more just and effective mode of operation. He suggests specific areas where secrecy in a democracy can be justified—advice privilege that is part of the decision-making process, national security narrowly limited to military matters, some aspects of foreign affairs, collective bargaining, and personnel matters where rights of privacy is involved.

———. *The System of Freedom of Expression*. New York, Random House, 1970. 754p. **1E67**
"This book attempts to formulate the legal foundations for an effective system of free expression in the United States. Based on the principles underlying such a system, the dynamics of its operation, and the role of law and legal institutions in maintaining it, the author develops a comprehensive theory of the First Amendment designed to achieve a workable system attuned to present-day conditions. Professor Emerson contends that the Supreme Court has failed to produce such a theory. The court has at different times experimented with the bad-tendency test, the clear-and-present danger test, the incitement test, and various forms of a balancing test. But it has never settled on any coherent approach. . . . The theory of the First Amendment advanced in this book rests upon making a basic distinction between 'expression' and 'action'—between holding a belief, uttering an opinion, or communicating an idea on the one hand, and other forms of conduct on the other. 'Expression,' it is argued, must be given full protection by the law. 'Action' may be regulated, but not by suppressing expression. The main portion of the book is devoted to applying this full-protection theory of the First Amendment to the concrete problems that arise in the operation of the system."

———. "Where We Stand: A Legal View." *Columbia Journalism Review*, 10(3):34–39, September–October 1971. (Reprinted in *Bill of Rights Journal*, December 1971) **1E68**
Some of the questions answered by Professor Emerson in an interview: Would you trace the roots in law of the *New York Times* case? What influence do you believe the Court's 1971 decision will have on the freedom of U.S. news media? Did the Government ask for secret proceedings that would exclude the press? Would you place this case on a level with the John Peter Zenger case in its implications for journalistic freedom? Would you comment on recent cases of subpoenas of journalists' notes and films? Where do the news media stand in other areas such as libel laws? Where do we stand in assuring broadcast media First Amendment protection?

——— *et al.* "First Amendment and the Right to Know: A Symposium." *Washington University Law Quarterly*, 1976:1–36, 1976. **1E69**
"The question to which I address myself is

whether the right to know can be effectively incorporated into our legal structure, through development of an adequate constitutional theory and workable operating rules." The concept includes two closely related features—the right to read, to listen, to see, and to otherwise receive communications; and the right to obtain information as a basis for transmitting ideas or facts to others. The author concludes that the issue involves both the negative force of the First Amendment in protecting against government interference, but also the affirmative use of expanding the whole system of freedom of expression. The former embraces traditional doctrines, the latter involves "formulating government controls to allocate scarce facilities, to provide mandatory access to the means of communication, or to compel disclosure" and calls for new doctrine. "The use of the right to know in obtaining information from government sources, its significance in analyzing the extent of reporter's privilege, and the reconciliation of the right to know with the right of privacy, all take us into uncharted fields." Walter Gellhorn (pp. 25–28) and James C. Goodale (pp. 29–36) respond to Emerson's lecture. Gellhorn concludes that the First Amendment is being overworked and that "whether the right to know should take precedence over other rights is not to be determined by dogma, but by hard thinking and debate in a proper forum. The proper boundaries of the right to know cannot be fixed by recourse to a single abstract principle." Goodale questions the right of the courts to judge communications before they are made. "Such prejudgments are likely to erode the distinction between prior restraint and subsequent punishment." He fears that "the right to communicate may be eroded if the courts perform too many of the functions that have historically been performed without court help."

Emerson, Tony. *Mass Communication—Or Deception*. London, Key Issue Publications, 1975. 18p. **1E70**
"The object of this pamphlet is to show how, in the absence of direct censorship, the ₍British₎ establishment uses its power to exercise control over the minds of men: more precisely, to show who has control over the media of mass communication, how this control is used, and finally, to look at the political, social, and economic consequences of the masses being at the receiving end of a 'controlled' (i.e., distorted, as I shall show) supply of information."

Emery, Alfred C. *An Oath of Freedom*. Salt Lake City, Division of Continuing Education, University of Utah, 1971. 36p. (Thirty-fifth Annual Frederick William Reynolds Lecture) **1E71**
A discussion of the meaning of the First Amendment, particularly as it applies to universities. The author traces the development of the concept of freedom of expression in British and American history, and shows how the meaning has been interpreted over the years by the courts. "The right to speak, the right to hear, and the right to peacefully assemble, are protected by both academic freedom and the

First Amendment, and, in case of doubt, the university, like the state must weigh the scales in favor of free expression." The concept of academic freedom is broader than the First Amendment which was designed as a limitation on government power. Academic freedom places "an affirmative obligation on the institution and its members to encourage the free exchange of ideas."

Emery, Edwin. "Freedom of the Press, the New Deal, and the Guild." In his *History of The American Newspaper Publishers Association*. Minneapolis, University of Minnesota Press, 1950, pp. 218–46. **1E72**
Long a staunch defender of the freedom of the press, the American Newspaper Publishers Association during the thirties opposed a large portion of the New Deal legislative program and also the unionization of editorial employees by the American Newspaper Guild, on grounds that both government and guild were encroaching on constitutional freedoms.

———. "John Peter Zenger and the End of Seditious Libel." *Scholastic Editor*, 55(1):25–27, September 1975. **1E73**
A recounting of the events in the John Peter Zenger trial and their significance, prompted by a visit to the Zenger Museum in New York.

Emery, Michael C. "Can Fairness Be Achieved Through Forced Access?" *Review of Southern California Journalism*, 12:10, September 1974. **1E74**
A discussion of the pros and cons in the debate over forced access to the media, a debate which has brought together strange bedfellows.

———, *ed.* *Pentagon Papers*. 36 slides, 2 × 2 mount. Minneapolis, Vis-Com, 1975. Printed guide. **1E75**
"The nation's leading dailies portray the courtroom and pressroom drama of June 1971 ending with the Supreme Court decision upholding press freedom."

———, and Ted C. Smythe, *eds*. *Readings in Mass Communications*. Dubuque, Iowa, Brown, 1972. 502p. **1E76**
Chapter 1, Increasing Access to the Mass Media: Multiplying Media Voices by Edwin Diamond. Access to the Press: A New Concept of the First Amendment by Jerome A. Barron. Right of Access and Reply by Clifton Daniel. What the FCC Must Do by Nicholas Johnson. Broadcast Regulation by Contract by Richard Jencks. Asleep at the Switch of the Wired City by Fred Friendly. Chapter 2, Increasing Control of the Mass Media: How

Community Press Councils Work by Donald E. Bregnolo. The Credibility Gap and the Ombudsman by Norman E. Isaacs. "Reporter Power" Takes Root by Edwin Diamond. Newsmen and Their Confidential Sources by Abraham S. Goldstein. The Selling of the Pentagon by Frank Stanton. Is Muckraking Coming Back? by Carey McWilliams. Chapters 9 and 10 carry speeches on news bias and responses, editorials on the use of classified material, and an article on media monopoly, Let's Protect Our Dying First Amendment by Bryce W. Rucker.

Emery, Michael C. *et al.* "Press Freedom: Maintaining Fragile Guarantee." *Publishers' Auxiliary*, 110(12):11–18, 25 June 1975.   **1E77**
Part I of a twelve-part series on Journalism Bicentennial History deals with press freedoms: Press Freedom; Maintaining Fragile Guarantee by Michael Emery. British Control Weakened by Zenger Flap. England Attempted to Constrain the Press by Mary Ann Yodelis. Feud Leads to Death for "Uncle Wes" by Joe Snyder. Most of the articles were written by members of the Association for Education in Journalism, under the direction of Michael C. Emery.

Emery, Walter B. "A Cross-Media Orientation in the Teaching of Freedom of Speech." In Speech Association of America. *Abstracts, 54th Annual Meeting*, Chicago, The Association, 1968, pp. 18–19.   **1E78**
"The emphasis in this presentation will be on freedom and responsibility as they relate to the print and broadcast media, motion pictures, and other systems of mass communications."

———. "Selected Studies of Broadcast Censorship in Five Countries." *Quarterly Journal of Speech*, 57:259–65, October 1971.   **1E79**
This study of broadcast censorship in Russia, China, Spain, Portugal, and France, indicates the comparative freedom in broadcasting enjoyed in America.

Endore, Guy. "War Yes, Sex No." *Push Pin Graphic* 43:1–6, 1963. (Condensed from talk given before the graduating class of the School of Library Service, University of California at Los Angeles, 25 May 1962)   **1E80**
An essay on the irony of looking upon sex as shameful, while glorifying the killing of men in war, a fact reflected in the library's card catalog which indicates most military books are on the open shelf, many sex books are locked in special collections. He tells the story of the Marquis de Sade, one of the most sexually profligate men of all times, speaking of Napoleon

who had been responsible for jailing him and destroying his writings: "I never killed a man." "So vile is still the name of Sade that when Eichmann, a year ago, was much in the news, reporter after reporter spoke of him as a sadist. But Eichmann killed millions whereas Sade never killed anyone. Should not Eichmann have been called Napoleonic rather than sadistic?"

Engberg, Edward. " 'A Free and Responsible Press': Where Are They Now?" *Center Magazine*, 1(1):22–25, 98–102, October–November 1967.   **1E81**
On the twentieth anniversary of the publication of the report of the Commission on Freedom of the Press, largely ignored at the time by the press it criticized, the author reconsiders the various recommendations on establishing "a free and responsible press." "The threat which the Commission saw coming to freedom of the press proceeds from its belief in an axiom in political physics I have characterized elsewhere as the 'rise-up theory' of reform. If those with the power over mass communication continue to abuse it, society, recognizing the impotence of the First Amendment to guarantee the flow of ideas, will rise up to seek redress by exercise of Government."

Engdahl, David E. "Requiem for Roth: Obscenity Doctrine Is Changing." *Michigan Law Review*, 68:185–236, December 1969.   **1E82**
Since recent obscenity decisions of the U.S. Supreme Court "indicate that the regime of *Roth* [*Roth v. United States*, 1957] has ended, it is important to determine what approach will arise to replace it. This Article has, through an analysis of existing constitutional law, suggested a possible approach. According to that approach, obscene expression should be treated no differently from nonobscene expression, and the only important matter for examination is the application of familiar constitutional standards to the particular dangers posed by obscenity. Since the legitimate federal interest in regulating obscenity is extremely limited, the primary concern of this Article has been an examination of the bases of permissible state regulation." The author proposes a framework on which to develop state obscenity legislation. Stanley K. Laughlin, Jr., responds to the author's views in the June 1970 issue.

Engelhardt, Robert W. *Freedom of Information Laws in New York State: Status and Recent Developments*. Milwaukee, Marquette University, 1974. 409p. (Unpublished Master's thesis)   **1E83**
"New York is one of a handful of states which have failed to enact a statewide 'open meetings law.' " The thesis "analyzes open meetings proposals before the State Legislature and studies development of a complex 'Freedom of Information bill'—originally modeled after the 1966 federal law, but revised substantially."

Engelman, Stephen B. "First Amend-

ment Prospective: The Gag Rule and Free Speech." *Chicago-Kent Law Review*, 51:597–611, 1974.   **1E84**
"The constitutionality of the gag rules [which prohibit judicial personnel from making extrajudicial statements which are likely to interfere with a fair trial] has recently been upheld in *Chicago Council of Lawyers v. Bauer*, (N.D. Ill. 1974). This note will analyze the reasoning of the district court in determining the constitutionality of the gag rules and their limit on free speech, assess the soundness of the court's decision to narrow the old standard defining the limits of free speech, and point out the alternatives available to the Seventh Circuit on appellate review."

Enger, Isadore, Guy T. Merriman, and Ann L. Bussemey. *Automatic Security Classification Study. Final Report*. Hartford, Conn., Travelers Research Center, 1967. 61p. (Defense Documentation Center, Report no. AD 660 120)   **1E85**
A study made for the Department of Defense of the feasibility of using computers to assign the security classification (unclassified, confidential, secret) to textual material.

England, Claire. *The Climate of Censorship in Ontario: An Investigation into Attitudes Toward Intellectual Freedom and the Perceptual Factors Affecting the Practice of Censorship in Public Libraries Serving Medium-Sized Populations*. Toronto, University of Toronto, 1974. 270p. (Unpublished Ph.D. dissertation)   **1E86**
The study embraced an analysis of attitudes of public librarians in six Ontario cities toward intellectual freedom and censorship. "Using a specifically developed method, it was found that, after allowing for the budget, a librarian's attitude toward intellectual freedom is the single best predictor of actual censorship in library collections."

———. "Comments on Obscenity: A Review of Recent Reform Commissions." *Canadian Library Journal*, 30:415–19, September–October 1973.   **1E87**
Comments on the reports of the U.S. Commission on Obscenity and Pornography, the British Longford Report, and the Canadian Law Reform Commission report, *Criminal Law—Obscenity*.

———. "The Librarian as Censor." *IPLO Quarterly* (Institute of Professional Librarians of Ontario), 15:5–11, July 1973.   **1E88**
A review of library literature on censorship with special attention to Canadian commentary. The author notes that "overall, Canadian librarians seem relatively unconcerned about censorship issues," and there is less coverage of

these events in library literature than similar events in the United States.

An Englishman. *Liberty of the Press in India; A Review of the Code of Bengal Regulations, Founded on an Enactment of Marquis Cornwallis, in 1793, Tracing the Influence of Discussion and its Nature at certain Periods, and Examining Some of the Most Prominent Measures of Civil Polity, with a Reference to their Actual Result.* London, William Davis, 1826. 66p. (Dedicated to Richard Hume, M. P., from An Englishman, On the Banks of the Ganges, 1825) **1E89**

Enoch Pratt Free Library, Baltimore. *How Baltimore Chooses: Selection Policies of the Enoch Pratt Free Library.* 4th ed. Baltimore, The Library, 1968. 58p. **1E90**
A comprehensive guide to selection of library materials, including policy on controversial materials, books on sex, religion, drugs, and pseudoscientific works. Separate sections deal with selection of materials for children and young adults.

Epstein, Daniel. *The Anatomy of AIM.* Columbia, Mo., Freedom of Information Center, School of Journalism, University of Missouri at Columbia, 1973. 6p. (Report no. 313) **1E91**
"Washington, D.C. pressure-group 'Accuracy in Media' (AIM) persistently criticizes media imbalance, distortion and bias. Some of AIM's critics claim the organization has a flourishing right wing bias of its own, a charge AIM's executive secretary Abraham Kalish denies."

Epstein, Edward J. "Bias of Network News." *Human Events*, 34:552–65, 15 June 1974. **1E92**
"The New York view, through which all network news is percolated, tends to stress the need for reform and change; the geographic contours of network news tend to focus attention on a few metropolitan areas which have been the drumhead for causes and movements challenging the status quo; the need to create national news tends to amplify local problems into apparent national crises; and the action requisite tends to direct the camera toward violent confrontations. Not all stories, or all newsmen, follow these underlying directions, but the attraction is sufficient so as to produce a unique version of national news on television." The result is not the product of willful bias, but the system.

———. "What Happened vs. What We Saw; The War in Vietnam." *TV Guide*, 21(39):6–10, 29 September 1973; 21(40):20–23, 6 October 1973; 21(41): 49–54, 13 October 1973. **1E93**
"It is no doubt true that television was to a large extent responsible for the disillusionment with the war, as those in the media take relish in pointing out. But it is also true that television must take the responsibility for creating—or, at least, reinforcing—the illusion of American military omnipotence on which much of the support of the war was based." The Tet offensive of 1968 shattered the invincibility of American progress and put correspondents into immediate contact with the horrors of war, the destruction, the atrocities—which they passed on to the American people. The military no longer were able to control the movement of the press or conceal the nature of the conflict.

Epstein, Julius. "Epstein v. Resor, or the Emasculation of the Freedom of Information Act." *Lincoln Law Review*, 7:82–99, December 1971. **1E94**
The plaintiff in the case *Epstein v. Resor* (1970), discusses his suit against the Secretary of the Army under the Freedom of Information Act to get access to the army's "top secret" file on Operation Keelhaul, concerning forced repatriation of anti-Communist replaced persons during and after World War II. The U.S. Supreme Court upheld a lower court decision in favor of the army's claims of exemption, a decision which the author believes has emasculated the Freedom of Information Act.

Epstein, Lisa, *comp. Newsman's Privilege: An Annotated Bibliography, 1967–1973.* Sacramento, Calif., California State Library, Law Library, 1973. 19p. Processed. **1E95**

Epstein, William H. *John Cleland; Images of a Life.* New York, Columbia University Press, 1974. 284p. **1E96**
A considerable portion of this biography of Cleland is devoted to his work, *Memoirs of a Woman of Pleasure (Fanny Hill)*, first published in England in 1749—the arrest and trial of the author, subsequent attacks on the book, ending in 1963 when the New York State Supreme Court cleared the work of charges of obscenity, making the first legal publication of the work in the United States.

Ernst, Morris L. "Introduction" to Radclyffe Hall, *The Well of Loneliness.* Victory edition. New York, Covici-Friede, 1929, pp. xiii–xix. (The Victory edition consists of two hundred and twenty-five copies, signed by the author) **1E97**
The attorney for the defense in the case of *The Well of Loneliness* before the New York Court of Special Sessions in 1928 writes of the events which began with the seizure of 815 copies of the book from the publisher at the instigation of John S. Sumner of the New York Society for the Suppression of Vice. Included is the text of Judge Salomon's decision for a unanimous court freeing the work. In his general observations on the work of the Vice Society and the nature of censorship and obscenity, Ernst states: "The attack on *The Well of Loneliness* by

the Vice Society is important to the citizens of the United States because it represented a new line of offense. Even while admitting that the work was pure in words, and beautifully written, its suppression was demanded because the theme was said to be objectionable. This was the first case in America where basic concepts had been attacked. . . . The charges rested on the opinion that adults should not be allowed to read any serious discussion of the social problems that accompany inversion or perversion, for reading means knowledge and knowledge might lead to sympathy and understanding."

[———.] "The Relationship of Literacy to Standard of Living and Censorship Activity." *Soundings* (University of California Library at Santa Barbara), 3(2):23–29, December 1971. **1E98**
An interview with Morris Ernst when his collection of banned books was presented to the library in April 1968.

———. "Sex Wins in America." *Nation*, 135:122–24, August 1932. **1E99**
The story of censorship of sex in the United States that began with its discovery in the 1870s by Anthony Comstock. "For nearly fifty years, from 1870 to 1920, campaigns were waged aginst everything connected with sex." Then the picture began to change as one effort after another to suppress works of literature with sex themes was thrown out by the courts. The author played a part in this effort, serving as lawyer for Joyce's *Ulysses* and other works. "The campaigns of the sex-hunters in the United States are virtually at an end unless the vendor of the picture or the tract enters the courtroom with an air of guilt and with the taint of stealth."

———, and Hallock Hoffman. *Ideas in the Marketplace.* 26 min. tape recording. Santa Barbara, Calif., Center for the Study of Democratic Institutions, 197?. **1E100**
In a conversation with Hallock Hoffman of the Center, Morris Ernst, internationally famous lawyer and civil liberties defender, talks about censorship and the need to enlarge the channels for disseminating a diversity of ideas. He speaks out against monopoly practices in the media, the surfeit of violence on television which, unlike obscenity, may have a causal relationship to behavior. He criticizes college students who use violence to silence speakers whose views they do not approve of, and college administrators who fail to take disciplinary action to protect the exercise of the First Amendment freedom of speech.

Errera, Roger. "A 'Secrets Act' for the USA?" *Index on Censorship*, 5:50–56, Spring 1976. **1E101**
The article studies the content of present and

proposed legislation concerning freedom of the press in the United States, particularly in matters relating to espionage and the disclosure of information on national security. A point-by-point examination is made of those sections of the Criminal Justice Reform bill (S. 1) and of a more strict version proposed by the Nixon Administration (S. 1400). Both bills reflect annoyance in the administration with both the press and Congress. In the present climate, an aftermath of Watergate, provisions curtailing freedom of the press are not likely to pass.

Erskine, Hazel. "The Polls: Freedom of Speech." *Public Opinion Quarterly*, 34:483–96, Fall 1970.   **1E102**
"Americans believe in free speech in theory, but not always in practice. . . . Very few have ever accorded complete freedom of expression to political extremists, at least since formal public opinion polls began their inquiries." The article reports on the polling by the seven major research groups from 1936 to 1970 in the area of freedom of speech, recording the response to forty-four questions.

Ervin, Sam J., Jr. "Advertising: Stepchild of the First Amendment." *Advertising Age*, 43(29):43–44, 17 July 1972.
          1E103
"Questions about freedom of speech, particularly 'commercial speech' (advertising) and its importance, or lack of it, in the American social and economic structure, are raised by Senator Ervin. From that, the senator from the tobacco-growing state of North Carolina leads into his objections to rulings, upheld by the U.S. Supreme Court, outlawing TV and radio commercials for cigarets and disallowing tobacco industry replies to anti-smoking announcements under the 'fairness doctrine.'"

———. "In Pursuit of a Press Privilege." *Harvard Journal on Legislation*, 11:233–78, February 1974. **1E104**
"This article attempts to explain why Congress was drawn to the press privilege issue and how Congress subsequently dealt with that issue. Part I describes the evolution of the controversy from before the beginning of the Republic to the opening of the 93d Congress in January 1973. It traces historical precedent, as well as the trappings of recent controversies, to give the reader a better understanding of why, after two hundred years of inaction, Congress was finally motivated to join the fray. Part II details the development of the issue, once seized upon by Congress, focusing particularly on its treatment in the Senate."

———. "Is the Press Being Hobbled?" *Popular Government*, 39(5):14–17, February 1973.   **1E105**
"The actions of the present administration appear to go beyond simple reactions to incidents of irresponsible or biased reporting to efforts at

wholesale intimidation of the press and broadcast media." Senator Ervin discusses in detail the issues of reporter's privilege and the shield bills before Congress.

———. "Secrecy in a Free Society." *Nation*, 213:454–57, 8 November 1971. (Also in *Current*, January 1972) **1E106**
The chairman of the Subcommittee on Separation of Powers of the U.S. Senate Judiciary Committee discusses the increased use of "executive privilege" by the president in keeping vital information from the Congress and the American people.

Erwin, David J. "Conflict of Laws: Defamation by Radio and Television." *Oklahoma Law Review*, 11:61–64, February 1958.   **1E107**
"With the advent of nation-wide television, the problems of the courts in relation to radio and multi-state defamation were again raised and the necessity of some semblance of a uniform or concrete law became readily apparent."

Esbin, Martha. *Sources of Information on Censorship in Iowa*. Iowa City, Iowa, School of Library Science, University of Iowa, [1970?]. 17p. Processed. **1E108**
Includes a list of organizations having information on censorship in Iowa and references to Iowa censorship in books and articles.

Escott, Richard H. *et al*. "Reality and Reason: Intellectual Freedom and Youth." *Top of the News*, 31:296–312, April 1975. (Also in *Intellectual Freedom Newsletter* [IFC-ALA], September 1974)   **1E109**
With the emergence of more realistic fiction, the nature of the children's and young people's collections in libraries has changed. In a conference sponsored by concerned units of the American Library Association, a panel addressed the question: Do librarians have an obligation to present to youth of all ages the gamut of what's being written? Participants: Richard H. Escott, Elaine Simpson, Patricia Finley, and Norma Klein.

Eshelman, David. "The Development of Shield Law for Newsmen: Acceleration in 1973." *Mass Communications Review*, 1(2):3–10, April 1974.   **1E110**
"During 1973 six states enacted legislation to shield newsmen from the compulsory disclosure power of the courts. Twenty-five states now recognize and have in force statutory protection for this aspect of the newsgathering process." The author lists five concepts that should be embodied in any shield law: protection should be afforded to any person connected with news gathering, eschewing any categorization and licensing; any medium disseminating information or opinion should be included; only two waivers should be allowed—a voluntary waiver by the newsgatherer, and waiver by an appeals court upon

an adequate showing of compelling need; protection should be afforded before any branch of government; and both the source of material and unpublished information should be protected.

———. "The First Amendment Argument for Newsmen Concealing Their Sources." In Speech Association of America. *Abstracts, 57th Annual Meeting*. San Francisco, The Association, 1971, pp. 11–12.   **1E111**
"In this presentation the arguments for a constitutional provision and the philosophical basis for legislative guarantees are traced in scholarly studies and legal cases."

———. *The Law of Compulsory Disclosure of News Source: The Status and Implications for a Federal Statute*. Warrensburg, Mo., The Author, 1973. 265p. Processed.
          1E112
"The purpose of this study was to investigate the status and implications of the law of compulsory disclosure on the right of newsmen to gather and report news. Existing limitations on newsmen, including the heritage of common law, statute law, and case law were examined to determine the legal issues and perimeters of the newsman's privilege and compulsory disclosure. Legal and communication theory was the basis for the analysis of the implications of the perimeters of the newsman's privilege and compulsory disclosure upon the flow of information in society." The study was financed by a research grant from the National Association of Broadcasters.

———, *comp*. "Freedom of Speech Bibliography: July 1973–June 1974. Articles, Books, and Court Decisions." In *Free Speech Yearbook, 1974*. Speech Communication Association, 1975, pp. 95–117.   **1E113**

———. "Freedom of Speech Bibliography: July 1974–June 1975. Articles, Books, and Court Decisions." In *Free Speech Yearbook, 1975*. Speech Communication Association, 1976, pp. 85–113.   **1E114**

Eshelman, David, and Alton Barbour. "Legal References on Newsmen and Compulsory Disclosure." *Journal of Broadcasting*, 17:37–50, Winter 1973.
          1E115
A list of books, journals, articles, state statutes, court cases, and other documents.

Eshelman, William R. "The Behemoths and the Book Publisher." *Library Trends*, 19:106–14, July 1970.
          1E116
A discussion of the recent movement of con-

glomerate corporations taking over book publishing, and the possible dangers to freedom of publishing. Countervailing forces are the vigor of other publishing companies, the activity of university presses, the risk of new independent publishers, and the realization by some conglomerates that publishing may not be as lucrative as they thought.

[————.] "Missouri Quicksand: An In-Depth Survey." *Wilson Library Bulletin*, 44:266–68, November 1969.
1E117

A chronology of events leading to and subsequent to the firing of Joan Bodger, consultant to children's services, Missouri State Library Commission, for her defense of an underground newspaper. Editor Eshelman criticizes the failure of the Missouri Library Association and its journal to come to the defense of Ms. Bodger.

Eshenaur, Ruth M. *Censorship of the Alternative Press: A Descriptive Study of the Social and Political Control of Radical Periodicals (1964–1973).* Carbondale, Ill., Southern Illinois University at Carbondale, 1975. 371p. (Ph.D. dissertation, University Microfilms, no. 76–13,235)
1E118

"The major purpose of this study was (1) to ascertain and measure the frequency and severity of controls on 'more radical' and 'less radical' alternative periodicals in the United States from 1964 through 1973 and the types of censorial agents, censorial actions, and their relationship to the urbanism of communities and the political liberalism of states and regions; (2) to identify all reported state and federal cases involving alternative periodicals during the period; and (3) to present significant findings together with case citations as to whether the decisions abridged the press freedoms of alternative periodicals."

Esplin, Fred C. "Looking Back: Clay Whitehead's OTP." *Public Telecommunications Review*, 3(2):17–22, March–April 1975.
1E119

"Because of his criticism of the news media, he will probably best be remembered as one of the White House crowd that tried to intimidate the press, and failed." The author believes Whitehead was motivated by principles as well as ambition and made a number of useful contributions before he and the Office of Telecommunications Policy became entangled in Nixon political fights.

[Esquire Magazine.] *Meet the Censor; A Summary of the Second Phase in the Case of Esquire v. Postmaster General, Together With a Complete Copy of the Decision in the U.S. District Court.* New York, Esquire, 1944. 23p.
1E120

Judge T. Whitfield Davidson of the Federal District Court in Washington, D.C., sustained Postmaster General Walker's contention that *Esquire Magazine* had violated the postal laws and therefore was not entitled to second-class mailing privileges. The U.S. Supreme Court overruled lower courts in 1946, limiting the power of the Postmaster General to censor magazines by means of withdrawing second-class mailing privileges. An earlier pamphlet on the case was listed in E150.

"Ethics and the Press." *Wall Street Journal*, 25 July 1967, p. 1. (Reprinted in David G. Clark and Earl R. Hutchison, eds. *Mass Media and the Law*, pp. 320–31)
1E121

An exposé of practices within the newspaper industry which have subverted newspaper integrity—undue influence of advertisers and politicians, personal interests and friendships of publisher, conflict of interest of reporters, and blackout of news unfavorable to the paper or even its competitors. He cites specifically the cases of the *Boston Herald*, the *Philadelphia Daily News*, the *Dallas Times Herald*, and columnist Bob Considine.

Etnyre, Robert H. *The Texas Open Records Act: A History and an Assessment.* Austin, Tex., University of Texas, 1975. 188p. (Unpublished Master's thesis)
1E122

"A history of the Texas Open Records Act was examined to judge the success of the Act in transforming the substantive concept of 'freedom of information' into a constructive, workable procedure."

Eubank, Royal C., Jr. "Libel and the Press—Are Sections One, Two, and Three of Article 5432 Absolute or Qualified Privileges?" *Baylor Law Review*, 23:648–55, Fall 1971.
1E123

Re: *Denton Publishing Company v. Boyd*, 460 S.W.2d 881 (Tex. 1970), in which the Texas Supreme Court ruled that the sections of the Texas statute which provide a privilege for fair trial and impartial reports of certain proceedings by newspapers and periodicals, could be overcome by proof of malice.

"Evaluation of Basis for and Effect of Broadcasting's Fairness Doctrine." *Rutgers-Camden Law Journal*, 5:167–84, Fall 1973.
1E124

Re: *Brandywine-Main Line Radio, Inc. v. FCC*, 473 F.2d 16 (D.C. Cir. 1972).

Evans, Harold. "Does the Label 'Confidential' Bind the Press?" *IPI Report* (International Press Institute), 17(8):10–11, December 1968.
1E125

The editor of the *Sunday Times* (London) discusses a case involving a court injunction on their publication of a "confidential" document. The *Times* won their case, but he believes there is a danger in the misuse of "confidential," so that it could prevent exposure of some of the worst scandals of our time. British newspapers

publish at their own risk and if they are wrong they are subject to a rigorous law of libel.

————. "The Half-Free Press." In William Haley *et al.*, *The Freedom of the Press. Granada Guildhall Lectures, 1974 . . .*, London, MacGibbon, 1974, pp. 21–47. (An abridged version appears in *New Statesman*, 8 March 1974)
1E126

The British press is restricted by comparison with several other countries, including the United States. Threat of contempt in discussing a matter before the courts would likely have prevented the British press from exposing a Watergate scandal. The author calls for reform in the contempt law to permit a defense "in the public interest," and for the abolition of the doctrine of "imminence," requiring press silence even when a criminal charge is suspected. "Our philosophy and, in turn our law and our attitudes have been conditioned to defend free speech rather than free inquiry. I have shown how in the House of Lords judgment it has been ruled that it is all right to utter opinion but not to publish the evidence that one believes sustains the opinion. We have a press which is half free, I believe, because its needs and the needs of the society it serves have outgrown a philosophy rooted in the simpler virtues of free expression."

————. "The Half-Free Press: A Report on Regression." *New Review*, 2(22):3–6, January 1976.
1E127

The British press is less than half–free, having retrogressed since the author's Granada Guildhall lecture in 1974. The main threats are in the areas of confidence and contempt, official secrets and libel, and "a ragbag of other restrictions" including parliamentary privilege, the Rehabilitation of Offenders Act, the law of privacy, and the voluntary moratorium on routine kidnapping reports. The law of libel is not a serious threat to newspapers, but is inhibiting to book publishing.

————. "Is the Press Too Powerful?" *Columbia Journalism Review*, 10(5):8–16, January–February 1972.
1E128

Do the media manage power? How do totalitarian and democratic presses differ? How might criticism of the information industry be improved? The author is editor of the *Sunday Times* of London.

Evans, M. Stanton. "Court's Pornography Ruling: Return to the Constitution." *Human Events*, 33:12, 4 August 1973.
1E129

"The long and the short of it is that, in previous High Court rulings, the federal government had sought to impose a single, permissive and essentially pro-pornography standard on the nation—usurping an area of law enforcement reserved by our system to the several states. Last month's decision is a reversal of this centralizing trend, and a welcome return to constitutional restraint."

————. "How to Silence Dissent." *Human Events*, 33:8, 17 November 1973. **1E130**

Comments on the recently uncovered Jeb Magruder *aide memoire* to President Nixon which suggests executive methods available for silencing the hostile press and a 1961 Victor Reuther memorandum to Attorney General Robert Kennedy, urging the use of federal resources to head off and dry up conservative critics of the administration.

————. "The Political Odyssey of Spiro T. Agnew." *National Review*, 24:894–900, 914, 18 August 1972. **1E131**

Included in a laudatory article on Vice-President Spiro T. Agnew as a spokesman for American conservativism is a section on his attack on the press and an assessment of the response from the media and the public.

————. "Pornography: Blue Art and Red Revolution." *American Opinion*, 13(11):31–40, December 1970. **1E132**
A critique on the report of the U.S. Commission on Pornography and Obscenity—an attack on the so-called experts who "want pornography freely distributed precisely because such distribution outrages the public. The public they feel needs to be shook up." The author believes "the report is fundamentally a lie, or a concatenation of lies. It misrepresents, one can only suppose deliberately, the nature of pornography, the consequences of its widespread distribution, and the attitude of the majority of the American people toward it." He charges pornographers with contributing to "the disordered consciousness" and with the power to "eunuchize the morale" of the people, particularly those who should provide leadership—a prelude to revolution.

————. "The Silencers"; "Censorship and Muzzling"; and "Managing the News." In his *The Liberal Establishment*. New York, Devin–Adair, 1965, pp. 277–317. **1E133**
In his attacks on the Liberal establishment, the author charges a systematic and considered effort by a number of Liberals to silence the Conservative dissent, giving as an example the Reuther Memorandum calling for the use of the FBI, FCC, and private groups against the radical right. He cites the use of Group Research, Inc. "To censor Communist propaganda is verboten. But to censor the *anti*-Communist remarks of American military men, that is an entirely different matter." He discusses the action taken against Major General Edwin A. Walker. "The performance of the Kennedy administration in the realm of 'news management' by common testimony, surpassed anything seen in Washington before." But Lyndon Johnson is upholding the standard. Evans describes the use of the "stick and carrot" with newsmen and broadcasters, and the distortion and deception in official news releases.

Everett, J. Diane. "Broadcast Media Regulation: Death Knell of the Fairness Doctrine." *University of Florida Law Review*, 27:607–13, Winter 1975. **1E134**
Re: *National Broadcasting Co., Inc. v. FCC*, 516 F.2d 1101 (D.C. Cir. 1974).

Everett, Mildred L. "FCC License Renewal Policy: The Broadcasting Lobby Versus the Public Interest." *Southwestern Law Journal*, 27:325–39, May 1973. **1E135**
"This Comment examines the significant developments, both substantive and procedural, in license renewal policy [of the Federal Communications Commission] which have followed the 1965 Policy Statement. It is submitted that none of these policies and proposals adequately protect the public interest while assuring sufficient stability to the broadcasting industry. A proposal which would better balance these diverse interests is presented."

Evers, Mike. *Pressure Groups and Sex Education*. Columbia, Mo., Freedom of Information Center, School of Journalism, University of Missouri at Columbia, 1970 7p. (Report no. 241) **1E136**
"With varying degrees of intensity, the controversy over sex education in public schools continues across America. Opponents, coalesced into militant pressure groups drawing on ultra-conservative political organizations, have brought their objections to the school house door. Educators and psychologists disagree as to the effects of sex education. Much clearer is the role of these conservative national political groups, which is to be seen almost wherever the issue is raised."

Eves, Vicki. "The Effects of Violence in the Mass Media." *Screen*, 11(3):31–42, Summer 1970. **1E137**
An examination of "available evidence on the effects of media-depicted violence, to see whether the attack on the mass media as a major cause of violence, is justified." The author finds no conclusive research evidence to show that media is an important reinforcing agent or that violence in the media renders people more likely to commit violent acts. "It may well be that violence in the media does not lead to physical violent behavior but . . . is a symptom of more general social conflict."

Ewbank, H. L. "Who's In Charge?" *AAUP Bulletin* (American Association of University Professors), 55:455–57, Winter 1969. **1E138**
A review board studied *The Purdue Exponent*, a controversial student newspaper, issuing a report that made a number of advances in free speech, determined "who's in charge?" and how to make things work better.

"Exclusion of Children from Violent Movies." *Columbia Law Review*, 67:1149–68, June 1967. **1E139**
"Society's interest in protecting the freedom of expression to children—more specifically, in allowing children to see movies despite the portrayals of violence therein—is great; the need to protect them against this form of expression cannot be shown to exist at all. The court in the instant case [*Interstate Circuit, Inc. v. City of Dallas*, 1966] wisely decided that the provisions of the Dallas ordinance which excluded children from movies showing crime and violence violated the first amendment to the Constitution."

"The Exercise of First Amendment Rights in Privately Owned Shopping Centers." *Washington University Law Quarterly*, 1973:427–35, Spring 1973. **1E140**
Re: *Lloyd Corporation v. Tanner*, 407 U.S. 551 (1972).

"The Expanding Constitutional Protection for the News Media from Liability for Defamation: Predictability and the New Synthesis." *Michigan Law Review*, 70:1547–80, August 1972. **1E141**
A review of the U.S. Supreme Court's recent resolution of the conflict between the law of defamation and the First Amendment in favor of First Amendment values, and an "exploration of the complex synthesis worked out by *New York Times Co. v. Sullivan* and its progeny." The author believes that the Brennan judicial standard for balancing First Amendment interests appears to be the most appropriate one, and calls for further court guidance for determining the dividing line between matters of public interest and those in the private sphere.

"Expansion of the *New York Times Co. v. Sullivan* Standard to Include State Civil Libel Action Brought by a Private Individual Involved in an Event of General or Public Interest." *Fordham Law Review*, 40:651–66, March 1972. **1E142**
Re: *Rosenbloom v. Metromedia, Inc.*, 403 U.S. 29 (1971).

"Extension of the *Sullivan* Rule to Non-Official Public Figures." *Washington Law Review*, 42:654–62, March 1967. **1E143**

The author believes that the U. S. Supreme Court should establish a definition of "public figure," and suggests various categories that might be established.

Eysenck, H. J. "People Have a Right to Know." *Index on Censorship*, 2(4):59–63, Winter 1973.

1E144
The text of a suppressed speech which Professor Eysenck was unable to give at the London School of Economics when he was assaulted, injured, and sent to the hospital. He was reporting on scientific findings in the field of genetics and was criticizing the American notion of affirmative action.

F

Fabian Society of New South Wales. *Toward a Free Press*. Sydney, Australia, The Society, 1949. 24p. (Pamphlet no. 3) **1F1**

"This pamphlet attempts to show what is wrong with the Australian Press. It also suggests a number of reforms which could be carried out without in any way impairing the principles of freedom of the Press. In particular, it urges the Labour Movement to make every effort towards the establishment of a daily newspaper of its own." Criticisms involved slanting of news to favor advertisers and views of owners, misuse of headlines, "burying" stories, and "blackout" treatment of items favorable to labor.

Fader, Carole. *The FOI Act and the Media*. Columbia, Mo., Freedom of Information Center, School of Journalism, University of Missouri at Columbia, 1973. 7p. (Report no. 303) **1F2**

"Since the Freedom of Information Act was signed into law, only a small number of requests for information have been filed by the news media under the law's provisions. Some reasons for this surprising situation are presented in this report."

Fadiman, Clifton *et al*. *Vulgarity and Obscenity*. 27 min. tape recording. North Hollywood, Calif., Center for Cassette Studies, 1971. **1F3**

A panel consisting of Charles A. Siepmann, Jacques Barzun, and Clifton Fadiman, moderator, attempt to define the terms "vulgarity" and "obscenity" by tracing their meanings through various cultural and historical periods.

Fagan, Edward R. "Censorship: Word Storm." *Journal of Research and Development in Education*, 9(3):76–83, Spring 1976. **1F4**

The author views censorship incidents as surface signs of value conflicts between communities and schools—sacred and secular societies. The community (sacred society) seeks to preserve its rituals, status quo, and heritage; the school or academy (secular soci-

ety) seeks to initiate change, progress, and novelty. The author suggests that "a balanced perspective which does justice to the sacred and the secular, the state and the academy, the school and the community should be pivotal to censorship decisions."

Fager, Christopher B. "FCC License Renewal Policy and the Right to Broadcast." *Boston University Law Review*, 52:94–148, Winter 1972. **1F5**

"This Note will outline the events and policies leading up to the *Citizens* decision [*Citizens Communications Center . . . v. FCC*, 1971] and examine the basis and impact of the holding specifically in light of past Commission practice giving preferred status to existing licensees. . . . This Note will also consider first amendment limitations that affect the scope of legislative choice in any effort to alter the present system of competitive challenge."

Fague, Anthony C. "Right of Privacy in California." *Santa Clara Lawyer*, 7:242–56, Spring 1967. **1F6**

The author calls for a more precise formulation of the limited right of privacy, including a realistic classification of the news event participants. He calls for a distinction to be made between a person who voluntarily seeks publicity, whose right of privacy is limited, and one who was a private person up to the time of a particular newsworthy event and was thrust into the public eye because of his participation in the event, whose right of privacy should be much broader.

Fahnstock, Jeanne R. "Geraldine Jewsbury: The Power of the Publisher's Reader." *Nineteenth-Century Fiction*, 28:253–72, December 1973. **1F7**

As a reader in the 1860s and '70s for the British publisher Bentley & Son, Geraldine Jewsbury advised on what subject matter and treatment was proper in novels of that period. Bentley followed her advice unless it obviously countered his business interests. "In the following discussion I have looked at Miss Jewsbury's debating the propriety of religious material in fiction, at her shocked reaction to a new frank-

ness and concentration on lovemaking, at her dislike at sadistic detail in the handling of anything from childbirth to corpses, and at her feeling that if everyday life is to be the subject of a novel, it must be the everyday life of spinsters, not of swindlers."

Fahringer, Herald P. "Seizure of Obscene Material." *Search and Seizure Law Report*, 1(8):1–4, June 1974. **1F8**

A discussion of U.S. Supreme Court protection against unlawful search and seizure of suspected obscene matter, particularly the requirement of a prior adversary hearing.

———, and Michael J. Brown. "Rise and Fall of Roth—A Critique of the Recent Supreme Court Obscenity Decisions." *Criminal Law Bulletin*, 10:785–826, November 1974; and *Kentucky Law Journal*, 62:731–68, 1973–74. **1F9**

"The specific issue here is the official regulation of communicative material deemed obscene. The larger issue is the freedom of consenting adults to view or read material in an enclosed setting when that material is sexually explicit. Beyond that is the question of censorship in a free society. By now most readers are aware of the recent Supreme Court decisions which once again attempt to resolve these issues. [*Miller v. California*, *Paris Adult Theatre I v. Slaton*, *Kaplan v. California*, *United States v. Orito*, and *United States v. 12 200-Ft. Reels of Super 8 mm Film* (1973).] Using the device of a careful analysis of the decisions, and adding actual and anticipated consequence the authors are deeply disappointed and gravely concerned." The majority of the Court concluded that the community standards used to judge a work should be "local" rather than "national" and that no expert advice was needed to prove a book or film's obscene character, and the requirement that a work be "utterly without redeeming social value" was renounced.

Faigley, Lester L. "What Happened in Kanawha County." *English Journal*, 64(5):7–9, May 1975. **1F10**

An essay based on observations of the school

textbook dispute, made by a member of the English faculty of the University of Washington, during a recent visit to Charleston, W. Va. The author does not agree with some observers who charged that in the attempt by school authorities to present divergent views from various ethnic groups, they neglected whites.

"Fair Trial and Free Press." *Law in Transition Quarterly*, 4:44–51, March 1967.   **1F11**

The article deals with the dilemma faced by the American Civil Liberties Union in the conflict over the issue of fair trial or free press, both guaranteed by the Constitution. The ACLU recommends that the first effort in combating prejudicial publicity should be aimed at law enforcement officials, members of the bar, and the court itself to prevent release of information that will prejudice the trial. A guideline of information standards and appropriate sanctions for their violation is presented by the author.

"Fair Trials, Judicial Gag Rules, and Freedom of the Press." *Free Speech* (Commission on Freedom of Speech, Speech Communication Association), 37:1, 3–9, February 1976.   **1F12**

An account of the broad "gag order" issued by a district court judge in Lincoln County, Nebr., prohibiting almost all reporting of a murder trial. The story is told through a series of newspaper stories, papers outside the jurisdiction of the court. The gag order was eventually overturned by a ruling of the U.S. Supreme Court.

Fairfield, Cicily I. [Rebecca West]. "Concerning the Censorship." In her *Ending in Earnest: A Literary Log*. New York, Doubleday, Doran, 1931, pp. 6–12.   **1F13**

Personal comments about the suppression of Radclyffe Hall's *Well of Loneliness* by Rebecca West. The "curiously muted tone" of the defense of the book, Miss West contends, is because it is not a very good book and difficult to defend on its merit. While joining the many literary figures who opposed the censorship, she wishes it could have been in behalf of a work of literary quality instead of an unworthy polemic. *Well of Loneliness* would have been forgotten in four months if the authorities had not unwisely decided to ban it.

Fairfield, William S. "The High Cost of Scientific Secrecy." *Reporter*, 18:22–25, 9 January 1958.   **1F14**

Summary of testimony of scientists before the U.S. House Special Subcommittee on Government Information. "The idol of security through secrecy, the scientists stated, is not merely a false one; it is a menace to the very national survival its worshipers hope to protect."

"The Fairness Doctrine and Broadcast License Renewals: *Brandywine-Main*

Line Radio, Inc." *Columbia Law Review*, 71:452–65, March 1971.   **1F15**

"This Comment will discuss the content of the fairness doctrine and its application in the instant case [*Brandywine-Main Line Radio, Inc. v. FCC*, 1970], and will examine the alternatives available to the FCC for enforcing the public interest as embodied in the fairness doctrine."

"The Fairness Doctrine and the Alaskan Pipeline." *Boston University Law Review*, 51:698–703, Fall 1971.   **1F16**

Comment on the case, *In re Wilderness Society*, 30 F.C.C.2d 643 (1971), in which the Federal Communications Commission held that the fairness doctrine applied to three commercials that asserted the need to develop Alaskan oil reserve while at the same time claiming that such development can take place without serious ecological harm.

"Fairness Doctrine Does Not Require Regular Presentation of Antipollution Announcements." *Vanderbilt Law Review*, 24:131–40, December 1970. **1F17**

The author objects to the FCC's decision in the case of the complaint from the Friends of the Earth Society, that a radio station was not required under the "fairness doctrine" to require regular free time for antipollution spot announcements. Such regular presentations, the author asserts, would effectively implement expressions of our national policy.

"Fairness Doctrine—Evaluation of Basis for and Effect of Broadcasting's Fairness Doctrine." *Rutgers Camden Law Journal*, 5:167–84, Fall 1973. **1F18**

In analyzing the *Brandywine* decision (*Brandwine-Main Line Radio, Inc. v. FCC*, 1970), "this Comment will examine two issues: (1) whether scarcity of broadcast stations still exists; and (2) whether the fairness doctrine fulfills its function of promoting an uninhibited marketplace of ideas."

"Fairness Doctrine: Personal Attacks and Public Controversies: Red Lion Broadcasting Co. v. FCC." *Georgetown Law Journal*, 56:547–56, January 1968.   **1F19**

Re: *Red Lion Broadcasting Co., Inc. v. FCC*, 1969, the first case before the U.S. Supreme Court to uphold the fairness doctrine of the FCC.

"Fairness Doctrine: Television as a Marketplace of Ideas." *New York University Law Review*, 45:1222–50, December 1970.   **1F20**

This note deals with four problem areas of the fairness doctrine: (1) the proper standards for compliance with the doctrine; (2) licensee censorship; (3) the right of access for the expression of controversial opinions; and (4) the applicability of the fairness doctrine to commercial advertising.

"The Fairness Doctrine: Time for the Graveyard?" *Fordham Urban Law Journal*, 2:563–86, Spring 1974.   **1F21**

"This comment will examine the rationale for the fairness doctrine, the obligations arising under it, and the FCC's administration of the doctrine. The judicial construction of the doctrine will be analyzed with emphasis on the doctrine's functional role and Constitutional ramifications. Finally, the future of the doctrine in light of recent trends within the FCC and the courts will be discussed."

"Fairness, Freedom and Cigarette Advertising: A Defense of the Federal Communications Commission." *Columbia Law Review*, 67:1470–89, December 1967.   **1F22**

An examination of the FCC ruling "that cigarette commercials, by giving a favorable image to smoking, present one side of a controversial subject, and that consequently, stations showing these commercials are obliged to present the other side" under the fairness doctrine.

A Faithful Report of a Genuine Debate concerning the Liberty of the Press. Addressed to a Candidate at the ensuing Election. Wherein a sure and safe Method is proposed of restraining the Abuse of that Liberty, without the least Encroachment upon the Rights and Privileges of the Subject. London, Reprinted for T. Becket and P. A. DeHondt, 1764. 45p. (First published in 1740)   **1F23**

An imaginary classical debate among four friends (Phileleutherus, a Whig; Constantius, a Tory; Nestor, a neutral elder statesman; and the author) on the use and abuse of a free press. While disagreeing in form of expression, the four agree in substance that whoever shall write, print, or publish any work "with a wicked and malicious Intent and Purpose to blaspheme God, to profane the Christian Religion, to affront the Person, or vilify the Authority of the King, or to stir up Mutiny, Sedition, and Rebellion against the Government" shall, upon conviction, be punished. Following discussion they agree to add "lewd and obscene Writers" to cover the "impudent merchants of Lust and Impurity, those forensick Detailers of contagious Poison in printed Packets." The scheme proposed would provide certain safeguards. It would be lawful for a person to defend his own opinions, provided they were "written in a Manner serious and decent, without taking the Liberty of Lies and Defamations, without any witty Affectations of Profaneness, or any Seditious Reflections." It would be lawful for any person to reveal information on any maladministration, wickedness, or corruption among public officials or ecclesiastics, provided the charges could be proved. It would also be lawful for any man to publish true copies of the speeches made in Parliament. The scheme called for a special high tribunal to administer cases on freedom of the press.

Falk, Adrian. "A Rhetorical Question about Censorship." *Meanjin Quarterly*, 29:365–69, Spring 1970. **1F24**
"I have tried to advance considerations which show that the idea of morality is misunderstood if it is thought that the enforcement of morality could suffice to preserve a social system. . . . So to try to justify censorship on these grounds is altogether wrong-headed." Falk cites as the basis of present censorship ideology the views of Lord Devlin who maintained that "society cannot ignore the morality of an individual any more than it can his loyalty."

Falk, Gerhard. "The *Roth* Decision in the Light of Sociological Knowledge." *American Bar Association Journal*, 54:288–92, March 1968. **1F25**
"Pointing out the confusion which has arisen with regard to obscenity cases since the *Roth* decision, Mr. Falk, a sociologist, applies some of the findings and concepts of sociology to such issues as the conflict between art and censorship and the effect of obscenity on the individual. He devotes particular attention to the concepts 'average person' and 'community standard' which are essential to the test for obscenity enunciated by the Supreme Court in *Roth*."—Editor

Fallaci, Oriana. "What Does Walter Cronkite Really Think?" *Look*, 34:57–62, 17 November 1970. **1F26**
In an interview with an Italian correspondent, the CBS newscaster comments, among other topics, on issues of press freedom. He speaks of the demagoguery of Spiro Agnew, in his attempt to exploit the public against a free press, of the implied threats in licensing renewal, and indicates that he would refuse to respond to a subpoena. He believes the reporter should "never, never, never consider the consequences that our information will have on the people or on ourselves."

"Fall-Out in Niagara Falls." *Trans-action*, 6(6):2–4, April 1969. **1F27**
Controversy over demands that the magazine *Trans-action* be removed from a Niagara Falls high school because of articles that used language that was alleged to be obscene. The Board of Education upheld the use of the magazine.

Fanning, David. "Rising Anger Over Censorship." *News/Check* (Johannesburg), 9(8):22–24, 16 October 1970. **1F28**
"While the rest of the western world has be-

come progressively freer of censorship and outcries from moralists, the Republic has simply grown accustomed to its watered-down diet of sliced movie and half-baked fiction." The author details the censorship activities of the Publications Control Board of South Africa, concluding that there is need for "a blanket system of appeal directly to the judiciary. It is only in this way that valid artistic expression is going to be allowed out of the bounds which constrict it."

Farber, Alan J. "Reflections on the Sedition Act of 1798." *American Bar Association Journal*, 62:324–28, March 1976. **1F29**
"This article will look at an extremely narrow area of First Amendment jurisprudence, the Sedition Act of 1798, and attempt to show that even the First Amendment has significant chinks in its historical armor." The author describes the struggle over the role of public criticism in a representative government that took place during the Adams Administration and led to the enactment of the Sedition Act; the trials of Republican editors Matthew Lyon, Anthony Haswell, Thomas Cooper, and James T. Callender; and the continuation of prosecution of Federalist editors under state law during the Jefferson Administration. "The Sedition Act," the author notes, "was never directly tested in the Supreme Court." He concludes that "until the possibility of prosecution for seditious libel has been eliminated from our system of jurisprudence, the fundamental right to criticize our government and its leaders freely and without fear of sanctioned reprisal remains unrealized."

Farber, Stephen. "Censorship in California." *Film Comment*, 9(1):32–33, January–February 1973. **1F30**
Commentary on forms of censorship faced by the motion picture industry—the antismut campaign for Proposition 18, the industry rating system, and the demands of black groups to precensor "Blaxploitation" films.

———. *The Movie Rating Game*. Washington, D.C., Public Affairs, 1972. 128p. **1F31**
A former liberal member of the Code and Rating Administration of the Motion Picture Association of America reports on rating practices and procedures and the daily debates that took place among members of the rating board. While the board is not a censor and cannot ban a movie or declare it obscene, it does limit what film producers can produce and what audiences can see. The author believes that the rating system must be either drastically overhauled or abolished completely. In the final chapter he gives alternatives to the present system.

Farberow, Norman L., *ed. Taboo Topics*. New York, Atherton, 1963. 140p. Foreword by Gordon W. Allport. **1F32**
"Eleven distinguished behavioral scientists discuss the occasional successes and frequent frustrations of conducting scientific research

on topics often considered not only socially, but also professionally, taboo: death, sex, suicide, homosexuality, parapsychology, graphology, religion, hypnosis, and politics."

Farley, John J. "The Reading of Young People." *Library Trends*, 19:81–88, July 1970. **1F33**
The article deals with the complexity of the concept of intellectual freedom as applied to young people—"the inherent paradoxes of the idea of freedom of the intellect for young people of high school age," who are neither clearly child nor clearly adult.

Farmer, R. G. "Censorship and Sex Education in the Home." *Australian Psychologist*, 8:148–49, July 1973. **1F34**
Summary of a paper given before a symposium on Psychological Impacts of Censorship at the 7th annual conference of the Australian Psychological Society.

Farmer, Thomas. *The Plain Truth: Being a Genuine Narrative Of the Methods made use of to procure a Copy of the Essay on Woman. With several Extracts from the Work itself, given as a Specimen of its astonishing Impurity*. London, Printed for the Author and sold by I. Pottinger, 1763. 16p. (Reprinted in John Wilkes, *An Essay on Woman* . . . , 1871 (W263) **1F35**
An account of the intrigue in the unauthorized circulation of copies of John Wilkes's privately printed *Essay on Woman* as told by the printer "into Whose Hands the Original Copy accidentally fell." Following the example of a similar pamphlet published by the dissolute clergyman, John Kidgell, who told his story of the affair (K96), Farmer signed every copy. He disclaimed any intention of hurting Mr. Wilkes, but the affair became a cause célèbre for freedom of the press and resulted in Wilkes's expulsion from Parliament.

Farr, William. "Notes from a Jail House Journal." *Bulletin of the American Society of Newspaper Editors*, 565:3–5, January 1973. **1F36**
The author wrote this article during his first week in jail on a contempt of court sentence. At the time of the original complaint action Farr was a reporter for the *Los Angeles Herald-Examiner*. He had refused to disclose to a Los Angeles county court judge the names of the prosecuting attorneys who had given him a copy of a witness' deposition in the Manson murder trial.

Farrell, Dianne. "CSD Intellectual Freedom Committee: Statement to the CSD Board January 21, 1976." *Top of the News*, 32:223–35, April 1976. **1F37**
A statement prepared by Dianne Farrell and approved by the Children's Services Division of the American Library Association, rescind-

ing a 1973 CSD Statement on Reevaluation of Library Materials for Children's Collections. The 1973 statement had proposed weeding of children's collections to remove works which, in light of changing social criteria, reflected racist, sexist, and puritanical attitudes. The statement had been objected to by the Intellectual Freedom Committee of the ALA as conflicting with the *Library Bill of Rights* and the statement on the Free Access to Libraries for Minors. The present statement grew out of considerable discussion and debate within the Association. "Admittedly, books in our children's collections reflect racist, sexist, and puritanical attitudes. But removing these books from our shelves will not eradicate racism, sexism, or puritanism. Should we not devote our energies to broadening our collections to include materials that will counteract stubborn prejudice and bias—materials produced by alternative, third-world, radical, and feminist presses? . . . CSD cannot, with logic, endorse ALA's *Library Bill of Rights* and ALA's statement on 'Free Access to Libraries for Minors' and, at the same time, maintain that as adults we have a responsibility and a right to make value judgments about which materials are 'appropriate' to give to children." The statement concludes: "The ALA Council has adopted a series of policy statements which provide librarians with a substantial defense against censorship. Unless and until we can make, justify, support, and defend a special case for treating children and children's collections in a wholly different manner (and, in a climate of growing concern about the legal rights of children, this may be impossible to do), let us accept ALA policy as CSD policy."

Farrell, Guy. "Publishers, Printers, & Obscenity: A Growing Web of Entrapment and Censorship." *Book Production Industry*, 46(4):36–41, April 1970.   **1F38**
"Changing standards of obscenity and the threats caused by ambiguous new censorship laws are creating growing concern and legal problems for printers and publishers. Shifting trends are beginning to flash danger signs of increased liability within a framework of bewildering laws." Topics covered: The Supreme Court, Federal legislation, state and local activities, the President's Commission, and an account of the dilemma faced by the printer of *Kaleidoscope* in Port Washington, Wis. An editorial (p. 35) also deals with the question of obscenity or censorship.

Farrell, James T. "A Censorship Case." *American Book Collector*, 21(6):8–9, March–April 1971.   **1F39**
The novelist recounts his "first big censorship case," the hearing in the Police Magistrate Court of New York at the instigation of the New York Society for the Suppression of Vice on his *A World I Never Made*. The work had been charged with being immoral, obscene, blasphemous, and contributing to the delinquency of minors. Chief Magistrate Henry M. Curran cleared the work of all charges against it.

———. "Literature, Law, Censorship." *Thought* (Delhi), 21(32):14–16, 9 August 1969; 21(33):20, 16 August 1969.   **1F40**
Farrell objects to arbitrary categorizing of works into literature or non-literature; it is more important to know what a work does for us than what it is in a logical sense. To be effective, literature must be free. "Formally and in terms of the law, there is great cultural freedom in America." But there are also economic restrictions in the mass media that are culturally and politically dangerous. Another danger to a free literature is the uncritical passivity that has developed in the mass audience. In the second installment Farrell rejects the myth of a mass mind, arguing against the requirement of conformity in literature. "Liberty and freedom require a free literature." We need to work for a democratic culture that accepts in literature the reflection of individual differences and the concept of change.

Faulk, John H. *Vigilantism, HUAC, and the Spirit of Dissent*. 65 min. tape recording. Berkeley, Calif., Pacifica Tape Library, 1967.   **1F41**
In a lecture given at the University of California, this humorist and radio personality tells of his suit against Aware, Inc., the red-baiting group that blacklisted him and others in the broadcasting industry during the McCarthy era, and about the continued threat of blacklisting and other action against dissenters.

"The FCC and Broadcasting License Renewals: Perspectives on WHDH." *University of Chicago Law Review*, 36:854–82, Summer 1969.   **1F42**
"In *WHDH Inc.*, the Federal Communications Commission ignored traditional considerations and refused to renew a television license despite faultless operation by the broadcaster. . . . After a brief review of the communications policies endorsed by the Commission, this comment will examine the development, rationale, and weakness of the traditional renewal system. It will then propose a method of securing the advantages of comparative hearings without occasioning the widespread losses predicted by the industry in the aftermath of WHDH."

"FCC Fairness Doctrine—Applicability to Advertising." *Iowa Law Review*, 53:480–91, October 1967.   **1F43**
Comments relating to the FCC's ruling in the complaint against WCBS–TV "that the fairness doctrine is applicable to cigarette advertising and that the broadcast licensee must exercise his own judgment in deciding whether or not sufficient time is being allocated for the presentation of contrasting viewpoints."

Federal Council of Churches of Christ in America. Department of Research and Education. *Broadcasting and the Public; A Case Study in Social Ethics*. Cincinnati, Abingdon, 1938. 220p.   **1F44**

"The report undertakes to answer the question, How can a nation-wide industry, 'heavily impressed with a public interest' and having a natural monopoly of a particular medium of communication, best be made to serve the public welfare, with a maximum of freedom from government interference and yet within a framework of democratic control?" There are chapters on Federal Regulation Since 1927, Control of Broadcasting in Other Countries, The Question of Monopoly, Advertising, Religious Broadcasting, and the Broadcasting of Controversial Issues.

"The Federal Freedom of Information Act As an Aid to Discovery." *Iowa Law Review*, 54:141–59, August 1968. **1F45**
The author considers three major problems the courts will confront in interpreting the Freedom of Information Act—the so-called "housekeeping" statute of 1789, the doctrine of executive privilege, and Section 3 of the Administrative Procedures Act of 1946, which agencies have interpreted as authority for withholding information. While the FOI Act states that records be made available to any person, it is likely that the courts will take into consideration the qualification and need of the person requesting the information, balanced against the agency's grounds for withholding the information.

"Federal Regulation of Radio Broadcasting—Standards and Procedures for Regulating Format Changes in the Public Interest." *Rutgers Law Review*, 28:966–85, Spring 1975.   **1F46**
"This note will examine the case law and will suggest more definite standards to govern programming in the public interest, giving consideration to the role of the courts and the FCC."

"Federal Statutes Prohibiting Importation and Mail Distribution of Obscene Materials Do Not Violate First Amendment." *Vanderbilt Law Review*, 25:196–206, January 1972.   **1F47**
In the two obscenity cases, *United States v. Reidel* (1971) and *United States v. Thirty Seven (37) Photographs* (1971), the Supreme Court "has quelled all speculation that the concept of privacy includes some forms of commercial distribution. Instead, the Court has thrust all commercial activity into the forbidden realm of public action, which may be proscribed by federal and state regulation."

Fedler, Frederic E. *Access to the Mass Media: A Case Study*. Minneapolis, University of Minnesota, 1971. 331p. (Ph.D. dissertation, University Microfilms, no. 72–391)   **1F48**
Information gathered in this study of twenty

"minority" and twenty "established" groups in Minneapolis failed to support the hypothesis that minority groups are denied access to the media. Instead, minority groups seem to receive a disproportionately larger share of publicity, although the publicity is not always favorable.

———. "The Media and Minority Groups: A Study of Adequacy of Access." *Journalism Quarterly*, 50:109–17, Spring 1973. **1F49**
"A study of Minneapolis media finds that minority groups receive more, not less, publicity than comparable established groups."

Fee, Walter. *Privacy and State Action*. Columbia, Mo., Freedom of Information Center, School of Journalism, University of Missouri at Columbia, 1976. 7p. (Report no. 357) **1F50**
The author examines the constitutional background of privacy and reports on state privacy laws.

Feis, Herbert. "The Shackled Historian." *Foreign Affairs*, 45:332–43, January 1967. **1F51**
A historian criticizes the policy of the U.S. and British governments for withholding public records from historians, while participants in the events are free to use them in writing their selective memoirs. The twenty-two-year period of internment of presidential records is too long; ten years would be sufficient. The decisions are not controlled by the professional archivists but by heads of executive agencies, and by library trustees.

———. "Unpublic Public Papers." *New York Times Book Review*, 21 April 1968, pp. 2, 58. **1F52**
An attack on the concept that presidential papers are held to be "personal" not "public" property. Privileged narratives of public officials, by their very nature biased and selective, appear in best-seller lists, while the original records of these same matters remain locked up in the archives, unavailable for possibly a quarter of a century or more, to historians. "Has not the time come—in view of the vital need for full and accurate historical knowledge—to correct the bias in favor of privileged history? I believe the American nation could stand the shock of being adequately informed about its past in time for possible improvement and correction."

Feldkamp, Fred. "The Sloughs of Secrecy; At Odds with the British Official Secrets Acts." *Harper's*, 243:79–82, December 1971. **1F53**
An American film producer writes of his experiences with the British Official Secrets Acts

which he found unrelenting and inflexible. The case involves a film about a British double agent in World War II. Information about the case (Eddie Chapman) had already appeared in print. Despite nine unsuccessful years of struggle for clearance in England and threats of prosecution, the film (*Triple Cross*) was produced in France and played all over the world, including Britain, without incident.

Feldman, Charles, and Stanley Tickton. "Obscene/Indecent Programming: Regulation of Ambiguity." *Journal of Broadcasting*, 20:273–82, Spring 1976. **1F54**
"This article reviews two important FCC decisions. Sonderling (WGLD–FM) and Pacifica (WBAI–FM), to discern and describe FCC policy trends and attempts to define just what obscenity and indecency is and what standards for broadcasting should exist."

Feldman, Samuel. "To Publish Underground Newspapers. Freedom or License?" *Communication: Journalism Today*, 23:7, 18, Fall 1968. **1F55**
"A survey of more than 400 high schools in southern California reveals that the threat of an underground paper forces wavering principals to grant more editorial freedom and motivates staffs to do a better job."

———. *The Student Journalist and Legal and Ethical Issues*. New York, Richards Rosen, 1968. 186p. **1F56**
The book is intended as a practical guide to students and teachers in the application of press law to student journalism. Written before the rendering of court decisions extending the First Amendment freedom of the press to the public schools, the author cites specific school cases, problems arising from the underground press, issues of censorship, the right to report, and ethical issues faced by student editors and faculty advisors.

Felker, Donald W. "An Historical Investigation of the Assumption that Theories of the Nature of Man and Theories of Freedom of the Press Are Related." *Gazette*, 13:261–73, 1967. **1F57**
"The pamphlet writers in England from 1640–1653 were chosen as suitable authors for this investigation. These authors were divided into three groups, the Levellers, the Independents, and the Conservatives. These three groups are fairly clearly differentiated as to their views of the nature of man. They are also similarly differentiated in their advocacy of press freedom. This finding would tend to confirm the assumption investigated."

Felker, Randolph B. "Libel in New Mexico—*Reed v. Melnick*." *New Mexico Law Review*, 1:615–29, July 1971. **1F58**
"This comment will examine the recent New Mexico Supreme Court decision of *Reed v. Mel-*

nick, in which the court adopted new rules concerning libel in New Mexico. A discussion of the historical treatment of defamation will enable the reader to familiarize himself with certain terms analogous to the study of libel."

Fellmeth, Robert C. "The Freedom of Information Act and the Federal Trade Commission: A Study in Malfeasance." *Harvard Civil Rights-Civil Liberties Law Review*, 4:345–77, Spring 1969. **1F59**
An examination of the information disclosure policies and practices of the Federal Trade Commission as revealed by an investigation under the direction of Ralph Nader. The author concludes that the people who are administering the Act are the very people who opposed the enactment and have most to lose by its proper administration. "The more reluctant the agency is in revealing information about its actions, the more probable the need to find out why."

Felsenthal, Steven A. "Free Speech on Premises of Privately Owned Shopping Center." *Wisconsin Law Review*, 1973:612–21, 1973. **1F60**
Re: *Lloyd Corp. v. Tanner*, 407 U.S. 551 (1972).

Feltman, Lee. "Cartoonists and Publishers Beware!" *Impact*, 11:5, November 1976. (Reprinted in *Newsletter on Intellectual Freedom* [IFC–ALA], 26:31, 59, March 1977.) **1F61**
A California case involving a political cartoon, charged with libeling an official of Union Oil Co. The California Court of Appeals, according to the author, "turned *New York Times v. Sullivan* upside down."

Fenson, Melvin. "Group Defamation: Is the Cure Too Costly?" *Manitoba Law School Journal*, 1:255–81, 1964–65. **1F62**
A survey of issues in the dilemma presented in Canada by the prospect of antihate legislation. Current Criminal Code provisions and judicial interpretations render the likelihood of successful prosecutions remote. Canadian lawmakers will be asked to draw "the fine line between the ordinary friction that is the condition of life in any plural society, and the sort of vilification that no group should be forced to tolerate."

Fenton, Bruce S. "The Federal Communications Commission and the License Renewal Process." *Suffolk University Law Review*, 5:389–425, Winter 1971. **1F63**
"The subject of this inquiry is the role of the Federal Communications Commission's broadcast licensing procedures in the regulation of broadcast stations, and the application of standards in the approval of (1) license applications of broadcast stations, (2) broadcast license renewals, and (3) transfers of license control."

Ferguson, Paul R. "A Judicial Farce." *Wilson Library Bulletin*, 43:653–56, March 1969. **1F64**
Account of an obscenity trial involving a Los Angeles underground newspaper, *Open City*.

Ferlemann, Mimi. "Pornography." *Menninger Perspective*, 2(3):2–7, April 1971. **1F65**
An interview with a member of the U.S. Commission on Obscenity and Pornography, Dr. Edward Greenwood of the Menninger Foundation. Dr. Greenwood discusses the scientific work of the Commission, which he notes is not definitive, but significant. He believes that adults should make individual decisions in these matters, juveniles should have some protection, but it is mainly a responsibility of parents. He scoffs at the accusation that sex education in the schools is a Communist plot, noting that in the Soviet Union it is considered a capitalist plot. He believes that older people are more concerned with pornography than are young people, whose interest is with more real threats—violence, racism, poverty, and war.

Ferman, Irving. "Congressional Controls on Campaign Financing: An Expansion or Contraction of the First Amendment?" *American University Law Review*, 22:1–38, Fall 1972. **1F66**
The author suggests that Congress face the issue of undue influence of the wealthy on campaign expenditures, consistent with the First Amendment. Instead of prohibiting contributions from the wealthy, they should encourage financing from as many diverse sources as possible. "Such a mechanism would receive strong philosophical support from the first amendment because it would foster greater political expression without unconstitutionally restricting political expression of the wealthy."

Fernando, Erique M., and Emma Quisumbing-Fernando. "Freedom of Expression in the Philippine and American Constitutions." *Philippine Law Journal*, 23:801–28, December 1948. **1F67**
"The Philippine and American constitutions in almost identical language prohibit the passing of any law 'abridging the freedom of speech, or of the press.' Freedom of expression is thus constitutionally safeguarded from abridgement by the government. A comparison will be here attempted of the scope of this constitutional right as deliniated in judicial decisions, both Philippine and American, in the light of the problems which it gives rise to and the goals it is intended to serve."

Ferril, Thomas H. "Persecution by Post Office." *Grassroots Editor*, 9(5):26–27, September–October 1968. **1F68**
An account of the quarrel between the publisher of a 108-year-old weekly paper and the United States Post Office over auditing of circulation records. The publisher considers the post office auditing ritual a form of harassment.

Ferris, Timothy. "Is the Press in Danger?" *Rolling Stone*, 133:1, 24–26+, 26 April 1973. **1F69**
A detailed account of numerous government threats to press freedom during the Nixon Administration, including the verbal attacks of Spiro Agnew, the schemes of Clay T. Whitehead, the Congressional investigation of *The Selling of the Pentagon*, White House pressures against CBS to censor a Watergate documentary, and the broadcast license challenge to unfriendly television stations. A major portion of the article deals with the case histories of individual reporters who were under attack, and some of whom were jailed: Earl Caldwell, Paul Branzburg, Bill Farr, Brit Hume, Les Whitten, and John Lawrence. The media managers, with notable exceptions, did not come to the support of the embattled reporters and the general public also did not rush to support freedom of the press.

Ferry, Anthony. "Eroticism in the Arts." *Performing Arts in Canada*, 6(4):8–9, Fall 1969. **1F70**
The author applauds the new sexual permissiveness in the theater but believes that after another five years "taste for this kind of thing will have grown jaded and the fuzz will see that our audience-boredom is a far more devastating weapon then censorship or summonses on charges of 'consentual' sodomy."

Feuilleton, *pseud.* "Twak Road." *Contrast*, 15:90–94, Autumn 1967. **1F71**
An examination of the South African censor's marks and underscoring in a copy of *Tobacco Road* "may throw some light on the mores of local censorship." "Twak" is the colloquial word in Afrikaans for tobacco; it also means "nonsense, rubbish, piffle."

Fichenberg, Robert G. "Do Voluntary Guidelines Work?" *Seminar (A Quarterly Review for Newspapermen by Copley Newspapers)*, 16:33–37, June 1970. **1F72**
"Twenty states now have voluntary fair trial–free press agreements and the author finds they work in an atmosphere of mutual understanding, respect, and confidence." Included is the text of the Joint Declaration Regarding News Coverage of Criminal Proceedings in California, proposed for endorsement of bench, bar, and media organizations in that state—a product of negotiations between the State Bar of California and the California Freedom of Information Committee.

———. "The Price of Liberty." *Albany Law Review*, 32:317–36, Winter 1968. **1F73**
The basis for the present deliberations on free press vs. fair trial which led to the report of the Reardon Committee were the U.S. Supreme Court's decision in the Sam Sheppard case and criticisms of the press on the report of the Warren Commission. In the former case the criticism was not against the press but the trial judge's handling of the case; in the latter the criticism was directed largely against the Dallas police and not the press for their "free and easy conduct." "The basic and fatal weakness in the Reardon Committee's proposal is the assumption that the pre-trial reporting of facts in criminal cases is itself prejudicial to a defendant. . . . Are we to believe, as the arguments of some segments of the bar would have us believe, that the only objective juror is a juror who hasn't read the newspapers, listened to the radio and watched TV, has little knowledge and no opinions, in other words, is totally ignorant, totally uninformed and totally neutral about the case?" The author also criticizes the Reardon report for carrying "the implication that the bar is the only profession interested in a fair trial. . . . Since we in journalism have our code of ethical practices, as the lawyers have theirs, the cause of justice in our free society will be served best when we newspapermen follow our code, which requires us to report all the news, fully, fairly and impartially, and when members of the bar faithfully follow all 47 canons of their professional ethics. . . . We need no new restrictive codes."

Field, James A. "Publicity by Prosecution; A Commentary on the Birth Control Propaganda." *Survey*, 35:599–601, 19 February 1915. **1F74**
"The prosecutors of William and Margaret Sanger presumably hoped to check the propaganda of birth control. . . . The obvious effect of the prosecutions has been to provoke a more widespread, outspoken and sympathetic discussion of this crucial subject than had before been ventured in the United States." The author reviews the consequences of previous attacks upon the partisans of birth control, going back to the eighteenth century. Included are the prosecution of Richard Carlile, Charles Bradlaugh, Annie Besant, and Charles Watts.

Fielding, Derek. "Censorship and Permissiveness." *Australian Library Journal*, 20(4):33–36, May 1971. **1F75**
A review of the report of the United States Commission on Obscenity and Pornography, with observations on the Australian scene and the situation in South Africa and Rhodesia.

———. "Does Australia Need Freedom to Read or the Blue Pencil of Big Brother?" *Australian Library Journal*, 19:90–93, April 1970. **1F76**
A comparison of American and Australian censorship, little of the latter appearing in professional journals. "Overwhelmingly the threat to Freedom to Read in Australia comes from the Commonwealth Department of Customs."

Fielding, K. R. "How to Prevent Censorship: Cultivate Local Politicians." *American Libraries*, 7:623–25, November 1976.   **1F77**
Our traditional weapons in fighting censorship—relying on professional ethics, enlisting outside help, relying on the intellectual elite in the community—have only served "to isolate us from the community without really confounding the censor. Consequently, to prevent censorship crises, we must turn to our own community for the best defense against restrictions in the freedom to read and think." The author recommends that the library identify with populist rather than aristocratic groups in the community, provide additional library services to local officials and legislators, and expand the library's base of support by developing positive relationships with potential censoring groups by expanding the collection to include material of interest to them, and by encouraging staff members to gain political expertise.

Fielding, Raymond. "Mirror of Discontent: The 'March of Time' and Its Politically Controversial Film Issues." *Western Political Quarterly*, 12:145–52, March 1959.   **1F78**
The March of Time series constituted "a dazzling display of controversial material which provoked the most intense and unrelenting program of censorship ever inflicted upon a motion picture film series."

Fields, James E. *Press Access: Rationale and Response*. Columbia, Mo., Freedom of Information Center, School of Journalism, University of Missouri at Columbia, 1973. 7p. (Report no. 296) **1F79**
"Jerome Barron's ideas about granting public access to the media as a right guaranteed by the First Amendment continue to foment widespread debate more than five years after their initial presentation. But the limelight is now shared by proposals from other sources and implementation seems increasingly farther away."

Fiene, Donald M. "From a Study of Salinger: Controversy in the *Catcher*." *Realist*, 30:1, 23–25, December 1961.   **1F80**
A review of the long history of controversy and suppression involving J. D. Salinger's *The Catcher in the Rye*. The novel was objected to for high school reading because of alleged blasphemy and obscenity, but most especially for the use of one phrase, "fuck you," which had also shocked the central character of the novel, Holden Caulfield. The author of the article cites numerous cases of banning and considers the reception of the work abroad—it has been translated into more than a dozen languages. The work was banned by Customs in Australia and South Africa but the ban was later lifted. He concludes with an account of his own experience in attempting to use the book in a Louisville high school English class, and being prohibited by the Board of Education.

Fifer, Samuel. "Musical Expression and First Amendment Considerations." *DePaul Law Review*, 24:143–64, Fall 1974. (Reprinted in *Advertising Law Quarterly*, Fall 1975)   **1F81**
"This Comment will review and analyze the administrative and judicial history of the Notices [FCC's drug-related lyrics] and suggest that lyrics and music be accorded protection under the first amendment."

Figg, Robert, Jr. "Free Press versus Fair Trial." *Arkansas Law Review*, 22:607–20, Fall 1968.   **1F82**
A member of the Reardon Committee defends the report of fair trial and free press and believes that the press has overreacted to the recommendations. "I believe that the news media will be on a sounder ground if they will give the Reardon standards a fair chance to function as intended and see whether in actual operation their fears are justified. They may well find that in so doing, they have served both their own and the public's interest." He calls for bar and press to "do battle side by side" for free press and fair trial, not against each other.

"Fight over Freedom and Privilege." *Time*, 101(10):64–65, 5 March 1973.   **1F83**
A review of the recent incidents against reporters and their newspapers, resulting in a Supreme Court rejection of some reporters' claims that the First Amendment gave them an absolute right to withhold confidential sources from grand juries, and subsequent efforts in Congress to pass a shield law.

Filvaroff, David B. "Conspiracy and the First Amendment." *University of Pennsylvania Law Review*, 121:189–253, December 1972.   **1F84**
Three interests are involved in the appraisal of the conspiracy doctrine as applied to speech: protection of society from the consequence of advocacy, protection of the individual from unwarranted prosecution, and the risk of loss to society from inhibited free flowing of ideas. Resolution of the conflict has almost always been in favor of suppression of speech. The combination of conspiracy with speech crimes should be held unconstitutional.

Finch, J. D. "Conspiracy, Society and the Press: The Recent Experience in English Law." *Canadian Bar Review*, 50:522–31, September 1972.   **1F85**
"In a recent case in England, the Court of Appeal (Criminal Division) held the editor of an 'underground' or 'alternative' newspaper to have committed the crimes of conspiracy to corrupt public morals and conspiracy to outrage public decency." The author examines recent developments in the English common law relating to conspiracy to see if the courts have been successful in their professed objectives. Related legal developments in Canada and the United States are also examined.

Finegold, Alan H. "Julian Bond and the First Amendment Balance." *University of Pittsburgh Law Review*, 29:167–209, December 1967.   **1F86**
"The author discusses the various standards which the [Supreme] Court has used in resolving free speech issues, and concludes, on the basis of his analysis of *Bond v. Floyd* [1966], that the Court does not follow any consistent theory as to the application of the first amendment. Rather, the various standards which have been employed in the past are all considered, and the issue is resolved by an over-all balancing technique."—Editor

Fink, Bobbie A. *Mass Murder in the Redwoods: A Comparative Analysis of the Press Coverage Given to the Three Mass Murders in Santa Cruz, California, and an Inquiry into the Effectiveness of News Gags*. San Jose, Calif., California State University, 1974. 202p. (Unpublished Master's thesis)   **1F87**
"In Santa Cruz County, California, there were three mass murders in a four-year period [1970–73]. After each suspect was apprehended, a news gag was issued. This thesis examines the need and effectiveness of each news gag."

Fink, Richard. "The Single Publication—Which One?" *Temple Law Quarterly*, 44:400–409, Spring 1971.   **1F88**
An attempt to clarify the concept of "single publication" for purposes of defining when and where an alleged libel offense in a periodical took place.

Finkel, David B. "Protection or Censorship?" *Los Angeles Bar Journal*, 51:534–38+, May 1976.   **1F89**
"The purpose of this article is to present the contrast in analysis of legal principles and underlying social issues, made by the Federal Communications Commission and a Radio Broadcasting Foundation, respectively, concerning the propriety of governmental restraint of broadcasters' use of sensitive language on the airwaves."

Finkelstein, M. Marvin. "Traffic in Sex-Oriented Materials and Criminality and Organized Crime: The Relationship." *Technical Report of the [U.S.] Commission on Obscenity and Pornography*, 5:61–79, 1971.   **1F90**
A study of bookstore operators and employees in five major cities—New York, Los Angeles, Chicago, Boston, and San Francisco, to gather evidence regarding the relationship between

the pornography industry and "organized crime."

―――. "The Traffic in Sex-Oriented Materials in Boston." *Technical Report of the [U.S.] Commission on Obscenity and Pornography*, 4:99–154, 1971.   **1F91**
"The project was concerned with an examination of the adult bookstore traffic in sex-oriented materials in the City of Boston and in developing preliminary information concerning the possible involvement of organized crime in the distribution of such materials."

Finlay, J. F. "Defamation by Radio." *Canadian Bar Review*, 19:353–74, May 1941.   **1F92**
"The radio is, so far as the law of defamation, nothing more nor less than a form of the press. Accordingly, it has been submitted, with deference, that actionable calumny broadcast should constitute libel rather than slander, whether delivered extemporaneously or from a written script, that the broadcaster should be liable as a primary publisher; and that the defences of privilege and fair comment should be available to the station."

Finnegan, Owen E. *An Historical and Metaphysical Study of Natural Law Theory Applied to Questions of Freedom of Expression in the United States.* East Lansing, Mich., Michigan State University, 1965. 195p. (Ph.D. dissertation, University Microfilms, no. 66–6122)   **1F93**
"The purpose of this thesis is to develop through empirical investigations and historical study an ethic of the media of mass communication proper to the American political philosophy rooted as this is in natural law theory. . . . The historical study traces the theory of natural law through a complex of significant authors. And from a posture of veritable criteria, an attempt is made to distinguish the several currents of natural law thinking that exercised discoverable influence in the political and philosophical formulations of the American experiment."

[Finnerty, Peter.] *Case of Peter Finnerty, including A Full Report of All the Proceedings which took place In the Court of King's Bench . . . Comprehending an Essay Upon the Law of Libel and Some Remarks Upon Mr. Finnerty's Case; to which Is Annexed, an Abstract of the Case of Colonel Draper, Upon which Precedent Mr. Finnerty Professed to Act.* 2d ed. London, Printed by J. M. Creery for M. Jones, 1811. 32p., 72p.   **1F94**
Finnerty was charged with a libel against the Rt. Hon. R. Stewart (Viscount Castlereigh), in an anonymous letter appearing in the *Morning Chronicle and Statesman*, 23 January 1810. Finnerty authorized the editors to reveal his name so that he, not the editors, would stand trial. He was convicted and given an eighteen-

month sentence. As the basis for his defense he had used the case of Edward A. Draper, 1808. In the thirty-two-page preface Finnerty criticizes the law of libel and its interpretation by the courts: truth ought not to be deemed a libel; juries should be allowed to receive evidence as to the truth or falsehood of the allegations before passing judgment; juries, not judges, should have the power of defining a libel.

Finnis, John M. " 'Reason and Passion': The Constitutional Dialectic of Free Speech and Obscenity." *University of Pennsylvania Law Review*, 116:222–43, December 1967.   **1F95**
The aim of the article is to sketch the intellectual basis of the idea that obscene utterances "are no essential part of any exposition of ideas," as expressed in *Chaplinsky v. New Hampshire* (1942) and quoted in *Roth v. United States* (1957). The article indicates the way in which the concept has shaped constitutional law on obscenity.

Firestein, Charles L. "*Red Lion* and the Fairness Doctrine: Regulation of Broadcasting 'In the Public Interest.' " *Arizona Law Review*, 11:807–21, Winter 1969.   **1F96**
"The purpose of this Comment is to examine the background of the fairness doctrine and FCC regulation of the communication industry in an effort to assess the impact of *Red Lion* on future claims by broadcasters of unconstitutional Commission action." *Red Lion Broadcasting Co. v. Federal Communications Commission* (1967).

"The First Amendment and Commercial Advertising: Biglow v. Commonwealth." *Virginia Law Review*, 60:154–62, January 1974.   **1F97**
Comments on the case *Bigelow v. Commonwealth* (1973), involving an abortion advertisement in a Charlottesville, Va. newspaper. The author believes the Virginia Supreme Court erred in finding the editor guilty, basing their decision on the notion that commercial speech is unprotected by the first amendment, a principle inconsistent with U.S. Supreme Court decisions which have considered the public value of speech not the "commercial" aspects as a basis for protection.

"The First Amendment and Regulation of Television News." *Columbia Law Review*, 72:746–71, April 1972.   **1F98**
"This Note explores the constitutional issues raised by proposals to regulate and prevent the willful broadcasting of distortions or misstatements of fact as 'news.' Considerations that may require broadcast media to be treated differently from others are then discussed. Finally, the constitutional implications of different forms of regulation will be examined, to determine whether some types of governmental intrusions may be consistent with the first amendment."

"The First Amendment and the 'Abridgeable' Right of Self-Expression." *Columbia Law Review*, 72:1249–71, November 1972.   **1F99**
This comment is concerned primarily with "the reasoning and constitutional underpinnings" of the U.S. Supreme Court decision in *Business Executives' Move for Vietnam Peace v. FCC* (1972), in which the Court found that the refusal of a broadcaster to air "controversial" editorial advertisements while accepting commercial announcements violated the first amendment rights of the listening public. Following consideration of the merits of the case there is a brief discussion of the regulations necessary to effect the policy announced by the court.

"The First Amendment Does Not Preclude State Regulation of Material Which, According to Contemporary Community Standards, As a Whole Appeals to Prurient Interest in Sex, Depicts or Describes in a Patently Offensive Way Sexual Conduct Specifically Defined by Applicable State Law, and Lacks Serious Literary, Artistic, Political or Scientific Value." *Brooklyn Law Review*, 40:442–60, Fall 1973.   **1F100**
Re: *Miller v. California*, 413 U.S. 15 (1973).

"First Amendment Prohibits Prior Restraint of Distribution of Underground Newspaper." *Indiana Law Review*, 6:583–89, 1973.   **1F101**
Re: *Fujishima v. Board of Education*, 460 F.2d 1355 (7th Cir. 1972), involving a high school paper, *Cosmic Frog*.

"First Amendment Protection of the News Media: *Caldwell v. United States*." *Rutgers-Camden Law Journal*, 3:46–97, Spring 1971.   **1F102**
A discussion of the use of subpoena power as a means to force a journalist to disclose confidential information received in the course of reporting the news. "In striking a first amendment balance in favor of a journalist's privilege, the courts have implicitly recognized the following syllogism: (1) drying up of news sources will have a 'chilling effect' on freedom of press; (2) compulsory disclosure will dry up news sources; (3) compulsory disclosure will have a 'chilling effect' on freedom of press."

"First Amendment's Role in Determining Place of Trial in Libel Actions." *Michigan Law Review*, 66:542–52, January 1968.   **1F103**
This note attempts an analysis of the rules formulated in three cases involving jurisdiction

over out-of-state defendants in a libel action: *New York Times v. Connor* (1964), *New York Post v. Buckley* (1967), and *Curtis Publishing Co. v. Golino* (1967).

"First and Fifth Amendments—Grand Jury Witnesses May Assert First Amendment Rights of Press and Association as a Basis for Refusing to Answer Questions—Immunity Extends Only to Subjects Specifically Mentioned in a Grant of Immunity." *New York University Law Review*, 48:171–96, April 1973.　　　　　**1F104**
Bursey v. United States, 466 F.2d 1059 (9th Cir. 1972).

Firth, Tony. "Freedom in Broadcasting." *Political Quarterly*, 47:169–79, April–June 1976.　　　　**1F105**
A review of various pressures exerted on radio and television over the years by government, unions, professional managers, and consumers. Current demands for more access "may well lead to more control and less initiative" and "Government . . . can then only be restrained from direct intervention by the evident exercise of greater control by the statutory broadcasting authorities." The most serious threats to freedom are "the combination of economic problems, social aspirations and the growing power of the government and abuse." Democratization is a solution favored by almost all who believe in greater accountability, but the long term effect will be "not permanently to radicalise and liberate the broadcasting institutions, but to hasten the day when they come more directly under governmental control."

Fischer, James F. "Florida Statute Requiring Equal Space Reply by Any Newspaper Attacking a Political Candidate Violates the First Amendment." *University of Kansas Law Review*, 23:300–308, Winter 1975.　　　**1F106**
Re: *Miami Herald Publishing Co. v. Tornillo*, 418 U.S. 241 (1974).

Fischer, John. "The Perils of Publishing: How to Tell When You Are Being Corrupted." *Harper's*, 236:13–14, 16, 18–20, May 1968. (The Easy Chair column)　　　　**1F107**
Looking back over his career in publishing the contributing editor sees little evidence of bribery, coersion, advertiser dictation, or "payola" in magazine publishing, but recognizes the power of editors and the subtle tendencies for corruption.

―――. "A Threat of Death by Mail."

Harper's, 246:30–33, May 1973. (The Easy Chair column)　　　**1F108**
The threat to the existence of some 10 thousand magazines and small newspapers by rising postal rates.

Fischer, Madeleine. "Commercial Speech Is Not Protected by the First Amendment." *Tulane Law Review*, 48:426–32, February 1974.　　**1F109**
In the case of *Pittsburgh Press Co. v. Pittsburgh Commission on Human Relations* (1973), the U.S. Supreme Court ruled that petitioner's sex-designated want-ad columns constituted commercial speech not protected by the First Amendment.

Fischman, Bruce D. "*Miami Herald Publishing Co. v. Tornillo*: Editorial Discretion v. the Electorate's Right to Know—Freedom of the Press for Whom?" *Ohio Northern University Law Review*, 2:562–68, 1975.　　**1F110**
The author criticizes the U.S. Supreme Court decision in *Miami Herald Publishing Co. v. Tornillo* (1974), which invalidated Florida's right of reply statute. "A 'right of reply statute' reasonably constructed, would not restrain editorialization. Rather, it would encourage a responsible press in communities where irresponsible journalism is recognized. . . . The Supreme Court's application of a rudimentary notion of freedom of the press to the facts presented in *Miami Herald Publishing Co. v. Tornillo*, unfortunately fosters an uninformed electorate and ignores the opportunity to encourage responsible journalism in the newspaper industry."

[Fishbein, Morris.] *The Case of Brinkley vs. Fishbein. Proceedings of a Libel Suit Based on an Article Published in Hygeia*. Chicago, American Medical Association, 1939. 194p.　　　**1F111**
The case involved an article by Dr. Fishbein entitled Modern Medical Charlatans, which questioned the ethical practices of Dr. John R. Brinkley of Del Rio, Texas, who used the radio to advertise cures for certain ailments. Judge R. J. McMillan, in his charge to the jury, recognized the validity of medical ethics as established by the profession. The jury found for the defendant and *Hygeia* carried the proceedings of the case in installments.

Fisher, Barbara. "Get By With a Little Help from My Friends." *Focus on Indiana Libraries*, 22:67–69, June 1968.　　**1F112**
A public librarian reports on a successful experiment with putting on the open shelves all of the controversial books formerly shelved behind the desk. The action was accompanied by a board-approved book-selection policy and a procedure for dealing with complaints.

Fisher, Donald C. *An Analytical Study of Harry S. Truman's Concept of Free Speech During the McCarthy Era*. Murray, Ky., Murray State University, 1973. 172p. (Unpublished Master's thesis)　　　　**1F113**

Fisher, John. "Censorship in Australia." *International Literature*, 10:86–91, 1935. (Organ of the International Union of Revolutionary Writers)　　　**1F114**
The issue also contains an account of the circumstances of publishing Henri Barbusse's *Under Fire* and the action of the censor.

Fisher, Jon E. *Photographic Invasion of Privacy*. Baton Rouge, La., Louisiana State University, 1972. 82p. (Unpublished Master's thesis)　　**1F115**
"The purpose of this study was to investigate the knowledge of the professional journalist and the average individual in the area of photographic invasion of privacy. In addition, the study was designed to learn the judicial and historical background of this form of privacy invasion."

Fisher, Paul. "Experience with State Access Legislation: An Overview of the Battle for Open Records." *Grassroots Editor*, 13(2):14–18, 37, March–April 1972.　　　　**1F116**
The director of the Freedom of Information Center at the University of Missouri reviews the history of the freedom of information movement in the United States since World War II, the contributions of such organizations as the American Society of Newspaper Editors and Sigma Delta Xi, and the resulting state open-records legislation. He calls for a reexamination of existing laws and proposed bills in light of experience and comments from the critics, and calls for continuing efforts of newsmen to keep the laws operating.

―――, and Ralph L. Lowenstein, *eds. Race and the News Media*. [Columbia, Mo.] Sponsored by Anti-Defamation League of B'nai B'rith and Freedom of Information Center, University of Missouri at Columbia, 1967. 158p.　　　**1F117**
Talks and summaries of discussions of newsmen from all parts of the country participating in a four-day conference at the University of Missouri on the topic of news coverage of the racial crisis. There are numerous references throughout to bias in reporting, pressures to suppress news in the interest of preserving the peace, and the role of the media as observer or participant. In the introduction the editors write: "The news media respond quickly and with keen interest to the conflicts and controversies of the racial story but for the most part disregard the problems that seethe beneath the surface until they erupt in the hot steam that is a 'live' news story."

Fisher, Robert. "Film Censorship and Progressive Reform: The National Board of Censorship of Motion Pictures, 1909–1922." *Journal of Popular Film*, 4:143–56, April 1975. **1F118**
One of the experiments in cultural reform initiated and administered by the People's Institute of New York City was the National Board of Censorship of Motion Pictures, the first private film-censorship body in the United States. At the time, the motion picture was the subject of widespread condemnation and the Board was an attempt to improve the quality of the motion pictures as well as to stave off a more severe official censorship. Between 1914 and 1922 the Board, which had changed its name to National Board of Review to play down the negative aspects, experienced alternating success and failure in its contests with the advocates of state censorship. Board decisions after 1916 grew increasingly permissive, passing on films dealing with such issues as birth control, capital punishment, and socialism. In 1922 the film industry, sensing the public demand for greater controls, set up its own industry code, leaving the National Board as a clearing house for information on the motion pictures.

Fisher, Roy M., and Paul A. Freund. *The Trial of the First Amendment*: *Miami Herald v. Tornillo*. Columbia, Mo., Freedom of Information Center, School of Journalism, University of Missouri at Columbia, 1975. 46p. **1F119**
Commentary on the case of *Miami Herald v. Tornillo* (1974) in which the U.S. Supreme Court in a unanimous decision ruled unconstitutional the Florida right of reply statute. "The issue in this case," the Court ruled, "is whether a state statute granting a political candidate a right to equal space to reply to criticism and attacks on his record by a newspaper violates the guarantee of a free press." Roy M. Fisher, dean of the University of Missouri School of Journalism, in an article entitled And Who Will Take Care of the Damrons, describes the dramatic events leading to the *Tornillo* case, the arguments before the U.S. Supreme Court, which revolved around the issue of a compulsory right of access to the newspaper press. He describes the legal reasoning in both the Florida Supreme Court decision upholding the right and the U.S. Supreme Court decision denying it. "The Damrons" refers to an earlier Florida libel case in which a politician was falsely accused. Paul A. Freund, Harvard law professor, in The Legal Framework of the Tornillo Case, discusses the legal philosophy of the decision and its implications, concluding that "for a multivocal local press we cannot turn to legal coercion but must look to changes in the economics of publishing that would make entry into the field more feasible, to measures of self-policing on the part of the press through agencies like the recent National News Council, and to self-discipline through generous use of letters columns, a spectrum of columnists, and a department of corrections."

Fitch, Robert E. "The Impact of Violence and Pornography on the Arts and Morality." In Victor B. Cline, *ed.*, *Where Do You Draw the Line?* Provo, Utah, Brigham Young University Press, 1974, pp. 15–24. **1F120**
The author attempts to answer four questions in relation to the impact of violence and pornography on the arts and morality, noting that they cannot be answered with scientific precision, but rather with "functional generalizations which are pragmatically feasible and which appeal to our common sense." (1) Do literature and the arts affect morals? (2) What effect have violence and pornography on the arts? (3) What is a definition of violence and of pornography? and (4) What can we do about it? He found that "literature and the arts most certainly have an important impact on morals" and that "violence and pornography assuredly are deleterious to the arts themselves."

Fitzgerald, Anthony F. "First Amendment Limitations on the Connecticut Law of Defamation." *Connecticut Bar Journal*, 43:175–85, March 1969. **1F121**
"Public officials, public disputants and propagandists, institutions in the conduct and management of which the public has a legitimate interest, and individuals prominent in those institutions must all prove publication with actual malice of a defamatory falsehood in order to recover in defamation."

Fitzgerald, Patrick. "Misleading Advertising: Prevent or Punish?" *Dalhousie Law Journal*, 1:246–64, December 1973. **1F122**
A look at Canadian law protecting the consumer from misleading advertising—from the seller, the advertiser, and media. "From the seller he needs protection against dishonesty and deceit. From the advertiser he needs protection against manipulation stultifying freedom of choice. From the media he needs protection from advertisement pollution. Of these three needs Canadian law satisfies only the first. Whereas in the United States both the informative and persuasive aspects of the content of any advertisement may be questioned, in Canada the law deals basically only with false information."

Fitzgerald, R. V. "The Threat to Freedom." *Library Journal*, 96:1429–30, 1 April 1971. **1F123**
The chairman of the American Civil Liberties Union of Toledo and Northwest Ohio discusses the reaction of two libraries to pressures from the policemen's association to remove the children's book, *Sylvester and the Magic Pebble*, from library shelves. The Toledo Board of Education removed the book; the county public library refused.

Fitzpatrick, John R. "Domestic Availability of Certain United States Information Agency Program Materials."

Virginia Journal of International Law, 11:71–96, December 1970. **1F124**
Caution on the part of the United States Information Agency against being accused of using its overseas propaganda programs to propagandize the American public "has hardened into Agency policy which prohibits the USIA from making its program materials available on request to interested Americans." The author proposes new guidelines so that congressional, public, and media oversight will more than adequately safeguard the American public from any form of domestic proselytization by the USIA.

Fitzsimons, Edward J. B., and John B. Fitzsimons. *Catholic Committee Persecutions. Reports of Two Trials for Libels . . . in which Mr. Michael Maley and George Bryan, Esq. were Plaintiffs, Edward J. B. Fitzsimons, Esq. Barrister at Law, and His Father, John Bourke Fitzsimons, Esq. Defendants*. Dublin, Espy & Cross, 1813. 35p. **1F125**
The father, proprietor of the *Hibernian Journal* and involved in a personal feud with the plaintiff, had unwisely drawn his lawyer-son into the affair. The judge, Lord Norbury, found the defendants not guilty but warned the son henceforth to stick to law and to leave newspapers to the "pandemonium of Printers Devils."

Fixx, James F., *ed. The Mass Media and Politics*. New York, Arno (New York Times), 1972. 636p. (Great Contemporary Issues series) **1F126**
A collection of news stories from the *New York Times* relating to the mass media and politics. Includes the following topics: Use and Abuse of the Media, The Fight for Fairness, Regulating the Media, and in the Appendix, the cases of Goldwater and *Fact* magazine, Spiro T. Agnew's criticism of the media, CBS-TV's *Selling of the Pentagon*, and press coverage of Vietnam.

Flackett, John M. "Newspaper Mergers: Recent Developments in Britain and the United States." *Antitrust Bulletin*, 12:1033–55, Winter 1967. **1F127**
"The decline of competition and trend toward concentration of ownership in the newspaper industry has been a troublesome phenomenon on both sides of the Atlantic." The author believes that "active antitrust enforcement in this country and further utilization of the Monopolies and Mergers Act in Britain may arrest the trend toward newspaper amalgamation," but that these measures are not likely to solve the fundamental problems facing the industry.

Flaherty, Daniel L. "Intellectual Freedom in the Catholic Press in the United

States." *Catholic Library World*, 38:95–99, October 1966. **1F128**
The editor of *America*, a Catholic paper established in 1909, discusses the role of the Catholic press in light of the recent Church Decree on the Instruments of Social Communication issued by the Second Vatican Council of 4 December 1963. He points out that the early Catholic press in America "was largely concerned more with combating error and answering criticism against the Church, than it was in undertaking any criticism of the Church on its own." The Council document reflects to some extent that tradition, but, he believes, it also contains echoes of the American tradition of a free and responsible press. "By and large, the practical freedom of the Catholic press today falls somewhere between its inherited position as a *Catholic* press and its inherited tradition of a Catholic *press*."

Flamm, W. H., Jr. "Further Limits on Libel Actions—Extension of the *New York Times* Rule to Libels Arising from Discussion of 'Public Issues.' " *Villinova Law Review*, 16:955–82, May 1971. **1F129**
"The purpose of this Comment is to show the emergence of a new standard for the application of the actual malice rule to all libels which arise from the publication of material which has been termed 'newsworthy,' 'in the public interest,' or 'concerning public issues.' "

Flanagan, Leo N. "Defending the Indefensible; the Limits of Intellectual Freedom." *Library Journal*, 100:1887–91, 15 October 1975. **1F130**
Criticism of the introduction to the American Library Association's *Intellectual Freedom Manual* as "a dangerous document" and one which reflects the confusion in the profession over intellectual freedom. While praising the rest of the *Manual* and particularly the article on Historical Overview, the author believes the introduction oversimplifies the issues, fails to recognize constitutional limitations on freedom of expression, confuses the concept of expression versus action, is irrational in asserting that only good ideas are effective and evil ones are not, and abrogates the responsibility of librarians in selection and rejection of materials, and counseling of readers. "The simplicity of the Introduction's definition, its failure . . . to make realistic distinctions in addressing intellectual freedom, diminishes community respect for the intelligence of librarians." He hopes that "the limitations of many of the documents contained in the *Manual* will provoke a more enlightened examination of intellectual freedom and censorship amongst librarians."

Fleisher, Richard E., and Edward Eckhart. "At Your Own Risk and Beyond: Developments in the Law of De-famation." *Arkansas Law Review*, 29:385–405, Fall 1975. **1F131**
This article examines the constitutional developments in the "public officials" and "public figures" areas of the law of defamation.

Fleishman, Stanley. "Censorship: The Law and the Courts." *Library Trends*, 19:74–80, July 1970. **1F132**
Beginning with the decision of Judge Curtis Bok in *Commonwealth v. Gordon et al.* (1949), the first obscenity case to be decided on the basis of the protection of the First and Fourteenth Amendments, the author traces the recent legal history of obscenity: *United States v. Roth* (1956), *Jacobellis v. Ohio* (1964), *Redrup v. New York* (1967), *Ginzburg v. United States* (1966), *Stanley v. Georgia* (1969), *United States v. Thirty-Seven (37) Photographs* (1970), and *Karalexis v. Byrne* (1969). The author is a constitutional lawyer who has argued a number of censorship cases before the Supreme Court.

———. "Introduction" to Oscar Peck, *Sex Life of a Cop*. n.p., Saber Books, 1967. pp. i–v. **1F133**
A Los Angeles attorney traces the legal history of the book from its conviction of obscenity by a federal court in Grand Rapids in 1963 to the reversal by the U.S. Supreme Court in 1967.

———. "Mr. Justice Douglas on Sex Censorship." *Los Angeles Bar Journal*, 51:560–62+, May 1976. **1F134**
Justice Douglas "has consistently taken the position that the First and Fourteenth Amendments deny Congress, the State Legislatures, and the judiciary the power to act as censor and determine what books our citizens may read and what pictures they may watch." While Douglas "has written enough opinions on sex censorship to fill a good-size book" they have been either dissenting or concurring opinions. The author reviews Douglas's views in the cases of *Roth v. United States* (1957), *Ginzburg v. United States* (1966), *Mishkin v. New York* (1966), *Memoirs v. Massachusetts* (1966), *Ginsberg v. New York* (1968), *Byrne v. Karalexis* (1969), *Dyson v. Steen* (1971), and *Miller v. California* (1973).

———. "Movies, Politics and the Supreme Court." *Journal of the Producers Guild of America*, 10(3):35–38, September 1968. **1F135**
The author reviews U.S. Supreme Court decisions on press freedom for the past twenty years, noting that "had the Supreme Court not intervened, the censor would have suppressed ideas relative to politics, religion, government, entertainment, race relations, and a vast gamut of opinions which a self-governing society must be free to consider if it is to endure."

———. "Obscenity and the Supreme Court." *Censorship Today*, 1(1):4–13, [June–July] 1968. **1F136**
Beginning with the *Roth* decision of 1957 (*Roth v. United States*) the author traces the U.S. Supreme Court's efforts to protect sexual ex-pression, while holding that obscenity did not fall within the protection of the First Amendment. The Court upset lower court decisions in cases involving nudist and homosexual magazines, movies (*Lady Chatterley's Lover* and *The Lovers*) and books (*Tropic of Cancer* and *Fanny Hill*). Only in the cases of *Ginzburg v. United States* (1966) and *Mishkin v. New York* (1966) did the Court uphold the obscenity conviction, the former largely on the basis of its offensive advertising campaign which was sufficient to tip the scales against Ginzburg.

———. "Overview." In *The Supreme Court Obscenity Decisions*. San Diego, Calif., Greenleaf Classics, 1973, pp. 7–20. **1F137**
An analysis of the U.S. Supreme Court decisions, rendered 21 June 1973, in *Paris Adult Theatre I v. Slaton*, *Miller v. California*, *Kaplan v. California*, *U.S. v. 12 200 Ft. Reels of Super 8mm. Film*, and *U.S. v. Orito*. Text of the decisions and dissents are reproduced along with petitions for rehearing by the American Library Association, the Association of American Publishers, and the Council of Periodical Distributors Association.

———. "The Seamy Side of Life." *Journal of the Beverley Hills Bar Association*, 2(11):10–14, December 1968. **1F138**
Criticism of the attack on Associate Justice Abe Fortas and the Supreme Court for giving constitutional protection to a harmless "girlie" film, prompts a review of the fine line of constitutional protection between the "seamy" and the criminally obscene.

———. "Smothering the Smothers Brothers." *Censorship Today*, 2(4):25–30, August–September 1969. **1F139**
"Now that the dust has settled, it is crystal clear that CBS cut the Smothers Brothers loose because the network disapproved of the sharp social satire the Smothers Brothers brought into their entertainment program." The author suggests economic interests of the networks as the basic factor in much of the censorship.

———, ed. *Selected Obscenity Cases*. Los Angeles, Blackstone, 1969. 127p. **1F140**
"This book has been written to help the general practitioner meet the prosecutor on more equal terms in obscenity cases." It contains the text of leading decisions that have protected books and magazines dealing with sex and nudity. It also includes a number of more obscure but significant cases. The work is also intended to assist the lawyer, the court, and booksellers make informed judgments on challenged materials based on lists of materials "held not-to-be-obscene." Included are Judge Jerome Frank's concurring decision in *U.S. v. Roth* (1956), Mr. Justice Black's dissenting opinion in *Ginzburg v. United States* (1966), Judge van Pelt Bryan's decision in the *Lady Chatterley's Lover* case (1959), *Grove Press, Inc. v. Christenberry* (1959), and the decisions freeing *Tropic of*

Cancer, Fanny Hill, Candy, and a group of pulp sex books, "girlie" magazines, nudist magazines, and homosexual magazines. Lists of titles cleared by the courts are included under the various categories.

[Fleishman, Stanley, Arthur Gauer, and Richard Harmetz.] *Sex, Pornography & Censorship*. 44 min. tape recording. Berkeley, Calif., Pacifica Tape Library, 1961. **1F141**
A panel discussion that took place at a meeting of the Hollywood Young Democrats. Participants were attorney Stanley Fleishman, active in many court battles against censorship; Arthur Gauer, executive director of the Citizens for Decent Literature; and moderator Richard Harmetz, president of the Hollywood Young Democrats.

Fleming, Horace W., Jr. *Administrative Regulation of Obscenity; A Comparison of Four State Literature Commissions*. Nashville, Vanderbilt University, 1973. 504p. (Ph.D. dissertation, University Microfilms, no. 73-25,046) **1F142**
"This study compares the Georgia Literature Commission, the Massachusetts Obscene Literature Control Commission, Oklahoma Literature Commission, and Rhode Island Commission to Encourage Morality in Youth. These commissions were established during the 1950's and vested with authority to review questionable publications, make 'findings of fact' on their literary merit, and recommend prosecution of those titles judged by the commissioners to be obscene. . . . As a result of cases reviewed by the United States Supreme Court procedures of the Rhode Island and Oklahoma commissions were declared unconstitutional. Subsequently, both boards were abolished." The constitutionality of the Georgia and Massachusetts commissions have not yet been determined.

―――. "The Georgia Literature Commission." *Mercer Law Review*, 18:325-36, 1967. **1F143**
A discussion of the creation of the Georgia Literature Commission in 1953 and how it has dealt with problems of obscenity, first through enlisting the voluntary cooperation of wholesale and retail news dealers in removing questionable material from the market and, secondly, through programs of community action.

―――. "The Oklahoma Literature Commission: A Case Study in Administrative Regulation of Obscenity." *Oklahoma Law Review*, 29:882-907, Fall 1976. **1F144**
An analysis of the work of the Oklahoma Literature Commission (1957-68), a state board "vested with authority to review questionable publications, hold formal hearings and make findings on their literary merit, recommend prosecution of those items found by the board to be obscene, and enter orders restraining

further sales of these materials." Oklahoma was one of only four states to attempt this approach to obscenity regulation. Based on the author's doctoral dissertation, *Administrative Regulation of Obscenity* (1973).

[Fleming, John G.] "Defamation." In *Encyclopaedia Britannica*, Chicago, Encyclopaedia Britannica, 1970, vol. 7, pp. 167-71. **1F145**
A discussion of British and, to a lesser extent, American law under the topics: publication, libel and slander (justification and fair comment), absolute and qualified privilege, privileged reports, apology, damages, libel insurance, and criminal law.

Fletcher, Homer L. "Intellectual Freedom. Bills in Legislature Dealing with Obscenity and Pornography in California." *ALA Bulletin*, 62:1354-57, December 1968. **1F146**

Fletcher, Sam G. *A Study of Public Access to Government Sessions and Records in Texas and Its Effect on Newsmen*. Lubbock, Tex., Texas Tech University, 1972. 154p. (Unpublished Master's thesis) **1F147**

[Flindell, Thomas.] *The Trial, Defence and Sentence, of Thomas Flindell, of Exeter, for a Libel on the Queen, Published in His Newspaper (The Western Luminary,) 11th July 1820*. Exeter, England, T. Flindell, 1821. 28p. **1F148**
The editor was convicted of publishing a libel on the Queen in a lengthy account in *The Western Luminary*, reporting on the charges made against the Queen by the House of Lords and on her impending trial. In a lengthy statement in his own behalf, Flindell argued that he was only publishing what was in the public record and that he bore no malice. The Court felt that he had gone beyond this with intemperate personal remarks and the jury found him guilty. Despite his plea for mercy (he had a wife and 12 children) he was given an eight-month jail sentence.

Flinn, Robert F. "The National Security Exception to the Doctrine of Prior Restraint." *William and Mary Law Review*, 13:214-25, Fall 1971. **1F149**
The author discusses cases involving the publication of the Pentagon Papers, *United States v. New York Times* (1971) and *United States v. Washington Post* (1971), giving historical perspective and evolution of the doctrine of prior restraint. He concludes that the Supreme Court's denial of an injunction to the Government "was a soundly based decision strongly supported by the central thrust of the first amendment. A prior restraint on the press for reasons of national security should be allowed only when the publication would create immediate, inevitable, direct and irreparable harm to the

United States. The burden of proof on the Government in such situations is extremely difficult to overcome, but the first amendment demands nothing less."

Flippen, Charles C., *ed. Liberating the Media: The New Journalism*. Washington, D.C., Acropolis, 1973. 212p. **1F150**
A collection of articles on the so-called "new journalism" which covers such topics as literary journalism, advocacy journalism, underground journalism, democracy in the newsroom, and public access.

Flippo, Chet. "Gushing Over Oil in Houston." *MORE*, 4(1):10-11, 14-15, January 1974. **1F151**
"In this company town, the two local newspapers—the *Post* and the *Chronicle*—are so busy flacking for the oil industry that house organs may become obsolete."

―――. "Time Inc.'s Sticky Thicket." *MORE*, 4(4):20-21, April 1974. **1F152**
"Henry Luce's empire is now increasingly under the influence of its East Texas stockholders. One result is that the company's magazines are studiously ignoring a major conservation story in the area."

Flood, F. J. "*Playboy* in Libraries." *Missouri Library Association Quarterly*, 29:197-200, September 1968. **1F153**
Despite the growing popularity of *Playboy* and the increased number of literary and socially significant articles it publishes, few libraries subscribe and for reasons that the author finds contradictory.

Flood, John C. H. *A Treatise on the Law Concerning Libel and Slander*. London, W. Maxwell, 1880. 471p. **1F154**
The object of this work, the author writes, is to set forth the law concerning individual defamation in a compact and readable form for the use of laymen as well as lawyers.

Florence, Lella S. *Birth Control on Trial*. With a Foreword by Sir Humphry Rolleston, Bart . . . and an Introductory Note by F. H. A. Marshall. . . . London, Allen & Unwin, 1930. 160p. **1F155**
An investigation into birth-control methods, undertaken at a Cambridge clinic under the auspices of the Cambridge Women's Welfare Association. Chapter 2 deals with the historical speculations, including references to the Bradlaugh-Besant trial. Throughout the book are references to the appalling ignorance of and the serious need for birth-control information. The work is well protected in the British Library.

Florence, William G., and Ruth Matthews. *Executive Secrecy: Two Perspectives*. Columbia, Mo., Freedom of Information Center, School of Journalism, University of Missouri at Columbia, 1975. 7p. (Report no. 336) **1F156**

Part I, a general view with specific cases was written by William G. Florence, former security classification policy officer with the Department of the Air Force and presently a consultant on government security policies with the Center for National Security Studies. Part II, which focuses on the Interagency Classification Review Committee, was written by Ruth Matthews, a graduate student in the School of Journalism.

Flynn, John J. "Anti-trust and the Newspapers; A Comment on S. 1312." *Vanderbilt Law Review*, 22:103–25, December 1968. **1F157**
A discussion of the failing-newspaper bill before Congress. While recognizing the peculiar competition problems faced by the nation's newspapers, the author believes that Congress should reject the bill, should investigate the means of breaking the advertising-circulation relationships, should restore competition to the industry, and should provide adequate support to the Federal Communications Commission in carrying out its responsibility with respect to newspaper monopoly.

Flynn, John T. *The Smear Terror*. New York, The Author, 1947. 30p. (Appeared serially in the *Chicago Tribune*, beginning 12 January 1947) **1F158**
"This pamphlet tells the story of one of the strangest chapters in our history—the story of private gestapos formed to terrorize citizens who differ with the objectives of the operators." The three organizations accused are: Non-Sectarian Anti-Nazi League to Champion Human Rights (an anti-Nazi group charged by the author with attempts to stir up fears of anti-Semitism among American Jews), the *Protestant* (anti-Catholic paper), and Friends of Democracy, set up by the Rev. L. M. Birkhead to fight Fascist threats to religion. The Friends sponsored the book, *Under Cover*, which Flynn charges was intended to discredit the political opponents of the Roosevelt war policy. He accuses the three groups of employing a combination of propaganda and censorship tactics. He calls on Congress to investigate the action of these "private gestapos," for the protection of the American people from use of the radio in smear campaigns, and for Jewish, Catholic, and Protestant groups to repudiate these organizations.

———. *The Thought Police: An Episode in Radical Bigotry*. New York, The Author, 1946. 8p. **1F159**

An attack on Rex Stout, head of the Writers' Board, for his efforts to get authors to boycott the *Chicago Tribune's* Literary Supplement by refusal to permit their books to be advertised in the publication. The majority of authors contacted did not support Stout's boycott.

Flynn, Leo J. *Fair Trial and the Mass Media: The Burden of Liberty in an Open Society*. Santa Barbara, Calif., University of California, Santa Barbara, 1971. 383p. (Ph.D. dissertation, University Microfilms no. 72-7458) **1F160**
"The purpose of this study is to examine the fair trial–free press controversy in order to determine whether or not there are any satisfactory measures for resolving the tension between our desire to promote the impartiality of criminal proceedings and our desire to promote the independence and vigor of the news media in reporting public affairs, including matters related to the administration of criminal justice."

Flynn, Thomas J. "Incarceration of Newsperson for Refusal to Disclose Confidential Sources Does Not Abridge First Amendment." *Santa Clara Lawyer*, 16:379–90, Spring 1976. **1F161**
Re: *Farr v. Pitchess*, 522 F.2d 464 (9th Cir.).

Fogel, Howard H. "Colonial Theocracy and a Secular Press." *Journalism Quarterly*, 37:525–33, Autumn 1960. **1F162**
"The American colonial press won its freedom from interference by religious authorities in a gradual process, highlighted by the experiences of William Bradford in Pennsylvania and of James Franklin in Massachusetts."

Fogel, Richard. "A Long Look at the Pentagon Papers." In Speech Association of America. *Abstracts, 57th Annual Meeting*. San Francisco, 1971, p. 36. **1F163**
The author suggests that who is right and who is wrong in the complex Pentagon Papers affair be left to the judgment of history.

———. "Newsmen v. Courts: A Case for the People." *Grassroots Editor*, 14(2):19–21, March–April 1973. **1F164**
In the conflict between the rights of a free press and the rights of an individual to get a fair trial, the author suggests a course that newsmen might follow which includes taking their case to the people.

Fohr, Bruce. *War: FTC vs. Advertisers*. Columbia, Mo., Freedom of Information Center, School of Journalism, University of Missouri at Columbia, 1976. 6p. (Report no. 355) **1F165**
"The antagonism between the advertising industry and the Federal Trade Commission is increasing as members of the industry are balking at the Commission's latest regulation 'tactics.' Advertisers call it overregulation and say the situation has reached the point of warfare."

Foley, Joseph M. "Broadcast Hearing Issues." In Don R. Le Duc, *ed.*, *Issues in Broadcast Regulation*. Washington, D.C., Broadcast Education Association, 1974, pp. 10–17. **1F166**
The author "uses statistics to isolate the issues which have caused the Federal Communications Commission to convene public hearings in broadcast license application cases. In essence [his article] is an effort to discover possible behavioral patterns in Commission procedures which might not emerge from intensive case by case analysis."

Folger, Peter M. "The Availability of Preliminary Injunctions Against Trade Libel." *University of San Francisco Law Review*, 6:418–29, April 1972. **1F167**
"It is the purpose of this Comment to review the law of preliminary injunctions against personal and trade libel, to trace the development of the *New York Times* rule and to discuss whether, in light of the expansion of the *New York Times* rule, the prohibition against preliminary injunctions in personal libel cases is now applicable to trade libel cases as well."

Folkard, Henry T. *Suggested Blacking-Out of Racing News: Summary of Returns*. Wigan, England, Wigan Public Library, 1905. 14p. **1F168**
The librarian of the Wigan Public Library, Wigan, England, proposes that public libraries black-out reports of racetrack gambling from newspapers in their reading rooms.

Follett, Robert J. R. "Freedom to Read and the Self-Renewal of Society." *Illinois Libraries*, 53:450–54, September 1971. **1F169**
A book publisher discusses the problem that publishers and distributors face when authors and publishers attempt to challenge the order of society. He believes the publisher "has a special responsibility to affect the communication of the ideas that will bring self-renewal and progress to our society."

Fong, Harold M. "Fair Trial-Free Press." *Women Lawyers Journal*, 61:13–15, Winter 1975. **1F170**
The effectiveness of any voluntary code covering media coverage of trials will depend on how fully the media agree to abide by it. It is up to the press and the parties "to assume the responsibility of guaranteeing the accused a fair trial by reporting factually what is brought out on record in the courtroom."

Fong-Torres, B. "Radio: One Take Behind the Line." *Rolling Stone*, 80:10, 15 April 1971. **1F171**

"Interpreting the ₁Federal Communications₁ Commission's indirectly-worded notice as a warning to ban all pro-drug songs, many station managers have appointed themselves censors and are pulling dozens of songs."

Foot, *Sir Dingle*. "The Relationship and Interplay Between the Law, the Government, Press and Parliament." *Journalism Today*, 1(1):47–70, Autumn 1967. **1F172**
Paper presented for discussion at the annual Conference of the Institute of Journalists at Ostend, 31 May 1967.

Foote, Edward B. *The Radical Remedy in Social Science; or Borning Better Babies Through Regulating Reproduction or Controlling Conception. An Earnest Essay on Pressing Problems*. New York, Murray Hill, 1886. 122p. **1F173**
This early essay on birth control by a New York doctor refers throughout to efforts by Anthony Comstock and the New York vice society to suppress information on the use of contraceptives.

——— *et al. Dr. Foote's Replies to the Alphites Giving Some Cogent Reasons for Believing that Sexual Continence Is Not Conducive to Health*. New York, Murray Hill, 1883. 126p. **1F174**
A collection of letters appearing in issues of *Dr. Foote's Health Monthly*, debating the issue of sexual continence versus artificial methods of birth control, the former position taken principally by Dr. Caroline B. Winslow, publisher of the *Washington Alpha*, thus "Alphites"; the latter by Dr. Foote, a New York physician. Throughout are references to the problems faced by Dr. Foote with the Post Office Department in permitting such freedom of discussion in matters dealing with sex. When his journal was suppressed by the Post Office on obscenity charges in 1881, he moved distribution to Whitby, Canada, but U.S. postal inspectors threatened to exclude it from Canadian mail. The arrival of a new and enlightened Postmaster General, Timothy O. Howe, reversed the policy, ruling that such journals should not be excluded without orders from the courts.

Foote, George W. *The "Freethinker" Question: An Appeal to the People of West Ham*. London, The Freethinker [1899?]. 8p. **1F175**
Editor Foote defends himself and his freethinker paper against "libelous" charges made by members of the Town Council of West Ham—that it was corrupting the people by its blasphemies and indecencies and should be banned.

———. *Reminiscences of Charles Bradlaugh*. London, Progressive Publishing Company, 1891. 46p. **1F176**
Personal recollections of the British reformer

and freethinker by a friend and associate. References are made to the 1869 trial of Bradlaugh for having failed to give sureties of £400 against the appearance of blasphemy and sedition in his paper the *Freethinker*. Bradlaugh won the case. The author also writes of Bradlaugh's role as defense attorney in the author's 1882 trial for blasphemy in the *Freethinker*, in which Foote was convicted and given a one-year sentence.

———, and Charles Watts. "Richard Carlile." In their *Heroes & Martyrs of Freethought*. London, Watts, 1874, pp. 145–60. **1F177**
A biography of the London printer-bookseller whose lifelong battle for press freedom frequently landed him in jail.

Forbes, Randall J., Lance A. Pool, and John F. Thompson. "Federalization of State Defamation Law." *Washburn Law Journal*, 15:290–310, Spring 1976. **1F178**
"It is the purpose of this article to examine the extent of this federal intervention and discuss the ramifications of it in the related areas of right of reply and retraction statutes in defamation actions."

Forcade, Thomas K. "Obscene Scene." *Countdown; a Subterranean Magazine*, 2:186–66 ₁sic₁, 1970. (Paged from back to front.) **1F179**
An account of the underground press in America, with exhibits, written by a member of the staff of the Underground Press Syndicate.

Fordham, Robert. "Censorship and the Law." In Raymond Astbury, *ed., Libraries & the Book Trade. Papers Delivered at a Symposium Held at Liverpool School of Librarianship, May 1967*. London, Clive Bingley, 1968, pp. 117–29. **1F180**
A Liverpool barrister discusses British obscenity law as it evolves over the years from the Lord Campbell Act of 1857, through numerous court decisions, to the Obscene Publications Act of 1959. He considers how the courts have interpreted the 1959 act in such cases as *R. v. Clayton and Halsey* (1963), *Mella v. Monahan* (1961), *Powell v. John Calder* (1965), and *Shaw v. DPP* (1962).

Fore, William F. "The Nixon Administration and the First Amendment." *Christianity and Crisis*, 33:23–28, 5 March 1973. **1F181**
The executive director of the Broadcasting and Film Commission of the National Council of Churches reports on the threats to First Amendment rights that have appeared in every branch of government under the Nixon Administration—"an attack more serious and insidious today than at any time since the McCarthy era, and possibly in our history." He discusses the Agnew attacks on the news media, Attorney General Mitchell's proposed

"guidelines" on the subpoena of newsmen, the Pentagon Papers case, the Supreme Court ruling against reporters' testimonial privilege, the Congressional investigation of *The Selling of the Pentagon*, the Whitehead doctrine, and threats to public television.

Forkosch, Morris D. "Freedom of Information in the United States." *DePaul Law Review*, 20:1–175, Autumn 1970. **1F182**
A comprehensive study of the history and political-legal basis of freedom of information in the United States. The author concludes that "almost-absolute freedom of information is a necessity for nation and individual and, it may be added, for the family of nations. It is not only a right of all persons themselves to seek out and obtain, edit, publish, and distribute all forms and types of information, but also a duty of all governments to make available and cooperate in all of this, and a coin-face right of all persons to receive, discuss, dissent, reply, and otherwise engage in a free and untrammeled debate concerning the substance and merits of such information." He recognizes the obligations attached to exercising such rights, but believes that the government, except in the direst of emergencies, should not restrict this freedom.

———. "Obscenity, Copyright, and the Arts." *New England Law Review*, 10:1–24, Fall 1974. **1F183**
"Works of art, whether visual or non-visual, may, because of the problems raised by the Supreme Court's obscenity guidelines . . . , run afoul of copyright laws, regulations, or administrative officials or employees; i.e., these works may be refused copyrights; or, at least, be required to meet (conform to) questionable interpretations and applications of laws and judicial decisions so as also to result in a form and degree of censorship. It is this overall thesis which is here to be explored at length."

Forman, Denis. "Television's Conscience." *Listener*, 78:737–39, 7 December 1967. **1F184**
The threat to television in Britain does not come from the danger of licensing. "The threat which we in television fear most is the threat of dullness; of a lazy conformity to notions of wholesome family viewing; the threat of political discussions emasculated in the interests of good public relations; the danger of adopting a comfortable style of reporting the world which leaves every disturbing avenue unexplored and every dubious stone unturned."

Forsman, John. "The Dangers of Being Honest with Yourself." *Virginia Librarian*, 16(4):5–8, Winter 1969/70. **1F185**
A librarian relates his own experience and those of others with the censor. Even if you

win, your ability as a library administrator may be greatly impaired if the fight has been bitter. He calls for association financial as well as moral support of embattled librarians. The author was involved in the Richmond (Calif.) Public Library censorship case.

Forster, Joseph. *The Rejected Address to the Editor of the Weekly Dispatch of Sunday, October 5, 1834, on Being Sentenced to Three Months' Imprisonment in That Horrible Bastile, the House of Correction, Cold Bath Fields, for Selling Unstamped Newspapers, Called the Man, Police Gazette, Twopenny Dispatch, Pioneer, etc. . . . to Which Is Added, a Few Remarks on the Present Awful and Momentous Crisis.* London, Howlett [1835]. **1F186**

Forston, Robert F. *How Communications Theory Could Be Used to Improve Judicial Decisions on Freedom of Expression.* n.p., The Author, 1972. 10p. (ED 71, 115) **1F187**
"The author considers the current position of the Supreme Court on the First Amendment and the right of free speech. There are questions of distinction between what constitutes lawful or unlawful expressions of opinion, including the use of symbolic conduct, with respect to the communicator's intent, his effectiveness, and the clear and present danger of the act. The author proposes use of a communications game theory to assist in distinguishing between lawful and lawless communication. Using sports events as analogies, he discusses rules, tactics, and customs and their functions in games. He concludes that this game model could serve as a 'unique, flexible perspective' for analysis of communication situations, particularly in making decisions about protection under the First Amendment and violations of free speech."

Fortin, Jacques. "Criminal Law Project: Obscenity." *IPLO Quarterly* (Institute of Professional Librarians of Ontario), 15:17–20, July 1973. **1F188**
Comment and interpretation with respect to the study paper on Obscenity, prepared by Richard G. Fox for the Law Reform Commission. "The purpose of the study paper is to inform the public, and give it the opportunity to reflect on the issue of obscenity and determine the kind of society in which, in terms of personal and collective liberties, it would like to have." Professor Fortin was director of the Prohibited and Regulated Conduct Project which produced the report on Obscenity for the Commission.

"Forum on Censorship." *Bookseller*, 3193:1442–46, 4 March 1967. **1F189**

A forum on censorship with panelists Brigid Brophy, John Calder, R. Davis-Poynter, Sydney Hyde, Robert Pitman, and David Holloway. The purpose was to discuss a proposal made by Robert Maxwell, M.P. that the Publishers Association set up a censorship or policing committee. The vast majority of those in attendance, including all but two of the speakers, rejected the proposal.

Foster, *Sir* John, and Paul Sieghart. "Libel, Privacy and English Law." *Index on Censorship*, 1(3/4):67–82, Autumn–Winter 1972. **1F190**
"The English law of libel, for all that it began—centuries ago—as an instrument of censorship devised by an autocratic government, performs no such function today. For this, as for so many others of our freedoms, we have to thank the Parliamentarians and judges of the past. Instead, it serves to regulate the balance between one man's right to publish the truth—or at least his honest opinion about the truth—and another man's right to be compensated if his reputation is unjustly attacked in public. Perhaps in one or more details it needs reform, but the very fact that different interests are calling for quite different reforms makes one suspect that it probably balances the many conflicting interests with a reasonable degree of fairness." This is the conclusion reached by the authors after surveying the numerous criticisms of British Libel laws and proposals for reform, with particular references to the proposals made in Michael Rubinstein's book, *Wicked, Wicked Libels.*

Foster, Retha K. "Censorship and Arizona High Schools." *Arizona English Bulletin*, 8:63–70, May 1966. **1F191**
A survey of English teachers and librarians in ninety-six public schools in Arizona revealed that 41 percent experienced censorship incidents and in 24 percent the efforts at suppression were successful. A list of the books under attack is appended, with objector (parent, teacher, superintendent), reasons for objection, and action taken.

Fought, Jack. "Bessie Stagg: The Fight Is Over." *Grassroots Editor*, 15(6):12, November–December 1974. **1F192**
The publisher of the *Bartonville* (Ill.) *News* quits after seventeen years because of a continuing campaign of harassment, boycotts, and threats to bomb her shop and kidnap her children.

———. "The Hutchins Report: Twenty Years After." *Grassroots Editor*, 8(6):20–21, 34, November–December 1967. **1F193**
Despite the fact that the 133-page report which criticized the American press was rejected by most of the newspaper profession when it was released in 1947, a generation later it is considered standard reading in journalism schools and "has undoubtedly influenced some of the prevailing attitudes in the communications industry."

"Four-Letter Words: A Symposium." *Humanist*, 29(5):7–8, 30, September–October 1969. **1F194**
"Magazines have often discussed what should be their policies concerning four-letter words. In some cases there have been protests from readers; some printers have attempted to censor magazines by not setting them in type; and dealers and booksellers have often refused material that they considered 'obscene.' Interested in the question of what should be the appropriate policy concerning the use of four-letter words, *The Humanist* sent out the following three questions to editors and authors, and to the A.C.L.U.: 1. What do you think should be the policy of magazines, newspapers and journals on the use of four-letter words? 2. Do you have an individual policy? 3. Have you encountered any restrictions from printers, newsdealers, booksellers, or readers on this matter?" Replies are printed from the following: Daniel Schwartz (*New York Times*), Cary McWilliams (*Nation*), John Barth (author), B. J. Stiles (former editor of the Methodist magazine, *Motive*), Alan Reitman (ACLU), and William Phillips (*Partisan Review*).

Fox, Donald R. "Obscenity: A Step Forward By a Step Back?" *Albany Law Review*, 38:764–97, 1974. **1F195**
After considering briefly the history of obscenity, the author examines the *Roth* decision (*Roth v. United States*, 1957) and refinements of *Roth*, and analyzes the latest contribution of *Miller v. State of California* (1973).

Fox, *Sir* John C. "*The King v. Almon.*" *Law Quarterly Review*, 24:184–98, April 1908; 24:266–78, July 1908. **1F196**
Comment on a judgment in *Rex v. Almon*, prepared by Justice Wilmot in 1765 but never delivered because the prosecution was dropped. Almon was accused of publishing a libel on Chief Justice Lord Mansfield in connection with the case of John Wilkes. Justice Wilmot's decision in favor of the plaintiff was published by his son in 1802 and widely used beginning in 1821 and up until the present day (1908). Justice Fletcher, however, in *Taaffe v. Downes* (1813) severely criticized the decision, noting that Lord Mansfield had been responsible for denying the rights of juries and freedom of the press and that Justice Wilmot considered Almon's attack on a friend and patron as little less than sacrilege and that his judgment might have been biased.

Fox, Richard G. *The Concept of Obscenity.* Melbourne and Sydney, Australia, Law Book Co., 1967. 193p. **1F197**
A detailed examination of the Australian law relating to obscenity. The author follows four broad objectives: "to describe the phenomenon of obscenity; to trace the development of the current law and to analyze its main features; to examine the justifications presented for the legal prohibitions on obscenity; and finally to express my views as to the proper function of the criminal law in this battleground of conflicting interests." Three basic problems must be resolved in order to apply the legal concept

of obscenity in any given situation: "to define the potential audience; to determine the likely effect of a given publication on the potential audience; and to decide whether this effect is sufficiently adverse to warrant suppression of the publication by way of criminal sanctions." The author explores the ramifications of each problem, noting that any obscenity law must take into consideration public policy and the varying demands of public opinion. "Ideally, at any given time, obscenity law should reflect, as accurately as possible, the relative importance assigned by the community to the need to avoid risk of harm; to the social values of individual liberty, freedom of expression, literary, artistic and scientific merit; and to the demands of public decency. But the literati, libertarians and social scientists are not the only ones who have drums to beat; the censorially-minded and religiously zealous also have their special claims to make. When these different groups clash over the issue of obscenity the immediate function of the law must be to seek passable compromises in order to keep the peace. . . . Whatever form the law takes, it is essential that it always recognizes the existence of competing values and that it provides, within its framework, some means for constantly reassessing and redressing the balance between them."

――――. "Obscenity and Indecency." *Adelaide Law Review*, 3:392–402, May 1969.   **1F198**
An interpretation of the Obscene and Indecent Publications Act, 1901–1955 (New South Wales). The article deals largely with the case, *Crowe v. Graham and Others* (1968), a prosecution which arose out of the publication in Sydney of the second issue of each of two magazines—*Censor* and *Obscenity*, works purporting to lampoon the irrationality of Australian censorship and reproducing portions of works prohibited by the Customs Act.

――――. *Study Paper on Obscenity. Prepared for the Law Reform Committee . . . June 1972*. Ottawa, Law Reform Commission, 1972. 134p. (Published as part of the report of the Prohibited and Regulated Conduct Project. Reprinted in *Alberta Law Review*, 1974, pp. 172–235)   **1F199**
"In his introduction, Professor Fox elaborates on the two fundamental difficulties at the root of the problem: first, that obscenity is an inescapably subjective phenomenon; and second, the law's own indeterminacy of aim. He then scrutinizes the plethora of possible subject matter for obscenity and its dissemination; and he proceeds to a consideration of whether the suspect material is obscene *per se* or variable according to susceptibility of the audience. Six possible justifications are offered for legislative prohibitions on obscenity; each of these are very closely examined and most are found to be tenuous at best. After a rather detailed examination of the cases on the Criminal Code provisions, other Federal legislation touching on the subject of obscenity, and the necessarily incidental consideration of defences and expert

witnesses, Professor Fox weighs the possible alternatives to the present law. There cannot, of course, be any definitive answers."—Editor's introduction, *Alberta Law Review*.

――――. "Survey Evidence of Community Standards in Obscenity Prosecutions." *Canadian Bar Review*, 50:315–30, May 1972.   **1F200**
R. v. Prairie Schooner News Ltd. and Powers (1971), C.C.C. (2d) 251, 75 W.W.R. 585 (1970), 12 C.L.Q. 462 and *R. v. Times Square Cinema, Ltd.* (1971), 4 C.C.C. (2d), 229, [1971] 3 O.R. 688.

Fox, Victor J. *The Pentagon Case*. New York, Freedom Press, 1958. 247p.   **1F201**
A fictional account of "the terrifying helplessness of this country in opposing the insidious saturation of its magazines, books, entertainment media, and educational system with subversive propaganda." Brett Cable, the hero, suggests a solution: a campaign against subversive literature patterned after the women's club drive against obscene magazines, including boycott of retailers who refuse to cooperate. "But how will the public know which magazines, books, or programs are subversive?" asks Jane. "The public isn't dumb," Brett responds. "All the public needs is a little guidance—just as it now gets from the Decency League in the case of immoral movies. There are plenty of patriotic organizations which could start the ball rolling, once they learn what's going on." He suggests that subversive books and movies be given a "patriotic rating," a term less controversial than "blacklisting."

Fox, W. J. *The Duties of Christians toward Deists: A Sermon Preached . . . on Occasion of the Recent Prosecution of Mr. Carlile for the Re-publication of Paine's "Age of Reason."* London, George Smallfield, 1819. 48p.   **1F202**
"If Deists will listen to you, persuade them; if they will reason, argue with them; if they write and publish, reply to them; if they misrepresent, expose them; but in the name of Christ, do not persecute them, do not abet or sanction persecution." The prosecution of Mr. Carlile is a libel on Christianity.

Fraenkel, Osmond K. "The Right to Express Oneself." In his *The Rights We Have. A Handbook of Civil Liberties*. New York, Crowell, 1971, pp. 26–71. **1F203**
Areas discussed include: sedition, disorderly conduct, obscenity, contempt of court, distribution of leaflets, the use of loudspeakers, maintaining anonymity, maintaining silence, defamation, invasion of privacy, academic freedom, symbolic speech, use of the mails, and the press.

Frakt, Arthur N. "The Evolving Law of Defamation: *New York Times Co. v. Sullivan* to *Gertz v. Robert Welch, Inc.*

and Beyond." *Rutgers-Camden Law Journal*, 6:471–513, Winter 1975. **1F204**
This article presents a brief examination of the development of the constitutional limitations on defamation law from *New York Times v. Sullivan* (1964), to *Rosenbloom v. Metromedia, Inc*. (1971), analyzes the new test for determining the constitutional limitations on the law of defamation under *Gertz v. Robert Welch, Inc.* (1974), and suggests an alternative test. The article discusses the effect of the *Gertz* fault requirements on the law of private defamation, examines the damages issues raised by the *Gertz* decision, and presents a brief examination of the effect of *New York Times* and *Gertz* upon nonmedia defamation.

Franck, Thomas M., and Edward Weisband, *eds. Secrecy and Foreign Policy*. New York, Oxford University Press, 1974. 453p. **1F205**
A collection of articles dealing with various points of view on the issue of the government need for secrecy in matters of defense and foreign affairs and the people's right to know, issues which are delineated in a foreword by Maxwell Cohen. The scope of the work encompasses United States, Great Britain, and Canada. Articles are grouped under four headings: The Executive Examines Its Secrecy Policies, The Legislators Confront the Security Managers, The Media Confront the News Managers, and The Individual Confronts the State. Of particular relevance to press freedom are the following articles: The Cannikin Papers: A Case Study in Freedom of Information by Patsy T. Mink. The Irreconcilable Conflict Between Press and Government: "Whose Side Are You On?" by Haynes Johnson. The American Espionage Statutes and Publication of Defense Information by Benno C. Schmidt, Jr. Cabinet Secrecy, Collective Responsibility, and the British Public's Right to Know About and Participate in Foreign Policy Making by William Clark. Secrecy, News Management, and the British Press by Anthony Sampson. Disclosure, Discretion, and Dissemblement: Broadcasting and the National Interest in the Perspective of a Publicly Owned Medium by Kenneth Lamb. Access to News in a Small Capital: Ottawa by Anthony Westell. Enforcing the Public's Right to Openness in the Foreign Affairs Decision-Making Process by Richard A. Frank. The Ellsberg Case: Citizen Disclosure by Leonard B. Boudin. Official Secrecy and External Relations in Britain: The Law and Its Context by Stanley de Smith. Secrecy and the Citizen's Right to Know: A British Civil Libertarian Perspective by Harry Street. Reform of the British Law Pertaining to Secrecy: A Rejoinder to Professor Street by Stanley de Smith. Secrecy in Law and Policy: The Canadian Experience and International Relations by Maxwell Cohen.

Francois, William. "Can the Press

Police Itself?" *America*, 124:433–35, 24 April 1971.   **1F206**
"A number of signs point to first-time preparations by America's Fourth Estate to formalize self-criticism in its use of the great powers of the press." A consideration by press associations of press councils.

————. "Law and the Writer." *Writers Digest*, 53(7):28–29, July 1973.   **1F207**
Re: *Rosenbloom v. Metromedia Inc.* (1971) and subsequent libel cases which indicate a tendency for "stories judged to be of general public concern or in the public interest [to be] constitutionally privileged even though they contain defamatory falsehoods—except when the plaintiff can show malice."

————. *Mass Media Law and Regulation*. Columbus, Ohio, Grid, 1975. 470p.
1F208
Content: Early Press Controls & First Amendment. First Amendment Theory & Practice. Injunction—Prior Restraint. Libel. Privacy. Freedom of Information vs. Secrecy. Free Press vs. Fair Trial. Subpoena Power vs. Newsmen's Privilege. Pornography. Advertising. Radio & TV: Overview. Radio & TV: Section 315. Radio & TV: Access to the Media. Radio & TV: Advertising, and Fairness Doctrine & Access.

————. "Media Access: Romance and Reality." *America*, 129:186–88, 22 September 1973.   **1F209**
"The public's right of access to mass media is threatened by a trend in the FCC and Supreme Court to see the broadcaster as a journalist with the journalist's right to decide what he will or will not print."

————. "New Libel Ruling." *Writers Digest*, 54(10):42–44, October 1974.
1F210
The author finds the U.S. Supreme Court's ruling in the libel case, *Gertz v. Robert Welch, Inc.* (1974), unsettling as it pertains to private citizens and the public news media.

Frandsen, Kenneth D., and James G. Backes. "Canon Thirty-Five: Televising Courtroom Proceedings." *Quarterly Journal of Speech*, 49:389–94, December 1963.   **1F211**
"After careful investigation, the writers have concluded that under certain common-sense limitations, broadcasting would seem to have a place in the courtroom."

Frank, Reuven. "An Address." *TV Quarterly*, 10(2):34–40, Winter 1973. (Also in *Vital Speeches*, August 1972)
1F212

The president, National Broadcasting Company News, comments on federal controls of television which, if applied to newspapers, would be thrown out of court as violations of the First Amendment. "Television news has been held not to fall within the protections of the First Amendment . . . [and] representation of all three branches of Government intrude into the news most Americans get, television news." He cites numerous instances of government intrusion. "If the Government should not be in news, it should not be in television news." The physical differences between the media is not a convincing reason for different treatment.

————. *An Answer to Television Critics*. Columbia, Mo., Freedom of Information Center, School of Journalism, University of Missouri at Columbia, 1971. 6p. (Report no. 0011)   **1F213**
Speaking before members of the Missouri Broadcasters Association, the president of NBC criticizes the critics of newscasting, emphasizing that the First Amendment guarantees the right to speak, not the right to be heard by a particular audience; that it is a guarantee to the people that they have a right to a free press. He comments on the political critics of the right and left (if the networks gave air time to a full presentation of every political and ideological point of view there would be no time for anything else); the social scientists who analyze the judgment of the news editors; the rash of content analysts; the Congressional investigators including the analysis of NBC and CBS video tapes of the Laos incursion to prove the networks hierarchy intentionally made the Laos operation appear to be a military and political disaster; and, until recently when their own interests coincided, newspaper colleagues.

————. *And Who Shall Censor the Censors?* Washington, D.C., National Broadcasting Co., 1971. 15p. (Also in *Nieman Reports*, November 1971, and in *Vital Speeches*, December 1971)   **1F214**
"The First Amendment does not protect newspapers against government supervision. It protects the American people from having their news supervised." This should include news supplied by radio and television. Concentrated ownership of the media is less a danger to freedom of the press than "leaving to a few government officials the power to decide what can be discussed and what cannot." Frank criticizes the critic in high places who wants television to "engineer for him the society he would prefer to this one." The role of the press is to inform society about problems, not to solve them.

Frankel, Max. "The 'State Secrets' Myth." *Columbia Journalism Review*, 10(3):22–26, September–October 1971
1F215
A veteran Washington correspondent describes the "very loose and special way in which classified information and documenta-

tion is regularly employed by our government. . . . The government's complaint against the *Times* [Pentagon Papers] comes with ill grace because government itself has, regularly and consistently over the decades, violated the conditions it suddenly seeks to impose upon us." Taken from the author's testimony in the Pentagon Papers case.

Frankino, Steven P. *et al.* "The FCC's Role in Television Programming Regulation. A Symposium." *Villanova Law Review*, 14:581–663, Summer 1969.
1F216
"The Editors asked the participants to discuss a number of significant issues: What constitutional questions are raised by the FCC effort to obtain balance and diversity in programming? Do present FCC requirements for balanced programming contravene proscriptions against FCC censorship? Do they contravene the first amendment guarantee of free speech? Is it desirable for the Commission to obtain balance and diversity in programming? Are efforts in this area necessary to insure service to minority interests and less dominant needs and tastes of the general viewing audience? What effect should diversity within the total spectrum of the communication media have on the overall judgment of program diversity? Should there be different free speech patterns for television than have been established for other media? Do the technical characteristics and psychological effects of television broadcasting constitutionally distinguish it from other media? How adequate and effective are FCC guidelines concerning the program policies of broadcasters? Does the use of these guidelines result in undesirable 'sameness'? Can and should the Commission concern itself with conglomerate ownership of broadcasting stations? Is the common ownership of several media within a given area a sufficient justification to deny issuance or renewal of a broadcasting license?" Participants: Kenneth A. Cox, FCC Commissioner; Ben C. Fisher, chairman, American Bar Association Section on Administrative Law; Louis L. Jaffe, Harvard Law School; and Edmund A. Barker, president, Radio Television News Directors Association.

Franklin, Marc A. *Case and Materials on Mass Media Law*. Mineola, N.Y., Foundation Press, 1977. 878p.   **1F217**
"The purpose of this book is to acquaint students with major aspects of media law and to provide an extended look at the tensions between legal regulation and the First Amendment. The materials have been organized functionally, in terms of gathering, publishing and distributing the product." Chapter 1, The Development of the Concept of Freedom of Expression; chapter 2, Business Aspects of Mass Media Enterprise; chapter 3, Legal Problems of Gathering Information (including newsmen's privilege, government information); chapter 4, Restrictions on Content of Communication (including libel, fair trial v. free press, privacy, state secrets); chapter 5, Distribution Problems of Non-broadcast Media; chapter 6, Introduction to Broadcasting; chapter 7, Broadcast Licensing; and chapter 8,

Legal Control of Programming (including fairness doctrine, access, political campaigns).

————. *The Dynamics of American Law. Courts, the Legal Process and Freedom of Expression*. Mineola, N.Y., Foundation Press, 1968. 803p.   **1F218**
The volume is intended "to give the reader an understanding of the role that the courts play in shaping our law, with particular attention to the law as it relates to freedom of expression." Chapter 1 follows an actual suit for libel, step by step to the decision that concluded it; chapter 2 studies the judicial decision-making process in common law, using defamation cases as examples; chapter 3 shows the relation between courts and legislatures, using as topics the privilege to report official proceedings and the law of privacy; chapter 4 studies the tripartite relationship among the legislative, administrative, and judicial branches in the context of the regulation of broadcasting; chapter 5 is concerned with the relationship between the courts and the Constitution with respect to the First Amendment.

————, and Ruth K. Franklin. *The First Amendment and the Fourth Estate; Communications Law for Undergrduates*. Mineola, N.Y., Foundation Press, 1977. 727p.   **1F219**
"The goals of this book are to clarify the major legal doctrines that affect mass media, to explain their origins and asserted justifications, and to evaluate their soundness. In these efforts we focus upon the language of the Supreme Court of the United States, whose interpretations of the First Amendment provide the essential starting part."

Fransecky, Roger B. " 'The Right to Read: Adults Only'?" *English Record*, 21(1):88–96, October 1970.   **1F220**
A review of the use of controversial literature in a sex-affirming culture with emphasis on the rights of the high school student. "The Freedom to Read is a freedom that is shared by all—by teacher and pupil—and it can never be a right we label 'For Adults Only.' "

Frantz, Laurent B. "Is the First Amendment Law?—A Reply to Professor Mendelson." *California Law Review*, 51:729–54, December 1963.
                                         1F221
An answer to Professor Wallace Mendelson's response to the author's "criticism of the Supreme Court's use of an *ad hoc* 'balancing of interests' test in free speech cases (M297)."

————. "Meiklejohn's Theory on Freedom of Speech." *Rights*, 12(1/2): 4–8, February 1965.   **1F222**
A tribute to the "wise, genial, and clear-headed teacher and philosopher who spent his autumn years trying to help us understand the meaning of our constitutional heritage." The author summarizes Meiklejohn's views as expressed in his book *Free Speech and Its Relationship to Self-Government*, noting that "Meiklejohn derived his concept of the meaning of the First Amendment, not from the natural or legal or constitutional rights of the individual, but from the necessities of self-government."

Franz, Jay L. *TV Self Regulation: Smothers Brothers*. Columbia, Mo., Freedom of Information Center, School of Journalism, University of Missouri at Columbia, 1970. 6p. (Report no. 238)   **1F223**
The quarrel over the canceling of the Smothers Brothers Comedy Hour by CBS "has served to draw attention to one of television's continuing dilemmas: presentation of social commentary within an entertainment vehicle."

[Fraser, Harry M., and Henry H. Beamish.] *Mond v. Fraser and Beamish*. London, Printed by C. F. Roworth, 1919? 7p.   **1F224**
Sir Alfred Moritz Mond, a member of the Privy Council and an international Jewish financier, charged defendants with libeling him in a poster in which he was described as "a traitor" who "allotted shares to Huns during the War." The pamphlet gives brief statements of plaintiff and defendants. Beamish was founder of Britons, an anti-Semitic publishing house.

Fraser, John. "The Erotic and Censorship." *Oxford Review*, 9:21–39, Michaelmas 1968.   **1F225**
The author relates the difficulties among the critics in separating the erotic from the pornographic. He believes that the notion that erotic violence in literature will lead to violence in real life is remote, but it may alter people's images of reality, which is harmful. He believes there should be no censorship of erotica for adults, probably none for children. Removing censorship will remove the temptations to sample the forbidden; will bring greater freedom to serious artists and art; and "the more that certain intensities can be found in intelligent work, the less one will be driven to look for them in stupid work. . . . Erotic art . . . has always been with us and presumably will be with us for a long time to come; and within the erotic there seem to me to be no regions that by their very nature are unreachable by art." He hopes that there will come a day when such discussions of censorship and pornography will "come to seem as quaint and remote" as the theological fussings of the nineteenth century.

Fraser, Peter. *The Intelligence of the Secretaries of State & Their Monopoly of Licensed News, 1660–1688*. Cambridge, England, Cambridge University Press, 1956. 177p.   **1F226**
The secretaries of state from 1666 to 1688 exercised a monopoly on licensed news, continuing it even after the expiration of the Licensing Act in 1679. Unlicensed news, the courts ruled, was illegal because it encouraged a breach of peace. Much of the book deals with the methods used by the various secretaries of state to gather news for their official newsletters, both foreign and domestic—the use of spies, the Post Office, and regular correspondents. With the expiration of the Licensing Act, independent, unlicensed newsbooks began to be issued, the coffee house became a center for news distribution, the first Whig newspapers emerged along with the institution of the Penny Post. One section deals with the restrictions on printing of parliamentary proceedings.

Fraser, Russell. *The War Against Poetry*. Princeton, N.J., Princeton University Press, 1970. 215p.   **1F227**
"The subject of this book is the attack on secular verse and the theatre in England in the sixteenth and seventeenth centuries."

Frasier, George E. "An Alternative to the General–Damage Award for Defamation." *Stanford Law Review*, 20:504–37, February 1968.   **1F228**
"This Note demonstrates that the conflict between these interests [the personal interest in reputation and the societal interest in the free flow of accurate information] in cases involving the mass media can be reduced by replacing the general-damage remedy with the remedies of retraction and reply in connection with making certain changes in the substantive law of defamation."

Free Art Legal Fund . . . London, The Fund, 1967? 4p.   **1F229**
This brochure solicits funds for the defense of Hubert Selby, Jr.'s *Last Exit to Brooklyn* and for a permanent legal fund for the defense of the arts. The inside pages contain an English translation of Émile Zola's On the Question of Morality in Literature.

Free Communications Group. *Free the Press: The Case for Democratic Control*. [London, Free Communications Group, 1970?] 32p. Processed. **1F230**
This pamphlet, bearing no publisher's imprint or date, is believed to have been circulated clandestinely among Fleet Street journalists in the early 1970s. Citing the decline in numbers and the decay of British newspapers as a threat to democracy, the author proposes that journalists "help to combat this danger in the press by refusing the role of opinion-manipulators, by abandoning the self-pity of the pub, and—in co-operation with other newspapers' workers—by taking control of policy, content and management increasingly into their own hands. Work through the Union, where you can . . . help convert the Union to the idea of democratic control."

"Free Press and Fair Trial—Trial

Judge May Not Close Courtroom to Press and Public Without Showing of Serious and Imminent Threat to the Integrity of the Trial." *Fordham Urban Law Journal*, 1:308–22, Fall 1972. **1F231**
Re: *Oliver v. Postel*, 30 N.Y.2d 171, 282 N.E.2d 306, 331 N.Y.S.2d 407 (1972).

"Free Press and TV—Fair Trial: A Panel." *Publishing, Entertainment and Law Quarterly*, 5:419–70, March 1966. **1F232**

A panel discussion held at the annual meeting of the Bar Association of the Seventh Circuit. Participants: Judge J. Skelly Wright; Justice A. T. Goodwin; Norbert A. Schlei, Assistant Attorney General of the United States; Edward V. Harahan, U.S. Attorney for the Northern District of Illinois; John Charles Daly, television commentator; and Norman E. Isaacs, executive editor, *Louisville Courier Journal*.

Free Press versus Fair Trial by Jury: The Sheppard Case. 16 mm b/w or color movie, 27 min. Chicago, Encyclopaedia Britannica Educational Corp., 1969. **1F233**
Conflict between freedom of the press and the right of the accused to a fair trial as seen in the case of Dr. Samuel Sheppard. Includes excerpts from the U.S. Supreme Court's decision in 1961, reversing the original verdict.

Free Speech. Newsletter of the Commission on Freedom of Speech, Speech Association of America. 1962–date. Three times a year. (Place of publication varies with location of the editor; Falls Church, Va. in 1976) **1F234**
Edited 1962–67 by Franklyn S. Haiman; 1967–70 by Thomas L. Tedford; 1970–73 by Haig A. Bosmajian; since 1973 by Peter E. Kane. The newsletter deals largely with issues involving freedom and suppression of oral communications, but sometimes with broader issues of freedom of expression. Lengthy articles are listed separately in this bibliography under the name of the author.

"Free Speech in the Marketplace—Accommodating 'Speech Plus' Activity and Property Rights." *University of Colorado Law Review*, 44:259–72, December 1972. **1F235**
Re: *Lloyd Corp. v. Tanner*, 407 U.S. 551 (1972), involving the distribution of antiwar handbills in a shopping center. The U.S. Supreme Court reversed a lower court and upheld the property claim of the shopping center owners who sought to prevent the distribution.

Free Speech Yearbook. A Publication of the Commission on Freedom of Speech of the Speech Communication Association. 1970–date. Annual (The Committee on Freedom of Speech issued a limited number of yearbooks in processed form from 1962 through 1969) **1F236**
Edited by George P. Rice and Nancy G. McDermid, 1968; George P. Rice, Haig A. Bosmajian, and Alvin A. Goldberg, 1969; Thomas L. Tedford, 1970–72; Alton Barbour, 1973–74. Papers presented deal largely with issues involving freedom and suppression of oral communications. Those pertaining to the mass media are listed in this bibliography under the name of the author.

Freedom at Issue; A Periodical of Comment and Review. New York, Freedom House, 1970–date. Bimonthly. **1F237**
Issues frequently report on international conditions of press freedom.

[Freedom Defence Committee.] "Freedom Defence Committee: [Statement of Purpose]." *Socialist Leader*, 18 September 1948. (Reprinted in George Orwell, *Collected Essays* . . . . New York, Harcourt, Brace, 1968, vol. 4, pp. 446–47) **1F238**
The Committee was set up in 1945 "to uphold the essential liberty of individuals and organisations, and to defend those who are persecuted for exercising their rights to freedom of speech, writing and action." The statement was signed by Benjamin Britten, E. M. Forster, Augustus John, George Orwell, Herbert Read, and Osbert Sitwell. The Committee also published a bulletin.

Freedom House. "The News Media and the Government: Clash of Concentrated Power." *Freedom at Issue*, 21:3–10, September–October 1973. **1F239**
Leading newsmen and present and past government officials took part in a two-day News Media/Government Consultation, sponsored by Freedom House. "The call to the consultation posed the question whether 'the press' and/or 'the government' has each in its own way hardened its adversarial position; whether there is now a closing of ranks on both sides, producing a *de facto* war of the worlds (press vs. government). The meeting was asked to define the real areas of press/government conflict, setting forth the operative Constitutional rules, and recommending specific common sense procedures by which to maximize the flow of information to the public without destructive confrontations." The result was a statement and guidelines entitled "The News Media and the Government: The Clash of Concentrated Power," which consists of recommendations for government and the news media in directing their relationship in judicial and other processes, and specific guidelines applied to government officials and to journalists. In addition the report contains a colloquy between Pentagon Papers adversaries, Whitney North Seymour, Jr., who prosecuted the *Times*, and Alexander M. Bickel, the *Times* attorney. Also included are statements by Erwin D. Canham (The Human Factor), Leo Cherne (Institutional Revolt), and Alexander M. Bickel (Aspects of the Constitutional Position). A brief reporting of the session is presented in a twenty-page pamphlet with the same title as the full report, also published by Freedom House.

"Freedom of Discussion of Controversial Issues Over the Air." *Air Law Review*, 12:372–78, October 1941. **1F240**
"The essential concern of this article is to investigate the effect of the Code adopted by the National Association of Broadcasters and the rules and regulations of the Federal Communications Commission upon freedom of discussion over the airwaves." Press reports rather than statistics are the basis of the analysis.

"The Freedom of Information Act: Access to Law." *Fordham Law Review*, 36:765–82, May 1968. **1F241**
The analysis is limited to those provisions of the Freedom of Information Act of 1967 "which affirmatively require disclosure of information amounting to law—documents through which agencies express policy and interpretation of law."

"The Freedom of Information Act and the Exemption for Intra-Agency Memoranda." *Harvard Law Review*, 86:1047–67, April 1973. **1F242**
"This Note will examine, with reference to these [FOIA] policies, the judicial attempts to date to define the scope and limits of the exemption for intra- and inter-agency memoranda."

"Freedom of Information Act—Commercial or Financial Information 'Confidential' If Disclosure Would Impair Government Access to Information or Harm Competitive Position of Informant." *Harvard Law Review*, 88:470–77, December 1974. **1F243**
Re: *National Parks & Conservation Ass'n. v. Morton*, 498 F.2d 765 (D.C. Cir. 1974).

"Freedom of Information Act: File Classified 'Top Secret' Is Within National Security Exemption for the Act and Is Not Obtainable Unless the Classification Is Arbitrary and Unreasonable." *Harvard Law Review*, 83:928–35, February 1970. **1F244**
Re: *Epstein v. Resor*, 296 F. Supp. 214 (N.D. Cal. 1969). "An historian associated with Stanford University's Hoover Institution on War, Revolution and Peace, brought suit under the Freedom of Information Act to enjoin the Secretary of the Army from withholding a World War II file generated by the Allied Force Headquarters. The file described as 'Forceful Repatriation of Displaced Soviet Citizens—Operation Keelhaul,' concerned the forcible removal of about 900,000 anti-communist

Russians from Germany to the Soviet Union, allegedly to execution or slave camps."

Freedom of Information Center. *Conference on Censorship*, *7 February 1969*. Columbia, Mo., The Center in cooperation with the Missouri State Library, the Missouri Library Association, and the Extension Division of the University of Missouri, 1969. 61p. (ED 38,428)   **1F245**
Speakers: Milton Meltzer, author and editor; Enid Olson, National Council of Teachers of English; Irving Levitas, Temple Emanu-el, Yonkers, N.Y.; Joan Bodger, consultant, Missouri State Library; Morris Ernst, lawyer and author; and Anson Mount, *Playboy*.

————. *Freedom of Information Committees*. Columbia, Mo., Freedom of Information Center, School of Journalism, University of Missouri at Columbia, 1970. 7p.   **1F246**
A current listing of membership in various national information organizations including the American Newspaper Guild, American Newspaper Publishers Association, American Society of Newspaper Editors, Motion Picture Association, Sigma Delta Chi, and so forth.

————. *The Pentagon Papers and the Public*. Columbia, Mo., Freedom of Information Center, School of Journalism, University of Missouri at Columbia, 1971. 5p. (Report no. 0013)   **1F247**
An opinion paper re: *U.S. v. the New York Times and the Washington Post*, 1971.

————. *State Access Statutes*. Columbia, Mo., Freedom of Information Center, School of Journalism, University of Missouri at Columbia, 1968. 32p. (Report no. 202)   **1F248**
The text of open meeting and access to public records statutes in the various states.

————. *World Press Freedom*, *1967*. Columbia, Mo., Freedom of Information Center, School of Journalism, University of Missouri at Columbia, 1968. 6p. (Report no. 201)   **1F249**
An abridged report of the survey of press freedom in eighty-four independent countries, indicating that the broad picture did not change from the 1966 report (°L41). This report presents the methodology of the study, criteria used, and a summary of the findings according to seven classifications (degrees of freedom) for both 1966 and 1967.

"Freedom of Information in Arizona: An Antidote for Secrecy in Government." *Arizona State Law Journal*, 1975:111–35, 1975.   **1F250**
"Complex and bureaucratic government has

made open public meetings and reasonable access to public records crucial to the survival of informed democracy. Appraisal of several legislative efforts to insure open government at the federal and state levels afford an educative comparison to present Arizona standards. The author suggests meaningful statutory protection of the Arizona public's right to know."

"Freedom of Information: The Statute and the Regulations." *Georgetown Law Journal*, 56:18–57, November 1967.
                                                1F251
Deals largely with categories of materials exempted from the Act: national defense and foreign policy, personnel rules and practices, statutory exemptions, confidential information, internal memoranda, personal privacy, investigatory files, reports on financial institutions, and geological data.

Freedom of Speech. 63 frame filmstrip: 35 mm., color and phonodisc; 1 side, 12 in., 33⅓ rpm., 17 min., microgroove. Pleasantville, N.Y., Warren Schloat Productions, 1969. (Fight for Our Rights, Set 2; with script and teacher's guide)   **1F252**
"Documents the history of free speech from Supreme Court Justice Oliver Wendell Holmes's idea of 'clear and present danger' to today's concept of 'symbolic speech,' presenting case histories, such as the 1968 demonstration at Columbia University and Dr. Benjamin Spock's crusade."

"Freedom of Speech and the Individual's Right of Access to the Airwaves." *Law and the Social Order*, 1970:424–36, 1970.   **1F253**
The author analyzes the rights of both the broadcaster and the individual citizen in terms of First Amendment guarantees of free speech and suggests that individuals be given a right of access to broadcast air time through utilization of traditional advertising time space.

Freedom of Speech Newsletter. Western Speech Communication Association, Pasadena, Calif., 1975–date.   **1F254**
This publication contains articles, news notes, and announcements of events relating to freedom of speech. Winfred G. Allen, Jr., is editor.

Freedom of the Press. 24 frame filmstrip: 35 mm., color. New York, Jones and Osmond; released by Modern Learning Aids, 1968. (Critical Thinking Aids; with teacher's guide)   **1F255**
"Part 1 describes the political tensions of the 1730's and the events leading to John Peter Zenger's decision to publish a newspaper attacking the English governor. Part 2 covers the trial of Zenger from the point of view of one of the jurors. For elementary grades. With captions."

Freedom of the Press. 53 frame filmstrip: 35 mm., color and phonodisc; 2 sides, 12 in., 33⅓ rpm., 13 min. (Also issued with phonotape in cassette) Tulsa, Okla., Learning Resources Division, Educational Development Corp.; made by Imperial Film Co., 1973. (Great Court Trials in U.S. History)   **1F256**
"Shows how the legal concept of freedom of the press embodied in the United States Constitution evolved from decisions applied to particular conflicts. Recounts interpretations of some of the nation's jurists concerning these conflicts and the United States Constitution."

Freedom of the Press. 81 frame filmstrip: 35 mm., color and phonodisc; 1 side, 12 in., 33⅓ rpm., 17 min., microgroove. Pleasantville, N.Y., Warren Schloat Productions, 1968. (Our Living Bill of Rights; with script and teacher's guide)
                                                1F257
"Describes freedom of the press as guaranteed by the Bill of Rights, using as an illustration the trial of John Peter Zenger for factual reporting of an election in colonial times, and the trial of the *New York Times* in 1964 for inaccuracies in an advertisement concerning civil rights."

"Freedom of the Press." *Senior Scholastic*, 107(9):6–11, 13 January 1976. **1F258**
Includes a discussion of current issues on press freedom; a cartoon strip, Superscoop; excerpts from pertinent court decisions; and a problem for students to solve: To Print or Not to Print.

"Freedom of the Press: A Menace to Justice?" *Iowa Law Review*, 37:249–61, Winter 1951.   **1F259**
Both the court and the press are responsible for fair trial. The court should control its officers and appeal to the press to observe certain standards of conduct. If a change in venue is required, the court should explain the matter frankly to the community, placing whatever blame on the press that it deserves. On the other hand, the press has a primary duty to inform, not sway, the public, to report facts and to indulge in respectable editorials. In the final analysis the press requires an uncoerced and fair judiciary to maintain its own freedom.

Freedom of the Press, and Privileges of the Commons Considered: In a Letter to a Country Friend. London, Printed for J. Bell, 1771. 61p.   **1F260**
An attack on the newspaper press for its unreliable, ignorant, and malicious coverage of public affairs, particularly the Parliament. The author calls on Parliament to exercise its historic powers of contempt, and cites the recent case of the House of Commons summoning printers before it who had maligned the dignity and

authority of the House, only to have a city magistrate interfere, illegally he believes, and release those arrested.

"Freedom of the Press: Confrontation at Press Club." *Vidura*, 6(4):5–11, November 1969. **1F261**
A report of a seminar on press freedom conducted by the Press Club of India, 18 September 1969. Participants: Frank Moraes, B. G. Verghese, Ram Singh, Pran Chopra, Chanchal Sarkar, and A. Raghavan.

"Freedom of the Press Does Not Justify the Invasion of Privacy through Subterfuge." *Texas Law Review*, 50:514–20, March 1972. **1F262**
Re: *Dietemann v. Time, Inc.*, 449 F.2d 245 (9th Cir. 1971). The court ruled that First Amendment freedom of the press does not include the right to invade an individual's privacy by gaining access to his home through subterfuge and taking photographs without his consent. The case involved an article in the 1 November 1963 issue of *Life*, entitled Crackdown on Quackery.

"The Freedom of the Press: Editorial." *St. Croix Review*, 7:2–8, February 1974. **1F263**
An editorial attacking American television for its instant commentary after President Nixon's speeches, in which the suggestion was made that he may have lied. "We should loathe and ignore such indescribably rude creatures" who assert their political philosophy and have no appreciation of "the majesty of the presidential office." The editor recommends legislation that would prohibit the publication of sensational stories and stories about an individual without his approval. He concludes that "democratic" movements for the reduction of the armed forces are against the best long-term interests of the people and should be resisted.

"Freedom of the Press; Symposium." *Vidura*, 6(3):12–15, August 1969. **1F264**
"Recent events have raised questions about the future of the Indian Press and its freedom. In the context of the attacks on newspapers in Calcutta, the Prime Minister's recent utterances about the Press, or sections of it, and demands for 'nationalization' and 'control' of the Press, we asked some veteran journalists for their views on the subject." Comments of the following journalists are published: B. Shiva Rao, D. R. Mankekar, and M. Chalapathi Rau.

Freedom of the Press Today. 2 filmstrips (pt. 1, 92 frames; pt. 2, 67 frames): 35 mm., color and 2 phonodiscs; 2 sides each (one side for manual projector, one side for automatic projector), 12 in.,

33⅓ rpm., pt. 1, 16 min., pt. 2, 13 min., microgroove. (Also issued with phonotape in cassette) Pleasantville, N.Y., Associated Press and Guidance Association, 1969. (An AP Special Report; with teacher's manual) **1F265**
"Examines government and military limitations on freedom of the press in the United States. Follows reporters and photographers who are working on stories about Vietnam and civil rights. Includes comments by Herb Klein and J. R. Wiggins."

"Freedom to Communicate versus Right to Privacy: Regulation of Offensive Speech. Limited by 'Captive Audience' Doctrine." *Washington Law Review*, 48:667–85, May 1973. **1F266**
"This note examines the conflict between free expression and privacy, focusing on the effect of privacy interests on the definition of obscenity and on the possibility of regulating nonobscene, sex-related expression through legislation designed to protect the individual's right to privacy from offensive contact." The case involved is *State v. Rabe* (1972) in which an outdoor movie operator was convicted for showing an alleged obscene movie, *Carmen Baby*, on grounds that the screen was visible to non-customers and the movie invaded their privacy. The Washington Supreme Court upheld the conviction as "an assault on individual privacy," but the U.S. Supreme Court reversed the decision on technical grounds that did not test the constitutionality of the Washington state law.

The Freedom to Read Committee (Canada). *Brief to the Task Force on Policing in Ontario, Regarding Police Enforcement of Obscenity Provisions of the Criminal Code.* [Toronto], The Committee, 1973. 23p. Processed. **1F267**
"It is the opinion of the Freedom to Read Committee that Police are not equipped to, and should not make the decision of whether or not to prosecute, where reading material is concerned. By permitting the subjective decision of morality officers to signal the start of prosecution proceedings, we have created a dangerous encroachment on our freedom to read, and have subverted the meaning of Canadian obscenity law."

———. *Report* . . . Toronto, The Committee, 1972. 46p. Processed. **1F268**
"The Committee has the following aims: to establish that the freedom to read is the rightful prerogative of Canadians and to focus public attention on the disturbing scope and inherent dangers of censorship. The philosophy of the Committee is that the selection of an individual's reading material is a personal matter and is not the proper subject of interference by the state in a free society." The report discusses existing Canadian censorship laws and how they have been administered; it considers the effect of pornography, citing the work of the

U.S. Commission on Obscenity and Pornography. It concludes that "the Obscenity provisions of the Criminal Code have created a crime without victims, and should be repealed," that Customs censorship be eliminated, and that "only a positive, healthy approach to the problem of pornography," as outlined in the report, "will improve the quality of contemporary literature and the taste of many Canadian readers."

Freedom to Read Foundation News. Chicago, Freedom to Read Foundation, 1971–date. Four times a year. **1F269**
Reports on news of the Foundation, created in 1969, in part, "to support the right of libraries to include in their collections and to make available to the public any creative work which they may legally acquire"; and to supply legal counsel to librarians who request help in their defense of freedom of speech and the press.

"Freedom vs. Fear." *Screen Writer*, 3:1–26, December 1947. **1F270**
A special section of this issue deals with the threat against freedom of the screen posed by hearings of the Un-American Activities Committee of the House of Representatives. Includes statements by Thomas Mann, Robert Sherwood, Bennett Cerf, Edward R. Murrow, Max Lerner, and others, and articles by Norman Corwin, Henry Seidel Canby, William Wyler (Censorship Through Fear), Emmet Lavery (Freedom of the Screen) and Howard Koch (The Cost of Silence).

The Freeholder's Magazine; Or, Monthly Chronicle of Liberty. By A Patriotic Society. London, Isaac Fell, 1769–70. (Issued monthly, September 1769–December 1770) **1F271**
The character of this short-lived Whig journal was set in the first issue by a frontispiece of John Wilkes, a dedication to friends of freedom in England, Ireland, Wales, and America, and a statement by the publisher that he would never reveal the name of any contributor without his expressed consent. The first issue also featured a petition of 1,565 freeholders of Middlesex County protesting to the king, among other things, the imprisonment of printers without trial, the seizure of private papers, and illegal action in libel trials. Subsequent issues included numerous references to the trials of John Wilkes—letters, poems, and songs; duties of jurymen in libel cases; accounts of the libel trials of H.S. Woodfall, John Horne Tooke, John Almon, and John Miller; and an article by "B.L." On the Late Encroachment of the Liberty of the Press (vol. 2, pp. 202–4). There are portraits of Serjeant Glyn, defense attorney, and John Horne Tooke, defendant, in several libel trials. The editor practices his own form of censorship in one article, Anecdote of Lady M——y W—— M—— from the Mouth of Her only Son W—— W—— M——. Beginning with the September 1770 issue, the journal degenerated into an organ of entertainment (scandal, anecdotes, and bons mots), according to the editor, in response to readers who preferred this to

politics. The final issue (December 1770) combined politics with sex in a letter to the editor from "Claudia," who defends prostitutes and attacks the men who patronize them.

Freeman, Dorinda E. *Newsmen's Privilege*. Chapel Hill, N.C., University of North Carolina, 1974. 48p. (Unpublished Master's thesis) **1F272**
A series of five articles introducing the major issues in the controversy over newsmen's privilege, written with emphasis on the North Carolina scene.

Freeman, Gillian. *The Undergrowth of Literature*. Foreword by David Stafford-Clark. London, Panther Modern Society, 1967. 220p. (First published in Great Britain by Thomas Nelson, 1967) **1F273**
"A survey of current fantasy literature which overtly, or covertly, supplies the stimulus which so many people need, from the romance of Woman's Own to the sado-masochism of Man's Story." The author concludes that "pornography is a real necessity in the lives of many people. So much so, in fact, that . . . it should be on open sale—with the proviso that, as with alcohol and tobacco, it is not available to minors."

[Freeman, Les.] "The People's Right to Know." *Municipal Journal* (London), 79:1305–8, 1313, 24 September 1971. **1F274**
A report on an investigation of closed committee meetings of public bodies in Britain. The author concludes that "the closing of committees puts too much real power into too few hands and tends to frustrate the development of progressive and imaginative policies . . . [and] smacks more of the oligarchist and totalitarian regimes we (as a nation) condemn than the sort of democracy we take pride in."

[Freilicher, Lila P.] "Story Behind the Book: 'The Little Red Schoolbook.'" *Publishers' Weekly*, 200(24):32–33, 13 December 1971. **1F275**
"Though 'The Little Red Schoolbook' was supposedly banned in England on sexual grounds, many people, including its authors, the Danish publisher, and Pocket Books Executive Editor Bernard Shir-Cliff, believe that the real reason for the banning was that the book sides with students on the matter of education."

Fremont, Ernest H., Jr. "Free Press, Fair Trial: A Constitutional Quandry." *Missouri Bar Journal*, 26:520–26, October 1970. **1F276**
The former chairman of the Missouri Advisory Committee on Free Press–Fair Trial addresses University of Missouri journalism students during Journalism Week, May 1970. Most, if not all, of the problems involved in the free press–fair trial controversy, the Committee

found, could be solved through a program of education and rededication.

French, Roberts W. "Milton's Areopagitica." *Humanist*, 28:15, March–April 1968. **1F277**
"This work transcends the immediate occasion to achieve a timeless universality; it is at once a classic defense of man's right to freedom of inquiry, thought, and expression, an eloquent assertion of the individual mind and conscience, and a noble statement of human dignity."

French, Roderick S. *The Trials of Abner Kneeland: A Study in the Rejection of Democratic Secular Humanism*. Washington, D.C., George Washington University, 1971. 382p. (Ph.D. dissertation, University Microfilms, no. 72–8,998) **1F278**
A study of the life and career of Abner Kneeland (1774–1844), leading American spokesman for democratic, secular humanism, with emphasis on the evolution of Kneeland's philosophy. "In January, 1834, Kneeland was indicted for blasphemy under a 1782 statute. On June 18, 1838, after four nationally notorious jury trials and an appeal hearing before the full bench of the state supreme court, he began serving a sixty-day sentence. In the course of the trials the ambiguities and compromises in American social theory and political practice were brought into the open. The Massachusetts courts, through the prosecuting attorney and the judges, repudiated Kneeland's secular republicanism in favor of an explicitly theocratic interpretation of American democracy." The author corrects errors in chronology made by Commager in his article on The Blasphemy of Abner Kneeland (C475) and perpetuated in the 1968 edition of this bibliography (K147–55).

Freund, Paul A. "The Great Disorder of Speech." *American Scholar*, 44:541–59, Autumn 1975. **1F279**
On the occasion of the 500th anniversary of the introduction of printing into England by William Caxton (1476) the author considers the sense of community and order and, at the same time, the threat of dissolution the device has brought to society. "How the promise and the threat have been assessed by those who think and those who govern is the subject of this synoptic sketch."

———. "Political Libel and Freedom of the Press." *American Philosophical Society Proceedings*, 112:117–20, 15 April 1968. **1F280**
A Harvard professor traces the historical events in England and the United States that led to the case of *New York Times v. Sullivan* (1964), which tested for the first time "the extent to which the constitutional protections for speech and press limit a State's power to award damages in a libel action brought by a public official against critics of his official conduct."

The Court "turned for support to the rules of privilege in libel as they had been developed in the state courts, not as constitutional mandates but as features of the law of torts." The author suggests two countervailing powers for the victims—a special jury verdict identifying their findings on truth or falsity and on legal malice, and, if finding for the plaintiff, the recovery of costs of litigation.

[———.] "The Supreme Court, 1973 Term: Freedom of Speech and Press." *Harvard Law Review*, 88:139–80, November 1974. **1F281**
Under the heading Libel Action by Private Individuals, the survey considers the case of *Gertz v. Robert Welch, Inc.*; under the heading Prohibition of Political Advertising on Public Mass Transit Systems, the survey considers the case of *Lehman v. City of Shaker Heights*; under Restriction on Speech of Members of the Military, the case of *Parker v. Levy*; under Bans of Press Interviews of Prisoners, the case of *Pell v. Procunier*; under Political Candidate's Statutory Right of Reply to Newspaper Editorials, the case of *Miami Herald Publishing Co. v. Tornillo*.

———, and Richard H. Kuh. "Political Libel and Obscenity." *Federal Rules Decisions*, 42:491–517, 1968. **1F282**
Professor Freund notes a difference in the order of problems in the two areas of political libel and obscenity. In libel the problem is that of "accommodation between the latitude of public debate and the danger to reputation from falsehoods." In obscenity there is a question as to whether there is a victim and why the law should be concerned with the matter at all. After reviewing the trend in libel decisions begun with *New York Times v. Sullivan*, Freund makes these suggestions: (1) "that the victim, if not a public officer or one in public authority, ought to be able to recover, subject to the defense of fair comment"; (2) that even when public officers are plaintiffs, the judge ought to instruct the jury in the meaning of malice and recklessness in light of the gravity of the charge; (3) an official should be able to request a special verdict in order to receive a vindication of his character by finding the libel untrue; and (4) there ought not to be punative damages in cases of political libel. Following a discussion of obscenity in which he notes the achievements thus far made in defining the meaning, scope, and purpose of the law, Freund suggests certain principles be established: (1) place the focus on the juvenile market, (2) deal with the problem of public affront, and (3) concentrate efforts on "hard core pornography." He finds a "disquieting element" in the recent Supreme Court emphasis on the "mode of marketing" of obscenity. Lawyer Kuh discusses what he believes a true liberal would accept as "the thinking man's censorship." He agrees with the three areas of legislative restraint on obscenity suggested by Professor Freund, but adds that a

pandering test could be sustained as an honest marketing statute. The discussion took place at the 29th annual judicial conference, 3d Judicial Circuit of the United States, and was presided over by Judge William H. Hastie.

₍Friedman, David.₎ "The Fairness Doctrine and Presidential Appearances." *New York Law Forum*, 19:398–407, Fall 1973. **1F283**
Consideration of the controversy over the right of response to noncampaign presidential broadcasts.

Friedman, Jane M. "Erotica, Censorship, and the United States Post Office Department: An Anti-Pollutant for Our Nation's Mailstream." *Michigan Academician*, 4:7–16, Summer 1971. **1F284**
"The present paper is an attempt to explore the ramifications of some of the information gathered while serving on the Commission ₍on Obscenity and Pornography₎ staff." During that period the author "interviewed a large number of federal, state, and local law-enforcement officials, as well as several attorneys for private parties who were in the business of producing and/or disseminating erotic materials."

———. "The Motion Picture Rating System of 1968: A Constitutional Analysis of Self-Regulation by the Film Industry." *Columbia Law Review*, 73:185–240, February 1973. **1F285**
"Spokesmen for the industry maintain that the rating system fulfills two functions: first, it gives 'parents reliable information to enable them to make informed judgments in guiding the attendance of their children'; second, and more importantly, it has allegedly forestalled censorship by federal and local governments. It is the thesis of this Article that the rating system has accomplished neither of these goals; and furthermore, in exercising editorial judgment with respect to the vast majority of films commercially exhibited in the United States, the motion picture industry is abridging the rights of film-makers to disseminate, and of moviegoers to receive, communications in unexpurgated form."

———. "Regulation of Obscenity by Federal Agencies." *Technical Report of the ₍U.S.₎ Commission on Obscenity and Pornography*, 5:15–34, 1971. **1F286**
A description of the law enforcement policy regarding obscenity in various federal agencies—Post Office (mail covers, seizures, purchase under pseudonyms, suppressions and discontinuances, denial of second-class mailing privileges, declarations of nonmailability, "unlawful" orders and mail-block statute,

and the Anti-Pandering Act), Customs Bureau (classics and books of literary and scientific merit, role of the courts, motion pictures, sealed mail), and the Federal Bureau of Investigation.

———. "State Obscenity Statutes: Description and Analysis." *Technical Report of the ₍U.S.₎ Commission on Obscenity and Pornography*, 2:37–61, 1971. **1F287**
"This paper attempts to describe and analyze the obscenity statutes of the 50 states plus the District of Columbia."

Friedman, Leon, *ed. Obscenity: The Complete Oral Arguments before the Supreme Court in the Major Obscenity Cases. Introduction by Charles Rembar.* New York, Chelsea House, 1970. 342p. **1F288**
"This volume," writes Rembar in his introduction, "shows the Warren Court at work, in one of the fields where change occurred—freedom of speech and press." While freedom of political expression had been acquired earlier, literature worked free in the seven years between 1959–66. "The law of obscenity constructed in the age of Victoria and Comstock had survived, almost intact, until this period." The volume gives the stenographic transcript of oral argument in a series of Supreme Court cases that helped to establish comparable freedom in the area of obscenity. The decisions were not popular at the time, notes Rembar, and would probably have been disapproved if put to a popular vote. "The pages of this book reflect sensitivity and obtuseness; agility and rigidity; creative legal thinking and failures of imagination." There is also high and low comedy, suspense, and evidence of the advocate's art and lack of it. The following cases are reported: *Roth v. United States* (1957), *Alberts v. California* (1957), *Kingsley International Pictures Corp. v. Regents* (1959), *Manual Enterprises v. Day* (1962), *Jacobellis v. Ohio* (1964), *Freedman v. Maryland* (1964), *Ginzburg v. United States* (1965), *Mishkin v. New York* (1965), *Memoirs v. Massachusetts* (1965), *Ginsberg v. New York* (1968), and *Stanley v. Georgia* (1969).

Friedman, Milton. "How to Free Television." *Newsweek*, 74(22):82, 1 December 1969. **1F289**
To free television from the present monopoly, the author proposes that the FCC sell television channels to the highest bidder and give them the full protection of the Bill of Rights now enjoyed by the press. Monopolies would be subject to the antitrust laws. He believes there would be greater diversity in type of financial support—advertiser supported, fee supported, or combination of the two—and that the bill of fare would be much richer.

Friend to Liberty. *A Serious Remonstrance to the Publick. In Regard to the many bold uncommon Insults and Reflections lately publish'd against the Govern-

ment by the Writers for the Malcontents; with a Hint upon the Use and Abuse of the Press . . . .*London, Roberts, 1740. 44p. (Part of the *Craftsman* controversy, possibly written by John Hervey) (Reprinted in Stephen Parks, *ed., The English Book Trade, 1660–1853.* New York, Garland, 1974. Vol. 9) **1F290**
Freedom of the press was not intended to protect scandal, defamation, falsehood, and to poison minds of mankind with idle thoughts; nor was it intended to teach disrespect and disobedience of law. The freedom of the press was given to instruct, not to destroy.

Friendly, Fred W. "Asleep at the Switch of Wired City." *Saturday Review*, 53(41):58–60, 10 October 1970. (Reprinted in Michael C. Emery and Ted C. Smythe, *eds., Readings in Mass Communications*, pp. 55–61) **1F291**
"The major, restrictive and malevolent force ₍in broadcast journalism₎ is the absurd shortage of air time," and that "a single organization, no matter how responsible, should be the gatekeeper, principal user, rate-maker, and adjudicator of who shall ride." The author sees as a potential solution to the problem of access, the development of the coaxial cable in the concept of the wired city.

———. "The Campaign to Politicize Broadcasting." *Columbia Journalism Review*, 11:9–18, March–April 1973. (Reprinted in *Current*, May 1973) **1F292**
Criticism of the policies of Clay T. Whitehead, director of the White House Office of Communications, which represent an attempt to politicize broadcasting. Friendly is answered on page 32 of the *Current* article.

———. "A Crime and Its Aftershock." *New York Times Magazine*, 21 March 1976. p. 16. **1F293**
A report on the reporting of a crime—the murder case against Erwin Charles Simants. "Chance and politics would combine to make it the focus of a major constitutional debate, one that pits the defendant's right to a fair trial, embodied in the Sixth Amendment to the Constitution, against the press's First Amendment right to print the news, and the public's right to know."

———. *Due to Circumstances Beyond Our Control.* New York, Random House, 1967. 325p. **1F294**
"Because television can make so much money doing its worst, it often cannot afford to do its best." The former director of Columbia Broadcasting System News who resigned after sixteen years with the network because of CBS failure to televise the 1966 Senate hearings on Vietnam, running instead a rerun of *I Love Lucy*, offers an inside story and critique of the broadcasting industry and the financial interests that control television programming. He is also critical of the Federal Communications

Commission for its failure to regulate the industry.

———. "Gag . . . Free Press vs. Fair Trial." *Southern Illinoisan*, 25 April 1967, p. 29. **1F295**
In a syndicated article appearing in a number of newspapers, the author considers the issues of free press vs. fair trial in light of the "gag order" imposed by a county judge in Sutherland, Nebr.

———. *The Good Guys, the Bad Guys and the First Amendment: Free Speech vs. Fairness in Broadcasting*. New York, Random House, 1976. 268p. **1F296**
A pioneer in broadcast journalism examines the controversy between freedom of speech and press as guaranteed by the First Amendment and the fairness doctrine which requires broadcasters to devote a reasonable amount of time to the discussion of controversial issues, with presentation of opposing viewpoints. "Can the Fairness Doctrine and the First Amendment coexist? Do the regulatory powers of the Federal Communications Commission constitute government censorship, endangering our eroding freedoms by setting up a kind of Big Brother as editor? How should—and how *can*—a democratic nation properly balance the conflicting rights of a free press, the public right to hear robust, uncensored debate on the airwaves, and the individual's right to be heard?" The author traces the court decisions that have addressed the issue—*Red Lion Broadcasting Co. v. FCC* (1969), *Miami Herald Publishing Co. v. Tornillo* (1974), and *Brandywine-Main Line Radio, Inc. v. FCC* (1972), devoting considerable attention to *Red Lion* because of its impact on broadcasting and because "it dramatizes the method by which a well-intentioned law can be manipulated to mute 'noxious views,' as perceived by one group of politicians." The book grew out of the author's contacts with students in the Columbia School of Journalism. Friendly draws upon his own experience in television, upon an "excursion through the fifty-year thicket of regulatory history," and "a search through the murky record of the 1964 presidential election."

———. "Justice White and Reporter Caldwell: Finding a Common Ground." *Columbia Journalism Review*, 11(3):31–37, September–October 1972. **1F297**
While resistance of newsmen to subpoenas is often justified, there are times when it is not, and the author cites as an example of the latter the case of the films of the 1937 Memorial Day massacre. "The subpoena impasse will not be broken without hard work, nor will the fair trial–free press problem be solved merely by unleashing platitudes about the First Amendment against those about the Fifth and Sixth, and vice versa. We need a new breed of journalism under law and a new kind of law that reckons with twentieth-century communications—and that might emerge from the two

professions talking with each other, not at each other." Views of Norman E. Isaacs and Benno C. Schmidt, Jr., are also given.

———. "Some Sober Second Thoughts on Vice-President Agnew." *Saturday Review*, 52:61–62, 75, 13 December 1969. **1F298**
The author charges Vice-President Agnew with attempting to create doubts in the minds of the American public about motivation and background of those charged with responsibility of explaining the controversies of our time—Vietnam, race, and youth. The vice-president has forgotten history in his criticism of the practice of critique of a president's speeches—it happened under Kennedy and Johnson. There needs to be more rather than less interpretive reporting.

———. "Television and the First Amendment." *Saturday Review*, 55(2):46–47, 55, 8 January 1972. **1F299**
The First Amendment is a cornerstone, not a completed building. While licensing of broadcasting is a form of prior restraint, technical factors have made it necessary. Congress and the FCC have an obligation to see that licensees live up to their promises. Friendly is not so much concerned with the restrictive practices of the FCC ("a tower of Jell-O") as he is with the threats of Vice-President Agnew and members of Congress and with the "chilling hand" of the profit drive in the broadcast industry. The latter is the real censor. He believes the fairness doctrine imposed by the FCC is counter-productive, an ineffective substitute for an industry "bill of responsibility." He calls for a citizens committee to study and develop a long-range communications policy which would establish both an electronic Bill of Rights and a Bill of Responsibility for broadcasting, replacing the piecemeal and improvised policies now in effect.

———. "The Unselling of *The Selling of the Pentagon*." *Harper's*, 242:30–33, 36–37, June 1971. **1F300**
The storm created by the showing of the Columbia Broadcasting System documentary, *The Selling of the Pentagon*, was predictable, writes this veteran producer of television documentaries. "When documentaries find their mark, pressure groups such as the cigarette or pesticide industry, the American Medical Association, the Farm Bureau, the National Rifle Association—and the military-industrial complex—take action." He follows with a description of the five steps in the "demolition manual" of pressure groups. The unique factor in this case was the involvement of high government officials and agencies. Friendly analyzes some of the specific complaints against the documentary, noting where CBS was at fault, but giving the network high marks, on the whole, for its production. The implied threats of the executive branch and Congress against the network in the affair indicate the need for a strong, independent public television.

———. "What's Fair on the Air?" *New*

York Times Magazine, 30 March 1975, pp. 11–12+. **1F301**
An account of the Red Lion broadcast which triggered a legal battle over whether the government had a right to order a broadcaster to grant reply time to a person or group that claims to have suffered from a broadcast over the public airwaves. Friendly concludes: "The basic issue is whether the Government will encourage or discourage broadcasters from the probing, hard-hitting journalism that their financial interests resist but the public interest demands. In this sense, the proper definition of the fairness doctrine will influence the essential quality of broadcast programming."

Friends, Society of. Philadelphia. *An Address on Some Growing Evils of the Day, Especially Demoralizing Literature and Art, from the Representatives of the Religious Society of Friends, for Pennsylvania, New Jersey, and Delaware, Second Month, 10, 1882*. Philadelphia, To Be Had at Friends' Book Store [1882]. 16p. **1F302**
An attack on the demoralizing literature of the day—seductive novels, "trashy" magazines displayed on the newsstands and sold by train vendors. Even professors of religion, the author charges, have on their shelves works of immoral poets. Children and females especially are susceptible to corruption from these "abuses of the printing press." Instead of censorship, however, he calls for personal religious commitment. "We firmly believe that the corrective for this and every other injurious tendency which threatens the highest interest of our beloved country, is to be found in a fuller and more practical acceptance of the teachings of our Lord Jesus Christ."

[Friends to the Abuse of the Liberty of the Press.] *Proceedings of the Friends to the Abuse of the Liberty of the Press; on December, the 22d, 1792, and January 19th, and March 9th, 1793*. London, Printed by Order of the Committee, 1793. 15p. **1F303**
This document, possibly written by John Reeves, is a satire on the *Proceedings of the Friends to the Liberty of the Press* (F360), which had met in December 1792 and in January and March 1793 at Free Mason's Tavern, London, to organize in opposition to the vigilante activities of the Association for Preservation of Liberty and Property against Republicans and Levellers. Thomas Erskine, who had defended Paine's *Rights of Man*, was a leader in the organization. The mythical Friends to the Abuse of the Liberty of the Press passed resolutions to make it illegal to defend the libel laws or to support efforts to maintain the public peace. This pamphlet, which follows in format and style the libertarian pamphlet, twists the intent of the latter in such a way as to support the cause of the *Liberty and Property* association whose

goal was to "check the circulation of seditious publications of all kinds whether newspapers or pamphlets, or the invitations to club members," and apprehend the author, printer, or bookseller. John Reeves was the leader in that association.

Friessen, Gordon. *Oklahoma Witch Hunt*. Oklahoma City, Okla., Oklahoma Committee to Defend Political Prisoners, 1941. 23p. **1F304**
The case of Ida Wood, sentenced to prison by an Oklahoma judge for possession and sale of Communist books.

Frome, Michael. "Freedom of the Press—For Those Who Own One." *Center Magazine*, 8:12–24, July 1975. **1F305**
A former columnist of *Field & Stream*, dismissed for his espousal of environmental causes which offended hunters and the hunting industry, writes of his experience with the policy of the magazine after it has been taken over by a conglomerate of Columbia Broadcasting System. "As I read the First Amendment, protection goes to the owner or operator of the press. Nevertheless, there is a need for Congress to enunciate a sound public policy to insure that the media themselves do not restrict the avenues of truth through the influence of conglomerate control or non-media-related business activities. A medium of communication should not be owned by another corporation, certainly not by a corporate conglomerate, because of the strong possibility that the medium's undertakings will be subverted to the service of interests other than the dissemination of truth."

Fromkin, Howard L., and Timothy C. Brock. *Erotic Materials: A Commodity Theory Analysis of the Enhanced Desirability Which May Accompany Their Unavailability*. West Lafayette, Ind., Institute for Research in the Behavioral, Economic, and Management Sciences, Krannert Graduate School of Industrial Administration, Indiana University, 1973. 16p. (Paper no. 421) **1F306**
"The present paper analyzes one dimension of the pornography control issue, namely, the probable reactions of individuals who are confronted by information that is not freely or easily available to all. After a review of commodity theory (Brock, 1968) and related research, it is concluded that making erotic materials more difficult to obtain, harassing and punishing pornographers and purveyors of pornography, restricting certain materials to certain age groups, etc., may increase interest in the materials and render them more desirable than would have been the case without the restriction, harassment, or difficulty."

Fromson, Murray. "Dateline Moscow: Censorship of Our TV News." *Columbia Journalism Review*, 14(3):32–34, September–October 1975. **1F307**
"In spite of the much-talked-about spirit of détente between the Soviet Union and the West, it is harder than ever for a foreign television reporter to work in Russia. Much of the blame for this lies with the Novosti Press Agency, on which all foreign television correspondents must depend for camera crews and, frequently, access to news sources." The author is a foreign correspondent for Columbia Broadcasting System News.

Frum, Austin P. *et al. Obscenity and Pornography*. 27 min. tape recording. Washington, D.C., Forum Associates, 1970. **1F308**
Two Washington, D.C., attorneys, Jacob Stein and Richard Ward, discuss the limits to the freedom of expression in the area of sex in light of recent court decisions. The moderator is attorney Austin P. Frum.

Fry, *Sir* Edward. *Betting Newspapers and Quakerism: A Letter Addressed to Members of the Society of Friends*. [London, 1911.] 17p. **1F309**
An attack on Quakers connected with the management of four British newspapers for permitting the papers to carry betting news. The Friends against whom Sir Edward Fry's criticisms have been directed replied in a pamphlet addressed to Members of the Society of Friends.

Fryer, David R. "Group Defamation in England." *Cleveland-Marshall Law Review*, 13:33–94, January 1964. **1F310**
"This article will attempt to sketch briefly the extent of the remedies in tort and the restraint in criminal law which can be invoked in English law when defamatory matter is written or spoken of a group of persons associated either voluntarily or involuntarily on the basis of race, religion, vocation, political views, or in any other way."

Fryer, Peter. "The Death of Censorship. (The Abuses of Literacy—6)." *Times Literary Supplement*, 3,651:195, 18 February 1972. **1F311**
The author believes that censorship is virtually dead in Britain, that there is "a tacit recognition that we are now living in a morally pluralistic society; that attempts by one group to impose its morality on another are futile; and that those unfortunate enough to be made anxious or angry or sick by words or images suggesting or depicting sexual pleasure have a simple, effective personal remedy, such as switching off the television set." And now that censorship is virtually dead, the author believes that pornography (as opposed to erotic realism), in turn, is doomed.

———, *comp*. British Birth Control

Ephemera, *1870–1947*. A Catalogue Compiled by Peter Fryer With an Introduction by Professor D. V. Glass. Syston, England, Barracuda Press, 1969. 42p. **1F312**
An annotated list of scarce pamphlets and other ephemera dealing with birth control, accompanied by an introduction that discusses the social significance of the works and the circumstances under which they were produced and distributed. The collection was assembled by David Collis.

Fryer, Peter, *ed. Forbidden Books of Victorians*. Henry Spencer Ashbee's Bibliographies of Erotica Abridged and Edited, With an Introduction and Notes. London, Odyssey, 1970. 239p. **1F313**
As an introduction to this abridged edition of Henry Spencer Ashbee's (Pisanus Fraxi, *pseud*.) three volumes "bio-biblio-iconographical" study of erotica (A258–60), the editor contributes a biography of Ashbee and describes the circumstances surrounding his work. He states that there is "not a shred of evidence" to support the claim (made by Gershon Legman) that Ashbee was "Walter" who wrote the anonymously published *My Secret Life*.

Fugard, Athol. "Challenging the Silence." *Index on Censorship*, 3:85–88, Spring 1974. (Reprinted from *Plays and Players*, November 1973) **1F314**
"The problems created by the policy of apartheid for the theatre in South Africa are discussed by the playwright, actor and producer Athol Fugard in this interview with Michael Coveney, assistant editor of *Plays and Players*."

Fulbright, J. William. "Fulbright on the Press." *Columbia Journalism Review*, 14(4):39–45, November–December 1975. **1F315**
While commending the nation's press for "renewed awareness of its great power and commensurate responsibility" that grew out of the tragic mistakes of the Vietnam war and the scandals of Watergate, he criticizes it for moving from extreme orthodoxy to sweeping iconoclasm. The new inquisitorial style tends to be vindictive, less concerned with uncovering and correcting mistakes in public affairs than in embarrassing and punishing those who make them. "The media have thus acquired an unwholesome fascination with the singer to the neglect of the song." He calls for a halt to media inquisitions and for greater self-restraint. "There is no one to restrain the press except the press itself—nor should there be."

———. "The High Cost of Secrecy." *Progressive*, 35(9):16–21, September 1971. **1F316**
The term "credibility gap" is a tame euphemism for a deep malady of our society. The people have lost faith in the truthfulness of

our government. Senator Fulbright, then chairman of the Foreign Relations Committee, discusses the secrecy in the conduct of foreign affairs in the Nixon Administration. The administration keeps the facts from the American people and prevents Congress from exercising its constitutional responsibility in formulating foreign policy and performing legislative review. He recommends legislation which would limit the exercise of executive privilege.

Fuld, Stanley H. "Free Press–Fair Trial Principles and Guidelines for the State of New York." *New York State Bar Journal*, 42:13–19, January 1970. **1F317**
A statement by the chief judge of the New York Court of Appeals "sets forth the approved guidelines resulting from the cooperation of judges, lawyers, and representatives of the press to achieve the twin goals of fair trial and a free press."

Fuller, Ralph N. "Texbook Selection: Burning Issue?" *Compact*, 9(3):6–8, June 1975. **1F318**
The controversy over textbooks in Kanawha County, W.Va., has died down without any state or federal action, leaving the local community to settle the broad issues of student rights, the public role in school policy, and integrity of education programs.

Fullmer, Mark A. "Obscenity Regulation." *Louisiana Law Review*, 35:601–8, Spring 1975. **1F319**
As part of a 1974 legislative symposium the author discusses the Louisiana obscenity statute in light of the U.S. Supreme Court decision in *Miller v. California* (1973), considers the definition of obscenity, regulation of material harmful to minors, and regulation of obscenity through nuisance statutes.

Funderburk, Raymond E. *News Coverage in Vietnam: An Analysis of the Barriers in the News Gathering Process*. University, Ala., University of Alabama, 1970, 127p. (Unpublished Master's thesis) **1F320**

"In a study of the restrictions imposed on newsmen reporting on military operations in Vietnam, the author concludes that (1) accreditation of newsmen in Vietnam is necessary and justifiable; (2) 'ground rules' are necessary because censorship has not been imposed and certain vital military information must be withheld from the enemy; and (3) logistical support is the greatest problem facing the correspondent."

Funk, Roger L. "Now It's 'Serious Value' and 'Gullible Citizens.' " *Ohio Library Association Bulletin*, 45(3):4–9, July 1975. **1F321**
A review of the role of the American Library Association in intellectual freedom and the special problems raised by recent court decisions on obscenity. The author, assistant director of the ALA Office of Intellectual Freedom, recommends a legislative watch in each state to prevent legislation that will cripple libraries, and calls for state and local workshops on intellectual freedom.

———. "Our (Slightly Abridged) First Freedom." *Newsletter on Intellectual Freedom* (IFC-ALA), 22:26, 39, 42, March 1973. **1F322**
Comment on the U.S. Supreme Court decision denying reporters' right of testimonial privilege (*Branzburg v. Hayes*, 1972) and the Nixon Administration's "mandate" to end permissiveness and to impose his concept of objectivity on the news media, as demonstrated in the attacks of Vice-President Agnew and the proposals of Clay T. Whitehead.

———, and Judith F. Krug. "Whose Freedom to Read?" *Top of the News*, 31:289–92, April 1975. **1F323**
A discussion of the rights of children and young adults with respect to reading matter in libraries and the role of the librarian vis-à-vis children and parents.

Funston, Richard "Pornography and Politics: The Court, the Constitution and the Commission." *Western Political*

Quarterly, 24:635–52, December 1971. **1F324**
In light of the report of the U.S. Commission on Obscenity and Pornography, "it may be of profit to reconsider this body of judge-made law and to analyze its philosophic and political implications." The author notes two central or generic constitutional issues in obscenity decisions—the imprecision of the term "obscenity" and the question of what evils obscenity legislation is intended to combat.

Furgurson, Ernest B. "Fire on the Mountain." *MORE*, 4(10):14, 16–18, October 1974. **1F325**
"Appalachia's *Mountain Eagle* crusades— against strip mining, secrecy in government and police harassment of youths. Its bite has drawn boycotts, physical threats and now, perhaps, arson."

Furman, Fred D. "Commonwealth v. Armao; the End of Pennsylvania's Criminal Libel Law." *Temple Law Quarterly*, 46:162–68, Fall 1972. **1F326**
The Pennsylvania Supreme Court in *Commonwealth v. Armao* (1972) declared the state's libel law unconstitutional and observed that criminal libel laws are obsolete and nugatory in our modern society.

Further and Still More Important Suppressed Documents. ₍Boston, Russell & Cutler, Printers, 1808.₎ 24p. **1F327**
"The right which every Government possesses to keep secret its intercourse and negotiations with foreign nations, so long as they are still pending, has been grossly abused by the present Administration." The anonymous writer, in a preface to the publication of the suppressed correspondence, accuses the Madison Administration of suppressing documents that were favorable to Britain and critical of France and that might involve the nation in war. Contains letters of James Madison, John Armstrong, and William Pinkney.

G

Gadd, Dale A. *Advertising & the Fairness Doctrine*. Columbia, Mo., Freedom of Information Center, School of Journalism, University of Missouri at Columbia, 1974. 7p. (Report no. 323) **1G1**
"This report reviews the rise and fall of the *Banzhaf* ruling [*Banzhaf v. FCC*, 1968] and explains the altered relationship between radio and television advertising and the Fairness Doctrine."

Gaddy, Wayne. "Obscenity Muddle." *PNLA Quarterly* (Pacific Northwest Library Association), 39:4–9, July 1975. **1G2**
A review of modern obscenity law, with a discussion of the landmark cases, *U.S. v. Ulysses* (1933), *Roth v. U.S.* (1957), *Kaplan v. State of California* (1973), and the 1973 cases, *Miller v. California* and *Paris Adult Theatre I v. Slaton*. Recent decisions "have left not only publishers and distributors, but also librarians, uncertain as to what are their legal rights and responsibilities." The author recommends the legal adoption of the ACLU standard: "Any governmental restriction or punishment of any form of expression on the grounds of obscenity must require proof beyond a reasonable doubt that such expression would directly cause, in a normal adult, behavior which has validly been made criminal by statute." A similar test would apply when children are the target.

Gaines, Ervin J. "Censorship and What To Do About It." *Minnesota English Journal*, 5(1):5–8, Winter 1969. **1G3**
The author considers the legal issues in treating literature dealing with sex in the classroom. Unlike the legal freedom granted in the area of politics, "the law is not always clearly on the side of the educator when sex is the issue surrounding a book or a classroom subject."

———. "The Crucial Error in Censorship." *Library Journal*, 92:3377–79, 1 October 1967. (Also in *Minnesota Libraries*, Summer 1967) **1G4**
"The crucial error in censorship, whether by government or by volunteer groups, is that it presumes that there is an inferior segment of

society that requires protection. Censorship is, *a priori*, undemocratic because it runs counter to the fundamental assumption that all men have a right to be heard and that, in the marketplace of ideas, all thoughts are permissible. A free society is literally egalitarian. To the degree that it is not egalitarian, it is not free." The author deals with the various arguments given by the moralists who believe individuals and society need to be protected against bad ideas in areas of politics and sex. The real threat to freedom of expression is the "corruption of the wells of information"—the manipulation of public opinion both by commercial and governmental agencies.

———. "Intellectual Freedom from *Roth* to the Presidential Commission on Obscenity and Pornography." In Eric Moon, *ed.*, *Book Selection and Censorship in the Sixties*. New York, Bowker, 1969, pp. 237–50. **1G5**
"In retrospect, the lively decade 1957–1967 generated attitudes which enlarged the boundaries of intellectual freedom, and promoted a growth of that freedom which is continuing even further in the present day. The variety and the boldness of controversial material increased; its availability to young people visibly extended. If prophecy has any merit, one might venture to predict that the United States may achieve in the next 10 years what it has struggled so long to establish: the complete freedom of the interchange of ideas, with restrictions by government removed once and for all. And if the prophecy proves accurate, librarians will have played a large part in making it an actuality."

———. "Libraries and the Climate of Opinion." *Library Trends*, 19:39–46, July 1970. **1G6**
A brief history of censorship in America as it has fluctuated with the social tensions of the times. "As fears of social danger rise, censorship activity rises with it; when the one subsides, so does the other." The censorship pressures on libraries are greatest where tax money is involved; public and school libraries are in the most exposed position because they are accessible to public control and because they are closely involved with children. The author

believes the climate has improved in recent years now that the American Library Association is bolder and more librarians are willing to risk their jobs over intellectual freedom.

———. "Moderation in Minneapolis." *Library Journal*, 96:1681–83, 15 May 1971. **1G7**
The librarian of the Minneapolis Public Library discusses the controversy between the mayor and the Library Board over two "filthy" books and underground newspapers which the mayor charged were available to children. Following a public hearing the Board decided to restrict the underground papers to adult use. Librarian Gaines defends this action against some librarian critics, noting that the Library Bill of Rights did not address itself to the question of rights of minors as distinguished from rights of adults. Gaines, long an advocate of freedom of access to materials in libraries, believes "it to be folly to press too rapidly against substantial public fear and hostility. To ignore public opinion is to invite the kind of retaliation that would severely cripple the library's ability to operate." The mayor had threatened to cut the library's budget. "The only librarians who can be openly contemptuous of such a position are those who do not have to live with the consequences of the decision."

———. "The New Censorship—Social Responsibility and Moral Righteousness." *Minnesota English Journal*, 12(1):3–8, Winter 1976. **1G8**
The author believes that "the long war to establish freedom of expression about sex was essentially won in the 1960's, following the *Roth* decision in 1957" and, while there may be local setbacks, the disease of obscenity censorship is under control. We should now be turning our attention to the more serious areas of political censorship, which has taken subtle forms since World War II "reflecting the inordinate complexity of modern society." Among the dangers to freedom are the attempts to alter our language patterns and to rewrite history to conform to present perceptions of social justice. "Social control exercised through the manipulation of information," is not only immoral, but it does not work. He accuses liberal intellectuals, including some librarians, with advocating

techniques, in the interest of certain social goals, "that have always been the chief stock in trade of the repressive right wing. . . . Any suppression of ideas, however unselfish and nobly motivated the censorship may be, and however obnoxious the opinion for which suppression is sought, ultimately diminishes us all."

Gale, Mary E. "An Obscene Case?" *MORE*, 6(2):23–24, February 1976. **1G9**
The conviction and imprisonment of William L. Hamling and Earl Kemp on obscenity charges for publishing *The Illustrated Presidential Report of the Commission on Obscenity and Pornography* was virtually ignored by the big media.

Gallagher, Donald A., Jr. "The Right to Inspect Public Records in Oregon." *Oregon Law Review*, 53:354–66, Spring 1974. **1G10**
"After providing an overview of Oregon's initial statutory attempts to solve the problem [right of inspection versus possible public harm] and the two major cases which dealt with it, *MacEwan v. Holm* [1961] and *Papadopoulos v. State Board of Higher Education* [1972], this comment analyzes the effects of the 1973 Act."

Gallagher, Robert S. "Peter Bridge Goes to Jail." *Saturday Review (Science)*, 55(44):7–8, 28 October 1972. **1G11**
A New Jersey reporter goes to jail for refusing to divulge his news sources to a grand jury.

Gallagher, Wes. "Are We Getting the Truth from Vietnam?" *Seminar (A Quarterly Review for Newspapermen by Copley Newspapers)*, 20:14–16, June 1971. **1G12**
"While there has never been censorship in Vietnam, there are other difficulties, but the truth gradually emerges, says the general manager of the Associated Press."

———. "Truth Is in the Eye of the Beholder." *Nieman Reports*, 22(3):3–7, September 1968. **1G13**
The general manager of the Associated Press discusses two growing dangers that threaten the concept of a free press in a democracy: the tendency of many in our society to read and hear only the news that reinforces their opinions; and another group that seizes upon conspiracy theories to explain the complex events of our times. "Both groups strike at the root of the free flow of information essential to our way of life."

———. *What Halo? We Never Had One!* Tucson, Ariz., University of Arizona Press, 1968. 18p. (John Peter Zenger Award Lectures) **1G14**
The newspaperman has never had a halo. "Every emotional news era in our history has brought out distrust and criticism of the press; . . . attacks upon the news media will rise in

direct proportion to the intensity of public frustration in meeting the problems of the day." The author offers a critique of the present-day critics of the press—those who want to stifle dissent and retain the status quo and those who want more representation of minority and unorthodox views. The solution is not in forced access, advocacy reporting, or a press council to adjudicate grievances. The press needs to continue its historic independence of government control, to be guided by the sense of duty and conscience of its editors, who should stop worrying about their image.

Gallogly, Edward P., Jr., and George E. Meng. "Television: the Public Interest in License Renewals." *Catholic University Law Review*, 20:328–42, Winter 1970. **1G15**
"This article will evaluate the 1970 Policy Statement [*FCC Public Notice*, Jan. 15, 1970 (FCC 70–62)] in relation to prior case law, the statutory means offered and available for FCC policy enforcement, and the public goals desirable in television broadcasting to determine whether this policy constitutes a breach of FCC authority. As an alternative to the 1970 Policy Statement, the article proposes the proper public goal for television broadcasting and its effective implementation within the boundaries of the FCC's regulatory authority."

Gallup, George. "Stricter Obscenity Laws Favored." *Washington Post* (and other papers carrying his syndicated column), 26 June 1967. (Also in U.S. House of Representatives, Committee on Post Office and Civil Service, Subcommittee on Postal Operations, *Obscenity in the Mails, Hearings, 5 and 6 August 1969*, pp. 83–84) **1G16**
Eighty-five of every 100 adults interviewed in a Gallup survey favor stricter laws against obscenity sent through the mail; 75 of 100 want stricter control of obscenity on the newsstand.

Gambill, Joel T. "Arkansas Editor Accused of Criminal Libel." *Grassroots Editor*, 13(6):11–15, November–December 1972. **1G17**
The story of the crusading editor of *Sharp Citizen* of Cave City, Ark., who had been critical in his paper of local and state politicians and office holders and of the FBI. He was shot at, attacked on the street, had his home searched, and was brought to trial on charges of criminal libel.

———. *Hugo Black: The First Amendment and the Mass Media*. Carbondale, Ill., Southern Illinois University, 1973. 287p. (Ph.D. dissertation, University Microfilms, no. 74–6200) **1G18**
"The purpose of this study was to examine Mr. Justice Black's First Amendment opinions dealing with the mass media and to determine the significance of his service on the Supreme Court in this regard. The problem necessarily

centered on Mr. Justice Black, the Supreme Court, the First Amendment, and the mass media. The interrelation of these elements was examined by compiling and analyzing Black's opinions and the relationship of these opinions to those of other justices and to the times."

Gandy, Oscar H., Jr. *et al. Media and Government: An Annotated Bibliography*. Stanford, Calif., Institute of Communication Research, Stanford University, 1975. 93p. **1G19**
"Although most research focuses on the impact of the media on the public or on the election process, we try here to encourage more research on the relationships between journalists and officials." In addition to annotations, the compilers supply a brief description of the research methodologies. Joint compilers are Susan Miller, William L. Rivers, and Gail Ann Rivers.

Ganek, Jeffrey P. "Consideration of Only Selected Presidential Speeches Is Arbitrary, and Therefore Impermissible, Where 'Responsiveness' to Prior Presidential Speeches Is the Criterion for Granting Time Under the Fairness Doctrine." *Journal of Public Law*, 22:257–70, 1973. **1G20**
Re: *Columbia Broadcasting System, Inc. v. Federal Communications Commission*, 454 F.2d 1018 (D.C. Cir. 1971).

Gangloff, John A. *Safeguarding Defense Information*. Columbia, Mo., University of Missouri at Columbia, 1971. 206p. (Unpublished Master's thesis) **1G21**
A formal system for withholding defense information from the public was created following World War II, prompted by the Cold War. The system enabled officials to hide their shortcomings, to enhance the significance of their work, as well as to provide necessary protection for sensitive defense information. The secrecy system not only hampered the press in reporting to the public but it restricted congressmen in their ability to legislate intelligently. A major problem in the system is the lack of an adequate program for declassifying information for which there is no longer a need for secrecy.

Gard, Robert R. "Censorship and Public Understanding." *English Journal*, 60:255–59, February 1971. **1G22**
A discussion of the dilemma faced by high school teachers in using or not using contemporary reading materials: "If a teacher clings to an unassailable rectitude in subjects for classroom treatment, his students see his class as irrelevant; if he allows reading and discussion in a contemporary vein, he is subject to per-

sonal attack from a suspicious public." The author calls for the laying of groundwork for better understanding with the public by means of an advisory committee made up of representatives of the faculty, librarians, supervisors, and administrators. "But responsible and trusted citizens from outside the professional staff—preferably members of the community power structure—should also be present."

Gard, Spencer A. "Free Press v. Fair Trial: Another Tempest in the Teapot." *American Bar Association Journal*, 54:669–71, July 1968. **1G23**
"Judge Gard contends that if standards ⌊concerning the withholding of information about a criminal prosecution prior to trial⌋ are considered from an evidentiary point of view it will be recognized that they have raised no new issues and are not unprecedented. He points out that under the rules of evidence certain types of information have long been privileged and that under certain circumstances in criminal prosecutions the state has had the privilege of not revealing certain information."

Gard, Stephen W. "Obscenity and the Right to Be Let Alone: The Balancing of Constitutional Rights." *Indiana Law Review*, 6:490–508, 1973. **1G24**
"Recognition of the right to be let alone and the right to direct the upbringing of one's children for what they are—fundamental constitutional rights—would free the United States Supreme Court from the problems of dealing with obscenity on a case-by-case basis and give it a conceptual framework with which it could consistently deal with the cases. Obscenity cases could be decided in the same manner the Court handles cases of conflicting constitutional rights in other areas of constitutional law—by balancing the rights involved and deciding which should take precedence in a given situation."

Gardiner, Harold C. "Censorship." In *Catholic Encyclopedia*, New York, McGraw-Hill, 1967, vol. 3, pp. 391–92. **1G25**
The article discusses two forms of censorship—prior and repressive (after the fact)—both coming under the justifying norm, "the protection of the common good through the coercive power of authority." Limitations of freedom, the author believes, "are at times as essential for the attainment of the common good as are extensions of freedom." He considers the concept of criticism vs. censorship and the conditions for the exercise of sane censorship. He concludes: "Censorship in practice is one of the most difficult problems in modern society, for it is a most sensitive area in the whole field of the proper balance between authority and freedom."

Gardner, John D. "Friends of the Earth

v. FCC: Environmentally Oriented Fairness Doctrine Complaints." *Environmental Law*, 5:159–74, Fall 1974. **1G26**
"Friends of the Earth v. FCC ⌊1971⌋ was a novel attempt by a public interest group to gain access to the television airways through the employment of the FCC's fairness doctrine in order to present environmental views to counter commercial product advertising which clashed with ecological concerns." While upheld by the appeals courts, the decision has not led to an extension of the doctrine by the FCC.

Gardner, Martin R. " 'He That Hath Eyes to See, Let Him See'; He That Is Offended, Let Him Look the Other Way—Obscenity Law and Artistic Expression." *Utah Law Review*, 1972:503–10, Winter 1972. **1G27**
"This note examines the conflict between the right of artistic expression and the public's right to be free from offensive material, and concludes with suggestions for the resolution of the conflict." The author suggests that the two-level theory basic to the *Roth* decision on obscenity be abandoned in order to make obscenity law more consistent with other First Amendment interests.

Gardner, Ro. "How to Get Rid of Your Hometown Editor." *Grassroots Editor*, 15(5):2, 28–29, September–October 1974. **1G28**
An appeal for help for the courageous editors of small-town newspapers who are being run out of town because they have "the guts to be unpopular and speak out about something that is rotten in their hometown."

Garnett, Edward. "Preface ⌊on Censorship⌋." In Norah C. James, *Sleeveless Errand; A Novel*. Paris, Henry Babou and Jack Kahane, 1929, pp. 1–3. **1G29**
A brief account of the suppression of Norah C. James's *Sleeveless Errand*, by the British Home Office, "a perfect example of official blundering."

Garnham, Nicolas. "Press Freedom or Social Justice: Take Your Choice." *Journalism Studies Review*, 1(1):15–17, June 1976. **1G30**
"The question facing the Royal Commission on the Press, the Annan Committee on the Future of British Broadcasting, the Government and each one of us, is whether we allow the myth of press freedom to stand in the way of our active pursuit of social justice."

Garrison, Dee. "Immoral Fiction in the Late Victorian Library." *American Quarterly*, 28:71–89, Spring 1976. **1G31**
American public libraries served as genteel guardians of reading during the latter part of the Victorian age. "Amid the whirl of social change in the late nineteenth century, the small literary flurry over book selection in the public

library serves to dramatize not only aesthetic problems but important questions of morality and religion that perplexed the age." The author analyzes the "immoral" best sellers, often rejected by public libraries, whose themes were in opposition to convention, whose heroines were sensual, active, and defiant. "By 1900 public library leaders had all but given up an attempt to discredit best-selling fiction. When the mass literary movement aided the nineteenth-century trend toward individualized morality which women novel readers strengthened, the decline of library paternalism became a sign of the times."

Gartner, Michael. "A New Cloud for the First Amendment." *Wall Street Journal*, 182(20):10, 30 July 1973. **1G32**
The threat of the courts upholding the Florida right of reply law prompts the author to consider the common concerns of both the newspaper and broadcast news in application of varying aspects of the fairness doctrine.

Gartrell, Richard B. "Syllabus and Bibliography for Issues in Freedom of Speech." In *Free Speech Yearbook*, *1971*. Speech Communication Association, 1971, pp. 1–27. **1G33**
An outline for an undergraduate college course, together with a list of concerned organizations, library resources, and bibliography.

Garvey, Daniel E. "Secretary Hoover and the Quest of Broadcast Regulation." *Journalism History*, 3:66–70, 85, Autumn 1976. **1G34**
The author discovers that Herbert Hoover, when Secretary of Commerce from 1921 to 1928, "was a staunch and unceasing advocate of strong federal regulation for broadcasting. Some of the power he sought for federal regulators far exceeded the powers finally granted in the Radio Act of 1927 and reconfirmed in the Communications Act of 1934. Many of the provisions of our present law of broadcasting were called for by Hoover years before Congress finally put them into law. Nothing in the record suggests that Hoover ever considered industrial self-regulation as anything but a stop-gap measure, useful only until strong federal legislation could be obtained."

Gaskin, Mary J. "The First Amendment: Blanket Protection for the Performance Arts?" *University of Pittsburgh Law Review*, 37:551–75, Spring 1976. **1G35**
"This Comment will analyze the language courts have used in treating the arts in order to uncover the problems judges have faced in formulating a consistent approach to the regulation of these art forms. In addition, the various tests used and proposed for use within the body of legal opinion will be examined for effectiveness in dealing with these problems. An attempt will be made to correlate factors which might help distinguish protected artistic

expression from conduct only purportedly artistic." Includes consideration of the motion picture.

Gasperini, Edwin L. "New Shift in the Libel Law." *Public Relations Journal*, 30(12):6–9, December 1974. **1G36**
"The recent Supreme Court case of *Gertz v. Robert Welch, Inc.* [1974] has significantly reduced a publication's defenses to a libel action by a private citizen. However, the case also places a heavier burden of proof on the plaintiff and limits his potential recovery; thus, it is difficult to assess whether the decision will encourage a substantial number of new plaintiffs."

Gastil, Raymond D. "The Moral Right of the Majority to Restrict Obcenity and Pornography Through Law." *Ethics*, 86:231–40, April 1976. **1G37**
"The majority has a moral right to legislate outside of the political realm" as to what should be permitted in public in a moral society. The author argues that "the presentation or acting out of sex or violence in public, or advertising such activities in public, will tend to popularize and familiarize a view of man and an attitude toward the self that will diminish the view that people have of the significance through specialness of human life and also divert creative artists from creative activity through the diversion of the time and money of the public toward an art world whose standards have been undermined. . . . by pornography."

Gatton, Edwin R. "Free Speech Regulated in Shopping Centers." *Wake Forest Law Review*, 8:590–97, 1972. **1G38**
Re: *Lloyd Corp. v. Tanner*, 407 U.S. 551 (1972).

Gauer, Raymond P. "National Director Tours Stockholm, Copenhagen and London." *National Decency Reporter*, 7(1–2):4–9, January–February 1970. **1G39**
The director of the Citizens for Decent Literature reports on his tour of Stockholm and Copenhagen where pornography is legalized and where it flourishes, and to London. In each city he visited with leaders of antipornography movements and public officials. In Copenhagen he visited with Professor Berl Kutschinsky, selected by the U.S. Commission on Obscenity and Pornography to report on Legalized Pornography in Denmark. He considered Kutschinsky as a biased observer who would be expected to have nothing but glowing praise for legalized pornography. In both Sweden and Denmark the director was shocked by the openness of pornography displays and sales and the promotion in the press. In a meeting with a Danish police official he learned of the misleading nature of statistics on the reduction of sex crimes since the legalization of pornography. In London he visited with Mary Whitehouse, leader against sexual promiscuity in England, John Trevelyan, then director of the British Film Censor Board, and

Malcolm Muggeridge, author and critic. A summary of his trip was presented in testimony before the U..S. Commission on Obscenity and Pornography (*National Decency Reporter*, May–June 1970).

Gaumer, F. T. "Police, Jurists, Newsmen Work 'As Usual.'"*Grassroots Editor*, 13(2):29–32, March–April 1972. **1G40**
A recent survey of Ohio newspaper editors, police reporters, and court reporters assessed the effect at the local level of the recommendations of the Reardon Report, the U.S. Supreme Court decision in *Sheppard v. Maxwell*, and other progeny of the free press–fair trial conflict. "The data reveal, in general, that there have been relatively few or only minor changes in court or police procedures in recent years, and few or only minor instances of interference in news gathering." This may have resulted from increased cooperation between press and bar, plus being overshadowed by such issues as the Pentagon Papers, the report on shield laws, and the Justice Department's clumsy attempt to force reporters to surrender their notes, tapes, and other materials.

Gaylin, Willard M. "The Prickly Problem of Pornography." *Yale Law Journal*, 77:579–97, 1968. (A revised version appears in Harry M. Clor, *ed.*, *Censorship and Freedom of Expression*, pp. 153–75 under the title, Obscenity Is More Than a Four-Letter Word) **1G41**
In this essay on pornography and obscenity, presented in the form of a review of Richard H. Kuh's *Foolish Figleaves*, a psychiatrist explores the confusion in the thinking that exists among judges, psychiatrists, and the general public. He raises many of the issues that have been faced by the courts and by writers in the area, including the basic question as to whether obscenity law serves a useful purpose; whether obscenity is capable of being defined. He notes the controversy over whether obscenity is "disgusting" or "prurient," or in fact, both. He explores the use of expert witnesses in court— the literary critic and the psychiatrist. If sex is really a healthy thing, as the medical profession suggests, what is wrong with literature that stimulates it? The production of great quantities of pornographic literature of a perverted nature suggests that there is a considerable audience for it. The author believes that the often criticized *Ginzburg* decision, which considered the purpose, intention, and motive of the publisher, "actually represents a new measure of sophistication in the law, and is, psychologically speaking, the soundest statement of the day." The author explores the dichotomy between thought and expression, on the one hand, and action, on the other, noting the difficulties of separating them. Can literature and art corrupt and harm? The danger of pornography may not be in the effect of an individual work on an adolescent, but the cumulated effect on the pattern of growth. While the reading of pornography may not be harmful, making it legal may be potentially dangerous because it gives it the sanction of

society. What about addiction to pornography, if it is made legal? Is sex expression innocuous, but portrayal of violence harmful, as argued by some liberals? Is the area of sex the only area of morality we are concerned in suppressing, a question also raised by liberals? Is law the best way of controlling obscenity or should this be left to the family? We must weigh the danger of pornography against the danger to freedom if we suppress it.

Gaynes, Martin J. "Trends in the Fairness Doctrine and Access: The Process of Free Speech." In Don R. Le Duc, *ed.*, *Issues in Broadcast Regulation*, Washington, D.C., Broadcast Education Association, 1974, pp. 75–79. **1G42**
The fairness problem in broadcasting during the past decade reflects the fact that "we face some very severe tensions in our society for a lot of reasons (imbalance, income, discrimination) which people believe are susceptible to some kind of rational solution to which people want to get their ideas across."The author believes there is no right of personal access, but rather a right of "issue access." Issues have to be aired in some way. One of the most pressing problems faced by the Federal Communications Commission under the fairness doctrine is the treatment of commercial advertising.

Gaynor, Michael J. "Obscenity Law: Après *Stanley*, le Deluge?" *Catholic Lawyer*, 17:45–62, Winter 1971. **1G43**
The article analyzes the *Stanley* opinion (*Stanley v. Georgia*, 1969), presents the diverse constructions of *Stanley*, and predicts the scope of constitutional protection that will be offered to obscene matter under the decision; and what view the U.S. Supreme Court will take when it determines the constitutionality of absolute bans on the public dissemination of obscene material.

———. "Obscenity Law: Le Deluge Postponed." *Catholic Lawyer*, 17:255–66, Summer 1971. **1G44**
"The purpose of this article is presentation and analysis of two major obscenity cases. First, the history of the constitutional status of obscenity is reviewed; second, the *Thirty-Seven Photographs* case [*United States v. Thirty-Seven Photographs*, 1971] is examined; third, the *Reidel* case [*United States v. Reidel*, 1971] is considered; finally, the present state of this aspect of obscenity law is summarized and possible modification is discussed."

Gebhard, Paul H. "Why 'Chant d'Amour' Was Banned." *Censorship Today*, 2(4):17–19, August–September 1969. **1G45**
An account of the banning of the French film, *Chant d'Amour*, written and produced by Jean Genêt, by the U.S. Supreme Court in 1966.

The author of the article, former executive director of the Kinsey Institute, analyzes the reasons for the rejection of this film which deals with homosexuality.

Gegan, Bernard E. "The Twilight of Nonspeech." *Catholic Lawyer*, 15:210–20, Summer 1969.   **1G46**
The author examines two categories of constitutional nonspeech, libel and obscenity—how they came to be exempt from First Amendment guarantees and how they are now breaking out. "It is worth noting that libel and obscenity left the category [nonspeech] in opposite directions. Libel became protected in so far as it is public. Obscenity acquired protection in so far as it is private."

Gehring, Durward J. "Comparing the Incomparable: Toward a Structural Model for FCC Comparative Broadcast License Renewal Hearings." *University of Chicago Law Review*, 43:573–612, Spring 1976.   **1G47**
"The comment concludes that the comparative renewal hearing as it is currently administered is inherently incapable of choosing between incumbent licensees and challengers. Finally, the comment proposes a procedure designed to enable the Commission to make selections between incumbents and challengers on the basis of objective policies and demonstrates that such a procedure could avoid the objections that led the court to invalidate the Commission's previous approach."

Geis, Gilbert. "Publication of the Names of Juvenile Felons." *Montana Law Review*, 23:141–57, Spring 1962.   **1G48**
A consideration of the assets and demerits of the 1961 Montana law "allowing newspaper publication of the name of any youth proceeded against as, or found to be, a delinquent child where a hearing or proceeding is had in the juvenile court on a written petition charging him with the commission of any felony."

———, and Robert E. L. Talley. "Cameras in the Courtroom." *Journal of Criminal Law, Criminology, and Police Science*, 47:546–60, January–February 1957.   **1G49**
The authors have attempted to assemble the various viewpoints on Canon 35 of the American Bar Association's Canons of Judicial Ethics, dealing with photographic coverage of trials: press photographers and editors on one side and lawyers and judges on the other. The evidence assembed points out the sharp disagreement between the two sides.

Geldmacher, John L. *"Rosenbloom" and Libel*. Columbia, Mo., Freedom of In-formation Center, School of Journalism, University of Missouri at Columbia, 1973. 8p. (Report no. 297)   **1G50**
"This report explains the U.S. Supreme Court's 'Rosenbloom v. Metromedia' decision, extending the 'actual malice' libel standard to private individuals involved in matters of public interest and concern. Arguments spawned by 'Rosenbloom' are examined, and future implications for libel are explored against a background of subsequent lower court decisions."

Gelfand, Ravina. *The Freedom of Speech in America*. Minneapolis, Lerner, 1967. 63p. (In America series)   **1G51**
In this book written and illustrated for young people the author considers the meaning of free speech, how the concept came about and was developed in English and early American history, and the various interpretations that the U.S. Supreme Court has given to the First Amendment. The author concludes with a chapter, What You Can (and Cannot) Do Under Your Right to Free Speech.

Geller, Evelyn. "Intellectual Freedom: Eternal Principle or Unanticipated Consequence?" *Library Journal*, 99:1364–67, 15 May 1974.   **1G52**
A discussion of the origin and history of the American Library Association's concern with intellectual freedom. Noting the disparity of views among library historians, she concludes: "The concepts embodied in the Library Bill of Rights were not part of the professional leadership's views of library selection and services in the years after the American Library Association was founded, and for a significant time to come. Essentially, the idea of intellectual freedom was an unanticipated consequence of library practices intended to embody older, and very different, views of library selection and service. In other words, it was a reversal of a former policy, and a reversal of an earlier social role."

———. "The Librarian as Censor." *Library Journal*, 101:1255–58, 1 June 1976.   **1G53**
In an examination of the history of library censorship the author found that "the current position of the American Library Association on intellectual freedom was not a development and refinement of its earlier positions, but a reversal of an older posture. . . . This analysis will attempt to show how librarians viewed their mission, and the areas of literature they concentrated on, the selection and exclusion policies they had developed, to provide a picture of what the concepts of selection and censorship were like 80 to 100 years ago."

———. "Two Cheers for Liberty: The Preconference on Intellectual Freedom and the Teenager." *Library Journal*, 93:3109–13, 15 September 1967; *School Library Journal*, 14:41–45, September 1967. (Reprinted in Eric Moon, *ed.*, *Book Selection and Censorship in the Sixties*, pp. 322–32)   **1G54**
"Librarians at the preconference on intellectual freedom and the teenager took the position that adolescents should have free access to adult literature. What was the background of the conference? What were the issues? How strong was the agreement?" The editor concludes that "whatever good emerges from the conference will not come from the program itself, but from whatever agency decides to bring the most crucial conflicts out into the open. For it seemed, in the end, that while librarians were very brave about sex—lauding their own liberality (or liberation?)—it was 'censorship,' in turn, that had become a dirty word, symbol of a ubiquitous and unmentionable phenomenon, best left unacknowledged, undiscussed, and unresolved."

Geller, Henry. "The Comparative Renewal Process in Television: Problems and Suggested Solutions." *Virginia Law Review*, 61:471–514, April 1975. **1G55**
"The article focuses on the effort to improve service through comparative hearings on renewal [of television licenses]. The basic issue is the governing criteria in such a hearing. How do we best strike a balance between providing a competitive stimulus to service in the public interest and ensuring reasonable stability also necessary to such service?" The author concludes with a proposal for a new standard for renewal.

———. "Does *Red Lion* Square with *Tornillo?*" *University of Miami Law Review*, 29:477–81, Spring 1975.   **1G56**
The author finds a direct conflict between the U.S. Supreme Court decision in *Miami Herald Publishing Co. v. Tornillo* (1974), denying the right of reply in the newspaper press and *Red Lion Broadcasting Co. v. F.C.C.* sustaining the right of reply over broadcast facilities. He proposes that the Federal Communications Commission "refer the fairness complaint to the licensee but take no action on it" until time for license renewal. "If it does not find a pattern of bad or reckless disregard of the fairness doctrine, it should not intervene."

———. *The Fairness Doctrine in Broadcasting: Problems and Suggested Courses of Action*. Santa Monica, Calif., Rand, 1973, 149p. (Prepared under a grant from the Ford Foundation)   **1G57**
This report offers analysis and suggested courses of action for resolving the overall inquiry of the Federal Communications Commission into the fairness doctrine. The report suggested these policies: (1) return to the practice of applying fairness doctrine only at the time of license renewal, (2) continue the policy of issuing prompt rulings in regard to personal attacks and political broadcasts, (3) require the licensee to show in a general fashion that he has afforded reasonable opportunity for contrasting viewpoints to be presented, (4) require that the TV licensee list annually the ten issues, local and national, to which he gave the most

coverage in the prior year, (5) implement the first part of the licensee's "two-fold duty"—the discussion of controversial issues—by adopting time percentage guidelines in television, (6) revise the complaint procedure so that it is fair to the complainant and yet not burdensome to the licensee, and (7) revise the rules pertaining to personal attacks and political editorializing in accordance with the basic notion of providing the licensee with wide latitude in fulfilling his fairness objectives.

Gellhorn, Walter. "Dirty Books, Disgusting Pictures, and Dreadful Law." *Georgia Law Review*, 8:291–312, Winter 1974.   **1G58**
A review of recent obscenity decisions of the U.S. Supreme Court. The author observes that the Court erroneously assumed that at the time of the adoption of the Constitution obscenity had been outlawed; that there is some confusion over the definition of "community" in establishing obscenity standards; and "the evidence of a nexus between pornography and anti-social acts is slim." Two areas of control may be justified: prohibition of pornography to minors (witness the New York state law), if for no other reason than "to enhance parental peace of mind"; and forbidding "imposing of sexual expression on unwilling adults." He cites five reasons for concern over efforts to censor pornography: (1) enforcement of the law has a chilling effect on freedom of expression; (2) the First Amendment protects the hearer's and viewer's freedom of choice as well as that of the writer and speaker; (3) prosecutors may use sex as a convenient peg upon which to hang suppression of political ideas; (4) it diverts the time of law enforcement officers and the courts from more serious matter; and (5) it places the emphasis on sexual morality to the disregard of other moral issues.

Gelman, David *et al.* "Counter-Spy." *Newsweek*, 87(1):41, 5 January 1976.   **1G59**
The death of a CIA agent in Athens has been attributed by U.S. intelligence officials to "publicity generated in spy-ferreting books by former CIA agents Victor Marchetti and Philip Agee, by Congressional probes of CIA operations, and most doggedly, by a quarterly called *Counter-Spy*."

Gent, George. "Pornography: Its Peril to Youth." *Columbia*, 46(2):16–19, February 1966.   **1G60**
"Many authorities who have studied the problem of obscenity feel certain it has noxious effects on youth, but they admit they have not yet come up with massive scientific proof to convince the doubters."

George, Thomas W., *comp.* "Coming to Grips with the Underground Press." *Nation's Schools*, 89(4):59–61, April 1972.   **1G61**
Three examples of guidelines for student publications are offered which conform to current legal thinking on what school officials can do in

regulating student printed materials. The guidelines were issued by the California State Department of Education, the Seattle Public School System, and the New Jersey Commissioner of Education.

Georgia Library Association. "Intellectual Freedom in Libraries: A Statement of Policy." *Georgia Librarian*, 7(1):13–15, March 1970.   **1G62**
The statement expresses four areas of concern of the Georgia Library Association: state, local, and school district legislation; restrictions imposed by individuals, voluntary committees, or administrative authorities on library materials or book selection; liaison with other groups supporting the Freedom to Read; and continuing education of librarians and the general public in the area of intellectual freedom.

Geraghty, Tony. " 'But No One Said Why It Was Dirty.' " *Bulletin* (Australia), 91:48–49, 27 December 1969.   **1G63**
"Inquiries into the background of both the Dobson and the Wrate ₁obscenity₁ cases reveal that in so-called permissive Britain there is a growing, if secret, army of official and unofficial Censors who work in private, intercept the mail and are answerable to virtually no one."

Gerald, J. Edward. "Press—Bar Relationships: Progress Since Sheppard and Reardon." *Journalism Quarterly*, 47:223–32, Summer 1970.   **1G64**
"Major changes in attitudes are permitting cooperation of press, bar and bench in voluntary committees working to influence news reporting that might prejudice criminal cases. Efforts are led by the ASNE and the ABA."

Gerber, Albert B. "Obscenity—And Chief Justice Warren." *Censorship Today*, 2(1):4–11, February–March 1969.   **1G65**
The author, on an examination of Chief Justice Earl Warren's decisions on obscenity, finds that Warren, who was the originator of the theory that obscenity as a crime must be based upon the conduct of the defendant, has been completely inconsistent in his position concerning noncriminal problems in obscenity. Also he has given "little inkling as to what he really regards as obscene."

————. "The Right to Receive and Possess Pornography; An Attorney Foresees the End of Legal Restrictions." *Wilson Library Bulletin*, 44:641–44, February 1970.   **1G66**
The author believes that the U.S. Supreme Court in *Stanley v. Georgia*, which ruled that mere possession of pornography was not a crime, represents a retreat from the strict interpretation of the *Roth* case (*Roth v. United States*, 1957). When the right of "mere possession" is combined with the right to receive, have, and possess material in the field of ideas

without Congress burdening that right unduly (*Lamont v. Postmaster General*, 1965), a new legal position is established. There would still remain controls over distribution and sale to juveniles, pandering, involuntary subjection of a captive audience to pornographic materials, and pornography in the flesh.

Gerbner, George, and Larry Gross. "Living with Television: The Violence Profile." *Journal of Communications*, 26:172–99, Spring 1976.   **1G67**
Using a new approach to the study of violence on television—Cultural Indicators—the authors conclude: "A heightened sense of risk and insecurity (different for groups of varying power) is more likely to increase acquiescence to and dependence upon established authority, and to legitimize its use of force, than it is to threaten the social order through occasional non-legitimized imitations. Risky for their perpetrators and costly for their victims, media-incited criminal violence may be a price industrial cultures extract from some citizens for the general pacification of most others."

Gerdts, Charles W., III, and Kevin J. Wolff. "State Court Reactions to Gertz v. Robert Welch, Inc.: Inconsistent Results and Reasoning." *Vanderbilt Law Review*, 29:1431–47, November 1976.   **1G68**
The article will "examine the state court reaction to Gertz ₁*Gertz v. Robert Welch, Inc.* (1974)₁, describe the reasons for the lack of uniformity in their conclusions, and suggest an approach to balancing the first amendment and reputational interests."

Gerlach, John C., and Lana Gerlach. *The Critical Index: A Bibliography of Articles on Film in English, 1946–1973, Arranged by Names and Topics.* New York, Teachers College Press, 1974. 726p.   **1G69**
Includes articles on blacklisting and censorship.

Gertz, Elmer. "Censorship in Chicago." *ICarbS* (Southern Illinois University), 3(1):49–59, Summer–Fall 1976.   **1G70**
The Chicago attorney for Henry Miller and Grove Press in the *Tropic of Cancer* litigation discusses the trial and the broader personal relationship between lawyer and client as seen through their extensive correspondence. "The correspondence between Miller and myself reflected the haze, frustrations, and anger over the delays, ignorance, and bigotry," and "the vicissitudes of the legal warfare strengthened the friendship between us."

————. "The *Chicago Seed* Case." *Censorship Today*, 2(4):20–23, August–September 1969. **1G71**
The case of the Chicago bookseller, arrested for the sale of *Chicago Seed*, an underground newspaper charged with carrying a two-page obscene illustration. The case was dismissed without resolving the constitutional issue of *scienter*, much to the disappointment of the author of this article who defended the bookseller.

————. *For the First Hours of Tomorrow: The New Illinois Bill of Rights*. Urbana, Ill., Published for the Institute of Government and Public Affairs by the University of Illinois Press, 1972. 178p. (Studies in Illinois Constitution Making) **1G72**
The chairman of the Bill of Rights Committee of the Sixth Illinois Constitutional Convention writes of his personal recollections of the deliberations of that body. Section 4 of the adopted Bill of Rights reads: "All persons may speak, write and publish freely, being responsible for the abuse of that liberty. In trials for libel, both civil and criminal, the truth, when published with good motives and for justifiable ends, shall be a sufficient defense."

————. "Henry Miller and the Law." In George Wickes, *ed. Henry Miller and the Critics*. Carbondale, Ill., Southern Illinois University Press, 1963, pp. 177–86. (Reprinted in Eleanor Widmer, *ed.*, *Freedom and Culture*, pp. 120–23) **1G73**
The attorney who successfully defended Henry Miller's *Tropic of Cancer* in the Chicago censorship trial before Judge Samuel B. Epstein, discusses that case, one of sixty suits of various kinds brought against the book in courts across the country. He concludes: "It seems to me that our day is witnessing the last gasp of legal censorship of literary materials." Text of the testimony of Mark Schorer and Harry Levin in *McCormack v. Tropic of Cancer* appears on pages 161–76.

————. "I Am No Longer a Mere Person; I Am a Legal Landmark." *Student Lawyer*, 4(2):12–16, October 1975. **1G74**
The subject of the U.S. Supreme Court landmark libel decision, *Gertz v. Robert Welch, Inc.* (1974), discusses the case and its implications. A brief biography of Lawyer Gertz by Charles Flynn is appended.

————. "A Lawyer 'Uses' the Press." In David G. Clark and Earl R. Hutchison, *eds.*, *Mass Media and the Law*, New York, Wiley-Interscience, 1970, pp. 161–80. **1G75**
A Chicago attorney illustrates some subtle ways in which lawyers use, and are used by, the press, writing from "many years' first-hand experience with sensational murder and obscenity cases, as well as from wide acquaintance with the workings of the mass media."

————. *To Life*. New York, McGraw-Hill, 1974. 252p. **1G76**
Memoirs of the Chicago civil rights lawyer who was successful in the reversal of Jack Ruby's death sentence, who defended Henry Miller's *Tropic of Cancer* in the successful Chicago case before Judge Epstein, and who more recently won his own libel suit against the John Birch Society before the U.S. Supreme Court.

"The *Gertz* Case: Unbalancing Media Rights and Reputational Interests." *Western State University Law Review*, 2:227–41, Spring 1975. **1G77**
Re: *Gertz v. Robert Welch, Inc.*, 418 U.S. 323 (1974).

"*Gertz v. Robert Welch, Inc.*: Redefining Defamation for a Private Citizen." *New England Law Review*, 10:585–98, Spring 1975. **1G78**
"The immediate impact of *Gertz* was that the States were no longer constitutionally compelled to apply the malice standard to a private citizen's action for defamation. In essence, the States must at least require a litigant to prove negligence and, if they so deem fit, actual malice. . . . It is the purpose of this article to discuss the factual context within which this case was adjudicated, its departure from prior case law and the ultimate significance of this decision."

Gest, John B. "Responsibility of State Supreme Courts in Obscenity Cases." *National Decency Reporter*, 6(7–8):8–9, July–August 1969. **1G79**
"State Supreme Courts should accept their responsibility under the direct mandate of the United States Constitution . . . and interpret the Constitution themselves in deciding obscenity cases under State statutes. . . . The courts should recognize that a decision of the Supreme Court of the United States is not considered as a precedent unless principles of law are clearly announced in an opinion definitely concurred in by a majority of the court."

————. "Speaking Out: On Censorship." *PLA Bulletin* (Pennsylvania Library Association), 25:70, 72, January 1970. **1G80**
Librarians should exercise their best professional judgment in selection of books, striving to promote the best taste in literature. They should not be intimidated by a cry of censorship when they reject a book which they believe unsuitable. Just because a work has been cleared by the courts of obscenity does not make it worthy of library purchase.

Gewirtz, Joel, Judith Krug, and Janet Cooper. *Censorship and the Schools*. 3 tape recordings: 24 min., 29 min., 30 min. West Haven, Conn., National Education Association, 1974. (Accompanying discussion questions and transcript) **1G81**
Tape 1, Academic Freedom—The Law and Censorship in the Schools by Joel Gewirtz, an NEA attorney; Tape 2, Intellectual Freedom—Censorship and an Enlightened Public by Judith Krug, director of the American Library Association's Office of Intellectual Freedom; Tape 3, Controversial Issues and the Classroom Teacher by Janet Cooper, a nontenured junior high school history teacher. The tapes have been produced "for reference and motivational use for in-service workshops and independent study; and for course material in schools of education."

Ghiglione, Loren. "The Case for the British Press Council Revisited." *Bulletin of the American Society of Newspaper Editors*, 586:9–11, April 1975. **1G82**
A member of the National News Council who had studied the British experience, discusses the British Press Council, noting three lessons for American editors: (1) A press council can serve both the best interests of the public and the press. (2) The development of a press council is a process that takes many years. (3) Preconceived notions about the usefulness of a press council may be totally inaccurate.

Ghosh, Kedar. *Freedom or Fraud of the Press*. Calcutta, Rupa, 1973. 126p. **1G83**
Using symbolical characters—Democ (for democracy), Fop (freedom of the press), and Sos (security of the state), the author presents his case against the proprietors of the Indian press and develops the theme that freedom of the press is given to individuals and cannot be transferred to newspaper publishers. He charges editors as being literary agents of the newspaper owners and guilty of fraud against the people. The public has been concerned with infringement of press freedom by the government, while tolerating control by a monopolistic press.

Giampietro, Wayne B. "The Constitutional Rules of Defamation: Or, It's Libel But Is He Liable?" *Illinois Bar Journal*, 64:10–15, September 1975. **1G84**
"The United States Supreme Court has stepped into the field of defamation law under the aegis of the First Amendment and has made drastic revisions in that law as it has been traditionally developed by the states." After an examination of recent cases, the author concludes that the Supreme Court has now given a measure of recognition to both privacy of the individual and the right of the public to be made aware of matters of importance.

"Neither the individual nor the press are subjected to an intolerable burden."

———. "Evening the Odds in Defamation—Troman v. Wood." *Loyola University of Chicago Law Journal*, 7:621–27, Summer 1976. **1G85**
Re: *Troman v. Wood*, 62 Ill. 2d 184 N.E. 2d 292 (1975), in which the Illinois Supreme Court responded to the delegation of authority in defamation cases by the U.S. Supreme Court (*Gertz v. Robert Welch, Inc.*) and set forth rules applicable to defamation actions between private individuals and the media.

Giannella, Donald A. "Agency Procedures Implementing the Freedom of Information Act; A Proposal for Uniform Regulations." *Administrative Law Review*, 23:217–70, May 1971. (Also in U.S. Senate. Committee on the Judiciary. *Freedom of Information Act Source Book*, pp. 296–349) **1G86**
This article is based on research undertaken by the Committee on Information, Education and Reports of the Administrative Conference of the United States to determine the existence and extent of problems in implementing the Freedom of Information Act. "On the basis of this research a proposal was drafted recommending that agencies adopt certain regulations governing procedures for the handling of requests for records." These guidelines appear in an appendix to the article.

"A Giant Step Backwards: The Supreme Court Speaks Out on Prisoners' First Amendment Rights." *Northwestern University Law Review*, 70:352–71, May–June 1975. **1G87**
The note analyzes the U.S. Supreme Court case, *Procunier v. Martinez* (1974), dealing with censorship of prisoners' mail, and *Pell v. Procunier* (1974), dealing with a prisoner's right to interviews with the press.

Gibbs, Annette. *Guidelines for the Chief Student Personnel Administrator in Implementing Editorial Policies Relating to Freedom of Expression in Sanctioned Student Newspapers of State Colleges*. Tallahassee, Fla., Florida State University, 1970. 114p. (Ph.D. dissertation, University Microfilms, no. 71–7017; ED 54,181) **1G88**
"The study was designed to answer three questions: (1) What should be the function of the state college's sanctioned student newspaper? (2) What are the legal boundaries which pertain to editorial policies of the student newspaper in relation to student freedom of expression and with which the state college must be concerned? and (3) What, if any, journalistic ethics or obligations should pertain to the student newspaper?"

[Gibson, John.] *Trial for Libel. State of Louisiana vs. John Gibson. Before the Hon. the Criminal Court of the First District of the State of Louisiana; Faithfully Reported by T. W. Collens, Esq. & W. G. Snethen.* . . . New Orleans, John Gibson, 1839. 70p. **1G89**
The editor of the weekly *True American* was charged with libeling Dr. James Monroe Mackie by questioning his moral behavior, accusing him of seducing a young woman and engaging in a fight. The jury found the incidents as reported in the paper so amusing that they laughed during the reading. Both prosecution and defense cited British and American precedent in issues of press freedom. The judge ruled that malice must be proved for a conviction. The jury could not reach an agreement and the case was dismissed.

Gibson, Martin L., Jr. *Freedom of the Press: Foundations and Attitudes*. Austin, Tex., University of Texas, 1974. 301p. (Ph.D. dissertation, University Microfilms, no. 74–14694) **1G90**
"This dissertation reports the results of a national survey of the attitudes of five demographic groups toward freedom of the press. The groups are: newsmen, state legislators, high school teachers, high school students and the general public. The survey found significant differences in attitudes between and in some cases within groups. Generally, all groups see in the press many flaws that they would correct. Legislators and newsmen stand apart from the other groups in opposing legislation that would correct those flaws but in so doing would restrict freedom of the press."

Gieber, Walter. "The Underground Press Viewed with Disenchantment." *Grassroots Editor*, 11(2):5–14, March–April 1970. **1G91**
An exposé of the underground press which the author believes is prey to all the flaws of the established press which it opposes, as well as to its own problems. The underground press is not a true or legitimate press of dissent nor a muckraking press; and it has never been underground. It is a deviant bourgeois press seeking a good market in a permissive American society. Its free sex is often "sheer exploitation" and "blatant commercialism." The political radicalism is secondary to sexuality and sexual fantasies. Many of the serious issues raised by the underground press—women's liberation, racial equality, and ecology have been taken over by the established press or drawn off by subsequent events. The laws of economics will, in the end, dictate the future of the underground press.

Giel, Lawrence A. *George R. Dale—Crusader for Free Speech and a Free Press*. Muncie, Ind., Ball State University, 1967. 157p. (Ed.D. dissertation, University Microfilms, no. 68–5,935) **1G92**
The story of the editor of the *Muncie* (Ind.) *Post-Democrat* who battled political corruption, Klan bigotry, and fought for free speech and

press. "He was repeatedly brought to court on 'trumped up' charges, assaulted, shot at, and, through pressure, deprived of all advertisement." When he criticized the local court for being negligent in its duties concerning corruption, the circuit judge ordered his paper off the streets of Muncie. The judge was impeached by the Indiana legislature for violating the principle of free speech and a free press, among other charges. Dale figured in both volumes of the *Middletown* studies by Robert S. and Helen M. Lynd.

Gielgud, Val. "Death of the Censor." *Contemporary Review*, 219:10–12, July 1971. **1G93**
Comments on censorship of the British theatre on the occasion of the abolition of the censorship role of the Lord Chamberlain.

Gies, Dianne, and Donna Polhamus. "Sex and the Workingclass Child: A Look at Sex Books and Services in Ten Hub Libraries." *Bay State Librarian*, 63(5):8–10, December 1974. **1G94**
"What kind of response does a thirteen-year-old get when he asks for sex education books in a public library? A survey of ten public libraries in workingclass communities in metropolitan Boston indicates an amazing range in the quality of service."

Gilbert, Michael. "The Lessons of PQ 17." *Author*, 83:55–60, Summer 1972. **1G95**
What can be learned about the British law of defamation by authors and publishers from the successful libel case against Cassell & Company, Ltd., publishers of David Irving's *The Destruction of Convoy PQ 17* (*Broome v. Cassell & Co., Ltd. and Irving*).

Gill, Brendon. "Blue Notes." *Film Comment*, 9(1):7–11, January–February 1973. **1G96**
A devotee of blue movies chides the "bourgeois" movie critics who ignore the genre. The author discusses the porn movies and the audiences that attend them. "The threat to freedom of the press and the threat to a continued easy access to pornography are scarcely to be spoken of in the same breath, but they occupy the same ground and will often be found to have the same defenders."

[Gill, Charles.] *The Recent Prosecutions for Blasphemy, and the Debate in the House of Commons on the Affirmation Bill. By the Author of "The Evolution of Christianity."* London, Williams & Norgate, 1883, 31p. **1G97**
Commenting on the blasphemy prosecutions of Foote, Ramsey, and Kemp, the author, while deploring the publication of the work,

believes that there should be a recognition that "as there is a fanaticism of faith, so also there may be a fanaticism of unbelief. . . . In thus avowing all sympathy with actively aggressive scepticism, I do not the less disapprove of all prosecutions for blasphemy, as survivals of medieval intolerance, far more prejudicial to all which is best in the teaching of Christianity than that confidence in the final triumph of truth, which fears not the expression of any form of religious or irreligious opinion. I regret that a British jury, controlled by our legal heritage from generations which conscientiously burnt heretics, should have felt the obligation to record a conviction on that ill-omened charge of blasphemy, inseparably associated with the trial and condemnation of Socrates and of Jesus." In the second part of the pamphlet the author calls for support in Parliament of a bill on religious freedom.

Gillers, Stephen. "Information Control: Secret Government." *Civil Liberties*, 297:3–4, July 1973.   **1G98**
An attack on the Nixon Administration's secrecy policy which "apparently believes that the security of the nation depends on his [Nixon's] unrestricted ability to control the flow of information about government, to keep secret what he wants to keep secret, and to leak what he wants to leak." The article lists some of the secrecy techniques employed.

———. "Secret Government and What To Do About It." *Civil Liberties Review*, 1:68–74, Winter–Spring 1974.
                                          1G99
Reporting on a conference on government secrecy sponsored by the Committee for Public Justice and New York University Law School, the author reached these conclusions on what might be done: restrict executive privilege, define security classification and regulate classifiers, establish the Justice Department as an independent agency of government, provide congressional review of the intelligence network, decriminalize press release of overclassified information, and provide guidelines for control of computerization and other technological devices that might threaten civil liberties.

Gillespi, Hal K. "Federal Statute Allowing Prosecution for Mailing 'Nonmailable' Obscene Material to Requesting Adults Is An Unconstitutional Infringement of First Amendment Free Speech." *Texas Law Review*, 49:575–81, March 1971.   **1G100**
Re: *United States v. Lethe*, 312 F.Supp. 421 (E.D.Cal. 1970).

Gilliam, Thomas B. *Newsmen's Sources and the Law*. Columbia, Mo., Freedom of Information Center, School of Jour-

nalism, University of Missouri at Columbia, 1971. 7p. (Report no. 259)
                                          1G101
"Despite the fact that the Supreme Court has not yet decided the issue of the first amendment's protection of a newsman's sources, there have been recent instances where the first amendment freedom of the press guarantee has been presented to the courts. It is therefore concluded that there is at least a limited constitutional protection afforded the media against compulsory disclosure of information upon which published material is based."

Gilligan, Carol *et al.* "Moral Reasoning About Sexual Dilemmas: The Development of an Interview and Scoring System." *Technical Report of the [U.S.] Commission on Obscenity and Pornography*, 1:141–73, 1971.   **1G102**
The authors develop concepts and methods to describe moral reasoning by adolescents about sexual issues.

Gillmor, Donald M. *Judicial Restraints on the Press*. Columbia, Mo., Freedom of Information Foundation, 1974. 28p. (Freedom of Information Foundation Series, no. 2)   **1G103**
"If the *Pentagon Papers* case was a setback for the government, it was no more than a Pyrrhic victory for the press; and it demonstrated for all time the fragility of *Near v. Minnesota* as an absolute barrier to prior restraint." According to the author, the Reardon Report of the American Bar Association and the United States Supreme Court decision in *Sheppard v. Maxwell* (1966), were misinterpreted "as a green light for use of the contempt power against offending news media and as an excuse to deny court and crime news to reporters." Examples of this "threatening progeny" are cited. On the brighter side, the author cites court rulings bringing out-of-court publications relating to judicial proceedings under the protection of the First Amendment and in support of the public monitoring of the judicial process. He concludes that "it is clear from this review of recent cases that the weight of judicial authority is on the side of the healthier progeny of *Near v. Minnesota*, and of the more liberal interpretations of the purposes of the First Amendment. . . . Future constitutional struggles then will revolve around the definition of postpublication accountability and the degree to which such accountability, when it is imposed upon the press, has the very same effect as an actual prior restraint."

———, and Jerome A. Barron. *Mass Communication Law; Cases and Comment*. 2d ed. St. Paul, Minn., West, 1974. 853p. (American Casebook Series. The first edition was published in 1969)
                                          1G104
This casebook, the product of interdisciplinary collaboration between a professor of journalism and a professor of law, presents the major First Amendment issues as interpreted

by the U.S. courts. The text of significant cases is given, prefaced by editorial comment. Content: Chapter 1, The First Amendment Impact on Mass Communication: The Theory, the Practice and the Problems. Chapter 2, Libel and the Newsman. Chapter 3, Privacy and the Press. Chapter 4, The Puzzle of Pornography. Chapter 5, Free Press and Fair Trial. Chapter 6, Newsman's Privilege. Chapter 7, Freedom of Information: Access to Governmental Information—Federal and State. Chapter 8, Selected Problems of Law and Journalism. Chapter 9, The Regulation of Radio and Television Broadcasting: Some Problems of Law, Technology, and Policy.

Gilluly, Richard H. "Secrecy and Elitism in Science and Government." *Science News*, 100:82–83, 31 July 1971.
                                          1G105
In the environmental, scientific, and technical areas there is an assumption that the experts possess special keys to truth and that they cannot function well if their activities are subjected to public and news media surveillance. The new Populists charge that the citizenry have been intimidated into accepting these assumptions.

Gilman, Richard. "There's a Wave of Pornography, Obscenity, [and] Sexual Expression." *New York Times Magazine*, 8 September 1968, pp. 36–37+. **1G106**
"The openness about sexual and scatalogical description in books by recognized writers is backed up by a more or less furtive and anonymous literature of outright sexuality at whose extreme end absolutely nothing is held back and no narrative or aesthetic justification whatsoever is sought." A discussion of events—legal and literary—that led to the present freedom, and ways in which the problem can be dealt with. "A society mustn't organize its general moral system on the basis of what applies only to children. We have to be permitted our adulthood with all its risks. Sexuality is a risk and so is sexual expression."

Gilman, William. "Viewpoint: A Flip of the Censorship Coin." *Newsletter on Intellectual Freedom* (IFC-ALA), 22:4–5, 22–23, January 1973.   **1G107**
"While a publisher confronted by government censorship can invoke the First Amendment right to publish, the same constitutional guarantee leaves no recourse for an author muzzled by a publisher." The author of this article reports on a longstanding feud with Harper (a part of the Cowles conglomerate) over the publication of his book, *Sharp Language*. He had received an advance royalty but Harper refused to publish the work until he had made numerous changes, which he refused to do, considering it a request for censorship. He reports that neither the ACLU nor the Authors Guild would support him in a legal challenge of the publisher.

Gilmer, Walker. *Horace Liveright: Pub-*

lisher of the Twenties. New York, David Lewis, 1970. 287p.   **1G108**
In this story of the rise and decline of one of the most colorful figures in American publishing, the author devotes two chapters to Liveright's conflicts with the censor: John Sumner's Vice Society and Two Censorship Trials. The former is an account of efforts by the New York Society for the Suppression of Vice to suppress works of modern literature. The attack on works published by Boni and Liveright began with the seizure of Hutchins Hapgood's *The Story of A Lover* in 1920 and followed two years later with an attack on an English translation of Petronius' *The Satyricon*. The author describes the alliance between John S. Sumner of the vice society and New York Supreme Court Justice John Ford, who was shocked at his daughter's reading D. H. Lawrence's *Women in Love*. The two launched a campaign for stronger state obscenity laws. Liveright led the efforts against their Clean Books bill, a cause supported by numerous authors but by only a few publishers. The bill was defeated. The Two Censorship Trials involved Maxwell Bodenheim's *Replenishing Jessica* and Theodore Dreiser's *American Tragedy*. Liveright was acquitted by a New York court over the Bodenheim book, after a sensational trial in which the entire book was read to a bored jury. Dreiser's *The American Tragedy*, which was the object of a trial in Boston, instigated by the Watch and Ward Society with the support of the Boston Bookseller's Committee, did not fare so well. In a celebrated trial (*Commonwealth v. Friede*, 1930) with distinguished counsel on both sides, Donald S. Friede, who represented Liveright in selling the book to the Boston police, was found guilty and the Supreme Judicial Court of Massachusetts refused to overturn the verdict. The case brought nationwide acclaim for Liveright from those who opposed censorship and stirred an interest in Boston which led eventually to the liberalizing of the state's obscenity laws.

Gilmore, Donald H. *Sex and Censorship in the Visual Arts*. San Diego, Greenleaf Classics, 1970. 2 vols. 416p.   **1G109**
An illustrated history of pornography, from its beginning in historical static art through such media as the comic books of the '30s and '40s, playing cards, art films, nudies, and stag-party movies. Includes discussions of pornography and the law and the Danish experiment.

Gilmore, Michael S. "From Roth to Miller: The Continuing Redefining of Obscenity." *Idaho Law Review*, 10:193–211, Spring 1974.   **1G110**
Content: A brief history of past obscenity standards; holdings and standards of the 1973 obscenity cases; an examination of the *Miller* test (*Miller v. California*, 1973) and related holdings; Idaho law and obscenity decisions; an attempted extrapolation from *Miller*.

Gimlin, Hoyt. *Credibility Gaps and the Presidency*. Washington, D.C., Editorial Research Reports, 1968. (*Editorial Research Reports*, 1:83–100, 1968) **1G111**

Content: Debate over government credibility; credibility question in other times; and the public's right to know in a democracy.

————. *First Amendment and Mass Media*. Washington, D.C., Editorial Research Reports, 1970. (*Editorial Research Reports*, 1:43–60, 1970)   **1G112**
Content: Debate over the fairness of the news media; the historical development of press freedom and the various interpretations given to the First Amendment by the courts; present-day problems of government and media, including equal-time and fairness rules in broadcasting; proposals for broader access to public forums; and government news management.

Ginger, Ann F. "Freedom of the Press." In her *The Law, the Supreme Court and the People's Rights*. Woodbury, N.Y., Barron's Educational Survey, 1973, pp. 52–69.   **1G113**
"This chapter describes two fairly common free press cases: obscenity charges against two booksellers ₍*Roth v. United States*, 1957₎ and libel charges against the *New York Times* and several ministers arising out of an ad taken by a civil rights group ₍*New York Times Company v. Sullivan*, 1964₎."

Ginsberg, Robert. "In Favor of Crying 'Fire' in a Crowded Theater." *Southwestern Journal of Philosophy*, 3(2):91–98, Fall 1972.   **1G114**
The author, considering the platitude that freedom of speech does not mean that a person has the right to cry "fire" in a crowded theater, suggests eight arguments in favor of crying "fire" as an exercise in the complexity of justifying speech acts. Examples: (1) the action takes place on the stage in the course of a play; and (2) there is no fire, but evidence that the walls are about to collapse. Justice Oliver Wendell Holmes used the phrase in his opinion in *Schenck v. United States*, 1919. John B. Moore wrote a critique of the article in the Fall 1975 issue.

Ginter, Donald E. "The Loyalist Association Movement of 1792–93 and British Public Opinion." *Historical Journal*, 9:179–90, 1966.   **1G115**
An analysis of the work and influence of the loyalist movement in England, led by John Reeves, and instituted to offset the propaganda and activities of the British radical and reform groups that were spreading over England in the aftermath of the French Revolution. This conservative movement enjoyed considerable success in suffocating the efforts for parliamentary reform.

Ginwala, Frene. "The Press in South Africa." *Index on Censorship*, 2(3):27–43, Autumn 1973.   **1G116**
In a paper prepared for the United Nations Unit on Apartheid the author described the state of the South African press. The Black

people have no press, neither one of their own nor one that reflects their views. The press, in general, is the mouthpiece of the dominant economic and political interests. Press policy is often controlled by the owner, not the editors. "The Government has wide powers to control the press: it can ban particular newspapers, or all publications of particular organisations or views. It can also act against individuals by preventing what they say or write from being published. It can prevent particular persons from continuing as journalists, or even from entering premises concerned with the publication of newspapers." The author concludes that "apartheid has tried to divide and segregate the country. But it can never place 'Black Freedom' and 'White Freedom' into separate compartments, for the very attempt to divide, to exclude one from the other, to remove either from the totality, extinguishes freedom itself. It is at this point that the South African press surrendered its freedom. It can only begin to regain it when it recognises that there can be no freedom for the press in a society where the majority of the people are not free."

Ginzburg, Ralph. *Castrated; My Eight Months in Prison*. New York, Avant-Garde Books, 1973. 35p. (Also published in *New York Times Magazine*, 3 December 1972)   **1G117**
The personal account of the publisher's imprisonment which climaxed a ten-year literary cause célèbre stemming from the U.S. Supreme Court's suppression of his quarterly magazine, *Eros* (*Ginzburg v. United States*, 1966). The volume includes brief statements about the case by Arthur Miller, James Jones, Sloan Wilson, I. F. Stone, Harry Golden, and others.

Girand, Dan. "Whither Thou Obscenity?" *New Guard*, 15(4):27–29, May 1975.   **1G118**
The "liberal legal juggernaut" has been responsible for federal court decisions that have brought confusion in the area of obscenity laws and have permitted pornography to flourish. The author believes the recent rulings of the Burger Court have finally come to grips with the obscenity issue by returning the responsibility for control of obscenity to the states and local communities where conservatives have advocated it belongs. "Anti-porn legislation could be the vehicle to bond conservatives together and motivate them to action. Let the tocsin sound."

₍Girodias, Maurice.₎ "Apology." *New Olympia*, 3:1–2, 1962.   **1G119**
An account of the ban of *Olympia* no. 2 by the governments of France, Italy, and Lebanon, and the determination of the publisher to fight for freedom of expression. "The purpose of this review is to push the demonstration even further, and suppress once and for all the old beliefs that certain things can be said and

others not; that art should coincide with morality; and that governments are qualified to play the role of spiritual mentors." *Olympia* is an English language publication printed in France by the Olympia Press. Issue no. 3 also carried excerpts from the *Lady Chatterley's Lover* case before the British House of Lords.

————. "Lolita, Nabakov, and I." *Evergreen Review*, 9(37):44–47, 89–91, September 1965.   **1G120**
The original publisher of *Lolita* writes of his difficult relationship with the author and his fight with the French authorities over the ban of the English version of the novel.

Gish, Thomas E. "Crusading Editor Tells of Free-Press Obstacles." *Egyptian* (Southern Illinois University at Carbondale), 10 December 1975, p. 5.
                                                          1G121
Excerpts from a Lovejoy Lecture in Journalism in which the publisher of the *Mountain Eagle* of Whitesburg, Ky., describes his experiences in publishing a crusading newspaper in a town controlled by mining interests—boycotts, threats of physical violence, social isolation, and arson.

————. *The Whitesburg Bridge*. Tucson, Ariz., University of Arizona Press, 1974. 19p. (John Peter Zenger Award Lectures)   **1G122**
The editor and publisher of the *Mountain Eagle* of Whitesburg, Ky., whose exposé of corruption and malpractice in and out of government resulted in the burning of his newspaper office, attacks the secrecy of regional government agencies. He charges that the Appalachian Regional Commission and the Tennessee Valley Authority held their "public" meetings in secret until the *Mountain Eagle* ("It screams") forced admission. The TVA, which "operates like a King presiding over a colony," continued to make it difficult and expensive for the press to get information about its operations, even under the Freedom of Information Act, leading the author to conclude: "Freedom of the press, freedom of information, obviously is only for those who can afford to pay."

Glaessner, Verina. "Censorship in London." *Film Comment*, 9(1):30–31, January–February 1973.   **1G123**
A report on the status in London of films dealing with sex and violence. With the liberalization of rulings by the British Board of Film Censors (an industry-sponsored agency with no legal authority) approving more and more films that deal seriously with sex, there has been a wave of protests from local groups. This led to the study of pornography by Lord Longford's Committee, whose report the author terms "an amateurish, contradictory hodge-podge of ideas and prejudices wrapped

up in some quaint language." The Longford Report recommended tighter controls on films shown both in public houses and in private clubs. The author notes that hard-core pornographic films are not generally available in London, not even in the private film clubs; many films billed as pornographic are severely cut to escape police prosecution.

Gleason, Ralph J. "Obscenity—Who Really Cares?" *Rolling Stone*, 187:28+, 22 May 1975.   **1G124**
Comment on the increased permissiveness in the use in recordings and on the air of words and phrases formerly considered taboo. "People who listen to today's music simply do not give a shit about things like this and it is a great social freedom that has come about."

Gleaton, John E. "Defamation: The Texas Approach." *South Texas Law Journal*, 13:159–93, 1971–72.   **1G125**
"This comment, after tracing the historical development of the law of libel and slander generally, and the law in Texas particularly, will be devoted to the procedures which should be followed in proving up a libel or slander action in Texas and the problem areas which will be the most troublesome. This comment will concentrate on the rights of the private citizen and will intentionally omit any reference to the 'public figure' concept of the law of defamation."

Gleaves, Edwin S. "Intellectual Freedom in Tennessee: *Tres Pasos Adelante*." *Kentucky English Bulletin*, 24(2):15–21, Winter 1974/75.   **1G126**
The three steps forward were taken in response to an antiobscenity resolution of the Tennessee General Assembly and an impending antiobscenity state law prompted by the U.S. Supreme Court's June 1973 obscenity ruling which turned responsibility in the matter to the states: (1) a recommendation to the Commissioner of Education for the adoption of the guidelines of the American Association of School Librarians; (2) a Tennessee Library Association statement asking that any antiobscenity law exclude libraries (the exemption was enacted); and (3) a series of workshops on intellectual freedom conducted by the Association in cooperation with local groups.

Glessing, Robert J. *The Underground Press*. Bloomington, Ind., Indiana University Press, 1970. 207p.   **1G127**
A pioneering study of the underground press in America, its origin, nature, and development, based on interviews with participants, and a detailed examination of 30 of the 457 papers listed in the appendix. Richard G. Gray, in an introductory statement, points out that the underground press typically speaks out against the establishment, against the decline of individualism, is basically spiritual in a broad sense, and is innovative in layout and design. It practices deliberate bias in behalf of its particular creed, and makes indiscriminate use of sexual materials and vulgar language. The author gives attention to the underground

press on the campus, the military post, and the influence it has on styles in dress, customs, sexual behavior, and the established press, as its circulation continues to grow.

Glicksberg, Charles I. "The Problem of Censorship." In his *The Sexual Revolution in Modern American Literature*. The Hague, Nijhoff, 1971, pp. 244–49.   **1G128**
An attack on efforts to censor works of literary worth on the basis of sex expression. The author quotes Maxwell E. Perkins as writing that sex cannot be suppressed and efforts to do it generally result in more damage than sex can do. "After all, it was not the invention of man, but of God."

Glide Foundation. "Effects of Erotic Stimuli Used in National Sex Forum Training Courses in Human Sexuality." *Technical Report of the [U.S.] Commission on Obscenity and Pornography*, 5:354–68, 1971.   **1G129**
"The Glide Foundation's paper presents a description of the rationale and content of a newly developed program for training professionals in such areas as social work, counseling, religion, and education to deal with sex, and a description of some of the trainees' responses to the program."

Glover, Jerry W. *The Question of Newsman's Privilege in Oklahoma*. Norman, Okla., University of Oklahoma, 1972. 144p. (Unpublished Master's thesis)
                                                          1G130
Research conducted in three Oklahoma cities to determine the attitude of journalists, attorneys, and state legislators on the question of newsmen's privilege.

Glucksmann, André. *Violence on the Screen; A Report on Research Into the Effects on Young People of Scenes of Violence in Films and Television*. London, British Film Institute, 1971. 78p. (Translated from the French by Susan Bennett)
                                                          1G131
A republishing of a 1966 summary of research on the effects of television violence on young people, "the clearest and most systematic account not only of research findings but of the different approaches with their attendant limitations and problems." Dennis Howitt summarizes research since 1966 (pp. 68–75).

Godofsky, Stanley. "Protection of the Press from Prior Restraint and Harassment under Libel Laws." *University of Miami Law Review*, 29:462–76, Spring 1975.   **1G132**
An account of the U.S. Supreme Court's protection of the press by establishing First Amendment limitations on libel and prior restraints. The author analyzes the implications of *New York Times v. Sullivan* (1964) and *Gertz v.*

Robert Welch, Inc. (1974) with respect to libel law, and *Near v. Minnesota* (1931) and *New York Times v. United States* (1971) with respect to prior restraint. He finds disturbing the increased willingness of courts to grant injunctions against the press, on whatever theory or purpose, including some social interest which the injunction would serve.

Goerke, Sara, and Betty Gay. "Harm—in the Mind or in the Matter?" *California Librarian*, 33:98–99, April–July 1971.   **1G133**
Uncertainty about the meaning of "harmful matter" in the revision of the California laws on obscenity and distribution to minors.

Goines, M. Douglas. "The Application of the Fairness Doctrine to Editorial Advertising." *Wake Forest Law Review*, 10:621–34, October 1975.   **1G134**
"The purpose of this note is to set forth the basic statutory framework and case law background for this decision [Columbia Broadcasting System, Inc. v. Democratic National Committee, 1973] and to analyze the Court's holding on the right of a broadcast licensee to impose an absolute ban on editorial advertisements. Because of the multiple opinions involved in this decision, this note will summarize each of the various positions taken by the Justices in order to provide a clearer presentation of the Court's position. . . . This note will also consider the Court's discussion of the issue of whether actions by a broadcast licensee are governmental actions within the meaning of the first amendment."

Goldberg, Arthur J. "The Bar and the Press." *Illinois Bar Journal*, 53:716–21, April 1965.   **1G135**
An associate justice of the U.S. Supreme Court believes the bar and press have a joint responsibility for the protection of all the rights and liberties of Americans. "A Constitution which commands freedom for the press should inspire responsibility by the press. . . . The press must measure up to this responsibility, and the bar should help it do so." Justice Goldberg suggests that press and bar get together for mutual education for themselves and the general public and that a joint standing committee of press and bar be established.

———. "Mr. Justice Brennan and the First Amendment." *Rutgers–Camden Law Journal*, 4:8–43, Fall 1972. **1G136**
Justice Brennan has established his preeminence on the U.S. Supreme Court in cases involving the First Amendment. He has been "a major figure in shaping solutions which satisfy the twin requirements of constitutional adjudication, harmony with the purposes of that document and pragmatic, flexible standards. . . . Mr. Justice Brennan has eschewed both the 'absolutist' and the 'ad hoc balancing' approaches to resolving conflicts between the essential freedoms of expression and other societal interests. Rather, his method has been one of 'definitional balancing,' a testing of the

societal need for a certain class of expression against the policy reasons advanced to curtail it."

Goldberg, Henry, and Albert H. Kramer. "FCC Broadcast License Renewal Reform: Two Comments on Recent Legislative Proposals." *George Washington Law Review*, 42:67–114, November 1973.   **1G137**
These comments "present differing views regarding current renewal policies and opposing views regarding the need for legislative revision of these policies." Goldberg argues that the Administration bill is needed to prevent additional government interference with broadcast licensee; Kramer argues that both the Administration bill and the Broyhill-Rooney bills are fatally defective because they would eliminate existing opportunities for public intervention at renewal. Text of the bills are given on pp. 69–72.

Goldberg, Isaac. "Sex Studies—The Bedborough Trial." In his *Havelock Ellis; A Biographical and Critical Survey*. New York, Simon & Schuster, 1926, pp. 151–68.   **1G138**
An account of the trial of George Bedborough for the sale of Ellis's *Sexual Inversion*, based largely on Ellis's own account, *A Note on the Bedborough Trial* (E68), and private letters.

———. "Upton Sinclair's Book Fight in Boston." *Haldeman-Julius Monthly*, 6:105–10, 6 September 1927.   **1G139**
A play-by-play account of the banning of Upton Sinclair's novel, *Oil!*, in Boston, Sinclair's visit to that city for the purpose of showing the absurdity of the obscenity law and defending what he considered a moral story, and his unsuccessful attempt to goad the authorities into arresting him for the sale of the book. The author of the article was a friend of Sinclair's, on hand for the episode. "Any person who can discover obscenity in *Oil!* is morally unbalanced." It was the mention of birth control in the novel that caused the trouble in Boston.

Golden, Aubrey E. "Concepts of Censorship." *IPLO Quarterly* (Institute of Professional Librarians of Ontario), 13(4):189–93, April 1972.   **1G140**
A discussion of nonlegal censorship (parental discipline, educational selection, social pressure, and individual choice) and legal censorship (contempt of court, libel, sedition, and sexual censorship), with a recommendation that certain forms of legal censorship should be removed to the nonlegal sphere.

Golden, Patrick G. "Absolute Privilege in California: The Scope of California Civil Code Section 47 (2)." *University of San Francisco Law Review*, 7:176–88, October 1972.   **1G141**
"This article will consider whether section

47(2) [of the California Civil Code] confers an unconditional immunity to defamatory remarks made in legislative or judicial proceedings."

Goldfarb, Ronald L. *Legal Restraints on Crime News*. Columbia, Mo., Freedom of Information Center, School of Journalism, University of Missouri at Columbia, 1967. 16p. (Report no. 185)
                                              1G142
An analysis of the legal history of restraints on press coverage of crime and trial news, taken from the appendix of Friendly and Goldfarb, *Crime and Publicity*.

Goldman, Albert. "The Old Smut Peddler." *Life*, 67:53, 29 August 1969.
                                              1G143
A "close-up" of Barney Rosset of Grove Press. "In 10 years of charging the forces of censorship and the devil, Rosset has never missed a chance to pick up a little yardage by publishing a banned book or straight-arming some local censor in the courts or backing some other freedom fighter like Lenny Bruce, say, or Malcolm X. The result has been a total liberation of the printed word."

———. "Witnessing Obscenity for Fun and Profit." *New York*, 5(15):47–53, 10 April 1972.   **1G144**
The confessions of a professional obscenity witness, a professor of English who is frequently called on as an "expert" witness for the defense. "Here he relates, in lurid but printable detail, what he often runs into, a nightmarish mélange of legalistic pettifoggery and non-communication."

Goldman, David J. *The Freedom of the Press in America*. Minneapolis, Lerner, 1967. 71p. (In America series) **1G145**
An illustrated work intended for young people, giving the background leading to the passage of the First Amendment, including an account of the John Peter Zenger trial. The book recounts challenges to press freedom and interpretation by the courts from the Alien and Sedition Acts of 1798 to the present day, concluding with a chapter on protection against libel.

[Goldman, Emma.] "The Confiscated Picture." *Mother Earth*, 1(5):34–38, July 1906.   **1G146**
A mock reverie of Anthony Comstock contemplating suicide "because he could endure the thought no longer that every human being stood naked in his boots." Instead, the vice crusader continues with renewed determination to defeat the devil. He confiscates an immodest postcard, which to his horror, turns out to be a trick card—one twist and Comstock's own face appears.

Goldman, Eric F. *et al. Literature or License.* 57 min. tape recording. North Hollywood, Calif., Center for Cassette Studies, 1971. (Distributor's title: Publishing and Purity) **1G147**
  Where in the literary field does liberty become license? A debate moderated by Eric F. Goldman, Princeton historian. Panelists: Ernest van den Haag, psychoanalyst; Arnold Gingrich, publisher of *Esquire*; John E. Lawler, counsel for Operation Yorkville; Barney Rosset, president of Grove Press; and Ephriam London, attorney.

Goldstein, Abraham S. "Newsmen and Their Confidential Sources." *New Republic*, 162(12):13–15, 21 March 1970. (Reprinted in Michael C. Emery and Ted C. Smythe, *eds.*, *Readings in Mass Communications*, pp. 95–99) **1G148**
  "The current controversy between the prosecutors and the news media serves to remind us once again that our confidences are protected far less than we realize, and that a more sensitive law of confidential communication is long overdue."

Goldstein, Mark L. "Prison Regulation Prohibiting Interviews Between Newsmen and Inmates Held Constitutional." *Cornell Law Review*, 60:446–66, March 1975. **1G149**
  Re: *Saxbe v. Washington Post Co.*, 417 U.S. 843 (1974).

Goldstein, Michael J. "Exposure to Erotic Stimuli and Sexual Deviance." *Journal of Social Issues*, 29(3):197–219, 1973. **1G150**
  The paper describes the results of a research project designed to assess whether relationships exist between experience with pornography and the development of normal or abnormal sexual behavior. Sex offenders reported less exposure to erotic stimuli both during adolescence and adulthood. "The hypothesis that the extent of exposure to erotica during adolescence is positively associated with the later emergence of sexual pathology is not borne out by this study. The control groups sampled had significantly greater exposure to erotic materials during adolescence than the deviants, convicted sex offenders, or heavy adult users of pornography." One of the studies stimulated by the U.S. Commission on Obscenity and Pornography.

———, and Harold S. Kant, with John J. Hartman. *Pornography and Sexual Deviance: A Report of the Legal and Behavioral Institute.* Berkeley, Calif., University of California Press, 1973. 194p. **1G151**

The book reports on a research program inspired by the need for scientifically obtained data on pornography and its effect. The study developed as an extension of a pilot study supported by the U.S. Commission on Obscenity and Pornography. Chapter 1 discusses the various approaches to defining obscenity and pornography; chapter 2 reviews previous research; chapters 3 through 11 constitute the body of clinical research; and chapter 12 deals with the legal and political issues involved in the censorship of pornography and relates the findings of the study to the legal process. A review of the book by Jay Mann appears in *Stanford Law Review*, June 1974.

Goldstein, Michael J., and W. Coty Wilson. "Introduction" to special issue on "Pornography: Attitudes, Use, and Effects." *Journal of Social Issues*, 29(3):1–5, 1973. **1G152**
  A purview of papers in the issue which represent a sample of the studies stimulated by the U.S. Commission on Obscenity and Pornography. Individual papers are entered under the name of the author in this bibliography.

Goldstein, Michael J. *et al.* "Exposure to Pornography and Sexual Behavior in Deviant and Normal Groups." *Technical Report of the [U.S.] Commission on Obscenity and Pornography*, 7:1–89, 1971. **1G153**
  "The present investigation was carried out to determine whether sex deviates, users of pornography, and representatives of a cultural group (Blacks) differed from a randomly selected group of Caucasian controls. Evidence concerning differential history of exposure and reaction to exposure could then provide some clues as to the effects of pornography on the development of sexual attitudes and behavior."

Goldstein, Paul. "Copyright and the First Amendment." *Columbia Law Review*, 70:983–1057, June 1970. **1G154**
  "This article will assess the extent to which copyright's statutory and enterprise monopolies presently conflict with the first amendment and will identify methods for reconciling the competing interests involved in these conflicts. Two principles will be relied upon for analysis and accommodation of the conflicting interests in infringement cases." The first principle "requires that copyright infringement be excused if the subject matter of the infringed material is relevant to the public interest and the appropriator's use of the material independently advances the public interest." The second principle "requires that only 'original' literary property be protected against unauthorized use, that actual damages be demonstrated by the plaintiff, and that the granting of legal, not equitable, relief be the general rule when the plaintiff prevails."

Goldsworthy, Peter J. "The Claim to Secrecy of News Source: A Journalistic Privilege?" *Canadian Communications*

Law Review, 3:151–72, 1971. (Also in *Osgoode Hall Law Review*, August 1971) **1G155**
  The article reviews the status of the newsman's claim to secrecy of news source in Great Britain, Canada, and the United States. The author finds that "a persuasive case can be made for the legal recognition of the claim, subject to limitations in the best interests of public policy." While there is lack of empirical evidence that freedom of information is advanced by the privilege, "some part at least of the newsman's fear of emasculation occasioned by the absence of the privilege may be justified." He believes the matter should not be left entirely to judicial discretion as it is in the United Kingdom and Canada. He believes that any privilege statute should be limited to restricting the name of the informant and any material tending to disclose his identity, but the news should not in itself be privileged. The privilege should be granted to the informant, not the newsman.

Gompertz, Kenneth. "A Bibliography of Articles about Broadcasting in Law Periodicals, 1956–1968." *Journal of Broadcasting*, 14:83–132, Winter 1969/70. **1G156**
  Topics: Background of legislation, basic law of broadcasting, administration, problems in regulation, and control of program content.

Goodale, James C. "*Branzburg* and the Protection of Reporters' Sources." *University of Miami Law Review*, 29:456–58, Spring 1975. **1G157**
  The author attempts to clarify the considerable misunderstanding concerning the subpoena of reporters' notes, sources, and out-takes surrounding the U.S. Supreme Court's decisions in *Branzburg v. Hayes* (1972), and analyzes the four cases involved. He argues that the *Branzburg* decision recognizes a qualified privilege and that any legislation drafted should reflect the treatment which the courts are currently giving to reporters' privilege.

———. "*Branzburg v. Hayes* and the Developing Qualified Privilege for Newsmen." *Hastings Law Review*, 26:709–43, January 1975. **1G158**
  "The enigmatic concurring opinion of Justice Powell in the 5–4 *Branzburg v. Hayes* decision [1972] left the question of a qualified newsman's privilege unsettled. The author finds support for such a privilege, based upon a tripartite balancing test, in the numerical majority of the *Branzburg* Court. He analyzes the relevant post-*Branzburg* case law—as he feels the Court will do when called upon to reconsider the qualified privilege issue—in an effort to articulate further the nature of the privilege."

———. "The Press 'Gag' Order Epidemic." *Columbia Journalism Review*, 12:49–50, September–October 1973. **1G159**
  While approving the press's voluntary compliance with fair trial–free press guidelines, the

author, a *New York Times* lawyer, objects to the use of the guidelines as granting powers to the courts to stop the presses from printing what they want to print.

————. "Senate Bill No. 1 and the Freedom of Information Act: Do They Conflict?" *Administrative Law Review*, 28:347–62, Summer 1976. **1G160**
The basic problem in the conflict between the Freedom of Information Act and proposed Senate bill 1 is in "our inability as a society to articulate what we want kept secret by the government and what we want to know. If we could limit classification to a few narrow categories such as troop movement, cryptographic codes, photographs of defense installations and weapons systems and perhaps only these categories, the problems of disclosure, communication and access to government documents would all solve themselves."

————. "Subpoenas of News Reporters to Compel Disclosure of Confidential Information: An Analysis of Recent Legal Developments." *Los Angeles Bar Bulletin*, 49:133–41, February 1974. **1G161**
The author believes that there has been some judicial disposition in recent months to limit the holdings on subpoenas since *United States v. Caldwell* (1970), and that "the law of communications subpoenas will develop on a case-by-case basis providing reporters with some protection in the event Congress does not pass a reporter's privilege bill."

Goode, Mort. *"Censored": Martha Wright Sings. The Original Versions of 12 Songs Presented on Broadway, Not Cleared for Broadcasting.* New York, Jubilee Records, n.d. Phonodisc: 2 sides, 12 in., 33⅓ rpm. microgroove. (Notes by Mort Goode on back of jacket) **1G162**
Songs dated from 1928 to 1946, include works by Cole Porter, Irving Berlin, and Rodgers and Hart. Goode defends these love songs from the charges of the censors. "It is time for reappraisal . . . for the censor to justify calling these a 'dirty dozen' and allowing our broadcast air to be profaned by choice kid stuff—with guns, violence, murders."

Goodman, Arnold A., *baron.* "The Freedom of the Press." *Political Quarterly*, 47:129–36, April–June 1976. **1G163**
The chairman of the Newspaper Publishers Association criticizes the amendment to the Trade Union and Labour Relations bill before Parliament which would permit the decision of a union to prevent a newspaperman from the employment of his pen.

Goodman, Marjorie J. "When Trouble Comes—Booksellers and Censorship." *Publishers' Weekly*, 193:55–57, 20 May 1968. **1G164**

A university bookstore manager gives advice on how to respond to efforts by individuals and groups to censor through political pressures, economic boycott, and prosecution.

Goodman, Reuben, and Timothy F. Fidgeon. *"Avatar*: Brief of *Amicus Curiae." Bay State Librarian*, 59(3):20–23, October 1970. **1G165**
The text of the *amicus curiae* brief filed by the Civil Liberties Union of Massachusetts in behalf of an underground newspaper published in Cambridge, Mass. *Avatar* was accused of obscenity.

Goodman, Walter. *The Committee: The Extraordinary Career of the House Committee on Un-American Activities.* Foreward by Richard H. Rovere. New York, Farrar, Straus and Giroux, 1968. 564p. **1G166**
A chronological account of the hearings of the House Un-American Activities Committee, presented in the context of the political and economic climate of the times. The author, writing with detached irony, considers the work of the Committee as a reflection of the deep fear and insecurity in American life.

Goodwin, H. Eugene *et al. The Hutchins Commission Revisited.* Iowa City, Iowa, Mass Communications and Society Division, Association for Education in Journalism, 1967. 26p. Processed. **1G167**
On the twentieth anniversary of the issuance of the report of the Commission on Freedom of the Press, a panel of five considers such questions as whether the recommendations are still valid in 1967, in view of the changes in the mass media, and whether there is need for a new Hutchins-type study of American mass communications in the context of contemporary society. Panel members: H. Eugene Goodwin, presiding; William E. Ames, Harry S. Ashmore, Ben H. Bagdikian, and Wayne A. Danielson.

Gora, Joel M. *The Rights of Reporters. The Basic ACLU Guide to a Reporter's Rights.* New York, Discus Books, 1974. 254p. **1G168**
The purpose of the book is to inform reporters of their legal rights. The information is presented in the form of questions and answers under the following topics: First Amendment Principles, Protecting Your Source, Gathering the News, Publishing the News, Covering the Courts, Libel and Invasion of Privacy, and Special Problems of the Underground Press. The appendix contains summaries of state shield laws and the text of the Department of Justice Guidelines.

————. "Who Owns the News?" *Civil Rights Journal*, 2(2):4–7, Spring 1975. **1G169**
In this guest editorial the writer discusses

the suppression by major newspapers, newsmagazines, and networks of "the story of the *Glomar*, the CIA–Howard Hughes ship that set out to recover an outmoded Soviet submarine from the floor of the Pacific Ocean." He points out the irony of the press, which argued in the case of the Pentagon Papers its obligation to inform the public, yet in the *Glomar* affair, "acted more like a government censor than an agent of the public. In censoring the story, the press ignored the purposes and principles of the First Amendment as well as its obligations to us."

Goralski, Robert. "How Much Secrecy Can a Democracy Stand?" *Lithopinion*, 7(3):78–81, Fall 1972. **1G170**
Criticism of the federal government's "security overkill" in classifying records. There are over 160 million World War II classified documents alone which would take 800 man-years to review. President Nixon's new Executive Order is only a nudge in the right direction.

Gorden, William I. *Nine Men Plus; Supreme Court Opinions on Free Speech and Free Press; An Academic Game-Simulation.* Dubuque, Iowa, Brown, 1971. 254p. Plus Appendix. **1G171**
A unique textbook on free speech and press designed to be used as a game to encourage dialogue among college students in various disciplines—political science, law, journalism, or speech. The text consists of quotations from notable free speech and press decisions of the United States Supreme Court, with cases arranged in one of six categories: academic freedom, censorship, defamation and libel, political dissent, privacy, and provocation and demonstrations.

Gordimer, Nadine. "Literature and Politics in South Africa." *Southern Review* (Adelaide, South Australia), 7:205–27, November 1974. **1G172**
The author, in an address before the Adelaide Festival of Arts, speaks of the history of suppression of books and the banning of authors in South Africa in the area of race relations. Every South African writer "black or white, writing in English, Afrikaans, Zulu, Sesuto, what-have-you, even if he successfully shoots the rapids of bannings and/or exile, ⌞if he attempts to⌟ present in South Africa a totality of human experience within his own country is subverted before he sets down a word."

————. "98 Kinds of Censorship." *American Pen*, 5(4):16–21, Fall 1973. **1G173**
"South Africa has a Censorship Act that lists no less than 97 definitions of what it considers undesirable in literature." The 98th restriction is the policy of apartheid which prevents writers from becoming aware of the total society in which they live.

———. "A Writer's Freedom." *Index on Censorship*, 5(2):53–55, Summer 1976. **1G174**
"To me it is his right to maintain and publish to the world a deep, intense, private view of the situation in which he finds his society. If he is to work as well as he can, he must take, and be granted, freedom from the public conformity of political interpretation, morals and tastes." Text of a paper delivered at a Conference on Writings from Africa: Concern and Evocation, held by the South African Teachers Association in Durban in September 1975.

Gordon, David. "The Confidences Newsmen Must Keep." *Columbia Journalism Review*, 10(4):15–20, November–December 1971. **1G175**
"Tying the privilege to the First Amendment would seem to keep its use more flexible and responsive to changing circumstances than would shield laws." Such a privilege would not represent class legislation, could not be removed by legislative whim, would give confidentiality enough legal respectability to stand on its own merits in court challenges, and "would provide the assumption of constitutional protection unless highly compelling reasons were found to deny it and require disclosure."

———. *The 1896 Maryland Shield Law; The American Roots of Evidentiary Privilege for Newsmen*. Minneapolis, Association for Education in Journalism, 1972. 44p. (*Journalism Monographs*, no. 22) **1G176**
A history of the passage of the first statute in the United States which granted newsmen the right to protect the identity of their confidential sources of information.

———. "Newsman's Privilege and the Free Marketplace of Ideas." *Northwestern Report*, 4:21–25, Fall 1973. **1G177**
Developments since 1970 have extended some measure of First Amendment protection to the newsman's privilege; the courts have passed the responsibility to the legislatures. The best hope for the future lies in an alert public demanding the "public's right to know."

———. *Newsman's Privilege and the Law*. Columbia, Mo., Freedom of Information Foundation, 1974. 52p. (Freedom of Information Foundation Series, no. 4) **1G178**
"This monograph will trace the recent legal developments on newsman's privilege—reported and unreported—and will attempt to synthesize the somewhat equivocal status of newsman's privilege in mid-1974. It will review briefly some of the current arguments for and against a journalist's privilege, in regard to both constitutional and statutory approaches to it. And it will report on a pilot survey of the attitudes of selected law enforcement personnel, which showed decidedly mixed opinions toward the whole complex issue of newsman's privilege, and whether and how it should be implemented."

———. *Protection of News Sources: The History and Legal Status of the Newsman's Privilege*. Madison, Wis., University of Wisconsin, 1971. 937p. (Ph.D. dissertation, University Microfilms, no. 71–16078) **1G179**
This dissertation attempts "to examine critically the background of the newsman's privilege question, and the arguments on all sides of it. It attempts to strip away some of the legalistic rigidity which has produced negative reactions to past claims of newsman's privilege, and to draw a parallel between an evidentiary privilege for newsmen and the one frequently granted by the government to protect the names of confidential informers. The dissertation proposes a newsman's privilege formula aimed at attracting support from open-minded people in both law and journalism."

Gordon, Edward. "The Teacher and the Censor." In Alexander Butman *et al.*, eds., *Paperbacks in the School*. New York, Bantam, 1963, pp. 62–72. **1G180**
"English teachers do not ask a license to put sensationalism in the hands of students, but they do ask that they may be allowed to teach to mature students the books that reputable critics feel make up our literary heritage." Censorship is of two types, the isolated attack against individual books and, more serious, the national pressures against textbooks. The censor conceives education as indoctrination, the educator as teaching students to apply reason in solving problems. The author suggests ways of meeting the censor, including the use of book-evaluation forms.

[Gordon, George, *Lord*.] *The Whole Proceedings on the Trials of Two Informations . . . against George Gordon, Esq. commonly Called Lord George Gordon: One for a Libel on the Queen of France and the French Ambassador. The Other for a Libel on the Judges, and the Administration of the Laws in England. Also of Thomas Wilkins for Printing the Last-Mentioned Libel. Tried in the Court of King's Bench, Guildhall, on Wednesday the 6th of June, 1787; before the Hon. Francis Buller, Esq. . . .* London, Sold by M. Gurney, 1787. 100p. (Also in *Howell's State Trials*, vol. 22, pp. 175–236, 1253–56; and in George Borrow, *Celebrated Trials*, vol. 5, pp. 138 ff.) **1G181**
Lord Gordon was tried for writing and distributing a pamphlet, *The Prisoners Petition to the Right Honourable Lord George Gordon, to Preserve Their Lives and Liberties, and Prevent Their Banishment to Botany Bay*. The pamphlet purported to be written by a group of convicted prisoners awaiting transportation to Botany Bay to Lord Gordon, asking his help in getting their release. Actually, the pamphlet was the work of the eccentric Lord Gordon who believed the sentences for theft were too severe. Lord Gordon, better known for his involvement in the anti-Catholic riots some years before, pled his own case. He was found guilty of a gross libel on the judges and the administration of law. At a subsequent trial he was accused of having written a libel against the French Ambassador to England, published in Henry Woodfall's *Daily Advertiser*, for which he was also found guilty. At both trials the jurors were instructed to consider only the fact of publication and not the substance of the work, which was left to the decision of the judge. Gordon, who was placed on bond awaiting sentence, escaped to Holland. On his return to England he was imprisoned in Newgate, where he is said to have lived in comfortable quarters. At the end of his term he was unable to obtain securities required by the court and remained in Newgate until his death in 1793. In that same year the Fox Libel Act was passed, permitting juries to consider the substance of the alleged libel. Thomas Wilkins, the printer of the libelous pamphlet (text on pp. 26–36) was also brought to trial, found guilty, and sentenced to two years imprisonment. Editor Woodfall, who had earlier been tried for libel, was not prosecuted in this case.

Gordon, Gerald. "The Right to Write." *Contrast, South African Quarterly*, 9(3):15–23, December 1974. (Reprinted in *Index on Censorship*, Summer 1975) **1G182**
An outline of the new system established to control "undesirable" publications in South Africa. Under the earlier controls (Publications and Entertainments Act of 1963) some 7,000 publications were banned. While only sixteen cases were appealed to the Supreme Court, the availability of the appeal is believed to have held down censorship. Under the new law the Supreme Court is replaced by an appointed appeals board. The author concludes that "the outlook for literature—and especially Afrikaans writers—is dark indeed."

Gordon, Michael, and Robert R. Bell. "Medium and Hard-Core Pornography: A Comparative Study." *Journal of Sex Research*, 5:260–68, November 1969. **1G183**
A discussion of literary pornography which has become widely distributed in the United States with the decline of censorship.

Gore, Daniel. "A Skirmish with the Censors." *ALA Bulletin*, 63:193–203, February 1969. Summary, 62:821–22, July–August 1968; comments, 63:553–56, May 1969; 63:889–90, July–August 1969; 63:1512–13, December 1969. **1G184**
A summary of a censorship episode which oc-

curred in the MacMurry College Library where the author recently terminated a brief period as director. The episode that provoked the censorship issue was the library's subscription to the *Evergreen Review*. The author concludes that if the *Evergreen Review* is to be excluded because of the obscenity of a portion of its contents we must be ready to ban works of such authors as Aristophanes, Ovid, Boccaccio, Chaucer, Montaigne, Shakespeare, Swift, Sterne, Joyce, and Hemingway. He makes four suggestions for curtailing the actions of library censors: (1) Make academic administrators and faculty aware of the dimensions of the library censorship problem and that it is a necessary cognate to academic freedom in the classroom. (2) Append to the Library Bill of Rights a formal procedure to follow when the censor strikes. (3) Prompt reporting of library censorship to the appropriate professional agency as a matter of professional ethics. (4) Adoption by the profession of an effective system of sanctions.

Gormley, William T., Jr. *The Effects of Newspaper-Television Cross-Ownership on News Homogeneity*. Chapel Hill, N.C., Institute for Research in Social Science, University of North Carolina, 1976. 276p.   **1G 185**
"In certain cities, cross-ownership may involve the deliberate distortion or suppression of the same stories by jointly owned newspapers and television stations (the equivalent of a 'smoking pistol'). However, the effects of cross-ownership on news content which we have discovered are more subtle. By contributing to 'pack journalism,' cross-ownership interferes with diversity in the flow of news. By reducing the willingness of television stations to editorialize, cross-ownership interferes with the diversity in the flow of opinions. The homogenizing effects of cross-ownership which we have identified are so circuitous as to be invisible to the casual observer. Nevertheless, homogenizing effects of cross-ownership need not be blatant, deliberate, or spectacular to warrant remedial action."

Goss, Patricia. "The First Amendment's Weakest Link: Government Regulation of Controversial Advertising." *Women Lawyers Journal*, 60:112–22, Summer 1974. (Also in *New York Law Forum*, Winter 1975, and in Speech Communication Association, *Free Speech Yearbook*, 1975, pp. 21–34)   **1G 186**
"This article will examine the legal basis for distinguishing commercial expression from that directed at public decision-making. Government efforts at regulating commercial speech will be discussed. Possible solutions to the inadequacy of legal safeguards in this area will then be presented."

Gossage, Howard L. "Freedom of the Press . . . Is There Such a Thing?" *Media-Scope*, 13:71–74, May 1969.   **1G 187**

"Freedom of the press is only guaranteed to those who own one. The reader lost his freedom of the press the day the advertiser's dollar became more important than the reader's preferences. . . . The most worthwhile thing publishers could to to restore a reader's freedom of the press would be to take the same responsibility for the advertising matter in their pages as they do for the editorial matter."

Gothberg, Helen M. "The Semantics of Obscenity." *Statement: The Journal of the Language Arts Society of Colorado*, 9(3):7–14, May 1974.   **1G 188**
The author reviews the attempts and difficulties over the years in defining obscenity. "The difficulty appears to lie in the nature of obscenity itself, which is relative. . . . What is obscene to an individual depends on a number of variables, including a person's culture and sub-culture, religious affiliations, sex and overall attitude characteristics and personal idiosyncrasies."

Gotshalk, D. W. "A Note on the Future of Censorship." *Journal of Aesthetic Education*, 4(3):97-100, July 1970.   **1G 189**
"Censorship in the old-fashioned sense—the imposition on art and education of the moral proclivities of an external agency—seems unnecessary when the artist and educator know their business. . . . The artist who roams the off-color area must incise a vision of its features that is an honest portrayal of its stature, and the educator must communicate this achievement."

Gottschalk, Earl C., Jr. "Border-line Cases: Hollywood Frets About Foreign Censorship; Some Lands Ban Sex, Some Outlaw Violence." *Wall Street Journal*, 182:22, 28 December 1973.   **1G 190**
The response of Hollywood to the various demands for censorship of American films abroad.

———. "A Dirty Deal? Pornography Ruling of Supreme Court Causing Confusion and Chaos . . ." *Wall Street Journal*, 182:28, 16 July 1973. (Also in *U.S. News & World Report*, 30 July 1973)   **1G 191**
A news account of reaction in the motion picture industry to the U.S. Supreme Court's decision to give states and communities broader powers over control of pornography.

Gould, Jack. "Control by Advertisers." In Harry J. Skornia and Jack W. Kitson, eds., *Problems and Controversies in Television and Radio*, Palo Alto, Calif., Pacific Books, 1968, pp. 417–21. (Reprinted from the *New York Times*, 12 July 1959)   **1G 192**
"How advertising agencies operate in

television—their strict supervision of shows and the business factors that influence or limit the choice of programs that the public sees." A summary of a report of agency executives to the FCC.

Gould, Martha, and Joseph J. Anderson. "Special Report on the Issue of Obscenity Legislation Proposed during the 58th Session of the Nevada Legislature, 1975." *Nevada Libraries Highroller*, 12:1–10, June 1975.   **1G 193**
A week-by-week account of action on Assembly bill 722 to revise Nevada's obscenity laws, including library association opposition, press reports, and editorials.

Gould, Stanhope. "Coors Brews the News." *Columbia Journalism Review*, 13(6):17–29, March–April 1975. **1G 194**
The story of Television News, Inc., "the only non-network source of national and international newsfilm for the nation's commercial TV stations," an organization backed by Adolph Coors Company, Colorado brewers. The company got into the business, according to Joe Coors, "because of our strong belief that network news is slanted to the liberal side of the spectrum and does not give an objective view to the American public." The author charges the news service with putting partisan pressure on its news staff to reflect a right-wing social philosophy. Those who refused to slant the news lost their jobs.

Goulding, Phil G. *Confirm or Deny. Informing the People on National Security*. New York, Harper and Row, 1970. 369p.   **1G 195**
The Assistant Secretary of Defense for Public Affairs in the Johnson Administration discusses his month-by-month relations with the press during the Vietnam war and four years of "total traffic in crisis."

[Gourlay, Robert Fleming.] *Liberty of the Press Asserted, in an Appeal to the Inhabitants of Wilts. and a Letter on the Corn Laws*. Bath, England, Sold by Meyler and Son, [1815]. 16p. (His Early Publications, 1831)   **1G 196**
The author protests the refusal of the proprietors of the *Salisbury Journal* to permit him to advertise his pamphlet, *An Apology for Scotch Farmers*, which the proprietors had decided was too violent. He threatens to start a competing journal and appeals to the citizens of the county of Wiltshire to support his right of access.

"Government Information and the Rights of Citizens." *Michigan Law Re-*

view, 73:971–1340, May–June 1975. **1G197**

A report on a project which delineates federal and state response to two fundamental societal concerns: the right of citizens' access to government-held information and the concurrent recognition of the need to protect individual privacy.

"The Government vs. the Press." *Newsweek*, 78:17–19, 5 July 1971. **1G198**

The case of the Pentagon Papers. "Whoever instigated it, the case of the U.S. vs. the *Times* et al. was clearly a bad idea."

Gower, Calvin W. "Conservatism, Censorship, and Controversy in the CCC, 1930s." *Journalism Quarterly*, 52:277–84, Summer 1975. **1G199**

An account of the action of the leaders of the Civilian Conservation Corps in banning certain books and periodicals from the Corps. Much of the controversy was over Director Robert Fechner's ban of *You and Machines*, a book written for the Corps by University of Chicago sociologist William Ogburn, and the periodical *Champion of Youth*, which the officials considered controversial.

Graburn, Lloyd. "Excerpts from Lecture to School for Crown Attorneys Delivered at the Centre of Criminology, Toronto, August 19, 1969." *Performing Arts in Canada*, 6(4):6–7, Fall 1969. **1G200**

The Crown Attorney of Metropolitan Toronto and the County of York advises Crown Attorneys how to proceed against obscenity in books, films, art, and stage plays. He counsels seeking advice from a cross-section of community leaders.

Grady, William R. *Prejudicial Pretrial Publicity: Its Effects on Jurors and Juries*. Evanston, Ill., Northwestern University, 1972. 103p. (Unpublished Master's thesis) **1G201**

An analysis of newspaper coverage of forty-six criminal cases indicated that "there was no strong relationship between guilty jury verdicts and publicity that was prejudicial and frequent." A second part of the study involved questioning of former jurors. Only about 25 percent were aware of media coverage. The 12 percent of respondents who presumed guilt were more aware of media coverage than were those who did not.

Graf, Edward L., *ed*. "Newsmen's Privilege—Where To From Here?" *Publishing, Entertainment, Advertising and Allied Fields (PEAL)*, 11:479–84, Spring 1973. **1G202**

A reprinting with introduction, of two articles which appeared more than ten years apart. The first, Reporter's Privilege Under the First Amendment (*Albany Law Review*, Winter 1972) is an analysis of the state of the law after the Ninth Circuit had ruled in *Caldwell* (*United States v. Caldwell*, 1972), but before the Supreme Court decision. The second, The Reporter's Right to Shield His "Reliable" Source by Judith S. Smith (S481), appeared in *PEAL*, June 1961, after the *Torre* case (*Garland v. Torre*, 1958). The two read in conjunction with the recent *Branzburg v. Hayes* case (1972) provide an historical survey of the law.

Graf, George F. "Liability of Station Owners for Political Broadcasts." *Marquette Law Review*, 42:417–22, Winter 1959. **1G203**

Re: *Farmers Educational & Cooperative Union of America No. Dakota Division v. WDAY, Inc.* (ND), 89 N.W.2d 102.

Graf, William S. "Stern's Victory over FBI Shows FOI Act Potential." *Journalism Quarterly*, 52:131–34, Spring 1975. **1G204**

An account of the twenty-six-month effort by National Broadcasting Company newsman Carl Stern to force the FBI by legal means (Freedom of Information Act) to release information on its use of agent provocateurs for political espionage. "Stern's efforts to free information from bureaucratic paperjams have far reaching implications for the press which, surprisingly, has made little use of the Freedom of Information Act."

Graham, Fred P. "Will Earl Caldwell Go To Jail?" *MORE*, 2(6):1, 14–16, June 1972. **1G205**

The *New York Times* correspondent covering the U.S. Supreme Court, explores the various issues, some of them unique, involved in the case of the *New York Times* reporter who refused to obey a subpoena to give a grand jury inside journalistic information about the Black Panther Party. Caldwell has become the press's symbol of resistance to subpoenas.

Graham, Fred P. *et al*. "Newspapers under Fire." In *Problems of Journalism; Proceedings of the 1976 Convention, American Society of Newspaper Editors*. Washington, D.C., ASNE, 1976, pp. 216–42. **1G206**

A panel discussion moderated by Clayton Kirkpatrick of the *Chicago Tribune*. Panelists: Fred P. Graham, Harold Andersen, James C. Goodale, and Judge William J. Bauer. The discussion revolved around the attacks on the press and the struggle to preserve press freedom. Graham (CBS legal reporter) commented on the work of the Reporters' Committee for Freedom of the Press of which he is a trustee, including the issues of gag orders and the increased secrecy in the courts; Andersen (Omaha publisher) reviewed the facts in the Nebraska gag-order case presently before the U.S. Supreme Court; Goodale (*New York Times*

executive) discussed the *Times* experience with gag orders and subpoenas; Judge Bauer pointed out that it was the courts that had extended the First Amendment to include the idea of the people's right to know; he expressed the belief that pretrial publicity had little effect on trials and should concern neither the media nor the court, but that publicity covering the trial itself was of considerable importance to a fair trial.

Graham, Fred P., and Jack Landau. "The Federal Shield Law We Need." *Columbia Journalism Review*, 11(6):26–35, March–April 1973. (Reprinted in Robert Blanchard, *ed.*, *Congress and the News Media*, pp. 447–55) **1G207**

The authors comment on five problems faced in the drafting of shield laws: (1) Which members of the "press" should qualify? (2) Which proceedings should be covered by a shield law? (3) What types of information should be protected? (4) Should there be any specific exceptions to the privilege to refuse to reveal confidential and nonconfidential information or sources? (5) Should the shield bill apply only to newsmen involved in federal legislative, executive, and judicial proceedings?

Graham, Hugh D., and Ted R. Gurr. *Violence in America: Historical and Comparative Prospectives. A Report to the National Commission on the Causes and Prevention of Violence by Hugh Davis Graham and Ted Robert Gurr*. Washington, D.C., National Commission on the Causes and Prevention of Violence, 1969. 2 vols. 644p. (A Task Force Report to the National Commission on the Causes and Prevention of Violence, nos. 1 and 2) **1G208**

This Task Force report, the result of the work of numerous scholars, "provides substantial insights into the causes and character of violence in America." Questions addressed: What have been the patterns and extent of violence by private individuals and groups in the United States, and what, by comparison, have been in Western Europe? What are the historical conditions that have contributed to different kinds of violence in the American past and present? How do group protest and violence in the United States compare with similar activism elsewhere in the world? What are the general conditions of group violence? What are the processes of violence, and what are some alternatives to it?

Graham, Katharine. *The Faith of a Free People*. Tucson, Ariz., University of Arizona Press, 1973. 16p. (John Peter Zenger Award Lectures) **1G209**

The publisher of the *Washington Post* defends the nation's press in uncovering and exposing the scandals of Watergate and the Agnew affair and the relentlessness of the press in getting at the facts, despite "the government's willingness to lie" and its campaign of vilification. She defends the concept of reporter's privilege which is in fact, "not a private license for the press but an essential instrument in fulfilling the public's right to know." To curtail the ability of the press to protect confidential sources would constrict, if not cut off entirely, the flow of information. She concludes: The Founding Fathers gave the press the mission to "inform the people and promote the free flow of facts and ideas, however untimely or challenging or disagreeable those facts and ideas may be." This is the faith of a free people.

————. "The Freedom of the American Press." In William Haley *et al*, *The Freedom of the Press*, London, MacGibbon, 1974, pp. 75–91.   **1G210**
In a Granada Guildhall Lecture, Publisher Graham discusses the contrasts between the British and American ideas of freedom of the press—"ideas which are grounded in two very different concepts of democratic government." She discusses the issues in the context of American press coverage of Watergate.

————. "Growth Threats Against Freedom to Dissent." *Nieman Reports*, 24(3):6–8, September 1970.   **1G211**
In a talk before the American Jewish Congress the publisher of the *Washington Post* notes the efforts of the Nixon Administration to stifle dissent. She calls on the nation's press to accept the fact that they will be caught in a withering cross-fire from the right and left, and to continue to carry out their historic and constitutional role to inform the public.

————. "A Vigilant Press: Its Job to Inform." *Vital Speeches*, 40:460–62, 15 May 1974.   **1G212**
The press should be considered not as a fourth branch of government but as "an essential counterweight to government, the basic check against abuses of official power." In an address at Colby College in accepting the Elijah Lovejoy Award, the publisher details numerous examples where the nation's press uncovered scandals and abuses of presidential power. Watergate shows how essential it is for the press to be vigorous, persistent, and free.

Graham, Roger D. "Disclosure of Journalist's Confidential News Sources." *West Virginia Law Review*, 73:318–25, September 1971.   **1G213**
Re: *Caldwell v. United States*, 408 U.S. 665 (1972).

Granato, Leonard A. "Obscenity Law: A Quagmire." *Grassroots Editor*, 13(2):33–36, March–April 1972. **1G214**
Among the various inconsistencies in obscenity rulings of the U.S. Supreme Court, the author refers to *Stanley v. Georgia* (1969) which permits a man to possess obscene matter in the privacy of his home, while *United States v. Thirty-Seven Photographs* (1971) permits Customs to seize obscene matter from a man's luggage when he is en route to his home.

————. "Press Access Case Raises Prior Restraint Issue." *Grassroots Editor*, 15(3):16–19, 27, May–June 1974.   **1G215**
A discussion of the issue of prior restraint in the case of the Florida compulsory right of reply law before the U.S. Supreme Court in *Tornillo v. Miami Herald* (1974). The Court subsequently declared the law unconstitutional. Reference is made to the Court's invasion of the advertising columns of the *Pittsburgh Press* in upholding a law forbidding help-wanted ads in columns designating sex.

————. *Prior Restraint: Resurgent Enemy of Freedom of Expression*. Carbondale, Ill., Southern Illinois University, 1973. 538p. (Ph.D. dissertation, University Microfilms, no. 74–6202) **1G216**
"The purpose of this study is (1) to trace the evolution of the governmental use of prior restraints from Fourteenth-Century England to the present United States, to explain the present-day status of prior restraints and to determine what to expect in the future; (2) to determine what modifications occurred in post-Revolutionary America that permitted the process to permit periods of increased governmental control, and how, when, and why these modifications occurred; (3) to identify the trends in the use of prior restraints for their historical importance, for understanding of present law, and for their future relevance; and (4) to provide a comprehensive study in an effort to call attention to the resulting dangers to freedom of expression."

"Grand Jury Witnesses May Assert First Amendment Rights of Press and Association as a Basis for Refusing to Answer Questions—Immunity Extends Only to Subjects Specifically Mentioned in a Grant of Immunity." *New York University Law Review*, 48:171–96, April 1973.   **1G217**
"In *Bursey v. United States* [1972] the United States Court of Appeals for the Ninth Circuit expanded fifth amendment rights by restricting the ability of grand juries to compel testimony by means of a federal transactional immunity statute. The court also recognized the right of witnesses to refuse questions infringing on first amendment freedoms."

[Grange, James Erskine, *Lord*.] *The Doctrine of Libels and the Duty of Juries, fairly stated, . . . The fatal Consequences of Ministerial Influence, &c and several other pieces in favour of our Constitution*. London, M. Cooper, 1752. 46p.   **1G218**
Comment on the role of juries in libel cases, part of the debate which led eventually to the passage of the Fox Libel Act in 1792, which permitted juries to judge whether or not the work was libelous as well as the mere fact of publication.

Granitsas, Spyridon. "UN Moves

Slowly on Codes for Freedom of Information." *Editor & Publisher*, 103(29):17–18, 18 July 1970.   **1G219**
The article deals with efforts to arrive at an international agreement on press freedom. Two other articles by the same author in the series deal with press freedom within the UN: Downgrading of the Press Continues a UN Problem (4 July 1970) and Status of Press at UN Hangs on a Preposition (1 August 1970).

Grannis, Chandler B. [Editorials on Censorship and Intellectual Freedom.] *Publishers' Weekly*, various issues, 1968–73.   **1G220**
Examples: Do We Face Censorship? (16 September 1968), Shifting Winds that Affect Censorship (1 July 1968), FTC Backs Away from the Censor's Role (20 January 1969), Where Do We Draw the Line? (14 April 1969), Bookseller's Stake in Intellectual Freedom (16 June 1969), and Postal Rates & Freedom of the Press (19 February 1973).

Grant, Alan. "Pre-Trial Publicity and a Fair Trial—A Tale of Three Doctors." *Osgoode Hall Law Journal*, 14:275–85, October 1976.   **1G221**
"The experience of these three doctors living in three different jurisdictions provides an opportunity to examine the concept of pre-trial publicity and to observe how it has been dealt with in societies, which, despite sharing a common law tradition, clearly differ in cultural terms." The three doctors: Samuel Holmes Sheppard (United States), John Bodkin Adams (England), and Henry Morgentaler (Canada). Sheppard and Adams were tried for murder, Morgentaler for abortion.

Grant, Alec. "Censorship—A Perennial Problem." *Socialist Commentary*, 1966:25–27, October 1966.   **1G222**
"A joint committee of both Houses of Parliament on censorship in the theatre is now at work—the fifth committee on this subject since 1943. Alec Grant, who is chairman of the Licensing Committee of the Greater London Council, which deals with censorship, gives a personal view of the problem."

Grant, J. H. "Pornography." *Medicine, Science, and the Law*, 13:232–38, October 1973.   **1G223**
In a paper presented as part of a program on the Role of the Law in a Permissive Society, a British law enforcement officer describes the kinds of pornographic materials being distributed in England and what police and court action has been taken against them. He cites examples of pornography serving as a release for sexual gratification and as a stimulant to sexual crime.

Grant, Lawrence. "Incitement to Disaffection." *Index on Censorship*, 3(3):3–9, Autumn 1974.   **1G224**
The case of the conviction and eighteen months' imprisonment of Pat Arrowsmith under the 1934 Incitement to Disaffection Act, for distributing to soldiers a fact-sheet on how to leave the army. This was part of a campaign for the withdrawal of British troops from Northern Ireland.

[Grascome, Samuel.] *An Appeal of Murther from certain unjust Judges, lately sitting at the Old Bailey, to the righteous Judge of Heaven and Earth; and to all sensible English-men, containing a Relation of the Tryal, Behavior and Death of Mr William Anderton, Executed June 16, 1693. At Tyburn, for pretended High-Treason.* London, 1693. 41p.   **1G225**
The anonymous author accuses Robert Stephens, messenger of the press ("whose Malice much outweighs his Brains"), of false arrest of William Anderton and of plundering his house. At the trial for treason, Stephens testified to finding seditious books in Anderton's desk. The author claims the books were planted and that there was no proof that the accused was the printer of two objectionable pamphlets, *Remarks* and *French Conquest*. The jury found the defendant guilty not because of the evidence against him but because he was a Jacobite. The jury was coerced into a verdict of guilty, although the foreman objected. The petition of William Anderton to the Lord Mayor of London protesting his innocence is attached. It asked for arrest of judgment. Also included is William Anderton's speech on the scaffold, which he was prevented from delivering by interruption by the Ordinary.

Graves, Alexander, Jr. "The 'Clear and Present Danger' Rule as Applied to Contempt by Publication." *New York Law School Student Law Review*, 1:63–76, Spring 1952.   **1G226**
The most serious class of contempt by publication involves not the applying of pressures on judge or jury but prejudicing an entire community by broad media coverage. Change of venue would have no value and the situation "practically precludes the showing of a clear and present danger." Perhaps the solution can be found in the stricter rules of the British courts against prejudicial publicity.

Graves, Thornton S. "Notes on Puritanism and the Stage." *Studies in Philology*, 18(2):141–69, April 1921.
                                         1G227
The article presents a few minor contributions to the struggle between the Puritans and the theater which have not been indicated in recent discussions. It also reviews a few phases of the controversy subsequent to the closing of the theaters in 1642, showing that the defenders of the stage were not so idle during the years 1642–60 as is sometimes supposed. Finally, the article presents evidence that "the objectors to the stage were by no means silent after the return of Charles II, even if it took a Jeremy Collier to make the morality of the playhouse a matter of considerable flurry and excitement."

Gray, C. B. "Prejudicial Publicity in Criminal Proceedings." *North Carolina Law Review*, 45:183–206, December 1966.   **1G228**
Comment on *Sheppard v. Maxwell* (1966), with particular attention to the Court's suggestions for limiting prejudicial publicity. "The rule recently set down by the Wake County Superior Court of North Carolina represents an attempt to follow *Sheppard*, by subjecting to contempt of court any statement after arrest by counsel, police, witness, or accused concerning any confession, prior criminal record, results of any tests, evidence, credibility of any witness, or any opinion as to the guilt or innocence of the accused." The author criticizes the Wake ruling as having misinterpreted the Supreme Court opinion by failing to acknowledge the distinction between prejudicial and nonprejudicial matters and setting up a flat rule of prohibition.

Gray, John R. *et al.* "GUM Symposium on Censorship." *Glasgow University Magazine*, no vol.:12–28, April 1966.   **1G229**
A Protestant clergyman, a Catholic priest, a cinema manager, a publisher, and a philosopher discuss censorship issues.

Great Britain. Cabinet Office. *The "D" Notice System.* London, H.M. Stat. Off., 1967. 16p. (Cmnd. 3312) **1G230**
A White Paper from the Prime Minister incorporating a report of the Radcliffe Committee which had been appointed "to examine the circumstances surrounding the publication of an article in the *Daily Express* of 21 February entitled 'Cable Vetting Sensation' in relation to the 'D' notice system; and to consider what improvements, if any, are required in that system in order to maintain it as a voluntary system based on mutual trust and confidence between the Government and Press in the interests alike of the freedom of the Press and of the security of the State." While the Committee approved the system, it recommended a re-writing of the "D" notice of 27 April 1956 "to clarify its application, bearing in mind the Committee's view that some wider restriction would be justified."

———. *Report of the Committee of Privy Counsellors Appointed to Inquire Into "D" Notice Matters. Presented to the Prime Minister by Command of Her Majesty, June 1967.* London, H.M. Stat. Off., 1967. 288p. (Cmnd. 3309)   **1G231**

This report of the Radcliffe Committee was summarized in the Prime Minister's White Paper, *The "D" Notice System*.

Great Britain. Charles II. *A Proclamation for the better Discovery of Seditious Libellers. 7 Jan 1675.* London, Assigns of Bill & Barker, 1675–76. Broadside (Wing C3451)   **1G232**
The proclamation urged action against surreptitious printing which criticized the government, and encouraged informers.

Great Britain. Civil Service Department. *Information and the Public Interest.* London, H.M. Stat. Off., 1969. 12p. (Cmnd. 4089)   **1G233**
This White Paper from the Prime Minister transmits some of the recommendations of the Fulton Committee's Report on the Civil Service (Cmnd. 3638) which investigated secrecy in government. "We think," the Report states, "that the administrative process is surrounded by too much secrecy. The public interest would be better served if there were a greater amount of openness. . . . We suggest that the Government should set up an inquiry to make recommendations for getting rid of unnecessary secrecy in this country." The White Paper concluded: "The Government agree with the Fulton Committee in wishing to see more public explanation of administrative processes, a continuing trend towards more consultation before policy decisions are reached, and increasing participation by civil servants in explaining the work of Government to the public."

Great Britain. Home Office. *Departmental Committee on Section 2 of the Official Secrets Act 1911, Chairman Lord Franks. Vol. 1. Report of the Committee . . . September 1972.* London, H.M. Stat. Off., 1972. 90p. (Cmnd. 5104)   **1G234**
The Franks Committee was appointed in 1971 by the Home Secretary to review the operation of Section 2 of the Official Secrets Act of 1911 and to make recommendations. The report discusses the operation of Section 2, how it came about and developed, and what people think about it; other safeguards for official information ("D" Notice, security classification, the Public Records Act of 1958); experience of the United States and Sweden; lines of reform; official information requiring the protection of criminal sanctions (national security, law and order, government and the cabinet, and the use of official information for private gain). The Committee found the present law unsatisfactory and proposed that it be changed "so that criminal sanctions are retained only to protect what is of real importance." A new Official Information Act should apply only to "official information which (a) is classified information relating to defence or internal security, or to foreign relations, or to the currency or to the reserves, the unauthorised disclosure of which would cause serious injury to the interests of the nation; *or* (b) is likely to assist criminal

activities or to impede law enforcement; *or* (c) is a Cabinet document; *or* (d) has been entrusted to the Government by a private individual or concern." Detailed recommendations follow.

————. *Report of the Committee on Privacy . . . Presented to Parliament by the Secretary of State for the Home Department, the Lord High Chancellor, and the Secretary of State for Scotland by Command of Her Majesty, July 1972.* London, H.M. Stat. Off., 1972. 350p. (Cmnd. 5012)   **1G235**
The report of the Committee on Privacy headed by Kenneth Younger, which was charged "to consider whether legislation is needed to give further protection to the individual citizen and to commercial and industrial interests against intrusion into privacy by private persons and organizations or by companies and to make recommendations." The Younger Committee considered the concept of privacy, the aspects of invasion of privacy by means of unwanted publicity from press and broadcasting, the misuse of personal information, the intrusion on home and business life, and the use of modern technical devises such as computers and electronic surveillance. With respect to the press the Committee recommended a number of changes in the membership and operations of the Press Council and suggested that magistrates be readier to ask the press not to publish identities of an offender where this "might involve a risk of severe mental disturbance to him or members of his family." In the area of broadcasting the Committee recommended that the British Broadcasting Corporation "extend the terms of reference of its Programme Complaints Commission to empower it to handle complaints about invasion of privacy . . . ," and that the Independent Television Authority publish the adjudication of its Complaints Review Board and extend its procedure to commercial radio.

Great Britain. Lord High Chancellor's Office. *Report of the Committee on Contempt of Court. Presented to Parliament by the Lord High Chancellor and the Lord Advocate by Command of Her Majesty, December 1974.* London, H.M. Stat. Off., 1974. 109p. (Cmnd. 5794)   **1G236**
The Committee, under the chairmanship of Lord Justice Phillimore, recognized the need to preserve the principles of the law of contempt, while making substantial reforms to take account of modern conditions, particularly in those parts of the law affecting the press. The report recommends more precise definition of press conduct which should amount to contempt of court, and more precise regulations with respect to procedure and appeals. Included among the suggested changes and clarifications: definition of publication; types of publications which may give rise to a risk of prejudice (crime reports, trial proceedings, "investigative journalism," publications incidentally affecting legal proceedings); use of "gagging writs"; tests of contempt; time for application of the law; defenses; and indi-

vidual, editorial, and employers' responsibility.

————. *Report of the Committee on Defamation. Presented to Parliament by the Lord High Chancellor and the Lord Advocate by Command of Her Majesty, March 1975.* London, H.M. Stat. Off., 1975. 307p. (Cmnd. 5909)   **1G237**
The Committee, chaired by Mr. Justice Faulks, was charged "to consider whether in the light of the working of the Defamation Act 1952, any changes are desirable in the law, practice, and procedure relating to actions for defamation," applying the study to England, Scotland, and Wales. The Committee did not recommend codification, but proposed numerous changes to remove or reduce complexities and technicalities in the defamation law, in response to widespread criticism of the Act of 1952.

Great Britain. Parliament. . . . *Expresse Commands From both the Honourable Houses of Parliaments containing These particular Heads following: I ⸤concerns administering of oaths⸥. II ⸤defense of forts⸥. III That the abuses of Printing, be likewise Reformed, and the publishing of obnoxious matters in Pamphlets be severely punished.* London, Printed for Robert Cotton, 1641. 8p.   **1G238**
In the third part of this Parliamentary command, warning is issued that those who issue printing falsely purported to be done by order of the House or by the king will be severely punished.

————. *An Order of the Lords and Commons Assembled in Parliament. For the Regulating of Printing, and for Suppressing the Great Late Abuses and Frequent Disorders in Printing Many False, Scandalous, Seditious, Libellous and Unlicensed Pamphlets, to Great Defamation of Religion and Government.* . . . London, Printed for I. Wright, 1643, 8p.   **1G239**

————. *Votes of Parliament touching Two Books; The one Entituled, The Accuser sham'd, or A Pair of Bellows to blow off that Dust cast upon John Fry a Member of Parliament, by Colonel John Downs, likewise a Member of Parliament; The other Entituled, The Clergy in their Colours, or A Brief Character of them.* London, John Field, Printer to the Parliament of England, 1650, pp. 1293–97.   **1G240**
The Committee for Plundred Ministers took exception to two books written by Fry (F369). The first was a breach of the privilege of Parliament since it was critical of a fellow member; the second was considered a scandalous attack on the clergy. Both books were ordered to be burnt by the Sheriff of London and Middlesex

and Fry was disallowed to sit in the present Parliament.

Great Britain. Parliament. House of Commons. *Copy of the Information, Evidence and Conviction, before Mr. Chambers, at the Marlborough-street Police office, the 16th June 1834, of Joseph Forster, for Selling Unstamped Publications.* . . . London, H.M. Stat. Off., 1835, 1p. (Report 555, 1835, vol. 46)   **1G241**
Brief account of the arrest, conviction, and sentencing to the House of Corrections of a crippled news vender for selling *The Man* and the *Weekly Police Gazette*, and a petition from area tradesmen urging his release.

————. *Minutes of Evidence Taken at the Bar of the House of Commons in the Matter of, and on the Consideration of the Petition, of Messrs Hansard.* London, Ordered by the House of Commons to be printed, 1840. 19p. (Report 3, 1840, vol. 45)   **1G242**
The case of *Stockdale v. Hansard* raised the question whether the printer of Parliamentary proceeding was protected against charges of libel when printing official reports. Parliament decided that he was (H69), and passed an act to this effect.

————. *Political Libel and Seditious Conduct. A Return of the Individuals Prosecuted for Political Libel and Seditious Conduct in England and Scotland, since 1807; with Sentences passed on them.* London, H.M. Stat. Off., 1821. 5p. (Report 379, 1821, vol. 21)   **1G243**
A tabulation of cases before the Court of King's Bench and other jurisdictions, from 1807 to 1821, a total of 101 prosecutions. A similar tabulation of returns of the ex-officio informations for political libel appears in a two-page report issued the same year (Report 438, 1821, vol. 21).

————. *Prosecutions for Libel, &c.* London, Printed by George Maule by Order of the House of Commons, 1830. 2p. (Report 608, 1830, vol. 30)   **1G244**
A listing of all prosecutions during the reigns of George III and IV either ex-officio informations or indictments under the direction of the Attorney or Solicitor General, for libels or other misdemeanors against individuals as members or officials of his Majesty's government. Covers the period 1761–1829.

————. *A Return of the Number of Persons Committed by the Magistrates of Great Bri-*

tain . . . *for Selling Unstamped Publications, from March 1834 to the Latest Period.* London, H.M. Stat. Off., 1836. 21p. (Report 21, 1836, vol. 41) **1G245**

————. *Return of the Number of Persons who have been Committed by the Magistrates of the Metropolis, within the last Year, for selling Unstamped Publications. . . .* London, H.M. Stat. Off., 1831–32. 3p. (Report 40, 1831–32, vol. 34) **1G246**
Most of those found guilty were fined; Henry Hetherington refused to pay his fine and was given a six months sentence.

————. *Return of the Number of Persons who have been Committed by the Magistrates for Selling Unstamped Publications, from 10th and 12th December 1831 . . . .* London, H.M. Stat. Off., 1831–32. 5p. (Report 711, 1831–32, vol 34) **1G247**
Includes the imprisonment of John Thompson and John Williams.

————. *Stockdale versus Hansard. Petition of James Hansard, Luke Graves Hansard, and Luke James Hansard, Printers to the Honourable the House of Commons, in the Matter of Stockdale versus Hansard, and Proceedings Therein. (Presented to the Honourable the House of Commons 16 January 1840.)* London, Ordered by the House of Commons to be Printed, 1840. 67p. (Report 1, 1840, vol. 45) **1G248**
Publisher Hansard had been threatened with a libel suit for publishing the proceedings of the House of Lords. The petition was intended to exempt Hansard, the official printer of the proceedings, from prosecution except on authorization by the Parliament. The case involved reference to a book, *The Generative System* by John Robertson, as being obscene. Stockdale was the publisher.

————. "Suppression of the 'Daily Worker'and the 'Week'." *Parliamentary Debates . . . Official Report,* 368(17): 463–534, 28 January 1941. **1G249**
Debate in the House of Commons over government suppression of two newspapers, under 2C of the Emergency Powers Act, for "steadily and systematically" sabotaging the war effort. The members overwhelmingly passed a resolution approving the action: "That this House expresses its detestation of the propaganda of the 'Daily Worker' in relation to the war, as it is convinced that the future of democratic institutions and the expanding welfare of the people everywhere depend on the successful prosecution of the war till Fascism is

finally defeated; and while anxious that the principle of freedom for the expression of minority opinions shall be maintained so far as possible and that the minimum use shall be made even in time of war of powers of repression, recognises that special and effective measures must be taken against the habitual and persistent publication of matter which is calculated to impede the national war effort and thus to assist the enemy, and approves the action of the Home Secretary in relation to the 'Daily Worker' and the 'Week'."

Great Britain. Parliament. House of Commons. Select Committee on Dramatic Literature. *Report from the Select Committee on Dramatic Literature with the Minutes of Evidence. . . .* London, Ordered by the House of Parliament to be Printed, 1832. 250p. (Report 679, 1831–32, vol. 7) (Reprinted with introduction and index by Irish University Press, *British Parliamentary Papers, Stage and Theatre,* vol. 1, 1968) **1G250**
The report recommended giving the sole authority to license theaters to the Lord Chamberlain; that the office of the censor be held at the discretion of the Lord Chamberlain; that he be authorized to approve additional theaters upon petition from the people (there was concern over theater monopoly); and that the legal right of the author to his play be guaranteed. Among the numerous witnesses before the Select Committee were J. Payne Collier, who preferred licensing to protection under common law; and Francis Place, who rejected all licensing of plays, preferring to leave the matter to the judgment of the audience.

Great Britain. Parliament. House of Commons. Select Committee on Newspaper Stamps. *Report from the Select Committee on Newspaper Stamps; Together with the Proceedings of the Committee, Minutes of Evidence, Appendix and Index.* London, Ordered by the House of Commons to be Printed, 1851. 659p. (Report 558, 1851, vol. 17) (Reprinted by Irish University Press, *British Parliamentary Papers, Newspapers,* vol. 1, 1968) **1G251**
The Committee was appointed "to inquire into the present state and operation of the law relative to newspaper stamps; also, into the law and regulations relative to the transmission of newspapers and other publications by post, and to report their opinion thereon to the House." Among the witnesses appearing before the Committee were Thomas Hogg, lawyer; Frederick K. Hunt, editor; Collet Dobson Collet, secretary of the Association for Promoting the Repeal of the Taxes on Knowledge; and Horace Greeley, American editor. The Committee found that "apart from fiscal considerations, they do not consider that news is of itself a desirable subject of taxation." The newspaper tax was abolished in 1855.

Great Britain. Parliament. House of Commons. Select Committee on Publication of Printed Papers. *Report . . . with the Minutes of Evidence, and Appendix.* London, H.M. Stat. Off., 1837. 99p. (Report 286, 1837, vol. 13) **1G252**
This committee was appointed following the arraignment of Hansard for publishing a libel. The Lord Chief Justice had informed the jury that "the fact that the House of Commons directed Messrs. Hansard to publish all their Parliamentary Papers is no justification for them, or for any bookseller who publishes a part containing a Libel against any man." Hansard was caught in the middle of a controversy between Parliament and the Courts and Parliament was concerned with defending its independence. The report contains an extensive history of Parliamentary printing and legal precedent. It concludes that "Printing of Publication should exist without restriction, and that the authority to determine the extent of that Privilege and the occasion for exercising it should rest exclusively with Parliament." It recommends, however, that Parliament take such precautions as possible against inflicting injury on individuals. Appendix: Chronology of printing orders, documents, legal decisions; extracts from the trial of *Stockdale v. Hansard,* and trial documents.

Great Britain. Parliament. House of Lords. "Pornography in Britain." *Parliamentary Debates,* 317 (5th ser.):639–754, 21 April 1971. **1G253**
Lord Longford, who subsequently headed a private inquiry into pornography in Britain, introduced the issue into the House of Lords and there followed a discussion over the seriousness of the situation and the need for legislative action.

Great Britain. Parliament. Joint Committee on Censorship of the Theatre. *Report, Together with the Proceedings of the Committee, Minutes of Evidence, Appendices and Index.* London, H.M. Stat. Off., 1967. 204p. (H.L. 255; H.C. 503) **1G254**
"The effect of the recommendations of the Committee will be to allow freedom of speech in the theatre subject to the overriding requirements of the criminal law which generally speaking applies to other forms of art in this country. The anachronistic licensing powers of the Lord Chamberlain will be abolished and will not be replaced by any other form of pre-censorship, national or local. The theatre will be subjected to the general law of the land, and those presenting plays which break the law will be subjected to prosecution under the relevant procedure. The penalties for offences will be realistically severe, but the author and producer will have the right to defend themselves before a jury and to plead the defence of artistic merit. Political censorship of any kind will cease."

Greater London Council Film Viewing

Board. *Exercise of the Council's Powers of Film Censorship for Adults*. London, The Board, 1974. 21p., 15p., 1p., 1p., 6p. Processed. **1G255**
A report of a study on film censorship for adults prepared for the Film Viewing Board. The report "describes and summarises the consultations, discusses research findings and goes on to consider some of the main issues. The report consists of a section covering the background to the question of film censorship for adults; this section deals with the Council's powers, the Council's requests for an inquiry, the position of cinema clubs, the Council's rules of management criteria since 1965, and particulars of films submitted to the Film Viewing Board and of decisions thereon. A second section deals with the GLC's inquiries and covers a summary of consultations with interested organisations and individuals with fuller particulars in an appendix; research on harmful effects; public attitudes to censorship; and the practice in other countries. A third section looks at the question of advertising and information about cinema programmes and deals specifically with the problem of offensive advertising and the need to convey adequate information about the content of films. A fourth section looks at the various statutes applying to the display of films to the public and reviews the current situation with regard to court proceedings in relation to a number of individual films. A fifth section considers the difficulty of enforcing age limits in respect of X films."

————. *The Future of Film Censorship for Adults*. London, The Board, 1974. 5p. Processed. **1G256**
A paper prepared by the chairman of the Film Viewing Board, Enid Wistrich, and approved by the Board, recommending to the Greater London Council that the Council no longer exercise its power to censor films for persons over the age of eighteen and that it permit adults to see films not passed by the British Board of Film Censors. Ms. Wistrich notes that there is no longer prior censorship of theaters in Britain and that there is no reliable evidence to indicate that explicit sex and violence causes criminal or deviant behavior. The Council would continue to exercise its power to regulate the viewing of adult films by children and would continue to regulate cinema advertisements. The Council rejected the request of the Film Viewing Board to remove controls over adult viewers and Ms. Wistrich resigned as chairman of the Board.

Green, Alan B. *Mother of Her Country: A Comic Novel About Pornography and Censorship*. New York, Random House, 1973. 210p. **1G257**
Most of the issues over freedom of expression in the area of sex are discussed in this witty novel involving a book brought to trial on charges of obscenity, the campaign of a mythical organization known as Americans for Clean Entertainment, a small-town librarian under attack for her book selection, the publisher of erotica, and a young lawyer dedicated to freedom of expression. When a moviescript is dis-

covered which cast aspersions on the marital fidelity of a revered American forefather, an organization is formed known as Defend America's Founders from Slander (DAFFS). To counteract the would-be censors, another group was formed entitled Don't Inhibit Legitimate Scholarship (DILS).

Green, Frances M., and Warren L. Lewis. "A Fair Break for Controversial Speakers: Limitations of the Fairness Doctrine and the Need for Individual Access." *George Washington Law Review*, 39:532–69, March 1971. **1G258**
"This note will analyze recent Commission actions as they illustrate the inability of the fairness doctrine, as presently applied, to protect the right of the public to be informed. It is suggested that operation of the media in a manner consistent with the 'public convenience, interest, or necessity' cannot be achieved unless the fairness doctrine is extended to include a limited right of individual access. This limited right of access may, in fact, be compelled by the Constitution."

Green, Lewis C. "The *New York Times* Rule: Judicial Overkill." *Villanova Law Review*, 12:730–37, Summer 1967. **1G259**
Criticism of the Court's decision in the *New York Times* case as an overreaction to the breakdown of law enforcement in certain segregation cases. The author believes that the situation called for "fair and adequate enforcement of our libel laws, not for a new law of libel. The remedy selected by the Court was not shaped to the need, and has already begun to produce unfortunate results."

Green, M.E. "The Librarian and Censorship: An Administrative View." *South African Libraries*, 38:224–27, January 1971. **1G260**
"To the librarian in South Africa operating at the ordinary everyday level, censorship is more of an administrative than an ideological issue. We have a state censorship exercised by the Publications Control Board, which has to be implemented regardless of our private opinions, and this implies constant checking of official lists to ensure that regulations are not contravened. . . . We have to watch not only for banned books and periodicals, but also for the publications of banned persons." A university librarian describes how this day-to-day censorship is performed and how the librarian is caught between government decrees and the demands for intellectual freedom in the university.

Green, Mark J. "Talking Back to the Hucksters." *MORE*, 3(10):6–9, October 1973. **1G261**
"The very idea of 'counter-commercials' has advertisers and the broadcast industry petrified. But something has to be done to rebut the misleading claims drilled into us by Madison Avenue."

Green, Stephen. "Enigma of DINFOS." *Quill*, 58(5):20–21, May 1970. **1G262**
A discussion of the conflict between free journalism and public relations in the army as seen in the joint-service Defense Information School (DINFOS) and the news censorship hassle in Vietnam.

Green, Wayne E. "Policing the 'Fairness' of Television." *Wall Street Journal*, 53(50):4, 26 December 1973. **1G263**
Comment on the proposal of Clay T. Whitehead, director of the White House Office of Telecommunications, to sponsor legislation lengthening the term of a station's license to five years from the present three, while making it tougher for citizen groups to oppose license renewal. In return, local stations would have to monitor and somehow change the bias of network programs. He notes a growing suspicion that the proposal was intended to frighten the networks into more friendly coverage of the Nixon Administration.

Greenberg, Rachel H. *A Study of Political Broadcasting under Section 315 of the Communications Act*. Philadelphia, Annenberg School of Communications, University of Pennsylvania, 1972. 159p. (Unpublished Master's thesis) **1G264**
"The study analyzes the consequences of Section 315 of the Communications Act upon the Presidential campaign process. The rising costs of political campaigning on the broadcast media and the near blackout of minority candidates' views are attributed to the 'equal opportunities' provision of Section 315."

Greenburg, Dan. *Porno-graphics; The Shame of Our Art Museums*. New York, Random House, 1970? 22p. **1G265**
A mock diatribe against nude paintings in art museums, accompanied by a group of famous nudes, with plastic overlays which clothe them properly.

Greene, Stuart C. *Public Attitudes Toward Free Press–Free Trial*. Columbia, Mo., University of Missouri, 1967. 187p. (Unpublished Master's thesis) **1G266**

[Greenspan, Lou, *ed.*] "The Journal Looks Again at Classification—What Now?" *Journal of the Producers Guild of America*, 10(2):1–44, June 1968. **1G267**
Content: Self-Regulation, Not Legal Coercion by Jack Valenti. Classification—A Middle Ground by Richard S. Randall. Classification or Pacification by Bosley Crowther. Who Will Guard the Guards? by James R. Webb. The

Catholic View of Classification by Rev. Patrick J. Sullivan. Film Classification—Whither Away? by Anne Childress. Keeping the Young People Moral After School by Bishop Gerald Kennedy. The Silliness and Pathos of Film Classification by G. William Jones. The How and Why of Classification in Britain by John Trevelyan. Caveat Emptor—Or Let the Movies Alone by George Slaff. Censorship and Classification in B. C. by R. W. McDonald. Exhibition's Position on Film Classification by Philip F. Harling. An earlier review of film classification appeared in the September 1961 issue (G274).

————. "The Journal Looks at Television Censorship." *Journal of the Producers Guild of America*, 11(2):1–46, June 1969. **1G268**
Content: The Public Interest and the Private Responsibility by Frank Stanton. Challenge and Change in Television by John O. Pastore. Television: Censorship, Politics and the New Comedy by David Levy. Smothering the Smothers Brothers by Stanley Fleishman. Television and Censorship by Nicholas Johnson. Violence on Television—Who Is Responsible by Goerge Edwards. Censors and Sensibility: A Television Content Analysis by Charles Winick. Public Commission or Government Intervision by Harry S. Ashmore. TV Depiction of Violence: If and How by Stockton Helffrich.

————. "The Journal Looks At the Film Rating Race." *Journal of the Producers Guild of America*, 11(4):1–36, December 1969. **1G269**
Content: Classification Is a Cop Out by Robert Steele. The Range of the Rating System by Anne Childress. The Sound of the Trumpet by Fredric Wertham. A Film Critic Looks at the Rating System by James M. Wall. Classified Matter by Martin S. Dworkin. Fair Warning by Bishop Gerald Kennedy. The Film Rating System—Is It Worth Continuing by Frank K. Kelly. The Rating System by Richard L. Coe. A Realistic View of the Rating System by Bernard R. Kantor.

————. "The Journal Looks at Violence in Films." *Journal of the Producers Guild of America*, 9(4):1–38, December 1967. **1G270**
A group of articles which reflect various areas of conflict and shades of opinion with respect to the issue of violence in motion picture films: The Exhibitor and Violence by Sherrill C. Corwin. An Appraisal by Judith Crist. Features, Violence and Television by David Levy. A Look at Violence by Malvin Wald. The Three "E's" of Screen Violence: Ethics, Esthetics, and Economics by G. William Jones. Violence and the Film Critic by Charles Champlin. A Church Critic Looks at Violence by James M. Wall. What Price Screen Violence? by Jay Emanuel.

Greenwood, Edward D. "Pornography/Obscenity and Intellectual Freedom." *Mountain Plains Library Association Quarterly*, 18(2):14–16, 1973. **1G271**
A member of the U.S. Commission on Obscenity and Pornography comments on various studies of the effect of pornography on the reader and the use of sex education materials.

Greer, Gordon. "Pornography: What Can We Do to Protect our Kids." *Better Homes & Gardens*, 49:16, 100, December 1971. **1G272**
How can we protect children from the onslaught of pornography within the existing laws? By returning unsolicited advertising to the sender and by filling out a postal form asking that your name be removed from the pornographer's mailing list. Picketing and confrontation with proprietors of porn shops or movies is ineffective. Enforcement of rules on legal age, however, can be insisted upon by local groups. In the long run, giving children more attractive alternatives to porn, is the most effective weapon.

Gregory, David D. "Substantive Issues of the Supreme Court's Method of Dealing with Obscenity Regulations." *Maine Law Review*, 18:284–96, 1967. **1G273**
The author concludes that "in the decisions from *Roth v. United States* [1957] to *Ginzburg v. United States* [1966], the Supreme Court has been faced with the task of reconciling and giving positive effect to antithetical values, confronting difficulties far-reaching in their effect, but has evolved a theoretically sound, politic method of regulating obscenity."

Grenier, Judson. "Upton Sinclair and the Press: *The Brass Check* Reconsidered." *Journalism Quarterly*, 49:427–36, Autumn 1972. **1G274**
Some fifty years after the publication of Upton Sinclair's *The Brass Check*, a vitriolic attack on the nation's press, the author looks at the events in Sinclair's life that prompted the work, its numerous faults (bias, overstatement, naïveté, etc.), the silence that the publication met in the contemporary press, and the significance of the work as a catalyst. The author interviewed Sinclair in his research for the article.

Grey, Charles G. *The Speech of Earl Grey in the House of Lords, May 12, 1817, on Lord Sidmouth's Circular*. London, Printed for Ridgways, 1817, 89p. **1G275**
Arguments against a proposal by Lord Sidmouth, Secretary of State, to give English justices of the peace the power to hold to bail, or commit to prison for want of bail, any persons accused of publishing blasphemous or seditious libels. Grey objects to the power being given either to justices or the Secretary of State.

Griest, Guinevere L. "The Circulating Censorship." In her *Mudie's Circulating Library and the Victorian Novel*. Bloomington, Ind., Indiana University Press, 1970, pp. 140–55. **1G276**
For more than a half century Mudie's Circulating Library served as a major source of book reading for middle- and upper-class Victorian families. By selecting books that would appeal to the British matron and the young girl, Mudie's had a profound effect not only on what was read but on what was published. "Mudie's censorship was directed primarily against works which depicted violations of the established Victorian sexual code, a code which was generally accepted by members of the established church as well as by those of other denominations." Mudie's selection was also influenced by the amount of discount he received from publishers. Numerous writers, including Charles Reade and George Moore, spoke out against the Mudie censorship.

Griffin, Hugh C. "Prejudicial Publicity: Search for a Civil Remedy." *Notre Dame Lawyer*, 42:943–56, Symposium 1967. **1G277**
"This note first investigates the possibility of finding relief for a victim of prejudicial publicity in one of the civil remedies presently afforded by the law. Next, the need for the creation of a remedy of this type is fully explored. Finally, a model statute, designed to meet this need and to fill the void in existing law, is proposed."

Griffith, Arthur. *When the Government Publishes Sedition*. Dublin, Irish Publicity League, 1915? 11p. (Tracts for the Times, no. 4) **1G278**
The Sinn Féin leader who later (1919) became President of the Irish Republic, writes in this satirical pamphlet that "so long as Mr. Ponsonby flourishes in Grafton Street, Dublin, bravely distributing his Britannic Majesty's Census Reports on Ireland and Finance Accounts, so long will sedition prosper." These official British bluebooks, Griffith charges, despite their dull statistical nature, are filled with damning facts about the British treatment of Ireland and are more seditious than the works of newspapers that have been suppressed and whose editors have been imprisoned or shot.

Griffiths, Richard. *Art, Pornography and Human Value; a Christian Approach to Violence and Eroticism in the Media*. London, Grove Books, 1975. 24p. (Grove Booklet on Ethics, no. 7) **1G279**
"This discussion aims to isolate standards applicable to any material, and to provide guidelines to help Christians evaluate its worth. We shall, therefore, discuss the relevant aesthetic and moral principles, and apply

them to the media generally before going on to give particular attention to pornography." The author concludes that "the best Christian approach to pornography should be on the basis of responsible criticism rather than of a less adequately considered emotional reaction. The problem that we are dealing with is not just whether this or that film should be shown at the local cinema, but is one which concerns our own and our families' exposure to the mass media that find their way into our homes: books, magazines, television and the newspapers. Any opportunity that we have for public protest should come as part of a continual critical response to the media." An Anglican Church publication.

————. *Censorship and the Arts*. London, Grove Books, 1975. 24p. (Grove Booklet on Ethics, no. 11)   **1G 280**
The author believes "the biblical approach to the problem [of obscenity] seems to be in shifting the emphasis of the law away from moral issues of obscenity and corruption to the injustice of exploitation." The law ought to be concerned in three areas: requirement that participants in the making of pornographic pictures are adults who have taken part without coercion; protection of children from participation in the making of pornography and from its use without parental consent; and prevention of pornography from being forced on unwilling adults.

Grigg, John. "India's Clampdown." *Index on Censorship*, 4(4):5–11, Winter 1975.   **1G 281**
A detailed analysis of the press censorship imposed in India by Prime Minister Indira Gandhi, including text of the edicts and the June 1975 Guidelines for the Press, "Not to Be Published." "The indiscriminate censorship that Mrs. Gandhi imposed was in no sense justified, and was almost certainly a grave mistake even from her own point of view. If newspapers had been left free they might have been, on balance, her allies in the struggle to uphold constitutional government, though of course there would have been some criticism. As it is, liberal opinion throughout the world has been alienated, and at home she faces the danger of proliferating rumor and the development of an underground press more hostile and damaging than the legitimate press she has muzzled."

Grist, John. "I Am a Censor." *Journal of the Society of Film and Television Arts*. 43/44:18–19, Spring–Summer 1971.   **1G 282**
The head of the Current Affairs Group, British Broadcasting Company television, describes his role as editor-censor in the area of news, features, documentaries, and religious broadcasting.

Griswold, Erwin N. "The Standards of the Legal Profession: Canon 35 Should Not Be Surrendered." *American Bar Association Journal*, 48:615–18, July 1962.   **1G 283**

"Dean Griswold [Yale Law School] writes that it is a matter of real professional concern that the possibility of modifying Canon 35 is even a subject for serious consideration within the organized Bar of the United States. Every factor of professional responsibility, and of the concern of lawyers for the fair and equal administration of justice, indicates clearly that the Bar would be acting contrary not only to its best traditions but to its real and vital obligations if it should weaken in this matter."—Editor

Groombridge, Brian. "Two Cheers for Access." *EBU Review* (European Broadcasting Union), 25(2):14–17, September 1974.   **1G 284**
The head of Educational Programme Services of the British Independent Broadcasting Authority states the case both for and against "access television," concluding with strong support for access.

Gros, Eugene. "A Libel Case as Seen by a Successful Plaintiff." In Michael Rubinstein, *ed.*, *Wicked, Wicked Libels*. London, Routledge & Kegan Paul, 1972, pp. 100–121.   **1G 285**
A technical writer and translator describes his experience in the British courts in a successful libel suit against the *Times Literary Supplement* for an article attacking the plaintiff and his scientific and technical information firm.

Gross, Edward. "Not for Publication." *Science News*, 95:508–10, 24 May 1969.   **1G 286**
The U.S. government has a hidden mine of consumer information on products from cars to floor wax, the result of government testing, but it is not available to the public unless there is a shift in national policy.

Gross, Gerald, *ed. Publishers and Publishing. Selected and Edited, with Commentary and an Introduction by Gerald Gross. Preface by Frank Swinnerton.* London, Secker & Warburg, 1961. 495p. **1G 287**
In addition to numerous brief references to censorship episodes, there are three essays on censorship: Sir Geoffrey Faber's opposition to establishing a Literary Censorship agency, pages 231–34, taken from his *A Publisher Speaking* (F1); George Palmer Putnam II's account of his brush with sex censors, pages 321–25, taken from his *Wide Margins* (P365); and Donald Friede's account of the cases of *An American Tragedy* and *The Well of Loneliness*, pages 343–53.

————. *The Responsibility of the Press.* New York, Fleet, 1966. 416p. **1G 288**
An anthology of articles relating to ethical and moral issues in the American press, including the television and motion picture industries. Includes text of various codes of ethics.

Gross, Jeanne. "*Rosemont v. Random House* and the Doctrine of Fair Use."

Journalism Quarterly, 50:227–36, 277, Summer 1973.   **1G 289**
An analysis of the 1966 decision of Judge Leonard B. Moore of the Second Circuit Court of Appeals in the case of an unauthorized Howard Hughes biography. Judge Moore ruled for the publisher, stating that "the public interest should prevail over the possible damage to the copyright owner," and the decision should turn on whether the distribution of the materials "would serve the public interest in the free dissemination of information." The author believes that the *Rosemont* decision, if followed, will lead to a more liberal interpretation of copyright law by the courts.

Gross, Stephen G. *Military News Censorship*. Columbia, Mo., Freedom of Information Center, School of Journalism, University of Missouri at Columbia, 1970. 7p. (Report no. 243)   **1G 290**
"By directive and tradition, the authorized military news media should be free of military control. Yet charges that the military is attempting to censor its media remain constant. Now a development has arisen—'underground' serviceman-produced newspapers—to trouble the armed forces. A case now working its way up to the military high court may determine the extent to which a member of the service must sacrifice his First Amendment rights, while the older battle, within the authorized media, continues unabated."

Grossman, Harvey M. "Freedom of Expression in India." *UCLA Law Review*, 4:64–80, December 1956. **1G 291**
Commentary on the freedom of speech and expression article in the Indian Constitution as interpreted by the Supreme Court.

Grosvenor, Peter. " 'Lord Porn' vs. Obscenity." *Publishers' Weekly*, 201(16):26, 17 April 1972.   **1G 292**
An account of the antipornography crusade of Lord Longford and his self-appointed pornography commission of fifty members, of which the author was one.

Grotta, Gerald L. "Attitudes on Newspaper Accuracy and External Controls." *Journalism Quarterly*, 46:757–59, Winter 1969.   **1G 293**
The preliminary study reported here indicates that "certain types of people—perhaps a majority—think that newspapers are inaccurate and are indeed tolerant of suggestions to 'regulate and control' those practices of the press involving accuracy." The study is also reported in Editors Living in Sin, *Grassroots Editor*, July–August 1970.

Grover, Stephen. "Banning Ads for Dirty Movies." *Wall Street Journal*, 179:16, 15 May 1972. **1G294**
"A recent decision of the *Detroit News* to ban all display advertising and editorial mention of x-rated movies has touched off a bitter controversy over the effectiveness and meaning of the movie rating system."

———. "Running Scared: Many in Broadcasting Fear the Rising Attitude from the Government." *Wall Street Journal*, 177:1+, 28 April 1971. **1G295**
"The broadcasters, both local and national, cite a seemingly endless list of happenings to back up their case that never before has the government tried harder to intimidate a medium and control its contents."

———. "The Wages of Sin: Pornography Business Experiences a Decline, Despite Liberal Laws." *Wall Street Journal*, 178:1, 23, 12 August 1971. **1G296**
Pornography business throughout the country is suffering from the combined effects of police pressure and public apathy.

Groves, Cy. "Book Censorship: Six Misunderstandings." *Alberta English*, 11(3):5–7, Fall 1971. **1G297**
The author dispels six false assumptions made by would-be censors of high school reading: (1) Use of rough language in a book suggests approval of its use; (2) the objectionable word is repeatedly used in class; (3) the English classroom is a sheltered sanctuary; (4) students are offended or embarrassed by frank expressions in contemporary literature; (5) literature inevitably mirrors life; and (6) students do not weigh in balance and reject what they consider worthless.

Gruenstein, Peter. "Press Release Politics: How Congressmen Manage the News." *Progressive*, 38:37–40, January 1974. **1G298**
"Too little public attention has been paid to how press coverage—or the lack of it—affects public policy."

Grundberg, Andy. "What's Legal?" *Modern Photography*, 39(9):92–96, September 1975. **1G299**
Which pictures do you have a right to take? Which pictures can you safely publish? Which pictures require a release? A sample release form accompanies the article.

Gruntz, Louis G., Jr. "Obscenity 1973: Remodeling the House that *Roth*

Built." *Loyola Law Review* (New Orleans), 20:159–75, 1974. **1G300**
An analysis of the U.S. Supreme Court's decision in *Miller v. California* (1973), and the way in which it modified the standards for obscenity established by *Roth v. United States* (1957). "The 1973 obscenity cases seem to have three basic objectives: (1) restrict the denial of first amendment protection to a very small class of material (hard-core pornography), (2) reduce the prosecution's burden of proof with respect to material clearly within this class, and (3) once material is classified pornographic, broaden governmental power to regulate and control it."

Guest, James A., and Alan L. Stanzler. "The Constitutional Argument for Newsmen Concealing Their Sources." *Northwestern University Law Review*, 64:18–61, March–April 1969. **1G301**
"Courts should protect the free flow of news by granting to newsmen a privilege under the first amendment to conceal their confidential sources. . . . It seems clear, however, that courts are not going to find a newsman's privilege under the common law. . . . Courts should start with the presumption that there is a constitutional privilege and make an exception only if the free flow of news will not be seriously impaired and the interest in more effective judicial administration will not be enhanced sufficiently by enforcing the exception."

Guhin, John P. "Flight of the Phoenix; The Censor Returns." *South Dakota Law Review*, 19:121–42, Winter 1974. **1G302**
Miller v. California (1973) repudiated the libertarian rationale in the area of obscenity in favor of a conservative rationale. "This comment has suggested that the *Miller* definition [of obscenity] is highly susceptible to abuse. Most of the danger arises from its acceptance of the 'local community standards' test which allows a jury to apply its own standards of 'patent offensiveness,' 'appeal to the prurient interest,' and 'serious literary, artistic, political, or scientific value.' Further, the local verdicts do not appear to be open to effective review by the United States Supreme Court. A final objection to the *Miller* test arises from its abolition of the 'utterly without redeeming social value' test. This raises most serious questions about the function of the first amendment and the policy of that amendment in supporting vigorous public debate."

Guimary, Donald L. "The Press of South Vietnam: A Recent Perspective." *Gazette: International Journal for Mass Communications Studies*, 21:163–69, 1975. **1G303**
By silencing the press in South Vietnam, President Thieu "silenced not only opponents but also constructive criticism and alternate sources of ideas." Freedom of expression in South Vietnam was never allowed to develop. Even after independence from France the press

was no better off than during the colonial era. "Since their inception, newspapers have been confiscated, reporters beaten and jailed, publishers fined, and newspaper plants vandalized."

Gulliver, *pseud.* "In Defence of Censors." *Bell*, 5:323, January 1943. **1G304**
A six-stanza poem poking fun at Irish censorship:
Since first the censors' work began,
I feel a nicer better man,
No longer do I read my Proust,
My private lust is much reduced.

Gummer, John S. *The Permissive Society*. London, Cassell, 1971. 181p. **1G305**
Chapters bearing on freedom of the press: literature and the permissive society; pornography on stage, film, and television; and the stand of the church.

Gunaratne, Shelton A. "Government—Press Conflict in Ceylon: Freedom versus Responsibility." *Journalism Quarterly*, 47:530–43, 552, Autumn 1970. **1G306**
"Mrs. Bandaranaike's United Front Coalition, defeated in 1965 after 13 attempts to take over major newspaper groups, was recently returned to power. The fate of the free press remains uncertain in spite of government declarations to the contrary."

Gunn, Donald L. *Moral Censorship of the Los Angeles Stage, 1966–1968: Two Case Studies*. Los Angeles, University of California, Los Angeles, 1970. 215p. (Ph.D. dissertation, University Microfilms, no. 71–9229) **1G307**
The case studies involve productions of *The Devils* and *The Beard*.

Gunther, Gerald. "Learned Hand and the Origins of Modern First Amendment Doctrine: Some Fragments of History." *Stanford Law Review*, 27:719–73, February 1975. **1G308**
"My main purpose is to put into print significant portions of the largely unpublished correspondence between Judge Hand and two other major contributors to the evolution of first amendment doctrine, Justice Oliver Wendell Holmes and Professor Zechariah Chafee, Jr. Sixteen of their letters—the first group between Hand and Holmes, the second between Hand and Chafee—constitute the Appendix to this Essay. Here I want not only to sketch the background and describe the substance of the exchanges, but also to offer my tentative interpretation of their meaning and impact."

[———.] "The Supreme Court, 1971 Term: Freedom of Speech, Press, and Association." *Harvard Law Review*,

86:122–30, 137–48, November 1972.
1G309
Under the heading Protection of First Amendment Activities on Private Property, the survey considers the case of *Lloyd Corp., Ltd. v. Tanner;* under Newsmen's Privilege to Withhold Information from Grand Jury, the case of *Branzburg v. Hayes.*

Gunther, Max. "All That TV Violence: Why Do We Love/Hate It?" *TV Guide*, 24(45):6–10, 6 November 1976; 24(46):34–35+, 13 November 1976.
1G310
The first article examines "what appears to be a central paradox: that people have always found violent TV material appealing, and watched it—as the ratings show—even while piously decrying it." The second article asks whether "any progress at all has been made, or if there is any hope of progress, in elucidating just how video violence affects adults and kids."

——. "But First, A Word Against Our Sponsor." *TV Guide*, 20(25):6–13, 17 June 1972; 20 (26):26–29, 24 June 1972; 20(27):14–17, 1 July 1972. **1G311**
An account of the movement for counter-advertising which threatens the broadcasting industry and the critical role of the Federal Communications Commission which must make and enforce the rules.

——. "The Great Sex Movie Scandal." *TV Guide*, 21(30):6–10, 28 July 1973. **1G312**
The story of a false rumor that Columbia Broadcasting System was about to show X-rated movies on the late show flooded the network offices with more than 400 thousand letters of protest. While the rumor didn't start with him, the Rev. Billy James Hargis passed it on to subscribers of his *Christian Crusade.*

——. "TV and the New Morality." *TV Guide*, 20(42):8–10, 12, 14 October 1972; 20(43):27–28, 31–32, 21 October 1972; 20(44):50–52, 54, 26 October 1972. **1G313**

America's greater tolerance toward sex, nudity, and language is beginning to show up in more frank and daring movies on television and there has been a strong reaction from some members of Congress, many individuals, and such organizations as Stop Immorality on TV and Morality in Media, Inc. Some of the rumors of the use of X-rated movies have been unfounded, witness the account circulated by the fundamentalist *Christian Crusade.* Television executives and those who police the TV Code are watching the situation carefully but do not see serious problems; most major religious groups have not shown great concern. Most critics agree that government censorship is not the answer to the problems raised by increasing adult fare on television. Greater experimentation can be expected, particularly on public television and in the later evening programs, but always within the range of toleration of the viewing audience on whom the industry depends for support.

——. "There Is a Man Who Can Do Something About Commercials." *TV Guide*, 19(13):6–8, 10, 12, 27 March 1971. **1G314**
The story of the TV Code Authority, headed by Stockton Helffrich, which reviews television commercials for compliance with the industry's TV Code. This is a forty-page pamphlet of rules and policies, first promulgated in 1952, and reviewed and revised as changing times dictate by a nine-member Review Board. The three major networks and two-thirds of the nation's television stations subscribe to the Code.

Gutkind, Lee A. "Censorship and the Cinema." *Cimarron Review*, 11:21–33, April 1970. **1G315**
A history of film censorship in the United States, beginning with the first municipal censorship ordinance, adopted in Chicago, 1907, and closing with the controversy over film classification. The author concludes with pros and cons on whether the cinema influences our society or merely reflects it.

"Gutter Politics and the First Amendment." *Valparaiso University Law Review*, 6:185–212, Winter 1972. **1G316**

A look at state laws containing provisions relating to "dirty" campaign tactics as seen in the light of a decade of Supreme Court decisions expanding the scope of protection of freedom of speech and press.

Guy, Daniel S., and Jack McDonald. "Government in the Sunshine: The Status of Open Meetings and Open Records Law in North Dakota." *North Dakota Law Review*, 53:51–80, 1976.
1G317
A history and analysis of the North Dakota open meetings and open records laws and the relevant court decisions.

Gwin Louis M., Jr. *Use of Federal Freedom of Information Legislation by Tennessee Newspapers to Obtain Government Information: A Historical and Survey Study.* Knoxville, Tenn., University of Tennessee, 1972. 111p. (Unpublished Master's thesis)
1G318
"The purposes of this study were (1) to determine the knowledge Tennessee newspaper publishers and editors have of the Freedom of Information Act, (2) to detail specific court cases where individual Tennessee newspaper publishers and editors have demonstrated their knowledge of the legislation and have implemented it successfully, and (3) to provide a set of guidelines for Tennessee newspaper publishers and editors to assist them in using the Freedom of Information Act for the purpose of obtaining non-classified public information from the various agencies of the federal government."

Gwyn, Robert J. "Opinion Advertising and the Free Market of Ideas." *Public Opinion Quarterly*, 34:246–55, Summer 1970. **1G319**
"This study assesses how well the advertising policies and practices of the major market mass media correspond to the standards set by the Commission on Freedom of the Press and the American Civil Liberties Union."

H

Haan, Jacques Den. *De Lagere Hartstochten; Meditaties over Pornografie*. The Hague, Bert Bakker, 1962. 172p. **1H1**

A collection of essays on pornography in England and the United States with references to action taken against various works of literary merit.

Haas, Sharon. "First Amendment Rights of Prisoners To Have Access to the News Media in Relation to Administrative Policy Bans Upon Such Access." *Pepperdine Law Review*, 1:382–403, 1974. **1H2**

The article looks at the problem from the point of view of the courts, prison administrators, the press, and the prisoners.

Hachten, William A. *The Supreme Court on Freedom of the Press: Decisions and Dissents*. Ames, Iowa, Iowa State University Press, 1968. 316p. **1H3**

A collection of decisions and dissents of the United States Supreme Court that relate to freedom of expression. The book "is not primarily concerned with the current state of the law of the press; it is concerned with the ideas and principles underpinning the freedom of our system of mass communication as they have been enunciated in decisions of the Supreme Court of the United States. It is an effort to pull together the Court's major statements and comments concerning the communication of information and ideas in a free and self-governing society." Some seventy excerpted decisions from twenty-eight justices relate to the areas of prior restraint and censorship, licensing and discriminatory taxation, contempt of court, pretrial publicity, libel immunity, freedom to report the news versus the right of privacy, press freedom and the post office, freedom of motion pictures, freedom of broadcasting, government regulation of the business aspects of the press, and the press and antitrust laws.

Hadley, Edwin W. "Bias and Prejudice or the Case of the Seven Bishops." *Bos-*

ton University Law Review*, 32:265–86, June 1952. **1H4**

How James II in 1688 attempted to control the judiciary in the case of seven bishops charged with seditious libel, but the jury refused to be intimidated. The account is presented as a crisis in English law.

Hagelin, Theodore M. "The First Amendment Stake in New Technology: The Broadcast–Cable Controversy." *University of Cincinnati Law Review*, 44:427–524, 1975. **1H5**

"The thesis of this article is that a technological solution to the first amendment dilemma in the electronic mass media is possible and that coaxial cable is the most likely prospect."

Hagens, William J. "The Moss Committee and Freedom of Information." *Michigan Academician*, 4:205–16, Fall 1971. **1H6**

"This paper presents an account of the House Government Information Subcommittee (Moss Committee), Congress' major vehicle against executive news censorship, and its struggle for freedom of government information. The study covers the creation of the Subcommittee and its first 11 years of operation which culminated in the passage of the 'Freedom of Information' Act of 1966 (FOI Act). Following the discussion of the creation of the Act is an analysis of its impact and effectiveness, concluding with some insight into the future of the issue."

Hagglund, Clarence E. "The Law of Libel: A Balance Between Personal Reputation and Freedom of the Press." *Federation of Insurance Council Quarterly*, 26:27–41, Fall 1975. **1H7**

"This article will attempt to review case law that deals with the subjects of malice and truth, personal reputation, and constitutional privileges and limitations relating to the law of libel. The article will deal essentially with the issues of liability as to newspapers or other publications that have allegedly printed libelous statements."

Hague, Mary A. "The Radical Right and the Library." In Mary L. Bundy and Sylvia Goldstein, *eds.*, *Library's Public Revisited*. School of Library and Information Service, University of Maryland, 1967, pp. 60–84. **1H8**

The author discusses the antidemocratic movements in America, the character of the radical right, the groups identified as rightist today, and efforts at library censorship of rightist literature and rightist group efforts to purge libraries of works they dislike.

Hague, Thomas. *A Letter to the Rt. Hon. S. Percival; Being a Statement of the Conduct of H.R.H. Duke of Sussex, Towards Mr. Hague, and of The Causes Which Led to the Prosecution of Woodfall*. London, W. Horseman, 1809. 42p; 9p. **1H9**

The author presents in boring detail his quarrel with the Duke of Sussex over falsely accusing him of writing libelous articles about His Royal Highness for Hunt's *Examiner*. Hague also complains that the Duke had hired the printer Woodfall to print anonymous handbills, which were posted throughout London, charging Hague with libel. Hague preferred charges against Woodfall, but the case was not brought to trial.

Haight, Anne L. *Banned Books; Informal Notes on Some Books Banned for Various Reasons at Various Times and in Various Places*. 3d ed. New York, Bowker, 1970. 166p. **1H10**

An up-dating of a work, first published in 1955, "a chronological list of books banned from 387 B.C. into the 1960's, compiled only with the idea of showing the trend ₍rather than comprehensive coverage₎ of censorship throughout the years and the change in thought and taste. It is a handbook, a quick reference work which touches upon most of the famous episodes in our sorry censorship history."

Haiman, Franklyn S. "The Fighting Words Doctrine: From Chaplinsky to

Brown." *Iowa Journal of Speech*, 3:4–28, Fall 1972. **1H11**
Traces the U.S. Supreme Court's opinions on the use of "fighting words" from the *Chaplinsky v. New Hampshire* decision in 1942 in which the Court upheld the conviction of a Jehovah's Witness member who used abusive language to a police officer, to *Brown v. Oklahoma* (1973) in which the majority of the court gave greater freedom to use of "fighting words."

————. *The First Freedoms: Speech, Press, Assembly*. New York, American Civil Liberties Union [1971]. 30p. **1H12**
Following an introduction which emphasizes the importance of freedom of expression in American society and notes the changing nature of the legal doctrine supporting it, the author describes the status of First Amendment freedoms: Where and when one may speak and what one may or may not say, the rights of students and teachers, the conflict between security of the state and the individual's right to criticize, and the legal status of libel and obscenity. He concludes that while the range of freedom of speech and press for American citizens is probably greater today than ever before, largely due to the courts' acceptance of dissent, these gains have not always been understood and accepted by the public at large.

————. *Freedom of Speech*. Skokie, Ill., National Textbook Company in Conjunction with the American Civil Liberties Union, 1976. 221p. **1H13**
The volume traces the development of the concept of freedom of speech and the press in our legal system, "explores the controversies and points of view that surround that issue in contemporary America, and provides the reader with a collection of key excerpts from landmark U.S. Supreme Court opinions and other historic documents which most eloquently explain these rights." Chapter 1 addresses those problems where the justification put forth for curbing speech is a concern for the security of the state; chapter 2 deals with limitations allegedly designed to maintain a peaceful and orderly public forum; chapter 3 surveys issues involving speech that is thought harmful to other persons; chapter 4 considers government regulations that purport to expand and purify the marketplace of ideas; and chapter 5, Why Freedom of Speech? presents the views of such diverse thinkers as Harold C. Gardiner, Harry M. Clor, Walter Berns, Thomas I. Emerson, Alexander Meiklejohn, John Stuart Mill, and Zechariah Chafee, Jr. Each chapter is introduced by a statement of the issues and a series of pertinent questions and concludes with a summary of the views and answers to some of the questions raised.

————. "Freedom of Speech and Its Relationship to Dissent." *National Association of Secondary School Principals Bulletin*, 54(350):22–29, December 1970. **1H14**
"Since time immemorial, teachers have complained about student apathy, lack of motivation, lack of interest in serious social problems. At last students are 'turned on.' But their manner of expressing themselves turns off people in authority. If we are to save and improve what we have of the democratic process and improve society, says Mr. Haiman, we must find a way to capitalize on the new motivation of the young. He lists a number of essential preconditions, some of which will surprise you."—Editor

————. "Freedom of Speech and the Repressive Backlash." *Civil Liberties*, 276:1, 6, March 1971. **1H15**
The massive backlash which has endangered freedom of speech and press is not so much a response to the escalation of violence but "is primarily an expression of intolerance toward the views being expressed, rather than to their particular mode of expression. What is at stake here, I think, is an attempt to suppress the growing advocacy of a counter-culture—a culture which rejects many of the basic values of the status quo—and it is for this reason that I see the problem as essentially a problem in freedom of speech."

————. "How Much of Our Speech Is Free?" *Civil Liberties Review*, 2(1):111–37, Winter 1975. **1H16**
A comprehensive survey of the changing interpretations of the First Amendment, recording the views of Mr. Justice Black who believed the Founding Fathers meant absolutely and literally what they said, and Professor Zechariah Chafee, Jr., who believed the original purpose of the Amendment was "to wipe out the common law of sedition," Professor Leonard Levy who found little support in history to either Black or Chafee, Mr. Justice Holmes and his "clear and present danger" doctrine, and Alexander Meiklejohn, who disagreed with the doctrine of Holmes, arguing that so long as speech contributed to the process of self-government, it was absolute. Professor Haiman devotes the major portion of his survey to an examination of three areas in which changing communication mores have placed strains upon the traditional interpretations of the First Amendment. They are: (1) nonverbal communications—picketing, sit-ins, flag desecration, topless dancing, and stage productions; (2) speech without political, religious, or social ideas—epithets and personal abuse, obscenity, "fighting words," and speech that is "utterly without redeeming social value"; and (3) the intrusion of the state into the communications marketplace including the idea of access expounded by Professor Jerome Barron. Haiman also comments on the status of commercial speech and the efforts to require counter-commercials. He concludes with comments on the ideas of philosopher Herbert Marcuse "who questions the widely accepted libertarian doctrine that freedom of speech is the *sine qua non* of all our other rights and freedoms," but is rather an opiate of the people and fails to provide a genuine avenue to social change.

————. *The Relationship of Age, Sex,*

Education and Urbanization to Free Speech Attitudes. Chicago, Speech Communication Association, 1972. 8p. (ED 77,052) **1H17**
"This paper reports the findings of two surveys, compares them to previous research, and discusses the combined implications. Both surveys (the first, conducted in Denmark in 1969, and the second, in Chicago and Evanston, Illinois, in 1971) reinforced previous findings of significant correlations between attitudes toward freedom of speech and the variables of age, sex, education, and urbanization. The author further discusses liberality of attitude as correlated with intravariable differences such as was found among younger and older adults, and suburban and central city residents, etc. From the collective research data a hypothesis is derived, namely, that levels of tolerance increase or diminish as the modes of expression in question appear to serve or threaten vested interests."

————. "Speech v. Privacy: Is There a Right Not To Be Spoken To?" *Northwestern University Law Review*, 67:153–99, May–June 1972. **1H18**
"By way of summary, what is proposed here is that in the clash of free speech and privacy interests surrounding claims of a right not to be spoken to, we must be careful not to allow our natural sympathy for tender psyches to beguile us into accepting serious erosions of the First Amendment. The human psyche, whether adult or juvenile, is tougher than most of its would-be protectors are inclined to admit. It is generally quite capable of taking care of itself. . . . Privacy will be adequately safeguarded if our right to escape from one another after the first exposure to unwelcome communication is made secure."

————. "Statement of the Speech Communication Association for the National Commission on Obscenity and Pornography." *Free Speech*, 21:3–5, November 1970. **1H19**
The statement, prepared by Professor Haiman and endorsed by the Association, addresses itself to the four questions raised by Congress in appointing the Commission: (1) The gravity of the situation. "The only gravity we perceive in the present situation in the United States with respect to so-called obscenity and pornography is not in any harm that the communicators of such material may do to those who read and listen, but rather in the repressive reaction to these who so lack confidence in the democratic process that they would substitute their own judgment or that of some governmental agency for the judgment of the natural marketplace in responding to such communication." (2) Definition. "The very difficulty, if not impossibility, of arriving at negotiable definitions of these terms by those who attempt the task, including our courts, is one of

the best reasons we know for abandoning the effort and abiding by the French proverb, 'chacun à son goût' (each to his own tastes)." (3) Harmful effects. "Since we believe in the principle of innocence until guilt is proven, we feel that the burden of proof is on those who maintain that there is such a causal connection and that this burden has not been met. . . . So-called obscene and pornographic communications are not 'overt acts against peace and good order' and there is no clear proof that they lead to such acts." (4) Adequacy of existing laws. "We do not think the situation can or will be improved by new legislation or further court opinions, for it is an area in which government control is inherently inappropriate."

———— *et al*. "Affirmative Means of Promoting Freedom of Expression." In Speech Communication Association, *Abstracts, 59th Annual Meeting*. New York, 1973, pp. 14–15. **1H20**
Abstracts of proposed solutions by Franklyn S. Haiman, Harriet Pilpel, and Richard Wright.

Haimbaugh, George D., Jr. "Obscenity: An End to Weighing?" *South Carolina Law Review*, 21:357–73, 1969. **1H21**
A review of and extensive commentary on the ideas expressed in two books: *The End of Obscenity* by Charles Rembar and *Tropic of Cancer on Trial* by E. R. Hutchison. Both books deal with the extensive litigation over Henry Miller's *Tropic of Cancer*. Rembar also considers the cases against *Lady Chatterley's Lover* and *Fanny Hill*. In addition the author looks at the Customs case against the Swedish film, *I Am Curious (Yellow)*.

————. "The Second Front: Free Expression versus Individual Dignity." *William and Mary Law Review*, 9:126–48, Fall 1967. **1H22**
"This article is concerned with the emergence, constitutional justification and scope of this new privilege [prohibiting a public official from recovering damages for a defamatory falsehood relating to his official conduct unless he proves that the statement was made with "actual malice"] which, as adapted, is serving as the workhorse or jeep of the Supreme Court's offensive in the Second Front area of state protection of individual dignity."

Haines, Rush T., II. "The Aftermath of Sheppard: Some Proposed Solutions to the Free Press–Fair Trial Controversy." *Journal of Criminal Law*, 59:234–47, June 1968. **1H23**
The purpose of the article is to examine the effects of the Supreme Court's suggestions in *Sheppard v. Maxwell* (1966) of means by which

prejudicial material in a criminal trial could be suppressed before resulting in the harm which necessitates remedial measures. "Of all the proposed solutions . . . the one that seems best suited for countering the constitutional arguments of the free press advocates while at the same time insuring fair trials is the statutory scheme." This would proscribe with specificity the dissemination of publication of certain material and the penalty for violation. The text of such a statute is offered, along with the text of a Recommended New Canon 20, proposed by the Medina Committee, and A Suggested Code of the Chicago Police Department.

Haldane, J. P. S. *Hands Off the Daily Worker*. [London, Daily Worker, 1941?] 16p. **1H24**
A protest against the threat to suppress the *Daily Worker*, under wartime Regulation 2D.

Haldeman-Julius, Emanuel. *My First 25 Years; Instead of a Footnote; An Autobiography*. [Gerard, Kans.], Haldeman-Julius Publications, 1949. 47p. (Also appears in *Critic and Guide*, May 1949) **1H25**
In this frank autobiography of the publisher of the Little Blue Books there are a number of references to censorship: pressures from the Catholic hierarchy in New York, Philadelphia, Detroit, and Fort Wayne, Ind., against newspapers to refuse advertisements for Little Blue Books, which were considered obscene and blasphemous; pressures from Christian Scientists, through Clarence Darrow, to stop publication of a critical biography of Mrs. Mary Baker Eddy; and a lengthy account of a lecture by Anthony Comstock and the confrontation by Emma Goldman, Alexander Berkman, and Ben Reitman.

Haldeman-Julius, Marcet. *Clarence Darrow's Two Great Trials; Reports of the Scopes Anti-Evolution Case and the Dr. Sweet Negro Trial*. Girard, Kans., Haldeman-Julius, 1927. 74p. (Big Blue Book, B-29; Reprinted from the *Haldeman-Julius Monthly*, September 1925, June 1926, and July 1926) **1H26**
Mrs. Haldeman-Julius gives her personal impressions of the Scopes evolution trial which she and her husband attended. The Sweet trial was a murder case.

————. "Is Arkansas Civilized?" *Debunker*, 9(1):3–16, 113–20, December 1928. **1H27**
The author describes her crusade in behalf of Charles Smith, arrested in Little Rock, Ark., for the distribution of atheist literature. The trial and conviction of Smith is reported in the January issue of *Debunker*, Arkansas Defends Its God (pp. 3–15).

Hale, G. E., and Rosemary D. Hale. "Competition or Control II: Radio and

Television Broadcasting." *University of Pennsylvania Law Review*, 107:585–620, March 1959. **1H28**
"The evils which result from the failure of the competitive mechanism to operate smoothly and equitably in an imperfect market have given rise to two theoretically distinct bodies of law, one aimed at strengthening the competitive forces which drive the self-regulating mechanism, and the other founded on an abandonment of the competitive principle in favor of direct government control. As a rule where industries generally considered 'public utilities' are involved, government attitudes and policies have tended toward the latter course. Often, however, elements of both 'competition' and 'control' appear in the pattern of laws applying to a particular utility. This Article explores the phenomenon as it occurs in the field of radio and television broadcasting."—Editor

Hale, Matthew. *The Moore Libel Suit. Argument of Hon. Matthew Hale, of Counsel for Plaintiff, Before the Jury, September 19, 1889*. Albany, N.Y., G. H. Reynolds, 1889. 19p. **1H29**
The case of Amasa R. Moore against New York editor James Gordon Bennett. Moore, a bank clerk, had charged the *Herald* with making false statements about him in articles on the run on the Manufacturers' National Bank of Troy. The jury found for the plaintiff.

Hale, Robert D. "Censorship: What A Bookseller Can Do About It." *Publishers' Weekly*, 200:26–28, 26 July 1971. **1H30**
A bookseller offers practical suggestions for avoiding censorship, for handling complaints, and for facing the issues. "The best way for the average bookseller to avoid censorship problems is to establish a positive bookstore image."

Haley, William *et al*. *The Freedom of the Press. Granada Guildhall Lectures, 1974, by Harold Evans, Lord Windlesham and Katharine Graham*. London, MacGibbon, 1974. 91p. **1H31**
Content: The Half-Free Press by Harold Evans. Government and the Media by Lord Windlesham. The Freedom of The American Press by Katharine Graham. Introduction by the chairman, Sir William Haley.

Halim, Abdul. *Law of Defamation and Malicious Prosecution. Revised by Vindeshwari Prasad and J. P. Bhatnagar. With a Foreword by Iqbal Ahmad*. 3d ed. Allahabad, Hind, 1960. 268p. **1H32**

Hall, Frank H. "Colorado's Six Years' Experience Without Judicial Canon 35." *American Bar Association Journal*, 48:1120–21, December 1962. **1H33**
"In 1956, the Colorado Supreme Court adopted a rule permitting judges in that state,

at their discretion, to permit the taking of pictures in court or the broadcasting or televising of courtroom proceedings. In this article, Justice Hall reports that the new rule is working well and that there have been none of the dire consequences that were predicted when the rule was adopted."

Hall, Grover C., Jr. "Reconciling Fair Trial and Free Press." *Alabama Lawyer*, 18:404–11, October 1957. **1H34**
A newspaper editor believes that conflicts between the two basic constitutional rights will be eased more adequately through the growing responsibility of the press than by devising new restrictions.

Hall, James, and Sandra Hall. *Australian Censorship: The XYZ of Love*. Sydney, New South Wales, Jack de Lissa, 1970. 148p. Illustrations by Bettan. **1H35**
A guide to sexual censorship in Australia consisting of definitions of terms, explanation of concepts, and identification of individuals and organizations concerned—from A (Academics, as agents of censorship) to Z (Zones, erogenous). Includes such entries as: banned books, breasts, Donald Leslie Chipp (Minister for Customs and Excise), Customs Department, graffiti, hair (pubic) and hair (public), Norman Lindsay, marriage manuals, National Literature Board of Review, nipple, obscenity, *Oz*, *Playboy*, *Portnoy's Complaint*, radio, Sir Arthur Rylah, standards (community), television, theatre, UBU (Sydney underground film-making cooperative), violence, Welfare and Decency Society, Eric Archibald Willis, words (four-letter), wowsers, and X-certificate (for films). Accompanied by humorous cartoons. The work was printed in Hong Kong.

Hall, James A., and Stephen C. Jones. "Pappas and Caldwell: The Newsman's Privilege—Two Judicial Views." *Massachusetts Law Quarterly*, 56:155–70, June 1971. **1H36**
"Since the *Pappas* decision [In the Matter of Pappas, 1972], denying newsmen a constitutional privilege to protect their confidential sources and information appears to be in conflict with *Caldwell* [United States v. Caldwell, 1972], and both cases are presently before the United States Supreme Court, this note will attempt to examine the facts and opinions of the respective cases to determine whether the facts are significantly distinguishable and, if not, whether the *Caldwell* approach to the issue of a newsman's privilege should have been more persuasive on the Supreme Judicial Court in *Pappas*."

[**Hall, Radclyffe.**] "Publisher's Note." In her *The Well of Loneliness*. New York, Covici-Friede, 1929. Four unnumbered preliminary pages. **1H37**
In this first American publication of Miss Hall's novel on a homosexual theme, the publisher recounts the events of the suppression of the British edition published by Jonathan

Cape, the court action, and the widespread support of the book by leading British and American literary figures and some of the most eminent journals.

[**Hall, Rebecca W.**] "Contempt of Court by Newspaper Publication." *Connecticut Bar Journal*, 24:366–72, September 1950. **1H38**
The evolution of contempt action against the press from the case of *State v. Howell* (1908) to *Maryland v. Baltimore Radio Show* (1949). In the Howell case the press was held in contempt; in the Maryland case the court found no clear and present danger to the accused's right to a fair trial.

[**Hall, Robert.**] *Correspondence between the Rev. R. Hall . . . his friends and the writer of the review, which appeared in the Christian Guardian for Jan. 1822, of "Mr. Hall's Apology for The Freedom of the Press and for General Liberty." Reprinted in London from the Leicester Journal, together with a conclusion by the Reviewer*. Leicester, England, J. Price, 1822. 74p. (Numerous other editions appeared in Leicester and London) **1H39**
The reviewer writes in the *Christian Guardian*: "It is with sorrow that we observe the republication under his own immediate sanction, of Mr. Hall's 'Apology for the Freedom of the Press.' Since its publication about 30 years ago, remembered only as 'one of the sins of the author's youth' the whole pamphlet argues for the supremacy and infallibility of the people, and of the necessity of paying the utmost obedience to the least expression of their will." Hall answers his critic with a vigorous statement: "There is not a principle in it which I can conscientiously retract." He had reissued the *Apology* with some corrections and alterations.

Hall, Ted. *The Censors; Who Are They?* Newark, N.J., Newark News, 1954. 16p. **1H40**
A series of seven articles reprinted from the *Newark News* deal with censorship efforts in a number of North Jersey communities—pressures in the name of patriotism brought by the New Jersey Anti-Communist League.

Hall, Walter L. "Right of Access: How Has It Fared in Court?" *Editor & Publisher*, 106:24, 26, 10 November 1973. **1H41**
"The decisions most favorable to Prof. Barron's theory [of access] and which tend to support the Florida Supreme Court Decision follow the 'dedicated to public use' theory. . . . The second line of decisions follow the more conventional path in which newspapers are private in nature and follow the *Amalgamated* line." [Chicago Joint Board, Amalgamated Clothing Workers of America v. Chicago Tribune Co., 1970.]

Halliwell, Leslie. "Censorship." In his

The Filmgoer's Book of Quotes. London, Hart-Davis, MacGibbon, 1973, pp. 20–23. **1H42**
A collection of quips about censorship in the American and British film industry, such as: Bob Hope's 1962 wisecrack, "Nowadays when a film is awarded the Production Code seal the producer cries: 'Where have we failed?' " The Chicago Chief of Police's remark in the thirties: "Any film that isn't fit to be shown to my youngest child isn't fit to be shown to anybody." The deletion of the remark by Marlene Dietrich in *Destry Rides Again* as she tucked money down her bosom: "There's gold in them thar hills."

Halloran, J. D. "Clear Responsibilities." In his *Control or Consent?* London, Sheed & Ward, 1963. 246p. **1H43**
The author deals with what he calls Catholics' preoccupation with censorship of sex materials, a practice which is self-defeating, ineffectual, and detracts from more serious moral issues. "Basically, censorship is nothing but a fraudulent substitute for personal judgment, and our efforts should be directed to producing an environment where judgments may develop rather than one in which decisions are made for us."

Halpern, Harold M. "Defamation via Television Ad Lib; Libel and Slander Distinctions." *Buffalo Law Review*, 6:325–28, Spring 1957. **1H44**
Re: *Shor v. Billingsley*, 158 N.Y.S.2d 476 (1957), in which the court held that defamatory matter not read from a prepared script constitutes libel and not slander.

Hamalian, Leo. "Nobody Knows My Names: Samuel Roth and the Underside of Modern Letters." *Journal of Modern Literature*, 3:889–921, April 1974. (A revised and expanded version of his article in *Journal of Popular Culture*, Spring 1968) **1H45**
The career of Samuel Roth, who was "without question the biggest booklegger who ever ripped off a legitimate author." Roth is, perhaps, best known today for the obscenity case, *Roth v. United States* (1957) in which the U.S. Supreme Court ruled that obscenity was not guaranteed under the First Amendment. The article describes Roth's fabulous career as legitimate publisher and bookseller, associate of numerous literary figures, literary pirate and plagiarist, and publisher of exposés (Hoover and Harding). He is also considered as publisher of a mild form of pornography that, alongside present-day hard-core pornography, "seems about as exciting as a filthy sock." A photograph of Roth appears on the cover.

——. "The Secret Careers of Sam Roth." *Journal of Popular Culture*,

1:317–38, Spring 1968. (A revised and expanded version appear in *3 × 3*, published by Harion Press, Saratoga Springs, N.Y., 1969, pp. 65–110, and as a separate reprint by the same publisher.) **1H46**
An account of the "pseudo-publishing" world of Samuel Roth, pornographer, pirate, ghost writer, talent tracker, and aspiring artist. He is known for his pirating of *Ulysses* and *Lady Chatterley's Lover*, which brought him into difficulty with the law as well as the literary world; for his publication of the fake autobiography, *I Was Hitler's Doctor*; and for the celebrated U.S. Supreme Court obscenity case, *Roth v. United States* (1957). Appearing before the Kefauver Committee to study pornography (1955) Roth testified to having been arrested seven times for his publishing activities and being imprisoned four times, sentences ranging from sixty days to three years. One of his jail sentences was for publishing *Waggish Tales of the Czech* (Gesta Czechorum), falsely attributed to Alexander Woollcott.

Hames, Peter. "Censorship—Stafford Style." *Film: British Federation of Film Societies Monthly Journal*, 34:1–2, February 1976. **1H47**
An account of the threatened censorship of the Stafford Film Society's showing of *Blow Out* and *Trash*.

Hamilton, Adrian. *The Infamous Essay on Woman, or John Wilkes Seated Between Vice and Virtue*. London, Deutsch, 1972. 256p. ("Of this book there are two thousand numbered copies. Each copy is accompanied by a special reading copy, identical in content and also limited to two thousand copies, to form a [boxed] set of two volumes.") **1H48**
A facsimile reproduction of a contemporary edition of John Wilkes's *Essay on Woman*, interleaved with a facsimile of Pope's *Essay on Man* of which the Wilkes poem was a risqué parody. In addition, the compiler has published a facsimile of Wilkes's controversial political paper, *North Briton*, number XLV (N207) and a facsimile of a number of contemporry pamphlets for and against Wilkes, including the Rev. John Kidgell's attack on Wilkes (K96), *A Letter to J. Kidgell Containing A Full Answer to His Narrative*, attributed to John Almon and J. Musgrave, and numerous pieces of correspondence between Wilkes and various figures in the affair. Also reproduced are many illustrations of persons and places figuring in the controversy. The compiler has also retold the Wilkes story from an examination of official papers as well as from contemporary and later accounts.

Hamilton, David C. *Advertising: The Right to Refuse*. Columbia, Mo., Free-dom of Information Center, School of Journalism, University of Missouri at Columbia, 1967. 6p. (Report no. 187) **1H49**
"With the exception of *Uhlman v. Sherman*, decided in 1919 in the Defiance County, Ohio, Court of Common Pleas, judicial opinion has held that the publishing of a newspaper is a private business, as distinguished from a business affected with the public interest, and that a publisher is under no obligation to accept advertising from all who apply for it."

Hamilton, Douglas C. "As Times Goes by: Gertz v. Robert Welch, Inc. and Its Effect on California Defamation Law." *Pacific Law Journal*, 6:565–89, July 1975. **1H50**
"This comment reviews the development of the constitutional privilege and the status of the California law of civil defamation prior to the *Gertz* decision, and then analyzes how that law is affected by this recent case, examining in turn the impact of *Gertz* upon the cause of action and upon the defenses."

Hamilton, Mary Ann. "Modern Movies Are Corrupting My Children." *St. Anthony Messenger*, 77:20–23, November 1969. Reply by James W. Arnold, 77:24–27, November 1969. **1H51**
"Erotic stories that were once read in the seclusion of one's room are now wide-screen spectacles, and millions who never would have read the book are flocking to theaters. An increasing number of these movie-goers are teenagers whose moral ideas are put in peril." *St. Anthony Messenger*'s movie critic, James W. Arnold, discusses the art of contemporary cinema, providing practical guidelines in his reply to Mrs. Hamilton.

Hamilton, William. "The First Amendment Does Not Relieve a Newspaper Reporter of the Obligation that All Citizens Have to Respond to a Grand Jury Subpoena and Answer Questions Relevant to a Criminal Investigation." *Texas Southern University Law Review*, 2:369–82, Winter 1973. **1H52**
Re: *Branzburg v. Hayes*, *In the Matter of Paul Pappas*, and *United States v. Caldwell*, 408 U.S. 665, 1972.

Hamilton, William "Obscenity, Protest, and War." *New Mexico Quarterly*, 37:363–67, Winter 1968. **1H53**
Obscenity is the only kind of moral language that rightly expresses the moral horrors of the war in Vietnam. Nothing sexual or anal are as obscene as war. Those who sponsor the war have preempted the grand old words of "commitment" and "sacrifice."

Hamlin, Peter R. *A Case Study of the*

Fairfax County, Virginia, Censorship Controversy, 1963. Urbana, Ill., Graduate School of Library Science, University of Illinois, 1968. 22p. (Occasional Papers, no. 95) **1H54**
"Censorship advocates in Fairfax County exerted considerable pressure for removal of offending films and books, but [librarian Mary] McCulloch's firmness, the public response, and the desire of the Board of Supervisors to stay out of the fracas effectively defeated the censors."

Hamling, William L., *ed. Obscenity: Censorship or Free Choice*. San Diego, Calif., Greenleaf Classics, 1971. 367p. **1H55**
A collection of prize-winning essays in a national college competition, introduced by remarks from the judges, Martha Boaz, Donald Cheek, Arthur Knight, James Powers, William Shinto, and the editor and publisher, William L. Hamling. Essay winners: Del Lane, David W. Gossett, and Lloyd R. Trussell, grand prize winners; Steven J. Bagby, William Fowler, Richard Sigler, Norman J. Fulco, Bradley M. Stanley, Mark Hicks, Russ A. Rueger, Mark T. Backman, Michael Cunningham, Kenneth D. Hoffman, Michael D. Gose, Elizabeth H. Sullivan, Monte W. Gast, Curtis Philips, Carl S. Sparkman, Hannah Sampson, John D. Merrill, Daniel G. Russell, Madeline A. Crosby, and Clarence R. Schmidt. Prizes ranged from $500 to $5,000.

Hammitt, Harry. *Advertising Pressures on Media*. Columbia, Mo., Freedom of Information Center, School of Journalism, University of Missouri at Columbia, 1977. 7p. (Report no. 367) **1H56**
"The author offers a review of instances in which advertisers have exerted either subtle or blatant pressures on editorial policies of newspapers and magazines."

Hammond, Edward H., and Thomas A. Dawes. "Student Press and the First Amendment." *NASPA Journal* (National Association of Student Personnel Administrators), 10:168–77, October 1972. **1H57**
"The purpose of this article is to review some recent developments in the law with reference to student publications at public institutions of higher learning. It represents a summary of recent legal activity in this field, and makes an attempt to isolate established precedent and to project trends in legal thought which bear upon the problems raised by the ever growing student press. The paper is limited to public institutions, where the regulation of student publications constitutes a clear case of state action and is thus liable to judicial scrutiny for conformation to constitutional principles."

Hammond, Herbert J. "*Gertz v. Robert Welch, Inc.*: New Contours on the Libel

Landscape—A Pyrrhic Victory for the Plaintiffs." *New York University Review of Law and Social Change*, 5:89–114, Winter 1975. **1H58**
"This Comment will analyze the ₁U.S. Supreme₁ Court's new doctrinal approach and *Gertz*'s three far-reaching results: the abandonment of strict liability in libel, the requirement that plaintiffs prove actual damage, and the proscription on the award of punitive damages except upon proof of malice. Finally, this Comment will suggest a modification of the *Rosenbloom* model which it is believed is better tailored to protecting both the individual's reputation and society's interest in a free press."

Hand, Learned. *The Arts and Craft of Judging; the Decisions of Judge Learned Hand*. Edited & Annotated, with an Introduction, by Hershel Shanks. New York, Macmillan, 1968. 335p. **1H59**
Among Judge Hand's decisions reproduced in this volume are two in the area of obscenity (*United States v. Kennerly*, 1913, and *United States v. Levine*, 1936); one decision on libel (*Burton v. Crowell Publishing Co.*, 1936); and two on the limits of political speech (*United States v. Dennis*, 1950, and *Masses Publishing Co. v. Patten*, 1917).

Handler, Joel F., and William A. Klein. "The Defense of Privilege in Defamation Suits Against Government Executive Officials." *Harvard Law Review*, 74:44–79, November 1960. (Reprinted in *PEAL Quarterly*, March 1962) **1H60**
"Using a recent Supreme Court decision as a point of reference, the authors reexamine the basis for and proper extent of the privilege granted an executive officer for defamatory statements made in his official capacity. Their analysis suggests that the traditional analogy to the absolute privilege accorded judges is not sufficiently defined, and that, barring government acceptance of liability for the torts of its officers, a new approach to privilege would often provide a more satisfactory resolution of the conflicting interests involved."

Handler, Michael. "The Expanding Right to Publish." *University of Pittsburgh Law Review*, 32:450–56, Spring 1971. **1H61**
Re: *Greenbelt Cooperative Publishing Assn'n., Inc. v. Bresler*, 1970. The U.S. Supreme Court reversed a decision of the Court of Appeals of Maryland which had awarded the plaintiff compensatory and punitive damages in a libel case against a weekly newspaper.

Handley, W. Scott. *Sheppard v. Maxwell: A Study of Impact*. Madison, Wis., University of Wisconsin, 1975. 193p. (Unpublished Master's thesis) **1H62**
"Major conclusions of this study are that the

Sheppard guidelines for controlling problems of prejudice and publicity are performing well and that their performance has been satisfactory to the U.S. Supreme Court. This study also concluded that there is little or no chance of their being amended."

Handlin, Joseph J. "Communications Law." *Annual Survey of American Law*, 1974–75:623–39, Summer 1976. **1H63**
Topics: cross-ownership, role of minorities in the licensing process, the prime time access rule, and the fairness doctrine.

Hanks, William E. "Mass Media and the First Amendment." *Speech Teacher*, 24:107–17, March 1975. **1H64**
"This article presents a series of five classroom exercises based on recent Supreme Court decisions on the First Amendment and mass media. Each case is discussed, and critical questions are listed for the instructor's use in post exercise discussion." The five cases are: (1) *Pittsburgh Press Company v. Pittsburgh Commission on Human Relations* (1973), on the issue of sex labeled want ads for employment; (2) *Paris Adult Theatre I v. Slaton* (1973), a recent Supreme Court decision on obscenity; (3) *United States v. Caldwell* (1972), a decision denying constitutional immunity from prosecution to reporters who refuse to appear before a grand jury; (4) the 1971 Pentagon Papers cases (*New York Times v. United States* and *United States v. Washington Post*), in which the Court attempted to determine whether prior restraint of classified information could be justified on national security grounds; and (5) *Miami Herald v. Tornillo* (1974), in which guaranteed right of reply by political candidates was declared unconstitutional."

Hanks, William E., and Martin Lazar. "Using the Fairness Doctrine: Case History of a Learning Project." *Journal of Broadcasting*, 16:475–83, Fall 1972. **1H65**
"The purpose of this paper is to describe those efforts to present a convincing case that anti-Army recruitment ads should be aired under provisions of the Fairness Doctrine."

Hannaker, Michael J. "Misinterpreting the Supreme Court: An Analysis of How the Constitutional Privilege to Defame Has Been Incorrectly Expanded." *Idaho Law Review*, 10:213–22, Spring 1974. **1H66**
Criticism of the United States Supreme Court's decision on defamation in *Rosenbloom v. Metromedia, Inc.* (1971) and the "misinterpretation" of the decision by courts and commentators.

Hannigan, Michael J., and Francis J. Nealon. "The Freedom of Information Act—The Parameters of the Exemptions." *Georgetown Law Journal*, 62:177–207, October 1973. **1H67**

"This Note will review, exemption by exemption, the courts' interpretation of the Freedom of Information Act and draw the parameters of exemptions under the Act." The author finds that the nine exemptions establish withholding standards that are too general to provide clear guidance to this issue. The courts have relied on the legislative history of the Act and their own notions as to what should be made public.

Hansen, C. J. "Contempt Power in Montana; A Cloud on Freedom of the Press." *Montana Law Review*, 18:68–85, Fall 1956. **1H68**
"This paper will outline the current federal view of contempt by publication and explore the Montana decisions on the subject. Our purpose is to show that the Montana cases, while in harmony with federal law at the time they were rendered, would, if followed today, be struck down as unconstitutional."

Hanson, Arthur B. *Libel and Related Torts*. New York, American Newspaper Publishers Foundation, 1969. 2 vols. (Issued with pocket part supplements) **1H69**
Vol. 1. Case and Comment: Defamation, Publication, Complete Defenses, Remedies, Actions, Criminal Defamation, Related Torts (including Right of Privacy), and Prognosis in The Newsroom. Vol. 2. Defamation Statutes of the United States and Canada—Texts of State and Provincial Statutes.

———. "The Right to Know: Fair Comment—Twentieth Century." *Villanova Law Review*, 12:751–63, Summer 1967. **1H70**
While, historically, libel laws existed before guarantees of free speech, "conceptually, it must be recognized that libel is carved out of the right of free speech—freedom of speech is not simply that which remains after the application of the laws of libel." The author believes that the *New York Times* decision enlarged free speech in two ways—by including "false statements of fact in the qualified privilege for discussion of public officials" and by redefining "malice" to require that "the plaintiff must show that the speaker knew that the statement was false or that he was reckless."

Hanson, Elisha. "Canon 35—Press, Radio and Television Coverage of the Courts." *Alabama Lawyer*, 16:248–67, July 1955. **1H71**
A review of the history of Canon 35, first adopted by the American Bar Association in 1937, with evidence of a need to modify it in light of modern broadcasting and photographic technology.

Hanson, Gillian. *Original Skin: Nudity*

and Sex in Cinema and Theatre. London, Stacey, 1970. 192p.   **1H72**
A look at the contemporary phenomenon of sex and nudity on the screen and the stage—how it came about in England, the United States, and certain other nations, and what has happened to censorship. The author considers the two-way play between theater and cinema, the serious erotica and the sexploitation pieces, and the debate among the critics over pornography and the arts. The merits of total freedom in the arts which has produced such vigor and excitement in recent years, the author observes, can also lead to a degradation of the arts.

Hanson, Wallace. "Pornography for the People." *Popular Photography*, 70:77–79, February 1972.   **1H73**
Advice to amateur photographers who are considering making pictures that may be considered obscene. "The evidence of one's senses notwithstanding, porne in the U.S. is, in the long run, unprofitable and dangerous from a legal point of view. Better see a lawyer before trying it yourself."

Harcourt, J. M. "The Banning of 'Upsurge.' " *Overland*, 46:30–33, Summer 1970–71.   **1H74**
The author of *Upsurge* gives an account of the 1934 banning of his novel in Australia. It was one of the first works to be placed on the *Index Expurgatorius Australianus*, but was recently removed from the list.

Harding, Ronald. "Freedom of Speech: One Step Backward: *Columbia Broadcasting Sys. Inc., v. Democratic National Comm.*" *New England Law Review*, 9:321–31, Winter 1974.   **1H75**
"On May 29, 1973, the United States Supreme Court ruled that radio and television licensees did not violate the Federal Communications Act or the First Amendment by refusing to sell editorial advertising to all who sought it. The ruling leaves the sale of such air time to the discretion of licensees, as long as they meet the minimum requirements of the fairness doctrine."

"Hard-nosed about Hard-core." *Time*, 102(1):42, 45, 2 July 1973.   **1H76**
News and commentary on the U.S. Supreme Court's decision shifting the responsibility for judging obscenity to the jurisdiction of state and local communities.

Hardt, Hanno. *Shield Legislation for Journalists: A Bibliography*. Iowa City, School of Journalism, University of Iowa, 1973. 37p.   **1H77**
The bibliography includes a listing of secondary sources, extracts of state laws, and decisions of recent court cases; it lists states having shield laws and those currently debating their adoption.

Hardy, Ashton R. "What the FCC's Fairness Doctrine Report Means to Grass-roots Station Management." *Television/Radio Age*, 22(8):32–33, 64, 11 November 1974.   **1H78**
This and a subsequent article, The Fairness Doctrine: How Much Opportunity Should Be Provided for Contrasting Views? (December 1974) were prepared by the FCC's General Counsel and an attorney in his office.

Hardy, Clifford A. "Censorship and the Curriculum." *Educational Leadership*, 31:10–11, 13, October 1973. **1H79**
"The persistent efforts of a handful of persons can often result in the banning of a particular text or in its alteration or modification," as shown by examples in various states and communities.

———, and Paul J. Cowan. "Science and Censorship." *Science and Children*, 12:26–27, September 1974.   **1H80**
The theory of evolution is the target of textbook censors in California, Texas, and Tennessee, where laws and state board regulations govern the treatment of the subject in secondary and elementary schools.

Hardy, Forsythe. "Censorship and Film Societies." In Charles Davy, *ed.*, *Footnotes to the Film*. New York, Oxford University Press, 1937, pp. 264–78.   **1H81**
The author charges the film censor with deliberate censorship of political ideas to avoid controversial issues, as evidenced by the case of *The Peace of Britain*, held up by the British Board of Film Censors, until public opinion forced its release. The Film Society, founded in London in 1925, was given permission by the London County Council to show films not submitted to the censor. Societies outside London have been handicapped by "the whimsies and perversities" of local licensing councils.

Hardy, Frank. *The Hard Way: The Story Behind "Power Without Glory."* Sydney, Australia, 1961. 256p.   **1H82**
An account of the prosecution of the author for criminal libel for his novel, *Power Without Glory*, by Ross Franklyn, *pseud.* "This book, *The Hard Way*, is the inside story of *Power Without Glory*: How it was conceived, how the material was gathered, how it was written, printed and published; of the courts and jails and how named and nameless people rallied to defend their rights and liberties." Despite Hardy's acquittal by the jury, efforts continued to suppress the book, to persecute the author and discredit him as a Communist. In the prologue, Hardy also refers to the difficulty in publishing *The Story Behind "Power Without Glory."*

[Hardy, Thomas, and John Horne Tooke.] ["The Treason Trials."] In Roland Bartel, *ed.*, *Liberty and Terror in England; Reactions to the French Revolution*. Boston, Heath, 1965, pp. 81–105.   **1H83**
A collection of documents relating to the treason trials of Thomas Hardy (H89–92) and John Horne Tooke (T153) in the period of hysteria that swept England during the French Revolution. The source material, arranged for use in preparing college research papers, includes Royal proclamations on seditious meetings and writings, excerpts from the trial proceedings, and contemporary press accounts.

Hargis, Billy J. *The Death of Freedom of Speech in the U.S.A.* Tulsa, Christian Crusade, 1967. 40p.   **1H84**
An attack on the fairness doctrine of the Federal Communications Commission as acting primarily against conservative and right-wing groups. The fundamentalist preacher charges Franklin H. Littell and the Institute for American Democracy which he heads as "fronts for an inspired attack against freedom of speech for Christian conservatives which began when President John F. Kennedy entered the White House in 1961." Also, behind the scenes in the attack, Hargis charges, are Walter Reuther, the National Council of Churches, and the Anti-Defamation League.

[Harman, Moses.] "More Legalized Robbery—The Govan Case." *Lucifer: The Light Bearer*, 5(2):9–10, 26 January 1901.   **1H85**
Deals with the prosecution of Charles L. Govan, editor of *Discontent*, a weekly paper published at Home, Wash. Govan was a philosophical anarchist and his arrest reflected a nationwide concern with the spread of political radicalism. In the 14 September issue, appearing a week after the assassination of President McKinley, Editor Harman comments on the tragedy and the aftermath in which the editor of *Free Society* was arrested in Chicago for possible complicity with Czolgosz, the assassin. Subsequent issues dealt with the anarchist movement in the United States and the opposition of the government and the press.

———. *The Next Revolution: Or Woman's Emancipation from Sex Slavery* (No. 2). Valley Falls, Kans., Lucifer Publishing Co., 1890? 72p.   **1H86**
A collection of articles by Moses Harman and others denouncing the double standard of sexual morality and promoting the cause of sexual freedom for women and the case for birth control. A number of the articles attack Anthony Comstock and the vice societies for their attempt to suppress the movement on grounds of obscenity. Instances of persecution are cited, including the trial of Harman for publishing *Lucifer, the Light Bearer*, which appears on pages 49–54.

Harmonay, Maureen. "Broadcast Re-

sponsibility and Children's Rights." *Journal of Current Social Issues*, 12(3):30–34, Summer 1975. **1H87**
"The seesaw juggling of corporate responsibility and broadcast profitability should be balanced so that children's rights, and thereby the future of society, are protected." Much of the discussion deals with the work of Action for Children's Television (ACT) and its voice against overcommercialism in television directed to young children.

Harper, Jerry L. "Kansas Open Meetings Act of 1972." *Journal of the Kansas Bar Association*, 43:257–62+, Winter 1974. **1H88**

₍Harrington, Leicester Fitzgerald Charles Stanhope, 5th earl.₎ *Sketch of the History and Influence of the Press in British India; Containing Remarks on the Effects of a Free Press on Subsidiary Alliances; on the Delays of Office; on Superstition; on the Administration of Justice; on Flogging; and on Agriculture. Also, on the Dangers of a Free Press, and the Licentiousness of a Censorship. . . . By Leicester Stanhope.* London, C. Chapple, 1823. 194p. **1H89**
"All history demonstrates that nothing tends so much to avert revolutions, as those timely and temperate reforms which result from free discussion." Content: State of the Press in India, Previous to the Establishment of a Censorship. Establishment of Press Censorship in British India. Military Disturbances at Madras. Abolition of the Censorship. Summary Transportation Without Trial. Effects of a Free Press on the Governments of the Subsidiary States. Effects to be Expected from a Free Press in Goa. Effects of a Free Press on Superstition, on the Administration of Justice, and in Preventing Flogging. Dangers of a Free Press. The Licentiousness of a Press under Censorship.

Harris, Max. *The Angry Eye*. Sydney, Australia, Pergamon, 1973. 254p. **1H90**
A number of the essays in this collection from the writings of an Australian literary journalist deal with issues on freedom *in* and *of* the press: Opinion Journalists in Australia. The Groves of Erotica. The Sad Decline of Varsity Satire Into Unfunny Pornography. The Fragile Right of Personal Privacy. An article, Should Our Censors Be Censored, appears in the January 1952 issue of *Ern Malley's Journal* (Melbourne).

Harris, R. H. "Florida Right of Reply Statute Held Unconstitutional." *Cumberland-Samford Law Review*, 5:535–42, Winter 1975. **1H91**
Re: *Miami Herald Publishing Co. v. Tornillo* (1974), in which the U.S. Supreme Court held that Florida's right to reply statute was unconstitutional, a violation of the First Amendment guarantee of a free press.

Harris, Sara. *The Puritan Jungle: America's Sexual Underground*. New York, Putnam, 1969. 193p. **1H92**
Chapter 1 contains interviews with Maryland movie censors; several chapters deal with erotic and pornographic movie production; chapter 11 discusses the way mailing lists are compiled for pornography; and chapter 12 consists of an interview with lawyer Stanley Fleischman and testimony from a Houston obscenity trial, a forerunner to the *Redrup* decision on obscenity before the U.S. Supreme Court.

Harris, Sydney J. "Censorship Satisfies Only Ruling Group." *Arizona English Bulletin*, 11:12, February 1969. (Reprint of 25 June 1968 syndicated column) **1H93**
Columnist Harris rejects as false the analogy between traffic signs which restrict our freedom of movement and censorship which restricts our freedom to read.

Harris, Wilson. "Influences and Restraints." In his *The Daily Press*. Cambridge, England, Cambridge University Press, 1943, pp. 70–91. **1H94**
The author believes that, while there is need for "unsleeping vigilance, encroachments on freedom ₍in Britain₎ amount to extremely little." Any restraints needed should be self-imposed, but an actual code of behavior "would be neither easy nor desirable."

Harrison, Brian. "Underneath the Victorians." *Victorian Studies*, 10:239–62, March 1967. **1H95**
In this critique of Steven Marcus's *The Other Victorians*, the author surveys the available contemporary accounts on "the underside of Victorian culture," and considers the suppression of information on prostitution, sexual perversion, venereal disease, and birth control. He attempts to answer the questions: Why is research on Victorian sexuality so scanty? What is the present state of knowledge of the area? What are the possibilities of future research?

₍Harrison, Donald C.₎ "Freedom to Communicate Versus Right to Privacy: Regulation of Offensive Speech Limited by Captive Audience Doctrine." *Washington Law Review*, 48:667–85, May 1973. **1H96**
"This note examines the conflict between free expression and privacy, focusing on the effect of privacy interests on the definition of obscenity and on the possibility of regulating nonobscene, sex-related expression through legislation designed to protect the individual's right to privacy from offensive contact." *State v. Rabe*, 1972.

———. "In Quest of a 'Decent Society': Obscenity and the Burger Court." *Washington Law Review*, 49:89–135, November 1973. **1H97**

"It is the thesis of this Comment that the Burger Court, in its search for constitutional certainty and structure, and for neutral principles of constitutional adjudicature, has seized upon the Meiklejohn model and applied it to the area of obscenity. It has done so gropingly and in an effort to restrict, not to expand, openness of expression; nevertheless, as a repository of constructive constitutional theory, *Miller* ₍*Miller v. California*, 1973₎ and its companion cases may prove more beneficial to future first amendment adjudication than all the confusing obscenity decisions of the Warren years."

Harrison, Gilbert A. "What's Fit to Print?" *Writer's Digest*, 50:54–55, January 1970. **1H98**
A reexamination of literary freedom, censorship, and good taste in relation to the people's right to know. What is to be printed, what is to be left out, and when and where should a journalist censor himself?

Harrison, Richard A. "Self-Censorship in Community Theatre." *Players Magazine*, 45:71–73, December–January 1970. **1H99**
The author attempts to define categories of themes that may be "censurable" in community theaters: attempted relevancy, "hard" theatre, and "let it all hang out" category. "The potential power of community theatre will ultimately be realized only when the professional director says 'no' to the self-censorship imposed by his boards, actors and audiences."

Harrison, Stanley. *Poor Men's Guardians: A Record of the Struggle for a Democratic Newspaper Press, 1763–1973*. London, Lawrence and Wishart, 1974. 256p. **1H100**
An editor of the *Daily Worker* traces the story of the radical and working-class press in Britain from "Wilkes and Liberty" agitators of the eighteenth century, through the prosecutions of William Cobbett and Richard Carlile, the revolt against the "taxes on knowledge," and the labor and militant Communist press of the present day. "This survey describes the struggle for a free press, the conflict of definitions of freedom that marked it from the beginning and the always tremendous stakes in the outcome of these struggles for the labor and progressive movement over a period of two centuries. It will show that the liberty flag beneath which the Fleet Street baronage operates is a stolen one; and that the achievements of generations of working people's effort and sacrifice, heroic in many of its phases, require for their preservation and further advancement, a more fundamental democratic new deal in the ownership and control of the press."

Hart, Harold H., *ed. Censorship: For &*

Against. New York, Hart, 1971. 255p. **1H101**
"Outstanding critics, lawyers, and publicists present their arguments for and against the control of books, magazines, movies, the stage, and government data." Contributors: Hollis Alpert, Judith Crist, Nat Hentoff, Joseph Howard, Charles H. Keating, Jr., Arthur Lelyveld, Max Lerner, Eugene McCarthy, Carey McWilliams, Charles Rembar, Ernest van den Haag, and Rebecca West.

Hart, Jim A. *Views on the News: The Developing Editorial Syndrome*. Carbondale, Ill., Southern Illinois University Press, 1970. 238p. **1H102**
In this history of the development of the newspaper editorial in England and in Colonial America are frequent references to the struggles of writers and printers to express their views on religion and politics, particularly views that were critical of Church or State. There are references to John Wilkes's *North Briton*, the *Craftsman* controversy, the Cato letters, the pamphleteering of Danial Defoe, the alternate pamphleteering and censoring of Roger L'Estrange, and Thomas Paine, whose ideas met with resistance on both sides of the Atlantic. In Colonial America, there are references to the cases of John Peter Zenger and Daniel Fowle and, in the early Federal period, to William Cobbett's *Porcupine Gazette*, and the pamphleteering of John T. Callender and William Duane.

Hartenberger, Werner K. "After Estes, What . . . ?"*Journal of Broadcasting*, 12:43–55, Winter 1967/68. (Reprinted in John M. Kittross and Kenneth Harwood, eds., *Free and Fair*, pp. 104–16) **1H103**
The United States Supreme Court's decision in the Billie Sol Estes case, *Estes v. Texas* (1965), has effectively diminished the position of the broadcast media in its arguments to televise trials. The author believes, however, that "as the role of the broadcast media becomes even more entrenched in the everyday activities of all the people, a change in emphases may well occur that will lead the Court to embrace the media as legitimate participants in trial proceedings."

———. *Cameras in the Courtroom: The Role of the Broadcast Media in the Free Press–Fair Trial Controversy*. Detroit, Wayne State University, 1966. 419p. (Ph.D. dissertation, University Microfilms, 69–11,542) **1H104**
The study includes the nature of the constitutional conflict, landmark cases in the controversy, a review of legislative, judicial, and self-imposed factors of restraint, and an examination of the major factors in contention,

with pertinent supporting and dissenting comment.

Harter, Stephen, and Charles Busha. "Libraries and Privacy Legislation." *Library Journal*, 101:475–81, 1 February 1976. **1H105**
In light of the Federal Privacy Act of 1974, the author reviews the complex issues involving the confidentiality of records of patron reading habits over against the concept of public access to files of a public institution. "The library profession is in need of an exacting legal code which outlines responsibilities of practicing librarians in protecting the privacy and confidentiality of library records belonging to its employees as well as its users."

Hartman, Harry. "The Comstock Lewd: 'Jurgen' and the Law—Updated." *Kalki*, 3:16–19, 1969. **1H106**
The author considers how James Branch Cabell's *Jurgen* would have fared in court under present obscenity rules where contemporary critics could be called upon to testify to its literary and social significance. The obscenity case against *Jurgen* in 1919 was summarily dismissed by the judge.

Hartman, William E., Marilyn Fithian, and Donald Johnson. "Nudism and the Law." In their *Nudist Society: An Authoritative, Complete Study of Nudism in America*. New York, Crown, 1970, pp. 211–37. **1H107**
The chapter deals with (1) opposition to the importation into the United States of nudist books, magazines, and other material—particularly if illustrated; (2) opposition of the Post Office Department to the distribution by mail of nudist publications; and (3) local opposition to the operation of nudist facilities. A chapter on the mass media, pages 201–11, discusses the treatment of nudism by the press.

Hartmann, John E. "The Minnesota Gag Law and the Fourteenth Amendment." *Minnesota History*, 37:161–73, December 1960. **1H108**
An account of the publishing activities of Howard A. Guilford and Jay M. Near, which led to the enactment of the Minnesota Act providing for injunction against obnoxious newspapers and magazines. The law was declared unconstitutional by the U.S. Supreme Court which ruled that the Fourteenth Amendment extended the First Amendment to the states.

Hartmann, Sadakichi. "Sadakichi on Censorship." *Sadakichi Hartmann Newsletter*, 5(2):1–2, Winter 1974/75. (Reprinted from *Art Critic*, March 1894) **1H109**
Hartmann describes his arrest at the instigation of the New England Watch and Ward Society for publication of his play, *Christ*. He calls for a revision of the Massachusetts obscen-

ity laws which would protect art and literature from arbitrary guardians of public morals.

Hartogs, Renatus. *Four-letter Word Games: The Psychology of Obscenity*. New York, Dell, 1967, 158p. **1H110**
A psychologist is convinced that obscenity is "a sub-language which, however primitive, reveals important and still mostly unexplored areas of personality and its interaction with the surrounding culture." He describes how four-letter words are used for ulterior aims: "omnipotence, aggressive self-assertion, displacement of anxiety, narcissistic prestige, and sexual power."

Harum, Albert E. "Broadcast Defamation: A Reformation of the Common Law Concepts." *Federal Communications Bar Journal*, 21:73–91, 1967. **1H111**
The Federal Communications Commission does not have the power to adjudicate private rights involving broadcast licensees; this is left to the state courts, subject to one preemptive prerogative exercised by Congress which immunizes broadcast licensees from action for defamatory broadcasts by legally qualified candidates for public office. The author suggests federal preemption in the matter of multistate libel cases.

———. "Choice of Law in Broadcast Defamation." *Florida Bar Journal*, 38:266–72, May 1964. **1H112**
Consideration of the complications arising in locating the tort and in fixing its legal consequences of a defamatory broadcast because the states where the broadcast is heard have nonuniform laws of defamation.

———. "Federal Occupation of Political Defamation." *American Bar Association Journal*, 49:1096–1100, November 1963. **1H113**
"Common law concepts have been virtually excluded from the law of defamation as it relates to radio and television broadcasts in the political arena, Mr. Harum states, as he reviews the equal-time provision of the Communications Act of 1934 and the problems it has raised for the Federal Communications Commission and the courts."

Harvell, Michael C. "Government Photocopying of Medical Journals Does Not Infringe Journal Copyright." *Boston University Law Review*, 54:689–701, May 1974. **1H114**
Re: *Williams & Wilkins Co. v. United States*, 1973.

Harvey, C. J. D. "The Problem of Censorship by an Ex-Censor." *Bolt* (South Africa), 1(2):8–13, August 1970. Comments: 1(3):48, November 1970. **1H115**
A former member of the South African Publi-

cations Control Board reflects on his experience in censoring works dealing with sexual immorality, obscenity, and nudity. He believes that those who are opposed to censorship in all forms are in a very small minority.

Harvey, Gregory M. "Protection of News Sources in Pennsylvania." *Pennsylvania Bar Association Quarterly*, 35:197–205, March 1964. **1H116**
"In Pennsylvania the newsman's privilege is only one of several statutory privileges applicable to certain occupational groups, including lawyers, physicians, clergymen and certified public accountants. Like the other occupational privileges, the statutory newsman's privilege is absolute, in that a court may not decline to apply the statute merely because the court believes that in a particular case the privilege should yield to some other interest. Such discretionary statutes have been suggested, but none has been adopted."

Harvey, James. *Pornography for Fun and Profit*. Los Angeles, Edka Books, 1967. 156p. **1H117**
A salacious exposé of the production of hardcore pornography, with references to difficulties with post office and police.

Harvey, James A. "Acting for the Children?" *Library Journal*, 98:602–5, 15 February 1973; also in *School Library Journal*, February 1973. Comments: *Library Journal*, 98:581, 15 February 1973; 98:1323, 15 April 1973; *School Library Journal*, 19:5, February 1973; 19:3, April 1973. **1H118**
The author challenges the proposals for reevaluation of children's books suggested by Sara Fenwick (*The Calendar*, January–April 1972) and Dorothy Broderick (*Library Journal*, 15 November 1971). "Both speak of discarding materials, not on the basis of traditional weeding considerations, but on the basis of highly subjective value judgments. That, then, seems to be the thrust of reevaluation. And, it becomes apparent that it is not synonymous with 'collection building.' It is more likely synonymous with censorship: the exclusion of literary materials because of the *views* of the authors."

————. "1971, with Hindsight." *Newsletter on Intellectual Freedom* (IFC-ALA), 21:1, 12–14, January 1972. **1H119**
A review of 1971 events involving intellectual freedom: The Pentagon Papers case, the developing conservatism of the U.S. Supreme Court and possible narrowing of free speech interpretations, episodes of book censorship in schools and libraries, censorship of motion pictures and stage plays, and the blackout of television programs.

————. "A Plowhorse in Thoroughbred's Clothing." *PLA Bulletin*

(Pennsylvania Library Association), 27:184–86, July 1972. **1H120**
The idea of intellectual freedom is not "a classy thoroughbred to be trotted out for study in library schools, for discussion at conventions, and occasionally for debate at cocktail parties in lieu of sex, politics, or religion" but "is more akin to a plowhorse" serving as a secure basis for the library's entire book-selection policy, as well as almost every other aspect of a library's functioning. "Put the plowhorse to work!"

————. "The Sky-Blue Tangled Web and How It Came To Be." *Focus on Indiana Libraries*, 26(1):32–34, Spring 1972. **1H121**
"Thinking that children are naive and they ought to be kept that way has resulted in an increasingly tangled web of restrictions on access to library collections for minors."

————, comp. *Librarians, Censorship, and Intellectual Freedom; An Annual Annotated Comprehensive Bibliography, 1968–1969*. Chicago, American Library Association, 1970. 42p. **1H122**

Harvey, James A., ed. *Intellectual Freedom and School Libraries; An In-Depth Case Study*. Chicago, American Library Association, 1973. 23p. (Reprinted from *School Library Media Quarterly*, Winter 1973) **1H123**
The case deals with a controversy over the book *Slaughterhouse Five* by Kurt Vonnegut, selected as recommended reading in an English class in Adams High School, Rochester, Mich. A parent lodged a complaint with the Board of Education, demanding that the book be banned. When the Board backed the school administrators in retaining the book, the objector filed a suit against the Board to have the book removed on the ground that it was "anti-religious." The controversy polarized the community and presented the school with a public relations dilemma because of a pending vote for increased school funds. The judge of the Circuit Court ruled for the plaintiff and ordered the book banned, but the Michigan Court of Appeals, by a 3–0 vote, reversed the decision. The story is told in seven phases: Phase 1, Selection of the Book (Harry Jones and Ray Lawson); Phase 2, Initiation and Handling of the Complaint (Harry Jones and Ray Lawson); Phase 3, Pressure on the Administration (Richard H. Escott); Phase 4, Pressure on the Board of Education (Dorothy A. Beardmore and Peter Vernia); Phase 5, Assessing and Handling Community Reaction (William J. Banach); Phase 6, Taking Legal Action (Michael J. Charbonneau); Phase 7, Enlisting Support from Professional Organizations (James A. Harvey). The report concludes with a statement on Intellectual Freedom and the Rights of Children by Judith F. Krug.

Harvey, James A., and **Patricia R. Harris,** comps. *Librarians, Censorship, and Intellectual Freedom; An Annual Anno-*

tated Bibliography, 1970. Chicago, American Library Association, 1970, 52p. **1H124**

Harvey, Sir Paul. "Censorship and the Law of the Press." In his *Oxford Companion to English Literature*. 4th ed., rev. Oxford, England, Oxford University Press, 1967, pp. 911–20. **1H125**
A brief history of press and theater censorship in England from the sixteenth century through the abolition of the newspaper tax in 1855 and the 1909 Parliamentary inquiry into theater censorship. There is also a summary of existing British law of press and drama.

Haselden, Kyle. *Morality and the Mass Media*. Nashville, Tenn., Broadman, 1968. 192p. **1H126**
An attempt to relate the demands of Christian morality to the mass media. "Control and censorship of knowledge, ideas, and feelings—though required under certain circumstances [e.g. protection of young children]—must be viewed generally as hostile to that human freedom that is indispensable to authentic morality." In a chapter on Obscenity Beyond Sex, the author concludes that, while sexual obscenity is one evil threatening the moral character of man, there are more subtle and destructive forces—religious and racial bigotry, brutality that feeds on human suffering, and the degeneracy of modern war. These must not be lost sight of in a preoccupation with sexual obscenity. He cites seven conditions (pp. 180–83) under which the law should prevent the mass media (especially radio and television) from offending the rights of the people: protection of children, broadcasting in the public interest, control over advertising, attention to the right's of minorities, protection against slander, promotion of pay-TV and public TV, and the requirements that the Federal Communications Commission may be more responsive to the public interest.

Hass, Sharon. "First Amendment Rights of Prisoners to Have Access to the News Media in Relation to Administrative Policy Bans Upon Such Access." *Pepperdine Law Review*, 1:382–403, 1974. **1H127**
An overview, in light of recent court cases, dealing with the right of the press to have access to prisoners, particularly those incarcerated in maximum security institutions. The author looks at the issues from the point of view of the rights of prisoners, the problems of prison administrators, and the media.

Hastie, William H. "Free Speech: Contrasting Constitutional Concepts and Their Consequences." *Harvard Civil*

Rights-Civil Liberties Law Review, 9:428–48, May 1974. **1H128**
"I intend to focus primarily upon constitutional problems created by the content of speech or publication as distinguished from the circumstances in which an otherwise protected communication occurs or is proposed—what may be said rather than where or when." The author concludes with these questions: Does a distinction between expression relevant to the people's governing function and all other self-expression lend itself to undesirable and systematic elaboration in case after case? Is this distinction any sounder or more practical than a distinction drawn in terms of redeeming social value? Would its utilization clarify and encourage the now evident judicial disposition to find that the Constitution guarantees greater freedom to expression about public affairs than to other types of expression?

Hastings, H. L. *A Few Cold Facts Concerning Preaching on Boston Common, Presented at a Public Hearing in the City Hall, Before a Committee of the City Council, on the Petition to Repeal the City Ordinance Prohibiting the Unlicensed Preaching of the Gospel on the Public Grounds of the City of Boston, Wednesday Evening, February 29, 1888*. Boston, Scriptural Tract Repository, 1888. 12p. (The *Monthly Message*, No. 4). **1H129**
A Protestant minister charges the City of Boston with violation of the First Amendment in requiring a license for preaching in a public park, making it virtually impossible to get a license, and in arresting and jailing ministers in violation of an unconstitutional ordinance. Only in Boston and Dublin has the writer been prohibited from speaking.

Hatch, Carl E. *The Charles A. Briggs Heresy Trial; Prologue to Twentieth Century Liberal Protestantism*. New York, Exposition, 1969, 139p. **1H130**
An account of the battle between liberals and conservatives in the 1890s that split Presbyterianism and other Protestant groups in the United States and led to a heresy trial of the Reverend Mr. Briggs, Bible scholar of Union Theological Seminary.

Hatfield, Robert M. *The Theater: Its Character and Influence. An address by Rev. R. M. Hatfield, delivered at the Clark Street Methodist Episcopal Church of Chicago, Monday Evening, December 11, 1865, . . . with an introduction by Rev. C. H. Fowler. . . .* Chicago, Methodist Book Depository, 1866. 40p. **1H131**
Quoting from numerous writers over the years, the speaker charges the theater with having been a pest for centuries, having cursed the location in which it has been situated, having cursed its actors, and having an affinity with crime. The theater cannot be reformed; various persons and groups have tried unsuccessfully. Young persons should boycott the theater because it is a waste of time and money; it surrounds them with bad company and keeps them from Christ.

Hauptman, William. "The Suppression of Art in the McCarthy Decade." *Artform*, 12(2):48–52, October 1973. **1H132**
The author records that "an almost pathological fear of communist infiltration in the first decade after World War II resulted in one of this country's most shameful endeavors to deny artists their basic freedom of expression." An account of the efforts of Michigan Congressman George A. Dondero and others to suppress exhibitions of modern art, to censor and destroy murals in public buildings, that were suspected of being Communist-inspired.

Hausman, Linda W. *Criticism of the Press in U.S. Periodicals, 1900–1939: An Annotated Bibliography*. Austin, Texas, Association for Education in Journalism, 1967. 49p. (Journalism Monographs, no. 4) **1H133**
Topics: The press as a society institution (including freedom of the press in wartime), the press in business, the newspaper, the periodical press, radio, the news services, and press personalities.

[Havens, Shirley.] "Intellectual Freedom at Dallas." *Library Journal*, 96:2447–49, August 1971. **1H134**
A summary of discussion and action dealing with intellectual freedom at the 1971 annual conference of the American Library Association held in Dallas.

[———.] "Intellectual Freedom in Chicago." *Library Journal*, 97:2531–34, August 1972. **1H135**
A summary of discussion and action dealing with intellectual freedom at the 1972 annual conference of the American Library Association held in Chicago. Included is the condemnation of the government's injunction against the CIA book by Victor L. Marchetti, the Beacon Press case over the *Pentagon Papers*, and the ALA's policy on Reevaluating Library Collections.

[———.] "Intellectual Freedom in Detroit." *Library Journal*, 95:2623–26, August 1970. **1H136**
A summary of discussion and action on intellectual freedom at the 1970 annual conference of the American Library Association held in Detroit. "While there are still vast differences of opinion over tactics and armament, the intellectual freedom campaign has come a long way from Atlantic City [1969 conference]. The Intellectual Freedom Committee has been one of the more responsive arms of the Association.

With a considerably strengthened program, and now a defense fund—whatever its deficiencies—perhaps the Association can translate mere action into true progress."

Haward, L. R. C. "Admissibility of Psychological Evidence in Obscenity Cases." *British Psychological Society Bulletin*, 28:466–69, December 1975. **1H137**
The author discusses the precedence for expert testimony in obscenity cases as defined in British common law.

Hawke, David F. *Paine*. New York, Harper & Row, 1974. 500p. **1H138**
This new full-length biography of Thomas Paine, propagandist in the American and French Revolutions, contains numerous references to the suppression of his works, including the London trials against his *Rights of Man* and *Age of Reason*.

Hawkins, Gordon J. *The Problem of Pornography*. Sydney, Australia, Society of Legal Philosophy, 1965. 25p. Processed. (Preliminary Paper no. 1, 1965) **1H139**

Hawks, Tad H. "Every Library Needs Tall Windows." *Canadian Library Journal*, 32:187–89, June 1975. **1H140**
A summary of the brief prepared by the Canadian Library Association on the Canadian Law Reform Commission's report on obscenity. The brief generally opposed restricted access of materials to both adults and children. "Every library needs tall windows: to let the sun shine in, to let freedom shine out."

Haworth, H. E. " 'The Virtuous Romantics'—Indecency, Indelicacy, Pornography and Obscenity in Romantic Poetry." *Papers on Language & Literature*, 10:287–306, Summer 1974. **1H141**
How the extreme Puritanism of critics censored the literature of such writers as Keats, Moore, Burns, and Byron, or encouraged self-censorship. "In this self-censorship, imposed for the purpose of protecting pure and innocent minds, the Romantics anticipated the Victorians."

Hayden, Martin S. "Newspaper and the Law: Where They Meet." *Kentucky State Bar Journal*, 36:38–43, January 1972. **1H142**
The editor of the *Detroit Free Press* considers three areas of common interest between press and bar: immunity privileges for reporters, fair trial and free press, and the Pentagon Papers case.

———. "Pentagon Papers: And Freedom of the Press." *Reader's Digest*, 99 (9):133–34, September 1971. **1H143**
An editorial from the *Detroit News* charging the

New York Times with irresponsibility in publishing the Pentagon Papers.

———, and Don Shoemaker. "The Movie Rating Dispute." *Bulletin of the American Society of Newspaper Editors*, 561:7–9, July–August 1972.   **1H144**
The policies of three newspapers—*Detroit News*, *Miami Herald*, and *New York Times*, with respect to the rejection of advertising for X-rated films.

Haydock, Roger. "Permissive Bounds of Prior Restraint of Movies." *DePaul Law Review*, 17:597–613, Summer 1968.   **1H145**
The author suggests the basis for drafting municipal film censorship ordinances, taking into consideration the rulings of the U.S. Supreme Court in *Freedman v. Maryland* (1965), and *Cusack v. Teitel Film Corp.* (1968).

Hayes, John C. "Obscenity: The Intractable Legal Problem." *Catholic Lawyer*, 15:5–22+, Winter 1969. **1H146**
The author analyzes "two 1968 decisions of the United States Supreme Court, each dealing with the constitutionality of local criminal laws prohibiting the dissemination *to youth* of materials obscene *for youth* though not obscene *for adults*. In the one case, a New York statute met the test of constitutionality ₍Ginsberg v. New York, 1968₎, but in the other, a Dallas ordinance failed that test ₍Interstate Circuit, Inc. v. City of Dallas, 1968₎." The author finds that the two cases are not inconsistent, either with each other or with *Gault* (*In re Gault*, 1967).

Hayes, Paul J. "The Correlation Between Modern Communications Media and Social Behavior." *National Decency Reporter*, 4(4):9–12, September–October 1967.   **1H147**
The director of the Christian Communications Apostolate, Archdiocese of Newark cites evidence of the harmful effect of obscenity and sadistic printed matter as determined from a nationwide survey conducted by his office: 92 percent of law enforcement officials questioned felt that pornographic, obscene, violent or crime-centered movies or reading had a relationship to delinquency; 83 percent of the psychologists felt that obscene and sadistic matter had a relationship to delinquency. The survey showed that "the question of the specific relationship between the communications media and behavior or character formation should not be dismissed lightly and that thorough investigation should be pursued in the field."

Hayes, Robert A. "The Defamatory Broadcast and Section 117a of the Broadcasting and Television Act." *Australian Law Journal*, 44:310–28, July 1970.   **1H148**
"One reason for the enactment of S.117a of the Broadcasting and Television Act 1942–1969 which requires that records in writing, or sound recordings, of broadcast matter relating to political subjects and current affairs be made and retained by the Australian Broadcasting Commission and by licensees of commercial broadcasting stations—was to obviate some of the evidentiary difficulties associated with legal proceedings in respect to broadcast defamatory matter." The article discusses the procedures that a plaintiff must follow to obtain use of these documents.

———. "Injunctions Before Judgment in Cases of Defamation." *Australian Law Journal*, 45:125–38, March 1971; 45:181–93, April 1971.   **1H149**
Unlike American courts which have repeatedly refused to enjoin publication of defamatory matter on the ground that it would interfere with freedom of speech, English and Australian courts "have accepted that in limited circumstances equitable relief may be granted in cases of defamation; that there is jurisdiction to grant injunctions protecting individuals from defamatory attack, and in particular, that the plaintiff to an action for defamation may be granted an injunction protecting him from repetition of the matter in dispute until the trial." The article deals with this practice in England and Australia.

———. "The Jury Verdict in Defamation: Commonsense or Conniption?" *University of Western Australia Law Review*, 11:140–68, December 1973.   **1H150**
Criticism of that section of the Report on Defamation of the New South Wales Law Reform Commission which recommends that the jury's inexperience and comstockery disqualify it as a disciplinarian of the wanton defamer, and ill-equipped it for decisions in many judgments as to the propriety or otherwise of the conduct of the defendant's case.

———. "Newspaper Libel—the Deterrent and Vindicatory Effects of General Damages Awards." *University of Queensland Law Journal*, 5:370–91, August, 1967.   **1H151**
Re: *Uren v. John Fairfax & Sons Pty. Ltd.*, 1966. The author concludes that "the law should aim first to prevent libel and, as a subsidiary aim, to punish—but only where there is good reason to believe that punishment will deter other wrongdoers. Large awards of damages may thus be justified as a preventative measure more appropriate than the injunction, in that they induce care into the self-regulatory procedures of newspapers. Exemplary damages may be justified, in that they serve a useful social purpose, providing a deterrent from conscious wrongdoing, where the criminal prosecution is inappropriate."

Hays, Arthur Garfield. *City Lawyer: The Autobiography of a Law Practice*. New York, Simon & Schuster, 1942, 482p.   **1H152**
Throughout these reminiscences of the civil

liberties lawyer, are references to cases involving freedom of the press, libel, and literary rights, including the Scopes evolution trial, the H. L. Mencken "Hatrack" case, and the attacks on Theodore Dreiser's *American Tragedy*.

Hayward, Jack. "The Crossman Diaries." *Index on Censorship*, 4(4):26–30, Winter 1975.   **1H153**
The author discusses the constitutional and political background and other issues raised by the doctrine of cabinet confidentiality in the publication of Richard Crossman's *The Diaries of a Cabinet Minister* (*Attorney General v. Jonathan Cape Ltd.* and *Attorney General v. Times Newspapers Ltd.*).

Hayward, John T. "Military Responsibility and Freedom." *Strategic Review* (United States Strategic Institute), 1:46–50, Fall 1973.   **1H154**
"I believe the highest national interest would be served if all present regulations and procedures governing review by the Department of Defense of publications by military people be reviewed in detail and redirected to encourage free expression by military professionals. Certain considerations regarding classified information and positions held in the Defense organization would limit some publication; but we should lift the dead hand of bureaucracy which now has everyone in its grip." The author is a retired vice admiral.

Healy, Allan. "Australian Censorship Under a Labour Government." *Index on Censorship*, 3(2):55–60, Summer 1974.   **1H155**
Little progress has been made by the Labour Government to combat censorship in Australia despite preelection promises, although efforts have been made. Attempts to recognize the rights of adults to read, hear, and view what they wish ran into opposition from several Australian states where Puritanism was strong. The libel laws remain severe and the Australian Broadcasting Commission "continues to be a muzzled and frightened organization."

———. "Letter from Australia: Censorship as a Nineteenth-Century Survival." *Index on Censorship*, 1 (3/4): 185–95, Autumn–Winter 1972.   **1H156**
"Australia ranks with Eire as one of the most censor-ridden societies in the Western world," according to the author, who attributes the situation to the historical liaison of the Australian colonial government with the Roman Catholic Church. The isolation of the country and the obsession with social homogeneity have also contributed to ethical and political conservatism. The author discusses the kinds of censorship that have prevailed over the

years, giving examples including the suppression of the author's doctoral thesis in 1962 by a major Australian university under instructions from a Federal government department, and the Customs controversy over Marcus's *The Other Victorians*, on the list of banned books. "Despite some recent moves toward the rationalisation of procedures and liberalisation of attitudes . . . , the diehard traditionalism of Australian society can still be expected to surface in a variety of ways."

Heap, Jane. "Art and the Law." *Little Review*, 7(3):5–7, September–December 1920. **1H157**
In protesting the government attacks on James Joyce's *Ulysses* (serialized in the *Little Review*) the author asks: "Can merely reading about the thoughts he thinks corrupt a man when his thoughts do not? All power to the artist, but this is not his function."

Heard, Alexander. "Relevant Thoughts on a Basic Freedom." *Tennessee Librarian*, 21:62–65, Winter 1969. **1H158**
"In the United States our belief in the importance of the freedom of the mind is symbolized by the First Amendment to the Constitution" which prohibits laws abridging freedom of speech and the press. "Inherent in the right to write and publish freely is the obligation to let others do likewise, and to read them closely." He notes that the right of free expression carries inherent obligations: willingness to change and the ability to be wrong, temperateness in opinion and debate, the obligation of humility, the obligation to competence and honor, and the hard work of civilization. An address by the chancellor of Vanderbilt University.

Hearn, Ron. "Working Class Approach to Censorship." *Australian Marxist Review*, 2:10–13, July 1973. **1H159**

Hebert, Elsie S. "How Accessible Are the Records in Government Records Centers?" *Journalism Quarterly*, 52:23–29, 60, Spring 1975. **1H160**
An analytical overview of "open record" laws and regulations, both federal and state, that govern access of the public and media to official records in government record centers.

Hebert, Hugh. "The Press Button Up War." *Guardian* (Manchester), 26 January 1973, p.12. **1H161**
British journalists feel threatened in the areas of "the right to publish, and the right of newspapers to garner by whatever means the information in the first place." The author looks at the Vassall case of 1962 which involved the jailing of journalists who refused to identify

their news sources; the 1967 D-notice affair; the more recent *Railway Gazette* raid; the dispute over press coverage of the National Industrial Relations Court; and the injunctions against the thalidomide articles and the Warhol film. Not one of the stories that produced a row was as serious as the affair of the Pentagon Papers whose publication was upheld by the U.S. Supreme Court.

Hébert, Jacques. *Obscénité et Liberté. Préface de Me Claude-Armand Sheppard. Plaidoyer contre la censure des livres, suivi d'extraits de plaidoiries et de jugements dans quelques causes célèbres: Lady Chatterley's Lover, Histoire d'O et cinq oeuvres du Marquis de Sade.* Montreal, Éditions du Jour, 1970. 191p. **1H162**

[Hecht, Ben.] "Fantazius Mallare Walloped for One Row of Ash Cans." *Ben Hecht's Chicago Literary Times*, 1(24):1–2, 15 February 1924. **1H163**
An irreverent account of the trial of Ben Hecht, author, and Wallace Smith, illustrator, of the erotic fantasy *Fantazius Mallare*, in federal district court on charges of obscenity, lewdness, and depravity. They were found guilty and fined $1,000 each, but given three months to pay. The *Chicago Literary Times* (*Modern Sardonic Journal*) frequently reported on news of censorship of the bold and risqué literature that appeared during the twenties.

Hechtlinger, Adelaide. "Introduction." In *Creative and Sexual Science: Or Manhood, Womanhood, and their Mutual Interrelations: Love, Its Laws, Power, etc. . . . as taught by Phrenology and Physiology. By Prof. O. S. Fowler. . . .* Edited and with an introduction by Adelaide Hechtlinger. Chicago, Follett, 1971. 255p. (Abridged facsimile edition) **1H164**
A brief essay introducing an abridged version of Professor Fowler's thousand-page book, "first published in 1870, in the midst of the Victorian era, written about the one topic supposedly taboo at that time—sex."

Hedley, Peter, and Cyril Aynsley. *The "D" Notice Affairs.* London, Michael Joseph, 1967. 144p. **1H165**
An account of the "cable-vetting" affair. The *Daily Express* for 21 February 1967 had announced: "Thousands of private cables and telegrams sent out of Britain from the Post Office or from commercial cable companies are regularly being made available to the security authorities for scrutiny." This bombshell set off an investigation both of the alleged practice of "cable vetting" and also the newspaper's propriety in publishing the information. The "D" notice is a deferred notice from a Services Press and Broadcasting Committee, warning the press to keep clear of certain "sensitive" subjects—a practice involving mutual agree-

ment without force in law. A committee headed by Lord Radcliffe was appointed to investigate the affair. (Great Britain, Cabinet Office. *The "D" Notice System.*)

Heerden, E. van. "Sensuur soos 'n skrywer-akademikus dit sien." *South African Libraries*, 38:228–31, January 1971. **1H166**
Censorship in the eyes of an author academician.

Heffernan, Michele O. "Board of Education Rule Requiring Prior Review of All Student Literature Distributed in High Schools Declared Unconstitutional." *Buffalo Law Review*, 22:611–24, Winter 1973. **1H167**
Re: *Fujishima v. Board of Education*, 460 F.2d 1355 (7th Cir. 1972). The author suggests that the courts need to clarify the parameters of school authority and the schools need "to define the conditions which would give a school sufficient cause to implement a regulated system of prior review."

Heffner, Richard D. *et al. Censorship on Television.* 30 min. tape recording. North Hollywood, Calif., Center for Cassette Studies, 1971. (Distributor's title: Television and Substance) **1H168**
Panel discussion moderated by Richard D. Heffner. Panelists: J. Nelson Tuck, Marya Mannes, and Philip H. Cohn.

———. *The Courts and a Free Press.* 2 tape recordings: part 1, 27 min.; part 2, 25 min. North Hollywood, Calif., Center for Cassette Studies, 1970. (Constitutional Issues Series; Distributor's title: Free Speech; Threat to Liberty) **1H169**
Author and historian Richard D. Heffner, editor Norton Mockeridge, attorney Florence Kelley, attorney Edward Bennett Williams, and L. E. Lipsky discuss the inequities of trial by press and television.

———. *Do We Have a Responsible Press?* 28 min. tape recording. North Hollywood, Calif., Center for Cassette Studies, 1957. (Distributor's title: The Responsible Press) **1H170**
A panel discussion by moderator Richard D. Heffner, historian; James A. Wechsler, editor of the *New York Post*, and John Fischer, editor of *Harper's Magazine*.

———. *Television and the Courtroom.* 27 min. tape recording. North Hollywood, Calif., Center for Cassette Studies, 1971. (Distributor's title: Television and Trials, Part I) **1H171**
A discussion of the pros and cons of televising trials. Moderator, Richard D. Heffner;

panelists: Robert Sweezy, chairman of the Freedom of Information Committee of the National Association of Broadcasters; Florence Kelley, Legal Aid Society; and Telford Taylor, former general counsel for the Federal Communications Commission.

Heilemann, Don. "NPPA Files Supreme Court Brief for Newsmen's Privilege." *National Press Photographer*, 26(10):6–7, October 1971. **1H172**
"We believe that any standard which recognizes First Amendment rights must be such that it will protect the newsmen and photographers in the ₁privilege₁ cases presently before the court." National Press Photographers Association.

Hein, Ed. *Accuracy in Media: Another Look.* Columbia, Mo., Freedom of Information Center, School of Journalism, University of Missouri at Columbia, 1976. 6p. (Report no. 360) **1H173**
This report attempts to present an objective picture of AIM, and details developments in the organization since the earlier reports by Daniel Epstein and Reed J. Irvine. "Though initially dismissed by journalists as a right-wing quack, Irvine ₁founder of AIM and chairman of the board₁ has survived their onslaught and continues to preach the gospel of balanced reporting. With limited victories, he has demonstrated that one man with brains, energy and a minimum of money can make the media listen to his message."

Hein, Hilde. "Obscenity, Politics, and Pornography." *Journal of Aesthetic Education*, 5(4):77–97, October 1971. **1H174**
A philosophical analysis of obscenity and pornography, considering definitions, classification, and the dilemma between the rights of free expression and the concern with the evil influence of the obscene. "I can think of few good purposes which are served by pornography. The obvious suggestions, that it relieves tensions, amuses, corrects impotence, prevents actual abuses and excesses, are severely undermined by the fact that unlike obscenity which merely offends, pornography implants and glorifies perverse and inhuman values and what is more, does so deceptively. That is a serious challenge to the civil libertarian argument and raises legitimate questions concerning the limits of pure toleration. At the same time, suppression at the hand of the system itself, the very source and maintainer of these perverse values, is also counter productive."

Heintz, Ann. "The Kennedy Report." *Communication: Journalism Education Today*, 7:2–8, 9–13, Summer 1974. **1H175**
Part 1 of the report of Robert F. Kennedy Memorial Commission of Inquiry into High School Journalism dealt with censorship. The report recommended that "the student staff should have ultimate authority over and responsibility for high school media, which

means the right to know and to produce and disseminate information free of interference or restrictions."

Helfand, Esther. "Love and Humanity—Not Intellectual Freedom." *Top of the News*, 24:47–54, November 1967. **1H176**
"I think librarians make a grave mistake when they, in an effort to be safe and avoid controversy, take the easy way out and virtually renege, avoiding their responsibilities. It is a fallacious policy, for example, to insist that parents give written permission regarding the materials that young people may borrow from adult shelves without guidance, on the theory that parents are the best judges of the maturity level of their teenagers. Those who are qualified to judge have no fear about the frank and explicit book that the youngster brings home. They need not have fear. They recognize that young people respond to books on exactly the same level that their experience and maturity enable them to approach life."

Helffrich, Stockton. "The Broadcast Code." In Don R. Le Duc, *ed.*, *Issues in Broadcast Regulation*. Washington, D.C., Broadcast Education Association, 1974, pp. 89–92. **1H177**
Highlights from his remarks at a Broadcasting Regulation Seminar in which the director of the National Association of Broadcasters' Code Authority shows how his organization attempts to aid broadcasters in making responsible decisions about program content.

———.₁ "A Conversation with Television's Chief Censor." *TV Guide*, 17(34):4–9, 23 August 1969. (Reprinted in Barry G. Cole, *ed.*, *Television: A Selection from TV Guide Magazine*. New York, Free Press, 1970, pp. 345–49) **1H178**
The director of the NAB Code Authority answers questions about the work of his office: Are the networks living up to the Code? Does the Code need updating? Was the Code office a factor in reducing violence? What is the NAB's position on Senator Pastore's proposal that networks submit their programs to the Code Authority for prescreening? Do movies present many Code problems? The censor is interviewed by Richard K. Doan.

———. "Self-Regulation in TV Advertising." *Television Quarterly*, 3:74–77, Summer 1964. **1H179**
"Self-criticism, implemented by courageous and meaningful action, is the ultimate test of effective broadcast self-regulation. The choice still exists; broadcasters have only to make it."

———. "TV Depiction of Violence: If and How." *Journal of the Producers Guild of America*, 11(2):43–46, June 1969. **1H180**
The author reports on the efforts of the indus-

try at self-regulation, noting that broadcasters, in light of recent Senate hearings, "are restudying the effects of media-depicted violence as revealed in findings based either on survey research or on laboratory experiments." He concludes that "broadcast material of artistic integrity should comprise its own best defense against petty censorship."

Heller, Melvin S., and Samuel Polsky. *Studies in Violence and Television.* New York, American Broadcasting Co., 1976. 503p. **1H181**
A report on eleven empirical studies, representing a set of coordinated, but independently pursued projects, conducted over a five-year period to determine the effects of television violence upon normal and disturbed children. The studies were conducted with the financial support of the American Broadcasting Co., but with complete research independence. Project I, Responses of Emotionally Vulnerable Children to Television. Project II, Responses to Cartoon and Human Portrayed Television Violence in Emotionally Vulnerable Children. Project III, Television Studies with Youthful and Violent Offenders (Pilot). Project IV, Television Viewing, Anti-Social Development and Violent Behavior—An Examination of One Hundred Young Male Offenders. Project V, Measurements of Aggression in Responses of Adolescent and Young Adult Offenders to Television Violence. Project VI, Prosocial Behavior, Violence and Television Viewing Habits: A Pilot Comparative Study of Non-Offender Adolescents and Young Adults. Project VII, Responses of Children to Action-Adventure Television Dramas With and Without Prosocial Content. Project VIII, Cognitive Style and Its Relationship to Perception of Violent or Prosocial Aspects in Television Programs. Project IX, Responses of Susceptible Children to Violent vs. Prosocial Television Programs. Project X, Behavioral Aggression and Television Viewing in Children: Psychological, Developmental and Clinical Factors. Project XI, Testing and Application of Guidelines. Tests and questionnaires used in the studies are included in the appendix. The American Broadcasting Company also issued: *Overview. Five Year Review of Research (on Children and Television) . . . September 1970 Through August 1975* (1976, 69p. 40p.).

Hellman, Lillian. *Scoundrel Time.* Boston, Little, Brown, 1976. 155p. **1H182**
The playwright describes the experience she and her friends endured during the McCarthy era of the early 1950s and the harassment by the Un-American Activities Committee. When she refused to act as an informer before the Committee, she was blacklisted.

Henderson, Hazel et al. "The Contemporary First Amendment." *Columbia Journalism Quarterly*, 8(1):4–22, Spring 1969. **1H183**

"The First Amendment is enjoying a revival of sorts" to fend off ambushing government regulators, to guarantee access of the public as a whole, not simply those who acquire the instruments of the press, and to remove the threat embodied in laws of libel and privacy. These issues are discussed in four articles: Hazel Henderson "sets the 'right of access' controversy in the context of the struggle for more open, democratically based media"; Ben H. Bagdikian "offers a professional journalist's analysis of the access proposition, acknowledging the problem but resisting the suggested solutions"; William B. Blankenburg "reviews a leading experiment in enhancing press responsiveness to the public—the local press councils funded by the Mellett Fund"; Donald L. Smith "describes the failure of the right of privacy to emerge as a well-defined legal concept."

Henderson, James D. "Protection of Confidences: A Qualified Privilege for Newsmen." *Law and Social Order*, 1971:385–406, 1971.   **1H184**
"This Comment, after surveying a selected cross section of the largest American newspapers to determine the importance of their confidential sources, examines the legal and practical problems involved in fashioning a non-disclosure privilege based upon the Constitution and suggests an approach to be taken by the courts." An appendix contains data on the frequency of stories based on confidential sources which are published each year in a selected cross-section of the nation's largest newspapers.

Hendrix, Jerry, and Theodore O. Windt, Jr. "The Speech Communication Classroom and the First Amendment." In *Free Speech Yearbook*, *1972*. New York, Speech Communication Association, 1973, pp. 85–91.   **1H185**
Two professors of speech express differing views over the latitude of social responsibility in teaching freedom of speech in the classroom.

Henegan, John, and James M. Hall. "First Amendment Gives Newsmen Limited Right of Access to the News of State Government." *Mississippi Law Journal*, 45:1064–72, September 1974.
1H186
Re: *Lewis v. Baxley* (1973), in which the Court held unconstitutional the section of the 1973 ethics statute requiring newsmen to file economic disclosure statements in order to be permitted to the press area in the legislative assembly.

Henkin, Louis. "The Right to Know and the Duty to Withhold: The Case of the Pentagon Papers." *University of*

Pennsylvania Law Review, 120:271–80, December 1971.   **1H187**
"The *Pentagon Papers Case* has dramatized issues, admonished bureaucrats, and created an atmosphere receptive to a major effort to increase public and scholarly knowledge even while reinforcing secrecy where it is necessary."

[———.] "The Supreme Court, 1967 Term: Freedom of Speech and Association." *Harvard Law Review*, 82:124–38, November 1968.   **1H188**
Under the heading Obscenity, the survey considers the case of *Ginsberg v. New York;* under Picketing in a Privately Owned Shopping Center, the case of *Food Employees Local 590 v. Logan Valley Plaza, Inc.*

Henn, Harry G. " 'Libel-by-Extrinsic-Fact.' " *Cornell Law Review*, 4:14–49, Fall 1961.   **1H189**
"Published written matter, innocent on its face, when coupled with extrinsic facts which render it defamatory, may in some jurisdictions constitute actionable libel." The author reviews statutory and case law in this confusing area of libel, suggesting needed reforms.

Henning, Albert F. *Ethics and Practices in Journalism*. New York, Ray Long & Richard R. Smith, 1932. 204p. **1H190**
Written for journalism students, the book contains chapters on freedom of the press, news boundaries and values, sacred cattle, suppression of news, faking news and making news, sensationalism, and freedom of journalists.

Henry, D. H. W. "The Combines Investigation Act and Mass Media." *Osgoode Hall Law Journal*, 8:147–58, August 1970.   **1H191**
"Mr. Henry describes the rationale and scope of the Combines Investigation Act and its application to the mass media, particularly to the press, to date."

Henshaw, David. *An Address Delivered Before an Assembly of Citizens . . . at Faneuil Hall, Boston, July 4, 1836*. Boston, Beals and Greene, 1836. 39p.
1H192
In a speech in behalf of the presidential candidacy of Martin Van Buren, the speaker criticizes the present action of the courts against libel as neither based on the statutes nor English common law. The only warrant for sustaining prosecution for libel is the decision of former judges, "as guilty as themselves in violating the Constitutional rights of the press and the citizens."

Hentoff, Nat. "Another Look at 'The Times.' " *Civil Liberties*, 280:4, September 1971.   **1H193**
The U.S. Supreme Court *Pentagon Papers* decision upheld the right of the *New York Times* to

publish the particular documents at the particular time without prior government restraint but was not a victory for First Amendment freedom.

———. "Are There Any Defenses Against a Free Irresponsible Press?" *Social Policy*, 7:51–53, May–June 1976.
1H194
An attack on the "leaking entente" between law enforcement officials and the press, which endangers defendants' chances of a fair trial. The author also objects to giving the press access to prior arrest records, where no conviction has taken place. He opposes any legal sanctions against the press as a violation of the Constitution; on the other hand, he has no faith in voluntary self-restraint by the press. As a possible defense against irresponsible reporting of criminal trials, he suggests civil action against prosecutors who "commit contempt of defendants' civil liberties, by leaking to the press."

———. "Covering Civil Liberties; The Somnolent Press." *Civil Liberties*, 290:1, 7, October 1972.   **1H195**
Hentoff accuses the press of ignoring civil liberties issues arising from the nation's courts. He proposes a work-study program for journalists for the coverage of the courts.

———. "Deepening Chill; Print and Broadcast Journalists and the First Amendment." *Commonweal*, 95:486–88, 25 February 1972.   **1H196**
There is a growing anxiety in the "straight" press about the state of the First Amendment under the Nixon Administration. He refers to the unprecedented use of the subpoena power, the use of secret police pretending to be reporters, and the use of prior restraint. The chill has been especially noted in the reluctance of public broadcasting to offer any controversial programming.

———. "Free Press/Fair Trial." *Civil Liberties*, 293:4–5, February 1973.
1H197
A discussion of the case of Harry Davidoff and the coverage of his trial by the New York press, as evidence of the "civil libertarian's nightmare" in the clash between First Amendment rights of the press and Sixth Amendment rights of a defendant for a fair trial.

———. "Government vs. Press; A New Round?" *Civil Liberties*, 288:2, July 1972.   **1H198**
Discussion of a new policy of the New York Civil Liberties Union—to oppose the subpoenaing of news items even though they have been previously published or broadcast "unless radical changes are made in the way subpoenas are presently granted." Hentoff cites three cases in point involving the *Village Voice*, New York radio station WBAI, and the Los Angeles *Free Press*.

———. "How 'Fair' Should TV Be?"

Lithopinion, 9:25–31, Summer 1974.
1H199
Criticism of the fairness doctrine as having a negative and chilling effect on broadcasting. Hentoff objects to government interference with programming in the interest of fairness. "I am persuaded, but obviously cannot yet prove, that the broadening omnipresence of the Fairness Doctrine *does* indeed effect the state of mind of some reporters, some editors, some news executives, if only because they know that if they don't watch out they're going to have to spend an enormous and unfruitful amount of time and money . . . " in answering complaints. References are made to the decision of Judge David Bazelon in *Brandywine-Main Line Radio, Inc. v. FCC*, 1972.

————. "How Much Freedom? A Journalist's Speech." *Civil Liberties*, 291:1, December 1972. **1H200**
The case of a New York television journalist, Geraldo Rivera, who was given forced leave during the Presidential campaign because of his speaking in behalf of George McGovern during off-duty hours, raises the question of advocacy journalism, which the author supports, within reason.

————. "How to Make the First Amendment Obscene." *Village Voice*, 21(26):27–30, 32, 35, 28 June 1976; 21(27):36–38, 41, 5 July 1976. **1H201**
The case of actor Harry Reems who appeared in the porno-movie, *Deep Throat*, convicted in Memphis for conspiring to transport across state lines "an obscene, lewd, lascivious, and filthy motion picture." The judge, in his charge to the jury, ruled out the First Amendment as a basis for defense and instructed the jurors to employ contemporary community standards. The author sees the case as a part of an antiobscenity campaign in Memphis and is concerned with the chilling effect of using conspiracy as a basis for obscenity prosecutions (*United States v. Perains et al.*).

————. "Librarians and the First Amendment after Nixon." *Wilson Library Bulletin*, 48:742–47, May 1974. **1H202**
"Until the Nixon Administration was diverted by its own desperate struggle for survival, the Nixon years have been characterized by the most systematic attempt by government in American history to subvert the Bill of Rights, certainly including the First Amendment." The author reviews the areas in which suppression and harassment of intellectual freedom has taken place—prior censorship of publications (Pentagon Papers), FBI requests for library circulation records, subpoenas, and enforced fairness (fairness doctrine) on TV.

————. "The Press & the Prisons: The Right to Know." *Civil Liberties*, 282:1, 4, December 1971. **1H203**
The denial of media access to information about prison affairs and of a prisoner's access to the media.

————. "Scholars' Civil Liberties." *Civil Liberties*, 283:5, January 1972. **1H204**
The article concerns the claim of academic immunity for scholars from forced testimony that could cause academicians to lose their confidential sources. References are made to the case of Richard Falk of Princeton, subpoenaed in the Pentagon Papers case.

————. "The Smothers Brothers: Who Controls TV?" *Look*, 33(13):27–29, 24 June 1969. **1H205**
"Were the Smothers Brothers unduly censored, or was the CBS Television Network management merely exercising its proper responsibility to see that material possibly offensive to a sizable minority of viewers not be permitted on the air?"

————. "Survey of Publishers." *Business and Society Review*, 14:9–13, Summer 1975. **1H206**
How strong are the commitments of American newspaper editors and publishers to freedom of the press? The author analyzes the responses to a survey of 100 papers as to whether they would run an ad of a Citizens Council of America which he deemed "racist." He finds it disturbing that so many papers would reject the ad because it disagreed with the sentiments (quotation from Abraham Lincoln) or made evasive answers.

————. "The War on Dissent." *Playboy*, 15:155, 170+, September 1968. **1H207**
"How the establishment's artillery of suppression—harassment, reprisal, physical force—is deployed against those who would exercise their constitutional right to activist disagreement." The author describes his own experience and that of others who have opposed the Vietnam war in speech and writing. In the war on dissent the greatest support comes from the apathy of the majority.

————. "Winding Down the First Amendment with Harper & Row." *Village Voice*, 17(34):21–22, 55, 24 August 1972. **1H208**
A criticism of Harper & Row for letting the CIA have an advance proof of Alfred McCoy's *The Politics of Heroin in Southeast Asia*. "Because his publisher would not fight for him McCoy fought for himself and for the integrity of his book. . . . ₍He took his case to the media.₎ If there has been a victory over the CIA in this case the credit is due McCoy."

————, and Herbert Biberman. *Debate at the Gate: Free Speech Radio*. 105 min. tape recording, Berkeley, Calif., Pacifica Tape Library, 1966. **1H209**
The role of a free speech radio staff is discussed by Nat Hentoff, staff writer for *New York* magazine and contributor to the *Village Voice*, with Herbert Biberman, author and motion picture director (*Salt of the Earth*). The moderator is

Ephraim London, civil liberties attorney. The conversation was recorded at The Village Gate.

Hepburn, Mary A. "A Case of Creeping Censorship, Georgia Style." *Phi Delta Kappan*, 55:611–13, May 1974. **1H210**
A right-wing group, the Georgia Basic Education Council, has succeeded in banning Edwin Fenton's social studies inquiry series from Georgia public schools. A case study in "creeping censorship."

Hepple, Alexander. *Press Under Apartheid*. London, International Defence and Aid Fund, 1974. 67p. **1H211**
Content: The Long War in South Africa Against the Press. Laws Which Restrain and Control the Press (15). Distributors as Censors. Police and the Press. The Press Powers. The Role of the Press in the Apartheid Society. Circulation and ownership of South African newspapers are given in the appendixes.

Herbert, Nicholas. "The British Press and the Closed Shop." *Index on Censorship*, 4(2):72–75, Summer 1975. **1H212**
A consideration of the issue of the closed shop in journalism and its likely effect upon the free flow of information and opinion.

Herd, Harold. *The March of Journalism. The Story of the British Press from 1622 to the Present Day*. London, Allen & Unwin, 1952. 352p. **1H213**
In this general history of British journalism several chapters deal with issues of press freedom: The Rebels (nineteenth-century fighters for press freedom). End of the "Taxes on Knowledge" (the newspaper tax). The Press in the Second World War. Parliament and the Press.

Herdman, Francis W., Jr. "Who Shall Silence All The Airs?" *Ohio Library Association Bulletin*, 45:10–13, July 1975. **1H214**
A brief historical review of efforts at censorship. "The war against censorship is an extremely complex one. The issues under attack vary, and the troops themselves change. Personal sensitivity differs, and who can tell a man what he should or should not be sensitive to? But to deny the opportunity of free choice—to writer or reader—in fear that it may be unwisely used is to destroy the freedom itself."

Heringer, Carl S. "Censorship in School—The Controversy Over Learning Materials." *Certiorari: A Journal of Law Student Research*, 2:17–23, 1976. **1H215**

Herron, Matthew. "The Law of Libel—Constitutional Privilege and the Private Individual: Round Two—*Gertz v. Robert Welch, Inc.*" *San Diego Law Review*, 12:455–74, March 1975.
1H216
"*Gertz* is an equitable solution to the conflict between the first amendment and a private plaintiff's interest in his reputation. It remains to be seen, however, if private individuals have really gained anything, considering the new burden of proving fault and damages, coupled with the limitations on punitive damages."

Hersh, Seymour M. *Cover-Up: The Army's Secret Investigation of the Massacre at My Lai 4*. New York, Random House, 1972. 305p. **1H217**
The newspaperman who disclosed the massacre at My Lai 4 in the Vietnam war describes how the facts were suppressed by the Army, from private to general. He charges complicity of the CIA, the destruction of files, and the distortion of official records.

————. "The Story Everyone Ignored." *Columbia Journalism Review*, 8(4):55–58, Winter 1969/70. (Reprinted in Michael C. Emery and Ted C. Smythe *eds.*, *Readings in Mass Communications*, pp. 434–39; and in Alfred Balk and James Boylan, *eds.*, *Our Troubled Press*, pp. 119–24) **1H218**
The author tells how he got the story on the My Lai massacre, "the story that everyone ignored," although rumors of the episode had been widely circulated in Saigon and at the Pentagon. "I honestly believe that a major problem in newspapers today is not censorship on the part of editors and publishers, but something more odious: censorship by the reporters."

Hertzberg, Hendrick. ["Monty Python v. American Broadcasting Company, Inc."] *New Yorker*, 52(6):69–70+, 29 March 1976. (Reprinted in revised form in London *Sunday Times*, 6 June 1976) **1H219**
The case involves a controversy over American Broadcasting Company's editing without permission of the producer, the British film series, Monty Python's Flying Circus. The producers asked a million dollars damages and a permanent injunction against ABC. The case is still in the courts.

Hertzog, Mary Beth M. *Privileged Communications for Journalists*. Austin, Tex., University of Texas, 1970. 87p. (Unpublished Master's thesis). **1H220**
The study covers a discussion of privileged communications for various professional groups, laws granting newsmen's privilege, related cases, opinions of journalists on shield laws, and a proposed solution.

Hess, John L. "The Real Danger to Civil Liberties." *MORE*, 6(3):28–29, March 1976. **1H221**
The author defends investigative reporting against recent charges that it can be dangerous and that it threatens the right of privacy and due process. "With freedom of speech the rest of the Bill of Rights may be dependent; without it there is no Bill of Rights. So let's worry a bit less about the dangers of investigative journalism and a bit more about the danger of *non*-investigative journalism."

Hettlinger, Richard F. "Sex, Religion and Censorship." In Harry M. Clor, *ed.*, *Censorship and Freedom of Expression*, Chicago, Rand McNally, 1971, pp. 73–96. **1H222**
"My reaction to those who defend the existing censorship, or wish to see it strengthened, on the ground that relaxation will lead to a serious degeneration in the civility and decency of our society is to ask what is so admirable, civil and decent about the existing order? The society we are being asked to preserve or to strengthen by the enforcement of restraints on private sexual activity, and the society to which the churches have for long given their blessing, has been (at least on the surface) decent and civil, but it has also been basically oppressive and unjust. Would a society which allowed the free circulation of sexually exciting literature be necessarily a worse society than one which preserved 'decency' together with segregation and poverty?" The author concludes that "the interest of religion in the achievement of personal and sexual maturity will not be advanced by censorship."

Heussenstamm, F. K. "An Analysis of a High School Underground Paper." *Educational Leadership*, 28:20–22, October 1970. (Condensed in *Educational Digest*, January 1971) **1H223**
An analysis of a complete file of one high school underground paper, the *Loudmouth*, which dealt with such controversial issues as race relations, abortion, capital punishment, loyalty oaths, economic inequality, drug use, and the Vietnam war.

Heuston, R. F. V. "Damages in Libel." *Dublin University Law Review*, 1(1):23–27, Winter 1969. **1H224**
A discussion of the issues in Irish and English cases in assessing monetary damages in libel cases.

Hevron, Ken. "Pretrial Restrictive Order Imposing Limitations on Public Media Violates First Amendment's Guarantee of Freedom of Press." *Texas Tech Law Review*, 8:476–89, Fall 1976. **1H225**
The author examines *Nebraska Press Association v. Stuart* (1976) with the conclusion that "circumstances *will rarely exist* in which a pretrial restrictive order would be justified."

[Hewitt, Cecil R.] "Background to the Law." *Author*, 79:119–25, Autumn 1968. **1H226**
A history of the work of the Herbert Committee, which resulted in the 1959 Obscene Publications Act. The Act introduced the concepts of "taken as a whole," "the public good," and the use of expert testimony. The author discusses the first test case, *Lady Chatterley's Lover*, the various court modifications, and the revisions in the Obscene Publications Act of 1964. There is still cleaning up to be done in the law. Hewitt writes under the pseudonym, C. H. Rolph.

————.] "A Backward Glance at the Age of 'Obscenity.'" *Encounter*, 32:19–28, June 1969. **1H227**
One of England's foremost authorities on obscenity reviews the history of the offense in English society from early stage censorship under the Lord Chamberlain; action against the eighteenth-century novel, *Fanny Hill;* Victorian morality, with efforts of Thomas Bowdler to purify literature; the flourishing of pornography including importation from France; and the efforts at control by Customs and the vice societies. The author discusses the early court cases (*R. v. Read*, 1708; *Curll*, 1727) and the passage of the Lord Campbell Act in 1857 "to apply exclusively to works written for the single purpose of corrupting the morals of youth, and of a nature calculated to shock the common feelings of decency in a well regulated mind." The act was rendered more rigid by the decision of Judge Cockburn in the *Hicklin* case ten years later. Finally, the author refers to the occasional rebellion as seen in Henry Vizetelly's publishing of the works of Zola, in Havelock Ellis's *Studies in the Psychology of Sex*, in Radclyffe Hall's *Well of Loneliness*, and D. H. Lawrence's *Lady Chatterley's Lover*.

————.] "Books and Juries." *New Statesman*, 74:838, 840, 15 December 1967. **1H228**
In his critique of the guilty verdict in the obscenity trial of *Last Exit to Brooklyn*, Hewitt questions the use of juries, preferring a judge with the support of a "lay" element.

————.] *Books in the Dock*. By C. H. Rolph [pseud.]. London, Deutsch, 1969. 144p. Foreword by John Mortimer. **1H229**
The secretary of the Herbert Committee which drafted the Obscene Publications Act of 1959, bringing reform to British obscenity law, discusses the operation of the Act and its shortcomings. He reviews the swift developments in literary frankness that have taken place in recent years and the resulting dilemma faced by lawmakers. He raises such

questions as: Should freedom of expression be absolute? Can a society do without disgust and indignation? Would total freedom weaken established morality, and if so would this be a good or bad thing? The author concludes with a consideration of various proposals, good and bad, for reforming the obscenity laws. Excerpts from the book appear in *Bookseller*, 29 March and 12 April 1969.

[————.] "Censorship and Juries." *Author*, 79(1):11–15, Spring 1968.   **1H230**
In the aftermath of the 1967 obscenity conviction of *Last Exit to Brooklyn*, the author proposes a number of reforms in the Obscene Publications Act, including a requirement that interception of imported books by customs officials be confined to books already condemned in British courts, that the right of a jury trial be made statutory, and that in a book prosecution the jury or magistrate having read the book should declare at once whether or not it is obscene, and only when it is declared obscene should experts be brought in.

[————.] "Deprave, Corrupt Or Enrage." *New Statesman*, 76:162, 9 August 1968.   **1H231**
Comments on the British case against *Last Exit to Brooklyn* by Hubert Selby, Jr.

[————.] "The Last Censor." *Author*, 78:105–8, Autumn 1967.   **1H232**
The author considers the deliberations of the Joint Committee on Censorship of the Theatre and the recommendation for the abolition of the censorship of plays by the Lord Chamberlain. References are made to the evasive actions of the theater clubs to avoid censorship.

[————.] "The Law and Its Application. (Abuses of Literacy-1)," *Times Literary Supplement*, 3, 646:33–34, 14 January 1972.   **1H233**
Consideration of the operation of the British Obscene Publications Act of 1959 after twelve years of enforcement. "There is a strong case for a complete overhaul of the law on this constantly-changing problem, involving a quite new exercise in semantics; and it should find issue in a consolidating statute taking in every aspect—publishing and bookselling, printing and distributing, posting and importing, inertia selling, and public entertainment of every kind." The author suggests two safeguards: the only sanction against publisher or distributor of condemned pornography should be the destruction of the condemned material, not fines or imprisonment; any such Act should expire after five years unless it is continued following parliamentary debate. This is the first of a series of seven articles on pornography.

[————.] "Libel Law: Money Is the Root." *New Statesman*, 79:281–82, 27 February 1970.   **1H234**
"In a libel action, unless the successful plaintiff can prove that he has sustained material damage or loss . . . the law ought to consider him

justly recompensed by a prominently published recantation and apology."

[————.] "The Literary Censorship in Britain." *British Book News*, 1969:495–98, July 1969.   **1H235**
The statutes of British censorship under the Obscene Publications Act of 1959 and 1964 and efforts by a working party of the Arts Council of Great Britain to produce a more rational obscenity law.

[————.] "Porn and the Police." *New Statesman*, 84:895–96, 15 December 1972.   **1H236**
The author discusses police seizure of publications under the Obscene Publications Act as learned from a visit to porn shops. Police operate under the direction and advice of the Director of Public Prosecutions, and it is the latter who should bear the brunt of any criticism. He notes that the police "go out of their way to avoid trouble in relation to art galleries, expensively published books with reputable imprints, theatres, and blue film shows in private houses and clubs."

[————.] "Porn on Display." *New Statesman*, 86:727–28, November 1973.   **1H237**
Commentary on the Cinematograph and Indecent Displays Bill. Further comment in *Author*, Summer 1974.

[————.] "Prison for Publishers." *New Statesman*, 77:355–56, 14 March 1969.   **1H238**
An examination of the New Zealand Indecent Publications Tribunal as an alternative to sending publishers to prison. A similar system in Great Britain "might be an undertaking of impossible size."

[————, ed.] *The Trial of Lady Chatterley:* REGINA V. PENGUIN BOOKS LTD. The Transcript of the Trial Edited by C. H. Rolph [pseud. for Cecil R. Hewitt] With Illustrations by Paul Hogarth and a Selection of Cartoons To Which Is Added the Report of a Debate in the House of Lords. [London?], Privately printed, 1961. 293p.   **1H239**
A limited edition of a Penguin Special, issued as a keepsake and signed by publisher Allen Lane for his friends. The debate in the House of Lords, as reported in Hansard, has been added to the Penguin Special (H239).

Heywood, Ezra. *An Open Letter to Walt Whitman*. Princeton, Mass., The Author [1882]. Broadside.   **1H240**
Heywood's letter describes his persecution by Anthony Comstock for publishing excerpts from Whitman's *Leaves of Grass* in his paper, the *Word*, after Boston publishers had withdrawn their edition from sale.

Heywood, Thomas, and I. G. *An Apol-*

ogy for Actors (1612) By Thomas Heywood; A Refutation of the Apology for Actors (1615) By I. G. With Introductions and Bibliographical Notes by Richard H. Perkinson. New York, Scholars' Facsimiles & Reprints, 1941. Various paging.   **1H241**
The first work by Thomas Heywood is a temperately written defense of the theater, largely, as the title indicates, of the players and not the plays. While recognizing some of the abuses of the theater, he rejects the charges of the Puritan attackers that the theater was an evil in itself. The second work, by I. G. (probably John Green or Greene), was written as a reply to Heywood's *Apology* and condemns the theater on moral grounds.

Hibbert, James. *The Stoneleigh Abbey Case. A Report of the Trial of Charles Griffin, Esq. on the Prosecution of Lord Leigh, for Libel . . . 1849, before Lord Chief Justice Wilde*. London, W. Strange, 1849. 88p.   **1H242**
Griffin was convicted and sentenced to two years in prison for remarks about the family of Chandas Baron Leigh, residents of the Abbey, in a book entitled *Stoneleigh Abbey Thirty-Four Years Ago*.

Hibschman, Harry. "Liability of News Vendor or Distributors for Libel." *John Marshall Law Quarterly*, 5:416–21, April 1940.   **1H243**
Re: *Summit Hotel Co. v. National Broadcasting Co.*, 8 Atl. (2d) 302, in which the Pennsylvania Supreme Court ruled that a broadcasting company is not liable for an interjected defamatory remark where it appears that the lessee that carried on the program was selected with due care.

Hickey, Edward J., Jr. "Radio Defamation—Libel or Slander?" *Georgetown Law Journal*, 26:475–84, January 1938.   **1H244**
A discussion of the conflict within the courts over whether radio defamation constitutes the tort of libel or that of slander.

Hickey, Neil. "Does TV Go Too Far; Result of a Nationwide Poll on the Medium's Morality." *TV Guide*, 21(41):7–9, 13 October 1973.   **1H245**
A nationwide poll commissioned by *TV Guide* revealed that almost 40 percent of Americans believe television is too frank; 41 percent believe too much time is devoted to sex; two-thirds believe there is too much violence; over half feel there is no significant number of racial or religious jokes; more than half favor a screening board to keep programs of "questionable taste" off the air.

Hickey, Philip E. "Why Not An Absolute Privilege? Rosenbloom Doctrine in Washington." *Gonzaga Law Review*, 7:344–65, Spring 1972. **1H246**
Re: *Miller v. Argus Publishing Co.*, 79 Wn. 2d 816, 490 P.2d 101 (1971). In a case charging a news magazine with libeling an advertising firm in an election campaign, the Washington Supreme Court found for the defendant holding "(1) that the constitutional privilege did apply, under the recently established 'public issue' test, but (2) that the proper burden of proof to overcome the constitutional privilege is actual malice shown by 'clear and convincing evidence,' not by absolute or conclusive proof. . . . The First Amendment is a two-edged sword. It extends a qualified privilege to protect the institutionalized speech of individuals through the press, from the censoring powers of libel law; at the same time it prevents the press from waging deliberate campaigns of untruth against the individual."

Hickman, Paula H. "A New Standard of Fault for the Reportorial Privilege." *Louisiana Law Review*, 37:247–55, Fall 1976. **1H247**
Re: *Time v.* Firestone, 424 U.S. 448 (1976).

[Hickson, William E.] "Proposed Reduction of the Stamp Duty on Newspapers." *London and Westminster Review*, 25:264–70, January 1836. (Also issued as a twenty-page pamphlet, London, C. Ely) **1H248**
An attack on Mr. Spring-Rice, chancellor of the exchequer, for his proposal to reduce the tax on newspapers. Hickson demands the total abolition of the tax which, he said, operates unfairly against the workingman. "The proposed measure of relief will therefore not enable a single person among the whole body of the working classes or among the classes of poor shopkeepers to purchase a daily paper, even one of small size." He recommends these actions: abolish the stamp duty on newspapers, abolish the tax on advertisements, reduce the paper duty, reduce postage for circulation of pamphlets and books, and extend copyright to newspapers to prevent piracy and put an end to anonymity.

Higginbotham, Robert. *The Case Law of Open Meetings Laws.* Columbia, Mo., Freedom of Information Center, School of Journalism, University of Missouri at Columbia, 1976. 9p. (Report no. 354) **1H249**
"An overview of the case law of state open meetings laws shows how the statutes are being interpreted in the courts to insure public access, and how, at times, judicial interpretation works against such access."

Higgins, Stephen B. "The Press and Criminal Record Privacy." *St. Louis University Law Review*, 20:509–30, 1976. **1H250**
"The basic issue is whether the people's right to know about the administration of justice, a right protected by first amendment guarantees of freedom of the press, takes precedence over the individual's right of privacy, a concept legally recognized [in Missouri] eight-six years ago and given constitutional status only eleven years ago. This comment will explore this dilemma by examining the competing demands of criminal history record privacy and the prevention of secrecy within the system of justice. The focus is on Missouri's law and the constitutional rights it affects."

Hightower, Paul. "Canon 35 Remains Same Despite Courtroom Tests." *Journalism Quarterly*, 52:546–48, Autumn 1975. **1H251**
"In 1937 the American Bar Association at its 60th annual national convention passed a resolution discouraging the taking of photographs during courtroom trials. This paper will explore the historical rationale for the rule, ideas of judges, attorneys, photojournalists and court cases involving the use of cameras."

Hill, I. William. "A History of the First Amendment." *Editor & Publisher*, 109(7):15, 14 February 1976; 109(8):14, 23, 21 February 1976; 109(9):16–17, 28 February 1976. (Reprinted in *Bookman's Weekly*, 22 March 1976) **1H252**
A brief history of the development of press freedom in the English-speaking world, leading to the establishment of the First Amendment to the U.S. Constitution.

Hill, J. Graham. "Gertz v. Robert Welch, Inc.: Defamation and Freedom of the Press—The Struggle Continues." *Southwestern University Law Review*, 28:1043–50, Winter 1974. **1H253**
Re: *Gertz v. Robert Welch, Inc.* (1974), in which "the U.S. Supreme Court restricted the application of the *New York Times* doctrine to public officials and public figures. The states are free to adopt appropriate standards for private individuals, as long as those standards do not include liability without fault." The author does not foresee a dramatic increase in number of defamation suits instituted by private citizens, but believes there will be an increase in the percentage of successful litigants, if the states lower the standards for establishing liability.

————. "Houston Chronicle Publishing Co. v. City of Houston: Public Has Limited Access to Criminal Records." *Southwestern Law Journal*, 30:514–20, Spring 1976. **1H254**
The media, under the Texas Open Records Act, have a limited right to review information maintained by state law enforcement agencies.

————. "Texas Open Records Act: Law Enforcement Agencies' Investigatory Records." *Southwestern Law Journal*, 29:431–53, Spring 1975. **1H255**
"The purpose of this Comment is analysis of the countervailing policy considerations of the personal right of privacy, the governmental need for secrecy, and the public's right to know in the context of TORA's [Texas Open Record Act] exemption from disclosure of the records of law enforcement agencies."

Hill, Lawrence H. "*State v. Rabe:* No Preseizure Adversary Hearing Required Under Nuisance Theory of Obscenity." *Utah Law Review*, 1971:582–93, Winter 1971. **1H256**
In *State v. Rabe* (1971), the Supreme Court of Washington held that an allegedly obscene movie may be seized without a prior adversary hearing and that motion pictures, not obscene under Roth, may be suppressed when the film is exhibited in a manner that intrudes upon the privacy of nonconsenting citizens who cannot avoid being exposed to the film. The U.S. Supreme Court reversed the conviction because the statute failed to give fair notice that the location of the outdoor film showing was a vital element of the offense.

Hill, Matthew D. *Speech . . . on Mr. Bulwer's Motion for a Repeal of the Stamp Duty on Newspapers, in the House of Commons, on Thursday, May 22, 1834: Extracted from the Mirror of Parliament.* London, Mirror of Parliament, 1834. 12p. **1H257**
Among the arguments used in support of abolishing the tax on periodicals is that they carry day-to-day reports on Parliament, "furnishing all cases, high and low, with materials for forming a correct judgment on public affairs" at a cheap rate.

Hill, Mavis M., and L. Norman Williams. *Auschwitz in England: A Record of a Libel Action.* New York, Stein and Day, 1965. 293p. (Introduction by Alan U. Schwartz; foreword by Lord Denning) **1H258**
A documentary reporting of a celebrated British libel trial that took place in 1964. A man who had served as a prisoner-doctor at Auschwitz during World War II and was, at the time of the trial, engaged in a profitable medical practice in London, sued Leon Uris, the author of *Exodus* and his English publishers. He claimed he had been libeled because he was referred to in the book as having performed sexual surgery, without benefit of anesthetic, on young Jewish men and women prisoners. Lord Denning refers to the trial as a model of how to conduct a libel action and praises the press for voluntarily protecting the anonymity of the witnesses who had suffered the grievous and humiliating operations. "The issues raised by the trial," write the compilers, "went far beyond the right of a man to claim compensation for damage done to his reputation by the

publication of a defamatory statement; they pose for everybody basic questions of morals and ethics and human behavior in adversity."

Hill, Morton A. "On Obscenity: A Jesuit Replies to Father Riga." *Catholic World*, 206:105–8, December 1967. **1H259**
Father Hill, executive director of Operation Yorkville, answers the views of Father Peter Riga (*Catholic World*, September 1967) on obscenity and obscenity law. Father Riga had argued that the real problem of our society was not obscenity but the meaning and significance of human love, and that it was doubtful if obscenity law had any moral value. Father Hill stated that "obscene material is a very real problem, and a dangerous one, causing growing concern among responsible people who cannot be lumped with Puritans or Comstockians, or Father Riga's 'Sacredizers.'" He cites various authorities to back his views. "Obscenity law does not attempt to dictate what a man will read or not read. It does attempt to hold responsible the purveyor of an instrument which contributes to the destruction of another's rational freedom."

———, James Lloyd, and Julius Neumann. "*Pornography: A Bad Companion; Three Clergymen Discuss the Impact of Obscene Material*. 28 min. tape recording. North Hollywood, Calif., Center for Cassette Studies, 1971. (Today's Mores series) **1H260**
Fathers Hill and Lloyd and Rabbi Neumann discuss the importance of parental guidance in children's exposure to pornographic material.

Hill, Morton A., and Ernest A. Villas. ₍Morality in Media Goals.₎ 28 min. tape recording. New York, Morality in Media, n.d. **1H261**
The president and vice-president of Morality in Media, Inc., discuss the aim of the organization which is to stamp out pornography, proposals for a national clearing house of legal information to assist prosecuting attorneys in prosecuting obscenity cases, and the procedure for organizing local chapters of Morality in Media.

Hill, Norman. "The Growing Phenomenon of the Journalism Review." *Saturday Review*, 54(37):59–60, 11 September 1971. **1H262**
An account of the rise of the so-called "journalism review," established by news reporters in a dozen cities as an outlet for criticizing the establishment press. The first such publication was the *Columbia Journalism Review*, begun in 1961.

Hill, Peter P. "Law, Libel and the Press: Sedition Act." *New Republic*, 170(14):7–8, 6 April 1974. **1H263**
President Nixon's call for a stiffer federal libel

law recalls to the author "this country's first foray into the thicket of press control, in 1798."

Hill, Robert, Sharon Perry, and Elizabeth Wolcott, comps. *Intellectual Freedom: A Bibliography*. Sacramento, Calif., California Library Association, 1972. 12p. Processed. **1H264**
Annotated list of seventy-six books and periodicals, published between 1966 and 1971, dealing with intellectual freedom events.

Hill of Luton, Charles Hill, baron. *Freedoms of the Communicators; A Speech Given by the Rt. Hon. The Lord Hill of Luton . . . at the Spring Conference of the Guild of British Newspapers, Scarborough, 27th April 1968*. London, British Broadcasting Corp. ₍1968.₎ 16p. **1H265**
"The only way that we, as communicators, can retain ₍our freedoms₎ is by exercising them responsibly." The author is chairman of the British Broadcasting Corporation and his comments relate largely to the broadcasting industry.

Hillerman, Tony. "The Budville Murders: Reardon Rules in Action." *Quill*, 56(10):12–15, October 1968. **1H266**
The author charges that enforced police security under bar association rules that prevented the exercise of a free press worked to the disadvantage of a defendant falsely suspected of murder.

₍Hilliard, David E.₎ "'Balance and Objectivity' in Public Broadcasting: Fairer than Fair?" *Virginia Law Review*, 61:643–78, April 1975. **1H267**
"In analyzing the statutory provision aimed at keeping public broadcasting programs untainted by bias, this note initially focuses on the history and structure of public radio and television in the United States; it then examines fairness standards imposed upon noncommercial broadcasting, application of a rigid requirement of balance and objectivity, and enforcement of such a strict criterion."

Hilpert, Fred P., Jr. "The Influence of a Course in Ethics and Free Speech in Changing Student Attitudes." *Free Speech Yearbook, 1972*. New York, Speech Communication Association, 1973, pp. 66–75. **1H268**
The investigation was designed to assess what influence the completion of a university course in Ethics and Free Speech might have on students' attitudes toward these issues.

Himes, Jay L. "Of Shadows and Substance: Freedom of Speech, Expression, and Action." *Wisconsin Law Review*, 1971:1209–35, 1971. **1H269**
"The conclusion of this comment is that the present approach adopted by the Supreme

Court of separating expressive activity into speech and nonspeech elements is misdirected. It is further suggested that unless a new method of legal analysis is used to handle questions of expressive activity, the first amendment will never allow the robust and vigorous expression of ideas that it is fully capable of permitting. The analysis posited is one which contrasts the effects of expressive activity with those of speech activity. Succinctly stated, the thesis is that all expressive activity, whether speech or nonverbal, can be subjected to the same analytical framework to determine the extent to which restrictions on the activity are consistent with the first amendment. Finally, an attempt will be made to apply the analysis derived to the problem of flag desecration."

Himes, Norman E. *Medical History of Contraceptives*. With a New Preface by Christopher Tietze, M.D., Medical Foreword by Robert Latou Dickinson, M.D. New York, Schocken Books, 1970. 521p. (First published in 1936 by Williams and Wilkins) **1H270**
This history of birth control includes not only an account of medical techniques of contraception from earliest times to the present (1930s), but records efforts of the birth control movement in England and the United States and the frequent difficulties with the law. Included are accounts of the work of such British pioneers as Francis Place, Richard Carlile, Richard Hassell, and William Campion; the early American crusaders Robert Dale Owen and Dr. Charles Knowlton; the trials of Knowlton in Massachusetts in 1833 and Charles Bradlaugh and Annie Besant in England in 1877 for publishing Dr. Knowlton's *Fruits of Philosophy*, an early birth control tract; also the trial of Edward Truelove in England in 1878. Also included are accounts of the efforts of such nineteenth-century crusaders as Dr. Edward Bliss Foote and his son Dr. Edward Bond Foote, and Dr. William J. Robinson; and the long career of Margaret Sanger, both in the United States and abroad, and the numerous efforts to suppress her books and lectures.

———. "The Rarissima of Birth Control." In *The Colophon*, Part 20. 12p. (Walpole Printing Office, New Rochelle, N.Y. 1935) **1H271**
The author writes of his adventures in collecting early birth control pamphlets, provides bibliographical information on Charles Knowlton's *Fruits of Philosophy*, and recounts the efforts to suppress the work in England and America.

Hinchey, John W. "The First Amendment Freedom of Speech: A Rediscovery of Absolutes." *Mercer Law Review*, 23:473–518, Spring 1972. **1H272**

The purpose of this article is "(1) to restate and examine the underpinnings of this 'absolute' view of the first amendment, (2) to test its viability as a rule for decision through application to typical problem cases decided by the Supreme Court within the past decade, and (3) to demonstrate that this 'absolutist' approach offers the greatest protection to the type of speech the first amendment was designed to protect, while at the same time allowing for protection of all other legitimate governmental interests such as peace, order and security, etc."

[Hindmarsh, Joseph *et al.*] *The Tryal and Condemnation of Several Notorious Malefactors, at a Sessions of Oyer and Terminer Holden for the City of London . . . April 13th, 1681.* London, 1681. 2p.
1H273
Hindmarsh was brought to trial on blasphemy charges for printing the *Presbyterian Paternoster*.

Hines, William. "News Under New Management." *Bulletin of Atomic Scientists*, 25:38, 42, March 1969. **1H274**
"There is no reason to expect that information policies in the science-oriented agencies of government will be any more sensible under Nixon-Klein than Eisenhower-Hagerty, Kennedy-Salinger or Johnson-Moyers/Christian. In fact, the whole history of public administration strongly suggests that the opposite will be true."

[Hinton, Frederick J.] "Open Meetings in Virginia: Fortifying the Virginia Freedom of Information Act." *University of Richmond Law Review*, 8:261–75, Winter 1974. **1H275**
"This comment will review the public meeting aspect of the Virginia [Freedom of Information] Act, indicating some possible problem areas, and recommend certain changes."

Hinton, Isaac T. *A Discourse delivered at the Baptist Church, Chicago, November 26, 1837, by Isaac Taylor Hinton. Occasioned by the Murder of the Rev. E. P. Lovejoy.* Chicago, Published by B. H. Clift, at the Chicago Bookstore, 1837. 14p. **1H276**
Lovejoy, an abolitionist editor of Alton, Ill., was murdered in an attempt to defend his press from destruction by a mob. Byrd (*Illinois Imprints*) notes that Hinton was an English-born, Oxford-educated scholar of the classics who in 1835 became the second pastor of the First Baptist Church of Chicago. He held strong antislavery views. Clift and Russell opened the first bookstore in Chicago in 1834.

Hipp, David W. "Attorney Comment on Pending Trial." *Wayne Law Review*, 22:1233–42, July 1976. **1H277**
Critical comment on *Chicago Council of Lawyers v. Bauer*, 522 F.2d 242 (7th Cir. 1975) which challenged a disciplinary rule of the American Bar Association Code of Professional Responsibility, the purpose of which was to minimize prejudicial effect of publicity before and during trials.

Hipps, G. Melvin. "Holden Caulfield Is Alive and Unwell in South Carolina." *South Carolina Librarian*, 17(2):7–8, Spring 1973. **1H278**
A reappraisal of the often-banned *The Catcher in the Rye* and its significance in today's schools and among present-day adolescents.

Hirsch, Jane K. *The Critical Reception of Three Controversial Children's Books.* Washington, D.C., Catholic University of America, 1966. 82p. (Unpublished Master's thesis) **1H279**
"This paper will attempt to see if an analysis of three 'controversial' juvenile novels and the reviews made of them, by professional critics and librarians, will lead to a better understanding of the nature of these books and the antithetical reactions they provoked. The three books chosen are *Harriet The Spy*, by Louise Fitzhugh, *Ring the Judas Bell* by James Forman and *Drop Dead* by Julia Cunningham."

Hirsch, Richard G., and John L. Ryan. "I Know It When I Seize It: Selected Problems in Obscenity." *Loyola University of Los Angeles Law Review*, 4:9–82, February 1971. **1H280**
The article deals with these questions in obscenity law: "Does the general rule that the prosecution must affirmatively plead and prove all elements of a criminal case apply to the 'redeeming social value' standard . . . ? Must there be a prior judicial determination on the issue of obscenity before the search for or seizure of allegedly obscene material is undertaken? Assuming such a determination is necessary, is there a violation of the Fifth Amendment right against self-incrimination when the court orders the individual to produce a copy of the questioned material for use by the prosecution in a subsequent criminal procedure? Are the concepts of res judicata and collateral estoppel available to either party in obscenity cases involving a subsequent action concerning the identical material?"

Hirsh, Michael. "The Sins of Sears Are Not News in Chicago." *Columbia Journalism Review*, 15(2):29–30, July–August 1976. **1H281**
The Chicago press coverage of the Sears, Roebuck trial before the Federal Communications Commission on charges of systematically engaging in bait-and-switch selling tactics was largely ignored by the Chicago press.

Hirshfield, David. *Report on Investigation of Pro-British History Text-Books in Use in the Public Schools of the City of New York At The Direction of Hon. John F. Hylan, Mayor.* New York, Office of the Commissioner of Accounts, 1923. 75p. **1H282**
At the petitioning of a number of patriotic organizations, New York's Mayor John F. Hylan requested Commissioner of Accounts, David Hirshfield, to "make a thorough investigation and report to me with regard to the new history readers and text-books alleged to contain anti-American propaganda, which have been introduced in the public schools of this city. . . . The school children of this city must not be inoculated with the poisonous virus of foreign propaganda which seeks to belittle illustrious American patriots." The Commissioner conducted hearings on the offending books at which twenty-one witnesses, mostly representing patriotic societies, spoke against the books and two witnesses spoke in favor. Authors and publishers did not appear to testify, nor did school officials. The objections were to modern historical (revisionist) scholarship which they claimed was pro-British and debunked the contribution of American patriots in the American Revolution. Objection was centered on the books of five authors: David S. Muzzey, Willis M. West, Albert B. Hart, Andrew C. McLaughlin, and Charles H. Van Tyne, the last two collaborating on a single text. Another author, William B. Guitteau had revised his book in 1923 to meet some of the criticism; Everett Barnes, a Brooklyn school superintendent and not a professional historian, in 1922 had obligingly rewritten his textbooks for grammar schools to the complete satisfaction of the critics, "having heard the rumbling of the storm of American patriotic protest." Commissioner Hirshfield concluded that "these text–books should not be permitted to be used in our schools."

Histoire de la Tyrannie du gouvernment Anglais exercée envers le Célèbre Thomas Muir, Écossais; sa déportation à Botany-Bay, son séjour dans cette île, son évasion, son séjour à Bordeaux, son arrivée à Paris; avec une description de Botany-Bay, des renseignements acquis par Thomas Muir sur la fin tragique du Voyageur Lapeyrouse, et une notice sur le continent appelé Pays de Galles Meridional. Paris, Prudhomme, 1798. 60p. **1H283**

"The History and Future of the Legal Battle over Birth Control." *Cornell Law Quarterly*, 49:275–303, Winter 1964. **1H284**
"This comment will review the legislative and judical history of the birth control controversy in this country, focusing particularly on the activities of the legislatures and courts of the federal government and the states of New York, Massachusetts, and Connecticut in the birth control area."

Hitchens, Gordon, *ed.* "Hollywood Blacklisting." *Film Culture*, 50–51:1–84, Summer–Fall, 1970. **1H285**
The entire issue is devoted to Hollywood blacklisting, including portions of the testimony of Nedrick Young before the Committee on Un-American Activities, articles by Alvah Bessie, Edith Tiger, Dalton Trumbo, John Howard Lawson, Abraham Polonsky, Joseph Strick, Joseph Losey, and Lew Irwin.

Hoak, Jon. "Court Upholds the Activities of the Federal Communications Commission in Curtailing Sex-Oriented Talk Show on Radio." *Drake Law Review*, 25:257–65, Fall 1975. **1H286**
The case, *Illinois Citizens Committee for Broadcasting v. Federal Communications Commission* (D.C. Cir. 1975), involved a penalty ($2,000) imposed on a radio broadcaster (Sonderling Broadcasting, Inc.) for failure to exercise proper self-restraint in a daytime radio call-in show. The U.S. Circuit Court of Appeals sustained the FCC's action as not infringing on the right of the public where the Commission determines that the broadcast is obscene.

Hoar, J. R. *Mississippi Newspapers and the Law. A Handbook of Mississippi Statutes, Case Law, and Other Material Related to Editing and Writing.* 2d ed. University, Miss., Department of Journalism, University of Mississippi, 1968. 74p. Processed. **1H287**
Chapters: The Constitutions and Freedoms of the Press, The Right to Gather and Print News, Civil Libel, Criminal Libel, Slander, Campaigns and Political Parties, Offenses against Chastity, Advertising, etc. Includes text of three bills on freedom of information considered by the Mississippi legislature in 1968.

Hoar, William P. "Parents Revolt: When Textbooks Are Propaganda." *American Opinion*, 17:1–8, 63–72, November 1974. **1H288**
A spirited defense of the parents and others who objected to the use of "liberal" textbooks in the schools of Kanawha County, W.Va. The books were objected to because they contained "a liberal sprinkling of obscenities, atrocious language passed off as 'non-standard' grammar; numerous subversive and Communist authors; inflammatory racial tracts; openly radical polemics; promotion of narcotic drugs; and, even detailed and explicit glamorization of prostitution." The author also attacks the radical "educrats" of the eastern cities, along with local citizens from the "radical chic" parts of the country where some of the wealthier families live and the high school is "progressive."

Hobhouse, John Cam, *Baron* Broughton. *Proceedings in the House of Commons, and in the Court of King's-Bench, Relative to the Author of the "Trifling Mistake," Together with the Argument Against Parliamentary Commitment, and The Decision Which the Judges Gave Without Hearing the Case.* London, Steuart and Steuart, 1820. 39p., 132p. **1H289**
Hobhouse's work had stated that relief of the people could only come from government reform. The House of Commons found him "guilty of a high contempt of the privileges and constitutional authority of the House." Hobhouse cited precedence to show that the House of Commons had no jurisdiction over inflammatory libel, could not serve as a court of record, could not fine or imprison, could not try in the absence of the accused, might detain in custody for future hearing, but could not pass sentence or imprison. The remedy is a discharge upon writ of habeas corpus. Lord Chief Justice Abbott ruled that the court had no authority to overrule the House of Commons.

Hobson, Julius W. *The Damned Information: Acquiring and Using Public Information to Force Social Change.* Washington, D.C., Washington Institute for Quality Education, 1971. 63p. (ED 54,794) **1H290**
Legal discussion and analysis of the Federal Freedom of Information Act and similar laws in fifty states. The author attempts to bring together information needed by the public to acquire and use public data available under the Act.

Hoch, Paul. *The Newspaper Game; The Political Sociology of the Press. An Inquiry into Behind the Scenes Organization, Financing and Brainwashing Techniques of the News Media.* London, Calder & Boyars, 1974. 217p. **1H291**
The book is an attack on the mass media and newspapers in particular in Great Britain and the United States for serving as propaganda agents for a capitalist society. Part 1 deals with the role of the established press in creating and fueling the fires of the Cold War; part 2 considers how news is selected and distorted to reflect the interests and concerns of the corporate class; part 3 discusses the impact of publishers and business considerations on editors and editorial policies, and the relationship between big press and big corporations; part 4 describes "how the economic organization of the press and of society generally has turned notions like Freedom of the Press, and indeed Freedom generally, into a facade behind which to hide what amounts to a class dictatorship."

Hochberg, Stephen. "Dedication to Morris Leopold Ernst." *New York Law Forum*, 20:447–51, Winter 1975. **1H292**
A preface to a First Amendment symposium issue of the *New York Law Forum*, entitled Confrontation: A Free Press in a Free Society and dedicated to Morris L. Ernst, "a most distinguished alumnus, whose legal career is synonymous with the courageous and successful defense of the rights created by that amendment."

Hochstettler, David. "On Rejecting Censors." *Arizona Teacher*, 57(2):9–10, 20–22, November 1968. **1H293**
The controversy over the removal of the book, *Major American Poets*, from Phoenix high schools prompts this broader discussion of how to deal with censorship. Schools are legally compelled to recognize the parent's "preeminent right to control his child's reading. Equally important, we are professionally and morally compelled to resist his efforts if he attempts to restrict the reading of other children." The Phoenix controversy "passed through all of the seven phases identified here: silence, informal talk, informal assistance from outside the school, filing of a formal written complaint, review by a committee of educators, formal debate featuring the whole range of attacks and defenses, and finally, election of a board member . . . who declared himself more sensitive to students' right to read. Educators lost each of the first six rounds but won the seventh."

Hoddeson, Bob. *The Porn People.* Watertown, Mass., American Publishing Co., 1973. 124p. **1H294**
"An in-depth, photo-illustrated, inside look at the performers, makers, sellers, and users who make up America's erotic marketplace."

Hodges, Clem. "Crisis in Publishing: Burning Books, Banning Authors." *Masses & Mainstream*, 4(11):1–7, November 1951. **1H295**
The author accuses Little, Brown and Company with capitulating to *Counterattack* charges of Communist-front activities.

Hodgin, R. W. "Defamation in East Africa." *Journal of African Law*, 17:66–92, Spring 1973. **1H296**
"The purpose of this article is to review the application of the English law of defamation in the East African countries (Uganda, Kenya, Tanzania), and to assess the possible contribution of the Kenya Defamation Act, 1970."

Hodgson, Beverly J. "Sex, Texts, and the First Amendment." *Journal of Law and Education*, 5:173–95, April 1976. **1H297**
"This article examines the purposes of Title IX [of the Education Amendments of 1972], the need for regulation in this area, and the applicable First Amendment doctrines and concludes that sex discrimination in instructional materials may be regulated without violating the First Amendment. . . . The School boards which select instructional material have, as government entities, no First

Amendment rights, nor has the right to academic freedom of elementary and secondary school teachers been held to allow independent choice of materials in the face of proof of harm to students." Even if First Amendment claims were supportable, the author concludes, sexist textbooks could be excluded from schools because "they conflict with students' rights to be free from government-imposed discrimination, the government's obligation to allow maximum access of ideas in a limited forum, its obligation not to infringe the rights and interests of a captive audience, and the general purposes of the First Amendment to promote circulation of ideas and information." The author proposes regulations requiring balanced presentation in the depiction of the sexes in instructional materials.

Hodierne, Robert. "How the G.I.'s in Vietnam Don't Learn About the War." *New York Times Magazine*, 12 April 1970, pp. 28–29+.　　　**1H298**
"The military's ban on giving out the news limits a soldier's view of his own war to little more than what he can see down the sights of his rifle." While civilian media are free to report most of the distasteful aspects of the Vietnam war, they are being hidden only from the G.I.'s in Vietnam. "When a unit gets in a tough fight with lots of people hurt, it comes out sounding like a tea party in the division newspaper and on A.F.V.N."

Hoduski, Bernadine E. "Federal Libraries and Intellectual Freedom." In American Library Association's *Intellectual Freedom Manual*, Chicago, ALA, 1974, pt. 3, pp. 17–18.　　　**1H299**
The librarian of a federal library makes eight suggestions for insuring intellectual freedom and avoiding censorship in libraries serving federal agencies.

————. "Recall Without Just Cause: Government Documents and Depository Libraries." *Newsletter on Intellectual Freedom* (IFC-ALA), 21:151–54, November 1972.　　　**1H300**
The article deals with the failure of federal government agencies to comply with the laws relating to the distribution of publications and the recall by the Superintendent of Documents of certain publications already distributed to libraries. The article asks: What should be the librarian's response when a government agent appears to take back a document from the library's shelf?

Hoellrich, Gene R. "Stanley v. Georgia: A First Amendment Approach to Obscenity Control." *Ohio State Law Journal*, 31:364–70, Spring 1970. **1H301**
Re: *Stanley v. Georgia*, 394 U.S. 557 (1969) in which the U.S. Supreme Court ruled that the First and Fourteenth Amendments prohibited making mere private possession of obscene material a crime.

Hoerster, John K. "The 1966 Freedom of Information Act—Early Judicial Interpretations." *Washington Law Review*, 44:641–86, Spring 1969.　　　**1H302**
"The purpose of this comment is to appraise the Act in light of its interpretation by agencies and by federal courts, and to demonstrate that these early interpretations do not accurately reflect legislative intent or sound policy considerations." The comments address themselves to interpretations of the Act's substantive provisions, its procedural provisions, and agency rules and regulations promulgated under the Act.

Hoets, Pieter J. "Symposium on Group Defamation: Symposium Conclusion." *Cleveland-Marshall Law Review*, 13:111–17, January 1964. **1H303**
In a summary of the symposium, the writer calls for legislation—criminal and civil law—to deal with group defamation. It is needed to protect the American people "from the sick and evil souls who would poison our society with hatred." While recognizing the need to respect freedom of expression guaranteed by the First Amendment of the Constitution, he points out that freedom of expression is not absolute and should not permit malicious defamation of large groups of American citizens. He cites German and Dutch laws as models. Referring to the classic difficulty in proving specific damages when a group or class is involved, he notes that medical experts now have substantial evidence to show damage done to the psyche and emotional stability of the individual, even if he is only identified as a member of a group or class. He calls also for legal measures "to keep hate propaganda out of the United States mails, radio, television, and other communications avenues." Participants in the symposium were: Senator Thomas H. Kuchel (Fright Peddlers), James J. Brown and Carl L. Stern (Group Defamation in the U.S.A.), David R. Fryer (Group Defamation in England), Manfred Zuleeg (Group Defamation in West Germany), Jean Peytel (Group Defamation in France), W. H. Bijleveld (Group Defamation in the Netherlands), Louis J. Bloomfield (Defamation of Corporations), and Richard J. Quigg (Defenses to Group Defamation Actions).

Hoffer, Thomas W., and Gerald A. Butterfield. "The Right to Reply: A Florida First Amendment Abberation." *Journalism Quarterly*, 53:111–16, Spring 1976.　　　**1H304**
Florida's right of reply statute, declared unconstitutional by the U.S. Supreme Court in 1974, had been passed in 1913 as part of the Corrupt Practices Act, and when the largely rural press "was either susceptible to demagogues or political party influence." A history of the passage of the law and the environment in which this took place.

Hoffman, Carl. *A Psychiatric View of Obscene Literature*. Cincinnati, Citizens for Decent Literature, n.d. 6p. Processed.　　　**1H305**
Evidence gathered from medical literature, examination of case files of patients and prison records, and testimony of a number of psychiatrists (including Frederick Hacker, Winfred Overholser, Fredric Wertham, Marcel Frym, and Courtney Ryley Cooper) concludes that there is ample evidence that pornography is a contributing factor in delinquency and sex crimes.

Hoffman, Elizabeth P. "School Libraries and Intellectual Freedom." *PLA Bulletin* (Pennsylvania Library Association), 27:187–90, July 1972.　　　**1H306**
Parents, teachers, and sometimes school librarians—seldom the students—have created the problems of censorship in school libraries. The author recommends that school librarians preserve objectivity in the selection of materials, that they follow a written selection code, involve teachers and students in the selection process, and acquaint the entire school community with the procedure.

Hoffman, Eunice M. *An Analysis of English and American Blasphemy Law*. Madison, Wis., University of Wisconsin, 1966. 234p. (Unpublished Master's thesis)　　　**1H307**

Hofsess, John. "The Witchcraft of Obscenity; A Canadian Director Tells How His Movie Was Charged and Found Guilty." *Saturday Night*, 85:11–16, August 1970.　　　**1H308**
"Public officials of a censorious, repressive nature do not trust the public; those who represent the world of art do. It is out of this conflict—an artist's trust in people, and the mistrust and cynicism of police and public officials—that the *Columbus of Sex* obscenity case was born."

Hofstadter, Samuel H. "Wanted: Jury Trials in Obscenity Cases." *National Decency Reporter*, 5(3–4):4–5, March–April 1968.　　　**1H309**
A justice of the New York Supreme Court believes the U.S. Supreme Court is floundering in the area of obscenity. He believes that the problem of obscenity is one of municipal order—a domestic one—and not primarily a constitutional matter. It should be decided not at the summit, but at the base, recognizing cultural pluralism and the differing outlooks in various localities. "To impose a single unitary rule" in the area of obscenity is not feasible. "Jury determination as a national method, however, is salutary and practical. As a constant, it can resolve the dichotomy, if any, between state standard and Federal constitutional sanction. Under such a dispensation, what the Supreme Court has found insoluble becomes soluble."

Hogan, Paul M. "Ohio: Printing *the Obscenity*." *Columbia Journalism Review*, 14(2):15–17, July–August 1975. **1H310**
The story of the resignation of the editor and publisher of the Dayton, Ohio, *Journal Herald* over a controversy with the owners for allowing an obscenity to be published in excerpts from an affidavit in the investigation of a killing. "The word was that most explosive of obscenities, 'fucking,' a word which remains taboo despite the changed standards of the past decade."

Hogan, Robert F. "Censorship Cases May Increase." *College English*, 35:27–31, January 1974. **1H311**
Testimony of the executive secretary of the National Council of Teachers of English before a New York joint legislative committee considering problems brought on by the U.S. Supreme Court's obscenity decision.

———. "State of Censorship." *Senior Scholastic*, 93(11):25, 42, 22 November 1968. **1H312**
In our democratic, pluralistic society the only form of censorship that is tenable is "each man serving as his own censor, each parent seeing to the rearing of his children." The author discusses the motives for censorship of school materials and how efforts to censor can best be met.

Hoge, James F., Jr. "Lessons of the Pentagon Papers." *Bulletin of the American Society of Newspaper Editors*, 553:1, 13–14, September 1971. **1H313**
An examination of the performance and credibility of the nation's press in light of the Supreme Court decision on the Pentagon Papers.

Hoggart, Richard. "Controls and Shocks." *New Statesman*, 77:837–38, 13 June 1969. **1H314**
A review of Donald Thomas, *A Long Time Burning*, and C. R. Hewitt (C. H. Rolph), *Books in the Dock*.

Hoglund, John A., and Jonathan Kahan. "Invasion of Privacy and the Freedom of Information Act: *Getman v. NLRB*." *George Washington Law Review*, 40:527–41, March 1972. **1H315**
The case (*Getman v. NLRB*, 1971) involves "balancing" between citizens' interest in access to government-held records and the interests of individual privacy and governmental efficiency and security.

Hogue, Richard W. *Censorship and the U.S. Senate*. Washington, D.C., 1930. 8p. **1H316**
A spirited attack on proposals by Senator Reed Smoot of Utah to reopen the question of imposing censorship on "obscene" literature in the tariff act, a measure already voted down in a fight led by Senator Bronson Cutting of New

Mexico. The author argues: "It is the same issue that was before the Senate on October 11th. It was not then and is not now a question of obscenity and immorality versus decency and purity. It is a question of whether the American reading public shall be controlled by the literary censorship of a Federal Bureau; whether Congress shall delegate to customs clerks this sort of guardianship over the minds of the American people. That is the fundamental issue, and no amount of outraged sentiment stirred by fresh Senatorial contact with indecent literature can banish or obscure this issue. . . . Even if there were unanimous agreement on a policy of the very strictest literary censorship, there would still be no need of enacting tariff legislation on the subject. The matter is amply covered in the laws of the separate states. These laws are rigid, comprehensive, entirely adequate, and with ample provisions for enforcement."

Hohenberg, John. *Free Press/Free People: The Best Cause*. New York, Columbia University Press, 1970. 514p. (Excerpts in *Current*, June 1971; *Bulletin of the American Society of Newspaper Editors*, March 1971; and *Saturday Review*, 13 December 1969 and 14 March 1970) **1H317**
A history of the development of press freedom presented in broad panorama, from its roots in ancient Athens to the present day, in the Eastern world as well as in the West, with numerous references to people, events, and changing concepts. The author is concerned not only with the expansion of freedom but the way in which the press has responded to the increased freedom over the centuries. He sees the need for improvement in today's press if the public's confidence in it is to be restored.

———. *The News Media: A Journalist Looks at His Profession*. New York, Holt, Rinehart and Winston, 1968. 320p. **1H318**
A series of essays on the ethics of the journalist, his outlook on society, and his duties to the nation. Includes chapters on: The Limits of Power; The Credibility Gap; War; Truth, and Vietnam; Free Press and Fair Trial; and Right to Know vs. Need to Know. In the last mentioned chapter the author notes that the burden of the campaign for the right to know is being carried by a small group of journalists, with no all-consuming interest on the part of the persons benefited.

[Holahan, Frank.] "Freedom of the Press and Reply Statutes." *New York Law Forum*, 20:645–54, Winter 1975. **1H319**
Re: *Miami Herald Publishing Co. v. Tornillo*, 418 U.S. 241 (1974), involving the rejection of Florida's right of reply law.

Holbrook, David. "Against 'Enlightenment.'" *New Blackfriars*, 52:149–58, April 1971. **1H320**

An attack on the dogmatic intolerance of the "enlightenment"—those who believe that the cultural depiction of sex can do no harm. His remarks are prompted by participation in a panel on censorship sponsored by the Young Publishers Group. He comments favorably on the book *Love and Will* by Rollo May, a psychoanalyst, who points out that sexual "enlightenment" has not solved the emotional problems attributed to sex. The major complaint of Dr. May's patients is not sex inhibition but lack of enjoyment of it. "Sex has become a drug to 'blot out our awareness' of our needs for passion and for relationship. In 'ostensibly enlightened discussions of sex, particularly those about freedom from censorship, it is often argued that all our society needs is full freedom for the expression of eros' (Eros Denied!). But what is revealed under the surface is just the opposite: 'We are in a flight from eros—and we use sex as the vehicle for the flight.' "

———. "Counter-Censorship." *Tablet: The International Catholic Weekly*, 227:844–46, 8 September 1973. (Reprinted in *Catholic Mind*, February 1974) **1H321**
An attack on the pseudo liberalism that not only tolerates widespread pornography in the mass media, but endorses it, and even goes so far as to suppress opposition to it. The author complains of the censorship by the British press of articles or letters that make it plain "that the essential act of watching sex is aggressive and rapacious."

———. "Lessons in Pornography." *Twentieth Century*, 179:36–40, October 1972. **1H322**
A satire on the virtues of bringing pornography into the schoolroom, the argument that complete freedom for pornography will lead to eventual boredom and indifference, and will permit indulgence in sex "without any of the messiness of being human."

———. "Little Red Schoolbook Again." *Index on Censorship*, 2(2):102–6, Summer 1973. **1H323**
Criticism of the partial treatment of *The Little Red Schoolbook* issue in *Index*, Autumn–Winter 1972. The *Index* had reprinted the New Zealand Indecent Publications Tribunal's decision declaring the Danish book "not obscene." The editor responded to the criticism, noting that opposition to censorship of a work did not represent endorsement of it.

———. "Mass Law—Breaking in the Mass Media." *New Law Journal*, 123:701–3, 26 July 1973. **1H324**
The author accuses British magistrates of serious dereliction of duty in not prosecuting the cinemas for showing pornographic films that

"offend against good taste or decency or would be likely to encourage or incite to crime or lead to public disorder or to be offensive to public feeling."

———. "Pornography and Death." *Critical Quarterly*, 14:29–40, Spring 1972. **1H325**
Pornography is seen as a means of deadening emotion, love, and creativity, as being full of hostility and nihilism. It introduces forms of violence parallel to racism and aggression. Instead of leading to true liberation, pornography encourages violence as socially acceptable and, therefore, is not the harmless form of expression that has been suggested.

———. "Pornography and Fascism." *Patterns and Prejudice*, 6(2):5–8, March–April 1972. **1H326**
Those who seek to use pornography for political purposes to subvert or overthrow society by destroying its moral values indulge in a form of sexual fascism. Society has found it possible to discriminate in the matter of racism; it should be able to judge whether the effects of a cultural work are human or antihuman and to apply controls. More important than censorship, however, "is the development of an alert and critical public opinion. When, at last, people see how degrading and full of hostility pornography is, then they will renounce it, reject it, and use their democratic institutions to thrust it back into the shadows."

———. *Pornography and Hate*. Sydney, Australia, Australian Festival of Light, n.d. 14p. (Group Resource Paper, no. 5) **1H327**
The author, an agnostic, humanist, and existentialist, challenges the propagandists for the "sexual revolution" who offer the new sex as leading to realms of joy. Holbrook believes that pornography is rather a form of perversion, full of sadism, meanness, and envy. It threatens the meaning of love, and thus the point of life. In this article he is critical of the Church's guilty silence in the matter and challenges those churchmen and others who have been persuaded that pornography is innocuous or even beneficial.

———. "Pornography and Its Effect." *Assistant Librarian*, 64:184–86, December 1971. **1H328**
The author rejects the commonly held notion that it is a myth that exposure to explicit sexual material has not corrupted or depraved anyone. He deplores the deterioration of the debate on pornography which fails to distinguish between erotic works of art and public obscenities. "I don't think censorship is the answer; but I am sure that if man is continually given a certain kind of picture of himself, by 'explicit sexual material,' then he may well come to become less responsible—and less cre-

ative in his living in consequence. Because of this, I believe the question of pornography is a most important one to consider, with deep political implications."

———. "Seduction of the People: Pornography Under Labour." *Spectator*, 7605:384–85, 30 March 1974. **1H329**
"What, I wonder, will the Labour Government do about the deliberate debauchery of public taste by pornography and sadism?" The author sees a changing attitude among left-wing intellectuals toward a permissive society. He presents a case for controls over obscenity and violence in the mass media just as we control the use of adulterated foods and work in dangerous and unsanitary factory conditions. In an accompanying article Leo Abse presents a different point of view.

———. " . . . So That Evil Things May Be Done With a Clear Conscience?" *Books*, 8:7–12, Summer 1972. **1H330**
The author concludes that "(a) pornography has an effect (b) the effect is to evoke distress, feelings of aggression and fear (c) these are mental, and tend to negate relationship, likely to make it less possible for people to love and fulfill themselves sexually (d) it can thus lead to withdrawal from life, decline of the capacity to perceive and deal with the world, and (e) it can possibly, in a disturbed minority cause 'acting out,' by the dynamics of hate. It can be unethical: and it can deprave and corrupt. . . . The best way of containing pornography would be by an alert and emphatic public opinion. . . . But because of the economic pressures towards greater and greater debasement of humanness for money, and because of the ruthlessness of the fanatical immoralist, we also need to make our law and our courts capable of effectively deciding where the line shall be drawn, and how the impulse to harm others through culture shall be restrained, without putting limits on the genuine forms of exploration of the darker depths of the human soul, or on the expression of sexual joy. But 'joy' is hardly the word to use for the general aspect of the present Sadist Revolution."

———, ed. *The Case Against Pornography*. London, Tom Stacey, 1972; LaSalle, Ill., Open Court, 1973. 294p. **1H331**
These essays on pornography are intended to keep the debate open, to examine the dehumanization and brutalization of sex in our culture. They "support the view that we urgently need a 'social psychology' capable of looking seriously at the problem and invoking appropriate ethical considerations. They certainly all convey the impression that in its implicit denial of love and tenderness, pornography threatens meaning and has in it somewhere a 'hatred of man.' " Rational debate on the subject will "sustain psychic health in the face of a subtle disease of spirit." Essays are by Walter Berns, David Boadella, Ronald Butt, Dr. Leslie H. Farber, Viktor Frankl, David Holbrook, Storm Jameson, Pamela Hansford

Johnson, Moira Keenan, Masud R. Khan, Irving Kristol, Rollo May, E. J. Mishan, Dr. Mary Miles, John MacMurray, Ian Robinson, Dr. Benjamin Spock, Dr. George Steiner, Tom Stacey, Dr. Robert J. Stoller, Dr. Erwin Straus, Ernest van den Haag, and D. W. Winnicott. Many of the essays are reprinted from books and journals.

Holbrook, Lanny R. "To Recover for Libel a Person Who Is Not a Public Figure Must Prove with Convincing Clarity That False Statements Which Involve a Matter in the Public Interest Were Made with Actual Malice." *University of Cincinnati Law Review*, 39:363–69, Spring 1970. **1H332**
Re: *Cerrito v. Time, Inc.*, 302 F. Supp. 1071 (N.D. Cal. 1969).

Holicky, Bernard H. "Recommend a Dirty Book?" *Focus on Indiana Libraries*, 26(1):36–37, Spring 1972. **1H333**
Confessions of a librarian who, as a library page, developed an interest in reading, through sampling the works in the locked case.

Holland, Norman N. "Pornography and the Mechanisms of Defense." *Technical Report of the [U.S.] Commission on Obscenity and Pornography*, 1:115–29, 1971. **1H334**
"Pornography defends against all unconscious fantasies save one, which is: 'phallic gratifications need not be feared.' Readers who enjoy this fantasy will respond to pornography by either sexual arousal or a lack of interest. Readers who cannot enjoy such a fantasy will need to add defensive measures of some kind. If government adds defenses on their behalf, it weakens their own adaptive capacity."

Holland, Vyvyan. "Introduction" to Oscar Wilde, *De Profundis; being the first complete and accurate version of "Epistola: in Carcere et Vinculis" the last prose work in English of Oscar Wilde*. London, Methuen, 1949, pp. 7–12. **1H335**
An account of the history of Oscar Wilde's manuscript, written in Reading Gaol in 1897– "how its publication was prevented during the lifetime of Lord Alfred Douglas, and how it finally became possible to present to an English public for the first time this complete, unexpurgated edition of Oscar Wilde's masterpiece."

Hollihan, J. P., III. "The Federal Election Campaign Act Amendments of 1974: The Constitutionality of Limiting Political Advertising by Non-Candidates." *Florida State University Law Review*, 3:266–89, Spring 1975. **1H336**
"Judicial determination of the constitutionality of subsection 608 (e) will necessarily depend on

the subjective balancing of many of the factors discussed in this article. However, it is this author's opinion that subsection 608 (e) is unconstitutional."

Hollinger, Robert. "Can a Scientific Theory Be Legitimately Criticized, Rejected, Condemned, or Suppressed on Ethical or Political Grounds?" *Journal of Value Inquiry*, 9:303–6, Winter 1975. **1H337**

"The real dilemmas which we face are in just those cases where a view is *both* scientifically acceptable *and* morally objectionable." If any kind of suppression is to be defensible, there is need for "a moral position which is not logically tied to the scientific legitimacy of any theory, and which does not stand or fall with the scientific acceptance of them."

Hollis, Patricia. *The Pauper Press: A Study in Working-Class Radicalism of the 1830's*. London, Oxford University Press, 1970. 348p. (Oxford Historical Monographs) **1H338**

The book is about popular journalism and working-class radicals in London during the 1830s. It is about the hundreds of "unstamped" papers that sprung up in defiance of the 1815 stamp tax, or "tax on knowledge" as it was known, under such titles as *Poor Man's Guardian*, *Slap at the Church*, and *Working Man's Friend*. For selling such papers some 740 men, women, and children went to prison. Chapter 5 deals with the prosecution of publishers, proprietors, and vendors, and the establishment of relief societies to support the victims of government prosecution. The emphasis of the work is on the relationship of the "pauper press" to the working-class radical movement. Among the original sources consulted by the author were the papers of Richard Carlile on file in the Huntington Library. The appendix includes biographical notes of leading publishers and authors of the London unstamped press, including William Benbow, Richard Carlile, William Carpenter, Henry Hetherington, and James Watson, all of whom figured in court cases.

Hollow, Richard L., and Rudolph L. Ennis. "Tennessee Sunshine: The Public's Business Goes Public." *Tennessee Law Review*, 42:527–55, Spring 1975. **1H339**

An examination of Tennessee's new open meetings act which "can give this state the brightest of government sunshine," but requires voluntary implementation by elected representatives and coercive enforcement by the courts on the petition of a watchful citizenry.

Holmes, Geoffrey. *The Trial of Doctor Sacheverell*. London, Eyre Methuen, 1973. 338p. **1H340**

The eminent English minister and Oxford don was brought to trial before Parliament in 1710 for a political sermon which had attacked the

Whigs. It was estimated that a hundred thousand copies of the sermon had been distributed throughout England. Dr. Sacheverell was found guilty and prohibited from preaching for three years and his sermons were burned. The celebrated trial contributed to the fall of the Whig government.

Holmes, Paul. *Retrial: Murder and Dr. Sam Sheppard*. New York, Bantam, 1966. 240p. **1H341**

On 6 June 1966 the U.S. Supreme Court's decision (*Sheppard v. Maxwell*) ordered a new trial for Dr. Sam Sheppard, convicted and serving twelve years in prison for murdering his wife. The new trial was ordered "because of the trial judge's failure to protect Sheppard sufficiently from the massive, pervasive, and prejudicial publicity that attended his prosecution." This is the story of the legal events leading to the Supreme Court decision and the retrial in which Sheppard was acquitted. The story involves the issue of free press versus fair trial.

Holmgren, Rod, and William Norton, eds. *The Mass Media Book*. Englewood Cliffs, N.J., Prentice-Hall, 1972. 421p. **1H342**

In this book of readings the following articles, entered under their authors' names in this bibliography, deal with aspects of press freedom: Why We Need Press Councils by Norman E. Isaacs. The Marketplace Myth: Access to the Mass Media by Robert K. Baker and Sandra J. Ball. Pretrial Crime News: To Curb or Not to Curb? by John Lofton. The Power of the Press by Spiro Agnew. Some Sober Second Thoughts on Vice-President Agnew by Fred W. Friendly. The Happy Ending (Maybe) of "Selling of the Pentagon" by Robert Sherrill. The Silent Screen by Nicholas Johnson. A Psychiatrist Looks at Television and Violence by Ner Littner. Social Comment and TV Censorship by David Dempsey. Pornography Revisited: Where to Draw the Line by Ruth Brine. Censorship of Pornography? Yes by Reo Christenson.

Holroyd, Michael. "Censorship." In his *Unreceived Opinions*. London, Heinemann, 1973, pp. 68–71. **1H343**

A review of Donald Thomas, *A Long Time Burning* and C. R. Hewitt (C. H. Rolph), *Books in the Dock*.

Holt, Hamilton. *Commercialism and Journalism*. Boston, Houghton Mifflin, 1909. 105p. (University of California, Weinstock Lectures) **1H344**

A study of commercialism "at present the greatest menace to the freedom of the press" by reason of the dependence of newspapers on their advertising business.

Holtzoff, Alexander *et al.* "Fair Trial and Freedom of the Press: A Panel Discussion." *Federal Rules Decisions*, 19:16–43, May 1956. **1H345**

Panelists: Florence E. Allen, judge, U.S. Sixth Circuit; James R. Wiggins, managing editor, *Washington Post* and *Times Herald*; and Richard P. Tinkham, chairman of the Committee on Public Relations, American Bar Association. Moderator was Alexander Holtzoff, judge for the U.S. District of Columbia. The panel was sponsored by the Section of Judicial Administration and the Junior Bar Association at a meeting of the American Bar Association, 11 June 1955.

Holzman, Sheridan V. *et al.* "Freedom to Read Workshop." *Michigan Librarian*, 41:5–16, Summer 1974. **1H346**

An American Civil Liberties Union attorney discusses the immaturity of American society about sex which has formed the bases for the major object of the censor. "The fact that the Supreme Court finds it necessary to declare obscenity outside of the realm of the First Amendment, and having no First Amendment protections is one manifestation; and the inability of the Supreme Court to fabricate a syntactical test or distinction between the artistic and the salacious is another manifestation." The author discusses recent decisions of the Court, particularly the *Miller* decision (*Miller v. State of California*, 1973) and its aftermath. He contends that "we should oppose any restraint, under obscenity statutes, on the right to create, publish or distribute materials to adults, or the right of adults to choose materials they read or view." Other remarks made at the workshops include: Facing the Censorship Issue by Judith F. Krug, Shopping for a Selection Policy by Lee Lebbin, Censorship and the Credibility of the High School Library by Marilyn L. Miller, The Trustee and Intellectual Freedom by Jane Cameron, Is There Obscenity in Your Neighborhood? Or, Current Legislation Reviewed by Bernard Margolis.

Homan, Robert. "Newspaper Control in America." Arlington, Va., National Socialist Publications, [1967?] 12p. (Reprinted from *National Socialist World*, Spring 1967) **1H347**

"It is the purpose of this article to demonstrate how an influential minority, which constitutes only 2.9 percent of the total U.S. population, has effectively achieved domination over America's newspaper industry. . . . This disproportionately powerful political and economic control of the news media by the Jews has allowed them to choose presidential candidates, swing elections, control foreign and domestic policy, and determine generally what is to be considered acceptable in every aspect of American culture."

Homer, Jack. "Censorship by Printers? Reflections on a Bad Idea." *Inland Printer/American Lithographer*, 169(4): 32–34, July 1972. **1H348**

While noting that the printer has a legal right to

accept or turn down any job, he questions the use of "antiobscenity" clauses in printing contracts. "By inserting that clause, the printer is expressly setting himself up as a censor," a radical change in the traditional relationship between printer and customer. "So far, we have been able to uncover only one example" of a printer being held responsible for content of publication and "we have yet to hear of a customer successfully suing a printer for refusing to produce material he feels is objectionable."

Hood, Stuart. "Mass Media: The Right to Be Heard." In *Toward an Open Society . . . Proceedings of a Seminar Organized by the British Humanist Association.* London, Pemberton Books, 1971, pp. 73–80.   **1H349**
While British broadcasting, unlike American broadcasting, has not been abandoned to commercial interests and gives greater coverage of political affairs, there are certain restrictive influences. Both in religion and politics, broadcasting in Britain is dedicated to the mainstream of thought and there is a curtailment of the spectrum of views and difficulty for dissident opinion to be given an adequate hearing.

———. "Television, Muck and Politics." *Index on Censorship*, 2(2):19–22, Summer 1973.   **1H350**
Britain's Independent Broadcasting Authority and the banning of the TV films on Andy Warhol, John Poulson and Michael Collins.

Hood, William F. "Liability of Broadcaster." *Michigan Law Review*, 39: 1002–10, April 1941.   **1H351**
The article deals with two problems: Should radio broadcast of defamatory matter be treated as libel or slander? and which of the several parties to a defamatory broadcast should be held responsible?

Hopkin, Deian. "Domestic Censorship in the First World War." *Journal of Contemporary History*, 5:151–69, October 1970.   **1H352**
Working from documentary sources, the author traces Britain's World War I censorship through its various phases: the early voluntary system; the operation of the government press bureau with its twofold mission of controlling dissemination of government information and screening press cables and telegrams; establishment of "D" notices; defining what categories of news were not to be published; instituting a more formal control under the Defence of the Realm Act; and action by police, military, and vigilanti against pacifist and revolutionary press. The author concludes that despite the occasional harassment and overreaction by government agencies, no serious or permanent damage was done to British

liberties, and censorship was allowed to die in July 1919.

Hopkins, Jeannette. *Books that Will Not Burn—Four Centuries of Books of Religious Liberalism. The First Century of Official Unitarian Book Publishing in the U.S. (1854–1954).* Boston, Beacon, 1954? 22p.   **1H353**
"John Biddle, the first Englishman to publish Unitarian books, spent most of his life in prison for his ideas. The books of this man, who was known as the 'father of English Unitarianism,' were burned by the common hangman—as though an idea could be killed like a man—but new copies kept appearing."

Hornadge, Bill. *Chidley's Answer to the Sex Problem; A Squint in the Life and Theories of William James Chidley, and the Reactions of Society Towards His Unorthodox Views.* Dubbo, Australia, Review Publications, 1971. 90p.   **1H354**
The story of the life and views of William James Chidley, eccentric Australian sex reformer whose work, *The Answer*, was the widespread subject of controversy in Australia, 1911–16(C317). Police in Sydney arranged for Chidley's arrest and, after getting a certificate of insanity, they committed him to an asylum. He was released only after public criticism of the action and an investigation in Parliament. Chidley continued to preach and publicize his unorthodox views on sex and spent the last few years of his life in and out of jail and mental hospitals. A Sydney conviction for the sale of *The Answer* in 1914 reached the Supreme Court which, in a divided decision, upheld the lower court's conviction under the Obscene Publications Act. Sir William Cullen, in a dissenting judgment, rejected the views of his fellow judges that sexual intercourse could never be the subject of any book except a medical text. He also defended the right of an author to be controversial, including ridiculous, which Chidley theories were generally considered. Briefly stated, Chidley preached that most of the world's social ills could be attributed to the erect male penis and its forcible entrance into the female vagina. In a native and wholesome state, he argued, the female organ "has the power of sucking the *unerect* penis in, there manipulating it naturally to erection and emission." One of the many versions of *The Answer* is reproduced on pp. 53–90 of this booklet.

Hornby, W. H. "Secrecy, Privacy, and Publicity." *Columbia Journalism Review*, 13(6):10–11, March–April 1975.   **1H355**
"When the press isn't told who is in jail, the protection of individual privacy has gone too far."

Horton, Frank. "The Public's Right to Know." *North Carolina Central Law Journal*, 3:123–42, Spring 1972. (Reprinted in *Case and Comment*, January–February 1972)   **1H356**

A Congressman criticizes Executive Order 10501, which governs official secrecy, the currently applied doctrine of executive privilege, and the administration of the Freedom of Information Act. He offers proposals for improving various aspects of the flow of public information.

Horton, Guy M. *Application of the "N. Y. Times" Rule.* Columbia, Mo., Freedom of Information Center, School of Journalism, University of Missouri at Columbia, 1968. 5p. (Report no. 205)   **1H357**
"The 1964 Supreme Court ruling in *New York Times v. Sullivan* has been applied to the area of privacy and extended to include 'public figures' as well as 'public officials.' Indications are that the high court has developed a position favoring expanded comment and unfettered interchange of ideas on public issues, perhaps at the expense of the individual. The endless flow of libel cases, however, suggests that conflicts between individual and societal rights will continue, but that additional guidelines will be determined."

———. *Fairness Doctrine Under Fire.* Columbia, Mo., Freedom of Information Center, School of Journalism, University of Missouri at Columbia, 1968. 4p. (Report no. 206)   **1H358**
"Questions regarding the constitutional status of the fairness doctrine are due interpretation by the Supreme Court in *Red Lion* [*Red Lion Broadcasting Co. v. FCC*, 1969] and other cases which may be considered with it late this year or early in 1969. The need for clarification is evident from the growing dissent of broadcasters. The fuzzy terms in the fairness doctrine and the 'personal attack' rules are subject to varied interpretations."

———. *Minority Groups and News Media.* Columbia, Mo., Freedom of Information Center, School of Journalism, University of Missouri at Columbia, 1968. 4p. (Report no. 209)   **1H359**
"Countless examples in America's past can be cited to illustrate that American news media, sometimes partisan themselves, have been victims of attacks by citizens and citizen groups. Today, efforts of so-called pressure groups to manipulate the news may be directly addressed to the reporters—sometimes through use of violence—or handled by such indirect means as boycotts."

Houde, Danièle. "La Liberté de la Presse en Droit Anglais, Américain et Canadièn." *Les Cahiers de Droit*, 13:121–93, 1972.   **1H360**
A study of liberty of the press in the three most important common law countries—England, United States, and Canada.

Hough, George, III. "Felonies, Jury

Trials, and News Reports." In Chilton R. Bush, *ed.*, *Free Press and Fair Trial*, Athens, Ga., University of Georgia Press, 1970, pp. 36–48. **1H361**
"The main objective of this study was to analyze the disposition in one criminal court [Detroit's Recorder's Court] and the reporting of one newspaper [Detroit's *Free Press*] of all felony cases for which warrants of arrest had been issued over a six-month period." "Mr. Hough," the editor reports, "found that of the 9,140 felony cases disposed of by the Recorder's Court in the calendar year of 1967, only 3.4 percent had gone to jury trial and only 2.4 percent resulted in a verdict of guilty. He also found that of the felony cases for which warrants had been issued in a six-month period, only 7 percent had been reported in the Detroit *Free Press*, and that nearly one-half of all crimes reported in that paper were from outside the state of Michigan."

Hough, Maxine L. "Censorship: Where Will You Be When It Hits the Fan." *Michigan Librarian*, 39(2):5–7, Summer 1973. **1H362**
Practical advice to librarians on action to take before the censor arrives: creation of a materials selection committee, and preparation of a selection policy adopted by the library board and understood by community leaders.

"Householder's Right to Restrict Commercial Obscenity Sent Through the Mails." *Rutgers-Camden Law Journal*, 3:144–54, Spring 1971. **1H363**
Re: *Rowan v. United States Post Office Department* (397 U.S. 728, 1970) in which the Supreme Court upheld the law empowering the householder to restrict the delivery of unsolicited advertisements deemed to be "erotically arousing and sexually provocative."

Houser, Thomas J. "The Fairness Doctrine—An Historical Perspective." *Notre Dame Lawyer*, 47:550–701, February 1972. **1H364**
Following an historical review of the fairness doctrine in broadcasting, the author discusses the problems the Federal Communications Commission faces in enforcing it. He concludes that a major review of the doctrine is needed to strike a balance "between the growing desire of our national citizenry to gain access to mass broadcasting channels," and the limited frequency availabilities requiring "a reaffirmation of the trustee relationship which underlies a broadcast licensee's discretion and decision-making function."

Housley, Roger, and William G. Lee. "Criminal Law: Pretrial Publicity—Threat to Trial By Jury." *Oklahoma Law Review*, 22:165–74, May 1969. **1H365**
A discussion of the present state of the law concerning two approaches to pretrial publicity: (1) providing a fair trial in spite of public-

ity, and (2) affirmative judicial action to counter adverse publicity.

Houston, Judith A., and Samuel R. Houston. "Identifying Pornographic Materials with Judgment Analysis." *Journal of Experimental Education*, 42(4):18–26, Summer 1974. **1H366**
Judgment analysis was used as a methodology for determining what is pornographic by testing this technique with three groups concerned with this issue: doctoral students majoring in psychology, counseling, and personnel guidance; lawyers; and police officers.

Houston, R. F. V. "Recent Developments in the Law of Defamation." *Irish Jurist*, 1(n.s.):247–70, Winter 1966. **1H367**
Changes in the Irish law of defamation since the Committee on the Law of Defamation made its report in 1939 and a defamation bill was passed. The article focuses on court decisions since 1952 and problems that have developed and criticism leveled against present law, both from within and outside the legal profession.

"How Far Should Censorship Extend?" *Bulletin of the Atomic Scientists*, 4:163–65, June 1948. **1H368**
The Committee on Secrecy and Clearance, Federation of American Scientists, in conducting an inquiry into problems of security and personnel clearance ran into opposition from a number of agencies that claimed that what the committee sought was classified information. The article suggests that military security was being used to suppress public discussion of administrative malpractice.

"How Much Censorship Is Too Much?" *Christianity Today*, 19:21–22, 8 August 1975. **1H369**
The editorial concludes: "There is a real question as to whether laws can be drafted to give a society the best of two worlds, openness and freedom of expression on the one side and privacy and protection on the other. The better route might be that which falls within the province of the churches, the persuasive, educative approach. The effect will be more lasting if people can be persuaded rather than coerced to refrain from anti-social behavior."

Howard, A. E. Dick, and Sanford A. Newman. *Fair Trial and Free Expression. A Background Report Prepared for and Presented to the Subcommittee on Constitutional Rights of the Committee on the Judiciary, United States Senate . . . .* Washington, D.C., Govt. Print. Off., 1976. 84p. (Committee Print, 94th Cong., 2d sess.) **1H370**
"This report on fair trial and free expression was undertaken at the request of the Subcommittee on Constitutional Rights of the Senate Judiciary Committee. Its purpose is to explore

fair trial–free expression issues and to aid the Subcommittee in determining whether hearings or legislation would be useful. The report considers relevant case law, proposals, and reports (such as those of bar associations and other groups) and offers commentary and recommendations for the Subcommittee's consideration." Content: State of the Law (direct restraints on publicity, constraints on trial participants, closing judicial proceedings to the press and public, review of restrictive orders, and First Amendment due process). Proposals and Reports (proposed legislation and hearings, other major reports including reports of the American Bar Association, Association of the Bar of the City of New York, United States Judicial Conference, Department of Justice Guidelines, American Newspaper Publishers Association, American Civil Liberties Union, and Twentieth Century Fund). Commentary and Recommendations (What body should formulate fair trial–free expression guidelines? Accommodating the interest of fair trial and freedom of expression). Recommendations (direct restraint on the press, orders restricting extrajudicial statements by trial participants, secrecy and closure of judicial proceedings, reviewability of restrictive orders, and procedural due process). Addendum: Comments on *Nebraska Press Association v. Stuart* (1976).

Howard, Edward A. "Obscenity and the Law." *Focus on Indiana Libraries*, 26(1):38–41, Spring 1972. **1H371**
Practical guidelines in book selection and access to controversial materials for public libraries.

Howard, Edward N. "Intellectual Freedom." *ALA Bulletin*, 62:1073–75, October 1968. **1H372**
When a petition was presented to the Vigo County Public Library protesting against "obscene paperbacks in our public library," the public came to the library's defense in great numbers and the library board unanimously supported the director. The strong public response was the result of an earlier staff study of the library's role in the community, which was followed by an aggressive program to develop good community-library relations. The text of the board's response to the petition is included.

[Howard, G. S., *plaintiff*.] *Report of the Trial of the Libel Suit of Dr. G. S. Howard of Carleton Place, Ont. against the "Montreal Star." Reprint from the "Star", 1898. . . .* [Montreal, Montreal Star, 1898.] 136p. **1H373**
The *Star* was accused of libeling Dr. G. S. Howard, known as the "sage of Aru," founder of a new religion, hypnotist, and manufacturer of patent medicines. Howard had been accused of swindling Mrs. Joseph H. Specht of Gunston Hall, Va., wife of a wealthy St. Louis clothing dealer, of $5,000. He fled to Canada

and Mrs. Specht joined him. The paper had called Howard's religion "a mixture of Brahminism, Eastern Philosophy, Christianity and Religious Quackery," and hoped that the work had not been transplanted to Canada. It advised husbands to warn their wives against the study of Eastern Philosophy. Four years after the alleged libel appeared in the paper Howard brought suit and the case was tried in Perth, Ont. He lost.

Howard, Herbert H. "Cross-Media Ownership of Newspapers and TV Stations." *Journalism Quarterly*, 51:715–18, Winter 1974.   **1H374**
Based on research done during preparation of his 1973 doctoral dissertation, Multiple Ownership in Television Broadcasting: Historical Development and Selected Case Studies at Ohio University.

———. "Multiple Broadcast Ownership: Regulatory History." *Federal Communications Bar Journal*, 27:1–70, 1974.   **1H375**
Content: The Report on Chain Broadcasting. The "Duoply" Rule. Television and FM Station Ownership Limits. Formulation of Present Multiple-ownership Rules. The Storer Case. Comparative Hearings and Media Diversification. Congressional Investigations into Television. The Broadcast Network Study. The Anti-Trafficking Rule. Multiple-ownership Rules Reviewed. FCC's Top-Fifty Market Policy. The "One-To-A-Customer" Rule. The Conglomerate Study. FCC Regulatory Philosophy.

Howard, James L., Clifford B. Reifler, and Myron B. Liptzin. "Effects of Exposure to Pornography." *Technical Report of the [U.S.] Commission on Obscenity and Pornography*, 8:97–132, 1971. **1H376**
"Twenty-three experimental and nine control subjects (young adult college males) were studied to evaluate the hypotheses that repeated exposure to pornography causes decreased interest in it, less response to it, and no lasting effect from it. . . . Results confirmed the hypotheses and it was concluded that exposure to pornography was a relatively innocuous stimulus without lasting or detrimental effect on the individual or his behavior."

———. "Is Pornography a Problem?" *Journal of Social Issues*, 29(3):133–45, 1973.   **1H377**
The study of sex satiation suggests that pornography loses its interest when it is no longer forbidden. One of the studies stimulated by the U.S. Commission on Obscenity and Pornography and reported in vol. 8 of the *Technical Reports*.

Howard, W. Corbin. "*Miller*, *Jenkins*

and the Definition of Obscenity." *Montana Law Review*, 36:285–99, Summer 1975.   **1H378**
"The purpose of this note is to analyze *Miller's* definition of obscenity [*Miller v. California* (1973)] in relation to the definitions of obscenity contained in current Montana law."

Howard, William J. *Literature and Regulation: A Study of the Development of Literature and Literary Practice in Relation to the Laws Regulating Publication in the First Half of the Eighteenth Century.* Leeds, England, University of Leeds, 1965. 552p. (Ph.D. thesis, School of English)   **1H379**
Content: The Law: Historical and Philosophical Background. Copyright and Trade Practice. The Author's Bid for Control. Libel Law as a Creative Stimulus. The Expansion of Traditional Rhetoric. Mystery as a Method. Libel and Functional Characterization. The Trade Adopts the Method. Conclusion: A Theory Sketched. Bibliography, pp. 5127–52.

Howe, Gregory J. "An Antitrust Challenge to the GGPRX Movie Rating System." *Harvard Civil Rights-Civil Liberties Law Review*, 6:545–57, May 1971.   **1H380**
"This Comment considers whether the market distortion [created by the movie industry's film rating system] causes injuries actionable under the antitrust laws, outlining arguments for attacking censorship practices of private organizations sheltered from direct constitutional attack by the state action doctrine and focusing on the significance of first amendment considerations in antitrust analysis."

Howells, Ronald F. *An Analysis of Editorial Freedom and Administrative Control of the Student Newspaper in the Four-Year Colleges and Universities in New York State.* Albany, N.Y., State University of New York, 1973. 195p. (Ed.D. dissertation, University Microfilms, no. 73-24,359).   **1H381**
"The study was designed to investigate judicial decisions of state and federal courts, concerning editorial freedom of the college and university student press to determine emerging legal rules, precedents, and trends in judicial decisions and to analyze the extent of editorial freedom and administrative control of the student press as perceived by student editors in colleges and universities in New York State."

Howes, John. "Censorship: Some Philosophical Issues: (3) Is Berlin Right about Mill's Arguments Against Censorship." *Philosophical Papers*, 5(1):85–98, May 1976.   **1H382**
A point-by-point refutation of Sir Isaiah Berlin's contention that the arguments of John Stuart Mill dealing with liberty of thought and

expression in his *Essay on Liberty* were defective. The author presents his case for Mill's logic in terms of the system of censorship in South Africa. Berlin had presented his views in a Robert Waley Cohen Memorial Lecture, first published in 1959.

Howitt, Dennis, and Guy Cumberbatch. *Mass Media, Violence and Society.* New York, Wiley, 1975. 167p. **1H383**
"The central theme of this book is that the Mass Media do not have any significant effect on the level of violence in society. This view arises from our consideration of the available social scientific research from social psychology, experimental psychology, sociology, and psychiatry. However, in arguing that the weight of the evidence is against any adverse effects of the media, we violate what would appear to be the established wisdom of social science and that of popular mythology."

Hoyt, Edwin P. *The Palmer Raids, 1919–20: An Attempt to Suppress Dissent.* New York, Seabury, 1969, 137p.   **1H384**
The dramatic events of the "red scare" that swept the nation in the years immediately following World War I resulted in action taken by President Wilson's Attorney General A. Mitchell Palmer, who sent his agents to sweep down on thousands suspected of political radicalism. Homes and offices were searched, books and papers seized, and suspects were carted off to jail. Much later it was discovered that the vast majority of those seized were innocent of any wrongdoing. The "Palmer Raids" did not stem from the Justice Department, the author notes in his epilogue, but from alarmed citizenry fanned by a hysterical press. "Had the press exercised the judicious restraint in matters of civil liberties and constitutionality which is one of its major reasons for being, then the Department of Justice and its agents and local police would never have dared violate the American Constitution."

Hoyt, Olga G., and Edwin P. *Censorship in America.* New York, Seabury, 1970. 127p.   **1H385**
A book written for young people, tracing the path of cultural freedom and censorship in the United States from Puritan days to the present. The authors consider books, stage, motion pictures, and television, emphasizing the changing attitudes toward censorship held by citizens and the courts.

Huard, Leo A. "The 1966 Public Information Act: An Appraisal Without Enthusiasm." *Public Contract Law Journal*, 2:213–24, January 1969.   **1H386**
The author finds that the law requires the generation of more records, is ambiguous, and that the public's access to the courts is neither quick nor certain.

Huckaby, James, Jr. "Denial of a Right of Public Access to the Press." *Emory*

Law Journal, 24:217–35, Winter 1975. **1H387**

Re: *Miami Herald Publishing Company v. Tornillo* (1974). The author believes that "the Court's refusal to impose on the press a fiduciary duty to insure a variety of views and opinions reflects a fidelity to the language but not the spirit of the First Amendment. By changing to the idealistic and totally unreal conception of the press as a still-effective forum for free discussion, the Court places the quality of public debate at the mercy of a powerful industry that is accountable only to itself."

Hudgins, H. C., Jr. "Academic Freedom and the Student Press." *Wake Forest Intramural Law Review*, 6:40–62, December 1969. **1H388**

"To what extent should college officials control student publications? Should there be any controls at all? Does attempted university control clash with first amendment rights of the student?" The author recommends a governing board to supervise student publications and lists six broad areas of board action.

Hudon, Edward G. "Freedom of the Press versus Fair Trial: The Remedy Lies with the Courts." *Valparaiso University Law Review*, 1:8–39, Fall 1966. **1H389**

The author concludes that there is no simple solution to the problem through codes of ethics or an inflexible formula for measuring "trial by newspaper." "A more realistic approach is the recognition that Anglo-American judicial machinery is adequately equipped with procedural safeguards designed to assure anyone accused of a crime of a fair and impartial trial—that when 'trial by newspaper' takes place, as often as not, it is because this judicial machinery is not used to the extent that it should be, or is misused. And when this happens, the blame must be placed on the courts rather than on the news media."

Hudson, Peggy. "How Will TV Handle Sexy Movies?" *TV Guide*, 15(29):22–26, 22 July 1967. (Reprinted in Barry G. Cole, *ed.*, *Television: A Selection from TV Guide Magazine*. New York, Free Press, 1970, pp. 350–55) **1H390**

Hudson, Robert V. "FOI Crusade in Perspective: Three Victories for the Press." *Journalism Quarterly*, 50:118–24, Spring 1973. **1H391**

"In this historical study, the author examines the press side of the war against executive privilege and the three major victories of the 1950's and 1960's."

Hudson, W. M. F. "Pornography and the Law." *Medicine, Science, and Law*, 13:244–45, October 1973. **1H392**

The question of obscenity has been clearly stated by the superior courts of England to be one of fact and not law and in England facts in the courts are decided either by magistrates who are not lawyers or by juries who reflect the climate of public opinion and taste. This paper was presented as part of a special program on The Role of the Law in a Permissive Society, International Bar Association, Monte Carlo, September 1972.

Huey, Rodney. "The People's Access to the Press." *Grassroots Editor*, 15:11–13, January–February 1974. **1H393**

Unless readers, regardless of their views, are granted access to the press through letters to the editors, then freedom of the press will not fully be realized.

Huffman, Laurence M. "Confidentiality of Newsmen's Sources." *Oklahoma Law Review*, 27:480–87, Summer 1974. **1H394**

"This note will examine the issue of whether some form of first amendment constitutional privilege for newsmen's sources should be recognized. The arguments for and against such a privilege will be examined in the context of the *Branzburg v. Hayes* trilogy of cases [1972] and in the somewhat broader context of the public policy considerations involved."

Huggins, Ira M. "Obscenity and the Law." *Utah Libraries*, 17(1):10–14, Spring 1974. **1H395**

A lawyer reviews the current status of obscenity law following the U.S. Supreme Court decision in the *Miller* case (*Miller v. State of California*, 1973), and how this relates to the Utah code. He points out some of the difficulties public librarians in Utah will face in applying contemporary standards, determining the limits of candor, who is the "average adult," and who is a minor under the age of eighteen. "You have a fickle public among fickle communities, and a fickle law to deal with. The only thing that is constant is change."

Hughes, Arthur E. "Contempt of Court and the Press." *Law Quarterly Review*, 16:292–300, July 1900. **1H396**

The evolution of the use of contempt of court as a means of protecting the courts from criticism and prejudicing the due administration of justice. The power of the court, the author argues, should not be used to protect the personal and judicial reputation of the judge, which "is no greater and no less than that of every subject of the Queen."

Hughes, Catharine. "Nudity, Obscenity and all That." *Christian Century*, 86:1349–50, 22 October 1969. **1H397**

"Here as elsewhere the New Theater and films too often seem to be employing nudity and sexual freedom in ways that are gratuitous rather than integral—and, being gratuitous, they are in the end degrading. . . . For better or for worse, cinematic and theatrical voyeurism is by its nature impermanent; short of

inviting repression, the professional's only alternative is to assume responsibility."

Hughes, Clarence. "Underground Newspaper: What's It All About?" *Clearing House*, 46:155–57, November 1971. **1H398**

A study of high school underground newspapers indicates that more papers are started because of dissatisfaction with the regular paper, and to focus on important social issues as well as school issues in order to achieve reform or change. Reaction by high school administrators is generally adverse; investigations and bannings have sometimes taken place, but the general pattern is for a school to tolerate the paper once the initial controversy has passed. Teachers and parents tend to be more tolerant than school administrators toward underground papers.

Hughes, Douglas A., *ed. Perspectives on Pornography*. New York, St. Martin's, 1970. 223p. **1H399**

Content: Eroticism in Literature by Alberto Moravia. What Is Pornography? by Anthony Burgess. The Unbanning of the Books by Harry Levin (L201). Master Percy and/or Lady Chatterley by Vivian Mercier. In Defense of Pornography by Stanley E. Hyman (H442). Pornography, Art, and Censorship by Paul Goodman (G172). An Apology for Pornography by Peter Michelson. Against Pornography by George P. Elliott (E64). Night Words: High Pornography and Human Privacy by George Steiner (S614). Dirty Books Can Stay by Kenneth Tynan. The Case for Pornography Is the Case for Censorship and Vice Versa by Ernest van den Hagg (°V4). The Pornographic Imagination by Susan Sontag. Pornography: A Trip Around the Halfworld by Felix Pollak. Write About Sex by William Phillips. Introduction by the editor. Articles are entered under authors in the 1968 volume (where number is cited) or in this ten-year supplement.

Hughes, T. E. F. *A Commentary on Some Aspects of Censorship*. Canberra, Australia, Attorney-General's Department, 1971. 10p. Processed. **1H400**

An address by the Attorney-General of Australia, the Honourable T. E. F. Hughes, Q.C., to the Fourth Commonwealth and Empire Law Conference, New Delhi, India, January 11, 1971.

Hugo, Leon H. *Authority, Literature, and Freedom*. Pretoria, University of South Africa, 1970. 16p. (Communications of the University of South Africa, A.65) **1H401**

"The censorship of literature, or of any cultural form, is an offense against the intellect. Exercise censorship whatever manner we may, apply it through the most enlightened of means, it remains a flouting of the historical process. . . . Censorship is practically if not theoretically a short-circuiting of the protective powers of the judiciary." It is an "arrogation of a person's hard-won freedom to decide for himself what he will or will not read, what he will or will not write. The best that can be said of censorship is that it is doomed to failure." Commenting on South African censorship particularly, the author states: "We do not need the censorship board. It does far more harm than good. Admitting the need of control, we can best find it in a virile, open-minded education policy." An inaugural lecture on the author's appointment to a professorship in the Department of English at the University of South Africa.

―――. "Milton and the Board." *South African Libraries*, 38:250–55, January 1971. **1H402**
One by one the author takes John Milton's eloquently worded arguments for a free press contained in *Areopagitica* and shows how the South African Publications Control Board has flouted or twisted them in its censorship policies. Milton notes that the ancients tolerated everything except blasphemy and libel; the Publications Control Board "bestows the largesse of plus-minus 998 further bookish and cinematic offences on us, and what's more, it will save authors and publishers the wearisome burden of legislation by settling matters for them out of court, without dispute and for nothing." The Board, while enunciating a Protestant tradition, applies one of the most questionable devices in the history of Catholicism—the Inquisition, which Milton cites as the basis for censorship. The author concludes: "As long as we tolerate the Board's inquisition, Milton's vision will not be ours."

Hulett, Mary. "Privacy and the Freedom of Information Act." *Administrative Law Review*, 27:275–94, Summer 1975. **1H403**
"Neither privacy nor access can ever be considered alone; both must be considered in relation to other needs and in relation to each other. Unfortunately, the Congress has not clearly addressed this conflict. The result is conflicting requirements on government agencies and a statutory pattern that does not clearly provide for the needs of either access or privacy."

Hult, Steve. "Sex, Morals and Pornography in the Printing Business." *Printing Impressions*, 10(6):10, 15, November 1967; 10(7):10, 13, December 1967; 10(8):24–25, January 1968; 10(9):22–23, February 1968. **1H404**
"Our changing standards have made a clear-cut legal definition of obscenity more elusive than ever. Printers must be aware of rapidly chang-

ing values in a society where virtually anything can be printed. Latest court actions regarding printed erotic materials do little to unravel guidelines for printer and publisher. The courts still eye the publisher, not the printer. In the final analysis if the printer becomes timid, who dares be bold."

Hulteng, John L. *Messenger's Motives: Ethical Problems of the News Media*. Englewood, N.J., Prentice-Hall, 1976. 262p. **1H405**
A "case-study examination of practical ethical problems that confront journalists every hour of every working day." The issues encompass self-imposed restrictions, concern for libel, abuses of trust, and the pervasive responsibility to the public. Signs of optimism with the continuation and upgrading of ethical behavior of the press are seen in "the reviews, the analyses provided by the academy, the in-house ombudsmen, and above all the stubborn persistence of the appeal of the central ethic of serving the public by getting and disseminating the news as fully and honestly as possible."

―――, and Roy P. Nelsen. *The Fourth Estate: An Informal Appraisal of the News and Opinion Media*. New York, Harper & Row, 1971. 356p. (A 32-page instructor's manual is available to accompany the textbook) **1H406**
This general appraisal of the communications industry covers many areas relating to press freedom, including the editing process, effect of monopolies, influence of advertisers and owners, objectivity or lack of it, ethics of the newsroom, news under licensing, libel, and codes of ethics.

Hume, Brit. "A Chilling Effect on the Press." *New York Times Magazine*, pp. 13, 78–79+, 17 December 1972. **1H407**
How the action of the U.S. Supreme Court in the *Caldwell* case, in denying newsmen protection of their news sources, has resulted in caution and self-censorship by the media; and clamming up by former sources of information. Hume cites cases where newsmen have been imprisoned for refusal to reveal sources of information. He sees the *Caldwell* decision the beginning of a protracted controversy over First Amendment protection of the source of news.

―――. "The Cult of Censorship." *MORE*, 4(4):9, April 1974. **1H408**
A discussion of the legal and censorship issues involved in the battle with the CIA over the book, *The CIA and the Cult of Intelligence*. The same issue carries an article by the authors Victor L. Marchetti and John D. Marks, adapted from material gathered for their book.

―――. "Now It Can Be Told . . . Or Can It?" *MORE*, 5(4):6–8, 11, April 1975. **1H409**
"Wilbur Mills and Fanne Fox wound up on page one across the country because they were

caught. More often, the press knows about such exploits [by public figures] but avoids putting them in the paper. Why?"—Editor

Humphrey, Thomas E. "The Newspaper Preservation Act: An Ineffective Step in the Right Direction." *Boston College Industrial and Commercial Law Review*, 12:937–54, April 1971. **1H410**
"It is the purpose of this comment to examine the nature of joint newspaper operating arrangements and their rejection by the Supreme Court. The legislative response to the situation, the Newspaper Preservation Act, will be considered with special emphasis on the antitrust and constitutional questions which may be raised by its enactment."

Humphreys, James. "Textbook War in West Virginia." *Dissent*, 23:167–70, Spring 1976. **1H411**
The people of West Virginia "are the victims of powerful and cunning outsiders, of themselves and their own kind, and of social and historical forces with regard to which they have no control or understanding." An analysis of the textbook controversy in Kanawha County, W.Va.

Humphreys, Thomas W. " 'Free Television Act' Passed by California General Electorate Held Violative of Free Speech Guarantee." *San Diego Law Review*, 4:162–72, June 1967. **1H412**
Re: *Weaver v. Jordan* (1966). The California Supreme Court held that Proposition 15, prohibiting subscription television was an unconstitutional abridgement of the guarantee of free speech.

Humphries, Charles W. "The Banning of a Book in British Columbia." *British Columbia Studies*, 1:1–12, Winter 1968/69. **1H413**
An account of the spirited debate in British Columbia in 1920 over the banning of W. L. Grant's *History of Canada* from use as a high school textbook. The work was considered disloyal to Great Britain.

Hunnings, Neville. " 'And Loss of Paradise . . .': The Origin of Censorship in England." *Sight and Sound*, 27:151–54, Winter 1957/58. **1H414**
An account of the early controls over the motion picture in England, beginning with the Cinematograph Act of 1907.

―――. "Censorship." *Sight and Sound*, 44:81–82, Spring 1975. **1H415**
A recent vote by the Greater London Council on the issue of discontinuing film censorship for adults came close to passage, suggesting that some such reform may be in the offing.

―――. "Censorship: On the Way

Out?" *Sight and Sound*, 38:201–2, Autumn 1969. **1H416**
A review of worldwide efforts to abolish censorship, dealing largely with the experience in Denmark, but including other European countries and India.

Hunsaker, David M. "The 1973 Obscenity–Pornography Decisions: Analysis, Impact and Legislative Alternatives." *San Diego Law Review*, 11:906–56, June 1974. **1H417**
"On June 21, 1973, the United States Supreme Court announced a series of decisions which inevitably will have far-reaching consequences. [*Miller v. State of California*; *Paris Adult Theatre I v. Slaton*; *Kaplan v. State of California*; *United States v. 12 200-ft. Reels of Film*; and *United States v. Orito.*] The purpose of this article is to assess their actual and potential impact."

———. *The Print Media and Equal Time*. Columbia, Mo., Freedom of Information Center, School of Journalism, University of Missouri at Columbia, 1975. 7p. (Report no. 0016) **1H418**
The U.S. Supreme Court in the *Red Lion* case (*Red Lion Broadcasting Co., Inc., v. FCC*, 1969) affirmed the fairness doctrine in broadcasting; five years later, in *Miami Herald v. Tornillo*, it rejected the Florida right of reply law as unconstitutional. The author believes the Court's reasoning was inconsistent and argues for access to be mandatory in the newspaper press as well as in broadcasting. "Our choice is either to break up the monopolies which dominate the print media, or make them socially responsible. I endorse the latter option and suggest an 'equal time' provision for the print media." He offers a Model Right of Access Statute.

Hunt, Chester F. *Attitudes of Texas District Judges and District Attorneys Toward Electronic Media and Photographic Coverage of Trials*. Austin, Tex., University of Texas, 1966. 94p. (Unpublished Master's thesis) **1H419**
The study examines the attitude of Texas judges and district attorneys following the U.S. Supreme Court decision in *Estes v. State of Texas* (1965) which altered media coverage of trials in the Texas courts.

Hunter, Frederic. "Violence on TV: What It Is Doing to Our Children." *Christian Science Monitor*, 9 November 1973, p. 11. (Reprinted in *Barrister*, April 1974) **1H420**
Interviews with two psychologists, Robert Liebert and Daniel Anderson. On the whole, they believe that entertainment television has been undesirable not only for children but socially because of the heavy focus on violence. Children who watch violence content on television are worse off than those who watch no television. The best government action would be the support of alternative programming on educational networks; the best audience action would be to express dissatisfaction in letters to the networks and the sponsors.

Hunter, Ian A. "Strange Passion in the County Court." *Criminal Law Quarterly*, 13:184–95, March 1971. **1H421**
The author views with "ribald amusement" the court procedure and decision in the obscenity case against a play, *An Evening with Fritz*, given in Toronto in 1969 (*R. v. O'Reilly and Four Others*, 1970). He notes the innate subjectivity of the issues involved in such a case and views the court as a singularly inadequate forum for their resolution.

[Hurdy Gurdy.] *Report of the Trial of the King versus Hurdy Gurdy, Alias Barrel Organ, alias Grinder, alias the Seditious Organ, for publishing and causing and procuring to be published a certain false, wicked, malicious and scandalous noise, clamour, sound, uproar, vibration, cussion, concussion, percussion or repercussion of the Air, which came on to be tried at the Bar of the King's Bench on the—day of—1794, with Arguments of Council and the Charge of the Judge, taken in Short-hand*. Dublin, 1794. 48p. (A New York edition appeared in 1806.) **1H422**
A farcical work which pokes fun at the current British trials for seditious libel. The musical composition, Ca Ira, threatened the King, the Constitution, and the Church. French Horn was a witness and the jury consisted of such names as Whig Tallyho Turncoat, Guzzle Tunbelly, and Tremble Cautious Panic. Hurdy Gurdy, the defendant, was pronounced guilty. The New York edition indicated that "the idea of the Hurdy Gurdy probably originated from a circumstance in the trial of Mr. Thomas Muir, in Scotland, where the music of such an instrument was made a material point of evidence to support his sentence of banishment to Botany Bay."

Hurley, Timothy. "The New Legislation on the Index." *Irish Ecclesiastical Record*, 4(4th ser.):423–37, 1898; 5(4th ser.):61–76+, 1899; 6(4th ser.):49–69, 242–66, 1899. **1H423**
In 1897 "a bull with a set of rules on the Index was promulgated by Leo XIII, which have completely changed the old legislation on the Index. By the bull all legislation made by previous pontiffs on the Index has been annulled, with the exception of one sole bull of Benedict XIV; the working of the Index has been rendered more simple and effective; and the rules have been made so lenient that no one, except indeed he be of bad disposition, can find it onerous or difficult to observe them. To a consideration of this bull, and the annexed rules we now invite the readers of the *I. E. Record*."

Hurst, William S. "How *Branzburg* Buried the Underground Press." *Har-*

vard Civil Rights-Court Liberties Law Review, 8:181–97, January 1973. **1H424**
"Failure to recognize a right of special access for the press would not necessarily defeat an underground newspaper's claim for treatment equal to that of established newspapers. Establishing the right of access is only one way of bringing the claim more clearly under the first amendment and, therefore, a stricter standard of judicial scrutiny. . . . Yet, the right of special access is crucial because the underground press has a unique interest, perhaps more intensive than that of the established press, in ferreting out information which the government seeks to hide." Re: *Branzburg v. Hayes*, 1972.

Hurt, Ronald. *A History of Texas Open Meetings Law*. Commerce, Tex., East Texas State University, 1973. 54p. (Unpublished Master's thesis) **1H425**
A study based on an examination of newspaper files, interviews with legislators and lobbyists, and those involved in court cases stemming from the 1967 Open Meetings Law.

Hurt, Walter. "Freedom of Press." *Paladin*, 1(1):3, 12 January 1918. **1H426**
A poem by the editor in this first issue of *Paladin*, a St. Louis newspaper devoted to opposing oppressive legislation and unjust administration. A cartoon on page 1 shows the bloody hand of bureaucracy knifing a free press represented by a maiden.

Hurwitz, Howard L. "Freedom of the Press in Schools: Civil Liberty vs. Simple Civility." *Human Events*, 35:122, 8 February 1975. **1H427**
A review of recent court decisions on rights of high school students to publish and distribute underground papers, considered by school officials to be obscene and disruptive. The issue is brought up by the case of *Corn Cob Curtain*, an Indianapolis high school paper, now before the U.S. Supreme Court.

Huston, Alice. "*Miller v. California*: A Search for a New Community." *University of West Los Angeles Law Review*, 5:63–67, Fall 1973. **1H428**
An examination of the U.S. Supreme Court's decision in *Miller v. California* (1973), and its use of community standards to identify obscene material. "Until the courts decide whether the post-*Miller* community is the entire state or only the jury, the dealer in questionable materials may be able to assert that he is not given fair notice of the proscribed conduct under the standard set forth in *Harris* [*United States v. Harris* (1954)]."

Huston, Luther A. "Conflicting Views Presented at House News Shield Hear-

ings." *Editor & Publisher*, 106(7):9, 11, 17 February 1973.   1H429
Reporters, spokesmen for media groups, and Department of Justice lawyers gave conflicting opinions on whether shield laws for newsmen should be absolute or qualified.

————. "Editors Split Over Need for Absolute Shield Laws." *Editor & Publisher*, 106(19):9–10, 12 May 1973.   1H430
Although the American Society of Newspaper Editors has endorsed legislation giving reporters absolute protection against forced disclosures to grand juries, judges, and other investigating bodies, editors attending the Society's 1973 convention were divided as to the need for enactment of a federal shield law.

————. "Mitchell Imposes Limitation on Dragnet Subpoena Process." *Editor & Publisher*, 103(33):9–10, 15 August 1970.   1H431
Report of Attorney General Mitchell's address to House Delegates of the American Bar Association, St. Louis, 10 August. The Attorney General stated "there is no constitutional or common law privilege for the press to refuse to produce evidence requested in a properly drawn subpoena."

————. "SDX Backs College Editors' Battle Against Censorship." *Editor & Publisher*, 101(48):11, 43, 45, 30 November 1968.   1H432
"Censorship of college newspapers and punishment of editors who publish stories containing four-letter words and other things displeasing to university authorities provided a theme for spirited discussion at the final session of the Sigma Delta Chi convention here [Atlanta] last week."

Hutchins, Robert M. *et al.* "Limits of Dissent." *Center Magazine*, 1(7):3–7, November 1968. (Also 29 min. tape recording, Center for the Study of Democratic Institutions, Santa Barbara, Calif., 1968)   1H433
"If sit-ins and demonstrations are the poor man's printing press and therefore subject to all the protections of the First Amendment—then what are the limits of dissent?" Five statements from Robert M. Hutchins, Harry S. Ashmore, Harrop A. Freeman, James A. Pike, and Rexford G. Tugwell. All statements except that of Rev. James A. Pike, deceased, were read at a later date for the tape.

Hutchins, Walter. "America Declares War on Pornography." *Saga*, 53(2): 18–21, November 1976.   1H434
"After literally being inundated by a tidal wave

of smut, Americans are beginning to fight back—and they're winning." The author calls on those opposing smut to "stop, look and listen" for evidence of pornographers moving into a community; complain; organize; petition; and picket.

Hutchison, Earl R. *Henry Miller and* TROPIC OF CANCER: *From Paris to Wisconsin—On the Censorship Trail*. Madison, Wis., University of Wisconsin, 1966. 646p. (Ph.D. dissertation, University Microfilms, no. 67,9005) 1H435
The basis for the author's book, *Tropic of Cancer on Trial*.

————. *Tropic of Cancer on Trial: A Case History of Censorship*. New York, Grove, 1968. 300p.   1H436
A documented study of the censorship of Henry Miller's *Tropic of Cancer*, the most censored novel in American history. When it was first published in the United States by Grove Press in 1961, the novel was already thirty years old. *Tropic* was on trial in the United States from 1961 to 1964 when it was cleared by the U.S. Supreme Court, *Grove Press, Inc. v. Gerstein et al.*, 327 U.S. 577(1964). During those years more than sixty legal proceedings had been filed against the book. Following a brief biography of Miller and critical reviews of the work, the author traces the censorship trail against *Tropic*, focusing on the banning in Milwaukee as part of a large-scale extralegal censorship program. The Wisconsin Supreme Court ultimately reversed a Milwaukee court's ban, which led to a political fight over the election of judges and, many believed, threatened the independence of the judiciary. There is a foreword by Elmer Gertz, attorney for the defense in the Grove Press case.

————, and David G. Clark. "Self-Censorship in Broadcasting—The Cowardly Lions." *New York Law Forum*, 18:1–31, Summer 1972. 1H437
"This article will treat first the role of a free press in a democratic society and those forces pushing social responsibilities onto the fledgling broadcasting industry. It will also examine governmental pressures being exerted on broadcasting, commercialization and self-censorship in the industry, and finally, some of the changes, technologically and otherwise, particularly cable television (CATV), which will help bring about resolutions to broadcasting problems."

Huth, Mary J. *The Birth Control Movement in the United States*. St. Louis, St. Louis University, 1955. 930p. (Unpublished Ph.D. dissertation)   1H438
Includes section on the legal and extralegal efforts to suppress birth control information on moral, religious, medical, eugenic, and economic grounds. The text of the original Comstock Act of 1873 is given in the appendix.

Huxford, Gary. "The English Lib-

ertarian Tradition in the Colonial Newspaper." *Journalism Quarterly*, 45:677–86, Winter 1968.   1H439
The American colonial editor "found in the natural rights doctrine of the Old Whigs [of England] the most popular form by which to express their arguments" in the political arena. The author traces the influence on opinion in colonial America of "Cato" (John Trenchard and Thomas Gordon) and other British libertarian writers, through the first half of the eighteenth century.

Huxley, Aldous. "To the Puritan All Things Are Impure." In his *Music at Night*. New York, Doubleday, 1931, pp. 153–62; reprinted in his *On Art and Artists*.   1H440
A satirical attack on Grundyism "the only deity officially recognized by the English State." Vice crusaders and home secretaries, regardless of what party is in power, react to frank expressions of sex (sexual blasphemy) in literature and art like Pavlov's dogs. Huxley defends D. H. Lawrence's *Lady Chatterley's Lover*, recently banned in England, as a welcome attack on sexual bigotry.

Hvistendahl, J. K. "The Reporter as Activist: Fourth Revolution in Journalism." *Quill*, 58(2):8–11, February 1970. (Reprinted in Michael C. Emery and Ted C. Smythe, *eds.*, *Readings in Mass Communications*, pp. 116–23)   1H441
The first revolution was the freeing of the American Press from threats of government control; the second revolution was the growth of the "objective press," brought about largely by the press associations; the third revolution was interpretive reporting, in which facts were reported objectively but with an attempt to explain or interpret them; the fourth revolution (now upon us) is journalistic activism, in which the reporter covers the news from the viewpoint of his own intellectual commitment. The author argues the case for harnassing the concerns of this new breed of journalists in the interest of a more meaningful press.

Hyde, H. Montgomery. "Echoes of Oscar Wilde in the Courts." In his *Cases that Changed the Law*. London, Heinemann, 1951, pp. 148–203. 1H442
Three libel trials took place in England as "echoes" of the celebrated trial of Oscar Wilde. In the first, Lord Alfred Douglas, a friend of Wilde, sued Arthur Ransome over statements made in his book, *Oscar Wilde: A Criticl Study*, published by Secker. Ransome won but voluntarily deleted the offending passages in the new edition. In the so-called "Black Book" trial, Noel Pemberton Billing, editor of *The Vigilante*, which had exposed alleged sexual immorality among prominent persons, was sued for libel by one of the persons named. Much to the displeasure of the judge, the jury found the defendant "not guilty." In the third libel case a literary critic was convicted of libeling a pub-

lisher by unwitting use of the word "foist" in charging that a work (*For Love of a King*) by Oscar Wilde was spurious.

———. "A Look at the Law." In Michael Rubinstein, *ed.*, *Wicked, Wicked Libels*. London, Routledge & Kegan Paul, 1972, pp. 3–39.   **1H443**
A look at the British law of libel—how it came about, how it has been modified over the years by action of Parliament (Fox Libel Act, 1792; The Libel Act, 1843; The Defamation Act, 1952), how it has been interpreted by the courts, the various proposals for change, and the complications and subtleties that characterize the law today.

———. *Their Good Names: Twelve Cases of Libel and Slander with Some Introductory Reflections on the Law*. London, Hamilton, 1970. 406p.   **1H444**
Cases: A Woman's Virtue (*Travers v. Wilde*), An Artist's Reputation (*Whistler v. Ruskin*), Scandal in a Bordello (*Reg. v. Parke*), A Game of Baccarat (*Gordon-Cummings v. Wilson and Others*), Libel by Waxwork (*Monson v. Tussaud's*), The Soap Trust Libel (*Lever v. Associated Newspapers*), The "Black Book" Trial (*R. v. Pemberton-Billing*), Winston Churchill and the Battle of Jutland (*R. v. Douglas*), The Birth Control Libel (*Stopes v. Sutherland*), Libel on a Dead Prime Minister (*Wright v. Gladstone*), The Princess and Rasputin (*Youssoupoff v. Metro-Goldwyn-Mayer Pictures Ltd.*), and The Limits of Criticism (*Liberace v. Daily Mirror Newspapers Ltd. and Connor*).

I

"If You Print My Name I May Be Killed!" *MORE*, 6(2):14–15, February 1976. **I11**
MORE poses a hypothetical case of a reporter undercovering a CIA involvement in financing Italian political parties and asks twenty newspaper or television editors whether or not they would publish the name of the agent in the story. Only eight responded in the affirmative.

Iglar, John L. "A Case for Censorship?" *Focus on Indiana Libraries*, 26(1):26–31, Spring 1972. **I12**
A report on a censorship controversy over the student newspaper, *Shavings*, at Calumet College, East Chicago, Ind. The author debates the issues involved in guidelines for student publications at this Catholic college.

Ignatius, David. "Dan Schorr: The Secret Sharer." *Washington Monthly*, 8:6–20, April 1976. **I13**
A detailed reconstruction of the story of Daniel Schorr and the publication in *Village Voice* of the secret report of the House of Representatives investigation of the CIA. What began as a sincere effort to open up the cult of intelligence to public scrutiny and discussion erupted into a "dismal chain of events in which each participant seems to be wearing blinders," and may have marked the end of an "extraordinary period in American history—in which the power and secrecy of the executive branch had, for a moment, been challenged; in which the scourge of CIA dirty tricks had, for a moment, been lifted; in which the lassitude of the Congress had for a moment, been dispelled."

Illinois. Governor's Commission on Individual Liberty and Personal Privacy. *Final Report. . . .* Chicago, The Commission, 1976. 136p. **I14**
Includes a proposal of an Illinois Public Records Access Act, and suggested text.

Illinois Obscenity Laws Study Commission. *Report . . . to the 76th General Assembly.* [Springfield, Ill., The Commission], 1969. 27p. Processed. **I15**

The Commission, established by the Illinois General Assembly to examine the adequacy of state obscenity statutes, made the following recommendations: that the existing general Illinois statute on obscenity be retained; that the statute dealing with harmful material for minors be replaced with a law based on the 1965 New York law, but with a stronger Illinois penalty; and that the former Illinois statute prohibiting tie-in sales be reenacted.

Illinois State Library. *Supreme Court Decision on Pornography: The First and Fourteenth Amendments As They Support Libraries, Librarians, Library Systems, and Library Development.* Springfield, Ill., Illinois State Library, 1974. 22p. (Reprinted from *Illinois Libraries*, January 1974) **I16**
Includes an article by Alex P. Allain, president of the Freedom to Read Foundation, on the First and Fourteenth Amendments as they support libraries. He argues for the exemption of libraries under any laws involving First Amendment rights to read, for standards that are statewide, and state laws that must preempt local ordinances. Also included is the ALA resolution on the 1973 U.S. Supreme Court decisions on obscenity, and an introduction on the implications of the Supreme Court decision on obscenity by Michael J. Howlett, Secretary of State and State Librarian.

Illo, John. "Pornography & Personality." *Cultural Affairs*, 12:20–22, Fall 1970. **I17**
Pornography, by isolating the excrementitious elements of sexuality, is a sin against communication. "The disintegrating effects of pornography are consistent with general patterns of disintegrations in the United States." To resolve the social dilemma of securing the freedom of the adult and the integrity of the child, the author proposes that pornography be distinguished from valid literature of sexuality by a council or consensus of readers—adult and adolescent, expert and lay, in arts, letters, law, medicine, and the sciences, having an advisory authority in law or privately, establishing principles of discrimination, if not specific evaluations.

An Impartial Briton, *pseud. A Sixth and Last Letter, or, Address to the Parliament, as well as to the People of Great Britain; with a Retrospection to All that has been Offer'd on the Case and Cowardice of Admiral Bing: and Several New and Interesting Circumstances. . . . By An Impartial Briton!* London, The Author [1756?]. 30p. **I18**
In defending the government's action against Admiral Bing the author deals extensively with freedom of the press and libel, charging the press with abuse of press freedom. "The Liberty of the Press, can only Merit our Encouragement, and regard, in matters of Truth, Justice, Entertainment, Instruction, and all General or Particular Topics, tending to the Universal Happiness, and Right Knowledge of Mankind: as on the other Hand it should, by every Honest Loyal Man, be discountenanc'd, Curtailed, and properly Detected, wherever the Propagations of Vice, Immorality, Scandal, and Disaffection against Government, or Wrong Suggestions against Those in Power, appears Dispersed either in Books, Papers, or Pamphlets, as before Observ'd."

Imperial Fascist League. *Jewish Press-Control.* 3d ed. London, The League, 1939. 8p. **I19**
"In democratic countries, the transmission of news to the public is controlled by the Jewish Money Power to such an extent that hardly anything unfavourable to the Jewish interest is allowed to appear in a journal."

"Implications of *Citizens Communications Center v. FCC.*" *Columbia Law Review*, 71:1500–1520, December 1971. **I110**
After examining the law governing television station license renewals and the historical development of comparative hearings between an applicant for renewal and a competing applicant, the author discusses the effects that *Citizens Communications Center v. FCC* (1971) is likely to have on the license renewal process. The Court had ruled that the FCC's 1970 Policy Statement on renewals violated the Federal Communications Act of 1934 by denying the challenger of an incumbent a full hearing.

Imwinkelried, Edward J., and Donald N. Zillman. "An Evolution in the First Amendment: Overbreadth Analysis and Free Speech Within the Military Community." *Texas Law Review*, 54:42–88, December 1975.   **1111**
"Two recent Supreme Court adjudications of first amendment challenges to military penal statutes evince an evolution both of the over-breadth analysis technique and of substantive first amendment rights accorded servicemen. The authors first suggest that the Burger Court has developed its own analytical framework for statutes that are purportedly overbroad, re-flecting the Court's particular philosophical bent. In a separate treatment the authors then define the emerging parameters of substantive first amendment rights afforded servicemen."

In Fact; for the Millions Who Want a Free Press. New York, 1940–50. Weekly.   **1112**
Edited by George Seldes and Victor Weingarten, this weekly newsletter reported on news events that were ignored or suppressed in the established press. It frequently criticized controls exercised by the "press lords," government news management, efforts by pressure groups to control the content of the mass media, and "sacred cows" who were exempt from press criticism. Examples of stories: Press kills criticism of NAM; unreviewed book attacks the ads of tobacco men; displaced radio commentators; press protects price gouging firms; American press suppresses news of anti-Semitic report of Un-American Activities Committee; strike news suppressed; advertisers protected by press silence; press hides record of Churchill; *Chicago Tribune* slants the broadcasts; press kills Attorney General Clark's speech; food news the papers won't print; second campaign of Vatican to censor the U.S.; suppressed report assails U.S. policy in Greece; and reactionaries propagandize high schools.

"In the Courts: The Government vs. the Press." *Newsweek*, 77:27, 30–31, 28 June 1971.   **1113**
The case of the Pentagon Papers. The Nixon Administration's action threatens not only the right of journalists, but the free flow of information the public requires to keep watch on its government.

Inabnit, Linza B. "The Possible Prejudicial Effects of Newspaper Articles on Juries in Criminal Cases." *Kentucky Law Journal*, 47:225–43, Winter 1959.   **1114**
"The general rule laid down by the courts is that an opinion of a juror as to the guilt or innocence of an accused based on newspaper or other accounts of the crime with which he is charged will not disqualify him from serving as a juror provided it appears to the reasonable satisfaction of the court that such person can and will, notwithstanding such opinion, fairly and impartially try the case on the evidence presented at trial."

Independent Briton: or, Free Thoughts on the Expediency of Gratifying the People's Expectations; as to Securing the Liberty of the Press; restoring the Freedom of the Stage; preventing Bribery in Elections; excluding Place-Men from Seats in the House of Commons; repealing the Septennial Act, Etc. . . . London, T. Cooper, 1742. 71p.   **1115**
The author argues for greater freedom of the press, every Briton's birthright, calling for a "clear and explicit declaration" from the government. He counters arguments against further securing press freedom: (1) Even the best government may be destroyed by a licentious press. "No good Government can be in Danger from any Writings whatsoever. . . . If Men write Falsities against the Government, they may be refuted either in legal or in a rational Way. . . . But if a thing cannot be proved either false or mischievous, I do not think that publishing of it ought to be criminal." (2) There is no need for better established press freedom; we already have more freedom than ever before. "The Liberty of the Press is at present very precarious . . . the Way should be left open, of informing the Nation, their Representatives, and the Crown, of any Grievances that are either felt or suspected, because this is the only way to have them examined and removed. To punish Men for complaining when they are injured, is unnatural as well as unjust. . . ."The author deplores the lack of freedom of expression on the stage where wit and humor, one of the great characteristics of a free people, are no more. "Let us not lose another, too, lest Sense and Reason should follow the Track of Humour and Wit, and the British Genius be reduced to the French, Spanish and Italian Employment, of spinning out new Systems of Philosophy or labouring in Defence of Tyranny and Suppression."

Independent Broadcasting Authority. *The IBA Code of Advertising Standards and Practice*. London, IBA, 1972. 20p. **1116**
Includes policies on advertising directed at children, financial advertising, advertising of medicines and treatments, and statutes affecting broadcasting advertising.

Index on Censorship. London, Writers & Scholars International, 1972–date. Quarterly.   **1117**
A journal devoted to the defense of freedom of expression, under the editorship of Michael Scammell. *Index* is international in scope and publishes poetry and articles that have been suppressed by various governments in addition to articles about censorship throughout the world. A regular feature is the "*Index* Index," which is a country-by-country chronicle of events "published to illustrate the ways in which freedom of expression is being variously curtailed or denied." A review of *Index* appears in the *New Yorker*, 18 August 1975. Individual articles from *Index* are entered under the name of their authors in this bibliography.

India. Cinematograph Committee,

1927–28. *Report, 1927–1928*. Calcutta, Government of India, Publications Branch, 1928. 226p.   **1118**
The present (1928) system of film censorship in India was introduced by the Indian Cinematograph Act, 1918, which set up boards of film censors in Bombay, Calcutta, Madras and Rangoon. The 1927–28 Committee dealt with the widespread criticism of the system (e.g., it allowed too many offensive western films to be seen), held a series of hearings in various parts of India (four volumes of *Evidence* were published), and concluded that a Control Board of Censors for the whole of British India was the best solution. Such a board would establish general principles, to be followed by provincial boards.

India (Republic). Enquiry Committee on Film Censorship. *Report*. New Delhi, Ministry of Information and Broadcasting, Government of India, 1969. 202p.   **1119**
The report includes a history of film censorship in India and an estimate of the present status, experience with film censorship in other countries, the legal aspects of film censorship, the effect of films on the audience, and an analysis of the criticism of film content and the present mode of censorship as received in oral interviews and written statements. In conclusion the report rejects voluntary self-regulation by the film industry as "wholly impracticable and impossible of achievement" due to the chaotic state of the industry and its profit-orientation. State censorship, the report maintains, must be kept within the reasonable restriction clause of the Constitution. An independent, self-supporting Control Board of twenty fully paid members drawn from various regions and familiar with regional languages is recommended. Guidelines for censorship are proposed. Controls should also be imposed on both import and export of films. On the positive side the report recommends greater freedom be given to Indian film producers in the theme content of films to improve the artistic and aesthetic quality of Indian films.

India (Republic). Parliament. Advisory Committee on the Press Council. *Report of the Advisory Committee on the Press Council, 1968*. New Delhi, Ministry of Information and Broadcasting, Government of India, 1969. 102p.   **1120**
In 1954 the Press Commission recommended the establishment of an All-India Press Council to safeguard the freedom of the press and to maintain the independence and standards of newspapers in India. In pursuance of that recommendation, the Press Council Act, 1965, was passed. In 1968 the government set up an Advisory Committee on the Press Council to study the existing Act and make recommendations. The Committee recommended con-

tinuance of the Council in reorganized form and membership. It disagreed with the Council's suggestions that newspapers be required to publish Council decisions, that it be empowered to make judicial inquiries, and that it advise the government of action to be taken against a newspaper that had been repeatedly censured.

India (Republic). Parliament. Joint Committee of the Houses of Parliament on the Press Council Bill. *The Press Council Bill, 1963. Report of the Joint Committee. . . .* New Delhi, Government of India, 1965. 41p.   **1121**
A bill to establish a Press Council "for the purpose of preserving the liberty of the Press and of maintaining and improving the standards of newspapers in India." Majority report favoring the bill together with a minority report opposing it.

India (Republic). Press Commission, 1954. *Report of the Press Commission, Part I.* New Delhi, Manager of Publications, Government of India, 1954. 538p.   **1122**
The Commission recommends formation of an All-India Press Council, and changes in the Press (Objectionable Matter) Act, the Press and Registration of Books Act, Official Secrets Act (1923), and the laws of contempt of court, defamation, and other acts relating to press freedom. Part II consists of a history of Indian journalism by Jagadish Nataranjan.

"An Individual Involved in an Event of General or Public Interest and Who Is the Target of Defamatory Remarks May Not Recover Damages for Libel Unless Actual Malice Is Shown." *Brooklyn Law Review*, 38:822–31, Winter 1972.   **1123**
Re: *Rosenbloom v. Metromedia, Inc.*, 403 U.S. 29 (1971).

Ingelhart, Louis E. *The College and University Campus Student Press: An Examination of Its Status and Aspirations and Some of the Myths Surrounding It.* Terre Haute, Ind., National Council of College Publications Advisers, 1973. 20p.   **1124**
A preliminary report of an ad hoc Committee on Legal Status of the Campus Press, issued at this time to counteract what the author calls the myths about the campus student press. In particular, the author criticizes the report prepared by Julius Duscha and Thomas C. Fischer (*The Campus Press: Freedom and Responsibility*) and issued by the American Association of State Colleges and Universities. Among the "myths" rejected by the present report are

those dealing with independence, incorporation, publisher, libel, censorship, and antagonistic administrators. In the matter of libel the author concludes: "Libel or losses do not pose a threat to universities or to student journalists who know what they are doing." On censorship: "Censorship or prior approval of copy for the campus press is not the standard procedure in American colleges and universities, public or private." On antagonistic administrators: "Truthfully, the student press on most campuses enjoys considerable understanding, support, and freedom." The Report was prepared for the National Council of College Publications Advisers and its Committee on the Legal Status of the College Press.

Ingersoll, Robert G. "Colonel Ingersoll Talks About his Threatened Indictment in Delaware for Blasphemy." *Truth Seeker*, 8:170–71, 12 March 1881. (Reprinted from the *Brooklyn Eagle*) **1125**
In an interview with a reporter from the *Brooklyn Eagle*, Ingersoll comments on blasphemy laws in general. "These laws were passed when our honest ancestors were burning witches, trading Quaker children to the Barbadoes for rum and molasses, branding people upon the forehead, boring their tongues with hot irons, putting one another in the pillory, and generally in the name of God, making their neighbors as uncomfortable as possible. We have outgrown the laws without repealing them." The chief justice of Delaware, in a public address, had suggested that a grand jury indict Ingersoll, presumably for a speech he had made in Wilmington which was objected to by local ministers. "It is easier to kill two Infidels than to answer one. . . . No theologian ever called for the help of the law until his logic gave out."

[———.] *The Great Ingersoll Controversy Containing the Famous Christmas Sermon by Colonel Robert G. Ingersoll, the Indignant Protests Thereby Evoked from Ministers of Various Denominations, and Colonel Ingersoll's Replies to the Same. Reprinted in Full from the Correspondence on the Subject by Special Permission of "The Evening Telegram."* New York, Edward Brandus, 1892. 213p.   **1126**
Many of the letters to the editor published herein challenge the press's right to publish the "blasphemies" of Colonel Ingersoll. The preface refers to the effort of a Methodist clergyman to organize a boycott against the *New York Evening Telegram* for printing Ingersoll's Christmas sermon which had touched off the controversy.

———. *. . . The Great Jersey Heresy Case . . . Speech in the Trial of the Rev. Charles B. Reynolds for Blasphemy, at Morristown, New Jersey, May 22, 1887.* Chicago, G. S. Baldwin, 1887. 14p. (Col. R. G. Ingersoll's Lectures, no. 46)   **1127**

Ingersoll defended Reynolds on charges of distributing a blasphemous pamphlet entitled *Blasphemy and the Bible*. Ingersoll made an eloquent plea in behalf of freedom of speech, denying that the defendant's paraphrasing the Bible, although in bad taste, was blasphemy. "Blasphemy is injustice. The man who knowingly contradicts the truth is a blasphemer. The man who violates his own conscience is a blasphemer. The jury who gives an unjust verdict and the judge who pronounces an unjust sentence are blasphemers, and a man swayed by public opinion against his better judgment is a blasphemer." Despite the eloquent address Reynolds was found guilty and fined $25. An advertisement in this pamphlet offers for sale *Fruits of Philosophy*, "the book the English Government is trying to suppress."

———, Frederic R. Coudert, and Stewart L. Woodford. *The Limitations of Tolerance; A Discussion*. New York, The Truth Seeker, 1889. 44p.   **1128**
Colonel Ingersoll, an agnostic, debates with a Catholic and a Protestant over the right to think and express opinions.

Inglis, K. S. *The Stuart Case*. Melbourne, Australia, Melbourne University Press, 1961. 322p.   **1129**
The book deals with the controversial rape-murder case in South Australia including the defamatory libel charges against the *Adelaide News*. An account of the libel trial is given in chapter 21. The jury found the defendants in the libel trial "not guilty."

Ingram, William. "The Closing of the Theaters in 1597: A Dissenting View." *Modern Philology*, 69:105–15, November 1971.   **1130**
An account of the political intrigue involving an allegedly seditious play, *The Isle of Dogs*, the proprietor of the Swan Theatre (Francis Langley), and the Privy Council which led to the closing of the London theaters in 1597.

Ingrams, Richard. "Eye Witness." In Michael Rubinstein, *ed.*, *Wicked, Wicked Libels*, London, Routledge & Kegan Paul, 1972, pp. 85–92.   **1131**
The editor of *Private Eye* discusses his ten-year experience at the receiving end of libel writs. The average citizen, he notes, tends to support the individual who has been libeled by the rich and powerful press. He asks the pundits to consider the plight of the small and relatively penniless papers such as *Private Eye*. Present libel laws serve as a useful excuse for apathy and inaction on the part of the established press that could afford to run the risk of libel in the interest of public service; the smaller papers that are willing to expose injustice and hypocrisy are faced with extinction under threat of the law of libel.

The Injured Iphigenia; A True History. In which the Nature of Libellous Paragraphs, Calculated To Disturb the Peace of

Families, Is Set in a Proper Light; And the Necessity of Preventing them by An Express Law, Is candidly enquired into, and impartially considered. In a Letter to a Friend in S—. London, J. Roberts, 1748. 27p. **1132**

The imaginary Iphigenia, virtuous wife of Nearchus, has been libeled both verbally and in print and a bachelor friend of the couple has appealed to the author for advice. After a long discussion on envy, frequently the root of libeling a woman, the author advises the husband to "sit down silently under an Insult" rather than bring the offenders to account and thereby "keep up the Memory of the Scandal" which would otherwise be buried in oblivion. He rejects the suggestion of more strict libel laws, as too great a price to pay for occasional misuse of freedom. Men and women of honor will rise above the evil of malicious libel. Virtue and good sense will not prevent us from being overturned in a coach or splashed in the street, but it will enable us to live with misfortune.

Insh, George P. *Thomas Muir of Huntershill (1765–1799).* Glasgow, Golden Eagle Press, 1949. 19p. **1133**

This essay was written to mark the 150th anniversary of the death of Thomas Muir, Scottish martyr to a free press, who was exiled in 1793. The author indicates his intention of publishing a life of Muir. The cover of the pamphlet reproduces a miniature of young Muir, once owned by biographer MacKenzie, but given to Insh by a colleague.

Institute of Professional Librarians of Ontario. "IPLO Statement of Intellectual Freedom (Adopted by the Membership at the Annual Meeting, April 22, 1972)." *IPLO Quarterly*, 15:4, July 1972; 17:87–88, July–October 1975. **1134**

The statement asserts that librarians will not reject material "because of the race, nationality, or political, religious or unpopular views of the creator or because the materials may be considered as depicting the ugly, shocking or unedifying in life." It rejects censorship as a valid activity for library staff or board, and recommends resistance of individuals or groups to curtail access to library materials.

Institute of Professional Librarians of Ontario. Board of Directors. "IPLO Findings on Conestoga College: A Report to the Membership." *IPLO Quarterly*, 12:117–20, January 1971. **1135**

Report of a committee of the Institute appointed to study the problems of intellectual freedom in the library of Conestoga College. While the committee found insufficient evidence to support a charge of censorship, it recommended that the college administration prepare a written statement on the role of the library and that the librarian prepare a statement on its book selection policies. The report deplored the fact that the college administration refused to cooperate in the investigation.

Interesting Papers Relative to the Recent Riots at Baltimore. Philadelphia, n.p., 1812. 90p. (Sabin 34899; Shaw-Shoemaker 25720) **1136**

An antiwar article in the 20 June 1812 issue of the *Baltimore Federal Republican* resulted in the destruction of the newspaper office and the press. The editors and supporters, including General H. Lee and General Lingan, took over a house in Baltimore, fortifying it against attack, and from there issued a further publication supporting their antiwar cause. A mob threatened the building, shots were fired, the militia arrived and arrested the occupants and ignored the destructive mob. The contents of the house were destroyed. The group was taken to jail, but given inadequate protection resulting in the death of General Lingan. General Lee, John Thomas, and others managed to escape to Yorktown, Pa. Newspapers in Boston and elsewhere came to the support of the editors and viewed the Baltimore affair with alarm. John Thomas wrote his experience in a twelve-page pamphlet, *Narrative of John Thomas, One of the Persons Intended to Be Massacred with Gen. Lingan and Others, in the Goal of Baltimore, on Tuesday, July 28th, 1812* (Boston, Nathaniel Coverly, 1812). In September 1812 George W. P. Custis delivered *An Address Occasioned by the Death of General Lingan, who was murdered by the Mob at Baltimore* (Boston, Bradford & Read, 1812. 16p.). (Sabin 18151.)

International Federation of Free Journalists. *Report on the Freedom of the Press in the World, 1963.* [New York, The Federation, 1964.] 33p. (Researcher: Oton Ambroz) **1137**

In this survey of the state of press freedom in countries that are members of the United Nations, references are made to Great Britain, Union of South Africa, Rhodesia, and the United States. "In publishing the enclosed report, the International Federation of Free Journalists wishes to draw the attention of freedom-loving people everywhere to the challenges faced by communist and authoritarian governments to the freedom of the press."

International Neo-Malthusian Bureau of Correspondence and Defence. *Memorandum concerning the prosecution of Mrs. Margaret H. Sanger of New York, U.S.A., for her advocacy of Birth Control and her issue of a Pamphlet entitled "Family Limitation," describing various methods of restricting families.* [London, The Bureau, 1914?] 6p. **1138**

An account of the prosecution and an appeal to "all true citizens of the United States to band together in [Mrs. Sanger's] support and in the determination to have this law [declaring birth control information obscene] repealed and the Comstock censorship destroyed."

International Organization of Journalists. *South Africa, Apartheid, Mass Media; A Report on the Present State of Official Restrictions and Persecutions.*

Prague, The IOJ, 1973. 28p. (IOJ Documents, Reports, Studies, Bibliography) **1139**

International Press Institute. *The Flow of the News; A Study By the International Press Institute.* Zurich, IPI, 1953. 266p. **1140**

The study deals with the flow of news into the United States, Western Europe, and India—the nature and extent of news flow, areas of ignorance in one country about another, possible causes of ignorance, methods of improving the flow of news, and cooperation among editors and between editors and news agencies.

International Typographical Union. *Federal Responsibility for a Free and Competitive Press. Presented Before the Antitrust Subcommittee of the House Committee on the Judiciary Investigation of Monopoly Practices in the Newspaper Industry. . . .* Colorado Springs, Colo., International Typographical Union, 1963. 170p. **1141**

"The ITU firmly believes that the time has come to halt the corrosive effects of monopoly and centralized absentee ownership in the newspaper industry. Appropriate action should be taken to guarantee competition and freedom of the press. Time is running out as chain ownership and the blight of monopoly overtakes the few remaining cities in which competition exists." Restriction on freedom of the press is caused by economic concentration in the newspaper industry. Newspapers cannot hide behind a claim of immunity from application of the antitrust laws based on freedom of the press. The ITU urges Congress to pass remedial legislation.

Iowa. University. School of Journalism. *Shield Legislation for Journalists: A Bibliography.* Iowa City, University of Iowa, School of Journalism, 1973. 36p. Processed. **1142**

Text of state statutes, pages 2–20, bibliography, pages 21–36.

"The Iowa Open Meetings Act: A Right Without a Remedy?" *Iowa Law Review*, 58:210–20, October 1972. **1143**

The article outlines the provisions of Iowa's Open Meetings Act and evaluates the Iowa Supreme Court's construction of the remedies available under the statute as given in *Dobrovolny v. Reinhardt*, 173 N.W.2d 837, 840 (Iowa 1970).

"Iowa's Freedom of Information Act: Everything You've Always Wanted to

Know About Public Records But Were Afraid to Ask." *Iowa Law Review*, 57:1163–89, April 1972.   **1144**
An analysis of the Iowa Public Records Act of 1967, which repudiated the common law concept of public records that balanced the interest of the litigants and ignored the public's right to know. Inspection under the new law is allowed unless no public interest is clearly promoted or unless substantial harm would accrue to any individual.

Irani, C. R. "The Indian Press Under Pressure." *Freedom at Issue*, 30:7–8, 14–21, March–April 1975.   **1145**
"Is the right of dissent being obliterated in India? A leading publisher spells out the threats and controls—ingenious and endless—by which Indira Gandhi's ministers target the press. The moral of this important case history of the abuse of democratic power: Journalists must not 'pay heed to the sensitivities of governments.' " The Freedom House citation to Mr. Irani is reported in the November 1976 issue.

———. "Killing the Press: The Indirect Approach." *Quest*, 87:29–32, March–April 1974.   **1146**
The author describes the various threats to a free press in India—efforts of the Gandhi government to require worker determination of newspaper policies, to control newsprint allocations, to regulate the price of papers and of advertising, and to dominate schools of journalism. If the Indian people do not resist these pressures the Indian press will not be the only casualty; "what the Government is about will not even be known to the citizens."

———. "Who Decides Our Freedom?" *Index on Censorship*, 5(4):22–25, Winter 1976. (Reprinted from the *CPU Quarterly*, Commonwealth Press Union, June 1976)   **1147**
A discussion of Indian censorship under the emergency powers granted the Gandhi government and under the specific law, Publication of Objectional Matter Act, whose objective is "to further emasculate and render much more difficult any worthwhile criticism of acts of omission and commission of those wielding political power." The author discusses the editor's code of conduct imposed upon the press by the Information Ministry, the encroachment of government in press management through appointment of directors of the major newspapers, and the establishment of a government-controlled monopoly in the news agency field. In a brief accompanying article, T. K. Ghosh defends the action against the Indian press as necessary to save the country from chaos and anarchy.

The Irish Times. "Censorship." In *The*

Liberal Ethic. Dublin, The Irish Times, 1950, pp. 57–88.   **1148**
Reprinting of a series of letters to the editor giving pro and con arguments on Irish censorship. The controversy was stimulated by the Censorship of Publication Board's banning of the *Report of the British Royal Commission on Population* because it advocated use of contraceptives and the banning of Vogt's *Road to Survival*. The Appeal Board subsequently removed the ban on the report of the Commission on Population.

Irvine, Reed J. *"AIM" Corrects Errors in Report*. Columbia, Mo., Freedom of Information Center, School of Journalism, University of Missouri at Columbia, 1975. 4p. (Report no. 0018)   **1149**
The chairman of the board of Accuracy in Media, Inc. responds to "serious errors and distortions" in the Center's report no. 313, *The Anatomy of "AIM"* by Daniel Epstein.

Irvine, Stanley G. "Neck Deep in the Big Muddy: The Underground Press and the Law." *Missouri Library Association Quarterly*, 30:184–90, September 1969.   **1150**
The author concludes that "the exact legal status of the underground press cannot be clearly defined in view of the present state of both obscenity and libel law," although much greater latitude in both areas has been allowed in recent years.

"Is the Supreme Court Soft on Pornography?" *Playboy*, 20(12):153–59, December 1973.   **1151**
A bawdy spoof of the U.S. Supreme Court's 1973 rulings on obscenity. "Like many well-intentioned Americans, you may feel that the recent Supreme Court decisions on obscenity were a crackdown on hard-core pornography. But we here at *Playboy*, where chastity has long been a primary concern, aren't so easily misled. It's obvious that the decisions are merely a more insidious way of encouraging other, new forms of filth to flourish. Nine monkeys with enough gavels could have come up with the same decisions."

Isaacs, Charles. "Free Speech for William Shockley?" *Chronicle of Higher Education*, 8(11):24, 3 December 1973. **1152**
" 'No,' says a professor, 'because Shockley's views are not legitimate dissent; they are inhumane lies.' " "Shockley," a controversial lecturer on the subject of racial differences, "is no dissenter, whatever his academic standing may be. His message is, in fact, that of the monopolists: Freedom of thought and discussion can only be created by breaking the monopoly, by destroying it, not by allowing it to hide in some fictional 'marketplace of ideas.' "

Isaacs, Norman E. "The Credibility Gap and the Ombudsman." *Bulletin of*

the American Society of Newspaper Editors, 527:1–3, 11, February 1969. (Reprinted in Michael C. Emery and Ted C. Smythe, eds., *Readings in Mass Communications*, pp. 77–83)   **1153**
How one newspaper, the *Louisville Courier-Journal*, met external criticism of the paper by creation of an internal critic, an ombudsman, to serve as a watchdog over the paper's accuracy and fairness, and to investigate complaints of readers.

———. "Standards Relating to Fair Trial and Free Press." *Harvard Law Review*, 82:960–66, February 1969. **1154**
While applauding the American Bar Association's Reardon Report on fair trial and free press for its major accomplishments and for its "sobering and salutary effect on the press," this newspaper editor is critical of various portions, particularly the move to have police departments impose internal regulations for release of information—a form of censorship which no newspapers will accept. He concludes that it is now "time for the bar to exchange its canon for a carrot."

———. "There May Be Worse to Come from This Court." *Columbia Journalism Review*, 11(3):18–24, September–October 1972.   **1155**
The 29 June 1972 ruling of the U.S. Supreme Court that the power of a grand jury took precedence over the heretofore presumed protection of the First Amendment. "These cases and the Pentagon Papers decision of last year—which involved temporary prior restraint—leave adherents of a free press no reason to be sanguine. The best hope for protection of news sources now appears to lie in passage of federal and state 'shield' laws." The author calls for major improvements in American journalism to help win back the trust of the American public. Views of Fred W. Friendly and Benno C. Schmidt, Jr. are also given.

———. "Why We Lack a National Press Council." *Columbia Journalism Review*, 9(3):16–26, Fall 1970. (Reprinted in Alfred Balk and James Boylan, eds., *Our Troubled Press*, pp. 343–59)   **1156**
The author reviews the idea of press councils from the suggestion made in the Hutchins Report to the present, noting the opposition of the press and the limited experience of local councils. "The need remains for some kind of agency to appraise press performance, or at least to consider grievances against it. For a yawning credibility gap was widening year by year." The matter should come before the American Society of Newspaper Editors. If it does, a secret ballot should be taken so that editors may vote their conscience rather than the views of their publishers.

——— *et al*. "Agnew, the National Mood and the Media." *Bulletin of the American Society of Newspaper Editors*, 537:1–3, January 1970.   **1157**

The president of ASNE calls for a "sensible, temperate program of intelligent self-examination" of the press in the wake of Spiro Agnew criticisms. This article is followed (pp. 4–5) by a defense of Agnew's criticisms by James J. Kilpatrick, editor of the *Richmond News Leader*, and by an article, A Matter of Image: Was Agnew Right About TV News, by Dick Cheverton of *Chicago Today* (pp. 6–7, 13).

Isbister, Clair, and G. R. Christmas. *The Menace of Pornography*. Sydney, New South Wales, New South Wales Council of Churches, 1973. 11p. **1158**
In a talk, Let Us Raise Community Standards, Isbister appeals to Christians to protect all children from the harmful effects of salacious literature and entertainment which depicts abnormal behavior as permissible and standard. Christmas, in The Price of Pornography Is Too High, sees the spread of pornography as a debasement and abuse of freedom, a commercialized exploitation of a human weakness. Those who seek to legalize it "are, I believe, making an attack upon society."

Isenberg, Barbara. "Harassing the Underground." *Columbia Journalism Review*, 10(2):54–56, July–August 1971. **1159**

A detailing of charges against the *Los Angeles Free Press*—court conviction on "receiving stolen property" for publishing a secret list of undercover narcotics agents, and refusal of accredited press status by the Los Angeles police. The author notes the indifference of the established press toward harassment of the underground press.

Isham, Duane L. "Libel Per Se and Libel Per Quod in Ohio." *Ohio State Law Journal*, 15:303–10, Summer 1954. **1160**

Israel, Callie. "Intellectual Freedom and Children." *Ontario Library Review*, 56:73–74, June 1972. **1161**
A children's librarian explores some of the issues relating to selection and censorship of books for children, an area formerly secure and isolated but now subject to controversy. "Selection means worrying about how words are used, not what the words are. Censorship is discarding the works of John Donovan, John Steptoe and others because of the occasional 'hell' or 'damn' even though the literary excellence of the books is undisputed. Selection means deciding on literary merit and integrity of purpose of a book and letting a child's parents decide on the moral issues. Censorship is deciding to be a pseudo-parent who knows best what values every child must hold." The author debunks the myth that comic books, abridged classics, and series books should be used as a come-on to get children into the library. "Children are not that stupid."

Israel, Jerold H., and Rita A. Burns. "Study Report on Juvenile Obscenity Laws." In Michigan Law Revision Commission. *Tenth Annual Report, 1975*. Ann Arbor, Mich., University of Michigan Law School, 1975, pp. 133–297. **1162**
"The Report analyzes various issues presented in drafting a juvenile obscenity statute and notes the treatment of those issues in various statutes and proposed statutes. Among the provisions considered are the current Michigan statutes, the statutes of various states (including California, Florida, Hawaii, Illinois, New York, Ohio, Oregon, Utah, Washington, and Wisconsin), the Detroit Obscenity Ordinance, and proposals advanced in the Michigan Bar Committee Report on Proposed Changes in the Criminal Code, the Proposed Criminal Code of Massachusetts, and the majority and dissenting reports of the Presidential Commission on Obscenity and Pornography. Accompanying the Report is a 'model statute' prepared by the authors. The statute is not presented as a specific legislative recommendation of the Com-

mission. It is designed solely to supplement the Study Report by providing a framework for the drafting of any legislation that might be introduced by the subcommittee or individual members of the subcommittee. The model statute covers the elements that might be included in a juvenile obscenity statute and provides alternative drafts on most areas of controversy." An analysis of the model statute by the authors appears in *University of Michigan Journal of Law Reform*, Spring 1976.

Ives, Almon P. "Freedom of Speech: Concepts of the Courts." In Speech Association of America. *Abstracts, 54th Annual Meeting*. Chicago, 1968, p. 18. **1163**
This paper presents a brief report of an effort to develop an undergraduate course exploring the First Amendment freedom.

Ivey, David. "Obscenity—The Definitional Dilemma." *Georgia Bar Journal*, 10:327–35, November 1973. **1164**
The author favors the rejection of the labeling process in obscenity cases as exemplified in *Roth v. United States* (1957) and *Miller v. State of California* (1973) and a return to a traditional First Amendment approach, "looking to the activity and resulting evil."

Ivory, James. "Hollywood versus Hollywood." *Index on Censorship*, 5(2):10–16, Summer 1976. **1165**
An American film director "describes his experiences with *The Wild Party* and explains how it is that his version of the film has still not been released to the public, one year after its completion, and probably never will." A case history of how internal commercial pressures serve as a film censor.

J

Jacklin, Phil. "Access to the Media; A New Fairness Doctrine." *Center Magazine*, 8(3):46–50, May–June 1975. **1J1**
The author argues for a regulatory strategy in the mass media which is fundamentally different from the present fairness doctrine in broadcasting and would apply to the newspaper press as well. "We can choose to regulate access rather than content, to insure fairness about who is heard rather than fairness in what is said." He describes how this concept could be applied and what changes in the communications law are needed to make it effective without violating the spirit of the First Amendment.

Jackson, Nancy B. "The Politics of Revenge." *MORE*, 4(2):5–8, February 1974. **1J2**
"Four separate groups are now trying to take away the licenses of the *Washington Post's* two Florida TV stations. Odd how many of the challengers can be linked to President Nixon."

Jacqueney, Theodore. "Nibbling at the Bureaucracy." *MORE*, 3(10):15–17, October 1973. **1J3**
"The Freedom of Information Act is an enormously powerful tool for investigative journalists, but in the seven years since it became law few reporters have bothered to use it."

Jacob, Joseph. "Some Reflections on Governmental Secrecy." *Public Law*, 1974:25–49, 1974. **1J4**
"A discussion of the working of official government secrecy in Britain, including the apparently minor role played by the Official Secrets Acts." The article also discusses how the government handles other people's secrets.

Jacobs, David H. "The Control of Obscenity in Connecticut." *Connecticut Bar Journal*, 41:172–200, June 1967. **1J5**
A review of the treatment of obscenity cases by the Connecticut courts in light of the *Roth v. United States* (1957) and *Ginzburg v. United States* (1966) decisions of the U.S. Supreme Court.

ᵣJacobs, Michael A.ᵧ "First Amendment Permits Showing Obscene Film in Public Theater to Paying Adult Audience That Was Forewarned of Film's Nature." *Albany Law Review*, 34:708–15, Spring 1970. **1J6**
In the case of *Karalexis v. Byrne* (1969) involving the showing of *I Am Curious (Yellow)*, the federal district court in Massachusetts ruled that the freedom of speech clause of the First Amendment protects restricted public dissemination of obscene films, and that the Massachusetts obscenity statute was unconstitutional.

Jacobs, William J. "Movies Are Dirtier Than Ever." *National Decency Reporter*, 4(3–4):6–9, March–April 1967. **1J7**
"It definitely is not an 'in' thing to complain about dirty movies, but there are some around that you wouldn't believe. They're bad enough to shock some pretty hard-boiled people, and they can't be justified on artistic or educational grounds. A little investigation shows that police can't do anything about them anymore. They blame the Supreme Court. New production standards promise to make things even worse, since all former restrictions are removed in favor of broad guidelines. You've probably never seen a film like the one described here, but you should know about it. You may even want to do something about it." The film described is *Mondo Freudo*.

Jacobson, Beverly. "Bookstore Perishes in Wake of Utah Obscenity Legislation." *Publishers' Weekly*, 205(25):49–51, 24 June 1974. **1J8**
An eighteen-page tough and explicit obscenity ordinance in Orem, Utah, was used against a new bookstore when a policeman found copies of *Last Tango in Paris* and *The Idolators* on the shelves. One of the provisions of the ordinance was the creation of a Commission on Public Decency to locate trouble areas and report them to the police; another provision prohibits teachers from assigning certain reading matter to pupils.

Jacobson, Donna L. "A Semi-

Analytical Plea for Understanding, Not Censorship." *Bay State Librarian*, 58(3):23–27, October 1969. **1J9**
A plea to understand what is taking place in protest music—evolution of folk to protest, and now to folk-rock. "Keeping the air clean will not remove the pollution if there is something driving man to sully." If you don't understand what is happening, "at the very least listen and let others listen with you."

Jacobson, Nancy G. "Restricting the Public Display of Offensive Materials: The Use and Effectiveness of Public and Private Nuisance Actions." *University of San Francisco Law Review*, 10:232–51, Fall 1975. **1J10**
"This Comment will analyze the effectiveness of both public and private nuisance actions in restricting public exposure of periodicals portraying front page nudity on sidewalk newsracks." Consideration of a San Francisco ordinance in light of the recent Supreme Court decision of *Erznoznik v. Jacksonville* (1975), and suggestion of the advantages of a private nuisance action.

Jaffary, K. D. "An Approach to the Criminal Provisions Regarding Obscenity." *University of Toronto Faculty of Law Review*, 20:5–19, April 1962. **1J11**
"It is the object of this article to look briefly at the principles underlying our ᵣCanadian obscenityᵧ law, their embodiment in the statute, and the reasonable interpretation or approach to the statute which the principles dictate." Special attention is given to the Brodie case, *Brodie v. The Queen*, presently before the Supreme Court of Canada.

Jaffe, Brett. "Freedom from Defamation: A Constitutionally Protected Right?" *Capital University Law Review*, 6:299–314, 1976. **1J12**
The author examines in some detail the defamation aspects of *Paul v. Davis* (1976), concluding that "the Supreme Court has effectively eliminated a person's reputation from either

the procedural safeguards guaranteed under the Fourteenth Amendment, or from a general right of privacy recognized by the Court as a constitutionally protected right."

Jaffe, Carolyn. "The Press and the Oppressed—A Study of Prejudicial News Reporting in Criminal Cases." *Journal of Criminal Law, Criminology, and Police Science*, 56:1–17, March 1965; 56:158–73, June 1965.   **1J13**
In part I "the author first examines the applicable standards of impartiality which a jury must meet in order for a trial to be constitutionally 'fair,' and then defines that 'prejudicial publicity' which can render a jury unconstitutionally partial and hence a trial not constitutionally fair. Finally, existing methods which have been used in an attempt to prevent defendants from being convicted by juries rendered partial by publicity are critically examined, with emphasis on the effect of each of these methods upon the co-existing interests of the press, the defendant, and the Government which are sought to be preserved." In part II "the author examines the possibility of expanding some of the existing solutions, with emphasis on the importance of formulating and making known to the press, Bar, and police a set of standards delineating the kinds of material which are likely to deprive a defendant of a fair trial. After examining the sources of prejudicial publicity and noting the probable futility of internal control by the press, the author proposes a remedial statute. Results of a poll of lawyers, police officials, and newsmen conducted by the author are tabulated in appendices to part II."—Editor

Jaffe, Louis L. "The Editorial Responsibility of the Broadcaster: Reflections on Fairness and Access." *Harvard Law Review*, 84:768–92, February 1972. (Reprinted in 1U100)   **1J14**
"Professor Jaffe explores the soundness of the recent application of the fairness doctrine to broadcast advertising and of the recent decision of the Court of Appeals for the District of Columbia creating a first amendment right to purchase broadcast time for political advertising. He concludes that since broadcasting has only a marginal impact on the public's political consciousness and that since extension of the fairness and access doctrines may exact significant costs in terms of other important values, the logic of those recent decisions must be carefully limited."—Editor

———. "The Fairness Doctrine, Equal Time, Reply to Personal Attacks, and the Local Service Obligation: Implications of Technological Change." *University of Cincinnati Law Review*, 37:550–57, Summer 1968.   **1J15**
Do the unique characteristics of television make the four doctrines listed in the title necessary? If there is value of one or another, what are the counterbalancing considerations, and do they finally outweigh the value of the doctrines? The author examines each doctrine,

noting that the answer is not the same for all four.

———. "WHDH: The FCC and Broadcasting License Renewals." *Harvard Law Review*, 82:1693–1702, June 1969.   **1J16**
"The Federal Communications Commission has recently caused the broadcasting industry considerable consternation by refusing to renew the license of Boston television station WHDH, granting the license instead to a competing applicant. Professor Jaffe argues that the Commission demonstrated in that decision a regulatory approach which is deficient as a means of improving programming and which gives insufficient protection to the legitimate reliance interest of broadcasting licensees. He suggests alternative methods of regulation which would be substantively more effective and would not threaten the stability of existing investments."—Editor

———, and Nicholas Johnson. "Two Views on the Regulation of Television." *New Republic*, 161(23):14–19, 6 December 1969.   **1J17**
Louis L. Jaffe, Harvard Law School professor, favors "something like the Pastore bill" which forbids the FCC to consider new applicants for station license unless it first finds that the present licensee has failed to measure up to its responsibilities. "Without such a bill, the licensee must compete with new applicants, so that he can be defeated on a merely comparative basis . . . thus, the Commission would have an easy opening for censoring the licensee and keeping him in constant terror." Commissioner Nicholas Johnson disagrees. The Pastore Bill "will remove from the people the only thin small reed to which they now cling in their self-defensive struggle against the combined force of the broadcasting industry and the FCC."

James, Beatrice M. "Testimony of the New Jersey Library Association Before the Obscenity Study Commission of New Jersey." *New Jersey Libraries*, 3(1):16–18, Spring 1970.   **1J18**
The president of the Association appeals to the Commission "to reject further moves for legislation in this field. The potential injury to freedom of ideas in the United States is greater than supposed 'protection' of the young from materials which they know of and have access to in any event."

James, Clive. "Where Do We Go After 'Oz'?" *Times Literary Supplement*, 3,624:698+, 13 August 1971. (Reprinted in his *The Metropolitan Critic*. London, Faber, 1974, pp. 199–204)   **1J19**
A critique of the British obscenity trial involving the periodical *Oz* by an Australian journalist. "It's the law that's at fault. It centers on a concept that nobody has ever been able to define, and once a charge has been brought under

it there is no defence against the ordinary prejudices of prosecution, judge and jury except to introduce a counterbalancing, equally undefinable concept, such as literary merit." In the *Oz* case the counterbalancing concept was a version of the public good—the right to criticize and the necessity for evolutionary change. "It didn't have a chance."

James, Howard A. "Why Has the Press Let the Courts Become Sacrosanct?" *Bulletin of the American Society of Newspaper Editors*, 502:7–9, 12 June 1968. **1J20**
The courts do not belong to the professionals, but to the people. The press has a responsibility for monitoring the work of the bench and bar—the lawyers, prosecutors, policemen, probation officers, and prison officials as well as the courts themselves.

James, Max H. "Propaganda or Education?" *Arizona English Bulletin*, 13:37–41, October 1970. (ED 45,675) **1J21**
The author reports on a survey that reveals that Arizona school newspapers are caught in the crosscurrent of two divergent streams of thought, whether papers should exist as propaganda organs for the school and should avoid controversial issues, or whether they should be given responsible freedom to publish all the news (pleasant or unpleasant) in the interest of education.

Jameson, Kay C. *The Influence of the United States Court of Appeals for the District of Columbia on Federal Policy in Broadcast Regulation, 1929–1971.* Los Angeles, University of Southern California, 1972. 566p. (Ph.D. dissertation, University Microfilms, no. 72–26,022) **1J22**
The study concludes that the influence of the U.S. Court of Appeals for the District of Columbia, "which has almost total jurisdiction over radio and television litigation," on federal policy in broadcast regulations remained fairly constant from 1929 to 1971; that the major industry criticism of judicial review since 1966 was to the encouragement of public involvement in broadcasting regulation; that the Court has not acted as a "super-Commission"; that the Court's major influence has been on procedures and not substance; that the Court has not usurped the rights of Congress and the commissions; that the system of checks and balances created by Congress in radio legislation with respect to rights and responsibilities of the Congress, commissions, and the courts, has worked extremely well over the four decades studied, to protect the public, the broadcasters, and the government.

Jameson, Storm. "The Retreat from the Pleasure Principle." In her *Parthian*

Words. London, Collins and Harvill, 1970, pp. 77–104. (Reprinted in David Holbrook, *ed.*, *The Case Against Pornography*, pp. 206–26)   **1J23**
A prominent novelist attacks the flood of pornography and pornographic novels which has brought on boredom and mental nausea. Pornography is a "depersonalizing of the human beings involved, a showing up of human lust as nothing but an affair of the genitals. Reduced to a conjunction of bodies, a display of faintly ridiculous sexual athletics," it becomes inconceivably silly. The author is torn between a dislike of censorship and a loathing for the dehumanizing nature of pornography. "The advocates of total freedom are sure they are right, the would-be censors are sure. I find it impossible to feel so sure that novels filled with accounts of tortures, beatings, sexual cruelties and humiliations of every sort, are fit for anything but burning. And as impossible to be better than uneasy about bureaucratic censorship. . . . Censorship by a government official is repugnant. Is it naïve to think that we might be able to rely on the evolution of a habit of moral responsibility among publishers? Even among writers?"

Janis, Robert K. *Privacy vs. the Right to Know: An Analysis of the Nation's Privacy Laws and Their Effect on the Freedom of the Press*. Kent, Ohio, Kent State University, 1974. 103p. (Unpublished Master's thesis)   **1J24**
"Thirty-four states plus the District of Columbia recognize a common law right of privacy, four states recognize the right by statute and four states have rejected the right. . . . The courts, in interpreting the common law right of privacy have relied on the following traditional legal principles: (1) Unfair competition, (2) Property rights. (3) Contract, (4) Natural Law, and (5) Constitutional Law." Ultimately, the author concludes, "privacy, as it effects the Freedom of the Press, is unconstitutional."

Jarrett, James L. "On Pornography." *Journal of Aesthetic Education*, 4(3):61–67, July 1970.   **1J25**
The author considers criticism of pornography as divided into two categories—internal and external. Internal criticism examines specifics—taboo words, extent, degree, and proportion; external criticism considers tendencies—to "stir the sex impulses" or to deprave and corrupt. Pornography is also considered favorably for its aphrodisiacal value, and as a literary genre.

Jaxa-Debicki, Andrew A. "Problems in Defining the Institutional Status of the Press." *University of Richmond Law Review*, 11:177–207, Fall 1976.   **1J26**
The focus of the comments "will be in the areas of the law dealing with defamation, testimonial

privilege and the fair trial–free press controversy. The purpose will be to discern whether the Supreme Court is developing a concept of freedom of the press which is distinguishable from the general guarantee of freedom of speech and which derives its rationale from the recognition of the special function of the press in a democratic society. The conclusion will summarize the results of this analysis, point out tendencies to limit the recognition of a differentiated guarantee of freedom of the press."

Jeffery, Paul. *California's "Open Meeting" Fight*. Columbia, Mo., Freedom of Information Center, School of Journalism, University of Missouri at Columbia, 1968. 8p. (Report no. 210) **1J27**
"The country's first significant right-to-know legislation, California's Ralph M. Brown Act, enacted in 1953, struggled through 12 years of amendments and attempted amendments before its basic intent—that the 'public's business' is the public's business—was realized. In September 1967, California Assembly Bill 495 finally provided uniform open meeting requirements for all state-level agencies."

Jeffrey, Francis.] "*Wat Tyler* and Mr. Southey." *Edinburgh Review*, 28:151–74, March 1817.   **1J28**
The editor of the *Edinburgh Review* attacks Poet Laureate Southey's poem, *Wat Tyler*, written in his youth, and Southey's letter of defense which Jeffrey finds unacceptable. He assails Southey's proposal for the enactment of stricter laws to put down seditious writing. "Now nobody, of course, can patronize sedition—or object to its being repressed. But, considering the extreme difficulty of ascertaining what sedition is, and the great hazard of having free and salutary discussion repressed along with it, we confess we think it better, in general, to leave it to the castigation of the antiseditious press— and let it be laughed or reasoned down by the ordinary operation of sound reason, and animated debate."

Jeffries, John A. *Legal Censorship of Obscene Publications: Search for a Censoring Standard*. Bloomington, Ind., Indiana University, 1968. 200p. (Ph.D. dissertation, University Microfilms, 69–7,690)   **1J29**
"The primary issue in this thesis is whether the threatened danger posed by allegedly obscene publications is sufficient to warrant use of police and judicial power for its suppression. Also examined is the unsolved problem faced by courts and legislators in formulating a workable censoring test to be used to identify that which is to be proscribed. These issues are presented in context of the historical attempts to censor to maintain a religious, political or social *status quo*. The censoring attempts of the past are utilized to show the abuses to which apparently all censorship is subject."

Jellenik, Stephen. "Freedom of the Press Versus the Right to a Fair Trial."

New York University Intramural Law Review, 16:169–82, March 1961.   **1J30**
The author suggests as a realistic approach to control over the abuses of the press that the courts "utilize the powers given to them to secure an individual's right to a fair trial. These powers include the contempt power which is so effective in England, and the power to grant certain motions made by a defendant which would either remove the trial from the sphere of influence created by a newspaper, or grant the defendant another opportunity to prove his innocence before a more receptive and impartial body."

Jellicorse, John L. "Some Historical Essentials of Teaching Freedom of Speech." In *Free Speech Yearbook*, *1972*. New York, Speech Communication Association, 1973, pp. 76–84.   **1J31**
A critique of existing teaching of freedom of speech which tends to place the emphasis on legal concepts, with the philosophy and history given secondary emphasis. "Historical research and historical approaches to course content may make an extremely important contribution if one of our purposes is to promote greater public acceptance of free speech."

———, and Robert D. Harrison. "The Historical Dimension of Free Speech: Suggested Readings." In *Free Speech Yearbook*, *1973*. New York, Speech Communication Association, 1974, pp. 60–65.   **1J32**
"This list of suggested readings is designed to supplement legally oriented works such as the textbooks authored or edited by Haiman, Bosmajian, and O'Neil; the contemporary legal-philosophical treatises such as those by Chafee, Meiklejohn, and Emerson; and the standard anthologies of cases such as those by Konvitz; and Freund, Sutherland, Howe, and Brown." Topics: overviews, general histories of civil liberties, the English and Colonial background, framing of the Constitution and adoption of the Bill of Rights, the Alien and Sedition Acts, nineteenth-century movements prior to the Civil War, the Civil War, controversy and conflict from the Civil War to the Espionage Acts, and civil liberties in other nations.

Jellison, Charles A. "That Scoundrel Callender." *Virginia Magazine of History and Biography*, 67:295–306, July 1959.   **1J33**
A brief biography of the unsavory pamphleteer who was convicted under the Sedition Act of 1798 for publication of a libel against President Adams. Callender was released from jail by President Jefferson whom he attacked in a subsequent pamphlet.

Jencks, Richard. "Broadcast Regulation By Contract: Some Observations on 'Community Control' of Broadcasting." In Michael C. Emery and Ted C.

Smythe, *eds.*, *Readings in Mass Communications*, Dubuque, Iowa, Brown, 1972, pp. 49–55.   **1J34**
A Columbia Broadcasting System vice-president discusses the consumer movement which seeks to "substitute for government regulation a novel kind of private regulation" of broadcasting through contracts with broadcast licensees which proscribes programming. The author charges that such contracts encourage fragmentation of programming to serve local groups which may or may not be representative of the community interests.

Jenkins, Gladys G. "Censorship and the Schools." *Iowa English Bulletin: Yearbook*, 25(3):18–24, November 1975.   **1J35**
A discussion of the role of parents and their children in the selection of instructional material and their relationship to the professional staff. "If a school has been open to parents, if parents have been listened to, if new methods and materials have been clearly discussed and explained, there is less likely to be angry controversy."

Jenkins, Roy. *Government, Broadcasting and the Press*. London, Hart-Davis, MacGibbon, 1975. 29p. (Grenada Guildhall Lecture, 1975)   **1J36**
Britain's Home Secretary considers "a society with a free press . . . comparable with a garden which is free from weeds. It is desirable but it is unnatural, and it is neither achieved nor maintained without almost unremitting care and effort." He notes that "the United States is almost the only country which has operated on a self-conscious philosophy of press freedom." In Britain, with its "instinctively private, discreet and secretive society there has been little spontaneous acclaim for the virtues of the Fourth Estate, and still less tendency to construct an accepted theory of journalistic rights." Nevertheless, in practice the history of Britain's press independence is second only to that of America and, in the absence of metropolitan monopoly, is superior. "Choice is as essential to a free press as is the prestige of journalists and the protection of resounding constitutional declarations." While proposing the replacement of the Official Secrets Act with a less restrictive statute, he does not favor a law comparable to the American Freedom of Information Act. Among the restraints needed on the freedom of the press, he believes, are protection against defamation, protection of the consumer against fraudulent advertising, prevention of incitement to violence and disorder, assurance of the right of an accused person to an unprejudiced trial, regulation of broadcasting because it is not subject to free entry, and (more controversial) control over grossly obscene publications devoid of literary or other merit.

Jenks, George. "Censorship or Privacy: The U.S. Mails." *R.Q.* (American Library Association), 10:205–6, Spring 1971.   **1J37**

A discussion of the 1967 law against using the U.S. mails for pandering, which was upheld by the U. S. Supreme Court in *Rowan v. U.S. Post Office Department*, 1970.

Jenner, William A. *The Publisher Against the People. A Plea for the Defense. An Examination of the Proposed New Copyright Law*. Cooperstown, N.Y., Crist, Scott & Parshall, 1907. 110p.   **1J38**
The author suggests that a conspiracy exists between the publishing industry and the librarian of Congress (Herbert Putnam) to prohibit importation by American citizens of works of foreign authors that have been printed and published abroad.

Jennings, David G. "Newsman's Privilege and the Constitution." *South Carolina Law Review*, 23:436–62, 1971.   **1J39**
The author concludes that "the public's right to be informed as well as the rights of those such as dissident groups to communicate their views anonymously requires constitutional recognition and implementation of a newsman's privilege of confidentiality."

Jennings, Mary. "Freedom of Information in Arizona: An Antidote for Secrecy in Government." *Arizona State Law Journal*, 1975:111–35, 1975.   **1J40**
"Complex and bureaucratic government has made open public meetings and reasonable access to public records crucial to the survival of informed democracy. Appraisals of several legislative efforts to insure open government at the federal and state levels affords an educative comparison to present Arizona standards. The author suggests meaningful statutory protections of the Arizona public's right to know."—Editor

Jennison, Peter S. "Censors Never Sleep." *American Pen*, 4:52–54, Winter 1972.   **1J41**
A summary of recent censorship events in America and England to indicate that censorship is not moribund.

Jensen, Jay. "The Tradition of Freedom in American Journalism." In Hansjürgen Koschwitz and Günter Pötter, *eds. Publizistik als Gesellschaftswissenschaft. Internationale Beiträge*. Konstanz, Federal Republic of Germany, Konstanz Universitätsverlag [1973], pp. 247–60.   **1J42**
"Since its birth in England centuries ago, the American tradition has grown slowly, drawing on experience on both sides of the Atlantic, adjusting itself to changes in the political, economic and social order, accommodating itself to shifts in the intellectual climate. Freedom of the press emerged not just from the struggle of idealists motivated by unselfish principle, al-

though they played a part, but also in large measure from the clash of contending classes, causes and factions, each claiming it to promote their own special interests. From a faith that the marketplace of ideas would best be served by a free play of individual rights against a natural harmony of interests, the tradition has moved to a joining of freedom with responsibility, of rights with obligations, enforceable not by law but by moral persuasion and social pressure."

Jentz, Gaylord A. "Federal Regulation of Advertising: False Representations of Composition, Character, or Source and Deceptive Television Demonstrations." *American Business Law Journal*, 6:409–27, Spring 1968.   **1J43**
A history of federal regulation of advertising; patterns and areas of deception; deceptive representations as to composition, character, or source of product; and deceptive television demonstrations.

Jess, Paul H. *Antitrust Law: A New Approach to Access to the Media*. Minneapolis, University of Minnesota, 1972. 357p. (Ph.D. dissertation, University Microfilms, no. 72–32,300)   **1J44**
The study examines the nature and extent of media ownership and posits the probable effects of such concentration on a partially pluralistic society. "Antitrust law, particularly case law, is examined as a possible tool to use in creating the potential for rival local newspapers. The captive newspaper printing plant is postulated as the most significant barrier to entry into the local market; hence its divestiture or metamorphosis into 'common carrier' status is perceived as necessary to encourage potential rivals to enter the market."

Jewett, Peter E. S. "Censorship of Movies for Canadian Television." *Canadian Communications Law Review*, 3:1–30, 1971. (Also in *Faculty of Law Review* [University of Toronto], August 1972)   **1J45**
The paper discusses philosophies underlining Canadian television censorship, traces the history of movie censorship legislation in Ontario and the law of obscenity, outlines the legal controls on the content of television programs and in particular of movies as television programs, discusses the policies and practices of television broadcasters in the Toronto area in relation to movie content in television, and suggests possible solutions to the broadcasters' movie censorship dilemma.

Jha, Shiva Chandra. *A Concept of Planned Free Press*. Calcutta, Bookland Private, 1958. 92p. (Appeared in serial

form between January and June 1957 in the *National Herald*, Lucknow) **1J46**
Following a review of British and American press freedom which the author states is based on a private property concept, he discusses the planned Soviet press, accessible to all *except* "foes of socialism." The author proposes a government owned and operated press to supply information to the people, plus a party-supported press free to criticize the government. Jha complains of his inability to get his book published in the United States (it was an outgrowth of graduate work at the University of California) because of the "present hysterical atmosphere in America." (This work was incorrectly entered in the 1968 edition under °S22.)

John, Alun. "Thomas Bowdler: Surgeon to Shakespeare." *Anglo-Welsh Review*, 18:124–32, Summer 1969. **1J47**
A biographical sketch of the doctor, who along with other members of his family, are credited with removing improper language from the plays of Shakespeare and other works of literary merit.

Johns, Jacqueline. "Is My Censorship Showing?" *Ohio Library Association Bulletin*, 40(4):18–19, October 1970. **1J48**
With the passage of a new state censorship law, the author calls for the state association to be ready to investigate complaints, apply sanctions, and allocate 20 percent of its budget to the cause of intellectual freedom.

Johns, Patricia *et al*. "Defamation on Cable Television Systems: The Legal and Practical Problems." *Canadian Communications Law Review*, 2:15–20, 1970. **1J49**
A study of the legal and practical implementations of Canadian defamation law in regard to the cable television system. The report summarizes the law of defamation in each province, the protection afforded by insurance, and some of the practical controls that can be instituted by the industry, which are not included in the defamation coverage of radio and television.

Johnson, Dick. "Pornography Decision Infringes on Constitutional Guarantees." *Engage/Social Action*, 1(9):51–53, September 1973. **1J50**
The author believes the U.S. Supreme Court's obscenity decision of June 1973 "is not an appropriate way to deal with pornographic material." He calls for regulation rather than suppression, the latter being impossible to achieve short of totalitarian controls.

Johnson, Donald. *The Challenge to American Freedoms; World War I and the*

Rise of the American Civil Liberties Union. [Lexington, Ky.] University of Kentucky Press for the Mississippi Valley Historical Association, 1963. 243p.
1J51
This study of the defense of civil liberties during and immediately following World War I includes discussions of prosecutions under the Espionage and Sedition Acts and the Post Office censorship of socialist and pacifist publications and others critical of the war. Action was taken against *Masses*, *International Socialist Review*, *Appeal to Reason*, *American Socialist*, *Milwaukee Leader*, *World Tomorrow*, and numerous publications of the Civil Liberties Bureau—*War's Heretics*, *The Price We Pay*, etc. The book also treats the Palmer raids during the "red scare" following the war.

———. "The Political Career of A. Mitchell Palmer." *Pennsylvania History*, 25:345–70, October 1958. **1J52**
In the aftermath of the McCarthy "red scare" the author considers an earlier "red scare" which followed World War I and in which Attorney General A. Mitchell Palmer was the principal force. Historians consider both periods of hysteria unjustified; in both cases "suppression went beyond the radical to include the liberal and even the conservative."

Johnson, Frank W. *The Octopus*. Omaha, The Author, 1940. 256p. **1J53**
This anti-Semitic work charges B'nai B'rith with "*national control*, through coercion or inducements, of speakers, books, articles, sermons, radio preachers, renting of halls for public meetings—in brief, of American freedom of speech, press and assembly."

Johnson, J. Peter. *The Practice of Maintaining a Restrictive Collection in the Public Libraries of Nassau County, New York*. Brookville, N.Y., Graduate Library School of Long Island University, 1967. 46p. **1J54**

Johnson, James W. "Freedom of Information Act: Its Application in the Air Force." *Air Force Law Review*, 16:54–63, Spring 1974. **1J55**
"The conscientious application of the Freedom of Information Act should be viewed as offering an opportunity to enhance the public image and integrity of the Government in general and the Department of the Air Force in particular."

Johnson, Kaye D. K. *Confidential Communications: A Newsman's Pledge to Protect His News Sources*. Eugene, Ore., University of Oregon, 1969. 125p. (Unpublished Master's thesis) **1J56**
The thesis deals with the case of Annette Buchanan, managing editor of the University of Oregon student newspaper who was convicted of contempt of court for refusing to reveal her confidential sources of news.

Johnson, Lee Z. *Christian Science Committee on Publication: A Study of Group and Press Interaction*. Syracuse, N.Y., Syracuse University, 1963. 632p. (Ph.D. dissertation, University Microfilms, no. 64–2,288) **1J57**
A study of the role of organized pressure groups as they interact with and impact on the media, using as a basis for investigation the Christian Science Committee on Publications, founded by Mary Baker Eddy in 1893 "to correct in a Christian manner impositions on the public in regard to Christian Science."

Johnson, Michael L. *The New Journalism; The Underground Press, the Artists of Nonfiction, and Changes in the Established Media*. Lawrence, Kans., The University Press of Kansas, 1971. 171p. **1J58**
An account of a "new journalism" that evolved during the late 1960s to respond with greater honesty and frankness than the established media to the issues of the times. Included are the underground press, rock journalism, and the new muckrakers.

Johnson, Nicholas. "Beyond the Fairness Doctrine." *New Republic*, 166(3):24, 37, 15 January 1972. **1J59**
"In finding the Fairness Doctrine constitutional [*Red Lion Broadcasting Co. v. FCC*, 1969] the [Supreme] Court went beyond to lay the groundwork for the newly emerging doctrine of 'access'—allowing individual citizens to get on the air and express themselves." All the present doctrine achieves is to prevent the grossest abuses.

———. "Electronic Media: Increasing and Protecting Access." *Columbia Journalism Review*, 8(4):28–33, Winter 1969/70. (Reprinted in Michael C. Emery and Ted C. Smythe, *eds*., *Readings in Mass Communications*, pp. 29–38) **1J60**
The FCC Commissioner reiterates ideas on citizen control of broadcasting expressed before a Congressional hearing. The present system of broadcasting does not operate in the public interest and neither the government (FTC) nor the broadcast industry is providing adequate program and performance standards. He recommends the encouragement of competition in program proposals at the time of license renewal and calls on citizens to take an active part in reviewing station performance and competitive proposals.

———. *Freedom to Create: The Implications of Antitrust Policy for Television Programming Content*. San Francisco, Trade Regulation Roundtable, Association of American Law Schools, 1969. 89p. Processed. (Also in *Osgoode Hall Law Journal*, August 1970) **1J61**
"The concentration of television ownership in

the hands of a few persons, corporations or networks; the power exercised by the networks over every step of programming production; the bureaucratic desires for orthodoxy, uniformity and mediocrity; the self-censorship conformism of talented creators who have been drawn inside these monolithic structures; and the constant strivings for profit, high audience ratings and commercial acceptability—all tend to shrink the latitude of freedom necessary for true creativity."

———. "Government by Television; A Case Study, Perspectives and Proposals." In Sidney Wise, *ed.*, *Issues 71, 72; Documents in Current American Government and Politics*. New York, Crowell, 1971, pp. 73–88. **1J62**
In a speech before the International Association of Political Consultants, an FCC Commissioner charges that the Nixon Administration has engaged in government by television. He details the reach of the use of television and its implications to American democracy. Among other reforms, he calls for establishing ground rules for presidential commandeering of television time, and for the right of reply from the "loyal opposition."

———. *How to Talk Back to Your Television Set*. Boston, Little, Brown, 1970. 228p. **1J63**
Criticism of the performance of American television by a member of the Federal Communications Commission who believes the industry which uses the airwaves as a public trust is not performing in the public interest. He discusses the growing concentration of broadcasting and newspaper ownership; he attacks the amount of violence in television programming. He calls for reexamination of the total communications system in the United States and suggests the creation of a Citizens Commission on Broadcasting to evaluate broadcasting priorities and program standards, to evaluate the effectiveness of existing government agencies, and to sponsor interdisciplinary research. He concludes with a chapter on what citizens can do to improve television, individually and in groups. A number of the chapters appeared earlier as periodical articles.

———. "The Media Barons and the Public Interest: An FCC Commissioner's Warning." *Atlantic*, 221(6): 43–51, June 1968. (Reprinted in David G. Clark and Earl R. Hutchison, eds., *Mass Media and the Law*, pp. 103–24) **1J64**
"Local monopolies, regional baronies, nationwide empires, and corporate conglomerates are more and more in control of the nation's communications media—newspapers, TV, radio, magazines, books, the electronic 'knowledge industry.'" Commissioner Johnson protests against the trend and suggests ways to combat it. "In general, I would urge the minimal standard that no accumulation of media should be permitted without a specific and convincing

showing of a continuing countervailing social benefit."

[———.] "Nicholas Johnson on Censorship, Violence, Propaganda." *Mademoiselle*, 74:174–75+, March 1972. **1J65**
Commissioner Johnson, outspoken critic of television, in an interview conducted by Peter Collier, answers questions on such topics as TV violence and its effect on children, commercial control of programming, censorship, the role of public and cable TV, and the work of citizen reform groups and their demand for change.

———. "Out of the Wasteland." *Chicago Journalism Review*, 3(5):7–10, May 1970. **1J66**
"The FCC today has cast itself adrift upon a 'boundless sea,' to borrow the Supreme Court language, in a search for decency without compass or pole star for guidance, with only the obscure charts of the orthodox, presumably represented by a majority of commissioners to guide us on our way. . . . The Commission today enters a new and untested area of federal censorship, censorship over the words, thoughts, and ideas that can be conveyed over the most powerful means of communication known to man, the broadcasting media."

———. "Public Channels & Private Censors." *Nation*, 210:329–32, 23 March 1970. **1J67**
"Television networks censor themselves (and their guests)—while asserting their commitment to free speech and denying self-censorship. The Nixon Administration attempts to control the broadcasters' comments—while professing abhorrence of government censorship."

———. "The Silent Screen." *TV Guide*, 17(27):6–13, 5 July 1969. (Reprinted in his *How to Talk Back to Your Television Set* and in Barry G. Cole, *ed.*, *Television: a Selection of Readings from TV Guide Magazine*. New York, Free Press, 1970, pp. 322–29) **1J68**
Johnson charges that discussion of vital public issues are suppressed by the television industry because of its dependence on advertising. Rebuttal by Richard S. Salant, president of Columbia Broadcasting System News in *TV Guide*, 20 September.

———. *Subpoenas, Outtakes, and Freedom of the Press: An Appeal to Media Management*. Washington, D.C., Federal Communications Commission, 1970. 20p. Processed. (Reprinted in 1U100) **1J69**
Johnson believes that "this wave of government subpoenas, together with other manipulations of the press, have placed the freedom and integrity of this country's news media in serious jeopardy." He deplores the chilling ef-

fect of such government threats on the media and the too often willingness of news management to cooperate or negotiate with government in order to protect their financial interests. "I believe we must all appeal to the leaders of the broadcasting industry to put aside their self-serving lust for corporate profits and power politics—at least long enough to defend those precious freedoms of a free press upon which all of us are so utterly dependent."

———. "Television and Violence—Perspectives and Proposals." *Television Quarterly*, 8(1):30–62, Winter 1969. (Abridged in *Journal of Producers Guild of America*, June 1969) **1J70**
Portions of a statement prepared by FCC Commissioner Johnson at the invitation of the National Commission on the Causes and Prevention of Violence. He affirms that the Federal Communications Commission has the responsibility to insure fairness in broadcasting and that the industry operates in the public interest. The Commission should not engage in censorship of program content or revoke the license of a station "because of its coverage of a political convention, a war, a riot, or a governmental official," or for using "excessive violence in action dramas, children's cartoons, and other programming in an effort to secure greater audiences," or for showing "movies that large segments of the populace find objectionable." He calls for the creation of an "independent entity" to investigate and report to the people on the impact of radio and television entertainment programming. Despite protests from the broadcasting industry, Commissioner Johnson believes that government is not the greatest threat to freedom in broadcasting; economic and corporate power is a much greater threat. Among the proposals he offers for improving broadcasting's contribution to society are: the strengthening of public television, greater citizen access and participation in local programming, greater diversity in programming, and the establishment of a Citizens Commission on Broadcasting.

———, and Tracy A. Westen. "A Twentieth-Century Soapbox: The Right to Purchase Radio and Television Time." *Virginia Law Review*, 57:574–634, May 1971. **1J71**
The authors explore the rationale of two FCC decisions which "rejected the request of a national political organization that had sought to purchase radio and television airtime at existing commercial rates for the discussion of timely public issues, including the course and conduct of the Vietnam war." The authors state that "by failing to apply established first amendment precedent to the forum of broadcasting, the Commission has erected an unconstitutional barrier against use of the broadcast spectrum to communicate protected political ideas." Commissioner Johnson had issued dissenting opinions in both cases. The article con-

stitutes, in part, a development of ideas contained in Johnson's opinions and in his testimony before a Senate Committee.

Johnson, Pamela Hansford. "Peddling the Pornography of Violence: Further Thoughts on 'Iniquity.' " *Encounter*, 34:70–76, February 1970.   **1J72**
The "catharsis" theory concerning pornographic violence is naïve and unsupported by scientific study. The author of *On Iniquity* (°J17) criticizes the report of the Working Party of the Arts Council of Great Britain which recommended the repeal of the obscenity law, favoring censorship of "the pornography of violence" in television, films, plays, and books.

Johnson, Paula, and Jacqueline D. Goodchilds. "Comment: Pornography, Sexuality, and Social Psychology." *Journal of Social Issues*, 29(3): 231–38, 1973.   **1J73**
"The purpose of this comment is not to critique the articles in this volume ₁Pornography: Attitudes, Use, and Effects, edited by W. Cody Wilson and Michael J. Goldstein₁ but to look at some additional issues which are or should be raised by these papers, in particular the interrelated and not necessarily conceptually equivalent questions: pornography in the context of individual and societal sexual trends, the importance of content, pornography and women's and men's roles, and the possible utility theory." Articles, representing studies stimulated by the U.S. Commission on Obscenity and Pornography are listed under the names of their authors in this bibliography.

Johnson, R. Christian. *Vice Reform and Visions of Socio-Economic Mobility: 1872–1900. A Paper Presented at the Convention of the American Historical Association, December 1971.* ₁Green Bay, Wis., The Author, 1972.₁ 15p. Processed.   **1J74**
The author looks at the nineteenth-century American vice reform movement as an attempt to preserve and protect a new and growing middle-class way of life. "It was necessary to suppress the vice that tempted young men away from the middle-class way of life in order to extend opportunity to more people and to protect existing opportunity. This way of life, although it could not guarantee success, was the only way in which it could be achieved. Those who were tentatively on the road to material prosperity and social esteem had to avoid the traps which were set by the vicious, the traps that Comstock sprung throughout his career and against which he warned the public. Vice reform was the vehicle in which he sought to convey a generation of Americans toward their visions of socio-economic mobility."

₁Johnson, Robert.₁ *Report of the Trial at*

Bar of the Hon. Mr. Justice Johnson, one of the Justices of His Majesty's Court of Common Pleas in Ireland, for a Libel: In the Court of King's-Bench, on Saturday the 23d Day of November, 1805. . . . London, Printed by B. McMillan, 1806. 122p.   **1J75**
Justice Johnson was accused of libeling the government of Ireland and its officials in an article, Affairs of Ireland, appearing in two letters signed "Juverna" in *Cobbett's Register*. Cobbett had earlier been tried and convicted for the same libel, but released the manuscript of the article to the authorities. The case revolved upon identification of the handwriting. Thomas Erskine, who worked both sides of the street in libel cases, was one of the prosecutors. Justice Johnson was found guilty.

Johnson, T. Page. "The First Amendment and Distribution of Literature in High Schools: A Case of Advice Not Taken." *Bulletin of the National Association of Secondary School Principals*, 55(352):74–78, February 1971.   **1J76**
Many schools have failed to follow the advice on distribution of literature on school grounds contained in Robert L. Ackerly's *Reasonable Exercise of Authority* (NASSP, 1969), as indicated by recent decisions of the courts. The publication states that "freedom of expression cannot legally be restricted unless its exercise interferes with the orderly conduct of classes and school work."

Johnson, Wayne A. "Libel: The *New York Times Standard* in Reports of Judicial Proceedings." *Southwestern Law Journal*, 25:800–805, December 1971.   **1J77**
Re: *Jones v. Commercial Printing Co.*, 463 S.W.2d 92 (Ark. 1971), in which the Arkansas Supreme Court refused to apply the *New York Times* rule to the case involving reports of judicial proceedings.

Johnson, Weldon T. "The Pornography Report: Epistemology, Methodology and Ideology." *Duquesne Law Review*, 10:190–219, Winter 1971.   **1J78**
A sociologist on the staff of the U.S. Commission on Obscenity and Pornography analyzes the *Report* of the Commission and the public's reaction to it, taking into consideration certain "delimiting political and emotional conditions," which were "not only responsible for the creation of the Commission in 1967, but helped shape the actual work of the Commission, its *Report*, and the manner in which we respond to it now." He addresses himself to three issues that have been raised with respect to the effects of pornography: (a) the investigation of effects is irrelevant to dealing with the pornography problem; (b) the actual effects of exposure to erotic materials are not measurable within the framework of social science research; and (c) the effects, particularly the presumed pernicious effects, are obvious but have not been recognized generally or in the

Report. The author also considers criticism of the methodology of the various studies and the role of ideology of Commission members in the work of the Commission.

————, Lenore R. Kupperstein, and Joseph J. Peters. "Sex Offenders' Experience With Erotica." *Technical Report of the ₁U.S.₁ Commission on Obscenity and Pornography*, 7:163–71, 1971.   **1J79**
"The present study attempted to examine more closely the experience with erotic materials of a relatively small sample of sex offenders, and to compare these experiences with an age-matched group of males drawn randomly from the general population."

Johnston, Bonita. "Postal Rates Threaten a Free Press." *Grassroots Editor*, 14(4):12–14, July–August 1973.   **1J80**
"If counter legislation is not implemented, government will be able to sit back and watch diverse opinion die a 'natural' death as did *Look* and *Life*. Then instead of 70 million mourners, 200 million Americans can reminisce about the free press and wonder what happened."

Johnston, Richard F., and Kay Marmorek. "Access to Government Information and the Classification Process—Is There a Right to Know?" *New York Law Forum*, 17:814–40, 1971.   **1J81**
"It is the authors' contention that there should be a recognition of a constitutional 'right to know' based on contemporary as well as historical interpretation of the Constitution. Recognition of this right would engender investigations into the decision-making process of our government and increase the participation of the people in that process." The authors find that the Freedom of Information Act has failed to increase public access to government information. By the use of the classification system numerous statutes prohibit or restrict the dissemination of information to the public. In spite of the bureaucratic wall of secrecy however, a vast amount of classified material still manages to reach the public through a complex relationship between government officials and the working press. Classification should be subject to judicial review and the burden of proof of a need for classifying should be placed on the classifying agencies. The authors call for an independent panel or commission to safeguard the public's right to know, by reviewing the classification action of agencies.

Johnston, W. T. "The Red Book Truck and Other Purple Passions." *Georgia Librarian*, 10(2):5–12, October 1973. **1J82**
An essay on the dilemma of librarians in attempting to determine what level of taste is acceptable in the community.

₁Johnston, William.₁ *The Petition and Complaint ₁to the Justice General, Lord Jus-*

tice Clerk, and Lords Commissioners of Justiciary₁ of Robert Dundas ₁His Majesty's Chief Advocate₁. Edinburgh, 1793. 14p.

1J83

The Advocate asks the Court to forfeit the good behavior bond of William Johnston, publisher of the *Edinburgh Gazette*. Johnston had served three months in prison for contempt of court for criticizing in his paper the conviction verdict in the libel case of John Morton, James Anderson, and Malcolm Craig. Johnston was further placed under a three-year bond for good behavior. The Advocate charged that Johnston violated his probation by attending a meeting of radicals and by corresponding with a convicted radical, William Skirving. A thirteen-page *Answer for Captain William Johnston, to the Petition and Complaint of Richard Dundas* was filed by Johnston's lawyer, Henry Erskine, dated Edinburgh, 1794.

Johnstone, James M. "The Freedom of Information Act and the FDA." *Food, Drug, and Cosmetics Law Journal*, 25:296–306, June 1970.

1J84

Suggestions as to the future significance of the Freedom of Information Act for the Food and Drug Administration and its industry and public constituency.

Jonas, Gerald. "The Story of Grove." *New York Times Magazine*, 21 January 1968, pp. 28–29+.

1J85

An interview with Barney Rosset, avant garde publisher (Grove Press, *Evergreen Review*), including his experiences with the censor and his comments about censorship.

Jones, Barry. "Some Aspects of Theatre Censorship in Australia." In *Civil Liberty; Civil Liberty Convention Papers*. South Yarra, Victoria, Australia, Victoria Council of Civil Liberties, 1969, pp. 42–47.

1J86

Censorship of the theater in Australia has taken place largely under three state laws—the Police Offenses Act, the Vagrants, Gaming and Other Offenses Act, and the Theatres Act which prescribes licensing. Little official censorship took place before 1960 because theater managers were very cautious and the "quiet word" from police was sufficient warning, and because Customs kept out offending scripts. The author cites a number of censorship cases, with special attention to the 1936 banning of an anti-Nazi play by Clifford Odets, *Till the Day I Die*, banned at the request of the German Consul-General, and the recent (1970) banning of *Oh! Calcutta!*

———, and Peter Coleman. "Porn: The Pleasures and Perils." *Forum, the International Journal of Human Relations*, 1(6):34–41, August 1973.

1J87

Jones states the case for pornography; Coleman the case against pornography.

Jones, D. A. N. "Silent Censorship in

the British Theatre." *Theatre Quarterly*, 1:22–28, January 1971.

1J88

A look at the extent and nature of managerial control of the theater in Britain.

Jones, *Sir* Elwyn. "The Law and the Press; The Release of Official Information, and the Public Interest." *Journalism Today*, 2:41–62, Spring 1970.

1J89

In an address before the Institute of Journalists, the Attorney-General discusses the Freedom of Publication bill before the House of Commons, the law of contempt as applied to tribunals of inquiry, the Official Secrets Acts, and the law of libel.

Jones, J. Clement. *Background Paper on Press Councils*. Paris, Collective Consultations on Mass Media Councils, 1974. 19p.

1J90

Meeting paper on professional associations of the press and their work with communication ethics to ensure freedom of information; presents draft models for national media council and includes notes from twenty-two countries describing their press councils.

———. "The Battle of Britain's Libel Laws." *Nieman Reports*, 24(1):12–13, March 1971.

1J91

An analysis of the Freedom of Publications (Protection) Bill before the British House of Commons, which would go a considerable way toward helping British newspapers in respect to contempt of court, official secrets, and libel.

———. "The Battle to Prune Britain's Libel and Contempt Laws." *IPI Report* (International Press Institute), 18(7):4–5, November 1969.

1J92

"Everyone agrees that Britain's press laws need overhauling, but . . . the House of Commons has a curious way of not getting things done."—Editor

———. "British Approach to Privacy." *Grassroots Editor*, 11(1):14–17, 29, January–February 1970.

1J93

"There is no law in Britain to protect an individual against the infringement of his or her privacy, as such. If character is defamed or if there is risk of miscarriage of justice in a court of law, there are remedies in the laws of libel and contempt, but there is only the good sense of all concerned to prevent publication of details about a person's private life." The author, chairman of the Parliamentary Committees of the Press Council and the Guild of British Newspaper Editors, compares British and American treatment of privacy.

———. "The Law and the Press in Britain." *Grassroots Editor*, 10(1):24–26, January–February 1969; 10(2):18–19, 30, March–April 1969.

1J94

There is no direct control of the press in Britain

and "newspapers may print and publish whatever their editors and proprietors see fit, so long as it doesn't contravene the laws of the land." These laws include contempt of court, defamation, obscenity, and probably, in the near future, will include the right of privacy. The author discusses the strict laws governing contempt of court, which range from scandal to interference with justice—anything that tends to bring the administration of law into disrespect or might prejudice a pending trial. This law "makes it difficult if not impossible for newspapers to run stories exposing certain kinds of malpractices." Contempt laws are currently under review. The British law of defamation is also strict in comparison with American law and many newsmen believe it is unfair to the press because there is no complete defense for unintentional defamation. Revision of libel laws is badly needed. The press is also unhappy over the lack of legal rights of admission to public meetings.

Jones, Lawrence A. "*Time, Inc. v. Firestone*: Is *Rosenbloom* Really Dead?" *University of Miami Law Review*, 31:216–25, Fall 1976.

1J95

The author "suggests that the Supreme Court has redefined the once discarded subject matter analysis for determining the applicability of the constitutional privilege in defamation suits and incorporated it into a new, two-pronged test for determining whether a defamation plaintiff is a public figure."

Jones, Marjorie. *Justice and Journalism: A Study of the Influence of Newspaper Reporting Upon the Administration of Justice by Magistrates*. London, Barry Rose, 1974. 180p.

1J96

"The author outlines the development of the relationship between justice and journalism in England, showing how newspapers have provided magistrates' courts with a public record and a channel of communication, and how reporters have acted as representatives of the public, as defenders of the defenceless, and as critics of the administration of justice." She describes the regulations that have restricted the press coverage of juvenile and domestic courts and the impact of newspaper reporting on the proceedings of police courts, magistrates' closed courts, and magistrates' criminal courts in recent years.

———. "Punishment by Publication." *Grassroots Editor*, 11(6):2–9, November–December 1970.

1J97

In an address before the Guild of British Newspaper Editors a Justice of the Peace argues that the current practice of the British press in reporting the proceedings of magistrates' courts is socially undesirable and detracts from the administration of justice. The random reporting of cases, she believes, constitutes cruel and harmful punishment by publication. It is based upon a faulty notion of the press "fulfilling its age-old function of ensuring that justice is not only done but seen to be done." She urges the press not to "degenerate into jackels, or the hyenas of justice. In your reports of judicial proceedings can you not cease to be the hounders of humanity, at least for its minor crimes, yet still continue to watch over and record the processes of justice?"

Jones, Mary G. "The Cultural and Social Impact of Advertising on American Society." *Osgoode Hall Law Journal*, 8:65–85, August 1970.   **1J98**
A member of the Federal Trade Commission "questions the appropriateness and adequacy of present regulatory patterns both public and private to deal with social problems raised by the cultural and value content of advertising." She "proposes several means by which freedom and diversity of ideas would be promoted so that television would reflect a wider variety of values, cultures and life styles."

Jones, Mervyn. "Great Obscenity Farce." *New Statesman*, 82:640–41, 12 November 1971.   **1J99**
Commentary on the *Oz* case. "In an ordinary trial, everyone agrees that the action (theft or murder) is reprehensible and the question is whether the accused did it. In an obscenity trial, everyone agrees that the action (publication) was committed by the accused and the question is whether it's reprehensible. . . . The outcome is chancy for many reasons, but primarily because the offence rests on definitions that can never be clarified and must be a matter of opinion."

————. "Political Indecency." *New Statesman*, 87:72–73, 18 January 1974.   **1J100**
Criticism of the Cinematograph and Indecent Displays bill before Parliament which the author terms "nasty, absurdly irrelevant, politically motivated, badly drafted, and potentially dangerous."

————. "Reporters and the Public." *Twentieth Century*, 170:18–28, Spring 1962. (Reprinted in Mervyn Jones, *ed.*, *Privacy*, pp. 122–26)   **1J101**
A British journalist describes some of the ways in which journalists invade the privacy of individuals to get a story: simple intrusion, pursuit, deception, bribery, bad faith, lack of respect for confidences, threats, and exploitation of silence.

————, *ed*. "The Mass Media." In his *Privacy*. London, David and Charles, 1974, pp. 122–34.   **1J102**
In a general work on the issue of privacy in Great Britain—the new technology, the power

of the state, and the debate over legislation—this section deals with the intrusion of the mass media (newspapers, radio, and television) into private lives. "It is the press that comes in for most of the criticism, partly because it is in private hands and unashamedly conducted for profit, partly because charges of triviality and sensationalism are easily made, and partly because journalists themselves are aware . . . of the dubious methods sometimes used in news gathering." In addition to the editor's own comments he includes appropriate sections from the Younger Report (*Report of the Committee on Privacy*, 1972).

Jones, Philip G. "A Clash Over 'Dirty Books' Is Shattering a School System." *American School Board Journal*, 161(11):31–32, 41–43, November 1974.   **1J103**
The controversy over school textbooks in Kanawha County, W.Va.

Jones, Roger A. "Notes from the New Underground." *Oklahoma Librarian*, 22(1):4–5, 30 January 1972.   **1J104**
"It is frightening that the printed materials of an entire social and political movement [the underground press] have been ignored by most libraries. . . . Will the library, as a social and intellectual force, allow itself to serve only the 'silent majority'? *Now* is the time for all librarians to stand firmly behind the American Library Association's continued opposition to any form of censorship and to serve equally both the 'majority' and the 'minority.' " A suggested reading list of the alternative press is attached.

Jones, Teddy M., Jr. "Obscenity Standards in Current Perspective." *Southwestern Law Journal*, 21:285–305, Spring 1967. (Conclusions reprinted in Donald B. Sharp, *ed.*, *Commentaries on Obscenity*, pp. 309–10)   **1J105**
A consideration of recent Supreme Court decisions on obscenity reveals the difficulties in defining obscenity and applying the definition to specific materials. The author concludes that regardless of the careful judicial review of state and federal statutes, most cases of literary suppression never come before the courts. They are acted upon by coercive forces in the community, by subsurface censorship, and by action of private, extralegal groups. "Operating through the use of fear and coercion and playing on ignorance, the damage they have done to the intellectual climate in this nation is incalculable."

Jones, W. R. " 'Actions for Slander'—Defamation in English Law, Language, and History." *Quarterly Journal of Speech*, 57:274–83, October 1971.   **1J106**
An account of the development of the English law of slander or spoken defamation. "As a matter of law rather than of morals or social propriety, slander was the artificial creation of

the various jurisdictions to which plaintiffs might appeal, and it was shaped more by the preconceptions and prejudices of competing legal systems than by canons of morality, etiquette, or good taste. Particular words and phrases reflected the capabilities or incapabilities and the interests or disinterests of the laws and courts of medieval and early modern England."

Jordan, Lynwood D. "The People's Right to Know in Georgia." *Georgia State Bar Journal*, 10:598–615, May 1974.   **1J107**
"The provisions of the Georgia Sunshine Law are examined here by going beyond a mere recomposition of the statutory language to embrace the public policies and social currents which coalesce to form the very genesis of open meeting laws. Particular attention is given to the open meeting laws of Florida, and the judicial interpretation thereof."

Jordon, Robert W. "Libel and Slander: Constitutional Standards Challenge Oklahoma Law." *Oklahoma Law Review*, 26:94–100, February 1973. **1J108**
"As a result of decisions by the United States Supreme Court over the past decade, the Oklahoma law of defamation does not provide the constitutional safeguards of free speech and press required by the first and fourteenth amendments. This note will examine the manner in which Oklahoma statutes and court decisions are affected by the new standards, as well as the implications of these standards for the future of the law of defamation."

Jose, Alhaji B. "Press Freedom in Africa." *African Affairs*, 74:255–62, July 1975.   **1J109**
The author notes that the early fifties was a period of nationalist agitation all over Africa; the late fifties to early sixties was a period of independence celebrations; the mid to late sixties was a military era. "Throughout this period, examined continentally, the press has been under seige with increasingly waning influence and freedom. With advancement in the fields of education and business . . . and industrial and economic prosperity increasing the quality of life of the individual . . . more and more people will then come to realize the nobility of the ideals which the press stands for and be ready to pay the price of pursuing these ideals." The African press will come into its own as governments become less authoritarian.

Joseph, Frank S. "City News Bureau Censors . . . Statements to Walker Report." *Chicago Journalism Review*, 1(2):1, 4, November–December 1968.   **1J110**
A charge that the Chicago City News Bureau censored reporters' statements about disorders in Chicago during the Democratic convention before they were submitted to the National Commission on Violence.

Joshi, K. C. "Freedom of Speech, Press and Assembly in America." *International Journal of Legal Research*, 3(1):47–51, June 1968. **1J111**
A general review of court interpretation of the First Amendment. "The trend of the development of freedom of speech and assembly in the U.S.A.," the author concludes, "is progressive save where the basic conflict is between communism and Americanism."

"Journalists and Their Sources: The First Amendment Privilege in Constitutional Libel Actions." *Iowa Law Review*, 58:618–37, February 1973. **1J112**
"Although the journalist's privilege received no common law recognition, courts in recent years have increasingly come to acknowledge that some degree of first amendment protection is desirable for reporters who seek to maintain a confidential relationship with their sources. This recognition has stemmed from an increasing awareness that the journalist's privilege protects the public's interest in an unimpeded flow of information on matters of general concern and is not merely a shield for the personal benefit of the reporter or his source. Through the proper application of procedural safeguards such as the summary judgment, courts can permit sanctioning of the press in appropriate cases, without endangering the interests sought to be protected in the first amendment."

Judd, Walter, *comp. Newspapers and the Law of Libel. Press Comments and Correspondence*. London, Heywood, 1910. 64p. **1J113**
The chairman of the board of a large number of trade papers presents pleas for revision of the newspaper libel laws of England. A collection of editorials and letters to the editor.

"Judicial Canon 35 . . . Revise or Retain?" *Florida Bar Journal*, 37:16–39, January 1963. **1J114**
A series of articles pro and con on the American Bar Association's Judicial Canon 35, banning radio and television coverage of court trials, written by judges, lawyers, journalists, and legislators. The series is introduced by a history of Canon 35 in Florida.

The Judicial Conference of the United States. Committee on the Operation of the Jury System. "Report of the Committee on the Operation of the Jury System on the 'Free Press–Fair Trial' Issue." *Federal Rules Decisions*, 45:391–415, 1968. Supplemental Report, 51:135–38, 1971. (Reprinted in Donald M. Gillmor and Jerome A. Barron, *Mass Communication Law*, 1st ed., pp. 763–86) **1J115**
Text of the Committee's Report on measures which might be taken by the federal courts to meet the problem of prejudicial publicity in criminal cases. Following a statement on the nature and background of the problem, the Report makes recommendations in four areas: (1) release of information by attorneys in criminal cases, (2) release of information by courthouse personnel in criminal cases, (3) conduct of judicial proceedings in criminal cases, and (4) use of photography, radio, and television equipment in the courtroom and its environs.

"Judicial Relief for the Newsman's Plight: A Time for Secrecy?" *St. John's Law Review*, 45:484–90, March 1971. **1J116**
The author believes that the most salutary test of the newsman's contended First Amendment right to conceal his confidential information is offered in the *Caldwell* case (*United States v. Caldwell*, 1972)—national compelling interest plus inaccessibility. "The test provides an acceptable form of protection for newsmen while at the same time serving the needs of justice when the situation necessitates disclosure. *Caldwell* is a vehicle for persuasion that should be adopted by other jurisdictions. A national standard must be established by the Supreme Court to resolve current non-uniformity in this area."

Judson, Horace. "The Critic Between." *Encounter*, 30:57–60, March 1968. **1J117**

A literary critic protests the use of his unfavorable review of *Last Exit to Brooklyn* for *Time Magazine* being used as evidence against the work in a British court. "The law which threatens the novelist, gags the critic. One way or another, by the existence of this censorship, every man of letters is inhibited in the judgments he may express."

Julian, Joseph V. "The First Amendment: Free Expression for All Citizens." *Maxwell Review*, 9(2):71–80, Spring 1973. **1J118**
"This piece will focus on [New York Times v. United States and Branzburg v. Hayes] and related cases in order to examine the arguments for and against the extension of the testimonial privilege and to determine how the courts have balanced these conflicting views in recent times. The analysis will reveal that, at one extreme, the trend of the courts is to give the investigative scholar and the reporter no protection at all, while at the other extreme, advocates of extension call for security through the creation of a privileged class. It will be suggested that the way out of this dilemma is to grant every citizen the First Amendment immunity that is currently given to doctors, lawyers, and clergymen and is now being advocated for the academic and the newsman."

Junger, Peter D. "Down Memory Lane: The Case of the Pentagon Papers." *Case Western Reserve Law Review*, 23:3–75, November 1971. **1J119**
"The case of the Pentagon Papers has been accused of 'greatness' and appears initially to be an important interpretation of the first amendment. The author contends, however, that the major issue in the case concerns the doctrine of separation [of] powers. He argues that the limited holding of the case is completely foretold by the steel seizure case of the 1950's, and he suggests that the protection it affords from unauthorized action by the Executive may be more fundamental to our liberties than the first amendment protection of the press."—Editor

K

Kaelin, E. F. "The Pornographic and the Obscene in Legal and Aesthetic Contexts." *Journal of Aesthetic Education*, 4(3):69–84, July 1970. **1K1**
The author believes that the social problem involving obscenity may be solved in theory at least, if not in legal practice, by clarifying the following aesthetic and moral distinctions: (1) initial judgments of artistic obscenity are primarily moral and fail to take into account both subject matter and treatment; (2) within aesthetic judgment there is no way of giving an absolute significance to any part of an artistic context; (3) the intent of an author is apparent in context only as a function of artistic design; (4) whether the response to a work is appropriate or not is dependent upon the artist's treatment of his subject; (5) a work is pornographic when a morally obscene subject matter goes "unredeemed" through artistic treatment; (6) directness of sexual response may be a function of the viciousness of the artist's treatment; (7) a "consensus of informed inquirers" may be an appropriate base for judging pornography; and (8) pornographic works, representing the pursuit of morally obscene subject matter for the effective value of that matter, obviously lack aesthetic value and so go "unredeemed" in context.

Kagen, Richard C. "Introduction." In Ross Y. Koen, *The China Lobby in American Politics*. New York, Harper & Row, 1974, pp. ix–xvii. **1K2**
"Ross Y. Koen's book was first printed in 1960, but its distribution was enjoined owing to pressures from the China lobby; over 4,000 copies were destroyed by the publisher [Macmillan]; less than eight hundred circulated. Many of these were stolen from libraries by right wing groups which literally replaced them with *The Red China Lobby*. Others were placed under lock and key in rare book rooms in university libraries throughout the country."

Kahn, Ellison. " 'Dirty' Books That Have Been Banned." *Standpunte* (South Africa), 20(4):33–42, April 1967. **1K3**
Between the erotic classics that are generally permitted to circulate in South Africa and the "hard-core pornography" which circulates freely in the United States but is beyond the pale in South Africa, "there is a host of literary works of this century and particularly of the postwar years, that may meet with disfavor of the censoring authorities." The author gives a brief description of the mechanism of South African censorship and calls for change. "The censorious are permitted freely to have their say. Is it not time that a group of counter-vigilantes be formed, to seek to vindicate, by protest, all arbitrary bannings of works of merit" and to secure the right of South Africans to have access to the literary product of this age, "misbegotten though some may think it be?"

———. *"When the Lion Feeds*—and the Censor Pounces; a Disquisition on the Banning of Immoral Publications in South Africa." *South African Law Journal*, 83:278–336, August 1966. **1K4**
A study of censorship in South Africa, beginning with historical background, leading up to the 1963 Publications and Entertainments Act which created a Publications Control Board. The Board was given powers over all types of reproduced matter but newspapers and over any work that could be termed an "undesirable publication." The article discusses the work of the Board and its predecessors, citing specific cases of banned works. He discusses in detail the case of the banning of Wilbur A. Smith's *When the Lion Feeds*, a novel dealing with life in the early pioneer days in Natal and in the Transvaal, and the decision of the court sustaining the ban.

Kahn, Frank J. "From 'Fairness' to 'Access' and Back Again: Some Dimensions of Free Expression in Broadcasting." In *Free Speech Yearbook, 1974*. New York, Speech Communication Association, 1975, pp. 1–10. **1K5**
A review of two significant cases involving freedom of expression and the broadcast media—*Red Lion Broadcasting Co., Inc. v. FCC* (1969) and *Columbia Broadcasting System, Inc. v. Democratic National Committee* (1973), and their implication to the fairness doctrine.

———. "A Proposal to Regulate Broadcasting as a Public Utility." In Don R. Le Duc, *ed.*, *Issues in Broadcast Regulation*, Washington, D.C., Broadcast Education Association, 1974, pp. 104–6. **1K6**
The author advances the argument that broadcasting regulated as a public utility might avoid many of the destructive competitive elements in the industry today.

———, *ed. Documents of American Broadcasting*. 2d ed. New York, Appleton-Century-Crofts, 1973. 684p. **1K7**
In addition to documents on the development of broadcasting, the collection includes statements on the regulation of programming (including the *Brinkley*, *Shuler*, *Suburban*, *Pacifica*, and *WUHY* cases), the "Blue Book," the controversy over drug lyrics, the various codes of self-regulation, documents on the regulation of broadcast journalism (including the Mayflower Decision, the Fairness Doctrine and its interpretations), "The Selling of the Pentagon," the great debates law, fair trial versus free press, and defamation and broadcast news. There are also a number of documents relating to the regulation of competition.

Kaiser, Ronald, Harry R. Olsson, Jr., and John V. Shute. "Notes on United States Privacy Law." *EBU Review* (European Broadcasting Union), 170 (119B):55–59, January 1970. **1K8**
These notes on the status of privacy law in the United States with respect to radio and television broadcasting are based on replies from the several networks and are presented under the following headings: right to a person's likeness, right to a person's voice, right to a person's name, the individual's right to safeguard his reputation, and the right of psychological integrity.

Kait, Richard E. "Withdrawal of Funding of Campus Newspaper." *Wisconsin Law Review*, 1973:1179–91, 1973. **1K9**
Re: *Joyner v. Whiting*, 341 F. Supp. 1244 (M.D.N.C. 1972). The case involves the suspending of financial support to the student

newspaper, *Campus Echo*, at North Carolina Central University, for the editors' announced policy of refusing white advertising. The author disagrees with the district court's decision upholding the action of the University, as constitutionally unsound. "The district court should have shaped a more equitable and practicable remedy to meet the requirements of both the first and fourteenth amendments."

Kalanadhabhatla, Rama R. *Freedom of Speech and Press: A Study of Their Nature and Location in Canadian Law*. Kingston, Ont., Queen's University, 1973. 267p. (L.L.M. thesis; Canadian theses on microfilm, no. 13,005)   **1K10**

Kalaw, Teodoro M. *The "El Renacimiento" Libel Suit*. Foreword by Pura Villanueva Kalaw. Manila, Philippines, Pura Villanueva Kalaw, 1950. 48p.   **1K11**
A personal account of the trial of the late editor of *El Renacimiento*, charged with libeling the U.S. Commissioner to the Philippines Dean C. Worcester. Kalaw had published an allegorical editorial, Birds of Prey, which is republished in this booklet. The trial began in 1906 and it was 1914 before the U.S. Supreme Court upheld the verdict for the government and Kalaw was sentenced to imprisonment and a fine. He was pardoned by the Governor-General under the newly elected Wilson Administration without having to spend time in prison. The booklet also contains memorial messages honoring the late editor for his efforts in behalf of a free press.

Kalijarvi, June D. W., and Don Wallace, Jr. "Executive Authority to Impose Prior Restraint upon Publication of Information Concerning National Security Affairs; A Constitutional Power." *California Western Law Review*, 9:468–96, Spring 1973.   **1K12**
"The Article considers the extent to which the Federal Executive's independent constitutional responsibility for the maintenance of the national interests in the external order and his constitutional duty to refrain from interference with freedom of the press allow nonstatutory imposition of prior restraint upon publications of internal government documents." The issue is considered in light of litigation over the Pentagon Papers.

Kalil, Earl L., Jr. "Florida Sunshine Law—Is Florida Sunshine the Most Powerful of Disinfectants?" *Florida Bar Journal*, 49:72–82, February 1975. **1K13**
"The goal of this article is to provide suggestions on how the Florida law can be amended so as to accomplish the political and democratic advantages envisioned by the law's authors, while at the same time minimizing any harmful or disadvantageous effects that an open meeting statute may entail. Finally, a proposed statute will be advanced."

Kalish, Abraham H. "Truth in the News Media; The Public's Right to Know." *AIM Report* (Accuracy in Media), 2(4):8–11, April 1973.   **1K14**
The executive secretary of Accuracy in Media, Inc., in an address at Harding College, discusses the work of his organization in serving as a watchdog over the nation's news media.

Kallen, Horace M. " 'Group Libel' and Equal Liberty." In his *What I Believe and Why—Maybe*. New York, Horizon, 1971, pp. 76–85.   **1K15**
"The law if libel . . . assures the poor the revolutionary right to invoke the law in public defense against the hurts of libel; it sets them free to fight back and to demand amends. But it frees them sheerly as individuals, not as members of a group who have been made the victims of libel because they are members of this group and identified by traits attributed to it. . . . What is lawfully open to him is to join together with others libelously so described and to watch for, challenge, and refute the libels as they appear; to expose their origins, their supporters and their motivations."

———, *et al*. "Race Defamation: A Symposium." *New York Law Forum*, 14:1–59, Spring 1968.   **1K16**
Content: "Group Libel" and Equal Liberty by Horace M. Kallen. English Law and Race Defamation by Anthony Dickey. Can the Law Provide a Remedy for Race Defamation in the United States? by John de J. Pemberton, Jr. International Definitions of Incitement to Racial Hatred by Natan Lerner.

Kalven, Harry, Jr. "Broadcasting, Public Policy and the First Amendment." *Journal of Law and Economics*, 10:15–49, October 1967.   **1K17**
"This essay proposes to explore the relationships between broadcasting and the traditions of the First Amendment, in the hope of inducing a wider confrontation of the anomaly of having at the moment in the United States two traditions of freedom of the press—that of the written and spoken word and that of the broadcast word." The essay is based largely on a memorandum prepared for the Columbia Broadcasting System.

———. "The Reasonable Man and the First Amendment: Hill, Butts, and Walker." In Philip B. Kurland, *ed*., *Supreme Court Review, 1967*. Chicago, University of Chicago Press, 1967, pp. 267–309.   **1K18**
A discussion of the new sequence of libel cases before the U.S. Supreme Court that have extended *New York Times v. Sullivan* (1964): *Time, Inc. v. Hill*, *Curtis Publishing Company v. Butts* and *Associated Press v. Walker*, all reported in 1967. Kalven concludes that (1) "the free speech issue etched in the sequence from *Times* to *Butts* and *Walker* of public speech interlaced with comment on individuals is a new issue never really confronted before in legal theory

about freedom of speech and press," (2) "all members of the Court care deeply about free speech values and about their proper wording of the law," and (3) "it shows a special respect for the potential of *New York Times* as a precedent on the First Amendment."

———. "The Right to Publish." In Norman Dorsen, *ed*., *The Rights of Americans*. New York, Pantheon, 1971. pp. 253–75.   **1K19**
"Neither obscenity nor libel can be said in any simple sense to present a clear and present danger of anything, yet there remains a strong momentum for subjecting them both to some degree of control."

[———.] "The Supreme Court, 1970 Term: Freedom of Speech, Press, and Association." *Harvard Law Review*, 85:199–212, 222–37, November 1971.   **1K20**
Under the heading National Security and Freedom of the Press, the survey considers the case of *New York Times Co. v. United States* (Pentagon Papers); under Media Privilege to Report Events of a Public Interest, the case of *Rosenbloom v. Metromedia, Inc.*

———. " 'Uninhibited, Robust and Wide-Open'—A Note on Free Speech and the Warren Court." *Michigan Law Review*, 67:289–316, December 1968. (Reprinted in Kenneth S. Devol, *ed*., *Mass Media and the Supreme Court*, pp. 347–56)   **1K21**
An assessment of the Warren Court's record in the area of the First Amendment, emphasizing how much the Court has contributed to constitutional doctrine, the high level of concern, the willingness to face the issues, and the eloquence and freshness of expression. The last is exemplified by the title of the article, a quotation from Justice Brennan's decision in *New York Times v. Sullivan*.

———, and Douglas H. Ginsburg. "Ernest Freund and the First Amendment." *University of Chicago Law Review*, 40:235–47, Winter 1973.   **1K22**
Fifty-four years after the event, Professor Kalven discusses the circumstances surrounding the case, *Debs v. United States*, 249 U.S. 211 (1919), in which Justice Holmes, who had expressed the "clear and present danger" doctrine the week before (*Schenck v. United States*), failed to follow the doctrine and joined with the other justices in upholding Debs's conviction. University of Chicago Law School Professor Ernest Freund criticized the decision in the *New Republic*, 2 May 1919. Freund's article is reprinted on pages 239–42. "The Freund article makes it clear that the outcome in *Debs* was perceived as dangerously unsound by sophisti-

cated legal intelligence of the day. If read with hindsight, *Debs* . . . now makes little sense and impeaches claims to serious freedom of speech." Douglas H. Ginsburg, in an Afterword (pp. 243–47) comments further on Holmes's action: "It is both plausible and intriguing to think that the criticism of *Debs* in the Freund article and in Hand's correspondence ⌊Judge Learned Hand⌋ with Justice Holmes throughout the period between *Debs* and *Abrams* compelled Holmes to recognize the dangers of *Debs's* casual approach and influenced his thinking about the value of political speech, even in time of war." In *Abrams v. United States* (1919) Holmes, in a dissenting opinion, made an eloquent plea in behalf of free speech, eight months after Debs had gone to prison.

Kamenka, Eugene. *"Pornography," Law and Culture*. Sydney, Australian Society of Legal Philosophy, 1965. 9p. Processed. **1K23**
The author comments on Preliminary Working Paper No. 1, prepared by Gordon J. Hawkins and issued by the Society. In reviewing the development of the British law of pornography, Kamenka fails to find a basis for defining or suppressing pornography. He believes that any change in the existing obscenity laws in Australia should be by common law rather than by legislation, by a "gradual extension of concepts and policies at a rate that permits each stage to become the 'accepted' and tested before the next is reached." He sees no value in making a distinction between pornography and erotic realism, which is merely a distinction between bad and good literature. He concludes that "sex cannot simply be isolated from human relations and the fabric of society generally, and then treated at the level of discussing whether four-letter words should or should not be banned; I have no doubt that four-letter words as such should not be banned; I have no doubt that if every school-child old enough or educated enough to follow it were to read *The Group*, culture and society would benefit; I have no doubt that if the present circulation of banned 'hard-core pornography' were to be multiplied ten-fold, there would be no public mischief, or even minor harm. But just as the banners want to ban 'pornography' without looking at the character of contemporary culture generally, so the liberals often talk as though one could delete the admittedly utterly confused conceptions of obscenity and indecency from our law, without looking at the character of contemporary culture generally, and of commercialisation in particular."

Kamp, Joseph P. *Will President Eisenhower Join the ADL Book Burners?* New York, Constitutional Educational League, 1953? 24p. (Reprinted from *Headlines*, 18 November 1953) **1K24**
An attack on the Anti-Defamation League of B'nai B'rith, charging it with exerting pressures to suppress the publication of the author's address before the Women's Patriotic Conference on National Defense and stifling the sale of the book, *The Conquest of a Continent* by Madison Grant. The author criticizes President Eisenhower for accepting an award from the League after he had appealed to the public in the McCarthy affair not to join the book burners.

Kampen, Julie D. "Limitations on Damages Awarded to Public Officials in Defamation Suits." *Wisconsin Law Review*, 1972:574–83, 1972. **1K25**
"This note will attempt to demonstrate that the Wisconsin Supreme Court's treatment of the damages issue (*Dalton v. Meister*, 52 Wis. 2d 173) was inadequate in light of a recent United States Supreme Court decision, *Rosenbloom v. Metromedia* (403 U.S. 29, 1971) which brought into question the constitutionality of certain types of damage awards in defamation suits."

Kane, Peter E. "Erosion of the First Amendment: Freedom of Speech and the Nixon Court." *Free Speech* (Commission on Freedom of Speech, Speech Communication Association), 38:7–9, May 1976. **1K26**
After reviewing the First Amendment decisions of the Nixon Court, the author suggests that "it is hard to speak with either clarity or hopefulness about the future. As a general principle it might be a wise course not to place a First Amendment issue before the Court because a negative ruling is almost assured."

——. "Freedom of Expression in Shopping Centers." *Today's Speech*, 22:45–48, Summer 1974. **1K27**
"Although the Supreme Court appeared to be moving in the direction of total recognition of the public character of a shopping center ⌊as proper locations for the exercise of the range of First Amendment rights⌋, the most recent decision in this area ⌊*Lloyd Corporation v. Tanner*, 1972⌋ affirms the private and exclusionary view of these commercial centers."

——. "Freedom of Speech for Public School Students." *Speech Teacher*, 20:21–28, January 1971. **1K28**
An analysis of the First Amendment rights of students as established by the courts, including editing, producing, and distributing underground newspapers, the availability of educational materials, and the provision of guest speakers.

——. "The Group Libel Law Debate in the Canadian House of Commons." *Today's Speech*, 18(4):21–25, Fall 1970. **1K29**
The paper examines the recently enacted Canadian group libel law and the arguments presented for and against it. Despite the strong case against it, Liberal Party discipline insured its passage. Discussion focused on the specific details of the bill rather than on the desirability of the concept of group libel.

Kanowitz, Leo. "Love Lust in New Mexico and the Emerging Law of Obscenity." *Natural Resources Journal*, 10:339–52, April 1970. **1K30**
This article is adapted from a chapter of the author's *Poem Is a Four-Letter Word* and involves the controversy over the use of the book of poems, *Love Lust* by Lenore Kandel, in a University of New Mexico English class. This article deals primarily with some of the legal aspects of the controversy.

——. *Poem is a Four-Letter Word*. Lawrence, Kans., Coronado, 1970. 280p. **1K31**
The story of the controversy touched off by the use of a book of poems, *Love Lust* by Lenore Kandel, in a freshman English class in the University of New Mexico. The author is a member of the law faculty who represented the suspended teaching assistants involved. The account treats with the relationship between the instructor and his teaching assistants, the response of the university community and the community outside the university to the affair, and the involvement of the governor and the state legislature which conducted an investigation of the New Mexico state universities and proposed "remedial" legislation. The author writes of the evolution of his own thinking as well as about the events themselves. Appended is the text of the report of the faculty advisory committee appointed to advise the university president in the matter and which solicited views of the faculty, students, and administrators. Also included is the response to the report by the president who, after prescribing future conduct, reinstated the teaching assistants.

Kant, Harold S., and Michael J. Goldstein. "Pornography." *Psychology Today*, 4:59–61, 76, December 1940. **1K32**
Two psychologists report on results of research done for the U.S. Commission on Obscenity and Pornography which strongly indicates that fears of parents that exposure of children to erotic materials will lead to depravity and encourage sex crimes, are groundless; that some exposure to pornography may be salutary. They found that a sample of rapists had seen less pornography as teen-agers than a comparable group of normal adults had; and that steady customers of an adult bookstore had seen less erotica than the control group had: "One's family background and his current attitudes—and his access to partners—seem much more likely to determine his sexual behavior."

——, and Derek J. Lepper. "A Pilot Comparison of Two Research Instruments Measuring Exposure to Pornography." *Technical Report of the* ⌊*U.S.*⌋ *Commission on Obscenity and Pornography*, 7:325–40, 1971. **1K33**
"This is a report on a pilot study to compare the function and effectiveness of two interview instruments, each designed to elicit information

concerning experience with and attitudes regarding pornography."

Kanter, Elliot. "The NBC Documentary You Never Got to See." *Ramparts*, 13:28, 57–60, August 1974. **1K34**
The case of the suppression of the documentary film, *Powers That Be*, produced by Don Widner for KNBC, Los Angeles. The film, which took a harsh, frightening look at the danger of atomic reactors, met with opposition from government and industry.

Kaplan, John. "Free Press–Fair Trial: Freedom of the Press and the Rights of the Individual." *Oklahoma Law Review*, 29:349–60, Spring 1976. **1K35**
The author calls for balancing of constitutional rights in the matter of free press v. fair trial. He sees a serious problem for fair trial in the press publishing accounts of the past criminal record of defendant's confessions, and other evidence not permitted as evidence in the criminal trial. While he supports the right of newsmen to confidentiality in the matter of investigations involving government corruption and maladministration, he believes the right should be denied in the case of a crime.

Kaplan, Nancy F. "Beyond Branzburg: The Continuing Quest for Reporter's Privilege." *Syracuse Law Review*, 24:731–73, 1973. **1K36**
"This article will briefly examine the history of the quest for reporter's privilege; discuss the context in which the recent Supreme Court decision arose ₍Branzburg v. Hayes, 1972₎; analyze the decision itself and the policy considerations behind it; and assess the future for reporter's privilege now that the court has spoken." The author concludes that "by declining to establish reporter's privilege as a matter of constitutional law, the Supreme Court has tossed the problem into the laps of other political institutions and, perhaps, this is where it belongs."

"*Karalexis v. Byrne* and the Regulation of Obscenity: 'I Am Curious (*Stanley*).'" *Virginia Law Review*, 56:1205–22, October 1970. **1K37**
"The problem, which *Karalexis* directly confronts, is whether the validity of obscenity regulation depends upon the context of the home or merely upon the nonexistence of unrestricted public distribution." *Karalexis v. Byrne* (399 U.S. 922, 1970).

Karam, Edward. *The FOI Act Gets Teeth*. Columbia, Mo., Freedom of Information Center, School of Journalism, University of Missouri at Columbia, 1975. 8p. (Report no. 337) **1K38**
"When the Freedom of Information Act was amended over President Ford's veto, expectations for improved access to federal agency records were high. Some of that optimism was justified, but problems remain."

₍Karowe, Marjorie E.₎ "Discrimination in Classified Advertising—Pittsburgh Press Company v. Pittsburgh Commission on Human Relations." *Albany Law Review*, 38:847–65, 1974. **1K39**
The U.S. Supreme Court upheld a municipal human relations ordinance which prohibited newspapers from publishing sex-segregated want ads for nonexempt job opportunities.

Karpatkin, Marvin M. "En Route to 'A Gross Conforming Stupidity': Lamentations on the Systematic Suffocation of Civil Liberties in the Declining Days of the Nixon Administration, As Aided and Abetted by the Supreme Court." *Today's Speech*, 22:7–14, Winter 1974. **1K40**
In a speech before the Speech Communication Association this New York lawyer discusses attacks on freedom of the press, the redefinition of obscenity, military surveillance over civilian dissenters, presidential secrecy, and chilling freedom of speech by government employees.

Karre, Richard A. "*Stanley v. Georgia;* New Directions in Obscenity Regulations?" *Texas Law Review*, 48:646–60, February 1970. **1K41**
"Although the *Stanley* opinion ₍Stanley v. Georgia, 1969₎ contains all the elements necessary for a repudiation of the two-level theory and the enunciation of a straightforward danger test for speech relating to sex, the Court failed expressly to reject the doctrine."

Karst, Kenneth L. "Equality as a Central Principle in the First Amendment." *University of Chicago Law Review*, 43:20–68, Fall 1975. **1K42**
"The principle of equality, when understood to mean equal liberty, is not just a peripheral support for the freedom of expression, but rather part of the 'central meaning of the First Amendment' . . . the principle lies at the heart of first amendment protection against government regulation of the content of speech. Proper appreciation of the importance of the equality principle in the first amendment suggests the need for a reconsideration of the results reached by the Supreme Court in several doctrinal subspheres. Just such a reconsideration is the aim of this article. When the equality principle is applied to content regulation, it demands a rethinking of several lines of decision. In the 'public forum' area, where the equality principle made its first appearances, a clear understanding of the principle should encourage the Court to abandon inconsistent precedents. The principle of equal liberty of expression also calls for a new look at the problem of access to the communications media. Finally, the first amendment's equality principle implies further constitutional progress toward equalization of the electoral process."

Kassner, Herbert S. "Obscenity Leads

to Perversion." *New York Law Forum*, 20:551–68, Winter 1975. **1K43**
With the 1973 obscenity decisions of the U.S. Supreme Court (*Miller v. California* and *Hamling v. United States*) "obscenity legislation has undergone a most extraordinary constitutional pretesting. Only with a change in the composition of the Court will the constitutional perversions wrought by *Miller* and *Hamling* be reviewed." In the meantime, First Amendment cases will be fought in the trial courts in individual communities across the country. "We now enter an era of 'thought prohibition.' It will undoubtedly meet the same fate as 'drink prohibition.' How long the process will take is unpredictable."

Katz, Al. "Free Discussion v. Final Decision: Moral and Artistic Controversy and the *Tropic of Cancer* Trials." *Yale Law Journal*, 79:209–53, December 1969. (Appeared in abridged form in *Midway*, Spring 1969) **1K44**
The author examines eight of the more than sixty local legal proceedings against Henry Miller's *Tropic of Cancer* in an investigation of the actual operation of the constitutional test of obscenity established by *Roth v. United States* in 1957. "The discussion generated by *Tropic of Cancer* involved issues of moral and aesthetic significance. Neither the censor nor the liberal can dismiss the *Tropic of Cancer* case as being atypical and therefore irrelevant to the main issue of free artistic expression. The book is atypical only in that it is more complex and 'contains' more ideas than most, but it also attracted more legal harassment than most. How is that to be explained in view of *Roth*? These trials make it very difficult for liberals to say that suppression of the 'hard-core' is tolerable—apparently the censors regarded *Tropic of Cancer* as more offensive than the hardest of the core. On the other hand, in the face of these trials, the censors cannot maintain that they are only after smut and not ideas."

————. "Privacy and Pornography: *Stanley v. Georgia*." In Philip B. Kurland, *ed. The Supreme Court Review, 1969*. Chicago, University of Chicago Press, 1969, pp. 203–17. **1K45**
An analysis of the Supreme Court's decision in *Stanley v. Georgia* (1969), ruling that mere possession of obscene materials cannot be punishable by the state. "The case is significant for its revelation of the difficulty that the Court has in shaping a conceptually defensible rationale for its judgments in the obscenity area."

Katz, Alan M. "Government Information Leaks and the First Amendment." *California Law Review*, 64:108–45, January 1976. **1K46**
"This Comment analyzes the extent to which

the first amendment protects government employees who leak government information and the press that publishes such information. After setting out the interests of the parties involved when an unauthorized leak occurs, the author suggests tests to determine the extent of first amendment protection in this area."

Katz, Joan M. "The Games Bureaucrats Play: Hide and Seek Under the Freedom of Information Act." *Texas Law Review*, 48:1261–84, November 1970. (Also in U.S. Senate. Committee of the Judiciary. *Freedom of Information Act Source Book*, pp. 350–73)   **1K47**
"The purpose of the Federal Freedom of Information Act is to permit private citizens access to government files, access that the Act's legislative history indicates was intended to be quite broad. The Act provides that information is to be available unless covered by specific exemptions. Mrs. Katz notes that the broad interpretations placed on the Act's exemptions by federal agencies have virtually rendered the Act a nullity. She argues that courts should reject attempts to constrict public access to government files and should instead read the exemptions in light of the purpose of the Act: to make the inner workings of the Government more visible to the private citizen."

Katz, John S. *Controversial Novels and Censorship in the Schools*. Cambridge, Mass., Harvard University, 1967. 201p. (Ph.D. dissertation)   **1K48**
"This thesis will examine ways in which censors view four novels. It will also examine how literary critics look at the same novels, how the opinions of each group are alike and how they are different, and what each group implies about the function of literature in the schools. In this thesis the term censor is broadly defined as a person who attempts to have certain books removed from the public school curriculum or library or who wishes to deny a teacher the right to teach or assign to his students certain books and materials." The four books examined are: *The Catcher in the Rye* (J. D. Salinger), *The Adventures of Huckleberry Finn* (Mark Twain), *The Grapes of Wrath* (John Steinbeck), and *1984* (George Orwell).

Katz, William A. "The Pornography Collection." *Library Journal*, 96:4060–66, 15 December 1971.   **1K49**
Following a general discussion of librarians as censors, the author examines the major cause for the lack of even basic dissident publications in public libraries—the language, which is sometimes offensive, irreverent, and obscene. Instead of librarians adopting the conventional defense for selecting controversial works, a defense recommended by the ALA Intellectual Freedom Committee, why not take a positive or lateral approach (one suggested by Edward de Bono). Such a positive approach would be to establish a pornography collection in the public library, an action which would be legal if the collection were out of the hands of children and not prominently displayed. His purposely one-sided argument for such a collection "is planned to give pause to the librarian who thinks he has reached the last intellectual and mass media frontier with Henry Miller and the *Reader's Digest*."

Kauffman, Bruce A.. *Fairness in TV News*. Columbia, Mo., Freedom of Information Center, School of Journalism, University of Missouri at Columbia, 1970. 5p. (Report no. 235)   **1K50**
"Congressmen who replied to a recent FOI Center survey consider Walter Cronkite the 'most fair' television network newsman and David Brinkley the 'least fair.' A majority of the respondents agree generally with Vice-President Spiro T. Agnew's criticism of TV network news."

Kauffmann, Stanley. "On Censorship: Freedom for What?" *Performance*, 3:44–49, July–August 1972.   **1K51**
A drama critic charges that some TV writers who complain of network and sponsor censorship want freedom to exploit themes for their own financial interest, without regard to quality or the public interest. While writing off most TV drama as beneath contempt, he defends the networks for their high quality documentaries and specials and news reporting of social problems. Considering the facts of advertiser domination of TV and government complicity with advertisers, "American TV is surprisingly good." David W. Rintels, whose testimony before the Senate Subcommittee on Constitutional Rights prompted Kauffmann's article responds on pp. 49–55. In a brief rejoinder Kauffmann notes that his argument is aesthetic, Rintels's is libertarian.

———. "On Obscenity." *New Republic*, 163:22, 35, 17 October 1970.   **1K52**
Commentary on the report of the U.S. Commission on Obscenity and Pornography. Unlike the Kerner report on civil disorders and the Scranton report on campus unrest, both of which spoke to expressed American principles, "the Lockhart report runs *counter* to a dominant strain in the American temperament," and is unlikely to meet wide acceptance. He observes that "a lot of radical nonsense has been published about the esthetics of pornography, particularly its literature. Discussion of style in porno books is affectation, I think. *Fanny Hill* is elegantly written, but the point of *Fanny Hill* is to make the reader masturbate if no partner is available which is not the point of the last section of *Ulysses*. The elegance only makes the masturbation more snobbish."

———. "On Pornography." *Public Interest*, 22:28–32, Winter 1971.   **1K53**
Commenting on an essay on pornography by Walter Berns in the same issue (pp. 3–24), the author asserts his dislike for both pornography and censorship. Pornography represents a "phoney emancipation—in fact, a negation of the very fullness of life that is ostensibly being offered." Censorship is "anticivil and anti-civilized." He suggests one way to cure his uneasiness on the subject of pornography is "to repeal all the laws restricting it except possibly the ones forbidding the advertising and sale to minors."

———. "Sex Symbols." *New Republic*, 159(18):30, 48–49, 2 November 1968.   **1K54**
Comments on the forthcoming moral rating of films by the Motion Picture Association of America. The film critic sees the rating system as a workable buffer against much worse restriction, which is very much in the wind.

Kaufman, Irving R. "A Free Speech for the Class of '75." *New York Times Magazine*, 8 June 1975. pp. 36–37+.   **1K55**
A federal judge deplores the lack of tolerance for free speech on college campuses, which should be bastions for expression of First Amendment rights. This new intolerance grows in part from the notion that free speech is only a means to an end and that if censorship would further advance the good of equality or social welfare it should be preferred to liberty of expression. He sees the root of the new morality as stemming from mass education where dialogue and diversity is frowned upon and doctrination is substituted for free exchange of views. Criticism of the mass media for its lack of uniformity is also a symptom of the new morality. "Tolerance of beliefs—even that we despise—does have a role to play in our continuing education, and must not be stifled. We value freedom of thought, freedom of speech, freedom of the press because they furnish vehicles for the new and provocative, and serve as barriers to tyranny."

———. "The Judges and the Jurors: Recent Developments in Selection of Jurors and Fair Trial—Free Press." *University of Colorado Law Review*, 41:179–200, May 1969.   **1K56**
Judge Kaufman discusses two recent developments which he believes will greatly improve the quality of federal juries—the Federal Jury Selection Act of 1968 and the recommendations of the Judicial Conference of the United States concerning the problems of fair trial and free press.

———. "The Medium, the Message, and the First Amendment." *New York University Law Review*, 45:761–84, October 1970.   **1K57**
"Drawing a crucial distinction between speech's 'message' or content and the medium through which it is conveyed, the Judge considers the permissible limits on regulation of each. He concludes that the most perplexing constitutional problems arise from regulation of the 'media' and the courts must be diligent in guarding the free and open channels of com-

munication whenever public safety and order permit."

Kaul, Donald. "Trouble with a Capital T." *Arizona English Bulletin*, 11:9–10, February 1969. (Reprint from Kaul's column, Over the Coffee, in the *Des Moines Register*, 9 February 1967) **1K58**
A humorous report of an imaginary street-corner harangue delivered by an antipornography crusader.

Kavaler, Lucy. "The Right to Write in Prison—U.S.A." *American Pen*, 4(3): 28–39, Summer 1972. **1K59**
An account of the problems faced by writers in American prisons, as investigated by the Writers in Prison Committee of P.E.N. One of the difficulties is lack of adequate libraries.

Kavanagh, Patrick. "The Wake of the Books." *Bell*, 15(2):4–16, November 1947. **1K60**
A mummery having as its theme Irish censorship. In the prologue he says:

"This little drama that I introduce
Is no great licker to excite my muse,
For howsoever I try I can't but feel
The censorship of books is not a real
Problem for writers of this land:
There's much that's insincere in what is banned—
And Time if left the Corpse would bury it deeper
In ten years than our bitterest conscience-keeper."

Kaye, J. M. "Libel and Slander—Two Torts or One?" *Law Quarterly Review*, 91:524–39, October 1975. **1K61**
The purpose of this article is to suggest certain modifications in Sir William Holdsworth's analysis of libel and slander as recorded in his *History of English Law* (1937).

Keating, Charles H., Jr. "Green Light to Combat Smut: Supreme Court Decision." *Reader's Digest*, 104:147–50, January 1974. **1K62**
In the wake of the U.S. Supreme Court's 21 June 1973 decision giving communities freedom to enforce their own standards of obscenity, the author gives advice on action to be taken by community groups.

———. "The Report That Shocked the Nation." *Reader's Digest*, 98(1):37–41, January 1971. (Reprinted in *Congressional Record*, 22 December 1970) **1K63**
"A much-distressed member of the Commission on Obscenity and Pornography examines the panel majority's bizarre proposal for handling the pornographic problem."—Editor

———. "Who Says Pornography Is Harmless." *National Decency Reporter*. 4(1–2):8–9, January–February 1967. (Condensed in *Family Digest*, 3 August 1967) **1K64**

"Keating Dissents! Commission Findings Blasted." *National Decency Reporter*, 7(7–8):1, 8–9, July–August 1970. **1K65**
The dissenting views of Charles H. Keating, Jr., a member of the U.S. Commission on Obscenity and Pornography, the only member appointed by President Nixon, his conflict with the chairman of the Commission, and his effort to alert the Nixon Administration to the permissive trend of the Commission and to have the president replace the membership with those who would stop the deluge of pornography.

Keck, William C. "A Search Warrant Must Particularly Specify Any Obscene Materials to Be Seized So That the Court's Function of Determining What Material Is Obscene and Therefore Outside the Protection of the First Amendment Is Not Delegated to Police Officers." *Notre Dame Lawyer*, 43:601–9, April 1968. **1K66**
Re: *People v. Rothenberg*, 20 N.Y.2d 35 (1967).

Keeley, Joseph C. *Left-Leaning Antennae: Political Bias in Television*. New Rochelle, N.Y., Arlington, 1971. 320p. **1K67**
A former editor of *American Legion Magazine*, following a month of intensive television watching and interviews with scores of persons involved in television, charges left-wing bias in the industry. This results, he believes, in a monopoly of licensed opinion, in effect if not in intent, enforced by the government. It constitutes a serious threat to free expression. He calls on conservative television viewers to express their disapproval in letters to networks, advertisers, and local stations. Appendixes include Vice-President Agnew's attack on media bias, the NAB Code, the fairness doctrine, and a proposal presented by Thomas Petry of WCNY–TV Syracuse, N.Y., to National Educational Television to counteract the present preponderance of leftist and liberal thought in NET and public television.

Keenan, Joseph C. *Prosecutions of the English Press during the Early Nineteenth Century*. Washington, D.C., Georgetown University, 1932. 105p. (Ph.D. dissertation) **1K68**
"It is the purpose of the author to point out the manner in which editors and publishers of the early nineteenth century were made to suffer from the strict enforcement of obnoxious press laws; and how, in spite of their many prosecutions, they succeeded in making such remarkable progress in their struggle to bring about a free press. It is a too common belief that Eng-

land at the time enjoyed a freedom of journalistic discussion that was the admiration of the Continent; and historians of English journalism themselves pass lightly over the narrow limits given to the right to publish, and the wholesale prosecutions of journalists for the violation of the law of libel."

[Keenan, Lawrence R.] "Broadcasting's Fairness Doctrine—An Illogical Extension of the Red Lion Concept." *University of Richmond Law Review*, 6:448–56, Spring 1972. **1K69**
A review of the District of Columbia Court of Appeals decision in *Business Executives' Move for Vietnam Peace v. FCC*, 1971, in which the Court reversed the FCC decision giving the right of a broadcasting station to refuse an editorial advertisement. The author holds that this was an illogical extension of the *Red Lion* decision upholding the fairness doctrine in broadcasting. A wiser approach would have been to evaluate the network's total performance in airing controversial issues.

———. "The Clear and Present Danger Standard: Its Present Viability." *University of Richmond Law Review*, 6:93–115, Fall 1971. **1K70**
"It is the purpose of this Note to evaluate the 'clear and present danger' test, to analyze its past applicability, and to determine whether or not it is still an effective device for measuring challenges to first amendment guarantees of freedom of expression."

Keenan, William H. "Erotica For Your Kiddies?" *National Decency Reporter*, 4(1):14–16, March–April 1967. (Reprinted from *Greater Saint Louis Magazine*, February 1967) **1K71**
The author describes the saturation of pornography in the St. Louis area in a question-and-answer session with Roy T. Dreher, a member of the Citizens for Decent Literature's staff, and attempts to arrive at a solution to the problem.

Keeton, Robert E. "Some Implications of the Constitutional Privilege to Defame." *Vanderbilt Law Review*, 25:59–77, January 1972. **1K72**
Because of the relatively complex rules in matters of libel, which may discourage free expression, and the increased scope of the constitutional privilege to defame under recent Supreme Court decisions, the author suggests that "a revised body of state law confining privilege in defamation cases to the minimum constitutional requirement might serve the interests of free expression about as well as a combination of the constitutional privilege with varied state-law privileges, some purportedly broader than constitutionally required."

He also suggests that a chosen degree of protection for free expression and a corresponding limitation of protection for security of good name might be achieved "by eliminating all state-law rules of privilege and broadening the federal law privileges as needed to accomplish the chosen accommodation."

Keeton, W. Page. "Defamation and Freedom of the Press." *Texas Law Review*, 54:1221–59, August 1976. **1K73**
The author "compares the English and American defamation principles, including the various privileges to defame and defenses to liability; he suggests that the law of defamation can be simplified without upsetting the proper balance between protecting personal reputations and encouraging the free interchange of ideas. To recover for defamatory falsehoods, Keeton argues, all plaintiffs should have to demonstrate that defendants knew of the falsity of their statements or had no reasonable basis for believing the statements to be true. He also rationalizes the principle that no liability should result from the publication of defamatory opinions as opposed to facts."

Kefauver, Estes. *A Senator Speaks on Salacious Literature*. Nashville, Tenn., Christian Life Commission of the Southern Baptist Convention, n.d. 4p. **1K74**
Senator Kefauver speaks out against "this insidious traffic in filth that has been undermining the morals of our youth" and calls for federal legislation.

Kehde, Ned. "The Hip Corporations and Anti-Establishment Press of the Left." *Missouri Library Association Quarterly*, 30:197–220, September 1969. **1K75**
A bibliography with introductory remarks.

Keith, Sara. "Literary Censorship and Mudie's Library." *Colorado Quarterly*, 21:359–72, Winter 1973. **1K76**
The author reviews the book selection policies of Mudie's Select Library, which began in the 1840s, defending it from the frequent charges of censorship—first by High Church authorities who charged Mudie with religious discrimination in the 1860s because it carried too much worthless and false, and in 1885 because it didn't carry George Moore's *A Modern Lover* (M493). Mudie's was a commercial organization and its selection merely reflected, rather than dominated, the reading interests of its subscribers. If the public demanded a work, Mudie bought it. The author considers the philosophy of Carlylean paternalism in judging the goodness or rightness of reading vis à vis the Millsian *laissez faire* doctrine applied to book selection.

Kelleher, Terry. "Phone-Tapping and Postal Censorship." *Hibernia*, 34(15): 8–9, 7 August 1970. **1K77**
Details on how government wire-tapping and postal censorship works in Ireland. "Despite the comprehensive machinery in existence, the whole system of ₁mail₁ censorship is carried out with a remarkable degree of amateurishness."

Kelley, Clarence. "Television Is Armed and Dangerous." *TV Guide*, 23(10):6–8, 8 March 1975. **1K78**
The director of the Federal Bureau of Investigation argues that TV publicity can produce a chain reaction of crime.

₁Kells, John?₁ *The Rights of Juries, Legal and Constitutional, in Cases of Libel, Considered in a Letter to the Jurors of Ireland. By a Barrister*. Dublin, Henry Watts, 1794. 61p. **1K79**
The author draws a distinction in the handling of criminal and civil cases; calls for vindicating the freedom of the press by punishing licentious misuse of freedom. The barrister describes eight degrees of press freedom, the first four are clearly permissible—forming ideas in our minds, expressing opinions in the abstract, arguing in behalf of abstract ideas, and temperate discussions of men and measures. The next four involve possible civil or criminal libel—imputing criminal acts punishable by law, inciting evasion of law, reducing respect for law by condemning ordinance and constitution, and advocating resistance to law. The National Library of Ireland attributes the anonymously published pamphlet to John Kells.

Kelly, Alfred H. "Constitutional Liberty and the Law of Libel: A Historian's View." *American Historical Review*, 74:429–52, December 1968. **1K80**
A comprehensive analysis of the development of libel law beginning with English common law and libel law in the early years of the republic. With the declining significance of state and federal prosecution of criminal libel during the nineteenth century, "the law of civil libel assumed increasing importance as a means of controlling false, reckless, and defamatory utterances, both in politics and public life and in the private affairs of men." He reports on recent efforts of the U.S. Supreme Court to bring criminal and civil libel within the scope of the First Amendment. The author shows the significance of the development of libel law to the writing of history. "In spite of the welter of legal details, it is clear that the mantle of constitutional right that the newer interpretation of the law of libel places around authors and publishers affords the historian a considerable degree of protection. . . . Probably the largest danger from libel prosecutions that the responsible historian faces is that of harassment."

Kelly, John J., Jr. "Contempt by Publication: Necessity of Clear and Present Danger to the Administration of Jus-

tice." *Cornell Law Quarterly*, 32:413–17, March 1947. **1K81**
The article discusses the historical development of the clear and present danger rule as applied to contempt by publication, including the current case, *Pennekamp et al. v. State of Florida*, 1946, in which the U.S. Supreme Court in a unanimous decision reversed a lower court decision against the *Miami Herald*, cited for contempt for an editorial and cartoon criticizing certain judges of the Circuit Court of Dade County.

Kelly, John M. "Freedom of Expression." In his *Fundamental Rights in the Irish Law and Constitution*. 2d ed. Dublin, Figgis, 1967, pp. 124–42. **1K82**
Content: Control in the Interest of State Authority. Control in the Interest of Judicial Authority. Control in the Interest of Private Reputations. Control in the Interest of Public Morality: Blasphemy, Obscenity, Censorship of Films, and Censorship of Publications. General Control of Certain Means of Communications: Postal and Telephone Services, Broadcasting.

Kelsey, Elizabeth J. "Defamation in New Zealand—An Alternative Approach." *Victoria University of Wellington Law Review*, 8:130–47, February 1976. **1K83**
"This paper is an attempt to present a viable alternative to the recognized approach, by abolishing the need for such controversial areas of defamation as privilege and fair comment, and modifying also that most ineffectual remedy which seems to pervade the most inappropriate areas of our law: damages."

Kemp, Karl H. "Recent Obscenity Cases." *Arkansas Law Review*, 28:357–72, Fall 1974. **1K84**
Following a summary of recent U.S. Supreme Court decisions on obscenity, the author concludes that, while the Justice Douglas approach of no obscenity is tempting, there is a legitimate interest in protecting children and the privacies of unconsenting adults, and, therefore, favors the intermediate approach taken by Justices Brennan, Stewart, and Marshall and by the majority of the U.S. Commission on Obscenity and Pornography.

Kemp-Ashraf, P. M., *ed*. "Selected Writings of Thomas Spence, 1750–1814." In *Essays in Honour of William Gallacher*. Berlin, Humbolt University, 1966, pp. 267–354. **1K85**
A London bookseller and radical reformer, Spence "was arrested and examined several times for selling his own and other seditious books; was imprisoned for six months without trial in 1794, and sentenced to three years for his *Restorer of Society to Its Natural State* in 1801 (S544–45)." The editor provides a biographical sketch of Spence and an account of his economic and social ideas, followed by a Spence bibliography and excerpts from his controversial writings.

Kempton, Murray. "A Feelthy Commission." *New York Review of Books*, 15(9):24–25, 19 November 1970. **1K86**
A review of *The Report of the U.S. Commission on Obscenity and Pornography*. "It is surely odd," writes Kempton, "that the only bequest of President Johnson's to be repudiated by the votes of all but five senators and to be denounced as 'morally bankrupt' by Mr. Nixon should be not his war but this report of his Commission on Obscenity and Pornography." The reviewer criticizes the "dubious research" of the social psychologists who "adjusted their methods to their motives." He believes it strange that the Commission, although headed by a law professor, "in defending its recommendations against statutory restraints on pornography, nowhere seems to mention the First Amendment."

[Kendall, Benjamin F.] *The Ex-Chief Justice, and the Printer: Being a Report of a Trial for Libel, Titus Hutchinson vs. B. F. Kendall. Had Before the Honorable County Court, for the County of Windsor, and State of Vermont, May term, 1836; Including Plaintiff's Declaration, Pleadings, Testimony, Arguments, Charges, and Verdict!!! With an Appendix containing Many Interesting Reminiscences, Morceaus, and Incidents, with which the Public Life and Meandering Course of the Late "Everlasting Candidate," Are So Profusely Variegated. . . . By the Defendant.* Woodstock, Vt., J. B. & S. L. Chase, 1836. 72p. **1K87**
A former justice of the Vermont Supreme Court, known as the "everlasting candidate" for having run unsuccessfully for U.S. senator three times, for congressman, and for town council, sued the editor of the *Woodstock Courier* that had opposed him. The charges involved reporting on the judge's handling of a case in Circuit Court. The jury found for the plaintiff and assessed a fine of $100. Judge Hutchinson had asked for $25,000.

Kennedy, David M. *Birth Control in America: The Career of Margaret Sanger.* New Haven, Conn., Yale University Press, 1970. 320p. (Yale Publications in American Studies, no. 18) **1K88**
"This book explores the relation between Margaret Sanger's character and the nature of the movement she led in America between 1912 and the Second World War. . . . It tries to describe the context in which Mrs. Sanger worked, the attitudinal and institutional responses she evoked." Included are the incidents of her arrest for distribution of birth control information and for her publication, *The Woman Rebel*.

———. *Birth Control: Its Heroine and Its History in America—The Career of Margaret Sanger.* New Haven, Conn., Yale University, 1968. 428p. (Ph.D. dissertation, University Microfilms, no. 69–8372) **1K89**
The dissertation was the basis for the book, *Birth Control in America: The Career of Margaret Sanger.*

Kennedy, J. de N. "Libel—Newspapers; Fair Comment on a Matter of Public Interest." *Chitty's Law Journal*, 16:42–46, February 1968. **1K90**
The author disagrees with the decision of the English Court of Appeal in the case of *Vitamins Limited, et al. v. The Daily Telegraph et al.* (1968) in which the judge held that letters to the editor published in the paper were defamatory but that since the letters contained a fair comment on a matter of public interest the defendants were not liable.

Kennedy, Marie M. "Censorship and the Young Adult Reader." *Catholic Library World*, 46:122–24, October 1974. **1K91**
A review of contemporary views on the role of the librarian in selecting material for young adults, including the issue of book selection versus censorship.

Kennedy, Robert P. *Expunged. Speeches of Hon. Rob't P. Kennedy, of Ohio, in the House of Representatives, Wednesday, Sept. 3, 1890, Wednesday, Sept. 24, 1890. . . .* Washington, D.C., R. O. Polkinhorn, printers, 1890. 16p. **1K92**
A speech critical of his own (Republican) party over failure to pass a fair election law led to a House resolution expunging the congressman's speech from the *Congressional Record.* Text of Kennedy's suppressed speech and his plea against such suppression.

Kent, Kurt E. "Freedom of the Press: An Empirical Analysis of One Aspect of the Concept." *Gazette: International Journal for Mass Communications Studies*, 18:65–75, 1972. **1K93**
"The aspect of press freedom investigated in this paper is government–press relations. More specifically, the study concerns itself with actual or potential governmental pressures on the press." Fifteen variables across ninety-four countries, taken from Lowenstein's 1966 survey of world press freedom, were used. "Support was found for the position that this aspect of press freedom is empirically as well as theoretically unidimensional."

Kenyon, Kathryn. *Advocacy Comes to the Newsroom.* Columbia, Mo., Freedom of Information Center, School of Journalism, University of Missouri at Columbia, 1970. 4p. (Report no. 250) **1K94**
Advocacy journalists in the United States as well as Europe are seeking more autonomy in the handling of the news, including participa-

tion in policy-making decisions in their news organization.

———. *FCC v. "Overcommercialization" II.* Columbia, Mo., Freedom of Information Center, School of Journalism, University of Missouri at Columbia, 1970. 4p. (Report no. 247) **1K95**
The threat of even more commercials per hour to meet the rising costs has caused the FCC to study again proposals to limit TV advertising.

Keogh, James. *President Nixon and the Press.* New York, Funk & Wagnalls, 1972. 212p. **1K96**
A former member of President Nixon's news staff writes a sympathetic account of the Nixon Administration news policies and describes the president's long-time battle with a liberal press which he considered hostile, antagonistic, and biased. He criticizes the superpower of the TV networks and the big newspapers, and is concerned with increased journalistic obsession with the negative, and with the rise of advocacy journalism. The appendix contains the text of President Nixon's address to the nation on Vietnam, 3 November 1969, and the controversial commentary by ABC, NBC, and CBS immediately following. Also included are the texts of Vice-President Agnew's speech about network television news, at Des Moines, Iowa, 13 November 1969, and his speech about news media at Montgomery, Ala., 20 November 1969.

Keough, Donald, ed. *Legislative Openness: A Special Report on Press and Public Access to Information and Activities in State Legislatures.* Kansas City, Mo., Citizens Conference on State Legislatures, 1974. 141p. **1K97**
"This study provides information, for state legislators and for the public, on the theory and practice of openness in the 50 state legislatures. . . . Part I of this book consists of four position papers commissioned by the CCSL. The first paper, written by Alfred W. Baxter, CCSL program advisor, considers the entire topic of legislative openness. The other three papers deal with information availability from the point of view of—the news media, by Henry Holcomb . . . ; public interest groups, by Nan F. Waterman . . . ; the businessman, by R. Allan Hickman. Part II is comprised of research papers on the various aspects of openness and information availability: openness of committees and caucuses, regulation of openness, advance public notice of legislative activities, record keeping, roll call voting, bill status reporting systems, and legislative facilities and procedures for providing news media and public access to legislative information."

Kerbec, Matthew J. "The Public In-

formation Act." *Library Journal*, 95: 4229–31, 15 December 1970. **1K98**
A discussion of the provision of the Act and its usefulness to librarians seeking information from the federal government. Includes text of the Act.

Kerby, Phil. "Tom, Dick and the Censors." *Nation*, 207:563–64, 25 November 1968. **1K99**
The experience of the Smothers Brothers show with Columbia Broadcasting System censors, with examples of some of their controversial dialogue.

Kermode, Frank. "Obscenities—Frank Kermode on the Question of Limiting What Can Be Read or Staged." *Listener*, 82:98–99, 24 July 1969. **1K100**
Views developed in the course of reviewing three books: *Books in the Dock* by Cecil R. Hewitt ₍C. H. Rolph₎, *A Long Time Burning* by Donald Thomas, and *The End of Obscenity* by Charles Rembar.

Kerr, Walter B. "Newspapers and Monopoly: S1312 and All That." *Saturday Review*, 52(19):77–78, 10 May 1969. **1K101**
A survey of the issues before the Congress in considering legislation which would exempt newspapers from the full weight of the antitrust laws.

Kessler, Jascha. "The Censorship of Art and the Art of Censorship." *Literary Review*, 12:409–31, Summer 1969. **1K102**
"The art that is necessary to a society is subject thereby to the editing of the Censor because Censorship is, even in the most freely conceivable of free worlds, the means of delimiting the utility of mental controls, and utility, as primitive art shows us, need not exclude beauty."

Kester, John G. "Soldiers Who Insult the President: An Uneasy Look At Article 88 of the Uniform Code of Military Justice." *Harvard Law Review*, 81:1697–1769, June 1968. **1K103**
The author, relying on original records of army general courts-martial, presents "a brief genealogy of Article 88 ₍of the Uniform Code of Military Justice, which prohibits a commissioned officer from using contemptuous words against the president and certain other officials₎, a compilation and discussion of past prosecutions under it, and some thoughts as to whether it is merely a bizarre atavism in the military code, or rather a restriction on members of the armed forces which can have useful and constitutional application today."

Kesterton, Wilfred H. *A History of Journalism in Canada*. With a Foreword by Wilfred Eggleston. Toronto, McClelland and Stewart, 1967. 304p. **1K104**
In this general history of Canadian journalism the author deals extensively with the development of press freedom: From 1752–1807 the press in British North America served largely as agents of the government, was pallid, neutral, and harmless; from 1807–58 a libertarian movement began to grow, with numerous conflicts between newspapers and authorities, including the famous libel trial of Joseph Howe in 1835; the period 1858–1900 saw the development of laws of libel which outlined the limits of press freedom. The development of press freedom in the twentieth century is reported under the following headings: philosophical background, Alberta Press Act (1938), the "Babies for Export" trial (1948), Quebec Padlock Law (1919), the libertarian system and law of the press, censorship in wartime (World Wars I and II), some cold war restrictions, and press freedom and responsibility in the 1960s (printed and electronic media).

————. *The Law and the Press in Canada*. Toronto, McClelland and Stewart in Association with the Institute of Canadian Studies, Carleton University, 1976. 242p. (Carleton Library no. 100) **1K105**
The book is intended to give Canadian journalists a "feel" for the law of the press, with emphasis on general precepts. Following a brief history of Canadian press law, the author deals with contempt of court, free press–fair trial, revealing the sources, civil defamation, criminal libel, obscenity and censorship, copyright, privacy, and government secrecy and the press. The appendix contains summaries of cases discussed in the book.

Key, Francis Scott. *A Part of a Speech Pronounced by Francis S. Key, Esq. on the Trial of Reuben Crandall, M.D. before the Circuit Court of the District of Columbia, at the March Term thereof, 1836, On an Indictment for Publishing Libels with Intent to Excite Sedition and Insurrection among the Slaves and Free Coloured People of Said District.* ₍From the *African Repository*, November 1836.₎ Washington, 1836. 15p. **1K106**
The man who is better known as the author of the *Star Spangled Banner* served as prosecuting attorney in the case of Dr. Reuben Crandall, charged with seditious libel for an antislavery tract which suggested that the black man had equal rights with the white and urged immediate emancipation of all slaves. Key refuted the defense arguments that more famous Americans—Jefferson, Patrick Henry, Pinckney, and Breckenridge—had expressed similar sentiments. These men, Key argued, were southerners and not outsiders like Dr. Crandall; also they didn't recommend the madness

of immediate emancipation. Dr. Crandall was acquitted. The report of the Crandall trial is entered under C627–28.

Keyser, Lester J. "The Watergate Scandal and the Mass Media: The Early Phases." In *Free Speech Yearbook*, *1974*. New York, Speech Communication Association, 1975, pp. 54–63. **1K107**
An account of the epic battle between the Nixon Administration and the press in the period from early spring 1972 to the fall of 1973. The account begins with Vice-President Agnew's "blazing attack on televised news, an attack to be followed at a later date with antitrust actions, prosecution of both print and broadcast journalists for failure to divulge sources, and massive cuts in funding of public television. Agnew was merely the spearbearer, however, for a policy of press harassment which was directed by the White House."

Khan, Masud R. "The Politics of Subversion and Rage (The Abuses of Literacy—4)." *Times Literary Supplement*, 3,649:121–22, 4 February 1972. (Reprinted in David Holbrook, *ed.*, *The Case Against Pornography*, pp. 129–36) **1K108**
A psychoanalyst looks at pornography as a perverted mind game that has little to do with ordinary sexual experiences and is pathetically bad literature. "It negates imagination, style, and the tradition of man's struggle to use language to know and enhance himself." The only true achievement of pornography is that "it transmits rage into erotic somatic events . . . it negates the person through its somatic expertise." Pornography tries "to make of the human body an idea machine, which can be manipulated to yield maximum sensation."

Khosla, Gopal D. "Censorship and Law." *Times of India*, 11 May 1969, p. 3. **1K109**
"The State cannot take upon itself the task of improving public taste by means of censorship because any law or regulation drawn up for this purpose would be unconstitutional. Measures can, however, be validly taken for the protection of children and adolescents. The easiest and the simplest way of affording such protection is by the classification of literature, films, plays, etc. as suitable for adults only."

————. "Obscenity and the Law." *Illustrated Weekly of India*, 90(43):6–9, 26 October 1969. **1K110**
The chairman of the India Films Censorship Inquiry Committee finds the law against obscenity "vague, ambiguous, uncertain, inconsistent and ineffective, in short, everything that a law should not be. Though the decision of what is and what is not obscene should rest with the courts and ultimately with the Supreme Court, decisions are frequently taken by officials who know little or nothing of art and aesthetics. This results in inconsistencies and

the application of double standards. There is no yardstick of the depraving influence of obscenity, indeed no evidence at all that what is called obscene, in fact depraves. The whole question is one of taste and this is a matter which should be left to the judgment of the public."

──────. *Pornography and Censorship in India*. New Delhi, Indian Book, 1976. 168p.   **1K111**
Justice Khosla examines the subject of pornography in the context of historical, social, and cultural backgrounds. Among the questions he raises and answers are: Is sex a proper subject for treatment in literature and the visual and performing arts? Is pornography harmful and, if so, to what extent? What is the effect of pornography on children? Do the sex mores of a particular society provide any indication of its integral strength and its capacity for survival? Are pornography and the treatment of sex in art and literature fit subjects for legislation or should the matter be left to the forum of public taste? What is the state of the law relating to censorship in India today?

Kidwai, M. Saleem. "Supreme Court and Freedom of Speech and Expression." *Modern Review*, 130(2):110–13, February 1972.   **1K112**
A review of action by the Supreme Court of India in interpreting the Constitution, attempting to maintain balance between freedom and social control.

Kiefer, George G. "Minors and Variable Obscenity." *Loyola Law Review*, 15:97–107, 1969.   **1K113**
Re: *Ginsberg v. State of New York*, 1968, in which the U.S. Supreme Court affirmed and held that it was constitutionally permissible for the New York legislature to accord minors under seventeen a more restricted right than that assured adults in determining for themselves what material they may see or read. The right to employ this "variable concept of obscenity" was held to be within the power of the state to protect the well-being of its youth.

Kies, Cosette. "Copyright Versus Free Access: CBS and Vanderbilt University Square Off." *Wilson Library Bulletin*, 50:242–46, November 1975. **1K114**
A review of the case of *CBS v. Vanderbilt*, in which the network charged the university with violating network copyright by renting copies of newscast tapes, preserved in the Vanderbilt Television News Archive, to persons requesting them. According to the author the case involved the issue of copyright control as opposed to the public's right to free access, as expressed in the First Amendment.

Kies, David. "Equal Time for Political Candidates." *New York University Intramural Law Review*, 23:266–91, May 1968.   **1K115**
"The purpose of this paper is to see how the

Congress has attempted to regulate the broadcast media in its use by political candidates during election campaigns." The author finds that the law has resulted in insuring the public and candidates a fair presentation of views, but that changes in the law should minimize bureaucratic discretion.

Kifer, Allen F. *The United States Congress and Censorship of Literature, 1929–1952*. Madison, Wis., University of Wisconsin, 1954. 166p. (Unpublished Master's thesis)   **1K116**

Kilander, H. Frederick. "The Dissemination of Offensive and Obscene Material." In his *Sex Education in the Schools*. New York, Macmillan, 1970, pp. 205–16. (Also in *School and Society*, Summer 1969)   **1K117**
Content: What constitutes pornography and obscenity. The legal testing of obscenity. Authoritative viewpoints. Freedom of the press and obscenity. The role of the mass media (magazines, books, paperbacks, mail solicitation, greeting cards, records, television, and motion pictures).

Kiley, Roger J. "The Supreme Court, Angst and Justice Black's Dissent." *Critic*, 25:45–49, December 1966–January 1967.   **1K118**
An analysis of the U.S. Supreme Court decision in the *Ginzburg* obscenity case (*Ginzburg v. United States*, 1966) in which pandering rather than the erotic nature of the material cited was the issue. "The law presumes that Ginzburg, at the time he mailed the publications, knew the *Roth* rule of obscenity and knew from the Warren concurring opinion that the 'central issue' in a criminal obscenity case was the conduct of the person, not the book."

Killefer, Constance. "Intellectual Freedom and the Post-Modern Generation: Double Standards." *Top of the News*, 25:392–99, June 1969. (Reprinted from *Bay State Librarian*, October 1968)   **1K119**
A discussion of the "post-modern kids" who "have both impatient feet running for tomorrow" while their modern parents have one foot in yesterday. The biggest schism is over morality, the parents hang-up being sex, the post-moderns being violence. They are challenging society's dishonest double standard saying one thing and doing another. "Censorship epitomizes the double standard against which the post-modern generation is rebelling."

Killenberg, George M. "Free Expression Implications of New Federal Election Law." *Journalism Quarterly*, 50:527–32, Autumn 1973.   **1K120**
"Campaign Act of 1971 may be in conflict with First Amendment because restrictions and

criminal penalties apply to media as well as politicians."

──────. "Working Journalists Say Confidential Sources Necessary." *Grassroots Editor*, 13(6):16–20, November–December 1972.   **1K121**
The author cites three surveys, one which he conducted, which show that "reporters rely heavily on confidential sources and newspapers publish a large number of stories based on information from informants." The threat of jury subpoenas and the loss of newsmen's privilege would have a chilling effect on the gathering of news.

Killits, J. M. . . . *Opinion of Hon. J. M. Killits on the Law of Newspaper Contempt of Court*. Toledo, Ohio, n.p., 1914. 82p.   **1K122**
In the case of *U.S. v. Toledo Newspaper Co. and Negley D. Cochran* Judge Killits of the District Court of the United States, Northern District of Ohio, Western Division, held the *Toledo News-Bee* and its publisher in contempt of court for publishing articles on a case pending before that court. The information charged that the articles were intended to influence the court's consideration of the pending traction case "by attempting an impression that a decision contrary to the wishes of the paper would not only be very unpopular in the community but likely to be met with active opposition." The publisher was fined and ordered to jail until the fine was paid. Another Toledo paper, the *Times*, applauded the decision.

Kim, Chin. "Constitution and Obscenity: Japan and the U.S.A." *American Journal of Comparative Law*, 25:255–83, Spring 1975.   **1K123**
"The primary purposes of this paper are to study Japanese constitutional solutions to the issue of obscenity by focusing on the *Koyama* and *Shibuzawa* cases and to put Japanese and American obscenity decisions into comparative perspective. . . . The Japanese Supreme Court decisions from the beginning established a trend favorable to censorship of 'obscene' material. Development of the standards to define obscene material did not reflect the same concern with a balancing of the state interests in censorship and individual interests in free speech and press as did the initial American decisions. Although the Japanese courts recognize the new rights granted in the new constitution, they seem to favor a preferred position for the public welfare standard and the concepts of the prevailing ideas of society and the art/obscenity two-dimensional approach."

──────. "Librarians and Copyright Legislation: The Historical Background." *American Libraries*, 2:615–22, June 1971.   **1K124**

A history of copyright, including the role of the library profession in the drafting of the 1905 Act, the issues which call for a revision of the Act and the position taken by the Joint Libraries Committee on Copyright.

Kim, Holim. *Free Press and Fair Trial: An Attitudinal Study of Lawyers and Journalists in a Conflict Between Two Professions.* Carbondale, Ill., Southern Illinois University, 1972. 279p. (Ph.D. dissertation, University Microfilms, no. 73–6222) **1K125**
"A general hypothesis of this study is that there may exist identifiable systems of beliefs and attitudes for certain professional groups. To empirically test it, two professional groups, lawyers . . . and journalists . . . were selected on an issue that concerned them both—the 'free press–fair trial' conflict. The conflict between the press and the bar was viewed as an effect of psychological sources rooted in their respective belief systems."

Kimball, Clark. "Patriots vs Dissenters: The Rhetoric of Intimidation in Indiana During the First World War." In *Free Speech Yearbook, 1972.* New York, Speech Communication Association, 1973, pp. 49–65. **1K126**
An account of vigilante action against suspected disloyalists in Indiana during World War I.

Kimber, William. "Libel—A Book Publisher's View." In Michael Rubinstein, *ed., Wicked, Wicked Libels,* London, Routledge & Kegan Paul, 1972, pp. 66–84. **1K127**
The trials and tribulations of a publisher under the British libel laws, related by a member of the Libel Committee of the Publishers' Association. He offers five measures that would provide a fairer basis for the publisher's accountability in libel cases: (1) damages and costs should be awarded separately against multiple defendants, reflecting the degree of responsibility; (2) "malice" should be precisely defined; (3) a greater margin of freedom should be given to creative works than to works purporting to state facts; (4) where an "innocent" libel has occurred the publisher should be entitled to the procedure of offering amends; and (5) authors and publishers would be protected against ill-founded claims.

Kimbrell, Edward M. *The Staging of the News.* Columbia, Mo., Freedom of Information Center, School of Journalism, University of Missouri at Columbia, 1970. 5p. (Report no. 249) **1K128**
Staging of the news by the media has opened the door to legislation codifying the boundaries of coverage, which, if enacted, may be declared unconstitutional.

———. *The Trumpets of Government.* Columbia, Mo., Freedom of Information Center, School of Journalism, University of Missouri at Columbia, 1969. 7p. (Report no. 231) **1K129**
An analysis of the growing government-publicity activities, including the so-called "indirect" forum which employ questionable public relations practices to influence public opinion.

Kindelan, Gilbert E. *A Study of United States Government Controls on Combat News from Vietnam: January 1, 1962, through January 1, 1967.* University Park, Pa., Pennsylvania State University, 1968. 138p. (Unpublished Master's thesis) **1K130**
"The U.S. Government's information policy in Vietnam has been severely questioned by journalists and critics of the administration. This thesis investigated the policy as it existed during the period January 1, 1962, through January 1, 1967. The purpose was to study to what extent, if any, the U.S. Government controlled combat news from Vietnam, whether it practiced prepublication censorship or news management, whether such actions were necessary, and to what extent it helped or hindered news media in reporting war news from Vietnam."

King, A. C. "Copyright." In Melbourne University, *The Law and the Printer, the Publisher and the Journalist. The Collected Papers of a Seminar at Melbourne University on August 12, 1971.* Melbourne, Antony Whitlock, 1971, pp. 47–57. **1K131**
A survey of Australian copyright law (Copyright Act of 1968) as it concerns the printer, publisher, and the journalist, with special attention to protection of literary and artistic work. The author concludes with reference to a unique concept in Australian law (borrowed from the French) to protect an author's reputation and the integrity of his work even after he no longer holds copyright.

King, Cecil H. "News and Abuse." In Michael Rubinstein, *ed., Wicked, Wicked Libels,* London, Routledge & Kegan Paul, 1972, pp. 93–99. **1K132**
A newspaper publisher charges that British libel law during his lifetime has become increasingly restrictive in practice, making it more and more difficult to make any adverse criticism of anyone. Almost any criticism may be held to be defamatory and the damages are generally high. He also observes that the libel law is being used as a form of censorship. "If Dickens were to write his novels today he would be crippled with libel actions and injunctions. . . . The same is true of foreign authors from Dante to Proust. If they wrote in England today they would either have to water down their creative talent or alternatively maintain a discreet silence on the living and only base their characters on persons now dead. . . . It is now not the dead but the living about whom only good may be said."

King, Daniel P. "A Proposal for an Obscenity Ordinance." *Police*, 8(6):41–42, 1964. **1K133**
The article outlines methods for drawing up an ordinance that will be effective in combating obscenity with the least restriction on freedoms of speech and press.

King, Rory P. "The Continuing Erosion of the Libel Remedy Against the Press: 'An Evil Inseparable from the Good.'" *South Dakota Law Review*, 17:350–73, Spring 1972. **1K134**
"It is the purpose of this comment to probe the reaches of the constitutional privilege espoused in the *New York Times* line of cases by an analysis of the present and possible interpretations of those concepts."

"King Kong Was a Dirty Old Man." *Esquire*, 76:146–49, September 1971. **1K135**
An illustrated account of the censoring of the 1933 *King Kong* movie and the recent search for the censored frames.

Kingsley, Robert G. *An Historical Study of Cooperation Between Press and Bar Associations.* Columbia, Mo., University of Missouri at Columbia, 1967. 148p. (Unpublished Master's thesis) **1K136**
"This study traces efforts of cooperation between press and bar associations at the national level, from 1924 to present. The thread is followed through the only major joint effort, in the late 1930s, when the three prominent associations then in existence—American Bar Association, American Society of Newspaper Editors and American Newspaper Publishers Association—wrote a statement on handling trials and pretrial news. The enactment of Canon 35 by the bar at this time virtually rendered the agreement worthless."

———. *Press–Bar Cooperation.* Columbia, Mo., Freedom of Information Center, School of Journalism, University of Missouri at Columbia, 1967. 4p. (Report no. 184) **1K137**
"In the last few years, unilateral research projects have replaced joint action as the press and bar groups seek solutions to problems relating to the handling of pre-trial and during-trial news. At the state level, cooperation has resulted in a number of agreements which have served to lessen the tension between the professions of law and journalism."

Kinzie, Charles E. "Swastika at Hof-

stra." *Midstream; A National Jewish Review*, 18(5):21–27, May 1972. **1K138**
The Protestant chaplain at Hofstra University discusses the dilemma over civil liberties when the student newspaper carried a paid advertisement of the National Socialist White People's Party, and a student displayed the swastika in his dormitory window.

Kirk, Russell. "Librarians and 'Fahrenheit 451.' " *National Review*, 19:1124, 17 October 1967. **1K139**
A complaint against "librarian-bureaucrats" who dispose of gift books, generally those classified as conservative, "because of doctrinaire prejudice against the views of the authors." He cites, by way of example, his own gift to a village library. "Most librarians, of course, are sensible and fairly tolerant people. . . . But watch out for local ideologues and bigots. They can be the very people who hang up posters in praise of the Freedom to Read."

Kirkpatrick, Clayton. "Free and Fair." *Chicago Bar Record*, 50:139–43, December 1968. (Also in *Nieman Reports*, March 1969 and *Current*, June 1969) **1K140**
A newspaper editor urges a moratorium on the debate between editors and lawyers over free press–fair trial, and substituting it with a joint press and bar effort to improve the quality of justice in the overwhelming majority of cases in which publicity is not a factor.

Kirkpatrick, R. B. "The Right to Dissent in a Free Society." *Quill*, 57(10):20–23, October 1969. **1K141**
Beginning with an account of the trial of John Peter Zenger, the author traces legal high points in preserving the freedom for dissent in America.

Kirkpatrick, Robert G. "Collective Consciousness and Mass Hysteria: Collective Behavior and Anti-Pornography Crusades in Durkheimian Perspective." *Human Relations*, 28:63–84, February 1975. **1K142**
"The present paper is an attempt to develop a Durkheimian formulation of collective behavior, while trying to describe, explain and predict the relative intensity of two public obscenity crusades. . . . We conclude that it is not the content of a law which determines the severity of the community reaction to violation of it, but the style of the deviant who breaks the law and the public designation of that act. We have developed a collective behavior theory from Durkheim's *Division of Labor in Society* which predicts the severity of a collective outburst according to the degree to which the crime is publicly designated a flagrant threat to the collective consciousness."

———. *The Socio-Sexual Dialectics of Decency Crusades*. Austin, Tex., University of Texas, 1971. 391p. (Ph.D. dis-

sertation, University Microfilms, no. 72–19,619) **1K143**
"This dissertation is an analysis of the historical context of two social movements, a natural history of events of each movement as examples of collective behavior, and the ideology and social and psychological motivation of the participants in these two social movements—two anti-pornography movements, in two cities."

Kirsh, H. J. "Film Censorship: The Ontario Experience." *Ottawa Law Review*, 4:312–17, Summer 1970. **1K144**
The author concludes that film censorship in Canada, now exercised by provincial censorship boards, may not be within provincial legislative power. It is even questionable whether Parliament itself has power to restrict such freedom of discussion.

Kirtz, William. "For the Record: A Reporter's View of the Media-Bar Relationship." *New England Law Review*, 11:371–81, Spring 1976. **1K145**
The author considers some of the problems in the relationship between attorneys and the media, offering suggestions to lawyers how they can improve their relationships with reporters. Included is the reporter's understanding of "off the record" and "background information."

Kirvan, John J. "Rating the New Movie Ratings." *Catholic World*, 210:15–18, October 1969. **1K146**
The system provides "some final proof for the impossibility of devising a rating system, either voluntarily or legislatively, that is going to end up anywhere except in the land of the absurd." Practically, however, it is probably our best safeguard against even more gross vagaries of local police inspectors.

Kister, Kenneth F. "Educating Librarians in Intellectual Freedom." *Library Trends*, 19:159–68, July 1970. **1K147**
"The combined force of these relatively recent developments—verification and general acceptance of [Marjorie] Fiske's conclusions about self-censorship tendencies among librarians [F134], emergence of an articulate group of young librarians who apparently value principle above expediency, and recognition of the central position of intellectual freedom in the expanding world of librarianship—could result in more and better teaching of intellectual freedom in the library schools during the next several years if library educators are at all responsive to contemporary professional trends. From this perspective, the curricular innovations at Simmons, UCLA, USC, and Minnesota are clearly indicative of future trends in the teaching of intellectual freedom." Reference is made throughout to the study by Dorothy Bendix on Teaching the Concept of Intellectual Freedom.

———. *Social Issues and Library Prob-*

lems: *Case Studies in the Social Sciences*. New York, Bowker, 1968. 190p. **1K148**
A number of the case studies pose situations involving censorship vs. book selection: Case 2 concerns a reference question involving the library's books on racial superiority and/or inferiority; case 4 deals with the propriety of selecting books on parapsychology; case 8 presents a controversy over the display and distribution of birth control literature in the public library; case 9 relates to demands from the local press that certain "dirty books" be removed from the public library shelves; case 13 presents demands for the removal of works containing ideas or words offensive to racial minorities; and case 18 is a debate over the public libraries' responsibility in providing ideological balance in its collection.

———. "A Unique Course on Intellectual Freedom and Censorship." In Eric Moon, *ed.*, *Book Selection and Censorship in the Sixties*, New York, Bowker, 1969, pp. 395–415. **1K149**
With preliminary comments, the author presents the syllabus of a course on Intellectual Freedom and Censorship offered at Simmons Library School. The fifteen topics, representing as many as two-and-one-half-hour class sessions, are as follows: (1) historical background, (2) roots of modern concepts, (3) majority power and minority rights, (4) religious liberty, (5) freedom of speech, (6) freedom of the press, (7) loyalty and freedom of association, (8) academic freedom, (9) political freedom and censorship abroad, (10) conformity v. freedom in the modern world, (11) moral censorship, obscenity, and the law, (12) the nature of pornography and hard-core censors, (13) moral censorship and the visual media, (14) "violence" the new "obscenity," and (15) summing up: the librarian in a censorious world. Methods of teaching are suggested along with sample discussion questions and a reading list.

Kitchen, Laurence. "The Trial of Dr. Bowdler." In his *Three on Trial: An Experiment in Biography*. London, Pall Mall, 1959, pp. 61–114. Line drawings by Arthur Horner. **1K150**
Using the device of a hypothetical trial the author of this drama (originally produced for the BBC Third Programme) examines the character and work of Thomas Bowdler, who "has come to symbolize narrow puritanism which equates morality with prudery and haunts the theatre." Bowdler is best known for his surgery on the works of Shakespeare and the Bible, to remove objectionable passages and words, usually with sexual implications. The other two figures dramatized are Byron and Machiavelli.

[Kitchens, W. H.] "Broadcasting and the Right of Access to Public Forums:

Business Executives' Move for Vietnam Peace v. FCC." *Georgia Law Review*, 6:208–20, Fall 1971. **1K151**
The United States Court of Appeals for the District of Columbia reversed the decision of the FCC, ruling that an absolute refusal to broadcast editorial advertisements contravenes the First Amendment when the licensee accepts commercial messages. The author concludes that, despite problems for the FCC in implementing the holding, answers can be reached within the present scheme of broadcast regulations.

Kittross, John M., and Kenneth Harwood, *eds. Free & Fair (Courtroom Access and Fairness Doctrine)*. Philadelphia, Association of Professional Broadcasting Education, 1970. 202p. **1K152**
A collection of articles on access to courtrooms and legislatures by broadcast media and the application of the fairness doctrine, which have appeared in the *Journal of Broadcasting*.

Klassen, Albert D., Jr. "Connoisseur and Gatekeeper of the Erotic in Print: The Public Librarian." *Focus on Indiana Libraries*, 28:6–11, Spring 1974. **1K153**
A sociologist discusses the meaning of "obscenity" and "pornography" and considers a variety of problems which arise in connection with three kinds of sex-related literature—the factual, the philosophical, and the fictional. He concludes with four observations that relate to the librarian, both personally and professionally: (1) The more knowledge we have about human sexuality the better we are able to cope with the fear of it. (2) The employment of literature for the purpose of stirring human feelings in many areas (religion, politics, black power, as well as sex) is an ancient phenomenon. (3) Literature can be evaluated not only by literary standards but by its effectiveness in stirring feelings. (4) Victimless "crimes" are not sufficient grounds to impose restrictions on the constitutionally guaranteed liberty of expression, whether sexual or nonsexual in nature.

Klausler, Alfred P. *The Christian Encounters Censorship, Obscenity, and Sex*. St. Louis, Concordia, 1967. 104p.
1K154
A study of the problems of censorship, obscenity, pornography, freedom, and the church's role in relation to these matters.

Klement, Alice M. "Shaping the Contours of the Newsperson's Privilege." *DePaul Law Review*, 26:185–96, Fall 1976. **1K155**
Critical examination of *Gilbert v. Allied Chemical Corp.*, 411 F. Supp. 505 (E.D. Va. 1976).

Klempner, I. M. "The Concept of 'National Security' and Its Effect on Information Transfer." *Special Libraries*, 64:263–69, July 1973. **1K156**
"The application of the concept of 'national security' within Federal agencies has had profound and unforeseen effects on national information transfer capabilities, dissemination, and use. Examined is the evolving definition and interpretation of this concept as it is applied to the control of security-classified documents and as it manifests itself in Federal government employee attitudes toward the dissemination of nonsecurity classified documents. The role of the special librarian or information scientist, who often serves as an intermediary in the information transfer process, is also examined."

Kline, F. Gerald, and Paul H. Jess. "Perjudicial Publicity: Its Effect on Law School Mock Juries." *Journalism Quarterly*, 43:113–16, Spring 1966.
1K157
A controlled experiment in four mock jury trials at the University of Minnesota Law School measured the effect of prejudicial publicity on the deliberation of the juries and their ultimate verdict.

Kloman, William. "The Transmogrification of the Smothers Brothers." *Esquire*, 72:148–53, 160, 199, October 1969. **1K158**
An account of the cancellation of the Smothers Brothers Comedy Hour by Columbia Broadcasting System and the broader issue of that network's standards of taste and decency and censorship practices. The network's Program Practices Office in New York, the author reports, "regularly chopped the Smothers show to shreds—tampering, the brothers say, with seventy-five percent of the show's material over a two-year period."

Klos, Thornton A. *FCC Programming Regulations Since 1960*. Austin, Tex., University of Texas, 1973. 283p. (Ph.D. dissertation, University Microfilms, no. 73–26,032) **1K159**
"The significance of this study is that it pulls into focus the extent of proscribed programming that has grown in the last twelve years as a result of the 1960 Policy Statement [Network Programming Inquiry]. . . . If the trend indicated in this study continues toward more regulation, there is ample room to fear that whatever freedom is left for the broadcaster to offer programming which criticizes the government, the mores and ways of society, the icons and vested interests, the military, the courts, and even the FCC itself, will disappear entirely."

Klosik, Frank. "Prejudicial News Coverage and Locking Up the Jury." *Police*, 11:55–58, March–April 1967.
1K160
"If the newspapers cannot be kept from the jury, maybe the answer should be to keep the jury from the newspapers by making them prisoners of the court during the trial. . . . In reviewing both press and jury, the court has failed to check the source of the problem, the source of the adverse publicity. . . . [News] is supplied to the reporters by the prosecutors, the police, and the individual attorneys. . . . Only when the courts act against officers under their control, may a solution be found, albeit partial, to a problem of growing complexity."

Knappman, Edward W., *ed. Government & the Media in Conflict: 1970–74*. New York, Facts on File, 1974. 202p.
1K161
An examination of major government–media conflicts, 1970–74: Pentagon Papers and government security; Watergate; confidentiality and the courts; fairness and equal-time doctrines; and broadcast programming and ownership. Under each topic there is a summary of the news events followed by a selection of newspaper editorials reflecting the various points of view on the issue.

Kneeland, Abner. *An Oration Delivered July 4, 1826, Being the Semicenturial Anniversary of the Independence of the United States of America. . . .* New York, J. Finch, 1826. 34p. **1K162**
Nine years before his conviction for blasphemy by the Massachusetts Supreme Court, Kneeland, the pastor of the First Universalist Church of New York City, speaks of the liberties of Americans under the Constitution and Bill of Rights. "The freedom of the press, under a benign Providence, is the great bulwark of our civil as well as our religious liberties." Kneeland complains of newspaper editors who refuse to provide fair argumentation on both sides of a question for fear of offending their patrons. He calls for "at least one free press, where all matters of opinion, whether in relation to religion or politics shall be brought to the test of that precious gift of heaven—reason and common sense!"

———.] *Review of the Rev. S. K. Lothrop's Sermon, delivered in the Brattle Street Church on Sunday, June 17th, 1838*. Boston, 1838? **1K163**
A detailed critique of Lothrop's sermon attempting to justify Abner Kneeland's prosecution for blasphemy.

Knight, Alfred B. "The Sherman Act and News Gathering Agencies." *George Washington Law Review*, 14:461–79, April 1946. **1K164**
Comments on the U.S. Supreme Court decision in *Associated Press et al. v. United States* (1945), which treats the press associations as quasi-public agencies which justify their being regulated in the interest of First Amendment rights and the free flow of information.

Knight, Arthur. "Sex in Cinema, 1973." *Playboy*, 20(11):150–60+, Nov-

ember 1973. (A separate paperback edition of the article was issued by Playboy Press)   **1K165**
Beginning with an assessment of the effect of the U.S. Supreme Court 21 June obscenity rulings on soft and hard-core pornography in the movies, the author examines the sex movies of the year. Special attention is given to the reception of *Deep Throat* and *Last Tango in Paris*. "On balance, 1973 may have produced a bumper crop of films, but it was hardly a vintage year."

————. "Sex in Cinema, 1974." *Playboy*, 21(11):144–55+, November 1974. (A separate paperback edition of the article was issued by Playboy Press)   **1K166**
A double standard permeates our society "where a President mouthed sanctimonious platitudes in public and conducted expletive-ridden vendettas in private. Never before has an American President concerned himself so directly—and vocally—with morality in the media. . . . Nixon's 'stop-the-smut' lead was assiduously followed up by the Congress, the Supreme Court, the FBI, the Postal Service . . ." while erotic movies hit all-time records.

————. "Sex in Cinema, 1975." *Playboy*, 22(11):130–42+, November 1975.   **1K167**
The language of the movies "is more explicit than ever used to be heard in first-run movie-houses; but the sexual activity itself is more suggested than carried out before the camera. . . . As far as industry officialdom is concerned, apparently, you can talk about sex all you want to; just don't show it."

————. "Sex in Cinema—1976." *Playboy*, 23(11):144–55+, November 1976.   **1K168**
"There can be little doubt that 1976 will go down in the annals of cinema as the year in which movie companies exploited the peculiar links between sex and violence for all they were worth. As successful prosecutions of sexually oriented fare made the forthright approach to sex that was visible only five years ago in *Carnal Knowledge* increasingly problematical, film makers sought a safer, yet commercially sound means of heating up their product. Seemingly, they found it in rape, murder and mutilation."

————, and Hollis Alpert. "Sex in Cinema, 1969." *Playboy*, 16(11):168–81+, November 1969.   **1K169**
Pictures "have become by sex possessed and, considering those still in production, the end is nowhere in sight." A profusely illustrated review of erotic film production, 1969.

————. "Sex in Cinema, 1970." *Playboy*, 17(11):152–64+, November 1970. (A separate paperback edition of the article was issued by Playboy Press)   **1K170**

"Without question, as far as sex in cinema is concerned, 1970 has been the crucial year. The big studios, the independents and the underground alike have pushed their new freedom to the limits, always testing to see how much further they can go, largely ignoring the silent majority implacably building up on the right. Meanwhile, the push for national movie censorship continues to grow. . . . Will these pro-censorship forces succeed or will audiences grow tired of the sexual excesses in so many films and cause them to fail through lack of attendance? The pendulum has already begun its reverse swing—and it's bound to hit somebody." Commentary on "a year of erotic abandon," in the cinema with 107 photographs.

————. "Sex in Cinema, 1971." *Playboy*, 18(11):162–75+, November 1971. (A separate paperback edition of the article was issued by Playboy Press)   **1K171**
"Despite the renascent romanticism of 'Love Story,' the last barriers fall before a wave of totally explicit erotica and uncensored language." An illustrated review of sex film production for the year 1971.

————. "Sex in Cinema, 1972." *Playboy*, 19(11):158–71+, November 1972. (A separate paperback edition of the article was issued by Playboy Press)   **1K172**
This illustrated review of film production in 1972 considers in detail the operation of the film rating system particularly with respect to X-rated films. Special attention is given to the film, *Portnoy's Complaint*, which epitomizes what happened to sex on the screen in 1972. The authors note that while "the tides of sex are receding, the temperature of violence in our movies—and particularly of sick, sadistic violence—seems to be mounting." They also consider the development and status of low-budget porno films in relation to the production emanating from the established film industry.

Knight, Charles. *The Case of the Authors As Regards the Paper Duty.* London, n.p., 1851. 24p.   **1K173**
Opposition to the tax on paper from the standpoint of the author whose sale of books is restricted and whose profits are thereby curtailed. In attempting to use the tax to restrict cheap literature, it also operates against the best British literature and favors invasion of foreign copyrights.

[————.] *The Newspaper Stamp, and the Duty on Paper, Viewed in Relation to their Effects upon the Diffusion of Knowledge. By the Author of "The Results of Machinery."* London, C. Knight, 1836. 64p. **1K174**
"If the evils of the Stamp upon newspapers, and the evils of the excise duty upon paper, cannot be removed without an entire abolition of these taxes, the taxes ought to be abolished. . . . The time, we think, has arrived

when it will be no longer possible to resist the demand of the people for cheaper newspapers." Knight favored repeal of the paper duty and reduction of the newspaper tax to 1d.

————. *The Struggle of a Book against Excessive Taxation.* London, The Author [1850]. 15p.   **1K175**
The publisher of *The Penny Cyclopaedia* (Society for Diffusion of Useful Knowledge) complains that paper duties (3 half-pence per pound) have taken the profits out of producing inexpensive educational works and have prevented the reprinting of his cyclopaedia. The paper duties are a fatal enemy to the diffusion of knowledge in Britain.

[Knight, John S.] *The Press Is Free. The Principal and Concurring Opinions Making up the United States Supreme Court's Unanimous Decision Involving the Miami Herald of Contempt Charges and Defining the Rights of Newspapers and of Free Men under the Court.* [Miami, 1946.] 39p.   **1K176**
The U.S. Supreme Court overruled the Florida Supreme Court's judgment against the *Miami Herald* for publishing editorials and cartoons critical of the administration of justice in Dade County, Fla. The issue involved the right of a newspaper "to inform its readers of what is going on in the courts without fear that an annoyed judge would use his contempt power to silence the newspaper or its editor." Text of the offending matter is included, together with the decision of the Supreme Court.

————. *To Speak One's Mind.* Tucson, Ariz., University of Arizona Press, 1967. 15p. (John Peter Zenger Award Lectures)   **1K177**
The American press, despite the recent threats and blandishments of government has performed well. It has exposed public grafting, demanded that public business be transacted in the open, fought extravagance and waste in government, laid bare land frauds, and insisted on justice through the courts. In referring to the Nixon Administration's criticism of the press, the speaker notes that the government spent $425 million on public relations and information—more than the combined amount spent by the two news services, the three television networks, and the ten largest newspapers; and the press carried five times as much government news as news of its critics. The Nixon Administration "in trying to put itself in the best possible light . . . has resorted to distortions of fact and half-truths of history."

Knight, Robert P. *The Concept of Freedom of the Press in the Americas: An Exploratory Study.* Columbia, Mo., University of Missouri at Columbia, 1968.

511p. (Ph.D. dissertation, University Microfilms, no. 68–12,497)   **1K178**
"The purpose of the investigation was to explore the concept of freedom of the press, primarily as that concept is held by journalists and future journalists in the Americas. . . . The conclusions drawn from this study were that subtle regional distinctions appear to exist among journalists in the Americas as to their concepts of freedom of the press . . . and that any programs to promote press freedom should take these differences into account."

Knightley, Phillip. "Aldington's Enquiry Concerning T. E. Lawrence." *Texas Quarterly*, 16(4):98–105, Winter 1973.   **1K179**
An account of the campaign in England by the friends of T. E. Lawrence to suppress Richard Aldington's book, *Lawrence of Arabia*, which was an exposé of the Lawrence legend.

Knoll, Steve. "Fair or Foul? Can TV Call a Spade a Spade?" *New Republic*, 171(9):16–18, 31 August 1974.   **1K180**
"The Fairness Doctrine has nothing to do with the truth; it simply requires that if a broadcaster presents one side of what is deemed 'a controversial issue of public importance,' he must—at the same time or at some other time—present the other side. . . . Unhappily for the Fairness Doctrine, the truth is not always, or even usually, equi-distant from opposite poles." The article takes issue with the Federal Communications Commission's ruling against the National Broadcasting Company in the case of the network's documentary program on pensions and with the *Red Lion* decision of the U.S. Supreme Court (*Red Lion Broadcasting Co. v. FCC*, 1967) which upheld the fairness doctrine.

———. "When TV Was Offered the Pentagon Papers." *Columbia Journalism Review*, 10(6):46–48, March–April 1972.   **1K181**
"Had TV dared to break fresh disclosures after the [New York] *Times* was gagged, the offending network would have incurred not only the risks facing the *Times*—grand jury investigation and followup indictments—but also the possibility of investigations by the FCC and by TV's many enemies on Capitol Hill. License renewals might have been held up pending these investigations."

Knowlton, Charles. *History of the Recent Excitement in Ashfield*. Ashfield, Mass. [The Author], 1834. 24p.   **1K182**
Dr. Knowlton, physician of Ashfield, Mass., fellow of the Massachusetts Medical Society, and contributor to scholarly medical journals, became the first person in birth control history to be imprisoned for his opinions. This is Dr. Knowlton's own account of the persecution against him in Ashfield, Mass., for his agnostic views and his advocacy of birth control in the publication and sale of his booklet, *Fruits of Philosophy*. He was tried three times. In Taunton, Mass., he was fined; at Concord he was given a three-month jail sentence at hard labor; and in Greenfield there was a hung jury. Included in his account is a reprint of an article from the *Boston Investigator* for 19 April 1833 reporting on a public meeting in Pittsburgh, Pa., in protest of Dr. Knowlton's imprisonment. Other references to the Knowlton case appear in the 1968 edition of this bibliography (K165–66).

Knox, John. "Production of Obscene Play." *Journal of Criminal Law and Criminology*, 23:479–82, September–October 1932.   **1K183**
Re: *People v. Wendling, et al.* (258 N.Y. 451) involving a 1932 production of the play, *Frankie and Johnnie*, prosecuted under the New York obscenity law.

Knox, Robert L. "Anti-trust Exemptions for Newspapers: An Economic Analysis." *Law and the Social Order: Arizona State University Law Journal*, 1:3–22, 1971.   **1K184**
An examination of the economic basis for the Newspaper Preservation Act. The author finds that it is difficult to make an economic case for protection of the newspaper industry, "particularly when the antitrust authorities appear willing to allow newspapers to take advantage of scale economies in production and distribution by sanctioning joint-operation agreements for these purposes." The case must be made on sociopolitical grounds. The sanctioning of a form of quasi-monopoly organization defeats the major purpose of the Sherman Act.

Knudson, Rozanne. "*Catcher* in the Wrong." In Bill L. Turney, *ed.*, *Catcher in the Wrong: Iconoclasts in Education*. Itasca, Ill., Published for Phi Delta Kappa by F. E. Peacock, 1968, pp. 183–87.   **1K185**
Writing in the lingo of young Holden Caulfield in *The Catcher in the Rye*, an English teacher tells how she lost her first high school teaching job in a row over quoting a paragraph from the J. D. Salinger book.

———. "The Censor's Horoscope." *American Libraries*, 2:180–85, February 1971. Illustrated by Jan Zibas.   **1K186**
This salty satire on the censor suggests, under the various signs of the zodiac, such thoughts as: down with Gutenberg movement; ALA's links with Castro and the Weathermen; Panthers in periodicals; founding an Anthony Comstock Chair in the state university; no-knock inspection of library accession lists; textbook burning. Aquarius, understandably, has been dropped from the zodiac because of *Hair*.

———. "Excerpts from *A Censor's Rhetoric*." *R. Q.* (American Library Association), 10:209–11, Spring 1971.   **1K187**
A satire on an imaginary censor's handbook quoting euphemisms for the term "censorship" and recommending the use of redundancies, triteness, and ambiguity, and the avoidance of conventional logic.

———. "Knudson's Complaint." *American Libraries*, 1:776–78, September 1970.   **1K188**
A montage of complaints that a classroom teacher hears against the use of certain books—complaints from students, parents, and school administrators, generally relating to issues of sex, race, or communism.

———. "To Corrupt? To Ennoble? To Anything? The Impact of Reading As Described by School Librarians." *California School Libraries*, 38(2):9–12, January 1967.   **1K189**
Forty-nine school librarians attending a meeting were asked to respond "yes" or "no" to the question: "Do you believe that reading matter—books, periodicals, newspapers, etc.— causes behavior, that, for example, 'good' books cause 'good' behavior, that 'bad' books cause 'bad' behavior on the part of their readers?" There were forty-seven "yes" and two "no" answers; twenty-three "yeses" were qualified.

Koch, Charles H., Jr. "The Freedom of Information Act: Suggestions for Making Information Available to the Public." *Maryland Law Review* 32:189–225, 1972. (Also in U.S. Senate. Committee of the Judiciary. *Freedom of Information Act Source Book*, pp. 374–410)   **1K190**
"This article will seek out interpretations of the [Freedom of Information] Act which will transcend the needs of individual applicants and provide effective ways to open the government both to parties involved in its proceedings and to the electorate. In addition, the article will venture more ambitious revisions, less closely related to the present Act, which should implement the goals of a public information system."

Koenig, Robert. *Community Press Councils—II*. Columbia, Mo., Freedom of Information Center, School of Journalism, University of Missouri at Columbia, 1974. 9p. (Report no. 331)   **1K191**
"Experiments with press councils at the local level have earned mixed evaluations, yet proponents of the idea remain optimistic that these and similar bodies can play important roles in improving press–public relationships."

Kohlmeier, Louis M. "Obscenity: Testing the Supreme Court." *Wall*

Street Journal, 176:14, 9 November 1970. **1K192**

As the U.S. Supreme Court considers several obscenity cases, the author reviews the Court's record in the area of obscenity, noting that the future of grown men and women to decide what they read and see hangs in the balance. The real issue before the Burger Court is not really obscenity, but "whether the Court now and in the years ahead will stand sufficiently above politics and beyond the crowd to preserve its delicate role in balancing majoritarian power against private rights in all areas, including obscenity, crime, student disorder and racial injustice."

————. "Press Decision: The Joy Is Premature." *Wall Street Journal*, 178:6, 2 July 1971. **1K193**

The Pentagon Papers decision of the U.S. Supreme Court may have been of temporary significance since the opinion "said nothing about the value of a free press or an informed public to a democratic society. It said nothing about constitutional limits on presidential power, or about the historic clash between rights and powers."

————. "Restraining the Press: Sheppard Case Ruling Will Limit Access to Crime News." *Wall Street Journal*, 167:18, 15 June 1966. **1K194**

"When the Supreme Court threw out the conviction of Dr. Samuel H. Sheppard for murdering his pregnant wife, it entered a conviction against the American press. Newspapers, radio and television had so abused their First Amendment freedom that Dr. Sheppard had been denied a fair trial, the court ruled."

Kohn, Richard I. "Cable Television: To What Extent May the State Regulate?" *Los Angeles Bar Bulletin*, 49:513–16, 536–43, October 1974. **1K195**

"It is the object of this article to attempt to define the extent to which the state may regulate cable television, within the framework of the federal regulations." The author concludes that since the states' role in the relationship to FCC rules is often unclear, "it must be defined by a continual testing of the rules. The state must carve out its own authority to regulate cable television."

Kohn, William I. "State Tort Actions for Libel after *Gertz v. Robert Welch, Inc.*: Is the Balance of Interest Leaning in Favor of the News Media?" *Ohio State Law Journal*, 36:697–720, 1975. **1K196**

"This note will first outline the common law remedies for libel, using Ohio law as a typical example, and place special emphasis on culpability and damage considerations. Thereafter, decisions by the Supreme Court requiring first amendment consideration for actions in libel will be reviewed. The purpose of this note is to follow the Supreme Court's attempts to balance the state interest in protecting the reputation of private persons against the interest of the news media in protection from unconstitutional censorship."

Kondracke, Morton. "The CIA and 'Our Conspiracy.'" *MORE*, 5(5):10–12, May 1975. **1K197**

"The almost lockstep cooperation of the media with William Colby's 'national security' campaign in the submarine case suggests that the lessons of Vietnam and Watergate still need to be driven home to most editors and publishers."

Koning, Hans. "Did the Pentagon Papers Make Any Difference?" *Saturday Review*, 55(24):13–15, 10 June 1972. **1K198**

A year after the release of the Pentagon Papers, the author interviews the participants in the event. The war continues, and the government continues to deceive the people and pursue vigorously through investigation and the courts everyone who had any remote connection with letting the people know the truth.

Konvitz, Milton R. "Censorship." In *Encyclopaedia Britannica*, Chicago, Encyclopaedia Britannica, 1970, vol. 5, pp. 161–67. **1K199**

Following an historical account of censorship from the Greek and Roman civilizations through the Christian era, the article discusses the development of ideas of freedom of expression in Britain and the United States. He covers the following topics: obscenity, policing the comics, motion pictures, the stage, broadcasting, school textbooks, libraries, freedom of information about the government, birth control literature, postal censorship, libel, privacy, and censorship of criminal justice.

————, ed. *Bill of Rights Reader*. 5th ed., rev. Ithaca, N.Y., Cornell University Press, 1973. 748p. (First edition [K181] published in 1954) **1K200**

An expanded chapter on Freedom of Speech and Press includes text and commentary on cases dealing with fighting words, speech that is a threat, symbolic speech, freedom of anonymous publication (*Tally v. California*, 1960), and First Amendment rights of students (*Healy v. James*, 1972), and libel (*New York Times v. Sullivan*, 1964). The chapter on Prior Restraint and Censorship includes the cases of the Pentagon Papers (*New York Times Co. v. United States* and *United States v. Washington Post*, 1971). An expanded chapter on Obscenity and Censorship of Literature and the Arts includes recent cases on obscenity and the First Amendment, obscenity and minors, and obscenity and the right of privacy.

Koop, Theodore F. "The News Media: Fair Trial and Free Press." *Oklahoma Law Review*, 22:144–54, May 1969. **1K201**

"At this stage it is important to develop and continue state-by-state conversations between media and bar. Opposing viewpoints must not be allowed to harden. Any reasonable solution—even a partial solution—of the fair trial–free press problem is bound to be a compromise that can be freely accepted by all concerned. The common goal—improvement of the American judicial system—requires unfettered reporting by responsible newsmen."

Kops, John M. "The First Amendment and Advertising: The Effect of the 'Commercial Activity' Doctrine on the Media Regulation." *North Carolina Law Review*, 51:581–92, January 1973. **1K202**

Re: *Mitchell Family Planning, Inc. v. City of Royal Oak*, 335 F. Supp. 738 (E.D. Mich. 1972). The case involved billboard advertising of an abortion message.

Kornfeld, Leo. "New York's Highest Court Lifts Injunction of Dacey's 'How to Avoid Probate' Book." *Trusts & Estates*, 107:104–6, February 1968. **1K203**

"On December 29, 1967, the New York Court of Appeals with one dissent, reversed two lower courts in that state, and ruled that Norman F. Dacey was not engaged in an unauthorized practice of law in New York via sale of his book on probate avoidence and that the book may once again be placed on booksellers' bookcases for public sale."

Koschwitz, Hansjürgen. "The Case 'New York Times': The Pros and Cons of Freedom of the Press." *Gazette: International Journal for Mass Communications Studies*, 18:235–44, 1972. **1K204**

A discussion of the case of the Pentagon Papers and its implications for the future relationship between the press and the federal government. "The dispute waged beyond the *New York Times* controversy, essentially aimed at both a more liberal Government information policy and a clearer demarcation between state-secrets worthy of protection and the freedom of the press to inform and be informed." The author believes the dispute enhanced the image of the American press abroad and emphasized American "democracy's capacity for regeneration."

Kosinski, Jerzy. "Against Book Censorship." *Media & Methods*, 12:20–24, January 1976. **1K205**

The novelist whose book, *Being There*, was removed from a high school readings list at the demand of a group of parents, discusses the overall danger that school censorship of books poses and what educators can do when confronted by demands that a book be banned.

Kostelanetz, Richard. *The End of Intelligent Writing: Literary Politics in*

America. New York, Sheed & Ward, 1973. 480p.   **1K206**
"The argument of this book is that 'intelligent writing' might come to an end, not because such writing is no longer produced—quite the contrary is true—or that it is not read—also untrue—but because the channels of communication have become so clogged and corrupted." The New York literary mob (critics and publishers) operates to the detriment of an indigenous cultural pluralism. To break this hold on American letters the author calls for the creation of a second literary industry (new periodicals, alternative book publishing) different from the editorial–industrial complex, both in its devotion to better books and in its awareness of the cultural abysses that must be filled.

———. " 'Freedom of the Press.' " *American Pen*, 5(3):36–40, Late Summer 1973. (Also appears in slightly modified form in the mid-summer issue of *Newsletters, Beyond Baroque;* in *Humanist*, January–February 1974; in *Newsletter on Intellectual Freedom* [IFC-ALA], March 1974, and in *Index to Censorship*, Spring 1975)   **1K207**
Commentary on the essay, The Freedom of the Press, written by George Orwell in 1944 as an introduction to his political satire, *Animal Farm*. The essay was never published because it was critical of the subtle and voluntary censorship of British publishers, fearful of offending public opinion that was then favorable to the Soviet. Kostelanetz observes that the publishers' censorship may have been more for fear of colleague reaction if they were to publish a distinguished work that was presently unfashionable. "It is obvious that, as American publishing becomes more and more commercialized, good writing is progressively more difficult to get into public print, and talented newcomers have as much chance of cracking the editorial–industrial complex as an experimental rat his academic maze." He proposes a subsidized Open Literary Press that would operate similar to the Public Broadcasting Corporation. The author's ideas were more fully developed in his book, *The End of Intelligent Writing*.

Kosterman, Donald J. *Kaleidoscope: An Underground Newspaper and the Law*. Madison, Wis., University of Wisconsin, 1975. 226p. (Unpublished Master's thesis)   **1K208**
"This thesis takes a look at one particular Milwaukee underground paper, *Kaleidoscope*, and concentrates on its legal problems. . . . Vendors were denied permits to sell or were hassled by repeated arrests; editor John Kois was arrested twice on obscenity charges; and pressure in the form of a boycott was placed on the paper's publisher. What followed, and what

becomes the major concern of this thesis, were a series of lengthy court battles as well as numerous small legal incidents."

Kovner, Victor A. "Disturbing Trends in the Law of Defamation: A Publishing Attorney's Opinion." *Hastings Constitutional Law Quarterly*, 3:363–72, Spring 1976.   **1K209**
The author reviews the adverse implications of the principal defamation decisions of the courts affecting the press since the 1974 decision, *Gertz v. Robert Welch, Inc.* The recent trend away from *New York Times Co. v. Sullivan* (1964) is seen as ominous.

Kozyris, Ph. John. "Advertising Intrusion: Assault on the Senses, Trespass on the Mind—A Remedy through Separation." *Ohio State Law Journal*, 36:299–347, 1975.   **1K210**
"The fact that advertising at its best plays some useful role in our economy is no reason why advertising's more blatant excesses should not be regulated in the public interest. . . . Intrusive overcommercialization and the propagandizing of unwilling, essentially captive audiences is a tyranny that need not be endured provided that there is a will to take the simple basic step of separation. The proposed role which would require the media to take reasonable measures to segregate advertising from non-advertising matter would go a long way in protecting the public interest without unduly burdening the industry or the sponsors."

Kramer, Aaron J. "New Reflections on Fair Trial–Free Press: Sheppard v. Maxwell and the American Bar Association Proposals." *University of Illinois Law Forum*, 1966:1063–80, Winter 1967.   **1K211**
The author examines the two theories of the press—"absolute" and "balancing"—in coverage of criminal trials, and examines in detail the implications of *Sheppard v. Maxwell*, and the American Bar Association solutions to prejudicial publicity. He concludes that freedom of the press is not an absolute right that justifies the American judiciary to abdicate its obligation to protect defendants accused of major crimes. The American Bar Association statement does not go far enough since it does not place restrictions on the news media. He would require the news media to refrain from disseminating prejudicial information during the pretrial period.

Kramer, Daniel C. "The Right to Denounce Public Officials in England and the United States." *Journal of Public Law*, 17:78–102, 1968.   **1K212**
"It is clear that the individual who denounces or threatens public officials on this side of the Atlantic is on safer ground than his English counterpart. It will be the purpose of this paper to prove this particular point: that instances of abuse or intimidation of agents of the govern-

ment protected by the first amendment here would be the basis of civil or criminal liability in Britain. This will be followed by an explanation of why the American rules in this area are more libertarian and an assessment of the relative merits of these differing policies."

Kramer, Rita. "The Dirty Book Bit." *New York Times Magazine*, 9 June 1968, pp. 99–100+.   **1K213**
The effect of violence and pornography on children and the role of parents in "reconciling two seemingly contradictory needs a child has—the need for security and protection and the need for independence and privacy of thought and judgment." The quotation is taken from statement of Dr. Bernard L. New.

Kramer, Victor H., and David B. Weinberg. "Freedom of Information Act." *Georgetown Law Journal*, 63:49–67, October 1974.   **1K214**
An analysis of the twelve decisions of Chief Judge David Bazelon (District of Columbia circuit) involving interpretation of the Freedom of Information Act. The author believes Judge Bazelon "has had a vital impact in strengthening the FOIA as a tool for the concerned citizenry and has laid the groundwork for judicial interpretations that will preserve the high purpose the Act seeks to achieve."

Krasnow, Erwin G. "The Process of Broadcast Regulation." In Don R. Le Duc, *ed.*, *Issues in Broadcast Regulation*, Washington, D.C., Broadcast Education Association, 1974, pp. 5–9. **1K215**
The author emphasizes the human element in government regulation of communications, pointing out that we often speak of Federal Communications policy when we are really describing the views of a small group of FCC administrators at a particular period of time.

———, and Lawrence D. Longley. *The Politics of Broadcast Regulations*. New York, St. Martin's, 1973. 148p. **1K216**
"By focusing on the very real case histories of regulation—of FM broadcasting, of UHF television, of proposed limits on broadcast commercial time, and of license renewal politics—the authors have shown us how the regulatory process actually works, how it is influenced by political realities, and how decisions are really made"—from introduction by Newton Minow.

Krause, Kristin. "Pornography or Literature." *Southeastern Librarian*, 20:141–46, Fall 1970.   **1K217**
A consideration of the assessment of "high pornography" by public librarians—works that tolerate obscene four-letter words, that contain explicit description of manifold sexual activity, and treat unnatural sexual themes, but are sold across the counter and reviewed by serious book critics. The author conducted a study of the critical reviewing of ten such works to determine whether the review had

"set forth the theme and content of each book in terms specific and meaningful enough for a reader to decide if he wished to buy the book" and whether he had "argued his considered judgment of the book's worth in sufficient depth so that an estimate of the book's qualities could be made from the reviewer's judgment of it."

Krebs, A. V., Jr. "Love in California: Catholics and Four-Letter Words." *Commonweal*, 86:359–61, 16 June 1967. **1K218**
Catholic overtones in the obscenity trial involving *The Love Book* by Lenore Kandel, which "opened a pandora's box within the Catholic community."

Krieghbaum, Hillier. "Government–Media Conflict; Presidential Relations." *Saturday Review*, 51(28):59–60, 13 July 1968. **1K219**
Following a brief history of news management in the federal government, the author refers to three recent developments: (1) the passage of the Freedom of Information Act, (2) the adoption by the American Bar Association of recommendations of the Reardon Report to curb press coverage of trials, and (3) the critique of news coverage of the 1967 riots in the report of the National Advisory Commission on Civil Disorders.

———. "The 'Op-Ed' Page Revisited." *Saturday Review*, 54(46):91–93, 13 November 1971. **1K220**
An old newspaper idea of giving space to opposition commentary (opposite the editorial page, i.e. "op-ed") has been revived in response to rising criticism of the press for ignoring minority views.

———. *Pressures on the Press*. New York, Crowell, 1972. 248p. **1K221**
An account of the rising tide of criticism of the press from government, pressure groups, and the general public. Chapters deal with The Nixon Administration and the Media; Freedom—and Responsibility—for Media; Pressure Points for Managing the News; Mass Media as Big Business; The Threat of One-Newspaper Towns; The Impact of Pressure Groups; and Right of Privacy Versus Publicity for Profit. The final chapter discusses the use of the press council and other forms of media review boards as a means of keeping the media's conscience.

Krislov, Samuel. "From Ginzburg to Ginsberg: The Unhurried Children's Hour in Obscenity Legislation." *Supreme Court Review*, 1968:153–97, 1968. **1K222**
A broad review of the developing legal concepts on obscenity as established by the U.S. Supreme Court. The author analyzes the decisions of *Ginzburg v. United States* (1964), which introduced the concept of pandering; the case of *Ginsberg v. New York* (1968), which intro-

duced the concept of "variable obscenity," i.e. drawing a distinction between children and adults; and the case of *Interstate Circuit, Inc. v. City of Dallas* (1968), involving a classification board to determine what materials were unsuitable for sale to minors. According to the author, the Court has outflanked the issue of morality by employing the concept of pandering; control of youthful access is another flank attack. "By thus controlling the most objectionable aspects of obscenity, the Court undoubtedly hopes to minimize the pressures for censorship with respect to adults." He concludes that "of all possible applications of variable obscenity, juvenile control promises the fewest problems with the most gain."

———. *The Supreme Court and Political Freedom*. New York, Free Press, 1968. 239p. **1K223**
A consideration of the changing role of the U.S. Supreme Court in the political process and in its support of First Amendment freedom, followed by examination of specific issues and dilemmas. These are discussed under the headings: (1) limitation of time and space, (2) regulation of content, (3) the competing value of law and order (and privacy), and (4) federal standards and state action.

Kriss, Ronald P. "The Anemic First Amendment." *Saturday Review*, 55(43): 28, 21 October 1972. **1K224**
Need for Congressional action to grant newsmen at least limited immunity in disclosing news sources.

———. "The National News Council at Age One." *Columbia Journalism Review*, 13(4):31–38, November–December 1974. **1K225**
The National News Council, patterned after the British Press Council, to monitor complaints against the news media, "made no major blunders, and few minor ones. All told, it fielded some 250 complaints, handling a number of them with considerable deftness." Public unawareness of its existence and lack of concern seem to be its major problem.

Kristol, Irving. "Pornography, Obscenity and the Case for Censorship." In his *On the Democratic Idea in America*, New York, Harper & Row, 1972, pp. 31–47. (Also appears under various titles in *New York Times Magazine*, 28 March 1971; *Quadrant*, September–December 1973; *Newsletter on Intellectual Freedom* [IFO-ALA], September 1971; David Holbrook, *ed.*, *The Case Against Pornography*, pp. 187–94; Victor B. Cline, *ed.*, *Where Do You Draw the Line?* pp. 45–55; and in condensed form in *Catholic Digest*, August 1971) **1K226**
The author argues for enlightened and liberal censorship of pornography and obscenity as a means to a better quality of life. While difficult, it is possible to regulate harmful excesses

in these areas without ending up with censoring political opinions. He subscribes to a liberal view of enforcing obscenity laws; while making obscenity illegal, he would allow it to be available "under the counter" as it has been for centuries for those who want to make a strenuous effort to get it. "I think the settlement we are living under now, in which obscenity and democracy are regarded as equals, is wrong; I believe it is inherently unstable; I think it will, in the long run, be incompatible with any authentic concern for the quality of life in our democracy." Eli M. Oboler responds to Kristol in an article entitled The Case Against Liberal Censorship in the January 1972 issue of *Newsletter on Intellectual Freedom* (IFO-ALA).

Kritzer, Paul E. "Copyright Protection for Sports Broadcasts and the Public's Right of Access." *Idea: The Patent Trademark & Copyright Journal of Research & Education*, 15:385–404, Fall 1971. **1K227**
The paper considers two thrusts in American copyright law—the angry demand of citizens for access to see or hear sports events of paramount public interest on the commercial airwaves and the plea of sports promoters, who sell broadcast rights to their events, for protection against cable television.

Kroch, Arthur. "Mr. Kennedy's Management of the News." *Fortune*, 67:82, 901–2, March 1963. **1K228**
A veteran journalist charges that the Kennedy news management policy "has been enforced more cynically and boldly than by any previous administration in a period when the U.S. was not in war or without visible means of regression from the verge of war. In the form of *indirect but equally deliberate* action, the policy has been much more effective than direct action in coloring the several facets of public information, because it has been employed with subtlety and imagination for which there is no historic parallel known to me." For any degree to which this public relations job is successful the principal onus rests on the purveyors of the news, the press itself.

Kroll, Paul W. *Agnew Versus the Media; A Symbolic Confrontation on Constitutional Freedoms*. Northridge, Calif., California State University, 1975. 364p. (Unpublished Master's thesis) **1K229**
"This thesis analyzes the thrust of the reaction to Agnew's criticism of the press by leading authors who wrote political biographies of Agnew, three leading American newspapers, the views of editorial writers from other American dailies, the thoughts contained in the more important magazines and the stance of electronic media executives and commentators."

Kronenberger, Louis. *The Extraordinary Mr. Wilkes: His Life and Times*. Garden City, N.Y., Doubleday, 1974. 269p.   **1K230**
A biography of the celebrated John Wilkes, libertine, reformer, member of Parliament, Lord Mayor of London, but best known for his championship, early in life, of press freedom. For his political attacks (*North Briton*) and his risqué poem (*Essay on Woman*) he was brought to trial, expelled from Parliament, and imprisoned. The affair stirred public opinion on both sides. This biography of Wilkes, the first by an American, emphasizes the political and social events of the times.

Kropf, C. R. "Libel and Satire in the Eighteenth Century." *Eighteenth-Century Studies*, 8:153–68, Winter 1974/75.   **1K231**
The eighteenth century was a litigious age and pamphlets and newspapers record frequent cases of libel before the courts. Since the licensing law in England was allowed to lapse in 1694, libel was the chief form of control of the press. Two works on the law of libel—March (M176) and Sheppard (S323)—were available to eighteenth-century authors as guides through the legal thicket. Until the passage of the Fox Libel Act in 1792, a jury was limited to deciding whether or not a work had been published by the defendant; the court decided whether it was libelous. And "no judge ever ruled against the Crown." Despite these restrictions the eighteenth century was an age of satire and this was possible because of a legal loophole involving the use of innuendo. A defendant in a libel case involving satire could plead "the rule that held that an innuendo, of itself, could not be used to identify its referent." While libeling of government and its officials was a serious crime, the satirist had a relatively free hand with respect to an individual. "At the very least we may conclude that were it not for the legal tolerance of innuendo the eighteenth century could hardly have been known as the age of satire."

Krotter, Mark M. "The Censorship of Obscenity in British Columbia: Opinion and Practice." *University of British Columbia Law Review*, 5:123–63, June 1970. (Reprinted in *Canadian Communications Law Review*, 1971)   **1K232**
"In this article, the focus is on the main exercisers of censorship powers in British Columbia, emphasizing Vancouver. In order of treatment, these censors are the Chief License Inspector of the City of Vancouver, the Vancouver City Prosecutor, the Vancouver Post Office, Canadian Customs, the Canadian Broadcasting Corporation, and the British Columbia Film Censor. In treating each censor, I have first set out the legislation conferring his powers, second, his policies and views, and last, a brief critique of his office."

Krueger, Robert. "Proposition 16—The Hell You Say." *Los Angeles Bar Bulletin*, 42:39–44, November 1966.   **1K233**
Proposition 16 is the California initiative sponsored by CLEAN, Inc. to stamp out smut in California. The author describes the referendum as a "blundering, obviously unconstitutional, approach to the subject of speech regulation." He concludes that "somewhere H. L. Mencken is rolling his greasy cigar from one side of his mouth to the other and having a ghostly belly laugh on the good people of the State of California and their Proposition 16." The Proposition was defeated.

Krug, Judith F. "Censorship in School Libraries: National Overview." *Journal of Research and Development in Education*, 9(3):52–59, Spring 1976.   **1K234**
Watergate has become a catalyst in school library censorship. Disillusioned with their ability to exercise effective control over their national government, many persons across the nation have turned their attention and energies to local problems including schools and libraries. Many parents were shocked by what they found. They saw in the new curriculum and the materials that supported it a threat to their way of life. "There are new teaching philosophies, and the textbooks reflect these. Society, as a whole, is more open, and school and library materials reflect this in terms of new themes, formats, and styles of writing. Textbooks even have new descriptors: multicultural and multi-ethnic. The new materials resulted, in part, from the influence other pressure groups have been exerting not only on publishers but on administrators in Washington." The controversy in Kanawha County, W.Va. was one of the results of the confrontation of parents and educators. Similar, if less violent, versions of the episode occurred across the country and can be expected to continue. One of the consequences has been a demand for parent review of both curriculum and materials. On the other hand, pressures on the schools have come from civil rights and women's liberation proponents, objecting to alleged racism and sexism in textbooks. "Unfortunately, the censorship pressures today are being exerted by and on a fearful citizenry unable to cope with a complex and uncontrollable society. The pressures are focused on the soft underbelly of the republic, the school system, and through the school system the children on whom the next 200 years depend." Regardless of where or how the pressures for censorship begin, society loses every time they succeed. The author sees the current situation as a "golden opportunity" for libraries. "Perhaps the library's time has come—for libraries remain the only public institutions in the United States where materials representing all points of view are available. Libraries do not require attendance, nor point of view, nor required reading, nor even acceptance. . . . The library is still the one and only place where the dictates of the First Amendment can be fulfilled and where society may eventually express its confidence in itself."

———. "Censorship of Library Materials." *PMLA* (Publications of the Modern Language Association), 86:1042–48, October 1971.   **1K235**
The director of the Office for Intellectual Freedom, American Library Association, reports on the efforts of the ALA to combat censorship and what services it offers to individuals or institutions under attack. There follows the text of the Library Bill of Rights and the Program of Action in Support of the Library Bill of Rights.

[———.] ["Comments on the U.S. Supreme Court's Obscenity Decision."] *NBC Today Show*. 10 min. tape recording. Evanston, Ill., Radio–TV Reports, 1973.   **1K236**
Bob Hale of WMAQ–TV, Chicago, interviews Judith Krug, director of the Office of Intellectual Freedom, American Library Association, on the implications to libraries of the 21 June 1973 obscenity decisions of the U.S. Supreme Court. The decisions, *Miller v. State of California* and four others, called for local community standards rather than national standards for judging obscenity. The Association had petitioned for a rehearing of the cases.

———. "The Curse of Interesting Times." *PLA Bulletin* (Pennsylvania Library Association), 29:250–55, November 1974.   **1K237**
In the wake of Watergate and the attendant secrecy in government, the librarian has a special responsibility as "defender and promoter of the concept of intellectual freedom."

———. "Intellectual Freedom." In *The Bowker Annual of Library and Book Trade Information*, 1975, pp. 78–81.   **1K238**
A review of the work of the Intellectual Freedom Committee of the American Library Association during 1974 and the national and local issues and events that affected intellectual freedom. Special attention is given to the Freedom to Read Foundation, the California case, *Moore v. Younger*, and the school textbook case in Kanawha County, W.Va.

———. "Intellectual Freedom: Anatomy of a Concept." *Connecticut Libraries*, 12(3):9–12, Summer 1970.   **1K239**
"Intellectual freedom [in libraries] becomes meaningful only in relation to the tangible activities undertaken by librarians in performance of their duties: material selection, reference service, a public relations program, weeding. The main goal of every librarian is to provide a balanced and useful collection for his library. Through this resulting collection the principles of intellectual freedom will, or should be reflected." The author urges libraries to be institutionally neutral, although librarians as individuals may be politically and socially active. "Once an institution takes a side—ceases to be neutral—intellectual freedom is destroyed. Our job as librarians is to make all points of view concerning all ques-

tions and issues of our times easily accessible to all people."

———. "Intellectual Freedom: Freedom to Read Foundation." *American Libraries*, 1:336–37, April 1970. **1K240**
An account of the Freedom to Read Foundation and its purposes: to promote and protect freedom of speech and freedom of press; to promote the recognition and acceptance of libraries as the repositories of the world's accumulated wisdom and knowledge and the right of public access; to support the right of libraries to include in their collections any creative work which they may legally acquire; to supply legal counsel to libraries and librarians in defense of freedom of speech and press.

———. "Intellectual Freedom: The Struggle Continues." *NJEA Review* (New Jersey Education Association), 46:16–17, November 1972. (Reprinted in *Education Digest*, January 1973) **1K241**
"Censorship is increasing and the focal point, more often than not, is the public school—both curriculum and libraries." Pressures are exerted both in the areas of sex and politics. Students who are protected by censorship will have an inadequate education: they will not be encouraged to develop judgments and make their own decisions.

———. "Intellectual Freedom [Would-be Censors]." *ALA Bulletin*, 63:446–48, April 1969. **1K242**
A discussion of some measures that can be undertaken once the censor comes to visit the library. They include the use of forms to require the complainant to formalize his objections in writing, countering of petitions of would-be censors, and letter-writing campaigns. Reproduced is the complaint form developed by the Missouri Library Association, entitled A Citizen's Request for Reconsideration of Library Material. Reference is also made to an analysis of local obscenity laws, to be assured that libraries are exempt. An exemption clause, developed by the Minnesota Library Association, is quoted.

———. "Professionals Polled on Pornography, Violence, Censorship." *Kansas Library Bulletin*, 38(3):23–25, Fall 1969. **1K243**
"Most psychiatrists and psychologists who have experience working with patients have found no cases in which exposure to pornography has caused antisocial behavior. This is the conclusion of a research project of the Department of Psychiatry of the University of Chicago's Pritzker School of Medicine, following a poll on pornography, violence, and censorship. More than 3,400 professionals in the mental health field responded to the questionnaire." A statistical breakdown of answers in the poll is provided.

———. "Statement of the American Library Association Prepared for the Commission on Obscenity and Pornography, May 4, 1970." In *Newsletter on Intellectual Freedom* (IFC-ALA), July 1970, pp. 59–62. **1K244**
The statement affirms the Association's opposition to censorship and denies that the situation regarding obscenity and pornography is a grave one and requires legislative controls. The suppression of allegedly obscene materials, the statement notes, leads easily to the suppression of other kinds of ideas and dissenting opinions. It urges the Commission "not to recommend any further controls on the population's access to materials of any kind."

———, *ed.* "Intellectual Freedom." Column in *American Libraries* (formerly *ALA Bulletin*), February 1968–June 1972. (James A. Harvey, coeditor, May 1970–June 1972) **1K245**
The column, appearing in most of the monthly issues, reported on new developments in intellectual freedom of interest to librarians—court cases and pending legislation, library censorship episodes, activities of state intellectual freedom groups, and official statements and actions of the Association. The column also discussed such topics as insurance protection against intellectual freedom problems (February 1970), access to library user records (September, October, and December 1970), The Dogma of Absolute Truth (June 1971), restricted shelves (July–August 1971), bias and balance in library collections (February, March 1971, March 1972), and "sex" as a smokescreen to veil other bases for censorship (October 1971). From time to time advice was offered to librarians facing threats of censorship or loss of jobs. A number of the columns by guest contributors are separately listed in this bibliography.

Krug, Judith F., and Roger L. Funk. "Pressure Groups vs. Library." *Wisconsin Library Bulletin*, 69:66–68, March–April 1973. **1K246**
The article deals with the kinds of pressures exerted on public and school libraries from individuals and groups and how to respond. "The librarian's best defense is a strong offense: a materials selection statement, an established procedure for handling complaints, and an active public relations program."

———. "Q & A with the Supreme Court." *California Librarian*, 34:4–9, July 1973. **1K247**
A series of questions and answers designed to allow the U.S. Supreme Court to speak for itself in an attempt to clarify the issues in their 1973 decisions on obscenity which changed First Amendment law regarding works with sexual content.

Krug, Judith F., and James A. Harvey. "Intellectual Freedom and Librarianship." In *Encyclopedia of Library and Information Science*. Allen Kent, Harold Lancour, and Jay E. Dailey, *eds.* New

York, Dekker, 1974, vol. 12, pp. 169–85. (A revised version appears in American Library Association, *Intellectual Freedom Manual*, pp. xv–xxx) **1K248**
A review of the history, status, and future of intellectual freedom in libraries. The authors conclude that the American Library Association's "positions and programs provide one of the few gauges for measuring the profession's response to the problems of defining, promoting and defending the concept. ALA's gradually shifting position reflects the steady emergence of a philosophy from among the entire library community."

———. "An Ox of a Different Color." *American Libraries*, 2:532–34, May 1971. **1K249**
A discussion of the double standard practiced by some librarians, illustrated by their willingness to remove *Little Black Sambo* from library shelves while resisting pressures to remove *Sylvester and the Magic Pebble*. The issue suggests a lack of understanding of the real meaning of intellectual freedom. "No matter how strong a librarian's personal commitment to a particular cause, it must not influence the decision to retain or remove materials from the library collection or intellectual freedom becomes merely a question of whose ox is being gored."

Kruger, Frederick. *Group Libel*. Columbia, Mo., Freedom of Information Center, School of Journalism, University of Missouri at Columbia, 1967. 12p. (Report no. 188) **1K250**
"There is now constant pressure on state and federal lawmakers to enact group libel legislation to enable groups or members of groups to bring action against professional hate-mongers and other defamers and inflamers. That such laws, admittedly a restraint on freedom of speech, may be constitutional if carefully drafted has already been established by the United States Supreme Court. It is the purpose of this monograph . . . to set forth the background, existing law, and implications for the immediate future of group libel protection vis à vis freedom of speech and press."

Kruger, J. J. "The Publications Control Board: The Rules by Which It Works." *South African Libraries*, 38:236–37, January 1971. **1K251**
The chairman of the Board describes the work of his organization which attempts to decide what books can be legally read in South Africa—"what is *bona fide* and what is *mala fide*." He declares that "this unenviable function is exercised in an enlightened manner within the compass of the provisions of the Act."

Kruse, James L. "FCC's Fairness Doc-

trine in Operation." *Buffalo Law Review*, 20:663–89, Spring 1971. **1K252**
"The focus of this comment will be the nature of a licensee's obligation to provide fair broadcasting of controversial issues under the fairness doctrine. The question will require an inquiry into the general powers and limitations of the FCC under the Communications Act of 1934, the development of the so-called 'fairness doctrine' in the broadcast industry, and the relation of its most recent formulation to the first amendment and the possibility of granting access rights to the airwaves."

Kruse, Karyn. *Censored! The Story of Book Censorship in the United States*. Madison, Wis., The Author, 1974. Ninety color slides with taped dialogue and fourteen-page script. **1K253**
A popular cartoon presentation, from the adoption of the First Amendment to the 1973 obscenity decision of the U.S. Supreme Court with numerous examples of cases of censorship.

Kruse, M. Russell, Jr. "From Logan Valley Plaza to Hyde Park and Back: Shopping Centers and Free Speech." *Southwestern University Law Review*, 26:569–88, August 1972. **1K254**
"This Comment will first examine traditional and fundamental property notions and then explore the constitutional impact of free speech upon those notions." Re: *Lloyd Corp. v. Tanner* (1972) and earlier cases.

Krutch, Joseph W. "Governmental Attempts to Regulate the Stage After the Jeremy Collier Controversy." *Publications of the Modern Language Association*, 38:153–74, March 1923. **1K255**
The study attempts to show the relationship between Jeremy Collier's attacks on Restoration drama and the subsequent reform of the stage in the direction of propriety and dullness. The author concludes that the situation is complex and that, while the tendency toward reform was present before Collier wrote, he was the most effective mouthpiece for the reformers. "He formulated the argument which was the result of the opinion of his time, and he led the people where they were ready to go. Without him Restoration comedy would inevitably have died, but he hastened its death."

Kubin, Karen J. "The Antitrust Implications of Network Television Programming." *Hastings Law Journal*, 27:1207–29, May 1976. **1K256**
"It is the purpose of this note to examine the challenged network practice against the framework of the antitrust laws to explore the applicability of the antitrust laws to television

as a regulated industry, and to assess the possible outcome of the suits on the merits."

Kuczun, Sam. "Times Rule Extended to Public Issues and Matters." *Journalism Quarterly*, 48:748–50, Winter 1971. **1K257**
Re: *Rosenbloom v. Metromedia, Inc.*, 403 U.S. 29 (1971) which extended the limitations of state libel law covering private individuals involved in events of public interest.

Kuh, Richard H. "Censorship *with* Freedom of Expression." In Harry M. Clor, *ed., Censorship and Freedom of Expression*, Chicago, Rand McNally, 1971, pp. 131–46. **1K258**
The author argues that a little censorship is not inconsistent in a democracy, but that the laws need to be unambiguous. "By combining . . . lucid and law-enforced censorship *with* free expression, and limiting the censorship to those areas in which pornography is most exacerbating, the law would strip extremists *on both sides* of their most strident claims. The vigilantes would find that their solicitousness for the young and for our public sensibilities had been catered to. The libertarians would find adults free to read anything privately and to see almost anything publicly, the expression of unpopular ideas remaining wholly unimpeded." The author proposes specific antiobscenity legislation that would deal with the protection of children, would prohibit public displays of sexual materials, and, where adults were concerned, would be so specific in proscribing hard-core pornography as to eliminate subjective judgment of the courts.

———. "Obscenity, Censorship, and the Nondoctrinaire Liberal." *Wilson Library Bulletin*, 42:902–9, May 1968. **1K259**
Is censorship—any antiobscenity legislation—inconsistent with the liberal mind? Perhaps not to the doctrinaire "liberal" to whom the Bill of Rights transcends all other issues in society, but it is consistent to the true liberal who can support censorship in three areas: (1) sale of offensive matter to children, (2) public display of offensive matter, and (3) adult viewing of hard-core pornography, coupled with restrictions on the tasteless public huckstering of borderline items—a pandering standard. The author suggests legislation that would support such a "thinking man's censorship."

———. "A Plan to Keep Pornography Away from Children." *Ladies' Home Journal*, 85:70, September 1968. **1K260**
The author suggests four well-defined features of a good obscenity statute: (1) The law should concentrate on *sales* to children rather than possession in homes, schools, and libraries. (2) The law should specify the age when minors would no longer be forbidden to buy what they please. (3) The law should include precise definition of what cannot be sold to minors. (4) Mail-order shippers should be compelled to label their packages.

———. "A Rational Approach to Pornography Legislation." *Brooklyn Law Review*, 37:354–64, Winter 1971. **1K261**
This discussion of pornography and the law's efforts to contain it focuses on three aspects of antipornography legislation: (1) a consideration of aspects of the pornography controversy that are unique to this particular area of criminal justice, (2) a suggestion as to our appropriate congressional approach to pornography—the main concern of the article, and (3) comment on legislation presently before Congress.

Kuhle, Roger. *Counter Advertising: Boon or Bogey?* Columbia, Mo., Freedom of Information Center, School of Journalism, University of Missouri at Columbia, 1973. 6p. (Report no. 302) **1K262**
"Should something like the 'Fairness Doctrine' be applied to advertising? Advocates of counter advertising think so; but many others think any such application would destroy much of broadcasting as it exists today. This report puts the arguments into perspective."

Kuhn, Harold B. "Right to Leer." *Christianity Today*, 21:89–90, 5 November 1976. **1K263**
The author notes the change taking place among liberal religion editors who had previously opposed censorship of pornography as ineffective and dangerous, preferring to "let such material die of its own shallowness." But when it did not die but rather flourished and expanded, editors were giving second thoughts to the need for some controls to explicit depiction of sexual activities on the screen and in books.

Kumar, Girja. "Book Censorship in India." *Mainstream*, 6(25):29–30, 17 February 1968. **1K264**
While there may be some ground for restricting the sale of obscene books on moral grounds, there is little justification for banning books on political, social, or ethical grounds. Few books have been banned under the Indian Penal Code, but rather through the more subtle device of the Sea Customs Act. While the government doesn't maintain a list of banned books, the author notes some of the books confiscated by Customs in recent years. These include all imports from China and North Korea.

[Kunz, David F.] "Obscenity Standards." *Albany Law Review*, 31:143–52, January 1967. **1K265**
With the conflicting obscenity decisions of *Memoirs v. Massachusetts*, *Ginzburg v. United States*, and *Mishkin v. State of New York*, the U.S. Supreme Court in 1966 further confused the issue of obscenity. "The case approach adopted by the Court allegedly enables it to balance the conflicting interest of censorship and freedom of expression, but it has the disadvantage of establishing the Supreme Court as a supreme censor board."

Kuper, Leo. "A Matter of Surrogate Censorship." In his *Race, Class and Power*. London, Duckworth, 1974, pp. 289–314. (Also reported in *Index on Censorship*, Autumn 1975) **1K266**
The case of the exclusion of the author's chapter on African nationalism from the South African edition of volume II of the *Oxford History of South Africa*. "The censorship was imposed by the Clarendon Press and the editors of the *History* so as to comply with the South African Suppression of Communism Act." The action was taken against the wishes of the author.

Kuper, Theodore F. "Jefferson and the Freedom to Print." *Thistle*, 13:85–92, September 1969. **1K267**
Mostly about the 1931 dedication of the Monticello Free Press shrine. The author was at that time national director of the Thomas Jefferson Memorial Foundation.

Kupperstein, Lenore R. "The Role of Pornography in the Etiology of Juvenile Delinquency: Review of the Research Literature." *Technical Report of the [U.S.] Commission on Obscenity and Pornography*, 1:103–11, 1971. **1K268**
"This paper reviews some of the voluminous professional theoretical and research literature on delinquency in order to answer the question: What do the major empirically based studies of juvenile delinquency have to say about the relationship between pornography and delinquency?"

———, and W. Cody Wilson. "Erotica and Antisocial Behavior: An Analysis of Selected Social Indicator Statistics." *Technical Report of the [U.S.] Commission on Obscenity and Pornography*, 7:311–23, 1971. **1K269**
"This paper will focus on . . . the assertion that the heightened availability of erotica during the past decade has been accompanied by a parallel rise in the rates of juvenile delinquency and crime, especially sex crimes. The general strategy will be to examine social indicator statistics for the past decade in order to determine whether there is a correlation between indices of availability of erotica and indices of sex crimes and illegitimacy."

[Kurland, Philip B.] "The Supreme Court, 1963 Term: Freedom of Speech and Association." *Harvard Law Review*, 78:201–5, 207–11, November 1964. **1K270**
Under the heading Privilege to Criticize Public Officials, the survey considers the case of *New York Times v. Sullivan;* under State Censorship of Obscenity, the cases of *Jacobellis v. Ohio* and *A Quantity of Copies of Books v. Kansas.*

———, ed. *Free Speech and Association: The Supreme Court and the First Amend-ment*. Chicago, University of Chicago Press, 1976. 444p. **1K271**
Content includes: The First Amendment Is An Absolute by Alexander Meiklejohn (M275). The New York Times Case: A Note on "The Central Meaning of the First Amendment" by Harry Kalven, Jr. (K15). The Concept of the Public Forum: Cox v. Louisiana by Harry Kalven, Jr. The Reasonable Man and the First Amendment: Hill, Butts, and Walker by Harry Kalven, Jr. Fifty Years of "Clear and Present Danger": From Schenck to Brandenburg—and Beyond by Frank R. Strong. Fora Americana: Speech in Public Places by Geoffrey R. Stone. Civility and the Restriction of Speech: Rediscovering the Defamation of Groups by Hadley Arkes.

Kurnit, Richard A. "Enforcing the Obligation to Present Controversial Issues: The Forgotten Half of the Fairness Doctrine." *Harvard Civil Rights-Civil Liberties Law Review*, 10:137–79, Winter 1975. **1K272**
"This Comment proposes that the active involvement of citizens' groups can provide the input into broadcasters' programming decisions which is necessary to enforce the obligation to broadcast controversial issues. Citizens' groups can perform this function supported by only a limited regulatory framework that does not significantly increase the potential censorial role of government."

Kurtz, Julia J. "Newspaper Reporter's Right to Attend a Trial." *Kentucky Law Journal*, 57:759–63, 1968–69. **1K273**
Comment on *Johnson v. Simpson*, 433 S.W.2d 644 (Ky. 1968) in which the circuit court held that a county judge may not condition a reporter's presence at the public trial of an adult on the reporter's agreement not to publish names of juveniles involved.

Kutner, Luis. "Freedom of Information: Due Process of the Right to Know." *Catholic Lawyer*, 18:50–66, Winter 1972. **1K274**
"A public demand for full disclosure of essential facts for public scrutiny is all important. Too often, military and diplomatic excuses tend to cover up bungling or failure. The American public is entitled to decide its own fate, and open and candid presentation of pertinent facts—within the bounds of national security—is essential to the process of freedom."

Kutschinsky, Berl. "The Effect of Easy Availability of Pornography on the Incidence of Sex Crimes: The Danish Experience." *Journal of Social Issues*, 29(3):163–81, 1973. **1K275**
The paper analyzes a statistical phenomenon—the drop in sex crimes in Denmark which followed the release of all censorship in that country. It attempts to present data from various sources in order to test alternative hypotheses regarding the meaning of the statis-

tics. One of the studies stimulated by the U.S. Commission on Obscenity and Pornography.

———. "The Effect of Pornography: A Pilot Experiment on Perception, Behavior, and Attitudes." *Technical Report of the [U.S.] Commission on Obscenity and Pornography*, 8:133–69, 1971. **1K276**
"This article is a report on an exploratory study of the immediate and short term effects of a one-hour exposure to hard-core pornography. The study was carried out in February 1970, in Copenhagen, as part of a series of investigations concerning pornography and sex crimes. . . . The subjects were 72 university students of both sexes, mostly married couples. . . . The purpose of this study was an exploratory one: to try out the usefulness of some questionnaires, a procedure, and a stimulus material to be used in subsequent studies of pornography and attitudes towards sex crimes."

———. "Pornography in Denmark: Pieces of a Jigsaw Puzzle Collected Around New Year 1970." *Technical Report of the [U.S.] Commission on Obscenity and Pornography*, 4:263–88, 1971. **1K277**
"This article is a report on an effort to gather information on the topic of pornography in Denmark. We have tried to answer questions such as: Who makes pornography, and what is the product like? Who sells it and who buys it? What do people in general think about pornography, and what was their reaction to the repeal of the ban? How much pornography is used, and what is it used for?"

———. "Towards an Explanation of the Decrease in Registered Sex Crimes in Copenhagen." *Technical Report of the [U.S.] Commission on Obscenity and Pornography*, 7:263–310, 1971. **1K278**
This is a study intended to explain the dramatic decrease in the number of offenders in four different types of sex crimes in Copenhagen since the repeal of laws relating to obscenity. "Concerning three of these types of crimes—exhibitionism, peeping, and (physical) indecency towards girls—it was possible, without restraint or ad hoc constructions, tentatively to explain this registered decrease as being due to the influence on either the victims or the potential offenders of one single factor, namely the development in the availability of pornography. . . . For two types of sex crimes—peeping and (physical) indecency towards girls—the analysis led to the tentative conclusion that the abundant availability of hard-core pornography in Denmark may have been the direct cause of a veritable decrease in the actual amount of crime committed."

Kutten, Joseph. "Radio Defamation —Libel or Slander." *Washington Uni-*

---

versity Law Quarterly, 23:262–70, February 1938. **1K279**
"The problem of radio defamation is one in which the elements of libel and slander are both present. It is the purpose of this note to determine whether or not radio defamation can unequivocally be held to be libel or slander." The author recommends that "the distinction between libel and slander be abolished and that the law of slander be assimilated to that of libel."

Kuttner, Bob. "Look Before You Leak." *MORE*, 6(3):6–7, March 1976. **1K280**
An account of Daniel Schorr's leak of the House Committee's report on the CIA to the *Village Voice*, and the subsequent suspension of the CBS newsman by the network. "Thus, CBS management—admittedly with an assist from the headstrong correspondent himself—has succeeded in doing what Richard Nixon was unable to do—get Dan Schorr off the air."

[Kutzschbach, George F.] "The Fairness Doctrine Requires Rebuttal to Air Pollution Policies Implicitly Espoused by Car and Gasoline Commercials." *Texas Law Review*, 50:500–509, March 1972. **1K281**
Re: *Friends of the Earth v. FCC*, 449 F.2d 1164 (D.C. Cir. 1971).

Kvapil, Charline R., and Louise S. Schellenberg. "The Right to Read." *Arizona English Bulletin*, 11:1–4, February 1969. **1K282**
Two members of Arizona's Right to Read, Inc. discuss that organization's work combating censorship in Arizona's schools.

L

Lacher, M. David. "The Freedom of Information Act Amendments of 1974: An Analysis." *Syracuse Law Review*, 26:951–93, Summer 1975. **1L1**

Lachman, Andrea S., Thomas B. Stoddard, and Max Von Hollwig. "First Amendment Rights." In *Annual Survey of American Law, 1976*. New York, New York University Law School, 1977, pp. 501–68. **1L2**
Includes sections on obscenity (pp. 521–41) and libel (pp. 541–68).

La Conte, Ronald T. *The Relationship Between Book Selection Practices and Certain Controversial Elements of Literature in Bergen County, New Jersey Public Senior High School English Departments*. New Brunswick, N.J., Rutgers—The State University, 1967. 202p. (Ed.D. dissertation, University Microfilms, no. 67–12,022) **1L3**
"It was the purpose of this study (1) to describe the book selection practices of certain English Departments in Bergen County, N.J. public high schools, (2) to investigate the relationship between these book selection practices and certain controversial elements of literature, and (3) to present the beliefs and opinions of the chairmen of these departments concerning controversial literature."

——. "Who Are the Real Censors?" *English Education*, 1:166–70, Spring 1970. (Condensed in *Education Digest*, October 1970) **1L4**
"Censorship can be practiced only by those who have the authority to censor," not the members of the community who protest, but "people in the school, or some other governmental agency, who either agree with these objectors or yield to their pressures."

Lacson, Arsenio H. "The Bell Case and Freedom of Speech and Freedom of Press." *Lawyers Journal* (Manila), 24:80–82, 31 March 1959. **1L5**
Criticism of the Garcia Administration in the Philippines by the mayor of Manila for the banning of James Bell, *Time-Life* correspondent, which the author charges is a violation of press freedom.

Lacy, Dan. "A Statement on H.R. 2223: The General Copyright Revision Bill." *Publishers' Weekly*, 208(21):25–27, 24 November 1975. **1L6**
A publisher discusses the doctrine of "fair use" and the provisions for it in the copyright bill before Congress. He takes issue with the demands of librarians and educators that restrictions on multiple copying and systematic copying be removed, believing that the doctrine of "fair use" as expressed in the bill is a generous one. He also recommends removal or modification of the manufacturing clause in the present copyright law which has given copyright protection to American authors only if their work was manufactured in the United States. He concludes: "It is distressing to hear copyright sometimes referred to as a restriction or barrier to the free flow of ideas and knowledge. On the contrary, the First Amendment and the Federal copyright law, both coming into effect in the same year—1791, are the twin pillars of free communication in this country, which have combined to give America the fullest and freest flow of ideas and knowledge the world has known."

——. "Suppression and Intellectual Freedom: Two Decisive Decades." *American Libraries*, 3:807–10, July–August 1972. **1L7**
In a festschrift essay for David H. Clift who retired after twenty years as executive director of the American Library Association, the author recounts the threats to intellectual freedom posed by McCarthyism and the fear of communism of the 1950s and the political censorship of the Nixon Administration. "Thanks to David Clift's leadership over the last twenty years and the encouragement he has given a vigorous Intellectual Freedom Committee, ALA is in a far stronger position, in organization and in commitment, to oppose oppression than it was in 1952."

Ladd, Bruce. *Crisis in Credibility*. New York, New American Library, 1968. 247p. **1L8**
The author analyzes the current secrecy, news management, and lying on the part of the United States government which has created a "crisis in credibility." To support his thesis he examines government statements and actions, including the United States occupation of the Dominican Republic and the role in Vietnam. The decline in government credibility began, according to the author, with the necessary censorship in World War II, continuing after the war in the name of national defense during the administrations of Truman, Eisenhower, Kennedy (except for a brief period), and reaching alarming proportions under President Johnson, whom the author considers "the most intensely secretive President in history."

Lader, Laurence, and Milton Meltzer. *Margaret Sanger: Pioneer of Birth Control*. New York, Crowell, 1969. 174p. **1L9**
A biography of the crusader for birth control, written for young readers.

Ladof, Nina S. "Censorship—the Tip and the Iceberg." *American Libraries*, 2:309–10, March 1971. **1L10**
A personal check of bookshops in the St. Louis area and elsewhere suggests that police harassment and fear of prosecution have prevented many booksellers from stocking certain works considered dangerous.

——. "The Dirty Word Smokescreen." *Library Journal*, 95:2424–26, July 1970. **1L11**
The story of the trial of four University of Missouri students for the sale of copies of an underground newspaper, *Free Press*, the champion of whose cause cost a Missouri librarian her job. "The dirty word controversy makes an ideal smokescreen for suppressing political and social ideas. Removing books with dirty words or offending pictures leads to caution on the part of the librarian. And caution can lead to self-censorship without any direct threat ever being made."

——. "Freedom to Read: A Battle-

field Report." *ALA Bulletin*, 63:903–5, July–August 1969. **1L12**
An account of the attack on the St. Charles (Mo.) County Library for subscribing to *Ramparts*, including a demand for labeling. After receiving legal advice which suggested the possibility of libel action, the library board issued a firm seven-point statement rejecting labeling.

———. "Intellectual Freedom, 1970." In *Bowker Annual Library and Book Trade Information*, *1971*. New York, Bowker, 1971, pp. 309–12. **1L13**
A chronology of events of the year including the release of the report of the U.S. Commission on Obscenity and Pornography, laws and court decisions, censorship efforts against libraries (including the case of *Sylvester and the Magic Pebble*), subpoenas against newsmen, and the intellectual freedom accomplishments of the American Library Association.

"Lady Chatterley in Ottawa." *Canadian Forum*, 42:11–13, April 1962. **1L14**
The case of the conviction of three Montreal newsdealers for selling *Lady Chatterley's Lover*. The Supreme Court of Canada reversed the lower court decision.

Lahey, John H. "Restrictions on Dissemination of Information in Criminal Trial." *Ohio State Law Journal*, 31:388–93, Spring 1970. **1L15**
Re: *Hamilton v. Municipal Court for the Berkeley–Albany Judicial District*, 76 Cal. Rptr. 168 (1969), which involved a court order restricting the dissemination of information concerning the trial of four demonstrators on the Berkeley campus.

Laird, Jean E. "Smut Peddlers: They Prey on the Youth of America." *Congressional Record*, 116:8830–31, 24 March 1970. (Reprinted from *VFW*, March 1970) **1L16**
Deals with the wave of pornography flooding the mails. The author states that everyone in America with a mailing address is on the pornographer's list and that 80 percent of the more than 100 million items of objectionable material mailed each year ends up in the hands of children.

Lambert, J. W. "Pornographers & Censors." *Encounter*, 30(3):55–57, March 1968. **1L17**
In a continuation of the dialogue beginning with a review of Pamela Johnson's *On Iniquity* (°J16), the author criticizes the views on pornography and censorship expressed by Ernest van den Haag in the December 1967 issue, which he terms "disguised authoritarianism." He discusses the British case of censorship of *Last Exit to Brooklyn*.

Lamont, John M. H. "Public Opinion Polls and Survey Evidence In Obscenity Cases." *Criminal Law Quarterly*, 15:135–59, February 1973. **1L18**
The paper outlines the development of the emerging Canadian law with respect to the tendering in evidence of public opinion polls and surveys in obscenity cases, some possible difficulties inherent in such evidence, and the judicial attitude toward it.

Lamotte, Charles. "An Appendix concerning Obscenity in Poetry and Painting." In his *An Essay upon Poetry and Painting, with Relation to the Sacred and Profane History*. . . . London, F. Fayram, 1730, pp. 184–202. (Reprinted by Garland, New York, 1970) **1L19**
An historical account of obscenity and lewdness in painting and poetry, which the author deplores. He includes not only the crude and filthy, but works of artistic and literary importance that are cleverly obscene—works of La Fontaine and Rousseau. He disagrees with William Law that the stage should be wholly suppressed, but suggests proper regulation to prevent such works as Farquhar's "loose compositions." The author is chaplain to the Duke of Montague.

Lampell, Millard, and Herbert Biberman. "Blacklisted." *Take One*, 1(5):10–15, June 1967. **1L20**
Hollywood blacklisting during the McCarthy era.

Lamson, Newton. "Aural Sex and the FCC." *MORE*, 3(6):5–6, June 1973. **1L21**
Controversy over the Federal Communications Commission's actions in the control of women's call-in programs dealing with sex-related subjects in a tasteless and vulgar manner.

Landau, Jack C. "Fair Trial and Free Press: A Due Process Proposed." *American Bar Association Journal*, 62:55–60, January 1976. **1L22**
"With restrictive orders being entered more frequently and with the news media tending to obey even the most unconstitutional orders on fear of contempt until an appellate court decision, the time has come to provide the public and the news media with due process rights to be heard and to appeal before the entry of orders restricting public access to the comment about criminal justice proceedings." The author's proposal is answered in an accompanying article by Judge Paul H. Roney.

———. "Harassing the Press." *MORE*, 2(12):8–9, December 1972. **1L23**
"In the following pages Jack C. Landau, who covers the U.S. Supreme Court for the Newhouse Newspapers and is a trustee of the Reporters Committee for Freedom of the Press, outlines the widening dimensions of the cen-

sorship trend nationwide and illustrates the unwillingness of most publishers and broadcasters to do much about it." He concludes with a case-by-case rundown on William T. Farr and many other reporters facing government harassment.

Landauer, Jerry. "Federal Secrecy." *Wall Street Journal*, 172:1, 28, 23 October 1968. **1L24**
Some federal agencies adhere to the Freedom of Information Act of 1967; others, including the Federal Trade Commission, are charged with improper restrictions.

Landers, Jim. "Court-Ordered Silence Aids Accused by Gagging Sources." *Editor & Publisher*, 105(14):24–25, 1 April 1972. **1L25**
Controversy over restriction of news coverage of a murder trial in Madison County, Ill.

Landis, Robert M. "Fair Trial and a Free Press." *Federal Rules Decisions*, 44:85–90, May 1968. **1L26**
In proceedings of the Thirtieth Annual Judicial Conference, Third Judicial Circuit of the United States, Atlantic City, N.J., 1967. Brief historic background and recent efforts of the organized bar to reach an accommodation in the objectives of the First, Sixth, and Fourteenth Amendments of the Constitution.

———. "Urges Keeping Alive Press-Bar Alliance." *Editor & Publisher*, 102(45):18, 20, 8 November 1969. **1L27**
An address by the chairman of the Bench-Bar-Press Committee of the Philadelphia Bar Association, made at a meeting of the Pennsylvania Newspaper Publishers Association.

Landis, Simon M. *The Prohibited Lecture! on Woodhull and Beecher, Analyzing Free-Love! By S. M. Landis, M.D. This is the Lecture that was advertised to be delivered at the Assembly Buildings, Phila., Sunday, April 13, 73, but Mayor Stokley, Threatened to arrest Dr. Landis should he deliver it. Everybody must know it must have been "very bad" to arouse him. Buy It, and Read It Quickly Before He Finds It Out.* Philadelphia, Published by the "Indignation League" [1873]. 18p., 14p. **1L28**
Landis, a controversial Philadelphia physician, pleads for sexual love for procreation only, denouncing free love ("free lust") as espoused by Victoria Woodhull in her weekly newspaper and in periodic lectures. Dr. Landis, likewise, denounces the preachings of Henry Ward Beecher for his secular views which could create false attitudes toward sex and lead to lust. He ignores Beecher's private sex life, which Mrs. Woodhull had denounced in her paper as hypocritical, but which Landis said should be left to the judgment of God. According to Landis, both Woodhull and Beecher had departed from the Scriptures in dealing with

sexual love. Landis combines his campaign for sexual purity with a Scripture-based plea for eating natural foods, avoiding meat, liquor, and drugs. Landis's book on sex education, *Secrets of Generation*, had sent him to prison three years earlier (L34). The present pamphlet is prefaced by an account of a citizens' indignation meeting held in Philadelphia on 22 April 1873, protesting the action of the mayor in suppressing free speech. Following the text of the speech are fourteen pages of advertisements for Dr. Landis's medical and sex education books, and for a patent device for use in Turkish baths.

Lane, George E., Jr. "The 'Public' Death of Civil Libel?" *Portia Law Journal*, 3:245–49, Spring 1968.   **1L29**
Comments on *New York Times v. Sullivan* (1964) and subsequent decisions on the libeling of public officials.

Lane, Roger F. *In Re Turner: A Study in Abuse of the Power of Contempt to Stifle Exposure of Wrongdoing by Bench and Bar*. East Lansing, Mich., Michigan State University, 1970. 114p. (Unpublished Master's thesis)   **1L30**
"The study analyzed a contempt of court charge brought against a small town newsmagazine publisher for out-of-court spoken and written criticism of the local court system. It considered the setting and nature of the alleged offenses, the constitutional theory and case law of contempt of court, the editor's trial and conviction, coverage and reaction within the Michigan news community and the reversal of the conviction on appeal. The end purpose was to test whether the citation was a reasonable and plausible act by the judge, consistent with proper historic use of the contempt power, or was clearly an abuse of judicial authority to stifle criticism. The author concludes that it was a gross abuse of judicial power."

Lane, S. [of Charing Cross]. *Food for the Head and None for the Body; or, the Newspaper Tax Taken Off*. Norwich, England, Walker, printers [1836?]. Broadside.   **1L31**
A page of doggerel on the occasion of the reduction of the newspaper tax in 1836, written by a wag who was unsympathetic to the press and would have preferred the tax removed from tobacco and food: "Oh blessed be the name of the Chancellor of Exchequer, / Why the deuce didn't he take the Tax off Tobacco [er] / What matters to a man that cannot tell B from A, / How much duty a nonsensical Newspaper pay."

Lang, Jovian P. "Do We Limit Children's Freedom to Read?" *Catholic Library World*, 46:125, October 1974.   **1L32**
The author raises questions about the efforts of children's librarians to eliminate sexism in children's literature. In their attempt to en-

courage portrayal of nonstereotyped sex roles in books for children, they may be wiping out "cultural and psychological differences between men and women as if they did not exist."

Lange, David L. "The Role of the Access Doctrine in the Regulation of the Mass Media: A Critical Review and Assessment." *North Carolina Law Review*, 52:1–91, November 1973.   **1L33**
"The net effect of the proposals for an enforceable right of access to the press will not be to increase effective public debate in a meaningful way. On the contrary, as a practical matter, access will be enforced only in those cases in which the discussion is relatively 'safe.' What we will get will not be diversity; we will only get a somewhat broadened spectrum of essentially mainstream thinking. We will hear both sides—but only both sides of the conventional wisdom. Meanwhile, real dissent—the serious disaffections, the genuine calls for revolution—will routinely be excluded from the press for reasons already embodied in the law: obscenity, 'clear and present danger' tests, and other similar grounds for preserving the established order intact."

————. "The Speech and Press Clauses." *UCLA Law Review*, 23:77–119, October 1975. Brief reply by M. B. Nimmer.   **1L34**
The author rejects the idea of the "duality" of the speech and press clauses of the First Amendment as suggested in an article by Melville B. Nimmer and a speech by Mr. Justice Stewart (*Hastings Law Journal*, January 1975). He bases his case on the evidence of history, common law, and the contemporary scene. "The goal of first amendment theory should be to equate and reconcile the interests of speech and press, rather than to separate them."

Langguth, Jack. "Doctor X." *Saturday Review: The Arts*, 55(49):6, 10–12, 2 December 1972.   **1L35**
Interviews with Dr. Aaron Stern, head of the rating board of the Motion Picture Association of America, and the author's unsuccessful efforts to sit in on a screening session.

Lanouette, William J., and Michael T. Malloy. "A Reporter's Jailing Sends Shock Waves Through Press." *National Observer*, 11(42):7, 14 October 1972.   **1L36**
"A New Jersey newspaper reporter named Peter Bridge went to jail in Newark last week amid debate and testimony on Capitol Hill on bills that would have shielded the reporter and all newsmen from such imprisonment."

Lansdale-Ruthven, Hugh P. *The Law of Libel for Journalists*. With a Foreword by R. D. Blumenfeld. London, Blandford, 1934. 208p.   **1L37**
Content: Construction of libels; persons libeled; publication; injurious falsehoods; de-

fenses; damages; practice in a civil action; criminal libel; blasphemous, obscene, and seditious libel; and contempt of court.

La Penta, Philip S. "Motion Picture Seizures and the Adversary Hearing: Settled Law or Fertile Ground for Change?" *American University Law Review*, 21:444–55, April 1972.   **1L38**
The article deals with procedural problems of search and seizure of obscene materials, particularly the question as to whether an adversary hearing is required prior to seizure of allegedly obscene films.

Lapham, Lewis. "The Temptation of a Sacred Cow." *Harper's*, 247:43–46+, August 1973.   **1L39**
The author debunks the romantic idea of a press as watchdog of democracy. "The real press must be understood as an institution, no more or less courageous than any other institution in the country. . . . The real press discovers injustice largely by accident. . . . The government and the press entertain inflated opinions of one another, and each flatters the other by exaggerating the importance of their mutual interests." The author objects to shield laws which would "encourage the press in its most cowardly instincts and so disembowel it." The more the press secrecy, the more the balance of power shifts in favor of bureaucracy. He objects to Congress legislating on First Amendment freedoms for what Congress can grant it also can take away. "The press grossly exaggerates its harassment and for the most part was frightened by its own editorials."

La Pota, Margherite E. "Seven Men Came for the English Teacher." *English Education*, 7:159–65, Spring 1976. **1L40**
A high school English teacher in Tulsa, Okla., describes the grand jury investigation of alleged misuse of school funds for purchase of obscene materials (no ground for an indictment was found); a countercharge from the other camp, accusing teachers of censoring books; and a campaign with notorized "documents" threatening teachers who failed to remove pupils from exposure to sex education and other objectionable subjects. She describes the constructive reaction on the part of the school and affirms that, despite the unpleasantness and sometimes ugliness in the parent-teacher confrontation, dissent is an essential part of the democratic process. The reference in the title is to the seven Russian policemen who came to arrest Alexander Solzhenitsyn.

————, **and Bruce P. La Pota.** "Textbook Censorship: Some Socio-Psycho-Political Implications." *Journal of Research and Development in Education*, 9(3):84–92, Spring 1976.   **1L41**
An examination of the textbook controversy in

West Virginia and elsewhere to consider the character of the participants, their motives, and the broad socio-psycho-political implications. Are the attacks on the schools merely a concern over "dirty books" and anti-Christian and anti-American materials, or do they represent a clash between two value systems, a challenge to the right of the professional educator to control the schools, efforts to thwart a Communist plot, or a manifestation of class warfare? Special attention is given to the controversy in Tulsa, Okla., where objection to "dirty books" resulted in a grand jury investigation of the schools for alleged misuse of funds. The jury found no ground for indictment, but the protesting group—Parents for Quality Education, benefitted by the publicity. Subsequently a Committee for Responsible Education circulated a document warning that school administrators and teachers utilizing materials offensive to them would be subject to prosecution. Text of the document is included.

Lardner, George, Jr., "The Battle of Watergate TV." In Robert O. Blanchard, *ed.*, *Congress and the News Media*, New York, Hastings House, 1974, pp. 460–64. (Reprinted from the *Washington Post*, 11 June 1973)   **1L42**
Commentary on the debate between Watergate prosecutor Archibald Cox and the Senate Watergate committee headed by Senator Sam Ervin, over the extent of television coverage of the affair.

Lardner, Ring, Jr. "My Life on the Blacklist." *Saturday Evening Post*, 234(4):38–44, 14 October 1961.   **1L43**
Deals with the blacklisting of the "Hollywood Ten," by one of them.

Large, Douglas B., and Kristopher Kallman. "Losing the Struggle to Define the Proper Balance Between the Law of Defamation and the First Amendment—Gertz v. Robert Welch, Inc.: One Step Forward, Two Steps Back." *Pepperdine Law Review*, 2:383–416, 1975.   **1L44**
"The objective of this comment is threefold: *first*, to examine from a historical perspective the nature of the coexistence between a free press and an individual's vindication for injury to reputation; *second*, to provide an analysis of the *Gertz* decision and dissent with an eye toward the extensive modification of the substantive law of defamation resulting from the Court's 'equitable balancing'; and *finally*, to offer a critical appraisal of the holding in *Gertz* in light of its abandonment of historical reason and precedent and failure to correctly weigh the opposing interests at stake."

Larry, Lionel C., and Harvey J. Kirsh.

"The Men with the Scissors." *Chitty's Law Journal*, 19:73–83, March 1971; 19:111–18, April 1971.   **1L45**
Content: History of Motion Picture Censorship and the Development of Boards in Canada. The Ontario Board of Censors. The Powers of the Board. Test Cases: *Ulysses*, *Woman in the Dunes*, and *High*. Concluding Alternatives—the Future of the Board. Further comments on the problem are given by S. B. Shah in the October 1971 issue.

Larsen, Otto N., *ed. Violence and the Mass Media*. New York, Harper & Row, 1968. 310p.   **1L46**
"Within this framework, there is specific material on the individual and social effects of media violence, on the history, scope, and character of violent content in mass communication, on methodological problems in studying effects, on the mechanisms of local and national protest that lead to control efforts, and on the nature and impact of various forms of censorship." Articles on regulation and control include: New Forms of Social Control Over Mass Media Content by John E. Twomey. The Greater Cincinnati Committee on Evaluation of Comic Books by Jesse L. Murrell. The Morality Seekers: A Study of Organized Film Criticism in the United States by Jack Schwartz. Crime Shows on TV—A Federal Crackdown Coming (*U.S. News & World Report*). Congressional Interrogation of the Creator of Horror Comics (U.S. Senate). A Public Commission on Mass Communication as an Alternative to Government Intervention by Harry S. Ashmore. New Movie Standards: General Film Code, Not Specific Bans by Louis Chapin. The Role of the Code Administrator and Applying the Comic Book Code (Comic Magazine Association of America). Censor and Sensibility: A Content Analysis of the Television Censor's Comments by Charles Winick.

Larson, Bruce L. *Lindbergh of Minnesota: A Political Biography*. New York, Harcourt Brace Jovanovich, 1973. 363p.   **1L47**
Account of the attacks and possible destruction of Charles A. Lindbergh, Sr.'s book, *Why Is Your Country at War*, on charges of disloyalty, appears on pages 211–12, 224, 229–35, and 252–53.

[Larson, Earl R.] "Homosexuality and Obscenity—An Unreported Court Opinion." *Censorship Today*, 2(1):12–17, February–March 1969.   **1L48**
The text of Justice Earl R. Larson's unreported decision in *United States v. Spinar and Germain*, U.S. District Court, District of Minnesota, Fourth Division. He found a number of homosexual pictorial magazines to be protected by the free speech and press provisions of the Constitution.

Larson, Milton R. "Free Press v. Fair Trial in Nebraska: A Position Paper."

Nebraska Law Review, 55:543–71, 1976.   **1L49**
The article explains why judicial restraint was imposed on the news media by a Nebraska district court in a murder trial—a decision reversed by the U.S. Supreme Court—and explores the problems facing a prosecutor in a sensational trial. The author concludes that "a narrow limitation on the press, confined to the shortest fixed period compatible with sound judicial determination, is a moderate price to pay for the preservation of justice and public confidence in the judicial system."

Laseter, Ernest P. "Texas and the 'Right to Read': The Ector County Case." *Texas Library Journal*, 52:4–5, January 1976.   **1L50**
A newspaper editor's demands to examine the circulation records of the Ector County Library under the Texas Open Records law led to an opinion from the Attorney General excepting these records from the law.

Lasher, Lawrence. *James Cheetham, Journalist and Muckracker*. College Park, Md., University of Maryland, 1965, 222p. (Ph.D. dissertation, University Microfilms, no. 66–930)   **1L51**
A biography of the editor of the Republican newspaper, *New York American Citizen*, whose vituperative articles against Aaron Burr, Thomas Paine, Maturin Livingston, and others within the ranks of the Republican Party, led to his conviction for libel. One conviction was for his *Life of Thomas Paine*, a scurrilous attack on the patriot in the year of his death (C295); another was for his attack on Maturin Livingston (C296).

Lashner, Marilyn A. "Privacy and the Public's Right to Know." *Journalism Quarterly*, 53:679–88, Winter 1976.   **1L52**
"As the states have continued to expand their definitions of privacy as a tort, the United States Superior Court, by using the doctrine of balancing, has cautiously embarked on a path limiting the use of the First Amendment as a complete defense of this relatively new tort, and as such has reversed the trend toward absolute press immunity which began [with *New York Times v. Sullivan*] in 1964."

Laski, Harold J. "Freedom of the Mind." In his *Liberty in the Modern State*. New York, Viking, 1949, pp. 72–128. (First published in 1930)   **1L53**
The author makes a case for freedom of thought and speech in a democracy. Those who exercise authority cannot be truly informed about the wants of the people, he argues, unless the mass of men are free to report their experience. While most people agree with the concept of freedom, they recoil from its implications, for it includes both "the right to sanctify the present social order, but the right also to condemn it with vigour and completeness. . . . The heresies we may suppress

today may be the orthodoxies of tomorrow." He discusses the issue of suppressing dangerous ideas in the areas of obscenity, blasphemy, and political subversion, concluding that unless we can show that a particular idea or conduct will destroy the will-power of those who practice it or will, unquestionably, injure the rest of society, government prohibition is an unwarranted interference with freedom.

Lasky, Michael S. "Libel." *Folio* (The Magazine for Magazine Management), 2:23–27. January 1973. **1L54**
Advice to magazine editors on how to avoid being sued for libel, compiled from the experience of many editors. Knowing the law (each state has its own) and careful "lawyerizing" every article before publication, is the best assurance of avoiding libel. He suggests a three-pronged test to use in detecting potential libel: Is the material defamatory to an identifiable individual or group? If it is, then, is the information privileged? If it is not, then, is it fundamentally true? And finally, "Would the target feel obligated to sue to demonstrate denial of the libel?"

Lasswell, Harold D. "The Library as a Social Planetarium." *American Libraries*, 1:142–43, February 1970. **1L55**
Following some personal observations of attacks on libraries, Professor Lasswell analyzes the bases of pressures for censorship. "When value norms and aspirations are perceived as threatened, value deprivations are sought to be imposed on the threatened." He concludes that "the library profession and the library institution can live up to their commitment to freedom of the mind by grasping the initiative, wherever possible, to supplement the historic role of print by integrating it more effectively in a social planetarium and in a center of continuing policy-seminars on the several choosing and deciding roles of society."

" 'Last Exit' Conviction Quashed." *Bookseller*, 3267:358–62, 3 August 1968. **1L56**
The text of the judgment of Lord Justice Salmon, reversing the conviction of Calder & Boyars, Ltd. for publishing "an obscene article" in the novel *Last Exit to Brooklyn* by Hubert Selby, Jr.

Latham, Frank B. *The Trial of John Peter Zenger, August 1735: An Early Fight for America's Freedom of the Press*. New York, Watts, 1970. 64p. (A Focus Book) **1L57**
An account of the Zenger trial, written for children and illustrated with contemporary prints.

Laturno, Gary M. "Freedom of the Press Versus Presidential Power." *Loyola Law Review* (New Orleans), 18:151–67, 1971–72. **1L58**
An analysis of the issues in the Pentagon Papers case. The author criticizes the U.S. Su-

preme Court for acting with undue haste and without obtaining all the facts. The case should have been remanded to the lower courts.

Laughlin, Michael J. "New Standards in Media Defamation Cases: Gertz v. Robert Welch, Inc." *California Western Law Review*, 12:172–90, Fall 1975. **1L59**
"The purpose of this Note is to examine *Gertz* in order to determine its effect on defamation law. The decision will first be given historical perspective, and then will be analyzed to ascertain what constitutionally acceptable standards may be adopted by the states."

Laughlin, Stanley K., Jr. "A Requiem for Requiems: The Supreme Court at the Bar of Reality." *Michigan Law Review*, 68:1389–1408, June 1970. **1L60**
A response to David Engdahl's Requiem for Roth (*Michigan Law Review*, December 1969). Professor Engdahl had suggested abandonment of the "incorporation" approach to the Fourteenth Amendment in favor of a return to a "substantive due process." "In my opinion, such dubious revisionism is neither a proper response to the obscenity problem nor at all called for at this critical juncture in American history."

Law, Ernestine B. *The Law of Libel and Public Officials in South Carolina*. Columbia, S.C., University of South Carolina, 1973. 116p. (Unpublished Master's thesis) **1L61**
An examination of the law of libel as it evolved in the United States from Colonial time up to the recent Supreme Court decision in *New York Times v. Sullivan* (1964), with special attention to political libel in South Carolina. Since few cases reach the state's highest court, evidence was gathered from questionnaires to newspapers and through interviews with the state's leading libel lawyers.

Law, Robert E. "Lloyd v. Tanner: Death of the Public Forum?" *University of San Francisco Law Review*, 7:582–95, April 1973. **1L62**
Re: *Lloyd Corp. v. Tanner* (1972). "The purpose of this case note is first to examine the similarities between shopping centers and central business districts in order to show why the shopping center is an appropriate forum for regulated first amendment activity. Second, the reasoning of the majority opinion in *Lloyd* will be examined and contrasted with the dissent's reasoning so that the case can be more easily understood. With this examination of opinions, it should be possible to accurately assess the impact of the decision on the citizen's ability to disseminate information to the public."

Law, Thomas, and Joseph Kramer. "The Reality of a Fair Trial in a Democratic Society." *Journal of Urban Law*, 47:399–426, 1969–70. **1L63**

"The American law should face up to the need to frame properly articulated and enforced legal controls over the acts of publication and broadcasting which are prejudicial to the conduct of a fair trial. . . . Nothing will be remedied by exhorting all parties involved to good behavior."

The Law of Libel, as Affecting the Newspaper Press, with Proposed Amendments. London, E. Marlborough, 1867. 71p. **1L64**
The work deals with libel cases arising from newspaper reports of public meetings, past efforts to amend the libel law to provide relief for the press and a current amendment proposed by Sir Colman O'Loghlin. Included are remarks of the *Times* and the *Leeds Mercury* on the claims of the press to immunity for reports of public proceedings.

"The Law of the Stage in Dublin." *Irish Law Times and Solicitors' Journal*, 43:209–10, 28 August 1909. **1L65**
Comparison of control of stage plays in England, where the Lord Chamberlain must approve each play, and in Ireland where control is achieved through government licensing of theaters.

"The Law Relating to Obscene Publications." *Irish Law Times and Solicitors' Journal*, 73:27–28, 21 January 1939. **1L66**
A detailed explanation of how the Censorship of Publications Board in Ireland operates under the Censorship of Publications Act of 1929 and a rebuttal of the criticism of Irish censorship contained in Alec Craig's *The Banned Books of England*.

Lawford, Hugh. "Privacy versus Freedom of Information." *Queen's Quarterly*, 78:365–71, Autumn 1971. **1L67**
In Canada "a single-minded concentration on regulating the computer's impact on privacy distracts us from the greater danger of the computer's threat to freedom of information. . . . If Great Britain, Sweden, and the United States have all been able to provide by law for rights of access to government documentation, Canada should be capable of making a similar provision to protect freedom of information."

Lawhorne, Clifton O. "Advertising Controls Shackle Free Discussion." *Grassroots Editor*, 14(1):31–32, January–February 1973. **1L68**
"Section 104 of the Federal Elections Campaign Act may be correcting political office-seeking abuses, but it also is placing restrictions on freedom of speech and the press."

———. *Defamation and Public Officials: The Evolving Law of Libel*. Carbondale, Ill., Southern Illinois University Press, 1971. 356p. **1L69**
A study of the evolution of the law of libel in the United States, based upon the examination of some 500 cases from Colonial days to the present. The study is limited to the libeling of public officials and reveals that the courts, over the years, have tended to give greater latitude of freedom to the press to discuss public officials, leading to the current broad interpretation of the rule of libel established by the Supreme Court in *New York Times v. Sullivan* (1964). Here the Court held that the press has a Constitutional right in the absence of actual malice, to publish even defamatory falsehood about the public conduct of public officials. In his conclusion, the author cautions that "abuses of the right to discuss public officials could lead to curtailment of our present level of liberty." He calls on the press to accept the ethical responsibility "to deal fairly with all, including public officials, in reporting the news truthfully, accurately, and sincerely."

———. *Newspapermen Versus Public Officials: The Evolving Law of Libel*. Carbondale, Ill., Southern Illinois University, 1968. 649p. (Ph.D. dissertation, University Microfilms, no. 69–6280) **1L70**
This study of the evolution of the law of libel as it relates to public officials is divided into four parts: Part I focuses on the Colonial background; part II examines the formation of libel laws in the United States from the nation's inception through the nineteenth century; part III details the development and divergency in the law of libel as it pertains to public officials, including the division of thought in the various state courts; part IV centers on the decisions of the U.S. Supreme Court that initiated a constitutional privilege to discuss public officials.

———. "Truth May Be Bygone Standard in Libel Suits." *Grassroots Editor*, 13(2):11–13, March–April 1972. **1L71**
The U.S. Supreme Court in the case of *Rosenbloom v. Metromedia, Inc.* (1971) "for all practical purposes, may have set a new uniform standard for libel, requiring those bringing suit, regardless of who they are, to prove convincingly and clearly that falsehoods were published knowingly and recklessly."

[Lawrence, D. H.?] *Dirty Words*. n.p., [1931?]. 6p. **1L72**
A defense of D. H. Lawrence's *Lady Chatterley's Lover*. "There are no dirty words. There are only dirty minds and tongues, and these have imparted a foul odor to what originally were mere descriptive terms for quite common experiences." Warren Roberts, *A Bibliography of D. H. Lawrence*, page 370, disclaims this as a work by Lawrence or by Aldous Huxley, although it has sometimes been attributed to Huxley because of a statement on the final page: "One hundred and fifty copies printed for A. H."

Lawrence, Elwood P. "Happy Land: W. S. Gilbert as Political Satirist." *Victorian Studies*, 15:161–83, December 1971. **1L73**
In 1873 the Lord Chamberlain banned W. S. Gilbert's satire on Gladstone and the Liberal government of the day after one performance. The author discusses the nature of the satire, why it was banned, and the reaction of the press and public. Photographs of the actors in costume were sold as were copies of the printed play. "A by-product of the Lord Chamberlain's interference with *Happy Land* was a short-lived but vigorous debate concerning censorship and the stage."

Lawrence, Thomas A. "Eclipse of Liberty: Civil Liberties in the United States During the First World War." *Wayne Law Review*, 21:33–112, November 1974. **1L74**
"The World War I war hysteria in the United States was ubiquitous and intense. It was fed by nativist impulses in Americans which resulted from the immigrant's rising political power and a distrust of that which was foreign and dissimilar. Immigrants seemed especially susceptible to ideas which powerful and influential groups condemned at every opportunity. Thus the nefarious doctrines of socialism, pacifism, radicalism, Bolshevism, syndicalism, and even unionism were given an alien tinge. . . . The war offorded an opportunity to Americanize these alien elements. . . . The Espionage Act and state loyalty act prosecutions helped to give effect to these goals. . . . The courts were both unwilling and unable to interfere with this process. The legal establishment was also infected with the war clamor. . . . The result was a judicial establishment which became the tool of political suppression. The law became the codification of intolerance, wartime policy, and political expediency."

Lawson, Elizabeth. *The Reign of Witches: The Struggle Against the Alien and Sedition Laws, 1798–1800*. With an Introduction by William L. Patterson. New York, Civil Rights Congress, 1952. 64p. **1L75**
A popular account of the Alien and Sedition Acts of 1798, written in light of the Smith and McCarran Acts of the 1950s.

Lawson, Linda. *President Johnson and the Press*. Columbia, Mo., Freedom of Information Center, School of Journalism, University of Missouri at Columbia, 1969. 6p. (Report no. 229) **1L76**
Deals largely with the charges of excessive secrecy, news management, and lack of credibility in the Johnson Administration. "The term 'credibility gap' spelled out the essence of President Lyndon B. Johnson's problems with the press."

Lazarus, Simon, "The Right of Reply." *New Republic*, 159(14):16–17, 5 October 1968. **1L77**
The Federal Communications Commission's personal attack rules were held unconstitutional by a Chicago federal court.

Lazenby, Beth. "The Right to Information and the FOIA: Shredding the Paper Curtain of Secrecy." *Houston Law Review*, 11:717–24, March 1974. **1L78**
Re: *Ethyl Corp. v. Environmental Protection Agency*, 478 F.2d 47 (4th Cir. 1973). "The instant case clearly restricts governmental use of executive privilege to maintain secrecy over those matters within the purview of the FOIA."

Leab, Daniel J. "Response to the Hutchins Commission." *Gazette: International Journal for Mass Communications Studies*, 16:105–13, 1970. **1L79**
An analysis of the "little acclaim and much criticism" that greeted the report of the Commission on Freedom of the Press when it appeared in 1947. "On the whole the press treated the Commission and the report harshly, and except for learned journals, a few newspapers, and some liberal magazines, quite prejudicially."

Leach, Michael. *I Know It When I See It. Pornography, Violence, and Public Sensitivity*. Philadelphia, Westminster, 1975. 153p. **1L80**
An exploration of pornography in the motion pictures and the paradoxes it poses in the treatment of violence and sex. "My hope was not to narrow down the concept of obscenity in order to help eliminate pornography but to stretch it in order to increase awareness of ourselves." On censorship the author observes: "The best censorship is not to take something away from everybody, but to maintain an atmosphere that provides everyone with alternatives and to support those that are positive. . . . If we don't like the reflections of obscenity . . . the solution is not to break the mirror but to face up to the face in front of the mirror."

League for the Abolition of Postal Censorship. *You Must Help Fight the New McCarthyism Now*. Washington, D.C., The League [1960?]. Broadside. **1L81**
An attack on the Post Office Department which has a "messianic complex" about sex which runs like this: "America is engulfed in an ocean of obscenity, obscenity is anything which the POD does not like, all who oppose the actions of the POD are Communists and/or perverts, this is a Communist-inspired activity to demoralize America, we cannot depend upon the Courts to save America from this

'Red Menace' because the Courts, particularly the Supreme Court, are too liberal." Therefore, the Post Office Department has taken matters into its own hands to "save America from the identical evils of obscenity and the Red Plot to undermine America." The broadside calls on all those who wish to see democracy triumph over demagoguery, to join the League and help in the financial support of court fights against action of the Post Office Department.

Leahigh, Alan K. *Press Passes; Patent or Privilege?* Columbia, Mo., Freedom of Information Center, School of Journalism, University of Missouri at Columbia, 1971. 7p. (Report no. 262) **1L82**
"Law enforcement agencies, particularly in the larger cities, have utilized the press pass as a means of controlling and limiting newsmen at the scenes of crimes, accidents and disasters."

Leamer, Laurence. *The Paper Revolutionaries: The Rise of the Underground Press.* New York, Simon & Schuster, 1972. 220p. **1L83**
"As yet the 'counter culture' has produced only one broad, unifying institution. It is not a political party or an organization at all, but a medium: The underground press." Beginning with the *Masses*, an early twentieth-century precursor, *Village Voice*, *Berkeley Barb*, and the *Los Angeles Free Press*, the author traces the development of the underground press. He looks at a number of papers associated with the Underground Press Service as well as two service institutions that hold the papers together. He views the underground press "on its own native grounds, as an organic part of radical-youth culture," and follows that culture and movement as it developed in the last half of the 1960s and early 1970s.

Leaper, W. J. *The Law of Advertising.* 2d ed. London, Butterworth, 1961. 353p., 39p. **1L84**
Includes chapters on defamation, independent television, and statutes and regulations relating to advertising. Rules governing codes of standards in the newspaper press and television are given in the appendix.

Leary, William M., Jr. "Books, Soldiers and Censorship During the Second World War." *American Quarterly*, 20(2): 237–45, Summer 1968. **1L85**
An account of the censorship of reading matter for soldiers, the result of an amendment to the Soldiers Voting bill introduced by Senator Robert A. Taft to prevent soldiers from reading any materials that might favor the democrats in the 1942 presidential elections. The bill was passed despite objections from the Council on Books in Wartime. The Army interpreted the ruling strictly, banning such books as *Yankee from Olympus* (a biography of Oliver Wendell Holmes), Charles A. Beard's *The Republic*, and even the *Official Guide to the Army Air Force*, which carried a picture of President Roosevelt as Commander in Chief. These events

triggered a nationwide storm of protest and the Act was amended to drastically liberalize the original provisions.

Leavitt, Jack. "Splendid Ignorance: The Mainspring of a Fair Trial." *Crime & Delinquency*, 14:207–15, July 1968. **1L86**
This article examines the seeming conflict of the Constitution's free press provisions in the First Amendment and the fair trial safeguards in the Fifth and Sixth. The author, a San Francisco lawyer, concludes: "We can hope, perhaps by adroit cancellations of our subscriptions, to make fairness profitable. Some day a Pulitzer Prize might be awarded to a story that, for reasons of basic justice, never saw print."

Ledbetter, Rosanna. *The Organization That Delayed Birth Control: A History of the Malthusian League, 1877–1927.* DeKalb, Ill., Northern Illinois University, 1972. 356p. (Ph.D. dissertation, University Microfilms, no. 72–22,792) **1L87**
The Malthusian League, "the first organization in the world to advocate voluntary family limitation as the solution to the problem of poverty," was founded in England in 1877, the result of a legal suit brought against Charles Bradlaugh and Annie Besant for publishing Charles Knowlton's *Fruits of Philosophy*. The organization based its views on the theories of Thomas Malthus who believed that overpopulation was a major cause of poverty. The movement was opposed by the labor movement and socialists who viewed concentration of the nation's wealth as the chief cause of poverty, by the medical profession that believed that contraceptive practices were injurious to health, by the Christian churches that saw birth control as immoral and contrary to the Scriptures, and by politicians who believed sex was a matter of bedroom or brothel and not a safe political issue. The League, under the domination of Dr. C. R. Drysdale and his family, also introduced the idea of eugenics or limitation of the "unfit," further anathema to many. It was not until the formation of the family planning organizations of the 1920s, which stressed advantage of birth control to the individual, that the movement began to gain widespread acceptance.

Lederman, S. N. "Interpretation and Application of Section 150 (8) of Criminal Code: Regina v. C. Coles Co., Ltd." *University of Toronto Faculty of Law Review*, 24:106–14, April 1966. **1L88**
An analysis of the case of *Regina v. C. Coles Co., Ltd.*, involving the sale of John Cleland's eighteenth-century work of fiction, *Fanny Hill*. While the Ontario Court of Appeals reversed a lower court decision, holding that *Fanny Hill* was not obscene, there is confusion in the Court's interpretation and application of section 150(8) of the Canadian Criminal Code, covering obscenity.

Le Duc, Don R. "Control of Cable Television: The Senseless Assault on States' Rights." *Catholic University Law Review*, 24:795–812, Summer 1975. **1L89**
Following an examination of the so-called "three-tier cable control," the author concludes that "if any tier of cable regulation could be said to be superfluous, it would be the federal tier, which seems at the moment bent upon betraying the promises it made to the public in its *Cable Report and Order* issued only three years ago."

———, ed. *Issues in Broadcast Regulation.* Washington, D.C., Broadcast Education Association, 1974, 151p. (Broadcast Education Association Monograph no. 1) **1L90**
A collection of papers presented at the 1969 and 1972 Broadcast Regulation Seminars sponsored by the Broadcast Education Association. The papers, modified to some extent by their authors, are introduced with comment by the editor. Part I, The Regulatory Process: The Process of Broadcast Regulation by Erwin G. Krasnow. Broadcast Hearing Issues by Joseph M. Foley. Procedures Involved in License Renewal by Robert Rawson. Part II, The Broadcast License: The Myths of Broadcast License Renewal by Lawrence W. Lichty. The WMAL Case by Howard Roycroft. WHDH: Two Issues by Robert Smith and Paul Prince. A Broadcaster's View of Audience by Thomas Bolger. Ascertainment Procedures: Rule and Reality by Herschel Shosteck. License Renewal and Reform by Barry Cole. Part III, The Broadcaster and Content Control: The FCC and Content Control by Lee Loevinger. The Fairness Doctrine by Kenneth Cox. Trends in the Fairness Doctrine and Access by Martin J. Gaynes. Broadcast Regulation and the News by J. W. (Bill) Roberts. 315 and the Political Spending Bill. The Broadcast Code by Stockton Helffrich. Part IV, The Broadcaster and Competition: Problems in Maintaining Competition in Broadcasting by Marcus Cohn. A Proposal to Regulate Broadcasting as a Public Utility by Frank Kahn. NAB Report: Pattern of Media Ownership by Christopher H. Sterling. Implications of the Third Report and Order by Roger Zylstra. Cable Beyond the Third Report and Order by Robert W. Coll. Copyright: Quo Vadis by Charles E. Sherman. Citizen Rights and Cable by Robert Pepper. Part V, The Study of Communication Law: Broadcast Regulation—Charting Course for the Future by Don R. Le Duc. Uses of Pike & Fisher by Henry Fisher. How a Broadcast Attorney Researches Law by Russell Eagen.

[Lee, Charles.] *Defence of the Alien and Sedition Laws, Shewing Their Entire Consistency with the Constitution of the United States and the Principles of Our Govern-*

ment. *Addressed to the People of Virginia*. *By Virginiensis*. Philadelphia, Printed by John Ward Fenno, 1798, 47p.   **1L91**
The author defends the constitutionality of the Alien and Sedition laws. "The freedom of the press differs from the licentiousness of the press, and the laws which prohibit and restrain the latter, will always be found to affirm and preserve the former." He makes reference to the Blackstone concept of press freedom, which consists of freedom from prior restraint. Oliver Wolcott attributes the work to Charles Lee.

Lee, James M. *History of American Journalism*. Boston, Houghton Mifflin, 1917. 462p.   **1L92**
This general history of journalism contains frequent references to issues of press freedom, censorship, libel suits, wartime controls, and the trials and imprisonment of editors.

Lee, Richard. "New York Times v. Sullivan: Defined or Shackled?" *De-Paul Law Review*, 21:248–62, Autumn 1971.   **1L93**
"The purpose of this note will be to examine these decisions [*Monitor Patriot Co. v. Roy* (1971) and *Ocala Star-Banner Co. v. Damron* (1971)] in terms of the development of the doctrine of constitutional privileges of fair comment, and to assess their impact in light of post *New York Times* trends."

———. "The Pornography Report." *Cresset*, 34(3):16–17, 1971.   **1L94**
Comment on the Report of the U.S. Commission on Obscenity and Pornography which has been widely denounced and might yet get as wide a reading as books banned in Boston. The author is concerned with the fate of such reports that seem to go against popular belief.

Lee, Richard W., ed. *Politics & the Press*. Washington, D.C., Acropolis, 1972. 191p.   **1L95**
A series of lectures on freedom of information and the public's right to know: Role of the Press in Presidential Politics by Elmer E. Cornwell, Jr. Appraising Press Coverage of Politics by William L. Rivers. Politicians and Biased Political Information by David S. Broder. A Publisher's View of Credibility by Otis Chandler. The Administration's View of Press and Politics by Herbert G. Klein. Political Reporting: The Criteria of Selection by Philip Potter. Politics, Blacks, and the Press by William Raspberry. The Influence of Polling on Politics and the Press by George Gallup, Jr. Television Distortion in Political Reporting by Kurt Lang. Politics and the Press: A Final Comment by Irving Dilliard.

Lee, Robert E. "Inquiry into Chil-

dren's Programming—A Call for Action?" *Notre Dame Lawyer*, 47:230–46, December 1971.   **1L96**
"The purpose of this paper is to investigate whether current children's programming practices are in the public interest; whether the specific ACT [Action for Children's Television] proposals are within the authority of the [Federal Communications] Commission to adopt; and whether any action should be taken by the Commission and, if so, what action."

———. "Self-Regulation or Censorship." In *Obscenity in the Mails*. Hearings before the Subcommittee on Postal Operations of the Committee on Post Office and Civil Service, U.S. House of Representatives, pp. 71–74. (Also in *Vital Speeches*, 15 September 1969)   **1L97**
Address by a member of the Federal Communications Commission before the Association of Broadcasting Executives of Texas, Dallas, 31 July 1969

[Leech, Edward J.] *What Next?* [Memphis?], 1918. 29p.   **1L98**
Leech, the young editor of the *Memphis Press*, was jailed for contempt of court for an editorial in the 20 July 1918 issue. The editorial had criticized corruption in Memphis politics, which the court considered an indirect criticism of the judiciary.

Leeds, Josiah W. *Concerning Printed Poison*. Philadelphia, The Author, 1885. 42p.   **1L99**
An attack on "flash literature," police papers, indecent posters, and show bills, and their evil effect on the young. Leeds calls for municipal censorship by a board of twelve examiners. He places blame on the purveyors of the pernicious literature, the city fathers who permit it, and the indifference or negligence of parents.

———. *The Theatre: An Essay upon the Non-Accordancy of Stage-Plays with the Christian Profession*. Philadelphia, The Author, 1884. 85p.   **1L100**
"It will be the scope of this essay to show the adverse estimation in which stage-plays have been held by the best of men of ancient and modern times, and how local communities and states have, in very self-defense, forbidden them . . ."; that theater-going corrupts youth and promotes crime; and invites the righteous judgment of the Almighty. The author's historical account begins with William Prynne's attack on the stage in seventeenth-century England. He assures the reader that, unlike some attacks on the theater, his work does not treat "the abounding wickedness of the stage with so much fidelity that, although very useful in certain hands, they are not exactly fitted reading aloud in families or for perusal by the young generally," and "stimulate a marked interest" in the evil they are attacking.

Leefe, Richard K. "Free Press v. Fair Trial." *Loyola Law Review* (New Or-

leans), 19:332–40, 1972–73.   **1L101**
Re: *United States v. Dickinson and Adams*, 465 F.2d 496 (5th Cir. 1972). The case involves a newspaper's contempt of court.

———. "Free Press v. Fair Trial: A Constitutional Dichotomy." *Loyola Law Review* (New Orleans), 20:148–52, 1974.   **1L102**
"By limiting the sources of his information, rather than placing direct limitations on what the newsman may publicize, the *Sheppard* decision [*Sheppard v. Maxwell*, 1966] represented a revelation in the free press–fair trial dichotomy."

Lefever, Ernest W. *TV and National Defense; An Analysis of CBS News, 1972–1973*. Boston, Va., Institute for American Strategy, 1974. 209p.   **1L103**
This study was commissioned by the Institute for American Strategy to examine the fairness of CBS–TV News in reporting national defense and foreign policy. The study covered the period of 1972–73 and analyzed patterns and themes, events covered and not covered, viewpoints of commentators, and in particular, coverage of the Vietnam war. The conclusions reached were that "CBS national security news was so spotty and lopsided that it failed to provide the essential facts for understanding U.S. defense and military issues, the Soviet definition of détente, or the forward surge in Soviet military might" and that "CBS Evening News was seriously deficient in presenting a fair, full, and meaningful picture of national security developments." The study further concluded that CBS Evening News was an active advocate on several national issues, but that it did not comply with the fairness doctrine by actively balancing these views with opposing views.

Le Fevre, Ronald E. "Professional Price Advertising Set Free?—Consumers' 'Right to Know' in Prescription Drug Price Advertising." *Connecticut Law Review*, 8:108–28, Fall 1975. **1L104**
Re: *Virginia Citizens Consumer Council, Inc. v. State Board of Pharmacy*, 373 F. Supp. 683 (W.D. Va. 1974).

Leflar, Robert A. "The Free-ness of Free Speech." *Vanderbilt Law Review*, 15:1073–84, October 1962.   **1L105**
"In this article Professor Leflar discusses the freedom of speech requirement of the first amendment and determines that this constitutional guarantee is not absolute. The author concludes that the courts should weigh the conflicting societal values of the present day in reaching a decision as to whether the particular speech in issue is protected."

Legman, Gershon. "Introduction." In *My Secret Life*. New York, Grove, 1966, pp. 15–57.   **1L106**
In his introduction to the first public edition of

this classic pornographic autobiography of a wealthy Victorian gentleman who lived for sex alone, Legman analyzes the work, speculates on the circumstances of original publication (about 1890), and develops the theory that the anonymous author is the bibliographer of erotica, Henry Spencer Ashbee (A257–60). This is an "abridged but unexpurgated" edition of a complete two-volume edition published by Grove Press. *My Secret Life* was first published in Amsterdam in only six copies for and at the expense of the author. One of the three known copies is in the Kinsey Institute.

————. "Sex-Censorship in the U.S.A.; A Letter from America from G. Legman." *Plan* (The Progressive League), 11(1):2–9, January 1945.
1L107
"Censorship of sex in the American press is almost entirely instigated and directed by the Catholic church acting through the post-office." The New York and Boston vice societies, once powerful Protestant censorship bodies, are now moribund.

Leibensperger, Patricia K. "The Sherman Act and the American Bar Association's Ban on Advertising: Madison Avenue Will Have to Wait." *Suffolk University Law Review*, 10:557–81, Spring 1976.
1L108
The author reaches the conclusion that under section one of the Sherman Act, the advertising ban imposed by the American Bar Association Code of Professional Responsibility does not constitute a violation.

Leigh, Peter R. "Advice to School Boards and Superintendents: Don't Overreact to Student Newspapers." *American School Board Journal*, 160:53–55, May 1973.
1L109
Guidelines for school administrators in their relations with school publications.

————. *The Implementation of Obscenity Decisions in the State of California*. Los Angeles, University of Southern California, 1969. 331p. (Ph.D. dissertation, University Microfilms, no. 69–19,383)
1L110
"The purposes of this study were to review major federal and state obscenity decisions and to measure the impact of such judicial decisions upon relevant actors." The actors in the obscenity drama examined consisted of enforcement personnel, citizens groups concerned with the proliferation of sexually-oriented materials, and members of the California legislature. "The inability of the Supreme Court to develop any common position on the obscenity issue is reflected in the confused and anxious responses made by many enforcement personnel, and in the virulent criticism aimed at the judicial system by numerous citizens groups. This confusion and disaffection with the Court, in turn, tends to

undermine confidence in, support of, and a positive affective orientation toward the United States Supreme Court."

[Leighton, Alexander.] *A Shorte Treatise Against Stage-Playes*. [Middleburgh, England?], 1625. 28p.
1L111
The author believes stage plays to be unlawful because they originated with the Heathen, they deal with sinful subjects, the actors are wanton and pursue an unlawful trade, and the playgoers submit themselves to evil. He cites the judgment that God has inflicted upon players and playgoers throughout history. Lowe attributes the work to Leighton who referred to his treatise against stage plays in his *Speculum Belli Sacri*.

Leighton, J. M. "Censorship: One or Two Points in Favor and Some Against." *Index on Censorship*, 5:41–45, Spring 1976.
1L112
A former member of the South African Publications Control Board defends censorship. "I remain convinced, after four years of censorship service, that freedom is better served by enlightened censorship than by total absence of censorship." He believes it is not possible for a society to exist without some form of censorship. It is easy to argue against fundamentalist censorship; but equally as unacceptable in society is the person who upholds no values at all. He favors banning of pornography (it denies what is essentially human) and conditioned propaganda, which "denies me the right to think and feel in relation to my fellow man." He appeals for "a battery of serious and balanced criticism of those decisions that limit human choice, that reduce man to a fundamentalist puppet, or a body without a heart."

Leland, Theron C. "Definitions—Obscenity." *Truth Seeker*, 5:420, 6 July 1878.
1L113
"Obscenity, as applied to the conduct of adult persons, is excess or intemperance in sex relations. Conduct or relations of sex that cause disease are obscene. The mental, orderly, and temperate manifestations of sex in adults are healthy, appropriate, and not obscene." Comstock is not qualified to judge.

————. "Two Phases of Repeal." *Truth Seeker*, 5:644–45, 12 October 1878.
1L114
An attack on the views of the Reverend Francis E. Abbot, president of the National Liberal League, who equivocated in his opposition to the Comstock obscenity laws. Leland calls for the repeal of the laws which he charges are unconstitutional.

Lemov, Michael R. "Administrative Agency News Releases: Public Information Versus Private Injury." *George Washington Law Review*, 37:63–81, October 1968.
1L115
"A recent decision of the Court of Appeals for the District of Columbia highlights a sharp

conflict between the policy of maximizing the flow of government information to the public and the need to protect private business against injury from administrative agency charges of illegality that are later disproved." *FTC v. Cinderella Career and Finishing Schools, Inc.*, 1968.

Lenes, Mark S., and Edward J. Hart. "Influence of Pornography and Violence on Attitudes and Guilt." *Journal of School Health*, 45:447–51, October 1975.
1L116
"The results of this study suggest that exposure to sexually explicit material will have some immediate impact on one's emotional response, at least for some people. The reaction is much stronger when one is exposed to violent scenes. Long-range effects and the impact of continued exposure may be quite another matter. There is needed research to explore the impact of this latter issue." The authors suggest that "if concern is to be leveled at the media for the quality of material and programs they present to the public, the focus of the issue ought to be centered upon violence."

Lent, John A. *Philippine Mass Communications Bibliography*. Manila, Philippine Press Institute, 1965. 102p. (Reprinted from *Silliman Journal*, 1965)
1L117
Extensive references to newspaper articles on press freedom and censorship in the Philippines, most of which are not included in the McCoy bibliography.

————. "The Philippine Press under Martial Law." *Index on Censorship*, 3:47–58, Spring 1974.
1L118
The Philippine press, which had been the freest in Asia, since September 1972 has become one of the most controlled presses. Under President Marcos martial law has resulted in the killing off of entire presses and the imprisonment of a large proportion of journalists. "Censors are still physically in the newsrooms; editors are intimidated by being threatened with the loss of their publications' printing permits; newsmen are still in prison . . . ; and released detainees are extremely limited in their day-to-day activities, not being allowed to leave the Manila area without permission." The text of the 25 September 1972 decree on the Philippine press follows.

————. "Press Freedom in the Commonwealth Caribbean." *Index on Censorship*, 2(3):55–70, Autumn 1973. **1L119**
Former British colonies in the Caribbean are in the process of redefining the concept of press freedom that they inherited from their mother countries. Leaders of such new governments tend to have authoritarian personalities; they ask the mass media to show restraint in criticizing government and at the same time promote

Gershon Legman – John A. Lent

national goals. Recognizing the risk of criticizing government, a number of mass media have initiated self-regulating guidelines.

———. "The Press of the Philippines: Its History and Problems." *Journalism Quarterly*, 43:739–52, Winter 1966. **1L 120**
"Legally, Philippine newspapers three times have gained their freedom, only to find themselves restricted today by handicaps partly of their own making. One promising step is the founding of the new Press Institute."

———. "Underground Press Fills the Gaps in the Philippines." *IPI Report* (International Press Institute), 23(12): 3–4, 9, December 1974. **1L 121**
The Philippine press is owned by friends and relatives of President Marcos and the government maintains tight control through legislation, guidance, and ownership. To get another side of the news, Filipinos must depend on the thriving, well-organized underground press.

Lentczner, Joan. *Struggle in Press Freedom*. La Cross, Wis., Journalism Education Association, 1975. 33p. (ED 105,459) **1L 122**
"This paper is a personalized account of one high school journalism faculty advisor's dismissal from her teaching position because she allowed students to publish a series on sex-related problems in the high school newspaper."

Leon, S. J. "Book Selection in Philadelphia." *Library Journal*, 98:1081–89, 1 April 1973. (An abridged account appeared in *PLA Bulletin* [Pennsylvania Library Association], July 1972) **1L 123**
A questionnaire survey of all major libraries in the Philadelphia area measures the extent of holdings of controversial materials (race, radical politics, changing sexual mores, and drugs), both fiction and nonfiction, and the libraries' selection policies and responses to censorship. Among the conclusions reached are that "books that challenge conventional sexual mores meet with more caution, anxiety, and defensiveness from our selection and/or administrative librarians than books that challenge prevalent political values and practices," that favorable book budgets are no guarantee of inclusion of more controversial materials, and that the overall description of the situation is neither "good" nor "bad," but rather "indifferent."

Leonard, John. "Kid Porn v. the Burger Five." *New York Times Book Review*, 8 July 1973, p. 31. (Also in William A. Katz and Sherry Gaherty, *eds.*, *Library Literature. 4—The Best of 1973*. Metuchen, N.J., Scarecrow, 1974, pp. 327–30) **1L 124**
A caustic attack on the U.S. Supreme Court's June 1973 decisions which turned over to the states and local communities the responsibility for defining obscenity. "Kid Porn must be gunned down. Librarians, bar the doors: here comes your average vigilantes."

Leopold, Richard W. "Crisis of Confidence: Foreign Policy Research and the Federal Government." *American Archivist*, 34:139–55, April 1971. **1L 125**
Based on an address to the Society of Historians of American Foreign Relations. Historian Leopold discusses "the crisis of confidence between those engaged in research in foreign policy and those administering the records of the Federal Government," and suggests some things that the Society can do to meet the challenge and help rebuild the confidence necessary for all those who engage in historical research.

Lépine, Normand. "La Liberté de L'information dans le Droit Canadien." *McGill Law Journal*, 14:733–56, December 1968. **1L 126**
The historical development of the law of press freedom in Canada, including law of cinema, and radio and television broadcasting,

Lester, Julius. "The Black Writer and the New Censorship." *Evergreen Review*, 14:18–21, 73–75, April 1970. **1L 127**
The author describes the difficulties of militant blacks to get their books published, and when published, to have them adequately promoted and reviewed. "So long as white reviewers interpret black writing for white readers, the result can only be another manifestation of blacks filtered through the white mind."

A Letter to a Friend in the Country, upon Occasion of the Many Scurrilous Libels, which have been lately publish'd. London, J. Roberts, 1743. 55p. **1L 128**
The writer argues that the widespread abuse of the freedom of the press is a threat against that freedom. He considers the vicious attacks on persons in government to be libelous, and believes the present government has been very patient with such libelers.

Letwin, Leon. "Regulation of Underground Newspaper on Public School Campuses in California." *UCLA Law Review*, 22:141–218, October 1974. **1L 129**
The author considers three general questions: "(1) What prohibitions may school officials legitimately impose on the substantive content of such publications? (2) Is prior censorship a permissible technique for enforcing them? and (3) How should such crucial incidents of newspaper distribution as time, place, and manner regulations and the right to sell such papers, be dealt with in the school setting?"

Leuchter, Linda I. "Media Cross-Ownership—The FCC's Inadequate Response." *Texas Law Review*, 54:336–71, January 1976. **1L 130**
"This conflict between the social goals implicit in the regulation of media ownership leaves some uncertainty with respect to the best regulatory approach to implement the social policies. Three possible approaches exist: deal with individual abuses on an ad hoc case-by-case basis; leave the problem to the Antitrust Division of the Department of Justice; or promulgate a general rule with across-the-board applicability and provide for waivers in appropriate cases. The FCC has chosen the last approach."

Leventhal, Harold. "The 1973 Round of Obscenity: Pornography Decisions." *American Bar Association Journal*, 59:1261–66, November 1973. **1L 131**
A review of the 1973 obscenity-pornography decision of the U.S. Supreme Court, noting to what extent questions have been settled, and what significant issues remain for consideration.

Leventhal, Lionel. "When They Tried to Tax Books." *Books; The Journal of the National Book League*, 337:171–75, September–October 1961. **1L 132**
Unsuccessful efforts during wartime Britain in 1940 to tax books, which were met by great opposition and were not tried again.

Leventhal, Norman P. "Caution: Cigarette Commercials May Be Hazardous to Your License—The New Aspect of Fairness." *Federal Communications Bar Journal*, 22:55–124, 1968. **1L 133**
The study is concerned with the extension of the fairness doctrine in the Federal Communications Commission's cigarette ruling.

Levin, Bernard. "The 17 Steps to Press Freedom." *Times* (London), 10 March 1976, p. 14. **1L 134**
The author reports the text of a seventeen-point Press Charter developed by parliamentary supporters of "closed shop" legislation to safeguard the rights of a free press in the case of entirely unionized papers.

Levin, Harry. " 'A Matter of National Concern': The Report of the Commission on Obscenity and Pornography." In Joseph P. Strelka, *ed.*, *Literary Criticism and Sociology*. University Park, Pa., Pennsylvania State University Press,

1973, pp. 107–23. (Yearbook of Comparative Criticism, vol. 5) **1L135**
In this critique of the Report of the Commission on Obscenity and Pornography, the author traces the historic concern over obscenity in Britain and the United States which led to the appointment of the Commission. He discusses the deliberations of the Commission, the scuttling of its Report by Congress and the White House (Congress "had wanted dogma and was offered dubiety"), and analyzes the findings. "If everything is permissible at the level of publication," the reviewer observes, "then at the level of criticism we must bear a new responsibility. If we shift our value judgments from ethics to esthetics, it is still our duty to discriminate art from trash. This is the critical consequence of the report; the other, perhaps the major consequence is scientific." He notes a curious contradiction between this report which found no causal relation between pornography and behavior, and the report of the Commission on the Causes and Prevention of Violence, which expressed concern for the effect of violence on children and proposed some curbs. "Are we to infer that violence is more contagious than sex, or merely it is more dangerous and less desirable?"

Levin, Harvey J. "Competition, Diversity, and the Television Group Ownership Rule." *Columbia Law Review*, 70:791–835, May 1970. **1L136**
A critique of the Federal Communications Commission's Television Group Ownership Rule, intended to encourage local diversified ownership and to insure interstation competition for network affiliations, advertiser income, and audience attention and, in addition, to preserve competition between network and non-network advertisers and program suppliers. The author questions the wisdom of using the present Rules as an instrument to safeguard competition and diversity in television. He sees a need "to recast the present numerical limitation in a form less likely to restrain competition; and second, to give even greater attention than hitherto to implementation of an *affirmative* strategy to diversify program choice."

———. *The Invisible Resource: Use and Regulation of the Radio Spectrum*. Baltimore, Published for Resources for the Future, Inc. by Johns Hopkins Press, 1971. 432p. **1L137**
The author "has attempted to describe and analyze the economic characteristics of the radio spectrum—that portion of electromagnetic waves used to transmit information through the air. In addition he identifies the participants in this industry and their roles, analyzes the economic efficiency with which the radio spectrum is utilized, and suggests some alternatives for management." The article is included here as representing the physical limits and control of the air as a medium of communication.

———. *The Policy on Joint Ownership of Newspapers and Television Stations: Some*

Assumptions, Objectives, and Effects. New York, Center for Policy Research, 1971. 58p. Processed. **1L138**
Statement before the Federal Communications Commission hearing (Docket no. 18110) evaluating the Commission's proposed "newspaper rule," that no new TV grants or transfers shall be approved to applicants owning daily newspapers in the same market, and that within five years, all ninety-four co-located cross-media enterprises must sell off either their newspaper or their TV holdings. The report strongly endorses the Commission's proposal.

Levin, Max. "The Medical Case Against Pornography." *Catholic Educator*, 37:124–26, August 1967. **1L139**
A professor of neurology believes that "pornography is more than just a social evil. Insofar as it can affect health (both mental and emotional health) it is also a medical evil, and therefore deserves as much attention as the physical effects of typhoid germs in the water supply." It produces crime and antisocial behavior, but worse, sick minds and hearts.

———. "Pornography and Social Pollution." *National Decency Reporter*, 9:7, January–February 1972. **1L140**

Levin, Meyer, "A F——R–Letter W——D Man Protests." *Signature* (The Diners Club), 4:40–42, 70–74, September 1969. **1L141**
A participant in the four-letter-word revolution finds relief at the liberation of the arts, but deplores the unimpressive lack of valid literature and art and the deluge of smut. He fears the abuse and commercial exploitation of the hard-fought freedoms may lead to demands for suppression. Nevertheless, the author would rather err on the side of permissiveness. "It is precisely because we do not want to lose this new freedom that we must take educative measures against what is false. . . . The only real defense against vulgarity and obscenity is education of popular taste."

———. *The Obsession*. New York, Simon & Schuster, 1973. 316p. **1L142**
"At the heart of his narrative is Meyer Levin's twenty-year battle over the rejection and suppression of his dramatization of *The Diary of Anne Frank*—a case that involved literary, legal and ethical questions of the highest importance."

Levin, Steven M. "Libel and Slander—A State Is Precluded from Imposing Liability Without Fault or Presumed or Punitive Damages in the Absence of *New York Times* Malice." *Loyola University Law Journal* (Chicago), 6:256–81, Winter 1975. **1L143**
Re: *Gertz v. Robert Welch, Inc.* (1974), in which "the Supreme Court still finds itself grappling to strike the proper balance between the

legitimate interests served by the law of defamation and the constitutionally protected freedoms of speech and press."

Levine, Alan H. " 'Impressionable Minds' . . . 'Forbidden Subjects': A Case in Point." *Library Journal*, 98:595–601, 15 February 1973; *School Library Journal*, 19:19–25, February 1973. **1L144**
A discussion of the banning of Piri Thomas's autobiography, *Down These Mean Streets*, from school libraries in Queens, N.Y., and the ACLU-sponsored suit that ensued. The U.S. District Court in Brooklyn upheld the school board as did the Appeals Court and the U.S. Supreme Court refused to consider the case. The author asks: "If we concede to school boards the power to exclude all but the current orthodoxy from the classrooms and libraries of our schools, will we not be granting them awesome power over the minds of our future citizens?"

Levine, George D. "Sexual Sensationalism and the First Amendment: The Supreme Court's Questionable Regime of Obscenity Adjudication." *New York State Bar Journal*, 42:193–206, April 1970; 42:308–15, June 1970. **1L145**
"The thesis here propounded stands in uncompromising hostility to all those forms of doctrinaire absolutism which would affirm an unstinting right of sexual publication and deny society as a whole any recourse against its disruptive effects." The author argues that "the extreme liberal approach is not really the methodology of freedom and that, in the field of obscenity, a Gresham's Law of expression has been seen to operate: bad expression drives out good expression, i.e. the torrent of sexually oriented films, plays, pictorial materials and books and magazines has diverted public attention from the more staid and subtle appeals of the great works of art, literature, drama and contemplation." In the end, such an ultraliberal approach may stifle creativity. He believes that it may be desirable to compromise sexual sensationalism to a limited extent "in order to attain a better balance of achievement which gives due recognition to the possibilities of artistic expression other than its shock and sensation-inducing potentialities." Such sexual sensationalism, "divorced from the context of any meaningful human relationship or any suggestion of the humanity and dignity of the object of sexual desire, does not enhance the quality of the emotional life or educate the imagination toward a more effective role in the promotion of individual creativity, personal growth, or social empathy."

Levine, James P. *The Bookseller and the Law of Obscenity: Toward an Empirical*

Theory of Free Expression. Evanston, Ill., Northwestern University, 1968. 207p. (Ph.D. dissertation, University Microfilms, no. 69-1882)   **1L146**
"The purpose of the study is to discover some empirical requisites of the open society, which is conceptualized as one in which external restraints on individual speech and behavior are at a minimum. Social freedom, the dependent variable, is operationalized as bookseller forbearance from self-censorship of literature dealing with sex. . . . The primary hypotheses explaining variance in social freedom are not verified. The impact of appellate courts remains unclear. Constitutional guidelines . . . are not comprehended by the majority of respondents, and the specific decisions . . . do not induce changes in bookseller behavior. The low correlation between state court policy-making and bookseller self-censorship attests to the remote relationship between judicial behavior and freedom of speech. . . . These rather negative results are overshadowed by the high correlation between respondents' attitudes toward sex expression and their self-censorship practices."

————. "An Empirical Approach to Civil Liberties: The Bookseller and Obscenity Law." *Wisconsin Law Review*, 1969:153–69, 1969.   **1L147**
"It is often hypothesized that civil liberties are directly dependent upon the relative permissiveness of political and legal governing elites as expressed through such things as court opinions and enforcement practices. To test this hypothesis, Professor Levine designed an empirical study focusing upon the behavior of booksellers in relation to the freedom to acquire literature dealing with sexual behavior. His findings not only speak to this freedom, but also suggest the determinants of civil liberties in general."

Levine, Jeffrey L. "Judicial Review of Classified Documents: Amendments to the Freedom of Information Act." *Harvard Journal on Legislation*, 12:415–46, April 1975.   **1L148**
"This Comment examines the relationship between the FOIA and the classification system, and the problems that have arisen in defining that relationship. The new amendments to the FOIA are evaluated in light of these problems and the likelihood the ambiguities under the old law will be clarified."

Levine, Stephen. "Pornography and Law—Latest U.S. Developments." *New Zealand Law Journal*, 1973:497–502, 20 November 1973.   **1L149**
An analysis of the June 1973 obscenity decisions of the U.S. Supreme Court and their implications for New Zealand. "It would be nothing less than disastrous for New Zealand to permit uneven, arbitrary application of vague and ill-defined standards of law. It may be 'unfair' for the people of Wairarapa to be inflicted with materials acceptable in Auckland or Wellington, but the development and enforcement of a system of local controls—where words and deeds are permissible in one area, punishable in another—removes from the citizen that sense of certainty about the law essential in a society committed to legal justice. It seems clear, too, that criminal proceedings should not be sustained without a prior finding that specific materials are obscene and that commerce in them is punishable."

Levings, Darryl W., and Patricia Murphy. *A U.S. "Official Secrets Act"?* Columbia, Mo., Freedom of Information Center, School of Journalism, University of Missouri at Columbia, 1973. 6p. (Report no. 311)   **1L150**
"The Nixon Administration's proposed revision of the Federal Criminal Code contains secrecy-tightening provisions which would, in effect, create a U.S. 'Official Secrets Act' akin to Great Britain's. Enactment of the revisions would have a serious impact, limiting investigative reporting practices and results."

Levita, *Sir* Cecil, and Edward Shortt. *Model Conditions for Cinema Licenses. A Report of Speeches at Caxton Hall, London, May 29, 1933. The Joint Cinema Committee of The Mothers Union, The National Council of Women, The National Federation of Women's Institutes, The Public Morality Council.* London, The Joint Committee, 1933. 11p.   **1L151**
Levita was chairman of the Film Censorship Consultative Committee and Shortt was president of the British Board of Film Censors.

Levitt, Eugene E. "Pornography: Some New Perspectives on an Old Problem." *Journal of Sex Research*, 5:247–59, November 1969.   **1L152**
Consideration of definition and classification of pornography and efforts at logical analysis of its effects. "At the moment no one can say with any degree of assurance that visual erotica, or a particular form of it, are guilty or innocent of any charge."

Levy, Alan D. *Censorship Laws in Canada.* [Kingston, Canada, Ontario Library Association, 1972.] 15p. Processed.   **1L153**
Includes censorship under the Customs Tariff Act, the Post Office Act, the Broadcasting Act, and libel, obscenity, and hate propaganda under the Criminal Code.

————. "The Freedom to Read Committee." *IPLO Quarterly* (Institute of Professional Librarians of Ontario), 15:25–31, July 1973.   **1L154**
"The Freedom to Read Committee consists of a group of Canadians who believe that censorship which has been instituted in Canada to screen out harmful literature constitutes a far greater harm to individual freedom and development than any of the materials which it was designed to eliminate." The author, a lawyer and coordinator of the Freedom to Read Committee, reports on the activities of the Committee, summarizing its report, which identified areas of censorship in Canada and recommended changes in the law. He also refers to a brief submitted to the Task Force on Policing in Ontario and dealing with the wave of police attacks on book and magazine sales in Toronto and southern Ontario.

————. "Open Line Radio Programs and the Law." *Canadian Communications Law Review*, 1:160–81, 1969.   **1L155**
The policy of the Board of Broadcast Governors not to interfere with open-line programming is well accepted. The author suggests removing antiquated restrictions on topics to be covered. Text of the BBG policy (Circular 51) is included.

————. *Psychological Aspects of "Dirty" Books.* [Toronto, Institute of Professional Librarians, 1972.] 11p. Processed.   **1L156**
The author considers the effect of pornography on the reader, finding no objective scientific evidence causally linking pornography with crime. He also considers the effect of pornography on the enforcer—the police morality squad, the prosecutor, the judges, and juries.

Levy, Benn W. "On Fig Leaves." *Encounter*, 35:64–70, July 1970.   **1L157**
The author of the British Arts Council's report on obscenity, responds to Pamela Hansford Johnson's article on pornography (February issue) which he considers more emotional than rational. He defends the views of the Arts Council's Working Party, which he believes has been misinterpreted by Miss Johnson. He expresses his conviction that the problem of violence is "the central and eternal problem of civilization," and is impatient with "the proffered remedy of a fig leaf for the arts."

Levy, David. "Television: Censorship, Politics and the New Comedy." *Journal of the Producers Guild of America*, 11(2):11–14, 24, June 1969.   **1L158**
The introduction of political and social humor on television, the author believes, is a refreshing change but has within it the seeds of a dangerous boomerang—network censorship if it gets out of hand.

Levy, Doran. *Agnew's Criticisms: How Much Support.* Columbia, Mo., Freedom of Information Center, School of Journalism, University of Missouri at Columbia, 1970. 4p. (Report no. 248)   **1L159**
College students interviewed tend to agree

with Vice-President Agnew's criticism of the media but consider with disdain any attempt to control the media's handling of the news.

Levy, Joyce C. *A Study of Press Freedom in South Africa*. Denton, Tex., North Texas State University, 1974. 77p. (Unpublished Master's Thesis) **1L160**
"The problem of the study was to analyze conditions and problems of the South African press, including effects of apartheid legislation on the free flow of information. The method of research was mail questionnaires to editors of twenty-two South African daily newspapers. The study showed that the South African press is restricted by legislation, and additional laws are expected."

Levy, Leonard W., *ed*. "Freedom in Turmoil, Era of the Sedition Act: The Crisis of 1797–1800." In *Major Crises in American History:Documentary Problems: I (1689–1861)*. New York, Harcourt, Brace and World, 1962, pp. 188–262. **1L161**
Documents include: The Sedition Act, Trial of Thomas Cooper, The Kentucky Resolutions, Madison's Argument for Freedom of the Press (from the Virginia Report of 1799–1800), and several contemporary newspaper accounts relating to press freedom, including an unintentionally humorous note on Jacobinism in children's books.

Lewels, Francisco J. *Critical Attitudes Toward the Media*. Columbia, Mo., Freedom of Information Center, School of Journalism, University of Missouri at Columbia, 1972. 7p. (Report no. 281; reprinted in Lee Brown, *The Reluctant Reformation*, pp. 147–66) **1L162**
The analysis concludes that the seeds have been planted for an era of stricter governmental control of the mass media. Criticism falls under six categories: the revolutionary, the pro-media critics, the silent majority, the critical intellectual, the traditional journalist, and the staunch defender.

———. *Expansion of the Fairness Doctrine*. Columbia, Mo., Freedom of Information Center, School of Journalism, University of Missouri at Columbia, 1970. 4p. (Report no. 251) **1L163**
"Historically defined as a policy designed to insure airing of divergent opinion on controversial issues, the FCC's fairness doctrine has been broadened to include rebuttals of televised commercial and presidential claims. The doctrine's expansion is being challenged by a deeply troubled television industry which claims the extension is another step toward increasing governmental control."

———. *The Newspaper Preservation Act*.

Columbia, Mo., Freedom of Information Center, School of Journalism, University of Missouri at Columbia, 1971. 5p. (Report no. 254) **1L164**
"A recent law suit, challenging the constitutionality of the newly enacted Newspaper Preservation Act, may eventually settle a question plaguing the newspaper industry—Does the law preserve failing newspapers, thereby maintaining a multiplicity of editorial voices, or does it stifle new competition in cities with joint agreement newspapers?"

Lewin, Nathan. "Gagging the Press." *New Republic*, 173(26):15–19, 27 December 1975. **1L165**
An account of the court's gag order against the press in a Nebraska murder trial, the action of the Nebraska Supreme Court, the interim opinion of Supreme Court Justice Blackmun, and the consideration of the full court. "The issue that exercises constitutional lawyers and should be the principal concern of press advocates is not whether this kind of information ⌊confessions⌋ should be printed, but whether courts should have the power to order the press not to print it."

———. "The Right to Publish: The Great Case That Made Great Law." *New Republic*, 165(2):11–13, 10 July 1971. **1L166**
A critique of the Pentagon Papers decision of the U.S. Supreme Court, a great case because it raised extraordinarily important issues of constitutional law and engaged an enormous amount of public concern and interest. "By any token, it is a resounding constitutional triumph for the press and a defeat for the increasingly suppressive position taken by the Department of Justice in the Nixon Administration."

———. "Sex at High Noon in Times Square." *New Republic*, 169(3052–53):19–21, 7 and 14 July 1973. (Reprinted in *Student Lawyer*, October 1973) **1L167**
"What the court, speaking through Chief Justice Burger, has done is to announce a rule ⌊21 June 1973⌋ that substantially strips publications or films describing sexual conduct of constitutional protection in all but exceptional cases." The new rule "encourages prosecutions under local laws and does not require . . . that any criminal prosecution be preceded by actual judgment that a work is 'beyond the pale.' " This "creates a serious danger of self-censorship, at least by those who would not be comfortable as defendants in criminal cases."

Lewis, Anthony. "Bad Time for Civil Liberties." *MORE*, 2(12):9–10, December 1972. **1L168**
An address delivered at a fund-raising rally for Peter Bridge, under sentence for contempt of court for refusing to divulge his journalistic sources, deals with the journalist's responsibilities as well as his rights.

———. "Cantankerous, Obstinate, Ubiquitous: The Press." *Utah Law Review*, 1975:75–94, Spring 1975. **1L169**
"My conclusion is that, just as the press needs a deeper understanding of the function of law, so should judges come to understand the extraordinary role of the press in this country—understanding that it is meant to be cantankerous, obstinate, even disrespectful. The press does not as a rule relish that role itself; it prefers to be comfortable and complacent. But in the extreme situation—a lawless President—the press, or enough of it, can rise to its great function and together with the law, protect the Constitution."

———. "Press, Freedom and National Security." *Journalism Today*, 1(2):51–61, Spring 1967. **1L170**
The chief London correspondent of the *New York Times* compares the freedom of American press with that of the British in matters of security affairs, contempt of court, and libel. He is critical of the British D-Notice system for guarding national secrets.

———. "Press Power and the First Amendment." *Civil Liberties Review*, 1:183–85, Fall 1973. **1L171**
A newspaper columnist finds it incongruous for the press, which traditionally questions others, to claim a broad immunity from being questioned itself. He is dubious about reporter's privilege bills and believes a press council would be a good thing for both the public and the press. "We think criticism strengthens governments and other institutions; why will it weaken ours?"

Lewis, Constance M. "Private Defamation: 'Mary Firestone, Mary Firestone?' " *North Carolina Central Law Journal*, 8:109–22, Fall 1976. **1L172**
Re: *Time, Inc. v. Firestone*, 424 U.S. 448 (1976).

Lewis, David L. "Henry Ford, Publicity and a One Million Dollar Libel." *Public Relations Journal*, 25:21–24, August 1969. **1L173**
The author reconstructs Henry Ford's famous libel suit against the *Chicago Tribune* in which the jury found the newspaper guilty of libel (it had called Ford an anarchist) and assessed a fine of six cents. Both Ford and the *Tribune* claimed victory and vindication. The famous industrialist organized his own news bureau to tell his side of the court battle.

Lewis, Denslow. *The Gynecologic Consideration of the Sexual Act. . . . Reprinted from Transactions of the Section on Obstetrics and Disease of Women at the Fiftieth Annual Meeting of the American Medical*

Association, Held at Columbus, Ohio, June Six to Nine, Eighteen Hundred and Ninety-Nine. Together with a Statement of Facts Incident to the Refusal of the Publication Committee to Publish This Paper in the Journal of the American Medical Association. Chicago, Henry O. Shepard, 1900. 49p. (Reprinted *With an Account of Denslow Lewis, Pioneer Advocate of Public Sexual Education and Venereal Prophylaxis* by Marc H. Hollender, M.D., M & S Press, Weston, Mass., 1970) **1L174**

The editor of the *Journal of the American Medical Association* refused to publish this scientific paper, delivered at their annual convention because of his "personal views in reference to this class of literature," and because he feared postal authorities would judge it obscene. Dr. Lewis argued his case before the Association, citing opinions of five leading jurists, including Clarence Darrow, that the work, addressed to physicians did not come under obscenity laws, but the Association backed the editor. Dr. Lewis arranged for private publication of the work, including correspondence relating to the censorship. Only three copies of the pamphlet are known to exist.

Lewis, Felice F. *Literature, Obscenity, and Law.* Carbondale, Ill., Southern Illinois University Press, 1976. 297p. **1L175**

This book "offers the reader a broad retrospective view of literature's involvement in the obscenity question by presenting a systematic, comparative investigation of (1) works of imaginative literature (novels, short stories, poetry, and plays) that are known to have been the subject of obscenity litigation in the United States; (2) trends in sexual content, explicit langauge, and moral values that are reflected in that fiction; and (3) judicial opinions concerning that fiction, and the literary implications of the opinions." In the discussion the author has "tried to present facts rather than opinions on the theory that the facts when known speak for themselves, and that the plethora of opinions offered has been less illuminating than is our experience with literary censorship in this country. It is clear, however, that censors have not discriminated between outstanding cultural contributions and what might be called worthless pornography in attacking literature, for the fiction that has been involved in litigation includes works by many important American writers of this century, as well as by prominent English and European authors both past and present. Thus one indisputable fact is that the threat to freedom of expression embodied in the censorship of literature is not an insignificant one, to be passed over lightly. And in spite of the increased freedom of recent years, the obscenity issue has not yet been resolved; indeed, the innate complexity of the problem has been increased by the latest rulings of the highest court in the land."

Lewis, Howard T. "Censorship." In his *The Motion Picture Industry*. New York, Van Nostrand, 1933, pp. 365–92. **1L176**

An historical survey of censorship of motion pictures in the United States, from 1909 when the National Board of Censorship was established in New York to the 1930 adoption of the code of moral principles by the Motion Picture Producers and Distributors of America. There are also chapters on block booking and chain theater control.

Lewis, J. William. "The Information Act: Judicial Enforcement of the Records Provision." *Virginia Law Review*, 54(3):466–90, April 1968. **1L177**

A discussion of Subsection (c) of the Information Act "which gives the public a right to receive certain information held by federal agencies, provides a judicial remedy, and authorizes a sanction for disobedience."

Lewis, Jane. *Access to Congressional Committees.* Columbia, Mo., Freedom of Information Center, School of Journalism, University of Missouri at Columbia, 1970. 5p. (Report no. 252) **1L178**

"Overturning the Rayburn doctrine barring live radio-TV coverage of House hearings this year is seen as another milestone in media's battle for greater access to government."

Lewis, Mason C. "The Individual Member's Right to Recover for a Defamation Leveled at the Group." *University of Miami Law Review*, 17:519–36, Summer 1963. **1L179**

"This paper will deal with the plaintiff specifically as a member of a defamed group and will attempt to indicate the various factors that the courts have considered significant in arriving at their conclusions as to the sufficiency of the identification."

Lewis, R. Fred. "A Newsman's Privilege—The First Amendment." *University of Miami Law Review*, 25:521–27, Spring 1971. **1L180**

Re: *Caldwell v. United States* (1970). "Where it is shown that the public's first amendment right to be informed would be jeopardized by requiring a journalist to submit to secret grand jury interrogation, the government must demonstrate a compelling need for the witness' presence before the judicial process properly can issue to require attendance."

Lewis, Robert. "Free Speech and Property Rights—Re-equated: The Supreme Court Ascends from Logan Valley." *Labor Law Journal*, 24:195–200, April 1973. **1L181**

The counsel for the Logan Valley shopping center analyzes the U.S. Supreme Court's decisions subsequent to *Food Employees v. Logan Valley Plaza* (1968), noting the *Lloyd Corp. v. Tanner* (1972) decision which favored property rights over First Amendment rights, reinterpreted *Logan Valley* and drained it of its vitality. The case involved the right to distribute printed matter in shopping centers.

Lewis, Roger. *Outlaws of America: The Underground Press and Its Context.* London, Heinrich Hanau, 1972. 204p. **1L182**

How the underground or alternative press movement came about in America during the 1960s; how the papers operate; and the numerous interest groups and shades of opinion represented—women's liberation, black liberation, gay liberation, communes, rock and roll, drug culture, mystic impulse, counter-culture, anti-war alliance of the oppressed, and alternative media of college campuses.

Lewis, Scott M. "The Reporter's Privilege: Perspectives on the Constitutional Argument." *Ohio State Law Journal*, 32:340–54, Spring 1971. **1L183**

An examination of the nature of the newsman's privilege with particular emphasis on the U.S. Supreme Court decision in *Caldwell v. United States* (1970). The author concludes that "Constitutional protection of a qualified privilege for newsmen may be justified under proper circumstances in order to maximize the free gathering and reporting of news without sacrificing the vital interests which are served by enforcing the duty of citizens to give testimony. . . . It is for the courts to determine whether there are events, circumstances, and conditions which necessitate extending such a broad and important privilege to members of the news media."

Lewis, Walter, and Richard A. Sprague. "Witness for the Prosecution (and) Objection!" *TV Guide*, 22(48):5–7, 30 November 1974. **1L184**

One district attorney (Walter Lewis) testifies that television is brainwashing juries; another (Richard A. Sprague) disagrees.

Lewis, William H., Jr. " 'Cross-Media' Ownership and the Antitrust Laws—A Critical Analysis and A Suggested Solution." *North Carolina Law Review*, 47:794–815, June 1969. **1L185**

"The purpose of this comment is to discuss how cross-media ownership has been handled in the past by the Federal Communications Commission, to point out and discuss possible modes of attack under the existing antitrust laws, and to suggest a possible solution to this major problem."

[Leyland, Roberts *et al.*] *A Full Report of a Trial for Libel, Browne v. Leyland & Others, at York Spring Assizes, April, 1835, Before Mr. Baron Parke, and a Spe-*

cial Jury; also the Verdict of a Trial for Assault, Waddington v. Browne & Another. . . . Halifax, England, Leyland & Son, 1835. 123p. **1L186**
The case, decided for the defendants, publishers of the *Halifax Guardian*, involved publication of a letter to the editor.

L'Heureux, Nicole. "La Liberté de Presse et la Concentration du Enterprises." *Les Cahiers de Droit*, 15:719–26, 1974. **1L187**
Deals with the issue of press monopoly in the Canadian case of *Regina v. K. C. Irving Ltd. et al*.

"Libel and the Corporate Plaintiff." *Columbia Law Review*, 69:1496–513, December 1969. **1L188**
"This note will examine several recent developments in the law of corporate libel subsequent to *Sullivan* [*New York Times Co. v. Sullivan*, 1964]. It will address itself to three basic issues. First, what is the traditional basis for the right of a corporation to sue in libel and how is this right distinguished from the allied business tort of product disparagement? Second, what policy considerations underlie the expansion of the *Sullivan* rule and why might these considerations support the proposition that the freedom to make reasonable error when criticizing economic institutions should be as great as that allowed for criticism of governmental institutions and 'public figures'? Finally, does the present direction in the development of the law of corporate defamation imply a future merger between corporate libel and product disparagement?"

"Libel Per Se and Epithets Imputing Disloyalty." *Washington University Law Quarterly*, 1968:118–35, Winter 1968. **1L189**
"This note will examine the kinds of epithets that are actionable on their face—libelous per se—with no requirement that the plaintiff plead or prove special damages."

"The Liberty of the Press and Contempt of Court." *Commercial & Municipal Law Reporter* (Port Elizabeth), 22:34–41, March–April 1969. **1L190**
The article examines the "well-defined limitations" placed on the press in order to maintain the dignity of the court and ensure a fair trial. These include publication of matter calculated to bring a court or a judge into contempt or to prejudice a judicial procedure which is pending.

Liberty of the Subject and the Press. Three Letters, Addressed to John Lord Eldon on the Subject of His Having Excluded Gentlemen Who Have Written for the Public Journals from the English Bar. By One Who Was a Writer for the Newspapers. London,

Printed for C. Chapple, 1810. 27p. **1L191**
Lord Eldon was a reactionary Tory who had prosecuted John Horne Tooke and other reformers for seditious libel.

Library Association of Australia. "Statement on Freedom to Read." *Australian Library Journal*, 20(9):43–44, October 1971. **1L192**
The statement reflects the belief of the Association "that freedom can be protected in a democratic society only if its citizens have access to information," and states the consequent obligations and responsibilities of librarians.

Lichty, Lawrence W. "The Myths of Regulation." *Chicago Journalism Review*, 6(7):11–13, July 1973. (Reprinted in Don R. Le Duc, *ed.*, *Issues in Broadcast Regulation*, pp. 22–27) **1L193**
"Broadcast regulation is little more than pious theories and bureaucrats." At license renewal time the Federal Communications Commission virtually never compares a station's past performance with its promises; no station has ever had its license denied or revoked solely because it did not fulfill its programming promises. Most station employees have never seen the promises.

———, and William B. Blankenburg. "Challenging a TV License: The Madison Story." *Chicago Journalism Review*, 5(10):10–13, October 1972. **1L194**
Two Wisconsin professors file petitions to force the Federal Communications Commission to enforce their own rules with respect to the renewal of the license to WISC–TV.

Lichty, Lawrence W., and Malachi C. Topping. "Regulation." In their *American Broadcasting; A Source Book on the History of Radio and Television*. New York, Hastings House, 1975, pp. 527–643. **1L195**
Content: The National Radio Conferences by Edward F. Sarno, Jr. Regulation of Broadcasting by the Department of Commerce, 1921–1927 by Marvin R. Bensman. John R. Brinkley: His Contribution to Broadcasting by Maurice E. Shelby, Jr. TNT Baker: Radio Quack by Thomas W. Hoffer. Regulatory Influences Upon Television's Development: Early Years Under the Federal Radio Commission by Robert H. Stern. Radio's Censorship "Code" by J. H. Ryan. Reaction to the "Blue Book" (FCC's 1946 Report, Public Service Responsibility of Broadcast Licensees) by Richard J. Meyer. Development of Television: FCC Allocations and Standards by Roscoe L. Barrow *et al*. Members of the Federal Radio Commission and Federal Communications Commission, 1927–1961 by Lawrence W. Lichty. The Impact of FRC and FCC Commissioners' Backgrounds on the Regulation of Broadcasting by Lawrence W. Lichty. The FCC: A Theory of Regulatory Reflex Action by Don R. Le Duc.

Licker, Jessica A. "Constitutionality of Federal Obscenity Legislation: *Roth* and *Stanley* on a Seesaw." *Boston University Law Review*, 52:443–63, Spring 1972. **1L196**
"By upholding 19 U.S.C. section 1305(a) and 18 U.S.C. section 1461, and simultaneously reaffirming *Stanley v. Georgia*, the Supreme Court has indicated that it would like to allow state and federal legislatures to place a comprehensive ban on obscenity, with criminal sanctions for distribution, but with the narrow exception that a reader-purchaser may not be prosecuted for possession. Although this broad rule may be desirable social policy, the argument that it is compelled by the Constitution is untenable."

Lieberman, J. Ben. "Freedom of the Press." In *Encyclopedia Americana*, New York, Grolier, 1970, vol. 22, pp. 554–55. **1L197**
Topics considered: Constitutional right (licensing, seditious libel, taxes on knowledge, absolute [negative] freedom, minimum limitations, harassment, intimidations and reprisals, and limitations on means of production or distribution), balanced rights, freedom of information, positive guarantee, Communist concept of press freedom, "constructive" freedom of information, and freedom of the student press.

Liebert, Robert M., Emily S. Davidson, and John M. Neale. "Aggression in Childhood: The Impact of Television." In Victor B. Cline, *ed.*, *Where Do You Draw the Line?* Provo, Utah, Brigham Young University Press, 1974, pp. 113–28. **1L198**
A summary of the present state of knowledge of the effects of television on children. The authors recommend the adoption of a code defining "prosocial" behavior, a more extensive exploration of the effects of prosocial programming, and learning more about children's preferences and reactions to programs as a guide for television producers.

Liebman, James S. "Search and Seizure of the Media: A Statutory Fourth Amendment and First Amendment Analysis." *Stanford Law Review*, 28:957–1003, May 1976. **1L199**
"Media searches lie at the crossroads of crucial first and fourth amendment interests. This Note surveys that vital intersection, through which also pass important societal interests in criminal investigation and judicial acquisition of knowledge, generally. The analysis turns in Part II to a consideration of the best constitutional accommodation of the colliding interests and in Part III concludes with a discussion of several alternative constitutional standards

that would restrict or prohibit press searches." Part I examines state shield laws.

[Liebowitz, Martin.] "The St. Louis *Free Press*: An Interview with Editor Martin Liebowitz." *Missouri Library Association Quarterly*, 30:191–96, September 1969. **1L200**

The editor discusses the role of the underground press and its accomplishments.

Lietzen, Walter E. *The Legal Process through Which Freedom of Publication Became Constitutionally Accepted Doctrine*. Lawrence, Kans., University of Kansas, 1973. 141p. (Unpublished Master's thesis) **1L201**

"This thesis examines historical documents of the colonial and constitutional periods of the United States and traces the judicial concept of liberty until the Supreme Court interpreted liberty to include freedom of the press in 1925."

"Lifting the Curtain from Government Secrets: Freedom of Information Act." *U.S. News and World Report*, 74(6):47–50, 5 February 1973. **1L202**

"It's easier now to get a look into those official papers that bureaucrats try to hide under 'Secret' stamps. A federal law and a Nixon order have expanded the public's 'right to know.' But problems remain."

"Light on the Darkness of Pornography." *PTA Magazine*, 65(3):16–17, November 1970. **1L203**

Comments on the findings of the U.S. Commission on Obscenity and Pornography, endorsing the ideas for sex education and for continuing open discussion of the issue, but disapproving of removing all bans on pornography for adults. "To make pornography available to adults and at the same time inaccessible to children and youth is an impossible feat."

[Liles, Gary F.] "Tennessee Grants Newsmen a Qualified Disclosure Shield." *Memphis State University Law Review*, 4:143–52, Fall 1973. **1L204**

The author believes that on balance the Tennessee shield law is a good one. "It grants a general protective shield to newsmen in the interest of preserving an unburdened stream of information to the public, while withholding or divesting the privilege in those civil and criminal cases in which disclosure is deemed essential to the public interest in the administration of justice."

Lim-Chun, Lily Y. *U.S. v. Nixon and Executive Privilege*. Columbia, Mo.,

Freedom of Information Center, School of Journalism, University of Missouri at Columbia, 1975. 8p. (Report no. 345) **1L205**

"The Supreme Court decision in *U.S. v. Nixon* focused on specifics and left the greater problems of executive privilege largely untouched. The author summarizes the events leading up to the historic confrontation and then looks at the future of executive privilege."

"Limited Access to Purchase Public Issue Advertising Time." *Rutgers Law Review*, 27:738–62, Spring 1974. **1L206**

"This Comment examines the bases of 'journalistic discretion' identified by the Court [*Columbia Broadcasting System, Inc. v. Democratic National Committee*, 1973] to determine whether, contrary to the Court's conclusion, broadcasters are indeed required to grant access to the medium through the sale of air time to some people who wish to express their views on some issues of public importance. It also explores whether the FCC policy of sharing program responsibilities with licensees, coupled with the first amendment, requires broadcasters to provide limited access for editorial advertising."

"The Limits of Literary Criticism." *Irish Law Times and Solicitors' Journal*, 75:47–49, 22 February 1941. **1L207**

Comment on the perils of literary criticism where the critic "is torn between the Scylla of outspoken and fearless criticism, where it is called for, and the Charybdis of cowardly commendation and faint praise." The occasion for the note was a recent libel trial in England, *Sitwell and Others v. Co-operative Press, Ltd., and Elliott*, which involved literary criticism.

Lincoln, Anthony. "Reading between the Lines—The Lawyers and the News Desk." In Michael Rubinstein, *ed.*, *Wicked, Wicked Libels*, London, Routledge & Kegan Paul, 1972, pp. 54–65. **1L208**

The author writes on the role of the newspaper lawyer in protecting the British press from libel charges. "The Press, guided by their lawyers, are inevitably tight-rope walking when they probe scandals. . . . If government and bureaucracy become oppressive, there is no problem. Civil servants cannot or do not sue, nor do administrators. It is the private tyrants in industry, trade and the professions who have to be watched carefully."

Linde, Hans A. " 'Clear and Present Danger' Reexamined: Dissonance in the *Brandenburg* Concerto." *Stanford Law Review*, 22:1163–86, June 1970. **1L209**

"The present Article shows that, 50 years after the birth of 'clear and present danger,' the Court's position remains ambivalent about the relationship between external circumstances and the intrinsic content of expression in first amendment analysis. The Article concludes

that the circumstances accompanying the expression—whether phrased as 'clear and present danger' or otherwise—can have no bearing on the validity of legislative restraints directed in terms against specified kinds of speech or press."

Linden, Kathryn B. *The Film Censorship Struggle in the United States from 1926 to 1957, and the Social Values Involved*. New York, New York University, 1972. 513p. (Ph.D. dissertation, University Microfilms, no. 72–20,646) **1L210**

"The purpose of this study is to show through the history and words of film censors and non-censors the significant social values each espouses, and to indicate each has ideological commitments involving value that cannot be ignored." The author recommends that a national advisory committee of responsible citizens and producers, directors and actors be established to formulate a realistic code, act as a clearing house for criticism, and expand the uses of the screen. She also recommends that the Motion Picture Association be restructured on a professional level. The study holds that "a code is as important in the area of film as in law and medicine."

Lindsey, Michael K. "Public Broadcasting: Editorial Restraints and the First Amendment." *Federal Communications Bar Journal*, 28:63–100, 1975. **1L211**

"This article will sketch the history of non-commercial television, review the general problem of broadcast editorializing, and examine justifications for and constitutional problems in the different standard applied to noncommercial broadcasters."

Lingeman, Richard R. "The Last Word: Freedom to Read (1)—Porno." *New York Times Book Review*, 76(43):71, 24 October 1971. **1L212**

Comments on the increased number of "fully accredited intellectuals" who have been expressing concern over the rising tide of pornography and have been espousing some form of controls.

———. "The Last Word: Freedom to Read (2)—Politics." *New York Times Book Review*, 76(44):63, 31 October 1971. **1L213**

A review of individual and organizational efforts in recent years to suppress books. In the complaints it is "difficult to tell where obscenity leaves off and fear of political and cultural ideas begins."

Linsley, William A. "The Supreme Court and the First Amendment: 1971–1972." In *Free Speech Yearbook*, *1972*. New York, Speech Communication Association, 1973, pp. 92–114. **1L214**

The review of court decisions includes cases in the areas of language, press, libel and slander, obscenity, and postal service.

―――. "The Supreme Court and the First Amendment, 1972–1973." In *Free Speech Yearbook*, *1973*. New York, Speech Communication Association, 1974, pp. 66–86. **1L215**
Includes a summary of cases on obscenity (*Miller v. State of California*, *Paris Adult Theatre v. Slaton*, *U.S. v. Orito*, *Kaplan v. California*, and *U.S. v. 12 200-ft. Reels of Super 8 mm Film*); radio and television (*Columbia Broadcasting System, Inc. v. Democratic National Committee*), and newspapers (*Pittsburg Press v. Pittsburg Commission on Human Relations*).

―――. "The Supreme Court and the First Amendment: 1973–1974." In *Free Speech Yearbook*, *1974*. New York, Speech Communication Association, 1975, pp. 74–94. **1L216**
Areas of special interest: symbolic speech, schools, fighting words, obscenity, loyalty oaths, prisons, newspapers, and defamation.

―――. "The Supreme Court and the First Amendment: 1974–1975." In *Free Speech Yearbook*, *1975*. Speech Communication Association, 1976, pp. 67–84. **1L217**
The review considers a number of cases involving newspapers (*Cantrell v. Forest City Publishing Co.* and *Bigelow v. Commonwealth of Virginia*), radio and television (*Cox Broadcasting Corp. v. Cohn* and *U.S. v. New Jersey State Lottery Commission*), and motion pictures and the stage (*Erznoznik v. City of Jacksonville* and *Southeastern Promoters v. Conrad*).

Lippert, David J. *The Enactment and Legal Interpretations of Wisconsin Access Laws to Public Records and Proceedings*. Carbondale, Ill., Southern Illinois University, 1969. 613p. (Ph.D. dissertation, University Microfilms, no. 70–437) **1L218**
"This is an historical and exploratory study of public access to public records and proceedings in Wisconsin. An examination is made of: (1) the enactment of legislation at the state level, and (2) legal decisions and opinions on this legislation. The study focuses on Section 14.90, a general open meetings law enacted by the Wisconsin Legislature in 1959; this has been known as the 'anti-secrecy law,' or the people's 'right to know' law. A major finding in the study is the existence of more than 100 other access laws, all but a few of which were enacted before the passage of Section 14.90. Several were enacted by the first State Legislature in 1848."

[Lippman, Marshall.] "Speech or Debate Clause Held No Bar to Declaratory Judgment and Injunction Against Publication of Congressional Committee Report by Public Printer." *New York Law Forum*, 16:934–41, 1970. **1L219**
Re: *Hentoff v. Ichord* (1970), in which the Court issued a permanent injunction barring publication or distribution of an official Congressional Committee report, which was charged by the plaintiff as being libelous, declaring the Congressional Committee report to be "without any proper legislative purpose." While recognizing the repugnance of an official "blacklist," the author concludes that the Court's remedy may be worse than the original wrong.

Lippmann, Walter. *American Inquisitors: A Commentary on Dayton and Chicago*. New York, Macmillan, 1928. 120p. (Barbour-Page Lectures, University of Virginia) **1L220**
Observations on the predicament faced by the modern teacher and others whose business it is to popularize ideas, while working under popular government during a period of conflict over religious fundamentalism and political tradition. The Scopes evolution trial at Dayton, Tenn., and the trial of William McAndrew in Chicago over the use of textbooks on American history, serve as the bases for a philosophical discussion.

―――. *A Free Press*. [London, International Press Institute, 1965.] 11p. (Printed by Berlingske Tidende of Copenhagen) **1L221**
In an address before the fourteenth International Press Institute Assembly, held in London, 27 May 1965, Lippmann noted that "a free press is not a privilege but an organic necessity in a great society." He cites as some of the problems of a free press—the conflict between the public's right to know and government's need for confidentiality, the reporting of crime and punishment versus the fair administration of justice, and the conflict between the journalist's duty to seek the truth and his human desire to get on in the world, to be on good terms with the powerful, and to be loyal to his country's government. The growing professionalism in journalism is "the most radical innovation since the press became free of government control and censorship."

―――. "The Public Philosophy and Freedom of Speech." In his *Essays in the Public Philosophy*. Boston, Little, Brown, 1955, pp. 124–31. (Reprinted in Clinton Rossiter and James Lare, eds., *The Essential Lippmann*, New York, Random House, 1965, pp. 193–96) **1L222**
"In the public philosophy, freedom of speech is conceived as the means to a confrontation of opinion," not as a trial of strength but as a means of elucidation. Because the purpose of confrontation is to discern truth, there are codes of fair dealing and fair comment. "For the right to freedom of speech is no license to deceive, and willful misrepresentation is a vio-

lation of its principles." Freedom of speech can never be maintained, according to the public philosophy, "merely by objecting to interference with the liberty of the press, of printing, of broadcasting, of the screen. It can be maintained only by promoting debate."

Lipsky, Abbott, Jr. "Reconciling *Red Lion* and *Tornillo*: A Consistent Theory of Media Regulation." *Stanford Law Review*, 28:563–88, Fall 1976. **1L223**
"This Note examines the Court's justification for this difference of treatment [in regulation of the newspaper press and the broadcast media]. Part I discusses the leading cases on the constitutionality of media regulation. These cases generally involve disputes concerning the allocation of editorial power—the power of the publisher or broadcaster to determine the contents of the message which he conveys. Part II argues that the existing constitutional rationale for broadcast regulation is based on inadequate distinctions between the print and broadcast media, and examines the sources and consequences of editorial power in each medium. Part III proposes a test for the constitutionality of media regulation which would shift the focus of the Court's approach from a concern with the allocation of editorial power to the equally important issue of how editorial power arises. The test is then applied to current and proposed regulatory schemes for several media institutions."

Liston, Robert A. *The Right to Know: Censorship in America*. New York, Franklin Watts, 1973. 150p. **1L224**
This book explores two conflicting ideas to rational consideration: censorship and total freedom of expression. "These two opposing ideas strike at the essential meaning of freedom in our society. Part of our much-observed American malaise lies in our confusion over what should be censored and by whom." The author deals with the area of obscenity in print, movies, and television, and in the area of public information—government secrecy, and censorship of newspapers and broadcasting. Whatever controls are necessary, he believes, can be carried out through methods other than nineteenth-century censorship. In the area of obscenity, for example, he suggests the use of taxation and a massive educational campaign.

Litman, Julius I. *News Bias: Perceived and Identified By Professional Reporters and Audience Members*. Philadelphia, University of Pennsylvania, 1973. 52p. (Unpublished Master's thesis) **1L225**

Little, Joseph W., and Thomas Tompkins. "Open Government Laws: An Insider's View." *North Carolina Law Review*, 53:451–89, February 1975. **1L226**

A look at open-meeting laws from the point of view of public officials and managers of public enterprises and the problems such legislation poses in both policy making and efficient day-to-day management. The authors propose a model open-meeting law which would take into consideration the internal problems of public administration.

"The Little Red School-Book Reconsidered." *Index on Censorship*, 1(3/4): 210–14, Autumn–Winter 1972. **1L227**
Text of the New Zealand Indecent Publications Tribunal's decision in the case of the book, *The Little Red School-Book* by Søren Hansen and Jesper Jensen. The Tribunal classified the book as "not indecent within the meaning of the Indecent Publications Act of 1963."

Littner, Ner. "A Psychiatrist Looks at Television and Violence." *Television Quarterly*, 8(4):7–23, Fall 1969. (Excerpted in Rod Holmgren and William Norton, *eds.*, *The Mass Media Book*, pp. 343–56) **1L228**
The author believes that the vast amount of violence on television is a reflection of the violent interests of the viewers, that honest portrayal of violence does not endanger viewers of any age who are not violent already; that for some who are already violently disposed, TV violence may provide a *modus operandi*, that dishonest violence does not have any marked pathological impact on the average adult; and that "instead of wasting their efforts on such red herrings as censorship, violence, sex, or nudity I think that both the viewing public and the television industry should devote its considerable talents and energies to creating conditions that would make it possible to develop and screen television shows specializing in such qualities as excellence, artistic value, creativity, originality, honesty, and integrity."

Liveright, Horace B. "The Absurdity of Censorship." *Independent*, 10:92–93, 17 March 1923. **1L229**
"A censorship over literature and the arts is stupid, ignorant, and impudent, and is against the fundamental social principles of all intelligent Americans."

Lloyd, Edward D. "Some Aspects of Contempt of Court." In Melbourne University, *The Law and the Printer, the Publisher and the Journalist. The Collected Papers of a Seminar at Melbourne University on August 12, 1971*. Melbourne, Antony Whitlock, 1971, pp. 3–11. **1L230**
The author traces the history of contempt of court in British law, giving special attention to the effect on journalists. While present-day contempt practices do not protect the judge

from reasonable criticism, they do protect jurymen from pretrial publicity that might be prejudicial to a fair trial. The author contrasts the situation in Britain and the Commonwealth with that in the United States.

Lloyd, Herbert. *The Legal Limits of Journalism*. Oxford, England, Pergamon, 1968. 121p. (Library of Industrial and Commercial Education and Training) **1L231**
A guide to the British law of libel and slander—written and spoken, camera, caption, or criticism—for those starting a career in journalism. Includes chapters on absolute and qualified privilege and text of the Defamation Act of 1952. Table of cases.

Lloyd, James *et al*. *Is Pornography Really Harmful?* 28 min. tape recording, North Hollywood, Calif., Center for Cassette Studies, 1971. (Publisher's title: Pornography—A Bad Companion) **1L232**
Rabbi Julius Neumann and Father Morton A. Hill, from Operation Yorkville, an organization to combat pornography, discuss the nature of pornography, its extent, its harmful influence, and methods of combatting it. Father James Lloyd is moderator.

Lloyd, Peter. *Not for Publication*. London, The Bow Group, 1968. 80p. **1L233**
A survey of restrictions on the mass media in Britain—the theater, books, newspapers, and broadcasting—prepared for the Bow Group, an independent organization of conservatives. While acknowledging the liberalization of censorship of films, books, and theater, the report shows that restrictions on libel, contempt, and official security remains much the same. Recommendations call for abolishing theater censorship, abolishing cinema censorship for adults, liberalizing the obscenity laws, reforming libel and contempt laws operating against newspapers, taking the government out of program control in broadcasting, and repeal of the existing Official Secrets Act. The report also recommends establishment of a permanent Institute of Communications Research.

Lloyd, Robert M. "Free Press and Fair Trial: An Evolving Controversy." *University of Florida Law Review*, 19:660–79, Spring 1967. **1L234**
The author calls for affirmative action by the bar to discipline itself to prevent members from releasing prejudicial information to the news media and for the press to "resist temptation to hide irresponsible criminal news behind the cliché: 'the public has a right to know.' " Trial courts can also help reduce the possibility of a prejudicial jury "by liberalizing existing trial level remedies."

"Lloyd Corp. v. Tanner; A Shopping Center Open for Business But Not for

Dissent." *Maine Law Review*, 25:131–46, 1973. **1L235**
The author attempts to show that in *Lloyd Corp. v. Tanner* (1972), and two earlier decisions considering the relationship between free speech and public property "the Court has begun to develop a constitutional doctrine based on the concept of essential community forums." He calls for a further delineation of the doctrine.

"Lloyd Corp. v. Tanner: The Demise of Logan Valley and the Disguise of Marsh." *Georgetown Law Journal*, 61:1187–1219, May 1973. **1L236**
Re: *Lloyd Corp. v. Tanner* (1972), a case involving distribution of handbills in a privately owned shopping center. The decision "is a departure from recent Supreme Court and lower court rulings involving first amendment rights on private property open to the public."

Lobdell, Robert, and Cecil Hicks. "Subpoena Power; A Legal Discussion." *National Press Photographer*, 26(1): 8–9, January 1971. **1L237**
The general counsel for the *Los Angeles Times* (Robert Lobdell) and the district attorney for Orange County (Cecil Hicks) conclude that new legal guidelines will evolve in the next two or three years to clarify the lawyer's subpoena powers and the newsman's rights to protect the sources of his information.

Lobenfeld, Eric J. "The Commercial Speech Doctrine: The First Amendment at a Discount." *Brooklyn Law Review*, 41:60–90, Summer 1974. **1L238**
"This note will explore the doctrinal basis for distinguishing commercial and noncommercial expression, and evaluate the appropriateness of 'commercial speech' as a discrete principle of constitutional law."

"Local Censorship—Beginning or End?" *Film; Monthly Magazine of the British Federation of Film Societies*, 24:1–2, March 1975. **1L239**
Criticism of the Greater London Council Film Viewing Board for continuing to prohibit adults from seeing films denied a license by the British Board of Film Censors.

Locke, Edward. "Access to Materials." *Bookmark* (New York State Library), 31:111–16, March–April 1972. **1L240**
Censorship is selection or refusal to select for the wrong reasons—pressure from a person or group or a desire to protect the reader from harm. Obscenity, not politics or blasphemy, is the major issue today. Librarians must know their legal rights. One of the greatest concerns of librarians today is the concept of "variable obscenity" which involves the access or denial to children and teen-agers those works considered appropriate for adults. Perhaps a law suit by a teen-ager denied access would clarify the issue.

Lockhart, William B. "Escape from the Chill of Uncertainty: Explicit Sex and the First Amendment." *Georgia Law Review*, 9:533–87, Spring 1975. **1L241**
"In *Miller v. California* [1973] the Supreme Court rewrote much of the law of obscenity and, in the process, engendered confusion as to the manner in which its standards should be applied. The logical result of this confusion is evident in the subsequent prosecutions of individuals who disseminated material which is at least arguably not obscene. Professor Lockhart analyzes these cases in terms of their probable, ultimate consequences—a 'chilling effect' on the dissemination of any material which may be violative of the *Miller* standards. After identifying the vagueness inherent in the *Miller* test as the cause for the confusion and its resulting 'chilling effect,' Professor Lockhart suggests several proposals for avoiding such consequences while maintaining the framework pronounced by *Miller*. He concludes by urging others to analyze his suggestions and promulgate still better solutions for the present situation."—Editor

——. "The Findings and Recommendations of the Commission on Obscenity and Pornography: A Case Study of the Role of Social Science in Formulating Public Policy." *Oklahoma Law Review*, 24:209–23, May 1971. (Reprinted in *Mountain Plains Library Quarterly*, May 1972) **1L242**
The chairman of the Commission, in an address delivered at the University of Oklahoma College of Law, discusses the collaboration of social scientists, lawyers, and citizens trained in neither law nor the social sciences in their attempt to develop public policy on the little understood area of obscenity and pornography.

[——.] " 'I Don't Want Anyone Telling Me What I Can Read or View': A Deep-Rooted Desire for Freedom: An Interview with William B. Lockhart, Chairman, President's Commission on Obscenity and Pornography." *Minnesota Journal of Education*, 51:19–21, May 1971. **1L243**
Dean Lockhart answers questions about the work of the Commission, its findings, and public reaction to the report.

——, Yale Kamisar, and Jesse H. Choper. *Cases and Materials on Constitutional Rights and Liberties*. 3d ed. St. Paul, Minn., West, 1970. 1074p. (4th ed., 1975, 1664p.) **1L244**
Chapter 6 deals with Freedom of Expression and Association: The Emerging Principles; Freedom of Expression and Association vs. National Security, Loyalty; Freedom of Expression vs. the Fair Administration of Justice; Freedom of Expression and Association vs. Preservation of Local Law and Order; Mass Protests and Demonstrations in the Context of

the Current "Negro Evangelism"; "Speech Plus" vs. the State's "Public Policy"; Freedom of Expression vs. Protection Against Damage to Reputation and Invasion of Privacy; Freedom of Expression and Association vs. Standards of Decency, Morality.

Lockhart, William B., and Robert C. McClure. "Obscenity Censorship: The Core Constitutional Issue—What Is Obscene?" *Utah Law Review*, 7:289–303, Spring 1961. (Reprinted in Donald B. Sharp, *ed.*, *Commentaries on Obscenity*, pp. 131–52) **1L245**
"While the Court has not provided much direction—yet—on the core problem of obscenity, it has made a great deal of progress and some very significant law on the collateral problems involved in the administration of obscenity laws." It has established that material must be judged by the dominant theme of the whole work, the bookseller must be charged with knowledge of the alleged obscenity to be convicted criminally, and considerable freedom is allowed for advocating ideas and behavior considered "immoral" by current standards. The authors believe that the Supreme Court has moved in the right direction toward protection of freedom of expression while at the same time protecting the immature from the evils of pornography.

Loevinger, Lee. "Advertising Abuses and the Worse Cure." *Vital Speeches*, 39:114–20, 1 December 1972. **1L246**
The author opposes present efforts to expand the power of the Federal Trade Commission to control advertising and counter-advertising. "The combination of these powers would enable the FTC to determine which media should receive or be denied the indispensable economic support of advertising." No currently charged abuses are sufficiently grave to warrant the dangers inherent in such power.

——. "The FCC and Content Control." In Don R. Le Duc, *ed.*, *Issues in Broadcast Regulation*, Washington, D.C., Broadcast Education Association, 1974, pp. 60–72. **1L247**
A former member of the Federal Communications Commission shows how court decisions and FCC rulings have gradually encroached upon First Amendment guarantees of freedom of speech in broadcasting. "Since the First Amendment commands government neutrality with respect to the content of all types of expression, government action to control the content of expression on limited and licensed facilities seems peculiarly inappropriate. Unfortunately, First Amendment principles are usually tested in situations where the natural sympathies of normal and decent people tend to be engaged by the noble aims and decent purposes of the government officials seeking to exercise control, and to be repelled by the ignoble goals and unworthy purposes of those whose freedom is at issue." The acceptance of the fairness doctrine, the public's right of access, and program evaluation in connection

with license renewal have created widening gaps between First Amendment treatment of broadcasting and the newspaper press. "While the scarcity of broadcasting facilities may support Fairness Doctrine rules, it does not, on the other hand, justify general broadcasting standards." The courts and the Commission have a responsibility to determine the balance of fairness and the bounds of fiduciary duty in broadcasting and "to say what the ideal of free speech means, and how it may be achieved in the confused groping society of our present turbulent and technological world."

——. "Free Speech, Fairness, and Fiduciary Duty in Broadcasting." *Law and Contemporary Problems*, 34:278–98, Spring 1969. **1L248**
Content: FCC License Renewal Denied; Licensee Editorialization; The Fairness Doctrine; The Licensee as a Fiduciary. Under the last heading the author discusses how fiduciary duties would be enforced, the fiduciary duty circumscribing FCC action, and the scarcity argument and fiduciary theory.

——. *The Politics of Advertising*. New York, Television Information Office, 1973, 12p. **1L249**
The author attacks proposals for counter-advertising as fallacious, discriminatory against broadcasting, and unfair to honest advertisers. Increasing the power of government over broadcasting would threaten the economic basis of the industry, would solve no important problems, but would create a host of new problems relating to free speech under the First Amendment.

Loewy, Arnold H. "Abortive Reasons and Obscene Standards: A Comment on the Abortion and Obscenity Cases." *North Carolina Law Review*, 52:223–43, December 1973. **1L250**
The author considers the U.S. Supreme Court's 1972 term approving abortion and defending antiobscenity legislation as being "wrongly decided in the abstract, but when juxtaposed together, they reflect a strangely convoluted concept of constitutional values for the Supreme Court to be espousing."

——. "Free Speech: The 'Missing Link' in the Law of Obscenity." *Journal of Public Law*, 16:81–106, 1967. **1L251**
In question and answer format, the author presents his views on "balancing" as a solution to the dilemma between control of obscenity and protection of free speech and press. He suggests the kinds of restrictions that would likely be constitutionally acceptable. These include legislation protecting children from obscenity, while precluding punishment for private viewing of obscenity or for selling it to a willing adult buyer.

Lofton, John. "Pretrial Crime News: To Curb Or Not to Curb?" *Current History*, 61:71–74, 112, August 1971. (Reprinted in Rod Holmgren and William Norton, eds., *The Mass Media Book*, pp. 63–70) **1L252**
A journalist discusses the case for and against curbing the news media in covering felony offenses subsequent to arrest and pending a verdict. "Under the American system of checks and balances," he concludes, "the courts and the media both play roles which are given high priority in our constitutional system—the courts, the function of insuring justice for individuals; the press, the function of securing for the public an independent scrutiny of governmental agencies, including the courts. Neither of these vital institutions should hold pervasive sway over the other."

Loftus, Joseph A. "New Freedom of Information Law: Fact-Seekers Testing Its Effectiveness." *New York Times*, 18 February 1968, p. 61. (Reprinted in U.S. Senate, Judiciary Committee, *The Freedom of Information Act* ₁Ten Months Review₁, pp. 183–86) **1L253**
The author reports on numerous cases where individuals or organizations have pressed government agencies, sometimes through the courts, to secure public information under the Freedom of Information Act. "The mere threat of a suit, in some cases, has influenced the Government agencies to take a second look at their information practices, and the second look often resulted in disclosure."

Logsdon, Guy. "Censorship in Oklahoma." *Oklahoma Librarian*, 19(1):13–16, January 1969. **1L254**
An historic view of censorship in Oklahoma, beginning with the humorous action in 1910 when the president of a state teachers college personally "denatured" three Greek statues that were "fully sexed instead of fig-leaved." A local poet immortalized the event by a poem that ended: "Now the moral of this isn't hard to find; / The nastiness is all in the mind; / So unless for sculpture you have a knack, / Don't take things off that you can't put back." There was the case of the Free Love Edition of the *Social Democrat*, issued 10 July 1912 by editor Hobart Commer, which sent the editor to jail for sixty days; there was the "Red scare" following World War I, the case against Robert and Ina Wood, Oklahoma City booksellers, imprisoned for selling Communist literature. Approximately ten thousand items from their shop were seized, including Sandburg's *Abraham Lincoln*, Tolstoi's *War and Peace*, and the Constitution of the United States. In 1950 Ruth Brown was discharged as librarian of the Bartlesville Public Library after thirty years of service for refusal to ban the *Nation* and the *New Republic*. In 1959 a Citizens for Decent Literature set up a "smutmobile" as part of a drive for "smut" legislation.

Logue, Cal M. "Free Speech: The Philosophical Poles." In *Free Speech Yearbook*, *1972*. New York, Speech Communication Association, 1973, pp. 40–48. **1L255**
A comparison of the thoughts of Thomas Hobbes, who believed that for man to have security he had to be governed by authority, and John Stuart Mill, who advocated a libertarian philosophy.

Londner, Mark. *Commercial Advertising Restrictions*. Columbia, Mo., Freedom of Information Center, School of Journalism, University of Missouri at Columbia, 1973. 6p. (Report no. 299) **1L256**
"Since the 1911 U.S. Supreme Court decision in *Fifth Avenue Coach Co. v. New York City*, government regulation of commercial advertising has increased significantly. Denied the same protection 'editorial' advertisers have enjoyed, commercial advertisers are fearful of further legislated bans similar to that which has eliminated cigarette commercials on television."

London, Ephraim *et al. Obscenity and the Law*. 56 min. tape recording. North Hollywood, Calif., Center for Cassette Studies, 1966. (Publisher's title: Freedom to Read) **1L257**
A review of the historical development of obscenity law in the United States as interpreted by the U.S. Supreme Court in such cases as *Butler*, *Ulysses*, *Roth*, *Lady Chatterley's Lover*, *Tropic of Cancer*, and *Ginzburg*. Following a background statement by the moderator, four lawyers discuss the meaning of obscenity as interpreted by the courts: Ephraim London, Alan U. Schwartz, Richard H. Kuh, and Robert L. Tofel.

London. Public Morality Council. *The Censorship of Films. Joint Report presented to the Council on 27th March 1930 by the Chairman of the Cinema and Stage Plays Committees*. London, The Council, 1930. 4p. **1L258**
The report reiterates support of film censorship by local authorities rather than by the State. The most powerful control force is the rejection of a theater license by local citizens.

———. *Report of the Stage Plays Committee, Adopted by Council, on October 21st, 1929*. London, The Council, 1929. 4p. **1L259**
Review of the work of the Committee for the past thirteen years. Recommends that licensing of plays should be separate from licensing of theaters. A fine should be imposed as a possible penalty as well as revocation of license. The report notes that the present advisory committee to the Lord Chamberlain in censoring drama now includes a drama critic, and a religious and educational member. A woman has been added to the censorship staff.

———. *A Report on Cinema Films Presented by the Special Sub-Committee to the Public Morality Council at their Meeting, 29th October 1931*. London, The Council, 1931. 23p. **1L260**
The report recommends that the film censor be requested to publish a classified list of subjects of films objected to and an unofficial list of specific titles; that a conference be held between the film censor and religious and educational organizations, dealing with the theme and tendency of certain films; that there be closer cooperation between film censor and licensing authorities; and that the censorship power of local authorities be strengthened. "The censorship of films is primarily in the hands of the British Board of Film Censors, but its decisions are always subject to revision, if necessary, by the local Licensing Authorities, who are the ultimate and, therefore, the real Censors of Films."

Long, Charles. "A Career in Jeopardy—Peter Bridge Goes to Jail." *Quill*, 60(11):48–50, November 1972. **1L261**
The case of the Newark reporter who was jailed when he refused to tell a grand jury, not the source of his information about a criminal case, but about what might be in his private notebooks on the case. References are made to the Sigma Delta Chi legal defense fund used to aid Bridge.

Long, Howard R. "The Commission Has Served Well the Interest of Press Freedom." *Bulletin of the American Society of Newspaper Editors*, 540:8–9, 16, April 1970. **1L262**
"The National Commission on the Causes and Prevention of Violence has served well the interests of press freedom. Offered here is another warning that what those who control the press refuse to do for themselves in some way may be done by others. . . . What the members of the commission are telling us is that, of all our institutions, the press is the one nearest to bankruptcy as measured by service to the public interest." The author cites the successful operation of local press councils, and the success of self-regulation in the motion picture industry and in organized sports.

———. "In Contempt of the Public." *Grassroots Editor*, 9(3):1, 3, May–June 1968. **1L263**
While a newspaper strike creates a crisis for readers, merchants, and journalists, it may not be a catastrophe for the owner because of the tax angle and strike insurance. A case in point is that of John S. Knight and the *Detroit Free Press*.

₍———.₎ "Newspapers Write Own Li-

censing Laws." *Grassroots Editor*, 13(1): 2–3, January–February 1972. **1L264**
"By arrogating to themselves privileges denied to other businessmen the publishers who seek the immunities of the Newspaper Preservation Act have come very close to creating a system of federal licensing. In fact by means of this law they may actually have caused themselves to be licensed."

———, ed. *Main Street Militants: An Anthology from Grassroots Editor*. Carbondale, Ill., Southern Illinois University Press, 1977. 157p. **1L265**
A collection of twenty-eight personal experiences of investigative journalists, taken from accounts appearing in *Grassroots Editor*, some of which have been entered separately in this bibliography. The accounts deal with "weekly newspaper editors who have fought, bled, and suffered a thousand agonies in fulfillment of our Bill of Rights' guarantees of free speech and free press"—Irving Dilliard. Included are the stories of Hazel Brannon Smith, the Mississippi editor whose crusade against political corruption resulted in her newspaper building being burned; J. R. Freeman, the Colorado editor who was fired upon by snipers during his crusade against rape of federal oil shale lands; Gene Wirges who lost his paper and was sentenced to prison on trumped-up charges of perjury for investigating corrupt election practices in Arkansas; Penn Jones, Jr., The Texas newsman whose paper was fire-bombed during his crusade for equal rights.

Long, Joseph C. "The Dawn of a New Era in Freedom of Government Information?" *Grassroots Editor*, 8(5):15–17, 30, September–October 1967. **1L266**
The author analyzes the 1966 amendment to the Federal Public Records Law which eliminates the requirement that a person, in order to get information, must be properly and directly concerned with it, and which closes many loopholes that have allowed government agencies to withhold information improperly "in the public interest."

Long, Laura. *John Peter Zenger: Young Defender of a Free Press*. Indianapolis, Bobbs-Merrill, 1966. 200p. **1L267**
A biography of the Colonial editor, centering around the famous libel trial. Written for children.

[Longford Committee Investigating Pornography.] *Pornography: The Longford Report*. London, Coronet [1972]. 520p. **1L268**
A report of an unofficial committee of some fifty members, appointed by the chairman, Lord Longford, and including a broad spectrum of British business and professional leaders, "to see what means of tackling the problem of pornography would command general support." The report deals with the growth of the pornographic trade and public concern about it, the relationship of violence and pornography, the work of the U.S. Commission on Obscenity and Pornography and the Danish experiment, and a Jewish view as expressed by Rabbi Raymond Apple. Seven subcommittees reported as follows: The Effects and Control of Pornography (Chairman, Norman Anderson); Broadcasting (Chairman, Malcolm Muggeridge); Cinema and Theatre (Chairman, James Sharkey); Books, Magazines, Newspapers (Special report), Advertising (Chairman, Ronald H. Kirkwood); Sex Education (Chairman, Thomas Corbishley); Legal Considerations and Recommendations, Scotland (Chairman, Herbert Kerrigan). In addition, eight individual members submitted statements, with widely varying points of view: Peregrine Worsthorne, Sir Frederick Catherwood, Kingsley Amis and Elizabeth Jane Howard, David Holbrook, Peter Grosvenor, Dr. Peter Scott, and Trevor Huddleston (Bishop of Stepney). Specific changes in the Obscene Publications Act, 1959 and 1964, and the Theatres Act, 1968 were proposed. The report recommended that cinema, television, and sound broadcasting be brought within the purview of the Obscene Publications Act, 1959; penalties under both the Obscene Publications Act and the Theatres Act should be increased; and a new statute be enacted to cover exhibiting material that fell short of being "obscene" but was "indecent." David Holbrook's article on Historical Perspective and Maurice Yaffé's article on Research Survey are included. The latter is an account of the empirical findings concerning the consequences of exposure to pornographic stimuli and gives some directions for future research. The Committee and its report was the subject of considerable controversy in the British press. Lord Longford, onetime member of the Labour Government and an outspoken foe of pornography in the House of Lords, has been popularly referred to as "Lord Porn."

Longley, Laurence D. "The FCC's Attempt to Regulate Commercial Time." *Journal of Broadcasting*, 11:83–89, Winter 1966/67. **1L269**
"The Commission had tried in 1962 to institute a bold policy for the regulation of broadcasting. That it failed to implement this policy, however, can be attributed less to industry pressure, or even to the massive Congressional opposition which developed, than to the inability of the majority of four in 1963 to convert any of their fellow Commissioners." The article is based on the author's doctoral dissertation, *The Politics of Broadcasting*, Vanderbilt University.

Lonnborg, Barbara A. *The First Amendment on the Classified Page: Commercial Speech and the 1973 Supreme Court*. Madison, Wis., University of Wisconsin, 1974. 130p. (Unpublished Master's thesis) **1L270**
"This study concluded that prior to *Pittsburgh Press* [*Pittsburgh Press v. Pittsburgh Commission on Human Relations et al.*, 1973] the Supreme Court used a financial motive test to determine whether speech was commercial or constitutionally protected. In *Pittsburgh Press*, however, the Court used a content test (the

outward form and appearance of the speech) to determine commerciality. Secondly, the study concluded that *Pittsburgh Press* appeared to reduce the scope of First Amendment protection for commercially related speech and might threaten further governmental regulation of quasi-commercial aspects of newspapers."

Loper, Merle W. "Media Access and the First Amendment's Romantic Tradition: A Commentary on Jerome A. Barron, Freedom of the Press for Whom?" *Maine Law Review*, 26:415–33, 1974. **1L271**
A review of Professor Barron's book which, the reviewer believes, "is much more persuasive of the need for access to the contemporary media than it is of the prospects for establishing such a right." He concludes: "The first amendment guarantees neither that the public discussion will be marked by quality, nor that truth will triumph in a fair debate with falsehood. Nor, of course, can a constitutionally guaranteed right of access assure every speaker of an audience. Nothing in a free society can guarantee these things. Rather, free speech in the constitutional sense—as democracy in our national political structure—is an opportunity which the government cannot deny, and which is to be used among the same imperfections and travails that accompany all of the other endeavors of life."

Loring, Mary C. *Burning Ice: The Moral and Emotional Effects of Reading*. New York, Scribner's, 1968. 303p. **1L272**
A questionnaire study of opinions of high school students regarding their perceived effect on themselves of reading books and magazines. The author concludes that "we do have evidence that reading effects and affects behavior for good or evil. The effect may result in socially acceptable behavior or anti-social behavior." The work stems from her 1945 study, *The Effect of Reading on Moral Conduct and Emotional Experience*, done as a doctoral dissertation at Catholic University of America.

Lord, Daniel A. *I Can Read Anything? All Right! Then Read This!* Dublin, Catholic Truth Society of Ireland, 1964. 24p. (Reprinted from Queen's Work edition, St. Louis) **1L273**
A fictional account of a discussion between a Catholic priest and a young man and woman (twins) on the effect of reading—good and bad—on people. The priest discusses anti-Catholic propaganda and dirty books—books intended to destroy religious faith and to make the reader love sin. "Dirt is dirt," Father Hall observes, "whether it is written by Boccaccio, or James Joyce or Cabell, and all the smug hypocrisy in the world will never make it anything but dirt." The story ends with a tiny bonfire in the garden.

————. *What Is Decent Literature?* St. Louis, The Queen's Work, 1940. 40p.
                                                            1L274
This Catholic tract emphasizes the harmful effect of immoral literature. "To the pure all things are pure," is simply nonsense. "To imply that because a man is pure he is not subject to temptation, not subject to the same biological reactions that are common to the rest of humanity, that he is not aroused by that very thing which God and nature meant to arouse him is to talk the most arrant stuff and nonsense." As long as men write dirt for dirt's sake we have to protect ourselves and others.

Lord, Richard A. "Film Is A Four Letter Word." *Memphis State University Law Review*, 5:41–58, Fall 1974. **1L275**
"The purpose of this note is to determine if municipal [motion picture] boards of review such as that existing in Memphis are constitutionally valid. Its scope will include a brief history of obscenity control, a comparison between censor boards and review boards, a look at self-regulation, and an in-depth study of the Memphis municipal legislation."

"A Lordly Look at Obscenity and the Public Good." *Bookseller*, 3262:2826–28, 29 June 1968.   **1L276**
Commentary on the debate in Parliament on the Theatres Bill.

Lorenz, Alfred L. "Does a Printer Have a Right to Print What He Chooses?" *Grassroots Editor*, 10(6):8–11, November–December 1969.   **1L277**
The case of a Port Washington, Wis., printer, the target of an economic boycott that threatened to drive him out of business because he refused to stop printing *Kaleidoscope*, a Milwaukee underground newspaper.

————. *Hugh Gaine: A Colonial Printer-Editor's Odyssey to Loyalism*. Foreword by Howard R. Long. Carbondale, Ill., Southern Illinois University Press, 1972. 192p.   **1L278**
A biography of the Colonial New York printer who was involved in various issues over press freedom, more with an eye on business profit than political ideology. His militant opposition to the Stamp Act and the Townshend Act resulted from a threatened livelihood. While he at first supported the Revolution, his economic conservatism became political and he defected to the British when they occupied New York. Based on the author's doctoral dissertation, Southern Illinois University, 1968 (University Microfilms, no. 69–1752)

Lorenz, Milton C., Jr. "Fairness Doctrine Extended to Product Commer-

cials." *Tulane Law Review*, 46:321–29, December 1971.   **1L279**
Re: *Friends of the Earth v. FCC*, No. 24,556 (D.C. Cir., Aug. 16, 1971).

Lo Sciuto, L. *et al*. "Public Attitudes Towards and Experience with Erotic Materials: Methodologic Report." *Technical Report of the [U.S.] Commission on Obscenity and Pornography*, 6:139–256, 1971.   **1L280**
"This is a report on the methodological procedures employed in conducting a national study of adults and adolescents for the Commission on Obscenity and Pornography during the winter of 1969 and the spring of 1970." Joint authors were: A. Spector, E. Michels, and C. Jenne.

Loshak, David. "India's Sterile Press." *Index on Censorship*, 5(4):20–21, Winter 1976.   **1L281**
"In the year since the Prime Minister, Mrs. Indira Gandhi, proclaimed a state of emergency, the once vivid and stimulating press of India has been reduced to a rapid sterility. Her censorship is as severe as any in the world. . . . It was Mrs. Gandhi's father, Jawaharlal Nehru, who said: 'I would rather have a completely free press with all the dangers involved in the wrong use of that freedom than a suppressed or regulated press.' In his daughter's India, that comment cannot be published."

[Lossing, Benson J.] "Freedom of the Press Vindicated." *Harper's New Monthly Magazine*, 57:293–98, July 1878.   **1L282**
The story of John Peter Zenger's fight for press freedom in Colonial New York.

[Lovejoy, Elijah P.] *Emancipator Extra. The Judgment of Freedom Against The Massacre, November 7, 1837, At Alton, Ill*. New York, American Anti-Slavery Society, 12 February 1838. 4p. (Issued with the *Emancipator*, 12 February 1838)   **1L283**
The entire "extra" edition of the *Emancipator* is devoted to the "outrage" over the murder of Elijah Parish Lovejoy, abolitionist editor, by a mob in Alton, Ill., on 7 November 1837. There is a biography of Lovejoy taken from the *Cincinnati Journal*, articles and editorials from various newspapers across the nation, statements from prominent citizens, the text of resolutions passed at public protest meetings, and calls for action by the American Anti-Slavery Society. The editor challenges the People of Illinois: "The case is before you, and your fellow-countrymen of all the free States are anxiously waiting to see what you will do in the matter. . . . The Legislature of the State ought to be convened, a competent court directed to sit in some other county, where an impartial jury and a peaceful trial may satisfy the world that justice is done." A black-

bordered edition of the *Emancipator*, 23 November 1837, carried the first account of Lovejoy's murder: "The First Martyr Has Fallen in the Holy Cause of Abolition!"

Lovelady, Steven M. "Censoring the Mail: Direct-Mail Advertisers Fear New Federal Law Will Cripple Operations." *Wall Street Journal*, 171:1, 8 February 1968.   **1L284**
A report on the new federal law which allows citizens to bar further mail from anyone who sends offensive ads.

————. "The Smut Industry." *Wall Street Journal*, 169:1, 13, 26 June 1967. (Reprinted in *National Decency Reporter*, July–August 1967)   **1L285**
An account of pornography publishing, including an interview with the self-styled "king of the pornographers," Martin Lehrmoss of Los Angeles, the center of the smut industry.

Loveland, David C. *Citizen Groups Challenge Radio-TV*. Columbia, Mo., Freedom of Information Center, School of Journalism, University of Missouri at Columbia, 1971. 5p. (Report no. 256)   **1L286**
Citizen groups are challenging the licenses of television and radio stations in an effort to make them more responsive to the needs of the community. This paper focuses on the groups which have been instrumental in these challenges and outlines the methods and procedures they used in challenging the broadcasting industry."

————. *Dept. of HEW Implements the FOI Act*. Columbia, Mo., Freedom of Information Center, School of Journalism, University of Missouri at Columbia, 1971. 5p. (Report no. 273)   **1L287**
Documentation of what one federal agency has done to live up to the spirit of the Federal Public Records Law (FOI Act) of 1967.

Loveland, Genevra K. "Newsgathering: Second-Class Right Among First Amendment Freedoms." *Texas Law Review*, 53:1440–82, November 1975.   **1L288**
"It appears highly unlikely that the Supreme Court will recognize a special press right in the near future even though *Branzburg* [Branzburg v. Hayes, 1972] and *Saxbe* [Saxbe v. Washington Post, 1974] do not necessarily preclude recognizing such a right in situations in which the Court might see government interests as less compelling. At the least, however, the Court must redefine its *Saxbe* position to make clear that it will not countenance wholesale exclusion of press and public. The Court must establish the public right it has extolled on a firmer constitutional basis. In addition, the dialogue regarding the meaning of the free press and

speech guarantees, emerging not only from cases asserting newsgathering rights, but also from those urging a public right of access to the media itself, raises an expectation that the Court may eventually reappraise the relationship of the two first amendment rights and accord them each independent significance."

Lovell, Colin R. "The 'Reception' of Defamation By the Common Law." *Vanderbilt Law Review*, 15:1051–71, October 1962. **1L289**
"Professor Lovell outlines the historical background of libel and slander and traces the separate conception and development of the two torts through the various courts of early England, explaining the reasons for ultimate division of defamation into two distinct actions."

Lowe, Michael. "The Ellsberg Trial." *New Statesman*, 8:262–65, 23 February 1973. **1L290**
A British writer reports on the trial of Daniel Ellsberg and Antony Russo and the events leading to the trial over the Pentagon Papers. While the Vietnam war touched everything in the case, the trial was presented as a legal confrontation over release of the classification of secret documents.

Lowenstein, Ralph L. *The Case Against a Press Council*. Columbia, Mo., Freedom of Information Center, School of Journalism, University of Missouri at Columbia, 1969. 4p. (Report no. 008) **1L291**
The author believes the Association for Education in Journalism, which adopted a resolution expressing an interest in a national press council but not binding the organization, would be unwise to go on record at this time in favor of a national press commission because of the lack of research, the danger to press relationships, and the danger to the Association since journalism schools will come under review of a national press council.

————. *Measuring World Press Freedom As a Political Indicator*. Columbia, Mo., University of Missouri, 1967. 437p. (Ph.D. dissertation, University Microfilms, no. 68–3630) **1L292**
"This dissertation describes an effort to design, execute and test a measurement system for placing all independent nations of the world with more than one million population in classifications on a free-controlled continuum. Called the Press Independence and Critical Ability (PICA) Index, the system utilized a questionnaire containing 23 criteria of press freedom. Each criterion was followed by a five-point verbal scale."

————. *National News Council Appraised*. Columbia, Mo., Freedom of Information Center, School of Journalism, University of Missouri at Columbia, 1974. 9p. (Report no. 0015; reprinted in *St. Louis Journalism Review*, January 1976, together with a response from the National News Council) **1L293**
"The track record of the National Press Council, after one year of operations, is rather lackluster. . . . It has failed to attract the kind of significant cases that could prove the NNC's value to the media and the public." The author examines in detail seven of the fifty-one officially docketed cases, listing all in the appendix. Only four of the fifty-one cases were upheld. He notes the Council's plans to expand its purview beyond the national suppliers of news, to every newspaper, magazine, and radio and television station in the country, and suggests that it can expect less cooperation and more hostility and resentment from the smaller dailies and local radio and television stations. "The NNC and the press have not yet come to terms with each other under the old set of rules. It is difficult to conceive what sort of adjustment will take place if the NNC goes 'national' and has to design a whole new set."

————. *Press Councils: Idea and Reality*. Columbia, Mo., Freedom of Information Foundation, 1973. 23p. (Freedom of Information Foundation Series, no. 1) **1L294**
"This paper will attempt to give a summary of the press council's history and the arguments that have been presented both for and against its existence in the United States."

————. "Press Freedom as a Political Indicator." In Heinz-Dietrick Fischer and John C. Merrill, *eds.*, *International Communications Media, Channels, Functions*. New York, Hastings House, 1970, pp. 129–40. **1L295**
The author of the Press Independence and Critical Ability (PICA) test of world press freedom describes how the survey technique operates.

————. *Why Network TV News Is Criticized*. Columbia, Mo., Freedom of Information Center, School of Journalism, University of Missouri at Columbia, 1970. 3p. (Report no. 0012) **1L296**
Criticism of network television "derives from the fact that it is at once different and more powerful than the newspapers which traditionally provided the main news source for the American public." The author lists ten differences between newspaper journalism and network TV news: Television (1) has greater impact, (2) is a licensed medium, (3) communicates non-verbally, (4) messages are highly condensed, (5) news has a feature structure, (6) messages are not renewable, (7) news must have sponsors, (8) network newsmen are a new elite, (9) audience is highly diverse, and (10) news is susceptible to manipulation.

Lower, Elmer W. "Fairness and Bal-

ance in Television News Reporting." *Quill*, 58(2):12–15, February 1970. **1L297**
To refute charges made by Vice-President Agnew that network news was biased, the president of American Broadcasting Company News cites results of a content analysis survey of ABC news made by a team headed by Dr. Irving E. Fang. He also rejects the recommendation of Frank Shakespeare, Nixon's appointee to the U.S. Information Agency, that networks select their news staff on the basis of their personal ideologies. Abridged from an address to Phi Delta Phi, School of Law, Columbia University.

————. "The First Amendment Under Attack: A Defense of the People's Right to Know." *Notre Dame Lawyer*, 42:896–906, Symposium 1967. **1L298**
The president of ABC News discusses the implications of the American Bar Association's report on fair trial and free press (Reardon Report) and appeals to the Bar Association to call a summit conference of news media and bar, where efforts will be made to work out some kind of mutually agreeable set of principles and guidelines.

————. *Freedom of the Press: A Basic Right Under Assault*. New Britain, Conn., Central Connecticut State College, 1971. 7p. Processed. **1L299**
"In 38 years as a professional journalist, I have never encountered such a wave of criticism of mass media as we have today." This criticism has come as a continual barrage both from spokesmen for the Nixon Administration who charge unfairness to the president, and from Nixon opponents who believe the media are handmaidens of the administration. The goal of both appears to be to cast a shadow of doubt on the believability of the news media. The author reports on a 1970 survey, commissioned by the American Broadcasting Company, to test the objectivity of its news programs. Professor Irving Fang of the University of Minnesota, and two colleagues found: 31.1 percent favorable to the Nixon Administration; 33.9 percent unfavorable; 35 percent neutral. The author attacks the congressional investigations. "ABC News opposes the principle of the Congress or any other legislative body subpoenaing untelevised material. The same holds true with respect to reporter's notes and sources of news information. . . . We do not have to answer to Congress. The First Amendment makes that perfectly clear."

————. "Freedom of the Press and Our Right to Know." *Nieman Reports*, 28(1/2):32–37, Spring–Summer, 1974. **1L300**
The author sounds a warning against the political erosion of the guarantee of the First Amendment in this country in five specific

areas: access to information, secrecy in government, harassment of reporters, unwarranted subpoenas by prosecutors, and undercover agents posing as reporters.

Lowman, Matthias P. *D. H. Lawrence and His Publishers: The Influence of the Changing Concept of Obscenity*. Chicago, University of Chicago, 1968. 95p. (Unpublished Master's thesis) **1L301**

Lowman, Walker B. "Federal Pandering Advertisements Statute: The Right of Privacy Versus the First Amendment." *Ohio State Law Journal*, 32:149–63, Winter 1971. **1L302**
A discussion of the case, *Rowan v. United States Post Office Department* (1970) in which the U.S. Supreme Court upheld the constitutionality of the law which permits an individual to determine whether or not he wishes to receive through the mail advertisements which he believes to be erotically arousing or sexually provocative. "The *Rowan* decision appears to have raised the right of privacy to the status of a constitutional imperative and paved the way for further federal endorsement of reclusion."

Lowry, Dennis T. "Agnew and the Network TV News: A Before–After Content Analysis." *Journalism Quarterly*, 48:205–10, Summer 1971. **1L303**
"Analysis of newscasts before and after [Vice-President Spiro] Agnew's criticism shows networks increased proportion of attributed sentences, a 'safe' response to a perceived threat of government interference."

[Lucas, Charles.] *The Tryal of Mr. Charles Lucas, on Certain Articles of Impeachment, exhibited against Him, before the Citizens of Dublin*. Dublin, Peter Wilson, 1749. 24p. **1L304**
A political pamphleteer and publisher of the *Censor*, Lucas was charged by the House of Commons with writing and publishing seditious and scandalous papers and for violating the privileges of the House. Lord Chief Justice Marley denounced Lucas as an "impudent scribbler, who has dared in print to menace His Majesty" and called upon the jury to "free us from these insolent libellers, these abandoned printers and publishers, these Jack Straws, Wat Tylers, and Jack Cades of the age." Munter writes in his *History of the Irish Newspaper* that "it was during the Lucas controversy that 'freedom of the press' was added to the Irish journalistic vocabulary, and during the 1750s the phrase was the subject of numerous essays and publications." The pamphlet was written as an attack on Lucas by his enemies.

Lucoff, Manny. "Broadcasting and

Cigarette Advertising: A Breakdown in Industry Self-Regulation." *Today's Speech*, 21(2):39–46, Spring 1973. **1L305**
The author reviews the events leading to the action by Congress in 1970 striking cigarette advertising from radio and television after the industry had rejected self-regulation. "Broadcasters fought that decision to the U.S. Supreme Court, although it is quite possible that the airing of cigarette commercials would still be permissible but for a critical industry decision ten years ago."

Luebke, Barbara F. *Textbook Censorship: New Aspects*. Columbia, Mo., Freedom of Information Center, School of Journalism, University of Missouri at Columbia, 1976. 8p. (Report no. 349) **1L306**
"Today, the textbook censorship movement has taken on new dimensions. While the traditional 'isms' continue to come under attack, there also is firing from the other side, from those who seek to have textbooks thrown out not for what is in them but for what is not in them." The author examines textbook censorship efforts throughout the country, with particular attention to the Kanawha County, W.Va. case.

Lukas, J. Anthony. "An Old and Seamy Story." *MORE*, 5(9):2–3, September 1975. **1L307**
All India is one vast "embattled zone" as Mrs. Gandhi has abolished press freedom in order to keep her office.

Lumpp, James A. *High School Press Restrictions*. Columbia, Mo., Freedom of Information Center, School of Journalism, University of Missouri at Columbia, 1974. 9p. (Report no. 329) **1L308**
"Legal precedents governing high school students' First Amendment rights are relatively recent and somewhat inchoate. As such, cautious interpretation is strongly advised, especially across federal court boundaries." The report deals with high school students' press freedoms, including precedent-setting court cases, and experience and incidents in schools across the country, and is intended to clarify the situation and to help schools shape their policies.

Lundy, L. Leonard. "Obscenity: A New Direction in Regulation." *John Marshall Journal of Practice and Procedure*, 4:268–315, Spring 1971. **1L309**
Roth v. United States (1957) was once thought to foreclose all constitutional protection to obscenity but more recent cases have opened up the issue. "*Stanley v. Georgia* [1969] mitigated the [*Roth*] effect by extending First Amendment protection to private possession of obscene material and *Freedman v. Maryland* [1965] regulated its effect by requiring adher-

ence to strict procedural requirements in its application. . . . *Redrup v. New York* [1967] clarifies the situation in which this state interest will take precedence over the individual's interest: circumstances involving juveniles, situations burdened with pandering, and publication designed so that an unwilling person cannot avoid exposure to it. . . . To secure its legitimate interests, state and federal legislation need only incorporate two factors: (1) a classification of persons to whom publications may or may not be distributed and (2) methods of advertising and dissemination which will infringe upon the sensitivities of unwilling persons."

Lunn, Betty. "From Whitest Africa— A Dark Tale of Censorship." *Library Journal*, 95:131–33, 15 January 1970. Comments: 95:1679, 1 May 1970; 95:2399–400, July 1970. **1L310**
An account of the oppressive censorship in South Africa under provisions of the Publications and Entertainments Act of 1963 which controls publications, films, art exhibitions, plays, entertainment, and certain objects deemed "undesirable." Publications imported are subjected to scrutiny by a Publications Control Board. The author accuses South African librarians of joining the general public in "their supine attitude" toward censorship. Many libraries subscribe to lists of books banned by the government, to make censorship easier.

Lunsford, Paul C. *A Study of Governmental Inquiries into Alleged Staged News Practices of Two Television News Documentaries*. Columbus, Ohio State University, 1972. 364p. (Ph.D. dissertation, University Microfilms, no. 72-27,058) **1L311**
"The purpose of this study was to examine the process, validity and reliability of governmental inquiries into two landmark cases of alleged staged news: WBBM–TV's 'Pot Party at a University,' and CBS' 'Project Nassau.' " The focus of the study was placed within the framework of traditional journalistic concepts of objectivity, interpretation, professional codes and ethics.

Luskin, John. *Lippmann, Liberty, and the Press*. University, Ala., University of Alabama Press, 1972. 273p. **1L312**
The major theme of this book is Walter Lippmann's continuing preoccupation with the natural and "proper" function of the press and the media. The author has brought together this journalist's many writings on freedom of the press and speech, news management, censorship, and credibility of government and the press, culled from his writings over half a century. His comments on press freedom extend from reaction to the suppression of the nonconformist press during World War I to applause for the publication of the Pentagon Papers, an action which he compared with the American patriots staging of the Boston Tea Party. Not all of his ideas of press

freedom were libertarian, as evidenced by his views expressed in *The Public Philosophy*, published in 1955.

Lusky, Louis. "Censorship." In *Encyclopedia Americana*. New York, Grolier, 1970, vol. 6, pp. 161–67.   **1L313**
A discussion of judicial control of censorship in the United States, including the British heritage, the role of the Supreme Court, the legal status of the mass media, individual expression, organizational activity, libel, creative expression, and the conflict between free press and fair trial. In the area of extralegal censorship the author discusses postal and customs censorship, control of government secrets, pressures for censorship of books in public libraries, textbook censorship, and self-censorship of the motion pictures.

Lutheran Research Society. *The Sedition Case*. Lowell, Ariz., Lutheran Research Society, 1953. 123p.   **1L314**
"There have been just two mass sedition trials in the history of the United States—one in the latter part of the eighteenth century [under the Sedition Act of 1798] promoted by the Federalist party, the other during the last war, promoted by the New Deal administration." This work is a critical account of the World War II sedition trial (1942–44) against twenty-eight persons who had been prominent in anti-Communist or pro-Nazi activities. The one woman, Mrs. Elizabeth Dilling, had published blacklists of alleged American Communists and fellow-travelers (C591); William Griffin was publisher of the New York *Inquirer*, and several were pamphleteers. The book accuses the Department of Justice of using entrapment schemes, by ordering copies of books, pamphlets, newspapers, and magazines from some of the defendants. The trial was long and heated, taking place in a hostile wartime atmosphere. "Supernatural intervention" in the sudden death of the presiding judge resulted in the dismissal of the case. The trial itself ended 7 December 1944; the case was officially dismissed 22 November 1946 by Chief Justice Bolitha J. Laws who called the trial "a travesty on justice."

Lydon, Michael. "The Word Gets Out." *Esquire*, 68(3):106–7+, September 1967.   **1L315**

The story of the underground press on college campuses and in major cities and the role of the Underground Press Syndicate, a loose federation of papers. Students have two options if they want to rebel: "write for the Underground Press, which many of them do and for which some are punished; or publish on campus and be damned, and they usually are."

Lynch, Charles D. "Burger Court's Crunch on 'Hard Core.' " *Ohio Northern University Law Review*, 1:97–110, 1973.   **1L316**
The author examines the Supreme Court's 1973 obscenity decisions in *Miller v. California*, *Paris Adult Theatre I v. Slaton*, and *Heller v. New York*, concluding that "there is now a new, carefully drawn obscenity test in *Miller*, and an equally carefully drawn rationale for the Court's position established in *Paris*. The Court has said that it does not like prior adversary hearings or expert testimony in obscenity cases, but it does favor explicitly drawn state obscenity statutes, civil proceedings to determine the issue of obscenity without criminal punishment, and prompt judicial action." The author sees more obscenity trials in the future and more zealous attempts at enforcement, which will temporarily repress some literary, artistic, political, and scientific material.

Lynch, John J. "Church Regulations in Reading." In Sister M. Regis, *ed.*, *The Catholic Bookman's Guide*. New York, Hawthorn, 1962, pp. 75–87.   **1L317**
Content: The Church's right to control reading, code of canon law, scriptural works, writings destructive of faith, writings contrary to morals, publications lacking approval, Index of forbidden books, and obtaining permission to read condemned literature.

Lynd, Robert D. "Banzhaf v. FCC: Public Interest and the Fairness Doctrine." *Federal Communications Bar Journal*, 23:39–56, 1969.   **1L318**
The article discusses cigarette advertising and the FCC's responsibility under the fairness doctrine to present other points of view on controversial issues of public importance. The essay won first prize in the 1969 Communications Essay contest sponsored by the Federal Communications Bar Association.

Lynd, Stoughton. "*Brandenburg v. Ohio*: A Speech Test for all Seasons?" *University of Chicago Law Review*, 43:151–91, Fall 1975.   **1L319**
"This comment first examines the *Brandenburg* formula [*Brandenburg v. Ohio*, 1969] in light of the earlier Supreme Court cases and demonstrates how *Brandenburg* significantly increases the protection of advocacy. It then critically examines the instances in which the Court has divided over or been uncertain about *Brandenburg*'s applicability. Finally, the comment argues that the concern that moved some of the Justices to relax the *Brandenburg* requirements in those cases can be amply protected under *Brandenburg* itself."

Lynn, Harlan. *Public Television in Transition*. Columbia, Mo., Freedom of Information Center, School of Journalism, University of Missouri at Columbia, 1973. 8p. (Report no. 301)   **1L320**
"The Public Broadcasting Act of 1967 was meticulously drafted to insure the new medium's freedom from conflict and interference engendered by political considerations. Despite the preventive measures, public television has been anything but free from such pressures and prospects for the future look no different."

Lyons, Louis M., *ed. Reporting the News; Selections from Nieman Reports*. New York, Atheneum, 1968. 443p.   **1L321**
Includes the following articles relating to press freedom: A Free and Responsible Press by Louis M. Lyons (L396). The Press under Pressure by Zechariah Chafee, Jr. (C257). Free Press and Fair Trial by Simon E. Sobeloff (S505). Managing the News by Clark R. Mollenhoff (M421). The Press Lives by Disclosures by Joseph Pulitzer, Jr. (°P24). The Newsmen's War in Vietnam by Stanley Karnow. Censors and Their Tactics by Jack Nelson (F311).

M

M., J. G. "Art and Prudence." *Irish Monthly*, 74:428–34, October 1946. (Reprinted from *The Advocate* [Australia]) **1M1**
An attack on "left-wing literati" who are all for the common man until he expresses his opposition to what is filthy and obscene in art and literature and then he is stupid and incompetent. As a case in point the author cites the Australian police ban on *We Were the Rats*. "Censorship admittedly is a dangerous weapon, but the principle involved is as sound as that of the Pure Food Acts. No one complains against protection from poisons that destroy the body. Why reject the protection against poisons that destroy the mind?"

Mabon, James M. "Encore for Roth: United States v. Reidel; United States v. Thirty-Seven Photographs." *University of Pittsburgh Law Review*, 33:367–78, Winter 1971. **1M2**
The author believes that these two cases "signal a definite return to the views [on obscenity] expressed by the Court in *Roth v. United States* [1957]."

McAllister, Gilbert, *ed. The Book Crisis . . . .* London, Faber & Faber, for the National Committee for the Defence of Books [1940?]. 58p. **1M3**
A wartime proposal in Britain to treat books as taxable merchandise has brought forth this collection of articles in defense of a free literature. The following contributed: Sir Hugh Walpole, J. B. Priestly, Geoffrey Faber, J. J. Mallon, Kenneth Lindsay, and Henry Strauss. Gilbert McAllister has written an introduction. "The defenders of a free literature," McAllister writes, "dare no more relax their vigilance against this danger from within, than the defenders of free Britain can relax their vigilance against the invaders from without."

MacAonghusa, Proinsias. "The Unbanned Books." *Bookseller*, 3219:1568–71, 2 September 1967. **1M4**
A listing of 110 of the thousands of books that had been banned in Ireland, some for as long as thirty-seven years, but now "unbanned" by the passage of the 1967 Censorship Bill. Some of the books are among the best written in the twentieth century.

McAuley, James. "Textbooks and Morals." *English in Australia*, 23:5–11, January 1973. **1M5**

McBath, James H. "Parliamentary Reporting in the Nineteenth Century." *Speech Monographs*, 37:25–35, March 1970. **1M6**
An account of the long struggle of the press for full reporting of the proceedings of Parliament, originally kept secret in an effort to avoid royal persecution.

McBride, Patrick. "Mr. Justice Black and His Qualified Absolutes." *Loyola of Los Angeles Law Review*, 2:37–70, April 1969. **1M7**
The author considers three topics: (1) Looking at the general problem of making any Bill of Rights provision an absolute, he comments on the problem of defining the *scope* of a particular provision. (2) He comments on Black's contention that the First Amendment does not include "conduct" and that "conduct" might be constitutionally regulated. (3) He examines Black's qualification that only direct abridgments of the First Amendment freedoms are absolutely protected, while "indirect" restrictions on free expression may be approved subject to a balancing test. He concludes that Mr. Justice Black's theory of First Amendment absolutes "even though it has some admirable features, is nevertheless to be found wanting when judged by his own criteria of assuring a strong and certain set of freedoms."

McBrier, Frederick P. "The EPA's Proposed Rule for Freedom of Information Act Disclosures: A Model for Orderly Agency Determinations." *Utah Law Review*, 1975:943–61, Winter 1975. **1M8**
"The Environmental Protection Agency (EPA) recently proposed a rule which would establish specific substantive and procedural guidelines for the analysis of certain information requests. This Note will analyze the proposed rule to determine the extent to which it will achieve [the Freedom of Information Act's] objective of maximum disclosure."

MacCafferty, Maxine, *comp. The Right to Know.* London, Aslib, 1976. 81p. (Aslib Bibliography no. 1) **1M9**
"This bibliography contains 669 selected references, mostly annotated, from the monograph, newspaper, periodical, and report literature on the right to know, covering the period 1971 January to 1976 February." In an introduction, James Michael notes that the term *right to know* "reflects not only a change in attitude toward free speech which acknowledges that freedom of speech is as much the right to hear as the right to speak, but also a growing interest in a right of access to information which has previously been regarded as confidential to government or business. To some extent this overlaps with the right to privacy, which may include both the individual's right to keep his private life secret and his right to know what information is being kept or circulated about him."

McCaffrey, J. "Reporter: A Campaign to Intimidate." *Vital Speeches*, 37:478–80, 15 May 1971. **1M10**
Discussion of the "concentrated campaign of intimidation against reporters" directed by Vice-President Agnew. "When the criticism is directed by the second highest ranking elected official in the nation's government there is a fine, if not indiscernible line between criticism and censorship."

MacCann, Donnarae. "Children's Books in a Pluralistic Society." *Wilson Library Bulletin*, 51:154–62, October 1976. **1M11**
The author argues for the exclusion or restriction of books in children's collections that reflect racist, sexist attitudes, as disregarding the rights of children in a pluralistic society. She differentiates treatment of such books from the treatment of books with puritanical attitudes, the latter dealing with a mutable philosophy, the former "connected with irrevocable physi-

cal conditions." She proposes an additional article to the *Library Bill of Rights* calling for the relegation to research collections children's books presenting demeaning images relating to race and sex.

———. "Sambo and Sylvester." *Wilson Library Bulletin*, 45:880–81, May 1971.
1M12
The International Conference of Police Associations has suggested that the book *Sylvester and the Magic Pebble* damages the image of policemen just as the image of black Americans is damaged by the book *Little Black Sambo*. The author believes this is not a valid comparison; the *Sylvester* book would not damage the image of the police in the mind of the child; *Little Black Sambo* would be damaging to the black American child.

MacCann, Richard D. *Film and Society*. New York, Scribner's, 1964. 182p. (Scribner Research Anthologies) **1M13**
Three sections of this anthology relate to freedom of the motion pictures: Part 5, Should the Screen Be Controlled? Part 6, Should Film Distribution Overseas Be Restricted? Part 7, Should Films for Television Be Controlled?

MacCarthy, Desmond. "Obscenity and the Law." *Life and Letters*, 2:327–35, May 1929. **1M14**
The recent successful prosecutions of *The Well of Loneliness* and *Sleeveless Errand* under the Lord Campbell Act suggest the need for a new definition of obscenity to replace the Hicklin rule and a more accurate application of the law, which was intended to suppress the crude pornography flourishing in Holywell Street. The law was never intended to harass and suppress works of literary merit and this freedom, the author argues, should apply to modern literary efforts as well as to the established classics. He cites eminent judges who have upheld this view in the past.

McCartney, Hunter P. "English Writer Leigh Hunt: Victim of Journalistic McCarthyism." *Journalism Quarterly*, 50:48–53, Spring 1973. **1M15**
As a journalist Hunt and his brother, John, flirted with libel in their weekly papers. After winning three cases, they were fined and imprisoned for libel against the Prince Regent. The author finds a parallel between the England of Hunt's time and America in McCarthy's time. Some of the characters in the McCarthy era had their antecedents in Hunt's England. "By comparing these similarities, we can perhaps understand administrative pressure vis-à-vis the press and see how to translate these pressures by means of a political barometer to ascertain the reasons for oppressive administrative press attitudes."

McCartney, James. "Must the Media Be 'Used'?" *Columbia Journalism Review*, 8(4):36–41, Winter 1969/70. (Reprinted in Alfred Balk and James Boylan, *eds.*, *Our Troubled Press*, pp. 141–51) **1M16**
"In the age of public relations, 'managed news,' and pseudo-events, the media must revise coverage procedures or continue to be exploited."

———. "What Should Be Secret?" *Columbia Journalism Review*, 10(3):40–44, September–October 1971. **1M17**
Criticism of the security classification system in which there is a maximum premium on secrecy and no adequate control of classification or provisions for declassification. Classified information "has become the plaything of Government administrators, who use inside knowledge as power in attempting to sell causes, stop projects they oppose, or otherwise manipulate public opinion." In fact, "the classification system today is so far out of control that the results frequently are a threat to 'national security.'"

McCartney, James L. "The Social Effects of Pornography." *Missouri Library Association Quarterly*, 29:187–96, September 1968. **1M18**
A review of existing social science research on the effects of pornography indicates that the evidence is inconclusive. "So long as humans maintain an interest in sex and differ about what is appropriate sexual response, we can expect that pornography will survive."

McCarty, Bryan K. "Obscenity from *Stanley* to *Karalexis*: A Back Door Approach to First Amendment Protection." *Vanderbilt Law Review*, 23:369–87, March 1970. **1M19**
This note reexamines government regulation of obscene material in the light of the First Amendment right of free speech and particularly in the light of two recent cases, *Stanley v. Georgia* (1969) and *Karalexis v. Byrne* (1970). "In spite of existing restrictions on the manner of public distribution, the rationale of *Stanley* and *Karalexis* clearly leaves open at least one more step in the development of constitutional protection for obscene material. Having created a right of possession, it seems inevitable that the court will also afford constitutional protection to the supplier."

McCauley, James H. "Political Defamation: The Price of Candidacy." *West Virginia Law Review*, 71:360–67, April–June 1969. **1M20**
It may be reasonably argued, the author notes, that the burden of proving malice should not be thrown on the plaintiff if he can establish the falsity of a defamatory publication. "Proof of malice could be reserved for those cases in which the plaintiff is unable to definitely establish the falsity of the communication and the defendant is likewise unable to definitely establish the truth of the matter."

McClain, Wallis. *Implementing the Amended FOI Act*. Columbia, Mo.,

Freedom of Information Center, School of Journalism, University of Missouri at Columbia, 1975. 10p. (Report no. 343) **1M21**
"The FOI Act amendments, which became effective in February, 1975, have so far yielded mixed results. The author provides an account of how different federal agencies are implementing the amended statute."

———. "Sunshine Law Works in Missouri—Most of the Time." *Focus/ Midwest*, 11(68):14–15, January–February 1975. **1M22**
"Although numerous complaints have resulted from uncertainty about the requirements of the law, most of those complaints have been resolved locally without resorting to judicial interpretation."

McClellan, John L. "Controversial Motion Pictures on Television." *National Decency Reporter*, 6(9–10):8–10, September–October 1969. **1M23**
In a speech in the U.S. Senate, 22 September 1969, Senator McClellan expresses concern that some of the obscene films currently being produced will eventually be shown on television where there is no effective way to restrict access to minors.

———. "McClellan on Obscenity." *Spectra* (Speech Communication Association), 7(3):2, June 1971. **1M24**
Senator McClellan's response to the Coalition Statement (April issue of *Spectra*) on the Report of the U.S. Commission on Obscenity and Pornography, reaffirming his criticism of the report and taking issue with the Association's stand.

——— *et al*. "Resolution Declaring that the Senate Reject the Findings and Recommendations of the Commission on Obscenity and Pornography." *Congressional Record*, 116:36459–78, 13 October 1970. **1M25**
Senator McClellan spoke at length in favor of the resolution and introduced the text of the Commission's minority report (pp. 36463–72). Senators Stennis, Griffin, Allott, and Hruska spoke briefly in defense of the resolution and Senator Mondale in opposition, submitting an editorial favorable to the Commission's majority report taken from the *Minneapolis Tribune* and two analytical feature articles by Austin C. Wehrwein from the *Minneapolis Star*. Senator Case spoke against the resolution and Senator Mathias, while objecting to the work of the Commission, opposed the resolution, preferring instead, the redelegation of the assignment. The resolution was passed 60–5.

McClelland, Doug. *The Unkindest Cut:*

The Scissors and the Cinema. New York, Barnes, 1972. 220p.   **1M26**
A lively account of an apparently widespread practice of cutting scenes from motion pictures, not as a necessary and routine process of editing, not by the censor, but by an arbitrary action of a producer, director, or exhibitor, and often after the picture has been released. The action may be for financial reasons, to oblige a powerful star who has been upstaged, in response to the blacklist, or for no apparent reason. The result, the author shows, has been damaging to cinema art as well as to the creative artists.

McClernan, David E. "The New York Times Rule Expanded." *Journal of Urban Law*, 48:982–88, June 1971.
                                          1M27
Re: *Farnsworth v. Tribune Co.*, 43 Ill. 2d 286, 253 N.E.2d. 408 (1969). The Illinois Supreme Court upheld the lower court's decision for the defendant, the *Chicago Tribune*, charged with libel in labeling the plaintiff a "quack." "Dr. Farnsworth must have been denied relief under the basic rationale of *Times* [*New York Times v. Sullivan*, 1964] and its progeny: that the first amendment protects the idea that 'debate on public issues should be robust and wide-open.' "

McCloskey, H. J., and D. H. Monro. "Liberty of Expression; Its Grounds and Limits." *Inquiry*, 13:219–37, Autumn 1970.   **1M28**
"Can those interferences with liberty of expression which are necessary and desirable be indicated in some simple, general way, e.g. in terms of some principle or principles of the kinds with which J. S. Mill sought to delimit the interferences with freedom of action." McCloskey fails to find a useful summarizing principle defining limits of freedom of expression that take into consideration all the kinds and degrees of interference which ought to be noted. Monro argues against McCloskey, maintaining that there is a general principle, that "an atmosphere of free inquiry is hard to maintain, and that any suppression, even one apparently justified, will have the indirect effect of helping to destroy that atmosphere, and is consequently likely to do more harm than good."

McCormack, Thelma. "Censorship and 'Community Standard.' " In Benjamin D. Singer, *ed.*, *Communications in Canadian Society*. Toronto, Clark, 1972. 24p. Processed. (Paper presented at annual meeting, Canadian Sociology and Anthropology Association, St. John's, Newfoundland, June 1971)
                                          1M29
An examination of "the censorship controversy

with a view to proposing a more sociological perspective on censorship generally, and on the concept of 'community standards' in particular."

———. "Obscenity; A Critique." *IPLO Quarterly* (Institute of Professional Librarians of Ontario), 15:21–24, July 1973.   **1M30**
Criticism of the work and findings of the Law Reform Commission in the area of obscenity, particularly for its failure to take into consideration the research of social psychologists done for the U.S. Commission, and for too heavy reliance on the legal approach.

McCormick, Kenneth. "Freedom of Expression." *American Pen*, 4(4):35–43, Fall 1972.   **1M31**
The author contends that a proposed price freeze on books would have the effect of censorship by interfering with the reprinting of books out of stock. He cites other government attacks on the press which affect book publishing—prior censorship (Pentagon Papers), subpoenas, post office censorship, inadequate copyright protection, and increase in postal rates.

———. "Freedom to Read—Not Censorship." *American Pen*, 4(3):1–10, Summer 1972.   **1M32**
A discussion of four aspects of censorship: the case of *Ulysses* ban by U.S. Customs; public and school library censorship and the American Library Association's effort to combat it; the U.S. Commission on Obscenity and Pornography and the reception of its report; and newspaper restrictions on book advertising.

McCormick, Kenneth D., and W. L. Smith. "The Guardians of Virtue Mount New Offensive." *Saturday Review*, 55(30):24–25, 22 July 1972. **1M33**
An editorial urging those who oppose censorship to back one of the various organizations fighting censorship, in order to combat the pro-censorship efforts of the large-budgeted Citizens for Decent Literature and Morality in Media, Inc.

McCormick, Marilyn G., *comp. The Williams & Wilkins Case: The Williams & Wilkins Company v. the United States*. New York, Science Associates/ International, 1974. 275p. (Vol. 1, Preface by Nicholas L. Henry) **1M34**
The volume brings together documents in the dispute over fair usage of copyrighted materials by libraries and educational institutions and reflects the divergent views of the publishing industry and the educational community. Part 1 covers the case before the U.S. Court of Claims; part 2 covers the case before the U.S. Supreme Court. Volume 2, to be issued, will contain the U.S. Supreme Court decision and all pertinent documents.

McCormick, Robert R. *The Free Press Fight*. New York, Editor & Publisher, 1935, 16p.   **1M35**
In an address before members of the Advertising Club of New York City, the editor of the *Chicago Tribune* discusses the implications for press freedom of the NRA (National Recovery Act) codes.

———. ["Freedom of the Press."] In *Addresses by Colonel Robert McCormick*. Chicago, Radio Station WGN, 1941–44. (Published as separate addresses and in various collected editions) **1M36**
In a series of brief weekly addresses over WGN and the Mutual Broadcasting System during 1941–44, the editor of the *Chicago Tribune* discussed various public issues, none more frequently than the topic Freedom of the Press. Examples: On 18 October 1941 his address dealt with the history of press freedom in America; on 25 April 1942, with the wartime British press; on 12 September 1942, with the contrast in press freedom between Britain and the United States; on 26 September 1942, with recent efforts to restrain the U.S. press, including the Minnesota gag law; on 13 February 1943 he traced the concept of press freedom as one of the "natural rights of man"; on 6 March 1943 he discussed the adoption of the First Amendment and subsequent related events; on 13 March 1943 and again on 8 April 1944 he considered the implication on press freedom of the cases of *Near v. Minnesota* and *City of Chicago v. Chicago Tribune*; on 6 May 1944, he argued that the First Amendment should operate the same in war as in peace: "The fangs of these [sedition] laws will be muzzled, if the Supreme Court continues to hold that alleged seditious utterances must constitute a clear and present danger to the existence of our institutions."

———. [*Freedom of the Press*.] Monticello, Va., Thomas Jefferson Memorial Foundation, 1931. 8p.   **1M37**
Opening address at the dedication of the study room of Thomas Jefferson at Monticello, Va., to the liberty of the press. McCormick discusses the recent (1 June 1931) decision of the U.S. Supreme Court in *Near v. Minnesota*, rendered by Chief Justice Hughes, which overturned the state's newspaper gag law.

———. [*Freedom of the Press*.] Waterville, Me., Colby College, 1935. 13p.   **1M38**
In an address at Colby College, McCormick criticizes the attempt to restrain freedom of the press in the NRA codes and objects to the reasoning of Lindsay Rogers who was designated to draw the code for the newspaper industry. He cites words of Alexander Hamilton in support of his argument.

———. [*Freedom of the Press in Wartime*.] *An Address . . . Before the Members of the Indiana Republican Press Association, Indianapolis, Indiana, February 27, 1943*.

Chicago, Chicago Tribune, 1943. 12p. **1M39**
Comment on the press in wartime, criticism of the handling of the espionage trials, and an attack on the New Deal. "The fate of the republic depends on our courage and our constancy . . . . Are we not the successors of the men who wrote the Constitution and who wrote the Bill of Rights?"

————. *How Stands the Constitution?* Topeka, Kans., 1934. 16p. **1M40**
In an address delivered at a dinner given by William Allen White in honor of Colonel Ed Howe, McCormick defends the introduction of a free-press clause in the NRA code and refers to various recent efforts to restrain the press.

————. *The Newspaper.* Charleston, S.C., The Citadel, 1932. 23p. **1M41**
An address dealing with the development of press freedom in the English-speaking world, given to the graduating class of the Military College of South Carolina, The Citadel, 3 June 1932.

————. *Newspapers and the Law.* Chicago, Chicago Bar Association, 1938. 22p. **1M42**
In an address before the Chicago Bar Association McCormick discusses the lack of press freedom in Britain, particularly in the coverage of public trials, and deplores the fact that some would change the American Constitution to import the English system of restraining press coverage of trials to the United States. He denies that the press interferes with the administration of justice and urges that public trials be covered both by photography and radio, enabling more people to witness and hear justice at work.

————. *The Powers of the National Government and the Rights of Americans.* Chicago, The Chicago Tribune, 1943. 64p. **1M43**
The second half of the pamphlet deals with the development of press freedoms from the Zenger case in 1731 to recent court decisions in which the *Chicago Tribune* was a party.

McCoy, Alfred W. "A Correspondence with the CIA." *New York Review of Books*, 19(4):26–35, 21 September 1972. **1M44**
An exchange of letters between the author (Alfred W. McCoy) and the publisher (Harper & Row) of *The Politics of Heroin in Southwest Asia*, and officials of the Central Intelligence Agency. McCoy's book, implicating the CIA in the international heroin traffic, was held up by the publishers pending a review of the galley proofs by the CIA, which had requested prior review. The publishers subsequently issued the book without change, despite objections from the CIA. "Considered collectively," writes McCoy, "this exchange of letters provides us with another important re-

minder . . . of the contempt this most clandestine of our government agencies has for the integrity of the press and the publishing industry. . . . [The CIA] tried to impose prior censorship in order to avoid public scrutiny of its record."

McCoy, Ralph E. *Freedom of the Press; An Annotated Bibliography.* With a Foreword by Robert B. Downs. Carbondale, Ill., Southern Illinois University Press, 1968. 600p. **1M45**
"This is an annotated bibliography of some 8,000 books, pamphlets, journal articles, films, and other material relating to freedom of the press in English-speaking countries, from the beginning of printing to the present. 'Press' is used generically to include all media of mass communications: books, pamphlets, periodicals, newspapers, motion pictures, phonograph records, radio, television, and, to a limited extent, stage plays. Subjects include heresy, sedition, blasphemy, obscenity, personal libel, and both positive and negative expressions on freedom of the press."

————. *Theodore Schroeder, A Cold Enthusiast: A Bibliography.* Carbondale, Ill., Southern Illinois University Libraries, 1973. 86p. (Bibliographic Contributions, no. 8) **1M46**
A bio-bibliography of one of the founders of the Free Speech League (1902) and a lifelong crusader for freedom of speech and the press, particularly in the areas of blasphemy and obscenity. His libertarian views on free speech, highly controversial when he first expressed them at the turn of the century, are widely accepted today. The annotated bibliography of this prolific writer is arranged under the five topics that interested him: religion, sex, psychology, law, politics, and Puerto Rico. A biographical sketch, based on the Schroeder papers at Southern Illinois University, is presented by Dennis L. Domayer; personal impressions of Schroeder are presented by a long-time friend, Arnold Maddaloni.

McCray, Stephen. *Press Access: A Growing Movement.* Columbia, Mo., Freedom of Information Center, School of Journalism, University of Missouri at Columbia, 1971. 6p. (Report no. 269) **1M47**
"Growing public sentiment towards enforced access to newspapers is causing publishers and editors to re-evaluate their public service commitments in order to stave off government controls. This trend has had the more important effect of advancing a new interpretation of the first amendment in which freedom of the press means free access to the press for everyone."

————. *Privacy: A Chilling Tort.* Columbia, Mo., Freedom of Information Center, School of Journalism, University of Missouri at Columbia, 1972. 7p. (Report no. 275) **1M48**

"The courts have given the press considerable ammunition for use in future privacy battles, but recent court action has shown that the 'breathing space' provided by the *Time, Inc. v. Hill* [1967] decision is not infinite."

McCrimmon, Barbara. "Victoria Woodhull Martin Sues the British Museum for Libel." *Library Quarterly*, 45:355–71, October 1975. **1M49**
In 1892 Victoria Woodhull Martin, who had enjoyed a notorious career in New York as a spiritualist, free-love advocate, stock broker, woman suffragist, and publisher of the sensational *Woodhull and Claflin Weekly*, but who was now married to a respectable British banker, sued the British Museum for libel. Mr. and Mrs. Martin charged that the Museum possessed books and pamphlets about the famous Beecher-Tilden adultery case which had taken place in Brooklyn in 1875 and which libeled Mrs. Martin. This article is an account of the Martin-British Museum libel trial, which was resolved in favor of the British Museum. Richard Garnett, Keeper of the Printed Books, backed by the Trustees of the Museum, agreed to remove certain of the offensive books, but disclaimed any responsibility for libel or any obligation to withdraw a book merely because it was objected to, a situation which, Garnett pointed out, would result in "the possibility of wholesale despoiling of the library." Garnett subsequently led efforts to provide a statutory base for protecting future librarians from such liability. Such a clause was written into a public library bill in 1900.

[McCulloch, John R.] *Observations, Illustrative of the Practical Operation and Real Effect of the Duties on Paper, Showing the Expediency of Their Reduction or Repeal.* London, Longman, Rees, Orme, Brown, Green, and Longman, 1836. 38p. **1M50**
The author bases his arguments on the exorbitancy of the duties, the mode in which the duties are imposed, and the oppressive and unjust operation of the paper duties on authors, publishers, and the interests of literature. Included is a petition of the paper manufacturers to the House of Commons.

[————.] *Report of the Trial by Jury of the Action of Damages for a Libel in the Scotsman Newspaper; William Aiton, M.D., against John Ramsay M'Culloch of Auchengoul, Editor of the Scotsman, and Others.* Edinburgh, Printed for J. Robertson, 1823. 72p. **1M51**
John R. McCulloch, editor, and Alexander Abernathy and James Walker, publishers of the *Scotsman*, were charged by Dr. Aiton with printing libelous statements about his behavior at a public meeting which tended to destroy his reputation as a physician. The defense claimed

the remarks were "not beyond the fair limit of observation and discussion to which every person who makes himself conspicuous at such a meeting virtually subjects himself." The plaintiff had asked for £5,000 damages; he was awarded £100.

[————.] "The Taxes on Literature." *Edinburgh Review*, 53:427–37, June 1831.   **1M52**
The taxes on literature (books) are glaringly unjust. The author proposes that publishers be taxed only on the books they sell, not in advance on the paper they use, since many volumes remain unsold. The advertising tax, about one-third from book ads, should be abolished.

McCullough, Dan H. "The History of the First Amendment and the Acts of September 24, 1789 and March 2, 1831." *South Dakota Law Review*, 12:171–257, Spring 1967.   **1M53**
An historical survey of the development of the contempt power of the American courts in relation to the guarantee of a free press. The account begins with the passage of the Judiciary Act of 1789 which established the English common law doctrine that the courts have the inherent power to punish as contempt all conduct which would tend to influence or prejudice judicial proceedings. The Act of 1831 gave federal judges the right to punish summarily for contempt only against misconduct committed "in the presence of said courts, or so near thereto as to obstruct the administration of justice." The account ends with the report of the American Bar Association's Reardon Committee and its reception by Bar and Press.

McDonald, Donald. "The Media's Conflict of Interests." *Center Magazine*, 9:15–35, November–December 1976.   **1M54**
"The premise of democracy is that a people can govern themselves." And this requires the rational dialogue of an informed electorate. While government challenges to press freedom have not been insignificant, "in some respects the most interesting and formidable threat to consistently responsible journalism comes not so much from government as from the mass media themselves." To promote the freer flow of information and ideas and more vigorous media competition, the author calls for "(1) deconcentration of ownership of the media, (2) facilitation of the entry of new, competitive media in the life of the national community, (3) opening up existing communication channels, expanding the public's access to them, and (4) developing the ethical and legal grounds for asserting the individual journalist's claim to a protected professional status vis-à-vis not only the government but also the institution that employs him or her." Except for the recom-

mendation calling for strict enforcement of the FCC's fairness doctrine, all the remedies proposed "keep government at arm's length from the content of newspapers and broadcasting. They seek, instead, to promote maximum diversity of media ownership, maximum competition in the task of informing the American citizens of public affairs and issues, and maximum protection for journalists so that they may, in fact, perform as professionals without fear of reprisal from any sources. When such diversity, competition, and protection are achieved, there will be no need for a Fairness Doctrine of any kind."

Macdonald, I. A. "Censorship: Some Philosophical Issues: (2) The 'Offence Principle' As a Justification for Censorship." *Philosophical Papers*, 5(1):67–84, May 1976.   **1M55**
The author makes a case "for the claim that an appropriate reason for restricting a person's behavior is that it gives offence to others, and that this general reason does have certain implications for legislation concerning pornographic literature or films and the advertising of such objects." Throughout the article he uses the concept of "offensive nuisances" suggested by Joel Feinberg in his work, *Social Philosophy*.

McDonald, Joseph. *"Rights in Conflict and Rights in Conflict." RQ* (American Library Association), 9:124–27, Winter 1967.   **1M56**
Comment on the public's response to the report of the U.S. Commission on the Causes and Prevention of Violence, *Rights in Conflict*, and the refusal of the Public Printer to print the report for public sale, ostensibly because it contained numerous obscenities.

Macdonell, Ian. *The Hair Controversy! Full Transcript of the Trial Plus Explanatory Comment*. Auckland, New Zealand, Comil Publications, 1972. 32p.   **1M57**
" 'Hair' polarized New Zealand as few other issues have done in recent years. People were either vehemently for it or violently against it. The controversy became a background for a new morality against traditional values."

McDougald, William W. *Federal Regulation of Political Broadcasting: A History and Analysis*. Columbus, Ohio, Ohio State University, 1964. 327p. (Ph.D. dissertation, University Microfilms, no. 65–3889)   **1M58**
"This study was an attempt to analyze the current regulatory position toward political broadcasting and to determine where such may logically lead. As a conclusion the study points to the need for a new approach to broadcast regulation and shows the necessity for the development of a new public policy toward broadcasting."

MacDougall, A. Kent. "Muting the

Message: Advertising Is Subject to Stricter Censorship Than Editorial Matter." *Wall Street Journal*, 173:1, 21 May 1969.   **1M59**
Both newspapers and broadcasters have been more restrictive of the content of advertising than editorial matter. *Playboy*, which specializes in nudes and spicy editorial matter is persnickety about what ads it accepts. "Various courts and the Federal Trade Commission repeatedly have upheld a newspaper's right to reject advertising, so long as it acts independently," but a number of authorities are challenging this broad discretion.

————, ed. *The Press: A Critical Look from the Inside*. Princeton, N.J., Dow Jones, 1972. 172p.   **1M60**
A collection of critical articles on the nation's press which have appeared in issues of *Wall Street Journal*, including such issues as concentration of media ownership, editorial and news bias, unethical practices, the "new journalism," and reporter activism.

MacDougall, Curtis D. *News Pictures Fit to Print*. Stillwater, Okla. Journalistic Services, 1971. 136p.   **1M61**
Deals with the ethical considerations on whether or not to print a news picture, involving such issues as public taste, morals, invasion of privacy, encouragement of crime, or embarrassment of the U.S. government at home or abroad.

McDowell, William M. *Mad Dog Killer: A Case Study of Pretrial Publicity*. Washington, D.C., American University, 1967. 113p. (Unpublished Master's thesis)   **1M62**
The study deals with the U.S. Supreme Court case, *Irvin v. Dowd* (1961), and traces the news coverage by two Evansville papers from the time of the first of the six murders of which Irvin was accused to his trial. The author concludes that newspaper coverage contributed to the atmosphere of hostility and prejudice in which the trial was conducted.

MacEacheron, James F. "On Intellectual Freedom [and the Law]. Address" *Canadian Libraries*, 23:173–83, November 1966.   **1M63**
This article traces the legal basis for intellectual freedom under Canadian law, federal and state, as interpreted by the courts. References are made to the Alberta Press Code case in 1938, the Quebec Padlock case in 1957, the report of the Special Committee on Hate Propaganda in Canada, and various cases involving obscenity. The author discusses two activities of prior restraint by the federal government: the Customs Tariff Act, which prohibits import of obscene or seditious publications, and Section 153 of the Criminal Code which gives the Postmaster General the right to deny use of the mails to obscene or scurrilous materials. Finally, the author discusses the Canadian Bill of Rights, 1960, its strengths and weaknesses.

McElreath, Mark P. "Right to Know and Employee Cognitions on Communications." *Journalism Quarterly*, 50:773–76, Winter 1973. **1M64**
"This study will use the concept (social psychological communications research) to answer this question: Does the public's right to know affect the public employee's attitude toward information in his organization?"

McGaffey, Ruth M. *An Analysis of the Origin and Development of Selected Freedom of Speech Concepts*. Evanston, Ill., Northwestern University, 1970. 458p. (Ph.D. dissertation, University Microfilms, no. 71–10,161) **1M65**
"The purpose of this study was to analyze the origin and development of four closely related freedom of speech concepts. Those concepts were 'symbolic speech,' 'the streets as a public forum,' 'right of access,' and 'the hecklers' veto.'" Part I is an analysis of some of the traditional and modern literature describing the judicial process; part II involves an investigation and description of the development of each of the four concepts; and part III concludes that the development of these concepts support the description of the judicial process contained in the first part of the study.

———. *Developments in the Law: Freedom of Speech Under the Nixon Court*. [Milwaukee, The Author, 1973.] 75p., 15p. Processed. **1M66**
This essay examines the decisions in the area of freedom of speech made by the U.S. Supreme Court with the four Nixon-appointed justices. "It will also be the purpose of this essay to describe the developments in the lower federal courts as they relate to the overall development of First Amendment law, particularly to Freedom of Speech. Some of these lower court cases may eventually reach the Supreme Court; many will not. It may be possible to see what effect the new makeup of the court has had thus far in influencing the actions of the lower courts or to what extent these decisions have been sustained or overruled in the High Court. In many areas of freedom of speech law, there appear to have been substantial changes made or implied. This essay will attempt to describe those changes. While an attempt will be made to discuss these developments under specific categories, it is obvious that there is considerable overlapping in many instances." Categories: obscenity, symbolic speech, loyalty oaths, libel, right of access, exclusion of aliens, confidentiality of news sources, picketing, leaflets and noise ordinances, and commercial speech.

———. "Freedom of Speech for the Ideas We Hate." *English Journal*, 64(5):14–15, May 1975. **1M67**
The author argues that all ideas must be protected, no matter how repulsive they might be—anti-Jewish, anti-black, or anti-Catholic. "These ideas we hate must be constitutionally protected if the marketplace of ideas is to survive for those ideas we love."

———. "Local Option on the First Amendment." In *Free Speech Yearbook*, 1974. New York, Speech Communication Association, 1975, pp. 11–17. **1M68**
"In this essay I shall explore the idea of local option versus national standards [in obscenity] in an attempt to determine what will be meant by 'community standards' and what effect those community standards will have on freedom of speech."

———. "A Realistic Look at Expert Witnesses in Obscenity Cases." *Northwestern University Law Review*, 69:218–32, May–June 1974. **1M69**
This article briefly reviews the controversy surrounding the proposition put forward by the U.S. Supreme Court in *Paris Adult Theatre v. Slaton* (1973), that expert testimony is not needed by jurors in obscenity cases and, in fact, has "often made a mockery out of the otherwise sound concept of expert testimony." The author argues that "both practical experience and communication research support the conclusion that experts probably have little effect in value-oriented areas such as obscenity."

———. "Toward a More Realistic View of the Judicial Process in Relation to Freedom of Speech." In *Free Speech Yearbook*, 1972. New York, Speech Communication Association, 1973, pp. 8–19. **1M70**
"This essay will attempt to show that constitutional interpretation and related judicial decision-making are chancey, subjective processes. The first way to observe this subjectivity is to examine the very factor which is thought to secure orderly, logical legal development, *stare decisis*." The author concludes that "neither our historical experience in the development of First Amendment law, nor the literature in the field of jurisprudence gives much support to the thought that constitutional interpretation is a logical and rational procedure immune from societal or personal pressure."

McGaffin, William, and Erwin Knoll. *Anything But the Truth: The Credibility Gap—How the News Is Managed in Washington*, New York, Putnam, 1968. 250p. **1M71**
Two Washington newsmen write of the critical problem of government secrecy, deception, and distortion of news that has prevented the American people and the Congress from knowing what was taking place in their national government. The events were dramatically exposed in recent years in President Eisenhower's U-2 Affair, in President Kennedy's fiasco at the Bay of Pigs, and most notably during the Johnson Administration in the Vietnam war and the Tonkin Gulf affair. They cite examples from the White House, the State Department, the Department of Defense, the Poverty Program, the Bureau of the Budget, and other agencies, to show how socializing,

public relations gimmicks, distortions, and outright lies have become a way of life in the course of managing the news in Washington,

———. "The White House Lies." *Progressive*, 31(9):13–18, September 1967. **1M72**
The article is adapted from the author's book on President Johnson's "credibility gap."

McGeady, Paul J. "Obscenity Law and the Supreme Court." In Victor B. Cline, *ed.*, *Where Do You Draw the Line?* Provo, Utah, Brigham Young University Press, 1974, pp. 83–106. **1M73**
The author reviews obscenity law as interpreted by the U.S. Supreme Court: The Hicklin test, based on an eighteenth-century British decision; the Roth test (*Roth v. United States*, 1957); and the decision on *Fanny Hill* (*A Book Named Memoirs of a Woman of Pleasure v. Attorney General of Massachusetts*, 1966). In 1973 the Court in *Miller v. California* "gave the United States a new frame of reference for deciding obscenity cases. These decisions will, without doubt, inhibit the flow of hard-core pornography and restore the right of the 'community' to be protected if it chooses from offensive assaults on its standards of morality in the sexual field." The author discusses the implications of *Miller* under the headings: new standards; appeal to pruriency; patently offensive descriptions or depictions; and lack of serious literary, artistic, political, or scientific value. "Perhaps the most important contribution of *Miller* and its sister cases is the reaffirmation of the state's right to protect and promote public morality in relation to its adult population as well as to its nonadult members and to use this concept as the philosophical underpinning of its obscenity legislation."

McGovern, George S. "The Pentagon Papers: A Discussion." *Political Science Quarterly*, 87:173–84, June 1972. **1M74**
Whether the press was justified in publishing the Pentagon Papers cannot be separated from their substance. The senator summarizes the papers' disclosures of government deception, the illegitimacy of the Vietnam war, clandestine and illegal action by the CIA, and a debasement of constitutional government. John P. Roche presents a different point of view in an accompanying article.

McGranery, Regina C. "Exemptions from the Section 315 Equal Time Standard: A Proposal for Presidential Elections." *Federal Communications Bar Journal*, 24:177–205, 1970–71. **1M75**
The author calls for the Federal Communications Commission to adopt a ruling for radio and television which would provide strict application of the fairness doctrine in presidential campaigns.

292 **1M76—90**

Tim McGraw–Donald McLachian

McGraw, Tim. *NARB: Impossible Dream?* Columbia, Mo., Freedom of Information Center, School of Journalism, University of Missouri at Columbia, 1973. 6p. (Report no. 300) **1M76**

"Many of the difficulties surrounding media self-regulation efforts in general are well illustrated in this account of the advertising industry's experience in particular. Even when intentions are impeccably honorable, a multitude of conflicts and paradoxes almost invariably emerges." This report follows the National Advertising Review Board (NARB) plan of self-regulation from 1970 to the present, showing the problems the organization has encountered in its policing role.

MacGregor, John. "The Modern Machiavellians: The Pornography of Sexual Game-Playing." In Ray C. Rist, *ed.*, *The Pornography Controversy*, New Brunswick, N.J., Transaction, 1975, pp. 175–202. **1M77**
The author analyzes a particular form of softcore pornography, books on sexual seduction and sex game-playing, which he considers Machiavellian in intent and method.

MacGuigan, Mark R. "Proposed Anti-Hate Legislation; Bill S-5 and the Cohen Report." *Chitty's Law Journal*, 15:302–6, November 1967. **1M78**
A member of the Cohen Committee that recommended Canadian anti-hate legislation discusses the issues involved and supports the legislation. He believes the bill balances the conflicting interests of protecting minorities against defamation and preserving free speech without substantial diminution.

McGuire, Harry D. *Photography and Broadcasting in the Courts: An Examination of Canon 35 of the American Bar Association.* Berkeley, Calif., University of California, 1965. 162p. (Unpublished Master's thesis) **1M79**

McHam, David. *Law and the Press; A Handbook for Newsmen.* [Austin, Tex.?], Texas Association of Broadcasters, Texas Daily Newspaper Association, and Texas Press Association, 1972. 83p. **1M80**
Chapter 5 deals with the law of libel; chapter 7 with the open meetings law, press shield laws, the right of privacy, public records, Canon 35 of the American Bar Association, the ABA's Reardon Report, and press councils.

McIlvenna, Ted, and Phyllis Lyon.

"What Do We Say About Pornography?" *Church and Society*, 60(4): 64–69, March–April 1970. **1M81**
Staff members of the National Sex and Drug Forum polled persons related to the Forum on their attitudes toward pornography. The authors conclude: "Each person should ask a very simple question of himself: Am I against pornography because it is crude, poorly done, or misrepresents the value and meaning of sexuality, or am I against pornography because it deals with sexuality?"

MacIver, Robert M. *Academic Freedom in Our Time.* New York, Columbia University Press, 1955. 329p. **1M82**
A political scientist, under the auspices of the American Academic Freedom Project, Columbia University, analyzes the contemporary climate of freedom in American schools and colleges, including the freedom to read. He discusses the numerous pressures on schools and libraries to censor textbooks, particularly in the area of government, American history, United Nations, and sex education. He discusses the State Department's censorship of American libraries overseas during the Eisenhower Administration, and action taken against student publications.

McKay, Robert B. "One Nation, Divisible—With Pornography for Some." *Bulletin of the Copyright Society of the U.S.A.*, 21:73–88, December 1973. **1M83**
The author looks at the U.S. Supreme Court's obscenity decision in *Miller v. California* (1973) and finds it "harmful, foolish, and probably unworkable," and will not accomplish its intended purpose—to bring relative stability and certainty into a troubled field and to relieve a weary Court of an unpleasant burden. He suggests that state legislatures "provide for the determination of community standards on a state-wide basis, foreclosing the patchwork of conflicting local ordinances," and that any statute "contain a narrow and specific definition of hard-core pornography."

McKeever, Joyce. "Publication of True Information on the Public Record." *Duquesne Law Review*, 14:507–20, Spring 1976. **1M84**
Re: *Cox Broadcasting Corp. v. Cohn*, 420 U.S. 469 (1975) in which the U.S. Supreme Court "held that a state may not base a cause of action for invasion of privacy on the publication of accurate information obtained from judicial records open to the public, because crime, criminal prosecutions and judicial proceedings are events of legitimate concern to the public which fall within the media's duty of responsible news coverage."

McKenna, Donald J. "Time, Inc. v. Firestone: More Than a New Public Figure Standard?" *Saint Louis University Law Journal*, 20:625–39, 1976. **1M85**
The U.S. Supreme Court decision in the libel

case, *Time, Inc. v. Firestone*, 1976, "raises serious questions about the nature of the public figure criterion, the public's legitimate concern with significant events such as judicial proceedings, and the degree of accuracy required for 'truth' in news."

Mackenzie, J. B. "Section 98, Criminal Code and Freedom of Expression in Canada." *Queen's Law Journal*, 1:469–83, November 1972. **1M86**
A history of the administration of section 98 of the Criminal Code which prevailed from 1919 to 1936 and was "a substantial encroachment on the traditional freedoms of speech and assembly."

McKey, Arthur D. "Defamation Law After *Time, Inc. v. Firestone.*" *Idaho Law Review*, 13:53–65, Winter 1976. **1M87**
The author concludes that "in the wake of *Firestone* [*Time, Inc. v. Firestone*, 1976] it seems clear that the media will be held to an extremely high standard of reportorial accuracy—a standard which may function to impose implicit prior restraints on the exercise of freedom of the press."

Mackie, William E. *The "Curious" Controversy.* Columbia, Mo., Freedom of Information Center, School of Journalism, University of Missouri at Columbia, 1969. 5p. (Report no. 224) **1M88**
"Controversy has followed the Swedish film 'I Am Curious (Yellow)' since its arrival in this country 18 months ago. U.S. Customs declared the film obscene and refused it entry. A federal district court concurred that the film was obscene. However, an appeals court overturned the verdict, thus allowing the film to be shown in the U.S. Now the film is in limited release and a new wave of debate will certainly develop wherever it is shown."

McKnight, C. A. "The Primacy of Press Freedom." *Bulletin of the American Society of Newspaper Editors*, 555:16–17, November–December 1971. **1M89**
Excerpts from the testimony of the president of the American Society of Newspaper Editors before the Senate Subcommittee on Constitutional Rights. He expresses concern over recent trends under the Nixon Administration to impose prior restraint on the press and to force newspaper reporters to reveal their news sources.

McLachian, Donald. "The Lohan Affair." *Spectator*, 218:700, 16 June 1967. **1M90**
This article and an editorial (pp. 697–98) deal with the "D" Notice controversy over a "cable vetting" story in the *London Daily Express*. An article by Colonel L. G. Lohan, principal figure in the affair, Slandered Out of Business, appears in the 30 June issue.

McLachlan, Bruce, and W. J. Scott. *C*NS*RSH*P; A Study of the Censorship of Books, Films and Plays in New Zealand.* Auckland, New Zealand, Heinemann, 1973. 41p. **1M91**
"In this book our main concern will be with the control exercised by the state censorship system [New Zealand] over the publication and exhibition of factual and fictitious matter dealing with human behavior." The authors have assembled facts about censorship under New Zealand law, concluding with the point of view that New Zealanders are not prepared to accept the free choice of reading argued by John Milton in his *Areopagitica*: "The judgments that Milton said we ought to be free to make for ourselves are made for us by the film censor, the Indecent Publications Tribunal, the Controller of Television Programmes, and the Courts. And there is no doubt that a large majority of us, with varying degrees of willingness, accept this situation and wish it to continue. We agree that a line must be drawn and that others must draw it for us, though we continue to argue where to draw it."

MacLaine, Shirley. "Eros and the Nixon Administration." *Newsweek*, 81(19):13, 7 May 1973. **1M92**
"Buried in the Nixon Administration's 680 pages of proposed changes in the Federal Crime Statutes is a new Federal bill dealing with 'disseminating Obscene Material.' Passed on to Congress by Attorney General Kleindienst, these recommendations could wipe out the film and publishing industries as we know them. . . . As a citizen I resent being told what I can or cannot see, read or enjoy. These choices belong to me. Not to the FBI. Not to the Justice Department. Not even to the President of the United States. There are more fundamental and profound obscenities occurring where there are real victims and real crimes."

McLane, Eugene G. "Censor—Who?" *Wisconsin Library Bulletin*, 67:247–48, July 1971. **1M93**
The author, a public librarian, accuses the American Library Association of violating intellectual freedom by its Policy on Sanctions, by providing for the expulsion of a censorial librarian. "It is ironic that the Intellectual 'Freedom' Committee now has the power to review and impose by vote its interpretation of an individual's intellectual freedom of choice."

MacLatchy, Edward S. "Contempt of Court by Newspapers in England and Canada." *Canadian Bar Review*, 16:273–85, 1938. **1M94**
A discussion of two kinds of contempt under British and Canadian law: "scandalizing the court," i.e., publishing anything tending to bring the court or judge into contempt; and publishing anything deemed to interfere with a fair trial by prejudicing the jury or witnesses. The author advises on appropriate methods for handling each type of offense, noting that Canada should enforce more vigorously its

contempt laws in order to bring the practice more nearly to British standards.

MacLauchlin, Robert K. *Freedom of Speech and the American Educational Television Station*. East Lansing, Mich., Michigan State University, 1969. 289p. (Ph.D. dissertation, University Microfilms, no. 69–20,887) **1M95**
The study raises the question of how free are the educational television stations to program "in the public interest, convenience and necessity?" A mail survey of managers of all stations affiliated with National Educational Television showed little agreement on the extent of freedom, but revealed a number of restrictions, including government rules and regulations, and the timidity of managers to program through fear of agitating financial supporters.

McLaughlin, Blaine D. "The Psychiatrist as Expert Witness in Pornography Prosecutions." In Victor B. Cline, *ed.*, *Where Do You Draw the Line?* Provo, Utah, Brigham Young University Press, 1974, pp. 271–82. **1M96**
Presented in the form of a cross-examination of an expert witness, a psychiatrist states his views on pornography. He believes that "the rights of the individual to see the sort of sexual material that he wishes and which would appear to be his Constitutional right, should be set aside because of the danger that badly presented material might be injurious to the population in general." He disagrees with the findings of both the Commissions on Pornography and on Violence.

MacLeish, Archibald. *Remarks at the Dedication of the Wallace Library, Fitchburg, Massachusetts, June 3rd, 1967*. Worcester, Mass., Achille J. St. Onge, 1967. 63p. **1M97**
The former Librarian of Congress observes that during the McCarthy era the dedication of a new library was "an act of defiance and protest" against "the whole miasma of suspicion and censorship and fear" that McCarthy had let loose on the country.

MacLeod, Lanette. "Censorship History of *Catcher in the Rye*." *PNLA Quarterly* (Pacific Northwest Library Association), 39:10–13, July 1975. **1M98**
The censorship history of J. D. Salinger's novel, the focus of many bitterly fought school and library controversies and sometimes regarded as the most censored book in the United States. Such a survey "can lead to an understanding of the facets of censorship as it occurs and of the methods of defending such works of literary merit and controversial explosiveness."

McLeod, Richard. "Dissent and Reaction in Missouri." *Wilson Library Bulletin*, 44:269–76, November 1969. **1M99**

A former teaching assistant at the University of Missouri at Columbia charges that "the recent free speech conflict in Missouri which led to the ouster of Joan H. Bodger as consultant to Children's Services of the State Library is the direct result of statewide suspicion and distrust of dissenting social and political thought at the University of Missouri in Columbia." He discusses the *Free Press Underground* controversy of three years previous. The chancellor and the deans and faculty of the Schools of Journalism, Law, and Library Science "either failed to take action, or based their negative response on the ground that the literature in question contained obscenities."

MacLoskey, P. *Trial and Conviction of a Franciscan Monk at Mayo, Spring Assizes, 1852, for Burning and Blaspheming the Holy Scriptures*. Dublin, George Herbert, 1852. 55p. **1M100**
Protestants had established missions in the parish of Ballyoull where Franciscan monks had long held an ecclesiastical monopoly. In response to this proselytizing the monks held five public burnings of the Protestant Bible and other religious literature. John Syngian Bridgman (Brother John) was found guilty of the offense, but no punishment was meted provided he kept the peace for seven years.

McLoughlin, Emmett. *American Culture and Catholic Schools*. New York, Lyle Stuart, 1960. 288p. **1M101**
A former Franciscan priest describes his twenty-one years of Catholic schooling, including the influence of the Index of forbidden books and the propaganda in Catholic texts. He charges that censorship warps the school books, suppresses the facts of the Inquisition and the Council of Trent, and distorts world history.

McMahon, Patricia D. "Sheppard v. Maxwell: A Challenge to Trial Judges." *Journal of Public Law*, 16:215–27, 1967. **1M102**
Re: *Sheppard v. Maxwell*, 382 U.S. 916, 333 (1966), in which the U.S. Supreme Court ruled that the petitioner had been deprived of that "judicial serenity and calm to which [he] was entitled." The massive publicity was held to be sufficient to deny the defendant a fair trial without proof of specific malice. The author believes the courts will find it difficult to justify limiting publicity which is not prejudicial *per se*.

McMullen, W. A. "Censorship and Participatory Democracy." *Analysis*, 32:207–8, June 1972. **1M103**
An "informed extreme participatory democracy" runs into difficulty over making judgments in the matter of pornography and state secrets without letting everybody see and read

what might be harmful. H. M. Jones's response appears in the March 1973 issue.

McNair, Sherwyn. *Lottery News in the Press.* Columbia, Mo., Freedom of Information Center, School of Journalism, University of Missouri at Columbia, 1969. 6p. (Report no. 233) **1M104**
Should lotteries legalized by a state be subject to normal advertising and coverage by newspapers and broadcast media? The recent establishment of lotteries in New York and New Hampshire has brought demands from the media to liberalize Post Office and FCC rules.

Macnamara, Michael. "The Pasquino Society." *South African Libraries*, 38:256–59, January 1971.   **1M105**
One of the founders of the South African Society whose purpose is to promote the discussion of, and access to, literature and the arts, discusses the Society's opposition to South African censorship.

McNaught, Carlton. "Censorship and Propaganda in Peace and War." In his *Canada Gets the News. A Report in the International Research Series of the Institute of Pacific Relations.* Toronto, Ryerson, 1940, pp. 147–74.   **1M106**
A discussion of the peacetime censorship measures in effect in Canada—the Quebec Padlock Act, the Bill to Ensure Publication of Accurate News and Information in Newspapers of Alberta (declared by the Supreme Court of Canada as beyond the power of the legislature), the portion of the Criminal Code of Canada providing a penalty for false news, and the effective self-censorship as practiced by the Canadian Press in censoring news from the United States (witness the abdication crisis). There are also references to wartime censorship under Defence of Canada Regulations, and voluntary action of newspapers.

McNeal, Archie L. "Librarians As Enemies of Books: Or, How to Succeed in Censorship Without Really Trying." *Southeastern Librarian*, 19(1):30–35, Spring 1969.   **1M107**
While the university, college, and school libraries relate their book selection policies to the curricular needs of their institutions, public libraries serve a public that is widely disparate in cultural background, education, political interests, and religious convictions, placing a greater responsibility on the professional staff in providing the right mix in book selection within the limitation of public funds. The article discusses the various issues and problems involved in wise selection and the professional standards of intellectual freedom that should prevail.

McNearney, Clayton L. "The Kanawha County Textbook Controversy." *Religious Education*, 70:519–40, September–December 1975. **1M108**
The controversy in Kanawha County, W.Va., over school textbooks involved four areas of concern: profanity, street talk and bad grammar often used to reflect varying life styles and minorities, sex education, and the views that God is a myth. This last, according to the writer, is the most important of protesters' objections. The controversy was basically religious and we can expect a replay of these events in other locales.

McNeil, Gerard. "Taking the Censor to Court." *Index on Censorship*, 5(2):21–22, Summer 1976.   **1M109**
A newspaperman describes his efforts to bring movie censorship in Canada before the courts.

MacNeil, Robert. "Government Regulation." In his *The Influence of Television on American Politics.* New York, Harper & Row, 1968, pp. 259–91.   **1M110**
Includes a discussion of the fairness doctrine, broadcast editorials, and Section 315 (equal time) of the 1934 Communications Act. "If television wants more ˌjournalisticˌ freedom it needs only to exploit the opportunities that lie before it. Kicking the Fairness Doctrine will not strengthen TV news coverage. . . . Broadcasting has not proved that present regulations are an infringement of its journalistic freedom."

McPhee, Neil. "Defamation." In Melbourne University. *The Law and the Printer, the Publisher and the Journalist. The Collected Papers of a Seminar at Melbourne University on August 12, 1971.* Melbourne, Australia, Antony Whitlock, 1971, pp. 34–46.   **1M111**
Australian libel laws are "a jungle of complexity and difficulty and uncertainty," and libel trials are among the most lengthy and costly trials known. The author reviews the defenses for libel—truth (a complete defense in Victoria but not in all Australian states), privilege (absolute or qualified), and fair comment. He discusses recent cases in detail.

McQueen, Thomas K. "No Right to Interference—Free Television Reception." *DePaul Law Review*, 22:870–86, Summer 1973.   **1M112**
Re: *People ex rel. Hoogasian v. Sears, Roebuck and Co.*, in which the Illinois Supreme Court ruled that injunctive relief was not warranted for television reception interference because it did not constitute an actionable nuisance. The case involved the construction of the 110-story Sears building in Chicago which, it was charged, would distort television reception.

McQuigg, Bruce. "The Librarian." In Billy L. Turney, *ed., Catcher in the Wrong: Iconoclasts in Education.* Itaska,

Ill., Published for Phi Delta Kappa by F. E. Peacock, 1968, pp. 219–20. **1M113**
A humorous account of a fictional high school librarian who used a felt pen to ink out offensive sex words before putting new books on the shelf.

McShean, Gordon. "Are There Disturbed Librarians?" *Wilson Library Bulletin*, 43:340–44, December 1968.   **1M114**
A criticism of professional librarians for lack of adequate resistence to censorship pressures when they become specific. "What justification can we give for permitting a continued adherence to the principles of intellectual freedom to be called 'extremism,' by rightists, leftists, 'concerned mothers,' 'decent literature' groups—and by ourselves?"

——. "From Roswell to Richmond . . . to Your Town." *Library Journal*, 95:627–31, 15 February 1970. Comments: 95:2035+, 1 June 1970; rejoinder, 95:2585–86, August 1970.   **1M115**
A librarian cites his experience with censorship in Roswell, N.Mex., where the principal thrust was made against a public reading of "hippie" poetry; and in Richmond, Calif., where the case centered around the *Berkeley Barb* and *Avant Garde.* He also refers to the case in Martinsville, Va., where he asserts the librarian was attacked not for what he had in his library but for his stand on the teaching of religion in the schools. The author concludes that "what we need is an invasion force to confront the censors on their own grounds, a massive army of dedicated freedom fighters who will attack the censors and deny them every parcel of community consciousness that they seek to control. . . . We need only tell the truth about their backgrounds, their motives, and their tactics."

McWilliams, W. Carey. "Is Muckraking Coming Back?" *Columbia Journalism Review*, 9(3):8–15, Fall 1970. (Reprinted in Michael C. Emery and Ted C. Smythe, *eds., Readings in Mass Communications*, pp. 106–15)   **1M116**
The editor of the *Nation* reviews turn-of-the-century muckraking and the various efforts in subsequent years that have kept reform journalism alive. The bright vision of life after World War II was never realized as the cold war intervened and, instead of muckraking, red-baiting was the order of the day. The *Nation* was one of the few organs of dissent and reform that survived. The scene began to change in the 1960s, ushering in a new era of reform journalism, made possible by new technology, an active breed of investigative reporters, and a new social concern.

——. "On Pornography." *Public Interest*, 22:32–38, Winter 1971.   **1M117**
Commenting on an essay on pornography by Walter Berns in the same issue, the author

notes that "there are offenses against civic virtue in America which are both more serious and more worthy of censorship than is obscenity." The problem of obscenity is "part of the generally grim and decadent character of modern politics," and obscenity becomes socially visible, emerging from the underground, "only when it has reason to expect a welcome." Moral standards and civic virtue "require construction as much or more than they do maintenance, and either may demand the remaking of modern society not the tinkering of the censor."

Macy, Christopher, *ed*. *The Arts in a Permissive Society*. London, Published for the Rationalist Press Association by Pemberton Books, 1970. 103p. **1M118**
Content: Introduction by D. J. Stewart. The Historical Perspective by Peter Faulkner. The Novel by John Calder. Cinema and Television by Roger Manvell. Is Social Theatre Possible? by Daniel Salem. The article by Faulkner examines sexual permissiveness in relation to artistic achievements in three societies—Roman, English Restoration, and Victorian. It was reprinted in *Books and Bookman*, March 1972.

Macy, John W., Jr. *The Rise and Fall of Public Broadcasting*. 29 min. tape recording. Santa Barbara, Calif., Center for the Study of Democratic Institutions [197–?]. **1M119**
"There is a growing fear that what has happened to public broadcasting under the Nixon administration may hint at the fate of national commercial television. Here the former president of the Public Broadcasting Corporation, John W. Macy, Jr., gives a step-by-step account of the process by which public broadcasting was established, flourished, and was finally brought to its present enfeebled state."

[Madden, Terrence J.] "Freedom of Information Act—Enjoining Administrative Proceedings Pending a District Court Resolution of a Demand for Information." *University of Illinois Law Forum*, 1973:180–92, 1973. **1M120**
Re: *Bannercraft Clothing Co., Inc. v. Renegotiation Board*, 466 F.2d 345 (D.C. Cir. 1972).

Maddock, Larry. "The Perilous Pedestal." *Candida*, 1(3):21, 56–57, 1958. **1M121**
"The difference between women's roles here and abroad is partly responsible for and partly reinforced by the current ridiculous censorship standards in this country." American women have been placed on a pedestal by Puritan doctrine, "a pedestal she never deserved."

Madgwick, Donald, and Tony Smythe. *The Invasion of Privacy*. London, Pitman, 1974. 197p. **1M122**
Throughout the book and particularly in chapter 11, The Media, the authors consider the apparent conflict between the people's right to know and the individual's right of privacy. While the British press has been free to expose personal scandal it has been greatly restricted in the coverage of news about public affairs. "Most of our newspapers have become willing partners in the conspiracy of silence, submitting alike to the external pressure of D-Notice, libel, contempt, and Official Secrets, and the internal one of editorial whim and borrowed control." The British press would have been virtually powerless in facing a Watergate affair. The authors criticize the Press Council and the findings of the Younger Committee on Privacy (chapter 2) and make their own recommendations in chapter 13.

Madison, A. P. "The Printer and Obscenity." *Montana Journalism Review*, 16:33–36, 16 November 1973. **1M123**
The director of printing services at the University of Montana discusses the implications for printers in printing obscenity, dealing largely with his experience with the student daily newspaper at the University of Montana, *Montana Kaimen*.

Maeder, Gary W. "Right of Access to Broadcast Media for Paid Editorial Advertising—A Plea to Congress." *UCLA Law Review*, 22:258–322, October 1974. **1M124**
"Although the Supreme Court found that a limited right of access to the broadcast media for paid editorial advertising was not compelled by either the first amendment or the Communications Act of 1934, it did keep the door wide open for Congress to legislate such a right. In drafting and urging Congress to pass such an act, this Comment has sought to show first, that providing limited access for paid editorial advertising would produce important benefits for the nation which are not otherwise attainable; and second, that the objections which have been raised to a limited right of access can be answered adequately and that the problems which such a right might produce can be solved."

Magaziner, Fred T. "Corporate Defamation and Product Disparagement: Narrowing the Analogy to Personal Defamation." *Columbia Law Review*, 75:963–1008, June 1975. **1M125**
The author examines the kinds of statements which are actionable as corporate defamation and product disparagement; addresses the question of the extent to which the commercial speech doctrine places corporate defamation and product disparagement outside the sphere of First Amendment protection. The final sections of the article "focus on two areas where distinctions must be developed between corporations and individuals: commercial privilege and equitable relief."

Mahaffie, Charles D., Jr. "Mergers and Diversification in the Newspaper, Broadcasting and Information Indus-

tries." *Antitrust Bulletin*, 13:927–35, Fall 1968. **1M126**
The chief of the General Litigation Section, Antitrust Division, Department of Justice, describes some of the activities taking place in the mass media industry that are of concern to the Antitrust Division and the kind of analysis the Division is conducting of the mergers in the media.

"Mailer, McLuhan, and Muggeridge: On Obscenity." *Realist*, 83:5–12, October 1968. **1M127**
Transcript of a Toronto television broadcast, The Way It Is. Panel: Norman Mailer, Marshall McLuhan, and Malcolm Muggeridge. Moderator: Bob Fulford.

Maine, Colin. "Is Pornography a Valid Form of Amusement?" *Australian Humanist* (Council of Australian Humanist Societies), 17:22–25, March 1971. **1M128**

Maines, Patrick. "Shielding the Press." *National Review*, 25:574–76, 25 May 1973. **1M129**
The author discusses the *Caldwell* decision of the U.S. Supreme Court (*United States v. Caldwell*, 1972), denying constitutional privilege to withhold information from grand juries, and the efforts to provide such guarantees through federal legislation. He writes of the complexity of the issue, the divided opinion within the press, noting four areas of controversy: (1) whether federal legislation should preempt state law, (2) whether legislation should give newsmen "absolute" or "qualified" immunity, (3) whether the immunity should apply only to working journalists or to other authors, scholars, pamphleteers, etc., and (4) whether immunity should apply only to his sources, or both his sources and his information.

"Major Moves to Rip up Broadcasting." *Broadcasting*, 78:27–30, 30 March 1970. **1M130**
News and commentary on the Federal Communications Commission attacks on radio and television network ownership and programming, including a cut-back on the amount of programs the networks may supply in prime time.

Makuch, Stanley. "Controlling Obscenity by Administrative Tribunal; A Study of the Ontario Board of Cinema Censors." *Osgoode Hall Law Journal*, 9:385–413, November 1971. (Reprinted in *Canadian Communications Law Review*, 1971) **1M131**
The author examines the stated goals of the

Ontario Cinema Censor Board both in 1911, when it was first instituted, and today. "The Censor Board's original goal was unattainable; it thus responded by choosing the goal of classification which is unimportant. The Board should be discarded for its dream of a distinctive Canadian society is surely an impossible dream."

Malakoff, Louise R. "The First Amendment and the Public Right to Information." *University of Pittsburg Law Review*, 35:93–114, Fall 1973.
                                          1M132
The author examines the present vitality of the public right of access to facts and competing ideas, protected through the personal liberties guaranteed by the First Amendment, in the context of current decisions of the Supreme Court. She concludes that the several decisions of the Burger Court, while not likely to cause a readily apparent decline in information available to the public, "contain no promise of the open, responsive government demanded in recent years by varying social, economic and political sectors of the population and envisaged by the concept of self-government."

Mallamud, Jonathan. "The Broadcast Licensee as Fiduciary: Toward the Enforcement of Discretion." *Duke Law Journal*, 1973:89–133, April 1973.
                                          1M133
"The thesis presented in this article is that, building on the fairness doctrine, a doctrine can be developed that would enable the Federal Communications Commission to enforce a positive duty of the licensee to use good faith efforts to present controversial issues of public importance."

Malleson, Miles. "Preface to the 2nd Edition." In his *"D" Company and Black 'Ell: Two Plays*. London, Hendersons, 1925, pp. 5–6.   **1M134**
A brief account of the seizure of copies of the first edition (1916) by Scotland Yard, because of "a deliberate calumny on the British soldier" and the raising of the issue in the House of Commons.

Mallette, Malcolm F. "Should These News Pictures Have Been Printed?" *Popular Photography*, 78(3):73–75+, March 1976.   **1M135**
The author discusses the ethical responsibilities of editors and photographers in choosing which photographs to run in the pages of family newspapers, giving examples of questionable pictures.

Malmgren, Lynn C. "Freedom of the Press to Gather News." *Villanova Law*

Review, 20:189–201, November 1974.
                                          1M136
"This note will explore both the recent developments in the judicial evolution of a right to gather news and the practical problems which may arise if courts continue to recognize and expand this arguable new first amendment protection."

Maloff, Sam. "Comstock's Complaint." *Commonweal*, 91:362–63, 19 December 1969.   **1M137**
The reissue of Anthony Comstock's *Traps for the Young* prompts the author of the article to recount some of Comstock's crusade in behalf of purity in print.

Malone, Donald M. "Broadcasting, the Reluctant Dragon: Will the First Amendment Right of Access End the Suppressing of Controversial Ideas?" *Journal of Law Reform*, 5:194–277, Winter 1972.   **1M138**
"The scope of this article will be limited to one aspect of electronic media programming—the extent to which the public is and should be exposed to an accurate cross section of public opinion and a broad range of controversial ideas. Many people, including the Federal Communications Commission (FCC), have acknowledged that a desirable goal for the broadcast media, particularly television, is to provide a marketplace for controversial ideas. Part II of this article will identify the principal reasons why that goal has not been achieved. Part III will examine the fairness doctrine, the antecedents of which have been traced back to 1929. While generally requiring that a broadcast licensee's programming cover issues of public importance in a manner fairly presenting conflicting points of view, the broad discretion given to licensees in applying the doctrine has significantly lessened its impact. Moreover, a raging debate continues over whether the effect of the fairness doctrine has been more to suppress than to enhance the expression of controversial ideas. Part IV will describe a new legal doctrine—the first amendment right of access—which has recently been applied to the broadcast media, and whose effect may be to thrust controversial programming upon *all* electronic media. Finally, Part V will discuss additional ways to encourage the broadcasting of controversial ideas."

Malone, Ronald H. "Obscenity: The Pig in the Parlor." *Santa Clara Lawyer*, 10:288–300, Spring 1970.   **1M139**
"This comment will explore the traditionally offered constitutional, practical and philosophical arguments supporting obscenity regulation and reveal their manifest inapplicability to the present American socio-political setting. The author will also examine the impact of *Stanley v. Georgia* [1969] on state regulation of obscenity and show why this decision heralds the arrival of the 'nuisance theory' as the only constitutionally permissible approach to obscenity regulation."

Maltbie, William M. "Courts and the Press." *Connecticut Bar Journal*, 10:270–76, October 1936.   **1M140**
Chief Justice Maltbie criticizes the press for coverage of trials and lays down a set of rules to be observed, including exclusion of reporters from outside the state, prohibition of runners during sessions, no pictures or drawings, no radio equipment, and no crowding of reporters around the court house. An editorial by M. S. Sherman from the *Hartford Courant* (pp. 277–81), while agreeing with Judge Maltbie's disapproval of melodramatic reporting, objects to his suggested code, which "sets up a series of discriminations quite unnecessary to the effective control of the evils under discussion."

[Maltz, Gerald S.] "The Substantive Law of Obscenity: An Adventure in Quicksand." *New York Law Forum*, 13:81–133, Spring 1967.   **1M141**
"Obscenity censorship has never been justified and thus exemplifies the rule of taboo and not the rule of reason. Social inutility is not a reason, but an excuse. The accusation that obscenity causes crime or 'corrupts' is unfounded. All expression is potentially influential, including the 'hate' literature and the war glorification that we do not censor. To censor expression that we fear might be persuasive . . . is to censor all unorthodox expression. . . . The best regulation is self-regulation. The applause or rejection of the audience will always be the ultimate censor, no matter what the state of the law. . . . The choice is admittedly difficult but unavoidably personal and it is high-time that we stop imprisoning men for selling books, and lift the distasteful task of the censor from the Court, and from government and make our own decisions as to what we are to read, to see, and to think."

Manchester, William. "Controversy." In his *Controversy and Other Essays in Journalism*, 1950–1975. Boston, Little, Brown, 1976. pp. 1–76.   **1M142**
The author's account of the controversy over the writing and publishing of *The Death of a President*, the story of the assassination of John F. Kennedy.

Manchikes, Alice W., *ed.* "Issue on Censorship." *Kentucky English Bulletin*, 24(1):3–31, Fall 1974.   **1M143**
Content: Foreword by Alice W. Manchikes. How to Burn a Book by Richard Armour. A Professional Approach to Censorship by William H. Peters. Case Study I: The Student as Censor by Doris G. Sutton. Case Study II: The Religious Community as Censor by Carole Shetler. Case Study III: The Parent as Censor by Jacqueline Walker. Censorship in Kentucky: KCTE Questionnaire by Alfred L. Crabb, Jr. and Alice W. Manchikes. Censorship and Academic Freedom in the Classroom by Priscilla Robertson. Protection Granted to Educators under Kentucky Obscenity Law by Michael R. Moloney.

Mander, A. E. *Public Enemy the Press*. Melbourne, Australia, International Book Shop, 1944. 94p.   **1M144**
The author challenges the right of press proprietors to special privileges of freedom for their "loud speakers." Using examples from the Australian press, he shows how the monopoly press, while fighting any outside controls as censorship, employ their own internal censorship by means of omission and distortion of news. He shows the interlocking directorships which foster monopoly practices. To prevent the present abuse of press freedom, the author recommends separating business ownership from editorial policy, the latter to be conducted by a staff appointed by and responsible to a Newspaper Commission. The Commission would consist of distinguished persons nominated by the University Senate, the Premier, the leaders of Parliament, the editors, and members of the Australian Journalists' Association. The Commission would report directly to Parliament.

Mangione, Anthony R. "Implications of Censorship: Past, Present, and Future Threats." *Ohio English Bulletin*, 15(3):24–31, September 1974.   **1M145**
Students can be trained to be "discriminating, sensitive users of language, distinguishing between rational and irrational examples . . . ; able to scrutinize the peculiar Newspeak of the courts, schools, governmental agencies and protest movements . . . ; alert to the rhetoric of politics and its characteristic euphemism, question-begging, and vagueness. Teachers of English, in turn, should be free to employ books, classic or contemporary, which do not lie to the young about the perilous but wondrous times we live in, books which talk of the fears, hopes, joys, and frustrations people experience, books about people not only as they are but as they can be. If the worst is realized, and teachers are forced through the pressures of censorship to use only safe or antiseptic works, then future man may well progress toward the nightmare fearfully outlined by Huxley, Orwell, and Toffler in their predictions of the future."

Mankekar, D. R. *The Press under Pressure*. New Delhi, Indian Book Co., 1973. 167p.   **1M146**
An Indian journalist examines the nation's press to determine the extent of freedom. He finds that "the Indian press is indeed the freest in the 'Third World'—but then that is not saying much. Press freedom has been extinguished in one developing country after another as dictatorships and 'limited democracies' have taken over." He acquits the press of charges leveled against it by the government—that it is being used to further property interests. He convicts the Indian press of the charge of failure to discharge its public duty—of retreating in the face of government threats and pressures.

———. "Why No Watergates Here?" *Quest*, 87:33–36, March–April 1974.   **1M147**

The Indian press does not enjoy the same immunity as that imparted to the American press by the First Amendment. The Indian press is further handicapped by the prevailing rigid laws of libel and contempt of court and an Official Secrets Act, which, he charges, the government misuses to protect itself from embarrassment.

Mann, Jay. *Data Is a Four Letter Word: Some Problems of Obscenity Research*. [San Francisco, The Author, 1971.] 12p. Processed.   **1M148**
A paper presented at a symposium, Western Psychological Association, San Francisco, April 1971.

———. "Experimental Induction of Human Sexual Arousal." *Technical Report of the [U.S.] Commission on Obscenity and Pornography*, 1:23–60, 1971.   **1M149**
The paper explores the technical problems of experimental research and served as a guide to the Commission in developing its research program.

———, Jack Sidman, and Sheldon Starr. "Effects of Erotic Films on Sexual Behavior of Married Couples." *Technical Report of the [U.S.] Commission on Obscenity and Pornography*, 8:170–254, 1971. (Also reported in the *Journal of Social Issues*, no. 3, 1973)   **1M150**
"Eighty-five married couples were studied in order to investigate the effects upon sexual and marital attitudes and behavior of viewing erotic films as compared with viewing nonerotic films or no films. . . . No sustained changes in behavior were found for subjects who viewed erotic films relative to other subjects; however, they exhibited significantly greater activity on film-viewing nights than did subjects who viewed nonerotic films. Some subjects in all conditions reported that participation in the study benefited their marital and sexual relationship. Film rating data are discussed."

Manners, George. *Vindiciae Satiricae, or A Vindication of the Principles of the Satirist, and the Conduct of Its Proprietors . . . to which is Added, a Correct Report of an Action Brought by Peter Finnerty, Against the Publisher of the Satirist, for a Libel. . . . London, Printed by Thomas Plummer for Samuel Tipper* [1809]. 90p.   **1M151**
A principal conductor of the *Satirist* writes of the formation of that journal as an answer to the wave of malicious libels being directed against innocent persons by unscrupulous, often anonymous, authors who "threatened to destroy all social confidence, who annihilate domestic happiness, and bring into contempt our monarch and our altars." The names of Charles Sedley (*pseud.* for Elrington), Thomas Hague, William Cobbett, and Peter Finnerty are held up to scorn. The editor accuses the

libelers of praising the blessings of the liberty of the press when it protects their own libels, but when those who are libeled attempt to counteract the falsehoods, the libelers scream "libel" and want the work suppressed. Much of the complaint is against William Cobbett and Peter Finnerty, and an account of the latter's libel case against *Satirist* publisher Samuel Tipper (1809) is presented in full. Finnerty had asked for a £25,000 judgment. The jury found Tipper guilty and, in obvious disgust over the actions of the plaintiff, awarded Finnerty damages of one shilling.

Mannes, Marya. "Pressures in the USA." *Index on Censorship*, 4:47, Winter 1975.   **1M152**
Comments on the social, unofficial, and unacknowledged pressures in the United States against individuals who dare to question motives or policies of certain ethnic groups.

[Mansel, Robert.] *A Struggle for Stage or No Stage; originating in a Sermon, Preached by the Reverend Thomas Best, in St. James Church, Sheffield*. Sheffield, England, Printed by W. Todd [1818]. 16p.   **1M153**
A collection of three letters from Robert Mansel, appearing in *Sheffield Mercury*, to the Reverend Mr. Best, objecting to his attacks on the local theater of which Mansel was manager, challenging the minister to produce one biblical interdict. He threatens to sue Best if he can prove that one person was kept from the theater because of Best's sermon. Other letters are included from the Sheffield, Leeds, and Bristol papers either in support of Mansel or Best.

Manvell, Roger. "Censorship: The Changing Mood." *Journal of the Society of Film and Television Arts*." 43/44:1–3, Spring–Summer 1971.   **1M154**
In an introduction to an issue devoted to assessing the current status of censorship in Britain, Manvell raises a number of major issues: (1) While there is a general liberalization of outlook on censorship, should society accede to the "fashionable pressures" for a vague goal of "total freedom?" (2) As the law and regulating authorities withdraw ancient sanctions, what, if anything, should take their place? (3) Should similar freedom be extended to all media? (4) Should regulation of the audience rather than the work, as presently exists with the cinema, be extended to other media? (5) What is the future of the so-called "club system," now operating in the cinema trade?

———. "The Cinema and Society." In his *The Film and the Public*. Harmondsworth, England, Penguin, 1955, pp. 241–52. (Reprinted in Richard D. MacCann, *ed.*, *Film and Society*, pp. 93–96)   **1M155**

A description of the system of film censorship in Britain and America. "If the Censor suddenly decided to abolish himself," the author observes, "it would almost certainly be necessary to re-create him again in one form or another."

———. "Porn Stop: A Humanist Approach." *New Humanist*, 88:364–65, January 1973.   **1M156**
A humanist comments on the views expressed in the Longford Report on obscenity. "The Humanist approach to the nature of pornography and obscenity and the rights and wrongs of their availability to the public must be conditioned initially by the Humanist's attitude to people, their rights as individuals, and any limitations they should be prepared to accept for the good of the community of which they are members." He concludes that "the Humanist must allow for the needs of others up to the limits of what is endurable in terms of our common civil rights, avoiding all unnecessary restriction and censorship."

Manwaring, David R. "The Impact of Mapp v. Ohio." In David H. Everson, *ed., The Supreme Court as Policy-Maker: Three Studies on the Impact of Judicial Decisions.* Carbondale, Ill., Public Affairs Research Bureau, Southern Illinois University, 1968, pp. 1–43.   **1M157**
Mapp v. Ohio (1961), which involved the testing of Ohio's novel statute punishing mere possession of obscene literature, is discussed here as a "showcase example" of a search and seizure case.

[Manwaring, Roger.] *The Proceedings of the Lords and Commons In the Year 1628. Against Roger Manwaring, Doctor in Divinity, [The Sacheverell of those Days] For Two Seditious High-flying Sermons, intitled, Religion and Allegiance.* London, Printed for Ben. Bragge, 1709. 24p.   **1M158**
Manwaring, the king's chaplain, was convicted by Parliament of sedition for sermons justifying the king's right to impose taxes without consent of Parliament. He was fined, sentenced to prison, and his books were ordered burned. The king's ministers, however, refused to carry out the punishment. The proceedings of the trial are republished with a new preface citing the Manwaring case as a precedent for Parliament's taking action against a minister, and suggesting that this procedure be followed in punishing the current offenses of Dr. Sacheverell.

Marble, Kenneth R. "Lloyd Corporation, Ltd. v. Tanner: Property Rights in a Privately Owned Shopping Center v. the Rights of Free Speech." *Willamette Law Journal*, 9:181–91, March 1973.   **1M159**
Re: *Lloyd Corporation, Ltd. v. Tanner*, 92 S.Ct. 2219 (1972).

Marble, Manton. *Freedom of the Press Wantonly Violated, Letter of Mr. Marble to President Lincoln, Reappearance of the Journal of Commerce, Opinions of the Press on This Outrage.* [New York, 1864?] 8p. (Papers from the Society of Political Knowledge, no. 22)   **1M160**
A contemporary reprinting of a letter to President Lincoln dated New York, 23 May 1864, in which the editor Manton Marble of the *New York World* accuses President Lincoln of ordering his arrest and the search and seizure of his paper by the military forces because of the publishing of a proclamation on the draft, purportedly issued by Lincoln but later proved to be a forgery planted by a rival newspaperman. Marble defends his action in recalling the papers as soon as the forgery was detected and in cooperating with the authorities in locating the culprit. He charges Lincoln with ruthless suppression of the freedom of the press on political grounds. In addition to the Marble letter, the pamphlet reprints other newspaper accounts of the affair which had resulted in the suspension of both the *World* and the *Journal of Commerce* which had also printed the spurious document. The confessed forger was Joseph Howard, Jr., prominent Republican and former city editor of the *New York Times*.

———. *Letter to Abraham Lincoln by Manton Marble, Editor of "The World."* New York, Privately Printed, 1867. 25p. (Edition of 99 copies)   **1M161**
A reprinting in book form of the Manton Marble letter to President Lincoln criticizing the military seizure of the *New York World*.

Marcello, David A. "Freedom of the Press: the Journalist's Right to Maintain the Secrecy of His Confidential Sources." *Tulane Law Review*, 45:605–26, April 1971.   **1M162**
The author calls for a clear constitutional mandate to protect freedom of the press, especially essential during a period when the news media are under vigorous attack by high public officials. "A first amendment freedom of the press to resist disclosure of confidential sources is presently emerging as the most recent development of our evolving system of constitutional protection."

Marchetti, Victor, and John D. Marks. *The CIA and the Cult of Intelligence.* Introduction by Melvin L. Wulf. New York, Knopf, 1974. 26p., 398p. 21p.   **1M163**
"This book, the first in American history to be subject to prior government censorship, began making news even before it was written. From the time it was no more than an outline to the present, the Central Intelligence Agency has been trying to prevent its publication. To a degree, the agency has succeeded. Legal proceedings and injunctions delayed publication for more than a year. One hundred and sixty-eight passages actually censored by the agency continue to be unavailable and are thus missing from the text as published here (although nearly two hundred more, first cut and then yielded up by the CIA following insistent demands by lawyers for the authors and the publishers, will be found in boldface type). Ironically, however, in a broader sense the agency has failed. In recent months, *The CIA and the Cult of Intelligence* has become a public issue of great symbolic importance—as a test of free speech and as a valuable and effective challenge to a particularly odious concept: the idea that any government body—even the CIA—should be permitted to exist beyond the reach of the Constitution and public control." Melvin L. Wulf, legal director of the American Civil Liberties Union, in his introduction describes the legal battle in the courts. Throughout the book are references to the CIA's efforts to control information and on pages 363–64 is an account of the CIA's "anti-book mission" against Alfred McCoy's *The Politics of Heroin in Southeast Asia*. The censored portions of the text are represented by white spaces.

Marcuse, F. L. "Some Reflections on Pornography and Censorship." *Canadian Forum*, 53:13–16, March 1975.   **1M164**
A psychologist writes of the psychological awareness of some of the factors involved in pornography, and with a broad humanistic orientation. He concludes: "The intimate relationship between the so-called pornographic and our socio-economic system cannot be ignored. Neither can one overlook the fact that no simple cause and effect relationship has ever been clearly demonstrated between the sexually obscene (however defined) and any form of sexual delinquency. Employing operational definitions, what data exist would suggest that psychological factors operate in different ways, with different effects, in the area of sex as compared with that of violence. One can plausibly, then, make a case for censorship of violence while supporting no censorship of sex."

Marcuse, Herbert. "Repressive Tolerance." In Robert P. Wolff, Barrington Moore, Jr., and Herbert Marcuse, *A Critique of Pure Tolerance.* Boston, Beacon, 1965, pp. 81–117. (Excerpted in Eleanor Widmer, *ed., Freedom and Culture; Literary Censorship in the 70's.* Belmont, Calif., Wadsworth, 1970, pp. 27–37)   **1M165**
Tolerance, as it is practiced today, serves the cause of oppression by supporting prevailing social and political attitudes and opinions. Marcuse calls for the liberalizing of tolerance which would mean "intolerance against movements from the Right, and toleration of movements from the Left." Such tolerance and intolerance "would extend to the stage of action as well as of discussion and propaganda, of

deed as well as of word. The traditional criterion of clear and present danger seems no longer adequate to a stage where the whole society is in the situation of the theater audience when somebody cries: 'fire.' " He acknowledges that such a point of view would incorporate censorship, even precensorship, but it would be "openly directed against the more or less hidden censorship that permeates the free media."

Marier, Charles. *Handbills and Shoppers: Idea Markets*. Columbia, Mo., Freedom of Information Center, School of Journalism, University of Missouri at Columbia, 1972. 8p. (Report no. 294) **1M166**

"Local regulations limiting distribution of handbills and shopper publications often threaten First Amendment rights, accidentally or by design. This report traces the evolution of such regulations through 'Green River ordinances' up to the present, while analyzing relevant constitutional questions."

Marino, Ralph J. "The New York Freedom of Information Law." *Fordham Law Review*, 43:83–92, October 1974. **1M167**

New York's law, patterned after the Federal Freedom of Information Act, "will promote free and open disclosure by government at all levels, thereby clarifying the public's right to information which is constitutionally theirs."

Markel, Lester. *What You Don't Know Can Hurt You. A Study of Public Opinion and Public Emotion*. Washington, D.C., Public Affairs, 1972. 288p. (Paperback issued by Quadrangle/New York Times) **1M168**

The author's thesis is that "the forces which mold opinion are not functioning as they need to function; that the nation's leaders and the media are not educating the ignorant and stirring the lethargic." Because a large part of the electorate does not have reliable information and is too prone to emotion to make sound judgments, opinion is formulated by a minority elite.

Markham, David. "Federal Censorship of National Open Forum Radio." In *Free Speech Yearbook, 1971*. New York, Speech Communication Association, 1971, pp. 36–42. **1M169**

"The Vice-President [Agnew] seems to view American society as a governmental monolith which broadcasting should reflect; but the United States Senate, at least in broadcasting matters, seems to view the society as a commercial monolith. This paper is a report of this conflict of attitudes concerning broadcasting between important legislative and administrative figures."

Markham, James W., *ed.* "Journalism Editors and the Press Council Idea: A

Symposium." *Journalism Quarterly*, 45(1):77–85, Spring 1968. **1M170**

Content: Association for Education in Journalism Efforts at Formal Press Appraisal by James W. Markham. The Mellett Fund's Activities by H. Eugene Goodwin. The Press Council Experience in Britain by Edmund M. Midura. What the AEJ Can Do with the Press Council Idea by J. Edward Gerald.

Marks, Herbert S., and George F. Trowbridge. "Control of Information under the Atomic Energy Act of 1954." *Bulletin of the Atomic Energy Scientists*, 11:128–30, April 1955. **1M171**

"The combination of monopoly plus secrecy has insulated atomic energy from the normal processes of public and official examination and criticism. . . . The Atomic Energy Act of 1954 represents a shift in the mood of Congress. The lawmakers have attempted to moderate government monopoly by enlarging opportunities for business and other private institutions, and to loosen somewhat the tight restrictions of secrecy."

Marks, John D. "The Story That Never Was." *MORE*, 4(6):20, 22, June 1974. **1M172**

"Did the *Times* at Kissinger's request kill a piece exposing U.S. plans to invade Cambodia in 1970? Absolutely not, says the paper's top editors. Yes, says the man who says he wrote the story."

Marks, Richard D. "Broadcasting and Censorship: First Amendment Theory After Red Lion." *George Washington Law Review*, 38:974–1005, July 1970. **1M173**

The author concludes that "the *Red Lion* decision [*Red Lion Broadcasting Co. v. FCC*, 1967] created confusion and, by upholding the Personal Attack Rules, injected an unnecessary impediment to the broadcast industry's coverage of public affairs. To remedy the present unsatisfactory state of the law the Commission and the courts should adopt a theory of broadcast regulation which incorporates first amendment doctrines previously applied only to the non-electronic media. . . . Applying general first amendment theory to broadcasting would yield sensible results for both the licensee and the community. Broadcasting could be conducted freely, efficiently and profitably, yet service obligations could still be expeditiously enforced."

Marks, Thomas C., Jr. *First Amendment Freedoms and the American Military*. Gainsville, Fla., University of Florida, 1971. 239p. (Ph.D. dissertation, University Microfilms, no. 72–16,633) **1M174**

"This paper attempts to place the question of the limitations on the First Amendment freedoms in the interest of military discipline in perspective by looking at the history of the relationship between the two from 1775 to the

present. The freedoms of speech and press are considered together as are the freedoms of petition and assembly. The freedom of religion is considered separately."

Marler, Charles. *Magazines and Postal Rates*. Columbia, Mo., Freedom of Information Center, School of Journalism, University of Missouri at Columbia, 1973. 10p. (Report no. 306) **1M175**

"Though increased second-class postal rates have been widely thought of as a serious threat to the lives of numerous magazines, a close examination of the situation reveals that such may not be generally the case. Postal rate hikes have not been cited as contributing causes of failure by the publishers of more than one now defunct major magazine."

———. *Sequester the Country*. Columbia, Mo., Freedom of Information Center, School of Journalism, University of Missouri at Columbia, 1972. 13p. (Report no. 277) **1M176**

"Trial court justices too often hand down restrictive orders and rulings prejudicial to freedom of the press and public trials under the First, Fifth and Sixth Amendments. To the credit of the judiciary, reform and educational programs are being aggressively pursued, and such institutions as the National College of Trial Judges seem to offer . . . most promise for progress. Press-bar-bench guidelines, although no panacea, have improved the coverage of criminal news."

———. *State Houses v. Unsigned Opinions*. Columbia, Mo., Freedom of Information Center, School of Journalism, University of Missouri at Columbia, 1973. 8p. (Report no. 316) **1M177**

"Anonymous writings helped win Bill of Rights liberties, including the right of the press to determine its journalistic practices and editorial policies. Recently many legislatures have attempted to require newspapers to sign editorials. Some states would extend the requirement to all content of all information mediums. The constitutional issues and newspaper practices are examined as related to anti-anonymity legislation."

Marler, Charles, and Bill Cloud. *Pro Sports: Super Blackout?* Columbia, Mo., Freedom of Information Center, School of Journalism, University of Missouri at Columbia, 1974. 8p. (Report no. 319) **1M178**

"The Great American Sports Complex—professional leagues, television and government—helped create Super Spectator, only to find he resents blackouts and pay TV. Pro football, unlike minor league baseball and boxing, has grown prosperous via the tube and federal exemptions. In 1973 Congress struck a blow for the preservation of 'electric democracy' by banning local blackouts of sellout games, checking team sports on pay TV for the time being."

Marnell, William H. *The Right to Know: Media and the Common Good*. New York, Seabury, 1973. 221p.   **1M179**
The author examines freedom of the press from the point of view of the citizen, noting that "a free press is one functioning aspect of the life of a free nation, a necessary and vital aspect that cannot be viewed apart from the framework within which it operates and the limits by which it is determined." He considers the right of a citizen to a fair trial, his right to protect his privacy and his reputation, and his right to control the moral climate in which he lives. He sees increased permissiveness in print as a threat against the stability in society which can only lead to more rigid controls.

Marple, Annette. "Plaintiff Must Meet *New York Times* Standard of Proof to Recover If the Alleged Defamatory Misstatement of Fact Concerns a Matter of Public Interest." *Texas Tech Law Review*, 3:159–68, Fall 1971.   **1M180**
Re: *Rosenbloom v. Metromedia, Inc.*, 403 U.S. 29 (1971).

Marrow, Frank A. "Speech, Expression, and the Constitution." *Ethics*, 25:235–42, April 1975.   **1M181**
The author concludes that (1) "the First Amendment protects speech . . . and not expression generally"; (2) it protects political speech absolutely, but not private speech; (3) private speech can be protected as a liberty analogous to a property right or as a Ninth Amendment right; and (4) "expression generally, although not protected by the First Amendment, may yet be a right secured by the Ninth, and that the Ninth Amendment—not the First—is the appropriate place in which to seek protection for such nonspeech expression as the wearing of unusual hairstyles or unorthodox clothing."

Mars, Newman F. " 'Freedom of the Press' and 'Freedom of Speech.' " In his *Tools of Freedom*. New York, Vantage, 1964, pp. 28–43.   **1M182**
An attack on concentration of ownership of the press which subverts the intent of the First Amendment. The author proposes a publicly supported news service.

Marsh, John L. "That Line Is Cut." *Peabody Journal of Education*, 45:359–62, May 1968.   **1M183**

Concerns censorship and editing of playscripts to bring mature plays within the range of a high school audience.

Marshall, Joan K. "Prejudice Through Library of Congress Subject Headings." *Newsletter on Intellectual Freedom (IFC-ALA)*, 20:126–27, November 1971.   **1M184**
A library cataloger charges that Library of Congress subject headings contain prejudicial "labeling" of certain groups such as women, blacks, and homosexuals.

Marshall, Max L. *Broadcasting and Self-Regulation*. Columbia, Mo., Freedom of Information Center, School of Journalism, University of Missouri at Columbia, 1968. 10p. (Report no. 193)   **1M185**
"This report describes the self-regulatory program of the broadcasting industry and points to the past success of the National Association of Broadcasters in warding off new and substantial government control."

——. *FTC and Deceptive Advertising*. Columbia, Mo., Freedom of Information Center, School of Journalism, University of Missouri at Columbia, 1967. 8p. (Report no. 183)   **1M186**
"The Federal Trade Commission's role in policing advertising has become increasingly pervasive. . . . The FTC has moved beyond its historical 'Thou shalt not!' function into a newer sphere, encompassing 'Thou shalt!' concepts of accuracy and additional information."

——. *The Impact of Television on Politics*. Columbia, Mo., Freedom of Information Center, School of Journalism, University of Missouri at Columbia, 1969. 10p. (Report no. 203)   **1M187**
A section of the report deals with regulation of political broadcasting.

——. *The "Right-to-Read" Controversy*. Columbia, Mo., Freedom of Information Center, School of Journalism, University of Missouri at Columbia, 1968. 14p. (Report no. 199)   **1M188**
This paper deals with the actions of individuals and opposing pressure groups in promoting or opposing legal, quasi-legal, or extralegal censorship. Included among those organizations opposing censorship are the American Library Association, the National Council of Teachers of English, and the American Book Publishers Council. Among those favoring some form of censorship are the National Organization for Decent Literature and Citizens for Decent Literature.

Marshall, Norman. "Banned!" *Drama*, 85:30–33, Summer 1967.   **1M189**
Comments on Richard Findlater's book, *Banned!* The author comments on his own experience with the British stage censor (Lord Chamberlain) and considers the most serious effect to be the number of plays never written because of the edict against depicting recent events and persons.

Marszalek, John F., Jr. "The Knox Court-Martial: W. T. Sherman Puts the Press on Trial (1863)." *Military Law Review*, 59:197–214, Winter 1973.   **1M190**
"Few generals on the northern side matched General William T. Sherman in his distaste for the press. Therefore, when an enterprising New York *Herald* correspondent aroused Sherman's ire, his response was military and direct. He court-martialed him." The article reviews the case of Thomas W. Knox.

——. *W. T. Sherman and the Press, 1861–1865*. Notre Dame, Ind., University of Notre Dame, 1968. 342p. (Ph.D. dissertation, University Microfilms, no. 69–4070)   **1M191**
"The aim of this dissertation was to study this acrimonious relationship ₍General William T. Sherman and the press₎ during the period of the Civil War. The approach was to follow Sherman through these years to gain an insight into his personality and determine the reasons for his anti-press feelings and his consequent actions. The main northern newspapers were also studied to determine their feelings toward Sherman and their treatment of him both in failure and success. . . . The importance of the Sherman-press imbroglio was that it prevented the two extremes that each represented from becoming dominant. Either complete censorship or complete liberty would have seriously hurt the nation, and the Sherman-press struggle, a microcosm of military-press struggle in general, helped prevent either from happening."

Martell, Edward, and Ewan Butler. *The Murder of the News Chronicle and the Star. Killed by Trade Union Restrictive Practices, October 17, 1960*. London, Christopher Johnson, 1960. 112p.   **1M192**
"The sudden merging of the *News Chronicle* with the *Daily Mail* and the *Star* with the *Evening News* on Tuesday, October 18, came as a tremendous shock, not only to Fleet Street, but to the country as a whole. The authors, both experienced newspapermen, claim that because of restrictive practices insisted upon by the trade unions both papers were paying out so much in salaries and wages that it was economically impossible for them to continue. They support their claim with detailed facts and figures . . . and they reveal how all national newspapers, with one exception, are under the constant threat of strike blackmail by the unions."

Martin, Allie B. "Decision in Tulsa: An Issue of Censorship." *American Libraries*, 2:370–74, April 1971. **1M193**
A documented, day-by-day account of the censorship threat to the Tulsa Public Library over two magazines, *Ramparts* and *Evergreen Review*, and an analysis of how the issue was resolved by the Library Commission.

Martin, Ernest. *FRC Program Regulation, 1927–34.* Columbia, Mo., Freedom of Information Center, School of Journalism, University of Missouri at Columbia, 1969. 7p. (Report no. 218) **1M194**
The author examines the Federal Radio Commission, created by the Radio Act of 1927, and its attempts to regulate radio programming by the standard of "public interest, convenience, or necessity." The FRC was superseded by the Federal Communications Commission in 1934.

Martin, Phil. "Fair Trial and Free Press: Oklahoma's Compact of Understanding and Guidelines for Reporting." *Oklahoma Law Review*, 22:174–80, May 1969. **1M195**
"This note will analyze Oklahoma's approach to the problem in light of the American Bar Association's conclusions and recommendations." A joint Oklahoma Bar-Media Relations Committee had formulated a Compact of Understanding and Guidelines for Reporting applicable to both professions.

Martin, Sandra. "Limits to Freedom?" *Oklahoma Librarian*, 26(1):6–28, January 1976. **1M196**
"*Limits to Freedom?* is a statewide project sponsored by the Public Library Systems of Oklahoma and supported by a grant from the Oklahoma Humanities Committee and the National Endowment for the Humanities. The project provides Oklahomans with an opportunity to explore their private values and public policies on the right to read." This report reflects and summarizes views of Oklahomans on freedom and censorship in the areas of politics, minors and minorities, religion, and obscenity/pornography. A four-page brochure, *Limits to Freedom?*, describing the program and its project, was issued by the project office in Norman, Okla.

Martin, Thomas. "How to Get Fired by a TV Station." *TV Guide*, 18(28):22–25, 11 July 1970. **1M197**
A Texas newscaster who received a national award for his television editorials, tells how he was fired by his station when the editorials offended local business interests. If editorials are to achieve credibility and success station owners and managers must recognize free editorial expression as a necessary ingredient of the democratic process and "not as a gimmick that may hypo ratings to lure advertisers."

Marting, Leeda P. "British Control of Television Advertising." *Journal of Broadcasting*, 17:159–72, Spring 1973. **1M198**
The author describes the unique approach to the problem of controlling quality and quantity of television advertising taken in Britain by the Independent Broadcasting Authority.

Martz, Carlton S. "Moot Court: Parducci v. Rutland, 316 F. Supp. 352 (1970)." *Social Education*, 39:212–13, April 1975. **1M199**
Outlines for a moot court exercise involving the question: What kind of literature is inappropriate for high school students to read? The simulation is adopted from a discussion of the Parducci case in chapter 3 of Louis Fischer and David Schimmel's *The Civil Rights of Teachers*.

Marwick, Christine M., *ed. Litigation Under the Amended Federal Freedom of Information Act*. 2d ed. Washington, D.C., The Project on National Security and Civil Liberties of the American Civil Liberties Union Foundation in Cooperation with the Freedom of Information Clearinghouse of the Center for the Study of Responsive Law, 1976. 171p. **1M200**
A handbook prepared for use at the Conference on Litigation Under the Amended Federal Freedom of Information Act, but also intended for use by attorneys and related professions seeking to secure government information under the provisions of the Act.

Maryland Crime Investigating Committee. *Youth, Obscene Materials, and the United States Mails*. Baltimore, The Committee, 1963. 19p. Processed. (The second report of a continuing study) **1M201**
Content: Mail Order Obscenity—the Problem. The Pornographer's Right to Sell Your Daughter's Name, Age and Address to Sexual Perverts. Statistical Data. Obscenity and the Interpretation of the Law. Summary and Recommendations.

Mason, John "Obscenity in Broadcasting and Motion Pictures." *Journal of University Film Producers Association*, 23:54–61, 1971. **1M202**
A discussion of the implications of the *Roth* decision (*Roth v. United States*, 1957) on the administration of the obscenity statutes with respect to motion pictures, with citations of such cases as *I Am Curious (Yellow)*, *Aroused*, and *The Female*. "The consistent theme in the response of the film industry to the trends of today has not been to wage an all-out war for absolute freedom of expression, but to advocate responsible, voluntary self-regulation." The author assesses the role of the FCC in monitoring controversial programs in the area of obscenity, where guidelines are unclear. Ul-

timately, "the courts will have to sharpen the legal constructs of obscenity; the self-regulating codes and classification mechanisms of the two industries will have to become something other than mere devices to ward off external control; and the FCC will have to be amended, abolished, or replaced by an agency equipped to operate in this electronic age."

Mason, Roy L., and Robert E. Ganz. "Columbia Broadcasting: Public Access to the Media Denied." *Catholic University Law Review*, 23:339–58, Winter 1973. **1M203**
An analysis of the U.S. Supreme Court decision in *Columbia Broadcasting System v. Democratic National Committee* (1973), involving a conflict between public access to the media and journalistic freedom in the field of electronic communication.

Massachusetts Library Association. Intellectual Freedom Committee. "Massachusetts Library Association and Intellectual Freedom: An Interview with the Intellectual Freedom Committee." *Bay State Librarian*, 60(1):6–8, February 1971. **1M204**
Discussion of the role of the Committee in censorship cases.

Massey, Morris E. "A Marketing Analysis of Sex-Oriented Materials; a Pilot Study in Denver, August 1969." *Technical Report of the [U.S.] Commission on Obscenity and Pornography*, 4:3–98, 1971. **1M205**
A marketing economist made this study "to collect and interpret information related to the marketing activities, environment, and community climate directly related to sex-oriented materials in Denver, Colorado."

"Materials May Be Obscene for Minors Without Being Obscene for Adults." *Vanderbilt Law Review*, 21:844–50, October 1968. **1M206**
In *Ginsberg v. New York* (1968), the U.S. Supreme Court upheld the New York Court of Appeals which validated a New York statute prohibiting the sale to minors under seventeen of material defined to be obscene on the basis of its appeal to minors without regard for whether the material would be obscene to adults. The Court also held that the statute was not an invasion of the minor's constitutionally protected rights.

Mathews, John. "Texts for Our Times." *New Republic*, 172(1/2):19–21, 4 January 1975. **1M207**
The controversy over school textbooks in the

Kanawha, W.Va. County school system. "The book banners are winning, for although the books officially are back in the schools, they are not being used. The protesters' school boycott has generally failed, but a vacillating school board has agreed to a new screening heavily stacked in favor of local community representatives and a set of criteria for book selection that may exclude all but the most bland and noncontroversial materials."

Mathews, William R. *A Responsible Press Is a Free Press*. Tucson, Ariz., University of Arizona Press [1967]. 16p. (The John Zenger Award for Freedom of the Press and the People's Right to Know, 1966)   **1M208**
Comments on press freedom in Arizona by the editor and publisher of the *Arizona Daily Star* on the occasion of his acceptance of the John Peter Zenger Award on behalf of *New York Times* columnist Arthur Krock. He speaks of three laws protecting journalists: the open records and open meeting laws and the shield law.

Mathis, Robert N. "Freedom of the Press in the Confederacy: A Reality." *Historian*, 37:633–48, August 1975.   **1M209**
The author maintains that the Confederacy permitted freedom of the press "to an extent unsurpassed in the wartime annals of the American people." The preservation of press freedom was widely debated and proclaimed by the Confederate Congress and defended by various leaders of the Confederacy, and the press remained virtually unfettered throughout the war. The most ominous threat to press freedom came from military commanders over the breach of military secrecy by certain editors, but this conflict was adjudicated by efforts of a Press Association of the Confederate States of America, which attempted to balance the conflicting need for wartime military secrecy and free political expression.

Matlack, Linda S. "A Martyrdom Recalled." *A.D. 1973*, 2(6):36–37, June 1973.   **1M210**
A brief account of the murder of Presbyterian pastor-editor Elijah Parish Lovejoy. On page 35 of the same issue is an announcement of a Freedom of the Press Award to be given by the publisher of *A.D.*, concerned with present-day attacks on press freedom by every branch of government. The cover of the issue bears a portrait of Lovejoy.

Matthew, Sidney L. "Government in the Sunshine: Judicial Application and Suggestions for Reform." *Florida State University Law Review*, 2:537–57, Summer 1974.   **1M211**

"This note first will survey recent judicial developments concerning application of the [Florida] Sunshine Law and then will offer suggestions for reform. It is the contention of this note that certain refinements could improve the law significantly, without damaging the open meeting principle."

Matthews, A. S. "Responsibility of a Free Press in South Africa." *South African Outlook*, 104:149–51, September 1974.   **1M212**
The author, in an address before the South African Society of Journalists, speaks of "the paradox of a press that is substantially free in a society that is not." He refers to two special difficulties faced by the press—the comprehensive restrictions of the law and the adequate reflection of "the black aspect of our social reality through a press that is white owned, white managed and white oriented." He believes that "there are signs that the Press is overimpressed by the obstacles that frequently, and quite humanly, exist in the situation, it is so mesmerized by the land-mines that it overlooks the safe avenues between them."

Matthews, Curt. [Freedom of the Press.] *St. Louis Post-Dispatch*, 10 October 1976, pp. 1–12D; 11 October 1976, p. 3C; 12 October 1976, p. 3B; 13 October 1976 p. 3E.   **1M213**
In this four-part series the paper's Washington correspondent deals successively with the crisis of litigation posing danger to the nation's free press, the confidential sources dilemma, gag orders and fair trials, and the threat of libel which subdues the press.

[Matthews, James N., and James D. Warren.] *The Great Libel Suit. The Hon. David S. Bennett, M.C. versus the Buffalo Commercial Advertiser. Damages Claimed, $100,000. A Complete History of the Trial. . . .* Buffalo, Matthews & Warren, 1890. 235p.   **1M214**
The *Buffalo Commercial Advertiser*, published by James N. Matthews and James D. Warren, was charged with libeling the defendant by charges of fraudulant financial transactions. The jury found for the defendants.

Mattson, Marylu C. *Censorship and the Victorian Drama*. Los Angeles, Calif., University of Southern California, 1969. 426p. (Ph.D. dissertation, University Microfilms, no. 69–9034) **1M215**
"Censorship of stage plays prior to public performance in England has long been a function of the Examiner of Plays, a deputy of the Lord Chamberlain. The Theatre Licensing Law of 1843 empowered him to ban plays or to order changes in them to assure that they did not offend political, religious, or moral sensibilities. During the seventeenth and eighteenth centuries court-fostered values established standards for the drama. With the nineteenth-century rise of the middle class, however, propriety became a major considera-

tion. Plays then were considered suitable if they did not offend against 'decorum.' Mid-Victorian drama, more a commercial enterprise than a serious art form, underwent official censorship, and few objected to its extensive control." During the last quarter of the nineteenth century, however, playwrights began to resist the censorship, but no official change took place in the system. "In combating the censorship, the authors articulated a philosophy of the drama which indicated that the English stage had found a new maturity."

Maverick, Maury, Jr. "Douglas and the First Amendment—Visiting Old Battlegrounds." *Baylor Law Review*, 28:235–48, Spring 1976.   **1M216**
An account of the struggle of Supreme Court Justice William O. Douglas in defense of First Amendment rights against government encroachments, reflecting Douglas's belief in the doctrine of absolute rights in First Amendment issues, a philosophy of limited government, and demonstration of personal courage.

Mawer, W. *Plain Reasons Why Prosecution for Blasphemy Should Be Abolished*. London, Freethought Publishing Co., 1884. 14p. (Printed by Annie Besant and Charles Bradlaugh)   **1M217**
Subtitle: "The Substance of a Speech Delivered in the Wood Green Parliamentary Debating Society." The arguments deal with the obscurity of the blasphemy laws, the danger of their uneven and vindictive application, charges that blasphemy is a priest-made offense, that it is anachronistic and insults the intelligence of the age, that prosecutions fail of their objective, and that real blasphemers are not interfered with.

Max, Alan. *What Do You Read?* New York, Workers Library, 1941. 15p.   **1M218**
An attack on the nation's capitalist press as favoring the advertisers, suppressing news that is critical of big business, and supporting the British empire in the war. Written by a member of the Editorial Board of the *Daily Worker* before the Soviet Union was attacked by Hitler's armies.

Maxwell, John. "Books in the Schools: The Adoption Controversy. Now Is the Time to Conspire Against the Censors." *Publishers' Weekly*, 208(15):33–34, 13 October 1975.   **1M219**
English teachers and publishers are involved in a meaningful partnership in the production of useful textbooks. The author, representing the National Council of Teachers of English, calls on textbook publishers to refuse to "whitewash" books for schools and to be influenced by the extreme conservative protests of the censors. And these publishers should be supported by the education community.

Maxwell, Robert. "Obscenity Regulation in Kansas—A New Standard."

Washburn Law Journal, 16:204–11, Fall 1976. **1M220**
Re: *State v. A Motion Picture Entitled "The Bet,"* 219 Kan. 64, 547 P.2d 760 (1976), in which the Kansas Supreme Court enjoined the showing of the film, but refused to padlock the theater, finding the statutes on this matter unconstitutional and overbroad.

May, Charles. "Pornography: The Divine Whore." *MAG*-6, pp. 4–21, Summer–Fall 1973. **1M221**
The paradoxical attitude of man toward pornography and whores is that "he doesn't like them, yet he runs to them; and when he runs to them, he feels guilty for liking them. The lies he has told himself about this have done much hurt to both men and women and therefore much hurt to literature and love. . . . To better show that it is the whorishness of pornography which has made it condemned by all levels of society, I propose a generic approach to the form which I hope will illustrate and challenge many of the reasons for this condemnation." The author considers three basic elements of pornography: thematics (man as body), the technique (fantasy), and intent (to arouse). On the effect of pornography he comments: "Society wishes to ban pornography because it thinks that if a man becomes sexually aroused he will want to go out and rape society's pure white daughter. . . . The truth of the matter is, this assumption is not only unproven; practically all studies indicate just the opposite. Men who rape women do not read porn, or much of anything." Those who argue that pornography can cause antisocial acts because "good literature can cause social acts are attributing more power to pornography than they have to claim for legitimate literature." He believes that the resistance to pornography has been caused by irrational fears, that we should accept pornography with "irrational joy." "I do not say that pornography is not the whore of literature; she is, but she does not have to be the scabby and vulgar whore of our nightmares, but rather the beautiful and divine whore of our daydreams."

May, Gunnar R. *The Minimum Requirements for a World Agreement on Standards for Press Freedom: Guidelines.* [Zurich, International Press Institute], 1974. 14p. **1M222**
Meeting paper (International Press Institute, General Assembly, Kyoto, Japan, 1974) presenting general guidelines for the development of freedom of information and the press, particularly in view of the advances in communication technology.

May, Kenneth R. *A Study of Pre-Trial Reporting in Selected Florida Newspapers Published in 1965–66.* Gainsville, Fla., University of Florida, 1968. 75p. (Unpublished Master's thesis) **1M223**
"The study showed that a considerable amount of potentially prejudicial information was conveyed in the stories surveyed and that a majority of the assertions coded were unfavorable to the accused. The writer concluded that although newspapers should exercise greater care in the publication of potentially prejudicial information, inflexible rules governing press coverage would hamper the press in its function of reporting public affairs."

Mayer, Julius M. "The Law of Free Speech." In National Security League, *Our Charter of Liberty . . . Prepared for the Celebration of Constitution Day. . . .* New York, The League, 1919, pp. 58–72. **1M224**
Free speech is for the law-abiding and does not encompass anarchist thought. Mayer defends the limitations on First Amendment freedoms imposed during wartime, citing U.S. Supreme Court decisions.

Mayer, Martin. "The Challengers." *TV Guide*, 21(5):5–8, 10, 12–13, 3 February 1973; 21(6):33–40, 10 February 1973; 21(7):18–21, 17 February 1973. **1M225**
A series of articles dealing with the movement for public participation in television broadcasting and the fact that "anyone who lives within range of a station signal" can challenge the station's right to continue in operation when its license is up for renewal. The author reports on what has happened in various communities across the nation when individuals and groups have challenged local stations and the role of the FCC and the courts in support of the challengers. The author believes that "the antics of the professional protesters might become more tolerable if their result was to force the local television stations to spend more money on more carefully planned, better produced, and more varied local programming."

———. "A Clash of Rights: How TV News Shows Are Aggravating a Basic Conflict in Our Constitution." *TV Guide*, 22(33):3–8, 17 August 1974; 22(34):28–33, 24 August 1974. **1M226**
The case of convicted bank robber and murderer, Joseph Subilosky, is cited as an "example of complexities, legitimate concerns and foolishness that are usually buried in abstract discussions of the conflict between First Amendment right of a 'free press' and Sixth Amendment right of a 'fair trial.' " The article deals with specifics in exploring the ramification of the problem.

———. "The FCC." *TV Guide*, 14(47):6–10, 19 November 1966; 14(48):16–18, 26 November 1966; 14(49):32–36, 3 December 1966. (Reprinted in Barry G. Cole, *ed.*, *Television; a Selection of Readings from TV Guide Magazine*, pp. 290–302) **1M227**
A review of the history of the Federal Communications Commission, its charge from the Congress, the problems it has faced and is presently facing, and the differences in opinion of the members over the years as to the extent

of controls that should be exercised over program content.

———. "Freedom of the Press Can Be A Matter of Self-Interested Definition." *Harper's Magazine*, 243:40, 42–44, December 1971. **1M228**
A critique of the widely publicized furor over the Columbia Broadcasting System documentary, *The Selling of the Pentagon*.

———. "In All Fairness." *TV Guide*, 18(41):6–10, 10 October 1970; 18(42):36–40, 17 October 1970; 18(43):36–40, 24 October 1970. **1M229**
The first part describes the *Red Lion* case which led to the U.S. Supreme Court upholding the FCC's fairness doctrine, providing for radio and television response to controversial issues, and the experience of the industry that followed the decision. The second part deals with the relative rights of the president and his critics in the use of television. Part three deals with the difficulty in imposing fairness. "The Fairness Doctrine is reasonable enough as a floor, but it would be a terrible ceiling." The author believes the answer lies in professional commitments and competent news staffs.

Mayer, Michael F. *Rights of Privacy.* New York, Law-Arts, 1972. 253p. **1M230**
The work considers the case of *Stanley v. The State of Georgia* (1969), involving obscenity in the privacy of the bedroom; the case of the movie, *John Goldfarb Please Come Home* (*Notre Dame v. 20th Century Fox*, 1964–65); the publication of misleading information as a form of privacy invasion; fictionalizing as an invasion of privacy in the case of *Time, Inc. v. Hill* (1967); and privacy vs. common law copyright as a source of protection.

———. *What You Should Know About Libel & Slander.* New York, Arco, 1968. 173p. Introduction by Morris L. Ernst. **1M231**
Through a popular discussion of recent libel cases against newspapers, magazines, and television the author brings out the essential nature of the libel laws and how they are being interpreted by the courts. In his introduction Ernst notes that the mass media "have engaged in a virtual conspiracy of silence by failing to report most of the amusing and often socially significant libel suits" brought against themselves—a form of "managed" news.

Mayer, Stanley D. "The Editor As Critic and Censor." *PLA Bulletin* (Pennsylvania Library Association), 30:47, 61, May 1975. **1M232**
The former editor of *Fantasy* criticizes the critics for praising works of little literary worth

and authors and publishers who have in the past produced quality works but, in the interest of sales, issue tasteless works of little literary value. He asks that librarians "use the discrimination and the literary background in which they have been trained" to decide between good and bad writing without fear of charges of censorship. "Over-zealous liberalism need not become an occupational disease of the librarian."

Mayer, Steven E. "The Freedom of Information Act: A Branch Across the Moat?" *Drake Law Review*, 22:570–83, June 1973.   **1M233**
The author finds that the movement toward greater accessibility to public documents under the Act has been thwarted to some extent by a combination of drafting infirmities, agency practices, judicial interpretations, and a lack of momentum on the public's part.

Mayes, Herbert R. "From Denmark with Love." *Saturday Review*, 54(27): 8–9, July 1971.   **1M234**
A review of the book, *The Little Red Schoolbook*, translated from the Danish and published in England. The work has been subjected to prosecution on the basis of contributing to the delinquency of children.

[Mayka, Stephen P.] "Reporter's Privilege under the First Amendment." *Albany Law Review*, 36:404–15, Winter 1972.   **1M235**
The author concludes that, under the First Amendment "the Court should forbid the practice of converting newsmen into government investigators by means of the subpoena power." Re: *Caldwell v. United States*, 1970.

Maynard, Richard A. "Obscenity Is a Four-Letter Word." *Scholastic Teacher, Junior/Senior High*, pp. 26–28, September 1974.   **1M236**
A discussion of the four stages in the recent development of vulgarity, pornography, and sadism in motion pictures, which poses a problem for use of commercial films in the classroom.

[Mayo, Robert, *plaintiff*.] *The Affidavit of Andrew Jackson, Taken by the Defendants in the Suit of Robert Mayo vs. Blair & Rives for a Libel, Analysed and Refuted.* Washington, D.C., Printed for the plaintiff, 1840. 23p.   **1M237**
The case involves charges made in the *Globe* newspaper, Washington, D.C., that the plaintiff had stolen a confidential letter from the then President Andrew Jackson. The pamphlet consists of Dr. Mayo's denial of the charge and an accusation of falsehood against the former president.

Mazer, Norma F. "Comics, Cokes, and Censorship." *Top of the News*, 32:167–70, January 1976.   **1M238**
The author of children's books who is also a parent describes how she resisted the strong temptation to censor her children's reading. She concludes that "children are people with as much sense and ability to sort out things for themselves as adults."

Mazzei, W. G. "Criminal Contempt: Necessity and Procedure Versus Fairness and Justice." *Saskatchewan Law Review*, 36:295–329, 1971–72.   **1M239**
A look at the sweeping power of the courts to cite for criminal contempt, the nature of contempt, and the issues that need to be solved. "It seems our courts have chosen to impose a moderate impingement on the freedom of the press in order to maintain the sanctity of respect for our judicial system and the right to a fair, unbiased trial."

Mead, Margaret. "Can We Protect Children from Pornography?" *Redbook*, 13(5):74, 76, 79–80, March 1972. **1M240**
An anthropologist writes that in a complex society such as ours, some minimal public control over obscenity is necessary to protect children, while permitting adults freedom of choice. By exposing children to pornography we are exposing them to lewd and covert attitudes toward sex that sex education is designed to prevent. Parent and community groups should direct their efforts not to the investigation of school libraries, but to the open display and sale of pornography in stores that are accessible to children. They should also take action against television programs that bring crime and violence into the home.

Meadley, Thomas D. "Attack on the Theatre (Circa 1580–1680)." *London Quarterly and Holborn Review*, 178(6th ser., vol. 22):36–41, January 1953.   **1M241**
Largely an account of the so-called "Puritan" attack on stage plays, a term loosely used to include those ecclesiastical and political Puritans, but also those allying themselves with the Puritans who qualified as fanatics against the arts and against drama in particular.

——. "The Second Attack on the English Stage, Preliminary Skirmishes." *London Quarterly and Holborn Review*, 178(6th ser. vol. 22):279–83, October 1953.   **1M242**
The controversy over stage censorship that broke out following the Protestant Revolution of 1688 and the activities of Jeremy Collier.

Medawar, Charles. "A Public Right to Know." *Aslib Proceedings*, 28:69–75, February 1976.   **1M243**
Because of the British Official Secrets Act and some sixty other statutes "it is impossible to obtain legitimately from anywhere a great deal of hard and relevant information" about the performance of the government, the expenditure of public funds, and many aspects of commercial and corporate activity of public interest. In the abuse of secrecy, the British people and, in fact, members of Parliament, get only the information that government officials want them to have. The author recommends the abolition of the Official Secrets Act and, in its place, one of three substitutes, ranked in ascending order of attractiveness: (1) a similar but more credible law, as recommended by the Franks Committee, (2) no law, but reliance on less formal measures and on existing laws such as that relating to conspiracy, and (3) a "public right to know" law along the lines of the Swedish and American models.

"Media and Freedom." *Senior Scholastic*, 103:6–17, 8 November 1973.   **1M244**
In this special issue students are challenged to consider press freedom and responsibility in three current issues: (1) the press handling of three murders in Boston, (2) Daniel Ellsberg and the Pentagon Papers, and (3) press treatment of President Nixon in the Watergate affair. In an article entitled Can the Press Call You a Creep and Get Away with It? the author traces the history of conflict between government and press from Colonial times to the present day.

"Media and the First Amendment in a Free Society." *Georgetown Law Journal*, 60:871–1099, March 1972.   **1M245**
The entire issue deals with the topic. Part 1, Evolution of Printed Communication, introduced by Senator Sam Ervin, consists of: The First Amendment in 1791; The Evolving Legal Concept of Free Expression; The Newspaper Industry Today; Governmental Control of the Press; and Books, Magazines and the Publishing Industry. Part 2, Media of Technical Revolution, introduced by Reuven Frank, consists of: Television Journalism; Television as Entertainment; Broadcast Advertising; Cable Television; and Federal Regulation of Broadcasting. Part 3, Points of Conflict— Legal Issues Confronting Today, introduced by Walter Cronkite, consists of: Diversity of Media Ownership; Analysis of the Fairness Doctrine; Federal Policy Toward Fine Arts as Media; Free Press v. Fair Trial; and Confidentiality of News Sources.

Media and the First Amendment, 1974; The Changing Patterns of Conflict. Conference Proceedings, May 3–4, 1974. East Lansing, Mich., Michigan State University, 1974. 160p. (A publication of the Journalism/Law Institute, School of Journalism, College of Communication Arts, Michigan State University)   **1M246**
Content: First Amendment Overview, 1974 (Panel: Vincent Blasi, John W. Reed, and Fred S. Siebert). Judicial Responsibility or Restraint (Panel: Richard W. Cardwell, Joel D. Weisman, John Feikens, and Frank J. Kelley). Leaks and the Law (Panel: John W. Hushen,

John Thompson, and J. Edward Murray). A Defense of the Fairness Doctrine by Benjamin L. Hooks, member of the Federal Communications Commission. Libel and Privacy (Panel: Bronson Murray, George E. Brand, Jr.). Access to Media (Panel: Jerome Barron, Daniel Paul, and William B. Arthur). Adversary Journalism and the Regime by Peter B. Clark.

Media Law Reporter. Washington, D.C., Bureau of National Affairs, 1977–date. Loose-leaf.   **1M247**
A reporting service on court decisions involving the mass communications and covering the following fields: (1) regulation of media content (prior restraints, fair trial–free press, obscenity, defamation, privacy, commercial speech/advertising, copyright, broadcast media regulations, and student media regulations); (2) regulation of media distribution (print, electronic); (3) newsgathering (authority to gather news, access to places and people, statutory right of access, restraints on access to information, press accreditation, forced disclosure of information, and criminal or tortuous newsgathering); (3) media ownership (print, electronic, and cross-ownership).

"A Media Publisher of an Apparent Libel Is Subject to All But Strict Liability for Actual Injury Caused a Private Individual, Who, in the Absence of Actual Malice, May Recover Neither Presumed Nor Punitive Damages." *Brooklyn Law Review*, 41:389–406, Fall 1974.   **1M248**
A review of the case of *Gertz v. Robert Welch, Inc.* (1974), in which the U.S. Supreme Court reversed a decision of the lower court, ruling that a private individual who has been the target of a news medium's libel may recover actual damages when the defamation is grounded in at least some degree of fault, and punitive damages, additionally when "actual malice" is proved. The author suggests that the *Gertz* ruling "appears to reflect the Court's concern that expansion of the *Times* privilege might in the end, virtually eliminate private libel suits."

Media Watch; Newsletter of the National Citizens Committee for Broadcasting. Washington, D.C., The Committee, 1976–date. Monthly.   **1M249**
"It is the purpose of the NCCB to effectively and responsibly represent the public interest [in broadcasting], to develop this audience constituency, and to create a voice for media reform issues at the national level." The first issue, published in March 1976, deals largely with violence on television.

Medina, Harold R. "The Press Should 'Fight Like Tigers': A Judge's View." *Bulletin of the American Society of Newspaper Editors*, 565:6–7, January 1973.   **1M250**
Judge Medina defends the right of the press and criticizes its being muzzled by the courts in the interest of a fair trial. He believes that the U.S. Supreme Court decision in the *Caldwell* case is not the final word in the matter of press subpoenas and that the press should "fight like tigers right down the line and not give in an inch."

Meek, Oscar. *Pornography, Obscenity, and Censorship; a Selected Bibliography*. Sante Fe, N.Mex., Research Library of the Southwest, 1969. 35p.   **1M251**
An essay on the development and present nature of obscenity censorship with special reference to New Mexico. The author also reports on a continuing survey being taken in Sante Fe, which revealed that "most of the respondents' individual actions and views seem to be at variance with their religiously-based group actions and attitudes . . . as far as obscenity, censorship and sexual activity are concerned."

Meeske, Milan D. "Broadcasting and the First Amendment." In Speech Association of America, *Abstracts, 55th Annual Meeting*, New York, 1969, p.80.   **1M252**
The paper proposes three alternative ways to deal with broadcasting and the First Amendment: (1) retain the status quo giving the Federal Communications Commission limited powers on programming and giving broadcasters the right of appeal to the courts; (2) give the FCC definitive powers in program regulation; and (3) limit the power of the FCC to technical matters, giving broadcasters the same freedom as the print media.

———. "Broadcasting and the Law of Defamation." *Journal of Broadcasting*, 15:331–46, Summer 1971.   **1M253**
"The purpose of this paper is to review the law of defamation, to trace the development of the *Times* doctrine [New York Times Co. v. Sullivan, 1964] in Supreme Court decisions extending from 1964 to June 1971, and to evaluate the implications of the *Times* doctrine for broadcasters."

———. *Broadcasting in the Public Interest: The Supreme Court and the First Amendment*. Denver, Colo., University of Denver, 1968. 218p. (Ph.D. dissertation, University Microfilms, no. 69–6387)   **1M254**
"The purpose of this study was to investigate the impact of five landmark Supreme Court decisions on the right of broadcasters to comment on public affairs. Existing limitations on broadcasting, including those encompassed by tort law and those embodied in government regulations, were examined to determine the major legal issues that confronted broadcasters prior to the Supreme Court's action. An attempt was then made to see how the decisions affect those issues."

———. *Counterads: Broadcasting and the*

First Amendment. n.p., 1972. 10p. (ED 72,502)   **1M255**
In a paper presented at the annual meeting of the Speech Communication Association, Chicago, 27–30 December 1972, the author raises three issues that are involved in counteradvertising: "the extent to which editorial advertising can logically be extended, the price of counteradvertising and the proportion of counterads to a given commercial, and the effect of counterads as a prior restraint that would force stations to reject some advertising."

———. "A Course in Freedom of Speech." In *1969 Yearbook of the Committee on Freedom of Speech of the Speech Association of America*. [New York], The Association, 1970, pp. 45–53.   **1M256**
Includes content of a course, boundaries of free expression, structure of a course, and a list of appropriate textbooks.

———. "Editorial Advertising: A New Form of Free Speech." In *Free Speech Yearbook, 1973*. New York, Speech Communication Association, 1974, pp. 51–59.   **1M257**
In recent years individuals and citizen groups have made use of paid "editorial advertisements" to express opinions on controversial public issues. The courts have been faced with the question: Is advertising protected by the freedom of speech and press provisions of the First Amendment? This article traces the case law on the subject.

———. "Editorial Advertising and the First Amendment." *Journal of Broadcasting*, 17:417–26, Fall 1973.   **1M258**
"One aspect of the recent pressure for greater public access to the airwaves is the attempt by several individuals and groups to buy air time for expression of opinion on often controversial subjects. The legal ramifications of this issue are explored in the following paper."

———. "A New Interpretation of the First Amendment: Access to the Press." In Speech Association of America. *Abstracts, 57th Annual Meeting*. San Francisco, 1971, p.11 **1M259**
"This paper traces the development of a new First Amendment right—the right of 'access' to the press, particularly broadcasting. Development of the 'access' theory is traced in scholarly studies and in landmark Supreme Court decisions."

Meeske, Milan D., and Roger Handberg, Jr. "News Directors' Attitudes Toward the Fairness Doctrine." *Jour-*

nalism Quarterly, 53:126–29, Spring 1976. **1M260**

News directors of all commercial television stations in Florida were surveyed to measure their attitudes toward the fairness doctrine imposed on television by the Federal Communications Commission, specifically how they have implemented the doctrine in the coverage of public affairs.

Meiklejohn, Alexander. "Dissent—and the First Amendment." *Censorship Today*, 1(1):15–25 ₁June–July₁ 1968.
1M261

In remarks before the U.S. Senate Committee on Constitutional Rights in 1956, Dr. Meiklejohn expounds his views on the First Amendment. "The First Amendment seems to me to be a very uncompromising statement. It admits of no exceptions. It tells us that the Congress and, by implication, all other agencies of the Government, are denied any authority whatever to limit the political freedom of the citizens of this Nation. It declares that with respect to political belief, political discussion, political advocacy, political planning, our citizens are sovereign, and the Congress is their subordinate agent." If Americans are to pass judgment upon public policy "unwise ideas must have a hearing as well as wise ones, dangerous ideas as well as safe, un-American as well as American." He objects to the balancing of conflicting claims between national security and freedom of speech. This balancing "was carefully done when, 170 years ago, the Constitution was adopted and quickly amended. . . . Whatever may be the immediate gains and losses, the dangers to our safety arising from political suppression are always greater than the dangers to that safety arising from political freedom." He draws a distinction between "advocacy of action," and "incitement to action." "To advocacy the amendment guarantees freedom, no matter what may be advocated. To incitement, on the other hand, the amendment guarantees nothing whatever."

₁———— et al.₁ *Brief of Alexander Meiklejohn, of Cultural Workers of Motion Pictures and Other Arts, and of Members of the Professions, as Amici Curiae . . . ₁in the cases before the U.S. Supreme Court₁ No. 248, John Howard Lawson vs. United States of America; Dalton Trumbo vs. United States of America. . . .* Los Angeles, Max Radin, Counsel for Petitioner, 1949. 36p. **1M262**

In this *amici curiae* brief Alexander Meiklejohn, former president of Amherst College, is joined by scores of persons from the motion picture industry and other arts and professions, in opposing the action of the House Un-American Activities Committee to impose censorship on the motion picture industry. The brief contends that: (1) Congress cannot impose a direct censorship on the motion picture industry since motion pictures enjoy the same protection under the First Amendment as the press and radio. (2) The hearings out of which appellant's conviction for contempt arose involved an attempt by Congress to impose censorship on the motion picture industry in violation of the First Amendment; it involved an abuse of power, and the petitioner was, therefore, not required to lend his assistance to the Committee's unconstitutional purpose.

————. *The Continuing Concern: Freedom of Speech.* 102 min. tape recording (two cassettes). Berkeley, Calif., Pacifica Tape Library, 1962. **1M263**

Speakers: Part 1—Alexander Meiklejohn, Clyde Doyle, Charles Garry, Frank Tavenner, Gordon Scherer, Benjamin Dreyfus, Dale Minor, Erwin Goldsmith, and Albert Bendich. Part 2—Hugo Black, Alexander Meiklejohn, Lewis Hill, Harold Winkler, James Sears, and Raymond Cope. Narrated by Elsa Knight Thompson.

Meiklejohn, Donald. "Public Speech in the Supreme Court Since New York v. Sullivan." *Syracuse Law Review*, 26:819–65, Summer 1975. **1M264**

"The purpose of this article is threefold: (1) to describe the public speech theory of first amendment interpretation and to illustrate its use in cases over the past decade since *New York Times* and *Garrison;* (2) to advocate the theory as the best perspective from which to determine the scope of first amendment freedoms; and (3) to speculate upon the theory's future in the Supreme Court as a functioning tool of interpretation."

Meiklejohn Civil Liberties Library. *Civil Liberties Docket:* Vols. I (1955)–XIV (1968–69). Berkeley, Calif., Meiklejohn Civil Liberties Library, 1955–1970. (Frequency of vol. I was five times a year; vols. X–XII, three times a year; vols. XIII ₁1967–68₁ and XIV ₁1968–69₁, annually. Edited by Ann Fagan Ginger and Kathleen Kahn) **1M265**

A summary of the issues and decisions in significant court cases involving First, Ninth, and Fourteenth Amendment liberties. Topics on freedom of speech and press include: licensing of motion pictures, censorship of books and magazines, customs and postal censorship, government secrecy, contempt by publication, and criminal sanctions against obscenity, sedition, and defamation. The docket includes numerous cases not reported elsewhere and important cases not yet tried. Vol. XIV contains 232p.

————. *Human Rights Casefinder; 1953–1969: The Warren Court Era.* Edited by Ann Fagan Ginger. Berkeley, Calif., Meiklejohn Civil Liberties Library, 1972. 281p. **1M266**

One of the three major areas covered is that of freedom of expression and association. A subject classification scheme is given and cases are indexed by subject with an alphabetical index.

Meisenheimer, James W. "The Pentagon Papers Case: *The New York Times Co. v. United States* & *United States v. Washington Post Co.*" *Loyola of Los Angeles Law Review*, 5:392–416, April 1972. **1M267**

Re: *New York Times Co. v. United States* and *United States v. Washington Post Co.*, 403 U.S. 713 (1971).

Melly, George. "Pornography and Erotica." *Art and Artists*, 5(5):4+, August 1970. **1M268**

"Erotic art may contain elements of pornography, but pornography can be churned out without reference to either eroticism or, except in the most superficial sense, art. Our permissive climate is unfavorable to erotic art but ideal for the spread and growth of pornography."

Meltzer, Milton. "Four Who Locked Horns with the Censors." *Wilson Library Bulletin*, 44:278–86, November 1969. **1M269**

A biographer writes of the experience of four authors with censorship: Langston Hughes, Mark Twain, Lydia Maria Child, and Margaret Sanger.

Mencher, Melvin. "Freeing the Student Press." *Columbia Journalism Review*, 13(3):49–53, October 1974. **1M270**

"Courts have extended Constitutional guarantees to student newspapers on public campuses; publications at private schools may be next."

————. "Student Journalists Have Constitutional Rights, Too." *Quill*, 60(10):9–13, October 1972. **1M271**

A summary of recent legal developments which have given the high school and college press greater freedom.

Mencken, H. L. *The Bathtub Hoax and Other Blasts & Bravos from the Chicago Tribune by H. L. Mencken.* Edited with an Introduction and Notes by Robert McHugh. New York, Knopf, 1958. 286p. **1M272**

In this collection is a group of essays under the heading, Land of the Free, which deal with issues of freedom of speech and the press: The Bill of Rights, The Comstockian Imbicility (an attack on the post office ban on *Judge*, the comic weekly), the Anatomy of Wowserism, Padlocks (ban on Sunday newspapers and movies), The Battle of Ideas, and The Birth Control Hullabaloo ("any one who tries to silence them by force is the common enemy of all of us").

————.] "Mencken as Missionary." Edited by Frank Durham. *American Literature*, 29:478–83, January 1958. **1M273**

Two lengthy letters from Mencken to Henry Sydnor Harrison of Richmond, urging Harrison to support the protest of writers against attempts to suppress Theodore Dreiser's *The Genius*.

Menninger, Karl A. "Violence Is Not Increasing; We're Just More Aware Of It." *Los Angeles Times*, 24 November 1968, Section G, pp. 1–2. **1M274**

"I don't really think violence is increasing. I think people are increasingly aware of violence." Violence is becoming more conspicuous, according to Dr. Menninger, because there are more people living closer together, we have a greater sense of injustice, persons rebel when they see others doing it, and the media has made us more aware of violence. They give the public what it wants to read and hear about. Knowing about violence may be a warning to some, may diminish the violence of others, may suggest methods to others, and is alarming and distressing to most.

Menninger, W. Walter. *The Panic Generation*. New York, Television Information Office, 1969. 12p. **1M275**

In an address before the American College Public Relations Association and American Alumni Council, Kansas City, 30 March 1969, Dr. Menninger places television in the role of mirror of unrest rather than an instigator. He was a member of the National Commission on the Causes and Prevention of Violence. He cites ways in which citizens can help to resolve the problems of violence in our society.

Menza, Alexander. "Movie Censorship in New York." *Intra-Mural Law Review* (New York University), 13:270–85, May 1958. **1M276**

The author, following a review of court decisions involving New York censorship of motion pictures by the State Department of Education, concludes that "there appears to be no justification for subjecting motion pictures to prior restraint."

Mercer, Joan B. "Innocence Is a Cop-Out." *Wilson Library Bulletin*, 46:144–46, October 1971. **1M277**

The author considers children's reading interests in sex and the response of children's librarians to the issue.

Mercier, Vivian. "Master Percy and/or Lady Chatterley." In Douglas A. Hughes, *ed.*, *Perspectives on Pornography*, New York, St. Martin's, 1970, pp. 21–34. **1M278**

The author describes his own adolescent experience with pornography and his reaction to it. He believes that "pornography may be valuable as a substitute for normal sex or for antiso-

cial sex activities, but as an adjunct to sex it may create more problems than it solves."

Merin, Jerome L. "Libel and the Supreme Court." *William and Mary Law Review*, 11:371–423, Winter 1969. (Extracts in Kenneth S. Devol, *ed.*, *Mass Media and the Supreme Court*, pp. 252–58) **1M279**

"This article attempts to reconcile the law of libel with the First Amendment guarantee of freedom of the press. Libel law, ideally, is a manifestation of society's concern for the individual's reputation, while the guarantee of a free press represents society's interest in encouraging new ideas, peaceful reform and political awareness. This article focuses on the Supreme Court's treatment of the law of libel in the context of the history and underlying theories of both the First Amendment and libel law. The bulk of the Court's rulings concerning libel have been rendered since 1964. The conflict between libel and a free press, however, goes back to the days of Coke. The Supreme Court's decisions, therefore, like the law of libel itself, represent the continuing attempt to reconcile two important and often competing values: freedom of communication and the individual's concern for his reputation."—Editor

Merrick, David. "Must Smut Smother the Stage?" *Reader's Digest*, 95(575): 103–5, March 1970. **1M280**

"When the shock at seeing nudity and explicit sexual acts in some of today's theater wears off, the scenes reveal themselves for what they really are: a pallid substitute for the imagination, style and wit that are the stage's true lifeblood."

Merrill, John C. "Access to the Press: Who Decides?" *Freeman*, 18:48–53, January 1968. **1M281**

A defense of the publisher's freedom to publish as opposed to the interpretation of the First Amendment as imposing upon the press an affirmative responsibility to publish minority views. He draws a distinction between freedom of information which "refers to the right of the reader to have all material available for reading" and freedom of the press which "denotes the right of the publisher to publish or not to publish without external compulsion." He explores the complexities of determining what shall or shall not be published, if the matter is taken out of the hands of individual publishers and editors. "A forced-publishing system will take root only when our society has proceeded much further along the road toward Orwell's *1984*."

————. *The Imperative of Freedom: A Philosophy of Journalistic Autonomy*. New York, Hastings House, 1974. 228p. (Studies in Public Communications) **1M282**

"This whole book has attempted to stress the importance of freedom or journalistic auton-

omy—not only for the individual journalist, but also for the individual media and the press systems themselves." The author argues that freedom of the press belongs to the press, not to the people. The First Amendment provides other freedoms for the people: expression, assembly, redress of grievances, and religion, but the explicit provision is made that *freedom of the press* shall not be abridged. He debunks three popular libertarian myths: (1) that the "people have a right to know," (2) that the people have "a right of access to the press," and (3) that the press is a "fourth branch of government." He rejects the concept of social responsibility as proposed by the Hutchins Commission, the idea of egalitarianism in journalism, and the libertarian assumption that a free press must be pluralistic. The "imperative of freedom" is journalistic autonomy.

————. "The 'People's Right to Know' Myth." *New York State Bar Journal*, 45:461–66, November 1973. **1M283**

"The contention of this article is that the 'right to know' is no more of a valid right than the 'right not to know' and that it has no standing either in law or in actual practice."

Merrill, John C., and Ralph Barney, *eds. Ethics and the Press; Readings in Mass Media Morality*. Edited with Special Introductory Notes and Bibliography. New York, Hastings House, 1975. 338p. (Humanistic Studies in the Communications Arts) **1M284**

A collection of articles on ethics of journalists, newspaper credibility and bias, self-criticism, fairness in television, and the "new journalism and the old."

Merrill, Samuel. "The Law of Libel." *Writer*, 1:10–12, April 1887; 1:25–28, May 1887. **1M285**

In the first issue of this journal "to interest and help all literary workers," the author gives practical advice on avoiding libel, citing numerous newspaper and magazine cases that have come before the courts.

Merrill, Thomas W. "First Amendment Protection for Commercial Advertising: The New Constitutional Doctrine." *University of Chicago Law Review*, 44:205–54, Fall 1976. **1M286**

The author examines the constitutional status of commercial advertising before and after *Bigelow v. Virginia* (1975) and *Virginia State Board of Pharmacy v. Virginia Citizens Consumer Council* (1976) and argues that a distinction between commercial and noncommercial speech remains valid.

Merritt, Le Roy C. *Book Selection and*

Intellectual Freedom. [New York], Wilson, 1970. 100p. **1M287**
The author discusses "those sensitive areas of book selection where librarians are divided in theory and in practice, where they find a conflict between selection theory and legal requirements, and where their selection policies and practices have been challenged": obscenity, sex education, religion, politics, health and medicine, and books as news. He also considers the use of closed shelves and the age of the reader as factors in selection. "Acting in good conscience and without fear of intimidation, the librarian must select each book as being in fact a positive contribution to the collection and of potential benefit or usefulness to some portion of the library's clientele. He must select each book not because it will do no harm but because it may do some good. . . . It is important also that the librarian harbor no fear that he is engaging in censorship himself when a title is rejected as not belonging in the library according to established policy." Chapters follow on writing a selection policy, evaluating the policy, and the role of professional associations in defending intellectual freedom of libraries. The appendix contains the text of the following basic documents: Library Bill of Rights, Resolution on Loyalty Programs, Statement on Labeling, Freedom to Read Statement, School Library Bill of Rights, How Libraries and Schools Can Resist Censorship, Citizen's Request for Reconsideration of a Book, and Intellectual Freedom in Libraries.

————. "Informing the Profession about Intellectual Freedom." *Library Trends*, 19:152–58, July 1970. **1M288**
"An account of the media of communication about intellectual freedom available to the profession, arranged in a rough progression from the general and retrospective to the particular and current."

————. "Intellectual Freedom." In *Bowker Annual of Library and Book Trade Information, 1969.* New York, Bowker, 1969, pp. 120–22. **1M289**
A review of legislation, court decisions, and censorship cases during 1968. "Probably the most far-reaching impact on the climate of intellectual freedom during the year . . . may be attributed to the U.S. Supreme Court's April 22, 6–3 decision upholding a 1965 New York statute establishing a 'variable' obscenity statute. The Court thus opened the way for states to prohibit sales of 'border-line' materials to minors, even though the same materials are protected when sold to adults."

————. "Intellectual Freedom." In *Bowker Annual of Library and Book Trade Information, 1970.* New York, Bowker, 1970, pp. 298–303. **1M290**
A review of legislation, court decisions, and censorship cases during 1969. Major progress in the cause of intellectual freedom during the year was made by the American Library Association through a strong Program of Action in support of the Library Bill of Rights.

Merryman, John H. "The Fear of Books." *Stanford Today*, 1(17):14–17, Autumn 1966. (Reprinted in Grant S. McClellan, *ed.*, *Censorship in the United States*, New York, Wilson, 1967, pp. 14–20; and in *Arizona English Bulletin*, February 1969) **1M291**
In this essay on book burners and censors the author finds that "logic and experience contradict the censorious on every point: on causation, on the social value of obscenity, and on the wisdom and effect of censorship legislation." He urges that a distinction be made between criticism, in which the critic is exercising his constitutional rights in seeking to persuade others to alter their reading habits, and censorship which violates the free marketplace of ideas by instituting state control and deprives others of the right of choice.

Merton, Robert K. *et al*. *Censorship: Should Books Ever Be Banned?* 57 min. tape recording. North Hollywood, Calif., Center for Cassette Studies, 1971. **1M292**
In a Court of Reason, Anne Fremantle, novelist and critic, speaking as a Catholic laywoman, presents the case for censorship; Morris L. Ernst, attorney, speaks "against all governmental control of the mind unless there be proof of some causal relationship between ideas and human behavior." Both speakers favor efforts of private organizations to recommend books to be read or not to be read, while questioning the action of the state as censor. Both speakers also see a danger in strong groups—minority or majority—imposing their views on others through influencing state action. Members of the Court: Eric Larrabee, Robert B. McKay, and Robert K. Merton, presiding.

Mertz, Neil. "Constitutional Limitations on Libel Actions." *Baylor Law Review*, 28:79–108, Winter 1976. **1M293**
The U.S. Supreme Court's holdings in *Gertz v. Robert Welch, Inc.* (1974) are "examined against the backdrop of the Court's decade of struggle to define the proper accommodation between the law of defamation and the freedom of speech and press."

Mervis, Joel. "Government and the Press." *Communications in Africa*, 1(2):1–5, 1972. **1M294**
"I do not believe that the standards of press freedom in South Africa are as absolute and inviolable as they are in the United States. . . . Yet I think it can honestly and validly be claimed that South Africa enjoys a very high standard of Press freedom." The author traces the tradition of press freedom from the assurance that John Fairbairn received from the British government in 1827—

"The Press in the Colony will be placed under the control and protection of the law, and no arbitrary suppression will be allowed in the future"—to the present day.

Methodist Church. General Board of Christian Social Concerns. *A Plan for Pornography Control*. Washington, D.C., The General Board, 1963. 4p. (Reprinted from *Concern*, 1 February 1963) **1M295**
The following principles are offered to define the role of the Church toward open expression of sex: (1) The Church must bear positive witness to a Christian view of sex. (2) Censorship violates the Protestant conscience. (3) The Church needs to develop a Christian critique of the arts. (4) Effective community action should be taken to control hard-core obscenity and questionable literature. Suggestions are offered for action against questionable literature and hard-core pornography.

Methvin, Eugene H. "The Hypocrisy of Absolute Privilege." *Seminar: A Quarterly Review for Journalists*, 30:17–20, December 1973. **1M296**
"Most journalists and newspapers were demanding 'absolute privilege' for themselves last spring. Now they are denouncing the President for daring to claim 'executive privilege' for himself and his White House tapes. . . . I find it hard to see why a reporter should be allowed to refuse a subpoena while the President of the United States should be required to answer it. . . . I confess to being puzzled at the journalistic outrage over the Watergate break in. Journalists ought to have considerable sympathy for the burglars. It was, after all, the *New York Times* and *Washington Post* that made the first wholesale theft of documents in this town stylish by making much hoop-la over Jack Anderson's subordination of the burglary of Sen. Tom Dodd's office." The author recommends more journalists study law to better understand the Constitution and the balancing of conflicting rights.

Meyer, Agnes E. *Freedom of the Mind; Address Delivered at the Convention of the American Association of School Administrators, Atlantic City, New Jersey, Tuesday Morning, February 17, 1953.* Stamford, Conn., Overbrook Press, 1953. 21p. **1M297**
An attack on McCarthyism as a threat against the freedom of the mind, and suggestions to school administrators on how to build a strong defense against Congressional threats of intimidation and local self-styled "patriots" who want to dictate what should be taught and what textbooks should be used.

Meyer, Bernard S. "News Reporting and Fair Trial." *Oklahoma Law Review*, 22:135–43, May 1969. **1M298**
"The purposes of this paper are three: first, to discuss the content of the Reardon Report [of the American Bar Association] and what it does

and does not recommend; second, to assess the current climate, as I see it; third, to suggest that the time is ripe for the establishment of an organized, permanent and continuing Media-Bar Conference to give shape to the dialogue between the two professions that now exists only in occasional and haphazard meetings."

———. "The Trial Judge's Guide to News Reporting and Fair Trial." *Journal of Criminal Law*, 60:287–98, September 1969. **1M299**
This article is intended as a guide for trial judges confronted by free press–fair trial dilemmas in actual practice. The author, a justice of the Supreme Court of the State of New York, describes the trial process from the prearraignment point to ultimate conclusion of the trial, with emphasis on those types of free press–fair trial problems a trial judge may have to deal with. He suggests alternative solutions to assure both the prosecution and the defendant a fair trial. He advises judges to examine each particular case rather than attempting to adopt orders entered by other judges in other cases.

Meyer, Karl E. "Fear on Trial at CBS." *MORE*, 5(5):16–17, 22, May 1975. **1M300**

"Almost 20 years ago, CBS helped destroy John Henry Faulk's career by refusing to fight the McCarthyite blacklisters. Now the network will present a portrayal of his travail. Only the names of the CBS executives will be changed."

Meyer, Paul R., and Daniel J. Seifer. "Censorship in Oregon: New Developments in an Old Enterprise." *Oregon Law Review*, 51:537–52, Spring 1972. **1M301**
While the Oregon legislature removed obscenity censorship on material for "consenting adults," they failed to deal with the "obtrusive thrusting of sexually explicit material upon an unwilling public" as an invasion of privacy. The author also points out the difficulties in any attempt by the state to censor what minors see or hear. To be constitutionally acceptable such legislation must set standards and have a pandering requirement.

[Meyler, Mary, and Thomas Mulligan.] *Report of the Trial in an Action for Libel in the Court of Exchequer Before Sir William Alexander . . . on Wednesday the 20th of February, 1828. Patrick Mathias Cumming, Clerk, Plaintiff, and Mary Meyler and Thomas Mulligan, Defendants. . . .* Bath, England, Printed by M. Meyler [1828]. 76p. + **1M302**
The case involved publication of a pamphlet, *A Full Account of the Anonymous Libel on the Reverend Patrick Mathias Cumming*. The issue concerned the business affairs of the Reverend Mr. Cumming, thus the involvement of the Court of Exchequer. The defendants were publisher and editor, respectively, of the *Bath Herald*.

Michael, Richard, *ed. A.B.Z. of Pornography*. . . . Cartoons by John Kent. London, Panther, 1972. 171p. **1M303**

[Michelman, Frank I.] "The Supreme Court, 1968 Term: Freedom of Speech and Association," *Harvard Law Review*, 83:133–54, November 1969. **1M304**
Under the heading Federal Communications Commission Editorializing and Personal Attack Rules, the survey considers the case of *Red Lion Broadcasting Co. v. FCC* (1967); under Private Possession of Obscene Material, the case of *Stanley v. Georgia* (1969).

Michelson, Peter. *The Aesthetics of Pornography*. New York, Herder, 1971. 247p. **1M305**
This study by a poet-critic is "a descriptive attempt to examine why and how some modern aesthetic concepts accommodate the pornographic in literature. Aesthetics refer to theories of beauty in the arts; the aesthetics of pornography refer to those theories of 'beauty' that incorporate the pornographic and its companion the obscene. This book, then, is more a study of literary aesthetics than it is a study of literary criticism." The author argues for the legitimacy of pornography as a distinctive literary genre, and as a form of writing which provides insight into man's demonic side. Chapters deal with Pornography as Poetic Genre, Decadence and the Poetics of Obscenity, Pornography as Moral Rhetoric, Tragedy and Pornography, Pornography and Moral Anarchy, Pornography as Comic Catharsis, How to Make the World Safe for Pornography (taken from an article in *Antioch Review*), and Censorship and Human Dignity.

———. "An Apology for Pornography." *New Republic*, 155:21–24, 10 December 1966. (Reprinted in Douglas A. Hughes, *ed.*, *Perspectives on Pornography*, pp. 61–71; and in Eleanor Widmer, *ed.*, *Freedom and Culture*, pp. 177–81) **1M306**
"The representation of life as all passion or all idyll or all sexuality is a delusion but not one that will determine the behavior of any but an already pathological personality. A *preoccupation* with pornography or any other kind of romance may be an index of mental imbalance or even potential criminality, but it is certainly not a cause."

———. "Censorship and Human Dignity." *Ave Maria*, 105(20):6–8, 20 May 1967. **1M307**
The intent of censorship—protection of moral and ethical values, of social and cultural order, and of psychological health—is good; the act of censorship violates its ideal. It takes away choice, which is a form of freedom. "The social and human risk of censorship turns out to be far greater than the risk of allowing one another our moral eccentricities."

———. " 'Lascivious, Ungodly Love'."

Nation, 210:245–47, 2 March 1970. **1M308**
A review of *A Long Time Burning* by Donald Thomas, *Art and Pornography* by Morse Peckham, and *Dr. Bowdler's Legacy* by Noel Perrin.

———. "The Pleasures of Commodity, or How to Make the World Safe for Pornography." *Antioch Review*, 29:77–90, Spring 1969. (Reprinted in Ray C. Rist, *ed.*, *The Pornography Controversy*, pp. 140–58; and, in revised form, in the author's *The Aesthetics of Pornography*, pp. 207–32) **1M309**
"The way to make the world safe for pornography is to show it that sex is good for business . . . if one can provide instruction while celebrating commodity, as both *Playboy* and *Cosmopolitan* do; then one has not only an acceptable but even a socially redemptive license for pornographic fun. The trick, quite simply, is to make it slick."

Michener, James A. "GMRX: An Alternative to Movie Censorship." *Reader's Digest*, 94(1):87–93, January 1969. **1M310**
"A noted novelist and ardent film fan, explains how all the sex and violence came to U.S. motion pictures—and describes the new rating system by which the industry is establishing 'acceptability' guidelines for children and their parents."

———. "South African Boycott: Necessary Pressure." *Index on Censorship*. 4(4):31–32, Winter 1975. **1M311**
The American novelist responds to the journal's questionnaire on South African censorship and proposals of an intellectual boycott.

———. "The Weapons We Need to Fight Pornography." *Reader's Digest*, 93(12):125–30, December 1968. (Reprinted in U.S. House of Representatives, Post Office and Civil Service Committee, *Hearings on Obscenity in the Mails*, pp. 185–87) **1M312**
While defending the frank use of sex in literature, the novelist calls for the stopping of traffic among teen-agers of books of perverted sex and violence, even if it means a change in the laws or the Constitution. He recommends that the U.S. Supreme Court refuse to review individual works, leaving it up to the supreme court of each state to serve as the court of last resort on whether a work is pornographic, and that each state return to the *Roth* rule of "applying contemporary community standards." Trials would be by juries of citizens who would be able to judge community standards.

Michigan Library Association. Com-

mittee on Intellectual Freedom. *Handbook*. n.p., The Committee, 1973. 28p. Processed. **1M313**
Documents include: Freedom to Read Statement; Library Bill of Rights; School Library Bill of Rights; How Libraries Can Resist Censorship; and a Statement of Policy of the Intellectual Freedom Committee, Michigan Library Association.

Mickelson, Sig. "The First Amendment and Broadcast Journalism." In Roscoe Pound–American Trial Lawyers Foundation, *The First Amendment and the News Media*, Cambridge, Mass., The Foundation, 1973, pp. 54–63. (Reprinted in Ted C. Smythe and George A. Mastroianni, eds., *Issues in Broadcasting*, pp. 230–47) **1M314**
A former president of National Broadcasting Company News discusses and appraises the controls on television broadcasting imposed by the Federal Communications Commission. He believes that there is nothing wrong with the principle of a fairness doctrine provided it is fairly imposed to maintain objectivity and balance but not as a vehicle for broadening government controls over all phases of broadcasting. "The main dangers involving the 'Fairness Doctrine' arise from the tendency of the Doctrine to encourage timidity on the part of broadcasters, the bracketing of 'fairness' with 'public access' and the decision in the *Red Lion* case."

Middleton, Edgar. "The Censor and the Author." In his *Banned by the Censor*. London, Laurie, 1929, pp. 7–8. **1M315**
The introduction to a collection of plays, three of which had been refused a license by the Lord Chamberlain. Of the banning of *Mussolini's Lunch* because it insulted a foreign statesman, Middleton writes: "I never felt so flattered in my life. The idea of Mussolini's fate trembling in the balance because I have poked fun at him in a little revue out at Hampstead!"

Middleton, Kent R. *The Need for a Guaranteed Right of Access to the Press Through Advertising*. East Lansing, Mich., Michigan State University, 1971. 113p. (Unpublished Master's thesis) **1M316**
"This thesis argues that there is an access problem in the press; that a guaranteed right of access to the press should be established; and that it can be done without impairing the editorial autonomy so important if the press is to be free to criticize a democratic government. This thesis argues that large, general circulation newspapers offer their advertising pages to the general public on a nondiscriminatory, commercial basis, and should therefore be required to accept all lawful, paid, advertisements prof-

fered to them. A partial solution based on market fairness, then, is proposed for a problem of free speech."

Mihevc, Nancy J. *et al. The Censorship of "Maude." A Case Study in the Social Construction of Reality*. n.p., 1973, 15p. (ED 81,055) **1M317**
In a paper presented at the annual meeting of the International Communication Association, Montreal, 25–28 April 1973, the authors consider the concept of reality held by individuals and societies by examining the reaction to the censorship of the two-part show in the "Maude" series that dealt with abortion and vasectomy. The television stations in Peoria and Champaign-Urbana, Illinois, had exercised their option not to broadcast the programs, which resulted in local controversies between citizens and the station. In Peoria, the issue revolved around the moral right of the station to censor programs; in Champaign-Urbana the controversy was over the station's legal right.

Milam, Lorenzo W. *Sex and Broadcasting—A Handbook on Starting a Radio Station*. 3d ed. [Los Gatos, Calif.], Dildo, 1975. 351p. **1M318**
There is a basic conflict between commercial broadcasting, which the author attacks, and community broadcasting which is daring, creative, irreverent, and controversial. The book offers advice in setting up, programming, and operating a community station. "Sex" in the title, the author confesses, was for the purpose of selling the book.

[Mill, James?] "Liberty of the Continental Press. Review of M. Benjamin de Constant *De la Responsabilité des Ministres* (Paris, 1815) and Joseph Rey *Addresse à l'Empereur* (Paris, 1815)." *Edinburgh Review*, 25:112–34, June 1815. **1M319**
From these works the reviewer conjectures what is likely to be the future of a free press in France during the years ahead, a not very sanguine view. He believes the French exaggerate the dangers of a free press and are apathetical toward its importance. He discusses Constant's ideas (C513) on press freedom in France in relation to English principles, Justice Holt's and his own. He comments on English libel law in relation to religion, political institutions, political officials, and private individuals. Houghton's *Wellesley Index to Victorian Periodicals* is unable to establish authorship but suggests it is possibly by James Mill since Mill is established as author of another article on press freedom in France in the May 1811 issue.

[Mill, John Stuart.] "The Taxes on Knowledge." *Monthly Repository*, 85(n.s.):103–9, April 1834. **1M320**
Mill, writing under the pseudonym "Theta," argues that violent words would not lead to violent action but would act as a "safety-valve" for popular protest. If the government wanted to purify the press it should take action against all papers that indulged in falsehood and libel,

not just the cheap ones or those that were written in less refined language.

Millard, Steve. "Broadcasting's Pre-Emptive Court." *Broadcasting*, 81(9):17–19, 22–23, 30 August 1971. **1M321**
The U.S. Court of Appeals for the District of Columbia Circuit, the author charges, "with dizzying regularity, has reversed the [Federal Communications] Commission on most issues of importance to come before it in recent years," constituting a principal force in regulation of broadcast policy.

Miller, Arthur *et al*. "The Law, the Press and the First Amendment." *Nieman Reports*, 28(4):8–33, Winter 1974. **1M322**
A Harvard Law School professor leads a discussion of a hypothetical case of Ned Nosy, investigative reporter for the *Tombstone Titillater*, at the annual Nieman Assembly, which covered journalistic ethics, press freedom, public records, invasion of privacy, and other legal issues.

Miller, Arthur S. "Watergate and Beyond: The Issue Is Secrecy." *Progressive*, 37(12):15–19, December 1973. **1M323**
Watergate and the controversy over Mr. Nixon's tapes and files raises the question of executive privilege. "But it does more: it reveals, with dramatic and frightening impact, the extent to which ours has become a government by secrecy." The public must become aroused and insist on change or it will continue to be a danger.

Miller, Beverly G. "Miller v. California: A Cold Shower for the First Amendment." *St. John's Law Review*, 48:568–610, March 1974. **1M324**
Following a review of the history of obscenity legislation and court decisions, the author analyzes the "new test" applied by the U.S. Supreme Court in *Miller v. California* (1973), which allocates to the local community the power to determine obscenity. She recommends that further efforts be made to arrive at a definitive answer. "It may very well be that the detrimental effects of pornography are not nearly as severe as the Supreme Court presumes them to be."

Miller, C. J. *Contempt of Court*. London, Elek, 1976. 279p. **1M325**
Includes sections on publicizing and reporting judicial proceedings in camera, in chambers, or in open court; reporter liability for publications; and reporters nondisclosure of sources of information.

———. "The Freedom of Publication (Protection) Bill." *Criminal Law Review*, 1969:177–84, April 1969. **1M326**
Comment on changes in the law of contempt of

court proposed in a bill before the British Parliament. "In the view of the present writer there is in fact no need for radical alterations in the law, but a real necessity for a more courageous attitude on the part of publishers."

—————. "Recent Developments in the Law of Obscenity." *Criminal Law Review*, 1973:467–83, August 1973. **1M327**

"In this article it is proposed to review some of the major changes and points of clarification in the law, especially those associated with cases such as *Anderson* (the 1971 *Oz* case), *D.P.P.v. Whyte* [1972], and *Knuller v. D.P.P.* [1972], and to note some developments and proposals in related areas."

Miller, Edwin. "G, M, R and X." *Seventeen*, 28(7):18–20, July 1969. **1M328**

A panel of nine young people (age from thirteen to nineteen) saw films falling into each of the four categories in the new rating system of the Motion Picture Association of America. They discuss their reaction to the films and the rating code. The readers of *Seventeen* are asked whether or not they agree.

Miller, Hannah. "Why Children's Films Are Not Rated 'R'." *Wilson Library Bulletin*, 46:183–84, October 1971. **1M329**

The author deplores the fact that sex has been excluded from most children's films.

[Miller, Henry.] "Letter from Henry Miller." *Censorship Today*, 1(2):4–9 [August–September] 1968. **1M330**

The author of *Tropic of Cancer* writes to attorney Stanley Fleishman of the circumstance and intentions surrounding the writing of the novel, the trials it has provoked, and the role the book has played in the freeing of literature.

Miller, Howard, and William Rusher. "The Advocates." *Quill*, 60:18–21, January 1972. **1M331**

Highlights from a debate on the question: Should television news be exempt from the fairness doctrine? Howard Miller, law professor, assisted by attorney Theodore Pierson favor exemption; William Rusher, publisher of *National Review*, assisted by Edith Efron, author of *News Twisters*, are opposed to the exemption.

Miller, Howard, William Rusher *et al.* *Pornography in America.* 56 min. tape recording. North Hollywood, Calif., Center for Cassette Studies, 1971. **1M332**

A debate on the question: Should the legislative recommendations of the President's Commission on Obscenity and Pornography be adopted? Pro: Howard Miller, Otto N. Larsen, and Dr. and Mrs. Marvin E. Wolfgang. Con: William Rusher, Charles H. Keating, Jr.,

and Ernest van den Haag. Larsen, Keating, and Marvin Wolfgang were members of the Commission.

Miller, J. G. "Some Obscene Thoughts." *University of Toronto Faculty of Law Review*, 25:128–41, May 1967. **1M333**

A critique of Canadian obscenity law as stated in the Criminal Code and interpreted by the courts. The author suggests a "completely different set of criteria to be used in judging whether or not any particular material is obscene," following the line of thinking suggested by Drs. Eberhard and Phyllis Kronhausen in their book, *Pornography and the Law*, in which they attempt to distinguish between pornography and erotic realism.

Miller, James N. "This Law Could Give Us Back Our Government; Freedom of Information Act." *Reader's Digest*, 104(4):109–13, April 1974. **1M334**

The need for the Freedom of Information Act is dramatized by the case of a Seattle couple's difficulty in getting information on how the Internal Revenue Service operated.

Miller, Jonathan. *Censorship and the Limits of Permission. The Sixth Annual Lecture under the "Thank-Offering to Britain Fund" by Jonathan Miller, 20 October 1971.* London, Oxford University Press for the British Academy, 1972. 24p. **1M335**

A philosophical analysis of the reasons for favoring or opposing censorship of pornography. The lecturer finds conflicting moral priorities and competing principles in force. He examines the three basic arguments raised in justifying censorship of pornography; moral justification, social harmfulness, and offense to the public. The spread of pornography, Miller believes, is part of a broader social and physical upheaval the world is facing. In facing the hazards of this upheaval "we must identify the genuine risks and exorcise the phantoms."

Miller, Justin, J. R. Wiggins, and R. P. Tinkham. "Should Canon 35 Be Amended? A Question of Fair Trial and Free Information." *American Bar Association Journal*, 42:834–86, September 1956. **1M336**

Three writers consider Canon 35 of the American Bar Association Canons of Judicial Ethics which condemns the presence of broadcasters and photographers in the courtroom. Justin Miller of the California Bar and J. R. Wiggins, managing editor of the *Washington Post* and *Times-Herald*, urge that the Canon be changed; Richard P. Tinkham, chairman of the Public Relations Committee of the ABA, summarizes arguments of Bench and Bar in support of the Canon.

Miller, Leo. "The Italian Imprimaturs in Milton's *Areopagitica*." *Papers of the*

Bibliographic Society of America, 65:345–55, Fourth Quarter 1971. **1M337**

A study of the identity of the several unidentified books referred to in Milton's *Areopagitica*, published in Italy, whose imprimaturs testified that they had been "approv'd and licenc't under the hands of 2 or 3 glutton Friers."

Miller, Merle. "Ralph Ginzburg, Middlesex, N.J., and the First Amendment." *New York Times Magazine*, 30 April 1972, pp. 18–19, 64–70. **1M338**

An interview with the former publisher of *Eros* whose jail sentence on obscenity charges was upheld by the U.S. Supreme Court. The author reports that the Post Office Department had received 35,000 complaints against the magazine and its methods of promotion, the largest in history. He discusses Ginzburg's life and career, the events leading up to the trial, the trial itself, and the subsequent appeals. He quotes an old acquaintance of Ginzburg as saying: "He is a loud and obnoxious man, and the reason he is going to jail is that he acts badly in courtrooms." Despite the innocuous nature of the content of *Eros* and the revolution in sexual permissiveness, Ginzburg went to jail, largely because of his pandering methods. He was prosecuted at the recommendation of Robert Kennedy.

Miller, Peter G. "Freedom of Information Act: Boon or Bust for the Press?" *Editor & Publisher*, 105(28):20, 22, 24, 8 July 1972. **1M339**

"The Freedom of Information Act—the legal wonder that was supposed to open many government files to newsmen—has turned out to be a boon for lobbyists and an infrequent formal weapon for journalists."

—————. "Newsman's Privilege: An Issue of Press Freedom." *Quill*, 59(7):14–15, July 1971. **1M340**

"Differing state statutes, contradictory court decisions and nebulous federal directives have all pointed to a need for uniform legislation, legislation that would give newsmen in every sector of the country equal protection before the law."

Miller, Peter P. "Freedom of Expression Under State Constitutions." *Stanford Law Review*, 20:318–35, January 1968. **1M341**

"It is the purpose of this Note to inquire into the protection afforded free speech and press by state courts interpreting state constitutions, in the past and at the present time; to examine the relationship of this protection to the federal courts' interpretation of federal guarantees; and to evaluate the role the state courts should play in the development of safeguards for free expression."

Miller, Robert H. "Commonwealth Broadcasting Power and Defamation by Radio or Television." *Tasmania University Law Review*, 4:70–85, 1971–72. **1M342**

Mills, Charlotte, and Donald E. Thompson. "Wabash College Library Project." *Library Occurrent*, 23:311–16, 332, February 1971. **1M343**
One of the seminars in an experimental program on coordinating the library with the educational program of the college was on censorship. The article deals in large part with the way the seminar was organized, student participation in discussion, and bibliographic critiques of censored titles.

Mills, Kay. "The Broadcast Will Be Delayed." *MORE*, 4(4):5–7, April 1974. **1M344**
"The Pacifica Foundation, which now operates freewheeling FM stations in New York, Houston, Los Angeles, and Berkeley, has been trying to land an outlet in Washington for six years—but its political style makes the FCC nervous."

Mills, Robert W. "Radio, Television and the Right of Privacy." *Journal of Broadcasting*, 13:51–62, Winter 1968/69. **1M345**
The author concludes, in part, that radio and television have not been a serious threat to privacy; most news programs can be presented without violation of the right of privacy; the courts must decide whether a fictionalized presentation is an invasion; where a person seeks public patronage he has no cause for complaint; and truth of the matter and absence of malice are not defenses in privacy invasions.

Millstein, Ira M. "The Federal Trade Commission and False Advertising." *Columbia Law Review*, 64:439–99, March 1964. **1M346**
This article traces the development and use of the powers of the Federal Trade Commission over advertising. "Along the way attention will be given to the standard employed by the FTC for ascertaining the meaning of the promise in an advertisement—a standard that may embody a limitation upon freedom of speech. And the need will be considered for a new approach to deal with the situation ten years hence when advertising is no longer the 12.5 billion dollar business it was in 1962, but a 25 billion dollar business."

Milton, John. *Areopagitica*. Edited by J. C. Suffolk. London, University Tutorial Press, 1968. 147p. **1M347**
A new edition of this classic on freedom of the press, prepared to make *Areopagitica* easier to study in English classes. It is presented in terms of English history rather than antiquity. A synopsis of the text is provided as an aid to understanding, and explanatory notes are given on pages opposite the text. Other editions are listed under M378.

———. *Areopagitica; A Speech of Mr. John Milton for the Liberty of Unlicensed Printing to the Parliament of England*. Cambridge, England, Deighton, Bell, 1973. 49p. Folio. (Of this edition of *Areopagitica* five hundred copies have been printed of which one hundred have been bound in full morocco numbered I–C and four hundred in buckram numbered 1–400.) **1M348**
"The introduction and notes, and the editing of the text are by Isabel Rivers." This fine edition of Milton's classical statement on press freedom was designed by Sebastian Carter and printed by him and Will Carter at Rampant Lions Press, Cambridge.

———. *For the Liberty of Unlicensed Printing: Areopagitica. Pour la liberté de la presse sans autorisation ni censure: Areopagitica*. Edited and translated by Oliver Lutaud. Paris, Aubier-Flammarion, 1969. 255p. (Bilingue Aubier-Flammarion, 24) **1M349**

Minhinette, Babs, and David Madden. [*Textbook Censorship Debate*.] 28 min. color videotape. Baton Rouge, La., Station WBRZ, 1976. (Inside Area 2 Series) **1M350**
A debate between Babs Minhinette, East Baton Rouge foe of "dirty" books, and David Madden, Louisiana State University professor, over the removal of a textbook, *Mass Media and the Popular Arts*, from the high school after threat of an obscenity prosecution by the district attorney. The debate begins with the issue of obscenity, but soon moves to consideration of left-wing and racial minority propaganda, and the broader issues of educational philosophy, the "new morality," humanism, and the rights and obligations of parents in the education of their children.

Mink, Patsy T. "The Mink Case: Restoring the Freedom of Information Act." *Pepperdine Law Review*, 2:8–27, 1974. **1M351**
"*Environmental Protection Agency v. Mink* [1973] presented the first opportunity for the Supreme Court to interpret the Freedom of Information Act of 1966. The court had previously denied certiorari to other cases. By its ruling in *Mink*, the court dealt such a severe blow to the purposes of the Act that it might better be titled the 'Executive Secrecy Act.'"

Minnick, Wayne C. "Teaching Free and Responsible Speech: A Philo-sophical View." In *Free Speech Yearbook*, 1972. New York, Speech Communication Association, 1973, pp. 1–7. **1M352**
"If we take it for granted that tolerance for freedom of expression has to be cultivated [evidence in polls suggests this is the case], do we have a right and/or an obligation to try to inculcate attitudes favorable to freedom of expression in our schools? The purpose of this paper will be to examine the philosophical implications of an affirmative answer to that question."

Minor, Dale. *The Information War*. New York, Hawthorn, 1970. 212p. (Published as paperback by Tower Public Affairs Books) **1M353**
The term "information war" is used by the author to describe the conflict between reporters and government officials when the former attempt to get accurate and full information about the Vietnam war; the term is also used in a broader sense to describe the "more profound conflict, that between the democratic imperative of full public disclosure and those forces and tendencies which act to constrict, control, and manipulate." He deals with specific efforts at manipulation, censorship, and deception in Vietnam (Khe Sanh, for example), at the highest levels in Washington, at the Democratic National Convention in Chicago, and within the press itself, both newspaper and broadcasting.

Mintz, Morton. "Spiro Agnew's Candles." *New Republic*, 162:13–15, 17 January 1970. **1M354**
Criticism of the press, particularly the Hearst, Scripps-Howard, and Newhouse newspapers, which "virtually ignored or blacked out significant and revealing aspects" of the attempt of Vice-President Agnew to intimidate the news media. These news chains are highly active proponents of the proposed Newspaper Preservation Act. The news media should have criticized Agnew's attack on the *New York Times* and the *Washington Post*, given in Montgomery, Ala., a monopoly newspaper town.

Mirsky, Jonathan. "High Drama in Foggy Bottom." *Saturday Review*, 55(1):23–26, 76–77, 1 January 1972. **1M355**
A comparison of the three editions of the Pentagon Papers, the censored government edition, the Senator Gravel edition (Beacon Press), and the *New York Times* (Bantam) edition.

Mishan, Edward J. "The Economic Steam Behind Pornography." In David Holbrook, *ed.*, *The Case Against Pornography*, La Salle, Ill., Open Court, 1973, pp. 157–60. **1M356**
"Although drawing support from writers and liberals, the steam behind the movement for the abolition of all forms of censorship, and more specifically in favor of complete freedom

of erotic subjects, is predominantly commercial. So-called men's magazines and postwar cinema have accustomed the public to tolerate new forms of bowdlerized pornography. The only question now is should the public succumb to the pressure of interested groups—well-meaning liberals as well as Peeping Toms and enterprising publishers—for the removal of all legal restraints."

—————. "Making the World Safe for Pornography." *Public Interest*, 24:33–61, Summer 1971. (Reprinted in *Encounter*, March 1972, and in the author's *Making the World Safe for Pornography—and Other Intellectual Fashions*. La Salle, Ill., Library Press, 1973, pp. 107–50) **1M357**

In this comprehensive argument for controls over the permissive sexual revolution that is sweeping the Western world, the author begins by indicating some of the varied manifestations of the revolution and the emotional attitudes of those who welcome it: (1) writers must have freedom to explore all aspects of human sexuality; (2) obscenity is in the eye of the beholder; (3) to be shocked is part of living; and (4) every man to his taste. "Those less happy at the turn of recent developments, however, seem unable as yet to reconcile their libertarianism with a return to stricter censorship. Despite all evidence to the contrary, they continue to hope for a reaction by the public arising from disgust or, in the last resort, from eventual boredom—a reaction, however, that would not need to invoke legal prohibitions." After examining some of the more familiar arguments against the censorship of sexually obscene matter, and finding them wanting in substance, he affirms the view that the law is ultimately an expression of the moral sentiments of society. "Though the law cannot instill virtue it can discourage vice." The author dismisses the argument that great art can never be obscene, also the idea that just because it can stir people's emotions, pornography should qualify as a legitimate art form. He also challenges the notion that pornography has a theraputic value. He raises the question about the provision for children in a "pornographic society," the ability to love, care, cherish, and trust one another. He concludes that failure to check the commercial pressures impelling a society into a pornographic maelstrom can be regarded as "but one more insidious form of distraction added to the many that already blind the fast-scurrying members of the affluent society to the impending holocaust of the human species."

Mishan, Ezra. "A Modest Proposal: Cleaning Up Sex Pollution." *Harper's* 245:54–56, July 1972. **1M358**

The author proposes that "all major cities designate a large single area, or a number of adjacent districts, where the avantest of avant-garde theaters may flourish unmolested; where no literature, drawing, painting, or work of art will be proscribed, no matter how obscene or shocking; where nude shows and misnomered 'adult' cinemas can flower; where artists, hippies, and every sort of exotic or

adventurous group could congregate and dwell and, if they wish, enact their fantasies." Such areas would be designated "X" areas, as opposed to the "U" areas where such activities would not be permitted or would be under special license. A similar arrangement would be made for X-rated television channels, with access only by use of a key, to prevent children from viewing. "Under such a situation no adult person need feel himself aggrieved."

[Mishkin, Paul J.] "The Supreme Court, 1964 Term: Freedom of Speech and Association." *Harvard Law Review*, 79:149–52; 154–59, 162–68, November 1965. **1M359**

Under the heading Censorship of Motion Pictures, the survey considers the case of *Freedman v. Maryland*; under Detention of Mail Deemed "Communist Propaganda," the case of *Lamont v. Postmaster General*; under Privilege to Criticize Public Officials, the case of *Garrison v. Louisiana*; and under State Legislation: Anti-Birth Control Statute, the case of *Griswold v. Connecticut*.

Misra, R. K. "Freedom of Speech and the Law of Sedition in India." *Journal of the Indian Law Institute*, 8:117–31, January–March 1966. **1M360**

A brief survey of the history of the law of sedition in India on the occasion of the Supreme Court's decision in *Kedar Nath Singh v. The State of Bihar* (1962), which the author criticizes as upholding the law of sedition without making a clear-cut distinction between an incitement to action and an incitement to ideas.

"Mississippi Textbook Censorship Challenged in Court." *Interracial Books for Children*, 6(8):1–2, 1975. **1M361**

This article and Textbook Battle in Mississippi in the subsequent issue—7(1)—discuss the refusal of the Mississippi History Textbook Committee to approve the use of a book, *Mississippi: Conflict and Change*, "as an alternative to the traditional, racist presentation of the state's history," and the suit by teachers and school officials against the Committee to force adoption of the alternative text.

Missouri Library Association. Intellectual Freedom Committee. *Guidelines for Insuring Intellectual Freedom in Missouri Libraries*. n.p., The Association, 1968. 5p. Processed. **1M362**

Adopted by the Association, 11 October 1968.

"Mrs. Gandhi's Taming of the Scribes." *Far East Economic Review*, 86:33–34, 8 November 1974. **1M363**

An account of attempts by the Gandhi government to stamp out dissent in the media, including the firing of the editor of the *Hindustan Times* following an editorial critical of Mrs. Gandhi.

Mitcham, Carl. "Reflections on Freedom of Speech." *Colorado Quarterly*, 18:277–87, Winter 1970. **1M364**

An analysis of the concept of freedom of the press by the New Left, who doubt, if not reject, the absolute value and support freedom only in the context in which it can have practical material consequences.

Mitchell, Austin. "The Association Movement of 1792–93." *Historical Journal*, 4:56–77, 1961. **1M365**

An account of the formation of protective associations in England in response to the fear of the French Revolution and the movement for parliamentary reform. Among the activities of the associations (e.g., the Crown and Anchor Association) was the control of seditious publishing and the bringing to prosecution authors, publishers, and booksellers who dealt with radical political and social ideas.

Mitchell, Douglas P. "Public Access to Governmental Records and Meetings in Arizona." *Arizona Law Review*, 16:891–919, 1974. **1M366**

"This Note will analyze Arizona's statutes, placing primary emphasis on their effect on county and municipal governments." Model legislation is offered as an alternative to the present Arizona public records statute.

Mitchell, John N. "The First Amendment and Dissent." *New York State Bar Journal*, 42:687–92, December 1970. **1M367**

The Attorney General of the United States outlined some of the guidelines followed by the Department of Justice in dealing with demonstrators who came to Washington, D.C., that "protect and confirm the First Amendment rights."

—————. "Free Press and Fair Trial: The Subpoena Controversy." *Illinois Bar Journal*, 59:282–97, December 1970. **1M368**

Adapted from an address by the Attorney General before the American Bar Association. Text of the Department of Justice Guidelines for Subpoenas to the News Media is included.

Mitchell, Keith. "Sense and Censorship." *Tablet: The International Catholic Weekly*, 229:223–24, 8 March 1975. **1M369**

Comments on the Catholic Church's involvement in the area of British film censorship. The pornographic cinemas "have their root cause in avarice, not lust. . . . It is bad that commercial exploitation of a God-given human instinct should be allowed on such an unprecedented scale. But it seems unlikely that censorship can be a more effective weapon against this than, say, prohibition is against alcoholism."

Mitchell, Lee M. "Background Paper." In Twentieth Century Fund Task Force on Broadcasting and the Legislature. *Openly Arrived At: Report*. . . . New York, The Fund, 1974, pp. 31–104. **1M370**
Content: Congressional Television. The Opposition. Congressional Television and the Balance of Power. Congressional Television and the Right to Know. Television in Other Legislatures. Televising Congress.

Mitchell, W. G. C. "Needed—Freedom of Information." *North Carolina Law Review*, 52:417–31, December 1973. **1M371**
Implications of the decision in *Environmental Protection Administration v. Mink* (1973), including the extent of privilege for internal memoranda contained in executive files.

Mitford, Jessica. *The Trial of Dr. Spock, the Rev. William Sloane Coffin, Jr., Michael Ferber, Mitchell Goodman, and Marcus Raskin*. New York, Knopf, 1969. 272p. **1M372**
First among the nine "overt acts" in support of the government charges of conspiracy to abet violation of the Selective Service law was the distribution of a statement, A Call to Resist Illegitimate Authority. Text of the document appears on pages 255–59.

Mithoff, Richard, Jr. "Open Meetings Act Has Potentially Broad Coverage But Suffers from Inadequate Enforcement Provisions." *Texas Law Review*, 49:764–80, April 1971. **1M373**
"Recent alleged violations of the Texas Open Meetings Act have focused attention on the inefficacy of that legislation and have prompted this Note, which will review the Act, suggest possible judicial constructions, and propose several amendments."

Mitnick, Judith A. "Judicial Discretion and the Freedom of Information Act: Disclosure Denied: Consumers Union v. Veterans Administration." *Indiana Law Journal*, 45:421–34, Spring 1970. **1M374**
Re: *Consumers Union v. Veterans Administration*, 301 F. Supp. 796 (S.D. N.Y. 1969) in which the Court "held that under the Freedom of Information Act a court may refuse to enjoin an agency from nondisclosure of information even if an agency fails to establish that the information sought falls within exemptions specifically provided by Congress." The au-

thor believes that in light of the statute's history, this decision is open to question.

Mobley, Gary S. "Bans on Interviews of Prisoners: Prisoner and Press Rights after *Pell* and *Saxbe*." *University of San Francisco Law Review*, 9:718–37, Spring 1975. **1M375**
"This comment will examine the Court's reasoning as it related to the claims raised by the prisoners and the press. In regard to the prisoner's freedom of speech argument, this comment will compare the Court's approach in *Pell* [*Pell v. Procunier*, 1974] to conventional first amendment analysis and the approach of the modern trend of prisoner rights cases. As to issues raised by the press, this comment will analyze the arguments for a special newsgathering right of the press and for a public right to receive information. In conclusion the ramifications of these two decisions as they relate to a possible new approach by the Burger Court to first amendment rights will be examined."

"Model Movie Censorship Ordinance." *Harvard Journal on Legislation*, 5:395–412, March 1968. **1M376**
The ordinance proposed is believed to be acceptable in light of recent Supreme Court decisions, and is designed so that it can be revised to meet subsequent definitions of obscenity, provided there is no radical change.

Moffett, Hugh. "Sexy Movies? Chardon, Neb. Tries Gentle Persuasion." *Life*, 66:52B–52D, 55–57, 30 May 1969. **1M377**
The "Chardon Plan," as a substitute for censorship, consists of a locally prepared and published preview of all movies with ratings, plus a careful checking of ages at the box office. There are also efforts to bring more quality films to the community.

Mohan, John J., Jr. "First Amendment Protection of Public Commercial Dissemination of Obscene Material." *Saint Louis University Law Journal*, 14:732–40, Summer 1970. **1M378**
In *Karalexis v. Byrne* (1969), the U.S. District Court in Massachusetts expanded the *Stanley v. Georgia* decision of the U.S. Supreme Court in the matter of private possession of obscene material to include the commercial distribution of certain admittedly obscene material.

Mohr, Hans. "On-Scene, Off-Scene." *Performing Arts in Canada*, 6(4):14–15, Fall 1969. **1M379**
"The theatre cannot be content to have conflict confined to the stage. . . . It can expect, however, that once a conflict has been opened, society will also not repress it, but give it a hearing."

Molchen, William E., II. "New York Times Standard Is Inapplicable to a

Defamed Individual Who Is Neither a Public Official Nor a Public Figure: and Only Actual Injury Is Compensable Absent Showing of Actual Malice." *Villanova Law Review*, 20:867–83, March 1975. **1M380**
Re: *Gertz v. Robert Welch, Inc.*, 418 U.S. 323 (1974).

Mollenhoff, Clark R. "Let's Take a Closer Look at 'Shield Laws.' " *Human Events*, 33(8):14–15, 24 February 1973. **1M381**
The author questions the value of shield laws in promoting responsible journalism. He believes that "it is impossible to define or limit those covered by the 'freedom of the press' clause without doing serious violence to the full meaning of the Constitution." He asks: "How can it [a shield law] be written so it covers only 'newsmen' entitled to protect their confidential sources and eliminates the possibility of its use by extremist groups or gangsters as a cover for illegal operations? . . . If reasonably competent, responsible and understanding of their job, [newsmen] do not need shield laws to be effective in exposing government corruption and mismanagement or repressive measures."

———. *Life Line of Democracy*. Lawrence, Kans., William Allen White School of Journalism, University of Kansas, 1964. 22p. (15th William Allen White Memorial Lecture) **1M382**
A criticism of the American press for failing in its responsibility to serve as the lifeline of democracy, through superficiality, partisanship, laziness, and incompetence. He calls for tough self-criticism and for the press to fight government secrecy and misinformation and to go beyond the public relations handouts.

———. "Meeting the Reardon Report at the Local Level." *Bulletin of the American Society of Newspaper Editors*, 519:7, 15, May 1968. **1M383**
A report on a panel discussion on press-bar relations presented at the convention of the American Society of Newspaper Editors. The Reardon report of the American Bar Association came under attack. "But the equally important theme that played in the background dealt with lack of understanding by editors of the importance of the coverage of the nation's courts and of the need for assigning better qualified men to coverage of crime news and the courts."

———, and Edwin A. Lahey. *Secrecy in Government*. New York, The Fund for the Republic, n.d. 13p. (The Press and the People, no. 4) **1M384**
A television program, moderated by Louis Lyons, dealing with the people's right to know.

Molz, R. Kathleen. "Burning Yourself Out: The Prisoner's Right to Read."

Newsletter on Intellectual Freedom (IFC-ALA), 21:143–46, September 1972. **1M385**

"Several significant issues have been brought to public attention in recent months regarding the rights of prisoners in the area of intellectual freedom: (1) the right of a prisoner to have access to reading materials without prior screening or censorship . . . ; (2) the right of a prisoner to publish his own writings or speeches without restraint or levy on his profits and royalties; (3) the right of a prisoner to correspond with or be interviewed by the public press; (4) the right of a prisoner to have access to legal research materials." The author cites recent court cases relating to each of these rights.

————. "The Test of Civilization." *North Carolina Libraries*, 32:12–18, Spring 1974. **1M386**

The author reviews the actions of the American courts toward obscenity, indicating the growing latitude, up until the 1973 series of decisions. In *Miller v. California* nationwide standards for judging obscenity were replaced by local community standards. The American Library Association has taken a strong stand against the ruling and against restrictive legislation at state and local levels, a consequence of the ruling. The author raises unanswered questions that these changes in common law pose to libraries and librarians.

[————, ed.] "Concerning the Obscene: A Symposium." *Wilson Library Bulletin*, 42:894–929, May 1968. **1M387**

Papers by New York attorneys Charles Rembar and Richard H. Kuh, and British author, C. H. Rolph (*pseud.* for Cecil R. Hewitt). These are followed by a panel discussion on censorship and pornography. In the introduction to this special issue (pp. 894–95) the editor notes that "libraries, which to all intents and purposes are an exempt group where legal censorship is involved, are nonetheless among the most susceptible of all book distribution agencies to the harassment of community pressure groups." While not questioning the current libertarian stand of the American Library Association, "what we do question is the absolutism (sometimes amounting to intolerance toward any other view) with which it is held." The papers presented are intended to present both sides of the issue, leaving the readers to decide.

Moltz, R. Kathleen *et al*. "Reality and Reason; Intellectual Freedom and Youth." *Newsletter on Intellectual Freedom* (IFC-ALA), 23:105–33, Summer 1974. (Also available as a tape recording in cassette form) **1M388**

A panel discussion at the American Library Association's 1974 annual meeting, intended to explore aspects of intellectual freedom in library service to young people. Particular emphasis is placed on self-censorship and the role of the librarian in preserving intellectual freedom. The panel considers the questions: Is

realism conveyed by four-letter words? Is it rational to expect children to remain innocent of sex when it is exploited in the mass media? Is it rational to expect the ghetto or the barrio to be depicted without giving offense? Richard H. Escott suggests ways to avoid some of the pitfalls of controversy and describes procedures developed for the school system of Rochester, Mich., to deal equitably with complaints. Elaine Simpson insists that "feeding children and young adults a steady book diet of the false, the trivial, and the phony will produce adults who will believe lies and cheap sentimentalities because they do not know truth." Patricia Finley "urges children's librarians to spend more time developing critical awareness in the child and less time selecting books to be included in the safe corner of the library. . . . Treating a child as if he were responsible leads to more responsible behavior as an adult." Norma Klein describes the background and philosophy of her controversial book, *Mom, the Wolfman, and Me*. "Breakdown of some traditional values does not mean the breakdown of all, merely the substitution of more intelligent or rational values."

Monaghan, Henry P. "First Amendment 'Due Process.' " *Harvard Law Review*, 83:518–55, January 1970. **1M389**

"A number of recent Supreme Court opinions primarily in the obscenity area, have fastened strict procedural requirements on governmental action aimed at controlling the exercise of first amendment rights. Professor Monaghan believes that there are two basic principles that can be distilled from these cases: that a judicial body, following an adversary hearing, must decide on the protected character of the speech, and that the judicial determination must either precede or immediately follow any governmental action which restricts speech."

[————.] "The Supreme Court, 1974 Term: Freedom of Speech, Press, and Association." *Harvard Law Review*, 89:111–31, November 1975. **1M390**

Under the heading Commercial Speech, the survey considers the case of *Bigelow v. Virginia*; under the heading State Power to Impose Restrictions Based on Content of Drive-In Motion Pictures, the survey considers the case of *Erznoznik v. City of Jacksonville*.

Monahan, Michael. "In Re Colonel Ingersoll: The Trial for Blasphemy." *Papyrus*, 4(2):1–3, February 1905. **1M391**

Editorial comment on the C. B. Reynolds blasphemy case in New Jersey in which Ingersoll served as defense attorney. "The result of this now famous trial for blasphemy proves that a law on the statute-book—no matter how antiquated, bigotted and absurd—outweighs with a jury the utmost logic and eloquence of the ablest advocate."

Money, John, and Robert Athanasiou. "Pornography." *American Journal of*

Obstetrics and Gynecology, 115:130–46, January 1973. **1M392**

A review of forty studies dealing with pictorial and written erotic material and related topics.

Monk, Carl C. "Applicability of Fairness Doctrine to Television Gas and Automobile Advertisements." *Howard Law Journal*, 16:380–90, Winter 1971. **1M393**

A review of the Federal Communications Commission's decision that the fairness doctrine as applied to cigarettes did not apply to television auto-gas advertisements or to any other commercial products. The author concludes that "if this decision is allowed to stand, not only will television be a vast wasteland, but our whole environment may rapidly become an even vaster wasteland."

Monroe, Bill. "The Crumbling First Amendment." *Bulletin of the American Society of Newspaper Editors*, 564:21–23, December 1972. **1M394**

An attack on the gradual encroachment of the federal government on the freedom to broadcast, particularly the threats of nonrenewal of license, equal time, and program interference.

Monroe, Hamilton. "What If? The Librarian and Texas Law." *Texas Library Journal*, 52:6–8, January 1976. **1M395**

"An important element in the statement [American Library Association's Statement of Professional Ethics, 1975] is the following: '(a librarian) must protect the essential confidentiality relationship which exists between a user and the library.' In Texas, in a landmark decision and in an impressive legal support for this ethical principle, the Attorney General of Texas has issued a formal opinion that 'information which would reveal the identity of a library patron in the connection with the object of his or her attention is excepted from disclosure . . . as information deemed confidential by constitutional law.' " It is the purpose of this paper "to explain possible restrictions inherent in the ruling that might possibly be overlooked by administrators, practicing librarians, and staff members. Overlooking these possible restrictions could well result in legal actions."

Monroe, William B., Jr. "The Case for Television in the Courtroom." *Notre Dame Lawyer*, 42:920–24, Symposium 1967. (Reprinted in *Federal Communications Bar Journal*, 1967) **1M396**

"The notion that a medium that covers church services, the Senate Foreign Relations Committee, and the United Nations cannot cover courtrooms quietly and unobtrusively, without affecting the proceedings, is absurd almost on its face." The director of National Broadcasting Company News believes that covering the courts would not be financially profitable for the broadcasting industry, but that the courts themselves, in the interest of improving the process of justice, should be actively exploring the possibilities of introducing television and radio coverage.

Montagno, George L. "Federalist Retaliation: The Sedition Trial of Matthew Lyon." *Vermont History*, 26:3–16, January 1958. Comments: 26:136–38, April 1958. **1M397**
An account of the trial, conviction, imprisonment, and political martyrdom of a Jeffersonian editor under the Sedition Act of 1798, assembled from original sources.

Montagu, Ivor. "The Porn Gang." *Labour Monthly*, 54:504–7, November 1972. **1M398**
Comment on the Lord Longford report on pornography.

Montgomerie, John. "Should There Be Obscenity Laws?" *Books: Journal of the National Book League*, 8:13–15, Summer 1972. **1M399**
"There is gradually evolving a consensus of opinion that the areas in which [British] obscenity laws may be appropriate relate only to the protection of juveniles, public display, and unsolicited mailing, and that general obscenity laws which produce censorship rather than protecting privacy should be abolished."

[Montgomery, James.] *The Trial of James Montgomery for a Libel on the War, By Reprinting and Republishing a Song originally Printed and Published long before the War began; at Doncaster Sessions, January 22, 1795.* Sheffield, England, J. Montgomery, 1795. 44p. **1M400**
Montgomery, a printer, had made and distributed copies of A Patriotic Song by a Clergyman of Belfast, a work originally written to celebrate the French Revolution's liberation of tyranny. It contained the phrase: "If France is subdued, Europe's liberty ends; if France triumphs the World will be free." The counsel for the defense, Mr. Vaughan, presented a strong argument for freedom of the press. The judge agreed with the defense that the work was not libelous when it first appeared in 1789, but he ruled that now that England and France were at war the same work could be libelous in 1794. Montgomery was found guilty, sentenced to three months in prison and fined £20.

Moody, Randall J. "The Armed Forces Broadcast News System: Vietnam Version." *Journalism Quarterly*, 47:27–30, Spring 1970. **1M401**

"The former news director of the American Forces Vietnam Network explains how the military command there is able to violate Defense Department regulations and censor news for G.I.s in the interest of 'image.' "

———. *Preserving the Image in Vietnam*. Columbia, Mo., Freedom of Information Center, School of Journalism, University of Missouri at Columbia, 1970. 4p. (Report no. 0010) **1M402**
The author "tells of his experiences at AFVN [American Forces Vietnam Network] and charges that regulations prohibiting existing news censorship practices by the military exist but are flaunted and twisted to such a degree they are ineffectual. He calls for full enforcement of these military laws and an end to news suppression by the military."

Moon, Eric. "The Blue and the Grey: Theory and Practice in Book Selection." In his *Book Selection and Censorship in the Sixties*, New York, Bowker, 1969, pp. 3–11. **1M403**
An essay "intended to undermine the certainties of those who think book selection can be done by rote or formula, of those who believe themselves 'safe' in their decisions if only they have a written policy, of those who ascribe fallibility or prejudice only to others." While the librarian can always defend the selection of a book under the general rubric of "intellectual freedom," it is more difficult to defend the rejection of a book. It is difficult for the reader to understand the distinction between book selection and censorship. The author examines with scepticism such common book selection terms as "needs of the community," "literary quality," "public demand," and "balance"; he suggests that many librarians practice a double standard by giving greater scrutiny to controversial books than those that are insipid.

———, ed. *Book Selection and Censorship in the Sixties*. New York, Bowker, 1969. 421p. **1M404**
"This book is primarily an anthology of articles written in *Library Journal* during the decade of the 1960s. . . . That so much material on the subject of book selection and censorship should have appeared in such a comparatively short span of time is testimony to the problems that surround this central discipline in librarianship in this period." Part I deals with Book Selection. Part II deals with Book Censorship: Views on Censorship—Outside the Profession; Library Associations Debate Censorship; Case Histories; The Politics of Censorship; and The Library School's Responsibility. Most of the articles have been included in the 1968 edition of *Freedom of the Press*.

Moon, Gordon A., II. "Military Security vs. the Right to Know." *Army*, 18(7):22–25, 65–66, July 1968. **1M405**
"The Army has always been proud of its friendship with the press. But even the best of pals have differences, and things could get cool if the Fourth Estate should decide that the

Pentagon is becoming overly taciturn. Incidents of alleged censorship, recent restrictions on the release of war information—and even the American Bar Association's controversial Reardon Report—are seen by some newsmen as signs that the candor that feeds the friendship is in jeopardy."

Moore, Charles B. "Censorship of AFVN News in Vietnam." *Journal of Broadcasting*, 15:387–95, Fall 1971. **1M406**
"The 'Pentagon Papers' amply demonstrate that the American public didn't get very much background of our involvement in Southeast Asia. Recent books and other writings attempt to show that we didn't get much of the foreground, either. But what of American servicemen in Vietnam, supposedly receiving all the news they need from the Armed Services Vietnam Network? The extent to which this information was censored for political reasons is explored in the following article." The author was formerly an officer in the Army Information Officers Program.

———. *Informal Censorship of the Press in Vietnam by the U.S. Military*. Lubbock, Tex., Texas Tech University, 1972. 211p. (Unpublished Master's thesis) **1M407**
This survey of newsmen and military information officers in Vietnam revealed, in part, that unofficial censorship did take place, but that it did not seriously interfere with the mission of the press; MACV ground rules were more of a hindrance to the military than to the press; 64 percent of the newsmen believed security classification was sometimes used to hide politically embarrassing information, while 69 percent of the information officers denied this; 68 percent of the information officers admitted giving preferential treatment to certain newsmen, but for personal reasons and not because they favored the U.S. policies.

[Moore, Charles W., and Edwin Sevey.] *Trial of Moore and Sevey for a Libel on Samuel D. Greene, in the Municipal Court, Boston, July Term, 1833. Reported by Charles H. Locke.* Boston, Moore & Sevey, 1833. 78p. **1M408**
Moore and Sevey were accused of maliciously composing and causing to be printed in the *Boston Mirror* a false, scandalous, and defamatory libel on Samuel D. Greene. The defendants were found not guilty.

Moore, Everett T. "The Evergreen Tempest: Eye of a Storm." *ALA Bulletin*, 63:1527, December 1969. **1M409**
Controversy over the Los Angeles Public Library having *Evergreen Review* on open shelves stirred up a tempest, but it ended with the Board supporting the judgment of the library staff.

———. "Intellectual Freedom." In Jerrold Orne, *ed., Research Librarianship*.

New York, Bowker, 1971, pp. 1–17.
1M410
In this volume dedicated to Dean Robert Bingham Downs, the author tells the story of the purge of United States libraries as part of the anti-Communist campaign of Senator Joseph R. McCarthy. The purge, which took place in the early 1950s, challenged the principles of free selection and free access to ideas, long cherished by American librarians. The State Department's censorship of overseas libraries (some forty authors and hundreds of titles) led to the adoption of the now famous joint statement of the American Library Association and the American Book Publishers Council on *Freedom to Read*. Shortly thereafter, President Eisenhower, who had silently tolerated the action of the State Department officials, made his famous statement, "Don't join the book burners" in a talk at Dartmouth College. In June of 1953, President Robert B. Downs of the American Library Association, opened the Association's annual conference with an address which denounced censorship of American overseas libraries; at the same conference the ALA Council adopted a resolution condemning the censorship. A letter from President Eisenhower to Dean Downs was read to the conference; it praised libraries' defense of intellectual freedom and condemned book burning. Shortly after the conference Robert L. Johnson, chief of the State Department's International Information Administration, who had carried out the book purge, resigned and the State Department attempted to clarify its new opposition to book burning. The author, while teaching in a Japanese library school, observed the State Department's censorship of U.S. information libraries in that country (*ALA Bulletin*, October 1953).

———. "The Intellectual Freedom Saga in California: The Experience of Four Decades." *California Librarian*, 35:48–57, October 1974. **1M411**
A tribute to the pioneering efforts of Helen E. Haines to alert librarians to the threats to intellectual freedom, particularly in the area of politics. Her own book, *Living with Books*, was attacked by right-wing groups and she was unjustly charged with being a dupe of subversive propaganda. The article surveys the work of the California Library Association and particularly its Intellectual Freedom Committee in fighting censorship.

———. "Threats to Intellectual Freedom." *Library Journal*, 96:3563–67, 1 November 1971. **1M412**
Despite the liberalizing influences of the past decade and tremendous anticensorship progress in the courts, there remain serious threats to intellectual freedom. The author writes of government attacks on the news media, comparing the climate with that of the McCarthy era. New and hopeful ingredients, however, are the awareness of youth and the flourishing of the underground press and the new breed of little magazines.

Moore, George. *A Communication to My Friends*. London, Nonesuch, 1933.

86p. (Edition limited to 1,000 copies)
1M413
In Moore's last work he recounts his publishing experiences with Tinsley and Henry Vizetelly and the banning of his works by Mudie's and Smith's Circulating Libraries. He also writes of the prosecution of Henry Vizetelly, at the instigation of the Vigilance Society, for publication of English translations of the works of Zola. He notes that the crusader, W. T. Stead, threatened to resign from the Council of the Society when it threatened action against the *Heptameron* and Flaubert's *Madame Bovary*.

———. "A New Censorship in Literature." *Pall Mall Gazette*, 40:1–2, 10 December 1884. **1M414**
The novelist Moore complains of the stranglehold the British circulating libraries have on English fiction. "What it disapproves of comes into the world, as it were, stillborn; for no book is reissued in a cheap form that has not been in the first instance a success at the libraries. At the head, therefore, of English literature sits a tradesman." Moore writes of his experience with the censorship of the circulating libraries in the case of his *A Modern Lover*.

Moore, Hugh, Jr. "A Newspaper's Risks in Reporting 'Facts' From Presumably Reliable Sources: A Study in the Practical Application of the Right of Privacy." *South Carolina Law Review*, 22:1–33, 1970. **1M415**
The article deals with the news media and "the right of a person to be free from needless embarrassment or harassment through publication of his name, photograph, or details of his personal life in a nonnewsworthy context."

Moore, John B. "On Philosophizing About Freedom of Speech." *Southwestern Journal of Philosophy*, 6(3):47–73, Fall 1975. **1M416**
"The gravamen of this article is for philosophers who aspire to influence legal thought. I propose to illustrate these counsels by a critical analysis of Professor Ginsberg's contributions to this journal in 1972 [In Favor of Crying "Fire" in a Crowded Theater, Fall 1972]. . . . I offer reasons for rejecting his claim that his work should be emulated by philosophers who seek to influence legal developments. I am more interested in arguing against his methodological claim than against the substantive conclusions he proposes." The author concludes: "Philosophy in law, particularly that concerned with the First Amendment, involves a most important set of issues. It deserves and needs the finest efforts of the philosophical community. But in order to merit being taken seriously, philosophers must understand legal materials which they discuss, they must make it clear to the lawyers that they understand them, and they must use the best tools in their philosophical repertoire. A rich and influential traffic in ideas awaits those philosophers who seek to work at the crossroads between law and philosophy at the First Amendment."

Moore, John C. "Advertising and Recent Developments in the Fairness Doctrine." *Washington and Lee Law Review*, 29:80–100, Spring 1972. **1M417**
A review of court decisions rising out of the application of the fairness doctrine to broadcast advertising. Includes consideration of the *Banzhaf*, *Chevron*, *Esso*, *Friends of the Earth*, and four military advertising cases.

Moore, Ray N. "Intellectual Freedom Workshop." *North Carolina Libraries*, 31(4):7–11, Conference issue, 1973.
1M418
The workshop dealt with problems facing librarians in the new guidelines set by the 21 June 1973 Supreme Court ruling on obscenity. Alex P. Allain and R. Kathleen Molz were guest speakers.

Moorhouse, John C. "Censorship, Revenue, and X-Rated Movie Taxes." *Quarterly Review of Economics and Business*, 13:83–89, Summer 1973. **1M419**
The author looks at South Carolina's use of a 20 percent excise tax on X-rated movie admissions, which "strikes a blow against sin, and on the other hand, provides an additional source of tax revenue. . . . In this note the tax-revenue-maximizing tax rate is derived in terms of the price elasticities of supply and demand, thereby establishing the critical ranges, then the usefulness of the concept is illustrated by exploring the economics of the South Carolina X-rated movie admissions tax; and estimates are made of the regulatory and revenue effects."

Moorman, William A. "Comments on the Current State of the Law in the United States—Protection of the Defamatory Falsehood and the Careless Liar." *Trial Lawyer's Guide*, 15:40–65, February 1971. **1M420**
A review of recent libel cases including *New York Times v. Sullivan* (1964), *Rosenblatt v. Baer* (1966), *Curtis Publishing Co. v. Butts* (1967), *Associated Press v. Walker* (1967), *Pauling v. Globe Democrat Publishing Co.* (1966), *Time, Inc. v. Hill* (1967), and *Gertz v. Robert Welch, Inc.* (1970). The author believes the scale is now "heavily weighted in favor of unbridled journalistic fervor. . . . Surely, the framers of the Constitution did not intend the First Amendment to protect the defamatory falsehoods of careless liars when they are directed at the ordinary private citizen under the guise of 'public interest.' "

Moos, Rudolf H. "The Effects of Pornography: A Review of the Findings of the Obscenity and Pornography Commission." *Comments on Contempo-*

rary Psychiatry, 1:123–31, January 1972. **1M421**
"This review will follow the Commission report in summarizing the most recent findings on a) behavioral responses, b) sexual responses, c) attitudinal, emotional, and judgemental responses, and d) anti-social and criminal behavior." The reviewer notes the "surprising and somewhat disconcerting fact that there has been some differential handling of the research on the effects of obscenity and pornography on the one hand, and that on the effects of violence and aggression on the other," suggesting that the evaluation of the data may have introduced philosophical assumptions about the general beneficial effects of sexuality and the general harmful effects of aggression and violence.

The Moral and Political Evils of the Taxes on Knowledge; Expounded in 1. The Speeches Delivered at the City of London Literary and Scientific Institution, on the Subject of a Petition to Parliament against the Stamps on Newspapers, the Duties on Advertisements, and on Printing Paper; 2. The Petition Presented to Parliament from the Members of the Institution; 3. A Letter of the Editor of "The Scotsman" to the Chancellor of the Exchequer: to Which is Appended an Abstract of the Parliamentary Returns of the Amount of Stamps Purchased, and of the Advertisement Duty Paid by the Leading Metropolitan Journals. London, Effingham Wilson, 1830. 16p. **1M422**

"Morality and the Broadcast Media: A Constitutional Analysis of FCC Regulatory Standards." *Harvard Law Review*, 84:664–99, January 1971. **1M423**
Content: Federal Communications Commission Regulation of "Morally Offensive" Programming. The Applicability of Constitutional Standards to Broadcasting (Current Constitutional Standards for Morally Offensive Material, The Unique Characteristics of the Broadcasting Media, the Constitutional Boundaries for Broadcasting Media Regulation). The Regulatory Approach of the FCC and Its Consequences for Programming Standards.

Morality in Media, Inc. *National Obscenity Law Center*. New York, Morality in Media, 1976. 4p. Folder. **1M424**
A brief statement of the purposes and accomplishments of the clearinghouse established to assist in the prosecution of obscenity cases. The Center, originally called the National Legal Center on the Law of Obscenity, was recommended by the minority report of the U.S. Commission on Obscenity and Pornography; it was initially funded by the U.S.

Department of Justice but when further funds were denied, was taken over by Morality in Media, Inc. An *Obscenity Law Bulletin*, issued six times a year, began in January 1977. The Center also issues a *Brief Bank Index* of obscenity cases.

———. *Newsletter*. New York, 1962–date. Published eight times a year by Immanuel Evangelical Lutheran Church, Congregation Zichron Moshe, and St. Nicholas Church, Greek Orthodox. **1M425**
Morality in Media, Inc. is an "interfaith organization working to stop the traffic in pornography constitutionally and effectively, and working toward media based on the principles of love, truth, and taste."

———. *Parents' Coalition Kit*. New York, Morality in Media, 1974. Various paging. **1M426**
The kit contains: Instructions on how to form your coalition, issues of the organization's newsletter, posters publicizing the U.S. Supreme Court's June 1973 obscenity ruling, suggested ads for newspapers and radio spots, complaint sheets, cliché questions and how to answer them, and a sheet of stamps (Parents Coalition Against Pornography).

———. *Smut and the Nation's Youth*. New York, Morality in Media, [1972?] 8p. **1M427**
A statement of the aims of Morality in Media, Inc. and its interfaith program to combat pornography.

Morawski, Stefan. "Art and Obscenity." *Journal of Aesthetics and Art Criticism*, 26:193–207, Winter 1967. **1M428**
"My frame of reference is aesthetics and, accordingly, the problem of art and obscenity interest me primarily in terms of the structure of art works. . . . (1) Can art be pornographic or, in other words, is the aesthetic phenomenon compatible with those products of culture commonly branded as filth? (2) Even if the answer is no, can obscenity arise in art and, if so, what place does it occupy in the artistic structure as a whole?"

MORE. New York, Rosebud Associates, 1971–date. Monthly. **1M429**
One of the major "journalism reviews," the independent voice of professional journalists in New York who examine with a critical eye the policies and practices of the city's major newspapers. News stories and articles frequently expose efforts at censorship, deception, or favoritism in the established press. A collection of articles appearing in *MORE* is contained in *Stop the Presses*, edited by Richard Pollak and published by Random House, 1975.

Morgan, Ernest. *Informal Methods of Combatting Secrecy in Local Government*. Columbia, Mo., Freedom of Informa-

tion Foundation, 1976. (Freedom of Information Foundation Series, no. 6) **1M430**
The paper reports on a survey of newspaper city editors on the issue of access to local public news; it suggests a program for newspapers to follow aimed at preventing or attacking official secrecy; and it reaches four conclusions: (1) "When fighting official secrecy, newspapers' arguments gain greatest force when they keep the high ground of the democratic ideal—a voting public able to govern itself because it is informed about public affairs." (2) "The closing of a public meeting or record must become NEWS, an atypical event." (3) "Newspapers, like all mass media, share in the blame for governmental secrecy." Superficial, sensational, and inaccurate reporting contributes to distrust of the media. (4) "Stave off open war with officials as long as possible."

Morgan, Harmon *et al.* "The Failing Newspaper Act—Testimony from behind the Front Page." *Grassroots Editor*, 8(6):7–13, November–December 1967. **1M431**
A compilation of comments pro and con on the proposed Failing Newspaper Act, taken from testimony before the U.S. Senate Antitrust and Monopoly Subcommittee.

Morgan, Hugh. "Censorship in the Military: Managing the News." *Civil Liberties*, 287:1, 6, May 1972. **1M432**
The author was formerly a Pentagon correspondent for the American Forces Radio and Television Service and, before that, a network newscaster in Saigon.

Morgan, Robert S. *The Television Code of the National Association of Broadcasters: The First Ten Years*. Iowa City, Iowa, University of Iowa, 1964. 385p. (Ph.D. dissertation, University Microfilms, no. 64–7933) **1M433**
"This study is an historical-critical report of the first ten years (1952 to 1962) of the Television Code of the National Association of Broadcasters. The Code oversees the advertising and programming practices of nearly four hundred Subscribers including approximately eighty percent of the commercial television stations on-the-air and the three networks. . . . The central questions which the writer attempts to answer are: (1) What factors have shaped the development of industry-wide television self-regulation in what ways? (2) How effective has the Television Code been in implementing standards for programming and advertising? and (3) How can television self-regulation be made more meaningful?"

Morgan, Stewart S. "The Damning of Holcroft's *Knave or Not?* and O'Keeffe's *She's Eloped*." *Huntington Library Quarterly*, 22:51–62, November 1958. **1M434**
During the political unrest in England following the French Revolution, these two comedies

were censored "not because of their artistic merit or their value as theatrical entertainments but because the censors did not see eye to eye with the political views that they attributed to the authors." Holcroft's plays had been a great favorite with London audiences, but on opening night for *Knave or Not?* (25 January 1798) the audience shouted down the play because its author was suspected of liberal tendencies. A peaceful reformer and dedicated humanitarian, Holcroft had three years earlier been brought to trial for treason as one of twelve leaders in the Corresponding Society. After three defendants were acquitted, charges were dismissed against Holcroft and the others (H298).

Morgan, Thomas B. "When Is a Book Obscene?" *Cosmopolitan*, 147(2):56–59, August 1959. **1M435**
"Can Hemingway, Faulkner, and D. H. Lawrence write anything they please, in the name of art? If an unknown writer says the same thing, less artfully, is it pornography? The answers to these questions continue to cause a bitter battle between censors and liberals, both of whom are convinced they qualify to determine what is fit reading for the American public."

Moriarty, Kathleen P. *The Irish Parliament and George William Russell on Censorship, 1928–1929: A Study of the Contraction and Amplification of an Issue*. Lafayette, Ind., Purdue University, 1972. 309p. (Ph.D. dissertation, University Microfilms, no. 72-30,942) **1M436**
"This study analyzes the 1928–29 censorship debates in both the Parliament and in an Irish journal of opinion edited by George William Russell, *The Irish Statesman*. . . . The study was designed to contrast not merely the types of arguments and evidence used in each debate, but especially to demonstrate how each group contracted or amplified the censorship question. . . . The study reveals the strengths and the inadequacies of the debate in the Parliament, a debate which gave inordinate emphasis to practical considerations of how to develop censorship machinery, while eschewing the responsibility to discuss the philosophical underpinnings of the censorship issue."

Morreale, Justin P. "Obscenity: An Analysis and Statutory Proposal." *Wisconsin Law Review*, 1969:421–68, 1969. **1M437**
"It is the thesis of this article that an acceptable and desirable interpretation of the first amendment and recent Supreme Court decisions provides substantial support for the contention that the only interest a state can legitimately protect by censorship of obscene representations to adults is the interest of persons to avoid an unwilling confrontation with obtrusive, obscene representations. If this thesis is valid, then the obscenity statutes of the states, all of which prohibit the commercial distribution of 'obscene' materials to willing

adults, are unconstitutional. A model statute designed to replace existing state statutes and to implement the obtrusiveness approach is included in this article."

Morris, C. H. "Views of a Trial Lawyer in Regard to Photographing, Televising and Electronic Transmission of Court Proceedings." *Inter-American Bar Association. Proceedings*, 11(1):234–44, 1959. **1M438**
A favorable view toward experimentation in televised coverage of court proceedings.

Morris, Earl F. "The Reardon Report—Where Now?" *Louisiana Bar Journal*, 16:11–16, July 1968. **1M439**
The president of the American Bar Association considers five questions with respect to the recommendation of the Association's Reardon Report on fair trial and free press: Why did the ABA adopt these standards? What does the Reardon Report do? What does the Reardon Report not do? To the last the author responds that the recommendations "do not impose any restrictions on the news media themselves; they only apply to lawyers, judges and law enforcement officers."

Morris, Marilyn L. *Reporter Immunity in State and Federal Law*. Berkeley, Calif., University of California, Berkeley, 1973. 92p. (Unpublished Master's thesis) **1M440**
The author reviews the development of the concept of journalist's immunity through common law and legislative enactments. She concludes that "the last resort for a newsmen's privilege seems to be in statutory formulation of which nearly 30 have been proposed."

Morris, Richard B. "The Case for the Palatine Printer: Zenger's Fight for a Free Press." In his *Fair Trial*. New York, Knopf, 1953, pp. 69–95. **1M441**
The long-standing freedom to criticize public officials "goes back to the courageous battle put up against the Royal government in America by a New York printer named John Peter Zenger. The Zenger case destroyed once and for all the notion that government officials were entitled to unqualified allegiance and support, that they were untouchables immune from criticism." Professor Morris also wrote the brief biography of Zenger for the *Dictionary of American Biography* (vol. 20, pp. 648–50).

Morris, Robert J. "The CHNS Case: An Emerging Fairness Doctrine for Canada." *Canadian Communications Law Review*, 4:1–54, 1972. **1M442**
"The purpose of this paper is to examine what the U.S. fairness doctrine is and then, in light of this analysis and a study of recent developments in Canadian broadcasting, try to determine whether such a principle now operates here. Two cases—an American, a Canadian—exemplify the 'fairness' problem

and, in the similarity of their solutions, underscore the legitimacy of this inquiry." The U.S. case: *Red Lion Broadcasting Co. v. FCC*; the Canadian case: The Canadian Radio-Television Commission's ruling on fairness in the case of radio station CHNS, Halifax.

Morris, Robert T. *Editorial Silence: The Third Era of Journalism*. Boston, Stratford, 1927. 256p. **1M443**
Much of this curious, discursive book consists of criticism of today's newspapers for devoting so much space to crime, divorce, scandal, and other sensational news which the author believes is harmful to the reader. He calls for a new era in journalism to replace the Second Era of "manufactured excitement." In this Third Era there would be "editorial silence" for antisocial news; emphasis would be on human achievements rather than human error.

Morris, Roger. "Taking AIM at Jack Anderson." *Columbia Journalism Review*, 14(1):19–23, May–June 1975. **1M444**
An account of the attacks on muckraker Jack Anderson by AIM (Accuracy in Media, Inc.) in complaints before the National News Council. While pointing out the ultra-conservative bias of AIM, the author blames the press for its unwillingness to accept criticism. AIM and Anderson, despite their mutual rancor, have something in common. "In a larger sense, the mentality that automatically dismisses AIM is similar to the mentality that regards Anderson as an unwelcome troublemaker. Both AIM and Anderson run up against self-protection and self-interest, a reluctance to admit error, and a fear of publicity in the literal meaning of that word."

Morrison, Brian A. "Newsman's Privilege to Refuse Disclosure of Confidential Sources in Criminal Trial." *Washington Law Review*, 51:1005–24, October 1976. **1M445**
Re: *Farr v. Pitchess*, 522 F.2d 464 (9th Cir. 1975). "This note will suggest that the court's overreliance upon the fair trial interest and its failure to analyze the newsman's testimonial privilege precluded the court from effectively utilizing the balancing test it stated to be applicable. . . . Evaluation of the first amendment interest, when weighed against the opposing need for disclosure, should have led to a contrary decision in *Farr*."

Morrissey, Michael J., and John L. Smith. "The Federal Communications Commission: Fairness, Renewal, and the New Technology." *George Washington Law Review*, 41:683–758, May 1973. **1M446**
"The focus of this study will be on the major

activities of the FCC in regulating the commercial broadcast industry from October 1971 to January 1973. Two of the areas studied pertain to the Commission's statutory authority to review a licensee's performance to assure that his operation is in the public interest. . . . In addition to this periodic scrutiny of licensee practice and policy, the Commission may at any time initiate an inquiry to determine whether a licensee's programming is in compliance with the 'fairness doctrine,' which requires broadcasters to afford a reasonable opportunity to qualified spokesmen to present contrasting viewpoints on controversial issues of public importance."

Morrow, Anne C. *Birth Control and Publicity; a Survey of the Periodical Coverage of the Birth Control Movement in the United States in the Twentieth Century*. Seattle, University of Washington, 1970. 148p. (Unpublished Master's thesis)   **1M447**
"The conclusion is that the media reported events considered newsworthy in the birth control movement but did very little to promote it. Only in scientific publications, which have limited circulation, has it been suggested that unless rich and poor alike limit their families population growth will force the United States as well as the rest of the world to accept a standard of living quite different from the present ideal."

Morse, Leon. "Attitudes Are Changing on Fairness Doctrine." *Television/Radio Age*, 23(6):39–41, 96–97, 13 October 1975.   **1M448**
While the fairness doctrine has come under fire from an increasing number of "liberals" on the grounds that it restricts First Amendment rights of broadcasters, ironically, conservative pressure groups are making use of the doctrine to force accuracy in news and documentaries and the redressing of alleged liberal bias.

Mortenson, Robert. "Copyright of Byron's *Cain*." *Papers of the Bibliographical Society of America*, 63:5–13, January 1969.   **1M449**
Cain, published by John Murray in December 1821, was attacked for its supposed blasphemy. William Benbow issued a pirated edition in January 1822 and, after much hesitation, Murray sought a copyright injunction against Benbow in Chancery. Lord Chancellor Eldon, after reading the work, refused to issue an injunction on grounds that the work might "vilify and bring into discredit that portion of the Scripture history on which it is founded. . . . " Earlier scholarship had reported that Murray took the matter before a jury trial which declared the work was not blasphemous and thus secured the copyright. Mortenson finds no evidence of such a trial and believes it

did not take place and that the copyright of *Cain* was never protected. Subsequent to Lord Eldon's decision various other publishers pirated the work with no apparent punishment.

[Mortimer, John.] "Obscenity Law As It Works Today." *Bookseller*, 3283: 1722–24, 23 November 1968.   **1M450**
A summary of a talk on the legal situation in Britain under the Obscene Publications Act, by the attorney in the *Last Exit to Brooklyn* case.

——. "Talking About Censorship— 2: After the Chamberlain." *Author*, 81:71–73, April 1971.   **1M451**
With the abolishing of the stage censorship of the Lord Chamberlain, "an impeccably arbitrary nanny has been dismissed and the theatre must now be prepared to face the so-called adult world of the British law courts." The next step should be the removal of all legal censorship.

Moscone, George R. "Freedom and the Pressures of Censorship." *California Librarian*, 30:23–27, January 1969. **1M452**
An address by a California State senator at a joint meeting of the Intellectual Freedom and Legislation Committees of the California Library Association, challenging librarians to keep up the good fight in the never ending war against censorship. Tom Bowdler, who expurgated Shakespeare and the Bible is not dead, Senator Mascone reported. "He is alive and a member of the State Board of Education. Now that the Board has completed its sanitation chores on contemporary literature, I understand they are turning their attention to United States History."

Moseley, Sydney A. *The Truth About a Journalist*. London, Pitman, 1935. 352p.   **1M453**
Chapter 7, Sense and Censorship, deals with British censorship during World War I. Chapter 17, Under the Libel Yoke, attacks the prevailing British libel laws which have resulted in "more miscarriages of justice" than any other form of legal action. Though "no man can gag a newspaper with a bribe, many a man has been able to silence one with a writ, or even the threat of one."

Mosher, Donald L. "Psychological Reactions to Pornographic Films." *Technical Report of the [U.S.] Commission on Obscenity and Pornography*, 8:255–312, 1971.   **1M454**
"The study was designed to answer a number of questions. How sexually arousing is the viewing of explicitly sexual films? What sorts of affective states accompany the viewing of such films: Are the films viewed as pornographic, disgusting, offensive, or enjoyable? Are there any changes in sexual behavior attributable to increased levels of erotic arousal in the 24 hours following viewing? Are there changes in emotional and vegetative states during a 24-hour period after viewing the films?

Are there any changes in opinions toward sex which are influenced by viewing films and persist over a two-week period?"

——. "Sex Callousness Toward Women." *Technical Report of the [U.S.] Commission on Obscenity and Pornography*, 8:313–25, 1971.   **1M455**
"A newly constructed measure of sex-calloused attitudes towards women as well as measures of guilt and sex experience was completed by 256 single college males; these measures were correlated with reported sex aggression and other exploitative tactics used to gain intercourse with dates."

——. "Sex Differences, Sex Experience, Sex Guilt, and Explicitly Sexual Films." *Journal of Social Issues*, 29(3): 95–112, 1973.   **1M456**
The paper reports on results of an experiment to determine the immediate effects of sexually explicit films on the viewers in relation to their sex, previous sexual experience, and sex guilt. One of the studies stimulated by the U.S. Commission on Obscenity and Pornography.

——, and Harvey Katz. "Pornographic Films, Male Verbal Aggression Against Women, and Guilt." *Technical Report of the [U.S.] Commission on Obscenity and Pornography*, 8:357–79, 1971.   **1M457**
"The present experiment was an analogue developed to begin the exploration of the questions: Does sexual arousal from viewing a pornographic film increase the likelihood of aggression against women? When sexual stimulation or continued sexual stimulation is contingent upon aggressive behavior against women, does aggressive behavior increase? What is the influence of guilt as a personality disposition on aggression against women?"

Moss, Donald D. "Public Domain and a Right of Access: Affect upon the Broadcast Media." *Loyola University of Los Angeles Law Review*, 3:451–74, April 1970.   **1M458**
Re: *Red Lion Broadcasting Co. v. Federal Communications Commission* (1969) and *U.S. v. Radio Television News Directors Association* (1969).

Moss, Frederick C. "The Effect of the First Amendment on Federal Control of Draft Protests." *Villanova Law Review*, 13:347–69, Winter 1968. **1M459**
"This comment will seek to deal briefly with the history of government prosecutions against those who have spoken out against the draft, describe the wide variety of anti-draft activity in this country today, and seek to distill from the first amendment a workable principle or test to be used in drawing the line between that form of protest which is protected from governmental censure and that which need not be tolerated. Finally, an attempt will be made to draw that line."

Moss, Harold G. "Satire and Travesty in Fielding's the Grub-Street Opera." *Theatre Survey*, 15:38–50, May 1974. **1M460**

By the use of thinly disguised satire on the administration of Sir Robert Walpole in his *Grub-Street Opera*, Henry Fielding hoped to avoid the suppression of his work that had befallen John Gay's *Polly* a few years earlier. But Fielding's opera was nonetheless mysteriously withheld from the stage in 1731 and Fielding began to write progressively bitter political satire which eventually resulted in the passage of the Theatre Licensing Act of 1737. The *Craftsman* pamphleteering controversy during this period further reflected the sensitivity of Walpole to criticism.

Moss, John E. "The Crisis of Security." *Bulletin of the Atomic Scientists*, 17:8–11, 35, January 1961. **1M461**
The chairman of the Special Government Information Subcommittee of the House Committee on Government Operations describes the growing trend of secrecy in the executive branch of government, particularly in the military establishment. Secrecy is often used as a shield for incompetence, and, in fact, becomes an impediment to progress. He calls for citizens to demand justification for secrecy, for the vast Washington bureaucracy to reexamine both procedures and policies that keep information from the people.

Moss, Norman. "The Narrow Confines of British Crime Reporting." *Reporter*, 37(9):29–31, 30 November 1967. **1M462**
"In reporting crime and court news, British papers operate within limits so narrow that they make the restraints on the American press, police, and legal profession proposed last year by a special panel of the American Bar Association seem mild indeed." References are made to the *London Daily Mirror* (Bolam) case of 1949 and other contempt cases against the British press.

Moss, Robert. "The Supreme Court, Artistic Freedom and the Movies: No, Dear Critic, Sex Is Not the Answer." *Film Heritage*, 10:37–42, Fall 1974. **1M463**
The author hopes that "the forces of reaction are turned back and filmmakers win their battle for sexual freedom—in order that they may then get on to more important things." Sexual frankness and profanity—two targets of censorship—are only two dimensions of cinematic art and perhaps the least important two.

Moss, Sidney P. *Poe's Major Crisis: His Libel Suit and New York's Literary World*. Durham, N.C., Duke University Press, 1970, 238p. **1M464**
A collection of documents relating to Poe's libel suit against the owners of the *New York Mirror*, and the ensuing controversy that contributed to the shortening of his life. The

documents reveal the sensitivity of Poe to criticism, the literary coteries that were formed to attack and defend the man, and the defamatory techniques employed by editors.

Motion Picture Association of America. *How the Public Has Accepted the Motion Picture Industry's New Code and Rating Program*. New York, The Association, 1969, 24p. **1M465**
A selection of favorable comments from national religious and civic organizations and reprints from newspaper and magazine articles.

———. *The Motion Picture Code and Rating Program; a System of Self-Regulation*. New York, The Association [1968]. 16p. **1M466**
An audience suitability rating system, devised by the motion picture industry went into effect 1 November 1968. Under the system films are given one of three ratings: "G" (general audiences), "M" (mature audiences), "R" (restricted to persons sixteen or over, unless accompanied by parent), and "X" (person under sixteen not admitted). The purpose of the system is to prevent children from seeing films that might be harmful, while preserving the right of adults to enjoy adult entertainment.

Moudry, Mary T. "Newsmen's Privilege Protects People's Access." *Grassroots Editor*, 13(2):23–24, 28, March–April 1972. **1M467**
A discussion of the three cases on newsmen's privilege under consideration by the U.S. Supreme Court: Earl Caldwell, Paul Pappas, and Paul Branzburg, together with arguments for privilege, particularly because it affects the ability of minority and radical groups to gain access to the press by assuring them that their confidences will be protected.

"Movie Censorship Standards Under the First Amendment." *Publishing, Entertainment, Advertising and Allied Fields Law Quarterly*, 2:129–37, June 1962. (Reprinted from *DePaul Law Review*, Autumn–Winter 1959) **1M468**
A review of Supreme Court cases involving censorship of motion pictures suggests that no adequate standard for assessing obscenity exists. The author believes that the only type of movie that can be banned under existing laws is one which displays obscene or pornographic acts.

Mowbray, A. Q. "Free Press & Fancy Packages." *Nation*, 205:621–23, 11 December 1967. (Reprinted in David G. Clark and Earl R. Hutchison, *eds.*, *Mass Media and the Law*, pp. 312–19) **1M469**
The author of a book on truth in packaging describes how the food lobby managed to arrange "a near blackout of information" about the Fair Packaging and Labeling Act before

Congress, resulting in a watered-down law that satisfied objections from the industry. "Although much lip service is paid in this country to the principle of an informed electorate, it seems clear that to an unhealthy degree the electorate depends for its information upon those who have a vested interest in influencing their judgments."

[Moye, Robert J. *et al.*] "The American Bar Association Suggests an Answer to the 'Fair Trial–Free Press' Dilemma." *Duke Law Journal*, 1967:593–631, 1967. **1M470**
"In order to secure a 'fair trial' the American Bar Association *Standards* place the major burden of nondisclosure on the legal profession and the law enforcement officials. . . . Whatever the desirability of any particular remedy may be, it would seem that the tide is turning toward compulsory nondisclosure in some form. Should this result without a prior exhaustion of the possibilities of liberalized trial and appellate remedies and self-restraint by both press and bar, a great disservice will have been done to society. . . . While the threat of contempt action may stimulate press reform, it is suggested that trial, appellate, and professional ethical standards first be thoroughly tested before resorting to the use of contempt."

Moyers, Bill D. "Press or Government: Who's Telling the Truth?" *Television Quarterly*, 7(3):17–31, Summer 1968. **1M471**
Both the press and government suffer from a "credibility gap." The author suggests several ways that the press can improve its image: (1) act with the same candor about itself as it expects of public officials; (2) either live apart from alliances with officialdom or be prepared to give up that illusion; (3) make accuracy the first rule in reporting; and (4) establish basic rules for the use of "backgrounders" and respect those rules.

———, Mike Gravel, and Gordon L. Shull. "The People's Right to Know." *Social Action*, 38(9):3–29, May 1972. **1M472**
Content: The Right and the Need to Know: An Interview with Bill Moyers. The Secrecy System by Senator Mike Gravel. The Necessity and Perils of Secrecy by Gordon L. Shull.

Mphahlele, Ezekiel. "Censorship in South Africa." *Censorship Today*, 2(4):4–16, August–September 1969. (Reprinted in his *Voices in the Whirlwind* . . . . New York, Hill & Wang, 1972, pp. 199–215) **1M473**
"An exiled African novelist writes sadly of a homeland where free speech is dying and the

inquiring mind is banned." Suppression takes place under the Suppression of Communism Act, the Prisons Act (*Rand Daily Mail* case), the Publications and Entertainment Act, the Customs Act, and other acts of Parliament.

Muchnik, Melvyn M. "Responsibility and Survival: Free Expression and Political Broadcasting on Public Radio and Television Stations." In *Free Speech Yearbook*, *1973*. New York, Speech Communication Association, 1974, pp. 38–50.   **1M474**
"This article seeks to identify the mission of public broadcasting with respect to political coverage, the history and regulations which both support and impinge on this mission, and the assault on public broadcasting as a result of attempts to fulfill its promise to enlighten the electorate."

Mueller, Rebecca S. "Intellectual Freedom." In *The Bowker Annual of Library and Book Trade Information*, *1976*. New York, Bowker, 1976. pp. 90–94.   **1M475**
In this review of the work of the Intellectual Freedom Committee of the American Library Association are reports of censorship incidents, ties with outside agencies with common interests, libraries and privacy, the Committee and legislation, and the work of the Intellectual Freedom Foundation.

Muhlen, Norbert. "Comic Books and Other Horrors: Prep School for Totalitarian Society?" *Commentary*, 68:80–87, January 1949.   **1M476**
"This education to violence, while hardly presenting the 'clear and present danger' of causing juvenile crime waves, breaks the ground for a future criminal society. Individual insecurity and social anxiety, the common roots of both the murder trend in entertainment and increasing juvenile delinquency, can lead to brute force and terror as a normal basis for society where today it is only an abnormal individual behavior pattern. If that is the case, the comic books may be helping to educate a whole generation for an authoritarian rather than a democratic society."

Mullally, Donald P. "The Fairness Doctrine: Benefits and Costs." *Public Opinion Quarterly*, 33:577–82, Winter 1969.   **1M477**
An examination of the potential consequences of the fairness rules adopted by the Federal Communications Commission in 1967 and upheld by the U.S. Supreme Court. The author concludes: "(1) We *are* restricting the freedom of the broadcaster when we burden him with an obligation triggered by his statement or the statement he allows to be broadcast; (2) if we do

not place this burden on him, we allow the broadcaster himself to restrict the freedom of others to express their opinion, and on an entirely arbitrary basis."

―――. *A Legislative*, *Administrative*, *and Judicial History of the Fairness Doctrine in Television and Radio Broadcasting*. East Lansing, Mich., Michigan State University, 1968. 328p. (Ph.D. dissertation, University Microfilms, no. 68-17,114)   **1M478**
Content: A Definition of the Fairness Doctrine. The Historical Development of Free Speech Concepts in the Early Days of Broadcasting. The Mayflower Decision, Chain Broadcasting Regulations and Other Decisions of the Period, 1941–49. Promulgation of the Fairness Doctrine and a Paragraph-by-Paragraph Examination of the Statement. Developments of the Doctrine, 1950–60. Developments in "Fairness," 1960–68. The Future of the Fairness Doctrine.

[Mullaly, John.] *Suppression of the Metropolitan Record in St. Louis. By Order of General Rosecrans. Letter to the Editor.* [New York? Editor and Publisher of the Record, 1864?] 12p.   **1M479**
General Rosecrans, in Special Order no. 84, issued from his headquarters in St. Louis, 26 March 1864, ordered the ban and seizure of the 26 March issue of this New York paper. The *Metropolitan Record*, a Catholic family paper, opposed conscription.

Mullen, John C. "*Troman v. Wood*: A Landmark Libel Decision in Illinois." *Chicago Bar Record*, 58:86–88+, September–October 1976.   **1M480**
In response to the U.S. Supreme Court decision (*Gertz v. Robert Welch, Inc.*, 1974) which allowed each state to choose its own standard for libel within conditional boundaries, the Illinois Supreme Court has adopted a negligence standard in libel cases involving statements made against private citizens who are not public officials or public figures.

Müller, Robert. "Nahum Tate's 'Richard II' and Censorship During the Exclusion Bill Crisis in England." *Salzburg Studies in English Literature*, 26:40–51, 1975.   **1M481**
The writer contends that the play was banned by the Lord Chamberlain for political reasons resulting from the curious situation surrounding the Exclusion Bill Crisis.

Mulvihill, Dennis J. "*Caldwell v. United States*: The Newsman's Constitutional Privilege." *University of Pittsburgh Law Review*, 32:406–15, Spring 1971. **1M482**
"This Note will analyze the rationale of *Caldwell* (*Caldwell v. United States*, 434 F.2d 1081 [9th Cir. 1970]), in light of prior case law, and discuss the scope and validity of the decision as it affects the average newsman seeking to protect his source."

"Municipal Transit District's Refusal to Accept Anti-War Advertisements While Permitting Commercial and Election-Related Advertising Violates First Amendment." *Harvard Law Review*, 82:1379–91, April 1969. **1M483**
Re: *Wirta v. Alameda-Contra Costa Transit District*, 434 P.2d 982, 64 Cal. Rptr. 430 (1967).

Munneke, Allen S. "You (Expletive Deleted) Mary." *English Journal*, 64(4):69–71, April 1975.   **1M484**
A high school English teacher discusses his experience with freedom of expression (or lack of it) in a student composition class.

Munro, Paul. "Official Secrecy and Freedom of Information." *Australian Academic and Research Libraries*, 2:101–8, September 1971.   **1M485**
The author considers Australia's law on release of official documents and the effect the regulations have on library access. While the availability of published matter has greatly improved in recent years, access to unpublished documents is unsatisfactory. "The relative apathy in Australia to reforms in this area of administrative law and practice is in stark contrast to developments in overseas democracies. . . . The editor of any Australian newspaper attempting publication, without Government authorization, of official documentation as significant as the Pentagon Papers would find that in addition to injunction restraining further publication he would quite likely be charged with the criminal offense of aiding in a breach of Section 70 of the Commonwealth Crimes Act."

Munro, William B. *A Free Press and a Free People; An Address at the Fiftieth American Convention of the California Newspaper Publishers Association*, *January 22, 1938*. n.p., [1938]. 12p. **1M486**
"It is the newspaper press that has made modern democracy possible." The author, in a radio broadcast, outlines the long struggle for a free press in England and America. Dictatorships, he observes, are formed by deluding the people and this is achieved by control of the press. "Limitations upon the freedom of the newspapers are always preceded by attacks upon the press as an institution. The governmental authorities begin by assailing the press as inimical to the public welfare, or casting aspersions upon its integrity." Hitler blasted the German press for editorials that impeded economic recovery; the Roosevelt government has recently criticized the press for fostering a fear psychology. What is happening in Russia, Germany, and Italy can happen here, if the press is considered a public utility to be regulated by law.

Munter, Robert. *The History of the Irish Newspaper*, *1685–1760*. Cambridge,

England, Cambridge University Press, 1967. 217p. **1M487**
A summary of the Government and Press Prosecutions appears in the appendix (pp. 189–91), and throughout the volume are references to licensing, libel cases, prosecutions of particular newspapers, and restrictions on parliamentary reporting.

Murasky, Donna M. "The Journalist's Privilege: *Branzburg* and Its Aftermath." *Texas Law Review*, 52:829–917, May 1974. **1M488**
"The focus of this article is on the propriety of the present judicially created balance of the public interests promoted by granting a privilege to journalists to protect their confidences and the public interests advanced by compelling disclosure of those confidences." The author concludes that "the Supreme Court in the *Branzburg* cases failed to consider the importance, from a first amendment standpoint, of the content of the information involved, held the press to a stringent and unprecedented standard of proof of chilling effect, and did not articulate with sufficient precision the nature of the state's justification for compelling disclosure."

Murnaghan, Francis D. "From Figment to Fiction to Philosophy—The Requirement of Proof of Damages in Libel Actions." *Catholic University Law Review*, 22:1–38, Fall 1972. **1M489**
The author reviews the conflicting views of William L. Prosser and Laurence H. Eldredge (P336) over damages in libel cases, which resulted in the suspension of efforts by the American Law Institute to bring up to date its pronouncements on the American law of defamation. He attempts to find a workable solution to the dilemma.

Murphy, Andrew P., Jr. *et al.* "Executive Privilege: The Public's Right to Know and the Public Interest." *Federal Bar Journal*, 19:iv–xi, 1–84, January 1959. **1M490**
Content: Introductory Remarks by Andrew P. Murphy, Jr. A Legislator's View of Executive Privilege by John E. Moss. An Executive Branch View of Executive Privilege by Leonard Niederlehner. The Executive Privilege and the People's Right to Know by Thomas C. Hennings, Jr. The Right to Know and Enforcement Problems in a Regulatory Agency (SEC) by Daniel J. McCauley, Jr. A Problem for Press and Bar: A Journalist's View by Clark Mollenhoff. The Public's Right to Know and the Public Interest—A Dilemma Revisited by Conrad D. Philos. Government Operations and the Public's Right to Know by J. R. Wiggins.

Murphy, C. B. "Censorship: Principle and Practice." and ["Replies."] *Bell*, 3:293–301, January 1942; 3:470–75, March 1942. **1M491**
A lawyer, Louis J. Walsh, had attacked Father

S. J. Gosling for his favorable review of Kate O'Brien's *Without My Cloak* in the *Clergy Review* and criticized C. B. Murphy's opposition to Irish censorship which had appeared in the *Bell* for September 1941. The Walsh article appeared in the November 1941 issue of *Irish Rosary*. Walsh had charged the O'Brien novel with flaunting "sexual sin in all its seductive details." In this article Murphy replies to Walsh's charges that hardly anyone in Ireland supports Murphy's case against Irish censorship except "dilettanti, mere poseurs, and literary lap-dogs . . . who claim for their writings and for the stage the abandonment of all the decencies and reticences wisdom of ages have set up." Murphy denies he is opposed to censorship inspired by the Church but only to its "silly" practice of banning everything that is not suitable to all classes of readers. In the March issue of the *Bell* Mr. Walsh replies and Mr. Murphy comments on the reply.

———. "Sex, Censorship, and the Church." *Bell*, 2(6):65–75, September 1941. **1M492**
"When the matter of sex is relevant then the writing that contains it is clean, even though it deals with sex frequently and in full detail." The test of whether a work can be read in the "family circle" is not a Catholic test but a Puritan one. Modern Irish squeamishness about sex is a Victorian hangover, and not native to Ireland; not part of the Gaelic tradition.

Murphy, James T. "Freedom of Speech in the Military." *Suffolk University Law Review*, 9:761–82, Spring 1974. **1M493**
"This Note will discuss the standards adopted by the courts in determining what speech may be legitimately curtailed by the armed forces and will focus on an application of these standards to the various articles of the Uniform Code of Military Justice which purport to restrict free expression."

Murphy, John F. "Knowledge Is Power: Foreign Policy and Information Interchange Among Congress, the Executive Branch, and the Public." *Tulane Law Review*, 49:505–54, March 1975. **1M494**
The author considers the issues of security classification, executive privilege claims with respect to Congress, and the availability of criminal sanctions against those who disclose classified information, advancing proposals which "may serve to increase the flow of meaningful information from the executive branch to the public and Congress," which should "result in a more informed and democratic, as well as a more effective, foreign policy."

Murphy, Patricia. *Pornography on the Local Level*. Columbia, Mo., Freedom of Information Center, School of Journalism, University of Missouri at Columbia, 1973. 7p. (Report no. 315) **1M495**

"The recent U.S. Supreme Court ruling on obscenity has left many citizen groups and media representatives in fear that the courts have once again become the nation's 'sex censor.' They now wonder how effective local laws will be in controlling the production and sale of pornographic works."

Murphy, Paul J. "Pornography." *Homiletic and Pastoral Review*, 67:657–61, May 1967. **1M496**
A priest attacks the lethargy among Catholics—laymen and priests—to the serious problem of pornography. While recognizing that private and public censorship can go to extremes, he believes it is "Christian treachery, if we tolerate a septic sinfulness infecting the body politic and poisoning family life."

Murphy, Paul L. *The Meaning of Freedom of Speech: First Amendment Freedoms from Wilson to FDR*. Westport, Conn., Greenwood, 1972. 401p. (Contributions to American History, no. 15) **1M497**
An examination of events of the twenties and early thirties, the years between the wars, which began with an extension of wartime restrictions on the press and radical thoughts, and ended in the early thirties with the U.S. Supreme Court redefining and strengthening the First Amendment. The year 1931 is seen as a legal turning point in the area of civil liberties. The action of individuals and organizations, particularly the American Civil Liberties Union, in behalf of freedom of expression—in the press and in the courts—is reported. The author analyzes the general ambivalence of life and the attitude toward freedom during the period.

Murphy, Vernon. "Media and Defamation: The Remedy for Character Assassination." *New York State Bar Journal*, 47:13–17, 45–46, January 1975. **1M498**
The author looks at newspaper libel of public officials as a citizen who supports freedom of the press, as a lawyer who recognizes the necessity of "limited and even absolute privileges extended to witnesses, legislators, judges, pornographers, and others," and as a public official who was a victim of newspaper libel (*Murphy v. Daily News*, 12 N.Y. 2d 1092) and won his case. He challenges the interpretation by the press of the *New York Times v. Sullivan* decision as granting the press a license to defame public officials or any newsworthy individual.

Murphy, Walter F. "Mr. Justice Jackson, Free Speech, and the Judicial Function." *Vanderbilt Law Review*, 12:1019–46, October 1959. **1M499**

"Jackson would have had the Court move cautiously, exercising a maximum of self-restraint in those areas where elected officials had to balance competing rights of individuals or groups. But where the judiciary possessed primary responsibility for decision, i.e., where he visualized the conflict as between liberty and authority, Jackson would have brought to bear all the carefully hoarded powers of the Court as well as his own plentiful supply of sarcasm to drive government officials off the sacred preserve. His was the strident voice of the judicial realist."

Murphy, William P. "Prior Restraint Doctrine in the Supreme Court: A Reevaluation." *Notre Dame Lawyer*, 51:898–918, July 1976.   **1M500**
"It is the purpose of this article to scrutinize the Court's use of the prior restraint doctrine and to propose a more realistic definition of a prior restraint—one that will consistently include subsequent-in-form restraints which have a substantial chilling effect on free expression, and exclude prior-in-form restraints which are not accompanied by such an inhibitive effect."

Murray, David. "Sense and Censorship." *Edge*, 2:6–15, Spring 1964.   **1M501**
The author considers the validity of statements commonly made about censorship of films, with special attention to the Canadian scene: censorship is undemocratic; censorship can spare viewer from the unpleasant; there is no evidence of the harmful effect of watching sex films; there is a greater impact of film than of the printed word; there is a difference in showing between the sophisticated city and the less sophisticated provinces; sadistic violence should be censored even if sex is not; and literary works must be given wide license.

Murray, George. *The Press and the Public: The Story of the British Press Council*. Foreword by Howard R. Long. Carbondale, Ill., Southern Illinois University Press, 1972. 243p.   **1M502**
A prominent British journalist presents an insider's view of the British Press Council, established in 1953 at the recommendation of the Royal Commission on the Press, to curb misuse of press freedom and power and to defend the press when it deserved to be defended. Its main duty has been to serve as a court of honor, acting independently of either government or the press. The author traces the development of the Council from its conception in "a welter of confused issues and contending interests," through its adolescence in the 1950s, to its coming-of-age during the 1960s.

Murray, J. Edward. *The Editor's Right to Decide*. Tucson, Ariz., University of Arizona Press, 1969. 19p. (John Peter Zenger Award Lectures)   **1M503**
A principal spokesman for the nation's press in the press–bar controversy and in the creation of the Freedom of Information Act defends the press against the critics. Spiro Agnew's main complaint is that the press is too liberal and does not reflect the "silent majority"; at the opposite end are the critics who believe the press has ignored the views of minorities and stifled dissent. The greatest threat posed by Mr. Agnew, the author believes, is the implied threat of licensing, which was eliminated in America even before the First Amendment. He attacks the new concept of forced access to the newspaper press, following the fairness doctrine of broadcasting, which would replace the judgment of the editor with that of the courts, the legislature, and the politicians—would "put the government in the saddle." The concept has attracted strange bedfellows—Mr. Agnew who sees it as insuring more good news; Professor Barron who believes it will insure more space for minority points of view. "The editor, fallible as he is, can still do his job better than anyone else in a free society. And he cannot be compelled by judges, lawyers, policemen, or politicians without doing more damage than good."

——. "The Free Press and the Watergate Scandal: Credibility Has Been Enhanced." *Grassroots Editor*, 14(4):16–17, July–August 1973.   **1M504**
In remarks made at a meeting of the American Society of Newspaper Editors, the associate editor of the *Detroit Free Press*, stated that he believed that the general credibility of the nation's press has been enhanced by its behavior in the Watergate affair.

——. "Pretrial Reporting: Hardly One of the *Real* Obstacles to Fair Trial." *Bulletin of the American Society of Newspaper Editors*, 514:9–11, December 1967.   **1M505**
"The more I study the Reardon Report [on fair trial and free press] the more I see it as a massive, misdirected effort to solve a minor, undefined problem by attacking it in the wrong places."

——. "The Reardon Press Formula; Threat to Our Open Society." *Journalism Education*, 22(4):1–7, Fall 1967.   **1M506**
Because the conflict between free press and fair trial is a conflict in social values, the goal of maintaining both cannot be realized if either the press or the bar insists on absolutes for its own side. "We must be satisfied with the *virtual* security of defendants' rights and with the *virtual* freedom of the press." The author makes six suggestions that the journalist can act upon to aid equal justice.

——. "The Reardon Report." *Nieman Reports*, 21(4):16–19, December 1967.   **1M507**

Comments on the American Bar Association's report on free press v. fair trial, by the chairman of the Freedom of Information and Press–Bar Committee of the American Society of Newspaper Editors.

Murray, J. Edward *et al.* "Caldwell Aftermath: A National Shield Law?" *Bulletin of the American Society of Newspaper Editors*, 562:12–15, September 1972.   **1M508**
Four views on a national shield law.

Murray, John. *Report of the Trial of Mr. John Murray, in the Court of King's Bench, at Westminster-Hall, the 19th December, 1829, on an Indictment for a Libel on Messrs. Lecesne and Escoffery of Jamaica*. London, Bagster and Thoms, 1830. 46p.   **1M509**
The publisher, John Murray, was brought to trail for libel by two Negro Jamaican merchants who objected to statements in the book, *The Annals of Jamaica*. Murray offered to withdraw the offending book and, though convicted by the court, was fined only one shilling.

Murray, Kathleen. *Moves to Legalize Drug Ads*. Columbia, Mo., Freedom of Information Center, School of Journalism, University of Missouri at Columbia, 1976. 8p. (Report no. 352)   **1M510**
"The once irreconcilable conflict between consumer groups and pharmaceutical associations over drug advertising bans, is being resolved in the courts. Almost without exception judges are striking down the bans, in favor of advancing a more informed public."

Murray, Marshall H. "The Contempt Power in Montana: A Cloud on Freedom of the Press." *Montana Law Review*, 18:68–98, Fall 1956.   **1M511**
"This paper will outline the current federal view of contempt by publication and explore the Montana decisions on the subject." The author believes that the Montana cases "while in harmony with federal law at the time they were rendered, would, if followed today, be struck down as unconstitutional."

Murray, Michael D. "J. B. Stoner and Free Speech: How Free Is 'Free'?" *Western Speech*, 38:18–24, Winter 1974.   **1M512**
A decision of the Federal Communications Commission upheld the right of a U.S. Senate aspirant from Georgia, J. B. Stoner, to use language in his radio ads that was flagrantly offensive to blacks. "If there is to be free speech, it must be free for speech that we abhor and hate as well as for speech that we find tolerable or congenial." The American Civil Liberties Union supported the Commissions' findings and the First Amendment right of any

citizen, regardless of any personal disdain for his position. The candidate lost the election.

Murray, William. "The Porn Capital of America." *New York Times Magazine*, 3 January 1971, sect. 6, pp. 20–25. **1M513**
An account of the making and selling of pornography in San Francisco and the movement led by the president of the Board of Supervisors to curb the booming industry. "The reform efforts have failed, primarily because the courts have consistently championed freedom. . . . The legal maneuverings have prevented almost all cases from even reaching the trial stage. . . . Whatever the courts may eventually rule in the case of dirty movies, San Francisco seems certain to survive as the country's most tolerant metropolis or, if you wish, porn capital."

Murrell, Jesse L. "The Greater Cincinnati Committee on Evaluation of Comic Books." In Otto N. Larsen, *ed.*, *Violence and the Mass Media*, New York, Harper & Row, 1968, pp. 182–89. **1M514**
An account of the organization of the Committee and how it works; the formulation of evaluation criteria; and a report on what other communities and agencies are doing to rate comic books.

Murty, B. S. *Propaganda and World Public Order: The Legal Regulation of the Ideological Instrument of Coercion*. New Haven, Conn., Yale University Press, 1968. 310p. **1M515**
"Concern over the effect of propaganda on international peace has spurred discussion in various international forums, but attempts to evolve a pattern of regulation by treaty have met with little success. . . . Mr. Murty has employed a policy-oriented jurisprudential approach to seek solutions to the tangled problems of propaganda regulation, bringing to bear the allied disciplines of psychology, communications research, and international politics. New policies, he suggests, must aim at promoting freedom of information and maintaining minimum world public order, and he emphasizes the present and potential role of the United Nations in regulating the use of propaganda."

Musiker, R. "Some Thoughts on Censorship: A Librarian's Point of View." *Communications in Africa*, 1(2):17–19, 1972. **1M516**

The deputy librarian of Rhodes University describes the rigid censorship existing in South Africa which had led to the ban of some 40,000 books between 1956 and 1970 and poses serious problems for librarians trying to keep abreast of the banning. The crux of the problem is that "a mature individual in a civilized society should have the right to make his own decisions" as to what books he wishes to read.

Muskie, Edmund S. "Government Secrecy Control Act of 1975." *Congressional Record*, 121:S16723–24, 25 September 1975. **1M517**
A speech in the U.S. Senate in behalf of himself and Senator Javits, supporting Senate Bill 2420 designed to curb government secrecy.

Musson, A. E. "Parliament and the Press: An Historical Survey." *Parliamentary Affairs*, 9:151–59, Spring 1956; 9:277–88, Summer 1956; 9:404–17, Autumn 1956. **1M518**
"Our history is of a gradually broadening freedom: freedom from monarchical absolutism, freedom from aristocratic, oligarchic, and plutocratic government, freedom from arbitrary arrest, freedom of speech, of religion, and of the press. The history of the press fits into the general trend: our modern freedom of the press has grown up with our modern parliamentary democracy, each contributing to the growth of the other. . . . The position of a capitalist press in a parliamentary democracy, especially in a State which is half Socialist, is a very delicate one. It is best observed against the historical development of the freedom of the press over the preceding centuries." The author discusses these developments from the earliest controls of printing in Tudor England to the recommendations of the Royal Commission on the Press made in 1949 and the establishment of the Press Council in 1953.

Myers, Charles. "Libel and Public Figures: Extension of the Rule of *New York Times Co. v. Sullivan*." *University of Missouri at Kansas City Law Review*, 36:132–50, Winter 1968. **1M519**
"It would now seem that through its most recent decisions [*Curtis Publishing Co. v. Butts* and *Associated Press v. Walker* (1967)], the [Supreme] Court has come very close to applying a 'public theory of speech' as espoused earlier by Dr. Meiklejohn. Although he would have insisted on an absolute freedom of expression as regards matters in the public interest, the Court, at this point, speaks of a qualified privilege of actual malice."

Myers, James S. "A Public Right of Access to the Broadcast Media: Its Present and Future State After Columbia Broadcasting System, Inc. v. Democratic National Committee." *South Dakota Law Review*, 19:167–206, Winter 1974. **1M520**
"A public right of access to the mass media has been advanced as a practical and constitutional necessity for the protection of the public's right to free expression. . . . As will be seen, some progress toward access to the media has been achieved through the courts, especially in the last half decade." But proponents of a right of access received a setback in the decision, *Columbia Broadcasting System, Inc. v. Democratic National Committee* (1973), denying right of access to the broadcast media for editorial advertising. "The implications of this decision will be investigated in this comment, as will the general area of access to the broadcast media."

Myers, John G. "Legislative Controls and Freedom of Speech: The Case of Commercial Advertising." *Public Affairs Report*, 13:11–51, August 1972. **1M521**
"This paper considers the question: How does one bring a measure of control on the *content* of speech (in this case, advertising or 'commercial speech') without at the same time abrogating the free speech provisions of the First Amendment."

Myers, Joseph S., *comp*. *The Journalistic Code of Ethics: A Collection of Codes, Creeds, and Suggestions for the Guidance of Editors and Publishers*. Columbus, Ohio State University, 1922. 35p. (*Ohio State University Bulletin, Journalistic Series*, vol. 1, no. 4) **1M522**
Includes the text of state codes from Kansas, Missouri, Ohio, Oregon, and Washington; individual newspaper codes from *Detroit News*, *Dayton Journal*, *New York Globe*, *Sacramento Bee*, *Tampa News*, and the Hearst papers; the code of journalism students, Ohio State University; Walter Williams's Journalist's Code; President Harding's code (*Marion Star*); and statements from William Allen White, Charles A. Dana, George Edward Graham, and Washington Gladden.

N

Nader, Ralph. "Freedom from Information. The Act and the Agencies." *Harvard Civil Rights–Civil Liberties Law Review*, 5:1–15, January 1970. (Also in U.S. Senate. Committee of the Judiciary. *Freedom of Information Act Source Book*, 1974, pp. 411–25) **1N1**
"Although the Freedom of Information Act was intended to compel agency openness, Mr. Nader argues that the agencies are still unresponsive to citizen inquiry; they are, in effect, baronies beyond the law. This disparity between aim and achievement of the Act is discussed in the context of empirical studies led by the author and conducted by, in the poetry of journalism, 'Nader's Raiders.' "—Editor

Nagel, Stuart, Kathleen Reinbolt, and Thomas Eimermann. "Free Press–Fair Trial Controversy: Using Empirical Analysis to Strike a Desirable Balance." *St. Louis University Law Journal*, 20:646–53, 1976. **1N2**
A report of results of a national survey of newspaper editors, police chiefs, prosecuting attorneys, and defense attorneys "to determine for each of several cities how much free press is allowed in terms of the tendency of the newspaper to publish various kinds of information concerning pending criminal cases. One of the main objectives of the study was to establish a free press scale ranging from zero percent for the lowest level of free press in a particular community to 100 percent for the highest level." The survey revealed that 2 percent do not regularly publish name and charge; 13 percent do not regularly publish details of arrest; 36 percent, evidence seized at arrest; 50 percent, criminal records; 64 percent, statements by the accused; 65 percent, witness testimony; 65 percent, test results; 74 percent, editorial opinions on cases; and 77 percent, information on plea negotiations. The questionnaire is reproduced.

————. "A Linear Programming Approach to Problems of Conflicting Legal Values Like Free Press Versus Fair Trial." *Rutgers Journal of Computers and Law*, 4:420–61, 1975. **1N3**

The purpose of the article is to provide some empirical data on the relation between (1) the degree of the free press present in various communities, and (2) the degree of satisfaction expressed by various interested types of persons within those communities, using what is known as a linear programming approach.

Nagy, Alex. *Federal Censorship of Communist Political Propaganda and the First Amendment, 1941–1961*. Madison, Wis., University of Wisconsin, 1973. 394p. (Ph.D. dissertation, University Microfilms, no. 74–9193) **1N4**
"This study has been an effort to trace U.S. suppression of Communist political propaganda from abroad during 1941–1961. A major part of the study focused on the Post Office Department and the Bureau of Customs since these two agencies were responsible for the censorship operations at various times in varying degrees. The attitude of Congress toward Communist propaganda and its perception of the harmful effects of propaganda also were investigated. Efforts were made to assess the role of the State Department and the Justice Department in policy considerations involving the suppression of Communist propaganda."

Nahmod, Sheldon H. "First Amendment Protection for Learning and Teaching: The Scope of Judicial Review." *Wayne Law Review*, 18:1479–1514, September 1972. **1N5**
"It has been seen that cases upholding students' first amendment rights indicate that student judgments as to the importance of particular kinds of expression, in absence of disruption or interference, override board determinations that such expression will have a deleterious educational effect. An important result of such decisions is that the board has the burden of justifying any prohibitions of student expression. Similarly, a school board must justify its decision to prohibit a teacher from assigning controversial literature or subjects which are relevant to the teacher's curriculum assignment and are reasonably balanced."

Nam, Sunwoo. *A Comparative Study of*

Freedom of the Press in Korea, Taiwan and the Philippines in the 1960s. Madison, Wis., University of Wisconsin, 1969. 214p. (Ph.D. dissertation, University Microfilms, no. 70–3641) **1N6**
"It was found, through rearrangement of both primary sources, mostly statutes, and secondary materials along [nine] categories, that the Philippines had a free press, quite comparable to the Anglo-American model, and Taiwan a controlled press with Korea in between but leaning toward the Taiwan side."

————, and Inwhan Oh. *Freedom of the Press As a Function of Subsystem Autonomy and As an Antithesis of Development*. n.p., The Authors, 1973. 20p. (ED 84,555) **1N7**
"The essential nature of political structures of developing nations appears to generate an opposition to criticism. Since most of the developing nations see no alternative but to regard freedom of the press as an antithesis to industrial development, many such nations suppress press freedom. The relationship between developmental efforts and curtailment of press freedom can be observed in the degree of subsystem autonomy rather than the economic indices." Paper presented at the annual meeting of the Association for Education in Journalism, Fort Collins, Colo., August 1973.

Namurois, Albert. "Broadcasting and Privacy: Notes on the Invasion of Privacy by the Broadcasting Media and Its Limits." *EBU Review* (European Broadcasting Union), 116B:51–59, July 1969; 117B:50–56, September 1969. **1N8**
Content: Protection of the Individual's "Psychological Personality." Protection of the Personality in Relation to External Manifestations of the Person. Liability of Broadcasting Organizations. The Need for a Code of Standards, Statutory and Otherwise.

Nannes, Michael E. "Gag Order Protection for Civil Trials." *Georgetown*

"Although few civil trials present a threat of prejudicial publicity sufficient to justify gag orders, a proper procedure must be provided for accommodating competing interests when a conflict cannot be avoided. The court must assure that all interested parties are given the opportunity to present their particular concerns. The constitutional right to a fair trial, to freedom of expression, and to freedom of the press will be paramount, but the court should also consider the business and personal interests of litigants and third parties."

Nash, Frank E. "The Application of the Law of Libel and Slander to Radio Broadcasting." *Oregon Law Review*, 17:307–13, June 1938. **1N10**
The author concludes that "in the interest of freedom of discussion, we should not compel the broadcaster to stand as an insurer of a risk for which he is not responsible and over which he has no control. If he must assume the risk, personal interest would force him to deny the public that which is salutary, and perhaps even vital, to government by the people."

Nassau Broadcasting Co. *Americans . . . One of Your Freedoms Is Missing!* Princeton, N.J., Nassau Broadcasting Co., 1974. 100p. **1N11**
"There are two standards of Communications in the United States: the free press and the encumbered, restricted electronic press. While the First Amendment presumably guarantees free speech, Congress and the Federal Communications Commission have imposed both laws and regulations which prevent the American public from being informed by broadcasters in the same fashion as the free press. . . . WHWH Princeton and WPST Trenton decided to create a practical test of the Equal Time and Fairness Doctrine provision to demonstrate that it is coercive, inhibiting, grossly one-sided, impractical, and costly." This is a documentary record of the test.

Nassau County Library Association. ["Intellectual Freedom."] *Odds and Bookends (NCLA)*, Summer 1966. 14p. **1N12**
Content: Association's Statement on Intellectual Freedom. Censorship in New York today by Joseph Covino. The Courage to Do Either by Martha Boaz. Censorship in the Library by Walter W. Curley. Historians Bid U.S. Halt Suit on Book by Harry Gilroy (Sylvester K. Stevens's *Pennsylvania–Birthplace of a Nation*).

Nathan, Manfred. *The Law of Defamation (Libel and Slander) in South Africa.* Johannesburg, South Africa, Hortors, 1933. 398p. **1N13**
A comprehensive treatise on the law of defamation in South Africa, arranged under headings: Nature of Defamation, Defences, Law of Procedure, and Injuries Other Than Defamation.

National Ad Hoc Committee Against Censorship. *Proceedings of the December 9, 1975 Censorship Conference.* New York, The Committee, 1976. 52p. Processed. **1N14**
Content: Censoring "Obscenity" by Franklyn S. Haiman. Textbook Censorship: Role Play of Open School Board Meeting. Reading by Melvyn Douglas from "Inherit the Wind" to Commemorate the 50th Anniversary of the Scopes Trial. Government Secrecy—Two Views and a Question Period by Morton H. Halperin and Frank N. Trager. Closing Remarks by William F. Fore, presiding. The National Ad Hoc Committee Against Censorship: What, Why, How, Who? The organization's name was changed in 1976 to the National Coalition Against Censorship.

National Association of Broadcasters. Code Authority Office. *Broadcast Self-Regulation: Radio Code, Television Code, Guidelines and Interpretation.* Washington, D.C., NAB, 1971. Loose-leaf binder. **1N15**

———. *Code News.* Washington, D.C., The Code Authority, 1968–date. Monthly. **1N16**
A reporting of news with respect to regulations and interpretation of the NABC Code, activities of the Code Review Board, and compliance by stations.

———. *Some Thing of Value.* [New York, The Code Authority, 1967.] 28p. **1N17**
A brochure containing comments on the issue of self-regulation in general and the NAB Radio and Television Codes in particular, made by leaders in various walks of life.

National Association of Broadcasters. Television Code Review Board. *Report.* Washington, D.C., The Board, 1952/53–date. Annual. **1N18**

National Association of Educational Broadcasters. *CBS and Congress: "The Selling of the Pentagon" Papers. . . .* Washington, D.C., National Association of Educational Broadcasters in Cooperation with the Ohio State University under the auspices of the EBR Editorial Board, 1971. 144p. (A special issue of the *Educational Broadcasting Review*, Winter 1971/72) **1N19**
Publication of the documents relating to the Congressional investigation of the Columbia Broadcasting System documentary, *Selling of the Pentagon*, with an introduction by Jerome Barron. Chapter 1 contains letters and official statements; chapter 2, Committee Reports; chapter 3, background and commentary, including articles by Tom Wicker, William J. Buckley, Jr.; chapter 4, remarks from the floor of the House of Representatives.

National Association of Manufacturers of the United States. *Throttling the Nation's Press.* New York, NAM, 1912. 58p. (Booklet no. 31) **1N20**
"How the arch grafters of the allied printing trades, the Typographical Union, propose to acquire complete newspaper control, as shown in the stranglehold it now has on the papers of New York City."

National Citizens Committee for Broadcasting. [*Violence on Television.*] Washington, D.C., The Committee, 1976. 4p. **1N21**
A television monitoring study conducted during a twelve-week period, indicating names of advertisers who sponsored the most violent programs on prime time television and rating the level of violence on prime time network programs. The Committee also issues a periodic newsletter, *Media Watch*, reporting on the movement to reform violence on television and indicating how members can apply public pressure on the networks and program sponsors. Former FCC commissioner Nicholas Johnson, is chairman.

National Committee on Federal Legislation for Birth Control, Inc. *A New Day Dawns for Birth Control; Summary of Seven Years Which Led to Legalization and Cleared the Way for an Epoch-making Advance.* New York, The Committee, 1937. 47p. **1N22**
The final report of the committee founded by Margaret Sanger to lobby for birth control legislation. With the U.S. Supreme Court decision in *United States v. One Package* (1936), the goal of the committee was met without recourse to Congress, and the committee was disbanded.

National Council for Civil Liberties. *Against Censorship.* London, The Council, 1972. 47p. **1N23**
"This pamphlet is about censorship and the law. It assumes that freedom of expression is desirable in itself and that limitations on freedom are potentially more harmful than any benefit likely to accrue. But while it is the NCCL's policy to secure the abolition of virtually all existing constraints, we have concentrated on the defects in the law which has further deteriorated as a result of recent judgments—and on some of the more inane suggestions to fall off the anti-pornographic bandwagon"—Tony Smythe in the introduction. Following a chronology of the development of the law of obscenity, the pamphlet deals with three recent cases in the area of obscenity: *Oz*, *IT* (International Times), and *Director of Public Prosecutions v. Whyte.* There follows: Censorship and the Limits of Permission, an extract from a lecture by Jonathan Miller; proposals for strengthening the obscen-

ity laws coming from the Society of Conservative Lawyers and the Longford Commission; and the NCCL Case for Reform by Alan Burns, which presents findings and recommendations of The Arts Council Working Party (Great Britain), and the U.S. Commission on Obscenity and Pornography.

—————. *"Non-Flam" Films: Some Observations on the proposed new Home Office regulations relating to non-inflammable films—together with the substance of a correspondence reprinted from "The Manchester Guardian."* London, The NCCL, [1935]. 19p. **1N24**
The Home Office proposal would extend the 1909 fire safety regulations to non-flammable films. This would, in effect, provide a basis for film censorship, unrelated to the threat of fire. Text of the Cinematograph Act of 1909 is included.

National Council for Civil Liberties and the Defence of Literature and the Arts Society. *The Arts and Censorship. A Gala Evening Concerning Depravity and Corruption.* [London, The Society, 1968?] 40p. **1N25**
A lavish souvenir program of a "gala entertainment" of music, poetry, film, art, and essays, contributed by prominent artists for the benefit of the two sponsoring societies. The program includes an essay on censorship by Stuart Hood, chairman of the Defence of Literature and Arts Society; a report of recent censorship activities by Tony Smythe, secretary of the National Council for Civil Liberties; a humorous poem, *lessons fr boys & girls* by Alexander Trocchi; a "dramaticule," *Come and Go* by Samuel Beckett; and numerous appropriate advertisements.

National Council of College Publications Advisors. *Student Press in America Archives, Fall–Winter 1973–74.* Terre Haute, Ind., The National Council, 1973. 41p. (ED 85,704) **1N26**
A collection of 100 entries providing information on incidents involving censorship of campus newspapers—suspension of the paper, ousting of the editor, and charges of libel or obscenity. Sources of information about each episode is provided.

National Council of Teachers of English. "NCTE Resolutions on Censorship." *English Journal*, 63(2):3-page insert, "For the Members." **1N27**
Two major resolutions on censorship were approved at the annual business meeting of the Council in June 1973. The first called for an exploration of steps to provide specific help in censorship incidents—and to inform member-

ship of basic issues and actions on freedom to read. The second resolution called for development of information and guidelines for teachers and school districts to use in making wise choice of materials.

—————. *The Right to Read: An Open Letter to the Citizens of Our Country from the National Council of Teachers of English.* Champaign, Ill., NCTE, 1962. 7p. (ED 29,864) **1N28**
"To preserve the unity of Western thought and culture, American citizens who care about the improvement of education are urged to join teachers, librarians, administrators, boards of trustees, and professional and scholarly organizations in supporting the students' right to read."

—————. *The Students' Right to Read.* Urbana, Ill., The Council, 1972. 24p. **1N29**
A revised edition of an earlier (1962) statement, including an introduction by Kenneth L. Donelson, which recounts incidents of censorship in the schools of classics, modern works of adult literature, and works written especially for young people.

—————. Committee to Report on Case Studies of Censorship. *Meeting Censorship in the School: A Series of Case Studies.* Champaign, Ill., The Council, 1967. 54p. **1N30**
Nine case studies are presented as examples of objections made by individuals to certain books in English classrooms and libraries. For each case information is provided, anonymously, on the community, the school, the nature of the complaint, and how the matter was resolved. Case I, Paperbacks; Case II, *A Pictorial History of the Negro in America* and *The Negro Heritage Library;* Case III, *The Catcher in the Rye;* Cases IV and V, *To Kill a Mockingbird;* Case VI, *The Good Earth;* Case VII, *1984;* Case VIII, *The Bedford Incident;* Case IX, Literature in Classroom and Library. Appendix: Book Selection Procedure, English Department, Junior and Senior High Schools, Wappingers Central School, Wappingers Falls, N.Y. The sponsoring Committee was headed by John Hove.

National Defense Association. *Brief for Argument for the Repeal of Section 3893, Title XLVI, United States Revised Statutes* (Obscenity Law). [New York, National Defense Association, 1886?] 38p. **1N31**
The law against obscenity (Comstock law) is unnecessary; it is unconstitutional; it is mischievous and dangerous and should be repealed. Included are excerpts from the Boston address of T. B. Wakeman in 1878 in defense of Ezra H. Heywood, convicted under the Comstock law (W16).

National Education Association. Teacher Rights Division. *Inquiry Re-*

port. *Kanawha County, West Virginia. A Textbook Study in Cultural Conflict.* Washington, D.C., The NEA, 1975. 87p. **1N32**
At the request of a local teachers organization, the Teacher Rights Division of the National Education Association conducted an investigation of all facets of the textbook controversy of Kanawha County, W.Va. This report is the result. The investigating panel did not attempt to evaluate the textbooks in the dispute nor mediate the problem which had divided the community. The purpose of the report was "to analyze the differences that have divided [the citizens of Kanawha County] and to suggest alternative courses of action—and the probable consequences of each alternative—that might be considered by the citizens themselves . . . in the effort to reach some eventual settlement of these differences."

National Federation for Decency. *Newsletter.* Tupelo, Miss., The Federation, 1977–date. Monthly. **1N33**
The Federation was formed "to promote decency in our American society based on the Judeo-Christian ethic." Its major emphasis has been to combat obscenity and violence on television and it has organized a boycott against Sears, Roebuck and Co., which it singled out as a major sponsor of objectionable programs. The organization is headed by the Rev. Donald E. Wildmon.

National Lawyers Guild. *National Lawyers Guild Presents the Case for the Prosecution of "Social Justice" and Charles E. Coughlin under the Espionage Act of 1917.* n.p., The Guild, 1942? 88p. **1N34**
In April 1942 Postmaster General Walker withheld copies of Father Coughlin's paper, *Social Justice*, from the mails upon notification from Attorney General Francis Biddle that the paper had violated the Espionage Act of 1917. Since Pearl Harbor the paper had made "a substantial contribution to a systematic and unscrupulous attack upon the war effort of our nation, both civilian and military," and "reproduces in this country the lines of the enemy propaganda war being waged against this country from abroad." The National Lawyers Guild presents a documented case of the paper's disloyalty and urges the government to prosecute.

The National News Council. *By-Laws and Rules of Procedure.* New York, The Council, 1973. 22p. **1N35**
Includes a statement (section 36) on the role of the Committee on Freedom of the Press and the Grievance Committee, including rules of procedure relating to public and media complaints.

—————. *In the Public Interest. A Report by the National News Council, 1973–1975.* New York, The Council, 1975. 164p. **1N36**

A report on activities during the first two years of the National News Council, an unofficial agency founded to serve the public interest in preserving freedom of communication and advancing accurate and fair reporting of news. The Council acted upon fifty-nine complaints against newspapers, news services, and television networks, upholding five complaints, finding thirty-three unwarranted, and dismissing twenty-one. The report details a Council investigation of President Nixon's charge in 1973 that television networks were responsible for "outrageous, vicious, distorted reporting." The investigation was dropped when the White House failed to cooperate by providing supporting evidence. Included is a Statement on General Ethics arising from cases in which reporters or columnists allegedly were involved in possible conflicts of interest.

————. *NNC Appraises an Appraisal.* Columbia, Mo., Freedom of Information Center, School of Journalism, University of Missouri at Columbia, 1975. 6p. (Report no. 0017; reprinted in *St. Louis Journalism Review*, January 1976, together with Ralph L. Lowenstein's criticism) **1N37**
The National News Council defends the record of its first year of operation against criticism made by Ralph L. Lowenstein in FOI Center Report no. 0015.

————. *Report.* New York, The Council, 1974. 18p. **1N38**
The National News Council was established in August 1973 on recommendation of a study of the Twentieth Century Fund, as a private, nonprofit organization "to serve the public interest in preserving freedom of communication and advancing accurate and fair reporting of news." This is a report of Council actions during the first eight months of its existence. Of the 160 complaints against the news media received, 28 (13 network broadcasts, 8 news syndicates, 3 wire services, 3 newspapers, 1 news magazine) were taken up by the full Council. The report gives brief descriptions of the 28 complaints and the action taken by the Council. The Council regularly issues news releases on its decisions.

————. ₍Report of Action Taken.₎ New York, The Council, 1973–date. Bimonthly. Processed. **1N39**
Report of action taken at the bimonthly meetings of the Council on complaints filed: nature of complaint, response of the news organization, conclusion of the Council.

————. *Report on President Nixon's Charges Against the Television Networks.* New York, The Council, 1974. 15p. Processed. **1N40**
"We believe it is seriously detrimental to the public interest for the President to leave his harsh criticisms of the television networks unsupported by specific details that could then be evaluated objectively by an impartial body." On 26 October 1973 President Nixon at a news conference had charged television networks with "outrageous, vicious, distorted" reporting. The National News Council offered to investigate the charges. Networks agreed to cooperate. The White House refused.

National Political Union. Taxes on Knowledge. Debate in the House of Commons, on the 15th June 1832, on Mr. Edward Lytton Bulwer's Motion "For a Select committee to consider the propriety of establishing a cheap postage on Newspapers and other Publications." With a Comment in the Form of Notes, and the Article from the "Examiner" Newspaper, of Sunday, 17th June 1832. Southwark, England, W. Barnes, 1832. 48p. **1N41**
One of the objects of the Union was "to obtain the abolition of all taxes on knowledge, and to assist in the diffusion of sound moral and political information."

National School Boards Association. *School Board Policies on Academic Freedom. Educational Policy Development Kit.* Waterford, Conn., Educational Policies Service, 1973. 30p. (Report no. 73–20) **1N42**
Samples of policy statements in use in schools, including textbook selection and adoption, library book selection, study of controversial issues, and handling of complaints about instructional materials.

"National Security and the Public's Right to Know: A New Role for the Courts Under the Freedom of Information Act." *University of Pennsylvania Law Review*, 123:1438–73, June 1975. **1N43**
"This comment will explore the scope of the courts' newly authorized powers under the FOIA amendments; the probable judicial response to this authorization, given the judiciary's traditional reluctance to intervene in the conduct of foreign affairs; and the need for a tempering of that reluctance in the interests of a vigorous, open, and democratic polity."

Naughton, James M., and Eric R. Gilbertson. "Libelous Ridicule By Journalists." *Cleveland State Law Review*, 18:450–55, September 1969. **1N44**
"Proof of actual malice, or even establishing that an attack in ridicule bears no relation to public conduct, seems at best, extremely difficult to bring out. The public interest in protecting itself, through criticism of those in prominence, weighs much more heavily on the scales of justice than does the interest of public figures in protecting themselves from personal attack. So go ahead and draw your cartoons, Conrad. Keep sticking pins in the kewpie dolls of America, Art Buckwald. And tell it like it is, Pogo."

Nawy, Harold. "In the Pursuit of Happiness? Consumers of Erotica in San Francisco." *Journal of Social Issues*, 29(3):147–61, 1973. **1N45**
A study of the consumers of erotica in San Francisco reveals that the average is "a white, middle-aged, married male, neatly attired and shopping alone. Questionnaire data reveal that these patrons are also well-educated, highly paid and employed in white-collar or above occupations." Most respondents report an active sex life and that erotica increases their social and sexual interaction. One of the studies stimulated by the U.S. Commission on Obscenity and Pornography.

————. "The San Francisco Erotic Marketplace." *Technical Report of the* ₍U.S.₎ *Commission on Obscenity and Pornography*, 4:155–224, 1971. **1N46**
"The present report contains a detailed summary of our research findings on the San Francisco erotic marketplace. The main objectives of the research study were as follows: (1) To determine the extent and nature of the distribution of sex-oriented material in San Francisco . . . . (2) To describe and analyze the sociological and psychological attitudes, experiences, and behaviors of the consumer population of the San Francisco marketplace for erotic literature and films."

Naylor, Alice P. "Intellectual Freedom and the Public Library." *Phi Delta Kappan*, 52:459–61, April 1971. **1N47**
An account of how public librarians across the nation, encouraged by the professional associations are resisting pressures for censorship, and some of the problems they are facing in "the never-ending juggling act" in an effort to maintain intellectual freedom.

Neary, John. "Pornography Goes Public." *Life*, 69(9):18–25, 28 August 1970. **1N48**
An illustrated article emphasizing the rising national concern over the wave of pornography spreading across the country.

Neef, Marian, and Stuart Nagel. "Judicial Behavior in Pornography Cases." *Journal of Urban Law*, 52:1–23, August 1974. **1N49**
"The first part of this article deals with some of the historical background of the question of obscenity and sets out certain decisions of the Supreme Court in its attempts to formulate guidelines for the lower courts concerning the control of or access to certain types of pornographic materials. The second part of the article describes a quantitative study undertaken by the authors in an attempt to determine how pornography rulings over the years have been affected by certain variables."

Neiger, Stephen. "Conversation with Dr. Stephen Neiger, M.D., Ph.D." *Performing Arts*, 6(4):20–21, 23–24, Fall 1969. **1N50**
A psychologist and coeditor of *Journal of Sex Research* discusses censorship. Because of mounting evidence to support the theory that being exposed to violent stimuli makes for violence, some censorship in this realm might be wise. Institutional censorship of sex expression, however, is totally unwarranted on the basis of evidence of harm done to the person. We should spend less effort in worrying about "perverted literature" than about understanding the perverted mind of the censor. If we maintain a freedom of expression, "a proper balance will be created by a free selection by individuals of various tastes, views and opinions."

Neill, S. D. "Censorship and the Uncertain Librarian." *Canadian Library Journal*, 32:345–48, October 1975. **1N51**
Despite strong opposition to censorship by professional library associations, individual librarians continue to censor. While they may agree in principle that censorship is wrong, they are uncertain about the specific. In the final analysis the individual librarian must make a judgment and to condemn such a person is "quite simply and unjustly, censorious."

Neilson, William. "Obscenity—A Change in Approach." *Loyola Law Review* (New Orleans), 18:319–34, 1971–72. **1N52**
"In the development of constitutional law the Supreme Court must develop and succinctly write opinions that are a reflection of the constitution rather than their own political or moral beliefs. This concept seems to be lacking in the field of obscenity. While the last 15 years since *Roth* has been a confusing era, the Court has now in *Reidel* and *Thirty-Seven Photographs* an opportunity to tread a new path in this jungle which everyone can understand and follow. However, if it reverts to the indefinite and absurd approach as set out in *Roth*, it will only be inviting more litigation and confusion in a field of law that already has too much of both."

Nejelski, Paul, and Kurt Finsterbusch. "The Prospector and the Researcher: Present and Prospective Variations on the Supreme Court's *Branzburg* Decision." *Social Problems*, 21:3–21, Summer 1973. **1N53**
"The confidentiality of research data and the testimonial privilege of newsmen's sources are similar issues and are legally tied together in the *Branzburg* decision [1972]. This decision, therefore, directly affects the social sciences. The present article attempts to outline the *Branzburg* decision and to speculate about its impact on American social science—especially on the ability of researchers to protect their data from grand jury subpoena. This article concludes that the inertia which has dominated the social sciences on the issue of confidentiality must now be replaced by vigorous action."

Nejelski, Paul, and Lindsey Millerherman. "A Researcher—Subject Testimonial Privilege: What To Do Before the Subpoena Arrives." *Wisconsin Law Review*, 1971:1085–1148, 1971. **1N54**
"This article concentrates upon the question: Under what circumstance, if any, should a researcher be compelled to reveal confidential information about individuals in his study? In attempting to answer this relatively narrow question, the article raises broader issues such as the proper relationship of government to its critics. Although the article focuses on the recognition of a testimonial privilege as the major shield in resisting outside demands, other available alternatives are discussed as well."

Nelkin, Dorothy. *Science Textbook Controversies and the Politics of Equal Time.* Cambridge, Mass., Massachusetts Institute of Technology Press, 1977. 174p. **1N55**
The author describes the numerous science textbook controversies that have erupted in all parts of the United States in recent years. In particular she "traces the response to two projects funded by the National Science Foundation: the creationist's opposition to the Biological Sciences Curriculum Study, with its emphasis on evolution as the central hypothesis of modern biology, and the crusade against the social program titled 'Man: A Course of Study,' which relates man's behavior to that of (other) animals. One of the more interesting findings of this study is the discovery of increasing pressure from the 'new left,' in addition to the more often predicted reaction by religious conservatives." A brief account of the controversies appears in the April 1976 issue of *Scientific American.*

Nelson, Christine J. "CBC Commercial Acceptance Policy." *Canadian Communications Law Review*, 2:21–26, 1970. **1N56**
The author studies the advertising screening operations of Canadian Broadcasting Company policies which have been kept confidential.

Nelson, Elwood F., Jr. "Juvenile Names: To Print or Not to Print." *Quill*, 57(12):16–18, December 1969. **1N57**
The author cites ten arguments in support of publishing names of juvenile offenders, commenting on the merit or lack of merit of each.

Nelson, Eva. "Overdue—Take Cuss Words Out of Kids' Books." *Wilson Library Bulletin*, 49:132–33, October 1974. **1N58**
Protest against the growing use of swear words in books for children eleven years of age and younger, often in what appears to be a contrived and unnecessary use.

———. "Why We Hardly Have Any Picture Books in the Children's Department Anymore; a Brief Fantasy." *Top of the News*, 29:54–56, November 1972. **1N59**
The fantasy describes a library where virtually all of the children's picture books have been removed or not purchased because of patron objections, including *A Visit From St. Nicholas* which some found objectionable because Santa Claus was associated with Christmas, and *The Tale of Peter Rabbit*, because Peter was sent to bed without supper for being naughty, an unacceptable form of punishment. Only the alphabet books remained.

Nelson, Harold L. "Newsmen and the *Times* Doctrine." *Villanova Law Review*, 12:738–50, Summer 1967. **1N60**
Two factors might help newsmen measure the "reckless disregard of falsity" as prescribed in the *New York Times* ruling on libel of public officials: the credibility of the news source and the extent of investigation by the news media. The author finds little change in the attitude of the vast majority of reporters toward writing about public officials, following the *New York Times* ruling.

———. "The Newsmen's Privilege against Disclosure of Confidential Sources and Information." *Vanderbilt Law Review*, 24:667–81, May 1971. **1N61**
An examination of court decisions since April 1970 and implications flowing from them, particularly as they bear on constitutional issues. As a prelude, the author summarizes the state of the law of newsmen's privilege prior to April 1970 when the U.S. District Court for the Northern District of California in the *Caldwell* case granted constitutional protection under the First Amendment's freedom of the press clause. The U.S. Supreme Court subsequently (after the article) reversed the decision.

———. "Seditious Libel in Colonial America." *American Journal of Legal History*, 3:160–72, 1959. **1N62**
"This study is offered to suggest in part the place of seditious libel as one of a group of controls over the press; to isolate the libel cases in the hope of finding regularities; and to make suggestions as to further study of the subject."

———, and Dwight L. Teeter, Jr. *Law of Mass Communications: Freedom and Control of Print and Broadcast Media.* 2d ed. Mineola, N.Y., Foundation Press, 1973. 713p. **1N63**

Content: Principles and Development of Freedom of Expression (freedom and control; historical background). Rights in Conflict with Free Expression (defamation: libel and slander; constitutional defense against libel suits; traditional defenses in libel; the law of privacy and the media; copyright; free press–fair trial; criminal words: libel, contempt, obscenity, and blasphemy). Communications Law and the Public Interest (access to government information; public access to mass media; regulation of advertising; antitrust law and the mass media; taxation and licensing). The work is a successor to Frank Thayer's *Legal Control of the Press* (T61).

———. *Notes to Update Nelson & Teeter: The Law of Mass Communications*. 2d ed. Mineola, N.Y., Foundation Press, 1975. 33p.　　　　**1N64**

Nelson, Jack A. *The Underground Press*. Columbia, Mo., Freedom of Information Center, School of Journalism, University of Missouri at Columbia, 1969. 6p. (Report no. 226)　　**1N65**
"In recent years, there has been a dramatic rise in the number of underground newspapers published and the number of people who read them. Factors accounting for the phenomenon of the underground press may be: (1) the advent of photo-offset printing which affords an inexpensive means of publishing the tabloids, and (2) the increasing disaffection among the young with the 'establishment' and its traditional press."

Nelson, James A. "Intellectual Freedom: Local Issues." *Kentucky Library Association Bulletin*, 34(1):11–14, January 1970.　　　　**1N66**
The writer urges the Association to take a more active role in intellectual freedom. Incidents that have occurred in other states can also happen in Kentucky.

Nelson, Jerome L. *Libel: A Basic Program for Beginning Journalists*. Ames, Iowa, Iowa State University Press, 1973. 89p. Processed.　　**1N67**
Content: Libel Defined, Necessary Conditions, Liability, Malice, Damages, and Defenses. Includes review quizzes and answers.

Nelson, Kristen C. " 'Offensive Speech' and the First Amendment." *Boston University Law Review*, 53:834–57, July 1973.　　　　**1N68**
"This Note will seek to demonstrate that offensive speech is entitled to first amendment protection, largely because the risks incident to state regulation in this area far outweigh any potential benefits to society." The author concludes that "Nixon appointees [to the Supreme Court] have sought to read a good measure of majoritarianism into the first amendment. In their attempt to protect the majority from what are perceived to be verbal assaults on their

sensibilities, the Nixon appointees have persistently disregarded the legitimate free speech claims of minority groups."

Nelson, Mark. *Newspaper Ethics, Codes, and the NLRB*. Columbia, Mo., Freedom of Information Center, School of Journalism, University of Missouri at Columbia, 1976. 8p. (Report no. 353)　　　　**1N69**
"The conflict between newspaper management and employees over journalistic codes of ethics is more intense than ever after a recent ruling by the National Labor Relations Board which stated that the Madison (Wis.) *Capital Times* code was not subject to bargaining by members of the local guild."

Nelson, Marlan D. *Free Press–Fair Trial: The Effects of "Sensational" and "Non-Sensational" Pre-Trial News Stories and of a Judge's Admonition upon "Juror" and "Non-Juror" Guilt Assessment*. Norman, Okla., University of Oklahoma, 1972. 110p. (Ed.D. dissertation, University Microfilms, no. 73–15,200)　　　　　　**1N70**
"Sensational pre-trial news-exposure resulted in respondents' assessing a significantly higher mean guilt score for the defendant than did non-sensational pre-trial news. In and of itself, pre-trial news was a factor in influencing prospective jurors. After assignment to a juror role to hear a case and being admonished by the judge, respondents rated the guilt of the defendant significantly lower than they did on a pretest after exposure to news."

———. *Free Press vs. Fair Trial; An Annotated Bibliography*. Stillwater, Okla., Journalism Services, 1971. 89p. Processed.　　　　**1N71**

Nelson, Robert J. *Judicial Interpretation of Freedom of Press Since 1919*. Bronx, N.Y., Fordham University, 1959. 136p. (Unpublished Ph.D. dissertation)　　　　**1N72**
An empirical study of U.S. Supreme Court decisions involving press freedom from the end of World War I to 1959, in an attempt to determine the principles that have guided the thinking of the Court. The author found a certain unevenness and even confusion in the decisions as the Court attempted to discover a satisfactory working formula for dealing with press freedom. He discusses in detail the various devices and dicta employed by the Court in seeking solutions to constitutional dilemmas in a complex and pluralistic society. No formula appears to have been found, although the "preferred position" doctrine may be regarded as an attempt to expand and complement the limited concept of no previous censorship originally enunciated by Blackstone.

[Ness, Leland S.] "Libel—'Official

Conduct' Concept Extended to Include Criminal Activity, No Matter How Far Removed in Time or Place." *New York Law Forum*, 17:869–74, Spring 1971.　　　　**1N73**
"In *Monitor Patriot Co. v. Roy* [1971] the United States Supreme Court further extended the rule set down in *New York Times v. Sullivan* [1964] concerning libel actions brought by public officials."

Nessel, William J. "Prior Censorship and Human Rights." *Jurist*, 27:58–76, January 1967.　　　　**1N74**
The writer "seeks to glean insights from American constitutional law, which may help Canon lawyers to resolve the question of prior censorship within the cultural framework of modern times."

———. "Prior Censorship for Young Readers." *Jurist*, 29:199–201, April 1969.　　　　**1N75**
"We are fortunate that both Church officials and state authorities concur in the need for special legal protection for youth below eighteen years of age. That each body arrived at this judgment independently strengthens the validity of this judgment for the American cultural environment." Re: *People v. Tannenbaum*, 18 N.Y. 2d 268 (1966).

Neubauer, Mark. "Newsman's Privilege after *Branzburg*: The Case for a Federal Shield Law." *UCLA Law Review*, 24:160–92, October 1976.　**1N76**
"The proposed federal shield law—despite several weaknesses in drafting—does nevertheless assist the newsman in protecting these confidences by lessening the pressures from the courts. It expands the protection currently afforded to newsmen under the first amendment in areas such as grand jury subpoenas and demonstrates a national commitment to protecting confidential news sources and their contribution to the free flow of information. . . . By basing their privilege on *both* the proposed federal shield law and the first amendment, reporters should be able to develop the best possible protection for confidential relationships while still accommodating the occasional public need to violate those confidences."

Neuburg, Victor E. "Introduction." In *How William Hone, the Persecuted Publisher of Fleet Street, Beat the Bigots on His Three Trials for Blasphemy. . . .* London, H. A. Kemp [1883?]. Reprinted in facsimile by Frank Graham, Newcastle Upon Tyne, 1970, pp. 5–7.　**1N77**
The author reviews the three blasphemy trials of William Hone (1817) in light of the political climate of the day. The trials were essentially

political rather than religious. The real charges against Hone were for his lampoon of the Castlereagh government, but religious impiety seemed surer ground for conviction. Hone spoke eloquently in his behalf and the jury, sensing the blatant action of the prosecution, refused to convict. "Hone's acquittal did much to discomfit the Government, and at the same time strengthened the hands of those who wished to see a free press." The text consists of the three offending publications: *The Late John Wilkes's Catechism* . . . , The Political Litany . . . , and *The Sinecurist's Creed* . . . . The title page of the 1833? edition bears this note: "I dedicate this Story of a Successful Fight for the Freedom of the Press and the Liberty of Free Thought and Discussion— without permission—to Sir Henry Tyler, in the hope that he may see three modern Trials for Blasphemy terminate in a manner equally creditable to the common sense of his countrymen. J.F.B." The three modern trials probably refer to the cases of G. W. Foote, W. J. Ramsey, and H. A. Kemp, the publisher (F200).

————. "The Reading of the Victorian Freethinkers." *Library*, 28(3):191–214, September 1973. **1N78**
The article deals with the popular ephemeral literature of freethought, the product of the working men who formed the militant freethought movement in Victorian England. Among those writers and publishers discussed are George J. Holyoake, Charles Bradlaugh, James Watson, G. W. Foote, Edward Truelove, and Charles Southwell, all of whom, along with such freethought periodicals as *Freethinker* and *Oracle of Reason*, were involved in censorship cases.

"New Approach to Censorship." *Round Table*, 58:89–91, January 1968. **1N79**
An account of the work of the New Zealand Tribunal which has exercised its power of censorship with prudence, thus attracting criticism from those who favor more strict bans.

"The New Concerns About the Press." *Fortune*, 91:121–23, April 1975. **1N80**
Many Americans are increasingly hostile to the press, despite (or because of) its present power and prestige, and journalists fear that this hostility may lead to restrictions on journalistic freedom. The change from a decentralized press to a national one, the increased number of intellectuals in journalism, the pressures for advocacy journalism and politicizing the news, are some of the reasons for concern. Add to these factors the general distrust of all institutions. The author calls for the development of responsibility among journalists to accompany the new power of the press. In its concern for minorities and causes, he urges the press not to neglect the establishment in politics and business.

New England Association of Teachers of English. "Censorship Issue." *The Leaflet*, 68(2):1–47, May 1969. (ED 31,495) **1N81**
Content: Censorship Is Disrupting Our Schools by Edward J. Gordon. Choosing Literature by Linwood A. Hanson. The Textbook Publisher As Censor and Critic of Censorship by Richard L. Nelson. Public School Superintendents and the Question of Censorship by Sayre Uhler. The NEA Looks at the Censorship Question by Joseph Devlin. A Thumbnail Social History of Free Expression by F. X. Shea. Notes on the "Appropriateness" of Censorship by Thomas J. Cottle. So What's Dirty? by Kathy Decker. Censorship: A School Problem by Lynda Billings. Literature and Censorship: A Statement of Belief by Lee E. Allen. The Right to Be a Reader by Bud Church. The English Department Chairman—Selector or Censor? by Ronald T. LaConte.

"New Irish Censorship Bill: Prohibition Order to Expire After 12 Years." *Bookseller*, 3209:2622–24, 24 June 1967. **1N82**
An account of criticism of Irish censorship that took place in the Dáil Éireann over the new Irish Censorship Bill, which provided that books banned on the grounds of obscenity would be removed from the ban after twelve years. Birth control works were not included.

New Jersey. Attorney General's Committee on the Right to Know. *New Jersey's Right to Know; a Report on Open Government*. Trenton, N.J., The Committee, 1974. 202p. **1N83**
The Committee recommends a new public information act for New Jersey and suggests principles and provisions. The open meetings law should be modified to encourage maximum disclosure of the deliberative process of government agencies. The Committee examined the New Jersey experience and the experience in other states as well as under the Federal Act. Text of a Proposed Public Information Act of 1974 is given on pages 43–54.

New Jersey. Commission to Study Obscenity and Depravity in Public Media. *Report to the Governor and Legislature . . . May 19, 1970*. Trenton, N.J., 1970. 119p. **1N84**
This legislative commission was created to study obscenity and depravity in the public media, to assess the effectiveness of existing controls, to review legal, psychological, and sociological knowledge bearing on the subject, and to recommend appropriate legislative action. The Commission considered three basic areas, all related to the commercial exploitation of obscene materials: (1) obscenity and minors, (2) offensive public displays, and (3) obscenity and adults. They recommended a new tripartite statute to cover the three areas. (1) Since there was evidence that exposure to certain types of sexual material might have a harmful effect on children and since use of it ran

counter to the wishes of most parents, legal restrictions should be placed on sale of pornography to minors. (2) Displays of obscene material which obtrude upon the public should be prohibited. (3) An unlimited freedom for adults to read what they choose, including pornography, should be preserved. Options were given for prohibition of the sale of morbid sexual materials. Text of the proposed statute is included. A list of public hearings and witnesses is given on pages 88–95. These are published in five volumes.

New Jersey. Senate. Committee on Education. *Report . . . Regarding the Alleged Distribution of Lewd and Obscene Literature to Students at Patterson State College, Persuant to Senate Resolution Number 12*. [Trenton, N.J., The Committee], 1969. 14p. Processed. **1N85**
Includes text of the offending story, Tea Party, by Robert L. Terrell.

New South Wales. Law Reform Commission. *Working Paper on Defamation*. Sydney, Australia, 1968? 231p. **1N86**
The Commission was asked by the Attorney General to review the law and practices of the Courts in relation to libel and slander, particularly as contempt, libel and similar legislation hamper the press in publishing facts of public interest and in editorially commenting thereon. The working paper was circulated to interested persons for their consideration and comments.

New South Wales Fabian Society. *Toward a Free Press*. Sydney, Australia, The Society, 1949. 24p. (Pamphlet no. 3) **1N87**
Fabian criticism of press ownership and control in New South Wales.

"A New Standard for Recovery of Damages by Private Individuals Libeled in a Report of Public Interest." *Brigham Young University Law Review*, 1975:159–71, 1975. **1N88**
Re: *Gertz v. Robert Welch, Inc.* (1974). "The court in *Gertz* set about to clarify the constitutional ramifications of libel that have arisen from *New York Times* and its progeny. This objective may not have been achieved as *Gertz* now presents additional problems of determining what type of evidence is competent to establish actual injury and how courts will apply the discretion accorded them in limiting unjustified jury awards."

New York (State). Law Revision Committee. *Report and Study Relating to Problems Involved in Conferring Upon Newspapermen a Privilege Which Would Legally Protect Them from Divulging*

Sources of Information Given to Them. Albany, Williams Press, 1949. 146p. (Legislative Document [1949], no. 65 (A) **1N89**

The report examines the history of the journalist's privilege in New York and analyzes provisions of shield laws in other states. "After weighing the conflicting interests involved, the Commission has unanimously concluded (1) that an unconditional privilege should not, in the public interest, be granted to newsmen to refuse to divulge the sources of information on which news stories are based; (2) that a privilege, with safeguards essential to the protection of the public interest, may safely be granted."

New York County Lawyers Association. Committee on Civil Rights. "Television and the Accused: Report of the Committee on Civil Rights." *New York County Lawyers Association Bar Bulletin*, 21:166–74, 4 November 1964. **1N90**

To balance television's freedom of the press with the right of the accused for a fair trial the Committee recommends: (1) the disciplining of any official who permits the interview of accused without being represented by counsel, or who makes public statements of information gained from such interviews; (2) no information gained by such methods will be admissible as evidence; and (3) the Canons of Ethics should proscribe as misconduct extrajudicial public statements of prosecutors concerning the guilt of accused or the evidence against him.

New York Fair Trial–Free Press Conference. "Guidelines in Criminal Cases." *Editor & Publisher*, 102(18):16, 44, 3 May 1969. (Reprinted in *Editor & Publisher*, 29 December 1973) **1N91**

Representatives of the news media, the law, and law enforcement agencies have developed this set of guidelines on press coverage of civil and criminal trials and have submitted the document to their parent organizations for adoption.

[New York Publishers Committee.] *An Analysis of the Letter of the Third Assistant Postmaster-General, April 13, 1901; Report of Committee Sent to Washington by Publishers of New York City; A Protest of New York Publishers.* [New York, The Committee, 1901.] 8p. **1N92**

New York publishers protest a proposal of the Post Office Department to exclude from second-class mailing privileges, those magazines which offer premiums for subscriptions, despite the fact that Congress has three times refused to pass such legislation.

New York State Freedom Train Commission. *Official Document Book, New York State Freedom Train.* Albany,

N.Y., The Commission, 1949. 63p. **1N93**

In the section on freedom of speech and press are included the following facsimiles: Section 8 of the New York State Constitution (1846) dealing with freedom of speech and press, records of the trial of John Peter Zenger, and a painting of the Zenger trial.

New York State Society of Newspaper Editors and New York State Bar Association. *Law & the Press: A Conference Sponsored Jointly by the New York Fair Trial/Free Press Conference, New York State Society of Newspaper Editors, New York State Bar Association.* Albany, N.Y., New York Bar Association, 1975. 88p. **1N94**

"The conference was designed to explore the most pressing problem areas which generate misunderstandings and confrontations when the law and press come into conflict, in hopes of producing constructive ideas leading to better law-media relations." There were three panel discussions: (1) How Not to Cover the Courts, led by Robert Kasanof, attorney. (2) How Not to Handle the Press, led by Mark Monsky, television news director. (3) Privacy and Privilege, led by Benno C. Schmidt, Jr., law professor. Background papers prepared by the discussion leaders are included, along with a conference summary and the following documents: New York Fair Trial Free Press Conference Guidelines in Criminal Cases; Lawyers Code of Professional Responsibility (Disciplinary Rule 7–107); NYS Administrative Board Rule 33.3; Federal Court Rules Relating to Press Coverage and the New York State Shield Law.

New York Times Company, *petitioner. The New York Times Company v. United States. A Documentary History. The Pentagon Papers Litigation.* Compiled and with an introduction by James C. Goodale, General Counsel of the Times. New York, Arno Press, 1971. 2 vols. 1298p. **1N95**

"A complete record of this case, arranged chronologically, starting with the motion by the Government on June 15, 1971, in Federal Court, for a temporary restraining order, and ending with the opinion of the Supreme Court on June 30, 1971. Contains all the legal papers and briefs filed in the District Court, Court of Appeals and Supreme Court, as well as transcripts of all arguments except for those proceedings held in camera. Also included are reprints of articles in the *Times* covering this case and the companion case, *United States v. The Washington Post Company et al.* The only complete record of this case, since, because of pressure of time, no printed record was filed with the Court."

"New York Times Rule: An Analysis of Its Application." *Minnesota Law Review*, 55:299–319, December 1970. **1N96**

"This Note will critically examine the post-*Times* cases in the state and federal courts and will suggest the directions in which this constitutional tort rule seems to be developing. The cases will be considered with especial reference to the two thorniest problems posed by *Times* [*New York Times v. Sullivan*, 1964]: first, who is disabled by the constitutional immunity; second, what kind of conduct defeats this immunity. While this juristic lode has felt many a jurisprudent's mattock, it is hoped that the more recent cases, by giving content and direction to the ambiguous words of the enunciated constitutional standards, may amply justify the enterprise."

"New York's 'Minor' Obscenity Statute Held Constitutional." *Catholic Lawyer*, 13:159–66, September 1967. **1N97**

In *People v. Tannenbaum* (1966), the Court of Appeals upheld the constitutionality of Section 484-i of the New York Penal Law which prohibits the sale or delivery of pornographic material to minors under the age of eighteen.

New Zealand Library Association. "New Zealand Library Association (Inc.) Statement of Policy on Censorship of Books and Other Printed Material for Library Use." *New Zealand Libraries*, 31:66, April 1968. **1N98**

Adopted by Council, 14 February 1968.

Newhouse, Andrew J. "Defamation by Radio: A New Tort." *Oregon Law Review*, 17:314–19, June 1938. **1N99**

The author concludes, on the basis of recent court decisions, that "the common law of libel and slander cannot appropriately be applied to defamation by radio. . . . Defamation by radio is properly neither slander nor libel . . . [but] should be regarded as a new wrong in the field of torts, which should be given a place of stability and certainty in our law by adequate legislation."

[Newman, John Henry.] *Achilli v. Newman. A Full and Authentic Report of the Prosecution for Libel, Tried before Lord Campbell and a Special Jury, in the Court of Queen's Bench, Westminster, June 1852. With Introductory Remarks, by the Editor of "The Confessional Unmasked."* London, W. Strange [1852?]. 65p. **1N100**

The sensational case between a defrocked Roman Catholic priest, G. G. Achilli, and a Church of England priest turned Roman Catholic, John Henry (later Cardinal) Newman. Achilli, who had been lecturing on the sexual immorality of the Catholic clergy, accused Newman of libeling him in an article which charged Achilli with numerous instances of gross immorality and debauchery. Newman documented his charges with dates, places, and names. The jury, after hearing a considerable number of witnesses testifying to the truth of the charges, sometimes in intimate detail, decided that all but one charge were unsubstantiated, and found Newman guilty of libel.

Newmyer, Jody. "Art, Libraries and the Censor." *Library Quarterly*, 46:38–53, January 1976. **1N101**
"This article examines the ambiguities of copyright legislation in regard to art, the origins and intractability of the attitude toward the graphic arts of the American public, and the ways in which librarians, individually and through their professional organizations, can attempt to meet the problem of censorship."

"News Twisters—Trouble Ahead?" *Broadcasting*, 81:32–36, 27 September 1971. **1N102**
A lengthy review of Edith Efron's *The News Twisters*, which charged liberal bias in TV network news, including references to the countercharges by network officials.

"The Newsman's Privilege After Branzburg v. Hayes: Whither Now?" *Journal of Criminal Law & Criminology*, 64:218–39, June 1973. **1N103**
"Section one will outline the decision in *Branzburg v. Hayes* [1972], isolating the arguments addressed by the Court and delineating the limits of the holding. Section two will put the question of a newsman's privilege in historical perspective, suggesting that the Supreme Court's reasoning in *Branzburg* is in accord with that history. Section three will present an argument in favor of a limited newsman's privilege which differs in crucial respects from the arguments heretofore presented to the courts, which is consistent with the historical considerations that properly proved persuasive to the majority in *Branzburg*, and which, accordingly, is likely to garner judicial acceptance."

"Newsmen Held to Possess No Testimonial Privilege with Respect to Confidential Communications." *Fordham Law Review*, 41:1024–34, May 1973. **1N104**
Re: *Branzburg v. Hayes*, 408 U.S. 665 (1972). The author of the note believes the the U.S. Supreme Court's decision in Branzburg "is perhaps most disturbing because it comes at a time in which the vitality and effectiveness of a free press are more necessary than ever before. . . . Clearly, matters such as official corruption or lassitude, social decay, and rising crime are problems which might well remain hidden without an effective press."

"Newsmen's Privilege: A Challenge to

Branzburg." *Boston University Law Review*, 53:497–512, March 1973. **1N105**
"As part of the developing law in this area [newsmen's privilege], a recent decision by the Second Circuit, *Baker v. F. & F. Investment* [470 F.2d 778 (2d Cir.)], recognized a limited right of confidentiality for newsmen and their sources. The opinion is significant not only as one of a small number of cases actually giving the requested protection to newsmen, but also as an early interpretation of Branzburg."

"Newsmen's Privilege Against Compulsory Disclosure of Sources in Civil Suits—Toward an Absolute Privilege?" *University of Colorado Law Review*, 45:173–93, Winter 1973. **1N106**
"This Comment will analyze the contention that a qualified newsmen's privilege is not sufficient. Furthermore, the question whether a 'limited absolute' constitutional privilege should be granted to newsmen in civil cases claiming the confidentiality of their sources will be addressed." The author concludes that the added certainty of application and any consequent encouragement to news gathering is worth the denial of access to the informer's identity to potential civil litigants.

"Newsmen's Privilege: Shield or Citizen's Duty." *Congressional Quarterly Weekly Report*, 31:355–57, 17 February 1973. **1N107**
Following a summary of the issue, there are statements (pro and con) from various public figures.

Newspaper and Periodical Press Association for Obtaining the Repeal of the Paper Duty. *The Tax Upon Paper: The Case Stated for Its Immediate Repeal.* . . . London, The Association [1858]. 48p. **1N108**

The Newspaper Stamp and Advertisement Duties: A Form of a Petition to Parliament, Accurately Setting Forth, as is Presumed, the Merits of Much of the Present Newspaper Press; and Suggesting with Respect to the Above Duties, an Entirely Novel Mode of Proceeding. London, Roake and Varty, 1836. 10p. **1N109**
The author proposes that the established daily papers in England that have not objected to the newspaper and advertising taxes continue to pay the tax, but that it be removed from papers published less frequently and those dealing with a specific topic.

Newspaper Stamps: Deputation to Lord Viscount Melbourne, to Procure the Total Repeal of the Stamp Duty on Newspapers: From Cleave's Gazette, of the 20th of Feb., 1836. London, C. Ely, 1836. 16p. (Also in the *London Review* for January 1836) **1N110**

George Birkbeck and a deputation which included Joseph Hume, John A. Roebuck, Francis Place, Henry S. Chapman, John Crawfurd, and William E. Hickson, appeared before the Chancellor of Exchequer to request total repeal of stamp duties on newspapers, arguing the case on moral, political, and financial grounds.

Newton, Peter M. "Restricting the Pandering of Obscenity: A Case of Legislative Overkill." *Pacific Law Journal*, 1:373–88, January 1970. **1N111**
Criticism of California legislative attempts to provide stricter controls on obscenity by codifying Supreme Court decisions, including *Ginsburg v. New York* (1968). The author calls for the repeal of the evidentiary section of the law, enabling a trial jury to be instructed to disregard any evidence of pandering when deciding the obscenity of the work in question.

Newton, Sally H. "The Commercial Speech Doctrine: *Bigelow v. Virginia.*" *Urban Law Annual*, 12:221–32, 1976. **1N112**
The article examines the doctrine of commercial speech as treated and affected by the Supreme Court in *Bigelow v. Virginia* (1975).

Nicholas, David. " 'We Regret That *Maude* Will Not Be Seen . . . ' " *TV Guide*, 21(9):6–8, 3 March 1973. **1N113**
Blackout of the Columbia Broadcasting program, "Maude," in Peoria and Champaign, Ill. because of objection to the abortion theme.

Nichols, Thomas L. *Journal in Jail, Kept During a Four Months Imprisonment for Libel, In the Jail of Erie County.* Buffalo, N. Y., A. Dinsmore, 1840. 248p. (Reprinted by Arno Press, 1970) **1N114**
Account of the celebrated libel case against the editor of the *Buffalonian*, whose paper had attacked the financial manipulations of a local banker, H. J. Stow, and others for mismanagement of an estate. Nichols had been threatened with kidnapping, his office wrecked by friends of the plaintiffs. Despite the fact that he had been out of town and had not written the offensive news story, Nichols was convicted and sentenced to four months in prison and fined $150. In his jail journal he continues to discuss the case, expose corruption in Buffalo, charge the judge and jury with unscrupulous conduct, and to comment on freedom of the press. Local citizens raised funds for him and James Gordon Bennett supported him in his *New York Herald*. A huge party celebrated his release.

Nilson, Jerril. "Censorship and the High School Press." *Communication: Journalism Education Today*, 8:4–6, Fall 1974. **1N115**
Based on a paper written by the author when editor of a high school newspaper.

Nimmer, Melville B. "Does Copyright

Abridge the First Amendment Guarantees of Free Speech and Press?" *UCLA Law Review*, 17:1180–1204, June 1970. **1N116**
Nimmer attempts to reconcile the interests of the author under the Copyright Act and the freedom of speech and press as guaranteed by the First Amendment, considering the device of definitional balance and the creation of an idea-expression line between copyright and free speech interests.

———. "Is Freedom of the Press a Redundancy: What Does It Add to Freedom of Speech?" *Hastings Law Journal*, 26:639–58, January 1975. **1N117**
"In this introduction, the author explores the fundamental question of whether the First Amendment press clause confers different or additional freedoms from those conferred by the speech clause. Focusing on the relevant First Amendment cases decided by the Supreme Court in its October 1973 term, he argues that speech and press are physically and conceptually distinguishable, and that the Supreme Court, by failing to acknowledge this distinction, has not yet properly analyzed the critical areas in which the freedoms overlap or conflict."—Editor

———. "National Security Secrets v. Free Speech: The Issues Left Undecided in the Ellsberg Case." *Stanford Law Review*, 26:311–33, January 1974. **1N118**
"The purpose of this Article is to explore the statutory and constitutional status of penalties for the disclosure of official secrets—the issues that were raised but left unanswered in the Ellsberg case. . . . What follows is an attempt to reduce that chill [chilling effects] by showing that the statutes Ellsberg was charged with violating either cannot be interpreted to make criminal his conduct or if so interpreted, are unconstitutional."

———. *Nimmer on Copyright; A Treatise on the Law of Literary, Musical and Artistic Property, and the Protection of Ideas*. Albany, N.Y., Matthew Bender, 1966. 1220p. Loose-leaf. **1N119**
Chapters on the Constitutional basis of copyright, the subject matter, derivative works, publications, persons entitled to copyright, statutory formalities, nature and rights protected by copyright, duration and renewal, transfer of rights, infringement actions, criminal actions, and the law of ideas. Appendices include: text of the Copyright Act, Copyright Office Regulations, the Universal Copyright Convention, the Buenos Aires Convention, the Berne Convention, and a table of cases.

———. "The Right to Speak from *Times* to *Time*: First Amendment Theory Applied to Libel and Mis-

applied to Privacy." *California Law Review*, 56:935–67, August 1968. **1N120**
"The Supreme Court's decision in *New York Times v. Sullivan* [1964] implicitly recognized the need for definitional balancing and drew a definitional line which on the whole establishes a felicitous equilibrium between antithetical interests in speech and reputation. The Court's subsequent decision in *Time, Inc. v. Hill* [1967] is unfortunate in that it assumes that the definitional balance appropriate to the speech and reputation context is equally applicable in balancing competing interests in speech and privacy. A recognition of the manner in which the privacy interest differs from the reputation interest requires a markedly different definitional balance in determining the constitutional limits of the right of privacy."

Niro, William L. "New Challenges to Newspaper Freedom of the Press— The Struggle for Right of Access and Attacks on Cross-Media Ownership." *DePaul Law Review*, 24:165–84, Fall 1974. **1N121**
In light of the U.S. Supreme Court's decision in *Tornillo v. Miami Herald Publishing Co.* (1974), the author reviews the historic First Amendment rights and the challenge posed by demands for the right of access. "The basic questions presented are: Can the American public have a right of access and reply in the nation's newspapers without abridging the fundamental constitutional guarantee of freedom of the press? Would such a statutory right of reply implement or restrain freedom of the press? Does the first amendment of its own force provide any right of access and reply to the public, especially in light of the media's present status as a large political, social, and economic institution?"

Nisely, Robert L. "New York Press Shield Law Applies Only When Confidential Relationship Exists Between a Newsman and His Source." *Buffalo Law Review*, 23:529–48, Winter 1974. **1N122**
Deals with the case, *WBAI–FM v. Proskin* (42 App.Div. 2d 5, 344 N.Y.S.2d 393), which arose under the New York press shield law which was enacted in 1970.

Nixon, Raymond B. "Trends in U.S. Newspaper Ownership; Concentration with Competition." *Gazette: International Journal for Mass Communications Studies*, 14:181–93, 1968. **1N123**
A discussion of the historical background of ownership concentration, growth of local press monopolies, the rise of inter-media competition, and the effect of local monopolies on groups and chains. The author notes three major paradoxes in concentration of ownership: (1) keen competition for readers and advertisers, despite the fact that 97 percent of the nation's dailies enjoy local monopoly; (2) certain government policies seem to encourage still further concentration of ownership; and

(3) the newspaper industry as a whole was never more prosperous.

Nixon, Richard M. "Classification and Declassification of National Security Information and Material." *Weekly Compilation of Presidential Documents*, 8:542–50, 13 March 1972. **1N124**
Statement by President Richard M. Nixon upon establishing a new classification system and directing the acceleration of publication of the "Foreign Relations" series, 8 March 1972.

———. "Commission on Obscenity and Pornography: Statement by the President on the Commission's Report, October 20, 1970." *Weekly Compilation of Presidential Documents*, 6:1454–55, 2 November 1970. **1N125**
Statement by President Richard M. Nixon denouncing the findings of the Commission on Obscenity and Pornography as "morally bankrupt," and having performed a "disservice" to America. "So long as I am in the White House, there will be no relaxation of the national effort to control and eliminate smut from our national life."

———. *Legislative Proposals to Deal with the Flow of Sex-Oriented Mail; Message from the President of the United States*. Washington, D.C., Govt. Print. Off., 1969. 3p. (Also in U.S. House of Representatives. Committee on Post Office and Civil Service. Subcommittee on Postal Operations. *Obscenity in the Mails. Hearings . . . on H.R. 10867 . . .*, pp. 127–29 and in *Weekly Compilation of Presidential Documents*, 5 May 1969) **1N126**
President Nixon asks the Congress (1) "to make it a federal crime to use the mails or other facilities of commerce to deliver to anyone under 18 years of age material dealing with a sexual subject in a manner unsuitable for young people," (2) "to make it a federal crime to use the mails, or other facilities of commerce, for the commercial exploitation of a prurient interest in sex through advertising," and (3) "to extend the existing law to enable a citizen to protect his home from any intrusion of sex-oriented advertising—regardless of whether or not a citizen has ever received such mailings."

"Nixon and the Media." *Newsweek*, 81(3):42–48, 15 January 1973. **1N127**
A struggle between President Nixon and the media that is in many ways "without precedent in the history of the United States." Television complains of increasing harassment from Washington, local stations fear for their licenses, public television is being cut back, the White House is sniping at the likes of the *Wash-*

ington Post and the *New York Times*, huge scheduled increases in the postal rates threaten the existence of many magazines, reporters have been thrown into jail for refusing to hand over confidential information to courts or grand juries, other reporters are threatened for engaging in investigative reporting that embarrasses politicians, and Daniel Ellsberg and Anthony Russo face trial for publishing the Pentagon Papers.

Nizer, Louis. "Headlines vs. Justice: Can We Have a Fair Trial and a Free Press at the Same Time?" *Journal of Beverly Hills Bar Association*, 2(9):18–23, October 1968.   **1N128**
On the eve of the Kennedy assassination trial, a prominent trial lawyer attacks the American practice of "trial by newspaper" which, he charges, hinders the judicial process and denies a fair trial for the accused. The press does not have a constitutional "right to know," only a "right to publish." He recommends the barring of certain statements and disclosures by all participants in an impending trial prior to the trial; he calls for voluntary agreements by the press to publish only certain basic data about the trial and accused before and during the course of the trial. Newspapers would merely be delaying the publication of details, not repressing them. Papers that violated the code should be punished by the courts, following the British doctrine of constructive criminal contempt.

————. "Trial by Headline." *McCall's*, 94(5):93, 182–84, February 1967.
1N129
The author charges that after reading the newspapers an impartial jury is not possible in today's sensational cases. He calls for reform in two directions. Law enforcement officers must not, prior to trial, issue statements or disclose confessions, criminal records of accused, opinions as to his guilt, or what witnesses will testify to. Newspaper, radio and television should pledge that before a trial begins they would publish only the following data: name, age, and address of the accused; how, where, and when the arrest was made; the charge and the identity of the complainant; and the fact that a grand jury has returned an indictment and that a trial date has been set.

Noll, John F. *Manual of the National Organization for Decent Literature*. Huntington, Ind., Our Sunday Visitor Press [1946?]. 222p.   **1N130**
Content: Too Much Emphasis on Sex; Attitude of National Organizing Committee Towards Filth in Print; Survey Confirms Committee's Position; A Secular Magazine Endorses Drive; The N.O.D.L. Code; Many Questions Answered; The Law; New Bills to Curb Lewd Literature; Mayors of Cities Enforce the Law; Druggists; An Appeal to Par-

ents; School Teachers Could Help Immensely; Youth Should Show Its Resentment; An Appeal to Editors and Writers; A Word to Every Christian; To People Professing No Religion; Comics; Death on the Newsstands; How to Organize the Drive Against Lewd Literature; Magazines Banned by the N.O.D.L.; Diocesan Directors.

Nolte, M. Chester, *ed. School Communications; Duties and Dangers. A Legal Memorandum*. Washington, D.C., National Association of Secondary School Principals, 1974. 8p. (ED 89,463)
1N131
"School administrators face increasing risks in the field of school communications. While a school administrator acting in the line of duty and without malice is protected by conditional privilege against libel and slander, it is easy to step outside this protection, and become liable for false or misleading statements. Knowing the results of the cases cited herein can hopefully prevent some wrong steps."

Noorani, A. G., *ed. Freedom of the Press in India. Proceedings of a Seminar Held in Srinagar, May 1970*. Bombay, India, Nachiketa, 1971. 143p. (Leslie Sawhny Programme of Training for Democracy)   **1N132**
Articles relating to press freedom: The Press in Free India by S. Mulgaokar. Freedom of the Press and the Constitution by A. G. Noorani. Monopolies in the Press and Newspaper Chains by Frank Moraes. The Importance of a Free Press in a Democracy by M. R. Masani. News Agencies—Their Role and Need for Independence by C. R. Irani. Several of the articles also appeared in *Quest*, July–September 1970.

[Norbury, John T.] *A Report of the Lord Chief Justice on the Trial of Charles Boulton Johnston and Joseph Timothy Hayden, for a Libel against . . . Richard Marquess Wellesley, Lord Lieutenant of Ireland*. Dublin, Ireland, Richard Milliken, 1825. 19p.
1N133
Johnston was proprietor and Hayden editor of *The Star and Fashionable World*. Justice Norbury told the jury that freedom of the press "does not authorize any man to defame his fellow creatures, or endanger the peace of society. . . . No man has a right to vilify or defame a public man, any more than he has a right to defame or vilify a private individual." The right to criticize public policy does not include the right to impute base nature or expose officials to contempt.

Nord, Nancy. "Red Lion Broadcasting Co., Inc. v. FCC—Extension of the Fairness Doctrine to Include Right of Access to the Press." *South Dakota Law Review*, 15:172–83, Winter 1970. **1N134**
"The Court's decision in *Red Lion* [*Red Lion Broadcasting Co., Inc. v. FCC*, 1969], upholding

the regulations implementing the FCC's fairness doctrine, points the way to the redefining of the first amendment to include right of access to the mass media."

Norman, Andrew E. "The Last To Censor." *Bookmark* (New York State Library), 29:128–30, January 1970.
1N135
Public libraries should be the last institutions to be allowed to act as censors. "Unlike many other public and semipublic agencies, which represent and serve the community as a whole, the library is created and supported to serve us all one at a time, each in our own way. Its very nature, then, demands that the persons responsible for it must ignore their own tastes and opinions, their own hopes and fears. When a question of censorship arises, the library's proper role is that of counsel for the defense, not prosecutor and not judge and jury." The author is both a publisher and a public library trustee.

Norman, Charles. *The Case of Ezra Pound . . . with Opinions by Conrad Aiken, E. E. Cummings, F. O. Matthiessen, William Carlos Williams, Louis Zukofsky*. New York, Bodley, 1948. 71p.   **1N136**
A brief biography of the poet, excerpts from his Rome propaganda broadcasts, and views of various writers on the eve of his treason trial. Included is a statement from Random House which deleted Pound's poems from a Modern Library anthology.

Norris, William C., Jr. *An Evaluation of Federal Court Decisions on Religion in Broadcasting in the Light of the First Amendment*. Los Angeles, University of Southern California, 1971. 259p. (Ph.D. dissertation, University Microfilms, no. 72–17,496)   **1N137**
"The general problem of this study was to describe, analyze and evaluate the Federal Appellate Courts and Supreme Court broadcast decisions, 1927–1969, which contained considerations of religion. Four criteria were derived from the First Amendment and the Communications Act of 1934." Twenty-six of the 770 decisions on broadcasting during the period dealt with religion among the issues.

North, Gary. "Pornography, Community, Law." *National Review*, 25:943–44, 31 August 1973.   **1N138**
The U.S. Supreme Court's reversal of a trend toward permissiveness in the area of obscenity (21 June 1973) and the return to the *Roth* standard of 1957, is applauded by the author. He rejects the "half-truth" that you can't legislate morality. "All law is legislated morality; each law will infringe on somebody. . . . There is hardly an issue more fundamental to a community than the regulation of its family structure and sexual behavior," and exposure to pornography has a serious effect on this behavior. He calls for censorship of pornography

which is "a subtle form of cultural nihilism. . . . It is quite possible to have censorship of obscene literature and wide freedom to publish anti-establishment newspapers and journals. . . . Local censorship over a few dirty bookstores and theaters, in the name of a familiar morality rather than some new brand of perfectionism, is a cheap form of insurance for the preservation of a seriously liberal society."

North, John H. *Speeches Delivered by Mr. North, on Behalf of Mr. James Magee, Proprietor of the Dublin Evening-Post: One in the Court of King's Bench, Dublin, On the 14th Day of December, 1815, in the Cause of James Magee against Nicholas Purcell O'Gorman, Barrister at Law; The Other in the Court-House of Galway, On the 2d of April, 1816, in a Cause Wherein Mr. O'Gorman Was Plaintiff, and Mr. Magee Defendant.* Dublin, Ireland, Printed for R. Milliken, 1816. 41p., 53p. **1N139**
James Magee, proprietor of the pro-Catholic paper, the *Dublin Evening Post*, sued O'Gorman for delivering to him and inducing him to publish a report knowing it to be false. O'Gorman was fined 977 pounds, 13 shillings, and 10 pence. James Magee had taken over operation of the *Post* two years earlier when his brother John was imprisoned for publishing articles in defense of the Catholic cause (M147).

North, William D. "Intellectual Freedom." *ALA Bulletin*, 62:948–50, September 1968. **1N140**
The legal counsel of the American Library Association notes that "the struggle between the forces of intellectual freedom and the forces of intellectual repression is, and probably always will be, a contest of wills, a test of motivation and inspiration. Victory will be decided not by the number of martyrs but by the number of converts." He calls for moderation and compromise in the effort to establish "legal rights."

North Carolina. Bench-Bar-Press Broadcasters Committee. *The News Media and the Courts: A Handbook.* Chapel Hill, N. C., The Committee, 1968. 60p. **1N141**
The guidebook, intended to familiarize newsmen with North Carolina courts and court procedures, includes a statement of principles on free press and fair trial adopted by the Committee.

North Carolina Associated Press Members. *Freedom of Information Conference. Minutes.* Raleigh, N.C., North Carolina Associated Press Members, 1954. 56p. Processed. **1N142**
Talks and discussions covered such topics as relations between the press and the judiciary, rights of reporters in covering trials, the covering of the legislature (J. W. Wiggins), withholding of information by law enforcement

agencies, and the right of inspection of police records.

[Northcott, William A.] *The Dedication of the Elijah P. Lovejoy Monument, Alton, Illinois, November 8, 1897.* Greenville, Ill., Illinois Advocate, 1897. 14p. **1N143**
Includes news reports of event from Alton *Republican*, historical notes, as well as address of Illinois Lieutenant Governor Northcott. Frontispiece of Lovejoy.

Northrop, David E. "Injunctive Proceedings Against the Display or Sale of Obscene Materials." *Ohio State Law Journal*, 33:236–46, Winter 1972. **1N144**
An examination of two Ohio obscenity cases in light of U.S. Supreme Court precedent—*State, ex. rel. Keating v. A Motion Picture Entitled "Vixen,"* 27 Ohio St. 2d 278, 272 N.E.2d 37 (1971) and *State, ex. rel. Sensenbrenner v. Adult Book Store,* 26 Ohio App. 2d 183, 271 N.E.2d 13 (Franklin County, 1971). The author concludes that the Ohio courts were incorrect in reasoning and conclusion.

Norton, David R. "Access to the Printed Media by Political Candidates: Miami Herald Publishing Co. v. Tornillo." *Southwestern Law Journal*, 28:1038–43, Winter 1974. **1N145**
The author concludes that the *Tornillo* decision of the U.S. Supreme Court (1974), supports the original intent of the First Amendment which guaranteed the freedom of newspapers to discuss public issues, but did not require the discussion to be fair or representative of both sides. The *Red Lion* decision (*Red Lion Broadcasting Co. v. FCC,* 1967), is inconsistent with *Tornillo* in that it requires the broadcasting industry to provide access. Inconsistent treatment of the two media will become more acute as scarcity of airways disappears and economic barriers to the press remain.

[Norton, John H., III.] "Private Defamation Plaintiff Allowed Recovery Based Upon Showing of Negligence in Reporting." *Memphis State University Law Review*, 5:285–91, Winter 1975. **1N146**
Re: *Gertz v. Robert Welch, Inc.* 94 S. Ct. 2997 (1974).

Norwick, Kenneth P. *Lobbying for Freedom: A Citizen's Guide to Fighting Censorship at the State Level.* New York, St. Martin's Press, 1975. 158p. (Excerpted in a 72-page pamphlet published in 1974 by Playboy Press, Chicago, which provided a grant to the author for his study) **1N147**
The work gives general background information on state legislatures and the legislative process. This is followed by a section on Censorship, the Supreme Court and State Legisla-

tures, answering the following questions: How should obscenity be defined? What is the appropriate "community"? Should there be prior court proceedings on the issue of obscenity? What kind of civil proceedings should there be? The final section gives guidelines and suggestions for effectively lobbying the legislature and the governor.

———. *Pornography: The Issues and the Law.* New York, Public Affairs Committee, 1972. 28p. (Public Affairs Pamphlet no. 477) **1N148**
A popular presentation of the issue—historical background, Supreme Court decisions, the case for and against suppressing pornography, recommendations of the Commission on Obscenity and Pornography, and what lies ahead.

Norwin, W. P. "Patrioteers in Action: The Strange Case of William H. Bridge." *Debunker*, 9(1):33–42, December 1928. **1N149**
The unsuccessful libel case against a columnist of the *Boonton* (N.J.) *Times Bulletin* by a local member of the Daughters of the American Revolution.

Notson, Robert C. "Newsmen Stand Naked Before the Courts." *Bulletin of the American Society of Newspaper Editors*, 522:9–10, September 1968. **1N150**
"For the first time in 180 years of Oregon's history, an editor has been punished for refusing to divulge the names of persons who provided published information." A discussion of the case of Annette Buchanan and its implications. The author would prefer no privilege law, "but now that all legal safeguard has been swept away, I believe it is necessary to restore the protections that we always thought existed."

Novak, John P. *The Legal Status of Sexually-Oriented Material in the State of Illinois.* Charleston, Ill., Eastern Illinois University, 1973. 133p. (Unpublished Master's thesis) **1N151**

Novak, Robert M. "The New Journalism." In Harry M. Clor, *ed.*, *The Mass Media and Modern Democracy.* Chicago, Rand McNally, 1974, pp. 1–14. **1N152**
A discussion of the deepening change in the mass media that has taken place in the last twenty-five years, the result of two basic developments: "First, the journalists working for the television networks, the big news magazines, and the important metropolitan press had now become part of the liberal establishment, both in their manner of living and in

their ideological commitment. Second, in a later and less fully developed trend, these journalists were increasingly advocating causes of the moment rather than functioning as neutral observers. Taken together, the developments widened the gap between the mass media and the great mass of citizens, a gap that can result only in diminished credibility of the media, and therefore the inadequate fulfillment of the necessary function of the press in a democratic society."

Noyes, Richard P. "The ABA's Involvement in the Long Struggle Against Censorship." *Publishers' Weekly*, 207 (20):129–30, 19 May 1975. **1N153**
A review of censorship legislation and court decisions since the *Ulysses* case in the 1930s and the role played by the publishing industry (American Booksellers Association). The author finds increasing banding together of book distributors, librarians, teachers, and others in the communications industry to fight censorship. He refers particularly to the Media Coalition in New York. The best advice to booksellers is "to run a truly first-rate, responsible bookshop . . . carrying a wide assortment of books representing a variety of points of view; then you have a good chance in your community to weather what local storms may come."

Nugent, H. P. *H. P. Nugent's Reply to the Calumnies of the Honorable F. X. Martin, one of the Judges of the Superior Court of the Territory of Orleans. . . .* Natchez, Miss., Printed for the Author, 1811. 60p. **1N154**
Nugent had written a critical review of Judge Martin's translation of the work of the eighteenth-century French jurist Robert J. Pothier. Judge Martin accused Nugent of being an atrocious libeler; Nugent retorted that Martin was a "lecherous, treacherous, bloody, bawdy villain," notorious for his libidinous amours. For this Nugent was brought to trial, found guilty of libel, and sent to jail.

Nyberg, Janet. *Minnesota's Press Council*. Columbia, Mo., Freedom of Information Center, School of Journalism, University of Missouri at Columbia, 1974. 5p. (Report no. 327) **1N155**
"The experiences and operations of Minnesota's press council are looked upon by many as demonstrating the basic soundness or folly of the press council concept. This report provides some evidence the reader may use in making a judgment of his own."

———. *Testing the FOI Act*. Columbia, Mo., Freedom of Information Center, School of Journalism, University of Missouri at Columbia, 1974. 7p. (Report no. 318) **1N156**

"In its first case involving the FOI Act, the Supreme Court upheld total secrecy of security papers. Despite this set-back, lower courts have ruled in favor of freedom of information in roughly half the cases argued under the Act. Proposed legislation could increase its successes by closing loopholes in the Act."

Nyren, Karl. "A Dime-Store Paul Revere. A New Trustee Plunges a Thriving Young Library on Long Island Into Chaos." *Library Journal*, 92:3380–84, 1 October 1967. (Reprinted in Eric Moon, *ed.*, *Book Selection and Censorship in the Sixties*, pp. 347–55) **1N157**
The case of a John Birch Society member who, upon election to the board of the Farmingdale Public Library, conducted a campaign of harassment and vilification of the library staff in his effort to stamp out liberal and obscene materials. At the time of writing, he had been charged with petty larceny, stemming from the confiscation of the Library's copy of *Paris Review*, and with assault against the children's librarian, when she attempted to prevent him from interrupting a children's program.

[———.] "Intellectual Freedom, ALA Midwinter." *Library Journal*, 95:997–99, 15 March 1970. **1N158**
A report of discussion and action relating to intellectual freedom at the Atlantic City conference of the American Library Association, the first priority of the Association for the year.

O

Oakley, Robert L. "Access to the Law." *Bookmark*, 32:7–10, September–October 1972.   **101**
Comments on the current interest, under due process, to give prisoners access to basic legal materials in order to take their cases back to the courts. A list of basic law books for a New York correctional facility is appended.

Obermier, Duane A. *A Study of Press Law in High School Journalism*. Manhattan, Kans., Kansas State University, 1971. 77p. (Unpublished Master's thesis)   **102**
This study analyzes the teaching of press law in high schools and the influence press law has on the content of high school publications—yearbooks and newspapers.

Oboler, Eli M. "Congress as Censor." *Library Trends*, 19:64–73, July 1970.   **103**
The author traces the history of federal censorship legislation in the United States from the Comstock Acts of 1873 through the 91st Congress when more than one hundred obscenity laws were introduced and President Nixon made obscenity the issue in a special message to Congress.

———. "Everything You Always Wanted to Know About Censorship (but were afraid to ask), Explained." *American Libraries*, 2:194–98, February 1971.   **104**
An essay on the anthropological basis for censorship of sex writings and the reasons for fear of sex words and symbols.

———. *The Fear of the Word: Censorship and Sex*. New York, Scarecrow, 1974. 362p.   **105**
Content: The Bases for Censorship. Taboo: The Primitive Censor. The Word and the Flesh. Portrait of a Censor: Cato. Hellenism, Stoicism, and Censorship. Portrait of a Censor: Savonarola. The Judeo-Christian Influence. The Puritan and the Censor. Today's Religion and Tomorrow's Censorship. The Psychology of Repression: The Motivations of the Censor. The Censor, the Creative Artist, and the Literary Critic. Portrait of a Censor: Anthony Comstock. The Community as Censor. The Law Says, "No!" Portrait of a Censor: Charles H. Keating, Jr. The New Morality and the Old Librarian. After the C.O.P. (Commission on Obscenity and Pornography) Report: Has Censorship a Future in America? The Censor, the Individual, and Morality. The Supreme Court, Censorship, and Eros. Epilog: Portrait of the Censor. Included in the appendix are Recommendations of the Commission on Obscenity and Pornography; Recommendations of the British "Working Party"; a collection of quotations on censorship, entitled An Anti-Censorship Chrestomathy; a bibliography.

———. "The Free Mind: Intellectual Freedom's Perils and Prospects." *Library Journal*, 101:237–42, 1 January 1976.   **106**
In an essay on the development of the concept of intellectual freedom, the author expresses concern for the future of libraries, faced by a "double onslaught" of Big Brother government and "a new nemisis in the form of a self-labeled 'information industry.' " He raises the question: "Is copyright a form of control of intellectual property whose value transcends the rights of students and researchers to 'reasonable' (whatever that is!) use of published materials in copied format?" In whatever format the library of the future may take, "whoever makes the decisions on *what* is to be stored, *what* is to be communicated, and *how*, must, if the free mind is to remain free, be equally free."

———. "The Freedom to Choose: A Reply to 'Freedom from Filth.' " *Intellect*, 103:263–64, January 1975.   **107**
A reply to an editorial by William W. Brickman in the December 1973 issue. "Censorship—any censorship—cannot be justified in a democracy if we really believe in man's freedom to choose for himself, in man's God-given right to motivation by his own conscience, and, finally, in the ability of man to learn only when he is given an opportunity to learn by seeing all knowledge spread out before him."

———. "The Grand Illusion." *Library Journal*, 93:1277–79, 15 March 1968.   **108**
"Parents are fooling themselves by limiting children's reading experiences. A librarian speaks out for intellectual freedom for teenage readers, underscoring flaws in current book selection guides." There follows a list of books on sex education compiled by Dorothy S. Jones, and a list of audio-visual material on sex education for the adolescent compiled by Abraham Cohen.

———. "Intellectual Freedom and Idaho Libraries." *Idaho Librarian*, 25:3–4, January 1973.   **109**
Introduction to an issue which reprints the various American Library Association statements on intellectual freedom together with a statement drafted by the Intellectual Freedom Committee of the Idaho Library Association in 1968.

———. "The New Morality and the Old Librarian." *ALA Bulletin*, 62:1369–73, December 1968.   **1010**
The author suggests that librarians need to take into consideration the "new morality" of sex in making book selections.

———. "Paternalistic Morality and Censorship." *Library Journal*, 98:2395–98, 1 September 1973.   **1011**
A discussion of public versus private morality and the implications for library book selection and censorship. The best reply to the question of what restraints should be exercised by the librarian in book selection is "that the self-respecting librarian must live by both public morality (as conveyed in laws and attitudes) and by his own private morality, his morality as a professional—his morality, finally, as a librarian."

———. "The Politics of Pornography." *Library Journal*, 95:4225–28, 15 December 1970.   **1012**

"A librarian's reaction to the U.S. Senate's rejection of the report of the Commission on Obscenity and Pornography."

————. "Public Relations and Intellectual Freedom." *PNLA Quarterly* (Pacific Northwest Library Association), 38:17–21, April 1974. **1013**
Advice and exhortation on how to create the kind of intellectual climate in the community before a censorship crisis arises. "If we can't sell the importance of intellectual freedom for all at least as well as the life insurance salesman sells his policies, we deserve to be forgotten, neglected, overlooked, and stepped on."

O'Brien, Josephine. "Sex, Saints and Censors." *Bell*, 8:23–33, April 1944. **1014**
Literary censorship in Ireland is dead, according to the author, because it has lost the confidence of the public. "The Censorship depended upon the support of the Roman Catholic Church for its hold on the public conscience; it lost that support as soon as the public lost its belief that the Censorship was conducted on Catholic principles. The precise time when that belief was lost must have been when the daily papers published the fact that the Censorship Board had banned as being in its general tendency indecent a book which had been approved by the highest Roman Catholic authority in England. The public would not swallow that." Some Irish priests may still support the censorship, but they do not represent the views of the Church.

"Obscenity." *Journal of Criminal Law & Criminology*, 65:499–504, December 1974. **1015**
"This note will explore *Hamling* [*Hamling v. United States*, 1974] and *Jenkins* [*Jenkins v. Georgia*, 1974] in the light of *Miller* [*Miller v. California*, 1973], examining the decisions to see if *Miller* has made the obscenity question more manageable."

Obscenity. An Australian Survey. Redfern, Australia, Goldeneye [1965?]. 50p., 30p. (Nos. 1 and 2) **1016**
This collection of facts and commentary includes a survey of the Australian obscenity law; who's who on literature censorship boards; a list of works banned as imports by the Literature Censorship Board; reviews of recently banned books, including, *Candy*, *Nexus*, and *Naked Lunch*; John Power's account of the banning of *The Ginger Man*; text of the *Tharunka* trial involving a University of New South Wales student publication; and a Statement of Principles on Freedom to Read adopted by the Library Association of Australia. The publishers of the journal were brought to trial, convicted, and the decision upheld by the High Court.

"Obscenity Law: Après Stanley." *Catholic Lawyer*, 17:45–62, Winter 1971. **1017**
"This article hopefully will perform three functions: (1) summarization and analysis of the *Stanley* [*Stanley v. Georgia*, 1969] opinion; (2) presentation of the diverse constructions of *Stanley*; and (3) prediction of the scope of constitutional protection that will be afforded in obscene matter." The author makes two predictions: "(1) Protection of children and of the privacy of unwilling adults will be held to outweigh any interest in its unrestricted dissemination; and (2) The decision will not be unanimous. As a result, controlled distribution, i.e. distribution which will not endanger children and invade the privacy of others, may eventually gain legal protection, but obscenity is not yet an 'idea whose time has come.' "

The Obscenity Report; The Report to the Task Force on Pornography and Obscenity. New York, Stein and Day, 1970. 130p. **1018**
A parody on the impending report of the U.S. Commission on Obscenity and Pornography, purportedly being submitted to President Nixon. *The Obscenity Report* finds that "greater frequency of sexual intercourse produces greater possibility of conception," that "the lust motive seems to appear more frequently among the young than among the old," and, as one evidence of the harmful influence of pornography, cites the case of a seventy-year-old woman who raped the mailman after receiving an obscene advertisement. The report recommends, among other things, suppressive legal measures and "compulsory federal regulation of pornography readers." It is filled with statistical documentation, footnotes, and contains an index that combines serious references to statements of Justices Black and Douglas, Sigmund Freud, and Representative Katherine Granahan, along with such humorous references as: Cherubim, private parts of, deplored by authors; Eve, treacherous but desirable valley of; and Texas, can't show nipple in. The publishers claim the report was a typescript leaked to them by a confidential source and that, since the official report might be suppressed, they were publishing this in the interest of a free press.

"Obscenity '73: Something Old, A Little Bit New, Quite a Bit Borrowed, But Nothing Blue." *Maryland Law Review*, 33:421–60, 1973. **1019**
The purpose of this Note is to examine the new guidelines formulated by the U.S. Supreme Court in five opinions handed down on June 21, 1973 (*Miller v. California, Paris Adult Theatre I v. Slaton, U.S. v. Orito, Kaplan v. California, U.S. v. 12 200-Ft Reels of Film*) and, "by comparison of these guidelines to the previously defined standards, to indicate what, if any, real changes have been made."

Observer, *pseud*. "Censorship in Australia." *Bulletin* (Australia), 92:39–42, 21 February 1970. **1020**

A review of Australia's *Censorship Crisis*, edited by Geoffrey Dutton and Max Harris, with comments on the censorship movement in Australia that began in the 1930s. The reviewer suggests what reforms of Australian censorship might be acceptable to a conservative country—limitation of controls to protection of children and consideration of "public decency."

O'Connell, Kevin, Justin Miller *et al*. *Should Television Be Allowed to Broadcast Criminal Trials with the Consent of the Defendant? A Debate.* 53-min. tape recording. North Hollywood, Calif., Center for Cassette Studies, 1971. (Publisher's title: Television and Trials, Part II) **1021**
Speakers for: Kevin O'Connell, Thomas Brennan, and Richard W. Jencks. Speakers against: Justin Miller, Grant Cooper, and Dr. Charles Wall. Judge: Joseph Ball.

[O'Connor, Arthur.] *Beauties of the Press; with an Appendix, Containing the Speech of Arthur O'Connor on the Catholic Question in the House of Commons of Ireland . . . May 4, 1795: Also, his Letter to Lord Castlereagh.* London, 1800. 602p., 48p. **1022**
A compilation of essays and letters to the editor (O'Connor) appearing in the *Press*, a paper established to give the people of Ireland an opportunity to express themselves, not afforded in the existing press, which, the author charges, was engaged in public prostitution. Numerous references to freedom of the Press: Thoughts on Printing and Liberty of the Press by William Caxton; On the Liberty of the Press by Marcus; On the Liberty of the Press by Sidney; and John P. Curran's speech on the trial of Peter Finnerty. There is also an account of the arrest and jailing of the printer (John Stockdale) and editor (Arthur O'Connor) of the *Press*. O'Connor's letter to Lord Castlereagh was written from prison.

[————.] *Extracts from the Press: A Newspaper Published in the Capital of Ireland, during part of the Years 1797 and 1798. Including Numbers sixty-eight and sixty-nine, which were suppressed by Order of the Irish Government, before the usual time of publication.* Philadelphia, William Duane, Aurora Office, 1802. 400p. **1023**
This American collection of extracts from the *Press* contains a number of the articles on press freedom that appeared in *Beauties of the Press*, including the essays of Caxton and Marcus, and numerous references to the arrest and trial of printer Peter Finnerty and the persecution of other Irish editors and publishers. The American publisher, William Duane, had himself been a victim of censorship under the Sedition Law of 1798.

O'Connor, Craig R. "Obscenity vel

None!" *Law and Social Order*, 1972: 300–312, 1972. **1024**
"The writer concludes from study of these cases, as well as others of like nature, that the Supreme Court is attempting to divorce itself from the burdensome task of protecting citizens of low 'obscenity tolerance.' . . . The Court will protect children and the sensibilities of citizens who seek privacy. But the Court will no longer pass judgment as the ultimate censor of the nation's reading and viewing matter. . . . In the immediate future, however, the impact of *Redrup* [Redrup v. New York, 1967] will continue to dominate the development of obscenity law."

[O'Connor, Feargus.] . . . *Trial of Feargus O'Connor, Esquire, and 58 Other Chartists, on a Charge of Seditious Conspiracy. Nisi Prius Court, Lancaster, Wednesday, March 1st, 1843. . . .* London, 1843. 451p. **1025**
O'Connor was founder and publisher of the weekly radical paper, *Northern Star*, which was practically the official organ of the Chartists. In 1840 he was sentenced to eighteen months imprisonment for seditious libels published in his paper. The 1843 trial was for a seditious conspiracy. Although he was convicted, a technicality in the indictment prevented sentencing.

O'Connor, John J. "What's Off at the Pictures?" *Wall Street Journal*, 176 (107):16, 30 November 1970. **1026**
A view of the motion picture self-rating system and the increased sexual permissiveness in films.

O'Connor, Neal W. "The Freedom to Communicate. An Advertising Man Re-Reads the First Amendment." *Vital Speeches*, 42:179–83, 1 January 1976. **1027**
An advertising executive discusses "freedom of expression which the journalist, the advertiser, the business executive and the just plain citizen in this country have the right to share." He remarks on the antibusiness bias in broadcasting which he attributes to a simplistic view of the complexities of business, a tendency toward cynicism, and the attempted manipulation of the media by professional advocates. He discusses the movement for counter-advertising and its serious consequences and argues for the extension of freedom of speech and press to advertising under the First Amendment.

O'Dell, Sherry. "Victorian Censorship." *Arkansas Libraries*, 28(3):24–27, Winter 1972. **1028**
A brief view of censorship in Victorian England, including the work of the vice societies and the Bowdlerizing of the classics.

Odgers, W. Blake. *Should the Existing Law as to Blasphemy be Amended, and, if so, in what Direction?* London, Spottiswoode, 1883. 17p. **1029**
The author is content with the existing law of blasphemy and believes it "permits the frankest avowal and the warmest advocacy of all opinions, however heretical, which the writer or speaker sincerely entertains. It only interferes where our religious feelings are insulted and outraged by wanton and unnecessary profanity." A paper read at the meeting of the Social Science Congress, Huddersfield, October 1883.

O'Donnell, James J. "Censorship and the Publishers." *NASSP Bulletin* (National Association of Secondary School Principals), 59:59–63, May 1975. **1030**
Publishers of controversial textbooks face a dilemma: they want to defend good texts against unwarranted criticism, but do not want to inject themselves into local controversies that might compromise the school's position. A textbook editor discusses threats against a particular textbook, *Communist China*, against the broader issue of pressure groups and the role of publishers and authors who must face the demands of educational adoption committees.

O'Donnell, Peadar. "The Dumb Multitudinous Masses." *Bell*, 2(4):67–69, July 1941. **1031**
"Censorship is the screen the dying order sets up to hide its weakness and shame."

Oettinger, Anthony. "Merging Media and the First Amendment." *Nieman Reports*, 28(4):3–7, Winter 1974. **1032**
"More recognition should be accorded the motion that investment transfers, as from over-the-air broadcasting operations in urban areas to cable, could provide in electronic media something of the much stronger—however flawed—First Amendment structure which we've become accustomed to in the print media."

Oettinger, Elmer. "A Shield Law for the Press. What Is the Free-Press Guarantee of the First Amendment?" *Popular Government*, 39(7):6–10, April 1973. **1033**
A resolution of the issue of a shield law for journalists has been hampered by differences in opinion among the professionals as to which alternative is desirable (1) an absolute shield law, (2) a qualified shield law, or (3) no shield law.

Oettinger, Mal. "Whitehead and License Renewal: Will His Speech Backfire in the Congressional Arena?" *Television/Radio Age*, 20:43–44, 95–96, 8 January 1973. **1034**
An interview with Clay T. Whitehead, President Nixon's spokesman on broadcasting, in which Whitehead's controversial speech on license renewal and network news bias was discussed.

"Offensive Speech and the FCC." *Yale Law Journal*, 79:1343–68, June 1970. **1035**
"Under the theory which currently justifies broadcast regulation, governmental power over this type of programming—which may be labelled quasi-obscene or offensive—is virtually unlimited. [References were made to complaints about a poem, Jehovah's Child, broadcast over stations licensed to the Pacifica Foundation.] Attempts to exercise this power raise important free-speech questions which the current theory of regulation ignores. A governmental role may be appropriate in the broadcast industry, but it should be a carefully limited one. After delineating the failings of the current approach to governmental regulation, this Note suggests a set of First Amendment standards for determining the validity of FCC action in the area of offensive speech."

O'Faolain, Sean. "The Dangers of Censorship." *Ireland Today*, 1(6):57–63, November 1936. **1036**
The author, whose own work, *Bird Alone*, was banned by the Irish censor, believes that the main objections to the working of the Censorship of Publications Act is not primarily concerned with the wisdom or unwisdom of banning certain individual books. "While it is, undoubtedly, an indignity to be publicly proclaimed as a pornographer, we could bear with that, confident of our own integrity as artists, and indifferent, as artists, to a form of insult which is rapidly becoming quite meaningless by indiscriminate use, if we did not believe that the chief results of the Censorship are to debase the public conscience, to bring the law into disrepute, and to limit, not the growth of the author, but the growth of the nation."

O'Flaherty, Wendy. "Obscenity in Religion (The Abuses of Literacy—3)." *Times Literary Supplement*, 3,648:91–92, 28 January 1972. **1037**
A comparative study of religion reveals that there is no innate quality in the "obscene" object which embodies obscene thoughts. " 'Obscene' is a pejorative term expressing moral disapprobation, yet the obscene element may be purposely used by worshippers to achieve their spiritual ends."

Oglesby, Dwayne L. "Freedom of the Press v. The Rights of the Individual—A Continuing Controversy." *Oregon Law Review*, 47:132–45, February 1968. **1038**
"It is the thesis of this paper that the press should be more readily held accountable for the publication of a false article in the field of entertainment news than for falsity in the publication of a political advertisement or a news dispatch."

O Hannracháin, Fachtna. "Privacy and Broadcasting." *EBU Review* (European Broadcasting Union), 1970(119B): 50–55, January 1970.   **1039**
The legal advisor of Irish radio reviews the existing laws on invasion of privacy by broadcasting in the United Kingdom and the United States, noting various offenses that are considered: intrusion, disclosure, false light in the public's eye, and appropriation of the plaintiff's identity. He suggests that broadcasters could best avoid enactment of overrestrictive legislation by voluntarily adopting codes of conduct which recognize the right of privacy.

O'Higgins, Paul. "Blasphemy in Irish Law." *Modern Law Review*, 23(2): 151–66, March 1960.   **1040**
The author finds that the Irish Constitution and Irish law leave considerable doubt as to the meaning of the term "blasphemous" and that the matter lends itself to confusion and obscurity.

————. *Censorship in Britain*. London, Nelson, 1972. 232p.   **1041**
"The main aim of this book is to make people aware of the different kinds of censorship operating in Britain; and to suggest that censorship poses a number of basic problems for those who are concerned to maintain and increase the area within which freedom of thought and expression operate in the community." The author describes the laws and regulations which govern official censorship; the extent and methods of extralegal censorship; and how censorship has operated against the various media: books, libraries, theater, advertising, newspapers, and broadcasting. One chapter deals with the relationship between employment and censorship; another deals with government secrecy. The appendix includes: the text of the Earl of Chesterfield's 1737 speech attacking stage censorship; the Independent Television Authority's Code of Violence; the British Code of Advertising Practices; Objectives of the Press Council; BBC's Television Policy Governing Violence; and the 1969 Freedom of Publication Bill, which amended the libel law.

Ohio Library Association. "Intellectual Freedom Policy Statement." *Ohio Library Association Bulletin*, 41(1):22–25, January 1971.   **1042**
Authority of the Ohio Library Association in the area of intellectual freedom, areas of concern, mechanism "for handling complaints about specific material which has been acquired by libraries in accordance with the basic policy and selection procedures adopted above."

O'Keefe, Daniel F., Jr. *et al.* "The FDA's Freedom of Information Act Regulations." *Food Drug Cosmetic Law Journal*, 30:312–80, June 1975.   **1043**
The entire issue is devoted to Freedom of Information Act Regulations issued by the Food and Drug Administration. The material presented resulted from a briefing session on the regulations held by the Food and Drug Law Institute, 12 March 1975.

Oklahoma Library Association. "Statement of Policy on Intellectual Freedom." *Oklahoma Librarian*, 21(3): 40–41, July 1971.   **1044**
Adopted by the Association, 16 April 1971.

[Oklahoma Public Library Systems.] *The Limits to Freedom? Oklahoma's Private Values and Public Policy on the Right to Read. Research Papers.* [Oklahoma City, Okla., Oklahoma Public Library Systems, 1975?] 121p. Processed.   **1045**
A collection of papers prepared under a project sponsored by the Oklahoma Public Library Systems and supported in part by a grant from the Oklahoma Humanities Committee and the National Endowment for the Humanities. Since the U.S. Supreme Court ruled in June 1973 that in matters of obscenity the arbiter of freedoms is to be the community standard, "the research of this committee," writes Peter Denman in the introduction, "has sought to uncover just what those standards are in a number of communities in Oklahoma. Another question which the researchers have investigated is the nature of the community itself. . . . Where are lines to be drawn where we can justly say, 'Here is the community and here are the standards'? . . . Perhaps the political and social life of a town is dominated by a self-perpetuating elite; shall the standards of that elite prescribe the standards of all people in town? Can we expect the prohibitive standards of a newspaper publisher to speak for its readership?" The papers are as follows: A Report on Legal Research Related to Limits to Freedom by Mary Lu Gordon. A Bibliographical Summary of Oklahoma Law by Mary Lu Gordon. The Limits of Individual Freedom by D. Duane Cummins. Film Censorship: Some Notes and Observations by John C. Pickard, Jr. Censorship in the History of the Modern Age of Western Civilization with the Focus on the Arts of the United States of America Now by John C. Pickard, Jr. Minors and Minorities: A Tape Recorded Discussion Summarized by Barbara Hillyer Davis (director of the project). The Double Impact of Censorship on Minorities by Elwyn B. Welch. Criteria for Evaluation of Minorities and Women in Textbooks and Other Materials by Mae F. Nolan. Appendices: A Survey of Adult Attitudes Concerning Nude Dancing in Oklahoma County. Censorship and Community Standards: A Collection of Newspaper Reports on Oklahoma's Private Values and Public Policy. Towards a Sane Look at Censorship and Obscenity by Donald E. Hayden. A library lending copy of the papers is on file at the American Library Association, Chicago.

O'Leary, J. Dennis. "Libel of the Public Figure: An Unsettled Controversy." *St. Louis Law Journal*, 12:103–18, Fall 1967.   **1046**
"This comment will trace the development of the public official exclusion and its subsequent application to the public figure generally." The author concludes that the Supreme Court "must reach an agreement upon a workable test applicable to public figures in the field of libel. Otherwise, as Justice Black suggests, the Court will find itself 'in the same quagmire in the field of libel in which it is now hopelessly struggling in the field of obscenity.' "

O'Leary, John F. "The Right to Be Informed." *Massachusetts Law Quarterly*, 54:63–75, March 1969.   **1047**
The author focuses on the difficulty of access to much of the "Executive Legislation" of the Commonwealth. "Taking note of the fact that the administrative rules and regulations of the Commonwealth are not readily accessible to persons whose lives are affected by them, the author proposes a statute which would go a long way toward curing the defects in the present system."

[Olick, Alice D.] "Fairness Doctrine." *New York Law Forum*, 21:455–64, Winter 1976.   **1048**
Re: *National Broadcasting Co. v. FCC*, 516 F.2d 1101 (D.C. Cir. 1974) in which "the court of appeals held that broadcasting licensees have far more power in determining program content than ever before, and consequently, it limited the powers of the FCC. The controversy in this case arose out of the presentation of a National Broadcasting Company television program entitled 'Pensions, A Broken Promise.' " Acting on a complaint from Accuracy-in-Media, Inc. the FCC found that the program violated the fairness doctrine, but the court reversed the ruling.

Oliver, Richard, and Burton B. Roberts. "Free Press vs. Fair Trial." *Senior Scholastic*, 108:30–31, 23 March 1976.   **1049**
A newsman (Richard Oliver) and a judge (Burton B. Roberts) express their views on the controversy between the First and Sixth Amendments.

Oliver, William I. "The Censor in the Ivy." *Drama Review*, 15:31–55, Fall 1970.   **1050**
A survey and analysis of censorship of the campus theater. The author concludes that campus "censorship is more a problem of social differences than of legal actions," a difference of "taste between the theater and the community that surrounds it." He gives advice on how to have a vigorous, honest, theater and to meet controversy rationally and wisely.

[Olivereau, Louise.] *The Louise Olivereau Case. Trial and Speech to the Jury in Federal Court of Seattle, Wash., November*

1917. Seattle, Minnie Parkhurst [1917?]. 64p.   **1051**
The trial of an American anarchist under the wartime espionage act for circulation of anti-war pamphlets.

Olson, Enid M. "Kids Know When They Are Being Conned." *English Journal*, 62:779–83, 816, May 1973. **1052**
Despite a dark past and an uncertain future, students, with backing from the courts are being granted more and more rights, including the right to read. Accordingly, many students have rejected some of the smug and all-knowing educational materials being offered in high schools. "The kids know when there's a gap of truth." The author offers advice for broadening and liberating the instructional material made available to high school students.

Olson, Paul E. "The Texas Harassment Statute, Is It Constitutional?" *South Texas Law Journal*, 17:283–300, 1976. **1053**
"The purpose of this comment is to look at the provisions of the Texas Harassment Statute, dealing with obscene telephone calls in light of *Walker v. Dillard*," and a review of some of the basic concepts which underlie the court's reasoning.

O'Mahony, T. P. "The Press and Democracy." *Studies: An Irish Quarterly Review*, 63:47–58, Spring 1974. **1054**
Freedom of the press is an essential to a democracy, but it is more than just the absence of government control: we need to understand the set of social forces—governmental, societal, and commercial—which bear upon press freedom in order to make the press more accessible and responsive to communal needs. The constitutional caveat that the press "shall not be used to undermine public order or morality or the authority of the State" should be applied with extreme caution, recognizing the shifting meaning of the terms.

O'Malley, William J. "How to Teach 'Dirty' Books in High School." *Media and Methods*, 4:6–11, 46, November 1967. **1055**
A priest considers how English teachers can prepare adolescents for realistic reading and realistic life. "As long as their exposure is gradual, aiming more at compassion for persons than knowledge of sexual variations, and governed by that elusive virtue, prudence, high school seniors should be able to read more and more sexually and literarily sophisticated novels and be prepared to look into the lives of other human persons—to care rather than to snoop." He offers a chart entitled, Literary Sophistication Demanded of Reader, classifying books by amount and kind of sex and by the extent of reader background required.

Omu, Fred I. A. "The Dilemma of Press Freedom in Colonial Africa: The West African Example." *Journal of African History*, 9:279–98, 1968. **1056**
"One of the most striking features of the African nationalist movement is the great effort that was made to safeguard the freedom of the press. As British subjects, most of whom were trained in Britain, educated Africans assumed that they were entitled to enjoy a free press, which was an essential ingredient in the British political tradition. Their newspapers were almost unavoidably highly critical, and colonial administrators sought to control them. A variety of factors contained official repressive enthusiasm, and these provide the key to the relatively small number of prosecutions and the seeming reluctance to enforce press legislation."

O'Neil, Robert M. "Libraries, Liberties and the First Amendment." *University of Cincinnati Law Review*, 42:209–52, 1973. **1057**
The article attempts to analyze three central questions: First, does a prospective reader have any constitutional right to withdraw and read a particular book or does he have any legal remedy against a library that denies him the book? Second, does the librarian, himself, have any constitutional claims and interests apart from those of the prospective reader or the author? Third, does a library, as a public institution, have constitutionally valid interests in withholding material that is constitutionally protected—material which, in other words, a private lending library could circulate with impunity?

————. "Libraries, Librarians and First Amendment Freedoms." *Human Rights Review*, 4:295–312, Summer 1975. **1058**
"Few professions more clearly deserve the protection of the first amendment than librarians. Yet few groups—perhaps none engaged in sensitive intellectual activity—have gained fewer constitutional safeguards. Decisions comparable to those defining the free expression of professors, teachers, reporters, theatrical performers, authors and others simply do not exist in the library field. As a consequence, professional librarians understandably fear censorship and repression—not only in 'book burning' communities but in more tranquil and civilized parts of the country as well." The author considers the reasons for the paucity of constitutional protection, and examines the untested legal bases for a new and much needed First Amendment freedom.

————. "Shield Laws: Partial Solution to a Pervasive Problem." *New York Law Forum*, 20:515–50, Winter 1975. **1059**
"The resolution of the resulting conflicts will be aided only in small part by the enactment of shield laws protecting the journalist's source. Such laws are of limited value for several reasons—courts tend to construe them rather narrowly; they protect only one type of confidential information holder; and their presence diverts attention from the more basic constitutional and public policy questions. . . . The

most serious threats to the journalist's first amendment interests have, after all, occurred in shield law states. Therefore, it would be wise to look to the Constitution for protection."

————. "The Supreme Court and the First Amendment: The 1970 Term." In *Free Speech Yearbook, 1971*. New York, Speech Communication Association, 1971, pp. 80–96. **1060**
A review of decisions which seek to place the Pentagon Papers controversy in the context of a series of related decisions.

————, and Sanford Kadish. "Freedom and Four-Letter Words." *California Monthly*, 58:18–21, May 1965. **1061**
Consideration of the issue of freedom of speech as it applies to four-letter words used in the recent Berkeley Campus demonstrations. "The four-letter language used out of context may be largely treated in non-speech terms even though words have been spoken." Use of obscenity is regulated "for the purpose of preventing deeply offensive or disgusting experiences, and perhaps in part to preserve a certain level of public morality. . . . The audience, too, has rights that must be protected by those who have power to regulate. If that can be done without restricting anyone's constitutional rights to speak and to publish, or to read for his own pleasure, then an intelligent balance is much to be preferred to an uncritical insistence upon absolutes."

O'Neill, Frank. "Censorship: In the South the Means of Resisting Are Weak." *South Today*, 2(6):4–6, January–February 1971. **1062**
"A study of the Southern press shows that while the day of mob attack is fading, censorship is practiced in quieter, equally venal and effective ways. The conclusions underscore the ambivalence of some of the most venerated Southern newspapers and their failure to cover history-making events."

O'Neill, James R. "The Freedom of Information Act and Its Internal Memorandum Exemption: Time for a Practical Approach." *Southwestern Law Journal*, 27:806–36, December 1973. **1063**
The author proposes "means of overcoming practical difficulties experienced in interpreting and implementing the Act," which would require relatively minor revisions.

Oppenheim, Jerrold N. "White House Media Czar Threatens Fairness, Public TV." *Chicago Journalism Review*, 5(6): 11–13, June 1972. **1064**
The work of Clay T. Whitehead, director of

the Office of Telecommunications Policy in the White House.

Oppenheimer, Harry F. "The Press and South African Society." *Communications in Africa*, 1(4):1–5, December 1972.   **1065**
"South Africa is the only country in Africa—and I am not excluding Rhodesia—with a truly free press; and it is the only country in Africa with an effective parliamentary system. The connection between the suppression of freedom of the press and the growth of dictatorships or one-party systems is a close one." The author believes, on the whole, the country is well-served by its press, but regrets the fact that it is divided along language lines in the matter of race relations—the Afrikaans press supporting the government and separation of the races, the English-language press supporting the opposition and the belief that all races should be united as citizens of the republic.

Oppenheimer, Stephen. "Implications of the New Obscenity Law: *Miller vs California* Comes to New York." *NYLA Bulletin* (New York Library Association), 22:1, 4, 7, October 1974. **1066**
An analysis of the changes in the New York obscenity law in light of the U.S. Supreme Court's 1973 decision in *Miller v. California*, the new standards established for finding a work obscene and the problems that they impose on libraries.

Orchard, William H. "Censorship: 1) A Psychiatrist's View." *Meanjin Quarterly*, 28:385–90, Spring 1969.   **1067**
The author, a practicing psychiatrist in Melbourne, views book censorship as a relatively recent sadomasochistic social game, employed by persons who seek a scapegoat on which to vent their wrath and bolster their own righteousness. "Censorship is an institutional form of childlike denial designed to preserve equanimity at the expense of reality." It is often employed to resist social change. He defends the use of socially taboo words in literature, pleads for the same tolerance for vicarious enjoyment of sex in literature that we allow for other themes, such as violence. "The person who vicariously gratifies himself sexually with books is psychologically probably an inhibited rather than an anti-social person." He rejects the notion that books and films significantly corrupt the adult or even the adolescent, since the modern psychiatric view holds that character is formed in the early years. Most criminal and deviant persons need no protection of censorship since they seem to have little interest in books with sexual themes. Book censorship in Australia, he notes, "betrays a very insecure view of Australian society."

"Ordinance Regulating Commercial Use of Streets Declared Uncon-

stitutional As Applied to Prohibit Newspaper Vending Machines." *Rutgers-Camden Law Journal*, 6:610–22, Winter 1975.   **1068**
Re: *Philadelphia Newspapers, Inc. v. Borough Council of Swarthmore*, 381 F. Supp. 228 (E.D. Pa. 1974).

O'Reilly, James T. *FOI and the "Secret Seven" Affair*. Columbia, Mo., Freedom of Information Center, School of Journalism, University of Missouri at Columbia, 1975. 5p. (Report no. 335)   **1069**
A report on the bizarre case involving efforts by the staff of a University of Virginia Law School publication to obtain documents from the U.S. Army pertaining to an improper expenditure of government funds in behalf of a secret society, The Secret Seven, on the University of Virginia campus.

———. "Government Disclosure of Private Secrets under the Freedom of Information Act." *Business Lawyer*, 30:1125–47, July 1975.   **1070**
"The rise of the 'public's right to know,' as reflected in decisions and statutes within the last several decades, conflicts with the traditions of equitable protection [of trade secrets] when the information to be protected is within the power of the Federal Government as well as that of its owner. . . . There is need for re-examination of the courts' performance under recent legislation in balancing public disclosure against private business confidentiality. This article will review the legislation, its history and case development, and suggest strategies for the proper application of the existing protections."

———. *The Privacy Act of 1974*. Columbia, Mo., Freedom of Information Center, School of Journalism, University of Missouri at Columbia, 1975. 6p. (Report no. 342)   **1071**
"The comprehensive Privacy Act of 1974, which goes into effect on Sept. 27, 1975, will have a major impact on the federal government's collection, use, and dissemination of information on individual citizens."

Orlik, Peter B. "Under Damocles' Sword—the South African Press." *Journalism Quarterly*, 46:343–48, Summer 1969.   **1072**
"While the Nationalist government lately exhibits greater tolerance toward the opposition papers, such tolerance is neither demanded nor insured by law. No guarantees exist that the press will not be further circumscribed."

Orr, Eloise. *Challenges to TV License Renewals*. Columbia, Mo., Freedom of Information Center, School of Journalism, University of Missouri at Co-

lumbia, 1970. 4p. (Report no. 253)   **1073**
Two stations have lost licenses to challenges by citizen groups. Worried broadcasters are turning to Congress for protection as the power of citizen groups increases.

———. *News Management in the Media*. Columbia, Mo., Freedom of Information Center, School of Journalism, University of Missouri at Columbia, 1969. 4p. (Report no. 230)   **1074**
"The credibility of the nation's news media is being questioned by a public that has been barraged by what some critics call canned news and slanted, biased reporting. Citizens' groups are challenging several broadcasters' license renewals on the grounds that the stations manage news and legislation is being proposed to curb news management by the media."

Ortega y Gasset, José. "The Mission of the Librarian." *Antioch Review*, 21: 133–54, Summer 1961. (Excerpted in *Wilson Bulletin for Librarians*, January 1936)   **1075**
The Spanish philosopher believes that the book, which is indispensable to man, has also become a danger. Too many books are being produced, beyond man's capacity to control and assimilate their contents. He sees a new mission for librarians as "the tamer of the raging book," who will, in time, be charged not only with selection and cataloging books, but with producing them. The future librarian will "make difficult the output of useless and harmful books and facilitate that of works whose absence does harm." The future librarian will be "a filter between books and man." An address before the second International Library and Bibliographical Congress, Madrid, May 1935. Translated and edited by James Lewis and Ray L. Carpenter. The full Spanish text appears in *Revista de Accidente*, no. 143.

Ortwein, Bernard M. "Privileged Communication—*In re Pappas*." *Suffolk University Law Review*, 6:184–95, Fall 1971.   **1076**
An analysis of the Massachusetts Supreme Court decision *In re Pappas*, 266 N.E.2d 297 (1971), involving a reporter's privilege of protecting a news source. Appended is the text of the Department of Justice Guidelines for Subpoenas to News Media.

Orwell, George. "The Freedom of the Press." *Times Literary Supplement*, 3,680:1–3, 15 September 1972. (Also in *New York Times*, 8 October 1972) **1077**
Text of a hitherto unknown and unpublished introduction to Orwell's *Animal Farm*, a book which appeared during World War II after having been rejected by four publishers for fear of offending the Russians. Orwell criticized the self-imposed censorship in Britain based on an uncritical loyalty to the USSR. The chief danger to freedom of thought and speech is not official interference but fear of public opinion.

"In this country intellectual cowardice is the worst enemy a writer or a journalist has to face. . . . Anyone who challenges the prevailing orthodoxy finds himself silenced with surprising effectiveness." Bernard Crick, in the same issue, tells How the Essay Came to Be Written.

Osborne, John W. *John Cartwright.* Cambridge, England, Cambridge University Press, 1972. 174p. (Conference on British Studies, Biographical Series) **1078**
A biography of Major Cartwright (1740–1824), a leader in British radical reform and a fighter for press freedom.

Osing, Gordon T. "Pornography; Our Concern Also." *Missouri English Bulletin*, 27:20–26, January 1970. (ED 38,427) **1079**
The classroom is an appropriate place for a frank discussion of pornography, for an examination of its nature as a fantasy in cheating the reader about the true nature of a complex phenomenon.

Oster, Patrick R. "Free Press vs. Fair Trial; a Classic Collision." *U.S. News and World Report*, 80:44–45, 23 February 1976. **1080**
An analysis of the press gag order case pending before the U.S. Supreme Court.

Ostro, E. "Lord Longford's Pornography Report." *St. Anthony's Messenger*, 80:14–19, January 1973. **1081**

[Oswald, Eleazer.] *The Case of the Commonwealth Against Eleazer Oswald for a Contempt of the Supreme Court of Pennsylvania . . . July, 1788. With A Brief Account of the Proceedings in the General Assembly upon the Memorial of the Defendant Against Three of the Justices of That Court, for the Judgment and Sentence Pronounced Against Him. Reported by a Gentleman of the Law.* Philadelphia, William Spotswood, 1788. 16p. **1082**
Oswald, the publisher of the *Independent Gazette*, had refused to give the name of the author of an anonymous article, criticizing Andrew Browne, master of a female academy. When the editor commented on the proceedings of the trial he was cited for contempt of court. The legislature failed to impeach.

Otto, Ulla. *Die Literarische Zensur als Problem der Soziologie der Politik.* Stuttgart, Fernand Enke, 1968. 168p. (Bonner Beiträge zur Soziologie, Nr. 3) **1083**
Numerous references throughout to censorship cases and conditions in Great Britain and United States.

Oudes, Bruce J. "The Press-Card Disguise." *Nation*, 211(18):561–64, 30 November 1970. **1084**
"Either an increasing number of public officials [police and military] are posing as newsmen in order to gather intelligence, or newsmen are becoming more willing to expose such imposters." The author suggests legislation to forbid such impersonation to protect the credibility of the press.

Our Boys; Its Mission. Dublin, Our Boys Office [1927?]. 4p. **1085**
A prospectus for the wholesome fortnightly paper for boys and an attack on the practice of reading filthy novels and impious newspapers which will please the devil and bring joy in hell. Irish boys are urged to burn filthy literature, keep away from immoral movies, and avoid smoking. Enclosed is a two-page list of books, pamphlets and newspapers "quite sufficient to change an angel into a devil." The "Black List" contains Class I (habitually rankly immoral) and Class II (extremely undesirable). There is also a list of suitable books.

"Our Son Was Reading Pornography." *Good Housekeeping*, 174(3):20+, March 1972. **1086**
How one mother coped with the problem of finding her thirteen-year-old son reading pornography.

Our Sunday Visitor. *Defamers of the Church.* 19th ed. [Huntington, Ind., Our Sunday Visitor, n.d.] 112p. **1087**
An attack on anti-Catholic papers, promoters, and organizations, including the *Menace* and *Appeal to Reason;* fake and real ex-priests and fake and real ex-nuns who have written defamatory books and articles. The book charges that most publishers of anti-Catholic publications are in the work for revenue only, that to make it appear that the Catholic Church opposes free speech, anti-Catholic lecturers often deliberately have their followers stir up a disturbance at their meetings; and it raises questions about the burning of the *Menace* newspaper plant in 1919, for which the insurance company refused to pay the insurance.

"Outer Limits of Free Speech: Proposed Revision of the Criminal Code." *Christian Century*, 90:499–500, 2 May 1973. **1088**
Consideration of the proposed revision of the U.S. Criminal Code with respect to pornography. "We do not find it pleasant to defend hard-core pornography, especially when we recognize that the huge profits the trade receives come as a result of human weakness. But until the supporters of the bill can make a convincing case that the dangers of hard-core pornography are such that it ought to be withheld from adults, we will continue to affirm the principle that a democracy thrives best when its avenues of free speech remain unfettered."

[Oviatt, James.] *James Oviatt Files Suit*

for $10,200,000.00 Against the Anti-Defamation League, Its Director, Milton A. Senn, and the Jewish Press for Libel and Invasion of Privacy. [Los Angeles? The Author, 1964?] 24p. **1089**
An account of a suit filed in Superior Court of California by a Los Angeles haberdasher against the Anti-Defamation League, accusing the latter of carrying on a conspiracy to discredit him through printed and published works. Oviatt, according to the League, had been distributing anti-Semitic literature, including the spurious *Protocals of the Learned Elders of Zion.* Oviatt's pamphlet charges the League with "book stifling" and "quarantine treatment"—devices "designed to destroy literary works of which they disapprove by discouraging favorable book reviews, and by pressuring all news media to withhold favorable publicity from any individual or organization," with which the League disagrees. He further complains that the press has ignored reporting the libel suit.

Owen, Bruce M. *Economics and Freedom of Expression: Media Structure and the First Amendment.* Cambridge, Mass., Ballinger, 1975. 202p. **1090**
This monograph deals with the ways in which mass media economic structure and public policy affect freedom of speech and press. The author argues that these public policies are based on "erroneous technical and economic assumptions, conceived in a climate of emotional preconception, and detrimental to the realization of free expression." A correct assessment of the economic structure of the mass media must embody a distinction between "editorial newsgathering" and "production-transmission" functions. In reaching public goals, economic incentives are more effective than political regulation of behavior. Among the policy changes the author advocates in recognition of the economics of freedom of expression are: (1) the legal separation of the editorial and newsgathering service from newspaper printing and distributing service; (2) rejection of the right of access to the editorial functions of the newspaper (as in the *Tornillo* decision) but acceptance of the right of paid access to the means of transmission; (3) prohibition of newspaper-television cross-ownership in a city; (4) the auctioning off to the highest bidder rights in the electromagnetic spectrum; (5) abolition of FCC licensing and regulatory authority over broadcast content; (6) encourgement of pay television; (7) abolition of public television to be replaced by federal subsidies for cultural and educational programming; (8) strict enforcement of the antitrust decision in the motion picture industry as laid down in 1948 in *United States v. Paramount Pictures;* and (9) postal subsidies to small circulation periodicals.

———. "Newspaper and Television

Station Joint Ownership." *Antitrust Bulletin*, 18:787–807, Winter 1973.
1091
The paper examines "some of the problems of industry structure which give rise to a public policy dilemma in the communications media," and "presents some empirical results on the actual price effects of joint ownership."

Owen, W. C. "Plazas, Parking Lots, and Picketing: *Logan Valley Plaza* Is Put to the Test." *Labor Law Journal*, 23:742–59, December 1972.   **1092**
The author examines court decisions on picketing or handbilling in privately owned shopping centers subsequent to *Food Employees v. Logan Valley Plaza*, 1969.

Owens, Jesse S., Jr. "Miller v. California: A Mandate for New Obscenity Legislation." *Mississippi Law Review*, 45:435–53, April 1974.   **1093**
"This comment will focus on the impact of this new decision [*Miller v. California*, 1973] and the resulting need for contemporary legislation in Mississippi." As background, the author reviews the history of obscenity legislation in the United States.

"Owners' Fifth Amendment Property Rights Prevent a State Constitution from Providing Broader Free Speech Rights Than Provided by the First Amendment." *Harvard Law Review*, 86:1592–1607, June 1973.   **1094**
In *Lenrich Associates v. Heyda*, 504 P.2d 112 (Ore. 1972), the Oregon Supreme Court, following the U.S. Supreme Court decision in *Lloyd Corp. v. Tanner* (1972), ruled that the distribution of printed matter, chanting, etc., in a private shopping center, infringed upon owners' property rights.

Oxton, Charles. *Smut in the Mail*. Techny, Ill., Divine Word, 1960. 22p.
1095
To stamp out the traffic in pornography, the author of this Catholic tract recommends stricter federal postal regulations and vigorous community action.

Oz Obscenity Trial, Old Bailey, London, 1971. Trial Begins 22 June. London, Friends of *Oz*, 1971. 9p. (Leaves) in a portfolio.   **1096**

P

Packard, William. ["Pornography and Eroticism."] *New York Quarterly*, 16:3–19, 1974. **1P1**
The editor discusses the issue of eroticism in literature in light of recent court decisions on obscenity, citing examples of eroticism in literature and quoting the censorship views of various authors.

Packer, Herbert L. "The Pornography Caper." *Commentary*, 51(2):72–77, February 1971. Discussion: 52:30, 33–36, July 1971. **1P2**
The article deals with the U.S. Commission on Obscenity and Pornography—its creation, deliberations, the leaking of its findings, efforts to prevent its publication, and the violent reaction to it from President Nixon and the Congress, which rejected it. The author sees no chance that the Commission's recommendations will be enacted into law, but rather the contrary—tougher laws against pornography. He believes that the U.S. Supreme Court should get out of the obscenity business and leave it to local boards of censorship. "In place of the First Amendment, I would suggest that the opponents of anti-pornography law should rely instead on the doctrine of 'substantive due process'" and that "it is to the courts rather than to legislatures that we must look to begin the process of reforming our substantive criminal law to bring our commitments into balance with our capacities."

Packman, Martin. *Cameras in Court*. Washington, D.C., Editorial Research Reports, 1956. (*Editorial Research Reports*, 1:159–75, 1956) **1P3**
Content: Moves to Lift Courtroom Ban on Cameras. Restrictions on Taking Pictures in Court. Disputed Aspects of Courtroom Photography.

Padden, Preston R. "The Emerging Role of Citizens' Groups in Broadcast Regulation." *Federal Communications Bar Journal*, 25:82–110, 1972. **1P4**
The rise in citizens' groups and their private contracts with broadcast licensees, which may result in the restructuring of the commercial broadcasting system. Depending upon the point of view and the particular instance the technique may be termed "community control" or "extortion."

Page, Robert L. "Holden Caulfield Is Alive and Well and Still Causing Trouble." *English Journal*, 64(5):27–31, May 1975. **1P5**
A former high school teacher and textbook author writes an imaginary account of book censorship in high school, in the style of Holden Caulfield, the young man in J. D. Salinger's often-suppressed book, *The Catcher in the Rye*.

Page, Roger. "Censorship and Customs Control." In his *Australian Bookselling*. Melbourne, Australia, Hill of Content, 1970, pp. 122–31. **1P6**
An account of the workings of Australian Customs censorship which has great powers over entry and inspection of all books. A National Board of Review serves as an ultimate arbitrator, although its decisions may be reversed by the Minister of Customs. The bookseller finds himself in a vulnerable position "subject to criticism from both sides: from the people who think certain books objectionable and report him to police . . . and from the people who think he should be a crusader for freedom and defiantly sell every book at which the authorities cast a querulous eye." While individual booksellers resent the censorship controls and the amount of paperwork involved, the Australian Booksellers' Association has accepted the fact that the community approves of censorship and the trade has to operate within that public attitude. One of the examples of the excessive zeal of Customs officials cited was the withholding of *Fun in Bed*, a book on pastimes for bedridden youngsters.

Pai, M. R. "Is Freedom of the Press in Danger?" *Thought*, 31(37):11–12, 13 September 1969. **1P7**
Favorable to press freedom in India are the great diversity of newspapers and periodicals, the presence of the Press Council, and the traditions of responsible journalism. Unfavorable to press freedom are the monopoly of All India Radio, government controls of the means of communication and transportation, the intimidation of demonstrators, and self-censorship by the press.

[**Pakenham, Francis A., 7th earl of Longford (Lord Longford).**] "Expert Witness—An Interview with Lord Longford." *New Law Journal*, 123:1171–74, 20 December 1973. **1P8**
The chairman of the British committee investigating pornography (The Longford Report) discusses the obscenity laws and their application, the use of expert testimony in obscenity trials, standards of sexual morality, and reforms proposed in the Longford Report. The Report is entered in this volume under Longford Committee Investigating Pornography.

Palisades (N.J.) Free Library. "A Bylaw on Censorship." *ALA Bulletin*, 63:1042–43, September 1969. **1P9**
An unusual and provocative statement on censorship adopted by the Palisades, N.J. Free Library. Examples: "If any idea or expression is truly dangerous or evil, the best protection against it is a public that has been exposed to it and has rejected it, and the least protection is a public that has been shielded from it by official or self-appointed guardians. . . . In the event that any person or group shall object to the library's acquisition, display, or retention of any book or other material on political, moral, philosophical, patriotic, religious, or esthetic grounds, the objection shall be recognized as an indication that the book or material in question may well be more than routine interest and may be likely to be desired by persons who wish to judge the merits and demerits for themselves. Objectors shall be notified of the library's policies, either by provision to them of a copy of this Bylaw or by other suitable means."

Palmer, Anthony. *The Trials of OZ*. London, Blond and Briggs, 1971. 275p. **1P10**
Proceedings and commentary on the British obscenity trial of three defendants charged with publishing an obscene magazine, *OZ*—

issue number 28, School Kids Issue. The trial at Old Bailey lasted six weeks, the longest obscenity trial in British history. The defendants were acquitted of charges of conspiracy to corrupt the morals of young children, but were found guilty of violation of the obscenity law and of sending obscene matter through the mails. The account is based on the author's personal attendance at the trial and on an approved tape recording of the proceedings. The author criticizes the trial as a parody of justice and the press coverage of it as prejudiced and badly informed. What was ultimately on trial, the author concludes, "was not the artistic merits or otherwise of the magazine; not the freedom to express minority opinions which the majority might find distasteful; not the ultimately feeble-minded defence by the accused of their belief in children's rights; not the obscenity or otherwise of *OZ* 28; not the extent to which the so-called permissive society should be allowed to flourish; not even the simple need to disagree. What was on trial was the Law itself, the machinery of justice, and its ability to comprehend ideas as opposed to facts. And on this particular occasion, the Law and its administration was found not only wanting, but guilty."

Palmer, Fredrick D. "Arizona Fair Trial–Free Press Dilemma at the Preliminary Hearing Stage." *Arizona Law Review*, 9:466–76, Spring 1968.   **1P11**
A discussion of the alternatives before the Arizona Supreme Court relating to the case of Walter W. Meek, a reporter for the *Arizona Republic*, held in contempt of court for refusal to comply with an order excluding the press from attending a preliminary hearing.

[Paltrowitz, Joel L.] "Procedural Problems in the Seizure of Obscenity." *Albany Law Review*, 37:203–27, 1972.   **1P12**
The purpose of this note is to "discuss the framework established by the Supreme Court concerning search and seizure requirements; discuss some of the federal approaches in dealing with procedural problems; and then focus on New York's attempt to handle properly the procedural questions connected with search and seizure of allegedly obscene material."

Paneth, Donald, and Robert L. Bishop. "Free Enterprise of a 'Free Press.' " *Nation*, 214:588–91, 8 May 1972.   **1P13**
The first article, Newspapers in Chains by Donald Paneth, deals with press monopolies in the United States. "Freedom of the press? The [newspaper] chains cannot accommodate it. Their approach is intended to sustain the prosperity of the enterprises." The second article, The Profit of Fusion by Robert L. Bishop, deals with the tax system—high income tax rates, coupled with extremely low capital gains

rates, overgenerous depreciation schedules, free reinvestment of capital gains, and corporate retention of surplus profit—which has driven the independent papers into the "tax-sheltering arms of the chains."

Paraschos, Emmanuel. *The Corrective and Challenge*. Columbia, Mo., Freedom of Information Center, School of Journalism, University of Missouri at Columbia, 1972. 6p. (Report no. 283)   **1P14**
The Federal Trade Commission's new aggressive stance is reflected in its present emphasis on corrective advertising, designed to correct previous claims made by the advertiser. Although several advertisers have faced the possibility of running such corrective campaigns, only one has accepted the order.

Parham, Paul B. *Criminal Law and the Press*. Columbia, Mo., Freedom of Information Center, School of Journalism, University of Missouri at Columbia, 1971. 5p. (Report no. 255)   **1P15**
"The reporter has traditionally tried to report criminal news by getting as close to the source as possible. In some cases, he has gotten too close and has faced criminal prosecution. The author searches the law and documents the legal and ethical restraints on reporting criminal acts."

Parker, Eugene F. *Fair Trial and Free Press: Balancing Two Fundamental Rights*. Athens, Ga., University of Georgia, 1969. 99p. (Unpublished Master's thesis)   **1P16**
"This study investigates the landmark decisions of the Supreme Court concerning both of these rights and attempts to characterize and delineate the major features of the environment in which both rights could be maintained through balance."

Parker, Everett C. "Can Freedom of the Press Survive?" *Engage/Social Action*, 1(9):6–17, 17 September 1973.   **1P17**
The Nixon Administration has made a concerted effort "to inculcate the public with the view that the news media—print or broadcast—cannot be trusted." Prior restraint on publication, subpoenas of newsmen, and other devices have been used to intimidate the press. Broadcast journalism is particularly vulnerable to intimidation because of license renewal requirements. There is also a threat to First Amendment freedom of the press from the concentration of ownership of the media and by the failure of the networks in particular to ensure a diversity of viewpoints in their programming. This has been challenged by the Office of Communication of the United Church of Christ of which the author is director. "Regulation of programming is properly directed at increasing diversity of program content, not at censoring or inhibiting it. No one could or should be penalized for broadcast-

ing any idea or opinion. The remedy for unfair utterances is the right to present opposing viewpoints, not the avoidance of debate by prior restraint of the initial statement. No subject matter is 'too controversial.' "

Parker, Frank M., Jr. "Shopping Centers and the 'Quasi-Public' Forum." *North Carolina Law Review*, 51:123–34, November 1972.   **1P18**
Re: *Lloyd Corp. v. Tanner* (1972), and related decisions involving distribution of handbills in shopping centers.

[Parker, G. E.] " 'Girlie' Magazines Are Not Meant for Boys." *Criminal Law Quarterly*, 10:394–98, August 1968.   **1P19**
Re: *Ginsberg v. State of New York* (1968), in which the U.S. Supreme Court sustained the right of the state to regulate the sale of sex materials to minors.

———. "History as Libel." *Chitty's Law Journal*, 18:62–64, February 1970.   **1P20**
The article is prompted by a recent case in which two editors of a "hippie newspaper" were convicted of criminal libel for likening a magistrate to Pontius Pilate.

———. "Regina v. McAuslane." *Criminal Law Quarterly*, 10:373–75, May 1968.   **1P21**
The case involved conviction under section 150 of the Canadian Criminal Code for having in possession obscene matter for the purpose of publication, distribution, or circulation.

Parker, Graham, ed. *Collision Course? Free Press and the Courts*. Toronto, Communications Department, Ryerson Polytechnical Institute, 1966. 77p.   **1P22**
A symposium of lawyers and journalists at Osgoode Hall Law School, 15 April 1966. Content: The Problem of Fair Trial by Graham Parker. Is a Free Press Compatible with the Concept of a Fair Trial? Comments by Bora Laskin, Ivan C. Rand, H. H. Bull, Arthur Maloney, Beland Honderich, and E. U. Schrader. Can the Press Be Both Free and Responsible? Comments by R. J. Doyle, J. Sedgwick, Charles B. Templeton, E. Patrick Hartt, and Douglas Leithermann. An Essay on Fair Trial–Freedom of the Press by Norman J. Freedman.

Parker, John. "Rhodesia—No Censors But . . . " *IPI Report* (International Press Institute), 22(3):1, 3–4, March 1973.   **1P23**
The story of the arrest and imprisonment of Rhodesian journalist Peter Niesewand for alleged violation of the Official Secrets Act.

[Parker, Theodore.] *The Trial of Theodore*

Parker, for the "Misdemeanor" of A Speech in Faneuil Hall against Kidnapping, before the Circuit Court of the United States, at Boston, April 3, 1855. With the Defence, by Theodore Parker. Boston, The Author, 1855. 221p. **1P24**
Text of the speech of antislavery crusader Theodore Parker, to have been given in his own defense at a trial for a "misdemeanor" for having made a speech against the enforcement of the fugitive slave law in Boston. The case was dismissed without a jury trial, but Parker published his intended remarks, together with the Boston incident that prompted them and his offending speech at Faneuil Hall. The lengthy defense includes a history of the British law of seditious libel and the development of the concept of free speech and press which formed the basis of American law.

Parks, Stephen, ed. The English Book Trade, 1660–1853. New York, Garland, 1974–75. 42 vols. **1P25**
One hundred and fifty-six titles (pamphlets, broadsides, memoirs) relating to the early history of English publishing, bookselling, the struggle for a copyright, and the freedom of the press, reprinted in photo-facsimile, with bibliographical notes by Stephen Parks. Many of the titles were included in the 1968 edition of this bibliography. They include works by L'Estrange, Defoe, Erskine, Almon, Bowles, Blount, Tindal, Addison, and Asgill, and pamphlets relating to the Craftsman controversy and the Friends of the Liberty of the Press. A sixteen-page brochure issued by the publisher lists the content of each volume.

Parmelee, Steven G. "Commercial Speech Falls Within the Protections of First Amendment." Creighton Law Review, 10:362–77, December 1976. **1P26**
"The test emerging from Virginia State Board of Pharmacy is that there is no test beyond that traditionally employed by the Court to harmonize the police and welfare interests of the state with the right of the public to receive and exchange information in a free and open marketplace of ideas."

[Parsons, John.] The Trial of Mr. John Parsons, Bookseller of Paternoster-Row for a Libel against John King, of York-Place, Portman-Square, in a Publication Entitled Authentic Memoirs, &c. Taken from the Journal of the King of the Swindlers; Wherein the Speeches of Both Counsel Are Fully Stated, as also Evidence, and Lord Kenyon's Charge to the Jury. London, Printed for J. Parsons, 1799. 46p. **1P27**

Partain, Eugene G. "The Use of Broadcast Media in Congressional Legislative and Quasi-Judicial Proceedings." Journal of Broadcasting, 4:123–39, Spring 1960. (Reprinted in John M.

Kittross and Kenneth Harwood, eds, Free and Fair, pp. 11–27) **1P28**
A survey of existing laws, regulations, and precedents for electronic coverage of legislative and quasi-judicial proceedings, and arguments for and against the practice.

Partridge, Eric. "Literary Censorship." In his The Old and the New: Christmas and New Year Greetings, 1929–30. . . . London, The Scholartis Press, 1929, pp. 9–19. (Edition limited to 150 copies) **1P29**
The legal definition of obscenity in England "is an insult to our sense of justice, while the interpretation of the law depends on the whim of the repressors." While pornography flourishes in England many good books are subject to suppression. The obscenity law is antiquated; it perpetuates a tyranny of the incompetent few over the intelligent many. The author attacks journalists who, while upholding the rights of the newspaper press, "arrogate to themselves the right to prejudice a book, even to ally themselves with the Law by taking steps perhaps before publication to suppress a book." The author concludes: "It is properly not books but actions which are censurable: Such acts as prostitution, exhibitionism, dissemination of disease, offences against children. Books merely set forth opinions, points of view. The world is not so corrupt that it needs a literary censorship: if it were, such a censorship would do no good; but most important of all, a literary censorship would be a grave infringement of liberty and, viewed from the standpoint of morality, an impertinence and an insult to human worth."

Pash, C. Grey, Jr. "Federal Communications Commission's Fairness Doctrine and Personal Attack Rule." Kentucky Law Journal, 58:392–403, Winter 1969/70. **1P30**
Re: Red Lion Broadcasting Company v. Federal Communications Commission (1969). "The Red Lion decision is important because of its strong support of the FCC's Fairness Doctrine. It would have been a more important decision if it had decisively opened the door for a reassessment of the function of the first amendment in relation to the communication media in contemporary society."

Pastore, John O. "Challenge and Change in Television." Journal of the Producers Guild of America, 11(2):7–9, June 1969. **1P31**
"Senator Pastore, chairman of the Subcommittee on Communications of the Senate, raised the hackles of many individuals in the television industry by calling for more stringent regulations of video sex and violence. The following article, based on a speech he made before the National Association of Broadcasters, shows his position on the subject."

Pate, William C., and Alan M. Winterhalter. "Monopoly Newspapers:

Troubles in Paradise." San Diego Law Review, 7:268–88, May 1970. **1P32**
The authors have attempted to illuminate the main constitutional and economic problems involved in newspaper monopoly and to demonstrate that "the government has the power to formulate a substitute for the checks that were once provided by the competitive economic system. If the citizen's right to a free press is to be more than just an historical oddity, the government must begin regulation of the newspaper industry to insure that no powerful interests have the power to suppress the free interchange of ideas."

Paterson, Adolphus A. "Why Africa Needs a Free Press." Africa Review, 16(4):22–24, April 1971. **1P33**
"To secure a free press in Africa it is necessary that the mass media at present owned by the state be 'weaned' and taken away from government control," according to the author, a Ghanaian journalist. "While politicians will continue to express their faith in press freedom and newsmen's liberties, it is up to African newsmen themselves to secure that freedom."

Patner, Marshall et al. "Public Access to Information." Northwestern University Law Review, 68:285–462, May–June 1973. (Entire issue.) **1P34**
Content: Information Disclosure Policies and Practices of Federal Administrative Agencies by G. Larry Engel. An Overview of the Law Governing Access to Information Held by Public Agencies in the State of Illinois and the City of Chicago. Public Access to Governmental Information: A Field Experiment by Stanley Divorski, Andrew C. Gordon, and John P. Heintz. Public Information and Public Access: A Sociological Interpretation by Andrew C. Gordon, John P. Heintz, Margaret T. Gordon, and Stanley W. Divorski. Factors Affecting Accessibility of Information Held by Public Agencies: The Case of the City of Chicago Building Department. Access to Information in the Office of the State's Attorney of Cook County, Illinois, the Chicago Board of Education, Office of the Chicago Department of Environmental Control, the Office of the Secretary of State, and the Cook County Assessor. Public Access to Government-Held Computerized Information.

Paton, Alan. "Pornography and Censorship." In his Knocking on the Door. New York, Scribner's, 1975, pp. 274–77. **1P35**
South Africa being what it is, some form of censorship of sex expression is inevitable. It is better for such decisions to be made by a judge who is too judicial than a moralist who is too moralistic. Any censorship board ought to include publishers and booksellers and there must be the right of appeal to the courts.

Patterson, Lyman R. *Copyright in Historical Perspective*. Nashville, Tenn., Vanderbilt University Press, 1968. 264p.   **1P36**
The author traces the legal concept of copyright from its first use as a censorship device in sixteenth-century England (Stationers' Company) to the present day in England and the United States, where the emphasis is on the protection of property rights. There are three basic but forgotten ideas in an integrated concept of copyright—"the danger of monopoly from the publisher rather than the author, the differing interests of the publisher and the author, and the rights of the individual user." The positive use of copyright "for the encouragement of learning" and "to promote science and useful arts"—as guaranteed in England under the Statute of Anne and in the United States by the Constitution—has been secondary to its use in controlling property rights. The text of the Star Chamber Decrees on the Licensing of Printing (1586 and 1637) are given in the appendix.

Patton, Lloyd H., Jr. *"Variable Obscenity" Legislation*. Columbia, Mo., Freedom of Information Center, School of Journalism, University of Missouri at Columbia, 1969. 7p. (Report no. 223)   **1P37**
"One of the most vigorous arguments forwarded by those favoring the censorship of obscene literature is that such material is harmful to children. The 'variable obscenity' concept, formally endorsed by the Supreme Court in *New York v. Ginsberg*, provides a means of keeping pornography out of the hands of children while still allowing adults to read what they please. Since the *Ginsberg* decision, many states have enacted variable obscenity statutes. Indications are that more such statutes will be passed in the future."

Paul, Daniel. "Why a Shield Law?" *University of Miami Law Review*, 29: 459–61, Spring 1975.   **1P38**
Support for a shield law to protect reporters from being forced to reveal news sources. Such a law should be short, simple, and absolute.

Paul, Noel S. "Why the British Press Council Works." *Columbia Journalism Review*, 10(6):20–26, March–April 1972.   **1P39**
An interview with the secretary of the Press Council.

Paull, H. M. "Censorship." In his *Literary Ethics: A Study in the Growth of the Literary Conscience*. New York, Dutton, 1929, pp. 171–83.   **1P40**
A general look at the history of literary censorship in England from the days of the Star

Chamber to action taken by the Lord Chamberlain against contemporary drama.

Paulu, Burton. "The 'Red Lion' Decision: A Landmark in American Broadcasting History." *EBU Review* (European Broadcasting Union), 117B:40–46, September 1969.   **1P41**
The U.S. Supreme Court held that the fairness doctrine and the related personal attacks rules were a proper use of the authority of the Federal Communications Commission. This permitted the FCC to prescribe certain program policies without violating the First Amendment. "Even more basically, it declared that the free speech concept long accepted for the printed press may be modified for application to the electronic communications media."

Pazar, Clara H. *Judicial Decisions in Censorship Cases of the New York Court of Appeals, 1933–1967*. Brookville, N.Y., Graduate Library School, Long Island University, 1969. 76p. (Unpublished Master's thesis)   **1P42**

Peabody, Frederick W. "Suppression." In Woodbridge Riley, Frederick W. Peabody, and Charles E. Humiston, *The Faith, the Falsity, and the Failure of Christian Science*. London, Allen & Unwin [1925?], pp. 205–25.   **1P43**
An account of the role of the Christian Science Committee on Publications with its local agencies in suppressing works unfavorable to the Christian Science religion or its founder, Mary Baker Eddy. Included is an account of the suppression of Georgine Milmine's *The Life of Mary Baker Eddy and the History of Christian Science*, written under the guidance of Willa Cather, and the Christian Science article written for the *Cambridge History of American Literature* by Dr. Riley. The latter was removed from printed copies, and volumes already distributed were recalled upon threat of a nationwide boycott of the work.

Pearce, Edward H., *baron*. "Council Assures Free But Fair Press." *Grassroots Editor*, 13(5):27–29, September–October 1972.   **1P44**
The chairman of the British Press Council since 1969 describes the work of the Council in an address to the Commonwealth Press Union, London, 1 June 1972.

Pearce, W. Barnett, and Dwight L. Teeter. "Obsc*n*ty: Historical and Behavioral Prospects." *Intellect*, 104: 166–70, November 1975.   **1P45**
"The current mess in obscenity regulation stems from a misreading of history and from a reluctance to employ the findings of behavioral science." The authors conclude that "privacy must be protected against unwanted intrusion by sexually explicit materials, and such materials may be withheld from juveniles. Beyond

that, any test—including the hardcore pornography and pandering sales notion—is dangerous."

Pearson, George. "How Free Should Student Publications Be?" *National Association of Secondary School Principals Bulletin*, 55:50–58, September 1971. **1P46**
The author cites two compelling justifications for freedom of the student press: The First Amendment rights of students as defined by the courts, and the "need for a free flow of information and commentary on the issues and problems which confront not only the education community but all humanity." He recommends the creation of an advisory board for student media, consisting of students, faculty, and administrators.

Peckham, Morse. *Art and Pornography: An Experiment in Explanation*. New York, Basic Books, 1969. 306p. (Studies in Sex and Society)   **1P47**
A study in the "interdependence of art, pornography, and sexual behavior, and in the function of pornography in the various modes of human behavior we name personality, culture, and society." Chapters on: What Is Pornography? The Art in Pornography. An Explanation for Pornography. Pornography and Culture. The study was sponsored by the Institute for Sex Research, Indiana University.

[Pedder, Sir John.] "The Roman 'Index.'" *Cornhill Magazine*, 69(o.s.): 257–64, March 1894.   **1P48**
"In spite of the pains bestowed on its compilation, and the weight supposed to attach to its pronouncements, the influence and use of the *Index* is very problematical. Very few besides students know anything of its contents and Dr. Murray, Archbishop of Dublin, went even further in his evidence before a Committee of the House of Commons to inquire into the state of Ireland. He said, 'the *Index Expurgatorius* has no authority whatever in Ireland: it has never been received in these countries; and I doubt very much whether there be ten people in Ireland who have ever seen it.'" The author discusses the history of the compilation of the *Index*.

Pedigo, Jess L. *X-Rated Movies—Hollywood's Scheme to Corrupt America*. Tulsa, Okla., Christian Crusade, 1970. 57p.   **1P49**
"How 'stag' movies have become regular fare in neighborhood theaters across America. And how you can be certain these same filthy movies will be featured as the 'Monday Night at the Movies' on network television one year from today." The new sexual freedoms have enslaved the people rather than set them free.

Pedrick, Willard H. "Publicity and Privacy: Is It Any of Our Business?" *University of Toronto Law Journal*, 20: 391–411, 1970.   **1P50**
A review of the state of privacy law and court

decisions in Canada and the United States and its relationship to press freedom. "What we seek for our media of information is a balance between the social interest in protecting the individual's private life and the social interest in the free publication and circulation of information and views on matters essential to the development of an informed, enlightened, open society. What we want and need for our press is a wide measure of freedom, exercised with responsibility. Is it too much to ask that the courts should, in the most extreme cases, enforce the American Society of Newspaper Editors' canon that 'A newspaper should not invade private rights or feelings without sure warrant of public right as distinguished from public curiosity.' "

Peebles, Thomas H. "The Preferred Position Re-Examined: An Emotive Justification." *Journal of Urban Law*, 51:255–84, November 1973.   **1P51**
"The view of this paper is that free expression is an important means of maintaining societal stability—that in a world of vanishing absolutes, free expression can have a therapeutic value and should be protected as a safety valve for expressing pent-up emotions more than as a guarantee that men might be free to search for truth. In this view, a guarantee of free expression for emotions and feelings as well as for more 'rational' thoughts and ideas provides a useful and acceptable (although only partially satisfactory) outlet for the unique psychological pressures and frustration which our largely urban, often volatile society imposes upon us. This view I have brazenly labeled the 'emotive' justification for the first amendment's preferred position."

———. "State Regulation of 'Fighting Words.' " *Journal of Urban Law*. 50:498–504, February 1973.   **1P52**
Re: *Gooding v. Wilson*, 405 U.S. 518 (1972).

Peers, Frank W. *The Politics of Canadian Broadcasting, 1920–1951*. Toronto, University of Toronto Press, 1969. 466p.   **1P53**
In this general history of the politics of Canadian broadcasting, there are numerous sections dealing with the issue of state control, controversial broadcasting, control of program content, broadcasts offensive to religious groups, libel, the recommendations of the Parliamentary Committee on Broadcasting (1942), and wartime broadcasting policies.

Peirce, Clyde. *The Roosevelt Panama Libel Cases: A Factual Study of a Controversial Episode in the Career of Teddy Roosevelt, Father of the Panama Canal*. New York, Greenwich, 1959. 150p.   **1P54**
An account of the libel suits brought by the federal government at the instigation of President Theodore Roosevelt against Delavan Smith of the *Indianapolis News* and Joseph Pulitzer of the *New York World*. The case involved alleged fraud in the purchase of rights for the Panama Canal. The federal judge dismissed the suits as violating the First Amendment. Included in the account is reference to the freedom of the press campaign conducted by the newspapers.

Pekkanen, John. "The Obstinacy of Bill Schanen." *Life*, 67(13):59, 26 September 1969.   **1P55**
Deals with the attacks on the man who printed *Kaleidoscope*, the Wisconsin underground newspaper.

Pelkington, Robert. "Obscenity: Legal and Moral Aspects." *Dominicana*, 53:136–44, Summer 1968.   **1P56**
Authority in a free society should not only be respected but should be loved. "Freedom of the press and of expression can be as legitimately subject to restriction as any other type of freedom when it is necessary and directed to the common good." This is the legitimate basis for censorship of obscenity.

Peltier, Linda J. "A Private Citizen Involved in an Event of Public or General Concern Must Show Actual Malice to Recover Damages in a Libel Action Against the News Media." *George Washington Law Review*, 40:151–61, October 1971.   **1P57**
Re: *Rosenbloom v. Metromedia, Inc.* (1971). While the decision "is sound in light of the important social interest in unfettered news dissemination," the author believes that "it is imperative that the legislatures act to ensure that effect is given to the spirit of the first amendment by providing improved opportunities for access to the 'marketplace of ideas.' "

———. "The Public Interest in Balanced Programming Content: The Case for FCC Regulation of Broadcasters' Format Changes." *George Washington Law Review*, 40:933–63, July 1972.   **1P58**
The article deals with issues raised by a ruling in *Citizens Comm. v. FCC* (1970), that a balanced programming content on television was a legitimate factor in broadcasting in the public interest. The affirmative requirements of both the Communications Act of 1934 and the First Amendment, the author concludes, "impose a broad mandate upon the Commission to consider balanced programming, including the impact of mid-term program format changes, in vindicating the public interest."

Pember, Don R. "The Broadcaster and the Public Interest: A Proposal to Replace an Unfaithful Servant." *Loyola of Los Angeles Law Review*, 4:83–111, February 1971.   **1P59**
The article attempts to show that the present system of regulating American broadcasting has not worked. The author examines the history of Federal Communications Commission regulatory policies, considers the 1968 case of WLBT to "spotlight the basic weaknesses in the present system of regulation," and outlines a plan for reforming broadcast regulation which involves a major realignment of broadcast ownership.

———. *Freedom and Privacy: The Law, the Media, and the First Amendment*. Madison, Wis., University of Wisconsin, 1969. 365p. (Ph.D. dissertation, University Microfilms, no. 70–3660)   **1P60**
The dissertation was the basis for the author's book, *Privacy and the Press*.

———. "Newspapers and Privacy: Some Guidelines." *Grassroots Editor*, 13(2):3–7, March–April 1972.   **1P61**
The author covers such aspects as the use of names and photographs for advertising purposes, publication of private affairs, publication of nondefamatory falsehoods, newsworthiness as a defense, and illicit methods used to obtain information.

———. "The 'Pentagon Papers' Decision: More Questions Than Answers." *Journalism Quarterly*, 43:403–11, Autumn 1971.   **1P62**
"The Supreme Court's 6–3 decision upholding the *New York Times* and *Washington Post* will be remembered far longer for its political implications than for its legal stature."

———. "Privacy and the Press: The Defense of Newsworthiness." *Journalism Quarterly*, 45(1):14–24, Spring 1968.   **1P63**
"After examining *Time, Inc. v. Hill* [1967] and 62 other cases involving a definition of newsworthiness in privacy suits, the author offers seven guidelines. But he warns that knowledge of intricate details is the journalist's best friend."

———. *Privacy and the Press: The Law, the Mass Media, and the First Amendment*. Seattle, University of Washington Press, 1972. 298p.   **1P64**
A broad study of the law of privacy and how it applies to the mass media. The author charts the growth of the law during the past eighty years and provides "a theoretical interpretive foundation for placing the law of privacy in its proper perspective to the First Amendment to the Constitution." It attempts to present the law in a manner which makes it understandable to laymen. Important cases and events in the development of the law of privacy, the status of the law in the states, and the text of privacy laws in New York, Virginia, Utah, and Oklahoma are given in the appendix.

———. *The Smith Act As a Restraint on the Press.* Austin, Tex., University of Texas, Association for Education in Journalism, 1969. 32p. (Journalism Monographs, no. 10) **1P65**
The Smith Act, passed in 1940, was the nation's first peacetime sedition law since the Alien and Sedition Laws of 1798. While there has been no seizure of printed materials and no printers or publishers have been arrested, the government, nevertheless, has used the Smith Act to restrict the printed word. The author cites numerous sedition cases in which ideas in books, pamphlets, and newspapers were used as evidence of the intent to overthrow the government. Although the law has been dormant for almost ten years, it still stands on the books as a threat for some future national panic, Red Scare, or alleged conspiracy.

———, and Dwight L. Teeter, Jr. "Privacy and the Press Since *Time Inc. v. Hill.*" *Washington Law Review*, 50: 57–91, November 1974. **1P66**
The authors trace developments in the law of privacy, with particular emphasis on how the law has affected the mass media since the Supreme Court decided its first privacy case, *Time, Inc. v. Hill*, in 1967.

Pemberton, John de J., Jr. "Constitutional Problems in Restraints on the Media." *Notre Dame Lawyer*, 42:881–87, Symposium 1967. **1P67**
The executive director of the American Civil Liberties Union, after an examination of the report of the American Bar Association's Advisory Committee on Fair Trial and Free Press, concludes that "the Committee's recommendations are constitutional insofar as they serve the historic purpose of the sixth amendment by protecting against state interference with the impartiality of judicial tribunals; insofar as the recommendations curtail the right of the private press to comment on litigation, they are constitutionally suspect. The judicial process needs the criticism of informed political opinion, and this criticism should not be lightly suppressed."

———. "The Right of Access to Mass Media." In Norman Dorsen, *ed., The Rights of Americans*, New York, Pantheon, 1971, pp. 276–96. **1P68**
"All those concerned for the democratic utility of a right to be heard should focus on the growth of First Amendment law pertaining to structure of the media rather than on the content of any particular program or set of programs."

[Pemberton-Billing, Noel.] *Verbatim Report of the Trial of Noel Pemberton Billing, M.P. On a Charge of Criminal Libel Before Mr. Justice Darling at the Central Criminal Court, Old Bailey With Report of the Preliminary Proceedings at Bow Street Police Court, an Appendix of Documents Referred to in the Case, Reference Index, &c....* London, "Vigilante" Office, 1918. 526p. (Published by subscription only; copies numbered) **1P69**
In January 1916 a member of Parliament, Noel Pemberton-Billing, founded a weekly paper in support of a more vigorous imperialist policy by the British government, particularly in prosecuting the war with Germany. The paper was first named the *Imperialist* and later the *Vigilante*, to serve as an unofficial organ of a society by that name (not to be confused with the vice societies). In the issue of 26 January 1918 the paper's leading article reported on the existence in Germany of a "black book of sin," compiled by German spies, describing alleged homosexual debauchery in England and listing 47,000 names of men and women, many in high places. The article implied that the book served as a blackmail device to prevent a more vigorous prosecution of the war. On 16 February 1918 the paper carried a brief paragraph entitled The Cult of the Clitoris, which again referred to the 47,000 homosexuals and mentioned "Maud Allen's [i.e. Allan] private performances in Oscar Wilde's 'Salome.' " It was this paragraph which gave rise to the trial, *Maud Allan, J. T. Grein v. Noel Pemberton-Billing*, under a charge of criminal libel at Old Bailey. The trial lasted six days and probed the espionage system, British sexual morality, the decadence of contemporary art, literature, and the theater, and the issue of obscenity and censorship. The jury found the defendant "not guilty," to the obvious displeasure of the presiding judge. The Vigilante Office published the proceedings of the trial in all its salacious detail, together with articles from the paper referred to in the trial, and a curious glossary of terms and phrases.

Pendergast, William R. "The Responsibility of the FDA to Protect Trade Secrets and Confidential Data." *Food, Drug, Cosmetic Law Journal*, 27:366–75, June 1972. **1P70**
A discussion of the issue from the point of view of the law governing the Food and Drug Administration and the broader question of public policy.

Penetar, Michael P. "Pornography and Censorship." *Social Justice Review*, 60: 412–13, March 1968. **1P71**
The author sees the spread of salacious literature as a contributing factor in rising delinquency, drug addiction, divorce, illegitimacy, and a decline in morality. He urges protection of the home from the invasion of pornography.

[Penn, William, and William Meade.] *The Tryal of William Penn & William Mead for Causing a Tumult. At the Sessions Held at the Old Bailey in London the 1st, 3d, 4th, and 5th of September 1670. Done by Themselves. Transcribed from the Compleat Collection of State Tryals First Published in 1719 and Edited by Don C. Seitz.* Boston, Marshall Jones, 1919. 37p. **1P72**
William Penn and an associate were brought to trial for preaching in a public area and causing "a great Concourse and Tumult of People in the Street." Penn demanded to know what law he was accused of violating and was told it was the Common Law, which did not satisfy the persistent Quaker. After much threatening by the Recorder and the Mayor, the jury brought in a "not guilty" verdict. The officers of the court were furious and locked up the jurors along with the accused for contempt of court. The case was cited some forty years later in the trial of John Peter Zenger in New York when Mr. Justice De Lancy threatened the twelve jurors. Attorney Andrew Hamilton read from the record of Penn's trial: "It is established for Law," Hamilton told the court, "that the Judges, how great soever they be have no Right to Fine, imprison, or punish a Jury, for not finding a Verdict according to the Direction of the Court."

Pennington, John. "Dan Hicks—Pistol Packing Editor." *Bulletin of the American Society of Newspaper Editors*, 545:4–9, October 1970. **1P73**
An account of the crusading editor of the *Monroe County Democrat*, Madisonville, Tenn., who had been assaulted, shot at, threatened, robbed, and his newspaper office burned down by persons in the community who resented his investigative reporting.

Pennybacker, John H., and Waldo W. Braden, *eds. Broadcasting in the Public Interest.* New York, Random House, 1969. 175p. (Issues and Spokesmen Series) **1P74**
A collection of readings followed by discussion topics and questions. Includes: Reevaluating the Regulatory Role [of the Federal Communications Commission] by Nicholas Johnson. Broadcasters as Revolutionaries by Kenneth A. Cox (deals with FCC Commissioner Cox's views on the positive obligations of broadcasters for public service programs). Masscom as Guru by W. H. Ferry (the mass communications bear social and cultural responsibilities of much greater weight than they have been willing to shoulder). Equal Time's Misfire by William E. Blundell, Julian Goodman, and Nathan Karp. Five Steps for Quick Relief When You (or Your Church or School or Club) Are Attacked by the Institute for American Democracy (adapted from *How to Combat Air Pollution: A Manual on the F.C.C.'s Fairness Doctrine*).

The Pentagon Papers: As Published by the New York Times. Based on Investigative Reporting by Neil Sheehan. Written by Neil Sheehan, Hedrick Smith, E. W. Kenworthy and Fox Butterfield. Articles and Documents Edited by

Gerald Gold, Allan M. Siegal and Samuel Abt. New York, Bantam, 1971. 677p. **1P75**

This controversial report on the background of U.S. involvement in the Vietnam war (1940–68) was commissioned by Secretary of Defense Robert S. McNamara and resulted in forty-seven volumes of which only fifteen copies were prepared. The report was "leaked" by Daniel Ellsberg and Anthony Russo to the *New York Times* which, along with the *Washington Post* and a number of other newspapers, published a substantial portion of the report in edited form in their daily papers, beginning 13 June 1971. Ellsberg and Russo were charged with conspiracy for dissemination of classified material and the Justice Department sought a permanent injunction against publication of the documents which they claimed violated U.S. security. The press contended that the papers should be in the public domain. The case was decided by a 6 to 3 vote of the U.S. Supreme Court (*New York Times v. U.S.* and *Washington Post v. U.S.*) on 30 June 1971, in favor of the newspapers. Justice Hugo L. Black, in a concurring opinion, stated: "The *New York Times*, the *Washington Post* and other newspapers should be commended for serving the purpose that the Founding Fathers saw so clearly. In revealing the workings of government that led to the Vietnam War, the newspapers nobly did precisely that which the founders hoped and trusted they would do." In addition to the Bantam and Quadrangle editions, which were based on the edited version published in the *Times*, Beacon Press issued an edition based on the version of the Pentagon Papers read into the *Congressional Record* by Senator Mike Gravel, which action brought both the Senator and the Beacon Press into litigation. An official version of the papers, issued by the Government Printing Office is entered under *U.S.* in this bibliography.

The Pentagon Papers as Published by the New York Times. The Pentagon History Was Obtained by Neil Sheehan. Written by Neil Sheehan [and Others.] New York, Quadrangle [1971]. 810p. **1P76**

The Pentagon Papers: The Defense Department History of United States Decision-making on Vietnam. The Senator Gravel edition. Boston, Beacon, 1971–72. 5 vols. **1P77**

Volume 5 includes Critical Essays edited by N. Chomsky and H. Zinn, and an Index to vols. 1–4.

"The Pentagon Papers: An Exchange of Views." *Index on Censorship*, 1:75–77, Spring 1972. **1P78**

Mostly a reprinting of the correspondence between Peter Calvocoressi and Anthony Lewis appearing in the Sunday *Times* between 11 and 25 July 1971 with respect to the significance of the U.S. Supreme Court decision in the Pentagon Papers case.

"Pentagon Papers: The Secret War"

and "The Legal Battle Over Censorship." *Time*, 97(26):11–19, 28 June 1971. **1P79**

A news account of "the most massive leak of secret documents in U.S. History," and the Nixon Government's "historic step of seeking to suppress articles before publication, and threatened criminal action against the nation's most eminent newspaper."

Pentecost, Hugh O. *A Good Man Sent to Prison*. New York, n.p., 1890. 14p. (Twentieth Century Library, vol. 1, no. 14) **1P80**

The case of Moses Harman, sentenced to jail on an obscenity charge for advocating sexual emancipation for women (H100–103).

"The People's Right to Know." *Trial Magazine*, 8(2):12–31, March–April 1972. **1P81**

A series of articles written "from the standpoint of the executive, the legislator, the lawyer, the broadcaster, and the newspaperman." The Spirit of Freedom of Information by Congressman John E. Moss and Benny L. Kass. What Should the People Know by Assistant Attorney General Robert C. Mardian. Secrecy: Democracy's Achilles' Heel by Senator Mike Gravel. The Road to Erosion by Elmer W. Lower, president of ABC News. It's Our Times, Not the Tube by Reuven Frank, president of NBC News. The Fatal Flaw by author Sidney Zion. "The Truth, the Whole Truth" by editor Paul Solman.

Pepper, Robert. "Citizen Rights and Cable." In Don R. Le Duc., *ed.*, *Issues in Broadcast Regulation*, Washington, D.C., Broadcast Education Association, 1974, pp. 126–29. **1P82**

An outline of recommendations made by various studies, intended to help protect and/or enforce cable related citizen-consumer rights.

"A Per Se Ban on All Editorial Advertisements by a Broadcast Licensee Violates the First Amendment." *Vanderbilt Law Review*, 24:1273–81, November 1971. **1P83**

A Washington radio station had refused to sell time to an organization opposed to the Vietnam war for announcements urging immediate withdrawal of American forces from Vietnam. The FCC upheld the station, holding that the exclusion of all editorial advertisements was a broadcaster's option. The U.S. Court of Appeals for the District of Columbia reversed the decision, holding that when a licensee accepts noncontroversial paid announcements, its absolute refusal to sell any advertising time to applicants seeking to present controversial public issues is violative of the First Amendment. *Business Executives' Move for Vietnam Peace* (1971).

The Periodical Press of Great Britain and Ireland: Or an Inquiry into the State of the

Public Journals, Chiefly as Regards Their Moral and Political Influence. London, Hurst, Robinson, 1824. 219p. **1P84**

This history of the periodical press in Britain and Ireland considers the enactment of laws and regulations over the years restricting the press—licensing, prosecution for libel, stamp duties on papers and advertisements, and restrictions on reporting the proceedings of Parliament and the courts.

Perrin, Noel. *Dr. Bowdler's Legacy: A History of Expurgated Books in England and America*. New York, Atheneum, 1969. 296p. **1P85**

An account of voluntary emasculation of literature in the name of taste and morality, from its obscure eighteenth-century beginnings up to the present. The practice bears the name "bowdlerizing" from Dr. Thomas Bowdler (1754–1825) who, with other members of his family, brought out a chaste edition of Shakespeare intended for family reading. One chapter deals with the assault on the Bible by such editors as John Bellamy, Dr. Benjamin Boothroyd, John Watson, William Alexander, and the American, Noah Webster.

Perry, John W. *Recent Developments in the Law of Censorship of Literature*. Melbourne, Australia [Victoria Council for Civil Liberties?], 1968. 4p. Processed. (Also in *Civil Liberty Convention Papers*. South Yarra, Australia, Victoria Council for Civil Liberties [1969?], pp. 13–16) **1P86**

Comments on the obscenity case of *Crowe v. Graham and Others* (41 A.L.J.R. 402) decided by the Supreme Court of New South Wales under the Obscene and Indecent Publications Act. The decision achieved "a new definition of obscenity which . . . departs radically from that which was previously believed to be the Hicklin test."

Perry, Stuart H. "The Face of the Censor Today." *New Zealand Libraries*, 30: 98–99, August 1967. **1P87**

A public librarian and member of the Indecent Publications Tribunal comments on the role and operation of the Tribunal under the Indecent Publications Act of 1963. "The chance to attain equal consistency in the field of literature is one of the arguments of the tribunal system."

———. "The Judiciary and the Press." *Texas Law Review*, 11:477–501, June 1933. **1P88**

"The paths of the press and the bar are not identical, but discrete and parallel. It is neither possible nor desirable to merge or intimately coordinate their efforts. . . . Each should stick to his plow; but when their lines are contiguous or in the rare instance coincident, they should work together with the fullest understanding and cordiality."

Persky, Joel. "Family Viewing Time: The Issue and Implications of the U.S. District Court Ruling in Los Angeles." *FOI Digest*, 18(6):4–5, November–December 1976.   1P89
Comment on the decision by a California federal court that the Federal Communications Commission's ruling on family viewing time was unconstitutional. The author defends the principle of family viewing time, a legitimate device for protecting the viewing audience, particularly children, from programs permeated by gratuitous sex and violence. "The real question to be discussed and debated is not whether family viewing time should be abolished but whether or not it should be expanded."

"Peter Bridge." *New Yorker*, 48:41, 4 November 1972.   1P90
The case of the reporter of the *Newark Evening News*, jailed for refusal to divulge the source of a news story, and a rally sponsored in his behalf by *MORE*.

[Peterkin, Alexander.] *The Editor of the Kelso Mail, and Mr. Peterkin. From the Kelso Mail of Monday, July 8*. Kelso, Scotland, n.p., 1833. 11p.   1P91
Peterkin, a well-known Scottish lawyer and an associate of Edinburgh men of letters, charged George Jerdan, editor of the *Kelso Mail* with libelous statements made in his paper. The Chronicle Office, Kelso, issued two other pamphlets related to the case: *Letter to George Jerdan, Esq., Proprietor and Editor of the Kelso Mail* (8p.) and *Reply to the Editor of the Kelso Mail, July 8, 1833* (7p.).

Peters, Charles, and Taylor Branch. *Blowing the Whistle: Dissent in the Public Interest*. New York, Praeger, 1972. 305p.   1P92
A collection of articles dealing with public employees who have risked their jobs and their reputations in order to reveal to the public through the press, dishonesty, mismanagement, and dangerous and deceptive practices in the federal bureaucracy. Most of the cases involve military espionage, excessive spending, and Vietnam policies under the Nixon Administration. Included are the cases of A. Ernest Fitzgerald who exposed the cost overrun on the C-5A plane, Daniel Ellsberg who leaked the Pentagon Papers, and Christopher Pyle who revealed the army's surveillance of civilians. Most of the articles are taken from *Washington Monthly*, a magazine to encourage such risk takers, men and women who are willing to "blow the whistle" on bureaucratic evils.

Peters, Charles C. *Motion Pictures and Standards of Morality*. New York, Macmillan, 1933. 285p.   1P93
"This monograph undertakes to give factual evidence on the question of the amount of divergence of commercial motion pictures from current standards of morality in respect to the conduct exhibited in them."

Peters, Robert S. "The FCC's Requirement of Reply to Personal Attack: The Bite in Red Lion." *Tennessee Law Review*, 37:383–400, Winter 1970. 1P94
"It will be the purpose of this Comment to examine critically the first amendment challenge to one aspect of the [Federal Communications] Commission's regulatory power, namely the requirement of reply time to personal attacks and editorial endorsements. It was this requirement that brought forth the constitutional attack in *Red Lion* [*Red Lion Broadcasting Co. v. FCC*, 1969]."

Peterson, C. Donald. "Press Councils—A Look Towards the Future." *University of Miami Law Review*, 29:487–90, Spring 1975.   1P95
The chairman of the Minnesota Press Council, created in 1972 at the invitation of the Minnesota Newspaper Association, discusses the history, development, and accomplishments of the Council. "The Minnesota Press Council is experimental. It is an idea whose time has arrived. It should remain if we are concerned about the credibility and the freedom of the press which we value so highly."

Peterson, Morris. "Shouldn't We Identify the Source?" *Grassroots Editor*, 12(3): 18–20, May–June 1971.   1P96
The author argues that while the editor has the right to determine the content of a paper, the public has the right "to demand complete and accurate details plus the full disclosure of the sources supplying those facts and the opinions related to those facts."

Peterson, R. G. "To Repeal the Obscenity Law." *Freethinker*, 88:276–78, 30 August 1969.   1P97
A favorable review of the *Report* of the Working Party set up by the British Arts Council's Conference on the Obscenity Laws. "All who want the state to stop trying to enforce a private sexual morality useful only for keeping its citizens out of the Christian Hell, who want instead a society that is both rational and humane, should get the *Report* and do what they can to help."

Peterson, Theodore, Jay W. Jensen, and William L. Rivers. *The Mass Media and Modern Society*. 2d ed. New York, Holt, Rinehart and Winston, 1971. 342p.   1P98
In this textbook the authors consider the structure and ownership of the media and the methods of control both historically and at

present; the role of the press in modern society and the various theories supporting this role—libertarian and social responsibility. They also examine and appraise the major criticisms of the media.

Petrick, Michael J. *Inspection of Public Records in the States: The Law and News Media*. Madison, Wis., University of Wisconsin, 1970. 362p. (Ph.D. dissertation, University Microfilms, no. 71–314)   1P99
"This study of the development of the legal right to inspect government records in the fifty American states analyzes the conditions which fostered legal support for a notion that government records should be inspectable by members of the general public. Particular attention is given to participation by journalists in the formal policy-making processes through which a guaranteed right of access developed."

———. "The Press, the Police Blotter, and Public Policy." *Journalism Quarterly*, 46:475–81, Autumn 1969. 1P100
"While 42 states do have 'public records' statutes, few such laws apply specifically to the police blotter. The judiciary and the state attorney general can play a key role in attaining statewide policy which favors access."

———. "When You've Got a Law, Use It." *Quill*, 60(3):16–17, March 1972.   1P101
More than a year after its passage, the Maryland Freedom of Information law was still relatively unknown and unused.

Pettengill, Samuel B. "This Is Tyranny." *Talk* (Columbia Broadcasting System), 5(1):53–56, January 1940.   1P102
The speaker opposes the recently adopted National Association of Broadcaster's Code of Standard Practices. The same issue includes excerpts of favorable comment by Neville Miller.

Pettijohn, C. C. *The Case Against Federal Regulation of Motion Pictures. Arguments in Opposition to Political Censorship of the Screen*. Washington, D.C., Motion Picture Producers and Distributors of America, 1934. 66p.   1P103
Brief of the general counsel of the organization in opposition to the enactment of H.R. 6097 to create a Federal Motion Picture Commission. Presented at a hearing before the House of Representatives, Committee on Interstate and Foreign Commerce.

Pettit, E. P. "Plastic Dolls, Pornography, and the Longford Report." *Liberty*, 68(4):8–10, July–August 1973.   1P104
A summary of the findings of the British report on pornography: "Pornography is harmful. It

is as addictive as benzedrine, exploits human weakness, dehumanizes men and women into sex objects, is linked with violence and therefore leads to debasement of human beings." The British public appears to be prepared to support some kind of crackdown on hard-core pornography.

Pew, Marlen E. "U.S.A. War Time Censorship Regulations." In Walter Williams, *ed.*, *The Press Congress of the World in Switzerland*. Columbia, Mo., E. W. Stephens, 1928, pp. 196–99.
1P105

A brief description of the voluntary press censorship in the United States during World War I, including a list of the eighteen rules issued by the Committee on Public Information (Creel Committee).

Pfaff, Daniel W. *The First Amendment and Symbolic Speech: Toward a Rationale of the Public Forum*. Minneapolis, University of Minnesota, 1972. 343p. (Ph.D. dissertation, University Microfilms, no. 72-27,791)
1P106

"This study attempts to assess the significance of the so-called 'symbolic speech' cases primarily by analysis of first amendment case law developed by the Supreme Court of the United States within the last decade."

——. "Race, Libel, and the Supreme Court." *Columbia Journalism Review*, 8:23–26, Summer 1969.
1P107

The author considers the racial undertones in the U.S. Supreme Court's decision in *New York Times v. Sullivan* (1964).

——. *The Supreme Court, Civil Rights, and Press Freedom: Another Look at the Negro Revolution*. University Park, Pa., Pennsylvania State University, 1968. 179p. (Unpublished Master's thesis)
1P108

"Two celebrated Supreme Court opinions were the root of the study—*Brown v. Board of Education*, the 1954 public school desegregation decision, and *New York Times v. Sullivan*, the 1964 libel decision. Philosophical linkage was established between the two by noting the growth of judicial policy bolstering Negroes' rights and press freedom in subsequent cases which used those decisions as precedents."

Pfaff, Ellen O. "Gag Orders on Criminal Defendants." *Hastings Law Journal*, 27:1369–99, July 1976.
1P109

"The primary purpose of this note is to analyze the legal justification for including a criminal defendant in a gag order. It will be contended that no legal justification exists for limiting the defendant's first amendment right to speak freely on any issue, including the facts and circumstances surrounding the crime for which he has been indicted. A subsidiary purpose of this note is to examine the procedural and substantive standards presently being used

by the courts in determining whether a gag order covering the defendant is needed or required. The author's conclusion in this regard is that even if a legal justification for the order is established, the current procedural and substantive standards are inadequate, given the nature of the defendant's rights which are involved."

Pfeiffer, Immanuel. "Lucifer and the Post-Office Department." *Our Home Rights*, 4(2):7–11, March–April 1904.
1P110

The editor of this magazine of political and social reform recounts his successful efforts in Washington to clear Moses Harman's paper, *Lucifer, the Light-Bearer*, with the U.S. Post Office. The same issue carries a lengthy article on the deportation case of John Turner, attacked for his anarchist beliefs.

Phelan, John M. *The National Catholic Office for Motion Pictures: An Investigation of Policy and Practice of Film Classification*. New York, New York University, 1968. 364p. (Ph.D. dissertation, University Microfilms, no. 69-3191)
1P111

The dissertation examined film classification policies and practices of the National Catholic Office for Motion Pictures, formerly titled the Legion of Decency. The study showed that taste of individual reviewers rather than Catholic dogma dictated the classification and that only 1 percent of the films found objectionable were on religious grounds. Two out of three films objected to were because of their treatment of sex. The author concluded that the ratings were of doubtful value in guiding those who chose to use them; short reviews would have been preferable.

——, *ed. Communications Control: Readings in the Motives and Structures of Censorship*. New York, Sheed & Ward, 1969. 238p.
1P112

A collection of writings "about the phenomenon of censorship, the sources from which it springs, the forms that it assumes, and the manner in which it operates." Part I, Censorship and Social Structure, deals with the social and institutional aspects of censorship; part II, Censorship and Aesthetics, "shows how individuals allow their own needs, philosophies, and aspirations to shape and color the messages they send and the messages they receive"; part III, Censorship and Conflict, shows the exercises of censorship in concrete laws and actual cases, introduced by an essay by Walter Ong on the nature of verbal communications and human conflict. The editor believes that "the censorious mind will always be present in men," that there is a human necessity and social inevitability of censorship rising from "the fear of combat and the fear of communion."

Phelps, Dawson. *The Freedom of the Press in the North During the Civil War*. . . .

Chicago, University of Chicago, 1921. 49p. (Unpublished Master's thesis)
1P113

Phelps, Guy. "Censorship and the Press." *Sight and Sound*, 42:138–40, Summer 1973.
1P114

"The current debate about film censorship in this country has brought to public attention the important part played by the local authorities, some of whom have interpreted their role to include the moral guardianship of their electors by asserting more extensively their statutory rights to allow or prevent the exhibition of films in their areas. This increased council activity has exposed a number of weaknesses in the structure of censorship, one of which is discussed in this article." Deals with British censorship of *Last Tango in Paris*.

——. *Film Censorship*. With an Introduction by Alexander Walker. London, Gollancz, 1975. 319p.
1P115

A study of the recent history of film censorship in Great Britain, particularly the work of the British Board of Film Censors (BBFC), which gave the author access to their files. He considers the history of the Board; how it operates; pressures upon it from the industry, the politicians, and the general public; and the "terrible" dilemmas faced by individual censors in particular films involving sex and violence. In a final chapter on the future of film censorship he concludes that the vast majority of the public (including the film industry) wants some form of censorship, at least for the protection of children. He considers two possible alternatives to the present system—control under the Obscene Publications Act, with the Board reduced to mere classification; and an expansion of the Board's scope and power to replace local authority. He believes that the BBFC, with all its faults, is still the best solution, and suggests a number of reforms in its organization and procedures. He endorses the device of "private clubs" for the showing of uncensored films, and concludes that the "real problem is not how to eradicate ⌊sick material⌋ from the screen, but how to produce a society in which such needs are less pervasive." In his introduction, Alexander Walker discusses his experience in the London obscenity trial of *Last Tango in Paris*, and notes that films should not be subjected to controls by both the administrative censor *and* the courts.

——. "The Role and Problems of Local Government Film Censorship." *Local Government Studies*, 9:11–20, October 1974.
1P116

This paper deals with problems under the British system that gives local authorities statutory responsibility for film censorship. There is a need for some changes, the author concludes, if the system is to be adapted to modern conditions. He finds "a high degree of unanimity" between the statutory authorities and the British Board of Film Censors, whose role is merely advisory. This is true despite the fact that the former are elected amateurs and rely on "gut reactions" while the latter consists of a small group of sophisticated professionals. The Cinematograph Act of 1952 imposes upon local councils a "duty" to control films shown to children; only a "right" to control films shown to adults. "It is perhaps curious that local authorities should pay so much more attention to that part of their role which is a 'right' than to that which is a 'duty.' "

Phelps, Robert. "Law and the Press: Unused Rights." *IPI Report* (International Press Institute), 17(7):5–6, November 1968.   **1P117**
The author believes that U.S. journalists make little use of their freedom under the landmark *New York Times* rule and must prove worthy of it by robust, responsible reporting.

[**Philagatharches,** *pseud.*] "On the Liberty of the Press." In his *Hints on Toleration: In Five Essays.* . . . London, Cadell and Davies, 1810, pp. 257–330. **1P118**
"By granting the free exercise of the press, the reasoning powers of men will be cultivated and thus the public mind will be fortified against the insidious attacks of sophisticated politicians. . . . By the freedom of the press, the publick are constituted a tribunal, to which we may appeal, as a last resort upon the merits of a case. . . . " Blasphemous crimes against God are not proper subject for a magistrate's concern; corrupt politics is best counteracted by argument in the press; only seditious libel is suppressible. Portrayal of vice is not a crime per se, unless it constitutes palpably contrived obscenity. The only legitimate restraints to a free press lie in the realm of sedition, personal libel, and inculcation of vice.

Philanthropos, *pseud. A Dissection of the North Briton, Number XLV. Paragraph by Paragraph. Inscribed to the Right Honourable Earl Temple.* London, G. Burnet, 1764. 52p.   **1P119**
The author charges the *North Briton* with being "the most daring piece that ever was publicly printed, in this or any other, well-governed state in the world." He accuses John Wilkes, the author, of being a traitor and seditious liar, but leaves the recommendation of punishment to the courts.

Phillips, A. A. "Censorship: 3) Confessions of an Escaped Censor." *Meanjin Quarterly*, 28:508–13, Summer 1969.   **1P120**
A former censor describes the frustrations faced by a state board in the absence of objective standards of obscenity. He comes to the conclusion that the state is not the right in-

strumentality to enforce the mores of society. Until such a libertarian stage is reached in Australia he recommends that censorship boards consider the reception of a book abroad and only take action against a work when there is a "reasonable probability that the circulation of the work would contribute to an erosion of essential moral standards." He cites the considerable liberalization of Australian censorship in the last decade.

Phillips, Gene D. "No More Ratings?" *America*, 117:560–61, 11 November 1967.   **1P121**
"The Catholic film office in French Canada no longer assigns a moral rating to films. It offers, instead, a capsule review, giving their artistic and entertainment value—and moral worth. Should NCOMP [National Catholic Office for Motion Pictures], the U.S. Catholic film office, follow suit?"

Phillips, Jerry J. "Defamation, Invasion of Privacy, and the Constitutional Standard of Care." *Santa Clara Law Review*, 16:77–102, 1975.   **1P122**
Re: *Gertz v. Robert Welch, Inc.* 418 U.S. 323 (1974).

[**Phillips, Josiah.**] *The Trial of Josiah Phillips, for a Libel on the Duke of Cumberland, and the Proceedings Previous Thereto Arising Out of the Suicide of Sellis, in 1810 (From the Short-hand Notes of Mr. Gurney.) to Which is added In An Appendix, the Republication of the Pamphlet (Out of Print.) Called "A Minute Detail of the Attempt to Assassinate the Duke of Cumberland."* London, J. Hatchard, 1833. 131p.   **1P123**
Josiah Phillips was brought to trial for printing and publishing a book, *The Authentic Records of the Court of England for the Last Seventy Years*, in which the Duke of Cumberland is charged with murdering his valet who had surprised him in unnatural practices with another servant. The event occurred twenty-two years earlier and was judged a suicide. A young barrister, sensing the strong case against his client, makes a number of observations on libel: it is unfair to try the publisher when it is the author who is responsible for the truth or falsity; such a case only gives greater publicity to the charges in the book; and even if truth could be established after so many years have passed, the work could still be a libel. The jury returned an immediate verdict of guilty. The title page of the Library of Congress copy reads "Josiah Phillips"; the bibliographer's copy, acquired from the library of Judge Samuel Seabury, reads "Joseph Phillips," obviously in error since "Josiah" is used in the text of both copies.

Phillips, Kevin. "An Argument to Regulate TV Networks." *TV Guide*, 22(39):A5–A6, 28 September 1974.   **1P124**
"Given the obvious bias writ large in network

actions over the last decade, plus seeming responsiveness to private interests as opposed to national welfare, can we afford to let the networks go their unregulated merry way? Barbers who shape our hair are regulated; why not people who shape our minds? Politicians who shape our destinies are subject to increasing conflict-of-interest regulation; and why not TV networks who shape a much larger amount of our destiny?"

———. " 'Guns of Autumn' Misses Bull's-eye But Still Scores." *TV Guide*, 23(39):3–4, 27 September 1975. **1P125**
A scoring of the pluses and minuses in "fairness" for the Columbia Broadcasting System's antihunting documentary, a program that created a tremendous opposition from the gun lobby and efforts at suppression.

———. "Is the First Amendment Obsolete? The Press and the Government." *Human Events*, 33:37, 13 January 1973.   **1P126**
"If the 1st Amendment can't stop the Adversary Culture, we need a new sociojurisprudential approach that can solve the problem before the government throws the baby out with the bathwater of the Liberal Establishment bias."

Phillips, Stephen M. "Concentration of Ownership of the Media of Mass Communication: An Examination of New FCC Rules on Cross Ownership of Co-located Newspapers and Broadcast Stations." *Emory Law Journal*, 24:1121–63, Fall 1975.   **1P127**

Phillips, Wayne. "Jamming the Fairness Doctrine." *Nation*, 220:532–34, 3 May 1975.   **1P128**
A report on the campaign of the networks, newspapers, and "a lot of otherwise well-meaning people," including Senator William Proxmire, to abolish the fairness doctrine in broadcasting. If such action is taken, the author believes: "Issue advertising would no longer be threatened; cigarette advertising might be regained; no affiliate would ever again be asked to carry a 'counter-commercial' or redress a network documentary; no station would ever have to notify those it had attacked; no station would have to provide time for those it had attacked to reply; no station would have to carry views on a controversial public issue which conflicted with its own."

Phillips, William. "Writing About Sex." *Partisan Review*, 34:552–63, Fall 1967. (Also in Douglas A. Hughes, *ed.*, *Perspectives on Pornography*, pp. 197–211; and in Eleanor Widmer, *ed.*, *Freedom and Culture*, pp. 192–200) **1P129**
A critique of the views of critics who deplore the excesses of sex in modern literature, with special references to the articles by George P. Elliott (E64) and George Steiner (S616).

Phillpotts, Eden. "The Censor." In his *From the Angle of 88*. London, Hutchison, 1951, pp. 77–82. **1P130**
The novelist, at the age of eighty-eight, recounts an incident in 1912 when he refused to accede to the demand of the theater censor that two sentences be deleted from his play, then in rehearsal. As a result the play, according to a quirk in the law, could only be given without charging admission. Protest over the censor's action came from prominent British authors, and Phillpotts quotes from some of them. Shaw wrote, in part: "The pleasure of defending Mr. Eden Phillpotts is a pure luxury to me, because I am entirely out of sympathy with his choice of subjects, his scenery and his treatment of women. I dislike country folk, I hate Dartmoor, which is one of the worst places for motoring that I know of; Devonshire cream always disagrees with me and Devonshire was the home of those buccaneering malefactors who invented Imperialism, despoiled the courteous Spaniards and were spiritual progenitors of Rhodes and Kipling. Then Phillpotts' women are strong, masculine, meat-eating viragoes. But all of these grounds of antipathy are as nothing compared with the fact that his play has been banned and therefore must be moral, instructive and salutary. If Mr. Brookfield would have the sense to ban the revival of *Dear Old Charlie*, I should be the first to lead a crusade in his favor."

Phinazee, Annette. "Report on the Report: A Series of Reviews on the *Technical Reports* of the Commission on Obscenity and Pornography." *Newsletter on Intellectual Freedom* (IFC-ALA), 21:135–38, September 1972. **1P131**
A review of the Commission's volume I, *Preliminary Studies*, which describes research on the effect of pornography, done prior to and during the initial phase of the Commission's existence. This review summarizes the literature reviews.

Pickerell, Albert G. "Access to News in the United States." *Gazette: International Journal for Mass Communications Studies*, 4:65–80, 1958. **1P132**
"The past decade represents a period during which there has undoubtedly been more secrecy in government than at any other time in our history. It is a policy that has clearly contributed to America's failure to maintain leadership in scientific achievement; it has played a part in diplomatic failure abroad; it is an important element in growing uneasiness at home." Legislation requiring open access to government is needed along with a continuous educational campaign.

————, and Michel Lipman. *The Courts and the Mass Media*. [Berkeley, Calif., Project Benchmark], 1975. 118p. **1P133**
This publication is the product of the Conference of California Judges, through its education program, Project Benchmark, and is intended to help bridge information gaps among the bench, the bar, and the media. The publication contains material about court organization and jurisdiction, pretrial civil procedure, pretrial criminal procedure, civil and criminal trial procedure, legal bibliography, a history of the free press–fair trial controversy in the United States, and an article on the current newsmen's shield law controversy. Copies of the book have been distributed to all members of the Conference of California Judges, to every daily and weekly newspaper, and to every radio and television station in the state.

Pienaar, L. A. "Freedom of the Press." *New Nation*, 1973–74:8–10, December 1974. **1P134**
A South African member of Parliament calls for greater self-discipline and patriotic responsibility on the part of the English language press if more stringent government controls are not to be imposed. The press code should be tightened and the Press Reference Council should deal more effectively with complaints against the press.

Pierce, Mary E. *The Right of Access to the Media: Trends and Implication*. Austin, Tex., University of Texas, 1972. 154p. (Unpublished Master's thesis) **1P135**
"This thesis is a study of the concept of a right of access to the mass media. It reviews legal and agency decisions involving broadcast and print media, popular commentary, and the results of interviews with journalism and law professors and journalists and lawyers."

Pigott, Charles. *Persecution. The Case of Charles Pigott: Contained in the Defence He Had Prepared and Which Would Have Been Delivered by Him on His Trial, If the Grand Jury Had Not Thrown Out the Bill Preferred Against Him. . . .* London, D. I. Eaton, 1793. 52p. **1P136**
Pigott, a radical journalist, was arrested along with a friend for uttering seditious words in a London coffee house. He had also written two objectionable books, *The Jockey Club* and *Political Dictionary*. A year later he escaped prosecution for the latter by dying in jail, but Daniel I. Eaton was brought to trial for publishing the *Political Dictionary* (E18). Pigott wrote: "Freedom of speech is an Englishman's prerogative, engraved in our Constitution, by the Magna Charta and the Bill of Rights. Let us beware lest arbitrary, vindictive ministers supported by the wretched sophistry of lawyers wrest it from us." He attacked the heinous practice of arrest and imprisonment of dissenters under ex-officio information warrants.

Pike, Chan P. "No Testimonial Privilege for Newsmen." *North Carolina Law Review*, 51:562–73, January 1973. **1P137**
This note examines the U.S. Supreme Court decision in *Branzburg v. Hayes*, *In re Pappas*, and *Caldwell v. United States* (1971) which held that the First Amendment does not grant to news-

men a testimonial privilege that other citizens do not enjoy.

Pilati, Joe. "The Underground GI Press." *Commonweal*, 90:559–61, 19 September 1969. **1P138**
A brief account of the Fort Dix *Shakedown* and other soldier antiwar papers.

Pilpel, Harriet F. "Birth Control and a New Birth of Freedom." *Ohio State Law Journal*, 27:679–90, Fall 1966. **1P139**
The author analyzes *Griswold v. Connecticut* (1965) and other recent developments in the birth control movement and explains their significance for constitutional theory.

————. "The Challenge of Privacy." In Alan Reitman, *ed.*, *The Price of Liberty*. New York, Norton, 1968, pp. 19–44. **1P140**
The development of the concept of privacy in the United States and various court decisions that have helped to mold the common law.

————. "Freedom of Expression: Matrix of All Freedoms." *Publishers' Weekly*, 192(22):24–25, 27 November 1967. **1P141**
A consideration of the thesis presented by Professor Jerome Barron that unless government intervenes, freedom of speech and the press will prove more theoretical than real.

————. "Freedom of the Press—American Style." *Publishers' Weekly*, 203(11):26–29, 12 March 1973. **1P142**
The author looks at seven constituent parts of freedom of the Press: freedom to speak, freedom to listen, the right not to speak, the right not to listen, the right to speak anonymously, the right to know, and the right of access. She also considers against whom the prohibition of the abridgment of speech and press applies and the current status of that guarantee.

————. "Freedom of the Press: How Does It Look Today?" *Publishers' Weekly*, 208(9):31–33, 1 September 1975. **1P143**
"On the brink of the Bicentennial, one of our most important guarantees is reasonably intact, but encroachments on it bear constant watching." In addition to the limitations placed on obscenity there are restrictions on libel, privacy, fraud, fighting words, commercial speech, speech limited by contract, and liability of publishers and booksellers, the former who may suffer harassment by facing multiple state suits against the same books—all of which have a "chilling effect" on freedom of the press.

————. "A Legal Bridge Should Exist Between Privacy and Obscenity." *Publishers' Weekly*, 190(25):54–55, 26 December 1966. **1P144**
Comment on the right of privacy of sexual conduct between consenting adults as upheld by the U.S. Supreme Court in *Redmond v. U.S.* (1966). The case involved the mailing of husband and wife nude films to an out of state firm for developing.

————. *Obscenity and the Constitution.* New York, Bowker, 1973. 25p. (First of the R. R. Bowker Memorial Lectures, New Series, under the Joint Sponsorship of the School of Library Service, Columbia University and the R. R. Bowker Company. A condensed version appears in *Publishers' Weekly*, 10 December 1973) **1P145**
A review of the good and bad news with respect to obscenity law: the good news was the *Roth* decision and its three-part test before a work could be held obscene, the report of the U.S. Commission on Obscenity and Pornography, and *Stanley v. Georgia* (1969) in which the Court held that a man had a constitutional right to enjoy obscenity in the privacy of his home. The bad news was the U.S. Supreme Court decisions of 21 June 1973, which weakened the *Roth* decision and shifted responsibility for standards in matters of obscenity to local communities. The author outlines what steps can be taken "to blunt the edges of the June 21 obscenity decisions and bring them more rationally into the framework of our Constitution." Charles Rembar presents a different opinion in the 14 January 1974 issue.

————. "Three Legal Issues." *Publishers' Weekly*, 193(5):47–48, 29 January 1968. **1P146**
A look at 1967 court decisions in the areas of obscenity, libel, and privacy.

————, and Kenneth P. Norwick. "Actual Malice Libel Test Applied to Public Figures." *Publishers' Weekly*, 193(26):43, 24 June 1968. **1P147**
Re: *Thompson v. The Evening Star Newspaper Company*, U.S. Court of Appeals for the District of Columbia, 1968.

————. "Can You Publish Data Improperly Obtained?" *Publishers' Weekly*, 195(13):32–33, 31 March 1969. **1P148**
"What are the legal consequences if an author and publisher publish material they know was 'improperly obtained'?" *Pearson and Anderson v. Dodd*, U.S. Court of Appeals for the District of Columbia, 1969.

————. "Content No Longer Sole Fac-

tor in Obscenity." *Publishers' Weekly*, 195(13):33, 31 March 1969. **1P149**
"We agree with the approach of the New York Criminal Court that determinations of obscenity—if they must be made—should not depend solely upon a police or judicial evaluation of the *content* of the material in question but that its target audience and mode of distribution should be considered."

————. "Courts Again Seek Definition of Obscenity." *Publishers' Weekly*, 198(22):17, 30 November 1970. **1P150**
Comment on the decision of the U.S. Court of Appeals for the Second Circuit in *United States of America v. Motion Picture Film Entitled "Language of Love,"* in which a lower court's ruling of obscene was reversed. The decision made a contribution to the meaning of "prurient interest."

————. "Crux of Obscenity: How, to Whom, and Where." *Publishers' Weekly*, 194(5):36–37, 29 July 1968. **1P151**
"It begins to look as if, from now on, our principal censorship battles will have to do with how, to whom and where allegedly obscene material is distributed." Re: *Reed Enterprises v. Clark* (1968) and *People ex rel. Weiss v. Menna* (1968).

————. "Federal Court Ruling Democratizes Obscenity." *Publishers' Weekly*, 197(5):65, 2 February 1970. **1P152**
A liberal obscenity ruling concerning the movie, *I Am Curious (Yellow)* by the U.S. District Court of Massachusetts (*Karalexis v. Byrne*, 1969).

————. "Flip Is Not Actual Malice." *Publishers' Weekly*, 196(14):33, 6 October 1969. **1P153**
Can a published report which is otherwise privileged, i.e. not recoverable-on though libelous, lose that protection because of the "flippant" and "smart-alecky" manner in which it is presented? Re: *Sellers v. Time, Inc.*, U.S. District Court, Eastern District of Pennsylvania, 1969.

————. "The Goldwater Case: Actual Malice Asserted." *Publishers' Weekly*, 196(9):31–32, 1 September 1969. **1P154**
Re: *Barry M. Goldwater v. Ralph Ginzburg*, U.S. Circuit Court of Appeals for the Second Circuit, 1969.

————. "Is 'Public-Interest' Discussion Libel-Proof?" *Publishers' Weekly*, 195(5):37–38, 3 February 1969. **1P155**
Re: *United Medical Laboratories, Inc. v. Columbia Broadcasting System, Inc.*, U.S. Court of Appeals for the Ninth Circuit, 1968.

————. "Lawyers Fail To Stop Anti-

Lawyer Promotion." *Publishers' Weekly*, 196(22):19, 1 December 1969. **1P156**
The case involved advertising of a book, *How to Avoid Lawyers*, by a Florida attorney: *Schutzman & Schutzman v. News Syndicate Co., Inc.*, Supreme Court of New York, Nassau County, 1969.

————. "Libel and Privacy Cases Explore Free Speech Limits." *Publishers' Weekly*, 196(18):27–28, 3 November 1969. **1P157**
The libel case: *Arizona Biochemical Co. v. Hearst Corp.* (1969); the privacy case: *Pagan v. New York Herald Tribune, Inc.* (1969).

————. "Supreme Court Approves Variable Obscenity Law." *Publishers' Weekly*, 193(22):32, 27 May 1968. **1P158**
Re: *Ginsberg v. State of New York*, 390 U.S. 629 (1968), upholding New York's law protecting minors from obscenity.

————. "*Times* Libel Rule Is Issue In Recent Court Cases." *Publishers' Weekly*, 197(9):54–56, 2 March 1970. **1P159**
"As things now stand . . . it would appear that although all courts seem to agree that the *New York Times* rule does in fact apply to discussions of 'matters of public interest and concern,' the courts do not necessarily agree on just what constitutes such a discussion."

————. "Two Faces of Malice." *Publishers' Weekly*, 198(5):31–32, 3 August 1970. **1P160**
"The Supreme Court has ruled that even a harsh statement, or accusation, if made in a context where it is 'rhetorical hyperbole,' may not be the basis for a libel recovery—even if the publisher of the statement knows that it is literally not true." Re: *Wasserman v. Time, Inc.*, U.S. District Court of Appeals for the District of Columbia, 1970.

————. "The Two Faces of Obscenity." *Publishers' Weekly*, 198(1):30–31, 6 July 1970. **1P161**
Comment on two recent obscenity cases: In *United States of American v. "Language of Love"* the U.S. District Court, Southern District of New York, ruled the Swedish movie obscene (it met the *Roth* standards for obscenity); in *United States of America v. Various Articles of "Obscene Merchandise"* a three-man court in the same district held the importation law unconstitutional as applied to importation of obscene materials even for private use. The latter decision "is a preview of what we hope will be a wave of the future as far as the obscenity law is concerned."

Pilpel, Harriet F., and Marjorie T. Parsons. "Dirty Business in Court." *Civil Liberties Review*, 1(4):30–41, Fall 1974. **1P162**
A review of recent events in the control of

obscenity—the report of the U.S. Commission on Obscenity and Pornography which recommended the repeal of all obscenity regulations involving consenting adults, and the rejection of the Commission's findings by President Nixon and the Congress; the 1973 decisions of the U.S. Supreme Court (*Miller v. California et al.*) which passed the buck in obscenity matters to the states and local communities and brought about general confusion; the Supreme Court case of *Jenkins v. Georgia* which ruled that the film, *Carnal Knowledge*, was not obscene; and *Hamling v. U.S.*, involving the illustrated edition of *The Report of the Commission on Obscenity and Pornography*. The authors note that three states—South Dakota, West Virginia, and Iowa repealed their obscenity statutes relating to adults, but Nebraska enacted a more oppressive new obscenity bill. The authors also consider the forces for and against obscenity legislation and their activities and results in various states.

————. *Obscenity and Censorship*. New York, American Civil Liberties Union, 1974. 9p. Processed. **1P163**
Background of the 1973 Supreme Court decisions on obscenity: What are their effects? What has been done about them? What can be done? A paper prepared for discussion at a policy-implementation workshop at the June 13-16, 1974 biennial conference of the ACLU, University of Wisconsin, Milwaukee. The authors conclude: "We must continue to litigate in the hope that good decisions will strike down bad laws. We must press for good laws, or better still, none at all in the obscenity area. We must, above all, educate, since in the final analysis, an informed and alert citizenry is the only true guarantee of a free society."

Pilpel, Harriet F., and Laurie R. Rockett. "Libel, Advertising and Freedom of the Press." *Publishers' Weekly*, 209(9):46-48, 1 March 1976. **1P164**
"It looks as if the United States Supreme Court has enunciated such ambiguous rules applicable to libel in relation to the First Amendment, that authors, publishers and their lawyers are at best hazarding informed guesses when they decide what can be published with the cloak of First Amendment protection. . . . For the writer or publisher trying to find some firm guidelines on which to avoid a libel claim, the situation is at least as vague today as it was before *Gertz* [*Gertz v. Robert Welch, Inc.*, 1974]." In the area of advertising which has been traditionally considered outside the protection of the First Amendment, recent decisions have indicated that some "commercial speech" may be protected, but protection will likely be of a lesser order.

————. "Supreme Court Libel Ruling in Firestone Case Is a New Danger to Press Freedom." *Publishers' Weekly*, 209(13):39-40, 29 March 1976. **1P165**
The case of *Firestone v. Time, Inc.* (1976), involving a brief news item on a divorce case "plunges the field of libel . . . into the cold certainty of self-imposed censorship. . . . In

effect, the Court said that people generally regarded as public figures can recover for libel when involved in court cases of great public interest if they can satisfy a jury that the press, through simple common law negligence, reported such an event inaccurately."

Pilpel, Harriet F., and Alan U. Schwartz. "A Deep Legal Look Into the Crystal Ball; Crisis of the Book in the 21st Century." *Publishers' Weekly*, 201(15):82-85, 10 April 1972. **1P166**
In the year 2025 the authors subject an imaginary manuscript which has been electrically coded in a data bank to a test for possible violations for libel, invasion of privacy, obscenity, and violation of government security classification.

————. "How Free Is the Free Press? Notes On a Number of Cases of Interest to the Book Trade." *Publishers' Weekly*, 202(13):32-34, 25 September 1972. **1P167**
Is advertising part of the free press? Can boiler-plate blow up? How free is the free press under the *New York Times* libel rule? Are fighting words worth fighting for?

————. "Obscenity Revisited: Supreme Court Cases." *Publishers' Weekly*, 200(5):37-38, 2 August 1971. **1P168**
While the president's Commission on Pornography and Obscenity has recommended repeal of most present obscenity legislation, except that which would protect minors and restrict public display of pornography, the Supreme Court is moving back toward increased censorship. "The Court by so explicitly stating that the *Roth* three-pronged test was its current word on obscenity seems to have walked away from *Stanley v. Georgia* and its privacy theory."

————. "Privacy, Publishing and You." *Publishers' Weekly*, 201(1):30-32, 3 January 1972. **1P169**
The authors discuss the European legal concept, *Droit Moral*, a group of rights which protect an author's work product as an aspect of his creative individuality, from distortion, theft, and mislabeling. "We think it likely that as courts look for additional ways to protect individuality from the ubiquitous voyeurism of modern urban civilization, we will see the further development and recognition of elements of the *Droit Moral*, albeit under an Americanized 'privacy' label."

————. "Truths and Untruths." *Publishers' Weekly*, 200(5):38, 2 August 1971. **1P170**
Re: *Rosenbloom v. Metromedia*, in which the U.S. Supreme Court held that a private person cannot win a libel suit against someone who may have damaged him by untruthful statements so long as the statements were in connection with matters of public interest, were non-malicious, and not made with "reckless disregard for the truth."

————. "When Is a Libel Not a Libel?" *Publishers' Weekly*, 206(25):29-30, 16 December 1974. **1P171**
Discussion of the implications of two 1974 libel cases: *Letter Carriers v. Austin* and *Gertz v. Robert Welch, Inc.* "The libel cases decided by the Court just one day after the obscenity cases [*Carnal Knowledge and Hamling*] are just as confused—but in the opposite direction. Here the Court appears to be dedicated to the proposition that there *should* be a national pattern, regardless of the desires of the individual states or 'vicinages.' " The obscenity case, on the other hand, had called for an increased reliance on state and local standards. "In the final analysis the Court seems in the *Gertz* decision to have, with one fell swoop, eroded First Amendment freedoms for publishers and authors while at the same time depriving private litigants in libel cases involving public issues of certain kinds of general and punitive damages to which they were previously entitled—a 'Judgment of Solomon' which, we submit, basically helps no one and heaps more confusion on the present state of the law of libel in this country."

Pincher, Chapman. "Press Freedom and National Security." *Journalism Today*, 1(2):37-50, Spring 1968. **1P172**
The author concludes that the onus should be on those who insist on secrecy under British law to justify each case, either to the reporter, his editor, or the "D-Notice" press members. Instead, the prevailing attitude is that a piece of information or a document is "secret because we say so." One of two papers presented for discussion at a meeting of the Institute of Journalists, by the defense correspondent of the *London Daily Express*.

Pincus, Walter. "After the Tornillo Decision." *Bulletin of the American Society of Newspaper Editors*, 578:6-9, May-June 1974. **1P173**
Commentary on the Florida right-to-reply statute, declared unconstitutional by the U.S. Supreme Court in a reversal of the Florida Supreme Court. Newspapers, concludes the author, should not draw back from editorializing or reporting fully and frankly on controversial issues because they have become monopoly news sources.

————. "Fairness in the News: The Right of Reply." *New Republic*, 170:11-14, 23 March 1974. **1P174**
Comment on the Florida right of reply statute, tested by the courts in the *Tornillo* case. As alternatives to the right of reply, the author suggests the reduction of press monopolies, aggressive newspaper efforts to seek opposing points of view, and a healthier attitude in the press toward self-criticism.

Pines, Burt. "The Obscenity Quagmire." *California State Bar Journal*, 49:509–12+, November–December 1974. **1P175**

An examination of the obscenity laws of California which practical experience with enforcement has demonstrated are virtually unworkable. The author proposes "more narrowly drawn statutes that would allow forewarned adults to read or see whatever they wish."

Pinkus, Philip. *Grub St. Stripped Bare. The scandalous lives & pornographic works of the original Grub St. writers, together with the bottle songs which led to their drunkenness, the shameless pamphleteering which led them to Newgate Prison, & the continual pandering to public taste which put them among the first almost to earn a fitful living from their writing alone.* Hamden, Conn., Archon Books, 1968. 312p. **1P176**

The story of the literary hacks of London during the last years of the seventeenth and the first years of the eighteenth centuries, told largely through their own accounts, with some commentary and historical background. Their unique way of life, their salacious works, and the penalties they paid for violation of controls on the press, are brought out in the book. Among those individuals who were subject to prosecution for their writing and publishing were: Daniel Defoe, Benjamin Harris, John Twyn, John Tutchin, and Edmund Curll.

Piraino, Thomas A., Jr., "Public Disclosure of Confidential Business Information under the Freedom of Information Act: Toward a More Objective Standard." *Cornell Law Review*, 60:109–30, November 1974. **1P177**

Under the Freedom of Information Act of 1966, nine specific instances were delineated in which government agencies would be exempt from disclosure. This article examines one such exemption, "trade secrets and commercial or financial information obtained from a person and privileged or confidential." He suggests "a possible judicial resolution of its inherent ambiguities in a manner consistent with the public's interest in disclosure and the individual's right of privacy."

Pitcairn, Robert A., Jr. "Licensee's Refusal to Sell Broadcast Time for Editorial Advertising Based on Its Policy of Selling Time Only for Commercial Advertising Is a Denial of Free Speech." *University of Cincinnati Law Review*, 40:870–76, 1971. **1P178**

Re: *Business Executives' Move for Vietnam Peace v. FCC*, 25 F.C.C. 2d 242 (1970).

Pitt, G. J. "Report of the Committee on Defamation." *Modern Law Review*, 39:187–95, March 1976. **1P179**

A review of the report of the Faulks Committee on Defamation which, "although succeeding in its aim of simplifying the law . . . has not taken the opportunity for any radical reform." The review discusses the report under the following headings: What Is Defamatory? Defences (justification, fair comment, privilege). Publishers Conduct of Action. Miscellaneous Reforms.

Pitt, Valerie. "Why the Church Should Not Play the Censor." *Times* (London), 26 July 1969, p. 10. **1P180**

"There is, of course, a responsibility on the church to make its way plain, and to ensure that the law does not make it impossible for Christians to follow a Christian way. There is no responsibility on us to argue for law which would force all citizens not to do anything we would not do. Indeed our faith, which lays so much emphasis on the right of men to choose even when they choose wrongly, and on the rightness of the heart, really forbids us to compel men to do good, or to read 'good' books merely because they cannot get anything else."

Pivar, David J. *Purity Crusade; Sexual Morality and Social Control, 1868–1900.* Westport, Conn., Greenwood, 1973. 308p. (Contributions in American History, no. 23) **1P181**

In the decade following the Civil War the mainstream of American reform movement focused on a crusade against prostitution and social impurity. It was a quasi-religious movement of women and former abolitionists. It paved the way for urban Progressivism at the turn of the century and the modification of the sexual attitudes of the twentieth century. "The basic objective of this book is to trace the major contours of the movement, including its accomplishment, the events in which purity reformers participated, the social functions of purity reform in the woman's movement and urban Progressivism, and its effects upon the development of the social hygiene movement." The antiobscenity crusade headed by Anthony Comstock was a part of this larger movement.

Place, Francis. "*Age of Reason:* The Case of Thomas Williams; the Conduct of Mr. Erskine." In *The Autobiography of Francis Place (1771–1854).* Edited with Introduction and Notes by Mary Thale. Cambridge, England, Cambridge University Press, 1972, pp. 159–72. **1P182**

Place, who had encouraged Thomas Williams to publish an edition of Thomas Paine's *Age of Reason*, gives his account of Williams's trial (1797), including criticism of Thomas Erskine, a leading exponent of press freedom, for serving as prosecutor. Four years earlier Erskine had defended Paine when he was tried for his *Rights of Man*.

[———.] *The Examiner and the Tax on Newspapers* . . . . London, G. Morgan, 1836. 15p. (Extracted from the *Radical*, 26 March 1836) **1P183**

One of the efforts of this early nineteenth-century British reformer was in behalf of the campaign to abolish the newspaper tax. Place wrote articles against these "taxes on knowledge" for any paper that would take them. Other articles by Place are entered in the 1968 edition of this bibliography.

[———.] *The Stamp Duty on Newspapers. From the Radical of Saturday, March 19, 1836.* London, G. Morgan [1836?]. 14p. **1P184**

[———.] *The Stamp Tax Bill. No. 1 [and No. 2].* London, G. Morgan [1836?]. 16p. (Reprinted from the *Radical*) **1P185**

———. *The Whigs and the Penny Stamp [Extracted from the London Dispatch, December 4, 1836],* London, Hetherington, 1836. 8p. **1P186**

"Plague of Censorship: Worse Things Than Cigarettes Threaten the Body Politic." *Barrons*, 50:1, 8, 21 December 1970. **1P187**

An attack on the FCC's prohibition of cigarette advertising. "What began as a well-intentioned, if perhaps misguided, effort to educate the citizen thus has escalated into an exercise in authoritarianism, the effects of which threaten to ripple far and wide."

Planned Parenthood Association, Chicago Area. *Chronological History of the Birth Control Controversy in Chicago.* Chicago, The Association, 1964. 11p. Processed. **1P188**

Planned Parenthood League of Massachusetts. *Birth Control and the Massachusetts Law.* Boston, The League, 1959. 5p. Processed. **1P189**

Playton, Vernon P. "Obscenity Control: A Search for Validity." *Land and Water Law Review*, 4:575–85, 1969. **1P190**

The conclusion to be drawn from studies of obscenity is that "at best, no good will come of holding obscenity illegal for children. It would also seem that regulations of what minors are to see and hear are not proper functions for the judicial system, but that any regulation should be left to the child and his parents based on their reason, social identity and religion. . . . If no cause and effect relationship can be established or if the courts determine that their function is not qualified to handle the problem effectively, then they should say so and leave obscenity control to more adequately equipped institutions."

"Plea Against Film Censorship." *Times of India*, 17 December 1969, p. 13.
1P191
"The consensus at today's three-hour session at the International Film Symposium was that there should be no censorship of films. India's film censor came in for severe drubbing." According to K. A. Abbas, "the censors presume to be guardian of morality but are actually the guardian of the status quo."

Plesser, Ronald L. "The When and How of the Freedom of Information Act." *Practical Lawyer*, 21:61–68, April 1975.
1P192
How to request information, fees and administration, judicial review, and a discussion of the nine exemptions. "Though these exemptions may seem broad and all encompassing, the courts have interpreted them narrowly."

Plevin, Cynthia H., and Steven M. Plevin. "Journalists in the Courts: Toward Effective Shield Legislation." *University of San Francisco Law Review*, 8:664–701, Spring 1974.
1P193
"This comment will examine the need for shield legislation [to protect journalists from compelled disclosure of confidential sources], discuss alternative components and propose a model federal statute. It will then trace the evolution of California's shield law and propose a revision of the statutory scheme."

Plotkin, Robert. "Ohio Criminal Syndicalism Act Which Punishes Mere Advocacy of Lawless Action Rather Than Incitement to Imminent Lawless Action Is Unconstitutional." *University of Cincinnati Law Review*, 39:210–15, Winter 1970.
1P194
Re: *Brandenburg v. Ohio*, 395 U.S. 444 (1969).

[Plotnik, Arthur.] "Enemies of Porno —and of Reason: An Analysis." *Wilson Library Bulletin*, 45:232–33, 332, November 1970.
1P195
Comment on the irrational response of the Congress to the report of the U.S. Commission on Obscenity and Pornography, with references to the dissenting report of Commissioner Charles H. Keating, Jr., who, the author charges, represents a "regression" of intellectual freedom.

Plowdon, William. "The Hidden Machine." *New Society*, 9:912–13, 22 June 1967.
1P196
"The row over the [British] D-Notice System raises wider questions about government secrecy. The incident is, in many ways, trivial: is that how constitutional things strike the public?"

Plowman, Edward E. "McIntire's Navy." *Liberty*, 69:2–9, January–February 1974.
1P197

An account of some of the legal difficulties encountered by the fundamentalist radio preacher, the Reverend Carl McIntire, has had with the Federal Communications Commission in that agency's efforts to enforce the fairness doctrine in controversial broadcasting. When his station WXUR lost its license, McIntire set up an unlicensed station in a converted World War II minesweeper off the New Jersey coast. Mr. McIntire's response to this article, charging numerous errors, is published in the July–August 1974 issue along with Mr. Plowman's reply. Mr. McIntire's article had been edited by *Liberty*'s editor, Hegstad, but Mr. McIntire insisted on the article being printed as submitted, which *Liberty* has done, but with the suggested editorial changes indicated by gray bars.

Plummer, Niel. "The Publication of Ghastly Photographs: Recipe for Judicial Restraints Possible." *Grassroots Editor*, 13(2):38–40, March–April 1972.
1P198
The author suggests ways in which the courts can act to prevent the publication of shocking photographs of victims of accidents or violent crimes.

———, and Frank Thayer. "The Press and Out-of-Court Contempt." *Notre Dame Lawyer*, 14:258–69, March 1939.
1P199
The authors conclude that despite abuses by the press, an outside control agency—legislative or executive—is not called for and that there has been a dangerous and unnecessary extension of judicial power to punish contempt for publications outside of court. They believe the administration of justice needs the disciplinary and reforming influence of the press.

Plumptre, James. *Four Discourses on Subjects Relating to the Amusement of the Stage. Preached at Great St. Mary's Church, Cambridge, on Sunday September 25, and Sunday October 2, 1808; with Copious Supplementary Notes.* Cambridge, England, Francis Hodson, 1809. 284p.
1P200
While professing a love for the drama, the Reverend Mr. Plumptre, recommends purifying the plays, removing the heathenism to make them proper for public presentation. In the dedication he admits to encountering two prejudices in his efforts to reform the stage—persons who think the stage does not stand in need of any reformation and those who think the stage incapable of amendment. Discourse I, The Lawfulness of the Stage Considered. II, Abuses and Uses of the Stage Pointed Out. III, On Wit and Ridicule. IV, On the Most Probable Means of Improving the Stage. References are made in notes to productions censored by the Lord Chamberlain.

Poe, Douglas A. "The Legal Philosophy of John Marshall Harlan: Freedom

of Expression, Due Process, and Judicial Self-Restraint." *Vanderbilt Law Review*, 21:659–96, October 1968. **1P201**
The author attempts to analyze the theoretical approach of one member of the U.S. Supreme Court to certain basic First and Fourteenth Amendment problems. A spokesman for "judicial restraint," Justice Harlan has often spoken for the majority, but has also been willing to take a far more advanced position. He has generally favored the balancing of interests rather than a more absolute approach, but his opinions fail to reveal a concise or consistent theory of the First Amendment.

Pogrund, Benjamin. "The South African Press." *Index on Censorship*, 5(3): 10–16, Autumn 1976.
1P202
"The press is free and yet unfree. It is a press choked by restrictions imposed by the Afrikaner Nationalist government yet it enjoys an extraordinary degree of freedom. It is often a courageous press; it is also often cowardly. . . . There is no direct censorship; censors do not sit in newspaper offices. There is also no censorship in the sense that reports must be submitted to the authorities in advance of publication—except in the notable case of military matters. Instead, a network of laws exists and it is up to the newspapers to ensure that they remain within the limits. The press is made to act as its own censor." The author fears that "the freedom that exists is likely to be increasingly less used and applied out of fear of the consequences. It remains to be seen whether the press will be emasculated—or emasculate itself to the point where meaningful reporting and commenting will no longer be possible."

———, and Slater Layton. "Two Views on the Press in South Africa." *IPI Report* (International Press Institute), 23(10):2–4, 10, October 1974.
1P203
Comments on the newspaper industry's self-imposed Code of Conduct in South Africa.

[Poles, Stefan, *plaintiff*.] *Stefan Poles v. The Times Newspaper. Action for Libel in Reference to the Secret Papers of M. Adolphe Thiers and Mademoiselle Félicie Dosne. . . . Court of Queen's Bench, Westminster. February 9 and 10, 1874 . . . (before Mr. Justice Blackburn).* London, Stefan Poles, 1874. 32p. **1P204**
The case involved a Paris dispatch to the *Times* (London) which charged the plaintiff, Stefan Poles, with attempted blackmail of M. Thiers over a manuscript taken from his home. The charge was proved false and the *Times* was required to pay £50 damages.

Politella, Dario. "Campus Censorship

Cases, Fall 1970." *Seminar (A Quarterly Review for Newspapermen by Copley Newspapers)*, 19:27, 30–32, March 1971. (Also published in *College Press Review*, Spring 1971)   **1P205**
In this paper, presented at the 1970 conference of the Associated Collegiate Press and NCCPA in Minneapolis, a journalism professor discusses recent college press censorship cases.

Pollack, Harriet. "*An Uncommonly Silly Law": The Connecticut Birth Control Cases in the U.S. Supreme Court*. New York, Columbia University, 1967. 240p. (Ph.D. dissertation, University Microfilms, no. 67-14,080)   **1P206**
An analysis of three Connecticut birth control cases, *Tileston v. Ullman* (1943), *Poe v. Ullman* (1961), and *Griswold v. Connecticut* (1965), as they reflect on the judicial process and on the desirable limits of majoritarian control. The author considers the role of the pressure groups which brought the cases to court and suggested the line of legal argument embodied in the decisions. The cases also raise "the question of the virtues of judicial activism v. judicial self-restraint."

Pollack, Terry. "Slow Leak in the Pentagon (and the CIA, and the State Dept., and the White House, and . . .)" *Ramparts*, 11:21–26, 49–50, January 1973.   **1P207**
"Leaking has become effective as ordinary, loyal, hard-working bureaucrats . . . increasingly take it on themselves to blow the whistle on official plans and actions which offend their sense of decency." The author describes in detail some of the "leaking" in agencies of the Federal government.

Pollak, Felix. "Pornography: A Trip Around the Halfworld." *Tri-Quarterly*, 12:121–38, Spring 1969. (Also in Douglas A. Hughes, *ed.*, *Perspectives on Pornography*, pp. 170–96, and Eleanor Widmer, *ed.*, *Freedom and Culture*, pp. 181–87)   **1P208**
"To me, the only acceptable view and practice of sex is the hedonistic one, and the divorce of the mutual pleasure from sex the only perversion." The author criticizes the typical liberal who uses the argument in defending pornography that "no girl has ever been seduced by a book. . . . If one denies the power of the word to do evil, one denies the power of the word to do good. . . . I prefer the healthy fear and awe of the written and spoken word." Pollak likewise criticizes the liberals who "instead of frankly admitting that a book may be pornographic and in spite of it, or even because of it, a good book, they endeavor to argue pornography away altogether." He deplores the

openness and widespread availability of pornography, preferring the former excitement of the forbidden. "As long as freedom can fight against limits, there is freedom; unlimited freedom negates itself, is merely an aimless tumbling in outer space. Pornography, in a climate of utter permissiveness, is *ipso facto* obliterated." Taboo words are less effective today since they have become commonplace and a new set of words may have to be created to fill the need. He argues that "the wholesale bestowal of permissiveness is more deadly to pornography as a genre than the barbs of ostracism and the shackles of censorship."

Pollak, Louis H. "Thomas I. Emerson, Lawyer and Scholar: *Ipse Custodiet Custodes*." *Yale Law Journal*, 84:638–55, March 1975.   **1P209**
An appraisal of the career and writing of the Yale law professor and author of *The System of Freedom of Expression*, "the major treatise on free speech written in our time."

Pollak, Richard. "A Case Against Press Councils." *MORE*, 3(2):3, February 1973.   **1P210**
Opposition to the Twentieth Century Fund's formation of a national press council, preferring fundamental reform from within the profession by "opening up the decision-making process to the men and women in the newsroom."

Pollard, James S. "The Kennedy Administration and the Press." *Journalism Quarterly*, 41:3–14, Winter 1964. **1P211**
While the late president enjoyed a degree of accessibility and warmth unmatched by any previous administration, these gains were offset by certain criticisms of his news policies: an effort to manage the news, an attempt to "unify" government news sources, suppression and distortion of the news as exemplified by the Cuban crisis, harassment of reporters and government officials by the FBI, and the play to White House favorites among the correspondents to serve administration purposes.

Pollock, John. *Anatole France & Mrs. Grundy. With passages hitherto unpublished from Anatole France en Pantoufles by F. F. Brousson.* Kensington, England, Cayme Press, 1926. 32p. (Edition limited to 750 copies)   **1P212**
Why were some ten pages suppressed in the English translation of *Anatole France Himself* by J. J. Brousson, published by Butterworth in London and Lippincott in New York? It was the work of the gentlemen representing the circulating libraries and following the standards of Mrs. Grundy. The author attacks the censorship of legitimate literature imposed by the circulating libraries in which "grown men and women must be content with current literature fit for girls in their teens." While defending the Anatole France work, the author would not accept putting into print everything in a man's mind. He cites Joyce's *Ulysses* as an example of a disgusting work, "portentiously

dull" and "flatly indecent" which should never have been written or published.

[Pollock, John C.] *Kansas City Post v. State of Kansas. The Anti-Cigarette Advertising Law and Judge Pollock's Decision.* Kansas City, Kans., [The Post?], 1917. 11p.   **1P213**
The U.S. District Court ruled unconstitutional the Kansas law against cigarette advertising on the grounds that Kansas City newspapers operated in interstate commerce and were not subject to state law.

Pollock, Merle, and Fred Cohen. "Problems of Pretrial Publicity." *Criminal Law Bulletin*, 11:335–49, May–June 1975.   **1P214**
"The relationship of the news media to the administration of justice is the subject of this article. A seminar, sponsored by the Institute of Judicial Administration, brought together working reporters and assignment editors from across the country, along with a battery of legal scholars, to discuss the 'free press–fair trial' complex of issues. What is reported here is not limited to the narrow question of what and when to report about a criminal event and trial. Rather, we learn of the reporters' 'right to know' in the context of a system where vital decisions—such as plea bargaining arrangements—never surface; where the Supreme Court itself functions in a veil of secrecy; where media representatives are selectively used for selective advantage by counsel; and where the media itself may be a stranger in that exotic land of law it is to describe and analyze."—Editor

Polsky, Ned. "On the Sociology of Pornography." In his *Hustlers, Beats, and Others*. Chicago, Aldine, 1967, pp. 186–202. (Also in paperback edition, Anchor Books)   **1P215**
Pornography is seen as a major functional alternative to prostitution. "Pornography's main function at the societal level . . . is to help preserve society's double institutionalizing of legitimate sex—within marriage and within a specified few of the possible sex acts—by providing sexual depictions that literally drain off the other, socially illegitimate sexual desires of the beholder." The author considers as pornographic any sexual depiction (written, recorded, pictorial) that facilitates such masturbatory involvement, whether it is labeled hard-core or erotic art. Society permits the dissemination of pornography as a safety-valve, just as it permits prostitution, although it officially denounces and harasses both.

Polur, Sam. "From Gitlow to Epton —New York's Resurrected Criminal Anarchy Statute—The First Amendment and National Policy." *New York Law Forum*, 16:93–118, Spring 1970.   **1P216**
"The inauguration of the progressive absorption of the Bill of Rights into the fourteenth

amendment in response to the New York Court of Appeals in *Gitlow* [*People v. Gitlow*, 1922]; the limitation of the scope of the New York Criminal Anarchy Statute by the application thereto of the 'clear and present danger' test as an absolute necessity for the affirmance of the conviction in *Epton* [*People v. Epton*, 1968]; and the prolific emergence of novel and critical issues surrounding the constitutionality of the process used to indict and try Epton and subsequent defendants under this same enactment or its re-adoption under the new Penal Law, reveal the total futility of the provisions of Criminal Anarchy Statutes together with those of the parallel congressional resolution and enactment of like import and design."

Pomeroy, Wardell B. "Kinsey and the Press, I and II." In his *Dr. Kinsey and the Institute for Sex Research*. New York, Harper & Row, 1972, pp. 252–60, 340–59.   **1P217**
The two chapters deal with conflicts between Dr. Alfred C. Kinsey, director of Indiana University's Institute for Sex Research, and the press over publicity of the findings revealed in the volumes on male and female sexuality. Dr. Kinsey was faced with sensational and often inaccurate reporting on the one hand, and newspaper censorship on the other. (The *New York Times* refused to accept advertising for the Kinsey books.) His request to see all reviews and stories prior to publication was not favorably received by the press. For the most part, however, the nation's press did a good job of covering the results of the Kinsey research.

Pontaut, Alain. "Passe la Censure, Restent les Navets." *Magazine Maclean*, 10(5):22–25, May 1970.   **1P218**
"Montréal, aujourd'hui sélectionne hardement les sous-produits pornos de tous les cinémas du monde."

Pooley, Beverly. "Librarians and Intellectual Freedom." *Microcosm*, June 1970, pp. 1, 3, 5.   **1P219**
A law librarian poses a dilemma faced by law librarians in providing "free access to knowledge and the human consideration of a decent respect for privacy," referring to the use of records and briefs of cases heard before the Michigan Supreme Court.

Pope, Michael. *Sex and the Undecided Librarian: A Study of Librarians' Opinions on Sexually Oriented Literature*. New York, Scarecrow, 1974. 219p.   **1P220**
A study of the opinions of school, public, and college librarians concerning the acquisition of nonfiction sexual materials. The findings are correlated with the personal, institutional, and professional characteristics of librarians and their libraries.

"Porn: The Vice Goes on Ice." *Newsweek*, 82(4):44–45, 47, 23 July 1973.   **1P221**
Reaction of the porn industry to the U.S. Su-

preme Court decision of 21 June 1973 which opened the way for tough new restrictions on the publication of obscene materials.

"Pornography and Censorship." *Western Review*, 4:5–16, Winter 1967. **1P222**
A compilation of some of the answers to a questionnaire sent to a group of lawyers, authors, editors, college professors, and literary critics. The questions: What is your definition of pornography? What limits would you place on the publication of pornography? How is pornography detrimental to society? Is pornography in the classics less detrimental than that in contemporary works? What would you nominate as the most pornographic work now available to the reading public? Whom, if anyone, would you trust to determine what constitutes pornography? If all censorship were ended, do you think pornography would abate to any degree?

"Pornography and the Court Presuppositions." *Christian Century*, 90:747–48, 18 July 1973.   **1P223**
Comment on the implications of the U.S. Supreme Court's 5–4 decision on obscenity made in June 1973. "We do not have to condone material to defend its right to a hearing. The public has a right to insist that children be protected from pornography and that such material not be pushed upon the public in offensive ways. . . . In the long run, our society is better off to leave pornography at the mercy of the adult marketplace, where, in time, we suspect, it will lose much of its so-called prurient appeal."

"The Pornography Explosion." *Tablet: The International Catholic Weekly*, 230:329–31, 3 April 1976.   **1P224**
Although cautioning that legal intervention is not necessarily the answer to the "pornography explosion" that plagues the country, the editorial supports efforts to prevent the thrusting of blatant erotica in public places. While the plague may "work itself out of society's system," the author fears moral values may be irreparably debased before it does.

"Pornography Goes Public." *Newsweek*, 76(25):26–28, 31–32, 21 December 1970.   **1P225**
"Smutty books and filthy pictures that used to be the exclusive preserve of a few big-city merchants are now available from coast to coast." An examination of the pornography industry.

"Pornography in a Free Society." *Christianity Today*, 14:20–21, 22 May 1970.   **1P226**
An editorial calling for an indignant citizenry to speak up in the fight against pornography. Hope is seen in the recognition of the danger of pornography to society by such authorities as Dr. Benjamin Spock and in the campaign of the Women's Liberation Movement against sexual exploitation.

"Pornography: It's A Legal Big Busi-

ness." *Marketing/Communications*, 298(4): 34–36, April 1970.   **1P227**
"By the standards of public morality that are still held up, pornography is obscene. By the standard of dollar flow, obscenity is obsolete and pornography is legal. It is an incredible double standard that has lawyers, communicators and marketers wondering what really reflects the public taste."

"Pornography Report—Official Findings That Set Off a Furor." *U.S. News & World Report*, 69(15):60–64, 12 October 1970.   **1P228**
Excerpts from recommendations in the report of the U.S. Commission on Obscenity and Pornography and comments on the reception of the report.

"Pornography Report Stirs Criticism." *Editorials on File*, 1:1017–28, 1–15 October 1970.   **1P229**
Complete text of editorials from thirty-one newspapers commenting on the report of the U.S. Commission on Obscenity and Pornography.

"Pornography Report Survives." *PTA Magazine*, 65:14–15, October 1970.   **1P230**
An editorial discusses the controversy over the report of the U.S. Commission on Obscenity and Pornography, welcoming its publication which will permit widespread, rational discussion of the issues.

Porter, Alexander. *Speech of the Hon. Mr. Porter, of Louisiana, on the Expunging Resolution delivered on Tuesday, March 22, 1836*. Washington City, Duff Green, Printer, 1836. 28p. (Abridged in the *Congressional Globe*, 22 March 1836)   **1P231**
The speech is against the proposal of Senator Thomas Hart Benton to expunge certain "offensive material" from the journal of the Senate, an action which Senator Porter believes would be unconstitutional and create a dangerous precedent.

[Porter, John G. V.] *The Right Hon. The Earl of Erne, Plaintiff: John Grey Vesey Porter, Esq., Defendant. Report of the Trial of an Action for Libel . . . before the Lord Chief Justice and a Special Jury. On the 12th and 14th February, 1859. . . .* Dublin, Goodwin, Son & Wethercott, 1859. 115p.   **1P232**
The director of a railway company charged Porter with libeling him in a pamphlet which discussed the business affairs of the company. The question revolved on whether the author

intended merely to expose error and mistake or to suggest dishonest, immoral, or hypocritical action. The judge encouraged the jury to read and study the pamphlet and to make their own decision. They found for the plaintiff, assessing damages of £300.

Porter, William E. *Assault on the Media: The Nixon Years*. Ann Arbor, Mich., University of Michigan Press, 1976. 320p.   **1P233**
"This book is an account of the wide-ranging efforts of governmental authority, over a period of five and one-half years, to intimidate, harass, regulate, and in other ways damage the news media, in their functioning, as part of the American political system. It is subtitled 'The Nixon Years' because most of these initiatives came directly from the White House during Richard Nixon's administration, and the remainder derived, at least in part, from a spirit generated through those top-level attacks." Following the final chapter is a collection of Documents of Significance which "give, as can no amount of retelling, something of the feel of the confrontation and the minds and spirit of the men central to carrying it on. It includes once-confidential White House memoranda, speeches, and excerpts from court decisions." From a White House conversation, 15 September 1972: *"The President:* . . . the main thing is the *Post* is going to have damnable, damnable problems out of this one. They have a television station . . . and they're going to have to get it renewed. *Haldeman:* They've got a radio station, too. *The President:* Does that come up, too? . . . it's going to be goddam active here.'"

Posner, Richard A. *Cable Television: The Problem of Local Monopoly*. Santa Monica, Calif., Rand, 1970. 35p. (Rand Corporation Memorandum, RM-6309-FF. Prepared for the Ford Foundation)   **1P234**
"Generally speaking, since only one supplier of cable service operates in any given local area, state and local governments are becoming increasingly concerned about whether cable television companies should be subject to the rules and practices developed for the control of public utilities and common carriers. The purpose of this brief discussion paper is to present a number of provocative ideas about the advantages and disadvantages of alternative forms of local regulation."

———. *Regulation of Advertising by the FTC*. Washington, D.C., American Enterprise Institute for Public Policy Research, 1973. 40p.   **1P235**
The author "examines the efforts of the Federal Trade Commission to prevent misrepresentations in advertising. He shows that these efforts are to a great extent misdirected due to (1) the Commission's failure to develop a theory of the

circumstances under which harmful misrepresentations are likely and (2) the limitations of the Commission's powers to prevent misrepresentations effectively. Reforms aimed at improving the Commission's performance are suggested."

Postgate, Raymond. "The Morning Star of American Liberty." In his *Murder, Piracy, and Treason*. London, Cape, 1925, pp. 126–43.   **1P236**
An account of the John Peter Zenger trial, 1735, for an alleged libel on the English governor.

Potocki, Count Geoffrey W. Vaile (of Montalk). *Dogs' Eggs; a Study in Powysology*. Chemin de St. Martin, Draguignan, France, 1971–72, 2 vols. (Pirated edition of vol. 1 was published in Draguignan by the Shack Press) **1P237**
This work consists of an attack on the Powys family, charged by Potocki with owing him £500. In a legal settlement, Potocki agreed not to publish or distribute further copies of the book. While he was in Italy, however, two friends broke into his villa in Draguignan and seized unbound sheets and the type of volume one. They issued a pirated edition (Shack Press) which included the text of the legal agreement and an account of their conspiracy.

———. *Snobbery with Violence: A Poet in Gaol*. London, Wishart, 1932. 53p. (Here and Now Pamphlets, no. 10)
                                    1P238

An account of life in prison (Wormwood Scrubs). Potocki had been sentenced to six months for publishing an obscene poem, *Here Lies John Penis* (P269).

Potter, Elaine. *The Press as Opposition: The Political Role of South African Newspapers*. London, Chatto & Windus, 1975. 228p.   **1P239**
A former South African journalist "describes how the Press, Afrikaans and English, exercised its extraordinary opportunity of preserving a degree of openness within the country and a means by which the Government's shortcomings could be exposed to the outside world." She traces the history of South African newspapers and the political framework within which they developed. She examines the financial structure of the press and the relationship between the press and the government, and assesses the extent of press opposition to the government since 1948. She sees more repressive government regulation of the press in the area of racial matters for the future as the white newspapers attract more and more nonwhite readers.

[Potts, Joseph T.] *Action for Libel against Saunder's News-Letter. Major Hugh Brabazon versus Joseph T. Potts, Esq. Tried before the Honourable Baron Hughes and a Special Jury of the County of Galway. . . .*

1st and 2nd August, 1862. Dublin, Hodges and Smith, 1862. 50p. **1P240**
The case involved the reporting of a land eviction episode in County Mayo. The newspaper had offered Major Brabazon the right of reply, but he refused, taking the case to court instead. The jury found for the defendant.

Pound, Ezra. "Historically Joyce (and Censorship)." *Tri-Quarterly*, 15:108–14, Spring 1969. (Translated from the Italian by Forrest Read.)   **1P241**
The poet discusses briefly the censorship of James Joyce's *Ulysses* in the United States and Great Britain, "two barbarian countries." He finds the American censorship "ridiculous, laughable, a demonstration of a failure to grow up," British censorship "much more sinister and oblique."

Powe, L. A., Jr. "Evolution to Absolutism: Justice Douglas and the First Amendment." *Columbia Law Review*, 74:371–411, Spring 1974.   **1P242**
The article describes the evolutionary process undergone by Justice William O. Douglas over the years in interpreting the First Amendment —from a willingness to weigh and balance individual rights against governmental powers to an approach bordering on absolutism.

———. "The *Georgia Straight* and Freedom of Expression in Canada." *Canadian Bar Review*, 48:410–38, September 1970.   **1P243**
"This article is intended to provide one opinion on the proper scope of freedom of expression in a democratic society in so far as that scope can be illustrated within the confines of the three *Georgia Straight* cases." *Georgia Straight* was an underground newspaper in Vancouver whose license to publish was suspended by the city's chief license inspector. The paper eventually had the suspension voided. Upon winning its case, the paper announced in a newspaper column the awarding of the "Pontius Pilate Certificate for Justice," for which it was found guilty of defamatory libel. *Hlookoff et al. v. City of Vancouver et al.* (1967 and 1968), and *R. v. Georgia Straight Publishing Ltd.*, *McLeod and Cummings* (1969).

Powell, Cheryl R. *Campus Press—Help Is At Hand*. Columbia, Mo., Freedom of Information Center, School of Journalism, University of Missouri at Columbia, 1976. 8p. (Report no. 363)
                                    1P244
"The author reports on the problems facing students and advisers of college publications, and lists centers and organizations which exist to assist in combating censorship in this area. The paper also includes summaries of court cases involving the First Amendment free expression right of students."

Powell, Edward M., and Robert Byrne. "Battling Censorship: A Case

Study." *NASSP Bulletin* (National Association of Secondary School Principals), 60:101–5, January 1976. **1P245**
"Community censorship of school instructional materials can be successfully combatted with a firm policy that delineates guidelines for both school and community action." Two school administrators in Dover, Del., tell how they won a censorship battle.

Powell, Jon T. "Broadcast Advertising of Medical Products and Services: Its Regulation by Other Nations." *Federal Communications Bar Journal,* 25:144–76, 1972. **1P246**
The article examines the policies of seventeen nations in imposing specific conditions on broadcast advertising, particularly in the area of medical products and services. The nations studied are Australia, Barbados, Canada, Cyprus, Finland, Great Britain, Hong Kong, Ireland, Kenya, Kuwait, Malaysia, Malta, New Zealand, Northern Nigeria, Singapore, Southern Yemen, and Trinidad and Tobago.

———. "Protection of Children in Broadcast Advertising: The Regulatory Guidelines of Nine Nations." *Federal Communications Bar Journal,* 26: 61–75, 1973. **1P247**
The author reviews the provisions regarding advertising and children of the broadcasting codes of nine nations: Australia, Cyprus, Finland, Great Britain, Hong Kong, Ireland, Malta, The Netherlands, and New Zealand. The purpose of the study is "to examine the themes and patterns underlying the regulations of other nations which have been able to formulate some precise regulations restricting broadcast advertising which might influence children."

Power, Edmond. *An Accurate and Faithful Report of a Trial Held Before the Rt. Hon. Lord Norbury, and a Special Jury, at Clonmel, in the County of Tipperary, Summer Assizes, 1804 Wherein John Bagwell, Esq. was Plaintiff, and Edmond Power, Esq. Defendant for a Libel. . . .* Clonmel, Ireland, Printed by Edmond Power [1804]. 89p. **1P248**
The defendant, printer of the *Clonmel Gazette and Munster Mercury,* was found guilty of libeling Colonel Bagwell of the Tipperary Militia.

Power, Richard W. "The Candy Case: A Defense of the Intellect." *St. Louis Law Review,* 13:544–63, Summer 1969. **1P249**
A critique of the case, *State v. Smith,* 422 S.W.2d 50 (Mo. 1967) in which the Missouri Supreme Court reversed an obscenity decision against the book *Candy.*

Powers, Murray. "Is There a Case for TV Censorship?" *Our Sunday Visitor,* 62:7, 31 March 1974. **1P250**

Prime television time has been invaded by dirty comedy routines which are seen by children. Because of this bad judgment more and more persons are urging censorship.

Powers, Thomas. "Right-to-Reply Laws." *Commonweal,* 100:255–57, 17 May 1974. **1P251**
While the Constitution guarantees the "right of reply" it does not guarantee a forum. Right of reply laws would tend to undermine the very freedom they are intended to enhance. The best cure for the failing of newspapers would be more newspapers, admittedly a difficult problem. "In the meantime we must protect the independence of the newspapers that survive, even as we criticize their performance, because if they cannot publish without let or hindrance, who can?"

———. "The Rights of Reporters." *Commonweal,* 98:280–83, 25 May 1973. **1P252**
"The subpoena of reporters ought to be seen as only one facet of a wider attack on the press, and that in turn part of a still broader effort to assert the authority of government, secure its freedom to act and quiet, if not altogether silence, its critics. For this reason the attempt to drive a wedge between reporters and their sources ought to be resisted as if it were an attempt to repeal the First Amendment entirely." The author believes there is a trusting tendency among journalists not justified by the accumulation of facts about what Walter Cronkite refers to as a virtual "conspiracy" in high places.

———. "Schorr and a Free Press." *Commonweal,* 103(8):241–43, 9 April 1976. **1P253**
"The investigation of Daniel Schorr by the House Ethics Committee is . . . only one more step in a broader government campaign to reimpose discipline on its employees, to protect its freedom to act as it thinks fit, and to prevent the truth of its actions from becoming public."

———. "Stop the Presses: Judges and the Rights of Reporters." *Commonweal,* 102:563–64, 21 November 1975. **1P254**
Comment on the banning of the movie, *Manson,* by a California judge to prevent possible prejudice of a jury in the trial of Lynette Fromme.

Powledge, Fred. *An ACLU Guide to Cable Television.* New York, American Civil Liberties Union, 1972. 46p. **1P255**
The impact of cable television on American society, with "special emphasis on the capacity of cable to serve the First Amendment interest in diversity of expression."

———. *The Engineering of Restraint; the Nixon Administration.* Washington, D.C., Public Affairs Press, 1971. 53p. **1P256**

From a sampling of opinion of a variety of experts in the field, the author concludes that "the First Amendment is being lost a little each day" through the chilling effect on the news media that began with Vice-President Agnew's Des Moines speech attacking television. "The decision *not to do a story* appears to be multiplying all over the nation, and before long there will just not be very much interpretation of complex events and social movements. What will be left will be the relatively safe 'hard' news of speeches and statements, and that can be easily manipulated." The appendix includes brief statements on the Agnew Attacks, The Caldwell Case, Drug Lyrics, Freedom of Information, Jack Nelson and the FBI, The Underground Press, The Campus Press, and Policemen Posing as Newsmen.

———. *Public Television: A Question of Survival. A Report of the American Civil Liberties Union.* Washington, D.C., Public Affairs, 1972. 46p. **1P257**
The report indicates that public television is "seriously in danger of disappearing as a relevant force in American society" because Congress and the Nixon Administration have been unwilling to provide long-range financing that would insulate the institution from the pressures of politics. "A cynical exercise in White House manipulation of a communications medium," the report charges "threatens to reduce the medium to even worse pap than commercial television's diet."

Practicing Law Institute. *Communications Law, 1975.* New York, The Institute, 1975. 837p. (Course Handbook Series, no 67) **1P258**
Content: Prior Restraints, Fair Trial–Free Press by James C. Goodale. Subpoenas by James C. Goodale. Pending Legislation Affecting Media by Richard M. Schmidt, Jr. Post-*Gertz* Libel Law by Carleton G. Eldridge, Jr. Post-*Gertz* Libel Practice and Tactics by Robert W. Meserve. Developing Liability of Media in the Law of Privacy by Melville B. Nimmer. Media Liability for Advertising by P. Cameron DeVore and Robert D. Sack. Merging Media and the First Amendment by Henry Geller. Suing to Get the News (Access) and Related Rights and Risks by Floyd Abrams. The bulk of the volume consists of court decisions and other documents relating to cases on prior restraint, subpoenas, libel, privacy, commercial speech, and the First Amendment.

———. *Communications Law, 1976.* New York, The Institute, 1976. 816p. (Course Handbook Series, no. 78) **1P259**
Content: Subpoenas by James C. Goodale, Access by Media to the News by Daniel Paul, Broadcasting and the First Amendment by Henry Geller, Commercial Speech by P. Cameron DeVore and Robert D. Sack, Privacy and the Freedom of Information Act by

Ronald L. Plesser, Defamation and Privacy under the First Amendment by Alfred Hill, Counseling on Libel and Privacy by Heather G. Florence and Victor A. Kovner, Pretrial Practices in Libel Cases by Robert S. Warren, Trial of Libel Cases by Don H. Reuben, Legislative Roundup by Richard M. Schmidt, Jr. The bulk of the volume consists of court decisions and other documents relating to cases on access, subpoenas, fair trial v. free press, commercial speech, privacy and freedom of information, and privacy and libel.

Pradka, Diana C. "Testimonial Reprieve for Newsmen in Civil Litigation." *North Carolina Law Review*, 51: 1550–63, October 1973.   **1P260**
An analysis of the decision, *Baker v. F & F Investment*, 470 F.2d 778 (2d Cir. 1972), 93 S. Ct. 2147 (1973), in which the court declined to extend the *Branzburg* rule to civil cases, one of the first circuit court decisions clearly to recognize a First Amendment claim to a reportorial privilege.

Pragnell, Anthony. "Contempt of Court: Some Recent U.K. Developments." *EBU Review* (European Broadcasting Union), 26(6):40–45, November 1975.   **1P261**
In light of increased interest in investigative reporting of malpractice and abuse in government, the Phillimore Committee was appointed to inquire into Britain's contempt of court laws. The deputy director general of Britain's Independent Broadcasting Authority discusses the Committee's recommendations. "Until the law is changed, the broadcasters, like the press, will continue to be uncertain where the line lies between what is and what is not permissible, and there will undoubtedly continue to be occasions when the law will be in conflict with what responsible journalists consider to be in the public interest."

"Prejudicial Publicity in Trials of Public Officials." *Yale Law Journal*, 85: 123–35, November 1975.   **1P262**
"If a reasonable likelihood of prejudice exists after all the applicable procedural requirements have been met, a fundamental question arises: does this residual prejudice deny the defendant a fair trial? This Note contends that it does not, at least in trials of public officials for crimes related to their office."

Preminger, Otto, Jerry Wald, and William Morring. *Censorship and Cinema*. 26 min. tape recording. North Hollywood, Calif., Center for Cassette Studies, 1971.   **1P263**
A spirited debate over regulation and control of motion pictures, particularly over the legitimacy of the motion picture production code. Panelists: producer Otto Preminger, who op-

poses the code; and producer Jerry Wald and critic William Morring, who defend it.

"Presidential Politics and Political Prerequisites: The Application of Section 315 and the FCC's Fairness Doctrine to the Appearances of Incumbents in Their Official Capacities." *Fordham Law Review*, 39:481–99, March 1971.   **1P264**
The article discusses the applicability of the fairness doctrine in broadcasting in the situation where an elected official, not presently a candidate for any public office, appears on television, ostensibly in his official capacity.

"Press and the Critical Fusillade." *Magazine Wall Street*, 128:11–13, 16 August 1971.   **1P265**
An analysis of the current attacks on the American press, newspaper and broadcasting, from the government, consumer activists, and individuals and organizations cutting a wide swath of economic and political persuasions.

"Press Besieged." *Economist*, 243:58–60, 13 May 1972.   **1P266**
The United States press is harassed by the Nixon Administration for its allegedly anticonservative bias, attacked by many working journalists for its hidebound ways, and viewed with distrust by the reading and viewing public.

"Press Comments About College Coach Within Libel Protection of Associated Press v. Walker." *Washington Law Review*, 44:461–73, Winter 1969.   **1P267**
Re: *Grayson v. Curtis Publishing Co.* (1967). The case involved an article, Basketball Bullies, in the *Saturday Evening Post*.

The Press Council (Great Britain). *The Aberfan Inquiry and Contempt of Court: A Statement by the Press Council*. London, The Council, 1968. 20p. (Press Council Booklet, no. 1)   **1P268**
Following the conclusion of the inquiry into the Aberfan mine disaster by a special tribunal, the Press Council issued this memorandum to clarify the issue of contempt of court by publication and the application of the 1921 Act to Tribunals. The Attorney General had complained of a television interview with one of the potential witnesses at the inquiry as being undesirable and possibly illegal.

[————.] "Official Secrets Act 1911; Memorandum of the Press Council to the Chairman and Members of the Departmental Committee on Section 2 of the Official Secrets Act 1911." *Index on Censorship*, 1:65–68, Spring 1972. **1P269**
The Press Council recommended that section 2 of the Official Secrets Act, long criticized by

the press as providing unnecessary secrecy in the workings of the government, be abolished.

————. *Outline of Practice and Principles*. London, The Council [1973?]. 16p. (Press Council Booklet, no. 3)   **1P270**
Content: History, Constitution, Complaints. Policies on Contempt, Hospitals, Local Government, Buying-up, Pictures, Confidentiality, Readers' Letters, Intrusion, Mis-Reporting, Embargoes, Advertising, Sex Crime, Schools, and Politics.

————. *Press Conduct in the Lambton Affair; A Report by the Press Council*. London, The Council, 1974. 37p. (Press Council Booklet, no. 5)   **1P271**
The Press Council reports on its investigation of the conduct of *News of the World*, the *Times*, *Sunday People*, and the *Daily Mail*, in connection with the Lambton Affair, which involved an alleged prostitution scandal among high British officials. This followed an official investigation of the affair by a security commission, under the chairmanship of Lord Diplock.

————. *Privacy, Press and Public; A Memorandum by the Press Council*. London, The Council, 1971. 52p. (Press Council Booklet, no. 2)   **1P272**
In 1971 the British Government set up a Committee of Inquiry (Younger Committee) "to consider whether legislation is needed to give further protection to the individual and to commercial and industrial interests against intrusion into privacy by private persons or private organizations or by companies and to make recommendations." In this pamphlet the Press Council considers the issue, taking into consideration the press's freedom to publish and the people's right to know. The memorandum also reports on the privacy cases investigated by the Press Council, 1953–70, including photographic intrusion, physical intrusion, medical cases, figures in the public eye, and cases of "hounding."

————. *Reforming the Law of Defamation; A Memorandum by the Press Council*. London, The Council, 1973. 43p. (Press Council Booklet, no. 4)   **1P273**
"In May 1971 the Government announced the setting up of a Committee of Inquiry, under the chairmanship of Mr. Justice Faulks, into the law of defamation. It would consider whether, in the light of the Defamation Act 1952, changes were necessary in the law, practice and procedure relating to actions for defamation. In this pamphlet the Press Council sets out the written memoranda which it submitted to the Committee of Inquiry and an appendix dealing with the defence of qualified privilege in connection with matter published in the public interest."

Press Council of India. *Annual Report*. New Delhi, The Council, 1969–date. Annual.   **1P274**

Press Freedom Committee (Great Britain). *A Statement of Aims and Purpose.* London, The Committee, 1941? 4p. **1P275**

An independent committee of nineteen Britons, later to become advisory to the National Council for Civil Liberties, was organized to protest against suppression of dissent. "Recent instances of suppression and intimidation have created a widespread uneasiness in the country." While recognizing the need for censorship during wartime, this can be done at the front. "The suppression of periodical publications or books or pamphlets expressing some particular point of view that may not be in accordance with the ideas of the party in power is an altogether different affair." John White is listed as secretary. Members of Parliament, authors (including H. G. Wells), trade unionists, and the Dean of Canterbury are among the members.

Die Pressfreiheit in England, mit besonderer Bezugnahme auf das Libell. Berlin, Nicolaischen Buchhandlung, 1841. 63p. **1P276**

Pressly, James B., Jr. "Freedom of Expression and the Censor." *South Carolina Law Review*, 22:115–25, 1970. **1P277**

"While the Supreme Court has not abolished censorship theoretically, the practical effect of its decisions has rendered the censor virtually powerless. The increasing restrictiveness of the test for obscenity is indicative of the Court's present philosophy toward censorship. . . . In the atmosphere of this philosophy, the censor will find it extremely difficult to litigate obscenity cases successfully."

Preston, Ivan L. *The Great American Blow-up; Puffery in Advertising.* Madison, Wis., University of Wisconsin Press, 1975. 368p. **1P278**

"This book you are about to read is a superior piece of work. It demonstrates the sheerest true excellence in its treatment of one of the outstandingly important topics of our time." Thus does the author introduce his book with an example of puffery—"purest baloney." He traces the history of puffery in advertising—statements that are not illegal but cannot be proved to be true; gives examples of the practice and shows how the Federal Trade Commission has avoided facing the issue of regulation. "He mounts a frontal assault on the given wisdom that puffery cannot be deceptive," and urges that the FTC provide tighter control to eliminate false puffery from the American marketplace.

Prettyman, E. Barrett, Jr. "Nebraska Press Association v. Stuart: Have We Seen the Last of Prior Restraints on the Reporting of Judicial Proceedings?" *St. Louis University Law Journal*, 20:654–62, 1976. **1P279**

Despite some equivocal language in the decision [Nebraska Press Association v. Stuart (1976)] suggesting that direct gags on the press might be appropriate in some situations, the author concludes that the barriers erected against the Nebraska order "will necessarily be applicable to all prior restraints of the reporting of judicial proceedings that can reasonably be perceived for the future."

Prévost, Yves. "Le Phénomène de la Violence au Cinéma en Regard de la Jeunesse." *Revue du Barreau* (Quebec), 30:59–66, January 1970. **1P280**

Consideration of the problem of violence in the cinema, the possible effect on children, and methods of control.

Price, Monroe E. "The First Amendment and Television Broadcasting by Satellite." *UCLA Law Review*, 23:879–903, June 1976. **1P281**

"International control that classifies, that protects existing distributors of information, that shelters young viewers from obscene programming, that selects among competing applicants on the basis of merit—all this can dwell in the test of the first amendment. But heavy-handed censorship will not work where there is a specific content control that touches upon ideas relevant to the political structure of the state and its relationship to other states. That is the heart of the first amendment. If the international community is to institute such restrictions on the free flow of information, it must not ask the United States to enforce the rule."

Price, Warren C., and Calder M. Pickett, *comps. An Annotated Journalism Bibliography, 1958–68.* Minneapolis, University of Minnesota Press, 1970. 285p. **1P282**

A ten-year supplement to the general bibliography on journalism (P315). Entries are arranged alphabetically by author, with a detailed subject index.

Price, William A. "Why I Took the First Amendment." *Nieman Reports*, 11(2):25–27, April 1957. **1P283**

A newspaperman, charged with contempt of Congress for invoking the First Amendment in refusing to answer questions of a Senate Committee, discusses the rationale for his action.

Priestly, J. B. "Taking the Lid Off." *Twentieth Century*, 170:29–33, Spring 1962. **1P284**

In discussing the intrusions of the press on private lives, Priestly remarks: "What I dislike is the idea that some people's private lives are sacred and other people's are there for show. . . . Either more lids should be removed, so that a lot of private lives now supposed to be sacred should be given the treatment, or all lids, outside criminal courts, should be respected and left untouched. And, of course, I prefer the latter."

Printing Historical Society. *Freedom of the Press: Four Broadsides, with notes by Berthold Wolpe, printed for the members of the Printing Historical Society.* [London, The Society, 1969.] Five broadsides (P.H.S. Publication, no. 7) **1P285**

The first broadside describes the four reproductions that follow: (1) William Hone's *The Printers Address to the Queen, & Her Magisty's Tribute to the Press in Answer*, 1820. (2) A lithograph by Charles Philipon, taken from *La Caricature*, 24 November 1831, showing a Stanhope press encumbered with a multitude of iron weights, representing repressive measures against the French press, despite the constitution of 1814. (3) A lithograph designed by Grandville and drawn by Desperret, 1832–34, showing agents of the government of Louis Philippe attacking the printing press. (4) A broadside in *Commemoration of the Enactment of Parliamentary Reform, Derby, 7 August 1832*, in which tribute is paid to a free press.

The Prior Adversary Hearing: Solution to Procedural Due Process Problems in Obscenity Seizures?" *New York University Law Review*, 46:80–119, March 1971. **1P286**

"In view of the controversy regarding the definition and need for regulation of obscenity as well as the judicial trend toward restricting the scope of such regulation, procedural due process is vital to insure that only those items lawfully subject to seizure will be confiscated. The adversary hearing prior to seizure or suppression offers a reasonable method of assuring that neither the public nor the owner will be deprived of material which is beyond the scope of valid regulation."

"Prior Adversary Hearings on the Question of Obscenity." *Columbia Law Review*, 70:1403–25, December 1970. **1P287**

The author examines court cases establishing the requirement of an adversary hearing to determine whether allegedly obscene material is indeed obscene prior to any governmental action making the material unavailable to the public.

"Prior Restraint—A Test of Invalidity in Free Speech Cases?" *Columbia Law Review*, 49:1001–6, November 1949. **1P288**

"The prior restraints doctrine would not appear to furnish a reliable criterion for determining the validity of legislation affecting freedom of expression. . . . Whatever the value of the prior restraints doctrine in the past, it has outlived its usefulness."

"Prior Restraints in Public High

Schools." *Yale Law Journal*, 82:1325–36, May 1973.   **1P289**
"This Note argues that *Tinker* [*Tinker v. Des Moines Independent Community School District* (1969)] does not authorize the imposition of prior restraints in high schools. Properly understood, the case is fully consistent with the general principle that speech may be regulated because of its potential for producing disorders; but such regulation cannot take the form of prior restraints."

"Prior Restraints in the Military." *Columbia Law Review*, 73:1089–1119, May 1973.   **1P290**
In the American armed forces a system of prior restraints is imposed upon many of the speech activities of servicemen, including a review of materials authored by servicemen before they can be distributed on bases or published in the civilian community. "This Note considers the extent of the military review system and the justifications and criticisms made of it, and suggests alternatives more in keeping with the fundamental principles of constitutional law."

"Prior to High Court Ruling: 58 Pct. Supported Publication of Controversial 'Pentagon Papers.'" *Gallup Opinion Index*, 74:19–22, August 1971.   **1P291**
Questions asked: Have you heard or read about the articles first published in the *New York Times* about how we got involved in the Vietnam war? In your opinion, did the newspaper do the right thing or the wrong thing in publishing these articles?

Pristin, Terry. " 'Deceptive Practices' at WPIX." *MORE*, 3(9):6–9, September 1973.   **1P292**
"In what may be a landmark document, the FCC's Broadcast Bureau has condemned the behavior of New York's Channel 11 and recommended that its license be denied."

Pritchard, Allan. "*Abuses Stript and Whipt* and Wither's Imprisonment." *Review of English Studies*, 14(n.s.):337–45, 1963.   **1P293**
An inquiry into the reasons for George Wither's imprisonment for four months in 1614 on orders from the Privy Council for authorship of *Abuses Stript and Whipt*, which had already been passed by the official licenser.

Pritchett, C. Herman. *Civil Liberties and the Vinson Court*. Chicago, University of Chicago Press, 1954. 297p.
                    1P294
Three chapters deal specifically with freedom of speech and the press: Chapter 2, Free Speech before Vinson; chapter 3, Free Speech: Previous Restraints; and chapter 4, Free Speech: Subsequent Punishment.

"Privacy, Defamation and the First Amendment: The Implications of *Time, Inc. v. Hill*." *Columbia Law Review*, 67:926–52, May 1967. (Excerpted in Kenneth S. Devol, *ed.*, *Mass Media and the Supreme Court*, pp. 272–80)
                    1P295
"It appears that the major impact of the *Hill* case [*Time, Inc. v. Hill* (1967)], with its emphasis on the informing function of the first amendment, may be on the law of defamation. The formulation of the 'public interest' test can be viewed as indicating the readiness of the Court to look away from the status of the individual being defamed and to focus instead upon the legitimacy of public interest in the subject discussed."

"Privacy in the First Amendment." *Yale Law Journal*, 82:1462–80, June 1973.   **1P296**
"Although the First Amendment analysis of the public disclosure tort generates a conception of privacy which comes closer than the conceptions of current tort and constitutional law to describing what privacy is and to making it susceptible to the application of legal doctrine, the claim which results is limited. The analysis discovers only a constitutional *interest* in privacy, not a constitutional *right* to have it protected in all cases. It does not yield a 'First Amendment right to privacy' which can be placed next to the constitutional privacy rights which already exist."

"Privacy of Mental Hospital Inmates Will Be Protected by an Injunction Prohibiting Open Public Exhibition of a Motion Picture Depicting Hospital Conditions." *Harvard Law Review* 83:1722–31, May 1970.   **1P297**
Re: *Commonwealth v. Wiseman*, 249 N.E.2d 110 (Mass. 1969), involving a film, *Titicut Follies*, depicting conditions at Massachusetts Correctional Institution at Bridgewater.

"Privacy, the Press and Mrs. X." *New Law Journal*, 122:666–67, 20 July 1972.
                    1P298
Criticism of the report of the British Younger Committee on Privacy which, in so far as press violations of privacy are concerned, "count upon the varied pressures—educational, cultural and social—employed in a democratic society to persuade particular sections of the community to behave in an acceptable manner." The author cites the case of Mrs. X, who would, under the Younger Committee recommendations, have no redress for her suffering at the hands of the press.

"Private Ratings of Motion Pictures as a Basis for State Regulations." *Georgetown Law Journal*, 59:1205–36, May 1971.   **1P299**
This discussion analyzes attempts by state legislatures to employ private ratings for motion pictures in statutory regulations, and

questions the constitutional validity of these and future attempts at regulation.

"Privilege Not to Appear and Testify Before Grand Jury Granted to Reporter Seeking to Protect Sensitive Source Where Government Fails to Establish Compelling Need." *New York University Law Review*, 46:617–33, May 1971.   **1P300**
Re: *Caldwell v. United States*, 434 F.2d 1081 (9th Cir. 1970). The decision was subsequently reversed by the U.S. Supreme Court.

"Privilege of *New York Times v. Sullivan* Held Applicable to Statements Made Of and Concerning a Non-Public Official." *Ohio State Law Journal*, 28:502–9, Summer 1967.   **1P301**
Re: *Pauling v. Globe-Democrat Publishing Co.* (1966) in which the court ruled that the newspaper had the privilege of making critical comments on a public figure, including false statements of fact, made without malice.

Proal, Louis. *Passion and Criminality: A Legal and Literary Study*. Translated from the French by A. R. Allinson. Paris, Charles Carrington, [1903]. 679p.   **1P302**
Three chapters deal with the contagion of literature (erotic and violent novels and plays) on suicide and criminal behavior. In a concluding chapter the author, a French judge, holds authors responsible for the damage done to the lives of their readers. "It is not the delineation of evil, if done with proper reserve, that constitutes a work immoral, that book may still be chaste, if its inspiration is lofty, and is described only to be branded hateful." The government should exercise a stricter surveillance over works displayed in stands and booksellers' windows and available in popular lending libraries. The publisher of this moralistic study, Charles Carrington, was a notorious English pornographer (C106). The work is believed to have been printed in England, despite the Paris imprint.

Probert, Walter. "Defamation, A Camouflage of Psychic Interests: The Beginning of a Behavioral Analysis." *Vanderbilt Law Review*, 15:1173–1201, October 1962.   **1P303**
"Does the law of defamation need to be reformed? The author thinks so. Professor Probert rejects the doctrine of libel per se and questions the courts' understanding of the use of the term 'reputation.' It is his belief that plaintiffs on an individual basis should have increased benefit of the knowledge accumulated by the various social sciences in proving the harm done by the alleged defamation, with more liberalization in the requirements of pleading and proof than is now generally countenanced by the courts."

A Problem for Parents: Pornography.

Washington, D.C., Division of Temperance and General Welfare, General Board of Christian Social Concerns of the Methodist Church, n.d. 4p. **1P304**
Content: The Problem. Parents Case. What Is Pornography? Enforcement of the Law Is Difficult. Can Pornography Harm the Child? The Unduly Absorbed Child. Sex Stimulants Abound in Current Culture. As Parents Strengthen the Foundation of Christian Love They Fight the Major Battle Against Pornography.

Proctor, S. K. "Henry Dumaresq on the Sydney Press in 1829." *Journal of the Royal Australian Historical Society*, 57: 172–81, June 1971. **1P305**
Dumaresq, secretary to Governor Darling of New South Wales, pleaded for the Colonial Office to initiate in the House of Commons legislation to stifle the Australian press.

Procuniar, Pamela E. "The Intellectual Right of Children." *Wilson Library Bulletin*, 51:163–67, October 1976. **1P306**
A lawyer writes of her concern over the abridgment of children's rights to read and learn. "To give democracy a chance of success, we need to develop adults who are capable of choice and decision-making. The more we protect and shelter our children, the less they will be able to participate meaningfully in the democratic process. . . . We must decide to risk exposing our children to knowledge of mankind's ideas and history, its mistakes and successes."

"Professional Associations and the Right to Free Expression: Constitutional Limitations on Control of Members." *Georgetown Law Journal*, 58: 646–56, February 1970. **1P307**
In *Firestone v. First Dist. Dental Soc'y* (N.Y., 1969), which involved an association requiring prior approval of its members professionally related publications and broadcasts, the New York Supreme Court ruled that the Association's conduct was in violation of the First Amendment.

"Professional Ethics and Trial Publicity: What All the Talk Is About." *Suffolk University Law Review*, 10:654–76, Spring 1976. **1P308**
Re: *Chicago Council of Lawyers v. Bauer*, 522 F.2d 242 (7th Cir. 1975).

"A Proposed Statutory Right to Respond to Environmental Advertisements: Access to the Airways After CBS v. Democratic National Committee." *Northwestern University Law Review*, 69:234–62, May–June 1974. **1P309**
"This comment has attempted to demonstrate that, at least in the area of environmental advertising, the fairness doctrine is not

adequate." A consideration of the U.S. Supreme Court decision in *CBS v. Democratic National Committee* (1973).

Prosser, William L. "Defamation." In his *Handbook of the Law of Torts*. 4th ed. St. Paul, Minn., West, 1971, pp. 737–801. (The Hornbook Series) **1P310**
Content: Defamation, libel and slander, basis of liability, absolute and qualified privilege, other defenses.

———. "Privacy." *California Law Review*, 48:383–423, August 1960. (Reprinted in *PEAL Quarterly*, December 1961) **1P311**
Beginning with the classic statement on the right of privacy by Warren and Brandeis presented in the *Harvard Law Review* in 1890, the author traces the development of the concept in common law under these headings: (1) intrusion, (2) public disclosure of private facts, (3) false light in the public eye, (4) appropriation, (5) common features, (6) public figures and public interest, (7) limitations, and (8) defenses.

Proudfoot, Merrill. "Censorship in South Africa." *New Letters*, 43:27–35, October 1976. **1P312**
On learning that a *Dennis the Menace* cartoon booklet is banned in South Africa, the author further investigated the status of censorship in that country. He comments on *Jacobsen's Index of Objectionable Literature*, a loose-leaf volume containing an estimated 15,000 titles illegal under South Africa's numerous censorship laws. The *Index*, kept up-to-date by periodic addenda, provides librarians and book dealers with titles of banned books, enabling them to keep out of jail.

Proxmire, William. "Abandon the Fairness Doctrine." *TV Guide*, 23:(15):11–12, 12 April 1975. **1P313**
Senator Proxmire considers the Federal Communications Commission's fairness doctrine and the equal-time provision for political candidates as major abridgments of the First Amendment. He favors extending to radio and television the same constitutional rights now afforded the newspaper press.

———. "The FCC's Fairness Report." *Congressional Record*, 120:S14272–74, 5 August 1974. **1P314**
Criticism of the fairness doctrine, recently reaffirmed by the Federal Communications Commission, which Senator Proxmire believes "violates the spirit and the letter of the first amendment." The text of Judge Bazelon's dissent in the case of *Brandywine-Main Line Radio, Inc. v. FCC* (1972) is given as Exhibit 1.

"Public and Press Rights of Access to Prisoners after *Branzburg* and *Mandel*." *Yale Law Journal*, 82:1337–54, May 1973. **1P315**
Re: *Branzburg v. Hayes* (1972) and *Kleindienst v. Mandel* (1972).

"Public Information Act and Interpretive and Advisory Rulings." *Administrative Law Review*, 20:1–54, December 1967. **1P316**
A panel discussion by Ogden R. Reid, Frank M. Wozencraft, Manuel F. Cohen, Philip Elman, and Thomas G. Meeker. Moderated by Kenneth C. Davis.

"Public Official and Actual Malice Standards: The Evolution of *New York Times Co. v. Sullivan*." *Iowa Law Review*, 56:393–407, December 1970. **1P317**
Re: *New York Times Co. v. Sullivan* (1964). "The decision established a new constitutional privilege in the law of defamation which attached upon the showing that defamatory statements concerning themselves with the official conduct of a public official and were published in the absence of actual malice."

"Public Participation in License Renewals and the Public Interest Standard of the FCC." *Utah Law Review*, 1970:461–67, June 1970. **1P318**
Re: *Hale v. FCC*, 425 F.2d 556 (D.C. Cir. 1970).

"The Public's Right of Access to the Broadcast Media for Airing of Editorial Advertisements." *Valparaiso University Law Review*, 8:125–39, Fall 1973. **1P319**
The author objects to the decision in *Columbia Broadcasting System, Inc. v. Democratic National Committee* (1973) because it avoided the issue of discrimination within a public forum and relied heavily on the belief that implementation of the right of access would entail countless administrative obstacles. The author attempts to show that these fears are largely unfounded. "The CBS decision is troublesome when one considers that radio and television are now the primary source and forum for public news and debate. If the public is refused a limited right to purchase time to voice its views, then it is true that the public's free speech interests are diminishing as the age of technology and mass communication moves onward."

Publisher's Auxiliary. Washington, D.C., National Newspaper Association, 1865–date. Semimonthly. **1P320**
Issues frequently contain news articles, editorials, and features dealing with freedom of the press.

Puechner, Ray. *The LSD & Sex & Censorship & Vietnam Cookbook*. Jacksonville, Ill., Harris-Wolfe, 1968. 165p. **1P321**
Aside from the title, based on the "Lincoln's Doctor's Dog" principle, this book of humor is included for the essay, Out, Damned Smut!

which describes the activities of the fictitious Mrs. Grundoon who glued together the dirty pages in books at Kroch's and Brentano's bookstore.

Pullen, Frances K. *Changing Dimensions of Press Freedom: A Study of* New York Times Co. v. Sullivan *and Its Impact.* Minneapolis, University of Minnesota, 1968. 161p. (Unpublished Master's thesis) **1P322**
The study is intended to determine what expansions or limitations the case of *New York Times v. Sullivan* (1964) offers to the concept of freedom of the press.

Pullen, Ricky D. *A Comparison and Contrast of the Libertarian and Social Responsibility Theories of the Press Based on United States Supreme Court Decisions.* Carbondale, Ill., Southern Illinois University, 1973. 344p. (Ph.D. dissertation, University Microfilms, no. 74–6238) **1P323**
"The idea that the press is in any way responsible to the government or society is in direct contrast to the libertarian idea incorporated in the First Amendment that government and society should have no control or power to manipulate the press. Hence, it was the purpose of this study to identify any emerging trends of legal rationale in United States Supreme Court decisions which imply that newspapers actually do have a responsibility to society and government, whose duty is to protect societal interests. A concomitant purpose was to identify libertarian trends in Court opinions establishing newspapers as independent and free from controls."

[Pulley, J. Waverly, III.] "The Emerging Constitutional Privilege to Conceal Confidential News Sources." *University of Richmond Law Review*, 6:129–40, Fall 1971. **1P324**
"The purpose of this Comment is to evaluate the constitutional privilege to conceal confidential news sources, as expressed in *Caldwell v. United States* [1970] and to assess the probable impact of that decision upon the further development of a journalistic privilege."

Pulliam, Eugene C. *The People and the Press: Partners for Freedom.* Tucson, Ariz., University of Arizona Press [1966]. 8p. (The John Peter Zenger Award for Freedom of the Press, 1965) **1P325**
Among the issues which the author considers threatening to the freedom of the press are: the government policies of secrecy and deception, the lack of competition in the media, the resistance of unions to new technology, and the conflict over trial by newspaper.

———. "We Can't Tolerate Government Control of TV." *Grassroots Editor*, 14(2):31–32, March–April 1973. **1P326**
"Unless the Congress of the United States takes decisive action to halt it, the total takeover of U.S. radio and television by the government will be finalized within the next few years. There will be but one radio and TV system. It will be operated, censored, programmed—in short, completely dominated—by an elite group of Washington bureaucrats." Of the fairness doctrine, he comments: "it has nothing to do with fairness, but it has everything to do with the power of government to harass people whose opinions the bureaucrats don't like."

[Pulton, Andrew.] *Some Reflections upon the Author and Licenser Of a Scandalous Pamphlet; called, The Missioners Arts Discover'd. With the Reply of A. Pulton to a Challenge Made Him in a Letter Prefix'd to the said Pamphlet.* London, Mary Thompson for the Author, 1688. 14p. **1P327**
An attack on the licenser, Mr. Needham, who placed his imprimatur on an anonymous "defamatory libel," thereby becoming party to the libel—"though not a Legitimate Parent, a Step-Father at least." The offending pamphlet, *The Missioners Arts Discovered . . . ,* charged Catholics with implication in the murder of Charles I.

Purdon, Richard L. "Pornography in the Dormitories: A Commander's Dilemma." *U.S. Air Force Judge Advocate General Law Review*, 14:146–54, May 1973. **1P328**
"The scope of this article is limited to an examination of the constitutional test for obscenity and the application of this test to military commanders as related to the dormitories under their control." The author suggests what might and might not be permitted on dormitory walls, advising a minimum of interference and noting that mere possession of pornography, if not displayed, cannot be prohibited.

The Purdue Opinion Panel. *Does Youth Believe in the Bill of Rights?* West Lafayette, Ind., Purdue Opinion Panel, Division of Educational Reference, Purdue University, 1947. 16p., 15p. (Report of Poll no. 30) **1P329**
A poll of some 15,000 high school students across the nation reveals that "youth does not apparently believe wholeheartedly in the Bill of Rights." Only 55 percent would give newspapers freedom to print anything except military secrets; only 53 percent support the principles of freedom of speech. The text is prepared by H. H. Remmers, R. E. Horton, and R. E. Mainer.

———. *Freedom to Read Issues.* West Lafayette, Ind., Purdue Opinion Panel, Measurement and Research Center, Purdue University, 1974. 22p., 24p. (Report of Poll no. 100) **1P330**
This nationwide poll of high school students' attitudes toward censorship reveals that three-fourths believe that censorship violates principles of American freedom but a sizeable minority would be willing to let outsiders screen the books they use in school. Five percent approved of burning "objectionable" books; 15 percent would "probably approve" burning books. Two questions sought student reactions to profanity in assigned readings; nine questions referred to attitudes toward censorship. A. C. Erlich summarizes the results. A review of the poll appears in *Intellect*, March 1975.

"The Purloined Pentagon Papers and Prior Restraint: The Press Prevailed!" *St. John's Law Review*, 46:81–103, October 1971. **1P331**
A detailing and analysis of the chain of legal events following the *New York Times* release of the first installment of the so-called Pentagon Papers, 13 June 1971. The author believes a temporary restraining order should be issued when the matter in question has been classified in the national interest. The courts then must delineate between government embarrassment and grave danger in each case.

Purrett, Louise A. *Trade Libel's Special Damage Rule.* Madison, Wis., University of Wisconsin, 1972. 85p. (Unpublished Master's thesis) **1P332**
"This thesis examines trade libel cases in state and Federal courts for the period from 1940 to 1972 to see if the rule is in fact being mitigated. The conclusion is that the rule is not being systematically changed. Some courts have required naming of lost customers, others have not, but there is no discernible pattern—chronological, geographic or in fact situation—to the mitigations, and they occur no more frequently now than they ever did."

Pushkar, Raymond S. E. "Criminal Libel and Slander in the Military." *U.S. Air Force Judge Advocate General Law Review*, 9:40–44, November–December 1967. **1P333**
"The purpose of this article is to discuss an offense which is often heard of but seldom litigated. It is punishable, at least in part under the common law, under the criminal codes of many states, and under military law. Rarely is it before a criminal court, or a court-martial." The offense is criminal libel and slander.

Putnam, George H., *comp. The Question of Copyright; Comprising the Text of the Copyright Law of the United States, A Summary of the Copyright Laws at Present in Force in the Chief Countries of the World Together With a Report of the Legislation Now Pending in Great Britain, A Sketch of the Contest in the United States, 1837–*

1891, in Behalf of International Copyright, and Certain Papers on the Development of the Conception of Literary Property, and On the Results of the American Act of 1891. 2d ed., rev. New York, Putnam's, 1896, 486p.   **1P334**

Putz, C. Delos, Jr. "Fairness and Commercial Advertising; A Review and a Proposal." *San Francisco Law Review,* 6:215–51, April 1972.   **1P335**
"This article (1) reviews the history of the application of the Fairness Doctrine to commercial advertising by the FCC and the courts, (2) considers alternatives such as an expanded right of paid access and (3) offers a proposed basis for compromise between the broadcasting industry and the proponents of counter-advertising."

Q

Quality Educational Development, Inc. "Sex Education Programs in the Public Schools of the United States." *Technical Report of the [U.S.] Commission on Obscenity and Pornography*, 5:295–338, 1971. **1Q1**
"Included are the results of examination of research literature as it affects programs, curriculum materials and guides, common goals and purposes of sex education programs, and methods employed. Interest was expressed by the Commission in the examination of programs for their potential for reducing adolescent or later interest in nonlegitimate sexual materials (pornography); this is reported in the form of compilation of subjective opinions only. Incorporated in the report are limited studies of problems commonly involved in implementation of programs."

Quebec (Province). Commission Parlamentaire Spéciale sur les Problèmes de la Liberté de Presse. *Rapport Préliminaire: Les Travaux de la Commission de 1969; Rapport Préparé par Pierre Beausoleil, Directeur de la Recherche.* Quebec, 1972. 73p. (La Liberté de Presse au Québec, 1) **1Q2**
The Commission was appointed to study the problems of monopoly and abuse in the Quebec press. This progress report includes summaries of testimony received during a series of public hearings, the recommendation of the two British press commissions, the working of the British Press Council, and proposals for a Press Council for Quebec.

Queensland Literature Board of Review. *Annual Reports of Operations under the Objectionable Literature Act of 1954.* Brisbane, Australia, Govt. Printer. 1955–date. **1Q3**

"The Question of Federal 'Newsmen's Shield' Legislation." *Congressional Digest*, 52:131–60, May 1973. **1Q4**
The entire issue deals with the topic of shield laws: Past legislative actions and court cases, a summary of state shield laws presently in effect, recent executive and judicial developments, action in the 92d and 93d Congresses, and pro and con arguments. Those favoring shield laws: U.S. Representative Jerome R. Waldie; Stanford Smith, president of the American Society of Newspaper Publishers Association; John B. Summers, general counsel, National Association of Broadcasters; Edward M. Korry, president, Association of American Publishers; and Jack L. Bradley, president, National Press Photographers Association. Those opposed to shield laws: U.S. Senator Jesse Helms; U.S. Representative David W. Dennis; Robert G. Dixon, Jr., U.S. Assistant Attorney General; William H. Fitzpatrick, executive editor, Landmark Publications; and Clark Mollenhoff, Washington Bureau chief, *Des Moines Register*.

"Question: The President is coming to your city on Friday. . . . How Would You Respond to the Secret Service Request?" *MORE*, 5(11):14–15, November 1975. **1Q5**
Sixteen editors and television directors respond to the question: "The President is coming to your city on Friday. On Tuesday, one of your reporters tells you he understands the FBI has arrested five local radicals. They were arraigned before a U.S. Commissioner at midnight—with no reporters present—and held without bail on a numbered Federal Code offense. Your reporter is the only journalist who has bothered to look up the code and finds the radicals are charged with conspiring to assassinate the President. You tell him to go ahead and write the story, but that afternoon you get a call from a high-ranking Secret Service official urging you in the strongest terms to hold the story for three days until the President has left town. He argues that the radical group has many supporters in the area who, if alerted to the arrests, might try to do the job themselves. In light of the recent assassination attempts and the controversy over the role of the press in inciting violence, how would you respond to the Secret Service request?"

Quigg, Richard J. "Defenses to Group Defamation Actions." *Cleveland-Marshall Law Review*, 13:102–10, January 1964. **1Q6**
"Most past group defamation cases have held that language including *all* members of a given group, or positively identifying the plaintiff, must be used. Tort actions have been upheld when small groups are defamed; tort claims are generally disallowed in the defamation of large groups unless the public readily recognizes the defamation as being directed at one individual."

Quincy, Alpha. "Freedom to Read." *Language Arts*, 53:410–13, 427, April 1976. **1Q7**
Censorship is not the answer to reading matter in the schools that may be objected to as sexist or racist: it is a dangerous solution for it denies our right to read. Two solutions that enhance the right to read are: (1) education of teachers for awareness and sensitivity to materials, and (2) the building of a collection of teaching materials that will broaden the base of ideology.

Quinlan, Maurice J. "Swift and the Prosecuted Nottingham Speech." *Harvard Library Bulletin*, 11:296–302, 1957. **1Q8**
Discussion of the nature and authorship of the sham speech of the Earl of Nottingham, attributed to Jonathan Swift, but denied by him, and for which Andrew Hind, a printer, was falsely arrested.

Quinn, Alexander J. *Censorship of Obscenity: A Comparison of Canon Law and American Constitutional Law*. Rome, Catholic Book Agency, 1963. 134p. (Dissertation, Doctor of Canon Law, Pontificia Universitas Lateranensis) **1Q9**
The author finds that both the Catholic Church and the Supreme Court of the United States allow prior censorship when necessary for the common good; but the Church's mission calls for more frequent use of the devise. The Church's mission to teach divine truth requires protection from doctrinal errors: such errors would be protected under the First Amendment. The Church prohibits literature

when a notable part of the work is obscene; the Supreme Court restricts censorship to those publications which, taken as a whole, are obscene.

Quinn, Pamela P. "The Red Lion Case: An Opportunity for First Amendment Reappraisal." *University of Pittsburgh Law Review*, 29:691–720, June 1968.
1Q10
A discussion of implications of the *Red Lion* case, then before the U.S. Supreme Court, in the regulation of broadcasting to provide greater access. The author believes the decision will more than likely "take the form of a balancing . . . of first amendment freedoms, with the freedoms of participants in a public debate overriding those of the broadcasters." Re: *Red Lion Broadcasting Co. v. FCC* (1969).

Quinn, Stephen K. "The Freedom of the Press vs. the Confidentiality Provisions in the New Mexico Children's

Code." *New Mexico Law Review*, 4:119–26, November 1973.
1Q11
A 1972 law "removing certain confidentiality provisions in the Children's Code, achieves a compromise between those factions advocating constitutional guarantees of freedom of the press and those proponents of the concept of a complete separation of child and adult proceedings."

R

Rader, Brian, David Penn, and Ted Williams. "Community Values and Public Policy—Cooperation or Conflict." *Oklahoma Librarian*, 26(2):13–17, April 1976.   **1R1**
Report on a questionnaire study to determine the "contemporary community standards" for obscenity in Tahlequah, Okla. as defined by *Miller v. California* (1973).

Rader, Dotson. "Steal This Book." *New York Times Book Review*, 76(26):16, 18 July 1971.   **1R2**
A review of Abbie Hoffman's book, rejected by thirty publishers, "yet to receive a single review," and turned down for advertising in newspapers and radio. "In the Boston area bookstores organized a boycott against it, and in New York the Doubleday bookstore chain, among others, has declined to stock the book." The reviewer charges a "fearsome censorship by tacit understanding within allied industries has been established."

Rae, W. F. *Wilkes, Sheridan, Fox: The Opposition under George the Third*. London, W. Isbister, 1874. 462p.   **1R3**
Biographical accounts of three Whig leaders who contributed in some measure to press freedom: John Wilkes, Richard Brinsley Sheridan, and Charles James Fox. Wilkes challenged the laws of sedition and obscene libel; Sheridan supported the Friends of the Liberty of the Press; and Fox sponsored the Libel Act of 1792 which gave juries, rather than judges, the right to determine whether or not a work was libelous.

Rafferty, Max. "Crack Down on the Smut Kings!" *Reader's Digest*, 93:97–100, November 1968. (Reprinted in U.S. House of Representatives, Post Office and Civil Service Committee, Postal Operations Subcommittee, *Hearings on Obscenity in the Mails*, pp. 183–85)   **1R4**
An attack on the avalanche of pornography emanating from the author's state of California, much of which he believes finds its way

into hands of juveniles. He makes five recommendations for public action: (1) encourage judges to hand down more severe penalties to pornography peddlers; (2) elect a president who will appoint Supreme Court justices who will take action against pornography; (3) pick public prosecutors who will attack the obscenity racket; (4) support organizations such as the National Organization for Decent Literature; and (5) conduct neighborhood boycotts of stores selling pornography.

———. "The Other Side: Hardest of All Things to Come By." *Wilson Library Bulletin*, 42:181–86, October 1967. **1R5**
In an address to the American Library Trustees Association, the former California state school superintendent defends school librarians against charges made by an earlier speaker, affirming that librarians should decide what's good for children and what isn't. While opposing the censorship of books intended for adults only, he believes librarians must apply censorship in facing "the torrent of printed filth currently being poured into our society like sewage into a stream." He takes issue with the point of view that bad books do not instigate bad deeds. "Logic, it appears, would compel librarians to concede that if bad books don't do anybody any harm, then good books certainly don't do anybody any good."

Ragan, Fred D. "Justice Oliver Wendell Holmes, Jr., Zechariah Chafee, Jr., and the Clear and Present Danger Test for Free Speech: The First Year, 1919." *Journal of American History*, 58:24–45, June 1971.   **1R6**
"Holmes' early 1919 free speech opinions— *Schenck v. United States*, *Frohwerk v. United States*, and *Debs v. United States*—given in March for a unanimous Court, were based not upon a libertarian construction of the danger doctrine, but rather upon a construction which had the effect of sanctioning the common law crime of seditious libel. . . . By November 1919, however, Holmes had altered his position. Dissenting in *Abrams et al. v. United States*, he declared that he could not agree 'with the argument of the Government that the First Amendment left the common law of seditious libel in force.' . . . This transition in Holmes'

construction of the clear and present danger test of free speech—from a restrictive or conservative test in the early cases, to a permissive or libertarian one in the later case—is the subject of this analysis."

Ragan, Samuel T. "The ABA Recommendations: A Newspaperman's Critique." *Notre Dame Lawyer*, 42:888–95, Symposium 1967.   **1R7**
A member of the American Newspaper Publishers Association's Special Committee on Free Press and Fair Trial (°A20) comments on the report of the American Bar Association Advisory Committee on Fair Trial and Free Press. He believes that the report embraces several false assumptions: that pretrial news is inherently prejudicial, that objective jurors must be ignorant jurors, and that treatment of crime news is always detrimental to the accused. He is also concerned that the judiciary may preempt the power of the executive if it restricts the release of information by law enforcement officials. "A free press is not an enemy of a fair trial. As our historical experience bears witness, they are not incompatible, but dependent upon each other."

———. "Fair Trial with a Free Press: The Reardon Report Revisited." *Tennessee Law Review*, 37:215–19, Fall 1969.
                    1R8
"The first amendment and the sixth amendment are not incompatible. Instead, they go hand-in-hand in the search for truth and justice, and one cannot be diluted without damage to the other."

Ragsdale, J. Donald. "*Last Tango in Paris et al. v. The Supreme Court*: The Current State of Obscenity Law." *Quarterly Journal of Speech*, 61:279–89, October 1975.   **1R9**
"It is the purpose of this paper to determine the state of obscenity law as shaped by the U.S. Supreme Court's decisions and dissents of June 21, 1973 [*Miller v. California* and three others] and June 24, 1974 [*Jenkins v. Georgia*] and by litigation which principally involved *Last Tango In Paris*." The analysis shows that "a

new Comstock era has not emerged, for the number of obscenity prosecutions is still far greater than the number of convictions." There has been a chilling effect, however, on the production of high-quality X-rated films by reputable film makers and studios.

Raichle, William G. "If There Is to be an Abridgment of Pretrial Communication, Should It be Coupled with an Expansion of Trial Coverage by Radio and Television?" *Notre Dame Lawyer*, 42:915–19, Symposium 1967. (Reprinted in *Federal Communications Bar Journal*, 1967)   **1R10**
The author opposes the telecasting and broadcasting of trials. "A trial should be conducted for the ascertainment of truth and not for the purpose of entertainment. Every trial is an exacting test of the fidelity to conscience and the intelligence of jurors. The test should not be made more difficult by the distracting impact of radio and television coverage of the trial."

Raitt, Cecil. "Defamation by Broadcast or 'Defamacast' Is Actionable *Per Se*." *Wayne Law Review*, 9:391–96, Winter 1963.   **1R11**
Re: *American Broadcasting–Paramount Theaters, Inc. v. Simpson*, 1962. The court held that the common law classifications of libel and slander were inadequate and a new classification, "defamacast," was necessary.

"Ralph Ginzburg Begins Term for 1963 Porno Conviction: Issues & Court Decisions." *Library Journal*, 97:1650, 1652–54, May 1972.   **1R12**
A brief history of the case of Ralph Ginzburg, whose obscenity conviction was upheld by the U.S. Supreme Court.

Rampal, Kuldip. *The Concept of the Press Council*. Columbia, Mo., Freedom of Information Center, School of Journalism, University of Missouri at Columbia, 1976. 5p. (Report no. 350)   **1R13**
"The press council is a twentieth-century institution designed to balance press freedom against public complaints of press activity. This paper is an overview of the concept of the press council as seen in its development from the first press council in Sweden in 1916."

Ramsey, Edward S. *The Law of Retraction in Libel: An Examination of the Wisconsin Statute*. Madison, Wis., University of Wisconsin, 1969. 121p. (Unpublished Master's thesis)   **1R14**
The thesis is intended to show that the measure of the constitutionality of the Wisconsin retraction statute is drawn from the pattern established by cases where statutes were upheld because the courts interpreted 'actual damages' to include general damage recovery.

This project attempts to suggest the reasoning the Wisconsin Supreme Court is likely to adopt when it is called upon to decide the validity of the statute.

Ranchod, Bhadra. *Foundations of the South African Law of Defamation*. Leiden, Netherlands, Leiden University Press, 1972. 183p.   **1R15**
Content: Roman Law, Medieval Law, Dutch Law, English Law (history of defamation, defamation in modern law), African Law (including the differences between Roman-Dutch Law and English Law).

Randall, Peter. "The Banning of *Confused Mhlaba*." *Index on Censorship*, 5(4):3–5, Winter 1976.   **1R16**
An account of the banning in South Africa of the sale and distribution of copies of the play by a young black author, and prohibition of its performance as "prejudicial to the safety of the state, the general welfare or the peace and good order." The Directorate of Publications found the play "strongly emotionally loaded" and the police were "presented in a bad light."

Randall, Richard S. *Censorship of the Movies: The Social and Political Control of a Mass Medium*. Madison, Wis., University of Wisconsin Press, 1968. 280p.   **1R17**
The aim of this study of motion picture censorship in the United States is "to relate the legal doctrine of a mass medium to the operating controls of a mass society." In chapters 2, 3, and 4, the author examines the law of movie censorship in its procedural and substantive aspects; in chapters 5 and 6 he deals with the operations of government prior censorship. This latter analysis is based on interviews with censors on major state and city licensing boards, with officials of the U.S. Customs, and with film proprietors and lawyers who deal with them. "Chapters 7 and 8 explore the wider world of censorship in a mass society, which encompasses control through criminal prosecution, extra-legal action by officials, the pressures of private groups, and the film industry's efforts at self-regulation. An attempt to evaluate the state of free speech in motion pictures is made in chapter 9."

———. "Classification by the Motion Picture Industry." *Technical Report of the [U.S.] Commission on Obscenity and Pornography*, 5:219–92, 1971.   **1R18**
A history and appraisal of the film-rating system established by the American motion picture industry (Motion Picture Association of America, MPAA) in 1968 as an alternative to government censorship. The author examines the rating process (submission, viewing, appeal, and rating) and the criteria used in rating. He details the use of these criteria in applying its ratings to four specific films; he analyzes the films rated during the first eight months—both in quantity and substance; he compares the ratings of the MPAA with ratings by eight other organizations—governmental and

quasi-governmental systems, nationally known nongovernmental programs, and local nongovernmental programs—and also with evaluations by newspaper movie critics. He looks at the advertisements of ratings and at the practices in restricting admissions to R and X films and the enforcement of restrictions. Finally, the author examines the industry rating system as an alternative to censorship, concluding that "the rating system only partially defends the film medium from censorship and control. As such, it is only one control among several that operates on the medium and only one element in the public policy problem of managing the tension between freedom of speech and censorship in the medium."

———. *Control of Motion Pictures in the United States*. Madison, Wis., University of Wisconsin, 1967. 682p. (Ph.D. dissertation, University Microfilms, 67–512)   **1R19**
This study, later embodied in book form, "accepts the traditional libertarian concern with prior censorship, and sets out to examine that censorship systematically and to offer an evaluation of it in its modern form."

Randolph, Eleanor R. "Are Polish Jokes Hazardous to Our Health?" *MORE*, 6(2):18, 24, February 1976.   **1R20**
"Bob Einstein and Steve Allen told four Polish jokes on the Dick Cavett Show three years ago. ABC and the FCC have been in and out of court—with the Polish American Congress—ever since."

Ranjan, C. N. Chitta. "Editors and Press Freedom." *Mainstream*, 8(4):8–10, 32, 27 September 1969.   **1R21**
Charges that the editors of Indian papers are merely go-betweens between the industrialist owners and the government, and have no independence. Freedom of the press can only be assured by a change in the pattern of ownership of the news agencies and newspapers, enabling the employees of newspapers as well as representatives of public opinion to manage the papers.

Rankine-Galloway, Honora F. *The Impact of the 1961 "Tropic of Cancer" Publication on the American Literary Community*. Philadelphia, Pa., University of Pennsylvania, 1973. 552p. (Ph.D. dissertation, University Microfilms, no. 74-14,131)   **1R22**
"The most singular effect of the publication, largely ignored though part of the public record, can be found in the transcripts of *Tropic* trials, where the evaluations by critics, writers, and academicians were offered to prove *Tropic* a serious work of literature and, hence, not

obscene. The testimony of the spokesmen for the literary community first is analyzed with regard to the 'redeeming social importance' of *Tropic of Cancer*. To pass by the *Roth* test, it had to be proven that the book was motivated by a 'serious purpose' on Miller's part: his stature, motives, and intent in and by the book had to be considered. Then the literary evaluation by the critics could proceed in court. . . . Rather than adherents to a freer sexual order, the literary community showed that they had come to *Tropic*'s aid in court as intellectuals fighting for freedom of expression against a community, organized against social change. What the courts and the communities most had objected to was not Miller the pornographer, but Miller the iconoclast and liberator of the social order."

Ranly, Donald P. *Action for Children's Television*. Columbia, Mo., Freedom of Information Center, School of Journalism, University of Missouri at Columbia, 1976. 11p. (Report no. 364)   **1R23**

Detailed information on the origins and development of Action for Children's Television (ACT), one of the most successful citizen pressure groups to emerge from the sixties.

——. *Electronic Coverage of Congress*. Columbia, Mo., Freedom of Information Center, School of Journalism, University of Missouri at Columbia, 1975. 9p. (Report no. 334)   **1R24**

"The electronic media have long clamored for First Amendment rights equal to those enjoyed by the print media. Nowhere has their second-class citizenship been more apparent than in rules governing coverage of the U.S. Congress. Many in the Congress now realize it cannot be an equal branch unless it allows the microphones and cameras inside its halls and meeting rooms."

——. *NCCB—A Media Challenger*. Columbia, Mo., Freedom of Information Center, School of Journalism, University of Missouri at Columbia, 1976. 9p. (Report no. 362)   **1R25**

"The author traces the development of the National Citizens Committee for Broadcasting in its attempt to make broadcasting better serve the public interest."

Rao, P. Kodanda. "Freedom of the Press in India." *Times of India*, 14 January 1973, p.6.   **1R26**

The author applauds the action of the Indian Supreme Court in striking down the attempt of the government to control the press by controlling newsprint. "It is difficult to sympathise with the editor who loudly complains of the invasion of his freedom by the government but tamely submits to the invasion of his freedom

by subscribers, advertisers and proprietors. The former are on the whole much milder and presumably operate in the public interest and are open to public view and public criticism, while the latter are secret and in the interest of private profit and often unconscionable to a degree."

Ratcliffe, Temple L. "The End of the Line: Rosenbloom v. Metromedia." *University of Pittsburgh Law Review*, 31:734–41, Summer 1970.   **1R27**

Re: *Rosenbloom v. Metromedia* (1969), in which the Court held that the fact that the plaintiff is neither a public official nor a public figure (he was a distributor of nudist magazines) does not prevent the application of *New York Times* actual malice standard.

[Ratliff, Debora D.] "In Comparative Hearings for Broadcast Licenses, the FCC Must Award Merit for Minority Ownership of a Broadcast Applicant Where That Ownership Is Likely to Increase Diversity of Opinion and Viewpoint." *Texas Law Review*, 52: 806–15, April 1974.   **1R28**

Re: *TV 9, Inc. v. FCC*, No. 72-2049 (D.C. Cir., Nov. 6, 1973).

[Ratliff, Horace, and Max Thomas.] *The Case of Ratliff and Thomas: An Exposure and a Challenge. Hitlerite Technique in Democratic Australia*. Sydney, Australia, Australian Civil Rights Defence League, 1941. 12p.   **1R29**

The two trade unionists were convicted and jailed under the National Securities Act for possessing papers which did not bear the name and address of the printer and having a typewriter and a duplicating machine "with a view to making an endeavor to influence public opinion in a manner likely to prejudice the efficient prosecution of the war." The case became a cause célèbre among unionists and civil libertarians.

Ratliff, Ray E., Jr. "Fairness Doctrine: Its Limits and Occasions in West Virginia Advertising." *West Virginia Law Review*, 74:120–34, August–November 1971.   **1R30**

Standards must be fashioned to (1) categorically apply the fairness doctrine to all paid advertising, and (2) include the spot commercial in the format of fairness broadcasting.

Ratner, Leonard G. "The Social Importance of Prurient Interest—Obscenity Regulation v. Thought-Privacy." *Southern California Law Review*, 42:587–99, 1969.   **1R31**

"The Supreme Court has not articulated a clear test to distinguish regulable from nonregulable. Obscenity Tests which define obscenity as 'appealing to prurient interest,' 'patently offensive,' and 'without redeeming social impor-

tance' are contradictory and reflect an esthetic, moralistic judgment that is inconsistent with the thought and religious-freedom values underlying the first amendment. The author examines the social purposes of obscenity regulation and proposes a less intrusive method of implementing those purposes"—Editor. The article was developed in response to a letter from the U.S. Commission on Obscenity and Pornography, soliciting comments on the constitutional problems of obscenity regulation.

Rawlings, Maurice E. "A Constitutional Balance Between Fair Trials and Free Press." *Drake Law Review*, 17:1–10, December 1967.   **1R32**

The author urges "the formulation and adoption of a fair and reasonable code of conduct by the members of the bar and news media of this state," and proposes a group of principles to be followed by (1) arresting officers, prosecutors, members of the bench and bar, and (2) all members of the news media.

Ray, Royal H. *Concentration of Ownership and Control in the American Daily Newspaper Industry*. New York, Columbia University, 1950. 482p. (Ph.D. dissertation, University Microfilms, no. 2352)   **1R33**

"Daily English language newspapers of general circulation in the United States decreased from 2,202 units in 1909 to 1,748 units during 1948. Investigation of the economic causes and consequences of this decrease in units and the increased concentration of ownership and control in the industry constitutes the basis for this study. The study falls into three parts: First, basic statistical trends; second, field case studies; and third, analysis and interpretation. The third part is both statistical and economic in character."

[Raybin, David L.] "The Abolition of Anonymity: Distribution of Publications Act." *Tennessee Law Review*, 40: 301–7, Winter 1973.   **1R34**

Comment on a 1971 Tennessee law which prohibits anonymous publication and distribution of circulars, posters, handbills, newspapers, or magazines and makes such action a criminal offense. The author cites the U.S. Supreme Court 1960 decision in *Talley v. California*, declaring unconstitutional a similar Los Angeles ordinance.

Raymond, Jacquelynn O. *The Status of Administrative Censorship of, and Attitudes Toward, the Scholastic Press in Public Secondary Schools in Kansas: A Survey and Case Study of How Controversial Issues Are Covered*. Lawrence, Kans., University of Kansas, 1972. 169p. (Unpublished Master's thesis)   **1R35**

Interviews, surveys, and case studies "indicated that administrators in Kansas public high schools do wield a tremendous power over scholastic journalism and do stringently administer and curtail both editorial and news scope in school newspapers."

Razdan, C. K., ed. *Bare Breasts and Bare Bottoms: Anatomy of Film Censorship in India*. Bombay, Jaico, 1975. 158p. **1R36**
A panel consisting of Partap Sharma, G. D. Khosla, Vinod Mehta, K. A. Abbas, and C. K. Razdan, examines the work of the Indian Board of Film Censors and criticism leveled against it. Included is an itemized list of "censor cuts," and the text of two court decisions involving Indian film censorship, *Devendra Goel v. Union of India* (1952) and *Gimi Garewal v. Film World* (1974).

Rea, Robert T. " 'The Liberty of the Press' as an Issue in English Politics, 1792–1793." *Historian*, 24:26–43, November 1961. **1R37**
In the Spring of 1792 the Fox Libel Act was passed, giving juries the right to decide whether or not a work was libelous. During that year and the next English politics was in the state of near hysteria over events of the French Revolution. A royal proclamation called for severe action to stamp out sedition and the Pitt government, supported by constitutional societies, took action against radicalism in print, including Paine's *Rights of Man*. The Whigs, under the leadership of Charles James Fox, and with the support of the Friends of the Freedom of the Press, attempted to preserve press freedom.

Read, Allen W. "An Obscenity Symbol." *American Speech*, 9:264:78, December 1934. **1R38**
"It is my purpose here to trace the fortunes of the word that has the deepest stigma of any in the language. We shall deal with (1) the nature of obscenity, (2) the history of this word, with special reference to its appearance in dictionaries, (3) the recent vogue of the word, and (4) its possible future." In fourteen pages of scholarly, footnoted, discussion the author fails to mention the taboo word he is discussing, which is obviously "fuck."

"Reaffirming the Freedom of the Press: Another Look at Miami Herald Publishing Co. v. Tornillo." *Michigan Law Review*, 73:186–214, November 1974. **1R39**
The author discusses the *Miami Herald* right of reply case (1974). "In an effort to justify more fully the court's conclusion, this note will first present the underlying rationale of the pro-access argument. It will then analyze the constitutionality of statutes that would implement a right of access. Finally, the note will discuss several practical difficulties that access legislation would present."

Reardon, Paul C. "Fair Trial–Free Press." *Marquette Law Review*, 52:547–60, Winter 1969. **1R40**
A discussion of the current status of the fair trial–free press question after a year's experi-

ence with the recommendations of the Advisory Committee on Fair Trial and Free Press of the American Bar Association, of which the author was chairman.

————. "The Fair Trial–Free Press Controversy—Where We Have Been and Where We Should Be Going." *San Diego Law Review*, 4:255–68, June 1967. **1R41**
The chairman of the Advisory Committee on Fair Trial–Free Press, American Bar Association Project on Minimum Standards for Criminal Justice, discusses the work of his committee, the historical background, the committee's membership, its research program, recommendations, and public reaction to the report.

————. "The Fair Trial–Free Press Standards." *American Bar Association Journal*, 54:343–51, April 1968. **1R42**
The author discusses the standards recommended by the American Bar Association Committee to strengthen the right of an accused to a fair trial within the framework of the Constitutional rights of freedom of speech and the press.

————, and Clifton Daniel. *Fair Trial and Free Press. . . . Rational Debate Seminars*. Washington, D.C., American Enterprise Institute for Public Policy Research, 1968. 181p. (Fourth in the second series of Rational Debate Seminars sponsored by the American Enterprise Institute, held at George Washington University, Washington, D.C.) **1R43**
The conflicting issues between the First and Sixth Amendments which guarantee, respectively, freedom of the press and a fair public trial are debated by spokesmen for the bar and press. Paul C. Reardon was chairman of the American Bar Association Advisory Committee on Fair Trial and Free Press which issued a report recommending limitations on the release and publication of crime news; Clifton Daniel is managing editor of the *New York Times* and outspoken critic of the Reardon Report.

Reasons against the Intended Bill for Laying some Restraint Upon the Liberty of the Press, Wherein all the Arguments yet Advanced by the Promoters of it, are unanswerably Answered. . . . London, J. Wilkie, 1772. 58p. **1R44**
A dull and discursive essay opposing a bill before Paliament that would place restrictions on press freedom. Some of the arguments in favor of the bill which the author refutes are: (1) press freedom has served its purpose and now can be discontinued, (2) in England's glorious Elizabethan Age the press was not free, (3) licensing would suppress the immoral and treasonable writings now abounding, (4) no anonymous works should be permitted, and (5)

increase in the newspaper tax would make papers pay for their vilification.

Reaves, Lacy H. "The Fairness Doctrine: A Continuing Advance Into Product Advertising." *North Carolina Law Review*, 50:664–73, April 1972. **1R45**
In *Friends of the Earth v. FCC* (1971) the Court of Appeals for the District of Columbia Circuit overturned an FCC decision holding the fairness doctrine applicable to the presentation of television commercials advertising high-powered automobiles and leaded gasoline. Before the fairness principle can be applied to commercial advertising it must be determined that the issue is both "controversial" and "public."

Reay, Thomas M. "Ad Censorship, Rejection and the Public Welfare." *Bulletin of the American Society of Newspaper Editors*, 543:5–7, 14, July–August 1970. **1R46**
A review of newspaper practices in rejecting advertising, particularly for X-rated movies.

Reddy, John. "Are Dirty Movies on the Way Out?" *PTA Magazine*, 66(3):2–5, November 1971. **1R47**
"Apparently the majority of movie-goers have reached the saturation point in sex exploitation on the screen. . . . Despite such efforts at self-policing as the movie rating system, sex on the screen has been steadily proliferating for the past few years. . . . Now suddenly, the pendulum seems to be swinging the other way."

Reddy, Sigrid. "An Encounter with the Censors." *Bay State Librarian*, 59(3):8–10, October 1970. **1R48**
The Bedford (Mass.) Public Library has an encounter over the presence of *Evergreen Review* and *Modern Utopian*, including an investigation by a state trooper.

Redfield, Marion B. *Consumer Cycles to Control False Advertising, 1865–1972*. Northridge, Calif., California State University, Northridge, 1972. 151p. (Unpublished Master's thesis) **1R49**
"This study investigated the possibility of a cycle of consumer protection activity operating in the United States during the past century, spaced at approximately thirty-year intervals and followed by legislation to control false advertising."

Redish, Martin H. "Campaign Spending Laws and the First Amendment."

New York University Law Review, 46:900–934, November 1971.   **1R50**
"While applauding the ultimate good of these measures ⌐to limit campaign spending¬ Mr. Redish argues that they may contravene the right of free expression protected by the first amendment. Rather than attempting to artificially restrict the ability of the wealthy candidates to communicate with the public, he feels that we should reduce the importance of financial resources in political campaigns by devising measures which will provide all candidates with greater access to the media."

———. "The First Amendment in the Marketplace: Commercial Speech and the Values of Free Expression." *George Washington Law Review*, 39:429–73, March 1971.   **1R51**
"The first segment of this article will consider the justifications for omitting pure commercial speech from the scope of the first amendment protection in light of the purposes and theoretical foundations of that amendment. The position taken herein is that no adequate justification exists for omitting certain types of commercial speech from the scope of the first amendment; on the contrary, informational and artistic advertising are entirely consistent with many of the purposes of the free expression clause. The second portion will explore how the judiciary has dealt with the problem of commercial speech in the numerous legal situations in which it may arise."

Reed, John P., and Robin S. Reed. "Profile of the Student Censor: A Research Note on Pornography." *Sociological Symposium*, 5:53–60, Fall 1970. **1R52**
"It is the purpose of this research note to examine one aspect of that question. In a college population, it will seek to determine who labels experimental material 'pornographic.' "

Reed, Omer L., Jr. "The Psychological Impact of TV Advertising and the Need for FTC Regulation." *American Business Law Journal*, 13:171–83, Fall 1975.   **1R53**
When presented in a straightforward manner, advertising messages can be accepted or rejected in a rational manner, "but when it is obliquely conditioned into children and adults alike through the most powerful method of mass communication known to our culture it becomes unfair and deceptive and subject to FCC regulation."

Reedy, George E. "Why Does Nobody Love the Press?" In Harry M. Clor, *ed.*, *The Mass Media and Modern Democracy*, Chicago, Rand McNally, 1974, pp. 15–36.   **1R54**
A veteran newspaperman and special assistant

to President Johnson, 1964–66, debunks the charges that the American press is dominated by a "liberal elite," a notion which he likens to the charges in his boyhood that everything bad in American life could be attributed to the "Perfidious Albion." He believes "the American press arouses such heated controversy *because* of its high quality and *because* it is not dominated by consistent ideological viewpoints." He concludes that "those who value freedom as an absolute will also value the free and diverse press we have today. Those who look to what they regard as higher values will take a different approach. But if freedom is ever lost, it will be because enough people are convinced that at last they have found Albion, and when they place controls on the press, they will find that the controls will be exercised on themselves as well."

Reedy, Gerard. "That Obscenity." *America*, 123:371–73, 7 November 1970.   **1R55**
In this review of the report of the U.S. Commission on Obscenity and Pornography, the author, a Catholic priest, finds the majority report a brave attempt at "a cool-minded analysis of a heated, vastly controversial phenomenon in contemporary culture. It makes its greatest contribution by communicating the results of research it initiated into the production, distribution, uses and effects of pornography in the late 1960's." The minority confronts the majority with different data or with different readings of the same data. While recognizing the serious nature of the charges made by the minority, their case is marred by inflammatory language. The full report, majority and minority, deserves careful study.

Rees, Goronwy. *Brief Encounters*. London, Chatto & Windus, 1974. 193p.   **1R56**
Several essays deal with censorship issues, including commentary on the Moors murder trial, in which there were references to Marquis de Sade's *Justine* and literary censorship; a review of Pamela Hansford Johnson's attack on pornography in her book, *On Iniquity;* and comments on the *Oz* case and its reflection on the nature of society. "Both *On Iniquity* and its critical reception," the author writes, "illustrate the extraordinary confusion which surrounds all our ideas about censorship at the present time and how much we are in need of a thorough and comprehensive study on the subject."

Rees, Marnie. "Promoting Intellectual Freedom—Chapter Style!" *PLA Bulletin* (Pennsylvania Library Association), 27:191–94, July 1972.   **1R57**
How one library association chapter promoted intellectual freedom through exhibits, radio and newspaper publicity.

Rees, William J. "The First Amendment Does Not Protect the Publicizing of Unnewsworthy Private Facts." *Van-*

derbilt Law Review, 29:870–80, April 1976.   **1R58**
In *Virgil v. Time, Inc.*, 527 F.2d 1122 (9th Cir. 1975) the U.S. Court of Appeals, in an action for invasion of privacy, held that absent a showing that the facts publicized are newsworthy, the publicizing of true but private facts is not protected by the First Amendment.

⌐Reeves, John?⌐ *The Legal and Constitutional Principle of the Declaration of the Friends of the Liberty of the Press.* . . . London, 1793. 24p.   **1R59**
An attack on the Friends of the Liberty of the Press and the declaration of Thomas Erskine, made 19 January 1793 at the second meeting of that group. The anonymous author defends the work of the constitutional societies which had been attacked by Erskine and his group for their vigilant efforts to help the authorities stamp out sedition. Another attack on the Friends, An Answer to the Declaration of the Persons Calling Themselves Friends of the Liberty of the Press, appeared in publication No. 4 of the Association, pp. 1–8.

"Reflections on Justice Black and Freedom of Speech." *Valparaiso University Law Review*, 6:316–31, Spring 1972.   **1R60**
"Black's belief in the absolute protection of the content of expression concerned not only expression categorized as subversive, but applied to all subjects and ideas, even to expression which was regarded by most others as slanderous and obscene. . . . While he would afford absolute protection to the kinds of expression he called 'speech,' Black would grant only 'reasonable' protection to expression deemed 'conduct.' . . . Although Black realized that conduct after, if not always, includes an element of expression, he did not feel that such a mode of expression was 'essential' to the preservation of our individual liberties; he therefore believed that conduct could be regulated when confronted by substantial countervailing government interests."

"Reform in the Classification and Declassification of National Security Information: Nixon Executive Order 11,652." *Iowa Law Review*, 59:110–43, October 1973.   **1R61**
"The broad question this Note proposes to deal with is whether Executive Order 11,652 is an adequate solution to the problems of needless government secrecy and overclassification of documents no longer in daily use." The author examines the background and history of classification but does not consider related questions of freedom of the press and the propriety of investigative journalism.

"Reformulation of the Constitutional Privilege to Defame." *University of Kansas Law Review*, 24:406–21, Winter 1976.   **1R62**
The author discusses the nature and development of the constitutional privilege to defame,

examines the majority's objection to the privilege as it had developed prior to *Gertz* [*Gertz v. Robert Welch, Inc.*, 1974] and identifies the respects in which *Gertz* purports to reformulate the privilege.

Regan, John J. "Obscenity Problem: Time for a Truce?" *Catholic World*, 207:70–73, May 1968.   **1R63**
"The doctrinaire on either side would be wise to withhold their condemnation of the [Supreme] Court for its softness or toughness about legal control of obscenity. They would have to recognize that adults for the most part are, and should be, the masters of what they read and see, and the law can do little to change this. At the same time the moral instinct of the American people demands legal protection of the weak, the susceptible, and the unwilling person from the invasion of the purveyor anxious to trade on the sex instinct. Thus the proposed truce would require the warring parties to withdraw from combat over legal issues. They might better direct their efforts toward educating men to be morally responsible toward themselves and toward society."

———. "An Unhurried Look at Obscenity." *Catholic Lawyer*, 13:297–324, Autumn 1967.   **1R64**
The article attempts to summarize the evolution in the Supreme Court's handling of obscenity over the past decade and its significance as seen by some of the major commentators.

Regina, Maria T. "Broadcasting Obscene Language: The Federal Communications Commission and Section 1464 Violations." *Arizona State Law Journal*, 1974:457–84, 1975.   **1R65**
"The FCC recently has imposed penalties against broadcast stations for violating the statutory prohibition against broadcasting obscene language. This Commentary explores the propriety of the FCC's actions in these instances, and concludes that violations for broadcasting obscene language are better left to Justice Department proceedings."

"The Regulation of Advertising." *Columbia Law Review*, 56:1018–1111, November 1956.   **1R66**
Content: Federal Regulation (Federal Trade Commission, Post Office Department, Federal Communications Commission, Security and Exchange Commission). State Regulation (The Printers' Ink and other general statutes, specific regulations of commodities and services, occupational and professional advertising). Self-regulation (advertiser, advertising agency, the media, better business bureaus, the public). Statutory appendix.

"Regulation of Commercial Speech: Commercial Access to the Newspapers." *Maryland Law Review*, 35:115–33, 1975.   **1R67**

"Tornillo [*Miami Herald Publishing Co. v. Tornillo*, 1974] guarantees that as to political and social issues, responsibility [for access] will be left to the journalistic ethics and the whims of the publishing profession. But as a commercial medium, the newspapers' imperfections are not shielded by the first amendment. A limited right of commercial access could constitutionally require newspapers to act responsibly in their control role in the marketplace."

"The Regulation of Competing First Amendment Rights: A New Fairness Doctrine Balance After *CBS?*" *University of Pennsylvania Law Review*, 122:1283–1329, May 1974.   **1R68**
"It is the purpose of this Comment to propose standards which could aid the [Federal Communications] Commission in reaching principled decisions, while simultaneously protecting the first amendment rights of all the affected parties."

The Regulation of Corporate Image Advertising." *Minnesota Law Review*, 59:189–222, November 1974.   **1R69**
"This Note will outline the development and use of corporate image advertising, evaluate the extent of first amendment protection, and discuss possible FTC regulation."

"The Regulation of Televised Violence." *Stanford Law Review*, 26:1291–1325, June 1974.   **1R70**
The article summarizes studies which show the negative impact of television aggression on societal attitudes and behavior and as an instigator of aggressive acts; it attempts to determine the elements that increase the likelihood of viewer aggression; suggests a specific policy for eliminating the adverse effect while protecting the discussion of public issues and dramatic expression; examines the most effective means of enacting the proposed restrictions, and argues that new congressional legislation is necessary.

Rehbinder, Manfred. *Die Informationspflicht der Behörden im Recht der Vereinigten Staaten*. Berlin, Duncker & Humblot, 1970. 68p. (Berliner Abhandlungen zum Presserecht, Heft 10).   **1R71**
Historical development and operation of the Freedom of Information Act of 1966 in the United States.

Rehnquist, William H., and Anthony L. Mondello. "Rights in Conflict—Reconciling Privacy with the Public's Right to Know: A Panel." *Law Library Journal*, 63:551–63, November 1970.   **1R72**
Mr. Rehnquist, then Assistant Attorney General, discusses the role of the Department of Justice in administration of the Freedom of Information Act; Mr. Mondello addresses

himself to the policies and practices of one federal agency, the Civil Service Commission, concerning the protection of privacy of employees. Marvin P. Hogan is moderator.

Reid, de Lafayette. "The Teachers Versus Pornography." *Catholic Library World*, 38:513–14, April 1967.   **1R73**
The librarian and teacher have but one recourse in the defense against the assault of pornography on the young mind and that is in nonlegal modes of value reinforcement; they must give sound reason for morality in all human action.

Reid, Francis. *Prosecution and Committal to Jail of Mr. Francis Reid, at the Instance of the Glasgow Stamped Newspaper Press, Under a Charge of Selling Unstamped Newspapers*. Glasgow, John Thomson [1835?]. 8p.   **1R74**

Rein, Irving J. *et al.* "Pornography in Mass Communication: Some Test Cases." In Speech Communication Association. *Abstracts, 58th Annual Meeting*. Chicago, The Association, 1972, pp. 55–56.   **1R75**
Abstracts of comments by Irving J. Rein, Obscenity: The Problems of Form; William C. Donaghy, Statement of Central Issues and Positions Regarding Pornography in Mass Communications; and Edward DeRoo, Is Pornography in the Ear of the Beholder? Chairman: Frank E. Beaver.

Reische, Diana. "Censorship and Obscenity: What's Happened to Taste?" *Senior Scholastic*, 89(5):12–14, 14 October 1966. (Reprinted in Paul C. Holmes and Anita J. Lehman, *eds., Keys to Understanding, Receiving and Sending*. New York, Harper & Row, 1968, pp. 226–37)   **1R76**
The article raises questions considered by the courts in attempting to write a clear definition of obscenity and to protect freedom of speech and press, and still shelter the general public from blatant indecency and smut.

Reisner, Robert G. *Show Me the Good Parts: The Reader's Guide to Sex Literature*. New York, Citadel, 1968. 340p. **1R77**
A reference work which indexes and annotates the salacious sections of more than 700 novels. Works are classified under such headings as adultery, exhibitionism, homosexuality, incest, petting, rape, seduction, voyeurism, etc. He omits pornographic works but includes many novels that have been banned or subject to controversy over their sexual content.

Reitman, Alan. "The Pentagon v. The Press; Government Secrecy." *Newsletter on Intellectual Freedom* (IFC-ALA), 21:4–9, January 1972; 21:38–44, March 1972. **1R78**
The associate director of the American Civil Liberties Union charges the Nixon Administration with shamefully exercising prior censorship over the mass media. "The much-publicized *Pentagon Papers* case, which fortunately had a successful Supreme Court conclusion, is but the latest episode of a far-reaching campaign by the Nixon Administration to attack the journalistic function." In addition to this "flagrant abuse of government power," the author cites other threats to the freedom of information: the non-publishing of information of concern to the people, threats from the vice-president which have had a chilling effect on the media, action against broadcast licensees, pressure for subpoenas to disclose reporters' sources of news, the investigation of CBS for its documentary, *The Selling of the Pentagon*, and the misuse of security classification and "executive privilege" to cover up questionable government actions. He suggests that citizens take advantage of their constitutional right to protest, make use of the Freedom of Information Act to get information from government agencies, and join with other agencies such as the American Civil Liberties Union, in exposing all threats to liberty.

———. "The Public Information Law and Libraries." *New York Library Association Bulletin*, 15:166–69, 178–80, November–December 1967. **1R79**
The author discusses the features of the new Freedom of Information law, unsettled questions about its coverage and operation, some of which directly affect librarians.

———, ed. *The Pulse of Freedom: American Liberties: 1920–1970*. New York, Norton, 1975. 352p. **1R80**
In this collection of six articles on intellectual freedom are numerous references to censorship. Paul L. Murphy in Communities in Conflict refers to the Scopes trial, the trial of Mary Ware Dennett, and the *Ulysses* case; William Preston, Jr., in Shadows of War and Fear discusses the work of the Legion of Decency, the attacks on public school textbooks, and the crusades of Jehovah's Witnesses; John W. Caughey in McCarthyism Rampant considers the war against subversion; and Milton R. Konvitz in The Flower and the Thorne discusses such obscenity cases as *Roth v. United States*, *Tropic of Cancer* and *Fanny Hill*.

Reitman, Bob. *Freedom on Trial: The Incredible Ordeal of Ralph Ginzburg*. Foreword by Sloan Wilson. San Diego, Calif., Publishers Export, 1966. 218p. **1R81**

A spirited defense of Ralph Ginzburg, convicted by the U.S. Supreme Court on obscenity charges. Wilson, chairman of the Committee to Protest Absurd Censorship, asserts that Ginzburg is being "hounded and jailed by the sexually dispossessed."

Religious Society of Friends. *An Address on Some Growing Evils of the Day, especially Demoralizing Literature and Art, from the Representatives of the Religious Society of Friends, for Pennsylvania, New Jersey, and Delaware. Second Month, 10, 1882*. Philadelphia, The Society, 1882. 16p. **1R82**
Works of fiction, "whatever may be their claims to literary merit, often present false views of life, or aims that are far from elevating; and by stimulating the fancy with dreams which they cannot realize, the young of either sex are frequently led into unwise courses or improper connections. . . . It is to the evils growing out of these and kindred abuses of the printing-press that we feel the community needs to be thoroughly aroused." The corrective for this is to be found not in censorship but "in a fuller and more practical acceptance of our Lord Jesus Christ."

Relyea, Harold C. "Opening Government to Public Scrutiny: A Decade of Federal Efforts." *Public Administration Review*, 35:3–10, January 1975. **1R83**
A synopsis of efforts made during the past decade to make government information from the executive branch more accessible to other branches of government, to the press, and the public.

Rembar, Charles. *The End of Obscenity: The Trials of Lady Chatterley, Tropic of Cancer, and Fanny Hill*. New York, Random House, 1968. 528p. (The Bantam Books edition has an introduction by Norman Mailer) **1R84**
The personal account of a legal revolution, told by the principal attorney who defended *Lady Chatterley's Lover*, *Tropic of Cancer*, and *Fanny Hill* against the censors. The author tells the dramatic story of these trials, using actual testimony (including that of distinguished critics) and arguments of counsel. The trials show the rapid change that took place in the attitude of the courts toward obscenity since the celebrated *Ulysses* decision of 1933, which countenanced obscene passages and ideas if "submerged" in a great quantity of highly esteemed nonsexual material. Rembar, in court, frankly admitted the sexually exciting and lustful quality of the works he was defending, but argued for freedom of sexual expression. The freeing of *Fanny Hill*, he believes, marks the triumph of the idea—the "end of obscenity."

———. "First Amendment on Trial: The Government, the Press, and the Public." *Atlantic*, 231(4):45–54, April 1973. **1R85**

An epoch in the history of the First Amendment has ended and another begun. The Nixon Administration chants devotion to free press but does not support it in its actions. The momentous free press issues today, despite the preoccupation with obscenity, are political—not religious or literary. While the freedom to express opinion has long been established, freedom to express fact in a complex culture (witness the Pentagon Papers) is now a major issue. Another recent facet in press freedom is the emphasis on the right of access to the media, which would enable those who have facts to be heard. "While the information needed has become more extensive and more complex, the means of communicating it have become constricted." The author discusses the recent conflicts between the news media and the government over news sources, a conflict between guarding the government versus guarding the people. "Immunity for newsmen," the author believes, "should be the rule and if an exception is to be made, the burden of proving its necessity should be on the government." On the Nixon Administration, the author comments: "Our present law is not good enough, but it is pretty good. Our present channels of communications are not good enough, but they are, in significant numbers, pretty independent. The main trouble is a government that has no respect for either."

———. "Obscenity and the Constitution: A Different Opinion." *Publishers' Weekly*, 205(2):77–79, 14 January 1974. (Also in his *Perspective*, pp. 111–19) **1R86**
The author takes issue with Harriet Pilpel's comments on obscenity laws (*Publishers' Weekly*, 10 December 1973), finding the picture not so bright following the *Roth* decision (it held that obscenity was not protected under the First Amendment) nor as gloomy as Ms. Pilpel views the situation following the 21 June 1973 decision of the U.S. Supreme Court. He believes there is an unwarranted anxiety among writers and publishers that "can create a climate that, quite needlessly, may have a bad effect upon the Court's future decisions."

———. "The Outrageously Immoral Fact." In Harry M. Clor, *ed.*, *Censorship and Freedom of Expression*, Chicago, Rand McNally, 1971, pp. 27–48. **1R87**
"The outrageously immoral fact," according to the author, "is that the only morality for whose sake the law has been willing to suppress books is sexual morality. Even if the attempt held a promise of success—even if it were true (and to my mind it is not) that decent sexual behavior is retarded rather than advanced by freedom of expression—it would make no sense to deny free speech and a free press in order to deal with just one small corner of morality. . . . Unless we are ready to embrace censorship with the idea of promoting all virtue—not just one of its meaner aspects—we cannot justify censorship at all."

———. "Paper Victory: The United States v. The New York Times and the

Washington Post." *Atlantic*, 228(5): 61–66, November 1971. (Also in his *Perspective*, pp. 131–50) **1R88**
A critique of the Pentagon Papers decision of the U.S. Supreme Court. "There was no occasion for hurrahs at the decision. There was occasion for remorse. The publication was certainly important; the judicial victory was not. The legal arguments that the newspapers made were paltry. The Justices' opinions were too narrow and too broad, and in thought and writing far below the usual level of Supreme Court opinions. A great chance was fumbled." The author examines in detail both the arguments and the opinions. The December issue prints a letter to the editor from A. M. Rosenthal and a rejoinder from the author.

————. *Perspective*. New York, Arbor House, 1975. 264p. **1R89**
A series of essays dealing with the theme of individual freedom in a democratic society and the primacy of the First Amendment in protecting that freedom. Included are: an account of the trial of Dr. Spock for expressing opposition to the Vietnam war; the case of *Evergreen* [*Review*] *v. Cahn*, an obscenity trial involving prior restraint in which the author served as defense attorney; several observations on the state of obscenity laws and decisions on artistic and literary freedom; the case of the Pentagon Papers, involving the *New York Times* and the *Washington Post*; First Amendment issues in the Watergate affair, the impeachment process, and the Nixon tapes. Throughout, the author holds the optimistic view that, despite roadblocks and setbacks, recent events have affirmed the vitality of the First Amendment. A number of the essays had appeared as journal articles.

————. "You Can't Show That on TV." *TV Guide*, 22(41):4–9, 12 October 1974. **1R90**
Following a brief review of the history of obscenity censorship in England and the United States, the author discusses the progression of Supreme Court decisions that have set increasing liberal standards for assessing obscenity. He points out the difference between reading an obscene book, which is a private affair, and the public display of sex which may be thrust upon unwilling persons. He notes the greater impact of motion pictures and television, the latter which comes into the home and is seen by children. Television is an obtrusive medium and "the close-to-absolute freedom that is now enjoyed by writers and publishers of books will not be granted to television. . . . Television . . . can look forward to an increasing freedom of expression. But it will be a long time before you will see—if you will ever see—'Deep Throat' on network television at 6 o'clock in the evening."

Remelgas, Alexandra. *News Reporting and Editorial Interpretation of the Palmer Raids, 1919–1920 By Three Detroit Daily Newspapers: A Study*. East Lansing, Mich., Michigan State University,

1970. 141p. (Unpublished Master's thesis) **1R91**
This study examines three Detroit daily newspapers during the Palmer Raids that took place in the Wilson Administration: the *Free Press*, the *Journal*, and the *News*. News stories in the *Free Press* and *Journal* were written with a progovernment bias that assumed the arrested were guilty of conspiring to overthrow the government. The *News*, on the other hand, reported the affair objectively in its news stories and with understanding in its editorials.

"Removal of Supreme Court Appellate Jurisdiction: A Weapon Against Obscenity?" *Duke Law Journal*, 1969: 291–325, April 1969. **1R92**
"This comment intends to explore the limitations which may be placed upon congressional action based on the exceptions and regulations clause, particularly as that action is related to the review the Court has exercised and the tests it has sought to formulate to afford maximum first amendment protection in the area of obscenity."

Rendleman, Douglas. "Free Press–Fair Trial: Review of Silence Orders." *North Carolina Law Review*, 52:127–64, November 1973. **1R93**
"The problem to be described and analyzed in this article is how to obtain appellate review of a silence order issued in a criminal proceeding. . . . This article will examine the media's procedural routes from the criminal action into an appellate court: terminal review, interlocutory review, review by prerogative writ, and review of contempt."

Reno, Donald M., Jr. "Obscenity Revisited—1972." *American Bar Association Journal*, 58:736–39, July 1972. **1R94**
"The enigma posed by official attempts to use the criminal law to control or prevent the dissemination of obscenity has remained unsolved by the Supreme Court, which proclaimed the *Roth* doctrine in 1957, retreated from it but then apparently returned to it in 1971. Obscenity cases require an inordinate amount of law enforcement and court time. Perhaps a new Oregon statute points the way to rational dealing with obscenity."

————. "People v. Ridens: The Witchcraft of the Illinois Obscenity Law Survives." *Illinois Bar Journal*, 63:640–45, July 1975. **1R95**
"Despite bitter controversial, legal and philosophical arguments about the right of adults to read and view sexually oriented materials, the decision of *People v. Ridens* affirmed the Illinois obscenity law permitting imprisonment for those commercially disseminating 'obscene materials.' This article reviews the intractable obscenity quagmire and questions the continued criminal penalties of existing obscenity laws in Illinois."

"Reporter Has First Amendment Right to Refuse to Appeal and Testify Before Grand Jury About Confidential Sources and Information." *Harvard Law Review*, 84:1536–47, April 1971. **1R96**
The comment deals with the case of *Caldwell v. United States* (434 F.2d 1081) in which a U.S. Court of Appeals upheld the refusal of a newsman to appear and testify before a grand jury with respect to confidential news sources. The U.S. Supreme Court subsequently reversed the decision.

"Reporter Has No Constitutional Right to Preserve Anonymity of an Informer if Court Orders Disclosure." *Harvard Law Review*, 82:1384–91, April 1969. **1R97**
The case of *State v. Buchanan* (1968), in which the editor of the student newspaper at the University of Oregon was denied newsman's privilege to withhold news sources when ordered by a court.

"Reporters and Their Sources: The Constitutional Right to a Confidential Relationship." *Yale Law Journal*, 80: 317–71, 1970. **1R98**
"This Note will argue that, subject to carefully delineated exceptions applicable to criminal trials and certain libel actions, the First Amendment should guarantee a broad right to keep communications and the identities of informants confidential when news gatherers are summoned before courts, grand juries, and legislative committees. An evaluation of the conflicting positions will suggest that the First Amendment interest of the newsman and his source in knowing with *certainty* when the confidentiality of their relationship will be respected (and when it will not) should be accorded substantially greater weight than the government's claim for a roving commission to gain access to communications arising from this relationship. This evaluation also provides guidance in deciding the scope of protection, who may claim the right of nondisclosure, what types of information the right protects, and when the right may be invoked."

The Reporters Committee for Freedom of the Press. Legal Defense and Research Fund. *How to Use the New 1974 FOI Act*. Washington, D.C., The Committee, 1975. 8p., 11p. (Part 1 is a supplement to the April–May 1975 issue of *Press Censorship Newsletter*; part 2 is a supplement to the October–November issue) **1R99**
The guide is based on information compiled by the Committee, the Freedom of Information Clearinghouse of the Department of the Army,

more than thirty other federal agencies, and the staff of the Senate Judiciary Committee. Part 2 contains case summaries of 225 pending FOI Act cases involving twenty-three major federal agencies.

———. *Press Censorship Newsletter*. Washington, D.C., The Committee, 1973–date. Issued three times a year. **1R100**

The Committee was formed in 1970 in response to the threat by the Justice Department's subpoena policy. It is "the only legal research and defense fund organization in the nation exclusively devoted to protecting the First Amendment and freedom of information interests of the working press of all media." The *Newsletter* and a periodic *News Media Alert* report on legal actions affecting the First Amendment and freedom of information interests of the news media on federal, state, and local levels, and calls attention to new developments and trends in the following areas: confidentiality of news sources, prior restraints on publication, privacy and libel, freedom of information, fair trial–free press and access to the courts, the broadcasting media, antitrust and access to the media, high school and college press, and employment. In October 1977 *The News Media & The Law* (eight times a year) replaced the *Press Censorship Newsletter*.

"The Reporter's Privilege: A New Urgency." *Washington University Law Quarterly*, 1971:478–84, Summer 1971. **1R101**

Re: *Caldwell v. United States*, 434 F.2d 1081 (1970).

A Representation of the Impiety and Immorality of the English Stage. London, J. Nutt, 1704. 24p. **1R102**

This pamphlet and a similar version, *A Short Account of the Impiety and Immorality of the English Stage*, revived the Jeremy Collier attacks on the stage (1698), encouraged by a great storm on the night of 26 November 1703 which was interpreted as a sign of God's wrath on the city of London for disapproval of the stage. The later edition was distributed in churches. Graham D. Harley (*Notes and Queries*, February 1971) attributes the work to one or more members of the Society for the Reformation of Manners.

"Requirement of the Certification of Newspaper Campaign Advertisements Under Federal Election Campaign Act of 1971 Is An Unconstitutional Prior Restraint of Speech." *Harvard Law Review*, 87:1568–79, May 1974. **1R103**

Re: *American Civil Liberties Union, Inc. v. Jennings*, 366 F. Supp 1041 (D.D.C., 1973), *appeal docketed sub non. Staats v. American Civil Liberties Union, Inc.*, 42 U.S.L.W. 3542 (U.S. Mar. 20, 1974) (No. 1413).

Resneck, William A. "The Duty of Newspapers to Accept Political Advertising—An Attack on Tradition." *Indiana Law Journal*, 44:222–41, Winter 1969. **1R104**

"Distinguishing political from commercial advertisements and identifying inflammatory or obscene matter may be difficult in some cases, but differentiating 'public officials' and 'public figures' is no less difficult. Subways, terminal stations and shopping centers now serve as forums for public expression. The creation of a right of access to newspapers is long overdue. . . . If we should not hold newspapers liable for good faith judgment not to publish, neither is it equitable to force advertisers to undertake court actions seeking an injunction and/or damages in order to have their advertisements published."

Resnik, Solomon. "Black, Douglas, and Absolutes: Some Suggestions for a New Perspective on the Supreme Court." *Journal of Urban Law*, 47:765–95, 1969/70. **1R105**

The author suggests that "a categorizing of Black and Douglas as absolutists is completely inappropriate since they too are clearly searching for the requisite balance between liberty and order and are willing, if the circumstances are serious enough, to allow restrictions on First Amendment rights. What they seem to be doing is using absolutist terminology simply to emphasize the vital importance of First Amendment rights and to set up an ideal which the Court must strive for but not necessarily obtain."

"Resolving the Free Speech–Free Press Dichotomy: Access to the Press Through Advertising." *University of Florida Law Review*, 22:293–320, Fall 1969. **1R106**

"This note is an attempt to describe the increasing incidence of suppression of free expression in the nation's newspapers. This suppression gives rise to the free speech–free press dichotomy. It is asserted that a positive view of the first amendment requires that access to the press be afforded the individual. Further, the right declared by newspapers to decline to accept advertisements at will cannot apply where the advertiser is exercising his constitutionally protected freedom of expression. Free speech, as a preferred freedom, must not be allowed to be impaired by the capricious acts of press management."

Rettig, Salomon. "A Note on Censorship and the Changing Ethic of Sex." *Ethics*, 78:151–55, January 1968. **1R107**

"It would seem that any censorship of sexual expression today is largely an unwarranted form of control over individual conduct, made possible by the diffuse conscience of the zealot. The damage due to censorship is not only in the individual unfreedom it creates but perhaps even more in the greatly exaggerated importance of sex on the part of the cultural mass media as well as on the part of the individual. Freud notwithstanding, sex is basically not so serious as to justify the multimillion-dollar industry created for the purpose of circumventing obscenity laws."

"Reverse-Freedom of Information Act Suits: Confidential Information in Search of Protection." *Northwestern University Law Review*, 70:995–1019, January–February 1976. **1R108**

"That the FOIA's purpose is to provide for broad disclosure of Government-held information is undeniable. This mandate of openness, however, is tempered by the protective purposes served by the Act's exemptions and the congressional intent to protect the competitive position of information-submitting individuals. Reverse-FOIA actions, suits to prevent the release of certain information, are consistent with this congressional intent."

Reynolds, John R. "Four Years of FOI Law: Is Secrecy Gap Widened?" *Editor & Publisher*, 107(20):14, 36, 38, 16 May 1970. **1R109**

A review of the operations of the Freedom of Information Act after four years reveals some dissatisfaction with the broad exemptions, the lengthy process of judicial review, and widespread violations and evasions. Reference is made to Ralph Nader's efforts to enforce compliance.

Reynolds, Joseph H. "Gag Order, Exclusion and the Press's Right to Information." *Albany Law Review*, 39:317–35, 1975. (Reprinted in *PEAL Quarterly*, Fall 1975) **1R110**

"A survey of recent cases and contact with several district attorneys' offices have revealed only one case in which New York courts have issued the type of 'gag orders' sanctioned in *Sheppard v. Maxwell*. The courts have chosen to utilize the traditional methods available for protecting defendants against adverse publicity and maintaining their fair trial rights."

Reynolds, Margaret. "England Restricts Freedom to Publish." *Publishers' Weekly*, 200(4):27–28, 26 July 1971. **1R111**

The case of *The Little Red School Book*.

———. " 'Last Exit' Verdict Casts Doubt on U.K. Obscenity Laws." *Publishers' Weekly*, 192(24):20–21, 11 December 1967. **1R112**

An account of the obscenity trial at Old Bailey in which Hubert Selby Jr.'s *Last Exit to Brooklyn*, was judged obscene. "The verdict has thrown British publishing circles into confusion. Scarcely a major publisher is without one or more books on his list as liable to prosecution. The case not only points up the frightening randomness of obscenity prosecutions and the exorbitant costs of defense, but also leaves these unanswered questions: (1) Can a serious work now survive the 1959 Act? . . . (2) Although private citizens can no longer initiate obscenity prosecutions, what restraints exist against the police? . . . [and] (3) Can the United Kingdom and the United States, the two largest English-speaking nations, remain 'out of phase' as far as contemporary standards go? It is doubtful that the British reading public will long tolerate being held in tutelage. Cultural and tourist interchanges militate against any great differences in what is permissible."

Reynolds, Osborne M., Jr. "Defamation from the Grave: Testamentary Libel." *California Western Law Review*, 7:91–108, Fall 1970.   **1R113**
The problem "concerns the testator who uses his will as a final opportunity to heap abuse upon an enemy. The questions that here arise concern (1) the liability of the executor of the will; (2) the liability of the decedent's estate; (3) the power of the courts to delete defamatory passages from the will; and (4) the executor's duty to have deletions made."

Reynolds, Ransom P., Jr. "Self-defense in Defamation or 'Re-tort Not Reply.' " *Albany Law Review*, 34:95–106, Fall 1969.   **1R114**
A discussion of case law involving the right of reply to defamatory comments and the implications of such a counterattack being defamatory.

Reynolds, Richard R. "Our Misplaced Reliance on Early Obscenity Cases." *American Bar Association Journal*, 61:220–22, February 1975.   **1R115**
"Some courts are misplacing reliance on early English obscenity cases. A careful examination of four eighteenth-century obscenity cases reveals that the issues were largely political since the materials brought before the courts were chiefly political in nature and the prosecutions equally political." Cases considered: *The King v. Sir Charles Sedley* (1663), *The Queen v. James Read* (1707), *The King v. Edmund Curll* (1721), and *The King v. John Wilkes* (1770).

Rice, Elmer. "The Stranglehold of Censorship." In Alan Reitman, *ed.*, *The Price of Liberty*. New York, Norton, 1968, pp. 132–64.   **1R116**
A broad review of the development of censorship in the various media in the United States and Britain and, conversely, the growth of opposition to censorship. Special attention to the motion pictures and the theater.

Rice, George P., Jr. "Freedom of Access to Information: The Right to Privacy." *Vital Speeches*, 42:329–32, 15 March 1976.   **1R117**
An examination of the 1974 Freedom of Information Act as it makes government information more available to citizens at large, but

especially to teachers and publishing scholars and the legal profession.

———. "Freedom of Speech and the 'New Left.' " *Central States Speech Journal*, 21:139–45, Fall 1970.   **1R118**
"This article examines the role and responsibilities of the 'New Left' in current social contexts. It explores, specifically, the legal rights and obligations of any dissenting group and the part that these dissenting factions play in our society." Charles M. Rossiter, Jr. and Ruth McGaffey, criticize the analysis made by Rice in their article, Freedom of Speech and the "New Left": A Response, in the Spring 1971 issue.

———. "Survey of Cases and Controversies, July 1, 1967–June 30, 1968." In *1968 Yearbook of the Committee on Freedom of Speech of the Speech Association of America*. n.p., The Association, 1968, pp. 7–12.   **1R119**
Includes references to *Ginsberg v. State of New York* (1968), *Dickey v. Alabama State Board of Education* (1967), and *Commonwealth (Pa.) v. Dell Publishers, Inc.* (1968).

Rice, H. Hamilton. "The Youth-Obscenity Problem: A Proposal." *Kentucky Law Journal*, 52:429–47, 1964.   **1R120**
"While there is an absence of scientific authority to demonstrate adverse effects resulting from juvenile consumption of obscene and near-obscene, sex-oriented publications, the growing concern of parents, educators and law enforcement officials that there is a very real danger to our young as well as to society as a whole, should be accommodated by the enactment of special state antiobscenity statutes designed to protect only that class. It is believed that such legislation would be found to be a valid exercise of the police powers of the state."

Rice, Jan P. "The Sheppard Case: Twenty Years Later." *Grassroots Editor*, 15(6):16–23, November–December 1974.   **1R121**
In this review of the issue of free press v. fair trial, the author criticizes the *Cleveland Press* for its lack of ethical behavior in covering the trial. "The prosecution was intent on getting a guilty verdict because of fear of editorial criticism from the *Cleveland Press* if the state did not 'solve the case.' "

Richards, Benjamin A. "The Historical Rationale of the Speech-and-Press Clause of the First Amendment." *University of Florida Law Review*, 21:203–17, Fall 1968.   **1R122**
An inquiry into the thinking that went into the formulation of the speech and press clause of the First Amendment and how it was interpreted in the early years of the republic. "It

seems safe to conclude that the intended purpose of the speech-and-press clause was just what Republican critics of the Sedition Act said it was: to safeguard the free discussion of public characters and measures to the end that capable and honorable men should be elected to public office and governmental power be scrupulously and responsibly exercised." The author qualifies his statement with three points: (1) the framers may have expected the courts to have common law jurisdiction over seditious libel; (2) only Congress is limited from passage of laws abridging speech and press; and (3) concern over states rights may have been an important factor in the adoption of the Amendment.

Richards, Calud H., Jr. *Jehovah's Witnesses: A Study in Religious Freedom*. Durham, N.C., Duke University, 1945. 304p. (Ph.D. dissertation) **1R123**
Chapter 4 deals with the Distribution of Literature: theory of Jehovah's Witnesses concerning their beliefs, permits and the distribution of Witnesses' literature, application of licensing regulations to Witnesses' activities, prohibitions on the use of the streets for the distribution of Witnesses' literature, the law of trespass as applied to Jehovah's Witnesses, child labor laws and the distribution of Witnesses' literature, and the use of laws prohibiting the desecration of the Sabbath in the prosecution of Witnesses.

Richards, David A. J. "Free Speech and Obscenity Law: Toward a Moral Theory of the First Amendment." *University of Pennsylvania Law Review*, 123:45–91, November 1974.   **1R124**
"The purpose of this Article is to explain a contractarian theory of the first amendment and to apply it to the recent obscenity cases. This moral theory is part of a developing line of thought familiar, in the work of Locke, to the framers of the Bill of Rights and developed as well by other philosophers." The 1973 cases of *Miller v. California* and *Paris Adult Theatre I v. Slaton* are examined.

[Richards, G. A.] *Penalty for Patriotism. A Battle for Freedom of Speech*. [Los Angeles, n.p., 1950?] 24p.   **1R125**
An assemblage of articles, editorials, and testimonials in support of G. A. Richards and his television stations, KMPC (Los Angeles), WVR (Detroit) and WGAR (Cleveland) under investigation by the FCC for bias and news-slanting. Richards was an aggressive anti-Communist crusader. Support came from such diverse sources as the American Legion, the *Saturday Evening Post*, the *Washington Post*, all of which saw danger in the FCC embarking upon a policy of censorship.

Richardson, Elliot L. "Freedom of In-

formation." *Loyola Law Review* (New Orleans), 20:45–64, 1974.   **1R126**
The former attorney general of the United States discusses three major areas that bear directly on freedom of information: "(1) the Freedom of Information Act which governs the disclosure of information to the public and its proposed amendment, S. 1142 introduced by Senator Muskie; (2) the need to withhold certain information from the congressional testimony process, or on occasion from Congress, the furnishing of which would be contrary to the public interest (referred to as Executive privilege); (3) the classification system designed to protect information essential to our national security, S.1520 introduced by Senator Roth and the concepts under-lying those provisions in the proposed federal criminal code (S.1400) that provide a basis for the prosecution of those who wrongfully disclose national security information."

Richardson, James B., Jr. "Limitations on the Rights of Privacy—Privilege to Report Matters of Public Interest." *South Carolina Law Review*, 21:92–101, 1968.   **1R127**
The comments relate to torts committed in the invasion of the right of privacy by public disclosure of embarrassing private facts.

Richardson, James R. "What Constitutes Prejudicial Publicity in Pending Cases?" *Kentucky Law Journal*, 54:625–42, Summer 1966.   **1R128**
The author recommends that bar associations and media develop a mutual code of ethics and suggests seven items that should be included.

Richardson, John A. "Dirty Pictures and Campus Comity." *Journal of Aesthetic Education*, 4(3):85–96, July 1970.   **1R129**
The intensification of eroticism's role in art, which the author explores, brings problems in higher education. Displaying the academic nude can be defended on the basis of tradition alone; other things may be unacceptable on the grounds of quality alone. Between resides the area of the "questionable."

Richmond (Calif.) City Council. *Shall The Berkeley Barb and Other Underground Newspapers and Magazines be Banned from the Shelves of the Public Library?* Berkeley, Calif., Pacifica Tape Library, 1968. Phonorecord.   **1R130**
A record of a public hearing of the Richmond (Calif.) City Council called to discuss whether *Berkeley Barb* and *Avant Garde* should be removed from the shelves of the public library. "Sometimes absurd, often deeply moving, the arguments range from the academic to the hysterical and inarticulate." The meeting was

adjourned when a John Birch Society leader demanded the expulsion of an attorney from the American Civil Liberties Union and refused to be quieted. The Library Commission, which had at first supported the librarian's selection, bowed to political and personal pressures and by a vote of 3–2, removed the two items from the shelves.

Richstad, Jim A. *The Press and the Courts Under Martial Rule in Hawaii During World War II—From Pearl Harbor to "Duncan v. Kahanamaku."* Minneapolis, University of Minnesota, 1967. 425p. (Ph.D. dissertation, University Microfilms, no. 67–14,643)   **1R131**

————. *The Press Under Martial Law: The Hawaiian Experience.* Minneapolis, Association for Education in Journalism, 1970. 41p. (*Journalism Monographs*, no. 17)   **1R132**
A study of how the press in Hawaii operated under military rule during World War II. There was first direct censorship of news and advertising in the daily newspapers, and later, self-censorship by newspaper staff members under guidelines established by the army. No publication was permitted unless authorized or licensed by the military governor. There was no precedent for such licensing in American history. No legal challenges were made to military control of the press, and, in fact, the press cooperated fully and wholeheartedly with the military. Based upon the author's doctoral dissertation, *The Press and the Courts Under Martial Rule in Hawaii During World War II.*

Rickards, Maurice. *Banned Posters; Presented and Reviewed.* London, Evelyn, Adams & Mackay, 1969. 72p.   **1R133**
"Each of the posters reproduced has, at one time or another, for one reason or another, fallen foul either of respectable opinion or of law and order. The selection (40 posters) includes not only the more predictable nudities but a wide range of less expected lapses." Some of the illustrations show posters both before and after censorship. The compiler has provided an entertaining and informative commentary. Ironically, a blank space on page 57 indicates that a "before" illustration has been omitted "following representations from the Twentieth Century Fox Corporation."

Rickword, Edgell, ed. *Radical Squibs & Royal Ripostes: Satirical Pamphlets of the Regency Period, 1819–1821. Illustrated by George Cruikshank and Others.* New York, Barnes & Noble, 1971. 319p.   **1R134**
A reprinting of ten of the satirical pamphlets written and published by William Hone and illustrated by George Cruikshank during 1819–21. Two of the parodies included, The Political House that Jack Built (H333) and The Political Showman—at Home! (H334), satirize government attacks on the press. Hone was

charged with blasphemous libel for his parodies on the church catechism, but was acquitted. An account of the trial appears in the editor's introduction, pages 14–21.

Ridgway, James. "Mum's the Word; How Government and Industry Keep Secrets from the People." *New Republic*, 165 (8–9):17–19, 21 and 28 August 1971.   **1R135**
The difficulty experienced by citizen groups and the press in gaining basic information about the energy industry.

Ridley, Clifford. "If Dirty Art Is Censored, Who Will Do the Censoring?" *Newsletter on Intellectual Freedom* (IFO-ALA), 21:28–29, January 1972. (Reprinted from the *National Observer*)   **1R136**
The author takes issue with the arguments for censorship of obscenity presented by Irving Kristol in the *New York Times Magazine* (28 March 1971). In response to Mr. Kristol's assertion that if no one was ever corrupted by a book, no one was ever improved by one either, he comments: "Literary improvement, after all, is a function of the mind, while literary sexual corruption affects a quite different portion of the anatomy."

Riegel, Robert E. "The American Father of Birth Control." *New England Quarterly*, 6:470–90, September 1933.   **1R137**
The story of the backwoods Massachusetts physician, Charles Knowlton, largely responsible for the inception of the birth control movement in America. His book, *Fruits of Philosophy*, published in 1832, resulted in his prosecution and jail sentence (K165).

Riga, Peter. "The Catholic and Obscenity." *Catholic World*, 205:340–45, September 1967.   **1R138**
The real problem of our society is not obscenity but the meaning and signification of love. Obscenity in the broadest sense means a degradation of the human person and, in a society that is insidiously corrupting man's dignity in many other areas, we have singled out only aberration of the sexual sphere for castigation. Father Riga has written this following his defense in court of *The Love Book*, whose ideas are good and theological but which used four-letter words to describe human sexual activity. Father Morton Hill responded in the December 1967 issue.

"Right of Reply Statutes: Unconstitutional Abridgement of the Freedom of the Printed Press." *Northwestern University Law Review*, 69:143–65, March–April 1974.   **1R139**
"This comment examines the constitutionality of the most broad right of reply legislation; that

is, a statute which allows a candidate to reply to all newspaper articles, commentary or editorials concerning his fitness for public office. This analysis focuses on the permissibility of requiring newspapers to publish articles against the will of its editors; moreover, it considers whether right of reply statutes inevitably chill the freedom of the press protected by the first amendment. Finally, the comment considers whether reply statutes are justifiable by the state's interest in fair elections or by the analogy to the right of reply given individuals with respect to broadcast media."

"The Right of the Press to Gather Information." *Columbia Law Review*, 71: 838–64, May 1971. (Also in 1U100)

1R140

"This Note will argue that the first amendment does indeed include the right of the press to gather information, and that where important governmental or societal interests militate against the right—e.g., where a reporter is called to testify, where he is excluded from secret meetings, or where his travel abroad is restricted—existing first amendment standards provide a foundation for devising tests that accommodate these conflicting needs."

"The Right of the Press to Gather Information After *Branzburg* and *Pell*." *University of Pennsylvania Law Review*, 124:166–91, November 1975. **1R141**
"This Comment will examine the constitutional basis for a right of the press to gather information in the face of government restrictions. It will attempt to show that such a right is consistent both with the understanding of freedom of the press in the early United States and with traditional first amendment interpretation. The tentative recognition of that right in *Branzburg v. Hayes* [1972] and its limitation in *Pell v. Procunier* [1974] will then be analyzed, and a more expansive formulation of the right will be proposed."

"The Right to an Adversary Hearing on the Issue of Obscenity Prior to the Seizure of Furtively Distributed Films." *Michigan Law Review*, 69:913–40, April 1971. **1R142**
"This Note will discuss the procedural safeguards that must be provided when allegedly obscene materials are seized prior to distribution." The note also considers whether the same requirements also apply to films, particularly those intended to be distributed furtively.

"Right to Conceal Identity of News Sources—Difficulties in Formulating and Applying the Right to Actual Situations." *Wisconsin Law Review*, 1971: 951–62, 1971. **1R143**
"This note will analyze *Knops* (*State v. Knops*, 49 Wis. 2d 647, 183 N.W.2d 93, 1971) as an illustration of the difficulties in defining and applying a reporter's limited constitutional right to protect his news sources."

The Right to Know. 16 mm. color movie, 17 min. Chicago, Gilbert Allschul Productions, released by Journal Films, 1973. With teacher's guide. **1R144**
"Examines the history of the basic democratic principles of the people's right to know. Describes the personal and institutional obstacles to full freedom of information, and warns that democracy ceases to function unless citizens have access to information."

"The Rights of the Public and the Press to Gather Information." *Harvard Law Review*, 87:1505–33, May 1974. **1R145**
"This Note will . . . analyze the scope of the public and press right to gather news by identifying the weight of these interests in three general situations—when a source is unwilling to provide information, when a source is neutral and access to it is prevented by the state, and when a source would voluntarily provide information were it not for the state's interference."

Riley, David J., *ed. Freedom of Dilemma: Critical Readings in the Mass Media.* Glenview, Ill., Scott, Foresman, 1971. 295p. **1R146**
Chapter 2, Electronic Violence: Is TV Brutalizing Your Child? by Eliot A. Daley. More Violent Than Ever by Richard L. Tobin. When Nonviolence Hurts by Joseph Finnigan. TV Violence and Sports by Harry J. Cargas. Who Killed Benny Paret? by Norman Cousins. Violence in Television Entertainment Programs (Eisenhower Commission Report). The Battle Rages Again by Edith Efron. Chapter 3, The Media and the Courts: Trial by Headline by Louis Nizer. Justice, the Press, and My Lai (*Newsweek*). The Narrow Confines of British Crime Reporting by Norman Moss. For Fair Trial and Free Press by Alexander Bodi. Reason Dethroned (*Nation*). A Crack in Canon 35 by Herbert Brucker. Newsmen and Their Confidential Sources by Abraham S. Goldstein. Mitchell and the Media (*National Review*). Chapter 4, Fair Comment or Intimidation? Agnew at Des Moines by Spiro Agnew. Agnew at Montgomery by Spiro Agnew. Commentary on Agnew by James Reston. A Question of Television's Power by James J. Kilpatrick. A Question of Reporting by Herbert Brucker. Rampant on a Field of Skewered Snobs by Tom Wicker. Bull's-Eyes and Bombast by William Randolph Hearst, Jr. Speaking for Myself Alone by Howard K. Smith. Some Sober Second Thoughts on Vice-President Agnew by Fred W. Friendly. The Dangers of Television Sportscasting by Art Buchwald. Chapter 5, "Not to Be Released Until . . .": The Danger of Getting Used to Lies by Robert M. Shaw. The Government Has the Right to Lie by Arthur Sylvester. (But Don't Tell Anyone I Told You) by Seymour M. Hersh. Does the *Washington Post* Lie by Stewart Alsop. How to Make Things Worse by James Reston. Where TV Fails by Robert E. Kintner. The Credibility Myth by Kenneth Crawford. The Leakiest Winter on Record by Clayton Fritchey. Off-the-Record by TRB. Chapter 6, Politics and the Wired City: Why

Not Ban Political Broadcasting? by John Osborne.

Riley, Samuel G., III. *The Free Press–Fair Trial Controversy: A Discussion of the Issues Involved and an Examination of Pretrial Publicity by Survey Research.* Chapel Hill, N.C., University of North Carolina, 1970. 230p. (Ph.D. dissertation, University Microfilms, no. 71–11740) **1R147**
"This study has a twofold purpose: (1) to present the many points and issues in the controversy raised by both bar-bench and media without requiring the reader to ferret out the issues from a welter of court cases and other historical material and (2) to examine the effects of pretrial publicity on potential jurors in an actual, on-going criminal case."

———. "Pretrial Publicity: A Field Study." *Journalism Quarterly*, 50:17–23, Spring 1973. **1R148**
"In the MacDonald case, no evidence was found to support a change of venue or venire; yet what people know about a crime appears to influence prejudgment, and—again—mere arrest seems to predispose to 'guilt.' "

Ringel, William E. *Obscenity Law Today.* New York, Gould, 1970. 245p. **1R149**
"My purpose is to set forth the law pertaining to obscenity, and *a priori* of free speech, as presently interpreted and applied by our courts." The author examines the history, philosophy, and application of the First Amendment to the obscenity issue and sets forth tests which must be administered in judging material to be legally obscene. Appendix A, *New York v. Emilio Stabile* (1969), with the decision of Judge Ringel; Appendix B, Representative Obscenity Decisions, listed under the name of the offending publication or production.

Rintels, David W. "On Censorship: Not for Bread Alone." *Performance*, 3:49–55, July–August 1972. **1R150**
In response to criticisms by Stanley Kauffmann (July–August 1972), Rintels denies television is "surprisingly good." It is "godawful by any standard." Rintels believes television in its entertainment sector is presenting a distorted picture of American life and not in the public interest. Since "make-believe makes belief," greater attention should be given to realism in fiction. He cites network censorship of drama dealing factually with Vietnam.

Ripley, Joseph M., Jr. "An Argument for Television in the Courtroom." *Journal of Broadcasting*, 12(1):23–31, Winter 1967/68. (Reprinted in John M. Kit-

tross and Kenneth Harwood, *eds.*, *Free and Fair*, pp. 64–72) **1R151**
"Some of the materials used in this article were originally gathered for the purpose of gaining permission for University of Wisconsin's WHA-TV to televise the proceedings of the trial of *Jane C. Braun, et al. v. the City of Madison, Otto Festge, Mayor of the City of Madison, et al.*"

———. *The Practices and Policies Regarding Broadcasts of Opinions about Controversial Issues by Radio and Television Stations in the United States.* Columbus, Ohio, Ohio State University, 1961. 279p. (Ph.D. dissertation, University Microfilms, no. 62–805) **1R152**
"This is a report of two descriptive studies of the broadcasting stations of the United States concerning their practices and policies regarding broadcasts of viewpoints about controversial issues. . . . The major conclusions drawn from the data collected by questionnaires were (1) that a great many broadcasting stations failed to meet their obligation to devote an adequate amount of time to broadcasts featuring points of view about public issues during either of the two study periods; (2) that generally the respondents felt the station had a duty to treat both sides of an issue fairly."

Rist, Ray C. "Polity, Politics and Social Research: A Study in the Relationship of Federal Commissions and Social Science." *Social Problems*, 21:113–28, Summer 1973. (Reprinted in his *The Pornography Controversy*, pp. 244–68) **1R153**
An attempt to assess the political and cultural influences upon the U.S. Commission on Obscenity and Pornography. "Within the context of a natural history of the Commission, I shall examine the cumulative political response to the final Commission report." The aim is not to evaluate the findings but "to elucidate the public and political nature of commission-type policy research and decision-making."

———, ed. *The Pornography Controversy: Changing Moral Standards in American Life.* New Brunswick, N.J., Transaction, 1975. 279p. **1R154**
Content: Pornography as a Social Problem: Reflections on the Relation of Morality and Law by Ray C. Rist. Obscenity as an Esthetic Category by Abraham Kaplan. Beyond the (Garbage) Pale, or Democracy, Censorship and The Arts by Walter Berns. Legislative Recommendations: Report of the Committee on Obscenity and Pornography. Pornography—Raging Menace or Paper Tiger? by John H. Gagnon and William Simon. Obscenity Laws—A Shift to Reality by Earl Warren, Jr. Pornographic Theaters Off Times Square by Joseph P. Slade. The Pleasures of Commodity,

or How to Make the World Safe for Pornography by Peter Michelson. Moral Principles Toward a Definition of the Obscene by Harold J. Gardiner. The Modern Machiavelians: The Pornography of Sexual Game-Playing by John MacGregor. Night Words: High Pornography and Human Privacy by George Steiner. The Effects of Explicit Sexual Materials: The Report of the Commission on Obscenity and Pornography. Violence, Pornography and Social Science by James Q. Wilson. Polity, Politics and Social Research: A Study of the Relationship of Federal Commissions and Social Science by Ray C. Rist.

Ritter, J. A., and Matthew Leibowitz. "Press Councils: The Answer to Our First Amendment Dilemma." *Duke Law Journal*, 1974:845–70, December 1974. **1R155**
"The law can guarantee a free press, but it is incapable of guaranteeing a fair press. The journalism profession must recognize that while its enterprise is and should remain a private business, free from government regulation, its efforts to define and realize standards of performance are also a community concern. A mechanism is needed through which individuals who understand the complexities of modern journalism and members of the community can meet and discuss press performance and press responsibility. Their discussions should not be restrained by strict interpretations of the first amendment; elementary fairness and high journalistic standards should serve as their guides. A press council satisfies this need."

Rivers, William L. *The Adversaries: Politics and the Press.* Boston, Beacon, 1970. 273p. **1R156**
The theme of this work is that, in carrying out their respective responsibilities to society, the proper stance of government and the press is that of adversaries. Professor Rivers states his thesis based on history and political theory and his students at Stanford University support the thesis in a series of case studies taken from the real world of journalism and politics.

———. "How to Kill a Watchdog." *Progressive*, 37(12):44–48, February 1973. **1R157**
"The media are facing a mounting campaign of repression and harassment by a hostile government. Their greatest potential ally in resisting this pressure is the public, but a public that expresses only eighteen percent confidence in the media does not promise much support. An independent council that would help the media keep their own house in order could go far to restore public confidence and give the media the ally they need to combat government suppression." The author discusses at length the widespread criticism of the nation's press to the Twentieth Century Fund's proposal of a Council on Press Responsibility and Press Freedom. "The Council will have no coercive power, no relationship to government. To consider this a threat to freedom is absurd, and yet the ultra sensitivity of so much of the press

made acid reaction entirely predictable." The March issue of *Progressive* carried eight comments to Rivers's article from media executives.

———. "Who Shall Guard the Guards?" *Progressive*, 35(9):23–28, September 1971. **1R158**
The time has arrived, the author believes, to give the public a voice in freedom of the press through a national press council. He sees this as a logical answer to the mounting criticism of the nation's press both from readers and from newspaper staffs. He sees this as preferable to federal laws enforcing right of access to the press.

———, William B. Blankenburg, Kenneth Starck, and Earl Reeves. *Backtalk: Press Councils in America.* San Francisco, Canfield, 1972. 146p. Introduction by Ben H. Bagdikian. **1R159**
"Written by those who established and operated several local press councils under a grant from the Millett Fund for a Free and Responsible Press. *Backtalk* describes these exchanges between citizens and newspapermen and broadcasters, telling why press councils are needed, how they are formed, how they work, what their members say, and what effect they have on the media. The growth of state and regional councils and the development of plans for a national council are also discussed."

Rivers, William L., and Michael J. Nyhan, *eds. Aspen Notebook on Government and the Media.* New York, Praeger, 1973, 193p. (Sponsored by the Aspen Program on Communications and Society) **1R160**
A workshop on government and the media in which participants were top-level government officials, leading journalists and media executives, and distinguished communications educators and attorneys, many of them with both government and media experience. The book consists of a prologue by Douglass Cater, director, Aspen Program on Communications and Society; and six chapters, each introduced by an essay and followed by a record of the group discussion: (1) Newsmen and Statesmen: Adversaries or Cronies by Ithiel de Sola Pool. (2) Press Rights vs. Press Responsibilities: The Issues of the First Amendment by Roger Fisher. (3) The Public's Right to Know: Functions and Malfunctions of the Media by Roger Fisher. (4) Rules for the Regulators: A Rationale for Government's Role by Dan Lacy. (5) Citizen Access to the Media by Anne W. Branscomb. (6) Who Watches the Watchdog? The Crisis of Public Confidence by Lee M. Mitchell. An epilogue suggests proposals for government action in such areas as freedom of information, privilege for newsmen, reform of the presidential press conference, regulation of media ownership, government access to communications channels, media conglomerates and the tax structure, decentralizing broadcast regulation, counter-advertising, fairness doctrine, and postal rates;

proposals for media action including identifying news sources, background and unattributed news, anticipatory journalism; proposals for citizen action through press councils, systems study of the nation's media, and a communications policy institute.

Rivers, William L. and Wilbur Schramm. *Responsibility in Mass Communications*. Rev. ed., New York, Harper, 1969. 314p. **1R161**
A revision of the Schramm book (S107) updated to include recent developments in the relation of the mass media and the public. A chapter on the Negro and the News: A Case Study has been added. Appendix contains the Canons of Journalism, the Television Code, the Radio Code, the Code of Self-Regulation (Motion Picture Association of America), and the Public Relations Code.

Roach, William J., and Louis Kreisberg. "Westchester College Students' Views on Pornography." *Technical Report of the [U.S.] Commission on Obscenity and Pornography*, 1:185–89, 1971. **1R162**
Self-administered questionnaires regarding experience with and reactions to pornography filled out by 625 students in eight colleges in Westchester County, New York.

Rob, Enid. "Libraries and Censorship." *Humanist*, 81:108–11, April 1966. **1R163**
"Anomalies and disagreements about censorship of books in libraries is discussed by a former librarian."

Robbins, J. C. "Deciding First Amendment Cases: Part I." *Journalism Quarterly*, 49:263–70, Summer 1972. **1R164**
"With a prior estimate that the probability of the correctness of a decision in favor of constitutionality is very low, the Court must demand of those who would restrict expression a showing of evidence that overcomes the prior estimate."

———. "Deciding First Amendment Cases: Part II, Evidence." *Journalism Quarterly*, 47:569–78, Autumn 1972. **1R165**
"Few laws incorporate scientific terminology directly, hence few allow straightforward application of scientific evidence."

———. "Jefferson and the Press: The Resolution of an Antinomy." *Journalism Quarterly*, 43:421–30, 465, Autumn 1971. **1R166**
"The libertarian side and the darker side of Thomas Jefferson are profiles of the same man. Both suppression and freedom arise from one systematic philosophy."

———. "The Paradox of Press Free-

dom: A Study of the British Experience." *Journalism Quarterly*, 44:428–38, August 1967. **1R167**
The paradox is: "A press which is free in a Libertarian sense is at least in part a diverse, or atomistic press. But to be diverse, the logic of bigness must not be allowed to operate. It seems the press, to be diverse, must be regulated economically. But a press which is regulated under Libertarian theory, is not free. To restate the antinomic syllogism: a free press must be atomistic; to be atomistic it must be regulated; but if it is regulated it cannot be free." The author calls for the working out of some satisfactory balance between majority rule and minority rights. The author traces recent British experience through the pages of two Royal Press Commission reports and the 1967 Joint Board report.

———. *Social Science Information and First Amendment Freedoms: An Aid to Supreme Court Decision-making*. Minneapolis, University of Minnesota, 1970. 188p. (Ph.D. dissertation, University Microfilms no. 71–8208) **1R168**
This study examines the use of social science information by the courts in cases in which constitutional rights are involved. The author finds wide tolerance for low-accuracy fact-finding by the courts and suggests ways in which the social sciences can be usefully employed in gathering evidence concerning the effect of expression on action.

Robbins, Patricia V. *The Status of News Shield Legislation*. Madison, Wis., Legislative Reference Bureau, State of Wisconsin, 1973. 16p. (Informational Bulletin 73-IB-2) **1R169**
Content: 1973 Wisconsin Legislation, Legislation in Other States, Federal Legislation and Guidelines, Court Decisions.

Roberts, Donald L. " 'Printism' and Non-Print Censorship." *Catholic Library World*, 48:223–24, December 1976. **1R170**
The author criticizes the library profession for its devotion to "printism" while ignoring non-print material in defense of intellectual freedom. "The censorship of non-book material is the 'bête noire' of intellectual freedom."

Roberts, H. Buswell, Jr. "The Supreme Court Takes Another Look at Obscenity." *University of Toledo Law Review*, 5:113–32, Fall 1973. **1R171**
"An analysis of the U.S. Supreme Court's ruling in *Miller v. California* (1973), the rationale for the decision, and the new guidelines for the determination of obscenity. Rejecting first amendment privacy and due process arguments, the Court concluded that the Constitution does not preclude state and federal regulation in these areas."

Roberts J. W. "Broadcast Regulation

and the News." In Don R. LeDuc, *ed.*, *Issues in Broadcast Regulations*, Washington, D.C., Broadcast Education Association, 1974, pp. 80–84. **1R172**
A veteran broadcaster calls for resistance to the increasing pressures for regulation of news coverage on television. The intellectuals who once complained of the lack of objectivity in news coverage now want more interpretive reporting; the so-called "silent majority," on the other hand, complain of news bias and undue emphasis on violence and bad news. The FCC has encouraged stations to be more aggressive in exploring controversial issues, but when they do this they run into the danger of public criticism and FCC and congressional investigations. The author sees the *Red Lion* decision of the U.S. Supreme Court (*Red Lion Broadcasting Co. v. FCC*, 1967), regulation proposals emanating from Congress, and demands of certain intellectuals for right of access, as dangerous trends toward federal control of broadcast news.

Roberts, Keith. "Antitrust Problems in the Newspaper Industry." *Harvard Law Review*, 82:319–66, December 1968. **1R173**
"Mr. Roberts believes that the prevailing scarcity of new entrants into the industry is undesirable and can be attributed in large part to a variety of anticompetitive practices, ranging from vertical restrictions placed by newspapers on distributors, to refusal by wire and feature services to accommodate new newspapers, and horizontal agreements to share physical plants and management departments. He concludes that opportunities to compete will benefit greatly from vigorous enforcement of the antitrust laws and from recent advances in printing technology, which can substantially reduce costs and enhance circulation."

Roberts, Leila-Jane. "Censorship Is Evergreen." *Bay State Librarian*, 59(3): 24–25, October 1970. **1R174**
Controversy over *Evergreen Review* in the Winchester (Mass.) Public Library.

Roberts, S. A. "Recovery of Punitive Damages Held Unconstitutional in Defamation Action Where Plaintiff Is a Public Figure and Liability Is Based on Actual Malice." *Cumberland Law Review*, 6:267–74, Spring 1975. **1R175**
Re: *Maheu v. Hughes Tool Co.*, 384 F. Supp. 166 (C.D. Cal. 1974).

[Roberts, William.] *The Whole Proceedings on the Trial of an Action Brought by Thomas Walker, Merchant, Against William Roberts, Barrister-at-Law, for a Libel Tried by a Special Jury at the Assizes at*

Lancaster, March 28, 1791 Before the Hon. Sir Alexander Thomson. . . . Manchester, England, Falkner and Birch, 1791. 208p.   **1R176**
The case involved the distribution of a handbill (an outgrowth of a Guy Fawkes Day after-dinner speech) in which Roberts called Walker a bully, fool, scoundrel, coward, and blackguard. Roberts was found guilty and fined £100.

Roberts, William. *The Earlier History of English Bookselling.* London, Sampson Low, Marston, 1892. 341p.   **1R177**
Contains references throughout to government action taken against booksellers, including the case of Edmund Curll.

Robertson, David W. "Defamation and the First Amendment: In Praise of *Gertz v. Robert Welch, Inc.*" *Texas Law Review,* 54:199–270, January 1976.
                                    1R178
The author believes the U.S. Supreme Court in the *Gertz* decision (1974) has defined the relationship between defamation law and the First Amendment in a way which is likely to prove stable. While enlarging First Amendment protection in some respect, it rejected the knowing or reckless falsity requirement for the defamation of private individuals and substituted liability based on fault. He disagrees with some of the critical comment on the *Gertz* decision: "(1) concern over the difficulty or irrationality of distinguishing between public and private plaintiffs and (2) fear that application of negligence law to private-plaintiff defamation suits will bring unacceptable self-censorship and unnecessary complexities." David A. Anderson responds to Robertson in the same issue (pp. 271–84).

Robertson, Edward D. "The Fair Trial–Free Press Debate Continues." *UMKC Law Review,* 45:311–20, Winter 1976.   **1R179**
Re: *Nebraska Press Association v. Stuart,* 427 U.S. 539 (1976).

Robertson, Geoff. "Film Censorship Blues." *New Statesman,* 89:817–18, 27 June 1975.   **1R180**
Cinematic freedom in Britain, which has always lagged behind that achieved in the other arts, has long relied upon the licensing system. Under a recent court decision, it is now subject to common law and the cinema industry is faced with asking that films be placed on the same basis as plays and books.

———. "Film Censorship Merry-Go-Round." *New Statesman,* 87:912, 914, 28 June 1974.   **1R181**

"There is an urgent need to rationalise recent developments in film censorship. Either give the BBFC [British Board of Film Censors] exclusive statutory responsibility for all films imported, made or screened in England, or else abolish it entirely, along with local viewing committees. Customs and common law offences and private prosecutions make all films subject to the Obscene Publications Act. Otherwise the smell of burning celluloid will soon be unbearably pungent."

———. "Obscenity: A Jury Decides." *New Statesman,* 84:716–17, 17 November 1972.   **1R182**
Re: *Regina v. Gold,* a British obscenity case which "established three important precedents which will favor the defence in future obscenity cases." The judge excused jurors who held strong views against publication of explicit sexual matters, permitted "experts" to testify on the possible effects in relation to the public interest, and cleared up the issue of consideration of the value of the work as a whole.

Robertson, Gordon. "Official Responsibility, Private Conscience and Public Information." *Transactions of the Royal Society of Canada,* 10(4th ser.):149–62, 1972.   **1R183**
Discussion of the serious nature and implications posed by the increasingly frequent leaks of government secrets. The author notes that "in a context of values in which established authority and procedures are more to be rejected than respected, and in which government tends to be seen more as a threat to the individual than as his means of acting for shared needs and purposes, it is not surprising that many, even in the service of government, give scant weight to arguments about confidentiality or secrecy." It is important to work out the terms on which confidentiality in government can be preserved and respected. We must ensure that secrecy is kept to the minimum required for national security and good government, and we must "establish acceptance that the resulting situation is reasonable and is necessary for effective government in a free society."

Robertus, Patricia E. *Postal Control of Obscene Literature 1942–1957.* Seattle, University of Washington, 1974. 218p. (Ph.D. dissertation, University Microfilms, no. 75–28,433)   **1R184**
"This dissertation is an examination of postal control of obscene literature from 1942 to 1957. . . . The Post Office Department developed three principal non-criminal sanctions: nonmailable orders, limitations on second-class mailing privileges, and mail blocks. All three methods of postal control were used between 1942 and 1957 but each was applied against a particular type of material."

Robinson, Charles W. "From the Administrator's Desk." *Top of the News,* 31:313–16, April 1975.   **1R185**
A public librarian, recognizing the day-to-day

problems of children's librarians in meeting expectations of parents for good moral influence, suggests ways that administrators can establish better communications on issues of intellectual freedom.

Robinson, David. "Trevelyan's Social History; Some Notes and a Chronology." *Sight and Sound,* 40(2):70–72, 1971.   **1R186**
The article deals with the career of the able and urbane man who had for thirteen years, until his retirement in 1970, directed the British Board of Film Censors. John Trevelyan managed to balance the interests of the industry, the public, and the government during a period of rapid change in tastes and standards. "If there has to be censorship," the author quotes a film producer, "I can think of no better person to be the censor. But I hope there will never be another." The author reviews the work of the Board on a year-by-year basis from 1958 through 1971.

———. "When Is a Dirty Film . . .?" *Sight and Sound,* 41(1):28–30, Winter 1971/72.   **1R187**
An essay prompted by the author's impressions of an erotic film festival in Amsterdam which "probably represents as fairly as possible the limits of free expression which the cinema has currently reached." He found much that was pornographic, nothing that was obscene. His experience demonstrated how deeply subjective is any evaluation of obscenity. It is this factor which explains "the difficulties of rational discussion of obscenity and of arriving at or demonstrating a legal definition, and the degree of emotion that enters any such debate as the *Oz* trial."

Robinson, Glen O. "The FCC and the First Amendment: Observations on 40 Years of Radio and Television Regulation." *Minnesota Law Review,* 52:67–163, November 1967. (Also in 1U100)
                                    1R188
This article is "an attempt to discuss comprehensively the constitutional limits on governmental regulation of radio and television under the first amendment." The primary concern of the article is "to focus on those restraints on radio and television which are clearly extraordinary, to point out those restraints which, though they may appear to be of great moment, clearly are not extraordinary or are not, in any event, unique to radio and television, and to evaluate the first amendment implications of such restraints."

Robinson, Ian. "Pornography." In David Holbrook, *ed., The Case Against Pornography,* LaSalle, Ill., Open Court, 1973, pp. 169–86.   **1R189**
"Pornography doesn't *cause* depravity and corruption, it *is* depravity and corruption. In this way it is possible to see a tendency to corrupt and deprave connected with pornography not in a cause-and-effect way but as an internal

relationship: the corruption occurs in whatever reading allows pornography to be itself." The author sees pornography as "a work whose sexual content is left deliberately uncontrolled by the artist," and he quotes from D. H. Lawrence's disapproval of pornography as "the attempt to insult sex, to do dirt on it." The best way to deal with pornography is to recognize it for what it is; perhaps when recognized "it will slink away—pornography ought to die of contempt." He accuses liberal intellectuals who defend pornography as trying "to speak a language they palpably fail to understand."

Robinson, John. "Obscenity and Maturity." *Sunday Times* (London) 14 December 1969, pp. 45–46. (Extracted from his *Christian Freedom in a Permissive Society*)   **1R190**
The former Bishop of Woolwich suggests that most decent people have yet to recognize that to disapprove is one thing but to prohibit is another. "There is place for more voluntarily adopted professional codes to consider the so-called 'conspiracy to corrupt.' But standards must be exercised in the interests of personal freedom, not of anti-sexual repression. For the way a mature society functions is not, except in the very last resort, by suppression . . . but by encouraging values and relationships which will make people not want to do dirt on sex or anything else."

Robischon, Thomas. "Chronicle of a Rear-Guard Action." *Arts in Society*, 7(1):86–89, Spring–Summer 1970.
                                                      1R191
Review of Earl R. Hutchison's *Tropic of Cancer on Trial* and commentary on the event.

Robison, Proctor D. H. "The Plain Meaning of the Freedom of Information Act: NLRB v. Getman." *Indiana Law Journal*, 47:530–45, Spring 1972.
                                                      1R192
Re: *NLRB v. Getman*, 450 F.2d 670 (D.C. Cir. 1971), in which the Court "narrowed the scope of information which administrative agencies may withhold under the Freedom of Information Act."

Roche, John P. "CBS Special An Excellent Show—But 20 Years Late." *TV Guide*, 23(42):3–4, 18 October 1975.
                                                      1R193
Comment on Columbia Broadcasting System's portrayal of the blacklisting of John Henry Faulk.

———. "Fairness Doctrine: A Haven for Lunatic Fringes." *TV Guide*, 22(32):A3–4, 10 August 1974.   **1R194**
The author discusses various interpretations of the fairness doctrine in broadcasting, including the balancing of opinion "from one loony end of the spectrum to the other," which he describes as a "lazy producer's way of avoiding genuine community responsibility."

———. "The Pentagon Papers: A Discussion." *Political Science Quarterly*, 87:184–91, June 1972.   **1R195**
A former consultant to President Lyndon Johnson finds the Pentagon Papers to be "fundamentally a historical junkpile which provides neither proof nor disproof for any hypotheses about the origins and character of the war in Vietnam." There is no logical connection, however, between the substantive merits of the Pentagon Papers and the question of censorship, and he believes the attorney general was unwise to have moved against the *New York Times*. Senator McGovern presents a different point of view in an accompanying article.

———. "Shakespeare's Shylock." In his *The Quest for the Dream: The Development of Civil Rights and Human Relations in Modern America*. New York, Macmillan, 1963, pp. 94–98.   **1R196**
The controversy within Jewish organizations and between Jewish and non-Jewish civil liberties groups over anti-Semitic episodes in great literature—*The Merchant of Venice* and *Oliver Twist*.

Rockwell, Lawrence K. "Public's Right to Know: Pell v. Procunier and Saxbe v. Washington Post Co." *Hastings Constitutional Law Quarterly*, 2: 829–58, Summer 1975.   **1R197**
"This note focuses on the issue common to the *Pell* and *Saxbe* cases (Pell v. Procunier (1974) and Saxbe v. Washington Post (1974)): does a total ban on personal interviews with specific willing inmates by the press unconstitutionally abridge the First Amendment freedom of the press guarantees? The purpose of this note is to demonstrate that the evolution of the press' character and role in American society argues for the reasoning adopted by the dissenters on that issue."

Roddy, Joseph. "Judge Tyler's New Mature Courtroom." *MORE*, 3(4):13–15, April 1973.   **1R198**
An entertaining account of the New York trial of the movie *Deep Throat* before Judge Joel J. Tyler in which "expert" witnesses testified for both prosecution and defense. The exhibitor, Mature Enterprises, Inc., was found guilty.

Rodgers, Harrell R., Jr. "Censorship Campaigns in Eighteen Cities: An Impact Analysis." *American Politics Quarterly*, 2:371–92, October 1974.   **1R199**
"The purposes of this paper are to determine how effective the Supreme Court's decisions on obscenity have been in protecting the rights of newsdealers to sell and the public to buy certain types of publications, and to isolate those factors responsible for determining the extent of the Court's impact in this area." The author sought "to determine whether the liberal position of the Supreme Court on this topic had filtered down to the local community by restricting the ability of censorship groups

to coerce retailers and wholesalers into limiting their merchandise to nonerotic publications."

Rodriguez, Antonio J. "A New Focus in a Conditional Privilege." *Loyola Law Review*, 18:168–87, 1971–72.   **1R200**
Comments on the implications for state libel laws of the U.S. Supreme Court's decision in *Rosenbloom v. Metromedia, Inc.* (1961). It is conceivable, the author states, "that the result of this controversy will be the ultimate elimination of all state libel laws concerning the news media and the press as contrary to the basic tenets of the first amendment."

Rodwin, Roger M. "Freedom of Information Act: Public Probing into (and) Private Production." *Food, Drug, Cosmetic Law Journal*, 28:533–44, August 1973.   **1R201**
An officer of a pharmaceutical company examines the FOI Act, the Committee hearings, and recent regulations of the Food and Drug Administration to determine whether the regulations adequately protect the proprietary interest in information, whether they encourage unjustified probing, and discourage the initiative required to produce private information.

Rogal, Samuel J. "Principal Eighteenth-Century British Titles Included in the *Index librorum*." *Library Chronicle* (University of Pennsylvania), 39:67–75, Spring 1973.   **1R202**
A checklist of titles by British writers appearing in Catholic Indexes published between 1668 and 1827. The list includes works by such authors as Defoe, Locke, Berkeley, Hume, Gibbon, Pope, Sterne, Priestly, Darwin, and Goldsmith.

Rogers, Jimmie N., and Theodore Clevenger, Jr. " 'The Selling of the Pentagon': Was CBS the Fulbright Propaganda Machine?" *Quarterly Journal of Speech*, 57:266–73, October 1971.
                                                      1R203
An analysis of the script of the controversial television program shows a marked similarity of the CBS documentary and the case presented by Senator Fulbright in his book, *Pentagon Propaganda Machine*. "Since we share the position with CBS that the public has a right to know, we believe the public should be informed that the principal difference . . . is a difference in media; significant dimensions of the message in both cases are the same, and the primary source of that message is J. William Fulbright."

Rogers, Kurt, and Patricia Murphy. *Access to School Boards*. Columbia, Mo.,

Freedom of Information Center, School of Journalism, University of Missouri at Columbia, 1973. 6p. (Report no. 312)   **1R204**
"Should negotiations between school boards and teachers' organizations be open to the press and public when large sums of public money are at stake? Newsmen in Minnesota and elsewhere have challenged school officials on this issue. They are now waiting for the courts and state legislatures to resolve the question."

Rogge, O. John. "High Court of Obscenity." *University of Colorado Law Review*, 41:1–59, 201–59, 1968–69.   **1R205**
"In this two-part article Mr. Rogge examines the obscenity dilemma in which the courts of the United States are now mired. In Part I he follows the historical trend of obscenity legislation and litigation, particularly emphasizing the landmark decisions of the Supreme Court and their effect on legal thinking in the obscenity field. In Part II he first comments on youth-protective obscenity legislation and then turns his attention to the issue of governmental censorship of allegedly obscene materials." Appendix I lists films whose ban was lifted by the Supreme Court, and other material held non-obscene by the Supreme Court; Appendix II lists obscenity judgments reversed on authority of *Redrup*; Appendix III lists those items judged obscene; Appendix IV shows the disposition of a representative aggregation of cases concerning Henry Miller's *Tropic of Cancer*; and Appendix V lists items deemed to be obscene by postal or Customs Bureau administrative officials.

———. "The Obscenity Terms of the Court." *Villanova Law Review*, 17:393–462, February 1972.   **1R206**
The author presents an overview of the sixty-one obscenity cases which came before the United States Supreme Court in the 1970–71 docket and the forty-two obscenity cases which the Court faces in 1971–72. He suggests four alternatives for getting the Court out of the obscenity muddle: (1) abandoning legislation and regulations of morals, (2) approaching the First Amendment as an absolute, (3) repudiation of the incorporation theory, i.e., that the due process clause of the Fourteenth Amendment does not make the federal Bill of Rights applicable to the states, and (4) invoking due process, i.e., that consenting adults have the due process right to read, see, or hear whatever they like. Appendices: Obscenity Cases in the Court's 1970–71 Docket; *Redrup* Rulings [*Redrup v. New York* (1967)]; Other Rulings Comparable to *Redrup*; Items Held Obscene at Recent Terms; Obscenity Cases in the Court Docket, October 1971.

———. "The Right to Know." *Ameri-can Scholar*, 41:643–48, Autumn 1972.   **1R207**
An attack on the policies of government secrecy, particularly in the conduct of foreign affairs. Going back at least to the Administration of President Eisenhower and his secretary of state, John Foster Dulles, the government has failed to level with the American people, has lost faith in democracy. The right of the people to know about the work of their government can be defended not only under the First Amendment, as in the case of the Pentagon Papers, but under the due process clauses of the Fifth and Fourteenth Amendments. He cites the cases of *Meyer v. Nebraska* (1922) and *Lamont v. Postmaster General* (1965).

———. "Williams v. Florida: End of a Theory." *Villanova Law Review*, 16:607–709, April 1971.   **1R208**
In a comprehensive article dealing with incorporation doctrines in which he suggests that the U.S. Supreme Court will apply case-by-case due process protection to rights nowhere specifically mentioned in the Constitution, the author discusses the application to obscenity cases. "The writer's position with respect to state power over obscenity is that under the due process clause of the fourteenth amendment there should be no obscenity legislation as to adults, and only carefully drawn minimal legislation for the protection of youth. Adults have the due process right to read, see, or hear whatever they like. The author's preference aside, however; whatever constitutional power there is over obscenity resides in the states under the tenth amendment and not in the federal government."

Rollock, Barbara. "Caveat Lector: A Librarian's View of Controversial Children's Books." *Catholic Library World*, 46:108–10, October 1974.   **1R209**
The children's librarian in selecting and presenting books to children must resist pressures against certain books being retained in library collections, and "now more than ever, must formulate selection policies which acknowledge the rights of children to a wide and varied scope of the best available materials."

Romano, David J. "Defamation of Political Candidates." *West Virginia Law Review*, 78:247–58, Fall 1976.   **1R210**
Re: *Sprouse v. Clay Communication, Inc.*, 211 S.E.2d 674 (W.Va. 1975), a case involving articles published in the *Charleston Daily Mail* containing "misleading statements [about a gubernatorial candidate appearing] in over-sized headlines."

Romm, Ethel G. "**** Is No Longer a Dirty Word." *Esquire*, 71:135+, April 1969.   **1R211**
In light of liberalized court decisions on the use of certain objectional four-letter words, editors are cautiously reappraising their policies on printing these alleged obscenities.

Roney, Paul H. "Fair Trial and Free Press: A Due Process Proposal: The Bar Answers the Challenge." *American Bar Association Journal*, 62:60–64, January 1976.   **1R212**
"The American Bar Association's Legal Advisory Committee on Fair Trial and Free Press proposes a court procedure that would provide notice and a hearing to all parties, including the news media, when a judge is considering the entry of a fair trial–free press judicial restrictive order"—Editor. Judge Roney, chairman of the Committee, responds to an accompanying article by Jack C. Landau.

Rook, W. Alan. *Cutteslowe Walls Despute; Open Letter to Mayor of Oxford*. Oxford, England, Oxford Union Society, 1936, 4p.   **1R213**
An accusation of press censorship for refusal to publish the author's letter sent to the editors of the two Oxford papers.

Rooker, Robert A. "Court Decisions May Be Implementing Goals of Commission on Obscenity." *Journalism Quarterly*, 48:544–47, Autumn 1971.   **1R214**
A study of the evolution of the U.S. Supreme Court's approach to obscenity through the three eras—the Hicklin Era, the Roth Era, and the Ginzburg-Stanley Era—indicates that the common law is headed directly toward the sense of recommendations made by the U.S. Commission on Obscenity and Pornography.

Roper Research Associates. *Trends in Public Attitudes Toward Television and Other Mass Media, 1959–1974*. New York, Television Information Office, 1975. 26p.   **1R215**
Questions asked involved government control over television programming and government control over television news programs.

Ropes, Barbara A. "Freedom of the Press: The Constitutionality of Florida's Right of Reply Statute." *University of Florida Law Review*, 26:352–59, Winter 1974.   **1R216**
Re: *Tornillo v. Miami Herald Publishing Co.*, 287 So. 2d 78 (Fla. 1973) in which the Florida Supreme Court upheld that state's right of reply law. The decision was later reversed by the U.S. Supreme Court.

The Roscoe Pound–American Trial Lawyers Foundation. *The First Amendment and the News Media. Final Report. Annual Chief Justice Earl Warren Conference on Advocacy in the United States, June 8–9, 1973*. Cambridge, Mass., The Foundation, 1973. 88p.   **1R217**
A group of constitutional law professors, newspaper executives, journalists, television broadcasters, television executives, political

scientists, lawyers, journalism professors, clergymen, congressional counsels, and judges at a two-day conference explored the issues relating to three problems: journalist's privilege, broadcast journalism, and access to government information. The report presents the recommendations of the conference which favor keeping the press free with a legal privilege to journalists, freeing television of government control of the content of broadcasts, and establishing an agency independent of the Executive Branch to review national security documents and report to Congress on the use and abuse of the classification system and the operation of the Freedom of Information Act. The following background papers presented for discussion are published in the report. These papers are entered in this bibliography under the respective authors: Journalists' Privilege: One Year After Branzburg by Benno C. Schmidt, Jr.; The First Amendment and Broadcast Journalism by Sig Mickelson; Access to Government Information—The Right Before First Amendment by Samuel J. Archibald.

Rose, Arnold M. *Libel and Academic Freedom. A Lawsuit Against Political Extremists.* Foreword by Paul A. Freund. Minneapolis, University of Minnesota Press, 1968. 287p. **1R218**
The victim of a libel attack gives an account of the trial in the Hennepin District Court, Minneapolis (*Arnold Rose v. Gerda Koch et al.*). He had been charged in a published leaflet as being a collaborator with Communists and a "security risk." The plaintiff, a professor of sociology, on leave from the University of Minnesota while serving a term in the Minnesota legislature, discusses the law of political libel as it pertains to a public figure and analyzes the movement of right-wing extremism which prompted the attack. Despite the recent U.S. Supreme Court ruling in *New York Times v. Sullivan* which greatly restricted libel laws of the states as applied to public officials, the Court found for the plaintiff, awarding him $20,000. The decision was reversed by the Minnesota Supreme Court on procedural grounds; the plaintiff died before the case could be appealed to the U.S. Supreme Court.

Rosen, Lawrence, and Stanley H. Turner. "Exposure to Pornography: An Exploratory Study." *Journal of Sex Research*, 5:235–46, November 1969. **1R219**
"This paper will be concerned with the consumer of pornography. It will attempt to distinguish, by a series of demographic and attitudinal variables, between those who have seen pornography and those who have not." The study indicated that "attitudinal variables such as belief in censorship, social harm of pornography and orientation toward anti-smut organizations proved unable to discriminate between those who had seen pornography and those who had not."

Rosenberg, David A. "Civil Liberties and the Mass Media Under Martial Law in the Philippines." *Pacific Affairs*, 47:472–84, Winter 1974/75. **1R220**
Freedom of the press under the administration of President Ferdinand E. Marcos was abolished on the pretext of Communist influence in the media and in order to dismantle the oligarchic structure of the "old society" media and create a government-supervised "new society" media. "After two years of martial law, the curtailment of civil liberties seems less temporary than before. There is still no freedom of the press, no freedom of speech, no freedom of assembly, no freedom from arbitrary arrest, and no guarantee of a fair trial. Press freedoms have been restored only to the extent necessary to avoid the appearance of complete subservience. . . . The continued absence of freedom of the press and other civil liberties provides strong evidence that the Marcos government is still more concerned with strengthening its powers than implementing basic reforms."

Rosenberg, Max. "Evaluate Your Textbooks for Racism, Sexism!" *Educational Leadership*, 31:107–9, November 1973. **1R221**
A list of "20 criteria which can serve as significant guidelines for educators in the process of selecting textbooks and other curriculum materials."

Rosenberg, Norman L. *The Law of Libel and Freedom of Press: Criticism of Public Officials and Candidates, 1800–1917.* Stony Brook, N.Y., State University of New York, 1972. 270p. (Ph.D. dissertation, University Microfilms, no. 72-18,120) **1R222**
"Throughout the nineteenth and early twentieth centuries American jurists attempted to harmonize the law of libel, particularly its use in political disputes, with constitutional guarantees of a free press. Decisions which limited or broadened the boundaries for libelous publications rested, in large part, upon lawmakers' consideration of a number of competing social and political policies: encouraging exposure of corruption; protecting the reputations of individual politicians; and preventing unrestrained libels from driving good men out of public life or fooling voters into electing dishonest candidates. From 1800 to 1917 trends in the law of libel reflected alterations in the organizations and functions of political journalism, changes in the nature of partisan conflict, and judges' and lawmakers' fears about the stability of the American policy."

———. "The New Law of Political Libel: A Historical Perspective." *Rutgers Law Review*, 28:1141–83, Summer 1975. **1R223**
"This article will examine the history of political libel law, particularly during the nineteenth and twentieth centuries, suggesting how political and legal milieu helped shape legal policies and doctrines. It will also analyze the most recent Supreme Court decision, *Gertz v. Robert*

Welch, Inc. [1974], from this historical perspective."

Rosenblatt, Stephen W. "Adjusting the Defamation Standard." *Mississippi Law Journal*, 46:279–301, Spring 1975. **1R224**
"This comment will examine the development of the first amendment conflict with state defamation laws. Various approaches to the problem will be discussed, followed by an analysis of the Supreme Court's latest formulation in *Gertz v. Robert Welch, Inc.*"

Rosenfield, Harry N. "The Constitutional Dimension of 'Fair Use' in Copyright Law." *Notre Dame Lawyer*, 50:790–807, June 1975. **1R225**
"Fair use in copyright has constitutional protection under the first and ninth amendments and can assure the public of reasonable access to its heritage, notwithstanding the purported exclusive right of the copyright proprietor under statute. . . . In the balancing between the constitutional right of access through fair use and the copyright law, the balance must tilt toward the constitutionally protected right to reasonable access."

Rosenfield, Lawrence W. "Politics and Pornography." *Quarterly Journal of Speech*, 59:413–22, December 1973. **1R226**
"I shall contend that the consumption of pornography by a given public serves as a surrogate for freedom; erotica comes into being as some particular aspect of the spirit of freedom and sharing that once pervaded a community fades. As an individual despairingly renounces an intolerable world, he seeks the comfort and obscurity of an interior landscape, a 'phantasy realm' free of external coercion. But in spite of his efforts to flee such oppression, public realities will intrude upon and ultimately inform the pornographic artifacts that begin to attract him and other similarly oppressed members of his community."

Rosenthal, A. M. " 'Save the First Amendment!' " *New York Times Magazine*, 11 February 1973, pp. 16, 47–51, 54–60. **1R227**
"If confidentiality of news sources is really destroyed, it will mean that the press will be virtually dominated by the official version of what is taking place in American society wherever it touches upon government and that means just about everywhere—in the bureaucracy, the military, the judiciary, the police, the expenditure of funds, and on all levels of government." There is a need for public understanding of its own involvement and the threat to the First Amendment. Only then can federal or state laws to protect the newsman be enacted. The press needs a bumper sticker: "Save the First Amendment."

[Rosenwein, Sam.] "A White Paper on Justice Black." *Censorship Today*, 1(3):5–17 [October–November], 1968. **1R228**

An interview with a "critical admirer" of Supreme Court Justice Hugo L. Black reveals his interpretation of Justice Black's stand on freedom of speech and assembly and the fundamental difference between Black and his critics.

Roshco, Bernard. "Making the Incredible Credible: Cases in News Management." *Columbia Journalism Review*, 7(2):41–45, Summer 1968. **1R229**

Several cases of news management through false information in handouts are cited by way of example of how able and alert newsmen can get at the truth by using additional sources.

———. "The Phoney Issue of News Management." *Interplay*, 3(8):19–23, April 1970. **1R230**

An inquiry into the nature of news management, which is a fact of political and journalistic life in Washington. The press depends on it and usually assents, attributing news to the personalities who make it. Most events in government would not be reported if public relations spokesmen didn't perform their roles as news managers.

Ross, Terry D. "Expert Testimony in Obscenity Cases." *Hastings Law Journal*, 18:161–79, November 1966. **1R231**

The paper examines the role of the expert in obscenity cases, finding that, if properly focused and reasonably controlled by the court, the expert "will help to insure that the test of obscenity is met in a literal way."

Rossiter, Charles M., Jr. "Teaching Freedom of Speech in the Basic Course." In *1969 Yearbook of the Committee of Freedom of Speech of the Speech Association of America*. n.p., The Association, 1970, pp. 56–61. **1R232**

"This is a report of an effort by the author to include lessons dealing with problems and issues of freedom of speech in the basic speech course and to evaluate those lessons in terms of (1) students' reactions to the lessons, and (2) changes in students' attitudes toward issues concerning freedom of speech."

Rostenberg, Leona. *The Minority Press & The English Crown: A Study in Repression, 1558–1625*. The Hague, Nieuwkoop, B. De Graff, 1971. 263p. **1R233**

A study of the courageous Catholic and Puritan printers who served the cause of those religious minorities in the England of Elizabeth I and James I. "Chased by the 'lynx-eyed' pursuivants, members of a ruffian gang of official hirelings, and Messengers of the Press employed by the august Company of Stationers ever ready to placate the government—the minority printer was compelled to work in obscure areas of London and its suburbs." The relentless persecution which included prison, torture, and sometimes death, finally drove printers to the provinces and occasionally to pursue their professions abroad. Even in exile "the refugee printer could not completely elude the authority of the Crown whose diplomatic servant, alerted to subversive or critical publication, impounded the text and seized the offender." Despite government attempts at censorship, however, the minority press survived. While the Catholic printer continued to represent the foreign authority and a national threat, the Puritan printer was elevated to stature under the Commonwealth.

Roth, Edwin. "Acquittal in Old Bailey Nullifies Official Secrets Act for Press." *Editor & Publisher*, 104(7):56+, 13 February 1971. **1R234**

"In a summation to 12 jurors at the 'Old Bailey' criminal court in London, Judge Sir Bernard Caulfield has made legal history and press history by interpreting Britain's 'Official Secrets Act' so that the British press has now lost its previous fear of 'Official Secrets Act' criminal charges. Judge Caulfield's summation contained the most important declaration about press freedom in Britain for many years."

———. "Stricter Controls Are Put on British Press by Lords." *Editor & Publisher*, 106(31):10, 4 August 1973. **1R235**

"Five Lord Judges in the House of Lords, who together carried out the House of Lords' function as Britain's Supreme Court, have decided in a final verdict that publication by the *Sunday Times* of an article reporting how thalidomide was advertised and sold in Britain would be 'contempt of court' until all legal actions against its British producers, The Distillers Company, are concluded." The author concludes that any British Watergate scandal would be covered up either by the Official Secrets Act or by "contempt of court."

Roth, Jeffrey, and Kathy Riley. "The Bill of Rights and the Student Press." *Chicago Journalism Review*, 6:3–7, January 1973. **1R236**

A discussion of the rights of campus newspapers in light of the U.S. Supreme Court's ruling in *Tinker v. Des Moines School District* (1969).

Roth, Samuel. *Stone Walls Do Not: The Chronicle of a Captivity*. New York, William Faro, 1930. 2 vols. (Edition limited to 105 copies) **1R237**

"An account of the seventy-five days of imprisonment resulting from my arrest on June 21, 1928, at the instigation of the New York Society for the Suppression of Vice." Leo Hamalian, in his article on Roth, Nobody Knows My Name, describes this work as "an assortment of essays, poems, dramatic fragments, aphorisms, prejudices, and sketches of a biographical nature." In 1957 Roth was again sentenced to prison for distribution of obscenity following the U.S. Supreme Court decision, *Roth v. United States*.

Rothbard, Murray N. *For a New Liberty*. New York, Macmillan, 1973. 327p. **1R238**

The author applies his views of a new libertarianism, which rejects both liberalism and conservatism and holds that "no man or group of men have the right to aggress against the person or property of anyone else." In the area of freedom of the press he favors the abolition of the laws of libel which protect a man's reputation on the false premise that it is a form of property; he believes that radio and TV should be treated the same as the newspaper press, with no government controls; and that there should be no laws against obscenity since they invade the property rights of people to produce, sell, buy, or possess pornographic material. "The libertarian stands foursquare for what are generally known as civil liberties: for the freedom to speak, publish, assemble, and to engage in such 'victimless crimes'as pornography, sexual deviation, and prostitution, which the libertarian does not regard as 'crimes' at all."

Rothchild, John. "Finding the Facts Bureaucrats Hide." *Washington Monthly*, 2(11):15–27, January 1972. **1R239**

A review of the operating of the Freedom of Information Act and particularly the ploys used by executive agencies to keep from releasing information: "commingling," that is filing classified and nonclassified material together so that it is difficult to separate them; "no tickee, no washee," which means that the agency fails to provide the user with an index to extensive files and accuses him of "fishing"; charging a "small fee," which turns out to be prohibitive; "we don't service that," which attempts to deny the existence of certain data; and the "working paper," a claim that the information sought is for internal staff use only. The author discusses a number of cases involving legal efforts to force agencies to comply with the law. He believes that some agencies, rather than release information, may decide not to collect it in the first place.

———. "The Stories Reporters Don't Write." *Washington Monthly*, 3(4):20–27, June 1971. **1R240**

Some of the best reporters, specialists in their area, are prisoners of their sources. To tell all may cut off further contact or rapport with sources, whether it is the White House, the FBI, radical groups, or relationships in foreign countries. Self-censorship by reporters is one of the paradoxes in modern journalism.

"The Rothenberg Case: Fair Trial–Free Press Confrontation." *St. Louis Journalism Review*, 2(8):3, March 1972. **1R241**

Criticism of the press coverage of the trial of David Rothenberg for the murder of an insurance investigator, including a statement of the judge on the obligation of the press in a criminal case.

Rotherham, Brenda. "Does The High School Press Really Enjoy Freedom of the Press?" *Nebraska Newspaper*, 24:14–16, January 1972.   **1R242**
A review of the legal and actual statutes of press freedom of high school newspapers and the position taken by professional education and journalism associations.

Rottenberg, Dan. "Biting the Hand . . . Reviewing Journalism *Is* a Hazardous Occupation." *Chicago Journalism Review*, 5(6):3–4, June 1972.   **1R243**
What happens to reporters who have criticized their own papers in journalism reviews.

———. "Do News Reports Bias Juries?" *Columbia Journalism Review*, 15:16–18, May–June 1976.   **1R244**
The author cites the disturbing findings of a study conducted by Alice Padawer-Singer at Columbia University's Bureau of Applied Social Research. She conducted an experiment simulating real courtroom conditions and using jurors picked from an actual panel. The result suggested that publicity does have adverse effects on jurors. Eighty percent of those who had seen newspaper stories revealing that the defendant had a criminal background favored a guilty verdict; only 39 percent of those who had not seen the stories favored a guilty verdict.

———. "Messing with the News." *Chicago Journalism Review*. 3(12):3–6, 12, December 1970.   **1R245**
"How Chicago's biggest law firm uses—and misuses—its dual role as press adviser and establishment spokesman."

Rotunda, Ronald D. "The Commercial Speech Doctrine in the Supreme Court." *University of Illinois Law Forum*, 1976:1080–1101, 1976.   **1R246**
This note "examines the status of the commercial speech doctrine in light of . . . *Virginia State Board of Pharmacy v. Virginia Citizens Consumer Council, Inc.* [1976] . . . suggests that this decision, which rejects the traditional commercial speech doctrine, promotes majoritarian ideals."

Rourke, Francis E., *ed*. "A Symposium [on] Administrative Secrecy: A Comparative Perspective." *Public Administration Review*, 35:1–42, January–February 1975.   **1R247**
Content: Opening Government to Public Scrutiny: A Decade of Federal Efforts by Harold C. Relyea. The Freedom of Informa-

tion Act: A Governmental Perspective by Robert L. Saloschin. Corporate Secrecy and Political Accountability by Mark V. Nadel. A Comparative View: Administrative Secrecy in Britain by James B. Christoph. Government Secrecy: Exchanges, Intermediaries, and Middlemen by Itzhak Galnoor.

[Rous, George.] *A Letter to the Jurors of Great-Britain: Occasioned by an Opinion of the Court of King's Bench, Read by Lord Chief Justice Mansfield, in the Case of the King and Woodfall; And Said to Have been left by his Lordship with the Clerk of Parliament*. London, G. Pearch, 1771. 67p. 2d ed., London, John Stockdale, 1785. 93p. (Reprinted in Stephen Parks, *ed.*, *The English Book Trade, 1660–1853*. New York, Garland, 1974. Vol 14)   **1R248**
Justice Mansfield in the Woodfall trial had declared that juries in libel cases had no right to decide other than the fact of publication. Rous criticizes the decision, giving historical evidence in support of jury rights under common laws to pass judgment on whether or not the offending work was libelous. The original edition was signed by "A Friend to the Laws and Government of his Country." The second edition is published under Rous's name with a preface added.

Routt, Edd. *Dimensions of Broadcast Editorializing*. Blue Ridge Summit, Pa., Tab Books, 1974. 204p.   **1R249**
A textbook which encourages broadcasters to take advantage of their rights and obligations to editorialize. The text includes the origin and background of broadcast editorializing and the rights and regulations as established by the Federal Communications Commission.

Rowan, Archibald H. *Autobiography of Archibald Hamilton Rowan, Esq., With Additions and Illustrations by William Hamilton Drummond. . . .* Dublin, Thomas Tegg, 1840. 475p.   **1R250**
In his memoirs Rowan discusses his trial for publishing in the *Northern Star* a United Irishmen's Address to Volunteers. He was convicted and sentenced to two years in prison for seditious libel. He escaped to France where he was mistakenly imprisoned as an English spy. A friend of the French Revolution, Rowan was horrified by the excesses and shipped to America. He was prevented from a life of obscurity by attacks on him made by William Cobbett in his *Porcupine Gazette*. Rowan eventually returned to Ireland where he lived out his life. Following the libel trial, Judge Clonmel, upon learning that Peter Byrne planned to publish the proceedings in behalf of Rowan, warned Byrne that if he published anything that would inflame the mob, reflect on the judges or misquote him he would "lay him by the heels" (R286–87).

Rowe, Frederick M. *et al*. "Antitrust

and Monopoly Policy in the Communications Industries: A Symposium." *Antitrust Bulletin*, 13:871–997, Fall 1968.   **1R251**
Content: Role of Antitrust Policy in the Communications Industry by Donald F. Turner. Harnessing Revolution: The Role of Regulation and Competition for the Communications Industry of Tomorrow by Nicholas Johnson. Monopoly and Competition Issues Facing the Communications Industry by Horace P. Moulton. The Role of Competition and Monopoly in the Communications Industry by Rosel H. Hyde. Competition in and Among the Broadcasting, CATV, and Pay-TV Industries by Kenneth A. Cox. Mergers and Diversification in the Newspaper, Broadcasting and Information Industries by Charles D. Mahaffie, Jr. The Role of Spectrum Allocation in Monopoly or Competition in Communications by John D. Dingell. Competition and Monopoly Practices in Domestic Satellite Communication by Henry Geller. Competition Problems in International Communication by David C. Acheson. The Congressional Perspective of Competition in the Communications Industry by Philip A. Hart. The Limit of a Regulated Monopoly—Telephone Attachments, Interconnection and Use of Circuits by Lionel Kestenbaum. Competition and Monopoly in the Computer and Data Transmission Industries by Bernard Strassburg.

Rowley, Peter. "Serious U.S. TV Fights for Life." *New Statesman*, 77:500–501, 11 April 1969.   **1R252**
Brief account of the difficult struggle of public broadcasting in the United States, compared with the early struggle of British Broadcasting Corporation.

Rowse, Arthur E. "The Press Dummies Up." *Nation*, 208:816–20, 3 June 1969.   **1R253**
Criticism of the proposed Newspaper Preservation Act which would give newspapers immunity from antitrust prosecution when separately owned newspapers have joint operating arrangements, "a sort of half-way house between competition and monopoly of local papers. . . . The pressure that has pushed this little-known bill ahead of countless more important measures in the past few months is silent tribute to the power of big publishers to get almost anything they want from publicity-hungry politicians."

———. *Slanted News. A Case Study of the Nixon and Stevenson Fund Stories*. With a Foreword by Erwin D. Canham. Boston, Beacon, 1957. 139p.   **1R254**
"A chapter-and-verse case study of the way 32 leading American dailies treated the controversial Nixon and Stevenson fund stories on their front pages."

Roy, Barbeau A. "Movie Censorship: A Public and Private Concern." *St. Louis University Law Journal*, 15:156–80, Fall 1970. **1R255**
"This paper will examine two aspects of the censorship question—the attempt of the movie industry to impose a self-regulatory scheme of censorship and the development of governmental regulation, as reflected in major court decisions on movie censorship." The author believes legislators can expect Supreme Court guidance along the lines indicated in the report of the Commission on Obscenity and Pornography: protection of juveniles, assault on individual privacy, and pandering.

Roy, Somnath. "Repercussions of the Vernacular Press Act, 1878." *Journal of Indian History* (India), 45:735–48, 1967. **1R256**

The Act empowered district magistrates to discipline any English language publication that might displease the government of India. The Act, although never vigorously enforced, gave rise to middle-class nationalism.

Roycroft, Howard. "The WMAL Case." In Don R. Le Duc, *ed.*, *Issues in Broadcast Regulation*, Washington, D.C., Broadcast Education Association, 1974, pp. 30–33. **1R257**
Discussion of the license challenge to WMAL-TV (Washington, D.C.) by a group of blacks who felt the station did not adequately represent their interests in programming. The FCC and later the court (*Stone v. FCC*, 1972) ruled in favor of the station, asserting that the petitioners had not proved their broad allegations against the station.

Roylance-Kent, C. B. "Two Radicals of the Old School." *Macmillan's Magazine*, 78:32–40, May 1898. **1R258**
Brief biographical sketches of J. A. Roebuck and Francis Place on the occasion of the publication of the autobiography of Roebuck and Wallas's biography of Place. Both men were active in the fight against the British newspaper tax.

Royster, Vermont. *The American Press and the Revolutionary Tradition*. Washington, D.C., American Enterprise Institute for Policy Research, 1974. 21p. (Distinguished Lecture Series on the Bicentennial) **1R259**
"Among the many revolutionary ideas to emerge from the American Revolution, none proved more revolutionary than the idea of freedom of the press. None has proved more durable, for it has withstood two centuries of assault." The speaker traces the development of the concept of press freedom from English common law to the adoption of the First Amendment to the United States Constitution. The American press today has gone far beyond the concept of press freedom envisioned by the founding fathers. "It can seize upon secrets stolen from government archives and broadcast them to the world. It can strip the privacy of councils and grand juries. It can pillory those accused of crimes before they are tried. It can heap calumnies not only upon elected governors but upon all whom chance has made an object of public attention. It can publish the lascivious and the sadistic. It can advance any opinion on any subject, including the opinion that all our government is corrupt and that the whole of the social order proclaimed in 1776 should be swept away and another put in its place." Despite these abuses, freedom of the press as an institution in a democracy must be maintained. Changes wrought by time are inevitable. "Freedom of the press, once proclaimed, admits to no logical limit." All liberty is subject to abuse, but the author has faith that the American people will find their way amid the abuses. The American experiment in freedom "rests less upon logic than upon a faith that the danger of unbounded liberty is not so great as that of putting liberty in bondage. It is a faith so far justified."

Royston, Robert. "A Tiny, Unheard Voice; The Writer in South Africa." *Index on Censorship*, 2(4):85–88, Winter 1973. **1R260**
Observations on the helpless position of the black writer in the oppressive atmosphere of the apartheid system in South Africa. "*Apartheid* is not a catastrophe—it is a system of routine deprivation and disruption that affects every dark-skinned person. The treatment meted out to political prisoners, the harassment of dissidents, the abstract structure of the society are here the less harrowing issues; less harrowing than the dailiness of discrimination, the taken-for-granted miseries that form the South African way of life." A selected list of books banned in South Africa, compiled by the U.N. Unit on Apartheid, appears on pages 99–102.

Ruane, Don. *The ABA and Gag Guidelines*. Columbia, Mo., Freedom of Information Center, School of Journalism, University of Missouri at Columbia, 1976. 8p. (Report no. 348) **1R261**
"Voluntary agreements between the news media and state bench and bar associations have led to increased understanding of the problems of media coverage of trials, but they may also have resulted in acceptance by the media of prior restraint. The author examines the ABA's [American Bar Association] proposed guidelines on gag orders in the light of these voluntary agreements."

Rubin, Alfred P. "A Wholesome Discretion." *New York Law Forum*, 20:569–616, Winter 1975. **1R262**
The article deals with the division of responsibility in the handling of information necessary for the making of government policy between the career experts of the executive branch and the amateurs of the legislative. The first part deals with existing legislation and regulations regarding public information—the Freedom of Information Act, the Administrative Procedure Act, the Espionage Act, and export controls. Part two deals with the Congressional quest for operative information, and part three with the source of confusion in the release of information to the Congress by the executive branch. The confusion stems, in part, from "the penchant of the executive branch to regard the amateurs of the legislative branch—amateurs by virtue of the structure of government, if not in fact—as merely members of the public and not members of a branch of government."

Rubin, David M. "Anatomy of a Snow Job." *MORE*, 4(3):18–22, March 1974. **1R263**
"The media are hopelessly outclassed by the elite public relations corps of David Rockefeller and his Chase Manhattan Bank. By one estimate, the bank and its officials appeared in 18,215 print and broadcast stories in 1973."

———. "Nothing Succeeds Like Failure." *MORE*, 5(6):18–19, June 1975. **1R264**
Criticism of the Newspaper Preservation Act, about to be challenged in court after five years in operation. "At stake is nothing less than the restoration of an open marketplace of ideas and the continuation of newspaper competition in many of the larger cities of the United States."

———. "The Perils of Muckraking." *MORE*, 4(9):5–6, 8, 21, September 1974. **1R265**
"Filing a libel suit to cripple a book and its author is an effective weapon even though a public figure has almost no chance of winning a suit in the end."

———. "Screw Gets Screwed: Porn Peddler Al Goldstein Faces 60 Years in Jail." *MORE*, 6(9):34–35, September 1976. **1R266**
"On June 18, a Wichita jury convicted Goldstein and his partner, Jim Buckley, on 11 counts of distributing obscene material—*Screw* and *Smut*—through the mails, and one count of conspiracy." The defense attorney, Herald P. Fahringer, believes that if the verdict is not overturned it will mean "that the government can artifically create a jurisdiction and then pick where you stand trial. The enormous expense of defending such a case will crush or liquidate a publication. The government will be able to wipe out any organ that displeases it." *Screw* and *Smut* are published in New York.

———. "Who's Afraid of the NNC?" *MORE*, 6(3):8–12, March 1976. **1R267**
"After three years of lackluster performance, media opposition and virtual invisibility, the National News Council is out of money and out of steam—and likely to sink into the

obscurity of journalism textbooks." The author concludes that the press and the public in the United States are not ready for a press council, and one cannot be imposed with success.

Rubin, Richard A. "Foreign Policy, Secrecy, And the First Amendment: The Pentagon Papers in Retrospect." *Howard Law Journal*, 17:579–612, 1972.
1R268
The Pentagon Papers case "only narrowly affirmed the extension of the First Amendment protection to the press when the government seeks to have prior restraints imposed upon it, but left many subsidiary issues unresolved." These included the government's right to continue to classify information, despite evidence of massive overclassification, and the "monolithic security system which allows the government to decide matters of war and peace furtively and with minimum visibility." What gives this case landmark dimensions equivalent to the Zenger case of 1735 is that "it marks the first time the United States sought to enjoin a newspaper from publishing information in its possession."

Rubinstein, Michael. "The Writer and the Writ." In his *Wicked, Wicked Libels*. London, Routledge & Kegan Paul, 1972, pp. 122–45.
1R269
Books, according to the author of this article, represent a more serious libel in the eyes of the law because they last a lifetime whereas newspapers are discarded in a day and television is gone in a flash. Libel awards against a book publisher may represent a more serious financial loss than awards against other media for, in addition to any damages awarded, he may have to withdraw the book from sale. Authors have major responsibility for libels, but it is the publisher who generally has to bear the brunt of claims. He discusses the impact of libel claims on author and publisher, the use of indemnity claims, libel insurance, and legal negotiations. Most defendants prefer an out-of-court settlement to a court adjudication, not only because of costs, but because of the difficulty of proving the accuracy of statements in accordance with the law.

———, ed. *Wicked, Wicked Libels*. London, Routledge & Kegan Paul, 1972. 179p.
1R270
"The law of libel is the instrument of censorship by which dignity—too often pseudo-dignity—is to be upheld," writes the editor in the introduction. "Like the law of the land throughout its whole range, it is but a blunt instrument; it metes out that mean measure of justice which is the most perfect that imperfect man can offer to imperfect man." This is a collection of essays on the law of libel, selected both to enlighten and entertain: A Look at the Law by H. Montgomery Hyde; Free Speech and Privacy by Louis Blom-Cooper; Reading Between the Lines—The Lawyers and The News Desk by Anthony Lincoln; Libel—A Book Publisher's View by William Kimber; Eye Witness by Richard Ingrams; News and

Abuse by Cecil H. King; A Libel Case as Seen by a Successful Plaintiff by Eugene Gros; The Writer and the Writ by Michael Rubinstein; Defamation as Contempt of Parliament by Louis A. Abraham; My Day in Court by Harold Laski; and Punitive Damages and the PQ 17 Libel Case by "Justinian."

[Rubright, James A.] "Free Speech and the Mass Media." *Virginia Law Review*, 57:636–56, May 1971.
1R271
This Note examines FCC Commissioner Nicholas Johnson's argument and questions his conclusions with respect to the right of access to radio and television airtime as expressed in his article in the same issue. "The Constitution does not compel a right of access, policy does not support it, and Congress has foreclosed judicial innovation by adopting a regulatory scheme protecting the interests of the media and the public." The author concludes that "The FCC has acted within its power in denying a right of access."

Ruckelshaus, William, Elie Abel *et al.* *Freedom of the Press....* Washington, D.C., American Enterprise Institute, 1976. 101p. (An AEI Round Table held on July 29 and 30, 1975, at the National Press Club, Washington, D.C.)
1R272
Part I, First Amendment Protections. A panel, moderated by William Ruckelshaus, discusses three current controversies whose common theme is tension between the First Amendment and government's exercise of power through the judicial system: Should a reporter under any circumstances be forced by the courts to reveal his confidential sources of information? To what extent does, or should, the First Amendment to the Constitution protect the press from libel actions by private citizens who claim that they have been wronged? To what extent should the courts prohibit the publication of classified material? Panelists: Jack Nelson, Antonin Scalia, Floyd Abrams, Charles Seib, and Edward J. Epstein. Part II, Regulation of the Media. A panel, moderated by Elie Abel, discusses such questions as: Are the broadcast media too powerful? Do we need more regulations or less? Does the First Amendment which guarantees freedom of the press, apply to journalism on the air as well, or only to the printed word? If it does apply to broadcasting, how do we justify any federal regulations at all under the explicit injunction of the First Amendment? Panelists: Bill Monroe, Kevin P. Phillips, Ralph K. Winter, and Clay T. Whitehead. Questions from the audience are answered following each panel.

Rucker, Bryce W. "Let's Protect Our Dying First Freedom." *Grassroots Editor*, 9(5):3–6, September–October 1968. (Reprinted in Michael C. Emery and Ted C. Smythe, *eds.*, *Readings in Mass Communications*, pp. 363–68)
1R273
An attack on newspaper monopoly—chains,

local monopolies, cross-media monopolies—and control of media by industrial conglomerates.

———. "The Muzzled Watchdogs." *Grassroots Editor*, 12(4):11–14, July–August 1971.
1R274
Arguments for democracy in the newsroom which will enable the press to do a better job as watchdog. "Working newsmen are best prepared to elect editors, subeditors and a board which would determine news-editorial policy."

Ruddy, F. S. "American Constitutional Law and Restrictions on the Content of Private International Broadcasting." *International Lawyer*, 5:102–10, January 1971.
1R275
"This paper is concerned with the Constitutional issues presented by an [international] agreement by which the United States undertakes to restrict transmissions by its citizens."

Rude, George F. C. "Wilkes and Liberty, 1768–69." *Guildhall Miscellany*, 8:3–24, July 1957.
1R276
A discussion of the Wilkes and Liberty movement that took place in England when John Wilkes was arrested for his publication of *North Briton* and faced his judges at Westminster Hall; again when he returned from exile to France; and during various elections in which he stood.

Rudkin, Olive D. *Thomas Spence and His Connections*. London, Allen & Unwin, 1927. 256p.
1R277
A biography of the London bookseller, pamphleteer, and reformer, best known for his proposal for establishing self-contained communities organized along semisocialistic principles, considered a threat to British land ownership. For publication of his views on land ownership, known as the Spencean system, he was imprisoned for a year (S544–45). Chapter 5 deals with the trial.

Rumsfeld, Donald. "FOI Cleanup Hitters with Good Follow-through." *Bulletin of the American Society of Newspaper Editors*, 516:9–10, Feburary 1968.
1R278
"Whether or not the law will work as its advocates hope will depend not merely upon court enforcement and intelligent administration by the Executive Branch of the Federal Government, but even more important, on the degree of follow-through that the nation's news media is willing to provide. To date, the press role in assuring proper implementation of the law has been spotty."

[Rupe, Gregory L.] "Commercial Speech Doctrine: Ordinance Prohibiting Newspaper from Printing Sex-Designated Employment Advertising Held Constitutional." *University of Richmond Law Review*, 8:292–96, Winter 1974. **1R279**
Re: *Pittsburgh Press Co. v. Pittsburgh Commission on Human Relations*, 93 S. Ct. 2553 (1973).

Rush, Betsy. "Weeding vs. Censorship: Treading a Fine Line." *Library Journal*, 99:3032–33, 15 November 1974. **1R280**
Children's librarians must find a workable course of action in maintaining a balanced up-to-date collection "without succumbing to either the arguments of the purist critics of sexism and racism in children's literature or to those of the purist defenders of intellectual freedom." An account of how one library staff reevaluated its older children's books.

The Rush-Light. By Peter Porcupine [William Cobbett]. New York and London, 1800–1801? Nos. 1–6. **1R281**
Cobbett initiated this series as a means of retribution shortly after losing the libel case brought against him by Dr. Benjamin Rush. The first five issues were published in New York where Cobbett had gone to live following his defeat in Philadelphia. The first issue is a vitriolic attack on Rush, his supporters, and the conduct of the trial; the second issue deals with the subject of the libel case—Rush's policy of blood-letting during the Philadelphia epidemic of yellow fever; the third is Cobbett's hypothetical self-defense at the Philadelphia trial; the fourth issue discusses the judge's prejudicial charge to the jury and other legal matters in the Rush-Cobbett trial; the fifth issue contains letters from Cobbett to Joseph Priestly and Thomas Cooper; the sixth and seventh issues were published in London after Cobbett had returned to England and deal more generally with criticism of American political figures. A publication entitled *The Republican Rush-Light by William Cobbett* and purported to be the seventh issue, is probably spurious, according to Cobbett bibliographer Pierce W. Gaines, because it is not in Cobbett's style and espouses views opposite to his. Upon the appearance of the first issue of *Rush-Light* in Philadelphia bookstores, Dr. Rush's son, John, went to New York to challenge Cobbett to a duel. This dramatic account is told in William and Frances Neilson's *Verdict for the Doctor* (N96).

Rushdoony, Rousas J. *The Politics of Pornography*. New Rochelle, N.Y., Arlington House, 1974. 163p. **1R282**
"The new pornography differs from the old; it is now a crusade for a new freedom and an all-out war against God and his law. . . . In the politics of pornography, there is neither hindsight nor foresight. The Sadean thesis, that the natural is the normative, will reduce man and society to the level of barbarians, to a world in which all acts and practices are valid, because all occur in nature." The appendix includes a section on legislation against pornography.

———. "The Politics of Pornography." In his *Law and Liberty*. n.p., Craig Press, 1971, pp. 16–20. **1R283**
One of the central purposes of pornography is political. Pornography is "hostile to morality and law, and it encourages and favors rebellion against morality."

Ruskay, Joseph A. "Censorship by Taxation: New Muzzle for Churchmen." *Nation*, 215(9):266–69, 2 September 1972. **1R284**
The author finds "increasingly disturbing signs that some of the more outspoken churchmen who criticize Nixon's foreign and domestic policies are being pressured into silence by various government agencies, and particularly by the Department of Internal Revenue."

[Russel, Alexander.] "The Newspaper Stamp." *Edinburgh Review*, 98:247–62, October 1853. **1R285**
Comments prompted by the publication of the House of Commons *Report from the Select Committee on Newspaper Stamps*.

Russell, Albert H., Jr. "*Rosenbloom v. Metromedia, Inc.*" *Suffolk University Law Review*, 6:712–20, Spring 1972. **1R286**
Re: *Rosenbloom v. Metromedia, Inc.*, 403 U.S.29 (1971).

Russell, Bertrand. "Mr. Bowdler's Nightmare." In his *Nightmares of Eminent Persons*. New York, Simon & Schuster, 1955, pp. 11–16. **1R287**
A spoof on Thomas Bowdler's obsession with improper words, in which Mrs. Bowdler is discovered in her husband's library reading an unexpurgated copy of Shakespeare.

Russell, Charles C. *An Interpretive History of Citizen Pressure Groups in Their Efforts to Control Obscenity in Books*. Columbia, Mo., University of Missouri at Columbia, 1968. 244p. (Ph.D. dissertation, University Microfilms, no. 69-3408) **1R288**
A history of pressure groups from the early Christian era when anti-Christian writings were banned and burned, to the present day, with emphasis on the growth of organizations and movements to control obscenity. Men were the predominant force in the movement between 1802 and 1940; women assumed leadership thereafter, giving special attention to the welfare of youth. Since 1950 suppression has taken an added dimension with efforts directed against librarians and teachers. "The major unresolved issue is whether the suppression of objectionable literature is a cultural obstruction or a saving grace."

Russell, Norman. *Censorship*. London, Inter-Varsity, 1972. 16p. (Topical Issues) **1R289**
After giving the pros and cons of censorship of pornography, the writer concludes that while sustained exposure to pornography is harmful, censorship is not the answer. Censorship will not change the values of our society. "It is one thing to stifle freedom of speech but quite another to forbid public display on the streets of material which many find offensive." He supports laws to control such pandering.

Russell, Sandra. "Freedom of the Press." *Quill and Scroll*, 49(2):6–9, December 1975. **1R290**
The legal status and implications of First Amendment theory for the high school press. A listing of student press censorship cases in appendix.

Russell, Thomas B. "Obscenity—the Need for Legislative Reform." *Kentucky Law Journal*, 57:582–91, Spring 1969. **1R291**
"The purpose of this comment will be to give the history of obscenity via Supreme Court decisions; to discuss the purposes of the Model Penal Code; to examine pertinent provisions of Kentucky's proposed code; and to recommend what should and should not be included in an obscenity statute."

Russen, Joe. *Censorship of the Mass Media*. 15 min. tape recording. Berkeley, Calif., Pacifica Tape Library, 1970. **1R292**
A discussion of the implicit and explicit censorship of the mass media, including the role of the Federal Communications Commission. The speaker refers to his experiences while working in educational television and for *Time*.

Russo, Frank D. "A Study of Bias in TV Coverage of the Vietnam War: 1969 and 1970." *Public Opinion Quarterly*, 35:539–43, Winter 1971. **1R293**
The bias in television coverage of the Vietnam war is assessed through content analysis of a representative sample of evening newscasts shown by NBC and CBS during 1969 and 1970.

Rust, William. *Gagged by Grigg*. [London, Daily Worker, 1944.] 12p. **1R294**
The editor of the *Daily Worker* pleads for the lifting of the ban on appointment of a *Daily Worker* war correspondent. Sir James Grigg was Secretary of State for War. The story of wartime censorship of the *Daily Worker* is also told in Rust's *The Story of the Daily Worker* (London, People's Printing Society, 1949).

————. *32 Questions on Press Freedom*. London, People's Press Printing Society, n.d. 16p. **1R295**
The full questionnaire issued by the Royal Commission on the Press and the replies made by the *Daily Worker*.

Rutledge, W. Eugene. "The Law of Defamation: Recent Developments." *Alabama Lawyer*, 32:409–23, October 1971. **1R296**
"The net result [of recent Supreme Court decisions] is to abolish libel action against the news media. The review of the facts by the court in the cases cited clearly demonstrates the practical impossibility of the plaintiff meeting the burden of proof to the satisfaction of the Court. . . . Justice Black has his victory. The press may now say what it pleases about anyone it pleases. The only loser is the individual citizen of this country."

Ruttle, Margaret. *Limiting Media Ownership*. Columbia, Mo., Freedom of Information Center, School of Journalism, University of Missouri at Columbia, 1972. 5p. (Report no. 293) **1R297**
"The FCC's controversial 'one-to-a-customer' rule restricting multiple ownership of media outlets in a single market has created much confusion and frustration among broadcasters and publishers. Aggravating the situation is the FCC's delay in clarifying different aspects of the rule and plans for enforcement."

Rutzick, Mark C. "Offensive Language and the Evolution of First Amendment Protection." *Harvard Civil Rights–Civil Liberties Law Review*, 9:1–28, January 1974. **1R298**
"This article will review the original contours of the Supreme Court's offensive language model and the changes which have led to increased constitutional protection. It will then attempt to formulate the elements of the model as it stands today."

Ruvolo, Ignazio J. "Newsman's Immunity Statute—A Comparison of Legislative Intent to Statutory Form." *San Diego Law Review*, 8:110–25, January 1971. **1R299**
"To completely insure the public interest in obtaining information from confidential sources, the immunity statute needs to be legislatively expanded to provide a privilege for the informer as well. The ideals of a free press and a free people are paramount to any arguments against such an extension." The comments deal with *Lipps v. State*, 258 N.E. 2d 622 (1970), involving an Indiana statute granting immunity to newsmen.

Ryan, Alan. "The Right to be Left Alone." (The Abuses of Literacy—7) *Times Literary Supplement*, 3,652:223–24, 25 February 1972. **1R300**
The object of this essay is to defend John Stuart Mill's principle that "the sole end for which mankind are warranted, individually or collectively, in interfering with the liberty of action of any of their number, is self-protection," as this principle relates to the legal censorship of obscene literature and "the whole range of pressures which we collectively employ to ensure that each of us conforms to the expectations we have of each other."

Ryan, Frederick. "The Latest Crusade Against 'Immoral Literature.'" *Irish Review*, 1:521–26, January 1912. **1R301**
The author discusses the present crusade against immoral literature, which had its origin at the Conference of the Catholic Truth Society in Dublin. The movement attempts to establish an intellectual censorship masquerading as a campaign for cleanliness. Those who criticize the censorship, however sincere and public spirited, are "branded as supporters of indecency by some of the organs of the campaign, themselves among the most vulgar and degraded periodicals in the country."

Ryan, Geoffrey C. "A Threat to U.S. Security?" *Index on Censorship*, 5(4):10–19, Winter 1976. **1R302**
An account of the *cause célèbre* involving Daniel Schorr and the unauthorized publication of the report of the U.S. House of Representatives Committee investigating the CIA (Pike Papers) by the *Village Voice*.

————. "Un-American Activities." *Index on Censorship*, 2(1):25–38, Spring 1973; (2):77–90, Summer 1973; 2(3):81–93, Autumn 1973. **1R303**
In this three-part series the author describes and analyzes the role of the Un-American Activities Committee of the United States Congress from 1930 until it was disbanded in 1969.

Ryan, James J. "Seizure of Allegedly Obscene Films." *South Dakota Law Review*, 15:399–411, Spring 1970. **1R304**
"The exhibitor and the public's right to review nonobscene films can be sufficiently safeguarded through use of a preliminary adversary proceeding similar to that employed in the *Bonanza* decision." The author believes that the South Dakota statutes may be construed as the California statutes in *Bonanza* (*California v. Bonanza Printing Co., Inc.*, 1969).

Ryan, Paul M. *Crime News Regulation in England and America*. Austin, Tex., University of Texas, 1968. 116p. (Unpublished Master's thesis) **1R305**
"The thesis examines the possibilities of transporting the British Press Council system of press self-regulation to America to control and eliminate certain techniques of crime coverage which lead to criticism by the public. The author contends that the council has moderated British crime stories and that such a system of self-regulation would be effective in America."

Ryan, Paul R. ["Letter to Readers and Advertisers of *The Drama Review*."] *Drama Review*, 19(2):1+, June 1975. **1R306**
An account of the delay in publication of the March issue of *Drama Review* because the printer refused to print a manuscript containing objectionable four-letter words. Included are letters to the editor, mostly in support of the editor's refusal to permit the printer to censor the copy.

Ryan, William D. *The Development of the Federal Trade Commission's Authority to Regulate Advertising*. Urbana, Ill., University of Illinois, 1968. 304p. (Ph.D. dissertation, University Microfilms, no. 68-12,190) **1R307**
"This study was undertaken to investigate the results of fifty-three years of advertising regulation by the Federal Trade Commission, the federal agency implementing the broadest mandate to control this type of information flow. An historical approach is taken to the development of the FTC with a transition to case analysis to trace the development of the agency's now well-established authority to handle advertising it believes false or misleading through its quasi-judicial procedure. The study then focuses on the ramifications of self-developed FTC procedures which the agency has brought to bear on advertising and finally analyzes current and probably future regulatory trends."

S

Saalberg, Harvey. "The Canons of Journalism: A 50-Year Perspective." *Journalism Quarterly*, 50:731–34, Winter 1973. **1S1**
"Born in response to the sensationalism of Jazz Journalism, the ASNE code has stood the test of time, as journalism has become more professional."

————. "Don Mellett, Editor of the Canton *News*, Was Slain While Exposing Underworld." *Journalism Quarterly*, 53:88–93, Spring 1976. **1S2**
"Murdered 50 years ago, Mellett had attacked his city's ineffectual police and all-too-efficient criminal elements when he was shot to death." Canton seemed to have remained relatively unchanged despite the martyrdom of Mellett.

————. "Martyrs to the Press: James M. Lingan." *Editor & Publisher*, 109(25):7, 19 June 1976. **1S3**
A brief account of the "first martyr to the press," General James M. Lingan, who had served under Washington in the Revolutionary War and was co-owner of the *Baltimore Federal Republican*, a Federalist paper that opposed the War of 1812. When his paper was destroyed by a pro-war mob, the sixty-two-year-old Lingan and a young associate escaped to Georgetown. There they were joined by others, including General Henry "Light-Horse Harry" Lee. They returned to Baltimore and set up their press in a Baltimore home. Again the mob attacked, but the cavalry arrived and rescued the beseiged newspapermen and printers, removing them to the jail for protection. The cavalry failed to defend the jail, however, and the mob moved in, killing Lingan and severely wounding General Lee and others.

Sabine, William H. W. *A Letter About Distorted History from a Member of the New-York Historical Society to a Friend.* Hollis, N.Y., Colburn & Tegg, 1975. 23p. **1S4**
The author charges the New-York Historical Society with a conspiracy of silence with respect to the turncoat behavior of a revolutionary war general, Nathaniel Woodhull, and

with a cold reception to the author's book, *Murder 1776, and Washington's Policy of Silence*, in which he exposed the long-time cover-up.

Sacco, Thomas W. "Branzburg, Caldwell and Pappas—A Quick Lateral Pass to Congress." *New England Law Review*, 8:336–49, Spring 1973. **1S5**
"As a result of *Branzburg v. Hayes, In re Pappas, United States v. Caldwell* (1972), there exists today no visible restraint upon the power of a Grand Jury to force the revelation by newsmen of the sources which may include information related to the commission of a crime. In this five to four multiple decision, the Supreme Court held that the First Amendment did not afford newsmen the right to remain silent before a Grand Jury, which by its very nature has the right to every citizen's testimony in the investigation of a crime."

Sackett, Harvey P. "The *Gertz* Case: Unbalancing Media Rights and Reputational Interests." *Western State University Law Review*, 2:227–41, Spring 1975. **1S6**
Re: *Gertz v. Robert Welch, Inc.*, 418 U.S. 323 (1974).

Sackett, Henry W., and Harold L. Cross. *What You Should Know About the Law of Libel. How Editors, Copyreaders and Reporters May Guard Against Libel Suits.* New York, Herald Tribune, 1950. 28p. (Revision of a 1929 work by Henry W. Sackett, New York, Columbia University Press) **1S7**

Saddler, Virginia B. "Intellectual Freedom vs. the Community Values Dilemma." *Kentucky English Bulletin*, 24(2):10–15, Winter 1974/75. **1S8**
The author describes the apparent dilemma faced by librarians and teachers in following the U.S. Supreme Court's rule of community standards on obscenity and yet holding to the belief in intellectual freedom. She concludes that "community values can best be served if intellectual freedom is our goal. What we must

do as educators, then, is to convince our governing bodies that intellectual freedom becomes *the* community standard."

Sadowski, Robert P. *An Analysis of Statutory Laws Governing Commercial and Educational Broadcasting in the Fifty States.* Iowa City, Iowa, University of Iowa, 1973. 223p. (Ph.D. dissertation, University Microfilms, no. 73-980) **1S9**
"The purpose of this study was to determine the extent to which the states have exercised their rights in legislating statutory laws governing certain aspects of commercial and educational radio and television broadcasting." The author found that every state had at least one law governing broadcasting. "Most state legislative activity has focused on matters pertaining to broadcasting and individual rights, including defamation/libel/slander, the right of privacy, and the right to know."

————. "Broadcasting and State Statutory Laws." *Journal of Broadcasting*, 18:433–50, Fall 1974. **1S10**
"This paper summarizes the results of a study which was designed to answer one major question concerning broadcasting regulation: What role are states playing in the regulation of broadcasting in the United States?" The article is based on the author's doctoral dissertation at the University of Iowa, 1973. He found that states have exercised their rights to regulate broadcasting in some eighty-six different aspects of broadcasting. An accompanying table lists state regulation of broadcasting as of 1973.

————. "Defamation and Disclosure: A Broadcast Precedent for State Shield Laws." *Journal of Broadcasting*, 17:437–46, Fall 1973. **1S11**
The article shows that "a precedent for state legislative action to provide a solution to the newsmen's privilege controversy can be found in an analysis of the events that led to the 1959 *Farmers Union* Supreme Court decision with defamatory statements broadcast by political candidates."

Sagarin, Edward. "An Essay on

Obscenity and Pornography: Pardon Me, Sir, But Your Asterisk is Missing." *Humanist*, 29:10–12, July–August 1969. **1S12**
The author considers how the pornographic and the obscene have changed in character in recent years. He finds that it has not been demonstrated that pornography has any lasting effect on the user; nor has it been demonstrated "whether or not a generation that grows up with little secrecy and mystique surrounding sex will be able to integrate sexuality better into its life, will be able to derive from sex more enjoyment and less guilt." He concludes in his evaluation of the pornographic revolution that "the antisexuality of former days consisted of suppression of body and talk of it; today it consists of the depiction of the same body as gross and ugly in order to shock and offend. The generation that tore away the fig leaves was not content with that accomplishment; but proceeded to replace the lovely organs of man and woman by crudely constructed distortions. It is no wonder, then, that obscenity is a weapon against one's enemies."

———. "On Banning the Beautiful and Showing the Ugly." *Humanist*, 34(2):22–25, March 1974. **1S13**
Some reflections by a civil libertarian on pornography, censorship and the recent *Miller* decision of the U.S. Supreme Court (*Miller v. California*, 1973). The result of this decision, he believes, will encourage the inartistic, worthless hard-core pornography while serious erotic art will go into eclipse. "It will be a sad irony for the crusaders for decency, and perhaps it will sound a deathknell to the demands for local control over our lives."

Sage, Ray O. "Cameras in the Courtroom: A Modern Fable." *American Bar Association Journal*, 54(1):54–56, January 1968. **1S14**
"Once upon a time, in order to keep the press happy, the court agreed to let one man with an innocuous little telephoto lens sit in the back of the courtroom. . . . Soon radio and TV became envious. But that situation was well resolved. And even the problem of the district attorney being a bad actor was not insurmountable. But then came the fateful day when the TV stations asked the court to speed up the administration of justice!"

Sager, Donald J. "Libraries Enter the Wasteland: Controversial Materials in the Media." *Catholic Library World*, 46:102–6, October 1974. **1S15**
A review of programming questions faced by libraries in attempting to present both sides of controversial questions over radio or television: Federal Communications Commission regulations, local station standards, action by local pressure groups, and the copyright law.

St. Dizier, Byron J. *Confidential News Sources and the Florida Newspaper Reporter*. Gainesville, Fla., University of Florida, 1974. 94p. (Unpublished Master's thesis) **1S16**
A questionnaire study of reporters in Florida's ten largest daily newspapers revealed that almost all relied heavily upon confidential sources in their reporting; 10 percent had at one time been asked by a judicial body to reveal news sources, but only one-fourth complied. A slight majority favored no shield legislation, but of those favoring such a law, almost three-fourths wanted it to be absolute.

St. John, Jeffrey. "The Fragmentation of Freedom: The Economics of the First Amendment." *Vital Speeches*, 40:660–62, 15 August 1974. **1S17**
A columnist for the Copley News Service writes that the courts have generally upheld the editorial freedom of editors and publishers but the economic freedom of the printed and broadcast press remains in peril. He calls for reform in guarantees of the right to advertise, for tougher libel laws, and for a recognition by the media of the need for freedom of the marketplace for goods as well as for ideas.

St. John-Stevas, Norman. "A. P. Herbert and Obscenity Law Reform." *Tablet: The International Catholic Weekly*, 225:1120, 20 November 1971. (Periscope column) **1S18**
On the occasion of the death of A. P. Herbert, the author comments on Herbert's part in modification of English obscenity law. "The basic distinction which the Obscene Publications Act sought to draw was between the erotic which should be accepted as a part of life and the pornographic which should not."

———. "The Control of Contraception." In his *Life, Death and the Law: Law and Christian Morals in England and the United States*. Bloomington, Ind., Indiana University Press, 1961, pp. 50–115. **1S19**
Includes efforts in England and the United States to prevent the distribution of information on birth control under the obscenity laws.

Ste. Marie, Jean-Paul. "L'Obscénité." *La Revue Juridique Thémis*, 1969:125–32, 1969. **1S20**
A discussion of obscenity as proscribed by the Criminal Code of Canada.

Salant, Richard S. "The Broadcast Press and Vice-President Agnew." [New York, Columbia Broadcasting System, 1969.] 15p. Processed. **1S21**
The president of CBS News answers Vice-President Spiro Agnew's attacks on the press, beginning with a detailing of the errors in facts, faulty logic, and internal contradictions. He denies Agnew's charge that television enjoys a monopoly, citing the four fiercely competitive networks, the 800 television stations, and the 7,000 radio stations. He comments on "instant analysis" of the President's speeches: "It is not

the proper role and function of a free press merely to act as passive conduit, as cheerleader, or as an amplifier for official views or speeches of any group or individual." To Agnew's charge that "the views of this fraternity [the network newsmen] do not represent the views of America," he responds: "If by this he means, as he appears to mean, that it is a journalist's function to determine what the consensus is, and then report only what the majority wants to hear, in the way the majority wants to hear it, omitting all else, then the Vice-President has called for an end to all the nobility of a free and vigorous press." An address given to the Arizona Broadcasters Association, Phoenix, Ariz., 5 December 1969.

———. *CBS News Comment on "The News Twisters."* New York, Columbia Broadcasting System, 1971. 10p. Processed. **1S22**
The president of CBS News responds to charges of network bias contained in Edith Efron's book, *News Twisters*. "She sees sinister meanings where none were intended and none exist. Her conclusions are based, in large part, on non-existent facts." Attached are the text of pertinent portions of CBS broadcasts together with Efron's comments, intended to show the inaccuracy and unfairness of her conclusions.

———. "Challenge to Broadcasters." *Public Relations Journal*, 26(10):58–60, October 1970. **1S23**
The press, particularly the electronic press, may have entered a guerrilla war with government, brought into focus by the attacks of Vice-President Agnew. The vice-president "did not confine himself merely to suggesting that the media should reflect the Administration's views rather than inform people. He went out of his way . . . to remind us that broadcasters have lesser First Amendment protection than the print press and are licensed by the same government of which he is a ranking official." Salant is concerned with the apparent popular tolerance of attacks on press freedom. "The preservation of a free press rests not only in the hands of practicing journalists; it depends upon public awareness of its importance and the public's will to remain free."

———. "He Has Exercised His Right To Be Wrong." *TV Guide*, 17(38):10–11+, 20 September 1969. (Reprinted by Television Information Office, New York; also in Barry G. Cole, *ed.*, *Television: A Selection of Readings from TV Guide Magazine*. New York, Free Press, 1970, pp. 330–37) **1S24**
Salant answers charges made by Federal Communications Commission member Nicholas Johnson (*TV Guide*, 5 July 1969) that vital public issues are not discussed on television because of TV's dependence on advertising.

———. "The Power of Licensing." *Vital Speeches*, 38:659–63, 15 August 1972. **1S25**
The speaker discusses the relationship between the presidency and the press, citing the historical development of conflicts. Until the advent of broadcasting, these relationships were really no more than a game, though often deadly serious, but the press always had the First Amendment, which was a warm comfort. The electronic press is more vulnerable because of government licensing and Federal Communications Commission controls. An additional problem, of more recent years, has been the aggressive use of radio and television by presidents for their own ends. This gives the "ins" great advantages over the "outs," and gives the Office of the president advantages over the other branches in reaching the people. Salant proposes the latter inequity be redressed by broadcasting arguments of the U.S. Supreme Court and the proceedings of Congress. He believes that, while there is no one solution to insure balance and fairness, that it is far better for broadcasting itself to devise solutions than for the government to do the job.

Saletsky, Doria. "Advertising of Discount Prescription Prices Is Unprotected Commercial Speech the Regulation of Which is Rationally Related to the State's Interest in Preserving Local Pharmacies and Preventing Harmful Competition." *Hofstra Law Review*, 4:867–79, Spring 1976. **1S26**
"The issue of whether a pharmacist has the right to advertise discount prescription prices has been the subject of many state and federal lawsuits in recent years. In *Urowsky v. Board of Regents* [1975] the New York Court of Appeals adopted the minority view and declined to recognize such a right." The author concludes that the Urowsky decision is "detrimental to the interests of both the advertiser and the consumer."

Salisbury, Harrison. "Print Journalism." *Playboy*, 19(1):121–22, 254–55, January 1972. **1S27**
A *New York Times* correspondent assesses the Nixon-Agnew Administration's attacks on the press, finding the press guilty but not as charged.

———. "Why We Need a Watchdog Press." *TV Guide*, 22(48):14–16, 30 November 1974. **1S28**
A veteran newspaperman who spent five years in Communist countries is interviewed by Eric Levin.

Salomon, Kenneth D., and Lawrence H. Wechsler. "The Freedom of Information Act: A Critical Review." *George Washington Law Review*, 38:150–63, October 1969. **1S29**
"The Act is a much needed step in the right direction, but to date it has not worked a significant change on the disclosure of information policies of the Federal Government."

Saloschin, Robert L. "The Freedom of Information Act: A Governmental Perspective." *Public Administration Review*, 35:10–14, January–February 1975. **1S30**
A discussion of some of the difficulties encountered by executive departments in implementing the Freedom of Information Act, and what can be done to improve the processing of requests for information.

Salter, Kenneth W. *The Pentagon Papers Trial*. Berkeley, Calif., Justa Publications, 1975. 123p. **1S31**
An abridged account of the trial of Daniel Ellsberg and Anthony Russo, Jr., for conspiracy, espionage, and theft, in the case of the Pentagon Papers. The author has limited his reporting to the charge of theft of information.

Samek, R. A. "Pornography as a Species of Second-Order Sexual Behavior: A Submission for Law Reform." *Dalhousie Law Journal*, 1:265–93, December 1973. **1S32**
This paper was prepared by a professor of law, Dalhousie University, as a submission to the Law Reform Commission of Canada in response to its Study Paper on Obscenity. "My submission on the whole has taken a different line of approach from the Study Paper. While the thrust of the Study Paper is in favor of relaxing the existing controls on pornography as part of a general withdrawal of criminal law from the protection of private morals, the burden of my proposed submission has been that it should be controlled by administrative means on the basis of the new guiding concept of undue commercial exploitation of sex. . . . Undue commercial exploitation is immoral as such; it need not be connected with sex, and when it is so connected, it is the commercial exploitation of the connection, and not its sexual nature, that makes it objectionable." The author denies the soundness of the laissez faire argument that increasing the supply of pornography beyond a certain point and the law of diminishing returns will apply. The supply of pornography will eventually level off, but it will not dry up. "The waters of pornography run deep; for they have been effectively linked to the well-spring of sex."

Samoff, Bernard, and Jeffrey C. Falkin. "The Freedom of Information Act and the NLRB." *Boston College Industrial and Commercial Law Review*, 15:1267–90, July 1974. **1S33**
Content: An Overview of the Freedom of Information Act, Litigation Involving the Act and the National Labor Relations Board, Analysis of the Cases, and Emerging Themes.

Samore, William. "New York Libel Per Quod: Enigma Still?" *Albany Law Review*, 31:250–54, June 1967. **1S34**
A discussion of the issues involving the "libel per quod" rule under discussion by the American Law Institute in restating the law of torts.

Sampson, John J. "Commercial Traffic in Sexually Oriented Materials." *Technical Report on the [U.S.] Commission on Obscenity and Pornography*, 3:3–208, 1971. **1S35**
This report "is an attempt to describe the operation of the several industries that publish and distribute sexually oriented materials, and to estimate the volume of business in these materials. The descriptions of the several different industries [motion pictures, books and magazines, mail order, and "under-the-counter" or "hard-core" pornography] are based on personal observation, interviews with many of the major operators in the industries, and interviews with knowledgeable people outside the industries. The estimates of volume of business are based on interviews with people in the industries, examination of the records of individual enterprises, industry statistics, governmental statistics and records, questionnaire data, and analyses which compare and combine information from various sources."

Samuel, Peter. "Government Secrecy." *Australian Quarterly*, 44:5–8, June 1972. **1S36**
Australian journalists, the author suggests, "thoroughly enjoy the establishment's present repressive posture toward information. It isn't so repressive that anyone is actually in jail, and yet there is a titillating excitement of knowing your phone is probably tapped, that a colleague has been questioned by the police, that some carbon copies of a report disappeared in the night . . . ." The article suggests (1) publication of all departmental submissions to ministers and Cabinet, (2) abandonment of restraints on comment and issue of information by public servants, and (3) legal insistence on the public's right of access to government documents.

Samuels, Alec. "Obscenity and the Law." *Northern Ireland Legal Quarterly*, 20:231–54, September 1969. **1S37**
"Public indecency, pornography (literally the writing of prostitutes) and harmful license must be suppressed. Yet society must practice toleration, preserve the freedom to publish, avoid censorship, and protect literature. The conflict lies between repression and license. The law must seek to reflect contemporary values and reach an acceptable compromise."

Samuels, Deby K. *Judges and Trial News Challenges*. Columbia, Mo., Freedom of Information Center, School of Journalism, University of Missouri at Columbia, 1973. 8p. (Report no. 317) **1S38**
"Protective court orders, sometimes called 'gag orders,' are utilized with increasing frequency

by trial judges attempting to balance the rights of a free press and an impartial jury. Sometimes such orders achieve the desired effects; on other occasions they infringe the rights of the press without any redeeming assurance of more impartial juries."

Sanchez, Benjamin C. "Restrictions on Freedom of Expression By School Authorities." *Gonzaga Law Review*, 3: 227–36, Spring 1968. **1S39**
A review of court decisions involving First Amendment freedoms applied to high school students. The author concludes that "it is clear that school authorities must show definitely compelling reasons for the regulations before they may intrude upon the student's freedom of expression."

Sandage, Charles H. "The Right to Know." *Grassroots Editor*, 12(3):4–7, May–June 1971. **1S40**
The author suggests that we recognize the mass media as common carriers and expect them to adhere to the principles that apply to other transportation agencies; that through the means of renting white space, freedom of access is provided to all who have a message, whether commercial, political, or otherwise.

Sandall, Roger. "A Curious Case of Censorship." *Encounter*, 47:42, 44, July 1976. **1S41**
The author charges that certain anthropologists in Australia are using censorship to prevent revealing ancient secret rights of the aborigines they have been studying. He sees the new anthropologist and the ethnographic research institutes as tending to compromise their disinterested inquiry by identifying with the tribalism they have been studying. The author's film, made for the Australian Institute of Aboriginal Studies, has been widely shown and acclaimed abroad, but in Australia may only be seen by "mature males with impeccable *bona fides*" and never unchaperoned outside of Sydney.

Sander, Jerry R. *Freedoms in Collision*. Washington, D.C., American University, 1968. 78p. (Unpublished Master's thesis) **1S42**
A study of the issue of fair trial–free press, with a proposed solution.

Sandman, Peter M. *Eco-Pornography: Environmental Advertising and Advertising Acceptance in the San Francisco Bay Area*. Palo Alto, Calif., Stanford University, 1972. 298p. (Ph.D. dissertation, University Microfilms, no. 72-16,786) **1S43**
"This dissertation explores and defends the argument that the mass media should adopt more stringent advertising acceptance standards for advertisements with environmental implications. . . . Legal and ethical analysis of the putative right of access to the media leads

to the conclusion that the media are legally entitled to reject any advertisement, and ethically obligated to reject all advertisements whose publication they believe would be harmful to society. Procedures are suggested for insuring ideological access in the context of responsible advertising rejection, and for assessing the accuracy and environmental responsibility of environmental advertisements."

————. *The Legal Rights and Responsibilities of College Student Publications*. Pittsburgh, Pi Delta Epsilon, 1969. 10p. **1S44**
Content: Censorship (the facts, the student publisher, the student editor), Post-Publication "Censorship," Informal Controls, Delegated Authority, The Right to Report, Libel, Obscenity, Sedition, Copyright, Contempt of Court, Lotteries, Responsibility. "In all respects but one, the legal rights and responsibilities of student publications are identical with those of their commercial cousins. The one exception is censorship."

————. "Who Should Police Environmental Advertising?" *Columbia Journalism Review*, 10(5):41–47, January–February 1972. **1S45**
"The issue goes beyond puffery. Besides leading the consumer astray, environmental ads can distort public opinion on the vital topic of ecological survival."

Sands, Alexander P., III. "The Requirement and Techniques for Holding an Adversary Hearing Prior to Seizure of Obscene Material." *North Carolina Law Review*, 48:830–47, June 1970. **1S46**
The author proposes state legislative enactment of constitutionally acceptable procedure for seizure of obscene materials rather than reliance on random case-by-case judicial improvisation.

[Santangelo, Orazio D. G. de A.] *Santangelo's Trial for Libel Against Samuel McRoberts, a Senator of the United States from Illinois. Before the Court of General Sessions in the City of New York. Part I. Instructions Given by Mr. O. de A. Santangelo to His Counsel*. New York, n.p., 1842. 86p. **1S47**
The libel case involved a sixteen-page pamphlet issued by Santangelo during the 1842 senatorial campaign: *A Circular to the World. Is the Honorable McRoberts More Honorable Than the Honorable Mitchell?*

Saraf, D. N., and K. P. Sarathy. "Reflections on the Press Council Bill, 1963." *Journal of the Indian Law Institute*, 7:112–22, January–June 1965. **1S48**
A discussion of a bill pending before Parliament to establish a Press Council, on recom-

mendation of the India Press Commission. The authors recommend changes in the bill which would provide for a more effective Council that would regulate the profession of journalism in all its stages.

Sare, Richard. *Advertisement. Whereas there is published an Advertisement [by T. Basset and others] menacing an action against R. Sare for printing Sir R[oger] L'Estrange's Translation of Josephus: This is to tell the World that I am resolved to go on with it, etc.* [London, 1693.] Broadside. **1S49**
Bookseller Sare seemed to have gotten by with his *Josephus*, but was brought to trial in 1709 for selling Matthew Tindal's *Rights of the Christian Church Asserted* (H267).

Sarkar, A. K. *The Law and Obscenity*. Bombay, N. M. Tripathi, 1967. 132p. **1S50**
An assessment and criticism of the obscenity laws in India—"strewn in a number of statutes like the Indian Penal Code, the Post Offices Act, the Press (Malicious Matters) Act, the Sea Customs Act, etc."—and suggestions for reform. In the appendix are: *Ranjit D. Udeshi v. State of Maharastra* (*Lady Chatterley's Lover* case, 1964), an account of the *Fanny Hill* trial in New York, 1963, and the text of the British Obscene Publications Act, 1959, which Sarkar suggests as a guideline for forming an Indian statute.

Sarkar, Chanchal. *Press Councils and Their Role*. Delhi, Press Institute of India, 1965. 18p. **1S51**
A brief review of the experience of press councils in various countries, prepared for an Asian seminar. Twelve kinds of cases considered by press councils are described. A press council will soon start work in India.

Sarker, Subhash C. "The Editor and His Freedom." *Vidura*, 12:45–49, February 1975. (Reprinted in *Modern Review*, March 1975) **1S52**
Under Indian law the editor is responsible for anything appearing in a newspaper, including advertisements, although the management may lay down the newspaper's policies and the subordinate editorial staff may carry them out. The author recommends that the terms of the appointment of the editor be made public so that his relationship with the staff, the public, and the advertisers is clear. The Press Council should play a more active role in supporting ethical practices within newspapers.

————. "Freedom of the Press in India." *Modern Review* (Calcutta), 132: 17–22, January 1973. **1S53**
The Indian press is only free if it avoids criti-

cism of the powerful political and business interests.

Sarno, Edward F., Jr. "The National Radio Conferences." *Journal of Broadcasting*, 13:189–202, Spring 1969. (Reprinted in Lawrence W. Lichty and Malachi C. Topping, *eds.*, *American Broadcasting*, pp. 534–44)   **1S54**
An account of the four national conferences called by Secretary of Commerce Herbert Hoover, 1922–25, which led to the eventual enactment of the Radio Act of 1927.

Sarnoff, Robert W. "The Threat to Freedom of Information." *Vital Speeches*, 39:551–54, 1 July 1973.   **1S55**
The chairman of Radio Corporation of America speaks of the escalation of government intrusion into broadcasting which he believes has reached a danger point. He accuses high government officials with attacking the news media with the intent to impair its credibility. The source of much of the assault is the Office of Telecommunication in the White House that has used the pretext of "localism" in proposing measures to throttle network broadcasting. The Nixon Administration has adopted the tactics of intimidation to make the broadcasters docile and accommodating. He calls on newspapers and broadcasters to unite in facing common threats to press freedom.

Sarris, Andrew. "Censorship: A View from New York." *Sight and Sound*, 38:202–3, 219, Autumn 1969. (Reprinted in his *Primal Screen*. New York, Simon & Schuster, 1973, pp. 106–10)
          1S56
The author writes of the liberation of the motion pictures from censorship and the hedonistic tide sweeping the nation. "This longtime movieman can only regret that we didn't have a little less freedom a little earlier. . . . The censors allowed us nothing when we asked for so little, and so now it is only fitting that we allow the censors nothing no matter how base the screen becomes. There can be no compromise with censorship even when there is regret for some of the lost charm of repression and innocence."

Sasser, M. Michael. "The Journalistic Privilege: Newsgathering Versus the Public's Need to Know." *Idaho Law Review*, 10:234–44, Spring 1974.   **1S57**
"The question of a journalistic privilege necessitates a balancing of two competing interests—enhancing the administration of justice through compulsory testimony of all citizens versus promoting the free flow of news, and hence, the people's right to know. To be sure, both interests are basic to the American philosophy."

Sastri, V. Parabrahma. "The Right to Publish Testimony of a Witness." *Journal of the Indian Law Institute*, 9:102–6, January–March 1967.   **1S58**
Consideration of the practice of holding a trial or portion of a trial *in camera*, in which publication of the testimony of witnesses is prohibited. This practice, the author believes, is in conflict with the Indian Constitution which guarantees freedom of the press.

Saunders, Keith. *The Independent Man: The Story of W. O. Saunders and His Delightfully Different Newspaper*. ₁Washington, D.C.?₎, Saunders Press, 1962. 282p.   **1S59**
The son of the controversial editor of the *Elizabethtown, N.J., Independent* reminisces about the trials and tribulations in the newspaper career of his father. During Saunders's stormy and iconoclastic career which started before World War I and spanned the Prohibition Era and the Great Depression, he was subjected to numerous libel suits, boycotts, and threats against his press and his life. Through all his troubles he maintained his independence. Included is the text of Saunders's editorial on freedom of the press, which he charged was a "big American joke like the wisdom and integrity of bankers, the sound economic sense of our business leaders, and the honesty and intelligence of our lawmakers. The most dependent, servile, spineless, opinionless and fearstricken thing I know, with the exception of a certain class of ministerial brethren, is the average American daily or weekly newspaper." He describes how politicians and advertisers dominate the average newspaper. "Every yardstick for the measurement of moral, social, and political values is in most hands but the lengthened shadow of a bank note." Theodore Schroeder wrote an article on Saunders, An Amusing Criminal, which appeared in *Open Road*, August 1942.

Saunders, W. O. "The Spirit of the Declaration of Independence Gone to Hell. U.S. Postoffice Department Puts the Ban on Saunders' Weekly." *Saunders' Weekly National Independent*, 1(10):3–6, 8 July 1916.   **1S60**
A report on the action of the U.S. Post Office in banning the 17 June 1916 issue of the *Saunders' Weekly* from second-class mailing privileges. The ban was imposed, according to the postmaster, because Saunders had sent out too many free issues; according to the solicitor general, because of obscenity, which was not identified. Editor Saunders believed it was because of his attacks on the Wilson Administration as "smelling to high heaven with rottenness and corruption." In the article Saunders accuses "the rich, representing less than two percent of the population," of controlling both the press and the government, no matter which party was in power.

₁Savage, Richard.₎ *An Author to be Lett. Being A Proposal humbly address'd to the Consideration of the Knights, Esquires,* *Gentlemen, and other worshipful and weighty Members of the Solid and Ancient Society of the Bathos. By . . . Iscariot Hackney* ₁pseud.₎ *. . . Numb. 1. To be continued*. London, Alexander Vint, 1729. 12p.   **1S61**
Purported to be the reminiscences of a hack writer, the author boasts of writing libels, works falsely attributed to dead authors, ghosted articles, spurious autobiographies, and cribbing from works of others, especially official reports and state tracts. He is pleased that his books have been declared libelous and have been burnt by the common hangman. He especially enjoys a sales trick of clapping a new title page to the sale of every half-hundred books, a trick he learned from publisher Curll.

"Saving Society? A Discussion on Censorship." *New Nation* (South Africa), 4(7):14–15, 21, February 1971.   **1S62**
A recorded discussion on censorship between a group of professional men, members of the Pasquino Society whose general object is the promotion of access to and discussion of literature and the arts.

Sawer, Geoffrey. *A Guide to Australian Law for Journalists, Authors, Printers and Publishers*. 2d ed. Melbourne, Melbourne University Press, 1968. 121p.
          1S63
Chapters on defamation, contempt of court and of Parliament, obscenity, blasphemy, and sedition.

Sawicky, Robert K. *Free Press v. Fair Trial: The Origins and Implications of the Reardon Report*. Berkeley, Calif., University of California, 1958. 163p. (Unpublished Master's thesis)   **1S64**

Scalia, Antonin. "Don't Go Near the Water." *Federal Communications Bar Journal*, 25:111–20, 1972.   **1S65**
"I do not think the problem of the Fairness Doctrine can successfully be resolved without simultaneously grasping the thorny issues presented by new demands of access. The one will continue to undermine and subvert any rational solution devised for the other, unless they are both resolved together." At the time the author was general counsel, Office of Telecommunications Policy.

Scammell, Michael. "Notebook." *Index on Censorship*, 1(2):5–14, Summer 1972.
          1S66
The editor of this magazine dealing with censorship comments on the aims and intentions of the sponsors, the reception of the first issue, and the contents of the current issue.

Scanlon, Paul D. "The FTC, the FCC, and the 'Counter-Ad' Controversy: An Invitation to 'Let's You and Him

Fight?' " *Antitrust Law and Economic Review*, 5:43–58, Fall 1971.   **1S67**
The Federal Trade Commission has suggested to the Federal Communications Commission that counter-advertising might be in the public interest with respect to certain categories of advertising: (1) advertising asserting claims of product characteristics that explicitly raise controversial issues of public importance, (2) advertising stressing broad current themes, affecting the purchase decision in a manner that implicitly raises controversial issues of current public importance, (3) advertising claims that rest upon or rely upon scientific premises that are currently subject to controversy within the scientific community, and (4) advertising that is silent about negative aspects of the advertised product. The text of the FTC statement is included.

Scanlon, Thomas. "A Theory of Freedom of Expression." *Philosophy and Public Affairs*, 1:204–26, Winter 1972. **1S68**
"The theory of freedom of expression which I am offering . . . consists of at least four distinguishable elements. It is based upon the Millian Principle, which is absolute but serves to rule out certain justifications for legal restrictions on acts of expression. Within the limits set by this principle the whole range of government policies affecting opportunities for expression, whether by restriction, positive intervention, or failure to intervene, are subject to justification and criticism on a number of diverse grounds. First, on grounds of whether they reflect on appropriate balancing of the value of certain kinds of expression relative to other social goods; second, whether they insure equitable distribution of access to means of expression throughout society; and third, whether they are compatible with the recognition of certain special rights, particularly political rights."

Sceales, Robin. "What Is Obscenity?" *New Nation* (South Africa), 4(2):7–8, September 1970.   **1S69**
The author examines current obscenity legislation in South Africa in light of the situation in United States, Canada, and Great Britain. He calls for a reassessment of the situation by the legislature.

Schad, Lawrence W. "The News and the Accused." *Prospectus*, 3:95–138, December 1969.   **1S70**
"The author believes that the Reardon Standards, if implemented, would provide an effective solution to the problem of prejudicial information, and that this potential can be best realized through adoption and enforcement of the Standards by the Courts."

Schadeberg, Henry C. "A Bad Situation Concerning Smut and Other Pornographic Literature." *Congressional Record*, 115:31643–45, 27 October 1969.   **1S71**
The congressman suggests legislation to control the sale of mailing lists as a means of keeping pornography from being advertised to minors. He also includes an article on obscenity by Rev. Morton A. Hill, reprinted from *Morality in Media*, October 1969, and an editorial, Let's Clean Up the Mails from *Postal Record*.

———. "Pornography—The Rising Tide of Smut." *Congressional Record*, 115:1996–97, 28 January 1969. **1S72**
A report on the operation of the law which enables parents and others who wish to protest unsolicited obscene advertisements received through the mail to have their names removed from mailing lists. The Act has been difficult to enforce and he is introducing a bill making it a federal offense to use the name of an individual without his clear consent. The bill would require mailing-list brokers to register and buyers of such lists to furnish information of their identity and transactions.

———. "President's Commission on Obscenity and Pornography." *Congressional Record*, 116:10635–37, 7 April 1970.   **1S73**
An attack on the report of the Commission. Included is a letter from a dissenting member, Father Morton A. Hill, and two newspaper reports by Judson Hand *(New York News)* and Jack Anderson *(New York Post)* concerning Father Hill's dissent and the reaction of the chairman, Dean William B. Lockhart.

Schaffer, Edward M. *et al.* "A Look at the California Records Act and Its Exemption." *Golden Gate Law Review*, 4:203–38, Spring 1974.   **1S74**
"This survey begins with a study of the Federal Freedom of Information Act, the forerunner of the California Act. It is followed by a brief history of the California Act, and finally a section by section examination of the specific exemptions to the California Act's general requirement of disclosure."

Schanberg, Sydney H. "The Saigon Follies, or, Trying to Head Them Off at Credibility Gap." *New York Times Magazine*, 12 November 1972, pp. 38–39+.   **1S75**
"Escape and evasion about sum up the attitude that most American officials in Vietnam have taken toward newsmen most of the time—an attitude that notwithstanding areas of guarded coexistence, generally consists of suspicion, distrust and sometimes outright animosity." A *New York Times* correspondent in Southeast Asia accuses the American establishment there of continued efforts to suppress unhappy facts, of being secretive and obstructive, of almost daily distortion and omission of facts—"a practice which stems more from official embarrassment over the course of events than from reasons of military security." He backs his charges with personal experiences.

Schardt, Arlie. "Press Freedom: A Turning Point." *Civil Liberties*, 291:3, December 1972.   **1S76**
As hearings are being held in Congress on legislation guaranteeing newsmen's privileges, the author considers the issues of absolute vs. qualified privilege.

Scharff, J. Laurent. "A Moment of Truth for Broadcast Journalism—Will It Be One for the Print Media?" *Quill*, 57(4):20–21, April 1969.   **1S77**
Legal challenges to the fairness doctrine in broadcasting and the implications to newspapers.

Schatz, Andrew M. "Gagging the Press in Criminal Trials." *Harvard Civil Rights–Civil Liberties Law Review*, 10:608–52, Summer 1975.   **1S78**
"This Comment will endeavor to provide an analytical framework to which courts may look in determining whether a gag order should be issued and, if so, the content and timing of publication that should be proscribed." The author suggests four primary safeguards to insure that the First Amendment is neither needlessly nor inappropriately violated: "(1) that the danger of interference with a fair trial is imminent, (2) that the gag order be the least restrictive necessary to ensure the fair trial, (3) that the court carefully balance the competing interests in the particular case, and (4) that the full panoply of due process safeguards be applied."

Schauer, Frederick F. "Obscenity and the Conflict of Laws." *West Virginia Law Review*, 77:377–400, April 1975.   **1S79**
"The approach advocated by this article is . . . based on the assumption that the trier of fact can apply the [obscenity] standards of a community other than his own. The Supreme Court has indicated its acceptance of this assumption, and there seems no reason why a properly instructed jury could not also apply the standards of a community other than its own."

———. "School Books, Lesson Plans, and the Constitution." *West Virginia Law Review*, 78:287–314, May 1976.   **1S80**
The author explores the educational philosophy and political and constitutional issues underlying recent controversies over choice of school books, teaching methods, and curricula in the public schools.

Scheiber, Harry N. "The California Textbook Fight." *Atlantic*, 220(5):38, 40, 43–44, 46–47, November 1967.   **1S81**

The political controversy in California over the adoption of an eighth-grade American history textbook, *Land of the Free* by John Hope Franklin.

Schember, Daniel M. "Textbook Censorship—The Validity of School Board Rules." *Administrative Law Review*, 28:259–76, Spring 1976. **1S82**
The article suggests "that administrative law precedents—interpreted in light of the constitutional interests at stake—are valid and useful reference points for analyzing the textbook ₍selection₎ guidelines and the rule-making authority of school boards. . . . The constitutional questions raised by textbook guidelines such as those of Kanawha County ₍W. Va.₎ are strong reasons for exploring a new path."

Schenkkan, P. M. "Power in the Marketplace of Ideas: The Fairness Doctrine and the First Amendment." *Texas Law Review*, 52:727–72, April 1974. **1S83**
The U.S. courts have ruled that "technological scarcity of outlets exalts the first amendment rights of hearers over those of broadcasters and authorizes the government to regulate the latter to protect the former. . . . ₍This thesis₎ amounts to a belief that the power of the broadcast media presents a clear and present danger of oligopoly in the marketplace of ideas, and that this constitutes a substantive evil that Congress has a right to prevent by content regulation. The most suspect consequence of this belief is the fairness doctrine as applied to television. On examination, neither the power rationale nor its fairness doctrine corollary can withstand first amendment scrutiny."

Scherer, Howard B. "Broadcast Journalism: The Conflict between the First Amendment and Liability for Defamation." *Brooklyn Law Review*, 39:426–47, Fall 1972. **1S84**
"This Note will deal with station censorship of guests' remarks, designed to protect the broadcaster from liability for defamation. The problem will be discussed in the context of a recent incident involving Mark Lane ₍author of *Rush to Judgment*₎ which resulted in proceedings currently before the FCC." Re: Golden West Broadcasters, Inc., licensee of KTLA-TV, Los Angeles.

Schickel, Richard. "Porn and Man at Yale." *Harper's* 241:34–38, July 1970. **1S85**
A movie critic attends a Russ Meyer sex movie festival at Yale "to test the waters of popular culture," and finds that the only message in the films is that "sex should be fun," that there was no evidence of a foreign plot to sap our moral fiber or "a scheme of the far-famed effete Eastern snobs to pollute the provincial American

mind," but a case of "our own, our native idiocy."

Schiess, Mario. "Censorship and the Films." *New Nation* (South Africa), 4(2):11, 20, September 1970. **1S86**
The author sees the current wave of sex and violence on the stage and screen in the Western world as subsiding as it reaches a saturation point. This will usher in a new public morality, but "founded on the free choice of the individual instead of the fear of some vengeful authority." The South African system of censorship, he believes, "denies us this development."

Schiller, Patricia. "Effects of Mass Media on the Sexual Behavior of Adolescent Females." *Technical Report of the ₍U.S.₎ Commission on Obscenity and Pornography*, 1:191–95, 1971. **1S87**
"The purpose of this exploratory study is (a) to identify the various popular media which function as catalysts for evoking or reinforcing the 'love theme' and associated erotic feelings among adolescent females, and (b) to examine the ways and degree to which these stimuli affected their sexual behavior."

Schimmel, David. "To Risk on the Side of Freedom." *Phi Delta Kappan*, 54:542–45, April 1973. **1S88**
"How much 'academic freedom' do public school teachers have? Do they have the right to assign any book or article they believe appropriate? What should happen if parents object? What rights do parents have to determine the type of reading materials assigned to their children? When there is a conflict between teachers and parents concerning teaching materials and methods, should the decision of the administration or school board be final? This article looks at some controversial legal cases that have dealt with these questions and summarizes what three federal courts have said about pertinent law."—Editor

Schimmel, Nancy. "Reading Guidance and Intellectual Freedom." *Top of the News*, 31:317–20, April 1975. **1S89**
Even the most carefully selected children's collections in libraries contain questionable material of one kind or another and librarians feel some responsibility, in a free society, to prepare children to use their freedom wisely, to develop healthy scepticism. Reading guidance serves a useful purpose in the conflict between the impulse to protect and the reluctance to censor.

Schlaver, Clarence O. "The Reardon Report—Battle Moves to States." *Quill*, 56(4):12–17, April 1968. **1S90**
"The battleground of 'Press vs. Reardon Report' has been localized to the 50 states with the announcement by Sigma Delta Chi of plans to form news media committees in each state to oppose American Bar Association recommendations restricting release of pre-trial information."

Schlesinger, Arthur M., Jr. "Freedom of the Press: Who Cares?" *Wall Street Journal*, 53(56):6, 5 January 1973. **1S91**
The recent threats to freedom of the press by the Nixon Administration and decisions of the U.S. Supreme Court are a reflection of President Nixon's own philosophy. "If the Nixon Administration has its way, criticism of government will become far more difficult."

———. "The Politics of Violence." In Eleanor Widmer, *ed.*, *Freedom and Culture*, Belmont, Calif., Wadsworth, 1970, pp. 41–47. (A fuller version appears in Schlesinger, *The Crisis of Confidence*. Boston, Houghton Mifflin, 1969) **1S92**
The author criticizes the new leftist doctrine as proclaimed by Herbert Marcuse who "perceives the First Amendment as the keystone, not of liberty, but of a wicked apparatus of tolerance employed by an oppressive social order to thwart basic change." Schlesinger considers this new creed "a kind of existentialism in politics," a way of fakery and fallacy, preposterous and depraved. "The demand for the forcible suppression of 'false' ideas would be an enormously effective way of calling a halt to human progress."

———. "The Secrecy Dilemma." *New York Times Magazine*, 6 February 1972, pp. 12–13+. **1S93**
The recent publication of secret documents has produced a collision between two equally venerated principles—disclosure and confidentiality. While recognizing the various legitimate needs for secrecy—diplomatic negotiations, intelligence operations, war, data whose release would compromise foreign governments, personal data such as income tax returns given with the understanding that it would be kept secret, and plans that if known, would permit land or financial speculation—he believes that the government has been moving more and more from legitimate to illegitimate uses of secrecy, where deception and lying is made possible. The author considers the operation of the security classification system and suggests methods of systematic declassification. He quotes Harold Nicolson, as distinguishing sharply between negotiation and policy; the latter never should be secret.

Schmidt, Benno C., Jr. "Beyond the 'Caldwell' Decision: 2. 'The Decision Is Tentative.'" *Columbia Journalism Review*, 11(3):25–30, September–October 1972. **1S94**
A member of the faculty of law, Columbia University, believes that "despite the predictable cries of outrage against the Supreme Court's decision, it should be remembered that the Court's rejection of the journalists' privilege may not be as complete as it appears. Courts have traditionally opposed the creation of evidentiary privileges because such barriers clog necessary investigative and adjudicative processes." Legislative bodies should respond to the Court's invitation to find a legislative

solution. Views of Fred W. Friendly and Norman E. Isaacs are also given.

―――. *Freedom of the Press vs. Public Access*. New York, Praeger, 1976. 296p. (Published for the Aspen Institute Program on Communications and Society and the National News Council) **1S95**
An overview and analysis of the issue of guaranteed access to the newspaper press. The author "deals with the basic questions of First Amendment theory and journalistic function. He questions whether such sweeping goals as equality and fairness in mass communications can be achieved through access requirements without compromising a free press. The book presents the controversy over access against a background of related developments in constitutional law, in journalistic practices, in libel laws, and in the protection given to expressive activities in those public and private places treated by the courts as public forums. Finally, the author explores in detail whether access obligations sustained for the electronic media are constitutionally barred for the print media, and whether such variance could undermine the efforts of radio and television to appeal to traditional First Amendment protections in other areas." Stanley H. Fuld, chairman of the National News Council, has written the foreword.

―――. "Journalists' Privilege: One Year After Branzburg." In Roscoe Pound–American Trial Lawyers Foundation, *The First Amendment and the News Media*. Cambridge, Mass. The Foundation, 1973, pp. 41–53. **1S96**
The article covers the U.S. Supreme Court's *Branzburg* decision on journalists' privilege and the prospects for shield legislation: Is legislation needed? Constitutional questions. Should a federal statute bind the states? What information should be privileged? Scope of the privilege. To whom should the privilege extend?

―――. "The Nebraska Decision." *Columbia Journalism Review*, 15(4):51–53, November–December 1976. **1S97**
"The Supreme Court's unanimous decision on June 30 to strike down prior restraint of the press in *Nebraska Press Association v. Stuart* is the most important constitutional victory for freedom of the press since the Pentagon Papers case, decided five years earlier to the day. Yet, as in the Pentagon Papers decision, the court's majority opinion in the 'gag-order' case is so qualified and so chary of laying down general principles that the press's victory has some disturbing undertones."

―――. "A New Wave of Gag Orders." *Columbia Journalism Review*, 14(4):33–34, November–December 1975. **1S98**
A review of the recent wave of court orders limiting press coverage of trials, several of which are discussed, suggests an abuse of injunction powers by trial judges.

―――. "Why We Haven't Heard the Tapes." *Columbia Journalism Review*, 14(3):53–54, September–October 1975. **1S99**
Discussion of the refusal of the court to yield aural copies of the evidentiary portions of the Nixon tapes for the hearing by the general public. The author believes that the withholding of the tapes from the public "does not comport with our laws' experienced accommodation between openness and insulation of judicial proceedings."

―――, and Harold Edgar. "S. 1." *Columbia Journalism Review*, 14(6):18–21, March–April 1976. **1S100**
"S. 1, we believe, goes much too far in protecting national defense information from press disclosure. Indeed, in purporting to protect just about everything, S. 1, if enacted, would probably not protect much of anything. The press would not obey such broad strictures, the act would not be consistently and generally enforced. Any limited enforcement of such broad prohibitions would be seen as highly selective, playing politics with the criminal law. The notion of legitimate secrecy would be discredited." S. 1 was the Senate bill to revise the entire federal criminal code.

Schmidtchen, Paul W. "On Freedom of the Press." *Hobbies*, 78(8):135–36, October 1973; 78(9):134–36, November 1973; 78(10):134–36, December 1973; 78 (11):134, 136–37, January 1974; 78(12):134, 136–37, February 1974. **1S101**
A discursive five-part series in which the author takes the press to task for transmitting "adulterated events meant to foment discord and resentment against those for some reason detested by certain controllers of the air-waves or printed columns." He supports Spiro Agnew's criticism of the press and believes that the current fuming over threats to press freedom by the Nixon Administration is "a lot of balderdash . . . promoted largely by individuals who have been taking advantage of this basic freedom to unload their off-beat and irresponsible ideas or ambitions upon the republic." Throughout, there is defense of the Nixon Administration and criticism of the press for persecuting him. "This time in July, 1973, we are watching a man being condemned on hearsay allegation alone, before all the facts are in."

Schnall, Marc. "The United States Supreme Court: Definitions of Obscenity." *Crime & Delinquency*, 18:59–67, January 1972. **1S102**
The author is encouraged by the Supreme Court's attempt since 1957 to define and redefine obscenity. While its decisions have not always been consistent or complied with "it has managed to expand individual rights within the constitutionally accepted areas of free expression."

Schneider, Dan W. "Authority of the

Register of Copyrights to Deny Registration of a Claim to Copyright on the Ground of Obscenity." *Chicago-Kent Law Review*, 51:691–724, 1975. **1S103**
"It is not clear whether the Register of Copyrights has authority to deny registration of a claim to copyright when the claim is based on allegedly obscene material. . . . In this article, then, examination of the arguments raised and conclusions drawn to support the existence of . . . administrative authority is undertaken, and effort is made to demonstrate that the Register may not have the authority he is currently believed to have or that if he does, his exercise of that authority necessarily should be subject to substantial practical, constitutional and policy limitations."

Schoen, Rodric B. "Billy Jenkins and Eternal Verities: The 1973 Obscenity Cases." *North Dakota Law Review*, 50:567–91, Summer 1974. **1S104**
A brief review of U.S. Supreme Court decisions in obscenity cases, 1957–73, followed by a lengthy discussion of *Miller v. California* (1973). "For the sake of Billy Jenkins, the people of Georgia, and the first amendment, the Supreme Court should reverse Billy's obscenity conviction [*Jenkins v. State*, 230 Ga. 726, 199 S.E.2d 188 (1973)] for showing the film *Carnal Knowledge*."

Scholl, Peter A. "What's Obscene in Indiana? The New Law, the Miller Decision, and the Teaching of English." *Indiana English Journal*, 10(1):12–17, Fall 1975. **1S105**
The author discusses the revised Indiana Code as it pertains to obscenity guidelines laid down since the U.S. Supreme Court decision in *Miller v. California*, noting the advantages and weaknesses of the new law and the possible effect on the teaching of English.

Schonberg, Edward R. "Search Warrants and Journalists' Confidential Information." *American University Law Review*, 25:938–70, Summer 1976. **1S106**
"The comment will examine the various issues arising from governmental searches of journalists' files. Because the use of search warrants to seize reporters' notes and files raises serious first and fourth amendment problems these constitutional difficulties will be closely scrutinized. The thesis of this comment is that law enforcement officials should only be allowed to use search warrants to seize information from the press when there is no other method available to obtain the needed materials."

Schopler, Ernest H. "Applicability to Advertisements of First Amendment's

Guaranty of Free Speech and Press." *U.S. Supreme Court Reports, Lawyers Edition*, 37 L Ed 2d 1124–40. **1S107**
Annotation on: *Pittsburgh Press Co. v. Human Relations Commission* (1973). Background information, statement of general rules and application of rules to printed and electronic media. The case dealt with a city ordinance forbidding newspapers to carry help-wanted advertisements in sex-designated columns. The court held the ordinance was not denial of freedom of press.

Schorr, Burt. "Secret Study: U.S. Suppressed Data That Might Have Aided Farmers in Grain Deal; The Report on Russian Crop, If Revealed, Also Might Have Hurt U.S. Exporters." *Wall Street Journal*, 180:1, 14 September 1972. **1S108**

Schorr, Daniel. "Chilling Experience: The White House, the FBI, and Me." *Harper's*, 246:92–97, March 1973.
1S109
Following his own investigation of the Nixon Administration's efforts at harassment of the author through an FBI investigation, he concludes: "I am now left to ponder, when a producer rejects a controversial story I have offered, whether it is because of the normal winnowing process or because of my troublemaking potential. Even more am I left to wonder, when I myself discard a line of investigation, whether I am applying professional criteria or whether I am subconsciously affected by a reluctance to embroil my superiors in new troubles with the Nixon Administration."

———. "The FBI and Me." *Columbia Journalism Review*, 13(4):8–14, November–December 1974. **1S110**
The Columbia Broadcasting System correspondent pieces together, with the help of official FBI files, a comprehensive account of his "mini-Watergate experience as seen from within the Nixon Administration." The story relates how Richard Nixon ordered an FBI investigation of Schorr after he had made an unfavorable analysis of a presidential speech.

———. "Shadowing the Press." *New Leader*, 55:8–10, 21 February 1972.
1S111
The CBS correspondent reports on his investigation by the FBI.

Schrag, Peter. "Criminal Case 9373." *Saturday Review*, 55(29):12–14, 15 July 1972. **1S112**
An analysis of the case of Daniel Ellsberg, indicted on two criminal counts for releasing the Pentagon Papers: conversion of government documents, and violation of the Espionage Act.

———. "The Ellsberg Affair." *Saturday Review*, 54(46):34–39, 13 November 1971. **1S113**
"It is still difficult to describe his act, or what it means, or where it will lead. Five months have passed, and the ugly secret called the Pentagon Papers is now available in three different versions, one of them published by the government itself. The man who divulged the papers stands indicted for high crimes by the same government, and the war, militarism, and the deceptions go on. . . . Ellsberg's conversion did not begin with the immorality of the war but with its futility and with the lies that were used in its defense. . . . It was the systematic deception, which started at the lowest echelons and ran through the entire government structure from the platoon leader to the President of the United States, that began to place the daily brutality in its ugliest light."

———. "The Road to Yakima." *Saturday Review*, 55(35):5–6, 12, 26 August 1972. **1S114**
Justice William O. Douglas, hearing evidence in Yakima, Wash., on his way to his summer retreat, agreed to a stay of the Ellsberg trial in the Pentagon Papers case, until a wiretap issue could be resolved.

———. *Test of Loyalty: Daniel Ellsberg and the Rituals of Secret Government*. New York, Simon & Schuster, 1974. 414p.
1S115
An account of the Pentagon Papers trial in the larger context of allegiance versus individual conscience and the "poisoned political system" of the Nixon Administration.

———. "TV's New Chastity Belt." *MORE*, 5(8):6–7, August 1975. **1S116**
Criticism of the National Association of Broadcaster's new code regulation that "entertainment programming inappropriate for viewing by a general family audience should not be broadcast during the first hour of network entertainment programming in prime time and in the immediately preceding hour. Complaints about sex and violence on television share the assumption that television is a major influence on behavior, an assumption still under debate."

Schram, Glenn N. "The First Amendment and the Educative Function of the Law." *American Journal of Jurisprudence*, 20:38–45, 1975. **1S117**
"Historically, Western political thought believed that the law should perform an educative function, that of developing men's capacities for virtue. For reasons arising out of the Protestant Reformation and the development of modern thought, the idea that the law should try to make men good is not very widely accepted today. One's acceptance or nonacceptance of it influences one's interpretation of the First Amendment of the United States Constitution, as shown by a dialectical examination of the reinterpretations by Walter Berns and Alexander Meiklejohn. The argument is made that American constitutional law should reflect Berns' view (that the law should try to make men virtuous) while also embodying a large measure of Meiklejohn's tolerance. Specific areas are mentioned in which, in the author's judgment, debate ought at least to be reopened on the educative function of the law."—Editor

Schroeder, Stephen K. "An Analysis of the Nebraska Privilege Statute (Free Flow of Information Act)." *Creighton Law Review*, 7:329–55, Spring 1974.
1S118
"The purpose of this comment is to examine the new Nebraska statute and analyze similar state statutes. Also, consideration will be given to the problems posed by the very existence of a newsman's privilege."

Schroeder, Theodore. "An Amusing 'Criminal.' " *Open Road*, 42(8):3–7, August 1942. **1S119**
The story of the controversial Washington D.C. editor of *Saunders' Weekly* (W. O. Saunders), formerly editor of a weekly paper in Elizabeth City, N.C. Saunders's courageous editions and his amusing antics put Elizabeth City on the map and subjected him to numerous arrests for libel. The article was first published in *Saunders' Weekly*, 6 May 1916.

———. "The Ballad of Joseph." *Truth Seeker*, 45:163, 16 March 1918. **1S120**
An account of the long history of suppression of a poem, The Ballad of Joseph, by "Williams," because of its alleged blasphemous content. The text of the ballad, together with an essay by Max Eastman, editor of the *Masses*, in which the controversial poem first appeared, are printed as a twelve-page pamphlet, 1916.

———. "Comstock As a Psychologist." *Truth Seeker*, 34:179, 23 March 1907.
1S121
Schroeder criticizes Anthony Comstock for his failure to appreciate the author's ideas on obscenity and quotes a letter from Havelock Ellis in his behalf.

———. "The Growth of Judicial Despotism." *Twentieth Century*, 2:319–24, July 1910. **1S122**
Judges and their decisions should be subjected to the same frank criticism by lawyers and laymen as any other public official. Schroeder objects to the use of the contempt power of the court to muzzle criticism and cites a number of instances where this power has been abused.

———. "Laws for Pure Literature." *Purity Journal and Christian Life*, 21:18–19, July–September 1907. **1S123**
A brief appeal to the readers to suggest a legal test for obscene literature that would enable all persons to reach the same conclusion by apply-

ing the test to every conceivable book or picture. The editor responds, defending existing purity laws as necessary protection not only of children but of the average, normal adult. There follows a resolution, submitted by Schroeder, amending the obscenity laws to exempt literature for adults and to require a court decision before a work can be excluded from the mails.

———. "Murder and 'Obscenity' Investigated." *Sunshine & Health* (Mays Landing, N.J.), 17(2):13–14, 32, February 1948. **1S124**
"Murderers are always energetically sought, prosecuted, and most severely punished: while the literary and artistic incitements to murder are most honorable occupations for authors, actors, artists, publishers, and radio advertisers. This situation is reversed in relation to fornication. Probably millions of fornications are committed daily for which practically no one is ever punished unless other factors are involved. But literary and artistic inciters to fornication are diligently sought, vigorously prosecuted and severely punished, without any proof presented of actual and material injury to anyone." The same theme was developed by Gershon Legman in his book, *Love and Death*, 1949 (L155).

———. "Obscenity and the Pathetic Fallacy." *Sunshine & Health* (Mays Landing, N.J.), 15(5):12–13, 28, May 1946. **1S125**
Based on psychological evidence Schroeder argues that "obscenity exists only in the wishful or fearful thinking—wholly in the feelings and fantasies of the accusing persons . . . and never can be transmitted by mail, express, freight, or by any interstate commerce, with any book, picture or play."

———. "Obscenity Laws." In Charles T. Sprading, *Liberty and the Great Libertarians. An Anthology on Liberty: A Handbook of Freedom*. Los Angeles, The Author, 1913, pp. 517–21. **1S126**
"Obscenity is not a quality inherent in a book or picture, but solely and exclusively a contribution of the reading mind, and hence cannot be defined in terms of the qualities of a book or picture."

———. "Presumption and Burden of Proof as to Malice in Criminal Libel." *American Law Review*, 49:199–216, March–April 1915. (Reprinted as a seventeen-page pamphlet by Free Speech League, New York) **1S127**
Ignoring legal precedent, except to illustrate a point, Schroeder examines the issue of malice in criminal libel, analyzing the natural factors in the problem. He interprets the New York libel law with special attention to paragraphs on justified and excused publication.

———. "To the Glory of Jackasses."

Open Road, 42(1):6–9, January 1942. **1S128**
An account of Colonel Isaac M. Meekins's tribute to the jackass as presented in his defense of Editor W. O. Saunders of Elizabeth City, N.C. (1916). Saunders had been accused of libeling a local man by calling him a "jackass."

Schroeter, Thomas F. "Bursey v. United States: The First and Fifth Amendments in the Grand Jury Room." *Hastings Law Journal*, 24:915–34, April 1973. **1S129**
"This note will first examine the different approaches used by various courts in interpreting [newsmen's] immunity statutes and list the reasons for preferring the *Bursey* [Bursey v. United States (1972)] court's approach. Second, the court's disposition of the First Amendment issue will be analyzed in terms of its basic weaknesses and the recent United States Supreme Court decision of *Branzburg v. Hayes* (1972)."

Schuelke, L. David. "Measuring Student Attitudes: Basis for the Freedom of Speech Course." In his Speech Association of America. *Abstracts, 54th Annual Meeting*, Chicago, The Association, 1968, p. 19. **1S130**
"This paper deals with the measurement and experimental investigation of attitudes and values toward speech and communication."

Schults, Raymond L. *Crusader in Babylon; W. T. Stead and the Pall Mall Gazette*. Lincoln, Nebr., University of Nebraska Press, 1972. 277p. **1S131**
In 1885 this English editor entered upon a sensational crusade against prostitution by publishing in his *Pall Mall Gazette* a series of articles entitled The Maiden Tribute of Modern Babylon. While his crusade helped to secure the passage of a law against traffic in young girls, his investigative reporting led to an inquiry in Parliament and three month's imprisonment on charges growing out of the crusade. Chapters 5 and 6 deal with the Maiden Tribute affair.

Schultz, Franklin M. "A Primer on the Public Information Act." *Public Contract Law Journal*, 2:208–12, January 1969. **1S132**
The author finds that despite ambiguities, internal inconsistencies, and redundancies the act is an improvement in the area of public administration.

Schwab, Howard J. "Obscene But Not Heard." *Los Angeles Bar Bulletin*, 46:483–87, 509–10, October 1971. **1S133**
Recent developments in the very unsettled California law of obscenity.

Schwartz, Jack. "The Morality Seekers: A Study of Organized Film Criti-

cism in the United States." In Otto N. Larsen, *ed.*, *Violence and the Mass Media*, New York, Harper & Row, 1968, pp. 189–203. **1S134**
"The purpose of the present paper will be to examine the sensitivities of both the National Legion of Decency and the Film Estimate Board by a detailed analysis of the comments which each organization makes about films released in the United States. I will also examine the relationship between the audience classification of each organization and the box-office estimates for each film rated by both organizations. And finally, a comparison will be made between the ratings of both groups when rating the same film."

Schwartz, Louis B. "Morals Offenses and the Model Penal Code." *Columbia Law Review*, 63:669–86, April 1963. (Reprinted in Donald B. Sharp, *ed.*, *Commentaries on Obscenity*, pp. 215–25) **1S135**
Included in the author's comments on the rationale for the American Law Institute's model code, is a section on obscenity. The target here is not the "sin of obscenity," but "primarily a disapproval of economic activity—commercial exploitation of the widespread weakness for titillation by pornography."

———. ["Review of American Newspaper Publishers Association's *Free Press and Fair Trial* and the American Bar Association's *Standards Relating to Fair Trial and Free Press*."] *University of Pennsylvania Law Review*, 116:1118–24, April 1968. (Reprinted in the *Bulletin of the American Society of Newspaper Editors*, November 1968) **1S136**
The author argues that a line between free press and fair trial can be drawn "without infringing true freedom of the press."

Schwartz, Ronnie. "The California Approach to the Yielding of the Newsman's Shield Law." *Pepperdine Law Review*, 3:313–35, Spring 1976. **1S137**
"This comment will examine the standards applied by the California judiciary in balancing the basic interests involved in the confrontation between free press and fair trial: the First Amendment protection to newsmen, the scope of the privilege afforded by the California Newsmen's Shield Law, the Sixth Amendment right to a fair trial in criminal cases, and the inherent power of the judiciary to control its proceedings and officers in order to prevent prejudicial publicity from emanating from court officers."

Schwartzman, S. Howard. "Obscenity

in the Movies." *Loyola Law Review*, 18:354–74, 1971–72.   **1S138**
An historical review of significant court decisions on obscenity in the movies, including *Joseph Burstyn, Inc. v. Wilson* (1952), *Kingsley International Pictures Corp. v. Regents of the University of the State of New York* (1959), *Times Film Corp. v. City of Chicago* (1961), and *United States v. A Motion Picture Film Entitled "I Am Curious—Yellow"* (1968). The writer notes the progressively greater freedom of expression permitted the motion pictures and the increased tolerance and apathy to obscenity on the part of the public.

"Scope of First Amendment Protection for Good-Faith Defamatory Error." *Yale Law Journal*, 75:642–56, March 1966.   **1S139**
Comment on the "public official" test and the good faith statements about public issues expressed in *New York Times v. Sullivan* (1964) and applied in subsequent libel cases before the U.S. Supreme Court.

Scott, Barbara. "Censorship and/or Classification." *Journal of the Producers Guild of America*, 10(3):33–35, 37, December 1968.   **1S140**
Support of the film industry's classification system, by an attorney of the Motion Picture Association of America.

Scott, Claude L., *pseud. The Science of Pornography*. San Diego, Calif., Greenleaf Classics, 1970. 287p. Introduction by Donald H. Gilmore.   **1S141**
An examination of pornography as it has been expressed in ancient and modern art, cartoons, and photography, profusely illustrated. The author is both an historian and collector of this genre.

Scott, Gloria S. "Paperback Censorship: An Idea Whose Time Has Gone." *Media & Methods*, 11:14–15, May–June 1975.   **1S142**
On the state and local level, archaic laws and regulations discriminate against the use of paperbacks in schools, a carry-over from an era when the paperback was considered cheap and lurid.

Scott, Gordon H. "Sex and the Law." *New Law Journal*, 123:168–72, 22 February 1973.   **1S143**
In the matter of pornography the author believes that the British law is preoccupied with sex; that "events of recent years have disclosed that the so-called 'permissive society' is but one side of the coin, and that on the other side there lies a new and virulent puritanism. I do not believe that recent prosecutions have served any useful purpose. On the contrary, I believe

they have served merely to feed the sexual imagination and desires of many people." Have the police nothing better to do? "The prosecutor, whoever he may be, should have his list of priorities, and prosecutions for obscenity and 'conspiracies to corrupt, etc.' should take a lowly place indeed on that list."

Scott, Hugh. "Candidate Broadcast Time: A Proposal for Section 315 of the Communications Act." *Georgetown Law Journal*, 56:1037–49, June 1968. **1S144**
"After analyzing section 315 of the Communications Act and the comparable regulations of other nations, Senator Scott discusses his proposed amendments. He suggests an 'equitable time' concept, implemented by a fixed formula for allocating free broadcast time among political candidates for the same office."

Scott, Ralph. "Censorship and the Schools: Problem or Opportunity?" *Iowa English Bulletin: Yearbook*, 25(3): 24–33, November 1975.   **1S145**
"Censorship and the schools constitutes only a skirmish within a broader conflict which has broken out along the entire border of contemporary social life." There is strong evidence that the educational and media establishment are controlled by liberals and unless parents become involved educators will omit more traditional materials from the curricula. There is a widening gap between parents and educators. "If educators claim an unqualified right to select reading materials, they in effect seek censorship powers. Perhaps never before has it been more important for parents and educators to form an effective working team."

Scott, Stephen C. "Nevergreen in Groton: Special News Analysis." *Wilson Library Bulletin*, 45:818–24, May 1971.   **1S146**
The case of the banning of *Evergreen Review* from the Groton, Conn., Public Library.

Scoville, Stanley E. "Private Morality and the Right to Be Free: The Thrust of *Stanley v. Georgia*." *Arizona Law Review*, 11:731–48, Winter 1969.   **1S147**
An examination of the implications of *Stanley v. Georgia* (1969), in which the U.S. Supreme Court "delineated some limitations on state regulatory power when it intrudes into the area of individual freedoms in matters of personal morality." The decision stated that "the First and Fourteenth Amendments prohibit making mere private possession of obscene material a crime."

Scripp, John. "Controlling Prejudicial Publicity by the Contempt Power: The British Practice and Its Prospect in American Law." *Notre Dame Lawyer*, 42:957–68, Symposium 1967.   **1S148**
The author concludes that the quality of English newspaper reporting of trials has not become "tepid" under the restraints of the con-

tempt power nor has it proven socially harmful. But in America "the idea of punishing newspapers for publications that a judge reflectively considers likely to prejudice a fair trial, would be, if not constitutionally invalid, fatally objectionable on grounds of social policy and tradition."

Scudi, Abbie T. *The Sacheverell Affair*. New York, Columbia University Press, 1939. 170p.   **1S149**
An account of the impeachment by Parliament and trial of this eminent English minister for publishing two sermons offensive to the Crown. He was sentenced not to preach for three years and his sermons were ordered burned by the common hangman.

Scuse, Dennis. "British Television Overseas: Censorship and Exports." *Journal of the Society of Film and Television Arts*, 43/44:16–18, Spring–Summer 1971.   **1S150**
Some of the problems involved in meeting the likes and dislikes, local taboos, and censorship requirements in the overseas markets.

Scutari, Kenneth A. "Dissection of Theatrical Plays Into Speech and Conduct Components: An Exception to the *Roth* Rule?" *Seaton Hall Law Review*, 4:379–96, Fall/Winter 1972.   **1S151**
Re: *Southeastern Promotions, Inc. v. Conrad*, 341 F. Supp. 465 (E.D. Tenn. 1972), involving the production of *Hair* in which the court made a distinction between speech and "conduct, apart from speech or symbolic speech." The latter they found in violation of Chattanooga obscenity ordinances and the statutes of Tennessee.

Sears, Hal D. *The Sex Radicals: Free Love in High Victorian America*. Lawrence, Kans., Regents Press of Kansas, 1977. 342p.   **1S152**
An account of the pioneering efforts at sex reform in the United States during the Victorian era. Through unorthodox and sometimes iconoclastic publications these crusaders espoused their shocking views on free love, sex education, birth control, and the emancipation of women—views which often subjected them to prosecution and imprisonment. Among the principal figures in the movement were Ezra Heywood (H240–43); Victoria C. Woodhull and her *Woodhull and Claflin's Weekly* (B187, B550,°S1); Moses Harman (H100–103) whose paper, *Lucifer, The Light Bearer* (L378), was dedicated to sexual liberty; Drs. E. B. Foote, father and son (F187–94); Emma Goldman (G138–45); Elmina Slenker; Louis Waisbrooker (W10–11) D. M. Bennett (B187–92), editor of *Truth Seeker* (T197); and Edwin C. Walker (W23–26). Throughout the book are references to the counter-activities of the nemesis of the sex reform movement, Anthony Comstock (C487–99).

"Second-Class Postal Rates and the

First Amendment." *Rutgers Law Review*, 28:693–706, Winter 1975. **1S153**
"A subsidy for magazines and newspapers through low postal rates poses special constitutional and policy concerns. This Note will examine the question of whether there should continue to be such a subsidy, whether cutting off this subsidy would be incompatible with the first amendment objectives of an informed electorate, and wide-open debate of public issues will also be discussed."

"Secrecy and Dissemination in Science and Technology." *Science*, 163:787–90, 21 February 1969. **1S154**
A report of the Committee of Science in the Promotion of Human Welfare prepared at the request of the Board of Directors of the American Association for the Advancement of Science. "In our view it is not secrecy as such that threatens the integrity of the scientific process, but excessive and inappropriate uses of secrecy which are the outcome of the present overconcentration of power."

"The Secret Law of the Immigration and Naturalization Service." *Iowa Law Review*, 56:140–51, October 1970. **1S155**
A criticism of the Service for violation of the Freedom of Information Act in refusal to release information on aliens.

"Sectarian Books, the Supreme Court, and the Establishment Clause." *Yale Law Journal*, 79:111–41, November 1969. **1S156**
The article discusses the case, *Board of Education v. Allen* (1968), involving the constitutionality of the New York State's Textbook Loan Law, which allows pupils in private and parochial schools to borrow textbooks from public authorities for classroom use. The author finds that sectarian textbooks are being purchased despite constitutional standards, because statute and regulations fail to provide national standards for review, assign review responsibility to incompetent officials, and allow for purchase of unreviewed textbooks.

The Sedition Bill Exposed . . . . London, Workers' Bookshop, 1934? 24p. **1S157**
An attack on the proposed Incitement to Disaffection Bill before Parliament which, the pamphlet charges, provides for imprisonment for possession of literature and restricts the rights of publishing, writing, and circulating radical, pacifist, and working-class books. The bill was intended to keep seditious literature out of the hands of members of the armed forces. The pamphlet compares the bill with the Japanese Government's Law Against Dangerous Thoughts.

See, Carolyn. *Blue Money. Pornography and the Pornographers—an Intimate Look at the Two-Billion-Dollar Fantasy Industry*. Philadelphia, McKay, 1975. 234p. **1S158**

The author focuses on the private lives of those who operate in a two-billion-dollar sex fantasy industry: a "dirty books" pirate, a skin-flick movie magnate, a businessman who has made a fortune in pornography, and an attorney whose job it is to keep these merchants of smut out of jail.

———. "My Daddy, the Pornographer." *Esquire*, 78(2):110–13, 184–86, August 1972. **1S159**
A bawdy account of the life and works of "Hardy Peters" who, at the age of sixty-seven, found his métier as a writer of dirty books.

———. "Whither Smut." *Human Behavior*, 2:72–75, February 1973. **1S160**
A novelist and college teacher considers the open market for explicit sexual fantasy and the possibility of the emergence of a new art form.

Seely, John B. *A Voice from India, In Answer to the Reformers of England*. . . . London, G. B. Whittaker, 1824. 239p. **1S161**
A defense of restrictions on the press of India, written in answer to members of the British Parliament who have advocated a free press for India: J. G. Lambton, Joseph Hume, and J. S. Buckingham, late editor of the *Calcutta Journal*. He quotes from what he considers their mistaken defenses of a free press.

Segal, Alan. "Censorship, Social Control and Socialization." *British Journal of Sociology*, 21:63–74, March 1970. **1S162**
"The point of the discussion has been that the problem of censorship is of far wider proportions than the debate about the imputed undesirable consequences of the portrayal of sex and violence would suggest; and that the wider significance of the seemingly endless controversy over what should be censored and what should not be censored is in one important sense a dispute reflecting the structure of political and social relationships about how much worth we should ascribe to the conception of man, what meaning we wish to attribute to, and how far we are willing to admit what we regard as the dual aspects of human nature."

Segal, Erich. "On Obscenity." *Writer's Yearbook*, 42:20, 1971. **1S163**
"Obscenity . . . is a poor excuse for art, a kind of book-juggling to hide artistic bankruptcy. . . . Shakespeare, fortunately, was neither curious or yellow, because Shakespeare had the courage, and it takes courage, to attempt to say the ineffable instead of showing the indelicate. . . . Far more glorious than the human groin, and far more interesting, is the human heart." Segal rejects censorship, noting that the greatest blow to pornography is legalized freedom. From a talk given to American Booksellers' Association, New York, 13 October 1970.

Seiden, Martin H. *Who Controls the Mass Media? Popular Myths and Economic*

Realities. New York, Basic Books, 1974. 246p. **1S164**
"Entertainment, information, and advertising flow to the American audience in a great variety of print and broadcast packages. The audience is continually surveyed for its opinions and this information results in continual adjustment of media output. No other nation has a mass communications system so finely tuned to the desires of the audience it serves. . . . There is a clear link between the media's mode of operation and the fact that *no one* in mass communications in the United States is a government employee. The government is excluded by design from participating in the operation of the system. . . . America's mass communication system is rooted in the soil of commerce, not politics. Indeed there is not a single party network broadcasting station, or daily newspaper in the United States. The system is designed to fit into a consumer oriented economy."

Seifert, Herbert A. *What Books Are Catholics Forbidden to Read?* Liguori, Mo., Redemptorist Fathers, 1959. 22p. **1S165**
"The Church is not afraid of her enemies nor their books; she will permit anyone to read their literature and answer them who shows himself capable. But for the safety of those who have not studied deeply in matters of faith, who are not capable of discovering errors against it, she continues to enforce the laws." This small pamphlet is intended to explain to the average Catholic the laws of the Church on forbidden literature.

Seigenthaler, John. "A Crisis of Credibility." *Grassroots Editor*, 13(6):3–7, November–December 1972. **1S166**
The editor of the *Nashville Tennesseean* discusses what he considers "a crisis of credibility" within the nation's press, which has to do with self-image and self-confidence. "I question whether many of us really trust ourselves any more. And I am certain we do not trust others who use and are protected by the free press amendment as we are."

———. "Open Meetings: Without Qualification or Reservation." *Grassroots Editor*, 15(4)11–15, July–August 1974. **1S167**
A defense of open meetings laws given at a meeting of the Tennessee Municipal League.

Seitz, Reynolds C. "Responsibility of Radio Stations for Extemporaneous Defamation." *Marquette Law Review*, 24:117–25, April 1940. **1S168**
"Under facts analogous to the publication of defamatory matter in the newspaper (a defamatory statement in a radio manuscript) it is felt the radio station should be liable. On the

other hand, when confronted by the factual situation covered by this analysis [departure from a manuscript], it is believed that there is no need for the extension of the absolute liability coverage."

Selby, Hubert, Jr. *Last Exit to Brooklyn*. Foreword to the post-trial edition by the Publishers. Introduction by Anthony Burgess. London, Calder & Boyars, 1968. 234p.   **1S169**
The publisher's foreword to this second British edition reports on the prosecution of the publishers of *Last Exit to Brooklyn* under Section 2 of the Obscene Publications Act. Distinguished witnesses appeared for both prosecution and defense. The jury's verdict of "guilty" was overturned by the Court of Criminal Appeal, the judgment having been delivered by Lord Justice Salmon. Critic Anthony Burgess, who appeared as a defense witness at the trial, comments on the obscenity issue in his introduction to this edition of the novel.

Seldes, George. *The Facts Are. . . . A Guide to Falsehood and Propaganda in the Press and Radio*. New York, In Fact, 1942. 128p.   **1S170**
The book produces evidence that the nation's "press is corrupt, that it has usually perverted the war news as well as labor news, and all news of social and economic importance." It suggests precautions for reading the war news and ways of measuring propaganda.

———. *Never Tire of Protesting:* [*The Story of* IN FACT *and Other Revelations*]. New York, Stuart, 1968. 288p. **1S171**
The story of the life and death of *In Fact*, the exposé paper which Seldes cofounded and edited. Exposés involved cigarette-cancer links, the *Reader's Digest*, the National Association of Manufacturers, the American Medical Association, the John Birch Society, Senator Joseph McCarthy, the Vatican, Cardinal Spellman, the Vietnam war, Eisenhower's Freedom Foundation, and the House Un-American Activities Committee. Some of the exposés involved suppression of information, distortion, and falsification of news. In the appendix are an honor roll of distinguished newspapers and a statement on the Catholic *Index Librorum Prohibitorum*.

———. *Tell the Truth and Run*. New York, Greenberg, 1953. 293p. **1S172**
Beginning with an account of the suppression of news about the divorce trial of multimillionaire Andrew Mellon, the author tells of his forty-four-year fight for a free press. He experienced censorship in his coverage of World War I for the *Chicago Tribune* and for ten years he published his own weekly newspaper, *In Fact* (1940–50), in which he reported the news that the establishment daily press suppressed.

During his entire career, through articles and books, Seldes crusaded for a free press.

———. *The Truth Behind the News, 1918–1928*. London, Faber & Gwyer, 1929. 355p.   **1S173**
"In his search for facts the newspaperman on foreign service contends with much more censorship, intimidation and frequently terrorism in Continental Europe nowadays than in that supposedly dark journalistic age which preceded the world war. Progress has been made in the past ten years, but of all the liberties which were outlawed and debased during the great conflict, that of the press seems to have recovered the least." The author writes of his experience as a foreign correspondent struggling for the truth against government censorship, beginning with World War I and during the decade that followed in Italy, Russia, Arabia, Mexico, Germany, and other European countries.

Seldes, Gilbert. "The Censor." *Saturday Evening Post*, 202(12):16, 150, 153, 21 September 1929.   **1S174**
A report on the annual bout with the censors. After a hard winter suppressing books and closing plays, the censor turns to the annual spring tryouts—efforts to put through more effective censorship measures in the legislatures. The author discusses the various points of view of censors and anti-censors. "The tendency to abuse authority whenever you have it is what makes the fight against the censor necessary, and the tendencies to abuse a 'liberty' whenever you have it is what makes the censor himself necessary. . . . " Artists who object to the censor should agree among themselves on general principles—"how far they want their liberty to go, what respect they are prepared to pay to public morals, and how far their allegiance to the state will carry them. . . . Just at present the stupidity of the censor is matched by the excesses of the artists. One of which is the assertion that although the arts can do everything good, they are incapable of doing evil."

———. "Regulation and Control." In his *The New Mass Media: Challenge to a Free Society*. Washington, D.C., Public Affairs, 1968, pp. 68–80.   **1S175**
"We examine the means by which motion pictures and broadcasting are regulated. We ask whether the nature of these new mass media demands or justifies exceptional controls, and whether such controls can be exercised within the framework of our democratic society."

Seltzer, Curtis. "West Virginia Book War: A Confusion of Goals." *Nation*, 219:430–35, 2 November 1974. **1S176**
An analysis of the issues in the controversy over public school textbooks in which the books "symbolized a variety of concerns over which people felt they had no control"— inflation, drugs, abortion, "permissiveness," pornography, violence on TV, the "biased media," rebellious teen-agers, vandalism, the "death of God," antiwar protests, black mili-

tants, Communist subversion, Nixon, and littering. "The books had a little of everything that a lot of people didn't like: people felt they could do something about the books." The author notes that "a look through some of the books reveals that white working-class parents from the coal fields and southern mountains do have legitimate grounds for complaint. The editing reflects a value system that runs counter to most of what they cherish. . . . Some of the selections were unpatriotic, sacrilegious and pro-minorities, and they would, as the parents predicted, legitimize different values and raise heretofore taboo questions. Equally important was the almost total exclusion of people like themselves from the 'multicultural' texts."

Sen, P. K., *comp. The Press, Publications and Copyright Laws of India*. Calcutta, Sakar, 1958. 147p.   **1S177**
Includes text of the Press and Registration of Books Act of 1867 as modified; Registration of Newspapers; Parliamentary Proceedings (Protection of Publications); Young People (Harmful Publications) Act of 1956; and Copyright Act of 1957.

Senff, Mark D. " 'Public Event' Interpretation of New York Times v. Sullivan as Applied to a Candidate for Public Office." *Ohio State Law Journal*, 31:393–96, Spring 1970.   **1S178**
The result reached in *Roy v. Monitor-Patriot Co.* (1969) is a good example of the "public events" approach to the *New York Times* rule on libel of public officials. The case involved an alleged libel of a U.S. Senate candidate in Drew Pearson's column.

"Sense and Censorship." *Herder Correspondence*, 7:187–91, June 1970. **1S179**
General comment on the need for radical reform in Catholic censorship (Canons 1384–1394) and the imprimatur system which has become more of an irritant than a protector of the faith. Detailed comment on the Dublin censorship case over a textbook, *Beginnings* by David Konstant and John Cumming. "Irish Catholic schoolchildren in the archdiocese of Dublin are deprived of what could be an extremely valuable means toward bringing them to a full awareness of what is involved in the Christian birthright they have inherited."

Serebnick, Judith. "The 1973 Court Rulings on Obscenity: Have They Made a Difference?" *Wilson Library Bulletin*, 50:304–10, December 1975.
   1S180
A study for the National Book Committee and the Ford Foundation "to assess the impact of the June 1973 and subsequent U.S. Supreme Court obscenity decisions on public and school libraries and trade bookstores." Ten medium-sized cities were visited. The study revealed general awareness of the Supreme Court rulings. It also revealed that there had not been any recent increase in the number or intensity of complaints against either libraries or

bookstores, much to the surprise of many who had expected a wave of suppression. Reasons given for the lack of complaints: a higher level of tolerance, greater concern with adult bookstores selling hard-core pornography than with libraries, and continued caution in the book selection policies of librarians. While obscenity, after the 1973 decision, continued to be the major complaint against libraries and bookstores, it was found that other factors generally entered into the picture before censorious action took place. Most libraries continued with the same book selection policies; a few have relaxed them. The author found that the sense of caution, recognized in the earlier study by Marjorie Fiske, continues to exist in many libraries. A chart indicates how some libraries surveyed differed in their treatment of censorship as revealed in an examination of written book selection policies.

Sethi, Vinod. "Freedom of the Press: A Critique of the Bennett Coleman Case." *Indian Political Science Review*, 8:27–40, January 1974. **1S 181**
In a case involving the Indian government's rationing of newsprint, the Indian Supreme Court laid down a narrow interpretation of the freedom of the press. *Bennett Coleman and Co. vs. Union of India*, A.I.R., 1973, S.C. 106.

Settle, Mary L. *The Scopes Trial: The State of Tennessee v. John Thomas Scopes*. New York, Watts, 1972. 121p. **1S 182**
In an account written for young people, the author retells the story of the celebrated evolution trial held in Dayton, Tenn. in 1925 which pitted two legal giants against each other—William Jennings Bryan, speaking for the Fundamentalists and the literal interpretation of the Bible, and Clarence Darrow, the skeptic and defender of scientific knowledge and, incidentally, of John Scopes, the young high school teacher accused of violating the Tennessee law against teaching the theory of evolution.

Sevareid, Eric. "In Defense of TV News." *TV Guide*, 18(11):6–11, 14 March 1970. **1S 183**
In an interview the Columbia Broadcasting System news analyst denies there is a network liberal bias and that newsmen tend to distort news. He accuses Vice-President Agnew of resorting to demagoguery in his criticism of the media. Sevareid does not agree with spectrum commentary, preferring exploration and elucidation to advocacy. He disapproves of the suggestion of the National Commission on the Cause and Prevention of Violence that a national board of review be established to monitor the performance of the news media. "Television is already the most heavily monitored, scrutinized, criticized medium of communication there's ever been." He favors the same First Amendment protection for television news as granted the print medium.

———. *The Quest for Objectivity*. New York, Television Information Office, 1970. 11p. **1S 184**

In the fourth annual Elmer Davis Memorial Lecture at Columbia University, 29 April 1970, Sevareid compares the threat to news coverage and broadcasting which he and Elmer Davis faced during the Joseph McCarthy days with the attacks on broadcasting in the era of Spiro Agnew, applying the wisdom of Davis to the present. "It remains a question whether a press form that is not fully free can long endure. I believe that it will. But it depends upon others, even more than upon ourselves who work in this form. It depends upon whether or not this society, too, surrenders to what has been called the politics of hysteria, the social curse of this astounding century. And that depends very much upon our constitutional leaders, whether they choose to divide the people for short run political gain or try to draw the people together and heal our divisions."

"Sex and the Arts: Explosive Scene." *Newsweek*, 73(15):67–70, 14 April 1969. **1S 185**
"Sheer numbers tell the tale—there are more explicitly erotic films, more blunt-spoken novels, more nudity on stage, more appeals to the libido in advertising than ever before. This anarchic increase in sexual outspokenness has incalculable importance for the arts, for culture and for the community. For this reason *Newsweek* returns to a phenomenon that has caused perplexity among citizens throughout the country." An earlier story, Anything Goes: Taboos in Twilight, appeared in the 13 November 1967 issue (°A26).

Sexuality in the Media. Nutley, N.J., Roche Laboratories, Hoffmann–La Roche, 1972. 18p. (Psychiatric Viewpoints Reports; ED 7,110) **1S 186**
A questionnaire survey of psychiatrists, asking their views on the effect of frank sexuality in the media, pornography, and whether or not there should be a "decency code" in their community.

Seymour, Whitney N., Jr. "The Public's Right to Know—Who Decides What the Public Should Be Told?" *Record of the Association of the Bar of the City of New York*, 29:625–30, November 1974. **1S 187**
The author makes these suggestions for greater press objectivity and thoroughness in fulfilling the public's right to know: (1) find out what the public wants to know, (2) to insure greater objectivity in reporting, expose distortion or abuse of the reporter's role, and (3) more investigative reporting of the press itself.

———. "Trial by Television." *New York State Bar Journal*, 40:19–28, January 1968. **1S 188**
The author sets forth reasons for his belief that pretrial publicity prejudices the rights of defendants in criminal cases and that television has now gotten into the act and is making matters worse.

Seymour, William O. "The Judicial

Trend—More Restrictions." *National Press Photographer*, 23(12):14, 16, December 1968. **1S 189**
A survey of sixty chief federal judges reveals that more restrictions are likely to be placed on photographic coverage of criminal cases.

Shafer, Ronald G. "What Is Obscenity? Lack of a Definition Stymies a Crackdown Against Smut Dealers." *Wall Street Journal*, 176:1, 19, 19 August 1970. **1S 190**
"The widespread availability of increasingly explicit books and films here [Washington, D.C.] and elsewhere points up the frustration of Federal smut fighters. Although they're scoring gains in one battle—a crackdown against dealers who send unsolicited materials through the mails—they're making little headway in a number of others. They'd like more authority and tougher laws." A major problem has been that the courts haven't been able to agree on what obscenity is.

Shaffer, Helen B. *Violence in the Media*. Washington, D.C., Editorial Research Reports, 1972 (*Editorial Research Reports*, 1(19):377–94, 17 May 1972) **1S 191**
A summary of inquiries into media violence, including the disagreement of experts on the impact on children; proposals and prospects for control, including petitions and lawsuits by citizens' groups; effect of self-censorship in network TV; and the movie rating system.

Shaffer, Thomas L. "Direct Restraint on the Press." *Notre Dame Lawyer*, 42:865–80, Symposium 1967. **1S 192**
The author prefaces his remarks with a fable involving a crisis in the prospective marriage of the Princess of Ap and the Prince of Upi—a conflict involving the town crier's right to proclaim information about the bride's wedding gown—*Free Crier v. Fair Marriage*. The author accompanies his story with full legal documentation of actual cases. Following comment on fair trial and free press, the author proposes a statute that would make the premature publication of certain kinds of prejudicial information a crime. The proposal would include assurance of greater access by the press to information at various stages coupled with restraints on its use until after the verdict had been reached. The result would be more freedom, but on a delayed basis.

[Shah, Amritlal B.] "On Censorship." *Quest*, 100:7–8, March–April 1976. **1S 193**
An editorial plea for greater freedom for the Indian press and offering mild criticism of the press censorship imposed by the government of Indira Gandhi. "If the Government is serious in its desire to see a healthy and enterprising press capable of upholding democracy

[quoting the words of Mrs. Gandhi], develop in India it will have to demonstrate it in the realm of action. For instance, it would not do to penalize *Quest* for publishing this editorial—though, following the exhortation of the Chief Minister of Maharashtra, we are 'prepared to face the consequences' of our action." The consequence was a government notice to the printers asking them to show cause why their printing press should not be forfeited as a penalty for having printed the editorial. The printers, to stay in business, were obliged to apologize to the government and notify *Quest* of their inability to continue printing the journal which they had printed for more than twenty years. Failing to find another printer willing to chance government prosecution, the publishers announced that the May–June issue would be the last published. "We are compelled to be silent, but we hope that the values for which *Quest* stood will not perish from the land. The human spirit may be blocked, but not forever. We shall look forward to its having free play once again."

―――, ed. *The Roots of Obscenity: Obscenity, Literature, and the Law*. Bombay, Lalvani Publishing House, 1968. 148p. (For International Association for Cultural Freedom)   **1S194**
In this work, five authors (A. B. Shah, Dilip Chitre, Madhao B. Achwal, K. M. Sharma, and N. S. Ranganath Rao) discuss obscenity, literature, and the law from various angles and suggest a review not only of the law in force in India but the attitudes behind it. The article by Shah traces "the origin of the consciousness of obscenity" and formulates "a reasonably objective working criterion for identifying obscenity"; Chitre "attempts to link up pornography with a wider mutation in contemporary culture norms" in one article and in another "discusses the origins of linguistic taboos and stresses the need for separating them from conventional behavior in a multicultural and rational society"; Achwal "examines the nature of the gap between the aesthetic and the social context of literature and obscenity"; Sharma "discusses the legal aspect of obscenity and analyses the Indian Supreme Court's judgment on *Lady Chatterley's Lover* against the background of recent judgments in the U.S."; and Rao "recapitulates the history of literary censorship and points out the inadequacies of the present law in India. He also offers amendment; to it with a view to curbing pornography and, at the same time, allowing maximum freedom to creative writers."

―――. "What Price Freedom?" *Quest*, 89/90:5–135, July–August 1974. (Reprinted in a separate volume, *What Price a Free Press?* Edited by V. V. John and A. B. Shah. Calcutta, Nachiketa, 1974. 135p.)   **1S195**
The entire issue of *Quest* is devoted to the *Statesman* case involving the efforts by the

Government of India, through a Fact Finding Committee, to lay down fair prices to be charged by newspapers and salaries to be paid employees. The newspapers objected to the recommendations and challenged the Government's action as an attempt to demoralize further an already demoralized press.

Shaheen, Jack G. " 'The War Game' Revisited." *Journal of Popular Film*, 1: 299–308, Fall 1972.   **1S196**
The story of the British Broadcasting Corporation's censorship of Watkins's film about nuclear war.

Shainess, Natalie. "Pornography Report: Psychiatrist Disputes It." *Congressional Record*, 116:32269–70, 16 September 1970. (Reprinted from the *Washington Evening Star*, 2 September 1970)   **1S197**
"There are so many things wrong with this experiment [the effect of pornography on college students] that one hardly knows where to begin. . . . To think that we can saturate adults with pornography and effectively isolate their children from it is a fool's dream. . . . I think one week of work by a few profound thinkers would have been of greater value."

Shalit, Gene. "The Rating Game." *Look*, 34(22):82, 86–89, 3 November 1970.   **1S198**
Comment on the new rating system established by the motion picture industry—G, GP, R, and X. The author believes "the rating system can work *if*: reasonable people work at it, parents keep an eye on their children, theater operators keep an eye on their audiences." The alternative may be government censorship.

―――. "Violence: The New Obscenity" and "More Violence: Round Two." *Ladies Home Journal*, 91(4):10, 14, April 1974; 91(7):8+, July 1974.   **1S199**
The author makes three suggestions: (1) abolish the Motion Picture Association of America rating board. "It should not be beholden to the movie business. It should be responsible to the public." (2) have only two ratings—"X", not for children thirteen or under "even if accompanied by St. Francis of Assisi" and "A" for everyone. (3) parents should boycott violent movies. In the second article Shalit writes: "I am against any form of government censorship of movies. Censorship is the enemy of freedom, and I oppose censorship totally and unalterably. But I do believe, and the *Journal* believes, that some system must be instituted to protect impressionable young children from films that have what might be called 3-D scenes, debased violence, depravity, and degradation. An intelligent child-protecting system can work if rating boards have intelligent, professionally competent members who are responsible to the public—not to the Motion Picture Industry; if theater owners enforce the system honestly;

and if parents accept their responsibility for what they permit their young children to see." There follows letters from readers and a response from the film industry's Jack Valenti who defends the rating system.

Shamer, James G. *Changing Congressional Secrecy*. Columbia, Mo., Freedom of Information Center, School of Journalism, University of Missouri at Columbia, 1974. 5p. (Report no. 330)   **1S200**
"Congressional secrecy—especially in markup sessions—has long been a focus of critical attention. The Legislative Reorganization Act of 1970 was somewhat helpful in creating more openness, but other efforts were needed as well."

Shankman, Arnold. "Converse, *The Christian Observer* and the Civil War Censorship." *Journal of Presbyterian History*, 52:227–44, Fall 1974.   **1S201**
The *Christian Observer*, a Presbyterian newspaper, was published by Amasa Converse simultaneously in the Confederacy and the North from January to June 1861, when federal authorities forbade written or printed communication between the United States and the Confederate States. When government agents invaded his Philadelphia office and suppressed the journal, Converse moved to Richmond and reestablished the *Christian Observer* as a paper loyal to the Confederacy.

―――. "Freedom of the Press During the Civil War: The Case of Albert D. Boileau." *Pennsylvania History*, 42: 305–15, October 1975.   **1S202**
An account of the arrest and imprisonment of Albert D. Boileau, editor of the *Philadelphia Evening Journal*, for an editorial appearing in the 20 January 1863 issue of that Democratic paper which was critical of President Lincoln and called for an end to hostilities and a negotiated peace. The arrest was made by military authorities and Boileau was removed to Baltimore's Fort McHenry. The storm of protest against the arrest in Baltimore and elsewhere died down when Boileau apologized for the editorial, which he said had been inserted in the paper without his knowledge, and his Unionist backers considered him a "collapsed martyr." He was released and his paper resumed publication.

Shapiro, Andrew O. *Media Access: Your Rights to Express Your Views on Radio and Television*. Boston, Little, Brown, 1976. 297p.   **1S203**
"This book focuses upon one key aspect of broadcasting law: namely, those rules which require a broadcaster to provide air time to concerned citizens for self-expression. . . . An important goal of this book is to disabuse citizens of the notion that broadcasters enjoy complete autonomy in the selection of viewpoints to be expressed over the air." The work is a how-to-do-it guide for the use of concerned

Shapiro, David L. "Background and Development of the Recommendations of American Bar Association Advisory Committee on Fair Trial and Free Press." *Oklahoma Law Review*, 22:127–34, May 1969. **1S204**
A member of the Reardon Committee discusses the background of the Committee, the procedures used, and the rationale for its recommendations.

Shapiro, Lionel. "Freedom to Read." *Canadian Library Journal*, 31:296–300, August 1974. **1S205**
The roots of censorship lie deep in recorded cultural history and many countries today, especially the church states, the "peoples" democracies, and the supernationalistic Arab states. In the Western liberal democracies censorship is more likely to be directed against sexual immorality than seditious material. The author contends that "Canada provides scope for the expression of a variety of moral positions which are tolerable, provided their expression does not seriously threaten the social existence of other minority or majority groups in the community. Is there not a risk that if the criminal law attempts to enforce moral concepts, a serious threat to the civil liberties of all citizens will ensue?"

Shapiro, Martin. "Obscenity Law: A Public Policy Analysis." *Journal of Public Law*, 20:503–21, 1971. **1S206**
The author concludes that while the United States Supreme Court has been unable to frame and administer a full set of policies with respect to obscenity, state legislatures can do so and some have. He suggests five policies that might be adopted: prohibition of obscene materials to juveniles, prohibition of commercial distribution of hard-core pornography (except for scientific purposes), prohibition of the display of obscenity to captive audiences, prohibition of modes of advertising and sale "that appeal to prurient interest. . . ." and prior restraint or licensing of stage plays and motion pictures.

———, ed. *The Pentagon Papers and the Courts. A Study in Foreign Policy-Making and Freedom of the Press*. San Francisco, Chandler, 1972. 131p. **1S207**
"This book presents a wide range of materials bearing on [the political and legal] issues, ranging from testimony on the classification system and analyses of government management of the news to the opinions of the Supreme Court denying the Government's request for an injunction against the *New York Times* and *Washington Post*. The premise of the volume is that the ultimate issue involved is democratic control of foreign policy."

Shapiro, Sanford. "Big Brother Is Watching Your Kids." *ALA Bulletin*, 62:1089–92, October 1968. Comments: 63:26–27, January 1969. **1S208**
The author discusses New York's law of "variable obscenity" which imposes special restrictions on the sale and distribution of obscene matter to children while permitting freedom of reading for adults. He challenges the need for the state to provide this protection to children as an extension of the role of the parent. "Risk for risk, Big Brother's smugtown neatness in morality will wound more children more deeply than the titillation of any 'girlie' magazine."

Shapo, Marshall S. "Media Injuries to Personality: An Essay on Legal Regulation of Public Communication." *Texas Law Review*, 46:650–67, April 1968. **1S209**
"Essentially, I propose that although the famous decision in *New York Times v. Sullivan* may supply a needed beginning for serious discussion about the first amendment, future pronouncements should consider explicitly the power relationships between media and the injured parties." The author suggests further that legal recognition be given to the commercial nature of the medium in cases that have little relation to the political role of the citizenry, and that, if necessary, "the government should be prepared to insure financially a balance between the conflicting imperatives of first amendment freedom and of fundamental rights to redress against superior communications power."

Sharma, K. M. "Obscenity and the Law: The Indian Experience Through the American Looking-Glass." *Houston Law Review*, 6:425–53, January 1969. **1S210**
Content: The aesthetic relevance of obscenity in the works of art and literature and the borderlines where the literary aspect touches the sociolegal aspects. A brief sketch of the development of obscenity in Anglo-American jurisprudence as background material to appraise the Indian law. Section 292 of the Indian Penal Code, 1860, and relevant law showing the state of obscenity law in India. Juristic implication of problems of Indian law and the relevance of American experience to solve them.

Sharma, Vishnu D., and F. Wooldridge. "The Law Relating to Obscene Publications in India." *International and Comparative Law Quarterly*, 22:632–47, October 1973. **1S211**
"An attempt will be made in the present paper to consider the law of obscene publications in India, and its possible reform. Some comparisons will also be made with English law where such comparisons appear constructive."

Sharp, Donald B., *ed. Commentaries on Obscenity*. New York, Scarecrow, 1970. 333p. **1S212**
An anthology of sixteen commentaries by legal scholars on issues raised by recent U.S. Supreme Court decisions in the area of obscenity, together with an introduction by the author, Obscenity Law and the Intransigent Threat of Ginzburg. Articles are entered under the names of their authors in this bibliography.

Sharpe, Richard O. "The Newsman's Qualified Privilege under the First Amendment." *South Dakota Law Review*, 16:328–50, Spring 1971. **1S213**
"The purpose of this article is to enumerate and evaluate the various arguments [with respect to newsmen's qualified privilege] that have confronted the courts and the predominant reasons for rejection of these arguments."

Shaver, James P. "Diversity, Violence, and Religion: Textbooks in a Pluralistic Society." *School Review*, 75:311–28, Autumn 1967. **1S214**
A study of social science textbooks' treatment of three topics directly related to diversity in American society—nonconformity, civil disobedience and violence, and religion. The investigator concludes that "available textbooks do not provide the context of controversy."

Shaw, David. "Public Obscenity." *New Humanist*, 90:404, April 1975. **1S215**
The author objects to the "warped obscenity" of the crucifixion as depicted in art and literature and urges that such scenes of sadistic brutality not be displayed in public.

———. "Sexual Hypocrisy of the American Press." *Penthouse Forum*, 5(5):34–37, February 1976. **1S216**
The author discusses ways in which leading American newspapers have avoided the use of obscene words or phrases. "Editors and publishers who oppose the publication of 'obscene' words argue that by printing them they will not only offend readers but also sanction, if not encourage, the legitimation of the words."

Shaw, Donald L. "Surveillance vs. Constraint: Press Coverage of a Social Issue." *Journalism Quarterly*, 46:707–12, Winter 1969. **1S217**
A study of news coverage of population and family-planning coverage reveals that it is more closely related to available newshole and wire service material than to local environmental need or surveillance.

———, and Stephen W. Brauer. "Press Freedom and War Constraints: Case Testing Siebert's Proposition II." *Journalism Quarterly*, 46:243–54, Summer 1969. **1S218**
"Analysis of the threats against a North Carolina Civil War editor [William W.

Holden, *North Carolina Standard*₁ proves the proposition that official and unofficial pressures on press freedom increase in times of governmental stress."

Shaw, Eugene F. "The Press and Its Freedom: A Pilot Study of an American Stereotype." *Journalism Quarterly*, 49:31–42, 60, Spring 1972.　**1S219**
"This study compares and contrasts attitudes toward the press and its freedom in a probability sample of students preparing for various professions. Media and professional bias was indicated in the various profiles."

Shaw, George Bernard. "Censorship As a Police Duty." In Dan H. Laurence, *ed. Platform and Pulpit: Bernard Shaw*. New York, Hill & Wang, 1961, pp. 183–200.　**1S220**
Address delivered before the Special General Conference of the Chief Constables' Association, held at Harrogate, 8 June 1928. Published in the Conference *Reports*, 1928. Of all the impossible duties that could be put on the local constabulary, "the censorship of plays is the most impossible, and the most odious. . . . Plays, like political speeches and books, bring you up against those constitutional liberties which you are supposed to protect. . . . My advice to you is to resist any attempt to put on you the duty of the Lord Chamberlain. . . . I advise you to press for the licensing of theatres ₁not plays₁ by local authorities as a substitute for the censorship."

———. "Morality and Birth Control." *Independent Shavian*, 10:33–36, Spring 1972. (Reprinted from *Physical Culture*, July 1919)　**1S221**
Shaw argues for freedom to discuss and publish information on birth control.

Shaw, Steven J. "Colonial Newspaper Advertising: A Step toward Freedom of the Press." *Business History Review*, 33:409–20, Autumn 1959.　**1S222**
It was largely through the development of profitable advertising that the colonial editors were finally able to free themselves from the subsidies and control of governors and political parties. Such colonial editors as Benjamin Harris, James Franklin, and John Peter Zenger fought the all-important battles for a free press, but they were unable to finance their papers entirely from revenues from sales and advertising. They depended, in part, on job printing, retailing, and politicking.

"Shaw and Yeats and Their Tribe: Editorial on the First General Meeting of the Irish Academy of Letters, with Special Reference to the Suppression

Under the Censorship Act of George Bernard Shaw's 'Adventures of a Black Girl in Search for God' Reporting a Deputation to Mr. P. J. Rutledge, Minister for Justice on the Matter." *Catholic Bulletin*, 23:693–96, September 1933.　**1S223**

Shawcross, Hartley W., *baron*. "A Free Press." *Journal of the International Commission of Jurists*, 8:52–59, December 1967.　**1S224**
A member of the International Commission of Jurists discusses the universal aspects of press freedom—"the fundamental right of every person to have full and free access to facts on all matters that directly or indirectly concern him and to hear and read the opinions of others." He suggests basic principles of press freedom which all countries should observe and legitimate restrictions which might be imposed as a protection to society. Among the areas of concern are expression of political views, government secrets, public order and morals, treason and sedition, personal libel, and the right of privacy.

Shayon, Robert L. "Lion, Lion Burning Bright." *Saturday Review*, 54(37):18, 20, 11 September 1971.　**1S225**
Comment on the aftermath of the 1969 *Red Lion* decision ₁*Red Lion Broadcasting Co. v. FCC*₁ in which the U.S. Supreme Court in a unanimous decision upheld the Federal Communications Commission's fairness doctrine.

———. "Notorious v. Run-of-the-Mill." *Saturday Review*, 53(14):40–41, 4 April 1970.　**1S226**
Comments on *Trial—The City and County of Denver vs. Loren R. Watson*, a four-program series shown recently on the National Educational Television network, which "represents a commendable and fascinating effort to provide all who are concerned about the issue of free press versus fair trial with some of the necessary evidence that Justice White had in mind when he dissented in the Billie Sol Estes case."

———. "TV Without Terror." *Saturday Review*, 55(10):34, 4 March 1972.　**1S227**
In light of the report of the Surgeon General finding "a preliminary and tentative indication of a causal relationship between viewing violence on television and aggressive behavior," Congress is faced with a dilemma: censorship or personal corporate responsibility.

———. "Two Bites of the Apple." *New Republic*, 165:22, 33, 11 December 1971.　**1S228**
Commentary on the role of Nicholas Johnson, activist member of the Federal Communications Commission, particularly with respect to the FCC decision in *Columbia Broadcasting System, Inc., v. Democratic National Committee*.

———. "Very Cold Turkey." *Saturday Review*, 54(18):21–22, 1 May 1971.　**1S229**
Federal Communications Commission's instructions to broadcasters to review lyrics of songs referring to illegal drugs.

Shea, Kevin M. "While Zoning Ordinances Regulating the Location of Adult Bookstores and Theaters Require Strict Judicial Scrutiny, Neighborhood Preservation Is a Compelling State Interest Satisfying That Standard." *Journal of Urban Law*, 52:388–99, November 1974.　**1S230**
Re: *Nortown Theatre Inc. v. Gribbs*, 373 F. Supp. 363 (E.D. Mich. 1974).

Shea, Thomas F. " 'Don't Bother to Smile When You Call Me That,'—Fighting Words and the First Amendment." *Kentucky Law Journal*, 63:1–22, 1974–75.　**1S231**
Under the *Chaplinsky* decision (*Chaplinsky v. New Hampshire*, 1942), the Court held that "fighting words" were an instrument of assault and not communication protected by the First Amendment. "The current rationale, that fighting words may be punished only if there is a showing that a violent reaction is likely to result leads the court to absurd results." A person who verbally abuses a burly construction worker is penalized; a person who reviles a paraplegic in a wheelchair is not.

Shearer, Lloyd. "What Price Secrecy?" *Parade*, 22 August 1971, pp. 4–7. **1S232**
"What it boils down to is that the government's present secrecy classification system is an undeniable mess riddled with inequity, stupidity and inconsistency. . . . Reform is in order." Included is a comment on security classification by Arthur J. Goldberg and suggestions on how to cure the overclassification syndrome by William G. Florence, retired Pentagon classification officer.

Shecter, Rosalyn M. *Open Letter to the Supreme Court*. Baltimore, Four Star, 1970. 58p.　**1S233**
The chairman of the Maryland Board of Motion Picture Censors calls upon the U.S. Supreme Court to provide positive guidelines that will protect children and the immature from harmful pornography. "The state owes an obligation to citizenry to protect the young and immature from obscenity and shocking lewdness." Without legal backing parents alone cannot do the job.

Sheed, Frank J. "Nobody Loves Censors." *Ave Maria*, 105(19):6–9, 13 May 1967.　**1S234**
A Catholic author discusses the role of the *Index Expurgatorius* and the *imprimatur*. He concludes that "something like the *Index* ₁which is no longer maintained₁ will continue, not for prohibition but for information. Authors

perhaps will be under no obligation to withdraw 'indexed' books, readers under no obligation to shun them. But at least if a Catholic chooses to read one, he will have been warned: He will not be misled into thinking he is getting Catholic teaching. Something of the same sort may happen about the imprimatur—it may function more flexibly than in the past . . . and there may be no obligation."

Sheed, Wilfred. "The Good Word: Dirty Business." *New York Times Book Review*, 5 August 1973, p. 2. **1S235**
A witty essay on pornography. Example: "Presuming that the censors will try to censor a little bit more each year (because, like editors and other officious people, censors don't feel they are getting anywhere unless they are up and doing) and that each case will produce at least five letters to the *Times*, we may find ourselves spending more person-hours just talking about pornography than any society in history. . . . In time the reading of pornography trial-transcripts may replace the real thing, unless these, too, come to be censored." On writing of X movies: "It would be nice if mankind's need for pornography could somehow be met without commandeering whole art forms like this."

Sheehan, Dennis W. "Broadcasters' Immunity from Liability for Political Defamation." *Georgetown Law Journal*, 48:544–62, Spring 1960. **1S236**
The author argues that there is justification for assigning the risk of loss to the broadcaster: (1) it is socially desirable not to have the burden fall upon the individual, (2) the broadcaster is in the best position to absorb the cost and pass it on to the consuming public, and (3) there is a positive benefit to supplying the broadcaster with an economic impetus to exercise surveillance.

Sheehy, Edward. "A Survey of Attitudes (Dealing with Censorship)." *Ireland Today*, 2:77–78, January 1937. **1S237**
The author defends modern Irish novelists who have "suffered much at the hands of authority." The censor-critic would like to see novels avoid unpleasant views of Ireland and the Irish and serve as an "unofficial ministry of propaganda to glorify our present state."

Sheehy, Michael. "Irish Literary Censorship." *Nation*, 208:833–36, 30 June 1969. **1S238**
There is some evidence of a relaxing of official censorship of literary works in Ireland that has been responsible for banning many important Irish and foreign works. The Irish Catholic church has lost control of Irish literary life.

Shepard, Lansing R. "Pornography—Shabby Front for a Big Industry." *Congressional Record*, 116:13977–79, 1 May 1970. **1S239**
This article and two others on the growing problem of pornography and efforts to curtail its distribution in the United States appeared originally in the *Christian Science Monitor* in April 1970. They were reprinted in the *Congressional Record* during the House debate on H.R. 15693. The other two articles were: Judicial Hard Line on Smut? describing the difficulty in drafting legal definitions of obscenity; and Gargantuan Task: Pornography Probers Struggle, discussing the problems faced by the U.S. Commission on Obscenity and Pornography.

Shepard, Paul C. "Freedom to Defame." *Wake Forest Law Review*, 11:166–76, March 1975. **1S240**
A discussion of *Gertz v. Robert Welch, Inc.* (1974), in light of prevailing defamation law and its effect upon the North Carolina Law of defamation.

Sheppard, Samuel H. *Endure and Conquer: Dr. Sam Sheppard*. Cleveland, World, 1966. 327p. **1S241**
Dr. Sam Sheppard's own account of his trial and conviction for the murder of his wife and the ordering of a new trial because of the prejudicial publicity in the Cleveland press. The new jury found him not guilty.

Sher, Susan S. "Requiring Newsmen to Appear and Testify Before Federal and State Grand Juries Does Not Abridge Freedom of Speech or Freedom of Press Guaranteed by First Amendment." *Loyola University Law Journal* (Chicago), 4:227–55, Winter 1973. **1S242**
Re: *Branzburg v. Hayes* (1972). The author concludes that "if the Supreme Court does not act and if legislatures do not pass strong shield statutes, the current hostility between the government and the news media will not diminish. It is still possible that there may be a deterrent effect on the free flow of information to the public. Yet it is unfortunate that this will be due either to the government's not enforcing its rights under the law, or to the belief of newsmen that they must disobey the law and go to jail in order to uphold a free press."

Shera, Jesse. "Intellectual Freedom—Intellectual? Free?" *Wilson Library Bulletin*, 42:323, 344–45, November 1967. Comments: 42:458–59, January 1968; 42:565, February 1968. **1S243**
"If no one knows what effect reading has on the individual or on society, how can it be argued that 'bad' books are not harmful, while 'good' books are beneficial?" Librarians can't have it both ways.

Sheridan, John D. "Graham Greene and the Irish: Commentary on Greene's 'The End of the Affair.' " *Irish Monthly*, 81:211–16, June 1953; 81:291, July 1953. (Reprinted from *Books on Trial*, January–February 1953) **1S244**

While Greene's novel, *The End of the Affair*, was ignored by the Irish press as a book not fit for the Irish public, the novel won an award in America as the most distinguished Catholic novel of the year. The author of the article attempts to explain the differences in opinion between Catholic Ireland and Catholic America in the area of art and morality.

Sherlock, Norman R. *The Founding Fathers and Press Freedom*. Seattle, University of Washington, 1966. 243p. (Unpublished Master's thesis) **1S245**
The author examined the correspondence, public statements, and writings of framers of the Constitution to determine their concepts of press freedom. He found that none of the three theories advanced by scholars is wholly correct: (1) that the Founders intended no federal or state libel laws (Justice Hugo Black), (2) that they meant free examination and discussion of public policy and officials (Zechariah Chafee, Jr.), or (3) that they embraced the doctrine of seditious libel (Leonard Levy). "It is clear that the lack of a Bill of Rights in the original document cannot be traced to human rights by the Founders, the Founders intended no *federal* libel laws, but no immunity at state level, and major Founders stood on both sides of the issue. The deep division of opinion among them was because they intended no explicit definition, only a general framework. America was in a formative period and the concept was in the process of being shaped."

Sherman, Edward F. "The Military Courts and Servicemen's First Amendment Rights." *Hastings Law Journal*, 22:325–73, January 1971. **1S246**
"A distinctively military philosophy of the First Amendment still prevails in military courts which has severely limited the availability of judicial protection for servicemen's free speech rights." The author considers recent First Amendment cases decided by the Court of Military Appeals.

Sherman, Jeffrey G. "Constitutional Protection for the Newsman's Work Product." *Harvard Civil Rights–Civil Liberties Law Review*, 6:119–40, December 1970. **1S247**
"This comment will briefly examine the rationale for the creation of a newsman's constitutional privilege to conceal confidential sources and information, and sketch the contours of the privilege by examining the questions: Who is a newsman? When is a privileged relationship created? And what information is protected?"

Sherman, Kenneth S. "State Control of Political Advertisements." *Suffolk University Law Review*, 7:711–19, Spring 1973. **1S248**

In *Opinion of the Justices to the Senate*, 284 N.E. 2d 919 (1972), the Supreme Judicial Court of Massachusetts advised the Senate of the Commonwealth that a bill governing political advertising violated state and federal constitutions and constituted prior restraint on the freedom of the press.

Sherrill, Robert. "Freedom of the Press; What It Means; Whom It Serves." *Katallagete*, 3:5–14, Winter 1971.   **1S249**
"In coming to grips with the major problems that have troubled the [American] nation since World War II, the daily press has been consistently timid, reactionary and repressive. Efforts to expose their defects and thereby reform institutions which were either impotent or were actually destructive of the public welfare have virtually always been made first either by elitist groups and their members (professors, radical organizers, freelance social critics) writing for the small opinion magazines or by the same people producing books. Not only has the daily press usually failed to take the lead, it often has failed to even follow after it was 'safe' to do so."

———. "The Happy Ending (Maybe) of 'The Selling of the Pentagon.' " *New York Times Magazine*, 16 May 1971, pp. 25–27+.   **1S250**
How the controversial Columbia Broadcasting System documentary on the Pentagon came about, how it was produced, how it was received by the Pentagon, Congress, and the White House, and the war of nerves that ensued. The happy ending is that the episode may have upset the network sufficiently that they have decided to take a stand.

[Sherrin, Jeffrey J.] "Internal Conflict in the First Amendment: Panarella v. Birenbaum." *Albany Law Review*, 38: 281–300, 1974.   **1S251**
A "classic confrontation between two fundamental first amendment rights, the right of freedom of the press and the right of religion to be free from government establishment and interference." The case involved the suppression of two student newspapers that printed articles allegedly grossly offensive to religion. The court ruled that the colleges were not required to suppress the newspapers on grounds that, the author notes, "they did not exceed the limits of constitutional protection of freedom of the press and that the use of state moneys to support the papers did not violate the establishment clause of the first amendment."

Sherwood, John T., Jr. "The Freedom of Information Act: A Compendium for the Military Lawyer." *Military Law Review*, 52:103–39, Spring 1971. **1S252**
"The Freedom of Information Act is now five

years old. Yet many of the difficulties that plagued its predecessor hinder its full application. The author examines the history, provisions, and subsequent interpretation of the 1966 Act in order to provide guidelines for the military practitioner. He stresses the necessity of giving a liberal interpretation to the philosophy of the Act: that full disclosure should be the rule and not the exception."

Sherwood, Margaret. "The Newsman's Privilege: Government Investigations, Criminal Prosecutions and Private Litigation." *California Law Review*, 58:1198–1250, October 1970. (Also in 1U100)   **1S253**
"The recent widespread use of governmental and defense subpoenas for newsmen's testimony and films has posed a grave threat to the ability of the press to gather and disseminate the news. This Comment explores the need for a newsman's privilege and the legal precedent upon which such a privilege would be based. The possible scope of the privilege is examined in connection with governmental and defense subpoenas and court orders in private litigation."

Shesgreen, Sean. "Missing the Story in Northern Ireland." *Chicago Journalism Review*, 4(11):11–12, November 1971.   **1S254**
Charges bias of the U.S. press against the minority cause in Northern Ireland.

Shibi, Haim. *Presidential Television*. Columbia, Mo., Freedom of Information Center, School of Journalism, University of Missouri at Columbia, 1976. 7p. (Report no. 347)   **1S255**
"Some critics have argued that the presidential use of television has tipped the constitutional system of checks and balances in favor of the President. The author analyzes the real meaning of this modern forum for persuasion."

Shield Legislation for Journalists: A Bibliography. Iowa City, Iowa, School of Journalism, University of Iowa, 1973. 36p. Processed.   **1S256**
A comprehensive listing of secondary sources, state laws with an indication of states currently debating the adoption of shield laws, and relevant briefs outlining the holdings in recent court cases.

"The 'Shield' Statute: Solution to the Newsman's Dilemma?" *Valparaiso University Law Review*, 7:235–48, Winter 1973.   **1S257**
"This note examines the urgent need for adequate statutory protections which would limit the instances in which a newsman must disclose his confidential sources and the corresponding treatment such legislation may encounter from a judiciary which seems determined to scrutinize the legislation on a highly technical basis."

Shields, Gerald R. "The Comfort of Fear." *Connecticut Libraries*, 17(2):12–15 [April 1975?].   **1S258**
A discussion of the American Library Association statement on Free Access to Libraries for Minors, and the controversy over the librarian's role *in loco parentis*.

———. "Editor's Choice." *ALA Bulletin*, 63:561–62, May 1969.   **1S259**
An editorial on the censorship episode involving the Missouri State Library, a children's librarian, and an underground newspaper.

Shiff, Anne L. "The Freedom of Information Act—The Use of Equitable Discretion to Modify the Act." *Tulane Law Review*, 44:800–805, June 1970.   **1S260**
Re: *Consumers Union of the United States, Inc. v. Veterans Administration*, 301 F. Supp. 796 (S.D. N.Y. 1969). Despite a finding that none of the information requested was exempted from the Act, the court invoked its equity jurisdiction, weighing the benefits and detriments of disclosure, holding that public interest required only a portion of the information revealed.

Shifflett, Kizzie H. *The Fifth Seal, Rev. 6 Chap., 9 Verse.* . . . [Springfield, Ill., Printed by the Edward F. Hartmann Co., 1922.] 200p.   **1S261**
A curious fictionalized account of the martyrdom of Elijah Parish Lovejoy in defense of his antislavery newspaper. The title is taken from the Book of Revelations in which the opening of the Fifth Seal revealed "the souls of them that were slain for the word of God, and for the testimony which they held."

Shiffrin, Steven. "A Rhetorician's View on Dissent and the Mass Media." In Speech Association of America. *Abstracts, 56th Annual Meeting*, New Orleans, 1970, p. 94.   **1S262**
"Because access to the media is a necessary prerequisite for effecting significant political change, broader access for dissenters is necessary not only on grounds of fairness but equally for the sake of expediency."

Shifrin, Leonard E. "The Law of Constructive Contempt and the Freedom of the Press." *Chitty's Law Journal*, 14: 281–95, October 1966.   **1S263**
The author examines the collision between two sets of social interests—scandalizing the court or abusing the parties concerned and the right of the public and the press to write, speak and have their views published. He considers the legal status in four countries—the United Kingdom, United States, Australia, and Canada.

Shilton, Lance R. *et al*. *No No Calcutta*. Adelaide, Australia, Brolga Books, 1971. 96p.   **1S264**

An account of the battle in South Australia over the staging of *Oh! Calcutta!*: a journalist's account by Helen Caterer; a discussion of the philosophical and psychological justification of what was done by psychologist John Court, a member of the Moral Action Committee; a summary of the legal proceedings by Margaret Wells; and moral and spiritual issues by Lance Shilton, chairman of the Moral Action Committee.

Shirley, William J. "State v. Kavanaugh: An Interpretation of Canon 20 Versus the Reardon Recommendations." *Wayne Law Review*, 15:1581–1600, Fall 1969. **1S265**
"Recently, the New Jersey Supreme Court referred to Canon 20 in removing from a case an attorney who had released prejudicial material to the news media prior to trial (*State v. Kavanaugh*, 52 N.J. 7, 243 A. 2d 225, 1968). After putting the problem in perspective, this comment will endeavor to examine that case and relate it to the Reardon Committee Recommendations in an effort to determine their applicability and effectiveness."

Shoaf, George H. *Fighting for Freedom*. Kansas City, Mo., Simplified Economics [1954?]. 160p. **1S266**
The autobiography of a long-time radical reporter and field agent for *Appeal to Reason*, and "the first person to be arrested for violating the California criminal syndicalism law." He was arrested for distributing copies of John Reed's *Ten Days That Shook the World* in Pershing Square, Los Angeles.

Shoemaker, Thaddeus E. *Constitutional Conflict: Free Press–Fair Trial. A Problem in Democratic Theory*. Los Angeles, University of Southern California, 1969. 208p. (Ph.D. dissertation, University Microfilms, no. 69-9041) **1S267**
"The purpose of this study was to investigate the nature of the controversy and to develop a theory of conflict that would explain and describe the causes behind the alleged incompatibility of two Constitutional principles." The author finds, in summary, that "the free press–fair trial controversy is a pluralistic conflict arising from the inharmonious confrontations of free press–fair trial theories and practices with ideas on one hand and scientific and technological realities on the other."

Shooshan, Harry M., III. "Confrontation with Congress: Professional Sports and the Television Antiblackout Law." *Syracuse Law Review*, 25:713–45, Summer 1974. **1S268**
The enactment of the sports "antiblackout law" came just four months after introduction in the Senate and less than two months after introduction in the House. "Rarely does the legislative process operate with such speed. But rarely is there such overwhelming public support for legislation and such little partisan discord over its specifics."

"Shopping Center Not Open to First Amendment Activities Unrelated to Use." *Minnesota Law Review*, 57:603–20, January 1973. **1S269**
Re: *Lloyd Corp. v. Tanner*, 407 U.S. 551 (1972) and related cases.

Shores, Louis. "Dissent with Dissent." *Intellectual Freedom Newsletter* (IFC-ALA), 18:68–69, July 1969. **1S270**
The librarian of the year 2069 will look back on the decade of the 1960s and see it as more permissive than censored and more concerned with freedom than with responsibility.

Shortt, Edward. *Problem of Censorship; Paper Read at the Summer Conference of the Cinematograph Exhibitors Association of Great Britain and Ireland, Thursday, June 27th, 1935, by the Rt. Hon. Edward Shortt. . . .* [London, British Board of Film Censors, 1935.] 12p. (Also in the Board's *Annual Report*, 1934) **1S271**
The president of the British Board of Film Censors believes film should be allowed the same freedom as other forms of dramatic art, but it should be of a character "which will not demoralize the public, extenuate crime or vice, or shock the just susceptibilities of any reasonably-minded section of the community." He discusses horror films, gangster films, cruelty to animals, and religious films.

Shosteck, Herschel. "Ascertainment Procedures: Rule and Reality." In Don R. Le Duc, *ed.*, *Issues in Broadcast Regulation*, Washington, D.C., Broadcast Education Association, 1974, pp. 41–48. **1S272**
The author discusses his experience with methods of determining how television meets or fails to meet audience needs.

Shrapnel, Norman. "The Porn Market (The Abuses of Literacy—5)." *Times Literary Supplement*, 3,650:159, 11 February 1972. **1S273**
A description of the London trade in pornography—well over sixty porn shops with an estimated annual sales of 10 million pounds a year. Prosecution takes place on the average of once a week. The author considers the nature of the stock, the economics of the business, the kinds of customers, and the questions raised in Parliament and elsewhere about this flourishing industry.

Shufeldt, Robert W. "Science and Art Protective Society." *Medico-Legal Journal*, 37:3–6, January 1920. **1S274**
A physician, author of *Studies of the Human Form*, calls for the creation of a body of artists and scientists to advise the courts in the matter of portraying the nude figure for artistic and scientific purposes. He cites the case of a Dutch ethnologist (H. M. B. Moens) in the United States, who was arrested ostensibly as a

German spy but convicted for possessing nude photographs of various racial types which he had gathered for an ethnological study. The Washington Court of Appeals reversed the decision.

Shuford, Bill, Jr. "Defamation: 'Real' Public Concern—A 'More Apt' Test for Constitutional Privilege?" *University of Florida Law Review*, 26:131–37, Fall 1973. **1S275**
Re: *Firestone v. Time, Inc.*, 271 So. 2d 745 (Fla. 1972), a case involving the reporting of a decree of divorce in which the Florida Supreme Court ruled that divorce proceedings are not of "real" public or general concern, and news reports concerning them are not constitutionally protected.

———. "Newsmen's Source Privilege: a Foundation in Policy for Recognition at Common Law." *University of Florida Law Review*, 26:453–80, Spring 1974. **1S276**
Comment on the U.S. Supreme Court decision in *United States v. Caldwell* (1972), in which the Court ruled that the First Amendment does not provide newsmen with a privilege to refuse to disclose confidential facts and sources to federal and state grand juries engaged in the investigation of crime. The author believes the Court should reverse itself and "grant newsmen unqualified constitutional or *common law right* to protect sources. Although first amendment arguments have been rejected in criminal cases, a foundation in policy supports the recognition of the newsman-source privilege at common law."

Shugrue, Richard E. "An Atlas for Obscenity: Explaining Community Standards." *Creighton Law Review*, 7:157–81, Spring 1974. **1S277**
The article considers the following factors: (1) The U.S. Supreme Court has never adequately addressed itself to the question of "contemporary community standards." (2) The lower courts have interpreted the Supreme Court rulings in a variety of ways, producing no consistent body of law. (3) The Supreme Court decisions failed to define community standards and to outline an objective test which can be used to discover those standards. (4) It is suggested that the Court return to a standard articulated by the California Supreme Court, which calls for the use of expert testimony to establish community mores.

———. "An Inquiry Into a Principle of 'Speech Plus.'" *Creighton Law Review*, 3:267–91, Fall 1969. **1S278**
Concern with enforcement of First Amendment freedoms when speech is combined with action in the case of picketing, demonstrations,

marching, assembly, etc. "Whether these actions may be protected by the First Amendment doctrine of free speech is the major concern of this article."

Shultz, Gladys D. "What Sex Offenders Say about Pornography." *Reader's Digest*, 99(7):53–57, July 1971.
1S279

The author takes issue with the findings of the Commission on Pornography and Obscenity, citing opinions regarding the relationship of pornography and sex crimes advanced by medical authorities and offenders themselves. She concludes that "when so many questions about pornography remain unresolved, isn't it the part of wisdom to hold off on breaking down more barriers until we can get a clearer idea of what our sexually permissive society is doing to us?"

Shuman, Bruce A. "Practical Handling of Censorship Problems in Public Libraries." *Library Occurrent*, 24:145–48, November 1972.
1S280

Remarks made at a workshop on censorship conducted at Indiana University for librarians of small libraries.

Shuman, R. Baird. "Making the World Safe for What?" *Illinois Schools Journal*, 48:145–54, Fall 1968. (Reprinted in *Education Digest*, December 1968) **1S281**

The author discusses the work of pressure groups which "in the name of morality and patriotism . . . usurp the professional prerogatives which school people have gained through years of arduous specialized training."

Shurn, Peter J., and Jacqueline Y. Parker. "Reporter's Privilege—Guardian of the People's Right to Know?" *New England Law Review*, 11:405–62, Spring 1976.
1S282

Following a review of the recent history of the newspaper drive for federal shield legislation, the authors examine the various state privilege statutes and the decisions of courts both where shield laws exist and where they do not. They conclude that "the dangers of a federal statute outweigh any possible benefit achieved by national uniformity since a 'bottom line' is already created by case law. The legal support needed by reporters not only exists without a federal statute, but will better continue to flourish without one."

Siau, Sandra M. *The Impact of the Sheppard Case on Newspaper Coverage of Crime, Especially in the Cases of Richard F. Speck, James Earl Ray and Sirhan Bishara Sirhan.* Lawrence, Kans., University of Kan-

sas, 1970. 113p. (Unpublished Master's thesis)
1S283

"A major point in the thesis is that each of these cases, because of the *Sheppard* case, received both press and legal treatment quite different from what it would have been in an era less conscious of the free press–fair trial problem."

Siebert, Fredrick S. "Access by Newsmen to Judicial Proceedings." In Chilton R. Bush, *ed., Free Press and Fair Trial.* Athens, Ga., University of Georgia Press, 1970, pp. 106–10. **1S284**

A survey of 483 trial judges reveals that the "practice of denying permission to all types of photographers (still and TV) to take pictures in the courtroom during the progress of a criminal trial is practically universal."

———. "Trial Judges Opinions on Prejudicial Publicity." In Chilton R. Bush, *ed., Free Press and Fair Trial.* Athens, Ga., University of Georgia Press, 1970, pp. 1–35.
1S285

In this study of whether or not judges thought that pretrial publicity had resulted in miscarriage of justice, the survey reveals, by indirection, that the "most highly or moderate" effective safeguards for protecting a defendant from unfavorable publicity during a trial were the judges' admonition to the jury, sequestering the jury, continuance or postponement, and the *voir dir* examination of jurors. The survey also assessed the judges' views on publishing the prior criminal record of the defendant and "confessions." More than 50 percent of judges favored a press-bar code; only 14.9 percent reported such a code in operation in their communities.

Siegel, Alberta. "Alternatives to Direct Censorship." In Victor B. Cline, *ed., Where Do You Draw the Line?* Provo, Utah, Brigham Young University Press, 1974, pp. 289–91.
1S286

In testimony before a Senate Committee the author suggests five alternatives to direct censorship: (1) an independent monitoring agency to measure the level of violence in television, (2) consumer expression of disapproval of violence by refusing to purchase the advertised product or to purchase stock in the firm, (3) increased support for public broadcasting, (4) travel fellowships offered to writers and producers of children's television programs to visit countries where television has been successful in nonviolent programs for children, and (5) a child advocate to be appointed to the staff of the Federal Communications Commission.

Sieghart, Paul. "Observations on Obscenity." *Table: The International Catholic Weekly*, 225:1116, 20 November 1971.
1S287

The author defines a few terms as a prelude to the better understanding of the issues in obscenity debates—"erotica," "aphrodisiac," "obscenity," "pornography," "indecency," and "deprave." He finds the film *Sunday,*

Bloody Sunday is not aphrodisiac, obscene, or pornographic, while *The Devils* is totally obscene and indecent, yet both have "X" certificates. A letter to the editor, 4 December 1971, from the Reverend Edward Fitzgerald, objects to Sieghart's definitions as only adding to the current confusion.

Sigler, Ronald F. "A Study in Censorship: The Los Angeles '19'." *Film Library Quarterly*, 4:35–38, 40–46, Spring 1971.
1S288

"The following study is an attempt to clarify the successful management of [the Los Angeles County Library] recent film censorship problems that have come to the attention of all libraries." Local groups and individuals had objected to films shown to high school students as having communistic leanings, and being un-American and atheistic.

Sigma Delta Chi. "Code of Ethics." *Quill*, 61(12):27, December 1973. **1S289**

Adopted by the national convention, 16 November 1973, the Code establishes standards of practice for professional journalists in the areas of responsibility, freedom of the press, ethics, accuracy and objectivity, and fair play. The Code concludes with this pledge: "Journalists should actively censure and try to prevent violations of these standards, and they should encourage their observance by all newspeople. Adherence to this code of ethics is intended to preserve the bond of mutual trust and respect between American journalists and the American people."

[Signer, Myer *et al.*] "Censorship of Erotica." *Causeway*, 1:4–33, 1966.
1S290

This section of the Canadian quarterly consists of an article, He and She and Him and Her; a group of quotations on censorship from books and articles; an interview with psychiatrist Stephen Neiger on the subject of censorship and pornography; and remarks on the civil liberties issue by Sidney Linden, Canadian Civil Liberties Association.

Silver, Isadore. "Secrets and Security: Postscript to the Pentagon Papers." *Commonweal*, 94:399–402, 6 August 1971.
1S291

The author considers some of the issues with respect to the First Amendment and national security not addressed or not conclusively answered by the decision of the U.S. Supreme Court in the case of the Pentagon Papers.

Silver, Louise, *comp. Restrictions on Freedom of Publication in South Africa, 1948 to 1968: A Select and Annotated Bibliography.* Johannesburg, Department of Librarianship, Bibliography and Typography, University of Witwatersrand, 1972. 54p. **1S292**

The work includes documentation of statute and case law covering the preunion, union, republic, and provincial ordinances as well as books and periodical articles under the following headings: general articles on restrictions, effect of restrictions on literary expression and the book trade, restrictions concerning undesirable and obscene publications, politics and restrictions on freedom of publication, and procedural aspects of restrictions.

Silver, Ronald K. "National Security and Freedom of the Press: The Constitutionality of S.1's 'National Defense Information' Provisions." *Loyola of Los Angeles Law Review*, 9:323–49, March 1976. **1S293**
"Three of the eight sections [of the proposed Criminal Justice Reform Act] dealing with espionage have the potential to increase the power of the executive branch to control the flow of news concerning the federal government. These sections and their possible effect on constitutional freedom of the press are the focus of this Comment."

Silverstone, Samuel. "Access to Government Information: Administrative Secrecy and Natural Justice." *University of British Columbia Law Review*, 10:235–50, 1976. **1S294**
The author reviews the question of administrative secrecy in Canada, on the occasion of the decision in *Rossi v. The Queen* [1974] F.C. 531 (F.C.T.D.).

Silvis, Douglas K. "The Confidential Informant: Will His Views Still Make News?" *University of Miami Law Review*, 27:230–38, Fall/Winter 1972. **1S295**
Re: *Branzburg v. Hayes* (1972), involving testimonial privilege of newsmen to refuse to appear or testify before grand juries as to information gained through confidential sources. "The question unresolved by *Branzburg*, which leaves the critics for freedom of the press somewhat uncertain, is whether trial and appellate courts will truly take such applications for judicial protection on a case-by-case basis, or whether, in avoiding a solid shield of protection for all confidential relationships, the Supreme Court has left the news media in the exposed and unprotected position feared by the dissent."

Simmons, Steven J. "The Fairness Doctrine and Cable TV." *Harvard Journal on Legislation*, 11:629–57, June 1974. **1S296**
"It is the author's contention that if cable television develops to the extent predicted by its advocates, the nature of the medium will at some point become so different from traditional broadcast television that the fairness doctrine should not be constitutionally required in cable systems." At the point when at least half of all American households are linked by cable systems carrying twenty or more channels, the "uninhibited marketplace of ideas which the Supreme Court has held the

first amendment to require, will be achievable in a cable system without fairness regulations."

Simms, Abby P. "Sequestration: A Possible Solution to the Free Press–Fair Trial Dilemma." *American University Law Review*, 23:923–57, Summer 1974. **1S297**
"This comment will concentrate on the alternative of sequestration, i.e. the isolation of the jury during the trial and/or during its deliberations as a means of resolving the conflict between a free press and a fair trial in criminal actions. In so doing, the effect of prejudicial publicity on jurors will be discussed and emphasis will be placed upon the procedural aspects of sequestration."

Simons, G. L. *Pornography without Prejudice: A Reply to Objectors*. London, Abelard-Schuman, 1972. 169p. **1S298**
"The present book is, in part, an attempt to indicate that where the moral indignation is directed at 'pornography' it is largely misplaced, and that the 'anti-pornography lobby' has little or no logical or empirical support. Where social or 'factual' reasons are given for opposition they serve, in the main, as *rationalization* for a pre-arranged philosophy—a common ploy in efforts at justification. . . . As soon as empirical criteria are acknowledged the *facts* will decide the case—and the facts are that access to pornography is not shown to be harmful, and that it may even be beneficial. If we aim to be *liberal* and *democratic* then the repeal of obscenity legislation properly follows."

Simons, Howard, and Joseph Califano, Jr., *eds. The Media and the Law*. New York, Praeger, 1975. 225p. (Published in cooperation with the *Washington Post*) **1S299**
The edited proceedings of a Conference on the Media and the Law, sponsored by the *Washington Post* and the Ford Foundation to struggle with the most troublesome First Amendment problems. Participants in the informal conference, held at the Homestead in Virginia, were top journalists, jurists, lawyers, and government appointees. They confronted three hypothetical cases, presented by two professors from Harvard Law School, Charles Nesson and Arthur Miller: "Case I raises issues relating to national security, the methods by which the press gathers information, and the role of the courts in assessing the competing claims of national security and the public's right to know. Case II raises issues relating to rights of privacy, libel, the public's access to the media, and again, the methods by which information to be published is gathered. Case III raises the issues surrounding the judicially sanctified nature of grand jury proceedings, gag orders, and whether it is appropriate for the media to put cash on the line for news stories." The editors introduce the dialogue with an essay on The Jurists and the Journalists, covering gag orders, confidential sources, news gathering, privacy, access to the

media, the broadcast media, and economic, ethical, and moral considerations.

Simons, Paula R. *Freedom of the Press in High School Newspapers and Yearbooks: A Status Report*, 1973–1974. Manhattan, Kans., Kansas State University, 1974. 285p. (Unpublished Master's thesis) **1S300**
"The purpose of this study was to determine the extent of censorship existing in high school yearbooks and newspapers, which authority in the school system is mainly responsible for restrictions, whether community standards affect the coverage of controversial items in school publications, how student editors view the restrictions, and finally, the underlying reasons for press censorship on the high school level."

———. "How Much Editorial Freedom?" *Communication: Journalism Education Today*, 5:13–15, 17, Summer 1972. **1S301**
"Legal precedents have already been established in the past four years in answer to these questions: Issues and coverage 'suitable' to the high school press; distribution of student publications which are *not* school sponsored; editorial policy in student tax-supported media; advisor's liability and authority; school administrator's influence and liability in school-sponsored media."

Simonson, Solomon. "Violence in the Mass Media." *Catholic World*, 207:264–68, September 1968. **1S302**
The author answers the "telegogs" who defend violence in television, countering the arguments that (1) the people want it; (2) there is no proof of causal relationship between fictional violence and actual violence; and (3) the classics had all manner of violence.

Simpson, David. *A Discourse on Stage Entertainment*. Birmingham, England, M. Swinney, 1788. 88p. **1S303**
In this sermon against stage plays, the Reverend Mr. Simpson cites the opposition to the theater expressed by ancient authors, Church Fathers, Church councils, eminent Englishmen (including Jeremy Collier), and governments. "I will not say but there may be some few Plays that are chaste and moral throughout, but then the number is exceedingly small and they are seldom brought upon the stage."

Simpson, Imogene. "A Survey: The Influence of Censorship on the Selection of Materials in the High School Libraries in the Third Education Dis-

trict in Kentucky." *Southeastern Librarian*, 24(2):29–31, Summer 1974. **1S304**
A questionnaire survey of the thirty-four high school librarians in the district reveals that "there seems to be a tendency of the librarians in the Third District not to order many books about sex, race, and current social problems. This is either because of the librarian's prejudice, lack of funds, or lack of current book selection aids."

₍Sinclair, Upton.₎ "Abolish the Censorship." *Upton Sinclair's Monthly Magazine*, 1:5, February 1918. **1S305**
An editorial condemning Post Office suppression of an issue of the *Truth Seeker* which compared reputed offenses of the Kaiser with those of God in the Old Testament, and suppression of a pamphlet by Lenin circulated by the Rand School. "We stood for censorship so long as our country was at war. We stand for it no longer." In the May–June issue Sinclair writes of the difficulty in getting Post Office approval for his own magazine.

————. "Burning Books in Boston." *EPIC News*, 4(48):1–2, 26 April 1937. **1S306**
An open letter to a Massachusetts legislator who had introduced a bill to ban Sinclair's book from all libraries in the state on grounds that he had attacked religion in his book, *The Profits of Religion*. "I do not attack any religion," writes Sinclair, "I attack the abuses of it. . . . When you discover that a man is writing books to expose and denounce this travesty upon religion, the insult to the memory of Jesus, you propose to introduce the methods of Fascism and Nazism to America, and start the burning of books."

————. "Censor: Fool or Knave." *New Masses*, 3:16, August 1927. **1S307**
"We authors," writes Sinclair, "are using America as our sales territory and Boston as our advertising department." He reports on his experience with Boston's Watch and Ward Society in the case of his novel, *Oil*. He indicates that he is preparing a Fig Leaf edition for sale in Boston, in which the nine pages (out of 527) objected to will be blacked out by a fig leaf (S420).

————. *The Crime of the "Times." A Test of Newspaper Decency.* Pasadena, Calif., The Author ₍1920?₎. 31p. **1S308**
Sinclair attacks the *New York Times* and Professor James Melvin Lee of the New York University Department of Journalism for their criticism of his book, *Brass Check*, which had dealt harshly with American journalism (S418).

Singer, Harry. "Alternatives to Censorship of Multi-Ethnic Literature." In

Phil L. Nacke, *ed. Diversity in Mature Reading: Theory and Research.* Boone, N.C., National Reading Conference, 1973, pp. 211–18. (22d Yearbook, vol. 1) **1S309**
An alternative to eliminating children's literature that may offend a minority group, the author suggests, might be to broaden selection criteria "to include books which realistically portray minority groups and which represent the entire range of attitudes and values. Instead of eliminating biased books, put them into historical context and use them for teaching evaluation and critical thinking."

Singer, Richard G. "FCC and Equal Time: Never-Neverland Revisited." *Maryland Law Journal*, 27:221–51, Summer 1967. **1S310**
"It is the purpose of this article to explore the Federal Communications Commission's regulation of political broadcasting as affected by the 'equal time' provisions of the Communications Act. This evaluation will occur in the context of the dual purposes of protection of minority parties and their candidates and assurance of a politically astute and informed public, which the author believes justify government concern with political broadcasting. Specific attention will be turned to the recent (1959) amendments to the statutory scheme, after which questions of reform and repeal will be discussed."

Singh, Bakhsish. "Freedom of Speech and Expression and the Role of Supreme Court of United States." *Civil and Military Law Journal*, 3:111–18, January–June 1967. (Reprinted in *International Journal of Legal Research*, 1968) **1S311**
A bird's-eye view of decisions of the U.S. Supreme Court in upholding the right of free expression. The author observes that the Court, despite its vigorous support of freedoms, has sometimes been far behind public opinion and the needs of society.

Singh, J. D. "More Pornography in Britain: Censors Beat Retreat." *Times of India*, 15 February 1973, p. 6. **1S312**
Britain is in the process of agonizing reappraisal of its censorship of sex in the wake of the more permissive practices in Denmark, Sweden, West Germany, and the United States. The author cites evidence of the relaxation of the British censor.

Sisk, Larry. "California Test Proves Lens and Mike Coverage Need Not Intrude." *Quill*, 54(4):20–23, April 1966. **1S313**
A demonstration in the use of modern photographic techniques was made before a committee of the California State Legislature to prove that cameras and recording devices would not be obstructive in court.

————. "Reardon Report Results in Secrecy in California." *California Publisher*, 47(8):9–12, May 1968. **1S314**
Effect of the recommendations of the American Bar Association's Committee on Fair Trial and Free Press.

Siskel, Gene. "An Interview with the Censor." *Playboy*, 19(1):129–30+, January 1972. **1S315**
"As the century reaches its final reel ₍20 January 1999₎ the silver screen's grand old man of the blue pencil ₍Erwin Putz₎ recounts his battles with the dark forces of cinematic evil."

Sissman, L. E. "Sex Biz." *Atlantic*, 228:24, 26, August 1971. **1S316**
While opposing censorship, the author charges that "the sanctity of our private lives, not to mention that of our literature, is being increasingly threatened by the cynical commercial exploitation of secondhand sex." Instead of censorship "we must seek extralegal redress for this infringement of our personal rights. We can do this in two ways. First by working through consumerist means and consumer organizations to lodge a loud and continuing protest with producers and purveyors of obscenity. . . . Second, those of us who are writers, teachers, community leaders, makers of public opinion can . . . help to cramp and cripple the mass appeal of pornography by making it démodé, by pointing out its kitschy insipidity, by exposing its infantilism, by laughing it to scorn."

Skidmore, James R. *A Survey of Civic and Legal Maneuvers to Eradicate Obscenity Since 1945.* Morgantown, W.Va., West Virginia University, 1968. 180p. (Unpublished Master's thesis) **1S317**
A survey of circulation and distribution of obscenity in West Virginia indicated that hard-core pornography was almost nonexistent; few communities ever used their ordinance against pandering. Most pornography reaching West Virginia came from New York and California by mail.

Skinner, Gary P. "Constitutional Aspects of Television in the Courtroom." *University of Cincinnati Law Review*, 35:48–70, Winter 1966. **1S318**
The solution to the problem of a fair trial vs. free press does not lie in the banning of television cameras from the courtroom; television's presence is not inherently a denial of due process of law. The trial judge should regulate the conditions under which televising a court trial is permitted.

Skogen, Tony R. "An Extension of the Fairness Doctrine to Advertised Products?" *Arkansas Law Review*, 26:402–7, Fall 1972. **1S319**
Re: *Friends of the Earth v. FCC*, 449 F.2d 1164 (D.C. Cir. 1971), in which the Court of Appeal ruled that the fairness doctrine applied, and

remanded the cause to the Commission for a hearing on the question of the broadcaster's compliance with it.

Skornia, Harry J., and Jack W. Kitson, eds. *Problems and Controversies in Television and Radio. Basic Readings.* Palo Alto, Calif., Pacific Books, 1968. 503p. **1S320**

Included in the readings are the following relating to freedom of the press: Congress and the Control of Radio-Broadcasting by Carl J. Friedrich and Evelyn Sternberg (F357); Through the Regulatory Looking Glass—Darkly by Robert W. Sarnoff (S64); The Role of the Commentator as Censor by Gunnar Back; Control by Advertisers by Jack Gould; and Why Suppress Pay-TV? The Fight in California by Sylvester L. Weaver, Jr. (W99).

Skrabut, Paul A. "Constitutional Law: Obscenity: Evidence." *Cornell Law Review*, 51:785–94, Summer 1966. **1S321**

"*Ginzburg v. United States* [1966] and the other obscenity cases recently decided by the Supreme Court have made the legal definition of obscenity even more obscure than it was prior to these decisions. It is difficult to see what practical or constitutional basis can justify compounding the ambiguities in this area. Apparently, the Court is trying, on a case-by-case basis, to balance the interests of protecting society from obscene materials with the interests of protecting freedom of expression."

Sky, Theodore. "Agency Implementation of the Freedom of Information Act." *Administrative Law Review*, 20: 445–57, June 1968. (Reprinted in U.S. Senate, Committee on the Judiciary, *The Freedom of Information Act (Ten Month Review)*, pp. 186–92) **1S322**

"On the whole, the climate created by the FOIA appears to have already fostered a freer flow of administrative material. At the same time . . . complex issues of law and policy concerning the availability of certain types of material remain to be resolved. Their resolution in some cases may be aided by direct dialog between individual agencies and the administrative law section [American Bar Association] acting through its various committees."

Slaby, Ronald G. *et al.* "Television Violence and Its Sponsors." *Journal of Communications*, 26(1):88–96, Winter 1976. **1S323**

The first study ranking advertisers by the amount of television violence they pay for.

Slade, Joseph P. "Pornographic Theaters Off Times Square." *Transaction*, 9(1/2):35–43, 79, November–December 1971. (Reprinted in Ray C. Rist, ed., *The Pornography Controversy*, pp. 119–39) **1S324**

New York City is an up-and-coming center of pornography, but California is the source of most of the pornographic films. The author describes the Times Square scene and the nature of the pornographic films that are shown. He makes observations on the social and psychological significance of this form of sexual fantasy which now flourishes openly in most major cities.

[Slaughter, Nathaniel G., III.] "Extension of Sullivan's Actual Malice Standard to Defamation of Public Figures." *Georgia Law Review*, 2:393–432, Spring 1968. **1S325**

"The thrust of this Note will be directed toward a determination of whether or not the actual malice standard should be applied to public figures, in addition to public officials. In formulating this determination, the following will be examined: The law of defamation as viewed from the constitutional perspective of *New York Times Co. v. Sullivan* [1964]; the problems of conflict and confusion created by *Sullivan* and subsequent cases interpreting and applying that decision; and the effect of *Curtis Publishing Co. v. Butts* [1967] and *Associated Press v. Walker* [1967] on the law of defamation with respect to public figures."

Sloan, William. "Code Control, Film Library Information Council's Stand on the New Motion Picture Association of America Classification Scheme." *Film Library Quarterly*, 2(2):33–36, Spring 1969. **1S326**

The Council is opposed to the new code. "It is opposed to the whole idea of this kind of restrictive covenant and, moreover, it is opposed to some of the ways this code, in particular, is being implemented. At the same time, we recognize that the MPAA leadership has fought long and hard against censorship at the hearings of state legislatures and elsewhere, and feel they are protecting a freer cinema through their actions."

Sloane, David E. E. "Censoring for *The Century Magazine:* R. W. Gilder to John Hay on *The Bread-Winners*, 1882–1884." *American Literary Realism, 1870–1910*, 4:255–67, Summer 1971. **1S327**

The correspondence between author John Hay and *Century* editor R. W. Gilder represents "as clear a case of Victorian editing practices as we shall ever have."

Slough, M. C. "Miller v. California: An Attempt to Control Obscenity." *Journal of the Bar Association of Kansas*, 42:317–23, 360–74, Winter 1973. **1S328**

Content: Miller and Progeny; Paris Adult Theatre I and the Brennan Dissent; The Fate of the Dirty Book; Importation and Transportation of Obscenity; Some Procedural Implications; The Summing Up.

———. "Obscenity, Freedom, and Responsibility." *Creighton Law Review*, 3:218–66, Fall 1969. **1S329**

The author criticizes the libertarian creed that obscenity for normal adults has no social consequences and should be permitted. This concept disregards the total nature of obscenity. While it may not be the immediate cause of antisocial acts, it loosens personal restraints which, in turn, leads to a disruption of a stable personality. He questions the Supreme Court's rationale in placing freedom of expression ahead of unrestrained addiction to perverted sexuality. He favors not only protection of juveniles, but also some restrictions on the adult world. "If the literary and theatrical arts are to be reduced to the standards of the exploiter, the incentive and the ability of the truly creative artists to publish and excel will inevitably be suppressed."

———. "Pornography and Sane Legal Control." *Journal of the Bar Association of Kansas*, 40:25–29, 69–86, Spring 1971. **1S330**

A history of obscenity in the United States and efforts to control it through legislation and court decisions. The author distinguishes between erotic literature which makes a contribution to society and the "reckless commercial exploitation" of pornography. While difficult to prove direct antisocial behavior as the result of pornography, the author argues that "obscenity's overall effect lies in the deterioration of society's moral and intellectual fiber." He criticizes the efforts of the U.S. Commission on Obscenity and Pornography as amounting to "a nullity." He believes that "there is a definite need for more explicit legislation in terms of regulating the publication of literature as differentiated from the regulation of the theater, motion picture, and live entertainment. All legislative efforts should be aimed at the reckless commercial exploitation of any and all such media."

———. "Privacy, Freedom, and Responsibility." *Kansas Law Review*, 16: 323–47, April 1968. **1S331**

The roots of privacy; a legal right to privacy (the tort concept of privacy, First Amendment limitations on the right); intrusions by public authority.

———. "Swift Currents of Change in the Law of Defamation." *Journal of the Kansas Bar Association*, 45:17–31, Spring 1976. **1S332**

Following a survey of the early history of defamation in American law with special attention to Kansas, the author discusses the rapid changes in libel beginning with *New York v. Sullivan* (1964) and extending through *Gertz v. Robert Welch, Inc.* (1974), again noting the status of the law in Kansas. "In the future," he concludes, "damage to reputation will likely be recurringly difficult to prove. Requiring actual proof may seriously jeopardize chances for adequate compensation. If the constitutional aspects, now an integral part of the law of defamation, provoke as much disagreement and dissent currently so evident in the obscenity cases, the aura of judicial insecurity can only increase."

Small, Philip. " 'Public Interest,' 'Fairness,' and the First Amendment: A Broadcaster's Dilemma." *Suffolk University Law Review*, 4:509–32, Winter 1970.   **1S333**
"This Note will examine the development of the 'public interest' standard and analyze its progeny, the 'Fairness Doctrine.' Primarily it will focus on the First Amendment problems created by application of the doctrine with particular emphasis placed upon the recent Supreme Court decision of *Red Lion Broadcasting Co. v. F.C.C.* [1969]."

Small, William J. *Political Power and the Press*. New York, Norton, 1972. 423p.   **1S334**
"This book examines the pattern of government pressures on the press from the days of George Washington to those of Richard Nixon. It explores the techniques of news management, where they work and where they fail. There is a detailed exploration of the fight over the publication of the Pentagon Papers by *The New York Times* and other newspapers and a similar examination of the controversial television documentary 'The Selling of the Pentagon,' which climaxed in a congressional vote on whether or not to cite the CBS network for contempt of Congress. . . . The basic theme of the book deals with the adversary relationship, the imbred hostility between politicians and reporters, what this means today, and what it holds for the future of a democratic state." The author is Washington Bureau manager of Columbia Broadcasting System.

Smith, Albert, *ed. "Press Orders": Being the Opinions of the Leading Journals on the Abolition of Newspaper Privileges*. London, W. Kent, 1853. 91p.   **1S335**
An account of the abuse of "press orders" (free admission to representatives of the press) and a call for reform, supported by a number of London papers.

Smith, Alexander B., and Bernard Locke. "Problems in Arrests and Prosecutions for Obscenity and Pornography: Response of Police and Prosecutors." *Technical Report of the [U.S.] Commission on Obscenity and Pornography*, 5:35–60, 1971.   **1S336**
"The present survey is aimed at reporting the reactions of police and prosecutors in a repre-

sentative sample of [seventeen] major cities scattered throughout the United States with respect to laws regulating obscenity and pornography and some of the problems they encounter."

Smith, Anthony. *The Shadow in the Cave. A Study of the Relationship Between the Broadcaster, His Audience and the State*. Urbana, Ill., University of Illinois Press, 1973. 351p.   **1S337**
The purpose of the book is to point out the origins of the tensions between the broadcasters, the politicians, and the vast audience which they jointly share, comparing the experience in Britain, the United States, France, Japan, and the Netherlands. Issues of freedom and access to the medium are considered throughout.

———. "TV Coverage of Northern Ireland." *Index on Censorship*, 1(2):15–32, Summer 1972.   **1S338**
One of the means by which the existing social structure in Northern Ireland was held together was by silence with respect to controversial issues on the part of radio and television; in turn this silence was partly responsible for perpetuating the social wrongs. Tight controls within the industry have seen to it that radio and television reflected the news and did not provoke it. "The 'real' meaning of the censorship argument in regard to Northern Ireland was thus a struggle between old and new attitudes towards television journalism." The well-established idea of "fairness" in British broadcasting was difficult to interpret in Northern Ireland in light of the "troubles." The author sees no likelihood of relaxation of controls over the media in the near future and suggests the most effective action in behalf of greater freedom in the media would be the development of professional organizations among program-makers to create their own counter-pressures.

———, *ed. The British Press Since the War*. Totowa, N. J., Rowman and Littlefield, 1974. 320p.   **1S339**
This collection of articles dealing with problems faced by the British press since World War II includes economic and financial restraints; legal restraints dealing with contempt, official secrets, privacy, libel, parliamentary privilege, and obscenity; the professional conduct of the press, including confidentiality of sources, the lobby system, and the efforts of the Press Council; the threat of press control within by worker participation in management. Documents include reports and recommendations from such groups as the Royal Commissions of the Press, the Monopolies Commission, the Radcliffe and Franks Committees on government secrecy, the Younger Committee on privacy, the Porter Committee on qualified privilege, the Select Committee on the Obscenity Bill of 1958, the Press Council, the Free Communications Group, and the Committee of "Justice" under the chairmanship of Lord Shawcross.

Smith, Anthony F. "Special Laws Covering the Press and Printers." In Melbourne University. *The Law and the Printer, the Publisher and the Journalist. The Collected Papers of a Seminar at Melbourne University on August 12, 1971*. Melbourne, Antony Whitlock, 1971, pp. 12–22.   **1S340**
The author deals with the following areas of Australian (Victoria) law relating to printers and journalists: registration of printing presses and newspapers dating back to 1864; no recognition of the right of journalists to refuse to disclose information or source of information to a court; the law against Sunday publications was repealed in 1969; false and deceptive advertising; protection of printer and publisher from responsibility for false statements unless they have violated a warning by a law officer.

Smith, B. L. "Censorship and Pornography." *Christian Lawyer*, 3(4):11–18, Spring 1971.   **1S341**
In a philosophical discussion, the author considers three objections frequently raised to censorship of written and visual material about sex: (1) censorship is hostile to morality because it deprives man of a free personal choice of alternate patterns of behavior, (2) it implies that the protected perspective is not true and the excluded alternatives are true, (3) the censor exposes himself to the very thing he seeks to protect others from.

Smith, D. V. "Pornography and the Law." *Weid: The Sensibility Revue*, 10:126–29, June 1976.   **1S342**
"Pornography which is innocent or experimental or inventive and amusing . . . ought to be encouraged by the law of the land. . . . But that which depicts violence, harm and hatred of persons and sex . . . ought to be discouraged; it should be outlawed and its practitioners incarcerated."

Smith, Don D. "The Social Content of Pornography." *Journal of Communication*, 26(1):16–24, Winter 1976. **1S343**
The study "seeks answers to several questions: What is the content of 'adults only' fiction paperbacks? How much sex is there in these books? What kind of sex? Who are the people portrayed in this literature and what characteristics are attributed to them? What else other than sex is in these books? What plots and themes dominate, if any?"

Smith, Donald L. *The New Freedom to Publish. Trends in Libel and Privacy Law—Effects on the Magazine Industry—New Challenges*. New York, Magazine Publishers Association, 1969. 79p.   **1S344**
"In preparing this monograph on press freedom in the 1960's, I have sought to achieve three main goals: to assess the extent to which free expression has been expanded by recent court decisions, notably those by the United

States Supreme Court, on libel and privacy; to find out how much magazine editors know about the decisions and if they think the rulings are having any effect on editorial decision-making and content; and to suggest possible meanings to be given the First Amendment in the future as courts interpret it in light of these rulings and changing social requirements."

Smith, Edward. *The Story of the English Jacobins: Being an Account of the Persons Implicated in the Charges of High Treason, 1794.* London, Cassell, Petter, Galpin [1881]. 184p. **1S345**
Includes an account of the trials of John Horne Tooke, Thelwall, Paine, and Muir; and the organization of the Association for Preserving Liberty and Property Against Republicans and Levellers, and Friends of the Liberty of the Press.

[Smith, Francis.] *An Account of the Injurious Proceedings of Sir George Jeffreys . . . against Francis Smith, Bookseller, with his arbitrary carriage toward the Grand-Jury at Guildhall, Sept. 16, 1680, upon an Indictment then exhibited against . . . F. Smith for Publishing a Pretended Libel: entituled, An Act of Common-Council for Retrenching the Expences of the Lord Mayor and Sheriffs of the City of London, etc.* London, [1681]. (STC 4024) (Reprinted in Stephen Parks, *ed., The English Book Trade, 1660–1853,* New York, Garland, 1974. Vol. 1) **1S346**

Smith, Frank H. "Can the 'Long-Arm' Reach Out-of-State Publishers?" *Notre Dame Lawyer,* 43:83–97, October 1967. **1S347**
An overwhelming legal burden faces the plaintiff "attempting to recover on an alleged libel by an out-of-state publisher under a single-act, long-arm statute."

Smith, Fred L. *The Selling of the First Amendment: An Analysis of Congressional Investigations of Four CBS Television Documentary Projects.* Tallahassee, Fla., Florida State University, 1972. 349p. (Ph.D. dissertation, University Microfilms, no. 72-32774) **1S348**
"During the period 1968 through 1971 two subcommittees of the United States Congress investigated four CBS television documentary projects. The Special Subcommittee on Investigations of the House Commerce Committee investigated CBS News' 'CBS Reports: The Selling of the Pentagon,' CBS News' never-broadcast 'Project Nassau,' and CBS-owned WBBM-TV's 'Pot Party at a University.' The Argiculture Appropriations Subcommittee of the House Appropriations Committee inquired into CBS News' 'CBS Reports: Hunger in America.' " The study sought to assess why the investigations occurred and what conclu-

sions could be drawn concerning the state of traditional First Amendment relationships among people, press, and government.

Smith, G. Roysce. "The Bookseller in Danger." *Publishers' Weekly,* 203(20): 35–36, 14 May 1973. **1S349**
"Booksellers everywhere are in clear and present danger as a result of a recent ruling of the New York State Court of Appeals in the case of *The People v. Charles Kirkpatrick and Peter Dargis.* It tested the validity of the statutory presumption that a seller of obscene materials knows the contents of what he sells." The author, executive director of the American Booksellers Association, indicates the Association's intent to file an *amicus curiae* brief in the appeal to the U.S. Supreme Court.

Smith, Godfrey. *Censorship, Monopoly, and the Working Newsman.* 28 min. tape recording. Berkeley, Calif., Pacifica Tape Library, 1970. **1S350**
The editor of the Sunday magazine section of the *Times* (London) talks to an audience of journalism students at the University of California about censorship and the efforts of radical newsmen in Britain, France, and Germany to control the publications they write for.

Smith, Hannis S. "A Position Paper on Anti-Pornography Legislation." *Minnesota Libraries,* 22:319–20, Autumn 1969. **1S351**
Opposition to a proposed Minnesota antipornography law on grounds that such legislation is irrelevant to the problems of society. If any obscenity law is passed, however, it should provide safeguards for literature and art, and should protect librarians and teachers from harassment.

Smith, I. Norman. "Freedom of the Press Is a *Public* Freedom, Not Just a Press Freedom." *Seminar (A Quarterly Review for Newspapermen by Copley Newspapers),* 25:21–22, September 1972. (Reprinted from Ottawa, Canada, *Journal*) **1S352**

Smith, Jerome R. "The FCC's Fairness Doctrine Not Applied to Advertisements for Commercial Products." *Emory Law Journal,* 25:479–500, Spring 1976. **1S353**
Re: *Public Interest Research Group v. FCC,* 522 F.2d 1060 (1st Cir. 1975).

Smith, John. *The Case of Mr. John Smith, Bookseller, Confined in the New Bastile, Clerkenwell.* [London, 1796.] Broadside. **1S354**
This London bookseller was charged with selling an anonymously printed sixpenny pamphlet entitled *A Summary of the Duties of Citizenship* which was critical of the government and, therefore, libelous. According to

Smith, the pamphlet, without his permission, bore his name on the title page as a bookseller where the work could be purchased, and copies were left at his shop and sold during his absence. Smith was, nevertheless, found guilty and, despite affidavits from two physicians attesting to his poor health, Lord Chief Justice Kenyon sentenced Smith to serve two years in Clerkenwell Prison, which the broadside describes as a cold, damp dungeon, a New Bastile. Another London bookseller, Joseph Burks, had already been sentenced to two years in Cold-Bath Prison for sale of the same pamphlet.

Smith, Kenneth V. *Newspaper Policies on the Publication of Names of Juvenile Offenders.* Reno, Nev., University of Nevada, Reno, 1975. 193p. (Unpublished Master's thesis) **1S355**
A twelve-year follow-up survey of a 1959 study to determine newspaper policies. The thesis includes a discussion of the origins of the controversy of confidentiality in juvenile court proceedings, a section of comments by newspaper editors, and statutes from each state regarding access by the news media to juvenile court records.

Smith, Larry V. "United States v. Reidel: Resolving an Ambiguity in Obscenity Control." *Southwestern Law Journal,* 25:819–23, December 1971. **1S356**
In *United States v. Reidel* (1971) the U.S. Supreme Court held constitutional the provisions of section 1461, title 18 of the U.S. Code which prohibits the knowing use of the mails for the delivery of obscene materials, even when the mailing was to a "consenting adult." The author finds *Reidel* a reaffirmation of *Roth.*

Smith, Lee H. "Is Anything Unprintable?" *Columbia Journalism Review,* 7:19–23, Spring 1968. (Reprinted in Michael C. Emery and Ted C. Smythe, *eds., Readings in Mass Communications,* pp. 419–26) **1S357**
A discussion of the increased candor in sex in the mass media, part of the sexual revolution that is taking place in America, and the censorship that is being practiced by newspaper and television editors in order to protect family readers and viewers. "The premise that mass publications must be edited for 'families' always seems to ignore the fact that families are growing up. . . . Furthermore, the 'family' standard is an unprofessional one that isn't applied to other areas or coverage. Any correspondent who filed from Saigon that he is witnessing a war that can't be talked about in a family newspaper would be hastily recalled." Editors should use their best judgments as to what is good taste without "trying to anticipate

the most hysterical reaction of the most sensitive reader."

Smith, Leonidas C., III. *Thirty Years of Federal Trade Commission Concern with Broadcast Advertising, 1938–1968.* Columbus, Ohio, Ohio University, 1970. 378p. (Ph.D. dissertation, University Microfilms, no. 71-4821)   **1S358**
"Over the years 1938 to 1968, the Federal Trade Commission has emerged as the primary source of regulation of deceptive broadcast advertising. In order to provide a key to the Commission's regulatory behavior, the present study examines and evaluates major cases of deceptive advertising heard before the Commission and the courts, as well as documents of the FTC and other agencies, and provides guidelines for selection of advertisements for broadcast."

Smith, Margaret Chase. "Why Women Must Speak Out Against Pornography." *Reader's Digest,* 101:235–36+, October 1972.   **1S359**
Senator Smith urges three effective ways that women can curb obscenity: (1) Keep informed of obscenity developments within your own community. (2) Urge your city, county and state to enact tough antipornography legislation. (3) Maintain constant pressures on local public officials to enforce obscenity laws.

Smith, Maurice T. "Living with the Censor." *Author,* 79:126–29, Autumn 1968.   **1S360**
A British publisher writes of the difficulties encountered by book publishers who cannot predict what the authorities and courts will, under the uncertain legal definitions, consider obscene. While violence may be more corrupting than obscenity, it is not interfered with. "What we need, more even than a change in the law, is to secure general approval for the fullest degree of freedom that the law allows. The public must be weaned away from its fears and inhibitions."

Smith, R. L. "Censorship and Permissiveness." *Australian Psychologist,* 8: 139–47, July 1973.   **1S361**
The author considers the findings of two United States commissions as they relate to censorship in their respective areas of concern: The Commission on Obscenity and Pornography and the Commission on the Causes and Prevention of Violence. He considers "the contrasting findings in a context of psychodynamic theory in order to seek some reconciliation of the respective conclusions of the two commissions."

[Smith, Ralph A.] "On the Third Domain—Art, Pornography, and Aesthetic Experience." *Journal of Aesthetic Education,* 4(3):5–8, July 1970.   **1S362**
"The question I will explore briefly is why hard-core pornography is not art." An introductory editorial to an issue dealing with pornography.

Smith, Robert, and Paul Prince. "WHDH: Two Issues." In Don R. Le Duc, *ed., Issues in Broadcast Regulation.* Washington, D.C., Broadcast Education Association, 1974, pp. 34–38.   **1S363**
The authors explore the issue of quality of broadcast in a television license renewal case which resulted in new ownership and management taking over an existing television channel.

Smith, Roger H. "Issues in the 'Probate' Verdict." *Publishers' Weekly,* 193(2):51, 8 January 1968.   **1S364**
Comments on the unsuccessful attempt of the New York County Lawyers Association to suppress Norman Dacey's *How to Avoid Probate.*

———. "Pleasantville's Velvet Trap." *Publishers' Weekly,* 193(24):49, 17 June 1968.   **1S365**
The case of the *Reader's Digest* ordering its subsidiary, Funk and Wagnalls, to cancel Samm Sinclair Baker's *The Permissible Lie.*

———. "Printer as Censor." *Publishers' Weekly,* 199(1):37, 4 January 1971.   **1S366**
The case of the October 1971 issue of *Scanlan's Monthly* which a New York printer refused to print because of political objection by union members to the content. A statement from the editors in the October issue indicates that the issue was printed in Quebec, after having been turned down by printers in New York, San Francisco, Colorado, and Missouri.

———. "The Suppression Business." *Publishers' Weekly,* 191(5):93, 30 January 1967.   **1S367**
Similarity in efforts of Jacqueline Kennedy to suppress Manchester's *The Death of the President* and Helen Clay Frick's efforts to stop publication of Sylvester Stevens's book with references to her father.

Smith, Shirley A. "Crisis in Kanawha County: A Librarian Looks at the Textbook Controversy." *School Library Journal,* 21:34–35, January 1975. **1S368**
A public librarian's account of the controversy over the supplementary language arts books adopted for use in the schools of Kanawha County, W. Va. Among the objections were to the use of profanity, "Damn the torpedos. . . ." A cartoon from the *Charleston Gazette,* 5 November 1974, shows John Paul Jones saying: "(Expletive deleted) the Torpedos! Full Steam Ahead!"

Smith, Stanford. "Freedom Is Everybody's Business." *Vital Speeches,* 33: 361–64, 1 April 1967.   **1S369**
The general manager of the American Newspaper Publishers' Association deplores the lack of public understanding of the essentiality of a free press. Too often the public sees the press as a special interest group rather than as their agent. He denies that it is necessary for the government to restrict the press in order to assure fair trial for the accused and believes that the equal time concept can be achieved in the press without the government applying regulations similar to those imposed upon broadcasting.

Smith, Thomas J. "How to Ban a Dirty Book." *U.S. Catholic,* 41(8):13–14, August 1976.   **1S370**
The author urges local control of pornography, giving the community an opportunity "to put the lids on the garbage cans of culture." Local control would "codify what a community considered permissible in books, films, photos, etc., and would spell out the consequences of violating these norms."

Smith, Warren S. *The London Heretics, 1870–1914.* New York, Dodd, Mead, 1968. 319p.   **1S371**
A study of the Christian and non-Christian seekers of the truth who spoke and published their views in Victorian England—secularists, positivists, theosophists, spiritualists, new Christians, Quakers, Catholic moderns, Unitarians, and Liberal Christians. Included in the study are accounts of various freethinkers whose views were under severe attack, whose publications were suppressed, or who suffered imprisonment: Annie Besant, Charles Bradlaugh, Havelock Ellis, George W. Foote, George J. Holyoake, and William T. Stead. References are made to the heretical societies that flourished during the period and to their controversial publications.

Smith, William H. T. "The Implications of the American Bar Association Advisory Committee Recommendations for Police Administration." *Notre Dame Lawyer,* 42:907–14, Symposium 1967.   **1S372**
The chief of police of Syracuse, N.Y. finds the recommendations of the Reardon Report "too vague and too susceptible to a variety of interpretations to serve as a useful guideline" on the release of information in criminal trials. He believes the proposed rules would create tremendous opposition to the police departments by the news media, and concurs with Frank Stanton of the Columbia Broadcasting System that the results would be less rather than more control of the climate of a trial. He prefers the adoption of voluntary canons of police ethics which would include guidelines for disclosure of criminal information.

Smoot, William R., II. "Uproar Hits

the Campus Press." *Look*, 33(4): 36, 38, 40, 18 February 1969. **1S373**
An account of the difficulties faced by editors of campus newspapers—firing, censorship, arrests—as they attempt to reflect changing student mores in sex and politics.

"Smut, Pornography, Obscenity—Signs the Tide Is Turning." *U.S. News & World Report*, 74(19):39–41, 44, 7 May 1973. **1S374**
"After years of growing license for eroticism, many people across the U.S. are fed up. Crackdowns are beginning on blatantly pornographic books, movies, stage shows—even radio programs. The battle, however, is far from over."

Smylie, James H. "Prudes, Lewds and Polysyllables." *Commonweal*, 89:671–73, 28 February 1969. **1S375**
This commentary is developed around the theories of Howard Moody's proposal in a 1965 article in *Christianity and Crisis*, recommending a new definition of obscenity as "that material, whether sexual or not, that has as its basic motivation and purpose, the degradation, debasement and dehumanizing of persons." The author applies his redefinition to the area of sexuality, particularly what has been considered sexual abnormality and perversion as expressed in such polysyllables as homosexuality, nymphomania, voyeurism, sadism, masochism, bestiality, etc. "What is and what is not permitted in a humane sexual relationship? What degrades? What debases? What dehumanizes? If we can come to some agreement about these questions, then, given the responsibility of a Christian to help mold the moral climate of the community, how are we to set 'community standards'—to use the Supreme Court terminology—for more humane sexual relations?"

Smyser, Jane W. "The Trial and Imprisonment of Joseph Johnson, Bookseller." *Bulletin of the New York Public Library*, 77:418–35, Summer 1974. **1S376**
An account of the 1799 trial and imprisonment of the prominent English publisher, Joseph Johnson, for publishing Gilbert Wakefield's *Reply* to a pamphlet written by Richard Watson, Bishop of Llandaff. Wakefield himself, along with booksellers Jeremiah Samuel Jordan and John Cuthell, were also found guilty. The Johnson trial does not appear in Howell's *State Trials* (he indicates he was unable to get a copy) and Erskine's speech in Johnson's defense does not appear in Erskine's collected speeches. The present account is taken largely from contemporary newspaper reports.

Smythe, Tony. "Britain's Civil Liberties—An Official Secret." *Civil Liberties Review*, 1:162–73, Fall 1973. **1S377**
Includes evidence of censorship of books, newspapers, and television programs taking place in England, belying the notion that "civil liberties are not in danger, despite any absence of written guarantee."

Snider, Clyde H. "The Public's Stake in Shield Laws." *Journal of the Missouri Bar*, 29:154–66, 188, April–May 1973. **1S378**
Unlike other common-law privileges of confidentiality (e.g., physician-patient, lawyer-client) which are for the purpose of maintaining what is considered socially desirable, the relationship between newsman and informer is based on the value to the public—the free flow of news. The author compares the newsman-informer relationship with that of police-informer. He discusses recent court decisions denying newsmen protection but passing the responsibility to state legislatures. He considers various proposals for shield laws—absolute and qualified—and advances arguments pro and con for each. "A shield law should be drafted with the purpose of making the public interest in administration of justice complement the public interest in a free flow of information to the public."

Snider, Paul B. *The British Press Council: A Study of Its Role and Performance, 1953–1965*. Iowa City, University of Iowa, 1968. 398p. (Ph.D. dissertation, University Microfilms, no. 69-8814) **1S379**
"This study proposed to examine the role and performance of the Press Councils in Great Britain since their inception in 1953 through 1965 in an effort to determine whether such a body has established itself as an institution successfully serving both Press and Public as well as to determine attitudes toward the Press Council." The study concluded that "the British Press Council is a force for good and is becoming increasingly effective in reducing Press excesses which in turn makes the Press more responsible. The Press generally has accepted the Council and looks to it for increased leadership."

Snyder, Gerald S. *The Right to be Informed: Censorship in the United States*. New York, Messner, 1976. 191p. **1S380**
Written for young people, grades seven and up.

Sobel, Lionel S. "Copyright and the First Amendment: A Gathering Storm?" *Copyright Law Symposium* (ASCAP), 19:43–80, 1971. **1S381**
In an analysis of two cases, *Rosemont Enterprises v. Random House* (1966) and *Time, Inc. v. Bernard Geis Associates* (1968), the author finds that the decisions "were incorrect in suggesting that the first amendment operates in some fashion to restrict the scope of copyright protection. They should not be considered sound precedent on that point or—since they incorrectly applied the fair-use doctrine also—on any other."

——. "Government Documents As 'Stolen Property': Reflections on the 'Free Press' Case." *Los Angeles Bar Bulletin*, 48:291–96, 315–20, June 1973. **1S382**
A critique of the California Supreme Court decision in *People v. Kunkin*, 9 Cal. 3d 245 (1973) involving the *Los Angeles Free Press* publication of a personnel roster of the Bureau of Narcotic Enforcement. The court ruled for the defendant, but the decision was on a narrow basis rather than for significant constitutional reasons.

——. "Television Sports Blackouts: Private Rights vs. Public Policy." *Los Angeles Bar Bulletin*, 48:169–74, 182–88, March 1973. **1S383**
Three issues are involved: the impact of federal antitrust law on the television policies of professional sports leagues, the significance of public ownership or other support of many sports stadia, and national television policy in general and the enormous revenue received by professional sports by virtue of its access to what are considered publicly owned airwaves.

Sobul, De Anne. *The Bill of Rights: A Handbook*. New York, Benziger, 1968. 264p. **1S384**
A teachers guide for Bill of Rights instruction in elementary and secondary schools.

The Social Morality Council (Great Britain). *The Future of Broadcasting; A Report Presented to the Social Morality Council, October 1973*. London, Eyre Methuen, 1974. 100p. **1S385**
This Report was commissioned by the Social Morality Council, a British organization which brings together humanists and religious believers of various faiths to undertake studies of contemporary social issues. "We have throughout," the report concludes, "accepted that broadcasting cannot and should not impose tastes and choices on listeners and viewers. But we believe it can and should make available to them all that is best in the range of human interests and activities—sometimes to solace, sometimes to challenge—but always with a profound respect for truth, and a serious regard for the human dignity and individual variety of its audience." One of the recommendations favored by a majority of the Commission was to create a Complaints Review Board to consider charges of inaccuracy and misrepresentation laid against the BBC and IBA, but only after the organizations had failed to satisfy the complaint, and without prejudice to their rights in law.

Socialist Party. *Court Rulings upon Indictments, Search Warrants, Habeas-Corpus, Mailing Privileges, Etc. Growing*

out of alleged offenses against Draft and Espionage Acts. Chicago, Socialist Party, National Office [1917?]. 54p.
1S386

Includes cases on the denial of second-class mailing privileges.

Society [Association] for Preserving Liberty and Property against Republicans and Levellers. *A Collection of Tracts . . . .* London, Printed and sold by J. Downes, 1793. Nos. 1–8. (Nos. 1–7 also bear the imprint of J. Sewell; the tracts were also issued separately)
1S387

The tracts are directed against the French Revolution, Thomas Paine, the Jacobins, and the "levelling of ranks," and in behalf of the king, the established religion, law and order, and protection of property. No. 1, Mr. Justice Ashhurst's Charge to the Grand Jury (the greater the truth, the greater the libel) (B203). No. 2, William Mainwaring's Charge to the Grand Jury (against seditious libel). No. 3, [John Bowles's] Protest against T. Paine's *Rights of Man*: addressed to the Members of a Book Society . . . . (B439). No. 4, An Answer to the Declaration of the "Friends of the Liberty of the Press"; Speech of the Lord President of the Court of Sessions addressed to the Lord Provost of Edinburgh. Plans for forming other [local] Liberty and Property societies. The organization was more frequently known as the Association rather than the Society (°A35).

Society for the Abolition of the Blasphemy Laws. *The Blasphemy Laws. Verbatim Report of the Deputation to the Home Secretary on April 16, 1924*. London, The Society [1924]. 15p.
1S388

The delegation from the Society presented the case for the repeal of the British blasphemy laws to Home Secretary Arthur Henderson, who assured the deputation of his sympathies for the cause, and of his intention to convey their views to the Prime Minister, but that they should not expect action before the next session of Parliament.

———. *The Blasphemy Laws. Verbatim Report of the Deputation to the Home Secretary (The Right Hon. J. R. Clynes, M.P.) on Thursday, November 7, 1929.* London, The Society [1929]. 15p.
1S389

A delegation from the Society presented to Home Secretary Clynes their arguments for abolishing the blasphemy laws. A similar presentation had been made in 1924. Chapman Cohen, Silas Hocking, Reginald Sorensen, and Mrs. Seaton Tiedeman were members of both delegations. Secretary Clynes failed to give the group any assurance of action, complaining how busy he was.

———. *Reasons for the Repeal of the Blasphemy Laws*. London, The Society, 1922? 4p.
1S390

The law of blasphemy is an attack on opinion; punishment for blasphemy becomes virtually a punishment for lack of education or taste; the law cannot prevent blasphemy; only the Church of England is protected by the law; many clergymen favor the repeal; and genuinely indecent language would still be subject to ordinary law relating to disturbance of the peace.

Society of Conservative Lawyers. *The Pollution of the Mind; New Proposals to Control Public Indecency and Obscenity*. London, The Society, 1971. 9p. Processed.
1S391

A sub-committee of the Society recommended the creation of a new offense of "public indecency" which they defined as any material displayed in any public place that "is grossly offensive to the public at large." The lawyers redefined obscenity as any material that "grossly affronts contemporary community standards of decency" *and* where "the dominant theme of the material taken as a whole (a) appeals to a lewd or filthy interest in sex *or* (b) is repellant." A person would not be convicted if it was proved that the material was "justified as being for the public good on the grounds that it is in the interest of science, literature, art or learning or of other objects of general concern."

Society of Film and Television Arts. "A Memorandum by SFTA to the Committee on Privacy at the Request of the Home Office." *Journal of the Society of Film and Television Arts*, 43/44:20–24, Spring–Summer 1971.
1S392

A report of a special subcommittee embodying the collective views of nine members on subjects of filming and recording people without their knowledge, publicity of true facts about private individuals, and violence and obscenity. The report concludes that private individuals have these safeguards against television's intrusion: existing laws of libel, trespass and contempt; codes of practices of BBC and the independent companies; and the public accountability of BBC and ITA to Parliament.

Society of Young Publishers. "When the Subject Is Censorship People Must Just Agree to Differ." *Bookseller*, 3259:2624–30, 8 June 1968.
1S393

Report on a panel discussion on Censorship and Books sponsored by the Society of Young Publishers. Panel members: John Bowen, playwright; Mrs. Mary Whitehouse, art teacher, housewife and "keeper of an eagle eye on the morals of TV"; Anthony Blond, publisher; Robert Maxwell, publisher and Member of Parliament; Richard Findlater (Kenneth B. F. Bain), author and chairman of the Society of Authors; Sir Basil Blackwell, bookseller and publisher; and David Holbrook, author and

journalist. The chairman was C. H. Rolph (Cecil R. Hewitt), author, journalist, and expert on the Obscene Publications Act. A wide variety of views were expressed, thus the title of the report.

Sohn, Ardyth B. "Determining Guilt or Innocence of Accused from Pretrial News Stories." *Journalism Quarterly*, 53:100–105, Spring 1976.
1S394

In an effort to find some empirical evidence to support arguments for either muzzling the press and its coverage of crime news or continuing and expanding its coverage, the investigator tests how a selected group of newspaper readers relate three typical crime story elements to belief in the guilt or innocence of the accused. The results showed that the kind of crime affects the opinions of some subjects, that is, there is a greater tendency to assess guilt when the subject is charged with a felony than with a misdemeanor.

Sokol, Daniel R. "United States Supreme Court Adopts A New Test. Miller v. California." *St. Louis University Law Journal*, 18:297–319, Winter 1973.
1S395

Re: *Miller v. California* (1973), in which the U.S. Supreme Court formulated a new obscenity test and directed that the new test be applied to meet local rather than national standards.

Solomon, Kenneth D., and Lawrence H. Wechsler. "The Freedom of Information Act: A Critical Review." *George Washington Law Review*, 38:150–63, October 1969.
1S396

The authors conclude that to date the act "has not worked a significant change on the disclosure of information policies of the Federal Government" because of vagueness of statutory language, the restrictive tenor given S. 1160 by the House Committee on Government Operations in its final report, the adoption of this interpretation by the Attorney General and federal agencies, and the compliance of the federal courts with the House interpretation.

Some Remarks Upon what is humbly supposed to be a Spurious Paper, intituled, Rules and Instructions by the Town-Council of———, to be observed by all who are permitted to cry Gazzettes and other Papers, or sell Roses and other Flowers, or to carry Links upon the Streets, Noblemen and Gentlemens Servants excepted. [Edinburgh?], 1734. 16p.
1S397

An attack on what the anonymous author believes (but is not quite sure) is a spurious tongue-in-cheek pamphlet setting up regulations of the press by a town council. The roguish pamphlet calls for the creation of a Society of no more than twenty persons who would wear badges consisting of an apron of blue linen. They would be given the exclusive right to publish and distribute pamphlets, subject to the prior approval of each item by the magistrates. This, the author charges, is a power no magistrates in Britain have a right to exercise. He calls upon the magistrates to repudiate the pamphlet as a fiction. There is apparently no reference in the text of the pamphlet to the sale of roses.

Some Thoughts on the Present State of the Theatres, and Consequences of an Act to Destroy the Liberty of the Stage. London [1735?]. 4p.   **1S398**
"Against the restoration of the number of playhouses with the resulting tyranny of managers; compares the freedom of the stage to the freedom of the press" (Lowe 171). The author concludes: "There is no Argument for the Liberty of the Press which will not hold in all its force and strength for the liberty of the stage."

Somers, Anne R. "Violence, Television and the Health of American Youth." *New England Journal of Medicine*, 29:811–17, 8 April 1976.   **1S399**
The "culture of violence" in America is a major health threat and one contributing factor is television's mass diet of symbolic crime and violence in "entertainment" programs. The medical profession is urged to concern itself with this complex health hazard.

Sommer, Michael H. *A Criticism of News Broadcasting and Regulatory Issues in the Richards Case.* Los Angeles, University of Southern California, 1969. 1612p. (Ph.D. dissertation, University Microfilms, no. 69-13083)   **1S400**
An examination of hearings records of the Federal Communications Commission in the case of the licensee-owner of radio station, FMPC, Los Angeles, revealed that the station was guilty of violating all six of the criteria examined.

Sonenschein, David. "Pornography: A False Issue." *Psychiatric Opinion*, 6:11–17, 1969.   **1S401**
"The problem of mental health lies not in pornography because it is far too minimal in its effect and marginal in its existence for that. The problem lies in the failure of the individual and his physician to responsibly confront human sexual behavior. Pornography will continue to survive—though not thrive—so long as these fundamental commitments are neglected by both groups."

Sontag, Susan. "The Pornographic Imagination." *Partisan Review*, 34:181–212, Spring 1967. (Also in her *Styles of Radical Will*. New York, Farrar, Straus & Giroux, 1966; and in Douglas A. Hughes, *ed., Perspectives on Pornography*, pp. 131–69)   **1S402**
A consideration of pornography as a literary genre rather than as a social and psychological phenomenon. The factors which make a work

of pornography part of art rather than trash are its "originality, thoroughness, authenticity, and power of that 'deranged consciousness' itself, as it is incarnated in a work." *Story of O* and *The Image* are cited as examples.

Soopper, Samuel. "The First Amendment Privilege and Public Disclosure of Private Facts." *Catholic University Law Review*, 25:271–98, Winter 1976. **1S403**
"This article will explore the competing interests of the right of society to a free and unhampered press and the right of the individual to be protected from unwanted and undesirable publicity. An attempt will be made to determine what kind of accommodation, if any, is possible between these rights under the United States Constitution and, if reconciliation is possible, whether the tort remedy for disclosure of private facts by the press is suitable."

Sorabjee, Soli J. *The Law of Press Censorship in India.* Bombay, Tripathi, 1976. 272p.   **1S404**
A survey of the law, followed by extracts from four key court decisions and other relevant documents, including the text of the Prevention of Objectionable Matters Act of 1976. Foreword by Justice Hidayatallah of the Indian Supreme Court.

Sorensen, Karen L. "Community Standards and the Regulation of Obscenity." *DePaul Law Review*, 24: 185–94, Fall 1974.   **1S405**
"A recent decision by the Supreme Court [*Miller v. California*, 1973] has strengthened the possibility of community control over the legal regulation of obscenity. Whether this form of control is necessary or desirable will be the focus of this Comment. The problem presented is whether the community's standards of morality and decency can be encouraged or enforced without abridging first amendment rights. And if so, should that enforcement be by informal or formal means?"

Sorensen, Thomas C. "Villains and Heroes." In his *The Word War: The Story of American Propaganda.* New York, Harper & Row, 1969, pp. 31–55.   **1S406**
This chapter deals with the McCarthy crusade against "subversion" during the Eisenhower Administration, which brought a wave of censorship of Voice of America and U.S. information libraries overseas.

Sorkin, Dan. "My Visit to the Citizens for Decent Literature." *Realist* (New York), 55:15–16, December 1964.   **1S407**
"The Citizens for Decent Literature is an insidious organization, because it advocates censorship. And censorship, in any form, to me is a 10-letter word." The writer describes with humor and ridicule his visit to a meeting of the CDL in Chicago where examples of pornography were on display, an obscene movie was

shown, and testimonials were given about successful community campaigns against pornography.

Soronow, Sidney G. "Judicial Process in the Law of Obscenity." *Manitoba Law Journal*, 4(2):380–92, 1971. **1S408**
In an examination of Canadian criminal law dealing with obscenity and recent cases coming before the Manitoba Court of Appeals, the author finds that "the concept of obscenity is evaluative and as such, cannot be the subject of definition. This being so the use of judicial notice cannot result in anything approaching objectivity. A judge cannot, by himself, distill a feeling of a Canadian consensus on objectivity. Such knowledge must derive from evidence."

"South Africa: Cultural Boycott—Yes or No?" *Index on Censorship*, 4(2):5–38, Summer 1975.   **1S409**
Responses to a survey circulated to six hundred artists around the world about a cultural boycott of South Africa, including extracts from some of the replies. There follows (pp. 38–40) a review of legislation curtailing press and artistic freedom.

South Africa. Parliament. House of Assembly. Commission of Inquiry Into the Publications and Entertainments Amendment Bill. *Report of the Commission of Inquiry into the Publications and Entertainments Amendment Bill, A.B. 61-'73.* Pretoria, South Africa, Govt. Print., 1974. 69p., 70p.   **1S410**
Continues the inquiry pursued by the Select Committee on the Publications and Entertainments Amendment Bill and published in its Report.

South Africa. Parliament. House of Assembly. Select Committee on the Publications and Entertainments Amendment Bill. *Report*. Pretoria, South Africa, Govt. Print. [1973]. 142p.   **1S411**
Evidence presented in an investigation of the work of the Publications Control Board. Professor R. E. Lighton, member of the Board, discusses the operation of the Board, including action taken against books and films that presented racial intermingling. Most of the testimony is in Afrikaans; Professor Lighton's report is in English.

South Australia. Law Reform Committee. *Relating to the Reform of the Law of Libel and Slander.* Adelaide, Govt. Print., 1972. 15p. (Fifteenth Report of the Law Reform Committee of South

Australia to the Attorney General)   **1S412**

Southwick, Ann. "Government Harassment of Newsmen." *Grassroots Editor*, 13(5):8–11, September–October 1972.   **1S413**
An account of the FBI's investigation of Columbia Broadcasting System correspondent Daniel Schorr and his statement before the Senate Subcommittee on Constitutional Rights.

Sovern, Michael I. *et al. Free Press and Fair Trial*. 28 min. tape recording. North Hollywood, Calif., Center for Cassette Studies, 1971. (Due Process for the Accused Series)   **1S414**
A panel discussion moderated by Michael I. Sovern, Columbia University law professor. Panelists: F. Lee Bailey, counsel for Dr. Sam Sheppard, and Russell Fairbanks, professor of law, Columbia University. The panelists discuss the unfair practices of trial judges and the sensation-seeking tactics of the press as illustrated by the case of Dr. Sam Sheppard.

Sowell, John H. "Commercial Speech Is Protected by the First Amendment." *Texas Tech Law Review*, 8:419–28, Fall 1976.   **1S415**
Re: *Virginia State Board of Pharmacy v. Virginia Citizens Consumer Council*, 423 U.S. 815 (1976).

[Spahn, Gary J.] "Obscenity Redefined." *University of Richmond Law Review*, 8:325–33, Winter 1974.   **1S416**
Re: *Miller v. California* (1973). "The majority of the [U.S. Supreme] Court in *Miller* made its decision in anticipation of tightening the reins of pornography, providing the proper authorities with clear guidelines for carrying out this design, and alleviating the Supreme Court's burden of reviewing a mass of pornography cases. Although it is too early to judge the success of *Miller*'s intentions, the immediate impact has been one of mass confusion and vigorous reaction. . . . At the risk of speculation, however, time will tell that *Miller* has failed to answer the hard questions it had anticipated and has unfortunately raised some harder ones."

Spain, Kenneth W. "Application of *New York Times* Standard to Libel Actions Brought by Private Individuals." *Kansas Law Review*, 20:299–310, Winter 1972.   **1S417**
Re: *Rosenbloom v. Metromedia, Inc.*, 403 U.S. 29 (1971).

Spangler, Eve. "Surveyor Finds Connecticut Libraries Avoid Controversial Books." *Connecticut Libraries*, 13(4):6–8, Autumn 1971.   **1S418**
A brief survey of Connecticut public libraries reveals that librarians do shy away to some extent from controversial titles, especially those of a "radical" nature; suggesting that the classical Fiske report (F134) is still relevant.

Spangler, Ray. "Right to Know." *California Publisher*, 49(3):16–17, December 1969.   **1S419**
The Reardon Report on fair trial versus free press has had the effect of "slamming doors in the faces of reporters from one end of the state to the other."

Sparks, Allister. "Mr. Vorster's 'Final Solution' for the Critical Newspapers?" *Atlas*, 17(4):62–63, April 1969. (Reprinted from *East African Standard*, Nairobi)   **1S420**
An account of the trial and attempted take-over of a South African newspaper chain. Charges were made under the Prisons Act of 1959, which makes it an offense to publish "false information" about prisons without taking "reasonable steps" to verify it. To the authorities this meant clearing the stories with the Commissioner of Prisons before printing it.

Sparrow, Gerald. *The Great Defamers*. London, Long, 1970. 175p.   **1S421**
A series of essays dealing with famous British libel cases, including the libel of George V by an article appearing in the *Liberator*; the case of *Richard Wootton v. Robert Sievier*, publisher of a racing paper; *Dr. Marie Stopes v. Dr. Sutherland* involving his book, *Birth Control*; Lord Alfred Douglas's libel of Winston Churchill; actress Hettie Chattell case against the London *Daily Mail*; the case against Metro-Goldwyn-Mayer over the film, *Rasputin, the Mad Monk*; Aleister Crowley against the publisher of Nina Hammett's *Laughing Torso*; and Lord Gladstone's attack on the author of a book he considered defamatory of his late father, the Prime Minister.

Sparrow, John. "Regina v. Penguin Books Ltd.: An Undisclosed Element in the Case" and "Afterthoughts on Regina v. Penguin Books Ltd." In his *Controversial Essays*. New York, Chilmark, 1966, pp. 40–70. (Reprinted from *Encounter*, February and June 1962) **1S422**
The "undisclosed element" in the obscenity trial of D. H. Lawrence's *Lady Chatterley's Lover* was, according to this literary critic, Lawrence's approval of the sexual offense known as "buggery." The two controversial articles, largely in the vein of literary criticism, contain numerous observations on pornography and censorship, as does the preface to the collection of essays. In another essay in the collection, The Press, Politics and Private Life, Sparrow considers the invasion of privacy by the British press in the Profumo Affair.

"Speaking Out on Book Banning."
School Library Journal, 23:82–84, October 1976.   **1S423**
Text of a WCBS radio editorial critical of the Island Trees School District (New York) Board of Education's book banning action, an editorial response by the president of the Board, and observations of the children's librarian of the Island Trees Public Library.

"The Speech and Press Clause of the First Amendment as Ordinary Language." *Harvard Law Review*, 87:374–94, December 1973.   **1S424**
"This Note pursues two ends, one through the other. Its ultimate purpose is to encourage close attention to the precise language of constitutional provisions by subjecting the speech and press clause of the first amendment to analysis like that of ordinary language philosophy. Its mediate purpose is to provide through analysis of the language of the speech and press clause a new approach to its interpretation."

Speech Communication Association. "Credo [on Freedom of Speech]." *Spectra*, 9(2):5, April 1973.   **1S425**
Composed by the Association's Commission on Freedom of Speech and adopted by the Legislative Assembly, December 1972.

Spence, Thomas. *The Case of Thomas Spence, Bookseller, Who Was Committed to the Clerkenwell Prison on Monday, the Tenth of December, 1792, for Selling the Second Part of Thomas Paine's "Rights of Man." To Which Is Added an Extract of a Letter from . . . the Duke of Richmond. . . .* London, 1792. (Reprinted in Stephen Parks, *ed. The London Book Trade, 1660–1853*. New York, Garland, 1974. Vol. 27)   **1S426**
At the instigation of John Reeves of the Society for Promoting Constitutional Information, a Bow Street runner bought a copy of Paine's *Rights of Man* from Spence who was promptly arrested and thrown into jail. Spence writes of his mistreatment by the runner and jailers. His arrest came ten days before the trial of Thomas Paine, author of the offending pamphlet, who was tried in absentia (he had escaped to France) and was found guilty. Spence was brought to trial in February 1793, but a flaw in the indictment saved him.

Spencer, Anna G. *Literature and Vice*. Chicago, Woman's Temperance Publishing Co., 1890. 20p.   **1S427**
The Woman's Christian Temperance Union maintained a Committee on Purity in Literature and Art, under the chairmanship of Mrs. Ada H. Kepley, Effingham, Ill. The Committee proposed changes in the postal laws to exclude the *Police Gazette* and other objectionable papers from the mails, and urged local chapters to support the establishment of free public libraries. This is one of the Committee's promotional pamphlets.

Spencer, Dale R. "Are You Liable to Publish Libel?" *Communication: Journalism Education Today*, 4(1):14–15, Fall 1970. **1S428**
Comments on libel in school newspapers.

———. *Law for the Newsman*. Columbia, Mo., Lucas, 1971. 149p. **1S429**
A textbook in communications law intended for students not trained in the law. The work begins with the historical position of First Amendment freedoms and follows with the many restrictions placed on these freedoms: libel, privacy, contempt, obscenity, copyright, broadcasting, advertising and business, and overall problems of access.

———. "Libel Privilege Spreads to Crime Reportings: Crime Source Protection Could Be Next." *Grassroots Editor*, 13(2):8–10, 37, March–April 1972. **1S430**
The author traces step-by-step the developments in the common law of libel which have extended the rights of the press to report freely on public issues and public figures.

Spencer, Harold. *The Right to Speak for Peace*. [Philadelphia, Pennsylvania Committee to Defend the Pittsburgh Six, 1952?] 16p. Preface by Howard Fast. **1S431**
"In the past year, three men in Pittsburgh, Pennsylvania—members of the Communist Party—have been convicted under the Pennsylvania State Sedition Act, charged with attempting to overthrow by force and violence the government of the United States. The main evidence against them was that they possessed and circulated literature."

Speranza, William J. "Reply and Retraction in Actions Against the Press for Defamation: The Effects of *Tornillo* and *Gertz*." *Fordham Law Review*, 43: 223–38, November 1974. **1S432**
"The *Gertz* and *Tornillo* decisions have seriously undercut arguments heretofore advanced in favor of providing the alternative remedies of reply and retraction in actions against the press for defamatory publications." Re: *Gertz v. Robert Welch, Inc.* (1974) and *Miami Herald Publishing Co. v. Tornillo* (1974).

Spetnagel, H. T., Jr. "Censorship in Colorado: A Survey Report." *Statement; The Journal of the Colorado Language Arts Society*, 4(1):21–24, October 1968. **1S433**
The author reports on results from a questionnaire sent to members of the Colorado Language Arts Society. Responses indicated that, while there was some censorship in Colorado schools at every level, it was the exception rather than the rule. Included is a list of thirty-two books reported to have been censored.

Spigelgass, Leonard. "Cassettes Censorship and a Planned Writers' Conference." *Dramatists Guild Quarterly*, 7(4):41–44, Winter 1971. **1S434**
A member of the Screen Writers Guild discusses two areas in which, he charges, the broadcasting companies and motion picture producers refuse to talk in contract negotiations: censorship and video cassettes.

Spigelman, James. *Secrecy: Political Censorship in Australia*. Sydney, Angus and Robertson, 1972. 194p. **1S435**
Content: The Mania of Secrecy. The Politics of Secrecy (including the role of Parliament, the role of the press, pressure groups). Political Responsibility. Effective Decision Making, Secrecy and the Individual Liberty. A Farrago of Secrecy and Deception. National Security: How Special a Case? Towards Reform. Two Indexes: An Inside Dopester's Index of One Hundred Examples of Secrecy. A Cynic's Index of Fifty Lies, Half-Truths, and Evasions. The text of the Security Classifications of Official Matter (top secret, secret, confidential, and restricted) is given in the appendix.

Spinrad, William. *Civil Liberties*. Chicago, Quadrangle Books, 1970. 355p. **1S436**
Includes chapters on McCarthyism, blacklisting, and censorship. The last deals largely with the efforts of pressure groups.

["Spiro Agnew's Attacks on Television and Newspapers."] *New Yorker*, 45(42):51–53, 6 December 1969. (Talk of the Town Department) **1S437**
Vice-President Agnew's idea of the role of the press in a democracy "is as strange as his concepts of rights and of censorship." The campaign of intimidation this Administration has launched against protestors and against the press "has set this nation on a dangerous course that will be hard to reverse."

Spitzer, Carlton E. "Public Information in Government Policy: Voice of Government Functions in Era of People's Right and Desire to Know." *Public Relations Journal*, 24(2):24–26, February 1968. **1S438**
"It is the job of the government information officer to respond to developing trends, anticipate public concern, and provide useful information, always protecting personal privacy and national security but opening all doors and all the avenues he can and should open."

Spock, Benjamin. "A Reactionary View of Obscenity and Brutality." In his *Decent and Indecent: Our Personal and Political Behavior*. New York, McCall, 1970, pp. 83–90. (Also in *Redbook*, January 1970, and U.S. House of Representatives. Committee on the Post Office, *Obscenity in the Mails*, pp. 407–10) **1S439**
A noted psychiatrist-pediatrician and civil libertarian writes that "recent trends in movies, literature, and art toward what I think of as shocking obscenity, and the courts' acceptance of it," have made him change his position about control of obscenity. It should not be necessary to prove that children or adults commit crimes as the result of reading or looking at pictures of sexual material in order to determine that the material has a harmful effect. Many pornographic works, particularly those involving perversion and brutality, "are unhealthy for society because they assault the carefully constructed inhibitions and sublimations of sexuality and violence that are normal for all human beings (except those raised without any morals at all) and that are essential in the foundations of civilization." Since it is not likely that people will refuse to support obscenity and that it can be kept out of the hands of children through voluntary means, he favors "new laws which would determine guilt simply on the basis of judges' and juries' sense of shock and revulsion. . . . I'd want such laws to specify that they are not intended to discourage the presentation of themes involving immorality, lawlessness, cruelty, or perversion (all of which have regularly been dealt with in great literature and art) but only to curb a shocking manner of presentation."

Sprading, Charles T. *Ruled by the Press*. Los Angeles, George Rissman [1917?]. 15p. **1S440**
An attack on the public press for control of news and opinion based on the economic interest of the owners. The press operates against the best interest of the public on three scores: it publishes only what will benefit the proprietors, it deceives the public as to its interests, and it prevents expression of contrary opinion. Newspaper-reading is more harmful than liquor or dope, for it keeps those who indulge in continuous intellectual bondage.

Sprague, William E. *Sex, Pornography & the Law*. San Diego, Calif., Academy Press, 1970. 2 vols. **1S441**
In a work illustrated with examples of pornography in art and photography, the author presents an analysis of the field, including discussion of the sociomedical effects of legalized pornography; the concept of "erotic" realism; erotic realism in historical perspective in the Christian and non-Christian world; the concept of "hard-core pornography"; and pornography, the law, and social evolution. Introduction by Donald R. Arbagian; foreword by Frank L. Annis.

Spreyer, Abigail. "First Amendment Retrospective: Free Speech and Defamation Law." *Chicago-Kent Law Review*, 51:612–32, 1974. **1S442**

Re: *Gertz v. Robert Welch, Inc.*, 471 F.2d 801 (7th Cir. 1972). "This discussion of the case will examine the facts upon which *Gertz* was based, the development and dimensions of the constitutional privilege to publish libel prior to *Gertz*, and the treatment of the case by the district court and the Seventh Circuit. An alternative disposition of the case by the Seventh Circuit will be proposed, and the Supreme Court decision and its potential effects will be described."

Sprigge, Samuel S. *The Life and Times of Thomas Wakley, founder and First Editor of the "Lancet".* . . . London, Longmans, Green, 1897. 509p. (Reprinted by Robert E. Krieger, Huntington, N.Y., 1974) **1S443**
A biography of the physician who founded and for many years edited the *Lancet*, a journal that crusaded for reform in British medicine. Wakley faced numerous libel suits for exposing medical quackery, malpractice in London hospitals, poor medical education, nepotism and monopoly practices among doctors, and autocratic policies of certain professional associations. Among the cases reported are: *Tyrrell v. Wakley*, *Cooper v. Wakley* (W18), *Macleod v. Wakley*, and *Wakley v. Johnson*. In the Johnson case Wakley was awarded £100 against Dr. James Johnson, editor of the *Medico-Chirurgical Review*. The journal had unjustly accused Wakley of arson in the fire which destroyed his home. Dr. Wakley also was a radical politician and member of Parliament for almost two decades. In Parliament he was a vigorous opponent of the tax on newspapers.

Spring, W. J. "Who Killed David McManus?" *Spectator*, 231:40–41, 14 July 1973. **1S444**
In a British murder trial in which a sixteen-year-old youth pleaded guilty, statements were made regarding a causal relation between the murder and the showing of the film *Clockwork Orange*. The author believes responsibility should be shared by the British film industry, the film critics, the politicians, and the British Board of Film Censors: "If you feed the public long enough with a diet of obscenity, perversion, pornography and violence it is not surprising that the young and impressionable whose heroes are often figures of the screen, should in the end finish up taking the thing seriously. With sometimes disastrous consequences."

Srivatsa, S. "Muzzling the Press." *Swarajya*, 15(15):5–6, 10 October 1970. **1S445**
"The free press of India is today functioning under great stresses and strains. This is because those who are expected to uphold the principles of democracy in India are becoming more and more intolerant of salutary criticism and are doing all in their power to curtail the freedom of the press, though Mr. V. V. Giri, the President of India, may spout the high sounding slogan that it is 'the true sentinel of democracy.' "

Stahle, Richard H. "Diversification in Communication: The FCC and Its Failing Standards." *Utah Law Review*, 1969:494–519, June 1969. **1S446**
"This Note examines the Commission's failure to effectively utilize its powers in licensing radio and television stations so as to protect the public interest in preserving diverse and antagonistic sources of public opinion. In the course of this discussion, a method of analyzing and applying existing licensing standards is offered as an alternative to those employed by the Commission in the past—one which will hopefully lead to more effective methods of combating concentration. Proposed rules for preventing concentration are then evaluated in light of the conclusions reached concerning administration of current licensing practices."

Staley, Anthony. "Parliamentary Privilege." In Melbourne University. *The Law and the Printer, the Publisher and the Journalist. The Collected Papers of a Seminar at Melbourne University on August 12, 1971*. Melbourne, Australia, Antony Whitlock, 1971, pp. 23–28. **1S447**
The Australian Parliament can call people to account but cannot in practice punish them for libel on the Parliament. So apologies are generally accepted.

Stallings, C. Wayne. "Local Information Policy: Confidentiality and Public Access." *Public Administration Review*, 34:197–204, May–June 1974. **1S448**
"This article outlines the basic provisions of a model policy which can be adopted by local governments to regulate the collection, storage, use, and dissemination of information in order to protect privacy while assuring that legitimate public access to government records is available."

Stallman, Robert W. "Stephen Crane's Revision of *Maggie: The Girl of the Streets*." *American Literature*, 26:528–36, January 1955. **1S449**
How the author expurgated the 1893 text of his work to make it suitable for publication by Appleton, removing "a goodly number of damns" and other offensive language.

Stambusky, Alan A., Jr. *Toward Modern Perspective: Political and Ecclesiastical Origins of Dramatic Censorship*. Madison, Wis., University of Wisconsin, 1960. 478p. (Ph.D. dissertation, University Microfilms, no. 60-3271) **1S450**
"This dissertation endeavors to determine the political and ecclesiastical origins of modern dramatic censorship and to trace their development from classical Greece and Rome, through the Christian Middle Ages, to the Protestant Reformation during the Renaissance, with particular attention to the evolvement of modern political censorship of the English drama during the English Reformation."

Stanbury, Robert. "The Government As Censor." *IPLO Quarterly* (Institute of Professional Librarians of Ontario), 15:12–16, July 1973. **1S451**
The Canadian Minister of National Revenue who has responsibility for enforcing the tariff restrictions on importation of treasonable, seditious, and immoral works, discusses the Tariff Act of 1879 and the various considerations involved in reform and revision. He notes that "if the Criminal Code were to be changed to give full freedom of choice to adults, while forbidding distribution of obscene materials to children then our Tariff Item might well be seen to serve little further purpose."

Stanga, John E., Jr. "Judicial Protection of the Criminal Defendant against Adverse Press Coverage." *William and Mary Law Review*, 13:1–74, Fall 1971. **1S452**
"This article deals with the remedies courts have at their disposal to protect the defendant whose case has received adverse press coverage before or during a trial. Because *Sheppard v. Maxwell* [1966] was a watershed in the development of case law on the fair trial–free press problem, this article first examines the major remedies developed prior to *Sheppard* and then assesses the consequence of *Sheppard* by examining the legal developments which have occurred in the fair trial–free press area since 1966."

———. *The Press and the Criminal Defendant: Newsmen and Criminal Justice in Three Wisconsin Cities*. Madison, Wis., University of Wisconsin, 1971. 483p. (Ph.D. dissertation, University Microfilms, no. 71-14,167) **1S453**
"This study attempts to discover how newsmen report crime news in ordinary cases, not just in notorious and highly publicized cases. The research approaches the fair trial and free press issue through (1) an extensive survey of the case and statutory law; (2) a study of Wisconsin newsmen's interactions with criminal justice news sources, based on interviews with newsmen, prosecutors, defense counsel, judges, and police in Madison, Kenosha, and Beloit; and (3) a content analysis of newspaper crime reporting in the three cities for 1966."

Stanhope, Charles Stanhope, *3rd earl*. *The Rights of Juries Defended. Together with Authorities of Law in Support of Those Rights. And the Objections to Mr. Fox's Libel Bill Refuted*. London, Printed by George Stafford for P. Elmsly, 1792. 164p. **1S454**

The 3rd Earl of Stanhope, chairman of the Revolution Society that expressed sympathy for the French Revolution, argues for the freedom of the press as he supports the Fox Libel Act then before Parliament. The Act, approved the following year, gave to juries the right to decide whether or not a work charged was in fact libelous. Previously, courts had held that juries could determine only whether or not the accused was guilty of publishing the work; it was left to the judge to determine whether or not the work was libelous. By examples from history, by hypothetical illustrations, and by logic, the author develops his case.

Stanley, C. M. "John Milton's Areopagitica and Today's Newspapers." *Alabama Lawyer*, 14:328–36, July 1953. **1S455**

The editor of the *Alabama Journal* quotes widely from Milton's work, relating his views to some of the present-day issues on press freedom.

Stanley, Robert H., and Charles S. Steinberg. *The Media Environment: Mass Communications in Modern Society*. New York, Hastings House, 1976. 306p. **1S456**

Chapters relating to press freedom: Motion Picture Self-Regulation, Broadcasting Law, Self-Regulation of Broadcasting, and Mass Communication and the Supreme Court.

Stanley, Sherry. "Torts: A Change in the Nature of the Libel Action." *University of Florida Law Review*, 28:1052–58, Summer 1976. **1S457**

In an analysis of *Time, Inc. v. Firestone* (1976), the author asserts that "the delicate balance between freedom of the press and libel law achieved . . . by the Court in *Gertz* has been upset."

Stanton, Frank. "The Courts and the Broadcast Media." *New Hampshire Bar Journal*, 7:12–18, October 1964. (Also issued as a separate ten-page pamphlet) **1S458**

It is in the interest of the people to televise the deliberation of the courts. He offers the television coverage of the United Nations as an example. The dignity of the UN has not suffered and "the force of these broadcasts in educating the people not only as to the issues but as to the United Nations itself has been incalculable."

———. "First Amendment: T.V. Coverage, Congress and the Supreme Court." *Vital Speeches*, 36:234–36, 1 February 1970. **1S459**

In an address to the Advertising Council, Stanton proposes the use of electronic communications "to give the American people greater access to significant proceedings of the Congress and of the Supreme Court—that is,

to allow television and radio to cover all proceedings of the House, the Senate and the Supreme Court to which the public and the press are admitted." He points out that this has been done for years in covering the United Nations and party conventions.

———. [*Freedom of the Press*] Speech before *American Council on Education*, 7 October *1971*. Washington, D.C., The Council, 1971. 5p. **1S460**

A discussion of academic freedom in universities in relation to the freedom of the press guaranteed under the First Amendment, both essential in a democratic system. Like freedom of the press which has recently been under attack by the Congress and the Administration, academic freedom requires constant vigilance.

———. "The Public Interest and the Private Responsibility." *Journal of the Producers Guild of America*, 11(2):3–5, June 1969. **1S461**

The president of Columbia Broadcasting System states the reasons for his network's refusal to accept the recommendation of the Senate Subcommittee on Communication, that the National Association of Broadcasters be given authority to police network programming. Stanton appraises the issue of the responsibility of television broadcasters for the content of programs.

———. "The Selling of the Pentagon: CBS vs. Congress." In Michael C. Emery and Ted C. Smythe, *eds.*, *Readings in Mass Communications*. Dubuque, Iowa, Brown, 1972, pp. 99–105. **1S462**

The CBS president defends the privacy of materials his network used in producing the documentary, Selling of the Pentagon, before a special Sub-Committee of the House of Representatives Interstate and Foreign Commerce Committee. Stanton was cited for contempt by the Committee for refusing to submit background material; the House refused to back the Committee.

Stapleton, John. *Communications Policies in Ireland*. Paris, Unesco Press, 1974. 73p. **1S463**

"Monograph on communication policy in Ireland considered within its social structure and economic structure: examines policies for the various mass media and considers their relations with the public sources of information and each other; deals with the communication professions with particular reference to journalist training and communication ethics; stresses the need for social participation in shaping mass communication systems; provides communication statistics."

Starck, Kenneth. "Design for Dialog with the People." *Grassroots Editor*, 12(6):4–12, November–December 1971. **1S464**

A report of the field director of local press council experiments in Cairo and Sparta, Ill., Redwood City, Calif., Bend, Ore., Seattle, and St. Louis, established under a grant from the Mellett Foundation. The director discusses the organization and operation of the councils and makes nine observations on the contribution of the councils to improvement of community-press relations.

———. "Needed: Two-Headed Watchdogs: Press Councils Here and Abroad." *Grassroots Editor*, 15(1):24–27, January–February 1974. **1S465**

Largely an account of the Finnish Council for Mass Media, with observations on press councils in general and the fledgling National News Council in the United States.

———. "Press Councils Revisited." *Grassroots Editor*, 12(5):10–13, 30, September–October 1971. **1S466**

A report reflecting the attitudes of participants in four newspaper-community press councils set up in Southern Illinois and on the West Coast, including interviews with two Illinois editor-publishers, Martin Brown (Cairo) and William Morgan (Sparta).

Stark, Kenneth B., Jr. *Letter Columns: Access to Whom?* Columbia, Mo., Freedom of Information Center, School of Journalism, University of Missouri at Columbia, 1970. 5p. (Report no. 237) **1S467**

"Coercive publishing is evoking heated controversy within the press. A key question in this debate with press critics is the role and effect letters-to-the-editor play. Research on this aspect of the argument, although inconclusive, seems to support proponents of guaranteed access."

Starnes, Richard. "New Mail-Order Smut Law—Ineffectual." *National Decency Reporter*, 7(11–12):7, November–December 1970. **1S468**

"A succession of Supreme Court decisions reaching back to World War II has so eroded the [antiobscenity] statutes that conviction under them has become almost impossible."

Starr, Don. "Hate Literature in Canada—A Civil Liberties Approach." *Manitoba Bar News*, 39:16–25, January 1973. **1S469**

Pros and cons of the recent amendment to the Canadian Criminal Code to deal with hate literature. The author believes that freedom of speech under the Bill of Rights is not an absolute, but the right must be interfered with only when there is a "clear and present danger" to society, and he is not convinced that publication of hate literature, odious as it is, presents such a danger.

"State and Local Censorship of Films Used on Television." *Federal Communications Bar Journal*, 10:193–200, Winter 1949.   **1S470**
Most of the material in this note is taken from the brief of plaintiffs in *Allen B. Du Mont Laboratories, Inc. et al. v. Carroll et al.*, 86 F. Supp. 813, 5 R.R. 2053 (E.D. Pa. 1949).

"A State May Not Impose Civil Liability for the Accurate Publication of a Rape Victim's Name Obtained from Publicly Available Judicial Records Maintained in Connection with a Public Prosecution." *Georgia Law Review*, 9:963–79, Summer 1975.   **1S471**
Re: *Cox Broadcasting Corp. v. Cohn*, 420 U.S. 469 (1975).

"State Prison Censorship Procedures Must Include 'Rudimentary' Elements of Procedural Due Process for Protection of Prisoners' First Amendment Right to Receive Literature and Magazines." *New York University Law Review*, 47:985–1011, November 1972.   **1S472**
Re: *Sostre v. Otis*, 330 F. Supp. 941 (S.D. N.Y. 1971).

"State Statute Allowing Injunction Against Dissemination of Allegedly Obscene Material Prior to Adversary Hearing Not Violative of First Amendment." *Vanderbilt Law Review*, 23:1352–59, November 1970.   **1S473**
Re: *ABC Books, Inc. v. Benson* (1970), a case involving two Tennessee statutes (civil and criminal) on obscenity.

"Statute Prohibiting the Importation of Obscene Matter into the United States Infringes the Right of Adults to Possess Such Matter." *Alabama Law Review*, 23:135–42, Fall 1970.   **1S474**
In *U.S. v. Thirty-Seven Photographs*, 309 F. Supp. 36, 37 (C.D. Cal. 1970), the district court ruled that a federal statute prohibiting the importation of obscene materials into the United States violates the First Amendment by depriving persons who may constitutionally possess such materials the right to receive them.

"Statute Requiring Newspapers to Furnish Free Reply Space to Candidates They Attack During an Election Campaign Does Not Violate the First Amendment." *Texas Law Review*, 51:1421–30, November 1973.   **1S475**
Re: *Tornillo v. Miami Herald Publishing Co.* Commentary on the Florida right of reply statutes, before the opinion of the Florida Supreme Court was reversed by the U.S. Supreme Court.

Stauber, Ruby R. *Freedom and the Military News Media*. Columbia, Mo., Freedom of Information Center, School of Journalism, University of Missouri at Columbia, 1969. 8p. (Report no. 222)   **1S476**
"*Stars and Stripes*, the military daily newspaper, and Armed Forces Radio and Television, strive to maintain the same standards of editorial independence as the civilian press. The Department of Defense is constantly accused of controlling the content of these two media. A series of events in 1967 illustrates the problems of editorial freedom faced by the military media."

———. *Vietnam's Controlled Press*. Columbia, Mo., Freedom of Information Center, School of Journalism, University of Missouri at Columbia, 1968. 8p. (Report no. 207)   **1S477**
"The South Vietnamese government has restricted newspaper freedom through licensing and the corollary power of suspension, censorship, control of newsprint and control of news through the national news agency (Vietnam Press). An additional control on the press is exercised by the Viet Cong. Radio and television are government-owned; however, foreign news broadcasts can be heard over the ubiquitous transistor radios."

Staves, Susan. "Why Was Dryden's *Mr. Limberham* Banned? A Problem in Restoration Theatre History." *Restoration and 18th Century Theatre Research*, 13:1–11, May 1974.   **1S478**
Various speculations are offered for the banning of Dryden's play, *Mr. Limberham* in 1677 after three performances, but there is no conclusive evidence. Obscenity, however, is ruled out as a basis for "not until the 1690's, was much fuss made over obscenity."

[Stead, W. T.] "The Maiden Tribute of Modern Babylon." *Pall Mall Gazette*, various issues in July, August, September, October, and November 1885. (A contemporary thirty-page reprint of the articles was issued by A. Roberts, of London)   **1S479**
In a series of articles in his London newspaper, *Pall Mall Gazette*, editor-crusader W. T. Stead shocked all England with his lurid accounts of the vicious white slave trade flourishing in London, particularly the trade in young female children. London officials, civic leaders, and churchmen took sides in the controversy. In the 9 July issue Stead reports on efforts by the City Solicitor to suppress his paper by arresting the newsboys and bringing them before the Lord Mayor. Stead challenges the authorities to bring him to court instead of persecuting the innocent newsboys. W. H. Smith and Son, leading news distributors then and now, refused to sell the *Pall Mall Gazette* during the controversy. Instead of prosecuting Stead for obscenity, which had been proposed, he was arrested for a questionable method used in gaining evidence. In the 28 September issue he published the text of the defense which he was not permitted to give in court. Stead was convicted and served three months in prison. The law on procurement of young women for prostitution was changed by Parliament as the result of his efforts.

Steamer, Robert J. "The Perimeters of Free Speech." *New York State Bar Journal*, 43:535–41, December 1971. **1S480**
Freedom of speech is a means for better government and better life and not an end in itself, as is the view of libertarians. Freedom of speech does not naturally involve search for the truth in the public interest. It may be used in a devisive way, to disseminate falsehood or to undermine government and law. The author takes issue with the views of Justice Hugo Black, favoring instead the views of Justice Robert Jackson that "society and the law need not tolerate evil words any more than they tolerate evil deeds. What Jackson understood clearly was that men do employ speech for other than good public ends, and if such men are permitted to harangue or misinform, deliberately or ignorantly, such free speech becomes destructive of self-government." The author concludes: "It has become difficult to preserve freedom because we have lost sight of the proper ends of government. Our central concern must be justice, and to approximate its goals, we must emphasize the need for virtue and make the agonizing judgment that an excessive preoccupation with free expression may bring the noble American experiment to an end."

Steel, John M. "Freedom to Hear: A Political Justification of the First Amendment." *Washington Law Review*, 46:311–75, January 1971.   **1S481**
"Since the guarantees for speech and press in the first amendment were intended to safeguard and promote effective self-government by the American people, then if our speech is to be effective to that end, our freedom of speech must embody the essential freedom to hear what is said or otherwise communicated on public matters, and to acquire the information needed for rational self-government."

Steele, Walter W., Jr. "The Impact of the New Penal Code on First Amendment Freedoms." *Texas Bar Journal*, 38:245–46+, March 1975.   **1S482**
An examination of sections of Texas's new Penal Code involving conduct conducive to violence, conduct inherently offensive to sensibilities, and conduct that inconveniences the public—against the backdrop of the First Amendment and doctrines of vagueness and overbreadth.

Stein, Aletha H., and Lynette K. Friedrich. *Impact of Television on Children and Youth*. Chicago, University of Chicago Press, 1975. 72p. **1S483**

The work summarizes research on the effect of television violence on aggressive behavior of children and youths (ages from 3 to 18)—"the conditions that enhance or reduce the likelihood that behavioral aggression will result from television violence." Other areas covered are "the relation of cognitive development, and prosocial behavior. . . . One principal theoretical basis for the research reviewed is social learning theory, particularly the refined conceptualization of observational learning developed by Bandura. One of the most important propositions of this theory is the distinction between acquisition and performance of behavior. Behavior observed on television may be learned without any immediate acting out by the child. This learned behavior is stored, however, and may be acted on later if appropriate circumstances arise."

Stein, Benjamin. "PBS Under Fire." *TV Guide*, 23(50):4–7, 13 December 1975; 23(51):24–27, 20 December 1975; 23(52):28–33, 27 December 1975. **1S484**

While underlining the need for public broadcasting in a pluralistic nation, the author criticizes its liberal bias and its dullness. He calls for the introduction of a broader spectrum of ideas and improved programming.

Stein, Herbert. "Media Distortions: A Former Official's Views." *Columbia Journalism Review*, 13(6):37, 39–41, March–April 1975. **1S485**

A former chairman of President Nixon's Council of Economic Advisors charges bias and negative reporting in radio, television, and newspaper coverage of the economic policies of the Nixon Administration. "Being misled by the media is one of the risks of democracy against which we can be protected only by the good sense of the people."

Stein, Leon S. *Editorializing by Broadcast Licensees: A Developmental Analysis of the Problem of Federal Regulation of Editorializing by Broadcast Licensees*. New York, New York University, 1965. 780p. (Ph.D. dissertation, University Microfilms, no. 66-5794) **1S486**

"The purpose of this study is to present a developmental analysis of the problem of Federal regulation of editorializing by broadcast licensees, as this relates to the fair and equal presentation of all sides of controversial issues." The study "serves to document the arguments for and against the right to editorialize and the principles of free speech on which these arguments rest. It serves, further, to test the effectiveness, irrespective of the right, of Commission measures directed toward securing fair play in controversy as represented in editorializing by licensees under the two successive regulations thereon imposed over the years by the Commission."

Stein, M. L. "Missouri's Freedom of Information Center." *Saturday Review*, 54(11):93–94, 100, 13 March 1971. **1S487**

A description of the work of the Center, "believed to be the world's largest clearing house for information on the public's right to know."

———. "News Access Isn't Only a Washington Problem." *Saturday Review*, 54(33):50–51, 56, 14 August 1971. **1S488**

Denial of access to public meetings takes place throughout the country at local, county, and state levels, as the author indicates by numerous incidents.

———. *Shaping the News: How the Media Function in Today's World*. New York, Pocket Books, 1974. 207p. **1S489**

Content: Free Country—Free Press. How News Gets Around. Media Ownership and Practice. Freedom Plus Responsibility. Free Press and Fair Trial. The Media and Government. The Media and the Law. A Matter of Ethics. The Media Watchers. The Future of the Media.

Stein, Richard H. "Freedom of the Press vs. the Public's Right to Know: Newspaper Right of Reply Statutes." *University of Cincinnati Law Review*, 43:164–74, 1974. **1S490**

A discussion of the arguments pro and con in the case of *Tornillo v. Miami Herald Publishing Co.* (1974), in which the Florida Supreme Court upheld a law requiring newspapers to publish a political candidate's response to a prior article. This was written prior to the U.S. Supreme Court reversal. The author fears that this may be a precedent for other more pervasive encroachments upon traditional freedom of the press guarantees. "Insuring the freedom of a newspaper's editorial content from governmental interference has been a hitherto demarcation line for determining whether a particular instance of governmental regulation of newspapers is permitted under freedom of the press. To breach this line once would be to destroy its inherent protections."

Stein, Robert. *Media Power: Who Is Shaping Your Picture of the World?* Boston, Houghton Mifflin, 1972. 265p. **1S491**

An analysis of the newly acquired power of the media to control access to ideas—a power formerly wielded by government officials, military men, and business leaders. Includes discussion of such issues as reporters' revolt, the underground press, attacks on the press by government officials, and arguments over equal time and access.

———. "The Punishment for Bad Taste Is Three Years." *New York*, 5(9):52–53, 28 February 1972. **1S492**

"American society, which has handsomely rewarded Hugh Hefner for his exertions on behalf of sexual enlightenment [*Playboy*], is putting Ralph Ginzburg in jail." The essential difference has been Ginzburg's indiscretion, the advertising of his publication, *Eros*, through the mails instead of selling it discreetly on newsstands and in bookstores.

Stein, Ruth M. "Confronting Censorship in the Elementary Schools." *Journal of Research and Development in Education*, 9(3):41–51, Spring 1976. **1S493**

The author reviews some of the problems faced by elementary school teachers and librarians in selecting textbooks and tradebooks for use in the schools, citing specific cases where legal requirements or community pressures have affected choice of reading material. One of the major issues is the treatment of minorities in textbooks. The California Education Code requires teachers to certify that the textbooks they are using do not reflect adversely upon persons because of their race, color, creed, national origin, ancestry, sex, or occupation and that they contain no sectarian or denominational doctrine or propaganda contrary to law.

———. "Preliminary Censorship Survey." *Minnesota English Journal*, 12(1):20–29, Winter 1976. **1S494**

Results of a questionnaire about book-selection policy and censorship conducted among Minnesota high school English teachers. Attached is a list of twenty-one titles of books and films objected to.

Steinbeck, John. "Introduction." In his *Once There Was a War*. New York, Bantam, 1960, pp. v–xiv. **1S495**

In his introduction to a collection of his World War II dispatches from abroad, Steinbeck recounts the censorship of anything which conceivably interfered with the war effort—self-censorship by the correspondent, military and political censorship, and censorship by the people back home. "Perhaps our miasmic hysteria about secrecy for the past twenty years had its birth during this period."

Steinberg, Marjorie S. "The FCC As Fairy Godmother: Improving Children's Television." *UCLA Law Review*, 21:1290–1338, June 1974. **1S496**

"This Comment will discuss various solutions which the FCC might direct at each problem individually. In addition, it will discuss a 'comprehensive' solution—elimination of the existing commercial system of children's broadcasting—which ACT [Action for Children's Television] feels will solve all four problems simultaneously [violence in shows which children watch, scarcity of programming for children, lack of affirmatively good programming for children, and exploitation of children by commercials]. . . . Finally, this Comment will propose an approach to the amelioration of children's programming which will avoid the competing uncertainties of the public interest standard in the area of program regulation and the conflict between the demands of that standard and the first amendment rights of broadcasters."

Steinen, Karl von den. "The Harmless Papers: Granville, Gladstone, and the Censorship of the Madagascar Blue Books of 1884." *Victorian Studies*, 14(2):165–76, 1970.   **1S497**
Efforts of the Gladstone government to appease France after British occupation of Egypt is evidenced by censorship of the 1884 Blue Books reporting the Anglo-French negotiations involving the French seizure of Madagascar.

Steiner, Susan. "Requiring Newsmen to Appear and Testify Before Federal and State Grand Juries Does Not Abridge Freedom of Speech or Freedom of Press Guarantees by First Amendment." *Loyola University Law Journal* (Chicago), 4:227–55, Winter 1973.   **1S498**
Comment on the 1972 decisions of the U.S. Supreme Court involving two newspaper reporters and one news photographer who refused to testify before juries concerning information they had acquired during the course of their employment as news gatherers: *Branzburg v. Hayes*, *Caldwell v. United States*, and *In re Pappas*.

Steinfels, Peter. "The Schorr Witchhunt." *Commonweal*, 103:199, 220–21, 26 March 1976.   **1S499**
While criticizing Daniel Schorr's action in leaking the CIA report, the author believes Congress should be devoting its time to the task of working out a reasonable system of intelligence oversight rather than in baiting the media.

Steingesser, Martin. "Diarrhea Is a Dirty Word: An Account of Censorship in the Public Schools." *American Poetry Review*, 5(2):16–17, March/April 1976.   **1S500**
What happened when a fifth grade student in a poetry workshop conducted by the author, composed a poem on diarrhea.

Steloff, Frances. "Censorship and the Gotham Book Mart." In Charles B. Anderson, *ed.*, *Bookselling in America and the World*. New York, Quadrangle/

New York Times, 1975, pp. 181–83.   **1S501**
The founder and long-time proprietor of New York's Gotham Book Mart discusses her encounters with John S. Sumner, secretary of the New York Society for the Suppression of Vice. She concludes: "I don't see how healthy-minded people could have their morals corrupted by reading a book, and for those without morals these books might even be some kind of therapy. After all, freedom to read need not mean freedom to disseminate vulgarity and obscenity. We should choose our books as we choose our friends. I wish there were a way to control pornography but censorship is too high a price to pay."

Stenerson, Douglas C. *H. L. Mencken: Iconoclast from Baltimore*. Chicago, University of Chicago Press, 1971. 287p.   **1S502**
Throughout the volume are references to Mencken's attacks on censorship and the mentality of the censor, including the workings of the Espionage Act against nonconformist newspapers and magazines (e.g. *The Masses*) during World War I, and the bigotry and prudery behind much literary censorship, exemplified by action against Dreiser's *The "Genius."*

Steng, William R. *Acceptance by Selected U.S. Editors of Proposals to Solve the Free Press–Fair Trial Controversy*. Gainesville, Fla., University of Florida, 1968, 102p. (Unpublished Master's thesis)   **1S503**
A questionnaire on solutions to the conflict between free press and fair trial sent to 209 American newspaper editors showed that editors approved five out of thirty-five proposals: "Continue the dialogue between press and bar to allow each side to explain its position; rely upon press and bar ethics; continue present content and presentation of pretrial and criminal trial news; investigate press coverage and court procedure for evidence of prejudicial effects upon jurors; and have courts act to lessen or resolve the controversy."

Stephen, *Sir* James F. "The Laws of England as to the Expression of Religious Opinions." *Contemporary Review*, 25:446–75, February 1875.   **1S504**
"If we look back upon what such prosecutions actually effected, I think the argument against them is as strong as if we look at the manner in which the law is now defined. That they did not check the open growth of scepticism or preserve the institutions which they are intended to defend, is obvious from the result. They had an effect, however. They threw open the advocacy of anti-Christian opinions, and the publication of open attacks upon Christianity, into the hands of men who had nothing to lose in character and position—authors like Paine, and booksellers like Eaton or Carlile. They helped to complete the alliance between religious and political disaffection and they forced serious and quiet unbelievers to take up

a line of covert hostility to Christianity which was injurious to their own honesty and directness of purpose on the one hand and doubly injurious to Christianity itself in the long run. It is impossible to imagine anything more paltry and wretched than the advantages which Christianity obtained by the law against blasphemous libels."

Stephens, Alfred G. "On Censorship." In Vance Palmer, *ed.*, *A. G. Stephens; His Life and Works*. Melbourne, Australia, Robertson and Mullens, 1941, pp. 218–21.   **1S505**
"Indecency, or even obscenity, simply cannot enter into the artistic question." A picture of a saint has no more artistic merit than a vile Pompeian fresco, and it may have less. "In art, as in nature, the fittest survives, and we cannot deny the reason for survival, however we dislike some of the subjects that survive." While defending the right of art to exist outside morality, he believes the community is justified in controlling where the art is exhibited and who is exposed to copies of a work considered indecent.

Stephensen, P.R., and Hal Collins. *The Well of Sleevelessness; A tale for the least of these little ones by P. R. Stephensen, with illustrations by Hal Collins*. London, The Scholartis Press, 1929. 27p.   **1S506**
A humorous illustrated poem on police censorship, taking its title from two banned books, *The Well of Loneliness* and *Sleeveless Errand*.

Stephenson, Donald G., Jr. "Can Judges Stop the Press?" *Intellect*, 105:171–73, December 1976.   **1S507**
"The legal outgrowth of Charles Simant's murder trial encouraged the Supreme Court to face for the first time the accommodation of the Constitutional guarantee of a free press with the promise of trial by an impartial jury." A discussion of the Supreme Court's rejection of the gag rule imposed on the press by a Nebraska Judge.

———. *Free Expression and the State Appellate Courts of Georgia and Florida: Constructive Contempt of Court, Written Obscenity, and the Public Forum*. Princeton, N.J., Princeton University, 1967. 426p. (Ph.D. dissertation, University Microfilms, no. 68-8966)   **1S508**
"This is a comparative study of the political functioning of the appellate courts of Georgia and Florida in certain fields of law, namely constructive contempt of court, written obscenity, and the use of streets and parks for political expression. The paper attempts to demonstrate the policy influence of state courts and to offer conclusions and hypotheses relating state courts to the American political system."

———. "State Appellate Courts and Written Obscenity: The Georgia Experience." *Mercer Law Review*, 19:287–311, Summer 1968.   **1S509**

A history of the development of Georgia's obscenity laws, beginning with an act of 1866 forbidding the use of obscene language in the presence of females and an 1878 act prohibiting the possession and sale of obscene matter, in part an outgrowth of the Comstock movement. In 1953 the Georgia Literature Commission was established as a quasi-judicial agency to rid the state of obscene literature. The author discusses the operation of the Commission over the years, its legal involvements, and the effect on the Commission's role brought about by the 1957 *Roth* decision of the U.S. Supreme Court and subsequent changes in the Commission's statutes by the legislature.

Sterling, Christopher H. "NAB Report: Pattern of Media Ownership." In Don R. Le Duc, *ed.*, *Issues in Broadcast Regulation*. Washington, D.C., Broadcast Education Association, 1974, pp. 107–11.   **1S510**

The author contends, on the basis of recent research, that neither the degree nor the magnitude of such concentration has increased during the past quarter of a century.

Stern, Arthur. *The Influence of the Clear and Present Danger Formula on Constitutional Law*. Tucson, Ariz., University of Arizona, 1968. 341p. (Ph.D. dissertation, University Microfilms, no. 68-11,835)   **1S511**

An examination of the use of the "clear and present danger" dictum in free speech and press issues, as expressed by Justice Oliver Wendell Holmes in the 1917 *Schenck* espionage case and employed in various subsequent decisions of the U.S. Supreme Court. "Although never specifically disavowed by the Court, the formula has been ignored in cases involving national security. Its inherent relativism and susceptibility to varying interpretations has rendered it useless as a protective device. . . . All our experience suggests that the formula has been detrimental to democratic values by allowing an exception to the First Amendment. These values can be ensured only by a legal rule which permits full public expression of all political opinions which are unaccompanied by seditious action."

Stern, Carl. "Free Press–Fair Trial: The Role of the News Media in Developing and Advancing Constitutional Processes." *Oklahoma Law Review*, 29:347–60, Spring 1976.   **1S512**

In the American constitutional system the press has a responsibility for informing the people what is happening in their government and to call attention when legal and moral standards are not being addressed by its officials. "So far, with only occasional exceptions, the courts have been an ally with the news media in ferreting out information to which the press is entitled."

Stern, Charles M. "Toward a Rationale for the Use of Expert Testimony in Obscenity Litigation." *Case Western Reserve Law Review*, 20:527–69, April 1969. (Excerpted in Donald B. Sharp, *ed.*, *Commentaries on Obscenity*, pp. 325–28)   **1S513**

"My thesis is that the word 'obscene' cannot be defined, and that as a result, experts are called upon to provide specific information about the challenged work so that under the guise of determining that the work is obscene, the court can legislate ad hoc by prohibiting further circulation. I wish to show, for a variety of reasons, that the only utility of expert testimony lies in providing information and that such testimony cannot be the sole basis for drawing legal conclusions that the challenged work is obscene—or, in other words, that such testimony merits legal proscription."

Stern, Laurence. "The Daniel Schorr Affair: A Morality Play for the Fourth Estate." *Columbia Journalism Review*, 15:20–25, May–June 1976.   **1S514**

Background and commentary on the case of Daniel Schorr, correspondent of Columbia Broadcasting System, who had leaked the report of the House of Representatives investigation of the CIA (Pike Report) to the *Village Voice*. "The Schorr Affair became a complex morality play from which each of the interested parties [CBS hierarchy, the intelligence establishment, anonymous leakers, the congressional hardliners, the columnists, the trustees of the Reporters Committee for Freedom of the Press, and Schorr] could extract the message it wanted to hear." The author concludes that, while CBS will pay the lawyer to keep Schorr out of jail, he awaits punishment under a different code of accountability—the law of the network hierarchy. Accompanying the article are brief statements by Professor Benno C. Schmidt, Jr. (Does Congress Have a Legal Case Against Schorr?) and I. F. Stone (Insufferable Hypocrisy), a criticism of CBS's treatment of Schorr.

Stern, Mort. "The Right to Know What Government Doesn't Tell." In *1968 Yearbook of the Committee on Freedom of Speech of the Speech Association of America*. n.p., The Association, 1968, pp. 29–41.   **1S515**

Criticism of the Kennedy and Johnson Administrations for their policies of secrecy, with detailed references to the withholding and distortion of news. At every level, the author believes, government has the obligation (with only a few exceptions) to tell us what we want to know about the affairs of government.

———, and Martin Shapiro. "The Right of Silence: Journalists and Scholars." *Nieman Reports*, 27(4):22–27, Winter 1973.   **1S516**

Two points of view are expressed in the matter of privilege for journalists. Stern concludes that "the only way I can see to resolve this

properly is for the courts, or the Congress, to spell out circumstances under which witnesses or potential witnesses will not be pressed to disclose their sources." Shapiro concludes that "a general reform of federal grand juries, particularly in giving them independent counsel and staff, would be a more promising approach to the specific problems that have arisen in recent years than would the assertion of either a constitutional or statutory newsman's or scholar's privilege."

Stevens, David H. *Party Politics and English Journalism, 1702–1742*. New York, Russell & Russell, 1916. 156p. (Reissued 1967)   **1S517**

The volume deals with Walpole's treatment of journalists—subsidies to favored papers, bribes or prosecution of troublesome writers, including the *Craftsman* group headed by Lord Bolingbroke. "It is easy to prove the part played by the *Craftsman* in enlarging the freedom of the press. Correspondence passing between state officials shows that the government was gradually relinquishing plans for prosecuting all party organs, simply because of the ineffectiveness of suits against that powerful journal."

Stevens, Frank A. "Where the Buck Stops." *Library Journal*, 93:4701–3, 15 December 1968.   **1S518**

The former head of the Bureau of School Libraries for New York State reports on three cases involving controversies over books brought to the attention of the Bureau.

Stevens, George E. "Defamation of Political Figures: Another Look at the *Times-Sullivan* Rule." *Federal Communications Bar Journal*, 27:99–107, 1974.   **1S519**

The article discusses four matters commonly overlooked in judging the actual malice rule of *Times-Sullivan*: (1) *Times-Sullivan* is not the exclusive property of the mass media or other critics of government. (2) There is no substantive evidence that *Times-Sullivan* discourages citizens from seeking office, or that it either encourages or discourages free debate. (3) Adequate remedies for injuried parties bound by *Times-Sullivan* already may be available. (4) If the *Times-Sullivan* rule is modified, priority should be given to protecting the reputation rights of those least able to defend themselves against false charges.

———. "Educators as Plaintiffs in Libel Suits: The Impact of the *Times-Sullivan* Rule." *Journal of Law & Education*, 3:81–91, January 1974.   **1S520**

"This article will examine how the [Times-Sullivan] rule has been applied to educators and educational matters, and will suggest some circumstances in which educators might be affected by *Times-Sullivan* and other circumstances in which the rule might not apply."

———. "Faculty Tort Liability for Libelous Student Publications." *Journal of Law & Education*, 5:307–16, July 1976.   1S521
"The purpose of this article is to investigate the possible liability of an adviser or administrator in this type of suit, and to attempt to determine how decisions on student free expression rights may have affected this liability."

———. "Journalists as Plaintiffs in Libel Suits Since 1966." *Journalism Quarterly*, 51:134–36, Spring 1974.   1S522
A study of journalists as plaintiffs shows that even relatively obscure newsmen may be bound by the *Times* rule if defamed in connection with the performance of their duties. "The *Times* rule may protect journalists when they are sued for libel, but also make it difficult for them to recover damages when they are defamed."

———. "Performing Artists as 'Public Figures': The Implications of Gertz v. Robert Welch." *Performing Arts Review*, 6:3–19, Spring 1975.   1S523
"The performing artist is not necessarily a public figure per se for purposes of *Times-Sullivan* [*New York Times v. Sullivan*, 1964], and there are portions of the lives of even the most prominent of persons that may be outside the protection of the actual malice rule. However, the performing artist faces many difficulties in any action for defamation and he should consider alternative remedies, including some form of self-defense."

———. "Shield Laws May Protect Student Journalists, Too." *Communications: Journalism Education Today*, 5:7–8, Summer 1972.   1S524
"In some states shield laws might protect student journalists from being forced by a court to disclose confidential news sources."

———. "Talking Back to the Business Critic: The Constitutional Privilege-of-Reply." *Business Lawyer*, 31:645–51, January 1976.   1S525
"While the operations of many American businesses are being severely criticized, the corporation's ability to recover damages for libel or slander has been adversely affected by United States Supreme Court decisions establishing a constitutional privilege in defamation actions. This defense prevents a damage award for discussion of business affairs of public interest if the plaintiff is unable to prove the defendant's 'actual malice.' "

———, and John B. Webster. *Law and the Student Press*. Ames, Iowa, Iowa State University Press, 1973. 158p.
                                         1S526
Includes chapters on censorship, libel, obscenity, contempt, advertising, copyright, access to information, privacy, and broadcasting. In the appendix are the text of the Joint Statement on the Rights and Freedoms of Students—Student Publications, the ACLU Statement on Freedom of the High School Press, the American Bar Association Statement on Freedom of the Campus Press, and various locally adopted campus policies.

Stevens, George S. "Private Enterprise and Public Reputation: Defamation and the Corporate Plaintiff." *American Business Law Journal*, 12:281–93, Winter 1975.   1S527
The author considers the impact of the "actual malice" rule of *New York Times Co. v. Sullivan* (1964) on the defamed corporation, finding that the decision impedes their defamation remedies, since many corporations "may be public figures because of their fame or notoriety and their involvement in public affairs."

Stevens, Jean. *Classification: Threat to Democracy*. Columbia, Mo., Freedom of Information Center, School of Journalism, University of Missouri at Columbia, 1971. 10p. (Report no. 270)
                                         1S528
"The controversy over the Pentagon Papers has focused attention once again on the continuing problem of the abuses of the classification system and the power of the executive branch to utilize 'executive privilege' to withhold anything it wants from the public as well as from the Congress. This paper discusses the threat that overclassification poses to our democratic nation."

———. *Exclusivity in Action*. Columbia, Mo., Freedom of Information Center, School of Journalism, University of Missouri at Columbia, 1973. 8p. (Report no. 304)   1S529
"Conflict between the interests of 'have' and 'have-not' newspapers is nowhere better illustrated than in the matter of competition for syndicated news services, features, and comic strips. The exclusive character of many contractual arrangements between papers and syndicates has engendered a continuing multifaceted dispute among the parties involved."

———. *Exclusivity: Pros and Cons*. Columbia, Mo., Freedom of Information Center, School of Journalism, University of Missouri at Columbia, 1973. 4p. (Report no. 305)   1S530
"Arguments for and against exclusive territorial agreements between syndicates and newspapers are by no means simple; even a cursory examination of the problem reveals a puzzling

lack of clear-cut rights and wrongs normally associated with such issues."

———. *The Free Market Place Dilemma*. Columbia, Mo., Freedom of Information Center, School of Journalism, University of Missouri at Columbia, 1971. 7p. (Report no. 261)   1S531
"Owners of the mass media, eager to invest in other communications properties, are being thwarted by a federal government that fears concentration of media ownership will stifle a diversity of voices and opinions. Cable television, which offers almost unlimited communications channels, seems to be the solution to the dilemma, but it in turn poses new problems."

———. *Leaks: Manipulating Secrecy*. Columbia, Mo., Freedom of Information Center, School of Journalism, University of Missouri at Columbia, 1971. 5p. (Report no. 274)   1S532
"The news 'leak,' a continuing source of irritation to government officials, has also been criticized by members of the press who feel that they are being manipulated. This paper analyzes the government-press relationship that has cultivated the leak system and discusses its effects on today's society."

———. *Privacy and the First Amendment*. Columbia, Mo., Freedom of Information Center, School of Journalism, University of Missouri at Columbia, 1973. 7p. (Report no. 0014)
                                         1S533
"This paper's brief discussion of privacy . . . suggests that the principles of press freedom and privacy have more in common than in opposition, and that by retarding the erosion of privacy, freedom of information advocates can serve both their own and the public's interests."

———. *Student Press Revisited*. Columbia, Mo., Freedom of Information Center, School of Journalism, University of Missouri at Columbia, 1971. 8p. (Report no. 260)   1S534
"More and more student editors are finding that legal action is the only way to prevent censorship by administration and faculty. In this area, the courts have been more liberal in their interpretation of the first amendment for college papers than for the high school press. Without the adoption of nation-wide guidelines, educational institutions will have to deal with each case on an individual basis."

Stevens, John D. "Freedom of Expression: New Dimensions." In Ronald T. Farrar and John D. Stevens, *eds.*, *Mass Media and the National Experience*. New York, Harper & Row, 1971, pp. 14–37.
                                         1S535

The author considers the two "propositions" on control of the press offered by Fredrick S. Siebert in his study of the English press, adding two more propositions of his own: (1) "The more heterogenous a society, the more freedom of expression it will tolerate," and (2) "the more developed a society, the more subtle will be the controls it exerts on expression." He discusses the following forms of control: government ownership, licensing, sedition and seditious libel, libel, contempt, subsidies, obscenity, access, and self-improvement.

————. "From Behind Barbed Wires: Freedom of the Press in W.W. II Japanese Centers." *Journalism Quarterly*, 48:279–87, Summer 1971. **1S536**
"Freedom among the papers varied from center to center. Some criticized internal camp policies, while others did not or could not. Readers probably underestimated the freedom that editors enjoyed."

————. "Press and Community Toleration: Wisconsin in World War I." *Journalism Quarterly*, 46:255–59, Summer 1969. **1S537**
The study revealed that Wisconsin editors as a whole did little to quell rising mob spirit during 1918 and showed little concern over threats to freedom of the press under the Espionage Act. A detailed study of eight counties, however, indicated that where papers were relatively tolerant of dissent, so were the citizens.

————. "Proposal to ACLU: Newspapers Must Carry All Viewpoints." *Journalism Educator*, 23(4):22–24, Fall 1968. **1S538**
An attack on the right of access doctrine, being considered by the national board of the American Civil Liberties Union, "a far cry from the traditional ACLU position" which has been an ally of journalists in the battle against governmental control. ACLU is being asked to bring suits to force print and broadcast media to sell advertisements and give editorial space and time to persons of all viewpoints.

————. *Suppression of Expression in Wisconsin During World War I*. Madison, Wis., University of Wisconsin, 1967. 364p. (Ph.D. dissertation, University Microfilms, no. 67-17,031) **1S539**
"World War I was one of the darkest hours in American history for civil liberties. In its crusade atmosphere, there was little tolerance for unpopular 'anti-war' views. In Wisconsin, the state with the nation's heaviest German population, federal, state and local officials cooperated with state and county defense councils and 'patriotic' organizations and individuals to silence dissenters. Most of their victims were socialists, Industrial Workers of the World, pacifists or backers of Senator Robert M. La Follette. . . . Ninety citizens were indicted under the federal wartime laws, most of them under the Espionage Act. . . . Another 81 individuals were indicted under the state sedition law and local disorderly conduct ordi-

nances. A survey of newspapers disclosed 105 incidents of extra-legal retaliation against 'disloyal' individuals. . . . The state's press did not champion minority rights. When the editors denounced extra-legal violence, they usually coupled such remarks with pleas for stronger sedition laws. Editors saw little danger to free expression from such laws, either at the time of their passage or later."

————. "When Sedition Laws Were Enforced: Wisconsin in World War I." *Transaction of Wisconsin Academy of Sciences, Arts and Letters*, 58:39–60, 1970. **1S540**
An account of the World War I enforcement of federal sedition laws in Wisconsin which had the nation's highest proportion of German descendants and one of the nation's most active and successful socialist parties. Action was taken under five major laws: Threats Against the President Act, Selective Service Act, Espionage Act, Trading-with-the-Enemy Act, and the Sabotage Act. Unlike World War II, Korea, and Vietnam, in World War I "men went to prison for chance remarks in bars, rooming houses and on street corners, when the Post Office hounded foreign language papers out of business, when wearing an Industrial Workers of the World pin made you, automatically, a disloyalist."

[Stevenson, Duncan.] *Report of the Trial by Jury of the Action, for Damages for a Libel in the Beacon Newspaper; Lord Archibald Hamilton, against Duncan Stevenson, Printer in Edinburgh*. Edinburgh, John Robertson, 1822. 154p. **1S541**
Stevenson, publisher of the *Beacon*, was brought to trial for publishing a letter to the editor abusive to Lord Hamilton's reform efforts. "A reformer is merely a person who is fit for nothing else; for every blockhead who is too stupid, or too lazy, to thrive as a tailor or shoemaker, forthwith imagines that the fault lies with the magistrates or the government, and that matters cannot possibly be set right until he tries his hand at politics." The jury found for the plaintiff and assessed a fine of one shilling.

Stevenson, Janet. *The Third President; a Play in Three Acts*. Hubbard Woods, Ill., The Author, 1975? Various paging. Processed. **1S542**
A fictionalized account of events during the administration of John Adams, involving the controversy between Federalists and Republicans over the philosophy of government, the odious Sedition Act of 1798, the trial of Matthew Lyon of Vermont, and climaxing in the election of Thomas Jefferson. The script was the winner in the American Bicentennial International Play Competition sponsored by the Theater Department of Southern Illinois University, Carbondale, where the premiere production was given in April 1976.

Stevenson, Robert L. *et al*. "Untwisting *The News Twisters*: A Replication of

Efron's Study." *Journalism Quarterly*, 50:211–19, Summer 1973. **1S543**
Four researchers, replicating Edith Efron's "documented analysis" of Columbia Broadcasting System's coverage of the 1968 presidential campaign, found coverage of each candidate was positive and there was no evidence of bias for or against any of the three candidates. Efron had concluded that coverage "was massively biased against Richard Nixon by all three major network news departments." The other members of the team were Richard A. Eisinger, Barry M. Feinberg, and Alan B. Kotok.

Stewart, Bruce. "Tangoes and Trashcans." *Month (A Review of Christian Thought and World Affairs)*, 6:217, June 1973. **1S544**
Comment on *Last Tango in Paris* and the "cinema of exploitation." The critic suggests that films be considered in their entirety. There is always a case for banning a film entirely; not much of a case for chopping it. "I would sooner for the moment [censorship boards] disbanded entirely and adopted the philosophy of the brown paper wrapper. A restriction of film advertising would help more than all the pruning and protesting to separate gold from dross."

Stewart, C. Jean. "Colorado Municipal Government Authority to Regulate Obscene Materials." *Denver Law Journal*, 51:75–94, 1974. **1S545**
"This note examines briefly the potential success of the new Denver ordinance [on obscene materials] in two possible areas of litigation: first, whether local governments in Colorado have the authority to regulate obscene materials under Colorado law; and second, to what extent the Miller decision [Miller v. California] should be interpreted as authorizing municipal control of pornography."

Stewart, Charles E., Jr., and C. Daniel Ward. "FTC Discovery: Depositions, The Freedom of Information Act and Confidential Informants." *Antitrust Law Journal*, 37:248–60, 1968. **1S546**
This paper discusses three topics: changes concerning the taking and use of depositions for purposes of discovery, the Freedom of Information Act and its impact of discovery of information in the Commission's files, and the problem of the status of the identity of confidential informers at the FTC.

Stewart, Donald H. *The Opposition Press of the Federalist Period*. Albany, N.Y., State University of New York Press, 1969. 957p. **1S547**
A comprehensive analysis of the Republican press of the 1790s, revealing the propaganda

techniques used by partisan editors to generate opposition to the Federalist party and support for Thomas Jefferson. The study also includes references to efforts by the Adams Administration to control the Republican press through the Sedition Act, and the prosecution of such editors as Thomas Adams, Benjamin Franklin Bache, Thomas Cooper, Charles Holt, Anthony Haswell, and Matthew Lyon.

Stewart, Potter. "Or of the Press." *Congressional Record*, 120:S19595–97, 19 November 1974. (Also in *Washington Post*, 11 November 1974; and in *Hastings Law Review*, January 1975) **1S548**
The First Amendment, according to Supreme Court Justice Stewart, "extends protection to an institution. The publishing business is, in short, the only organized private business that is given explicit constitutional protection. . . . The primary purpose of the constitutional guarantee of a free press was . . . to create a fourth institution outside the Government as an additional check on the three official branches." He believes that the press coverage of the Agnew affair was a legitimate function and in the public interest. He comments on the court's decisions on libel, shield laws, and right of reply. Senator Proxmire, who placed the text of the address in the *Congressional Record*, commented on the ideas expressed.

Stewart, Ronald B. "Trial By the Press." *Military Law Review*, 43:37–70, January 1969. **1S549**
"This article examines the problem of prejudicial news reporting in criminal trials. The author discusses the reports themselves, the standard of review, the existing safeguards, and the possibility of new ones. It is concluded that the best controls, consistent with both fair trial and free press, are those exerted internally by the courts and bar associations."

Stewart, Vilate D. "A Widening Crack in the Media's Shield Against Libel Suits." *Utah Law Review*, 1976:386–99, 1976. **1S550**
Re: *Time, Inc. v. Firestone*, 424 U.S. 448 (1976).

Stewart, William F. "The Newsman's Source Privilege—A Balancing of Interests." *University of San Fernando Valley Law Review*, 2:95–120, Summer 1973. **1S551**
While absolute privilege would satisfy the news media "it would also inure to society's detriment far beyond the extent necessary to further the legitimate objectives of the privilege. . . . If a newsman's privilege is enacted, it should be qualified. A qualified privilege, coupled with the continued concern of the courts for the protection of First Amendment rights by controlling the issuance

of subpoenas, will insure the existence of a vital, inquiring and responsible press."

[Stiglitz, Jan.] "Must the Telephone Company Censor to Avoid Liability for Libel? *Anderson v. New York Telephone Company*." *Albany Law Review*, 38:317–31, 1974. **1S552**
The case involved the telephone company's liability for defamatory communications transmitted over its lines. The author believes the telephone company should be accorded an absolute privilege, as a public utility, and freed of censorship of any type.

"Still More Ado About Dirty Books (and Pictures): *Stanley, Reidel*, and *Thirty-seven Photographs*." *Yale Law Journal*, 81:309–33, December 1971. **1S553**
"This note will suggest a doctrinal framework for future obscenity cases which reconciles *Stanley's* concern for protecting individual First Amendment interests with the governmental power to regulate obscene material, as upheld in *Reidel* and *37 Photos*." (*Stanley v. Georgia*, 1969; *United States v. Reidel*, 1971; and *United States v. Thirty-seven Photographs*, 1971).

Stillwell, James C. "Obscenity—The Wavering Line on Pornography—How Hard the Core?" *University of San Fernando Valley Law Review*, 1:210–52, January 1968. **1S554**
The elements and dynamics of judicially determining pandering, contemporary standards, and judicial procedure since *Ginzburg*. The author examines the case of *People v. Noroff* (1967), presenting an in-depth view of obscenity issues as contrasted in the actual litigation. He presents the arguments of counsel at the trial court hearing in a summarization of their respective briefs, together with the decisions of the various courts, "as the elements of a time oriented dialectic so that the reader may either select those specific elements suited to his own needs, or may obtain a more detailed picture of the entire *Noroff* conflict."

Stocker, Barbara L. "An Analysis of the Distinction Between Public Figures and Private Defamation Plaintiffs Applied to Relatives of Public Persons." *Southern California Law Review*, 49:1131–240, July 1976. **1S555**
The note considers the circumstances in which defamation plaintiffs who are related to public persons should bear the standard of proof required of public persons. The issue grew out of the U.S. Supreme Court's decision in *Time, Inc. v. Firestone* (1976).

Stone, F. F. "Damage by Mass Media." In John N. Hazard and Wencelas J. Wagner, eds., *Law in the United States of America. Reports from the United States of America on Topics of Major Concern as*

Established for the IX Congress of the International Academy of Comparative Law. Brussels, American Association for the Comparative Study of Law, 1974, pp. 141–57. **1S556**
Content: Trial by Press and Television. Invasion of Privacy. Abuse of the Right of Fair Comment. Defamation of Public Figures. The author concludes that whether, in the long run, the press and mass media are absolutely free to write and speak as they please (Justices Black and Douglas) or there is still a limited place for state law on defamation or some middle ground of compromise (Justices Brennan and White), "will ultimately be determined on the basis of whether the power is abused."

Stone, I. F. "The Crisis Coming for a Free Press." In *The I. F. Stone's Weekly Reader*, edited by Neil Middleton. New York, Random House, 1973, pp. 10–17. (Reprinted from the *I. F. Stone Bi-Weekly*, 12 July 1971) **1S557**
Criticism of the U.S. Supreme Court's decision on the Pentagon Papers, which "left a bigger loophole than before for prior restraint. . . . If the government can continue to abuse its secrecy stamp to keep the press, the Congress, and the people from knowing what it is really doing—then the basic decisions in our country are in the hands of a small army of faceless bureaucrats, mostly military."

———. "Nixon, Agnew and Freedom of the Press." *I. F. Stone's Bi-Weekly*, 18(11):1, 4, 1 June 1970. **1S558**
The editor recalls Richard Nixon's statement in 1965, when President Johnson first sent combat troops into Vietnam, advocating restrictions of speech and press in wartime; and Nixon's earlier (1948) efforts at restricting dissent when he introduced the Mundt-Nixon bill to create the Subversive Activities Control Board, justifying restricting liberty as a means of defending it. Citing the widespread opposition to the Vietnam war and the efforts at suppressing dissent, he concludes: "More and more, as anti-war dissent rises in every class and region, Nixon and Agnew are thrown back on an appeal to the Know Nothings of our time."

Stonecipher, Harry W. "A Boost for Censorship?" *Grassroots Editor*, 14(6):21–25, November–December 1973. **1S559**
An analysis of the recent obscenity rulings of the U.S. Supreme Court.

———. "The Government vs. the Press." *Grassroots Editor*, 12(4):4–5, 18, July–August 1971. **1S560**
An examination of the events leading up to the Pentagon Papers case and an analysis of the U.S. Supreme Court's decision. Many newspapers viewed the decision as "something less than the clear proscription of prior restraint which boosters of the First Amendment had hoped for . . . something less than an absolute

faith by the Supreme Court in the First Amendment." And there has been further concern about "threats of possible future action by the government under various criminal provisions of the federal statutes."

———. "Legal Status of Newsmen's Privilege." *Grassroots Editor*, 13(2):19–22, 36, March–April 1972. **1S561**
A review of legal developments which set the stage for the three cases on newsmen's privilege now before the U.S. Supreme Court. "Statutory protection is at present wholly inadequate. In the federal system, as well as in three-fifths of the states, reporters have no more right than other citizens to withhold information demanded by the subpoena of a court, grand jury or legislative committee. Past efforts of newsmen to reach a satisfactory solution to the problem through the courts have been largely unsuccessful."

———. "Should Newspapers Be Subject to Additional External Controls?" *Grassroots Editor*, 12(6):16–18, November–December 1971. **1S562**
A questionnaire study of newsmen and a cross-section of newspaper readers reveals that "readers do not view the press as being as socially responsible as newsmen apparently do. Readers, therefore, are more willing to see external controls imposed which might force the press to perform a role which they view as being more responsible."

———. "Supreme Court Requires Newsmen to Testify before Grand Juries." *Grassroots Editor*, 13(4):22–24, July–August 1972. **1S563**
Commentary on the U.S. Supreme Court's rulings in the *Caldwell*, *Pappas*, and *Branzburg* cases. "The Supreme Court's denial of even a conditional newsman's privilege under the free press clause of the First Amendment isn't likely to lower the blood pressure of a press faced with subpoenas and increasing governmental harassment. And of even more concern, the public's right to know may suffer as a consequence."

———, and Robert Trager. "The Impact of *Gertz* on the Law of Libel." *Journalism Quarterly*, 53:609–18, Winter 1976. **1S564**
"It is clear in examining the cases citing *Gertz* [*Gertz v. Robert Welch, Inc.*, 1974] that the already complex body of libel law is being made even more complex by imposing upon it one more special category—that of the private libel plaintiff, a category not clearly defined by federal or state courts. . . . The full impact of *Gertz*, however, will not be known until the state courts have had more opportunity to fully interpret the *Gertz* standards in light of the traditional common law principles of defamation."

———. *The Mass Media and the Law in Illinois*. Carbondale, Ill., Southern Il-

linois University Press, 1976. 207p. Foreword by Howard Rusk Long. **1S565**
"The purpose of this book is to define the present status of laws regarding the mass media, specifically as applied to the Illinois newsman-publisher-broadcaster. . . . The organizational focus of the book is upon the First Amendment guarantees of free speech and free press as they affect the various professional roles of Illinois newsmen. Chapter 1 provides an overview of the newsman's constitutional privileges and how these may be abridged when a sufficient governmental interest warrants it. The remaining chapters are divided into various 'conflict' areas": libel, privacy, free press–fair trial, contempt of court, newsman's privilege, obscenity, access to public information, copyright and the doctrine of fair use, advertising and business regulation, and regulation of broadcasting.

Stop Immorality on TV. *Newsletter*. Warrenton, Va., Stop Immorality on TV, 1972–? Occasional. **1S566**
A national organization, sponsored by the Society for the Christian Commonwealth, Inc., with the goal of halting the increased sexual immorality in television shows.

[Stormer, John.] *Anatomy of a Smear. An Analysis of the Attacks and Smears on the Book, "None Dare Call It Treason."* Florissant, Mo., Liberty Bell Press, 1965. 16p. **1S567**
An analysis of the attacks made on the anti-Communist book *None Dare Call It Treason* by John Stormer, chairman of the Missouri Federation of Young Republicans, showing "the lengths to which 'liberals' will go to discredit an effective anti-Communist book." Special responsibility for the attacks is credited to a Cleveland organization, National *Committee* for Civil Responsibility and a newly formed group, National *Council* for Civic Responsibility, headed by Arthur Larsen of Duke University.

Stottlar, James F. "A Victorian Stage Censor: The Theory and Practice of William Bodham Donne." *Victorian Studies*, 13:253–82, March 1970. **1S568**
As British stage censor from 1849 to 1874, Donne's rulings precluded any "serious treatment of life on the British stage," banning objectionable references to sex, religion, politics, royalty, and anything that would lower the Victorian standard of decorum.

Stouse, Jean. "The Battle Over 'Hearts and Minds.' " *MORE*, 4(12):5–6, 17, 19–20, December 1974. **1S569**
A highly acclaimed documentary on Vietnam has not been released by Columbia Pictures in a controversy over whether a film "that tells unpleasant truths about America in recessionary times, at a studio on the critical list," will be financially profitable.

Strackbein, O. R. *Tyranny of the Press*. Washington, D.C., The Author, 1968. 58p. **1S570**
The author calls for the creation of a public review board to consider cases involving abuse of press freedom.

[Strahan, Alexander.] "Bad Literature for the Young." *Contemporary Review*, 26:981–91, November 1875. **1S571**
An attack on the "penny dreadfuls" for the harm being done to the morals of youth, particularly in the literature published in America.

Strain, William S. "The Limits of 'Public Interest.' " *Louisiana Law Review*, 33:351–55, Winter 1973. **1S572**
Comment on the case of *Firestone v. Time, Inc.* (1972), in which the Fifth Circuit Court of Appeals reversed a lower court decision and held that the *New York Times* doctrine applied to defamatory statements concerning private individuals involved in matters "of public or general interest."

Straker, Jean, ed. *Censorship in the Arts; Freedom of Vision Teach-In held in Hampstead Old Town Hall, October 2nd 1966 from 3 p.m. till 10 p.m.* London, Academy of Visual Arts, 1967. 66p. (Freedom of Vision Report Series) **1S573**
The Freedom of Vision Society was formed in London in 1964, with photographer Jean Straker as a leading figure. Its primary purpose was to urge the British government to give statutory recognition to Articles 19 and 27 of the Universal Declaration of Human Rights, dealing with freedom of expression and participation in the arts, and to repeal the 1964 Obscene Publications Act. This is the transcript of a public meeting, convened under the chairmanship of Ben Whitaker, MP, at which members of the Society and others from most art media contributed to the symposium. In the report, a copy of which was sent to the Home Office, the point was made that, pursuant to Article 10 of the European Convention on Human Rights, "restrictive laws must describe beforehand, accurately and objectively, the nature of the offence, so that it shall be clear to all what constitutes an offence, and further that the law must have been shown, by sufficient objective evidence, to have been necessary 'for the protection of morals.' "

[———.] "Jean Straker in Cyril Black-Land." *Freethinker*, 88:76–77, 8 March 1968. **1S574**
In an address at the Wimbledon School of Art, the man whose nude photographs had been declared obscene, comments on photographing the human body and on the efforts of

Wimbledon's Member of Parliament, Sir Cyril Black, to support the Obscene Publications Act under which Straker was convicted.

———. "The Last Exposure." *New Statesman*, 75:546–47, 26 April 1968. **1S575**
A letter from the London photographer with respect to his campaign to legalize publication of unretouched nudes. Some 1,479 of Straker's negatives had been seized by the police.

———. *Letter to the Lord Chief Justice & Others, 3 May 1969, from Jean Straker.* London, Freedom of Vision, 1969. 17p. (Obscene Publications Papers) **1S576**
An appeal for a review of his obscenity conviction with a view to the granting of a Crown pardon and the return of his negatives of nudes that had been seized by the police.

"Strange Case of Michael Frome, Lover of Trees and Bête Noire of the Lumber Industry." *Living Wilderness*, 35:22–33, Autumn 1971. **1S577**
A documented account of the threatened censorship and ultimate firing of Micheal Frome as columnist for *American Forests*, because of his criticism of the U.S. Forest Service and the lumber industry.

Strauss, George. "Theatre Censorship: Exit the Lord Chamberlain." *Times* (London), 24 September 1968, p. 9. **1S578**
After 231 years, the Lord Chamberlain's censorship powers over the British theater have been abolished. The Member of Parliament who introduced the bill in the House of Commons discusses the events leading to the action and the controversy that was generated.

Street, Harry. *Freedom, the Individual and the Law.* Harmondsworth, England, Penguin Books, 1973. 324p. **1S579**
This survey of present civil liberties in England includes the area of freedom of expression—theater, cinema, broadcasting, the printed word and advertising, obscenity, defamation, contempt of court (restrictions on reporting cases), and contempt of Parliament.

———. "Privacy and the Law." *Twentieth Century*, 170:35–48, Spring 1962. **1S580**
A survey of the British law of privacy which, the author notes, protects the individual in an oblique way, whereas the American law is more explicit and encompassing. In Britain invasion of privacy by the press must be attacked under the law of trespass, the law of nuisance, injunctions against interference with another's property, the law of copyright, or under the law of libel and slander. Thus far efforts to pass a privacy law in Britain have been unsuccessful.

Streifford, Howard I. *An Axiological Analysis of the Rhetorical Implications in Selected Supreme Court Decisions.* Carbondale, Ill., Southern Illinois University, 1967. 429p. (Ph.D. dissertation, University Microfilms, no. 67-15,878) **1S581**
"The study was concerned with the relationships which maintain between (1) selected Supreme Court decisions affecting free speech and certain theories of free speech and (2) contemporary rhetorical theory."

Strick, Joseph. "Blacklisting of Men and Ideas; a Taped Conversation." *Film Culture*, 50–51:50–53, Fall/Winter 1970. **1S582**
Comments on blacklisting, the House Un-American Activities Committee, censorship, film rating, and the regimentation of men and ideas in American cinema. Conversation with James Pasternak.

Strick, Philip. "Talking About Censorship—3: Cinema Freedoms." *Author*, 81:74–77, Summer 1970. **1S583**
A description of the way in which the British Board of Film Censors, under the direction of John Trevelyan, deals with a motion picture script or final product submitted to them in advance. On themes where sex and violence is intermingled, the Board consults a team of psychiatrists to ensure that the chance of corruptive influence is avoided. With an enlightened Board, "the writer has more to fear from his financiers than from Trevelyan."

Stridsberg, Albert B. *Effective Advertising Self-Regulation: A Survey of Current World Practice and Analysis of International Patterns.* New York, International Advertising Association, 1974. 181p. **1S584**
Content: The Basic Issues of Self-Regulation. Organizing for Self-Regulation. The Future of Self-Regulation. Country Profiles (twenty-nine countries). The appendices include texts of the International Code of Advertising Practices and World Chart of Advertising Self-Regulation.

Stroll, Avrum. "Censorship and Repressive Tolerance." In Eleanor Widmer, *ed., Freedom and Culture*, Belmont, Calif., Wadsworth, 1970, pp. 37–41. **1S585**
An analysis and critique of the views on censorship held by Herbert Marcuse. "Basicly, what is wrong with Marcuse's argument is that it presupposes that censorship in a democratic society is a *legitimate* political device. But this posture is inconsistent with the fundamental model upon which self-government rests. Marcuse is convinced that in every society censorship in fact exists; his aim is directed toward using it for the benefit of society. But such a benevolent conception is not a benevolent form of democracy. It is a form of autocracy. It rests upon a conceptual model in which some persons in society exercise force over others, and it attempts to apply this model to a domain where it is inappropriate."

Strong, Catherine R. *Open Meeting Laws in the United States: An Analysis of Their Effectiveness and a Proposed Model Law.* Kent, Ohio, Kent State University, 1974. 174p. (Unpublished Master's thesis) **1S586**
Laws requiring governmental meetings to be open to the public currently exist in forty-six states, but only three score high in effectiveness.

Strong, Frank R. "Fifty Years of 'Clear and Present Danger': From Schenck to Brandenburg—And Beyond." In Philip B. Kurland, *ed., The Supreme Court Review, 1969.* Chicago, University of Chicago Press, 1969, pp. 41–80. (Also in Kurland's *Free Speech and Association*) **1S587**
"The fiftieth anniversary of the 'clear and present danger' test is not a happy one for it. Commentators no less than Justices have been undertaking to inter the test for some little time. Hailed at the outset as the interpretational device for effective realization of First Amendment liberties, the danger test has lost favor to the point where the Court only irregularly admits to its employment, and there are few who would grieve at its total demise." A comprehensive history of the employment of the "clear and present danger" test in freedom of expression cases, beginning with its formulation in the 1919 *Schenck* case to the case of *Brandenburg v. Ohio* (1969), where any reference to the test was assiduously avoided. The author quotes views on the test expressed by legal scholars over the years.

Strong, R. A., and J. A. Strong. *Mr. Chipp and the Porno-Push.* Melbourne, Australia, Minton Publishing Co., 1971. 40p. **1S588**
An attack on the views and actions of Australia's Customs censor, Donald L. Chipp, for his permissive and tolerant attitude toward explicit sex in books and films. Quoting Mr. Chipp as accusing Australians who are concerned with the harmful effect of the wave of sexual materials entering the country as being obsessed with the fear of sex, the author states: "Mature and responsible people who insist on standards being maintained that make for a sane, crime-and-problem-free society, not just now but in the next and future generations, who have the intellectual capacity to recognize the danger signs for the future, such people are not 'obsessed' with sex in any manner or form, but solely with maintaining social standards, social stability—society itself." Replying to

Mr. Chipp's statement that complaints to his office were more concerned with the expression of sex than with hate, envy, and jealousy, the author notes that the portrayal of a sexual event is itself a vigorous sexual experience and this artificially produces appetites that cannot be satisfied in an ordered society. The same is not true of the other passions.

Stroud, D. Michael. "Newspaper Regulation and the Public Interest: The Unmasking of a Myth." *University of Pittsburgh Law Review*, 32:595–606, Summer 1971.　　**1S589**
Relates to the case of *Chicago Joint Board, Amalgamated Clothing Workers of America, AFL-CIO v. Chicago Tribune Company* (1970) in which the Appellate Court affirmed the ruling of the trial court that the newspaper had the right to reject a paid editorial advertisement because (1) the relationship between a newspaper and its advertisers is one of private contract, and (2) that the lack of state involvement was jurisdictionally fatal.

"The Struggle Over Broadcast Access." *Broadcasting*, 81(12):32–43, 20 September 1971.　　**1S590**
A discussion of the nationwide growth of consumer interest in having greater access to local radio and television programming and the organizing of "coalition" groups. Following a general summary there is a story on the efforts by the United Church of Christ and other groups to take legal action on behalf of minority groups whose interests they felt were ignored.

Stuart, I. R. "Personality Dynamics and Objectionable Art: Attitudes, Opinions, and Experimental Evidence." *Journal of Aesthetic Education*, 4(3):101–16, July 1970.　　**1S591**
"Pornography in the form of singular concern with coitus, sexual organs, violence associated with sex, and similar presentations, has an inherent *attracting* value and needs no elaboration to establish its primacy in arousing sexual excitement. Its possession of intrinsic value via its supposed aesthetic elements, however, must be denied. It is still unverified that pornography has beneficial effects, nor has it been observed to have socially or politically desirable residuals, despite its defense by some vested (economic) interests. Some supporters base their claim upon its pretension to be a weathervane of political democracy. Politically, freedom from censorship pays a price in profits for those who sponsor sex in public, assured of a ready market by the curiosity of the young and the alarm of the senile."

Stuart, Lonnie D. *Youth Protection Laws and the History of Variable Obscenity*. Provo, Utah, Brigham Young University, 1969. 136p. (Unpublished Master's thesis)　　**1S592**
Analysis of recent obscenity decisions of the United States Supreme Court shows the Court moving toward acceptance of a theory of variable obscenity to protect children from questionable and obscene materials. "The variable obscenity theory says materials not considered obscene for adults may be obscene when viewed by children. . . . Examination of state statutes shows 22 states now have youth protection laws."

The Student Press Law Center. *Manual for Student Expression: The First Amendment Rights of the High School Press*. Washington, D.C., The Center, 1976. 30p.　　**1S593**
"The First Amendment to the Constitution of the United States guarantees all citizens, including high school students, the right to express themselves on topics of their choices free from official interference. This Manual is specifically designed to inform the high school press—writers, reporters, editors and publishers, and their broadcast counterparts—about First Amendment rights and how to protect them."

———. *Reports*. Washington, D.C., The Center, 1976–date. Occasional.　　**1S594**
The Center is a national organization which collects, analyzes, and distributes through its periodic *Reports* "information on the First Amendment as it affects student journalists and journalism teachers in high school and college. The SPLC also provides direct legal assistance and advice to students and journalism teachers experiencing censorship problems, and to attorneys defending student expression."

Studybaker, Deborah, and Stevan Studybaker. "Cox Broadcasting v. Cohn: A Finer Definition of the Publication Privilege." *Capital University Law Review*, 5:267–76, 1976.　　**1S595**
"The Supreme Court in *Cox [Cox Broadcasting Co. v. Cohn,* 1975] balanced the appellee's right to privacy against the freedom of the press and found the scales tipped in favor of the press. The Supreme Court's decision facilitates the press' function of informing the public and tends to discourage self-censorship by the press and the suppression of public information."

Stukas, William B. "The Federal Communications Commission and Program Regulation—Violation of the First Amendment?" *Nebraska Law Review*, 41:826–46, June 1962.　　**1S596**
"The purpose here is to comment upon the nature of the power Congress vested in the FCC pertaining to the programming area, to discuss the limitations upon that power, to discuss the criteria used by FCC in the regulation of the radio and television industry, and to analyze the various possible approaches to delineating the extent of regulation the FCC should have in this area."

Sturges, Gerald. "Congressional Clout and the FoI." *Editor & Publisher*, 102(26):7, 60, 28 June 1969.　　**1S597**
A review of compliance and lack of compliance among government agencies at the end of the first year of the Freedom of Information Act.

Sturm, Kathryn H. "Judicial Control of Pretrial and Trial Publicity: A Reexamination of the Applicable Constitutional Standards." *Golden Gate University Law Review*, 6:101–38, Fall 1975.　　**1S598**
"Protective orders should be issued only when it appears that in the absence of court control there exists a reasonable likelihood that the trial may be prejudiced. A finding of this nature should be sufficient to include attorneys, defendants and law enforcement officers within the ambit of a protective order. The news media, however, should rarely, if ever, be directly restrained by a protective order. A very strong showing of great and immediate prejudice is needed before a direct restraint can be imposed. . . . Because of the public's 'need to know,' and the quickly passing newsworthiness of events, the press should be included in the original discussion of the need for and the scope of a protective order."

Styron, William. "The Vice That Has No Name." *Harper's*, 236:97–100, February 1968.　　**1S599**
"A veil of obscurity, if not prudery, has been drawn over masturbation as over no other aspect of sexual behavior," probably because it was assumed, mistakenly according to the sex studies, that "self abuse" was a sin of schoolboys. This is a review of Grove Press's reprinting of *Light on Dark Corners*, a book on sex education first published in 1894 and which went through forty-one printings in forty years. The book "was considered in itself a shocker and was hounded by the minions of Anthony Comstock for the resemblance it bore to pornography."

Suber, Howard. *The Anti-Communist Blacklist in the Hollywood Motion Picture Industry*. Los Angeles, University of California, Los Angeles, 1968. 353p. (Ph.D. dissertation, University Microfilms, no. 69-7266)　　**1S600**
"For over a decade after 1947, people who were believed to be members of the Communist Party were excluded from the Hollywood motion picture industry through the process commonly known as blacklisting. This historical narrative traces the growth and development of that blacklist, the reasons why it came into being, the way in which those who were blacklisted survived during this period, the position of the motion picture producers in relation to the blacklist, and the forces and events that caused the blacklist to be abandoned."

———. "Hollywood's Political Blacklist." In Donald E. Staples, *ed.*, *The American Cinema*. Washington, D.C., Voice of America, 1974, pp. 289–99. (Forum series)   **1S601**
An account of the Hollywood blacklist, the film industry's boycott of the 1940s and '50s in response to anti-Communist crusaders. On the list were those persons in the industry—writers, producers, actors, and others—who were suspect of having Communist affiliations and who did not purge themselves.

Suddards, Roger W., and Dorothy White. *The Law and the Amateur Theatre*. London, Samuel French, 1962. 73p.   **1S602**
Sections deal with licensing the theater, licensing the play, copyright, and libel.

Suits, Alan P. "Current Crisis in Censorship." *AB Bookman's Weekly*, 43: 2276–78, 16 June 1969.   **1S603**
Talk given at the ABA annual business meeting by the chairman of the Freedom to Read Committee of the Bureau of Independent Publishers and Distributors. Suits describes the picture on obscenity since the *Ginsberg* decision.

Sullenberger, Lloyd. "Sheppard v. Maxwell: Free Speech and Press v. Fair Trial." *William and Mary Law Review*, 8:143–51, Fall 1966.   **1S604**
"The significance of the case [*Sheppard v. Maxwell*, 1966] lies in the fact that even though no confession was involved and even though the death penalty had not been imposed and even though no broadcasting was allowable from the courtroom, the Court took another step and let the courts and press know that interference and lack of control could deny due process."

[Sullivan, Alexander M.] *The Plot Discovered: Digest of the Action for Libel, Hardy v. Sullivan, Tried Before the Lord Chief Justice of the Queen's Bench, Dublin, in Dec. 1861. . . . By the Secretary, Armagh Protestant Association*. Armagh, Ireland, Published and printed for the Armagh Protestant Association by John Thompson, 1862. 34p.   **1S605**
The case involved publication in the defendant's newspaper, *Morning Post*, of charges that Hardy, a sub-sheriff had juggled a jury panel. The case had overtones of a Catholic-Protestant controversy. The plaintiff was awarded £50 damages.

Sullivan, Eileen S. "The Student's Right to Free Expression." *Wilson Library Bulletin*, 51:168–71, October 1976.   **1S606**

A discussion of the impact of the U.S. Supreme Court decision in *Tinker v. Des Moines Independent School District* (1969) and subsequent decisions on children's right to read and to express themselves under the First Amendment.

Sullivan, Francis C. "Prejudicial Publicity: A Look at the Remedies." *Suffolk University Law Review*, 1:77–104, Spring 1967.   **1S607**
"Faced with the present ineffectiveness of direct method of control over the production of prejudicial publicity, it can only be concluded that the curing of the effects of prejudicial publicity rests with the wise and fair use by the courts of those procedural devices presently available. . . . It is to the development of better internal procedural devices to which the courts must devote their resources and abilities if our system of the administration of criminal justice is effectively to implant the constitutional right of an accused to a fair and impartial trial."

Sullivan, Peggy. "Sylvester . . . Meets the Press." In her *Problems in School Media Management*. New York, Bowker, 1971, pp. 19–25.   **1S608**
This case study involves pressures from the local chief of police to ban the Caldecott award-winning children's book, *Sylvester and the Magic Pebble*, because two pigs in this animal story were dressed as policemen.

Sullivan, Robert J. "Let Them Write Responsibly: Freedom of the Press in the High School." *Education Digest*, 34(5):50–51, January 1969.   **1S609**
The author urges faculty advisors to encourage high school journalists to write responsibly on controversial subjects and to give them the necessary freedom.

———. "The Overrated Threat." *Bulletin of the National Association of Secondary School Principals*, 53:36–44, September 1969. (Reprinted in *Education Digest*, November 1969; *Communication: Journalism Today*, November 1969)   **1S610**
What to do about underground newspapers in high schools. There are three ways more desirable than a knockout punch to deal with high school underground papers: prevention, toleration, and preemption. "A banned paper is far more interesting than one that flourishes unnoticed."

Sumberg, Theodore A. "Privacy, Freedom, and Obscenity: Stanley v. Georgia." *Journal of Critical Analysis*, 3:84–96, July 1971.   **1S611**
A consideration of the issues in the U.S. Supreme Court ruling in *Stanley v. Georgia* (1969), in which the court held that no ban on obscenity can "reach into the privacy of one's own home." The author objects to the philosophy

of *Stanley*, finding that it is "soft to the governed and harsh to the government. . . . It is also soft in not keeping people to standards; the absence of standards for the people is the great void in the decision. It sets no standards because it believes in no standards: distinctions between virtue and vice, base and elevated, and decency and indecency are, all of them, foreign to *Stanley*."

Summers, David S. "The Commercial Speech Doctrine and the Consumers' Right to Receive." *Washburn Law Journal*, 16:197–203, Fall 1976.   **1S612**
Re: *Virginia State Board of Pharmacy v. Virginia Citizens Consumer Council, Inc.*, 423 U.S. 815 (1976).

Summers, John, "315 and the Political Spending Bill." In Don R. Le Duc, *ed.*, *Issues in Broadcast Regulation*. Washington, D.C., Broadcast Education Association, 1974, pp. 85–88.   **1S613**
The chief counsel for the National Association of Broadcasters outlines objections broadcasters have to recent legislation limiting spending for political advertising on radio and television.

Summers, Marvin, *ed. Free Speech and Political Protest*. Lexington, Mass., Heath, 1967. 136p. (Problems in Political Science)   **1S614**
Content: A Tradition of Suppression by Leonard W. Levy. The Common Law, Sedition and the First Amendment by John H. Kelly. The Clear and Present Danger Doctrine by Mr. Justice Oliver Wendell Holmes. The Danger Test in Retrospect by Edward G. Hudon. A Critical View of the Danger Test by Walter Berns. A Preference for the First Amendment Freedoms (*Thomas v. Collins*, 1945) by Justice Wiley Rutledge. The Preferred Position: A Mischievous Phrase (*Kovacs v. Cooper*, 1949) by Justice Felix Frankfurter. "The Preference for Freedom": A Rebuttal to Frankfurter by Robert B. McKay. The Balance-of-Interest Approach by Paul G. Kauper. Plain Words and Constitutional Absolutes by Justice Hugo L. Black. A Philosopher Dissents in the Case of Absolutes by Sidney Hook. Maintaining Wide-Open and Robust Debate (*New York Times v. Sullivan*, 1964) by Justice William J. Brennan, Jr. A New Look at the Central Meaning of the First Amendment by Harry Kalven, Jr.

Summers, Montagne. "The Censorship of Restoration Plays." *Drama* (Journal of the British Drama League), 8(n.s.):57–59, 21 June 1921.   **1S615**
The author cites numerous examples to show that the theater of Charles II "was not the reckless unlicensed saturnalia vulgar error has pictured it to be, but that a pretty close watch was kept upon the stage, and complaints not unseldom led to serious results for those concerned."

Sumner, John S., and Theodore

Schroeder. *Debate*: "*Is there any Social Value in the work of the New York Society for the Suppression of Vice?*" New York [Sunrise Club] 1916. 6op. (Typed report from recorder's shorthand notes) **1S616**
Mr. Sumner, the new secretary of the Society says "yes" and describes and defends the work of his organization, which from its founding immediately after the Civil War until 1915 had been directed by one man—Anthony Comstock. Eighty percent of the work of the Society is remedial, about 20 percent punitive. The former, less sensational, seldom gets into the newspapers. Theodore Schroeder, secretary of the Free Speech League, says "no" to the question, charging that the vice societies are attacking problems that don't exist. He debunks the psychology that motivates the work of vice societies—fear of sex.

Sunderland, Lane. *Obscenity: The Court, the Congress and the President's Commission*. Washington, D.C., American Enterprise Institute for Public Policy Research, 1975. 127p. **1S617**
An examination of the 1973 obscenity decisions of the U.S. Supreme Court in relation to earlier court decisions, First Amendment guarantees of press freedom, and the findings of the Commission on Obscenity and Pornography. The study finds that "determinations of obscenity are now dependent on subnational 'community standards' in some respects, but they are circumscribed by the Court's guidelines which protect First Amendment freedoms." The author concludes that "despite contemporary comment to the contrary, these decisions do not portend the end of literary, artistic, scientific, or political achievement. In making the landmark pronouncements, the 1973 opinions did not depart from earlier constitutional law laid down by a majority of the Court. In some respects, however, the recent decisions do allow more latitude in obscenity regulation than existed under prior plurality standards."

[Sundermeyer, Michael S.] "Filthy Words, the FCC, and the First Amendment: Regulating Broadcast Obscenity." *Virginia Law Review*, 61: 579–642, April 1975. **1S618**
"Do the FCC [obscenity] cases constitute firm and reliable precedent for future decisions? And what limits does the Constitution place on the FCC regulation of speech? To answer these questions, this note will first examine *Miller* [*Miller v. California*, 1973] itself to determine the changes it effected in obscenity law. Second, it will consider the constitutionality of 18 U.S.C., par. 1467—the federal criminal statute prohibiting the broadcasting of obscenity. Third, any answer to these questions must explore FCC compliance with the obscenity definitions and tests of the Supreme Court. Fourth, if the Commission has not complied with the tests, any justifications for noncompliance must be assessed. And fifth, if no justifications exist for FCC noncompliance,

the note must attempt to adapt the *Miller* definition to the broadcast media."

"Supreme Court Looks to Local Standards in Determining Obscenity." *Valparaiso University Law Review*, 8:166–79, Fall 1973. **1S619**
Comments on *Miller v. California* (1973), and companion cases in which the U.S. Supreme Court placed the burden of dealing with obscenity cases squarely on the shoulders of state and local authorities.

The Supreme Court Obscenity Decisions. San Diego, Calif., Greenleaf Classics, 1973. 232p. **1S620**
The text of the U.S. Supreme Court obscenity decisions of 21 June 1973, together with the dissents: *Paris Adult Theatre I v. Slaton*, *Miller v. California*, *Kaplan v. California*, *U.S. v. 12 200-Ft. Reels of Super 8mm. Film*, and *U.S. v. Orito*. Includes the text of the petition for rehearing. Stanley Fleishman has supplied an "overview" of the cases on pp. 7–20.

Sussman, Barry. "Limits of Advocacy: Newspapers." *Public Relations Quarterly*, 18(3):18–19, 26, Winter 1974. **1S621**
"Our position on advocacy [*Washington Post*] has been that it begins and ends in our editorial pages, among our columnists and with some occasional pieces of news analysis. . . ." The editor believes that people sometimes "confuse aggressive reporting with advocacy. With aggressive reporting we bring issues to people. That's our real job."

Sussman, Leonard R. "The American Press—Under Seige?" *Quadrant*, 16(6): 88–100, November–December 1972. **1S622**
The American press today believes it is in a state of seige laid down by the Nixon Administration. Complaints include over-classification of official documents; management of news of the federal government; harassment of newsmen through subpoenas, contempt power of the courts, and by police posing as newsmen; federal antitrust suits against the television networks; and attacks from high governmental officials. On the other side, courts have given the press greater freedom in the area of obscenity and libel of public officials. In the area of free press vs. fair trial no mutually satisfactory balance has yet been achieved. Restrictions on press freedoms generally relate to conflicts of rights, individual or body politic, and the author calls for a "calmer working out of middle road approaches to 'collision' issues" as the essence of the democratic method. Both government and the press face serious tests of credibility with the American people.

———. "A Fateful Year for the News Media." *Freedom at Issue*, 39:2–4, January–February 1977. **1S623**
Includes a report on the efforts at government control of the press—a Soviet proposal for

government-operated news agencies to provide adequate coverage of Third World news. The proposal, made at a UNESCO conference held in Nairobi, was referred to a committee. An earlier report on the proposal appeared in the September–October 1976 issue.

———. "Mass Communications and Press Freedom: A World View." *Mass Communications Review*, 1(1):18–22, August 1973. **1S624**
The director of Freedom House describes that organization's Comparative Survey of Freedom, which includes the ranking of the world's press. English language nations—Australia, Canada, New Zealand, and U.S.A.—were ranked in the first seven groups, noting greatest press freedom.

Sutherland, Halliday G. *Birth Control Exposed*. London, Cecil Palmer, 1925. 225p. **1S625**
An attack on the birth-control movement by a Roman Catholic doctor. Chapter 1 reviews the Bradlaugh-Besant trial (B468) and the libel case, *Stopes v. Sutherland*, in which birth-control advocate Dr. Marie Stopes sued Dr. Sutherland for a statement in his book, *Birth Control: A Statement of Christian Doctrine against the Neo-Malthusians*.

Sutherland, Janet R. "A Defense of Ken Kesey's *One Flew Over the Cuckoo's Nest*." *English Journal*, 61:28–31, January 1972. **1S626**
A high school teacher defends Kesey's novel against the charge that it is an improper and even evil book, fit only "to be burned."

Sutro, John A. "A Lawyer's View of Courtroom Broadcasting." *Journal of Broadcasting*, 12:19–22, Winter 1967–68. (Reprinted in John M. Kittross and Kenneth Harwood, *eds.*, *Free and Fair*, pp. 89–92) **1S627**
A defense of the principle of excluding broadcasting from the courtroom, based on California's Rule 980 rather than upon the American Bar Association's Canon 35.

[Sutter, E. Lloyd.] "Separate Obscenity Standards for Youth: Potential Escape Route From Its 'Supercensor' Role." *Georgia Law Review*, 1:707–31, Summer 1967. **1S628**
"The purpose of this note is to advocate an alternative approach to the obscenity problem, tailored to a specific and constitutionally justifiable purpose—the protection of youth. There would seem to be no reason why a separate standard for children could not be both constitutional and effective. If such be the case, a progressive and skillful legislature could si-

multaneously insure the welfare of its youth and eliminate the abridgment of adult constitutional rights. Moreover, a well-drafted statute might even provide the Supreme Court with an escape route from its current 'supercensor's' role." The author looks at two such schemes—the Dallas movie ordinance and the New York approach to the magazine rack problem. He concludes with an outline for a separate obscenity standard for youths under eighteen years of age.

Sutton, Shaun. "Television Drama and the Censor." *Journal of the Society of Film and Television Arts*, 43/44:15, Spring–Summer 1971. **1S629**
From the first, television has censored itself and, for the most part, it has worked. The complexity of television drama writing, recording, and transmitting makes formal censorship by an independent board virtually impossible.

Suzman, Arthur. "Censorship and the Courts: The Suggested Abolition of the Right of Appeal to the Supreme Court from Decisions of the Publications Control Board." *South African Law Journal*, 89:191–206, May 1972. **1S630**
"If the existing right of appeal from decisions of the Publications Control Board to the Supreme Court were to be abolished, the very necessary safeguards inherent in an appeal to the courts would disappear; freedom of expression would be further curtailed and we would witness a yet further encroachment on the Rule of Law." A memorandum from the chairman of the South African PEN. Court decisions are given in an appendix.

Swaim, Elizabeth A. "Owen Wister's *Roosevelt*: A Case Study in Post-Production Censorship." *Studies in Bibliography*, 27:290–93, 1974. **1S631**
An account of the bibliographical intricacies resulting from "Macmillan's last minute recall before publication of Owen Wister's *Roosevelt: The Story of a Friendship*, *1880–1919* (1930) and their hasty and expensive replacement of an entire sixteen-page section before redistributing the expected best-seller with a new publication date." The action was taken as the result of threat of a libel suit from the family of a person mentioned in the book. Copies of the original printing of the book had already gone out to reviewers.

Swan, Judith W. L. "Misleading Advertising: Its Control." *Alberta Law Review*, 9:310–30, 1971. (Reprinted in *Canadian Communications Law Review*, December 1971) **1S632**
"Misleading advertising is controlled both through legal measures and extra-legal organi-zations such as the Canadian Advertising Advisory Board. The writer of this article details existing legislation in this area, dealing particularly with Section 33C and 33D of the Combines Investigation Act, and considers the extent to which these laws, together with the extra-legal organizations, can successfully suppress false and misleading advertising."

Swan, Peter. "The Problem of Pornography." *Library Association Record*, 70: 275–77, November 1968. Comments: 71:20–24, January 1969. **1S633**
"The following article is an attempt to examine some of the human and social implications of obscene literature, and to highlight the principles at stake in this well-worn controversy, without becoming submerged in a discussion of the merits or otherwise of any particular book." The author declares at the outset his conviction that "the written word is capable of evoking the best in human nature—and the worst." The harm of pornography, he notes, cannot be proved or disproved; therefore the issue doesn't lend itself to a purely rational discussion. Librarians must exercise some discretion in book selection. Comments by John Calder, Alan Bevan, A. H. Rouse, C. Derek Robinson, and others appear in the January issue.

Swancara, Frank. *Separation of Religion and Government; The First Amendment, Madison's Intent, and the McCollum Decision: A Study of Separationism in America*. New York, Truth Seeker, 1950. 246p. **1S634**
The author states the case for the separation of church and state under the U.S. Constitution. In a chapter on Government Censorship in Aid of Religion he cites numerous historic cases of efforts by officials to censor works on grounds of heresy or blasphemy: refusal of copyright, postal and customs restrictions, and criminal prosecution of booksellers. In a chapter on Private Censorship in Aid of Orthodoxy, he discusses the Catholic *Index Prohibitorum*, the pressures of individuals and groups for censorship of school textbooks, and the efforts to prevent booksellers from selling books and libraries from buying them.

Swann, *Sir* Michael. *Freedom and Restraint in Broadcasting: The British Experience: The "Queen's Lecture" Given by Sir Michael Swann, Chairman of the BBC in the Kongresshalle, Berlin, 29 May 1975*. London, British Broadcasting Corporation, 1975, 32p. **1S635**

Swanson, Edward. "The New Obscenity Standard." *Connecticut Law Review*, 6:165–95, Fall 1973. **1S636**
Re: *Miller v. California* (1973). Among the significant differences between the *Miller* test for obscenity and the *Memoirs* test (*A Book Named "John Cleland's Memoirs of a Woman of Pleasure" v. Attorney General of Massachusetts*, 1966) are (1) the specific affirmation of the use of local community standards, (2) the changing of "utterly without redeeming social value" to "without serious literary, artistic, political, or scientific value," and (3) sexual material has been more precisely defined as "sexual conduct specifically defined by state law."

Swartz, John L. "Fairness for Whom? Administration of the Fairness Doctrine, 1969–1970." *Boston College Industrial and Commercial Law Review*, 14: 457–70, February 1973. **1S637**
An examination of the means used by the Complaints Branch of the Federal Communications Commission Broadcast Bureau to administer the fairness doctrine. This is done by examining several FCC rulings and by taking a systematic sampling of incoming correspondence.

Sweeney, Walter H. "Regulation of Television Program Content by the Federal Communications Commission." *University of Richmond Law Review*, 8:233–44, Winter 1974. **1S638**
The telecasting of programs with excessive violence and horror during hours when a substantial number of children are in the viewing audience suggests to the author the need for greater FCC supervision of the content of television programs. "As recognized by Congress, the Courts, and the Attorney General, the FCC possesses broad regulatory power over television content, but has exercised it sparingly. Whatever the reason for its abstinence, the FCC should re-examine its policies and practices with the view of becoming a more effective instrumentality of the public interest."

Sweeny, Conor. "The Faces of Censorship." *Hibernia*, 34(5):21, 6 March 1970. **1S639**
"Once sexual taboos begin to crumble censorship is eroded along with them." An account of the increased tolerance of sexual scenes in motion pictures and television in the United States and England. While the pressure for censorship has eased in Ireland, adult films are still being cut as if intended for children while films of violence and cruelty are cleared.

Swertlow, Frank S. "The Policy." *TV Guide*, 23(46):6–9, 15 November 1975. **1S640**
Criticism of the rigid network policy of rejecting news documentaries from outside sources.

Swietnicki, Edward M. "First Amendment Conflicts Concern Social Scientists." *Editor & Publisher*, 107(1):18–19, 5 January 1974. **1S641**
A report on discussions of the mass media at the annual meeting of the Allied Social Science Associations, which represented nine economic, financial, and statistical associations.

Swihart, Dale. "The Supreme Court

and Obscenity." *Missouri Library Association*, 29:176–86, September 1968.

1S642

"The landmark case of *Roth v. United States* (354 U.S. 476), decided in 1957, still provides the basic position of the United States Supreme Court in regards to the regulation by the State and Federal governments of 'obscene' expression." The author discusses the Court's definition of obscenity and the concept of "variable obscenity" and the protection of children. He observes that the Missouri obscenity statute, passed after *Roth*, does not take that ruling into consideration and that local prosecutors have not always followed the Court's rulings in obscenity matters.

Swing, Bradford. "Libel: A Two-Tiered Constitutional Standard." *University of Miami Law Review*, 29:367–72, Winter 1975. **1S643**

Re: *Gertz v. Robert Welch, Inc.*, 94 S. Ct. 2997 (1974).

"The Swinging Pendulum—Conflict of Interest in Renewal of Broadcast Licenses." *Northwestern University Law Review*, 65:63–92, March–April 1970.

1S644

The author discusses the rights and conflicts of the present licensee and his competitors, and the role of the Federal Communications Commission in resolving these conflicts in the interest of the listening public whose interest is central to the purpose of federal regulation of the mass media.

Syllabus: The Campus Press. Amherst, Mass., Commission on the Freedom and Responsibilities of the College Student Press in America, 1970–date. Quarterly. **1S645**

This "review of the collegiate journalism scene" carries frequent articles and reports on censorship and freedom of college publications.

Sylvester, Arthur. "The Government Has the Right to Lie." *Saturday Evening Post*, 240(23):10, 14, 18 November 1967. **1S646**

The former Assistant Secretary of Defense defends the government's right to lie in the interest of national security. His comments were the subject of widespread controversy.

———, Bill Monroe, and Charles L. Gould. "The Free Press: How Free?" *Human Rights*, 3:93–124, Summer 1973. **1S647**

In a symposium at the San Francisco meeting of the Section of Individual Rights and Responsibilities of the American Bar Association,

three speakers discuss the Free Press: How Free. Arthur Sylvester, former Assistant Secretary of Defense for Public Affairs; Bill Monroe, National Broadcasting Company correspondent; and Charles L. Gould, publisher of the *San Francisco Examiner*. SYLVESTER: "Given a sound financial foundation, the press is as free as it wants to be, assuming it has the courage of a few basic convictions and a decent respect for human shortcomings, including its own." MONROE: "I submit that the First Amendment must be restored. If it is not made whole again as a guardian of the press, it will lapse into weak old age—a sad relic of the confident America of 200 years ago." GOULD: "I am concerned that the reckless abuse of the freedoms we now possess could invite the use of these harsh, restrictive constitutional safeguards [e.g., suspension of writ of habeas corpus]. Do not casually discount the possibility of such an eventuality if the revolutionary excesses continue."

Symons, Michael. "The Australian Press Council Row." *Index on Censorship*, 5(2):41–44, Summer 1976. **1S648**

A proposal for an Australian Press Council along the lines of the British Council, under consideration by the new Minister of Media, was knocked down in a barrage of outraged opposition from the press. A monopolistic press, the author charges, intentionally distorted the idea to confuse it with newspaper licensing which was not seriously considered.

"Symposium on the 1974 Amendments to the Freedom of Information Act." *American University Law Review*, 25:1–130, Fall 1975. **1S649**

Content: New Opportunities for Open Government: The 1974 Amendments to the Freedom of Information Act and the Federal Advisory Committee Act by Ralph Nader. The Sanctions Provision of the Freedom of Information Act by Robert G. Vaughn. Judicial Review of National Security Classifications by the Executive Branch After the 1974 Amendments to the Freedom of Information Act by Morton Halperin. Amended Exemption 7 [law enforcement records] of the Freedom of Information Act by Larry P. Ellsworth. Veto by Neglect: The Federal Advisory Committee Act by Barbara W. Tuerpheimer. The Personal Accountability of Public Employees by Robert G. Vaughn.

"Symposium: Openness in Government—a New Era." *Federal Bar Journal*, 34:279–366, Fall 1975. **1S650**

Foreword by Jeffrey S. Edelstein. Remarks by Bella S. Abzug. Proper Disclosure and Indecent Exposure: Protection of Trade Secrets and Confidential Commercial Information Supplied to the Government by James H. Wallace, Jr. National Security and the Public's Right to Know by Paul C. Warnke. The Government's Security Declassification Program

by William L. Brown. Privacy Legislation: Yesterday, Today, and Tomorrow by Douglas W. Metz. Remarks by Carl F. Goodman. The Privacy Act of 1974—Exceptions and Exemptions by James H. Davidson. Government Contractors; and the Initial Steps of the Privacy Act by Robert P. Bedell. Enforcing the Right of Privacy through the Privacy Act of 1974 by Hope B. Eastman. Remarks by Lewis A. Engman; Constance B. Newman. Openness in Government: Protecting the Informant's Confidential Information against Discretionary Release by Irving Scher. Government in the Sunshine by Lawton M. Chiles, Jr. Agency Reform and the Public Interest by David Cohen and Andrew Kneier. Remarks by Richard K. Berg.

Symula, James F. "Censorship and Teacher Responsibility." *English Journal*, 60:128–31, January 1971. **1S651**

The author suggests a number of practical ways in which the English teacher might take the initiative in fighting censorship: an English department newsletter to all households, creation of a book evaluation committee, conducting of a censorship seminar with interested community leaders, and, finally, involving students themselves in the book evaluation process.

———. *Censorship of High School Literature: A Study of the Incidents of Censorship Involving J. D. Salinger's "The Catcher in the Rye."* Buffalo, N.Y., State University of New York, 1969. 162p. (Ed.D. dissertation, University Microfilms, no. 69-19,035) **1S652**

Four conclusions were drawn from the study: (1) Censorship is based on ignorance. (2) In choosing literature for classroom use the English teacher has a tremendous responsibility to the student. (3) English teachers must fight against censorship. (4) There is a great need for honest reporting of the facts which surround an incident of censorship.

Szilagyi, Richard. "How Far May Newspapers Go in Criticizing?" *Cleveland-Marshall Law Review*, 17:283–98, May 1968. **1S653**

"In light of recent United States Supreme Court decisions, it appears that the courts are so zealous in protecting this freedom [freedom of the press] that they are overlooking the need to protect the individual's right against carte blanche defamation which may be injurious to his reputation, as well as to his career. . . . Steps must be taken to allow legal redress for libelous injuries before our judicial decisions completely submerge this tort."

T

Tabb, Winston. *Sources of Information on the Pornographic Issue*. Washington, D.C., Congressional Research Service, Library of Congress. 1973. 5p.   **1T1**
A selected, annotated list of books and other sources.

Tadman, Martin. "Obscenity, Civil Liberty and the Law." *Manitoba Bar News*, 38:313–24, 1972.   **1T2**
The author believes existing Canadian obscenity laws "are an unwarranted and unjustifiable muzzle placed on our fundamental right of free speech, and as such should be repealed." He favors laws prohibiting use of the mail for distribution of unsolicited erotica and the public display of obscene posters.

Taft, Robert A., II. "Prisons and the Right of the Press to Gather Information: A Review of *Pell v. Procunier* and *Saxbe v. Washington Post Co*." *University of Cincinnati Law Review*, 43:913–21, 1974.   **1T3**
"These ₁1974₁ cases involved the right of the press to conduct face-to-face interviews with designated prison inmates. This Comment will discuss the Court's interpretation of the right of the press to gather news and the ensuing implications for the underlying interest of the public in being informed about the affairs of its government."

Taft, William H. *Newspapers as Tools for Historians*. Columbia, Mo., Lucas, 1970. 138p.   **1T4**
This book, which reviews the use of newspapers in the writing of history, deals with the accuracy and reliability of the press in relation to events of the time, the factor of bias, and the so-called "credibility gap."

Talansky, Jerry. "Extension of the *New York Times* Rule in Libel Actions Arising from Matters of Public Interest." *Journal of Public Law*, 20:601–14, 1971.   **1T5**
"While the *New York Times* case ₁*New York Times Co. v. Sullivan*, 1964₁ involved a 'public official,' *Rosenbloom* ₁*Rosenbloom v. Metromedia*, 1971₁ interprets the real thrust of that landmark decision as giving effect to the first amendment function—to encourage robust debate on matters of public or general interest 'without regard to whether the persons involved are famous or anonymous.'"

Talbot, David, and Barbara Zheutlin. "The Password Is Blacklist: George C. Scott, CBS & John Henry Faulk: The Way We Really Were." *Crawdaddy*, 53:44–48, October 1975.   **1T6**
A preview of the current CBS television show, *Fear on Trial*, the dramatic story of John Henry Faulk, radio commentator during the McCarthy era who was "tarbrushed as a Red sympathizer . . . and soon afterwards, his rising career takes a nosedive. One by one, the advertising sponsors desert his radio program. Alarmed by the controversy, the broadcasting network (CBS) drops him without a word of warning; old friends avoid him; his marriage dissolves under the pressure. But he has seen the spirit of too many people crushed by the witchhunt and he resolves to take a stand for civil liberties. He solicits the help of celebrated attorney Louis Nizer, and files suit against the anti-communist organization which defamed him. After years of legal battling, he triumphs. In a decision which marks the demise of the blacklist, a jury awards him the largest libel judgment in history." CBS, after eighteen years, airs the true story of the event, including a frank exposé of their own complicity. The authors interview actor George Scott, who played the part of Nizer, and a number of CBS officials who figured in the original event.

Talmage, T. De Witt. "Immoral Literature." In his *Social Dynamite; or, the Wickedness of Modern Society*. Chicago, Standard Publishing Co., 1889, pp. 171–81.   **1T7**
A noted pulpit orator attacks evil books and their influence, particularly on the young. "Cursed be the books that try to make impurity decent, and crime attractive, and hypocrisy noble. Cursed be the books that swarm with libertines and desperadoes, who make the brain of the young people whirl with villainy. . . . Ye authors who write them ₁bad books₁, ye publishers who print them, ye booksellers who distribute them, shall be cut to pieces, if not by an aroused community, then, at last by the hail of divine vengeance, which shall sweep to the lowest pit of perdition all ye murderers of souls." If there is anything in your library that is evil, the author exhorts, "do not give it away, for it might spoil an immortal soul, do not sell it for the money you get would be the price of blood; but rather kindle a fire on your kitchen hearth, or in your back yard, and then drop the poison in it, and keep stirring the blaze until from preface to appendix there shall not be a single paragraph left." In the author's *The Masque Torn Off* (1887) he writes of impure literature as "the first gate of hell" (pp. 60–62) and agonizes over the "baneful literature" at popular watering places (pp. 178–79).

Tamblyn, Eldon W. *Censorship in North Carolina Public Libraries*. Chapel Hill, N.C., University of North Carolina, 1964. 154p. (Unpublished Master's thesis)   **1T8**

Tannenbaum, Percy H. "Emotional Arousal as a Mediator of Erotic Communication Effects." *Technical Report of the ₁U.S.₁ Commission on Obscenity and Pornography*, 8:326–56, 1971.   **1T9**
"This paper reports on research stemming from a theoretical model with a somewhat different focus—that many dramatic communications (such as erotic messages, which are of direct concern to us here) evoke varying degrees of general emotional arousal, and that it is the level of such nonspecific (to any one emotional state) arousal, more than the specific content of the message, that determines the degree of subsequent behavior."

Tanner, Eric. "The First Amendment Due Process and the University." *U.M.K.C. Law Review*, 42:390–95, Spring 1974.   **1T10**
Re: *Papish v. Board of Curators of the University of Missouri*, 410 U.S. 667 (1973), in which the U.S. Supreme Court reversed a lower court

ruling which had upheld the University in expelling a student for "obscene" matter in an undergraduate newspaper.

Tans, Mary D., and Steven H. Chaffee. "Pretrial Publicity and Juror Prejudice." *Journalism Quarterly*, 43:647–54, Winter 1966. **1T11**
"Experiment shows potential jurors do prejudge guilt on the basis of news stories, especially if a confession is reported. And the more information provided, the more willing they are to make such a judgment."

Tarnopolsky, Walter S. "Freedom of Expression v. Right to Equal Treatment; the Problem of Hate Propaganda and Racial Discrimination." *University of British Columbia Law Review*, Centennial edition: 43–68, 1967. **1T12**
"It is proposed to refer briefly to the events associated with the appointment of the Cohen Commission [Special Committee on Hate Propaganda in Canada], to summarize the findings of the Committee, to analyze its recommendations as well as the terms of Bill S-49, and finally to come to some conclusions as to whether the legitimate demands of minority groups for the protection of their dignity and right to equal treatment can best be served by legislation restricting 'hate propaganda,' and if so, whether the proposed text should be adopted."

Tarr, Joel A. "A Historian and the Federal Government." *Pacific Historical Review*, 38:329–35, August 1969. **1T13**
The difficulties of a historian attempting to use bank examiners' reports in the National Archives, suggests the need to modify the existing statutory situation regarding the availability of archival material.

Taubenhaus, Marsha. "Time, Inc. v. Firestone: Sowing the Seeds of Gertz." *Brooklyn Law Review*, 43:123–46, Summer 1976. **1T14**
An examination of the U.S. Supreme Court decision in *Time, Inc. v. Firestone*, 1976, "indicates that the Burger Court will locate the fulcrum between the freedoms of speech and press and the law of defamation closer to that end of the sliding scale favoring reputational interests than did the Warren Court before it. Although Supreme Court Justices may be dedicated to effecting a workable compromise, in fact, after *Gertz* and *Firestone*, they may find that, despite the best of intentions, they have obliterated the line between media circumspection and censorship."

Tauro, G. Joseph. "Fair Trial–Free Press Revisited." *American Bar Association Journal*, 55:417–19, May 1969. **1T15**
"Far from applying stricter bonds to the news media, the American Bar Association's Standards Relating to Fair Trial and Free Press will

serve to ameliorate the potential of the contempt power by adding the requirement that the publication alleged to be in contempt must be made with a willful intent. The news media should recognize that the standards are a reasonable base on which to balance the rights of fair trial and free press. If flagrant abuses are continued, more stringent measures may result."—Editor

Taylor, Arthur R. "Dangers in Our Midst." *TV Quarterly*, 11(3):54–59, Spring 1974. **1T16**
Some of the dangers seen by the president of Columbia Broadcasting System are: antitrust suits against the networks, trial balloons from FCC suggesting an inquiry into barring networks from producing entertainment programs, FCC's attempt to encourage diversity by restricting primetime access, proposals by FCC for percentage programming requirements for license renewals, Congressional proposals for compulsory allocation of air time for political candidates, FCC discriminatory protection of pay cable television, the Justice Department's urging of the FCC to challenge license renewals of television stations owned by newspapers, and subpoenas and contempt citations against newsmen and news organizations.

Taylor, Daniel B. "Books in the Schools: The Adoption Controversy; The Hazards of Selecting Textbooks." *Publishers' Weekly*, 208(15):32–33, 13 October 1975. **1T17**
In light of the recent controversy over school textbooks in West Virginia, the State Superintendent of Schools looks at the broader question: Who has responsibility for selecting textbooks? In addition to the professional educator, whose role is indispensible, there is room for lay citizens and parent assistance in textbook adoption procedures. Whether this can be accomplished without censorship and controversy is an unanswered question.

Taylor, H. A. "Morals and Myths." In his *Jix: Viscount Brentford* . . . . London, Stanley Paul, 1933, pp. 242–50. **1T18**
A chapter on censorship in this biography of William Joynson-Hicks, who, in his capacity as Home Secretary, was required to perform as British literary censor. "In no single instance did Joynson-Hicks himself act as censor. . . . The Home Secretary is little more than a channel of communication with the Director of Public Prosecutions, with whom it rests to decide whether the case is to be taken to Court."

Taylor, Hannis. *The Freedom of the Press. . . . In the Supreme Court of the United States. Ex Parte in the Matter of John L. Rapier, Publisher of the Mobile Daily and Weekly Register. Argument of Hannis Taylor Upon a Petition for Writs of Habeas Corpus and Certiorari, against the Constitutionality of the Recent Act of Con-*

gress Generally Known as the Anti-Lottery Law. [Mobile, Ala., The Petitioner (Rapier), 1891?] 48p. **1T19**
The brief argues the unconstitutionality of the federal law which prohibits sending through the U.S. mails any matter containing advertising of lottery. According to the brief the law violates the First Amendment by requiring a government imprimatur. "No new restraint upon the freedom of the press, which did not exist at the date of the First Amendment can be imposed by subsequent legislation."

Taylor, John. *The Whole Life and Progresse of Henry Walker the Ironmonger. First, the Manner of his Conversation. Secondly, the severall offenses and Scandalons [sic] Pampehlets [sic] the said Walker hath writ, and for which he is now a Prisoner in New Gate. Thirdly, the forme of the Indictment which is laid against him, by the Kings Sergeants at Law, and his learned Counsell. Fourthly, His Conviction by the Jury. Fifthly, His Recantation, and sorrow for the publicke wrong he hath done his Majesty and the whole Kingdome*. London, 1642. 8p. **1T20**
Walker was an ironmonger turned publisher. He produced some 300 titles in copies of 100 or 200—"such things as he supposed would vent or be saleable . . . that tended to rend or shake the piece of either Church or State." He employed itinerant booksellers ("mercuries" or "hawkers"). Legitimate booksellers complained that he paid no taxes. Walker was arrested once for selling offensive printed matter but was released by the magistrate when he agreed to return to ironmongering. Shortly thereafter, when the king came to London to dine, Walker, back to his old tricks, showered the king's coach with a batch of mischievous tracts—a petition based on biblical verse (Kings 12:16). Walker was arrested and jailed awaiting trial. On the way to court he was rescued by "a rabble" and eluded capture for some weeks, part of the time disguised as a priest. (A man of talents, he even conducted services at St. Mary Magdeline, Southwark.) The king was offended by Walker's insolence and sent two messages to Parliament on the suppression of libelous pamphlets. Walker was finally captured and taken to the Tower. He was convicted of writing, composing, and publishing a libel on the king. He readily admitted his guilt and begged the king's mercy. Surprisingly, the king recommended that Walker's act be considered a misdemeanor rather than treason. The pamphlet was published before the sentencing, so we do not know the fate of the ironmonger cum printer. One witness against Walker testified that Walker did not have "any word of God in his Shop above the bulk or size of a Horne-booke."

Taylor, Mark. "Censorship or Pornog-

raphy?" *Commonweal*, 99:260–64, 7 December 1973. **1T21**
"The main enemy of freedom of expression is not censorship but pornography. . . . Resistance to pornography is one important part of a hard battle for the survival of the human imagination, where freedom of expression begins and ends. . . . It is when joined to the imagination that sexuality becomes human, becomes more than the coupling of beasts—becomes, sometimes, an act of love."

Taylor, Richard C. *The Newsman's Privilege to Refuse to Disclose His Source of Information: An Analysis of Newsman's Privilege Statutes and Case Law*. Washington, D.C., American University, 1969. 307p. (Unpublished Master's thesis) **1T22**
"The existence of a newsman's legal privilege of source non-disclosure can most accurately be assessed through comparative analytical study of applicable shield statutes and reported cases. This thesis reports the findings of such a study."

Taylor, Telford. "Press and Prejudice: The Impact of News on Justice." *Proceedings of the American Philosophical Society*, 112:121–25, 15 April 1968. **1T23**
A review of the issues, historically and currently, between press and bar over pretrial publicity. "I suppose that if there is any consensus at all in the current state of professional thinking, it is that there should be administrative restrictions on the police, possibly backed by legal sanctions of some kind, and that the court and bar associations should seriously apply to the members of the bar the canons and other provisions which prevent disclosures which would be prejudicial to the conduct of trials." But since the press would still be free to print, the use of reporter wiles and anonymous attribution might defeat the purpose. Taylor cites the favorable experience with the New Jersey Supreme Court rules. "It seems to me that we must preserve the benefits of a curious and irreverent press which is not overly impressed by wigs and robes; that we must cut down the rough edges of publicity in ways which the decision in New Jersey and other comparable steps may do; and we must try to improve overall judicial administration so that these problems will not arise so frequently."

———. *Two Studies in Constitutional Interpretation*. Columbus, Ohio, Ohio State University Press, 1969. 225p. **1T24**
The first study, dealing with search, seizure and surveillance, traces the legal history of search and seizure from its use in Britain and Colonial America to reveal seditious publications to present-day interpretations by the U.S. Supreme Court. The second study, deal-ing with fair trial and free press, gives historical background in the conflict between the First and Sixth Amendments and reports on what is actually being done to resolve the issue.

Taylor, Wallace L. "The Status of Iowa's Obscenity Laws." *Drake Law Review*, 21:314–30, January 1972. **1T25**
"The purpose of this Note is to examine Iowa's obscenity statutes in light of the constitutional mandates imposed by the Supreme Court, and to explain the present law governing the regulation of obscenity."

Teach, William, *ed*. *Kiss, Screw, Pleasure and Sex*. San Diego, Calif., Greenleaf Classics, 1969. 158p. **1T26**
"A scholarly documentation of a new field of journalism that dares to treat sex with unprecedented candor. The title is derived from the names of three notable New York publications, sold currently at newsstands: *Kiss, Screw*, and *Pleasure*."

Teague, Bernard G. "Defamation: A Plea for Bold Reforms." *Law Institute Journal* (Melbourne), 47:254–57, July 1973. **1T27**
The author reviews the present concern with reform of the libel laws in Britain and Canada. "Can the Victorian Press be judged on present performances and the experience of the past 40 years, as sufficiently responsible to be permitted freedom akin to that permitted in the United States? If so, the gain to the public in being fully informed and therefore less likely to be duped will far outweigh the loss to the few individuals who in the process may be the subject of false imputations to their discredit."

Tebbel, John. *The Media in America*. New York, Crowell, 1975. 407p. **1T28**
A comprehensive history of the communications media in America—newspapers, books, magazines, and broadcasting—from the first Colonial press in Cambridge, Mass., in 1638 to the investigative reporting of Watergate. "His dominant theme is the struggle to define the idea of a free press and then to make the idea a reality. He shows how the early presses in the colonies gradually emerged from strict governmental regulation only to become propaganda organs of political parties. Not until the nineteenth century, under such editors as Horace Greeley of the *Tribune* and Henry Raymond of the *Times*, did the concept of a fair and accurate press, as well as a free one, begin to blossom." In a final chapter the author denounces the Nixon Administration critics of the press and the "new journalists," both of whom have lost sight of the idea of a free press and the people's right to know.

———. "The Prospect Before Us." *Saturday Review*, 52(17):19–22, 26 April 1969. **1T29**
"We have reached the point in the development of television where the private monopoly in programming enjoyed by the networks has come into direct conflict with the public inter-est on a number of fronts." The article considers this area of controversy and the kind of broadcasting pattern that is likely to emerge.

———. "What's Happening to the Underground Press?" *Saturday Review*, 54(46):89–90, 13 November 1971. **1T30**
Following an examination of the underground (alternate) press of the 1960s, the author concludes that this genre may change in size, content and even tone, but it will survive. "And that is a good thing, because the diversity of the press in a democracy is one of the best guarantees of the system's good health."

———. "Who Owns Television?" *Saturday Review*, 52(19):75–76, 10 May 1969. **1T31**
Criticism, organized and unorganized, of television raises questions about the role of government in controlling broadcasting content. "The time has come for both the public and the private sectors to think seriously about the purpose of TV, about the ownership of the air, about the First Amendment in its relation to broadcasting. Television is a medium so important to the political and cultural life of America that it cannot be left in the hands of a few entrepreneurs or politicians to decide its ultimate fate."

Tedford, Thomas L. *Freedom of Speech: A Selected Annotated Basic Bibliography*. New York, Speech Communications Module, ERIC Clearinghouse on Reading and Communication Skills, 1974. 13p. **1T32**
Books on freedom of speech are arranged by historical studies, First Amendment "classics," anthologies, paperback "texts," and studies on particular topics.

———. "Freedom of Speech: The Students' Right to Read (and Speak): Sources for Help in Formulating Policy." *English Journal*, 63(9):14–16, December 1974. **1T33**
Includes text of the Credo for Free and Responsible Communication of the Speech Communication Association, resolutions on censorship adopted by the American Theatre Association, references to the Library Bill of Rights, and statements of the Association of University Professors and the American Civil Liberties Union.

———. "Freedom of Speech: What Every Teacher Should Know About the Supreme Court Obscenity Decisions." *English Journal*, 63(7):20–21, October 1974. **1T34**
The author asserts that the U.S. Supreme Court "(1) Has never held that 'obscenity' presents a clear-and-present-danger to society. (2) In its 1973 decisions made it easier to successfully prosecute the artist-communicator by asserting that only 'serious' materials are protected by the Constitution, and that explicit

sexual materials accused of being 'obscene' are guilty until proven innocent. (3) Admits that no conclusive scientific proof exists to support censorship. (4) Says that it is legal for a state to have no censorship regulations, or no censorship for consenting adults; it is legal to provide procedural safeguards such as a mandatory hearing followed by fair warning prior to an arrest; it is permissible to provide special protection to parents, teachers, librarians, etc."

————. "Teaching Freedom of Speech through the Use of Common Materials." *Speech Teacher*, 16:269–70, November 1967. (Symposium on Using Common Materials, III)   **1T35**
"While teaching at Appalachian State Teachers College the writer assigned his class in group discussion the following question of policy for study throughout the course: What restrictions, if any, should be placed on freedom of speech? The teaching of the theory and practice of group discussion through the use of a single question on freedom of speech enabled the students to master group methods and to learn appreciation for freedom of speech."

Teeter, Dwight L. *Legacy of Expression: Philadelphia Newspapers and Congress During the War for Independence, 1775–1783.* Madison, Wis., University of Wisconsin, 1966. 349p. (Ph.D. dissertation, University Microfilms, no. 66–9975)   **1T36**
"The study describes economic and political controls exerted by the Continental Congress over Philadelphia's English-language newspapers during the War for Independence. Congress, along with the government of Pennsylvania, was a major source of revenue for Philadelphia's printers from 1775 to 1783, and did, from time to time, attempt to control the newspapers. However, attempts to control the actions of independent-minded and sometimes unruly printers were not often successful. . . . The freedom which Philadelphia's newspapers enjoyed appears to have been based largely upon factional divisions in Pennsylvania and in Congress. These contending factions turned repeatedly to the newspapers to air their arguments, and printed statements deplored by one faction were often defended by another. In Philadelphia during the War for Independence, 'freedom of the press' in practice meant simply the right to publish what a printer wished the public to see, including criticisms of government. Given the Quakers and Tories in exception, this crude standard amounted to a legacy of expression."

————. "The Printer and the Chief Justice: Seditious Libel in 1782–83." *Journalism Quarterly*, 45:235–42, 260, Summer 1968.   **1T37**
Criticism of Pennsylvania's Chief Justice Thomas McKean in the Philadelphia *Independent Gazetteer* led to attempts to punish printer Eleazer Oswald for seditious libel. "The prosecution was ultimately thwarted by a balky grand jury, but only after the *Gazetteer* had

published many columns complaining about the use of 'the English doctrine of libels' in America. These arguments, published late in 1782 and early in 1783, prefaced the development of a home-grown American theory of press freedom."

————. *The Supreme Court and Obscene Literature.* Berkeley, Calif., University of California, 1959. 66p. (Unpublished Master's thesis)   **1T38**

————, and Don R. Pember. "Obscenity, 1971: The Rejuvenation of State Power and the Return to *Roth*." *Villanova Law Review*, 17:211–45, December 1971.   **1T39**
In this article the authors attempt to answer whether the U.S. Supreme Court is moving in a new direction or merely returning to some of its earlier standards. "By outlining the several developmental stages in which the law has moved since 1957, and by viewing more recent Supreme Court decisions in that context, it is hoped that a pattern will emerge from which conclusions may be drawn as to the state of the law of obscenity. To those ends, it may be seen that the development of the law of obscenity has, to date, passed through five distinct stages." These stages are conceived as: defining obscenity, controlling conduct, concepts of "overbreadth" and "private possession," back to the states, and reemphasizing *Roth*. The article is divided into sections which follow this five-stage development.

————. "The Retreat from Obscenity: *Redrup v. New York*." *Hastings Law Journal*, 21:175–89, November 1969.   **1T40**
"The purpose of this article is to discuss briefly the rather confusing tangle of obscenity cases prior to *Redrup* [*Redrup v. New York*, 1967] and then to describe the Supreme Court's use of the *Redrup* language to redefine and clarify this area of the law."

Teeters, Negley K. *Censorship as a Control Device Regulating Sex Behavior.* Columbus, Ohio State University, 1931. 180p. (Unpublished Ph.D. dissertation)   **1T41**
Following a discussion of the anthropological origin of sex censorship, the types imposed, and the early history of censorship, the author proposes a rational program of control over sexual expression in literature, art, and the cinema. It consists of restricting children from certain movies, controlling most objectionable features of sex from public gaze, and a program of sex education. The proposal closely resembles the recommendations of the U.S. Commission on Obscenity and Pornography made some forty years later.

"Televised Presidential Addresses and the FCC's Fairness Doctrine." *Columbia Journal of Law and Social Problems*, 7:75–106, Winter 1971.   **1T42**

"After briefly analyzing the various components of Presidential access to television, and contrasting it to the access available to those representing different political viewpoints, the FCC's current positions on the question of fair coverage are discussed. Finally, alternative proposals are put forth."

"Television Counteradvertising: 'And Now a Word Against Our Sponsor . . .'" *Rutgers-Camden Law Journal*, 3:516–32, Spring 1972.   **1T43**
The author suggests that the consumer interest in accurate product information may be achieved by counteradvertising, which allows public interest groups to combat the effects of product misinformation. "The evolution of the fairness doctrine [in broadcasting] has created a right of access to the media for counteradvertising. . . . Licensee and advertiser fears of the adverse effect of counteradvertising should not deter its immediate implementation."

Templin, Don C. "Newspaper Publicity of Criminal News in Oklahoma." *Oklahoma Law Review*, 22:180–96, May 1969.   **1T44**
A survey of the amount and types of pretrial and trial publicity of criminal cases in Oklahoma reveals that "neither the Oklahoma Accords nor the Reardon Report have affected the criminal news situation very significantly in Oklahoma. Those groups that released or published possibly prejudicial information before the reports do so now and those with prior restrictive policies have continued with them."

Teplitzky, Sanford V., and Kenneth A. Weiss. "Newsmen's Privilege Two Years After Branzburg v. Hayes: The First Amendment in Jeopardy." *Tulane Law Review*, 49:417–38, January 1975.   **1T45**
"Since *Branzburg* was decided by the Supreme Court more than two years ago, there have been several attempts to enact a newsmen's privilege statute on the federal level, but proposed legislation died in committees of both houses of Congress at the end of the 93d session." Future legislation must direct itself to such questions as: Which workers of the press would qualify? What proceedings should be covered? What type of information ought to be protected? Should there be specific exemptions to the privilege? Should the legislation apply to state as well as federal proceedings?

terHorst, J. F. "Government and a Free Press." *Current*, 170:26–29, February 1975.   **1T46**
"The press is constitutionally required to live in a kind of no man's land, subject to constant criticism of both government and public and loved by neither." This concept of a free press

as an adversary should be more understood by government, public, and media.

"Term Paper Companies and the Constitution." *Duke Law Journal*, 1973:1275–1317, January 1973. **1T47**
The article deals with the legal problems associated with efforts of state legislatures to curtail the activities of companies selling term papers to college students. The author concludes that: "It is not only unlawful but unnecessary to curtail first amendment freedoms in order to control a problem capable of being resolved by colleges and universities themselves."

Terp, Thomas T. "Federal Communications Commission Fairness Doctrine—Applicability to Commercial Advertising." *William and Mary Law Review*, 13:519–24, Winter 1971. **1T48**
Re: *Friends of the Earth v. FCC*, 449 F.2d 1164 (D.C. 1971).

Terry, Bernis J. "The Effect of Recent Obscenity Cases." *Washburn Law Journal*, 13:26–32, Winter 1974. **1T49**
"The decisions in *Miller v. California* 93 S. Ct. 2607 (1973), and several companion cases mark a significant change by the Supreme Court in its efforts to deal with the obscenity issue. These cases reject the former standard that before material allegedly obscene can be regulated it must be found to be utterly without redeeming social value. They also hold contemporary community standards and not national standards are to be applied to determine whether material is obscene." The author concludes that Kansas is "left in the anomalous position of having a more liberal obscenity statute than is constitutionally required by *Miller*."

Tessier, André. "L'Obscénité, Sujet Controversé en Droit Criminel." *Revue du Barreau* (Quebec), 26:671–75, December 1966. **1T50**
Recommendations for changes in the obscenity section of the Canadian Civil Code.

Texas Library Association. Intellectual Freedom Committee. *Intellectual Freedom Handbook*. Houston, The Association, 1972. 17p. **1T51**
Content: Texas Library Association Intellectual Freedom Statement. Library Bill of Rights. Free Access to Libraries for Minors. How Libraries Can Resist Censorship. Nonremoval of Challenged Library Materials. Statement on Labeling. Policy on Confidentiality of Library Records. School Library Bill of Rights. Freedom to Read Statement. Librarians' Form—Request for Advice and Assistance (from Texas Library Association).

Citizen's Form—Request for Reconsideration of Library Material.

"Textbook Battles: They's Brewing and Bubbling . . . ." *American School Board Journal*, 162(7):21–28, July 1975. **1T52**
"If you think the 1974–75 school year was scarred by a rash of textbook controversies, just wait until this fall. That is plainly the admonition of the many veteran school board members, administrators, civil libertarians and censorship advocates from the U.S. and Canada who were interviewed for this article."

Thelwall, John. *The Tribune; A Periodical Publication. Consisting Chiefly of the Political Lectures of J. Thelwall . . . .* London, Printed for the Author, 1795–96. 3 vols. **1T53**
In addition to extracts from the author's suppressed *Political Lectures* (T68), the volumes contain accounts of Thelwall's trial for seditious libel and documents relating thereto: Narrative of the Proceedings of the Messenger, &c. on the Seizure of J. Thelwall's papers, with his Examination before the Privy Council, Treatment of the Messengers, &c. (vol. 1, pp. 85–96, 301–28). To the Right Honourable William Pitt, Henry Dundas, William Wyndham, and Thomas, Lord Grenville; to Sir John Scott, Sir John Mitford, and the Majority of the Two Houses of Parliament, who, Deluded by the Misrepresentations of Government Reporters, Voted in Favor of the Bill for Suppressing These Lectures (vol. 3, pp. i–v). A Civic Oration in Commemoration of the Acquittal of Thomas Hardy . . . (pp. 201–20). A Civic Oration in Commemoration of the Acquittal of John Horne Tooke . . . (pp. 221–38). Civic Oration on the Anniversary of the Acquittal of the Lecturer, Being a Vindication of the Principles, and a Review of the Conduct that placed him at the Bar of the Old Bailey (pp. 239–62). The First Lecture on the Political Prostitution of our Public Theatres . . . (pp. 279–98).

Thirkill, Clive E. *The History and Development of Obscenity Law*. Provo, Utah, Brigham Young University, 1971. 120p. (Unpublished Master's thesis) **1T54**
"The study concludes that the judgment of the [Supreme] Court in the case of *Roth v. United States* is the only law of the land defining obscenity in the judgment of cases involving *general* prohibitions against pornographic materials."

Thody, P. M. W. *Four Cases of Literary Censorship*. Leeds, England, Leeds University Press, 1968. 26p. **1T55**
The lecturer discusses the 1857 Parisian censorship of Gustave Flaubert's *Madame Bovary* and Charles Baudelaire's *Les Fleurs de Mal*, comparing and contrasting these cases with action against Jean Genêt's works and the 1959 case against *Lady Chatterley's Lover* in England. "Literary censorship, though ostensibly limited in our society to ensuring that certain decencies be observed in literary discussion of sexual matter, can be used to give expression to the views which certain members of society hold on a wide variety of topics which are not necessarily related to sex or literature." This inaugural lecture was delivered before the University of Leeds on 27 November 1967.

Thomas, D. S. "Prosecutions of *Sodom: Or, the Quintessence of Debauchery*, and *Poems on Several Occasions by the E of R*, 1689–1690 and 1693." *Library*, 24:51–55, March 1969. **1T56**
A discussion of the unpublished case of *Rex v. Hill*, involving obscenity charges against printer Hill (possibly Henry Hills, Jr.) in 1698 for publishing the poems of the Earl of Rochester. The case was the first prosecution in the Court of King's Bench for obscene libel. The defendant fled so that the outcome was inconclusive. In 1708 in the case against James Read, the Court found obscenity to be the prerogative of the ecclesiastical courts; and in 1725–28, in the case of Edmund Curll, that obscene libel was, in fact, a crime to be dealt with by the state.

Thomas, Donald. "Fat Men on Thin Ice." *Studio*, 175:224–30, April 1968. **1T57**
Account of the rise of the political satirist in eighteenth-century England who attacked his enemies through caricatures. A certain amount of tolerance was exhibited by authorities for fear prosecution might subject the politician to ridicule, and by a realization that under a two-party system the "ins" would eventually become the "outs" and the same caricature device would be available to them. A vigilante group was formed to take action against political satire—the Constitutional Association, headed by Dr. John Stoddart (known to his enemies as Dr. Slop). This "Bridge-street banditti," took action against publishers William Benbow and Mary Anne Carlile. William Hone was among the most prominent publishers of satirical cartoons, and he was brought to trial on three occasions, but acquitted in each. In January 1941 the *Daily Worker* was suspended for its cartoon, Their Gallant Allies, which allegedly violated national defense regulations. Thomas's article is illustrated with eighteenth-century caricatures.

———. *A Long Time Burning: The History of Literary Censorship in England*. London, Routledge & Kegan Paul, 1969. 546p. **1T58**
"The present study is an account of the political, religious and moral censorship of literature, in the context of English literary history. It is principally concerned with the evolution of a modern pattern of censorship between the abolition of licensing in 1695 and the late Victorian period." Content: The Fear of Literature. Censorship before Publication: 1476–1695. Enemies of the State: 1695–1760. Blasphemy in an Age of Reason. Obscene Libel and the Reformation of Manners. Liberty versus Licentiousness: 1760–1792 (including the

Wilkes affair and Parliament and the press). Guardians of Public Morality (The Proclamation Society). Political Censorship: A Fight to the Finish, 1792–1832. Guardians of Public Morality (The Society for the Suppression of Vice). Victoria: Politics and Blasphemy. Victoria: Sex. The Twentiety Century: "Plus Ça Change . . . ."

————. "*My Secret Life:* The Trial at Leeds." *Victorian Studies*, 12:448–51, June 1969. **1T59**
The trial of Arthur Dobson at Leeds assizes for publication of *My Secret Life*.

————. "*Ulysses* and the Attorney-General, 1936." *Library*, 5th ser. 24:343–45, December 1969. **1T60**
An account of the decision of the Attorney General and Director of Public Prosecutions to allow James Joyce's *Ulysses* free circulation in Great Britain.

————, *ed. State Trials.* London, Routledge & Kegan Paul, 1972. 2 vols. **1T61**
Includes accounts of the following trials dealing with libel: John Bastwick, Henry Burton, and William Prynne (1637); Richard Baxter (1685); Edmund Curll (1727); Henry Sampson Woodfall (1770); John Horne (1777): John Hatchard (1817). The text from Howell's *State Trials* plus introductory comment by Thomas.

Thomas, Geoffrey L. "The Listener's Right to Hear in Broadcasting." *Stanford Law Review*, 22:863–902, April 1970. **1T62**
"The thesis of this Note is that despite the Supreme Court's encouragement in *Red Lion* [*Red Lion Broadcasting Co. v. FCC* (1967)], it will be extremely difficult for listeners to force broadcasters or the FCC to fashion an adequate regulatory remedy, giving the present advertiser-dominated nature of the industry. Only by converting the economic structure of the industry from over-the-air television broadcasting to cable television (CATV) on a common-carrier basis can the listeners exercise their right to hear with minimal interference from advertisers, broadcasters, or the Government."

Thomas, Howard. "Taste or Taboos." *Journal of the Society of Film and Television Arts*, 43/44:12–14, Spring–Summer 1971. **1T63**
The managing director of Thames Television Ltd. describes the actual working of program controls. "There is a responsibility on the television producer to be aware of the changing audience he is serving at varying times of the day, and he cannot willfully expose to susceptible people of all ages, scenes of violence and permissiveness, or language unfamiliar and embarrassing in the home." He contrasts television with the theater and cinema, where the audience seeks out the particular performance.

Thomas, Isaiah. [“Liberty of the Press.”] *Massachusetts Gazette*, 237:1, 24 April 1786. **1T64**
In a letter to the editor of the *Gazette*, the publisher of the *Massachusetts Spy* announces his decision to discontinue publication of his paper because of the new Massachusetts tax on newspaper advertisements. He charges that the law is a violation of the liberty of the press as guaranteed in the Massachusetts Bill of Rights. "The tax on News-Paper Advertisements has a direct tendency not only to restrain, but to destroy, those necessary vehicles of publick information, by taking away their only support . . . ." To replace the *Spy*, Thomas indicates he will start a monthly "pamphlet" entitled the *Worcester Magazine* since "magazines" are not subject to the tax. The same issue reprints a letter from A Loyal Republican, defending the tax on newspapers and condemning Thomas's subterfuge. "I always thought that the constitution, in asserting that 'the liberty of the press is essential to the security of freedom in a State, and ought not therefore to be restrained in this Commonwealth' intended to guard the freedom of our citizens; but not to give an exclusive right to any set of men to exempt themselves from burthens which fall generally on most branches of business in the community." In the 15 May issue of the *Gazette*, Impartialitas comes to the support of Isaiah Thomas and calls for the repeal of the newspaper tax.

[Thomas, Lowell S., Jr.] "Federal Communications Commission: Control of 'Deceptive Programming.'" *University of Pennsylvania Law Review*, 108:868–93, April 1960. **1T65**
"The purpose of this Note is to inquire into the nature of the revealed broadcasting practices, into the propriety of their regulation, and into some of the problems which may be encountered in pursuing the alternative regulatory methods suggested."

Thomas, P. W. *Sir John Berkenhead, 1617–79: A Royalist Career in Politics and Polemics.* London, Oxford University Press, 1969. 298p. **1T66**
A biography of the Royalist editor and satirist who, along with Roger L'Estrange, served as Restoration censor. Chapter 6, "No man must print or write Books," deals with press restrictions on Royalist publishing during the Commonwealth; chapter 7, "Commented upon by Sir Jo. Berkenhead," is an account of his work as Restoration censor and propagandist.

[Thomas, William.] *The Enemies of the Constitution Discovered, or, an Inquiry into the Origin and Tendency of Popular Violence. Containing . . . the Dispersion of the State Anti-Slavery Convention by the Agitators, the Destruction of a Democratic Press, and of the Causes Which Led Thereto . . . By Defensor.* New York, Leavitt, Lord, 1835. 183p. **1T67**
The first portion of the volume deals with (1) condemnation of Postmaster General Amos

Kendall for permitting the seizure and destruction of antislavery publications by Southern postmasters (and the New York postmaster), thus serving as censors of the press, and (2) an account of a Cincinnati Bible salesman, arrested in Nashville, Tenn., for possessing and selling abolitionist literature and tried by a Committee of Vigilance and sentenced to twenty lashes and expulsion. Copies of the letters of Postmaster General Kendall to the Charleston and New York postmasters, authorizing censorship, are given in the appendix.

Thomason, Tommy G. *Arkansas' Freedom of Information Act; A Landmark in American Access Legislation.* Commerce, Tex., East Texas State University, 1972. 61p. (Unpublished Master's thesis) **1T68**
"Arkansas' 1967 Freedom of Information Act has been hailed as one of the broadest and strongest pieces of state access legislation. The purpose of this study was to document the history of the Arkansas Act and assess its present effectiveness. The study reviews earlier Arkansas access legislation, the conditions which caused Arkansas journalists to push for a new freedom of information law, and the events surrounding the passage of that law."

Thompson, Anthony H. *Censorship in Public Libraries in the United Kingdom During the Twentieth Century.* New York, Bowker, 1976. 236p. **1T69**
A study of public library censorship in Britain, arranged chronologically, with numerous cases cited. The author considers censorship by local public libraries widespread, with the vast majority of cases of attempted suppression resulting from action of council members. Efforts at censorship have also come from individual readers, organized groups, and from librarians themselves who refuse to purchase books, limit the number of copies, or restrict their circulation. Sex is the first offender, with politics second, and religion a distant third. The author notes that the censor generally claims altruistic motives, that there is confusion between erotic literature and pornography, and that local censorship in the realm of sex "may be regarded as contrary to the intentions of the Obscene Publications Act 1959."

Thompson, Charles A. H. "The New York Times Versus the United States Government." *World Affairs*, 134: 243–56, Winter 1971. **1T70**
The author considers the moral positions of the press and government in releasing or withholding publication of the Pentagon Papers, and their future relationship. "Both press and government need to improve practices for promptness of disclosure and, far more important, for the full and fair interpretation of the

meaning of facts, whether embodied in classified documents or not." The press "must accept and should acknowledge its own share of responsibility for protecting official secrets." He suggests an impartial board to advise in matters of classified information. "Both press and government need to consider the extent to which they can improve their moral position—and their consequent influence—by closer adherence to simple standards of truth-telling."

Thompson, Fred. *Right-Wing Censorship of Books*. Columbia, Mo., Freedom of Information Center, School of Journalism, University of Missouri at Columbia, 1968. 6p. (Report no. 194) **1T71**
"This paper discusses the tactics of right-wing pressure groups in their efforts to control the books used in schools and available in bookstores and libraries. A special emphasis is given to the well-organized efforts of the Daughters of the American Revolution, Texans for America, and America's Future. . . . The paper also includes a discussion of the criticism made by counter-protest groups and individuals."

———. *Textbooks and Racial Pressure Groups*. Columbia, Mo., Freedom of Information Center, School of Journalism, University of Missouri at Columbia, 1968. 8p. (Report no. 195) **1T72**
"During the first half of the 20th century, Negro pressure groups were involved principally in obtaining civil and economic rights. It was not until after the Supreme Court decision of 1954 that they and other groups became concerned about the 'integrated textbook.' Whether by coercion, law or sympathy to the cause, more and more publishers have produced books which depict the Negro as playing an active and important part in society."

Thompson, John. "Pornography and Propaganda." *Commentary*, 48:54–57, August 1969. (Reprinted in Michael C. Emery and Ted C. Smythe, *eds.*, *Readings in Mass Communications*, pp. 426–33) **1T73**
Commentary on the nature of current pornographic fiction published by Maurice Girodias, the porn shops, who buys the dirty books, and for what reasons. "It is difficult to imagine them doing any harm unless you believe that masturbation is harmful." *Barbara* by Frank Newman is singled out for special comment as an example of the genre of sexual-political fantasy.

[Thompson, T. Perronet.] "Taxes on Literature: The Six Acts." *Westminster Review*, 12:416–29, April 1830. (Re-

printed as a separate pamphlet by William Strange, London) **1T74**
Two of the so-called "Six Acts" of 1819 affected the radical press: one defined and controlled "Blasphemous and seditious libels"; the other defined more tightly a newspaper that was subject to the fourpenny tax. Thompson, owner of the *Westminster Review*, was one of the radical members of Parliament who fought for repeal of the newspaper tax. He sold off-prints of articles from his journal at a minimum price as a means of educating those too poor to subscribe.

Thompson, Thomas. "Film Ratings Flunk Out." *Life*, 71(7):50B, 54–57, 20 August 1971. **1T75**
"As they now stand, even with corrective surgery planned this month, hardly anybody likes, follows, or even understands the confusing, misleading alphabet soup of G, GP, R and X." The author suggests a two-rating system —family films for everybody and adult films for selected audiences. And perhaps a third— "SA," stay-away.

Thompson, Thomas N. "Defamation: Constitutional Standards and Utah Law." *Utah Law Review*, 1974:805–18, Winter 1974. **1T76**
"This Note will analyze the constitutional standards pertaining to personal defamation, will examine Utah civil and criminal defamation law in light of those standards, and will suggest areas where Utah law is constitutionally deficient or otherwise inadequate."

Thompson, W. H. "Freedom of Expression" and "More Freedom of Expression." In his *Civil Liberties*. London, Gollancz, 1938, pp. 17–37. **1T77**
Among the restrictions on free speech and free press in England are the common law offense of sedition (vague and subject to abuse by a reactionary government), blasphemy (it is not blasphemy to vilify the Jewish or any non-Christian religion), film controls under the Cinematograph Act of 1909 (originally intended to control the use of inflammable films, but sometimes used against radical and pacifist films), and the convenient device of "breach of peace."

Thompson, William N. *Access to Hospitals*. Columbia, Mo., Freedom of Information Center, School of Journalism, University of Missouri at Columbia, 1973. 5p. (Report no. 314) **1T78**
"A Statewide survey reveals that the extent of newspapers' access to hospital information in Michigan varies widely. The presence of public relations personnel on hospital staffs makes a positive difference."

———. *Attitudes Toward Open Meetings*. Columbia, Mo., Freedom of Information Center, School of Journalism,

University of Missouri at Columbia, 1976. 8p. (Report no. 358) **1T79**
"The attitudes of government officials toward secrecy are studied by the author. Questionnaires were sent to Michigan city managers to determine the validity of a number of hypotheses."

———. *FOI and State Attorneys General*. Columbia, Mo., Freedom of Information Center, School of Journalism, University of Missouri at Columbia, 1973. 14p. (Report no. 307) **1T80**
An examination of the opinions of states attorneys general to determine their attitudes toward freedom of information and the extent to which they have promoted openness in the conduct of public business.

Thomson, R. J. *Television Crime Drama: A Report to the Australian Broadcasting Control Board on Results and Findings of an Experimental Investigation By R. J. Thomson into the Effects on Adolescents and Children of Television Crime Dramas and Tension Films*. Melbourne, Australian Broadcasting Control Board, 1972. 272p. **1T81**
A report on research conducted in 1958–59 for the Board's Programme Research staff. "In the light of social-psychological research carried out during the sixties into problems of imitative social learning of aggressive patterns of behavior, and the recently renewed concern in a number of countries with the social problems of combatting aggression, crime and violence in the community, it now appears appropriate to make the contents of the report available to a wider audience."

Thomson, Samuel. *The Law of Libel; the Report of the Trial of Dr. Samuel Thomson, the Founder of the Thomsonian Practice, for an Alleged Libel in Warning the Public against the Impositions of Paine D. Badger, as a Thomsonian Physician Sailing under False Colors . . . .* Boston, H. P. Lewis, 1839. 52p. **1T82**

Thornberry, Terrence P., and Robert A. Silverman. "Exposure to Pornography and Juvenile Delinquency: The Relationship as Indicated by Juvenile Court Records." *Technical Report of the [U.S.] Commission on Obscenity and Pornography*, 1:175–79, 1971. **1T83**
"This study was designed to collect empirical data in order to assess the relationship between exposure to or experience with pornography and juvenile delinquency by examining the records of a selected sample of delinquents brought to the attention of the Neuropsychiatric Division of a large urban municipal court in the eastern United States during the calendar year 1968."

Thorp, Bruce. "Radio-TV Lobby Fights Losing Battle Against Rising Federal Control." *National Journal*, 2(34):1807–14, 22 August 1970. **1T84**
"With a staff of about 100, the National Association of Broadcasters works daily to fend off further government control by promoting self-regulation of the industry and by attempting to convince the public and the government that stations already are acting in the best public interest."

Thoughts on the Entertainments of the Stage. Leeds, England, Printed for J. Binns and sold by J. Wallis, 1786. 22p. **1T85**
The writer condemns stage plays for their immoral and profane tendencies, their waste of time and money, the evil of giving a bad example, their breach of divine commands, and the fear of judgment to come. He proposes the alternative use of leisure time in Bible reading and prayer.

"A Threat to Press Freedom." *The Tablet: The International Catholic Weekly*, 228:1153, 1155, 30 November 1974. **1T86**
Charges that through the weapon of the closed shop the National Union of Journalists in Britain threatens a free press by compelling editors of newspapers to join the union and thereby make them subject to union dictation of editorial policy.

Thurman, S. David. *The Right of Access to Information from the Government*. Dobbs Ferry, N.Y., Oceana, 1973. 113p. (Legal Almanac Series no. 7) **1T87**
The work is "designed to assist a layman, when dealing with a federal agency, in securing the documents and records to which he is entitled." Chapters deal with specific departments of the federal government.

Tiernan, Robert J. *New York's Access to Records Law*. Columbia, Mo., Freedom of Information Center, School of Journalism, University of Missouri at Columbia, 1975. 9p. (Report no. 340) **1T88**
"New York's open records law is unique in its provision of a Committee on Public Access, a group of individuals who 'interpret the law, oversee its implementation, establish procedures, and propose revisions.' "

₁Tigar, Michael E.₁ "The Supreme Court, 1969 Term: Freedom of Speech and Association." *Harvard Law Review*, 84:117–27, November 1970. **1T89**
Under the heading, Private Citizen's Power to Terminate Mailings from Specific Senders, the survey considers the case of *Rowan v. United States Post Office*.

Tiger, Edith *et al. Blacklisting: Will Our Past Become Our Future*. 55 min. tape record. Berkeley, Calif., Pacifica Tape Library, 1972. **1T90**
Excerpts from a spirited panel discussion about the blacklisting of figures in the movie industry during the McCarthy era. Thomas Bolan, Stephan Kanfer, Millard Lampell, and John Randolph are members of the panel; Edith Tiger is moderator.

Timmons, Durward E. "Clear and Present Danger—Full Circle." *Baylor Law Review*, 26:385–400, Summer 1974. **1T91**
A discussion of the evolution that has taken place in the doctrine of "clear and present danger" as originally put forth in 1919 by Justice Holmes in *Schenck v. United States*. Attention is directed primarily to the decision in *Schenck, Gitlow v. New York* (1925), *Dennis v. United States* (1951), *Yates v. United States* (1957), *Scales v. United States* (1961), *Brandenberg v. Ohio* (1969), and *Communist Party of Indiana v. Whitcomb* (1974).

Tingley, Donald F. "History and Freedom of Speech." *Dispatch from the Illinois State Historical Society*, 3(5):1, 3, November 1968. **1T92**
In a general discussion of protests in wartime, the author reports on the suspension and padlocking of Illinois newspapers during the Civil War and World War I.

Tinling, Nicholas G. "Newsman's Privilege: A Survey of the Law in California." *Pacific Law Journal*, 4:880–902, July 1973. **1T93**
"This comment will examine the claim that newsmen should be afforded testimonial privilege, review the relevant decisions bearing on the possible existence of a constitutional privilege, and determine the extent of California statutory protection afforded newsmen under the various circumstances in which they may be asked to testify."

Tish, Ronald I. "The Federal Communications Commission's License Renewal Policies—A Turn of Events, Some Unanswered Questions, and a Proposal." *St. Louis University Law Journal*, 15:94–125, Fall 1970. **1T94**
"It is the purpose of this article to determine the effectiveness of the policy statement ₁the FCC's 1970 policy statement involving regular renewal applicants₁ as a means of guaranteeing broadcasting which will serve the public interest."

" 'Titicut Follies' Case: Limiting the Public Interest Privilege." *Columbia Law Review*, 70:359–71, February 1970. **1T95**
"Nearly eighty years after two citizens of Massachusetts first articulated a right to privacy ₁Warren and Brandeis₁, with the explicit caveat that the right would 'not prohibit any publica-

tion of matter which is of public or general interest,' the highest court of that state has for the first time acted expressly to prevent an invasion of privacy by denying the general public access to information which cries out for disclosure. Ironically, this first judicial recognition of a right to privacy in Massachusetts is designed to protect the sensibilities of the criminally insane from the effects of a disclosure which can only improve the squalid circumstances of their lives. The only interests clearly protected are the dignity of the Commonwealth and the public image of her agents. Employing an ad hoc balancing test of the competing values, the court deemed the potential invasion of privacy so serious as to warrant restricting free speech on a public issue. Whether such a conclusion is justified on the facts of the case, whether another test would better serve the competing interests involved, and the practical effects of the decision are the principal considerations of this comment."

Tobin, Richard L. "Free to Speak, Free to Publish." *Saturday Review*, 53(13):53–54, 11 April 1970. **1T96**
"The inalienable right of an American citizen to speak and to publish what he wishes within the laws of libel and peaceful assembly are so fundamental that the recent incidents at Princeton and Amherst ₁harassment of speakers₁ are that much more shocking and in need of exposure and explanation to those of the new generation who hold a simplistic view of life."

———. "How Far Does Free Speech Go?" *Saturday Review*, 52(2):113–14, 11 January 1969. **1T97**
The author considers the apparently altered views of Justice Hugo Black on absolute guarantees of the First Amendment, as revealed in a television interview.

———. "On the Hour Every Hour." *Saturday Review*, 51(23):63–64, 8 June 1968. **1T98**
Concern with violence on television.

———. "On Violating the First Amendment." *Saturday Review*, 51(10):97–98, 9 March 1968. **1T99**
Newspaper strikes as restraints on freedom of the press.

———. "The People's Right to Know." *Saturday Review*, 50(2):109, 115, 14 January 1967. **1T100**
Comment on the American Newspaper Publishers Association report on free press–fair trial, "by all odds the most thorough expression of the people's right to know ever assembled and published in this country."

———. "Reporters, Subpoenas, Immunity, and the Court." *Saturday Re-*

view, 54(50):63–64, 11 December 1971. **1T101**

"The right of a newsman to protect his sources has come to the United States Supreme Court in three landmark cases, each of which involves the eternal conflict between the subpoena power of law enforcement agencies and the process of news gathering."

————. " 'Responsible for the Abuse of That Liberty.' " *Saturday Review*, 51(2):107–8, 13 January 1968. **1T102**

"Freedom of speech, press, or assembly will exist only as long as those lucky few granted this towering privilege exercise it while 'being responsible for the abuse of that liberty.' " The quotation is taken from the Constitution of the State of Connecticut, 1818.

————. "The Right to Know." *Saturday Review*, 54(15):41–42, 10 April 1971. **1T103**

Commentary on restrictions on news coverage of the Vietnam war.

————. "The Right to Protect a News Source." *Saturday Review*, 54(19):45–46, 8 May 1971. **1T104**

Comments on the drive of the American Society of Newspaper Editors for a federal shield law.

————. "The Right to Turn Down Advertising." *Saturday Review*, 54(24):55–56, 12 June 1971. **1T105**

Favorable comment on the U.S. Supreme Court's decision giving newspapers the right to turn down advertising, with or without explaining the reason for doing so.

————. "What We Don't Know Will Hurt Us." *Saturday Review*, 54(46):85–86, 13 November 1971. **1T106**

In the case of the Pentagon Papers what can he seen at long range "is that our federal government has been exposed as a bungler and a liar and that our news gatherers in recent years have been both incompetent and sanctimonious, generally lacking in those traits that made American journalism the envy of the world, both free and fettered."

————, *et al*. "The Coming Age of News Monopoly." *Saturday Review*, 53(41):51–65, 10 October 1970. **1T107**

In this special issue on the future of news monopoly in the United States Herbert Brucker considers monopoly in newspapers in a free society; Fairfax Cone considers how advertising will function; Fred W. Friendly looks at radio and television; Richard L. Tobin examines printing and broadcasting technology.

Tobolowsky, Edwin. "Obscenity: A Continuing Dilemma." *Southwestern Law Journal*, 24:827–37, December 1970. **1T108**

The article is intended to demonstrate the chaos spawned by the Supreme Court's approach to obscenity. Following an historical review of federal court decisions, the author discusses obscenity law in Texas under the Texas Penal Code. The President's Commission findings, coupled with the Supreme Court's holding in *Stanley v. Georgia* (1969), "are very persuasive support for permitting consenting adults to view pornography in any form as long as no unwilling viewer is exposed."

[Tobolowsky, Peggy M.] "Prison Superintendent Must Follow Written Standards Unrelated to Content of Speech When Deciding Whether to Grant Prisoner Requests for Personal Contact with Press." *George Washington Law Review*, 44:453–74, March 1976. **1T109**

Re: *Main Road v. Aytch*, 522 F.2d 1080 (3d Cir. 1975).

Todaro, Gerald J. "Piercing the Newsman's Shield: The Supreme Court and the States Assess Privilege Legislation." *Capital University Law Review*, 3:53–76, 1974. **1T110**

"This article will discuss briefly the Supreme Court decision of *Branzburg* [*Branzburg v. Hayes* (1972)]. Secondly, the infirmities inherent in state statutes providing absolute or qualified privileges will be considered. Finally, the case law interpreting the nineteen state statutes affording legislative protection to the news media will be reviewed. The purpose of this article is to identify statutory deficiencies impairing the effective operation of shield laws."

[Todd, Henry J.] *A Remonstrance Addressed to Mr. John Murray, Respecting a Recent Publication. By Oxoniensis*. London, Printed for F. C. and J. Rivington, 1822. 20p. **1T111**

The author pleads with John Murray, publisher of the works of Lord Byron, not to become "the agent of so much mischief as must result from a wide dissemination of works like 'Cain, A Mystery,' " which he terms "absolute trash" and blasphemous. Byron, he notes, "already resembles the wretched [Richard] Carlile in so many points." Carlile was at the time in jail for publishing obscene libels.

Todd, Judith. " 'Not In Rhodesia's Interest.' " *Index on Censorship*, 1(3–4):85–96, Summer–Winter, 1972. **1T112**

Censorship has existed in one form or another since the white occupation of Rhodesia in 1890, but the real watershed came with the unilateral declaration of independence in 1965. The most powerful censorship is authorized by the Law and Order (Maintenance) Act which provides for outright banning of publications. While formal censorship was lifted in 1968, self-censorship continued under threat of Government action. The author, whose name cannot be mentioned by the Rhodesia press while she is under a "detention order," describes some of the incidents of censorship.

————. *The Right to Say No*. London, Sidgwick & Jackson, 1972. 200p. **1T113**

This firsthand account of political suppression and detention in Rhodesia includes sections on the operation of the Suppression of Communism Act, the Emergency Powers Regulation which forbids publication of anything about people "detained" or "restricted," the censorship board, and newspaper and broadcasting self-censorship.

Toinet, M. F. "La Liberté de la Presse aux Etats-Unis: Des Documents du Pentagone au Scandale du Watergate." *Revue Françoise de Science Politique*, 23:1020–45, October 1973. **1T114**

An analysis of the constitutional issues involved in the case of the Pentagon Papers—the conflict between the rights of the press and the preservation of national security.

Tollefson, E. A. "Freedom of the Press." In O. E. Lang, *ed.*, *Contemporary Problems in Public Law in Canada; Essays in Honour of Dean F. C. Cronkite*. Toronto, Published for the College of Saskatchewan by University of Toronto Press, 1968, pp. 49–70 **1T115**

"The primary submission of this paper is that the *Press Bill* case [Alberta Press Bill, 1938] cannot be relied upon as authority for any rule relating to jurisdiction over the press. While it would be practically convenient for the federal government to have exclusive jurisdiction over the press because of the national nature of some publications and the boundless nature of news itself, it cannot be stated with any degree of confidence that the constitution so provides. It seems more likely that the jurisdiction over the press is divided between the federal and provincial governments. To those who suggest that there is nothing to worry about, the British experience may be cited as evidence that the press is either unable or unwilling to rectify its own shortcomings without some form of government regulation. Perhaps it is time that Canadians re-examine their century-old clichés about freedom of the press, with emphasis not on freedom of the press itself but on the goal to which that freedom is directed—an enlightened public. The task of the legislator and the lawyer alike is to consider what measures will best facilitate the attainment of this goal within the framework of Canadian constitution."

Tomlin, Harry H., III. "*Sellers v. Time, Inc.*: The Extension of *New York Times Co. v. Sullivan* to Commenting upon Judicial Proceedings." *Temple Law*

Quarterly, 43:250–59, Spring 1970. **1T116**

"The recent case of *Sellers v. Time, Inc.* (299 F. Supp. 582, E.D. Pa. 1969) indicates a further extension of this protection [against libel charges] by suggesting for the first time that *Times* should be applicable to comments upon judicial proceedings, heretofore sanctioned by the more limited doctrine of *fair comment*. It is submitted that this extension is undesirable from a practical standpoint and is inconsistent with both the principles underlying the *Times* decision and its past applications."

Toogood, Alexander F. *Canadian Broadcasting: A Problem of Control*. Columbus, Ohio, Ohio State University, 1969. 435p. (Ph.D. dissertation, University Microfilms, no. 70–6898) **1T117**

An historical and analytical study of Canadian broadcasting with emphasis on the regulatory and political aspects. The study examines the five attempts to establish agencies of regulation and control and the numerous investigations of broadcasting, including three Royal Commissions, a public Committee, and twenty Parliamentary hearings.

————. "How Independent Is New Zealand's Broadcasting Corporation?" *Journalism Quarterly*, 46:105–13, Spring 1969. **1T118**

"The [Broadcasting Corporation] Act of 1961 was supposed to remove all political controls, but this study shows the national government moving into programming, finance, personnel and other less blatant areas of authority."

Toohey, Daniel W. "The Avoidance of Offense: Observations on the Matter of Broadcast Censorship." *St. Louis University Law Journal*, 15:48–72, Fall 1970. **1T119**

Content: A Brief History. Techniques of Regulatory Censorship (the complaint process, review of programming performance, emerging direct censorship). The First Amendment—Censorship Conflict (the *Red Lion* decision, the gap in First Amendment theory, the fairness doctrine, and offensive programs). The author suggests three areas where some revision of policies and practices by the FCC might "reduce friction between programming regulation and First Amendment freedoms."

[Tooke, John Horne.] *The Genuine Trial Between the Rt. Hon. Geo. Onslow, Esq; and the Rev. Mr. John Horne, Tried at Guildhall the 18th of August, 1770 Before the Right Honourable Lord Mansfield for Printing Two Libels against, and speaking Defamatory Words of, George Onslow, Esq; one of the Representatives for the County of Surry. Together with the Two Libels, and All the Letters That Passed Relative to This Affair . . . .* London, I. Williams [1770?]. 43p. **1T120**

A second trial for publication of alleged libels in issues of the *Public Advertiser*, 14 and 18 July 1769. The first trial had been dismissed on technical grounds. Horne was found guilty and fined £400. On appeal the verdict was set aside.

————.] *The Whole Proceedings in the Cause on the Action Brought by the Rt. Hon. Geo. Onslow, Esq. against the Rev. Mr. Horne, on Friday, April 6, at Kingston, for a Defamatory Libel, Before the Right Honourable Sir William Blackstone, Knt. . . . Taken in Short-hand . . . by Joseph Gurney*. London, Printed for T. Davies and J. Gurney, 1770. 48p. **1T121**

The defendant, the Reverend Mr. Horne (later Horne Tooke), was accused of authoring a libelous letter appearing in the *Public Advertiser*, but because of a technicality (an error in the printing) the case was dismissed. The plaintiff, a Lord of the Treasury and Member of Parliament, had asked for £10,000 damages.

Toomey, Kevin J. "Access to the Press in Light of the Traditional Concept of Journalistic Freedom." *Suffolk University Law Review*, 8:682–727, Spring 1974. **1T122**

"This Note reviews the various theories upon which individuals have unsuccessfully attempted to justify the right [for a public access to newspapers], namely, that newspapers operate in the public interest, serve a public function within the state action concept, or are obligated by the first amendment itself to accept proffered articles. . . . Since implementation of the access right may be vexed with great administrative difficulties, and has been met with rejection in the context of broadcasting, the author concludes that a right to purchase space in newspapers will be viewed as too great a governmental encroachment on these 'critics of government.' Although a right of access, limited to political candidates, may pass the constitutional test, the traditional protection of editorial discretion will insulate newspapers from the duty of insuring individual access."

Topicator; Monthly Classified Article Guide to the Advertising-Broadcasting Trade Press. Littleton, Colo., Thompson Bureau, 1965–date. Monthly with annual cumulations. **1T123**

Indexes news articles on freedom of the press, censorship, and government regulation of the media, from eighteen trade journals that, because of their brevity or news character, are not included in this bibliography.

Torgrud, Richard D. "The Banning of a Book." *North Dakota Quarterly*, 39(4): 71–72, Autumn 1971. **1T124**

A brief note on the banning of *Huckleberry Finn* from twelfth grade English Literature because of charges that it was a racist book. "Although

much better educated than Huck Finn, present-day intellectuals seem unable to reject the nonsense of their own time. So they ban books in the name of social progress." The author observes that New Brunswick's action may do for *Huckleberry* what the city of Boston has done for so many books—increase the circulation.

Torrens, Thomas M. "Professional Football Telecasts and the Blackout Privilege." *Cornell Law Review*, 57: 297–312, January 1972. **1T125**

"The original purpose of the legislative antitrust exemption [which permitted the blackout of telecasting sports events in home territory] has been achieved and there are no new or alternative justifications for its existence. The exemption is neither necessary nor beneficial in 1971."

"Tort Liability of a University for Libelous Material in Student Publications." *Michigan Law Review*, 71:1061–88, April 1973. **1T126**

Despite an expansion of First Amendment rights and the greater potential of defamation in student newspapers, a concurrent expansion of protection afforded the press has reduced the likelihood of a successful suit. The lack of court precedent belies the significance of the problem. "The surest device for minimizing the risk of university liability is insurance against libel: Over fifty percent of the schools answering the author's inquiry carried some form of libel insurance."

Towery, Patricia. "Censorship of South Carolina Newspapers, 1861–65." In James B. Meriwether, *ed.*, *South Carolina Journals and Journalists*. Spartanburg, S.C., Reprint Company, 1975, pp. 147–60. **1T127**

An account of the long battle of South Carolina journalists against military censorship and control of news during the American Civil War. Included are references to the work of the Confederate Press Association which provided organized opposition to censorship restraints.

Towns, Rose M. "Proposition 16: One Year Later." *California Librarian*, 29: 21–24, January 1968. **1T128**

A report on unsuccessful efforts in the 1967 California legislature to pass obscenity legislation, one year after the so-called CLEAN proposition was rejected by voters.

Toy, Eckard V., Jr. "The Social Meaning of Television Censorship." In Roy B. Browne, Larry N. Landrum, and William K. Bottorff, *eds.*, *Challenges in American Culture*. Bowling Green,

Ohio, Bowling Green University Popular Press [1970?], pp. 111–33. **1T129**

The author examines television's response or lack of response to the changing mores of society. "As a mass medium, television tends to be conservative in its political and social content, partly because of the fear of offending any large portion of the audience and also because it is a business and its goals often clash with the role of the intellectual as a critic of society." The networks forestalled public demands for censorship by creating and reinforcing corporate controls. The article examines in detail some of the efforts at program control on network series, noting problems encountered by the "editors" in taking into consideration the audience, the sponsors, and the NAB Code.

Tracey, Ann M. "Minority Ownership Likely to Increase Diversity of Content Must Be Accorded Merit in FCC Licensing Hearing." *University of Cincinnati Law Review*, 43:669–78, 1974. **1T130**

Re: *TV 9, Inc. v. FCC*, 495 F.2d 929 (D.C. Cir. 1973).

Tracy, Donald J. "United States Supreme Court Reaffirms Its Decision in *Gertz v. Robert Welch, Inc.*, to Emphasize the Individual Injured in a Libel Action Rather than the Event Reported." *Creighton Law Review*, 10: 351–61, December 1976. **1T131**

"The importance of *Firestone* [*Time, Inc. v. Firestone*, 1976] lies in the almost total acceptance of the *Gertz* decision by a sizable majority of the Court."

Tracy, F. P. *A Sermon occasioned by the Alton Outrage and Murder of Rev. E. P. Lovejoy. Delivered in Newbury, Mass. December 22, 1837.* Newburyport, Mass., Charles Whipple, 1838. 16p. **1T132**

In his attack on the mob action which resulted in the editor Lovejoy's murder, the minister rebukes the nation's press for speaking against the rioters in the faintest tones, but castigating the victims in the voice of thunder.

Tracy, John P. "Fair Trial and Free Press." *Air Force Judge Advocate General Law Review*, 9:24–29, July–August 1967. **1T133**

"The most practical solution in the control of pretrial publicity seems to be in the implementation of voluntary codes on the part of the Press, the Bar, and the Police themselves. . . . The outlook is optimistic, however, because lawyers and newspaper men alike have finally realized that they each must 'put its own house in order.' "

Trager, Robert. "Freedom of the Press in College and High School." *Albany Law Review*, 35:161–81, 1971. **1T134**

"While freedom of the press in colleges has a better legal foundation than in secondary schools, neither is on solid ground. The courts are beginning to scrutinize more often administrative rulings that are violative of first amendment rights, but such violations are rarely brought to court; students and teachers generally comply with instructions rather than risk their student or professional positions. Many restrictions can be legally imposed. The first amendment is relative, not absolute, with libel, obscenity, and fighting words not protected."

———. "The Legal Status of Underground Newspapers in Public Secondary Schools." *University of Kansas Law Review*, 20:239–51, Winter 1972. **1T135**

"This article explores the legal rights of the high school underground press and of the students who write, publish, and distribute such publications. . . . In general, the contention here is that underground newspapers should be subject to the same students' rights as school-sponsored newspapers; that those students' rights include first amendment rights; and that, although certain administrative restrictions can be employed to discourage students from distributing underground papers, such papers cannot legally be barred from public high school campuses."

———. *Student Press Rights: Struggles in Scholastic Journalism.* Urbana, Ill., Journalism Education Association and ERIC Clearinghouse on Reading and Communication Skills, 1974. 84p. **1T136**

"The purpose of this monograph is to acquaint journalism teachers, faculty advisers to student newspapers, administrators, and students with the court cases and decisions which have been made concerning student publications and underground newspapers. The author, avoiding giving legal advice, discusses the implications of the court decisions with respect to the rights of students and the responsibilities of teachers and administrators."

———, and Donna L. Dickerson. *College Student Press Law.* Athens, Ohio, National Council of College Publications Advisers and ERIC Clearinghouse on Reading and Communication Skills, 1976. 87p. **1T137**

Content: The First Amendment on the College Campus. Colleges and Student Publications. Administrators: Permissible Control. Administrators as Censors (prior restraint, vagueness and overbreadth, the university and its image, postpublication punishment, disciplinary actions and due process, sanctions against publications, litigation and liability). Adviser: Teacher or Censor. A Publication's Responsibilities (libel, privacy, obscenity). Advertising. Contempt. Copyrights. Endorsements.

Trager, Robert, and Ronald Ostman. "Caging the Censorship Dragon . . . With a Good 'Bop.' " *Scholastic Editor*, 50(4):8–11, December 1970/January 1971. **1T138**

"The plan presented in this article gives high schools an alternative to the traditional structure of having the principal and/or adviser act as censor, a situation they should refuse to accept because it does not allow students to gain the full benefit of functioning in the best democratic tradition of a free and responsible press."

Trail, George Y. "Beardsley's Venus and Tannhäuser: Two Versions." *English Literature in Translation*, 18(1):16–23, 1975. **1T139**

The author studies expurgated and unexpurgated editions of Aubrey Beardsley's *Venus and Tannhäuser* in order to determine the original intent of the author, the circumstances of publishing, and the literary and moral standards of the time. He notes the difficulty in this liberal age of obtaining copies of expurgated editions of works for the purpose of study.

"The Trammels of the Press." *Westminster Review*, 18:474–93, April 1833. **1T140**

The author discusses "latent agents of mischief" that threaten the British press, including the law of libel, the law of copyright, corruption of patronage, high price of postage, and defective post office arrangements. "The press is a great spy-glass; and the grand debate is whether the public shall have the liberty of bringing it to the focus they can see with, or the government shall take measures to secure its being always an inch on one side."

Trapp, Mary E. "Americans Need Access to Today's Mass Media." *Communication: Journalism Education Today*, 5:9–12, Summer 1972. **1T141**

"Two suggestions for accomplishing public access: (1) federal government subsidy or public ownership, (2) legislative provision of a public right of access to the media and judicial enforcement of the legislation."

———. *Public Access to the Mass Media: The Political Meaning of Freedom of the Press.* Iowa City, University of Iowa, 1971. 142p. (Unpublished Master's thesis) **1T142**

"This thesis concludes that provision of access would not guarantee public utilization of the media, and stresses education as a possible remedy to public ignorance of First Amendment rights."

Traynor, Roger J. "Speech Impediments and Hurricane Flo; the Implications of a Right-of-Reply to Newspapers." *University of Cincinnati Law Review*, 43:247–66, 1974. **1T143**

The article deals with the case of *Tornillo v. Miami Herald Publishing Co.* in which the Supreme Court of Florida held that the Miami Herald Publishing Co. is bound by Florida's right-of-reply statute to publish the reply of a candidate for public office to two editorials allegedly attacking his personal character. The decision was later reversed by the U.S. Supreme Court, which held the statute unconstitutional. The author presents the case for and against the right-of-reply doctrine.

————. "What the National News Council Has In Mind." *Center Magazine*, 6:69–73, May–June 1973. **1T144**
An interview with a former Chief Justice of the California Supreme Court and presently chairman of the National News Council. Traynor is interviewed by Donald McDonald. "I cannot believe that a council, completely detached from government and without any power to impose any sanctions whatever other than publicity, can be in any way a threat to press freedom or encourage an atmosphere of regulation."

Trelford, Donald. "After the Chamberlain." *Observer*, 25 June 1967, pp. 11–12. **1T145**
"Is the Lord Chamberlain the only jailer of artistic freedom—or will his keys merely be passed on at his demise to the lawyer and the policeman? . . . By abolishing, instead of reforming the licensing system, will the men of the theatre not in fact be delivering themselves up, unarmed, to the courts, the legislators, the cautious commercial management, the watch-committees, the police, those old grey guardians of public morality?"

Trench, Charles C. *Portrait of A Patriot: A Biography of John Wilkes*. London, Blackwood, 1962. 412p. **1T146**
A biography of the eighteenth-century rake, agitator, and reformer, whose celebrated efforts in behalf of press freedom brought him expulsion from the Parliament, exile, imprisonment, and great popular support. "Wilkes and Liberty" became a rallying cry of his riotous supporters and the number "45," representing the issue of his offending publication, *North Briton*, was scrawled on doors and buildings. The abolition of the general warrant, which had been widely used to suppress dissenters, and the freeing of the press from political harassment of government were among his achievements. He ultimately became Lord Mayor of London.

Trendel, Robert. "The Expurgation of Antislavery Materials by American Presses." *Journal of Negro History*, 58:271–90, July 1973. **1T147**
"The attempt during the 1840s and 1850s to expose the influence of Slavepower through illustrating the expurgation and suppression of American and British literature was just one more weapon in the abolitionist arsenal to awaken moral sensitivity throughout the nation. Under the guidance and determination of evangelical abolitionists such as Lewis Tappan

and William Jay, Americans and antislavery friends in England were directed to specific mutilations that amounted to a censorship of the literature they read and a violation of the first amendment to the Constitution. School books for children and readers for youth were especially vulnerable."

Trevelyan, George O. "The Law of Libel, etc." In his *The Early History of Charles James Fox*. New York, Harper, 1900, pp. 289–347. **1T148**
Chapters in this general biography of the liberal British statesman and Parliamentary leader, deal with the free press cases of John Wilkes and Henry S. Woodfall and the attack on the use of the general warrant against publishers and booksellers. Fox's efforts to change the law of libel, which were successful in 1793, are beyond the time scope of this work.

Trevelyan, John. "The B.B.F.C. View." *Journal of the Society of Film and Television Arts*. 43/44:4–5, Spring–Summer 1971. **1T149**
In an issue devoted to an assessment of the current status of censorship in Britain, the former secretary of the British Board of Film Censors, describes the attitude and role of the Board, which is largely that of protecting children from harm in the areas of violence and sex, in that order.

————. "Censored!—How, and Why We Do It." *Film and Filming*, 4(10):8+, July 1958. **1T150**
The British film censor discusses the work of his office.

————. "Could We Become a Police State?" *Film* (British Federation of Film Societies), 2(9):1–2, December 1973. **1T151**
"The new Cinematograph and Indecent Displays Bill is a threat to Film Societies, and therefore a threat to the people who take films seriously and care enough about them to join clubs and societies."

————. "Disguising Pornography in a Plain Cover." *Times* (London), 4 December 1973, p. 16. **1T152**
Criticism of a Cinematograph and Indecent Displays Bill before Parliament which would go beyond the intent of protecting people from having sex thrust upon them in public places. The author fears the bill would discourage creative work in the arts, interfere with legitimate film societies, and increase the power of local censorship groups.

————. "Film Censorship in Great Britain." *Screen*, 11(3):19–30, Summer 1970. **1T153**
The secretary of the British Board of Film Censors discusses the history of British film censorship, the finances and composition of the Board, its methods of operation, policies and problems, and suggests future trends.

————. *What the Censor Saw*. Preface by Alexander Walker. London, Joseph, 1973. 276p. **1T154**
An account of Trevelyan's thirteen years as secretary of the British Board of Film Censors in which he describes the detailed workings of the Board. "The picture conveyed is of a liberal and concerned man, sympathetically conscious of the difficulties and paradoxes involved in reconciling censorship with artistic integrity. It was under his guidance that the Board was steered into the 'new permissiveness' of the early '70s and since his departure that the Board's authority has been increasingly challenged by the local authorities" (Jean Young in *Film*, December 1973).

————. "Who's Guarding Whose Morals?" *Guardian* (Manchester), 12 May 1973, p. 11. **1T155**
The former British film censor sees the public as the ultimate censor and "at the present time, in spite of protestations that the 'ordinary decent people' do not want sex and violence in films, the evidence seems to point the other way." Perhaps the time has come to free the film for adult audiences from censorship as the threater was freed five years ago. "Film censorship could not be abolished by getting rid of the British Board of Film Censors. It could only be abolished, or even substantially modified, by an Act of Parliament removing or modifying the powers of the local authorities."

Tribe, David. *One Hundred Years of Freethought*. London, Elek, 1967. 259p. **1T156**
Includes discussion of restrictions on birth control information; censorship of freethought literature and works considered blasphemous, seditious, or obscene; biographical information on such leaders in press freedom as Charles Bradlaugh, Annie Besant, and G. W. Foote.

————. *President Charles Bradlaugh, M.P.* Hamden, Conn., Archon, 1971. 391p. **1T157**
In this general biography of the nineteenth-century British freethinker are sections dealing with Bradlaugh's trial for publishing the *National Reformer;* his trial, with Annie Besant, for publishing Dr. Charles Knowlton's birth control pamphlet, *Fruits of Philosophy;* and his lifelong efforts to combat church and state restrictions against heresy and blasphemy.

————. *Questions of Censorship*. London, Allen and Unwin, 1973. 268p. **1T158**
An account of the forces that have exercised censorship down the years, viewed from the total concept of the continuing debate—psychological, sociological, political, and philosophical. The emphasis is on recent events in Britain, but comparisons are made with the scene in the United States, France, and the Soviet Union. Greatest attention is

given to the area of obscenity, but with appropriate references to censorship in politics and religion. Throughout, the author enlivens his account with quotations from original sources and contemporary documents. Illustrated.

[Tribe, Laurence H.] "The Supreme Court, 1972 Term: Freedom of Speech, Press, and Association." *Harvard Law Review*, 87:153–88, 221–33, November 1973.   **1T159**
Under the heading Prohibition of Newspaper's Sex-designated Help-Wanted Advertising Classification System, the survey considers the case of *Pittsburgh Press Co. v. Pittsburgh Commission on Human Relations;* under Obscenity, the case of *Miller v. State of California;* under Public Access to Broadcasting Media for Editorial Advertising, the case of *Columbia Broadcasting System, Inc. v. Democratic National Committee;* under Scope of Privileged Legislative Activity and Protection of Government Printing Officials, the case of *Doe v. McMillan.*

Triezenberg, George. "Student Communication Rights." *National Association of Secondary School Principals Bulletin*, 57(372):13–23, April 1973.   **1T160**
"Speech rights of students outside the classroom, school and underground newspapers, political speech on and off campus, and the right to hear political speakers are all treated in this article."

Trillin, Calvin. "Kanawha County, West Virginia." *New Yorker*, 50(32):119–22, 126–27, 30 September 1974.   **1T161**
"Some elements in a dispute [over school textbooks] that resulted in the closing of schools, the shutting down of industry, the wounding of men, and the cancellation of football games."

————. "U.S. Journal: Suffolk County, Long Island. Trying 'Green Door.'" *New Yorker*, 49:74+, 11 February 1974.   **1T162**
An account of the obscenity trial over the film, *Behind the Green Door,* including selection of jury, showing of the film, and testimony of expert witnesses—Ernest van den Haag for the prosecution, Charles Winick, Arthur Knight, and Wardell Pomeroy for the defense. The jury decided that under New York law the movie was obscene.

Tripp, Miles. "Pornography and Obscene Literature: An Outline of the Law." *Books; the Journal of the National Book League*, 302:115–19, June 1956.   **1T163**

The author traces the history of obscene literature and efforts to control it from the seventeenth century to the present. "Since [pornography] depends for its existence on the frustrated longings of its writers and readers, it can only be effectively stamped out by the satisfaction or sublimation of these longings. According to a person's needs and spiritual powers, this process requires an effort of will, medical or psychiatric treatment, or religious instruction and prayer."

Trotter, F. Thomas. "The Church Moves Toward Film Discrimination." *Religion in Life*, 38:264–76, Summer 1969.   **1T164**
The Film Awards Nomination Panel of the Broadcasting and Film Commission of the National Council of Churches has replaced the film censorship and boycott approach of church groups with a positive program of issuing annual awards to outstanding motion pictures. Despite heated controversy over some of the awards (e.g., *Who's Afraid of Virginia Woolf*), the author believes the program has "opened a new era of responsible, ecumenical, and theologically informed film criticism."

Trout, Greg. "Invasion of Privacy: New Guidelines for the Public Disclosure Tort." *Capital University Law Review*, 6:95–110, 1976.   **1T165**
The case of *Virgil v. Time, Inc.*, 527 F.2d 1122 (9th Cir. 1975) "offers guidelines for determining which of an individual's matters are inviolate and which are subject to the privilege of the press to report." The case involves an article in *Sports Illustrated*, 22 February 1971.

Trumbo, Dalton. "Blacklist Equals Black Market." *Nation*, 184:383–87, 4 May 1957.   **1T166**
The effect of the Hollywood blacklist after ten years, discussed by one of the blacklisted ten.

————. *The Time of the Toad. A Study of Inquisition in America.* By One of the Hollywood Ten. Hollywood, Calif., The Hollywood Ten, 1949. 38p. (Reprinted, along with his *The Devil in the Book* (T194) and *Honor Bright and All that Jazz.* New York, Harper & Row, 1972)   **1T167**
An attack on the Un-American Activities Committee, representing "the nation turned upon itself in a kind of compulsive madness." Trumbo, one of the "Hollywood Ten" who refused to testify to his political activities, writes of actions of the Committee, his trial, and the Committee's threat to intellectual freedom. One of the incidents described is the effort of the Committee to get some seventy American colleges and universities to submit to the Committee a list of "textbooks and supplementary reading, together with authors" in the various social sciences and American literature. In the end, writes Trumbo, "either the committee or the individual is bound to be destroyed."

Tuber, Richard "An Annotated Bibliography on Broadcast Rights, 1920–1955." *Journal of Broadcasting*, 2:263–72, Summer 1958. Reprinted, 14:147–55, Winter 1969/70.   **1T168**
Topics: Copyrights, defamation, right of privacy, sports, trademarks.

Tuchman, Barbara W. "The Courage to Stand for Standards in a Time When Pornography Masquerades as Literature. . . ." U.S. House of Representatives, Post Office and Civil Service Committee, Postal Operations Subcommittee, *Hearings on Obscenity in the Mails*, 5–6 August 1969, pp, 85–89. (Reprinted from *Philadelphia Bulletin*, 18 June 1967)   **1T169**
Deploring the wave of pornography sweeping across America under the guise of literature and art, this self-labeled liberal writes: "The dealers know it; the critics know it; the purveyors themselves know it; the public suspects it; but no one dares say it because that would be committing oneself to a standard of values and even, heaven forbid, exposing oneself to being called a square."

Tuck, George. *Post Office Controls of Obscenity.* Columbia, Mo., Freedom of Information Center, School of Journalism, University of Missouri at Columbia, 1970. 7p. (Report no. 234)   **1T170**
"Congress has passed bills limiting the mailing of pornographic material. Pressure from constituents could force Congress to take stronger steps against the indiscriminate mailing of such material. And a conservative stand by the Supreme Court could make it easier for judges to obtain convictions under postal regulations forbidding the mailing of obscene material."

Tucker, Benjamin R. "Walt Whitman and Comstock, or the Whirligig of Time." In Joseph Ishill, *ed., Free Vistas, Vol. II.* Berkeley Heights, N.J., Oriole Press, 1937, pp. 109–15.   **1T171**
Tucker recounts his part in the 1882 conflict with Anthony Comstock and Boston authorities over the suppression of Walt Whitman's *Leaves of Grass.*

Tucker, Edwin W. "The Law of Obscenity. Where Has It Gone?" *University of Florida Law Review*, 22:547–79, Spring–Summer 1970.   **1T172**
The law of obscenity is not dead, despite recent Supreme Court decisions. "During the past two decades a fragmented Supreme Court, time and again speaking through plurality rather than a majority, has haphazardly constructed a body of constitutional principles in the obscenity area. . . . The constitutional principles governing obscenity are loosely related but related they are." When assembled,

they "will present an appearance of oneness—interlacing, although not very neatly, with one another."

Tucker, Eliot P. "The Anti-Evolutionists of 1964." *Science Education*, 51:371–78, October 1967. **1T173**
A controversy in Texas over three high school textbooks "because they explain the theory of evolution and acknowledge that it is accepted by most scientists as the most plausible theory which attempts to explain the facts of biology." The Church of Christ waged an organized campaign against the books, led by the editor of *Firm Foundation*.

Tucker, John M. "An Analysis of Censorship News Reporting." *Newsletter on Intellectual Freedom* (IFC-ALA), 23:143, 159–61, November 1974. **1T174**
An analysis of censorship news as reported in the "Censorship Dateline" column of the *Newsletter*, November 1971 through March 1974, "to arrive at an assessment of the prominence of roles played by individual citizens in efforts to control the availability and use of print and non-print materials."

Tuite, Patrick A. "Seizure of Allegedly Obscene Materials." *Police Law Quarterly*, 2:15–19, October 1972. **1T175**
The author concludes that, in light of the U.S. Supreme Court decision in *Stanley v. Georgia* (1969), "it is quite possible that the future will bring decisions which will allow dissemination of even obscene materials to adults who are aware of what they are about to read or see and there is no evasion ₍sic₎ upon the privacy of unwilling or unsuspecting persons. If that day comes it will make the job of police officer a lot less complicated and allow him to concentrate on other major areas of law enforcement."

Tullock, Gordon. "A Note on Censorship." *American Political Science Review*, 62:1265–67, December 1968. **1T176**
"In *Toward a Mathematics of Politics* I presented a model of reciprocal interaction between information media and the opinions held by members of the community. It is the purpose of this note to apply a somewhat simplified version of this model to the specific problem of censorship."

Tunstall, Jeremy. *The Westminister Lobby Correspondents: A Sociological Study of National Political Journalism*. London, Routledge, 1970. 142p. **1T177**
A study of the "lobby system," the mechanism for national political reporting from Westminster to the British people, a system shrouded in almost complete secrecy until about 1960. The Lobby correspondents specialize in government policy and behind-the-scene politics; the Gallery reporters cover the debates in Parliament. Access to information is one of the issues considered.

Tuoni, Gilda M. "NEPA and the

Freedom of Information Act: A Prospect for Disclosure." *Environmental Affairs*, 4:179–201, Winter 1975. **1T178**
"This article discusses the overlapping public information functions of NEPA ₍National Environmental Policy Act of 1969₎ and FOIA ₍Freedom of Information Act of 1966₎. It evaluates both Acts as tools for the disclosure of the facts concerning the environmental effects of government action. Finally, it argues that information previously prohibited by the exemptions of the Freedom of Information Act may be required by NEPA to be made public."

Turan, Kenneth, and Stephen F. Zito. *Sinema: American Pornographic Films and the People Who Make Them*. New York, Praeger, 1974. 244p. **1T179**
A study of the burgeoning pornographic film industry and the changing mores of Americans that have made it possible. Includes interviews with film makers and actors and references to the problems of censorship and litigation.

Turkington, Richard C. "Foreseeability and Duty Issues in Illinois Torts: Constitutional Limitation to Defamation Suits Under *Gertz*." *DePaul Law Review*, 24:243–73, Winter 1975. **1T180**
The author "discusses the impact on Illinois law of a recent United States Supreme Court decision ₍*Gertz v. Robert Welch, Inc.* (1974)₎ examining defamation suits brought by private individuals."

Turnbull, George S. *An Oregon Crusader*. Portland, Oreg., Binfords & Mort, 1955. 246p. **1T181**
An enlargement of *An Oregon Editor's Battle for Freedom of the Press* (T205), which dealt with the editor George Putnam's libel fight in Medford, Oreg., in 1907–8. Two additional sections deal with Putnam's crusades against the Ku Klux Klan and lawless forces controlling some of the Oregon labor unions.

Turnbull, Robert. *The Theatre, in Its Influence Upon Literature, Morals, and Religion*. Hartford, Conn., Canfield and Robins, 1837. 58p. **1T182**
An attack on the theater as an unholy and dangerous institution which will only bring temptation, death, and woe to young people of the city. The essay was presented in two congregational meetings in Hartford by the pastor of the South Baptist Church on the occasion of a bill before the Connecticut legislature to repeal the law prohibiting the establishing of theaters.

Turner, A. J. "The Jeremy Collier Stage Controversy Again." *Notes & Queries*, 20(n.s.):409–12, November 1973. **1T183**
Comment on the role of the religious societies of London in support of the attack on the London stage after the great storm of 26–27 November 1703.

Turner, E. S. *The Shocking History of Advertising*. London, Michael Joseph, 1952. 303p. **1T184**
This popular account of the history of advertising in Britain and the United States includes sections on the various legal and moral restraints placed on the industry, such as taxes and laws and regulations dealing with fraudulant, misleading, and offensive "puffery."

Turner, Ralph E. "The Freedom of the Indian Press." In his *James Silk Buckingham, 1786–1855, A Social Biography*. London, Williams & Norgate, 1934, pp. 115–28. **1T185**
Buckingham was founder of the *Calcutta Journal* and crusader for a free Indian press.

Turner, Stephen. "Responding to Obscenity: Methodological and Conceptual Problems." *Kansas Journal of Sociology*, 6:178–87, Winter 1970. **1T186**
This study tests the hypothesis, held from two viewpoints—the sociocultural and the psychoanalytic—that anxiety responses to obscene stimuli indicate sexual frustration. A group of men substantially deprived of women were found to show significantly less anxiety in response to the "sexual deviant" stimuli, disconfirming the hypothesis.

Turner, Woodrow, Jr. "Private Distribution of Obscene Materials." *William and Mary Law Review*, 12:691–94, Spring 1971. **1T187**
In *United States v. Dellapia*, 433 F.2d 1252 (2d Cir. 1970), the court ruled that where there is no public distribution and when children are not involved the government cannot constitutionally prosecute an individual for mailing obscene material to adults who have requested it.

Turnstile, Magnus. "Managing the News in Ireland." *New Statesman*, 73:754–55, 2 June 1967. **1T188**
An account of government banning of Dublin television coverage of the Vietnam war and the Mao cultural revolution, believed to have been prompted by an American protest. "Ministers' use of their position to manage the news, to have commentators of whom they disapprove banned from the television screen, to score points off one another in the endless manoeuvering for power that is going on inside the cabinet, and police actions against newsmen are merely symptoms of much else that is happening in the Irish Republic at present."

Tushnet, Mark. "Free Expression and the Young Adult: A Constitutional Framework." *University of Illinois Law Forum*, 1976:746–62, 1976. **1T189**

"This article will provide general guidelines for the development of the first amendment rights of young adults without attempting to canvass all the cases that have been decided since *Tinker* [*Tinker v. Des Moines Independent School District*, 1969]. The general theme of the article is that both limitations on judicial competence and isolation from the schools preclude the court from developing workable standards."

[Tutchin, John.] *The Examination, Tryal, and Condemnation of Rebellion Observator, At a Session of Oyer and Terminer. . . . On the 24th of August, 1703 . . . .* London, 1703. 24p.　**1T190**
Burlesque of a trial for a publication that "stabbed the Church, Establish'd and Present Constitution, to the Heart, in order to bring in Anarchy and Confusion." The offending work was described as "a libel in Breadth six inches, and ten in Length." Tutchin had been brought to trial on charges of seditious libel for his publication, *The Observator*.

Twentieth Century Fund. Task Force for a National News Council. *A Free and Responsible Press. The Twentieth Century Fund Task Force Report for a National News Council. Background Paper by Alfred Balk.* New York, The Fund, 1973. 88p.　**1T191**

The report proposed: "That an independent and private national news council be established to receive, to examine, and to report on complaints concerning the accuracy and fairness of news reporting in the United States, as well as to initiate studies and report on issues involving the freedom of the press. The Council shall limit its investigations to the principal national suppliers of news—the major wire services, the largest 'supplemental' news services, the national weekly news magazines, national newspaper syndicates, national daily newspapers, and the nationwide broadcasting networks." The background paper by Alfred Balk explores the problems that news councils have considered and cites experiences of the British Press Council, the Minnesota Press Council, Honolulu's Community-Media Council, and other experiences with press councils and similar organizations in the United States and abroad. The report led to the establishment of the National News Council in 1973.

Twentieth Century Fund. Task Force on Broadcasting and the Legislature. *Openly Arrived At. Report of the Twentieth Century Fund Task Force on Broadcasting and the Legislature. Background Paper by Lee M. Mitchell.* New York, The Fund, 1974. 104p.　**1T192**
The Task Force recommended that (1) the United States Congress authorize the Corpora-

tion for Public Broadcasting to provide for the broadcast coverage and recording of all public sessions of the House and Senate; (2) House and Senate Committees with jurisdiction over broadcast coverage create a Congressional Television Advisory Committee consisting of officers of the existing press galleries and representatives of CPB, the commercial networks, independent broadcasters, and the public; (3) all committee sessions that are open to the public should be open to television coverage; and (4) each state legislature should work with state public broadcasting authorities to establish broadcast coverage of the legislative process. One member, William A. Rusher, dissented; another, Douglass Cater, made separate comments. The Task Force was chaired by James Rowe.

Twentieth Century Fund. Task Force on Justice, Publicity and the First Amendment. *Rights in Conflict. Report of the Twentieth Century Fund Task Force on Justice, Publicity, and the First Amendment. Background Paper by Alan Barth.* New York, McGraw-Hill, 1975. 112p.　**1T193**
The Task Force, under the chairmanship of Dean Abraham S. Goldstein of Yale Law School, and consisting of members mainly drawn from the bar and journalism, was formed for the purpose of examining and reporting on the conflict between the public's right to know and the individual's right to a fair trial. The Task Force "believes that the conflict between the courts and the press has intensified in the past two or three years in ways that seriously endanger the traditional freedom of the press in the United States . . . that current restraints imposed by some judges on the reporting of criminal proceedings constitute a growing threat to freedom of the press—that is, to the right of the public to know how justice is administered . . . [and] that fairness in the administration of criminal justice can be maintained without impairment of press freedom." The Task Force recommended the enactment by the states of legislation consistent with a model statute it prepared (pp. 23–30). The report suggests that "without abridging First Amendment rights, courts can maintain the Sixth Amendment's promise of a public trial by an impartial jury by the following means: vigorous administration of the *voir dire;* painstaking instructions to juries; resort, where necessary, to continuance, to a change of venue, or to sequestration; reasonable restrictions upon court officers and employees in regard to statements concerning any criminal proceedings; consultation with representatives of the press respecting the issuance of special orders in connection with trials; and testing the validity of challenged court orders through a special procedure in accordance with the standards of due process. These measures entail no sacrifice of independence either by the courts or by the press." The background paper by Alan Barth "provides the reader with documentation on the issues that, at this writing, are moving toward constitutional confrontation in the highest court in the land."

Twentieth Century Fund. Task Force on the Government and the Press. *Press Freedoms under Pressure. Report of the Twentieth Century Fund Task Force on the Government and the Press. Background Paper by Fred P. Graham.* New York, The Fund, 1972. 193p.　**1T194**
The Task Force (nine journalists and three lawyers) considered the major pressures restraining the American press, recommending that: (1) "An adequate newsmen's privilege should be incorporated into the law to protect the flow of information through the press to the public." (2) "The public's need—and the value of democracy—of the fullest possible information can be threatened by Congressional investigations of editorial judgments, as well as by the Federal Communications Commission's questioning of editorial content." (3) "The chief officers of all law enforcement and other public agencies that seek intelligence about domestic groups—and particularly those agencies that have permitted their agents to pose as journalists—should publicly disapprove of these masquerades and should take steps to ensure that they do not happen in the future. Law enforcement agencies should abandon the practice of employing journalists as informants." (4) "The underground press should be considered entitled to all legal and constitutional rights applicable to other elements of the press . . . ." In the matter of the Pentagon Papers case the majority of the Task Force found that "excessive secrecy is inimical to a free society and should be combatted . . . that an effective and essential instrument to achieve this end is a free and responsible press—free to investigate; free to interrogate; and free to publish. When we weigh the imperative of secrecy against the imperative of an effective government in a free society, we believe that the balance is more heavily weighted in favor of the latter." Fred P. Graham of the *New York Times* served as rapporteur for the Task Force and his background paper deals with the issues of rights of newsmen, press subpoenas, shield laws, police impersonation of newsmen, the underground press, and access to news. He played no part in the preparation of the recommendation on the Pentagon Papers, which involved his newspaper. The appendix includes the text of shield laws, Department of Justice Guidelines for Subpoenas to the News Media, and the Supreme Court's Pentagon Papers decision.

Twynam, Ella. *John Toland, Freethinker, 1670–1720.* [London?], Privately Printed, 1968. 31p.　**1T195**
An account of the life and ideas of a British freethinker whose earliest work, *Christianity Not Mysterious*, was condemned by the Lower House of Convocation and ordered by Parliament to be burned by the common hangman.

———. *Peter Annet, 1693–1769.* London, Pioneer Press, 1925. 16p.　**1T196**
The author deals with the prosecution of a deistical writer for publication of a blasphemous libel in 1763. The publication, entitled *The Free Inquirer*, it was charged, tended "to

blaspheme Almighty God, and to ridicule, traduce, and discredit the Holy Scriptures; and to diffuse and propagate irreligious and diabolical opinions in the minds of his Majesty's subjects, and to shake the foundations of Christian religion, and of the civil and ecclesiastical government established in this kingdom." Annet was convicted and sentenced to a month in prison, to stand twice in the pillory, to spend an additional year in prison at hard labor, and to find security for his good behavior for the rest of his life.

Tyerman, Donald. "Crying for the Moon; Sri Lanka's New Press Council Law." *Index on Censorship*, 2(2):37–42, Summer 1973. **1T197**
The passage by the Sri Lanka (Ceylon) National State Assembly of a Press Council Law "is the logical conclusion of a campaign against the press of Sri Lanka begun more than ten years ago. Equally it belongs in character to the Singapore government's campaign against the press (or, indeed, India's too). And its excuse of public safety and the national interest is, of course, Mr. Smith's excuse in Rhodesia, too, for incarcerating or expelling journalists and taking exceptional measures to ensure that press freedom should not be too 'free.' "

Tyler, John E. *Access to Presidential Materials*. Columbia, Mo., Freedom of Information Center, School of Journalism, University of Missouri at Columbia, 1975. 7p. (Report no. 346) **1T198**
"This paper is a brief review of the controversy between President Richard Nixon, the Congress and the courts over access to the now-famous presidential tapes. It will include a look at the attempts by the Senate Select Committee on Presidential Campaign Activities to gain access to the tapes; the efforts by the two special Watergate prosecutors, culminating in a Supreme Court decision; the role of the House Judiciary Committee during its impeachment investigation; and the current status of the tapes, who owns them and who controls them, in light of the recently passed Presidential Recordings and Materials Preservation Act. Its purpose is to generate a better understanding of the forces which were at play during the controversy—arguments for disclosure as opposed to arguments against disclosure."

Tyler, Robert L. "Pornos and Prudes Unite!" *Humanist*, 31:30–31, July 1971 **1T199**
The prude and the porno, the author argues, might have reason for political alliance. They may face a common danger from the center. "Granting the reflex opposition to our sexual utopia by the prude, does the honest porno really want to see the sexual revolution succeed under the leadership of the 'sexologists'? Does he really want his whole marvelous game reduced to such trampoline exercises?"

Tyler, Robert M., and Doris Kaufman. "The Public Scholar and the First Amendment: A Compelling Need for Compelling Testimony." *George Washington Law Review*, 40:995–1023, July 1972. **1T200**
"This note will examine the government's need for compulsory process to obtain information and the abridgment of first amendment interests which may result from insensitive use of the subpoena power as it is applied to scholars. Further, it will suggest a method of analysis in resolving the conflict between these interests which will help to assure that a proper balance is drawn."

Tyler, William R. "La libertad de prensa en los Estados Unidos." *Revista de Occidente*, 146:145–59, May 1975. **1T201**
The status of press freedom in the United States today under the First Amendment as interpreted by the courts.

Tynan, Kenneth. "Dirty Books Can Stay." *Esquire*, 70:168–70, 258–60, October 1968. (Also in Douglas A. Hughes, *ed.*, *Perspectives on Pornography*, pp. 109–21) **1T202**
A defense of hard-core pornography as a legitimate function of literature. "One inalienable right binds all mankind together—the right of self-abuse. That—and not the abuse of others—is what distinguishes the true lover of pornography. We should encourage him to seek his literary pleasure as and where he finds it. To deny him that privilege is to invade the deepest privacy of all."

———. "Pornography? And Is That Bad?" *Performing Arts: Canada*, 6(4):4–5, Fall 1969. **1T203**

In an interview, British drama critic and author of *Oh! Calcutta!* defends eroticism and good pornography on the stage.

Tyrmand, Leopold. "The Media Shangri-La." *American Scholar*, 45:752–75, Winter 1975/76. **1T204**
A Ford Foundation fellow, born in Warsaw and educated in Paris, considers the growing conflict between American society and its communication media which, he charges, have aligned with so-called liberalism and created a monopoly under the protection of the First Amendment to the Constitution. "By successfully identifying their freedom with freedom, the media have come closer to a hegemony than any element in this society, and neither the elective government, nor religion, nor big money can do anything about it. Once there was a belief that the free press was a self-regulatory mechanism, governed by free-market principles: not good, not bought. We know now that this is not true. A monopoly has imposed its rules, while the sturdy historic American tendency to break monopolies has become bogged down in sophistry this time. A dispute has been going on since the First Amendment, and only one specious dogma has reached the general awareness: that we can monitor everything from food to air quality, except the quality of the food for popular thinking. An obvious violation of the amendment, whose essence is that *everything* can and should be amended if need be. It all boils down to a choice. Either the free press will correct and censor itself by the open competition of variegated ideas, not bank accounts; or it must accept social supervision."

[Tytler, James.] [*Petition and Complaint*.] Edinburgh, 1792. 11p. **1T205**
Tytler is charged with giving William Turnbull, printer, the manuscript for a pamphlet, *To the People and Their Friends*, to print 500 copies. An undistributed portion of the printed pamphlet was returned to the printer to add a paragraph, which was charged as seditious. Tytler had urged the reader to refuse to pay his taxes until the king heeded the wishes of the people.

U

Uhlan, Edward. "The Tilted Fig Leaf." In his *The Rogue of Publishers' Row: Confessions of a Publisher*. New York, Exposition, 1956, pp. 161–73. **1U1**

A publisher reminisces about censorship, particularly in the area of sex. He concludes that, despite the fears of book censors and critics, the young are not likely to be corrupted by books.

Ulanov, Barry. "Criticism and Censorship." In his *The Two Worlds of American Art*. New York, Macmillan, 1965, pp. 449–65. **1U2**

"The proponents of a public philosophy in the arts tend to be censorious, however little they may want to invoke the machinery of censorship in support of their positions. The Scholar-critics, while far from a bland indifference to other men's points of view, tend to fight out their differences in comparatively recondite language, in the pages of journals somewhat remote from the interests or competency of the large reading public. . . . Can one hope in time to find censoriousness a matter of tone—as among serious critics—rather than a matter of public action—as in committees of censors?"

Ulin, Arnold A. *Small Station Management and the Control of Radiobroadcasting*. Cambridge, Mass., Littauer Center, Harvard University, 1948. 28p. (Radiobroadcasting Research Project. Studies in the Control of Radio, no. 6) **1U3**

A case study of one locally owned broadcasting station and its attempts to control programming standards. The author concludes that the practical difficulties and political implications of government "snooping" would impair any efforts toward control of program standards. "In its present attempt to regulate such standards the government may be moving beyond an effective degree of centralized control. We have, indeed, arrived at a crucial point in the regulatory history of this enterprise."

Umrigar, K. D. *Journalists and the Law*.

Allahabad, India, Law Book Co., 1969. 262p. **1U4**

In a section on press freedom the author discusses trial by newspaper, libel, official secrets, contempt of court, infringement of privacy, and fair comment. Emphasis is on Indian and British law, but there are references throughout to press law in other countries. The appendix includes text of the Freedom of Speech section in the Indian Constitution, Laws Regulating the Indian Press, the Indian Official Secrets Act (1923), and the Press Council Act (1965).

Underwood, Kenneth E. "Education Crisis in Kanawha County." *School Administrator*, 32(1):4–5, January 1975. **1U5**

The superintendent of Kanawha County Schools reports on the devastation wrought on that school system "by a calculated attack [on textbook adoption] initiated by a board member seeking to superimpose personal bias, ideologies, and political persuasion upon others who, in a democratic society, should be guaranteed the right to decide for themselves." He discusses the campaign of fundamentalist groups in the community, backed by influential and well-financed national groups, to control school textbooks through threats of reprisal and violence, leaving the children the real victims.

Ungar, Sanford J. "The Battle for Press Freedom." *Progressive*, 37:42–46, January 1973. **1U6**

Comment on the cases of Peter Bridge and William Farr and the issue of newsmen's privileges. "To deny newsmen the ability to operate with total freedom abrogates a constitutional heritage and also keeps information from the people. . . . Ultimately, it may be that the advent of an absolute newsmen's privilege would encourage some irresponsibility. But freedom of the press, in the last analysis, is freedom for the irresponsible press, freedom for everyone to get his or her message to the people. The privilege . . . might initially hamper the prosecution of a few 'crimes,' but the government can surely develop and improve its own constitutional investigative techniques without relying upon newsmen."

———. *The Papers & The Papers: An Account of the Legal and Political Battle Over the Pentagon Papers*. New York, Dutton, 1972. 319p. **1U7**

The author, who covered the story of Daniel Ellsworth and the Pentagon Papers for the *Washington Post* from the first scoop in the *New York Times* through the ruling of the U.S. Supreme Court, writes of this historic clash between freedom of the press and the federal government. He reports on behind-the-scene events, relying on information gathered from the mass of documents generated by the case and upon interviews with participants in newspaper and government offices. "This work," he writes in the preface, "is intended as a portrait of people and institutions under stress, a chronicle of what I believe to have been a period of critical importance in the relationship between the American government and the press."

———. "The Pentagon Papers." *Esquire*, 77(5):99–108+, May 1972. **1U8**

"The true inside story of how the *New York Times* and the *Washington Post* decided which government secrets were fit to print."

United Church of Christ. Office of Communication. *How To Protect Citizen Rights in Television and Radio*. New York, United Church of Christ, 1969. 18p. **1U9**

If a broadcaster does not live up to his responsibility to serve the public, the public has a right to demand that his license be taken away and be given to a licensee who will act in the public interest. A guide to how citizens can evaluate stations in their communities and act to improve programs.

———. *In Defense of Fairness. A Report of a Program to Defend the Public Interest in Broadcasting by Combatting the Practices of Some Radio and Television Stations that Air Extremist Viewpoints on Controversial Issues of Public Importance Without Counterbalancing Them with Other Prevailing Views. Conducted Under Grants from the*

Field Foundation ₍and₎ the American Federation of Labor—Congress of Industrial Organizations. New York, United Church of Christ ₍1969?₎. Unpaged. **1U10**

―――. *Racial Justice in Broadcasting.* New York, United Church of Christ ₍1970?₎. 16p. **1U11**
Report of a program to combat discrimination practices by broadcasting licensees against blacks and other minorities.

United Nations. *These Rights and Freedoms.* Lake Success, N.Y., The UN, 1950. 214p. (UN 1950.1.6) **1U12**
Includes chapters on the formation of the 1948 Universal Declaration of Human Rights, the Conference on Freedom of Information, and text of the 1949 Convention on the International Transmission of News and the Right of Reply.

―――. *Universal Declaration of Human Rights Adopted and Proclaimed by the General Assembly of the United Nations on the tenth day of December 1948. Final Authorized Text.* Lake Success, N.Y., The UN, 1952. 12p. (UN Document A/810) **1U13**
Article 19 guarantees the right to freedom of opinion and expression through any media; Article 27 guarantees the right to enjoy the arts and to share in scientific advancement.

United Nations. Educational, Scientific and Cultural Organization (UNESCO). *Meeting of Experts on a Draft Declaration Concerning the Role of the Mass Media. Report.* Paris, UNESCO, 1974. 11p. **1U14**
Meeting on the draft declaration concerning the use of the mass media for the promotion of international understanding and peace and the elimination of war propaganda, racial discrimination and apartheid; also mentions human rights and freedom of information; includes the text of the Draft Declaration of Fundamental Principles Governing the Use of the Mass Media.

United Nations. Educational, Scientific and Cultural Organization (UNESCO). Department of Mass Communications. *Removing Taxes on Knowledge.* New York, UNESCO Publications Center, 1969. 43p. (Reports and Papers on Mass Communications, no. 58) **1U15**
This study brings up to date the 1951 UNESCO publication, *Trade Barriers to Knowledge* (U32), suggesting both short and long-term solutions toward elimination of trade barriers to the free interchange of educational, cultural, and scientific materials.

United States. Attorney General. *Congress Has Not Abridged Freedom of Press, in Supreme Court, Oct. Term, 1912, nos. 818 and 819, Journal of Commerce and Commercial Bulletin v. Frank H. Hitchcock, as Postmaster General and George W. Wickersham, as Attorney General, et al.; Lewis Publishing Company ₍publishers of Morning Telegraph₎ v. Edward M. Morgan, as Postmaster for New York City, Appeals from Court of Southern District of New York; Brief in Behalf of United States.* Washington, D.C., Govt. Print. Off., 1912. 54p. **1U16**
The U.S. Supreme Court upheld the Post Office Department in cases where newspapers had charged that postal regulations on second-class matter were an abridgement of the First Amendment.

United States. Commission on Government Security. *Report Pursuant to Public Law 304, 84th Congress, as Amended.* Washington, D.C., Govt. Print. Off., 1957. 807p. (Senate Document no. 64, 85th Cong., 1st sess.) **1U17**
Established by Congress in 1955, the Commission was mandated to study and make recommendations on laws and regulations relating to national security, with particular emphasis on defense against agents of Soviet imperialism. The recommendations of the Commission included the establishment of a central security agency, the continuance of the Attorney General's list of proscribed organizations, loyalty programs for federal employees, and changes in the document classification system to abolish the "confidential" classification. This last mentioned action would eliminate the immense task of declassifying "confidential" documents. "The report of the Commission stresses the dangers to national security that arise out of overclassification of information which retards scientific and technological progress, and thus tend to deprive the country of the lead time that results from the free exchange of ideas and information." Lloyd Wright was chairman of the Commission.

₍United States. Commission on Obscenity and Pornography.₎ *The Illustrated Presidential Report of the Commission on Obscenity and Pornography.* Edited and with a Foreword by Earl Kemp . . . With an Introduction by Dr. Eason Monroe, Executive Director for Southern California, American Civil Liberties Union, and with Prefaces by Donald H. Gilmore . . . and Roger Blake . . . . San Diego, Calif., Greenleaf Classics, 1970. 352p. **1U18**
The publishers have included in this unofficial printing of the text of the *Report* "illustrative material as examples of the type of subject matter discussed and the type of material

shown to persons who were part of the research projects engaged in for the Commission as basis for their *Report*." The publisher of the edition was charged with violation of the obscenity law and the U.S. Supreme Court upheld the conviction (*Hamling v. U.S.*, 1974).

₍―――.₎ *The Obscenity Report, Containing an Edited Version of the Complete and Unexpurgated Findings of the Presidential Commission on Obscenity and Pornography, Followed by the Recommendations of the Commission and the Reports of the Panels to the Commission, with the Dissenting Report of Commissioner Charles H. Keating, Jr.; Incorporating the Report of the Arts Council of Great Britain (1969) on the Obscene Publications Acts; and, the Report from the Danish Forensic Medicine Council to the Danish Penal Code Council, 1966.* With an Introduction by John Trevelyan, O.B.E., a Preface by Maurice Girodias, and a Statement by President Richard M. Nixon. London, Olympia, 1971. 256p. **1U19**
"One cannot read these two (U.S. and British) reports without being impressed by the fact that in each case responsible people weighed the available evidence and reached the conclusion that we were unnecessarily worried about the sale of obscenity and pornography to adults who want to buy it" (from the foreword by John Trevelyan, former British film censor).

―――. *Progress Report, July 1969.* ₍Washington, D.C., The Commission₎, 1969. 26p. (Also published in U.S. House of Representatives, Committee on Post Office and Civil Service, Subcommittee on Postal Operations, *Obscenity in the Mails. Hearings. . . . ,* pp. 101–26) **1U20**
This interim report of the Commission, established in October 1967, makes no recommendations, but "reports the manner in which the Commission is carrying out its assignments, and the directions its studies, investigation and research are taking." A tentative draft of a statute regulating unsolicited mailings of potentially offensive materials is appended. Separate remarks of Commissioner Morton A. Hill are included.

―――. *Report.* New York, Bantam, 1970. 700p. (Introduction by Clive Barnes) **1U21**
This edition of the Report was set in type from materials released by the Commission to the press on 30 September 1970.

―――. *The Report of the Commission on*

Obscenity and Pornography. Washington, D.C., Govt. Print. Off., 1970. 646p.
1U22

The Commission on Obscenity and Pornography was established by Congress in 1967 to consider the traffic in obscenity and pornography which was "a matter of national concern." The Commission was charged with the "responsibility to investigate the gravity of this situation and to determine whether such materials are harmful to the public, and particularly to minors, and whether more effective methods should be devised to control the transmission of such materials." The Commission, appointed by President Johnson, initiated a program of research, solicited written statements from concerned organizations, and held a series of public hearings. Its final report is organized as follows: Part I, Overview of Findings (Volume of Traffic and Patterns of Distribution of Sexually Oriented Materials; The Effects of Explicit Sexual Materials; Positive Approaches—Sex Education, Industry Self-Regulation, and Citizens Action Groups). Part II, Recommendations (nonlegislative and legislative). Part III, Reports of the Panels. Part IV, Separate Statements of Commission Members: Irving Lehrman, Joseph T. Klapper, G. William Jones, Otto N. Larsen and Marvin E. Wolfgang, Winfrey C. Link, Morris A. Lipton and Edward D. Greenwood, Morton A. Hill and Winfrey C. Link, and Charles H. Keating, Jr. Nonlegislative recommendations: (1) promotion of a massive sex education effort; (2) continuation of open discussions on obscenity and pornography based on factual information; and (3) the organization of local, regional, and national citizens groups to implement these goals. Legislative recommendations: (1) repeal of all federal, state, and local legislation prohibiting the sale, exhibition, and distribution of sexual materials to consenting adults; (2) adoption by states of legislation (a draft is proposed) prohibiting the commercial distribution or display for sale of certain sexual materials for young people; (3) passage of state and local legislation prohibiting public display of sexually explicit pictorial materials; and (4) enactment of legislation authorizing prosecutors to obtain declaratory judgment as to whether particular sexual materials are actionable (a model statute is offered). A minority of the Commission (Morton A. Hill, Winfrey C. Link, and Charles H. Keating, Jr.) objected strongly to the recommendations and wrote separate reports criticizing the conduct of the Commission, the bias of its members, and the research which the Commission sponsored. They denounced the document as "a Magna Carta for the pornographer." Their reports are included, together with supporting data. On the other hand, two sociologist members (Otto N. Larsen and Marvin E. Wolfgang) wished to push the Commission findings further than the majority, and recommend "no specific statutory restrictions on obscenity or pornography," even for the protection of juveniles. The Commission report was denounced by President Nixon as "morally bankrupt." It was

rejected with equal vehemence by the Congress. Controversy over the recommendations and the research on which the recommendations were based has been the subject of widespread commentary in the press, both popular and scholarly. Much of the controversy was over the validity of the studies relating to effects of sexual materials. The report stated that "empirical research designed to clarify the question has found no evidence to date that exposure to explicit sexual materials plays a significant role in the causation of delinquent or criminal behavior among youth or adults."

[————.] *The Report of the U.S. Commission on Hardcore Porno*. Melbourne, Australia, Baker Publishing Co., 1973. 95p. (Volcano Books)
1U23
An edited version of the findings of the U.S. Commission on Obscenity and Pornography. "Sale to persons under 18 years of age strictly prohibited."

————. *Technical Reports*. Washington, D.C., Govt. Print. Off., 1971. 6 vols.
1U24
Vol. I, Preliminary Studies (literature reviews, theoretical analyses, preliminary empirical observations). Vol. II, Legal Analyses (obscenity law in the United States, historical and philosophical perspectives, comparative perspectives—other countries). Vol. III, The Marketplace: The Industry (motion pictures, books and magazines, mail order, "under the counter" or "hard-core" pornography). Vol. IV, The Marketplace: Empirical Studies (pornography in Denver, Boston, and San Francisco; characteristics of patrons; pornography in Denmark). Vol. V, Societal Control Mechanisms (law enforcement, citizen action groups, industry self-regulation, sex education). Vol. VI, National Survey of Public Attitudes Toward and Experience with Erotic Materials. Vols. VII and VIII, Erotica and Antisocial Behavior. Individual reports within the volumes are entered under the names of their authors in this bibliography. Reviews of the *Technical Reports* appeared in issues of the *Newsletter on Intellectual Freedom* (IFC-ALA) during 1973.

[————.] *To Deprave and Corrupt: Technical Reports of the United States Commission on Obscenity and Pornography*. Edited and Abridged by Alan Burns. London, Davis-Poynter, 1972. 191p.
1U25
In abridging the reports for the general British reader, the editor attempted to retain both the ideas and the preconceptions of the authors, omitting matters of exclusive interest to American citizens, substituting common terms for technical jargon, and deleting some of the methodology and bibliography.

United States. Congress. House of Representatives. Committee on the Armed Services. *Hearings on Investigation of National Defense Establishment; Study of Regulations and Procedures, Classification and Dissemination of Information*. *Special Sub-*

committee No. 6 . . . Under the Authority of H. Res. 67. Hearings held March 10, 11, 12, April 1, and July 9, 1958. Washington, D.C., Govt. Print. Off., 1958. 1144p. (85th Cong., 2d sess.)
1U26
In addition to testimony from officials of the Department of Defense, there are texts of documents relating to the classification of defense documents, including Executive Order No. 10501, Safeguarding Official Information in the Interests of the Defense of the United States; Department of Army Report on Scientific Information; Report to the Secretary of Defense by the Committee on Classified Information (1956); the Department of the Navy Security Manual for Classified Information; and various Army Regulations on dissemination of information.

————. *U.S.—Vietnam Relations, 1945–1967* [*Pentagon Papers*]. Washington, D.C., Govt. Print. Off., 1971. 12 vols.
1U27
The first forty-three of forty-seven volumes of the Pentagon Papers, declassified at the request of the House Armed Services Committee. The "official" publication of the report released after portions of the report had been published in the *New York Times* and the *Washington Post*. Other editions were published by Bantam/Quadrangle and by Beacon Press (Senator Gravel edition). None was complete.

United States. Congress. House of Representatives. Committee on the District of Columbia. *Exempt Theater Motion Picture Projectionists from Prosecution under D.C. Obscenity Law. Report to Accompany H.R. 2745*. Washington, D.C., Govt. Print. Off., 1970. 6p. (House Report 91-1723, 91st Cong., 2d sess.)
1U28
Because of the increase in the number and boldness of sex-type films being exhibited in the District of Columbia, the motion picture projectionists, who have no responsibility over what films are shown, have been exposed to an ever-growing risk of arrest and prosecution. The Moving Picture Machine Operators Union requested the law to exempt the operators and the Committee recommended that the bill be approved.

United States. Congress. House of Representatives. Committee on Education and Labor. Select Subcommittee on Education. *Creating a Commission on Obscenity and Pornography. Hearing, April 20 and 24, 1967, on H.R. 2525 . . . .* Washington, D.C., Govt. Print. Off., 1967. 95p. (90th Cong., 1st sess.)
1U29
Includes supportive statements from representatives of the National Council of Juvenile Court Judges, U.S. Post Office Department, American Legion, American Book Publishers Council, National Council of Catholic Women, National Council of Catholic Men, and the National Association of Evangelicals.

United States. Congress. House of Representatives. Committee on Government Operations. *Administration of the Freedom of Information Act. Twenty-First Report by the Committee on Government Operations Together With Additional Views.* Washington, D.C., Govt. Print. Off., 1972. 89p. (House Report 91-1419, 92d Cong., 2d sess.)   **1U30**
Content: Background. Introduction, Finding, and Conclusions. Freedom of Information Regulations and Administrative Requirements. Government Roadblocks Preventing Effective Use of the Act. Public Information Experts and the Act. The High Cost of Information. Public Information Versus Publicity. The Department of Justice's Role in Administration of the Act. Litigation under the Act, 1967–72. Administrative and Legislative Objectives to Strengthen the Freedom of Information Act.

——. *Amending Section 552 of Title 5, United States Code, Known as the Freedom of Information Act.* Washington, D.C., Govt. Print. Off., 1974. 29p. (House Report 93-876, 93d Cong., 2d sess.)   **1U31**

The report approved H.R. 12471, which seeks to strengthen the procedural aspects of the Freedom of Information Act to "clarify certain provisions of the Act, improve its administration, and expedite the handling of requests for information from Federal agencies in order to contribute to the fuller and faster release of information, which is the object of the Act."

——. *Executive Classification of Information—Security Classification Problems Involving Exemption (b) (1) of the Freedom of Information Act (5 U.S.C. 552). Third Report . . . .* Washington, D.C., Govt. Print. Off., 1973. 113p. (House Report 93–221, 93d Cong., 1st sess.)   **1U32**
Content: Historical Background. Previous Studies of Security Classification System. Security Classification and the Freedom of Information Act. Dimensions of the Classification Problem. Executive Order 11652 Issued by President Nixon. The Classification System—Historical Research Problems. Security Classification System—Executive Order Versus Statute. Conclusions. Recommendations. Text of Executive Orders Nos. 11652 and 11714.

——. *Freedom of Information Act (Compilation and Analysis of Department Regulations Implementing 5 U.S.C. 552); November 1968.* Washington, D.C., Govt. Print. Off., 1968. 314p. (Committee Print, 90th Cong., 2d sess.) **1U33**
A general analysis of regulations, a review of the Act after one year, and text of the Attorney General's Memorandum and regulations from

executive offices and independent agencies and commissions.

United States. Congress. House of Representatives. Committee on Government Operations. Subcommittee on Foreign Operations and Government Information. *Access by the Congress to Information from Regulatory Boards and Commissions.* Washington, D.C., Govt. Print. Off., 1970. 41p. (Committee Print, 91st Cong., 2d sess.)   **1U34**
Compilation of responses to a Committee questionnaire sent to regulatory boards and commissions to identify and clarify the appropriate statutes and current rules and regulations governing access to information by the Congress.

——. *Availability of Information to Congress. Hearings . . . on H.R. 4938 . . . H.R. 5983 . . . and H.R. 6438 . . . , April 3, 4, and 19, 1973.* Washington, D.C., Govt. Print. Off., 1973. 361p. (93d Cong., 1st sess.)   **1U35**
Statements from members of Congress, the General Accounting Office, Common Cause, and others with respect to bills to amend the Freedom of Information Act to require the executive branch to supply Congress with information when requested.

——. *The Freedom of Information Act. Hearings before a Subcommittee of the Committee on Government Operations . . . on H.R. 5425 . . . and H.R. 4960 . . . , May 2, 7, 8, 10, and 16, 1973.* Washington, D.C., Govt. Print. Off., 1973. 412p. (93d Cong., 1st sess.) **1U36**
The hearings were held on proposals to amend the U.S. Code to limit exemptions on disclosures of information, and to establish a Freedom of Information Commission. Statements were received from government officials, representatives of the press, and members of the Bar. Chairman William S. Moorhead noted that, while government secrecy has been greatly reduced in the seven years since the passage of the first Freedom of Information Act, the legislation did not become the weapon that the press needed in its fight against secrecy. Part of the blame must be shouldered by the press for not making greater use of the law, part on the administration of the law, and part on defects in the law itself, which the Congress now seeks to remedy.

——. *U.S. Government Information Policies and Practices—The Pentagon Papers. Hearings . . . [23 June 1971–1 June 1972].* Washington, D.C., Govt. Print. Off., 1971. 3758p. (9 pts.) (92d Cong., 1st and 2d sessions)   **1U37**
These hearings focus on the withholding of information by the claim of executive privilege, the misclassification of information, and prior restraint of publication by the executive branch. Testimony was received from

government officials, particularly those dealing with the classification of documents, Congressmen, university professors, and media representatives. The first three parts deal largely with the issues raised by the publication of the Pentagon Papers and the ensuing legal case; parts 4–6 deal with the administration and operation of the Freedom of Information Act; part 7 deals with the security classification problems under the Freedom of Information Act; part 8 deals with problems of Congress in obtaining information from the executive branch; part 9 deals with public access to information from executive branch advisory groups.

United States. Congress. House of Representatives. Committee on Government Operations. Subcommittee on Government Activities. *Use of the Postal Service for Unsolicited Advertisements of Hard-Core Pornographic or Otherwise Obscene Material.* Washington, D.C., Govt. Print. Off., 1969. 41p. (91st Cong., 1st sess.)   **1U38**
Testimony of Postmaster General Winton M. Blount and other officials of the Post Office Department.

United States. Congress. House of Representatives. Committee on Government Operations. Subcommittee on Government Information and Individual Rights. *Government in the Sunshine: Hearings . . . on H.R. 10315 and H.R. 9868 to Provide that Meetings of Government Agencies Shall Be Open to the Public . . . November 6 and 12, 1975.* Washington, D.C., Govt. Print. Off., 1975. 565p. (94th Cong., 1st sess.) **1U39**

United States. Congress. House of Representatives. Committee on Interstate and Foreign Commerce. *Political Broadcasting . . . . Conference Report to Accompany S. 3637, August 13, 1970.* Washington, D.C., Govt. Print. Off., 1970. 6p. (Report 91-1420, 91st Cong., 2d sess.)   **1U40**
A report of a Senate-House conference committee agreeing upon an amendment to Section 315 of the Communications Act of 1935 with respect to equal time requirements for candidates for public office.

——. *Proceedings Against Frank Stanton and Columbia Broadcasting System.* Washington, D.C., Govt. Print. Off., 1971. 272p. (House Report 92-349, 92d Cong., 1st sess.)   **1U41**
The Committee ruled that Frank Stanton,

president of Columbia Broadcasting System, was without legal justification when he refused to comply with the Committee's subpoena to supply film and related materials dealing with a CBS documentary, The Selling of the Pentagon. The refusal was based on the belief that the subpoena was in violation of the First Amendment to the Constitution. Specific arguments advanced by the CBS brief and answered by the Committee: (1) the legislative purpose and scope of the subpoena were improper; (2) the First Amendment is applicable to broadcasting; (3) the press has a right to criticize the government; (4) the subcommittee subpoena has a "chilling effect" on news reporting; (5) film "outtakes" are equivalent to reporters' notes; (6) reliance on the *Caldwell* case; and (7) absence of allegations of illegal conduct. The report of the minority members of the Committee who opposed the citation, is also included.

————. *Regulation of Radio and Television Cigarette Advertisements. Hearings . . . June 10, 1969 . . . .* Washington, D.C., Govt. Print. Off., 1969. 266p. (91st Cong., 1st sess.)   **1U42**
Includes the Broadcast Cigarette Advertising Report of the Code Authority, National Association of Broadcasters; and Cigarette Advertising Guidelines of the Radio and Television Boards of the National Association of Broadcasters.

United States. Congress. House of Representatives. Committee on Interstate and Foreign Commerce. Subcommittee on Communications. *Broadcast Advertising and Children. Hearings . . . on the Problems Associated with Broadcast Advertising Directed Toward Children, the Amount of Such Advertising and Its Content and the Regulatory Functions of the Federal Communications Commission and the Federal Trade Commission. July 14, 15, 16, and 17, 1975.* Washington, D.C., Govt. Print. Off., 1975. 495p. (94th Cong., 1st sess.)   **1U43**
Statements from representatives of the broadcasting and advertising industries and from such concerned groups as Action for Children's Television (ACT), Council on Children's Media and Advertising, Children's Television Workshop, Council of Better Business Bureaus, and Media Action Research Center, Inc. (MARC).

United States. Congress. House of Representatives. Committee on Interstate and Foreign Commerce. Subcommittee on Communications and Power. *Broadcast License Renewal. Hearings . . . on [12] Bills to Amend the Communications*

Act of 1934 with Regard to Renewal of Broadcast Licenses. Washington, D.C., Govt. Print. Off., 1973. 1209p. (2 pts.) (93d Cong., 1st sess.)   **1U44**
Statements from members of Congress, government officials, and representatives of the broadcasting industry and special interest groups.

————. *Films and Broadcasts Demeaning Ethnic, Racial, and Religious Groups. Hearings . . . on H. Con. Res. 262 and H. Con. Res. 304 . . . , September 21, 1970.* Washington, D.C., Govt. Print. Off., 1970. 97p. (91st Cong., 2d sess.)   **1U45**
The resolutions state "that the sense of Congress finds ethnic, racial, or religious defamation or ridicule existing in motion pictures or in programs produced for the electronic media, and that the producers of such so-called entertainment should develop and adhere to a code of ethics that would rule such material out of bounds." Among those testifying were representatives from the Congress of Italian-American Organizations, Japanese American Citizens League, National Association of Broadcasters, and the National Mexican American Anti-Defamation Committee.

————. *Films and Broadcasts Demeaning Ethnic, Racial, or Religious Groups—1971. Hearings . . . on H. Con. Res. 9 and H. Con. Res. 182 . . . April 27 and 28, 1971.* Washington, D.C., Govt. Print. Off., 1971. 67p. (92d Cong., 1st sess.)   **1U46**
A continuation of hearings on the resolutions "expressing the sense of Congress relating to films and broadcasts which defame, stereotype, ridicule, demean, or degrade ethnic, racial, and religious groups."

————. *Political Broadcasting, 1970. Hearings . . . on H.R. 13721 [etc.] June 2, 3, and 4, 1970.* Washington, D.C., Govt. Print. Off., 1970. 127p. (91st Cong., 2d sess.)   **1U47**
Hearings on seven House Resolutions and one Senate Bill which would amend the Communications Act of 1934 to provide candidates for Congressional offices with certain opportunities to purchase broadcast time from public television broadcasting stations, and for other purposes.

————. *Political Broadcasting, 1971. Hearings . . . on H.R. 8627, H.R. 8628 . . . Bills to Regulate the Use of Communications Media By Candidates for Elective Public Office, June 8, 9, 10, 15, and 16, 1971 . . . .* Washington, D.C., Govt. Print. Off., 1971. 299p.   **1U48**
President Nixon had vetoed a bill passed by the previous Congress to repeal the "equal time" provisions of broadcasting for presidential and vice-presidential general elections. He wished

the bill to apply equally to newspapers. The new bill was intended to meet those objections.

United States. Congress. House of Representatives. Committee on Interstate and Foreign Commerce. Special Subcommittee on Investigations. *Deceptive Programing Practices. Hearings . . . Staging of Marihuana Broadcast—"Pot Party at a University," April 15, 29; May 9, 10; June 17, 1968.* Washington, D.C., Govt. Print. Off., 1968. 364p. (90th Cong., 2d sess.)   **1U49**
An investigation of charges that Chicago station WBBM-TV may have violated the Federal Communications Act of 1934 and the Federal Trade Commission Act by staging a "pot party" for telecasting.

————. *Deceptive Programing Practices. Staging of Marihuana Broadcast—"Pot Party at a University." Report . . . .* Washington, D.C., Govt. Print. Off., 1969. 47p. (House Report 91-108, 91st Cong., 1st sess.)   **1U50**
The Congressional investigation involved charges that a television program entitled Pot Party at a University, broadcast by station WBBM-TV, Chicago, was staged. The issue involved possible violation of the Communications Act of 1934 and the Federal Trade Commission Act, and "whether the pertinent statutes and regulations contained provisions adequate to protect the public interest in light of the testimony and evidence received during the course of these proceedings."

————. *The Fairness Doctrine and Related Issues. Report . . . .* Washington, D.C., Govt. Print. Off., 1969. 159p. (House Report 91-257, 91st Cong., 1st sess.)   **1U51**
The report concludes that equal-time requirements should be amended so as to allow for a differential degree of access for major as opposed to minor political candidates; once the Supreme Court has acted, the Federal Communications Commission should conduct definitive rule-making hearings on the entire subject of the fairness doctrine; and the right of an individual to respond to derogatory or defamatory statements broadcast over the air should be definitely established by statute. Following a review of the issues, the report publishes a summary of panel discussions presented at the hearings of 5 and 6 March 1968.

————. *Fairness Doctrine. Hearings . . . . Panel Discussion on Fairness Doctrine and Related Subjects, March 5 and 6, 1968.* Washington, D.C., Govt. Print. Off., 1968. 245p. (90th Cong., 2d sess.)   **1U52**
The controversial fairness doctrine in broadcasting is discussed in eight papers: Paper 1—The Role and Influence of Radio and Television in the Formation of Public Opinion:

Comparison with Newspapers, Magazines, and Specialized Journals of Opinion by Elmer W. Lower. Paper 2—The Equal Time Requirements of Section 315 of the Communications Act of 1934 by Frank Stanton. Paper 3—The Fairness Doctrine, the Law, and Policy in Its Present Application by Glen O. Robinson. Paper 4—The Effect of the Fairness Doctrine on Broadcast News Operations by Reuven Frank. Paper 5—The Effect of Section 315 and the Fairness Doctrine on Educational Broadcasting by William G. Harley. Paper 6—The Effect of the Fairness Doctrine on the Broadcasting of Public Controversy by Vincent T. Wasilewski. Paper 7—The Fairness Doctrine: Its Use and Application by Jay Crouse. Paper 8—The Fairness Doctrine, Equal Time, Reply to Personal Attacks, and the Local Service Obligation; Implications of Technological Change by Louis L. Jaffe. Prominent authorities in the broadcasting field comment on each paper. In the appendix is a Legislative History of the Fairness Doctrine prepared by the staff of the Committee. The history is also issued as a separate twenty-nine-page committee print.

————. *Inquiry Into Alleged Rigging of Television News Programs. Hearings . . . May 17, 18, and 23, 1972.* Washington, D.C., Govt. Print. Off., 1972. 216p. (92d Cong., 2d sess.)   **1U 53**
The hearings relate to the issue of staging of events for the television camera without disclosure in the context of news programming. Witnesses include representatives of television news, police officials, and union representatives. Text of guidelines regarding news coverage practices of five major networks are included.

————. *Network News Documentary Practices—CBS—"Project Nassau." Hearings . . . July 17, 24, 30, September 11, 17, November 7, 1969; February 10, April 16, 1970.* Washington, D.C., Govt. Print. Off., 1970. 487p. (91st Cong., 1st and 2d sessions)   **1U 54**
An investigation to determine the extent of involvement of the Columbia Broadcasting System in the Haiti invasion.

————. *Subpenaed [sic] Material Re Certain TV News Documentary Programs. Hearings . . . April 20, May 12, June 24, 1971.* Washington, D.C., Govt. Print. Off., 1971. 373p. (92d Cong., 1st sess.)   **1U 55**
The hearings involved the subpoenaing of Frank Stanton, president of Columbia Broadcasting System, to provide the Committee with certain films, written transcripts, outtakes, recordings, and other materials relating to the CBS documentary entitled The Selling of the Pentagon; also the subpoenaing of Julian Goodman, president of National Broadcasting Company, to provide similar materials relating to a documentary entitled Say Goodby. The investigation involved issues of the fairness doctrine and freedom of broadcasting under

the First Amendment. NBC complied with the subpoena; CBS voluntarily submitted only the film and written transcripts, but refused to comply with the order to supply recordings, outtakes, and other materials, challenging the legality of the subpoena. "We believe Congress cannot constitutionally compel journalists to produce such a wide range of materials." The publication of the hearings contains numerous documents relating to the production of the documentaries as well as newspaper and magazine commentary. Mr. Stanton was cited for contempt of Congress, but subsequently cleared by the courts.

United States. Congress. House of Representatives. Committee on the Judiciary. *Newspaper Preservation Act. . . . Report Together with Individual Views (to Accompany H.R. 279).* Washington, D.C., Govt. Print. Off., 1970. 13p. (House Report 91-1193, 91st Cong., 2d sess.)   **1U 56**
The Committee reports favorably on the bill (H.R. 279) to exempt from the antitrust laws certain joint newspaper-operating arrangements. The bill was subsequently enacted into law.

————. *Postmaster General's Authority Over Mailable Matter . . . . Report.* Washington, D.C., Govt. Print. Off., 1863. 15p. (Report 51, 37th Cong., 3d sess.)   **1U 57**
The official report of the Committee embodying the information in Miscellaneous Document no. 16. A three-member minority disagreed.

————. *Postmaster General's Authority Over Mailable Matter . . . . Resolution.* Washington, D.C., Govt. Print. Off., 1863. 15p. (Miscellaneous Document 16, 37th Cong., 3d sess.)   **1U 58**
Following an investigation, the Committee affirmed the right and duty of the Postmaster General to exclude from the mails those newspapers in the north, mostly in New York, that were interfering with the pursuit of the war by expression of sympathies with the rebels. The Postmaster had reported the exclusion of twelve newspapers considered treasonable in time of war. The Committee recognized the inherent danger of such summary action but believed that under the watchful eye of Congress abuses would be prevented.

————. *Prohibiting Salacious Advertising . . . . Report to Accompany H.R. 11032.* Washington, D.C., Govt. Print. Off., 1970. 8p. (Report 91-1353, 91st Cong., 2d sess.)   **1U 59**
The Committee voted favorably on the bill (as amended) to prohibit the use of interstate facilities, including the mails, for the transportation of salacious advertising. Action was taken in response to President Nixon's 2 May 1969 message to Congress, Proposals on Sex-

Oriented Mail, the text of which is included in the report.

————. *Telegraph Censorship.* Washington, D.C., Govt. Print. Off., 1861. 14p. (Report 64, 37th Cong., 2d sess.)   **1U 60**
The government should not interfere with the free transmission of news by telegraph if not in the aid of the enemy, except when the government requires the exclusive use of the facility.

United States. Congress. House of Representatives. Judiciary Committee. Antitrust Subcommittee. *Newspaper Preservation Act. Hearings . . . on H.R. 19123 and Related Bills to Exempt from the Antitrust Laws Certain Joint Newspaper Operating Arrangements. Sept. 18–Oct. 3, 1968.* Washington, D.C., Govt. Print. Off., 1968. 500p. (90th Cong., 2d sess.)   **1U 61**
Testimony for and against the bills to exempt certain newspaper joint operating practices from the antitrust laws was given by members of Congress, newspaper publishers, representatives of labor unions, the National Newspaper Association, the Federal Trade Commission, and the Department of Justice.

————. *Newspaper Preservation Act. Hearings . . . on H.R. 279 and Related Bills . . . September 10, 24, 25 and October 1, 1969.* Washington, D.C., Govt. Print. Off., 1969. 536p. (91st Cong., 1st sess.)   **1U 62**
Continuation of testimony for and against bills to exempt from the antitrust laws certain joint newspaper-operating arrangements.

United States. Congress. House of Representatives. Committee on the Judiciary. Subcommittee on Courts, Civil Liberties, and the Administration of Justice. *Newsmen's Privilege. Hearings . . . on H.R. 215 . . . April 23 and 24, 1975.* Washington, D.C., Govt. Print. Off., 1976. 132p. (94th Cong., 1st sess.)   **1U 63**
A continuation of hearings (five days in the 92d Congress and ten days in the 93d Congress) on legislation to protect newsmen from revealing their news sources. Witnesses: Fred Graham, Arthur Hanson, Richard W. Jencks, Jack Nelson, Antonin Scalia, Len H. Small, and William Small. Included in the appendix are request sheets for newsmen's subpoenas, submitted to the Attorney General, 1 March 1973 to 8 May 1975.

United States. Congress. House of

Representatives. Committee on the Judiciary. Subcommittee No. 3. *Anti-Obscenity Legislation. Hearings before Subcommittee No. 3 . . . on H.R. 5171, H.R. 11009, H.R. 11031, H.R. 11032, and Related Measures . . . September 25 . . . April 16, 1970.* Washington, D.C., Govt. Print. Off., 1970. 1222p. (91st Cong.)   **1U64**

The hearings deal with the "large number of legislative proposals whose purpose is to control the great and apparently growing traffic in obscene materials, both through the mails and in commerce. The subcommittee has pending before it approximately 150 such bills. . . . A subcommittee of the Committee on Post Office and Civil Service has had referred to it on the order of 40 additional anti-obscenity bills and has been holding hearings on those." Testimony was heard from members of Congress sponsoring the bills, from representatives of Bar associations, the Citizens for Decent Literature, the Commission on Obscenity and Pornography, the Authors League of America, the Motion Picture Association of America, American Book Publishers Council, U.S. Catholic Conference, and the American Civil Liberties Union. The appendix includes: Danish regulations re sale of pornographic publications to minors, the president's message of 2 May 1969 with proposals on sex-oriented mail, a progress report from the Commission on Obscenity and Pornography, and texts of a number of bills being considered.

―――. *Newsmen's Privilege. Hearings . . . on H.R. 837, H.R. 1084 . . . H.R. 15891, H.R. 15972 . . . H.R. 16527, H.R. 16713 . . . H.R. 16542, September 21, 27, 28, October 4 and 5, 1972.* Washington, D.C., Govt. Print. Off., 1972. 275p. (92d Cong., 2d sess.)   **1U65**

The several resolutions protest nondisclosure of information and sources of information coming into the possession of the news media. In addition to the text of the resolutions there is testimony from representatives of the Pennsylvania Society of Newspaper Editors, the National Press Photographers Association, Radio Television News Directors Association, National Newspaper Association, American Society of Newspaper Editors, Associated Press Managing Editors Association, American Civil Liberties Union, Association of American Publishers, New York Press Club, Newspaper Guild, Sigma Delta Chi, American Newspaper Publishers Association, National Association of Broadcasters, and the several broadcasting networks. Peter Bridge, reporter for the now defunct *Newark Evening News*, jailed for refusal to divulge news sources, also testified as did a number of members of Congress.

―――. *Newsmen's Privilege. Hearings . . . on H.R. 717, To Assure the Free Flow of Information to the Public and Related Matters, February 5, 7, 8, 26, March 1, 5, 7, 12, 14, and 20, 1973.* Washington, D.C., Govt. Print. Off., 1973. 754p. (93d Cong., 1st sess.) **1U66**

The measures deal with creating a statutory privilege for newsmen to refuse to disclose information on the source of news. Testimony from members of Congress and representatives of such organizations as Reporters Committee for Freedom of the Press, National Newspaper Publishers Association, American Newspaper Publishers Association, American Society of Newspaper Editors, American Library Association, Association of American Publishers, National Association of Broadcasters, Newspaper Guild, Society of Magazine Writers, Association of the Bar of the City of New York, and various individual newspapers and television networks.

United States. Congress. House of Representatives. Committee on Post Office and Civil Service. *Obscene Mail Category for Minors and Potentially Offensive Sexual Material . . . . Report (to Accompany H.R. 8805).* Washington, D.C., Govt. Print. Off., 1971. 40p. (House Report 92-273, 92d Cong., 1st sess.)   **1U67**

The Committee reports favorably on a bill to amend title 39, United States Code, "to exclude from the mails as a special category of nonmailable matter certain material offered for sale to minors, to improve the protection of the right of privacy by defining obscene mail matter."

United States. Congress. House of Representatives. Committee on Post Office and Civil Service. Subcommittee on Postal Facilities and Mail. *Anti-Obscenity Legislation. Hearings . . . on H.R. 2159 . . . April 28, May 5, 1971.* Washington, D.C., Govt. Print. Off., 1971. 108p. (92d Cong., 1st sess.) **1U68**

Hearings on a "bill to amend title 39, United States Code, to exclude from the mails as a special category of nonmailable matter certain material offered for sale to minors, to improve the protection of the right of privacy by defining obscene mail matter, and for other purposes." Testimony was received from representatives from the American Civil Liberties Union, Morality in Media, Inc., and the U.S. Postal Service.

United States. Congress. House of Representatives. Committee on Post Office and Civil Service. Subcommittee on Postal Operations. *Obscenity in Mail . . . Hearings on the Report of President's Commission on Obscenity and Pornography and H.R. 19541, A Bill to Amend Title 39, United States Code, to Improve the*

Protection of a Person's Right of Privacy by Defining Obscene Mail Matter, and for Other Purposes, August 11, November 17 and 18, 1970. Washington, D.C., Govt. Print. Off., 1970. 185p. (91st Cong., 2d sess.)   **1U69**

Testimony was received from psychologists, psychiatrists, and medical doctors. Numerous periodical articles on the effect of pornography are included, some of which are entered in this bibliography under the names of the authors.

―――. *Obscenity in the Mails. Hearings . . . on H.R. 10867, A Bill to Amend Title 39, United States Code, to Exclude from the U.S. Mails as a Special Category of Nonmailable Matter Certain Obscene Material Sold or Offered for Sale to Minors, and for Other Purposes. August 5 and 6, 1969 [Part I]; October 1, 9, 22, December 10, 1969 [Part II].* Washington, D.C., Govt. Print. Off., 1969. 510p. (2 pts.) (91st Cong., 1st sess.)   **1U70**

Testimony was received from members of Congress, officials of the Post Office and the Commission on Obscenity and Pornography, representatives from the Direct Mail Advertising Association, the American Legion, Citizens for Decent Literature, and the American Civil Liberties Union. There are published statements from the Authors League of America, the American Book Publishers Council, and reprints of articles appearing in newspapers and magazines dealing with the subject of obscenity.

―――. *Privacy in the Mail. Hearings . . . . July 23 and 24, 1968.* Washington, D.C., Govt. Print. Off., 1968. 33p. (90th Cong., 2d sess.)   **1U71**

"In a society as complicated and as big as ours, we must provide new protections for our people against the panderer, the propagandist, and the unsolicited mailing of potentially dangerous products. . . . One of the responsibilities of this subcommittee is protection from invasion of privacy by mail. There is an attack on the mailbox. It is our position that the primary right in the mailbox as part of the home is in the homeowner. We are going to do what we can to protect that right" (Robert N. C. Nix, chairman).

United States. Congress. House of Representatives. Committee on Post Office and Civil Service. Subcommittee on Postal Rates. *Postal Revenue and Offensive Intrusion of Sexually Oriented Mail. Hearings . . . on H.R. 10877 . . . , June 24, 25, September 10, 12, 15, 16, 19, 24, October 17, 22, 29, November 12, 17, December 3, 10, 1969.* Washington, D.C., Govt. Print. Off., 1969. 343p. (91st Cong., 1st sess.)   **1U72**

H.R. 10877 adjusts the postal revenues and affords protection to the public from offensive intrusion into their homes of sexually oriented mail matter through the postal service.

United States. Congress. House of Representatives. Un-American Activities Committee. *Issues Presented by Air Reserve Center Training Manual. Hearings . . . .* Washington, D.C., Govt. Print. Off., 1960, pp. 1285–1321. (86th Cong., 2d sess.)   **1U73**

An inquiry into the withdrawal by the Air Force of an air reserve training manual which had referred to Communist infiltration of the National Council of Churches. The Christian Crusade reprinted and distributed copies of the hearing, with passages marked.

United States. Congress. House of Representatives and Senate. Joint Committees on Government Operations (House) and Judiciary (Senate). *Freedom of Information Act and Amendments of 1974 (P.L. 93-502). Source Book: Legislative History, Texts, and Other Documents.* Washington, D.C., Govt. Print. Off., 1975. 571p. (Joint Committee Print, 94th Cong., 1st sess.)   **1U74**

A compilation of materials relating to the legislative history of the Freedom of Information Act (5 U.S.C. 552) and the three-year investigative and legislative efforts to strengthen and improve the operation of the Act.

United States. Congress. Senate. "Resolution Declaring that the Senate Reject the Findings and Recommendations of the Commission on Obscenity and Pornography." *Congressional Record*, 116:36459–78, 13 October 1970.   **1U75**

The Senate rejected the findings of the Commission as "based on unscientific testing, inadequate review of such testing, and an attempted denial of the rights of the minority members of the Commission," and having "failed to carry out the mandate of Congress and its statutory duties by ignoring potential effects of long-term exposure to obscene and pornographic materials." Senator McClellan led the debate in favor of the resolution which passed with only five dissenting votes. The text of the minority report of the Commission is appended.

United States. Congress. Senate. Committee on Commerce. *Committee on Film Classification. Hearings . . . on S. Res. 9 to Create a Special Committee to be Known as the Committee on Film Classification . . . June 11, 1968.* Washington, D.C., Govt. Print. Off., 1968. 58p. (90th Cong., 2d sess.)   **1U76**

The proposed committee would conduct research and investigation into problems of film classification in this country and abroad and

would aid Congress in enacting legislation contemplating limitations upon the exhibition of certain motion pictures to minors.

United States. Congress. Senate. Committee on Commerce. Subcommittee on Communications. *Amended Communications Act of 1934. Hearings . . . on S. 2004 . . . .* Washington, D.C., Govt. Print. Off., 1970. 724p. (2 pts.) (91st Cong., 1st sess.)   **1U77**

The bill provides for the Federal Communications Commission, at the time it considers an application for renewal of a broadcast license, to first determine whether the public interest, convenience, and necessity has been and would be served by a grant of the application. If the answer is in the affirmative the license will be granted; if in the negative and after a hearing, it will be denied and applications for new licensees will be considered. Witnesses include representatives of the FCC and the broadcasting industry, Federal Communications Bar Association, American Newspaper Publishers Association, National Citizens Committee for Broadcasting, United Church of Christ, American Civil Liberties Union, Black United Front, Action for Children's Television, and a number of university professors. The Committee and FCC chairman Robert E. Lee also discussed obscenity in television (pp. 345–74).

——. *Analysis of the Character of Violence in Literature and Violence as Expressed through Television. Staff Report Prepared . . . by the Library of Congress.* Washington, D.C., Govt. Print. Off., 1969. 5p. (Committee Print, 91st Cong., 1st sess.)   **1U78**

"Violence in literature, if it is good literature, serves to place the human condition in perspective, to comment in some way upon the aggressive side of man's nature which is never far from the surface of human activity. Violence, when presented as the cause of human behavior to be followed by consequences, can be used to reflect constructively upon the nature of man. Violence presented for its own sake, however, serves no purpose but to desensitize the audience to which it is directed, to apotheosize aggression in such a way as to distort the truthful balance of life."

——. *Blackout of Sporting Events on TV. Hearings . . . on S. 4007 . . . S. 4010, October 3, 4, and 5, 1972.* Washington, D.C., Govt. Print. Off., 1972. 223p. (92d Cong., 2d sess.)   **1U79**

Testimony, statements and reprints of articles relating to two bills introduced to amend the act providing for an exemption from the antitrust laws, to terminate such exemption from blackouts of television of professional sports events under certain conditions.

——. *Broadcast License Renewal Act. Hearings . . . on [14 bills]. Miscellaneous*

Broadcast Renewal Legislation, June 18, 19, 20, 26, and 27, July 23, 24, 25, and 31, 1974. Washington, D.C., Govt. Print. Off., 1974. 906p. (2 pts.) (93d Cong., 2d sess.)   **1U80**

An extensive list of witnesses including members of Congress, government officials, professors, representatives of the broadcasting industry, and members of special interest groups concerned with amending the law for license renewal of radio and television stations. Additional statements, letters, and articles are given in part 2.

——. *Fairness Doctrine. Hearings . . . on S. 2 . . . S. 608 . . . S. 1178 . . . , April 28, 29, 30, May 1, and 6, 1975.* Washington, D.C., Govt. Print. Off., 1975. 451p. (94th Cong., 1st sess.)   **1U81**

S. 2 would provide for amending the Communication Act of 1934 to strengthen and further the objective of the First Amendment to radio and television broadcasting; S. 608 would amend Section 315 of the Act to exempt legally qualified candidates for the offices of president and vice-president of the United States from equal-time requirements during a presidential campaign; S. 1178 would guarantee all rights under the First Amendment to the Constitution to the electronic media and would terminate any discrimination between the print and broadcast media. Witnesses included members of Congress, representatives of the FCC, the broadcasting industry, citizens groups, and faculty members.

——. *Fairness Doctrine, Staff Report . . . on the FCC's Actions and the Broadcasters' Operations in Connection with the Commission's Fairness Doctrine.* Washington, D.C., Govt. Print. Off., 1968. 602p. (Committee Print, 90th Cong., 2d sess.)   **1U82**

Content: The Fairness Doctrine (the public interest, convenience or necessity; its content, its origin, and development). Enforcing the Fairness Doctrine (sanctions, administration). Applying the Fairness Doctrine (the stations, the major networks). Conclusions and Recommendations. The Appendices include: Selected Attitudes and Policies of Broadcast Licensees; Program Series Dealing with Issues of Public Importance; and Licensee Questionnaire. The report was prepared by Robert Lowe, special counsel to the Committee. Comment on the report appeared in *Broadcasting*, 13 May 1968.

——. *Federal Communications Commission Policy Matters and Television Programming. Hearings . . . on Review of Policy Matters of Federal Communications Commission and Inquiry into Crime and*

Violence on Television and A Proposed Study Thereof by Surgeon General. Washington, D.C., Govt. Print. Off., 1969. 517p. (2 pts.) (91st Cong., 1st sess.) **1U83**

Part 1 (March 4 and 5, 1969) includes testimony from members of the Federal Communications Commission and a table, Commercial Broadcast Stations Identified with Daily Newspaper Ownership in Same City. Part 2 (March 12, 19, and 20, 1969) includes testimony from officials of the broadcasting industry, a preliminary report of the National Commission on the Causes and Prevention of Violence, and other pertinent documents.

———. *Federal Election Campaign Act of 1973. Hearings . . . on S. 372, To Amend the Communications Act of 1934 to Relieve Broadcasters of Equal Time Requirement of Section 315 with Respect to Presidential and Vice Presidential Candidates and to Amend the Campaign Communications Reform Act to Provide a Further Limitation on Expenditures in Election Campaigns for Federal Elective Office.* Washington, D.C., Govt. Print. Off., 1973. 470p. (93d Cong., 1st sess.) **1U84**

———. *Impact of Television on Children. Hearing . . . February 13, 1976.* Washington, D.C., Govt. Print. Off., 1976. 62p. (94th Cong., 2d sess.) **1U85**
Testimony of broadcasters, educators, public officials, and church leaders on the impact of television on the nation's children, given at a hearing held in Salt Lake City. Includes a statement on the Effects on Children and Current Status of Sex, Violence and Anti-Social Content of Commercial Television Programming by Victor B. Cline, psychologist, University of Utah.

———. *Surgeon General's Report by the Scientific Advisory Committee on Television and Social Behavior. Hearings . . . March 21, 22, 23, and 24, 1972.* Washington, D.C., Govt. Print. Off., 1972. 525p. (including separate Appendix A). (92d Cong., 2d sess.) **1U86**
Testimony on the report was taken from members of the Committee, psychologists, educators, and representatives of the television networks, and the FCC. Appendix A includes The Violence Index and The Violence Profile, both prepared by George Gerbner. The text of the Report is entered in this bibliography under U.S. Surgeon General.

United States. Congress. Senate.

Committee on Foreign Relations. *Security Classification As a Problem in the Congressional Role in Foreign Policy. Prepared for Use of the Committee . . . by the Foreign Affairs Division, Legislative Reference Service, Library of Congress.* Washington, D.C., Govt. Print. Off., 1971. 41p. (Committee Print, 92d Cong., 1st sess.) **1U87**
"The purpose of this paper is to survey the security classification process to determine how it affects the work of Congress on foreign policy and to explore proposals for changing the process. It does not deal with the related problems of loyalty or censorship, and it attempts to differentiate the problem of security classification from the problem of executive privilege, that is the withholding of either classified or unclassified information from Congress by the Executive Branch on the grounds that it is the right of the President to do so."

United States. Congress. Senate. Committee on Government Operations. Subcommittee on Intergovernmental Relations. *Government Secrecy. Hearings . . . on S. 1520, S. 1726, S. 2451, S. 2738, S. 3393, and S. 3399, May 22, 23, 29, 30, 31, and June 10, 1974.* Washington, D.C., Govt. Print. Off., 1974. 907p. (93d Cong., 2d sess.) **1U88**
Consideration of six Senate bills dealing with the system of secrecy in the executive branch of government which, Chairman Edmund S. Muskie stated, "has not only denied the Congress information it requires to make effective judgments of policy, it has also withheld from the people the knowledge of the Government's behavior that is essential to popular understanding and democratic consensus." Witnesses appearing before the Committee include senators, government officials, professors, the Archivist of the United States, and persons involved with classification of records. Also included are comments from various government agencies, some in response to questions from the Committee; documents dealing with classification; and news articles on the topic of government secrecy.

———. *Legislation on Government Secrecy.* Washington, D.C., Govt. Print. Off., 1974. 265p. (Committee Print, 93d Cong., 2d sess.) **1U89**
A compendium and comparative analysis of five bills before the subcommittee dealing with government secrecy and the classification of information in the interests of national defense.

United States. Congress. Senate. Committee on Government Operations. Permanent Subcommittee on Investigations. *Negotiation and Statecraft. Hearings . . . Pursuant to Section 4, Senate Resolution 49 . . . Part 4, with Panel on the International Freedom to Write and*

Publish. November 18, 1975. Washington, D.C., Govt. Print. Off., 1975. 299p. (94th Cong., 1st sess.) **1U90**
The following representatives of the American literary community testified at this hearing which, according to the chairman Henry M. Jackson, "focuses on the American role in encouraging respect for freedom of the press and of publication, rights protected by international law and thus applicable to all societies": Robert L. Bernstein, Arthur Miller, Joseph Okpaku, Sr., Harrison Salisbury, Alan U. Schwartz, and Rose Styron.

United States. Congress. Senate. Committee on the Judiciary. *Amending the Freedom of Information Act.* Washington, D.C., Govt. Print. Off., 1974. 64p. (Senate Report 93-854, 93d Cong., 2d sess.) **1U91**
The Judiciary Committee recommended unanimously the passage of S. 2543, amending the Freedom of Information Act "to facilitate freer and more expeditious access to government information, to encourage more faithful compliance with the terms and objectives of the FOIA, to strengthen the citizen's remedy against agencies and officials who violate the Act, and to provide for closer congressional oversight of agency performance under the Act."

———. *Juvenile Delinquency. Hearings . . . Pursuant to S. Res. 342, Investigation of Juvenile Delinquency in the United States. Part 22. Pornography and Obscenity. September 23, 1970.* Washington, D.C., Govt. Print. Off., 1971, pp. 6947–7316. (91st Cong., 2d sess.) **1U92**
Three critics of the Final Report of the Commission on Obscenity and Pornography testify before the Committee: Dr. Victor B. Cline, a psychologist from University of Utah; Rev. Morton A. Hill, S.J., head of Morality in Media, Inc.; and Rev. Winfrey C. Link, administrator of a United Methodist retirement home, Hermitage, Tenn. Hill and Link were two of the three members of the Commission who submitted a minority report, the text of which is included. In it they charge that the majority report is "a Magna Carta for the pornographer." Included in the exhibits is a statement by Harry N. Hollis, Jr., director of Special Moral Concerns, Christian Life Commission, Southern Baptist Convention.

———. *Newspaper Preservation Act. Report Together with Individual Views . . . to Accompany S. 1520, November 18, 1969.* Washington, D.C., Govt. Print. Off., 1969. 18p. (91st Cong., 1st sess.) **1U93**
The Committee reports favorably on the bill (S. 1520) as amended "to exempt from the antitrust laws certain combinations and arrangements necessary for the survival of failing newspapers."

United States. Congress. Senate. Committee on the Judiciary. Subcommittee on Administrative Practice and Procedure. *Freedom of Information Act Source Book: Legislative Materials, Cases, Articles*. Washington, D.C., Govt. Print. Off., 1974. 432p. (Senate Document 93-82, 92d Cong., 2d sess.) **1U94**

Content: Legislative History of the Freedom of Information Act. Decided Court Cases Involving the Freedom of Information Act. Selected Bibliography and Articles. Freedom of Information Regulations of the Department of Justice.

―――. *The Freedom of Information Act (Ten Months Review)*. Washington, D.C., Govt. Print. Off., 1968. 252p. (Committee Print, 90th Cong., 2d sess.) **1U95**

A review of the operation of the Freedom of Information Act after its first ten months in force. Includes reports from various government agencies, court cases under the Act, and tables showing types of information presently being withheld.

United States. Congress. Senate. Committee on the Judiciary. Subcommittees on Administrative Practice and Procedure and Separation of Powers. Committee on Government Operations. Subcommittee on Intergovernmental Relations. *Freedom of Information, Executive Privilege, Secrecy in Government. Hearings . . . .* Washington, D.C., Govt. Print. Off., 1973. 537p., 325p., 620p. (3 vols.) (93d Cong., 1st sess.) **1U96**

In the wake of the Watergate affair two Senate committees considered legislation which would amend and strengthen the Freedom of Information Act to remove the curtains of secrecy from the business of the federal government. Chairman Edward Kennedy expressed hope that the new legislation would reduce the exemptions, facilitate appeals from information denials, and extend the Act to the Congress and the White House. Extensive testimony was received from government officials (including Senators Lawton Chiles and Frank Moss), representatives of the press, and from numerous consumer groups. Vol. 3 consists of published articles and reports, correspondence, memoranda, and other documents.

United States. Congress. Senate. Committee on the Judiciary. Subcommittee on Antitrust and Monopoly. *The Failing Newspaper Act. Hearings . . . Pursuant to S. Res. 233 on S. 1312, The Failing Newspaper Act . . . .* Washington, D.C., Govt. Print. Off., 1968. 3462p. (7 vols.) (90th Cong., 1st and 2d sessions) **1U97**

In opening the hearings on the proposed bill entitled The Failing Newspaper Act, the chairman, Senator Philip A. Hart, said: "Any legislation that proposes to grant antitrust exemptions will be approached with some caution. Particularly, I think, this is true where newspapers would be the subject of the exemption, because the product of newspapers, opinion and information, are essential to the kind of society that we undertake to make successful here. Other products—automobiles, steel, television sets—may be necessary, at least for the kind of society we have created, but information and opinion are indispensable. . . . If I were forced to name the one industry in which competition ought to be vigorous, it probably would be newspapers. But, we know that newspapers fail. And there may be special circumstances surrounding the newspaper business which would justify antitrust concessions not available generally to others. But, before such special treatment is provided for newspapers, the economic problems of the newspaper industry should be indentified with candor and completeness." There follows extensive testimony from the newspaper industry opposing and supporting the bill. Numerous journal articles and court decisions are reproduced as evidence.

―――. *The Newspaper Preservation Act. Hearings . . . on S. 1520, The Newspaper Preservation Act Pursuant to S. Res. 40, June 12, 13, and 20, 1969.* Washington, D.C., Govt. Print. Off., 1969. 703p. (91st Cong., 1st sess.) **1U98**

The declaration of policy of Senate Bill 1520: "In the public interest of maintaining the historic independence of the newspaper press in all parts of the United States, it is hereby declared to be the public policy of the United States to preserve the publication of newspapers in any city, community, or metropolitan area where a joint operating arrangement has been or may be entered into because of economic distress." Witnesses for and against the bill, which would modify the antitrust acts, include editors and publishers, labor leaders, law professors, businessmen, and public officials. News stories, editorials, and periodical articles on both sides are reproduced as is the text of three Supreme Court decisions—*Citizens Publishing Co. v. United States*, *Red Lion Broadcasting, Inc. v. Federal Communications Commission*, and *Simpson v. Union Oil*.

United States. Congress. Senate. Committee on the Judiciary. Subcommittee on Constitutional Rights. *Free Press–Fair Trial*. Washington, D.C., Govt. Print. Off., 1976. 22p. (Committee Print, 94th Cong., 2d sess.) **1U99**

"In this report, the subcommittee assesses the issues not conclusively resolved or, in some cases, not even addressed [by the U.S. Supreme Court] in *Nebraska v. Stuart* [1976]. It is our view that prior restraints on the press are never justified in the fair trial context. Nor is subsequent punishment of the press for publication where no restrictive orders have been issued. In some circumstances restrictive or-

ders on trial participants may be justified, but only if they conform to rigorous legislatively enacted guidelines. . . . The major portion of this report presents the case for, and substance of, legislative guidelines." A background report prepared for the Committee is listed under its authors, A. E. D. Howard and Sanford A. Newman.

―――. *Freedom of the Press. Hearings . . . September 28, 29, 30, October 12, 13, 14, 19 and 20, 1971 and February 1, 2, 8, 16, and 17, 1972.* Washington, D.C., Govt. Print. Off., 1972. 1332p. (92d Cong., 1st and 2d sess.) **1U100**

"These hearings, and the subcommittee study of which they are a part," according to Senator Sam J. Ervin, Jr., chairman, in an introductory statement, "have been organized because it is apparent that in today's America, many people doubt the vitality and significance of the First Amendment's guarantee of freedom of the press." He cites as examples the subpoenaing of journalists, the government's efforts to prevent publication of the Pentagon Papers, the use of false press credentials by government agents, and fear of government control of the broadcasting media. Testimony was received from representatives of a wide segment of the mass media, as well as from authors, scholars, and representatives of professional and consumer organizations. The appendix of this encyclopedic work on freedom of the press contains the text of important court decisions and administrative opinions, law review articles, legal briefs, newspaper and magazine articles, and reports of speeches. While the delay in the printing of this massive volume prevented a detailed listing of contents in this bibliocyclopedia, many of the items have been brought out in the index. A 4 hour, 51 minute tape recording—5 cassetts—condensation of three days of the hearings, was issued by Pacifica Tape Library, Berkeley, Calif., in 1971. It contains testimony from Ogden Reid, Frank Stanton, Richard J. Barnett, Senators Edward M. Kennedy, Hugh Scott, and Roman Hruska, Walter Cronkite, Jerome A. Barron, Julian Goodman, and Fred Friendly.

―――. *Newsmen's Privilege. Hearings . . . on S. 36, S. 158, S. 318, S. 451, S. 637, S. 750, S. 870, S. 917, S. 1128, and S. J. Res. 8, Bills to Create a Testimonial Privilege for Newsmen, February 20, 21, 22, 27, March 13 and 14, 1973.* Washington, D.C., Govt. Print. Off., 1973. 760p. (93d Cong., 1st sess.) **1U101**

Witnesses include journalists, lawyers, and members of Congress. Also included are the text of judicial decisions, pertinent newspaper and magazine articles, and speeches. Other material: A Department of Justice Memorandum, Activities Involving Subpoenas to Newsmen Since the Issuance of the Attorney General's Guidelines; An Analysis of Newsman's Privilege Legislation by the American Newspaper Publishers Association; A Position Paper on Protection of Confidential Sources and Information by the Citizens' Right to News Committee; the Department of Justice Memorandum to U.S. attorneys, Guidelines for Subpoenas to the News Media; a report of the Committee on Federal Legislation, the Association of the Bar of the City of New York, Journalists' Privilege Legislation; results of a poll of state attorneys general on confrontation between the press and investigative bodies, conducted by the American Newspaper Publishers Association; the Association's report on State Newsmen's Privilege Legislation and Cases Arising Thereunder; the Subpoena Log, A Compilation of Cases by the Reporters Committee for Freedom of the Press; and a synopsis of newsmen's privilege legislation pending before Congress.

United States. Congress. Senate. Committee on the Judiciary. Subcommittee on Separation of Powers. *Executive Privilege: The Withholding of Information by the Executive. Hearings . . . on S. 1125, July 27, 28, and 29, and August 4, 5, 1971*. Washington, D.C., Govt. Print. Off., 1971. 635p. (92d Cong., 1st sess.) **1U102**
The hearings center on S. 1125, a bill which would amend title 5 of the United States Code with regard to executive privilege—the doctrine by which the executive branch of the government refuses to divulge information requested by the Congress. The bill provides that no employee of the executive branch shall refuse to appear when summoned by Congress "on the grounds that he intends to assert executive privilege," and that executive privilege shall not be asserted without "a statement signed personally by the President requiring that the employee assert executive privilege as to the testimony or document sought." In addition to the opening statements of the chairman Sam J. Ervin, Jr. and Senator Charles C. Mathias, Jr. there is testimony from present and former government officials, professors of law and political science, and other members of the Senate. News articles and scholarly articles are reproduced as is the text of S. 1125, Executive Order 10501 (Safeguarding Official Information in the Interest of the Defense of the United States); the text of the Freedom of Information Act; and pertinent correspondence of government officials bearing on the doctrine of executive privilege.

———. *Refusal of the Executive Branch to Provide Information to the Congress, 1964–1973: A Survey of Instances in Which Executive Agencies of the Government Have Withheld Information from Members of the Congress and from the Comptroller General of the United States*. Washington, D.C., Govt. Print. Off., 1974. 571p. (Committee Print, 93d Cong., 2d sess.) **1U103**

United States. Congress. Senate. Committee on Post Office and Civil Service. *Obscenity. Hearing . . . on S. 3220 . . . , September 1, 1970*. Washington, D.C., Govt. Print. Off., 1970. 60p. (91st Cong., 2d sess.) **1U104**
Hearing on a bill to protect a person's right of privacy by providing for the designation of obscene or offensive mail matter by the sender and for the return of such matter at the expense of the sender.

———. *Pornographic Mail . . . Report To Accompany S. 3220, September 21, 1970*. Washington, D.C., Govt. Print. Off., 1970. 10p. (Senate Report 91-1217, 91st Cong., 2d sess.) **1U105**
"S. 3220 as amended adds to the procedures by which the privacy of the home may be protected from sexually oriented material by placing reasonable and enforceable restrictions upon sexual advertisements. The Committee believes that it is through advertisements of sexual material that privacy is most often invaded." The Committee recommends the passage of the bill.

———. *Postal Rates. Hearings . . . on H.R. 7977 . . . October 16, 17, 18, 19, 20, 23, 24, 25, 26, 27, and 30, 1967*. Washington, D.C., Govt. Print. Off., 1967. 679p. (90th Cong., 1st sess.) **1U106**
The bill included provisions to regulate the mailing of pandering advertisements (Title III). Testimony of Laurence Speiser of the American Civil Liberties Union (pp. 582–93) opposed this section. Most of the testimony, however, related to the serious effect of higher postal rates on the distribution of newspapers, magazines, and books.

United States. Defense Department. *Field Press Censorship*. Washington, D.C., Govt. Print. Off., 1967. 82p. (Army Field Manual, 45-25; Air Force Manual 190-5; Navy Regulation OP-NAVINST 5530.5A) **1U107**
A manual setting forth general principles of military field censorship in combat areas. Two controlling principles are cited: "The sole criterion for killing or temporary withholding of any information in material submitted for review is that it would be of value to the enemy in his prosecution of the war effort. All information which does not come under this specific heading is releasable and the field censor is enjoined to conduct his work in such manner that publication will be expedited. It is beyond his authority to suppress matter simply because it comes under the heading of 'unfavorable publicity.' "

United States. Federal Communications Commission. *Annual Report*. Washington, D.C., Govt. Print. Off. Published annually since 1934. **1U108**
The reports summarize the events of the year involving the Commission and generally include legislation and litigation, and changes in rules and regulations for broadcasting.

———. "Applicability of the Fairness Doctrine in the Handling of Controversial Issues of Public Importance." *Federal Register*, 29:10416–27, 25 July 1964. **1U109**
"It is the purpose of this Public Notice to advise broadcasting licensees and members of the public of the rights, obligations, and responsibilities of such licensees under the Commission's 'fairness doctrine,' which is applicable in any case in which broadcast facilities are used for the discussion of a controversial issue of public importance. For this purpose, we have set out a digest of the Commission's interpretive rulings on the fairness doctrine. This Notice will be revised at appropriate intervals to reflect new rulings in this area."

United States. Justice Department. *Attorney General's Memorandum on the Public Information Section of the Administrative Procedure Act. A Memorandum for the Executive Departments and Agencies Concerning Section 3 of the Administrative Procedure Act as Revised Effective July 4, 1967*. Washington, D.C., U.S. Department of Justice, 1967. 47p. **1U110**
A memorandum to federal agencies for implementing the section of the Administrative Procedures Act which provides guidelines for the public availability of the records of federal departments and agencies. In signing the legislation President Johnson noted that "the United States is an open society in which the people's right to know is cherished and guarded."

———. *Attorney General's Memorandum on the 1974 Amendments to the Freedom of Information Act. A Memorandum for the Executive Departments and Agencies Concerning the Amendments to the Freedom of Information Act (5 U.S. C. 552) . . . Effected by P.L. 93-502, Enacted November 21, 1974. . . .* Washington, D.C., U.S. Department of Justice, 1975. 26p. + **1U111**

United States. Justice Department. Criminal Division. Government Regulation Section. *Handbook for Federal Obscenity Prosecution*. Washington, D.C., Govt. Print. Off., 1972. 73p. **1U112**

The handbook lists the federal "agencies with whom we deal" in obscenity matters, describes the investigative techniques, the nature of proof, search and seizure problems, proof of obscenity, pretrial and trial practices, and cites pertinent federal cases.

United States. Library of Congress. Congressional Research Service. Foreign Affairs Division. *The Pentagon Papers as Described by the American Press: Summaries of Major Newspaper Articles.* Washington, D.C., Library of Congress, 1971. 268p. Processed. **1U113**
Summaries of articles appearing in eight newspapers, analyzing and interpreting the Pentagon Papers and the implications of their publication.

—. *The Pentagon Papers: Summaries of Documents Published in the American Press.* Washington, D.C., Library of Congress, 1971. 92p. Processed. (Prepared by Theodor Galdi) **1U114**
Abstracts of 152 Pentagon Papers documents in four newspapers, the majority (134) in the *New York Times*. Others are from the *Boston Globe*, the *St. Louis Post-Dispatch*, and the *Chicago Sun-Times*.

—. *Security Classification as a Problem in the Congressional Role in Foreign Policy. Prepared for the Use of the Committee on Foreign Relations, United States Senate . . . .* Washington, D.C., Govt. Print. Off., 1971. 41p. (Committee Print, 92d Cong., 1st sess.) **1U115**
Content: The Origin and Legal Basis of Present Classification Procedures. The Classification System in Practice—Executive Order 10501 and Agency Regulations. The Effect of the Classification System on the Congressional Role in Foreign Policy. Proposals for Changing the Classification System.

United States. National Advisory Commission on Civil Disorders. *Report of the National Advisory Commission on Civil Disorders.* Washington, D.C., Govt. Print. Off., 1968. 425p. (Also issued in hardcover by Dutton, New York, 609p. plus charts, and in paperback by Bantam, New York, 609p. plus charts) **1U116**
The Commission, headed by Governor Otto Kerner, was created by President Johnson following the racial disorders during the summer of 1967 to inquire into the cause of such disorders in America and to recommend what could be done to prevent them. A chapter in this final report of the Commission deals with the role of the news media. The Commission came to three conclusions: (1) despite incidents of sensationalism, inaccuracy, and distortion, the news media on the whole made a real effort to give factual and unbiased coverage of the 1967 disorders; (2) the overall effect, however, was

to exaggerate both the mood and events; and (3) the media failed to report adequately on the causes and consequences of the disorders and the underlying problems of race relations. The report recommends improvement of riot coverage, better liaison between police and press, establishment of central information centers, and the creation of voluntary codes of behavior for police and press. The Commission also recommends establishment of an Institute of Urban Communications to improve police-press relations through research and teaching. In the introduction the report states: "Freedom of the press is not the issue. A free press is indispensable to the preservation of the other freedoms this nation cherishes. . . . Only a free press unhindered by government can contribute to freedom."

United States. National Archives and Records Service. Office of the Federal Register. "Freedom of Information Act. Implementation Regulations. Various Government Agencies." *Federal Register*, 40:7231–7348, 19 February 1975. **1U117**
Official statements from thirty-five federal agencies are published under provisions of the Freedom of Information Act. References are also given (p. 7232) to other documents containing Freedom of Information implementation regulations previously published in the *Federal Register* or to be published at a later date.

United States. National Commission on the Cause and Prevention of Violence. *Mass Media Hearings. A Report to the National Commission on the Causes and Prevention of Violence.* Washington, D.C., Govt. Print. Off., 1969. 463p. (Vol. 9A, Staff Study Series, edited by Paul L. Briand, Jr.) **1U118**
A record of five days of hearings on the mass media, conducted by the Commission "in order to sound out the best minds in the communications media, especially in television; in the academic community, particularly communications specialists; and in the government agencies, notably the Federal Communications Commission. The record of the hearings that follow in this report center primarily on one basic question: Do media portrayals of violence cause violence? The networks, seeking a valid scientific methodology, claim no objective correlation between the two; the scholars are not that certain; and others argue that an obvious relationship exists, if we would but look at the evidence. . . . Rightfully, the media claim the protection of the First Amendment against censorship. But what protection can the mass audience claim against censorship by the media themselves?"

[—.] *Rights in Conflict. The Violent Confrontation of Demonstrators and Police in the Parks and Streets of Chicago During the Week of the Democratic National Convention of 1968. A Report Submitted by Daniel Walker, Director of the Chicago*

Study Team, to the National Commission on the Causes and Prevention of Violence. Special Introduction by Max Frankel of the *New York Times*. New York, Bantam, 1968. 362p. **1U119**
This task force considered three questions in studying the relationship of the police and the press during the period of violence (pp. 287–331): Was any news staged and manufactured by demonstrators and newsmen? Were newsmen calculated targets of violence by police? Were any police attacks on newsmen unwarranted and unprovoked? "The Government Printing Office in Washington," writes Max Frankel, "refused to publish a document containing so much outrageous language," so it had to be commercially published.

—. *To Establish Justice, To Insure Domestic Tranquility; Final Report of the National Commission on the Causes and Prevention of Violence.* Washington, D.C., Govt. Print. Off., 1969. 338p. (Also issued by Award Books, New York, 1969, 319p.) **1U120**
In the conclusion of the report of the Commission, appointed by President Lyndon B. Johnson and headed by Milton Eisenhower, there are these recommendations concerning the press: (1) the enactment of legislation that would give the United States District Court the power to grant injunctions against threatened or actual interference with the right of free speech and press; (2) that "private and governmental institutions encourage the development of competing news media and discourage increased concentration of control over existing media"; and (3) that "the members of the journalism profession continue to improve and re-evaluate their standards and practices, and to strengthen their capacity for creative self-criticism." The report also recommends that "the broadcasting of children's cartoons containing serious non-comic violence should be abandoned"; that the amount of time on TV devoted to crime and violence be reduced; that the television industry give serious attention to studying the effect of violence on viewers; and that the movie rating system be studied with respect to violence and admission standards for minors (pp. 187–207). Two staff reports prepared for the Commission are entered in this bibliography under the names of their authors: *Violence in America: Historical and Comparative Perspectives* by Hugh D. Graham and Ted R. Gurr; *Violence and the Media* by Robert K. Baker and Sandra J. Ball *et al.*

United States. Presidential Study Commission on International Radio Broadcasting. *The Right to Know. Report of the Presidential Study Commission on International Radio Broadcasting.* [Washington, D.C., Govt. Print. Off., 1973?] 91p. **1U121**

The report concludes that "Radio Free Europe and Radio Liberty by providing a flow of free and uncensored information to peoples deprived of it, actually contribute to a climate of détente rather than detract from it," and should be continued. The report "recommends the creation by Congressional action of a Board for International Broadcasting as a public institution to receive appropriated funds for allocation to Radio Free Europe and Radio Liberty," and to serve "as a nexus between the public, Congress, the Executive Branch, and the stations."

United States. Surgeon General. Scientific Advisory Committee on Television and Social Behavior. *Television and Growing Up; Impact of Television on Violence. Report to the Surgeon General, United States Public Health Service from the Surgeon General's Scientific Advisory Committee on Television and Social Behavior*. Washington, D.C., Govt. Print. Off., 1972. 279p.   **1U 122**
The report of the Commission, formed by the Surgeon General at the request of Senator John O. Pastore, to "help resolve the question of whether there is a causal connection between televised crime and violence and antisocial behavior by individuals, especially children." The findings summarized in the report derive primarily from research conducted under the program (detailed in five volumes of technical reports) but also take into account past research and other current research. "The experimental studies bearing on the effects of aggressive television entertainment content on children support certain conclusions. First, violence depicted on television can immediately or shortly thereafter induce mimicking or copying by children. Second, under certain circumstances television violence can instigate an increase in aggressive acts. The accumulated evidence, however, does not warrant the conclusion that televised violence has a uniformly adverse effect nor the conclusion that it has an adverse effect on a majority of children. It cannot even be said that the majority of children in the various studies we have reviewed showed an increase in aggressive behavior in response to the violent fare to which they were exposed. The evidence does indicate that televised violence may lead to increased aggressive behavior in certain subgroups of children, who might constitute a small portion or a substantial portion of the total population of young viewers. We cannot estimate the size of the fraction, however, since the available evidence does not come from cross-section samples of the entire American population of children. . . . There is evidence that among young children (ages four to six) those most responsive to television violence are those who are highly aggressive to start with—who are prone to engage in spontaneous aggressive actions against their playmates and, in the case of

boys, who display pleasure in viewing violence being inflicted upon others."

————. *Television and Social Behavior. An Annotated Bibliography of Research Focusing on Television's Impact on Children*. Edited by Charles K. Atkin . . . , John P. Murray . . . , and Oguz B. Nayman . . . . Rockville, Md., National Institute of Mental Health, 1971. 150p. (Public Health Service Publication no. 2099)   **1U 123**
Content: Television Content and Programming. Audience Viewing Patterns and General Effects of Television. The Impact of Television and Other Visual Media on Children and Youths.

————. *Television and Social Behavior. Reports and Papers, Volume I: Media and Control. A Technical Report to the Surgeon General's Scientific Advisory Committee on Television and Social Behavior*. Edited by George A. Comstock and Eli A. Rubinstein. Rockville, Md., National Institute of Mental Health, 1972. 546p.   **1U 124**
Content: New Research on Media Content and Control (Overview) by George A. Comstock. Violence in Television Drama: Trends and Symbolic Functions by George Gerbner. Trends in Violent Content in Selected Mass Media by David G. Clark and William B. Blankenburg. Perceptions of Violence in Television Programs: Critics and the Public by Bradley S. Greenberg and Thomas F. Gordon. The Role of the Producer in Choosing Children's Television Content by Muriel G. Cantor. Violence in Television: The Industry Looks at Itself by Thomas F. Baldwin and Colby Lewis. The Structure and Content of Television Broadcasting in Four Countries: An Overview by Michael Gurevitch; United States by George Gerbner; Great Britain by James D. Halloran and Paul Croll; Israel by Dov Shinar; and Sweden by Peter Dahlgren.

————. *Television and Social Behavior. Reports and Papers, Volume II: Television and Social Learning. A Technical Report to the Surgeon General's Scientific Advisory Committee on Television and Social Behavior*. Edited by John P. Murray, Eli A. Rubinstein, and George A. Comstock. Rockville, Md., National Institute of Mental Health, 1972. 371p.   **1U 125**
Content: Television and Social Learning: Some Relationships Between Viewing Violence and Behaving Aggressively (Overview) by Robert M. Liebert. Children's Responses to Television Violence by Aimée Dorr Leifer and Donald F. Roberts. Short-term Effects of Televised Aggression on Children's Aggressive Behavior by Robert M. Liebert and Robert A. Baron. Television Content and Young Children's Behavior by Aletha H. Stein and Lynette K. Friedrich with Fred Von-

dracek. Reality and Fantasy in Filmed Violence by Seymour Feshbach. Television and the Behavior of Preschool Children by Harold W. Stevenson.

————. *Television and Social Behavior. Reports and Papers, Volume III: Television and Adolescent Aggressiveness. A Technical Report to the Surgeon General's Scientific Advisory Committee on Television and Social Behavior*. Edited by Eli A. Rubinstein and George A. Comstock. Rockville, Md., National Institute of Mental Health, 1972. 435p.   **1U 126**

————. *Television and Social Behavior. Reports and Papers, Volume IV: Television in Day-to-Day Life: Patterns of Use. A Technical Report to the Surgeon General's Scientific Advisory Committee on Television and Social Behavior*. Edited by Eli A. Rubinstein, George A. Comstock, and John P. Murray. Rockville, Md., National Institute of Mental Health, 1972. 603p.   **1U 127**

————. *Television and Social Behavior. Reports and Papers, Volume V: Television's Effects: Further Explorations. A Technical Report to the Surgeon General's Scientific Advisory Committee on Television and Social Behavior*. Edited by George A. Comstock, Eli A. Rubinstein, and John P. Murray. Rockville, Md., National Institute of Mental Health, 1972. 375p.   **1U 128**

United States Catholic Conference. Communications Committee. "Freedom of the Media of News." In *Catholic Mind*, 71:6–8, June 1973.   **1U 129**
The statement expresses concern with press freedom in the United States—as it is impaired by government interference, by public apathy, and media bias. "Corrective action, when required, is in general best left to the news media themselves, working in concert, and to the free operation of public opinion. . . . We therefore urge the media industry to initiate prompt action leading to the development of whatever voluntary programs of self-regulation and enforcement of media responsibility may be necessary for the common good."

"United States v. CBS: When Sketch Artists Are Allowed in the Courtroom, Can Photographers Be Far Behind?" *Duke Law Journal*, 1975:188–205, March 1975.   **1U 130**
The Court held that, in the absence of a showing that sketching was obtrusive or disruptive, a blanket prohibition of sketching within the courtroom was constitutionally impermissible as an overbroad limitation of First Amendment

rights. The author believes the decision may have unlocked a Pandora's box of litigation.

The University Press, Ltd. "The Corruption of the Morals of Her Majesty's Subjects: Police Prosecution." In The University Press, Ltd., *List of Recent Publications*. London, The Press [1899?], pp. 1–3.   1U131
The publisher of Havelock Ellis's *Studies on the Psychology of Sex*, recently the subject of a British court case, reports on the seizure by the police of Watford, England, under authority of the Obscene Publications Act of 1857, of all copies of Ellis's book, Geoffrey Mortimer's *Chapters on Human Love*, A. Hamon's *The Universal Illusion of Free Will*, Ch. Féré's *The Pathology of Emotions*, *The University Magazine*, and other scientific and philosophical works issued by The University Press. As a consequence of these "prudes on the prowl," the publisher announces his intention, henceforth, to supply these works from Paris and Leipzig, and not to stock them again in Britain. The pamphlet includes the pages of contents of three of the censored volumes.

Uris, Leon. *QB VII*. New York, Doubleday, 1970. 426p. (Also in Bantam paperback edition)   1U132
A novel centered on a British libel trial in which an American novelist is sued by a highly respected British surgeon of Polish origin. The novelist had referred to Polish claims that the doctor had performed experimental sterilization surgery on Jewish inmates of a World War II concentration camp. The title of the book refers to Queen's Bench Number 7. In addition to providing a plot in which there are dramatic confrontations between characters and moral issues, the trial itself brings out the many and intricate facets of British libel law.

Usherwood, Robert C. "Issued on Request Only." *Assistant Librarian*, 60: 110, 112–13, June 1967.   1U133
The author objects to the closed shelves collections in libraries as a stupid form of censorship. Librarians should reject the idea because (1) the withdrawal of books means the visitor doesn't see a representative collection; (2) the librarian is making a moral decision; (3) books (sex manuals) that could be of help to people are kept from these people because of their natural shyness in asking; (4) public money is being used

for books not put to good use; and (5) the practice violates the principle of open access.

Uys, Stanley. "Nation Cut Off by the Censor." *New Statesman*, 78:854, 12 December 1969.   1U134
A detailing of the effect of mass censorship in South Africa. "South Africa's censors have banned at least 13,000 publications in the past 13 years, ranging across the whole literary spectrum. All publications from communist countries, for example, are automatically banned; nothing, not even the classics, like Lenin, Stalin and Trotsky, escape. Nearly all books critical of apartheid are banned, as are most publications dealing with race. Books and magazines on sex are suppressed wholesale. . . . South Africans have grown accustomed to the cultural deprivation and if they cannot lay their hands on a smuggled book, they go resignedly without it. . . . South Africa today is what the world was like 25 years ago, the country where time stood still."

V

Valdez, Reuben V. *A Case Study in Pretrial Criminal News Reporting: The Rio Arriba County Courthouse Raid of June 5, 1967, Involving Reies Lopez Tijerina*. Morgantown, W.Va., West Virginia University, 1970. 182p. (Unpublished Master's thesis) **1V1**
"The purpose of this investigation was to document the pretrial criminal news reporting of the June 5, 1967 armed raid of the Rio Arriba County Courthouse in Tierra Amarilla, New Mexico, involving Reies Lopez Tijerina. The Tijerina case synthesizes the aspects of a fair trial–free press dilemma and a civil rights case. A content analysis of more than 500 news articles and editorials which appeared in the *Albuquerque Journal* and the *Albuquerque Tribune* was conducted."

Van Alstyne, Arvo, Kenneth R. Hardy, and Stephen L. Tanner. "The Role of Church and State in Controlling Pornography." *Dialogue: A Journal of Mormon Thought*, 2(2):75–109, Summer 1967. **1V2**
"In this Roundtable three Latter-day Saints bring both their varied professional perspectives—as an expert on constitutional law, a social scientist, and a teacher of literature—and their common faith to bear on this problem." Obscenity and the Inspired Constitution: A Dilemma for Mormons by Arvo Van Alstyne (pp. 75–89); Controlling Pornography: The Scientific and Moral Issues by Kenneth R. Hardy (pp. 89–103); Toward a Positive Censorship by Stephen L. Tanner (pp. 103–9).

Vance, Ralph D. *The Federal Communications Commission's Fairness Doctrine: Its History and Its Impact on the Broadcast Newsman*. Los Angeles, University of California, Los Angeles, 1968. 196p. (Unpublished Master's thesis) **1V3**
"In an attempt to determine the true effect of the fairness doctrine, its history was traced from the 1927 concept of public interest broadcasting to its current court test by the Radio Television News Directors Association. Attitudes of radio and television news directors

were examined by a questionnaire mailed to all commercial licensees in California."

Vance, Stephen A. *What Did Agnew Really Say at Des Moines*? Berkeley, Calif., University of California, 1971. 98p. (Unpublished Master's thesis) **1V4**
This thesis examines the Des Moines speech of Vice-President Spiro Agnew, 13 November 1969, and the questions it raises including press control and freedom of the press.

van den Haag, Ernest. "Democracy and Pornography." In Victor B. Cline, ed., *Where Do You Draw the Line?* Provo, Utah, Brigham Young University Press, 1974, pp. 257–70. **1V5**
The author asks whether it is not odd that "having abandoned the defense of the social and political order against subversive ideas, the censor should make a stand on what appears to be a comparatively trivial and semiprivate cultural matter: sexual mores." He argues, however, that obscenity does threaten the social order. "By de-individualizing and dehumanizing sexual acts, which then become impersonal, pornography reduces or removes the empathy and the mutual identification which restrain us from treating each other merely as objects or means. . . . Pornography thus is antihuman and antisocial. . . . Censorship laws are, in the first place, a defense for those who fear temptation: they help restrain impulses of which the actor fears to become the victim before anyone else does. In the second place, they protect third persons who might be victimized." With respect to the work of the U.S. Commission on Obscenity and Pornography he concludes that "the Commission selectively and prejudicially initiated and presented investigations to bolster conclusions which were determined by its formulation of the problem and not by the evidence which a broader definition would have led to."

──────. "Free Speech and Censorship." *Newsletter on Intellectual Freedom* (IFC-ALA), 23:109, 135–37, September 1974. **1V6**
In a talk at the 1974 annual conference of the

American Library Association, the author states the view that librarians and teachers (or any professional) should not be vested with the power to select books, but this should be held by boards of trustees and laymen. Professionals have no valid basis for crying "censorship" when their selection is challenged. He considers it irrational for the public to expect government to protect it from deceptive and harmful products, while not trusting government to protect it from deceptive and harmful political ideas. He rejects the concept that we can separate ideas (free from control) from action taken on the basis of ideas (controlled). He calls for society to set perimeters for freedom of expression, one of which should be anything which offends public decency. Society, no less than individuals, is imperiled by pornography.

──────. "Is Pornography a Cause of Crime?" *Encounter*, 29(6):52–56, December 1967. (Reprinted in David Holbrook, ed., *The Case Against Pornography*, 161–68) **1V7**
"The influence of books varies from case to case; it can contribute to the formation of disposition (given the individual potential for the disposition) or can precipitate the action, once the disposition has been formed for whatever reason. . . . " Books can seldom be the only influence on behavior, but to conclude that they have no role is unwarranted. "I am against both censors and pornographers—but even more am I against one without the other. . . . If we indulge pornography, and do not allow censorship to restrict it, our society at best will become ever more coarse, brutal, anxious, indifferent, de-individualized, hedonistic; at worst its ethos will disintegrate altogether. . . . Why must society lead its members into temptation and then punish them when they do what they were tempted to do?" A continuation of the dialogue growing out of Pamala Hansford Johnson's *On Iniquity* (°J17).

──────. " 'The Pornography of Violence': John Calder's Illusions." *Encounter*, 35(2):84–87, August 1970. **1V8**
The author takes issue with Calder's criticisms of Pamala Hansford Johnson's defense of her *On Iniquity* (February and April issues of *En-*

counter), finding Calder's remarks "obscure irrelevancies." The alleged reduction of sexual crimes in Denmark following abolition of censorship is not a real reduction, but only a statistical reclassification. The author finds pornography damaging in three ways: it precipitates crimes which it makes inviting; it cheapens the quality of life; and it erodes social cohesion. Pushing liberty too far will call forth reaction in the form of repressive censorship. "Contrary to what so many defenders urge, I can see no loss to literature if pornography were prohibited."

Van den Heuvel, William J. "The Press and the Prisons." *Columbia Journalism Quarterly*, 11(1):35–40, May–June 1972. **1V9**
"The responsibility of the news media is to lift the veil of secrecy surrounding the nation's prisons, to give voice to both the victims of crime and of the criminal justice system, and to reveal the incredible waste that our jails and penitentiaries represent. The federal courts have been responsive to the First Amendment questions posed by prison secrecy. . . . The gates of the prisons are ajar for the media to enter, but the need is for aggressive initiative and creativity by the press to give substance to the Constitutional right the courts have protected."

Van Gelder, Lawrence. *The Untold Story: Why the Kennedys Lost the Book Battle*. New York, Award Books, 1967. 128p. **1V10**
The story of Jacqueline Kennedy's efforts to prevent the publication of William Manchester's *The Death of the President*.

Van Heerden, Ernst. "Sensuur—Soos 'n Skrywer-Akademikus dit Sien" [Censorship—in the eyes of an author-academician]. *South African Libraries*, 38:228–31, January 1971. **1V11**
"There is widespread concern among South African literary scholars about the manner in which censorship is applied in South Africa. . . . Each book banned diminishes our independent thought and increases the isolation of our literature. . . . The Publications Control Board should press for unrestricted access by literary men to the world's literature."

Vanocur, Sander. "TV's Failed Promise." *Center Magazine*, 4(6):44–50, November–December 1971. **1V12**
A former National Broadcasting Company news commentator sees TV as having formed an unnatural coalition with government, so that it becomes more and more a part of the selling process of government propaganda. "The caution that stultifies broadcasting is the product of fear—fear of government, fear of the medium itself." He calls for a dissolution of the coalition and a new independence and creativity in broadcasting.

Van Tassel, George N. "Obscenity." *Alabama Librarian*, 25(2):9–12, Spring 1974. **1V13**
Following a general discussion of obscenity law the author reviews Alabama law. "The Alabama law consists of three separate acts, one passed in 1961, and two passed in 1969, one of which deals with minors. The 1961 act basically enunciates the *Roth* test while the 1969 act seeks to utilize the *Memoirs* test." One of the 1969 acts was declared unconstitutional; the other is likely to be. The 1961 law is also questionable. Librarians, however, are unlikely to be prosecuted under the act which is intended for hard-core pornography.

Van Wageningen, Henry J. "The Right to Reply: A Challenge to Freedom of the Press." *University of Miami Law Review*, 28:219–26, Fall 1973. **1V14**
Re: *Tornillo v. Miami Herald Publishing Co.* (Fla. 1973). Comments on the Florida Supreme Court's decision in upholding the constitutionality of Florida's right of reply statute. "Both the constitutional and policy reasons set forth . . . appear to warrant reversal by the United States Supreme Court," which action subsequently took place.

Van Zyl, John. "Mr. Kruger and the Lord Protector." *New Nation* (South Africa), 4(9):12–13, April 1971. **1V15**
In the discussions of censorship in South Africa "what has not been discussed is the actual effect of media on morals and conduct; secondly, whether South Africa is a Cromwellian church state or not; and thirdly, whether the lessons of Prohibition have been learnt."

Varley, Douglas H. "Trends Abroad: South Africa." *Library Trends*, 19:139–51, July 1970. **1V16**
"There is in South Africa today a complex structure of laws and regulations which in the name of internal security impose a variety of restrictions on individual liberties, including in the present context the freedom to read literary material judged by a Publications Control Board to be 'undesirable,' and to publish any material that may undermine 'the traditional race policy of the Republic.' Since 1956 approximately 13,000 books have been banned, in terms of existing legislation, including the entire works of any person banned from public meetings by any previous legislation."

Vaughan, Robert. *Only Victims: A Study of Show Business Blacklisting*. With a Foreword by Senator George McGovern. New York, Putnam's, 1972. 355p. **1V17**
The work deals with the influence of the House Committee on Un-American Activities on the American theater, 1938–58. The Committee devoted much of its investigations to alleged Communist influence to the field of entertainment, beginning with the Federal Theater, which was eliminated as a result. After temporarily desisting from attacks on

alleged Communist activities during World War II, the Committee resumed its attacks on Hollywood, culminating with the jailing of the Hollywood Ten, authors who refused to answer questions about their personal political beliefs. They and scores of others, mostly writers, were blacklisted and kept out of jobs for almost a decade, except for operating in the blackmarket. The Committee's influence led to the persecutions by Senator Joseph McCarthy during the Eisenhower years. Unlike the employers in the film industry, the New York stage had no organized blacklist, but writers for the stage are believed to have been silenced by fear of punitive reprisals. No legislation came of the Committee's investigation, only twenty years of publicity and the damaging of scores of lives and careers.

Vaughn, Robert G. "The Freedom of Information Act and *Vaughn v. Rosen*: Some Personal Comments." *American University Law Review*, 23:865–79, Summer 1974. **1V18**
Personal commentary on the events which led to the litigation, *Vaughn v. Rosen* (1973), and the plaintiff-author's view of the effect of the litigation on freedom of government information.

Vaughn, V. G., and Susan E. Heberling. "Inland Printer Debate: Revolutionary or Obscene Material: Should We Print It?" *Inland Printer/American Lithographer*, 165:68–69, September 1970. **1V19**
The printer has no right to set himself up as a censor. Mr. Vaughn, president of a printing company, says "no." Ms. Heberling, editor of a university literary magazine, says "yes." The issue was over *Parchment Conch*, Indiana University of Pennsylvania.

"*Vaughn v. Rosen*: Toward True Freedom of Information." *University of Pennsylvania Law Review*, 122:731–44, January 1974. **1V20**
The Court of Appeals for the District of Columbia in *Vaughn v. Rosen* (1973), "scrutinized and significantly modified the nature of the procedure through which federal courts adjudicate government information denials under the Freedom of Information Act. . . . The comments examine *Vaughn's* assumptions, precedent upon which it relies, and its probable effect upon the future FOIA litigation."

Vedanta, Iengar H. R. "A Free Press, a Pre-Condition to a Free Society." *Swarajya*, 15(42):9–10, 17 April 1971. **1V21**
"The hope for Indian democracy now rests on how freely and fearlessly the Indian press will continue to function." The author warns of a government "inebriated by the consciousness

of a massive majority at its behest . . . with illusions of omniscience and infallibility," becoming intolerant toward honest press criticism.

Veitch, Russell, and William Griffitt. *"Community Standards" and Erotica: Personal and Attributional Determinants*. Manhattan, Kans., Department of Psychology, Kansas State University, 1974. 27p. Processed.   **1V22**
"Personal (self-rated) and attributions to same and opposite-sex persons of sexual and emotional responses to literary erotica and the relationships of such responses to restrictive decisions concerning erotica were examined in the present study."

Veix, Donald B. "Teaching a Censored Novel: *Slaughterhouse Five*." *English Journal*, 64(7):25–33, October 1975.
1V23
Following a general discussion of censorship, the author suggests ways of presenting controversial novels in general and *Slaughterhouse Five* in particular to high school English classes: Emphasizing the nature of tragedy; producing the work through transparancies and sound that can create the mood and reflect the period and theme of the novel; production of puppet and marionette shows; through motion picture film and still photography; examining the "myths" of American life suggested in the novel; a debate of the issues suggested in the work; and consideration of the charges of obscenity and blasphemy made by critics and the nature of these categories.

Velvel, Lawrence R. "Supreme Court Stops the Presses." *Catholic University Law Review*, 22:324–43, Winter 1973.
1V24
"In the final analysis, the decision in the newsman-subpoena cases represents a needless sacrifice of first amendment rights. . . . The majority has shown itself insensitive to the critical role of an independent press. It has created a situation in which newsmen and their sources will have to be very cautious. It has given government another tool with which to harass dissenters or unfriendly commentators. It has increased the pervasiveness of government power and the government's ability to stifle people and causes."

Ventgen, Carol. "Let's Hear It for Intellectual Freedom." *Oregon Library News*, 19(2):18–21, Fall 1973.   **1V25**
A discussion of a censorship bill passed by the Oregon legislature, "a reaction to 1971 legislation which restricted dissemination of pornography only to minors. . . ." The proliferation of porn shops, live sex shows, and so forth, caused the push for the bill which follows recent Supreme Court guidelines. A section

providing for local obscenity ordinances was deleted following testimony of the Oregon Library Association. Opponents of the law are seeking a statewide referendum for its repeal.

Ventresca, Michael A. "Freedom of the Press." *Suffolk University Law Review*, 6:174–84, Fall 1971.   **1V26**
Re: *New York Times Co. v. United States*, 403 U.S. 713 (1971).

Verghese, George. " 'Please Kill: Withdrawn by Censor.' " *MORE*, 6(2):10–12, February 1976.   **1V27**
"In a candid interview [with J. Anthony Lukas], Indira Gandhi's former press adviser and one of India's leading editors, describes the pivotal role of censorship as the former democracy falls increasingly under dictatorial rule."

Vermont Library Association. "Guidelines for Insuring Intellectual Freedom in Vermont Libraries." *Vermont Libraries*, 4:2–4, January–February 1975. Comments: 4:44–48, March 1975. **1V28**
The statement, adopted by the Executive Board of the Vermont Library Association, 5 March 1970, and amended by the Board, 6 November 1974, contains sections on legislation, censorship, materials selection policy, and liaison with other state and national organizations. Following the statement is the text of the recent revisions of the Vermont obscenity law.

Vickery, Diana. "Magruder Wrote Haldeman: Watergate Memo Shows Media Attack Planned." *Grassroots Editor*, 17(2):5–7, 13, Summer 1976.
1V29
"Here is a look at how, during the first two years of the Nixon Administration, the plans were laid and the tone set for the administration's 'war' with the press and how these [Agnew] speeches fit into the plan."

Victoria. State Library. *Literary Censorship*. Melbourne, Australia, State Library of Victoria, 1965. 37p. Processed. (Research Service Bibliographies, 1965, no. 4)   **1V30**
The emphasis of this bibliography is on current problems of censorship in Australia.

"Victory for the Press." *Newsweek*, 78(1):16–19, 12 July 1971.   **1V31**
A report on the U.S. Supreme Court decision in the case of the Pentagon Papers, with excerpts from opinions of five justices.

Vidal, Gore. "Pornography." In his *Homage to Daniel Shays: Collected Essays, 1952–1972*. New York, Random House, 1972, pp. 219–33. (Reprinted from *New York Review of Books*, 31 March 1966)   **1V32**

"Until recently, pornography was a small cottage industry among the grinding mills of literature. But now that sex has taken the place of most other games (how many young people today learn bridge?) creating and packaging pornography has become big business, and although the high courts of the American Empire cannot be said to be very happy about this state of affairs, they tend to agree that freedom of expression is as essential to our national life as freedom of meaningful political action is not. . . . Efforts must be made to bring what we think about sex and what we say about sex and what we do about sex into some kind of realistic relationship. Indirectly, the pornographers do this. They recognize that the only sexual norm is that there is none. Therefore, in a civilized society law should not function at all in the area of sex except to protect people from being 'interfered with' against their will."

Villano, Stephen. "Federal Newsman's Shield and the First Amendment." *Free Speech*, 31:3–9, February 1974.   **1V33**
A discussion of the implications of the U.S. Supreme Court's 1972 decisions in the *Branzburg*, *Pappas*, and *Caldwell* cases involving newmen's privilege.

Villard, Oswald G. "The Freedom of the Press." *American Scholar*, 3:28–39, January 1934.   **1V34**
The American press which was so indifferent to government censorship during and immediately following World War I has had a sudden revival of interest in protecting a free press now that their business affairs are being restricted by the code of the National Recovery Act. Had the press recognized their public responsibilities, had they championed the rights of free men in war and peace, had they been enlightened employers they would have had public sympathy at this time. As it is "an army of newspaper employees is rejoicing over the fact that the United States Government has come to their aid, and in so coming to their assistance has made the publishers realize that the newspapers of the country are entitled to no more consideration in this matter of business reorganization than any other commercial enterprise."

———. *How Stands Our Press?* Chicago, Human Events Associates, 1947. 18p. (Human Events Pamphlets, no. 19)
1V35
A veteran journalist criticizes the nation's press in its coverage of World War II and particularly for accepting the secret diplomacy that preceded the war and for lack of questioning of wartime policies. In the postwar period he sees the danger of unquestioning acquiescence in government policies, the trend toward monopoly, and the decreased number of daily papers. He does not believe that the Commission on the Freedom of the Press report offers any practical, immediate measures to improve the press, and criticizes both the American Society of Newspaper Editors and the American Newspaper Guild for their inaction. We

may have hope for the future "only if those who conduct our publications are men and women of conscience and ethical responsibility."

Villemez, Wayne J. *Attitude Research Concerning Freedom of the Press*. Austin, Tex., University of Texas, 1967. 106p. (Unpublished Master's thesis)   **1V36**
"To determine current attitudes toward freedom of the press, this investigation surveyed samples of the general public and of the following significant groups: Managing editors of newspapers, legislators, high school teachers, and high school students. The study was limited to the state of Texas."

"Vindication of the Reputation of a Public Official." *Harvard Law Review*, 80:1730–56, June 1967.   **1V37**
"This Note will discuss the constitutional permissibility of alternative remedies for the defamed public official and will consider whether such alternatives can eliminate the inadequacies and undesirable characteristics of the traditional damages suit as a device for vindicating reputation."

Vinson, Tony, and Arthur Robinson. "Censorship and the Australian Public." *Australian Journal of Social Issues*. 3:63–74, 1968. (Reprinted in Michael H. Prosser, *ed.*, *Intercommunication Among Nations and People*, pp. 519–29)   **1V38**
In a survey of public opinion to assess public tolerance, it was found that "three out of every four people questioned in Sydney and Melbourne supported the idea of public ventilation of opinions critical of organized religion, the monarchy, and censorship."

"Violence and Obscenity—*Chaplinsky* Revisited." *Fordham Law Review*, 42: 141–60, October 1973.   **1V39**
"*Chaplinsky v. New Hampshire* [1942], a decision almost totally ignored in its own day . . . emerges as a focal point of four of the most important doctrines which have been employed by the Supreme Court in its continuing attempt to find a workable definition of free expression in the areas of obscenity and political dissent."

"Violence on Television." *Columbia Journal of Law & Social Problems*, 6:303–24, May 1970.   **1V40**
The article examines possible methods of controlling television violence in light of *The Statement on Violence in Television Entertainment Programs* issued by the National Commission on the Causes and Prevention of Violence, and the U.S. Surgeon General's study on the violent nature of television programming.

Virginia. Commission on Constitutional Government. *Sex, the Supreme Court, and the States; the Supreme Court Deals With Dirt, What It Is, and Who Is to Say What It Is; Mr. Justice Harlan Dissents in the Case of Fanny Hill*. Richmond, The Commission, 1966. 6p.   **1V41**

Vitullo-Martin, Thomas W. "Political Religious Freedom and School Censorship: A Conundrum." In Phil L. Nacke, *ed.*, *Diversity in Mature Reading: Theory and Research*. Boone, N.C., National Reading Conference, 1973, pp. 232–37. (22d Yearbook, vol. 1)   **1V42**
The author proposes "ending geographic attendance districts and permitting the curriculum to be set and books to be chosen at the local school level," which would "eliminate the most destructive effects of censorship, and thereby greatly reduce the censorship movement we will otherwise witness in the near future." Parents would have a choice of schools for their children, which implies a diversity in the character and offering of the schools. There would be far less political resistance to "far out" public schools and less need for compromising with texts that would serve a heterogeneous constituency.

Vivian, Charles H. "Radical Journalism in the 1930s; The *True Sun* and *Weekly True Sun*." *Modern Language Quarterly*, 15:222–32, September 1954.   **1V43**
The story of a radical London paper and its frequent brush with the law in the matter of libel.

Vizzard, Jack. *See No Evil: Life Inside a Hollywood Censor*. New York, Simon & Schuster, 1970. 381p.   **1V44**
A member of the staff of the Motion Picture Production Code from the days of Joseph Breen to the end of the code and its replacement with the new classification, writes an entertaining inside story of what took place in the process of screening motion pictures.

Vlachos, Helen. "Freedom of the Press." *New Humanist*, 88:387–90, February 1973.   **1V45**
A leading Athens publisher, who voluntarily ceased publishing rather than accept censorship of the Greek dictatorship, writes of the efforts of press censorship wherever it exists. The degree of freedom in a country can readily be measured by the extent of dissent reported in the press. Even the free press in other countries suffers in reporting news of a country under press controls. Mrs. Vlachos criticizes the practice of the British and other free presses of "dropping the subject" syndrome, lack of coverage of news when it is no longer hot. She expresses alarm over the threat against the free press in the United States from the Nixon Administration. "The gap between Washington and the free press is positively frightening and gets wider all the time."

Vogel, Amos. *Film as Subversive Art*.
New York, Random House, 1974. 336p.   **1V46**
"This is a book about the subversion of existing values, institutions, *mores*, and taboos—East and West, Left and Right—by the potentially most powerful art of the century. It is a book that traffics in scepticism towards all received wisdom (including its own), towards eternal truths, rules of art, 'natural' and man-made laws, indeed whatever may be considered holy." Part 3, Forbidden Subjects of the Cinema, deals with the power of the visual taboo, the attack on puritanism, erotic and pornographic films, films dealing with homosexuality, birth, death, blasphemy and anticlericalism, and witchcraft. Numerous illustrations.

Vogel, Joe B. *Ethical Codes and Courts of Honor in the Press of the Free World*. Iowa City, Iowa, State University of Iowa, 1961. 433p. (Ph.D. dissertation, University Microfilms, no. 61-1939)   **1V47**
This study evaluates and compares the codes of ethics and courts of honor adopted by national journalism organizations among the "free-press" nations. Ethical controls for sixty-two countries are described and analyzed. "The author concludes that the national press council type of control—as found in Great Britain, Sweden, Norway, etc.—offers the best type of voluntary control for the press in the free world."

———. "International Search for Ethical Control." In Heinz-Dietrick Fischer and John C. Merrill, *eds.*, *International Communications Media, Channels, Functions*. New York, Hastings House, 1970, pp. 106–14.   **1V48**
A study of sixty-two "free press" countries to determine what the free press has done to define its own standards of conduct.

Voight, Harry H. "Public Access to Intra-Agency Documents: The *International Paper* Case." *Natural Resources Lawyer*, 4:554–68, July 1971.   **1V49**
"This article concerns itself with an examination and analysis of the right of an individual to inspect and copy inter-agency memoranda in light of the fifth exemption to the broad public-access requirements of the Freedom of Information Act." The exemption involves inter-agency or intra-agency documents and the case cited is *International Paper Co. v. FPC* (1971).

Vold, Lawrence. "The Basis for Liability for Defamation by Radio." *Minnesota Law Review*, 19:611–60, May 1935.   **1V50**
"It is the purpose of this paper to support the conclusion that radio stations are properly sub-

jected to the same basis for liability for publication of defamatory utterances that is applied to newspapers."

———. "Extemporaneous Defamation by Radio." *Marquette Law Review*, 25:57–65, February 1941.   **1V51**
The author takes issue with Professor Seitz (*Marquette Law Review*, April 1940) over liability for extemporaneous statements, holding that the radio broadcaster "who for his own profit carries on the activity and creates the risks should also bear the burden of damage which his activity inflicts upon his passive and innocent victim." Professor Seitz replies in the June 1941 issue, maintaining his earlier position.

Volner, Ian D. "Broadcast Regulation: Is There Too Much 'Public' in the 'Public Interest'?" *University of Cincinnati Law Review*, 43:267–89, 1974. **1V52**
"This article will consider some aspects of the role of the public in the formulation of communications policy affecting program content and quality. The first part of the article outlines the traditional view of the FCC and, to a lesser extent, of the courts, of the function of the public in the formulation and application of policy. In the second part, the sources and underlying reasons for broadening of the involvement of the public in the FCC's decisionmaking which began in the middle 1960s will be examined. Next, the application of the newer philosophy of expanded public participation and greater public control over radio and television programming will be explored."

Von Feldt, Elmer. "Vying for the Title of Sodom and Gomorrah. *Columbia*, 50(4):3, April 1970. (Reprinted in *Congressional Record*, 28 May 1970) **1V53**
An editorial criticizing the permissive character of the work of the U.S. Commission on Obscenity and Pornography, authored by the editor of *Columbia*, based on charges made by three members of the Commission in their minority report. Interviews with the dissenting commissioners are included.

von Stroheim, Erich. "Movies and Morals." *Decision*, 1(3):49–56, March 1941. **1V54**
The motion picture actor and director describes the hypocrisy in matters of sex that dominated the film industry from its beginning until the present (1941). He traces the treatment of sex from the early period of "pristine wishfulness and repression," through the important fling at sex following World War I and the subsequent industry controls. He writes of his own films that "offended Mrs. Grundy," *Blind Husbands* and *Foolish Wives*. At the time of writing, he finds that the films, despite the rigid and often illogical censorship, "have reached their 'age of consent,' and decided to recognize their sex instincts and live their own sex life."

Voorhees, John. "Development of New Public Interest Standards in the *Format Change Cases*." *Catholic University Law Review*, 25:364–79, Winter 1976. **1V55**
This article will explore the development of entertainment format regulations in broadcast media and the consequences of the U.S. Court of Appeals for the District of Columbia Circuit's decision in *Citizens Committee to Save WEFM v. FCC*, 506 F.2d 246 (D.C. Cir. 1974).

Vortrefich, Charles R. *Freedom of the Press in High School Newspapers: Federal Court Decisions and New York State Practices*. New York, Columbia University, 1974. 184p. (Ed.D. dissertation, University Microfilms, 74–11,813; ED 94,410) **1V56**
A questionnaire study of principles, faculty advisors, and student editors in New York State high schools to determine the congruence of practices of the student press with the developing body of judicial law.

Waas, George. "How Fair Is the Fairness Doctrine?" *Florida Bar Journal*, 49:246–49, May 1975. **1W1**
The author considers criticism of television's fairness doctrine under these headings: government control, issue avoidance, vagueness, license obligations, and noncontroversiality.

Waco-McLennan County Bar Association. "Courtroom Television." *Texas Bar Journal*, 19:73–74, 106–10, February 1956. **1W2**
An account of the televising of the Washburn murder trial (KWTX) in the 54th District Court, Waco, Tex. The American Bar Association Judicial Canon no. 35 prohibits the televising of trials, but such a canon has not been adopted in Texas. The judge stated that television coverage seemed to dignify the trial and that there was no "grandstanding" by the witnesses or attorneys and that the television camera was not distracting. The foreman of the jury did not believe the camera had affected jurors in any way. In a poll of all lawyers in the county bar association only 9.6 percent found television coverage disturbing and forty-eight of the sixty-one lawyers believed that television improved public opinion of our system of justice; forty-seven of sixty-one believed that the type of media coverage of trials should be left to the trial judge. KWTX-TV prepared a forty-five-minute film of interviews with various principals in the Washburn trial.

Wade, John W. "Defamation and the Right of Privacy." *Vanderbilt Law Review*, 15:1093–1125, October 1962. **1W3**
"In this article Dean Wade discusses the scope of the tort of unwarranted invasion of the right of privacy, comparing and contrasting it with the tort of defamation. He observes that the action for invasion of the right of privacy may come to supplant the action for defamation and that this development should be welcomed by the courts and writers. Finally, he concludes that the whole law of privacy may someday become a part of the larger, more comprehensive tort of intentional infliction of mental suffering."

———. "Defamation, the First Amendment and the Torts Restatement." *Forum* (Chicago), 11:3–17, Fall 1975. **1W4**
A discussion of the *Restatement (Second) of Torts* (in process) as it deals with defamation, the major changes reflecting the U.S. Supreme Court's "holding in 1964 ₁New York Times v. Sullivan₁ that defamation law, whether common law or statutory, is subject to the control of the free-speech and free-press provisions of the First Restatement."

Wade, Nicholas. "Freedom of Information: Officials Thwart Public Right to Know." *Science*, 175:498–502, 4 February 1972. **1W5**
A criticism of the operation of the Freedom of Information Act in the area of science and technology. The author calls upon Congress to exercise greater oversight on the operation of the act so that executive agencies do not limit public information to only what government officials do not mind revealing.

Wagner, Susan. "Congress, ANPA Join Fight to Protect Authors, Newsmen." *Publishers' Weekly*, 203(3):387, 15 January 1973. (Reprinted in *Current*, March 1973) **1W6**
The status of bills now before Congress on newsmen's rights regarding confidential sources.

———. "Copying and the Copyright Bill: Where the New Revision Stands on 'Fair Use.'" *Publishers' Weekly*, 210(16):20–30, 18 October 1976. **1W7**
This article and an earlier article (11 October) deal with freedom and limitation of copying of copyrighted materials.

———. "Obscenity Guidelines Threaten Widespread Confusion Over Local Standards." *Publishers' Weekly*, 204(1):53–54, 2 July 1973. **1W8**
A summary of the concerns expressed by publishers, authors, and lawyers over the signifi-

cance of the new U.S. Supreme Court ruling on obscenity which empowers states and local communities to apply their own community standards.

———. "Porno Report Becomes Political Football." *Publishers' Weekly*, 198(15):34–35, 12 October 1970. **1W9**
The report of the U.S. Commission on Obscenity and Pornography has "become part of a political scenario in which the Republicans are pushing the law and order issue in the current election campaigns."

Waisbrooker, Lois. *My Century Plant*. Topeka, Kans., Independent Publishing Co., 1896. 272p. **1W10**
The author demands "unqualified freedom for woman *as woman*, and that all the institutions of society be adjusted to such freedom." She is especially critical of the Church for its control of sex in the interests of males and of the Comstock postal laws for their suppression of information about sex and birth control. Anthony Comstock, she charges, is "a chosen medium for the church hierarchy" and the Comstock postal laws are "a deliberate plot . . . to destroy all whose purpose is to bless humanity instead of churchanity." She writes of the Comstock attacks on D. M. Bennett and Moses Harman on grounds of obscenity, and of her own arrest for sending "obscene" matter through the mails—a pamphlet entitled *The Lawyer's Letter*, offering free-love advice. The text of the offending publication is included.

Wakley, Thomas. *A Letter to the People of England, on the New Project for Gagging the Press*. London, G. Churchill at "The Lancet" Office, 1836. 32p. **1W11**
The author, a physician, medical reformer, and founder of the *Lancet*, was one of the leading Parliamentary crusaders against the newspaper tax. This pamphlet consists of a group of letters denouncing the tax and calling for public support of those members of Parliament who vote against it. "We are approaching a crisis. We are on the point of determining whether there shall, or shall not be a free press in this country. In reality, you must promptly

determine whether the political press of Great Britain and Ireland shall be chained to Somerset-House—under the delicate guardianship of a set of Censors, or Licensers, but nicknamed 'Commissioners of Stamps,'—during another half century, or whether it shall be protected from the new schemes which I preceive have just been devised for the annihilation of the last remnant of its liberty." Text of the odious new stamp duties bill is given with critical comment.

Waldchen, Alfred J. "The Serviceman's Right of Free Speech: An Analytical Approach." *San Diego Law Review*, 10:143–57, December 1972. **1W12**
"Although the ultimate objective of this article is to develop an approach applicable to the military, civilian free speech cases will be explored and their principles examined for possible application to the military speech cases. Then the military cases will be examined in this historical context. Finally, using principles extracted from cases of both types, an approach to the military cases will be suggested."

Walden, John C. "Student Press." *National Elementary Principal*, 53:69–71, March 1974. **1W13**
The author explores recent legal trends in the freedom of the student press and in the distribution of printed materials in elementary and high schools.

Waldrop, Bernard K. *Aesthetic Uses of Obscenity in Literature.* Ann Arbor, Mich., University of Michigan, 1964. 115p. (Ph.D. dissertation, University Microfilms, no. 65-5954) **1W14**
"The theory that pornography is fantasy while any other writing concerned with sex is 'erotic realism' (Kronhausen) is shown to be nonsense. Marcuse's premise, that a dualistic attitude is a *sine qua non* for obscenity, is accepted, but his conclusion that obscenity is not now possible is rejected. Manichaeism is presented, not as a dogma, but as a psychological syndrome, leading in philosophy towards transcendentalism, in religion towards soteriology, and in literature towards apocalyptic."

Walker, Brooks R., and Sandra R. Walker. "The Place of Pornography." In their *The New Morality.* New York, Doubleday, 1968, pp. 109–26. **1W15**
The role of pornography in the sexual revolution and the warfare among moral authorities on the significance of the increased permissiveness of society toward pornography.

Walker, C. Eugene. "Erotic Stimuli and the Aggressive Sexual Offender."

Technical Report of the [U.S.] *Commission on Obscenity and Pornography*, 7:91–147, 1971. **1W16**
"The purpose of the present research was to provide more definitive information regarding the relationship between pornography and sexual offenses. Specifically, answers were sought to two questions. First, 'Is the sex offender a person who has been exposed to pornography more frequently than the non-sex offender?' Secondly, 'Does the sex offender have different thoughts, fantasies, and ideas occur to him as he views pornography than those of the average person?' "

Walker, Thomas. *A Review of Some of the Political Events which have occurred in Manchester, during the Last Five Years: Being a Sequel to the Trial of Thomas Walker, and Others, for a Conspiracy to Overthrow the Constitution and Government of This Country.* . . . London, J. Johnson, 1794. 161p. **1W17**
Walker was one of several members of the Manchester Constitutional Society charged by the government with conspiracy and uttering of seditious words. One of the items in evidence was the alleged reading of the works of Thomas Paine. Thomas Erskine defended the members and they were acquitted, in part because a prosecution witness was found guilty of perjury. In this work Walker documents the events leading to, during, and after the trial, including the text of the offending publications.

Walklin, Larry J. *Federal Communications Commission. Regulation of Broadcast Programing in Historical Context, 1934–1965.* Iowa City, Iowa, University of Iowa, 1968. 175p. (Ph.D. dissertation, University Microfilms, no. 68-16,872) **1W18**
"The purpose of this study was to trace the evolution of the Federal Communications Commission programing regulatory philosophy between 1934 and 1965 and to discover what historical factors in the political and social milieu helped to shape this philosophy."

Wall, James M. "Cinema—Church Political Standoff." *Christian Century*, 91:198–99, 20 February 1974. **1W19**
Concerns the appeal by the Motion Picture Association for support of their film rating system "to help them exorcise local censorship demons."

———. "Film Anarchy Threatens the Rating System." *Christian Century*, 91:1003–4, 30 October 1974. **1W20**
Despite its shortcomings and the attacks on it, the voluntary film rating system "is certainly to be preferred to the sheriffs and small-town politicians who might otherwise determine the suitability of movies for the rest of us."

———. "Matter of Taste." *Christian Century*, 92:427–29, 30 April 1975. **1W21**
An editorial pointing out that "censorship is a presumptuous heresy, for it assumes that one can know with finality what is truth"; that it is self-defeating, increasing the popularity of forbidden fruit. "If censorship advocates really want to see pornography and tasteless literature recede from public view, their strategy should be to let such material die of its own shallowness."

———. "Which Films Are OK for Our Children?" *Together*, 13(2):2, February 1969. **1W22**
The editor of the Methodist Church's *Christian Advocate* concludes: "In a democracy, no protective system is perfect. The present classification system, however, is a good try at protecting both freedom of expression and the right of children to develop without undue exploitation."

Wall, Joseph E. "Fighting Words or Free Speech?" *North Carolina Law Review*, 50:382–403, Fall 1972. **1W23**
A look at the decision, *Cohen v. California* (1971), involving the concept of "fighting words." The author concludes that the determining factor is the manner in which the words are used. "When highly abusive words are used in a manner so provocative as to virtually assure retaliation, the 'fighting words' doctrine operates to exclude such expression from first amendment protection." In the case of *Cohen*, the passive use of fighting words did not qualify for exemption.

Wall, Thomas H. "Section 309 of the Communications Act—the Renewal Provision—a Need for Change." *Administrative Law Review*, 25:407–13, Fall 1973. **1W24**
The author proposes legislation that will permit an incumbent licensee to be judged on his past record and promises at the time of television station license renewal.

Wallace, Douglas H. "Obscenity and Contemporary Community Standards." *Journal of Social Issues*, 29(3):53–68, 1973. **1W25**
This article deals with the definition of obscenity—the criminal charge under which pornographic materials are prosecuted. It attempts to define the nature of stimuli that people consider obscene and the uniformity of community standards applied to these materials. One of the studies stimulated by the U.S. Commission on Obscenity and Pornography.

———, and Gerald Wehmer. "Pornography and Attitude Change." *Journal of Sex Research*, 7:116–25, May 1971. **1W26**
"The present study sought to investigate the relationship between exposure to erotic mate-

rials, some of which were legally obscene themes, and attitude/value change." The results indicated that such exposure "does not lead to a change in a person's attitudes toward such materials or in attitude toward their censorship. In addition, such exposure does not cause any significant disruption in a person's moral values. . . . Thus, the results are in contradiction to the hypothesis, derived from the obscenity statutes, that exposure to such materials would cause an increase in anti-social ideation and would promote a disruption of a person's morals."

[Wallace, Irving.] ["Interview with Irving Wallace."] *Penthouse*, 6:34–38, 96–97, March 1970.   **1W27**
Much of the interview covers Wallace's *The Seven Minutes*, a novel dealing with censorship of obscenity, and the author's own views on pornography and laws regulating it.

————. "Irving Wallace on Censorship." *Censorship Today*, 2(5):4–20, October–November 1969.   **1W28**
The author of *The Seven Minutes*, a novel dealing with censorship of obscenity, discusses his work—how he came to write it, the ideas that went into it, and the problems. He also relates some of his own experiences with censorship, including the rejection of his book, *The Chapman Report*, by many public libraries. "Despite the magnificent fight for freedom of the shelves fought by the American Library Association, its Council, its Intellectual Freedom Committee, there continue to exist various individual public library acquisition department and branch library personnel who censor according to their own tastes and prejudices and fears, to the detriment of free speech and communication. This library censorship of authors and their works is erratic but widespread—it is persistent, active, and generally unpublicized." He refers and quotes from his 1962 article in *Library Journal* (W38).

————. *The Seven Minutes*. New York, Simon & Schuster, 1969. 607p. **1W29**
A novel about pornography and the growing permissiveness in the United States; about the confrontation between the forces of censorship and a free press. In the novel a California bookseller is arrested for selling a copy of "the most obscene piece of pornography written since Gutenberg invented moveable type." The novel within the novel involved the thoughts inside a woman's head during the seven minutes she engaged in sexual intercourse. The Los Angeles obscenity trial that ensued became a cause célèbre; it involved a courageous young defense lawyer pitted against an honest but ambitious district attorney. As the trial progresses most of the obscenity issues unfold: sexual frankness, perversion, nudity, coarse language, the effect of pornography on behavior (a respectable college boy had committed brutal rape and murder), as well as hidden motivations and the activities of censors and anticensors. In real life the publisher of *The Seven Minutes* initiated a suit against Olympia Press, charging invasion of privacy and unfair competition for bringing out a paperback novel

entitled, *The Original Seven Minutes* by J. J. Jadway, the title of the censored work of fiction that was the subject of Wallace's novel.

Wallace, Paul S., Jr. *The Freedom of Information Act (5 U.S.C. Sec. 552): Background, Judicial Construction, Select Bibliography, and Pending Proposals to Amend the Act*. Washington, D.C., Library of Congress, Congressional Research Service, 1974. 52p.   **1W30**

————. *Regulation of Obscenity: A Compilation of Federal and State Statutes and Analysis of Selected Supreme Court Opinions*. Washington, D.C., Library of Congress, Congressional Research Service, 1972. 340p.   **1W31**
A Postscript on the Present and the Future of Obscenity Regulation. Definition of Obscenity. Provisions for the Protection of Minors. Text of Federal Statutes. Text of State Statutes. Appendix A: Recommendations of the U.S. Commission on Obscenity and Pornography. Appendix B: Statement by the President on the Commission's Report.

Wallahan, Franklin J. "Immorality, Obscenity and the Law of Copyright." *South Dakota Law Review*, 6:109–29, 1961. (Reprinted in *PEAL Quarterly*, June 1963)   **1W32**
The author seeks to answer such questions as: What is the status of an immoral or obscene work in the law of copyright? Can copyright be obtained on such a work? If so, will the courts afford such a work the same protection which is afforded other copyrighted works? What factors are given consideration by the courts when adjudging the morality of one's work? Do works which are immoral or obscene serve any purpose which is beneficial to society? Is it socially desirable that judicial protection be denied works of such a nature?

Wallis, C. Lamar. "Confrontation in Memphis." *Library Journal*, 94:4101–3, 15 November 1969. Comment: 95:189–90, 15 January 1970.   **1W33**
A report on the attack made in Memphis on Philip Roth's *Portnoy's Complaint* and the way in which the Public Library Board resolved the issue. Included is a strong letter of support for the library received from Henry Mitchell, editor of the *Delta Review*.

Wallis, Judith K. "Professional Ethics and Trial Publicity: What All the Talk Is About." *Suffolk Law Review*, 10:654–76, Spring 1976.   **1W34**
Re: *Chicago Council of Lawyers v. Bauer*, 522 F. 2d 242 (7th Cir. 1975) in which the plaintiff challenged the disciplinary rule of the American Bar Association's Code of Professional Responsibility, prohibiting any out-of-court statement regarding pending litigation by any attorney involved in the litigation if there is a

likelihood that the statement will interfere with a fair trial.

[Walpole, Horace, *Earl of Oxford*.] *A letter to the Whigs. Occasion'd by the Letter to the Tories*. London, M. Cooper, 1747. 54p. (Reprinted in Stephen Parks, *ed*., *The English Book Trade, 1660–1853*. Vol. 12)   **1W35**
Criticism of the daily hints thrown out by fellow Whigs in power to restrain the press. In striking at the liberty of the press they are behaving like Tories. *The Letter to the Tories* (George Lyttleton) had urged that the press be restrained because it is profligate and produces "license of the press." This is an old phrase often used, "a fripperry Art," by the enemies of liberty.

————. *A Second and Third Letter to the Whigs. By the Author of the First*. London, M. Cooper, 1748. 92p. (Reprinted in Stephen Parks, *ed*., *The English Book Trade, 1660–1853*, Vol. 12)   **1W36**
"The Press is dangerous in a despotic Government, but in a free Country may be very useful, as long as it is under no Correction, for it is of great Consequence that the People should be informed of every Thing that concerns them; and without Printing, such Knowledge could not circulate either so easily or so fast. And to argue against any Branch of Liberty from the ill Use that may be made of it, is to argue against Liberty Itself, since All is capable of being abused." Walpole criticizes his fellow Whigs for threatening suppression of the press.

Walter, David. *Censorship Is On the March*. Philadelphia, Society for Individual Freedom [1973?]. 6p. Processed.   **1W37**
An attack on all forms of censorship, issued by a society of libertarians, "resolved to resist all forms of involuntary collectivism and all programs and activities of government which violate our rights and attempt to take from us the ability to set our own goals and to determine our own destiny."

Walter, John. *Trial of Mr. John Walter, in the Court of King's Bench, for a Libel against his Royal Highness the Duke of York*. London, 1789.   **1W38**
The founder and publisher of the *Times* was brought to trial for a libel which tended to promote dissension between the king and his family in an article appearing in his paper. The duke and his two brothers were described as "insincere" in expression of joy at the king's recovery. Walter was fined £50, imprisoned in Newgate for a year, and ordered to appear in the pillory. While in prison he was brought to trial for further libels against other members of the royal family, convicted, fined, and given an

additional year in prison. He was pardoned by the king in March 1791. Thomas Erskine represented the plaintiff in the trial reported here.

———. *The Whole Proceedings on the Trial of an Action, brought by Mr. H. T. Hodgson against Mr. John Walter, for a Libel. Tried before Lord Chief Justice Abbott . . . 1821. . . .* London, Hodgson, 1821. 75p.   **1W39**
The publisher of the *Times* had complained of the misconduct of Mr. Hodgson, news vendor.

Walters, Robert. "Sharing the News with Justice." *Columbia Journalism Review*, 14(3):18–21, September–October 1975.   **1W40**
"The Justice Department has violated its own guidelines governing subpoenas for journalists."

Walterscheid, Edward C. "With Malice Toward One." *New Mexico Law Review*, 4:37–48, November 1973.   **1W41**
"This article will concern itself with the changing law of libel. . . . It will seek to give the New Mexico legal practitioner an overview of libel as seen under the common law, by the American Law Institute, by the New Mexico Supreme Court, and by the United States Supreme Court. In particular, consequences to New Mexico libel law as a result of the vigorous First Amendment attack on state libel laws by the United States Supreme Court will be indicated."

Waltz, Jon R. "Juries and the Mass Media." *Nation*, 219:495–98, 16 November 1974.   **1W42**
A review of the problems of pretrial publicity and the difficulties in selecting an impartial jury.

Waples, Dorothy. *The Whig Myth of James Fenimore Cooper.* New Haven, Conn., Yale University Press, 1938. 318p.   **1W43**
The book deals with the Whig myth of the disagreeable Mr. Cooper, who had the temerity to espouse the cause of the Democrats and to introduce some of his political views in his writing. The result was a war of vilification in the Whig press which Mr. Cooper answered with charges of libel. Between 1837 and 1845 he brought a total of fourteen civil libel suits and two criminal libel suits against newspapermen, including Horace Greeley, of the *New York Tribune*, winning most of the suits. "The politicians, though they did not break his spirit, ruined his reputation and his fortune in the prime of his life; indeed, they so blackened his character that for almost a hundred years we have had a damaged remembrance of him."

Waples, Gregory L. "Freedom of Information Act: A Seven-Year Assessment." *Columbia Law Review*, 74: 895–959, June 1974.   **1W44**
"The purpose of this Note is three-fold: (1) to clarify the congressional policies underlying the FOIA and to examine the Act as an instrument of these policies; (2) to explore significant problems the courts have encountered and to evaluate critically the case law applying and interpreting the Act against the policy backdrop; and (3) to encourage the development of more coherent judicial principles within the framework of the present statute in order to strengthen the FOIA as an effective tool for obtaining information buried within the bureaucracy."

"War Looms on Radio-TV Obscenity." *Broadcasting*, 77(23):58, 60–61, 8 December 1969.   **1W45**
The controversy over Pacifica's KPFK (FM) broadcast of a poem, Jehovah's Child, raises questions in the FCC and Congress about need for a tougher stand against allegedly obscene programming.

Warburg, Fredric. "A Slight Case of Obscenity." In his *All Authors Are Equal*. London, Hutchinson, 1973, pp. 173–97.   **1W46**
The publisher of Stanley Kauffmann's *The Philanderer*, writes of the obscenity trial (*Regina v. Warburg*, 1954) in which he stood in the dock at the Old Bailey. Mr. Justice Stable required the jury to read the entire book. His "summing-up" for the jury is published in the second edition of *The Philanderer* (K28) and in a limited edition pamphlet published by Blanche and Alfred Knopf (S569).

Ward, Nancy. "Feminism and Censorship." *Language Arts*, 53:536–37, May 1976.   **1W47**
The author suggests the book selection standards which will allow schools to have nonsexist material without book-banning. "We want balance, not censorship—not material taken away but material put in."

Ward, Rutherford. "Books in the Dock." *Books and Bookmen*, 16(12):32, 34–35, September 1971. (Reprinted from *New Society*, 6 May 1971)   **1W48**
A criticism of the present English obscenity law which places the responsibility on an enlightened jury, giving the defendant no better odds than a game of chance. The author proposes removing obscenity cases from the criminal courts and placing the book (not the publisher) on trial before a special tribunal similar to the New Zealand Indecent Publications Tribunal. He discusses the working of that body, noting that serious literary, artistic, or scientific books are seldom suppressed.

Warden, Karl P. "Canon 35: Is There Room for Objectivity?" *Washburn Law Journal*, 4:211–39, Spring 1965. **1W49**

The author brings together some of the landmark opinions in the dispute between press and bar over Judicial Canon 35 of the American Bar Association, barring photography from the courts, presenting the claims of both sides.

Wardlaw, Frank H. "Of Books and Truth." *Southeastern Librarian*, 17:69–73, Summer 1967.   **1W50**
The director of the University of Texas Press attacks the volunteer censors, "well-meaning patriotic people," who demand removal of books from public libraries and want to remove controversial material from school textbooks. "This sort of thing is an insult to our young people and an offense against America."

Wardroper, John. *Kings, Lords, and Wicked Libellers. Satire and Protest, 1760–1837.* London, Murray, 1973. 263p.   **1W51**
A lively account of the bawdy, bitter, and passionate work of balladeers, lampoonists, newsmen, and caricaturists who flourished in London from the accession of George III to the coming of Victoria. These impudent scribes, or their publishers and vendors, were sometimes brought to trial and served time in jail; sometimes they were bought over with government funds. The book also deals with the many devices used by the government to manage or subsidize official news. Among the authors, publishers, or vendors figuring in the story are: John Almon, William Benbow, Sir Francis Burnett, Richard Carlile, George Cruikshank, Isaac Eaton, John Wilkes (from an earlier period), W. T. Sherwin, William Hone, Thomas Wooler, Thomas Hardy, Thomas Spence, John Horne Tooke, Henry and John Hunt, Charles Pigott, "Peter Pendar," John Thelwall, and Junius. Among the periodicals referred to are: *Black Dwarf*, *Cosmopolite*, *Gorgon*, *Republican*, *Reformists Register*, *Political Register*, *John Bull*, and *Politics for the People*.

Ware, William M., and Gerard D. DiMarco. "Journalistic Media and Fair Trial." *Cleveland State Law Review*, 18:440–49, September 1969. (Reprinted in Donald G. Douglas and Philip Noble, *eds., Justice on Trial*, pp. 209–18)   **1W52**
Self-regulation among the professional groups involved is the answer to the conflict between a free press and fair trial. The lawyers and the journalists, through joint professional efforts, must establish a working code. The authorities that establish the code must also act as a unifying force in policing the operation of the code.

Waring E. M., and J. J. Jeffries. "The Conscience of a Pornographer." *Journal of Sex Research*, 10:40–46, February 1974.   **1W53**
"The clinical case presented gives insight into the dynamics of a professional pornographer, unconscious guilt feelings and anticipation of psychic disaster as the defense against such guilt, expressed in the man's work."

Waring, Houstoun. "The Murder of Elijah Parish Lovejoy." *Grassroots Editor*, 15(6):24–26, November–December 1974. **1W54**
A brief account of the murder of the abolitionist editor in Alton, Ill., 1837, and events that followed.

Warncke, Ruth. "Intellectual Freedom for Seminarians." *Catholic Library World*, 38:291–94, January 1967. **1W55**
"I am making a case for absolute intellectual freedom for seminarians. Unless it is granted, I think the world will be a poorer place, lacking the quality of leadership these men should give. . . . It seems to me that curtailment of intellectual freedom on the grounds that such a procedure will keep people morally upright, politically pure, and socially adjusted is fallacious. The morally upright man is not the man who has never encountered evil. He is the man who has seen evil, often in all of its seductiveness, and has chosen to reject it."

Warnock, Frank H. "The New York Times Rule—the Awakening Giant of First Amendment Protections." *Kentucky Law Journal*, 62:824–43, 1973–74. **1W56**
"With the advent of *New York Times v. Sullivan* [1964], the legal concept of freedom of the press in juxtaposition with the tort of defamation changed substantially. The purpose of this note is to analyze the scope of the change, the reasons for it, and the results stemming therefrom."

Warren, Earl, Jr. "Governmental Secrecy: Corruption's Ally." *American Bar Association Journal*, 60:550–52, May 1974. **1W57**
"When secrecy surrounds government and the activities of public servants, corruption has a breeding place. Secrecy prevents the citizenry from inspecting its government through the news media. The minimum amount of secrecy needed for the proper operation of government should be fixed by law, and no secrecy beyond that point should be countenanced."—Editor

———. "Obscenity Laws—A Shift to Reality?" *Santa Clara Lawyer*, 11:1–19, Fall 1970. (Reprinted in Ray C. Rist, *ed., The Pornography Controversy*, pp. 96–116) **1W58**
The former Chief Justice of the U.S. Supreme Court reviews the recent development of common law in obscenity, the basic *Roth* decision (*Roth v. United States*, 1957) with its elements of "prurient interest," "contemporary community standards," and "redeeming social value." He suggests a new approach based not on the concept of labeling, but within the context of how the material is employed. Further possible approaches are on the basis of laws of "nuisance," disturbing the peace, and assault and battery. He believes the landmark case of *Roth* has been appropriately expanded by *Ginzburg* (*Ginzburg v. United States*, 1966),

which added the element of pandering, and *Stanley* (*Stanley v. Georgia*, 1969), which protected mere possession of obscene matter. He believes the judiciary is on the true course in obscenity decisions and hopes that legislators and the executive branch will not "encumber or deter this trend by advocating and enacting unconstitutional or unworkable laws which run counter to it."

Warren, John H., III. "Judicial Review, State Secrets, and the Freedom of Information Act." *South Carolina Law Review*, 23:332–40, 1971. **1W59**
"The circuit court in *Epstein* [*Epstein v. Resor*, 1970] made a solid contribution to the area of the law concerning the discovery of state secrets. It did so by outlining specific criteria, as to the duration of the initial classification, type of filing system employed, and the attitude of the withholding agency, to be used by the courts in adjudging the propriety of executive classifications and by leaving the door open to future *in camera* review in such proceedings."

Warren, Robert S. *et al.* "The Press under Fire." *Bulletin of the American Society of Newspaper Editors*, 566:3–21, February 1973. **1W60**
In this special issue, a group of writers discuss current threats against press freedom: Robert S. Warren discusses court orders which gag the press in Examining the Erosion of a Basic Human Freedom; John Lawrence writes on Going to Jail Over the Watergate Tapes; Gordon Hanna, Almost Going to Jail over Shielding a Source; William F. Thomas, How Did We Get Into This Terrible Fix; and Joseph H. Weston, Facing Jail for Criminal Libel, a personal account of the editor-publisher of *Sharp Citizen*, Cave City, Ark., jailed for criticizing local politicians.

Warren, Robert S., and Jeffrey M. Abell. "Free Press–Fair Trial: The 'Gag Order'; A California Aberration." *Southern California Law Review*, 45:51–99, Winter 1972. **1W61**
The author criticizes the growing practice of the California courts to impose gags on the state's press by restricting the coverage of pending criminal trials. The author finds that the legal profession has failed to establish that a free press actually causes unfair trials. On evidence available he finds that (1) In the vast majority of cases, pretrial publicity will never reach members of a jury. (2) Even when potentially damaging publicity does reach the jury, there is a lack of empirical evidence that the publicity has any significant effect upon the deliberations. (3) The courts possess effective alternative means to prevent prejudice from pretrial publicity.

Warta, Darrell L. "The Newsmen's Privilege: A Need for Constitutional Protection." *Washburn Law Journal*, 10:387–402, Spring 1971. **1W62**
The courts should presume the newsman has a privilege to refuse to disclose confidential

sources until overcome by a compelling government interest. "This recommended procedure would provide the best means to ascertain in any given case whether the public is best served by allowing for full and complete disclosure of information through the news media absent the chilling effect of a grand jury interrogation or whether the public's interest would be better served by indirectly restricting the flow of news by requiring compulsory disclosure of confidential news sources at grand jury interrogations." The occasion for the commentary is the U.S. Supreme Court decision in *Caldwell v. United States* (1970).

Wasby, Steven. "The Pure and the Prurient: The Supreme Court, Obscenity and Oregon Policy." In David H. Everson, *ed., The Supreme Court as Policy Maker: Three Studies on the Impact of Judicial Decisions*. Carbondale, Ill., Public Affairs Research Bureau, Southern Illinois University, 1968, pp. 82–116. **1W63**
"The purpose of this paper is to examine the impact of the United States Supreme Court opinions on state policy, particularly policy concerning obscene literature in Oregon during the period January, 1958, through June, 1963." The relevant Supreme Court decisions were: *Roth v. United States* (1957), *Alberts v. California* (1957), *Butler v. Michigan* (1957), *Kingsley Books v. Brown* (1957), *Smith v. California* (1959), and *Manual Enterprises v. Day* (1962). "While the Oregon Obscenity controversy probably would have commenced even if the Supreme Court had not decided these cases, and while they were not the sole determinants of policy, the opinions played a substantial role in the process by which policy was developed and in the ultimate outcome of policy development."

———, *ed. Civil Liberties: Policy and Policy Making*. Carbondale, Ill., Southern Illinois University Press, 1976. 235p. **1W64**
Includes the following articles dealing with press freedom: Minority Access to the Media: The Free Marketplace Dilemma by Francisco J. Lewels. Television and Socialization to Violence: Policy Implications of Recent Research by Meredith W. Watts. Television, Children, and Censorship by Deanna C. Robinson. The Right to Know by Richard E. Morgan. Erotica and Community Standards: The Conflicts of Elite and Democratic Values by Richard S. Randall.

Washington (State) Library Association. "Intellectual Freedom in Libraries: Statement of Policy by the Washington Library Association." *Library News Bulletin*, 38:269–72, July–September 1971. **1W65**

The Washington Post Writers Group. *Of the Press, By the Press, For the Press (And Others Too). A Critical Study of the Inside Workings of the News Business. From the News Pages, Editorials, Columns and Internal Staff Memos of the Washington Post.* Edited by Laura Longley Babb. Washington, D.C., Washington Post Writers Group, 1974. 246p. **1W66**
Articles deal critically with such issues as newsroom discrimination, conflict of interest and ethics, pretrial publicity, advocacy, anonymous sources, and a tribute to George Seldes.

Wasserman, Leonard M. "*Caldwell v. United States*—Journalistic Privilege: A New Dimension to Freedom of the Press." *Brooklyn Law Review* 37:502–32, Spring 1971. **1W67**
"This Comment will explore the background and history of the journalistic privilege in light of case law and early constitutional arguments. It will also analyze in detail the *Caldwell* decision [*Caldwell v. United States* (1970)], discussing its weaknesses and ramifications."

Wassom, Earl. "Education and the Censorship Dilemma." *Kentucky Library Association Bulletin,* 35(3):11–16, July 1971. **1W68**
A rational approach to achieving the goal of intellectual freedom is to require a school to adopt: "(1) a standardized policy of book selection; (2) a sound philosophy for the utilization of these resources; and (3) an educational approach which encourages learning at the 'teachable moment.' "

"Watchdog, Stay Away from My Door." *Progressive,* 37:30–35, March 1973. **1W69**
Eight "media executives and other seasoned observers of American journalism," at the request of the editor, responded to William L. Rivers's article (February issue) advocating a national press council. Most of the responses were sharply critical of Rivers's "watchdog" concept.

Waters, Harry F. *et al.* "The Censors." *Newsweek,* 86(21):85–86, 24 November 1975. **1W70**
The work of the television network censors and the dilemma they face with the advent of the networks' new "family hour" programming. While "most of TV's creative community recognizes that the nation's networks, like its newspapers, have the right to edit the material they present," the television industry also "has the obligation to draw up clear cut standards for the people who design its product."

Watkins, Alan. "Obscenity: The Case for Repeal." *New Statesman,* 82:195, 13 August 1971. **1W71**
While disagreeing with the contentions that (1) no good writing can be produced under existing conditions, and (2) books and writing have no effect on the reader, the author argues for repeal of obscenity laws.

———. "A Slight Case of Obscenity." *New Statesman,* 77:210, 14 February 1969. **1W72**
An account of the trial and conviction of a British bookseller for the publication and sale of *My Secret Life*.

Watkins, Barry. "Captivity of an Audience Viewing Screen of Drive-in Theater Outside of Premises." *Arkansas Law Review,* 30:82–88, Spring 1976. **1W73**
Re: *Erznoznik v. City of Jacksonville* (1975), in which the U.S. Supreme Court found a Jacksonville, Fla., ordinance regulating a drive-in theater in violation of free speech as protected by the First Amendment.

Watkins, John J. "Newsgathering and the First Amendment." *Journalism Quarterly,* 53:406–16, 493, Autumn 1976. **1W74**
Is there a special First Amendment right of press access to government information? Is newsgathering constitutionally protected? While there is recognition that a right of special press access is desirable, "the full scope of protection afforded the press is still undefined." The Supreme Court has largely avoided formulating standards in information gathering. In *Branzburg v. Hayes* (1972) the Court explicitly recognized some kind of First Amendment status for news gathering and may have left the door open for further positive ruling. "The proper analysis would appear to be to recognize that the First Amendment protects the gathering of information by the news media and, since first amendment rights are not absolute, to evaluate the claim in its particular context according to the appropriate tests for restricting the exercise of first amendment right."

———. "The Status of Confidential Privilege for Newsmen in Civil Libel Actions." *Journalism Quarterly,* 52:505–14, Autumn 1975. **1W75**
The author considers two cases involving the right of newsmen to withhold the identities of confidential sources in civil proceedings: *Cervantes v. Time, Inc.,* 464 F.2d 986 (8th Cir. 1972) and *Carey v. Hume,* 492 F.2d 631 (D.C. Cir. 1974). Both plaintiffs argue that need to demonstrate actual malice required that they know sources. One claim was allowed, the other wasn't, but common points emerge.

———. *Texas Media Law; Libel, Privacy and Contempt.* Austin, Tex., University of Texas, 1971. 183p. (Unpublished Master's thesis) **1W76**
The thesis outlines Texas law, state court decisions, and controlling federal and U.S. Supreme Court decisions in the areas of libel, invasion of privacy, and contempt of court.

Watkins, Mark E. "Implications of the Extension of the Fairness Doctrine to Editorial Expressions Implied in Commercial Advertising." *Albany Law Review,* 34:452–64, Winter 1970. **1W77**
"The purpose of this comment is to examine briefly the validity of the FCC's efforts to first regulate and later prohibit cigarette advertising over radio and television, and to explore the possible contour of future policies designed to achieve fairness in advertising."

Watras, Joseph. "The Textbook Dispute in West Virginia: A New Form of Oppression." *Educational Leadership,* 33:21–23, October 1975. **1W78**
The real issue in the West Virginia textbook controversy is how can schools deal with divergent beliefs? "The school system that takes a chance and affirms genuine pluralism with both sides interacting, maintaining the possibility of one finally dominating, searching for the truth all within limits will revolutionize education. Just as the Appalachian people have to lose their paranoia, we have to lose our fear of strongly held values."

Watson, Eric R. "John Wilkes and the Essay on Woman." *Notes and Queries,* 9(11th ser.):121–23, 14 February 1914; 143–45, 21 February 1914; 162–64, 28 February 1914; 183–85, 7 March 1914; 203–5, 14 March 1914; 222–23, 21 March 1914; 241–42, 28 March 1914. **1W79**
The author finds further evidence of John Wilkes's authorship of the *Essay on Woman*, and from examination of numerous documents, sheds further light on the incident of publication, intrigue, and prosecution.

Waugh, Auberon. "My Father's Diaries." *New Statesman,* 85:528–29, 13 April 1973. **1W80**
The author discusses the possibility of libel in the publication of diaries in general and the diary of his father (Evelyn Waugh) in particular, currently being serialized in the *Observer*.

Waxman, Jerry J. "Local Broadcast Gatekeeping During Natural Disasters." *Journalism Quarterly,* 50:751–58, Winter 1973. **1W81**
"Public replaces newsman as primary gatekeeper for small and medium radio stations in time of major local disaster."

"We Pick 'Em, You Watch 'Em: First Amendment Rights of Television Viewers." *Southern California Law Review,* 43:826–47, Fall 1970. **1W82**
"It is the thesis of this Comment that certain

forms of censorship practiced by television networks violate the first amendment. This violation will be established by an examination of the role played by television in American society, and its relation to the values underlying the first amendment. After demonstrating that the structure of the television industry is such that network executives can, and do, thwart first amendment values by discouraging or removing controversial presentations from programming, it will be argued that recipients, as well as expressors, of television communication possess rights under the first amendment which are infringed by such programming practices. The Comment will conclude with a discussion of the means whereby the television-viewer, as a recipient of communication, may vindicate his rights."

Weart, Spencer R. "Scientists with a Secret." *Physics Today*, 21:23–26+, February 1976. **1W83**
"While the Nazi war machine was gearing up, a few physicists realized that a fission chain reaction was feasible—would they be able to get all groups to agree to hold back publication?" The author discusses a unique case of wartime scientific self-censorship.

Weaver, Paul H. "Is Television News Biased?" *Public Interest*, 1972:57–74, Winter 1972. **1W84**
Media are, by definition and of necessity, biased, according to the author; the question is how are they biased. He discusses the controversy over television bias, largely surrounding the publication of Edith Efron's book, *The News Twisters*, which he considers "an extensive and tolerably reliable body of evidence" of network bias in covering the 1968 presidential campaign. The personal political opinions of the newsmen "almost certainly influenced the content of television campaign coverage." Their depiction of the various candidates "were often in harmony with their liberal political sympathies." He finds that the format of television news endows it "with a strong preference for personifying and dramatizing, for representing institutions, situations, general developments, and the like, by means of the actions, predicaments, moods, or statements of individual people . . . the typical television news story will be far more interpretive than a newspaper news story." He concludes that, while "the biases of television news more often than not have their origin in the news form rather than in reporters' personal opinions, it is disconcerting in the extreme to discover, when one examines that form, how frivolous, mean-spirited, and intellectually impoverished a form it is. It clearly would be desirable for reporters to see *more* themes, developments, and phenomena in the campaigns and other events they cover. Thus, what is needed is a pluralizing of the themes of 'stories,' and an expansion and improvement of the 'vocabulary' of the television reporter and editor."

————. "The New Journalism and the Old—Thoughts After Watergate." *Public Interest*, 35:67–88, Spring 1974. **1W85**

In an analysis of the future of journalism in the United States, the author sees two general forms of behavior—partisan or ideological journalism and liberal or objective journalism. The former prevails in many European countries; the latter has been the traditional pattern in the United States. A major tension in traditional journalism is the conflict between access to the news and autonomy of the newspaper. In opting for access to government news the press must establish a certain cooperative and favorable relationship with the news sources which inevitably reduces the level of independence. In the aftermath of Watergate and the hostility of the Nixon Administration to the press, a new stance of "truculent independence from government and officialdom," has been growing among journalists, a mood for adversary journalism. The author sees a danger to press freedom in this retreat from liberal journalism. "When newsmen begin to assert they are positively the adversaries of government, access diminishes drastically, and with it not only the contribution journalism can make but also the openness and flexibility of government itself." Government officials threatened, will isolate themselves from the press and thus from the people. "Partisan journalism would not increase the openness of the system, it would sharply decrease it." The author believes there are ways to curb the abuses and still preserve the liberal tradition of the press. Government can increase the amount of information made available and reduce its public relations activities. The press can abandon its flirtation with the "oppositional" posture and refrain from exploiting public affairs for their sensational value. "The result, I believe, will be a journalism that provides more, and more useful information to the citizenry, and a political system that, in consequence, comes a bit closer than in the past to realizing its historic ideals."

————. "The Politics of a News Story." In Harry M. Clor, *ed.*, *The Mass Media and Modern Democracy*. Chicago, Rand McNally, 1974, pp. 85–111. **1W86**
The news media exercise a political influence but "this influence is not to be discovered in the explicit content of news, nor, apparently, can it be described by the conventional left-center-right nomenclature." The author seeks more subtle evidence of political implication of news through the analysis of a single news story—the 1964 sit-in demonstration at the University of California. He concludes that "this story presents the Berkeley events in a way that encourages the mobilization of partisans and liberals and the withdrawal of the indifferent, with the result that public discussion and action are dominated by the partisans and liberals, who act out their roles before the cynical indifferentists." He finds that the story "encouraged needless conflict (among the various parties) and mindless consensus (among the groups of partisans), and to this extent it was an instrument of political drift rather than of public mastery of events."

Weaver, Timothy A. "States May Regulate Material Depicting Obscene

Sexual Conduct Specifically Defined by Applicable State Law." *Illinois Bar Journal*, 62:218–20, December 1973. **1W87**
Re: *Miller v. California*, 413 U.S. 15 (1973).

Weaver, Warren, Jr. "Public's Right to Know: How Much? About Whom?" *New York Times*, 15 December 1974, p. 11. (Week in Review) **1W88**
A consideration of the conflict between freedom of the press as guaranteed by the First Amendment and right of privacy, that has attained constitutional stature through a series of judicial interpretations in the last half century. The occasion for the story is that three cases now before the U.S. Supreme Court turn on the question of whether the press can give true accounts of nonpublic figures where the accounts intrude into private lives.

Webb, Peter. *The Erotic Arts*. Boston, New York Graphic Society, 1975. 514p. (First published in England by Secker & Warburg) **1W89**
Chapter 1, Art and Pornography; Chapter 5, Sexual Attitudes in Victorian Art and Literature; Appendix II, The Restricted Collections of the British Museum and the Victoria and Albert Museum; Appendix IV, Censorship in the Cinema; Appendix V, Pornography: A Brief Survey. Generously illustrated; extensive notes and a critical bibliography of works relevant to the theme of eroticism in the arts.

Weber, George. "The Case Against *Man*: A Course of Study." *Phi Delta Kappan*, 57:81–82, October 1975. **1W90**
A widely used course of study for the fifth and sixth grades, developed with federal funds, "came under heavy fire from some parents, some teachers, some congressmen, and a section of the press."

————. "West Virginia Textbook Controversy." *Education Digest*, 40:14–15, March 1975. (Condensed from *CBE Bulletin* [Council for Basic Education], January 1975) **1W91**
The author discusses the lessons to be learned from the turmoil in West Virginia over use of textbooks, which includes awareness by school professionals of parental rights, adequate community review of textbooks, orderly complaint procedures, and a recognition of the rights of minorities as well as the majority, not only with respect to racial and ethnic groups but also to views on religion, politics, and sex.

Webster, George D. "How To Get the Information You Need From Government Agencies. . . ." *Association Man-*

agement, 26(10):89–95, October 1974.
1W92

"The Freedom of Information Act, passed in 1966, provides associations with a way to obtain rules, opinions, records, and proceedings of government agencies. Here is a background report on how the act can be used to get the information you need."

Webster, Owen. "Censorship and the Publisher." *Australian Author*, 1:30–35, October 1969. **1W93**

Wechsler, Andrew R., *comp. Economics and Freedom of Expression; A Bibliography*. Stanford, Calif., Department of Economics, Stanford University, 1974. 51p. Processed. (Studies in Industry Economics, no. 38) **1W94**

Part 1, Books, reports, and articles. Part 2, Court decisions and laws.

Wechsler, James A. *The Age of Suspicion*. New York, Random House, 1953. 333p. **1W95**

A political autobiography of the editor of the *New York Post*, a paper that had crusaded against both communism and McCarthyism. Editor Wechsler had been brought before Senator McCarthy's committee and accused of being a Communist, although he had quit the party many years before, and had a long record of subsequent anti-communism. "In this nightmare proceeding Wechsler fought back. He did not plead any privilege or immunity. He had nothing to hide. He answered every question—and his answers were a dramatic chapter in the battle for press freedom."

———. "Free Press versus Fair Trial." *Progressive*, 29(3):18–21, March 1965.
1W96

A discussion of some of the complexities in adopting into law an overall "code" of pretrial publicity.

Weclew, Robert G. "Fair Trial—Equal in Value to Free Press." *DePaul Law Review*, 16:353–73, Spring–Summer 1967. **1W97**

The author traces the development of the concepts of free press and fair trial and the conflicts between these two constitutional guarantees. He reviews various solutions proposed or attempted over the years, mostly without success. He recommends the passage of "a narrowly drawn contempt statute that would apply to employees of news media as well as prosecutors and defense counsel and their staffs, the accused, subpoenaed witnesses, enforcement officers, and government officers and employees. The Attorney General's Statement of Policy could furnish the direction for such a criminal contempt statute which

would delineate specific types of punishable publication. Any person in the above categories responsible for the publication would be subject to criminal contempt proceedings with the punishment including at least a fine."

Wedell, E. G. *Broadcasting and Public Policy*. London, Michael Joseph, 1968. 370p. **1W98**

"The first chapter attempts to set the broadcasting system within the context of the whole range of the mass media and of the public stake in them. Chapter two gives an account of the British system as successive governments have developed it. . . . Chapters three, four and five deal with the triangle of forces which determines the output of the broadcasting services: the controllers, the producers, and the consumers. Chapter six tries to look out from the present base, to discuss some of the choices open to us and to indicate some of the principles on which such choices might be based." The various studies and investigations of the broadcasting industry are discussed, including reports of the Beveridge Committee (1949) and the Pilkington Committee (1960). The ITV Code on Violence in Programmes is given on pages 343–45.

Wedgeworth, Robert. "Q & A with the Supreme Court." In American Library Association, *Memorandum Re: Supreme Court Decisions of June 21, 1973*. Chicago, The Association, 1973. 8p. Processed. **1W99**

A series of questions and answers relating to the U.S. Supreme Court's obscenity decisions of 21 June 1973 (*Miller v. California*, etc.) in which the wording of the Court is used in answers.

Wei, Michael Ta Kung. *Freedom of Information As an International Problem*. Columbia, Mo., University of Missouri, 1964. 355p. (Ph.D. dissertation, University Microfilms, no. 64-13,311) **1W100**

"As a result of the cold war and differing ideology, the progress in the United Nations [in the field of freedom of information] has been quite slow. This study traces the development and collects the arguments about and definitions of freedom of information by nations divided on the issue. The basic division seems obviously to be that some countries emphasize freedom while others concentrate chiefly on responsibility."

———. "Freedom of Information As an International Problem." In Heinz-Dietrich Fischer and John C. Merrill, *eds., International Communication Media, Channels, Functions*. New York, Hastings House, 1970, pp. 85–93. **1W101**

The author traces the efforts in behalf of international freedom of the press from the establishment of the International Union of Press Associations in 1893, to the United Nations

Conference on Freedom of Information in 1948, to the formation of the International Press Institute in 1951.

Weihe, Bruce A. "Procedural Compromise and Contempt: Feasible Alternatives in the Fair Trial Versus Free Press Controversy." *University of Florida Law Review*, 22:650–67, Spring–Summer 1970. (Reprinted in Donald G. Douglas and Philip Noble, *comps., Justice on Trial*, pp. 237–44) **1W102**

"This note will analyze the factors involved in the fair trial–free press controversy, discuss and evaluate the remedial procedures presently utilized, and suggest possible modifications to improve the guarantee of fair and impartial jury trials." The author believes the trial judge should use his contempt power when pretrial publicity is prejudicial to the defendant.

Weiler, Daniel A. "Gertz v. Robert Welch, Inc.: Constitutional Privilege and the Defamed Private Individual." *John Marshall Journal of Practice and Procedure*, 8:531–47, Spring 1975. **1W103**

Re: *Gertz v. Robert Welch, Inc.*, 418 U.S. 323 (1974).

Weiler, Joseph. "Controlling Obscenity by Criminal Sanction." *Osgoode Hall Law Journal*, 9:415–32, November 1971. **1W104**

"The purpose of this paper is to explore some of the problems that confront the [Canadian] legislators and courts in their attempts to enforce morals in obscenity legislation through the utilization of the instrument of criminal sanction." The study presents a brief summary of the philosophical debate over legislating morality, a statement of current statutory and common law form of obscenity law in Canada, an assessment of the legality of obscenity law using the analysis promulgated by Lon Fuller, the practical difficulties of administration and a discussion of the impropriety of such an enterprise, and an analysis of the enforcement costs.

Weiler, Paul C. "Defamation, Enterprise Liability, and Freedom of Speech." *University of Toronto Law Journal*, 17(2):278–343, 1967. **1W105**

Content: The Relevance of Fault to Liability in Defamation—a Critical Statement and Analysis of the Present Law. The Underlying Rationale of Tort Law. Freedom of Speech, Fault Liability, and Defamation—"Private Law" Considerations. "Freedom of Speech" and Fault in Defamation—"Public Law" Considerations. Limits on the Effectiveness of Tort Law—Appropriate Alternatives.

Weinberg, Steve. "You Still Need a Can Opener." *Nation*, 220:463–66, 19 April 1975. **1W106**

A report of a meeting of government bureaucrats to discuss the implications and operation of the amended Freedom of Information Act, followed by examples of how the Act can be used and abused.

Weinberger, Andrew D. *Freedom and Protection; the Bill of Rights*. San Francisco, Chandler, 1962. 180p.   **1W 107**
Chapter 11, The Doctrine of "Clear and Present Danger" (*Whitney v. California*, 1927, *Barenblatt v. United States*, 1959). Chapter 12, Opinion and Association (*Grosjean v. American Press Co.*, 1935, *Uphaus v. Wyman*, 1959). Chapter 15, Group Libel (*Beauharnais v. Illinois*, 1952). Chapter 16, Censorship (*Roth v. United States* and *Alberts v. California*, 1957, and *Times Film Corp. v. City of Chicago*, 1961). Appendix includes: U.S. Bill of Rights, Canadian Bill of Rights, Universal Declaration of Human Rights.

Weiner, Charles A. "Teaching 'Dirty' Literature: A Rationale." *Alberta English*, 12(1):24–28, Winter 1971/72.   **1W 108**
The author suggests a number of so-called "dirty" works of literature that might be used in high school English classes if properly presented—*Catcher in the Rye*, *The Sot-Weed Factor*, *Giles Goat-Boy*, and *Lolita*.

Weiner, Charles R. "Freedom of Speech vs. the Right to a Fair Trial." *Shingle*, 19:154–57, October 1956.   **1W 109**
A lawyer proposes regulation of the press by a board or commission similar to those regulating radio and television (Federal Communications Commission) and the food and drug industry (Pure Food and Drug Administration). The newspapers "might themselves act as their own overseers, in conjunction with a committee of the Bar Association."

Weingast, David. "Censorship: The Road to Nowhere." In David R. Bender, *ed.*, *Issues in Media Management*. Baltimore, Division of Library Development and Services, 1974, pp. 19–26.   **1W 110**
A school superintendent offers advice to school librarians in facing censorship issues. He recommends careful book selection, with group participation, and written guidelines and criteria. He discusses the various areas that are likely to be controversial and suggests ways of dealing with the critics. "The content of instruction under a censorious book policy would be drained of life. This would demean education while it exalts ignorance."

Weingrad, Ronald C. "Right of Newsmen Not to Reveal Confidential Sources of Information to a Grand Jury." *Duquesne Law Review*, 11:657–76, Summer 1973.   **1W 111**
Re: *Branzburg v. Hayes* (1972), in which "the Supreme Court has held that in a grand jury setting, a newsman's status is the same as that of any other citizen and therefore he must re-

spond to subpoena and answer all relevant questions relating to any investigation into the commission of crime."

Weinman, Howard M. "The FCC Fairness Doctrine and Informed Social Choice." *Harvard Journal on Legislation*, 8:333–57, January 1971.   **1W 112**
"This Note will focus on the present status of the law and recent developments in that part of the fairness doctrine which requires that broadcast licensees 'afford reasonable opportunity for the discussion of conflicting views on issues of public importance.'"

[Weinstein, Joel H.] "Broadcast Media Regulation—the Fairness Doctrine and the First Amendment." *New York Law Forum*, 19:639–52, Winter 1974. **1W 113**
Re: *Columbia Broadcasting System, Inc. v. Democratic National Committee*, 412 U.S. 94 (1973).

Weisberg, Elizabeth. "Don't Breed—Read: Sex Education Literature in the Library." *Bay State Librarian*, 58(3):20–22, October 1969.   **1W 114**
Consideration of the campaign against sex education and its literature, spearheaded by the John Birch Society and other ultraright groups, that equate it with Communist propaganda. When the controversy hits the library the first aim should be to collect information representing both liberal and conservative viewpoints; second, to have accurate, trustworthy materials for use of parents and children in learning and examining attitudes about sex and behavior. "Sex education literature and instruction is protected by the law of the land."

Weisberg, Michael. *The Daniel Schorr Investigation*. Columbia, Mo., Freedom of Information Center, School of Journalism, University of Missouri at Columbia, 1976. 6p. (Report no. 361)   **1W 115**
"After months of controversy and publicity, what has come to be known as 'The Daniel Schorr Affair' has ended. The author details events leading to the leak and the investigation by the House Ethics Committee, and provides some historical perspective of other reporters in conflict with the government." Schorr had leaked the secret report of the House Select Committee on Intelligence to the *Village Voice* which published it.

Weisman, Peter, and Andrew D. Postal. "The First Amendment As a Restraint of the Grand Jury Process." *American Criminal Law Review*, 10:671–99, Summer 1972.   **1W 116**
"This article examines the propriety of and the need for first amendment limitations on the grand jury process, with special emphasis on the problems posed to the separation of powers and to judicial integrity. Further, it attempts to define an appropriate standard for resolving

conflict. Finally, the discussion outlines the possible substantive and procedural obstacles the practicing attorney may encounter in raising these issues."

Weiss, Charles. *Copyright and Reprography*. Columbia, Mo., Freedom of Information Center, School of Journalism, University of Missouri at Columbia, 1976. 6p. (Report no. 351)   **1W 117**
A summary of the issue of copyright and photocopying in which authors and publishers are pitted against users—librarians and educators.

Weitzel, Stephen E. "Constituent Elements of Tripartite Definition of Obscenity to be Determined by Applying Contemporary Standards, Not National Standards." *Emory Law Journal*, 23:551–65, Spring 1974.   **1W 118**
Re: *Miller v. California*, 413 U.S. 15 (1973).

Weitzman, Lenore J., and Diane Rizzo. *Biased Textbooks: Action Steps You Can Take*. Washington, D.C., National Education Association, 1974. 16p. (Produced by the Resource Center on Sex Roles in Education)   **1W 119**
"Studies the images of males and females in elementary school textbooks in five subject areas, and suggests action to take in helping to bring about change."

Welch, Edwin W. "Classified Information and the Courts." *Federal Bar Journal*, 31:360–77, Fall 1972.   **1W 120**
"The paper attempts to pull together the law dealing with classified information in both criminal and civil litigation. Particular emphasis has been placed on the rules and procedures applicable to courts-martial. The paper will show that the courts do not blindly follow the decisions of the people who classify information and that there is a fairly well defined body of existing law to which the judge advocate may refer when he is confronted with a problem involving classified matter."

Welch, Susan. "Vietnam: How the Press Went Along." *Nation*, 213:327–30, 11 October 1971.   **1W 121**
The failure of the press to challenge administration assumptions about the Vietnam war "was due in part to the day-to-day demands of journalism; in part to the prevailing political climate; and in part to more complex kinds of human behavior, such as the tendency to ignore facts that do not fit existing notions about how things 'should be.'"

Weller, Francis G. "Freedom of the Press Report Résumé." *International Lawyer*, 3:122–28, October 1968. **1W122**

The source of the article is material presented by the Committee on Freedom of the Press of the Inter-American Press Association, giving the status of press freedom in the Americas. The report "charged Haiti and Cuba with news suppression, looked critically at Paraguay, accused the government of the United States of 'managed news' [particularly with respect to the Vietnam conflict] and labeled 'harsh and uncompromising' the American Bar Association's support of courtroom restrictions on news coverage."

Welles, Chris. "The Fairness Doctrine: Is it a fickle affront to the First Amendment? Or would its elimination be 'the worst single thing to happen in the history of U.S. journalism'?" *TV Guide*, 23(35):4–9, 30 August 1975. **1W123**

A presentation of the arguments pro and con of the fairness doctrine in radio and television, a basic philosophical issue with explosive implications.

Wells, E. F. "Your Trash Is Blowing in My Yard." *Liberty*, 68(4):2–7, July–August 1973. **1W124**

"Pornography, like trash, is difficult to confine. Unless there is a concerted effort to keep the lid on it, it is thrown into the faces of those who wish to be free from it, and this is an abuse of their liberty." The author suggests ways in which pornographic trash can be prevented from blowing into yards where it is unwanted.

Wells, Reese, and Gena Davidson. "Censorship and the Authors' Viewpoint." *Journal of Research and Development in Education*, 9(3):69–75, Spring 1976. **1W125**

A brief biographical sketch of and interview with William O. Steele and Mary Steele, married authors of children's books (they write independently) that have occasionally dealt with themes and situations considered taboo. The authors discuss the present character of children's books, the qualities that have made them controversial, and the efforts at censorship.

Welsh, David. "Censorship in South Africa: (1) Censorship and the Universities." *Philosophical Papers*, 5(1):19–33, May 1976. **1W126**

A member of the faculty of the University of Cape Town writes of the stifling of scholarship in South Africa by the rigid controls over what books libraries may acquire and scholars may read. Under the Publications and Entertainments Act works on the banned list may be acquired by a university library or read by scholars only under permits issued by the Publications Control Board. "The present system has been an endless source of irritation, annoyance and frustration." An even tighter control is exercised over works proscribed under the Suppression of Communism Act. Such works are almost totally unavailable for study and research. Likewise, the ban on many black writers means that "it is hardly possible today lawfully to make a scholarly, deep study of Black South African literature" or of black nationalism. The author documents his article with cases where books were denied to legitimate scholars.

[Welton, C. J.] *A Post Office Outrage and Medical Tyranny with Sidelights on Officialism*. Nottingham, England [1910?]. 97p. **1W127**

An attack on the medical profession for its opposition to herbal medicine, to the distribution of birth control and sex education information, and on the proposed Indecency Bill that would give the post office power to seize such publications and periodicals advertising them. The author cites with contempt the American experience with Comstock laws, and his own trial in England for the sale of *Marriage and Its Mysteries*. He also reports on the case of Dr. Henry A. Allbutt, ousted from the medical profession for his book, *The Wife's Handbook* (A 69–70). He also attacks ex-President Theodore Roosevelt for his prudery.

Welty, Joanne. "Listeners' Rights: Public Intervention in Radio Format Changes." *St. John's Law Review*, 49: 714–47, Summer 1975. **1W128**

"This note will analyze varying views of the [Federal Communications] Commission's responsibilities in overseeing format changes."

Wender, Faith. "Privacy Legislation: Protection of Individual Liberties or Threat to a Free Press?" *Hofstra Law Review*, 3:773–93, Summer 1975. **1W129**

The article examines proposed privacy legislation in light of the opposition from the press. The author concludes that "it is certainly in our best interest to ensure that the rights of the press are not infringed upon so that the press may continue to view with healthy skepticism and to criticize government agencies and their actions. It is equally important that individuals be protected from the serious invasion of privacy resulting from abuses of the criminal justice investigative intelligence systems. It appears, upon examination, that well drafted privacy legislation would meet both of these vital objectives."

Wenglin, Barbara N. *The Effects of the 1973 Supreme Court Obscenity Ruling on the Public Library; A Survey*. Tucson, Ariz., University of Arizona, 1974. 40p. (Master's thesis, available from Educational Resources Information Center, ED 105,880) **1W130**

Wenk, Joseph R. "Federal Communications Commission's Fairness Doctrine Is Constitutional." *Villanova Law Review*, 13:393–99, Winter 1968. **1W131**

Re: *Red Lion Broadcasting Co. v. FCC* (D.C. Cir. 1967), in which the United States Court of Appeals (and later the Supreme Court) upheld the Federal Communications Commission's fairness doctrine.

Wentz, William H. "The Aftermath of WHDH: Regulation by Competition or Protection of Mediocrity?" *University of Pennsylvania Law Review*, 118: 368–409, January 1970. **1W132**

"There are two possible consequences of WHDH [FCC decision of 1969 not to renew the license of the station]—regulation by competition or automatic renewal. The choice is presently before Congress. It is a choice between continuing tolerance of mediocrity and new incentives to responsible broadcasting."

Werner, Gary L. *The Credibility Gap—1966; Prestige Gatekeepers View Government Handling of Vietnam Information*. Madison, Wis., University of Wisconsin, 1967. 116p. (Unpublished Master's thesis) **1W133**

The study was an exploration of the "credibility gap" in Vietnam news as reflected in the views of the editors and executive producers responding. The study involved a mail survey of end-of-channel gatekeepers of forty-two daily newspapers and three daily network news programs.

Wertham, Fredric. "Are Comic Books Harmful to Children?" *Friends Intelligencer*, 105:395–96, 10 July 1948. **1W134**

Comic books are harmful. "You don't need experts to determine that. . . . All you need is to look at comic books. . . . Since self-regulation of the comic-book industry is so flagrantly insincere, outside regulation is absolutely necessary."

———. "Notes on Violence by a Psychiatrist." *Television Quarterly*, 5(1): 42–43, Winter 1967. **1W135**

Excerpt from comments made at the Conference on International Understanding Through Film, Television, and Radio. "There are many forms of hidden censorship. . . . But one subject is completely open and free from censorship: violence, sadism, brutality, and torture. You can do anything you want in this area. If a half-nude girl is tortured, the nudity might be objected to—but not the torture. That is accepted because 'it helps the kids get rid of their aggressions.'"

———. "School for Violence; Mayhem in the Mass Media." In his *A Sign for Cain: An Exploration of Human Violence*. New York, Macmillan, 1966, pp. 193–228. (Reprinted in Victor B. Cline, *ed.*, *Where Do You Draw the Line?* pp. 157–75) **1W136**
As part of a general attack on the harmful effect of violence on American life, a consulting psychiatrist at Queens General Hospital and formerly member of the faculty at Johns Hopkins and New York University, indicts the mass media for their disservice as a "school for violence." He challenges these arguments frequently given in accepting violence in the media: (1) an emotionally healthy and well-adjusted child is not harmed; (2) it is up to the family to shield the child; (3) the mass media give the public and the children what they want; (4) violence is a part of human life and children should learn to cope with reality; (5) violence enables children to get rid of pent-up aggressions vicariously; (6) the harm of violence on children has not been proven; (7) a critique of mass media violence may breed censorship; (8) only maladjusted and emotionally disturbed children will be affected; (9) violence already exists in classical literature and fairy tales; (10) good always triumphs in the end and therefore the effect can be only salutary; (11) children are so resilient that they can take it; (12) trouble doesn't come from the media but what a child brings to them; (13) the mass media cannot cause harm, but merely trigger it; (14) contacts with real people, not pictures and print, influence children; (15) when children say they are imitating something they learned from the mass media they are just using this as an excuse; (16) so many factors enter into a child's development that one cannot gauge the effect of a single element; (17) children are not affected by mass media violence because they know it is only make believe; and (18) the character of a child has "jelled" by the age of seven and later influences, therefore, are negligible.

Werts, John S. "The First Amendment and Consumer Protection: Commercial Advertising As Protected Speech." *Oregon Law Review*, 50:177–96, Winter 1971. **1W137**
"This comment will explore the possibility that there is within the present scope of the first amendment a protection from libel actions for advertisers who would be critical of competitors. . . . The inquiry is limited to whether a *competitor* should have a right to make critical rebuttals to a rival's advertising or criticize his product. It is likely that courts already recognize the right of consumers themselves to comment critically on commercial products."

Wesker, Arnold. "Casual Condemnations: A Brief Study of the Critic As Censor." *Theatre Quarterly*, 1(2):16–30, 1971. **1W138**
A playwright whose recent work, *The Friends*, was reviewed almost unanimously unfavorably, conducts a detailed critique of the judgment of his critics. "If this article has any value I would like it to be that of cautioning the theatre public to question the degree of authority with which a critic passes judgment, and to read with much greater care his words, made seductively omnipotent by print. Otherwise this man, who has always been the real censor although cloaked by the respectable legitimacy of his trade, will become the final arbiter of what people should or should not experience in art and will heap anguish and terror upon the terror and anguish already inherent in its creation."

Wesolowski, James W. "Obscene, Indecent, or Profane Broadcast Language as Construed by the Federal Courts." *Journal of Broadcasting*, 13(2):203–19, Spring 1969. **1W139**
The author examines relevant cases that have been adjudicated in the Federal courts in an attempt to define the hazy but perilous line between acceptable and unacceptable language in broadcasting.

West, Hortense H. "Censorship and Boards." *Iowa English Bulletin Yearbook*, 25:12–17, November 1975. **1W140**
Guidelines for the selection of school textbooks and library books and for resolving issues involving controversies over use of materials.

West, Robert N. "A Case of Intimidation." *Publishers' Weekly*, 201(21):28–29, 22 May 1972. **1W141**
The president of the Unitarian Universalist Association describes how his religious denomination was systematically harassed after its publishing arm, the Beacon Press, printed Senator Gravel's edition of the Pentagon Papers.

———. *The Pentagon Papers*. 40 min. tape recording. Chicago, American Library Association, 1973. (Tape cassette distributed by Development Digest, Los Angeles) **1W142**
At a conference on Media, Man, Material, Machine, the president of the Beacon Press discusses the events that followed the Press's publicaton of Senator Gravel's version of the Pentagon Papers. Justice Department agents went through the bank records of Beacon Press and the Unitarian Universalist Association. The speaker claims the action was a violation of the First Amendment and the people's right to know.

West, William L. "The Moses Harman Story." *Kansas Historical Quarterly*, 37:41–63, Spring 1971. **1W143**
A biographical account of the freethought journalist of Valley Falls, Kans., whose crusade for sexual freedom through the columns of his paper, *Lucifer, the Light Bearer* (L378) resulted in his prosecution and imprisonment under the Comstock obscenity laws (H100–103). Activities of Harman's son-in-law, E. C. Walker, are also included (W23–26).

Westen, Tracy A. "Fair Play on the Air." *MORE*, 2(1):8, 11–12, January 1972. (Reprinted in Ted C. Smythe and George A. Mastroianni, *eds.*, *Issues in Broadcasting*. Palo Alto, Calif., Mayfield, 1975, pp. 247–55) **1W144**
Criticism of the "Whitehead Doctrine," devised by Clay T. Whitehead, director of the White House Office of Telecommunications as part of the Nixon Administration's strategy for controlling the electronic media. "If the broadcast industry failed to provide favorable media coverage of White House spokesmen and policies, then the White House would take reprisals against their economic interests." This proposal, part of the White House bargain, called for abolishing the fairness doctrine and handing over radio licenses to their present owners to be operated in perpetuity. The author believes the proposal "leaves untouched the fundamental profit maximizing motive that drives broadcasters toward conformity and middle-of-the-road programming."

Western Australia. Law Reform Committee. *Defamation*, *Privileged Reports; Report*. Perth, Australia, 1972. 30p. (Project no. 8) **1W145**

Wettstein, Hermann. *An Exposure of Attempts Made by the Materialistic Freethought Inquisition to Suppress the "Undesirable Truths" Contained in the "Teleo-Mechanics of Nature and the Subconscious Minds." . . . Open Letter to Prof. Ernst Haeckel. . . .* Fitzgerald, Ga., The Author, 1908. 26p. **1W146**
The author charges the editors of leading freethought papers with censoring material from his manuscripts and with malicious mutilation of his articles to embarrass and subject him to ridicule and contempt.

Weyandt, Gregory M. "Privacy v. the Press: Inevitable Conflict?" *Marquette Law Review*, 59:573–83, 1976. **1W147**
"This article will examine the inadequacy of courts' analyses of this conflict, in particular, the failure to examine the rationale supporting freedom of the press and how this failure affects a fair appraisal of the 'right of privacy.' "

Weyant, Piers J. "The FCC's Fairness Doctrine and the First Amendment." *Journal of Public Law*, 19:129–37, 1970. **1W148**
A review of the Federal Communications Commission's interpretation and administration of the fairness doctrine and the support

from the U.S. Supreme Court in the decision, *Red Lion Broadcasting Co., Inc. v. FCC*, 1967.

Whale, John. *Journalism and Government: A British View*. Columbia, S.C., University of South Carolina Press, 1972. 120p.   **1W 149**
In chapters on Political Imperatives and the Liberty to Know the author examines the official concealment of news and the role of the press as the "enemy of unreason in public affairs." He sees the press not as an opponent of government but, in the broad sense, a partner.

Whalen, Charles W., Jr. *Your Right to Know*. New York, Random House, 1973. 205p.   **1W 150**
A Republican congressman and sponsor of a newspaper shield bill explains the meaning and implications of such legislation in insuring a free flow of information to the American public. "He traces the history of the challenges to the press, showing that in most cases journalists have gone to jail rather than reveal their sources. Those who did reveal them found their future effectiveness seriously curtailed. . . . He answers the arguments that have been raised against journalistic 'privilege,' analyzes the privilege statutes already in existence in nineteen states, and . . . underlines the need for legislative action, not for journalists' sake but for their readers."

Whaley, Elizabeth G. "What Happens When You Put the Manchild in the Promised Land? An Experience With Censorship." *English Journal*, 63(5): 61–65, May 1974. (Reprinted in *Newsletter on Intellectual Freedom* [IFC-ALA], November 1974)   **1W 151**
An account of the controversy in a small public academy in New Hampshire over the use of the book *Manchild in the Promised Land* by Claude Brown in a class on black literature.

Wheeler, Tom. "Drug Lyrics, the FCC and the First Amendment." *Loyola University of Los Angeles Law Review*, 5:329–67, April 1972.   **1W 152**
Comment on the binding effect of FCC Notice 71-205 to radio broadcast licensees to discourage or eliminate the airing of "drug lyrics" in the public interest. The author believes that the Commission has overstepped valid constitutional restraints in its broad and vague notice. "The chilling effect upon protected speech is manifested through widespread overreaction."

Wheelwright, Kevin W. "Parody, Copyrights and the First Amendment." *University of San Francisco Law Review*, 10:564–85, Winter 1976.
                    1W 153

Conflicts and problems involving parodies and copyright infringement, with proposals for resolving the conflicts that will preserve "the virtues of the parodist's art while safeguarding the sanctity of the copyrighted creation."

Whelan, Charles M. "Behind the Fig Leaf: A Legal Analysis." *America*, 129:84–87, 18 August 1973.   **1W 154**
A professor of constitutional law and an associate editor of *America* summarizes the facts of each of the principle obscenity cases before the U.S. Supreme Court and the reasons given by the majority for their rulings.

Wheldon, Huw. "BBC Television Programmes: Responsibility and Reference." *Journal of the Society of Film and Television Arts*, 43/44:6–9, Spring–Summer 1971.   **1W 155**
The managing director of British Broadcasting Corp. Television describes the system of control over subject matter in BBC programming. "In general it can be said that the processes of editorial control are more akin to similar processes in large newspapers than they are to the machinery of censorship in the theatre and the film industry."

"When In Doubt, Don't." *Newsletter on Intellectual Freedom* (IFC-ALA), 18: 19–21, March 1970. (Reprinted from *Operation LAPL* [Los Angeles Public Library], November 1969)   **1W 156**
Report of remarks on the implications of two new state obscenity laws on the operation of California public libraries, made at a meeting of the Library Commission.

Whipple, Charles L. "The People's Need to Know." *Computers and Automation and People*, 22(4):26–31, April 1973; 22(5):36–38, May 1973. (Reprinted from *Boston Globe*, 21–27 January 1973)
                    1W 157
In a series of editorials in the *Boston Globe*, the editor of the editorial page looks at the controversy over journalist's privilege, concluding that an unqualified federal shield law is needed.

[Whiston, William.] "Proceedings against William Whiston, for publishing divers Tenets contrary to the Established Religion: 10 Anne, A.D. 1711." In T. B. and T. J. Howell, *eds.*, *State Trials*, London, Hansard, 1816–28, vol. 15, cols. 703–16.   **1W 158**
The defendant had been ousted from his professorship of mathematics at Cambridge for heretical and blasphemous ideas expressed in his books and lectures. A Church commission found Whiston guilty and recommended censure to the Queen. But Queen Anne lost the document and "Whiston's affair sleeps."

White, Arthur P. *The Office of Revels and*

Dramatic Censorship. Cleveland, Western Reserve University, 1931. 45p. (Studies in English Literature, *Western Reserve Bulletin*, vol. 34 (n. s.) no. 13, 15 September 1931)   **1W 159**
"It is the purpose of this study to trace the history of the office of the Master of the Revels and the work of the Master as official censor of the drama during the Restoration Period." Working from official records that are fragmentary, the author attempts to show that, contrary to common belief, censorship of the stage existed and plays were frequently banned during the forty years after the restoration of Charles II.

White, David A. "Censorship and the Concept of Imitation." *New Scholasticism*, 48:464–80, Autumn 1974. **1W 160**
"The purpose of this essay is to evaluate one possible attitude toward censorship, i.e., that censorship is at least questionable because the majority of men are inadequately educated as far as understanding the artistic nature of (censurable) works. . . . The principal conclusion turns on the fact that censorship can be justified only if certain assumptions are made concerning an equivalence in properties between works of art and immoral actions as this equivalence is experienced through the pleasure of imitation."

White, David M., and Lewis D. Barnett. "College Students' Attitudes on Pornography: A Pilot Study." *Technical Report of the [U.S.] Commission on Obscenity and Pornography*, 1:181–84, 1971.
                    1W 161
Interviews of 300 college students enrolled in summer school at five universities.

White, Emil, *ed. Henry Miller: Between Heaven and Hell*. Big Sur, Calif., Emil White, 1961. 86p.   **1W 162**
Includes the text of Judge Louis Goodman's article (1951) on the importation into the United States of Henry Miller's *Cancer* and *Capricorn;* correspondence between Miller and Trygve Hirsch with respect to *Sexus;* and the opinion of Lord Chief Justice Wald and the dissenting opinion of Judge Thrap in the trial of *Sexus* before the Supreme Court of Norway.

White, Eula T., and Roberta Friedman. "How the Library Can Help Show that: Sex Is Not a Four-Letter Word." *Wilson Library Bulletin*, 46: 153–62, October 1971.   **1W 163**
The selection and use of library materials in support of the teaching of human sexuality.

White, Isaac D. *Accuracy and Fair Play in the New Journalism*. New York, The World, 1913. 16p. (Reprinted from the editorial section of the *Sunday World*, 29 December 1912)   **1W 164**
A discussion of the newspaper's responsibility

to be honest and accurate. "If what is published is true and fair, the writer need not worry about the Libel law, civil or criminal. . . . It insures the freedom of the press with the same certainty that it protects the citizen from abuse of the press's power."

White, Lucien. "The Censorship Dilemma." *Illinois Libraries*, 49:612–21, September 1967. **1W165**
A brief chronology of landmarks in legislation and court decisions that limit or interpret the First Amendment, from the Sedition Act of 1798 to the U.S. Supreme Court decision in the case of Ralph Ginzburg; followed by a review of censorship problems and practices in public libraries.

White, Mary L. "Censorship—Threat Over Children's Books." *Elementary School Journal*, 75:2–10, October 1974. **1W166**
The author discusses some of the disputes over the suitability of certain children's books in schools and libraries, disputes that have resulted in the denial of children the freedom to read. Some of the controversies involved: *Down These Mean Streets, Charlie and the Chocolate Factory, Sylvester and the Magic Pebble, Comeback Guy, In the Night Kitchen, Little Black Sambo,* and *The Little House.* Appended is a list of controversial children's books and articles about them.

White, Mike. "Connecticut Contraceptive Ban v. Right of Privacy." *University of Missouri at Kansas City Law Review*, 34:95–120, Winter 1966. **1W167**
I. The Comstock Act—History of Birth Control Legislation on a Federal Level. II. Birth Control Legislation in the States—the History of Connecticut's Statute. III. The Demise of 53-32 (Section of Connecticut Statutes prohibiting use of contraceptives). IV. Privacy —A Constitutional Right?

Whited, Roberta. *Leaks: Concern and Control.* Columbia, Mo., Freedom of Information Center, School of Journalism, University of Missouri at Columbia, 1976. 6p. (Report no. 356) **1W168**
"The leaking of classified information has been an increasing trend in the United States since the classification system was established. Although many public officials are outraged at the leaks, and express concern over national security, it seems apparent that many governmental abuses of power would have gone undetected without the unofficial disclosures."

Whitehead, Clay T. "Broadcasters and the Networks. The Responsibility of the Local Station." *Vital Speeches*, 39: 230–32, 1 February 1973. **1W169**
In an address before a chapter of Sigma Delta Chi, Whitehead describes the steps the Nixon

Administration is taking to increase freedom and responsibility in broadcasting and to shift responsibility (not production) of programming from networks to individual stations. In proposals for changes in requirements for license renewal, "the broadcaster's performance [is] evaluated from the perspective of the people in his community and not the bureaucrat in Washington. . . . The broadcaster must show that he has afforded reasonable, realistic, and practical opportunities for the presentation and discussion of conflicting views on controversial issues."

———, and Fred W. Friendly. "Both Sides of Debate Over Television News." *U.S. News and World Report*, 74(8):48–52, 19 February 1973. **1W170**
The director of the White House Office of Telecommunications Policy answers questions about proposals to make major changes in the licensing of TV stations and in network programming. Fred W. Friendly, former president of National Broadcasting Company News, reacts to the White House proposals in answer to questions.

"Whitehead Calls for a New Deal." *Broadcasting*, 81(15):14–16, 11 October 1971. **1W171**
The director of the Office of Telecommunications Policy in the Nixon Administration proposes to turn the broadcasting industry by eliminating the fairness doctrine and replacing it with a statutory right of paid access, change the license-renewal process to get the government out of programming, and de-regulate commercial radio.

Whitehouse, Mary. "Freedom or License?" *Books*, 8:16–19, Summer 1972. **1W172**
The author accuses the libertarian left, who have contempt for capitalism, of defending money-making pornographers. If sadism is directed against Negroes and Jews there are calls for censorship among the libertarians, but who is to protect the children? "Pornography and sadism are hate manifestations. That this hate should be directed against humanity as a whole rather than constituents of it, makes it more, not less, dangerous. . . . That the present obscenity laws are to a great extent unworkable in their existing form there seems little doubt. Neither, to my mind, is there doubt that they could be made effective, without being repressive. Quite the reverse, for the law can be a very liberating thing."

———. *Who Does She Think She Is?* Foreword by Malcolm Muggeridge. London, New English Library, 1971. 175p. **1W173**
An autobiography of the founder of Britain's National Viewers' and Listeners' Association which has conducted a vigorous crusade against "gratuitous sex and violence" in television. The campaign, widely known as "Clean-Up TV Campaign," is discussed in detail in the book.

——— *et al.* "Censorship: Just How Far Should We Go." *Sunday*, 1(6):7–12, October 1966. **1W174**
Four Christians, all with a special interest in the issue of censorship, present the case as they see it: Mary Whitehouse, founder of the Clean-Up TV Campaign; Roy Shaw, director of Extramural Studies, Keele University; John Cordle, Conservative MP for Bournemouth East and Christchurch; and Tom Driberg, Labor MP for Barking.

Whiteing, Richard. "Bowdler Bowdlerized." *English Review*, 23:100–111, September 1916. **1W175**
The author examines a copy of Bowdler's *Family Shakespeare*, commenting on the blue penciling of improper language. He notes a later Bowdlerizing of Gibbon for a "careful omission of all passages of an irreligious or immoral tendency," extending his efforts from modes of expression to modes of thought.

Whiteside, Thomas. "Annals of Television: Shaking the Tree." *New Yorker*, 51(4):41–48+, 17 March 1975. **1W176**
A detailed accounting of the Nixon Administration's systematic campaign against the news media.

"A Whitewash Commission: Presidential Body on Pornography." *Columbia*, 50:20–29, April 1970. **1W177**
Columbia reporters interview three members of the U.S. Commission on Obscenity and Pornography—Father Morton A. Hill, Rev. Winfrey C. Link, and Charles H. Keating, Jr.—who suggest that "the basic results of the commission's efforts will be two and a half precious years wasted, millions of dollars squandered in misdirected research and the probable conclusion there really is nothing wrong with pornography, hard-core or otherwise."

Whiting, Albert N. "The Campus Press: A Dysfunctional Entity." *North Carolina Central Law Journal*, 6:1–7, Fall 1974. **1W178**
The chancellor of North Carolina Central University discusses the quandry faced by university administrators in handling of a potentially dangerous student press. "Either they rely on commonsense judgment and hazard punitive action that may later, through litigation, be ruled censorship and therefore reversed, or risk disruption (immediate or eventual), loss of control, or other dire consequences before legally supportable punitive action is possible. In a sense, one outcome is as damaging as the other." He considers the North Carolina Central case, *Quarterman v. Boyd* (1971), and the legal and administrative issues that it raises.

Whitman, Ainsley A. "The Buncombe County Case." *North Carolina Libraries*, 31(4):12–18, Conference issue 1973.
1W179

A librarian's personalized account of the events in Buncombe County, N.C., when a member of the Board of Education conducts a one-woman crusade against what she considers "trash" in local school libraries. Books which she had students check for her and then refused to return included: *Of Mice and Men*, *Grapes of Wrath*, and *Catcher in the Rye*.

————. *The Buncombe County Case and Would-Be Censors*. Presented to: *The Intellectual Freedom Committee, North Carolina Library Association, Durham, N.C., May 17, 1973*. n.p., n.p., 1973. 47p. Processed.
1W180

"A case study of a well-organized movement to establish a continuing program of censorship of library materials in the Buncombe County Schools." Relates to the efforts of a fundamentalist organization known as the Christian Action League.

Whitmore, Harry. "Censorship of the Mass Media: The 'D' Notice System." *Australian Law Journal*, 41:449–53, 29 February 1968.
1W181

A discussion of the British system to protect official secrets ("D" Notice) as it has been in operation in Australia since 1952. The author believes that the public has never been properly informed that such informal censorship exists. "The 'right to know' in Australia goes then by default; the federal Government denies the right; the Parliament, the Press and the people are not sufficiently interested to demand the right."

[Whitmore, Ross W.] "Freedom of the Press Does Not Justify the Invasion of Privacy through Subterfuge." *Texas Law Review*, 50:514–20, March 1972.
1W182

Re: *Dietemann v. Time, Inc.*, 449 F.2d 245 (9th Cir. 1971).

Whitney, D. Charles. "Libel: New Ground Rules for an Old Ball Game." *Quill*, 62(8):22–25, August 1974. **1W183**

Comments on the law of libel in light of the U.S. Supreme Court's decision in *Gertz v. Robert Welch, Inc.* (1974). "A few things are clear about the case: private citizens will find it easier to sustain libel actions; punitive damages will, on the other hand, be difficult to recover; and the status of libel per se is questionable."

Whitney, Dwight. "I Want It on the Air." *TV Guide*, 18(27):5–9, 4 July 1970.
1W184

Why Truman Capote's documentary, *Death Row, USA*, praised by the critics who previewed it, has been refused by the networks.

Whyte, Frederic. " 'The Maiden Tribute of Modern Babylon.' " In his *Life of W.T. Stead*. London, Cape, 1925, vol. 1, pp. 159–86.
1W185

An account of Editor Stead's attack on prostitution in a series of articles in the *Pall Mall Gazette* in 1885, his subsequent trial at Bow Street and the Old Bailey, and his sentence to three months' imprisonment.

Whyte, Jean P. "Trend Abroad: Australia." *Library Trends*, 19:122–30, July 1970.
1W186

A look at intellectual freedom in Australia and the laws and agencies, both federal and state, that operate to censor books and control television. Most of the censorship of books in Australia has been exercised by the Board of Review in the Department of Customs and Excise. "Restrictions on public access to official records may be a greater impediment to the achievement of intellectual freedom than the haphazard seizing of books by the Department of Customs." Signs point to increasing restrictions on intellectual freedom in Australia, despite the vigorous role of the library profession.

Wickham, Douglas Q. "Let the Sun Shine In! Open-Meeting Legislation Can Be Our Key to Closed Doors in State and Local Government." *Northwestern University Law Review*, 68:480–501, Fall 1973.
1W187

Includes a model bill requiring state and local governmental bodies to open their meetings to the public.

————. "Tennessee's Sunshine Law: A Need for Limited Shade and Clearer Focus." *Tennessee Law Review*, 42:557–72, Spring 1975.
1W188

The author proposes amendments to the state's open-meeting laws to remedy four specific problem areas: a restrictive caption, inexact coverage definitions, a complete absence of exceptions, and an inappropriate enforcement provision.

Wicklein, John. "From Zenger to Bernstein; a Conversation with John Wicklein." *Journal of Current Social Issues*, 13:30–35, Winter 1976.   **1W189**

In an interview conducted by Paul Sherry, Dean Wicklein of the School of Public Communication, Boston University, comments on freedom of the press. He fears the nation's electronic press cannot be counted on to stand up under pressure because of the threat of government control. The charge that the press often distorts news because of liberal bias is a product of the propaganda campaign of the Nixon Administration; 93 percent of the newspapers supported Nixon in the last election. "The Nixon Administration deliberately tried to suppress freedom for its own devious

purpose." "National security" has been used as a device by the bureaucracy to manipulate public opinion. Control of news also takes place in newspaper offices through selection, placement, and editing of news stories. For the future he sees greater press freedom with more public awareness, a more vigilant and aggressive press, aided by "sunshine laws" which open up public records, shield laws to protect reporters' sources, and possible use of unofficial press councils.

Widmer, Eleanor, *ed. Freedom and Culture: Literary Censorship in the '70s*. Belmont, Calif., Wadsworth, 1970. 216p.
1W190

A complete revision of an earlier collection, entitled *Literary Censorship* by Kingsley and Eleanor Widmer, 1961 (W231). In addition to a number of classical texts such as Milton's *Areopagitica*, the following new articles appear: Repressive Tolerance by Herbert Marcuse. Censorship and Repressive Tolerance by Avrum Stroll (written for the volume to counterbalance the Marcuse argument). The Politics of Violence by Arthur M. Schlesinger, Jr. Can Reading Affect Delinquency? by William C. Kvaraceus. Censorship and the Public Schools by Lee Burress. The Freedom to Read and the Racial Problem by Charles Morgan, Jr. The Public Custody of High Pornography by Kathleen Moltz. Obscenity and the Supreme Court by Ralph L. Lowenstein. Pornography, Art, and Censorship by Paul Goodman. An Apology for Pornography by Peter Michelson. Pornography, a Trip Around the Halfworld by Felix Pollak. Against Pornography by George P. Elliott. Writing About Sex by William Phillips. Beyond Censorship? The Restrictive Processing of American Culture by Kingsley Widmer. Documentary materials are included on five censorship cases: James Joyce's *Ulysses*, D. H. Lawrence's *Lady Chatterley's Lover*, Henry Miller's *Tropic of Cancer*, John Cleland's *Fanny Hill*, and the Ralph Ginzburg case. A selected list of censored British and American books is given on pages 215–16.

Widmer, Kingsley. "Beyond Censorship? The Restrictive Processing of American Culture." In Eleanor Widmer, *ed., Freedom and Culture*. Belmont, Calif., Wadsworth, 1970, pp. 200–209.
1W191

"The basic restrictions of speech in our society find other forms than laws and officials, censors and cops. They must in the complexities of an advanced technical-mass-bureaucratic society. Practicalities rather than principles encourage the substitution of covert restrictions for direct controls. The exploitations of techniques and markets, the built-in exclusions of competitive institutions, and the tyrannies of repressive life styles provide the controlling processes." The author demonstrates in the field of television and publishing how the more subtle cultural restrictions limit real freedom of expression.

————. "Underground Press: Censorship by Harassment." *Nation*, 210: 366–69, 30 March 1970. **1W 192**

When the "underground" press fails to keep its place and threatens to trouble the controlling order it provokes new censorship ways. These operate in two antithetical directions: "the sophisticated structural controls of an indoctrinating institutional order, and when that approach falters, more gross illegal and quasilegal harassments."

Wiederholt, Kathleen. "Defending Right to Read in Oregon." *Newsletter on Intellectual Freedom* (IFC-ALA), 24(2): 37–38, 61–64, March 1975. **1W 193**

An account of the Oregon Library Association's vigorous campaign against the passage of Ballot Measure 13 in the 1974 general election. The measure was designed to restrict the availability of so-called obscene material to adults and minors and to outlaw certain sexual activities in massage parlors and live public shows. The measure passed, but efforts are now being made to amend the act, reinstating the freedom of adults from censorship and in defense of schools, libraries, and museums.

Wiener, Joel H. *A Descriptive Finding List of Unstamped British Periodicals, 1830–1836*. London, Bibliographic Society, 1970. 74p. **1W 194**

In 1830 British reformers began an illegal "war of the unstamped" in which hundreds of periodicals were illicitly published without payment of the newspaper tax, a protest against the increase in the tax. The war came to an end in 1836 when newspaper duty was reduced to 1d. This descriptive finding list of 562 titles is a by-product of the author's *The War of the Unstamped*.

———. *The Movement to Repeal the "Taxes on Knowledge," 1825–1840: A Study in British Working-Class Radicalism*. Ithaca, N.Y., Cornell University, 1965. 359p. (Ph.D. dissertation, University Microfilms no. 66-4687) **1W 195**

The result of this study was published as *War of the Unstamped*.

———. *War of the Unstamped. The Movement to Repeal the British Newspaper Tax, 1830–1836*. Ithaca, N.Y., Cornell University Press, 1969. 310p. **1W 196**

A study of the national campaign that took place in England during the years 1830 to 1836 to obtain the removal of the tax on newspapers. Besides describing the protest movement, the author analyzes its social and political effects and long-range implications for the reform movement. "Working-class reformers were in the vanguard of the struggle during these years, openly violating the press laws by publishing and selling large numbers of unstamped newspapers and tracts. Several hundred vendors and a smaller number of printers and publishers were imprisoned. Professor Wiener studies in detail many of the illegal papers and

the personalities behind them, and shows that an untaxed press became the symbol which rallied many groups of discontented workers."

Wiener, Valerie. *Reaction to Prime-Time Access*. Columbia, Mo., Freedom of Information Center, School of Journalism, University of Missouri at Columbia, 1972. 7p. (Report no. 276) **1W 197**

"Only a few months old, the FCC's Prime-Time Access Rule has caused considerable debate in the broadcast industry. Whether the effort to create program diversity and decentralization of network control over programming will succeed, however, will only be determined with the passage of time."

Wiesman, Melvyn W. "Obscenity—The Court Tries Again." *Journal of the Missouri Bar*, 30:81–92, March 1974. **1W 198**

The author examines the newly defined standards for obscenity handed down by the U.S. Supreme Court in three cases on 21 June 1973, and the effect of these changes on the obscenity laws of Missouri.

Wigg, George. "Press Monopoly in Britain." *Grassroots Editor*, 9(11):16–19, January–February 1968. **1W 199**

The British press has exchanged the tyranny of the political establishment for the tyranny of the commercial establishment. The author decries the growing commercialization of the newspapers and their concentration in the hands of a few large industrial organizations, "a process of centralisation and monopoly which is evident in its most advanced form in Britain." He also criticizes the government for excessive secrecy and the press for lack of objectivity, serious analysis of news, and insufficient attention to real news rather than the sensational, the trivial, and the non-event.

Wiggins, Bruce. "Applying the Fairness Doctrine to Environmental Issues." *Natural Resources Journal*, 12: 108–15, January 1972. **1W 200**

"The recent decision of the District of Columbia Court of Appeals in *Friends of the Earth v. FCC* (1971) may become a valuable tool for environmentalists in their struggle to secure a fair presentation by the broadcasting media of their views on pollution."

Wiggins, Gene. "Access Is Limited: Publishers Still Control." *Grassroots Editor*, 13(2):25–28, March–April 1972. **1W 201**

Courts have consistently maintained that commercial newspapers are functioning as part of private enterprise when they deny individuals access. "Whether or not state action is involved in denying access continues to be the decisive factor."

Wiggins, James R. "Inadequate Propo-

sals Based on Inaccurate History." *Bulletin of the American Society of Newspaper Editors*, 540:5–7, April 1970. **1W 202**

Criticism of the attack on the press in the report of the National Commission on the Causes and Prevention of Violence. The author concludes: "The country was never more in need of independent media, and it seldom has had before it proposals more likely to end the independence of the media."

———. "The Law of Credibility." *Bulletin of the American Society of Newspaper Editors*, 572:1, 13–14, October 1973. **1W 203**

There is "a powerful and persistent restraint and check" upon every newspaper. "It is a self-righting, self-balancing, self-adjusting mechanism from the impact of which no newspaper—and perhaps no publishing or news enterprise—can escape." It is the paper's credibility bank account.

Wiggins, James R. *et al.* ["Revolutionary Handbook for Editors."] *Bulletin of the American Society of Newspaper Editors*, 589:3–13, September 1975. **1W 204**

The entire issue "has been committed to a compendium of recent wisdom on the issues and arguments confronting the American editor, from within and without his/her newsroom. It is intended not to just fortify the defenses, but to project a constructive revolution in behalf of a new understanding of the free press." The Perspective by J. R. Wiggins. The Issue by William C. Heine. The Defense by Anthony Day. The Myth by Alvin P. Sanoff. The New World by Lester Markel.

Wiggins, Robert G. *Access to the Mass Media: Public's Right or Publishers' Privilege*. Carbondale, Ill., Southern Illinois University at Carbondale, 1973. 325p. (Ph.D. dissertation, University Microfilms, no. 74-6254) **1W 205**

"The hypothesis is that no constitutional right exists which proponents can utilize to formulate a public policy of access to the privately-owned print media. Furthermore, it is hypothesized that there is no guaranteed 'right of access' to any form of print media, whether privately owned or not. Finally, it is asserted that no legal foundation exists which would justify applying broadcast regulations, which have granted access to the electronic media in certain cases, to the print media."

Wiik, Susan L. "The Sexual Bias of Textbook Literature." *English Journal*, 62:224–39, February 1973. **1W 206**

In a study of current literature textbooks for secondary schools, the author discovered that it "perpetuates the female stereotypes which cruelly limit and define an adolescent female in terms of second-class status."

Wilcox, Dennis L. *Political Ads; American Dilemma*. Columbia, Mo., Freedom of Information Center, School of Journalism, University of Missouri at Columbia, 1972. 7p. (Report no. 287) **1W207**
"The need for some kind of regulation of political candidates' advertising expenditures is widely agreed upon in the United States. However, no single proposal for dealing with the problem has elicited universal agreement; even the recently enacted Federal Election Campaign Act raises serious Constitutional issues."

——. *Stolen Documents and the Press*. Columbia, Mo., Freedom of Information Center, School of Journalism, University of Missouri at Columbia, 1972. 6p. (Report no. 295) **1W208**
"Among the issues raised by the trial of Daniel Ellsberg and Anthony Russo for their roles in copying and leaking the Pentagon Papers is the matter of whether photocopies of the government documents are 'stolen property.' "

Wilcox, John. "under·ground, n." In *Countdown; A Subterranean Magazine*, 1:186–75, 1970. (Pages are numbered in reverse order, 186–1) **1W209**
A report on the underground magazine in America as a phenomenon of the times, written by one of the founding fathers. A current list of underground magazines, members of the Underground Press Syndicate, is given on pages 8–7. The Syndicate also issues a periodical, *The Alternative Journalism Review*.

Wilcox, Linda, and Pat Busch. "Two Levels of Tolerance: Is It Possible? A Chronological Study of Obscenity Censorship in Minnesota from 1949 to 1969." *Minnesota Libraries*, 22:307–18, Autumn 1969. **1W210**
In a senior research project in the Department of Library Science, College of St. Catherine, a study was made "to find the real spirit" behind the controversy over obscenity. This was done through wide reading and by interviews. "The whole obscenity question seems to center on symbolism. Librarians and others who take civil liberties stands have a long tradition of symbolism behind them. The tradition is inherent in the Constitution's First Amendment, which stands for the individual's right to free expression. . . . On the other side of the fence are the average, interested citizens. They are concerned with legislating morality and with protecting themselves from being exploited by uncontrolled use of 'free speech' in pornography. . . . Librarians and 'intellectuals'

should accept the fact that moral legislation is a very real necessity in the minds of many people. On the other hand, those who represent the general public should be more perceptive of what dilemmas legislation can easily bring to civil liberties. This mutual understanding would be the 'two levels of tolerance' in operation."

Wilcox, Walter. *The Press, the Jury and the Behavioral Sciences*. Austin, Tex., Association for Education in Journalism, 1968. 56p. (Journalism Monographs no. 9; reprinted in Chilton R. Bush, *ed.*, *Free Press and Fair Trial* . . . , pp. 49–105) **1W211**
A summary and evaluation of research which relates to the question of whether or not jurors are affected by crime news published in newspapers. The review attempts "to determine if indeed existing behavioral science theories, concepts, principles, postulates and experiments have the power to illuminate the question of fair trial v. free press and, if so, the extent of such power."

——. "Right of Reply in the United States." *Gazette: International Journal for Mass Communications Studies*, 14:1–6, 1968. **1W212**
The study is intended to probe public opinion toward a right of reply law, to determine the kinds of situations to which such a law might apply, and to alert the press and reply law advocates to the climate of public opinion in the matter.

Wilcoxon, Reba. "Pornography, Obscenity, and Rochester's 'The Imperfect Enjoyment.' " *Studies in English Literature*, 15:375–90, Summer 1975. **1W213**
"Using as a test case 'The Imperfect Enjoyment,' a poem blatantly shocking in sexual language and imagery, I shall attempt to clear Rochester of the blanket charge of pornography, to defend the obscenity in historical and aesthetic contexts, and to suggest a psychological and moral dimension in the poem that bears examining."

Wild, Raymond W. "Newspapers' Advertising Codes Aim to Keep Movie Ads Decent." *Editor & Publisher*, 101(33):18, 49, 1 June 1968. **1W214**
The results of a survey of fifty advertising directors of metropolitan dailies throughout the country appeared in *Editor & Publisher*, 23 March 1968. This article quotes from some of the twenty-four screening codes.

Wiley, Bradford. *The Essential Freedom—Speech and the Press*. New York, Association of American Publishers, 1971. 5p. Processed. **1W215**
A statement made by the chairman of the Board of Directors of the Association of American Publishers before the Subcommittee on

Foreign Operations and Government Information of the Committee on Government Operations, House of Representatives, 25 June 1971, expressing the Association's opposition to the action of another House Committee in the subpoena against the Columbia Broadcasting System in connection with their documentary, *The Selling of the Pentagon*, and affirming the historic principles of American press freedom.

Wiley, Richard E. "License Challenges." In Ted C. Smythe and George A. Mastroianni, *eds.*, *Issues in Broadcasting*. Palo Alto, Calif., Mayfield, 1975, pp. 255–62. **1W216**
The chairman of the Federal Communications Commission, in an address before the Florida Association of Broadcasters, discusses the various points of view on license renewals. He considers the five criteria for "superior performance" suggested by the court in the case of *Citizens Communications Center* in declaring the FCC's renewal policy statement unlawful. He also discusses the 1970 case of station WMAL-TV which "was a reaffirmation of the Commission's belief that responsibility and diligent license effort is the industry's best safeguard at renewal time." The author believes that "the broadcast industry has generally accepted the challenge of full public service as a part of its credo to make the dissemination of information, the advancement of our national interest, and the betterment of us all its life work."

Wilion, Allan E. "Invasion of Privacy by Intrusion: *Dietemann v. Time, Inc.*" *Loyola of Los Angeles Law Review*, 6:200–226, January 1973. **1W217**
In *Dietemann v. Time, Inc.* (1971) the Court held that "under California law a cause of action for invasion of privacy was established where employees of defendant [Time, Inc.] by subterfuge, gained entrance to plaintiff's home and without his consent photographed him and electronically recorded and transmitted his conversation, as a result of which he suffered emotional distress."

[Wilkes, John.] *A Complete Collection of the Genuine Papers, Letters, &tc. in the Case of John Wilkes, Esq. Elected Knight of the Shire for the County of Middlesex, March XXVIII, MDCCLXVIII*. Berlin, 1769. 246p. 15p. **1W218**
In addition to documents relating to Wilkes's sedition trial, this Berlin edition contains the text of No. 45 *North Briton*. A preface reads: "The Reception Mr. Wilkes's Letters have met with, on their separate Appearance, has induced one of his sincerest Friends to present the Public with an entire Collection of them, as a lasting Monument of the resolute Stand made for Liberty, against Ministerial Oppression and Tyranny, and of the unparalleled ill Usage of the Author; in a Country too, famed for Freedom from the earliest Records of Time!"

——. *English Liberty: Being a Collection of Interesting Tracts, From the Years*

1762 to 1769, Containing the Private Correspondence, Public Letters, Speeches, and Addresses, of John Wilkes, Esq. . . . London, T. Baldwin [1769]. 391p.
1W219

One of several contemporary collections of documents involving the case of John Wilkes including correspondence, account of trial, text of warrants, affidavits, reports of the House of Commons, and public addresses. There is a laudatory preface by the editor.

[————.] *An Expostulatory Letter to the Reverend Mr. Kidgell, Occasioned by His Late extraordinary Publication of the Genuine Narrative of a Scandalous, obscene, and exceedingly prophane Libel, intituled, An Essay on Woman. By A Layman. . . .* The Third Edition With Very Material Alterations. London, J. Burd, 1763. 11p. (Signed: Laicus)
1W220

"To pose a general censure upon such obscene and impious performances, would be sufficient; but to make a collection of the several passages in which Religion and Virtue are insulted, makes the Censor, in some measure, a partaker in the guilt of the censured; and barely repeating impieties and blasphemies, must bring a blemish upon a Divine, who should have too great an abhorrence for such things, even to mention them. . . . You have offended those laws, that Liberty and that Religion to which, contrary to all the rules of Common Sense, you have dedicated your execrable collection of blasphemous and obscene ribildry." An attack on the pamphlet by John Kidgell (K96), the dissolute clergyman who feigned shock at Wilkes's *Essay on Woman*, but had been involved in making the work public.

[————.] *A Full and Candid Answer to a Pamphlet Called A Genuine and Succinct Narrative of A Scandalous, Obscene, and exceedingly profane Libel, entitled, an Essay on Woman. By a Friend to Truth.* London, William Griffin, 1763. 11p.
1W221

In refuting the Reverend Mr. John Kidgell's account (K96), the anonymous author claims the *Essay on Woman* was never intended for publication, that the work was not written by one person but by a group of eminent men, that Kidgell's pamphlet was written only for his own vanity, that his advertising the work was more criminal than silence. The *Essay* was written "by a society of men mad with wine, and wanton with desire; designing, no doubt, to create a laugh among themselves. One, more hardy than the rest, ventures to print a dozen copies . . . and that with the utmost precaution possible; even to the seeing them struck off himself, in order to prevent the evil from spreading." Kidgell, by accident, discovers a few pages of the work and "tries by every means in his power to obtain a complete copy" for the purpose of making it public. Kidgell should have committed the work to the flames; he is the real criminal. The author suggests

Kidgell give the profits of the sale of his pamphlet to Magdalen charity.

[————.] "John Wilkes, Esq. against Wood. The Case of General Warrants." In Capel Lofft, *ed., Reports of Cases Adjudged in the Court of King's Bench. From Easter Term 12 Geo. 3, to Michaelmas 14 Geo. 3. . . .* Dublin, James Moore, 1790, pp. 1–20. **1W222**

The case involved a charge by Wilkes that Wood and an assistant, under a general warrant, has broken into and entered his home and seized papers. The jury found Wood guilty and fined him £1,000.

[————.] *The Lamentation of Britannia for the Two-and-Twenty Months Imprisonment of John Wilkes, Esq. in the King's-Bench Prison. . . .* London, H. Woodgate [1768]. 10p. **1W223**

An oration in the form of biblical lamentations: "Like as a bird that is confined within the walls of the King's-Bench."

[————.] *A Letter to the Right Honourable Earl Temple, Upon the Probable Motives and Conduct with regard to Mr. Wilkes.* London, W. Nicoll, 1763. 12p. **1W224**

Criticism of Temple for supporting John Wilkes.

[————.] *A Letter to the Right Honourable The Earl of T——e: Or, The Case of J—— W——s, Esquire: With respect to the King, Parliament, Courts of Justice, Secretaries of State, and the Multitude. Being A Detail of Facts, from May 5th, 1763, to 28th of March, 1768; and from thence to the present Time.* London, Printed for A. Johnson [1768]. 40p. **1W225**

A vicious personal attack on John Wilkes, his ancestry, his family, and his "sins of adultery, blasphemy, and sedition," addressed to the Earl of Temple, friend and supporter of Wilkes. The anonymous author details the case against Wilkes for publication of No. 45 *North Briton*, containing "an invidious commentary upon what the King had spoke from the throne!" He defends the use of the general warrant in the arrest of Wilkes. He also reports on the case against Wilkes for publication of *An Essay on Woman*, "a piece so shockingly base, impious and nonsensical, that my blood runs chill, while the very name drops from my pen!" The author writes with disgust of the wild acclaim Wilkes received from the London mob. He finds it beyond the pale that Wilkes is now standing for Parliament.

[————.] *A Letter to the Right Hon. the Earl of Temple, on the Subject of The Forty-fifth Number of the North Briton* [Containing a libelous article by J. Wilkes, dealing with the speech from the throne] *and on His Patronage of the Supposed Author of*

It. . . . London, J. Hinxman, 1763. 50p. **1W226**

Another attack on Wilkes and on Lord Temple who supported him.

[————.] *The Life and Political Writings of John Wilkes, Esq., Knight of the Shire for the County of Middlesex.* Birmingham, England, 1765. 522p. **1W227**

Biographical data; an account of the Wilkes trials; text of *North Briton* through no. 44; letters regarding the controversy.

[————.] *No. 45; A Comic Song (with Spirit).* London, 1768. Broadside.
1W228

A bawdy six-verse song in which Nell, a bride of six weeks complains that her husband, Ned, spends too much time away from home in the cause of John Wilkes, who had been arrested and jailed for publication of issue No. 45 of *North Briton*. It ended happily:
"Let's have no Jaw dear Nell said he,
    But lets make haste to Bed.
They stript in a Trice and to't they went,
    As hard as they could drive,
Ned cry'd WILKES for ever,
    And Nell cry'd FORTY FIVE."

[————.] *The Priest in Rhyme: A Doggerell Versification of Kidgell's Narrative, Relative to the Essay on Woman. By a Member of Parliament, A Friend to Mr. Wilkes, and to Liberty. . . .* London, Printed for the Author, 1763. 18p.
1W229

The attack on Chaplain Kidgell, responsible for making public Wilkes's *Essay on Woman* through his pious tract (K96), ends:
"When Parsons grave shall print Plain Truth
Determin'd to carry to our Youth;
When thus from decency we sever,
Farewel dear Liberty for ever!
No nation that the Sun does set on,
Will be so wretched as Great Britain:
And (grief of griefs!) the Devil will have his will,
When Reverend Priests in bawdy dip their quill."

[————.] *Serious Considerations on a Late Very Important Decision of the House of Commons . . . .* London, S. Bladon, 1769. 37p. **1W230**

Deals with the legal and constitutional aspects of Wilkes's expulsion from Parliament.

[————.] *Some Observations on the Late Determination for Discharging Mr. Wilkes from his Commitment to the Tower of London; for being the Author and Publisher of a Seditious Libel, called the North Briton,*

Number XLV. By a Member of the House of Commons. London, A. Millar, 1793. 114p. 8p.   **1W231**
"A Particular and exact Account of the Opinion of the Judges of the Court of Common Pleas, as delivered by the Lord Chief Justice Pratt, on Friday the 6th of May 1763, with respect to the Question, Whether Mr. Wilkes was or was not liable to be arrested for being the Author and Publisher of the *North Briton*, No. XLV. Faithfully transcribed from the Short-hand Notes of a Person who was in Court the whole Time, together with Observations on the principal Authorities on which the Opinion appears to be founded, will, in a Case so interesting, and big with Consequences so alarming to the Safety and Liberties of the Subject at large, merit the serious Attention and Perusal of the Public."

[———.] *Wilkes and Liberty. A New Song.* London, Sold by E. Sumpter, 1763? Broadside. (Reproduced in Adrian Hamilton, *The Infamous Essay on Woman*, p. 87)   **1W232**
One of numerous songs, poems, and prints issued to celebrate John Wilkes's release from prison where he had been sent as the result of a general warrant charging him with publishing a seditious issue (No. 45) of *North Briton*.

Wilkins, Barratt. "Censorship and Modernity." *South Carolina Librarian*, 15(2):15–17, 39, Spring 1971. **1W233**
A look at one of the greatest intellectual controversies of the nineteenth century caused by the publication in Paris in 1863 of Ernest Renan's *Life of Jesus*. "As a naturalistic life of Jesus it ran counter to the literal, orthodox interpretation of the Bible and added another chapter to the history of the war of science with theology."

Wilkins, Stan N. "The Obscenity Law's Application in Kansas: Issues and Procedures." *Washburn Law Journal*, 12:185–202, Winter 1973. **1W234**
"This article surveys obscenity law and its particular application in Kansas. Each obscenity issue is discussed briefly in general terms and as applied in Kansas."

[Wilkins, Thomas.] "The Trial of Thomas Wilkins for Printing and Publishing the Foregoing Libel." In George Gordon, *The Whole Proceedings on the Trials of Two Informations Against George Gordon, Esq. commonly Called Lord George Gordon . . . .* London, Sold by M. Gurney, 1787, pp. 61–69.   **1W235**
Wilkins was printer of the alleged libel in *The Prisoners Petition to the Right Honorable Lord George Gordon to preserve their Rights and Liberties,*

and prevent their Banishment to Botany-Bay, for which Lord Gordon, charged as the author, was convicted. Wilkins was also found guilty and given a two-year sentence.

Wilkinson, Jan. "Keeping the Censor at Bay: A Positive Approach." *Ohio Association of School Librarians*, 27:54–56, January 1975. **1W236**
Three Ohio librarians who have come under fire because of complaints regarding books from their libraries describe their experiences.

Will, Hubert. "A Free Press and a Fair Trial." *Mississippi Law Journal*, 40:495–506, October 1969. **1W237**
A U.S. District Court judge recommends that the Mississippi State Bar Association follow the recommendation of the Judicial Conference of the United States and adopt a state supreme court rule applicable to every member of the bar of the state which prohibits disclosures indicated in the Reardon Report. He notes that the press is also taking steps to improve the situation through the adoption of codes and upgrading the education of reporters.

Willett, Orville R. *Freedom of Speech and Press in England During the War.* Chicago, University of Chicago, 1919. 49p. (Unpublished Master's thesis) **1W238**
Content: Freedom of Speech at the Outbreak of the War (World War I). Access to Sources of News Closed. Organization of the Censorship. Suppression and Amendment of News and Opinion. The Creation of War Propaganda. Criticism of the Censorship. Defense of the Government. The Armistice and Relaxation of Censorship.

Williams, Charles C. "Public Figure Denied Recovery for Libel Absent Showing of Actual Malice." *Texas Southern University Law Review*, 2:173–79, Fall 1971. **1W239**
Re: *Monitor Patriot Co. v. Roselle Roy*, 91 S. Ct. 621 (1971).

Williams, Dwight A., Jr. "Regulation and Programming in the Broadcasting Industry: A Study in the Twentieth Century Conservative Counter-Revolution." In Speech Association of America, *Abstracts*, 57th Annual Meeting, San Francisco, The Association, 1971, pp. 12–13. **1W240**
"This study places the broadcasting industry's development in a context provided by social historian Rowland T. Berthoff. Special attention is given to development of regulation in the industry and its effect on the concept of 'freedom of speech.'"

Williams, Edward F., *Baron* Francis-Williams. "Libel & the Truth." *En-*

counter, 29:83–87, September 1967. Reply by Linton Andrews, 29:94–95, November 1967. **1W241**
The author argues for qualified privilege of newspapers in libel cases, citing instances where existing libel law prevented the press from publishing important information in the public interest. He takes issue with Sir Linton Andrews in the matter but supports Lord Shawcross. He favors the right of the jury to decide the issue of malice. Sir Linton responds with argument against proposals for qualified privilege.

———. *The Right to Know: The Rise of the World Press.* London, Longmans, 1969. 336p. **1W242**
A study of the press in a free society from the beginnings of editorial independence in the *Times*, in the 1820s, until the present day. He discusses the growing independence of the press, on the one hand, and the increased monopoly ownership on the other; he compares British and American patterns of controls in the newspaper press, radio, and television; he examines the present-day problems relating to controls, the "plague of secrecy" in government, and the maintenance of public interest under commercial ownership of the media. The author is a journalist and a television commentator; he has been a newspaper editor and a governor of the British Broadcasting Corp.; he was Controller of News and Information in Britain during World War II.

Williams, Howard S. "The Sirhan Trial: Courtroom TV." *Quill*, 57(7): 16–18, July 1969. **1W243**
"The Sirhan trial proved conclusively, in my opinion, that television can cover trials of public significance without disturbing in any way the course of justice. It was the first small step toward resurrecting courtroom television after its burial by the United States Supreme Court in the Estes decision."

Williams, J. Danvers. "Banned! Newsreels You Must Not See." *New Theatre*, 1(1):10–12, August 1939. **1W244**
A look at the unofficial political censorship of newsreels in Great Britain that encourages film companies to ignore big national and international events and concentrate on the launching of ships and the laying of cornerstones.

[Williams, John A.] "[Review of] Williams, John Ambrose. Trial of John Ambrose Williams, for a Libel on the Clergy, before Mr. Baron Wood and a Special Jury . . . London, Ridgway. 57p. 1822." *Edinburgh Review*, 37 (74):350–79, November 1822. **1W245**
The reviewer objects to the use of libel law to suppress reasonable criticism of clergy and their methods. The trial document is cited as W297.

Williams, Kathy. *Infiltration of the Press.* Columbia, Mo., Freedom of Informa-

tion Center, School of Journalism, University of Missouri at Columbia, 1972. 5p. (Report no. 286) **1W246**
"Police and other government agencies' infiltration of the working press for the purpose of gathering intelligence began to pose serious problems in the 1960's. Despite continuing controversy and debate, no universal, satisfactory solution has yet been implemented."

Williams, Patrick, and Joan T. Pearce. "Censorship Redefined." *Library Journal*, 101:1494–96, July 1976. **1W247**
"Constraints which impair or destroy a library's capacity to provide information and service in accordance with informational objectives constitute censorship. Censorship must however be distinguished from the controls which support fulfillment of library objectives. The most important of these controls are scope, redundancy, balance, and quality controls. Scope control is the most important and complex."

———. "Common Sense and Censorship: A Call for Revision." *Library Journal*, 98:2399–400, 1 September 1973. **1W248**
The authors criticize the library profession for its official position on intellectual freedom which fails to recognize that freedom of expression and inquiry are not absolutes, but relative to other values in society. Some degree of censorship is necessary and desirable as well as inevitable. The essay brought forth a barrage of letters of criticism leading the authors to a revision of their redefining censorship and introducing the term "communication controls" in subsequent articles.

———. "Communication Controls and Censorship." *Catholic Library World*, 46:116–18, October 1974. **1W249**
A discussion of two kinds of communication controls: controls which support and enable an institution to function and controls which damage or destroy the capacity of an institution to fulfill its social objectives. Censorship, a form of the latter, is defined specifically in relation to libraries, as consisting of "the removal from circulation, refusal to accept as a gift, or refusal to purchase with available funds, materials which are in-scope, not redundant, do not unbalance the collection, and which meet quality standards."

Williams, Raymond. *Britain in the Sixties: Communications*. Harmondsworth, England, Penguin, 1962. 134p. **1W250**
Communication systems in Britain are not limited to "controlled" and "free." There are four systems in practice, or in local experiments in Britain: authoritarian, paternal, commercial, and democratic. "The vestiges of authoritarianism are there, in certain kinds of censorship; the first experiments in democracy are also there, in local ways. But the main struggle, over the last generation, has been between the paternal and commercial systems,

and it looks as if the commercial has been steadily winning."

Williams, Robert H. *The Anti-Defamation League and Its Use in the World Communist Offensive*. Hollywood, Calif., The Author, 1949. 44p. (Copyrighted by Closer-Ups) **1W251**
An attack on the Anti-Defamation League for its alleged pro-Communist leanings and for its libeling of persons with whom it disagrees. The author, a former counter-intelligence officer, describes the League's positive propaganda program and its "negative, suppressive program ₍which₎ sets up a self-constituted censorship over public speech, fixing a watchful eye on every radio, every lecture platform, every publisher, every movie film producer, every school teacher, every political party, every public official and every citizen who becomes conspicuous or influential." The pamphlet is introduced by Upton Close.

₍Williams, Thomas.₎ *The Sentence of the Court of King's Bench Against Thomas Williams for the Infamous Crime of Publishing Paine's Age of Reason*. Edited by Robert M. Gutchen. Kingston, R.I., Biscuit City Press, 1973. 10p. (Limited to 60 copies) **1W252**
On 28 April 1798 Justice Ashhurst sentenced Thomas Williams to one year at hard labor for blasphemy, a crime "horrible, most horrible, to the ears of a Christian." Thomas Erskine represented the prosecution.

Williams, Walter. "Law and Journalism." *Missouri Bar Journal*, 1(12):10–12, December 1930. **1W253**
The president of the University of Missouri and former head of the School of Journalism, in an address before the Missouri Bar Association, speaks of the common interests of journalists and lawyers. The newspaperman, like the lawyer, is "an instrument for the establishment of justice or injustice." The newspaper as an agent of society, has a responsibility for speaking out against injustice in law enforcement and in the courts. Williams outlines the strict policies that should govern a newspaper's coverage of a criminal trial. Only after the termination of the trial are interviews and comments on the evidence proper. Then the action of the participants can be criticized. The lawyer and journalist should make common cause in behalf of higher ethical standards within their professions.

Williams, William P. "Sir Henry Herbert's Licensing of Plays for the Press in the Restoration." *Notes & Queries*, 22:255–56, June 1975. **1W254**
Less is known about this aspect of the Master of Revels than his control over the operation of the theaters producing the plays.

Williamson, Audrey. *Wilkes; "A Friend

to Liberty"*. New York, Reader's Digest–Dutton, 1974. 250p. **1W255**
A new biography of "that devil Wilkes," the eighteenth-century reformer, wit, rake, and champion of freedom of the press. For his *North Briton* paper Wilkes was expelled from Parliament for the crime of seditious libel.

Williamson, Bruce. "Porno Chic." *Playboy*, 20(8):132–39, 153–54, 158–61, August 1973. **1W256**
A look at the production and exhibition of pornographic movies, emphasizing the "tremendous cultural chasm between official attitude toward hard core—as a peril to the nation—and the general public's genial and fairly sophisticated tolerance to it."

Willis, Paul G. *Political Libel in the United States, 1607–1949*. Bloomington, Ind., Indiana University, 1949. 569p. (Unpublished Ph.D. dissertation) **1W257**
Following background on the development of English common law of libel and the history of libel in Colonial America, the author examines individual libel cases in chronological order: 1789–1830 (including Sedition Act cases), 1831–1860 (including abolitionist cases), and 1861–1949. In a final chapter, he takes a look at the future of libel law. The appendix includes a table of cases by period and state.

Willis, Susan C. "Today's Child, Yesterday's Standard: A Brief Look at Censorship." *Kentucky Library Association Bulletin*, 38:2–10, Fall 1974. **1W258**
Today's children have been exposed through the mass media to the complexities and problems of life in the twentieth century, but attempts by schools and libraries to provide meaningful interpretive materials have often met with resistance from well-meaning persons and groups that wish to judge the suitability of these materials according to yesterday's standards. The article discusses the child's right to read as interpreted by the courts and affirmed by professional library and education associations. Four areas of concern are: obscenity, politics, religion, and minorities.

Williston, Frank S. "A Philosophic Analysis of Pornography." *Journal of Thought*, 7:95–105, April 1972. **1W259**
"This essay is an attempt to develop the following two theses: (1) The cognitive aspects of pornography suggest its capacity to function as a dominant mode of social interaction. (2) The analysis of pornography illuminates the failure of dialectic historicism to clarify the problems inherent in the attempt to synthesize rationalism and empiricism."

Wills, J. Robert. "Olive Logan vs. The

Nude Woman." *Players*, 47:37–43, October–November 1971. **1W260**
An account of the campaign against nudity on the American stage conducted in the 1860s by actress-playwright Olive Logan.

Wilson, Clyde. "The Liberty and Responsibility of the Press." *Intercollegiate Review*, 6:113–21, Spring 1970. **1W261**
A critique of the "social responsibility" theory of press freedom, prevailing in American academic circles, indicating "contradictions and philosophical weaknesses." A solution to monopoly threats to a free press will not be found in concentrating "more power into the hands of men who already wield the coercive apparatus of the state," but rather by "the vicissitudes of time, technology, and the marketplace."

Wilson, Frank W. "If the Public Is To Know, the Press Must Be Free To Report." *Bulletin of the American Society of Newspaper Editors*, 513:11–14, November 1967. **1W262**
A United States district judge believes that existing legal remedies, voluntary codes of ethics for lawyers and journalists, plus a competent judiciary are sufficient safeguards for fair trial. While encouraging voluntary codes, he points out that "no publisher or groups of publishers and no member of the bar or bar association has the prerogative to bargain away the public's right to know." He finds it difficult to believe that the only choice we have is to sacrifice one constitutional right to preserve another.

Wilson, Gray W. "Right to Access to Broadcasting: The Supreme Court Takes a Dim View." *Georgetown Law Journal*, 62:355–76, October 1973. **1W263**
"In order to ensure the effectiveness of the first amendment in the twentieth century, the right of free speech guaranteed to all Americans must include a right of access, within reasonable limits, to the broadcasting media. . . . Because of the inability of the ₍Supreme₎ Court to reach agreement on the government action issue in *Columbia Broadcasting System, Inc. v. Democratic National Committee* (1973), the majority opinion is not decisive on the vital issue of protection of the first amendment rights of non-broadcasters."

Wilson, Hunter. "California's New Obscenity Statute: The Meaning of 'Obscene' and the Problem of Scienter." *Southern California Law Review*, 36:513–45, 1963. **1W264**
"This article will be limited to a discussion of the new ₍California₎ statute's impact on the regulation of obscene matter, such as writings, photographs, paintings, advertisements, and so forth, and will not deal with indecent acts as such. Moreover, the article will be further restricted to a consideration of the special problems created by the statute's definitions of obscenity and guilty knowledge."

Wilson, J. Dover. "The Puritan Attack Upon the Stage." In *Cambridge History of English Literature*. New York, Macmillan, 1933, vol. 6, pp. 421–61. **1W265**
Content: The attitude of the reformers toward the stage. Theological and moral objections. Beginnings of Puritan opposition in England. Attitude of the civic authorities in London. Systematic persecution of actors. Royal patronage. Attacks on the stage from the pulpit. Work of pamphleteers. Gosson's *Schoole of Abuse*. Lodge's *Defence*. Stubbes's *Anatomie of Abuses*. Waning interest in the struggle. The controversy at the universities. Effects of changes introduced under the Stuarts. Heywood's *Apology for Actors*. Prynne's *Histriomastix*. General aspects of the controversy.

Wilson, James Q. "Violence, Pornography and Social Science." *Public Interest*, 22:45–61, Winter 1971. (Reprinted in Victor B. Cline, *ed.*, *Where Do You Draw the Line?* pp. 293–307; in Ray C. Rist, *ed.*, *The Pornography Controversy*, pp. 225–43) **1W266**
"In the cases of violence and obscenity, it is unlikely that social science can either show harmful effects or prove that there are not harmful effects. It is unlikely, in short, that considerations of utility or disutility can be governing. These are moral issues and ultimately all judgments about the acceptability of restrictions on various media will have to rest on political and philosophical considerations."

Wilson, Jerome L. "The Fairness Doctrine: Big Brother in the Newsroom." *American Bar Association Journal*, 61:1492–94, December 1975. **1W267**
"From both ends of the political spectrum come pot shots at the fairness doctrine—the web of rules of the Federal Communications Commission that has its greatest effect in the radio and television newsroom. It is inhibiting sound journalistic coverage of the news, but it needn't be thrown out entirely. There is an appealing middleground good for both the broadcasters and the public."

———. "Justice in Living Color: The Case for Courtroom Television." *American Bar Association Journal*, 60(3):294–97, March 1974. **1W268**
"The American judicial system needs television, but limitations on its use in the courtroom, imposed by the American Bar Association's new Canon 3 (A) (7) of the Code of Judicial Conduct, restrict the contributions it can make. The problems with telecasting trials can be solved by setting up firm but practical guidelines for coverage and not by barring TV altogether."

Wilson, John A. B. "For Permissiveness with Misgivings." *New York Times Magazine*, 122:19–20, 1 July 1973. **1W269**
With certain aesthetic misgivings this British writer (Anthony Burgess, *pseud*.) is in favor of total permissiveness in sex expression in literature, believing that if any censorship is called for it "must operate only in the private sector—the sector, that is, of creation and distribution. The law must keep its nose out." The creative artist is his own best censor. The author calls for writers to practice greater discipline, reticence, and ingenuity to produce more aesthetic works, noting that the undisciplined freedom of recent years has produced fewer great works of literature than when sex expression was banned. With today's freedom served by more and more daring books and films, "appetites are growing coarser and ears deafer." A debasement of art, not morals, is the issue.

———. *Obscenity and the Arts*. Malta, Malta Library Association, 1973. 16p. **1W270**
In an attack on Maltese censorship, the author-literary critic discusses the nature and rationale of obscenity, suggesting three categories in the use of words: for teaching (didactic), for aesthetic or literary purposes (arousing emotions as a part of the rhythm of the work), and to inflame (pornographic). A critical review of the essay by John Sparrow appears in *Punch*, 26 June 1974.

———. "What Is Pornography?" In his *Urgent Copy*. New York, Norton, 1968, pp. 254–57. (Reprinted in Douglas A. Hughes, *ed.*, *Perspectives on Pornography*, pp. 4–8) **1W271**
In this essay the author describes a pornographic work as an instrument which encourages solitary fancy, which is usually quite harmlessly discharged in masturbation. It "rarely promotes the desire to achieve ₍sexual catharsis₎ through a social mode, an act of congress: the book is, in a sense, a substitute for a sexual partner." Pornography, he believes, "is harmless so long as we do not corrupt our taste by mistaking it for literature."

Wilson, Samuel S. "Chaos in the Courtroom: Adequate Press Facilities for Highly Publicized Trials." *University of Cincinnati Law Review*, 36:210–22, Spring 1967. **1W272**
"The values of wide news coverage are recognized by the legislative and executive branches of government. . . . Yet, the judiciary, while recognizing the value of a public trial, insists on conducting those of its activities in which there is great public interest in a journalistic closet and then clucking in dismay at the resulting chaos. Excess of journalistic enterprise certainly causes much of the confusion, but a constructive approach to providing fair trials covered by a free press requires a realistic recognition of the kind of facilities necessary to

allow both court and press to perform their proper functions."

Wilson, Stephen A. *Absolute Privilege in Judicial Proceedings: A Comprehensive General Survey.* Bloomington, Ind., Indiana University, 1967. 57p. (Unpublished Master's thesis) **1W273**
A study of communications that have been accorded an absolute privilege from civil libel action because they were part of a judicial proceeding.

Wilson, W. Cody. "The American Experience with Pornography." In George V. Coelho and Eli A. Rubinstein, *eds.*, *Social Change and Human Behavior.* Rockville, Md., National Institute of Mental Health, 1972. pp. 111–35. **1W274**
"In the discussion that follows, we will look at the background of the Commission [U.S. Commission on Obscenity and Pornography], its purposes, the way it went about its job, some of the conclusions it reached, and the consequences of reporting those conclusions. Then we will look at the research program set up by the Commission and some of the research findings." The author was executive director of the Commission.

———. "Belief in Freedom of Speech and Press." *Journal of Social Issues*, 31(2):69–76, 1975. **1W275**
"Data regarding belief in freedom of speech and press collected in early 1970 in face-to-face interviews with 2,486 respondents in a national probability sample of adults test several hypotheses derived from previous empirical research. The general findings were: (a) a minority of adults in the U.S. fully accept the principle of free speech and press; (b) belief in free speech and press is related to a variety of demographic variables; (c) people who label themselves as liberal, who are high consumers of written mass media, and who are more active in the political process are more likely to endorse freedom of speech and press; and (d) patterns of relationship between belief in freedom of speech and press and other social psychological and demographic variables are rather stable over time."

———. "Facts Versus Fear: Why Should We Worry About Pornography?" *Annals of the American Academy of Political and Social Science*, 397:105–17, September 1971. **1W276**
"Prior to the work of the U.S. Commission on Obscenity and Pornography, the discussion of pornography necessarily had to be based on fear because there were few facts available. As a result of the Commission's work there are now data to inform the discussion. Many of our cultural myths in this area are not borne out by empirical facts. Nearly everyone in our society has been voluntarily exposed to depictions of explicit sexual activity often referred to as pornography. Initial exposure generally occurs

before the end of high school; perhaps 50 percent are first exposed in junior high school. Viewing or reading sexual depictions generally produces sexual arousal but this does not necessarily eventuate in sexual activity. Sex criminals have had less experience with explicit sexual materials than have normal people. Exposure to explicit sexual materials does not produce bad moral character nor calloused sexual attitudes toward women. The gaining of information is perhaps the most common enduring consequence of exposure to sexual materials. But to many people these facts are irrelevant; and this poses a potential threat to our society."

———. "Law Enforcement Officers' Perceptions of Pornography As a Social Issue." *Journal of Social Issues*, 29(3):41–51, 1973. **1W277**
A questionnaire study of prosecuting attorneys reveals a wide variation in their perceptions of the degree to which pornography constitutes a community problem. "Concern about pornography is very correlated with size of community and with changes in the availability of pornography: concern is found in large urban situations and when the availability of pornography seems to be increasing." This is one of the studies stimulated by the U.S. Commission on Obscenity and Pornography.

———. " 'No Evidence Pornography Causes Crime.' " *U.S. News and World Report*, 70(4):74, 25 January 1971. Reply by Morton A. Hill, 70(8):78, 22 February 1971. **1W278**
An interview with a social psychologist who served as executive director of the U.S. Commission on Obscenity and Pornography. Reply by the Reverend Morton A. Hill, president of Morality in Media and a member of the Commission.

———. "Pornography: The Emergence of a Social Issue and the Beginning of Psychological Study." *Journal of Social Issues*, 29(3):7–17, 1973. **1W279**
"The emergence of pornography as a current social issue is associated with a series of Supreme Court cases beginning in the late 1950's, posing the question as to whether or not legal prohibition of obscenity violated the First Amendment guarantees of freedom of speech and freedom of the press. The ensuing discussion was based primarily on fear and speculation because there were few empirical facts to inform the discussion. In 1967 Congress declared that obscenity and pornography were matters of national concern, raised questions about the effects of these materials, called for a thorough study, and authorized the use of funds for the collection of relevant scientific data. Thus the beginning of extensive 'scientific' analysis of the social issue of pornography." This is one of the studies stimulated by the U.S. Commission on Obscenity and Pornography.

———, and Herbert I. Abelson. "Ex-

perience With and Attitudes Toward Explicit Sexual Materials." *Journal of Social Issues*, 29(3):19–39, 1973. **1W280**
A description of the results of a large-scale national public opinion survey designed to measure peoples' attitudes about pornography, their concern about this social issue, and the degree of personal exposure to erotica. "The data do not support a concept of a 'contemporary community standard' relating to the representation of sexual matters: There does not exist anything approaching consensus in attitudes regarding the availability of sexual materials; attitudes toward availability vary greatly according to the circumstances of availability; and attitudes vary considerably among groups formed on the basis of demographic characteristics." This is one of the studies stimulated by the U.S. Commission on Obscenity and Pornography.

Wilson, W. Cody, Jane Friedman, and Bernard Horowitz. "Gravity of the Pornography Situations and Problems of Control: A Survey of Prosecuting Attorneys." *Technical Report of the [U.S.] Commission on Obscenity and Pornography*, 5:5–14, 1971. **1W281**
The results of a mail survey of a stratified random sample of prosecuting attorneys throughout the United States soliciting their views on pornography.

Wilson, W. Cody, and Sylvia Jacobs. "Pornography and Youth: A Survey of Sex Educators and Counselors." *Technical Report of the [U.S.] Commission on Obscenity and Pornography*, 5:369–73, 1971. **1W282**
The results of a mail survey of sex educators regarding their perception of adolescents' experience with explicit sexual materials, the possible relationship between sex education and interest in pornography, and the consequences of exposure to such material.

Winchester, James H. "The Pied Piper of Smut." *New York Mirror Magazine*, 22 May 1960, pp. 3, 5. **1W283**
An account of "the purveyor of obscenity who is destroying youth in a rising epidemic of disease via mailbox," and what is being done about it in government and in local communities.

Winger, Howard W. *Regulations Relating to the Book Trade in London from 1357 to 1586. . . .* Urbana, Ill., University of Illinois, 1953. 257p. (Unpublished Ph.D. dissertation) **1W284**
An account of the regulations framed by the Church, State, and Stationers' Company of London relating to the book trade in London

between 1357 and 1586. Conclusions drawn: (1) The Church, the State and the Stationers' Company were alert throughout the period to control of the London book trade; (2) the efforts to regulate the book trade were based upon a tradition of restraint, a product of a society that feared change; (3) the attempt to suppress the publication of all books not acceptable to authorities resulted in failure; and (4) among the causes of failure were: the human will to resist, the wide distribution of books by amateurs, the increased efficiency in book production, the wide geographic area involved, division of thought and lack of resolution among officials, and division of authority among the three agencies.

Wingfield, William. "California's Dirty Book Caper: The Politics of Smut." *Nation*, 202:456–59, 18 April 1966.   **1W285**
All about the work of the California League Enlisting Action Now (CLEAN) and its campaign against pornography—the way in which it operates, the people behind it, and the censorship legislation it supports.

———. "California's New Vigilantes." *Progressive*, 32(2):30–33, February 1968.   **1W286**
A report on the various right-wing pressure groups active in Southern California in attacks on school textbooks (*Land of the Free*), the UCLA *Daily Bruin*, and radio talk shows. "The rightists in Southern California are battering at the Bill of Rights with increasing power and virulence."

Winick, Charles. *Critique of the Methodology of Edith Efron's The News Twisters*. New York, Columbia Broadcasting System, 1971. 15p. Processed. **1W287**
The News Twisters seems less interested in exploring alternate explanations and implications of its findings than on documenting network bias. It is more like a legal brief, organizing evidence to support a thesis, than a research study which seeks to explore all facets of a situation. . . . A comparison of 'the rules as set forth' with the established principles of content analysis raises serious questions about the validity of *The News Twisters*." The author is a professor of sociology at City College of the City University of New York.

———. "Some Observations on Characteristics of Patrons of Adult Theaters and Bookstores." *Technical Report of the [U.S.] Commission on Obscenity and Pornography*, 4:225–44, 1971.   **1W288**
"This report is concerned with characteristics of customers of movie theaters and bookstores which offer sexually explicit materials in a number of communities in the United States.

The study was undertaken in order to explore these characteristics at a time when public interest in them seems to be at an all-time high. The proliferation of these materials may have many meanings and implications. The content of sexually explicit publications and movies presumably reflects their creators' impressions of what consumers want, and the expansion of the market suggests that it is increasingly meeting some of these needs."

———. "A Study of Consumers of Explicitly Sexual Materials; Some Functions Served by Adult Movies." *Technical Report of the [U.S.] Commission on Obscenity and Pornography*, 4:245–62, 1971.   **1W289**
"This report presents interviews with consumers of explicitly sexual materials. . . . [It] identifies some of the functions which appear to be served by these materials as determined by intensive personal interviews with persons who had just seen an explicitly sexual movie."

Winokur, Dena. *The Influence of Legal and Voluntary Restraints Upon the Gatekeeping Function in the Regulation of Retail Advertising Copy: A Case Study of the New York Daily News and the New York Times*. Athens, Ohio, Ohio University, 1975. 370p. (Ph.D. dissertation, University Microfilms, no. 76-8872)   **1W290**
"There are few sectors of American business which are subjected to so many types of federal, state and local legislation as the business of advertising. . . . Through the use of focused interviews and a formal survey, the study examined the advertising acceptability standards of the *New York Times*, the nation's single most prestigious and informative newspaper and the *New York Daily News*, the biggest and most prosperous daily in the United States."

Winslow, Helen L. "The First Amendment Status of Commercial Advertising." *North Carolina Law Review*, 54:468–77, Fall 1976.   **1W291**
Re: *Bigelow v. Virginia*, 421 U.S. 809 (1975) in which the U.S. Supreme Court applied a standard that gives commercial speech first amendment protection if it contains "factual material of clear public interest."

Winthrop, Henry. "Sexuality in Literature." *Colorado Quarterly*, 21:337–38, Winter 1973.   **1W292**
"Winthrop examines the current uninhibited interest in sexual themes—pornotopia—as this interest is reflected in a limited sample of literature. This examination is undertaken by using Lynes's taxonomy of culture—highbrow, middlebrow, and lowbrow—and by suggesting aspects of taste in the erotic and pornographic, as these are displayed in the literature likely to be of interest to individuals classifiable within these three taxonomic levels. . . . The

relationship of differences in the tastes, values, and motivations of readers at the three levels, to their likely choices of reading material, is emphasized. Initial attention is focused upon the possible social and psychological consequences of the pornotopic revolution, as these are envisaged by writers like Norman Cousins or Pitirim Sorokin. Speculations are made on some of the factors that may be generating the rise of pornotopia."

Wintour, Charles. *Pressures on the Press: An Editor Looks at Fleet Street*. London, Deutsch, 1972. 276p.   **1W293**
The author deals with pressures on the newspapers of Great Britain arising from the clock, public opinion, advertisers, owners and managers, the Press Council, and workers. He also deals with such legal pressures as the libel laws, contempt of court, breach of privilege, official secrets, and obscenity. He concludes with an appeal for greater research in the role of the press and other media, taking into consideration "the varying pressures that are brought to bear on editorial judgment and the scope of the options available."

Wisconsin. University. Department of Journalism and Mass Communications. *The Future of Press Journalism: Journalism and Law Perspectives*. Madison, Wis., Department of Journalism and Mass Communications, University of Wisconsin, 1972. 60p. (Wingspread Report)   **1W294**
"A Wingspread Symposium to discuss conflicting views of the status of First Amendment press freedoms as our democratic society enters the final third of the twentieth century and approaches the bicentennial of its founding as a nation." Speakers and their topics: Freedom of the Press in American Constitutional Law by David Fellman. The Residual Rights of Reputation and Privacy by Donald N. Gillmor. Press Freedom: Can It Survive the Seventies? by Arville O. Schaleben. James Fosdick, moderator. Discussants: James P. Brody, Verne A. Hoffman, Gilbert H. Koenig, Edward Nager, Jay G. Sykes, and Harold L. Nelson, moderator.

Wise, D. Scott. "Growing Deference to the Broadcaster's First Amendment Rights." In *Annual Survey of American Law*, 1976. New York, New York University Law School, 1977, pp. 399–425.   **1W295**

Wise, Daniel M. "Military Censorship Is to Censorship As . . . : Prior Restraint in the Armed Forces." *New York University Review of Law & Social Change*, 2:19–41, Summer 1972. **1W296**
"This note will examine the constitutional issues raised by Army Regulation 210-10 (5-5). Principally, it is submitted that, contrary to the first amendment, the regulation imposes a prior restraint on the distribution of ideas, in-

corporates a standard in conflict with leading civilian precedent, and fails to provide constitutionally guaranteed procedural protections. These deviations from well-established constitutional principles have been justified primarily by the military's need to maintain discipline. This note will evaluate that rationale to determine whether it provides a constitutionally sufficient basis for a military censorship system." Under A. R. 210-10 military base commanders may establish a censorship system to prohibit the distribution of materials which, they determine, pose a clear danger to base loyalty, discipline, and morale.

Wise, David. "Hidden Hands in Publishing." *New Republic*, 67:17–18, 21 October 1967.   **1W297**
Concern over the secret subsidies paid by the U.S. Information Agency to American publishers to produce books sold not only overseas but in this country as well.

———. *The Politics of Lying: Government Deception, Secrecy, and Power.* New York, Random House, 1973. 415p. (Vintage Edition, paperback, 614p.)   **1W298**
"The consent of the governed is basic to American democracy. If the governed are misled, if they are not told the truth, or if through official secrecy and deception they lack information on what to base intelligent decisions, the system may go on—but not as a democracy. After nearly two hundred years, this may be the price America pays for the politics of lying." This volume chronicles the development of government deception, secrecy, and misinformation under at least four administrations, two Democratic and two Republican, climaxing with the totalitarianism of Richard Nixon as revealed in the corruption of Watergate. The totalitarianism "came in the guise of 'national security,' a blanket term used to justify the most appalling criminal acts by men determined to preserve their own political power at any cost. . . . The temptation to abandon the Bill of Rights and constitutional freedoms when dealing with 'enemies,' real or imagined, is the central issue of our time."

———. "The President and the Press." *Atlantic*, 231(4):55–64, April 1973.   **1W299**
A frank account of the hostility of the Nixon Administration toward the press and the systematic efforts at intimidation and harassment, particularly against Columbia Broadcasting System News and correspondents Daniel Rather and Daniel Schorr. "By applying constant pressure, in ways seen and unseen, the leaders of the government have attempted to shape the news to resemble the images seen through the prism of their own power."

Wistrich, Enid. "Censorship and the Local Authority." *Local Government Studies*, 9:1–9, October 1974.   **1W300**
A discussion of the powers of local authority, the role of the British Board of Film Censors,

and the legal position of film censorship in Britain. The author, a member of the Greater London Council and chairman of the Council's Film Viewing Board, argues for abolishing prior censorship of films, making the cinema subject to the same laws as publications. "The likely degree of harm caused by pornographic or violent films is insufficient to justify the repressive apparatus of censorship," and "adult citizens should be free to see the films which they choose, just as they similarly decide which books to read."

Witcover, Jules. "Civil War Over Smut." *Nation*, 210:550–53, 11 May 1970.   **1W301**
An account of the conflicts existing within the U.S. Commission on Obscenity and Pornography and the efforts of Nixon appointee Charles H. Keating, Jr., to get the new administration to make new appointments to the Commission which he felt was stacked against antipornography crusaders like himself.

———. "A Reporters' Committee That Works." *Columbia Journalism Review*, 12(1):26–30, 43, May–June 1973.   **1W302**
A small group of reporters, The Reporters Committee for Freedom of the Press, formed in March 1970, "has become a serious and constructive force in the growing fight against executive, judicial, and legislative encroachment on the press's First Amendment rights."

———. "Trial by Publicity?" In Robert O. Blanchard, *ed.*, *Congress and the News Media*. New York, Hastings House, 1974, pp. 482–85.   **1W303**
The author examines the charges that the Senate Watergate committee was conducting a trial by publicity.

Witcover, Jules *et al.* "The First Amendment on Trial." *Columbia Journalism Review*, 10(3):7–50, September–October 1971.   **1W304**
In this special section on the Pentagon Papers Jules Witcover traces the events of publication and court decision in Two Weeks That Shook the Press; A. M. Rosenthal of the *New York Times*, Benjamin C. Bradlee of the *Washington Post*, and Thomas Winship of the *Boston Globe* discuss Why We Published; Max Frankel discusses the "State Secrets" Myth; five Washington reporters, editors, and news bureau chiefs tell Where We Stand; Thomas I. Emerson, professor of law at Yale, answers questions involving the court case in Where We Stand: A Legal View; James McCartney discusses the issue of security classification in What Should Be Secret? and Ben H. Bagdikian completes the section in an article entitled What Did We Learn?

———. "Vietnam: What Lessons?" *Columbia Journalism Review*, 9(4):7–46, Winter 1970/71.   **1W305**
In this special section appraising press cover-

age of the Vietnam war, Jules Witcover writes on Where Washington Reporting Failed. Fred W. Friendly discusses TV at the Turning Point, noting that "the mistakes we journalists made in 1964 and 1965 almost outran those of the statesmen." Don Stillman considers Tonkin: What Should Have Been Asked? Nathan Blumberg discusses Misreporting the Peace Movement, noting that mass demonstrations were far more than hippie "happenings" and that the press was reluctant to report growth of dissent. James McCartney asks Can the Media Cover Guerilla Wars? Robert Shaplen concludes the series with an article on The Challenge Ahead.

Witham, Barry B. "Play Jury: Censorship in the 1920's." *Educational Theatre Journal*, 24:430–35, December 1972.   **1W306**
The story of the five-year history of New York's Play Jury, established in 1922 as the theater's answer to a possible city or state system of theatrical regulation. In the five years only a few cases were brought before this extra-legal jury: Eugene O'Neill's *Desire Under the Elms* and Sidney Howard's *They Knew What They Wanted* were acquitted by unanimous vote; in the case of Benvanute's *The Firebrand*, the jury recommended the reduction in the length of a kiss; Eduard Boudet's *The Captive*, was cleared by a split decision, but resulted in a subsequent legal battle; and *The Bunk of 1926*, which the jury banned, also came before the courts, which condemned the meddling by unofficial bodies, and paved the way for the final breakdown of the system.

Wittenberg, Philip. *The Protection of Literary Property*. Boston, The Writer, Inc., 1968. 267p.   **1W307**
In addition to information on copyright, the work deals with the protection of ideas, libel, the right of privacy, and literature and censorship.

[Wojcik, Walter S.] "Libel: Still Alive." *Albany Law Review*, 36:193–202, 1971.   **1W308**
A discussion of recent developments in the law of libel, growing out of the U.S. Supreme Court's decisions in *New York Times v. Sullivan* (1964) and *Rosenbloom v. Metromedia, Inc.* (1971), which recognized the doctrine that "debate on public issues should be uninhibited, robust, and wide-open." Two remedies are available under the *Times* doctrine: retraction and right of reply. The author believes a federal right of reply statute would "promote public discussion on public issues as well as provide a uniform standard for all news media." It would also "provide a partial remedy to the victim without the chilling effect of litigation on the press."

Wolf, Hazel C. *On Freedom's Altar: The*

Martyr Complex in the Abolition Movement. Madison, Wis., University of Wisconsin Press, 1952, 195p. **1W309**
The thesis of this study is that abolitionists of the pre-Civil War era were fanatics, capitalizing on a concept of martyrdom akin to that of the early Christians. Many of the abolitionists, including William Lloyd Garrison, James G. Birney, and Elijah P. Lovejoy, were editors or publishers and were the victims of persecution, Lovejoy losing his life in defense of his press.

Wolf, Steven M. "Obscenity: The Lingering Uncertainty." *New York University Review of Law and Social Change*, 2(1):1–19, Spring 1972. **1W310**
"The purpose of this Note is to analyze the constitutional tests employed in obscenity litigation since *Roth v. United States* [1957], examine the rationale behind their use, and evaluate the current relevance of the *Roth* doctrine."

Wolfe, Tom. "Pause, Now, and Consider Some Tentative Conclusions About the Meaning of this Mass Perversion Called Porno-Violence: What It Is and Where It Comes From and Who Put the Hair on the Walls." *Esquire*, 68(1):59, 110, 112, July 1967. **1W311**
The author finds that the discoveries of violence by the avant-garde press have been "preempted by the Establishment and is so thoroughly dissolved into the mainstream they no longer look original," and the old pornography is losing its kick because of overexposure.

Wolff, Geoffrey. "Pornography and Social Value." *New Leader*, 51(15):14–15, 5 August 1968. **1W312**
The author believes that "aside from banning certain books to children with the same energy that the states employ banning liquor to children, it seems clear that in the interest of reason all censorship of books should be abolished." He refers to Charles Rembar's defense of *Fanny Hill* before the U.S. Supreme Court in which Rembar argued that, because the book was well-written, it could by no means be without social value. "To argue that a book must be well-written to have the law's protection, and that a badly-written one is obscene, is to place the ignorant in double jeopardy. The courts can safely let the critics punish the hack."

Wolfson, Lewis W. "Whose First Amendment?" *Progressive*, 39(1):42–46, January 1975. **1W313**
Despite the fact that the nation's press has been vindicated in its First Amendment rights by Watergate, the Pentagon Papers case, and the rejection of the Florida right-of-reply statute, the press still faces a lack of public confidence. Right of access, monopoly control, and arrogance about their affairs call for reform. "They can show that their First Amendment freedom is everybody's freedom by spurring debate on their pages by all voices, and by leveling with the people about their own shortcomings. Then, when the press goes after the next ill-conceived war or Watergate rampage, we will all gladly get out bumper stickers that say, *Support Your Local Journalist*."

Wolkovich, William. *Bay State "Blue" Laws and Bimba. A Documentary Study of the Anthony Bimba Trial for Blasphemy and Sedition in Brockton, Massachusetts, 1926*. Brockton, Mass., Forum Press and The Village Offset of Sandwich, Mass., 1973. 141p. **1W314**
An account of the trial of Anthony Bimba in Brockton, Mass., in 1926. The native Lithuanian, a Socialist turned Communist, was charged on two counts of blasphemy and sedition, resulting from a speech made to an assemblage of Lithuanians, mostly Catholic. The case, coming soon after the more celebrated Sacco-Vanzetti case, "became a crucible for the issue of free speech, liberty of assembly, the socialist-communist fracture at the national and local level, and a furious dispute of two boisterous ethnic factions in the New England industrial city." The affair combined a consideration of a seventeenth-century statute forbidding expression of antireligious sentiments with a 1919 Massachusetts law outlawing seditious utterances.

Wood, Clement. "That Old Devil, Prudery." In his *Barnarr Macfadden: A Study in Success*. New York, Lewis Copeland, 1929, pp. 103–29. **1W315**
The efforts of Anthony Comstock and the vice society to suppress editor Macfadden's *Physical Culture*, on the grounds that articles on sex education were obscene. Macfadden was given a two-year sentence and fined $2,000.

Wood, Clive, and Beryl Suitters. *The Fight for Acceptance: A History of Contraception*. Aylesbury, England, Medical and Technical Publishing, 1970. 230p. **1W316**
In this general history of birth control are chapters dealing with the Fight for Acceptance and the Breakthrough in Britain, which report on the efforts in the United States and Britain to ban information on contraception and which discuss contributions of some of the crusaders who made the breakthrough—Francis Place, Richard Carlile, Robert Dale Owen, Charles Knowlton, Ezra Heywood, Charles Bradlaugh, Annie Besant, Edward Truelove, George Drysdale, Moses Harman, Edward Bliss Foote, Marie Stopes, and Margaret Sanger.

Wood, Donald N. "Trial and Ordeal of an ETV Sex Series in Hawaii." *Educational Television*, 1:14–16, 24, July 1969. **1W317**
A blow-by-blow account of the legal battle over a sex-education program in Hawaii schools, including a film, *A Time of Your Life*. The attacks were led by the Concerned Citizens of Hawaii. The court ruled in favor of the program. The author suggests nine guidelines for schools planning a sex-education series over television.

Wood, H. Curtis. *Book Banning in the Land of the Free*. [Washington, D.C.?, n.p., 1963.] 12p. (Speech delivered at the First National Congress on Health Monopoly Sponsored by the National Health Federation, Washington, D.C., October 25, 26, 27, 1963) **1W318**
An attack on the Food and Drug Administration for the seizure of the author's book, *Overfed But Undernourished*, in a raid of the home of a health food distributor who was allegedly making false claims for his products. Wood, a graduate of the University of Pennsylvania Medical School, had stressed the importance of vitamins and trace minerals in diet and the harmful effects of alcohol and tobacco. He charged the FDA with abridging the freedom of the press. Their answer: the book was "not in agreement with the informed medical and scientific consensus concerning the state of nutrition in this country and the value or necessity of the addition of vitamins and minerals to the ordinary diet."

[Wood, Henry H.] ["Suppressed and Censured Books."] *Edinburgh Review*, 134:161–94, July 1871. **1W319**
Expressing the need for a record of books suppressed or censured in England that would be comparable to Peignot's *Dictionnaire Critique* . . . for the French, the author (identified by the *Wellesley Index* as the Reverend Henry H. Wood) reports on information that he has collected. Beginning with the burning of the works of heretic John Wycliff at Oxford in 1412 and concluding with the persecution of John Wilkes in the 1760s, the chronicle includes action against the following authors and/or their works: William Tyndale (in 1523 his Bible was the first printed book to be burned in England), the works of Martin Luther by order of a Papal bull in 1520, Simon Fish (The Supplication of Beggers, 1531), Christopher Goodman (How Superior Powers Ought to be Obeyd, 1558), John Hales (1563), John Stubbes (1579), Gregory Martin (1578), W. Wilkinson and I. Knewstub (1579), John Penry and the Martin Marprelate tracts (1588–89), Bartholomew Legate (1612), Richard Montagu (1628), Roger Manwaring (1628), Alexander Leighton (1628), William Prynne (1633), John Lilburne (1638), Lawrence Clarkson (1646), John Milton (1649), Arthur Bury (1690), Anthony à Wood (1693), Charles Blount (1693), Henry Sacheverell (1710), Daniel Defoe (1702), John Tutchin (1704), and John Wilkes (1762).

Wood, Robert. "The Truth Shall Make

You Free—Or Will It?" *Focus on Indiana Libraries*, 26(1):11–18, Spring 1972. **1W320**

The writer assembles a collection of views on censorship, beginning with the Library Bill of Rights and closing with Justice Black's dissent in the *Ginzburg* case.

Woodall, Robert. "Before Hansard." *History Today*, 23:195–202, March 1973. **1W321**

Until comparatively recent times the British Parliament insisted in conducting its affairs in an atmosphere of secrecy and on punishing any journalist or printer rash enough to publicize its proceedings. The article recounts the struggle of the press for the right of Parliamentary reporting—the efforts in the eighteenth century of such printers as John Almon and William Woodfall, and the episode of the arrest and imprisonment of the Lord Mayor of London, Brass Crosby, for refusal to permit Parliamentary agents from taking action against London printers.

Woodberry, Joan. *Andrew Bent and the Freedom of the Press in Van Diemen's Land*. Hobart, Tasmania, Fullers Bookshop, 1972. 174p. (Limited to 750 copies) **1W322**

An account of the conflict between an early governor of Tasmania (Van Diemen's land), Colonel George Arthur (1825–36), and Andrew Bent, a convict-printer who became Australia's first martyr to a free press.

Woodfield, Denis B. *Surreptitious Printing in England, 1550–1640*. New York, Bibliographical Society of America, 1973. 203p. **1W323**

"This author deals with those books, pamphlets, and broadsides in contemporary foreign languages which were surreptitiously printed in England before 1640. . . . A book which was 'surreptitiously printed' was almost never illegally printed. On the contrary, most of these works were entered in the Stationers' Register in the normal manner. . . . It is doubtful if the English Government disapproved of the printing of any of the works included in this book, with the one exception ₁Le Prince₁ for which the bookseller, Whittacres (Whitaker) was brought to trial."

Woodford, Jack. *The Loud Literary Lamas of New York*. New York, Vantage, 1950. 94p. **1W324**

An attack on the New York publishing fraternity that turns down the work of talented writers, forcing them to publish their own work to reach the public. It accuses the publishers and the critics of limiting the reading public and thus ruining the writers' market.

Woodhouse, Peter. "Control of Television Advertising in Great Britain." *Food, Drug, Cosmetic Law Journal*, 26:328–33, August 1971. **1W325**

A lawyer associated with the British Independent Television Authority describes how advertising is controlled under the Television Act of 1964. Advertisers buy time on commercial stations but cannot sponsor programs. The ITA has the legal duty to prevent undesirable and misleading advertising and works through a comprehensive Code of Advertising Standards and Practice. The British system "offers the availability of help and advice from the television industry itself in clearing the way to imaginative, competitive, persuasive, but entirely credible, television advertisements."

₁Woodhull, Victoria?₁ "Law of Libel." *Woodhull & Claflin's Weekly*, 7(22):8–9, 9 May 1874. **1W326**

A review of the legal aspects of the obscene libel case against the Woodhull and Claflin sisters, brought by Anthony Comstock because of the sisters' exposé of the Beecher-Tilton affair in the issues of their paper. The author, presumably Mrs. Woodhull, rejects the validity of requiring "good motives" and "justifiable ends" in defense of an alleged libel. There can be no commonly agreed upon legal standard that juries can follow. "Motives" and "ends" are questions of morals and not of law, and might well enough enter into a cause in a religious controversy, but are not proper legal enactments. "The journalist must have the right to write and publish the truth about any individual; or else he must not be permitted to publish any thing whatever having a detrimental personal application. . . . To deprive the press, in this advanced age, of the right to criticize the private acts of individuals would be to encourage a return to the infamies that obtained socially under the old regime."

Woodhull & Claflin's Weekly. New York, 14 May 1870–10 June 1876. (Suspended 29 June–26 October, 9 November–21 December 1872) **1W327**

Victoria Woodhull and her sister Tennessee Claflin published this controversial weekly paper to promote such causes as women's suffrage, free love, spiritualism, socialism, freedom of expression, and Mrs. Woodhull's campaign for presidency of the United States. The two "lady brokers" on Wall Street gained national fame when they released the details of the Beecher-Tilton scandal in the pages of their paper. The issue of 2 November 1872, detailing the affair, was suppressed and the sisters were charged by Anthony Comstock with obscene libel. Subsequent issues deal with the Beecher-Tilton affair and the libel case. The issue for 14 June 1873 carried headlines—Woodhull and Claflin to be "Railroaded in Two Days"—and accounts of their prosecution; the issue for 28 June 1873 carried further information on the case including a lengthy editorial, U.S. Government Threatening the Freedom of the Press. The entire cover of the 5 July 1873 issue consisted of headlines on the case: The Freedom of the Press Threatened by the God-in-the-Constitution YMCA, who Attempt to Make Use of the U.S. District Court To Perpetuate Their Infamy. This is in reference to Anthony Comstock whose antiobscenity crusade was sponsored by the

YMCA. Comstock and his crusade are denounced throughout issues of the paper. Joseph Treat, M.D., attacks Comstock in the 9 August 1873 issue in an article entitled, The Great Jackal. Reformer Parker Pillsbury protests action of the vice society in various issues. An account of a New Bedford, Mass., case of arrest of an art dealer for exhibiting a nude statue in his window (Puritan Prudery vs. the Fine Arts) appears in the 15 November 1873 issue. Most issues carry advertisements of books on sex education, some of which have been suppressed by action of the vice societies. The Woodhull-Claflin sisters were acquitted of the obscene libel charge in New York General Sessions Court. A lengthy article on The Law of Libel appears in the 9 May 1874 issue, reviewing many of the legal aspects of the Woodhull-Claflin case.

Woodluck, Douglas P. "High Court Bars Newsmen's Privilege." *Chicago Journalism Review*, 5(8):6–9, August 1972. **1W328**

Commentary on the U.S. Supreme Court's ruling barring a reporter's privilege to refuse to answer grand jury questions to information gathered on a confidential basis. Text of the various opinions are given.

Woods, Julian. "Censors on Council, or The Case of Snugglepot and Cuddlepie." *Australian Library Journal*, 20(7):22–24, August 1971. **1W329**

An account of aldermanic debate in Ryde Council on censorship leading to a report from the librarian advising on book selection. The report makes the distinction between "(a) rejection of some printed matter by the librarian (book selection), and (b) rejection of some printed matter by the state acting on behalf of the people (book censorship)."

Woods, Winton D., Jr. "Suppression of the Press in Early Pennsylvania: The Penumbra of Bayard v. Passmore." *Arizona Law Review*, 10:315–46, Fall 1968. **1W330**

An account of early Pennsylvania trials involving press freedom: *Respublica v. Oswald* (1788), *Respublica v. Cobbet₁t₁* (1798), *Respublica v. Dennie* (1805), the case of William Duane of the *Philadelphia Aurora* (1799), and *Bayard v. Passmore* (1802).

Woodsworth, Ann, *comp. The "Alternative" Press in Canada: A Checklist of Underground, Revolutionary, Radical and Other Alternative Serials from 1960*. Toronto, University of Toronto Press, 1972. 74p. **1W331**

An alphabetical listing of 413 papers, followed by a geographical and subject listing. Bibliography.

Woodward, A. E. "Censorship." *Australian Law Journal*, 45:570–88, September 1971. **1W332**
"After a brief background consideration of the nature and purpose of censorship, the paper will selectively draw attention to what are suggested to be particular weaknesses in our present arrangements and will suggest changes ₍within the existing structure₎ which could be usefully made. . . . " The author follows with advocacy for a "far-reaching change in approach to the whole subject," which involves the establishment of an eminent advisory literary board. Discussion of the paper follows: Judge Jones (Western Australia), P. D. Connolly, Q.C. (Queensland), M. D. Broun (New South Wales), Lord Diplock, Justice Hart (Queensland), L. Davies (Western Australia), Justice Bray (South Australia), J. Cain (Victoria), T. Martin (New South Wales), and J. Perry (South Australia).

Woolf, Virginia. "The Censorship of Books." *Nineteenth Century*, 106:446–47, April 1929. **1W333**
The author argues that "it is desirable that the law should distinguish clearly between books that are written or sold for pornographic purposes and books whose obscenity is an incidental part of them—between Aristotle's works as they are sold in the rubber goods shops, that is to say, and Aristotle's works as they are sold in the shops of Messrs. Hatchard and Bumpus."

Wooll, Edward. *A Guide to the Law of Libel and Slander*. London, Blackie, 1939. 214p. **1W334**
"This book presents an attempt to review for the general public the nature and degree of the control exercised by English law over the expression of opinion in this country."

———. *Libel! A Play in Three Acts*. London, Heinemann, 1934. 123p. **1W335**
The play, founded on a combination of facts, deals with a libel charge against a London newspaper. The work also appears as a novel, published in 1935 by Blackie.

Worchel, Stephen, and Susan E. Arnold. *The Effects of Censorship and Attractiveness of the Censor on Attitude Change*. ₍Chapel Hill, N.C., The Authors₎, 1971. 26p. (ED 78,319) **1W336**
"This research studies the effects of censoring a communication, overriding the censor, and the attractiveness of the censor on the potential audience's attitude and desire to hear the communication."

World Peace Broadcasting Foundation. *Procedure Outline for Local Groups Seeking to Use the "Fairness Doctrine" of the FCC to Obtain Public Service Time on Radio and TV Stations for Broadcast On Peace Issues*. West Des Moines, Iowa, The Foundation, 1969. 2p. Processed. **1W337**

₍World's Press News Publishing Co., London.₎ *Freedom of the Press Vindicated; Libel Case, G.A. Hutt v. World's Press News Publishing Co., Ltd*. London, World's Press News, 1950? 64p. **1W338**
George A. Hutt, journalist and member of the National Executive Council of the National Union of Journalists, sued the *World's Press News* for libel because of a letter to the editor appearing in the 1 January 1948 issue. The jury found for the defendants.

Worrall, Thomas D. *Slander and Defamation of Character, the Great Crimes of the Nineteenth Century*. Washington, D.C., 1884. 207p. **1W339**
A spirited attack on slander which "causes more misery than theft, more than arson, and sometimes, even more than murder." The work is a collection of essays on slandering and slanderers—motives, method, effect, legal redress, slander in politics, slander and the rights of the press, pleading the truth of a libel in justification. The author calls for the formation of a Society for the Suppression of Slander to aid in "purifying the press and saving the nation from the terrible effects of reckless libeling." He urges more severe criminal laws against slander and more rigorous enforcement.

Worsnop, Richard L. *Cable Television: The Coming Medium*. Washington, D.C., Editorial Research Reports, 1970. (*Editorial Research Reports*, 2:669–86, 1970) **1W340**
Content: Challenge Posed by Cable Television. A New Medium—Its Origin and Growth. Debate on How to Regulate Cable TV (state and local controls, copyright problems, and issue as to whether cable TV is a common carrier).

———. *Secrecy in Government*. Washington, D.C., Editorial Research Reports, 1971. (*Editorial Research Reports*, 2:629–50, 1972) **1W341**
Content: Controversy over the Pentagon Papers. Information Practices of U.S. Agencies. Efforts to Counteract Secrecy Trends. The Overhauling of the Security Classification System. Leaks of Classified Data by Government Officials.

Worsthorne, Peregrine. "Porn & the Liberals: Thoughts after Longford." *Encounter*, 40(5):86–94, May 1973. **1W342**
A member of the Longford group studying pornography, attacks the Liberal Establishment for subjecting members to ridicule and ostracism just as the Conservatives had treated Marie Scopes a generation before when she advocated birth control. Liberals displayed a new variety of authoritarianism in the matter of pornography. The result is a society in which "a whole range of views that are currently unpopular and heretical do not get a fair and proper hearing, since as soon as they begin to appear on the horizon a barrage of moral abuse, and intellectual mockery falls upon them which makes rational debate virtually impossible."

Worton, Stanley N. *Freedom of Speech and Press*. Rochelle Park, N.J., Hayden, 1975. 131p. (American Issues in Perspective: A Documentary Approach) **1W343**
Content: Dissent Is Not Treason: Zenger trial and Alien and Sedition Acts, 1798. Clear and Present Danger: (*Schenck v. United States*, 1919; *Abrams v. United States*, 1919; *Gitlow v. New York*, 1925; and *Near v. Minnesota*, 1931). In the Library or Behind the Barn (*United States v. One Book Called "Ulysses,"* 1933; *Burstyn v. Wilson*, 1952; *Times Film Corp. v. Chicago*, 1961; testimony of Frank Askin before the New Jersey Commission to Study Obscenity; "Report of the Freedom to Read Committee"; *Miller v. California*, 1973; *Paris Adult Theatre v. Slaton*, 1973). Channels of Communication: I.T.T. and the San Diego Convention Are Just the Tip of the Iceberg by Nicholas Johnson; The Pentagon Papers; The Secrecy Dilemma by Arthur Schlesinger, Jr. Opportunities and Constraints: The Campaign to Politicize Broadcasting by Fred Friendly.

Wozencraft, Frank M. *et al*. "The Freedom of Information Act and the Agencies." *Administrative Law Review*, 23:129–67, March 1971. (Also in *Public Utilities*, 24 September 1970) **1W344**
A symposium introduced by Frank W. Wozencraft. The Freedom of Information Act and the Agencies: SEC No-Action Letters by Richard B. Smith; The Freedom of Information Act and the CAB by Secor D. Browne; The Journalist's Viewpoint by Louis M. Kohlmeier; The Work of the Freedom of Information Committee of the Department of Justice by Robert L. Saloschin; and The Federal Power Commission and Freedom of Information by Carl E. Bagge. Addresses given before the Public Utilities Law Section of the American Bar Association, 10–12 August 1970.

Wright, Andrew. *The Anti-Shepherd-Crat; Or, An Appeal to Honest Republicans. An Historical Sketch*. Northampton, Mass., The Author, 1811. 20p. **1W345**
Pertains to the interparty controversy between Wright and Shepherd. Wright was given a six-month sentence; he had charged Governor Strong with speculating in public securities and with irregularities in making appointments. The trial is reported in W399.

Wright, Christopher. *Libraries and*

Copyright. *A Summary of the Arguments for Library Photocopying.* Washington, D.C., American Library Association, 1974. 47p. **1W 346**
"This booklet is an attempt to provide librarians with a short summary of the arguments in favor of library photocopying, combined with a status report on how these arguments have fared in the courts and in Congress."

Wright, Donald R. "Fair Trial and Free Press: Practical Ways to Have Both." *Judicature*, 54:377–82, April 1971. **1W 347**
The Chief Justice of California suggests ways to improve press, bar, and bench relationships in the coverage of trials by way of introducing the text of a *Joint Declaration Regarding News Coverage of Criminal Proceedings in California*, adopted by the State Bar of California, the California Newspaper Publishers Association, the California Broadcasters Association, Radio and TV News Directors, and the executive board of the Conference of California Judges.

Wright, Francis B. *A Narrative of the Proceedings in the Court of King's Bench, against the Editor of the Liverpool Chronicle, for a Libel.* London, W. Minshull, 1809. 42p. **1W 348**
Wright was found guilty and given a six-month prison sentence.

Wright, J. Skelly. "Defamation, Privacy, and the Public's Right to Know: A National Problem and A New Approach." *Texas Law Review*, 46:630–49, April 1968. **1W 349**
The author finds the law of libel almost total confusion, and expresses the need for a national law of defamation—"a law that goes beyond establishing limitations on state actions for defamation and extends to the elements of the tort itself."

———. "Fair Trial–Free Press." *Federal Rules Decisions*, 38:435–39, February 1966. **1W 350**
A U.S. Circuit Court judge believes that "only a precious few cases" would be affected by the press exercising its First Amendment freedoms and that the press itself, by taking appropriate steps of self-discipline could avoid confrontation.

Wright, Keith, and Roy Alin. "Questions on Censorship: Junior High Books." *English Journal*, 62(12):1286–87, December 1973. **1W 351**
The authors discuss the NCTE pamphlet, *The Students' Right to Read*, and raise additional "questions that arise in our minds as a result of our attempt to answer the two questions—What is the relationship between power and moral responsibility? and How can man reconcile the conflict of duty between what he owes society and what he owes his own conscience?" One of the authors of the pamphlet, Kenneth

L. Donelson, attempts to answer some of the questions in an article in the April 1974 issue.

Wright, Vincent. *Suppressio Veri, or The Dangers of the Press by Vincent Wright Together with "A Foreign Correspondent Speaks" by Sisley Huddleston.* London, The Weekly Review [1939?]. 29p. (Reprinted from the *Weekly Review*) **1W 352**
"There is quite a lot of freedom and independence in the job [of news reporting]—within sharp limits imposed by the newspaper office atmosphere, its owners, its revenue side, and its circulation department." The real boss is circulation; the press follows the dictates of the "ill-informed masses." Wright accuses the British press of suppressing facts unfavorable to the Communists, especially in coverage of the Spanish Civil War. The press, he charges, is "a much graver danger to the country and to the Empire than a dozen Hitlers." It is a monopoly without responsibility.

Wright, William G. "Freedom of the Press vs. Protection of the Reputation: Actual Malice and the New Public Interest Test." *Arkansas Law Review*, 25:525–34, Winter 1972. **1W 353**
In *Rosenbloom v. Metromedia, Inc.* (1971) the U.S. Supreme Court declared: "We honor the commitment to robust debate on public issues, which is embodied in the First Amendment, by extending constitutional protection to all discussion and communication involving matters of public or general concern, without regard to whether the persons involved are famous or anonymous."

Wright, William R., II. "Open Meetings Laws: An Analysis and a Proposal." *Mississippi Law Journal*, 45:1151–84, November 1974. **1W 354**
"The purpose of this comment is not to reach a conclusion as to why Mississippi does not have open meeting legislation. Instead, this writer will attempt within a limited scope to examine the arguments for such laws, and to look at the experience of other states with regard to open meeting laws. To put the topic in perspective, the open meetings rationale and its historical and constitutional background will be examined; then the basic provisions of existing open meetings laws will be analyzed in terms of their relative strengths and weaknesses. Finally, the focus of this comment will return to Mississippi with proposed open meetings legislation based on the best—and, hopefully, eschewing the worst—to be found in the 46 existing state open meetings laws."

Wszolek, Dennis F. "The Application of Miller v. California in Ohio." *Capital University Law Review*, 4:315–24, 1975. **1W 355**
An examination of the new test for obscenity established by the U.S. Supreme Court in *Miller v. California*, 1973, with reference to its role in Ohio.

Wulf, Melvin L. "Excess Access." *Civil Liberties Review*, 1(2):128–30, Winter–Spring 1974. **1W 356**
"There is an idea in circulation whose time, I hope, will never come. Its purpose is to force newspapers by law to open their pages to dissenting or minority points of view and be compelled to publish material that they might otherwise choose to ignore." Wulf opposes the Florida right of reply law and the views of Professor Jerome A. Barron.

———. "A Soldier's First Amendment Rights: The Art of Formally Granting and Practically Suppressing." *Wayne Law Review*, 18:665–82, March–April 1972. **1W 357**
The author concludes that since members of the military force are properly citizens first and soldiers second their civil liberties as embodied in the First Amendment should be protected.

———. "What's Fit to Print: Tragedy of 'The Times.' " *Civil Liberties*, 280:1, 11, September 1971. **1W 358**
"The attempt of the Nixon administration to prohibit the publication of the Viet Nam papers was the first direct act of political censorship by the federal government since the founding of the nation. . . . That the courts refused to permit it says something about the independence of the judiciary and the extent to which the ideas embodied in the First Amendment have taken root in the law. I only wish it could be said with more confidence." The author notes that the public "won the case by only a little more than the skin of our collective teeth and we have no firm assurance that in some future case this Supreme Court would not tolerate the suppression of similar documents, under other conditions."

Wyatt, Wilson W. "The 'Right of Privacy' Doctrine: A Prime Newspaper Headache." *Bulletin of the American Society of Newspaper Editors*, 513:3–4, 7, November 1967. **1W 359**
The author summarizes the "complex of four" principles which form the basis for the legal doctrine of the "right of privacy." "The result of the *Griswold* case may be far-reaching, in that for the first time, the Supreme Court found basis in the Federal Constitution for a 'right of privacy.' . . . On the other hand, in the *Sullivan*, *Garrison*, *Hill* and *Walker* decisions, the Supreme Court has given significant new First Amendment protection to newspapers to print in the public interest."

[Wyman, Charles *et al.*] *Actions for Libel. Goldschmidt v. Wyman* (Printer of "*Public Opinion*"); *The Same v. Spottiswoode* (Printer of "*The American Register*"); *The Same v. Stiff* (Proprietor of "*The London*

Reader"). London, Printed by Wetherby and Co., 1871. 55p.   **1W360**

The printers of these three London papers were charged with libel by Otto Goldschmidt, husband of the famous singer, Jenny Lind. The three papers had reprinted statements from the New York paper, *Woodhull & Claflin's Weekly*, charging Goldschmidt with wanton waste of his wife's fortune and reporting their marital estrangement. Both husband and wife appeared at the trial to deny the charges. Although the printers had not read the copy of the paper submitted for printing and although the papers had printed retractions, all three printers were found guilty in successive trials before the same jury and fined heavily.

Wynd, Ian. *Censorship*. Melbourne, Australia, Australian Catholic Truth Society, 1970. 30p. (A.C.T.S. Publication no. 1589)   **1W361**

The author discusses the pros and cons of censorship of obscenity in Australia, concluding that while there is some uncertainty as to the effects of obscenity and violence, where there is a reasonable doubt a system of censorship should be maintained. The prime responsibility for censorship of children's reading and viewing should be that of parents. Wherever they see their community standards breached they should register protests to advertisers, newspapers, and to Mr. Chipp, the Australian minister of Customs.

Wyoming Library Association. Intellectual Freedom Committee. "Results of Survey Concerning Policy and Censorship in Wyoming." *Wyoming Library Roundup*, 27(2):23–24, June 1972.   **1W362**

A tabulation of answers to ten questions on censorship put to school and county librarians.

X

"X-Rated Motion Pictures: From Restricted Theaters and Drive-Ins to the Television Screen." *Valparaiso University Law Review*, 8:107–24, Fall 1973. **1X1**

"This note will examine whether—in light of current constitutional standards governing the dissemination of sexually explicit materials to a community—the Columbia Broadcasting System, or any American network or local station, could similarly exhibit unedited X-rated motion pictures over a medium to which potentially large numbers of children and unwilling adults might unavoidably be exposed. It will be argued that although precious first amendment freedoms are involved, X-rated motion pictures should remain limited to present areas of distribution rather than be extended to the commercial television medium."

Y

Yacavone, J. P. "Emerson's Distinction." *Connecticut Law Review*, 6:49–64, Fall 1973. **1Y1**
"This article shall offer some criticism of the central doctrine of [Thomas I. Emerson] *Toward a General Theory of the First Amendment* . . . [E89]. The focus will be on two of the concepts of central ideas upon which the theory is premised. These concepts of 'action' and 'expression' are in need of closer attention than the author has given them."

Yadlosky, Elizabeth. "U.S. Supreme Court Decisions on Pornography 1954 to February 1968." In U.S. Senate, Committee on Commerce, *Hearings on S. Res. 9. to Create a Special Committee on Film Classification*, pp. 6–30. **1Y2**
The *Roth* definition of obscenity (1957) marked the first significant change in the attitude of the Supreme Court in the area of obscenity; in the *Ginzburg* decision in 1966 the Court appeared to have departed somewhat from the *Roth* approach. This memorandum discusses these and other decisions during the fourteen-year period in chronological order. Alphabetical and chronological tables of cases are appended.

Yale University. Committee on Freedom of Expression. "Freedom of Expression at Yale." *Chronicle of Higher Education*, 10(8):15–16, 14 April 1975. **1Y3**
Excerpts from the report of a committee headed by historian C. Vann Woodward, formed following the disruption of a debate involving William Shockley, the Stanford physicist who believes that black persons are genetically inferior to white. The Yale governing board adopted the report. The Committee concluded that "the paramount obligation of the university is to protect their right to free expression. This obligation can and should be enforced by appropriate formal sanctions. If the university's overriding commitment to free expression is to be sustained, secondary social and ethical responsibilities must be left to the informal processes of suasion, example, and argument." One member of the thirteen-member panel dissented. In his report he con-

cluded: "I agree that free expression is an important value, which we must cherish and protect. But it is not the only value which we uphold, either in our society or in our universities. Under certain circumstances, free expression is outweighed by more pressing issues, including liberation of all oppressed people and equal opportunities for minority groups."

Yamhure, Patricia S. "Gertz v. Robert Welch, Inc." *Revista Juridica de la Universidad de Puerto Rico*, 44:175–94, 1975. **1Y4**
The article deals with *Gertz v. Robert Welch, Inc.* (1974) and its effect on the Puerto Rican civil law of defamation.

Yankwich, Leon R. "Certainty in the Law of Defamation." *UCLA Law Review*, 1:163–82, February 1954. **1Y5**
A discussion of the historical development of the legal concept of certainty in the law of defamation.

Yarbrough, Tinsley E. "The Burger Court and Freedom of Expression." *Washington & Lee Law Review*, 33:37–90, Winter 1976. **1Y6**
The Nixon appointments to the U.S. Supreme Court "have produced a pattern of gradual retrenchment in a number of first amendment issue areas. A showing of 'substantial' overbreadth is now required in cases involving facial review of statutes regulating communicative conduct rather than 'pure' speech alone, and the Nixon appointees favor a general curtailment of vagueness-overbreadth review. A 'serious value' obscenity guideline has replaced the 'no value' standard endorsed by the *Memoirs* plurality—a standard which had seemed to foredoom most obscenity controls." The Burger Court also applied a less expansive concept of the public forum and the First Amendment balancing doctrine appears to be undergoing change. On the other hand, the author cautions against exaggerating the conservative impact of the Nixon justices, noting that the Court has continued to lend a sympathetic ear to claims raised on speech-plus and symbolic speech cases, and where the content

of expression has been the subject of regulation; and it has required the same standards of freedom for the academic community as normally applied in free expression.

———. *Fair Trial Versus Free Press: Trial Publicity and Procedural Due Process*. University, Ala., University of Alabama, 1967. (Ph.D. dissertation, University Microfilms, no. 68–1075) **1Y7**
"It is the purpose of this dissertation to describe and analyze, in a comprehensive fashion, problems involved in attempting to reconcile the conflict between the right of fair trial and the freedom of the press to report criminal proceedings. Special attention is given in the study to procedural questions raised by prejudicial trial publicity and the approaches of judges to such questions." The author concludes that "reasonable limitations designed to prevent news media activity which may impair the right of an accused to a fair trial are not an unjustifiable invasion of freedom of expression."

———. "Justice Black and His Critics on Speech-Plus and Symbolic Speech." *Texas Law Review*, 52:257–84, January 1974. **1Y8**
The author concluded that "Justice Black's position on speech-plus and symbolic speech claims reflected several basic tenets of his judicial and constitutional philosophy": (1) He preferred clear, precise legal standards and opposed the Court's tendency to blur the distinctions between protected and unprotected behavior; (2) he desired to restrict the scope of judicial discretion; (3) he hesitated to interfere with governmental regulation in fields where government has general authority to act; and (4) he held an absolutist conception of the First Amendment.

———. "Justice Black, the First Amendment, and the Burger Court." *Mississippi Law Journal*, 46:203–46, Spring 1975. **1Y9**
"This article examines Justice Black's first amendment jurisprudence from the perspec-

Yarbrough, Willard. "Controversial Editor Burned Out." *Grassroots Editor*, 13(5):13–15, September–October 1972. **1Y10**
An account of the persecution of Dan Hicks, Jr., publisher of the *Monroe County Democrat*, Madisonville, Tenn., who has led a fight against racial intimidation by the Ku Klux Klan, against misconduct in the county highway department, and other local abuses, suffered two attempts on his life, and a torch to his newspaper office. Six months after he received the Elijah Parish Lovejoy Award for courage in journalism, his newspaper plant was burned out for a second time, leaving only the walls standing.

Yeager, Suzanne. *G-GP-R-X: Exercise in Ambiguity*. Columbia, Mo., Freedom of Information Center, School of Journalism, University of Missouri at Columbia, 1971. 6p. (Report no. 258) **1Y11**
"Neither the public nor the motion picture industry is satisfied with the motion picture rating system which is currently in use. The Code Administration, caught in the middle, is faced with the dilemma of having to satisfy both the filmmaker's right of artistic expression and the public's right to protect its youth from violence and obscenity."

———. *G-GP-R-X: Forced Self-Regulation?* Columbia, Mo., Freedom of Information Center, School of Journalism, University of Missouri at Columbia, 1971. 6p. (Report no. 257) **1Y12**
"The motion picture industry, historically in opposition to any form of regulation, is now attempting to head off forced regulation through implementation of the motion picture rating system. This move is seen as an effort to maintain the balance between freedom of expression and society's right to protect its youth."

Yergin, Daniel. "Muzzled Sheep: The British Press Today." *Nieman Reports*, 28(1-2):25–29, Spring–Summer 1974. **1Y13**
"The working journalist is so entangled in a web of legal restrictions and habits that he faces great difficulties merely in going about his day-to-day business of trying to report who is really doing what to whom. This web is not just the work of others; the press itself has helped in the weaving. The consequence of the entire situation is that much of the press often ends up as a house organ for The Way Things Are."

Yesner, Seymour. "Our Changing Censorship." *Minnesota English Journal*, 12(1):9–14, Winter 1976. **1Y14**
The author describes a new form of censorship of children's literature. "Though the new cen-

sors are not afraid of four letter words, explicit sex or un-American viewpoints, they are still afraid of certain words and descriptions, those that are 'sexist' or 'racist.' " The author concludes that what is needed instead of a "reverse ethnocentric perspective" is "a generic one that sees literature and stories as conveying through symbol, legend, myth, and metaphor the foibles, misconceptions, tragic attitudes and often horrendous behavior of all groups of human beings. For a while women and minorities seemed headed in this direction" and "forced us to look at the plight of the poor, the blacks, Indians, women, all the oppressed and forlorn folk of the world. . . . Suddenly the risks in this venture of dialogue seem too great, and, out of a desperation to maintain the momentum of a cause, coercion becomes the style, factionalism the trend, and exploitation of the young in captive classroom audiences the morality."

Yodelis, Mary A. "Boston's First Major Newspaper War: A 'Great Awakening' of Freedom." *Journalism Quarterly*, 51:207–12, Summer 1974. **1Y15**
"Although the tradition of supporting a free press did not originate in Boston, advocates of press freedom in the American colonies during the revolution may well have been inspired by a Bostonian, Thomas Fleet. One of the city's important printers from 1735 until his death in 1758, Fleet repeatedly expressed some generally libertarian attitudes during Boston's first major newspaper war in the 1740s."

———. "Courts, Counting House and Streets: Attempts at Press Control, 1763–1775." *Journalism History*, 1:11–15, Spring 1974. **1Y16**
"This study will summarize briefly the constraints exercised against all the Boston newspapers and publishers: legal, economic, violent, symbolic, and rhetorical. The study essentially documents the widening gap between the law of seditious libel in theory and the law in fact."

———. "The Rejection of Florida's Right to Reply Statute: A Setback for a 'New Right' of Access to the Press." *New York Law Forum*, 20:633–42, Winter 1975. **1Y17**
The U.S. Supreme Court's decision in *Miami Herald Publishing Co. v. Tornillo* (1974), has for the present at least, rebuffed the argument that there is a need for a new First Amendment right of access to the press.

Young, Brian. "The ITA and Censorship." *Journal of the Society of Film and Television Arts*, 43/44:10–12, Spring–Summer 1971. **1Y18**
The director-general of Britain's Independent Television Authority discusses the role of the Authority which stands "somewhere between the committed creators of programmes and the millions of diverse views" and "tries to balance assertion and protest."

Young, David M. "Security and the Right to Know." *Military Review*, 44:46–53, August 1964. **1Y19**
A journalist discusses the conflict between national security and the public's right to know, citing examples in the Cuban crisis and Vietnam. He concludes that "it is quite possible for a government to carry out a short-term news management campaign for the sake of national security, but it seems impossible for a government to perpetrate a long-term propaganda campaign. Under our system, the public may show disapproval by voting a particular administration out of office every four years."

[Young, George M., Jr. *et al.*] " 'Granite' Loses Its $750 Grant for Obscenity." *Granite*, 7/8:[i–viii], Spring 1974. **1Y20**
An exchange of correspondence involving the disapproval by the governor of New Hampshire of a grant to *Granite* magazine because of objections to a poem, "Castrating the Cat."

Young, J. C. *Study to Determine the Nationwide Pattern of Censorship in School and Public Libraries as Reported in Two Library Periodicals from 1962–1971*. Emporia, Kans., Kansas State College, 1974. 121p. (Unpublished Master's thesis) **1Y21**

Young, Ken M. "School Storm Centers: Charleston." *Phi Delta Kappan*, 56:262–66, December 1974. **1Y22**
An account of the school textbook controversy that has "ripped this school system and community apart over the past eight weeks." The author is associate superintendent, Division of Curriculum and Instruction, Kanawha County Schools, Charleston, W.Va.

Young, W. Winston. "Censorship: The Need for a Positive Program to Prevent It (Book Selection as Public Relations)." In Charles Suhor, *ed.*, *The Growing Edges of Secondary English: Essays by the Experienced Teacher Fellows at the University of Illinois, 1966–67*. Champaign, Ill., National Council of Teachers of English, 1968, pp. 201–17. **1Y23**
In this paper the author attempts to bring the school and community together in developing a rationale for the selection of literary works. He considers the nature of censorship pressures from individuals and groups and suggests a book selection procedure with careful advance planning which he believes will result in little or no objection to the books required for class use.

Younger, Evelle J. "Fair Trial, Free Press, and the Man in the Middle." *American Bar Association Journal*, 56:127–30, February 1970.   **1Y24**
"When the constitutional rights of fair trial and free press conflict, the public prosecutor is the man in the middle. If he is subjected to broad and restrictive orders regarding publicity, such as the order issued in the case of Sirhan Sirhan, the prosecutor is precluded from treating rumors with the antidote of truth and is isolated from the constituency to which he owes an accounting—his electorate. There must be a better way to reach the desired end than gagging the prosecutor."

Younger, Irving. "Pornography and Violence." *Nation*, 205:120–21, 124, 14 August 1967.   **1Y25**
The author discusses the issue of whether or not society should limit the freedom of the writer to write obscenity in order to lessen the risk of inciting crime. The essay is prompted by Pamela Hansford Johnson's book, *On Iniquity*, based on the case of British sadistic murders, known as the "Moors Murders" (°J17).

Youngs, Frederick A., Jr. "The Tudor Governments and Dissident Religious Books." In C. Robert Cole and Michael E. Moody, *eds.*, *The Dissenting Tradition: Essays for Leland H. Carlson.* Athens, Ohio, Ohio University Press, 1975, pp. 167–90.   **1Y26**
The author deals with control over dissident religious books by the Tudor governments— attempts to keep such books from being printed or imported from abroad, suppression of books which eluded the net, and punishment of those who wrote, printed, distributed or read the works.

Youngtypo, *pseud. Britannia's Intercession for the Deliverance of John Wilkes, Esq. from Persecution and Banishment to Which Is Added, A Political Sermon: and a Dedication to L*** B***.* 4th ed. London ₁H. Woodgate? 1768?₎. 17p.   **1Y27**
A defense of Wilkes, written as a parody in the form of the ritual of the Church of England and the Psalms: "O Give thanks unto Wilkes, for he is sensible and his sensibility continueth for ever. . . . I believe in Wilkes, the firm patriot, maker of number 45. Who was born for our good. Suffered under arbitrary power. Was banished and imprisoned. He descended into purgatory, and returned some time after. He ascended here with honour, and sittith amidst the great assembly of the people, where he shall judge both the favorite and his creatures. I believe in the spirit of his abilities, that they will prove to the good of our country. In the resurrection of liberty, and the life of universal freedom for ever. Amen." The following note appears on the verso of the title page of the issue in the British Museum: "Wheras the Word FORM, printed on the Title Page of some which were at first sold, has given Disgust to a few Individuals, we have in its room substituted that of BRITANNIA, as it is very far from the Intention of the Author to displease any of his Readers, even the most conscientious and devout." The dedication was probably to Lord Bute. Wilkes's trials for publishing *North Briton*, no. 45 and *Essay on Woman* are given in W256–67.

Yuill, Phyllis. "Little Black Sambo: The Continuing Controversy." *School Library Journal*, 22(7):71–76, March 1976.   **1Y28**
A review of the historical background and present controversy over Helen Bannerman's *Little Black Sambo*, first published in 1898, the simple story that "seems to remain a popular example of the dilemma faced by responsible librarians, teachers, and parents when reevaluating children's books in relation to today's heightened social awareness."

Z

Zack, Marilyn G. "F.C.C. and the Fairness Doctrine." *Cleveland State Law Review*, 19:579–94, September 1970. **1Z1**

A critique of the *Red Lion* decision (*Red Lion Broadcasting Co., Inc. v. F.C.C.*, 1969) in which the U.S. Supreme Court upheld the Federal Communications Commission's fairness doctrine.

Zafren, Daniel H. *Testimonial Privilege for Representatives of the News Media: A Summary of Recent Court Decisions. . . .* Washington, D.C., Congressional Research Service, Library of Congress, 1972. 67p. **1Z2**

Content: The Supreme Court Decision. Present Federal Practice. Arguments in Favor and Against Enactment of a Testimonial Privilege Act for Newsmen. Some Problems in Devising a Federal Bill. State Statutes. Some Federal Bills Introduced in the 92d Congress. Alternatives.

Zarnoch, Robert A. *The Attorney General's Guidelines: The Federal Government's Role in Preserving Fair Trials in the Face of Prejudicial Publicity.* Washington, D.C., American University, 1969. 232p. (Unpublished Master's thesis) **1Z3**

A study of the Justice Department's rules to guide its employees in the release of information relating to criminal proceedings.

[Zeidenberg, Leonard.] "How Nixon Administration Plans to Cut TV Networks Down to Size." *Broadcasting*, 84:24–26, 12 February 1973. **1Z4**

An interview with Clay T. Whitehead reveals the Nixon Administration's calculated policy to encourage cable TV as a means for reducing the power of the television networks.

Zeisler, Sigmund. *Reminiscences of the Anarchist Case.* Chicago, Chicago Literary Club, 1927. 37p. (Limited to 570 copies for members) **1Z5**

One of the lawyers who defended the anarchists who were convicted forty years ago in the Chicago Haymarket bombing tells his account of the affair, which he believes was a tragic miscarriage of justice. He concludes with Governor Altgeld that the men were found guilty not because they had been proved guilty of murder but because they were anarchists. Two were editors of anarchist papers: August Spies was editor of the *Arbeiter Zeitung*; Albert R. Parsons, editor of the *Alarm*. Both were hanged.

Zellick, Graham. "Films and the Law of Obscenity." *Criminal Law Review*, 1971:126–50, March 1971. **1Z6**

The author contends that, with one small exception, films fall outside the scope of the British Obscene Publications Act. They can be acted against under common law. The obscenity laws are in urgent need of review because of the confusion and complexity of their interpretation and enforcement.

———. "Libelling the Dead." *New Law Journal*, 119:769–70, 14 August 1969. **1Z7**

The author reviews the British law with respect to defamation of the dead, noting that there is now no adequate controls either under civil or criminal laws. The Theatres Act of 1968 swept away such controls over stage productions. "Parliament rightly swept away the controls: they must now give this matter urgent consideration."

———. "A New Approach to the Control of Obscenity." *Modern Law Review*, 33:289–98, May 1970. **1Z8**

The author recommends changes in the British obscenity laws along the lines of the Massachusetts law which places the book rather than the publisher or printer on trial. He also suggests the retention of a separate standard for children along the lines of the Children and Young Persons (Harmful Publications) Act, 1955, which deals with horror comics. He calls for consolidation in one statute of all laws concerning obscenity in the theater, literature, the mails, and customs.

———. "Offensive Advertisements in the Mail." *Criminal Law Review*, 1972:724–43, December 1972. **1Z9**

Criticism of the British criminal law against unsolicited publications as "rash" and "ill-conceived" and failing to address itself to protection of privacy. The U.S. law, on the other hand, operates only when an individual requests protection from invasion of his privacy.

———. "Two Comments on Search and Seizure under the Obscene Publications Act." *Criminal Law Review*, 1971:504–14, September 1971. **1Z10**

"This article seeks to explore two facets of the power conferred by section 3 of the 1959 [Obscene Publications] Act. The consultation that does and should take place before the power is activated; and the delay invoked once the power has been invoked." Both matters are illustrated by the case involving the showing of the Andy Warhol film, *Flesh*, at London's Open Space Theatre.

———. "Violence as Pornography." *Criminal Law Review*, 1970:188–200, April 1970. **1Z11**

An analysis of the law on violence as pornography in Britain and America. "In Britain the courts have extended the meaning of obscenity to include violence, while the United States courts have refused to do so, even when the legislature had expressly intended it." The only legislation on the point in Britain is the "Horror Comics" Act of 1955, which has been successful. There seems to be no problem in the area of theater or cinema, but "it is in television which is the great worry, and here the law scarcely intervenes at all."

[Zenger, John Peter.] *Trial of John Peter Zenger.* 22 min. tape recording. North Hollywood, Calif., Center for Cassette Studies, 1969. (Distributor's title: Spotlight on John Peter Zenger) **1Z12**

A dramatization of the historic trial of John Peter Zenger, newspaper editor arrested in New York in 1734 for his political views.

Zenor, John L. "The Fairness Doctrine, the Automobile and Ecological

Awareness: An Affirmative Role for the Electronic Media in the Pollution Crisis." *Cornell Law Review*, 57:121–36, November 1971. **1Z13**
The author believes that the fairness doctrine should be applied to advertising that ignores deadly ecological effects of the product, and presents only one side of controversial issues of economic policy and public health. "Such an application of the doctrine is commanded in policy and firmly based on the cigarette advertising precedent."

Zimmer, Dieter E., *ed. Die Grenzen Literarischer Freiheit. 22 Beiträge über Zensur im In- und Ausland Herausgegeben von Dieter E. Zimmer mit Zeichnungen von Paul Flora*. Hamburg, Nannen-Verlag, 1966. 227p. (Die Zeit Bücher) **1Z14**
Includes articles on Great Britain, Das Kontrollierte Chaos by John Calder; India, Zeit der Unsicherheit by Anand Mohan; Ireland, Nur die Blinden dürfan alles Lesen; and United States, Die Subversive Rolle der Pornographie by Fred Jordan.

Zimmer, Steven L. "How One Southern City Faced the Obscenity Standards Issue." *Christian Century*, 91: 884–86, 25 September 1974. **1Z15**
An analysis of the work of the Jefferson County (Ky.) Commission on Community Standards Related to Obscenity and the response to a request for citizen opinions.

Zimmering, Paul L. "Liability for Defamation of Private Persons—New Standards." *Tulane Law Review*, 49:685–91, March 1975. **1Z16**
Re: *Gertz v. Robert Welch, Inc.*, 418 U.S. 323 (1974).

Ziobert, Felix J., Jr. "Fair Trial and Free Press—State Court Contempt Power." *Western Reserve Law Review*, 18:1376–84, May 1967. **1Z17**
The Arizona Supreme Court in *Phoenix Newspaper, Inc. v. Superior Court*, 418 P.2d 594, Arizona (1966) held that the lower court could not, in advance of publication, limit the petitioner's right to print the news and inform the public of matters which had occurred in open court in the course of a judicial hearing. The contempt order of the lower court was held to violate the Arizona constitution.

Zive, Gregg W. "Prior Restraint and the Press Following the *Pentagon Papers* Cases—Is the Immunity Dissolving?" *Notre Dame Lawyer*, 47:927–58, April 1972. **1Z18**
The author believes that while the press still

enjoys freedom from the imposition of prior restraints, "the *Pentagon Papers* cases have opened avenues on which restraints might be able to travel in the future, resulting in a narrowing of the liberty of the press. . . . It is apparent that the Court will no longer find all manner of prior restraint to be invalid; the only question is how far the Court is going to go in shedding the doctrine of prior restraint as a constitutional shield for the press."

Zolna, Bruce. "The Continuing Problem of Prior Restraints." *DePaul Law Review*, 21:822–42, Spring 1972. **1Z19**
"It is the objective of this note to present a brief historical outline of the overall constitutional problem involved in *Sperry* [*State ex rel. Superior Court of Snohomish County v. Sperry*, 79 Wash. 2d 69, 483 P.2d 608 (1971)], to familiarize the reader with the legal reasoning used by the Washington Supreme Court in arriving at its decision, and to survey the recent major decisions which have dealt with various aspects of the constitutional problem involved." The case involved a contempt of court charge against two reporters for violating a pretrial order.

Zubras, Joan A. "Gertz v. Welch: Reviving the Libel Action." *Temple Law Quarterly*, 48:450–70, Winter 1975. **1Z20**
The author concludes that it is "unlikely that the revitalizing of the libel action under *Gertz* [*Gertz v. Welch* (1974)] as an effective private remedy for injury to reputation will cause the financial demise of newspapers. . . . If the situation arises in which small newspapers are not amply protected by *Gertz*, then the First Amendment can be utilized to eliminate punitive damages altogether."

Zuckerman, David. " 'Dirty Linen' at CBS." *MORE*, 3(7):3–4, July 1973. **1Z21**
"Some at the network [Columbia Broadcasting System] thought the public might like to know about the internal debate over 'instant analysis' following televised speeches by the President, but top management decided it was bad news."

Zuckerman, Marvin. "Physiological Measures of Sexual Arousal in the Human." *Technical Report of the [U.S.] Commission on Obscenity and Pornography*, 1:61–101, 1971. **1Z22**
The paper explores the technical problems of physiological measurement and served as a guide to the Commission in developing its research program.

Zuidema, Henry P. "Why Parent 'Minutemen' Are Taking Up Arms in Defense of Their Children." *Liberty*, 71:10–13, January–February 1976. **1Z23**
Criticism of the "fog of hypocrisy and hokum" surrounding the textbook controversy in West Virginia, in which local groups, outside investigators, and the media, and the publishers

shared. Legal and professional pressures to include multicultural and multiethnic materials in school textbooks, with values that conflicted with local mores was the central issue. Also at issue was the right of parents to have a voice in the selection of textbooks used by their children. The author accuses a group of multiethnic-text promoters who complained of book burning, of suppressing other texts that conflicted with their views.

Zurcher, Louis A. "Political Efficacy, Political Trust, and Anti-Pornography Crusading: A Research Note." *Sociology and Social Research*, 56:211–20, January 1972. **1Z24**
"Gamson's proposition [W. A. Gamson, *Power and Discontent*] that optimum conditions exist for the mobilization of citizen political action when citizens report a high degree of political efficacy and a low degree of political trust was tested with interview data from active and control participants in two anti-pornography crusades. The results are interpreted as supporting Gamson's proposition and as demonstrating that it applies to citizen-action which is change-resistant and to the right of political center." The article is based upon research conducted under contract with the [U.S.] Commission on Obscenity and Pornography. (W. A. Gamson, *Power and Discontent*. Homewood, Ill., Dorsey, 1968.)

———, and Robert G. Cushing. "Participants in Ad Hoc Antipornography Organizations: Some Individual Characteristics." *Technical Report of the [U.S.] Commission on Obscenity and Pornography*, 5:143–215, 1971. **1Z25**
The authors describe the characteristics of members of two ad hoc citizens' organizations, formed to combat pornography, and compare these with individuals in the same communities who oppose the organizations and others who are more neutral on the issue.

Zurcher, Louis A., and R. George Kirkpatrick. *Citizens for Decency: Antipornography Crusades as Status Defense*. By Louis A. Zurcher, Jr. and R. George Kirkpatrick with the Collaboration of Robert C. Cushing, Charles K. Bowman, Ronald D. Birkelback, Adreain Ross, Susan Lee Zurcher, Russell L. Curtis. Austin, Tex., University of Texas Press, 1976. 412p. **1Z26**
The book is based upon intensive case histories of two antipornography crusades and extensive interviews with their most central participants and opponents. The authors consider it the first systematic, comprehensive, comparative, and theory-oriented study of antipornography crusades. It provides an "in-depth analysis of antipornography efforts as symbolic-status and norm-oriented movements in a context of social change." It presents "a contemporary example of the process of citizens' attempts to

influence social legislation" and an example of citizen voluntarism. Among the important findings, the authors show that antipornography crusaders are people discontented with their status who have mobilized to protect the dominance and prestige of their traditional life styles.

———. "Collective Dynamics of Ad Hoc Antipornography Organization." *Technical Report of the ₍U.S.₎ Commission on Obscenity and Pornography*, 5:83–141, 1971.   **1Z27**
The investigators compare two ad hoc citizens' groups, organized to fight pornography and analyze the dynamics of their development and functioning. "The paper is based on detailed 'natural histories' of the two organizations, which in turn are based on personal observation, intensive interview, and examination of organization records."

Zurcher, Louis A. *et al.* "Ad Hoc Antipornography Organizations and Their Active Members: A Research Summary." *Journal of Social Issues*, 29(3):69–94, 1973.   **1Z28**
This paper summarizes an intensive field study of two ad hoc antipornography organizations, the campaigns they conducted, and their leaders and active participants. Comparative analysis of the two antipornography campaigns revealed the social structure of the "conporn" and "proporn" organizations involved in the campaigns.

———. "The Anti-Pornography Campaign: A Symbolic Crusade." *Social Problems*, 19:217–38, Fall 1971.
                                    1Z29
"The natural histories of the two antipornography campaigns (Midville and Southtown) are analyzed comparatively in the frameworks suggested by Smelser's (1962) theory of collective behavior and Gusfield's (1963) dramatistic theory of status politics. Both the Midville and Southtown campaigns are found, as hypothesized, to be norm-oriented social movements and symbolic crusades, and developmentally to fit the value-added stages of collective behavior. Active participants in the campaigns (Conporns) are found, again as hypothesized, to be status discontents defending the dominance and prestige of a life style to which they were committed, and to differ markedly from opponents to the campaign (Proporns) in selected demographic characteristics."

Zwerdling, Daniel, and David Sanford. "The Right to Be Seen and Heard." *New Republic*, 163(3):15–17 18 July 1970.   **1Z30**
Zwerdling discusses proposed restrictions on political candidate spending on television ads and Sanford discusses the right of antiwar groups to air their views under the fairness doctrine.

Zwerin, Michael. "London, My Favorite Censor." *Village Voice*, 16(2):35, 46, 14 January 1971.   **1Z31**
An interview with England's film censor, John Trevelyan, compassionate, intelligent, urbane, but super-establishment, and how the system works.

———. "London Obscenity Carnival." *Village Voice*, 16(30):19, 27, 29 July 1971.   **1Z32**
An account of the *OZ* obscenity trial at the Old Bailey. *OZ* is a British underground paper.

INDEX

ERRATA in the 1968 Edition

INDEX

THIS INDEX IS INTENDED to bring out the multifaceted nature of the entries, so that an article on customs censorship of an obscene book in Australia may be located under *Australia, Customs censorship,* and *Obscenity and pornography,* as well as under the title of the censored volume and, if appropriate, the name of the court case. Banned books are listed under their titles and not their authors, unless the author as well as his book, is under discussion. For the more important twentieth-century court cases a complete citation to the published decision is given in the index, for example, *Nebraska Press Association v. Stuart,* 423 U.S. 1319 (1976); for earlier cases and decisions of lower courts, only the date is given. The author of a book or article entered in the bibliocyclopedia is not generally included in the index since his work can be located alphabetically in the text. But joint authors of portions of a collected work are indexed.

Abbas, K. A., 1R36

ABC Books, Inc. et al. v. Benson, 315 F. Supp. 695 (D. C. Tenn. 1970), 1S473

Abel, Elie, 1R272, 1U100

Abell, Jeffrey M., 1W61

Abelson, Herbert I., 1A8, 1W280

Abolitionist press: 1D200; Beach (Thomas P.) imprisonment, 1B156; Cincinnati Committee of Vigilance, 1T67; Crandall (Dr. Reuben) trial, 1K106; expurgation of abolitionist ideas from literature, 1T147; libel cases, 1W257; Lovejoy (Elijah P.) martyrdom, 1H276, 1L283, 1M210, 1N143, 1S261, 1T132, 1W54, 1W309; martyr complex, 1W309; Parker (Theodore) case, 1P24; postal restrictions, 1T67

Abortion: advertisement of referral service, 1B24, 1C425, 1F97, 1K202, 1L217, 1M286, 1M390, 1N112, 1W291

Abrams, Floyd, 1A14, 1P258, 1R272

Abrams v. United States, 250 U.S. 616 (1919), 1K22, 1R6, 1W343

Abuses Stript and Whipt (George Wither), 1P293

Abzug, Bella S., 1S650

Academic freedom: 1D176; campus speakers, 1E144, 1I52, 1K55, 1T96, 1Y3; casebook, 1D177; First Amendment implications, 1E71, 1S460, 1T200; libel and, 1R218; MacIver (Robert M.) on, 1M82; Meyer (Agnes E.) on, 1M297; Russell (Bertrand) case 1D111; schools, colleges, and libraries, 1C346, 1M82; Shockley (William) dissent, 1I52, 1Y3; testimonial immunity, 1H204. *See also* College and university publications

Access of public to the mass media. *See* Public access to the mass media

Accuracy in Media, Inc. (AIM), 1A1, 1E91, 1H173, 1I49, 1K14, 1M444

Accuser Sham'd, The (John Fry), 1G240

Acheson, David C., 1R251

Achilli v. Newman (1852), 1N100

Achwal, Madhao B., 1S194

Actes and Monuments (John Foxe), 1C70

Action for Children's Television (ACT): 1E49, 1H87, 1L96, 1R23, 1S496; congressional testimony, 1U43, 1U77

Adams, Roy, 1D185

Adams, Thomas: trial of, 1S547

Aday v. United States, 388 U.S. 447 (1967), 1F133

Adler, Renata, 1D14

Administrative proceedings: broadcast of, 1B213

Adolescent reader, freedom for: 1D166, 1D169, 1F33, 1F220, 1F323, 1G54, 1H176, 1O8; constitutional basis, 1T189; moot court exercise, 1M199; opinions of high school students, 1L272

Adventures of the Black Girl in Her Search for God (G. B. Shaw), 1S223

Adversaries, The (William L. Rivers), review of, 1A223

Advertise, the right to: 1D108, 1D182, 1D220, 1E19, 1M316, 1P164; abortion, 1B24, 1C425, 1F97, 1K202, 1L217, 1M286, 1M390, 1N112, 1W291; book advertisements, 1M32, 1P156; British case (1815), 1G196; drug prices, 1A58, 1B2, 1B24, 1C341, 1D62, 1D215, 1L104, 1M286, 1M510, 1N112, 1P26, 1R246, 1S26, 1S415, 1S612, 1W291; First Amendment protection, 1B24, 1C425, 1F97, 1L238, 1M286, 1M390, 1P164, 1P258–59, 1R51, 1R67, 1W137, 1W291; professionals (lawyers, physicians), 1A199, 1L108. *See also* Advertising, political

Advertisers, control of media by: 1H56, 1H344; charges denied, 1S24; hunting industry, 1F305; patent medicine companies, 1A36; reader's freedom violated, 1G187; television programming, 1C171, 1C231, 1J68

Advertising, broadcast: 1M245; access rights, 1B159, 1B169, 1D220, 1F99, 1F253, 1K69, 1K151, 1M316, 1P83, 1R67, 1R104, 1R106, 1T122; Canadian Broadcasting Co., 1N56; children-oriented, 1B602, 1P247, 1S496, 1U43; cigarette commercials, 1E103, 1F22, 1L305, 1L318, 1P187, 1U42; code and standards, 1G314, 1I16; controls on, 1A191, 1H179, 1J43, 1K95, 1L246, 1L269, 1P335, 1S358; controls on (Canada), 1N56; criticism of intrusion, 1K210; cultural aspects, 1J98; fairness doctrine and, 1E19, 1E57, 1F22, 1F43, 1G1, 1G134, 1H65, 1J14, 1K262, 1L133, 1L163, 1M393, 1P335, 1R30, 1R45, 1S319, 1S353, 1W77, 1Z13; Great Britain, 1M198, 1O41, 1W325; liability, 1P258, 1W137; medical products and services, 1P246; political advertising restricted, 1G203, 1J71, 1S613, 1W207, 1Z30; programming influence, 1B142, 1C171, 1C231, 1G192, 1J68, 1S24; violence in programming, sponsorship of, 1S323. *See also* Advertise, the right to; Advertising, control of

Advertising, control of: 1H16, 1L256, 1M59, 1M521, 1R66; *Banzhaf v. FCC,* 1G1, 1L318, 1M417; British law, 1L84; *Business Executives' Move for Vietnam Peace v. FCC,* 1B159, 1F99, 1K69, 1K151, 1P83, 1P178; corporate image advertising, 1B283, 1R69; debaters' guide, 1C367; editors' attitudes toward, 1H206; environmental issues, 1S43, 1S45; Federal Trade Commission role, 1A62, 1D41, 1D61, 1D243, 1F165, 1J43, 1L246, 1M186, 1M346, 1P14, 1P235, 1R53, 1R66–67, 1R307, 1S358; First Amendment protection, 1B24, 1B151, 1E103, 1F97, 1G186, 1L217, 1L238, 1L270, 1M286, 1M390, 1O32, 1P164, 1P258–59, 1R67, 1W137, 1W291; history, 1T184; Independent Broadcasting Authority (Great Britain), 1M198; National Advertising Review Board, 1M76; pandering, 1A5, 1E20, 1H363, 1J37, 1L302, 1T89; *Pittsburgh Press Co. v. Pittsburgh Commission on Human Rights,* 1B326, 1B531, 1F109, 1H64, 1K39, 1L215, 1L270, 1R279, 1S107, 1T159; psychological impact, 1R53; rejection rights, 1B159, 1F99, 1K69, 1K151, 1P83, 1P178, 1R46, 1S43, 1S45, 1S353, 1T105; self-regulation, 1B25, 1G288, 1S584; state regulations, 1R66; worldwide practices, 1S584

Advertising, corrective: 1C338–40; Federal Trade Commission formula, 1A174, 1C339, 1D243, 1P14

Advertising, counter: 1C258, 1D55, 1E57, 1G261, 1G311, 1H16, 1H65, 1K262, 1L249, 1M255, 1O27, 1S67, 1T43, 1Z13; *Friends of the Earth v. FCC,* 1B94, 1C125, 1F17, 1G26, 1K281, 1L279, 1M417, 1R45, 1S319, 1T48, 1W200

Advertising, deceptive: 1D61; Canadian law, 1F122, 1S632; consumer cycles, 1R49; Federal Trade Commission regulations, 1A62, 1D41, 1M186, 1M346, 1S358; puffery, 1P278; self-regulations, 1B141

Advertising, editorial: 1B511, 1D220, 1M124, 1M257–58, 1M316, 1W77; *Business Executives' Move for Vietnam Peace v. FCC,* 1B159, 1F99, 1J71, 1K69, 1K151, 1P83, 1P178; *Chicago Joint Board, Amalgamated Clothing Workers of America v. Chicago Tribune,* 1H41, 1S589; *Columbia Broadcasting System, Inc. v. Democratic National Committee,* 1B486, 1C43, 1C337, 1G134, 1H75, 1K5, 1L206, 1L215, 1M203, 1M520, 1P310, 1P319, 1S228, 1T159, 1W113, 1W263; *Wirta v. Alameda-Contra Costa Transit District,* 1B584, 1M483

Advertising, motion picture: codes, 1W214; modification of, 1E11; rejection of X-rated film, 1G294, 1H144, 1R46

Advertising, newspaper: access, right of, 1B169,

1C287, 1C320, 1D9, 1D12–13, 1D15, 1D125, 1D217, 1D246, 1F106, 1F110, 1F281, 1F296, 1G215, 1H304, 1H319, 1H387, 1H418, 1J1, 1O90, 1S49, 1S95, 1T122, 1W201; anti-cigarette advertising law, 1P213; censorship of, criticizing British unions, 1A54; Colonial press (United States), 1S222; Great Britain, 1L84; influence on newspaper policy, 1A36, 1H56, 1H344, 1H406, 1S24; liability, 1P258; right to reject, 1D182, 1G294, 1H41, 1H49, 1H144, 1K9, 1M59, 1R46, 1S589, 1T105; standards, 1G319, 1W290; *Ublman v. Sherman*, 1H49. *See also Miami Herald Publishing Co. v. Tornillo; Pittsburg Press Co. v. Pittsburgh Commission on Human Relations*

Advertising, outdoor. See Billboards

Advertising, political: 1J71, 1W207; campaign financing restrictions, 1F66, 1H336, 1K120, 1L68, 1R50, 1R103–4, 1S613, 1W207, 1Z30; fairness doctrine, 1E19, 1F22, 1F43, 1G1, 1H65, 1J14, 1K262, 1L133, 1L163, 1M393, 1P335, 1R30, 1R45, 1S319, 1S353, 1W77, 1Z13; *Lehman v. City of Shaker Heights*, 1F281; Massachusetts, 1S248. *See also Business Executives' Move for Vietnam Peace v. FCC; Columbia Broadcasting System, Inc. v. Democratic National Committee; Reply, right of*

Advertising, salacious: movie ads touched up, 1E11; porn-film ads rejected, 1G294, 1H144, 1R46; prohibited from mails (bill), 1U59, 1U104–5

Advertising industry, criticism of: book rejected by Reader's Digest Association, 1B32, 1S365

Advertising tax (Great Britain): abolition of, favored (1831), 1M52

Advertising tax (United States): Thomas (Isaiah) on, 1T64

Advocacy journalism: 1B52, 1D117, 1F150, 1H441, 1J58, 1K94, 1M284, 1N80, 1N152, 1S491, 1W66; limits of, 1S621; muckraking, 1M116, 1S171; opposition to, 1B535, 1B556, 1C175, 1W85; support for, 1A224, 1A227, 1H200

African nations: freedom of the press in, 1J109. *See also* Rhodesia; South Africa

Age of Reason (Thomas Paine), 1H138

Agnew, Spiro (Vice-President): attacks on the news media, 1A47–51, 1B39, 1B100, 1B485, 1D27, 1F126, 1F181, 1K96, 1K107, 1K229, 1L159, 1L297, 1M10, 1M169, 1M354, 1P256, 1R78, 1R146, 1S21, 1S23, 1S27, 1S183–84, 1S437, 1S558, 1V4; *Baltimore Sun* article on, killed, 1C219; Boston talk (text), 1A48; criticizes attack on press, 1E12, 1F26, 1F298–99, 1F322, 1I57, 1M503, 1P256, 1R146, 1S21, 1S23, 1S27, 1S183–84; Des Moines talk (text), 1A49, 1R146; effect of attack on newscasts, 1L303; Jewish control of press charged, 1B286; Montgomery talk (text), 1A50, 1R146; relationship with press, 1B172; supports attack on press, 1D129, 1E131, 1I57, 1K67, 1S101. *See also* Nixon (President Richard M.) Administration

Ahmad, Iqbal, 1H32

Aiton v. McCulloch (1823), 1M51

Alabama: newsmen's financial disclosure law, 1A97; obscenity law, 1V13

Alberta, Canada: Padlock Act, 1K104; Press Code case, 1M63

Alberts v. State of California, 354 U.S. 476 (1957), 1F288, 1W63, 1W107

Aldrich, Robert, 1D132

Alien and Sedition Acts. See Sedition Act of 1798

Alien Registration Act of 1940 (Smith Act), 1B180, 1P65

Alin, Roy, 1W351

Allain, Alex P., 1A81–83, 1I6, 1M418

Allen, Florence E., 1H345

Allen, Lee E., 1N81

Almon, John, 1A93–94, 1C282, 1W51, 1W321

Alpert, Hollis, 1A95, 1H101

Alsop, Joseph W., Jr., 1C81

Alsop, Stewart, 1R146

Alternative (dissident) press: 1A224, 1F150, 1F179, 1L182, 1N65, 1T30, 1W209; accreditation of, 1T194; *Ativar*, 1G165; ban of establishment press reporters,

1D112; *Berkeley Barb*, 1R130; *Branzburg v. Hayes* effect on, 1H424; checklist, 1A28, 1K75, 1W209, 1W331; *Chicago Seed*, 1G71; college campuses, 1L11, 1L315; disenchantment with, 1G91; *Georgia Straight* (Vancouver), 1B595, 1P243; harassment of, 1E118, 1I59, 1W192; high school papers, 1B196, 1D138, 1F55, 1G61, 1H223, 1H398, 1H427, 1L129, 1S610, 1T135, 1T160; history and development, 1J58, 1L83; *Kaleidoscope*, 1B581, 1K208, 1P55; legal status, 1I50; libraries ignore, 1J104; *Los Angeles Free Press*, 1B299, 1I59; military camp, 1P138; Minneapolis Public Library, 1G7; Missouri librarian fired for defending, 1A133, 1E117, 1L11, 1M99, 1S259; *Open City* (Los Angeles), 1F64; *Papish v. Board of Curators*, 1B104, 1T10; *St. Louis Free Press*, 1L200; sex oriented, 1T26; social and political control, 1E118; study of, 1E118, 1G127

Alternative Journalism Review, The, 1W209

Amalgamated Food Employees Union Local 509 et al. v. Logan Valley Plaza, Inc. et al., 391 U.S. 308 (1968), 1H188, 1L181, 1O92

America Hurrah (J. C. Van Itallie), 1A279

American Bar Association: ban on lawyer advertising, 1L108; freedom of the campus press, 1S526; secrecy in government testimony, 1U96

American Bar Association, Canon 35. *See* Photography in the courtroom

American Bar Association, Reardon Report. *See* Fair trial v. free press

American Book Publishers Council: 1M188, 1U64; obscenity law testimony, 1U64, 1U70

American Booksellers Association, 1N153

American Broadcasting Co.: Monty Python editing suit, 1H219

American Broadcasting-Paramount Theaters, Inc. et al. v. Simpson, 126 S.E.2d 873 (1962), 1R11

American Civil Liberties Union: broadcast license renewal testimony, 1U77; fair trial and free press statement, 1A120, 1F11, 1H370, 1P67; Freedom of Information Act, 1A119; freedom of speech, 1M497; freedom of the press testimony, 1U100; obscenity law testimony, 1U64, 1U68, 1U70, 1U106; public access to media, 1C383, 1D15, 1S538; public broadcasting report, 1P257; secrecy in government testimony, 1U96; student publications, 1S526; wartime restrictions opposed, 1A116, 1J51

American Civil Liberties Union, Inc. v. Jennings, 366 F. Supp. 1041 (D.C. Cir. 1973), 1R103

American Legion: obscenity law testimony, 1U70

American Library Association: access of minors to library material, 1A136, 1F37, 1S258; Bodger (Joan) investigation, 1A133; challenged library material, 1A142; confidentiality of borrower records, 1A138; copyright statement, 1A131; Criminal Code revision statement, 1A134; expurgation of library material, 1A135; governmental intimidation of dissenters, 1A143; intellectual freedom role, 1A149, 1B240, 1C84, 1D22, 1F321, 1G52–53, 1H134–36, 1K235, 1K238, 1K248, 1L7, 1M188, 1M410, 1M475, 1N158; *Kaplan v. California* brief, 1A132; labeling, 1A146; newsmen's privilege testimony, 1U65–66; obscenity legislation, 1A132, 1A151–52, 1K244, 1M386; public records, policy on, 1A141; reevaluation of library collections, 1A140, 1F37; restricted access to library material, 1A144, 1B585; sanctions against violators of intellectual freedom, 1A139; sexism, racism, and other "isms" in library material, 1A145; state obscenity laws, 1A152; *Williams and Wilkins* brief, 1A131. *See also* Library Bill of Rights

American Newspaper Publishers Association: broadcast license renewal testimony, 1U77; fair trial v. free press statement, 1H370, 1R7, 1T100; freedom of the press testimony, 1U100; history, 1E72; newsmen's privilege testimony, 1U65–66, 1U101

American Revolution: newspaper censorship in Philadelphia, 1T36

American Socialist, 1J51

American Society of Newspaper Editors: 1A155, 1F116, 1H430, 1T104; newsmen's privilege testimony, 1U65–66

American Tragedy, An (Theodore Dreiser), 1B420, 1G287, 1H152

Ames, William E., 1A252

Ames v. Hazard (1862), 1B301

Amis, Kingsley, 1L268

Anarchist Cookbook (William Powell), 1B184

Anarchist publications, censorship of: Chicago Haymarket bombing case, 1Z5; favored, 1M224; Govan (Charles L.) arrest, 1H85; *Herald of Revolt*, 1A72; New York criminal anarchy law, 1P216; Olivereau (Louise) trial, 1O51

Anatole France Himself (J. J. Brousson), 1P212

Anderson, Burnett F., 1B583

Anderson, Daniel, 1H420

Anderson, Harold, 1G206, 1U100

Anderson, Jack, 1A177–78, 1M444

Anderson, Joseph J., 1A182, 1G193

Anderson, Margaret, 1A184–85, 1B420

Anderson v. New York Telephone Co., 345 N.Y.S.2d 740 (1973), 1S552

Anderson v. Rintoul (1824), 1B199

Anderton, William: trial of, 1G225

Andrews, Linton (Sir), 1W241

Animal Farm (George Orwell): introduction suppressed, 1C397, 1K207, 1O77

Annals of Jamaica, The, 1M509

Annet, Peter: trial of, 1T196

Ann Veronica (H. G. Wells), 1C366

Anonymity for journalist, publishers: Chester (G. K.) opposes, 1C137; state laws against proposed, 1M177; Tennessee law prohibiting, 1R34

Anonymity for juveniles. *See* Juveniles

Another Country (James Baldwin), 1B332

Answer, The (James Chidley), 1H354

Anthropologists: suppression of data on aborigines rites, 1S41

Anti-communist book: attack on, 1S567

Anti-Defamation League of B'nai B'rith: 1A272, 1K24; censorship activities criticized, 1W251; libel suit against, 1O89

Anti-Imperialist, 1A264

Anti-Universalist, 1B3

Appeal to Reason, 1J51

Apple, Raymond, 1L268

Archer, William, 1B148

Areopagitica (John Milton): 1C70, 1F277, 1M337, 1M347–49; modern implications, 1S455; South African censorship flouts, 1H402

Argentina: libel laws of, 1D32

Arizona: contempt of court case, 1P11; fair trial v. free press, 1B370, 1Z17; open meetings law, 1F250, 1J40, 1M208, 1M366; public records law, 1F250, 1J40, 1M208, 1M366; school library censorship, 1D153–54, 1D169, 1F191, 1K282; school newspapers (survey), 1J21; shield law, 1M208

Arizona Biochemical Co. v. Hearst Corp., 302 F. Supp. 412 (S.D.N.Y. 1969), 1P157

Arkansas: blasphemy, 1H27; Freedom of Information Act, 1T68; obscenity law, 1B66

Arkes, Hadley, 1A208, 1K271

Armour, Richard, 1M143

Arnold, Edmund R., 1A217, 1B196

Arnold, James W., 1H51

Arnold, Martin, 1D16

Arnold, Susan E., 1W336

Aroused (film), 1M202

Arrangement, The (Elia Kazan), 1B332

Art and morality. *See* Morality and art

Arthur, William B., 1A230–31, 1M246

Arts, censorship and the: 1H72, 1P47; copyright laws, regulations, 1F183; criticism and censorship, 1U2; Freedom of Vision Society, 1S573; moral aspects, 1B53; opposition to, 1B409; permissive society, 1M118, 1S185; philosophical issues, 1B474. *See also* Morality and art

Arts Council of Great Britain, report on obscenity laws: 1A233–34; British Society of Authors reaction to, 1A284; criticism of, 1J72; defense of, 1L157, 1P97

Art works, censorship of: 1C168; British museums, 1W89; Comstock (Anthony), 1B569, 1C279; Dondero (George A.) proposes, 1H132; Greek statues, 1L254; libraries, 1N101; Radich (Stephen) trial, 1B36; Rockford (Ill.), 1A86; social role performed, 1K102

Aryanization of the Jewish State (Michael Selzer), 1B514

Ashbee, Henry S.: bibliography of erotica, 1F313

Asher, Courtland M., 1A189

Butterfield, Gerald A., 1H304
Byrne, Robert, 1P245
Byrne et al. v. Karalexis et al., 401 U.S. 216 (1971), 1F132, 1J6, 1K37, 1M19, 1M378, 1P152
Byron, George Gordon. 6th Baron Byron: letters to his mother suppressed, 1D7; *Marino Faliero*, 1A246

CIA and the Cult of Intelligence, The (Victor Marchetti and John D. Marks), 1B281, 1E2, 1H408, 1M163
Cable television. *See* Radio and television broadcasting (United States)
Cahill, Robert V., 1A191, 1C7
Cain, J., 1W332
Cain (Lord Byron), 1M449, 1T111
Cairo, Ill.: press council, 1B310, 1S464, 1S466
Calcroft, John W. [pseud.], 1C247
Calder, John, 1C12–14, 1F189, 1M118, 1S633, 1Z14
Califano, Joseph, Jr., 1C19, 1S299
California: *Beard, The*, 1A196, 1C22; California League Enlisting Action Now (CLEAN), 1W285; evolution theory in textbooks, 1H80; fair trial v. free press, 1F72, 1S314, 1S419, 1W347; intellectual freedom in libraries, 1M411, 1M452; libel law, 1A80, 1G141; motion picture censorship, 1F30; newspaper gag orders, 1F87, 1W61; obscenity and pornography industry, 1B403, 1F90, 1L285, 1R4; obscenity decisions of courts impact on, 1L110; obscenity law, 1A7, 1A151, 1C20, 1C24, 1C59, 1C124, 1F146, 1G133, 1K233, 1N111, 1P175, 1S133, 1T128, 1W156, 1W264, 1W285; open meetings law, 1B340, 1J27; photography in courtroom, 1C21, 1S313; privacy, right of, 1F6; public records law, 1B57, 1B340, 1S74; rightist pressure groups, 1W286; shield law, 1B552, 1P193, 1S137, 1T93; stage censorship, 1A196, 1C22, 1D118; student newspapers, freedom for, 1C23, 1G61; syndicalist (criminal) law, 1S266; textbook controversy, 1S81, 1S493, 1W286
California v. La Rue, 409 U.S. 109 (1972), 1D118
Callender, James T.: libel case, 1H102, 1J33, 1S547
Calley, William (Lt.): trial of, 1C214
Calumet College: censorship of newspaper, 1I2
Cambridge History of American Literature, 1P43
Cameron, Jane, 1H346
Campion, William, 1H270
Canada: advertising, deceptive, 1F122, 1S632; Bill of Rights (1960), 1M63; copyright law, 1K105; foreign policy news, 1F205; freedom of information, 1C37, 1D103, 1L67; freedom of the press, 1A259, 1C115, 1H360, 1K10, 1K104, 1M63, 1M86, 1S205; Freedom to Read Committee, 1F267–68; government administrative secrecy, 1S294; government and the press, 1A283, 1C37, 1S294; hate propaganda, 1A232, 1B481, 1C39–40, 1C232, 1F62, 1K29, 1M63, 1M78, 1S469, 1T12; Law Reform Commission report on obscenity, 1F188, 1F199, 1H140, 1M30, 1S32; libel, 1A259, 1B136, 1B595, 1F62, 1K104–5, 1P243, 1W105; mass media study, 1C38; newsmen's privilege to withhold news sources, 1G155; obscenity law, 1B77–78, 1B482, 1C36, 1C41, 1D30, 1F188, 1F199–200, 1F267–68, 1G200, 1H162, 1J11, 1K104–5, 1K232, 1L88, 1L154, 1M30, 1M63, 1M106, 1M333, 1P21, 1S20, 1S32, 1S408, 1T2, 1T50, 1W104; Official Secrets Act, 1C385, 1F205, 1K104; press council proposed, 1B149; privacy, right of, 1K105, 1P50
Canada, censorship in: Alberta Padlock Act, 1K104; Alberta Press Code case (1938), 1M63; British Columbia, 1B482–83, 1H413, 1K232; Criminal Code on false news, 1M106; Criminal Code on obscenity, 1L88, 1M63; Customs office, 1F268, 1M63, 1S451; laws relating to, 1L153; librarians attitudes toward, 1B463, 1E88; motion picture classification, 1G267; motion pictures, 1B349, 1B483, 1C28, 1H421, 1J45, 1K144, 1M109, 1M131, 1P218; obscenity, 1B482, 1K232, 1L88, 1M63; Ontario, 1E86, 1H421, 1J45, 1K144, 1M131; police censorship, 1F267; public library censorship, 1B463, 1E86, 1E88; Quebec, 1C28, 1H162, 1L14, 1P218; Quebec Padlock Act, 1K104, 1M63, 1M106; Saskatchewan, 1B349; stage censorship, 1F70, 1M379; textbook ban (British Columbia), 1H413
Canada, motion picture censorship: 1B349, 1B483, 1C28, 1H308, 1H421, 1J45, 1K144, 1M109, 1M131,

1P218; classification, 1B483, 1G267, 1P121; violence in, 1P280
Canada, newspapers: alternative press (list), 1W331; contempt of court, 1M94, 1M239, 1S263; fair trial v. free press, 1A259, 1G221, 1K104–5, 1P22; government regulation essential, 1T115; history, 1K104–5; law, 1D103, 1K105, 1L126; monopoly control, 1B142, 1C38, 1H191, 1L187, 1Q2; "October Crisis" reporting, 1A283; *R. v. Georgia Straight*, 1B595, 1P243; self-censorship, 1M106
Canada, radio and television broadcasting: 1P53; advertising regulations, 1N56; cable television, 1B254; children-oriented advertising, 1P247; controversial issues, 1B140, 1B142; criticism, 1B423; defamation on cable television, 1J49; fairness doctrine, 1M442; law and regulations, 1B139–40, 1B142, 1B179, 1L126; medical products and services, 1P246; motion pictures on, censored, 1J45; open-line radio programs, 1L155; ownership and control, study of, 1C38, 1T117; Parliamentary debate, 1D33; public access, 1B254, 1C37; violence on, 1C35
Canby, Henry S., 1F270
Canby, Vincent, 1D14
Candy (Terry Southern and Mason Hoffenberg), 1B332, 1O16, 1P249, 1R119
Canham, Erwin D., 1C45, 1F239
Canons of Journalism: 1B524, 1E121, 1G288, 1H190, 1H406, 1R161, 1S1, 1V47–48; American Society of Newspaper Editors, 1A155, 1C392; Associated Press Managing Editors Association, 1A250; codes of sixty-two countries, 1V47–48; compilation of (1922), 1M522; fair trials protected by, 1F73; labor union bargaining and, 1N69; Sigma Delta Chi code, 1S289; voluntary press codes, 1C384, 1C392. *See also* Fair trial v. free press
Canons of Judicial Ethics, American Bar Association, Canon 20. *See* Fair trial v. free press
Canons of Judicial Ethics, American Bar Association, Canon 35. *See* Photography in courtroom; Radio and television broadcasting (United States)
Cantor, Muriel G., 1U124
Cantrell et al. v. Forest City Publishing Co. et al., 419 U.S. 245, 1L217
Captive, The (Eduard Bourdet), 1W306
Cardwell, Richard W., 1M246
Carey v. Hume, 492 F.2d 631 (D.C. Cir. 1974), 1W75
Cargas, Harry J., 1R146
Carhart, Thaddeus, 1B181
Carlile, Mary Anne, 1T57
Carlile, Richard: 1B207; association with radical surgeons, 1B498; birth control pioneer, 1H270, 1W316; trial, 1B207, 1C15, 1F177, 1F202, 1H100, 1H338, 1W51
Carlson, Rick J., 1A244, 1C105
Carnal Knowledge (film), 1A263, 1O15, 1P162, 1R9, 1S104
Carpenter, William, 1H338
Carpetbaggers, The (Harold Robbins), 1D238
Cartoons, caricatures: eighteenth-century England, 1T57, 1W51; Herblock on censorship, 1B327; libel case involving, 1F61
Cartwright, John (Major): 1C282, 1O78
Carus-Wilson, E. C., 1C255
Cassell & Co., Ltd. v. Broome and Another, (1972) 1 All E.R. 801, 1G95
Catcher in the Rye, The (J. D. Salinger), 1F80, 1H278, 1K48, 1K185, 1M98, 1N30, 1P5, 1S652, 1W108, 1W179–80
Cater, Douglass, 1C87, 1R160, 1T192
Catherwood, Frederick (Sir), 1L268
Catholic Church, censorship of: anti-Catholic literature, 1L273, 1O87; Australia, 1H156; birth control information, 1B313, 1D122; history, 1R288; *Index Librorum Prohibitorum*, 1C70, 1H423, 1P48, 1R202, 1S234; Ireland, 1C88, 1C315, 1H491, 1O14, 1R301, 1S238, 1S244; Legion of Decency, 1B51, 1C332–33, 1P111, 1R80, 1S134; *Love Book, The*, 1K218; obscenity, 1H147, 1H259, 1L107, 1M369, 1M496, 1P56, 1Q9, 1R138; opposition to, 1H43, 1S179, 1S634; prior censorship (civil and canon law), 1N74–75; reading by Catholics, 1L317, 1S165, 1S234, 1S244; review of film replaces ratings, 1P121; seminarians and intellectual freedom, 1W55; textbooks, 1M101; U.S.

Catholic Conference on press freedom, 1U129
Catholic press: censorship of priest-editor, 1A27; intellectual freedom in, 1F128; secret printing, 1A90
Catmull, Joan, 1D169
Cato's Letters (Thomas Gordon and John Trenchard): 1H102; American colonists influenced by, 1B379, 1H439
Caughey, John W., 1R80
Caulfield, Bernard (Judge Sir), 1R234
Cenci, The (Percy B. Shelley), 1E51
Censors and censorship: 1O5; anti-pornography crusader (spoof), 1K58; attitude changes affected by, 1W336; Berkenhead (Sir John) as censor, 1T66; blind man as film censor, 1B31; *Causeway* anthology on, 1S290; characteristics, 1D158, 1D161; comic cuts, 1B19; confessions of censor (Australia), 1P120; Faber (Sir Geoffrey) on, 1G287; fictional account, 1F210, 1S3, 1W29; individual his own censor, 1B182; interview with censor (year 1999), 1S315; Joynson-Hicks (William) as censor, 1E31, 1T18; librarians attitudes toward, 1B402, 1K189, 1O5; memoirs of motion picture censor, 1V44; memoirs of television censor, 1A103, 1G282; Putnam (George P. II) on, 1G287; quips on film censorship, 1H42; satire and whimsy on, 1B467, 1E31, 1G146, 1G257, 1K186–87, 1P321, 1S506; Seldes (Gilbert) on, 1S174; Trevelyan (John) as censor, 1G267, 1R186, 1S583, 1T149–50, 1T153–55, 1Z31
Censorship: 1D4, 1T158; absurdity of, 1D82; anthropological basis for sex, 1O4–5; attitude changes resulting from, 1A245; bibliography, 1D149, 1D160, 1D169, 1M45; children's books, 1D21; criticism v., 1G25, 1M291; debaters' guide, 1C367, 1D216; education preferred to, 1H369; fiction dealing with, 1D150, 1D208, 1W27–28; history, 1A9, 1B345, 1K199, 1O5, 1O45, 1T158; ideas feared as basis for, 1A268, 1O5; imitation, concept of, 1W160; international efforts to abolish, 1G140; legal and nonlegal, 1G140; liberals' interpretation of, attacked, 1B456; logic and experience refute, 1M291; mathematical model, 1T176; Mill (John Stuart) on, 1A24; Milton (John) on, 1A24; moral choice violated by, 1M307; need for, not shown by research, 1B155; New Jersey, 1H40; philosophical issues, 1B474, 1D93, 1P112, 1T158; private morality controlled by, 1C390, 1G37, 1W104; pro and con, 1D4, 1H101, 1M292, 1M501; "psychical distance" theory, 1C415; rationalization of, 1A9, 1B245, 1C390, 1F24; readings, 1P112, 1W320; sacred and secular societies, 1F4; symposium, 1N14; traffic signs not analogous, 1H93; undemocratic assumptions, 1G4, 1O7; world problems may prompt, 1B134. *See also* Censors and censorship; Literature, censorship of (Great Britain); Literature, censorship of (United States); Public library censorship; School library and classroom censorship
Censorship (Australia): 1A221, 1B210, 1B369, 1B412, 1B476, 1C398, 1F75–76, 1H74, 1H400, 1O20, 1W93, 1W186, 1W332; absurdity of, 1D82; attitudes toward, 1V38; Catholic Church, 1H156; Colonial period, 1P305; confessions of a censor, 1P120; conformity behavior v., 1C50; Customs, 1H156, 1S588, 1W186; essays, 1H90; guide to, 1H35; licensing system proposed, 1W332; obscenity, 1A276, 1B445, 1B495, 1B661, 1C31, 1D82, 1D96, 1D238, 1F75–76, 1F197–200, 1G63, 1H35, 1H139, 1H354, 1K23, 1O16, 1P86, 1W332, 1W361; opposition to, 1A180, 1H156; quality control favored, 1C361; Queensland Literature Board of Review, 1Q3; security restrictions, 1C31, 1S435, 1W181; stage, 1A279, 1B495, 1C356, 1D238, 1H35, 1J86, 1S264; working-class movement, 1A181, 1H159
Censorship (Canada): Alberta Padlock Act, 1K104; Alberta Press Code case (1938), 1M63; British Columbia, 1B482–83, 1H413, 1K232; Criminal Code on false news, 1M106; Criminal Code on obscenity, 1L88, 1M63; criticism of public official, 1B534; Customs, 1F268, 1M63, 1S451; laws, 1K105, 1L126, 1L153; librarians' attitudes toward, 1B463, 1E88; mo-

multi-ethnic literature, 1S309; obscenity and profanity in, 1B53, 1M240, 1N58; panel discussion, 1M388; parents' role in textbook selection, 1D165, 1D171, 1J35, 1M350, 1S88, 1S145, 1T17, 1Z23; "penny dreadfuls" deplored, 1S571; picture books banned (spoof), 1N59; realism in, 1B320–21, 1D167, 1M388; role of librarians, children, parents, 1M238; sex interest in, 1M277; sexism and racism in, 1B490, 1H118, 1L32, 1M11–12, 1R280, 1S309, 1S493, 1Y14; standards in modern society, 1W258. *See also* School library and classroom censorship; Textbooks and assigned readings

Childress, Anne, 1G267, 1G269
Childs, Marquis, 1C81
Chiles, Lawton M., Jr. (Sen.), 1S650, 1U96
China, People's Republic of: broadcast censorship, 1E79; censorship of news from, 1A236
China Lobby in American Politics, The (Ross Y. Koen), 1K2
Chipp, Donald L., 1C141, 1S588
Chitre, Dilip, 1C142, 1S194
Choice Not an Echo, A (Phyllis Schafly), 1B332
Chopra, Pran, 1C144, 1F261
Christ (Sadakichi Hartmann), 1H109
Christianity Not Mysterious (John Toland), 1T195
Christian Observer, The, 1S201
Christian Science censorship: 1H25, 1J57; *Cambridge History of American Literature*, 1P43; *Life of Mary Baker Eddy*, 1P43
Christmas, G. R., 1I58
Christoph, James B., 1R247
Chronicles of England, Ireland and Scotland (Raphael Holinshed), 1C86
Church, Bud, 1C152, 1N81
Church and censorship: 1H126, 1P17, 1R288, 1S634; broadcasting fairness, 1F44, 1U9–11; censorship will not advance religion, 1H222, 1P180; Christian Science, 1H25, 1J57, 1P43; Church of England, 1C154; criticism v. censorship, 1D210; educational approach preferred, 1H369, 1R190; film discrimination awards, 1T164; Mormon doctrine, 1B182, 1V2; obscenity, pornography, and violence, 1B150, 1C154, 1C352, 1G279–80, 1G313, 1H43, 1H126, 1H222, 1H327, 1K154, 1K263, 1L80, 1M295, 1M496, 1P223–24, 1P226, 1P304, 1S375; permissive society, 1G305; radio program banned, 1G305; religious broadcasts (court decisions), 1N137; sex exploitation, 1G280
Church trials. *See* Heresy
Cincinnati: abolitionist literature ban, 1T67; anti-pornography campaign, 1A211; bible reading in schools, 1C155; comic book evaluation, 1M514; public library censorship, 1D213
Circulating libraries (Great Britain): *Anatole France Himself*, 1P212; Bennett (Arnold) on, 1B200–202, 1D45; censorship by, 1C156, 1P212; Circulating Libraries Association, 1C366, 1G276; Moore (George) and, 1M413–14; Mudie's Select Library, 1G276, 1K76; Times Book Club, 1C366
Citizens Committee to Save WEFM v. FCC, 506 F.2d 246 (D.C. Cir. 1974), 1V55, 1W128
Citizens Communications Center, 1B5
Citizens Communications Center et al. v. FCC, 477 F.2d 1201 (D.C. Cir. 1971), 1F5, 1I10, 1P58, 1W216
Citizens for Decency Through Law: 1A210–11, 1C163, 1M188, 1O5; criticism of, 1S407; obscenity law testimony, 1U64, 1U70
Citizens for Decent Literature. *See* Citizens for Decency Through Law
Civil Aeronautics Board: public records, 1W344
Civil disobedience: domesticated, 1B268
Civil War censorship (United States): 1P113; Boileau (Albert D.) arrest, 1S202; *Chicago Times*, 1C140; *Christian Observer, The*, 1S201; Confederate States of America, 1M209, 1T127; Holden (William W.), harassment, 1S218; Illinois newspapers, 1T92; Indiana copperhead papers, 1D126; Knox (Thomas W.), court-martial, 1M190; *Metropolitan Record, The* (New York), 1M479; *New York Herald*, 1M190; *New York Journal of Commerce*, 1M160–61; *New York World*, 1M160–61; Post Office seizure of newspapers, 1U57–58; Rosecrans (Gen. William S.), 1M479; Sherman (Gen. William T.), 1M190–91; South Carolina newspapers, 1T127; telegraph transmission of news, 1U60

Civilian Conservation Corps: book bans by, 1G199
Clark, Blair, 1A244, 1C105
Clark, David G., 1C171–72, 1H437, 1U124
Clark, Peter B., 1C116, 1C175, 1M246
Clark, Susan H., 1C177, 1D169
Clark, William, 1F205
Clarkson, Lawrence, 1W319
Classification of films. *See* Motion picture censorship (Great Britain); Motion picture censorship (United States)
"Clear and present danger" dictum: 1A157, 1A235, 1B354, 1C33, 1K22, 1S614, 1W107, 1W343; Communist conspiracy, 1C33; contempt of court by publication, 1G226, 1K81; evolution of, 1T91; Holmes (Justice Oliver W.) and Zechariah Chafee, Jr., on, 1R6; India press application, 1B49; influence of, 1S511, 1S587
Cleavinger, Howard C., 1C286
Cleland, John: trial of, 1C186, 1E96
Clemens, Samuel L., 1C285, 1E38, 1M269
Clergy, libel of: Fry (John) trial, 1G240; Williams (John Ambrose) trial, 1W245
Clergy in Their Colours, The (John Fry), 1G240
Cleveland Press: coverage of Sheppard murder trial, 1R121. *See also Sheppard v. Maxwell*
Clevenger, Theodore, Jr., 1R203
Clifford, George, 1A178
Clift, David, 1L7
Cline, Rebecca J., 1C190
Cline, Victor B., 1C191–97, 1U85, 1U92
Clockwork Orange (film): crime attributed to influence of, 1S444
Clor, Harry M., 1C198–206, 1H13
Cloud, Bill, 1M178
Cobbett, William: 1C380, 1D197, 1H100, 1J75, 1M151; *Rush-Light*, 1R281
Codes, self-regulation. *See* Canons of Journalism; Comic books; Motion picture censorship (United States); Radio and television broadcasting (Great Britain); Radio and television broadcasting (United States)
Coe, James, 1D169
Coe, Richard L., 1G269
Coffin, William Sloane, Jr.: trial of, 1M372
Cogley, John, 1C105
Cohen, David S., 1C221–22, 1S650
Cohen, Fred, 1P214
Cohen, Manuel F., 1P316
Cohen, Maxwell, 1F205
Cohen, Morris R., 1D111
Cohen, R., 1A8
Cohen v. California, 403 U.S. 15 (1971), 1W23
Cohn, Marcus, 1C237–38, 1C267
Cohn, Philip H., 1H168
Coleman, Peter, 1J87
Coleridge, John D. (Judge): blasphemous libel opinion, 1B560
College and university campuses: freedom of speech on, 1I52, 1K55, 1T96
College and university library censorship: 1C249, 1C346; case studies, 1A168; Conestoga College investigation, 1I35; McMurry College, 1G184; South Africa, 1M516, 1W126
College and university publications: administrator's dilemma, 1W178; alternative press, 1G165, 1L11, 1L315, 1R130; American Bar Association statement, 1S526; art exhibits, 1R129; Buchanan (Annette) case, 1B165, 1J56, 1N150, 1R97; California (University of) report, 1C23; Calumet College, 1I2; censorship and freedom of the press news, 1S645; censorship of, 1D221, 1N26, 1P205, 1S373; *Dickey v. Alabama State Board of Education*, 1R119; freedom for, 1A3–4, 1B243, 1C118, 1D214, 1D236, 1E138, 1F56, 1H57, 1H381, 1H388, 1H432, 1I24, 1K138, 1M270–71, 1P244, 1T134; guidelines, 1G88, 1P244; Ithaca College (*Ithacan*), 1B177; *Joyner v. Whiting* (North Carolina Central University), 1C409, 1K9; *Keyishian v. Board of Regents of the University of the State of New York*, 1B243; legal status, 1H57, 1S44, 1S526, 1S534; libel, 1C330, 1I24, 1S521, 1T126; *Mackinlay v. Wiley* (University of Western Australia), 1D119; Missouri (University of) case, 1B104, 1E117, 1L11, 1M99, 1S259, 1T10; *Montana Kaimen*, 1M123; National Council of College

Publication Advisors, report, 1I24; *Norton v. Discipline Committee of East Tennessee State University*, 1B61; *Panarella v. Birenbaum*, 1S251; *Parchment Conch* (Indiana University of Pennsylvania), 1V19; shield laws, 1S524; *Tharunka* (University of New South Wales), 1O16; *Tinker v. Des Moines School District*, implications of, 1R236
Collier, J. Payne, 1G250
Collier, Jeremy: attack on the stage, 1K255
Collins, Hal, 1S506
Colman, John: trial, 1B364
Colonial press censorship (United States): 1D200, 1F162, 1H102; advertising helps free press, 1S22; Boston newspapers, 1Y15–16; Bradford (Andrew) trial, 1D53; Bradford (William) trial, 1F162; British libertarian traditions influence, 1B379, 1H439; Fleet (Thomas), 1Y15; Franklin (James) trial, 1F162; Gaine (Hugh), 1L278; Massachusetts newspaper tax, 1T64; Oswald (Eleazer) trial, 1T37; search and seizure practices, 1T24; seditious libel, 1N62, 1T37; Zenger (John Peter) trial, 1B79, 1C370, 1E73, 1E77, 1F255, 1F257, 1G145, 1H102, 1K141, 1L57, 1L267, 1L282, 1M441, 1N93, 1P236, 1W343, 1Z12
Colonial speech censorship (United States): Penn (William) trial, 1P72
Colorado: courtroom broadcasting and telecasting, 1A130, 1H33; obscenity law, 1S545; school library censorship survey, 1S433
Columbia Broadcasting System, Inc.: *Columbia Broadcasting System, Inc. v. Democratic National Committee*, 1B486, 1C43, 1C337, 1G134, 1H75, 1K5, 1L206, 1L215, 1M203, 1M520, 1P310, 1P319, 1S228, 1T159, 1W113, 1W263; *Columbia Broadcasting System, Inc. v. FCC*, 1G20; *Columbia Broadcasting System, Inc. v. Vanderbilt University*, 1K114; congressional investigation of, 1L311, 1S348, 1U41, 1U55; Efron (Edith) study replicated, 1S543; Faulk (John H.) case, 1M300, 1R193, 1T6; Friendly (Fred W.) on, 1F294; *Hunger in America*, 1S348; national defense reporting criticized, 1L103; *News Twisters, The*, 1E24, 1E26–27, 1S22, 1S543, 1W287; Nixon attack on, 1D115, 1S21, 1W299; Project Nassau, 1L311, 1S348, 1U54; Salant (Richard S.) defends television, 1S21–25; *Selling of the Pentagon*, 1B101, 1B117, 1C265, 1D142, 1F69, 1F126, 1F181, 1F300, 1K7, 1M228, 1N19, 1R203, 1S250, 1S334, 1S348, 1S462, 1U41, 1U55, 1W215; Smothers Brothers program, 1F139, 1F223, 1G268, 1H205, 1K99, 1K158; Stanton (Frank) defends, 1S462, 1U41, 1U55; *United Medical Laboratories, Inc. v. Columbia Broadcasting System, Inc.*, 1P155; *United States v. Columbia Broadcasting System, Inc.*, 1C223, 1U130
Columbia Broadcasting System, Inc. v. Democratic National Committee, 412 U.S. 94 (1973), 1B486, 1C43, 1C337, 1G134, 1H75, 1K5, 1L206, 1L215, 1M203, 1M520, 1P310, 1P319, 1S228, 1T159, 1W113, 1W263
Columbia Broadcasting System, Inc. v. FCC, 454 F.2d 1018 (D.C. Cir. 1971), 1G20
Columbus of Sex (film), 1H308
Comeback Guy (C. H. Frick), 1W166
Comic books: Cincinnati Committee on Evaluation, 1M514; code of ethics, 1C269; harmful effect of, 1M476, 1W134
Commager, Henry S., 1C81
Commer, Hobart: trial of, 1L254
Commission on Freedom of the Press, Report of: press response to, 1L79; reevaluated, 1A252, 1B421, 1E81, 1F193, 1G167; study of, 1B551
Commonwealth (Mass.) et al. v. Wiseman, 249 N.E.2d 610 (1969), 1C248, 1P297
Commonwealth (Mass.) v. Friede, 171 N.E. 472 (1930), 1G108
Commonwealth (Mass.) v. Horton, 310 N.E.2d 316 (1974), 1A229
Commonwealth (Mass.) v. Origen Bacheler (1829), 1B3
Commonwealth (Pa.) v. Armao, 286 A.2d 626 (1972), 1F326
Commonwealth (Pa.) v. Dell Publishers, Inc., 233 A.2d 840 (1968), 1R119

ing Corp. and Another, 1D134; *MacLeod v. Wakley* (1827), 1S443; Martin-British Museum trial (1892), 1M49; Meyler (Mary) and Mulligan (Thomas) trial (1828), 1M302; *Mond v. Fraser and Beamish*, 1F224; *Monson v. Tussaud's* (1894), 1H444; Murray (John) trial (1829), 1M509; *Palmer v. Bull* (1823), 1B568; Phillips (Josiah) trial (1810), 1P123; *Poles (Stefan) v. The Times Newspaper* (1874), 1P204; Porter (John G. V.) trial (1859), 1P232; Potocki (Count G. W. V.), 1P237; *Private Eye*, 1I31; *QB VII*, novel based on, 1U132; *R. v. Almon* (1765), 1F196; *R. v. Douglas*, 1H444; *R. v. Parke* (1890), 1H444; *R. v. Pemberton-Billing*, 1H442, 1H444, 1P69; *Sitwell and Others v. Co-operative Press, Ltd., and Elliott*, 1L207; *Stopes v. Sutherland*, 1B287, 1B406, 1H444, 1S421, 1S625; *Taaffe v. Downes* (1813), 1F196; Thomson (Dr. Samuel) trial (1839), 1T82; *Times Literary Supplement*, 1G285; Tipper (Samuel) trial (1809), 1M151; *Tyrrell v. Wakley* (1825), 1S443; *Vitamins Ltd. et al. v. The Daily Telegraph et al.*, 1K90; *Voice of Labour*, 1D8; *Wakley v. Johnson* (1826), 1S443; Walker (Henry) libel on the king (1642), 1T20; *Walker v. Roberts* (1791), 1R176; Walter (John) trials (1789, 1821), 1W38–39; *Webster v. Baldwin* (1816), 1B37; *Whistler v. Ruskin* (1878), 1H444; Williams (John Ambrose) trial (1822), 1W245; *Wootton v. Sievier*, 1S421; Wright (Francis B.) trial (1809), 1W348; *Wright v. Gladstone*, 1H444. *See also* Blasphemous libel cases (Great Britain); Seditious libel (Great Britain)

Libel cases (Ireland): *Bagwell v. Power* (1804), 1P248; *Brabazon v. Potts* (1862), 1P240; Byrne (Robert) trial (1845), 1B615; Fitzsimons (Edward J. B. and John B.) trial (1813) 1F125; *Hardy v. Sullivan* (1862), 1S605; Johnston (Charles B.) and Hayden (Joseph T.) trials (1825), 1N133; *Lavelle (Patrick) v. Bole (John)* (1860), 1B362; *Magee v. O'Gorman* (1815), 1N139; *Travers v. Wilde* (1864), 1H444

Libel cases (Scotland): *Aiton v. McCulloch* (1823), 1M51; *Anderson v. Rintoul* (1824), 1B199; *Hamilton v. Stevenson* (1822), 1S541; *Kelso Mail* case (1833), 1P91

Libel cases (United States): *Ames v. Hazard* (1862), 1B301; *Arizona Biochemical Co. v. Hearst Corp.*, 1P157; *Associated Press v. Walker*, 1B290, 1D100, 1E37, 1K18, 1M420, 1M519, 1S325; *Bennett v. Buffalo Commercial Advertiser* (1870), 1M214; *Bouligny (R. H.) Inc. v. United Steelworkers*, 1E56; *Brinkley v. Fishbein*, 1F111; Buckingham (J. T.) trial (1822), 1B559; *Buffalonian, The* case, 1N114; *Burton v. Crowell Publishing Co.*, 1H59; *Cerrito v. Time, Inc.*, 1H332; Cheetham (James) trial (1807), 1L51; *Chicago (City of) v. Chicago Tribune*, 1B523, 1M36; Cobbett (William) trials (1797, 1799), 1D197; Colman (John) trial (1720), 1B364; *Commonwealth (Mass.) v. Origen Bacheler* (1829), 1B3; *Commonwealth (Pa.) v. Armao*, 1F326; Cooper (James F.) suits filed (1837–45), 1W43; *Curtis Publishing Co. v. Butts*, 1B290, 1D100, 1D106, 1E37, 1K18, 1M420, 1M519, 1S325; *Curtis Publishing Co. v. Golino*, 1F103; *Denton Publishing Co. v. Boyd*, 1E123; *Doe v. McMillan*, 1T159; *Farnsworth v. Tribune Co.*, 1D29, 1M27; *Ford v. Chicago Tribune*, 1L173; *Frick v. Stevens*, 1B126; *Garrison v. Louisiana*, 1B452, 1M359; *Gertz v. Robert Welch, Inc.*, 1A171–73, 1A192, 1A275, 1B259, 1B504, 1B596, 1C66, 1C310, 1D56, 1D64, 1E8, 1F204, 1F210, 1F281, 1G36, 1G68, 1G74, 1G76–78, 1G132, 1H50, 1H58, 1H216, 1H253, 1K196, 1K209, 1L44, 1L59, 1L143, 1M248, 1M293, 1M380, 1M420, 1N88, 1N146, 1P122, 1P171, 1R62, 1R178, 1R223–24, 1S6, 1S240, 1S332, 1S432, 1S442, 1S523, 1S564, 1S643, 1T131, 1T180, 1W103, 1W183, 1Y4, 1Z16, 1Z20; *Gibler v. The Houston Post*, 1B507; *Grayson v. Curtis Publishing Co.*, 1P267; *Greenbelt Cooperative Publishing Association, Inc. v. Bresler*, 1H61; *Greene v. Moore and Sevey* (1833), 1M408; *Hutchinson v. Kendall* (1836), 1K87; *Jones v. Commercial Printing Co.*, 1J77; Kalaw (Teodoro M.) case (Philippines), 1K11; *Lewis v. Reader's Digest Association*, 1D40; *Louisiana v. John Gibson* (1839), 1G89; *McClellan v. Beattie* (1829), 1B163; *McRoberts v. Santangelo* (1842), 1S47; *Maheu v. Hughes Tool Co.*, 1A187, 1R175; *Martin v. Nugent* (1811), 1N154; *Maryland v. Robert J. Breckinridge* (1840), 1B449; *Mayo v. Blair & Rives* (1840), 1M237; *Miller v. Argus Publishing Co.*, 1H246; *Monitor Patriot Co. v. Roy*, 1L93, 1N73, 1S178, 1W239; *Moore v. Bennett* (1889), 1H29; *National Association of Letter Carriers v. Austin*, 1B532, 1E60, 1P171; *National Labor Relations Board v. Gissel Packing Co.*, 1B532; *New York Post v. Buckley*, 1F103; *New York Times v. Connor*, 1F103; *New York Times v. Sullivan*, 1A209, 1B256–57, 1B294, 1B324–25, 1B452, 1B504, 1B518, 1C57, 1D57, 1D65, 1D100, 1D106, 1D135, 1D193, 1D195, 1E8, 1E41, 1E141, 1F204, 1G113, 1G132, 1G259, 1H70, 1H357, 1K18, 1K134, 1K270, 1L29, 1M253, 1M420, 1M498, 1N60, 1N96, 1N120, 1P107–8, 1P159, 1P317, 1P322, 1S139, 1S325, 1S332, 1S519–20, 1S522–23, 1S525, 1S527, 1W56, 1W308; *Ocala Star-Banner Co. v. Damron*, 1L93; Oviatt (James) cases, 1O89; Panama Canal libel case, 1P54; *Pauling v. Globe Democrat*, 1M420, 1P301; *Paul v. Davis*, 1C151, 1J12; *People (N.Y.) v. Bennett* (1857), 1B209; *People (N.Y.) ex rel. Richard Bursteed v. Thomas N. Carr* (1858), 1C61; *Pike v. Beals & Greene* (1835), 1B160; Poe (Edgar Allan) trial, 1M464; *Powers v. Cary* (1874), 1C79; *Reed v. Melnick*, 1F58; *Rosenblatt v. Baer*, 1B452, 1C374, 1D106, 1M420; *Rosenbloom v. Metromedia*, 1B130, 1E142, 1F207, 1G50, 1H58, 1H66, 1H246, 1I23, 1K20, 1K25, 1K257, 1L71, 1M180, 1P57, 1P170, 1R27, 1R200, 1R286, 1S417, 1T5, 1W308, 1W353; *Rose v. Koch et al.*, 1R218; *Rush v. Cobbett* (1799), 1D197, 1R281; *St. Amant v. Thompson*, 1C11; Saunders (W. O.) trial, 1S59, 1S119, 1S128; *Sellers v. Time, Inc.*, 1P153, 1T116; *Shor v. Billingsley*, 1H44; *Sprouse v. Clay Communication, Inc.*, 1C371, 1R210; Stoner (J. B.) case, 1M512; *Stone v. Cheever* (1835), 1C133–35; *Stone v. Essex County Newspapers, Inc.*, 1D172; study of 500 cases, 1L69–70; *Summit Hotel Co. v. National Broadcasting Co.*, 1H243; *Thompson v. The Evening Star Newspaper Co.*, 1P147; *Time, Inc. v. Firestone*, 1C151, 1C188, 1D34, 1D174, 1H247, 1J95, 1L172, 1M85, 1M87, 1P165, 1S275, 1S457, 1S550, 1S555, 1S572, 1T14, 1T131; *Time, Inc. v. Hill*, 1B290, 1B518, 1D106, 1E37, 1K18, 1M48, 1M230, 1M420, 1N120, 1P63, 1P66, 1P295; *Troman v. Wood*, 1G85, 1M480; *Virgil v. Time, Inc.*, 1R58, 1T165; *Walker v. Colorado Springs, Inc.*, 1B596; *Wasserman v. Time, Inc.*, 1P160; *Wilkes v. Chamberlin* (1873), 1C117; Wright (Andrew) trial, 1W345. *See also* Seditious libel (United States)

Libel laws (Argentina), 1D32

Libel laws (Australia): 1C31, 1H155, 1M111; damages, 1H151; injunctions, 1H149; jury verdicts, 1H150; Law Reform Commission, New South Wales, 1N86; Law Reform Committee, South Australia, 1S412; Law Reform Committee, Western Australia, 1W145; Parliamentary privilege, 1S447; radio and television, 1H148, 1M342; reforms proposed, 1T27

Libel laws (Canada): 1A259, 1B136, 1F62, 1K104–5, 1W105; history, 1K104

Libel laws (Great Britain): book publishing, 1E127, 1R269; Carter-Ruck (Peter F.) on, 1C76; Collingwood (C. A.) on, 1C255; criticism of, 1C324, 1C421, 1F94, 1I31, 1J91–92, 1M453; dead, concerning the, 1Z7; defense of, 1D146, 1F190; Denning (Lord Alfred T.) on, 1D86; Duncan (Colin) and Hoolahan (A. T.) on, 1D228; eighteenth-century confessed libeler, 1S61; eighteenth-century restrictions, 1H379, 1K68, 1K231; Faulks Committee report, 1G237, 1P179; Flood (John) on, 1F154; Fox Libel Act (1792), 1R37, 1S454, 1T148; Freedom of Publications (Protection) Bill, 1J89, 1J91; German treatise on (1841), 1P276; guide to, 1L231; history of, 1H443, 1J106, 1L289; Holdsworth (Sir William) on, 1K61; Jones (J. Clement) on, 1J91–94; Jones (Sir Elwyn) on, 1J89; jury roles (1752, 1771), 1G218, 1R248; Lansdale-Ruthven (Hugh P.) on, 1L37; newspaper lawyers, 1L208; Parliamentary sketching, 1B218; Press Council memorandum, 1P273; printers' and publishers' guide, 1C207; privacy rights basis of, 1B330; public libraries exempt from, 1M49; public meetings reports, 1L64; publisher criticizes, 1K127, 1K132; reform called for, 1C189, 1E126, 1H234, 1H443, 1J91–92, 1J94, 1J113, 1K127, 1K132, 1L233, 1W241; *Treatise on the Offense of Libel*, review of, 1B508; United States law compared with, 1D32, 1E126, 1K73, 1K212; Wooll (Edward) on, 1W334. *See also* Blasphemy laws (Great Britain); Sedition laws (Great Britain)

Libel laws (India), 1H32, 1M147, 1U4

Libel laws (international), 1D32

Libel laws (Ireland), 1H224, 1H367

Libel laws (New Zealand), 1K83

Libel laws (South Africa), 1A106, 1B578, 1N13, 1R15

Libel laws (Sri Lanka), 1A106

Libel laws (United States): 1D101, 1L2, 1M231, 1P258–59; American Law Institute on, 1M489, 1W4; British law compared with, 1D32, 1E126, 1K73, 1K212; California, 1A80, 1G141; casebooks, 1D177, 1F217–19, 1G104, 1H69, 1L63–64, 1L244, 1P310; court decisions virtually repeal, 1C323; Eldredge (Laurence H.) on, 1E40–43, 1M489; evolution of, 1F204; federal intervention, 1F178, 1R224; Field (Marshall) on, 1D58; Florida, 1A274; Franklin (Marc A.) on, 1F218; Freund (Paul A.) on, 1F280, 1F282; German law v., 1A6, 1C83, 1D32, 1H303; Hand (Judge Learned) on, 1H59; historians affected by, 1K80; history, 1F280, 1K80, 1L61, 1L69–70, 1L289, 1M279, 1S332, 1W257; Illinois, 1S565, 1T180; Kalven (Harry, Jr.) on, 1K18–19; Kansas, 1S332; legislative-judicial community, 1G141; Louisiana, 1C376; Montana, 1D40; national law needed, 1W349; New Mexico, 1F58, 1W41; New York, 1C61, 1S34, 1S127; Ohio, 1B543, 1I60; Oklahoma, 1J108; Pennsylvania, 1F326; privacy law v., 1B330, 1E37, 1J12, 1L52, 1M246, 1R272, 1S299, 1W3; Prosser (William L.) on, 1M489, 1P310; South Carolina, 1L61; state, *Gertz* impact on, 1D64, 1R224; state law changes needed, 1K72; stricter penalties for libelous reporting, 1D58, 1W339; Texas, 1E123, 1G125, 1W76; Utah, 1T76; Wisconsin, 1R14

Liberace v. Daily Mirror Newspapers Ltd. and Connor (1959), 1H444

Librarians: attitudes toward censorship, 1B402, 1B605–8, 1D80, 1E88, 1K189, 1O5; attitudes toward sexually oriented literature, 1P220; censorship by, 1E61, 1K51, 1K139; constitutional protection, 1O57–58; danger in resisting censorship, 1F185; dismissal of Joan Bodger, 1A133, 1E117, 1M99, 1S259; producer and controller of books, role as, 1O75. *See also* Intellectual freedom in libraries

Libraries, college. *See* College and university library censorship

Libraries, public. *See* Public library censorship

Libraries, school. *See* School library and classroom censorship

Library Bill of Rights (American Library Association): 1A149, 1A153, 1B240, 1M287; attitude of public librarians toward, 1B605–8; donor restrictions clause proposed, 1B585; history, 1C147; interpretation, 1A137; labeling, 1A146; minors' access to materials, 1A136, 1F37, 1S258; reevaluating library collections, 1A140, 1F37; restricted access, 1A144, 1B585; sanction against violators, 1A139; School Library Bill of Rights, 1A108, 1A149, 1A153, 1M287; social responsibility v., 1B238. *See also* Intellectual freedom in libraries

Library book selection policies: 1A107, 1C73, 1H346, 1M287; Australia public library (Ryde Council), 1W329; board responsibility, 1A83; British public libraries, 1C68, 1T69; case studies, 1K148; censorship device, 1C422; censorship influence on, 1S304; censorship v. selection, 1D4, 1L240, 1M404, 1N81, 1W247–49; children's books, 1B600, 1C289, 1D21, 1D23, 1I61, 1K249, 1M388, 1R5, 1R185, 1R209, 1R280, 1W329; community standards v. intellectual freedom, 1S8; controversial materials, 1B492, 1C220, 1F112, 1H8, 1L123, 1M403; discrimination without fear of censorship charges, 1G80, 1M232, 1M403; donor restrictions, 1B585; Enoch Pratt Free Library (Baltimore), 1E90; erotica, 1K153; expurgation of library materials, 1A135; history of selection and censorship, 1G52–53; Indiana libraries, 1A30; intellectual freedom and, 1M287, 1M403, 1O6, 1W247–49; intellectual neutrality in, 1K239, 1K249, 1N135; lawyer's view, 1A238; legal implications, 1O57–58; librarian's fallibility, 1M403; librarian's inability to judge, 1E61; Minnesota survey, 1S494; multi-ethnic literature, 1S309; new morality in sex, 1O10–11; obscenity implications, 1A81, 1D163, 1H371, 1I6, 1S180, 1S633; Ortega y Gasset (José) on, 1O75; Philadelphia area,

1D106, 1M420

Rosenbloom v. Metromedia, Inc., 403 U.S. 29 (1971), 1B130, 1E142, 1F207, 1G50, 1H58, 1H66, 1H246, 1I23, 1K20, 1K25, 1K257, 1L71, 1M180, 1P57, 1P170, 1R27, 1R200, 1R286, 1S417, 1T5, 1W308, 1W353

Rosenthal, A. M., 1R227, 1W304

Rose v. Koch et al., 154 N.W.2d 409 (1967), 1R218

Ross, Leonard, 1C131

Rosset, Barney, 1G143, 1G147, 1J85

Rossiter, Charles M., Jr., 1R118, 1R232

Rossi v. The Queen, (1974) F.C. 531 (F.C.T.D.), 1S294

Roswell, N.M.: public library censorship, 1M115

Roth, Samuel: 1A194, 1H45–46; imprisonment, 1R237

Roth v. United States, 354 U.S. 476 (1957), 1B452, 1B555, 1C5, 1D106, 1E33, 1E82, 1F25, 1F95, 1F132, 1F136, 1F195, 1F288, 1G2, 1G113, 1G273, 1K44, 1L257, 1M73, 1P145, 1R80, 1S642, 1T38, 1T54, 1W58, 1W63, 1W107, 1W310

Rouse, A. H., 1S633

Rowan v. United States Post Office Department, 397 U.S. 728 (1970), 1A5, 1E20, 1H363, 1J37, 1L302, 1T89

Rowe, James, 1T192

Rubin, Isadore (Dr.), 1C401

Rubinstein, Eli A., 1U124–28

Ruckelshouse, William, 1R272

Rucker, Bryce W., 1E76, 1R273–74

Rueger, Russ A., 1H55

Rush, Benjamin: 1D197; Rush-Corbett controversy, 1R281

Rush, William, 1B372

Rusher, William, 1M331–32, 1T192

Rush v. Cobbett (1799), 1R281

Russell, Bertrand: 1R287; dismissal from College of City of New York, 1D111

Russell, Daniel G., 1H55

Russell, George W., 1M436

Ryan, J. H., 1L195

Ryan, John L., 1H280

Sacheverell, Henry: impeachment, 1H340, 1M158, 1S149, 1W319

Sachs, Howard F., 1B532

Sack, Robert D., 1P258–59

Sade, Marquis de, 1E80

St. Amant v. Thompson, 390 U.S. 727 (1968), 1C11

St. Charles (Mo.) County Library: labeling rejected, 1L12

St. Louis: Civil War censorship, 1M479; harassment of bookseller, 1L10; KWK license renewal case, 1B234; pornography flourishing in, 1K71; press council, 1B310, 1S464

Salant, Richard, 1A244, 1C105, 1J68, 1S21–25

Salem, Daniel, 1M118

Salinger, Pierre, 1C81

Salisbury, Harrison, 1S27–28, 1U90

Saloschin, Robert L., 1D178, 1S30, 1W344

Sampson, Anthony, 1F205

Sampson, Hannah, 1H55

Sanford, David, 1Z30

San Francisco: pornography traffic, 1F90, 1M513, 1N45–46

Sanger, Margaret, 1B420, 1C285, 1D122, 1D186, 1F74, 1H270, 1I38, 1K88–89, 1L9, 1M269, 1W316

Sanger, William, 1A184, 1F74

Sanoff, Alvin P., 1W204

Sarathy, K. P., 1S48

Sarkar, Chanchal, 1F261, 1S51

Sarkar, Kobita, 1D113

Saskatchewan: Board of Film Censors, 1B349

Satellite broadcasting: control of, 1A247, 1B173, 1B520; First Amendment implications, 1D131, 1P281

Satire: eighteenth-century Britain, 1K231, 1T57, 1W51

Satirist, The, 1M151

Satyricon, The (Petronius), 1G108

Saunders' Weekly, 1S59–60, 1S119, 1S128

Savannah, Ga.: school newspaper code, 1D49

Saved (Edward Bond), 1D47

Saxbe v. Washington Post Co., 417 U.S. 843 (1974), 1G149, 1R197, 1T3

Scales v. United States, 366 U.S. 978 (1961), 1T91

Scalia, Antonin, 1A244, 1C105, 1R272, 1S65, 1U63

Scanlan's Monthly, 1D148, 1S366

Scanlon, Simon, 1B53

Schaleben, Arville O., 1W294

Schellenberg, Louise S., 1K282

Schenck v. United States, 249 U.S. 47 (1919), 1K22, 1R6, 1T91, 1W343

Scher, Irving, 1S650

Scherer, Gordon, 1M263

Schlei, Norbert A., 1F232

Schmidt, Benno C., Jr., 1F205, 1N94, 1S94–100, 1S514

Schmidt, Clarence R., 1H55

Schmidt, Richard M., Jr., 1D189, 1P258–59

School library and classroom censorship: 1B469, 1D23, 1G81, 1H346, 1M32, 1N81, 1P245; *Adventures of Huckleberry Finn*, 1K48, 1T124; areas of concern, 1D158, 1D161, 1D168, 1G6, 1K188, 1K234, 1K246; Arizona, 1D153–54, 1D191, 1K282; Australia School Library Bill of Rights, 1A280; authority to censor, 1L4; banned author discusses, 1K205; Bennington, Vt., 1C428; bibliography, 1D232; book selection affected by, 1S304; Buncombe County (N.C.) case, 1W179–80; case studies, 1A168, 1H123, 1N30; *Catcher in the Rye, The*, 1F80, 1H278, 1K48, 1K185, 1M98, 1N30, 1P5, 1S652, 1W179–80; censorship increasing, 1K241; censorship necessary, 1R5; Colorado survey, 1S433; community relations and, 1Y23; controversial literature, 1B44, 1C152, 1D155–56, 1D158, 1D168–70, 1G22, 1G297, 1H215, 1K48, 1K185, 1L3, 1O55, 1S494, 1W108, 1W151, 1W166; *Down These Mean Streets*, 1L144, 1W166; ethical pluralism as issue, 1A239, 1K234, 1S309; federal controls favored, 1H297; fictional account of, 1D150, 1M113; *Grapes of Wrath*, 1K48, 1W179–80; Illinois, 1D169; Island Trees, N.Y., 1S423; Kansas, 1D169; Kentucky, 1M143; *Learning Tree, The*, 1B229; lists of books banned, 1D152, 1D154, 1D169, 1W258; *Little Red Schoolbook, The*, 1C85; Louisiana, 1D169; measures to combat, 1D155–56, 1D161, 1D167, 1D169, 1H312, 1K246, 1M388, 1N27, 1W110; Minnesota survey, 1S494; moot court exercise, 1M199; National Council of Teachers of English resolutions and statements, 1N27–29; New Jersey, 1L3; New York City, 1A79, 1L144; New York state, 1S518; Niagara Falls, N.Y., 1F27; *1984*, 1K48; nonprint material, 1D157, 1D162; obscenity, 1D163, 1N81, 1R73; Ohio, 1D169, 1W236; *One Flew Over the Cuckoo's Nest*, 1S626; parental role, 1H293, 1K234, 1S88; pattern of (1962–71), 1Y21; Pennsylvania, 1D169; Phoenix, Ariz., 1H293; picture books banned (spoof), 1N59; poetry-writing assignment, 1S500; policy statement on, 1A148, 1A153, 1D23, 1D156, 1D167, 1D191, 1E50, 1H293, 1H306, 1L3, 1M388, 1N20, 1N42, 1W68, 1W110, 1Y23; pressure groups and, 1S281; reading guidance, 1S89; readings, 1D169, 1M404, 1N81; reevaluating library collections, 1A140, 1B489–90, 1F37, 1H118, 1K249, 1R280; Rochester, Mich., 1H123; school board role, 1B50, 1D169, 1E50, 1L144; School Library Bill of Rights, 1A108, 1A149, 1A153, 1M287; school superintendent's role, 1N81; sexism and racism, 1A140, 1A145, 1C98, 1D169, 1F37, 1H297, 1K249, 1Q7, 1S493, 1T124, 1W47, 1Y14; *Slaughterhouse Five*, 1H123, 1V23; standards for modern society, 1W258; Students' Right to Read (NCTE), 1N28–29; survey (1966–68), 1D154; survey (1971–74), 1D169; *Sylvester and the Magic Pebble*, 1F123, 1K249, 1S608, 1W166; Texas, 1B72, 1D169; Tulsa, 1L40; Utah, 1D169; Virginia, 1D169; Wyoming, 1W362. *See also* Textbooks and assigned readings

School newspapers: alternative (underground) newspapers, 1B196, 1D138, 1F55, 1G61, 1H223, 1H398, 1H427, 1L129, 1S610, 1T135, 1T160; American Civil Liberties statement, 1S526; Arizona survey, 1J21; California State Department of Education, 1G61; censorship of, 1A43, 1B195–96, 1C262, 1N115, 1S300; Commission of Inquiry into High School Journalism, report of, 1C270; faculty advisor dismissed, 1L122; freedom for, 1A3–4, 1B196, 1C262, 1D92, 1D124, 1D169, 1F56, 1F101, 1H175, 1H427, 1J76, 1K28, 1L308, 1M271, 1P46, 1R242, 1R290, 1S39, 1S300–301, 1S609, 1T134, 1T136–38, 1T160, 1V56; Grosse Point (Mich.) policy statement, 1B612; guidelines, 1H167, 1L109, 1S593; Kansas survey, 1R35; legal status, 1F56, 1O2, 1S428, 1S526, 1S534,

1T136–37, 1V56, 1W13; New Jersey Commission of Education, 1G61; principals' attitudes toward press freedom, 1C32; rights and responsibilities, 1B196; Savannah (Ga.) policy statement, 1D49; Seattle Public School System, 1G61; shield laws, 1S524; Student Press Law Center, 1S593–94

School play: censorship of, 1C354

Schorer, Mark, 1A129, 1G73

Schorr, Daniel: CIA report case, 1D16, 1I3, 1K280, 1P253, 1R302, 1S499, 1S514, 1W115; harassment, 1S109–11, 1S413, 1U100, 1W299

Schrader, E. U., 1P22

Schramm, Wilbur, 1R161

Schroeder, Theodore: 1A270, 1B539, 1B541–42, 1E54–55, 1M46, 1S119–28; debate with John S. Sumner, 1S616

Schutzman & Schutzman v. News Syndicate Co., Inc., 304 N.Y.S.2d 167 (1969), 1K203, 1P156, 1S364

Schwartz, Alan U., 1L257, 1P166–71, 1U90

Schwartz, Albert V., 1D169

Schwartz, Herbert, 1C401

Schwartz, Murray L., 1C20

Scienter, element of: in sale of obscene works, 1A7, 1C59, 1S349, 1W264

Scientific and technical data: Freedom of Information Act and, 1B351, 1D144, 1D177, 1D199, 1W5; government secrecy, 1D178, 1D199, 1F14, 1G105, 1G286, 1H274, 1H368, 1S154, 1W5; wartime voluntary secrecy, 1W83

Scientific theories: suppression of, 1H337

Scopes, John T.: evolution trial, 1B350, 1B549, 1D59–60, 1H26, 1H152, 1L220, 1R80, 1S182

Scotland: libel cases, 1B199, 1M51, 1P91, 1S541; seditious libel, 1C208, 1E4, 1H283, 1I33, 1J83, 1S345, 1T53

Scott, Gloria S., 1D169, 1S142

Scott, Hugh (Sen.), 1S144, 1U100

Scott, Peter (Dr.), 1L268

Scott, W. J., 1M91

Scouten, A. H., 1A281

Screw, 1R266

Scuncio v. Columbus Theatre, Inc., 277 A.2d. 924 (1971), 1A197

Search and seizure: 1F8; First and Fourth Amendments, 1B590, 1L199; Food and Drug Administration seizes book, 1W318; history, 1T24; *Mapp v. Ohio*, 1M157; New York, 1P12; *People (N.Y.) v. Rothenberg*, 1K66; prior adversary hearing, 1C126, 1E14, 1H200, 1H280, 1L38, 1M389, 1P286–87, 1R142, 1R304, 1S46, 1S473; reporters' notes and files, 1S105; *Stanley v. Georgia*, 1C167, 1D106, 1D227, 1E1, 1E15, 1E33, 1F132, 1F288, 1G43, 1G66, 1G214, 1H301, 1K41, 1K45, 1L196, 1L309, 1M19, 1M139, 1M230, 1M304, 1O17, 1P145, 1S147, 1S553, 1S611, 1T108, 1T175, 1W58; *Tyrone, Inc. v. James B. Wilkinson*, 1C410

Sears, James, 1M263

Seattle: press council, 1B310, 1S464; student newspapers, policy on, 1G61

Secrecy, government. *See* News, management of; Public meetings, right of access to; Public records, right of access to; Security restrictions on news

Secret printing: Catholic books in English, 1A90

Securities, defamation in regulation of, 1B224

Securities and Exchange Commission: public records, 1W344; registration of magazines and newspapers by, proposed, 1B323

Security classification of documents: 1A261, 1D178, 1F156, 1R272, 1S650, 1U115; abuse of, 1A261, 1F215, 1G21, 1G99, 1G170, 1J81, 1M17, 1R217, 1R268, 1S232, 1S528; computer-assigned, 1E85; concept of, analyzed, 1K157, 1U115; congressional investigation, 1U26, 1U37, 1U87; courts martial, use of, in, 1W120; Criminal Code revision, 1A134, 1C388, 1C399, 1E101, 1L150, 1S100, 1S293; "D" Notice system (Great Britain): 1G230–31, 1G234, 1H161, 1H165, 1L170, 1M90, 1M122, 1P172, 1P196; declassification, 1D114, 1N124, 1R61, 1U32; Department of Defense documents relating to, 1U26; *Epstein v. Resor*, 1E94,

1F244, 1W59; foreign policy, 1F205, 1R268, 1S207, 1U87, 1U115; Freedom of Information Act and, 1A43, 1C104, 1F244, 1L148, 1S649, 1U32, 1U37; historical research, 1U32; history, 1U32, 1U115; leak of information, 1K46, 1W168, 1W341; libraries affected by, 1K156; maladministration hidden by, 1H368; moral obligation of government and press, 1T70; Navy Department security classification manual, 1U27; Nixon Executive Order 11652, 1D114, 1N124, 1R61, 1U32; photocopying of, as theft, 1W208; reforms proposed, 1B274, 1M494, 1S93, 1S232, 1U17, 1U115, 1W341; restrictions on, needed, 1B592, 1G160; Richardson (Elliot L.) on, 1R126; scholars' access affected by, 1A125, 1B65, 1B594, 1C51, 1C417, 1F51–52, 1L125; U.S. Commission on Government Security report, 1U17. See also Pentagon Papers case

Security restrictions on news: Australia, 1C31, 1S435, 1W181; Canada, 1C385, 1F205, 1K104

Security restrictions on news (Great Britain): 1A59, 1D178, 1O41; comparison with United States, 1L170, 1M122; criticism of, 1A59, 1H161, 1L170, 1M122, 1P172; "D" Notice system, 1G230–31, 1G234, 1H161, 1H165, 1L170, 1M90, 1M122, 1P172, 1P196; foreign affairs, 1F205; Franks Committee report, 1B28, 1B60, 1B288, 1D212, 1G234, 1M243, 1S339; Lohan (Col. L. G.) affair, 1M90; Radcliffe Committee report, 1G230–31; readings, 1F205; secrecy violations deplored, 1R183; Sunday Times publication of confidential document, 1E125. See also Official Secrets Act

Security restrictions on news (United States): 1D178, 1E66, 1K161, 1L244, 1N118, 1P132; atomic energy, 1A170, 1M171; Center for National Security Studies, 1C104; comparison with Great Britain, 1L170, 1M122; Criminal Code revision, 1A134, 1C388, 1C399, 1E101, 1L150, 1S100, 1S293; criticism of, 1F215, 1F316, 1G21, 1G98–99, 1H356, 1M461, 1S93; executive authority, 1K12; foreign policy, 1F205, 1R268, 1S207, 1U87, 1U115; Freedom of Information Act, 1A43, 1C104, 1F244, 1L148, 1N43, 1R247; Glomar affair, 1G169, 1K197; Internal Security Act of 1950, 1B180; Johnson Administration, 1D48, 1G195, 1L8, 1M71–72, 1M353; laws, 1E16; Madison Administration, 1F327; military security, 1M405, 1Y19; Muskie (Sen. Edmund S.) on, 1M517; Nixon Administration, 1A143, 1A227, 1F316, 1G98–99, 1K40, 1M353, 1M372, 1P256; policy matters v. negotiation details, 1S93; press conduct criticized, 1C116, 1G169; readings, 1F205, 1F217–19, 1P81; right to know v., 1M405, 1N118, 1S299, 1S650, 1Y19; Supreme Court, 1B168; U.S. Commission on Government Security report, 1U17; United States v. Marchetti, 1B281, 1E2, 1H408, 1M163; wartime, 1E65. See also Central Intelligence Agency; Pentagon Papers case; Security classification of documents; Vietnam war

Sedgwick, J., 1P22

Sedition Act of 1798: 1H263, 1L75, 1S547, 1W343; Bache (Benjamin Franklin) case, 1S547; Callender (James T.) case, 1H102, 1J33, 1S547; Cooper (Thomas) case, 1S547; defense of, 1A38; documents relating to, 1L161; Haswell (Anthony) case, 1S547; Holt (Charles) case, 1S547; libel cases under, 1W257; Lyon (Matthew) case, 1M397, 1S542, 1S547; play dealing with, 1S542; reappraisal, 1B248, 1F29; Republican opposition press, 1S547

Sedition laws (Great Britain): opposition to (1817), 1G275; Southey (Robert) favors, 1J28; strengthening urged (1809), 1C275

Sedition laws (United States): Alien Registration Act of 1940 (Smith Act), 1B180, 1P65; Internal Security Act of 1950 (McCarran Act), 1B180; Kramer sedition bill (1935), 1A115; mass sedition trial, 1942–44, 1L314, 1M39; Pennsylvania, 1S431. See also Espionage Act of 1917; Sedition Act of 1798

Seditious libel (Great Britain): 1T58, 1T61; abuse of freedom, 1L128; American heritage, 1P24; Bastwick (John) trial, 1T61; Baxter (Richard) trial, 1T61; Berry (Walter) and Robertson (James) trial, 1B255; Briellat

(Thomas) trial, 1B464; Burks (Joseph) trial, 1B588; burlesque of eighteenth-century trial, 1T190; Burton (Henry) trial, 1T61; Caunt (James) trial, 1C91; Charles II proclamation, 1G232; Cobbett (William) trial, 1C380, 1D197, 1H100, 1J75; Cook (Samuel) trial, 1C318; Cuthell (John) trial, 1S376; Duffy (Charles G.) trial, 1D225; eighteenth-century constitutional associations, 1B291, 1C282, 1F303, 1G115, 1M365, 1R37, 1R59, 1S345; Ellenborough (Lord) on, 1C380; English Jacobins, 1B526, 1C282, 1R37, 1S345, 1S387; "ex-officio information," use of, 1B107; Fox Libel Act (1792), 1R37, 1S454, 1T148; French Revolution influence on, 1B526, 1C282, 1G115, 1H83, 1M434, 1R37, 1S345, 1S387; Friends to the Abuse of the Liberty of the Press, 1F303; Friends to the Liberty of the Press, 1B291, 1C282, 1R59, 1S345; Gordon (Lord George) trial, 1G181, 1W235; Grub Street pamphleteers, 1P176; Hone (William) trial, 1C380; Hunt (John) trial, 1C380; Hurdy Gurdy trial (satire), 1H422; Johnson (Joseph) trial, 1S376; Jordan (Jeremiah S.) trial, 1S376; Lambert (John) trial, 1C380; Mainwaring (William) on, 1S387; Manwaring (Roger) trial, 1M158; Montgomery (James) trial, 1M400; O'Connor (Feargus) trial, 1O25; Paine (Thomas), 1C282, 1H102, 1H138, 1S345; Parker (Theodore) on, 1P24; "patriotic" song judged, 1M400; Peltier (Jean G.) trial, 1C380; Perry (James) trial, 1C380; Pigott (Charles) trial, 1P136; Prynne (William) trial, 1T61, 1W319; Sacheverell (Henry) trial, 1H340, 1M158, 1S149, 1W319; Seven Bishops trial, 1H4; Smith (Francis) trial, 1S346; Smith (John) trial, 1S354; Spence (Thomas) trial, 1C282, 1K85, 1R277, 1S426, 1W51; tabulation of cases (1821, 1830), 1G243–47; Thelwall (John), trial, 1C282, 1S345, 1T53, 1W51; Tooke (John Horne) trial, 1C282, 1S345, 1T53, 1T61, 1T120–21, 1W51; Tytler (James) petition, 1T205; Walker (Thomas) trial, 1W17; Wilkes (John) trial, 1F271, 1H102, 1K230, 1P119, 1R276, 1T58, 1T146, 1T148, 1W218–19, 1W224–27, 1W231, 1W255, 1Y27; Wilkins (Thomas) trial, 1W235; Woodfall (Henry S.) trial, 1H9, 1T61, 1T148, 1W321

Seditious libel (India): Kedar Nath Singh v. The State of Bihar, 1M360

Seditious libel (Ireland): Browne (Thomas E.) imprisonment, 1B282; Johnson (Robert) trial, 1J75; King v. Richard Barrett (1833), 1C381; Lucas (Charles) impeachment, 1L304; Rowan (Archibald H.) trial, 1R250

Seditious libel (Scotland): Johnston (William) trial, 1J83; Muir (Thomas) trial and exile, 1C208, 1C282, 1E4, 1H283, 1I33, 1S345, 1T53; Palmer (Thomas F.) trial, 1C208, 1C282

Seditious libel (United States): Colonial America, 1N62, 1T37; Crandall (Dr. Reuben) trial, 1K106; Oswald (Eleazer) trial, 1T37; search and seizure practices, 1T24; Zenger (John Peter) trial, 1B79, 1C370, 1E73, 1E77, 1F255, 1F257, 1G145, 1H102, 1K141, 1L57, 1L267, 1L282, 1M441, 1N93, 1W343, 1Z12

Segal, Ronald M., 1A244, 1C105, 1C109

Seib, Charles, 1R272

Seifer, Daniel J., 1M301

Seizure of papers. See Search and seizure

Seldes, George, 1I12, 1S170–73, 1W66

Sellers v. Time, Inc., 299 F. Supp. 582 (E.D. Pa. 1969), 1P153, 1T116

Selling of the Pentagon, The (documentary film), 1B101, 1B117, 1C265, 1D142, 1F69, 1F126, 1F181, 1F300, 1K7, 1M228, 1N19, 1R203, 1S250, 1S334, 1S348, 1S462, 1U41, 1U55, 1W215

September Morn (painting), 1C386

Sevareid, Eric, 1A244, 1C81, 1C105, 1C109, 1S183–84

Seven Bishops: trial of, 1H4

Seven Minutes, The (Irving Wallace), 1W27–29

Severy, Bruce, 1D169

Sevey, Edwin, 1M408

Sex education: Boston Public Library survey, 1G94; censorship and, 1F34; Christian Crusade, 1D204–5; Creative and Sexual Science, 1H164; eighteenth-century works attacked (Great Britain), 1C433; Hawaii school program controversy, 1W317; Landis (Dr. S. M.) lecture prohibited, 1L28; library book selection 1G94, 1O8, 1P220, 1W114; Light in Dark Corners, 1S599; Massachusetts public libraries, 1B506;

nineteenth-century advocates (United States), 1S152; Physical Culture, 1W316; pornography and, 1W282; pressure groups against, 1E136, 1W114; programs evaluated, 1G129, 1Q1. See also Birth control information

Sex expression in literature and art: 1B428, 1G128, 1K111, 1P1, 1W89, 1W292; abuse of freedom, 1L141, 1P129, 1W269; classification for high school English, 1O55; criticism of (1730), 1L19; defense of, 1F225; Dell (Floyd) on, 1D75; effect on reader, 1F120, 1M221, 1P129, 1R136, 1S633, 1V7, 1W269–71; erotica v. pornography, 1M268; erotic fiction in United States, 1960s, 1B444; Huxley (Aldous) on, 1H440; index to salacious passages, 1R77; India, 1S194; Jameson (Storm) on, 1J23; Levin (Meyer) on, 1L141; permissive society, 1G106, 1M118, 1S185, 1S357; Princeton University Press editorial policies on, 1B18; Romantics, Puritan censorship of, 1H141; Segal (Erich) on, 1S163; study, 1L175; Victorian hypocrisy, 1H95; war glorification v., 1E80. See also Literature, censorship of; Morality and literature; Obscenity and pornography

Sexism and racism in library and teaching materials: American Library Association policy, 1A140, 1A145, 1B490, 1C98, 1F37; balance, not censorship, 1W47; Brademas (Congr. John) on, 1B425; California law, 1S493; criteria for evaluation, 1O45; Epaminondas, 1B463; federal controls favored, 1H297; Huckleberry Finn, Adventures of, 1K48, 1T124; Little Black Sambo, 1D95, 1K249, 1M12, 1W166, 1Y28; reevaluation of library collections, 1A140, 1B490, 1F37, 1H118, 1L32, 1M11–12, 1R280; reverse ethnocentric perspective, 1Y14; textbooks, 1R221, 1W119, 1W206; use in classroom, 1B47, 1D169, 1Q7, 1S309. See also Library book selection policies; Textbooks and assigned readings

Sex Life of a Cop (Oscar Peck), 1F133

Sex radicalism and free love: Harman (Moses), crusade of, 1H86, 1P80, 1S152, 1W143

Sexual Inversion. See Studies in the Psychology of Sex

Sexus (Henry Miller), 1W162

Seymour, Whitney N., Jr., 1F239, 1S187–88

Shah, S. B., 1L45

Shakedown (Fort Dix), 1P138

Shakespeare, Frank, 1L297

Shanghaied into the European War (Daniel H. Wallace), 1C316

Shapiro, Martin, 1S206–7, 1S516

Shaplen, Robert, 1W305

Sharma, K. M., 1S194, 1S210

Sharma, Partap, 1R36

Sharp Citizen (Cave City, Ark.), 1G17, 1W60

Shattuck, John H. F., 1C284, 1D178

Shaw, George Bernard: birth control views, 1S221; English censorship views, 1P130; Irish censorship views, 1E45; stage censorship, 1S220

Shaw, Robert M., 1R146

Shaw, Roy, 1W174

Shaw v. Director of Public Prosecutions, (1961) 2 All E.R. 466, 1F180

Shea, F. X., 1N81

Shearer, David H. R., 1C336

Shelby, Maurice E., Jr., 1L195

Sheldon, R. C., 1D216

Shepherd, William G.: trial, 1A91

Sheppard, Claude-Armand, 1H162

Sheppard v. Maxwell, 384 U.S. 333 (1966), 1C374, 1D106, 1F73, 1F233, 1G221, 1G228, 1H23, 1H62, 1H341, 1K194, 1K211, 1L102, 1M102, 1R121, 1S241, 1S283, 1S414, 1S452, 1S604

Sheridan, Richard B., 1R3

Sherman, M. S., 1M140

Sherman, William T. (Gen.): quarrels with press, 1M190–91

Sherry, Paul, 1W189

Sherwin, W. T., 1W51

Sherwood, Robert, 1F270

She's Eloped (John O'Keefe), 1C306, 1M434

Shetler, Carole, 1M143

Shewing-up of Blanco Posnet, The (G. B. Shaw), 1E51

Shield laws (United States): 1A122–23, 1A255, 1C4, 1F83, 1G175–79, 1H222, 1M508, 1Q4, 1S96, 1S378, 1W150, 1Z2; American Society of Newspaper Editors, 1H430, 1T104, 1U65–66; Arizona, 1M208;

ERRATA IN THE 1968 EDITION, FREEDOM OF THE PRESS

B56	Oren [not Owen] Barber
B301	This work by the American [not British] critic, R. P. Blackmur, also appears in the *Nation* under the pseudonym Perry Hobbes (H284).
B322	Charles [not George] Bradlaugh
B622	Date omitted: 23 February 1962
C515	A review [not text] of an address.
D200	Doyle [not Dolye]
E70	Revaluation [not Revolution]
F188	obscenity [not blasphemy] trial of D. M. Bennett
F193	The author of *In the Matter of the Repeal. . . ,* according to Theodore Schroeder, is Edward Bliss Foote [not the son, Edward Bond Foote].
F216	Hugh Gaine [not Gaines]; also incorrect in the index
F239	1850 [not 1950]
G102–7	Donald M. Gillmor [not Gillmore]
G179	Nadine Gordimer [not Gordiner]
G244	John Hollingshead [not Hallinghead]
H101	Rev. Walter H. MacPherson was minister of People's Church, South Chicago.
H284	atheism [not theism]
H325	1842 [not 185?]
H423	Truelove's trial was for obscenity [not blasphemy].
K169	Theodore B. [not S.] Knudson
L68	vol. 3 [not 30] *Encyclopaedia of the Social Sciences*
M95	160p. [not 60p.]
O72	She [not he] argues.
P115–16	Stuart Perry and Stuart H. Perry are the same.
R182	*Medical Critic and Guide*
S67	W. O. [not W. C.] Saunders
S168	64th [not 66th] Congress
S330	"violent [not violation] partisan"

S681	J. Andrew Strahan [not Straham]
S743	Frank Swancara [not Swacara]
W69	D. M. [not D. W.] Bennett
W250	1964 [not 1940]
W288	Harold Williams, Jr. [not Willimas]
W360	Date omitted: 4 April 1855
°C35	Harriette [not Harriet] Wilson
°M17	Lenore Kandel [not Kendel]; also incorrect in index
Index	Paterson, N.J., E133; N112 [not N12]
Index	Spring-Rice [not Spring-Rue]

AUTHORSHIP IDENTIFIED

Authors for the following works, entered under titles in the 1968 bibliography, have been identified as follows:

B322	G. G. Greenwood (identified by Gordon Stein)
C40	Attributed to J. N. Marcie
C106	Charles Carrington is the pseudonym for Paul Ferdinando, according to Gershon Legman.
C129	J. Middleton Murry (Houghton's *Wellesley Index*)
C270	John Chandos is the pseudonym for John Lithgow Chandos McConnell.
C515	Henry Peter Brougham, Brougham and Vaux (Houghton's *Wellesley Index*)
L237	Attributed to Alfred Hill (Houghton's *Wellesley Index*)
L252	Henry Peter Brougham, Brougham and Vaux (Houghton's *Wellesley Index*)
L249	Attributed to James Mill (Houghton's *Wellesley Index*)
O82	Edwin Chadwick
S200	Theodore Schroeder
W180	Attributed to John Wilson (Houghton's *Wellesley Index*)